THIRTY-SIXTH EDITION

KOVELS'
ANTIQUES
& COLLECTIBLES

PRICE LIST

FOR THE 2004 MARKET
ILLUSTRATED

RANDOM HOUSE REFERENCE
NEW YORK TORONTO LONDON SYDNEY AUCKLAND

Published by Random House Reference, an imprint of the Random House
Information Group, 1745 Broadway, New York, New York 10019.
Distributed by the Random House Information Group, a division of
Random House Inc., New York, and simultaneously in Canada
by Random House of Canada Limited, Toronto.

Random House is a registered trademark of Random House, Inc.
www.randomhouse.com

Printed in the United States of America

Library of Congress Catalog Card Number: 83-643618

ISBN 1-4000-4664-5

10 9 8 7 6 5 4 3 2 1

THIRTY-SIXTH EDITION

BOOKS BY RALPH AND TERRY KOVEL

American Country Furniture, 1780–1875

A Directory of American Silver, Pewter, and Silver Plate

Kovels' Advertising Collectibles Price List

Kovels' American Art Pottery:
The Collector's Guide to Makers, Marks, and Factory Histories

Kovels' American Silver Marks, 1650 to the Present

Kovels' Antiques & Collectibles Fix-It Source Book

Kovels' Bid, Buy, and Sell Online

Kovels' Book of Antique Labels

Kovels' Bottles Price List

Kovels' Collector's Guide to American Art Pottery

Kovels' Collectors' Source Book

Kovels' Depression Glass & Dinnerware Price List

Kovels' Dictionary of Marks—Pottery & Porcelain

Kovels' Guide to Selling, Buying, and Fixing
Your Antiques and Collectibles

Kovels' Guide to Selling Your Antiques & Collectibles

Kovels' Illustrated Price Guide to Royal Doulton

Kovels' Know Your Antiques

Kovels' Know Your Collectibles

Kovels' New Dictionary of Marks—Pottery & Porcelain

Kovels' Organizer for Collectors

Kovels' Price Guide for Collector Plates, Figurines,
Paperweights, and Other Limited Editions

Kovels' Quick Tips—799 Helpful Hints
on How to Care for Your Collectibles

Kovels' Yellow Pages: A Resource Guide for Collectors

The Label Made Me Buy It: From Aunt Jemima to Zonkers—
The Best-Dressed Boxes, Bottles and Cans from the Past

INTRODUCTION

This is the 36th year *Kovels' Antiques & Collectibles Price List* has been published. And the book is still being written by the original authors, Ralph and Terry Kovel. It has changed from a book with no illustrations and typewriter-style letters to this edition with hundreds of pictures and logos, about 50,000 prices, and dozens of tips about care. It also has a special color insert, "A Menagerie of Collectibles," a picture-price report showing recently sold antiques and collectibles shaped like animals.

READ THIS BEFORE YOU USE THIS BOOK—IT WILL HELP

This is a book for the average collector. All year we check prices, visit shops, shows and flea markets, read hundreds of publications and catalogs, check the Internet, and decide what antiques and collectibles are of most interest. We concentrate on the average pieces in any category. Sometimes one or two high-priced pieces are included so you will realize that some rarities are valuable.

Examples of furniture, silver, Tiffany, or art pottery may sell for more than $50,000; we list a few of those examples. The highest price in this book is $51,750, for a Pairpoint puffy orange-tree lamp. The lowest is $1 for a red, white, and blue "I'm the Watergate Bug" cigar band or a Halloween paper napkin picturing a cat and pumpkins. Most pieces we list cost less than $10,000.

We also list the weird and wonderful. This year you can find prices for a contortionist's table of cast aluminum for $770; an 1890 Westclox combination pocket-watch and pistol for $4,100; and a cardboard box that holds waxed dental floss for $70. A large folk art chain made of beer-bottle caps has 11,764 caps in seven colors. The 45-foot–long chain sold for $3,000. The smallest object is a 5/16-inch butterscotch Catalin button that sold as part of a set of nine buttons for $6. The largest is an iron garden fence with spikes, terminals, and five posts, 42 inches by 31 feet, 6 inches, that sold for $2,640.

Prices are up in some categories. The biggest surprise is that Royal Doulton figurines are again attracting collectors and going up in price. Furniture by George Nakashima set records, including $95,600 for a dining table and chairs. Arts and Crafts and Art Pottery continue to rise. Roseville pottery is the most popular and is seen at every show. Early twentieth-century California potteries and Grueby pottery are selling for high prices, and so is nineteenth-century spatterware. A spatterware cup and saucer with a rainbow swirl auctioned for $24,150. Nippon is selling for high prices because it is popular with Japanese buyers. There is continued interest in garden antiques from old flowerpots to large fountains. Anything glass or pottery, especially perfume bottles, marked Czechoslovakia sells quickly. Vintage clothing and textiles sell at profitable prices. Less-than-perfect antiques and collectibles are selling at much higher than expected prices if they are rare. A broken covered pressed glass sugar bowl in a rare color of Acanthus Leaf and Shield sold for $950. An Australian offered a 1950s battery-operated toy of Popeye lifting a tank driven by Olive Oyl. The toy was really a box of the parts, but a collector paid $14,601 for it. A mint, boxed example is worth $35,000.

Antiques malls seem to be doing less business. Some have closed. Many offer items they also list on the Internet. We hear two stories from dealers: Business was off because of 9/11 and the war in Iraq, but is recovering. Dealers at shows with quality merchandise say sales are better than before these events. But dealers at flea markets and small shows say customers are showing less interest. Sales on the Internet are also influencing prices. A survey showed that Internet auction prices are still dropping. Prices on eBay are down this year by three percent; prices on that site are down 35 percent since 2000. The number of pieces listed on eBay that actually sold fell to 45 percent. But the online market is international and growing. This has changed the pricing of some collectibles. Objects that are known in most of the world, such as pens, cigarette lighters, toys, and ordinary '50s furniture, are selling at the same or slightly lower prices than last year. Only exceptional pieces are going for the extraordinary prices reported in the news media.

Each year categories are added or omitted to make it easier for you to find your antiques. There are many new categories this year: Blenko Glass, Clifton, Decorated Tumbler, Durant Kilns, Glidden, Heintz Art, Horn, Losanti, Metlox, Morgantown Glass, Poole Pottery, Swastika Keramos, Toothbrush Holder, University City, and Wall Pocket.

The book is kept at about 800 pages because it is written to go with you to sales. We try to have a balanced format—not too many glass, pottery, or collectible items, furniture from the eighteenth through the twentieth centuries, and not too many items that sell for over $5,000. The prices are from the American market for the American market. Few European sales are reported. We take the editorial privilege of not including prices that seem to result from "auction fever." The computer-generated index is so complete it amazes us. Use it often. An internal alphabetical index is also included. For example, there is a category for Celluloid. Most items made of celluloid will be found there, but if there is a celluloid toy, it will be listed under Toys and also indexed under Celluloid. There are also cross-references in the listings and in the paragraphs. But some searching must be done. For example, Barbie dolls are found in the Doll category; there is no Barbie category. And when you look at "doll, Barbie" you will see a note that Barbie is under "doll, Mattel, Barbie" because most dolls are listed by maker. We differentiate between doll furniture made to a scale suitable for display of dolls and dollhouse furniture made in the small scale meant for a dollhouse.

All pictures and prices are new every year, except pictures that are pattern examples shown in Depression Glass and Pressed Glass. Antiques pictured are items offered for sale, not museum pieces. Tips about care of collections, security, and other useful information are set in special type. Leaf through the book and learn how to wash porcelains, guard against theft, and much more.

Don't discard this book when it is time to buy a new one next year. Old Kovels' price books should be saved for future reference and for tax and appraisal information.

The prices in this book are reports of the general antiques market. Each year, every price in the book is new. We do not estimate or "update" prices. Prices are actual asking prices, although a buyer may have negotiated a price to a lower figure. We do not pay dealers and writers to estimate prices. Experience has shown that a collector of one type of antique is prejudiced in favor of that item, so estimated prices are rarely a true report. If a price range is given, it is because at least two identical items were offered for sale at different times. Price ranges are found only in categories like Pressed Glass, where identical items can be identified. If the price listed in this book is from an auction, it includes the buyer's premium, but does not include sales tax. Some prices in *Kovels' Antiques & Collectibles Price List* may seem high and some may seem low because of regional variations. But each price is one you could have paid for the object somewhere in the United States.

If you are selling your collection, do not expect to get retail value unless you are a dealer. Wholesale prices for antiques are usually 50 percent less than retail. Remember, the antiques dealer must make a profit or go out of business. Internet auction prices are less predictable. Because of the international audience and "auction fever," prices can be higher or lower than retail.

THE RECORD PRICES HYPE

The media loves to report record prices, amazing auctions, high-priced discoveries, and events that really have little to do with the antiques and collectibles market familiar to the average collector. An oil painting by Worthington Whittredge was stored in a closet for many years, then taken to an appraisal clinic, and finally auctioned for $103,500. A pewter porringer by Simon Pennock of Pennsylvania bought for $5 at an estate sale in South Bend, Indiana, auctioned for $3,250 on the Internet. Great stories, but—like winning the lottery—not likely to happen to everyone. Remember that these are the prices for the rarest and best.

RECORD-SETTING PRICES

ADVERTISING

Beer can: $19,299 for a steel Clipper Pale Beer flat-top can, Grace Bros. Brewing Co., picturing Boeing's transoceanic "flying boat," the Yankee Clipper, with stamped date 6-10-41.

Trade sign: $113,525 for a double-sided wooden cobbler's trade sign, elephant form, painted gray, red, yellow, white, and black, elephant wearing boots and carrying a banner in his trunk reading "John M. Dyckman," also wearing a blanket reading "Boots & Shoes," 19th century, 57 x 79 inches.

DECOY

Decoy by Crowell: $801,500 for an Elmer Crowell preening pintail drake with carved crossed wings, c.1915.

FURNITURE

Belter table: $86,250 for a John Henry Belter Cornucopia center table with marble top, carved rosewood, c-scrolls, and cornucopias forming the stretchers; pierced and carved apron with leaves, flowers and acorns; continuous s-scroll legs, made in New York, 1850-1860, 28½ x 36 inches.

Frank Lloyd Wright armchair: $104,750 for a Frank Lloyd Wright three-legged armchair designed for the Johnson Wax Co.'s Administration Building in Racine, Wisconsin, with original "Cherokee" red paint and original fabric upholstery, c.1936.

George Nakashima Frenchman's Cove dining table and New chairs: $95,600 for a George Nakashima "Frenchman's Cove" dining table and "New" chairs, black walnut table with rosewood butterfly keys, two signed armchairs and four side chairs of walnut and hickory; table, 28¾ x 79¾ x 78 inches; armchairs, 38⅝ inches; side chairs, 36 inches.

George Nakashima Minguren II dining table: $130,500 for a George Nakashima monumental "Minguren II" dining table, 1989-1992, Claro walnut with rosewood butterfly keys, signed "Mira Nakashima—best wishes," dated September 1992, 29½ x 172 x 72¾ inches. George Nakashima designed this table before he died; his daughter finished it.

Marshmallow sofa: $129,000 for a George Nelson Marshmallow sofa, c.1960.

GLASS

A.W. Buchan & Co. ginger beer bottle: $3,507 (£2,234) for an A.W. Buchan blue-print sample ginger beer bottle, labeled "Manufacturers of vitrified, weather & acid proof stoneware, Waverley Potteries, Portobello, Scotland."

Czechoslovakian glass perfume bottle: $17,000 for a Czechoslovakian glass perfume bottle with a clear, frosted, 3-dimensional stopper of a nude seated with her legs dangling over the bottle, black opaque base, 6¼ inches.

English ginger beer/English Hamilton bottle: $7,828 (£5,150) for a dark olive green Hodgsons pontilled Hamilton bottle, with coat of arms on shoulder.

English slab-seat bottle: $2,888 (£1,900) for a flat-bodied stoneware J. Salman's/Peterbourogh (sic) bottle.

Ink bottle: $40,700 for a deep cobalt blue Harrison's Columbian Ink bottle, 12-sided, with iron pontil and applied mouth, 1845-1860, 11½ inches (gallon size).

Martindale & Smythe, Liverpool, ginger beer bottle: $1,894 (£1,246) for a green-top champagne Martindale & Smythe Ltd./Liverpool ginger beer bottle.

René Lalique flacon: $100,550 for a René Lalique et Cie. flacon, clear & frosted glass, circular shape, decorated with a swimming siren with trailing hair and surrounded by small air bubbles, 5½ inches.

Scroll flask, pint size: $19,800 for a deep purple-amethyst pint Scroll flask (GI-14), pontil-scarred base, tooled mouth, 1845-1860.

Silloth mineral water bottle: $2,888 (£1,900) for a black-print Silloth Mineral Water Company bottle.

LAMPS & LIGHTING

Frank Lloyd Wright lamp: $1,900,000 for a Frank Lloyd Wright table lamp, identical double pedestals, with bronze and leaded glass shade, c.1903, 22¼ x 32¼ x 19⅛ inches.

Gustav Stickley table lamp: $80,500 for a Gustav Stickley forged iron table lamp, No. 755, with four-sided base and shaft, hammered copper, amber hammered-glass shade, pendant amber glass squares, 35½ x 27 inches.

Tiffany chandelier: $365,900 for a "flowering bouquet" leaded glass and bronze chandelier by Tiffany Studios, c.1910, with beaded rims, 11 x 28½ inches.

MISCELLANEOUS

Candy container: $22,425 for a tin and glass Kaleidoscope candy container, glass cylinder set vertically on a tin base, with a crank on the base that revolves the cylinder when turned, red and cream "Moving Pictures" decal with directions for use, "By West Bros. & Co., Grapeville, Pa.," c.1913, 6¾ x 2¾ in.

Candy container, Statue of Liberty: $7,975 for a Statue of Liberty candy container with gold painted lead figure on glass container, 5¾ inches.

Cash register, floor model: $11,000 for a restored NCR floor model "542-4F" cash register, with receipt writer, c.1910.

Mickey Mouse figure: $690,000 for a solid gold Mickey Mouse figure standing 2 feet tall, weighing 1,500 ounces (93 pounds, 12 ounces).

Pennsylvania stove plate: $12,375 for a Mary Anne Furnace Pennsylvania stove plate with Dutch-style tulips and the names George Ross and George Stevenson (Ross was a signer of the Declaration of Independence), dated 1763.

Shaker garment hanger: $18,700 for a cherry Shaker garment hanger, stamped on both sides "M.E.T. 1864," carved by Mary E. Todd (1852-1881), 7 x 12½ x ⅜ inches.

Slot machine, floor model: $88,000 for a restored Caille 5¢ floor model "Roulette" slot machine, mahogany case, c.1904 (less than ten are known to exist).

Tiffany copper vase: $276,300 for an enameled Tiffany copper vase, with wisteria vines and seed pods in relief, c.1901, 9½ in.

MUSIC

Classical guitar: $93,210 for a 1936 Hermann Hauser classical guitar.
Victor Victrola: $71,875 for a Victor Victrola floor model, inlaid allover in the Moorish style.

PAPER

Circus poster: $35,100 for a Barnum, Bailey & Hutchinson color-lithograph poster of Jumbo the elephant striding through London Zoo, a howdah strapped to his back and filled with children, led by a well-dressed Victorian gentleman, with the caption "The Largest Living Beast, The Children's Mute Friend, The Most Universal Favorite," along with a data sheet, c.1882, 40 x 30 inches.
Orville Wright poster: $19,550 for a Hans Rudi Erdt Wright/Flugvorführungen poster, Berlin, 1909, advertising Orville Wright's Model A bi-plane flying exhibition over Tempelhof Field in Berlin.
Scottish travel poster: $32,783 (£21,150) for a Scottish color-lithograph travel poster, by Henry George Gawthorn, "St Andrews, The Home of the Royal & Ancient Game," 1924, 40 x 50 inches.

PHOTOGRAPHY

Fred Thompson hand-colored lithograph: $880 for a Fred Thompson hand-colored lithograph, *Monument Square in 1869*, signed, matted, and framed, c.1905, 11 x 14 inches.
Fred Thompson hand-colored photograph: $743 for the rare Fred Thompson hand-colored photograph, *Faithful Oxen*, picturing a farmer and oxen, signed, matted, and framed, c.1910, 10 x 12 inches.

POLITICAL

Lincoln Banner: $124,000 for an 1864 Abraham Lincoln banner, focusing on slavery and the Emancipation Proclamation, depicting kneeling male and female slaves, 6 x 6 feet.

POTTERY & PORCELAIN

Charles Volkmar plaque: $8,625 for a Charles Volkmar plaque painted in barbotine with mallard ducks and a landscape of trees by a river, gilded frame, signed Chas. Volkmar, c.1880, 9¼ x 16 inches.
Clarice Cliff plate: $64,200 for a Clarice Cliff May Avenue pattern charger with printed marks and strong colors, 18 inches.
George Ohr teapot: $55,812 for a George Ohr teapot, red and pink on amber, 12½ inches.
Miniature spatterware cup and saucer: $16,100 for a miniature red, blue, green, and yellow rainbow spatterware cup and saucer in a drape pattern.
Sleeping lamb pottery doorstop—rare form: $58,000 for a Shenandoah Valley earthenware polychrome-glazed sleeping lamb molded doorstop

with lead, manganese, and copper glaze over a slip wash, 3¼ inches high x 12 inches long.

Spatterware cup and saucer: $24,150 for a spatterware cup and saucer in yellow, blue, red, and green rainbow swirl pattern.

Willson & Co. stoneware pitcher: $28,600 for a rare 2-gallon stoneware pitcher decorated with dark blue daisies and signed by the maker, "T.H. Willson & Co., Harrisburg, Pa.," 14½ inches.

Wright Teco vase: $250,000 for a Teco vase designed by Frank Lloyd Wright for Unity Temple, in the form of a skyscraper, 29½ inches.

SPORTS

Heddon Dowagiac casting bait: $17,600 for a 1903 model Heddon "Dowagiac" casting bait in original picture box, with brass cup, tail cap, and friction collar, 4⅛ inches.

Heddon wooden lure: $31,857 for a rare Heddon wooden bronze-orange fishing lure, with glass eyes, 5 inches long.

Soccer ball (football): $49,350 (£32,900) for the soccer ball used for the F.A. (Football Association) Cup final held at The Oval in 1888 when West Bromwich Albion defeated Preston North End 2-1; after the game, the segmented leather ball was gilded, painted, and inscribed "The Great Victory."

TOOL

Plow plane: $64,900 for an Israel White three-arm plow plane, with original paper label with Israel White imprint and serial number 138.

Wrench: $3,520 for a pre-Civil War quick-adjust nut wrench by E.S. Scripture, New Haven, Connecticut, marked with maker's name and patent date April 13, 1858.

TOYS

Lionel girl's train set: $16,240 for a 1957 Lionel No. 1587S girl's train set, boxed, including pink steam locomotive, tender, and gondola.

A NOTE TO COLLECTORS

You already know this is a great price guide for all sorts of antiques and collectibles. Each entry is current, every picture is new, all prices are accurate.

But in the collecting world, things change quickly. Important sales produce new record prices. Fakes appear. Rarities are discovered. To keep up with these developments, read *Kovels on Antiques and Collectibles*, a monthly newsletter with up-to-date information on collecting. It is filled with color photographs, about forty to an issue. The newsletter reports prices, trends, auction results, Internet sales, and other pertinent news for collectors *as it happens*. For a free sample of *Kovels on Antiques and Collectibles*, fill out and mail the postage-paid postcard at the back of this book. We also have a FREE informational website that gives pricing information, lists of important publications and sources for collectors, and excerpts from our newsletter. Visit www.kovels.com to learn more.

KEEP READING—
HOW TO USE THIS BOOK

There are a few rules for using this book. Each listing is arranged in the following manner: CATEGORY (such as Pressed Glass), OBJECT (such as vase), DESCRIPTION (information about size, age, color, and pattern). Some types of glass, pottery, and silver are exceptions to this rule. These are listed CATEGORY, PATTERN, OBJECT, DESCRIPTION. All items are presumed to be in good condition and undamaged, unless otherwise noted. If a maker's name is easily recognized, like Gustav Stickley, we include it near the beginning of the entry. If the maker is obscure, the name may be at the end. Because the descriptions are part of actual reports, we do not edit to make everything consistent in each category.

Many of the general glass entries are in special categories: Glass-Art, Glass-Blown, Glass-Contemporary, Glass-Midcentury, and Glass-Venetian. Major glass factories are still listed under the factory names, and well-known types of glass, such as cut, pressed, Depression, Carnival, etc., can be found in their own categories. The silver listings are also different. You will find silver flatware in either Silver Flatware Plated or Silver Flatware Sterling. You will also find a section for Silver Plate, which includes coffeepots, and other plated pieces. Solid or sterling silver is listed by country, so look for Silver-American, Silver-English, etc. Silver jewelry is listed under jewelry. Most pottery or porcelain is listed by factory name, such as Weller; or by item, such as Calendar Plate; or in sections like Dinnerware or Kitchen; or in a special section, Pottery-Art, Pottery-Contemporary, Pottery-Midcentury, etc.

Sometimes we make arbitrary decisions based on the number of entries or the amount of interest in a subject. Fishing has its own category, but hunting is part of the larger category called Sports. We have eliminated all guns except toys. It is not legal to sell weapons without a special license, so guns are not part of the general antiques market. Airguns, BB guns, rocket guns, and others are listed in the "Toy" section. Several idiosyncrasies of style appear because the book is printed by computer. Everything is listed according to the computer alphabetizing system. All numerals are before all letters; thus "2" comes before "A."

We made several editorial decisions. A bowl is a "bowl" and not a "dish," unless it is a special dish, such as a pickle dish. A butter dish is a "butter." A salt dish is called a "salt" to differentiate it from a saltshaker. It is always "sugar and creamer," never "creamer and sugar." Political collectors often refer to "pin-backs," the round celluloid or tin pins that are decorated with candidates' names and faces. The word "button" is sometimes used in this book instead of the word "pinback." Of course, the word "button" is also used when referring to the fasteners on clothing. Where one dimension is given, it is the height; or if the object is round, the dimension is the diameter. The height of a picture is listed before width. Glass is clear unless a color is indicated.

Every entry is listed alphabetically, but problems of language remain. Some antiques terms, such as "Sheffield" or "Pratt," have two meanings. Be sure to read the paragraph headings to know the meaning used. All category headings are based on the language of the average person, and we use terms like "mud figures" even if not technically correct.

This book does *not* include price listings of fine art paintings, antiquities, stamps, coins, or most types of books. *Big Little Books* and similar children's books *are* included. Comic books are *not* listed, but original comic art and cels *are* listed in their own categories.

Prices for items pictured can be found in the appropriate category. Look for the matching entry with the abbreviation "Illus."

We *do* use the computer. It alphabetizes, ranges prices, sets type, and does other time-consuming jobs. The last entries are added in June; the book is available in October. But it is human help that finds prices and checks accuracy. We read everything at least three times, sometimes more. We edit more than 60,000 entries to the 50,000 entries found here. We correct spelling, remove incorrect data, write category headings, and decide on new categories. We sometimes make errors. Information in the paragraphs is reviewed and updated each year. This year sixteen new paragraphs and forty-two corrections and additions were made in the category paragraphs.

Prices are from all the United States, Canada, and Europe, converted to U.S. dollars at the rate of exchange prevalent at the time of the sale. The average rate of exchange between June 2002 and June 2003 ranged from $0.65 to $0.75 U.S. to $1 Canadian. Prices are from auctions, shops, Internet sales, and shows. Every price is checked for accuracy, but we are not responsible for errors.

We cannot answer your letters asking for specific price information. But please write if you have any requests for categories to be included in future editions or any corrections to information in the paragraphs or prices.

When you see us at shows and flea markets, please stop and say hello. Don't be surprised if we ask for your suggestions for the next edition of *Kovels' Antiques & Collectibles Price List.* Or you can write to us at P.O. Box 22200-K, Beachwood, Ohio 44122 or visit us at our website, www.kovels.com.

RALPH & TERRY KOVEL
July 2003

ACKNOWLEDGMENTS

We give special thanks to those who helped us with pictures and deeds: Andre Ammelounx; Arte Primitivo; Auction Team Köln; Be-Hold (Larry Gottheim); Bertoia Auctions; Charlton Hall Galleries; Christie's; Collectors Auction Services; Conestoga Auction Co.; Cowan's Historic Americana Auctions; Craftsman Auctions; David Rago Auctions (David Rago & John Sollo); DeFina Auctions; Robert C. Eldred Co.; Fontaine's Auction Gallery; Garth's Auctions; Gary Metz's Muddy River Trading Co.; Glass-Works Auctions; Green Valley Auctions; Ivey-Selkirk Auctioneers; Jackson's International Auctioneers & Appraisers; James D. Julia, Inc.; Lang's Sporting Collectables; MastroNet; McMasters Harris Auction House; Mid-Hudson Galleries; New Orleans Auction Galleries; Northeast Auctions; Pacific Glass Auctions; Phillips, de Pury & Luxembourg; Pook & Pook, Inc.; Randy Inman Auctions; Robert C. Eldred Co.; Robert S. Brunk Auction Services, Inc.; Skinner, Inc.; Smith and Jones, Inc.; Sotheby's; Theriault's; Thomaston Place Auction Galleries; Treadway Gallery; Village Doll and Toy; William Doyle Galleries; Woody's Auctions; Wright Auctions; York Town Auction.

To the others in the antiques trade who knowingly or unknowingly contributed to this book, we say "thank you": A.S. Munn Auction; Aetna Gallery; Aleph-Bet Books; Amazing Visions Unique & Antique; American Social History & Social Movements; American Toys; Anderson Auction; Another Time, Another Place, Inc.; Antique Bottle & Glass Collector; Antique Stove Exchange; Asia House; Autopia Advertising Auctions; Baker's International Antiques & Collectibles; Beatles etc.; Best of Santa Fe; Bill & Joan Lennon; Bill Magee; Bob & Mary Kreimer; Braswells; Brown Auction; Butterfields Auctioneers Corp.; Butterfly Net; Carol Jean Reed; Collection Liquidations Auction; Copake Auctions; Crown Jewels of the Wire; Daguerreian Society Newsletter; Decoys Unlimited, Inc.; Du Mouchelle's Art Galleries Co.; Earlip Art Glass; El Alcazar Antiques; Faganarms, Inc.; Fiesta Collector's Club; Forever Heisey; Frank H. Boos Gallery; Frankoma Family Collectors Association; Freeman's (Samuel T. Freeman & Co.); Gisela Antiques; Glass from the Past; Gray Horse Emporium; Heisey Collectors of America; Henry Peirce Auctioneers; Hobstar; Hoosier Peddler; Hopalong Cassidy Fan Club; Hummel Collector's Club; Jackson & Wickliffe Auctioneers; James Hagenbuch Auctions; Jean Parrett; John Woytowicz; June Burke; Just Kids Nostalgia; Kay Fries; Kevin L. Shea; Kratzer Living Estate Auction; Lin's Antiques & Collectibles; Lloyd Ralston Gallery; Longbrook Antiques; Manhattan Art & Antiques Center; Manion's International Auction House; Maritime Antiques Auction; Mary Baker; Mary Jane & Don Carver Jr.; McCoy Lovers; McMurray Antiques & Auctions; Mickey Reichel; Mimi's Antiques; Monsen and Baer, Inc.; Mostly Heisey; Musical Box Society International; Nancy Alderson; Naomi Bornstein; National Cambridge Collectors, Inc.; National Sheet Music Society; Nita Kadwell; Oak Grove Antiques; Old Barn Auction; Old World Auctions; The Olde Touch; One of a Kind Antiques; Paper Collectors'

Marketplace; Past Time Pleasures; Phoenix Militaria Corp.; Phyllis Deal; Political Bandwagon; R.O. Schmitt Fine Arts; Red Barn Antiques; Red Wing Collectors Society; Reichel Auction Center; Rex Stark Americana; Reyne Gallery; Rich Penn Country Store and Advertising Auction (Fred Van Metre); Richard Opfer Auctioneering; Ron Smith; S. Campbell; S.J.'s Antiques & Collectibles; Scott J. Winslow Associates, Inc.; Shades of the Past by Nan; Shirley Dunbar; Showcase Antique Center; Sloan's Auctioneers & Appraisers; Smith House Toys; Society of Inkwell Collectors; Southern Folk Pottery Auction; Sweeney's Emporium; Sweet Inspiration; Tea Leaf Club International; Team's Tiffany Treasures; Three G Hobbies; TIAS; Toy Shop; Tradewinds Antiques; Trocadero; Wayne & Phyllis Hilt; Weschler's & Son Inc.; Winter Associates, Inc.; Yesterday for Tomorrow; Yesterday's South, Inc.

This year our books were moved to a different division of Random House, Random House Reference. That meant almost all new people were working on the book. We thank all of them for working through the peculiar ways we write a price book. Our longtime editor, Dorothy Harris, who moved with us, guided the book through all of its stages and made sure it was better than ever and on time. Jeanne Kramer, publisher; Bonnie Ammer, president and publisher of Random House Information Group; Sheryl Stebbins, publisher of Value Publishing; Beth Levy, managing editor; Pat Ehresmann and Lisa Montebello, production; and Tigist Getachew and Nora Rosansky, interior and cover art, all worked together to make the final book. Merri Ann Morrell at Precision Graphics once again solved the problems of forcing the data to create perfect, printed pages and clear photographs.

The hard work of recording prices, assembling pictures and information, checking and rechecking entries for accuracy and all the other details is done by our staff first. We thank Carmie Amata, Debbie Bedell, Linda Coulter, Grace DeFrancisco, Doris Gerbitz, Laura Goldberg, Marcia Goldberg, Evelyn Hayes, Katie Carrick, Kim Kovel, Liz Lillis, Heidi Makela, Tina McBean, Sara Puliafico, Nancy Saada, Julie Seaman, June Smith, Edie Smrekar, Cherrie Smrekar, and Katie Smrekar. The pictures seem to require new technology every year. Benjamin Margalit took many of the photographs and managed to show the details and styles that interest collectors. Karen Kneisley has conquered the problems of getting and reproducing pictures that come in all forms, from black and white glossies to digital images. But the person who keeps us all on schedule, reads and rereads the copy, keeps up-to-date information for the paragraphs, finds and solves hundreds of unexpected problems, and works around the computer glitches is Gay Hunter. This is her 23rd book and her knowledge is encyclopedic. We thank all of them because we know that even though our names are on the book, we couldn't do it without their expertise.

THIRTY-SIXTH EDITION

KOVELS'
ANTIQUES
& COLLECTIBLES
PRICE LIST

A. WALTER made pate-de-verre glass under contract at the Daum glassworks from 1908 to 1914. He started his own firm in Nancy, France, in 1919. Pieces made before 1914 are signed *Daum, Nancy* with a cross. After 1919 the signature is *A. Walter Nancy*.

Dish, Orange & Yellow, Amethyst Beetle Crawling Across, Signed, 5 1/2 In.	1568.00
Dish, Orange & Yellow, Green Lizard On Side, Signed, 3 x 6 3/4 In.	4144.00
Dish, Turquoise & Yellow, Glass Fish Crisscross, 2 1/2 x 5 1/2 In.	4480.00
Figurine, Chickadees, Lime Green, Marked, Pair	978.00
Paperweight, Butterfly, Multicolored, Oval Base, 4 x 1 1/2 In.	3000.00
Vase, Green Trees, Matte Green & Brown Ground, Cylindrical, Signed, 6 1/2 In.	1008.00
Vase, Polychrome, Trailing Leafy Vines, Yellow Ground, c.1900, 6 1/2 In.	690.00

ABC plates, or children's alphabet plates, were most popular from 1780 to 1860, but are still being made. The letters on the plate were meant as teaching aids for children learning to read. The plates were made of pottery, porcelain, metal, or glass. Mugs and other items were also made with alphabet decorations.

Pitcher, Schoolhouse, Alphabet Border, Verse, 6 1/4 In.	154.00
Plate, 2 Children In Garden, Green Transfer, Staffordshire, 6 In.	75.00
Plate, 3 Children & Dog, Embossed, Black, Green & Red, Staffordshire, 6 In.	125.00
Plate, Alphabet & Braille Letters, Green Glaze, Dog Center, c.1930, 6 In.	40.00
Plate, Cock Robin, Alphabet, 8 1/2 In.	120.00
Plate, Fox Hunt, White, Blue, 7 1/4 In.	285.00
Plate, Steeplechase, Diamond Center, White, Blue, 7 1/4 In.	247.00
Plate, The Fall, Polychrome, 8 1/4 In.	195.00
Plate, Village Blacksmith, Raised Alphabet Border, c.1820, 5 1/8 In.	150.00
Plate, Young Sergeant, Polychrome, Staffordshire, 8 1/2 In.	250.00

ABINGDON POTTERY was established in 1908 by Raymond E. Bidwell as the Abingdon Sanitary Manufacturing Company. The company started making art pottery in 1934. The factory ceased production of art pottery in 1950.

Bowl, Centerpiece, White, Sea Green, Marked, 15 x 9 x 2 3/4 In.	35.00
Bowl, Shell, Sea Green, Embossed, Marked, c.1940-1948, 11 1/4 x 8 In.	35.00
Bowl, Turquoise, 2 Handles, No. 632, 14 In.	45.00
Candlestick, White Matte Glaze, Marked, c.1940, 4 1/4 x 5 1/2 In., Pair	25.00
Cookie Jar, Jack-In-The-Box	250.00
Cookie Jar, Mammy, Little Old Lady, Marked, 9 In.	595.00
Planter, Fan Shape, Bow, Marked, Incised No. 484	40.00
Vase, Baden, Flowers, Gold Trim, Marked, c.1940-1948, 8 3/4 In.	30.00
Vase, Boyne, Peach, 9 In.	35.00
Vase, Delphite Blue, 2 Handles, Original Label, c.1935, 9 1/2 In.	45.00
Vase, Green, Ribbed, Ornate Handles, 8 3/4 In.	26.00
Vase, Pink, No. 312, 6 In.	25.00
Vase, Star Flower, Pink Cameo, No. 560, 6 1/4 x 6 1/4 In.	125.00
Vase, Tan, Salmon, 10 3/4 In.	30.00
Vase, White, Flared Top, 2 Handles, 7 In.	29.00
Vase, Yellow Glaze, White, Scroll Handles, Stamped, 8 1/4 x 4 In.	35.00
Vase, Yellow Matte Glaze, 4 x 5 In.	35.00

ADAMS china was made by William Adams and Sons of Staffordshire, England. The firm was founded in 1769 and became part of the Wedgwood Group in 1966. The name "Adams" appeared on various items through 1998. All types of tablewares and useful wares were made. Other pieces of Adams may be found listed under Flow Blue and Tea Leaf Ironstone.

Bowl, Flowers, Pearlware, Blue, White Transfer, c.1825, 9 1/2 x 4 In.	950.00
Cup & Saucer, Green Transfer, Handleless, c.1830	120.00
Cup & Saucer, Jeddo, Black Transfer, Handleless, c.1830-1840	125.00
Footbath, Maxstoke Castle, Blue, Leaves, Scrolled Border, c.1825, 20 x 9 x 14 In.	7200.00
Jug, Palestine, Damascus, Dark Pink, Feathery Handle, Red, White Transfer, 1835, 6 In.	275.00
Pepper Pot, Basket Of Flowers, Chinese Figure, Pearlware, Blue, White, c.1825, 4 1/2 In.	475.00

Pitcher, Bologna, Purple, c.1830, 11 In. 550.00
Pitcher, Palestine, Embossed Fruit, Flowers, Scallops, Brown Transfer, c.1836, 9 1/4 In. . . 475.00
Plate, Andalusia, Impressed, Green Transfer, c.1835, 10 1/2 In. 275.00
Plate, Andalusia, Man, Woman On Horseback, Dogs, Red, White Transfer, c.1830, 8 In. . 165.00
Plate, Andalusia, Pearlware, Green & White Transfer, c.1830, 8 1/4 In. 265.00
Plate, Andalusia, Spain, People, Horses, Dogs, Red, White Transfer, 1830s, 9 1/2 In. 225.00
Plate, Andalusia, Woman On Horse, Pearlware, Red, White Transfer, c.1830, 7 In. 125.00
Plate, Bamborough Castle, Cobalt Blue, Impressed, c.1804-1819, 10 1/4 In., 2 Piece 400.00
Plate, Beckenham Place, Kent, Cobalt Blue, c.1804-1840, 6 In. 265.00
Plate, Caledonia, Hunter In Kilt, Scottish Dress, Red, Green Transfer, c.1835, 10 3/4 In. . 345.00
Plate, Cattskill Mountain House, Women, Eagle, Flowers, Swirls, Pink, c.1830, 10 1/2 In. 225.00
Plate, Conway, New Hampshire, Pink, c.1804-1819, 9 In. 195.00
Plate, Cupids, Dark Blue, Roses, Ribbons, Pearlware, c.1825, 10 In. 375.00
Plate, English Scene, Cattle, Flower Border, 6 In. 35.00
Plate, Indian, Pink Transfer, Impressed, c.1830, 9 In., 2 Piece 175.00
Plate, Mitchell & Freeman's China & Glass Warehouse, Boston, Stoke, 1827, 10 1/4 In. . . 470.00
Plate, Monte Video, Connecticut, Red, White Transfer, 7 In. 85.00
Plate, Moulin Surlamarne Acharenton, Cobalt Blue, c.1804-1819, 9 1/8 In. 400.00
Plate, Mt. Vernon, Cobalt Blue, c.1896-1917, 10 1/4 In. 395.00
Plate, Palestine, Man On Horseback Talking To Men, Gazebo, Red, c.1835, 9 1/2 In. 125.00
Plate, Persia, 3 Men & Woman Sit, Stand Near Trees, Blue Transfer, 1819-1960, 9 1/4 In. 95.00
Plate, Railroad Scene, St. Clair Tunnel, Cobalt Blue, Impressed, c.1896-1917, 10 1/2 In. . 250.00
Plate, Villa In Regent's Park, London, 3 Figures, Dog, 1770-1820, 9 In. . . . . .180.00 to 345.00
Platter, Persia No. 2, 3 Figures On River Banks, Blue Transfer, 1819-1864, 13 x 10 In. . . 195.00
Platter, Persia, 3 Figures On River Bank, Stylized Flowers, Blue, 1850s, 15 1/2 x 12 In. . 225.00
Platter, Scottish Stag-Hunting, Caledonia, Red Transfer, 15 x 12 In. 510.00
Relish, Persia, Sailboats, Mountains, Blue Transfer, 1819-1864, 9 x 5 In. 125.00
Teapot, Palestine, Red Transfer, 1836-1864, 12 1/2 x 8 In. 650.00

ADVERTISING containers and products sold in the old country store are now all collectibles. These stores, with the crackers in a barrel and a potbellied stove, are a symbol of an earlier, less hectic time. Listed here are many of the advertising items. Other similar pieces may be found under the product name, such as Planters Peanuts. We have tried to list items in the logical places, so large store fixtures will be found under the Architectural category, enameled tin dishes under Graniteware, paper items in the Paper category, etc. Store fixtures, cases, and other items that have no advertising as part of the decoration are listed in the Store category.

Ashtray, Castles Ice Cream, China, Hexagon, c.1940, 4 1/2 x 7 1/2 In. 12.00
Ashtray, Chicken Charlie, Figure, Plaster, Glass, c.1960, 8 x 4 x 4 1/2 In. 65.00
Ashtray, McDonald's, Metal, Green, Raised Section, 1970, 3 1/2 x 6 In. 5.00
Ashtray, Michelin, Mr. Bib, Brown, White, Plastic, 5 1/2 x 5 In. 65.00
Ashtray, N. Brezner & Co., Mr. Cobbleright, Composition, Wood Base, c.1940, 5 In. 48.00
Ashtray, Pfaulder, Graniteware, Cobalt Blue, 5 1/2 x 1 1/2 In. 45.00
Ashtray, Piedmont Cigarettes, Green Background, Package Of Cigarettes, 8 1/4 In. 175.00
Ashtray, Richmond Gem Cigarettes, Glass, 5 1/2 x 3 5/8 x 1 In. 121.00
Ashtray Stand, Moxie Maid, Blue Dress, Painted Wood, Copper Ashtray, 28 In. 143.00
Badge, Reddy Kilowatt, People's Choice, Cello, Brass, c.1950, 4 In. 65.00
Banner, Angostura Bitters, Woman Served Bitters By Cherubs, 12 1/2 x 29 In. 2645.00
Banner, Arbuckle's Coffee, Cloth, Plastic Cover, 21 3/4 x 57 In. 110.00
Banner, Bill Anthony 5 Cent Cigars, Battleship Maine, Nautical Flags, 18 x 46 In. 1000.00
Banner, Cow Brand Baking Soda, Black & White Hunting Dog, Oilcloth, 21 x 30 In. 220.00
Banner, Enjoy Olympia Beer, It's The Water, Velveteen, 1940s, 10 x 11 In. 50.00
Banner, Everybody Shoots Better With A Winchester, Paper, Tube, 72 x 24 In. 187.00
Banner, Levi's, Cowboys, America's Finest Jeans, Corrugated, 1960s, 93 x 34 In. 745.00
Banner, Remington UMC, Indians Hunt Buffalo, Canvas, c.1910, 28 x 56 In. 4000.00
Banner, Schleegers Cigars, Cloth, Frame, 14 x 38 In. 44.00
Barrel, Alpine Bitters, Silver Plate, Spigot, 10 1/2 In. 275.00
Barrel, Cover, Dr. Hess Stock Tonic, Wooden, Label, 21 In. 14.00
Barrel, Cover, Tone Bros. Coffee, Des Moines, Iowa, Wooden, 25 In. 55.00
Bell, Counter, Perfect Tea & Coffee Co., Brass, Engraved, Gadrooned Edge, 8 In. 259.00
Bin, A & P Coffee, Bulk, Wooden, Painted Red 358.00

Bin, Baked Goods, Painted, Wooden, Octagonal, marked MMW, 11 x 12 In. 92.00
Bin, Beech-Nut Chewing Tobacco, Quality Made It Famous, 8 3/4 x 10 x 8 In. 129.00
Bin, Cremo Cones, Tin Lithograph, Hinged Lid, 17 In. 176.00
Bin, Griswolds, Cream Of Tartar, OK Brand, 10 x 8 x 6 1/2 In. 66.00
Bin, McLaughlin, Coffee, Kept Fresh, Metal, Glass, 3 Sections, Marquee, Red, 38 In. 154.00
Bin, Polar Bear Tobacco, Tin Lithograph, Hinged Lid, 18 In. 210.00
Bin, Sweet Cuba Tobacco, Tin Lithograph, Hinged Lid, Countertop, 9 1/2 In. 105.00
Blotter, Blue Bird Soda, Baseball Player, Wilson Equipment 4.00
Blotter, Clark Twins, Highest Quality, Great Sellers, Cardboard, 4 x 9 1/4 In. 110.00
Blotter, Diamond Fast Color Eyelets, Girl, Flowers, c.1900, 3 1/4 x 6 1/2 In. 20.00
Blotter, Green River Whiskey, Blots Out All Your Troubles, 1899 .... 28.00
Blotter, Texaco Motor Oil, Mechanic & Car, Paperboard, Lithograph, 6 x 3 1/2 In. 120.00
Books may be included in the Paper category.
Booklet, Regal Shoes, Regal Rhymes, c.1900, 3 1/2 x 6 1/2 In., 12 Pages 12.00
Booklet, Ronald McDonald, Travel Fun, Color, c.1970, 8 x 11 In., 12 Pages 15.00
Booklet, Wrigley's Spearmint Gum, Mother Goose, Spearman, 1915, 4 x 6 In., 24 Pages . 12.00
Bottles are listed in their own category.
Bottle Carrier, Welch's Grape Juice, Double As Doodyville Buildings, 4 Bottles 135.00
Bottle Openers are listed in their own category.
Bowl, Reddy Kilowatt, Ceramic, Syracuse China, c.1960, 6 1/2 x 1 3/4 In. 24.00
Bowl, Vita B, China, White, Blue, c.1930, 6 x 6 x 1 1/2 In. 8.00
Box, see also Box category.
Box, Atwood's LF Bitters, H.H. Hay Co., Wood, 10 1/2 x 8 x 7 1/2 In. 66.00
Box, Bear Brand Hosiery, Bear With Hosiery, 7 x 9 x 3 In. 149.00
Box, Cereal, Kellogg's, Sugar Smacks, Ringling Clown Paul Jung, 1953 .... 200.00
Box, Cigar, Big Run, Buck Ewing, Buffalo Bill & 4 Athletes, Color Label 1100.00
Box, Cigar, Cover, Pietra Dura, Black, Inlaid Smoking Accessories, 8 1/2 x 6 In. 633.00
Box, Cigar, Flying Dude, Wood, Passenger Train, 11 x 6 5/8 In. 229.00
Box, Cigar, Jack Horner, Wood, Label Inside, 1880s, 9 1/4 x 8 5/8 In. 145.00
Box, Cigar, Jenny Lind, Havana Cigars 175.00
Box, Cigar, Montana Sport, 2 For 25 Cents, 7 1/2 x 5 1/2 x 3 1/2 In. 55.00
Box, Cigar, Morning Sambos, 3 x 4 x 3 In. 200.00
Box, Cigar, Span Am, Dewey & Sampson, Color Label, Black 65.00
Box, Compound Oxygen Treatment, Wood, Dovetailed, 14 x 8 x 5 1/2 In. 60.00
Box, Dr. Herrick's Sugar Coated Pills, Sealed, Wood, Oval, 2 In. 154.00
Box, Dr. Strong's Vegetable Stomach Pills, Wood, Sealed, Wrapper, 2 1/4 In. 60.00
Box, Dwinell-Wright Coffee Co., Pine, 15 x 15 x 19 In. 80.00
Box, Fairbanks Fairy Soap, Wood, 16 x 8 1/2 x 17 In. 120.00
Box, Fountain Of Youth Mineral Crystals, Cardboard, Woman, Tennis, 5 x 3 x 2 In. 30.00
Box, Fun-To-Wash Soap, Washing Powder, Black Mammy, c.1910 .... 34.00
Box, Gibbs Hollow Suppositories, Wood, Dovetailed, Slide Lid, 6 x 4 1/2 In. 220.00
Box, Glycerin Tablets For The Teeth, Cardboard, 2 1/2 x 1 1/2 In. 39.00
Box, Hershey, Honeybar 2 For 5 Cents, Cardboard, 9 x 5 x 2 In. 139.00
Box, Indian Girl Oats, Cardboard, Round, 9 5/8 x 5 3/8 In. 1265.00
Box, Jos. A. Goddard & Co. Coffee, Muncie, Ind., Red Paint, Black Star, 50 Lb. 800.00
Box, Lash's Tonic Laxative Bitters, Wood, 13 x 10 x 10 1/2 In. 45.00
Box, Lion Coffee, Woolson Spice Co., Toledo, Ohio, Wood, 29 x 19 x 16 In. 55.00
Box, Marshmallow, Kraft, Star Trek, Plastic, 1989, 7 In. 18.00
Box, Mohican Brand Mince Meat, Indian, 2 1/2 x 3 3/4 x 1 3/4 In. 65.00
Box, Mother's Oats, Wood, Round, Chicago 39.00
Box, Pratts Poultry Regulator, Sealed, Color, Sample, 2 1/2 x 4 1/2 In. 85.00
Box, Prof. Hamilton's Sugar Coated Root & Plant Pills, Contents, Wood, Oval, 2 In. 155.00
Box, Sage Brush Hair Tonic, Nature's Own Remedy, Wood, 13 x 9 x 10 In. 95.00
Box, Santa Claus Soap, Fairbanks, 100 Bars, Wood, 10 1/4 x 14 x 21 1/4 In. 440.00
Box, Sawyers Laundry Bluing, Display, Wood, 1880s, 11 x 9 7/8 In. 105.00
Box, Seed Packet, Ferry Morse Seed Co., Box, 27 x 12 x 17 In. ....230.00 to 295.00
Box, Seed, D.M. Ferry & Co., Wood, Label Under Lid, 14 x 9 In. 45.00
Box, Shredded Wheat, Cereal, Lithograph, c.1920, 5 3/4 x 7 1/2 x 4 In. 106.00
Box, Tobacco, Gold Shore, Man On Flying Horse, 4 1/4 x 7 In. 85.00
Box, Tobacco, Solace, Cardboard, Stone Lithograph, 1880, 12 x 11 x 8 In. 205.00
Box, True's Elixir, The Old Standard, Wood, 5 1/4 x 6 1/2 x 6 1/2 In. 50.00
Box, Wm. Radam's Microbe Killer Cures All, Wood, 18 x 12 x 8 In. 165.00
Box, Wood Box Stove Polish, Lithograph, 17 x 11 1/2 In. 285.00

Box, Wrigley's Pepsin Chewing Gum, Cardboard, 3 1/4 x 8 In. 195.00
Box, Yager's Cream Chloroform Liniment For Man Or Beast, Wood, 13 x 9 x 8 In. 209.00
Broom Holder, DeLaval Cream Separators, Tin Lithograph, 3 1/2 In. 650.00
Broom Holder, Fresh Bond Bread, Metal Sign, 2 Sides, 19 x 39 In. 220.00
Cabinet, Cadbury's Chocolate, 2 Glass Shelves, Milk Glass, 32 x 28 x 17 In. 520.00
Cabinet, California Fruit Gum, Etched Carved Glass, Oak Frame, 9 1/2 x 17 In. 580.00
Cabinet, Carr & Co. Biscuits, Mahogany, 3 Glass Doors, 53 x 42 In. 690.00
Cabinet, Condon Bros. Cigars, Etched Cigars, Curved Glass, 11 1/2 x 21 In. 635.00
Cabinet, Diamond Dyes, Children With Balloon, Tin Lithograph, Embossed, 24 In. 1045.00
Cabinet, Diamond Dyes, Evolution Of Women, Tin Lithograph, 30 In. ....660.00 to 1035.00
Cabinet, Diamond Dyes, Governess, c.1906, 23 x 30 x 10 In. 1035.00
Cabinet, Diamond Dyes, Red Haired Fairy, Wooden, Tin Lithograph Panel, 30 In. 4070.00
Cabinet, Diamond Dyes, Washer Woman, Wooden, Tin Lithograph Panel, 30 In. 2915.00
Cabinet, Dr. Daniels' Animal Medicines, Oak, Tin Lithograph, Embossed, 29 In. 1870.00
Cabinet, Dr. Daniels' Veterinary Medicines, Doctor, Oak, Tin, 21 x 28 In. ......1650.00 to 2587.00
Cabinet, Dr. Meyers' Veterinary Medicines, Ash, Oak, Tin Lithograph Panel, 28 In. 1980.00
Cabinet, Hanfords Balm Of Myrrh, Oak, 2 Shelves, 24 In. 495.00
Cabinet, Harris Flavoring Extracts, Oak, Adjustable Shelves, 56 In. 990.00
Cabinet, Harvard Cigars, Pippins 5 Cents, Bell, Glass Top, 4 x 7 1/4 x 11 In. 140.00
Cabinet, Humphrey's Homeopathic, Masonite, 2 Doors, 11 x 11 In. 190.00
Cabinet, Humphrey's Specifics, 35 Remedies, Tin, 21 1/2 x 28 x 7 In. 575.00
Cabinet, Keen Kutter, Etched Emblem, Scissors, Shears, Revolving, 31 In. 1265.00
Cabinet, Lundborg Perfumes, Curved Etched Glass, Metal Frame, 7 x 17 In. 1430.00
Cabinet, Munyon's Homeopathic Remedies, Oak, Tin Price List, 17 x 24 In. 771.00
Cabinet, New York Knife Co., Etched Arm, Hammer, 13 x 18 In. 770.00
Cabinet, Nuns Needles, Slant Front, Mahogany, Glass, 11 1/4 x 7 1/2 In. 80.00
Cabinet, Perfection Dye, Chestnut, Tin Lithograph Insert, 2 Doors, 24 In. 578.00
Cabinet, Pratt's Veterinary Remedies, Oak, Tin Lithograph Panel, 33 x 17 x 7 In. 3245.00
Cabinet, Putnam Dye, Hinged Front, Contents, Tin Lithograph, 18 3/4 x 14 1/2 In. 310.00
Cabinet, Ribbon, H. Pauk & Sons, St. Louis, Wood, Glass, 37 In. 2420.00
Cabinet, Rit Dye, Cake, Flakes Or Powdered, 10 Cents, Tin Lithograph, 14 x 11 In. 190.00
Cabinet, Sophomore Cigar, Mahogany, Mechanical, Glass Lift Front, Trays, Counter 635.00
Cabinet, Spice, French's Pure Spices, Tin, 4 Back-To-Back Sections, 24 In. 2530.00
Cabinet, Spool, Belding's Silk, Oak, Glass Door Over 3 Drawers, Revolves 2420.00
Cabinet, Spool, Chadwick's, Ash, 9 Drawers, Black Glass Fronts 1128.00
Cabinet, Spool, Clark's O.N.T. Spool Cotton, Walnut, 2 Drawers, Ruby Glass Inserts 250.00
Cabinet, Spool, Clark's O.N.T., Oak, 4 Drawers, Red Glass Inserts, 24 x 15 In. 880.00
Cabinet, Spool, Clark's O.N.T., Oak, 6 Drawers, Red Glass Letters, 22 x 29 In. . .750.00 to 1155.00
Cabinet, Spool, Clark's Spool Cotton, 5 Over 2 Drawers, Ruby Glass Inserts 2750.00
Cabinet, Spool, Corticelli, 30 Drawers, Glass Front, 43 x 41 1/2 x 17 In. 2875.00
Cabinet, Spool, Crowley's, Oak, 6 Drawers, Red Glass Inserts, 22 x 12 In. 605.00
Cabinet, Spool, Heminway & Sons, Oak, 6 Drawers, Red Glass Inserts, 30 x 17 In. 880.00
Cabinet, Spool, J. & P. Coats', Oak, 4 Drawers, Inkwell For Writing, Counter 400.00
Cabinet, Spool, John Clark Jr., Oak, 9 Drawers, 25 1/2 x 22 In. 1320.00
Cabinet, Spool, Merrick's Cotton, Oak, Oval, Glass Ends, Mirrors, Drawer, 31 In. 3630.00
Cabinet, Spool, Richardson Silk, 7 Drawers, Mirrored Door, Clock Gallery 1705.00
Cabinet, Spool, Star Braid, 2 Glass Doors, 1 Drawer, Philadelphia, Late 1800s 434.00
Cabinet, Spool, Willimantic, Walnut, Dovetailed Drawers, Embossed Panels, 24 In. 825.00
Cabinet, Standard Paper Co., Milwaukee, Pull-Drawer, File, Wooden, 14 x 8 In. 3300.00
Cabinet, Winchester Cutlery & Tool, Oak, Glass Door & Sides, 26 x 17 In. 478.00
Cabinet, Zeno Gum, Slant Front, Stamped Wood Marquee, 8 In. 605.00
Calendars are listed in their own category.
Can, Mobiloil Aero, Gold Band, Qt. 209.00
Can, Texaco Outboard Gear Oil, Gulls, Speedboats, 2 Lb., 6 3/8 x 4 1/4 x 2 3/4 In. 120.00
Can, Texaco Outboard Motor Oil, Qt., 7 1/2 x 4 1/2 In. 17.00
Canisters, see introductory paragraph to Tins in this category.
Canteen, Bardwell's Root Beer, Stoneware, Dragonfly & Deer Design, 1800, 11 In. 500.00
Cards are listed in the Card category as card, advertising.
Case, Dalton's Sarsaparilla & Nerve Tonic, 12 Unopened Bottles, Boxes 470.00
Case, Display, Wrigley's Gum, Glass Panel, Hinged Door, Shelf, 16 x 10 3/4 x 14 3/4 In. . 150.00
Chair, Piedmont Cigarette, Folding, Wood, Porcelain, 31 1/4 x 16 1/4 x 18 In. 220.00
Chair, Sargent Floor & Furniture Enamel, Spindle Back, Plank Seat, Gilt 635.00
Chalkboard, Betsy Ross Bread, Tin, 28 1/4 x 20 In. 39.00

Chalkboard, Dad's Root Beer, Original Draft, Bottle Cap, Tin, Embossed, 20 x 28 In. 60.00
Chalkboard, Drink Dr Pepper, Tin Over Cardboard, Self-Framed, 17 1/4 x 23 1/4 In. 176.00
Chalkboard, Enjoy Squirt, Self-Framed, 1959, 28 x 19 3/4 In. 90.00
Chalkboard, Jersey Maid Dairy Products Menu, 23 3/4 x 16 In. 90.00
Chalkboard, Kickapoo Joy Juice, Speshuls, Tin, Embossed, 30 x 19 In. 330.00
Chalkboard, Sun Crest Beverages, Tin, Embossed, Self-Framed, 30 x 19 1/2 In. 65.00
Change Purse, Compliments Of First Nation Bank, Three Forks, Mont., Suede, 1909 . . . . 95.00
Change Receiver, see also Tip Tray in this category.
Chopping Block, Trexler's Grocery Store, Salisbury, 28 x 39 x 29 1/2 In. 400.00
Cigar Cutter, Ambrosia, Erie Specialty Co., Cast Iron, Embossed Lettering, 6 x 9 In. 550.00
Cigar Cutter, Hoffman House Bouquet Cigar, Iron, Wood Base, Erie Specialty, 1890 . . . . 440.00
Cigar Cutter, Ottina Cigars, E. Popper & Co., N.Y., 11 1/2 x 5 In. 1100.00
Cigar Cutter, Yocums, Spana-Cuba, Oak Base, 8 1/2 x 5 In. 525.00
Cigarette Case, Kool, Penguin, Metal, 3 1/4 x 2 5/8 In. 150.00
Clocks are listed in their own category.
Coffee Bin, A & P, Greek Key, Red, Fitted Lid, Trexler's Grocery Store, 30 x 18 x 18 In. . 425.00
Cooler, Maxwell House, Iced Tea, Wood Cover 66.00
Cooler, Moxie, Chest, Wheels 800.00
Crayon Set, Dr Pepper, Pad, Eraser, On Card, 1982 . . . . 10.00
Crock, Heinz, Apple Butter, Paper Decal, Engraved, 6 1/2 In. . . . . *Illus* 1155.00
Crock, Heinz, Baked Beans, Brown Glaze, Cover, Electric 116.00
Crock, Heinz, Ketchup, Octagon, Brown Top, Beige Bottom, 7 1/2 In. . . . . *Illus* 550.00
Crock, Heinz, Quince Jelly, Tin, Handle, Paper Decal, 4 1/2 In. . . . . *Illus* 600.00
Crock, Heinz, Raspberry Preserves, Label Shows Mixed Fruit, White Crock, 8 x 14 In. . . . 550.00
Crumb Set, C.F. Berquist & Co. Lumber, Farm Equipment, Tray & Scraper 650.00
Cup, F & F Mold & Die Works Inc., Yogi Bear, Dayton, Ohio, 3 3/8 x 3 3/4 In. 10.00
Decanter, Hamm's Beer, Figural, Bear, Holding Logo, Ceramic, 11 In. 55.00
Dice Roller, Sunshine Cigar, Metal Base, Globe Top, Crazy Dice, Brunhoff, 1890 . . . . 3080.00
Dish, C.T. Heisel Chewing Gum Co., Glass, Embossed, Cleveland, 5 1/2 x 5 1/4 In. 85.00
Dispenser, Boye Needles, Tin Lithograph, Countertop 235.00
Dispenser, Buckeye Root Beer Syrup, Cleveland, Ceramic, 8 1/2 x 12 In. 2090.00
Dispenser, Buckeye Root Beer, Black, Ceramic, 8 1/2 x 16 In. 880.00
Dispenser, Buckeye Syrup, Tree Stump Shape, Ceramic, 8 x 16 In. 525.00
Dispenser, Canada Dry, Frosted Glass, Embossed, Black Milk Glass Base, 12 3/4 In. 130.00
Dispenser, Cherry Smash Syrup, Always Drink Cherry Smash, 1900, 9 x 10 In. 1750.00
Dispenser, Cherry Smash, Ceramic, Painted, Pump, 13 1/2 In. 2420.00
Dispenser, Cigarette, Donkey, Sunshine Valley Pipe Creek Station, Tin, Wood, 10 In. 180.00
Dispenser, Dr. Swett's Root Beer, Ceramic, c.1900, 22 In. 800.00
Dispenser, Dr. Swett's Root Beer, Tree Stump, Boy, 14 1/2 In. 5460.00
Dispenser, Drink Green River, Porcelain, Yellow, Green, 8 x 16 x 10 In. 825.00
Dispenser, Drink Moxie, Milk Glass, Bowl, Spigot, Countertop, 1927, 9 1/2 In. 530.00
Dispenser, Grape Ola Syrup, 5 Cents, Grapes, Purple, Ceramic, 10 x 21 In. 1100.00
Dispenser, Hires Root Beer, Tin Lithograph, Embossed, Counter Clamp, 21 In. 230.00

Advertising, Crock,
Heinz, Apple Butter, Paper Decal,
Engraved, 6 1/2 In.

Advertising, Crock, Heinz,
Quince Jelly, Tin, Handle,
Paper Decal, 4 1/2 In.

Advertising, Crock, Heinz,
Ketchup, 8 Sides, Brown Top,
Beige Bottom, 7 1/2 In.

Dispenser, Hires Syrup, Drink Hires, It's Pure, Hourglass, Ceramic, 7 1/2 x 14 In. 770.00
Dispenser, Hires Syrup, Money Maker, Marble Base, Milk Glass Globe, 16 x 34 In. 5830.00
Dispenser, Hunter's Soda Fountain Syrup, Holds 1 Gal., 10 In. 55.00
Dispenser, Indian Rock Ginger Ale, Aromatic, Glass Barrel, 9 1/2 In. 2200.00
Dispenser, Lash's Real Orangeade, Tin, Painted, Decals, Fruit Finial, 23 In. 605.00
Dispenser, Mansfield's Pepsin Gum, Etched Glass, Celluloid Marquee, 12 In. 1018.00
Dispenser, Mansfield's Pepsin Gum, Wood Base, Countertop, 11 1/2 x 5 In. 3300.00
Dispenser, Orange-Julep Syrup, Orange, Ceramic, 10 x 14 In. ....1870.00 to 1980.00
Dispenser, Pulver Chewing Gum, One Cent, Porcelain, White, Clockwork 1185.00
Dispenser, Queen Dairy Chilled Buttermilk, Porcelain, White, Black Letters, 35 In. 3190.00
Dispenser, Smith Brothers Cough Drops, Tin, Hinged Lid, 9 3/4 x 4 In. 440.00
Dispenser, Ver-Ba, Drink Ver-Ba, 5 Cents, Ceramic, 8 x 15 In. 1980.00
Dispenser, Ward's Lemon Crush, Lemon Shape, Ball Pump, c.1918 .... 1430.00
Dispenser, Ward's Orange Crush, Color Added, Orange, Ceramic, 8 x 14 In. 990.00
Display, 7-Up, Infant In Red Playsuit, 1950, 5 x 8 1/2 In. 5.00
Display, A.C. Spark Plugs, Tin Lithograph, Back Door, 18 1/4 In. 187.00
Display, Acme Fly Killers, 5 Fly Swatters, Wood, Painted, 24 In. 255.00
Display, Ayer's Sarsaparilla, Deacon & Wife, Cardboard, Die Cut, 13 x 7 In. 265.00
Display, Baskin-Robbins Chocolate Mouse Royal, Mouse King, Throne, 1981, 15 In. 210.00
Display, Bickmores Gall Cure, 3 Panels, Cardboard, 49 x 32 In. 195.00
Display, Brown Bilt Shoes, Metal, Die Cut Open-Toe Shoes, Straps, Stand, 12 In. 165.00
Display, Camel Cigarettes, Wire Rack, Sheet Metal, 45 In. 65.00
Display, Card Seed Co., Seed Packet, Paper, Frame, 32 Vegetables, 24 x 32 1/2 In. 176.00
Display, Dr. C.W. Benson's Celery & Chamomile Pills, Cardboard, Sunflower, 8 In. 44.00
Display, Dr. Caldwell Syrup Pepsin, Dr. Holding Product, Cardboard, Die Cut, 15 In. 385.00
Display, Dr. Morse Indian Root Pills, Box, 42 x 27 In. & 20 x 9 3/4 In., 2 Piece 525.00
Display, Drysmoke, 12 Pipes, Dupont Nylon, National Briar, c.1955, 18 x 8 In. 38.00
Display, Durkees Ful-Milk Bread, Cow, Bell, Wooden, Metal Base, 19 x 14 In. 495.00
Display, Edison Mazda Light Bulbs, 12 Sockets, Parrish, 15 x 23 x 11 In. 3240.00
Display, Emilia Garcia Cigars, Cardboard, Fold-Out, 42 x 30 1/2 In. 95.00
Display, Eveready Batteries, Santa Claus, Cardboard, 15 x 10 1/2 In. 130.00
Display, Fehrs Beer, Indianapolis 500 Race, Cardboard, 1954, 20 x 18 In. 95.00
Display, Gem Damaskeene Razors, Man, Rocking Chair, Baby, 30 x 21 x 4 In. ..... *Illus* 4250.00
Display, General Electric, Figure, Wooden Band Major, Red Uniform, 19 In. 880.00
Display, Grants Hygienic Crackers, A Daily Regulator, Square, Box, 8 3/4 x 6 In. 55.00
Display, Grants, Chambray Shirt, Sanforized, 65 x 132 In. 1750.00
Display, Grolsch Holland Beer, Girl & Boy, Vinyl, Base, Dutch, c.1970, 9 1/2 In. 60.00
Display, Hamm's Beer, Electric, Moving, 19 x 16 In. 330.00
Display, International Distemper Cure, Box, Cardboard, 6 3/4 x 4 3/4 In. 380.00
Display, Iron Glad Hosiery, Woman, Easel Back, Cardboard, 10 1/2 x 13 In. 145.00
Display, Italian Swiss Colony, Plaster, Man, c.1950, 5 x 9 x 6 In. 30.00
Display, Jar, Borden's Malted Milk, Glass, Label, Metal Domed Lid, Knob 825.00
Display, Kraft Mayonnaise, Hand Holding Jar, Figural, 2 Sides, c.1930, 11 x 10 In. 55.00
Display, La Creme Disinfectine, Roman Soldier, 3 Soap Bars, 7 1/4 x 4 x 1 In. 44.00
Display, Lance Crackers, 4 Glass Jars, Metal Rack, 34 In. 330.00
Display, Larkin Co.'s Ocean Bath Soap, Cat, Red Ribbon, Die Cut, Cardboard, 12 x 9 In. . 230.00
Display, Lax-Fos Medicine, Children, Cardboard, Die Cut, 6 1/8 x 9 1/2 In. 300.00
Display, Lion Coffee, King Of Beast Holding 1 Lb. Of Coffee, 1900, 9 x 13 In. 315.00
Display, Log Cabin Syrup, Towles, 3-D, Woods, Cardboard, 16 x 28 x 10 In. 725.00
Display, Marquette Club Ginger Ale, Die Cut, Standup, Cardboard, 22 x 26 In. 77.00
Display, Martin Ware Chicken Feeders, Metal, Wood, c.1930, 60 In. 55.00
Display, Merkle's Blu-J Brooms, Tin Signs On Ends, Stand, 35 x 10 x 23 In. 470.00
Display, Michelin Tire Man, Ceramic, White Body, Black Boots, 16 x 33 In. 1760.00
Display, Miller High Life Beer, Silver Ice Bucket, Bottles, Light-Up, Revolves, 19 In. ... 99.00
Display, Neatip Shoelaces, Mirror Front, 6 Cardboard Drawers, 13 x 5 1/2 In. 195.00
Display, Nebraska Seed Co., Oak, Folding, 6 Shelves, Wire Separators, Stenciled, 46 In. .. 248.00
Display, Panama Chewing Gum, Blue, Cardboard, Helmet Co., 4 3/4 x 7 1/4 In. 198.00
Display, Patriot Beer, Good For Him & Good For You Since 1742, Metal, Painted, 16 In. . 415.00
Display, Poll-Parrot Shoes, 3-D Mechanical, Cardboard, Dr. Seuss, 13 x 34 x 6 In. 400.00
Display, Primly Chewing Gum, Oak & Glass, Curved, 18 1/2 x 12 x 9 1/2 In. 660.00
Display, Professors Laxative Tablets, Cardboard, 12 Tins, Countertop, 4 3/4 x 4 In. 80.00
Display, Ray-O-Vac Batteries, Tin, 9 1/2 x 7 1/2 x 11 In. 330.00
Display, Red Goose Shoes, Papier-Mache, Electric, Nodding Head, 21 3/4 In. 495.00

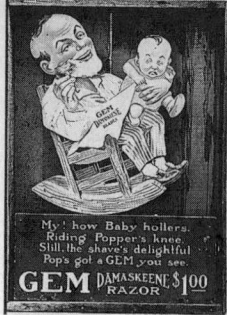

Advertising, Display,
Gem Damaskeene
Razors, Man,
Rocking Chair, Baby,
30 x 21 x 4 In.

Advertising, Display,
Wrigley's
Doublemint Gum,
Arrow Man, Metal,
Celluloid, 14 In.

Display, Redgate Orange Crush & Lemonade, Embossed, Cardboard, 10 x 14 In. 44.00
Display, Rogers Bros. Silver Plate, Precious, Cardboard, Easel Back, 1847, 10 x 14 In. . . . 44.00
Display, Schmidt's Of Philadelphia, Cast Metal, Waiter, Beer Mug, 1930s, 10 In. 975.00
Display, Scotch Heather, Scotsman, Plaster, Base, c.1950, 3 x 5 x 9 1/2 In. 35.00
Display, Vet Serum, Animal Health Products, Countertop, 1930s, 6 x 12 In. 185.00
Display, Viuna Wonder Medicine, Cardboard, Trifold, 13 1/2 x 11 In. 250.00
Display, Whistle, Sparkling Orange Goodness, Girl, Drinks From Straw, 6 1/2 x 17 In. . . . 44.00
Display, White Horse Whiskey, Metal, Wood, c.1950, 6 3/4 In. 24.00
Display, Whitlocks Renowned Remedies, Tin, Glass Front, 25 In. 3630.00
Display, Whitman's Chocolates, Santa Holds Candy, 38 x 36 In. 35.00
Display, Winchester Lawn Mowers, 13 x 9 In. 1540.00
Display, Wrigley's Chewing Gum, Tin, Curved, Countertop, 13 x 13 x 6 In. 2875.00
Display, Wrigley's Doublemint Gum, Arrow Man, Metal, Celluloid, 14 In. . . . . *Illus* 150.00
Display, Wrigley's Gum, Die Cut, Tin, 4 Gum Boxes, Countertop, 16 x 14 In. 770.00
Display, Wrigley's Gum, Moon-Faced Figure, Holding 4 Boxes, Die Cut, Tin, c.1920 . . . . 1265.00
Display, Zeno Gum, Oak, Glass, 3 Shelves, Molded Composition Marquee, 17 In. 300.00
Dolls are listed in their own category.
Door, Screen, Colonial Bread, Push Bars, Painted, 80 x 30 In. 330.00
Door, Screen, Noldes Bread & Cakes, Wood, Painted, 80 x 30 In. 100.00
Door Push, Edgeworth Tobacco, 14 x 4 In. 330.00
Door Push, Foley Kidney Pills, Embossed, Porcelain, Oval, Black Letters, 6 x 3 In. 375.00
Door Push, Freihofers Sonny Boy Bread, Tin Lithograph, 3 x 12 x 2 In. 150.00
Door Push, Salada Tea, Delicious Flavor, Porcelain Over Steel, 32 x 3 1/2 In. 65.00
Door Push, Smoke Buckingham, Throat Easy, Porcelain, 32 x 3 In. 220.00
Door Push, Stag Tobacco, Porcelain, Tin, Lithograph Of Stag, 6 x 3 In. 1760.00
Door Push, Sweet Heart Products, Hard Wheat Flour, Heart Shape, 5 x 5 In. 355.00
Dust Pan, Compliments Of Drake Mercantile, Tin, 6 1/2 x 9 3/8 In., 2 Piece 230.00
Egg Separator, Charles Chips, Plastic, Blue 10.00
Fans are listed in their own category.
Fan Pull, Old Dutch Cleanser, Multicolored, Lithograph, Cardboard, 5 1/4 In. 66.00
Figure, Blatz Man, Bottle Body, Holding Mug & Sign On Tray, 20 In. 55.00
Figure, Bulldog, Watta Pop 1 Cent Lollipops, Chalkware, 7 x 5 x 6 3/4 In. 170.00
Figure, California Raisin, Male, Microphone, Polyvinyl, Flex, 1987, 5 1/2 In. 8.00
Figure, Castle Hall Cigars, Stork, Chalk Over Cardboard, 23 1/2 In. 605.00
Figure, Cold Stream Guard, Exclusive Pipe Tobacco, Rubber, England, 19 In. 60.00
Figure, Conmar The Major Zipper, Cast Iron, Painted, c.1950, 4 1/2 In. 35.00
Figure, Don Q Rum, Composition, Wood, Base, Schieffelic & Co., c.1940, 12 1/2 In. 85.00
Figure, Dutch Boy Paints, Jointed, Original Coveralls, 24 In. 745.00
Figure, Eskimo Pie, Eskimo Holding Cooler, Arm Goes Up & Down, 32 In. 468.00
Figure, Fruit Kid, Penny Pineapple, Painted, Plaster, Base, 1942, 4 1/2 In. 40.00
Figure, Hamm's Beer, Bear, Styrofoam, 60 In. 165.00
Figure, Heinz 57, Tomato Head, Rubber, Painted, c.1940, 2 1/2 x 2 1/2 x 5 3/4 In. . .90.00 to 125.00
Figure, Hush Puppies, Dog, Die Cut, Styrofoam, 17 In. 20.00
Figure, Klondike Mike, Ceramic, Painted, 6 In. 15.00
Figure, KMPC Free Speech Mike, Plaster, Microphone, Base, c.1960, 5 3/4 In. 85.00
Figure, Kool Cigarettes, Penguin, Dr. Kool, Chalkware, 4 1/2 x 5 3/8 In. 260.00
Figure, McDonald's, Mayor McCheese, Action, 6 1/2 In. 18.00

Figure, Merito Rum, National Distillers Product Co., Composition, Base, 6 x 9 In. 120.00
Figure, Miss Dairylea, Vinyl, Painted, Base, c.1960, 6 In. 65.00
Figure, Mr. Clean, Vinyl, Proctor & Gamble, c.1961, 8 In. 48.00
Figure, Nabisco Award Statuette, Child In Rain Slicker, Base, c.1980, 9 1/2 In. 60.00
Figure, National Tailoring Co., Man In Tuxedo, Composition, Oak Base, 32 In. 1045.00
Figure, Reddy Kilowatt, Glow, Plastic, Base, c.1940, 5 x 1 1/2 x 3 In. 90.00
Figure, Sandler Of Boston, Colonial Man, c.1940, 8 1/2 x 13 In. 25.00
Figure, Tagamet, Flex, Vinyl, Pink, Base, 1988, 5 In. 14.00
Figure, Weatherbird Shoes, Rooster, Electric, Head Nods, Papier-Mache, 27 x 20 In. ... 495.00
Fire Screen, Winchester Flashlights & Batteries, Papier-Mache, c.1920, 48 x 100 In. 846.00
Flashlight, Reddy Kilowatt, Plastic, Brass, Chain, c.1950, 3 In. 24.00
Foam Scraper, Rainier Beer, Red, Silver .... 60.00 to 75.00
Funnel, Marked Forbes Quality Coffee, Tin, 3 In. 50.00
Globe, C.E. Goddard Optometrist, Etched Lettering, Milk Glass, 2 Sides, 14 In. 300.00
Hat, McDonald's Captain Crook Costume, Glossy Thin Cardboard, 1978 .... 12.00
Hat, McDonald's, Manager, Paper, Mesh, Cellucap Mfg., c.1950, 5 1/2 x 11 In. 25.00
Hat, Miss Dairylea Ice Cream, Red, White, Blue Spirals, c.1950 .... 18.00
Hat, Willie Wiredhand, Paper, Webbing, Tricorn, c.1940, 4 x 12 In. 15.00
Horseshoe, Take Simmons Liver Regulator, Brass, Patina, 6 x 5 In. 85.00
Keg, Storz Beer, Oak, Wooden Spigot, Omaha, Neb., 20 In. 132.00
Key, Ilco Lock & Key Products, Fitchburg, Mass., Steel, 2 Sides, 2 Top Holes, 32 In. 40.00
Key Fob, Duquesne, Good Luck, Penny, Plated, 1940s 8.00
Key Set, Texaco, Restroom, Women's, Men's, Metal, 12 x 9 In. 240.00
Knife, New England Road Machinery, Folding, Canton Cutlery, Boston 125.00
Label, Cigar, American Belle, Lady, Flowers, c.1900, 6 x 9 In. 30.00
Label, Cigar, Statue Of Liberty, Inner, c.1920, 6 x 9 In. 18.00
Label, Citrus, Moon Washington Navels, Greenspot Citrus Association, Calif., 10 In. 30.00
Label, Firecrackers, Buck A-Roo, Cowboy With Lasso, Chinese, 1920s 280.00
Label, Food, Abba Dabba Milk Chocolate, 1920s, 11 x 14 In. 50.00
Label, Food, Crane's Chocolates, Mother's Day, Cleveland, Oh., 3 7/8 x 2 In. 3.00
Label, Food, Defiance Alaskan Salmon, Associated Food Distributors, 4 1/2 x 10 In. 9.50
Label, Food, Dynamite Lettuce, F.J. McCann & Son, Salinas, Calif., 9 1/4 x 7 In. 8.50
Label, Food, Henry's Home Style Wheat Bread, Shippensburg, Penn., Wax Paper 6.00
Label, Fruit, Black Swan, Barrel, c.1920, 12 1/2 In. 8.00
Label, Fruit, Brownies Brand Oranges, Elves Drinking Juice, 11 x 10 In. 31.00
Label, Fruit, Outboard Apples, Chelan, Wash., 8 3/4 x 10 In. 30.00
Label, Fruit, Skookum Brand Apples, Wenatchee, Wash., 1940s, 8 3/4 x 10 In. 5.00
Label, Hotel, Excelsior, Casablanca, Morocco, 3 1/2 x 5 In. 30.00
Label, Hotel, Grotte Bleue, Capri, Italy, 1930s, 4 x 6 In. 55.00
Label, Hotel, Orchard, Singapore, 1950s 11.00
Label, Tea, New Orleans Import Co., Banzai Brand, 1920s, 3 x 9 In. 7.00
Lamps are listed in the Lamp category.
Ledger Marker, Vaseline Petroleum Jelly, Black Lettering, 3 x 12 In. 220.00
Lunch Boxes are listed in their own category.
Mask, Aunt Jemima Pancake Flour, Black Face, Yellow Bandanna, Paper, 9 x 11 In. 410.00
Mask, Good Humor Ice Cream, Truck Vendor, Smiling, Paper, c.1930, 9 x 11 In. 24.00
Match Striker, Sun Proof Paints, Man & Blackboard, Tin Lithograph, 6 x 2 1/2 In. 230.00
Matchbook, Bob's, Home Of The Big Boy, Blue, Folder, c.1950, 1 1/2 x 2 In. 12.00
Milk Can, Whitchurch Creameries Ltd., 21 In. 46.00

Advertising mirrors of all sizes are listed here. Advertising pocket mirrors range in size from 1 1/2 to 5 inches in diameter. Most of these mirrors were given away as advertising promotions and include the name of the company in the design.

Mirror, Anderson Soup, Each Can Makes 6 Plates, Celluloid, 1 3/4 In. 150.00
Mirror, Anheuser-Busch, Buschtee, Man On Horse, Jumping, Celluloid, 2 3/4 x 1 In. 227.00
Mirror, Benjamin Harris Advertising Novelties, N.Y.C., Pocket 150.00
Mirror, Big Boy Dominates, Soda Pop, Celluloid, 2 3/4 x 1 1/4 In. 100.00
Mirror, Buffalo Brewing Co., Beer, Cigar, Lithograph, 1906, 10 x 14 In. 523.00
Mirror, Cascarets, They Work While You Sleep, Pocket 85.00
Mirror, Club Saloon, Good For One Drink, S. Gobbi, Proprietor, Celluloid, 2 1/4 In. 578.00
Mirror, Congress Beer, Haberle Brewing Co., Syracuse, Celluloid, 2 3/4 x 1 3/4 In. 184.00
Mirror, Continental Cubes Pipe Tobacco, Lady On Box, Celluloid, 1 3/4 x 2 3/4 In. 275.00

Mirror, Dahm Leather Co., Woman, Celluloid, 2 1/4 In. 231.00
Mirror, Demottes Furniture Stores, Black, White, El Paso, Ill. 125.00
Mirror, Directory Hotel, Albany, N.Y., Good For 10 Cents In Trade, Celluloid, 2 In. 172.00
Mirror, Dr Pepper, Glass, Wood, Frame, 28 1/2 x 19 3/4 In. 44.00
Mirror, Dr. Caldwell's Syrup, Pepsin Cures, Oval, Celluloid, 1 3/4 x 2 3/4 In. 121.00
Mirror, Gates Hats, Chicago, Celluloid, 1 3/4 In. 83.00
Mirror, Gay-Ola, Woman With Cola, c.1910, 1 3/4 In. 422.00
Mirror, Hamilton Medical Assoc., Cancer & Tumor Care, Celluloid, 2 1/8 In. 89.00
Mirror, Imperial, Good For 10 Cents, Gloucester, Mass., Pocket 200.00
Mirror, International Tailoring Co., King Of Tailors, Lion, Tin, 1 5/8 In. 100.00
Mirror, King Tomato Filler, Red, White, Black, Salem, N.J., Pocket 135.00
Mirror, Louis James Cigar, Cast Iron, Tabletop, 10 1/2 x 12 In. 440.00
Mirror, Mohr Cafe & Pool Room, Multicolored, Celluloid, 2 1/8 In. 215.00
Mirror, Motley's Flour Co., Bag Of Flour, Celluloid, 2 3/4 x 1 3/4 In. 150.00
Mirror, Munsingwear Co., Deer Head, Celluloid, 1921, 1 3/4 In. 175.00
Mirror, Murine, For Your Eyes, Woman, Glass, Reverse Painted, 10 x 14 In. . . . . .920.00 to 1155.00
Mirror, Murphy Haberdasher, Silk Shirts, Brown, Green, White, Los Angeles, Pocket 100.00
Mirror, Northwestern School For Stammerers, Milwaukee, Pocket 150.00
Mirror, Old Manse Canadian Maple Syrup, Celluloid, 2 1/8 In. 207.00
Mirror, Old Player's Navy Cut Tobacco, 18 x 21 In. 460.00
Mirror, Omar Pearls, Woman, 3 Strands Of Pearls, Celluloid, 2 3/4 x 1 3/4 In. 165.00
Mirror, Ortman Hotel & Clinic, Blue, White, Canistota, S.D., Pocket 150.00
Mirror, Parisian Novelty Co., Factory Image, Celluloid, 3 1/2 In. 50.00
Mirror, Ponciana Gum, Celluloid, W.J. White., 4 1/2 x 2 7/8 In. 330.00
Mirror, Queen Quality Shoes, Lady, Blue Scarf, Celluloid, 2 3/4 x 1 3/4 In. 83.00
Mirror, Queen Shoes, Miss Liberty, Celluloid, 2 3/4 x 1 3/4 In. 89.00
Mirror, Royal Glue, Topless Girl With Bow & Arrow, Celluloid, 2 3/4 x 1 3/4 In. 423.00
Mirror, Spalding, Celluloid, 2 1/8 In. 330.00
Mirror, Standard Oil Co., Red Crown Gasoline, Barron, Wisconsin 350.00
Mirror, Surbrugs Tobacco, Celluloid, Oval, Topless Lady, Pocket, 2 x 1 In. . . . . . . .825.00 to 950.00
Mirror, Texaco, I See Myself, Metal, c.1930, 7 3/4 x 3 3/8 In. 171.00
Mirror, Uncle Sam Brewery, Elks Carnival, Wilmington, June 1900, Celluloid, 1 3/4 In. . . 231.00
Mirror, Watany Cigarette Co., Woman, Multicolored, 1 3/4 x 2 3/4 In. 132.00
Money Clip, Anheuser-Busch Golf Classic, Badge Form, Logo, Sterling Silver, 3 In. 115.00
Mug, Higbee Hot Or Cold Sanitary Vacuum Bottle, Hot 24 Hours, 2 1/8 x 2 1/8 In. 25.00
Mug, Hires Root Beer, Mettlach Stoneware, Boy With Bib, 5 x 4 1/4 In. 240.00
Mug, Keebler Elf, Plastic, Raised Feathers, R & F Mold & Die Works, 1972, 3 In. 8.00
Mug, Ovaltine, Captain Midnight, Shake-Up, Off-White, Blue Top 325.00
Mug, Ovaltine, Uncle Wiggily, Grandpa Goosey Gander, Ceramic, 1924, 3 In. 40.00
Mug, Richardson Root Beer Rich, Glass, c.1940, 4 x 6 1/2 In. 20.00
Napkin, Borden, Elsie The Cow, Paper, White Ground, 1950s, 6 x 6 In. 3.00
Necklace, Charlie Tuna, Charm, Figural, Metal, Gold, c.1970, 24 In. 8.00
Needle Threader, Prudential Insurance, Rock Of Gibraltar Logo, 2 In. 19.00
Needle Threader, Prudential Insurance, Tin, Wire Threader, 5 Needles, 2 3/4 In. 6.50
Night-Light, Bob's Big Boy, Plastic, Face, Red, White, c.1960, 2 x 3/4 In. 18.00
Night-Light, Elsie The Cow, Figural, Borden, Composition, 9 1/4 In. . : 198.00
Pack, Cigarette, One-Eleven, Sealed, Contents, 24-Cent Federal Tax Stamp 59.00
Pack, Cigarette, Philip Morris, Cellophane Wrapper, 1940s, 2 x 2 3/4 In. 48.00
Pail, Brotherhood Tobacco, Tin Lithograph, Orange & Black, 4 x 7 In. 220.00
Pail, Fashion Tobacco, Well Dressed Couple, 4 1/4 x 7 3/4 In. 244.00
Pail, Frontenac Peanut Butter, Tin Lithograph, Bail Handle, 3 1/2 In. 35.00
Pail, Mammy Coffee, Black Woman, Tin Lithograph, 4 Lb., 10 3/4 x 6 1/8 In. 248.00
Pail, Mayo's Tobacco, Tin Lithograph, Wood Bail Handle, Collapsible, 7 1/2 In. 165.00
Pail, Miners & Puddlers Tobacco, Early Miners, 6 5/8 x 5 1/4 In. 275.00
Pail, Monarch Popcorn, Children Popping Corn, 14 Oz., 3 3/4 x 3 3/8 In. 178.00
Pail, Morris Supreme Peanut Butter, Children At Beach, Tin Lithograph, 3 In. 120.00
Pail, Mosemann's Peanut Butter, Animals, Tin, 1 Lb., 3 3/4 x 3 3/8 In. 138.00
Pail, Red Seal Peanut Butter, Newton Tea & Spice Co., Cincinnati, Tin, 15 Oz. 85.00
Pail, Sanders Satin Candies, Children At Table, Cover, 2 1/2 Lb., 5 x 5 1/2 In. 145.00
Pail, Squirrel Peanut Butter, Tin Lithograph, Bail Handle, 3 1/2 In. 145.00
Pail, Sultana Peanut Butter, Boy, Girl, Tin Lithograph, 1 Lb., 4 x 4 In. 85.00
Pail, Tin, Sunny Boy Peanut Butter, Roundage Brothers, Toledo, Ohio, 15 Oz. 65.00
Pail, Toyland Peanut Butter, Circus Parade, 1 Lb., 4 x 3 1/2 In. 386.00

Advertising, Pin, Damon's, Go
Hog Wild, 3 1/2 In.

Advertising, Pin, Damon's, In
Your Face Sports Party
Place, 3 In.

Advertising, Pin, Damon's,
It's Mother's Day To Loaf,
3 In.

Pail, United Candy, Sugar Candies, Fancy Shapes, Tin, c.1920, 3 3/4 x 3 1/2 In. 196.00
Pail, White Clover Peanut Butter, For Amos-James Grocer's, 4 x 3 In. 495.00
Patch, Bob's Big Boy, Fabric, Stitched, Double Burger, c.1950, 2 3/4 x 4 1/4 In. 15.00
Patch, Burger Chef, Cloth, Hamburgers-Open-Flame Broiling, 4 x 4 In. 12.00
Patch, Frisch's Big Boy, Fabric, Title Bar, c.1950, 1 1/2 x 4 In. 15.00
Pencil, Reims Champagne, Bottle Shape, Amber Plastic, 1920s-1930s 45.00
Pin, Bond Bread, For Happier Health, Wiley Post, No. 2, Celluloid, 1 1/4 In. 25.00
Pin, Breyers 75th Anniversary, Red, White, Green, Oval, Celluloid, 1941, 2 3/4 In. 35.00
Pin, Ceresota, Best Flour Sold, Young Boy Wearing Hat, Celluloid, 1 1/4 In. 22.00
Pin, Cinderella Stoves & Ranges Never Fail, Celluloid, 1 1/4 In. 16.00
Pin, Columbia Flour, Miss Liberty, Celluloid, 1 1/4 In. 255.00
Pin, Crush Carbonated Beverage, Celluloid, Over Cardboard, Easel Back, 9 In. 198.00
Pin, Cub Shoe Polish, Bear, In Cub Uniform, Tin Lithograph, 1 1/2 In. 235.00
Pin, Damon's, Go Hog Wild, 3 1/2 In. . . . . *Illus* 2.00
Pin, Damon's, In Your Face Sports Party Place, 3 In. . . . . *Illus* 2.00
Pin, Damon's, It's Mother's Day To Loaf, 3 In. . . . . *Illus* 2.00
Pin, Duffy's Malt Whiskey, Makes The Weak Strong, Multicolored, 2 3/4 In. 119.00
Pin, DuPont Smokeless, Champion Powder, Dogs, Celluloid, 1896, 1 1/4 In. 120.00
Pin, Fisher's Flour, America's Finest Flouring Mills, Multicolored, 1 1/2 In. 18.00
Pin, Frenzel Brothers, Steamship, Multicolored, Celluloid, 1 1/4 In. 49.00
Pin, Globe Poultry Feed, Globe, Multicolored, Celluloid, 1 1/4 In. 40.00
Pin, Hires Root Beer, Red, Black, White, Celluloid, 2 1/8 In. 55.00
Pin, Hummer Plow Will Plow Anything, Celluloid, 7/8 In. 119.00
Pin, Kool Cigarettes, In Either Case Keep Kool, Penguin, Donkey, Elephant 18.00
Pin, LaFrance Shoes, Gottlieb's Department Store, Red, Green, White, 2 1/4 In. 35.00
Pin, Moxie, Woman Holding Bottle, Tin Lithograph, Die Cut, 2 x 1 7/8 In. 249.00
Pin, Pep Comics, G-Man Club, Shield Shape, Celluloid, 1944 . . . . 145.00
Pin, Peter Max, Paint Your Wagon, Multicolored, Celluloid, 1 3/4 In. 20.00
Pin, Reddy Kilowatt, Ohio Edison Co., Celluloid, Parisian Novelty Co., 3 1/2 In. 65.00
Pin, Tarita Cigars, Woman, Long Dark Hair 40.00
Pin, Thoroughbred Work Clothing, Celluloid, 1 1/2 In. 260.00
Pin, Vote For Philip Morris, Bellhop, Celluloid, 1 1/4 In. 16.00
Pin, Wattle Day, Multicolored, Celluloid, 1918, 1 1/4 In. 40.00
Pin, Wm. H. Whiting Co. Flag & Yacht Supplies, Red, Blue, Cream, Black, 1 3/4 In. 61.00
Pin Tray, Clover Brands Shoes Are Always Correct, 2 Pug Puppies, 2 5/8 In. 44.00
Pin Tray, Try Bee Candy, Black, White Dog, Scalloped, 3 3/8 x 2 1/4 In. 77.00
Plaque, Ives Toys Make Happy Boys, Commemorative, Bronze, 1959, 20 x 30 In. 8690.00
Plate, Anheuser-Busch, Malt Nutrine, Tin, Lady Gold, Cobalt Rim, Vienna, 10 In. 80.00
Plate, Ever-Ready Lighters, Tin Lithograph Of Arab & Water Pipe, Vienna Art, 10 In. . . . 300.00
Plate, Peter Rabbit's Radio Party, Thornton Burgess, Tin Lithograph, 7 7/8 In. 359.00
Plate, Reddy Kilowatt, Servant Of The Century, Ceramic, Metal, c.1960, 6 In. 25.00
Pot, Jackson Soap, Cast Iron, 5 In. 33.00
Pot Scraper, American Maid Bread, Loaf Shape, Tin, Red, White, Blue, 1 x 3 In. 220.00

Pot Scraper, Junket, Makes Milk Into Delicious Desserts, Metal, 2 Sides, 3 x 3 In. 215.00
Pouch, Tobacco, Hine & Co., Cloth, Tin, c.1870, 6 1/2 x 4 3/4 In. 409.00
Premium, Canada Dry Soda, Super Circus Punch-Out, 10 Sheets, 1950 . . . .   200.00
Premium, Insurance Pro-Rater, Peru, Indiana, Copyright 1948, 12 In. . . . . *Illus*   3.00
Rug, Buster Brown, Round, 48 In. 580.00
Ruler, American Line & Red Star Line, Multicolored, Lithograph, 12 In. 220.00
Ruler, Transylvania Printing Company, Lexington, Kentucky, 15 In. . . . . *Illus*   2.00
Sack, Flour, Jack Sprat, No. 98, Color Logo On Both Sides 66.00
Salt & Pepper Shakers are listed in their own category.
Scales are listed in their own category.
Scoop, Coffee, McLaughlin & Co., Tin, 13 In. 55.00
Scoop, Goelitz Confectionary Co., Butter Sweets, Tin, 3 7/8 x 1 3/4 x 3/8 In. 165.00
Scoop, Hungerford Star Brand Ice Cream, Aluminum, Plunger, 10 1/2 In. 525.00
Scoop, Prince Castle Ice Cream, Brushed Steel, Square Bowl, Squeeze Plunger, 5 In. 255.00
Scrubber, Crystal White Soap, Soap Box Image, Tin, 6 3/4 x 4 3/4 In. 150.00
Shoehorn, Schoenecker, Princess Comfort Shoe, Tin, 4 x 1 5/8 In. 177.00
Shoehorn & Buttonhook, Perry Shoe Repair Shop, Boston, Folds, Metal, 1915, 6 1/2 In. . .   10.00
Sign, 7 Sutherland Sisters Hair Grower, Overlay Mat, 1897, 29 3/4 x 24 In. 360.00
Sign, 7-Up, First Against Thirst, Tin, Canada, 28 x 20 In. 110.00
Sign, 7-Up, Fresh Up, Tin, Embossed, Self-Framed, 11 1/4 x 23 In. 230.00
Sign, A & W Root Beer, Frothy Mug, Diamond Shape, Metal, Embossed, 47 In. 77.00
Sign, AAA Root Beer, Red, Yellow, Tin, 28 x 20 In. 195.00
Sign, Adam Hats, From Coast To Coast, America's Famous, Neon, 21 x 7 In. 330.00
Sign, Alamo Beer, Lone Star Brewing Co., Frame, c.1907, 16 x 20 In. 1800.00
Sign, Allens Red Tame Cherry, Tin Lithograph, Die Cut, Stand-Up, 35 1/2 In. 10450.00
Sign, Allis-Chalmers, Red, White, Blue, Porcelain, 16 x 16 In.   195.00
Sign, Alpenkrauter Stomach Tonic, Feel Fine Thanks To, Masonite, 24 x 48 In. 120.00
Sign, American Express Co. Agency, Porcelain, Red, White & Blue, 18 x 16 1/2 In. 635.00
Sign, Ames Shovels, Lock Socket, Celluloid Over Metal, Over Cardboard, 12 x 8 In 83.00
Sign, Amorita Cigar, Your Old Favorite, Paper, Hanging, 2 Sides, 6 1/2 In. 4.00
Sign, Anheuser-Busch, Budweiser Girl, Orange Dress, Frame, 24 x 39 In. 825.00
Sign, Anheuser-Busch, Custer's Last Fight, Frame, 43 x 33 In. 440.00
Sign, Anker-Werke, Sewing Machine, Woman, Paper, Roll-Up, Frame, 20 1/2 x 31 In. . . .   220.00
Sign, Arbuckles Coffee, Pure Wholesome, Tin Lithograph, Embossed, 19 x 5 1/2 In. 385.00
Sign, Arden Dairy Co., Delivery Boy, Red, White, Black, Porcelain, Oval, 21 x 36 In. . . .   798.00
Sign, Arm & Hammer Baking Soda, Tree Stump, Birds, Paper, 16 x 22 In. 132.00
Sign, Armour & Co. Meats, Tin, 23 x 26 1/2 In. 1035.00
Sign, Armour & Co., Butcher Shop, Hams, Bacon, Tin, 21 1/2 x 27 In. 480.00
Sign, Armour's Old Black Joe Fertilizer, Tin, 42 x 18 In. 605.00
Sign, Atlantic & Pacific Tea Co., Columbia World's Fair Tower, Lithograph, 14 x 24 In. . .   175.00
Sign, Atlantic Coast Line, Yellow Ground, Black Letters, Round, Metal, 24 In. 220.00
Sign, Aunt Jemima Ready Mix, Aunt Jemima, Cardboard, 12 1/4 x 21 3/4 In. 1375.00
Sign, Ayer's Hair Vigor, Girl With Long Hair, Tin, Oak Frame, 16 x 23 In. 1650.00
Sign, Bank Note Cigars, 2 Men, Die Cut, Cardboard, Frame, 22 1/2 x 30 In. 275.00
Sign, Bardenhier Wine & Liquor, Take A Little Papa, Tin, 1890, 23 x 20 In. 1200.00
Sign, Bartels Beer, Blue, Round, Tin, 18 1/2 In. 285.00
Sign, Bartels Brewing Co., Factory Scene, Paper, 46 x 34 1/2 In.   2090.00

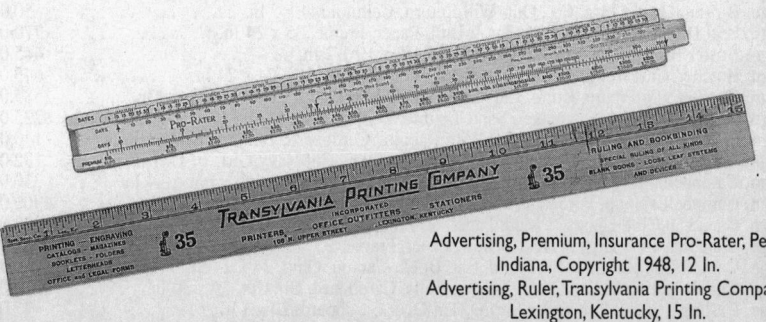

Advertising, Premium, Insurance Pro-Rater, Peru,
Indiana, Copyright 1948, 12 In.
Advertising, Ruler, Transylvania Printing Company,
Lexington, Kentucky, 15 In.

Advertising, Sign, Black
Cat Cigarettes, Matured,
Tin, England, 19th
Century, 36 x 25 In.

Advertising, Sign,
Boot, Shoes Shined,
Painted, Steel, 2 Sides,
32 x 21 In.

Sign, Baums Poultry Food, Black Leghorn Fowls, 1878, 9 x 11 In. 90.00
Sign, Becker's Fisherman's Grain Shoe, Man Fishing From Shoe, 26 x 20 1/2 In. 3278.00
Sign, Beech-Nut, Black Cough Drops, Cardboard, 26 x 16 In. 275.00
Sign, Belar Cigars, Perfection Of Quality, Tin Lithograph, c.1900, 10 x 7 In. 99.00
Sign, Bengal Cheroots, Tiger's Face, H. Ellis & Co., 1880s, 14 1/2 x 23 1/4 In. 1320.00
Sign, Bireley's, Keep Fit, Cool Jump Roper, Cardboard, Die Cut, 1941, 24 x 40 In. 550.00
Sign, Black Caps, Treatment Of Gonorrhoea & Gleet, Tin Lithograph, 7 x 9 In. 77.00
Sign, Black Cat Cigarettes, Matured, Tin, England, 19th Century, 36 x 25 In. .... *Illus* 1763.00
Sign, Blatz Old Heidelberg, Plaster Relief, Painted, 1933, 42 x 24 In. 385.00
Sign, Bludwine 5 Cents, Grape Drink, Bottle, Tin, 2 Sides, 12 3/4 x 9 1/2 In. 520.00
Sign, Blue Coal, America's Finest Anthracite, Flaming Lump Of Coal, Tin, 12 x 12 In. ... 240.00
Sign, Bo-Ko Cigars, Smoke Bo-Ko, Cardboard, Metal Frame, 42 x 15 In. 99.00
Sign, Boot, Metal, 2 Sides, Hanging, Bracket, 32 3/4 x 19 1/4 In. 375.00
Sign, Boot, Red, Zinc, Lyre Frame, Iron Wall Bracket, 38 x 37 3/4 In. 3525.00
Sign, Boot, Shoes Shined, Painted, Steel, 2 Sides, 32 x 21 In. .... *Illus* 1955.00
Sign, Bootmaker's, Woman's Shoe, Man's Boot, 17 x 21 1/2 In. 230.00
Sign, Boots & Shoes Repaired, Wood, Black & Red Lettering, 18 x 31 3/4 In. 1295.00
Sign, Borax Soap, Lady Of Quality, Meek Co., Tin Over Cardboard, 1904, 19 x 13 In. ... 490.00
Sign, Borden, Elsie The Cow, Tin, 1960s, 58 x 28 In. 300.00
Sign, Boschee's German Syrup, Wheatbelt Girl, Lithograph, Frame, 1904, 25 x 33 In. 1250.00
Sign, Bowers Batteries, White Ground, Black Letters, Tin, 16 x 65 In. 305.00
Sign, Brauns Bread, Eat Brauns Town Talk Bread, Tin, Rack, 14 1/2 x 38 In. 190.00
Sign, Brown's Household Panacea, Samaritan & Sick Man, Cardboard, 11 x 14 In. 385.00
Sign, Brownfield's Little Liver Pills, Cardboard, 17 x 12 1/2 In. 35.00
Sign, Brylcreem, For Smart Healthy Hair, Red, White, 16 x 18 In. 165.00
Sign, Buckeye Beer, On Draught Here, Picks You Up, Tin, Embossed, 3 x 14 In. 35.00
Sign, Buckshoe & Tiger Stripe Tobacco, Girl, Fishbowl, Lithograph, 32 x 18 In. 230.00
Sign, Bud Light, Star Wars Style Background, Light-Up, 1986, 66 In. 95.00
Sign, Budweiser, Anheuser-Busch, In Bottles, Tin Over Cardboard, 5 x 9 In. 112.00
Sign, Budweiser, Revolving Clydesdale Team, Light-Up, Hanging, 24 In. 525.00
Sign, Buffalo Brewing Co., Porcelain, Navy Blue On Light Blue, 20 x 14 1/2 In. 2420.00
Sign, Buffalo Club Rye Whiskey, C. Person's Sons, Bison, 23 1/2 x 33 1/2 In. 960.00
Sign, Buffalo Dental Mfg. Co., Out, Will Return, Celluloid, 4 x 5 In. 50.00
Sign, Bull Durham Tobacco, Matador & Bull, Paper, Frame, 35 x 24 In. 770.00
Sign, Buster Brown Bread, Girl, Dog, Tin, 28 1/2 x 19 1/2 In. 445.00
Sign, Butcher, Cast Iron, Steer Over Molded Tools, Painted, 19 3/4 x 24 In. 645.00
Sign, Butcher, Pig Figure, Knife, Carved, Painted, Wood, 19th Century, 32 x 39 In. 2585.00
Sign, C. Brandenstein, Bootmaker, Sand Texture, 2 Sides, 18 x 61 In. 8225.00
Sign, C.D. Kenney, Grocery Co., Girl With Rabbits, Cardboard, Trifold, 18 1/4 x 20 In. .. 140.00
Sign, Camel Cigarettes, Favorite Of Navy Canteens, Die Cut Navy Girl, 10 x 31 In. 132.00
Sign, Campbell's Horse Remedy, Black Stable Boy, Paper Lithograph, Frame, 24 In. 330.00
Sign, Campbell's Soup, Porcelain, Curved, 12 1/2 x 22 1/2 In. 4900.00
Sign, Canadian Club Cigars, 3 Men, Paper, c.1930, 11 x 16 In. 28.00
Sign, Canadian Club Cigars, Red, Yellow, Paper, Frame, 25 x 18 1/2 In. 187.00
Sign, Canton Iron Roofing Co., Child, Cat, Book, Canton, Ohio, 24 x 14 In. 140.00
Sign, Carborundum, Indian Chief, Niagara Falls, Cardboard, Die Cut, 39 x 30 In. 1210.00
Sign, Carling's Ale, 9 Policemen Sitting, Tin Over Cardboard, 20 x 13 In. 77.00

Sign, Carnation Ice Cream, Ice Cream Sundae, Logo, Porcelain, 22 x 23 In. 798.00
Sign, Carstairs Harmony Blended Whiskey, Cardboard, Frame, c.1940, 16 x 21 In. 25.00
Sign, Carter's Gossamer Carbon Paper, Judge, Multicolored, Tin, 11 1/4 x 17 In. 880.00
Sign, Case Modern Machines For Profitable Farming, Tin, Frame, 60 x 36 In. 1650.00
Sign, Cattle Crossing, Tin, Painted, Late 19th Century, 20 x 25 3/4 In. 645.00
Sign, Centiliver Tonic, Nurse Serves Dose, Cardboard Lithograph, 27 x 17 In. 460.00
Sign, Century Magazine, Lithograph, Maxfield Parrish, c.1898, 12 x 18 3/4 In. 920.00
Sign, Cetacolor Washing Product, Half Of Lady's Dress Faded, Paper, 35 x 24 In. 750.00
Sign, Chase & Sanborn, Old-Fashioned New England Grocery, Paper Lithograph, 24 In. . . . 242.00
Sign, Chesterfield Cigarettes, Ronald Reagan, Paper, Frame, 20 x 24 In. . . . . .28.00 to 55.00
Sign, Chew Red Man Tobacco, Porcelain, 2 Sides, 59 x 22 In. 440.00
Sign, Clabber Girl Baking Powder, Cardboard, 34 x 12 In. 44.00
Sign, Cleveland Plain Dealer Sold Here, Porcelain, Flange, Black & White, 18 In. Diam. . 360.00
Sign, Columbia Chainless, Pope Mfg., Lithograph On Linen, Roll-Up, 40 x 87 In. 2850.00
Sign, Columbia Grafonola, Folsom Music Co., Brainerd, Minn., Tin, 24 x 18 In. 605.00
Sign, Columbia Grafonola, Modern Phonograph, Lithograph, Tin, 23 3/4 x 18 In. 770.00
Sign, Columbia Saloon, Woman On Phone, Embossed, Die Cut, c.1900, 11 x 15 In. 490.00
Sign, Columbian Rope, Fisherman In Slicker, Cardboard, Frame, 34 x 54 In. 330.00
Sign, Consumers Lumber Co., Blue River, Wis., House, Tin, Wood Frame, 30 x 22 In. . . . 495.00
Sign, Continental Fire Insurance Co., New York, Patriot, Porcelain, 12 x 18 In. 240.00
Sign, Coor's Beer, A Quality Cargo, Riverboat, People, Tin Lithograph, 30 x 23 In. 145.00
Sign, Country Club Ice Cream, Cream Of Quality, Porcelain, 2 Sides, 20 x 28 In. 340.00
Sign, Cream Of Wheat, Children Watching Clock, Frame, 1906, 11 x 15 In. 175.00
Sign, Crescent Chick Feed, Superior Quality, Tin, Die Cut, Embossed, 13 x 9 In. 210.00
Sign, Crescent Watch Cases, Glass, Reverse Painted, Embossed, Frame, 25 1/2 In. 495.00
Sign, Cudahy's, Diamond C, Lady Slicing Bacon, Tin, Frame, 25 1/2 x 32 In. 665.00
Sign, Cunard Lines, Ocean Liner, Berengaria, Tin, Frame, 44 x 34 In. 1540.00
Sign, Dad's Old Fashioned Root Beer, Papa, Tin, 10 x 28 In. 205.00
Sign, Dad's Root Beer, Big Junior, Bottle, Tin, Embossed, 13 3/4 x 29 In. 305.00
Sign, David's & Black Ink, Graphics, Hand Colored, Lettering, 12 3/4 x 16 In. 2575.00
Sign, Deering Co., Man On Harvesting Machine, 2 Horses, Paper, 31 x 19 In. 470.00
Sign, DeLaval Cream Separators, Cow Cutout, Sheet Metal, 2 Sides, Lithograph, 5 x 4 In. . 214.00
Sign, DeLaval Cream Separators, Multicolored, Tin, Frame, 30 x 41 In. 2530.00
Sign, DeLaval, A.M. Kimball & Sons, Pine River, Tin, Yellow, 41 x 29 In. 1980.00
Sign, Delaware Rubber Co., Washington Crossing Delaware, Paper, 20 x 26 In. 165.00
Sign, Delco Radio, GM United Service Television Tubes, Tin, 27 x 19 In. 220.00
Sign, Dentist, Tooth Shape, Painted, Iron Hook, 19th Century, 17 1/2 In. 2420.00
Sign, Diamond Dyes, Busy Day In Dollville, Tin Lithograph, 1911, 17 x 11 1/2 In. 800.00
Sign, Diet-Rite Cola, Sugar Free, Bottle, Embossed, Tin, 31 x 12 In. 55.00
Sign, Doherty Organs, Victorian Parlor Scene, Paper, 28 x 19 1/2 In. 1550.00
Sign, Double Cola, Cardboard Lithograph, Frame, 29 1/2 In. 160.00
Sign, Dr Pepper, Good For Life, Girl, Flowers, Cardboard, Frame, 18 x 28 In. 165.00
Sign, Dr Pepper, I'd Give A Month Pay, World War II Army Tank, 24 x 20 In. 715.00
Sign, Dr Pepper, Smart Lift, Woman Wearing Bathing Suit, 1940, 6 1/2 In. 595.00
Sign, Dr. Bells Anti-Pain, Sutherland Medicine Co., Lithograph, Frame, 34 x 48 In. 1450.00
Sign, Dr. D. Jayne & Son, General Robert E. Lee, Frame, 1908, 15 x 19 In. 345.00
Sign, Dr. Duval's Superfluous Hair Destroyer, Gold, Black, Tin, 7 1/2 x 5 1/2 In. 275.00
Sign, Dr. Harris' Cramp Cure, For Every Ache, Paper, Lithograph, 11 x 46 In. 600.00
Sign, Dr. Harshorn's Aromatic Syrup Of Rhubarb, Buff Coated Stock, 12 x 8 In. 420.00
Sign, Dr. Leon's Infant Remedy, 4 Colors, Letterpress, Cardboard, 12 x 8 In. 345.00
Sign, Dr. McLean's Liver & Kidney Balm, Woman, Roses, Frame, 21 x 27 In. 875.00
Sign, Dr. Morse's Indian Root Pills, Cardboard, Die Cut, Trifold, Easel, 42 In. 210.00
Sign, Dr. Morse's Indian Root Pills, Cardboard, Die Cut, 24 x 13 In. 65.00
Sign, Dr. P. Hall's Catarrh Remedy, Cardboard, c.1900, 21 x 11 In. 130.00
Sign, Dr. P. Hall's Catarrh Remedy, Photo On Box, Paper, Frame, 45 x 31 In. 360.00
Sign, Dr. Pierce's Anuric Tablets, Paper Lithograph, 23 x 8 1/2 In. 805.00
Sign, Dr. Pierce's Purgative Pellets, Giant Looks Out Window At Jack, 27 x 32 In. 3680.00
Sign, Dr. Russell's Pepsin, Paper Lithograph, c.1880-1890, 15 x 21 In. 900.00
Sign, Dr. Warner's Coraline Corsets, Cardboard, Frame, 1915, 18 x 26 In. 415.00
Sign, Drake's Cake, Marble Cake On Plate, Tin, Cardboard, 13 1/2 x 9 1/4 In. 138.00
Sign, Drink Almond Smash, Bottle Topper, Cardboard, Die Cut, 13 x 10 3/4 In. 28.00
Sign, Drink Brownie, If You Like Chocolate Soda, Cardboard, Frame, 20 x 60 In. 495.00
Sign, Drink Genuine Nehi Beverages, Bottle, Lady's Legs, Cardboard, 20 x 11 In. 45.00

Sign, Drink Good Grape, In Bottles, Tin Lithograph, Embossed, 19 1/2 x 5 1/2 In. 165.00
Sign, Drink Nichol Cola, America's Taste Sensation, Tin, 1936, 8 x 24 In. 28.00
Sign, Drummond Tobacco, Victorian Woman, Paper Lithograph, Frame, 19 x 35 In. 275.00
Sign, Dubois Export Beer, Ask For, Tin, Wood Frame, 70 x 36 In. 110.00
Sign, Duplex Marine Engine Oil, Steel, Painted, Black & Red On Turquoise, 20 x 10 In. . . 242.00
Sign, Dutch Boy, Painting Wall, Paper, Frame, 16 x 29 In. 220.00
Sign, Dutchess Trouser Factory, Name, Prices, Tin Lithograph, Frame, 34 In. 440.00
Sign, Ebbert Wagons, Shade Of Old Apple Tree, Man, Woman, 37 1/2 x 25 In. . . .825.00 to 2100.00
Sign, Eberhardt & Ober Brewing Co., Factory Scene, Paper, Frame, 50 x 35 1/2 In. 1320.00
Sign, Eckles Ice Cream, Sheet Steel, 2 Sides, 18 x 24 In. 110.00
Sign, Eddies Everlasting Black Dye, Tin Lithograph, Hanging, c.1920, 6 1/2 x 8 1/2 In. . . 24.00
Sign, Egyptienne Luxury Cigarettes, Woman, Cardboard, 13 1/2 x 17 1/2 In. 230.00
Sign, Eight Ball Soda, Celluloid & Cardboard, 9 In. 193.00
Sign, Eisenlohrs Cinco Cigars, Cardboard, Die Cut, Frame, 47 x 33 In. 220.00
Sign, El Rancho Rankin Motel, Metal, Stenciled, c.1950-1960, 5 x 7 In. 28.00
Sign, Emerson's Ginger Mint Julep, Yellow Ground, Tin, 28 x 10 In. 61.00
Sign, Emilia Garcia Cigars, Cardboard, Die Cut, 3 Panels, 43 x 31 In. 240.00
Sign, Emmerling's Beer, German Lager, Tin Lithograph, 27 1/2 x 19 1/2 In. 540.00
Sign, Empress Chocolates, Woman, Cardboard, 14 x 17 3/4 In. 515.00
Sign, Eveready, Fresh Power, Brighter Light, Battery, Porcelain, 9 x 14 In. 220.00
Sign, Excelsior Pneumatic Tires, Tin, Embossed, 16 1/2 x 12 In. 120.00
Sign, Eye-Gene For Your Eyes, Blue, Porcelain Over Steel, 3 3/4 x 5 In. 187.00
Sign, F. Lozano Clear Havana Cigars, Glass, Reverse Painted, 14 x 10 In. 1760.00
Sign, Farley Funeral Home, Gold Leaf Finish, Taunton, Mass., Wood, Glass, 8 x 55 In. . . . 115.00
Sign, Feen-A-Mint, Chewing Laxative, Chew It Like Gum, Porcelain, 30 x 8 In. 690.00
Sign, Fels-Naptha, Get Fels-Naptha Here, Tin Lithograph, Self-Framed, 24 In. 44.00
Sign, Felton's Old Rum, Factory Scene, Tin, 28 1/4 x 22 1/2 In. 1920.00
Sign, Fenton Glass, Handmade In USA, Opalescent, Logo, 2 1/2 x 4 In. 45.00
Sign, Ferguson Farm, This Farm Uses The Ferguson System, Metal, 10 7/8 x 22 In. 175.00
Sign, Feuerhand Pillow, Porcelain, 15 1/2 x 11 3/4 In. 120.00
Sign, Fidelity-Phoenix Fire Insurance Company Of New York, Frame, 14 x 30 In. 100.00
Sign, Fleishmann's Yeast, For Health, Self-Framed, 5 5/8 x 8 5/8 In. 120.00
Sign, Foster Hose Support, Victorian Woman, Celluloid, 19 1/2 x 11 1/2 In. 405.00
Sign, Fountain Service, Porcelain, Dual Tap Graphics, c.1939, 14 x 27 In. 5850.00
Sign, Francis Frost Paint Co., Uncle Sam & Naval Admiral, 27 1/4 x 19 1/2 In. 2300.00
Sign, Franklin Fire Insurance Company Of Philadelphia, Porcelain, 12 x 18 In. 175.00
Sign, Frostie Root Beer, Light-Up, Plastic, Metal, 15 x 14 3/4 In. 145.00
Sign, Gardner Cigars, Indian In Tobacco Field, Brantford, Ontario, Tin, 10 x 14 In. 1650.00
Sign, General Electric Television Service, Tin, Flange, 1949, 16 1/2 x 12 In. 110.00
Sign, Genesee Lager Beer, N.Y. Brewery, Brewery In Gold, Glass, 34 x 24 In. 2010.00
Sign, Gold Bond Ham, A Masterpiece, Woman, Masonite, 44 x 24 In. 45.00
Sign, Gold Dust Twins, Heading Toward House, 25 x 14 1/2 In. 1200.00
Sign, Goodwin & Co. Chewing Tobacco, Paper, 13 3/4 x 9 3/4 In. 1035.00
Sign, Gorham, Maine, Fire Department, Red, Yellow, Black, 7 x 72 In. 635.00
Sign, Granger Pipe Tobacco, Keeps The Smoker Happy, Joe Heistand, 14 x 20 In. 55.00
Sign, Grape Ola, It's Real Grape, Tin, Embossed, 19 1/2 x 13 1/2 In. 495.00
Sign, Grape-Nuts, Girl & Dog, Tin Lithograph, 30 1/2 x 20 In. 1265.00
Sign, Grapette Soda, Thirsty Or Not, Woman In Pool, Cardboard, 31 1/2 x 20 In. 165.00
Sign, Green River Whiskey, Black Man & Horse, Tin, 41 x 31 In. 990.00
Sign, Greyhound Lines, Black Ground, Porcelain, 2 Sides, Oval, 24 x 26 In. 550.00
Sign, Griesedieck Bros. Brewery, Lady Holding Bottle, Paper, 19 x 25 In. 798.00
Sign, Griffith & Boyd Fertilizer Co., Paper, Roll-Up, Frame, 16 1/2 x 23 In. 220.00
Sign, Grocery Store, Wooden, Gilt Decoration, 13 x 106 In. 1670.00
Sign, Grover Soft Shoes, Gibson Girl, Wood, 11 x 19 In. . . . . *Illus* 316.00
Sign, Halls Hair Renewer, Nashua, N.H., Lithograph, Gilt Frame, 18 x 20 In. 850.00
Sign, Hamilton-Brown Shoes, Lady, Blue Dress, Paper, Roll-Up, 17 x 30 In. 110.00
Sign, Hamm's Beer, Waterfall, Motion Display, Light-Up, Plastic, Metal, 34 x 19 In. 385.00
Sign, Hanover Fire Insurance, Paper, 19 x 25 In. 1210.00
Sign, Hart, Schaffner & Marx, Reverse Painted, 21 x 26 In. 578.00
Sign, Harvester Cigars, Yellow, Red, Tin, Oval, Self-Framed, 9 x 13 In. 110.00
Sign, Hat, Cone Shape, Painted Red & Black, Henry In Gold, Tin, 22 1/2 x 25 In. 4400.00
Sign, Hawley & Company Perfumers & Chemists, 1860s, 16 x 18 In. 520.00
Sign, Headlight, Light From Train, Black, Red, White, Porcelain, 48 x 15 In. 330.00

Sign, Heinz Keystone Mixed Pickles, Embossed, Cardboard, 11 x 4 In. 99.00
Sign, Heinz Peanut Butter, Red & Green, Cardboard, Metal Frame, 1920s, 8 x 14 In. 305.00
Sign, Heinz Vinegar, 4 Kinds, Cider, White, Malt, Tarragon, Cardboard, 11 x 21 In. 275.00
Sign, Hendlers Ice Cream, The Velvet Kind, Paper, c.1950, 8 x 13 In. 5.00
Sign, Hercules Powder Co., Don't Fool Me Dog, F.M. Spiegle, 1920, 25 x 15 In. 2875.00
Sign, Hi-Plane Tobacco, Tin Lithograph, 12 x 36 In. 110.00
Sign, Hires Root Beer, Boy, Say Hires, Tin, Oval, Self-Framed, May 21, 1907, 20 x 24 In. 1760.00
Sign, Hoffman & Co. Tobacco, Lithograph, Red Hook, N.Y., 1906, 22 x 16 In. 1595.00
Sign, Hoffman Quality Beverages, White Ground, Red, Blue, Porcelain, 41 x 13 In. 110.00
Sign, Holsum Bread, Miller Patton Baking Co., Paper, Roll-Up, 11 1/2 x 34 In. 110.00
Sign, Honest Scrap Tobacco, Cardboard Lithograph, 1800s, 26 x 30 1/4 In. 1500.00
Sign, Hood's Sarsaparilla, Baby, With Box, Cardboard, Die Cut, 24 x 26 In. 140.00
Sign, Horlacher Beer, Betsy Ross Sewing Flag, Paper, Frame, 22 1/2 x 29 1/2 In. 175.00
Sign, Hotel Marlborough, New York City, Bold Image Of Hotel, 31x 26 In. 460.00
Sign, Howells Orange Julep, Lady Holding Bottle, Paper, Frame, 13 1/2 x 16 In. 35.00
Sign, Hudson River Day Line Cruise, Linen Backed, c.1910, 24 x 37 In. 240.00
Sign, Hudson Shop, Owner's Supplies, Blue Ground, Rack, Tin, 39 x 14 In. 330.00
Sign, Humphrey's Specific Homeopathic Remedies, Cardboard, 17 1/2 x 14 In. 525.00
Sign, Hunts Ice Cream, A Delicious Sundae, Celluloid, 9 In. 295.00
Sign, Hydrox Ice Cream, Sealtest, Porcelain, 2 Sides, 42 x 30 In. 330.00
Sign, I.W. Harper Whiskey, Grandpa, Children, Glass, Reverse Painted, 32 x 44 In. 688.00
Sign, Icy-Pi Ice Cream, Paper Lithograph, 19 In. 39.00
Sign, Illinois Springfield Watches, Conductor, Tin, 13 x 19 In. 1320.00
Sign, Imperial Club 5 Cent Cigars, Best For The Money, Tin Lithograph, 14 x 10 In. 149.00
Sign, Independent Truckers Assoc., Coal Truck, Aluminum, Embossed, 1920s, 12 x 9 In. . . 395.00
Sign, Ingersoll Watches, Blue, White, Porcelain, 7 x 16 In. 248.00
Sign, Iroquois Brewery, Indian Head, Porcelain, Die Cut, Embossed, 17 x 19 In. 4840.00
Sign, Ivory Soap, Lady In Bonnet, Purity, Paper, Frame, 25 1/2 x 33 1/2 In. 300.00
Sign, Jamesway Power Choring Equipment, Robot, Tin, 1956, 17 x 11 In. 225.00
Sign, John Deere Farm Implements, Yellow Ground, Tin, 24 x 12 In. 285.00
Sign, John I. Haas Hops, Malt, Washington, D.C., Hanging, 12 x 13 In. 200.00
Sign, Johnsons Chocolate, Cincinnati, Shield, Brown, Die Cut, 9 1/2 x 11 1/2 In. 440.00
Sign, Johnston Harvester Co., Mower, Globe, Paper, 26 x 19 1/2 In. 468.00
Sign, Julia Marlowe Shoes, Tin, Embossed, 13 1/2 x 19 1/4 In. 805.00
Sign, Just-See Beverages, Bakelite, Light-Up, 13 x 8 In. 99.00
Sign, Kamm & Schellinger Brewing Co., Lion, Globe, Paper, 26 x 36 1/2 In. 1760.00
Sign, Kaughran Clothing & Dry Goods, Purse Shape, Die Cut, 9 1/2 In. 65.00
Sign, Keds, Annual Wire-Haired Terrier & Bicycle Contest, Paper, 1935, 13 x 9 In. 45.00
Sign, Kellogg's Corn Flakes, Goldilocks & 3 Bears Offer, Multicolored, 18 x 24 In. 500.00
Sign, Kellogg's Corn Flakes, Scouts Today, Leaders Tomorrow, 1951, 23 x 30 In. 690.00
Sign, Ken-L Ration Biskit, Dog Food Of Champions, Tin, c.1950, 18 x 29 In. 275.00
Sign, Kerns Bacon & Sausage, Store Hours, Clocks, Tin Over Cardboard, 13 x 9 In. 55.00
Sign, Keystone Ice Cream, Girl, Tin, 27 3/4 x 19 3/4 In. 1980.00
Sign, King Of Soaps, Girl With Puppy, Tin Lithograph, 13 x 25 In. 240.00
Sign, Kingan's Smoked Ham, Sea Captain, Cardboard, 31 x 39 In. 805.00
Sign, Kingston Roller Skates, Kokomo, Ind., Tin, Embossed, 15 x 6 In. 44.00
Sign, Kool Cigarettes, Penguin, Tin, Embossed, 17 x 8 In. 45.00

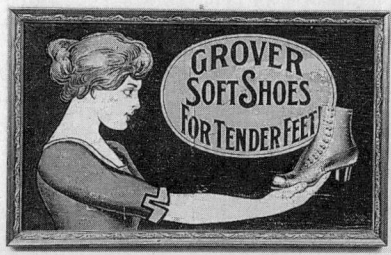

Advertising, Sign, Grover Soft Shoes,
Gibson Girl, Wood, 11 x 19 In.

Advertising, Sign, Red
Goose Shoes, Neon,
Red, Porcelain,
24 x 12 x 6 In.

Sign, Kool Cigarettes, Smoke Kool, Penguin, Tin, Embossed, 26 x 11 In. 50.00
Sign, Kow Kure, For Cows Only, Dairy Assoc., Lyndonville, Vt., Tin, 9 3/4 x 12 3/4 In. . . 204.00
Sign, Kruger Pilsner Beer, Porcelain, 18 1/2 x 38 1/2 In. 40.00
Sign, La Crosse Hat Works, La Crosse, Wis., Blue & White, Metal, 6 x 10 In. 22.00
Sign, La Preferencia Cigars, 30 Minutes In Havana, Paper, Frame, 25 x 35 1/2 In. 1540.00
Sign, Larkin Co. Perfumes, Woman Perfuming Bath Water, Frame, 13 1/2 x 9 In. 90.00
Sign, Lash's Bitters, The Perfect Laxative, Meyercord, Wood, 14 x 20 In. 475.00
Sign, Lawrence Barrett Cigars, Porcelain, 32 x 42 In. 300.00
Sign, Lehigh Valley Railroad, Schuykill, Wyoming, Susquehanna, 6 x 4 In. 6.00
Sign, Lenox Hotel, Buffalo, N.Y., Tin, Round, 24 In. 1380.00
Sign, Levi Strauss, Folds Into Shape Of Blue Jeans, Paper Lithograph, 22 x 7 In. 338.00
Sign, Libby McNeill & Libby, Factory Scene, Oak Frame, 35 1/2 x 23 1/2 In. 600.00
Sign, Lifebuoy Health Soap, Baseball Player Washes Hands, c.1915, 11 x 21 In. 135.00
Sign, Lion Brand Meats, Tin, Oval, 17 1/4 x 14 1/2 In. 1725.00
Sign, Lipton's Instant Cocoa, Woman, Tin, Beveled Edge, 9 x 13 In. 460.00
Sign, Little General, Painted Wood, Applied Letters, 2 Sides, Horse, Rider, 37 In. 310.00
Sign, Liverpool Tin Canister Co., Boy On Chair, Tin Lithograph, 19 x 13 In. 100.00
Sign, Locksmith, Skeleton Key, Brackets, Flat, Steel, 52 x 16 3/4 In. 175.00
Sign, Long Island Oysters, 6 Oysters On Red Plate, Green Ground, 11 x 21 In. 2300.00
Sign, Lorillard's Climax Plug Tobacco, Lady In Chair, Cardboard, 9 3/8 x 13 5/8 In. 305.00
Sign, Lucky Lager, Ice Cold, Beer Bottle, Tin, Embossed, 1950s, 17 x 43 In. 495.00
Sign, Lucky Strike, Luckies Taste Better, Paper Lithograph, 31 1/2 x 43 In. 60.00
Sign, Luden's Menthol Cough Drops, For Quick Relief, Tin, Embossed, 19 x 35 In. 520.00
Sign, Luxite Hosiery, Fulfilling Every Requirement, Cardboard, Easel, 13 x 17 In. 55.00
Sign, Lycoming Rubber Boots, Shoes, Lady & Fisherman, Frame, 1905, 25 x 33 In. 1760.00
Sign, Maestro Cigars, Man, Cardboard, Die Cut, 15 x 17 In. 60.00
Sign, Magnus Root Beer, Serving Station, Tin Lithograph, Flange, 18 x 13 1/2 In. 358.00
Sign, Mail Pouch Tobacco, Chew, Smoke, Porcelain, 2 7/8 x 12 In. 275.00
Sign, Marguerite Havana Cigars, Tin, Cardboard, Self-Framed, 11 1/4 x 14 1/4 In. 88.00
Sign, Marvels Cigarettes, Tin Lithograph, 15 x 10 In. 28.00
Sign, Massanutten Caverns, Porcelain, Stamped, 20 x 17 In. 405.00
Sign, Mayer Hungarian Wine, Process To The Festivities, 1877, 22 1/2 x 19 1/2 In. 920.00
Sign, McBurney's Dry Goods, Carpets & Cloaks, Tipton, Iowa, Wood, 36 x 48 In. 620.00
Sign, McCormick Dairy Equipment, Yellow Ground, Tin, 24 x 18 In. 165.00
Sign, McCormick Reaper, Families Coming Over Bluff, 37 x 27 In. 980.00
Sign, McLean's Liver & Kidney Balm, Forbes & Co., St. Louis, 1898, 27 x 21 In. 400.00
Sign, Meadow Gold Ice Cream, Metal, Flange, 2 Sides, 26 x 20 In. 176.00
Sign, Mentholatum, Till The Doctor Comes, Aluminum, 2 Sides, Hanging, 3 1/2 x 5 In. . . 99.00
Sign, Mercury Outboard Motors, Sales & Service, White Ground, Tin, 24 x 24 In. 580.00
Sign, Mestanke Brewery, Czechoslavakia, Self-Framed, c.1930, 14 3/4 x 10 In. 50.00
Sign, Mil-Kay Vitamin Drink, Black Waiter, Tin Lithograph, Embossed, 40 In. 580.00
Sign, Milken's Parlor Pride, Liquid Stove Enamel, 3-D, 21 1/2 x 17 1/2 In. 575.00
Sign, Milwaukee Brewery Co., Factory, Trolley, Paper, Frame, 40 x 30 In. 2970.00
Sign, Mission Orange Drink, Naturally Good, Bottle, Yellow, Tin, Embossed, 24 In. 95.00
Sign, Morse's Duchess Filled Candies, Lithograph, Frame, 31 x 41 In. 1075.00
Sign, Morton Salt, When It Rains It Pours, Salt Container, Cardboard, 13 x 20 In. 175.00
Sign, Mother's Own Tea, Yellow, Porcelain, 2 1/2 x 20 In. 275.00
Sign, Moxie, Drink Moxie, Tin Lithograph, Die Cut, 2 Sides, Flange, 18 In. 250.00
Sign, Moxie, It's A Hit, Says Ted Williams, Cardboard, Stand-Up, 8 x 13 In. 450.00
Sign, Moxie, Learn To Drink To Your Health, Man On Box, Tin, Die Cut, 5 5/8 x 3 In. . . . 110.00
Sign, Mr. Cola, 16 Oz., Yellow, Red, Embossed, 12 x 12 In. 55.00
Sign, Mt. Vernon Gold Dust Tobacco, George Washington, Paper, 22 x 18 In. 1150.00
Sign, Mullins Canoes, World's Best, Cardboard Lithograph, Die Cut, 31 x 14 In. 2970.00
Sign, Mumms Extra Rye, Lady, Black Dress, Sitting, Cardboard, Frame, 24 x 29 In. 440.00
Sign, Murad Cigarettes, Woman Holding Tray, Tin, Self-Framed, 28 x 39 In. 415.00
Sign, Murine Eye Medicine, Woman With Eye Dropper, Cardboard, 29 x 18 1/2 In. 260.00
Sign, Murphy's Varnishes, Bronze Color, Papier-Mache, Embossed 26 x 19 1/2 In. 270.00
Sign, Narragansett Suspender Co., Heroes Of 1776, 6 1/2 x 15 1/2 In. 860.00
Sign, Natural Chilean Soda, Uncle Natchel, Green, Tin, Flange, 15 x 21 1/2 In. 165.00
Sign, New England Brewing, Hunting Scene, Tin, Self-Framed, 33 x 23 In. 2750.00
Sign, New York Champion Hay Rakes, Boy Painting Fence, Die Cut, 8 In. 75.00
Sign, Niagara Fire Insurance Co., Niagara Falls, Cardboard, 20 x 14 In. 90.00
Sign, Nichol Kola, America's 5 Cent Taste Sensation, Tin, c.1936, 10 x 14 In. 19.00

Sign, Norwegian Brand Smoked Sardines, Statue Of Liberty, Embossed, 10 x 4 In. 85.00
Sign, Nourse Oils, Business Is Good, Viking, Tin, Embossed, 27 3/4 x 9 3/4 In. 635.00
Sign, Now Playing, Eleanor Cleveland, Pine, Paint, American, c.1885, 96 x 22 In........ 3600.00
Sign, NuGrape Soda, Figural, Tin Lithograph, 17 1/8 x 5 In. 110.00
Sign, Nutex Condoms, Baseball Players, Be Safe, Silk Screen Stand-Up, 11 x 14 In. 630.00
Sign, Octagon Soap, Premium Agency, Octagonal, 17 1/4 x 17 3/8 In. 248.00
Sign, Odin 5 Cent Cigars, Tin, Embossed, 19 1/4 x 27 1/4 In. 525.00
Sign, Ogden & Co., You Get Good Value In Goods At Our Store, Tin, 9 3/4 x 27 3/4 In. .. 97.00
Sign, Ohio Valley Piano Co., Paper, 25 x 14 1/2 In. 975.00
Sign, Old Chum Tobacco, White & Yellow On Cobalt Blue, Porcelain, 30 x 18 In. 495.00
Sign, Old English Tobacco, Man, Pipe, Paper, Roll-Up, 20 1/2 x 24 1/2 In. 165.00
Sign, Old Gold Cigarettes, America's Smoothest, Cardboard Lithograph, 44 In. 580.00
Sign, Old Gold Cigarettes, Woman, Fur Wrap, Cardboard, Die Cut, Frame, 29 1/2 x 40 In. 385.00
Sign, Old Kirk Whiskey, Enameled, Brass, San Francisco, Calif., 12 x 3 In. 149.00
Sign, Old Reading Beer, Men Around Table, Cardboard, Frame, 36 x 26 In. 55.00
Sign, Old Reliable Coffee, Girl, Blue Dress, Cardboard, 9 1/2 x 15 In. 66.00
Sign, Old Sailor's Drinking Society, Pub, Wood, Painted, 24 x 18 In. 29.00
Sign, Oliver Chilled Plows, 2 Men, Horse, Tin, Embossed, Self-Framed, 25 x 32 In. 1925.00
Sign, Omega, Stylized Watch Face, Enamel, 13 x 19 1/2 In. 310.00
Sign, Optician, Gold Eyeglass Frames, Carved Wood, 13 1/2 x 39 In. 4115.00
Sign, Optometrist, Eyeglass Rims, Red & Blue Lenses, 35 x 12 In. 3220.00
Sign, Orange Crush, New Flavor-Guarding Bottle, 54 In. 605.00
Sign, Orange Flower Cigars, Cardboard, c.1930, 6 1/2 x 11 In. 20.00
Sign, Orange-Ade, 5 Cents, Bottle, Green Spot, Tin, Embossed, 12 x 36 In. 175.00
Sign, Oscar's Beverages, Bigger & Better, Logo, Bottle, Tin, 32 x 12 In. 70.00
Sign, OshKosh B'Gosh, Work Clothes, Uncle Sam, Composition, Die Cut, 6 x 14 In. 275.00
Sign, Pabst Blue Ribbon Beer, Sheet Steel, 51 x 42 In. 35.00
Sign, Pacific Soft Water Laundry Agency, Sunrise Logo, Porcelain, 42 x 8 In. 1430.00
Sign, Palm Cigars, 3 For 5 Cents, That Different Smoke, Tin, Embossed, 19 x 6 In....... 176.00
Sign, Parke, Davis & Co., We Dispense Pharmaceuticals, Tin, 1890, 27 x 16 In. 500.00
Sign, Pawnbroker, 2 Wood Balls, Wire Posts, Gold Repaint Over Silver, 18 In. 110.00
Sign, Pear's Soap, Girl Making Soap Bubbles, 17 1/2 x 26 1/2 In. 200.00
Sign, Pee Gee Paint, Tin Lithograph, Embossed, Die Cut, 19 3/4 In. 99.00
Sign, Penn Club Beverages, 3 Smiling Men, Cardboard Lithograph, 15 In. 55.00
Sign, Penn Ester Stoves, Cardboard, 18 x 22 In. 1380.00
Sign, Pet Milk, Picture Of Fultz Quadruplets, Framed, 21 x 11 In. 20.00
Sign, Peter Pan Ice Cream, Tin Lithograph, Embossed, 28 In. 155.00
Sign, Peter Schuttler Wagons, Brownwood, Texas, 5 x 27 1/2 In. 325.00
Sign, Peter Schuyler Cigars, Black, Yellow, Porcelain, 36 x 12 In. 160.00
Sign, Petromax Kerosene Lamps, Black, Green, White, Porcelain, 13 x 26 In. 220.00
Sign, Pex Poultry Feed, I Get The Milk-Bank Boost, Metal, Die Cut, 19 x 13 1/2 In. ... 120.00
Sign, Pfluegers Fishing Tackle, Leaping Bass, c.1908, 9 3/4 x 14 In. 2420.00
Sign, Philip Morris, Bellboy Holding Tray, Die Cut, Cardboard, 20 x 44 In............ 495.00
Sign, Phillies Cigars, Only 5 Cents, Tin, Embossed, 17 x 10 5/8 In. 220.00
Sign, Pickwick Ale & Stout, Sold Here, Tin Lithograph, Embossed, 19 5/8 x 27 In. 176.00
Sign, Pied Piper Shoes, Graphics, Aluminum, 57 1/2 x 26 1/2 In. 115.00
Sign, Piedmont Cigarettes, Blue Central & White Side Panels, 52 x 15 1/2 In. 210.00
Sign, Piedmont Cigarettes, George & Martha Washington, Tin, 30 x 23 1/2 In. 290.00
Sign, Piedmont Tobacco, Lady With Cigarettes, Frame, 1908, 19 x 25 In. 330.00
Sign, Piedmont, For Cigarettes Virginia Tobacco Is Best, Porcelain, 30 x 46 In. 175.00
Sign, Pilgrim Fathers Cigars, Pilgrims, Gresh & Sons, Tin, Embossed, 27 x 19 In. 575.00
Sign, Pingree & Smith Fine Boots, Shoes & Slippers, Tin, 23 1/2 x 17 1/2 In. 518.00
Sign, Piper Heidsieck Chewing Tobacco, Champagne Bottle, Paper, 14 x 11 In. 460.00
Sign, Pittsburgh Paints, 8 Colors, Porcelain, 2 Sides, 16 x 25 In. 305.00
Sign, Players Tobacco, Cigarette Pack, Yellow, Black, Blue, Porcelain, 45 x 16 In. 440.00
Sign, Plymouth Rock Steamer, Chromolithograph, c.1850, 20 x 24 In. 470.00
Sign, Pocket Watch, Painted, Cast, Sheet Metal, Gilt, J.E. Rene, 27 x 19 1/2 In. 3080.00
Sign, Poland China Hog, Sheet Steel Lithograph, 2 Sides, 42 x 48 In. 580.00
Sign, Poll-Parrot Shoes, Parrot, Clown, Trees, Wood, 49 In. 130.00
Sign, Popsicle, Refreshing, Easy To Eat, Tin, Embossed, 35 1/2 x 11 3/4 In. 580.00
Sign, Prince Albert Tobacco, Chief Joseph, Nez Perce, R.J. Reynolds, 19 1/4 x 25 In. 5750.00
Sign, Prudential Insurance, Ship Passing Straits Of Gibraltar, 32 x 22 In. 290.00
Sign, Pulver Chewing Gum, Tasty Chew, Red, Porcelain, 5 x 22 1/2 In. 250.00

Sign, Quaker Puffed Wheat, Babe Ruth, 1, 000 Prizes, Frame, 1934, 28 x 39 In. 2500.00
Sign, R&G Corsets, Woman, Multicolored, Tin, Frame, 13 1/4 x 18 In. 1210.00
Sign, Raleigh Cigarettes, Elegantly Dressed Couple, Cardboard, Frame, 14 x 20 In. 39.00
Sign, RC Cola, Rita Hayworth Serves Bottles, Cardboard, 40 x 26 In. 248.00
Sign, RCA Radiotron Radio Tubes & Parts, 2 Sides, Flange, 15 3/4 x 22 In. 210.00
Sign, RCA Victor Records, His Master's Voice, Nipper Listening, Porcelain, 24 x 18 In. . . 1375.00
Sign, Red Cross Cotton, Blacks Picking Cotton, Cardboard Lithograph, 30 3/4 In. 95.00
Sign, Red Goose Shoes, Children Riding Bicycles, Cardboard, Die Cut, 40 x 30 In. 300.00
Sign, Red Goose Shoes, Neon, Red, Porcelain, 24 x 12 x 6 In. . . . . *Illus* 1955.00
Sign, Red Star Line, Antwerpen-New York, 34 x 24 In. 1150.00
Sign, Red Wing Grape Juice, Lemonade, Tin, Cardboard, Self-Framed, 13 x 9 1/2 In. 330.00
Sign, Redfern Co., Cop Chasing Child, Yellow, Porcelain, 48 x 20 In. 385.00
Sign, Regal Boot With Spur, Cast Bronze, 12 x 18 In. 60.00
Sign, Registered Holsteins, Cow In Pasture, Tin, 2 Sides, 36 x 24 In. 605.00
Sign, Reliance Batteries, Finest Built, Rely On Me, Tin, Embossed, 13 3/4 x 39 3/4 In. . . . 305.00
Sign, Restroom, Woman, Gentleman, Silhouettes On White, Porcelain, 9 x 11 In., Pair . . . 415.00
Sign, Rheingold Beer, Gold Metal Frame, Price Brothers, 7 1/4 x 7 1/4 In. 58.00
Sign, Richmond Cigarettes, Woman, Cardboard Lithograph, 15 1/2 x 12 1/2 In. 465.00
Sign, Rising Sun Stove Polish, Picture Hanging On Wall, Woman, Paper, 18 x 22 In. 405.00
Sign, Robert Burns 10-Cent Cigar, Glass, Curved Front, 22 1/2 x 15 1/2 In. 880.00
Sign, Rockland Company's Shoes, Foil Lettering, 37 1/2 x 23 3/4 In. 1380.00
Sign, Roebling Bar & Grill, 2 Sides, 72 x 16 In. 865.00
Sign, Roi-Tan 5-Cent Cigars, Glass, Reverse Painted, Gold Leaf, Frame, 84 x 45 In. 2420.00
Sign, Royal Crown Cola, My Mom Knows Best, Cardboard, F. Nawicke, 28 x 11 In. 99.00
Sign, Royal Crown Cola, Tin, Embossed, Wood Frame, 1939, 16 x 36 In. 415.00
Sign, S. Stokes Boot & Shoe Repairer, Green, Yellow, 13 1/2 x 21 In. 550.00
Sign, Saddle Shop, Horse Head Shape, Zinc, 19th Century, 15 x 12 In. 4115.00
Sign, Sam's Boot & Shoe Repairs, Painted, 2 Sides, 21 1/4 x 18 1/2 In. 495.00
Sign, San Felice Cigars, For Gentlemen Of Good Taste, Porcelain, 40 x 13 In. 385.00
Sign, Scandinavian-American Steamship, Tin Lithograph, c.1890, 41 x 31 In. 1020.00
Sign, Schlitz Tonic, Have You Tried It, Tin Lithograph, Over Cardboard, 9 1/2 x 13 In. . . . 85.00
Sign, School Crossing Guard, School Drive Slowly, Red Uniform, Tin, 18 x 64 In. 440.00
Sign, Seapure Oysters, Time To Eat, Clock Face, 12 Months, Card Stock, c.1930, 10 In. . . 28.00
Sign, Segars Bulldog, Paper Lithograph, Merrian, Framed, 1900, 9 1/2 x 13 1/2 In. 115.00
Sign, Selz Shoes, Make Your Feet Glad, Flange, 12 x 19 3/4 In. . . . . *Illus* 230.00
Sign, Sewall's Paints, For Best Results, Wood, 60 x 28 In. 120.00
Sign, Sherwin Williams, Paint Can, Porcelain, Die Cut, 44 In. 300.00
Sign, Shoe Repair, Figural, Luma Neon, Sheet Metal, 53 x 34 x 16 In. 360.00
Sign, Shoe Repair, Man's Shoe, Black, White, Red Ground, Tin, 17 1/4 x 18 In. 999.00
Sign, Shoe, Lacing Holes, Metal, 19th Century, 15 x 28 In. 230.00
Sign, Shoe, Pointing Hand, 2 Sides, 19th Century, 38 1/2 In. 2645.00
Sign, Silver Dime Beer, Blue, Silver, Tin, Over Cardboard, 5 x 10 In. 280.00
Sign, Singer Sewing Machines, Orange S, Woman Sewing, Porcelain, 16 x 22 In. 275.00
Sign, Slater's Cigars, Boss Stogies, Washington, Pa., Painted, Metal, Hanging, 7 x 10 In. . 245.00
Sign, Snow Boy Washing Powder, Boy & Sled, Cardboard, 23 1/4 x 29 1/4 In. 9775.00
Sign, Sober-Up, Drink Sober-Up, It's A Life Saver, Cardboard, c.1950, 14 x 19 In. 130.00
Sign, Spinner, Towles Log Cabin Maple Syrup, Celluloid, Brass, 2 Sides, 2 3/4 x 1 1/4 In. . 249.00

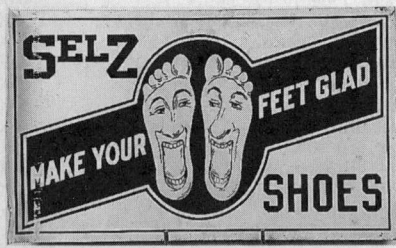

Advertising, Sign, Selz Shoes, Make Your Feet Glad,
Flange, 12 x 19 3/4 In.

Advertising, Sign, Tree Brand Shoes, Battreal
Shoe Co., 2 Sides, Die Cut, Flange, 13 In.

Sign, Spitting, Smoking, Prohibited By Law, Porcelain, 15 x 11 5/8 In. 255.00
Sign, Springfield Watches, Patriotic Design, Tin, Wells & Hope, 8 x 19 1/2 In. 1150.00
Sign, Squire's Pig, Ham, Bacon, Sausage, Tin, 20 1/4 x 24 1/4 In. 2760.00
Sign, Squirrel Brand Salted Peanuts, Squirrel, Cardboard, Die Cut, 11 x 12 In. 300.00
Sign, Squirt, Never An After-Thirst, Bottle, Tin, Embossed, 27 x 9 1/2 In. 190.00
Sign, SS Deutschland Steamship, Ship Entering N.Y. Harbor, 50 3/4 x 32 In. 175.00
Sign, Stafford's Ink, Ink Bottle, Figural, Tin, 12 x 16 In. 1035.00
Sign, Stafford's Universal Ink, Girls, Bands, 21 x 27 In. 800.00
Sign, Stag Smoking Tobacco, 12-Point Buck, Cardboard, Frame, 28 x 42 In. 660.00
Sign, Star Soap, Schultz & Co., Grandpa's Pets, Paper, 14 1/2 x 22 In. 890.00
Sign, Stephens Ink, Gold Cartouche, Black Lettering, 1840-1850s, 10 x 8 In. 460.00
Sign, Sterling Brand Seeds, Woman In Field, Ear Of Corn, Paper, 1912, 29 x 21 In. 475.00
Sign, Stickney & Poor Spices, Mustard, Pepper, Ginger Packs, Tin, 20 x 28 In. 230.00
Sign, Stoneware, Best Food Container, Boy, Dog, Doughnuts, Tin, 13 x 19 In. . . .935.00 to 1150.00
Sign, Stoudt's Dandelion Bitters, 28 1/4 x 22 In. 70.00
Sign, Stratton & Loveland Dentists, Wood & Iron, Shield Shape, 23 x 33 In. 560.00
Sign, Strauss & Co., Every Woman's Shoe Store, Glass, Copper Bound, 14 x 54 In. 315.00
Sign, Sunbeam Bread, Girl Eats Bread, Red Ground, Tin, Oval, 54 1/2 x 36 In. 935.00
Sign, Sunbeam Bread, Miss Sunbeam Holding Bread, Cardboard, Die Cut, 29 x 50 In. . . .   220.00
Sign, Sunbeam Energy-Packed Bread, Reach For, Tin, Embossed, 19 x 55 In. 1330.00
Sign, Sweet Caporal Cigarettes, Woman Clown, Paper, 18 x 28 In.   600.00
Sign, Sweet Heart Products, Hard Wheat Flour, Porcelain, Heart Shape, 5 In. 270.00
Sign, Sweet-Orr Pants, Shirts, Overalls, Porcelain, 23 1/2 x 10 In.   250.00
Sign, Swifts Pride Soap, Relief For Rubbers On The Washboard, Cardboard, 13 x 9 In. 146.00
Sign, Taco Bell, Join Bullwinkle Taco Crunch Club, Cardboard, 1993, 12 x 17 In. 25.00
Sign, Taft's Specific For Brain & Nervous Diseases, Die Cut, 9 x 6 In. 130.00
Sign, Texas & Southwestern Cattle Raisers, Member, Porcelain, 10 x 20 In. 215.00
Sign, The Times, Get The Best, All The News, 1 Cent, 15 1/2 x 8 1/2 In. 400.00
Sign, Tiger Brand, Cut Your Sanding Costs, Porcelain, 12 x 15 In.   99.00
Sign, Toy Manchester Terriers, Cutout Silhouette, Painted, Brown, Black, 20 x 21 In. 85.00
Sign, Tree Brand Shoes, Battreal Shoe Co., 2 Sides, Die Cut, Flange, 13 In. . . . . *Illus*   633.00
Sign, Turnbull's Scotch Whisky, Bottle, Tin, Embossed, Frame, 16 1/2 x 22 In. 155.00
Sign, Union Mills Flour, Baby In Basket, Matted, 20 x 16 In. 230.00
Sign, Union Pacific Tea Co., Woman, Doves, Rabbit, Roll-Up, 21 1/2 x 44 1/2 In. 288.00
Sign, United States Fur, Hunters Laughing, Black Boy, Paper, 1900s, 15 x 21 In. 210.00
Sign, Van Camp's Pork & Beans, Boy & Girl, Cardboard, Die Cut, 16 x 19 3/8 In. 575.00
Sign, Visiting Nurse Assoc., Pure Milk For Babies, Milk Station, Wood, 18 x 2 In. 940.00
Sign, W.A. Wilson Jeweler, Black Sand Paint, Gold Letters & Molding, 2 Sides, 60 In. 225.00
Sign, W.D. Grover, Undertaker, 115 Main Street, Dansville, N.Y., Tin, 5 x 19 1/2 In. 85.00
Sign, Walk-Over Shoes, Hanson Shoe Store, Winooski, Vt., 23 1/2 x 11 3/4 In. 180.00
Sign, Walter Beer, Glass, Red, White, Curved Front, Wood Frame, 22 1/2 x 16 In. 1210.00
Sign, Ward's Orange Crush, Like Oranges, Paper, Frame, 28 x 8 In. 120.00
Sign, Warner's Log Cabin Remedies, Glass, Walnut Frame, 13 x 11 In. 2200.00
Sign, Watchmaker, Gold Paint, Face, Hands, Cast Iron, Tin, C.W.I. Co., 34 In. 935.00
Sign, Watchmaker, Pocket Watch Shape, Cast Iron, Zinc, 23 1/2 x 52 In. 1760.00
Sign, Waterman's Fountain Pens, Santa Claus, Cardboard, Die Cut, 15 x 14 In. . . . .146.00 to 250.00
Sign, Wave Line Cut Plug Tobacco, Man Fishing & Smoking, 12 x 16 In. 1035.00
Sign, Wayne Feeds, Man On Horse, Red Stripes, Porcelain, 36 x 48 In. 935.00
Sign, We Sell Beasley, Hardwood Shoe Co. Shoes, Tin, Wood Frame, 16 1/2 x 97 In. 350.00
Sign, Welcome Soap, Curtis Davis Co., 2 Women, 16 1/4 x 31 1/2 In. 990.00
Sign, Wells Richardson & Co., Butter, Boy, Cow, Frame, 21 1/2 x 31 1/2 In. 330.00
Sign, Western Union Everywhere, Blue Ground, Porcelain, 2 Sides, 30 x 18 In. 330.00
Sign, Westinghouse Mazda Lamps, Die Cut, Easel Back, 11 3/8 x 16 In. 120.00
Sign, Whistle Soda, Thirsty, Just Whistle, Boy, Bottle, Cardboard, Die Cut, 14 x 27 In. . . .   330.00
Sign, White House Roasted Coffees, Black & White, Wood Frame, 13 x 10 In. 2970.00
Sign, White Leghorn Chickens, Paper Lithograph, 6 1/2 x 9 In. 70.00
Sign, White's Golden Tonic Horse Cure, Horse, Paper, Frame, 25 x 19 1/4 In. 230.00
Sign, Whiteley Harvesting Machine, 2 Harvesters, Paper, Frame, 19 x 34 In. 525.00
Sign, Wilson Whiskey, Horse & Buggy, People, Tin, Frame, 50 x 37 In. 4400.00
Sign, Winchester Lawn Mowers, Cardboard, Easel Back, 19 x 13 In. 1540.00
Sign, Wolf & Co. Flour Milling & Machinery Factory, Factory Scene, 31 x 22 In. 575.00
Sign, Wonder Bread, Builds Strong Bodies 8 Ways, Tin, Embossed, 20 x 12 1/2 In. 230.00
Sign, Woods First Premium Mowers, Horses & Cart, Paper, Frame, 31 x 22 1/2 In. 690.00

Sign, Woolworth & Co., Gold & Red Reverse Lettering, 2 Sides, 10 x 71 In. 250.00
Sign, Woonsocket Boots & Shoes, Fishing Scene, Paper, 17 x 25 In. 3850.00
Sign, World's Fair Cigars, Embossed, Paper, Hanging, 10 x 14 In. 125.00
Sign, Wrigley's Doublemint & Spearmint Chewing Gum, Cardboard, 21 x 11 In. 120.00
Sign, Wrigley's Doublemint Chewing Gum, Orange, Black, Frame, 27 x 17 In. 80.00
Sign, Wrigley's Juicyfruit Chewing Gum, After Every Meal, Frame, 27 x 17 In. 176.00
Sign, Yale Padlocks, Mounted, Plexiglas Cover, Wood Frame, 40 In. 275.00
Sign, Yorktown Cigarettes, Ship, Cigarette Pack, Blue Ground, Tin, 12 x 16 1/2 In. 55.00
Sign, Zenith Radio, Red Ground, White Letters, Neon, 36 x 60 In. 660.00
Sign, Ziegler's Beer, Tin Lithograph, Over Cardboard, 11 1/2 In.   165.00
Stringholder, Gold Dust, Tin Lithograph, Collapsible, 8 1/2 In. 495.00
Stringholder, Jaxon Soap, Cast Iron, Nickel Plated, Embossed, 4 1/2 In. 105.00
Stringholder, Lion Is The King Of Coffees, Painted, Stenciled, Sack 1100.00
Stringholder, Surprise Soap, Tin Lithograph, Figural Wash Barrel, 6 1/2 In. 190.00
Sugar Shaker, Chef Boy-Ar-Dee, Milk Glass, 5 In. 20.00
Sweetheart Soap Trade Stimulator, Automaton Baby In Bassinet 2500.00
Thermometers are listed in their own category.

Advertising tin cans or canisters were first used commercially in the
United States in 1819 and were called *tins*. The English language is
sometimes confusing. Today the word *tin* is used by most collectors to
describe many types of containers, including food tins, biscuit boxes,
roly poly tobacco containers, gunpowder cans, talcum powder sprin-
kle-top cans, cigarette flat-fifty tins, and more. Beer Cans are listed in
their own category. Things made of undecorated tin are listed under
Tinware.

Tin, 4 Roses Smoking Tobacco, Liggett & Myers, Embossed, 4 1/4 x 3 1/4 In. 428.00
Tin, After Dinner Peanuts, 10 Lb., 9 5/8 x 1/4 In. . . . . .99.00 to 118.00
Tin, Airedale Cigars, Dog, Embossed, Round, 5 1/4 x 5 1/2 In. 222.00
Tin, Allen's Sanitary Tooth-Ease, Image Of Allen S. Olmsted, Label, 4 In. 176.00
Tin, American Eagle Tobacco, Quill Smoking Tobacco, 3 3/8 x 4 3/8 x 2 1/4 In. 130.00
Tin, American Lady Coffee, Puts A Smile In Good Morning, 1 Lb., 4 1/4 x 6 In. 1815.00
Tin, American Powder Mills, Dead Shot Rifle, 1900, 1 Lb., 4 x 6 x 1 In. 275.00
Tin, Ariel Club Coffee, C.H. Kroneberger & Co., Steel Cut, 1 Lb., 6 x 4 In. 264.00
Tin, Aunt Dinah Molasses, Black Mammy, Gingerbread Recipe, 4 3/4 In. 110.00
Tin, Axle Oil, Buggy, Lithograph, Cleveland, Ohio, 6 1/2 x 3 1/2 In. 140.00
Tin, B & B Baby Talc, Toy Animal Scene, Lithograph, 2 1/4 In. 28.00
Tin, Bagdad Short Cut Tobacco, Pipe Smoking, 3 3/4 x 3 3/8 x 1 1/8 In. 227.00
Tin, Bagley & Buckingham Co., Vivid Colors, Lithograph, 4 1/2 x 3 1/8 In. 170.00
Tin, Battleship Coffee, Tin Lithograph, Slide Lid, 8 1/4 In. 110.00
Tin, Ben Franklin Cigars, Ben Franklin & American Eagle, Lithograph, 4 x 3 In. 85.00
Tin, Benzotol Tooth Powder, Butte, Montana, Price 25 Cents, 3 3/4 In. 175.00
Tin, Betsy Ross Tea, Betsy, Flag, Multicolored, Tin, Cardboard 18.00
Tin, Big Ben Tobacco, Black Horse, Lithograph, 4 1/2 x 3 1/8 In. . . . . .85.00 to 140.00
Tin, Bishops Candies, Eagle, Bear, Lithograph, Screw Top, 5 x 7 x 5 In. 99.00
Tin, Blackwell's Tobacco, English Flake Out, Lithograph, 4 1/2 x 6 1/6 x 4 In. 624.00
Tin, Blue Ointment Poison, Round, Skull & Crossbones, 1 1/2 In. . . . . .33.00 to 77.00
Tin, Bluehill Coffee, Milk Pail Shape, Blue, 5 Lb., 10 1/4 x 7 1/4 In. 300.00
Tin, Boardman's Putnam Coffee, Soldier On Horse, 1 Lb., 3 5/8 x 5 In. 72.00
Tin, Boldts Specials, Quality Mild Cigars, 1915, 3 x 5 1/2 x 1/2 In. 44.00
Tin, Bond Street Tobacco, Lithograph, Sample, 2 x 3 In. 147.00
Tin, Bonnie Bright Powder, Yellow, Child At Table, Paper Label, 4 3/4 x 3 In. 140.00
Tin, Boston Confectionary Co., Pencil, Jackie Coogan, 7 7/8 x 2 x 5/8 In. 75.00
Tin, Bowl Of Roses Tobacco, Man Smoking Pipe, Tin Lithograph, 4 3/8 x 3 1/8 In. 398.00
Tin, Bowl Of Roses, Pipe Mixture, Lithograph, 3 5/8 x 3 x 7/8 In. . . . . .221.00 to 304.00
Tin, British Army Foot Powder, Coat Of Arms, Round, 4 x 1 3/4 In. 70.00
Tin, Bucket Syrup, Pioneer Maple Products Co., Lithograph, 1920s, 3 1/2 x 4 In. 127.00
Tin, Buckingham Tobacco, Lithograph, Sample, 3 x 2 1/4 In. 195.00
Tin, Bunte Marshmallows, Lithograph, 5 x 12 3/4 In. 220.00
Tin, Buy-Roz Gum, Startup Candy Co., Rose Fragrance, 1 1/2 x 2 x 1/2 In. 195.00
Tin, California Perfume Soap, American Ideal Brand Soap, Hinged, 2 x 3 In. 95.00
Tin, Campfire Marshmallows, Supreme, Camp Scene, 8 x 2 1/4 In. 140.00
Tin, Caravan Condoms, Desert Caravan, 1/4 Dozen, 1 5/8 x 2 1/8 In. 170.00

Tin, Cels Condoms, Frank Aaronoff Co., 1 5/8 x 2 1/8 In. 160.00
Tin, Charles Thomson Cigar, American Patriot, Tin Lithograph, 5 1/4 x 3 3/8 In. 115.00
Tin, Charm Of The West Tobacco, Woman, Dog, Horse, Yellow, 2 x 3 3/4 x 5/8 In. 260.00
Tin, Chuck Wagon Coffee, Yellow Ground, Red Covered Wagon, 1 Lb. 185.00
Tin, Cleopatra Rose Palmolive Talc, 2 1/8 x 1 1/4 x 6 In. 85.00
Tin, Coach & Four Tobacco, English Pipe Blend, Pocket, Unopened, 3 x 4 1/2 x 1 In. 215.00
Tin, Colgans Taffy Tolu Chewing Gum, Red, Lithograph, 8 5/8 x 7 1/2 x 4 1/2 In. 170.00
Tin, Colgate Talc, Baby Holding Talc Tin, Lithograph, 6 x 2 1/4 In. 195.00
Tin, Columbia Coffee, Sealed Can, Original Key, 2 1/4 x 2 3/4 In. 230.00
Tin, Commander Baking Powder, General Robert E. Lee, Red Ground, 4 x 2 In. 330.00
Tin, Cornhusker Highway Cigar, State Map, Tin Lithograph, 5 1/4 x 4 In. 139.00
Tin, Country Club Cigars, Woman Golfer, Winston & Co., 6 x 4 In. 315.00
Tin, Court Royal Cigars, 2 For 15 Cents, Lithograph, 5 1/2 In. 49.00
Tin, Crawford Tea, Inlaid Satinwood, Tea Caddy Shape, c.1920, 6 x 4 3/4 In. 250.00
Tin, Daniel's Liniment Powder, Lithograph, 2 1/2 x 3 In. 67.00
Tin, Darko Coffee, Drake & Co., Lithograph Of Duck On Both Sides, 1 Lb. 1210.00
Tin, Dean's Peacock Condoms, Peacock, Reservoir Ends, 1 3/4 x 2 1/8 In. 39.00
Tin, Devoe's Tobacco Co., Sweet Smoke, Concave, 4 1/4 x 3 x 1 In. ....276.00 to 380.00
Tin, Dill's Best Tobacco, Yellow Ground, Lithograph, 4 3/8 x 3 In. 166.00
Tin, Dinsmore's Cough Drops, Woman, Somers Bros., 1810, 8 x 5 x 5 In. 520.00
Tin, Donald Duck Coffee, Goyer Coffee Co., Yellow Lithograph, 2 1/4 x 3 In. 550.00
Tin, Double Tip Condoms, Girl In Bathing Suit, Lithograph, 1 3/4 x 2 1/8 In. 210.00
Tin, Dr. E.L. Graves Unequaled Tooth Powder, Contents, 4 In. 95.00
Tin, Dr. Hammond's Nerve & Brain Tablets, For Men's Special Diseases, 3 x 1 5/8 In. ... 190.00
Tin, Dr. Herman's Foot Powder, Young Woman, Paper Label, 4 1/2 x 2 1/2 In. 150.00
Tin, Dr. Hess Udder Ointment, Cow, 4 x 1 1/2 In. 45.00
Tin, Dr. Hitchcock's Laxative Powder, Bearded Man, Contents, Domed Lid, 3 In. 50.00
Tin, Dr. Hobson's Eye Salve, Round, Box, 1 1/8 In. 130.00
Tin, Dr. I.W. Lyon's Perfect Tooth Powder, Woman, 4 In. 130.00
Tin, Dr. Robert's Dog Medicine, Roundworm, Paper Label, Flyer, 1 3/4 x 1 1/4 In. 145.00
Tin, Dr. Saymans Toilet Talcum Powder, Cardboard, Paper Label, 5 x 2 3/8 In. 108.00
Tin, Drako Coffee, Duck, 6 x 4 In. 1210.00
Tin, Epicure Tobacco, Man Lying On Ground Smoking, Lithograph, 4 1/8 x 3 In. 276.00
Tin, Fast Mail Tobacco, Bagley & Co., Train, 2 1/4 x 3 1/2 x 5/8 In. 550.00
Tin, Flick & Flock Cigars, Roby Cigar Co., Dogs, 5 5/8 x 6 1/8 x 4 1/4 In. 4750.00
Tin, Forest & Stream Tobacco, Man Fishing, Lithograph, 4 1/2 x 3 In. ....198.00 to 354.00
Tin, G.F. Hersh & Bros High-Grade Waldorf Coffee, Lithograph, 18 x 17 In. 95.00
Tin, Gail & Ax, Navy Tobacco, Sailor, Tobacco Pack, 3 1/8 x 5 5/8 x 1 1/2 In. 70.00
Tin, Girard Cigars, Stephen Girard, Tin Lithograph, 5 1/2 x 5 1/2 In. 60.00
Tin, Globe Tobacco Co., Cube Cut, Red Lithograph, 3 5/8 x 3 1/2 x 1 1/4 In. 359.00
Tin, Golden Bear Cookies, Silhouette Of Bear Eating Cookie, 5 1/2 In. 100.00
Tin, Golden Harvest Coffee, Key Wind, Lithograph, 1 Lb., 5 1/4 x 4 In. 90.00
Tin, Golden Vine Peanuts, Lithograph, 10 Lb., 11 x 7 1/2 In. 120.00
Tin, Golden Wedding Coffee, Pry Lid, Lithograph, 2 x 3 In. 95.00
Tin, Gray Dunn, Chinoiserie, Biscuit, Scotland, 1930s, 7 In. 25.00
Tin, Gypsy Boy Spices, Cloves, Boy On Horse, 1 Oz., 2 x 2 1/4 x 1 3/8 In. 106.00
Tin, Half & Half Tobacco, Lithograph, Sample, 3 x 2 1/4 In. 170.00
Tin, Half Spanish Cigars, Rooster, Lithograph, 5 1/8 x 4 3/4 In. 155.00
Tin, Harper's Mops, Woman Mopping Floor, Red Ground, Lithograph, 7 x 3 1/4 In. 85.00
Tin, Hatchet Coffee, Tin Lithograph, 1 Lb., 6 x 4 In. 145.00
Tin, Henalfa Hair Restorer, Girl, 4 Oz., 2 1/2 x 3 In. 99.00
Tin, Hi-Plane Tobacco, Single Engine Plane, Lithograph, 4 1/2 x 3 In. 195.00
Tin, Hi-Plane Tobacco, Twin Engine Plane, Lithograph, 4 3/8 x 3 In. 231.00
Tin, Himrod's Asthma Powder, Box, 2 x 3 1/2 In. 50.00
Tin, Hitt Fireworks Co., Red Danger Lights, Lithograph, 1931, 13 x 2 1/4 In. 130.00
Tin, Holmes & Coutts, Champagne Wafers, Biscuit, 3 1/2 x 5 In. 125.00
Tin, Honey Moon Tobacco, Man On Moon, Lithograph, 4 3/8 x 3 In. ....154.00 to 166.00
Tin, Hostess Holiday Fruitcake, Metal Pkg. Corp., c.1930, 3 1/2 x 6 x 3 In. 12.00
Tin, Hudson, Scott & Sons, Portrait Of Woman, Biscuit, Carlisle, England, 6 In. 65.00
Tin, Humpty-Dumpty Talc, Lithograph, 7 1/2 In. 55.00
Tin, Huntley & Palmers, Books Shape, 4 In. 300.00
Tin, Huntley & Palmers, Farm House, Biscuit, 6 1/2 In. 860.00
Tin, Huntley & Palmers, Fire Brigade, 6 1/2 In. 90.00

Advertising, Tin,
Loverin & Browne
Co. Wholesale
Grocers, Chicago,
8 1/2 In.

Remove rust from old tins by using an ink eraser. If you can't find an old one, use the type that comes on a ball-point pen.

Tin, Huntley & Palmers, Handbag, 1904, 8 In.	90.00
Tin, Huntley & Palmers, John O'Groats Shortbread, Scottish Tartan, Biscuit, 4 In.	50.00
Tin, Huntley & Palmers, Lion's Head Doorknocker, Bicsuit, c.1910, 8 1/2 In.	95.00
Tin, Hy Gee Prophylactic, Lithograph, 1 5/8 x 2 x 1/4 In.	385.00
Tin, Hyacinth Talc, 1920 Woman Tennis Player, Trees, Paper Label, 5 x 1 7/8 In.	130.00
Tin, India Tea Co., Gold, Silver, Nickel Polish, Paper Label, 1911, 2 1/2 x 5 In.	66.00
Tin, Indian Girl Brand Allspice, Jewitts, Sioux Falls, S.D., Paper Label, 2 x 3 1/2 In.	90.00
Tin, J & C Marshmallows, Building, Red, 2 3/8 x 6 x 3 7/8 In.	248.00
Tin, Jayne's Expectorant Tablets, Opium, 1 Grain To Ounce, 2 7/8 x 1 3/4 In.	130.00
Tin, John Paul Jones Tobacco, Image Of Naval Hero, Pocket, 4 x 3 In.	1870.00
Tin, John Ruskin Cigar, Image Of Ruskin, Tin Lithograph, 5 1/2 x 3 1/2 In.	100.00
Tin, Kamargo Coffee, American Indian Design, Lithograph, 1 Lb.	440.00
Tin, Kenny's Maid Coffee, Lithograph, Slip Lid, Bail Handle, 8 1/4 In.	275.00
Tin, King Cole Coffee, King & Servant, Tin Lithograph, 1/2 Lb., 3 x 4 1/4 In.	200.00
Tin, Kopper Kettle Klub Cigars, Black Kettle, Lithograph, 5 3/8 x 5 1/8 In.	295.00
Tin, Lax-Ets, A Bowel Laxative, From Dr. Shoop's Laboratories, 5 Cents, 2 1/4 x 1 In.	44.00
Tin, Laxo-Koko, When Nature Fails, Paper Label, Unopened, 2 1/3 x 4 x 1 1/2 In.	66.00
Tin, Le Transparent Trojan, Youngs Rubber Co., 1 7/8 x 2 5/8 x 5 1/16 In.	145.00
Tin, Lincoln Highway Cigar, U.S. Map, Tin Lithograph, 5 1/8 x 3 1/4 In.	70.00
Tin, Little Elf Coffee, Elf Carrying Tray, Bursley & Co., Fort Wayne, 1 Lb.	630.00
Tin, Log Cabin Syrup, Towles, Log Cabin Shape, Lithograph, 3 5/8 x 2 1/2 In.	88.00
Tin, Lorillard Tobacco, Lithograph, Lid, Swivel Handle, c.1900, 9 1/2 x 7 In.	28.00
Tin, Loverin & Browne Co. Wholesale Grocers, Chicago, 8 1/2 In. *Illus*	20.00
Tin, Luden Cough Drops, Lithograph, 1906, 2 x 3 7/8 In.	200.00
Tin, Luzianne Coffee & Chicory, Sample, c.1930, 2 1/2 x 3 In.	119.00
Tin, M.J.B. Coffee, c.1920, 1 Lb., 5 1/4 x 4 In.	29.00
Tin, Macarlane, Lang & Co., Heraldic Crests, Biscuit, 1930s, 6 In.	18.00
Tin, Macfarlane, Lang & Co., Hat Shape, Scottish Tartan, 8 In.	40.00
Tin, Maiden Herbs Nature's Own Remedy, 3 1/4 x 2 1/4 In.	50.00
Tin, Mammy's Favorite Brand Coffee, C.D. Kenny Co., 4 Lb., 6 x 11 In.	190.00 to 215.00
Tin, Maryland Club Tobacco, Maryland Club Building, Lithograph, 4 x 3 1/4 In.	440.00
Tin, Massasoit Coffee, Indian Chief, Paper Label, 5 3/8 x 4 1/4 In.	250.00
Tin, Master Mason Smoking Tobacco, Brick Layer, 4 x 3 x 7/8 In.	1760.00
Tin, McKesson Baby Powder, 2 Nude Children Standing By Fire, 6 x 3 x 1 3/8 In.	49.00
Tin, Messer's Charcoal Gum, Lithograph, 1 x 2 5/8 In.	500.00
Tin, Moses Cough Drops, Mr. Moses, Orange Ground, Lithograph, 8 x 6 In.	205.00
Tin, Napoleon's Condoms, Garanti Pour Cinq Ans, 1 7/8 x 2 5/8 In.	380.00
Tin, National Cocoa, Capital Dome, Children At Table, c.1920, 5 x 2 5/8 x 2 5/8 In.	130.00
Tin, Newton Horse Remedy Co., Heave, Cough, Distemper, 3 x 4 x 3 In.	88.00
Tin, Nigger Hair Tobacco, Yellow Lithograph, Slip Lid, 6 1/2 In.	350.00
Tin, North Pole Tobacco, Polar Bears & Walrus, Mountains, Lithograph, 9 x 6 In.	1100.00
Tin, Old Black Joe Grease Can, Lithograph, Bail Handle, 8 1/2 In.	99.00
Tin, Old Colony, Tobacco Mixture, Bagley & Co., Pocket, Sample, 3 x 2 x 5 In.	850.00
Tin, Old Dutch Coffee, Windmill, Key Wind, Lithograph, 1 Lb.	44.00
Tin, Old Mother Hubbard Popcorn, Cardboard, Metal, 6 1/2 Oz., 4 5/8 x 2 In.	75.00
Tin, Omar Cigarettes, Turkish Blend, Exceptional Quality, 4 1/2 x 6 5/8 x 1/2 In.	55.00
Tin, Page Borated Baby Talc, Mother & Baby, 5 1/4 x 3 x 1 1/8 In.	290.00
Tin, Peachey Double Cut Tobacco, Peach, Yellow, Red, 4 1/8 x 2 5/8 x 7/8 In.	180.00 to 220.00

Tin, Peacock Condoms, Peacock, Lithograph, 1 5/8 x 5/8 In. 249.00
Tin, Peerless Talcum Powder, Perfumed, Lithograph, 1 1/2 x 3 3/4 In. 99.00
Tin, Peter Pan Peanut Butter, Derby's, Screw Top, Sample, 2 Oz., 1930 . . . . .55.00 to 66.00
Tin, Peter Rabbit Baby Powder, Lithograph, 4 In. 190.00
Tin, Pipe Major Tobacco, Men Wearing Kilts, Lithograph, 4 1/2 x 3 1/8 In. 120.00
Tin, Pirates Condoms, Women Pirates On Ship, Light & Dark Green, 1 x 2 x 3 In. 850.00
Tin, Poehler King Jumbo Peanuts, Polar Bear, 8 x 8 In. 1155.00
Tin, Police Foot Powder, Policeman, Contents, 4 1/2 x 2 1/2 In. 415.00
Tin, Popper's Ace Cigars, Lithograph Of Bi-Plane, White Ground, 6 x 5 x 5/16 In. 415.00
Tin, Powers & Weightman Quinine Sulfate, Lithograph, 1 Oz., 3 1/2 x 2 1/2 In. 86.00
Tin, Princine Baking Powder, Cup, Handle, 8 Oz., 2 3/4 x 3 1/4 In. 150.00
Tin, Q-Boid Tobacco, Yellow Ground, Lithograph, 4 x 3 In. 4.00
Tin, Ramses Condoms, Egyptian Theme, Lithograph, 1 7/8 x 2 7/8 In. . . . . .165.00 to 250.00
Tin, Rawleigh's Talcum, Nursery Rhyme Images, Lithograph, 7 1/2 In. 176.00
Tin, Rawleigh's Veterinary Ointment, Round, Part Contents, 3 1/4 x 4 1/4 In. 45.00
Tin, Real Thing Condoms, Embossed, 1 3/4 In., 2 Piece 50.00
Tin, Red & Blue Tobacco, Lithograph, 4 3/8 x 3 In. 910.00
Tin, Red Jacket Tobacco, Jockey On Horse, Lithograph, 4 1/2 x 3 1/8 In. 165.00
Tin, Red Wolf Coffee, Ridenours-Bakers Co., 3 Lb., 9 x 6 In. 139.00
Tin, Roby Cigar Co., Sunset Trail, America's Finest, 6 x 5 1/2 x 4 In. 495.00
Tin, Roly Poly, Dixie Queen Tobacco, Singing Waiter, Lithograph, 6 x 6 1/2 In. 270.00
Tin, Roly Poly, Mayo's, Dutchman, 7 x 6 In. 345.00
Tin, Roly Poly, Mayo's, Mammy, Black Woman, 7 x 6 In. 520.00
Tin, Roly Poly, Mayo's, Satisfied Customer, Man In Red Jacket, 7 x 6 In. . . . . . . .280.00 to 520.00
Tin, Roly Poly, Mayo's, Scottish Lawman, 7 x 6 In. 460.00
Tin, Roly Poly, Mayo's, Singing Waiter, 7 x 6 In. 400.00
Tin, Roly Poly, Mayo's, Storekeeper Smoking Pipe, 7 x 6 In. 490.00
Tin, Romeos Condoms, Blue, Gray, Killian Mfg., 1 5/8 x 2 1/8 In. 170.00
Tin, Romeos Condoms, Yellow, Lithograph, 1 5/8 x 2 1/8 In. 139.00
Tin, Royal Quality Coffee, Lithograph, Fitch, Thomas Co., Pry Lid, 6 x 4 1/4 In. 70.00
Tin, Sally Lee Coffee, Key Wind, Lithograph, 1 Lb., 5 x 4 In. 100.00
Tin, Sanitol Tooth Powder, Saint Louis, 4 In. 95.00
Tin, Satin Tooth Powder, 25 Cent Label, Detroit, Michigan, Contents, 3 3/4 In. 155.00
Tin, Scotten Dillion Co.'s. Tobacco, Lithograph, 4 1/2 x 3 In. 120.00
Tin, Sheik Condoms, Sheik On Horse, Lithograph, Hinged Lid, 1930, 1 5/8 x 1 5/8 In. . . . 200.00
Tin, Shogun Mixture, 4 3/8 x 3 3/8 In. 5656.00
Tin, Silvertex Condoms, Killian Mfg, Co., Lithograph, 1 3/4 x 2 1/8 In. 55.00
Tin, Skookum Maple Syrup, Teepee, Indian, Symbols, Scully Co., 5 x 4 In. 450.00
Tin, Smith Bros. Cough Drops, 3 3/4 x 2 3/8 In. 385.00
Tin, Smith's Non-Irritant Adamantine Phosphate Cement For Filling, 3 1/2 x 2 In. 198.00
Tin, Somerville's Gum, Blood Orange Flavor, Lithograph, 1 1/8 x 3 1/8 In. 270.00
Tin, Sozodont Powder For Cleaning Teeth, 3 In. 385.00
Tin, Stag Tobacco, Large Buck, Lithograph, Sample, 3 5/8 x 2 3/4 In. 310.00
Tin, Suchard Cacao, Lithograph, Hinged Lid, 8 3/4 In. 60.00
Tin, Sunny Boy Peanut Butter, Child Eating Sandwich, Lithograph, 9 x 8 1/2 In. 430.00
Tin, Suprema Nail Polish, Victorian Girl, Lithograph, 2 x 1 In. 350.00
Tin, Swallow & Ariel, Trefoil Shape, Portrait Of Woman, Australia, 8 1/4 In. 60.00
Tin, Sweet Cuba Chewing Tobacco, Yellow Ground, Black, Red, 12 x 14 x 18 In. 240.00
Tin, Tastebest Coffee, Key Wind, 1 Lb., 3 1/8 x 5 1/8 In. 95.00
Tin, Tennyson Cigar, Man On 3 Sides, Tin Lithograph, 5 5/8 x 3 1/8 In. 90.00
Tin, Texaco New Airplane Oil, Airport, Planes, Logo With Wings, Qt. 635.00
Tin, Three Cadets Condoms, 3 Soldiers, Red Ground, 1 3/4 x 2 1/8 In. 145.00
Tin, Tiger Chewing Tobacco, 12 In. . . . . .88.00 to 95.00
Tin, Tiger Chewing Tobacco, Bright, Sweet, P. Lorillard Co., 2 7/8 x 3 x 7/8 In. 199.00
Tin, Tiger Tobacco, Basket Weave Pattern, Blue, 7 3/4 In. 50.00
Tin, Times Square Tobacco, Nighttime Broadway Scene, Lithograph, 4 3/8 x 3 In. 300.00
Tin, Tiny Tot Toilet Powder, Lithograph, 3 1/2 In. 110.00
Tin, Toyland Peanut Butter, Band, H.C. Derby Co., 1 Lb., 3 1/2 x 3 3/4 In. 270.00
Tin, Tuxedo Tobacco, Man Wearing Tuxedo, Lithograph, 4 3/8 x 3 In. 139.00
Tin, Union Leader Redi Cut Tobacco, Lithograph, 4 3/8 x 3 x 7/8 In. 100.00
Tin, Union Leader Tobacco, Uncle Sam, Red Ground, Lithograph, 4 1/2 x 3 1/8 In. 166.00
Tin, Valley Queen, Cloves, Wilson Mercantile, Paper Label, 1 3/4 x 3 x 1 In. 80.00
Tin, Velvet Tobacco, 8 Sides, Tin Lithograph, 3 7/8 x 4 5/8 In. 50.00

Tin, Vision Baking Powder, Paper Label, Unopened, 3 x 7 In. 160.00
Tin, Watkins Egyptian Bouquet Talcum Powder, Pyramid, Embossed, 5 x 3 In. ......55.00 to 95.00
Tin, Weldon Tobacco, Yellow Ground, Lithograph, 3 5/8 x 3 1/2 In. 428.00
Tin, White House Coffee, Tin Lithograph, 1907, 3 1/4 x 2 5/8 In. 99.00
Tin, White Nutex Condoms, Green & Black Ground, 1 x 2 x 3/16 In. 575.00
Tin, White Trojans Condoms, Red & White, Youngs Rubber Co., 1 3/4 x 2 1/8 In. 55.00
Tin, Whitman's, Salmagundi, Gold, c.1920, 2 x 4 x 7 1/2 In. 15.00
Tin, William Arnott, Geisha Scene, Biscuit, Australia 95.00
Tin, William Crawford & Sons, Fairy Tree, Biscuit, 14 x 5 In., 1935 .... 250.00
Tin, Williams Talc Powder, English Lilac, Glastonbury, Conn., 4 3/4 x 2 3/4 In. 65.00
Tin, Wilsons Co-Re-Ga, Hold Dental Plates Firmly In Mouth, Full, 1 1/4 x 2 1/4 In. 44.00
Tin, Woolsons Vienna Coffee, Toledo, Ohio, 2 3/4 x 3 In. 66.00
Tin, Woolworth & Co., Santa Claus, Airplane, Lithograph, Oval, 1 3/4 x 4 x 2 In. 72.00
Tin, Wrigley's Sam Toy Talcum, Lithograph, 1906, 2 x 4 1/4 x 1 3/4 In. 55.00
Tin, Yankee Boy Plug Cut Tobacco, Blond Yankee Boy, Burley, 4 1/4 x 4 x 1 In. 640.00
Tin, Yogi Spice, Paper Label, 2 1/4 x 2 In. 60.00
Tin, Young's Victoria Cream, Queen Of Complexion Creams, Dome Top, 2 In. 95.00
Tin, Zigzag Confection, Betsy Ross Home, Lithograph, 2 1/2 In. 140.00

Advertising tip trays are decorated metal trays less than 5 inches in
diameter. They were placed on the table or counter to hold either the
bill or the coins that were left as a tip. Change receivers could be made
of glass, plastic, or metal. They were kept on the counter near the cash
register and held the money passed back and forth by the cashier.
Related items may be listed in the Advertising category under Change
Receivers.

Tip Tray, American Perfect Beer, Man & Woman, Tin Lithograph, 1914, 5 In. 550.00
Tip Tray, Boss Coffee, Adm. Sampson, Drink The Best, 6 In. 135.00
Tip Tray, Buffalo Brewing Co., Bohemian Woman, Blue Dress, Tin Lithograph, 4 1/4 In. .. 400.00
Tip Tray, C.D. Kenny Teas, Drink & Enjoy, Woman With Roses, Tin Lithograph, 5 In. 250.00
Tip Tray, C.D. Kenny Teas, Soldier, Sailor, Round, 4 3/8 In. 300.00
Tip Tray, Carnation Milk, Cows In Pasture, Seattle, Wash., 5 1/2 x 3 1/2 In. 145.00
Tip Tray, Century Beer, Schneider Brewing, Man, Woman Toasting, 4 1/4 In. 385.00
Tip Tray, Cincinnati Gas Company, Woman Cooking, Tin Oval, 4 1/4 In. 490.00
Tip Tray, Cleveland & Buffalo Cruise Ship, Tin Lithograph, 4 1/8 In. 385.00
Tip Tray, Clysmic, King Of Table Waters, Lady, Buck, 4 1/4 x 6 1/4 In. ....385.00 to 410.00
Tip Tray, Consult Sheldon, Optical Specialist, Bear Rides Giraffe, 3 3/8 x 4 7/8 In. 358.00
Tip Tray, Domestic Sewing Machine, It Stands At The Head, Tin Lithograph, 5 In. 75.00
Tip Tray, Dr Pepper, Black & White Dog, Tin Lithograph, 3 1/2 x 2 1/2 In. 605.00
Tip Tray, Drink Dr Pepper, Black Boy Eating Watermelon, Tin, Oval, Scalloped, 3 In. 1320.00
Tip Tray, El Verso Havana Cigars, Man Reclining In Chair, 6 1/2 x 4 1/2 In. 99.00
Tip Tray, Emerson Hotel, Baltimore, Md., 4 3/8 x 6 1/8 In. 80.00
Tip Tray, Enterprise Meat & Food Choppers, 30 Sizes & Styles, Tin, 4 1/4 In. 78.00
Tip Tray, Fleischmann Compressed Yeast, Blue, Gold Border, 10 1/4 In. 1045.00
Tip Tray, Frank Jones Homestead Ale, 5 In. 75.00
Tip Tray, Franziskaner Pilsner, West End Brewing, Utica, New York, 4 1/8 In. 550.00
Tip Tray, Frost Wire Fence Co., 3 White Horses, Cleveland, Ohio, 4 In. 88.00
Tip Tray, General Arthur Cigars, Man, Flowers, Kerbs, Wertheim, 5 x 3 1/4 In. 550.00
Tip Tray, Globe-Wernicke, Sectional Bookcases, Tin Lithograph, 4 1/4 In. 105.00
Tip Tray, Hardy The Shoe Man, Woman, Black Ground, c.1907, 4 1/4 In. 525.00
Tip Tray, Heath & Milligan Paints, 2 Girls, Dog, Floor, Red Border, Round 175.00
Tip Tray, Home Treasure Stoves, Tin Lithograph, 5 3/4 In. 55.00
Tip Tray, Hyroler Whiskey, Louis Adler, Well-Dressed Man, Black, White, 4 1/4 In. 90.00
Tip Tray, Jap Rose Soap, Children Washing Doll, Lithograph, 4 1/4 In. 160.00
Tip Tray, Jenney Aero Gasoline, Black, Orange, White, 4 1/4 In. 145.00
Tip Tray, John Hampden Havana Cigars, Man, Curly Black Hair, Lithograph, 4 1/4 In. ... 55.00
Tip Tray, King Of Rochester Beers, Monroe Brewing Co. 135.00
Tip Tray, King's Pure Malt, Nurse Holds Tray, 4 1/2 x 6 1/8 In. 154.00
Tip Tray, La Ligera Y Suave Maquina, Woman Sews Boy's Pants, 4 1/4 In. 255.00
Tip Tray, Laxol, Castor Oil, Like Honey, Bottle, Tin Lithograph, Round, 4 1/4 In. 145.00
Tip Tray, Lewis 66 Whiskey, Man, Table, Whiskey Bottle, Round, 4 1/4 In. 255.00
Tip Tray, Maltosia, German American Brewing, Green, Red, White, 5 1/8 In. 130.00
Tip Tray, Monticello Special Reserve, It's All Whiskey, Oval, 6 1/4 x 4 3/8 In. 210.00

Tip Tray, Mount Vernon Evaporated Milk, Can, Tin Lithograph, 3 1/2 x 4 1/2 In. 88.00
Tip Tray, Moxie, I Just Love Moxie Don't You, Woman Drinks Moxie, 6 1/8 In. . . .385.00 to 550.00
Tip Tray, Muriel Cigars, Mild Blend Havana, Woman, Red Hair Scarf, 4 x 6 In. 176.00
Tip Tray, National Beer, Best In The West, Cowboy, Horse, 4 1/2 In. 770.00
Tip Tray, Northwestern National Bank, Portland, Ore., 4 1/4 x 6 In. 130.00
Tip Tray, Our Brands National Cigar Stands, Woman, Flowers, 6 1/8 In. 300.00
Tip Tray, Pippins Cigars, 5 Cents, Red Apple, 5 3/8 x 5 In. 410.00
Tip Tray, President Suspenders, Absolute Comfort, Crook & Meitz, 4 1/4 In. 90.00
Tip Tray, President Suspenders, Absolute Comfort, Tin Lithograph, Under Glass, 4 In. . . . 605.00
Tip Tray, Puritan Ham, First In Land, Puritan Boy, Ham, Round, 4 1/4 In. 90.00
Tip Tray, Red Raven Splits, Ask The Man, Pittsburg Exposition, 1905, 4 1/4 In. 226.00
Tip Tray, Resinol Soap & Ointment, For All Skin Diseases, 4 1/4 In. 250.00
Tip Tray, Rockford High Grade Watches, Woman, Blue Dress, 3 3/8 x 4 7/8 In. 130.00
Tip Tray, Ruhstaller's Gilt Edge Lager, California Invites The World, 4 1/4 In. 490.00
Tip Tray, Salvador Rull, Tin, Spain, c.1930, 3 x 5 In. 24.00
Tip Tray, Saratoga Star Spring Water, Round, 5 In. 100.00
Tip Tray, Sign Of The Bulldog, Real Habana Segars, Bulldog, Tin Lithograph, 5 x 7 In. . . 138.00
Tip Tray, Smith-Wallace Shoe Co., Lady, Chicago, Ill., 4 1/2 In. 140.00
Tip Tray, Southern Select Beer, Don't Gamble, Horse Race, Tin Lithograph, 4 In. 66.00
Tip Tray, Stephen A. Gottwall, Newark, N.J., Lady Holding Red Flowers, 1908, 4 1/4 In. . 275.00
Tip Tray, Stroh's Malt Extract, Weak People, Bottle, Yellow Ground, 4 1/4 In. 155.00
Tip Tray, Success Brand Manure Spreader, Kemp & Burpee Co., Farmer, Horses, 3 x 4 In. 440.00
Tip Tray, Taka-Kola Soda, Woman & Clock, Green Rim, Tin Lithograph, 4 1/4 In. 465.00
Tip Tray, Wolverine Mfg. Co., Factory, 4 1/2 x 6 In. 250.00
Tobacco Cutter, John F. Kelly Wholesale Grocer, Davenport, Iowa, Iron, c.1914 . . . . 145.00
Toothbrush Holder, Listerine Prophylactic, Skeezix, Tin Lithograph, Die Cut, 6 x 3 In. . . 77.00
Tray, Altes Lager, Tivoli Brewing, Man Pours Into Glass, 12 1/8 In. 360.00
Tray, Anheuser-Busch, Bevo, All Year Round Soft Drink, 6 3/4 x 4 1/2 In. 130.00
Tray, Anheuser-Busch, Factory Scene, Tin Lithograph, 18 1/2 In. 320.00
Tray, Borden's Ice Cream, Boy & Girl Eating Ice Cream, 13 1/2 In. 145.00
Tray, Budweiser Beer, Bottle & Glass Of Beer, Tin, Round, 1960s, 13 In. 50.00
Tray, Buffalo Brewing Co., Life Saver, Fireman, Sacramento, Calif., 1911, 13 In. 1625.00
Tray, Buster Brown, Child's Tea Set, Germany, 3 5/8 x 5 5/8 In. 100.00
Tray, Cascade Beer, Union Brewing & Malting, 17 1/4 x 12 1/4 In. 176.00
Tray, Chippewa's Pride Beer, Chippewa Falls, Wis., Indian, Round, 13 In. 99.00
Tray, Crescent Ice Cream, 2 Children, Tin Lithograph, 13 1/2 In. 495.00
Tray, Croft Cream Ale, Goes With The Best Of Everything, Green, Yellow, 12 In. 60.00
Tray, Doebler Beer Factory, Tin, 13 5/8 x 16 5/8 In. 2310.00
Tray, E. Robinson & Sons Pilsner Bottled Beer, 13 1/4 In. 300.00
Tray, East Side Beer, Los Angeles Brewing Co., Factory, Tin, 13 1/8 In. 800.00
Tray, Eidelweiss Beer, Woman Smiling, Metal, Round, c.1913, 12 In. 116.00
Tray, Falls City Brewing Co., Maid With Tray, Tin Lithograph, Round, 12 In. 138.00
Tray, Flynn's Ice Cream, Tin Lithograph, 13 1/2 In. 230.00
Tray, Frank Jones Bro., Portsmouth, N.H., Monk Drinking, c.1905, 10 1/8 In. 468.00
Tray, Graham's Ice Cream, Mother & Children, Tin Lithograph, 13 1/4 In. 635.00
Tray, Gretz Beer, Steinie Quarts & Pints, Tin Lithograph, 13 1/2 In. 195.00
Tray, Gypsy Hosiery, Girl With Harmonica, Tents, Tin Lithograph, Round, 6 In. 440.00
Tray, Hick's Capudine Medicine, Cherubs, Tin Lithograph, Box, 10 In. 850.00
Tray, Hopsburger Golden Beer, Woman, Tin, Round, 13 In. 300.00
Tray, Huser & Co. Shoes, Miss Liberty & Allegorical Females, 16 x 13 In. 375.00
Tray, John Hauenstein Beer, New Ulm, Minn., Bottle, Oval 16 In. 155.00
Tray, Marter Cigar Co., King Coin, Tin Lithograph, 10 1/4 In. 396.00
Tray, Menks Bottle Beer, Home Phone City 1912, Louisville, Ky., 13 1/2 x 16 In. 525.00
Tray, National Cigar Co., Our Brands, Lady Holding Flowers, 6 In. 220.00
Tray, NuGrape Soda, Girls At Fountain, 10 1/4 x 13 1/4 In. 360.00
Tray, Peter Doelger Bottled Beer, Eagle, Lithograph, 6 1/4 x 4 In. 300.00
Tray, Pittsburgh Ice Cream, Children's Party Scene, Tin Lithograph, 13 1/4 In. 715.00
Tray, Rainier Beer, Seattle Brewing & Malting Co., Evelyn Nesbit, 1903, 13 In. 1210.00
Tray, Rheingold Beer, Prosit, Chas. Lutz & Bro., Brooklyn, N.Y., 1910, 10 x 13 In. 300.00
Tray, Royal Bohemian Beer, Duluth, Minn., Metal, Round, 13 In. 50.00
Tray, Schnecksville State Bank, Woman, Fishing Outfit, 1920, 4 1/2 x 6 In. 190.00
Tray, Tip, see Tip Trays in this category.
Tray, Tom Moore Cigars, America's Favorite, Man's Bust, 13 1/8 In. 1595.00

Paper ephemera like trade cards, photograhs, books, signs, and letters that were made before 1950 rarely flouresce under a black light. Paper made after 1950 contained many bleaches and dyes and will fluoresce.

Advertising, Whirligig, Bub's Beer, Painted Iron, 27 x 49 In.

Tray, Walter Baker Chocolate, Lithograph, Tin, c.1905, 16 1/2 x 13 3/4 In.	290.00
Tray, White Rock Beer, Akron Brewing Co., Woman With Tiger, Tin, Round, 13 1/2 In.	690.00
Tray, Wm. J. Lemp Brewing, Tin Lithograph, 12 In.	495.00
Tumbler, Uneeda Milk Biscuit, Chocolate Glass, National Biscuit Company, 5 3/4 In.	120.00
Wallet, Reddy Kilowatt, Dancing, Vinyl, Black, c.1950, 4 x 6 3/4 In.	18.00
Whirligig, Bub's Beer, Painted Iron, 27 x 49 In. ....*Illus*	950.00
Window, Transom, Rexall, Thank You, 40 x 17 In.	198.00
Window Shade, Pollard Bros. Dry Goods, Boots & Shoes, Canvas, 102 x 74 In.	120.00

AGATA glass was made by Joseph Locke of the New England Glass Company of Cambridge, Massachusetts, after 1885. A metallic stain was applied to New England Peachblow and the mottled design characteristic of agata appeared.

Cuspidor, Woman's, Purple Stain, White To Pink Ground, 5 x 2 1/2 In.	1800.00
Tumbler, Amber & Blue Stain, White To Pink Ground, 3 3/4 In.	392.00

AKRO AGATE glass was made in Clarksburg, West Virginia, from 1932 to 1951. Before that time, the firm made children's glass marbles, which are listed in this book in the Marble category. Most of the glass is marked with a crow flying through the letter *A*.

Bowl, Stacked Disc, Interior Panel, Transparent Cobalt, 3 3/8 In.	60.00
Creamer, Stacked Disc, Interior Panel, 3 1/8 In.	50.00
Creamer, Stippled Band, Transparent Topaz, 1 1/2 In.	20.00
Cup, Chiquita, Lavender, 1 1/2 In.	35.00
Cup, Stacked Disc, Interior Panel, Cobalt, 3 1/8 In.	4.00
Cup, Stippled Band, Transparent, Green, 1 1/2 In.	15.00 to 20.00
Cup & Saucer, Stacked Disc, Interior Panel, Green, Marbleized	35.00
Cup & Saucer, Stippled Band, Transparent Topaz	20.00
Cup & Saucer, Transparent Topaz	20.00
Plate, Octagonal, Opaque Green, 3 3/8 In.	5.00
Plate, Stacked Disc, Interior Panel, Transparent Cobalt, 3 1/4 In.	24.00
Plate, Stippled Band, Transparent Topaz, 4 1/4 In.	10.00
Sugar, Cover, Interior Panel, Transparent Cobalt, 1 1/4 In.	100.00
Sugar, Cover, Strippled Band, Transparent Topaz, 1 1/2 In.	35.00
Tumbler, Stippled Band, Transparent Green, 1 3/4 In.	11.00

ALABASTER is a very soft form of gypsum, a stone that resembles marble. It was often carved into vases or statues in Victorian times. There are alabaster carvings being made even today. Because the alabaster is very porous, it will dissolve if kept in water, so do not use alabaster vases for flowers.

Bust, Dante, Italy, 19th Century, 12 In	681.00
Bust, Diana, Green Marble Base, Late 19th Century, 26 In	1192.00
Bust, Girl, Flowing Pigtails, France, c.1880, 17 In.	345.00
Bust, Girl, Short Hair, Scalloped, Collar, Yellow Tint, 19th Century, 4 In.	300.00

Bust, Gypsy, Italy, c.1900, 18 In. 1265.00
Bust, Plato, Greek Style, c.1890, 8 In. 379.00
Bust, Rosseau, Wood Pedestal, France, 19th Century, 9 1/2 In. 1192.00
Bust, Woman, Flowers In Hair, Art Nouveau Style, Square Marble Base, 21 In. 411.00
Bust, Woman, In Lace Hat, Signed, G. Pochini, Italy, c.1900, 23 In. 1380.00
Bust, Young Woman, Wearing Hat, Shaped Green Marble Base, 8 x 7 In. 235.00
Figurine, Child, 1 Praying, 1 Crying, 22 In., Pair 881.00
Figurine, Girl Feeding 2 Bronze Deer, Gold Hair & Wrap, Marble Base, 16 x 26 In. 2072.00
Figurine, Girl With Goat, P. Conti, Italy, 19th Century, 19 In. 1022.00
Figurine, Hawk, Perched On Rock, Polychrome Accents, c.1920, 17 1/2 In. 1035.00
Figurine, Little Red Riding Hood, I Am Going To Grandmama, 17 In. 2350.00
Figurine, Nude Woman, Rocky Base, Ribbed & Swirled Pedestal, c.1900, 19 x 45 1/2 In. . 1840.00
Figurine, Our Lady Of Lourdes, Marble Base, Italy, c.1920, 27 1/2 In. 518.00
Figurine, Woman, Placing Flowers In Hair, Diaphanous Gown, 28 In. 940.00
Figurine, Young Girl, Seated On Urn, Playful Cat, 27 In. 1960.00
Figurine, Young Woman, With Lute, Marble Base, Victorian, 19 In. 259.00
Group, Boy Consoling Girl, Barefooted, 23 In. 900.00
Group, Pieta, Full Round, 16th Century, 9 1/2 In. 1265.00
Pedestal, Column, 8-Sided Top, Round Base, Ivory, Gray Streaks, 30 x 14 In. 548.00
Pedestal, Round Top, Spiral-Reeded Body, Molded Base, 29 x 9 In., Pair 144.00
Urn, Leaf Tips & Scroll, Barbedienne, 19th Century, 22 In. 4780.00

ALEXANDRITE is a name with many meanings. It is a form of the mineral chrysoberyl that changes from green to red under artificial light. A
man-made version of this mineral is sold in Mexico today. It changes
from deep purple to aquamarine blue under artificial light. The
Alexandrite listed here is glass made in the late nineteenth and twentieth centuries. Thomas Webb & Sons sold their transparent glass shaded
from yellow to rose to blue under the name Alexandrite. Stevens and
Williams had a cased Alexandrite of yellow, rose, and blue. A. Douglas
Nash Corporation made an amethyst-colored Alexandrite. Several
American glass companies of the 1920s made a glass that changed
color under electric lights and this was also called Alexandrite.

Compote, Ruffled Edge, Ground Pontil, 4 1/2 x 2 In. 1725.00
Pitcher, Applied Handle & Foot, Rough Pontil, 6 3/4 In. 575.00

ALUMINUM was more expensive than gold or silver until the 1850s.
Chemists learned how to refine bauxite to get aluminum. Jewelry and
other small objects were made of the valuable metal until 1914, when
an inexpensive smelting process was invented. The aluminum collected today dates from the 1930s through the 1950s. Hand-hammered
pieces are the most popular.

Belt Buckle, DLV EM, 2 Piece, Pebble Finish, Steel Keepers 193.00
Plate, Morning Glories, Hearth & Home Scene, Farberware, 15 In. 55.00
Sandwich Tray, Handles, Berries, Farberware, 12 In. 55.00
Snack Tray, Hammered, Pinecones, Curled Handle, Fluted Sides, 8 In. 25.00
Tray, Grasshoppers, Wendell August Forge, 5 1/2 In. 155.00
Wastebasket, Pinecones, Wendell August Forge, 11 In. 215.00

AMBER, see Jewelry category.

AMBER GLASS is the name of any glassware with the proper yellow-
brown shading. It was a popular color just after the Civil War and
many pressed glass pieces were made of amber glass. Depression glass
of the 1930s–1950s was also made in shades of amber glass. Other
pieces may be found in the Depression Glass, Pressed Glass, and other
glass categories. All types are being reproduced.

Bowl, Blown, Lobed, Wide, Applied Cobalt Blue Rim, 16 1/2 x 3 3/4 In. 193.00
Pitcher, Honeycomb Optic, Cobalt Blue Rim, Threading, Handle, 5 3/4 In. 69.00
Vase, Amethyst Grape Vines, Leaves, 2 Open Handles, 19th Century, 9 1/2 In. 144.00

AMBERETTE pieces are listed in the Pressed Glass category under the pattern name
Amberette.

AMBERINA is a two-toned glassware made from 1883 to about 1900. It was patented by Joseph Locke of the New England Glass Company, but was also made by other companies. The glass shades from red to amber. Similar pieces of glass may be found in the Baccarat, Libbey, and Plated Amberina categories. Glass shaded from blue to amber is called *Blue Amberina* or *Bluerina*.

Berry Set, Daisy & Button, Oval, 8 Piece	150.00
Biscuit Jar, Diamond-Quilted, Polished Pontil, Victorian, 5 In.	35.00
Boot, Woman's, Victorian, 4 In.	460.00
Bowl, Daisy & Button, Square, 9 In.	230.00
Bowl, Diamond-Quilted, Ruffled Edge, Ground Pontil, 7 1/2 In.	863.00
Bowl, Finger, Ruffled Edge, 5 1/4 x 3 In.	86.00
Bowl, Inverted Thumbprint, Reeded Feet, Ruffled Edge, 4 1/2 In.	360.00
Bowl, Inverted Thumbprint, Rigaree Edge, Scalloped Rim, 3 3/4 In.	115.00
Butter, Cover, Inverted Thumbprint, Applied Reeded & Curled Knob, 5 In.	575.00
Celery Vase, Diamond-Quilted, Squared Rim, Polished Pontil, Victorian, 6 1/4 In.	144.00
Celery Vase, Inverted Thumbprint, Crimped Ruffled Edge, 7 In.	167.00
Celery Vase, Scalloped, Ribbed, Silver Plated Holder, 9 In.	1610.00
Cheese Dish, Underplate, Applied Clear Knob, 8 x 7 In.	173.00
Cordial, Lily Shape, 4 1/2 In., 4 Piece	2300.00
Creamer, Enameled, Flowers, Applied Reeded Amber Handle, 4 3/4 In.	290.00
Creamer, Inverted Thumbprint, Square Rim, Petticoat Shape, Applied Handle, 4 1/2 In.	460.00
Cruet, Diamond-Quilted, Applied Amber Handle & Stopper, 6 1/4 In.	207.00
Cruet, Gold Enameled, Victorian, 6 In.	86.00
Cruet, Inverted Thumbprint, Victorian, 6 In.	92.00
Decanter, Blown Stopper, Ground Pontil, 12 In.	1035.00
Decanter, Inverted Thumbprint, Ruffled Edge, Applied Clear Handle, Clear Stopper, 9 In.	145.00
Decanter, Reverse, Inverted Thumbprint, Amber Lapidary Cut Stopper, 12 1/2 In.	690.00
Decanter, Wine, Swirl, Amber Cut Stopper, 9 1/2 In.	175.00
Ewer, Diamond-Quilted, Handle, Lapidary Stopper, 10 In.	115.00
Ewer, Swirled Ribs, Amber Stopper, Applied Amber Handle, Pedestal Foot, 12 In.	630.00
Finger Bowl, Diamond-Quilted, Polished Pontil, Victorian, 4 1/2 In.	58.00
Finger Bowl, Pleated Rim, Ribbed, 2 1/2 x 4 1/2 In.	460.00
Goblet, Inverted Thumbprint, 6 1/2 In.	15.00
Ice Bucket, Inverted Thumbprint, Tab Handles, 5 1/2 In.	160.00
Ice Cream Set, Daisy & Button, Metal Holder, 13 Piece	2185.00
Jug, Inverted Thumbprint, Applied Amber Handle, Flared Foot, Victorian, 4 1/2 In.	80.00
Lamp, Cranberry Font, Thumbprint Optic, Ribbed, Swirled Chimney, 20 1/2 In.	460.00
Lemonade Set, Inverted Thumbprint, Ruffled Edge, 3 3/4 In., 7 Piece	690.00
Nappy, Enameled, Polished Pontil, Handled, Victorian, 6 In.	138.00
Nappy, Ice Cream, Daisy & Button, Square, Scalloped Corners, 5 3/4 In.	70.00
Pitcher, Enameled Rows Of Flowers & Leaves, Ruffled Edge, Reeded Handle, 7 1/4 In.	150.00
Pitcher, Enameled, Flowers, Tricorner Spout, Applied Amber Handle, 8 1/2 In.	58.00
Pitcher, Hobnail, Bulbous, Applied Amber Handle, 7 1/2 In.	375.00
Pitcher, Inverted Thumbprint, Applied Handle, 9 1/2 In.	575.00
Pitcher, Inverted Thumbprint, Polished Pontil, Hobbs & Brockunier, 7 3/4 In.	115.00
Pitcher, Inverted Thumbprint, Tricorner Spout, Applied Reeded Handle, 5 1/2 In.	115.00
Pitcher, Polka Dot, Square Top, Reeded Handle, Hobbs, Brockunier & Co., 6 1/2 In.	190.00

Don't keep identification on your key ring. If it is lost, it's an invitation for burglars to visit.

Amberina, Tumbler, Venetian
Diamond, Reverse, 3 1/2 In.

Pitcher, Ribbed, Applied Amber Handle & Foot, 8 1/4 In. 460.00
Pitcher, Swirled Optic, Applied Amber Square Handle, 7 In. 130.00
Pitcher, Swirled Ribs, Applied Amber Handle, Ground Pontil, 7 In. 345.00
Punch Bowl Set, Cover, Enameled Leaves, Birds, Ferns, Flowers, Paneled Cups, 9 Piece . 1725.00
Punch Cup, Diamond-Quilted 129.00
Rose Bowl, Applied Petal Feet, Lutz Style, Victorian, 4 1/2 In., Pair 300.00
Salt & Pepper, Inverted Thumbprint, Barrel Shape, Metal Tops, 3 1/2 In. 317.00
Salt & Pepper, Ribbed, Silver Plated Tops, 3 3/4 In. 403.00
Spooner, Swirled Ribs, Ground Pontil, 4 1/4 In. 288.00
Sugar, Diamond-Quilted, Crimped Edge, Ground Pontil, 4 1/2 In. 748.00
Sugar & Creamer, Inverted Thumbprint, Applied Handles, 2 3/4 In. 259.00
Syrup, Inverted Thumbprint, Silver Plated Hardware, Cover, 5 1/2 In. 2473.00
Tankard, Applied Amber Reeded Handle, Ground Pontil, 10 1/4 In. 173.00
Toothpick, Diamond-Quilted, Crimped Edge, 2 1/4 In. 173.00
Toothpick, Inverted Thumbprint, Crimped Edge, New England Glass Co., 2 1/4 In. 460.00
Tumbler, Dew Drop, Hobbs & Brockunier, 3 3/4 In., Pair 311.00
Tumbler, Enameled Daisies, 4 In. 60.00
Tumbler, Inverted Thumbprint, Ground Pontil, 3 3/4 In., 4 Piece 225.00
Tumbler, Ribbed Optic, Champagne, 4 1/4 In. 60.00
Tumbler, Ribbed, Applied Reeded Handle, 3 1/2 In., 4 Piece 230.00
Tumbler, Swirled Ribs, 3 3/4 In. 100.00
Tumbler, Venetian Diamond, Reverse, 3 1/2 In. . . . . *Illus* 100.00
Vase, Applied Rigaree Around Neck, Foot, 9 In. 110.00
Vase, Applied Swirling Rigaree, England, c.1900, 8 In. 135.00
Vase, Diamond-Quilted, Egg Shape, Corned Rim, Ground Pontil, Footed, 5 1/2 In. 518.00
Vase, Flower, Bird, Swirl, Applied Ruffled Edge, 9 1/2 In. 288.00
Vase, Inverted Thumbprint Pattern, Applied Flowers, Feet, Rim, Victorian, 6 In. 316.00
Vase, Inverted Thumbprint, Mounted On Crossed Scepter Frame, 12 1/2 In. 460.00
Vase, Lily, Silver Plated Holder, Flowers & Butterflies Cutouts, 9 In. 633.00
Vase, Square, Ribbed, Applied Amber Rim, Rough Pontil, 8 1/2 In. 173.00
Vase, Swirled Ribs, Applied Amber Rigaree, Polished Pontil, Victorian, 25 3/4 In. 345.00
Vase, Trumpet, Enameled Bluebird, Signed, 8 1/2 In. 175.00
Vase, Trumpet, Ribbed, Ground Pontil, 10 1/4 In. 259.00
Water Set, Diamond-Quilted, Pitcher, Applied Handle, 8 1/2 In., 7 Piece 420.00
Wine Set, Baby Thumbprint Optic, Decanter, 6 Tumblers, 14 In. 201.00

AMERICAN DINNERWARE, see Dinnerware.

AMERICAN ENCAUSTIC TILING COMPANY was founded in Zanesville,
Ohio, in 1875. The company planned to make a variety of tiles to com-
pete with the English tiles that were selling in the United States for use
in fireplaces and other architectural designs. The first glazed tiles were
made in 1880, embossed tiles in 1881, faience tiles in the 1920s. The
firm closed in 1935 and reopened in 1937 as the Shawnee Pottery.

Frieze, Stylized Flower, Cuerda Seca, Frame, 6 In., 2 Piece 200.00
Man, Sitting, Smoking, Brown, Ivory, Signed, Bruning, Frame, 6 In. 110.00
Tile, Bacchanalian Scenes, Polychrome Glossy Glaze, 18 x 6 In., Pair 430.00
Tile, Boy, Sheep Landscape, Terra-Cotta, 17 1/2 x 5 3/4 In. 144.00
Tile, Female Silhouette, Blue Glaze, Arts & Crafts Frame, 8 In. 175.00
Tile, Man In Colonial Dress, Glossy Burgundy Glaze, 18 x 6 In. 259.00

AMETHYST GLASS is any of the many glasswares made in the dark purple color of the gemstone called amethyst. Included in this category are
many pieces made in the nineteenth and twentieth centuries. Very dark
pieces are called *black amethyst* and are listed under that heading.

Saltshaker, Lid With Agitator, Christmas Type, 2 1/2 In. 50.00
Vase, Coralene Gold Flowers & Leaves, Blue Dots, White Flowers, Gold Trim, 4 1/2 In. . . 88.00
Vase, Crackle, Flared Top, Pinched Neck, 2 Openings, Mid 20th Century, 4 In. 75.00
Vase, Hyacinth, Panel Optic, 2 Bulges Around Base, c.1890, 6 3/4 In. 165.00
Vase, Spiral Optic, Egg Shape, Flared Rim, 12 In. 60.00

AMPHORA pieces are listed in the Teplitz category.

ANDIRONS and related fireplace items are included in the Fireplace category.

ANIMAL TROPHIES, such as stuffed animals, rugs made of animal skins, and other similar collectibles made from animal, fish, or bird parts, are listed in this category. Collectors should be aware of the endangered species laws that make it illegal to buy and sell some of these items. Any eagle feathers, many types of pelts or rugs (such as leopard), ivory, and many forms of tortoiseshell can be confiscated by the government. Related trophies may be found in the Fishing category. Ivory items may be found in the Scrimshaw or Ivory categories.

Deer, Hide Covered, Glass Eyes, Black Antlers, 10 1/2 x 11 In. 115.00
Planter, Moose Antlers, Urn Shape Holder, Rounded Base, 28 x 13 In. 193.00

ANIMATION ART collectibles include cels that are painted drawings on celluloid needed to make animated cartoons shown in movie theaters or on TV. Hundreds of cels were made, then photographed in sequence to make a cartoon showing moving figures. Early examples made by the Walt Disney Studios are popular with collectors today. Original sketches used by the artists are also listed here. Modern animated cartoons are made using computer-generated pictures. Some of these are being produced as cels to be sold to collectors. Other cartoon art is listed in Comic Art and Disneyana.

Cel, Alvin Show, Chipmunks, Mat, Frame, 14 3/4 x 17 1/2 In. 65.00
Cel, Bambi & Flower, 1942, 11 x 9 In. 3827.00
Cel, Bugs Bunny & Male Vaudeville Dancer, What's Up Doc, 1950 . . . . 1091.00
Cel, Bugs Bunny, Super Rabbit, 1943, 12 x 10 1/4 In. 2958.00
Cel, Cheerios, Honey Nut, Bee, c.1980, 10 1/2 x 12 1/2 In. 25.00
Cel, Cinderella, Gus & Jacques, 1950, 10 x 9 In. 629.00
Cel, Dennis The Menace, Joey Character, c.1960, 2 7/8 x 4 1/2 In. 20.00
Cel, Fantasia, Milkweed Pods, Toccata & Fugue In D Minor, 14 x 9 1/2 In. 2132.00
Cel, Frankenstein, Grinning Monster, Mat, c.1970, 7 1/2 x 9 1/2 In. 30.00
Cel, Fruit Roll-Ups, Flying Carpet Wizard, c.1980, 10 1/2 x 12 1/2 In. 20.00
Cel, Goofy Skiing, The Art Of Skiing, 1941, 8 1/2 x 9 In. 3215.00
Cel, How The Grinch Stole Christmas, Signed Photocard, Dr. Seuss, 1966 . . . . 4495.00
Cel, Lady & The Tramp, Lady Walking, 1955 . . . . 1091.00
Cel, Lady & The Tramp, Outside Of Tony's, 1955, 15 x 12 In. 1787.00
Cel, Mickey Mouse, Brave Little Tailor, 1938 . . . . 3827.00
Cel, Oscar Mayer, Li'l Oscar, c.1950, 4 1/2 x 5 1/2 In. 35.00
Cel, Peter Pan, Captain Hook, 1953, 13 1/4 x 9 1/4 In. 1360.00
Cel, Peter Pan, Tinker Bell, Starry Background, 1950s, 10 x 7 1/2 In. 1298.00
Cel, Pink Panther, Camera, Chinese Restaurant, 16 x 19 1/2 In. 75.00
Cel, Pinocchio, Under The Ocean, Signed Walt Disney, 1939, 12 x 9 In. 4591.00
Cel, Pluto Drooling, The Pointer, 1938, 10 1/2 x 9 In. 1378.00
Cel, Practical Pig, 1939, 11 1/2 x 9 1/2 In. 1853.00
Cel, Raggedy Ann, Andy, CBS Inc., Certificate, Frame, 1990, 12 x 15 In. 60.00
Cel, Sleeping Beauty, Sleeping Beauty & The Owl, 1959, 11 x 11 In. 1298.00
Cel, Smurf Holding Brown Measuring Tape, c.1970, 10 1/2 x 12 1/2 In. 50.00
Cel, Smurf, Azriel Cat, Brown, c.1970, 10 1/2 x 12 1/2 In. 25.00
Cel, Snow White & Prince, Frame, 1937, 7 1/2 In. 8310.00
Cel, Sylvester With Blue Bowl, Mel Blanc Collection, Warner Brothers, 1959 . . . . 557.00
Cel, Teenage Mutant Ninja Turtles, Head, Mask, Purple, c.1990, 11 x 14 In. 25.00
Cel, Wynken, Blynken & Nod, 1938, 15 x 12 1/2 In. 2470.00
Cel, Yellow Kid, Paint Brush, Lucca Comic Convention, c.1990, 12 x 16 In. 50.00
Cel, Yellow Submarine, Nowhere Man, 1968, 12 1/4 x 8 1/4 In. 603.00
Drawing, Art Of Bambi, Pencil, Signed Marc Davis, 11 x 8 1/4 In. 817.00
Drawing, Big Bad Wolf, 1933, 12 x 9 1/2 In. 543.00
Drawing, Dopey, Snow White & Seven Dwarfs, Lavender Pencil, 1937, 15 x 12 1/2 In. . . . 695.00
Drawing, Dumbo & Timothy Mouse, Pencil, 1941, 15 1/4 x 12 1/4 In. 842.00
Drawing, Mickey Mouse, Barn Dance, 1928, 9 1/2 x 8 1/4 In. 556.00
Drawing, Mickey Mouse, Dog Napper, Pencil, Some Coloring, 1934, 12 x 9 1/2 In. 449.00
Drawing, Mickey Mouse, Mickey's Melledrammer, 1933, 12 x 9 1/2 In. 334.00
Drawing, Mickey Mouse, Pencil On Paper, Signed Walt Disney, 13 x 16 In. 11245.00
Drawing, Mickey Mouse, Pencil, David Hand, 1931, 12 x 9 1/2 In., Pair 556.00
Drawing, Mickey Mouse, Puppy Love, Pencil, 1933, 9 1/2 x 12 In. 695.00
Drawing, Mickey Mouse, Touchdown Mickey, Pencil, 1932, 11 1/4 x 8 1/2 In. 817.00

Drawing, Mickey Mouse, Ye Olden Days, Pencil, 1933, 12 x 9 1/2 In. 303.00
Drawing, Peter Pan, Hook & Smee, 1955, 15 x 11 In. 974.00
Drawing, Society Dog Show, Mickey Holding Back Pluto, 1939, 12 x 9 1/2 In. 598.00
Drawing, Society Dog Show, Pluto Sniffing Microphone, 1939, 12 x 9 1/2 In. 250.00

APPLE PEELERS are listed in the Kitchen category under Peeler, Apple.

ARCHITECTURAL antiques include a variety of collectibles, usually
very large, that have been removed from buildings. Hardware, back-
bars, doors, paneling, and even old bathtubs are now wanted by collectors. Pieces of the Victorian, Art Nouveau, and Art Deco styles are
in greatest demand.

Backbar, Oak, Mirror, China Closet Top, 4 Glass Doors, 90 x 102 In. 4000.00
Baluster, Limestone, Square Cap, Foot, England, 21 1/4 In., Pair 173.00
Bathtub, Folding, Sheet Metal, Chestnut, c.1920, 16 x 58 x 21 In. 3850.00
Bracket, Wall, Wood, Carved, Winged Angel Face, Roses, 19 x 12 1/2 x 6 1/2 In. 375.00
Caryatid, Wood, Polychrome, Female Bust, Scrolls, Swags, Tapered, Italy, 64 In., Pair . . . 5980.00
Ceiling Rosettes, Rococo Revival Style, Cast Iron, Reticulated, 23 1/4 In., Pair 748.00
Column, Grained Pine, Blown, Cut Glass Globes, 90 In., Pair 2015.00
Column, Mahogany, Nude Female Figure, Art Nouveau, c.1890, 52 In., Pair 1400.00
Corbel, Pine Finish, Stripped, England, c.1885, 23 1/2 In., Pair 290.00
Corbel, Pine Finish, Stripped, Leaves, England, c.1885, 26 1/4 In., Pair 175.00
Cupboard, Corner, 2 Sections, 2 Paneled Doors, 1800s, 105 x 53 x 22 In. 2990.00
Door, Cast, Welded Metal, Goff, Price House, American, 1966, 33 1/4 x 92 3/4 In. 9200.00
Door, Furnace, Cast Iron, Arched Top, Lion, Haag, Kline & Co., 10 1/2 x 15 1/2 In. 120.00
Door, Granary, 3 Panels, Relief Carved Figures, Serpents, Lizards, Latch, 20 x 26 In. 305.00
Door, Leaded Glass, Beveled Edge, Frosted Panels, 78 1/2 x 36 In. 345.00
Door, Leaded Glass, Beveled Edge, Scrolled Shield, 78 x 35 3/4 In. 690.00
Door, Leaded Glass, Beveled, Stylized Flower, 79 1/4 x 29 3/4 In. 460.00
Door, Painted, Blue, Cream, Brown, 4 Fielded Panels, Wood Pull, 60 1/2 x 30 In. 717.00
Door, Steel, Enamel, Red, Orange, Purple, Kay Whitcomb, c.1971, 84 x 32 1/4 In. 1998.00
Door, Yellow Pine, Rectangular Panels, Iron Hinges, 72 x 19 In., Pair 275.00
Door Frame, Oak, Raised Panel, Carved Columns, Scrolled Fretwork, 104 x 108 In. 3360.00
Door Frame, Victorian, Gingerbread, Spindles, Cutwork, 48 x 13 In. 200.00
Door Knocker, Butterfly, Cast Iron, Waverly Studios, No. 70139, 3 1/2 In. 325.00
Door Knocker, Girl By Door, Cast Iron, Hubley, No. 143, 3 3/4 In. 300.00
Door Knocker, Man, Green, Acanthus Leaf Beard, Winged Hair, Iron, 21 In. 880.00
Door Knocker, Octagonal, Masonic Symbol, Wood, Cast Brass, 11 x 10 3/4 In. 170.00
Door Knocker, Parrot In Circle, Cast Iron, 3 1/4 In. . . . . .175.00 to 250.00
Door Panel, Iron, Art Deco, New York, 1928, 81 x 24 In., 2 Sets 5875.00
Drawer Pull, NHCO Logo, Cast Iron, 3 7/8 In. 78.00
Figure, Chimera, Wood, Carved, Mounted On Tin, 19th Century, 27 1/2 x 18 In. 235.00
Figure, Eagle, Spread Wing, Copper, Molded, Gilded, 19th Century, 44 x 55 In. 10575.00
Figure, Eagle, Zinc, 32 In., Pair 2255.00
Finial, Acorn, Wood, Turned, 20 x 11 In., Pair 1540.00
Finial, Spiral, Turned, Baluster Shaft, Wood, Painted, 17 In., Pair 825.00
Finial, Urn, Granite, Turned, 37 x 12 In., Pair 575.00
Grate, Medieval Style, Wrought Iron, 12-Square Grid, 2 Hinges, 17 x 16 In. 60.00
Hinge, Barn Door, Large Tulip, Cutout Heart, Forged, Iron, c.1780, 31 In. 1760.00
Hinge, Iron, Horseshoes, Flower Shape, Mid 1800s, 32 In., Pair 478.00
Hinge, Iron, Ram's Horn Shape, Heart, Tulip, 18th Century, 16 In., Pair 835.00
Hinge, Split Horn, Long Strap, Forged, Iron, Late 18th Century, 27 1/2 In., Pair 325.00
Hinge, Tulip Shape, Strap, Iron, 30 In., Pair 300.00
Letter Drop, Mailboxes, Window, U.S. Post Office, 1800s, 47 x 44 In. 850.00
Lintel, Carved Wood, Deities, Birds, Lion, 2-Headed Serpent, India, 1800s, 32 1/2 In. . . . 150.00
Lock, Door, Gilt Bronze, Louis XVI Style, Classical Maiden, c.1900, 7 In., Pair 1095.00
Lock Plate, Metal, Etched, Trefoil, Scrolls, Pierced, 3 Finials, 14 1/2 In. 118.00
Mantel, Faux Marble, Painted, Gray Green, White Veining, Shelf, 49 x 61 x 6 1/2 In. 999.00
Mantel, Faux Marble, Painted, White, Gray Veining, Shelf, Cove Molding, 48 x 60 In. . . . 705.00
Mantel, Folk Art, Grain Painted, Geometric Forms, 62 x 7 3/4 x 49 1/2 In. 2375.00
Mantel, George III, Pine, Composition, Marine Motifs, 58 x 68 In. 7170.00
Mantel, Louis XIV Style, White Marble, France, 44 x 53 1/2 In. 2530.00
Mantel, Louis XV Style, Marble, Canted Legs, Scrolling Pilasters, 42 x 36 In. 1725.00

Mantel, Louis XVI Style, Marble, Rectilinear Panels, Canted Legs, 40 x 37 In.	1610.00
Micro Mosaic, Our Lady Of Perpetual Help, Marble, Vatican Workshop, 5 1/2 x 4 1/2 In. .	460.00
Model, Staircase, Double, Flying, Mahogany, Italy, 16 x 13 In.	1035.00
Model, Temple, Column Enclosure, Balsa, 20th Century, 18 x 13 x 10 In.	405.00
Ornament, Eagle, Spread Wing, Cast Concrete, Late 19th Century, 18 x 17 1/2 In.	705.00
Ornament, Eagle, Spread Wing, Iron, c.1910, 15 x 31 x 12 In.	660.00
Ornament, Lion Head, Scroll, Sheet Copper, 19th Century, 22 x 37 x 12 1/2 In.	6325.00
Overmantel Mirror, Edwardian, Giltwood, 3 Beveled Plates, c.1900, 34 x 43 In.	2070.00
Overmantel Mirror, Federal, Frieze, Paterae, Anthemia, Garlands, Bows	4995.00
Overmantel Mirror, George III, Giltwood, c.1760, 35 x 58 In.	7768.00
Overmantel Mirror, George IV, Giltwood, Oblong, Side Panels, 27 x 57 1/2 In.	1150.00
Overmantel Mirror, Gilt, Mahogany, Eagle, Shield Pediment, 48 x 22 In.	200.00
Overmantel Mirror, Giltwood, Gesso, Leaf Swag Molded Frieze, 1800s, 51 x 54 In.	1380.00
Overmantel Mirror, Giltwood, Spread Wing Eagle Crest, c.1865, 73 x 52 In.	1955.00
Overmantel Mirror, Louis Philippe, Giltwood, Carved, Plaster, c.1835, 52 x 41 1/2 In. . . .	1840.00
Overmantel Mirror, Louis Philippe, Oblong, Giltwood, Plaster, c.1835, 51 1/2 In.	805.00
Overmantel Mirror, Louis XVI Style, Parcel Silver, c.1910, 81 1/2 x 41 In.	980.00
Overmantel Mirror, Majorelle, Giltwood, Carved, Overmantel, c.1900, 72 x 45 In.	9560.00
Overmantel Mirror, Napoleon III, Giltwood & Plaster, Bowknot, 66 x 52 1/2 In.	7475.00
Overmantel Mirror, Napoleon III, Giltwood, Carved, c.1865, 78 1/2 x 56 In.	5750.00
Overmantel Mirror, Napoleon III, Giltwood, Carved, Flower Heads, Leaves, 88 x 64 In. .	1725.00
Overmantel Mirror, Napoleon III, Giltwood, Serpentine Ribbon, Bead, 67 x 45 In.	1610.00
Overmantel Mirror, Oak, Carved, Standing Winged Griffins, Beveled, 66 x 60 In.	5600.00
Overmantel Mirror, Regency Style, Cabinet, Mahogany, Auspitz, York, 54 x 20 In.	506.00
Overmantel Mirror, Regency Style, Giltwood, Plaster, Oblong, France, 56 x 37 In.	748.00
Overmantel Mirror, Regency, Giltwood, Ebonized, Molded Crest, 36 x 59 In.	2300.00
Overmantel Mirror, Regency, Giltwood, Ebonized, Reeded Molding, 27 x 50 In.	1093.00
Overmantel Mirror, Rosewood, Rectangular, 19th Century, England, 36 x 58 In.	405.00
Panel, Door, Art Deco, Iron, Scroll, Hammered, New York, 1928, 81 In., Pair	5875.00
Panel, Louis XVI Style, Marble, Painted, Trompe L'Oeil, 81 x 36 In.	750.00
Panel, Oak, 4 Panels, Relief Carved Faces, Leaves, Scrolls, Cornice, 33 x 72 In.	1760.00
Panel, Oak, Carved, 2 Cartouches, Stylized Cupids, Leaves, 72 x 16 In.	660.00
Panel, Walnut, Relief Carved, Cherub, Swags, 13 x 47 In.	3190.00
Pedestal, Baroque Style, Wood, Continental, c.1900, 35 1/2 In.	1555.00
Pedestal, Napoleon III Style, Sarrancolin Scagliola, France, 45 In.	1955.00
Pediment, Copper, Lead, Broken Arch, Center Flame Finial, Weathered, 98 In.	2400.00
Pilaster, Louis XIV, Giltwood, Spiral, Grape Cluster, c.1685, 95 x 7 In., Pair	3220.00
Railing, Art Deco, Nickel Plated Brass, 1930s, 22 1/2 x 82 In.	980.00
Shelf, Gothic, 5 Carved Brackets, Graduated, France, 9 x 10 In.	260.00
Shelf, U.S. Postal Wall Unit, Metal, Painted, Early 20th Century, 49 x 48 In., 2 Sections . .	920.00
Shelf, Wall, Walnut, Drop Front, Chains, Flowers, Cincinnati Art, 16 x 16 In.	345.00
Stairs, Section, Pine, Red Paint, Enfield, N.H., 1840-1850, 29 1/2 In.	1150.00
Thumb Latch, Flat Finger Tab, Moravia, Early 18th Century, 10 In.	395.00
Thumb Latch, Wrought Iron, Indian Head Shape, 19th Century, 12 In.	1675.00
Window Frame, Arched, Gothic Pattern Mullions, 20th Century, 35 x 35 1/2 In.	55.00
Window Grate, Cast Iron, Fan Shape, Row Of Rosettes, 31 x 63 In., Pair	535.00
Window Grate, Cast Iron, Half Round, Scroll, Starburst, Ball Finials, 44 In.	113.00

AREQUIPA POTTERY was produced from 1911 to 1918 by the patients
of the Arequipa Sanatorium in Marin County, north of San Francisco.
The patients were trained by Frederick Hürten Rhead, who had worked
at the Roseville Pottery.

Vase, Bulbous, Blossoms, Leaves, Speckled Light Blue Matte Glaze, 6 1/4 In.	2530.00
Vase, Bulbous, Carved Abstract Design, Gunmetal Black Glaze, 4 3/4 x 3 3/4 In.	3819.00
Vase, Bulbous, Leaves, Seafoam Green Matte Glaze, Stamped, 5 1/4 In.	4315.00

ARGY-ROUSSEAU, see G. Argy-Rousseau category.

ARITA is a port in Japan. Porcelain was made there from about 1616.
Many types of decorations were used, including the popular Imari
designs, which are listed under Imari in this book.

Charger, Flying Phoenixes, Dragons, Blue, White, 14 1/2 In.	100.00
Charger, Polychrome, c.1912, 15 7/8 In., Pair	635.00

Art Deco, Percolator,
Electric, Sugar &
Creamer, Porcelain,
Royal Rochester

Charger, Polychrome, c.1912, 18 In. 259.00
Charger, Scholars, In Garden, Blue, White, Japan, 19th Century, 15 1/4 In. 1410.00
Dish, Fish Form, Carved Scales, Gilt Details, Early 1800s, 10 In., Pair 345.00
Dish, Flying Cranes, On Interior, Landscape Exterior, 4 x 17 In. 400.00
Vase, Teardrop Form, Blue, White, Arita, 11 In. 160.00

ART DECO, or Art Moderne, a style started at the Paris Exposition of
1925, is characterized by linear, geometric designs. All types of furniture and decorative arts, jewelry, book bindings, and even games were
designed in this style. Additional items may be found in the Furniture
category or in various glass and pottery categories, etc.

Dresser Set, Bakelite, Brown, Ivory Stripes, Signed Janeke, 6 Piece 170.00
Dresser Set, Geometric, Stylized Flowers, Candlestick, Perfume, Boxes, Ring Stand, Tray   896.00
Figure, Patinated Metal, Man Playing Pipes, Woman With Cymbals, Pair, 7 1/2 In. 269.00
Group, Bronze, Woman & Dog, Marble Base, Signed I. Gallo, 25 1/2 In. 1435.00
Ice Bucket, Silver Plate, 8 Lapis Lazuli Dots, 2 Ring Handles, 8 x 7 3/4 In. 220.00
Percolator, Electric, Sugar & Creamer, Porcelain, Royal Rochester . . . . *Illus*   350.00
Plate, Black Man, Winking At Chinese Girl, 8 Sides, Filigree Edge, England, 10 In. 60.00
Sculpture, Worker, On Horseback, Red Clay, Italy, 1930s, 16 x 16 In. 2233.00
Tray, Eggshell, Black Lacquer, Jungle Cat, Signed Sauvagnat, 15 1/2 In. 120.00
Tray, Plastic Laminate, Chrome, Handles, Geometric, Black, Red, Cream, 2 x 18 x 12 In. .   765.00
Vase, Lime Green, Mocha Pulled Designs, Stamped Made In Czechoslovakia, 8 1/4 In. . . 105.00
Vase, Opalescent, Stylized Centaur & Panther Hunting Gazelles, c.1925, 12 1/2 In. 635.00

ART GLASS, see Glass-Art category.

ART NOUVEAU is a style of design that was at its most popular from
1895 to 1905. Famous designers, including Rene Lalique and Emile
Galle, produced furniture, glass, silver, metalwork, and buildings in
the new style. Ladies with long flowing hair and elongated bodies were
among the more easily recognized design elements. Copies of this
style are being made today. Many modern pieces of jewelry can be
found. Additional Art Nouveau pieces may be found in Furniture or in
various glass categories.

Bust, Female, Turned Head, Flowing Hair To Base, Gilt Bronze, Gruber, 5 1/4 In. 75.00
Figurine, Robed Woman, Bronze, Ivory, Signed D Watrin, 15 In. 1960.00
Figurine, Woman, Flowing Hair, 2 Colors, Signed Peyre Louchet Paris Foundry, 13 In. . . . 1176.00
Frame, Silver On Copper, Carved Geometric & Chinese Dragon, 5 1/2 x 4 In. 400.00
Frame, Silver On Copper, Carved Peacocks, Feather Design, 7x 5 In. 430.00
Plaque, Enameled, Maiden, Brown Hair, Blue Dress, Frame, 7 1/2 x 5 3/4 In. 1668.00
Plaque, Sleeping Lady, Flowers, Cast Iron, Copper Patina, Late 19th Century, 10 3/4 In. . . 140.00
Tray, Ceramic Insert, Landscape Scene, Metal Frame, Impressed Mark, 21 In. 865.00
Vase, Girl, Braided Hair, Pink Flowers In Hair, Amethyst Glass, Bulbous, 6 1/4 In. 325.00
Vase, Jeweled, Threaded, Holly Band, Gold Highlights, Marked, Terex Austria, 13 1/2 In. . 1095.00
Vase, Oval, Flared Neck, Amber Iridescence, Pulled Design, 11 1/4 In., Pair 895.00
Vase, Pink Iridescence, String Design, Knopped Shape, Austria, 8 1/4 In. 155.00
Vase, Shape Cylindrical Shape, Stylized Flowers, Cranberry, Gilt Detail, 13 1/2 In. 478.00
Wallpaper Block, Carved, Border, Stylized Flowers, Leaves, 22 1/2 x 32 1/2 x 2 In. 350.00

ART POTTERY, see Pottery-Art.

ARTHUR OSBORNE plaques are found in the Ivorex category.

ARTS & CRAFTS was a design style popular in American decorative arts from 1894 to 1923. In the 1970s collectors began to rediscover Mission furniture, art pottery, metalwork, linens, and light fixtures from this period. The interest has continued. Today everything from this era is collectible, including jewelry, graphics, and silverware. Additional items may be found in the Furniture category, various glass categories, etc.

Candleholder, Brass, Carved Words, Symbols, Shade, 15 1/2 In.	144.00
Chair, Tabouret, Oak, Hexagonal, Michigan Co., Early 20th Century, 18 1/4 x 16 In.	94.00
Desk Set, Green Marble, Bronze Ship, Blotter, Inkwell, Letter Opener, 13 x 6 In.	127.00
Leather Work, Griffon Heads, W.E. Hentschel, Oak Frame, c.1914, 9 x 11 1/2 In.	230.00
Portrait, Wax, Girl In Green Dress Reading, Round, Relief, Frame, c.1916, 6 1/2 In.	264.00
Vase, Lavender Matte Glaze, 11 3/4 x 6 1/2 In.	88.00

AURENE glass was made by Frederick Carder of New York about 1904. It is an iridescent gold, blue, green, or red glass, usually marked *Aurene* or *Steuben*.

AURENE

Basket, Blue, Corset Shape, Ruffled Edge, Applied Loop Handle, Signed, 17 x 12 In.	2910.00
Bowl, Blue, 3-Footed, Rolled Rim, No. 2586, Signed, 2 1/2 x 10 In.	450.00
Bowl, Gold, Applied Pedestal Foot, Ribbed, Signed, 12 In.	1265.00
Bowl, Gold, Calcite Interior, Signed, 10 In.	259.00
Candlestick, Blue, Twisted Stem, Signed, 8 In., Pair	2040.00
Candlestick, Gold, Tulip, 8-Petal Foot, Loop Stem, 12 In.	3240.00
Compote, Blue Aurene, Bell Shape, 4 Ribs, Ruffled Edge, Signed, 6 x 8 In.	1900.00
Compote, Gold, Signed, 5 In.	575.00
Compote, Gold, Signed, 8 In.	1150.00
Cordial Set, Gold, Swirl, Pinched, Ruffled Decanter, Marked, 10 1/2 In., 7 Piece	2530.00
Darner, Gold, 6 1/4 In.	520.00
Flower Frog, Steuben, Engraved, Signed, 2 1/2 x 4 In.	207.00
Goblet, Gold, No. 2772, 4 1/2 In.	690.00
Goblet, Gold, Twisted Stem, No. 2361, Signed, 6 In.	290.00
Jar, Cosmetic, Gold, Melon Ribbed, Applied Scroll Feet, Stopper, Signed, 4 1/4 In.	578.00
Nut Dish, Gold, Blue Tones, Scalloped Rim, Signed In Silver, 3 1/2 In.	225.00
Salt, Gold, Ribs, Folded-In Ruffled Rim, 5 1/4 In.	560.00
Shade, Brown, Calcite, Fleur-De-Lis Mark, 4 3/4 In., Pair	345.00
Shade, Brown, Platinum Intarsia Border, Zigzag, Marked, 4 x 4 In.	750.00
Shade, Gold, Green Fishnet, Fleur-De-Lis Mark, 4 3/4 In.	430.00
Shade, Gold, Molded Flower, Fleur-De-Lis Mark, 4 1/4 x 4 3/4 In.	145.00
Shade, Gold, Pulled Feathers, Green Tipped, Fleur-De-Lis Mark, 5 1/2 In.	260.00
Shade, Gold, White Pulled Drapes, 6 1/2 In.	173.00
Shade, Gold, White Pulled Feather, Green Tipped, 4 3/4 In.	315.00
Shade, Green, Blue Broken Threading, 5 1/4 In.	1095.00
Shade, Green, Blue Pulled Feathers, Fleur-De-Lis Mark, 5 1/2 In., Pair	1725.00
Shade, Ribbed Body, Gold, c.1920, 4 3/4 In., Pair	115.00
Sherbet, Underplate, Gold, Steuben, Signed, 5 1/4 In.	345.00
Tumbler, Blue, Ribbed, Bulbed Foot, Inscribed, 20th Century, 4 1/8 In.	294.00
Vase, Blue, Applied Foot, 10 In.	1495.00
Vase, Blue, Fan, Circular Foot, c.1927, 8 1/2 In.	3345.00
Vase, Blue, Flared Rim, Signed, 5 In.	380.00 to 500.00
Vase, Blue, Ribbed, Flared Rim, Signed, 5 x 4 In.	977.00
Vase, Blue, Ruffled Rim, Metal Base, 10 3/4 In.	149.00
Vase, Blue, Stick, Applied Foot, Ground Rim, Signed, 8 1/4 In.	489.00
Vase, Blue, Tree Trunk, 3 Prongs, Signed, 6 1/4 In.	949.00
Vase, Blue, Urn, Pinched Neck, Flared Rim, c.1911, 5 1/2 In.	520.00
Vase, Blue, Urn, Signed, 8 In.	1380.00
Vase, Blue, Urn, Signed, 10 1/2 In.	1495.00
Vase, Brown, Red Gold Top To Blue Gold Foot, c.1920, 16 1/2 In.	3165.00
Vase, Brown, Ruffled Edge, Footed, c.1910, 5 3/4 In.	400.00
Vase, Double Gourd, Gold, Applied Foot, Signed, 5 1/2 In.	720.00 to 1000.00
Vase, Gold Iridescent, Flared Rim, No. 238, 4 1/4 In.	225.00

Vase, Gold, Baluster, No. 2683, 10 In. 1175.00
Vase, Gold, Chalice Shape, Applied Berry Prunts, Signed, 9 1/2 In. 2760.00
Vase, Gold, Flared, Ruffled Edge, Signed, 7 In. 660.00
Vase, Gold, Jack-In-The-Pulpit, Ruffled Top, Steuben, Signed, 7 3/4 In. 1495.00
Vase, Gold, Pulled Hearts & Vines, Fleur-De-Lis Mark, 9 1/2 In. 1840.00
Vase, Gold, Ribbed, Flared Rim, Signed, 5 In. 545.00
Vase, Gold, Ruffled Rim, 4 Applied Prunts, Signed, 5 3/4 In. 1680.00
Vase, Gold, Spiraled Ribs, Signed, 6 1/2 In. 600.00
Vase, Gold, Squat, Flared Rim, Applied Chain Link, c.1925, 5 1/8 In. 2350.00
Vase, Gold, Stick, Ground Rim, Signed, 10 1/2 In. 345.00
Vase, Gold, Tricorner Rim, No. 141, Signed, 6 In. 250.00
Vase, Gold, Trumpet, Rolled Edge, Ground Pontil, Signed, 6 In. 660.00
Vase, Gold, Urn, 3 Applied Swirled Handles, Footed, No. 6627, c.1924, 6 In. 410.00
Vase, Green, Gold Pulled Vines, Hearts, Flowers, Shouldered, Footed, 11 In. 8400.00
Vase, Jack-In-The-Pulpit, Gold, Ruffled Edge, Blue, Gold Body, Signed, 6 In. 230.00
Vase, Stick, Blue, Signed, 8 In. 400.00
Vase, Tree Trunk, Gold, 3 Prongs, 6 In. 1120.00
Vase, Urn Shape, Blue, Calcite, Rolled Rim, 5 x 5 1/2 In. 600.00

AUSTRIA is a collecting term that covers pieces made by a wide variety of factories. They are listed in this book in categories such as Royal Dux, or Porcelain.

AUTO parts and accessories are collectors' items today. Gas pump globes and license plates are part of this specialty. Prices are determined by age, rarity, and condition. Signs and packaging related to automobiles may also be found in the Advertising category. Lalique hood ornaments will be listed in the Lalique category.

Ashtray, Mobil Oil Co., Figural Pegasus, Cast Metal, 5 1/2 x 3 3/4 In. 253.00
Atlas, World, Mobilgas, Paper, 1942, 16 x 11 In. 17.00
Banner, Pennzoil Tiger Motor Oil, Puts A Tiger Under Your Hood, 34 3/4 x 77 1/2 In. ... 55.00
Blotter, Wayne Pump, 4 1/2 x 9 In. 17.00
Can, Red Indian H.P. Grease, McColl-Frontenac Oil Company Limited, Logo, 4 1/4 In. ... 385.00
Chalkboard, Capitol Motor Oil, Fiber Board, 15 x 17 In. 17.00
Chalkboard, Quaker State Duplex Outboard Oil, Tin, 23 1/2 x 17 1/2 In. 61.00
Charger, Mopar Trickle, Metal, 9 x 4 x 4 In. 66.00
Chart, Tiolene Motor Oil, Paper, Metal, 1934, 32 3/4 x 23 3/4 In. 17.00
Desk Set, Bearcat, Powerlube Motor Oils, Thermometer, 1936 Calendar, 6 1/2 x 6 1/2 In. . 170.00
Display, Mr. Goodwrench Works Here, Cardboard, Rolling Stand, 72 In. 330.00
Display, Pontiac Sales & Service, Glass, Metal, Countertop, 14 1/2 x 18 1/4 x 3 1/4 In. 1210.00
Display, Showroom, Knight Engine, Cutaway Picture, Electrified 3410.00
Figure, Champ Man, Champion Auto Stores, Flex, Vinyl, 1991, 6 In. 15.00
Funnel, A.R. Co., Embossed Letters, Metal, 19 1/4 x 9 3/4 x 9 3/4 In. 17.00
Gas Pump, Bennett 106 6-M-401 .... 220.00
Gas Pump, Bowser, Richfield Hi-Octane, Modern Globe, 2 Sides 2860.00
Gas Pump Globe, Aladdin, Illinois Farm Supply Company, 13 1/2 In. 550.00
Gas Pump Globe, Allied Premium, Plastic Body, 13 1/2 In. 185.00
Gas Pump Globe, Buffalo Gasoline, Charging Buffalo, Gill Lens, 13 1/2 In. 1815.00
Gas Pump Globe, Clark, 2 Sides, Glass Casing, Lens Inserts, 17 In. 110.00
Gas Pump Globe, Crown, 2 Sides, Glass Casing, Mirrored Gold Inserts, 17 In. 275.00
Gas Pump Globe, Deep Rock Green Gasoline, Glass Body, Metal Base Ring, 13 1/2 In. ... 715.00
Gas Pump Globe, Ethyl, Plastic, 13 1/2 In. 50.00
Gas Pump Globe, Fleet-Wing, Plastic Body, 13 1/2 In. 410.00
Gas Pump Globe, Imperial Refineries, 13 1/2 In. 198.00
Gas Pump Globe, Kanotex, Metal Base, 13 1/2 In. 990.00
Gas Pump Globe, Lion, 2 Lenses, Red, White, Black, 13 1/2 In. ....*Illus* 1430.00
Gas Pump Globe, Mohave Oil Co., Colorful Desert Scene, 13 1/2 In. 495.00
Gas Pump Globe, Pemco Premium, Plastic Body, 13 1/2 In. 145.00
Gas Pump Globe, Pennzoil Gasoline, Reverse Glass Lenses, 2 Sides, 16 1/2 In. 935.00
Gas Pump Globe, Purgo Radiator Service, 16 1/2 In. 1870.00
Gas Pump Globe, Red Crown, Milk Glass, Red, White, 16 x 16 In. ....*Illus* 275.00
Gas Pump Globe, Red Indian, Indian Head, Single Lens, 13 1/2 In. 990.00
Gas Pump Globe, Shell, Shell Shape, 17 In. 110.00
Gas Pump Globe, Sinclair Power-X, 2 Sides, Plastic Casing, Lens Inserts, 16 In. 154.00
Gas Pump Globe, Skelly, Fortified Gasoline, Red, White, Blue 220.00

Gas Pump Globe, Skelly, It's Better, 15 In. 935.00
Gas Pump Globe, Standard Oil, Flame, Glass, Red, White, 20 1/4 x 13 x 7 In. ..... *Illus* 385.00
Gas Pump Globe, Texaco Ethyl, Logo, 2 Gill Lenses, Copper Screw Base, Box 2640.00
Gas Pump Globe, Tony's Economy Gasoline, Red, Metal Body, 15 In. 520.00
Gas Pump Globe, USO, Travelers Aid Service, Reverse Glass Lenses, 2 Sides, 14 1/2 In. . 300.00
Gas Pump Globe, White Crown, Milk Glass, Metal Base, 16 In. 175.00
Gas Pump Globe, Wildfire, 2 Gill Lenses, Cobalt Blue & White 2970.00
Hood Ornament, Rolls-Royce, Emily, Polished Metal, Stepped Wooden Base, 9 In. 390.00
Hood Ornament, Studebaker, Chrome, Center Logo Design, 1940s, 10 x 4 1/4 In. 50.00
Jack, Cadillac, Metal, 1 1/2 In. 60.00
Kit, Esso Happy Motoring, Box, 6 x 6 x 1 1/2 In. 28.00
Kite, Zephyr Motor Oil Gasoline, Paper, Wood, 33 x 27 1/2 In. 28.00
License Plate, Alaska, 1982, 6 x 12 In. 44.00
License Plate, Massachusetts, 1914, Blue On White, Rich Mfg., Beaver Falls, Pa., 14 In. . 88.00
License Plate, New Jersey, 1912, Black Ground, Yellow Letters, Porcelain, 14 1/2 x 6 In. . 83.00
License Plate, Pennsylvania, 1915, Porcelain, White On Blue 30.00
License Plate, Virginia, 1912, Porcelain, White On Green 425.00
License Plate Attachment, 3 Star Beverage, 5 3/4 x 6 1/4 In. 55.00
License Plate Attachment, Farm Bureau Quality Insurance, 4 1/4 x 3 In. 22.00
License Plate Attachment, Fleet-Wing, Flying Bird, Tin, Self-Framed, 6 x 5 3/4 In. 132.00
License Plate Attachment, Harolds Club Or Bust, Reno, Nev., Metal, c.1950, 14 x 8 In. . 55.00
License Plate Attachment, Illinois Farm Bureaus, 4 1/2 x 3 3/4 In. 55.00
License Plate Attachment, Mobil Pegasus, Embossed Tin, 5 1/4 x 6 3/4 In. 88.00
Magazine, Texaco Star, Photos, Drawings, 1931, 11 1/4 x 8 In. 11.00
Mirror, Drive Slowly, Glass, 12 1/4 x 8 1/4 In. 303.00
Mirror, Jordan Auto, Southwest Motor Co., Kansas City 350.00
Oil Can, Anchor Precision Built Motor Oil, Anchor Logo, Qt. 130.00
Oil Can, Atlantic Quality Motor Oil, Metal, Qt. 40.00
Oil Can, Caltex Home Lubricant, Logo, Pour Spout With Dipper, 3 3/4 In. 365.00
Oil Can, Defender Motor Oil, World War II Soldier & Scene, 2 Gal. 88.00
Oil Can, Dixie Supreme Motor Oil, Oval Logo On Red Label, Qt. 190.00
Oil Can, Golden Leaf Motor Oil, Yellow Logo & Letters On Cobalt Blue Label, Qt. 55.00
Oil Can, Hancock Golden Scot Motor Oil, Logo, Red Ground, Qt. 55.00
Oil Can, Mobiloil Gargoyle A, Metal, Qt., 7 1/2 x 3 1/2 In. 77.00
Oil Can, Moly Black Gold, Heavy Duty Truck Motor, Metal, Qt., 5 1/2 x 4 In. 17.00
Oil Can, Oilzwel Motor Oil, 2 Gal., 11 1/4 x 8 1/2 In. 17.00
Oil Can, Old Dutch Motor Oil, Windmill Scene, Pour Spout, 5 Qt. 231.00
Oil Can, Oneida Motor Oil, Indian Scene, Pour Spout, Imperial Gallon, 9 1/2 In. 193.00
Oil Can, Peerless Motor Oil, 1/2 Gal., 6 1/4 x 8 In. 90.00
Oil Can, Penn's All American Motor Oil, Metal, 2 Gal., 12 x 8 1/2 x 5 1/2 In. 50.00
Oil Can, Pennstate Heavy Duty, Qt., 5 1/2 x 4 In. 33.00
Oil Can, Pennsyline Motor & Tractor Oils, 5 Gal., 13 x 11 3/4 In. 22.00
Oil Can, Pennzoil, Be Oil Wise, Pennzowls & Red Bell Logos, Qt. 72.00

Auto, Gas Pump Globe,
Lion, 2 Lenses, Red, White,
Black, 13 1/2 In.

Auto, Gas Pump Globe,
Red Crown, Milk Glass, Red,
White, 16 x 16 In.

Auto, Gas Pump Globe,
Standard Oil, Flame, Glass,
Red, White, 20 1/4 x 13 x 7 In.

Oil Can, Racing Stalube Motor Oil, Qt. 55.00
Oil Can, Rocket Motor Oil, Metal, 2 Gal., 11 1/2 x 8 1/2 x 5 1/2 In. 39.00
Oil Can, Shell Motor Oil, Logo, Pitcher Shape, Spout, Handle, Tin Lithograph, Pt., 5 In. ... 468.00
Oil Can, Sinclair Pennsylvania Motor Oil, Metal, 5 Qt., 9 1/2 x 6 1/2 In. 72.00
Oil Can, Sohio Sohikote 100, Gal., 10 1/4 x 6 1/2 x 4 1/8 In. 33.00
Oil Can, Speedwell Motor Oil, British Oil Turpentine Corp., 7 1/2 x 4 1/2 In. 175.00
Oil Can, Sphinx-Penn Motor Oil, Gal., 12 x 6 1/2 x 4 1/8 In. 22.00
Oil Can, Texaco Home Lubricant, Logo On Label, Squirt, 5 In. 715.00
Oil Can, Tiolene Motor Oil, Metal, Qt., 5 1/2 x 4 In. 61.00
Oil Can, Tiopet Motor Oil, Indian, Pointing, Imperial Gallon, 11 x 6 1/2 In. 688.00
Oil Can, Tomahawk Hi-Speed Motor Oil, Logo On Yellow & Black Label, Qt. 468.00
Oil Can, Wakefield Castrol Motor Oil, Metal, Foreign, Gal., 9 1/2 x 6 1/2 x 2 5/8 In. 22.00
Oil Can, Whippet Motor Oil, Dog Graphic, Metal, 11 1/2 x 8 1/2 In. 35.00
Oil Filler, Long Spout, Pump, Tin, Landers Frary & Clark, Conn., 3 1/4 x 9 1/4 In. 90.00
Oil Spout, Huffman, Metal, 17 x 4 3/8 In. 17.00
Pennant, Atlantic Motor Oil, 26 1/4 x 54 1/2 In. 99.00
Plaque, Shell Oil Company, 10 Year, Metal On Wood, 13 1/4 x 10 1/4 In. 44.00
Poster, Auto Show, Early Car, Madison Sq. Garden, Chromolithograph, 1903, 42 x 32 In. 1100.00
Poster, Bugatti, Blue, Violet, Black, White, Mounted, Frame, 51 1/2 x 37 In. 220.00
Poster, Goodyear, Rear Truck Tires, Paper Lithograph, Frame, 35 In. 176.00
Pump, Tokheim, Mobiloil Globe, Metal, Plastic, 59 x 27 1/2 x 19 In. 770.00
Radiator Ornament, Spirit Of St. Louis, 7 Flags, 48 Stars On Each, c.1927 .... 750.00
Radio, La Salle, General Motors, Loudspeaker, 5-Valve Set, c.1947 .... 55.00
Rain Gauge, Dodge, Plymouth, Metal, Glass, 7 x 5 In. 28.00
Sign, AAA Official Service Station, Porcelain, Oval, 2 Sides, 23 In. 121.00
Sign, ALA Automobile Green Book, Porcelain, Oval, 2 Sides, 24 x 18 In. 990.00
Sign, Aladdin Gasoline, We Use & Recommend, Metal, Embossed, 19 1/2 x 7 In. 231.00
Sign, Atlantic Premium, White Ground, Red, Porcelain, 13 x 11 In. 165.00
Sign, Automobile Owners Association Of America, 2 Sides, 14 x 16 1/2 In. 118.00
Sign, Canco, No Smoking, Tin, 9 1/4 x 19 1/2 In. 22.00
Sign, Champion Spark Plugs, We Clean & Check Spark Plugs, Tin, 26 x 12 In. 495.00
Sign, Chicago Motor Club, AAA, Bonded Service Station, Porcelain, 36 x 44 In. 385.00
Sign, Clean Rest Rooms, Porcelain, 2 Sides, Mounted, 54 x 19 In. 143.00
Sign, Conoco, Danger High Pressure Gas Line, Porcelain, 8 x 15 In. 30.00
Sign, Curb, Koolmotor Die Cut, Porcelain, Metal, 2 Sides, 57 x 24 x 19 In. 72.00
Sign, Curb, Wolf's Head Motor Oil, 2 Sides, 30 x 23 In. 110.00
Sign, Curtis Ethyl Pump, Red & Yellow, Metal Lithograph, Embossed, 1960s, 16 x 12 In. . 194.00
Sign, Danger Acid Area, Metal, 12 x 18 In. 72.00
Sign, Delco Battery, Die Cut Battery, Tin, 23 1/4 x 18 In. 198.00
Sign, Deshler Michelin Tires, Wood Sand Finish, Cross Sign Co., Chicago, 36 x 12 In. 1100.00
Sign, Firestone, Red Ground, White Letters, Tin, 48 x 12 In. 275.00
Sign, Fisk Tires, Yellow Letters, Black Ground, Porcelain, 1930s, 18 x 60 In. 385.00
Sign, Flying A Hydrogen Treatment, A With Wings, Tin, 11 x 14 In. 231.00
Sign, Fortune Ethyl Gasoline, Mercury, Logo, Tin, 12 x 9 In. 523.00
Sign, Gargoyle Mobiloil Arctic, Logo, Porcelain, 2 Sides, 9 x 10 3/4 In. 440.00
Sign, Gillette Tires, Embossed, Tin Lithograph, 72 In. 303.00
Sign, Goodrich Accessories, Does Your Car Need These, Roll-Up, 18 x 25 In. 135.00
Sign, Goodrich Tires, Cruikshank & Kollin, Pleasanton, Embossed, Tin, 35 x 12 In. 138.00
Sign, Gulf Diesel, Logo, Porcelain, 11 3/8 x 8 1/2 In. 121.00
Sign, Gulf No-Nox, Logo, Porcelain, 11 3/8 x 8 1/2 In. 143.00
Sign, Havoline Motor Oil, Metal, 30 1/4 In. 176.00
Sign, Humble Oil, Red Letters On White, Blue Rim, Porcelain, Oval, 14 x 7 1/4 In. 468.00
Sign, Irving Gas Oil, Porcelain, 2 Sides, Canada, 10 7/8 x 17 3/4 In. 475.00
Sign, Kendall, 2000 Mile Oil, Round, Red Ground, Tin, 24 In. .... 165.00 to 195.00
Sign, Lion Oil Company, Porcelain, 11 x 42 In. 360.00
Sign, Mercedes-Benz Service, Logo, Porcelain, 2 Sides, Round, 42 In. 525.00
Sign, Michelin Man, On Bicycle, Red Ground, Yellow Letters, Porcelain, 15 x 18 In. 358.00
Sign, Michelin Man, Tire, Yellow Ground, Porcelain, 18 x 24 In. 550.00
Sign, Mobil Premium, Logo, Porcelain, 9 3/4 x 8 1/2 In. 330.00
Sign, Mobil, Red Pegasus Horse, Cookie Cutter Sign, Porcelain, 72 In. 2200.00
Sign, Motor Repair, 2 Sides, Light-Up, 12 x 8 In. 165.00
Sign, Musgo, Indian Chief, Porcelain, 48 In. 5500.00
Sign, Oilzum Motor Oil Lubricants, Bakelite & Wood, 12 In. 825.00

Sign, Oldsmobile Service, Porcelain, Round, 12 In. 11.00
Sign, Penn Drake Oil, Double Mileage, Logo, Tin, Celluloid, 13 x 61 In. 495.00
Sign, Pennzoil, Costs Less Per Mile, Logo, Tin, 20 x 11 3/4 In. 176.00
Sign, Pennzoil, Safe Lubrication, White Ground, Bell, Porcelain, Round, 42 In. 1980.00
Sign, Pennzoil, Safety System Lubrication, Logo, Tin, Oval, 20 x 12 1/2 In. 85.00
Sign, Phillips 66 Shield, Embossed, Porcelain, 48 x 48 In. 515.00
Sign, Phillips 66 Shield, Metal, 25 x 25 1/2 In. 220.00
Sign, Pontiac, Indian Head, Die Cut, Metal, 37 x 53 In. 440.00
Sign, Prest-O-Lite, Embossed, Tin, 11 3/4 x 23 In. 121.00
Sign, Quaker State Motor Oil Bubble, Metal, 23 1/2 In. 187.00
Sign, Quality OK Used Cars, Orange Ground, Enamel, 16 x 28 In. 198.00
Sign, Red Crown Gasoline, Die Cut Logo, Porcelain, 14 x 12 1/4 In. 1760.00
Sign, Shell Motor Oil, Die Cut Shell, Tin, Flange, 21 5/8 x 17 1/2 In. 1210.00
Sign, Sinclair Opaline Motor Oil, Metal, 2 Sides, 25 1/2 In. 360.00
Sign, Sky Chief Supreme Gasoline, Sheet Steel, Painted, 18 x 12 In. 60.00
Sign, Sunoco Motor Oil, Die Cut, Porcelain, 29 In. 330.00
Sign, Super Shell Gasoline, Die Cut Shell, Porcelain, 12 x 12 1/4 In. 468.00
Sign, Texaco Gasoline Filling Station, Porcelain, 42 In. 1430.00
Sign, Texaco Motor Oil, Clean, Clear, Golden, Porcelain, Flange, 17 3/4 x 23 In. 578.00
Sign, Texaco Star, Figural, Porcelain, Red, No Words Or Logo, 15 1/4 x 16 x 2 In. 230.00
Sign, Texaco, T In Red Star Logo, Steel, Round, 8 In. 121.00
Sign, That Good Gulf Gasoline, Porcelain, 10 1/2 In. 176.00
Sign, Thermoid Hydraulic Brake Service, Embossed, Tin, Self-Framed, 24 x 18 In. 72.00
Sign, U.S. Tire, Black & White, Porcelain, 18 x 71 In. 248.00
Sign, United Service Motors, United For Service, Neon, 36 x 60 In. 1870.00
Sign, Valvoline, Pennsylvania Motor Oil, Logo, Green, Tin, Round, 2 Sides, 7 In. 231.00
Sign, Veedol Motor Oil, Tin, Self-Framed, 19 3/4 In. 990.00
Sign, Willys Knight Service Genuine Parts, Porcelain, 2 Sides 1430.00
Sign, Willys Overland, People In Green Car, Cardboard, Die Cut, N.Y., 1914, 9 x 6 In. 66.00
Spark Plug, Motormeter, Take-Apart, Patent 12-15-25 .... 4.00
Start-O-Scope, Mobil, Plastic, Metal, 8 x 3 3/4 In. 50.00
Thermometer, Advertising, Polarine Iso-Vis 1100.00
Thermometer, Fleet-Wing Petroleum, Metal, Self-Framed, 6 3/8 x 3 In. 55.00
Thermometer, Prestone Anti-Freeze, 36 1/2 x 9 1/4 In. 121.00
Thermometer, Texaco, Plastic, 7 x 2 1/2 In. 50.00
Thermometer, Yellow Cab, Wood, 15 x 4 In. 264.00
Tin, Mather Thousand Mile Axle Grease, Commercial Oil Co., 2 7/8 x 2 x 1 1/4 In. 230.00

AUTUMN LEAF pattern china was made for the Jewel Tea Company beginning in 1933. Hall China Company of East Liverpool, Ohio, Crooksville China Company of Crooksville, Ohio, Harker Potteries of Chester, West Virginia, and Paden City Pottery, Paden City, West Virginia, made dishes with this design. Autumn Leaf has remained popular and was made by Hall China Company until 1978. Some other pieces in the Autumn Leaf pattern are still being made. For more information, see *Kovels' Depression Glass & Dinnerware Price List*.

Bowl, Lug, 6 In. 15.00
Bowl, Oval 28.00
Bowl, Salad 28.00
Bowl, Soup, Cream, Handles 56.00
Bowl, Vegetable, Oval, Cover, 10 In. 56.00
Cake Plate, 9 1/2 In., 2 Piece 28.00
Casserole, Round, Cover, 1 1/2 Qt. 28.00
Coffeepot, China & Aluminum, 13 In. 42.00
Coffeepot, China, 10 1/2 In. 252.00
Creamer, Ruffled-D 30.00
Gravy Boat, Underplate, 9 In. 39.00
Jam Jar, Underplate, Cover, 3 1/2 In. 78.00
Jug, Ball 28.00
Mustard Jar, Underplate, Cover, 2 3/4 In. 56.00
Pepper Shaker, Range, Handle 20.00
Platter, Oval, 11 1/2 In. 22.00
Saucer 3.00

Sugar & Creamer, Cover, Ruffled-D	45.00
Teapot, Aladdin	67.00
Teapot, Porcelier, 6 Cup	35.00
Teapot, Rayed, Long Spout, 7 In.	67.00
Tray, Tin, Oval, 18 3/4 In.	84.00
Tumbler, Frosted Glass, Set Of 8, 5 1/2 In.	112.00
Vase, Bud, 6 In.	168.00

AVON bottles are listed in the Bottle category under Avon.

AZALEA dinnerware was made for Larkin Company customers from 1918 to 1941. Larkin, the soap company, was in Buffalo, New York. The dishes were made by Noritake China Company of Japan. Each piece of the white china was decorated with pink azaleas.

Butter, Liner, Square Handles, Wreath M Mark	100.00
Celery Dish, Open Handles, 12 3/4 In.	225.00
Dish, Mayonnaise, Underplate, Spoon, Footed, Rising Sun Mark	145.00
Dish, Pickle, No. 121, Plastic Fork, 5 1/2 In.	24.00
Sugar & Creamer, Gold Trim, Blue Mark, c.1915	45.00
Sugar & Creamer, Pink & Gold Beading & Trim, Crown Mark	150.00
Underplate, No. 3, 5 3/8 In.	12.00

BACCARAT glass was made in France by La Compagnie des Cristalleries de Baccarat, located 150 miles from Paris. The factory was started in 1765. The firm went bankrupt and began operating again about 1822. Cane and millefiori paperweights were made during the 1860 to 1880 period. The firm is still working near Paris making paperweights and glasswares.

Bonbon, Amberina, Swirl, Pedestal Foot, 5 3/4 In.	58.00
Bottle, Scent, Geometric Form, Lobed Stopper, Crystal, 3 3/4 In., Pair	120.00
Bowl Set, Intaglio Cut, Trellis & Star, c.1900, 5 1/4 In., 6 Piece	315.00
Candlestick, Putto Stem, Reeded Sconce, Molded Drops, Reeded Spread Foot, 14 In., Pair	590.00
Decanter Set, Harcourt, Acid Stamp, 1900s, 59 Piece	2530.00
Dresser Set, Chrysanthemums, Cranberry To Green Ground, Gilt Highlights, 2 Piece	615.00
Ewer, Charles X, Cut Glass, Fitted Box, c.1995, 13 1/2 In.	1095.00
Figurine, Bear, Walking, Clear, Signed, 11 In.	2300.00
Figurine, Cat, Black, Seated, Box, France, Late 20th Century, 2 3/4 In.	645.00
Figurine, Cat, Lying Down, Signed, 4 In.	70.00
Figurine, Horse's Head, 10 7/8 In.	1150.00
Glass, Wine, Ruby Overlaid, Acid Stamped Mark, 7 In., 6 Piece	975.00
Inkwell, Double, Clear, Swirl Inserts, Metal Stand	145.00
Paperweight, Floral, Purple, Yellow Pansy, Green Leaves, Star-Cut Base, 2 x 2 7/8 In.	450.00
Paperweight, Pansy, 8 Facets, Fluted Cuts, Star-Cut Base, c.1875, 2 3/4 In.	470.00
Paperweight, Pansy, Purple, Red, Blue, Yellow, Leaves, Star-Cut Base, 1 1/2 x 2 1/2 In.	400.00
Paperweight, Sulphide, Figures, Walking, Cobalt Blue, Signed	160.00
Paperweight, Sulphide, Harry Truman	120.00
Paperweight, Sulphide, John F. Kennedy	120.00
Paperweight, Sulphide, Napoleon	120.00
Perfume Bottle, Oriza Legrand, Stylized Enamel Flowers, Pedestal Base, 1917, 7 In.	3850.00
Perfume Bottle, Ybry, Femme De Paris, Cased Glass, Green, Box, Medallion, 2 1/2 In.	2090.00
Perfume Set, Atomizer, Swirl Mold, Silver Tops, 3 Piece	100.00
Pitcher, Water, Embossed, Swirl, Red To Clear Body, Clear Applied Handle, 9 x 7 In.	295.00
Pitcher, Water, Rose Teinte, Amberina, Round Couth, Clear Applied Handle, 9 In.	265.00
Sculpture, Crystal, Cubist Volumes, Original Box, Late 20th Century, 9 3/4 In.	529.00
Urn, Cut, Engraved, Flowering Baskets, Lid, Faceted Knop, Square Foot, 14 In.	460.00
Vase, Crystal, Green Overlay, Flared Rim, Fluted, Base Stamp, France, 1900s, 7 In.	295.00
Vase, Crystal, Holder, Bronze, Art Nouveau, Winding Stems, Signed, 7 1/4 In., Pair	2280.00

BADGES have been used since before the Civil War. Collectors search for examples of all types, including law enforcement and company identification badges. Well-known prison or law enforcement badges are most desirable. Most are made of nickel or brass. Many recent reproductions have been made.

Achievement, Bohemian & Mahren Protectorate, Brass, Lions, Eagles, 2 1/2 In.	370.00

Anti Partisan, Swastika, Serpents, Wreath, Gold, Zinc, Hollow Back, 2 1/4 x 2 In. 690.00
Bailiff, Lancaster Co. Courthouse, Shield, Pinback, 2 In. 44.00
Beach Security, Naval Weapons Station, Department Of Defense Seal, Pinback, 3 1/2 In. . 115.00
Captain, Fletcher Aviation, Shield, Double-Screw Back, 2 1/2 In. 40.00
Deputy Colonel, Pasco County, Florida, 5-Point Star, Gold Colored Finish, 2 3/4 In. 40.00
Deputy Constable, Bexar County, Texas Seal, Spring Pin, 1 1/2 x 2 In. 95.00
Deputy Sheriff, 6-Point Star, Wire Pin, Cover Plate, 2 3/4 x 3 1/8 In. 225.00
Detective, Lieutenant, Los Angeles Police Department, 2 3/8 x 3 3/8 In. 606.00
Driver, Loomis Armored Car Service, Safety With Dispatch, Star, Nickel Plate, 3 In. 45.00
Express Co., Brown, Blue, Rhodes & Lusk's Express, December 15, 1953 .... 150.00
Express Co., Oval, Gilt, Brass, Spring Pin, C-Catch, 2 1/4 x 2 1/8 In. 650.00
Fire Department, Dayton, Maltese Cross Shape, Nickel Plated, 1920s, 2 In. 35.00
Fireman, Eagle, Trumpets, 2 Ladders, Hose, Sterling Silver, Lowell Fire Dept. 325.00
GAR Encampment, Pennsylvania Delegate, Milwaukee, Bronze, 1889, 1 1/2 x 1 1/2 In. .. 95.00
Highway Patrol, 7-Point Star, California, Flower, State Seal, Sterling, 2 7/8 In. 390.00
Infantry Assault, Eagle, Rifle, Wreath, Die Struck, Solid Back, 2 3/8 x 2 In. 45.00
Iron Cross, 1st Class, Marked J. Wagner & S, 1870, 1 3/4 x 1 3/4 In. 900.00
Iron Cross, 2nd Class, Original Ribbon, 1870, 1 1/2 x 1 1/2 In. 338.00
KGB, Special Forces Merit, Bronze Wreath, Ukraine, 2 x 1 3/8 In. 30.00
Kriegsmarine, German Coastal Artillery, Gray Metal, Wreath, Gun, 2 1/4 x 1 1/2 In. 129.00
Luftwaffe, Ground Assault, Wreath, Eagle, Blitz, Gray Metal, 2 1/4 x 1 5/8 In. 170.00
Luftwaffe, Pilot Observer, Wreath, Eagle, Swastika, Nickel, Silver, Brass, 2 x 2 1/2 In. ... 679.00
Military, Bavarian Service Cross, 2nd Class, Swords, Ribbon 150.00
NASA, Exceptional Achievement, Medal, Globe In Triangle, Pinback, Ribbon 69.00
NASA, Space Flight, Space Shuttle In Triangle, Pinback, Ribbon 96.00
Panzer Assault, Tank, Eagle, Wreath, Die-Struck Zinc, Bronze Finish, 2 3/8 x 1 5/8 In. .. 106.00
Panzer Assault, Tank, Eagle, Wreath, Pot Metal, 1942, 2 3/8 x 1 5/8 In. 86.00
Pilot, Stylized Winged-Eagle Shape, Center Star, Starry Field, Bronze, 4 In. 35.00
Police, 6-Point Star, Wire Pin, 2 1/8 x 2 3/8 In. 130.00
Police, City Of Garfield, N.J., Eagle Shield, Nickeled Silver, Wire Catch, 3 1/2 In. 56.00
Police, Deming, New Mexico, Nickel, Silver, Cutout Center, 5-Point Star, 2 1/4 In. 67.00
Police, Ft. Worth, Crouching Panther, Black Enamel, Embossed Star, 2 1/8 x 2 7/8 In. ... 550.00
Police, Harris County, Texas, Badge Number, State Seal, Nickel Finish, 2 3/4 In. 85.00
Police, Naval Training Center, Chrome Finish, Orlando, Florida, 2 1/2 x 1 1/2 In. 30.00
Police, Portland, Circle Star, 5 Balls, Nickel Over Brass, Wire Pin, 2 5/8 In. 250.00
Police, San Jose, 7-Point Star, Nickel Plated, Spring Pin, 3 x 3 In. 350.00
Police, Shield, Eagle, 2 Figures, Nickel, Silver, New York, Hat, 1890s, 2 1/2 In. 37.00
Police, Special, Circle, 2 Stars, Wire Pin, 2 1/4 In. 190.00
Police, Special, Iron Cross & Scroll, 6-Point Star, Ball Tips, Wire Pin 105.00
Police, State Emblem, Nickel, Silver, Die Struck, St. Petersburg, 3 1/8 x 2 1/4 In. 58.00
Police, Topsham, Maine, Eagle On Shield, Nickeled Silver, Stamped, 3 In. 40.00
Police, Vancouver, Circle Star, 5 Balls, Wire Pin, 2 5/8 In. 270.00
Police Chief, Augusta, Maine, Eagle On Shield, Nickeled Silver, Stamped, 2 3/4 In. 40.00
Police Constable, Deep River, Canada, Nickel, Silver, Beaver, 2 1/8 x 1 5/8 In. 46.00
Prison, San Antonio, Brass, Wire Pin, 1 1/8 x 1 1/2 In. 110.00
Quarterman, Boston Navy Yard, Shield, Nickeled Brass, 2 1/2 In. 37.00
Salvation Army, Worker's, Cutout Letters, Eagle, Logo, Pinback, 1 3/4 In. 35.00
Security Guard, Fisher Body Works, Shield, Die-Struck Metal, GM Logo, 2 1/2 In. 35.00
Security Guard, Harley-Davidson, Shield, Stamped Nickel, Enamel Logo, 2 1/2 In. 60.00
Sheriff, Corporal, Marion County, 5-Point Star, Silver Finish, 2 3/4 In. 36.00
Special Deputy, Silvered Finish, Kansas, State Crest, 2 1/4 In. 30.00
Special Officer, 5-Point Star, Ball Tips, Wire Pin & Cover, 2 5/8 In. 110.00
Special Officer, 6-Point Star, Ball Tips, Dingbats, Wire Pin, 1 3/4 x 2 In. 110.00
U.S. Census, 1910, Eagle Shield, Nickeled Silver, Pinback, 1 3/4 In. 67.00
Watchman, Nantucket Steam Boat Co., Hat 425.00

BANKS of metal have been made since 1868. There are still banks, mechanical banks, and registering banks (those that show the total money deposited on the face of the bank). Many old iron or tin banks have been reproduced since the 1950s in iron or plastic. Some old reproductions marked Book of Knowledge or John Wright, or Capron are listed. Pottery, glass, and plastic banks are also listed here. Mickey Mouse and other Disneyana banks are listed in Disneyana. We have

added the M-numbers based on *The Penny Bank Book: Collected Still
Banks* by Andy and Susan Moore and the R numbers based on *Coin
Banks by Banthrico* by James L. Redwine.

Aberdeen Angus Bull, Aluminum, M 555, 4 1/8 In.	363.00
Acorn, Acorn Stoves, Ceramic, Brown Glaze, M 1282, 3 1/8 In.	39.00
Andy Gump, Cast Iron, Arcade, 1928, M 217, 4 3/8 In.	1375.00
Apple, On Branch, Attached Leaves, Cast Iron, Kyser & Rex, 1882, M 1621, 3 In.	3080.00
Aunt Jemima, Cast Iron, A.C. Williams, 1905, M 168, 5 7/8 In.	220.00 to 440.00
Baby In Egg, Lead, Bronzed Finish, Polychrome Paint, Key Lock, 7 1/4 In.	367.00
Bank Building, B & O Queen City Station, White Metal, Banthrico, 1986, R 535, 2 7/8 In.	143.00
Bank Building, Blackpool Tower, Cast Iron, Chamberlain & Hill, 1908, M 984, 7 3/8 In.	231.00
Bank Building, Citizen's Federal Centre, White Metal, Banthrico, 1989, R 969, 5 3/8 In.	70.00
Bank Building, Cupola Bank, Cast Iron, J. & E. Stevens, 1872, M 1146, 4 1/8 In.	525.00
Bank Building, Cupola Bank, Cast Iron, M 1145, 4 1/8 In.	1595.00
Bank Building, First National Bank Of Springfield, Banthrico, 1970, R 612, 3 5/8 In.	61.00
Bank Building, State Bank, Cast Iron, M 1633, 5 1/2 In.	743.00
Bank Building, Tower Bank, Combination Lock, Kyser & Rex, 1890, M 1198, 7 In.	660.00
Baseball Player, Cast Iron, A.C. Williams, 1909, M 20, 5 3/4 In.	140.00 to 165.00
Basket Of Fruit, Cast Iron, Nicol, 1894, M 919, 2 3/4 In.	440.00
Bear Stealing Pig, Cast Iron, M 693, 5 1/2 In.	825.00
Beehive Shape, Coin Slot, Stoneware, c.1850, 3 1/2 In.	88.00
Billiken, Cast Iron, A.C. Williams, 1909, M 74, 4 In.	100.00
Billy Bounce, Cast Iron, Hubley, 1906, M 15, 4 11/16 In.	550.00
Boy Scout, With Belt Buckle, Cast Iron, Hubley, 1912, M 47, 5 3/4 In.	126.00
Bozo The Clown, Figural, Vinyl, Play Pal Plastics, c.1960, 5 1/4 x 9 3/4 x 8 In.	25.00
Buffalo, Amherst Stoves, Cast Iron, 1930, M 556, 5 1/4 In.	385.00
Bugs Bunny, By Tree Trunk, White Metal, M 278, 5 1/2 In.	88.00
Bugs Bunny, Figural, What's Up Doc, Vinyl, 1972, 5 1/2 x 12 1/2 In.	25.00
Building, Eiffel Tower, Cast Iron, Sydenham & McDustra, 1908, M 1074, 8 3/4 In.	1265.00
Building, Flat Iron Building, Aluminum, Kenton, 1904, M 1159, 8 1/4 In.	2860.00
Building, Gingerbread House, Cast Iron, Key Locked Trap, France, M 1029, 3 7/8 In.	495.00
Building, Goodyear Zeppelin Hanger, Cast Iron, Jerrosteel, 1930, M 1430, 2 5/16 In.	550.00
Building, Independence Hall, Cast Iron, 1875, M 1243, 8 1/8 x 15 1/2 In.	10450.00
Building, Independence Hall, Cast Iron, M 1244, 8 7/8 x 6 11/16 In.	1760.00
Building, Lighthouse, Red Tower, Cast Iron, 1891, M 1115, 10 1/4 In.	5170.00
Building, Mosque, Yellow, Red, Cast Iron, Grey Iron Casting, 1903-1928, M 1177, 4 In.	470.00
Building, New England, Church, Cast Iron, Nickel-Plated Roof, M 986, 7 1/2 In.	1155.00
Building, Palace, Cast Iron, Ives, 1885, M 1116, 7 1/2 In.	8470.00
Building, Rutherford County Courthouse, White Metal, Banthrico, 1976, 5 1/4 In.	115.00
Building, Statue Of Liberty, Cast Iron, A.C. Williams, 1910, M 1164, 6 In.	88.00 to 94.00
Building, Westminster Abbey, Japanned, Cast Iron, England, 1908, M 973, 6 1/4 In.	825.00
Building, Woolworth, Cast Iron, Kenton, 1915, M 1041, 7 7/8 In.	138.00
Building, Wrigley Building, White Metal, Banthrico, 1980, 7 1/2 In.	70.00
Bullwinkle, Brown, Vinyl, Hong Kong, 1977, 10 In.	45.00
Calumet Baking Powder, Tin Lithograph, Boy On Top, 5 1/2 x 2 3/8 In.	220.00
Camel, Kneeling, Cast Iron, Kyser & Rex, 1889, M 770, 2 1/2 In.	605.00
Campbell Kids, Cast Iron, A.C. Williams, 1910-1920, M 163, 3 5/16 In.	180.00
Captain Kidd, Cast Iron, 1901, M 38, 5 5/8 In.	385.00
Car, Limousine, Yellow Cab, Cast Iron, Arcade, M 1480, 3 1/2 In.	4180.00
Cash Register, Junior, Cast Iron, J. & E. Stevens, 4 1/4 In.	55.00
Cat, Seated, With Bow, Cast Iron, Grey Iron Casting, 1922, M 364, 4 3/8 In.	264.00
Chicken Delight, Figural, Painted, Yellow, Brown, Vinyl, c.1960, 6 In.	45.00
Clown, Gilt Paint, Cast Iron, A.C. Williams, 1908, M 211, 6 1/4 In.	200.00
Composition, Kliban Cat, c.1980, 6 In.	35.00
Conoco, Figural, Fat Mechanic, Plastic, 5 In.	176.00
Deer, Reindeer, Painted Red, Cast Iron, M 736, 6 1/4 In.	308.00
Devil, 2 Faces, Cast Iron, A.C. Williams, 1904-1912, M 31, 4 1/4 In.	341.00 to 750.00
Dog, Bulldog, Seated, Made In Canada, Cast Iron, M 396, 3 7/8 In.	110.00
Dog, Fala, Painted Green, Cast Iron, 1930s, M 430, 3/4 In.	297.00
Dog, Fido, Cast Iron, Hubley, c.1946, M 417, 5 In.	50.00
Dog, Husky, Cast Iron, Grey Iron Casting, c.1910, M 411, 5 In.	265.00
Dog, Newfoundland, Cast Iron, Arcade, 1910-1930, M 440, 3 5/8 In.	70.00
Dog, Smoking Cigar, Red Bow, Cast Iron, M 415, 4 1/4 In.	3080.00

Dutch Girl Holding Flowers, Cast Iron, Key Locked Trap, Hubley, M 183, 5 1/4 In. 253.00
Elephant, On Bench On Tub, Cast Iron, A.C. Williams, c.1920, M 486, 3 7/8 In. 110.00
Elephant, Raised Coin Slot, Cast Iron, M 475, 4 1/2 In. 94.00
Elephant, With Howdah, Cast Iron, A.C. Williams, c.1905, M 477, 3 In. 35.00
Elmer Fudd, At Tree Trunk, White Metal, Metal Moss Mfg., c.1930, M 308, 5 1/2 In. . . . 60.00
Flintstones, Plastic, Fred, 1973 . . . . 25.00
Football Player, Cast Iron, A.C. Williams, c.1910, M 11, 5 7/8 In. 358.00
Foxy Grandpa, Cast Iron, Hubley, c.1920, M 320, 5 1/2 In. 240.00
Give Me A Penny, Cast Iron, Hubley, c.1902, M 166, 5 1/2 In. 495.00
Good Luck, Billiken On Throne, Cast Iron, A.C. Williams, 1909, M 73, 6 1/2 In. 50.00
Goose, Red Goose Shoes, Painted Red, Squat, Cast Iron, Arcade, 1920, M 612, 3 7/8 In. . 350.00
Halloween Hag, Witch Wearing Pointed Hat, Aluminum, Reynolds, 1981, M 243, 4 3/4 In. 70.00
Happy Days Barrel, Tin Lithograph, Chein, 4 In. 11.00
Horse, Good Luck, Standing, Encircled By Gold Horseshoe, Cast Iron, M 511, 4 1/4 In. . . 176.00
Horse, Workhorse, Applied Saddle & Bridle, Cast Iron, Arcade, c.1910, M 533, 4 1/8 In. . 220.00
Humpty Dumpty, Sitting On Wall, Cast Iron, 1930s, M 42, 5 1/2 In. 550.00
Ice Cream Freezer, Richmond, Cast Iron, Grey Iron Casting, c.1910, M 1370, 4 1/4 In. . . 308.00
Indian, Standing, With Tomahawk, Cast Iron, Hubley, c.1915, M 228, 5 7/8 In. 890.00
Indian Family, 3 Heads, Cast Iron, Chicago Hardware Backplate, M 224, 3 5/8 In. 2640.00
Jerry, Mouse, Figural, Vinyl, Box, MGM, 1978, 5 1/4 In. 20.00
Jewel Chest, Nickeled, Cast Iron, c.1889, M 952, 4 1/2 In. 165.00
Jukebox, Musical, 18 Keys, Brown & Pink Plastic Body, Ideola, 6 In. 111.00
Key, St. Louis World's Fair, Cast Iron, 1904, M 1665, 5 3/4 In. 195.00
Lindy, Lindberg, Bust, Aluminum, Grannis & Tolton, M 124, 6 1/2 In. 72.00
Mailbox, Airmail, Bank On Base, Red Paint, Cast Iron, Dent, 1920, M 848, 6 3/8 In. 340.00
Mailbox, Postal Savings Mailbox, Eagle, Pull Down, Silver Finish, Cast Iron, M 855, 4 In. 88.00
Mailbox, U.S. Mail, 4 Legs, Cast Iron, Hubley, 1928, M 842, 3 3/4 In. 45.00
Mailbox, U.S. Mail, Red Letters, Silver Finish, O.B. Fish, 1903, M 834, 6 7/8 In. 308.00
Mammy, With Hands On Hips, Cast Iron, Hubley, M 176, 5 1/2 In. 116.00
Mark Twain, Aluminum, Reynolds, 1982, M 246, 5 1/4 In. 39.00

Mechanical banks were first made about 1870. Any bank with moving
parts is considered mechanical. The metal banks made before World
War I are the most desirable. Copies and new designs of mechanical
banks have been made in metal or plastic since the 1920s. The condition of the paint on the old banks is important. Worn paint can lower a
price by 90%.

Mechanical, 2 Frogs, Cast Iron, J. & E. Stevens, 8 1/2 In. . . . . .2145.00 to 5500.00
Mechanical, Alms, Black Boy Nods Thanks, Painted, England, 14 In. 285.00
Mechanical, Artillery, Cast Iron, Book Of Knowledge 33.00
Mechanical, Artillery, Cast Iron, Shepard Hardware, 8 In. 220.00
Mechanical, Artillery, Civil War Figure, Copper Wash, Cast Iron, 8 In. 290.00
Mechanical, Bad Accident, Black Man, Cart, Cast Iron, Capron 205.00
Mechanical, Bad Accident, Black Man, Cart, Cast Iron, J. & E. Stevens 2000.00
Mechanical, Balancing Act, Clown Holding Balancing Rod, Aluminum, Reynolds, 1972 . . 285.00
Mechanical, Bill E. Grin, Cast Iron, J. & E. Stevens 2090.00
Mechanical, Birdhouse, Musical, Coin On Perch, Bird Appears, Bing, 12 In. 145.00
Mechanical, Bowling Alley, Man, Bell, Cast Iron, Kyser & Rex, 12 3/8 In. 16500.00
Mechanical, Boy On Trapeze, Cast Iron, Book Of Knowledge 70.00
Mechanical, Boy Robbing Bird's Nest, Cast Iron, J. & E. Stevens 7200.00
Mechanical, Bucking Buffalo, Cast Iron, Book Of Knowledge 50.00
Mechanical, Cabin, Black Figure, Cast Iron, Banjo, J. & E. Stevens, 4 1/4 In. 2415.00
Mechanical, Calamity, Football Players, Cast Iron, J. & E. Stevens 10450.00
Mechanical, Chinaman, In Boat, Lead, Charles Bailey, 7 1/2 In. 25300.00
Mechanical, Circus, Clown & Pony, Cast Iron, Shepard Hardware 9020.00
Mechanical, Clown On Globe, Cast Iron, J. & E. Stevens, c.1890 . . . . .2400.00 to 6800.00
Mechanical, Counter, Coffeepot Perks, Waitress, Tin Lithograph, Nomura, 1950s, 8 In. . . . 500.00
Mechanical, Creedmor, Man Shoots Target On Tree, Iron, J. & E. Stevens, 10 In. . .358.00 to 770.00
Mechanical, Darktown Battery, Baseball, Iron, J. & E. Stevens, 9 7/8 In. . . . . . . .6050.00 to 7500.00
Mechanical, Dentist, Cast Iron, Book Of Knowledge 70.00
Mechanical, Dinah, Black Woman, Rolls Eyes, Moves Tongue, Cast Iron, 4 1/2 In. 170.00
Mechanical, Dinah, Cast Iron, England, c.1911 . . . . 385.00
Mechanical, Dog On Turntable, Coins Into House, Cast Iron, Judd Mfg., 4 3/4 In. .138.00 to 218.00

Mechanical, Eagle & Eaglets, Silver, Green, Cast Iron, J. & E. Stevens, 6 11/16 In. 1100.00
Mechanical, Elephant, Cast Iron, Man Pops Out, Enterprise Mfg 935.00
Mechanical, Frog, Cast Iron, Round Base, J. & E. Stevens, 4 1/8 In. ....770.00 to 2420.00
Mechanical, Girl Skipping Rope, Cast Iron, J. & E. Stevens, 8 1/2 In. ....14300.00 to 34100.00
Mechanical, Goat, Frog, Man, Ram Moves, Rider Drops Coin, 7 1/2 In. 805.00
Mechanical, Hall's Excelsior, Carved Wooden Monkey Teller, Cast Iron, 5 1/4 In. 195.00
Mechanical, Hall's Excelsior, Cast Iron, Cashier Receives Deposit, John D. Hall, 5 In. 765.00
Mechanical, Home Bank, Cashier, Red, White, Blue, Cast Iron, J. & E. Stevens, 4 7/16 In. 1650.00
Mechanical, Humpty Dumpty, Cast Iron, Shepard Hardware, 7 1/2 In. 160.00
Mechanical, I Always Did 'Spise A Mule, Yellow, Iron, J. & E. Stevens Co. ....1320.00 to 2800.00
Mechanical, Indian & Bear, Cast Iron, Book Of Knowledge 60.00
Mechanical, Indian & Bear, Multicolored, Cast Iron, J. & E. Stevens, 10 1/2 In. .1650.00 to 2000.00
Mechanical, Jolly Nigger, Cast Iron, Shepard Hardware, 6 3/4 In. 495.00
Mechanical, Jonah & Whale, Book Of Knowledge 45.00
Mechanical, Jonah & Whale, Cast Iron, Shepard Hardware, 10 1/4 In. 5720.00
Mechanical, Kicking Cow, Cast Iron, Book Of Knowledge 50.00
Mechanical, Leap Frog, Cast Iron, Book Of Knowledge 50.00
Mechanical, Lion & Monkeys, Black, Yellow, Cast Iron, Kyser & Rex, 9 1/16 In. ..420.00 to 990.00
Mechanical, Lion Hunter, Cast Iron, J. & E. Stevens ....5720.00 to 7130.00
Mechanical, Little Joe, Black Face, Polychrome, Cast Iron, John Harper, 5 In. ....345.00 to 495.00
Mechanical, Mama Katzenjammer, Kids, Rolls Eyes, Cast Iron, Kenton, 3 1/2 In. 780.00
Mechanical, Mammy & Child, Blue Dress, Cast Iron, Kyser & Rex, 4 1/2 In. 6050.00
Mechanical, Mason, Cast Iron, Shepard Hardware, 7 3/8 In. ....3850.00 to 4290.00
Mechanical, Monkey, Organ Grinder, Cast Iron, Hubley, 8 7/8 In. ....1760.00 to 1870.00
Mechanical, Monkey, Organ Grinder, Cast Iron, Capron 116.00
Mechanical, Monkey, Tin, Tips Hat, Chein 45.00
Mechanical, Mule Entering Barn, Cast Iron, J. & E. Stevens, 5 1/8 In. 250.00
Mechanical, Novelty, Cashier, Red, Yellow, Cast Iron, J. & E. Stevens, 4 1/4 In. 2530.00
Mechanical, Organ Grinder & Bear, Cast Iron, Kyser & Rex 5500.00
Mechanical, Owl, Eyes Roll, Cast Iron, Kilgore Mfg., 5 1/2 In. 375.00
Mechanical, Paddy & Pig, Cast Iron, J. & E. Stevens, 7 1/8 In. 4180.00
Mechanical, Pelican & Rabbit, Cast Iron, Trenton Lock & Hardware 3500.00
Mechanical, Professor Pug, Frog, Bike, Boy, Girl, Cast Iron, J. & E. Stevens, 10 1/16 In. . 12650.00
Mechanical, Punch & Judy, Cast Iron, Large Letters, Shepard Hardware, 7 1/2 In. 358.00
Mechanical, Punch & Judy, Cast Iron, Medium Letters, Shepard Hardware .....4290.00 to 6050.00
Mechanical, Rooster, Moves Head, Cast Iron, Kyser & Rex, 6 1/4 In. 495.00
Mechanical, Santa Claus, At Chimney, Cast Iron, Shepard Hardware, c.1889 ....2310.00 to 2400.00
Mechanical, Speaking Dog, Cast Iron, Shepard Hardware, Pat. 1885 .... 2860.00
Mechanical, Stump Speaker, Cast Iron, Shepard Hardware, Pat. 1886 ....1250.00 to 2090.00
Mechanical, Tammany, Brown, Yellow, Cast Iron, J. & E. Stevens, 5 3/4 In. ......170.00 to 460.00
Mechanical, Teddy & The Bear, Cast Iron, Book Of Knowledge 105.00
Mechanical, Teddy & The Bear, Cast Iron, J. & E. Stevens, Pat. 1906, 10 1/8 In. ..1250.00 to 2860.00
Mechanical, Trick Dog, Jumps Through Hoop, Cast Iron, Capron 116.00
Mechanical, Trick Dog, Jumps Through Hoop, Cast Iron, Hubley, 8 1/2 In. 1155.00
Mechanical, Trick Dog, Jumps Through Hoop, Cast Iron, Shepard Hardware Co., c.1888 . 2400.00
Mechanical, Uncle Sam, Cast Iron, Book Of Knowledge, 11 1/2 In. ....132.00 to 440.00
Mechanical, Uncle Sam, Moves Jaw, Cast Iron, Shepard Hardware, c.1886 .....2970.00 to 5500.00
Mechanical, Uncle Sam, Whirligig, Aluminum, Reynolds, 1985 .... 242.00
Mechanical, William Tell, Cast Iron, J. & E. Stevens, Pat. 1896, 10 5/8 In. .....1092.00 to 2420.00
Mechanical, Zoo, House, Animals, Cast Iron, Kyser & Rex, c.1894 .... 1980.00
Merry-Go-Round, Cast Iron, Grey Iron Casting, c.1925, M 1611, 4 5/8 In. 465.00
Mexico Chili Pepper, Figural, Soccer Player, Sombrero, Vinyl, 9 In. 25.00
Mice, Kellugh Mice Krusties, Composition, Painted, c.1980, 2 1/4 x 3 1/4 x 5 In. 45.00
Michigan Wolverine, White Metal, Banthrico, c.1950, R 88, 5 3/8 In. 99.00
Money Bag, 100,000, Cast Iron, Key Locked Trap, M 1262, 3 5/8 In. 330.00
Money Is Time, Cast Iron & Tin 33.00
Monkey In Clothes, Porcelain, George Borgfeldt Corp., New York, 14 In. 83.00
Mutt & Jeff, Cast Iron, A.C. Williams, c.1912, 4 1/4 In. 25.00
Officer, Cadet, Cast Iron, Hubley, 1905-1915, M 8, 5 3/4 In. 385.00
Organ, Musical, Crank, Tin, Germany, 8 1/2 In. 145.00
Owl, On Branch, Be Wise, Cast Iron, A.C. Williams, c.1912, M 598, 4 7/8 In. 138.00
Pagoda, Cast Iron, England, 1889, M 1153, 5 In. 1018.00
Parlor Stove, Cast Iron, M 1357, 6 7/8 In. 120.00

Pelican, Cast Iron, Hubley, c.1930, M 679, 4 3/4 In. 1100.00
Pickaninny, Black Man, Red Shirt, Cast Iron, England, M 171, 5 1/8 In. 286.00
Pig, Brown Albany Glaze, Stoneware, c.1900, 4 In. 155.00
Pig, Decker's Iowana, Cast Iron, M 603, 4 1/4 In. 39.00
Piggy, Polka Dot, Wrisley Bubble Bath, Label, American Bisque, 6 x 3 1/4 In. 75.00
Piggy, Yellow, Blue Bow, Gold Trim, Ceramic, American Bisque, 6 x 3 1/4 In. 35.00
Pinocchio On Drum, Copper Over White Metal, M 252, 5 7/8 In. 17.00
Policeman, Cast Iron, Arcade, c.1920, M 182, 5 1/2 In. 240.00
Porky Pig, Cast Iron, Hubley, 1930, M 264 .... 110.00
Porky Pig, Figural, Vinyl, Dakin, 1976, 6 1/4 In. 35.00
Purdue Boilermakers, Holding Football, White Metal, Banthrico, c.1950, R 99, 6 3/4 In. . 66.00
Raggedy Ann, Plaster, Box, c.1970, 3 3/4 x 9 3/4 x 3 In. 25.00
Register, Benjamin Franklin Thrift, Cash Register, Marx, Tin, 4 In. 66.00
Register, Commonwealth, Tin Lithograph, Shonk, 3 Coin, c.1905, 5 In. 50.00
Register, New York World's Fair, 8 Sides, Tin, 2 1/2 In., Dime 50.00
Register, Pail, Bail Handle, Japanned, Cast Iron, Kyser & Rex, M 912, 2 3/4 In., 1 Cent .. 286.00
Rhinoceros, Silver Paint, Cast Iron, Arcade, c.1910, 5 In. 295.00
Richfield, Figural, Fat Mechanic, Plastic, 5 In. 242.00
Robert E. Lee, Bust, White Metal, Banthrico, 1955, R 33, 5 3/8 In. 83.00
Rooster, Painted Black, Cast Iron, M 548, 4 5/8 In. 286.00
Roy Rogers & Trigger, Ceramic, 7 1/2 In. 60.00
Safe, Black, Gold Pinstripes, Cast Iron, Wheels, 6 In. 28.00
Safe, Imperial Safe Deposit, Cast Iron, Tin, 8 5/8 In. 240.00
Safe, Moon & Stars, Cast Iron, 5 1/4 In. 240.00
Safe, Roller Safe, Square, Cast Iron, Kyser & Rex, 1882, M 880, 3 1/2 In. 400.00
Safe, Security Safe Deposit, Cast Iron, 4 5/8 In. 154.00
Safe, State, Cast Iron, Nickel Plated, 4 In. 120.00
Safe, Young America, Embossed Children, Cast Iron, 4 1/2 In. 286.00
Sailor Boy, Rides In Boat, Cast Iron, 4 1/2 In. 460.00
Santa Claus, Cast Iron, Harper, c.1907, M 63, 4 1/8 In. 2090.00
Santa Claus, Cast Iron, Hubley, c.1906, M 59, 5 7/8 In. 1320.00
Santa Claus, Cast Iron, Ives, c.1890, M 56, 7 1/4 In. 770.00
Santa Claus, Christmas Tree, Cast Iron, Hubley, c.1914, M 61, 5 7/8 In. 660.00
Santa Claus, Hanging, Aluminum, Reynolds, 1982, M 100, 6 In. 28.00
Seal, On Rock, Cast Iron, Arcade, c.1910, M 732, 3 1/2 In. 418.00
Semi-Mechanical, Presto, Cast Iron, 4 1/4 In. 85.00
Sharecropper, Cast Iron, A.C. Williams, M 173, 5 1/2 In. 132.00
Shawmut, Indian, White Metal, Banthrico, 1972, 6 5/8 In. 39.00
Shell Oil, Figural, Shell, Logo, Yellow Plastic, Red Letters, 4 x 4 x 2 In. 176.00
Ship, Battleship Maine, Cast Iron, Grey Iron Casting, M 1441, 5 1/4 In. 3630.00
Ship, Battleship Maine, Cast Iron, J. & E. Stevens, 1902, M 1439, 6 In. 2640.00
Ship, Steamboat, Cast Iron, A.C. Williams, c.1912, M 1459, 2 7/16 In. 319.00
Smokey The Bear, Help Prevent Forest Fires, Plastic, Box, c.1960, 3 x 5 x 8 In. 70.00
Smurfette, Plaster, 1980, 10 1/2 In. 10.00
Soldier, Cast Iron, Hubley, c.1905, M 44, 6 In. 440.00
Space Heater, 6 Sides, Cupids, Cast Iron, England, c.1895, M 1090, 6 1/2 In. 1210.00
Space Heater, Beehive Design, Japanned, Cast Iron, England, c.1890, M 1092, 6 1/2 In. . 1815.00
Squirrel, With Nut, Cast Iron, M 660, 4 1/8 In. 352.00
Sundial, On Pedestal, Cast Iron, Arcade, c.1910, M 1549, 4 5/16 In. 1760.00
Tank, Cast Iron, A.C. Williams, 1918, M 1435, 3 In. 407.00
Teddy, Theodore Roosevelt Bust, Cast Iron, A.C. Williams, 1919, M 120, 5 In. .....88.00 to 242.00
Transvaal, Money Box, Bearded Man, Cast Iron, England, 6 In. 258.00
Trolley, Rolling Wheels, Main Street, Cast Iron, A.C. Williams, c.1920, M 1469, 6 1/2 In. . 259.00
Turkey, Cast Iron, A.C. Williams, c.1905, M 585, 4 1/4 In. 231.00
Turkey, Original Paint, Cast Iron, A.C. Williams, c.1905, M 587, 3 1/2 In. ....72.00 to 283.00
Tweety & Sylvester, Talking, Action, Battery, Plastic, Box, 1978, 3 1/2 x 8 x 8 In. 30.00
Von Hindenberg, Bust, Lead, Germany, 1915, M 152, 9 1/4 In. 963.00
Washington, Standing With Scroll, Cast Iron, M 138, 6 1/4 In. 75.00
Waterwheel, Cast Iron, M 1606, 4 1/2 In. 1705.00
Weatherbird Shoes, Rooster, Plastic, c.1950, 2 x 3 x 4 In. 15.00
Wonder Bread, Wrapped Loaf, Plastic, c.1960, 1 3/4 x 1 3/4 x 4 1/4 In. 35.00
Yosemite Sam, Vinyl, Dakin & Co., 1971, 7 In. 25.00
Zeppelin, Graf, Cast Iron, A.C. Williams, c.1920, M 1428, 1 3/4 In. 160.00

BANKO, Korean ware, and Sumida are terms that are often confusing.
We use the names in the way most often used by antiques dealers and
collectors. Korean ware is now called *Sumida Gawa* or *Sumida* and is
listed in this book in the Sumida category. Banko is a group of rustic
Japanese wares made in the nineteenth and twentieth centuries. Some
pieces are made of mosaics of colored clay; some are fanciful teapots.
Redware and other materials were also used.

Tea Set, Bisque Teapot, Creamer, Sugar, Marbleized, 3 Piece	230.00
Wall Pocket, Bats, 3 In.	39.00

BARBED WIRE was first patented in 1867. Collectors want eighteen-
inch samples.

Briggs, Snake, 6 Barbs, 18 In.	1.50
Crandal, Double Twist, End Link, 18 In.	5.00
Hodge, Spur Rowel, Parallel, 4 Spurs, 18 In.	15.00
Kelly, Split Ribbon, 18 In.	5.00
Pooler-Jones, 3 Points On 2, 3 Barbs, 18 In.	4.00
Ross, Copper, 6 Barbs, 18 In.	2.00
Scutt, Wooden Block, 2 Blocks, 2 Barbs, 18 In.	20.00
Upham, Single Side, 4 Barbs, 18 In.	2.00

BARBER collectibles range from the popular red and white striped pole
that used to be found in front of every shop to the small scissors and
tools of the trade. Barber chairs are wanted, especially the older models with elaborate iron trim.

Chair, Edwardian, Walnut, Carved, Gooseneck Arms, Velvet, Kneeler, Late 1800s	790.00
Chair, Kochs, Oak, Nickel Plated Arm, Footrests, Columbia, 1891, 48 x 26 x 45 In.	1035.00
Chair, Koken, Oak, Cast Metal, Iron Leaf Mounts, Leaf Carvings, 4 Splay Legs	4600.00
Chair, Koken, Porcelain, Child's Size	1650.00
Chair, Porcelain & Vinyl, Carved Wood Horse Head, Emil Paidar, Child's, 44 In.	3300.00
Pole, Bronze, Porcelain, Leaded Glass Panels, 32 1/2 In.	4250.00
Pole, Koken, Electric, Wall Mount, 30 x 7 In.	120.00
Pole, Koken, Red, White & Blue Stripes, 6 Leaded Glass Panels, St. Louis, 1910, 33 In. ...	1760.00
Pole, Poplar, Half Round, Painted, Red, White & Blue, Gold Acorn Finial, 79 In., Pair ...	3820.00
Pole, Porcelain, Red, White & Blue Stripes, Milk Glass Globe, Electric, 77 In.	2245.00
Pole, Porcelain, Red, White & Blue Stripes, White Top, Bottom, 43 In.	715.00
Pole, Red, White & Blue, Electrified Top, White Glass Globe	4400.00
Pole, Wood, Gesso Undercoat, Red, White & Blue Repaint, On Base, 52 1/2 In.	385.00
Pole, Wood, Red, White & Blue, Polygon Base, Ball Finial, 83 x 16 In.	1670.00
Sign, Barber Shop Wildroot, Tin Lithograph, Embossed, 13 x 40 In.	130.00
Sign, Grand Union Barber Shop, Manicure, Pine, Painted, American, c.1900, 74 In.	5100.00

BAROMETERS are used to forecast the weather. Antique barometers
with elaborate wooden cases and brass trim are the most desirable.
Mercury column barometers are also popular with collectors. It is difficult to find someone to repair a broken one, so be sure your barometer is in working condition.

Aneroid, Magnifier, Footed, Circular Brass Case, Drawing Instruments, 1876, 4 1/2 In.	295.00
Aneroid, Short & Mason Division-Tycos, Life Buoy, Beveled Glass, 5 1/4 In.	175.00
Aneroid, Silvered Scale, Brass, Mahogany Case, England, c.1900, 5 1/4 In.	235.00
Aneroid, Taylor Instrument Co., Rochester, 8 1/4 In.	150.00
Banjo, H. Dallaway, Mother-Of-Pearl Inlay, Bonnet Top, 31 Milsom St., Bath, 40 In. ...	690.00
Banjo, J. Pensa & Son, Mahogany, Scrolled Pediment, Inscribed, 10-In. Dial, 44 In.	560.00
Banjo, J.J. Lockwood, Mahogany, Encased Thermometer, Engraved Brass Dial, Mirror ...	565.00
Banjo, Sheraton Style, Mahogany, Painted Vines, Convex Mirror, Silvered Dial, 43 In. ...	590.00
Banjo, Shortland Instrument Co., England, Ebonized, Mother-Of-Pearl Case	280.00
Bigelow, Kennard & Co., Boston, Brass Ship's Wheel Design, Clock, 5 x 4 1/2 In.	145.00
Black Forest, Carved, Dead Game Group Frame, c.1870, 46 x 29 In.	4000.00
Eagle, Crest Top, Wheat, Ribbon, Gilt, 36 x 20 1/2 In.	1955.00
Empire Style, Giltwood, Eglomise, Lyre Shape, Late 19th Century, 36 1/2 In.	575.00
Forecaster, I. Krick, 13 View Of Clouds, Instructions, c.1950, 11 In.	120.00
Fortin Pattern, Brass Body, Silver Scales, Vernier, Mahogany Base, 42 In.	235.00

Gimbal, Brass, Wooden Body, 20th Century 720.00
Hygrometer, Thermometer, M. Riva, Mahogany, Convex Mirror, Glasgow, 38 In. 530.00
Louis XVI Style, Gilt Wood, Leaves, 25 x 23 In. 1116.00
Pocket, J.J. Hicks, Gilt, Round Body, Leather Case, London, 2 1/2 In. 175.00
Pocket, Short & Mason, Silver Dial, Circular Case, 2 3/4 In. 150.00
Stick, Brass, Thermometer, Ivory, George III Style, Mid 19th Century, 42 In. 750.00
Stick, Charles Wilder, Mahogany, Arched Crest, Bracket Throat, c.1860, 38 1/2 In. 1175.00
Stick, Charles Wilder, Rosewood, Bracket Throat, c.1860, 39 In. 3290.00
Stick, E.C. Spooner, Storm King, Silver Scale, Thermometer, Sliding Cursor, 41 In. 650.00
Stick, Elm, Admiral Fitzroy's Remarks, 36 In. 575.00
Stick, James Murray, Rosewood, Thermometer, Brass End, Calcutta, 36 1/2 In. 2470.00
Stick, Oak, Brass Plates, Engraved Ivory Compass Insignia On Tail 85.00
Stick, Spencer & Son, Mahogany, Thermometer, Dublin, Ireland, c.1870, 37 In. 1060.00
Thermometer, Satinwood, F. Molton, St. Law Norwich, c.1830, 37 In. 3450.00
Thermometer, Wall, Carved Floral, Porcelain Dial, Germany, c.1880, 17 1/2 In. 115.00
Traveling, Mahogany, Scales, Sliding Vernier, Thermometer, 18th Century, 39 1/2 In. 2000.00
Wheel, A. Wherle & Co., Mahogany, Hygrometer, Thermometer, 44 In. 825.00
Wheel, Barnascone & Co., Mahogany, Inlaid, Shells, Thermometer, Leeds, 38 In. 380.00
Wheel, Ebonized, Brass, Mother-Of-Pearl Inlay, 37 In. 805.00
Wooden, Carved, 2 Birds, On Branches, Glass Eyes, Switzerland, c.1900, 23 x 11 In. 520.00

BASALT is a special type of ceramic invented by Josiah Wedgwood in
the eighteenth century. It is a fine-grained, unglazed stoneware. The
most common type is black, but many other colors were made.

Garniture, Figures, Horse Of San Marco, Elliptical Marble Pedestal, 9 1/2 In., Pair 575.00
Lamp, Candle, Composition, Regency, Gothic, Gilt-Edged Parchment Shade, 28 In. 490.00
Teapot, Black, Classical Relief Figures, Columns, Festoons, Oval, 9 3/4 In. 355.00
Teapot, Sybil Finial, Black, Red & Black Leafy Design, Squat, D-Shape Handle, 5 In. 2350.00
Vase, Cover, Black, Fluted, Pierced Shoulder, 2 Strap Handles, 8 3/4 In. 1116.00
Vase, Garniture, Black, Marble Base, England, 14 In., Pair 374.00

BASEBALL collectibles are in the Sports category, except for baseball cards, which
are listed under Baseball in the Card category.

BASKETS of all types are popular with collectors. American Indian,
Japanese, African, Shaker, and many other kinds of baskets can be
found. Of course, baskets are still being made, so the collector must
learn to tell the age and style of the basket to determine the value.

Apple, Splint, Tin Band Open Handles, 12 x 18 In. 165.00
Ash, Carved Hoop Handles, Rectangular, c.1860, 8 1/2 In. 320.00
Ash, Hickory, Handle, Rectangular, c.1860, 11 1/4 In. 630.50
Berry, Splint, Round, Carved Handle, 7 x 8 In. 95.00
Berry, Splint, Square Base, 7 3/4 x 9 In. 110.00
Berry, Splint, Squat Shape, 8 x 9 In. 65.00
Black Ash, Rectangular Base, Side Handles, Shirley, Mass., c.1840, 14 In. 860.00
Burl, Carved, Freeform, American, 19th Century, 5 3/4 x 10 3/4 In. 1115.00
Buttocks, 24 Ribs, Bentwood Handle, Wide Center Band, 9 x 14 1/2 In. 210.00
Buttocks, 26 Ribs, Arched Handle, Black, Red & Blue Splotches, 10 1/2 In. 385.00
Buttocks, 32 Ribs, 2 Lift Lids, Bentwood Handle, Paint Traces, 8 1/4 x 9 1/4 In. 140.00
Buttocks, Splint, Hickory, 19th Century, 12 x 10 x 9 In. 270.00
Cheese, D-Shape Handle, Round, Copper Tacks, 15 3/4 x 21 In. 750.00
Cheese, Hoop Handles, 17 1/4 In., Pair 690.00
Coil, Brown, Green Tree Design, 3 1/2 x 9 In. 25.00
Coil, Rye Straw, Splayed Side, 5 1/2 x 12 1/2 In. 230.00
Coil, Rye Straw, White Oak Skep, Honeycomb Support, 11 1/2 x 13 1/2 In. 660.00
Egg, Oak Splint, Tapering Ribs, Yellow Paint, 7 In. 1980.00
Feather, Split Lid, 10 1/2 x 8 1/2 In. 72.00
Field, White Oak, Rib, 14 1/2 x 15 1/2 In. 550.00
Fish, Splint Work, 2 Handles, Ada Miller, Provincetown, Mass., 22 In. 115.00
Gathering, Black Ash, Side Handles, Open-Weave Bottom, c.1840, 21 1/2 In. 1840.00
Gathering, Splint, Green Paint, 6 1/2 x 18 1/2 In. 60.00
Gathering, Splint, Oval, Tapered, Flared Splint Backplate, French Provincial, 34 In. 200.00
Laundry, 4 Handles, 14 In. 2070.00

Market, Splint, Carved Handle, Rectangular, 11 1/2 x 16 x 11 In. 198.00
Market, Split Oak, Side Handle, 10 x 6 1/2 In. 120.00
Melon, 18 Ribs, Eye Of God Design, Brown, 15 In. 305.00
Melon, Double, Green Paint, 12 1/2 x 17 In. 115.00
Melon, Splint, Double, 11 x 13 1/2 In. 69.00
Melon, Splint, Oval, 16 x 14 x 14 In. 169.00
Nantucket, Bentwood Handle, Brass Tabs, Paper Label, S.P. Boyer, 5 x 3 1/2 In. 1430.00
Nantucket, Bentwood Handle, Brass Tabs, Plaque, Wooden Disc Base, 3 1/2 x 5 3/4 In. . .   1870.00
Nantucket, Lightship, 2 Handles, Turned Wood Base, c.1890, 19 In. 10350.00
Nantucket, Lightship, Handles, By Mitchell Ray, 12 In. 1905.00
Nantucket, Lightship, Round, Swing Handle, c.1936, 11 x 10 1/2 In. 728.00
Nantucket, Oval, Carved Swing Handles, 20th Century, 10 1/4 In. 4115.00
Nantucket, Round, 2 Carved Handles, Light Caning, Dark Staves, 12 1/2 x 18 In. 3760.00
Nantucket, Round, Carved Ivory Relief, Dog's Head, Ivory Knobs, 8 1/2 In. 345.00
Nantucket, Round, Carved Swing Handle, Inscribed, Early 20th Century, 13 3/4 In. 176.00
Nantucket, Round, Carved Swing Handle, Turned Base, 19th Century, 11 3/8 x 9 3/8 In. .   1645.00
Nantucket, Round, Salmon Paint, Swing Handle, 19th Century, 10 5/8 x 14 1/2 In. 3055.00
Nantucket, Round, Swing Handles, Ferdinand Sylvaro, c.1944, 10 5/8 In. 2115.00
Nantucket, Round, Swing Handles, Wooden Base, 8 7/8 In. 1530.00
Nantucket, Round, Tall, Contrasting Cane Weaver, c.1927, 11 1/4 x 12 1/2 In. 2468.00
Nantucket, Round, Wooden Swing Handle, Turned Base, 19th Century, 8 1/2 x 11 3/4 In.   2115.00
Nantucket, Walnut Base, Swing Handle, Label, Mitchell Ray, 15 x 11 In. 1870.00
Nut, Splint, Tapered, 17 x 9 In. 60.00
Oak, Split, Scalloped Border, Caswell County, N.C., 11 x 13 1/2 x 12 In. 88.00
Picnic, Splint, Cover, 2 Wood Handles, 19th Century, 10 x 16 x 11 In. 90.00
Splint, 28 Ribs, Bentwood Handle, 10 1/4 x 5 1/4 & 12 1/4 x 7 1/2 In., Pair 193.00
Splint, Ash, 4-Color Weave, Porcupine Stitch, Late 19th Century, 11 In. 1060.00
Splint, Bentwood Handle, Weathered, 13 3/4 x 8 3/4 In. 105.00
Splint, Black Ash, Lid, Hoop Handle, c.1868, 13 1/2 In. 1725.00
Splint, Broad Bent Handles, 3 3/4 x 4 In. 190.00
Splint, Carved Handles, Salmon Paint, Lining, 19th Century, 3 x 4 x 5 3/8 In. 1060.00
Splint, Cheese Curd, 6 Sides, Round, Openwork, 22 In. 12.00
Splint, Cover, Rectangular, 6 x 14 x 9 In. 39.00
Splint, Handles, P.C. Quintaro, N.Y. State, 12 x 17 In. 460.00
Splint, Northeast, Handles, Rectangular Bottom, 2 Blue Dyed Bands, 17 In. 470.00
Splint, Oval, Painted, Upright Handle, Pine Base, 19th Century, 17 x 16 x 24 In. 765.00
Splint, Oval, Upright Handles, Red Paint, America, 19th Century, 4 1/4 x 6 7/8 In. 1175.00
Splint, Painted, Cover, Swollen Shape, Mustard Yellow, 19th Century, 8 1/8 In. 499.00
Splint, Rectangular, Open, 7 x 23 x 16 1/2 In. 46.00
Splint, Round, 2 Carved Handles, Painted, America, 19th Century, 5 x 6 3/4 In. 1880.00
Splint, Signed, James & Shirley Cook, 1978, 12 1/2 x 13 1/2 In. 55.00
Splint, Squat, Light Brown Patina, 10 x 13 x 13 In. 28.00
Split Oak, Lid, Bentwood Handles, Latch, Green, 30 x 22 x 23 In. 230.00
Straw, Red, Brown, Black, Swastika, 6-Point Stars, 3 3/4 x 6 3/4 In. 140.00
White Oak, Ribs, Checkerboard Handle, Overlay, 9 1/2 x 10 In.   330.00
Wirework, Stand, Norwich, c.1900, 18 1/2 x 29 In. 145.00

BATCHELDER products are made from California clay. Ernest
Batchelder established a tile studio in Pasadena, California, in 1909
and expanded until 1916. Then he built a larger factory with a new
partner. The Batchelder-Wilson Company made all types of architec-   **BATCHELDER**
tural tiles, garden pots, and bookends. The plant closed in 1932. In
1936 Batchelder opened Batchelder Ceramics, also in Pasadena, and   **LOS ANGELES**
made bowls, vases, and earthenware pots. He retired in 1951 and died
in 1957. Pieces are marked *Batchelder Pasadena* or *Batchelder Los
Angeles*.

Tile, 2 Eagles In Medallion, Brown & Blue Engobe, Marked, Frame, 12 In. Sq. 1380.00
Tile, Lion, Deer Scenes, Multicolored, 4 In., 24 Piece 865.00
Tile, Pine Trees, Hills, Blue & Brown Engobe, Marked, Frame, 6 x 6 In., Pair 518.00
Tile, Sequoia Trees, Ocher Slip, Blue Ground, Impressed, Frame, 6 In., 4 Piece 1650.00
Vase, Egg Shape, Purple, Mirror Black, 4 3/4 x 4 1/2 In. 764.00
Vase, Glossy Green Glaze, Mottled Rose, Marked, 9 7/8 In. 115.00

BATMAN and Robin are characters from a comic strip by Bob Kane that started in 1939. In 1966, the characters became part of a popular television series. There have been radio and movie serials that featured the pair. The first full-length movie was made in 1989.

Batmobile, Batman & Robin, Noise, Lights, Tin, Battery Operated, Taiwan, Box, 12 In. . . .	231.00
Batmobile, Bump & Go, Lights, Gun, Tin, Battery Operated, Alps, 12 In.	633.00
Batmobile, Lights, Tin, Battery Operated, Remote, Japan, Box, 8 1/2 In.	1540.00
Batmobile & Boat, Plastic, Chinese, c.1980, 10 In.	94.00
Clock, Alarm, Talking, Janex, c.1975, 9 1/2 In.	125.00
Coloring Book, Whitman, 1966	35.00
Mug, Glass, White, 2 Portraits In Black Of Batman, NPP, 1966, 3 In.	12.00
Scissors, Kiddy, On Card, 1973	15.00
Toy, Batmobile & Trailer With Boat, Corgie, 1950s	120.00
Toy, Rolykin, Plastic, Marx, Hong Kong, Box, 1 In.	72.00
Tumbler, Batmobile, Glass, Ultramar, 1989 . . . . .3.00 to 4.00
Tumbler, Pepsi-Cola, Super Series, Batgirl, NPP, 1976	40.00
Tumbler, Pepsi-Cola, Super Series, DC Comics, 1976	15.00
Tumbler, Pepsi-Cola, Super Series, Joker, NPP, 1976	45.00
Tumbler, Pepsi-Cola, Super Series, Riddler, NPP, 1976	20.00
Tumbler, Pepsi-Cola, Super Series, Robin, NPP, 1976	5.00
Tumbler, Robin, 1966	15.00
Wrapper, White Bread, 1966	25.00

BAUER pottery is a California-made ware. J.A. Bauer moved his Kentucky pottery to Los Angeles, California, in 1909. The company made art pottery after 1912 and dinnerwares marked *Bauer* after 1929. The factory went out of business in 1962.

Contempo, Cup, Indio Brown, 2 7/8 In.	12.00
Florist Ware, Flowerpot, Swirl, Yellow, 7 1/2 In.	30.00
Florist Ware, Planter, Swan, Blue, 6 In.	70.00
Florist Ware, Vase, Jade Green, Handles Below Flared Neck, Matt Carlton, 12 In.	500.00
Florist Ware, Vase, Jade Green, Twist Handles, Center Bands, 8 In.	600.00
Florist Ware, Vase, Turquoise, Pinched Waist, Fred Johnson, 6 In.	30.00
Gloss Pastel Kitchenware, Cookie Jar, Yellow	150.00
La Linda, Bowl, Fruit, Green, 5 In.	18.00
La Linda, Bowl, Fruit, Pink, 5 In.	18.00
La Linda, Creamer, Chartreuse	10.00
La Linda, Cup & Saucer, Turquoise	15.00
La Linda, Plate, Pink, 9 1/2 In.	20.00
Monterey, Bowl, 2 Tiers, Yellow, Green, 10 1/2 In.	45.00
Monterey, Bowl, Salad, 5 In.	8.00
Monterey, Pie Plate, Turquoise, 9 1/2 In.	35.00
Monterey, Plate, Gray, 9 1/2 In.	10.00
Monterey, Salt & Pepper, Orange, Blue	20.00
Oil Jar, Vase, Blue, 12 In.	400.00
Plainware, Coffee Carafe, Burgundy, 7 1/2 In.	60.00
Plainware, Coffee Carafe, Orange, 7 1/2 In.	30.00
Ring, Batter Bowl, Jade Green, 10 1/2 In.	90.00
Ring, Bowl, Vegetable, Black, 8 1/2 In.	100.00
Ring, Chop Plate, Yellow, 12 1/4 In.	15.00
Ring, Creamer, Burnt Orange, 2 3/4 In.	25.00
Ring, Cup & Saucer, Cobalt Blue	85.00
Ring, Custard Cup, Yellow, 2 1/2 In.	30.00
Ring, Mixing Bowl, Orange, 10 1/2 In.	50.00
Ring, Plate, Vase, Blue, 9 In.	45.00
Ring, Plate, Cobalt Blue, 6 In.	25.00
Ring, Plate, Cobalt Blue, 7 1/2 In.	15.00
Ring, Platter, Jade Green, 13 In.	75.00
Ring, Salt & Pepper, Green, Yellow, 3 1/2 In.	50.00
Ring, Saucer, Yellow	18.00
Ring, Sherbet, Orange, 4 In. . . . . .35.00 to 55.00

Ring, Sugar Shaker, Orange, 5 In. 400.00
Ring, Sugar, Cover, Yellow, 4 In. .... .60.00 to 90.00
Ring, Teapot, Cover, Orange, 7 3/4 In. 280.00
Ring, Teapot, Cover, Yellow, 7 3/4 In. 1026.00
Sand Jar, Vase, Yellow, No. 122, Straight Sides, 20 In. 100.00
Tumbler Set, Mixed Colors, Copper Holder, 4 3/4-In. Tumbler, 7 Piece 280.00

BAVARIA is a region in Europe where many types of porcelain were made. In the nineteenth century, the mark often included the word *Bavaria*. After 1871, the words *Bavaria, Germany*, were used. Listed here are pieces that include the name *Bavaria* in some form, but major porcelain makers, such as Rosenthal, are listed in their own categories.

Bowl, White, Rose Border, Petals, Crown Over Wreath Mark, 10 x 2 1/4 In. 88.00
Chop Plate, Pink Roses, Green Leaves, Yellow Flowers, Gold Border, 12 1/2 In. 110.00
Mug, Cherries, Hand Painted 55.00
Mug, Strawberries, Hand Painted 60.00
Pitcher, Water, Dutch Sailor, Landscape, 7 In. 230.00
Tray, Dresser, White, Portrait Of Queen Josephine, 12 1/2 In. 225.00
Tray, Woodbine, 15 In. 83.00
Vase, Portrait, Lady, Cobalt Blue, 8 In. 182.00

BEADED BAGS are included in the Purse category.

BEATLES collectors search for any items picturing the four members of the famous music group or any of their recordings. Because these items are so new, the condition is very important and top prices are paid only for items in mint condition. The Beatles first appeared on American network television in 1964. The group disbanded in 1971. Ringo Starr and Paul McCartney are still performing. John Lennon died in 1980. George Harrison died in 2001.

Banner, Black, White, Portraits, Rayon, 45 x 45 In. 175.00
Button, Fan Club, National Member, Celluloid, Red, Black, White, 1960s, 2 1/4 In. 254.00
Compact Disc Set, Get Back Journals, Cased Set, Fiberboard Case, 8 Piece 155.00
Cup Set, Paul, Ringo, John, George, Gold Rim, Box, 4 x 2 1/2 In. 2600.00
Display, Stand-Up, Sgt. Pepper's Lonely Hearts Club Band, Card Stock, 1988, 10 x 12 In. .. 40.00
Doll Set, Paul, John, Ringo, George, Remco, Box 1900.00
Figure, Paul McCartney, Old Fred, Yellow Submarine, McFarland Brand, On Card, 8 In. .. 35.00
Figure, Plastic, Beatlemania, George's Face Header, Package, Emirober, 4 Piece 12.00
Kaboodle Kit, Blue, Vinyl, Standard Plastic Products, 9 x 7 x 3 1/2 In. 760.00
Lunch Box, Brunch Bag, Aladdin, 1965 .... 870.00
Lunch Box, Yellow Submarine, Metal, King Seeley Thermos, c.1969 .... 535.00
Panels, 4 Individual Portraits, Painted, Signed, R. Callen, c.1973, 8 x 4 Ft. Each Panel ... 4200.00
Pennant, Group Image, Yeah, Yeah, Yeah, Collarless Jackets, 1964, 21 In. .... .425.00 to 605.00
Poster, Fan Club, Bulletin, 1969 .... 25.00
Program, Candlestick Park, San Francisco, 1966 .... 100.00
Ring, Flicker, 4 Beatles, I'm A Beatles Fan, Plastic, 4 Piece 25.00
Soaky, Paul McCartney, Soft Plastic Head, Nems Ltd., Copyright 1965, 9 In. 110.00
Ticket, Last Concert In San Francisco Candlestick Part, August 29, 1966, Full Ticket 955.00

BEEHIVE, Austria, or Beehive, Vienna, are terms used in English-speaking countries to refer to the many types of decorated porcelain bearing a mark that looks like a beehive. The mark is actually a shield, viewed upside down. It was first used in 1744 by the Royal Porcelain Manufactory of Vienna. The firm made porcelains, called *Royal Vienna* by collectors, until it closed in 1864. Many other German, Austrian, and Japanese factories have reproduced Royal Vienna wares, complete with the original shield or *beehive* mark. This listing includes the expensive, original Royal Vienna porcelains and many other types of beehive porcelain. The Royal Vienna pieces include that name in the description.

Bowl, Classical Figure Vignette, Cobalt Bands, Gilt, Royal Vienna, 12 x 10 In. 392.00
Charger, Gotterdammerung, Der Schalf, Liebestraum, Late 19th Century, 16 1/4 In., Pair . 2530.00

Charger, Mythological Scene, Mars & Venus, Octagonal, 19th Century, 20 1/2 In. 3885.00
Cup & Saucer, Silver Ground, Oxidized, Flower Band, Joseph Bloss, c.1821, 3 3/4 In. . . . 1435.00
Cup & Saucer, Sommer, Cobalt Blue, Gold Enamel, Blue Mark, Royal Vienna, 2 3/4 In. . . 201.00
Plaque, Allegorical Scene, Royal Vienna, c.1880, 13 In. 1725.00
Plate, Ayesta, Gypsy, Green Dress, Red Hat, Gold & Blue Enamel Rim, 9 1/2 In. 690.00
Plate, Classical Maiden, Jug, Cobalt Blue Border, Vienna, 8 1/4 In. 560.00
Plate, Cup, Cover, Stand, Achilles, Ulysses, Thetis, Diana, Gilt Border, 9 1/2 In. 2270.00
Plate, Girl In Hat, Butterfly On Flower, Burgundy Flange, Gold Vine, Green, 7 3/4 In. . . . 565.00
Plate, Liebesgeheimnis As Venus & Cupid, Ruby Border, Vienna, 10 In. 1116.00
Plate, Portrait, Amicitia, Cobalt Blue, Gold Enamel, Royal Vienna, Mark, 9 1/2 In. 288.00
Plate, Portrait, Woman, Hand Painted, Royal Vienna, 9 1/2 In. 8050.00
Plate, Portrait, Woman, Handles, Royal Vienna, 11 1/2 In. 205.00
Plate, Portrait, Young Woman, Blue Dress, Titled Rose, Mark, Germany, 8 In. 375.00
Plate, Scantily Clad Nymph, Kneeling By Pool Of Water, Barschneider, 9 1/2 In. 780.00
Powder Box, Cover, Maidens, Cupid, Green, Red, Gold, Signed, Green Beehive, 4 In. . . . 150.00
Stein, Flowers, Turquoise Ground, Hand Painted, Royal Vienna, 4 3/4 In., 1/4 Liter 1095.00
Stein, Ladies & Man, Hand Painted, Royal Vienna Type, Inlaid Lid, 1/2 Liter 4140.00
Tray, Quatrefoil Shape, Scroll Rim & Handles, Sleeping Cupid, Gilt, c.1900, 11 1/2 In. . . . 1019.00
Tray, Round, Classical Figures, Gilt Surround, Floral & Geometric Rim, c.1900, 15 1/2 In. 873.00
Urn, Hand Painted Scene, Snake Handles, 18 In. 45.00
Urn, Mantel, Gold Decoration, Trim, Austrian, Signed, A. Kauffman, 16 In. 200.00
Vase, Cottage Scene, Royal Vienna, 8 1/2 In. 358.00
Vase, Portrait, Art Nouveau Shape, Royal Vienna, Germany, 8 In. 201.00
Vase, Portrait, Ruth, Violet Luster Ground, Enamel Frame, 5 3/4 In. 430.00
Vase, Round Panels, Venus & Adonis, Aurora & Cephales, 8 3/4 In., Pair 1435.00
Vase, Woman Watching Putti, Cream, Blue, Gold, Floral, 2 Handles, 8 1/2 In. 170.00
Vase, Yellow, Portrait Of Girl, Gilded Laurel Leaves, Blue Pedestal, Cone Shape, 5 1/2 In. 135.00

BEER BOTTLES are listed in the Bottle category under Beer.

BEER CANS are a twentieth-century idea. Beer was sold in kegs or
returnable bottles until 1934. The first patent for a can was issued to
the American Can Company in September of that year; and Gotfried
Kruger Brewing Company, Newark, New Jersey, was the first to use
the can. The cone-top can was first made in 1935, the aluminum pop-
top in 1962. Collectors should look for cans in good condition, with no
dents or rust. Serious collectors prefer cans that have been opened
from the bottom.

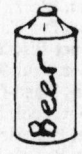

A-1 Pilsner, Flat Top, Arizona Brewing, Phoenix, Ariz. 1775.00
Aero Club, Cone Top, East Idaho Brewing, Pocatello, Idaho 196.00
Champagne Pilsener, Cone Top, Harold C. Johnson, Lomira, Wis. 210.00
Champagne Velvet, Cone Top, Terre Haute Brewing, Terre Haute, In. 76.00
Fitzgerald Beer, Cone Top, Fitzgerald Bros., Brewers, Qt., 7 1/2 In. 335.00
Gibbons Ale, Cone Top, Lions Inc. Brewers, Qt., 3 7/1/2 x 3 3/4 In. 305.00
Goetz Country Club, Cone Top, Pony Express Rider, St. Joseph, Mo. 25.00
Iron City Beer, Battle Scene, Pittsburgh, Pa. 13.00
Iron City Beer, Cone Top, Cover, Pittsburgh, Pa. 275.00
James Bond 007, Flat Top, Late 1960s 650.00
Jet Malt Liquor, Flat Top, Pull Tab, 1960 . . . . 15.00
Krueger's, Flat Top, G. Krueger Brewing, Newark, N.J. 2150.00
Mickey Gilley, Urban Cowboy, Unopened 13.00
Molson, Bubba, Toronto Maple Leafs, Canada, 9 3/4 x 6 1/2 In. 13.00
Primo, Hawaii, Unopened, 1958, 11 Oz. 245.00
Reisch Gold Top Beer, Crowntainer 250.00
Schwabenbrau, Flat Top, Germany, 1952 . . . . 1100.00
Spearman, Straight 8, Cone Top, 12 Oz. 3650.00
Uchtorff, Flat Top, Uchtorff Brewing Co., Davenport, Ia. 757.00

BELL collectors collect all types of bells. Favorites include glass bells,
figural bells, school bells, and cowbells. Bells have been made of
porcelain, china, or metal through the centuries.

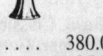

Buddhist, Dragon & Thunder, Brass, Japan, 19th Century, 14 In. 380.00
Ceramic, White, Frog On Front, 4 3/4 In. 35.00

Chrome, Art Deco, Bakelite Knob, Metal Clapper, 2 In. 50.00
Countertop, Hotel, Sunflower, 3 1/2 x 5 1/2 In. 50.00
Custard Glass, Fenton, 7 In. 25.00
Dinner, L. & J.G. Stickley, Brass, Peaked Roof Cabinet, Plaque, 13 x 7 x 22 In. 431.00
Dinner Gong, Arts & Crafts, Pagoda Frame, 36 x 29 1/2 In. 2875.00
Electric, Nickel Plated, 15 In. 77.00
Fenton, Log Cabin On Custard 50.00
Glass, Cobalt Blue, Folded Rim, Clear Applied Handle, Faceted Clapper, 10 1/2 In. 248.00
Harness, Parade, Engraved Center Plume, Scrolled Cast Frame, On Leather Strap, 2 Piece   96.00
Iron, Brass, Wrought Mounting, Hames, 14 x 17 In., 3 Piece 300.00
Milk Glass, Hobnail, Fenton 15.00
Napoleon, Brass, c.1850, 6 x 2 3/4 In. 225.00
School, Brass, Walnut Handle, Original Clapper, c.1920, 5 x 2 5/8 In. 80.00
School, Brass, Wooden Handle, 11 1/2 In. 90.00
School, Brass, Wooden Handle, c.1800s, 7 1/2 x 4 In. 280.00
Servant, Mother-Of-Pearl Shells, Flowers, Brass Cage, Alabaster, France, 3 1/2 x 4 1/2 In.   200.00
Sleigh, 4 Graduated Bells, Brass, Engraved, Leather Strap, 19th Century, 41 In. 114.00
Sleigh, 6 Graduated Bells, Brass, Leather Strap, 6 Piece 169.00
Sleigh, 10 Graduated Bells, Bronze, Leather Strap, England, 19th Century, 38 In. 104.00
Sleigh, 16 Graduated Bells, Cast Brass, Original Leather Strap, 1 1/2 To 2 1/2 In. 158.00
Sleigh, Graduated Bells, Brass, Engraved, Leather Strap, 44 In. 161.00
Store Counter, Brass, Spherical Shape, Marble Base, 6 1/2 In. 309.00
Tulips, Bronze, 1796, 4 In. 495.00
Wall, Brass, 2 Arms, Pull Cords, 17 In. 275.00

BELLEEK china was made in Ireland, other European countries, and the
United States. The glaze is creamy yellow and appears wet. The first
Belleek was made in 1857. All pieces listed here are Irish Belleek. The
mark changed through the years. The first mark, black, dates from
1863 to 1890. The second mark, black, dates from 1891 to 1926 and
includes the words *Co. Fermanagh, Ireland.* The third mark, black,
dates from 1926 to 1946 and has the words *Deanta in Eirinn.* The
fourth mark, same as the third mark but green, dates from 1946 to
1955. The fifth mark, green, dates from 1955 to 1965 and has an R in
a circle added in the upper right. The sixth mark, green, dates after
1965 and the words *Co. Fermanagh* have been omitted. The seventh
mark, gold, was used from 1980 to 1993 and omits the words *Deanta
in Eirinn.* The eighth mark, introduced in 1993, is similar to the second mark but is printed in blue. The word *Belleek* is now used only on
the pieces made in Ireland even though earlier pieces from other countries were sometimes marked *Belleek.* These early pieces are listed
by manufacturer, such as Ceramic Art Co., Haviland, Lenox, Ott &
Brewer, and Willets.

Basket, Woven Openwork, Twig Handle, Floral Trim, 3 3/4 x 11 3/4 x 9 1/4 In. 660.00
Biscuit Jar, Cover, Basket Weave, Shamrocks, 7th Mark, 6 In. 160.00
Biscuit Jar, Shamrock, Cross Weave, Bamboo Finial 265.00
Bowl, Heart Shape, Yellow Interior, Scalloped Edge, 6th Mark, 5 1/2 x 5 5/8 In. 95.00
Butter, Cover, House Shape, 7th Mark, 5 x 6 1/2 In. 250.00
Cup & Saucer, Ivory, Pink Handle, 6 Sides, Parian China, Ireland, 2nd Mark 375.00
Cup & Saucer, Shamrock, 2nd Mark, 2 x 5 1/8 In. 110.00
Cup & Saucer, Shamrock, Basket Weave, Vine Handle, 2nd Mark 230.00
Ewer, Wild Roses, Silver Overlay, Green Ground, Brown Ink Stamp, 9 x 5 1/2 In. 460.00
Mug, Flowers, Signed, L.C. Sherwood 132.00
Sugar & Creamer, Bacchanalian Design, 3rd Mark 200.00
Tea & Coffee Set, Blue Enameled Hobnails, Painted Flowers, 10 1/2-In. Pot, 4 Piece 1512.00
Teapot, Basket Weave, Shamrocks, Twig Handle, 6th Mark 280.00
Teapot, Limpet, Cob Handle, Trim, 5th Mark, 5 1/2 In. 295.00
Urn, Chrysanthemums, Green Ground, Signed, E. Orrison, 1912, 12 x 9 1/2 In. 431.00
Vase, Birds, On Branch, Over Pond, Oval, 12 x 4 1/4 In. 575.00
Vase, Dark Green, Christmas Poinsettia, Pedestal, Handles, 17 In. 250.00
Vase, Rose Bowl Shape, Applied Flowers, Shamrocks, Signed, 3 x 4 In. 100.00
Vase, Scrolled, Pierced, Handles, Applied Flower Bouquet, Ireland, c.1891, 9 In., Pair ... 690.00

BENNINGTON ware was the product of two factories working in Bennington, Vermont. Both the Norton Company and the Lyman Fenton Company were out of business by 1896. The wares include brown and yellow mottled pottery, Parian, scroddled ware, stoneware, graniteware, yellowware, and Staffordshire-type vases. The name is also a generic term for mottled brownware of the type made in Bennington.

Bottle, Figural, Rockingham Glaze, Man Holding Mug, 1849, 10 1/4 In. 325.00
Bottle, Figural, Rockingham Glaze, Tassels, Man Holding Bottle, 1849, 10 3/4 In. 375.00
Candlestick, Yellow, Cream, 4 1/2 x 4 1/4 In. 10.00
Casserole, Cover, Yellow, Handles, Marked, 9 x 3 3/4 In. 25.00
Churn, Cobalt Blue Bird, On Branch, Stoneware, E. & L.P. Norton, 5 Gal., 18 1/4 In. . . . 1980.00
Churn, Dotted, Stylized Flower, Blue, Stoneware, E. & L.P. Norton, c.1880, 4 Gal., 16 In. 470.00
Churn, Stylized Flowers, Blue, Stoneware, E. & L.P. Norton, Vt., c.1880, 3 Gal., 15 In. . . 605.00
Creamer, Cow, 19th Century 58.00
Crock, Bird On Fence, House, Stoneware, J. & E. Norton, 4 Gal. 8800.00
Crock, Blue Bird On Leaf, Stoneware, E. & L.P. Norton, c.1880, 3 Gal., 10 In. 415.00
Crock, Cobalt Blue Flower, Handles, Stoneware, E. & L.P. Norton, 3 Gal., 10 1/2 In. 330.00
Crock, Cobalt Blue Flowers, Sprigs, Ear Handles, Stoneware, E. Norton & Co., 2 Gal. . . . 250.00
Crock, Cobalt Blue Flowers, Stoneware, Ear Handles, E. & L.P. Norton, 4 Gal. 145.00
Crock, Cobalt Blue, Stoneware, Marked E. & L.P. Norton, Gal. 125.00
Crock, Cobalt, Flowers, Stoneware, E. & L.P. Norton, 2 Gal. 220.00
Crock, Flower Thistle, Benny Blue, Stoneware, J. & E. Norton, c.1855, 4 Gal., 11 1/2 In. . 660.00
Crock, Flowers, Benny Blue, Stoneware, E. & L.P. Norton, c.1880, 4 Gal., 11 1/2 In. 1980.00
Crock, Stylized Thistle Flowers, Blue, Stoneware, J. Norton & Co., c.1861, 2 Gal., 9 In. . . 120.00
Cuspidor, Rockinghm Glaze, 8 x 4 In. 150.00
Figurine, Poodle, Mottled Green, Brown Glaze, No. 367, c.1849, 9 x 8 x 4 1/2 In. 4900.00
Jar, Bird, Stoneware, J. & E. Norton, Gal. 449.00
Jar, Cobalt Blue Freehand Flower, Cover, Stoneware, J. Norton & Co., Salt Glaze, 3 Gal. . 480.00
Jar, Cover, Flint Enamel, Acorn Finial, 11 In. 900.00
Jar, Painted, Deer In Landscape, Marked J. & E. Norton, Bennington, 3 Gal. 17600.00
Jug, 2 Cobalt Blue Flowers, Stoneware, J. & E. Norton, 15 3/4 In. 590.00
Jug, Benny Flowers, Blue Stoneware, J. Norton & Co., c.1861, 2 Gal., 13 In. 1045.00
Jug, Bird On Branch, Stoneware, J. & E. Norton, c.1855, Gal., 11 1/2 In. 470.00
Jug, Butterfly, Blue, Stoneware, Julius Norton, c.1848, 2 Gal., 13 1/2 In. 935.00
Jug, Cobalt, Floral, Stoneware, E. & L.P. Norton, 2 Gal. 185.00
Jug, Flowers, Blue Accent, Stoneware, J. Norton & Co., c.1861, 3 Gal., 16 In. 990.00
Jug, Peacock On Stump, Cylinder Shape, Stoneware, J. & E. Norton, c.1855, 4 Gal., 17 In. 2420.00
Lamp, Flint Enamel, Square Blue Base, Olive Baluster Stem, Copper Font, 14 In. 2530.00
Paperweight, Dog, Seated, Rockingham Glaze, Lyman Fenton & Co., c.1849, 3 x 4 In. . . 850.00
Pitcher, Cupid, Psyche, White, Blue Stippled Ground, Leaf Handle, 10 1/2 In. 220.00
Pitcher, Rockingham Glaze, Embossed Medallion, Portrait, 9 In. 50.00
Pitcher, Rockingham Glaze, Embossed Peacock Mold, 8 1/2 In. 30.00
Pitcher, Syrup, Palm Street, Tan Ground, 7 3/4 In. 395.00
Pitcher, Water, Rockingham Glaze, Embossed Hunter With Dog, 9 In. 60.00
Pitcher, Water, Rockingham, Brown Glaze, Figural Dog Handle, 8 In. 110.00
Pitcher, Wild Rose, Graniteware, High Glaze, Octagonal, Rope Handle, 10 1/4 In. 125.00
Plaque, Lion, 8 1/2 In. 15.00
Plate, Whale Log, Yellow Glaze, No. 1629, 10 In. 11.00
Pot, Cream, Dotted Spray, Blue, Stoneware, J. Norton & Co., c.1861, 3 Gal., 12 1/2 In. . . 1045.00
Teapot, Brown Glaze, Acorn Finial, 5 1/2 x 9 In. 10.00
Teapot, Oriental Figures, Brown Glaze, 8 1/2 In. 125.00
Teapot, Rockingham Glaze, Embossed Rebecca At Well Scene, 7 1/2 In. 100.00
Tile, Sun Face, Yellow, Green, White Ground 8.00

BERLIN, a German porcelain factory, was started in 1751 by Wilhelm Kaspar Wegely. In 1763, the factory was taken over by Frederick the Great and became the Royal Berlin Porcelain Manufactory. It is still in operation today. Pieces have been marked in a variety of ways.

Bowl, Round, Dome Cover, Figures, Flowers, Bacchus Finial, Scepter Mark, c.1880 . . . . . 1383.00
Censer, Dome Cover, Egg Shape, Pierced, Late 19th Century 550.00
Figurine, Courting Couple, 18th Century, 8 x 9 1/4 In. 460.00
Figurine, Male, Female, Malabar, Floral Robes, Square Plinth, 14 1/2 In., Pair 2468.00

Figurine, Woman & Bachus Child, Grape Leaves, c.1850, 8 In. 1750.00
Plaque, Biblical Scene, 3 Men, 1 Holding Coins, Mahogany Frame, c.1880, 10 x 13 In. . . 1035.00
Plaque, Gypsy Woman, Holding Tambourine, By Stone Wall, Frame, 7 1/2 x 13 In. 3525.00
Plate, Das Wappen Der Familie Von Jaskowsry, 12 In. 95.00
Plate, Flower Spray, Scalloped Rim, Raised Scrolled Leaf Border, Gilt, 10 In., 12 Piece . . 590.00
Tureen, Cover, Oval, Flowers, Molded Borders, Handles, 19th Century, 10 In. 508.00
Vase, Handles, Mounted As Lamp, Gilt Brass Base, c.1885, 38 1/2 x 11 /12 In. 920.00

BESWICK started making earthenware in Staffordshire, England, in
1936. The company is now part of Royal Doulton Tableware, Ltd.
Figurines of animals, especially dogs and horses, Beatrix Potter animals, and other wares are still being made.

Animal, Dog, Pekingese, Begging, Gloss, No. 1059, 4 1/2 In. 175.00
Animal, Owl, Gloss, No. 1046B, 7 1/4 In. 48.00
Animal, Penguin, Chick, No. 800, 2 In. 40.00
Animal, Siamese Cat, Gloss, Seal Point, No. 1887, 4 1/4 In. 25.00
Character Jug, Jemima Puddleduck, No. 3088, 4 In. 225.00
Creamer, Pecksniff, No. 1117, 3 1/2 In. 70.00
Figurine, A Snack, Kitty McBride, No. 2531, 3 1/4 In. 100.00
Figurine, Aunt Pettitoes, No. 2276, 3B, 3 3/4 In. 75.00
Figurine, Benjamin Bunny Sat On Bank, Head Down, No. 2803/1 . . . . 125.00
Figurine, Benjamin Wakes Up, No. 3234, 2 1/4 In. 50.00
Figurine, Chippy Hackee, No. 26273C, 3 3/4 In. 110.00
Figurine, Cottontail, No. 2878, 3B, 3 3/4 In. 75.00
Figurine, Foxy Whiskered Gentleman, No. 1277, 4 3/4 In. 60.00
Figurine, Goody Tiptoes, No. 1675, 3A, 3 1/2 In. 100.00
Figurine, Guilty Sweethearts, Kitty McBride, No. 2566, 2 1/4 In. 175.00
Figurine, Hunca Munca Sweeping, No. 2584, 3 1/2 In. . . . . .40.00 to 100.00
Figurine, Hunca Munca, No. 1198, 3C, 2 3/4 In. . . . . .55.00 to 85.00
Figurine, Indian, Mounted, No. 1391, 8 1/2 In. 1555.00
Figurine, Jemima Puddleduck, No. 1092, 4 3/4 In. .50.00 to 175.00
Figurine, Jemima Puddleduck, No. 3373/2, 9C, 6 In. 100.00
Figurine, King Of Hearts, Alice In Wonderland, No. 2489, 3 3/4 In. 125.00
Figurine, Lady Mouse, No. 1183, 4 In. . . . . .40.00 to 100.00
Figurine, Little Pig Robinson, No. 1104, 4 In. . . . . .80.00 to 375.00
Figurine, Mallard, No. 756/2, 5 3/4 In. 95.00
Figurine, Miss Moppit, Brown Stripe, No. 1275/2, 3 In. 40.00
Figurine, Mock Turtle, Alice In Wonderland, No. 2478, 4 1/4 In. 300.00
Figurine, Mr. Alderman Ptolemy, No. 2424, 3 1/2 In. 175.00
Figurine, Mr. Benjamin Bunny, No. 1904, 4 1/4 In. . . . . .40.00 to 85.00
Figurine, Mr. Drake Puddle-Duck, No. 2628, 3, 4 In. 75.00
Figurine, Mr. Jeremy Fisher, No. 1157, 3B, 3 In. 75.00
Figurine, Mr. McGregor, No. 3506 . . . . 60.00
Figurine, Mrs. Flopsy Bunny, No. 1942, 4 In. 55.00
Figurine, Mrs. Rabbit & Bunnies, No. 2543, 3 3/4 In. 55.00
Figurine, Mrs. Tiggy Winkle, No. 1107 . . . . .65.00 to 275.00
Figurine, Mrs. Tittlemouse, No. 1103, 2, 3 1/2 In. 195.00
Figurine, Old Mr. Brown, No. 1796, 3 1/4 In. 40.00
Figurine, Old Woman Who Lived In A Shoe, No. 1545, 2 3/4 x 3 3/4 In. . . . . .60.00 to 85.00
Figurine, Peter In The Gooseberry Net, No. 3157, 2 In. 80.00
Figurine, Peter Rabbit, No. 3356, 6 3/4 In. . . . . .65.00 to 90.00
Figurine, Peter With Postbag, Royal Albert, No. 3591, 4 3/4 In. 45.00
Figurine, Pigling Bland, Lilac Jacket, No. 1365/2, 4 1/4 In. . . . . .55.00 to 65.00
Figurine, Pigling Bland, Purple Jacket, No. 1365/1, 4 1/4 In. 500.00
Figurine, Queen Of Hearts, Alice In Wonderland, No. 2490, 4 In. 125.00
Figurine, Racegoer, Kitty McBride, No. 2528, 3 1/2 In. 115.00
Figurine, Rebecca Puddleduck, No. 2647, 3 1/4 In. . . . . .40.00 to 65.00
Figurine, Ribby & Patty Pan, No. 3280, 3 1/2 In. 55.00
Figurine, Sir Isaac Newton, No. 2425, 3A, 3 3/4 In. 525.00
Figurine, Squirrel Nutkin, No. 1102, 3 3/4 In. . . . . .45.00 to 275.00
Figurine, Tailor Of Gloucester, No. 1108, 3 1/2 In. 40.00
Figurine, This Little Pig Had None, No. 3319, 4 In. 55.00
Figurine, Timmy Tiptoes, No. 1101, 3 3/4 In. . . . . .65.00 to 75.00

Figurine, Timmy Willie Sleeping, No. 2996, 1 1/4 x 3 3/4 In. 65.00
Figurine, Timmy Willie, From Johnnytown-Mouse, No. 1109-2, 2 1/2 In. 225.00
Figurine, Tom Kitten, Blue Trousers, Green Base, No. 1100, 3 1/2 In. 225.00
Figurine, Tom Thumb, No. 2989, 3 1/4 In. 55.00
Figurine, Tommy Brock, No. 1348, 3 1/2 In. ....45.00 to 65.00
Pepper Shaker, Sairey Gamp, No. 689, 2 1/2 In. 45.00
Saltshaker, Mr. Micawber, No. 690, 3 1/2 In. 45.00
Teapot, Sam Weller, No. 1369, 6 1/4 In. 400.00
Wall Mask, Blond Woman, Cocked Green Beret, Green Earring, 9 1/2 x 7 1/2 In. 529.00

BETTY BOOP, the cartoon figure, first appeared on the screen in 1931.
Her face was modeled after the famous singer Helen Kane and her
body after Mae West. In 1935, a comic strip was started. Her dog was
named Bimbo. Although the Betty Boop cartoons ended by 1938, there
was a revival of interest in the Betty Boop image in the 1980s and new
pieces are being made.

Cookie Jar, Carmen Miranda, King Features, 12 In. 325.00
Cookie Jar, McCoy, 11 x 7 In. 75.00
Doll, Jointed, Composition, Green Dress, Schoenhut, 12 In. 195.00
Doll, Red Dress, Composition & Wood, 12 In. 1238.00
Doll, Wood, Composition, Jointed, Green, 1930 .... 700.00
Game, Jigsaw Puzzle, Betty At Circus, Bonzo, Bimbo, Wilder Fleischer, 1932, Set Of 2 .. 385.00
Pin, For President, 1980 National Convention, Monarch Ski Resort, Tin, 1 3/4 In. 5.00
Stringholder, c.1940-1950, 7 1/2 In. 550.00
Tray, Change, Refrescos Lulu, Spanish, c.1950, 6 1/4 x 3/4 In. 30.00

BICYCLES were invented in 1839. The first manufactured bicycle was
made in 1861. Special ladies' bicycles were made after 1874. The
modern safety bicycle was not produced until 1885. Collectors search
for all types of bicycles and tricycles. Bicycle-related items are also
listed here.

Ariel, Pneumatic Safety, Man's, c.1898 .... 1700.00
Boneshaker, Hanlon, 39-In. Front Wheel, 35-In. Rear Wheels, Stamped, c.1868 .... 6500.00
Boneshaker, Hanlon, French Diagonal Pattern, c.1868 .... 7150.00
Boneshaker, Michaux, 36-In. Front Wheel, 30-In. Rear Wheel, c.1869 .... 4620.00
Boneshaker, Michaux, Diagonal Iron Frame, Paris, France, 1870, 33 In. 5530.00
Button, Chief Manufacturing, Milwaukee, Purple, Celluloid, 1 In. 14.00
Button, Eldorado, Chicago, Red, Black, Cream, Stud, 1 In. 17.00
Button, Halladay, Multicolored, Stud, 1 In. 17.00
Button, Napoleon, Blue, Cream, Celluloid, 1 In. 16.00
Button, Stahl's Puncture Proof, Multicolored, Stud, 1 In. 23.00
Clipper, Tandem, Man's, Wooden Wheels, c.1897, 28 In. 375.00
Colson, Girl's, Snap-In Tank, Fenders, Chain Guard, Drop Stand, Headlight, 1930s 110.00
Columbia, 3 Star Deluxe, Woman's, Headlamp, c.1949-1950 .... 100.00
Columbia, Century, Split Frame, c.1891 .... 950.00
Columbia, Expert, Spokes, Moustache Handlebars, Rank, Pedals, c.1885, 48 In. 2600.00
Columbia, High Wheel, Spokes, Handlebars, Wooden Grips, c.1880, 56 In. 2200.00
Columbia, Open Head, Spokes, Straight Handlebars, Wooden Grips, c.1879, 50 In. 1400.00
Columbia, Pneumatic Safety, Man's, Coaster Pegs, Headlamp Bracket, Hub Brake, c.1890 225.00
Columbia, Pneumatic Safety, Woman's, Chainless, Front Brakes, Skirted Fender, c.1890 .. 500.00
Columbia, Spokes, Drop Handlebars, Grips, Brakes, Saddle, Pedals, c.1880, 54 In. 2100.00
Columbia, Spokes, Straight Handlebars, Wooden Grips, Brake Hardware, c.1880 .... 2300.00
Columbia, Westfield, Girl's, Balloon Cruiser, Plain Jane Model, 1930 .... 35.00
Eagle, Altare, Pneumatic Safety, Man's, c.1894, 28 In. 900.00
Eagle, Ordinary, Safety, Direct Spoked, c.1889, 52 In. 11000.00
Elgin, Bluebird, Pennsylvania, 1930s 3520.00
Elgin, Pneumatic Safety, Man's, Pinstripe, c.1927-1928 .... 150.00
High Wheel, Columbia, Expert, 54-In. Drop Handlebars, Pear Grips, 1881 .... 2200.00
High Wheel, Eagle, c.1887, 52 In. 4200.00
High Wheel, Victor, Stirrup Handlebars, Brakes, c.1883, 50 In. 2200.00
Hillman, Herbert & Cooper, 28-In. Front Wheel, 36-In. Rear Wheels, c.1880 .... 4300.00
Humber, Man's, 3-Speed, Gears, Handbrakes, Bookrack, Pump, England, 1960s 100.00
Indian, Electric, Skirted Fender, Split Crank, Triple Crown Fork, c.1918 .... 2600.00

Iver Johnson, Girl's, Balloon Tires, Painted Fenders, Rims, Truss Rod Fork, c.1939 . . . . .   55.00
Iver Johnson, Pneumatic Safety, Woman's, Skirted Fenders, Chain Guard, c.1920 . . . .   75.00
Keystone, Pneumatic Safety, Man's, Wooden Rims, Ram's Horn Handlebars, 1915 . . . . . .   275.00
Meade, Windsor, Woman's, 1899, 28 In. 1300.00
Monark, Firestone, Boy's, Horn Tank, Pedestal Light, Rack, Spring Fork, Reflector, 1949 .   550.00
Montgomery Ward, Hawthorne, Girl's, Fenders, Chain Guard, Pinstripes, 1939 . . . .   45.00
Pierce, Cushion Frame, Kelly Bars, Lamp Bracket, Carbide Lamp, c.1903 . . . .   2640.00
Pierce, Dual Cushion Suspension, Wooden Rims, 1898, 28-In. Single-Tube Tires 10350.00
Punnett, Handlebars, Mesinger Seat, Name Badge, c.1897 . . . .   2900.00
Roadmaster, Fleet Wing, Girl's, Springer Forks, Tank, Light, Rack, 1941 . . . .   70.00
Schwinn, Debutante, Girl's, Middle Weight, c.1950, 26 In. 90.00
Schwinn, Fleet, Boy's, Speed Coaster Brake Hub, Speedometer, 1964 . . . .   350.00
Schwinn, Pea Picker, Stick Shift, High-Rise Handlebars, Spring Fork 3450.00
Schwinn, Super Deluxe Autocycle, Hanging Cantilevered Frame, 1938 . . . .   12650.00
Schwinn, Henderson Motorbike, Woman's, Royal Whitewall, Greyhound Fender, 1937 . . .   800.00
Silver King, Man's, Aluminum, Stainless Fenders, Light, Battery Tube, Whitewall, 1937 . .   525.00
Springfield Roadster, Model No. 3, Boston, Late 1880s, 46 In. 8800.00
Sterling, Shaft-Driven, 1897 . . . .   2530.00
Tricycle, Adult, Hillman, Herbert & Cooper, 36-In. Rear & 28-In. Front Wheel, 1880s . . .   4730.00
Tricycle, Aluminum, Wide-Spoke Wheels, Silver, Art Deco, 35 x 27 1/4 In. 115.00
Tricycle, Fairy, Child's, 1900-1910 . . . .   295.00
Tricycle, Pioneer, Gendron Wheel Company 1380.00
Tricycle, Victor, Overman Wheel Company, Adult, Chicopee, Mass., 1880s 18150.00
Waverly, Pneumatic Safety, Man's, Rear Brake, Wooden Handlebars, c.1890 . . . .   500.00

BING & GRONDAHL is a famous Danish factory making fine porcelains
from 1853 to the present. Underglaze blue decoration was started in
1886. The annual Christmas plate series was introduced in 1895.
Dinnerwares, stoneware, and figurines are still being made today. The
firm has used the initials B & G and a stylized castle as part of the
mark since 1898.

Bell, Christmas, 1980, Christmas In The Woods 39.50
Figurine, Come To Mum, Girl, Sitting, Arms Up, No. 2324, 4 3/4 In. 175.00
Figurine, Dickie, Crouching Boy, No. 1636, 4 1/2 In. 195.00
Plate, Christmas, 1895, Behind The Frozen Window 7500.00
Plate, Christmas, 1896, New Moon Over Snow-Covered Trees . . . . .1200.00 to 3185.00
Plate, Christmas, 1897, Christmas Meal Of The Sparrows 500.00
Plate, Christmas, 1899, Crows Enjoying Christmas 2250.00
Plate, Christmas, 1901, Three Wise Men From The East 600.00
Plate, Christmas, 1902, Interior Of Gothic Church 275.00
Plate, Christmas, 1903, Happy Expectations Of The Children 275.00
Plate, Christmas, 1907, Little Match Girl . . . . .125.00 to 145.00
Plate, Christmas, 1908, St. Peter Church Of Copenhagen 95.00
Plate, Christmas, 1909, Happiness Over The Yule Tree 95.00
Plate, Christmas, 1910, Old Organist 95.00
Plate, Christmas, 1912, Going To Church On Christmas Eve 95.00
Plate, Christmas, 1913, Bringing Home The Yule Tree 95.00
Plate, Christmas, 1917, Arrival Of The Christmas Boat 85.00
Plate, Christmas, 1919, Outside The Lighted Window 85.00
Plate, Christmas, 1921, Pigeons In Castle Court 85.00
Plate, Christmas, 1924, Lighthouse In Danish Waters 85.00
Plate, Christmas, 1926, Churchgoers On Christmas Day 95.00
Plate, Christmas, 1927, Skating Couple 85.00
Plate, Christmas, 1929, Fox Outside Farm On Christmas Eve 85.00
Plate, Christmas, 1933, Korsor-Nyborg Ferry 95.00
Plate, Christmas, 1935, Lillebelt Bridge 90.00
Plate, Christmas, 1937, Arrival Of Christmas Guests 85.00
Plate, Christmas, 1940, Delivering Christmas Letters 175.00
Plate, Christmas, 1942, Danish Farm On Christmas Night 175.00
Plate, Christmas, 1943, Ribe Cathedral 255.00
Plate, Christmas, 1944, Sorgenfri Castle 110.00
Plate, Christmas, 1947, Dybbol Mill . . . . .110.00 to 141.00
Plate, Christmas, 1948, Watchman, Sculpture Of Town Hall Of Copenhagen 85.00

Plate, Christmas, 1950, Kronborg Castle At Elsinore 95.00
Plate, Christmas, 1951, Jens Bang, New Passenger Boat 117.00
Plate, Christmas, 1952, Old Copenhagen Canals At Wintertime 85.00
Plate, Christmas, 1953, Boat Of His Majesty, King Of Denmark 85.00
Plate, Christmas, 1954, Birthplace Of Hans Christian Andersen 85.00
Plate, Christmas, 1956, Christmas In Copenhagen 147.00
Plate, Christmas, 1958, Santa Claus 85.00
Plate, Christmas, 1959, Christmas Eve 85.00
Plate, Christmas, 1960, Danish Village Church 200.00
Plate, Christmas, 1963, Christmas Elf 156.00
Plate, Christmas, 1966, Home For Christmas 60.00
Plate, Christmas, 1970, Pheasants In Snow 35.00
Plate, Christmas, 1975, Christmas At The Old Water Mill, Box 25.00
Plate, Christmas, 1982, Christmas Tree 55.00
Plate, Jubilee, Royal Palace, 1895-1970, 9 In. 30.00

BINOCULARS of all types are wanted by collectors. Those made in the eighteenth and nineteenth centuries are favored by serious collectors. The small, attractive binoculars called *opera glasses* are listed in their own category.

Carl Zeiss, 8 x 24, 5 1/2 In. 77.00
Carl Zeiss, 8 x 30, Leather Case, No. 1706451, 1938 .... 160.00
Field Glasses, Carl Zeiss, 7 x 50, Wehrmacht, Eagle, Swastika, No. 17750 ..... 424.00
Herters, 6 x 30, No. 162660 .... 52.00
Huet, Trinotix, 8 x 30, G Champ 65.00
Kanto, 7 x 35, Case, Japan 58.00
M16, 7 x 50, M1 Filter, Leather Case, American 127.00
Nash Kelvinator, 6 x 30, M3, Leather Neck Strap, American, 1942 .... 101.00
Prussian Army Field Glasses, Fernglas 08, Busch, Brown Leather Case, Strap ... 75.00
Sears, 7 x 50, Case, No. 6281 .... 45.00
Universal Camera, U.S. Navy, Model 0, Ships Mark 33, Leather Case, 1943 ...... 109.00

BIRDCAGES are collected for use as homes for pet birds and as decorative objects of folk art. Elaborate wooden cages of the past centuries can still be found. The brass or wicker cages of the 1930s are popular with bird owners.

Beechwood, Wire, Green, Dishes, Louis XVI, c.1890, 29 x 27 x 12 In. 532.00
Brass, Glass Holders, Stand, Hendryx, c.1900, 69 In. 340.00
Chicken Coop, Wood, Arkansas, 35 x 20 In. 185.00
Iron, Mounted Mesh, Chinese Pavilion, c.1900, 98 x 39 x 26 In. 1610.00
Metal, Light Green, House Shape, Dishes, Crown, 63 1/2 In. 155.00
Metal, Red, c.1930, 15 1/2 In. 85.00
Stained Glass, c.1960, 10 x 12 x 7 In. 55.00
Wicker, White, Victorian, 72 In. 650.00
Wire, Mesh, Forest Green, Domed, 3 Perches, 14 x 12 In. 50.00
Wireware, 37 1/2 x 17 x 44 In. 495.00
Wood, Wire, House Frame, Multiple Tiers, 4 Doors, Victorian, 28 x 37 In. 460.00
Wood, Wire, Round Cupola Center, Peaked Ends, Victorian, 35 In. 158.00

BISQUE is an unglazed baked porcelain. Finished bisque has a slightly sandy texture with a dull finish. Some of it may be decorated with various colors. Bisque gained favor during the late Victorian era when thousands of bisque figurines were made. It is still being made. Additional bisque items may be listed under the factory name.

Box, Cover, Car Driven By Cupid, Egg Shape, 4 In. 60.00
Bust, Lady, Sevres Style, Cobalt Blue Socle, 12 1/2 In. 149.00
Candy Dish, Chicks Emerge From Eggs, Basket Weave Base, 7 In. 295.00
Figurine, 2 Women, Umbrella, Fan, Man, Book, Dog, Glass Dome, Wood Base, 7 In. 40.00
Figurine, Boy & Girl, Pink Blankets, Pink & Cobalt Shorts, Pink Night Caps, 18 In., Pair . 100.00
Figurine, Boy In Nightshirt Holding Blanket, Fence, Creek, 15 In. 25.00
Figurine, Indian, Smiling, Young, c.1930, 3 1/2 In. 40.00
Figurine, Lady Godiva On Horseback, W.H. Goss, Stoke On Trent 1860, 7 In. 270.00
Figurine, Naughty Nellie, Girl Sitting, Holding Dress, Turns Over, 3 1/2 In. . 160.00
Figurine, New Haven Fishwife, 10 In. 40.00

Figurine, Nude, Lying On Side, Holding Book, 6 1/2 In. 230.00
Figurine, Romeo & Juliet, 19 In., Pair 160.00
Figurine, Sleigh, Swan Shape, Woman & Putti, 10 1/2 In. 10.00
Match Holder, Figural, Skull, Striker On Back, Blue Anchor Mark, 2 x 3 In. 79.00
Planter, Uncle Willie & Emmy, Moon Mullins' Group, 5 In. 295.00
Toothbrush Holder, Donald Duck With Arms Around Mickey Mouse, 1930s 350.00
Urn, Guilloche Circles, Flowers, Blossom Finial, Silver Mounts, 14 x 6 1/4 In., Pair 1725.00

BLACK memorabilia has become an important area of collecting since
the 1970s. The best material dates from past centuries, but many recent
items are also of interest. F & F is the mark used on plastic made by
Fiedler & Fiedler Mold & Die Works, Inc. in the 1930s and 1940s.
Objects that picture a black person may also be listed in this book
under Advertising, Tins; Banks; Bottle Openers; Cookie Jars; Salt &
Pepper; Sheet Music; Toys; etc.

Andiron, Male & Female, Elderly Couple, Painted Clothing, Cast Iron, 16 In. 1470.00
Ashtray, Figural, Minstrel Head, Mouth Is Tray, Head Knob Holds Matches, 1890s, 4 In. . . 185.00
Ashtray, Mammy, So You Think You've Been Thru The Wringer, Plastic, 6 In. 115.00
Ashtray, Nodder, Boy, Barefoot, Cigar In Mouth, Alligatored Tin Tray, 4 1/2 In. 180.00
Broadside, Runaway Slave, $100 Reward, March 7, 1860, Liberty, Mo., 12 x 9 In. 7475.00
Bust, Boy, Plaster, Polychrome, Early 20th Century, 20 In. 170.00
Cane, Root, Carved, Folk Art, Bone Inserts, Early 20th Century, 35 In. 1150.00
Cigar Holder, Girl, Sitting, Eating Melon Slice, Ceramic, Japan, 1940s, 5 In. 95.00
Cookie Jars are listed in the Cookie Jar category.
Deed, Slave, Gifting Of Child Named Moses, To Anson Gaskill, 1808 . . . . 206.00
Document, Manuscript Tax List, Slaves Of A. Feaster, Fairfield District, S.C., 1857 . . . . . 288.00
Doll, Abyssinian Baby, Composition, Sleep Eyes, Wool Wig, Open Mouth, c.1900, 11 In. . 65.00
Doll, Bisque Head, Googly Eyes, Watermelon Mouth, Mohair Wig, 1900s, 11 1/2 In. 205.00
Doll, Celluloid, Brown Glass Eyes, Lashes, Closed Mouth, Black Mohair Wig, 17 In. 380.00
Doll, Child, Crying, Papier-Mache Head, Glass Inset Eyes, Cloth Body, Leo Moss, 22 In. . 9500.00
Doll, Cloth, Woman, Calico Dress, Bandanna, Copper Tack Eyes, Folk Art, 13 In. 275.00
Doll, Golliwog, Red Jacket, Black Pants, Crocheted, Looped Hair, England, 13 In. 60.00
Doll, Mammy, Quilted Dress, Painted Face, Human Hair, Cloth, Stuffed, 14 In. 495.00
Doll, Man, Papier-Mache Head, Bald, Bearded, Glancing Eyes, Leo Moss, c.1900, 17 In. . 13500.00
Doll, Man, Red Tuxedo, Black Pants, Corduroy, Embroidered Face, Yarn Hair, 18 In. 495.00
Doll, Pete The Pickaninny, Startled Face, Cloth, Stuffed, 14 In. 100.00
Doll, Pumpkin-Shaped Head, Zigzag Eyebrows, Formed Ears, New England, c.1880 . . . . 795.00
Doll, Rag, Girl, Muslin, Dyed, Unjointed Neck, Glass Eyes, Fur Brows, 27 In. 1000.00
Doll, Rastus, Cream Of Wheat, Printed, Stuffed, White Apron & Hat, c.1890, 18 In. 100.00
Doll, Topsy, Turn Upside Down To Li'l Eva, Cloth, Stuffed, Embroidered Faces, 15 In. . . 110.00
Doll, Topsy-Turvy, Black Child, White Child, Painted Face, Composition, c.1910, 7 In. . . 125.00
Doll, Uncle Remus, Painted Face, Human Hair, Cloth, Stuffed, 14 In. 70.00
Figure, Dancing, Wire Rod, Turned Pole, Movable Paddles, 8 3/4 In. 380.00
Figurine, Boy, Barefoot, Sitting, Eating Ear Of Corn, Painted, Bisque, Austria, 1890, 4 In. 162.00
Figurine, Dice Player, Red Shorts, Base, c.1930, 1 1/4 x 2 1/2 In. 12.00
Figurine, Minstrel, Playing Banjo, Mahogany, Carved, 16 1/2 In. 305.00
Figurine, Shoeshine Boy, Standing Proudly By Box, Bisque, Box, Occupied Japan, 6 In. . 65.00
Figurine, Woman Wearing Bandanna, Stamped, 15 1/2 In. 495.00
Humidor, Barrel Head, Face, Green Cap, Ceramic, Austria, 1880s, 4 1/2 In. 367.00
Humidor, Boy, Smiling, Emerging From Melon, Terra-Cotta, Austria, 1880s, 7 1/2 In. . . . 587.00
Humidor, Chauffeur, Grinning, Removing Hat, Painted, Ceramic, Austria, 1880s, 6 In. . . . 375.00
Humidor, Stylized Slave Head, Majolica Style, Austria, 1990s, 6 1/2 In. 405.00
Mug, Boy, Sitting, Eating Watermelon, Majolica, 7 In. 95.00
Nodder, King, Sitting, Holding Arrows, Painted, Bisque, Austria, 1880s, 5 1/2 In. 267.00
Nodder, Queen, Cross-Legged, Painted, Bisque, Gilt Trim, Austria, 1880s, 5 1/2 In. 250.00
Painting, Folk Art, Comic Black Boy Crying, Goose Biting, J.R. Smith, 1925, 12 In. 145.00
Pattern, Aunt Jemima, Cloth, Quaker Oats, Mailer, 1929, 5 x 10 1/2 In. 125.00
Pencil Box, Comic Minstrel, Cardboard, Cylindrical, Tin Hat Lid, England, 10 In. 134.00
Pencil Sharpener, Black Uncle Sam, Exaggerated Features, Metal, Occupied Japan, 2 In. . 90.00
Plaque, Figure, Hot Pad Holder, Plaster, Screw Hook, Hanging, c.1950, 5 x 7 In. 36.00
Plate, Golliwog, Sitting With Teddy Bear, Alphabet, Numbers, 7 1/4 In. 30.00
Postcard, A Quiet Game, Blacks Playing Marbles, 1908 . . . . 7.50
Poster, Aunt Jemima Ready-Mix Buckwheat, Corn, Wheat Flour, Cardboard, 22 x 12 In. . 1375.00

Puppet, Hand, Female, Plaster Head, 1970s Clothing, 18 In. 52.00
Rug, Golliwog, Toy Soldier & Teddy Bear, On Locomotive, Wool, England, 1930s, 36 In. 222.00
Sampler, Uncle Tom & Eva's Foreboding, Wool, Muslin, 15 x 16 In. 750.00
Sheet Music, Come Out, Miss Dinah Lee, Woman Peeks, Door, 1911 .... 55.00
Sheet Music, Hap' Li'l Mose, Smiling Child, 1903 .... 100.00
Sheet Music, Keep A Coming Ma Honey, Fancy Dressed Woman, 1899 .... 102.00
Sheet Music, Nobody Knows Where John Brown Went, Man, Headstone, 1909 .... 40.00
Sheet Music, Old Black Joe, Stephen Foster, 1915 .... 20.00
Sheet Music, Rag-Time Skedaddle, Man, Straight Razor, 1899 .... 55.00
Sheet Music, Scramble Rag, Man Dancing, Banjo Player, 1911 .... 36.00
Sign, Minstrel, Folk Art, House Shape, Leroy Minstrels, Figure Playing Banjo, 35 x 40 In. 3450.00
Sign, Waiting Room, Whites Only, Reverse Painted, Gold On Black, 1920, 24 In. 267.00
Statue, Jockey, Holding Starter's Trumpet, Painted, Bisque, Austria, 1900s, 13 In. 100.00
Stringholder, Mammy, Plaid, Polka Dot Dress, Ceramic 175.00
Toothbrush Holder, Moorish Prince, Holder At Feet & Arms, Japan, 1930s, 5 1/2 In. 75.00
Towel Holder, Mammy, Hands Hold Dowel, Painted, Wooden, 12 1/2 In. 125.00
Toy, Golliwog, Leading Animal Marching Band, Tin Lithograph, 8 Sides, England, 5 In. .. 90.00
Toy, Hey Hey The Chicken Snatcher, Man Steals Chicken, Dog Bites Arm, Marx, 1920s .. 1920.00
Toy, Oh My Alabama Coon Jigger, Windup, Lehmann, 1912 .... 1150.00

BLACK AMETHYST glass appears black until it is held to the light, then
a dark purple can be seen. It has been made in many factories from
1860 to the present.

Ashtray, Match Holder, 4 3/4 x 3 1/4 x 1 1/2 In. 20.00
Bottle, 8 Panels, Polished Pontil, Qt. 1375.00
Cracker Jar, Cover, 6 1/2 x 5 In. 155.00
Cup & Saucer, Mt. Pleasant, L.E. Smith 15.00
Planter, Swan, 8 1/2 In. 65.00
Urn, 11 In., Pair 40.00
Vase, 6 Sides, Ruffled Edge, Art Deco, 4 7/8 x 4 11/16 In. 50.00
Vase, Bud, Figural, Athena Holding Vase, Silver Plated Holder, 13 1/2 In. 200.00
Vase, Fan, Ruffled Edge, Art Deco, 5 3/4 x 8 1/2 In. 20.00
Vase, Gold Floral Highlights, Ruffled Edge, 9 In. 150.00
Vase, Iridescent, 8 In. 30.00

BLENKO GLASS COMPANY is the 1930s successor to several glassworks
founded by William John Blenko in Milton, West Virginia. In 1933, his
son, William H. Blenko Sr. took charge. The company made a line of
reproductions for Colonial Williamsburg. They are still in business and
are best known today for their decorative wares and stained glass.

Bottle, Cone Shape, Red Orange, Bulbous Neck, Flame Stopper, 29 In. 700.00

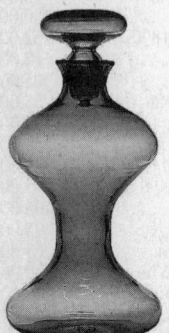

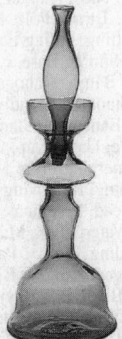

Blenko, Bottle,
Orange, Pinched Waist,
Mushroom Stopper,
c.1957, 19 In.

Blenko, Bottle, Orange,
Tapered, Cone Shaped,
Flame Stopper,
c.1950-1960, 26 1/2 In.

Blenko, Bottle,
Peacock Blue, Multilobed,
Open Pontil,
c.1959, 21 1/4 In.

Blenko, Bottle,
Ruby Red, Pinched
Waist, Ribbed,
1972, 40 In.

Bottle, Cone Shape, Red Orange, Long Neck, 27 1/4 In.	450.00
Bottle, Globular, Yellow, Stopper, Pontil, 29 1/2 In.	450.00
Bottle, Orange, Pinched Waist, Mushroom Stopper, c.1957, 19 In. . . . . *Illus*	800.00
Bottle, Orange, Tapered, Cone Shaped, Flame Stopper, c.1950-1960, 26 1/2 In. . . . . *Illus*	450.00
Bottle, Peacock Blue, Multilobed, Open Pontil, c.1959, 21 1/4 In. . . . . *Illus*	860.00
Bottle, Ruby Red, Pinched Waist, Ribbed, 1972, 40 In. . . . . *Illus*	1035.00
Bowl, Blue, On Clear Cone Shaped Pedestal, 14 In.	400.00
Bowl, Free-Form, Purple, Clear Base, Signed, 4 1/4 x 9 In.	225.00
Vase, Apricot Yellow, Long Neck, Witch's Ball Stopper, 28 In.	475.00
Vase, Green, Egg Shape, 12 Appliques, Pontil, 11 1/4 In.	525.00
Vase, Orange, Pinched Waist, Cylindrical, Flared Lip, Pontil, 24 In.	250.00
Vase, Pedestal, Green, 4 Appliques On Base, Pontil, 11 In.	400.00
Vase, Yellow, Fish Shape, Clear Base, 13 1/4 In.	265.00

BLOWN GLASS, see Glass-Blown category.

BLUE GLASS, see Cobalt Blue category.

BLUE ONION, see Onion category.

BLUE WILLOW, see Willow category.

BOCH FRERES factory was founded in 1841 in La Louviere in eastern Belgium. The wares resemble the work of Villeroy & Boch. The factory is still in business.

Bowl, Poppies, On Stoneware Body, Ruffled, Marked, 10 1/4 x 2 1/4 In.	150.00
Vase, Blue & Turquoise Drip Glaze, 9 In.	300.00
Vase, Buffalo, Earthenware, Charles Catteau, Signed, c.1929, 15 1/2 In.	6570.00
Vase, Bulbous, Enameled, Unglazed Outline, Flowers, Blue, Yellow, 15 x 13 In., Pair	1530.00
Vase, Diamonds, Intersecting, Teal, Royal Blue, Cream Crackle Ground, 12 1/2 In.	1225.00
Vase, Discs, Red, Blue, Turquoise, Black, On White Crackle Glaze, Catteau, 9 In.	315.00
Vase, Faceted, Stars & Moon, Black, Gold, White, Blue, 5 x 6 In.	489.00
Vase, La Maitrise, Oval, Flowers, Blue, Turquoise, White Ground, 14 x 5 In., Pair	1175.00
Vase, Matte Glaze, Veined Leaves, Green, Tan, 5 1/2 In.	295.00
Vase, Pink High Glaze, Red, White Blossoms, Leaves, Black Band, 10 In.	345.00
Vase, Potter Throwing Pot On Wheel, Ernest D'Hossche, c.1930, 17 3/4 In.	4180.00
Vase, Stalagmites, Green, Yellow, White, Bulbous, Catteau, 6 1/2 In.	320.00
Vase, Stylized Deer Grazing, Leaves, Ferns, Cream Crackled Glaze, c.1930, 9 In.	800.00
Vase, Stylized Flowers, Blue, Green, Orange, Marked, 12 1/2 x 6 In.	450.00
Vase, Stylized Flowers, Leaves, Blue, Yellow, Green, Flared Rim, Oval, 1900s, 10 In.	235.00
Vase, Stylized Flowers, Polychrome, White Crackled Ground, 9 1/2 In.	230.00
Vase, Yellow, Blue & White Drippings, Signed, 10 x 6 1/2 In.	150.00

BOEHM is the collector's name for the porcelains of Edward Marshall Boehm. In 1953 the Osso China Company was reorganized as Edward Marshall Boehm, Inc. The company is still working in England and New Jersey. In the early days of the factory, dishes were made, but the elaborate and lifelike bird figurines are the best-known ware. Edward Marshall Boehm, the founder, died in 1961, but the firm has continued to design and produce porcelain. Today, the firm makes both limited and unlimited editions of figurines and plates.

Candlestick, Holly, Berries, Leaves, c.1965, 3 1/2 x 10 In.	316.00
Figurine, Cygnet, Eyeing Insect On Lily Pad, Signed, 3 1/2 In.	150.00
Figurine, Cygnet, On Lily Pad, Signed, 4 1/4 In.	161.00
Figurine Set, 3 Wise Men, Kings Gaspar, Balthazar & Melchior, Signed, 9 To 12 In.	165.00
Sculpture, Black Throated Blue Warbler, No. 441, Signed, 10 1/4 In.	550.00
Sculpture, Bobolink, No. 473, Signed, 15 In.	525.00
Sculpture, Canada Warbler, Monarch Butterfly, Signed, 8 1/4 In.	715.00
Sculpture, Catbird & Hyacinth, No. 483, Signed, 14 1/2 In.	525.00
Sculpture, Downy Woodpeckers With Trumpet Vine, Signed, 13 In.	715.00
Sculpture, Golden Crowned Kinglets, Oriental Poppies, No. 419, Signed, 9 1/2 In.	605.00
Sculpture, Horned Lark, Signed, No. 400-251, 19 1/2 In.	1870.00
Sculpture, Hummingbirds On Icelandic Poppy, No. 4, Signed, 10 1/2 In.	770.00
Sculpture, Meadowlark, No. 435, Signed, 8 1/2 In.	308.00
Sculpture, Northern Water Thrush With Ferns, No. 490, Signed, 10 1/2 In.	415.00

Sculpture, Parula Warblers, Morning Glories, No. 48, Signed, 15 3/4 In. 1210.00
Sculpture, Sandpipers, No. 293, Signed, 13 1/4 In. 715.00
Sculpture, Tufted Titmice, No. 482G, Signed, 13 In. 660.00
Sculpture, Varied Bunting, No. 481, Signed, 22 3/4 In. 2090.00
Sculpture, Woodcock, Signed, 10 1/2 In. 550.00

BOHEMIAN GLASS, see Glass-Bohemian.

BONE DISHES were considered a necessary part of a table setting for
the Victorian table. The crescent-shaped dish was kept at the edge of
the dinner plate so the bones removed from the fish could be stored
away from the uneaten food. Some bone dishes were made in more
fanciful shapes and many resemble fish.

Autumn Tints, c.1880-1890, 6 5/8 x 4 In. 20.00
English Chippendale, Red Pink, Johnson Brothers, 8 x 5 1/4 In. 38.00
Flow Blue, Labelle China, Wheeling, W. Va. Pottery, c.1900 . . . .   60.00
Flowers, Pink, Yellow, On White Ground, Gold Trim 15.00
Ideal, Flowers, Gold, Flow Blue, W.H. Grindley & Co. 30.00
Martha, Flower Basket, Scrolls, Kidney Shape, 6 1/2 x 3 In. 20.00
Princess, Roses, Blue Ribbons, Vines, Haviland Limoges 30.00
Ranson Blank, Haviland Limoges, White 15.00
Vienna Woods, Blue Delft, 6 1/2 x 2 3/4 In. 15.00

BOOKENDS have probably been used since books became inexpensive.
Early libraries kept books in cupboards, not on open shelves. By the
1870s bookends appeared, especially homemade fret-carved wooden
examples. Most bookends listed in this book date from the twentieth
century. Bookends are also listed in other categories by manufacturer
or material. All bookends listed here are pairs.

Arts & Crafts Design, Rectangular Block Base, Green Matte Glaze, 5 In. 115.00
Bakers Cocoa, Figural, Girl Holding Tray, Cast Iron, 5 3/4 x 3 3/4 x 3 1/4 In. 198.00
Black Forest, Fruitwood, Folding, 30 In. 34.00
Borzoi, Figural, Glass, 7 1/4 In. 138.00
Butterfly, Brass Plated Metal, Stylized Stumps, Flowers, Swirls, 5 5/8 x 4 In. 155.00
Cat & Dog, Bronze, Signed, E. Norton, 7 In. 660.00
Cathedral Window, Vines, Cast Iron, Bradley & Hubbard, Mfg. Co., 6 1/4 x 6 In. 165.00
Concentric Arches, 2-Tone Metal, Walter Von Nessen, Chase, Art Deco, 6 x 4 x 3 In. 353.00
Cornucopia, Glass, New Martinsville, No. 651, 5 3/4 In. 45.00
Cowboy On Bronco, Ranch Background, OrnaWood, Sticker, 6 1/2 x 4 1/2 In. 28.00
Crane, Dodge Inc., Gray Metal, Copper, Brass Finish, c.1946, 6 3/4 x 4 3/4 In. 95.00
Deer, Metal, Gray, Kraftware, 5 1/2 x 5 In. 180.00
Dog, Bronze, Gorham Co., Signed, E.B. Parsons, Early 20th Century, 6 3/4 In. 777.00
Dog, Bulldog, Cast Iron, Bradley & Hubbard, Painted, Patina, 5 In., Pair 490.00
Dog, Pekingese, Ceramic, Japan 45.00
Dog, Poodle, Ceramic, Japan, c.1950, 6 1/4 In. 25.00
Dog, Pug, Crouching, Tail In Air, Brass, Marble Base, Red Striations, 6 In. 495.00
Dog, Scotty, Cast Iron, Hubley, No. 430, 4 1/2 x 4 x 4 3/4 In. 395.00
Dog, Scotty, Syroco Wood, Label, Made In USA, Syracuse, N.Y., 7 x 5 In. 40.00

Bookends, End Of The Trail, Plated & Painted White
Metal, Ronson, Weighted, 6 1/4 x 5 In.

Bookends, Viking Ship, Cast Iron, Painted,
Label, Lucas Incense, 5 x 4 1/2 In.

Dog, Setter, Cast Iron, Hubley, 8 x 1 3/4 x 4 7/8 In.	290.00
Dog, Whippet, Brass, Dilwyn & Harmonican, Marked	125.00
Don Quixote, Mounted, Carrying Lance, Cast Iron, Hubley, 6 x 5 In.	195.00
Eagle, Black, Red, White, Blue Shield, Cast Iron, 7 In.	30.00
Eagle, Brass, Onyx Base, Washington Guard	175.00
Eagle, Clutching Skull, Ceramic, Butterscotch Glaze, 5 1/4 In.	85.00
Elephant, Chase, Brass, Orange Bakelite, Art Deco, Stamp Mark, 4 3/4 x 5 x 3 1/2 In.	470.00
Elephant, Front Legs On Tree Stump, Syroco Wood, Label	16.00
Elephant, Metal, Gray, Gold Matte Finish, August 21, 1928	195.00
Elk, Brass, Hartford Insurance Co.	30.00
End Of The Trail, Plated & Painted White Metal, Ronson, Weighted, 6 1/4 x 5 In. .... *Illus*	45.00
Fireplace & Kettle, Cast Iron, 6 1/2 x 2 1/4 x 6 In.	125.00
Fish, Tropical, Cast Iron, Littco Mfg. Co., c.1925, 6 1/8 In.	250.00
Fish Head, Bronze, Art Deco, 4 1/2 In.	316.00
Flower Basket, Pink, Yellow, Green, White, Cast Iron, 6 1/2 x 5 In.	150.00
Flower Basket, Syroco Wood, U.S.A., Marked, Syracuse, N.Y., 6 1/2 In.	21.00
Galley Slaves, Cast Iron, Copper Painted, Littco Mfg. Co., 4 3/4 x 5 3/4 In.	220.00
George Washington National, J. Co., Masonic Memorial, No. 9667, 5 1/2 In.	145.00
Goose Head, Cast Iron, R. Madison Mitchell, 1983, 7 1/2 In.	281.00
Horse Head, Crystal, Jeanette	23.00
Horse Head, Green Crystalline Glaze, Amaco, 5 In.	201.00
Indian, Plateau, Elk Hide, Beaded, Flowers, Hearts, c.1930, 5 x 6 In.	275.00
Indian Chief, Cast Iron, Copper, A.C.W. Co., 4 x 3 5/8 In.	175.00
Indian Chief, Syroco Wood, Syracuse, N.Y.	33.00
Indian Profile, One Feather, Bronze, 6 3/8 x 4 x 2 In.	350.00
Infant Satyr, Goat, Spelter, Marble, Art Deco, France, c.1900, 7 In.	403.00
Jockey, On Base, Bronze, L.A. Web, Signed, 10 In.	460.00
Knight, Embracing Maiden, Village Ground, Cast Iron, 5 3/4 x 5 x 2 In.	110.00
Knights On Chargers, Bronze, 8 1/4 x 7 1/2 x 4 In.	285.00
Knute Rockne, Figural, Cast Iron, 1930s	295.00
Lighthouse, Cottage, Wood Carved, 6 x 4 x 6 In.	100.00
Madonna & Child, Relief, Cenotaph Form, Cast Iron, Bronze Patina, c.1900	35.00
Nude Man Climbing Rock, Bronze, Kileny, Signed, 7 1/2 x 4 1/2 x 3 5/8 In.	360.00
Owl, Brass, Expandable, Early 20th Century, 4 1/2 x 9 In., Closed	40.00
Owl, Glass, Dark Green, Viking Glass, 7 x 2 In.	68.00
Owl Face, Brass, Hammered, Roycroft, 4 x 6 1/2 In.	358.00
Parthenon, Brown Finish, Cast Iron, Bradley & Hubbard Co., 4 3/4 x 3 1/2 In.	80.00
Pelican, Open Mouth, Eating 3 Ribbons, Wrought Iron, Edgar Brandt, c.1925, 6 In.	9560.00
Pigeon, Fantails, Crystal, 6 In.	35.00
Praying Hands, Metal, 9 x 4 In.	65.00
Puppy With Bow, Red, Blue, Bronze-Clad Plaster, c.1920, 7 In.	160.00
Schoolchildren, F.F. Ziegler Sr., c.1921, 7 x 4 1/2 x 3 In.	374.00
Sorceress Reading Book, Figural, Bronze, Ivory, Gerald Style, Art Deco, 8 x 7 1/2 In. ...	353.00
Squirrel, Bronze Painted, Metal, 4 x 3 x 2 1/4 In.	110.00
Thinker, Copper, 8 In.	52.00
Toadstools, Toad, Bronze, 4 1/2 x 3 3/4 In.	281.00
Urn, Red Roses, Cast Iron, 5 1/2 x 3 3/4 In.	95.00
Verona Frigates, Iron, 1927, 5 1/4 x 4 1/4 In.	115.00
Viking Ship, Cast Iron, Painted, Label, Lucas Incense, 5 x 4 1/2 In. .... *Illus*	45.00

BOOKMARKS were originally made of parchment, cloth, or leather. Soon woven silk ribbon, thin cardboard, celluloid, wood, silver, tortoiseshell, and metals were used. Examples made before 1850 are scarce, but there are many to be found dating before 1920.

Abalone & Ivory, Tassel	20.00
Cecilian Player Piano, Bush & Lane	11.00
Claw, Holding Agate Ball, Brass, 3 1/4 x 1/2 In.	115.00
Coiled Snake, E.H.H. Sterling, 1904-1920, 3 1/2 x 1/2 In.	165.00
Copper, Silk Cord, Tassel, Blue	8.00
Cupid's Gum, Cardboard, Die Cut, 2 1/4 x 5 3/8 In.	330.00
Girl, Pink Dress, Roses, Victorian, Kirk Johnson & Co. Pianos, 2 x 6 In.	15.00
Goodyear, Zeppelin, Duralumin, 4 7/8 In.	35.00
Hires Soda Co., How To Take Care Of Books, 1941	5.50

**When shelving books, leave room for air
flow. The books should be about a half-inch
from the wall or back of the shelf unit.
They should not be packed together tightly.**

Bookmark, Statue Of Liberty,
Lafrance, L'Amerique, Silk,
Paris, 1878

Indian Totem Head, Celluloid, Carved, Summerside, P.E.I., 4 1/4 In. 28.00
Lucky Strike, 4 Mystery League Books, 2 1/2 x 7 In. 10.00
Montreal, Canada, Enamel, Sterling B M Co., 2 1/2 x 3/4 In. 6.00
Romeo & Juliet, Norma Shearer, Leslie Howard, Erlanger Theater, Chicago 20.00
Statue Of Liberty, Lafrance, L'Amerique, Silk, Paris, 1878 . . . . *Illus* 50.00
Yale Coffee, Victorian Woman, 6 x 2 1/4 In. 3.00

BOSSONS character wall masks, plaques, figurines, and other decorative pieces are made by W.H. Bossons, Limited of Congleton, England.
The company was founded in 1946 and closed in 1996. Dates shown
are the date the item was introduced.   **BOSSONS**

Plaque, Autumn Gold, 1982, 14 In. 155.00
Shelf Ornament, Baby Hippo, 1 3/4 x 4 1/2 In. 99.00
Shelf Ornament, Cupid, 1969-1973 . . . . 130.00
Shelf Ornament, Giraffe, Briar Rose, 1973-1979, 9 x 5 In. 275.00
Wall Figure, Fighting Cock, Fraser-Art, 1966-1968 . . . . 600.00
Wall Figure, Fox Cub, 1972, 7 In. 150.00
Wall Figure, Indian Chief, 1961, 10 In. 150.00
Wall Mask, Catherine Of Aragon, 1986, 6 In. 165.00
Wall Mask, Custer & Sitting Bull, 1990 . . . . 150.00
Wall Mask, Emiliano Zapata, 1991 . . . . 150.00
Wall Mask, Grenadier, Closed Eyes, 1965, 7 1/2 In. 115.00
Wall Mask, Sherlock Holmes, Chalkware, 1984, 6 1/2 In. 103.00
Wall Mask, Sir Lancelot, 1991, 8 In. 100.00
Wall Plaque, Market Day, 14 In. 100.00
Wall Plaque, Mayfair, 14 In. 100.00

BOSTON & SANDWICH CO. pieces may be found in the Lutz and Sandwich Glass
categories.

BOTTLE collecting has become a major American hobby. There are
several general categories of bottles, such as historic flasks, bitters,
household, and figural. ABM means the bottle was made by an automatic bottle machine after 1903. Pyro is the shortened form of the
word *pyroglaze,* an enameled lettering used on bottles after the mid-
1930s. This form of decoration is also called ACL or applied color
label. For more bottle prices, see the book *Kovels' Bottles Price List* by
Ralph and Terry Kovel.

Apothecary, 6-Sided, Tooled Mouth, Stopper, 1890-1910, 8 1/2 In. 670.00
Apothecary, Aeth. Butyr., Glass Label, Stopper, 6 3/4 In. *Illus* 16.00
Apothecary, Benzo-Napthol, Amber, Shield Label, Flat Stopper, 7 In. 45.00
Apothecary, Blue Milk Glass, Stopper, Pontil, 9 1/2 x 3 1/2 In., Pair 358.00
Apothecary, Cover, Applied Cobalt Blue Rings, Cobalt Button Finial, 9 In. 470.00
Apothecary, Cover, Applied Cobalt Blue Rings, Cobalt Button Finial, 11 1/4 In. 415.00
Apothecary, Cover, Cobalt Blue, Opaque White Rims, Footed, Finial, 13 1/2 In. 2530.00
Apothecary, Extract Triple Heliotrope, Enamel Shield, Fluted, Stopper, 9 In. 88.00

Bottle, Apothecary,
Aeth. Butyr., Glass
Label, Stopper, 6 3/4 In.

Bottle, Barber,
Cranberry,
Opalescent, Melon
Ribbed, 7 In.

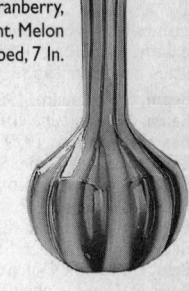

Commercial false teeth cleaners are good to use to remove scum and dirt from the inside of old glass bottles.

Apothecary, Extract Triple Wall Flower, Enamel Shield, Fluted, Stopper, 9 In. 220.00
Apothecary, F.E. Hydrast, Cobalt Blue, Glass Label, Stopper, Pontil, 8 1/2 In. 250.00
Apothecary, Tooled Mouth, Ground Glass Stopper, 1900-1910, 10 In. 420.00
Apothecary, Tooled Mouth, Stopper, Labels, Contents, 1900-1910, 13 In. 225.00
Apothecary, Vinum Aromatic, Amber, Tin Cap, Enamel Paint, Pontil, 9 In. 44.00

Avon started in 1886 as the California Perfume Company. It was not until 1929 that the name *Avon* was used. In 1939, it became Avon Products, Inc. Avon has made many figural bottles filled with cosmetic products. Ceramic, plastic, and glass bottles were made in limited editions.

Avon, Alaskan Moose Aftershave, 1974 . . . . 11.00
Avon, Wild Country Aftershave, 1923 Star Station Wagon, Box, 7 In. 35.00
Barber, A.W. Holsapple, Bay Rum, Milk Glass, Blue, Pretty Woman, 11 In. 2016.00
Barber, Acme Hair Vigor, Label Under Glass, Embossed Wildroot Top, 9 In. 425.00
Barber, Amethyst, Frosted, Ribs, Yellow Gold, Rolled Lip, 1890-1925, 8 In. 336.00
Barber, Amethyst, Gold & Enamel Design, 7 1/4 x 3 5/8 In. 195.00
Barber, Bay Rum, Milk Glass, Flowers, Multicolored, 1890-1925, 9 1/8 In. 672.00
Barber, Blue, Opalescent, Tooled, Flared Lip, Pontil, 12 In. 198.00
Barber, Brilliantine, Cranberry, Clear, White Design, Sheared Lip, Stopper, 1890, 3 3/4 In. 476.00
Barber, Brilliantine, Cranberry, Ribs, Sheared Lip, 1890-1925, 4 1/4 In. 448.00
Barber, Clear, Cranberry, White Splatter, Tooled Top, 10 In. 209.00
Barber, Clear, Diamond, Copper Wheel, Neck Band, Cap, 1885-1925, 7 In. 213.00
Barber, Clear, Label Under Glass, White, Blue, Yellow, Gold, 1890-1925, 8 1/4 In. 672.00
Barber, Clear, Lime Green, Ribs, Polished Lip, 1890-1925, 7 1/2 In. 269.00
Barber, Clear, Ruby Red, Ribs, Polished Lip, 1890-1925, 7 3/8 In. 280.00
Barber, Cobalt Blue, Flowers, Yellow, Gold, Rolled Lip, Ribs, 1890-1925, 7 3/4 In. 235.00
Barber, Coin Spot, Yellow Amber, Tooled Mouth, Pontil, 1890-1925, 7 In. 224.00
Barber, Cranberry Opalescent, Stars & Stripes, Rolled Lip, c.1905, 7 1/4 In. 196.00
Barber, Cranberry, Opalescent, Melon Ribbed, 7 In. . . . . *Illus* 200.00
Barber, Cranberry, Ribs, Boy, White, Cream, Brown, Polished Lip, 1890-1925, 10 5/8 In. 1568.00
Barber, Cranberry, Ribs, Girl, White, Cream, Brown, Polished Lip, 10 5/8 In. 1120.00
Barber, Cranberry, Swirl, Solid Stopper, 6 In. 185.00
Barber, George Clark, Bay Rum, Milk Glass, Pretty Woman On Label, 1890, 10 7/8 In. . . 1904.00
Barber, Girl, Boy Tennis Players, Original Metal Stoppers, Pontil, Pair 413.00
Barber, Hobnail, Turquoise, Rolled Lip, Pontil, 1890-1925, 7 In. 78.00
Barber, Latticinio, Multicolored Stripe, White, Porcelain Stopper, Open Pontil 176.00
Barber, Milk Glass, Cobalt Blue, Bird & Branch, 1890-1925, 8 1/8 In. 224.00
Barber, Milk Glass, Flowers, Multicolored, 1890-1925, 9 In. 392.00
Barber, Milk Glass, Opalescent, Black, Orange, Blue, Rolled Lip, Pontil, 1890, 7 3/8 In. . . 672.00
Barber, Milk Glass, Opalescent, Clover, Multicolored, Rolled Lip, Pontil, 1890, 9 3/8 In. . . 336.00
Barber, Opalescent Blue, Vine Pattern, Rolled Lip, c.1905, 7 5/8 In. 1008.00
Barber, Purple Amethyst, Ribs, Yellow, White, Orange, Tooled Lip, Pontil, 1890, 7 1/2 In. 235.00
Barber, Shampoo, Pretty Woman On Label, Rolled Lip, 10 1/4 In. 1680.00
Barber, Silver Overlay, Cobalt Blue, Leaf & Berry, Frosted, 1890-1925, 7 3/4 In. 672.00
Barber, Toilet Water, Milk Glass, Multicolored Flowers, c.1905, 9 In. 140.00
Barber, Turquoise, Flowers, White, Yellow, Flared Lip, 1890-1925, 8 1/2 In. 364.00

Barber, Witch Hazel, Milk Glass, Bird, Multicolored, 1890-1925, 9 In. 56.00
Barber, Witch Hazel, Milk Glass, Red Flowers, c.1905, 8 5/8 In. 190.00

Beam bottles were made to hold Kentucky Straight Bourbon, made by
the James B. Beam Distilling Company. The Beam series of ceramic
bottles began in 1953.

Beam, Car, Camaro, 1969 Model, Green 160.00
Beam, Car, Corvette, 1953 Model, Turquoise ....140.00 to 150.00
Beam, Police Car, 1929 Model A 100.00
Beam, The Big Apple, Statue Of Liberty, Building, 1979 .... 35.00
Beer, A. Palmtag & Co., Eureka, Cal., Amber, Stopper, Qt. 110.00
Beer, B. Whitcomb Sassaparilla Beer, Stoneware, Gray, c.1865, 9 1/2 In. 157.00
Beer, Barker Vroman & Co., Gray, Stoneware, Cobalt Slip Glaze Over Letters, 9 3/4 In. ... 146.00
Beer, California Beer, Stoneware, Albany Slip Glaze, 10 1/2 In. 73.00
Beer, Cowden & Wilcox, Stoneware, Light Gray, 9 3/8 In. 213.00
Beer, D. Davis, Cobalt Blue, 12-Sided, Applied Sloping Collar, 10 In. 1568.00
Beer, E. Tousley, Cronk's Beer, Cobalt Blue, 12-Sided, Applied Sloping Collar, 10 In. ... 448.00
Beer, Fredericksburg Bottling, S.F., Fern Green, Blob Top, Qt. 35.00
Beer, G.S. Smith, Stoneware, Tan, Dark Red Brown Glaze, 9 1/8 In. 90.00
Beer, Gambrinus, San Francisco, Cal., Amber, Stopper, Qt. 33.00
Beer, Great Northern, I.L. Lamm Co., Clear, White Enamel, Qt., 5 x 12 In. 259.00
Beer, Hansen & Kahler, Oakland, Ca, Amber, Original Stopper, Pt. 143.00
Beer, John Ryan Porter & Ale, Philada. XX, Cobalt Blue, Iron Pontil 55.00
Beer, P.C. Morris, Lemon Beer, Stoneware, Gray, 10 1/8 In. 67.00
Beer, R. Green, Toronto, Cobalt Blue, 12-Sided, Smooth Base, Applied Mouth, 10 In. ... 5200.00
Beer, S. J. Norkewicz, Mahanoy City, Pa., Crown Top, 9 1/4 In. 10.00
Beer, Schroeder's B.W.B. Co., St. Louis, Mo., Deep Yellow Green, Blob Top 675.00
Beer, Theodore Lutge & Co., San Jose, Cal., Green, Applied Blob Top, Qt. 495.00
Beer, Wunder Brewing Co., S.F., Amber, Split Blob Top, 7 1/2 In. 19.00
Bininger, A.M. & Co., 19 Broad St., N.Y., Barrel, Amber, 1860-1880, 12 1/2 In. 364.00
Bininger, A.M. & Co., Night Cap, Amber, Oval, Applied Collar Mouth, c.1870, 8 In. 269.00
Bininger, A.M. & Co., Old London Dock Gin, Yellow Olive Green, Sloping Collar, 8 In. . 92.00
Bitters, African Stomach Amber, Applied Top, 9 1/2 In. 77.00
Bitters, African Stomach, Amber, 9 5/8 In. 140.00
Bitters, Alpine Herb, TT&Co Shield, Amber, Square, 10 In. ....375.00 to 475.00
Bitters, Argyle, E.B. Wheelock, N.O., Amber, Applied Sloping Collar, 9 3/4 In. 190.00
Bitters, Atwood's Genuine N. Wood, Sole Proprietor, Aqua, 6 3/4 In. 39.00
Bitters, Atwood's Jaundice, Georgetown, Mass., Aqua, Paneled, Pontil, 6 1/16 In. .. 165.00
Bitters, Atwood's Quinine Tonic, Aqua, Rectangular, 8 7/16 In. 65.00
Bitters, Blue Mountain, Aqua, Rectangular, 7 7/8 In. 125.00
Bitters, Bourbon Whiskey, Strawberry Puce, Applied Mouth, 1860-1870, 9 1/4 In. 448.00
Bitters, Boyer's Stomach Bitters, Cincinnati, Amethyst Ribs, 10 1/8 In. 165.00
Bitters, Brown's Celebrated Indian Herb, Patented February 11, 1866, Amber, 12 1/4 In. .. 308.00
Bitters, C & C, P.R. Delaney & Co., Semi-Cabin, Aqua, Paneled, 10 1/2 In. 476.00
Bitters, Canton, Star, Lady's Leg, Amber, Applied Collar, 12 In. 364.00
Bitters, Clarke's Vegetable, Sherry Wine, Aqua, Open Pontil, c.1845, 11 1/4 In. 504.00
Bitters, Coco, Hartwig Kantorowicz, Posen, Germany, Green, Applied Top, 9 1/4 In. 240.00
Bitters, Columbo Peptic, L.E. Jung, New Orleans, Amber, Rectangular, 7 1/4 In. 85.00
Bitters, Curtis Cordial Calisaya, Great Stomach, Yellow Olive, 11 5/8 In. 1904.00
Bitters, Dingens Napoleon Cocktail, Buffalo, N.Y., Lady's Leg, Smoky Tint, 10 In. 4200.00
Bitters, Dr. Ball's Vegetable Stomachic, Northboro, Mass., Aqua, 6 5/8 In. 300.00
Bitters, Dr. Bishop's Wahoo, Yellow Amber, 7 5/8 In. 1100.00
Bitters, Dr. C.W. Robacks Stomach, Cincinnati, Barrel, Amber, Applied Top, 9 3/8 In. 330.00
Bitters, Dr. Doty's Celebrated Mandrake Freedom & Unity, Oval, Honey Amber, 8 1/2 In. .. 440.00
Bitters, Dr. Geo. Pierces Indian Restorative, Lowell, Mass., Aqua, Rectangular, 8 7/8 In. .. 60.00
Bitters, Dr. Green's Poleish, Yellow Amber, Iron Pontil, 11 In. 650.00
Bitters, Dr. J. Hostetter's Stomach, Amber, Front & Back Labels, Square, 8 3/4 In. 176.00
Bitters, Dr. Lovegood's Family, XX, Cabin, Deep Amber, 10 1/2 In. 2688.00
Bitters, Dr. Mampes Herb Stomach, Aqua, Rectangular, 6 3/4 In. 160.00
Bitters, Dr. Petzolds Genuine German, Oval, Amber, 10 5/8 In. 90.00
Bitters, Dr. Skinner's Sherry Wine, Aqua, Applied Mouth, OP, 8 1/4 In. 280.00
Bitters, Dr. Soule's Hop, Apricot, Embossed Hop Flowers, Leaf, Applied Top, 9 1/4 In. .. 132.00
Bitters, Dr. Stephen Jewett's Celebrated Health Restoring, Rindge, N.H., 7 1/4 In. 195.00

Bitters, Dr. Stover's, Kryder & Co., Lancaster, Pa., Amber, Applied Mouth, 9 1/2 In. 728.00
Bitters, Dr. W.H. Black's Rocky Mountain, Black & Richardson, Yellow Amber, 9 In. ... 476.00
Bitters, Drake's Plantation, 4 Log, Yellow, Amber, Olive, Sloping Collar, 10 1/4 In. 1120.00
Bitters, Drake's Plantation, 6 Log, Apricot Puce, 10 1/4 In. 450.00
Bitters, Drake's Plantation, 6 Log, Copper Puce, Sloping Collar Mouth, 10 1/4 In. 170.00
Bitters, Drake's Plantation, 6 Log, Red Amber, Applied Top, 10 1/4 In. 198.00
Bitters, Drake's Plantation, 6 Log, Salmon, Applied Top, 10 1/4 In. 770.00
Bitters, Fish, W.H. Ware, Gold, Fish Shape, Applied Mouth, Patented 1866, 11 3/8 In. ... 550.00
Bitters, Frisco Hop, Aqua, Applied Top, 9 1/4 In. 66.00
Bitters, Geo. A. Clement Niagara, Aqua, Oval, Strap Sides, 8 3/8 In. 1680.00
Bitters, German Balsam, Wm. Watson & Co., Milk Glass, Applied Top, 9 In. 605.00
Bitters, German Stomach, Amber, Sloping Collar, 9 5/8 In. 1120.00
Bitters, Greeley's Bourbon, Barrel, Amber Puce, Applied Top, 9 3/8 In. 415.00
Bitters, Greeley's Bourbon, Barrel, Smoky Olive Green, Applied Mouth, 9 3/8 In. 2240.00
Bitters, Griffith's Opera, Amber, Panels, Applied Mouth, 8 7/8 In. 200.00
Bitters, H.P. Herb Wild Cherry, Amber, Cabin, Embossed Tree, Tooled Top, 10 In. 410.00
Bitters, Hall's, New Haven, Barrel, Yellow Amber, 9 1/8 In. 235.00
Bitters, Halls, Yellow Amber, Barrel, Applied Mouth, 1842, 9 1/8 In. 275.00
Bitters, Harvey's Prairie, Amber, 1865-1875, 9 1/2 In. 15400.00
Bitters, Henley's Wild Grape Root, Aqua, Applied Band, 12 In. 413.00
Bitters, Hi-Hi, Rock Island, Ill., Amber, 3-Sided, Tooled Lip, Label, 9 3/8 In. 390.00
Bitters, Holtzermann's Stomach, Cabin, Yellow Amber, 9 1/2 In. 2800.00
Bitters, Hops & Malt, Sheaf Of Grain, Amber, 9 1/4 In. 650.00
Bitters, Hutchings Dyspepsia New York, Aqua, Iron Pontil, 8 1/2 In. 265.00
Bitters, Jno Moffat, Phoenix, Olive Green, 5 1/2 In. 1195.00
Bitters, Johnson's Calisaya, Burlington, Vt., Red Amber, Square, 10 In. 395.00
Bitters, Johnson's Indian Dyspeptic, Rectangular, Pontil, 6 5/8 In. 650.00
Bitters, Kaiser Wilhelm Bitters Co., Sandusky, O., 10 1/8 In. 44.00
Bitters, Kelly's, Log Cabin, Amber, Sloping Collar Mouth, 9 5/8 In. 896.00
Bitters, McConnon's Stomach, Winona, Minn., Red Amber, Tooled Mouth, 8 3/4 In. ... 392.00
Bitters, Mill's, A.M. Gilman, Honey Amber, Applied Top, 1874, 11 1/4 In. 6600.00
Bitters, Morning Call, Amber, Paneled, Applied Sloping Collar, 9 1/2 In. 616.00
Bitters, National, Ear Of Corn, Amber, 12 5/8 In. 448.00
Bitters, National, Ear Of Corn, Amber, Applied Collar Mouth, 1880-1900, 12 5/8 In. 560.00
Bitters, Normandy Herb & Root Stomach, Orange Amber, Rectangular, 7 3/4 In. 195.00
Bitters, Old Hickory Celebrated Stomach, J. Grossman, New Orleans, La., Amber, 9 In. .. 160.00
Bitters, Old Homestead Wild Cherry, Cabin, Amber, 9 7/8 In. ....892.00 to 1400.00
Bitters, Old Sachem & Wigwam Tonic, Barrel, Apricot Gold, 9 3/8 In. 1320.00
Bitters, Old Sachem & Wigwam Tonic, Barrel, Strawberry Puce, Yellow Amber, 9 3/8 In. 1568.00
Bitters, Pankin's Hepatic, New York, Amber, Applied Mouth, 8 5/8 In. 210.00
Bitters, Penn's Pony, H.W. Long, Philadelphia, Amber, Oval Panel, Tooled Lip, 9 In. 560.00
Bitters, Reed's, Lady's Leg, Amber, 12 1/2 In. 476.00
Bitters, Rising Sun, John C. Hurst, Philada., Yellow, Amber, 9 3/8 In. 448.00
Bitters, Rocky Mountain Tonic, Try Me, Yellow Amber, 9 7/8 In. 448.00
Bitters, S.O. Richardson, South Reading Mass., Aqua, 6 1/8 In. 195.00
Bitters, San Joaquin Wine, Red Amber, Round, 9 3/4 In. 395.00
Bitters, Sarasina Stomach, Amber, Square, 4 In. 99.00
Bitters, Sazerac Aromatic, Lady's Leg, Light Amber, 10 1/4 In. 467.00
Bitters, Shurtleff's, Blood & Dyspepsia, Lady's Leg, Amber, Applied Mouth, 12 7/16 In. . 952.00
Bitters, Simon's Centennial, Bust Of Washington, 9 3/4 In. 784.00
Bitters, Solomon's Strengthening & Invigorating, Savannah, Blue, Applied Top, 9 5/8 In. . 1210.00
Bitters, Suffolk, Philbrook & Tucker, Boston, Amber, Pig, Applied Top, 10 1/8 In. 990.00
Bitters, Sumter, Amber, Dowie Moise & Davis, Indented Panels, Applied Mouth, 9 7/8 In. 425.00
Bitters, Tyree's Chamomile, Yellow Amber, Tooled Lip, 6 1/2 In. 168.00
Bitters, W.R. Tyree's Chamomile, Semi-Cabin, Amber, Tooled Mouth, 9 1/2 In. 840.00
Bitters, Warner's Safe, Rochester, N.Y., Orange Amber, Applied Mouth, 9 1/2 In. 840.00
Bitters, William Allen's Congress, Aqua, Rectangular, Applied Mouth, 10 In. 2128.00
Bitters, Winter's Stomach, Red Amber, Square, Tooled Lip, 9 1/2 In. 135.00
Bitters, Yerba Buena, S.F., Cal., Gold Amber, Strap Flask, 9 1/2 In. 85.00
Black Glass, Kidney Shape, Olive Amber, String Lip, Pontil, Dutch, 1750-1770, 7 3/4 In. . 840.00
Black Glass, Storage, Cylindrical, Long Neck, 3-Piece Mold, Pontil, 8 3/4 In. 59.00
Blown, Beehive, Aqua, 24 Ribs, Swirled Right, Tapered Neck, Applied Lip, 8 1/2 In. 145.00
Blown, Chestnut, Amber, Applied Mouth, Pontil, 1783-1830, 8 1/8 In. 560.00

Blown, Chestnut, Forest Green, Applied Mouth, Pontil, 1783-1830, 6 3/4 In. 448.00
Blown, Cylindrical, Green, Applied Mouth, Pontil, 1797-1800, 7 In. ....'........ 264.00
Blown, Fly Trap, 3-Footed, Applied Ring Top, c.1850, 7 x 5 In. 415.00
Blown, Globular, 16 Ribs, Swirled Left, Aqua, Ohio, 6 In. 150.00
Blown, Globular, 24 Ribs, Swirled Right, Aqua, Ohio, 9 1/4 In. 575.00
Blown, Globular, Blue Green, Rolled Mouth, Pontil, 1780-1830, 7 1/2 In. 190.00
Blown, Globular, Yellow Olive, Applied Mouth, Pontil, 1780-1830, 7 1/2 In. 1120.00
Blown, Gold Amber, Puce Overtone, Painted Design, Applied Mouth, 1840-1860, 18 In. ... 950.00
Blown, Jenny Lind, Aqua, Fislerville Glass Works, 9 3/8 In. 165.00
Blown, Utility, Green, Applied Tooled Mouth, Tubular Pontil, 1800-1840, 7 7/8 In. 446.00
Blown, Utility, Yellow Amber, Sheared Mouth, Tubular Pontil, 1820-1860, 11 In. 1008.00
Coca-Cola bottles are listed in the Coca-Cola category.
Cordial, L.Q.C. Wishart's Pine Tree Cordial, Teal, 9 3/4 In. 220.00
Cosmetic, A. Grand Jeans, For The Hair, Fold & Flared Lip, Pontil, 1830-1845, 3 3/8 In. . 135.00
Cosmetic, Mrs. S.A. Allen's World's Hair Restorer, New York, Amber, 7 1/4 In. .....20.00 to 55.00
Cosmetic, Mrs. S.A. Allen's World's Hair Restorer, Amethyst, Flared Mouth, 1860, 7 In. . 246.00
Cosmetic, Oldridge's Balm Of Columbia, Aqua, 5 In. 160.00
Cosmetic, Pearson & Co., Circassian Hair Rejuvenator, Brooklyn, N.Y., Amber, 8 In. 50.00
Cosmetic, Seven Sisters Hair Grower, New York, Contents, Label, Aqua, 5 In. 65.00
Cosmetic, Swaynes London Hair Color Restorer, Cathedral, Panel, Aqua, 7 1/2 In. 65.00
Cure, Ayer's Ague, Lowell, Mass., Aqua, Applied Mouth, Pontil, 7 In. 269.00
Cure, Bishop's Reliable Cough, Aqua, Front & Back Label, Contents, 5 3/4 In. 90.00
Cure, Brown's Blood, Philadelphia, Green, Tooled Mouth, 6 1/8 In. 146.00
Cure, Brown's Blood, Philadelphia, Yellow Green, Square, Beveled Corners, 6 1/8 In. ... 179.00
Cure, Dr. Nywall's Family Medicine, Rheumatic Cure, Label, Amber, Square, 7 1/4 In. ... 66.00
Cure, One Night Cough Cure, Cannabis Indica, Sealed Wrapper, Baltimore, 6 In. 280.00
Cure, Warner's Safe Kidney & Liver Cure, Rochester, N.Y., Amber, 9 5/8 In. 35.00
Cure, Warner's Safe Rheumatic, Amber, Blob Top, Label, 9 1/4 In. 690.00
Decanter, 4 Openings, Sections, Whiskey, Gin, Brandy, Rum, Footed, 10 In., Pair 880.00
Decanter, 6-Pillar Mold, Cascading Drapes, Applied Neck Ring, Pittsburgh, 12 1/4 In. 385.00
Decanter, 8-Pillar Mold, Cobalt Blue, Applied Mouth, Neck Ring, 10 1/2 In. 2700.00
Decanter, 8-Pillar Mold, Pontil, Applied Mouth, Neck Band, 11 5/8 In. 78.00
Decanter, Backbar, Cobalt Blue, Dirigible, Brass Stand, Basket, Brass Holders, 14 In. ... 476.00
Decanter, Backbar, Opalescent, Stopper, 1880s, 13 In. 132.00
Decanter, Baroque Plume, 3-Piece Mold, Amethystine, Flared Rim, Stopper, 9 1/2 In. ... 235.00
Decanter, Baroque Plumes, Plain Neck, Ribbed Stopper, Qt. 200.00
Decanter, Baroque Ribbed Eyes, 3-Piece Mold, Plain Neck, 8 1/4 In. 330.00
Decanter, Blown, Cobalt Blue, Flared Out Tooled Lip, Glass Stopper, c.1870, 8 In. 350.00
Decanter, Blown, Lion, Shield, Pale Green, Pewter Base, 14 1/2 In. 375.00
Decanter, Blue, Clear, White Looping, Trefoil Spout, Applied Clear Handle, 10 In. 110.00
Decanter, Canary, Applied Mouth, Pontil, 1830-1860, 10 In. 7895.00
Decanter, Cathedral, Willington, Aqua, Green Swirl, Corinthian Columns, Pontil, 12 In. .. 195.00
Decanter, Concentric Sunburst & Diamond Diaper Band, 3-Piece Mold, Stopper, 10 In. .. 143.00
Decanter, Diamond Band Over Ribbed Band, 3-Piece Mold, Wheel Stopper, 9 In. 140.00
Decanter, Diamond Band, Ribbed, 3-Piece Mold, Flared, Cogglewheel Rings, 8 1/4 In. .. 190.00
Decanter, Emerald Green, 10 Sided, Pinched Waist, Tooled Mouth, Neck Ring, 11 1/2 In. 1905.00
Decanter, Engraved Flowers, Swags, 3 Neck Rings, Mushroom Stopper, 10 In., Pair 468.00
Decanter, Engraved Sailboats, Grape Clusters, Windmills, Neck & Shoulder Rings, 12 In. 180.00
Decanter, Faceted Band At Base, Stopper, 8 1/2 In. 240.00
Decanter, Flared Lip, Neck Rings, Umbrella Stopper, 8 1/2 In. 80.00
Decanter, Fluted Panels Over Convex Ribs, 3-Piece Mold, Flared Rim, Stopper, 8 3/4 In. . 156.00
Decanter, Grape Amethyst, Gold, Black, Tooled Mouth, String Lip, Backbar, 10 7/8 In. .. 140.00
Decanter, Purple Amethyst, 8 Sided, Applied Mouth, Pontil, 10 1/4 In. 785.00
Decanter, Ruby Red, Silver Overlay, Dancing Couple, 7 3/4 In. 125.00
Decanter, Silver Overlay, 3 Men In Bar, Stopper, 10 In. 110.00
Decanter, Sunburst & Diamond Diaper Band, 3 Double Rings, 3-Piece Mold, Qt., 10 In. . 150.00
Decanter, Teal Green, 8 Sided, Applied Mouth, Pewter Stopper, 10 1/4 In. 4200.00
Decanter, Truncated Cone, Tapered Neck, Olive Green 9 1/2 x 3 7/8 In. 1045.00
Decanter, Waffle Sunburst & Diamond Diaper Band, 3-Piece Mold, Wheel Stopper, 10 In. 80.00
Decanter, Wavy Daisies & Leaves, 2 Beaded Neck Rings, Sunburst Stopper, 9 1/2 In. ... 880.00
Demijohn, 3-Piece Mold, Olive Green, Monogrammed Silver Top, 1830-1860, 18 In. 560.00
Demijohn, Blue Aqua, Applied Sloping Collar Mouth, Pontil, 1850-1865, 3/8 In. 146.00
Demijohn, Blue Green, Widemouth, Ornately Applied Lip, Pontil, Continental, 13 In. 165.00

Demijohn, Blue, Flared Mouth, Rounded Square, Irregular Pontil, 12 1/3 In. 198.00
Demijohn, Globular, Dutch Gin, Olive Green, Applied Top Pontil, 10 In. 468.00
Demijohn, Heart Shape, Blue, Applied Top, Bubbles, Pontil, 10 1/2 In. 110.00
Demijohn, Molded, Amber, Hand Tooled Lip, 18 x 15 In. 226.00
Demijohn, Olive Green, Sloping Collar Mouth, Pontil, 1840-1870, 18 1/8 In. 85.00
Demijohn, Sapphire Blue, Applied Sloping Collar Mouth, 15 1/2 In. 235.00
Figural, Barney Google On Spark Plug, Clear, Sheared Lip, 1910-1925, 4 1/8 In. 235.00
Figural, Bear, Aqua, Applied Face, A.A.T., 8 In. 390.00
Figural, Bear, Dark Olive Green, Applied Face, Tooled Lip, A.A.T., 8 1/4 In. 364.00
Figural, Car, Aqua, Tooled Mouth, Embossed, Continental, 1900-1925, 3 In. 390.00
Figural, Cat, Clear, Frosted, Rolled Lip, France, 1890-1920, 1 7/8 In. 123.00
Figural, Cherubs, Holding Globe, Clear, Tooled Mouth, France, 1900-1920, 12 1/8 In. . . . 168.00
Figural, Child, Clear, Frosted, Sheared & Ground Lip, 1890-1910, 13 3/8 In. 215.00
Figural, Clam, Whiskey Nip, Cobalt Blue, Sheared & Ground Lip, 1890-1915, 5 3/8 In. . . . 280.00
Figural, Ear Of Corn, Cobalt Blue, 1890-1930, 8 3/4 In. 310.00
Figural, Ear Of Corn, Yellow Amber, Sloping Collar, 1875-1885, 10 3/8 In. 146.00
Figural, Flask, Liberty Dollar Coin, Ground Lip, 1885-1895, 4 1/2 In. 390.00
Figural, Hatchet, Clear, Sheared & Ground Mouth, 1890-1910, 6 5/8 In. 215.00
Figural, Hot Air Balloon Captif 1878, Tooled Mouth, France, 1890-1915, 9 1/4 In. 160.00
Figural, Joan Of Arc, Orange Amber, Tooled Mouth, Pontil, 1890-1915, 13 3/4 In. 670.00
Figural, Moneybag, My Liquid Assets, Porcelain, Cork Stopper, 6 In. 46.00
Figural, Moses, Poland Springs Water, Blue Aqua, Sloping Collar Mouth, 1870, 11 1/8 In. 123.00
Figural, Owl, Clear, Tooled Mouth, France, 1890-1910, 13 1/4 In. 235.00
Figural, Pear, Frosted, Lime Green, Ground Lip, Handle, France, 1890-1910, 6 1/8 In. . . . 190.00
Figural, Pig, Pure Old Rye, Stenciled 215.00
Flask, 18 Broken Ribs, Swirled, Cobalt Blue, Sheared Lip, Midwest, Pontil, 5 3/4 In. 2200.00
Flask, 20 Broken Ribs, Swirled, Diamond, Aqua Green, Midwest, Pt. 358.00
Flask, 24 Vertical Ribs, Olive Yellow, Pocket Type, Pontil, c.1830, 4 3/4 In. 1456.00
Flask, Andy Balich, 170 Pacific Ave., Santa Cruz, Cal., Pumpkinseed, Purple, Pt. 255.00
Flask, B.S. Hirsch, Uriah, Cal., Pumpkinseed, Clear, 1/2 Pt. 935.00
Flask, Balto & Fells Point, Pink Amethyst, Pontil, 1/2 Pt. 2688.00
Flask, Balto & Fells Point, Topaz, Sheared Lip, Pontil, 1/2 Pt. 4760.00
Flask, Byron & Scott, Yellow Amber, Olive Tone, Pontil, 1/2 Pt. 224.00
Flask, Cannon, A Little More Grape, Blue Aqua, Tooled Lip, Pontil, Pt. 560.00
Flask, Cannon, A Little More Grape, Yellow Amber, Sheared Lip, Pontil, Pt. 4480.00
Flask, Chestnut, 18 Ribs, Swirled To Right, Aqua, Flattened, 5 3/4 In. 468.00
Flask, Chestnut, 24 Broken Ribs, Swirled To Left, Midwest, Green Aqua, Pontil, 6 1/2 In. 210.00
Flask, Chestnut, 24 Ribs, Swirled To Left, Aqua, Midwest, 4 1/2 In. 440.00
Flask, Chestnut, 24 Ribs, Swirled To Right, Rolled Lip, Pontil, 2 3/8 In. 336.00
Flask, Chestnut, 24 Vertical Ribs, Amber, Flattened, Flared Neck, Midwest, 5 In. 305.00
Flask, Chestnut, 25 Ribs, Swirled To Right, Blue Green, Sheared Lip, Pontil, 6 3/4 In. . . . 190.00
Flask, Chestnut, Green, Applied String Lip, Pontil, c.1800, 7 1/2 In. 270.00
Flask, Chestnut, Olive, Applied String Lip, Pontil, c.1800, 7 3/4 In. 385.00
Flask, Chestnut, Olive, Flattened, Open Pontil, 5 1/4 In. 85.00
Flask, Chestnut, Pastel Green, Applied String Lip, Pontil, c.1800, 5 1/2 In. 358.00
Flask, Chestnut, Yellow, Applied String Lip, Pontil, c.1800, 5 3/4 In. 305.00
Flask, Chestnut, Yellow, Applied String Lip, Pontil, c.1800, 7 In. 358.00
Flask, Clasped Hands & Eagle, Citron, Applied Mouth, Qt. 784.00
Flask, Corn For The World, Olive Green, Sheared Lip, Pontil, Qt. 9520.00
Flask, Cornucopia & Medallion, Blue Aqua, Tooled Mouth, Pontil, 1/2 Pt. 2800.00
Flask, Cornucopia & Urn, Olive Amber, Plain Lip, Pontil, Pt. 110.00
Flask, Cornucopia & Urn, Olive Green, Pontil, 1/2 Pt. 132.00
Flask, Cornucopia & Urn, Olive Green, Pt. 77.00
Flask, Dark Brown Glaze, Flower, Children, Man, England, c.1875, 7 5/8 In. 100.00
Flask, Deep Claret Amethyst, Globular, Flattened, c.1800-1840, 6 1/2 In. 220.00
Flask, Double Eagle, Amber, Sheared Lip, Pontil, Pt. 440.00
Flask, Double Eagle, Aqua, Ribs, Sheared Mouth, Pontil, 1855-1860, Pt. 476.00
Flask, Double Eagle, Cornflower Blue, Applied Band, Pt. 660.00
Flask, Double Eagle, Deep Blue Aqua, Sheared, Tooled Mouth, Pontil, Qt. 235.00
Flask, Double Eagle, Green Aqua, Sheared Lip, Pontil, Pt. 224.00
Flask, Double Eagle, Medium To Deep Olive, Pt. 468.00
Flask, Eagle & Anchor, Resurgam, Blue Aqua, Applied Mouth, Pt. 134.00
Flask, Eagle & Cornucopia, Brown, Blown Molded, 19th Century, Pt. . . . . .200.00 to 345.00

Bottle, Flask, Flower & Heart, Light To Dark Blue Green, Sheared Lip, Pontil, c.1850, Qt.

Bottle, Flask, Masonic Arch & Eagle, Purple Amethyst, Tooled Mouth, Pontil, Pt.

Bottle, Flask, Washington Bust, Baltimore Glass Works, Yellow Olive, Pontil, Qt.

Flask, Eagle & Cornucopia, Dark Olive Amber, Tooled Mouth, Pontil, Pt. 145.00
Flask, Eagle & Cornucopia, Medium Olive, Pt. 330.00
Flask, Eagle & Cornucopia, Yellow Olive, Sheared Mouth, Pontil, 1815-1830, 1/2 Pt. 10080.00
Flask, Eagle & Flag, Light To Medium Yellow Green, Pontil, Pt. 4144.00
Flask, Eagle & Flag, Medium Yellow Green, Tooled Lip, Pontil, Pt. 4200.00
Flask, Eagle & Willington, Rounded Collar, Olive Green, 1/2 Pt. 495.00
Flask, Flag & Stoddard, Yellow Olive, Sheared Mouth, Pontil, 1860, Pt. 8400.00
Flask, Flora Temple, Yellow Topaz, Applied Mouth, Pt. 308.00
Flask, Flower & Heart, Light To Dark Blue Green, Sheared Lip, Pontil, c.1850, Qt. . . *Illus* 3575.00
Flask, Flower Basket, Olive Green, Blown, 19th Century, 1/2 Pt. 230.00
Flask, Flowers, Leaves, Stems, Enameled, Jeweled, 10 1/4 In. 1035.00
Flask, Franklin & Dyott, Aqua, Sheared Mouth, Bubbles, Pontil, c.1820, Qt. 532.00
Flask, Girl On Bicycle, Aqua, Applied Mouth, 1860-1870, Pt. 365.00
Flask, Grant & Eagle, Portrait, Aqua, Applied Collar, 1860-1880, Pt. 215.00
Flask, Horse Pulling Cart, Olive Green, Applied Mouth, Pt. 476.00
Flask, Hunter & Fisherman, Calabash, Orange Amber, Sloping Collar, Pontil, Qt. 308.00
Flask, J. Hayes & Co. Wholesale Dealers, Manchester, N.H., Amber, Qt., 9 3/4 In. 65.00
Flask, J.N. Kline & Co., Aromatic, Digestive, Amber, Pumpkinseed, 5 1/2 In. 308.00
Flask, J.N. Kline & Co., Aromatic, Digestive, Cobalt Blue, Pumpkinseed, 5 1/2 In. 560.00
Flask, Jenny Lind & Glasshouse, Yellow Olive Green, Double Sloping, Pontil, Qt. 7280.00
Flask, Jenny Lind & Lyre, Ice Blue, Sheared Lip, Pontil, Qt. 728.00
Flask, Jenny Lind, Blue Green, Applied Sloping Collar Mouth, Pontil, Qt. 2352.00
Flask, Leather Case, Dove, Seam Split, England, 1 1/2 Oz. 44.00
Flask, Log Cabin & Hard Cider, Blue Aqua, Sheared Lip, Pontil, Pt. 5600.00
Flask, Marbrie Loop, Clear, Red Loops, Tooled Lip, Oval, Open Pontil, 6 1/4 x 3 3/4 In. . . 225.00
Flask, Masonic & Eagle, Aqua Green, Sheared Lip, Pontil, Pt. 385.00
Flask, Masonic Arch & Eagle, Purple Amethyst, Tooled Mouth, Pontil, Pt. . . . . *Illus* 45100.00
Flask, Masonic, Aqua, Sheared Mouth, Pontil, Pt. 2688.00
Flask, Pitkin Type, 32 Broken Ribs, Swirled Right, Light Green, c.1810, 6 7/8 In. 700.00
Flask, Pitkin Type, 32 Broken Ribs, Swirled To Left, Yellow Green, Midwest, 6 1/2 In. . . . 145.00
Flask, Pitkin Type, 36 Broken Ribs Swirled To Right, Sheared Lip, Pontil, 6 5/8 In. 670.00
Flask, Scroll, Blue Aqua, Applied Mouth, Pontil, 1/2 Pt. 145.00
Flask, Scroll, Citron, Sheared Lip, Pontil, 1/2 Pt. 1344.00
Flask, Scroll, Gold Amber, Sheared Lip, Pontil, 1/2 Pt. 840.00
Flask, Scroll, McCarty & Torreyson, Blue Green, Sheared Lip, Pontil, Qt. 5600.00
Flask, Scroll, Yellow Green, Tooled Mouth, Pontil, 1/2 Pt. 1568.00
Flask, Sheaf Of Grain, Westford Glass Co., Amber, Double Collar, Pt. 257.00
Flask, Sheaf Of Grain, Westford Glass Co., Deep Olive Amber, Pt. 165.00
Flask, Stiegel Type, 18 Ribs, Swirled To Right, Amethyst, Flared Lip, 5 1/4 In. 90.00
Flask, Stiegel Type, Chestnut, Diamond & Daisy, Amethyst, 5 1/4 In. 4510.00
Flask, Stiegel Type, Horizontal Rows Of Diamonds, Amethyst, Flared Lip, 5 1/4 In. 120.00
Flask, Success To The Railroad, Olive Green, Amber, Pontil, Pt. 532.00
Flask, Success To The Railroad, Yellow Olive, Sheared Mouth, Pontil, Pt. 448.00

Flask, Summer & Winter, Blue Aqua, Applied Double Collar, Qt. 146.00
Flask, Sunburst, Deep Strawberry Puce, Tooled Lip, Pontil, 1/2 Pt. 5040.00
Flask, Sunburst, Light Green, Sheared Lip, Pontil, Pt. 1430.00
Flask, Sunburst, Yellow Amber, Tooled Lip, Pontil, Pt. 3584.00
Flask, Sunburst, Yellow Green, Sheared Mouth, Pontil, 1815-1830, 1/2 Pt. 3080.00
Flask, Traveler's Companion & Star, Yellow Amber, Sloping Collar, Qt. 112.00
Flask, Union, Clasped Hands & Eagle, Chocolate Amber, Applied Mouth, 1/2 Pt. 212.00
Flask, Union, Clasped Hands & Eagle, Yellow Green, Applied Mouth, Qt. 1904.00
Flask, Washington & Eagle, Aqua, Sheared Mouth, Pontil, Pt. 1904.00
Flask, Washington & Eagle, Blue Green, Pontil, Pt. 7280.00
Flask, Washington & Fells Point, Ruby Red, Pontil, Pt. 2090.00
Flask, Washington & Jackson, Gold Amber, Sheared Lip, Pontil, Pt. 440.00
Flask, Washington & Taylor, Blue Green, Double Collar, Iron Pontil, Qt. 224.00
Flask, Washington & Taylor, Cobalt Blue, Qt. 8400.00
Flask, Washington & Tree, Calabash, Aqua, Double Collar Mouth, Pontil, Qt. 2128.00
Flask, Washington Bust, Baltimore Glass Works, Yellow Olive, Pontil, Qt. . . . . *Illus* 24300.00
Food, Borden's Malted Milk, Glass, Metal Cover, 6 x 8 In. 605.00
Food, Buffalo Peanuts, Painted Label, 10 x 7 In. 440.00
Food, Gordon & Dilworth Preserved Tomatoes, Embossed Greek Key Bands 165.00
Food, Heinz Vinegar, Cork, Qt., 7 1/2 x 4 1/4 In. 580.00
Food, Heinz, Cider Vinegar, White, Original Labels, Cork, Handle, 6 x 4 In. 1155.00
Food, Heinz, Ground Stopper, Embossed Keystone, 12 In. 110.00
Food, Horlick's Malted Milk, Metal Cover, Blue Embossed Lettering, 6 x 5 In. 330.00
Food, Ketchup, Heinz Co., Glass, Paper Label, Tin Lithograph Lid, 9 1/2 x 2 5/8 In. 122.00
Food, Mustard, Barrel, Dark Olive Amber, Applied Mouth, 3 7/8 In. 90.00
Food, Sauce, Cobalt Blue, Burst Top, Smooth Base, 8 In. 90.00
Food, Storage, Olive Amber, Wide Mouth, Tooled Flared Lip, Pontil, 9 3/4 In. 532.00
Food, Storage, Yellow Olive Green, Wide Mouth, Tooled Flared Lip, Pontil, 12 In. 160.00
Food, Syrup, D. Miller & Co., Shaker Syrup, Canterbury, N.H., Aqua, Pontil, 7 1/4 In. . . .   575.00
Food, Syrup, No. 1 Shaker Syrup, Canterbury, N.H., Aqua, Applied Lip, Pontil, 7 5/8 In. . .   245.00
Food, Zatex Chocolate Candy, Glass, Letters, Gilt, Embossed, 17 In. 800.00
Fruit Jar, A Stone & Co., Philada, Aqua, Applied Wax Sealer Mouth, 1845-1860, Pt. 476.00
Fruit Jar, All Right, Patd Jan 28 1868, Aqua, Metal Dome Lid, Wire Clamp, Qt. 165.00
Fruit Jar, Atlas E-Z Seal, Aqua, Glass Lid, Closure, Qt. . . . . *Illus*   6.50
Fruit Jar, Ball Perfect Mason, Olive Amber, Zinc Lid, Qt. 145.00
Fruit Jar, Ball, Aqua, Ground Mouth, Wire Bail, Tin Lid, 1890-1900, Qt. 258.00
Fruit Jar, BBGM Co., Aqua, Ground Mouth, Glass Lid, Zinc Band, 1880-1890, Pt. 672.00
Fruit Jar, Flaccus Bros., Steers Head, Embossed Cow, Yellow Amber, Screw Top, Pt. 468.00
Fruit Jar, Fruitkeeper, Monogram, Sea Green, Ground Lip, Wire Clamp, Pt. 55.00
Fruit Jar, Gilberds Improved Jar, Star, Aqua, Glass Lid, Long Metal Clamp, 1/2 Gal. 330.00
Fruit Jar, Globe, Amber, Iron Clamp, Qt. 110.00
Fruit Jar, Globe, Amber, Metal Clamp, 1/2 Gal. 143.00
Fruit Jar, Globe, Deep Aqua, Wide Mouth, Iron Clamp, Qt. 110.00
Fruit Jar, Haines Combination, Aqua, Applied Collar Mouth, Glass Lid, 1870-1880, Qt. . . .   112.00
Fruit Jar, Huyett & Fridley, Ladies Choice, Aqua, Ground Mouth, 1860-1870, Qt. 1064.00
Fruit Jar, J.C Baker's, Patent Aug 14 1860, Aqua, Ground Mouth, Qt. 112.00
Fruit Jar, J.D. Willoughby, Patd Jan. 4 1859, Aqua, Wingnut Closure, Qt. 198.00
Fruit Jar, Kerr Self Sealing, Sky Blue, Metal Screw Lid, Qt. 45.00
Fruit Jar, Leader, Yellow Amber, Glass Lid, Wire Clamp, Qt. 230.00
Fruit Jar, Mason Fruit, Union Stoneware Co., Cover, Qt. 198.00
Fruit Jar, Mason's Improved, Yellow Amber, Ground Lip, 1/2 Gal. 365.00
Fruit Jar, Mason's Patent Nov 30th 1858, Aqua, Ground Mouth, Zinc Lid, 1865-1880, Qt.   532.00
Fruit Jar, Mason's Patent Nov 30th 1858, CFJCo, Yellow Olive, Qt. 336.00
Fruit Jar, Mason's Patent Nov 30th 1858, Yellow Green, Zinc Lid, 1/2 Gal. 168.00
Fruit Jar, Mason's Patent Nov 30th, 58, Pale Blue, Ground Lip, Metal Lid, Pt. 176.00
Fruit Jar, Mason's, Olive Streak, Ground Mouth, Zinc Lid, 1800-1900, Pt. 230.00
Fruit Jar, Patented Oct 19 1858, Green, Ground Lip, Lid, Qt. 123.00
Fruit Jar, Pet, Aqua, Glass Lid, Spring Wire Clamp, Qt. 55.00
Fruit Jar, Sun, Trademark, Aqua, Glass Lid, Wire Clamp, Pt. 130.00
Fruit Jar, The Howe Jar, Aqua, Ground Mouth, Glass Lid, Wire Bail, 1888-1900, Pt. 179.00
Fruit Jar, The Puritan, Aqua, Ground Mouth, Glass Lid, Iron Ring, 1870-1890, Pt. 365.00
Fruit Jar, The Rose, Machined Mouth, Glass Lid, Zinc Band, 1880-1900, Pt. 250.00
Fruit Jar, The Schaffer Jar, Rochester, N.Y., Aqua, Ground Mouth, Glass Lid, c.1879, Qt. .   315.00

If you collect old bottles that held herb remedies, don't throw out the contents. It adds to the value. But be sure no children will ever open the bottle and taste the herbs.

Bottle, Fruit Jar, Atlas E-Z
Seal, Aqua, Glass Lid,
Closure, Qt.

Bottle, Milk, Kaste's Dairy,
Milk Is Nature's Most
Perfect Food, Red ACL, Qt.

Fruit Jar, Trademark Lightning, Light To Medium Amber, 1/2 Gal.	55.00
Fruit Jar, Trademark Lightning, Yellow Amber, Ground Mouth, Glass Lid, 1880-1890, Pt.	336.00
Fruit Jar, Union, No. 4, Aqua, Ground Mouth, Wax Sealer, 1860-1880, Qt.	168.00
Fruit Jar, Van Vliet Jar Of 1881, Aqua, Glass Lid, Metal Yoke, 1/2 Gal.	825.00
Fruit Jar, Woodbury Packing, Co., Monogram, Aqua, Metal Clamp, 1/2 Gal.	110.00
Gin, A. Van Hoboken, A.V.H. Monogram On Seal, Applied Top, Olive Amber	55.00
Gin, Blown, Yellow Olive, Tapered Form, Applied Mouth, Pontil, 1770-1800, 17 3/4 In.	1456.00
Gin, C.A. Richards, Boston, Amber, Sloping Collar, 1865-1875, 9 1/2 In.	110.00
Gin, Case, Dip Mold, Medium Olive Green, Amber, Applied Lip, Pontil, 9 1/2 In.	2016.00
Gin, Case, Dip Mold, Medium Olive Green, Applied Mouth, Pontil, 9 1/2 In.	150.00
Gin, Case, Dip Mold, Tobacco Amber, Olive, Applied Mouth, Pontil, 9 3/4 In.	135.00
Gin, Daniel Visser & Zonen, Schiedam, Case, 11 In.	95.00
Gin, London Jockey Club House, Horse & Rider, Olive Green, Applied Top	990.00
Ginger Beer, Dolan L. Bros., Cobalt Top, 1902	125.00
Ginger Beer, F.B. Weeks, Gray, Cobalt Slip Glaze, 8 7/8 In.	56.00
Household, Ammonia MNFD, S.F. Gaslight Co., Blue, 10 1/4 In.	4840.00
Ink, Annular Rings, Olive Green, 1815, 1 5/8 In.	2585.00
Ink, Bertinguiot, Olive Amber, Tooled Lip, Pontil, 1845-1860, 2 1/4 In.	308.00
Ink, Cabin, Ground Lip, 1875-1890, 3 1/4 In.	1064.00
Ink, Carter's, 6-Sided, Cobalt Blue, ABM, 2 7/8 In.	168.00
Ink, Carter's, Green, Applied Top, 7 1/2 In.	120.00
Ink, Carter's, Yellow Amber, Applied Mouth, Tooled Pour Spout, Labels, 8 1/4 In.	125.00
Ink, Carter, Cathedral, Cobalt Blue, 6 1/2 In.	305.00
Ink, Carter, Cathedral, Cobalt Blue, 8 In.	176.00
Ink, Carter, Cathedral, Cobalt Blue, 9 3/4 In.	110.00 to 136.00
Ink, Caw's, Cobalt Blue, Tooled Mouth, 1890-1910, 6 5/8 In.	157.00
Ink, David's, Amber, Paper Label, New York Skyline, Glass, 9 1/2 x 4 In.	310.00
Ink, Diamond Diaper, Olive Green, Applied Disk Rim, c.1813, 1 7/8 In.	265.00
Ink, Emerald Green, 22 Ribs, Boston & Sandwich Glass Co., 1825, 1 3/4 In.	765.00
Ink, Emerald Green, Teakettle, 8-Sided, Brass Cap, 2 In.	590.00
Ink, Geometric, Olive Amber, Sheared Lip, Pontil, 1815-1835, 1 3/4 In.	179.00
Ink, Harrison's Columbian, 8-Sided, Igloo, Aqua, Sheared Lip, 1870-1880, 1 7/8 In.	308.00
Ink, Igloo, Teal Blue, Sheared Lip, 1 5/8 In.	218.00
Ink, Igloo, Yellow Green, Sheared & Ground Lip, 1870-1890, 2 In.	1456.00
Ink, J. & I.E.M., Igloo, Cobalt Blue, Tooled Mouth, 1875-1895, 1 3/4 In.	3920.00
Ink, J. & I.E.M., Igloo, Teal Blue, Tooled Mouth, 1875-1895, 1 3/4 In.	1345.00
Ink, J. & I.E.M., Igloo, Yellow Green, Tooled Mouth, 1875-1895, 1 3/4 In.	1232.00
Ink, J.J. Butler, Blue Aqua, Rolled Lip, Pontil, 1845-1855, 2 7/8 In.	90.00
Ink, Kirtland's, Igloo, Yellow Amber, Sheared Lip, 1875-1895, 1 7/8 In.	840.00
Ink, Liberty Bell, Tooled, Mouth, c.1926, 2 5/8 In.	168.00
Ink, Peacock Blue, Cylinder, Sloping Shoulders, 2 3/4 In.	79.00
Ink, R.F., Black Amethyst, Flared & Rolled Lip, France, Pontil, 1840-1855, 2 In.	365.00
Ink, Runge-Tinte, MF & R, Horse, Black Amethyst, Tooled Pour Spout, Germany, Master	258.00
Ink, Square, Olive Green, 36 Ribs, 1783-1830, 1 1/2 In.	1410.00

Ink, Teakettle, 6-Sided, Light Amethyst, Brass Collar, 2 1/4 In. 385.00
Ink, Teakettle, 8-Sided, Amethyst, Brass Cap, c.1850, 2 In. 470.00
Ink, Teakettle, 8-Sided, Cobalt Blue, 3 Vertical Ribs, 2 1/8 In. 395.00
Ink, Teakettle, 10-Sided, Cobalt Blue, Painted Flowers, Butterfly, Dots, 2 1/4 In. 385.00
Ink, Teakettle, 10-Sided, Milk Glass, Flowers, Vines, Yellow, Gold, 2 1/2 In. 350.00
Ink, Teakettle, Hinged Lid, Milk Glass, Embossed Flowers, Ground Lip, 1875-1890, 3 In. 560.00
Ink, Teakettle, Pear Shape, Lime Green, Lobed Panels, 2 1/4 In. 375.00
Ink, Teakettle, Turtle, Sheared & Ground Lip, 1875-1890, 2 In. 179.00
Ink, Umbrella, 12-Sided, Deep Blue Aqua, Rolled Lip, 2 3/4 In. 670.00
Ink, Umbrella, Medium Amber, Burst Top, 2 1/2 In. 176.00
Ink, Umbrella, Sapphire Blue, Rolled Lip, 2 1/2 In. 880.00
Ink, Umbrella, Stoddard Style, Plum Puce, Rolled Lip, 2 1/2 In. 1430.00
Ink, Umbrella, Teal Blue, Rolled Lip, Pontil, 2 1/2 In. 825.00
Ink, W.E. Bonney, Barrel, Aqua, Tooled Mouth, 2 3/4 In. 90.00
Ink, Ward's Ink, Emerald Blue, Drippy Applied Top, 7 3/4 In. 190.00
Ink, Yellow Olive Amber, Applied Sloping Double Collar, Tooled Spout, Master 224.00
Jar, Embossed Griffin, San Francisco, 10 In. 330.00
Jar, J.M. Clark & Co., Louisville, Ky., Tooled Top, 7 In. 88.00
Jar, Pomade, Figural, Bear, Black Glass, F.B. Strouse, N.Y., 1850-1887, 3 5/8 In. 265.00
Jar, Storage, Porcelain, Famille Rose Enamels, Courtesans, Chinese, c.1890, 9 1/2 In. 144.00
Jar, Utility, Green, Pontil, 1800-1830, 12 In. 154.00
Jar, Utility, Light Green, Pontil, 1800-1830, 11 1/2 In. 100.00
Medicine, A. McEckron's Ringbone Liniment, N.Y., Aqua, Pontil, 6 In. 165.00
Medicine, A. Mosher, Blue Green, Applied Collar Mouth, Iron Pontil, c.1850, 8 3/4 In. . . . 3360.00
Medicine, Acker's English Remedy, Cobalt Blue, 7 In. 179.00
Medicine, Alexander's Silameau, Bell Form, Sapphire Blue, Pontil, 1845-1860, 6 1/4 In. . . 532.00
Medicine, Allen's Dyspeptic Medicine, Philada., Pontil 110.00
Medicine, Alterative Chalybeate, Welden Springs, St. Albans, Vermont, c.1870 . . . . 3475.00
Medicine, Ayers Cherry Pectoral, Cloudy, Open Pontil, 6 5/8 In. 90.00
Medicine, Bach's American Compound, Auburn, N.Y., Aqua, Double Collar, OP, 7 3/4 In. . 110.00
Medicine, Balm Of X Thousand, Aqua, Applied Mouth, Pontil, 1845-1855, 5 1/8 In. 476.00
Medicine, Barry's Tricopherous For The Skin & Hair, New York, Aqua, Pamphlet, Pontil . 39.00
Medicine, C.W. Atwell, Portland, Me., Deep Blue Aqua, Open Pontil, 7 5/8 In. 145.00
Medicine, Carter's Spanish Mixture, Olive Green, Applied Top, Graphite Pontil, 8 In. 605.00
Medicine, Clark Stanley's Snake Oil Liniment, 6 1/2 In. 45.00
Medicine, Curtis & Perkins Cramp & Painkiller, Bangor, Me., Aqua, 5 In. 187.00
Medicine, Damascus, San Francisco, Arab Man & Camel, Yellow Amber, 4 1/2 In. 200.00
Medicine, Davis Vegetable Pain Killer, Aqua, Graphic Label, Open Pontil, 4 5/8 In. 440.00
Medicine, Davis Vegetable Pain Killer, Deep Blue Aqua, Iron Pontil, 8 3/4 In. 595.00
Medicine, Dr. A. Atkinson, New York, Aqua, Rectangular, Open Pontil, 8 In. 165.00
Medicine, Dr. Agnew's Cure For The Heart, Buffalo, N.Y., 7 3/4 In. 77.00
Medicine, Dr. Browder's, Compound Syrup, Sloping Collar, Blue Aqua, Pontil, 7 In. 392.00
Medicine, Dr. D. Jayne's Alternative, 84 Chest. St., Phila, Aqua, Open Pontil, 7 In. 59.00
Medicine, Dr. D. Jayne's Carminative Balsam, Aqua, Rolled Lip, 4 7/8 In. 24.00
Medicine, Dr. E.L Robertson, Lansing, Mich., Labels, Contents, 6 3/4 In. 385.00
Medicine, Dr. Henry's Botanic Preparations, Aqua, Applied Top, 6 1/4 In. 120.00
Medicine, Dr. J. Blackman's Genuine Healing Balsam, 6-Sided, Aqua, Pontil, 5 5/8 In. . . . 69.00
Medicine, Dr. Jackson's Pile Embrocation, Phila., Green Aqua, Flared Lip, Pontil, 4 In. . . 504.00
Medicine, Dr. Jas. C. Kerr's Great System Renovator, Amber, Square, Applied Top, 8 In. . 110.00
Medicine, Dr. Kennedy's Medical Discovery, Roxbury, Mass., Aqua, 8 1/2 In. 358.00
Medicine, Dr. Kennedy's, Prairie Weed, Roxbury Mass., Aqua, Rectangular, 8 1/4 In. 85.00
Medicine, Dr. Kilmer's Indian Cough Cure Consumption Oil, Aqua, 5 1/4 In. 132.00
Medicine, Dr. King's New Life Pills, Recessed Label Under Glass, Glass Stopper, 13 In. . 523.00
Medicine, Dr. Mile's Restorative Nervine, ABM, Label, Box, 8 1/4 In. 230.00
Medicine, Dr. Pedro's Sootherine, Aqua, Round, Label, 4 1/4 In. 44.00
Medicine, Dr. Perry's Last Chance Liniment, Aqua, Applied Top, 5 3/4 In. 80.00
Medicine, Dr. Pierce's Favorite Prescription, Buffalo, N.Y., Aqua, Box, 8 1/4 In. 240.00
Medicine, Dr. S. Feller's Eclectic Liniment, Aqua, Rolled Lip, Open Pontil, 4 3/8 In. 99.00
Medicine, Dr. S.F. Stowe's Ambrosial Nectar, Stemmed Glass In Vine Frame, Citron, 8 In. 125.00
Medicine, Dr. S.S. Fitch, 707 B.Way N.Y., Oval, Aqua, Open Pontil, 6 1/8 In. 69.00
Medicine, Dr. Shoop's Family Medicines, Racine, Wis., Aqua, Label, 7 In. 60.00
Medicine, Dr. Swayne's Panacea, Philada., Blue Green, Cylinder, c.1860, 8 In. 379.00
Medicine, Dr. Taylor's Chronothermal, Blue Aqua, Sloping Collar, Pontil, 1840, 6 7/8 In. . 420.00

Medicine, Dr. Tebbett's Physiological Hair Regenerator, Purple Amethyst, 7 1/2 In. 258.00
Medicine, Dr. Tobias Venetian Liniment, New York, Aqua, Rectangular, Pontil, 5 1/4 In. . . 45.00
Medicine, Dr. Townsend's Aromatic, Amber, Square, Applied Collar Mouth, 1860, 9 In. . . 146.00
Medicine, Dr. Townsend's Sarsaparilla, Amber Black, Collar Mouth, Pontil, 9 1/4 In. 1008.00
Medicine, Dr. Townsend's Sarsaparilla, Teal, Square, Applied Collar Mouth, 9 1/4 In. . . . 180.00
Medicine, Dr. Wood's Soothing Syrup, Aqua, Contents, Label, 5 1/4 In. 190.00
Medicine, Ely's Cream Balm, Amber, Label, Box, 2 1/2 In. 44.00
Medicine, F.J. Steinmetz Druggist, Carson City, Nev. Opp. Post Office, 7 5/8 In. 220.00
Medicine, Fish's Hair Restorative, B.F. Fish, San Francisco, Aqua, Applied Top, 7 1/4 In. . 825.00
Medicine, G.C. Taylor's Liniment, Oil Of Life, Fairport, N.Y., 10 In. 35.00
Medicine, G.W. Merchant, Lockport, N.Y., Aqua, Applied Mouth, Open Pontil, 5 In. 365.00
Medicine, Gargling Oil, Lockport, N.Y., Teal Blue, Applied Top, 7 1/8 In. 165.00
Medicine, Geo. W. Laird & Co., Oleo-Chyle, Cobalt Blue, Front & Back Labels, 9 7/8 In. . 468.00
Medicine, Great Shoshonees, Remedy Of Dr. Josephus, Aqua, 9 3/8 In. 157.00
Medicine, H. Lake's Indian Specific, Aqua, Applied Mouth, Pontil, 1845-1855, 8 1/4 In. . . 1680.00
Medicine, H.H. Warner & Co., Tippecanoe, Amber, 9 In. 358.00
Medicine, Hall's Balsam For The Lungs, Deep Aqua, Indented Panels, 6 3/4 In. 79.00
Medicine, Healy & Bigelow, Kickapoo Oil, Indian, Label, Contents, 7 In. 145.00
Medicine, Healy & Bigelow, Kickapoo Oil, Indian, Label, Cork, Contents, Box, 5 1/4 In. . 88.00
Medicine, Henshaw & Edmands Druggists Boston, Green, Stopper, Pontil, c.1855, 11 In. . 1120.00
Medicine, Herbine Co., St. Louis, Aqua, Label, Box, 6 7/8 In. 165.00
Medicine, Holden's Ethereal Cough Syrup, Stockton, Aqua, 5 In. 29.00
Medicine, Hunt's Remedy, Prevents & Cures Diseases, Aqua, Label, 8 3/4 In. 385.00
Medicine, J.B. Marchisi M.D., Utica, N.Y., Aqua, Oval, Square Collar Lip, 7 1/8 In. 49.00
Medicine, J.B. Wheatley's Compound Syrup, Dallasburg, Ky., Pontil, 6 In. . . . . . . .180.00 to 195.00
Medicine, J.S. Seabury, Jamaica, L.I., Aqua, Rectangular, Open Pontil, 3 3/4 In. 39.00
Medicine, Jewetts Stimulating Liniment, Aqua, Rolled Lip, Open Pontil, 3 7/8 In. 395.00
Medicine, Jno. Sullivan Pharmacist, Boston, Milk Glass, Logo, 5 In. 59.00
Medicine, Jos. Fleming Druggist, Ice Blue, Double Collar Mouth, Iron Pontil, 7 5/8 In. . . . 448.00
Medicine, L.P. Dodge Rheumatic Liniment, Newburg, Olive Amber, c.1850, 6 In. 3800.00
Medicine, L.Q.C. Wishart's Pine Tree Tar Cordial, Blue Green, Sloping Collar, 1859, 8 In. . 200.00
Medicine, L.Q.C. Wishart's Pine Tree Tar Cordial, Phila., Tree, Emerald Green, 8 1/4 In. . 185.00
Medicine, Leaven's English Vermin Destroyer, Aqua, Applied Top, Pontil, 8 In. 385.00
Medicine, Log Cabin Cough & Consumption Remedy, Amber, 6 7/8 In. 225.00
Medicine, Log Cabin Hops & Buchu Remedy, Amber, 10 In. 320.00
Medicine, Log Cabin Scalpine, Rochester, N.Y., Amber, Paneled, Label, 8 5/8 In. 1345.00
Medicine, Louden & Co.'s Carminative Balsam, Aqua, Flared Lip, Open Pontil, 5 1/4 In. . 77.00
Medicine, McIntosh & Kubon Druggist, Known Throughout Alaska, 7 1/2 In. 330.00
Medicine, McLean's Volcanic, Oil, Liniment, Aqua, Contents, Box, 6 1/2 In. 60.00
Medicine, McNutt & Hurlbut Druggist, Ogden, Utah, Monogram, 6 1/4 In. 55.00
Medicine, Mother Seigel's Curative, A.J. White, Ltd., Aqua, Label, Contents, 4 3/4 In. . . . 440.00
Medicine, Mother's Relief, Aqua, Pontil, Sloping Collar, 1845-1855, 8 1/2 In. 215.00
Medicine, Mrs. A. Allen's World's Hair Balsam, 355 Broom St., Aqua, Pontil, 6 1/2 In. . . . 120.00
Medicine, Murine Eye Remedy Co., Chicago, Milk Glass, 3 1/8 In. 176.00
Medicine, N. Wood, Portland, Me., Aqua, Applied Top, Graphite Pontil, 7 1/2 In. 415.00
Medicine, Newell's Pulmonary Syrup, Reddington & Co, Aqua, Applied Top, 7 3/8 In. . . . 55.00
Medicine, Norwood's Tinct. V. Viride, Label, Shakers, Mount Lebanon, 5 1/4 In. 176.00
Medicine, Nyal's Corn Remover, 52 Gram Indian Cannabis Per Ounce, Glass, Label, 3 In. . 66.00
Medicine, Owl Drug Co., Incorporated Valdez, Alaska, Embossed Owl, 5 1/8 In. 605.00
Medicine, Pike & Osgood, Alterative Syrup, Boston, Mass., Amber, Olive Tone, 8 5/8 In. . 12936.00
Medicine, Querus Cod Liver Oil, Jelly, Aqua Blue, Jar, Wide Mouth, Pontil, 5 3/8 In. 476.00
Medicine, Radium Radia, 2 Men On Front, Label, Contents, Box, 5 1/2 In. 165.00
Medicine, Rhode's Fever & Ague Cure, Smooth Base, Deep Aqua, 8 1/4 In. 55.00
Medicine, Rushton Clark & Co., Chemists, New York, Aqua, Open Pontil, 10 In. 195.00
Medicine, S.M. Kier Petroleum, Pittsburgh, Deep Aqua, Open Pontil, 6 1/2 In. 145.00
Medicine, Saratoga Aperient, Cobalt Blue, Contents, 4 3/4 In. 198.00
Medicine, Schenck's Pulmonic Syrup, 8-Sided, Green Aqua, Iron Pontil, 7 1/4 In. 250.00
Medicine, Scovill Blood & Liver Syrup, Cincinnati, O., Deep Aqua, 9 1/2 In. 39.00
Medicine, Smith's Green Mountain Renovator, Blue Aqua, Oval, 1855-1865, 7 5/8 In. . . . 504.00
Medicine, South Carolina Dispensary, Embossed Palm Tree, Tooled Top, 9 In. 209.00
Medicine, Swaim's Panacea Philada., Aqua, Vertical Panels, Sloping Collar, 1860, 7 In. . . 110.00
Medicine, Swaim's Panacea Philada., Yellow Green, Sloping Collar, Pontil, 1850, 8 In. . . . 896.00
Medicine, Swaim's Panacea, Genuine, Philada, Aqua, Rectangular, 1830-1860, 7 In. 550.00

Medicine, U.S.A. Hosp. Dept., Ice Blue, 7 In. 550.00
Medicine, U.S.A. Hosp. Dept., Olive, Applied Top, 5 13/16 In. 770.00
Medicine, Vaughn's Vegetable Lithotriptic Mixture, Buffalo, Aqua, Smooth Base, 8 In. 176.00
Medicine, Veno's Seaweed Tonic, Sapphire Blue, 5 In. 15.00
Medicine, Warner's Safe Cure, Yellow Olive, Oval, Collar Mouth, 1870-1890, 7 1/8 In. ... 95.00
Medicine, Warner's Safe Nervine, Rochester, N.Y., Amber, 7 1/4 In. 198.00
Medicine, Warner's Safe Remedies Co., Rochester, N.Y., Amber, 9 In. 50.00
Medicine, Wheeler's Nerve Vitalizer, Aqua, Albion, Michigan, Sealed, Box, 9 In. 232.00
Medicine, Winans Brothers Indian Cure For Blood, Blue Aqua, 1880-1890, 9 1/4 In. 308.00
Milk, Abbington Dairy, Scranton, Penna., Embossed, 1/2 Pt. 10.00
Milk, Adams Dairy, Rawlings, Colo., Bucking Horse, ACL, Tall, Round, Qt. 45.00
Milk, Blue-Bell Farms Milk, Irvington, N.J., Orange ACL, Cream Top, Round, Pt. 25.00
Milk, Blue-Bell Farms Milk, Irvington, N.J., Orange ACL, Cream Top, Round, Qt. 200.00
Milk, Cloverleaf Dairy Inc., Mass Seal, 4-Leaf Clover, Green ACL, Round, Qt. 35.00
Milk, Columbia Dairy, Col., S.C., Embossed, 1/2 Pt. 12.00
Milk, Cooperative Milk Bottle Association, Saint John, N.B., Embossed, Qt. 35.00
Milk, Crestall Dairy, Carlstadt, N.J., Maroon ACL, Cream Top, Round, Qt. 125.00
Milk, Evans Amityville Dairy Inc, Amityville, L.I., Orange ACL, Cream Top, Qt. 75.00
Milk, Farmville Creamery, Farmville, Va., Embossed, Tall, Round, Qt. 65.00
Milk, Fisher's Dairy, Crystal Falls, Mich., Black ACL, Tall, Round, Qt. 40.00
Milk, Grand View Dairy Farm, Canton, O., Embossed, 1/2 Pt. 15.00
Milk, Herlihy's Store, Orange ACL, Embossed, Pt. 35.00
Milk, Humboldt College, Arcata, Calif., ACL, Round, Qt. 125.00
Milk, J.F. Page, Potsdam, N.Y., Embossed, Qt. 30.00
Milk, Kaste's Dairy, Milk Is Nature's Most Perfect Food, Red ACL, Qt. .... *Illus*   18.00
Milk, Miller's Dairy, Watkins Glen, N.Y., Maroon ACL, Embossed, Pt. 35.00
Milk, Model Dairy, Wauken, Iowa, Red ACL, Tall, Round, Qt. 30.00
Milk, Mt. Lakes Dairy, Nevada, Qt. 330.00
Milk, Pleasant View Dairy, A.W. Croscut & Sons, Sherman, N.Y., Maroon ACL, Pt. 18.00
Milk, Pocahontas Dairy, Pocohontas, Ark., Blue ACL, Tall, Round, Qt. 50.00
Milk, Roland Abbott, Hudson, N.H., Embossed, Pt. 16.00
Milk, Seller's Creamery, Clearwater, Fla., Embossed, Tall, Round, Qt. 35.00
Milk, Slosek's Farm, Cow's Head, Orange ACL, Round, Qt. 35.00
Milk, Tom Houde's Dairy, Kankakee, Ill., Blue ACL, Tall, Round, Qt. 50.00
Milk, Walnut Hill Dairy, Jessup, Maryland, Embossed, Tall, Round, Qt. 50.00
Milk, Wauregan Co. Farm, Wauregan, Conn., Embossed, Pt. 18.00
Milk, Wilson Dairy Co., Atlantic City, Embossed, Tall, Round, Qt. 40.00
Mineral Water, Artesian Spring Co., Ballston, N.Y., Blue Green, Pt. 89.00
Mineral Water, Boyd & Beard, Olive Green, Applied Sloping Collar, IP, 6 7/8 In. 190.00
Mineral Water, C.A. Reiners & Co. Improved, San Francisco, Aqua, Blob Top, 7 1/8 In. . 220.00
Mineral Water, Clarke & Co., N.Y., Black Olive, Pt. 159.00
Mineral Water, E. McIntire, Emerald Green, Applied Tapered Collar, OP, 6 1/2 In. 2240.00
Mineral Water, Empire Spring Co., E. Saratoga, N.Y., Emerald Green, Pt. 59.00
Mineral Water, G.W. Weston & Co., Forest Green, Applied Collar Mouth, c.1860, 1/2 Pt. . 448.00
Mineral Water, Geyser Spring, Spouting Springs, Saratoga, Ice Blue, Pt. 69.00
Mineral Water, Hanbury Smith's Kissingen Water, Blue Green, Oval, Blob Top, IP, 8 In. . 840.00
Mineral Water, Hathorn Spring, Saratoga, N.Y., Deep Blue Green, Bubbles, Pt. 69.00
Mineral Water, Holmes & Co., New Orleans, Aqua, Fluted Neck, 7 1/4 In. 120.00
Mineral Water, Ideal, Newark, N.J., Embossed, Man With Flag, Excelsior, Blob Top, Qt. . 50.00
Mineral Water, J.C. Parker & Son, New York, Light Blue 88.00
Mineral Water, John Clarke, New York, Olive Amber, Applied Sloping Collar, Pontil, Pt. . 179.00
Mineral Water, Kissingen Water, T.H.D., The Spa Phila, Yellow Olive, Pt. 339.00
Mineral Water, Lynde Putnam, San Francisco, Blue, Blob Top, 7 1/2 In. 300.00
Mineral Water, Morgan Bros. & Co., New York, Blue Green, Blob Top, IP, 7 1/2 In. 308.00
Mineral Water, P. Conway, Superior, 8 Hunter St., Cobalt Blue, 8-Sided Base, 7 1/2 In. ... 728.00
Mineral Water, Saratoga Vichy Spouting Spring, Saratoga, N.Y., Aqua, Pt. 69.00
Mineral Water, Star Spring Co., Saratoga, N.Y., Embossed Star, Red Amber, Pt. 179.00
Mineral Water, Suydam & Dubois, N.Y., Superior, Cobalt Blue, 8-Sided Base, 7 1/2 In. . 1790.00
Pepper Sauce, Cathedral, 6-Sided, Applied Top, Open Pontil, 10 11/16 In. 295.00
Pepper Sauce, Durkee, Green, Embossed, 7 In. 88.00
Perfume bottles are listed in their own category.
Pickle, Aqua, 5 Flutes, 2-Piece Mold, Rolled Mouth, Pontil, 1860-1880, 10 1/2 In. 145.00
Pickle, Aqua, Square, Indented Panels, Scalloped Shoulders, Ring Neck, 11 1/2 In. 125.00

Pickle, Cathedral, Aqua, Rolled Lip, 1855-1865, 11 1/2 In. 135.00
Pickle, Cathedral, Aqua, Rolled Lip, Pontil, 1850-1860, 11 5/8 In. 336.00
Pickle, Cathedral, Aqua, Rolled Mouth, 1855-1870, 7 1/2 In. 125.00
Pickle, Cathedral, Blue Aqua, 6-Sided, Applied Mouth, 1855-1865, 13 1/4 In. 215.00
Pickle, Cathedral, Deep Blue Aqua, Applied Mouth, Embossed, 1855-1865, 14 In. 420.00
Pickle, Cathedral, Green Aqua, 6-Sided, Rolled Lip, 1860-1870, 13 In. 224.00
Pickle, Cathedral, Green Aqua, Rolled Lip, 1855-1870, 11 1/2 In. 170.00
Pickle, Cathedral, Green, Applied Top, Smooth Base, 8 3/4 In. 525.00
Pickle, Cutter Packing, S.F., Fire Aqua, Winged Griffin, 9 1/8 In. 225.00
Pickle, Goofus, Deep Blue Aqua, Embossed Rose, Sheared Rim, 1890-1920, 15 1/4 In. ... 160.00
Pickle, Goofus, Deep Cobalt Blue, Embossed Rose, 1890-1920, 15 1/8 In. 5100.00
Pickle, Goofus, Yellow Amber, Embossed Rose, Sheared & Tooled Rim, 15 In. 950.00
Pickle, J.J. Wilson, Chicago, Ill., Mixed, Label, 4 1/2 In. .... *Illus* 12.00
Pickle, R & F. Atmore, Cathedral, Aqua, Beveled Corners, 3 Panels, c.1860, 11 3/8 In. ... 310.00
Pickle, Skilton Foote & Co.'s, Bunker Hill, Light Amber, 7 1/2 In. 20.00
Poison, Amber, Tooled Top, 7 7/8 In. 415.00
Poison, Bliss Narive Balsam, ABM, 4 7/8 In. 145.00
Poison, Embossed Not To Be Taken, Poisonous, Ammonia, Beehive, Aqua, 6 1/2 In. 20.00
Poison, Embossed Poison, Glass Lid, Cream, Stoneware, 6 3/4 In. 224.00
Poison, Embossed Poison, Mercuric Chloride, Coffin Shape, Cobalt Blue, Label 60.00
Poison, Embossed Poison, Strychnia, Oval, 2 1/2 In. 40.00
Poison, Fowler's Solution, Purity Drug Company, Cobalt Blue, Fishnet, 4 1/8 In. .... *Illus* 85.00
Poison, Gift Flasche, Skull & Crossed Bones, Yellow Green, 6-Sided, 6 5/8 In. 90.00
Poison, Jno. Wyeth & Bro., Cobalt Blue, Panels, Round, 2 5/8 In. 40.00
Poison, Kurokol, ABM, Contents, 5 1/8 In. 240.00
Poison, Lattice & Diamond, Cobalt Blue, Tooled Mouth, Stopper, 1890-1910, 7 In. 125.00
Poison, Lyon's Powder, B & P, N.Y., Bug Killer, Amber 35.00
Poison, Owl Drug Co, Cobalt Blue, 3-Sided, Embossed Owl, 7 3/4 In. ....300.00 to 375.00
Poison, Quilted, Cobalt Blue, Original Stopper, 4 3/4 In. 90.00
Poison, Sauer's Extract Laudanum Poison Opium, Embossed, Label, 4 7/8 In. 285.00
Poison, Sulphuric Ether, Cobalt Blue, 6-Sided, Label, 4 1/2 In. 125.00
Poison, Vapo Cresoline, Contents, Label, 4 In. 20.00
Poison, Zewnetrznie, Aqua, 6-Sided, Germany, c.1900, 8 1/2 In. 170.00
Sarsaparilla, Ayers, Compound Ext., Lowell Mass U.S.A., Aqua, 8 1/2 In. 39.00
Sarsaparilla, Babcock's Gold Medal, Amber, 9 In. 89.00
Sarsaparilla, Dr. Henry's, Aqua, Applied Top, 9 1/4 In. 45.00
Sarsaparilla, Dr. Marshall's Extract Of Sarsaparilla, Rectangular, Aqua, 8 3/4 In. 85.00
Sarsaparilla, Dr. Townsend's, Albany, N.Y., Olive Green, Pontil, 9 1/2 In. 120.00
Sarsaparilla, Dr. Wood's Sarsaparilla & Wild Cherry Bitters, Aqua, Pontil, 8 3/4 In. 375.00
Sarsaparilla, Emerson's 50 Cts. Sarsaparilla, Applied Double Ring Lip, Aqua, 8 3/4 In. .. 59.00
Sarsaparilla, H.T. Helmbold Chemist Philadelphia, Genuine, Aqua, Open Pontil, 6 1/4 In. 154.00
Sarsaparilla, John Bull Extract, Louisville, Ky., Aqua, Pontil, 9 In. 395.00
Sarsaparilla, Kemp's, D.F. Woodward, Leroy, N.Y., Aqua, Label, Box, 9 1/2 In. 965.00

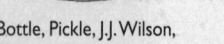

Bottle, Pickle, J.J. Wilson,
Chicago, Ill., Mixed, Label,
4 1/2 In.

**To remove a glass stopper stuck
in a narrow-necked perfume
bottle or decanter, put the
bottle in warm water, then
gradually add hot water and
gently try to loosen the stopper.**

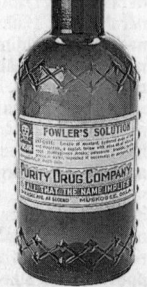

Bottle, Poison, Fowler's
Solution, Purity Drug Company,
Cobalt Blue, Fishnet, 4 1/8 In.

Sarsaparilla, Kenifick & Skrine, Green Aqua, Double Collar, 1850-1865, 9 1/4 In. 225.00
Sarsaparilla, Log Cabin, Rochester, N.Y., Amber, Label, Contents, Box, 9 In. 1375.00
Sarsaparilla, Mack's Sarsaparilla Bitters, Amber, Applied Top, 1880s, 9 1/2 In. 415.00
Sarsaparilla, Primley's Sarsaparilla, 9 1/4 In. 46.00
Sarsaparilla, Sand's Sarsaparilla Genuine, New York, Aqua, Open Pontil, 10 1/8 In. 375.00
Scent, Amethyst, White Looping, Tooled Mouth, Pontil, 1820-1840, 3 1/4 In. 260.00
Scent, Cameo, White & Yellow, Leaves, Silver Top, 2 1/2 In. 1150.00
Scent, Cut Glass, Green Over Clear, Gold Highlights, Silver Top, 6 1/4 In. 690.00
Scent, Flower, Bird, Carved Elephant Head Handles, Quartz, 4 3/4 In. 40.00
Scent, Ribs Swirl To Right, Purple Amethyst, Sheared Mouth, Pontil, 2 3/4 In. 179.00
Seal, 3-Piece Mold, Dark Green, Bristol, England, 19th Century, 8 3/4 In. 259.00
Seal, 3-Piece Mold, Medium Green, L. Thorndike, 19th Century, 10 1/2 In. 200.00
Seal, J.W. Chever, Black Glass, Rickett's Glass Works, Bristol, c.1830, 8 3/4 In. 550.00
Seltzer, California Natural, Embossed Bear, Aqua Blue, Blob Top 110.00
Snuff, Agate, Dragon Perusing Pearl, Brown Opaque Skin, 2 3/4 In. 175.00
Snuff, Agate, Figure Holding String Of Cash, Bats, Toad, Oval, Jadeite Stopper, 2 1/4 In. . 3220.00
Snuff, Agate, Pebble Form, Brown & White, Ivory Stopper, 2 In. 150.00
Snuff, Agate, Sage & Attendant Under Tree, Opaque Ocher, 2 1/2 In. 115.00
Snuff, Agate, Warrior Carrying Hammer, Wood Stopper, 2 1/4 In. 1840.00
Snuff, Amethyst, Prunus, Pebble, Coral Stopper, 2 1/4 In. 259.00
Snuff, Aventurine, Oval, Glass Stopper, c.1900, 1 3/4 In. 35.00
Snuff, Cinnabar, Red, Figural Landscape, Oval, Stopper, 20th Century, 2 1/2 In. 65.00
Snuff, Cloisonne, Pilgrim Flask Form, Flower, Blue Ground, Stone Stopper, 2 1/2 In. 200.00
Snuff, Doct. Marshall's Catarrh & Headache Snuff, Label, Pontil, 3 1/2 In. 145.00
Snuff, Enameled Leaf, Branches, Silver Filigree, Impressed, Chinese, 3 In. 29.00
Snuff, Fluorite, Green, Temple Jar, Flowers, Red Glass Stopper, c.1900, 1 3/4 In. 29.00
Snuff, Glass, Amber Crab Overlay, Yellow Ground, Spade Form, Agate Stopper, 2 1/4 In. . 345.00
Snuff, Glass, Bird & Landscape, Olive, Yellow, Red, Green, Stopper, 2 1/4 In. 345.00
Snuff, Glass, Olive Green, Wide Rolled Lip, Beveled Corners, Pontil, 6 1/8 In. 280.00
Snuff, Glass, Overlay, Buddha, Boy On Elephant, Blue, White Ground, 2 1/2 In. 58.00
Snuff, Glass, Overlay, Fisherman & Ducks, Glass Stopper, 2 1/4 In. 58.00
Snuff, Glass, Pebble Form, Black & White, c.1900, 2 1/4 In. 69.00
Snuff, Glass, Prunus On Snowflake, Oval, Stone Stopper, 2 1/2 In. 345.00
Snuff, Glass, Yellow Olive, Tooled Mouth, 1850-1870, 7 3/4 In. 225.00
Snuff, Ivory, Man On Horseback, Boy, Calligraphy, Flattened Oval, Chinese 230.00
Snuff, Ivory, Whaling Ship, Pear Shape, Stopper, c.1900, 2 3/8 In. 35.00
Snuff, Jade, Black & White, Figural Landscape, Pink Quartz Stopper, 2 1/4 In. 4140.00
Snuff, Jade, Celadon, Goldfish, Carved Scales & Fins, 19th Century 230.00
Snuff, Jade, White, Lotus & Beetle, Pear Form, Glass Stopper, 2 1/4 In. 230.00
Snuff, Jade, White, Rectangular, Quartz Stopper, 2 3/8 In. 520.00
Snuff, Jade, White, Tree & Grotto Carving, Pebble Form, Glass Stopper, 2 3/4 In. 5060.00
Snuff, Jade, Yellow, Dragon, Oval, Jadeite Stopper, 2 3/8 In. 1840.00
Snuff, Jade, Yellow, Mask, Mock Handles, Pear Form, Jadeite Stopper, 2 3/8 In. 1380.00
Snuff, Jadite, Leaves & Blossoms, Peach Form, Agate Stopper, 2 In. 635.00
Snuff, Lapis Lazuli, White Jade, Urn, Stopper, 1 7/8 In. 230.00
Snuff, Malachite, Leaping Carp With Waves, Stopper, 20th Century, 3 In. 115.00
Snuff, Milk Glass, Butterfly & Flower, Jadite Stopper, 2 3/8 In. 1265.00
Snuff, Milk Glass, Oval, Glass Stopper, 2 1/2 In. 460.00
Snuff, Mother-Of-Pearl, Stopper, Oval, 20th Century, 2 In. 40.00
Snuff, Palm Nut, Inlaid Mongolian, Coral, Turquoise, Stopper, 2 3/4 In. 230.00
Snuff, Porcelain, Blue, Fisherman On Rock, Cylinder, Stopper, 19th Century, 2 3/8 In. ... 160.00
Snuff, Porcelain, Blue, White, Landscape, 6 Characters, Yung Cheng, c.1800, 2 1/2 In. ... 160.00
Snuff, Porcelain, Carp & Sea Grass, Spade Form, Stopper, 19th Century, 1 1/4 In. 29.00
Snuff, Porcelain, Enameled, Magpie, Cylindrical, Amethyst Stopper, 1800s, 3 1/8 In. 575.00
Snuff, Porcelain, Erotic Figures, Cylindrical, Ceramic Stopper, Tao Kuang, 2 3/8 In. 230.00
Snuff, Porcelain, Figural Landscape, Red & Blue, Cylindrical, Coral Stopper, 3 1/2 In. ... 200.00
Snuff, Porcelain, Figural, 4 Characters, Red, Blue, Stopper, 19th Century, 2 3/8 In. 115.00
Snuff, Porcelain, Flask Form, Figural Medallions, Flower Ground, Agate Stopper, 2 1/8 In. 230.00
Snuff, Porcelain, Grasshopper, Flowers, Ivory Stopper, c.1900, 3 1/4 In. 230.00
Snuff, Porcelain, Horsemen, Grooms, Cylindrical, Aventurine Stopper, 3 1/4 In. 430.00
Snuff, Porcelain, Rooster, Songbird Landscape, Baluster, Tao Juang, 2 3/4 In. 288.00
Snuff, Porcelain, Stylized Lotus, Spearhead Lappet Border, Ch'ien Lung, 3 In. 635.00
Snuff, Porcelain, Yellow, Dragon, Stone Stopper, Purse Shape, 2 5/8 In. 345.00

Snuff, Pottery, Landscape, Pilgrim Flask Form, Agate Stopper, 2 In. 201.00
Snuff, Rock Crystal, Painted Inside, River Landscape, Signed, Wang, 20th Century 259.00
Snuff, Tourmaline, Pink, Bats & Dragon, Amethyst Stopper, 2 1/2 In. 1150.00
Snuff, Turquoise, Monkeys & Vines, Double Gourd Form, Stopper, 3 In. 345.00
Snuff, Wood, Carved, Renaissance Style, Oval, Hinged Lid, 3 x 7 x 2 1/2 In. 633.00
Snuff, Yellow Green, Beveled Corners, Tooled Flare Mouth, Pontil, 1780-1840, 7 In. 500.00
Soaky, Wolfman, Frankenstein, Mummy & Creature, Colgate-Palmolive, 1964 .... 200.00
Soap, Purex, Mr. Jinx, Pixie, Dixie, Vinyl, c.1960, 9 3/4 In. 25.00
Soda, Bay City Soda Water Co., S.F., Embossed Star, Cobalt Blue, Blob Top, 7 1/4 In. 145.00
Soda, C. Cleminshaw, Troy, N.Y., Sapphire Blue, Applied Mouth, IP, 7 In. 336.00
Soda, Carl H. Schultz, Pat. May 1868, New York, Green, Applied Blob Top, 6 3/4 In. 90.00
Soda, Champagne Mead, Aqua, 8-Sided, Blob Top, 7 3/8 In. 44.00
Soda, Congress & Empire Spring Co., Saratoga, N.Y., Dark Green, Pt. 44.00
Soda, Crump & Fox Superior, Bernardston, Mass, Blue Green, Blob Top, IP, 7 1/4 In. ... 1120.00
Soda, Daniel Ritter, Allentown, Pa., Medium Amber, Hutchinson, Tooled Mouth, 6 3/8 In. 530.00
Soda, Distilled Soda Water Of Alaska, Hutchinson, Aqua, 7 1/4 In. 130.00
Soda, Dixon & Carson, 41 Walker St., N.Y., Blue Green, Smooth Base, 6 7/8 In. 150.00
Soda, Dr. Cotton & Co., Barbados, Green, Torpedo, England, 1880-1910, 8 1/2 In. 336.00
Soda, E.Y. Cronk Root Beer, Chicago, Cobalt Blue, Monogram, 1870-1880, 7 3/8 In. 258.00
Soda, Emerald Green, Torpedo Shape, Applied Mouth, c.1855, 7 3/4 In. 2128.00
Soda, Gaffe's Potash, Cobalt Blue, Round Base, Applied Top, England, 9 In. 385.00
Soda, George Bibbey & Co., Glen Falls, N.Y., Emerald Green, 1870-1880, 10 In. 476.00
Soda, Geyser Spring, Saratoga Springs, N.Y., Blue Aqua, Double Collar Mouth, Qt. 125.00
Soda, Guilford Mineral, Guilford, Vt., Emerald Green, Double Collar, 1870-1880, Qt. ... 45.00
Soda, I. Sutton & Co., Covington, Ky, 12-Sided, Cobalt Blue, 1855-1865, 8 1/2 In. 840.00
Soda, J. Harvey & Co., Providence, R.I., H, Dark Green, Blob Top, 7 In. 209.00
Soda, J.A. Lomax, Medicated Aerated Waters, Green, Round Base, Blob Top, 9 In. .... /... 198.00
Soda, J.W. Harris, New Haven, Conn., Sapphire Blue, Applied Mouth, 7 1/2 In. 365.00
Soda, James Ray Ginger Ale, Savannah, Geo., Cobalt Blue, Applied Mouth, 7 7/8 In. 365.00
Soda, John Ryan, Excelsior Ginger Ale, Yellow Amber, 7 1/2 In. 336.00
Soda, Luke Beard, Blue Treen, Tenpin Shape, Applied Mouth, Pontil, 7 In. 160.00
Soda, M. McCormack's Celebrated Ginger Ale, Nashville, Tenn., Cobalt Blue, 8 1/8 In. .. 390.00
Soda, M.T. Crawford, Hartford, Conn., Teal Blue, Blob Top, Pontil, 1845-1855, 7 1/2 In. . 420.00
Soda, Neptune Glassworks, Apple Green, Sloping Blob Top, Pontil, 7 1/4 In. 505.00
Soda, Paul Jeenicke, San Jose, Amber, Hutchinson, 6 3/4 In. 1650.00
Soda, R.C. & T., New York, Blue Green, Embossed, Pontil, 1845-1855, 6 5/8 In. 168.00
Soda, S.S. Knickerbocker, Cobalt Blue, 8-Sided, Blob Top, 8 In. 448.00
Soda, Saratoga High Rock Spring, N.Y., Emerald Green, Double Collar, 1865-1875, Pt. ... 560.00
Soda, Saratoga Red Spring, Blue Green, Double Collar, 1865-1875, Pt. 125.00
Soda, Seitz & Bro., Easton, Pa., Teal Blue, Sloping Shoulders, Double Collar, 7 1/4 In.... 45.00
Soda, Stoddard Type, Yellow Olive Amber, Tenpin Shape, 7 7/8 In. 365.00
Soda, Union Glass Works, Philadelphia, Teal Blue, Blob Type Mouth, 7 1/4 In. 896.00
Soda, W. Dean, Newark, N.J., Blue Aqua, Blob Top, Iron Pontil, 6 3/4 In. 135.00
Soda, W.H. Burt, San Francisco, Green, Applied Blob Top, Graphite Pontil, 7 3/8 In. 120.00
Soda, W.H.H., Chicago, Cobalt Blue, Blob Top, Iron Pontil, 7 1/2 In. 146.00
Soda, W.P. Knickerbocker, Cobalt Blue, 10-Sided, Blob Top, Iron Pontil, 7 1/4 In. 1100.00
Soda, Wm. A. Carpenter's, Hudson, N.Y., Emerald Green, 8-Sided, 1845-1855, 7 In. 670.00
Stoneware, Jug, Keystone Rye, Tan, Cream, Painted Flowers, Gold Letters 65.00
Stoneware, Jug, New England Tomato Relish, Cream, Dark Brown Glaze, 1890, 6 3/4 In. 146.00
Syrup, Lemon Life, Glass, John Graf., 11 3/4 x 3 1/4 In. 415.00
Target Ball, Amber, Ribbed, 2-Piece Mold, 2 3/4 In. 165.00
Target Ball, Amber, Sheared Mouth, 1880-1900, 2 5/8 In. 5700.00
Target Ball, Bogardus, Cobalt Blue, Diamond, c.1890, 2 5/8 In. 1120.00
Target Ball, Bogardus, Pat'd Apr 10 1877, Amber, Hobnail, Sheared Mouth, 2 5/8 In. .. 3360.00
Target Ball, Bogardus, Pat'd Apr 10 1877, Yellow Amber, Sheared Mouth, 2 5/8 In. 670.00
Target Ball, Cobalt Blue, 7 Horizontal Bands, Sheared Mouth, 2 5/8 In. 505.00
Target Ball, Cobalt Blue, Square Pattern, Sheared & Flared Lip, 1880-1900, 2 5/8 In. 160.00
Target Ball, Composite, Patented Sept 3, 1879, March 3, 1880, Lockport, N.Y., 2 3/4 In. . 476.00
Target Ball, Diamond, Amber, Sheared Mouth, Germany, 1880-1900, 2 5/8 In. 530.00
Target Ball, Diamond, Apricot Puce, Sheared & Ground Mouth, 2 5/8 In. 225.00
Target Ball, Diamond, Cobalt Blue, 2 Circular Panels, FBH, Australia, 2 5/8 In. 896.00
Target Ball, Diamond, Cobalt Blue, Blank Center Band, Flared Mouth, France, 2 5/8 In. . 100.00
Target Ball, E. Jones Gunmaker, Backburn Lanc, Cobalt Blue, England, c.1890, 2 3/4 In. . 280.00

Target Ball, For Hockey's Patent Trap, Medium Green, England, 1880, 2 1/2 In. 1905.00
Target Ball, Glashutten Dr. A. Frank, Yellow Olive, Diamond, 1880, 2 5/8 In. 785.00
Target Ball, Glashutten F.W. Otte Jun Charlottenburg, Diamond, 2 5/8 In. 1065.00
Target Ball, Gold Amber, 3-Piece Mold Blown, c.1890, 2 5/8 In. 190.00
Target Ball, Ira Paine's, Pat. Oct. 23 1877, Yellow Amber, Sheared Mouth, 2 5/8 In. 392.00
Target Ball, Man, Shooting, Diamond, Purple Amethyst, England, 1880, 2 5/8 In. 672.00
Target Ball, Man, Shooting, Diamond, Purple Amethyst, Sheared Mouth, 2 3/4 In. 728.00
Target Ball, Man, Shooting, Moss Green, Diamond, Sheared Mouth, 2 5/8 In. 670.00
Target Ball, N.B. Glass Works, Perth, Pale Aqua, Diamond, 1880-1900, 2 5/8 In. 110.00
Target Ball, N.B. Glass Works, Perth, Sapphire Blue, Diamond, 1880-1900, 2 5/8 In. 135.00
Target Ball, Olive Green, Sheared Mouth, 3-Piece Mold, 1880-1895, 2 5/8 In. 728.00
Target Ball, Sapphire Blue, Squares, England, 1880-1900, 2 5/8 In. 125.00
Target Ball, Sheared Mouth, 1880-1900, 2 5/8 In. 365.00
Target Ball, Stacey & Co., London, Cobalt Blue, Squares, Sheared Mouth, 2 5/8 In. 730.00
Target Ball, W.W. Greeners, St. Marys Works, Cobalt Blue, Diamond, c.1890, 2 5/8 In. . . . 280.00
Target Ball, Yellow Amber, 5-Piece Mold, Sheared Mouth, 1880-1900, 2 5/8 In. 179.00
Target Ball, Yellow Amber, Stars & Bars, Sheared Mouth, 1880 1900, 2 5/8 In. 3360.00
Tonic, Hall's Wine, Light Amber, Tooled Top, Embossed Key Hole, Free Sample, 6 In. . . . 66.00
Tonic, Highland Bitters & Scotch, Barrel, Yellow Amber, 9 5/8 In. 2128.00
Tonic, Primley's Iron & Wahoo, Yellow, Amber, Square, Applied Mouth, 8 5/8 In. 275.00
Tonic, Reeds Gilt 1878 Edge, Rectangular, Amber, 8 5/8 In. 50.00
Whiskey, AAA Old Valley, Amber, Applied Single Roll Collar 1760.00
Whiskey, Albro & Bro's., 156 Bowery, N.Y., Olive Amber, Strap Side, Qt. 134.00
Whiskey, Auld Lang Syne, Weideman Company, 3 Men, Poem, Jug, 7 3/4 In. 90.00
Whiskey, Backbar, Guckenheimer Rye Whiskey Nothing Better, Embossed, Enamel 140.00
Whiskey, Backbar, Old Kirk A.P. Hotaling & Co, Original Stopper, Gold Paint 200.00
Whiskey, Backbar, Pittsburgh, Canary, 8 Panels, Bulbous Lip, Slide Stopper, 10 3/8 In. . . . 1540.00
Whiskey, Backbar, Red Amber, Recessed, Shield Shaped Label, c.1865, Qt., 11 1/2 In. . . . 189.00
Whiskey, Chestnut Grove, Embossed Seal, Amber, Applied Mouth, 1840-1860, 8 7/8 In. . . 258.00
Whiskey, Deerfoot Rye, Cylinder, Scallops, 10 1/2 In. 110.00
Whiskey, Durham, Standing Deer, Orange Amber, 11 1/2 In. 840.00
Whiskey, Fine Old Bourbon Whiskey, Philadelphia, Cylinder, Hand Cut, Flutes, 10 1/2 In. 125.00
Whiskey, Griffith Hyatt & Co., Flattened Label, Amber, Applied Handle, 7 1/2 In. 840.00
Whiskey, H. Brickwedel & Co., 208 & 210 Front St., S.F., Yellow Amber, Pt. 605.00
Whiskey, H.A. Graef's Son, Canteen, N.Y., Olive, Applied Square Collar, 6 5/8 In. 235.00
Whiskey, Hilbert Bros., Wine & Liquor Merchants, S.F., Red Amber, 1892-1895, 12 In. . . . 7700.00
Whiskey, I.W. Harper Gold Medal, Pottery, Blue Green Glaze, Square, Embossed Ropes . . 79.00
Whiskey, J.F. Cutter Extra Old Bourbon Trademark, Amber, Rolled Collar, Pt. 1980.00
Whiskey, J.H. Cutter, O.K. Whiskey, Orange Amber, Barrel, Glop Top, 11 7/8 In. 180.00
Whiskey, Jameson's Old Irish Whiskey Dublin Trademark, Brown, Tan, Jug, 2 Dragons . . 159.00
Whiskey, Jesse Moore & Co., Louisville, Ky., Amber, Fifth 66.00
Whiskey, Jesse Moore-Hunt Co., San Francisco, Oxblood Red, Fifth 350.00
Whiskey, Log Cabin, Red Amber, 6 7/8 In. 215.00
Whiskey, M. Rothenberg & Co., Game Cock, 1/2 Pt. 99.00
Whiskey, Meredith's Diamond Club Pure Rye, Jug, White China, 7 3/8 In. 79.00
Whiskey, Michael B. Wolfs, Schiedam, Aromatic Schnapps, Sloping Collar, Hinge Mold . 285.00
Whiskey, Millers Extra, E. Martin & Co., Green, 8 In. 1430.00
Whiskey, Mohawk Pure Rye, Feb. 11 1868, Figural, Indian Queen, Gold Amber, 12 In. . . . 3640.00
Whiskey, Old Continental, Yellow Amber, Applied Mouth, 1776, 9 1/2 In. 4760.00
Whiskey, Old Gilt Edge OK Bourbon, Wichman & Lutgen, Embossed Crown, Fifth 35.00
Whiskey, Old Linwood Whiskey, Cylinder, Flutes, 11 In. 100.00
Whiskey, Phoenix Old Bourbon, Naber, Alfs & Brune, S.F., Bird, Amber, 1880-1895, Fifth 1430.00
Whiskey, Pure Old Corn, Figural, Pig, Pottery, Cream, Brown Glaze Spots, 8 1/2 In. 170.00
Whiskey, Simmond's Nabob Pure Ky. Bourbon, Amber, 10 3/4 In. 1430.00
Whiskey, Thos. Taylor & Co. Importers, Virginia, NV, Amber, 1870-1880, 11 3/4 In. 5500.00
Whiskey, Udolpho Wolfe's Aromatic Schnapps, Green, Double Collar, Ball Pontil 175.00
Whiskey, Urse Beata Locke's Kilbeggan Irish Whiskey John Locke & Co. Ld., Jug 35.00
Whiskey, Voldner's Aromatic Schnapps, Yellow Olive Green, Applied Mouth, 10 In. 125.00
Whiskey, Wharton's, 1850, Chestnut Grove, Amber, Flask, 5 1/4 In. 235.00
Whiskey, Wharton's, Chestnut Grove, Cobalt Blue, Applied Mouth, 5 1/4 In. 365.00
Whiskey, Wise's Old Irish, Cream, Brown Glaze, Maroon Transfer, Handle, Jug, 7 3/8 In. . 310.00
Whiskey, Wm. H. Spears & Co., Old Pioneer Whiskey, Amber, Applied Top, Fifth 7150.00
Wine, Sake, China Incident War, Cherry Blossoms, Flag, Star, c.1930s, 5 1/2 In. 80.00

Zanesville, 24 Ribs, Swirled To Left, Gold Amber, Globular, Flat Collar, 7 3/4 In. 770.00
Zanesville, 24 Swirled Ribs, Gold Amber, Globular, Folded Over Lip, 8 1/4 In. 770.00

BOTTLE CAPS for milk bottles are the printed cardboard caps used during the past 85 years. Unusual mottoes, graphics, and caps from dairies that are out of business bring the highest prices.

Charles Lindbergh, First Non Stop Flight Across The Atlantic Ocean, 1927 . . . . 20.00
DeLaval Co., Seasons Greetings, Holly Leaves, Berries, Tree, Bow 19.00
Harold Radley, Angelica, N.Y. 9.50
Irvin Conder Dairy, Bloomington, In., Monroe County 16.00
Racine, Meigs County, Ohio, 1930-1940 . . . . 19.00

BOTTLE OPENERS are needed to open many bottles. As soon as the commercial bottle was invented, the opener to be used with the new types of closures became a necessity. Many types of bottle openers can be found, most dating from the twentieth century. Collectors prize advertising and comic openers.

Alligator, Aluminum 3.00
Ashtray, Cast Iron, Elephant, Figural, 3 In. 35.00
Bear Head, Open Mouth, Iron 24.00
Big Boys Saloon, Nickel Over Steel, Royalton, Illinois, 3 In. 85.00
Billy Goat, Cast Iron 2.00
Bird, Dodo, Aluminum 2.00
Black Boy & Alligator, Cast Iron, c.1940, 2 3/4 In. 145.00
Black Man, Face, Cast Iron, Wilton, c.1940, 4 1/2 x 3 3/4 In. 135.00
Black Man, Winking, Wham-Ee, Brass, c.1940, 4 In. 225.00
Boot, Corkscrew Inside, Sterling, 4 In. 175.00
Bottle, Figural, Wylres Holland Brand Beer, Plastic 5.00
Cactus Drunk, Cowboy & Cactus, Cast Iron 50.00
Dacro, Handy Way To Remove Dacro Milk Caps 5.00
Dog, Black, Metal, Scott Products, Newark, N.J., 5 x 2 1/4 x 4 In. 85.00
Dog, Brown, Metal, Scott Products, Newark, N.J., 6 1/2 x 2 x 3 In. 85.00
Dog, Bulldog, Open Mouth, Black, Cast Iron 10.00
Dog, Setter, Aluminum 2.00
Don's Service Station, Kingston, Ill., Plastic, 6 In. . . . . Illus 6.00
Donkey, Seated, Gold Painted, 3 3/4 x 3 1/2 In. 55.00
Donkey, Timberjack Machines Ltd., Brass 30.00
Duck Head, Brass, 4 x 3 1/4 In. 22.00
Elephant, Pink, Cast Iron, c.1960, 3 1/2 In. 20.00
Elephant, Trunk Up, Hamilton, Cast Iron 45.00
Fish, Largemouth Bass, Metal, Scott Products, c.1970, 3 7/8 x 2 1/4 x 6 1/4 In. 110.00
Fish, Rainbow Trout, Metal, Scott Prod Inc, Newark, N.J., 2 x 4 1/2 In. 95.00
Fisherman, Hollow Mold, Cast Iron 20.00
Foundryman, Aluminum 2.00
Fox, Metal, Scott Products Inc., Newark, N.J., c.1970, 3 x 5 In. 110.00
Goat, Seated, Cast Iron 20.00
Goose, Metal, Scott Products Inc., Newark, N.J., c.1970, 4 1/4 x 5 1/2 In. 85.00
Hand, Aluminum, c.1960, 8 In. 15.00
Henninger Beer, Globe, Black, Imported German Beer 16.00
Leg, Brass, 3 In. 25.00
Lobster, Cast Iron, Red, Black, Freeport, Maine, 3 1/2 In. 36.00
Mallard Duck, Metal, Scott Products, Green Head, Yellow Bill, c.1970, 5 3/4 In. 75.00
Marlboro, Adventure Team Tag & Key Ring, Box, 1 3/4 In. 7.00
Monkey, Seated, Aluminum 2.00
Mule, Cast Iron, c.1930, 3 In. 70.00

Bottle Opener, Don's Service Station,
Kingston, Ill., Plastic, 6 In.

Have an inventory of your collections and adequate insurance.

Norton Jack, Cast Iron 20.00
Nude, Arms Up, Holding Opener, Brass, Box 15.00
Orange, Figural, Magnetic, Wood, Metal, Florida, 5 3/4 In. 22.00
Parrot, Can Punch, Cast Iron 28.00
Parrot, Corkscrew, Cast Iron 5.00
Parrot, Iron, Art Deco, Painted, Blue, Gold, Orange, Black, 3 1/2 In. 250.00
Parrot, On Perch, Cast Iron, John Wright, 3 3/8 x 1 3/4 x 5 1/2 In. 75.00
Pelican, Cast Iron, Wilton Products 50.00
Pheasant, Cast Iron 2.00
Pretzel, Cast Iron, Brown, White Dots, 3 1/2 In. 88.00
Queen Elizabeth II, Key Fob, Blue, 1 3/4 x 2 1/2 In. 7.50
Rooster, Cast Iron, Red, Yellow, Black, 3 1/4 In. ....85.00 to 110.00
Royal Crown Cola, Better Taste Calls For RC 5.00
Scandinavian Airlines, Plastic, 3 1/2 In. 9.00
Seagull, Cast Iron, Gray, White, Pale Yellow, Black, 3 1/4 In. 55.00
Ship, Excursion Of Steamer Avalon, 4 In. 10.00
Shoe, High Heeled, Aluminum 60.00
Skull, Drink It Here, Not Hereafter, Painted White, Cast Iron, 1930s 145.00
Tennents Lager & Beer, Metal Crown Cork, 3 1/2 In. 4.00

BOXES of all kinds are collected. They were made of thin strips of
inlaid wood, metal, tortoiseshell, embroidery, or other material.
Additional boxes may be listed in other sections, such as Advertising,
Ivory, Shaker, Tinware, and various Porcelain categories. Tea Caddies
are listed in their own category.

Ballot, Fraternal, Walnut, Turned Wood Handle, 16 In. 127.00
Ballot, Softwood, Paint, Chamfered Peaked Top, 2 Drawers, Clay Marbles, 7 3/4 In. 225.00
Band, Wallpaper Covered, Blue Ground, Top Hat Design, 9 1/4 x 14 1/2 x 12 1/2 In. 578.00
Band, Wallpaper Covered, Blue, Tan Flowers, Jesse Baker, Phila., Oval, 10 x 14 x 11 In. .. 250.00
Band, Wallpaper Covered, Blue, Urns, Flowers, Green, Red, Pink, Oval, 10 x 7 In. 620.00
Band, Wallpaper Covered, Green Damask Pattern, 19th Century, 10 x 16 x 12 In. 115.00
Band, Wallpaper Covered, Hannah Davis, Jaffrey, N.H., c.1844, 8 x 12 x 9 In. 690.00
Band, Wallpaper Covered, Squirrels, Stag, Hounds, Label, Hannah Davis, Jaffrey, N.H. ... 4406.00
Band, Wallpaper Covered, Yellow Ground, Green Leaves, Cover, 9 x 6 1/2 In. 825.00
Band, Wood, Red & Black, Flower Baskets, Light Rays, Kidney-Shape Panels, 14 x 10 In. 664.00
Bible, Flowers, Leaves, Iron Strap Hinges, 18th Century, 6 1/2 x 13 3/4 x 9 1/2 In. 305.00
Bible, Oak, Carved Flowers, Circles, Scrolls, Scalloped Iron Binding, Stand, 27 In. 495.00
Bible, Oak, Dovetailed, Blue, Birds, Heart Wreath, Red Bow, Tulips, 18 x 15 x 6 In. 990.00
Bible, Pine, Slant Lid, Carved Scrolls & Leaves, Jacobean Style, 15 x 11 x 24 In. 110.00
Bible, Stuart, Oak, Carved, 17th Century Design, 28 x 18 In. 200.00
Blanket, Lift Top, Green Paint, Bootjack Ends, American, 44 x 18 In. 776.00
Blanket, Pine, Gray Paint, 15 x 43 x 18 In. 230.00
Bonbonniere, 18K Gold, Enamel, Micromosaic, Spirals, Austria, 20th Century, 2 3/4 In. . 2270.00
Book Form, Bird's-Eye, Tiger Maple, Pinstripe Border, Hex Design, Eagles, 6 x 4 In. 705.00
Book Form, Painted, Binding Slides Out, Early 19th Century, 13 x 9 x 3 In. 550.00
Brass, Iron Pyrite, Footed, 3 x 5 x 2 In. 175.00
Brass, Malachite, Victorian, Rectangular, Leaf Engraved Case, 5 3/4 x 8 x 4 In. 598.00
Brass, Wood, Slant Front, Rampant Lions, Eagle, Ladies Head Columns, 21 x 30 x 18 In. .. 405.00
Bride's, Bentwood, Oval, Cream Ground, Polychrome Flowers, 6 1/2 x 10 x 16 1/2 In. 350.00
Bride's, Bentwood, Polychrome, Decorated, Continental, Early 19th Century, 7 x 19 In. .. 920.00
Bride's, Painted, Bridge, Flower Wreath, Sun, German Verse, 17 In. 1100.00
Bride's, Pennsylvania Dutch, Red, Green Bands, Yellow Flowers, 12 x 18 x 7 In. 770.00
Burl, William & Mary Style, Inlaid, Secret Drawer, Ball Feet, 15 x 10 In. 1645.00
Burl Veneer, Zigzag, Banded, Inland, Hinged Lid, 4 x 10 x 6 1/2 In. 60.00
Candle, Curly Maple, Dark Stain, Ivory Inlay, Lid Carving, Matthesiee, Pa., 12 x 2 1/4 In. 19800.00
Candle, Mahogany, Inlay, Slant Lid, Geometric Border, England, c.1810, 14 3/4 In. 205.00
Candle, Pennsylvania Pine, Slide Lid, Dovetailed, 10 x 9 x 21 In. 475.00
Candle, Slide Lid, Painted, Blue, 19th Century, 4 x 10 x 4 1/2 In. 720.00
Candle, Softwood, Dovetailed, Flame Grained, Red Flame Paint, 11 x 6 1/2 x 5 1/2 In. ... 20.00
Candle, Softwood, Dovetailed, Slide Lid, Original Red Paint, 4 1/2 x 12 x 6 In. 165.00
Candle, Wall, Mahogany, Tapered Sides, Hinged Lid, Scrolled Crest, 18 1/2 In. 195.00
Candle, Wall, Poplar, Painted, Red, Cutouts, 12 x 7 x 6 In. 275.00
Candle, Wall, Walnut, Dovetailed Front, Scalloped Backboard, Drawer, 10 x 12 1/2 In. ... 340.00

Candle, Wall, Walnut, Poplar, Drawer, Hinged Lid, 14 x 7 1/4 x 8 3/4 In. 578.00
Candle, Walnut, Dovetailed, Chamfered Lid, Handles, Early 1800s, 8 1/2 x 6 In. 192.00
Candle, Walnut, Dovetailed, Slide Lid, Flared Molded Base, 1 1/2 x 4 3/4 x 2 In. 300.00
Candle, Walnut, Lap Joint Construction, Early 1800s, 11 x 9 1/4 x 4 3/4 In. 310.00
Candle, Walnut, Oak, Dovetailed, Slide Lid, 17 x 6 In. 230.00
Candle, Wood, Green Paint, Yellow Star & Bands, Inscribed S.A. Perry, 4 x 11 x 6 In. . . . 518.00
Candy, Figural, George Washington On Horse, Germany, c.1900, 13 In., 5 Piece 1200.00
Card, Dice, Cocktail, Exclusive Playing Card Co., Dice Set, Extra Stirrer, 8 1/4 In. 85.00
Cartridge, Silver, Wood Block, 21 Holes, Prussia, 18th Century 1850.00
Casket, Jewel, Brass Band, Calamander, Brass Plaque, 19th Century, 10 x 7 1/2 In. 575.00
Casket, Sandalwood, Hindu Images, India, 19th Century, 12 1/2 x 17 x 12 In. 920.00
Cherry, Dovetailed, Double Lid, Molded Base, Turned Feet, 14 x 13 In. 366.00
Cherry, Dovetailed, Slide Lid, Early 19th Century, 4 1/4 x 5 1/2 x 9 1/2 In. 110.00
Chest, Lift Top, Pigskin, Brass, Relief Rondels Of Bats, Bamboo, Chinese, 16 x 32 In. . . . 345.00
Chestnut, Open, 2 Compartments, Hanging Loop, 14 x 11 1/2 x 6 3/4 In. 235.00
Cigarette, Adolf Hitler Face, Bronzed, Hinged, Wood Lined, Pre 1934 . . . . 403.00
Cigarette, Benson & Hedges, Presentation, Silver, Cut Glass, c.1980, 9 3/4 In. 896.00
Cigarette, Half Log Shape, Bear Finial, OrnaWood USA, Foil Sticker, 2 x 4 1/2 In. 14.00
Coffer, Rosewood, Brass Scrolling, Lift-Out Tray, Inset Handles, 7 x 13 In. 690.00
Copper, Patina, Arts & Crafts, 6 x 2 In. 81.00
Cover, Bail Carrier, C.H. Slocum & Son, Orient, Iowa, 13 1/2 x 12 x 11 In. 275.00
Cover, Enameled Flowers, Leaves, Silver Filigree, Jeweled, 4 x 3 1/2 In. 518.00
Cover, Enameled, Red, Green, 8 Sides, Gold Design, France, 2 1/4 In. 259.00
Cover, Flowers, Enameled, Jeweled, Silver Filigree, Gilt Interior, Triangular, 3 x 2 1/2 In. . 345.00
Cowrie Shell, English Silver, Natural Shell Form, 19th Century, 3 1/8 In. 460.00
Curse, Brass, Cylindrical, Coin Slot, Scalloped Ends, Handle, England, 6 3/4 x 7 In. 440.00
Cutlery, Georgian, Mahogany, Urn Shape, Dome Top, Herringbone Inlay, 26 In., Pair 4406.00
Cutlery, Mahogany, Dovetailed, Whale's Tail Carvings, 19th Century 978.00
Cutlery, Mahogany, Inlay, Silver Detail, c.1780, 15 7/16 x 9 x 12 In., Pair 4780.00
Cutlery, Pine, Canted & Dovetailed Sides, Handle, Mt. Lebanon, N.Y., c.1840, 6 1/2 In. . . 690.00
Cutlery, Red Paint, Divided Interior, Cutout Handle 110.00
Cutlery, Rosewood, Lift Top, 19th Century, 2 x 13 x 9 In. 140.00
Cutlery, Walnut, Dovetailed, Shaped Center Divider, Cutout Handle, 15 x 10 In. 236.00
Desk, Brass Mounted, Elm, Engraved, Russia, 19th Century, 41/2 x 8 1/2 x 6 In. 290.00
Desk, Bronze, Onyx Cover, 2 Bronze Dogs, Early 20th Century, 4 3/4 x 3 3/4 x 6 1/2 In. . 240.00
Desk, Ebonized Wood, Oblong, Slide Lid, East India, 19th Century, 2 x 7 x 4 In. 92.00
Desk, Hardwood, Quill, Inlaid, Oblong, East India, 19th Century, 2 3/4 x 8 1/4 x 6 1/2 In. 230.00
Desk, Mahogany, Brass Bound, N. Middleton, Newcastle St., London, 7 x 10 x 20 In. 345.00
Desk, Mahogany, Brass Corner Mounts, Side Handles, Fitted Interior, 21 x 11 In. 355.00
Desk, Mahogany, Brass Mounted, Campaign Style, 19th Century, 4 x 11 x 4 1/2 In. 690.00
Desk, Marquetry, Rosewood, Satinwood, Mother-Of-Pearl, England, 4 x 10 1/2 x 7 1/2 In. 230.00
Desk, Pine, Lid Attached, Interior Hinge, Dovetailed Paper Holder, Drawer, 5 1/2 In. 9775.00
Desk, Quill, Bone Inlaid, Ebonized Wood, East India, 19th Century, 5 1/4 x 12 x 8 1/2 In. 805.00
Desk, Quill, Ebonized Wood, Oblong, Slide Lid, East Indian, c.1900, 2 x 6 3/4 x 4 In. 200.00
Desk, Regency, Penwork, Fruitwood, Florentine Papers, 4 x 12 1/2 x 11 In. 980.00
Desk, Rosewood, Brass Inlay, Lined, Brass Feet, 19th Century, 5 3/4 x 10 3/4 x 7 3/4 In. . . 316.00
Desk, Satinwood, Ebonized Trim, Pull-Out Front, Top Handle, Pen Rests, 11 x 13 x 9 In. . 715.00
Ditty, Wood, Carved, Painted, Cover, Lapped Bands, 19th Century, 3 5/8 x 7 3/8 In. 1530.00
Ditty, Wood, Painted, Cover, Lapped Bands, Yellow Compass Star, 3 1/8 x 7 3/4 In. 1060.00
Document, Leather Covered, Brass Tacks, Bail Handle Lid, James Riley, 5 x 10 In. 90.00
Document, Lift Top, Grain Painted, American, 19th Century, 9 1/2 x 21 In. 175.00
Document, Mahogany, Brass Corners, Shield, Hinged Lid, Fall Front, 14 3/4 x 10 In. 380.00
Document, Painted, Church, Dark Background, 19th Century 5500.00
Document, Painted, Square, Semicircles, Brass Handle, Brass Hinges, 5 1/4 x 9 1/2 In. . . 1440.00
Document, Pine, Dovetailed, Hinged Lid, Painted Blue, 6 3/8 x 13 1/2 x 8 In. 560.00
Document, Pine, Green Paint, Square Nails, Wrought Iron Chain Loop Hasp, 17 x 8 In. . . 275.00
Document, Rosewood, Regency, Inlaid Brass Initials, Paper Lining, 7 x 17 1/2 x 11 In. . . . 460.00
Document, Walnut, Cherry, Gold, Black, Tulips, W.F. Abram, 12 x 7 x 5 1/4 In. 470.00
Document, Walnut, Dovetailed, Iron Handle, Divided Interior, 18 In. 35.00
Dome Top, Green, Mustard, Initials, RVG, Iron Clasp, Hinges, 8 x 18 x 9 1/2 In. 635.00
Dome Top, Paint Decorated, Pink Birds, Branches, Ivory Background, 4 x 6 1/4 x 4 In. . . . 635.00
Dome Top, Pine, Grain Painted, Faux Bois Red & Black, Early 1800s, 12 x 29 x 13 1/2 In. 325.00
Dome Top, Pine, Poplar, Painted, Pegged Lid, Iron Strap Hinges, c.1808, 17 x 12 x 11 In. . 580.00

Dresser, Brass Bound, Lift Top, Burled Walnut, 2 x 12 x 7 In. 400.00
Dresser, Egyptian Revival, Sarcophagus Shape, Bentwood, Art Deco, c.1925, 12 In. 460.00
Dresser, Porcelain, Poppies, Gilt, Round, Late 19th Century, 3 x 6 In. 25.00
Dressing, Mahogany, 2 Dovetailed Drawers, Ogee Feet, 12 1/2 x 10 1/2 x 8 1/2 In. 420.00
Feed, Lift Top, Painted, Pine, Red Paint, Bootjack Ends, 24 1/2 x 79 x 17 In. 575.00
Feed, Walnut, Dovetailed, Slant Lid, Shoe Type Feet, 49 In. 1350.00
File, Oak, Roll Front, Cubby Holes, Slots, Tambour, Early 20th Century, 12 1/2 In. 60.00
Game, Pine, Carved, Painted, Playing Cards, Dice, Game Names, Pa., c.1900, 9 1/4 In. . . . 3000.00
Glass, Enamel, Flowers & Gilt Scrolls, Rectangular, Canted Corners, Napoleon III, 6 In. . 2115.00
Glove, Burl, Inlaid Nacre Dots On Ebony, Brass Trim, Serpentine Fall Front, 3 x 12 In. . . . 470.00
Glove, Sandalwood, Carved, Pierced, Deities, Flowers, Ducks, 19th Century, 13 1/2 In. . . . 345.00
Glove, Walnut, Veneered, Inlay, 1800s, 2 3/4 x 10 1/2 x 4 In. 150.00
Gold, 14K, Green Stones, 14 Diamonds, Lid, Seaman Schepps, 3 In. 1528.00
Gold, Ivory, Pierced Peach Branch & Butterfly Design, Tortoiseshell Base, 2 3/4 In. 1150.00
Heart Shape, Ladies & Cupid On Lid, Porcelain, Late 1800s, 3 1/2 x 6 1/4 x 7 In. 50.00
Heart Shape, Wallpaper Covered, Flowers, Fauna, Late 18th Century, 4 1/2 x 8 x 7 In. . . . 480.00
Horn Veneer, Ivory Straps, Carved, Pierced, Engraved Fruit, Bone Paw Feet, 3 x 8 x 6 In. 220.00
Humidor, Oak, Scrolled Brass Inlay, Cylindrical, Hinged Lid, 6 1/4 In. 235.00
Iron, Cover, Hexagonal, Seijo, Signed, Japan, 19th Century, 4 In. 1530.00
Iron, Hammered, Arts & Crafts, Applied Hinges, Handle, 2 Keys, 8 1/2 x 3 1/2 In. 430.00
Jewelry, Bird's-Eye & Curly Maple, Ring Turned Corner Posts, 2 Compartments, 7 In. . . . 825.00
Jewelry, Bone, Steel Tesserae, Fruitwood Inlay, Anglo Egyptian, c.1920, 3 x 8 x 6 In. 635.00
Jewelry, Burl Walnut, Hinged Lid, Spring-Loaded Drawer, Brass Trim, 7 x 12 In. 460.00
Jewelry, Casket, Brass Mounted, Mahogany, 3 Drawers, c.1900, 12 1/2 x 10 1/2 x 6 In. . . . 315.00
Jewelry, Casket, Ebony, Brass Inlaid, Ball Feet, 19th Century, 4 1/4 x 8 1/2 x 5 In. 575.00
Jewelry, Casket, Mahogany, Gilt, Ivory, Brass Mounted, 19th Century, 6 1/4 x 9 x 7 In. . . 520.00
Jewelry, Diamond Cut Crystal, Oval Cylindrical, Hinged, Bronze Mounted, 7 In. 646.00
Jewelry, Dome Top, Tortoiseshell, Silver, Engraved Zigzags, Griffons On Corners, 5 In. . . 770.00
Jewelry, Edwardian, Bird's-Eye Maple, Marquetry Borders, c.1900, 3 1/2 x 12 In. 259.00
Jewelry, Mahogany, Ebony & Rosewood Trompe L'Oeil Cube Marquetry, 6 x 13 In. 748.00
Jewelry, Malachite, Bronze Dore, Calla Lily & Leaf Mounts, Hinged Lid, Oval, 4 x 5 In. . 930.00
Jewelry, Pietra Dura, Panels, Inlaid Flowers, Chain Border, Guithon Bordeaux, 6 3/4 In. . 2015.00
Jewelry, Regency, Sarcophagus Form, Rosewood, Mother-Of-Pearl, Paw Feet, 4 x 13 In. . 375.00
Jewelry, Rosewood, Brass Feet, Lined, Lift-Out Tray, 19th Century, 6 x 11 x 7 3/4 In. 635.00
Jewelry, Walnut, Carved, Rosette, Fan, Lid Mirror, Whalebone Handles, 10 x 18 x 12 In. . 2350.00
Knife, George III Style, Brass Mounted, Inlaid Mahogany, Late 18th Century, 14 1/2 In. . 575.00
Knife, George III, Mahogany, Inlaid, Sloped Lid, Ogee Bowfront, Fitted Interior, 14 In. . . 440.00
Knife, Georgian Style, Mahogany, Brass Mount, Banded, England, 15 x 8 x 12 In. 1095.00
Knife, Georgian, Mahogany, Banded, Slope Front, Marquetry Shell, 15 x 9 x 12 In. 690.00
Knife, Mahogany, Carved, Vase Shape, Edwardian, c.1900, 34 1/2 x 11 In. 2530.00
Knife, Mahogany, Shaped Front, Sections, 2 Brass Handles, 3 Ball & Claw Feet, 14 x 9 In. 345.00
Knife, Satinwood, Inlaid Mahogany, c.1800, 12 3/4 In. 4600.00
Knife, Satinwood, Olivewood, Inlaid Mahogany, Serpentine, c.1800, 14 In. 575.00
Knife, Urn, Regency Style, Mahogany, Turned Pedestal, c.1910, 24 In., Pair 460.00
Knife Urn, Mahogany, Acorn Finials, Ribbon Inlay, c.1775, 28 In., Pair 5750.00
Lacquer, Birds, Floral, Chamfered Corners, Pierced Handle, 4 Trays, 19 x 14 1/2 x 8 In. . . 175.00
Lacquer, Landscape, Gold, Box, 4 x 6 1/2 In. 1725.00
Lacquer, Wheels, Waves, Tray, Black, Gold, 7 1/2 x 6 In. 1840.00
Letter, Georgian, Mahogany, Gilt, Brass, 19th Century, 22 x 14 x 12 In. 2160.00
Letter, Mahogany, Inlaid, Slanted, Hinged Lid, Interior Sections, c.1880, 7 x 10 x 5 In. . . 230.00
Letter, Oak, Coromandel Carved, 6 Shaped Feet, Figural Lock, Dutch, 1920s, 6 x 16 In. . 2020.00
Letter, Oak, Slant Lid, 2 Doors, Stepped-Down Letter Slot, Drawer, 12 x 11 In. 125.00
Lift Top, Bone Inlay, Hunting Scenes, 1800s, 10 x 17 x 13 In. 660.00
Lift Top, Pine, Modified Compass Rose Inlay, 19th Century, 5 1/2 x 14 x 10 In. 320.00
Lift Top, Wooden, Inlaid, Diamond Shape, 19th Century, 2 1/2 x 10 x 6 1/2 In. 69.00
Mahogany, Carved, Inlaid Exotic Woods, 4-Section Interior, 6 x 13 3/4 x 9 3/4 In. 410.00
Mahogany, Cedar Lined, Brass Inlay, England, Late 19th Century, 5 x 12 1/4 x 10 In. 265.00
Mahogany, Raised Panel, Inlaid Tiger Maple, Green Velvet Interior, Lid Mirror, 7 x 11 In. 325.00
Mahogany, Rectangular, 3 Escutcheons, Drawer, Hinged Lid, 19 3/8 x 13 In. 940.00
Maple, Swing Handles, c.1923, 8 In. 315.00
Marquetry, Wood, Ivory Floral Inlay, Blue Satin Lining, Lock, c.1870, 6 x 13 In. 2300.00
Metal, 4-Footed, Raised Design, Patina, Arts & Crafts, 6 1/2 In. 345.00
Metal, Handwrought, Goberg, Hammered Design, Austria, 6 1/2 x 3 In. 127.00

Mother-Of-Pearl, Inlaid, Round, Insects, Flowers, Indonesia, 13 1/2 x 5 1/4 In. 1555.00
Necessaire, Burlwood Veneer, Line Inlay, Brass Hexagon, Hinged Lid, 12 x 9 x 6 3/4 In. . . 380.00
Necessaire, Calamander, Victorian, Brass Inlaid, 19th Century, 7 1/2 x 12 x 9 1/2 In. 345.00
Oak, Pierced Double Lollipop Back, Rectangular, 19 Century, 16 1/4 In. 206.00
Pantry, Bentwood, Red Wash, Steel Nails, Lacing, H.H.S., Scandanavia, 8 1/2 In. 305.00
Pantry, Cover, Bentwood, Maple, Hickory, Pine, Wallpaper Lined, Iron Tacks, 18 x 9 In. . 56.00
Pantry, Nested, Wood, Lapped, Banded, 2 Green, 1 Brown, 1 White, 4 Piece 705.00
Pantry, Wood, Round, Lapped Construction, Painted Stars On Lid, 1 Within Other, 7 In. . 280.00
Patch, Battersea, Enamel, Naval Engagement Scene, Glorious Victory, 1794, 1 1/2 In. . . . 430.00
Patch, Cover, Enamel Flowers, Blue, Turquoise, Gold Wash Interior, Oval, France, 2 In. . 345.00
Patch, Fruitwood, Painted, Hinged Lid, Black & White Flower Compass, 1 7/8 x 3 In. 59.00
Patch, Glass, Light Amber, Enamel Flowers, 1 1/4 x 2 In. 100.00
Patch, Oval, Enamel, 2 Lovebirds On Lid, Mirrored Interior, Blue Base, 1 3/4 In. 520.00
Patch, Oval, Enamel, Bird In Nest, Jeweled Border, Green Ribbed Base, 1 5/8 In. 375.00
Patch, Oval, Enamel, Pink, Lady Light Foot On Lid, Bilston, 18th Century, 1 5/8 In. 290.00
Patch, Partridge Shooting Scene, Cobalt Blue Base, 19th Century, 2 1/8 In. 460.00
Pill, Fuchi, 14K Gold, Bronze, Potter Mellon, 1 x 7/8 x 1 1/2 In. 250.00
Pill, Lozenge Shape, Silver & Tortoiseshell, 2 In. 150.00
Pine, Dovetailed, Slide Lid, Painted, Blue, Red, White, Orange Tulips, 17 x 10 x 8 1/2 In. 250.00
Pine, Dovetailed, Slide Lid, Painted, Flower Band, Initials, Molded Edges, 18 x 12 x 8 In. 385.00
Pine, Dovetailed, Square Nails, Painted Green, American Eagle Plaque, 7 x 17 x 12 In. . . 385.00
Pine, Grain Painted, Lid, Brass Ring Pull, 19th Century, 3 x 10 1/2 x 6 1/2 In. 235.00
Pine, High Back, Shaped Ends, Shelf, Red Paint, 19th Century, 40 x 17 x 29 1/2 In. 200.00
Pine, Painted, Decoupage, Hinged Lid, Armorial Shield, Ball Feet, 5 x 13 1/2 x 9 1/8 In. . 440.00
Pine, Painted, Dovetailed, Slide Lid, Basket Of Strawberries, 19th Century, 4 x 12 x 8 In. 1880.00
Pine, Painted, Mustard, Wire Hinges, Linear Order, Early 19th Century, 6 x 16 x 8 3/8 In. . 590.00
Pine, Painted, Orange, Slide Lid, Black Eagle, Leaf Outlining, 3 1/2 x 5 x 9 In. 705.00
Pine, Stenciled Stars, Blue, Green, Yellow, Hinged Lid, 19th Century, 5 x 9 In. 355.00
Pipe, Curly Maple, Reddish Stain, Drawer, Scalloped Edge, Crest, 16 x 4 In. 165.00
Pipe, Wall, Stained Finish, Canted Sides, Early 20th Century, 9 1/2 x 4 1/2 x 21 In. 385.00
Pipe, Wood, Painted, Open, Flower Shape Hanger, Drawer, Mid 1800s, 15 x 5 x 4 In. 1795.00
Pipe, Wood, Red Stain, Shaped Rim, Hanging Hole, Drawer, Ring Handle, 18 x 5 In. 4310.00
Pocket Watch, Wood, Carved, Relief Flowers, Ribbed Sides, Velvet Lining, 3 1/2 x 2 In. . 60.00
Poker Chip, Oak, Insert, Chips, Arts & Crafts, 7 x 5 1/2 In. 175.00
Polychrome, Ivory, Shell, Rectangular, Chinese Export, c.1830, 3 3/4 x 3 In. 4945.00
Porcupine Quills, Poplar, Inlaid Baleen Trim & Ivory Dots, 3 1/2 x 6 1/2 x 9 In. 330.00
Powder, Copper Luster Finish, Butterflies, Lid, Marked, 8 x 4 In. 115.00
Puzzle, Mahogany, Slide Lid, Black, Red, Green, 19th Century, 2 x 6 3/4 x 3 7/8 In. 550.00
Quill Work, Birch Bark, Variegated Leaves, Oval, 6 x 4 1/4 x 2 3/4 In. 489.00
Reliquary, Cross Shape, Relief Crucifixion, Relics, 18th Century, 8 3/4 In. 690.00
Rosewood, Etched & Pierced Brass Trim, Arched & Hinged Lid, 3 x 9 x 5 In. 345.00
Rosewood, Marquetry Inlay, Mother-Of-Pearl Lock Plate, Fabric Lined, 11 x 9 x 5 In. . . . 240.00
Rosewood, Parquetry, Hinged Lid, Blue Paper Interior, 9 x 6 x 2 1/2 In. 230.00
Saffronwood, Blue Ground, Strawberries, Banded, Joseph Lehn, 4 1/2 In. 6050.00
Saffronwood, Painted, Salmon Ground, Pomegranate, Strawberry, 1879, 4 1/4 In. 4510.00
Salt, Pine, Spoon Rack Back, 1 Drawer, c.1800, 22 x 14 In. 220.00
Salt, Wall, Cherry, Slant Lid, Drawer, Painted, Inscribed, 1771, 11 x 9 x 8 In. 3080.00
Salt, Wall, Softwood, Shaped Backboard, Grain Painted, 8 In. 125.00
Set, Oval, Covered, Lapped Finger Construction, Painted, Green, Yellow, Brown, 3 Piece . 3408.00
Shaving, Mahogany, Hepplewhite, Fold-Out Mirror, Dovetailed Drawer, Macheis 259.00
Shoe Form, Maple, Chip Carved, Slide Lid, 9 In. 690.00
Silver, Embossed, Nike In Classical Scene, Rosettes, Gilt Lid & Trim, 3 In. 550.00
Softwood, Slide Lid, Single Piece, Original Red Finish, 1 x 3 3/4 x 1 In. 120.00
Spruce Gum, Chip Carved, Book Shape, Slide Lid, 2 3/4 x 12 x 8 1/2 In. 240.00
Spruce Gum, Painted, Pierced Heart Motif, Quatrefoil, 19th Century, 1 1/2 x 3 5/8 x 4 In. . 1175.00
Storage, Maple, Oval, Cover, Lapped, Pierced Heart Designs, 4 5/8 x 16 1/4 In. 2235.00
Storage, Vinegar Decoration, Blue Over Green, Pencil Post Legs, 17 3/4 x 13 1/2 x 17 In. . 660.00
Storage, Wood, Ivory Inlay, Marquetry, Pedestal, Chinese, 19 x 17 In. 259.00
Strong, Iron, Continental, c.1700, 19 x 34 x 19 In. 2030.00
Strong, Raised, Engraved Details, Applied Medallions, Iron, Persia, 7 x 8 1/2 In. 615.00
Sweetmeat, Silver Gilt, Sky & Lapis Blue Champleve Enamel, c.1900, 1/2 x 3 1/2 x 2 In. . 575.00
Sweetmeat, Tortoiseshell, Restauration, Maiden In Bed, Silver Plaque, 1 x 3 x 2 In. 980.00
Tea, Brass, Burlwood, Sarcophagus Shape, Bone Grips, George IV, 6 x 8 1/2 x 4 1/2 In. . . . 460.00

Tea, Burl, Brass Mounted, Yew Band, Casket Shape, Georgian, 5 1/2 x 8 x 4 1/2 In. 805.00
Tea, Ivory, 10 Sides, Inlaid Horn Border, Paneled, English Regency, 5 x 4 1/2 x 4 1/2 In. . .   4370.00
Tea, Mahogany, 2 Sections, Lids, Ball Feet, England, 19th Century, 6 x 7 1/2 x 4 1/2 In. . .   495.00
Tea, Mahogany, Band Of Ebony Inlay, Lid, 19th Century, 4 1/4 x 5 1/4 x 4 1/2 In. 210.00
Tea, Rosewood, Bowl, Sections, Cover, Inlaid, 19th Century, 6 1/2 x 12 1/2 x 6 1/2 In. . . .   520.00
Tea, Turned Wood, Alternating Light, Dark Woods, Laminated, 7 In. 489.00
Tinder, Tin, Finger Loop, Soldered Candle Socket, Round, 2 3/4 x 2 1/2 In. 495.00
Tobacco, Brass Hinged, Oval, Francis Armstrong, July 2nd, 1764, Dutch, 7 x 1 3/4 In. . . .   245.00
Tobacco, Brass, Copper Lid & Base, Relief Military & Naval Scenes, Dutch, 7 1/4 In. . . .   770.00
Tobacco, Brass, Lid, Cutout, Overlay, Inscription, Dutch, 18th Century, 6 In. 790.00
Tobacco, Copper, Brass, Mottos, Picture, Dutch, 18th Century, 6 1/2 x 2 1/4 In. 255.00
Tobacco, Cover, Brass, 6 Panels, Story Scenes, Captions, 18th Century, 6 1/2 In. 508.00
Tobacco, Cover, Brass, Flowers, Geometric Engraving, c.1800, 5 x 3 In. 135.00
Tortoiseshell, Abalone & Mother-Of-Pearl·Inlay, Turned Bun Feet, Lined, 2 x 6 In. 690.00
Tortoiseshell, Etched Oval, Ship At Sunrise, Ivy Covered Ruins, Brass Liner, 3 1/2 In. 165.00
Tortoiseshell, Gold Bound, Venus & Cupid Scene, France, 19th Century, 1 1/4 x 3 In. . . .   635.00
Tortoiseshell, Heart Shape, London, Victorian, 1860, 1 1/2 x 3 3/4 x 4 1/2 In. 575.00
Trompe L'Oeil, Metal, Painted, Stack Of Books Shape, 18 1/2 In., Pair 1675.00
Wall, Chip Carved, Geometric, Mirror Back, Candle Shelves, 21 x 14 In. 145.00
Wall, Cutout Stars, Sponge Painted, Late 20th Century, 6 3/4 x 10 1/2 x 4 1/2 In. 60.00
Wall, Drawer, Maple, Carved, Pierced Back, 19th Century, 14 x 7 3/8 x 4 In. 440.00
Wall, Pine, Blue Paint, Yellow Linear Decoration, 19th Century, 13 3/8 x 11 x 7 In. 1175.00
Wall, Softwood, Slant Lid, Scalloped Gallery, Molded Base, Black Paint, 17 In. 95.00
Wall, Wood, Carved, Painted, Pierced Shaped Back, Red Wash Finish, 9 x 14 x 6 3/8 In. .   500.00
Walnut, Arches, Molding, Recessed Tiger Maple Panels, 11 x 17 In. 480.00
Walnut, Dovetailed, Inlaid Maple Starflower, 11 1/2 x 6 3/4 x 5 1/4 In. 140.00
Walnut, Dovetailed, Slide Lid, Drawer, Virginia, Early 19th Century, 4 x 5 x 9 1/4 In. . . .   950.00
Walnut, Yellow Pine, Dovetailed, Inlaid Diamonds & Bands, Slant Lid, 8 1/2 x 14 In. . . .   145.00
Watch Safe, Mahogany, Rectangular, Lift-Off Top, Dovetailed Base, 5 1/2 In. 394.00
Wood, Brass Inlaid Design, Arts & Crafts, Germany, 6 x 3 1/2 In. 230.00
Wood, Hand Hammered Copper Corners, Tin Lined, Arts & Crafts, 10 1/2 x 5 In. 175.00
Wood, Painted, Blue Green, Compartmentalized, Slide Lid, 10 x 7 1/4 In. 210.00
Wood, Polychrome, Flute Player, Flowers, Square, Tibet, c.1850, 10 1/2 x 9 3/4 In. 470.00
Wood, Small Inlaid, Hinged Lid On Rectangular Box, 3 1/8 In. 499.00
Work, Gilt, Brass Mounted, Scored Leather, Ball Feet, 2 3/4 x 6 3/4 x 5 1/4 In. 430.00
Writing, Mahogany, Brass Bound, Felt Writing Surface, Segmented Tray, 18 In. 169.00
Writing, Pine, Lift Top, 2 Drawers, Heart Shape Pulls, 18th Century, 10 x 20 x 20 In. . . .   175.00
Writing, Wood, Carved, Inlaid, Heart, Stars, Diamonds, 1839, 1 1/2 x 9 x 1 3/8 In. 1116.00

BOY SCOUT collectibles include any material related to scouting, including patches, manuals, and uniforms. The Boy Scout movement in the United States started in 1910. The first Jamboree was held in 1937. Girl Scout items are listed under their own heading.

Bugle, Chrome Finish, Mouthpiece, Rexcratt, 16 3/4 In. 63.00
Camera, Kodak, Black Bellows, Logo On Face Plate, England, c.1930 . . . .   250.00
Camera, Kodak, Green, Boy Scout Logo, Case, England, 1929 . . . .   95.00
Certificate, Scoutmaster B.S.A., 1913 . . . . 220.00
Figure, 3 Hikers, 2 With Flags, 1 At Attention, Painted, Barclay, 3 1/2 In. 60.00
Fire Starter Kit, Flint & Steel, 3 Compartment Pouch, 1950s 29.00
First Aid Kit, Bauer & Black, 1930s 99.00
Handbook, 34th Printing, Norman Rockwell Cover, First Edition, Copyright 1940 . . . . . .   55.00
Handbook, Boy Scout Executive, Red Cover, 1921 . . . .   55.00
Insignia, Catholic Scout Retreat, Buttonhole, Brooklyn, New York, 1960, 2 x 3 5/8 In. . . .   5.00
Insignia, Continental Dist. B.S.A. First Aid Meet, Embroidered, 1978, 3 1/2 x 3 In. 5.00
Jacket, Khaki, 18 Merit Badges On Sleeve, 1920s, 13-In. Neck 885.00
Knife, Pocket, Keen Kutter, No. 6559 . . . . 200.00
Knife, Remington No. RH50, 4 1/2 In. 201.00
Knife, Utility, 5 Blades, Marked Imperial Prov. U.S.A., 3 3/8 In. 35.00
Literature, Merit Badge Series, Stamp Collecting, Illustrated, New York, 1931, 39 Pages .   10.00
Literature, Merit Badge Series, Wildlife Management, New Brunswick, 1958, 96 Pages . .   6.00
Magazine, Boy's Life, America's Pastime, Vol. 33, No. 06, June, 1943, 42 Pages 9.00
Magazine, Scouting, Scout Saluting, Rockwell Cover, Vol. 32, No. 02, 1944, 32 Pages . . .   12.00
Manual, Kerchief Jamboree Guide, 1950s 600.00

Medal, Eagle Scout, Type 1, Palm, Sterling, Bronze, Case, c.1920	217.00
Medal, Hornaday, Distinguished Service To Conservation, Engraved, June 1, 1964	1000.00
Merit Badge Sash, Folded Brown Twill, 24 Badges, Square Cut, 1930s	109.00
Patch, Arrowhead COPE, Philmont Ranch	550.00
Patch, Veteran Award, 10 Years Service, Green Twill, Blue & Gold Embroidery, 4 In.	360.00
Pencil Box, At Camp, Tin Lithograph, 3 1/2 x 8 In.	65.00
Pin, Eagle, B.S.A., On Ribbon, Be Prepared, Red, White, Blue, 3 In.	185.00
Ring, Eagle Scout, Sterling L, 1940s, Size 10	58.00
Shirt, Baseball Style, Short Sleeves, Patches, Olive Green, Size 14, 1970s	180.00
Uniform, Eagle Scout, National Jamboree 1935, Sash, Pants, Neckerchief, Badges	2100.00
Wristwatch, Comic Character, Ingersoll, 1920s	40.00

BRADLEY & HUBBARD is a name found on many metal objects. Walter Hubbard and his brother-in-law, Nathaniel Lyman Bradley, started making cast iron clocks, tables, frames, andirons, lamps, chandeliers, sconces, and sewing birds in 1854 in Meriden, Connecticut. The company became Bradley & Hubbard Manufacturing Company in 1875. Charles Parker Company bought the firm in 1940. Their lamps are especially prized by collectors.

Andirons, Hammered Iron, Square Top, Column, Patina, 10 x 16 x 24 In.	290.00
Andirons, Twisted Square Stem, Scrolling Feet, c.1915, 18 x 9 x 16 1/2 In.	315.00
Candlestick, Brass, Chamber, Bobeche, Bolted To Saucer, Ring, 4 3/4 In.	30.00
Desk Set, Brass, Geometric Bands, Pen Tray, Roller, Clip, Letter Holder, Marked	110.00
Desk Set, Brass, Stamped Geometric Bands, Stamped Mark, 4 Piece	110.00
Desk Set, Bronze, Garland, Ribbon, Shield, Letter Rack, Calendar, Blotter, 7 Piece	150.00
Lamp, 3-Light, Leaded Glass, Grape Cluster, Bronze, c.1910, 28 x 20 In.	2645.00
Lamp, 8-Panel Shade, Scroll & Leaves, Metal Overlay, 2-Light, c.1900, 19 In.	205.00
Lamp, Amberina, Inverted Thumbprint Shade, Electric, 16 In.	345.00
Lamp, Arabesques, Green Slag Glass, 8-Sided Shade, Bronze Base, 20 In.	805.00
Lamp, Bronze, Lotus Column Base, Striated Gold Shade, 24 In.	635.00
Lamp, Desk, Overlay, Slag Glass, Hexagonal Shade, 6 x 12 In.	1150.00
Lamp, Fluid, Organ, Brass, White Flower Shade, Griffin Head, Claw Feet, 1878	1240.00
Lamp, Hanging, Globe, Birds, Brown Stems, Metal Fittings, 17 In.	420.00
Lamp, Leaded Shade, Geometric, Caramel, Orange, 22 1/2 x 34 In. .... *Illus*	1960.00
Lamp, Metal Overlay, 4 Panels, Buildings, Trees, Incised Base, 23 In.	2520.00
Lamp, Oil, Rose Cameo Cut, Urn Body, Footed Base, 1890, 22 In.	345.00
Lamp, Patinated Brass, Russet Enamel Custard Glass Shade, Kerosene, 21 In.	315.00
Lamp, Slag Glass Panel Shade, Metal Overlay, Trees, 2-Socket Base, 19 In.	780.00
Parrot In Ring, Cast Iron, Painted, c.1900s	525.00

BRASS has been used for decorative pieces and useful tablewares since ancient times. It is an alloy of copper, zinc, and other metals. Additional brass items may be found under Bell, Candlestick, Tool, or Trivet.

Basin, Gray Green, Paw Foot, Beaux Arts Style, Italy, 8 x 20 1/4 In.	405.00
Bed Warmer, Engraved Flowers, Copper Rivets, Wooden Handle, 43 1/2 In.	220.00
Bed Warmer, Engraved Rooster On Hill, Flowers, Turned Wood Handle, 42 In.	385.00

Clean metal with a back-and-forth motion, not a circular motion. Use a soft, clean, lint-free cloth and turn it often to avoid reusing a soiled part. Wear cotton gloves when cleaning any type of metal. Oils in the skin will leave a mark.

Bradley & Hubbard, Lamp, Leaded Shade, Geometric, Caramel, Orange, 22 1/2 x 34

Bed Warmer, Hinged Cover, Iron Handle, Dutch, 18th Century, 43 In. 210.00
Bed Warmer, Pierced Decoration, Turned Wood Handle, Hinge Pin Cover, 46 In. 240.00
Bed Warmer, Pierced, Raised, Adam & Eve, Serpent, Plants, Beasts, 42 In. 4025.00
Bed Warmer, Tooled Floral Medallion Decoration, Turned Softwood Handle, 42 In. 135.00
Bed Warmer, Tooled Lip, Exotic Bird & Flowers, Turned Wood Handle, 1800, 43 In. 185.00
Bed Warmer, Turned Wood Handle, Chased, Pierced Cover, 34 In. 86.00
Bed Warmer, Wooden Handle, Copper, Hand Chased Cover, 1800s, 42 x 10 1/2 In. 110.00
Belt Plate, Soldier's, King George III, Initials GR, Crown, England 350.00
Bleeding Bowl, Barber's, Circular, Rolled Rim, Attached Ring, England, 1700s, 10 1/2 In. 220.00
Bowl, Cast, Turned, Wriggled Decoration, 18th Century, 7 3/4 In. 250.00
Box, Art Deco, Nude Relief, Goats, Grapes, Hinged Lid, Fluted, Marked Chase, 7 x 6 In. . 470.00
Box, Jarvie, Prairie Design, Inscribed AMPA, 1912, 4 1/4 x 1 3/4 In. 635.00
Bucket, Coal, Helmet Shape, Swivel Handle, Brass Rivets, 19 In. 110.00
Bucket, Peat, George III, Mahogany, Spiral Turned, Early 19th Century, 17 x 14 1/2 In. . . 26290.00
Bucket, Spun, Wrought Iron Handle, Copper Rivets, 14 x 12 In. 85.00
Caddy, Beehive, Swing Handle, 19th Century, 5 In. 15.00
Canister, Cover, Ring Turned Base, Cylindrical, France, 13 In., Pair 145.00
Card Press, Footed, 7 1/2 x 6 3/4 x 6 3/4 In. 431.00
Case, Clay Pipe, Dutch, 18th Century 250.00
Chimes, 5 Tubular, Mounted On Wooden Plaque, Sanctus, Communion, 21 In. 690.00
Chimes, Mahogany, Rosewood, 8 Chimes, 20th Century, 18 1/2 x 27 1/2 In. 220.00
Cigar Cutter, Figural, Ship's Wheel, On Column, Round Base, D. Munchen, 5 In. 115.00
Coal Hod, Relief Floral, Handle, Footed, c.1900, 12 3/4 x 13 x 22 3/4 In. 400.00
Coffee Service, Embossed Vertical Lines, Eagle, Snake Handle, Germany, c.1910 . . . . 200.00
Coffeepot, Lighthouse Form, Acorn Finial, Gooseneck Spout, Early 1800s, 8 3/4 In. 158.00
Crucifix, Oval, Silver Leaf, Frame, Italy, c.1865, 20 x 16 1/2 In. 518.00
Cup, Hand Hammered, Incised Swirling Design, Art Nouveau, Lalaounis, 4 In. 12.00
Cuspidor, Deep Patina, Trumpet, Embossed Cuspidors Made By Ireland, 2 In. 150.00
Desk Set, Brass, Pierced, Art Nouveau Style, Embossed Lid, Scrolled Pen Rest, 8 In. 25.00
Desk Set, Figures, Lions, Inkwells, Pen Tray, Footed, Renaissance, 7 x 12 x 8 In. 299.00
Dog Collar, Adjustable, Ring, England, 18th Century 1200.00
Door Knocker, Cutty Sark Sailing Ship, 7 In. 195.00
Door Knocker, Lion Head, c.1900, 5 In. 175.00
Door Pull, Round, Grimacing Figure, Arts & Crafts, 8 In. 270.00
Doorbell, Pull Chain, Victorian, 1890-1900 . . . . 350.00
Fern Stand, Lacquer, Gilding, Talon Feet, Leafing, Scrolling, 14 1/2 x 35 1/2 In. 440.00
Figure, Giraffe, Frederick Weinberger, Cast, Stylized, 12 x 3 In., Pair 265.00
Figure, Girl Standing On Ladder Back Chair Seat, Bronze Patina, c.1900, 12 In. 175.00
Figure, Musician, Seated With Stringed Instrument, India, c.1900, 6 In. 69.00
Flagon, Hinged Cover, Switzerland, 18th Century 1350.00
Foot Warmer, Diamond Panels On Sides, Tulip Fretwork Lid, Holland, c.1720 . . . . 595.00
Footman, Hanging, Iron, Pierced Sliding Tray, England, 1800s, 8 1/2 x 16 In. 79.00
Garniture Set, Silvered Metal, Chinoiserie, France, c.1900, 3 Piece 805.00
Girandole, Woman & Child, Arbor, Prisms, 16 In., Pair 69.00
Goblet, Coconut Shell, 5 1/2 In. 259.00
Horn, Automobile, Squeeze Ball, Black, Rubber, India, 19 In. 25.00
Humidor, Lid, Cylindrical, Openwork Border, Wood Base, 8 In. 405.00
Jamb Hooks, Oval Mounting, Swaged Assembly, 3 3/4 x 3 In., Pair 110.00
Jar, Chased Designs, Various Deities, Scrolled Field, India, 20th Century, 16 x 17 In. 415.00
Jardiniere, Urn Form, Copper Liner, Handles, Stem, Hexagonal Base, 1800s, 22 x 20 In. . 545.00
Mailbox, Brass, Steel, Cutler Mfg. Co., Rochester, N.Y., 45 x 21 1/2 x 14 In. 550.00
Mailbox, U.S. Mail Chute Equipment Co., St. Louis, Wall Mount, 26 x 15 In. 240.00
Mirror, Liberty & Co., c.1902-1905, 28 1/2 In. 8965.00
Money Box, Merchant's, National Cash Register Company, Oak, 1893, 19 x 10 x 8 In. . . . 675.00
Mortar & Pestle, Flared Rim & Handle, 3 1/4 In. 88.00
Pill Roller, Walnut, 2 Parts, 19th Century 120.00
Plaque, Last Supper, Embossed, Argente, Ebonized Frame, Relief Scrolls, 26 x 19 In. . . . 460.00
Rattle, Lid, India, 19th Century, 4 1/2 In. 59.00
Sculpture, British Lion, Half Figures, On Standard, Openwork Roses, 9 x 10 In., Pair . . . 305.00
Stencil, Nobscusett, Mounted On Board, 2 Part, 5 x 32 In. 80.00
Sundial, Italian, Square, Ludovici Lingery, 1659, 4 3/4 In. 880.00
Sundial, Pocket, Cover, Masonic Engraving, Case, 18th Century 275.00
Sundial, Universal Equinoctial, Johan Schrettegger, Augsburg, 2 In. 530.00

Tag, Baggage, 208 Bridgeton & Saco River RR, Robbins 310.00
Teapot, Ball Shape, Silvered Interior, England, c.1720 . . . .   4500.00
Tieback, Pressed, Victorian Scene, Tin Back, c.1852, Pair 475.00
Token Set, Trade, 17th Century, England 285.00
Tray, Calling Card, Continental, Art Nouveau, c.1900, 12 x 18 In. 375.00
Vase, Hammered, Slender, Rose Design, Arts & Crafts, 8 In. 127.00
Wall Plaque, U.S. War Office, Department Seal, 13 In. 235.00
Wall Pocket, Zigzag Front, Scalloped Crest, Cutout Star, 6 5/8 x 8 In., Pair 110.00
Weight Set, Nesting, Lid, Decorative Closure, Swing Handle 100.00
Wine Bucket, Cover, Fruit Band, Mahogany Handles, 14 x 13 In. 230.00
Writing Set, Traveling, 2 Inkwells, Brush, Pen, Candlestick, Brass Interior, 5 x 3 In. 650.00

BRASTOFF, see Sascha Brastoff category.

BREAD PLATE, see various silver categories, porcelain factories, and pressed glass
patterns.

BRIDE'S BASKETS OR BRIDE'S BOWLS were usually one-of-a-kind
novelties made in American and European glass factories. They were
especially popular about 1880 when the decorated basket was often
given as a wedding gift. Cut glass baskets were popular after 1890. All
bride's baskets lost favor about 1905. Bride's baskets and bride's
bowls may also be found in other glass sections. Check the index at the
back of the book.

BRIDE'S BASKET, Amberina Enameled, Gilt Bronze, Dragon Handle, Victorian, 10 1/2 In. . . .   690.00
Cameo, Pink Overlay, Winged Lion, Meriden Frame, c.1910, 9 1/2 In. 750.00
Cranberry Over White, Ruffled Edge, Enameled Flowers, Silver Plated Holder, 11 In. . . .   550.00
Opalescent, Clear Stripes, Beige Shaded To Rust Interior, Thorn Handle, 7 1/2 x 6 In. . . .   300.00
Opaline, Pink Over White, Enameled, Fruit Handles, 7 1/4 x 12 In. 520.00
Opaque White, Red Shaded Rim, Silvered Pedestal Base, 10 In. 145.00
Orange, Red Swirls, Ruffled Edge, Clear Thorn Handle, 7 x 6 In. 60.00
Pink, Satin, Herringbone, Ruffled Edge, Silver Plated Base, 11 1/2 In. 300.00
Purple, Satin, Cased, Ruffled Edge, Pairpoint Silver Plate Stand, 8 In. 275.00
White Ribbon Center, Ruffled Green Edge, Pink Thorn Handle, 7 In. 375.00
BRIDE'S BOWL, Blue & White Satin, Orange Enameled Flowers, 15 In. 250.00
Burmese, Enameled, Chrysanthemums, Silver Plated Holder, 14 1/2 x 11 1/4 In. 3680.00
Hobnail, Yellow Over Pink, Reed & Barton Holder, Figural Soldiers, 13 1/2 In. 500.00
Opaline Over Pink, Amber Rim, Ruffled Edge, Silver Plated Holder, 9 3/4 In. 145.00
Peachblow, Stylized Leaves, Flowers, Ruffled Rim, Silver Plated Base, Birds, Angel 1065.00
Pink, Enamel Daisies, Vines, Ruffled Edge 335.00
Pink Over Yellow, Girl & Veteran, Flowers, Ruffled Edge, Satin, 12 x 11 In. 5100.00
Spangled, Ruffled Rim, Yellow, White Mottled, Silver Mica, Blue Daisies, 10 1/2 In. 85.00
White, Light Blue Interior, Tricornered, Mt. Washington, 12 x 11 1/2 In. 460.00
White, Peg, Black Acorns, Green Enamel Leaves, Silver Holder, 13 x 8 In. 700.00

BRISTOL glass was made in Bristol, England, after the 1700s. The
Bristol glass most often seen today is a Victorian, lightweight opaque
glass that is often blue. Some of the glass was decorated with enamels.

Box, Hinged Lid, Courting Scene, Peachblow Colors, Bell Shapes, Label, 5 1/2 In. 150.00
Fingerbowl, Amethyst, 5 x 3 1/4 In., 12 Piece 748.00
Mug, Liberty Eagle, Polychrome, Painted, Barrel Shape, Opalescent White Glass, 3 3/4 In.   470.00
Spoon Tray, Armorial, Daniel Ludlow Of Camden, Gilt Edge, c.1775, 6 1/4 In. 10755.00
Urn, Parcel Gilt, Blue Band, Ribbon Swags, Vase Shape, c.1860, Pair 1250.00
Vase, Bird, Flower Garland, Spring Green, Footed, 7 In. 40.00
Vase, Blown, Robin's-Egg Blue, Applied Bird & Flowers, Polychrome, 16 1/2 In., Pair . . .   50.00
Vase, Blue, Rust Flowers, Gold Beading, 8 x 3 1/4 In. 35.00
Vase, Flared Neck, Enameled, Birds, Flowing Branches, Oval, 11 1/4 In., Pair 195.00
Vase, Flower Panels, c.1880, 10 In., Pair 920.00
Vase, Gold Decoration, Trim, Brass Connector, Footed, 13 1/2 x 5 In. 125.00
Vase, Orange & Blue Flowers, Green Leaves, Flared, Scalloped Rim, 10 3/4 x 4 1/2 In. . . .   115.00
Vase, Pink Roses, Gold Enamel, White Ground, Frosted Foot, 7 1/2 x 5 In. 100.00
Vase, White, Enameled Roses, 10 1/2 In., Pair 50.00
Vase, Yellow & Green, Enameled Chrysanthemums, 2 1/2 In. 50.00

BRITANNIA, see Pewter category.

BRONZE is an alloy of copper, tin, and other metals. It is used to make figurines, lamps, and other decorative objects. Bronze lamps are listed in the Lamp category. Pieces listed here date from the eighteenth, nineteenth, and twentieth centuries.

Ashtray, American LaFrance, Maltese Cross, Eagle	80.00
Ashtray, Bach, Oscar B., Standing, Ship Medallion Finial, 1925, 39 In.	645.00
Basket, Trompe L'Oeil, Folded Linen, Woven Handle, Applied Flowers, Insects, 10 1/4 In.	345.00
Bowl, Applied Lily Pads, Buds, Ruffled Edge, 4 x 11 In.	748.00
Bowl, Set In Base, 3 Elephant Trunk Feet, 6 3/4 x 12 In., 2 Piece	60.00
Box, Marble, Teak Lined Sections, Inscribed, c.1925, Austria, 7 1/4 x 16 x 8 1/2 In.	7170.00
Box, Vienna Bronze, Bird On Log, 3 In.	315.00
Bust, Aurili, H., Gladiator, Marble Base, France, 19th Century, 19 In.	650.00
Bust, Buddha, Draping, Cloud Tiara, Verdigris Finish, 9 1/2 In.	165.00
Bust, Duke Of Wellington, Gilt, 19th Century, 12 In.	1022.00
Bust, Ezekiel, Moses, Robert E. Lee, Bronze, Marble Base, 7 In.	3165.00
Bust, Man On Socle, Horse Jumping Hurdle, 7 In.	150.00
Bust, Moreau, Mathurin, Diana, Red Marble Socle, Title Plaque, 25 1/2 In.	1765.00
Bust, Napoleon, After Chaudet, 19th Century, 23 x 12 x 10 In.	5975.00
Bust, Pilon, Germain, Henri III, Patinated, 18th Century, 14 1/2 In.	750.00
Bust, Pina, Alfred, Beethoven, Signed, Italy, 7 1/2 In.	1190.00
Bust, Rolle, Marie, Woman, Flowers In Hair, Medieval Costume, Gilt, 25 In.	1530.00
Cannon, Scale Replica, Leaves, Cast Dolphins, Armorial Device, Wood, 1785, 17 x 7 In.	330.00
Censer, Pierced Cover, Relief Figures, Mounted Handles, Chinese, c.1810, 9 x 12 In.	750.00
Charger, Slavic Style, Relief Borders, Coat Of Arms, c.1887, 15 In.	805.00
Compote, Aesthetic Revival, Ivy Vines, Snails, 3 Twig Legs, Oval, 6 3/8 In.	1175.00
Compote, Nymphette Kneeling In Net, Gilt, Glass, 11 1/4 In.	978.00
Cruet, Gilt, Enamel, Engraved Glass, France, 19th Century, 10 1/4 In.	605.00
Desk Set, Louis XIV Style, Gilt, Stamp Box, Letter Holder, Pen Tray, 4 Piece	290.00
Desk Set, Onyx & Polychrome Branches, 3 Perching Parakeets, Pen Tray, Letter Holder	928.00
Frame, Napoleon III, Gilt Bronze, Double, Oval Opening, Leaves, 7 1/2 In.	590.00
Garniture Set, Art Deco, Clock, Onyx, Marble, France, 3 Piece	600.00
Garniture Set, Gilt, Handles, Malachite Pedestal, 13 x 5 1/2 x 5 1/2 In., Pair	5750.00
Garniture Set, Louis XV Style, Ormolu, Clock, 7-Light Candelabra, c.1900, 3 Piece	4140.00
Garniture Set, Louis XVI Style, Clock, Gilt Metal, Porcelain, Candelabra 17 In., 3 Piece	940.00
Garniture Set, Louis XVI Style, Clock, Marble, Columns, Lovebirds, 15 In., 3 Piece	705.00
Garniture Set, Louis XVI Style, Clock, Marble, Drum Shape Case, Candelabra, 3 Piece	1998.00
Garniture Set, Louis XVI Style, Onyx, Ormolu, Urns, c.1900, 3 Piece	2070.00
Garniture Set, Napoleon III, Clock, Marble, Allegorical Figure, 20 In., 3 Piece	2585.00
Garniture Set, Ormolu Mounts, Clock, Cathedral Shape, 3 Piece	405.00
Garniture Set, Restoration, Parcel Gilt, Patinated, Pedestal, 12 1/2 x 4 x 4 In., Pair	1955.00
Gospel Stand, Gilt, Winged Griffins, Fretwork, Footed, 19th Century, 14 x 14 1/2 In.	430.00
Holy Water Font, Guardian Angel, Cherubs, Clouds, 19th Century, 20 In.	1380.00
Holy Water Font, Our Lady Of Lourdes, Scrolling Foliage, Cherubs, Gilt, 17 1/2 In.	635.00
Incense Burner, Classical Figures, Child Masks, Gilt, 3-Footed, 7 3/4 In.	345.00
Incense Burner, Foo Dog, Japan, 5 1/4 In.	220.00
Incense Burner, Standing Woman, Striding Forward, Gilt, Marble Base, 23 1/2 In.	1790.00
Jardiniere, Flying Cranes, Phoenix, Flowering Branches, Japan, 23 In.	825.00
Jardiniere, Neoclassical Style, Round Basin Top, Continental, 35 x 19 1/2 In.	2235.00
Jardiniere, Oval, Flat, Flowers, Handles, 3-Footed, Chinese, 12 In., Pair	825.00
Letter Holder, Royal Seal, Merry Phipson & Parker, 1843, 1 1/2 x 2 x 1 1/2 In.	175.00
Loving Cup, Gilt, France, 19th Century, 5 1/4 In.	86.00
Mirror, Flower Form, Deities In Flight, Birds, Flowers, Insects, T'ang Dynasty, 6 In.	920.00
Mirror, Flowers & Birds, Insects, Stylized Dragons, T'ang Dynasty, 4 3/4 In.	460.00
Mirror, Phoenix & Dragon, Mother-Of-Pearl Inlay, Lacquered Ground, Ming, 6 In.	1065.00
Mold, Tablespoon, 2 Sections, 9 1/2 In.	330.00
Pedestal, Figural, Cherub, Holding Drapery, Silvered, 20th Century, 18 x 12 In.	460.00
Planter, Dragons, Lizard Handles, Scalloped Corners, Oblong, Foo Dog Feet, 11 In.	385.00
Planter, Zodiac, Blooming Tree, Rock, Pierced Design, Chinese, 1800s, 6 x 6 1/2 In.	259.00
Plaque, 2 Men Working, Hammered, Frame, Germany, 16 x 9 In.	748.00
Plaque, 2 Satyrs, Enamored Nude, Gilt, Relief, 19th Century, 10 In.	690.00
Plaque, Flight Into Egypt, Gilt, France, 19th Century, 14 x 11 In.	1265.00
Plaque, Mills, Clark, George Washington, Profile, 21 x 17 In.	2700.00
Plaque, Peregrine, Falmouth, Massachusetts, c.1930, 6 x 22 In.	325.00

Plaque, Prost, Maurice, Panther, Marble Base, c.1925, 11 5/8 x 24 In. 4780.00
Sculpture, 2 Infants, Polychrome, Marble Plinth, After Auguste Moreau, 18 In. 400.00
Sculpture, 2 Piggyback Cats, Vienna, 2 1/2 In. 375.00
Sculpture, 3 Leaping Frogs, By Pond's Edge, Austria, 6 1/2 x 3 3/4 In. 2235.00
Sculpture, Aarons, George, Nude Woman, Bending Down, Brown Patina, 1929, 8 In. 2875.00
Sculpture, Aizelin, Eugene, Marguerite, Woman Holding Book, Signed, 27 In. 129.00
Sculpture, Andre, Emile, Man, Women & Baby, Wooden Base, France, 24 In. 4770.00
Sculpture, Arab Reclining On Carpet, Austria, c.1900, 5 1/2 In. 1035.00
Sculpture, Avalokitesvara, Holding Lotus Branch, Tibet, c.1900, 18 In. 800.00
Sculpture, Bacchus Standing With Grapes & Vase, Marble Base, 12 In. 470.00
Sculpture, Balestrieri, Bernado, Nude Boy With Seashell, Italy, 19 In. 2897.00
Sculpture, Barbedienne, F., 2 Men Wrestling, France, 19th Century, 15 x 18 In. 2385.00
Sculpture, Barre, Jean A., Napoleon, France, 19th Century, 11 In. 680.00
Sculpture, Barye, A., Raptor, Perched On Rocky Outcrop, 1796-1875, 4 3/4 In. 1116.00
Sculpture, Barye, Alfred, Equestrian, Joan Of Arc, Signed, 34 1/2 In. 1998.00
Sculpture, Barye, Alfred, Lion & Lioness, Stamped, France, 1800s, 15 1/2 In., Pair 3875.00
Sculpture, Barye, Antoine-Louis, Eagle, On Rocky Outcrop, 10 In. 3885.00
Sculpture, Berge, Edward, Standing Nymph, Flower Frog, American Art Foundry, 7 In. . . 1610.00
Sculpture, Bergman, Horseman, Marble Base, Vienna, 5 1/2 In. 1615.00
Sculpture, Blake, Buckeye, Kid Russell & Monte, Signed, c.1986, 20 1/2 In. 1150.00
Sculpture, Bodendick, Jacob, Man Holding Lyre, Woman Leaning On Shoulder, 19 1/2 In. 1380.00
Sculpture, Boehm, J.E., Huntsman & Horse, England, 14 3/4 x 12 1/4 In. 4348.00
Sculpture, Bonheur, Isidore, Bull & Bear, Green Marble Base, 1900, 21 x 13 In. 520.00
Sculpture, Boulton, Joseph L., Mountain Lion, Crouching, 9 In. 460.00
Sculpture, Bourgouin, Eugene, Cupid, Silvered, Early 20th Century, 12 x 9 1/2 In. 805.00
Sculpture, Bronson, Clark E., A Lofty View, 3 Bighorn Sheep, c.1974, 14 x 13 In. 2590.00
Sculpture, Bronson, Clark E., Escape To The High Country, Stag, c.1975, 13 1/2 x 18 In. . 1150.00
Sculpture, Bronson, Clark E., It's Mine, Bear, With Fish, c.1975, 7 1/2 In. 805.00
Sculpture, Brown, Joe, Boxers, 2 Men Boxing, Dark Green Patina, 1935, 9 In. 3160.00
Sculpture, Buddha Standing On Lotus Base, Long Robe, Sash, Bangkok, Thailand, 9 In. . 172.00
Sculpture, Buddha, Seated On Lotus Throne, Gilt, 2 5/8 In. 690.00
Sculpture, Buddha, Seated, Coiled Snake, 7 Hands, Khmer Style, 21 1/2 In. 374.00
Sculpture, Buddha, Seated, Parcel Gilt, Early 20th Century, 21 1/2 In. 1150.00
Sculpture, Bureau, Leon, 3 Pheasants, Gilt, France, Late 1800s, 17 1/2 In. 3067.00
Sculpture, Cana, Louis Emile, Horse & Dog, France, 20th Century, 16 x 19 In. 5792.00
Sculpture, Cardona, J., The Miner, c.1900, 29 x 14 x 14 In. 3750.00
Sculpture, Centaur, Club, Lion Skin, Oval Marble Base, 17 1/2 In. 1295.00
Sculpture, Charpentier, Improvisateur, Brown Patina, c.1887, 31 In. 1725.00
Sculpture, Cherub, Brown Patina, Stepped Marble Base, 5 1/2 x 13 3/8 In. 1050.00
Sculpture, Chiparus, Harem Girl, Stepped Marble Plinth, 18 In. 230.00
Sculpture, Cipriani, Reclining Nude, 20th Century, 33 x 14 1/2 In. 230.00
Sculpture, Clara, Juan, Girl, Playing With 2 Cats, 12 1/2 In. 1230.00
Sculpture, Clark, James Lippit, Rhinoceros, Mottled Brown Patina, 6 1/2 x 14 3/4 In. 4025.00
Sculpture, Classical Maiden, Seated, Rococo Style Base, Pierced Leaves, Gilt, 16 In. 1528.00
Sculpture, Classical Maidens, Cymbals, Castanets, Wood Base, 65 In., Pair 10575.00
Sculpture, Classical Warrior Embracing Sculpture Of Athena, 21 1/2 In. 2115.00
Sculpture, Cleopatra, Sphinxes, Gilt, Ivory, Marble, After D.H. Chiparus, 18 1/2 x 12 In. . 575.00
Sculpture, Clodion, Man, Woman, 2 Children, 20th Century, 15 1/2 In. 980.00
Sculpture, Cornu, Vital, Whistling Boy, France, 1851-1927, 26 In. 1700.00
Sculpture, Coudray, Georges C., Arab, France, 19th Century, 24 In. 2900.00
Sculpture, Crucified Christ, Cast, Velvet Board Mount, France, 44 In. 575.00
Sculpture, Cupid Playing Drum & Horn, Stepped Marble Base, 16 In. 1645.00
Sculpture, D'Aste, Joseph, Stylized Dancer, Gilt, Ivory, Marble Base, 16 In. 4780.00
Sculpture, Dachshund, Vienna Bronze, 3 3/4 In. 355.00
Sculpture, Dancing Faun Of Pompeii, Verdigris Patinated, Late 19th Century, 18 1/4 In. . . 518.00
Sculpture, Debut, Boy Playing Hurdy Gurdy, 26 In. 1295.00
Sculpture, Debut, Standing Warrior Resting On Ax, 33 In. 2940.00
Sculpture, Deity Seated On Lion, Gilt, 7 In. 2415.00
Sculpture, DeLabriere, Edouard, Prowling Lion, Carved Stone Base, 6 x 8 In. 518.00
Sculpture, Deming, E.G., Woman, Standing, Wearing V-Neck Sweater, 1981, 7 3/4 In. 85.00
Sculpture, Drouot, 2 Cavaliers Playing Dice, Signed, 15 In. 1645.00
Sculpture, Drouot, Edouard, Egyptian Woman, With Harp, Dore, 26 In. 1625.00
Sculpture, Drouot, Edouard, Nude Women, France, 1859, 41 In. 2215.00

Sculpture, Drouot, Edouard, Victory, Gilding, Brown Patina, 40 In. 3450.00
Sculpture, Dubois, Paul, Florentine Lute Player, c.1865, 19 In. 2030.00
Sculpture, Dufour, Rooster, Black Marble Base, France, 19th Century, 5 In. 345.00
Sculpture, Durer, Albert, Rhinoceros, Louis XVI Style, Marble Base, 10 x 6 1/2 x 15 In. . 345.00
Sculpture, Dying Man, France, 19th Century, 10 x 19 In. 1190.00
Sculpture, Eagle, Spread Wings, Perched On Branch, c.1900, 74 In. 3920.00
Sculpture, Eros Victorious, Holding Arrow, On Marble Stepped Pedestal, 15 1/2 In. 175.00
Sculpture, Falconer, Renaissance Costume, Hooded Falcon, 20 1/2 In. 1434.00
Sculpture, Falguiere, Jean, Boy Running With Rooster, Red Marble Base, 20 1/2 In. 1765.00
Sculpture, Family Of Birds, Among Wheat Stalks, Art Deco, Marble Base, 23 In. 1435.00
Sculpture, Farnham, John, Life Force, Great Britain, 1975, 22 In. 6000.00
Sculpture, Faune & Bacchante, After E. Carrier-Belleuse, 24 In. 3286.00
Sculpture, Fighting Elk, Elliptical Gray & White Marble Base, 13 In. 978.00
Sculpture, Foo Dog, Glass Eyes, Front Foot Raised On Ball, c.1850, 16 x 15 In., Pair ... 1035.00
Sculpture, Fredericks, Marshall, Boy On Bear, Patinated, 11 1/2 In. 9775.00
Sculpture, Frishmuth, Harriet Whitney, Nude Maiden, Black Marble Base, c.1929, 11 In. . 14950.00
Sculpture, Gardet, Georges, Tiger Attacking Tortoise, Green Brown Patina, 18 x 7 3/4 In. . 1035.00
Sculpture, Gaudez, Adrien E., Woman, Marguerite, France, 19th Century, 24 In. 3410.00
Sculpture, Girls, Posing As If At Beach, Weathered Green Patina, 21 In., 3 Piece 2875.00
Sculpture, God Of Literature Standing On Sea Dragon, 8 In. 1095.00
Sculpture, Grachev, Vasily, Couple, In Troika, Signed Cyrillic, c.1905, 12 x 7 1/2 x 7 In. . 2875.00
Sculpture, Granet, Pierre, Court Jester, Oblong Terrain Base, Brown Patina, 36 In. 2990.00
Sculpture, Great Dane, Vienna, 4 3/4 In. 425.00
Sculpture, Gregoire, Boy Clipping Wings Of Bird, 26 1/2 In. 1765.00
Sculpture, Hagenauer, Johann, Golfer, Marble Base, 4 1/2 In. 525.00
Sculpture, Hallili, Standing Hunter, Holding Bow, Deer, After Marioton, 40 In. 1880.00
Sculpture, Houdon, Jean A., Standing Nude Woman, 19th Century, 38 In. 4260.00
Sculpture, Hunter With Young Lion Cub, Brown Patina, France, 26 3/4 In. 1380.00
Sculpture, Huntsman, Polychrome, Marble Plinth, After H.F. Moreau, 32 In. 1150.00
Sculpture, Jackson, Harry, Seeker, Indian, Headdress, Blanket, c.1978, 14 In. 1150.00
Sculpture, Jaeger, Gothilf, Nude, Male, Holding Sword, Marble Base, 28 In. 777.00
Sculpture, Kauba, Cowboy, American Indians, Horses, 27 In. 9625.00
Sculpture, Lady Justice, Dark Brown & Green Patina, Black Marble Base, 23 x 6 In. 195.00
Sculpture, Lama, Seated, Lotus Throne, Monastic Robes, Tibet, 18th-19th Century, 7 In. . 460.00
Sculpture, Lanceray, Couple On Sled Pulled By 2 Horses, 19th Century, 21 In. 3885.00
Sculpture, LeGrand, August Ernest, Ready For Battle, Green Patina, Embossed, 20 1/2 In. 290.00
Sculpture, Leopard, Ivory Accents, Gilt, Marble Base, After D.H. Chiparus, 21 x 19 In. .. 575.00
Sculpture, Levasseur, Henri, Nymph Perched On Eagle, Silvered, 18 1/2 In. 1765.00
Sculpture, Lieberich, Nicholai, Hunter, Horse, 3 Dogs, 19th Century, 21 1/4 In. 4180.00
Sculpture, Lieberich, Nicholai, Woodsman, Axe, Bear, Russia, 19th Century, 15 3/4 In. .. 8960.00
Sculpture, Lindenburg, Boy Standing With Hands In Pockets, 9 In. 355.00
Sculpture, Lion & Tiger In Combat, Inlaid Eyes, Japan, 20th Century, 8 In. 380.00
Sculpture, Lion, Striding, Signed, 17 In. 880.00
Sculpture, Lohan Reclining, Wearing Robe, Chinese, 8 In. 320.00
Sculpture, Lovet-Lorski, Boris, Mask, Creten God, Marble Base, 12 1/4 In. 5079.00
Sculpture, Madrassi, Diana Aux Bois, Shaped Marble Base, c.1890, 28 1/2 In. 3360.00
Sculpture, Malakala, Riding On Horse, Holding Vajra & Skull Cup, Asia, 12 1/4 In. 3105.00
Sculpture, Man, Kneeling & Manacled, Terra-Cotta Base, 25 In. 1795.00
Sculpture, Mars & Athena, Patinated, Slate Pedestal, France, 14 x 13 3/4 In., Pair 690.00
Sculpture, Masson, Clovis, Lion, Reclining, c.1905, 14 In. 2350.00
Sculpture, Masson, Jules E., Stag & Doe, Gilt, France, 27 In. 4940.00
Sculpture, Mene, Pierre, Horse & Jockey, Light Brown Patina, 9 5/8 In. 2705.00
Sculpture, Mene, Pierre, Horse, France, 19th Century, 15 In. 2385.00
Sculpture, Mene, Pierre-Jules, Mounted Falconer, Dark Patina, c.1870, 29 3/4 In. 3520.00
Sculpture, Mercie, Antonin, David, With Head Of Goliath, Sheathing Sword, 24 1/2 In. ... 2390.00
Sculpture, Moigneiz, Jules, Stallion, France, 19th Century, 10 1/2 In. 680.00
Sculpture, Moigneiz, Jules, Dogs On Rock Ledge, 6 x 10 1/4 x 4 1/2 In. 900.00
Sculpture, Moreau, Girl Holding Twig With Birds, Red Marble Base, 21 In. 1534.00
Sculpture, Moreau, Man, Woman, Carrying Baby, 19th Century, 17 In. 1725.00
Sculpture, Moreau, Mathurin, Mother & Child, France, 20th Century, 33 In. 5110.00
Sculpture, Moreau, Mathurin, Nymph, Seated On Rock, France, 20 In. 1398.00
Sculpture, Moreau, Whispering Children, Raised Marble Base, 16 In. 355.00
Sculpture, Muir, James N., Drummers, Confederate, Union, 1984, 9 1/2 In., Pair 1495.00

Sculpture, Muller, H., Woman With Tankard, Signed, 7 3/4 In. 290.00
Sculpture, Night & Day, After Michelanglo, 22 In., Pair 6465.00
Sculpture, Nude Athlete, Patinated, Marble Base, 10 x 13 In. 230.00
Sculpture, Nude Maiden Playing Cymbals, 20th Century, 7 3/4 In. 470.00
Sculpture, Nude, Antelope, Verdigris, Art Deco, Stepped Black Glass Base, 8 x 26 In. ... 500.00
Sculpture, Nude, Hands Crossed Over Chest, Modernist, Marble Base, 50 In. 345.00
Sculpture, Omerth, Dancer, Art Deco, Ivory, Onyx Standard, Signed, 11 1/2 In. 1765.00
Sculpture, Oxen Pulling Cart With Driver, Marble Base, Signed, Russia, 20 In. 3525.00
Sculpture, Panthers, Poised To Attack, Dark Patina, 20th Century, 41 x 29 In., Pair ... 1610.00
Sculpture, Parrot On Stump, Napoleon III Style, Patinated, Marble Base, 16 x 6 In. 290.00
Sculpture, Pautrot, Ferdinand, Dog With Bird In Mouth, 12 1/2 In. 1410.00
Sculpture, Pautrot, Ferdinand, Startled Finch On Perch, Gold Green Patina, 5 In. 259.00
Sculpture, Perraud-Harry, E., Sea Lion, Alabaster Base, France, 1878, 7 1/2 In. 426.00
Sculpture, Perry, Roland Hinton, Woman On Bench With Fan, 1911, 15 In. 1880.00
Sculpture, Picault, Emile, Man With Book, France, 26 In. 2555.00
Sculpture, Picault, Emile, Woman On Eagle, Allegorical, 24 In. 2938.00
Sculpture, Piron, Eugene Desire, Dancing Mythical Creatures, 13 1/4 x 11 In. 4370.00
Sculpture, Pollet, Joseph, Partially Nude Woman, Winged Putti, 20 In. 896.00
Sculpture, Preiss, Fritz, Russian Dancer, Ivory, Cold Painted, Marble Base, c.1920, 11 In. 1675.00
Sculpture, Procession Of Musicians, 35 In. 5993.00
Sculpture, Prowling Lion, Right Foot On Ball, Oval Base, Late 19th Century, 4 In. 259.00
Sculpture, Qilin, Ferocious Face, Bulging Eyes, Roaring Mouth, Qing Dynasty, Pair, 6 In. 1495.00
Sculpture, Rabbit, Meiji, 7 1/4 x 8 In. 3470.00
Sculpture, Reclining Nude, Black Marble Base, Onyx, After Emile Carlier, 26 x 15 In. ... 460.00
Sculpture, Rhinoceros, Signed, Japan, 19th Century, 20 In. 5170.00
Sculpture, River God Seated Holding Oar, Upturned Jug At Side, 17 In. 2645.00
Sculpture, Robed Woman, Marble Pedestal Base, 18 1/2 In. 450.00
Sculpture, Romulus, Remus, Roman Wolf, Patinated, Marble Base, 4 In. 200.00
Sculpture, Rooster, Monogram, Hebrard Foundry Mark, 11 3/4 In. 205.00
Sculpture, Rozet, Fanny, Exotic Dancer, With Scarf, Onyx Base, Art Deco, 12 1/2 In. ... 1195.00
Sculpture, Russell, Charles M., Silent Thunder, California Art Foundry, 6 1/2 In. 4600.00
Sculpture, Samson, Charles A., Bust Of Young Girl, Marble, Gilt, 6 3/8 x 6 1/2 In. 375.00
Sculpture, Satyr Carrying Off Nude Maiden, Marble Base, Greece, 14 1/2 In. 825.00
Sculpture, Schmidt-Hofer, Coal Miner, Holding Davey Lantern, 1920s, 24 In. 3500.00
Sculpture, Schoenewerk, Alexander, Woman, Gilt, France, 19th Century, 19 In. 3410.00
Sculpture, Scudder, Janet, Young Pan, Brown Patina, Gorham Co., 14 1/8 In. 8625.00
Sculpture, Sehring, Adolf, Jennie, Girl With Basket, 7 1/2 x 5 1/2 x 15 1/2 In. 345.00
Sculpture, Seifert, Archer, Marble Plinth Base, Austria, 12 1/2 In. 805.00
Sculpture, Semi-Draped Woman, Art Deco, Perched On Stool, 30 In. 1645.00
Sculpture, Shiva, 4 Arms, Dancing, Flaming Aureole, India, 20th Century, 31 In. 865.00
Sculpture, Silvertooth, Dennis, The Challenge, Indian Brave, Knife, c.1974, 12 1/2 In. ... 345.00
Sculpture, Soldier, Silvered, Standing, French Uniform, c.1898, 26 In. 1765.00
Sculpture, St. Marceaux, Jester Standing With Arms Crossed, 34 In. 1880.00
Sculpture, Stag, Standing, Fox Hiding In Stump, c.1893, 21 In. 3495.00
Sculpture, Standing Woman, In Headdress, Silvered, Square Base, Tibet, 14 1/2 In. 115.00
Sculpture, Swordsman, Black Marble Base, Dark Brown Patina, 12 1/2 In. 220.00
Sculpture, Sykes, Charles, Rolls-Royce, Art Nouveau, 25 1/2 In. 6720.00
Sculpture, Tara, Seated On Lotus Throne, Lotus Blossoms, Tibet, 18th Century, 5 1/8 In. . 2070.00
Sculpture, Tiger, Silvered, 20th Century, 42 In. 259.00
Sculpture, Tiger, Stalking, Glass Eyes, Late 19th Century, Japan, 18 In. 805.00
Sculpture, Trajan's Column, Black, Marble Base, 18 1/2 In. 940.00
Sculpture, Valton, Charles, Bull, Curved Horns, Marble Base, 8 1/2 x 8 In. 460.00
Sculpture, Vermare, Andre Cesar, Joan Of Arc, Gilt, Signed, c.1909, 14 1/2 In. 920.00
Sculpture, Vidal, Louis, Lioness, Patinated, France, 9 x 12 x 4 In. 1495.00
Sculpture, Vienna Bronze, Arab Praying, Cold Painted, 5 1/2 In. 1793.00
Sculpture, Vienna Bronze, Boston Terrier, 1 1/2 In. 265.00
Sculpture, Vienna Bronze, Go To Bed, Boy On Sawhorse, 3 1/4 In. 225.00
Sculpture, Vienna Bronze, Man, Sign, Eat At Joe's, 3 In. 355.00
Sculpture, Vienna, Arab Tea Vendor, Cold Painted, 4 In. 1795.00
Sculpture, Vienna, Diogenes, Marble Base, 2 1/2 In. 415.00
Sculpture, Villanis, Edouard, Bohemienne, Maiden Holding Lyre, 22 In. 2235.00
Sculpture, Villanis, Edouard, Woman Riding A Camel, Oval Marble Base, 18 In. 1435.00
Sculpture, Vishnu, Lotus Base, India, 18th Century, 22 In. 2875.00

Sculpture, Waagen, Whippet & Butterfly, Ormolu, Oval Terrain Base, 11 x 14 In. 1150.00
Sculpture, Warriors, Medieval, Armor, Gilt Details, Marble Base, 18 In. 3820.00
Sculpture, Wine Goddess, Cast, Green Patina, Stamped IWP, 1940s, 13 3/4 In. 230.00
Sculpture, Woman In Renaissance Costume, Ivory, 12 In. 1528.00
Sculpture, Woman With Dog, Art Deco, After Georges Coste, 26 In. 2585.00
Sculpture, Woman, Parcel Gilt, Patinated, Circular Base, 19th Century, 22 x 11 In. 690.00
Sculpture, Young Pharaoh, Marble Base, Inscribed Picault, 28 1/2 In. 316.00
Scultpure, Lemire, Charles B., Cupid Seated, Brown Patina, 10 3/4 In. 1265.00
Shrine, Pala Style, 3 Sections, Manjushri, Museum Style Display, 19th Century, 14 In. 865.00
Shrine Niche, Gilt, Filigree Canopy, France, 19th Century, 47 x 15 x 19 In. 750.00
Stirrup, Brass, Revolutionary War 225.00
Tazza, Acanthus Leaf, Circular Bowls, Scroll, Leaf, Gilt, 12 x 14 1/2 In., Pair 1150.00
Tazza, Napoleon III, Gilt, Onyx, Flowers, 13 In. 1175.00
Tobacco Box, Figural, Monkey, 13 In. 1645.00
Tray, Hand Hammered, Apollo Studios, c.1910, 9 In. 35.00
Tray, Matchbox Holder, Applied Scrolling, Dore, Arts & Crafts, c.1910, 6 1/4 In. 69.00
Tray, Presentation, Figural, Brown Green Patina, Signed, Charles Marey, c.1908, 17 In. . . 290.00
Urn, Chocolate Brown Patina, Applied Birds, Fish, 3 Legs, Foo Dog Knees, 21 In. 440.00
Urn, Classical Women, Silvered, Relief, Allegory, Late 20th Century, 19 In. 405.00
Urn, Cover, Garden, Rococo, Man & Woman Flanked By 2 Cupids, 43 In. 2415.00
Urn, Landscape Scenes, Foo Dogs, Leaves, Applied Dragons, Chinese, c.1900, 24 In. 750.00
Urn, Napoleon III, Grecian Style, Figures, Inscribed, 11 In., Pair 805.00
Vase, 3 Karako Holding Vase, Meiji Period, Japan, 9 1/2 In. 290.00
Vase, Cover, Louis XVI Style, Gilt Mounted, Marble, Oval, Handles, Swags, 19 1/2 In. . . 1795.00
Vase, Cranes, Phoenix, Dragon, Turtle, Relief, 27 5/8 In. 415.00
Vase, Fish, Oval, Meiji, Japan, 12 In. 880.00
Vase, Flared Rim, Paneled Shoulder, Flowers, Peacock, Peahen, 42 In. 3300.00
Vase, Floor, Green, Brown Patina, Japan, c.1912, 24 In. 316.00
Vase, Intricate Frog, Fish & Snake Design, Tree-Trunk Handle, Original Patina, 5 In. 265.00
Vase, Landscape Relief, 3 Elephants, Raised Trunks, Oval, Chinese, 6 1/4 In., Pair 209.00
Vase, Mt. Fuji, Silver Inlay, Japan, 20th Century, 9 In. 380.00
Vase, Stylized Dragons, Dragon Head, Tong-Form Handles, Qing, Chinese, 12 1/2 In. . . . 295.00
Vase, Swollen Cylindrical Shape, Flying Birds, Pierced Foliate Base, Chinese, 15 In. 840.00
Wall Bracket, Gilt, Marble Top, 1890, 10 x 11 1/2 In., Pair 1110.00
Water Font, Figural, Guardian Angel, Gilded, France, 8 1/2 x 6 1/4 In. 1265.00
Weight Set, Opium, Oriental Zodiac Figures On Square Base, 1 1/2 In., 10 Piece 69.00
Weight Set, Stylized Burmese Dragons, Tallest 2 1/2 In., 6 Piece 60.00

BROWNIES were first drawn in 1883 by Palmer Cox. They are characterized by large round eyes, downturned mouths, and skinny legs. Toys, books, dinnerware, and other objects were made with the Brownies as part of the design.

Block Set, Winter Scenes, Christmas Scenes, Set Of 6 . . . . 355.00
Book, Brownies & The Farmer, 1902, 6 3/4 x 8 3/4 In. 35.00
Cutouts, Paper, Lion Coffee Premium 35.00
Stamp Set, Hand Stamps, Wood Box, Paper Label, Rubber Stamp Co., Set Of 14 . . . . 120.00
Toothpick Holder, 1 Side With 3 Brownies Stealing Goat, Policeman In Pursuit, 2 In. . . . 490.00
Trade Card, Corn Stalks, Use Sleeper's Crescent Gloss & Corn Starch, 3 x 4 1/2 In. 10.00
Tray, Ice Cream, Brownies Scene, 13 1/4 x 10 1/2 In. 280.00

BRUSH Pottery was started in 1925. George Brush first worked in 1901 in Zanesville, Ohio. He started his own pottery in 1907, but it burned to the ground soon after. In 1909 he became manager of the J.W. McCoy Pottery. In 1911, Brush and J.W. McCoy formed the Brush-McCoy Pottery Co. After a series of name changes, the company became The Brush Pottery in 1925. It closed in 1982. Collectors favor the figural cookie jars made by this company. Because there was a company named Brush-McCoy, there is great confusion between Brush and Nelson McCoy pieces. See McCoy category for more information.

MARK

Ashtray, Double Croaking Frog, 3 x 7 In. 104.00
Bowl, Onyx Blue, No. 01, 7 In. 45.00
Bowl, Tree & Fence Scene, Ivory, Green, Brown, Marked, 3 1/2 x 8 In. 35.00

Cookie Jar, Cookie House, 10 3/4 In.	90.00
Cookie Jar, Formal Pig, Green Coat, 11 1/4 In.	375.00
Cookie Jar, Little Red Riding Hood, 10 1/2 x 6 1/2 In.	650.00
Cookie Jar, Teddy Bear, Feet In, 1940s, 11 In.	185.00
Cuspidor, Ivory, Green Design, c.1918, 5 1/2 x 7 1/4 In.	100.00
Custard, Nurock, No. 556, 5 Oz.	25.00
Figurine, Croaking Frog, 6 x 11 In.	220.00
Figurine, Duck, Ivory, Head Up, Brown Underglaze, 3 3/4 In.	9.00
Figurine, Frog Crouched On Lily Pad, Arms Around, 7 In.	219.00
Figurine, Frog, 1 1/4 In.	115.00
Figurine, Frog, 5 x 10 In.	185.00
Figurine, Turtle, Brown Over Green Glaze, 2 3/4 x 7 1/4 In.	58.00
Flower Frog, Froggie, 2 1/2 x 4 In.	69.00
Jardiniere, Brown & Green, Drip Glaze, 8 x 6 3/4 In.	90.00
Jardiniere, Gargoyle Faces, Ornate Arches, 7 In.	145.00
Mug, Kolorcraft Keg, No. 397, 15 Oz.	20.00
Planter, Brown, Glossy, Drip Glaze, Art Deco, 9 1/2 x 5 In.	22.00
Planter, Celadon, Ribbed, Oblong, Impressed, 3 1/2 x 7 1/8 In.	25.00
Planter, Dog, Standing, 4 1/2 In.	14.00
Planter, Donkey & Cart, Gold Trim, 4 In.	12.00
Planter, Frog, Green, 5 5/8 In.	25.00
Planter, Pie Crust Top, Orange Under Tan, Speckles, 10 x 3 1/4 x 4 In.	9.00
Planter, Reclining Frog, 5 x 10 In.	130.00
Planter, Swan, Yellow, Stamped, 6 1/4 x 9 1/2 In.	65.00
Planter, Tan, Hand Coiled, Low, 6 x 3 3/4 In.	18.00
Salt & Pepper, Cloverleaf, Pair	70.00
Teapot, Cloverleaf, 8 Cup, 6 1/2 In.	75.00
Urn, Cobalt, Light Blue, Mottled Glossy Glaze, 20 x 10 1/2 In.	295.00
Vase, Blue, White Spatters, Handles, Marked, USA, 1871, 8 In.	135.00
Vase, Brown Onyx, 6 1/2 In.	68.00
Vase, Bud, Green Onyx, Marked No. 745, 1930s, 6 In.	95.00
Vase, Green Onyx, Signed, Marked No. 050, 6 x 6 1/2 In.	55.00
Wall Pocket, Dog & Doghouse, 1952, 8 x 7 In.	79.00

BRUSH MCCOY, see Brush category and related pieces in McCoy category.

BUCK ROGERS was the first American science fiction comic strip. It
started in 1929 and continued until 1967. Buck has also appeared in
comic books, movies, and, in the 1980s, a television series. Any memorabilia connected with the character Buck Rogers is collectible.

Attack Ship, Fuselage, Fins, Exhaust & Nose Cone, Box, Tootsietoy, 1937, 4 3/4 In.	750.00
Badge, Solar Scouts Members, Brass, Signature, Cream Of Wheat, 1936, 1 1/2 In.	85.00
Badge, Space Ship Commander, Whistle, Cream Of Wheat, 1936, 1 3/4 In.	200.00
Battle Cruiser, Tootsietoy, Box	280.00
Battle Cruiser, Yellow, Nose Cone, Box, Tootsietoy, 1937, 4 7/8 In.	280.00 to 750.00
Belt, Leather, Buckle, Silhouette, Spaceships, Stars, Reliable Belt, 1937, 32 In.	500.00
Binoculars, Supersonic, Hard Plastic, Norton-Honer, Box, 1963, 5 1/2 In.	115.00
Book, Adventures Of Buck Rogers, 1934, 7 x 9 1/2 In.	100.00
Book, Buck Rogers In The 25th Century, Kellogg's, 1933, 6 x 8 In.	120.00
Book, Cutout Adventure, Full Color, Cocomalt, 1933, 9 x 13 In., 4 Pages	375.00
Book, In The City Below The Sea, Hardcover, Whitman, 1934, 3 5/8 x 4 1/2 In.	350.00
Book, On The Moons Of Saturn, Hardcover, Whitman, 1934, 3 5/8 x 4 1/2 In.	375.00
Book, Pop-Up, A Dangerous Mission, Hardcover, 1934, 4 x 5 In., 60 Pages	600.00
Booklet, Gum, No. 1, Thwarting Ancient Demons, 1934, 2 3/8 x 2 7/8 In., 8 Pages	400.00
Booklet, Gum, No. 4, The Fight Beneath The Sea, 2 3/8 x 2 7/8 In., 8 Pages	175.00
Booklet, Gum, No. 5, A Handful Of Trouble, 2 3/8 x 2 7/8 In., 8 Pages	150.00
Button, Buffalo Evening News Contest, Aviator Character, 1930, 1 1/4 In.	175.00
Button, Color, Chicago American Lithograph, Greenduck, 1934, 1 1/8 In.	165.00
Catalog, Color Cover, Premiums, Cream Of Wheat, 1936	300.00
Chemical Laboratory, Gropper Mfg. Co., 1937	1320.00
Game, Card, Full Color, All-Fair, Box, 1936, 4 x 5 In., 35 Piece	550.00
Game, Game Of 25th Century, Robots, Monsters, Board, 1934, 18 x 13 In.	350.00
Gun, Rubber Band, Blue, Red, Punch-Out, Targets, 1940, 5 x 10 In.	475.00
Helmet, 25th Century Inter-Planetary Navigation, Daisy, XZ-34, 1930s, Medium	560.00

Buffalo Pottery,
Plate, Christmas
Carol, Seasons
Greetings, 1958

Buck Rogers, Rocket Skates, Streamlined,
Pressed Steel, c.1934, 10 1/2 In.

Helmet, Leather, Robots, Space Ships, Premium, Box, Daisy, 1930, 8 x 6 In. 3900.00
Helmet, Suede Cloth, Navigation, XZ-42, 1930s, 7 In. 259.00
Holster, Buck Holding Gun, Felt, Studs, c.1930, 11 In. 292.00
Mask, Wilma Deering, 1930, 8 x 10 In. 225.00
Pencil Box, Buck, Wilma Riding Space Scooters, Cardboard, John Dille, 1936, 9 In. 138.00
Picture, Buck & Wilma, Sepia, Browntone, Cocomalt, 1933, 7 1/2 x 10 In. 125.00
Pistol, Atomic, Black, Muzzle, Blaster, Sparks, Box, Daisy 330.00
Popgun, 25th Century, Daisy, c.1932, 7 1/2 In. 330.00
Popgun, Color, 2 Sides, Cardboard, Cocomalt, 1934, 9 1/2 In. 350.00
Punch-O-Bag, Morton Salt, Envelope, 1935, 3 x 5 In. 40.00
Ray Gun, Sonic, Battery Operated, Hard Plastic, Norton-Honer, 1952, 7 1/4 In. 150.00
Ring, Ring Of Saturn, Red Stone, Alligator, Glows In Dark, Plastic 350.00
Rocket, Police Patrol, Space Noise, Windup, Tin, Marx, 1939, 12 In. 420.00
Rocket Ship, 25th Century, Box, Marx, 1934, 12 In. 5300.00
Rocket Ship, Police Patrol, Portholes, Fins, Blue, Green, Red, Marx, 1935 . . . . 1395.00
Rocket Skates, Streamlined, Pressed Steel, c.1934, 10 1/2 In. . . . . *Illus* 2860.00
Space Ranger Kit, 6 Punch-Out Sheets, Sylvania, 1952, 11 x 15 In. 144.00
Space Ranger Kit, Sylvania, Early 1950s, 10 3/4 x 8 In. 125.00
Spaceship, Bomb, Instruction, Morton Salt, 1942, 2 1/2 x 7 1/2 In. 60.00
Spaceship, Space Noise & Spark, Windup, Tin, Marx, 12 In. 300.00
Spaceship, Venus Duo-Destroyer, Deck & Nose Cone, Box, Tootsietoy, 1937, 4 5/8 In. 795.00
Telescope, Black, Pull-Out Lens, Japan, 14 In. 1020.00
Uniform, Space Playsuit, Sackman Brothers, 1934, Size 4, 3 Piece 1300.00
Walkie-Talkies, Decoder, Certificate, Remco, Box, 8 1/2 x 13 In. . . . . .230.00 to 418.00
Watch, Pocket, Box, 1935 . . . . 1025.00
Water Pistol, Liquid Helium, Yellow, Orange, Brass Nozzle, 1936, 7 1/2 In. . . . .300.00 to 1000.00
Water Pistol, Pressed Steel, Marked, Daisy Co., 7 1/2 In. 300.00

BUFFALO POTTERY was made in Buffalo, New York, after 1902. The
company was established by the Larkin Company, famous manufacturers of soap. The wares are marked with a picture of a buffalo and
the date of manufacture. Deldare ware is the most famous pottery
made at the factory. It has either a khaki-colored or green background
with hand-painted transfer designs.

BUFFALO POTTERY, Bowl, Pink, Willow, 8 In. 50.00
Pitcher, Chrysanthemum, Blue, Mark, 7 1/2 x 8 1/2 In. 275.00
Pitcher, Cinderella, Coach, Horsemen, Mark, 1906, 6 x 7 In. . . . . .275.00 to 460.00
Pitcher, Dutch, Castle In Landscape, Mother & Daughter Walking, 1907, 6 x 7 In. 248.00
Pitcher, Fox Hunt, Whirl Of The Town, Transfer Logo, 1906, 6 3/4 In. . . . . .345.00 to 825.00
Pitcher, Gaudy Willow, Mark, 1905, 6 3/4 x 7 In. 385.00
Pitcher, Gloriana, Field Of Flowers, Mark, 1907, 9 x 8 In. 605.00
Pitcher, Holland, Girls Knitting, Mark, 1908, 6 x 7 In. 550.00
Pitcher, Landing Of Roger Williams, Mark, 1907, 6 1/4 x 7 In. 413.00
Pitcher, Mason, Teal Flowers, 6 Panels, 1907, 8 x 8 In. 440.00
Pitcher, Pilgrim, Mayflower, Miles Standish, John Alden, Mark, 1907, 9 x 8 In. 413.00
Pitcher, Robin Hood Sounding Horn, Guarding Off Indians, 8 1/4 x 5 3/4 In. 660.00
Pitcher, Roosevelt Bears, At Home, Circus, School, Take A Ride, 1907, 8 1/4 x 8 In. 1100.00
Pitcher, Whaling City, New Bedford, Mass., Blue Green Transfer, 6 1/4 In. 355.00
Plate, Christmas Carol, Seasons Greetings, 1958 . . . . *Illus* 45.00
Plate, George Washington, Chesapeake Railroad Co., Mark, 10 3/4 In. 605.00

Plate, Gunner, Hunter Aiming, Dog In Hunt Position, 9 In.	66.00
Plate, Niagara Falls, Monochrome, Teal Green, 7 1/2 In.	95.00
Plate, Patriotic, V Medallion, Red, White, Blue Bands, Stars, 10 3/4 In.	1760.00
Plate, Roycroft, Oval, Squares On Border, White, Black, Red, Mark, 6 1/2 x 8 1/2 In.	358.00
Salt & Pepper, Cross Decoration, 3 x 2 1/2 In.	345.00
Tankard, Fallowfield Hunt, Supper, Ivory, Mark, 12 1/4 x 7 In.	1650.00
Tray, Buffalo Hunt Scene, Green, 14 x 11 In., Pair	400.00
BUFFALO POTTERY DELDARE, Bowl, Cereal, Fallowfield Hunt, The Start, 1908, 2 x 6 1/4 In.	330.00
Bowl, Fallowfield Hunt, Breakfast At The 3 Pigeons, 5 1/8 x 12 In.	770.00
Bowl, Fruit, Dr. Syntax Reading His Tour, 1911, 4 x 9 In.	1045.00
Bowl, Fruit, Ye Village Tavern, 1909, 3 3/4 x 9 In.	110.00
Bowl, Ye Lion Inn, 7 3/4 In.	374.00
Bowl, Ye Olden Days, Man Walking On Boardwalk, Mark, 1924, 2 1/2 In.	303.00
Candlestick, Scenes Of Village Life, Signed, 1925, 9 1/3 x 5 In., Pair	413.00
Card Tray, Fallowfield Hunt, Huntsmen Finish Meal, Mark, 1909, 8 In.	193.00
Creamer, Fallowfield Hunt, Breaking Cover, Huntsmen, Mark, 1908, 3 x 5 In.	110.00 to 275.00
Creamer, Village Life In Ye Olden Days, Saucer, 2 3/4 x 4 1/2 In.	150.00
Cup & Saucer, Fallowfield Hunt, Horseman, Dog, Mark, 1909, 2 x 6 In.	138.00
Cup & Saucer, Ye Olden Days, Mark, 1909, 2 x 5 3/4 In.	138.00
Cup & Saucer, Ye Village Street, Mark, 1909, 3 x 5 In.	440.00
Dresser Tray, Heirlooms, 3 Women Around Table, 1908, 14 x 10 1/2 In.	413.00
Humidor, Mariner, There Was An Old Sailor, 1909, 7 1/4 x 6 In.	605.00 to 1430.00
Humidor, Ye Lion Inn, 1924, 7 1/2 x 6 1/2 In.	770.00
Match Holder, Ye Olden Days, Scenes Of Village Life, 1925, 3 1/2 x 5 In.	825.00 to 990.00
Matchbox Holder, Ashtray, Fallowfield Hunt, Mark, 1909, 3 1/2 x 7 In.	715.00
Mug, Breaking Cover, Signed, L Anna, 1908, 3 2/3 In.	295.00 to 335.00
Mug, Breaking Cover, Signed, L. Streissel, 1909, 3 2/3 In.	335.00
Mug, Dr. Syntax Made Free Of The Cellar, Emerald, 1911, 4 1/2 x 5 In.	195.00
Mug, Fallowfield Hunt, At The 3 Pigeons, Mark, 1909, 4 1/2 x 5 1/4 In.	193.00
Mug, Fallowfield Hunt, Geaton & Rex, 1908, 4 1/2 x 5 In., Pair	660.00
Pitcher, Dr. Syntax Setting Out To The Lake, Emerald, 1911, 9 x 8 In.	1540.00
Pitcher, Fallowfield Hunt, Breaking Cover, Ball, 7 x 6 1/2 In.	595.00
Pitcher, Fallowfield Hunt, The Return, 1909, 8 x 7 1/4 In.	550.00
Pitcher, To Spare An Old Broken Soldier, 1909, 7 x 6 3/4 In.	275.00
Pitcher, Ye English Village, 3 Men, Lion Inn, Mark, 1908, 10 x 8 3/4 In.	413.00
Plaque, Dr. Syntax Sketching The Lake, Emerald, 1911, 12 In.	1045.00
Plaque, Fallowfield Hunt, The Start, 14 In.	330.00
Plaque, Lost, Sheep Huddled In Storm, Emerald, Mark, 1911, 13 1/2 In.	3575.00
Plate, At Ye Lion Inn, 1908, 6 1/4 In.	88.00
Plate, Dr. Syntax Disputing His Bill, Emerald, Mark, 9 1/4 In.	2310.00
Plate, Dr. Syntax Losing His Way, Emerald, 1911, 9 1/4 In.	770.00
Plate, Dr. Syntax Making A Discovery, Emerald, M. Broel, 10 In.	875.00
Plate, Dr. Syntax Pursued By A Bull, Chased Up Tree, Emerald, Mark, 1911, 9 In.	990.00
Plate, Dr. Syntax Sells Grizzle, Horse Buyers, Emerald, Mark, 1911, 14 In.	880.00 to 1045.00
Plate, Dr. Syntax The Garden Trio, Girls Playing Violin, Cello, Emerald, 1911, 9 In.	550.00
Plate, Fallowfield Hunt, Breaking Cover, 2 Horsemen, Mark, 1909, 7 In.	385.00
Plate, Fallowfield Hunt, The Death, 1909, 8 1/2 In.	220.00
Plate, John Alden & Pricilla, Marked, 1911, 10 In.	4675.00
Plate, Misfortune At Tulip Hall, Emerald, E. Dowlman, 8 1/4 In.	395.00
Plate, Misfortune At Tulip Hall, Emerald, M. Broel, 1911, 9 1/4 In.	995.00
Plate, Salesmen, Village Border, Mark, 1908, 6 1/2 In.	1210.00
Plate, Town Crier, Mark, Signed AR, 1909, 8 1/2 In.	99.00
Plate, Ye Village Gossips, 1924, 10 In.	165.00
Powder Jar, Bird Heads Peering Upwards, Emerald, 1911, 2 3/4 x 4 In.	715.00
Powder Jar, Cover, Ye Village Street, Mark, 1909, 3 x 4 1/2 In.	440.00
Punch Bowl, Hunt Scenes, Mark, 1909, 9 1/4 x 14 1/2 In.	5225.00
Sugar, Scenes Of Village Life In Ye Olden Days, 6 Sides, Mark, 2 3/4 In.	468.00
Tile, Traveling In Ye Olden Days, 1908, 6 In.	165.00
Tray, Calling Card, Dr. Syntax Robbed Of His Property, Emerald, 1911, 7 1/2 In.	358.00
Vase, 3 Women, Victorian, Deldare Ware Transfer Logo, 1924, 7 3/4 In.	288.00
Vase, American Beauty, Flowers, Butterflies, Cylindrical, Emerald, 1911, 14 In.	1100.00 to 1320.00
Vase, Ye Village Parson, Ye Village Schoolmaster, 1908, 8 1/4 x 7 In.	770.00
Vase, Yellow, Silver Overlay, Transfer Logo, 1910, 7 3/4 In.	2300.00

Vase, Abstract Feathers, Green, White, Gray, Emerald, 1911, 8 1/2 x 5 1/2 In. 935.00
Vase, Tapered, Bayberry, White Flowers, Vines, Emerald, Mark, 1911, 9 x 6 In. 1320.00

BUNNYKINS, see Royal Doulton category.

BURMESE GLASS was developed by Frederick Shirley at the Mt. Washington Glass Works in New Bedford, Massachusetts, in 1885. It is a two-toned glass, shading from peach to yellow. Some pieces have a pattern mold design. A few Burmese pieces were decorated with pictures or applied glass flowers of colored Burmese glass. Other factories made similar glass also called *Burmese*. Related items may be listed in the Fenton category, the Gunderson category and under Webb Burmese.

Bowl, Enameled Berries, Leaves, Earth Tones, 19th Century, 2 3/4 x 3 1/2 In. 316.00
Bowl, Jack-In-The-Pulpit, Crimped Edge, 5 3/4 In. 375.00
Bowl, Oval Bottom, Cornered Rim, 5 In. 196.00
Bowl, Star Shaped, Ruffled Edge, 4 In. 150.00
Bride's Basket, Diamond-Quilted, Ruffled Edge, Silver Plated Stand, Handle, 12 In. 220.00
Celery Vase, Squat, Bulbous, Scalloped Rim, Glossy, 6 1/2 In. 450.00
Condiment Set, Ribbed, Pairpoint Silver Holder, 3 Piece 325.00
Creamer, Enameled Pine Bow, Pine Cones, Applied Handle, Ruffled Edge, 2 1/2 In. 328.00
Rose Bowl, Flowers, 3 1/4 In. 180.00
Rose Bowl, Gundersen, 4 In. 60.00
Rose Bowl, Ribbed, Footed, 3 In. 225.00
Salt & Pepper, Melon, 4 Piece 270.00
Salt & Pepper, Ribbed, 4 In. 175.00
Salt & Pepper, Ribbed, Silver Plated Tops & Holder, 6 In. 805.00
Sugar Shaker, Flowers, Blue, Pink, Yellow, Fig Shape, 4 In. 2185.00
Sugar Shaker, Red & White Berries, Green Leaves, Satin, 4 1/2 In. 2130.00
Syrup, Blue & White Flowers, Applied Handle, Silver Plated Hardware, 6 In. 5405.00
Toothpick, Asters, Blue, White, Satin, Fold-In Rim, 2 In. 290.00
Toothpick, Top Hat, Glossy, 1 3/4 In. 365.00
Toothpick, White & Red Flowers, Green Stems, Tricornered Rim, 2 1/4 In. 670.00
Vase, Cylindrical, Applied V-Scroll Handles, 10 1/4 In. 1230.00
Vase, Enameled Leaves, Ruffled Edge, 6 1/4 In. 130.00
Vase, Fan Shape, Satin Feet, Ruffled Edge, 4 1/2 In. 50.00
Vase, Flared, Ruffled Edge, 19th Century, 4 In., Pair 316.00
Vase, Hobnail, Applied Rigaree, Ruffled Edge, 3 In. 375.00
Vase, Jack-In-The-Pulpit, Enameled Flowers, 9 1/2 In. 345.00
Vase, Pink To Yellow, Beaded Flowers, 9 3/4 In. 1035.00
Vase, Reverse Shaded, 3 Reeded Feet, 5 1/2 In. 60.00
Vase, Squared Rim, 19th Century, 2 1/2 In. 144.00
Vase, Stick, Bulbous, Beaded White & Yellow Daisies, 7 1/2 In. 2240.00
Vase, Stick, Yellow To Pink, 10 1/4 In. 1035.00
Vase, Trumpet, Enameled Daisies, Glossy, 7 3/4 In. 250.00
Vase, Trumpet, Glossy, Wooden Holder, 10 1/2 In. 155.00
Vase, Trumpet, Satin, Tricornered Rim, 9 In. 145.00

BUSTER BROWN, the comic strip, first appeared in color in 1902. Buster and his dog, Tige, remained a popular comic and soon became even more famous as the emblem for a shoe company, a textile firm, and others. The strip was discontinued in 1920, but some of the advertising is still in use.

Balloon Inflator, Figural Head, Vinyl Tank, Winking, 24 x 21 In. 150.00
Balloon Inflator, Plastic Head, Fabric Body Fits Air Tank, 48 In. 165.00
Bank, Black Horse, Good Luck, 4 1/2 x 5 In. 190.00
Bank, Cast Iron, A.C. Williams, 1910-1932, M 241, 5 1/2 In. . . . . .242.00 to 275.00
Bench, Figural, 4-Seat, Red, Wooden, 75 x 35 In. 2640.00
Bench, Shoe, Advertisements On Back, 36 x 60 x 18 In. 1980.00
Bench, White House, 60 In. 1800.00
Box, Company History On Lid, Buster, Tige On Floor, 1910 . . . .   600.00
Button, Bread, Multicolored, Celluloid, 1 1/4 In. 20.00
Candy Container, Nodder, Buster Brown & Tige, On Egg, Papier-Mache 170.00
Cards, Playing, Buster Brown & Tige, U.S. Playing Card Co., 52 Cards, 2 1/2 x 1 3/4 In. . .   100.00
Display, Figure, Shoe Shelves, 8 Sides, Masonite Lithograph, 60 In. 220.00

Display, Tige, Masonite Lithograph, 8 Sides, 2 Shoe Shelves, 30 In.	110.00
Doll, Tige, Cloth, 10 1/2 In.	100.00
Knife, Pocket, Brown, Bilt Shoe, 3/4 x 3 3/4 In.	40.00
Knife, Pocket, Buster Brown Shoes, White Store, Green Bay, Wisconsin	75.00
Mirror, Advertising, Shoes, The Little Girl On The Other Side Should Wear	250.00
Mirror, Buster Brown Shoes, For Boys & Girls, Buster, Pup, Celluloid, 1 1/4 In.	95.00
Pin, Tige, Celluloid, 1900s, 1 1/2 In.	149.00
Sign, Buster Brown & Tige, Plastic, Painted, Lights Up, 18 x 18 In.	230.00
Sign, Buster Brown Shoes, Boy, Dog, Neon, Case, Square, 54 In.	2475.00
Sign, Gilded, Circular Plaque, 17 In.	160.00
Tin, Spice, Buster & Tige, Red, Metal Top & Bottom, 2 1/2 x 1 3/4 In.	112.00
Tray, Child's, Germany, 5 1/4 x 3 1/2 In.	90.00
Whistle, Buster Brown & Tige, Buster Brown Shoes, Brown Bilt Shoes, 1 1/2 In.	60.00

BUTTER CHIPS, or butter pats, were small individual dishes for butter. They were the height of fashion from 1880 to 1910. Earlier as well as later examples are known.

Bleu De Four, Square, C. Field, Haviland, 2 3/4 In.	35.00
Blue Garland, Platinum Trim, Scalloped, Haviland, 3 5/8 In.	19.00
Blue Willow, Buffalo Pottery, 1916, 3 3/4 In.	39.00
Delta Airlines, White, 4 In.	8.00
Denmark, Blue, Franciscan	16.00 to 20.00
Diana, J. & C. Meakin, Hanley, England, 3 In.	10.00
Dresden Flowers, Empress, Schumann, 4 1/4 In.	30.00
English Rose, J. & G. Meakin, England, 3 1/4 In.	15.00
Floral Cartouche, Gold Trim, Fluted Rim	4.00
Flowers, Gold Highlights, Kelly Green Rim, Scalloped, Grindley, 1880s, 3 3/8 In.	18.00
Gold Flowers, GDA, Limoges, France, 3 1/2 In.	17.00
Orange Flowers, Gold Trim, M. Redon, Limoges, 3 1/2 In.	10.00
Orchid, Limoges, Jean Pouyat Mark 5, 3 1/4 In.	25.00
Parsifal, Austria	12.00
Pink Flowers, Gold Trim, Haviland, Mark 26, c.1893, 3 1/4 In.	30.00
Pink Roses, Scalloped Edge	10.00
Playing Card Designs, Wooden, 3 In.	9.00
Quail, Brown, Furnival, 3 1/4 In.	20.00
Restaurant China, Blue, Beaded Drape Border	10.00
Restaurant China, Dark Green Leaves, Berries Border	10.00
Roses, Gold Trim, Germany, 3 3/4 In.	10.00
Santa Fe Railroad, California Poppy, 1930s, 3 1/2 In.	35.00
Shakespeare Country, Homer Laughlin, 4 1/4 In.	20.00
Windmill, House By Lake, Ship Sailing By, Blue Trim	10.00
Yellow Crocus, Easterling, Bavaria, 3 1/4 In., 4 Piece	20.00

BUTTER MOLDS are listed in the Kitchen category under Mold, Butter.

BUTTON collecting has been popular since the nineteenth century. Buttons have been known throughout the centuries, and there are millions of styles. Gold, silver, or precious stones were used for the best buttons, but most were made of natural materials, like bone or shell, or from inexpensive metals. Only a few types are listed for comparison.

Brass, Agate, 5/8 In., 24 Piece	20.00
Brass, Cherub, Dragon, Tin Back, Victorian, 1 3/8 In.	25.00
Brass, Oval, Lavender Stone, 12 Amethyst & Gold Stones, Bar Shank, 2 x 1 5/8 In.	167.00
Butterscotch, Catalin, Drilled Shank, 5/16 In., 9 Piece	6.00
Celluloid, U-Shape, Golf Club, Ball, Metal Shank, 1 x 1 1/8 In.	34.00
Copper, Oval, Moonstone, Embossed Scrolls, 1 x 13/16 In.	34.00
Glass, Dog Holding Basket In Mouth, 9/16 In.	25.00
Glass, Mosaic, House Scene, 1/2 x 3/8 In.	14.00
Le Chic, Yellow, Flower Shape, 1/2 In., 10 Piece	5.00
Metal, 2 Children On Fence, Umbrella, Kate Greenaway, Loop Shank Back, 1 3/4 In.	6.00
Metal, Bronze Luster, Pigeon Eye, Set In Starburst, Wire Loop Shank, 9/16 In.	10.00
Milk Glass, Rose, Leaf Pattern, 1/4 In.	11.00
Nickel, Concho, Redskin Maid Jewelry, 6 On Card	6.00

BUTTONHOOKS have been a popular collectible in England for many years but are now gaining the attention of American collectors. The buttonhooks were made to help fasten the many buttons of the old-fashioned high-button shoes and other items of apparel.

Bakelite, Butterscotch, 7 3/8 x 11/16 In.	25.00
Bakelite, Tangerine, Art Deco	40.00
Brass, Broom Shape, 2 3/4 In.	33.00
Brass, Mother-Of-Pearl Handle, Fan Designs At Ends, 4 In.	5.00
Mother-Of-Pearl, Carved, France	65.00
Silver Plate, Chatelaine, Nursery Rhyme Characters On Both Sides, 4 1/4 In.	95.00
Sterling Silver, Grotesque & Eagle Mask, Birmingham, 1900, 5 In.	40.00
Sterling Silver, Repousse, Flowers, Folds, For Gloves, 3 In.	50.00
Sterling Silver, Steel Hook, Punch & Judy Design, England, c.1880	275.00
Sterling, Silver, With Shoehorn, Cherubs, Mark, Fitted Case, Birmingham, 1905, 5 3/4 In.	55.00
Tangerine Handle, Flared, Inverted Skyscraper Tip, Art Deco, 1920s	40.00

CALENDARS made to hang on the wall or to be displayed on a desk top have been popular since the last quarter of the nineteenth century. Many were printed with advertising as part of the artwork and were given away as premiums. Calendars with guns, gunpowder, or Coca-Cola advertising are most prized.

1876, Home Insurance Co., New York City, 5 x 7 1/2 In., 14 Sheets	75.00
1880, Brooks Coach Varnishes, Stereotype Black Comic Scenes	325.00
1888, Hood's Sarsaparilla, Girl In Bonnet, Advertisements, 11 x 13 In.	385.00
1892, Budweiser, Elegant Woman Sitting, Paper, Lithograph, Frame, 15 x 8 In.	1650.00
1893, E. Nister Angels, Landscape, Flowers, 4 1/2 x 3 1/2 In.	13.00
1896, Hood's Sarsaparilla, Frame, 10 1/2 x 13 1/2 In.	187.00
1898, Hood's Sarsaparilla, Coupon, Blond Baby, Flowers, Blue Ground	39.00
1903, Walter Wood Harvesters, Hoosick Falls, New York	125.00
1905, Metropolitan Life, 4 Girls, Lithograph, Frame, 8 x 25 In.	99.00
1906, Aetna, Winged Blond Angel, Hartford, 8 x 16 In.	125.00
1907, Hood's Sarsaparilla, Halcyon Days, Frame, 14 x 21 In.	121.00
1908, A. Hirschauer, Chicago, Girl In Red, Die Cut Cardboard, Embossed, 12 x 14 In.	220.00
1910, Ballistite & Empire Powders, Hunters, N.C. Wyeth, 19 x 12 1/2 In.	1495.00
1910, San Francisco Life Insurance Co., Boy & Flag, Celluloid, 10 Year, 3 x 5 In.	66.00
1911, Hood's Sarsaparilla Co., Lady, Rose Bouquet, Frame, 9 1/2 x 14 1/2 In.	275.00
1911, US Fidelity, Lady, Red Dress, Hat, Frame, 16 1/2 x 23 1/2 In.	525.00
1912, Wells Fargo, Nevada National Bank, Chinese Band & Emperor, 9 x 18 In.	385.00
1913, Aztec Mineral Water, Indian Woman, Paper, Roll-Down, Frame, 24 x 40 In.	635.00
1913, Ceresota Flour, Girl With Bread & Sack, Cardboard, Lithograph, 14 x 19 In.	99.00
1913, Dutch Boy Painter, Lithograph, Frame, 18 x 42 In.	275.00
1913, Heppell Bros. Insurance, Paper, Roll-Down, Frame, 16 x 33 In.	525.00
1914, Aztec Mineral Water, Indian Woman, Paper, Roll-Down, 15 x 30 In.	770.00
1914, E.P. Timmons, Fish & Oysters, Frame, 18 x 25 In.	520.00
1914, Hood's Sarsaparilla, Madonna, The Little Mother, 5 x 13 In.	77.00
1915, Peter Cartridge Company, Paper With Metal Edges, 20 In.	690.00
1916, L.L. Holden, Lady, Grapevine, Die Cut, Cardboard, Frame, 20 1/2 x 25 In.	440.00
1917, Nevins Candy, Portrait Of Lady, Paper, 3. 1/4 x 6 1/4 In.	15.00
1918, George Egret's Hell Gate Brewery, Factory Scene, Complete Pad, 28 x 21 In.	1430.00
1919, Edison Mazda, Night Is Fled, Maxfield Parrish, 9 x 4 In.	960.00
1920, Winchester, 2 Hunters, Ducks, 20 x 39 In.	908.00
1922, Overland & Willys, Edw. G. Bush, Cars, Washington, Missouri, 14 x 20 In.	110.00
1923, Mount Airy Tire & Battery Co., Frame, 19 1/4 x 10 3/4 In.	145.00
1923, Western Cartridge, Diplomats, 3 Men By Fence, 14 x 26 In.	745.00
1924, Red Goose Shoes, Getting His Goat, 8 x 19 In.	77.00
1926, A.F. Bullion, A Startling Moment, Bears, Men In Canoe, 5 1/4 x 10 1/2 In.	255.00
1926, Clintonville Implement Co., Girl With Basket, Frame, 18 x 30 In.	385.00
1926, Cudahays Puritan Meat Products, Priscilla & John Alden, 2 1/4 x 3 3/4 In.	10.00
1927, DeLaval, Lithographed Paper, Full Pad, Top Metal Hanger, Frame Under Glass	120.00
1927, Frarys Ford Garage, Men Canoeing, 14 1/2 x 11 1/2 In.	176.00
1928, J.C. Driscoll General Merchandise, Bear In Mind, 20 x 15 In.	305.00
1929, Cudahays Puritan Meat Products, Why Don't You Speak, 2 1/4 x 3 3/4 In.	10.00
1929, H.B. Hardenburg Corp., The Fish Story, C.M. Relyea Print, Frame, 25 x 42 In.	330.00

1929, Sharpe Bros. Milk, Lady Holding Roses, Paper, Roll-Down, 15 x 41 In. 110.00
1929, US Cartridge Co., Come On, What Ails Yer, 16 x 35 In. 825.00
1929-1930, Dutch Boy White Lead, Frame, 14 1/2 x 35 In. 330.00
1930, US Cartridge Co., Scarecrow, 16 x 31 1/2 In. 1075.00
1931, Edison Mazda, Waterfall, Maxfield Parrish, Girls On Rock, 41 x 22 In. 1485.00
1931, World's First Reaper, International Harvester, N.C. Wyeth, 13 x 20 1/2 In. 925.00
1932, Hercules Powder Co., Stowaways, 13 1/4 x 30 In. 385.00
1932, Trans-Canada Hotel, 2 Men, Pulling Boat From Stream, 19 x 29 In. 440.00
1933, Edison Mazda, Sunrise, Maxfield Parrish, Women At Canyon, 20 x 9 In. 770.00
1934, Nehi, Sophisticated Woman, Rolf Armstrong Artwork, 11 x 18 In. 905.00
1934, Wrigley's Spearmint Gum, Myrt & Marge, Frame, 14 3/4 x 8 3/4 In. 99.00
1936, Conradis Pharmacy, Season Greetings, Horse, Rider, 7 3/4 x 15 3/4 In. 110.00
1937, Corn Belt Serum, Inc., Boy Chasing Pigs On Scooter, Frame, 17 1/2 x 24 In. 88.00
1937, Ford, Scotty Dogs, Watch The Fords Go By, Cardboard, 15 x 23 In. 35.00
1938, Brown & Bigelow, Maxfield Parrish, The Glen, Blue Woods, 18 x 13 In. 210.00
1938, Hercules Powder Co., Alchemist, 13 x 30 In. 99.00
1939, NuGrape Soda, Lady, On Bench, Under Tree, 13 1/2 x 25 1/2 In. 303.00
1940, 7-Up, Pinup Girl, Seasons Greetings, 5 1/2 x 11 In. 99.00
1941, Bachelder's Service Station, Goodyear Tires, Boy Fishing, 10 x 9 1/2 In. 50.00
1942, Hercules Powder, Lithographed Paper, Oct. Showing, Wood Frame 132.00
1943, Greyhound Bus Co., 4 Foldover Sheets, New Frontier 40.00
1944, Corn Belt Laboratories, Boy Talking To Pig, 17 1/2 x 24 In. 88.00
1947, Crown Cola, Joan Caulfield, 11 1/2 x 25 In. 204.00
1947, Grey Van Lines, Blotter, 9 x 4 In. 10.00
1947, Kelly Springfield Tires, Carrs Tire Service, Lady Barbequeing, 16 x 33 In. 110.00
1948, Maas & Steffen Co., Wandering Herd, 13 1/2 x 26 In. 413.00
1951, B & B Plumbing & Heating Co., Minot, N.D., Frame, 13 x 21 In. 55.00
1952, Kinghon, Dog, Puzzling Pups, 8 1/4 x 10 In. 58.00
1953, Palace Club, Reno, Buffalo Hunt, 19 x 14 1/2 In. 176.00
1955, Firestone, Hunting Dogs, Oakland, California, 24 x 42 In. 30.00
1957, Simon Pure Beer, Dogs Playing Poker, 18 x 27 1/2 In. 33.00
1959, Napa Herminie Motor Company, 33 3/4 x 16 In. 17.00
1960, Harry Eckman, The Loot Has Been Good, Blotter 10.00
1961, Best Magazine, International Edition 30.00
1961, Best Magazine, Pinup Girls, Graphic 18.00
1961, Stockton Box Co., Pinup, Bill Randall, Original Envelope 35.00
1962, Winchester, Paper With Metal Edge, 29 In. 55.00
1963, Napa Herminie Motor Company, Paper, Metal, 33 3/4 x 16 In. 17.00
1968, Horlacher Brewing Co., Surfing Pinup Girl, 16 x 33 In. 35.00
1969, Playboy 25.00
1974, Marilyn Monroe 30.00
Perpetual, Dupont, Thomas Jefferson, Tin Lithograph Over Cardboard, 19 x 29 In. 330.00
Perpetual, Whitehead & Hoag, Portrait Of Lady, 4 1/2 x 6 In. 24.00

CALENDAR PLATES were very popular in the United States from 1906
to 1929. Since then, plates have been made every year. A calendar and
the name of a store, a picture of flowers, a girl, or a scene were featured on the plate.

1907, Metropolitan Life Ins. Co., Stages Of Life, Girl To Old Woman, 33 x 12 In. 345.00
1909, Flowers, Lake Scene, Pope Gosser China Co., 8 In. 11.00
1909, Williams Brothers Dealers, Morse Mill, Mo. 11.00
1911, Swan In Pond, Compliments Of A.H. Striegel 14.00
1911-1912, Compliments Of Henry Fauss, Craven, S. Dakota, 8 1/2 In. 50.00
1915, Bank Of Neck City, Mo., Panama Canal Digging, Harker Pottery 10.00
1924, Wrigley's Gum, 3 3/4 x 5 1/2 In. 23.00
1946, Dr Pepper, 13 1/2 x 22 In. 210.00
1962, Finke Monument Co., Wentzville, Mo. 8.00
1976, 200th Anniversary, Eagle, Shields, Flags, Spencer Gifts, 9 In. 25.00

CAMARK POTTERY started in 1924 in Camden, Arkansas. Jack Carnes
founded the firm and made many types of glazes and wares. The company was bought by Mary Daniel. Production was halted in 1983.

Candlestick, Ivory Matte Glaze, Landscape, Stamped Mark, 4 3/4 In. 144.00

Jug, Emerald Green, Brown, Flowers, Circular Mold Mark, c.1929, 3 3/4 In. 125.00
Strawberry Jar, Mottled Orange & Green Matte Glaze, 8 In. 175.00
Vase, Blue Flambe Glaze, Scalloped Shape, 8 In. 86.00
Vase, Green, Rose & Gray Flambe Glaze, 2 Handles, 7 In. 175.00
Vase, Mottled Brown Matte Glaze, Pinched Star Top, 5 In. 115.00
Vase, Pink Matte Glaze, 2 Molded Deer, Trees, 9 1/2 In. 173.00

CAMBRIDGE GLASS Company was founded in 1901 in Cambridge, Ohio. The company closed in 1954, reopened briefly, and closed again in 1958. The firm made all types of glass. Their early wares included heavy pressed glass with the mark *Near Cut*. Later wares included Crown Tuscan, etched stemware, and clear and colored glass. The firm used a C in a triangle mark after 1920. Some Cambridge patterns may be included in the Depression Glass category.

Apple Blossom, Compote, Willow Blue, 7 1/4 In. 275.00
Apple Blossom, Ice Bucket, Pink 295.00
Apple Blossom, Plate, 8 1/2 In. 20.00
Apple Blossom, Plate, Salad, Square, Emerald Green, 8 In. 45.00
Apple Blossom, Relish, 4 Sections, Gold Krystol, Center Handle 85.00
Apple Blossom, Relish, 5 Sections, Emerald Green, 10 x 12 In. 88.00
Apple Blossom, Tumbler, 8 Oz. 25.00
Azurite, Bowl, Gold Band, Seaweed Design, 8 In. 60.00
Bashful Charlotte, Flower Frog, 8 1/4 x 4 1/8 In. 175.00
Beehive, Perfume Bottle, Amber 75.00
Blossom Time, Relish, 8 1/2 In. 20.00
Cambridge Square, Relish, 3 Sections, 8 In. 25.00
Cambridge Square, Salt & Pepper 20.00
Caprice, Ashtray, Moonlight Blue, 5 In. 25.00
Caprice, Bonbon, Moonlight Blue, Oval, Footed, 6 In. 50.00
Caprice, Bonbon, Square, Handles, 4 In. 20.00
Caprice, Bowl, Crimped, 4-Footed, 13 In. 35.00
Caprice, Bowl, Midnight Blue, Crimped, 4-Footed, 10 1/2 In. 90.00
Caprice, Candlestick, 2-Light, Moonlight Blue, 6 In., Pair 200.00
Caprice, Candlestick, 3-Light, Pair 145.00
Caprice, Candlestick, Moonlight Blue, 2 1/2 In. 45.00
Caprice, Candlestick, Moonlight Blue, Prisms, 7 In., Pair 160.00
Caprice, Cigarette Box, Cover, Moonlight Blue, 3 1/2 x 2 1/4 In. 160.00
Caprice, Claret, Moonlight Blue, 4 1/2 Oz. 90.00
Caprice, Cocktail, Moonlight Blue, 3 1/2 Oz. 55.00
Caprice, Compote, Moonlight Blue, 7 In. 70.00
Caprice, Cup & Saucer, Mocha 32.00
Caprice, Dish, Bridge, Diamond, Moonlight Blue, 4 3/4 x 6 1/4 In. 125.00
Caprice, Dish, Mayonnaise, Underplate, Moonlight Blue . . . . .95.00 to 120.00
Caprice, Goblet, Moonlight Blue, Alpine, 10 Oz. 60.00
Caprice, Ice Bucket, Alpine, 5 3/4 x 6 1/2 In. 110.00
Caprice, Plate, Cabaret, 4-Footed, 14 In. 30.00
Caprice, Plate, Cabaret, Moonlight Blue, 4-Footed, 11 In. 55.00
Caprice, Plate, Moonlight Blue, 8 1/2 In. 38.00
Caprice, Plate, Moonlight Blue, 11 1/2 In. 90.00
Caprice, Plate, Moonlight Blue, Handles, 6 In. 20.00
Caprice, Plate, Silver 25th Anniversary, Alpine, Low-Footed, 8 In. 85.00
Caprice, Relish, 2 Sections, Moonlight Blue, 6 3/4 In. 30.00
Caprice, Relish, 3 Sections, Moonlight Blue, Alpine, 8 In. 60.00
Caprice, Rose Bowl, Moonlight Blue, 4 1/2 x 6 1/4 In. 168.00
Caprice, Sandwich Tray, Footed, 11 1/2 In. 60.00
Caprice, Saucer, Moonlight Blue 13.00
Caprice, Sherbet, Blown, 7 Oz. 60.00
Caprice, Sherbet, Moonlight Blue, Pressed, 7 Oz. 32.00
Caprice, Sherbet, Moonlight Blue, Tall, 6 Oz. 40.00
Caprice, Sherbet, Pressed, 7 Oz. 20.00
Caprice, Sugar & Creamer, Moonlight Blue, Individual 30.00
Caprice, Torte Plate, 4-Footed, 14 In. 20.00
Caprice, Torte Plate, Moonlight Blue, 4-Footed, 14 In. 60.00

Caprice, Tumbler, Footed, 10 Oz.	20.00
Caprice, Tumbler, Iced Tea, 12 Oz	60.00
Caprice, Tumbler, Juice, Moonlight Blue, Footed, 5 Oz.	55.00
Caprice, Tumbler, Moonlight Blue, Footed, 3 Oz.	125.00
Caprice, Tumbler, Mushroom, Moonlight Blue, 12 Oz.	55.00 to 65.00
Caprice, Tumbler, Old Fashioned, Moonlight Blue, 7 Oz.	100.00
Caprice, Tumbler, Water, Moonlight Blue, Footed, 10 Oz.	45.00
Caprice, Vase, Amethyst, 5 1/2 x 7 In.	95.00
Caprice, Vase, Ball, Moonlight Blue, 4 1/2 In.	200.00
Caprice, Vase, Ball, Moonlight Blue, 8 3/4 In.	345.00
Caprice, Vase, Moonlight Blue, Crimped, 4 1/2 In.	175.00
Caprice, Wine, Blown, 2 1/2 Oz.	20.00
Carmen, Urn, Cover, 12 5/8 x 6 1/2 In.	600.00
Cascade, Cocktail	11.00
Cascade, Compote, 5 1/4 In.	35.00
Cascade, Goblet	14.00
Cascade, Sugar & Creamer	15.00
Cascade, Tumbler, Footed, 12 Oz.	15.00
Chantilly, Candlestick, Martha, 4 In.	25.00
Chantilly, Candy Dish, Cover, Silver Foot, Marked, 7 In.	200.00
Chantilly, Champagne Sherbet, 5 3/4 x 3 x 3 1/2 In.	290.00
Chantilly, Cordial, 1 Oz.	40.00
Chantilly, Creamer	13.00
Chantilly, Decanter, Footed	165.00
Chantilly, Goblet, Water, 9 Oz.	25.00
Chantilly, Jug, Martini, Stir Stick, 8 3/4 x 6 In.	300.00
Chantilly, Relish, Martha 3 Sections, 9 In.	65.00
Chantilly, Sherbet, Low, 6 Oz.	15.00
Chantilly, Vase, Sterling Silver Base, 12 In.	215.00
Chesterfield, Nappy, Square, 8 In.	40.00
Chintz, Ivy Ball, Gold Encrusted, Crown Tuscan, 6 1/2 In.	70.00
Cleo, Bonbon, Emerald Green, 6 1/4 In.	20.00
Cleo, Bowl, Console, Peach-Blo, 1 5/8 x 8 3/8 In.	200.00
Cleo, Bowl, Pedestal, Peach-Blo, 4 5/8 x 10 3/4 In.	135.00
Cleo, Bowl, Vegetable, Cover, Oval, Emerald Green, 8 1/2 In.	325.00
Cleo, Plate, Emerald Green, Ringed, 6 1/2 In.	100.00
Cleo, Saucer, Emerald Green	15.00
Cleo, Wine, Pulled Stem, 3 1/2 Oz.	30.00
Corinth, Candlestick, 5 In., Pair	30.00
Corinth, Goblet, Water	8.00
Corinth, Sherbet	5.50
Corinth, Tumbler, 10 Oz.	5.50
Corinth, Tumbler, 12 Oz.	7.50
Crown Tuscan, Ashtray, Gold Trim, 3-Footed, 4 In.	20.00
Crown Tuscan, Bowl, Oval, Footed, Rolled Handles, 6 In.	130.00
Crown Tuscan, Bowl, Shell, Nude Woman, Clear Stem & Foot, 9 x 12 In.	325.00
Crown Tuscan, Candlestick, Nude Stem, 8 3/4 In.	125.00
Crown Tuscan, Cocktail, Nude Stem, 3 Oz., 8 Piece	1230.00
Crown Tuscan, Compote, Shell, 6 3/4 x 6 In.	70.00
Crown Tuscan, Dish, Cover, Shell, 6 In.	195.00
Crown Tuscan, Dish, Shell, Footed, 8 In.	185.00
Crown Tuscan, Ivy Ball, 5 In.	25.00
Crown Tuscan, Ivy Ball, Keyhole Stem, Footed, 7 1/2 In.	85.00
Crown Tuscan, Relish, 3 Sections, Keyhole Handles, 8 In.	100.00
Crown Tuscan, Shell, Enameled Roses, 7 1/2 In.	85.00
Crown Tuscan, Swan, 3 1/2 In.	50.00
Crown Tuscan, Tray, Shell, Silver Encrusted Seahorse & Band, 7 1/2 In.	275.00
Crown Tuscan, Vase, Cornucopia, Leaf Base, 9 3/4 In., Pair	100.00
Crown Tuscan, Vase, Keyhole, Stem Footed, 8 3/8 In.	130.00
Crown Tuscan, Vase, Keyhole, Stem Footed, 10 In.	60.00
Daffodil, Goblet, 9 Oz.	25.00
Decagon, Bowl, 5 1/2 In.	6.00
Decagon, Bowl, Moonlight Blue, 12 In.	60.00

Decagon,	Champagne, Moonlight Blue, 6 Oz.	25.00
Decagon,	Cocktail, Amber, 3 1/2 Oz.	12.00
Decagon,	Cordial, Amber, 1 Oz.	50.00
Decagon,	Creamer, Moonlight Blue	20.00
Decagon,	Cruet, Peach-Blo, 6 Oz.	155.00
Decagon,	Cup & Saucer, Amber	12.00
Decagon,	Cup & Saucer, Moonlight Blue	15.00
Decagon,	Dish, Soup, Emerald Green, Flat Rim, 8 1/2 In.	70.00
Decagon,	Goblet, Water, Moonlight Blue, 9 Oz.	30.00
Decagon,	Gravy Boat, Double Spouted, Amber	70.00
Decagon,	Ice Bucket, Peach-Blo, Handle, Tongs	60.00
Decagon,	Plate, 6 In.	4.00
Decagon,	Plate, Moonlight Blue, 8 3/8 In.	15.00
Decagon,	Platter, Amber, 11 In.	65.00
Decagon,	Sandwich Server, Moonlight Blue, Center Handle	50.00
Decagon,	Sugar & Creamer, Tray, Center Handle, Lightning, Handles, Moonlight Blue	130.00
Decagon,	Sugar & Creamer, Willow Blue	30.00
Decagon,	Sugar, Amber	15.00
Decagon,	Sugar, Moonlight Blue	20.00
Decagon,	Tumbler, Moonlight Blue, Footed, 8 Oz.	30.00
Diane,	Bowl, Pink, Handles, 10 In.	225.00
Diane,	Candlestick, 2-Light, Keyhole, Stem, Pair	85.00
Diane,	Candy Dish, Cover, 3 Sections	100.00
Diane,	Cocktail Icer, Insert	80.00
Diane,	Relish, 6 In.	25.00
Draped Lady,	Flower Frog, 9 In.	175.00
Draped Lady,	Flower Frog, Satin, 12 1/2 In.	325.00
Ebony,	Basket, 7 In.	95.00
Ebony,	Bowl, Fluted Rim	70.00
Ebony,	Candlestick, 2-Light, 5 1/2 x 8 In., Pair	135.00
Elaine,	Basket, 5 In.	150.00
Elaine,	Compote, 7 In.	75.00
Elaine,	Creamer, Sterling Silver Base	50.00
Elaine,	Cup	20.00
Elaine,	Saucer	3.50
Elaine,	Sherbet, High, 6 Oz.	19.00
Elaine,	Vase, Gold Flowers, 13 1/2 x 6 3/8 In.	470.00
Emerald Green,	Relish, Keyhole Handle, 6 In.	20.00
Everglade,	Bowl, Swan Handles, 14 In.	125.00
Everglade,	Creamer, Amber	50.00
Everglade,	Plate, 16 In.	125.00
Everglade,	Sugar & Creamer	90.00
Everglade,	Vase, Crown Tuscan, 7 1/2 In.	500.00
Gloria,	Relish, 3 Sections, Handles, 8 In.	40.00
Gold Krystol,	Turkey, Cover, 8 In.	1050.00
Helio,	Console, 5 x 9 3/4 In.	110.00
Heron,	Flower Frog, 8 3/4 x 4 In.	130.00
Imperial Hunt Scene,	Claret, Peach-Blo, Gold Encrusted, 5 1/2 In.	170.00
Imperial Hunt Scene,	Cocktail, Emerald Green, 2 1/2 In.	55.00
Imperial Hunt Scene,	Tumbler, Bulbous, Emerald, Green	70.00
Imperial Hunt Scene,	Wine, Peach-Blo, Emerald Green Foot, 2 1/2 Oz.	115.00
Inverted Feather,	Pitcher, Milk, Pt.	75.00
Jenny Lind,	Rose Bowl, Footed, Mocha	65.00
Larosa,	Ivy Ball, Keyhole Stem, 5 In.	70.00
Laurel,	Relish, 3 Sections, 8 In.	20.00
Lynbrook,	Cocktail, 3 Oz.	10.00
Lynbrook,	Sherbet, 6 Oz.	10.00
Lynbrook,	Tumbler, Iced Tea, Footed, 12 Oz.	15.00
Mandarin Gold,	Vase, Violet, 3 1/2 In.	45.00
Manor,	Cordial, Wisteria, 1 Oz.	145.00
Manor,	Tumbler, Gold Krystol, Footed, 10 Oz., 5 1/8 In.	30.00
Marjorie,	Punch Set, 13 Piece	175.00
Martha,	Candlestick, 5 In., Pair	20.00

Martha, Plate, Asparagus 30.00
Martha Washington, Dish, Fruit, Footed, 7 Oz. 105.00
Milk Glass, Urn, 7 1/4 In. 100.00
Mt. Vernon, Cake Plate, Yellow, 11 1/2 In. 50.00
Mt. Vernon, Compote, 7 1/2 In. 25.00
Mt. Vernon, Creamer, Footed 10.00
Mt. Vernon, Cup 6.50
Mt. Vernon, Goblet, 8 Oz. 15.00
Mt. Vernon, Goblet, 10 Oz. 15.00
Mt. Vernon, Plate, 8 1/2 In. 7.50
Mt. Vernon, Saucer 7.50
Mt. Vernon, Sherbet 10.00
Mt. Vernon, Sugar, Footed 10.00
Mt. Vernon, Tumbler, 14 Oz. 25.00
Mt. Vernon, Tumbler, Footed, 5 Oz. 12.00
Nearcut, Mug, Souvenir, Gold Band, White Enameled Dots, 4 Oz. 1585.00
No. 402, Vase, Amber, 12 In. 75.00
No. 628, Candlestick, Amber, Pair 20.00
Nude, Brandy, Mocha Bowl, Clear Stem & Foot, 1 Oz. 250.00
Nude, Brandy, Royal Blue Bowl, Clear Stem & Foot, 1 Oz. 295.00
Nude, Champagne, Heatherbloom Bowl, Clear Stem & Foot, 6 Oz. 650.00
Nude, Cocktail, Mocha Bowl, Clear Stem & Foot, 6 1/2 In. 200.00
Nude, Compote, 8 1/4 x 6 3/4 In. 195.00
Nude, Compote, Shell Shape, 5 1/2 x 5 1/4 In. 275.00
Nude, Cordial, 1 Oz. 375.00
Nude, Goblet, Smoke, Crackle Bowl, Clear Stem & Foot, 6 1/2 x 2 7/8 In. 1200.00
Nude, Ivy Ball, Amber, Clear Stem & Foot, 13 1/2 x 6 3/8 In. 485.00
Nude, Ivy Ball, Forest Green, Clear Stem & Foot 325.00
Nude, Wine, Gold Krystal Bowl, Crown Tuscan Stem & Foot, 6 1/2 In. 175.00
Pelham, Ladle, Cream, 1916 .... 10.00
Portia, Bonbon, Handles, 5 1/4 In. 25.00
Portia, Candlestick, 2-Light, Crown Tuscan, Gold Encrusted, Keyhole 150.00
Portia, Vase, Crown Tuscan, Gold Encrusted, 6 1/8 x 7 In. 230.00
Pristine, Dish, Corn 5.00
Pristine, Sherbet, Low, 6 Oz. 45.00
Rosalie, Cocktail, Icer, Liner 35.00
Rosalie, Sugar & Creamer 40.00
Rose Point, Basket, 10 x 6 3/4 In. 895.00
Rose Point, Basket, Wallace Sterling Silver Holder, 6 In. 195.00
Rose Point, Bonbon, Handles, 6 1/2 In. .... .40.00 to 65.00
Rose Point, Bowl, 4-Footed, 13 In. .... 110.00 to 145.00
Rose Point, Candlestick, 3-Light, 6 1/4 In. 250.00
Rose Point, Candlestick, Ram's Head, 4 1/2 x 4 3/4 In. 195.00
Rose Point, Candy Dish, Cover, 3 Sections, Gold Encrusted 150.00
Rose Point, Candy Dish, Cover, Footed, High, 5 1/2 In. 185.00
Rose Point, Celery Dish, 3 Sections, Moonlight Blue, 2 1/4 x 13 In. 250.00
Rose Point, Claret, 4 1/2 Oz. 110.00
Rose Point, Compote, 4-Footed, 6 In. .... .55.00 to 65.00
Rose Point, Cup & Saucer 50.00
Rose Point, Decanter, 28 Oz. 795.00
Rose Point, Decanter, Footed, 14 Oz. 525.00
Rose Point, Goblet, 10 Oz. 50.00
Rose Point, Parfait, 5 Oz., 6 1/4 In. 115.00
Rose Point, Pitcher, 20 Oz. 395.00
Rose Point, Pitcher, Ball, 80 Oz. 400.00
Rose Point, Pitcher, High Handle, 80 Oz. 575.00
Rose Point, Plate, 7 In. 15.00
Rose Point, Plate, Dinner, 10 1/4 In. 200.00
Rose Point, Plate, Handles, 11 In. 70.00
Rose Point, Plate, Shell, Crown Tuscan, 5 1/2 In. 35.00
Rose Point, Relish, 3 Sections, Gold Encrusted, Handles, 10 In. 100.00
Rose Point, Salt & Pepper, Ball Shape, Wallace Sterling Silver Base, 2 In. 495.00
Rose Point, Salt & Pepper, Egg Shape 195.00

Rose Point, Sandwich Server, Center Handle, Square, 5 1/4 x 10 3/4 In. 230.00
Rose Point, Saucer 7.00
Rose Point, Sherbet, Low, 6 Oz. . . . . .25.00 to 30.00
Rose Point, Sugar 18.00
Rose Point, Torte Plate, Gold Rim, 14 In. 55.00
Rose Point, Tumbler, Iced Tea, Footed 55.00
Rose Point, Vase, 5 In. 150.00
Rose Point, Vase, Bud, 6 1/8 In. 190.00
Rose Point, Wine, 4 1/2 Oz. 75.00
Rose Point, Wine, Amethyst, 4 1/2 Oz. 50.00
Rose Point, Wine, Forest Green, 4 1/2 Oz. 85.00
Roselyn, Celery Dish, 11 In. 45.00
Seashell, Dish, Oval, 4-Footed, Dark Emerald Green, 8 In. 50.00
Seashell, Sugar & Creamer 100.00
Stackaway, Ashtray Set, Blue, Emerald, Amber, Amethyst, Clear, 5 Piece 65.00
Star, Ashtray, 4 In. 10.00
Swan Dish, Emerald Green, 5 1/2 x 9 1/2 x 5 In. 200.00
Tally-Ho, Claret, Crystal, 4 1/2 Oz. 20.00
Tally-Ho, Cup & Saucer, Carmen 35.00
Tally-Ho, Ice Bucket 40.00
Tally-Ho, Ice Bucket, Catawba Etch 325.00
Tally-Ho, Mug, Amber, 16 Oz. 25.00
Tally-Ho, Mug, Forest Green, 16 Oz. 45.00
Tally-Ho, Plate, 8 In. 5.00
Tally-Ho, Plate, 9 1/2 In. 7.50
Tally-Ho, Punch Bowl, Footed, Amber, 13 In. 65.00
Tally-Ho, Salad Set, Underplate, Royal Blue Bowl, 2 Sections, Footed, 18 In. 325.00
Tally-Ho, Sugar, Carmen 20.00
Tally-Ho, Tumbler, Iced Tea, Carmen, Flat, 10 Oz., 5 5/8 In. 30.00
Tally-Ho, Tumbler, Royal Blue, 10 Oz., 5 5/8 In. 30.00
Tally-Ho, Tumbler, Water, Carmen 20.00
Tally-Ho, Tumbler, Whiskey, Carmen, 2 Oz. 30.00
Tally-Ho, Wine 20.00
Two Kid, Flower Frog, Boy & Goat, 9 1/4 In. 195.00
Virginian, Goblet 13.00
Virginian, Sherbet, Low 7.50
Waterlily, Jug, Cover, Emerald, 76 Oz. 200.00
Wildflower, Bowl, Salad, 11 In. 55.00
Wildflower, Candlestick, 2-Light, 6 In., Pair 65.00
Wildflower, Cheese Dish, Amber, Gold Encrusted, Footed 75.00
Wildflower, Compote, Keyhole Stem, 5 3/8 x 7 1/8 In. 100.00
Wildflower, Dish, Mayonnaise 75.00
Wildflower, Plate, Handles, Gold Encrusted, 13 1/2 In. 85.00
Wildflower, Relish, 2 Sections, Gold Encrusted, 7 In. 55.00
Wildflower, Sherbet, Low, 6 Oz. 15.00
Wildflower, Tumbler, Iced Tea, Footed, Gold Encrusted, 12 Oz. 28.00
Wildflower, Vase, Bud, Ebony, Gold Encrusted, 10 In. 495.00
Wildflower, Vase, Flip, 8 In. 195.00

CAMBRIDGE POTTERY was made in Cambridge, Ohio, from about
1895 until World War I. The factory made brown glazed decorated artwares with a variety of marks, including an acorn, the name
Cambridge, the name *Oakwood*, or the name *Terrhea*.

Tankard, Terrhea, Portrait, Smiling Monk, Impressed Mark, 15 3/4 In. 460.00
Vase, Geometric Design, Green Matte Glaze, Handles, 5 In. 115.00
Vase, Oakwood, Green Matte Luster Glaze, Squat, Acorn Stamp, 3 x 6 3/4 In. 440.00

CAMEO GLASS was made in much the same manner as a cameo in jewelry. Parts of the top layer of glass were cut away to reveal a different-
colored glass beneath. The most famous cameo glass was made during
the nineteenth century. Signed cameo glass pieces are listed under the
glasswork's name, such as Daum or Galle.

Bowl, Green, White Mistletoe, Frosted Textured Ground, Gold Rim, 4 1/2 x 9 In. 575.00

Decanter, Butterflies In Branches, Bulbous, Silver Mounted Neck, 9 1/4 In. 2000.00
Ewer, Green Flowers, Frosted Gray, Embossed Flip Top, 19th Century, 11 In. 490.00
Pitcher, Beetle Resting In Oak Tree, Earthtones Over Opaque White, 15 1/2 In. 175.00
Pitcher, Yacht Cecelle, Red Over Frosted Clear, Applied Handle, c.1901, 12 In. 1150.00
Vase, 2 Peaches, Leafy Stems, Feathered Rim, Red Ground, Oval, Shouldered, 5 In. 2200.00
Vase, Amethyst Flowers, Gray, Lavender, Yellow, Charder, c.1925, 5 In. 805.00
Vase, Berry Clusters, Enameled, France, c.1900, 12 In. 175.00
Vase, Black, Stylized Terriers, Bronzed, Silvered Ground, Art Deco, France, 8 1/2 In. 260.00
Vase, Burgundy, Rose, Castle, Mountain, Landscape, Touchard, c.1900, 7 3/4 In. 200.00
Vase, Flowering Branch, Frosted Glass, Urn Form, 20th Century, 5 5/8 In. 705.00
Vase, Flowers, Butterfly, White, Red, Yellow, 2 In. 860.00
Vase, Forest, Birds, Dark Blue To Pink Ground, French, 11 x 4 In. 3750.00
Vase, Forest, Meadow, Stream, Purple, White Streaked Sky, Footed, Lamartine, 10 In. . . . 2125.00
Vase, Green Leaves, Frosted Ground, Gold Highlights, Signed, 12 In. 345.00
Vase, Green, Iris Blossom, Olive Green Ground, Signed, 11 In. 2400.00
Vase, Irises, Red Over Frosted Clear, Shouldered Oval, Pantin, 12 In. 1410.00
Vase, Leaves, Branches, Flowers, Butterfly, Blue & White, 7 1/2 In. 840.00
Vase, Orange, Brown, Geometric & Floral, Bulbous, Charder Le Verre, c.1926, 7 In. 880.00
Vase, Pink & White Orchids, Gold, Pinwheels, Burgun & Schverer, 10 1/2 In. 9200.00
Vase, Pink, Flowering Branches, Alabaster Ground, Shouldered, 7 1/2 In. 195.00
Vase, Red Flowers, Leaves, Stems, Green Ground, Gold Enamel, Signed, St. Louis, 11 In. . 489.00
Vase, Roses, White & Red, 1 3/4 x 2 1/2 In. 860.00
Vase, Rubina Satin, Gold Flowers, Enameled, 12 In. 145.00
Vase, Ruby Thistle, Frosted, Rose Ground, France, c.1920, 3 1/4 In. 260.00
Vase, Sailing Vessels At Sea, 3 Colors, Petrache, c.1900, 5 1/4 In. 260.00
Vase, Stick, Honeysuckle, Daisies, Leaves, Yellow Ground, 5 In. 670.00
Vase, Trees, Stream, Blue, Green, Enamel, Lamartine, c.1910, 6 1/4 In. 1200.00

CAMPAIGN memorabilia is listed in the Political category.

CAMPBELL KIDS were first used as part of an advertisement for the
Campbell Soup Company in 1906. The kids were created by Grace
Drayton, a popular illustrator of the day. The kids were used in magazine and newspaper ads until about 1951. They were presented again
in 1966; and in 1983, they were redesigned with a slimmer, more contemporary appearance.

Bank, A.C. Williams, c.1910 . . . . 250.00
Button, I'm A Campbell Kid, Multicolored, Celluloid, 7/8 In. 31.00
Doll, Composition, Swivel Head, Jointed Shoulders, Hips, Clothes, 12 In. 600.00
Wristwatch, 1982 . . . . 25.00

CANDELABRUM refers to a candleholder with more than one arm to
hold many candles; a candlestick is designed to hold one candle. The
eccentricity of the English language makes the plural of candelabrum
into candelabra.

2-Arm, Brass, Scrolled, Tripod Base, Baluster Stem, 22 1/4 In., Pair 1155.00
2-Light, Art Deco, Faux Candles, Electrified, France, c.1930, 9 1/2 x 11 3/4 In. 546.00
2-Light, Bisque, Coral & White, Attached Figure, Removable Top, 8 1/2 x 7 In., Pair 295.00
2-Light, Brass, Tripod Base, Spiral Column, Drip Pans, Paw Feet, 16 In., Pair 330.00
2-Light, Bronze, Brass, Gilt, Patinated, Regency, 16 In. 2760.00
2-Light, Bronze, Ormolu, Louis XVI Style, Putto, Electrified, c.1900, 15 In., Pair 1150.00
2-Light, Chrome, U-Shape Shaft, Round Base, Stamped, Chase, 19 x 8 In., Pair 176.00
2-Light, Copper, Hammered, Faceted Base, Stamped, Karl Kipp, 8 In., Pair 1095.00
2-Light, Gilt Brass, Bronze, Girandole, Classical, Eagles, Prisms, 14 3/8 In., Pair 11750.00
2-Light, Gilt Bronze, Girl & Boy, Green Marble Base, L. Gregoire, 1870, 21 In. 5111.00
2-Light, Gilt Bronze, Malachite, France, 12 In., Pair 3918.00
2-Light, Gilt Bronze, Patinated, Restoration, c.1815, 23 1/4 In., Pair 5060.00
2-Light, Gilt Bronze, Scroll Leaf, Scroll & Shell Base, c.1880, 8 3/4 In., Pair 1019.00
2-Light, Hurricane, Opaline, Green, French Cut, c.1885, 26 3/4 x 14 1/2 In. 1610.00
2-Light, Silver Plate, Art Deco, Scroll Arms, 8 In., Pair 120.00
2-Light, Sterling Silver, Maiden, Serpent, Paw Feet, Prosper Bourg, c.1840, 17 In., Pair . . 10755.00
2-Light, Victorian, Molded, Domed, Faceted, Mid 19th Century, 28 x 18 In., Pair 5676.00
3-Light, Brass, Porcelain, Woman, Man, Prisms, Continental, 23 In., Pair . . . . *Illus* 1000.00
3-Light, Bronze, Bacchic Cherub, Beaded Urn-Shape Sconces, Chains, 25 In. 355.00

3-Light, Bronze, Heron, Gilt Bronze Roses, 24 In., Pair 1365.00
3-Light, Bronze, Patinated, Woman Figures, France, c.1885, 18 1/2 x 7 In. 2530.00
3-Light, Gilt Brass, Biblical Scene, Prisms, Molded Base, c.1870, 19 x 17 In. 290.00
3-Light, Gilt Bronze, Louis XV Style, Cupid, Cornucopia, Marble Base, 22 In., Pair 1175.00
3-Light, Gilt Bronze, Louis XVI Style, Swag Urn Finial, 18 1/2 In., Pair 777.00
3-Light, Gilt Bronze, Marble, Napoleon III, Leafy Arms, Hoof Feet, 15 1/2 In., Pair 2350.00
3-Light, Gilt Bronze, Napoleon III, Oriental Style, c.1875, 20 1/2 In., Pair 1610.00
3-Light, Sheffield Silver, George II Style, Flowers, T.J. & N. Creswick, c.1843 . . . . 9560.00
3-Light, Silver Plate, Baluster Stem, Crested, Waterhouse & Co., 19 In., Pair 1554.00
3-Light, Silver Plate, Baluster Stem, Round Base, 15 1/2 x 14 In., Pair 230.00
3-Light, Silver Plate, Convertible, England, 19 1/2 x 18 In., Pair 520.00
3-Light, Silver Plate, England, Late 19th Century, 18 1/2 In., Pair 865.00
3-Light, Silver Plate, Knave On Pillar, Scroll Feet, 18 x 13 In., Pair 1380.00
3-Light, Silver Plate, Rococo Style, Scroll Arms, Rogers, 12 1/2 In., Pair 50.00
3-Light, Silver Plate, Shell, Leaf, Borders, Marked, Boulton, c.1810, 21 In., Pair 2988.00
3-Light, Silver, Continental, Scrolling Arms, Knopped Standard, 19 1/2 In., Pair 780.00
3-Light, Silver, Epergne Marked, Mexico City, Mid 20th Century, 9 & 7 In., Pair 405.00
3-Light, Silver, William IV, William Bateman II, London, 1831, 30 1/2 In., Pair 29875.00
3-Light, Sterling Silver, Art Deco, Curved Stem, Oval Base, Germany, 8 1/2 In., Pair 1460.00
3-Light, Sterling Silver, Art Nouveau, Fluted Bulbous Shaft, Round Base, 11 In., Pair 169.00
3-Light, Sterling Silver, Bobeches, Impressed Mark, Gorham, 1942, 14 1/2 In., Pair 865.00
3-Light, Sterling Silver, Mueck Cary, New York, c.1950, 13 x 13 In., Pair 460.00
3-Light, Sterling Silver, Weighted, Removable Arms, Hamilton, c.1950, 13 In., Pair 288.00
3-Light, Sterling Silver, Weighted, Repousse Pattern, No. 3525, S. Kirk & Son, 3 In. 1555.00
3-Light, Wrought Iron, Turned Middle, 3 Shaped Legs, Diamond Feet, 58 In., Pair 230.00
4-Light, Brass, Amethyst Base, Cut Panels, Scrolled Acanthus, France, 11 1/4 In. 550.00
4-Light, Brass, Louis XVI, Glass Drops, France, c.1885, 15 1/4 In., Pair 460.00
4-Light, Bronze Dore, Ram's-Head Arms, Sphinx Base, 27 In., Pair 5040.00
4-Light, Bronze, Patinated, Napoleon III, Tripod, c.1865, 23 1/4 In., Pair 1495.00
4-Light, Flowers, Glass Drops, Draped Chains, Bead Accent, 21 In., Pair 3220.00
4-Light, Gilt Bronze, Cut Glass, Louis XV Style, Knops, Scroll Arms, 27 In., Pair 940.00
4-Light, Gilt Bronze, Figural, Footed Base, France, 19th Century, 41 In. 865.00
4-Light, Gilt Bronze, Green Marble, 1890, 15 1/2 In., Pair 1365.00
4-Light, Gilt Bronze, Louis XV Style, Leaf Cast Arms, 22 In., Pair 650.00
4-Light, Gilt Bronze, Louis XVI Style, Marble, 17 In. 3585.00
4-Light, Gilt Bronze, Louis XVI Style, Scroll Arms, Shaped Feet, 16 1/2 In., Pair 880.00
4-Light, Gilt Bronze, Napoleon III, Parcel c.1870, 15 1/4 x 8 In., Pair 1495.00
4-Light, Gilt Bronze, Patinated, Renaissance Style, Cupid On Dolphin, 26 In., Pair 2938.00
4-Light, Gilt Bronze, Scrolled, Marble Plinth, Claw Feet, 19th Century, 22 1/2 In. 520.00
4-Light, Porcelain, Child, Pitching, Swinging, Flowers, Voight Bros., 21 In., Pair 400.00
4-Light, Silver, Gadroon Edging, Empire Silver Co., 12 In., Pair 259.00
4-Light, Spelter, 3 Nude Children, Wreaths, Leaves, Flowers, Marble Base, 21 In., Pair . . 450.00
5-Arm, Bronze, Griffins, Minerva Heads, Pinecones, 3 Paw Feet, c.1867, 30 In., Pair 3080.00
5-Light, Art Nouveau, Round Base, Mexico, c.1900, 10 1/4 x 26 In., Pair 575.00

Candelabrum, 3-Light, Brass, Porcelain,
Woman, Man, Prisms, Continental, 23 In., Pair

To easily remove wax that has dripped on a candlestick, put the candlestick in the freezer for about an hour. The wax will flake off.

Candlesticks will crack if candles burn too low. Always support the arm of a candleabrum when putting in the candles.

5-Light, Bronze, Ormolu, Silver, George I Style, 8-Sided Baluster, c.1930, 18 In., Pair ... 6572.00
5-Light, Bronze, Patinated, Louis Philippe Style, France, 46 1/4 In. 1955.00
5-Light, Gilt Brass, Gothic, Band Of Religious Cameo Plaques, Chains, 34 In. 405.00
5-Light, Gilt Bronze, Champleve, Enamel, 4 Columns, Panels, 9 3/4 In., Pair 1555.00
5-Light, Gilt Bronze, Empire Style, Column, Tripod Base, Electrified, 27 In., Pair 1528.00
5-Light, Gilt Bronze, Louis XV Style, Leafy Cast Arms, 24 In., Pair .... ' 881.00
5-Light, Gilt Bronze, Louis XV Style, Patinated, Cupid Holder, 16 In., Pair 705.00
5-Light, Gilt Bronze, Louis XVI Style, Early 20th Century, 25 In., Pair 1955.00
5-Light, Gilt Bronze, Louis XVI Style, Leaves, Electrified, 32 In., Pair 1998.00
5-Light, Gilt Bronze, Marble, Leaf & Flowers, Putto, Step Base, c.1880, 24 1/4 In., Pair .. 2475.00
5-Light, Gilt Bronze, Marble, Louis XV Style, Flower & Leaf Arms, 26 In., Pair 2150.00
5-Light, Gilt Bronze, Patinated, Empire Style, Grotesque Heads, 30 In. 1795.00
5-Light, Gilt Bronze, Patinated, Marble, Cupid Holding Cornucopia, 23 In., Pair 1675.00
5-Light, Goberg, Handwrought Metal, Stylized Flowers, Austria, 13 1/2 In. 430.00
5-Light, Marble, Louis XVI Style, Cherubs, France, c.1885, 21 x 14 1/2 In., Pair 920.00
5-Light, Sterling Silver, Weighted, Miyata, Mid 20th Century, 18 In., Pair 865.00
5-Light, Wrought Iron, Art Deco, Stylized Cat, Trumpet Foot, 20th Century, 13 In. 999.00
6-Light, Brass, Champleve, Dolphins, Scrolled Leaf Arms, Rococo Base, 19 In., Pair 330.00
6-Light, Brass, Marble, Gilt, Glass Buttons, Prisms, France, c.1880, 20 1/2 In., Pair ... 1600.00
6-Light, Cut Glass, Ormolu, Louis XVI Style, Electrified, c.1900, 34 In., Pair 3220.00
6-Light, Gilt Bronze, Patinated, Louis Philippe, c.1835, 37 3/4 x 9 1/2 In. 1840.00
7-Light, Blackamoor, Polychrome, Step Plinth, Italy, 83 In., Pair 1600.00
7-Light, Brass, Double Cross Bar Arms, Stepped Base, 20 1/4 In., Pair 110.00
7-Light, Napoleon III, Bouquet, Glass Drops, c.1865, 53 1/2 In., Pair 4370.00
7-Light, Silver Plate, Flowerhead Serpentine Arms, Lobed Baluster Base, 29 In. 1645.00
8-Light, Bronze, Ormolu, Louis XV Style, Figural, Putto, c.1890, 26 1/2 In., Pair 2300.00
8-Light, Gilt Bronze, Baroque Style, Scrolling Leaves, Continental, 32 1/2 In., Pair 705.00
9-Light, Sheffield Silver, Acanthus, Paw Feet, c.1825, 32 In. 4480.00
10-Light, Brass, Knop Stem, Round Base, Turned Feet, Continental, c.1900, 27 1/2 In. 235.00
10-Light, Metal, Polychrome, Blackamoor, Cornucopia, Wood Base, 80 In., Pair 3335.00
10-Light, Ormolu, Louis XV Style, Classical Male, c.1890, 37 In., Pair 2530.00
10-Light, Silver, Grapevine, Entwined, Storr Mortimer & Hunt, 1846, 36 In. 19120.00
11-Light, Iron, Sockets & Prickets, Ring, Twisted, High Tripod Base, 58 In., Pair 550.00
12-Light, Gilt Brass, Shells, Scrolls, Square Ogee Base, 33 In., Pair 853.00
13-Light, Gilt Bronze, Scroll Arms, 3 Tiers, Leaf Wax Pans, Scroll Feet, c.1880, 34 In. ... 728.00
13-Light, Oak, Baluster & Ring Column, 3-Sided Top, Lead Sockets, X-Footed, 62 In. 248.00
Altar Stick, Giltwood, Carved On Front, 18th Century, 38 In., 4 Piece 2300.00
Bohemian Glass, Gilt Bronze Mounts, 20th Century, 27 In., Pair 1959.00
Brass, Pierced Horse & Dog, Stamped Marks, Hagenauer, 16 In., Pair 7768.00
Bronze, Marble Base, Signed H. Ferrat, France, 1880, 29 In., Pair 1534.00
Gilt Metal, Cut Glass, Ceramic Drum Socles, 25 x 18 In., Pair 5079.00
Girandole, 2-Light, George III Style, Giltwood, 55 x 31 In., Pair 17925.00
Girandole, 3-Light, Flower Basket Pattern, American, c.1850, 18 1/4 In., Pair 575.00
Girandole, Spelter, Brass Finish, Relief, Mary, In Arched Panel, Grapevines, 19 In., Pair . 75.00
Nickeled Bronze, Inscribed, L. Loebl, Brussel, Belgium, c.1890, 62 In., Pair 259.00
Sconce, 3-Arm, Brass, 8 Medallions, Faces, Beveled Glass Mirror, 17 1/2 x 23 In. 195.00
Sconce, Brass, Cast, Mirror, Openwork, Flowers, Medallions, Urn Crest, 23 1/4 x 8 In. 110.00

CANDLESTICKS were made of brass, pewter, glass, sterling silver, plated silver, and all types of pottery and porcelain. The earliest candlesticks, dating from the sixteenth century, held the candle on a pricket (sharp pointed spike). These lost favor because in times of strife the large church candlesticks with prickets became formidable weapons, so the socket was mandated. Candlesticks changed in style through the centuries, and designs range from classic to rococo to Art Nouveau to Art Deco.

Bell Metal, Federal, Round Base, Tapered Shaft, Bobeche, 9 1/2 In. 100.00
Bell Metal, Handle, Tapered, 4 3/4 In., Pair 489.00
Bell Metal, Regency, Classical Column, Square Base, England, c.1825, 7 In. 190.00
Bell Metal, Turned Shaft, Round Base, 4 In., Pair 11.00
Bisque, Nodder, Blackamoor, Woman & Man, Yes & No, 9 1/2 In., Pair .... *Illus* 200.00
Blown Glass, Leaded, Bulbous, Wafers & Knobs, Pittsburgh, c.1815, 10 In., Pair 1017.00
Brass, 12 Sides, Ringed Stem, Oversize Socket, Domed Base, 6 1/2 x 8 In. 220.00

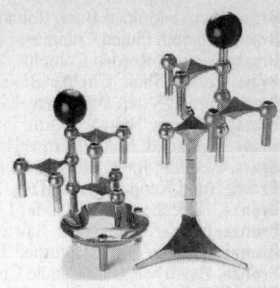

Candlestick, Bisque, Nodder, Blackamoor, Woman & Man, Yes & No, 9 1/2 In., Pair

Candlestick, Brass, Wood Knop, Signed AD/R, 7 3/4 In., Pair

Candlestick, Chrome, Interchangeable Tripods, Dish, Base, Ebonized Balls, Variente, Box, 5 In.

Brass, Acorn Shape Stem, Copper Color, Octagonal Base	149.00
Brass, Baluster Turned Stem, Mid Drip Pan, Domed Base, 16 In., Pair	935.00
Brass, Baluster Turned Stem, Mid Drip Pan, Round Base, Dutch, 11 In., Pair	280.00
Brass, Baluster Turned Stem, Stepped Triangular Base, Paw Feet, 11 1/2 In.	110.00
Brass, Beaded Details, Threaded Base, Side Push-Up, 7 In., Pair	250.00
Brass, Beehive, Diamond Shaft, Push-Up, Mid 19th Century, 9 3/4 In., Pair	120.00
Brass, Beehive, Push-Up, 19th Century, 8 In., Pair	150.00
Brass, Bell-Shaped Hurricane, Etched Flowers, Scroll Handle, Push-Up, 18 In., Pair	118.00
Brass, Brighton Bun, England, 19th Century, Pair	395.00
Brass, Capstan, Scalloped Edge Drip Pan, Ribbed Base, 3 1/2 x 3 1/2 In.	1155.00
Brass, Cast Bell Center Section, Wheel, Pull Chain, 11 1/4 In., Pair	220.00
Brass, Chamber, Engraved Drip Pan, Long Curved Handle, 18th Century, 7-In. Handle	226.00
Brass, Chamber, Keyhole Handle, England, 18th Century	495.00
Brass, Cloisonne, Figural, Blue Mythical Animals, 7 1/8 In.	195.00
Brass, Column Stem, Saucer Base, Detachable Oval Reflector, 20 In., Pair	110.00
Brass, Disc Bobeche, Egg Shape, Slender Stem, Jarvie, c.1905, 10 7/8 In.	940.00
Brass, Double Ring Handle, Drip Pan, Arts & Crafts, England, c.1890, 6 1/2 In., Pair	115.00
Brass, Edwardian, Barley Twist Standard, c.1900, 4 3/4 In., Pair	29.00
Brass, Faceted, Beaded Detail, Octagonal Base, Push-Up, 12 In., Pair	193.00
Brass, Faceted, Beehive, Push Rods, England, 8 3/4 In., Pair	248.00
Brass, Flared, Molded Edge, Baluster Stem, Domed Base, 7 In.	195.00
Brass, Flowers, Continental, c.1800, 9 1/2 In., Pair	460.00
Brass, George III, Engraved, England, c.1785, 9 In., Pair	960.00
Brass, Handwrought, Notched Shaft, Flat Base, 3-Footed, 1930s, 12 3/4 x 5 In., Pair	88.00
Brass, Middle Eastern Figural, Prisms, Marble Base, c.1880, 15 1/2 In., Pair	690.00
Brass, Molded Edge, Baluster Stem, Raised Rings, Domed Base, 8 1/4 x 5 7/8 In.	385.00
Brass, Octagonal Base, Georgian, c.1835, 9 In., Pair	90.00
Brass, Petal, Bobeche, Ruffled Swelling, Conforming Base, England, c.1740s, 9 In., Pair	470.00
Brass, Push-Up, England, 19th Century, 8 1/2 In., Pair	100.00
Brass, Queen Anne Style, England, 4 3/4 In., Pair	34.00
Brass, Queen Anne, 2 Bulbous Rings, 4-Petal Base, 18th Century, 7 In., Pair	345.00
Brass, Queen Anne, Baluster Stem, Octagonal Stepped Base, 7 1/2 In.	110.00
Brass, Queen Anne, Baluster Stem, Scalloped Base, 9 1/4 In., Pair	4950.00
Brass, Queen Anne, Baluster Stem, Turned & Faceted Base, 6 1/2 In., Pair	460.00
Brass, Queen Anne, Petal Base, Baluster Turned Stems, 7 3/4 In.	1760.00
Brass, Queen Anne, Scalloped Corners, Domed Ring, Baluster Turnings, 6 3/4 In., Pair	660.00
Brass, Queen Anne, Seamed, Turned Shaft, Shaped Base, 7 1/2 In.	309.00
Brass, Queen Anne, Turned Rings, Scalloped, Raised Base, 8 In., Pair	1540.00
Brass, Reeded Column, Raised Square Base, 11 In., Pair	130.00
Brass, Removable Bobeche, England, c.1760, 24 In., Pair	3200.00
Brass, Ring, Incised Line, Deep Socket, Mid Drip Pan, Domed Base, 9 In.	440.00
Brass, Seated Buddha, Brown Patina, Pricket, Early 20th Century, 22 1/2 In.	575.00
Brass, Sheet Iron, Hog Scraper, Spun Brass Bands, Early 1800s, 9 1/4 In., Pair	1295.00
Brass, Spring-Loaded, Hooded Reflector, Victorian, 14 1/4 In.	240.00
Brass, Square Base, Recessed Circle-Turned Column, 4 x 4 x 4 3/4 In.	195.00

Brass, Square Molded Base, Round Stem, Push-Up, 7 3/4 In. 140.00
Brass, Tapered, Fluted Columns, Square Base, England, c.1780, 10 1/4 In., Pair 440.00
Brass, Tapered, Reeded Columns, Baluster Base, Beaded Feet, 19th Century, 21 In., Pair . 242.00
Brass, Turned Shaft, Circular Base, Push-Up, 9 3/4 In. 50.00
Brass, Turned Shaft, Petal Base, 18th Century, 7 In. 127.00
Brass, Victorian, Baluster Form, Push-Up, 8 In., Pair 135.00
Brass, William & Mary, Domed Hexagonal Bases, Ring Turned, 7 1/2 In., Pair 990.00
Brass, Wedding Band, Hog Scraper, Push-Up, 5 1/2 In., Pair 4800.00
Brass, Wood Knop, Signed AD/R, 7 3/4 In., Pair .... *Illus* 150.00
Bronze, Bobeche, Patina, Jarvie, 13 In. 1150.00
Bronze, Cobra, Flared Neck, Sawtooth Bobeche & Holder, Chased, 8 In. 115.00
Bronze, Dolphin Form, Upturned Tail, Square Base, 5 In., Pair 265.00
Bronze, Engraved, Oval Candle Cup, Square Plinth, c.1790, 10 1/2 In., Pair 1998.00
Bronze, Flared, Brushed Patina, Flattened Foot, Jesse Preston, 14 In. 1610.00
Bronze, Flattened Socket & Base, Round Tapered Stem, Arts & Crafts, 12 In., Pair 330.00
Bronze, Gilt, Pricket, Fretwork, Footed Base, 19th Century, 25 In., Pair 980.00
Bronze, Lily Pad Shape, Applied Frog, Barye, Signed, 8 In. 200.00
Bronze, Marble, Louis XVI, Beading, Acanthus, Cup, Drip Pan, 19th Century, 9 In. 460.00
Bronze, No. 8, Jesse Preston, 13 In., Pair 9200.00
Bronze, Seahorse Shaft, Verdigris Patina, E.T. Hurley, 13 3/4 In. 1780.00
Chrome, Interchangeable Tripods, Dish, Base, Ebonized Balls, Box, 5 In. .... *Illus* 150.00
Copper, Brass, Arts & Crafts, 12 1/2 In., Pair 150.00
Copper, Double Cross, Arts & Crafts, 1 3/4 x 3 3/4 In., Pair 200.00
Copper, Hammered, Chamber, Applied Handle, Gustav Stickley, Marked, 9 In. 1035.00
Copper, Silver Overlay Leaf Design, Arts & Crafts, 14 1/2 In. 431.00
Cut Glass, Anglo-Irish, 19th Century, 13 In., 4 Piece 2510.00
Cut Glass, Gilt Brass, George III, Clear, Lemon Glass Drops, 13 3/4 In., Pair 7768.00
Cut Glass, Gilt Bronze Mount, Louis Philippe Style, France, c.1885, 30 1/4 x 5 In. 1495.00
Cut Glass, Regency, Prisms, 18th Century, 11 1/4 In., Pair 3220.00
Faience, 18th-Century Style, Late 19th Century, 9 In., Pair 405.00
Faience, Polychrome, Leaf Shape, Handle, 6 3/4 In. 35.00
Gilt Brass, Restoration, Column Shafts, 3 Paw Feet, 19th Century, 5 1/4 In., Pair 690.00
Gilt Bronze, Empire, Fluted Sconce, Paneled Stem, Reeded Base, Leaves, 9 In., Pair 646.00
Gilt Bronze, Louis XV Style, Late 19th Century, 16 In., Pair 2390.00
Gilt Bronze, Louis XVI, Ram's Heads, Flowers, Scrolls, Hoof Feet, 19th Century, 12 In. . 1095.00
Gilt Bronze, Napoleon III, Standing Pharaoh Holding Symbols, 11 1/4 In., Pair 1380.00
Gilt Bronze, Patinated Brass, Louis Philippe, Tripod, Paw Feet, 15 3/4 In. 690.00
Gilt Bronze, Patinated, Louis Philippe, Lamp Mount, c.1835, 14 3/4 In. 805.00
Gilt Bronze, Patinated, Restoration Style, Winged Men, France, 14 In., Pair 2300.00
Gilt Bronze, Patinated, Rococo Style, Cupid Riding Alligator, 8 3/4 In. 646.00
Gilt Bronze, Regency, Black Marble Base, 1815, 10 In., Pair 1535.00
Gilt Bronze, Tripod, Lion Masques, c.1815, 10 3/4 In., Pair 805.00
Gilt Bronze, White Marble, Louis XVI Style, 10 3/4 In., Pair 2030.00
Glass, Amber, Egg Shape Standard, Faceted Base, c.1925, 19 1/2 In., 4 Piece 4780.00
Glass, Bright Canary, Wafer Construction, Hexagonal, 9 3/4 x 4 1/4 In. 145.00
Glass, Canary Yellow, Hexagonal Socket, Column, 9 5/8 In., Pair 825.00
Glass, Clambroth, Hexagonal, Mid 19th Century, 8 3/8 In., Pair 325.00
Glass, Cobalt Blue, Hexagonal, 7 5/8 In. 440.00
Glass, Cobalt Blue, Hexagonal, Mid 19th Century, 9 1/4 In. 235.00
Glass, Deep Cobalt Blue, Hexagonal, 7 5/8 In. 440.00
Glass, Dolphin & Shell Socket, 9 1/2 In. 1320.00
Glass, Elongated Loop, Scalloped Edges, Pewter Inserts, 9 1/4 In., Pair 358.00
Glass, Iridized Blue, Stretched, 10 1/2 In., Pair 70.00
Glass, Pears, Grapes, Apples, Wheel Cut, Cobalt Blue, 12 1/2 In., Pair 920.00
Glass, Pewter Insert, Round, Domed Base, Pittsburgh, 9 1/2 In., Pair 275.00
Glass, Polychrome, Tulip Shape Cup, Memphis, Ettore Sottsass, 21 1/2 x 4 In. 1880.00
Glass, Ruby, Blue & Clear Prisms, Ruffled Shade, Stylized Flowers, 23 In. 115.00
Glass, Translucent Blue Socket, 6-Sided Clambroth Shaft, Stepped Base, 8 In., Pair 765.00
Glass, Turquoise Petal Socket, Clambroth Column Standard, Stepped Base, 9 In., Pair ... 1175.00
Iron, Carved Wood Base, Wire Cage, Stable, Mid 18th Century, 6 7/8 In. 558.00
Iron, Chamber, Handwrought, Goberg, 8 In., Pair 200.00
Iron, Hog Scraper, Brass Band, Octagonal Base, 18th Century 695.00
Iron, Hog Scraper, Brass Ring, Side Push-Up Tabs, Stamped, 9 1/4 In., Pair 180.00

Iron, Rushlight, Pricket, Arched Tripod Base, Penny Feet, 15 In. 525.00
Mahogany, Wrought Iron, George IV, Bone Mounted, Low Pricket, 9 In. 405.00
Oak, Saucer Socket, Round Turned & Tapered Stem, Floor, 42 In. 165.00
Ormolu, Louis XV Style, Baluster, Urn Socket, Bobeche, Flowers, c.1900, 8 In., Pair 1035.00
Parian, Composition, Regency Style, Kneeling Slave, 7 3/4 In., Pair 230.00
Pewter, Adjustable, Spiral Strip Forms Shaft, Domed Base, 18th Century, 8 In. 206.00
Pewter, Baluster Stem, Round Base, Homan & Co., Cincinnati, 7 3/4 In., Pair 220.00
Porcelain, Violets, Leaves, France, 19th Century, 4 3/8 In., Pair 40.00
Pottery, Black & Umber Mottled Glaze, Raised Mark, Wannopee, 7 In. 345.00
Pottery, Blue Flowers, Tan Ground, Saucer Base, 1978, 2 In., Pair 105.00
Pottery, Brown Sponge, Saucer Base, 1978, 3 1/4 In., Pair 105.00
Pottery, Mottled Green & Brown Patina, Arts & Crafts, 14 In. 375.00
Redware, Green, Brown Glaze, Barrel Back, Loop Handle, I.S. Stahl, 1941, 7 In. 187.00
Sheet Iron, Notched Tube Shaft, Adjustable, Footed Dish Base, Early 1800s, 6 5/8 In. . . . 265.00
Sheffield Silver, Georgian, Nozzle Shape, Scale-Banded Base, 19th Century, 9 3/4 In. 69.00
Sheffield Silver, Inverted Baluster Stem, c.1820, 12 3/4 In., Pair 200.00
Silver, 5 Sides, Daffodil Shape Cup, F.W. Lawrence, 4 1/2 x 4 5/8 In., 4 Piece 650.00
Silver, Baluster, Crested, 8-Sided Base, William Paradise, 1728, 5 7/8 In., Pair 9560.00
Silver, Beaded Border, Extinguishers, Marked, John Carter, 1759, 6 1/2 In., Pair 4780.00
Silver, Continental, Sabbath, Knopped Standard, Spreading Base, 13 In., Pair 720.00
Silver, Dog Roses, Detachable Nozzles, Baluster Form, Gorham, c.1919, 11 In., Pair 19200.00
Silver, Figural, Cupid With Bow & Quiver, Domed & Fluted Base, Spain, 8 1/4 In., Pair . . 294.00
Silver, Reeded Border, Extinguishers, Hampston & York, 1795, 5 3/8 In., Pair 2990.00
Silver, Rococo Style, Flower Design, Moscow, c.1860, 12 In. 316.00
Silver, Slender Shaft, Broad Circular Base, Shreve & Co., 9 1/2 x 4 In., Pair 2200.00
Silver, Tapered, Fluted, Beaded Border, Marked, John Scofield, 1792, 13 In., Pair 8960.00
Silver, Telescoping, Scrolled & Gadrooned Bands, 6 3/4 x 9 1/2 In., Pair 220.00
Silver, Telescoping, Urn-Shaped Socket, Leafy Bands, 8 To 10 3/4 In., Pair 495.00
Silver, Weighted, Corinthian Column, Hawksworth, Eyre & Co., c.1899, 10 In., Pair 1035.00
Silver Gilt, Enamel, Urn-Shaped Sconce, Torch, c.1893, 5 In., Pair 4200.00
Silver Plate, Cartouche, Flowers, Late 19th Century, 11 3/4 x 6 In., Pair 125.00
Silver Plate, Chamber, Scrolled Arms, Flower Feet, Art Nouveau, Pairpoint, 7 1/2 In. 235.00
Silver Plate, Flowers, Scroll, Pricket, 36 In., Pair 1265.00
Spinach Jade, Pricket, Standing Crane, Outstretched Wings, 9 1/2 In., Pair 2150.00
Steel, Modular, Germany, 1960s, 25 Piece 1725.00
Steel, Wrought, 2 Socles, Writhen Post, 49 In. 115.00
Sterling Silver, Athenic Pattern, Leaf, Bud Support, c.1905, 10 1/4 In., Pair 10160.00
Sterling Silver, Baluster Stem, Urn Shape Sconce, Octagonal Base, 10 In., 4 Piece 2530.00
Sterling Silver, Bulbous Shaft, Swags In Relief On Base, 9 In., Pair 310.00
Sterling Silver, Floral Band, American, First Half 20th Century, 12 1/4 In., Pair 345.00
Sterling Silver, Floral Bobeche, Mexico, Mid 20th Century, 13 1/2 In., Pair 375.00
Sterling Silver, Flower Form, Trefoil Base, Cellini, c.1930, 3 5/8 In. 1175.00
Sterling Silver, George II Style, Esko, Elgin, N.Y., 20th Century, 10 1/2 In., 4 Piece 6575.00
Sterling Silver, Kirk Rose, S. Kirk & Sons, 1828, 3 3/4 In., Pair 345.00
Sterling Silver, Repousse, Weighted, Low, S. Kirk & Son, c.1940, 3 1/2 In., 4 Piece 288.00
Sterling Silver, Stylized Shells, Shaped Square Foot, Kalo, 8 1/2 In., 4 Piece 1880.00
Sterling Silver, Tapering Square, Spreading Base, England, c.1896, 11 In., Pair 1075.00
Sterling Silver, Taperstick, Georgian Style, Bobeche, 5 1/4 In., Pair 863.00
Sterling Silver, Vase Form, Weighted, Gorham, Rhode Island, 1925, 10 1/2 In., 4 Piece . . 1675.00
Sterling Silver, Weighted, Revere Silver Co., 4 In., 4 Piece 175.00
Tin, Adjustable, Tall Notched Shaft, Mid Drip Pan, Applied Curved Handle, 16 3/4 In. . . . 118.00
Tin, Chamber, Crimped Saucer, Drip Flange, Deep Socket, 19th Century, 5 x 4 In. 300.00
Tin, Tinderbox, Cylindrical, Ring Handle, Early 19th Century, 3 In. 558.00
Wood, Open Twisting Form, Arts & Crafts, 15 In., Pair 1150.00
Wood, Painted, Gesso, Gilt Wings, Putto Holding Cornucopia Pricket, 10 In. 499.00
Wood, Painted, Mustard, Smoke, Baluster Turned, Early 20th Century, 11 1/4 In. 176.00
Wood, Pricket, Round Base, 12 In. 68.00
Wood, Woman, Classical Robes, Holding Candlestick, Step Base, 1800s, 21 In., Pair 800.00
Wrought Iron, Chamber, Arts & Crafts, Drip Pan, Strap Handle, Germany, c.1915, 8 In. . 100.00
Wrought Iron, Hog Scraper, Brass Ring, Push-Up, 9 1/2 In. 550.00
Wrought Iron, Spiral Iron Stem, Curled Finger Loop, Tab, 9 3/4 In. 160.00

CANDLEWICK items may be listed in the Imperial and Pressed Glass categories.

CANDY CONTAINERS have been popular since the late Victorian era. Collectors have long favored the glass containers, but now all types, including tin and papier-mache, are collected. Probably the earliest glass container sold commercially was the Liberty Bell made in 1876 for sale at the Centennial Exposition. Thousands of designs were made until the cost became too high in the 1960s. By the late 1970s, reproductions were being made and sold without the candy. Containers listed here are glass unless otherwise described. A Belsnickle is a nineteenth-century figure of Father Christmas. Some candy containers may be listed in Toy or in other categories.

Airplane, Spirit Of Goodwill, Glass, Closure, Painted	105.00 to 204.00
Airplane, Spirit Of St. Louis, Amber, Tin Closure	385.00
Airplane, T.M.A. 44, Glass, Closure	83.00 to 110.00
Baby Chick, Standing, Closure	121.00
Barney Google, Ball, Painted, Contents, Closure	550.00
Barney Google, Bank, Glass, Green, Closure	1650.00
Baseball Bank, Flying Horse Emblem, Glass, Tin & Plastic Mount	39.00
Baseball Player With Bat, Closure	286.00
Bear, On Circus Tub, Closure	341.00
Bell, Liberty Bell Bank, Milk Glass, Closure	220.00
Belsnickle, Fabric Coat, Fur Beard, Basket On Back, 1890s	795.00
Belsnickle, Yellow Coat, Hand Pressed, 11 1/2 In.	1250.00
Boat, Battleship On Waves, No Closure, Glass, 5 In.	193.00
Boat, Remember The Maine, Glass, 7 In.	39.00
Boat, Submarine F6, Glass, Tin, 5 1/2 In.	770.00 to 855.00
Boat, Submarine, Colorado 1914, Glass, 6 In.	145.00
Buddy Bank, Original Closure	330.00
Bus, Greyhound, Wheels, Luggage Rock, Victory Glass Co., 5 In.	340.00
Bus, Jitney, Glass, Pierced Tin Wheels, 4 1/4 In.	55.00
Bus, Victory Lines Special, Closure, Painted Blue, Silver, Glass, 5 In.	50.00
Camera, On Tripod, Donkey Picture, Original Box, c.1913, 5 In.	880.00
Candlestick, Original Label, Contents & Closure, Glass, 4 1/2 In.	440.00
Cannon, 2 Wheel Mount, No. 3, Glass Barrel, Iron Wheels, 4 1/4 In.	715.00
Cannon, Muzzle Loader, Closure, Tin, Glass, 4 3/4 In.	825.00
Cannon, Rapid Fire Gun, Glass, Metal, Instructions, 7 3/4 In.	385.00 to 660.00
Cannon, U.S. Defense Field Gun, No. 17, Closure, Glass, 1940-1945, 4 1/4 In.	385.00
Car, Amos 'n' Andy, Open Air Taxi, 4 1/2 In.	330.00
Car, Electric Coupe Pat Feb 18 1913, Original Closure, Vail Bros., 2 1/2 In.	120.00
Car, Flat Top With Tassels, 2-Line Hood, Closure, 4 3/8 In.	176.00
Car, Hearse No. 2, 15-Line Hood, 4 3/8 In.	100.00
Car, Limousine With Rear Trunk & Tire, Red Paint, No Closure, 4 3/4 In.	66.00 to 100.00
Car, Little Sedan, c.1939, 3 In.	39.00
Car, Sedan With 12 Vents, Glass, Tin, Victory Glass Co., 4 5/16 In.	44.00
Car, Streamlined, Original Closure, Blue, Paint, 3 Sections, c.1945, 4 1/2 In.	50.00
Car, West Bros. Co. Limousine, Original Closure, 1912-1914, 4 In.	198.00
Carpet Sweeper, Baby Sweeper, Handle, Closure, 2 3/4 In.	500.00 to 770.00
Carpet Sweeper, Dolly Sweeper, c.1914, 3 In.	143.00
Cash Register, Clear Glass, Original Closure	578.00 to 605.00
Chicken, Crowing Rooster, Closure, 5 In.	220.00 to 413.00
Chicken, On Oblong Basket, Glass, c.1930, 3 In.	204.00
Chicken, On Round Base, Closure, Glass, Metal, 2 3/4 In.	578.00
Chicken, On Sagging Basket, Closure, 3 1/8 In.	72.00 to 94.00
Chicken, On The Nest, Oval Base, c.1946, 4 5/8 In.	11.00
Clark, Alarm, Closure, c.1916, 3 5/16 In.	303.00
Clock, Lynne Clock, Plastic, Cardboard	40.00 to 99.00
Coal Car, N.Y.C., Closure	275.00
Coal Car, Overland Limited, Metal Wheels, Closure	385.00
Condiment Set, Rainbow Candy, White Glass, Original Closure	55.00
Dirigible, Los Angeles, Pressed Glass, 5 3/4 In.	90.00 to 253.00
Dog, Begging, 3 1/2 In.	110.00
Dog, Bulldog, Round Base, 4 1/2 In.	5.50
Dog, By Barrel, Closure, 1/4 In.	100.00
Dog, Circus, Hat, Cardboard Tube Hat, Tin Rim, c.1964, 3 1/2 In.	22.00

Dog, Kiddies Breakfast Bell, Original Contents & Paper Label, 2 3/8 In. 121.00
Dog, Looking Left, Screw Top, 3 5/8 In. . . . . .110.00 to 150.00
Dog, On Oblong Base, Amber, Glass, 3 3/4 In. 120.00
Don't Park Here No. 2, Bubbles In Glass, Original Closure 468.00
Duck, On Plain Top Basket, Closure, 2 3/4 In. 77.00
Duck, On Rope Top Basket, 3 1/4 In. 33.00
Elephant In Swallowtail Suit, Closure, 4 3/4 In. . . . . .187.00 to 468.00
Fat Boy On Drum, Closure, c.1914, 4 3/8 In. 385.00
Fire Engine, 1914 Stough, Original Wheels & Closure, 5 In. 105.00
Fire Engine, Ladder Truck, 5 In. 121.00
Fire Engine, Little Boiler No. 1, Glass, Blue, 4 3/4 In. 88.00
Flat Iron, 3 1/2 In. 330.00
Flossie Fisher's Chair, Cat & Rabbit Seat, 3 Piece . . . . .1210.00 to 1540.00
Flossie Fisher's Chair, Cat & Squirrel Seat 1210.00
Flossie Fisher's China Closet 1100.00
Flossie Fisher's Table, Round, 3 5/8 In. 2530.00
Girl, With 2 Geese, 5 3/4 In. 600.00
Hat, Uncle Sam, Painted . . . . .28.00 to 39.00
Hat, With Tin Brim, Closure . . . . .50.00 to 110.00
Helicopter, 2 Blade, Closure, Metal, 5 In. 220.00
Horn, Musical Clarinet No. 515A, 6 In. 187.00
Horn, Trumpet, White Glass, Closure, 5 1/2 In. 60.00
House, All Glass . . . . .198.00 to 275.00
House, Cabinet Bank, Glass, Large, 3 In. 17.00
Independence Hall, Closure, 7 In. 253.00
Indian Tomahawk & Gun, Original Closure, 12 In. . . . . .61.00 to 88.00
Jack-O'-Lantern, Pop-Eyed, Smiling, Original Closure, 2 1/2 In. 745.00
Kettle, On 3 Feet, Original Contents, Paper Strap & Closure . . . . .28.00 to 44.00
Lamp, Apothecary Jar, Closure 55.00
Lamp, Candlestick Base, Shade, T.H. Stough Co. 176.00
Lamp, Christmas, Shade, Glass, Paper, Closure, 8 In. 165.00
Lamp, George Washington, Paper Shade, 5 In. 715.00
Lamp, Kerosene, Closure, Metal, 4 5/8 In. . . . . .33.00 to 77.00
Lamp, Library, Closure, 4 1/4 In. 440.00
Lamppost, Pewter, Glass, c.1880, 6 In. 275.00
Lantern, Twins On An Anchor, Salt & Pepper, Original Closure, 4 In. 11.00
Liberty Bell, 1776 Liberty Bell Bank, Glass, No Closure 55.00
Locomotive, American Type, 4 3/4 In. 39.00
Locomotive, Lithographed Closure . . . . .44.00 to 60.00
Locomotive, Stough's Patent 115533 . . . .   22.00
Mailbox, Milk Glass, 3 1/4 In. 165.00
Man, On Motorcycle With Side Car, Closure 605.00
Midget Washer, 8 3/4 x 6 In. . . . . .50.00 to 61.00
Monkey Lamp, Closure 25.00
Moon Mullins 28.00
Mule Pulling 2 Wheeled Barrel With Driver, Closure 22.00
Opera Glasses, Plain Panels, Closure 75.00
Pencil, Baby-Jumbo, Closure . . . . .55.00 to 75.00
Pipe, Germany . . . . .39.00 to 50.00
Policeman's Night Stick No. 2, Closure 125.00
Pumpkin Head, Policeman, Original Closure 1100.00
Pumpkin Head, Witch, Bail 358.00
Rabbit, In Eggshell, Painted, Closure 130.00
Rabbit, Pushing Chick In Shell Cart, Painted, Closure 740.00
Rabbit, Running On Log, Painted, Closure 275.00
Rabbit, With Basket On Dome, Painted, Closure 520.00
Rabbit, With Feet Together, Round Nose, Closure 55.00
Rabbit, With Laid Back Ears, Painted, Closure 165.00
Rabbit, With Legs Apart, Painted, Closure, 5 1/2 In. 165.00
Rabbit, With Wheelbarrow, Glass, Closure, 4 1/4 In. 110.00
Radio, Tune In, Original Contents, Closure, 4 1/2 In. 145.00
Rocking Horse, With Clown Rider, Paint, Closure 315.00
Safety First, Closure, 3 3/4 In. 259.00

Santa Claus, By Square Chimney, Closure 300.00
Santa Claus, In Sleigh, Papier-Mache, 8 In. 22.00
Santa Claus, Leaving Chimney, Closure . . . . .50.00 to 193.00
Santa Claus, Leaving Chimney, Original Paint & Candy, 1940s, 5 1/2 In. 195.00
Santa Claus, On Skis, Plastic, 4 1/2 In. 22.00
Santa Claus, With Paneled Coat 66.00
Santa Claus Nodder, West Germany, 1950s, 10 In. 17.00
Skookum, By Tree Stump, 3 5/8 In. . . . . .83.00 to 120.00
Soldier, With Sword 578.00
Spark Plug, Horse, Painted, Closure 176.00
Spinning Top, Glass, Wooden Winder, Closure . . . . .77.00 to 110.00
Stop & Go, Closure 578.00
Tank, U.S. Army, T.H. Stough Co. 11.00
Tank, World War I, Closure 132.00
Taxi, Black & White, Westmoreland Glass Co., 4 1/4 In. 990.00
Taxi, Yellow, Metal Roof, Tin Wheels, Westmoreland Glass Co., 4 1/4 In. 1320.00
Telephone, Lynne Type, Sunken Dial, 4 5/8 In. 11.00
Telephone, Millstein's ToT, Cord & Receiver, Closure 33.00
Telephone, Pewter Top, Original Closure, 4 3/8 In. 50.00
Telephone, West Bros. Co., Original Closure, 1907 . . . . 44.00
Top, Glass Spinning Top, Wood Winder, Closure 90.00
Trunk, With Round Top, Opaque White Glass, Gold Detail, Closure 90.00
Turkey, Gobbler, Closure 165.00
Turkey, Plastic, Nov 18, 1953, 6 1/2 In. 15.00
U.S. Express Wagon, c.1914, 4 In. 165.00
Valentine, Clown, Clown Around With Me, Head Unscrews, 1970s, 4 3/4 In. 14.00
Village, 5 & 10 Cent Store, Tin 2310.00
Village, Engine Co. No. 23, Tin 110.00
Village, Princess Theatre, Tin 138.00
Village, Toys & Confectionary, Tin 165.00
Wheelbarrow, Red Tin Wheels, Closure . . . . .44.00 to 80.00
Windmill, Ruby Flash Glass, 5 Windows 440.00
Windmill, Teddy, c.1914, 4 In. 635.00

CANES and walking sticks were used by every well-dressed man in the
nineteenth century, but by World War I the style had changed. Today
canes are used by few but the infirm. Collectors prize old canes made
with special features, like hidden swords, whiskey flasks, or risqué pictures seen through peepholes. Examples with solid gold heads or made
from exotic materials, such as walrus vertebrae, are among the higher-
priced canes.

Bamboo, Justice Of The Peace, Brass Collar, c.1820, 35 1/2 In. 2350.00
Bamboo, Pebbled, White, Engraved Scrolls, Hidden Sword, O. Oldham, Paris, 34 In. 499.00
Bone, Carved, Polished, Hard Rubber, 1860-1870 . . . . 475.00
Bone, Carved, Woman Offering Man Apple, Snake, 3 1/2 In. 275.00
C-Scrolls, Blossoms, Wood Shaft, Oval Handle, Gold, Tiffany & Co., c.1920, 36 In. 3250.00
Dog Head, Horse, Eagle, Stag, Stars, Late 19th Century, 39 1/2 In. 1320.00
Glass, Ball, Blue, Silver Star Of David, Bamboo, c.1900, 34 1/4 In. 1680.00
Glass, Whimsy, Knob, Spiral, Cobalt Blue, White, Maroon, 45 In. 270.00
Handle, Nephrite, Gold, 10 Cabochons, Acanthus Band, Russia, c.1890, 2 1/4 In. 2300.00
Hardstone, Gold, Enamel, Hound Head, Diamond Set Eyes, 2 3/4 In. 4180.00
Ivory, Death & Maiden, Ebony, Silver Collar, France, c.1880, 38 In. 5040.00
Ivory, Donkey, Double Automata, Bamboo Shaft, 34 3/4 In. 3360.00
Ivory, Dragon, 3-Toed, Japanese, Partridgewood, c.1890, 37 In. 1680.00
Ivory, Eagle, E Pluribus Unum, Gold Collar, Malacca Shaft, c.1870, 35 1/2 In. 1120.00
Ivory, Elephant, Glass Eyes, Malacca Shaft, c.1880, 35 In. 1344.00
Ivory, Pipe, Gadget, Hardwood Shaft, c.1890, 34 In. 950.00
Knife, Hidden, Cruciform Blade, 36 In., 13-In. Blade 175.00
Man With Cane, Full-Bodied, Leo Turmel, Early 20th Century, 32 1/2 In. 715.00
Maple, People, Horses, Brass Tip, Mid 19th Century, 35 In. 3585.00
Sandalwood, Mythical Beast, Flowers, Animals, Burmese, c.1880, 36 In. 5320.00
Silver, 4 Eagles Holding Arrows, Hickory Shaft, Mourning, 34 1/4 In. 3250.00
Silver, Bird, Curved Beak, Amber Glass Eyes, Ebony Shaft, c.1900, 37 In. 560.00

Silver, Hammered Texture, Ebony Shaft, Tiffany & Co., c.1920, 36 In. 1120.00
Silver, President Andrew Jackson, Hickory Shaft, Presentation, c.1820, 34 1/2 In. 3360.00
Silver Knob, Rosewood, 5-Point Star, Marine Corps Symbol, 33 In. 690.00
Silver Plate, Chinaman Spitting, Siphon, Bamboo Shaft, c.1890, 36 In. 2240.00
Silver Plate, Pop-Up Pencil Racetrack, Bamboo, Brigg Of London, c.1920, 34 In. 1120.00
Snake, Burnt Design, 35 1/2 In. 85.00
Spear Thrower, Rattan-Mounted Wood Figure, North Coast, New Guinea, 33 1/2 In. 365.00
Staghorn, Rabbit & Turtle, Partridgewood Shaft, c.1890, 38 3/4 In. 1345.00
Staghorn Cigar Cutter, Malacca Shaft, London, 1909, 35 In. 1904.00
Sterling Silver, Whalebone, Seasick Mariner, Malacca, c.1830, 34 1/2 In. 1568.00
Walking Stick, Bamboo, Gold, Flower Panel, 19th Century, 33 1/2 In. 550.00
Walking Stick, Bird Handle, Cow Horn, Painted Black, 36 1/2 In. 165.00
Walking Stick, Boxwood, Inlaid Abalone, Tassel, Louis XVI Style, 34 1/2 In. 69.00
Walking Stick, Brass Knob, Oak, Stamped, c.1920, 35 In. 58.00
Walking Stick, Brass Mounted, Eagle's Head, Ebony, 36 1/4 In. 40.00
Walking Stick, Brass, Ebonized Wood, c.1920, 36 1/4 In. 58.00
Walking Stick, Brass, Rosewood, Compass Head, Germany, c.1900, 36 1/2 In. 382.00
Walking Stick, Bronze Ax-Shape Grip, Wood, Turned, Kaiser Eagle, Parade, 40 In. 168.00
Walking Stick, Burl Knob, Carved, Shield, Church, Inkwell Case Inside, 1906, 38 In. 495.00
Walking Stick, Cow, Eyes & Horns, 36 1/2 In. 193.00
Walking Stick, Ebonized Fruitwood, Gold Fill Mounted, Belle Epoque, c.1900, 34 In. . . . 145.00
Walking Stick, Ebony, Ivory Tip Continental, c.1900, 35 1/2 In. 431.00
Walking Stick, Fruitwood, Damascene Mounted, Spain, c.1900, 36 1/2 In. 69.00
Walking Stick, Gold Filled, Flowers, Late 19th Century, 36 In. 45.00
Walking Stick, Hardwood, Gold Head, Modern Gothic, 19th Century, 32 1/2 In. 316.00
Walking Stick, Ivory Knop, Wood, Silver Band, U.S. Frigate Constitution 1797, 35 In. . . . 1293.00
Walking Stick, Ivory, Antlers, Sterling Collar, Wood, 35 In. 173.00
Walking Stick, Ivory, Dogs Head, Applied Eyes, Wood, 39 In. 920.00
Walking Stick, Ivory, Hardwood, Gartered & Tasseled Lady's Thigh & Knee, 35 In. 259.00
Walking Stick, Ivory, Malacca, Sterling Silver Bands, Appliqued Fleur-De-Lis, 36 In. 288.00
Walking Stick, Ivory, Monkey Grip, Bamboo, Amber Eyes, Silver Bands, Germany, 36 In. 374.00
Walking Stick, Ivory, Skull Head, Glass Eyes, c.1860 . . . . 600.00
Walking Stick, Raccoon, Tack Eyes, Painted Mask & Tail, 36 In. 209.00
Walking Stick, Resin, Celluloid, Ivory, Amber Handle, Flying Bird, 37 1/2 In. 58.00
Walking Stick, Rolled Gold, Repousse Handle, c.1920, 36 1/2 In. 316.00
Walking Stick, Rosewood, Ivory, Rosebuds, Leaves, Stippled Silver Bands, 43 In. 288.00
Walking Stick, Silver, Bird Head, Applied Red Glass Eyes, Wood, 33 1/4 In. 489.00
Walking Stick, Wood, 2 Entwined Snakes, Man Frowning, 36 In. 316.00
Walking Stick, Wood, Alligator, Man Smiling, Sterling Ferrule, 36 In. 489.00
Walking Stick, Wood, Cedar, Snakes Chasing Birds & Frogs, 37 In. 193.00
Walking Stick, Wood, Rabbit, Glass Eyes, Brass Tip, 35 In. 240.00
Walking Stick, Wood, Snake Eating Bird, Glass Eyes, Metal Tip, 40 In. 605.00
Walking Stick, Wood, Snake, Cactus Plant, Eagle, Snake, Lizards, Mexico, 35 In. 165.00
Walking Stick, Wood, Snake, Tack Eyes, Lips, Wire Tongue, 50 In. 55.00
Walnut, Knob Top, Sawtooth Border, Relief Carved, 34 In. 339.00
Wood, Alligator, Eating Snake, Snake Eating Rabbit, 34 In. 270.00
Wood, Animals, Elephant, Deer, Horse, Lion, Cattle, 36 In. 550.00
Wood, Ball-In-Box, Whimsy, Twined Snake, Fraternal Emblem, 37 In. 275.00
Wood, Bird In Hand, Schtockschnitzler Simmons, 29 In. 2640.00
Wood, Brass Collar, Hidden Gun, Breech Load, c.1890, 35 In. 1176.00
Wood, Cannon, Francis Beach, Civil War 3450.00
Wood, Carved, Clenched Hand, Red, Black, Late 1800s, 36 1/2 x 3 x 4 1/2 In. 450.00
Wood, Carved, Hand With Ball, Snake, 35 3/4 In. 1181.00
Wood, Dog Head, Hidden Gun, Remington 4300.00
Wood, Dog, Horse, Eagle, Stag, Stars, Late 19th Century, 33 In. 1155.00
Wood, Eagle, Bull Fighting, Pullman Train, 35 1/2 In. 385.00
Wood, Eskimo Bust, Eureka Springs, Carol County, 39 In. 345.00
Wood, Fist, Snake Spiraling Up Shaft, Wooden, Engraved Silver Plaque, 1863, 36 In. 765.00
Wood, Human Head, Open Work Ball-In-Box Whimsies, Snake, 35 3/4 In. 1265.00
Wood, Indian Head, Dartmouth College, Names Around Shaft, 1926, 35 1/2 In. 240.00
Wood, Ivory Cue Ball Handle, Plastic Ferrule, Odd Fellows, 35 1/2 In. 635.00
Wood, Malacca, Turk Wearing Turban, Automaton, c.1880, 35 3/4 In. 1456.00
Wood, Man, With Beard, Signed, J. Hunt, c.1860, 37 1/2 In. 460.00

Wood, Rope Twist Shaft, C. Walker, 34 In. 340.00
Wood, Shaped Handle, Carved Free-Floating Balls In Boxes, Red Paint, 37 1/2 In. 145.00
Wood, Supreme Court Justice Portraits, Eagle, Shield, Liberty, Our Supreme Tribunal ... 1850.00
Wood, Whimsy, Open Spiral Snake, Lacquered, 36 1/2 In. 495.00
Wooden, Foot, Early 20th Century, 36 In. 140.00

CANTON CHINA is a blue-and-white ware made near the city of Canton, in China, from about 1785 to 1895. It is hand decorated with Chinese scenes. Canton is part of the group of porcelains known today as Chinese Export Porcelain.

Basket, Centerpiece, Reticulated Sides, 4 x 10 1/4 In. 400.00
Basket, Fruit, Reticulated Tray, Shell Handles, 9 1/2 x 8 1/4 In. 715.00
Basket, Fruit, Undertray, Oval, Reticulated, 19th Century, 3 3/8 x 8 7/8 In. 558.00
Basket, Undertray, Reticulated, c.1820, 4 x 10 1/2 In. 630.00
Bidet, Mahogany Stand, Mid 19th Century, 20 1/2 x 16 3/4 x 25 1/2 In. 1410.00
Bowl, Cut Corner, 9 1/2 In. 1100.00
Bowl, Edge, 5 x 10 In. 440.00
Bowl, Fruit, Oval, Undertray, Fenestrated, 11 In. 1150.00
Bowl, Lotus, Scalloped Edge, 9 1/4 In. 300.00
Bowl, Oval, Gilt Edge, 12 1/2 In. 165.00
Bowl, Shrimp, 10 1/2 x 9 1/4 In. 935.00
Bowl, Underplate, Oval, Reticulated, 10 In. 440.00
Bowl, Vegetable, Cover, Cut Corner, Rectangular, Peach Knob Finial, 9 1/4 x 8 In. .165.00 to 193.00
Bowl, Vegetable, Cover, Oblong, Shaped Edge, Peach Knob Finial, 12 x 9 1/2 In. . .220.00 to 330.00
Bowl, Vegetable, Cover, Rectangular, Cut Corners, 9 x 7 1/2 In. 259.00
Bowl, Vegetable, Cover, Undertray, Lozenge Form, 10 In. 575.00
Bowl Set, 6-Lobe, Scallop Rim, 19th Century, 7 5/8, 10 7/8, 10 3/8 In., 3 Piece 380.00
Butter, Cover, Pierced Insert, Finial, Tray, 5 x 7 In. 1870.00
Candlestick, 19th Century, 6 3/8 In., Pair 1760.00
Candlestick, Flared, 9 3/8 In., Pair 2530.00
Coolers, Food, 3 Sections, Nanking Border, Handle, 20th Century, 10 1/4 In. 920.00
Creamer, Bullnose, Spout With Flared Rim, Orange Peel Glaze, 4 In. 225.00
Creamer, Handle, 3 x 3 1/2 In. 110.00
Creamer, Helmet Shape, Oriental Porcelain, 3 In. 110.00
Creamer, Helmet Shape, Pagoda Landscape, 4 1/4 In. ....220.00 to 338.00
Cup & Saucer, 6 Piece 110.00
Dish, Condiment, 2 7/8 In. ....70.00 to 138.00
Dish, Leaf Shape, 7 x 5 1/4 In. ....220.00 to 276.00
Dish, Oval, Scallop Edge, Temple Scene, c.1820, 8 1/2 In. 145.00
Dish, Pagoda, Bridge, River, Square, 9 In., Pair 635.00
Dish, Pagoda, Bridge, Scenic Landscape, 18-Lobe Border, 8 1/2 In. 430.00
Dish, Shrimp, c.1840, 10 1/2 x 9 3/4 In. 1175.00
Ewer, Acanthus Leaf Design, 6 1/4 In. 2200.00
Garden Barrel, 18 1/2 In. 6900.00
Ginger Jar, 19th Century, 7 1/2 In. 127.00
Ginger Jar, 19th Century, 9 1/4 In., 6 Piece 1095.00
Ginger Jar, Cover, Late 19th Century, 8 1/4 x 8 1/2 In. 125.00
Ginger Jar, Turned Wood Lid, 7 In. 385.00
Jar, Brush, Cylindrical, 9 5/8 x 3 3/4 In. 1485.00
Jar, Cylindrical, Cover, 5 1/4 x 4 3/4 In. 470.00
Jardiniere, Scenic Panels, 20th Century, 13 In. 518.00
Jug, Cider, Barrel Shape, Cover, Double Leaf Handle, Foo Dog Finial, 5 1/2 x 5 In. 3025.00
Mug, Cider, Double Leaf Handle, 3 1/4 x 3 In. 330.00
Mug, Cider, Double Leaf Handle, 4 x 3 1/2 In. 385.00
Mug, Cider, Double Leaf Handle, 4 5/8 x 3 1/4 In. 440.00
Mug, Cider, Double Leaf Handle, 5 x 4 1/2 In. 550.00
Mug Set, Cylindrical Shape, Entwined Lapped Handle, China, 19th Century, 3 7/8 In. 470.00
Mustard Pot, Bulbous Shape, Handle, Cover, 3 1/4 In., Pair 300.00
Pie Plate, Scenic Center, c.1840, 1 1/2 x 10 1/4 In. 575.00
Pitcher, Milk, Octagonal, Molded Design, 7 1/4 In. 2070.00
Plate, Dinner, 19th Century, 10 1/4 In., 12 Piece 823.00
Plate, Figures In Garden, Flowers & Bird Border, c.1850, 8 In. 58.00
Plate, Orange Butterfly, 1800s, 9 3/4 In., 4 Piece 780.00

Plate, Soup, 19th Century, 8 1/2 In., 7 Piece	355.00
Platter, 11 1/4 x 8 1/4 In.	495.00
Platter, 13 3/4 x 10 1/2 In.	550.00
Platter, 16 x 12 3/4 In.	578.00
Platter, China, Octagonal, Oblong, 19th Century, 20 In.	1060.00
Platter, Fitzhugh, Chrysanthemum, Octagonal, 18 x 15 1/2 In.	690.00
Platter, Octagonal, 8 1/8 x 11 1/8 In.	110.00
Platter, Octagonal, Bridge, Houses, Boats, 13 3/4 In.	259.00
Platter, Octagonal, Deep, Bridge, Water, Buildings, 12 In.	145.00
Platter, Octagonal, Oblong, 19th Century, 18 3/8 In.	880.00
Platter, Pagoda, Boat, Bridge, Fish Scale, Scroll Borders, Greek Key, 12 3/4 x 16 In.	110.00
Platter, Pagoda, Figures On Bridge, Diaper, Flower Border, 20 In.	805.00
Platter, Pagoda, Scenic Landscape, Fenestrated Border, 11 In.	405.00
Platter, Riverscape, 19th Century, 15 1/2 In.	645.00
Platter, Well & Tree, Octagonal, Oblong, 19th Century, 15 1/8 In.	235.00
Punch Bowl, Wood Base, 9 x 16 3/4 In.	825.00
Sauceboat, Footed, Diamond Shape, 2 Spouts, 7 3/4 x 5 1/4 In.	440.00
Sauceboat, Handles, 6 3/4 x 3 1/2 In.	330.00
Server, Curry, Footed, Scalloped Edge, Diamond Shape, 13 1/2 x 10 In.	1100.00
Spoon Rest, Leaf Shape, 6 3/4 x 4 3/4 In.	130.00
Sugar, Cover, Strawberry Finial, 6 1/2 x 5 In.	550.00
Tea Caddy, Hexagonal, Footed, 19th Century, 6 1/2 In.	411.00
Teapot, Cover, Double Leaf Handle, Strawberry Finial, 6 1/2 x 5 In.	248.00
Teapot, Intertwined Branch Handle, Berry Finial, Individual Size, 5 1/8 In.	116.00
Tile, Square, 5 7/8 In.	495.00
Tray, Rectangular, 7 1/4 x 9 3/4 In.	360.00
Tureen, Cover, Underglaze, Mid 19th Century, 4 1/2 In.	259.00
Tureen, Cover, Undertray, Boar's Head Handles, 13 In.	1955.00
Tureen, Sauce, Cover, Boar's Head Handles, Melon Finial, 8 1/4 x 4 1/2 In.	990.00
Tureen, Soup, Cover, Pistol Grip Finial, Boars Head Handles, 8 x 13 x 9 1/2 In.	1320.00
Tureen, Soup, Undertray, Cover, Boar's Head Handles, Melon Finial, 11 3/4 x 8 1/4 In.	1650.00
Tureen, Undertray, Pagoda, Landscape, Boar's Head Handles, Leaf Finial, 14 In.	1856.00
Tureen, Undertray, Stem Shape Knop, Boar's Head Handles, 19th Century, 7 1/4 In.	411.00
Vase, Elongated Cylindrical Neck, Tapered Oval Shape, 19th Century, 21 5/8 In.	1410.00
Vase, Ku Shape, 19th Century, 13 3/8 In.	1058.00
Warming Dish, Dome Cover, Flower Bud Handle, 10 1/8 In.	198.00
Warming Dish, Hot Water Reserve, 2 3/4 x 10 1/4 In.	220.00
Washbowl & Pitcher, Handle	3105.00

CAPO-DI-MONTE porcelain was first made in Naples, Italy, from 1743
to 1759. The factory moved near Madrid, Spain, reopened in 1771, and
worked to 1834. Since that time, the Doccia factory of Italy acquired
the molds and is using the crown and N mark. Societe Richard
Ceramica is a modern-day firm often referred to as Ginori or Capo-di-
Monte. This company uses the crown and N mark.

Cabaret Service, Buildings, River Landscape, Ginori, G. Toccafonoli, 10 Piece	777.00
Charger, Napoleon's Retreat Scene, Signed, 19th Century, 14 In.	1265.00
Dresser Box, Porcelain, Painted, Gilt, Hinged Lid, 3 x 5 1/2 x 3 1/2 In.	520.00
Elf Band Set, Painted, Hats, Instruments, 3 1/4 In., 3 Piece	115.00
Figurine, 2 Ladies, 3 Men, Rococo Style, Marked, 18th Century, 13 1/4 x 18 In.	1150.00
Group, Couples Conversing Around Table, Violinist, Oval Base, 9 x 15 x 10 In.	805.00
Jewel Casket, Burgundy Lining, Lift Lid, Handles, Brass Feet, 14 x 13 1/2 x 7 In.	2640.00
Lamp, Partially Nude, Landscape, Acanthus Leaf, c.1840, 22 In.	460.00
Planter, Fruit Relief Band Under Rim, Flared Base, 9 In.	310.00
Urn, Snake Handles, Square Base, Classical Hunting Scenes, 13 x 10 In.	345.00

CAPTAIN MARVEL was introduced in February 1940 in Whiz comic
books. An orphan named Billy Batson met the wizard, Shazam, and
whenever he said the magic word he was transformed into a superhero.
A movie serial was released in 1940. The comic was discontinued in
1954. A second Captain Marvel appeared in 1966, a third in 1967.
Only the original was transformed by shouting *Shazam*.

Button, Celluloid, Shazam	7.00

Cap, Overseas Type, Off-White Felt, Red Trim, Picture Of Captain On Sides 300.00
Cup, Slurpee, Plastic, 1975 .... 10.00
Tie Clip, Brass, On Card, 1940s 100.00
Toy, Car, Racing, Windup, 4 In. 175.00

CAPTAIN MIDNIGHT began as a radio show in September 1940. The first comic book appeared in July 1941. Captain Midnight was really the aviator Captain Albright, who was to defeat the Nazis. A movie serial was made in 1942 and a comic strip was published for a short time. The comic book Captain Midnight ended his career in 1948. The radio premiums are the prized collector memorabilia today.

Badge, Magni-Matic Decoder, Plastic, Alphabet, 1945 .... 80.00
Big Little Flip Book, 1942, 4 1/2 In., 424 Pages 30.00
Book, Secret Squadron, Charts, Codes, Secrets, 1942, 6 x 8 3/4 In. 220.00
Coin, Brass, Flight Patrol Membership, 1940, 1 1/4 In. 12.00
Decoder Cipher Wheel, Ovaltine Premium, Brass, 1942, 2 3/4 x 1 7/8 In. 50.00
Medal, Flying Cross, Premium, Brass, Signature, 1942, 1 1/2 In. 140.00

CARAMEL SLAG, see Imperial Glass category.

CARDS listed here include advertising cards (often called trade cards), greeting cards, baseball cards, playing cards, and others. Color pictures were rare in the nineteenth century, so companies gave away colorful cards with pictures of children, flowers, products, or related scenes that promoted the company name. These were often collected and stored in albums. Baseball cards also date from the nineteenth century when they were used by tobacco companies as giveaways. Gum cards were started in 1933, but it was not until after World War II that the bubble gum cards favored today were produced. Today over 1,000 cards are issued each year by the gum companies. Related items may be found in the Postcard and Movie categories.

Advertising, A Twister, Boston 99 Cent Store, Baseball Goods, Baseball Pitcher 125.00
Advertising, Borden, Elsie Bottle Neck, Seasons Greetings, c.1940, 5 x 5 1/2 In. 14.00
Advertising, Cartridge Co., Elk, 1912, 3 1/4 x 6 In. 88.00
Advertising, Caswell, Hazard Coca Wine, Labeled Bottle, 5 1/2 x 4 1/4 In. 105.00
Advertising, Dr. Bloom's Tooth Powder, Woman Smiling, Moon, N.Y. 39.00
Advertising, Dr. S.B. Collins' Painless Opium Antidote, Laboratory, 5 1/8 x 3 In. 88.00
Advertising, Flexible Flyer, Die Cut, Figural, Sled That Steers, 3 1/4 x 6 In. 45.00
Advertising, French's Cream Salad Mustard, Recipes, Folded .... *Illus* 18.00
Advertising, Jersey Whiskey, Yellow, Red Box, c.1900 .... 45.00
Advertising, King Phiop Oyster, Kickemuit River, Orthodox Jewish Man Eats Oyster 150.00
Advertising, Mechanical Bank, Eagle & Eaglets, 5 1/4 In. 540.00
Advertising, Mechanical Bank, Punch & Judy, 5 1/2 In. 600.00
Advertising, Parker Gun, Live Bird Trapshooting, Multicolored, Prices On Reverse 200.00
Advertising, Parker Gun, Men Shooting At Birds, 5 3/4 x 3 1/2 In. 275.00
Advertising, Pemberton's French Wine Coca, Boat On Lake, Mountains, 4 1/2 x 6 3/4 In. .. 2640.00
Advertising, Penick & Ford Molasses, Recipes, Folded .... *Illus* 12.00
Advertising, Reve De Champion, Mechanical Bicycle, Moving Head, France, 1930s, 6 In. 75.00
Advertising, Score, Winchester, Excell At The Trap, 3 1/4 x 5 1/2 In. 330.00

Card, Advertising,
French's Cream
Salad Mustard,
Recipes, Folded

Card, Advertising,
Penick & Ford
Molasses, Recipes,

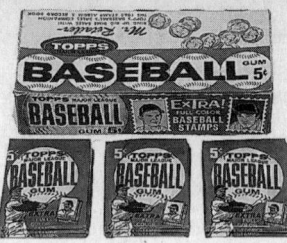

Card, Baseball, Topps, 1962 First Series,
24 Unopened Wax Packs, Box

Card, Movie Star, Three Stooges, Fleer,
24 Unopened Wax Packs, Box, 1966

Advertising, Sen-Sen Gum, Baseball Counter Back Side, 3 x 2 In. 12.00
Advertising, U.S Cartridge Co., Between 2 Fires, 1912, 5 1/2 x 3 1/4 In. 77.00
Advertising, US Ammunition, Hits Where You Aim, 2 Bears, Treed, 3 1/4 x 6 In. 120.00
Advertising, Wells Cigarettes, Tom Mix 40.00
Baseball, Cartoon Positions, Cosack & Co., 1882, 3 1/2 x 5 1/2 In., 9 Piece 250.00
Baseball, Donruss, 1986, 660 Cards, Factory Set 50.00
Baseball, Fleer, 1960, 79 Cards, Complete Set 3910.00
Baseball, Fleer, 1986, 660 Cards, Factory Set 40.00
Baseball, Topps, 1952, Black Back, Nos. 1-80 .... 1093.00
Baseball, Topps, 1954, 250 Cards, Complete Set 1380.00
Baseball, Topps, 1957, 407 Cards, Complete Set 6900.00
Baseball, Topps, 1958, Nos. 1-494 .... 7475.00
Baseball, Topps, 1962 First Series, 24 Unopened Wax Packs, Box .... *Illus* 20599.00
Basketball, Wilt Chamberlain, Rookie, 1961-1962 .... 2363.00
Buffalo Bill On Horse, 20th Century, 3 1/2 x 6 In. 75.00
Football, Bowman, 1954, 128 Cards, Complete Set 518.00
Football, Bowman, 1955, 160 Cards, Complete Set 1093.00
Football, Walter Payton, Rookie, 1976 .... 1909.00
Greeting, Anniversary, Blondie, Dagwood, Becomes Poster, K.F.S., 1943, 19 x 23 In. 65.00
Greeting, Birthday, Dr. Who, Police Call Box, c.1970, 5 x 7 In. 8.00
Greeting, Folding, Cat Show, Chromolithograph, England, 19th Century, 4 1/2 x 17 In. .. 411.00
Greeting, Valentine, Big-Eyed Girl, To Teacher, Scarf, Beret, Ruler, 1950s, 7 x 4 In. 11.00
Greeting, Valentine, Kitten, Googly-Eyed, Beret, Holding Doll, 1950s, 6 1/4 x 3 1/2 In. .. 10.00
Greeting, Valentine, Puppy, Tin Can Tied To Tail, String, 1950s, 8 1/4 x 4 1/4 In. 11.00
Greeting, Valentine, To Teacher, Girl, Scarf, Beret, Ruler, c.1950, 7 x 4 1/4 In. 11.00
Movie Star, Three Stooges, Fleer, 24 Unopened Wax Packs, Box, 1966 .... *Illus* 1180.00
Playing, Buffalo Bill, Pawnee Bill, 53 Cards, Box 800.00
Playing, Gamblers 999 Steamboat Cards, Blue, White Daisy Back, Revenue Stamp, 1932 . 75.00
Playing, Jersey Whiskey Bottle, Yellow & Red Box, c.1900 .... 45.00
Playing, Pocahontas, Joker, Ace 190.00
Playing, Poker, Blue, White Flower Scroll, Union Playing Card Co., New York 175.00
Playing, Poker, Hunter, Dog, c.1895 .... 50.00
Playing, Sitting Bull, Joker, Capitol Building, Ace, Congress, U.S. Playing Card Co. 175.00
Playing, Vanity Fair, Deck, No. 41, 3 3/4 In. 500.00
Playing, Western, Flower Borders, Wagon Train, U.S. Playing Card Co. 250.00
Playing, World War II Aircraft Spotter Cards, Axis & Allies, Box, U.S. Playing Card Co. . 2900.00

CARDER, see Aurene and Steuben categories.

CARLSBAD is a mark found on china made by several factories in
Germany, Austria, and Bavaria. Many pieces were exported to the
United States. Most of the pieces available today were made after
1891.

Dish, Flowers, Curved Sides, Rectangular, Marked, 9 1/4 x 6 1/2 In. 13.00
Dish, Irregular Shape, Pink Flower Spray, Hand Painted, C. Knoll, c.1900, 6 1/2 In. 25.00
Pitcher, Woman Seated Writing, Flowers, Marked, c.1891-1918 .... 100.00
Plate, Napoleon, Signed, Ferrier, 8 1/4 In. 35.00
Plate, Portrait, Mdle. De Montpensier, Victoria Carlsbad Mark, c.1905, 8 1/2 In. 125.00

Plate, Roses, Scalloped, Austria, 8 1/4 In. 30.00
Tureen, Cover, Underplate, Scalloped, Handle, Leaf, Berries, 6 x 12 & 15 1/2 x 9 1/2 In. . .   135.00

CARLTON WARE was made at the Carlton Works of Stoke-on-Trent, England, beginning about 1890. The firm traded as Wiltshaw & Robinson until 1957. It was renamed Carlton Ware Ltd. in 1958. The company went bankrupt in 1995, but the name is still in use.

Bowl, New Stork, Exotic Birds, Trees, Rouge Royale, Handles, 6 3/4 x 6 1/2 In. 450.00
Bowl, Oval, Handle, Pedestal Foot, Deco Tree, Orange Flowers, 7 1/8 x 12 1/4 In. 295.00
Dish, Leaf, Tomatoes, Salad Ware, No. 2095/2, Australian Design, 10 1/2 x 6 In. 60.00
Dish, Round, Currents, Light Green Ground, No. 1603, Australian Design, 4 In. 35.00
Dish, Springtime, Handle, Australian Design, 9 1/2 x 6 In. 60.00
Pitcher, Rouge Royale, Enameled Bird, Mother-Of-Pearl Interior, 6 3/4 x 5 In. 475.00
Vase, Babylon, Willow Branches, White Starflowers, Rouge Royale, 6 In. 450.00
Vase, Chevrons, Geometric Designs, Black & Green, 8 x 4 1/2 In.   660.00
Vase, Cover, Hand Craft, Tree, Flowers, Blue Ground, Foo Dog Finial, 8 3/4 x 3 1/2 In. . .   325.00
Vase, Deep Blue Ground, Oriental Man Paddling Boat, 2 Ladies, 11 In. 325.00
Vase, Dragon & Cloud, Black & Red, 8 1/4 In. 275.00
Vase, Fantasia, Exotic Plants, Dark Blue With Green Swallows, 7 x 5 In. 240.00
Vase, Red Flambe Glaze, Birds, Flowers, Gold Highlights, 8 In., Pair 764.00

CARNIVAL GLASS was an inexpensive, iridescent, pressed glass made from about 1907 to about 1925. More than 1,000 different patterns are known. Carnival glass is currently being reproduced. Additional pieces may be found in the Northwood category.

Acorn Burrs, Table Set, Butter, Sugar & Creamer, Spooner, Amethyst 350.00
Acorn Burrs & Bark pattern is listed here as Acorn Burrs.
American Beauty Roses pattern is listed here as Wreath of Roses.
Autumn Acorns, Bowl, Aqua, 8 1/2 In. 55.00
Autumn Acorns, Plate, Green, 9 In. 500.00
Banded Medallion & Teardrop pattern is listed here as Beaded Bull's-Eye.
Basket, Basket, Amethyst, Handle 90.00
Basket, Basket, Aqua Opalescent, Handle 250.00
Basket, Basket, Emerald Green, Handle 900.00
Basket, Basket, Ice Blue, Handle 300.00
Basket, Basket, Sapphire Blue, Handle 1000.00
Battenburg Lace No. 1 pattern is listed here as Hearts & Flowers.
Battenburg Lace No. 2 pattern is listed here as Captive Rose.
Battenburg Lace No. 3 pattern is listed here as Fanciful.
Beaded Bull's-Eye, Vase, Amethyst, 12 In. 200.00
Beaded Bull's-Eye, Vase, Green, 11 1/4 In. 75.00
Beaded Medallion & Teardrop pattern is listed here as Beaded Bull's-Eye.
Beaded Shell, Mug, White 750.00
Beaded Star & Snail pattern is listed here as Constellation.
Blackberry & Checkerboard pattern is listed here as Blackberry Block.
Blackberry B pattern is listed here as Blackberry Spray.
Blackberry Block, Water Set, Marigold, 2 Piece 500.00
Blackberry Spray, Bonbon, Red Amberina, 6 3/4 In. 350.00
Blueberry, Water Set, Blue, 7 Piece 900.00
Bouquet, Tumbler, Marigold 125.00
Bouquet, Water Set, Blue, 6 Piece 800.00
Boutonniere, Compote, Amethyst 95.00
Brocaded Acorns, Ice Bucket, Lavender 300.00
Brocaded Palms, Candlestick, Pink, 3 In., Pair 250.00
Brocaded Palms, Vase, Pink, 8 In. 170.00
Broken Arches, Punch Cup, Amethyst 240.00
Brooklyn Bridge, Bowl, Marigold 115.00
Bull's-Eye & Loop, Vase, Amethyst, 11 In. 325.00
Bushel Basket pattern is listed here as Basket.
Butterfly, Ornament, Marigold 800.00
Butterfly & Berry, Bowl, Blue, Footed, 10 In. 115.00
Butterfly & Berry, Butter, Cover, Marigold 210.00
Butterfly & Berry, Spooner, Green 225.00

Butterfly & Berry, Sugar, Cover, Blue 275.00
Butterfly & Berry, Tumbler, Marigold 15.00
Butterfly & Berry, Water Set, Blue, 7 Piece 325.00
Butterfly & Cable pattern is listed here as Springtime.
Butterfly & Fern, Pitcher, Blue 250.00
Butterfly & Grape pattern is listed here as Butterfly & Berry.
Butterfly & Plume pattern is listed here as Butterfly & Fern.
Butterfly & Stippled Rays pattern is listed here as Butterfly.
Butterfly & Tulip, Bowl, Purple, Square, Footed ....1100.00 to 1500.00
Butterfly Bush & Waratah, Compote, Amethyst 425.00
Buzz Saw, Cruet, Stopper, Green, 4 In. 300.00
Buzz Saw & File, Tumbler, Marigold 250.00
Cane & Daisy Cut, Vase, Marigold, 10 In. 300.00
Captive Rose, Bowl, Green, 10 In. 155.00
Captive Rose, Plate, Marigold, 9 In. 1600.00
Carolina Dogwood, Bowl, Cobalt Blue Opalescent, 8 1/2 In. 125.00
Caroline, Basket, Amethyst Opalescent 575.00
Castle, Shade, Marigold, Large 250.00
Cattails & Fish pattern is listed here as Fisherman's Mug.
Charlotte, Compote, Blue 290.00
Chatelaine, Tumbler, Amethyst 250.00
Cherry, Bowl, Amethyst, 10 In. 200.00
Cherry, Plate, Ruffled Edge, Peach Opalescent, 6 In. 175.00
Cherry Chain, Bowl, Blue, 10 In. 155.00
Cherry Chain, Plate, Blue, 6 In. 100.00
Cherry Wreathed pattern is listed here as Wreathed Cherry.
Christmas, Compote, Marigold 6000.00
Christmas Cactus pattern is listed here as Thistle.
Chrysanthemum, Bowl, Vaseline, Footed, 10 In. 325.00
Chrysanthemum, Water Set, Marigold, Enameled, 7 Piece 750.00
Circle Scroll, Tumbler, Marigold 475.00
Circle Scroll, Vase, Marigold, 8 In. 250.00
Cobblestones, Bowl, Marigold, 8 1/2 In. 195.00
Colonial, Tumbler, Marigold 225.00
Columbine, Pitcher, Blue, Enameled 475.00
Concave Diamonds, Tumble-Up Set, Vaseline 350.00
Concave Diamonds, Water Set, Celeste Blue, 8 Piece 700.00
Constellation, Compote, Amethyst 500.00
Constellation, Compote, Lavender 105.00
Constitution pattern is listed here as God & Home.
Coral, Bowl, Blue, 9 In. 255.00
Corinth, Vase, 9 In. 165.00
Corn, Bottle, Aqua 1600.00
Corn, Vase, Plain Base, Marigold 350.00
Cosmos & Cane, Butter, Honey Amber 300.00
Country Kitchen, Butter, Cover, Amethyst 200.00
Courthouse, Bowl, Amethyst, Ruffled Edge ....600.00 to 650.00
Courthouse, Bowl, Aqua, Ruffled Edge 800.00
Courthouse, Bowl, Ice Cream, Amethyst 1300.00
Curved Star, Chalice, Marigold, 7 In. 45.00
Dahlia, Tumbler, Marigold 105.00
Daisy, Bell, Marigold 175.00
Daisy & Drape, Vase, Aqua Opalescent 375.00
Daisy & Drape, Vase, White, Flared 225.00
Daisy & Lattice Band pattern is listed here as Lattice & Daisy.
Daisy & Plume, Compote, Marigold 85.00
Daisy & Plume, Rose Bowl, Amethyst 200.00
Daisy Band & Drape pattern is listed here as Daisy & Drape.
Daisy Squares, Compote, Crimped, Green 500.00
Daisy Web, Hat, Marigold 225.00
Daisy Wreath, Bowl, Cobalt Blue Opalescent 95.00
Dandelion, Mug, Amethyst 100.00
Dandelion, Mug, Green 850.00

To clean carnival glass, try using a mixture of ½ cup ammonia and ⅛ cup white vinegar.

Carnival Glass, Dragon & Lotus, Bowl, Ice Cream, Red, 9 In.

Dandelion, Mug, Knight Templer, Aqua Opalescent 400.00
Dandelion, Pitcher, Green 800.00
Dandelion, Tumbler, Green 120.00
Dandelion, Tumbler, White 50.00
Dandelion, Water Set, Amethyst, 2 Piece 575.00
Dandelion, Water Set, Ice Blue, 7 Piece 4500.00
Dandelion Variant pattern is listed here as Panelled Dandelion.
Deep Grape, Compote, Flared, Green 1450.00
Diagonal Band, Tankard, Amethyst 550.00
Diamond & Fan, Vase, Marigold, 8 In. 140.00
Diamond & Rib, Vase, Green, Swung, 22 In. 1500.00
Diamond & Rib, Vase, White, 7 In. 90.00
Diamond & Sunburst, Decanter, Marigold 105.00
Diamond & Sunburst, Wine Set, Marigold, 7 Piece 180.00
Diamond Band pattern is listed here as Diamonds.
Diamond Lace, Pitcher, Amethyst 175.00
Diamond Lace, Water Set, Purple, 7 Piece 300.00
Diamond Point & Daisy pattern is listed here as Cosmos & Cane.
Diamond Point Columns, Vase, Lavender, 7 1/2 In. 45.00
Diamond Points, Basket, Marigold 900.00
Diamonds, Water Set, Green, 5 Piece 475.00
Diving Dolphins, Bowl, Nut, Marigold 100.00
Dogwood & Marsh Lily pattern is listed here as Two Flowers.
Double Loop, Chalice, Aqua Opalescent 115.00
Double Loop, Creamer, Blue 235.00
Double-Stem Rose, Bowl, Celeste Blue, 8 1/2 In. 675.00
Double-Stem Rose, Plate, Amethyst 125.00
Dragon & Berry, Bowl, Footed, Green, 9 In. 1500.00
Dragon & Berry, Bowl, Footed, Marigold, 9 In. 400.00
Dragon & Lotus, Bowl, Amethyst Opalescent, 9 In. 850.00
Dragon & Lotus, Bowl, Amethyst, 9 In. 90.00
Dragon & Lotus, Bowl, Ice Cream, Red, 9 In. .... *Illus* 500.00
Dragon & Lotus, Bowl, Lavender, 9 In. 110.00
Dragon & Lotus, Bowl, Red 750.00
Dragon's Tongue, Bowl, Ruffled, Marigold, 11 In. 1700.00
Drapery, Candy Dish, Blue 225.00
Drapery, Rose Bowl, Aqua Opalescent 250.00
Drapery, Rose Bowl, White 175.00
Drapery, Vase, Blue, 7 In. 130.00
Drapery Variant, Vase, Ice Blue, 7 In. 325.00
Dugan Honeycomb, Rose Bowl, Peach, Opalescent 60.00
Egyptian Queen, Rose Bowl, Marigold 375.00
Elegance, Plate, Marigold 6500.00
Elks, Bell, Detroit, 1910, Amethyst 700.00
Elks, Plate, Atlantic City, Blue, 7 In. 900.00
Emaline pattern is listed here as Zippered Loop Lamp.

Embroidered Mums, Bowl, Blue, 9 In. 200.00
Enameled Chrysanthemum, Water Set, Blue, 7 Piece 300.00
Enameled Grape, Water Set, Blue, 7 Piece 105.00
Enameled Iris, Pitcher, Blue 400.00
Enameled Swallow, Tumbler, Marigold, 5 In. 185.00
Estate, Sugar & Creamer, Amethyst, Westmoreland, Child's 100.00
Fan-Tail, Bowl, Blue, Footed, 9 In. 205.00
Fanciful, Bowl, Amethyst, 8 1/2 In. 115.00
Fanciful, Plate, Amethyst, 9 In. 400.00
Farmyard, Bowl, Ruffled Edge, Amethyst 4250.00
Farmyard, Bowl, Square, Amethyst 5750.00
Fashion, Punch Cup, Blue 40.00
Fashion, Rose Bowl, Marigold 135.00
Fashion, Tumbler, Smoke 85.00
Feather & Heart, Tumbler, Amethyst 110.00
Feather & Heart, Water Set, Marigold, 5 Piece 200.00
Feather Stitch, Bowl, Amethyst, 10 In. 165.00
Feathered Scroll pattern is listed here as Feathered Serpent.
Feathered Serpent, Bowl, Aqua, 10 In. 65.00
Fenton's Butterfly pattern is listed here as Butterfly.
Fentonia Fruit, Bowl, Marigold, Footed, 10 In. 60.00
Field Flower, Pitcher, Aqua 110.00
Field Flower, Pitcher, Milk, Amber 120.00
Field Thistle, Plate, Marigold, 9 In. 425.00
File, Tumbler, Dark Marigold 145.00
File, Vase, Whimsy, Marigold, 5 In. 200.00
Fine Cut & Roses, Candy Dish, Ice Blue 140.00
Fine Cut & Roses, Rose Bowl, Horehound 155.00
Fine Rib, Vase, Amber, 10 In. 1500.00
Fine Rib, Vase, Red 10 In. 250.00
Finecut & Star pattern is listed here as Star & File.
Fisherman's Mug, Amethyst 145.00
Fisherman's Mug, Marigold ....160.00 to 200.00
Fisherman's Mug, Peach Opalescent 1150.00
Fishscales & Beads, Plate, Amethyst, 7 In. ....375.00 to 450.00
Fishscales & Beads, Plate, Marigold, 6 In. 165.00
Five Hearts, Bowl, Dome Foot, Marigold 85.00
Five Hearts, Rose Bowl, Marigold 725.00
Fleur-De-Lis, Bowl, Amethyst, 8 In. 230.00
Fleur-De-Lis, Bowl, Dome Foot, Tricornered, Marigold, 8 In. 500.00
Floral & Diamond Point pattern is listed here as Fine Cut & Roses.
Floral & Grape, Water Set, Amethyst, 7 Piece 500.00
Floral & Grapevine pattern is listed here as Floral & Grape.
Floral & Optic, Bowl, Footed, Flared, Amethyst 450.00
Floral & Optic, Cake Plate, Red, Footed 800.00
Floral & Sunburst, Vase, Marigold, 10 In. 675.00
Florentine, Candlestick, Ice Green, Pair 105.00
Florentine, Candlestick, Olive Green, 8 In., Pair 170.00
Flower Pot pattern is listed here as Butterfly & Tulip.
Flowers & Frames, Bowl, Dome Foot, Amethyst, 8 In. 200.00
Fluffy Bird pattern is listed here as Peacock.
Fluffy Peacock, Water Set, Amethyst, 5 Piece 700.00
Fluffy Peacock, Water Set, Marigold, 2 Piece 550.00
Folding Fan, Compote, Sides Rolled, Peach Opalescent 280.00
Formal, Hatpin Holder, Amethyst 525.00
Four Flowers, Bowl, Blue 175.00
Four Flowers, Plate, Amethyst 140.00
Four Flowers, Plate, Emerald Green 400.00
Four Pillars, Vase, Aqua Opalescent, 10 In. 145.00
Four Pillars, Vase, Aqua, 9 In. 500.00
Four Pillars, Vase, Sapphire Blue, 8 1/2 In. 250.00
Four Seventy Four, Pitcher, Marigold 145.00
Four Seventy Four, Punch Set, Marigold, 11 Piece 135.00

Four Seventy Four, Vase, Marigold, 8 In. 1400.00
Freefold, Vase, Purple, 10 In. 170.00
Fruit Salad, Punch Bowl, Base, Blue Opalescent 2600.00
Fruit Salad, Punch Bowl, Base, Peach Opalescent 1750.00
Fruits & Flowers, Bonbon, Aqua Opalescent 400.00
Fruits & Flowers, Bowl, Green, 10 In. 85.00
Fruits & Flowers, Plate, Green, 7 In. 210.00
Garden Path, Bowl, Vaseline, 9 1/2 In. 1000.00
Garland, Rose Bowl, Blue 40.00
God & Home, Tumbler, Blue 125.00
God & Home, Water Set, Blue, 7 Piece 2100.00
Golden Harvest, Wine Set, 7 Piece 185.00
Golden Harvest, Wine, Aqua 28.00
Good Luck, Bowl, Amethyst, 8 1/2 In. 215.00
Good Luck, Bowl, Blue, 8 1/2 In. 225.00
Good Luck, Bowl, Electric Blue, Ruffled Edge, 8 1/2 In. 450.00
Good Luck, Bowl, Ribbed Back, Ice Green, 8 1/2 In. 5000.00
Good Luck, Bowl, Ruffled Edge, Marigold, 8 1/2 In. 300.00
Good Luck, Bowl, Sapphire Blue, 8 1/2 In. 1500.00
Good Luck, Bowl, Smooth Back, Purple, 8 1/2 In. 575.00
Good Luck, Bowl, Stippled, Renninger Blue, 8 1/2 In. 425.00
Good Luck, Plate, Plain, Horehound, 9 In. 450.00
Good Luck, Plate, Ribbed, Horehound, 9 In. 1700.00
Gothic Arches, Vase, Marigold, 12 In. 160.00
Graceful, Vase, Ruffled Edge, Ice Blue 1300.00
Grand Thistle, Tumbler, Blue 175.00
Grape & Cable, Banana Bowl, Green 200.00
Grape & Cable, Banana Bowl, Stippled & Banded, Blue 400.00
Grape & Cable, Biscuit Jar, Amethyst, Handles 275.00
Grape & Cable, Bonbon, Aqua Opalescent, Stippled 1600.00
Grape & Cable, Bonbon, Blue 95.00
Grape & Cable, Bonbon, White 125.00
Grape & Cable, Bowl, Cobalt Blue Opalescent, Footed 1100.00
Grape & Cable, Bowl, Red 300.00
Grape & Cable, Bowl, Ruffled Edge, Aqua Opalescent 1950.00
Grape & Cable, Bowl, Ruffled Edge, Lime Green, Stippled 1800.00
Grape & Cable, Bowl, Ruffled, Green, 8 3/4 In. 65.00
Grape & Cable, Bowl, Stippled, Amethyst, 8 1/2 In. 70.00
Grape & Cable, Butter, Cover, Green 155.00
Grape & Cable, Candlelamp, Amethyst 800.00
Grape & Cable, Candlelamp, Green 575.00
Grape & Cable, Candlestick, Amethyst, Pair 275.00
Grape & Cable, Centerpiece, Ice Blue, Footed . . . . 1450.00 to 2100.00
Grape & Cable, Cologne Bottle, Amethyst . . . . 100.00 to 325.00
Grape & Cable, Cologne Bottle, Lavender 185.00
Grape & Cable, Cup & Saucer, Amethyst 175.00
Grape & Cable, Fernery, Ice Blue 2100.00
Grape & Cable, Fernery, White 800.00
Grape & Cable, Hatpin Holder, Marigold 175.00
Grape & Cable, Humidor, Amethyst 325.00
Grape & Cable, Plate, Marigold, Radium, 9 1/4 In. 105.00
Grape & Cable, Plate, Sapphire Blue, Stippled, 9 In. . . . . 2000.00 to 3600.00
Grape & Cable, Punch Set, White, 13 1/2 In., 11 Piece 3850.00
Grape & Cable, Tray, Dresser, Amethyst 175.00
Grape & Cable, Tumbler, Amethyst 35.00
Grape & Cable, Water Set, Aqua, 7 Piece 525.00
Grape Arbor, Water Set, Marigold, 2 Piece 600.00
Grape Delight pattern is listed here as Vintage.
Grape Wreath, Bowl, Aqua, 5 In. 125.00
Grapevine, Bowl, Lattice, Ruffled, White, 1 5/8 x 7 In. 85.00
Grapevine Diamonds pattern is listed here as Grapevine Lattice.
Grapevine Lattice, Plate, Amethyst, 7 In. 700.00
Greek Key, Plate, Blue, 9 In. 400.00

Greek Key, Water Set, Amethyst, 2 Piece 625.00
Harvest Time pattern is listed here as Golden Harvest.
Hattie, Chop Plate, Marigold 2000.00
Hearts & Flowers, Bowl, Ruffled Edge, Ice Blue, 8 1/2 In. 350.00
Hearts & Flowers, Compote, White 140.00
Hearts & Flowers, Plate, Amethyst, 9 In. 1500.00
Hearts & Flowers, Plate, Ice Blue, 9 In. 650.00
Hearts & Flowers, Plate, White, 9 In. 2400.00
Heavy Grape, Bowl, Marigold, 10 In. 25.00
Heavy Grape, Chop Plate, Smoke 700.00
Hobnail, Cuspidor, Marigold, Woman's 500.00
Hobnail, Pitcher, Amethyst 1100.00
Hobstar Band, Celery Dish, Handles, Marigold 65.00
Hobstar Fruit, Bowl, Amethyst Opalescent, Ruffled Edge, 6 In. 12.50
Holly, Bowl, Black Amethyst, 8 In. 170.00
Holly, Bowl, Marigold, 8 In. 95.00
Homestead, Plate, Marigold, 10 1/4 In. 350.00
Honeycomb Collar pattern is listed here as Fishscales & Beads.
Horse Medallions pattern is listed here as Horses' Heads.
Horse's Heads, Plate, Marigold, 7 In. 350.00
Horse's Heads, Rose Bowl, Marigold 100.00
Imperial Grape, Carafe, Amethyst 500.00
Imperial Grape, Plate, Marigold, 9 In. 80.00
Imperial Grape, Tumbler, Amber 250.00
Inverted Strawberry, Cuspidor, Marigold 800.00
Inverted Strawberry, Pitcher, Green 950.00
Kimberly pattern is listed here as Concave Diamonds.
Kittens, Bowl, Blue, Squared Edge 215.00
Kittens, Plate, Folded, Marigold, 4 1/2 In. 150.00
Kittens, Toothpick, Marigold 85.00
Labelle Poppy pattern is listed here as Poppy Show.
Labelle Rose pattern is listed here as Rose Show.
Lattice & Daisy, Water Set, Amethyst, 7 Piece 2100.00
Leaf & Little Flowers, Compote, Marigold, Radium Finish, Ruffled Edge 150.00
Leaf Chain, Bowl, Emerald Green, 9 In. 20.00
Leaf Medallion pattern is listed here as Leaf Chain.
Leaf Pinwheel & Star Flower pattern is listed here as Whirling Leaves.
Lined Lattice, Vase, Amethyst, 10 In. 185.00
Lion, Plate, Marigold, 7 In. 600.00
Lotus & Grape, Plate, Green, 9 In. 1900.00
Lustre Rose, Spooner, Marigold 25.00
Magnolia Drape, Pitcher, Marigold, Enameled 110.00
Maine Coast pattern is listed here as Seacoast.
Melinda pattern is listed here as Wishbone.
Melon & Fan pattern is listed here as Diamond & Rib.
Morning Glory, Vase, Green, 6 In. 115.00
Mums & Greek Key pattern is listed here as Embroidered Mums.
Nu-Art Chrysanthemum, Chop Plate, Marigold 450.00
Oak Leaf Brocade pattern is listed here as Brocaded Acorns.
Orange Tree, Mug, Amber 150.00
Orange Tree, Plate, Marigold, 9 In. 125.00
Orange Tree, Rose Bowl, Vaseline 375.00
Oriental Poppy, Water Set, Marigold, 2 Piece 525.00
Paneled Dandelion, Water Set, Green 500.00
Panther, Bowl, Ruffled Edge, Red, 5 In. 500.00
Panther, Centerpiece, Marigold 1400.00
Panther, Marigold, Footed, 9 In. 170.00
Peach, Pitcher, Tumbler, White 750.00
Peacock, Bowl, Aqua Opalescent 1100.00
Peacock, Plate, Amethyst 600.00
Peacock, Plate, Ice Blue, 9 In. 1600.00
Peacock & Dahlia, Plate, Marigold, 8 1/2 In. 650.00
Peacock & Grape, Plate, Marigold, Footed, 9 In. 175.00

Peacock & Urn, Bowl, Black Amethyst, Stippled, 10 In. 500.00
Peacock & Urn, Bowl, Ice Cream, Aqua Opalescent, Pink Iridescence, Master 22000.00
Peacock & Urn, Bowl, Ice Cream, Green, 6 In. 450.00
Peacock & Urn, Bowl, Ice Cream, Lime Green, 10 In. 1050.00
Peacock & Urn, Plate, Marigold, 9 In. 350.00
Peacock At The Fountain, Compote, Amethyst 450.00
Peacock At The Fountain, Compote, Ice Green 1100.00
Peacock At The Fountain, Orange Bowl, Amethyst 175.00
Peacock At The Fountain, Orange Bowl, Aqua Opalescent 11000.00
Peacock At The Fountain, Pitcher, Green 4000.00
Peacock At The Fountain, Spooner, Marigold 130.00
Peacock At The Fountain, Tumbler, Green 350.00
Peacock On Fence pattern is listed here as Peacock.
Persian Medallion, Bowl, Green, Ruffled Edge, 8 3/4 In. 158.00
Persian Medallion, Dish, Ice Cream, Red 450.00
Persian Medallion, Plate, Amethyst, 9 In. 5250.00
Persian Medallion, Plate, Blue, 6 In. 195.00
Persian Medallion, Plate, Light Marigold, 9 In. 2900.00
Persian Medallion, Plate, White, 9 In. 1800.00
Peter Rabbit, Plate, Green, 9 In. 2800.00
Peter Rabbit, Plate, Marigold, 9 In. 6000.00
Pine Cone, Plate, Blue, 7 In. 150.00
Pine Cone Wreath pattern is listed here as Pine Cone.
Plaid, Bowl, Blue, 3 Sections, Ruffled Edge, 8 3/4 In. 1000.00
Plaid, Bowl, Red, Ruffled Edge, 8 3/4 In. . . . . .1600.00 to 2250.00
Poinsettia & Lattice, Bowl, Footed, Aqua Opalescent 10500.00
Poinsettia & Lattice, Bowl, Footed, Ice Blue 1000.00
Poppy, Dish, Pickle, Aqua Opalescent 1800.00
Poppy, Dish, Pickle, Green 350.00
Poppy, Dish, Pickle, Marigold 225.00
Poppy Scroll pattern is listed here as Poppy.
Poppy Show, Plate, Amethyst, 9 In. 750.00
Poppy Show, Plate, Green, 9 In. 3000.00
Poppy Show, Plate, Ice Blue, 9 In. 1500.00
Raspberry, Pitcher, Water, Amethyst, 9 In. 290.00
Ribbon Tie, Bowl, Red, Ruffled Edge, 9 1/2 In. 10500.00
Ripple, Vase, Teal, 10 1/2 In. 175.00
Rose Show, Bowl, Amethyst, 8 3/4 In. 600.00
Rose Show, Plate, Blue, 9 1/2 In. 600.00
Rose Show, Plate, Ice Green Opalescent, 9 In. 9000.00
Rose Show, Plate, Marigold, 9 In. 800.00
Roses & Loops pattern is listed here as Double-Stem Rose.
Royal Lustre, Rose Bowl, Red, 3 1/4 In. 100.00
Scroll, Embossed, Plate, Green, 9 In. 100.00
Scroll-Cable pattern is listed here as Estate.
Seacoast, Pin Tray, Amethyst 800.00
Shell & Wild Rose pattern is listed here as Wild Rose.
Singing Birds, Mug, Aqua Opalescent 1450.00
Singing Birds, Mug, Marigold . . . . .25.00 to 30.00
Singing Birds, Tumbler, Green 75.00
Ski Star, Bowl, Peach Opalescent, 11 In. 65.00
Soda Gold, Tumbler, Smoke 105.00
Soldiers & Sailors Home, Plate, Blue, 7 In. 1900.00
Spider Web pattern is listed here as Soda Gold.
Spring Flowers pattern is listed here as Bouquet.
Springtime, Water Set, Marigold, 7 Piece 900.00
Stag & Holly, Bowl, Footed, Marigold, 11 In. 90.00
Stag & Holly, Chop Plate, Marigold 1000.00
Star & Fan, Cordial Set, Argentina, 5 Piece 140.00
Star & File, Compote, Marigold 135.00
Stippled Posy & Pods pattern is listed here as Four Flowers.
Stippled Rays, Compote, Ice Cream, Vaseline 300.00
Stippled Rays, Plate, Red, 7 In. 750.00

Stork ABC, Plate, Marigold, 7 1/2 In.	60.00
Strawberry, Bonbon, Amberina	100.00
Strawberry, Plate, Amethyst, 9 In.	140.00
Strawberry Wreath, Compote, Ruffled Edge, Marigold, Radium Finish	350.00
Sunflower pattern is listed here as Dandelion.	
Sunflower & Wheat pattern is listed here as Field Flower.	
Swirl Hobnail, Vase, Green	500.00
Swirl Rib, Cup & Saucer, Marigold	225.00
Thistle, Banana Boat, Marigold	410.00
Three Fruits, Bowl, Ice Cream, Marigold	60.00
Three Fruits, Plate, Aqua Opalescent, Stippled, 9 In.	1700.00
Three Fruits, Plate, Aqua, 9 In.	200.00
Three Fruits Medallion, Bowl, Aqua Opalescent, Footed	450.00
Tree Trunk, Vase, Dark Marigold, 9 1/2 In.	30.00
Two Flowers, Chop Plate, Marigold	650.00
Victorian, Bowl, Amethyst, 11 In.	325.00
Vintage, Bowl, Nut, Amethyst, Footed, 6 In.	50.00
Vintage, Plate, Marigold, 9 In.	750.00
Vintage Banded, Tumbler, Amethyst	5.00
Waffle Block, Basket, Marigold, 9 1/2 In.	20.00
Whirling Leaves, Bowl, Green, Tricornered	325.00
Wild Rose, Bowl, Green, Rayed Interior, Footed, 6 In.	17.50
Wild Rose, Syrup, Marigold	400.00 to 900.00
Wishbone, Pitcher, Amethyst, Bulbous	625.00
Wishbone & Spades, Bowl, Peach Opalescent, Ruffled Edge, 5 In.	50.00
Wishbone & Spades, Chop Plate, Amethyst	1500.00
Wreath Of Roses, Punch Bowl, Cups, Marigold, 7 Piece	350.00
Wreathed Cherry, Water Set, Marigold, 7 Piece	500.00
Zigzag, Pitcher, Water, Enameled, Ice Green	300.00

CAROUSEL or merry-go-round figures were first carved in the United States in 1867 by Gustav Dentzel. Collectors discovered the charm of the hand-carved figures in the 1970s, and they were soon classed as folk art. Most desirable are the figures other than horses, such as pigs, camels, lions, or dogs. A jumper is a figure that was made to move up and down on a pole; a stander was placed in a stationary position.

Billy Goat, Curved Horns, Carved String Of Bells On Harness, 41 x 47 In.	2310.00
Chariot, Sideboard, Deep-Relief Cherub, Herschell-Spillman	2750.00
Deer, Leaping, Real Antlers, Glass Eyes, 70 x 45 In.	2200.00
Elephant, Original Gray Paint, America, c.1860, 41 In.	10450.00
Giraffe, Leaping, Looff	13200.00
Giraffe, Wooden, Carved, Eagle Head On Saddle, 42 x 60 In.	7150.00
Horse, Dappled, Yellow Saddle, Green Blanket, c.1900, 42 In.	7200.00
Horse, Derby Racing Form, Polychrome, 2 Seats, 84 In.	748.00
Horse, Derby, Williams, Coney Island	1375.00
Horse, Jumper, Carved, Painted, Open Mouth, Inset Glass Eyes, 2 Seats, c.1910, 68 In.	1265.00
Horse, Jumper, Muller, c.1915	17600.00
Horse, Prancer, Riverside Park, New Jersey, Looff	4675.00
Horse, Rearing, Applied Stars On Saddle Blanket, 62 x 61 In.	1650.00
Horse, Rocking, Appaloosa, Gray, White, Painted Saddle, Blue Rockers, 36 x 48 In.	990.00
Horse, Rocking, Charles Dare, 47 1/2 x 55 x 32 In.	2245.00
Horse, Standing, Black & Gold Saddle, Carved Feathers Around Neck, 72 x 72 In.	880.00
Horse Head, White, Brown Flowing Mane, Glass Eyes, 22 In.	1375.00
Lion, Standing, Muller, c.1910	27000.00
Pig, Pink, Black, Red, Glass Eyes, 19 x 37 In.	358.00
Ram, Carved, c.1911	4675.00
Shorebird, Wooden, Carved, 50 In.	1553.00
Unicorn, Rearing, White, Gray, Brown & Blue Saddle, Tassels, 54 x 48 In.	1100.00

CARRIAGE means several things, so this category lists baby carriages, buggies for adults, horse-drawn sleighs, and even strollers. Doll-sized carriages are listed in the Toy category.

Baby Buggy, Victorian, 1880	165.00

Baby Buggy, Wicker, Cloth Parasol	248.00
Buggy, 3 Seats, Amish, Black Canvas Covering	440.00
Doctor's Buggy, Upholstered Seat, 1-Horse, McLaughlin Carriage Works	660.00
Sleigh, Push, Red, Gold Stenciling, Turned Wood Handle, Child's, 42 In.	340.00
Sleigh, Serpentine Front, Bentwood Runners, Blue, Red, Child's, 33 x 26 In.	770.00
Sleigh, Victorian, Push, Upholstered Velvet, Child's, 46 x 17 x 32 In.	1450.00
Sleigh, Wood, Push, Oak, Iron Runners, Needlepoint Back, Child's, 48 x 18 x 34 In.	275.00
Sleigh, Wood, Slats, Curved Runners, Child's, 14 1/2 x 49 1/2 x 15 In.	235.00
Sleigh, Wood, Swan's-Neck Front, Blue Paint, Upholstered, Child's, 33 x 15 x 25 In.	220.00
Sleigh, Yellow Painted, Farmers, Dogs, Signed, John L. Davis, Salisbury, Mass, 1810	6900.00
Surrey, Fringed Hood, Tufted Velvet Interior, Wood Handles, Spokes, Victorian, 48 In.	395.00
Wagon Seat, Wood, Splint, 18th Century	110.00

CASH REGISTERS were invented in 1884 because an eye on the cash was a necessity in stores of the nineteenth century, too. John and James Ritty invented a large model that resembled a clock and kept a record of the dollars and cents exchanged in the store. John Patterson improved the cash register with a paper roll to record the money. By the early 1900s, elaborate brass registers were made. About World War I, the fancy case was exchanged for the more modern types.

Grimme Natalis & Co., Spoke Wheel, Nickel Plated, Art Nouveau, Germany, 1900	1955.00
Mahogany, Slotted Shelves, Coin Slots, Mirror Back, England, 17 x 15 In.	385.00
McCaskey, No. 295 SC, Metal Case, Mahogany Drawer	60.00
National, Brass, Floor Standing, Raised Panel Oak, 62 x 29 x 21 In.	840.00
National, Model 91, Brass, Day & Night Clock, Marquee, Case	1760.00
National, Model 137 476770, Cast Iron Case, Bronze Placard, Oak Base, 21 In.	590.00
National, Model 311, Candy Store, Polished Brass, 21 In.	880.00
National, Model 312, Candy Store, Brass, Polished, Black Vitrolite Sill, 17 In.	798.00
National, Model 313, Candy Store, Polished Brass, 1970s	635.00
National, Model 332, 2-Row Keyboard, Brass Case, 17 In.	440.00
National, Model 333, Candy Store, Brass, Polished, White Marble Sill, 17 In.	660.00
National, Model 349-G, Brass	220.00

CASTOR JARS for pickles are glass jars about six inches in height, held in special metal holders. They became a popular dinner table accessory about 1890. Each jar had a top that was usually silver or silver plate. The frame, also of a silver metal, had a handle that arched above the jar and a hook that held a pair of tongs. By 1900, the pickle castor was out of fashion. Many examples found today have reproduced glass jars in old holders. Additional pickle castors may be found in the various Glass categories.

Pickle, Amberina, Hobnail, Silver Plated Metal Holder, Tongs, Mt. Washington, 12 In.	2070.00
Pickle, Blue & White Enameled, Silver Plated Holder & Tongs, 12 In.	350.00
Pickle, Blue, Satin, Enameled Flowers, Tongs, Rogers Frame, 11 3/4 In.	1006.00
Pickle, Clear Insert, Meriden Silver Plated Holder, Embossed Sunflowers, 11 In.	450.00
Pickle, Clear Insert, Paneled, Rockford Silver Plated Holder, 12 In.	650.00
Pickle, Clear Insert, Ruby Stripes, Meriden Silver Plated Holder, 12 In.	1000.00
Pickle, Cobalt Blue, Paneled, Enameled Flower Sprigs, Silver Plated Frame, 8 1/2 In.	778.00
Pickle, Coin Spot, Amber, E.G. Webster Bros., Quadruple Plated Frame, Tongs, 10 1/2 In.	405.00
Pickle, Coin Spot, Cranberry, Benedict Mfg. Co., Frame, 10 In.	600.00
Pickle, Cranberry Opalescent, Adelphi Silver Plate Co., Frame & Tongs, 12 1/2 In.	360.00
Pickle, Cranberry, Enameled Flowers, Derby Silver Plated Holder, 12 In.	800.00
Pickle, Cranberry, Silver Plated Holder, G-Clef Sides, 9 1/2 In.	600.00
Pickle, Crown Milano, Enameled Acorn & Leaves, Rogers Silver Plated Holder, 10 In.	1150.00
Pickle, Daisy & Button, Pairpoint, Silver Plated Holder, Spiral Twist, 11 In.	225.00
Pickle, Daisy & Button, Vaseline Glass, Meriden Silver Plated Holder, 11 In.	400.00
Pickle, Daisy & Fern, Cranberry Opalescent, Eagle Finial, Tongs, 11 In.	585.00
Pickle, Diamond-Quilted, Blue Satin, Silver Plated Holder, Medallion, Claw Feet, 13 In.	1200.00
Pickle, Diamond-Quilted, Opal, Silver Plated Holder, Fern Leaf, Bamboo, 10 1/2 In.	1200.00
Pickle, Homestead Medallion Insert, Meriden Silver Plated Holder, 13 In.	700.00
Pickle, Inverted Thumbprint, Cranberry, Embossed Silver Plated Frame, 10 In.	230.00
Pickle, Inverted Thumbprint, Cranberry, Enameled Daisies, Silver Plated Frame, 11 In.	575.00
Pickle, Inverted Thumbprint, Cranberry, Silver Plated Frame & Tongs, 10 1/2 In.	358.00

Pickle, Ruby, Ground Rim, Pairpoint Quadruple Plated Frame & Tongs, 10 1/4 In. 575.00
Pickle, Vaseline, Derby Silver Co. Silver Plated Frame & Tongs, 10 1/2 In. 495.00
Pickle, Wave Crest, Swirl Mold, Silver Plated Holder, Meriden, 9 1/2 In. 1900.00
Sweetmeat, Blue, Boston Silver Plated Holder, 11 In. 250.00

CASTOR SETS holding just salt and pepper castors were used in the seventeenth century. The sugar castor, mustard pot, spice dredger, bottles for vinegar and oil, and other spice holders became popular by the eighteenth century. These sets were usually made of sterling silver. The American Victorian castor set, the type most collected today, was made of silver plated Britannia metal. Colored glass bottles were introduced after the Civil War. The sets were out of fashion by World War I. Be careful when buying sets with colored bottles; many are reproductions. Other castor sets may be listed in various porcelain and glass categories in this book.

2 Bottles, Vaseline, Meriden Silver Plated Holder, 13 1/2 In. 2000.00
3 Bottles, Coach Shape, Oak, Silver Plated, Frame, England, 13 7/16 x 18 x 9 1/4 In. ... 2390.00
3 Bottles, Pansy Enameled, Mt. Washington, Metal Holder 270.00
6 Bottles, Button & Daisy, Amber Stain, Silver Plated Holder, 18 In. 350.00
Plated, Crystal, 4 Bottles, England, 9 In. 105.00
Victorian, 6 Bottles, Silver Plate, 17 In. 173.00

CATALOGS are listed in the Paper category.

CAULDON Limited worked in Staffordshire, Great Britain, and went through many name changes. John Ridgway made porcelain at Cauldon Place, Hanley, until 1855. The firm of John Ridgway, Bates and Co. of Cauldon Place worked from 1856 to 1859. It became Bates, Brown-Westhead, Moore and Co. from 1859 to 1862. Brown-Westhead, Moore and Co. worked from 1862 to 1904. About 1890, this firm started using the words *Cauldon* or *Cauldon ware* as part of the mark. Cauldon Ltd. worked from 1905 to 1920, Cauldon Potteries from 1920 to 1962. Related items may be found in the Indian Tree category.

Plate, Burgundy Border Band, Gilt Rim, Purple Transfer Label, 10 In., 8 Piece 165.00
Plate, Dessert, Game Bird In Landscape, Gilt Scalloped Rim, 8 1/2 In., 12 Piece 3175.00
Plate, Dinner, Cobalt Blue Border, Flower Baskets, c.1900, 10 1/2 In., 12 Piece 690.00
Punch Bowl, Floral, Pink, Green, Gold, On White Ground, 17 In. 500.00

CELADON is the name of a velvet-textured green-gray glaze used by Chinese, Japanese, Korean, and other factories. The name refers both to the glaze and to pieces covered with the glaze. It is still being made.

Bowl, Rice, Cover, Underplate, Animals, Figures, Flowers, 5 3/4 x 7 1/2 In. 380.00
Charger, Court Scene, 100 Antiques Border, Textured Ground, 10 1/2 In. 265.00
Charger, Court Scene, Animal Border, Flowers, Textured Ground, 13 In. 355.00
Charger, Mandarin Warrior, 100 Antiques Border, 19th Century, 10 In. 206.00
Dish, Kidney Shape, Dining Scene, 100 Antiques Border, 8 x 11 In. 235.00
Ginger Jar, Base, 3 Figures, Deer, Covered, Mahogany Stand, 11 In. 410.00
Platter, Butterflies, Birds, Flowers, Oval, Chinese, 16 1/2 In. 635.00
Shrimp Dish, Flowers, Birds, Butterflies, 19th Century, 10 1/4 x 9 3/4 In., Pair 646.00
Umbrella Stand, Raised Birds, Bamboo, Blue & White, 24 1/2 In. 165.00
Vase, Baluster Form, Blue Ornaments, Gold Highlights, Enameled, Bird, 9 1/2 In. 150.00
Vase, Double Gourd, Fishnet Pattern, Seto Province, Japan, 19th Century, 9 1/2 In. 550.00
Vase, Fish Shape, Brown Glazed Eyes, Japan, 19th Century, 13 In. 345.00
Vase, Hexagonal Paneled Form, Handles, Birds, Flowers, 12 3/4 In. 380.00

CELLULOID is a trademark for a plastic developed in 1868 by John W. Hyatt. Celluloid Manufacturing Company, the Celluloid Novelty Company, Celluloid Fancy Goods Company, and American Xylonite Company all used Celluloid to make jewelry, games, sewing equipment, false teeth, and piano keys. Eventually, the Hyatt Company became the American Cellulose and Chemical Manufacturing Company, the Celanese Corporation. The name *Celluloid* was often used to identify any similar plastic. Celluloid toys are listed under Toys.

Brush Set, Yellow, Engraved, Black, Horsehair, 5 x 2 1/2 In. 60.00

Buttonhook, Pearlized Green, Butterscotch, 6 3/4 In. 9.00
Cuticle Pusher, French Ivory, c.1930, 4 5/8 In. 7.50
Figurine, Black Cook, Mechanical Moving Eyes, 7 1/2 In. 185.00
Hairbrush, Green, Boar's Hair Bristles, Black & Taupe, Geometric Design, 9 In. 7.50
Mirror, Hand, Butterscotch, Amber, Pearlized, c.1930, 10 In. 12.00
Mirror, Pale Blue, Collapsible Handle, 9 3/8 In. 15.00
Nail Cleaner, French Ivory, c.1930, 3 1/4 In. 5.00
Powder Box, Green, Pearlized, Tan & Black Design, 4 1/2 In. 28.00
Powder Box, Ivory, Pyralin, c.1930, 2 3/4 x 4 1/4 In. 8.50
Powder Box, Roxana Cover, Nudes In Corners, Pink Frosted, c.1930, 3 3/4 x 2 3/4 In. 34.00
Purse Holder, Flowers, Dark Rose, Handbag Caddy, Lavie, Box, 1 1/2 In. 33.00
Scissors, Caramel, Faux Mother-Of-Pearl Exterior, Germany, 4 3/4 In. 13.00
Spoon, Make-Up, French Ivory, c.1930, 3 1/4 In. 5.00
Vanity Set, Butterscotch, Mottled Gray, Green, Beige, 11 In. 10.00
Vanity Set, Pearl Gray, Amber Tones, c.1920, 3 Piece 22.00

CELS are listed in this book in the Animation Art category.

CERAMIC ART COMPANY of Trenton, New Jersey, was established in 1889 by J. Coxon and W. Lenox and was an early producer of American Belleek porcelain. It became Lenox, Inc. in 1906. Do not confuse this ware with the pottery made by the Ceramic Arts Studio of Madison, Wisconsin.

Bouillon, Roses, Sterling Silver Holders, 2 x 6 1/2 In., 6 Piece 545.00
Coffee Set, After Dinner, Cobalt Blue, Mauser Silver Overlay, 13 Piece 545.00
Coffee Set, Blue Dot, Lenox, c.1905, 10-In. Pot, 3 Piece 865.00
Cup & Saucer, After Dinner, Roses, Shreve Silver Holder, Lenox, c.1905, 6 Piece 460.00
Ewer, Pink Cherry Blossoms, Gilt Painted, Ivory Ground, Gilt Handle, 10 x 5 In. 489.00
Pitcher, Polychrome, Belleek, c.1900, 6 In. 805.00
Tea Set, Apple Blossom Medallions, Gilt Swags, Lenox, 10-In. Teapot, 3 Piece 489.00
Toby Jug, George Washington, Gilt Trim, Lenox, 1896, 7 1/2 In. 265.00
Urn, Chrysanthemum Medallion, Gilt Flowers, Ribbons, Ivory, Flared, Lenox, 11 1/2 In. . 520.00
Urn, Empress Josephine, Gilt Flowers, Ribbons, Green, S. Werkner, Lenox, c.1905, 10 In. 980.00
Urn, Girl Portrait, Red, Green, Silver Overlay, Purple Stamp, c.1896, 9 In. .... *Illus* 1265.00
Urn, Girl, Gilt Flowers, Ribbons, Burgundy Ground, D. Campana, Lenox, 10 In. 980.00
Urn, Swags Of Pink & Yellow Roses, Brass Mount, 18 1/4 x 5 In. 920.00
Urn, White Roses, 2 Gilt Whiplash Handles, Bulbous, Signed, Malin, 11 x 8 1/2 In. 520.00
Vase, Chrysanthemums, Yellow Ground, Bulbous, W.H. Morley, 12 x 8 1/2 In. 999.00
Vase, Flowers, Gilt, Ivory Ground, Asymmetric Handles, Aesthetic Revival, 11 In. 2070.00
Vase, Gilt Chrysanthemums, Green Ground, Bulbous, Lenox, c.1905, 13 x 7 1/2 In. 520.00
Vase, Gilt Day Lilies, Bulbous, Tapered & Flared Neck, c.1905, 12 In. 489.00
Vase, Gilt Flowers, Pink Ground, Handles, Bulbous, Elongated Neck, Belleek, 10 In. 575.00
Vase, Maiden Picking Blossoms, Classical Style, H. Nosek, Lenox, 1905, 10 In. 1955.00
Vase, Tea Roses, Gilt Wreaths, Blue Dots, Pear Shape, c.1905, 8 x 4 3/4 In. 405.00
Vase, Tea Roses, Pastel Colors, Cylindrical, W. Morley, Lenox, 15 1/2 x 5 In. 1725.00
Vase, White Roses, Gold Trim, Delft Style, Gilt Whiplash Handles, Bulbous, 9 In. 865.00
Vase, Young Woman Reading Letter, Delft Painted, Oval, Signed Mim, 8 x 4 In. 489.00

CERAMIC ARTS STUDIO was founded about 1940 in Madison, Wisconsin, by Lawrence Rabbett and Ruben Sand. Their most popular products were expensive molded figurines. The pottery closed in 1955. Do not confuse these products with those of the Ceramic Art Co. of Trenton, New Jersey.

Candlestick, Woman In Flowing Gown & Scarf, Holding Basket, 6 7/8 x 3 In. 82.00
Candy Dish, Elf Lying Under Toadstool, Leaf Shape, 6 x 3 3/4 In. 112.00
Figurine, Autumn Andy, Carries ABC Book, 5 In. 130.00
Figurine, Bali Hai Dancer, 8 In. 50.00
Figurine, Bashful, Girl Earring Red & White Dress, 4 3/4 In. 27.00
Figurine, Bo-Peep, Green Dress, Brown Hair, 5 1/4 In. 40.00
Figurine, Colonial Boy & Girl, Blue, 5 3/4 & 5 In., Pair 165.00
Figurine, Colonial Woman, Blue, 6 3/4 In. 50.00
Figurine, Comedy & Tragedy, Women With Masks, 10 In., Pair 100.00
Figurine, Gypsy Musician, 6 3/4 & 7 1/2 In., Pair 40.00
Figurine, Little Boy Blue, Plain Shirt, 4 1/2 In. 40.00

Rearrange lamps, figurines, vases, and other knickknacks on tabletops. If you don't, the exposed wood will be lighter than the covered sections under the ornaments.

Ceramic Art Co., Urn,
Girl Portrait, Red, Green,
Silver Overlay, Purple
Stamp, c.1896, 9 In.

Figurine, Miss Lucindy, Green, 6 7/8 In.	30.00
Figurine, Mr. & Mrs. Skunk, 3 In., Pair	110.00
Figurine, Our Lady Of Fatima, 9 1/4 In.	210.00
Figurine, Peter Pan & Wendy, 5 1/2 & 5 In., Pair	170.00
Figurine, Skunk, Dinky, 2 In.	30.00
Figurine, Ting-A-Ling, Sung-Tu, Green, 5 1/2 & 4 In.	75.00
Figurine, Tragedy, Green, 10 In.	125.00
Salt & Pepper, Dutch Girl & Boy, 4 In.	50.00
Salt & Pepper, Siamese Cat & Kitten, 4 1/4 & 3 1/4 In.	90.00
Salt & Pepper, Wee Dutch Girl, 2 7/8 In.	30.00
Shelf Sitter, Cocker Spaniel, 5 In.	67.00
Shelf Sitter, Pete & Budgie, Marked, 5 1/2 & 9 In., Pair	46.00
Vase, Blue, Gray, 4 3/4 x 5 1/4 x 3 1/4 In.	180.00
Vase, Lotus & Manchu, Marked, c.1944-1955, 7 3/4 In., Pair	250.00

CHALKWARE is really plaster of Paris decorated with watercolors. One type was molded from Staffordshire and other porcelain models and painted and sold as inexpensive decorations in the nineteenth century. Figures of plaster, made from about 1910 to 1940 for use as prizes at carnivals, are also known as chalkware. Kewpie dolls made of chalkware will be found in their own category.

Bank, Dog, Painted Spots, Collar, 6 1/2 In., Pair	220.00
Bank, Fat Man Squatting With Lowered Trousers, 8 3/4 In.	44.00
Bank, Peach Shape, Red Highlights, 3 In.	176.00
Bank, Still, Apple, Red, Green, Black, 19th Century, 3 In.	358.00
Bust, Crying & Smiling Babies, Marble Base, Signed Moreau, 8 1/2 x 7 1/2 In.	110.00
Bust, Woman, Turban, On Round Plinth, Green, Yellow, Red, Flesh Tone, 7 1/2 In.	550.00
Dish, Pedestal, 3 Mermaids, 11 1/2 In.	30.00
Figurine, Baby, Naked, Crawling 5 x 5 3/4 In.	17.00
Figurine, Bird, On Flowers, Silver Flecks, 10 x 8 In.	14.00
Figurine, Bronco Rider, c.1940, 12 x 8 In.	275.00
Figurine, Cat, Gray, Tiger Striped Tabby, Yellow Eyes, Orange Collar, Smile, 15 1/2 In.	2640.00
Figurine, Clown, Holding Balloons, 9 In.	28.00
Figurine, Cowgirl Drum Major, 13 1/2 In.	22.00
Figurine, Dog, Collie, Seated, Bow On Breast, 11 In.	11.00
Figurine, Dog, Poodle, Standing, Black, Rectangular Base, 7 1/4 In.	44.00
Figurine, Dog, Pug, Seated, Black & White, 10 1/4 In.	11.00
Figurine, Dog, Pug, Smiling, Wearing Hat, 10 1/2 In.	17.00
Figurine, Dog, Seated, Long Haired, Yellow, Brown Spots, Blue Collar, 9 1/2 In.	275.00
Figurine, Dog, Seated, Painted, Brown, Black Ears & Tail, 8 1/4 In., Pair	193.00
Figurine, Dog, Seated, White, Curly Tail, Black Painted Ears, Muzzle, Yellow Eyes, 6 In.	121.00
Figurine, Dog, Spaniel, Standing, Mid 19th Century, 7 x 5 1/4 In.	30.00
Figurine, Dog, With Ball, Brown, 7 1/4 In.	22.00
Figurine, Dove, White, Red, Green Berry Branch, Yellow Feet, Eyes, Beak, 10 3/8 In.	495.00
Figurine, Drum Major, Blue, Silver, 13 1/2 In.	11.00
Figurine, Ewe, Reclining, Lamb, Polychrome, 19th Century, 9 In.	1100.00
Figurine, Girl, Wearing Crooked Hat, 16 In.	11.00

Figurine, Hobo, 11 In.	14.00
Figurine, Horse, Prancing, 11 1/4 x 8 1/2 In.	11.00
Figurine, Horse, White, Black Hooves, Muzzle, Tan Eyes, 9 1/2 In.	413.00
Figurine, Lion, Paw On Ball, 8 x 9 1/2 In.	17.00
Figurine, Pig, 3 Piglets, 12 1/2 x 4 1/2 In.	17.00
Figurine, Rooster, Freestanding Legs, Painted, Green, Yellow, Brown, 6 3/4 In., Pair	660.00
Figurine, Rooster, Hand Painted, Yellow, Green, Red, 8 1/4 In.	138.00
Figurine, Rooster, Standing, Open Center Tail, Polychrome, 19th Century, 6 3/4 In.	6325.00
Figurine, Sailor Boy, 9 In.	14.00
Figurine, Sailor Girl, 10 In.	14.00
Figurine, Snow White, Yellow Dress With Flecks, 14 1/2 In.	25.00
Figurine, Woman, With Dog, 11 In.	17.00
Humidor, Indian Head, Painted, 8 In.	440.00
Plaque, George & Martha Washington, Frame, 19th Century, 6 x 4 5/8 In., Pair	2090.00
Plaque, Poodle, Beige, Gold, Rhinestone Eyes, Prancing, Running, 9 & 12 In. Pair	50.00
Plaque Set, Seahorse Family, Dad, Mom, Baby Girl, Triple Bubble, 7 Piece	28.00
Statue, U.S. Army Paratrooper, Jumpsuit, Flag Patch, Ammo Can, Painted, 12 In.	58.00
Stringholder, Chef	25.00
Toothbrush Holder, Dutch Girl, Wall Plaque, Miller Studio, 1964, 6 3/4 In.	165.00
Wall Pocket, Basket, Flowers, Parrot, 5 3/4 x 7 1/2 In.	17.00

CHARLIE CHAPLIN, the famous comic and actor, lived from 1889 to 1977. He made his first movie in 1913. He did the movie *The Tramp* in 1915. The character of the Tramp has remained famous, and in the 1980s appeared in a series of television commercials for computers. Dolls, candy containers, and all sorts of memorabilia picture Charlie Chaplin. Pieces are being made even today.

Candy Container, Barrel, Glass, Smooth Base, American, c.1930, 3 7/8 In.	101.00
Condiment Set, No. 4578, Germany, 1920s, 5 1/2 In.	425.00
Figurine, Charlie With Cane, Celluloid, 3 In.	125.00
Figurine, Drinking From Bottle, Dog, Celluloid, 4 In.	135.00
Look Magazine, The Dictator, Vol. 4, No. 20, September 24, 1940	18.00
Tobacco Jar, Porcelain, 6 In.	900.00
Toy, Walker, Cane, Iron Shoes, Windup, Germany, 1920s	700.00

CHARLIE MCCARTHY was the ventriloquist's dummy used by Edgar Bergen from the 1930s. He was famous for his work in radio, movies, and television. The act was retired in the 1970s.

Coloring Set, Whitman No. 3927, 1938, 9 1/8 x 12 In.	65.00
Doll, Composition, Shoulder Head, Painted Face, Effanbee, c.1935, 19 In.	500.00
Dummy, Composition, Cloth Body, Jaw Attached To String, Effanbee, 20 In.	550.00
Dummy, Composition, Linen Suit, Tie, Monocle, 34 In.	230.00
Eggcup, Ceramic, Japan, c.1930, 1 3/4 x 2 1/2 In.	60.00
Figurine, Chalk, c.1930, 7 1/4 In.	40.00
Figurine, Wooden, Fun-E-Flex, c.1930, 5 1/2 In.	275.00
Game, Flying Hats, Canister, 1938	25.00
Game, Question & Answer, Card, 1938	30.00
Game, Radio Party, Figures, Paper, 4 1/2 In.	110.00
Perfume Bottle, Figural, Glass, c.1930, 3 1/2 In.	25.00
Radio, White, Figure, Metal, Majestic, c.1930, 6 In.	300.00
Toy, Benzine Buggy, Drives, Head Spins, Tin, Windup, Marx, c.1939, 7 1/2 In.	385.00
Toy, Charlie McCarthy Drives Car, Black, Windup, Tin, Marx, Box, 7 1/2 In.	715.00
Toy, Krazy Kar, Mortimer Snerd, Tin Lithograph, Windup, Marx, 8 1/2 In.	385.00
Toy, Rocks, Opens Mouth, Windup, Tin, Marx, 8 1/2 In.	305.00
Toy, Walker, Windup, Tin Lithograph, Box, 8 1/2 In.	470.00
Wrapper, Gum, 1930s-1940s	15.00

CHELSEA porcelain was made in the Chelsea area of London from about 1745 to 1784. Some pieces made from 1770 to 1784 may include the letter *D* for *Derby* in the mark. Ceramic designs were borrowed from the Meissen models of the day. Pieces were made of soft paste. The gold anchor was used as the mark but it has been copied by many other factories. Recent copies of Chelsea have been made from the

original molds. Do not confuse Chelsea porcelain with Chelsea Grape, a white pottery with luster grape decoration.

Bust, Minerva, Wearing Helmet, Coiled Serpent, c.1755, 5 1/4 In.	1675.00
Dish, Scolopendrium Leaf, Turquoise, Yellow Leaves, Shaped Rim, c.1752, 7 1/2 In.	8365.00
Plate, Botanical, Fruit, Flowers, Turquoise, Puce, Molded Rim, c.1760, 8 1/2 In., Pair	3286.00
Plate, Kakiemon, Quail In Flower Wreath, c.1755, 9 5/8 In.	1315.00
Punch Bowl, 3 Panels, Exotic Birds, Gilt, Blue Escutcheon, 11 1/4 In.	460.00
Saucer, Kakiemon Pattern, Octagonal, c.1752, 4 1/2 In.	600.00
Teabowl, Saucer, Bird, Perched On Branch, 1 5/8 x 5 In.	5080.00
Teabowl, Saucer, Woman In Pavilion, Octagonal, c.1752, 2 1/4 x 5 1/2 In.	3885.00
Teaware Set, Claret Ground, Flower Sprigs, Gilt Border, c.1765, 5 Piece	5380.00

CHELSEA GRAPE pattern was made before 1840. A small bunch of grapes in a raised design, colored with purple or blue luster, is on the border of the white plate. Most of the pieces are unmarked. The pattern is sometimes called *Aynsley* or *Grandmother*. Chelsea Sprig is similar but has a sprig of flowers instead of the bunch of grapes. Chelsea Thistle has a raised thistle pattern. Do not confuse these Chelsea patterns with Chelsea Keramic Art Works, which can be found in the Dedham category, or with Chelsea porcelain, the preceding category.

Cup & Saucer, Pate-Sur-Pate, Periwinkle Blue, Copper Luster, 3 In.	13.00
Pitcher, Cream, 20th Century, 6 In.	5.00
Plate, 8 1/2 In.	15.00
Plate, Embossed, Tab Handle, 9 3/4 In.	50.00

CHINESE EXPORT porcelain comprises all the many kinds of porcelain made in China for export to America and Europe in the eighteenth, nineteenth, and twentieth centuries. Other pieces may be listed in this book under Canton, Celadon, Nanking, and Rose Medallion.

Basket, Mandarins, Polychrome, Parcel Gilt, Footed, Handles, 6 1/2 x 14 In.	69.00
Basket, Oval, Blanc-De-Chine, Shell Handles, 1800s, 6 x 12 x 10 In.	145.00
Bottle, Ormolu Mounted, Blue Ground, Famille Verte, 8 7/16 In., Pair	2030.00
Bourdalou, Yellow Ground, Sepia Landscape, Cover, c.1800, 10 In.	3000.00
Bowl, 3 Dragons, Lobed Edge, Famille Jaune, 6 3/4 In.	240.00
Bowl, Centerpiece, Millefiori Design On Outside, 14 1/2 In.	805.00
Bowl, Famille Rose, Cafe Au Lait, Flower Reserves, 18th Century, 7 3/8 In.	269.00
Bowl, Famille Verte, Flared, Inscriptions, c.1722, 8 In., Pair	780.00
Bowl, Figures Of Children, Flared Sides, 9 1/2 In.	405.00
Bowl, Fish, Traditional, Polychrome, Stands, 21 x 18 1/2 In., Pair	865.00
Bowl, Fox-Hunting Scene, Flowers, Butterfly Border, Reds, Oranges, 5 1/2 In.	717.00
Bowl, Harbor Scene, Cobalt Blue Ships, Pagoda, Footed, 10 1/4 x 4 1/2 In.	110.00
Bowl, Pagoda & Landscape Design, Square, Cut Corners, Blue, White, 5 x 10 In.	1725.00
Bowl, Pagoda & Landscape, Floral Cavetto & Rim, Blue, White, Octagonal, 15 In.	1035.00
Bowl, Sages & Attendants In Garden, Fruits, Famille Rose, Octagonal, 6 3/4 In.	50.00
Bowl, Tea, Armorial, Center Arms Of Palmer, Spearhead Band, 1 1/4 x 6 In., Pair	489.00
Bowl, Tree With Birds & Flowers, Blue & White, Scalloped Rim, 10 3/4 In.	28.00
Bowl, Vegetable, Cover, Shield-Breasted Eagle, Olive Branch, Arrows, c.1815, 9 1/4 In.	620.00
Bowl, Wucai, Bird, Flowers, 18th Century, 7 1/2 In.	140.00
Bowl, Yellow, Iron Red, Grisaille, 5 1/4 In.	1410.00
Bowl Set, Famille Rose, Polychrome Birds, Butterflies, Fruit, 8 In., 6 Piece	358.00
Box, People On Cover, Sides, Famille Rose, Cylindrical, 1 1/4 x 2 1/4 In.	25.00
Box, Red Lacquer, 3 Tiers, Purple, Gilt Landscapes, Octagonal, Wood Handle, 24 In.	460.00
Candleholder, Foo Dog, Famille Rose, 9 In., Pair	529.00
Charger, Armorial, Center Arms Of Langton, Scalloped Rim, Leaf & Scroll, 14 In.	1035.00
Charger, Famille Rose, Central Peony Spray, Brown Whorl, c.1740, 14 In.	1560.00
Charger, Famille Rose, Songbirds, Peony Branch, Green Trellis, c.1740, 14 In.	4500.00
Charger, Flowers, Flower Medallions, Scalloped Rim, Gilt Trim, Famille Rose, 14 In.	275.00
Charger, Flowers, Scalloped Rim, Gilt Trim, Famille Rose, 12 1/2 In., Pair	605.00
Charger, Orange Fitzhugh, American Eagle, Marked 1815 China, 16 1/4 In.	165.00
Chocolate Pot, Cover, Pink Peonies, Blue Ground, c.1735, 7 1/4 In.	2160.00
Chocolate Pot, Lighthouse, Flared, Shaped Lid, Famille Rose, c.1735, 7 1/2 In.	575.00
Coffeepot, Lighthouse, Orange, Sepia & Gold, Strap Handle, 9 In.	345.00
Coffeepot, Lighthouse, Sepia Tea Leaves Design, c.1800, 7 1/2 In.	1175.00

Cooler, Fruit, Insert, Cover, Blue & White, Landscape, Pagoda, Handles, 14 In., Pair 1955.00
Creamer, Helmet Shape, Footed, Hard Paste, Polychrome Flowers, 1700s, 6 In. 180.00
Creamer, People, Birds, Gilt, Bulbous, 4 3/4 In. 75.00
Cup, Blue & White, Lovebird Decoration, Handleless 50.00
Cup, Wine, Nesting, Courtesans, Actors, 4 1/2 In., 10 Piece 175.00
Cup & Saucer, Family Scene, Baby, Dog, 3 1/4 In. 175.00
Cup & Saucer, Polychrome, No Handle, 9 1/4 In. 46.00
Dish, Blue & White, Leaf Shape, Fitzhugh Border, c.1870, 8 In. 230.00
Dish, Blue, Dragon Chasing Flaming Pearl, Iron Red, 7 3/4 In. 380.00
Dish, Cover, Scalloped, Oval, Famille Rose, Signed, 3 1/2 x 8 1/2 x 10 1/2 In. 125.00
Dish, Entree, Cover, Blue Fitzhugh, 9 3/4 In. 375.00
Dish, Footed, Nested, Famille Rose, 4 Piece, 1875-1908, 13 3/4 In. 545.00
Dish, Hot Water, Blue & White Fitzhugh, Oval, 12 1/2 In. 720.00
Dish, Pagoda & Bridge Design, Leaf Shape, Blue, White, 7 1/2 In. 276.00
Dish, Pagoda & Landscape Design, Leaf Shape, Blue, White, 6 1/4 In. 240.00
Dresser Box, Famille Rose, Hinged Lid, Armorial, Flowers, 1 1/2 x 4 1/2 x 3 In. 259.00
Figurine, Dog, Spotted, Seated, Neck Ribbon & Bell, 10 3/4 In., Pair 345.00
Figurine, Duck, Straw & Aubergine Glaze, Terrain Base, 1900s, 12 In., Pair 750.00
Figurine, Foo Dog, Ceramic, Polychrome, Rectangle Base, c.1940, 14 x 19 In., Pair 1265.00
Figurine, Foo Dog, Orange, Reclining, 1800s, 5 1/4 In., Pair 3600.00
Figurine, Guanyin, Seated, Long Robes, Necklace, Famille Rose, 1800s, 17 In. 4715.00
Figurine, Guanyin, Standing On Lotus Throne, Famille Rose, 9 1/4 In. 325.00
Figurine, Parrot, Green, Yellow, Ormolu Mount, 19th Century, 8 3/8 In., Pair 3286.00
Figurine, Phoenix, Standing, Famille Rose, Pink, Yellow, Green, 23 1/2 In., Pair 1840.00
Figurine, Spaniel, Parcel Gilt, Iron Red Glaze, Biscuit, 1900s, 5 5/8 In., Pair 345.00
Figurine, Wart Hog, Painted, Mid 19th Century, 3 x 6 3/4 In. 50.00
Fish Bowl, Floral, Butterflies, Insects, Interior Painted Goldfish, 16 x 19 In., Pair 805.00
Flower Basket, Reticulated, Birds In Branches, Leaf Ground, c.1775, 6 1/4 In. 2400.00
Ginger Jar, Cover, Birds, Flowers, Leaves, Famille Verte, c.1900, 9 1/2 In., Pair 920.00
Jar, Cover, Flowers, Geometrics, Greek Key Border, Oval, Flared, 17 In. 165.00
Jar, Dome Cover, Foo Dog Finial, Bulbous, Warrior Design, 1800s, 10 In., Pair 405.00
Jardiniere, Blue & White, Flowers, Leaves, 9 In. 410.00
Jug, Barrel Shape, Sepia Paint, Country House, Cover, c.1800, 11 In. 3600.00
Jug, Cider, Armorial, Center Arms Of Fitzhugh, Foo Dog Finial, Handle, 12 In. 2415.00
Jug, Famille Rose, Barrel Shape, Underglaze Diaper Pattern, c.1790, 9 3/8 In. 1080.00
Junk, Dragon Form, Dignitaries, Attendants, 2 Pagodas, Yellow Glaze, 9 1/2 In. 765.00
Lamp, Foo Dog, People, Birds, Famille Rose, 9 In. 225.00
Mug, Blue & White, Trees, Fencing, Mid 18th Century, 6 3/4 In., Pair 300.00
Mug, Continuous Landscape, Geometric Rim, Ovoid, 5 1/2 In. 520.00
Mug, Continuous Landscape, River, Floral Border, Cylindrical, Spread Foot, 6 In. 1035.00
Mug, Famille Rose, Barrel Shape, Sprays, Borders, Early 19th Century, 4 1/2 In. 690.00
Mug, Lion, Flowers, Bat, Straight Sides, Loop Dragon Handle, 4 1/2 In. 1380.00
Parrot, Giltwood Stand, Continental, 20th Century, 11 In., Pair 835.00
Plant Tub, Drain Tray, Alternating Mandarin & Floral Reserves, 14 1/2 In. 200.00
Plaque, 2 Hunters, Heavenly Beings, Famille Rose, Mother-Of-Pearl Frame, 11 In. 345.00
Plaque, Famille Rose, Landscape, Early 20th Century, 23 x 18 1/4 In., Pair 805.00
Plate, Armorial, Blue Fitzhugh, Dawe Quartering Moore Arms, c.1800, 11 5/8 In. 1320.00
Plate, Armorial, Center Arms, Marriage Of Royal Families, Lattice, Border, 9 In. 805.00
Plate, Armorial, Painted, Gilt Spearhead Band, c.1740, 10 In., Pair 6570.00
Plate, Armorial, Stewart Arms, Flowers, Medallions, c.1738, 8 5/8 In. 960.00
Plate, Famille Jaune, Reverse Famille Noire, Silk Covered Box, c.1800, 7 1/2 In. 115.00
Plate, Famille Rose, Scalloped Edged, Late 19th Century, 8 1/2 In. 69.00
Plate, Fish Design, Japanese Taste, c.1800, 9 In. 90.00
Plate, Flowers, Unscrolled Scroll, Famille Rose, 9 In., Pair 518.00
Plate, Hot Water, Mandarin Decoration, Garden Scene, c.1800, 10 1/4 In., Pair 2990.00
Plate, Imari Decoration, Polychrome, 18th Century, 9 In., Pair 230.00
Plate, Imperial Russian 2-Headed Eagle, St. George, Dragon, c.1785, 10 In., Pair 7200.00
Plate, Mandarin Figures, Famille Rose, Lattice Border, 9 1/2 In. 765.00
Plate, Marriage, Famille Jaune, Dragon & Phoenix, Kuang Hsu Mark, 9 1/4 In. 290.00
Plate, Parrots Perched Upside Down On Tree Branch, 8 3/4 In., Pair 369.00
Plate, Phoenix & Flower Design, Famille Jaune, 18th Century, 8 1/2 In. 68.00
Plate, Pictorial, Blue & White, 20th Century, Kangxi Marked, 12 Piece, 8 1/2 In. 375.00
Plate, Red Diapered Panels, Blue Swags, Center Flower & Wreath, 8 3/4 In. 107.00

Plate, Soup, Armorial, Chain Border, Shaped Rim, c.1760, 9 In., Pair 2270.00
Plate, Soup, Hope Figure, Anchor, Spero Motto, Monogram, c.1786, 9 In. 7800.00
Plate Set, Blue Fitzhugh, 9 5/8 In., 6 Piece 940.00
Platter, Armorial, Pope Arms, Flower Sprays, Spearhead Border, 16 In., Pair 7200.00
Platter, Blue & White, Garden Scene, Octagonal, c.1780, 14 In., Pair 1150.00
Platter, Blue & White, Pine Tree, Peonies, Brocade Border, 15 In. 765.00
Platter, Blue, Fitzhugh, Oval, 19th Century, 18 5/8 In. 1410.00
Platter, Famille Rose, Shaped, Flared, Butterflies, Flowers, Pheasant, 15 1/4 In. 345.00
Platter, Flowers, Ironside Arms, Latin Motto, Ch'ien Lung, c.1752 .... 865.00
Platter, Mandarin, Figures, Oval, Shallow, 2 x 15 In. 690.00
Platter, Orange, Fitzhugh, Oval, 12 3/4 In. 920.00
Platter, Pagoda & Lake Design, Fenestrated Border, Blue, White, 11 In. 405.00
Platter, Pagoda Scene, Swag With Hearts, Blue Transfer, 19 3/4 In. 280.00
Platter, Pagoda, Pine & Bamboo Trees, Octagonal, Scroll Border, 13 x 10 In. 415.00
Platter, Pagoda, Water, Octagonal, 14 1/2 In. 170.00
Platter, Quail, Reticulated, Blue Rockwork, Greek Key Rim, c.1760, 13 1/4 In. 1320.00
Punch Bowl, Cabbage Leaf, 20th Century, 7 1/4 x 16 In. 980.00
Punch Bowl, Famille Rose, Figures, Flowers, 16 In. 1645.00
Punch Bowl, Famille Rose, Flowers, Urns, Garlands, 4 3/4 x 11 1/4 In. 345.00
Punch Bowl, Flowers, Cobalt & Gilt Flowering Vine Band, 4 x 10 In. 316.00
Punch Bowl, Medallion, Flowers, People, Butterflies, 6 1/2 x 15 3/4 In. 2130.00
Punch Bowl, Scenes Depicting Sailor's Farewell & Return, Lotus Sprays, 8 In. 600.00
Salt, Figure, Holding Can & Sprig, Orange, Gilt, Octagonal, Footed, 3 1/2 In. 120.00
Sauce, Fitzhugh, Brown, Armorial Device, Indian, Motto, Monogram, 5 In. 3740.00
Sauceboat, Celadon, Famille Rose, Underplate, 8 In., Pair 575.00
Sauceboat, Oval, Nanking, Blue & White, Strap Handle, 7 1/4 In., Pair 400.00
Serving Dish, Footed Base, Lotus & Peonies, Famille Rose, 10 1/2 In., Pair 35.00
Soup, Dish, Famille Rose, Armorial, Coat Of Arms, Floral Border, c.1860, 9 In., Pair 260.00
Soup, Dish, Flowers, Scalloped Rim, Gilt Trim, 9 In., 6 Piece 165.00
Soup, Dish, Spread-Wing Eagle, 9 In., Pair 375.00
Sugar & Creamer, Square, Engraved, Repousse, Flowers & Dragon, c.1850, 3 In. 259.00
Tankard, Sepia Landscape, Branch Handles, 18th Century, 6 In. 265.00
Tea Caddy, Mandarin Palette, Mauve Design, Famille Rose, c.1770 .... 595.00
Tea Caddy & Cup, Bird Crest, 4 3/4 x 2 1/2 In. 175.00
Tea Set, Egg Shell Porcelain, Teapot, 6 Cups & Saucers, Painted Overglaze Design 215.00
Teapot, Aubergine, Peach, Green Leaves, Cadogan, 6 1/4 In. 380.00
Teapot, Famille Rose, Mandarin Decoration, Gilt, 19th Century, 4 In. 230.00
Teapot, Iron Red, Grisaille, Oval, Riverscape, 4 1/2 In. 380.00
Teapot, People, Birds, Gilt, Cylindrical, Metal Handle, 6 x 5 1/4 In. 100.00
Teapot, River Scene, Sampans, Pagodas, Cobalt Blue, 18th Century, 6 x 9 In. 900.00
Teapot, Sacred Bird & Butterfly, Double Barrel Shape, Orange, 5 1/4 In. 560.00
Tray, Ship Decoration, Cut Corner, Enameled Ship, 14 x 10 1/2 In. 720.00
Tureen, Cover, Roper Arms Impaling Grosvenor, c.1750, 13 3/4 In. 3600.00
Tureen, Cover, Stand, Figures, Landscape, Flowers, Mid 18th Century, 16 1/2 In. 5975.00
Tureen, Cover, Underplate, Bats, Gold Strap Handles, 7 7/8 In. 980.00
Tureen, Duck Shape, Yellow Ground, Blue, Red & Yellow Feathers, 10 In., Pair 3910.00
Tureen, Famille Rose, Handles, 1796-1820, 15 In. 460.00
Tureen, Sauce, Undertray, Cover, Oval, Famille Rose, Qianlong, c.1750, 8 1/2 In. 2185.00
Umbrella Stand, Green Fitzhugh, 20th Century, 23 1/8 x 10 In. 460.00
Urn, Cover, Egg Shape, Famille Verte, Floral & Birds, c.1890, 15 1/2 In., Pair 518.00
Urn, Landscape, Figures, Horses, Porcelain, 24 In. 374.00
Vase, Bird & Butterflies, Flowers, Bamboo, Urn Shape, Cat Handles, 8 In. 400.00
Vase, Birds Perched In Flowering Branches, Famille Rose, 16 In. 165.00
Vase, Blue & White, Children Playing, Seated Dignitary, Scholar, 17 In. 1645.00
Vase, Blue & White, Double Gourd, Birds, Flowers, 10 In. 765.00
Vase, Blue & White, Phoenix Birds, Flowering Branches, 30 In., Pair 1050.00
Vase, Cartouches, Flowering Vines, Trees, Red, White Geometric Urn Shape, 16 In. 300.00
Vase, Cover, Baluster, Painted, Flower Filled Vase, Sprays, c.1780, 18 1/4 In. 8960.00
Vase, Cover, Blue & White, Baluster, 19th Century, 15 In., Pair 2030.00
Vase, Double Gourd, Red Glaze, c.1910, 13 1/2 In. 375.00
Vase, Famille Rose, Bottle, Underglaze, Gilt, c.1855, 6 1/2 In., Pair 316.00
Vase, Famille Rose, Cylindrical, 4 x 1 1/2 In. 105.00
Vase, Famille Rose, Flat Hexagonal, Gilt Handles, 19th Century, 13 1/2 In. 1610.00

Vase, Famille Rose, Foo Dog Handles, c.1890, 24 In., Pair 1035.00
Vase, Famille Verte, Rouleau, Dignitary & Consort, 18 1/2 In. 2090.00
Vase, Figures, Red, Famille Rose, 23 In., Pair 410.00
Vase, Figures, Urn Shape, Elongated & Flared Neck, 17 1/2 In. 460.00
Vase, Foo Dog, Flowers, Wucai, 12 1/4 In. 529.00
Vase, Fruit & Flowers, c.1880, 17 1/2 In., Pair 705.00
Vase, Gilt Bronze Mount, Baluster Shape, Dragon Handles, c.1790, 13 In., Pair 3680.00
Vase, Immortals In Mountain Garden, Cylindrical Baluster Shape, 24 In. 290.00
Vase, Imperial, Yellow Glass, 1900s, 14 1/4 In. 520.00
Vase, Lion & Flower, Famille Rose, 19th Century, 6 1/2 In., Pair 115.00
Vase, Medallions, Figures, Famille Rose, 12 In. 400.00
Vase, Pear Shape, Lamp Mounted, Jade Finial, Mandarin Enamels, 20 1/2 In. 460.00
Vase, People, Birds, Butterflies, Gilt, Baluster, Famille Rose, 13 3/4 x 8 1/2 In. ... 125.00
Vase, Pheasant, Flowers, Blues, Applied Scroll Handles, 23 In. 110.00
Vase, Porcelain, Blue Glaze, Hu Formmdeer's, Head Handles, 12 In. 1265.00
Vase, Porcelain, Polychrome, Baluster Form, Leaves, Splayed Foot, 12 1/2 In. 65.00
Vase, Relief Dragons, Clouds Overall, Cobalt & Light Blue, 36 In. 305.00
Vase, Scroll, Flower, Famille Rose, Mid 19th Century, 17 In. 660.00
Vase, Wacai, Dignitaries, Flowers, Fruit, 17 In. 470.00
Vase, Yellow Ground, Dragons, Phoenixes, Bulbous, Guangxu, c.1880, 22 In. 4800.00

CHINTZ is the name of a group of china patterns featuring an overall
design of flowers and leaves. The design became popular with English
makers about 1928. A few pieces are still being made. The best known
are designs by Royal Winton, James Kent Ltd., Crown Ducal, and
Shelley. Crown Ducal and Shelley are listed in their own sections.

Anemone, Tray, 2 Tiers, Royal Winton, 8 3/4 In. 195.00
Bedale, Sauceboat & Liner, Royal Winton 135.00
Black Crocus, Lamp, Royal Winton, 26 In. 2065.00
Briar Rose, Jam Pot, Lord Nelson 85.00
Briar Rose, Tea Cup & Saucer, Lord Nelson 95.00
Briar Rose, Tray, Lord Nelson, 12 3/4 x 7 In. 125.00
Cheadle, Plate, Ascot Shape, Royal Winton, 8 3/4 In. 165.00
Crocus, Coffeepot, Royal Winton 440.00
Delphinium, Teapot Lid, Royal Winton 65.00
Dubarry, Ashtray, James Kent, 4 3/4 In. 95.00
Dubarry, Plate, James Kent, 9 In. 190.00
Dubarry, Vase, James Kent, 5 In. 495.00
Evesham, Sauceboat, Royal Winton 165.00
Florence, Snack Tray, Cup, Royal Winton, 12 Piece 412.00
Hazel, Bowl, Salad, Chrome Rim, Royal Winton 154.00
Hazel, Vase, Bud, Royal Winton, 5 In. 288.00
Heather, Teapot, Stacking, Lord Nelson, 6 1/2 In. 750.00
Marguerite, Breakfast Set, Royal Winton 575.00
Marguerite, Saucer, Royal Winton 15.00
Marina, Cheese Keeper, Lord Nelson, 6 x 5 In. 235.00
Marina, Cup & Saucer, Tea, Lord Nelson 55.00
Marina, Plate, Lord Nelson, 4 1/2 In. 35.00
Marina, Teapot, Lord Nelson, 6 Cup 545.00
Marina, Teapot, Stacking, Lord Nelson 660.00
Marina, Vase, Bud, Lord Nelson, 5 1/4 In. 245.00
May Festival, Tennis Set, Royal Winton 135.00
Old Cottage, Bowl, Vegetable, Square, Royal Winton, 8 1/4 In., 3 Piece 80.00
Old Cottage, Cake Plate, Royal Winton, 11 In. 235.00
Old Cottage, Coffeepot, Trivet, Royal Winton, 8 In. 275.00
Old Cottage, Condiment Set, Salt & Pepper, Undertray, Royal Winton 155.00
Old Cottage, Dish, Canoe, Royal Winton, 11 1/2 x 4 3/4 In. 325.00
Old Cottage, Jam Pot, Royal Winton, Rheims Shape, 4 1/2 In. 225.00
Old Cottage, Pitcher, Milk, Royal Winton, 4 1/2 In. 80.00
Old Cottage, Teapot, Stacking, Royal Winton 495.00
Old Cottage, Vase, Tudor Shape, Royal Winton, 4 1/2 In. 225.00
Pansy, Dish, Lord Nelson, 6 1/2 In. 85.00
Pansy, Saucer, Lord Nelson 32.00

Pansy, Sugar, Stacking, Lord Nelson	125.00
Rosetime, Cup & Saucer, Tea, Lord Nelson	85.00
Royalty, Jam Pot, Ascot, Lid & Liner, Royal Winton	225.00
Royalty, Sugar & Creamer, Royal Winton, Ascot Shape	215.00
Somerset, Breakfast Set, Royal Winton, 5 Piece	605.00
Spring Bouquet, Sugar & Creamer, Hammersley	95.00
Summertime, Basket, Royal Winton, 6 In.	358.00
Summertime, Bowl, Mayonnaise, Royal Winton	110.00
Summertime, Butter, Cover, Royal Winton	335.00
Summertime, Candy Jar, Royal Winton, 8 In.	550.00
Summertime, Pot, Hot Water, Royal Winton, 5 In.	358.00
Summertime, Sugar, Royal Winton, Ascot Shape	55.00
Summertime, Teapot, Royal Winton, 5 In.	240.00
Summertime, Teapot, Royal Winton, 6 3/4 In.	210.00
Summertime, Teapot, Royal Winton, 8 In.	525.00
Victorian Rose, Teapot, Royal Winton, 5 1/2 In.	660.00

CHOCOLATE GLASS, sometimes mistakenly called caramel slag, was made by the Indiana Tumbler and Goblet Company of Greentown, Indiana, from 1900 to 1903. It was also made at other National Glass Company factories. Fenton Art Glass Co. also made chocolate glass from about 1907 to 1915. More recent pieces have been made by Imperial and others.

Cactus, Biscuit Jar, Greentown, 8 In.	110.00
Cactus, Compote, High Stem, 8 1/2 In.	150.00
Cactus, Mug, 3 1/2 x 3 In.	25.00
Cactus, Tumbler, 4 In.	35.00
Cat On Hamper, Bowl, Vegetable	250.00 to 550.00
Chyrsanthemum Leaf, Compote, Jelly, 4 3/4 x 4 1/2 In.	300.00
Dolphin, Dish, Cover, Sawtooth Edge, 4 1/2 x 7 In.	80.00
Early Diamond, Tumbler, 3 3/4 In.	220.00
Fleur-De-Lis, Tumbler, 3 3/4 In.	60.00
Geneva, Compote, Jelly, 3 1/2 x 4 1/2 In.	110.00
Geneva, Tumbler, 3 7/8 In.	110.00
Indoor Drinking Scene, Pitcher, 8 1/4 In.	425.00
Leaf Bracket, Berry Set, 7 Piece	130.00
Leaf Bracket, Cruet, Greentown	308.00
Leaf Bracket, Tumbler, 3 3/4 In.	25.00
Pillar, Creamer, Indiana Tumbler Co., 6 1/2 In.	70.00
Sawtooth, Tumbler, 3 3/4 In.	60.00
Scalloped Flange, Tumbler, 3 7/8 In.	100.00
Shuttle, Creamer, Tall, 6 In.	170.00
Shuttle, Tumbler, 3 7/8 In.	50.00
Squirrel, Pitcher, Water, Scalloped Rim, 8 3/4 In.	700.00
Venetian, Tray, Dresser, 8 x 10 In.	425.00
Waterlily & Cattails, Tumbler, 4 In.	250.00
Wild Rose With Bowknot, Tumbler, 3 3/4 In.	100.00
Wild Rose With Scrolling, Creamer, Stippled Ground, Child's, 2 3/4 In.	150.00

CHRISTMAS collectibles include not only Christmas trees and ornaments listed below, but also Santa Claus figures, special dishes, and even games and wrapping paper. A Belsnickle is a nineteenth-century figure of Father Christmas. A kugel is an early, heavy ornament made of thick blown glass, lined with zinc or lead, and often covered with colored wax. Christmas cards are listed in this section under Greeting Card. Christmas collectibles may also be listed in the Candy Container category. Christmas trees are listed in the section that follows.

Bank, Santa Claus At Chimney, Mechanical, Shephard Hardware Co., c.1889	2400.00
Bell, Santa, Label, Josef Originals, 4 1/4 In.	35.00
Belsnickle, Feather Tree, Composition, Red Robe, Fur Beard, Germany, 1922, 16 In.	1375.00
Belsnickle, Papier-Mache, Blue, Paper Label On Base, Germany, c.1880, 8 1/2 In.	470.00
Belsnickle, Papier-Mache, Pink Robes, Carrying Evergreen, c.1880, 6 1/2 In.	500.00
Belsnickle, Papier-Mache, Red Robes, Paper On Base, Germany, c.1880, 11 1/4 In.	646.00

Christmas, Candle,
Snowman, Interpur,
Made In Korea, 5 In.

Christmas, Candle,
Santa, Interpur, Made
In Korea, 5 In.

Christmas, Paper Napkin,
Santa, Poinsettia, Holly Leaves,
Berries, Square, 6 3/4 In.

Belsnickle, Papier-Mache, Red, Blue Skirt, Germany, c.1880, 9 1/2 In.	825.00
Belsnickle, Papier-Mache, White Robes, Holding Evergreen, c.1880, 11 1/2 In.	645.00
Belsnickle, Papier-Mache, Yellow, Green-Gold Trim, 11 1/2 In.	1600.00
Box, Candy, Children & Christmas Scenes, Woven String Handles, c.1940	5.00
Box, Candy, Santa, Woven String Handles, c.1940	7.00
Button, Santa, Upside Down, Merry Xmas, Red, White, Blue, Celluloid, 3 1/2 In.	128.00
Candle, Santa, Interpur, Made In Korea, 5 In.	*Illus* 10.00
Candle, Snowman, Interpur, Made In Korea, 5 In.	*Illus* 10.00
Clock, Santa, Head Moves, Hour Hand Star, Ornament Numerals, Alarm, Bayard, 5 In.	156.00
Corsage, White Chenille Stems, Gold Glass Beads, Green Leaves, Pine Cones, Bea West	15.00
Corsage, White Christmas, Plastic Leaves, Red Ribbons, Bells, Deer, Violin	12.00
Cutout, Die Cut, Angel & Book Of Carols, Tree, Embossed, Germany, c.1890, 5 x 8 In.	28.00
Cutout, Die Cut, Children, Forest, Fire, Embossed, Germany, c.1890, 7 1/2 x 10 In.	26.00
Cutout, Die Cut, Santa, Girl, Toys, Raphael Tuck, No. 641, Germany, c.1890, 9 x 15 In.	195.00
Display, Kodak, Window, 3 Parts, For Cameras, Films, Projectors, 1950s	88.00
Doll, Santa In Sleigh, Composition, Felt Outfit, Wooden, Swan Neck Sleigh, 8 1/2 In.	50.00
Figurine, Church, Santa Claus As Steeple, Chalkware, 19th Century, 18 1/2 In.	3738.00
Figurine, Girl, Red Dress & Hat, White Boots, Holding Bell, Napco	15.00
Figurine, Santa Band, Cotton, Prewar France, 4 1/4 In., 8 Piece	135.00
Figurine, Santa Claus, Celluloid, 5 In.	17.00
Figurine, Santa Claus, Papier-Mache, 4 1/2 In.	17.00
Figurine, Santa Claus, Pressed Paper, Red Outfit, Signed, 12 In.	17.00
Figurine, Santa Claus, Stand-Up, Paper, 15 1/2 In.	99.00
Figurine, Santa Mouse, Fur Beard, Holding Present, Napco, 4 1/4 In.	20.00
Figurine, Santa Mouse, Holding Wreath, Napco, 4 1/4 In.	20.00
Greeting Card, Casper, Jimmy Murphy, Toots, c.1925, 4 1/4 x 6 3/4 In.	25.00
Greeting Card, Dick Calkins, Santa On Bike, 1946, 6 In.	75.00
Greeting Card, Pogo, Mandolin, Walt Kelly, 1958, 4 x 6 In.	75.00
Greeting Card, Ringling Bros & Barnum & Bailey Circus, 1920s	20.00
Lantern, Snow, Holly, Plastic, Electric, 1950s, 16 In.	45.00
Painting, Girl Mails Letter To Santa, Cutler Mail Chute, Loomis, 1928, 40 x 28 In.	6600.00
Paper Napkin, Santa, Poinsettia, Holly Leaves, Berries, Square, 6 3/4 In.	*Illus* 1.00
Pen, Float About, Santa Moves Gifts Into Chimney	3.25
Pen, Float About, Santa Moves In & Out Of Chimney	3.75
Pen, Float About, Santa's Train Goes Through Town	3.25
Pennant, Santa's Workshop, North Pole On Whiteface Mt., N.Y., Blue, White, 1950s	30.00
Pin, Santa Claus, Join Our Christmas Club, Kings Highway Bank, Celluloid, 1 1/4 In.	72.00
Pin, St. Nick's Animals, Lake Placid, N.Y., Santa, Reindeer, Celluloid, 1 3/4 In.	48.00
Plates that are limited editions are listed in the Collector Plate category or in the correct factory listing.	
Popeye Cheers Light Shades, Popeye, Swee' Pea, General Electric, 1929, Set Of 8	315.00
Postcard, Kewpies Preparing Yule Log, Christmas Tree, Windowpane Scene, 1913	20.00
Postcard, Lighthouse Ray From Behind Wheel, Mechanical, December 25, 1913	18.00
Puzzle, Santa Claus, Roll Metal Balls Into Eyes, Cardboard, Celluloid, 3 In.	45.00
Salt & Pepper, Santa & Mrs. Claus Waving, 4 In.	14.00
Salt & Pepper, Santa, Standing, Holding Bell & Candy Cane, 4 3/4 In.	12.00
Santa, Rocks, Rings Bell, Clockwork Driven, Battery Operated, Box, Alps, Japan, 10 In.	265.00
Stocking, E.T., Tree, Star, Felt, 1982, 15 1/2 In.	10.00
Stocking Holder, Nutcracker, Cast Iron, Hook, 6 In.	50.00

Stocking Holder, Snowman, Hook, Cast Iron, 4 1/2 In.	15.00
Tin, Candy, Santa, Tin Lithograph, Bail Handle, 4 1/2 In.	77.00
Tin, Candy, Tin Lithograph, Bail Handle, Tindeco, 4 1/2 In.	154.00
Towel, Santa & Reindeer, Linen, Hand Printed, Town & Country, 29 x 15 1/2 In., Pair	22.00
Toy, Car, Merry Xmas, Santa, Tin, Friction, Japan, c.1950, 5 1/2 In.	110.00
Toy, Foxy Grandpa Santa Claus, Mechanical, 1902, 10 x 14 In.	60.00
Toy, Lantern, Santa, Lights Up, Glass, Amico, Box, 6 In.	165.00
Toy, Marionette, Santa Claus, Composition, Cloth, Wooden X-Shape Control, 16 In.	75.00
Toy, Roly Poly, Santa, Papier-Mache, A. Schoenhut Co., 11 1/2 In.	800.00
Toy, Santa Claus, Bell Noise, Circular Motion, Tin, Windup, Box, Japan, 6 1/2 In.	320.00
Toy, Santa Claus, Celluloid, Windup, Lead Pendulum, Nodder, 7 In.	350.00
Toy, Santa Claus, Moves & Nods Head, Celluloid, Windup, Occupied Japan, Box, 4 In.	195.00
Toy, Santa Claus, On Reindeer, Windup, Japan	55.00
Toy, Santa Claus, Roly Poly, Composition, 1910, 8 In.	550.00
Toy, Santa Claus, Seesaw, Box, 1960s, 5 1/2 In.	450.00
Toy, Santa Claus, Skier, Tin, Vinyl Head, Windup, Japan, 1950s	150.00
Toy, Santa Claus, Sled, Celluloid, Tin, Box, Occupied Japan, 8 x 4 In.	265.00
Toy, Santa Copter, Multiple Actions, Battery Operated, Original Box, Illco, 1960s	145.00
Tumbler, Open Sleigh, Forest Green, Anchor Hocking Glass, 6 3/4 In.	16.00
Tumbler, Scenes Of Christmas, Wreath Theme, Federal Glass Co., 1950s, 4 3/4 In.	13.00

CHRISTMAS TREES made of feathers and Christmas tree decorations of all types are popular with collectors. The first decorated Christmas tree in America is claimed by many states, including Pennsylvania (1747), Massachusetts (1832), Illinois (1833), Ohio (1838), and Iowa (1845). The first glass ornaments were imported from Germany about 1860. Dresden ornaments were made about 100 years ago of paper and tinsel. Manufacturers in the United States were making ornaments in the early 1870s. Electric lights were first used on a Christmas tree in 1882. Character light bulbs became popular in the 1920s, bubble lights in the 1940s, twinkle bulbs in the 1950s, plastic bulbs by 1955. In this book a Christmas light is a holder for a candle used on the tree. Other forms of lighting include light bulbs. Other Christmas memorabilia is listed in the preceding section.

Kugel, Bell, White Glass, Victorian, 6 x 4 1/2 In.	75.00
Light, Cat, Bulb Cover, Red, Hand Painted, Plastic, 3 In.	10.00
Light, Cobalt Blue, Tapered, Pontil, France, 2 3/4 In.	80.00
Light, Milk Glass, Bulbous Base, Slightly Flared, Pontil, 8 In.	45.00
Light, Revolving, For Aluminum Tree, Evergleam, Box	260.00
Light, Ribbed, Ruby, Rolled Rim, 1890-1910, 3 In.	90.00
Light, Strawberry, Cobalt Blue, England, 1880-1900, 3 1/2 In.	475.00
Light Bulb, Frog, Hand Painted, Blown Glass, 3 In.	13.00
Light Bulb, Japanese Lantern, Hand Painted, Blown Glass, Clip-On, 5 Piece	40.00
Light Bulb, Santa, Hand Painted, Blown Glass, 3 1/2 In.	12.00
Light Set, Disney, 7 Different Characters, Paramount, Box, 1950s	210.00
Light Set, Opaque Cone Shape Bulbs, C6, Noma, Box, 1930s	16.00

Christmas Tree, Ornament, House, Attaches To Light Strand, Cardboard, Mica Snow, Japan, 4 1/2 In.

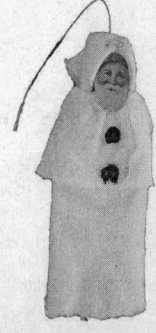

Christmas Tree, Ornament, Santa, Tissue Paper, Lithographed Face, Norway, 1940s, 4 1/2 In.

Lights, Mickey Mouse, Noma Electric, 1935 .... 310.00
Ornament, Angel, White, Gold Paint, Plastic, 1950s, 3 1/4 In. 6.00
Ornament, Ball, Shiny Brite, Blown Glass, American, Box, 1950s, 12 Piece 20.00
Ornament, Clip-On, Bird, Macaw, Hand Painted, Blown Glass, 6 In. 20.00
Ornament, Clown, Red & Yellow, Celluloid, 5 In. 60.00
Ornament, Coffeepot, Red, Hand Painted Leaves, Blown Glass 17.00
Ornament, Elf, Playing Banjo, Hand Painted, Blown Glass, 4 1/4 In. 10.00
Ornament, Flower Basket, Handle, Tinsel & Blown Glass 38.00
Ornament, Fox, 3-Dimensional, Glass Eyes, Dresden 695.00
Ornament, House, Attaches To Light Strand, Cardboard, Mica Snow, Japan, 4 1/2 In. *Illus* 5.00
Ornament, Man In The Moon, Crescent, Blown Glass, Germany, 1920s, 3 In. 45.00
Ornament, Moose, Full-Bodied, Dresden, Large 620.00
Ornament, Pear, Pink, Yellow, Cotton Batting, 3 1/4 In. 25.00
Ornament, Pig, Hat, Pink, Blown Glass, Hand Painted, Glitter, Italy, 7 In. 35.00
Ornament, Santa Claus, Red Robe With White Trim, 7 3/4 In. 33.00
Ornament, Santa, Hand Paint, Composition, Japan, 4 In. 10.00
Ornament, Santa, Tissue Paper, Lithographed Face, Norway, 1940s, 4 1/2 In. ...... *Illus* 12.00
Stand, Bronze, Raised Geometric Openwork Design, Square, 1928, 5 x 13 In. 150.00
Stand, Cast Iron, Floral, Bakelite Electrical Outlet, Early 1900s 350.00
Stand, Cast Iron, Mark's, Patented 1891, 12 In. 94.00
Stand, Electrified Base, Sockets, Cast Iron, 1920s 375.00
Stand, Flowers, Bakelite, Cast Iron, 1900s 350.00
Stand, Musical, Circular Nickeled Cover, Germany, c.1900, 14 In. 59.00
Stand, Receptacles, Outlets, Painted, Cast Iron, Peerless, 1930s 350.00
Stand, Square, Raised Geometric, Openwork Design, c.1928, 5 x 13 In. 150.00
Tree, Feather, Dresden Trim Base, 8 1/2 Ft. 4400.00
Tree, Feather, New-Growth Coloring On Branch Tips, Germany, 8 1/2 Ft. 4500.00
Tree, Feather, Synthetic Branches, White, Wooden Stand, 39 In. 23.00

CHROME items in the Art Deco style became popular in the 1930s. Collectors are most interested in high-style pieces made by the Connecticut firms of Chase Brass and Copper Company, and Manning Bowman.

Appetizer Stand, Art Deco, Swan Shape, Red Bakelite Head, Pierced, Dished Base, 7 In. 94.00
Ashtray, Art Deco, Chase, Spherical Sliding Top, Fluted Shaft, Enamel Base, 27 x 6 In. ... 323.00
Box, Cover, Dolphin Finial, Bakelite, Black, 3 1/8 x 3 1/2 In. 40.00
Breakfast Set, Chase, Art Deco, Concentric Circle Design, R. & W. Gerth, 3 Piece 82.00
Butter, Tray, Bakelite Handles, Burgundy, 1950s, 8 x 7 In. 16.00
Cake Server, Lid, Square, 11 In. 10.00
Candlestick, 2-Light, Art Deco, Chase, 4 3/4 x 8 1/2 In. 150.00
Candlestick, Nude Woman, Art Deco, Krome-Kraft Farber Bros., 8 1/2 x 3 1/2 In. 35.00
Cigarette Holder, Cover, Cylindrical, Chase 20.00
Coat Hanger, Midget, Collapsible, 1913 Patent, 15-1/2 In. Extended, Pair 59.00
Cocktail Shaker, 1/2 Circle Handle, Bakelite Finial, Stopper, Revere, 11 x 7 In. 1175.00
Cocktail Shaker, Penguin, Hinged Beak Spout, Napier, 12 x 6 In. 705.00
Cocktail Shaker, Rattan-Wrapped Handle, Finial, Footed, Manning-Bowman, 12 x 7 In. ... 176.00
Cocktail Shaker, Wooden Handle & Knob, Art Deco, 1930s, 6 1/2 x 11 In. 26.00

Chrome, Server, Penguin Hot & Cold, Bakelite
Handles, West Bend Co., 8 3/4 In.

Clean chrome with white vinegar or tea.

Bakelite needs special care. Avoid extreme heat sources like an electric stove or hot hair dryer. Wash by hand, never in a dishwasher.

Coffee Maker, Art Deco, Sunbeam, No. C20-B, Filter 20.00
Coffee Percolator, Bakelite Handles, Footed, Art Deco, Rowena, 10 1/4 In. 150.00
Coffee Service, Bakelite Handles, M.W. McArdle, Sunbeam, 1934, 4 Piece 155.00
Coffee Set, Art Deco, Sunbeam, Black, Pot, Cream, Sugar, Tray, Bakelite Handles 36.00
Coffeepot, Art Deco, Pyrex Silex 26.00
Console Set, Diana, Chase, Art Deco, H. Laylon, 3 Piece 95.00
Ice Bucket, Tongs, Chase, Art Deco, 6 In. 41.00
Lazy Susan, 4 Clear Crescent Shape Dishes, 14 In. 11.00
Mustard Pot, Undertray, Glass, Chase, 5 In. 25.00
Napkin Holder, 4 Ball Feet, Bakelite Handle 27.00
Pitcher, Glass Stopper, Manning-Bowman, Art Deco, c.1940, 9 In. 30.00
Ring Tray, No. 90058, Signed, Chase, c.1930, 11 3/4 In. 26.00
Server, Penguin Hot & Cold, Bakelite Handles, West Bend Co., 8 3/4 In. .... *Illus*   50.00
Sugar & Creamer, Tray, Embossed Handles, Art Deco 35.00
Toiletry Set, Brass, Soap Dish, Covered Boxes, Lotion Bottles, Hermes, 5 Piece 441.00
Tray, Wooden Legs, Revere, Art Deco, 12 3/4 x 2 1/2 x 9 In. 20.00

CIGAR STORE FIGURES of carved wood or cast iron were used as advertisements in front of the Victorian cigar store. The carved figures are
now collected as folk art. They range in size from counter type, about
three feet, to over eight feet high.

Indian, Brave, Tobacco Leaves, Pine, Painted, Pedestal Base, c.1850, 69 In. 8365.00
Indian, Headdress, Holding Box, Thomas Brooks Style, Chicago, c.1890, 69 In. 6930.00
Indian, Pine, Holding 12 Cigars, Mounted On Wooden Slab, c.1880, 37 3/4 In. 17600.00
Indian, Princess, Full-Length, Raised Arm, Painted, 20th Century, 76 In. 3585.00
Indian, Squaw, Feathered Headdress, Shotgun, Wooden, Carved, 18 x 73 In. 6050.00
Indian, Standing Cross Legged, Holding Knife, Cigars, Polychrome, 76 In. 525.00

CINNABAR is a vermilion or red lacquer. Pieces are made with tens to
hundreds of thicknesses of the lacquer that is later carved. Most
cinnabar was made in the Orient.

Box, Carved Scholars In Garden, Flowers, Greek Key Border, Brass Trim, 2 x 4 x 6 In. ... 55.00
Vase, Carved Chrysanthemums, Black Diaper Ground, Blue Base & Interior, 10 In. 35.00
Vase, Carved, Chinese, 18 1/2 In. 172.00

CIVIL WAR mementos are important collectors' items. Most of the
pieces are military items used from 1861 to 1865. Be sure to avoid any
explosive munitions.

Bandanna, Silk, Union Constitution, Flag, Cannon, Foster, Porter & Co., 29 x 32 In. 1450.00
Belt Buckle, Eagle Clutching An Anchor, Holder, 2 1/4 In. 184.00
Belt Buckle, Eagle, Leather Belt, 48 Brass & Pewter Buttons 230.00
Binoculars, Leather Case, Gutta Percha Thumb Wheel, Marked, Merchant Marine Parts .. 58.00
Boots, Cavalry, Leather, Square Toe, Pinstripe, Black 215.00
Bullet Holder, Linen Strap, 7 In. 375.00
Button, Raised Eagle, Wm. H. Smith & Co., New York Infantry, 3/4 In. 48.00
Cane, Burl Knob Handle, Tortoiseshell Like Shaft, 17th Connecticut Volunteers, 34 In. ... 248.00
Canteen, Confederate, Cedar, Iron Bands, Copper Strap Retainers, 7 1/2 In. 1785.00
Chair, Camp Folding, Slat Back, Oak Frame, Molded Stretchers, Carpet Seat 225.00
Desk, Field, Hinged, Slant Top, Compartments, Hand Made, 9 x 6 x 13 In. 275.00
Desk, Officer's Field, 2 Drawers, 10 Compartments, 30 x 19 3/4 x 11 In. 1495.00
Diary, Corporal Miles Littlefield, New York, 1864 .... 1670.00
Diary, George Ingersoll, Battles, Soldiers, Captures, March 1862 To August, 1863 ...... 1150.00
Drum, Compass Rose, Brass Tack, 16 x 16 1/2 In. 575.00
Extractor, Clamp, Swivel, Wood Handle 120.00
Kepi, Sons Of Veterans, 79 SV, Laurel Wreath, M.C. Lilly, Columbus, Size 7 .... 345.00
Knife, Bowie, Antler Handle, Oval Guard, 15 1/2 In. 550.00
Knife, Bowie, Spear, Motto, Sheath, Silver Handle, Barnett & Cone Of Sheffield, 7 In. ... 415.00
Knife, Pike, Confederate, Curved, 11 In. 248.00
Knife, Pocket, Folding, Fork & Knife, Iron Side Plates, Brass Pins 95.00
Knife, Side, Stiletto Type Blade, Scrolling Leavers, Pewter Hilt, W&S Horrabin, 4 In. 425.00
Pipe, Prisoner's, Confederate, Limestone, C.S.A. Shield, Flag, Cannon, Crossed Flags ... 460.00
Pitcher, Memorial, Embossed Union Soldier, Inscription, Earthenware, c.1870, 7 1/4 In. .. 190.00
Powder Horn, Prisoner Of War, Engraved, 1864, Red River, La., Eagle, Mermaid, 16 In. . 880.00

Saber, Iron Scabbard, Cast Brass Hilt, Leather Wrap, Confederate, 40 1/2 In. 6040.00
Sling, Carbine, Hook, Leather, O. North & C. New Haven, C.T. 145.00
Spurs, Brass, Sand Cast, Officer's, Pebbled Pattern 94.00
Sword, Artillery, Confederate, Cast Brass Hilt, Cast Grip, Wood Scabbard, 19 In. 1025.00
Sword, Musician's, Inspector Initials, Ames-Chicopee, Mass., c.1864 .... 395.00
Sword, Officer's, Scabbard, Chelmsford, Mass., Model 1852, 35 In. 259.00
Tobacco, Minne-Ha-Ha Cavendish, Paper Wrapped, Red Wax Seal, Contents, 3 x 2 In. ... 80.00
Walking Stick, Natural Branch, Dog Finial, Inscribed Band, Yorktown, 1862, 36 In. 765.00

CKAW, see Dedham category.

CLARICE CLIFF was a designer who worked in several English factories
after the 1920s, including A.J. Wilkinson Ltd., Wilkinson's Royal Staffordshire Pottery, Newport Pottery, and Foley Pottery. She is best known
for her brightly colored Art Deco designs, including the "Bizarre" line.
She died in 1972. Reproductions have been made by Wedgwood.

Apples, Lotus, Jug, Ribbed Body, Yellow Bands, Applied Single Strap, 11 1/2 In. 3819.00
Autumn, Tree, Plate, Blue, Green, Yellow, 8 3/4 In. 303.00
Chahar, Wall Mask, Asian Woman, 11 x 9 1/2 In. 1765.00
Chintz, Bowl, Orange, Deco, Black Flowers, 2 x 7 In. 300.00
Chintz, Candlestick, Blue, Mauve & Purple Flowers, 3 1/2 x 4 3/4 In. 550.00
Chintz, Lotus, Jug, Blue, Pastel Colors, Single Strap Handle, 11 3/4 In. 3055.00
Crocus, Bowl, 2 1/2 x 4 1/2 In. 100.00
Crocus, Cup & Saucer 100.00
Crocus, Honey Pot, Cover, 3 3/4 x 3 1/2 In. 350.00
Crocus, Lotus, Jug, Violet, Orange, Blue, 12 x 10 In. 1100.00
Crocus, Plate, 7 3/4 In. 100.00
Delecia Citrus, Lotus, Jug, Orange, Yellow, Green, 12 x 8 1/2 In. 1540.00
Etna, Vase, Squat, Ribbed Body, Mountains, House, 6 3/4 x 9 1/2 In. 8225.00
Gayday, Vase, Daisies, Yellow, Brown Bands, Lobed, Bulbous, 8 In. 940.00
Lotus, Jug, Pyramid, Bizarre, Geometrics, Handle, c.1930, 11 1/2 In. 1265.00
Morocco, Pot, Cover, Yellow, Honey Glaze, Orange, 6 x 6 3/4 In. 715.00
Picasso Flower, Pot, Green Bolts, Blue Circles, Orange Circles, 3 x 3 In. 500.00
Secrets, Honey Pot, Cover, 3 x 2 1/2 In. 575.00
Sliced Circle, Lotus, Jug, Abstract Circles, Single Strap Handle, 11 1/2 In. 9400.00
Sunray, Bowl, Broth, Bubbles, Green, Black, Red, Blue, 3 3/4 x 8 1/2 In. 590.00
Sunray, Bowl, Yellow, Orange, Purple, Black, 2 1/2 x 4 1/2 In. 235.00
Tennis, Creamer, Cone Shape, Geometric Design, 4 In. 1765.00
Tulips, Plate, Orange, Red, Green, Brown, Black, Octagonal, 7 1/4 In. 303.00
Tulips, Vase, Spherical, 6 In. 1060.00
Wheat, Tray, Flowers, Leaves, Handle, 12 1/2 In. 220.00
Woodland, Jug, Flowers, Trees, Orange, White, Black, Green, 4 1/4 In. 380.00

CLEWELL ware was made in limited quantities by Charles Walter
Clewell of Canton, Ohio, from 1902 to 1955. Pottery was covered with
a thin coating of bronze, then treated to make the bronze turn different
colors. Pieces covered with copper, brass, or silver were also made.
Mr. Clewell's secret formula for blue patinated bronze was burned
when he died in 1965.

Lamp, Copper Clad, Umbrella Shade, Cattails, Dragonflies, Flared Base, 16 x 10 In. 1035.00
Mug, Copper Clad, Hammered, Studs, Impressed, 4 1/2 In. 115.00
Pitcher, Copper Clad, 6 Panels, 6 x 3 1/2 In. 305.00
Vase, Charcoaled Bronze On Shoulder, Sea Green Patina, Oval, Mark, 5 1/2 x 4 3/4 In. .. 605.00
Vase, Copper Clad, Classic Shape, 11 3/4 x 5 In. 590.00
Vase, Copper Clad, Man & Woman, Egyptian Design, 12 1/2 In. 2300.00
Vase, Copper Clad, Melon Form, 3 3/4 In. 90.00
Vase, Copper Clad, Orange & Green Patina, 2 Handles, Incised, Marked, 5 1/4 In. 750.00
Vase, Copper Clad, Original Patina, Blue, Green Rim, Marked, 4 1/2 In. 635.00
Vase, Copper Clad, Patina, Cylindrical, Marked, 10 In. 1035.00
Vase, Copper Clad, Patina, Signed, 6 In. 460.00
Vase, Copper Clad, Poppies, Reticulated Collar, Patina, Marked, 13 1/4 x 5 1/2 In. 4900.00
Vase, Copper Clad, Raised Berries & Leaves, Flared, 8 In. 375.00
Vase, Copper Clad, Tapered, 15 1/2 In. 980.00
Vase, Copper Clad, Tapered, Original Patina, Incised Mark, 13 In. 1840.00

CLEWS pottery was made by George Clews & Co. of Brownhills Pottery, Tunstall, England, from 18906 to 1961. Additional pieces may be listed in the Flow Blue category.

Cup & Saucer, 2 Dogs, Flower & Leaf Border, 5 3/4 In.	150.00
Plate, Landing Of General Lafayette, 1819-1836, 7 3/4 In.	499.00
Plate, Landing Of General Lafayette, Dark Blue Transfer, 9 In.	395.00
Plate, Peace & Plenty, Dark Blue Transfer, 9 In. ....226.00 to	358.00
Platter, Landing Of Lafayette, Octagonal, Blue & White, 1835, 19 In.	2300.00
Soup, Dish, Blue Transferware, 9 3/4 In.	825.00

CLIFTON POTTERY was founded by William Long in Clifton, New Jersey, in 1905. He worked there until 1909 making lines including *Crystal Patina* and *Clifton Indian Ware*. Clifton Pottery made art pottery until 1911 and then concentrated on wall and floor tile. By 1914 the name had been change to Clifton Porcelain and Tile Company. Another firm, Chesapeake Pottery, sold majolica marked *Clifton Ware*.

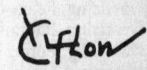

Bowl, Black Glazed Interior, Marked, 9 In.	145.00
Vase, Crystal Patina, Amber Matte Glaze, Celadon Ground, Bulbous, 1906, 6 1/2 x 5 In...	470.00
Vase, Crystal Patina, Amber, Celadon, Flared, Squat Base, 1907, 7 1/4 x 4 1/2 In.	440.00
Vase, Crystal Patina, Green, Beige Matte Glaze, Egg Shape, 1906, 8 1/2 x 6 In.	529.00
Vase, Crystal Patina, Silver Plated Poppy Overlay, Bulbous, 1906, 6 3/4 x 5 In.	1000.00
Vase, Crystal Patina, Sunburst, Matte Yellow, Celadon, Spherical, 1906, 5 1/4 x 7 In.	1058.00
Vase, Diamonds On Crosses, Squat, Little Colorado, Ariz., Marked, 5 In.	460.00
Vase, Double Gourd, Pale Green Glaze, 4 In.	460.00
Vase, Gourd, Wave Pattern, Arkansas, Marked, 6 In.	375.00
Vase, Green Crystalline Glaze, 2 Handles, Incised Mark, 7 In.	175.00
Vase, Indian Ware, Gourd, Ivory, Red, Black, Florida Tribe, No. 241, 10 x 12 1/4 In.	940.00
Vase, Indian Ware, Squat, Terra-Cotta, Greek Key Band, Pueblo Viejo, 9 x 15 1/2 In.	590.00
Vase, Indian Ware, Swirls, Brown, Stovepipe Neck, Bulbous, Marked, 12 In.	1093.00
Vase, Ivory, Taupe Matte Glaze, 4-Sided Flared Rim, Squat Base, 1905, 7 1/4 x 5 In.	650.00
Vase, Key Pattern, Tapered, 4-Mile Ruin, Ariz., Marked, 5 1/2 In.	290.00
Vase, Squat, Flared Rim, Arkansas, Marked, 4 3/4 In.	345.00
Vase, Squat, Stylized Feathers, 4-Mile Ruin, Ariz., Marked, 5 In. ....200.00 to	300.00
Vase, Tirrube, Baluster, Heron, Palm Fronds, A. Haubrich, 12 x 6 1/2 In...............	1295.00
Vase, Tirrube, Baluster, White Rose, Green Leaves, Terra-Cotta Ground, 7 3/4 x 5 In.	325.00
Vase, Tirrube, Bottle Shape, Nasturtium, Green Leaves, Terra-Cotta Ground, 9 1/4 x 5 In. .	440.00
Vase, Tirrube, Bottle Shape, White, Gray Tulips, Terra-Cotta Ground, 12 x 8 In.	705.00

CLOCKS of all types have always been popular with collectors. The eighteenth-century tall case, or grandfather's clock, was designed to house a works with a long pendulum. In 1816, Eli Terry patented a new, smaller works for a clock, and the case became smaller. The clock could be kept on a shelf instead of on the floor. By 1840, coiled springs were used and even smaller clocks were made. Battery-powered electric clocks were made in the 1870s. A garniture set can include a clock and other objects displayed on a mantel.

Advertising, 7-Up, Plastic Face, Round, Brass Spoke Trim, 1960s	105.00
Advertising, 7-Up, Plastic, Light-Up, Round, 1970s	22.00
Advertising, Abercrombie & Fitch, Desk, Chelsea, Brass, Barometer, Thermometer, 12 In.	423.00
Advertising, Boston Cigar, L.O. Grothe & Co., Montreal, Cast Iron, Figural, 16 x 12 In. . .	1540.00
Advertising, Chevrolet, Neon, Electric, 20 In.	990.00
Advertising, Cities Service, Metal, 14 1/2 x 14 1/2 x 3 In.	242.00
Advertising, Clapperton's Thread, Baird, 6-Cord Spool Cotton, 18 1/2 x 31 In.	1035.00
Advertising, Clyde Minich Jewelers, Allentown, Pa., Light-Up, Square, 15 In.	70.00
Advertising, Dr Pepper, Fiberglass, Turquoise Case, Round	176.00
Advertising, Fresca, Enjoy, White Ground, Red Edge, Light-Up, Square, 15 In.	138.00
Advertising, Gargoyle Marine Oils, Metal, 11 x 6 1/2 In.	550.00
Advertising, Grant Batteries, Metal, Plastic, Red & Green, Square	220.00
Advertising, Grapette Soda, White Ground, Blue Center Oval, Electric, Round, 10 In. ...	195.00
Advertising, Harley-Davidson, Chrome Frame, Round, 13 1/2 In.	40.00
Advertising, Harley-Davidson, Neon, Logo On Face, Aluminum Case, Round, 20 In.	825.00
Advertising, Iroquois Beer Ale, Glass, Metal, International Breweries, 15 1/2 In.	523.00

Advertising, John Deere, Quality Farm Equipment, Metal, Plastic, Light-Up, Round 340.00
Advertising, Jolly Tar Pastime, Roman Numerals, Baird, c.1890, 31 In. 3080.00
Advertising, Marigold Dairy Products, Double Bubble, Round, 15 In. 255.00
Advertising, Mark Twain Flour, Regulator, Roman Numerals, 36 In. 385.00
Advertising, Monroe Shock Absorbers, Metal, Plastic, Light-Up, Square 20.00
Advertising, Nestle Cookie, Alarm, Metal, Enamel, Wind-Up, Case, c.1940, 4 x 6 In. 35.00
Advertising, New Haven Sunshine Biscuits, School, Mahogany, 11 3/4-In. Dial 180.00
Advertising, NuGrape Soda, Metal & Glass, Electric, Light-Up, 16 x 13 x 3 1/2 In. 90.00
Advertising, Oilzum, Light-Up, Metal, Glass, 15 In. 660.00
Advertising, Old Mr. Boston Fine Liqueurs, Metal, Figural Bottle, 21 x 10 In. . . . .120.00 to 335.00
Advertising, Olga Genuine Pocahontas Coal, Red Center, Yellow Edge, Light-Up, 15 In. .   85.00
Advertising, Pennzoil Motor Oil, Logo On Face, Plastic, Light-Up, Round, 15 In. 495.00
Advertising, Peters Shoes, Gilbert, Cast Iron, 5 x 5 In. 30.00
Advertising, Phillips 66, Double Bubble, Glass, Metal, 16 In. 495.00
Advertising, Purina Chows, Sanitation Products, Double Bubble, Light-Up, 15 In. 358.00
Advertising, Quaker State Motor Oil, Painted Glass, Metal, Electric, 20 x 6 1/8 In. 715.00
Advertising, Reed's Gilt Edge Tonic Cures 1500.00
Advertising, Regal Premium Beer, American Brewing, Miami, Florida, 14 In. 110.00
Advertising, Remington Dupont, Embossed, Self-Framed, Tin, Wood, 24 x 18 In. 90.00
Advertising, Sauer's Extracts, New Haven Clock Co., 41 x 17 x 5 3/4 In. 1322.00
Advertising, Squirt, Happy Taste, Metal, Plastic, Light-Up, Square 145.00
Advertising, Star Brand Shoes Are Better, Metal, Art Deco, New Haven, 6 1/4 In. 25.00
Advertising, Texaco, Logo On Face, Plastic, Light-Up, Round, 14 3/4 In. 715.00
Advertising, Union Petroleum, Ingraham, Banjo, 36 x 10 x 4 In.   630.00
Advertising, Waterbury, Gallery, Oak, Bruce Stone Jeweler, c.1914, 25 1/2 In. 3658.00
Alarm, Bugs Bunny, Animated Bugs Smiling, Holds Carrot, Ingraham, 1940s, 2 x 4 In. . .   145.00
Ansonia, 8-Day, Time & Strike, Mirror, Cherubs, 1890 . . . .   265.00
Ansonia, Beehive, Mahogany Case, 8-Day Movement, 19 In. 115.00
Ansonia, Calendar, Rosewood Veneer Case, 25 In. 690.00
Ansonia, Carriage, Rococo Style, Swing Handle, Round Dial, 4 x 3 1/2 In. 115.00
Ansonia, Crystal Regulator, Apex, 19 In. 3450.00
Ansonia, Crystal Regulator, Roy, 8-Day, Time & Strike, c.1914, 11 1/8 In. 635.00
Ansonia, Cupids Holding Clock Face, Inkwell, 8 In. 325.00
Ansonia, Fisher & Hunter, Gilt Spelter Figures, White Enameled Base, 21 1/2 In. 1630.00
Ansonia, Flowers, Granite, Royal Bonn Case, 6 1/2 In. 215.00
Ansonia, Flowers, Royal Bonn, New York 555.00
Ansonia, Fortuna, Swing Arm, Seated Woman, Cupid, Gold-Painted Spelter 4800.00
Ansonia, Gloria, Bronzed Figure, Blue Enameled Swinging Ball, 8-Day, 28 1/2 In. 4500.00
Ansonia, Huntress, Swinger, Spelter, Bronze Finish, 18 1/2 In. 985.00
Ansonia, Mantel, Brass, Mercury-Filled Pendulum, Scroll & Leaf Corners, Urn Top, 15 In.   525.00
Ansonia, Mantel, Brass, Metal, Painted Faux Rosewood, 13 1/2 x 9 x 5 In. 58.00
Ansonia, Mantel, Cobalt Blue China Case, Flower Panels, Gilding, Royal Bonn, 17 In. . . .   2900.00
Ansonia, Mantel, Creamware, Polychrome, Parcel Gilt, Round Dial, Flowers, 12 x 12 In. . .   405.00
Ansonia, Mantel, Egyptian Revival, Faux Slate, Gilt Metal, Gong, c.1890, 10 In. 490.00
Ansonia, Mantel, Faux Slate, Gong, Enamel Dial, Roman Numerals, 1882, 14 In. 290.00
Ansonia, Mantel, Faux Slate, Gong, Rectangular, Griffins, Paw Feet, c.1880, 9 1/2 In. . . .   230.00
Ansonia, Mantel, Green Lacquer, Gilt Metal Mounts, France, c.1890 . . . .   259.00
Ansonia, Mantel, Ogee, Tin Dial, Lower Tablet Mirror 50.00
Ansonia, Mantel, Pizarro & Cortez, 8-Day, Time & Strike, c.1894, 20 1/2 In. 1430.00
Ansonia, Mantel, Porcelain Dial, Time & Strike, Royal Bonn, 12 In. 635.00
Ansonia, Mantel, Round Bezel, Beveled Glass, Brass Gallery, 4 Griffin Feet, 16 x 8 In. . .   235.00
Ansonia, Mantel, Science By August Moreau, c.1890, 24 In. 1265.00
Ansonia, Mantel, Senator, Female Figures, Silver Metal Dial, Oak, Brass Case, 22 In. . . .   3000.00
Ansonia, Mantel, Wyoming, Porcelain, Blue, Flowers, 11 3/4 In.   535.00
Ansonia, Mirror, Beveled, 8-Day, Roman Numerals, Time Only, c.1910, 30 In. 170.00
Ansonia, Ossipee, Cobalt Blue, Flowers, 8-Day, Time & Strike, c.1900, 11 1/2 In. 440.00
Ansonia, Rainbow, Green, Purple Flowers, 8-Day, Time & Strike, c.1901, 11 1/4 In. 550.00
Ansonia, Regulator, Crystal, 8-Day, Brass Case, c.1920, 10 In. 175.00
Ansonia, Regulator, Crystal, Pink, Blue China Case, Flowers, Beveled Panels, 18 1/2 In. .   3100.00
Ansonia, School, 8-Day, Time & Strike, Paper Dial, Oak Case, 20 1/2 In. 96.00
Ansonia, School, Mahogany, Pendulum, Key Wind, 32 In. 175.00
Ansonia, Shelf, Black Walnut, 8-Day, Time & Strike, c.1880, 24 In. 690.00
Ansonia, Slate, Polished Black, Pewter & Brass Mounted, Signed, 1882, 13 x 9 In. 490.00

Ansonia, Soldier, Green Faux Marble Base, Key Wind, 20 1/2 x 20 1/2 In. 220.00
Ansonia, Steeple, 30-Hour, Time & Strike, Mahogany Veneer, c.1850, 19 3/4 In. 285.00
Ansonia, Viscount, Regulator, Crystal, Jeweled Sash & Pendulum, 16 1/2 In. 845.00
Ansonia, Wall, Hanging, Oak Case, Brass Mounts, Pendulum, 46 In. 5500.00
Arthur Pequegnat, Wall, Regulator, 8-Day, Oak Case, Canada, 1905, 35 3/4 In. 1990.00
Arts & Crafts, Hammered Wrought Iron, Enameled Face, Dutch, 8 x 10 In. 805.00
Atmos, Art Deco, Black Enamel Case, Chrome Accents, 9 1/2 In. 2419.00
Atmos, Le Coultre, Art Deco, Brass, Polished, Jeweled, Open Escapement, 15 In. 425.00
Balloon, Edwardian, Mahogany, Marquetry, Dial Inscribed, c.1900, 10 1/4 In. 460.00
Balloon, Edwardian, Mother-Of-Pearl, Mahogany, Marquetry, c.1900, 9 In. 430.00
Banjo, Ansonia, Girandole, Etched Glass Panel 3600.00
Banjo, Burl Walnut, 8-Day, Germany, c.1950, 34 In. 230.00
Banjo, Curtis & Dunning, Federal, Mahogany, Brass Bezel, Paper Dial, Grapevines, 35 In. 4700.00
Banjo, Curtis, Lemuel, Concord, Federal, Constitution's Escape, Parcel Gilt, Inlaid, 33 In. 2990.00
Banjo, Curtis, Lemuel, Mahogany, Giltwood, Brass Eagle Finials, c.1815, 33 1/4 In. 7640.00
Banjo, Federal Style, Mahogany Inlay, Convex Glass, Metal Dial, Eagle, 34 1/4 In. 1528.00
Banjo, Federal Style, Mahogany, Parcel Gilt, Eglomise Panel, c.1890, 39 1/2 In. 575.00
Banjo, Federal, Mahogany, 8-Day, Brass Side Arms, Marine Scene, 1820s, 28 1/2 In. 1880.00
Banjo, Federal, Mahogany, Brass Bezel, Painted Metal Dial, Ball Finial, c.1825, 32 In. ... 2470.00
Banjo, Federal, Mahogany, Eglomise, Boston Massacre, 19th Century, 38 In. 980.00
Banjo, Federal, Mahogany, Eglomise, Man Near Mill, 19th Century, 31 In. 920.00
Banjo, Federal, Mahogany, Parcel Gilt, Eglomise Panel, c.1820, 40 In. 805.00
Banjo, Giltwood, Elgomise, Ship, Flowers, Scrolls, Mass., c.1815, 29 3/4 x 10 In. 16730.00
Banjo, New Haven Clock Co., Federal, Brass, Chimes, Key Wind, 1923, 39 1/2 In. 330.00
Banjo, New Haven, Waring, 8-Day, Time & Strike, 2 Ships, c.1923, 37 In. 385.00
Banjo, New Haven, Washington, Westminster Chime, 8-Day, c.1923, 41 In. 495.00
Banjo, Seth Thomas, Brookfield, 8-Day, Time & Strike, c.1958, 30 In. 165.00
Banjo, Simon Willard & Son, Alarm, Mahogany, No. 4696, 32 1/2 In. 3290.00
Banjo, Stennes, Elmer, Weight Driven, Mahogany Crossband, Bee, c.1966, 34 In. 2816.00
Banjo, Waltham, Federal, Reverse Painted On Glass, Wayside Inn, 1925 .... 2025.00
Banjo, Waltham, Mahogany, Brass Eagle, Side Rails, 8-Day, 21 In. 705.00
Banjo, Waltham, Weight Driven, Green, Gold Paint, c.1910, 42 x 10 In. 1008.00
Banjo, Waterbury Clock Co., Federal, Eglomise & Gilt, Ships In Harbor, 43 In. 825.00
Barwise, Carriage, Ebonized Case, Gilt, Acorn Feet, London, 18th Century, 8 In. .... *Illus* 14100.00
Becker, Gustav, Regulator, Vienna, Single-Weight 880.00
Benson, J.W., Bracket, 2 Fusee, Ebony Veneer, Streaks, England, c.1890, 14 In. 2167.00
Biedermeier, Temple Form, Eagles, Ebonized, Parcel Gilt, Onyx Mounted, Music, 22 In. . 470.00
Bigelow & Kennard, Black Marble, Bronze, Egyptian Style, Sphinx Finial, 18 In. 1035.00
Bigelow Kennard & Co., Wall, Recessed Pyrographic Face, 33 x 15 x 7 1/2 In. 490.00
Birge, Peck & Co., Shelf, Double-Decker, Mahogany, Locomotive Dial, 32 3/4 In. 405.00
Birge & Fuller, Steeple On Steeple, Gothic, Mahogany, Bristol, c.1848, 25 1/4 In. 1765.00
Birge & Fuller, Steeple On Steeple, Wagon Spring Movement 4840.00
Birge & Mallory, Mahogany, Eagle Crest, Reverse Painted, 8-Day, Time & Strike, 39 In. . 200.00
Black Forest, Cuckoo, Deer, Glass Eyes, Game Carvings, 61 x 25 In. 4760.00
Black Forest, Cuckoo, Hanging, 8-Day, Carved Eagle, Acorns, Stag, Dogs, 37 In. 1180.00
Black Forest, Cuckoo, Lindenwood, Dead Grouse, Rabbit, Game Bag, 25 x 25 1/2 In. ... 3910.00
Black Forest, Cuckoo, Oak, Bird In Nest, Acorn, Fox, 8-Day, c.1890, 22 In. 1150.00
Black Forest, Cuckoo, Quarter Strike, Cast Plate Movement, c.1910, 21 x 34 In. 1650.00
Black Forest, House, Music Box Base, Geneva, 1885, 17 x 18 x 10 In. 1230.00
Black Forest, Mantel, Carved Deer Ascending Rocky Ledge, Sleeping Under, 36 x 23 In. . 4760.00
Black Forest, Mantel, Stump, Eagle, Brass Movement, Porcelain Dial, 25 In. 2200.00
Black Forest, Wall, Antelope Crest, Birds, Leaves, Vines, Oak, 2 Weights, 46 x 19 In. ... 1624.00
Black Forest, Wall, Walnut, Eagle Attacking Antelope, Black Glass Dial, 8-Day, 47 In. ... 3600.00
Bloomer & Sperry, Shelf, Mahogany, 8-Day Movement, Brass, 25 3/4 In. 180.00
Bracket, Cherry Case, Gilt Brass, 3 Fusee, 8-Day, Paw Feet, c.1890, 26 In. 3450.00
Bracket, Ebonized, France, Early 18th Century, 11 In. 1076.00
Bracket, George III Style, Mahogany, 5 Gongs, Arch Dial, c.1910, 18 In. 635.00
Bracket, George III, Mahogany, 8-Day, 2-Train Striking Movement, 18 x 1 7/16 x 8 In. . 6570.00
Bracket, Louis XV Style, Ormolu Mounted, Boulle Marquetry, 20th Century, 41 In. 2300.00
Bracket, Rococo, Gilt Bronze, Scrolled Case, Portraits, 19th Century, 21 1/2 In. 635.00
Bracket, Walnut Marquetry, 8-Day, Time & Strike, Fusee, England, c.1880, 29 In. 2145.00
Bradley & Hubbard, Lion, Blinking Eye, Cast Iron, 10 1/2 In. 3080.00
Bradley & Hubbard, Sambo, Blinking Eye, Cast Iron, Polychrome, 16 In. 2195.00

Brewster, Beehive, 8-Day, Mahogany, Frosted Cut Flower Tablet, 19 In. 2815.00
Brewster, E.C., Shelf, Cornice, Mahogany, Silk-Screened Tall Ship, 30-Hour, 23 1/2 In. . . . 280.00
Brewster & Ingraham, Steeple, Mahogany, Rosewood, Flower Tablet, 30-Hour, 19 In. 180.00
Brillie, Electrique, Horseshoe Magnet, Oak Case, France, c.1930, 18 In. 865.00
Brocot, Achille, Mantel, Slate, Green Marble, 2 Train Movement, France, c.1880, 13 In. . . 230.00
Bronze, Gilt, Louis XV Style, Porcelain, Loving Couples, Egg Shape, Mounted, 21 In. . . . 1058.00
Bronze, Gilt, Patinated, Standing Male Nude, Round Clock, Marble Base, 10 In. 2645.00
Brown, J.C., Shelf, Mahogany, 8-Day, Time & Strike, Bristol, Conn., 15 x 9 In. 670.00
Bulle, Electric, Dome, Battery, Solenoid Pendulum, 16 In. 338.00
Burleigh, T.E., Wall, Girandole, Giltwood, Eglomise, Painted Metal Dial, 47 In. 9400.00
Caldwell & Co., Gilt Bronze, Man Holding Clock, Marble Base, Signed, 9 1/2 In. 5288.00
Caldwell & Co., Gilt Bronze, Round Dial, 2 Sea Monsters, Blue Lazuli Base, Signed, 8 In. . 5580.00
Calendar, Double Dial, Full Round Columns, Mahogany Veneer Case, c.1875, 31 In. 1325.00
Campos, F., Shelf, Mahogany, Barber Pole Inlay, Medallion, 8-Day, Time & Strike, 34 In. 2815.00
Carriage, 8-Day, Alarm, Painted Porcelain Sides, France, c.1900, 5 3/4 In. 2725.00
Carriage, Brass Corniche Case, Seahorses, Flowers, France, c.1900, 6 3/4 In. 740.00
Carriage, Brass, Beveled Glass Top & Sides, Toupie Feet, France, 20th Century, 4 In. 115.00
Carriage, Brass, Original Leather Case, Stamped Aiguilles 12532, c.1900, 3 In. 345.00
Carriage, Bronze Dore, Engraved, Cherub Head & Dolphin Tail Feet, 7 In. 4406.00
Carriage, Bronze, Blue Enamel, Scrolling Leaves, Birds, Butterflies, Art Nouveau, 6 In. . . 590.00
Carriage, Bronze, Engraved Birds, Blossoms, Black Ground, Aesthetic Movement, 7 In. . . 4700.00
Carriage, Bronze, Porcelain Faceplates, Repeating, Town Scene, Birds, Figures, 7 In. 4348.00
Carriage, French Renaissance Revival Style, Gilt Bronze, Late 19th Century, 5 In. . . *Illus* 4406.00
Carriage, Grand Sonniere, Alarm, Brass Case, Gilt Gorge, France, c.1890, 7 1/4 In. 1705.00
Carriage, Norman, Matthew, Brass, Crystal, Alarm, No. 1754A, 1987, 4 1/2 x 3 3/4 In. . . 405.00
Carriage, Oval, Round Face, Engraved Flowers, Bows, Roman Numerals, Key Wind 250.00
Carriage, Repeating, Bronze, Beveled Glass Panels, Alarm Dial, Tiffany & Co., 7 1/2 In. . 1060.00
Carriage, Sterling Silver, Enameled Face, Gilded Roses, S.O. & Co., 1907-1908, 3 x 2 In. 920.00
Carriage, Time, Strike, Repeat, Alarm, Lever Platform, France, c.1900, 7 In. 550.00
Carriage, Tortoiseshell, Pierced Silver Corner Mounts & Serpentine Handle, 6 1/2 In. 1410.00
Cartel, Art Nouveau, Walnut, 8-Day Movement, Gong Strike, France, c.1910, 23 In. 517.00
Cartel, Louis XV Style, Gilt Bronze, Lion's Head, Urn Shape, 30 In. 1135.00
Cartier, Carriage, Repeating, Enameled Silver, Purple, Turned Ground, Leather Box, 3 In. 7638.00
Character, Bugs Bunny, Alarm, Warner Bros., c.1940, 2 x 4 x 4 1/2 In. 145.00
Charles Oudin, Carriage, Brass, Glass, Enamel Dial, Late 19th Century, 3 3/4 In. 748.00
Chauncey & Ives, Shelf, Pillar & Scroll, Mahogany, Reverse Painted House, 32 x 17 In. . . 2127.00
Chelsea, Desk, Chinese Lacquer, 8-Day, Beveled Glass Door, c.1949, 6 3/4 In. 715.00
Chelsea, Sampson, Yacht Wheel, Bell, Electric, c.1932, 14 In. 1045.00
Chittenden, Austin, 30-Hour, Time & Strike, Wood Movement, c.1837, 34 In. 347.00
Dent, Carriage, Bronze Dore, Engraved, Flame Finials, Half Strike Movement, Paris, 7 In. 1528.00
Desk, Art Nouveau, Bronzed, Lily Pad Overlay, Triangular, Leather Covered, 3 1/8 In. . . . 96.00
Desk, Bronze, Seahorse Frame, Round Face, Key Wind, Patina, E.T. Hurley, 7 1/2 x 6 In. . 3405.00
Desk, La Esmeralda, 8-Day, Jeweled Lever, Fired Enamel Dial, Swiss, c.1935, 6 In. 1639.00
Digital Flick, Crystal, Regulator, Enamel, Display Case, France, c.1900, 10 In. 5500.00
Drocourt, Carriage, Grand Sonniere, Day, Date, Alarm, France, c.1895, 6 3/4 In. 10520.00
Dungan & Klump, Wall, Hickory Dickory Dock, 8-Day, Mouse, No. 2, c.1910, 43 In. 690.00
Eli Terry, Federal, Mahogany, Pillar & Scroll, Plymouth, Conn., c.1818, 30 1/4 In. 7640.00
Eli Terry, Mahogany, Pillar & Scroll, 20th Century, 31 In. 1035.00
Eli Terry, Mahogany, Pillar & Scroll, Reverse Painted Scene, Brass Finials, 31 x 18 x 5 In. 1595.00
Eli Terry, Mantel, Mahogany, Pillar & Scroll, Weights, c.1900, 31 In. 1035.00
Eli Terry & Sons, Mahogany, Pillar & Scroll, Reverse Painted, White House, 32 x 17 In. . . 1725.00
Eli Terry & Sons, Mahogany, Pillar & Scroll, Veneer, Weights, Key, Pendulum, 32 In. 6325.00
Eureka, Skeleton, Dome, Battery, London, c.1908, 14 1/2 In. 2310.00
Figural, Automobile, Woman, Steering Wheel, Bronzed, France, c.1890, 19 In. 2640.00
Figural, Cherub, Flute, Bronze, Spelter Case, France, c.1910, 16 In. 585.00
Figural, Female Dancer, Gilt, Marble Base, Ormolu, 8-Day, France, c.1890, 9 In. 1760.00
Figural, Huntress, Spelter, Swing Bracket, Circular Base, c.1890, 19 1/2 In. 460.00
Figural, Joan Of Arc, Gilt, Brass Movement, Bell Strike, France, c.1840, 22 In. 2550.00
Freeman, Carl, Shelf, Tiger Maple, Ogee Bracket Base, Glass Door, c.1931, 34 1/2 In. . . . 2160.00
French, Cathedral Form, Ormolu, 8-Day, Time & Strike, Silk Thread, c.1840, 24 In. 3520.00
French, Gilt Bronze, Champleve Enamel, Rectangular Case, Beveled Glass, 16 In. 1295.00
French, Gilt Bronze, Enamel, Hooved Feet, Maroon Panel, Cherubs, c.1900, 14 In. 2590.00
French, Louis XVI Style, Urn, Annular Dial, Black Snake, Gilding, c.1875, 17 In. 8278.00

Clock, Barwise, Carriage,
Ebonized Case, Gilt, Acorn Feet,
London, Late 18th Century, 8 In.

Clock, Carriage, French
Renaissance Revival Style, Gilt
Bronze, Late 19th Century, 5 In.

Clock, Lepine, Carriage,
Bronze, Grand Sonnerie,
Engraved Panels, Signed, 7 In.

French, Regimental, Steel, Gilt, Bronze, Late 19th Century, 22 3/4 x 16 1/2 In. 1790.00
French, Urn, Snake, Annular Dial, 4 Acanthus Swags, c.1880, 28 1/2 In. 7205.00
Gallery, Lacquer, Fruitwood, Mother-Of-Pearl Inlay, 8-Day, c.1890, 19 1/4 x 16 In. 196.00
Gallet & Co., Boudoir, Sterling Silver, 8-Day, Porcelain Dial, Swiss, 3 1/4 In. 158.00
George III, Mahogany, Bracket, 8-Day, 2-Train Strike, Thomas Green, Late 18th Century . 5080.00
Gilbert, Angel, Gilt Spelter, Trumpet, Scrolled Base, Porcelain Dial, No. 1025, 8 1/2 In. . . 280.00
Gilbert, Camel Back, Time & Strike, No. 1807 . . . . 99.00
Gilbert, Musicians, 30-Hour, Gilt Spelter Case, c.1905, 12 1/2 In. 160.00
Gilbert, Parlor, Altai, Walnut, 8-Day, Time & Strike, c.1885, 20 In. 450.00
Gilbert, Wm. L., Calendar, Walnut, Burl Veneer, Carved, Ebonized Bezel, c.1880, 31 In. . 1295.00
Gilt Bronze, Champleve Enamel, Rectangular Case, Urn, Porcelain Panel, 17 1/2 In. 2820.00
Gilt Bronze, Guilloche Enamel, Azure Blue Ground, 19th Century, 4 In. 575.00
Giltwood, Grand Sonnerie, Musical, Picture, Austria, Mid 19th Century, 21 x 17 In. 590.00
Globe, 30-Hour, Wood Base, Germany, c.1900, 15 In. 1485.00
Graham, George, Bracket, Mahogany Case, Carved, Gilt, 18th Century, 20 x 14 x 8 In. . . 10350.00
Guyerdet, Carriage, Bronze, Quarter Strike, Push Repeater, Silvered Dial, 6 3/4 In. 3525.00
Haddon, Multicolored Glass, Metal Hands, Marked, 11 1/2 In. 316.00
Hancock, C.F., Gothic Revival, Golden Oak, Musical, London, 1880, 30 x 25 x 12 In. . . . 7638.00
Harker Mfg., White Clover, Adobe Face, White Hands, Russel Wright, 1958, 8 x 8 In. . . . 118.00
Honore Pons, Mantel, Charles X, Bronze, Sienna Marble, Mid 19th Century, 22 1/4 In. . . 1380.00
Horolovar, Hickory Dickory Dock, Mahogany, Mouse, c.1970, 24 1/2 In. 230.00
Howard, Regulator, No. 70-3, Quartersawn Oak Case, c.1885, 41 In. 7700.00
Howard, Wall, Oak, No. 59, 6-In. Dial 9130.00
Howard Miller, Ball, Birch, Brass Dial, Black Metal Arms, G. Nelson, 1950, 23 In. 805.00
Howard Miller, Ball, Painted Black Balls, Brass Rods, Center, G. Nelson, 1950s 460.00
Howard Miller, Ball, Spun Brass Center, Spherical Numeral Marks, G. Nelson, 13 In. 588.00
Howard Miller, Brushed Chrome, Rosewood Face, G. Nelson, 13 In. 558.00
Howard Miller, Burst, No. 2240, Brass Fins, Orange, Black, G. Nelson, 31 1/2 In. 2115.00
Howard Miller, Enameled Metal, Walnut, c.1950, 5 x 7 In. 6900.00
Howard Miller, Exotic Face, White & Red Enamel Handles, Round, Marked, 13 1/2 In. . . 175.00
Howard Miller, Eye Shape, Brushed Brass Lids, Dowel Lashes, G. Nelson, 15 x 30 In. . . . 6465.00
Howard Miller, Oak Frame, Cork Face, Wood Marks, Enamel Hands, G. Nelson, 13 In. . . 118.00
Howard Miller, Orange, Yellow, Brown Matte Glazes, Enamel Hands, 13 1/2 In. 440.00
Howard Miller, Plexiglas Face, Brass Numbers, Pendulum, 15 In. 206.00
Howard Miller, Printed Face, Enamel Hands, Cork Back, G. Nelson, 11 1/2 In. 470.00
Howard Miller, Starburst, Black Rays, Hands, Orange, Yellow, White Face, 19 In. 499.00
Howard Miller, Sunflower, Walnut, Birch Plywood, Brass, G. Nelson, 29 3/4 In. 2185.00
Howard Miller, Tall Vertical Shape, Geometric Design, G. Nelson, 20 x 6 In. 255.00
Howard Miller, Wall, Ball, Model 4755, Irving Harper, 1950, 13 In. 6670.00
Howard Miller, Wall, Ball, Multicolored, Lacquered Wood, G. Nelson, 1950s, 13 In. 3105.00
Howard Miller, Wall, Oak Frame, Printed Round Face, Enamel Hands, 16 In. 80.00
Howard Miller, Wall, Rosewood, Aluminum, G. Nelson, 12 3/4 In. 1095.00

Howard Miller, Wall, Spike, G. Nelson, c.1947, 19 x 19 In. 323.00
Howard Miller, Wall, Spun Brass Components, G. Nelson, Original Box 380.00
Howard Miller, Wall, White Enamel Case, Black Face, Red Hands, Electric, 3 1/2 x 14 In. 118.00
Howard Miller, Walnut Spikes, White Enameled Metal Dial, G. Nelson, 1950s, 18 In. 575.00
Howard Miller, Walnut, Enameled Metal, 3 Legs, G. Nelson, c.1955, 8 x 4 3/4 In. 4600.00
Howard Miller, Zoo-Timer, Blue & Green Fish, G. Nelson, c.1965, 10 In. 46.00
Imhof, 2-Piece Glass Dial, 8-Day, Gilt Bronze Base, Swiss, c.1965, 7 In. 330.00
Industrial, Automaton, Beam Engine, Marble Base, France, c.1880, 7 1/4 In. 4620.00
Industrial, Horizontal Steam Boiler, 8-Day, Brass Base, France, c.1885, 11 In. 6985.00
Ingraham, Calendar, Lewis Perpetual, c.1890, 21 1/2 In. 1485.00
Ingraham, Calendar, Walnut, Roman Numerals, 24 In. 290.00
Ingraham, E., Wall, Figure Eight, Walnut Veneer, Reverse Painted, Time & Strike, 30 In. . 805.00
Ingraham, Gingerbread Shelf, Oak, Connecticut, Late 1800s, 14 1/2 x 5 In. 255.00
Ingraham, Ionic, Columns, 8-Day, Time & Strike, c.1880, 22 In. 290.00
Ingraham, Mantel, Draped Window, Lion's Head Handles, Time & Strike 105.00
Ingraham, Regulator, Oak, 8-Day, Roman Numerals, Time Only, c.1880, 37 In. 259.00
Ingraham, Shelf, Rosewood, 8-Day, Peacock Tablets, Metal Dial, 18 1/2 In. 2025.00
Ingraham, Shelf, Venetian, No. 3, Rosewood Case, 8-Day, c.1880, 16 In. 730.00
International Time Recorder, Wall, Mahogany, Electric, Self-Winding, No. 167, 63 In. . . 2080.00
Ithaca Calendar Clock Co., Double Dial, Walnut Case, 25 1/2 In. 575.00
J.R. Mills & Co., Torsion Pendulum, Mahogany, Cobalt Glass Tablet, Swans, 22 In. 2138.00
Jaeger-LeCoultre, Mantel, Wood, Copper, Brass, No. 285, 1950s, 5 1/4 x 8 x 2 1/4 In. . . . 325.00
Japy Fils, Mantel, Gilt Metal, Onyx, Child, Hammer, Roman Numerals, c.1860, 12 x 5 In. 575.00
Japy Freres, Bracket, 8-Day, Time & Strike, Crackle Finish, c.1900, 14 1/2 In. 809.00
Japy Freres, Bronze Bearded Scholar, Leaning On Movement, Black Slate Base, 24 In. . . 2350.00
Japy Freres, Champleve, Bronze Case, Enamel Panels, 19th Century, 12 3/4 In. 575.00
Japy Freres, Mantel, 2-Train Movement, Scroll Base, Slate, c.1875, 12 In. 405.00
Jerome, Chauncey, Cathedral, Iron Front, Flowers, 8-Day, 23 In. 416.00
Jerome, Chauncey, School, Mahogany, Roman Numerals, Reverse Painted, 1800s, 24 In. . 288.00
Jerome, Chauncey, Steeple, Mahogany Veneer, 8-Day, Fusee, c.1850, 20 In. 1270.00
Jerome, Cottage, Mahogany, 30-Hour, Flower Tablet, Metal Dial, 16 1/4 In. 125.00
John Birge & Co., Shelf, Split Column, Mahogany, Locomotive Engraving, 32 x 18 In. . . . 290.00
Junghans, Barmaid, Swinger, 30-Hour, Germany, c.1910, 13 In. 1595.00
Junghans, Batboy, Swinger, Germany, c.1910, 18 In. 2640.00
Junghans, Bracket, Mahogany, Swag, Ribbon Inlay, Westminster Chime, 8-Day, 17 In. . . . 255.00
Junghans, Carriage, Cylinder Music Box Alarm, Embossed Brass Plate, 6 In. 190.00
Junghans, Elephant, Swing, Bronzed Spelter, Ormolu Frame, Germany, c.1910, 11 In. . . . 1705.00
Junghans, Elephant, Swinger, Germany, c.1910, 11 In. 1100.00
Junghans, Mantel, Bull Elephant, Swinger, Spelter, c.1920, 11 In. 635.00
Junghans, Onion Boy, Swinger, 30-Hour, Bronzed Spelter, c.1905, 15 3/4 In. 1980.00
Junghans, Plato, Digital, Blue Pages, Brass & Glass, Round, 4 1/2 In. 70.00
Just, Mantel, Boulle Style, Brass, Red Tortoiseshell, 8-Day, France, c.1915, 12 In. 1375.00
Just, Mantel, Boulle Style, Brass, Tortoiseshell Inlay, France, c.1910, 19 In. 1110.00
Kitchen, Gingerbread, Oak, 8-Day, Time & Strike, 24 In. 96.00
Kitchen, Gingerbread, Walnut, Paper Dial, Roman Numerals, 8-Day, 24 x 15 x 5 In. 170.00
Knox, A., Liberty, Pewter, Enamel, Celtic Style Knots, c.1905, 8 In. 3585.00
Knox, A., Liberty, Pewter, Enamel, Tree, c.1905, 7 3/4 In. 8365.00
Kroeber, Shelf, Walnut, 8-Day, Time & Strike, No. 54, New York, c.1875 . . . . 670.00
Lalique, R., Art Deco, Frosted Glass Frame, Birds, Branches, Sepia Patina, c.1924, 6 In. . . 5520.00
Lalique, R., Blue & White Art Deco Face, Opalescent Glass Frame, Birds, c.1926, 4 In. . . 1955.00
Leavenworth, 30-Hour, Carved Column & Splat, Fruit Basket Crest & Tablet, 20 In. 1915.00
Leavenworth, Mark, Mantel, Mahogany, Pillar & Scroll, 3 Brass Urn Finials, 31 x 16 In. . 3819.00
LeCoultre, Art Deco, Bronze, Alarm, Swiss, c.1930, 3 1/2 x 3 In. 30.00
LeCoultre, J., Desk, Gilt Brass, Date, Keyless Wind, Swiss, Box, c.1970, 1 1/2 x 5 In. 206.00
LeCoultre, Mantel, Atmos, Brass Bound, Glass Case, 9 1/4 x 8 1/4 x 6 1/2 In. 320.00
LeCoultre, Mantel, Atmos, Brass, Lacquered, Glass Panels, Swiss Works, 9 x 8 In. 250.00
LeCoultre, Mantel, Atmos, Perpetual, Brass, Glass, c.1950, 9 1/2 In. 460.00
Lepine, Carriage, Bronze, Grand Sonnerie, Engraved Panels, Signed, 7 In. . . . . *Illus* 2233.00
LeRoy, Carriage, Brass, Fluted, Engraved Face, Beveled Glass Panels, 4 3/8 In. 646.00
LeRoy, Carriage, Bronze, Half Strike, Push Repeater, Engraved, White Enamel Face, 7 In. 2115.00
Liberty, Desk, Tudric, Pewter, Stylized Leaves, Blue, Green Enameled Face, 8 x 5 1/2 In. . 5175.00
Liberty, Tudric, Pewter, Enamel, Tapered Square, Blue Dial, Flowers, 7 1/2 In. 3495.00
Lux, Art Nouveau, Brass, Pinched Waist Case, Cherub, Flowers, 5 1/8 In. 56.00

Lux, Cuckoo, Wall, Bobbing Bird, 6 In. 56.00
Lux, Smiley Face, Have A Nice Day, Yellow, Plastic, c.1970, 7 In. 10.00
Lux, Sundial, 3 1/2 In. 45.00
Lux, Windmill, 30-Hour, 10 In. 56.00
Lyre, 8-Day, Mahogany Veneer, Gilt Mountings, France, c.1860, 14 3/4 In. 2805.00
Lyre, Inverted Cornucopia, Bronze, Ormolu, France, c.1825, 21 1/4 In. 4950.00
Lyre, Ormolu, Winged Boy Sides, Trumpets, Gilding, France, c.1870, 23 In. 8250.00
Malet, Mantel, Gilt, Brass, George Washington Bust, France, c.1820, 18 1/2 x 8 In. 41825.00
Manross, Elisha, Steeple, Painted Eagle On Door, 20 In. 200.00
Mantel, 2 Leopards, Slate, Bronze, Arch, Roman Numerals, France, c.1875, 16 In. 1610.00
Mantel, 2-Train Movement, Bronze Medallion, Pendulum, Slate, France, c.1875, 9 In. . . . 460.00
Mantel, 8-Day, Gong, Enamel Dial, Roman Numerals, Slate, France, c.1900, 48 3/4 In. . . 440.00
Mantel, Apollo & Athena, Floral, Porcelain, Germany, c.1900, 17 In. 635.00
Mantel, Art Deco, Green Variegated Onyx, Geometric Shape, c.1925, 16 In. 90.00
Mantel, Art Deco, Onyx, Marble Verdigris Bronze Gazelles, Triangle Face, 13 x 21 In. . . 295.00
Mantel, Art Nouveau, Bronze Case, Westminster Chime, Germany, c.1900, 14 In. 1650.00
Mantel, Arts & Crafts, Overhang Cap, Tapered Posts, Round Face, 20 x 13 x 7 In. 518.00
Mantel, Bronze Dore Base, Reclining Children, Basket Top, Cobalt Porcelain Urn, 27 In. . 2520.00
Mantel, Bronze, Gilt, Patinated, Temple Shape, Aesthetic, Oriental, 15 In. 1765.00
Mantel, Bronze, Marble, Woman Studying Globe, Enamel Dial, 1810, 14 1/2 In. 3750.00
Mantel, Bronze, Rococo Style, Figural Heads, Claw Feet, c.1880, 16 x 11 In. 785.00
Mantel, Charles X, Maiden, Lyre, Putto, Ormolu, c.1825, 22 1/2 In. 2415.00
Mantel, Copper, 2-Train Movement, Roman Numerals, Slate, France, c.1880, 15 1/2 In. . . 1095.00
Mantel, Copper, Hammered, Obelisk, Embossed Trees, 4 Iron Supports, 11 1/2 x 6 1/2 In. 1035.00
Mantel, Dome Top, Etched Designs, Slate, France, c.1890, 11 x 8 3/4 x 5 1/8 In. 115.00
Mantel, Empire, Gilt Bronze, Eagle & Snake, France, 17 x 8 x 5 In. 1095.00
Mantel, Empire, Gilt, Bisque, Molded Mythology Scenes, 1800s, 25 x 13 1/2 In. 2150.00
Mantel, Empire, Veiled Maiden, Marble, Ormolu, c.1810, 29 1/2 In. 4830.00
Mantel, Federal, Mahogany, Colored Stenciling, Paw Feet, Bristol, Conn., 29 1/2 In. 770.00
Mantel, French Restoration, Gilt Bronze, Terpsichore, 21 x 13 1/2 In. 3450.00
Mantel, French, Rococo Scroll Decoration, Enameled Face, Patina, Pendulum, 12 1/2 In. . 275.00
Mantel, George III, Gilt Metal, Fruitwood Veneer, Early 19th Century, 15 3/4 In. 1076.00
Mantel, Gilt Bronze, 2 White Biscuit Groups, Flowers, Leaves, 18 x 16 3/4 x 5 1/2 In. . . . 2300.00
Mantel, Gilt Metal, 1-Train Movement, Fast/Slow Lever, Slate, France, c.1880, 12 1/4 In. . 200.00
Mantel, Girl Picking Flowers, Spelter, 8-Day, 2 Putti, Roman Numerals, c.1890, 24 In. . . . 575.00
Mantel, Girl With Flowers, Roman Numerals, 8-Day, Gilt Base, 14 In. 2070.00
Mantel, Lavender Marble, Impressed Numerals, Slate, France, c.1875, 12 1/2 In. 375.00
Mantel, Louis Philippe, Autumn Goddess, Cornucopia, Slate, Ormolu, c.1850, 25 In. 3220.00
Mantel, Louis Philippe, Gilt Bronze, Brass, c.1835, 21 3/4 x 18 1/2 In. 2300.00
Mantel, Louis Philippe, Man, Books, Children Frieze, Slate, Bronze, c.1850, 22 In. 1495.00
Mantel, Louis Philippe, Man, Trophy, Gilt Metal, c.1850, 12 1/2 In. 375.00
Mantel, Louis Philippe, Praying Woman, Shrine, Ormolu, c.1840, 19 1/2 In. 490.00
Mantel, Louis Philippe, Seated Woman, Bronze, Sienna Marble, c.1850, 21 In. 2530.00
Mantel, Louis Philippe, Serpent-Handled Urn, Marble, Ormolu, c.1850, 19 In. 1150.00
Mantel, Louis XV Style, 3 Putti, Ormolu, c.1875, 21 In. 2300.00
Mantel, Louis XV Style, Bronze, Gilt, Patinated, c.1890, 22 1/2 x 17 1/2 In. 4480.00
Mantel, Louis XV Style, Ormolu, 2-Train Movement, Cartouche, c.1900, 14 In. 1495.00
Mantel, Louis XV Style, Seated Man & Woman, Bronze, Ormolu, c.1850, 23 In. 4600.00
Mantel, Louis XV Style, Seated Officer, Globe, Ormolu, c.1880, 12 In. 750.00
Mantel, Louis XV Style, Woman, 3 Putti, Bronze, Ormolu, c.1850, 19 In. 3220.00
Mantel, Louis XV, Gilt Metal, Flowers, Monogram, c.1913, 8 1/2 In. 430.00
Mantel, Louis XVI Style, 2 Reclining Women, Bronze, Marble, Ormolu, c.1850, 16 In. . . . 2760.00
Mantel, Louis XVI Style, Gilt Bronze Mounted, Flaring Urn, Marble, France, 16 1/2 In. . . 1912.00
Mantel, Louis XVI Style, Gilt Bronze, Marble, Venus, Cupid, Plaque Of Putti Base, 13 In. 1765.00
Mantel, Louis XVI Style, Maiden, Ewer, Slate, Metal, Gong, c.1880, 24 In. 403.00
Mantel, Louis XVI Style, Marble Columns, Urn, Ormolu Mount, Floral Swags, 15 In. . . . 353.00
Mantel, Louis XVI, Gilt Bronze, Marble Base, 12 In. 470.00
Mantel, Marble, Greek Temple, Gilt Flowers, Slate, France, c.1880, 13 x 12 x 5 3/4 In. . . 115.00
Mantel, Marble, Griotte D'Italie, 2-Train Movement, France, c.1860, 15 In. 290.00
Mantel, Marble, Slate, 8-Day, Time & Strike, France, c.1885, 12 1/4 x 10 3/4 In. 420.00
Mantel, Mercury, Hand Painted, Porcelain, Gilded Bronze, France, c.1890, 14 In. 1106.00
Mantel, Miniature, Tall Case, Faience, Landscapes, Flowers, 8-Day, France, 12 1/2 In. . . . 310.00
Mantel, Mission, Oak, Miniature Tall-Case, Early 20th Century, 15 x 4 1/2 In. 70.00

Mantel, Napoleon III, 2 Soldiers, Throwing Dice, Bronze, Ormolu, c.1875, 20 In. 4370.00
Mantel, Napoleon III, Angel, Child, Marble, Bronze, c.1875, 21 1/2 In. 1150.00
Mantel, Napoleon III, Bronze Mounted, Black Slate, Marble, c.1865, 15 3/4 In. 405.00
Mantel, Napoleon III, Gilt Bronze, Marble, Cartouche Base, Twisted Columns, 21 In. 1645.00
Mantel, Napoleon III, Gilt, Patinated Bronze, Enamel, Classical Maidens, Marble, 21 In. . 1528.00
Mantel, Napoleon III, Goddess Diana, Marble, Bronze, c.1875, 37 3/4 In. 2300.00
Mantel, Napoleon III, Leaning Scholar, Bronze, Slate, Ormolu, c.1875, 22 In. 1265.00
Mantel, Napoleon III, Mother-Of-Pearl, Inlaid, Ebonized Wood, Mid 19th Century, 24 In. 316.00
Mantel, Napoleon III, Seated Woman, Spool Of Thread, Slate, Ormolu, c.1875, 26 In. . . . 2070.00
Mantel, Napoleon III, Slate, Ormolu, 2-Train Movement, c.1880, 19 In. 405.00
Mantel, Napoleon III, Woman, Child, Slate, Bronze, c.1875, 18 In. 1090.00
Mantel, New Hampshire Type, Brass Works, Reverse Painted Glass, 30 x 16 In. 1035.00
Mantel, Onyx, Champleve, Brass Housing, Columns, Urn Finial, 18 1/2 x 10 x 5 In. 980.00
Mantel, Ormolu Finish, Painted Cherubs, Shell, Leaves, 13 x 8 x 5 In. 230.00
Mantel, Porcelain, Ormolu, Hand Painted, Bell Strike, France, c.1880, 14 In. 770.00
Mantel, Portico, French Empire, Black Marble, Gilt Brass, Eagle Pendulum, 17 1/4 In. . . . 394.00
Mantel, Portico, Louis Philippe, Mahogany, c.1835, 22 1/2 x 10 1/2 In. 1265.00
Mantel, Red Marble, 2-Train Movement, Slate, France, c.1880, 8 1/2 In. 230.00
Mantel, Roman God Mercury, Urn, Faux Slate, Gilt Metal, c.1875, 18 In. 460.00
Mantel, Tucker No. 2, 30-Hour Lever, Iron Case, c.1874, 8 In. 230.00
Mantel, Vienna Porcelain, Bronze, Gilt, Dome Top, Allegorical Scene, 17 1/2 In. 3110.00
Mantel, Walnut Case, Brass, Mirrors, Key Wind, Conn., c.1887 . . . . 895.00
Mantel, Woman, Putti, Pink Marble, Gilt Metal, France, c.1875, 20 1/2 In. 430.00
Marti, Incised Slate, Angled Edges, Inward Curving Sides, Enamel Bezel, 16 In. 355.00
Marti, Regulator, Oval, Glass, Brass, Coiled Wire Gong, France, c.1910, 12 In. 666.00
Marti, Samuel, Regulator, 8-Day, Porcelain Floral Dial, Brass Case, 11 In. 290.00
Mastercrafters, Duke, Bulldog, Molded Composition, 110v, c.1955, 7 3/4 In. 585.00
Mathey-Tissot & Co., Silver Gilt, Jade Green Enamel, Rose Quartz Repeater, 3 1/4 In. 5580.00
Mauch, Konrad, Louvre, Dome, Porcelain Dial, 400-Day, c.1955, 15 1/2 In. 328.00
Movado, Alarm, Travel, Stainless Steel, Green Leather, 17 Jewel, c.1920 . . . . 294.00
Movado, Ermeto, Travel, Stainless Steel, Alligator, c.1920 . . . . 380.00
Mystery, Bronzed Spelter Statue, Marble Case, France, c.1890, 24 In. 4978.00
Mystery, Spelter, La Farandole, Bronzed, France, c.1890, 39 In. 7590.00
Mystery, Square Glass Dial, Round Base, c.1880, 14 In. 10230.00
Nelson, G., Enameled Metal, Spikes, Herman Miller 575.00
Nelson, G., Wall, Ball, Herman Miller, 1950s 550.00
Nelson, G., Wall, Brass, Birch, Herman Miller, 1950s, 13 In. 635.00
Nelson, G., Wall, Sunburst, Herman Miller 255.00
Nelson, G., Wall, Walnut, Enameled Metal, Herman Miller, 1950s, 30 In. 3105.00
New Haven Clock Co., Calendar, Oak, Double Dial, 30-Day, 48 In. 1610.00
New Haven Clock Co., Calendar, Octagon, Striking Bell, 24 In. 230.00
New Haven Clock Co., Empire Style, Brass, Twisted Glass Columns, c.1913, 8 1/4 In. 195.00
New Haven Clock Co., Mantel, Mission, Ebonized Oak, 8-Day, 13 3/4 x 11 3/4 x 5 1/2 In. 106.00
New Haven Clock Co., Regulator, Oak, 2-Panel Glass Door, Pendulum, 36 In. 115.00
New Haven Clock Co., Shelf, Cut Glass, Daisy & Button, Porcelain Dial, 8 In. 140.00
New Haven Clock Co., Wall, China, Plate Shape, Applied Butterfly, Flowers, 8 1/2 In. 84.00
Nicholls, Gallery, Octgaon, 8-Day Fusee, Rosewood Veneer, Brass Inlay, c.1830, 17 In. . . . 1485.00
Novelty, Oswald, Dog, Rolling Eye, 30-Hour, Back Windup, Germany, c.1930, 7 1/4 In. . . . 605.00
Parker, Alarm, Brass Plated Bell, 2 1/2 x 3 1/2 In. 345.00
Patek Philippe, Desk, Bronze, Solar Power, Square Corner Posts, 1900s, 5 x 5 1/2 In. 1295.00
Patek Philippe, Mantel, Art Deco, Stainless Steel, Solar Power, Corner Posts, 5 x 8 In. . . . 825.00
Planchon, Tabernacle, 8-Day, Gilt Brass, France, c.1890, 24 In. 2420.00
Poole, Mantel, Electromagnetic, Battery, Glass Dome, c.1920, 11 In. 115.00
Regulator, Crystal, Gilded, Multicolored Enamel, France, c.1900, 14 1/2 In. 2805.00
Regulator, Crystal, Time & Strike, France, 6 3/4 x 5 1/4 x 10 3/4 In. 290.00
Regulator, Grand Sonnerie, 3 Weights, Walnut Case, Angel, Austria, c.1895, 54 In. 3519.00
Regulator, Half-Strike, Pull Repeater, Brass Bezel, Classical Women, 3 Finials, 55 In. 380.00
Regulator, Jewelers, Mahogany, Burl Panels, Urn Finials, 84 In. 3450.00
Regulator, Pinwheel, 8-Day, Mahogany, Finial, Porcelain Dial, 15 x 56 In. 3900.00
Regulator, Porcelain Dial, Roman Numerals, 8-Day, 2 Weights, c.1890, 46 x 19 x 8 In. . . . 520.00
Regulator, Vienna, Enamel Dial, Pendulum Weights, 49 In. 575.00
Regulator, Vienna, Walnut Case, Carved, Time & Strike, Porcelain Dial, 1860s 2895.00
Regulator, Vienna, Walnut Case, Serpentine Style, White Porcelain Dial, 1860s 1495.00

Regulator, Walnut, 8-Day, Brass Dial, c.1880, Austria, 44 In. 230.00
Regulator, Walnut, 8-Day, Porcelain Dial, Roman Numerals, 2 Weights, c.1880, 46 In. . . . 430.00
Self Winding Clock Co., Gallery, Walnut, Bronze Numerals, Battery, 24 In. 1406.00
Sembrich, Calendar, Walnut, Wales, 39 x 15 In. 896.00
Sessions, Mantel, Oak, Time & Strike, Columns 90.00
Sessions, Regulator, Oak, Mission Style, 31 In. 175.00
Sessions, School, Oak, Late 19th Century, 27 1/2 In. 150.00
Sessions Clock Co., Calendar, Pressed Oak, Octagon Bezel, 33 In. 420.00
Seth Thomas, Art Deco, Semicircular, Onyx Mounted, Brass Bezel, Crystal, 5 x 6 1/2 In. . 95.00
Seth Thomas, Art Nouveau, Lily, Bronze Face, 8-Day, Time & Strike, 11 1/4 In. 338.00
Seth Thomas, Bird's-Eye Maple, Mahogany, Baltimore Cemetery Scene, 26 In. 259.00
Seth Thomas, Character, Bugs Bunny, Metal, Plastic, 1970, 2 7/8 x 4 In. 30.00
Seth Thomas, Chronometer, 8-Day Lever Movement, Bronze Case, c.1920, 10 1/2 In. . . . 1073.00
Seth Thomas, Cottage, Mahogany, 8-Sided Top, Flower Tablet, Alarm, 9 1/2 In. 169.00
Seth Thomas, Cottage, Rosewood, 30-Hour, Time & Strike, Painted Metal Dial 115.00
Seth Thomas, Double Decker, Rosewood Veneer Case, Painted, Gilt, 32 1/2 In. 575.00
Seth Thomas, Federal, Maple, Inlaid Mahogany, Pillar & Scroll, c.1820, 29 3/4 In. 460.00
Seth Thomas, Gallery, Time & Strike, Tin Dial, 18 In. 220.00
Seth Thomas, Mahogany, Rosewood, Hummingbirds, Ogee, Flat, 30-Hour, 16 In. 169.00
Seth Thomas, Mantel, 4-Chime Bell Sonora Chime, Oak, No. 12, c.1910, 17 In. 670.00
Seth Thomas, Mantel, 8-Day, Painted Dial, Wreath Tablet, Walnut Case, 17 In. 113.00
Seth Thomas, Mantel, Adamantine, 8-Day, Brass Dial, Chimes, c.1920, 13 In. 345.00
Seth Thomas, Mantel, Adamantine, Green, 8-Day, Time & Strike, c.1910, 11 1/4 In. 205.00
Seth Thomas, Mantel, Art Nouveau, Pagoda Top, Glass Sides, Flat Leaf Base, 14 In. 590.00
Seth Thomas, Mantel, Art Nouveau, Woman In Flowers, Gold Finish 405.00
Seth Thomas, Mantel, Berkeley, 8-Day, Time & Strike, c.1909, 11 1/2 In. 520.00
Seth Thomas, Mantel, Column, Time & Strike, 30-Hour, 8-Day, 25 In. 149.00
Seth Thomas, Mantel, Navarre, Art Deco, 8-Day, Time & Strike, c.1930, 10 3/4 In. 435.00
Seth Thomas, Mantel, Navy, Oak, 8-Day, Time & Strike, c.1897, 14 3/4 In. 265.00
Seth Thomas, Mantel, New Sucile, Adamantine, 8-Day, Time & Strike, c.1909, 12 In. . . . 330.00
Seth Thomas, Mantel, Rosewood, 8-Day, Roman Numerals, c.1850, 16 1/2 In. 170.00
Seth Thomas, Mantel, Sonora Chime, 8-Day, 5 Bells, Mahogany, c.1916, 14 1/4 In. 910.00
Seth Thomas, Mantel, Sonora, Beehive, Mahogany, 8-Day, Brass Dial, Chime, 14 In. 400.00
Seth Thomas, Mantel, Tiffany & Co., Roman & Arabic Numerals, c.1890, 25 x 13 x 6 In. 3910.00
Seth Thomas, Mantel, Triple Decker, Painted, Gilt Detail, 32 1/2 x 18 3/4 In. 220.00
Seth Thomas, Pillar & Scroll, Mahogany Veneer, Painted Wooden Dial, 29 1/2 In. 1265.00
Seth Thomas, Railroad, Square Case, Round Dial, 30-Day, Pendulum, 19 In. 300.00
Seth Thomas, Regulator, Beveled Edge Windows, Enamel Dial, 14 1/2 x 6 1/2 x 6 In. . . . 420.00
Seth Thomas, Regulator, Empire, 8-Day, Time & Strike, No. 301, c.1913, 9 1/2 In. 360.00
Seth Thomas, Regulator, Oak, 8-Day, Roman Numerals, Second Hand, c.1880, 42 In. 1150.00
Seth Thomas, Regulator, Oak, Round Top, 8-Day, Second Hand, 1-Weight, c.1880, 36 In. 1035.00
Seth Thomas, Regulator, Walnut, Nickel Plated Weight, No. 18, c.1910, 54 In. 5170.00
Seth Thomas, School, Brass Buttons, Girl, Boy Decal, Label, 16 In. 240.00
Seth Thomas, School, Key Hole, Lift Pendulum Door, 18 In. 150.00
Seth Thomas, School, Oak Case, 24 In. 145.00
Seth Thomas, Shelf, Glass, Tambour, Pink Daisy & Button, 8-Day, Porcelain Dial, 14 In. . 85.00
Seth Thomas, Shelf, Lincoln, Ash, 8-Day, 2-Weight, c.1886, 27 In. 2420.00
Seth Thomas, Shelf, Rosewood, 8-Day, Reverse Painted Bird On Branch, 15 x 12 In. 195.00
Seth Thomas, Sonora Chime, Mahogany, 2 Chimes, No. 261, c.1918, 13 1/4 In. 2310.00
Seth Thomas, Sonora Chime, Mahogany, No. 264, c.1915, 14 In. 2739.00
Seth Thomas, Steeple, Pine Case, 8-Day, Time & Strike, Plainville, c.1970, 22 1/4 In. . . . 80.00
Seth Thomas, Wardroom, Ship's Bell, Round Oak Case, 8 5/8 In. 620.00
Shelf, Ansonia, Mahogany, Veneer, Ogee, Mid 19th Century, 26 x 15 1/2 In. 75.00
Shelf, Art Nouveau, Gunmetal Case, Rhinestones, Porcelain Dial, 3 1/8 In. 28.00
Shelf, Brass & Enamel Dial, Roman Numerals, Cherub Finial, Continental, 1800s, 24 In. . 1120.00
Shelf, Cottage, Double Dial, Walnut, 22 In. 920.00
Shelf, Eglomise, Panel, Landscape, Eagle On Cannons, c.1820, 34 In. 1150.00
Shelf, French Empire, Dore Bronze, Gilt Eagle, Pillars, 1810-1820, 16 In. 2200.00
Shelf, Mahogany, Garland, Starburst Spandrels, Landscape, c.1840, 33 In. 259.00
Shelf, Walnut Case, Bracket, Roman Numberals, c.1890, 15 1/4 x 4 3/4 x 24 1/4 In. 290.00
Shelf, Walnut, 8-Day, Roman Numerals, Mercury Pendulum, c.1890, 23 x 15 x 5 In. 115.00
Shelf, Walnut, 8-Day, Roman Numerals, Minerva Head Crest, c.1880, 23 x 14 x 5 In. 170.00
Ship's, Chelsea, Strike, Brass, Wood Base, 14 x 9 1/2 In. 350.00

Ship's, Quarter Deck, Automata, Bronze, Silver Case, Bayard, France, c.1890, 12 In. 7370.00
Ship's, Smith's, Brass, Convex Glass, Spherical, Pocket-Watch Shape, 4 1/4 x 5 In. 200.00
Skeleton, 1-Train Fusee, Marble Base, Roman Numerals, 1800s, England, 16 In. 460.00
Skeleton, Nickel Plated, Beveled Glass, France, 1885, 21 In. 770.00
Skeleton, Walnut Base, Dome, Single-Chain Fusee, England, c.1850, 11 In. 1595.00
Smith, Animated, Noddy, Alarm, 5 In. 39.00
Smith & Goodrich, Buckingham Palace, Ogee, 30-Hour, Alarm, 15 1/4 In. 395.00
Tall Case, Ansonia, Brass Mounts, Weights, 8-Day, Time & Strike, 90 In. 6200.00
Tall Case, Arts & Crafts, Staircase, Pyramid Posts, Crossgate, 78 1/4 x 18 x 15 In. 805.00
Tall Case, Arts & Crafts, Weight Driven, Brass Face, Glass Door, 21 x 14 x 69 In. 750.00
Tall Case, Birch, Butternut, Bracket Feet, Scalloped Apron, Tombstone Door, 87 1/2 In. . .   2200.00
Tall Case, Birch, Crotch Bonnet, Brass Finials, Brass Mounts, 85 x 19 x 10 In. 3520.00
Tall Case, Cherry, Flowers, American, c.1800, 86 In. 865.00
Tall Case, Chippendale, Cherry, Flat Top, Turned Columns, 30-Hour, 88 1/2 In. 2475.00
Tall Case, Chippendale, Walnut, Carved, Glazed Tombstone Door, c.1780, 86 In. 6465.00
Tall Case, Colonial Manufacturing Co., Mission, 29 x 18 x 83 In. 1265.00
Tall Case, Derry Manufacturing, Federal, c.1910, 51 In. 4400.00
Tall Case, Elm, Brass Face, Works, Engraved Landscape, Calendar Dial, 82 1/2 In. 1380.00
Tall Case, Federal, Inlaid, Cherry, Connecticut, c.1800, 89 x 21 In. 7800.00
Tall Case, Federal, Walnut, Broken Scroll, c.1800, 95 x 21 In. 4370.00
Tall Case, Frederick Heisley, Walnut, No Pendulum, 82 In. 2750.00
Tall Case, Gazo Clock Co., San Diegan, 86 In. 1725.00
Tall Case, George III Style, Mahogany, Brass Dial, Moon Phase, c.1950, 93 In. 1265.00
Tall Case, George III Style, Mahogany, Satinwood Inlay, Roman Numerals, c.1890, 87 In.   3220.00
Tall Case, George III Style, Stained Pine, John Simock, 19th Century, 74 1/2 In. 805.00
Tall Case, George III, Elm & Fruitwood, Inlaid, E. Smith, c.1800 . . . .   3750.00
Tall Case, George III, Mahogany Inlay, 8-Day Movement, 79 x 18 7/16 x 11 In. 14340.00
Tall Case, George III, Mahogany Inlay, Edinburgh, Scotland, 1760 . . . .   2475.00
Tall Case, George III, Mahogany Inlay, Swan's Neck, Painted Dial, 19th Century, 90 In. . .   1600.00
Tall Case, George III, Mahogany, 8-Day, 2-Train Strike, Pagoda Top, 90 x 20 In. 4780.00
Tall Case, George III, Mahogany, Banded Oak, 8-Day, Scroll Top, 89 x 23 x 9 In. 2645.00
Tall Case, George III, Mahogany, Brass Mounted, Late 18th Century, 91 In. 4830.00
Tall Case, George III, Oak, Inlay, Brass Dial, Chapter Ring, c.1790, 79 1/2 In. 1150.00
Tall Case, Georgian Style, Ebonized, Painted Flower Sprays, 77 In. 1410.00
Tall Case, Georgian, Mahogany, Marquetry, James Coates Wigan, 90 x 24 x 10 In. 4600.00
Tall Case, Georgian, Walnut, Inlaid, Swan's-Neck Crest, Painted Face, Gothic Door, 89 In.   1410.00
Tall Case, Gothic, Mahogany, Bonnet Top, 3-Weight, Westminster Chime, 93 In. 2800.00
Tall Case, Henry Wismer, Broken Arch, Carved Rosettes, Iron Dial, Plumstead, Pa., 95 In.   5875.00
Tall Case, Hepplewhite, Mahogany, 4 Seasons On Face, Jas. Black, Kirkaldy, 88 In. 2475.00
Tall Case, Hepplewhite, Mahogany, Poplar, Pine, Man-In-The-Moon, 91 1/2 In. 6325.00
Tall Case, Hepplewhite, Scottish, Inlay, Pine, Bird's-Eye Maple Veneer, 89 1/2 In. 4400.00
Tall Case, Herschede, Mahogany, 5-Tube, 3-Train Movement, No. 314, c.1930, 78 In. 3300.00
Tall Case, Herschede, Mahogany, 9-Tube, No. 86, c.1925, 92 In.   5500.00
Tall Case, Herschede, Sheffield, 9-Tube, No. 230, 1969, 86 x 24 In. 5000.00
Tall Case, J.C. Jennens & Sons, Mahogany, Marquetry, England, c.1780, 95 In. 6900.00
Tall Case, Jacob Hendel, Federal, Walnut, Pennsylvania, c.1800, 92 1/2 x 21 x 11 In. 14340.00
Tall Case, Jacob Hoff, Federal, Painted, Urn Finials, Arched Glazed Door, c.1815, 96 In. .   16730.00
Tall Case, Jacobean Style, Oak, Ebonized, Roman & Arabic, Brass Dial, c.1890, 94 In. . . .   1380.00
Tall Case, Leeming, Mahogany, Painted Face, 30-Hour, 69 x 20 In. 1610.00
Tall Case, Louis Philippe, Cherry, Scalloped Carving, c.1835, 101 x 21 In. 2990.00
Tall Case, Louis XV, Cherry, Paneled Door, c.1885, 94 x 17 1/2 In. 2070.00
Tall Case, Louis XV, Walnut, Oak, Carved, Enameled Dial, Signed, 95 x 18 x 10 In. 1060.00
Tall Case, Louis XVI Style, Red Tortoiseshell, France, c.1880, 17 3/4 In. 2970.00
Tall Case, Luman Watson, Cherry, 30-Hour Bell Strike, 19th Century, 92 1/2 In. 4805.00
Tall Case, Mahogany, 6-Tube, Chime, Strike, Providence, 101 In. 4140.00
Tall Case, Mahogany, Brass, Decorated Face, Shells, Second Hand, 93 In. 1035.00
Tall Case, Mahogany, Carved Columns, Masonic Symbols, Painted Arched Dial, 100 In. . .   1915.00
Tall Case, Mahogany, Flame Veneer, Brass Face, Cherubs, Crown, Calendar Dial, 92 In. . .   1045.00
Tall Case, Mahogany, Inlaid Conch Shell, Chinoiserie Panels, 8-Day, Moon Phases, 94 In.   7475.00
Tall Case, Mahogany, Moon Face Dial, Brass Movement, c.1810, 105 x 20 x 11 In. 3290.00
Tall Case, Mahogany, Shaped Cornice, Inlaid Frieze, Tapered Columns, 86 In. 2420.00
Tall Case, Mason & Hamlin, Chippendale, Mahogany, Swan's-Neck Crest, Moon Phases .   2940.00
Tall Case, Matlack, White, Chippendale, Mahogany, N.Y., c.1770, 92 3/4 x 20 x 9 In. 14340.00

Tall Case, Nathan Howell, Sarcophagus Top, Mahogany, 8-Day, New Haven, 95 In. 4725.00
Tall Case, Nathaniel Mulliken, Walnut, Arched Molding, Brass Dial, Bracket Feet, 87 In. .   7640.00
Tall Case, Nathaniel Munroe, Mahogany, Pierced Fretwork, Iron Dial, c.1810, 93 In. 5290.00
Tall Case, Oak, Broken Arch Bonnet, Paneled Door, 81 In. 1265.00
Tall Case, Oak, Carved, Brass Dial, Flat Reeded Columns, 78 In. 345.00
Tall Case, Painted, Yellow, Brown, Hudson River Scene, Lion, c.1820 . . . .   7900.00
Tall Case, Peter Brown Birmingham, Chinoiserie, Brass-Faced Works, 1725, 90 In. . . .   5175.00
Tall Case, Pine, Fluted Columns, Painted Face, 19th Century, 90 In. 1700.00
Tall Case, Pine, Red Over Yellow Grain, Line Inlay, Decorated, 82 1/2 In. 2475.00
Tall Case, Queen Anne Style, Custom Case, Window Front, 84 3/4 In. 230.00
Tall Case, Richard Rayment, Painted Dial, 30-Hour Brass Movement, Bury St. Edmunds .   2300.00
Tall Case, Rococo, Burl Walnut, Brass Dial, Date & Month, c.1850, 108 In. 3910.00
Tall Case, S. Hoadley, Mixed Wood, Arch Bonnet Top, Early 19th Century 1725.00
Tall Case, Samuel Higginson, Ahogany, 8-Day, Gilded Brass Dial, Calendar Dial, 70 In. . .   5625.00
Tall Case, Schreiner, Chippendale, Mahogany, No. 137, 94 1/2 In. 20900.00
Tall Case, Selfridge & Co., Oak, Arched Pediment, Divided Glazed Panel Door, 77 In. . . .   290.00
Tall Case, Seth Thomas, Tombstone, Eagle, War Trophies, 88 x 17 1/2 x 10 3/4 In. 2530.00
Tall Case, Silas Hoadley, 3 Plinths, Pierced Fretwork, Urn Finials, Arched Cornice, 89 In.   8815.00
Tall Case, Smith, George III, Elm, Fruitwood, Pierced Geometrics, 1800, 20 x 10 In. 2075.00
Tall Case, W. & G. Hutchinson, Mahogany, Changing Moon Dial, New Brunswick, 95 In.   2875.00
Tall Case, Walnut, 8-Day, Painted Moon Phase Dial, Fretwork Case, 100 In. 5850.00
Tall Case, Walnut, Beechwood, Banjo Shape, Scandinavia, 19th Century, 82 x 18 1/2 In. .   1175.00
Tall Case, Walter Durfee, 9-Tube, Mahogany, Arch Bonnet, J.E. Caldwell & Co., 96 In. . .   1700.00
Tall Case, William Cummens, Federal, Mahogany Inlay, Boston, c.1800, 91 In. 16450.00
Tall Case, Wooden Works, Painted Dial, Village Scene, Acorn Finials, 87 In. 4025.00
Telechron, Art Deco, Plexiglas Base, Smoke Mirror Face, c.1938, 6 1/2 x 12 In. 265.00
Terry, 30-Hour, Iron Case, c.1875, 8 1/4 In. 210.00
Terry, Silas, Cottage, Mahogany, 30-Hour, Ladder Movement, 10 1/2 In. 340.00
Terry & Andrews, Beehive, 8-Day, Brass Spring, Mahogany, Painted Dial, 19 In. 340.00
Terry & Andrews, Steeple, 30-Hour Brass Spring, Mahogany, Frosted Bluebirds, 20 In. . .   310.00
Tiffany clocks that are part of desk sets made by Louis Comfort Tiffany are listed in the
Tiffany category. Clocks sold by the store, Tiffany & Co., are listed here.
Tiffany & Co., Mantel, Enamel & Gilt Bronze, 19th Century, 18 1/2 In. 4780.00
Tiffany & Co., Regulator, Crystal, Brass, Pendulum Dial, 11 1/2 x 7 1/2 x 5 1/2 In. 805.00
Tiffany Electric Co., Regulator, Never Wind, Crystal, Battery, 9 1/2 In. 235.00
Time, Employee, Oak Case, c.1908, 67 In. 290.00
Tobey & Waltham, Tall Case, 9-Tube, Mahogany Veneer, Broken Arch, c.1905, 97 In. . . .   8745.00
Trend, Mantel, Westminster Chime, 8-Day, Time & Strike, c.1973, 18 1/4 In. 220.00
United Clock Corp., Guitar Shape, Spelter Case, Thermometer, 18 1/2 In. 160.00
Vincenti & Cie., Empire Style, Ormolu Mounted, Mahogany, Late 19th Century, 14 3/4 In.   690.00
Vitra, Orange Face, Balls, Black Hands, G. Nelson 155.00
Von Schierholz, Mantel, Couple, Porcelain, Cartouche, c.1885, 18 In. 690.00
Wall, Champleve Enamel, Onyx, Dial Set In Beveled Case, Love Birds, 21 1/2 In. 1315.00
Wall, Dutch Baroque Style, Birds, Landscape, Roman Numerals, Gilt Mask, 22 In. 175.00
Wall, Enamel, Gold Leaf, Music Box, Austria, 19th Century, 27 x 20 1/2 x 6 In. 3450.00
Wall, Gilt Bronze, Patinated Metal, Empire Style, Round, Bird Heads, 14 In. 1530.00
Wall, Louis XVI Style, Ormolu, Enamel Dial, Bell, Late 19th Century, 26 In. 1495.00
Wall, Owl, Eyes Move As Pendulum Swings, Wood, Carved, Metal Dial, 16 1/2 In. 160.00
Wall, Porcelain Dial, Gold Gilt, Gessoed Frame, Continental, 14 1/4 x 17 1/2 In. 205.00
Wall, Renaissance Revival, Walnut, Winged Griffins, Magazine Rack, 21 x 16 In. 670.00
Wall, Swiss Chalet, Brass Pendulum, Wood Front, Hand Painted, Germany, c.1950, 5 In. . .   29.00
Wall, Walnut, Grand Sonniere, 3-Weight, Square Dial, Austrian, c.1900, 49 In. 2200.00
Wall, Walnut, Grand Sonniere, Second Baroque, 3-Weight, Austrian, c.1885, 49 In. 3430.00
Wallace & Tiernan, Wall, Walnut, Brass Movement, See-Through Dial, Electric, 62 In. . . .   705.00
Waltham, Bracket, Brass, Gas Illuminated, Leather Case, Early 20th Century, 5 In. 410.00
Waltham, Gaslight, 30-Hour, Milk Glass, Gas Jet Mount, c.1910, 5 1/2 In. 480.00
Waltham, Regulator, Jeweler's, Walnut, Circular Face, Second Hand, 30-Day, 39 1/2 In. . .   770.00
Waterbury, Calendar, Octagon, Rosewood Veneer Case, 21 1/2 In. 178.00
Waterbury, Calendar, Peru, Walnut, Figure 8, Peru, Ill., 21 1/2 In. 896.00
Waterbury, Calendar, Rosewood Veneer Case, Pendulum, 24 In.   175.00
Waterbury, Carriage, Brass, Arched Top, Handle, 8-Day, Gong Strike 56.00
Waterbury, Carriage, Sage, Brass, Beveled Glass, Porcelain Dial, Alarm, 4 1/4 In. 215.00
Waterbury, Mantel, Falconer & Bird, Gilt Brass, Copper, Gong, c.1900, 24 In. 290.00

Waterbury, Mantel, Oak Case, Vine, c.1893, 16 In. 226.00
Waterbury, Mantel, Rosewood, Ogee, 19th Century 11 1/2 x 4 x 17 1/2 In. 175.00
Waterbury, Regulator, Pressed Oak, Decorated Window, 37 In. 173.00
Waterbury, School, Mahogany Case, 11 In. 86.00
Waterbury, School, Mahogany Case, Key Wind Holes, 19 In. 120.00
Waterbury, School, Oak Case, 8-Day, c.1914, 9 In. 330.00
Waterbury, Wall, Library, Mahogany Case, Carved, Finial, 17 x 44 In. 4100.00
Welch, E.N., Beehive, Mahogany, Scenic Transfer Tablet, 8-Day, Time & Strike, 21 In. ... 145.00
Welch, E.N., Gingerbread, Walnut, 8-Day, Silk Screened Knights In Armor, 24 In. 146.00
Welch, Little Grip, Suitcase, Bronzed Metal, Handle, 3 In. 395.00
Welch, Lucca, 8-Day, Walnut, Cast Pendulum, Sandwich Glass Insert, 23 In. 675.00
Welch, Wall, School, Verdi, Rosewood Case, 8-Day, Time & Strike, c.1885, 31 In. 1705.00
Whistler, Peddler, Clock Under Arm, Wood, Germany, 13 1/2 In. 1155.00
Whittington & Cambridge, Bracket, Mahogany, 8-Day, 3-Fusee, c.1890, 22 1/2 In. 6270.00
Willard, Aaron, Shelf, Downswept Cornice, Painted Dial, Boston, 1810-1820, 30 1/2 In. . 11950.00
Willard, Aaron, Shelf, Sailboat, Pink Sky, Painted, Stenciled Eglomise, 34 x 13 In. 4780.00
Wright, Thomas, George III, Mahogany, Bracket, c.1790, 22 1/4 In. 3585.00
Yale, Cast Iron Case, Mother-Of-Pearl Inlay, Pendulum, 4 1/4 In. 190.00

CLOISONNE enamel was developed during the tenth century. A glass
enamel was applied between small ribbons of metal on a metal
base. Most cloisonne is Chinese or Japanese. Pieces marked *China* are
twentieth-century examples.

Basin, Dragons, Pearls, Plants, Chinese, 19th Century, 30 In. 705.00
Bowl, Carp Swimming, Blue Sea, Shotai, 2 x 3 In. 100.00
Bowl, Enamel, Dragon, Polychrome, Green Ground, c.1912, 19 1/2 In. 545.00
Bowl, Flowers, Blue Ground, 4 3/8 In., Pair 460.00
Bowl, Prunus & Bird, 20th Century, 8 1/4 In. 80.00
Box, Bird, Butterfly, Flowers, Round, Japan, 9 1/2 In. 865.00
Box, Enamel, Flowers, Blue Ground, c.1900, 4 In. 46.00
Box, Enamel, Lift Top, Flowers, White Ground, 4 1/2 In. 175.00
Box, Oval, Flowers, Brass Stand, Russia, 1 3/4 In. 999.00
Cachepot, Gilt Metal Mounted, Blue, Elephant Head Handles, 5 7/16 x 9 In., Pair 7170.00
Candlestick, Brass, Bird & Flower, Blue Ground, 20th Century, 8 1/2 In. 69.00
Charger, Butterflies, Exotic Birds, Flowers, White Field, Japan, 18 In. 430.00
Charger, Enamel, Fuku Mark, Blue Fishscale Ground, c.1926, 17 7/8 In. 490.00
Charger, Leaves, Dragon, Brocade, Japan, Meiji, 23 3/4 In. 940.00
Egg Stand, Silver Gilt, Floral Enamel, 4 1/2 In. 1765.00
Figure, Horse, Gilt Bronze, Phoenixes, Scrolled Florals, 20th Century, 21 In. 405.00
Incense Burner, Flowers, Brocade, Goldtone Ground, Japan, Meiji, 7 1/2 x 8 1/2 In. 175.00
Incense Burner, Flowers, Butterflies, 3 Legs, Goldstone Ground, Japan, c.1925, 6 In. 1610.00
Incense Burner, Turquoise, Bird Shape, Scroll, Chinese, Qing Dynasty, 8 3/4 In., Pair ... 405.00
Jar, Cover, Butterfly & Flowers, 3 5/8 In. 175.00
Jar, Cover, Geese, Grasses, Fruit, Flowers, Japan, 19th Century, 13 In. 765.00
Jar, Cover, Peony, White Ground, Marked, China, c.1900, 9 1/2 In. 60.00
Jardiniere, Bronze, Design Bands, Yellow, Blue, Geometric, 13 x 10 In. 220.00
Jardiniere, Stand, Gilt Bronze Mounted, Bulbous, Dragon Handles, 43 In. 11355.00
Koro, Cover, Egg Shape, Gold Landscape, Brown Ground, 3-Footed, Signed, 5 1/2 In. ... 13800.00
Matchbox, Silver Gilt, Enamel, Moscow Hallmark, c.1900, 2 1/4 In. 345.00
Plate, 2 Fish, Dark Blue Ground, 7 1/8 In. 80.00
Plate, Multi-Carpet, Inlaid, Gold Stone On Black Ground, 8 3/8 In. 130.00
Teapot, Coin, Black Ground, 19th Century, 7 In. 105.00
Vase, 5-Claw Yellow Dragon, Black Ground, 20th Century, 10 In., Pair 230.00
Vase, Baluster, Dragon, Green, Brown, Black, Brocade, Signed, 5 7/8 In. 2300.00
Vase, Baluster, Phoenix, Blue, Black Ground, Adachi, 12 1/2 In. 430.00
Vase, Bird & Flowers, Red Foil Ground, 6 Sides, 3 3/4 In. 115.00
Vase, Bird, Plum Tree, Bamboo, Chrysanthemum, Japan, 9 In. 575.00
Vase, Birds On Bamboo, Blue Ground, Ando Jubei, Signed, Japan, 5 In. 1150.00
Vase, Bronze, Geometric, Animal Heads, 3 Bands, Stylized Flowers, 7 In. 55.00
Vase, Bronze, Geometric, Stylized Flowers, Turquoise Ground, 20th Century, 16 In. 230.00
Vase, Butterfly, Peonies, Blue Ground, Cylindrical, Tapered, c.1894, 18 1/8 In. 865.00
Vase, Crane, Iris, Blue Ground, 4 1/2 In. 380.00
Vase, Dragon, Black Figured Ground, Geometric & Floral Neck, 7 1/2 In., Pair 115.00

Vase, Firefly, Blue Ground, Kiriwood Box, Kumeno Teitaru, Box, 7 In. 230.00
Vase, Fish, Fantail, Red & Green Foil Ground, 4 5/8 In. 318.00
Vase, Fish, On Green, Egg Shape, Japan, 6 1/2 In. 1765.00
Vase, Flowers, Aventurine Black & Brown Ground, 5 In. 65.00
Vase, Flowers, Blue Ground, Marked, c.1900, 9 1/2 In. 80.00
Vase, Flowers, Goldstone Ground, Trumpet Mouth, Hexagonal, Japan, 10 In. 380.00
Vase, Flowers, Wooden, Pear Shape, 20th Century, 3 5/8 In. 150.00
Vase, Flying Cranes, Landscape, Leaves, Flowers, Oval, Chinese, 12 1/2 In., Pair 529.00
Vase, Foiled Ground, Forest Green, Flowers, Butterflies, 7 1/4 In. 226.00
Vase, Goldfish, Water Plants, Leaves, Lotus, Bottle Form, Japan, 19th Century, 13 1/2 In. . .   410.00
Vase, Inverted Pear Shape, Hydrangeas, Black Ground, Silver, Marked, 9 3/4 In. 2185.00
Vase, Inverted Pear Shape, Peony, Wisteria, Blue Ground, 12 In. 980.00
Vase, Iris, Oval, Red Ground, Japan, 24 In. 2300.00
Vase, Lowers, Square, Round Corners, Black Ground, Japan, Meiji, 29 1/2 In. 940.00
Vase, Medallions, Black Ground, Kyoto, Japan, 19th Century, 6 1/4 In. 295.00
Vase, Passion Flower, Blue Ground, c.1900, 6 1/2 In., Pair 58.00
Vase, Peacocks, Flowers, Elephant Handles, Chinese, 20th Century, 15 In., Pair 382.00
Vase, Peony, Blue, White, Rust Red Ground, 20th Century, 8 1/4 In. 35.00
Vase, Phoenix & Flowers, Baluster, 6 In., Pair 130.00
Vase, Prunus, Yellow Ground, Marked Ando, 20th Century, 7 In. 185.00
Vase, Reserves Enclosing Birds, Butterflies, Flower Branches, Japan, 10 In., Pair 978.00
Vase, Silver Wire, 3 Clawed Dragons, Navy Ground, Japan, c.1920, 5 In. 375.00
Vase, Silver Wire, Celadon Ground, 6 Fish, Signed, Japan, c.1920, 14 1/2 In. 6038.00
Vase, Silver Wire, Dragons, Bottle Shape, Black Ground, Japan, c.1925, 10 1/4 In. 575.00
Vase, Silver Wire, Flowers, Birds, Dark Blue Ground, Japan, Kumeno, c.1925, 10 In. 2990.00
Vase, Stick, Exotic Birds, Dragons, Blue Foil Ground, Signed, 4 3/4 In. 175.00
Vase, White Egrets, Leaves, Irises, Royal Blue Field, Chinese, 24 In., Pair 2185.00
Vase, White Iris, Pink Center, Green Ground, Thin Silver Wires, A. Jubei, 8 In., Pair 635.00
Wine Pot, Butterfly, Flower, Pear Shape, 3 1/2 In. 69.00

CLOTHING of all types is listed in this category. Dresses, hats, shoes,
underwear, and more are found here. Other textiles are to be found in
the Coverlet, Movie, Quilt, Textile, and World War I and II categories.

Belt, Buckle, Gold Colored, Faceted White Jewel, 3 3/8 In. 11.00
Belt, Gold Braid, Emerald, Amethyst, Cobalt Stones, Kenneth Jay Lane 1200.00
Belt, Marcasite, Imitation, Adjustable Link, 1920s, 48 1/4 x 5/8 In. 75.00
Belt, Stretch Fabric, Red, White, Blue, Doves, Metal Buckle, Peter Max, 1970, Size 10 . .   255.00
Beret, British Royal Irish Ranger, Badge, 1980s, Size 8 . . . .   35.00
Beret, Selous Scouts, Brown, Badge, Rhodesia, 1970s, Size 7 1/4 In. 76.00
Blouse, 100% Wool, Beaded, Iridescent Sequins, Light Blue, Faux Pearl Accents, Small . .   95.00
Blouse, Striped, Orange, Yellow, White, Back Zipper, 1960s, Large 11.00
Bonnet, Gordon Highlander, Wool, Badge, Checkered Band, Scotland, 1980s, 7 1/4 In. . . .   52.00
Bonnet, Mourning, Silk, Black, Feather & Chin Ties, Lined, Mid 1800s 175.00
Boots, Cowboy, Acme, Brown Pebbled Leather, White Stitching, c.1967, Size 6 1/2 C . . .   36.00
Bra, Lace, Pink, Solid Back Strap, National Recovery Act Label, 1930s, Size 38 . . . .   52.00
Cap, Visor, Army, Cavalry Officer, Yellow Band, Metal Slide, Vietnam, Size 7 1/8 . . . . . .   56.00
Cape, Wool, Blue, Kashmir Style, Embroidered, Gold Thread, Flowers, Sleeveless, 23 In. .   618.00
Chasuble, Brocade, Silver, Flowers, Cream Ground, 19th Century 288.00
Chemise, Silk, Blue, Equestrians, Horses, Hermes, Size 40 . . . .   235.00
Coat, Mink, Dyed Frosted, Chloe, Full-Length, Small 100.00
Coat, Mink, Ranch, Female, Black, Ankle Length, Tags, Michael Kors, Size 8 . . . .   5523.00
Coat, Mink, Red Sheared, Gathered Sleeves, Christie Brothers, Size 8 . . . .   1763.00
Coat, Pop Art, Pointed Lapel, Pearlized Front Snaps, Sash Belt, 1960s, Size 14 . . . .   45.00
Coat, Rabbit, Full-Length, Man's, Size 42 . . . .   100.00
Coat, Summer, Embroidered, Dragons, Flaming Pearls, Cloud Scrolls, Blue, Chinese 635.00
Coat, Swing, Faux Leopard, 3/4-Length Sleeves, 1950s, Size 8 . . . .   95.00
Coat, Wool, Dark Blue, Christ's Church School, England, Mid 19th Century, Girl's 195.00
Coat, Wool, Pendleton, Zane Grey's 881.00
Coat Dress, Wrap, Double Breasted, Black, 1950s, Medium 99.00
Collar, Lace, Crocheted, Pale Ecru, c.1910, 17 x 4 In. 20.00
Corset, Linen, Lace, White, R. Warner Coraline Health, Clasp, 1881, Large 510.00
Dress, Black Roses, Rose Buds, White Ground, Pouffe Skirt, Bow, Back Zipper, 1950s . . .   99.00
Dress, Black, Square Neckline, Rhinestones, Raised Stitching, Belt, 1950s, Medium 99.00

Dress, Bolero Jacket, Cotton, Side Buttons, Florida Fashion, 1940s, Large 99.00
Dress, Coat, Bonnet, Christening, Satin, Lace Flowers, Scalloped Edges 100.00
Dress, Cocktail, Green, 1960s, Medium 95.00
Dress, Cocktail, Polyester, Netting, Sweetheart Neckline Stacked Skirt, Sleeves 100.00
Dress, Cotton, Edwardian, White 95.00
Dress, Polished Cotton, Cap Sleeves, Belt, Hordmausen-Harz Label, 1940s, Large 99.00
Dress, Raglan Sleeves, English Lawn Cotton, c.1910, Child's 325.00
Dress, Rayon, Beige, Heart Shapes, Front Buttons, Doris Dodson Original, 1940s, Small . 98.00
Dress, Red Paisley Print, Long Sleeve, 1800s, Woman's 210.00
Dress, Red, Stiff Pockets, Collar, Rhinestone Button Accents, 1950s, Medium 98.00
Dress, Sheath, Crepe, Navy, Rhinestone Buttons, Eisenberg, c.1950, Medium-Large 99.00
Dress, Summer, Cotton, Bolero Jacket, Side Metal Closure, 1940s 100.00
Dress, Summer, Navy Blue Eyelet, Embroidered, Cuffed Sleeves, Belt, 1940, Size 14 . . . . 46.00
Dress, Waist, Blue, White, Victorian, Small 45.00
Dress, Wedding, Ecru, Lace Work, Train, Ribbon 409.00
Dress, White Muslin Cotton, Lace Embroidery, Tassels, Edwardian, Medium 100.00
Dress, Wrap, Chiffon Over Rayon, 1950s, Medium 99.00
Dress & Cape Ensemble, Wool Blend, Red Plaid, High Collar, Back Zipper, c.1970 . . . . . 100.00
Dress & Jacket, Suede, Leather Trim, Lord & Taylor, Size 8 . . . . 25.00
Gloves, Leather, Dark Brown Stitching, BACMO Stamp, 1800s, Toddler's 35.00
Hat, Boater, Straw, Woven, Empire State Hats, Man's 95.00
Hat, Bonnet, Jet Beading, 19th Century 95.00
Hat, Cowboy, Satin Band, Humorous, 7 3/8 In. 160.00
Hat, Faux Leopard, Bow Design, Black Lining, 1940s 45.00
Hat, Feathers, Ostrich, Pheasant, Edwardian 100.00
Hat, Felt, Rust, Gold Brocade, Side Large Covered Buttons, Back Brocade Drape, 1920s . 100.00
Hat, Flop, Velvet, Black, 3-In. Floppy Brim, Satin Bow, Lined, 1940s 45.00
Hat, Naval, 1-Piece Formed Jack Leather, Revolutionary War, 14 In. 7000.00
Hat, Silk, Beaver, Fitted Brass Mounted Leather Case, Dun & Company 325.00
Hat, Sombrero, Leather Hatband, Mexico, 1940, 18 1/2 In. 176.00
Hat, Wedding, Satin, Lace, Wide Brim, Victorian Style 45.00
Hat, Wool Felt, Gray, Feather, 1950s 10.00
Hat, Yellow Cab, Lancaster Brand, Size 7 1/2, 10 In. 143.00
Hat, Zane Grey's, Signature On Brim 3231.00
Jacket, Army AAF EM Type B-14 Flight, Patches, American, Size 40 . . . . 390.00
Jacket, Arrowhead Sportsmen's Club, Oak Lawn, Ill., Poplin, Patches, 1960s 30.00
Jacket, Baseball, Wool, Leather, Knit Collar & Cuffs, Blue, A's Logo, Box, 1960s, Size 38 53.00
Jacket, Denim, Big E, Indigo Blue, Button Front, Waist-Length, Levi's, Size 38 . . . . 40.00
Jacket, Denim, Big E, Levi's, Size 44 . . . . 100.00
Jacket, Denim, Indigo, 2 Flapped Pockets, Dickies, Mexico, 1960s, Size 16 . . . . 40.00
Jacket, Denim, Indigo, Acrylic Lining, Zipper Front, Big Ben, Wrangler, 1960s, Size 36 . . 78.00
Jacket, Denim, Indigo, Gray Blanket Lining, No. 785, Levi's, Size 40 . . . . 137.00
Jacket, Denim, Indigo, Lot 220, Lee Riders, 1960s 246.00
Jacket, Evening, Bolero, Velvet, Red, 3/4 Sleeves, 1940s, Small 99.00
Jacket, Flight, Air Force, Nylon, Sage Green, Orange Satin Lining, American, 1969, Large 69.00
Jacket, Flight, Leather, Shag Collar, Knit Cuffs & Waist, Talon Zipper, Size 52 . . . . 55.00
Jacket, Fox, Blue, 1970s, Medium 99.00
Jacket, Jungle, Army, Ripstop, Cotton, American, 1969, Large 56.00
Jacket, L-2B Pilot, Air Force, Major General Name Tag, American, 1974, Medium 235.00
Jacket, Nylon, Pile Lined, Knit Cuffs, CAT Patch, Caterpillar Tractor, Medium 58.00
Jacket, Rip Stop Poplin, Third Pattern, Vietnam, Etowah Industries, 1969, Medium 30.00
Jacket, Silk Brocade, Blue, Dragon Rondels, Lambskin Interior, Child's 230.00
Jacket, Silk, Flat Woven, 8 Dragons, 4 Claws, Foo Dog, Chinese, 19th Century 230.00
Jacket, Smoking, Rayon, Satin, Oriental Motif, 3 Pockets, Burgundy Belt, XL 100.00
Jacket, Suede, Mink Collar & Cuffs, Woman's 94.00
Jacket, Suit, Wool, Fitted, Plaid, Navy Collar, Cuffs, Woman's, 1940s, Medium 100.00
Jacket, Tuxedo, Yellow, Black Satin Lapels, 1 Button, Flap Pockets, Man's, Size 42 . . . . . 98.00
Jeans, Button Fly, Suspender Buttons, Powell, Late 19th Century, 36 x 32 In. 2011.00
Jeans, Denim, Indigo, Copper Rivets, Labels, Maverick, Blue Bell, 29 x 31 In. 90.00
Jeans, Denim, Indigo, Talon 42 Zipper Fly, Lot 109B, Lee Riders, 1960s, 24 x 23 1/4 In. . . 158.00
Jeans, Denim, Indigo, Zipper Fly, Maverick, Blue Bell, 1970s, 27 x 34 In. 40.00
Jeans, Denim, Indigo, Zipper Fly, Paper Tags, Tuf-Nut Westerns, 1950s, 31 x 30 In. 98.00
Jumpsuit, Black, Rhinestones, Shooting Star Design, Flared Sleeves, 1970s, Size 10 . . . . 45.00

Kimono, Shades Of Gold, Needlework, Vines, Flowers, Leaves 109.00
Kimono, Silk, Red, Needlework, Butterflies, Flowers, Trees, Blue Lining 57.00
Muff, Fur, Satin Lining, 1930s 45.00
Necktie, Famous Pioneer Club, Vegas Vic, c.1950, 4 x 50 In. 77.00
Overcoat, Leopard Pattern, Black Silk Trim, Knee Length, Lilli Ann, 1950s, Size 8 .. 410.00
Pants, Red, Green, Yellow, Blue Plaid, Tags, Blue Bell Jeanies, 1950s, Misses 20 .... 55.00
Pants, Work, Mustard Tan Twill, Button Fly, Suspenders, Imperial, 1915, 28 x 28 In. 906.00
Pantyhose, Off-Black, Flocked Tiger, Rhinestone Eyes, Sealed Package, Queen Size 11.00
Pantyhose, Smoke Colored, Flocked Tiger, Rhinestone Eyes, Tiffany's, Sealed Package .. 11.00
Parasol, Patriotic, Ink Decoration, Flag Day, Signed David Dunlap, 1901, 33 In. 58.00
Petticoat, 2 Bottom Ruffles, 4 Rows Lace, Tucks, 4-Button Back Closure, Victorian 99.00
Petticoat, Hand Woven Wool, Dyed In Shades Of Lavender, Mid 1800s, 34 In. 825.00
Playsuit, Strap Handles, Full Hips, Marissa, 1960s, Small 99.00
Raincoat, Brown Plastic, A-Line, Knee Length, Pierre Cardin, 1960, Size 10 .... 680.00
Robe, 8 Dragons, 4 Claws, Buddha Symbols, Chinese, 19th Century 288.00
Robe, 9 Dragons, 5 Claws, Buddha Symbols, Horse Hoof Cuffs, Chinese, 18th Century .. 3565.00
Robe, 9 Dragons, 5 Claws, Horse Hoof Cuffs, Chinese, 18th Century 1725.00
Robe, 9 Dragons, Cranes, Flowers, Horse Hoof Cuffs, Chinese 805.00
Robe, Blue, Silk Needlework On Gauze, Dragons, Buddhistic Symbols, Chinese, 1800s .. 3450.00
Robe, Dragon, Embroidered, Gold, Blue Ground, Chinese, 19th Century 1058.00
Robe, Embroidered, Flowers, Butterflies, Satin Stitch, Chinese, c.1900 .... 1840.00
Robe, Flat Woven, 8 Dragons, 5 Claws, Blue Ground, 19th Century 345.00
Robe, Kesi, Dragons With Flaming Pearls, Cloud Scrolls, Bats, c.1900 .... 6325.00
Robe, Priest's, Satin, Black, Embroidered Crosses, Symbols, Paste Jewel Set 175.00
Robe, Silk Brocade, Dragons, 5 Claws, Blue & Gold 805.00
Robe, Silk On Gauze, Blue Embroidered, 9 Dragons, Buddhist Symbols, 19th Century ... 3450.00
Robe, Silk, Blue, Foo Dog, Scrolling Leaves, Qing Dynasty, Chinese 980.00
Sandals, Lucite Heels, Clear Plastic, Open Toe, Rhinestones, Southern Charm, Size 7 1/2 . 110.00
Sandals, Lucite Heels, Clear Vinyl, Open Toes, Heel Strap, Jack Rogers, Size 7M 80.00
Scarf, Flowers & Leaves, Silk, Yellow & White Center, Baar & Beard 34 x 35 In. 35.00
Scarf, Holland, Michigan, Silk, Plain Weave, 28 x 28 In. .... *Illus* 15.00
Scarf, Horses & Cowboys, Western, Fuchsia, Blue, Yellow, 26 x 26 In. 45.00
Scarf, Leaves, Silk, Pink Center With Blue, Baar & Beard Inc., 32 x 32 In. 35.00
Scarf, Lighthouses, Chiffon, Blue & White Stripes, 33 x 33 In. 35.00
Scarf, Nautical, Anchors, Fish, Rope, Copper Color, Blue, White, 26 x 26 In. 11.00
Scarf, Silk Twill, Orange, Pink, Blue, Rainbow, Planets, Face, Peter Max, 42 In. ..... *Illus* 85.00
Scarf, Silk, Cashmere, Tapestries, Strapwork, Gold, Red, Green, Hermes 411.00
Scarf, Synthetic Fabric, Yellow, Blue, Green, Purple, Heart Centers, Peter Max, 1970 .... 70.00
Shawl, Paisley, Black Center, 68 x 72 In. 175.00
Shawl, Paisley, Interlocking Boteh & Leaves, Black, Blue, Rose, 72 x 65 In. 295.00
Shawl, Paisley, Wool, Woven 80.00
Shirt, Hawaiian, Kahanamoku, Fruit, Front Pocket, 1960s, Large 45.00
Shirt, Hawaiian, Rayon, Cotton, Birds, Flowers, Paradise Of The Pacific, c.1970, Medium .. 45.00
Shirt, Rock & Roll Style, Pullover, Brown, Black, Tan, 1950s, Large 48.00
Shoes, Alligator, T-Strap, Open-Toed, Shenanigans, Salesman's Sample, Box, 1940s, 5 In. .. 495.00
Shoes, Baby, Beige, Satin, Lace Appliqued, Original Box, Size 1 .... 11.00
Shoes, Evening, Blue, Soft Leather, c.1890 .... 95.00

Clothing, Scarf, Holland,
Michigan, Silk, Plain
Weave, 28 x 28 In.

Clothing, Scarf, Silk Twill,
Orange, Pink, Blue, Rainbow,
Stars, Planets, Face, Peter
Max, 42 In.

Shoes, Silk, White, Heart-Shaped Buckle, 18th Century 895.00
Shoes, Work, Roper Style, Brown Leather, Rubber Soles, Fringed Tongue Flap, Size 11E . 52.00
Skirt, Brocade, Dragon, 20th Century 184.00
Skirt, Chintz Cotton, Black, Tucks, Ruffles, Victorian, Large 99.00
Skirt, Rayon, Polyester, Mini, Plaid, Front Pleats, Side Button, Marmie West, c.1970 .... 11.00
Skirt, Silk, Peony & Butterfly, Chinese, c.1900 .... 575.00
Skirt, Silk, Yellow Embroidered, Butterflies, Peonies, Chinese, 19th Century 460.00
Skirt, Silk, Yellow Embroidered, Golden Peacocks, Peonies, Chinese, 19th Century 405.00
Slippers, Velvet, Silk, Black, Maroon Scrolls, Chinese, c.1900 .... 150.00
Stockings, Nylon, Dolly Madison, Taupe, Size 8 1/2, Original Box, 3 Pair 25.00
Stockings, Nylon, Seamed, Taupe, Reinforced Heels, Toes, Vanity, 3 Pair 20.00
Stole, Silk Brocade, Dragon-In-Cloud Design, Blue Ground, Japan, 60 x 11 In. 253.00
Stole, Silk Brocade, Peonies, Clouds, Gold Ground, Japan, 19th Century, 60 x 11 In. 230.00
Stole, Silk Brocade, Phoenix, Peonies, Salmon Ground, Japan, 19th Century, 63 x 11 In. . 175.00
Suit, 2-Piece, Wool, Polyester Blend, Tailored, Side Zipper, 1950s, Small 50.00
Suit, Double-Breasted, Fuchsia, Albert Grossman, Size 14 .... 95.00
Suit, Silk, Victorian Style, Anne Crimmins, Size 14 .... 45.00
Suit, Tailored, Rayon, Black Rhinestone Buttons, Davidow Of New York, 1950s 100.00
Sweater, Mohair, Modelia, St. Moritz, Zurich, Medium 45.00
Swimsuit, Back Closure, Back Button Straps, Belt, Elizabeth Stewart Of Calif., 1950s ... 99.00
Swimsuit, Elasticized Back, Back Closure, Pleated Neckline, Jantzen, 1960s, Medium ... 99.00
Swimsuit, Right Side Drape, Catalina, 1950s, Large 99.00
Swimsuit, Satin, Black, Wrapped At Hips, Halston, 1970s 1600.00
Swimsuit, Spaghetti Straps, Elasticized Sides, Plaid, Sea Waves, 1960s, Large 99.00
Tie, Bolo, Beige, Gold Metallic Lanyard, Silver Colored Tips, Awards By Kay, 1970s 11.00
Tie, Silk Jacquard, Yellow, Gray, Diagonal Stripes, Wavy Lines, Narrow, Late 1950s 11.00
Tie, Silk, Gray, Red, Green, White Leaves, Tiban Pearlman, 3 3/4 x 49 In. 11.00
Uniform, East German, General Officers Set, Tunic, Trousers, Cap, Belt, Aigulette, 1980s 863.00
Uniform, Harold's Club, Dealer's Outfit, Pants, Vest, Apron, Cummerbund, 1950s 55.00
Uniform, Jungle, Captain, Flight Surgeon, Jacket, Pants, Small 63.00
Uniform, US Army, 82nd Airborne, 80th Division, Dress, c.1945 .... 170.00
Uniform, US Special Forces, NCO Class A, Green Wool, 1957-1967 .... 506.00
Vest & Skirt, Dragons, Birds, Flowers, Navy Blue Ground, Chinese, 19th Century 764.00
Vestment, Jacket Style, Silk, Embroidered, Chinese, 1890-1910 .... 220.00

CLUTHRA glass is a two-layered glass with small air pockets that form
white spots. The Steuben Glass Works of Corning, New York, made it
in 1920. Kimball Glass Company of Vineland, New Jersey, made
Cluthra from about 1925. Victor Durand signed some pieces with his
name. Related items are listed in the Steuben category.

Vase, Clear, White, Orange Trim, Cylindrical, Flared Rim, 6 In. 70.00
Vase, Green, Shouldered, Wide Flared Rim, Signed, Steuben, 10 1/2 In. 1680.00
Vase, Green, White, Signed, Steuben, 6 1/2 In. 865.00
Vase, Pink, Urn, Steuben, 6 1/2 In. 1380.00
Vase, Pomona Green, Classic Form, Fleur-De-Lis Mark, Steuben, 10 1/2 In. 1495.00
Vase, Purple, Gray, Etched Mark, 6 3/4 In. 60.00
Vase, White, Classical Shape, Signed, Steuben, 12 In. 2860.00
Vase, Yellow, Opal, Signed, 4 1/4 In. 210.00

COALBROOKDALE was made by the Coalport porcelain factory of
England during the Victorian period. Pieces are decorated with floral
encrustations.

Burners, Pastille, Cup, Attached Saucer, Lid, 8 x 5 1/2 & 2 3/4 x 1 7/8 In. 50.00
Vase, Flowers, Stately Homes, Handles, 9 x 2 1/3 x 5 In. 320.00

COALPORT ware has been made by the Coalport Porcelain Works of
England from 1795 to the present time. Early pieces were unmarked.
About 1810–1825 the pieces were marked with the name *Coalport* in
various forms. Later pieces also had the name *John Rose* in the mark.
The crown mark has been used with variations since 1881. The date
1750 is printed in some marks, but it is not the date the factory started.
Some pieces are listed in Indian Tree.

BONE   CHINA
COALPORT
MADE IN ENGLAND
EST. 1750

Basket, Rectangular, Footed, Pink Dog Rose Border, Gilt Rim, c.1810, 10 1/4 In., Pair ... 5378.00

Bowl, Jeweled, Round, Blue On Gold, Marks, Covered, 5 In. 1295.00
Cachepot, Black, Gilt Ground Reserves, Flower Band, Greek Key Border, c.1810, Pair .. 4182.00
Compote, Blue & White Polychrome Design, 5 x 9 1/2 In., Pair 115.00
Compote, Stand, Turquoise, Pink Rose Border, Footed, c.1810, 5 1/2 In., Pair 5676.00
Cup & Saucer, Cabinet, Swirling Turquoise Jewels, Gilded Interior, 1900, 4 1/2 In. 695.00
Cup & Saucer, Demitasse, Landscape, Gilt, c.1885, 3 1/2 x 1 1/2 In. 520.00
Cup & Saucer, Footed, Cobalt Blue Leaf Pattern 55.00
Cup & Saucer, Swirling Turquoise Jewels, Gilded Interior, 1900, 4 1/2 x 4 1/2 In. 695.00
Dessert Dish, Lozenge Shape, Exotic Birds, Trellis Patterns, c.1825, 11 In., Pair 1675.00
Dessert Dish, Union Embossed, Flowers, Buff Ground, c.1825, 9 7/8 In., Pair 3884.00
Ice Pail, Cover, Flower Spray, Gilt, Green Border, Paw Feet, c.1820, 14 3/4 In., Pair 4480.00
Plate, Dessert, Flight, Barr & Barr, Cobalt Blue Ground, Flowers, c.1830, 10 In., Pair ... 3000.00
Plate, Dragon, c.1830, 9 1/4 In. 104.00
Plate Set, Dinner, Impressed Numerals, c.1825, 10 1/8 In., 14 Piece 2390.00
Platter, Enamel Flowers, Gilt Feather Edge Border, Scalloped Rim, 18 In., Pair 1645.00
Vase, Cover, Blue Ground, Oval Panels, Hummingbirds, Flowers, c.1870, 17 In., Pair 7170.00

COBALT BLUE glass was made using oxide of cobalt. The characteristic bright dark blue identifies it for the collector. Most cobalt glass found today was made after the Civil War. There was renewed interest in the dark blue glass in the late 1930s and dinnerwares were made.

Creamer, Diamond Optic, Applied Loop Handle, Footed, 3 1/2 In. 300.00
Dish, Fluted, Flared Edge, 1 1/4 x 3 1/2 In. 190.00
Salt, Diamond Point, Footed, 3 In. 415.00
Salt, Footed, 3 In. 248.00
Salt, Waffle & Sunburst, 3-Piece Mold, Footed, 1 1/2 x 2 3/4 In. 715.00
Vase, Trumpet Gallery Rim, Etched Vines, Conical Foot, 14 1/2 In., Pair 660.00

COCA-COLA was first served in 1886 in Atlanta, Georgia. It was advertised through signs, newspaper ads, coupons, bottles, trays, calendars, and even lamps and clocks. Collectors want anything with the word *Coca-Cola*, including a few rare products, like gum wrappers and cigar bands. The famous trademark was patented in 1893, the *Coke* mark in 1945. Many modern items and reproductions are being made.

Advertising Handbook, Embossed Cover, Colored Lithographs, 12 In. 192.00
Badge, Bottlers Conference, 50th Anniversary, Metal, Celluloid, c.1930, 2 x 3 In. 363.00
Badge, Bottlers Conference, Woman Drinking Coke, Metal, Celluloid, c.1930, 2 x 3 In. .. 77.00
Badge, Employee, Bottlers Conference, Metal Back, Celluloid, c.1930, 2 1/4 x 2 3/4 In. .. 149.00
Banner, Edgar Bergen & Charlie McCarthy, Canvas, 1950s, 40 x 60 In. 1325.00
Bottle, Altoona, Pa., Script, BIMAL Crown Top, Aqua 59.00
Bottle, Coca-Cola Bottling Wks., Martinsburg, W. Va., R.J. Shine, BIMAL, Blue Aqua .. 69.00
Bottle, Hobbleskirt, Patented Thanksgiving Day, Nov. 16, 1915 .... 25.00
Bottle, Salutes The Bicentennial, Green, Red, White, Blue Printing, 1976, 16 Oz. 9.00
Bottle, Straight-Sided, Script, Hygeia Bottling Works, Pensacola, Fla. 25.00
Bottle Holder, For Shopping Cart, 1950s 121.00
Bowl, Green, Artificial Ice In Bowl, Vernonware, 1930s, 10 In. 675.00
Box, Bottle, Logo, Wooden, Steel Corners, 12 x 18 In. 35.00
Box, Cardboard, Red, White, Unused, Flat, 1933, 12 x 15 In. 55.00
Button, Yes!, Coke Is Still 5¢, Coke Boy, Painted Aluminum, Decal, 16 In. 303.00
Calendar, 1914, Betty, Pink Dress, Frame, 19 1/2 x 39 1/2 In. 2420.00
Calendar, 1919, Girl With Knitting Bag, Pink Dress, Hat, Frame, 21 x 40 In. 1650.00
Calendar, 1926, Girl With Tennis Racquet, Frame, 15 1/2 x 23 In. 385.00
Calendar, 1936, 50th Anniversary, N.C. Wyeth, 12 x 24 In. 430.00
Calendar, 1943, Army Nurse, Holds Bottle, 13 1/2 x 19 3/4 In. 330.00
Calendar, 1958, Starts With December 1957, Santa Claus 193.00
Carrier, 6-Pack, Wood, Stenciled, Metal Trim, 8 In. 94.00
Chalkboard, Sign Of Good Taste, 27 3/4 x 19 1/2 In. 130.00
Clock, Fishtail Logo, Electric, Plastic, 11 x 12 In. 209.00
Clock, Ice Cold, In Bottles, Fluorescent, Metal, Plastic, Round, Black Face 990.00
Clock, Logo, Square, Wooden Frame, 1939 .... 303.00
Clock, Oak Case, Glass Bottom Panel, Reverse Painting, 33 1/2 In. 330.00
Clock, Reverse On Glass, Metal Frame, Light-Up, 19 1/2 In. 523.00
Clock, Silhouette Girl, Octagonal, Neon, c.1939, 18 x 18 In. 2025.00

Coin Changer, Vendo, Painted Metal Case, Debossed Front Panel, 15 1/4 In. 797.50
Coin-Operated Machine, Vendorlator, V.M.C., Model No. 33, Logo, 10 Cent 770.00
Cooler, Airline, Bottle Opener, Embossed, Red, 17 x 13 In. 220.00
Cooler, Picnic, Red Painted Galvanized Steel, Embossed, 1950s, 19 x 11 x 8 In. 280.00
Dispenser, Plastic, Metal, Dispenses 3 Products, Countertop, 25 In. 165.00
Display, Enjoy Frozen Coca-Cola, Light-Up, Plastic, Revolves, 35 In. 248.00
Display, Take Enough Home, Cardboard Lithograph, Die Cut, Battery Operated, 11 In. 176.00
Display, Window, Woman At Fountain, Cardboard, 1929, 24 x 25 In. 10969.00
Display Case, Coca-Cola Decal, Oak, Pine, Marble, 72 In. 248.00
Door Pull, Bottle Shape, Plastic & Metal, Have A Coke, 1950s, 8 In. 310.00
Envelope, Home Office, Atlanta, 1899 . . . .   200.00
Figure, Circus Clown, Carrying Popcorn & Coca-Cola, 1960 . . . .   50.00
Globe, Milk Glass, Logo In 4 Places Along Perimeter, 1930s, 14 In. 1115.00
Kick Plate, Drink Coca-Cola, Logo, 1931, 10 x 30 In. 633.00
Kick Plate, Man & Woman Sharing Bottle, Tin, 1942, 11 1/2 x 35 In. 2925.00
Kick Plate, Scrolling Factory Logo, 1923 Bottle Image, Tin, 1933, 11 1/2 x 35 In. 1975.00
Menu, Cardboard, c.1950, 27 3/4 x 22 In. 88.00
Mirror, Pocket, Drink Coca-Cola In Bottles, Cat, Cardboard, Glass, Germany, c.1925 . . . .   450.00
Napkin Dispenser, Have A Coke, Coke Boy, Metal, Cardboard Lithograph Insert, 9 In. 495.00
Pen, Float About, Olympic, 1996, Atlanta, Runner, Over Relay Map Of Race 2.75
Pencil, Mechanical, Metal, Celluloid, Clip, Eraser, c.1940, 5 1/4 In. 24.00
Plate, Refresh Yourself, Center Coke Bottle & Glass, Knowles, 7 1/4 In. 845.00
Playing Cards, Double Deck, 1 Deck Red Ground, 1 Blue Ground, 1939 . . . .   900.00
Premium, Clown Holding Bottle Of Cola, Circus Cutouts, 1932, 10 x 15 In. 200.00
Radio, Bottle Shape, Speaker, Dial, Tubes, Original Cord, 1930s, 24 In. 9565.00
Radio, Cooler Form, Red, 1950s 2530.00
Score Pad, Bridge, Logo, Woman Holding Bottle, 1940s, 7 1/2 x 4 In. 29.00
Shooting Gallery, 10 Cents, Test Your Skills, Have A Coke, 60 In. 546.00
Sign, 6-Pack, Delicious & Refreshing, Die Cut, 1951, 11 x 13 In. 1125.00
Sign, 6-Pack, Die Cut, 1951, 11 x 13 In. 1250.00
Sign, 6-Pack, Gold Highlights, Tin, Die Cut, 1962, 32 x 36 In. 1969.00
Sign, Cap, Bottle With Logo, Round, 36 In. 375.00
Sign, Cap, Coca-Cola, Bottle, Porcelain, 24 In. 470.00
Sign, Cap, Drink Coca-Cola In Bottles, Porcelain, 48 In. 210.00
Sign, Cap, Drink Coca-Cola In Bottles, Red Ground, 1955, 12 In. 479.00
Sign, Cap, Drink Coca-Cola, Sign Of Good Taste, Silver Arrow, 1951, 12 In. 1125.00
Sign, Cap, Drink Coca-Cola, Sign Of Good Taste, Silver Arrow, Embossed, 1948, 16 In. . . . 2250.00
Sign, Cardboard, 2 Sides, 1947, 20 x 41 In. 220.00
Sign, Coke Bottle, White, Porcelain, c.1950, 24 In. 2025.00
Sign, Come In, We Have Coca-Cola, Coke Boy, Paper Lithograph, 24 1/2 In. 85.00
Sign, Curb, School Zone Wood In Metal Base, 48 x 16 In. 660.00
Sign, Drink Coca-Cola Fountain Service, Porcelain, Green, 1950s, 28 x 11 3/4 In. 1125.00
Sign, Drink Coca-Cola Fountain Service, Porcelain, Yellow, 1950s, 50 x 10 In. 1690.00
Sign, Drink Coca-Cola Ice Cold, Red Circle, White Arrow, Flange, 1951, 22 1/2 x 18 In. .   550.00
Sign, Drink Coca-Cola, Fountain Service, Die Cut, Porcelain, 1930s, 24 x 24 In. 1155.00
Sign, Drink Coca-Cola, Ice Cold, Red Circle, Bottle, Tin, 1957, 18 x 22 In. 1125.00
Sign, Drink Coca-Cola, In Bottles, 5¢, Tin Lithograph, Embossed, 24 In. 635.00
Sign, Drink Coca-Cola, Red Ground, Bottle, Yellow Dot, Tin, 1946, 33 1/2 x 11 1/2 In. . . .   275.00
Sign, Drink Coca-Cola, Red Ground, White Lettering, 36 x 84 In. 80.00
Sign, Drink Coca-Cola, Red Ground, White Letters, Porcelain, c.1920, 12 x 30 In. 3825.00
Sign, Enjoy Coke, Metal, Self-Framed, 10 1/4 x 31 1/2 In. 44.00
Sign, Enjoy That Refreshing New Feeling, Cardboard, 1950s, 37 x 24 In. 120.00
Sign, Figure Skater Sits On Log, Holds Bottle, Cardboard, 1940s 1400.00
Sign, For Picnic Fun, Die Cut Picnic Scene, Cardboard, 1950s, 13 x 8 In. 165.00
Sign, Fountain Service, Drink Coca-Cola, Green, Yellow, Red, White, 1934, 42 x 60 In. . . .   375.00
Sign, Green Ground, White Letters, Die Cut, Porcelain, 1930s, 18 x 5 1/2 In. 790.00
Sign, Ham & Cheese Sandwich & Coca-Cola, Cardboard, Metal Frame, 13 x 17 In. 385.00
Sign, Hello Refreshment, Logo, Woman In Swimming Pool, Cardboard, 30 x 50 In. 575.00
Sign, Ice Cold Coca-Cola Sold Here, Red Ground, Embossed, Tin, 1933, 19 3/4 In. 816.00
Sign, Ice Cold Coca-Cola Sold Here, Tin Lithograph, Embossed, Wood Frame, 28 In. 468.00
Sign, Ice Cold Coca-Cola Sold Here, Tin, Embossed, 1931, 19 1/2 x 27 1/2 In. 330.00
Sign, Lady Drinking Glass Of Coke, Black, White, Paper, 1917, 12 1/2 x 24 In. 44.00
Sign, Lillian Nordica, Delicious Refreshing, Celluloid, Cardboard, 19 x 25 In. 20000.00

Sign, Lillian Russell, Cardboard, White Gown, Black Feather Fan, 1905, 2 1/4 In. 4510.00
Sign, Logo, Curved Ends, Porcelain, 68 x 24 In. 165.00
Sign, Now!, Family Size Too!, Same Sparkling Refreshment, Paper Lithograph, 36 In. . . .   176.00
Sign, Pause That Refreshes, Woman In Lounge Chair, Frame, 1942, 36 x 20 In. 880.00
Sign, Pause That Refreshes, Woman Skier, H.H. Sungblom, 29 1/2 x 21 1/2 In. 18700.00
Sign, Pick Up 6, For Home Refreshment, White Ground, Tin, 1954, 50 x 16 In. 1688.00
Sign, Rack, Have A Coke, Take Some Home, Coke Boy Decal, 23 1/2 In. 95.00
Sign, Radiator Grill, Drink Coca-Cola In Bottles, Aluminum, c.1930, 17 1/2 In. 730.00
Sign, Red Dispenser On White Field, 2 Sides, Porcelain, 1950s, 27 x 28 In. 1125.00
Sign, Santa On House, Holding Bottles, Die Cut Cardboard, 27 x 71 In. 154.00
Sign, Santa With Dog, Logo, Die Cut Cardboard, 32 x 48 In. 99.00
Sign, Serve Ice Cold, King, Bottle, 6-Pack, Die Cut, Cardboard, 1953, 13 1/2 x 21 In. 500.00
Sign, Smokey Says Prevent Forest Fires, Die Cut, Cardboard, 44 x 55 In., 3 Piece 495.00
Sign, Stock Up For The Holidays, Santa, Helicopter, Cardboard, 66 x 32 In. 176.00
Sign, Take A Case Home Today, Red Ground, Tin Lithograph, Wood Frame, 28 In. 330.00
Sign, Take Home A Carton, Drink Coca-Cola, Embossed, Tin, 1930s, 18 x 54 In. 440.00
Sign, Take Some Home Today, 6 Bottles 25¢, Paper Lithograph, Frame, 24 1/2 In. 94.00
Sign, Talk About Refreshing, Woman Holding Umbrella, Cardboard, Frame, 28 In. 855.00
Sign, Truck Cab, Drink Coca-Cola Ice Cold, Porcelain, 1950s, 50 x 10 In. 1240.00
Sign, When Friends Drop In, Santa, Logo, Cardboard, 66 x 32 In. 130.00
Sign, Work Refreshed, C.E. Heinzerling, 1941, 42 x 28 In. 225.00
Sign, You Can't Beat The Real Thing, Charlotte Motor Speedway, 1990, 22 x 34 In. 35.00
Stringholder, 6-Pack Of Coke, Take Home In Cartons, 2 Sides, 1940s 4500.00
Thermometer, Be Really Refreshed, Fishtail Logo, Pam, 12 In.   1070.00
Thermometer, Bottle, Tin Lithograph, Stick, 16 In. 35.00
Thermometer, Bottle, Tin, Embossed, 1950s, 30 In. 130.00
Thermometer, Cap Top, Tin, Round, Dial, 12 1/4 In. 176.00
Thermometer, Drink Coca-Cola, Gold Bottle, Red, Green, Round, Box, 1950s, 12 In. 1465.00
Thermometer, Logo, Round, Glass Front, c.1950s, 12 In. 110.00
Thermometer, Silhouette Girl, Porcelain, Thirst Knows No Season, Canada, 1939, 18 In. . .   5400.00
Thermometer, Things Go Better With Coke, Pam, c.1963 . . . .   730.00
Thermometer, Tin Lithograph, Glass, Die Cut, 16 In. 175.00
Tip Tray, 1909, Exhibition Girl, Sitting At Table, 4 1/2 x 6 1/4 In. 495.00
Tip Tray, 1914, Betty, White Bonnet, Lithograph, 4 1/4 x 6 In. 275.00
Tip Tray, 1916, Elaine, Yellow Dress, Holding Glass, 4 1/4 x 6 In. 275.00
Tip Tray, 1923 Flapper Girl, 8 1/2 In. 280.00
Tip Tray, 1989, Trolley Cars, 1905 Advertisement Sign, 4 5/8 x 6 5/8 In. 4.00
Toy, Car, Ford, Tin, Friction, Japan, 1959, 9 1/4 In. 395.00
Toy, Playtown Luncheonette, Wood, Cardboard, Coca-Cola Logo, Box, Accessories, 10 In.   220.00
Toy, Tractor Trailer, Buddy L, Box, 10 x 3 In. 28.00
Toy, Truck, Bottles, Dolly, Steel, Marx, c.1950, 13 In. 130.00
Toy, Truck, Buddy L, 1960s, 13 In. 475.00
Toy, Truck, Buddy L, Yellow, Red Decal, 1960s, 15 In. 160.00
Toy, Truck, Coca-Cola Bottling, 10 Bottles, Headlights, Metalcraft Co., 1930 . . . .   750.00
Toy, Truck, Metal With Plastic Windows, Buddy L Decals, 14 1/2 In. 255.00
Toy, Truck, Pressed Steel, Lights, Tires, Glass Bottles, Metalcraft, 1930s, 11 1/2 In. 1375.00
Toy, Truck, Pressed Steel, Wood, 10 Bottles, Metalcraft, 1930s, 35 In. 1100.00
Toy, Truck, Yellow, Cases, Bottles, Cab-Over, Smith-Miller, Box, 13 In. 2310.00
Toy, Truck, Yellow, White, Tin, Battery Operated, Sanyo, Box, c.1950, 12 1/2 In. 440.00
Tray, 1914, Betty, Bonnet, Lace Dress, 13 x 10 1/2 In. 825.00
Tray, 1916, Elaine, Holding Glass, 19 x 8 1/2 In. 715.00
Tray, 1922, Golfer Girl, 13 x 10 1/2 In. 600.00
Tray, 1923, Flapper Girl, 13 x 10 1/2 In. 358.00
Tray, 1925, Party Girl, With Fox Wrap, 13 x 10 1/2 In. 385.00
Tray, 1926, Golfer Pouring Coke For Lady, 13 x 10 1/2 In. . . . . .660.00 to 1300.00
Tray, 1927, Curb Service, 10 1/2 x 13 In. 523.00
Tray, 1929, Girl In Yellow Bathing Suit, 13 1/4 x 10 1/2 In. 550.00
Tray, 1930, Bathing Beauty, 13 x 10 1/2 In. . . . . .468.00 to 500.00
Tray, 1931, Barefoot Boy, Norman Rockwell, 13 x 10 1/2 In. 660.00
Tray, 1932, Girl In Yellow Bathing Suit, 13 x 10 1/2 In. 1265.00
Tray, 1934, Maureen O'Sullivan & Johnny Weismuller, 10 1/2 x 13 In. 605.00
Tray, 1936, Hostess, Holding Coke, 13 x 10 1/2 In. . . . . .105.00 to 165.00
Tray, 1937, Running Girl, 13 x 10 1/2 In. 121.00

Tray, 1939, Springboard Girl, 13 x 10 1/2 In. 264.00
Tray, 1940, Sailor Girl, 10 1/2 x 13 In. ....143.00 to 330.00
Tray, 1941, Skater Girl, 13 x 10 1/2 In. ....175.00 to 330.00
Tray, 1942, 2 Girls At Car, 10 1/2 x 13 1/4 In. ....187.00 to 305.00
Tumbler, 75th Anniversary Fountain, Buffalo, N.Y., White, 1977, 5 In. 7.00
Tumbler, Coke Flare Mobil, Philadelphia Eagles, 1992 .... 3.00
Tumbler, Dinosaurs, Plateosaurus, Continental, 6 7/8 In. 11.00
Tumbler, Holly Hobbie & Robbie, Merry Christmas, No. 2, 1978, 4 Piece 4.00
Tumbler, Kollect-A-Set, Wimpy, 1975, 5 7/8 In. 5.00
Tumbler, Pause That Refreshes, France, 6 1/4 In. 4.00
Tumbler, Sample, Indiana Jones In Turban, Round Bottom, 1982, 6 In. 535.00
Tumbler, Sample, Indiana Jones, Sand For Statue, Round Bottom, 1982, 6 In. 485.00
Tumbler, Sample, Raiders Of Lost Ark, Marion, Round Bottom, 1982, 6 In. 586.00
Vending Machine, Vendo V-39, Red, Hand Holding Bottle, 10 Cent 1815.00
Vending Machine, Vendo V-44, Bottle Rack, Key 2090.00

COFFEE GRINDERS, or coffee mills, of home size were first made about
1894. They lost favor by the 1930s. Large floor-standing or counter-
model coffee grinders were used in the nineteenth-century country
store. The renewed interest in fresh-ground coffee has produced many
modern electric and hand grinders, and reproductions of the old styles
are being made. See also the Kitchen category.

Adams, Box, Iron Hopper & Drawer 100.00
American, No. 14, Box Mill, Wooden Adjusters, Grind Adjusters, Paper Labels 70.00
American Duplex Co., Countertop, Coffeepot Shape, 29 In. 550.00
Arcade, No. 25, Wall Canister, Glass Jar, Tin Cover, Iron Grinding Body, 15 In. 150.00
Arcade Jewel, Wall Canister, Decorative Glass, Cover, Gold On Metal Parts, 14 In. 400.00
Box, Grind Adjustment, France, Mid 18th Century, 6 In. 1100.00
Box, Hand Craved, Brass Hopper, Crank, Continental, 18th Century, 6 In. 800.00
Cast Iron, Fruit Decals, Coin Medallions, 13 In. 300.00
Cast Iron, Wood, Glass Insert, Golden Rule, Wall Mount, Ohio 259.00
Crown, No. 20, Upright, Cast Iron, Lid, Original Black Paint, Decal 1000.00
D-E Koffie, Douwe-Egberts, 1930s, 13 x 5 In. ....*Illus*   195.00
Dr. Edwards, Side, Cast Iron, Wooden Back, 1859 .... 300.00
Elgin National, No. 10, Upright, Cast Iron, Wheels, Hopper, C.H. Woodruff 1800.00
Elgin National, No. 44, Decals, Eagle Finial, Countertop 605.00
Elgin National, Red, Eagle Finial, Late 19th Century, 28 x 66 In. 1400.00
Elma, Upright, Cast Iron, 2 Wheels, Black With Red & Gold Trim, 12 In. 660.00
Elma, Upright, Cast Iron, Crank Gears, Tin Dome, Wooden Drawer, Red, 13 In. 225.00
Enterprise, Cast Iron, Painted, Decals, Wooden Drawer, 27 In. 550.00
Enterprise, Cast Iron, Painted, Stenciled, Brass Eagle Finial, 25 In. 1210.00
Enterprise, Cast Iron, Painted, Stenciled, Brass Eagle Finial, 34 In. 1100.00
Enterprise, No. 00, Wall Mounted, Hopper, Iron Cup, Original Paint, Decal, 9 In. 350.00
Enterprise, No. 2, 1 Drawer, Cast Iron, 11 x 13 In. 605.00
Enterprise, No. 2, Size 9, Painted Wheel, Oak Base ....550.00 to 715.00
Enterprise, No. 4, Cast Iron, Brass Hopper, Eagle Finial, 21 In. 1760.00
Enterprise, No. 14, Cast Iron, Nickel Plated Hopper, Tin Catch Can, Flowers 1600.00
Enterprise, No. 650, Iron, Wall Mounted, Black & Gold Trim, 19-In. Wheel 325.00
Enterprise, No. 712, Brass Oval Plaque, 34 1/2 In. 935.00
Enterprise, Upright, Cast Iron, Cover, Original Red Paint, Decals, 1898 .... 1150.00
Grand Union, Table Top, Griswold 455.00
Hobart, No. 2020, Table Top, Red, Gold Trim, 30 In. 90.00
Hotel, Poplar, Brass Hopper, Wrought Iron Crank, Dovetailed, 8 1/2 x 8 x 13 In. 165.00
Iron Steamship, Wall Mounted, Crank In Front, Grind Adjustment, 6 In. 150.00
Landers, Frary & Clark, Box, Bronzed Black Iron, Twist-Off Base, Crank 550.00
Landers, Frary & Clark, Crown, No. 1, Box Mill, Tin, Hopper & Cover 140.00
Lightning, No. 23, Wall Canister, Cylindrical Tin, Green & White 325.00
National Specialty Mfg. Co., Cast Iron, 2 Wheels, Drawer, Painted, 27 In. 563.00
None-Such, Tin Lithograph, Wood Base, 10 x 5 1/2 In. 578.00
Parker, No. 44, Cylindrical Tin, Cover, Eagle Design 275.00
Parker Eagle, No. 70, Side, Grind Adjustment, Tin Hopper, Cover 120.00
Peugeot Freres, Upright, Cast Iron, Tin Dome, Wooden Drawer, 13-In. Wheel 550.00
Portable, Steel, Tall Cylinder Type, 18th Century 350.00

When away on a trip, lower the sound of your telephone bell so that it can't be heard outside.

Coffee Grinder, D-E Koffie,
Douwe-Egberts, 1930s,
13 x 5 In.

Coin-Operated Machine,
Strength Tester, Try Your Strength,
5 Cents, Lift, Grip, Pull, 71 In.

Queen Arcade, No. 9, Box, Wooden, Gold Design On Metal, Child's, 2 1/2 x 2 1/2 In. ... 150.00
Schilling & Co., Buck In Forest, Iron & Wood Handle, 10 x 6 In. 1018.00
Simmons Delmar, Side, Cast Iron, Bronzed, Wooden Back 200.00
Softwood, Brass Mounted, Lip Molded Drawer, 8 1/2 x 6 1/2 x 9 In. 105.00
Table Top, Grand Union, Griswold 495.00
Waddel, Box, Decorative Iron Cover & Handle, Side Door, Tin Cups, 1888 .... 140.00
York Co., Shelf, Case, Drawer, Pewter Collar, S & B, No. 4, Lewisberry, Pa., 1881 ...... 370.00

COIN SPOT is a glass pattern that was named by the collectors for the spots resembling coins, which are part of the glass. Colored, clear, and opalescent glass was made with the spots. Many companies used the design in the 1870–1890 period. It is so popular that reproductions are still being made.

Berry Dish, Frosted Seated Liberty Quarter, c.1892, 3 3/4 In. 175.00
Pitcher, Blue, Star Crimped Edge, Applied Translucent Blue Handle, 6 In. 90.00
Pitcher, Blue, Star Crimped Edge, Translucent Blue Handle, 9 1/2 In. 190.00
Pitcher, Clear, Bulbous, 8-Sided Ruffled Edge, 8 In. 90.00
Pitcher, Cranberry Opalescent, Ruffled Edge, Applied Satin Reeded Handle, 8 1/2 In. ... 345.00
Pitcher, Green, Ruffled Edge, 9 1/2 In. 240.00
Saltshaker, Cranberry, 3 3/4 In. 90.00
Shade, Hanging, Cranberry, Brass Mounts, 13 In. 315.00
Sugar Shaker, Blue, 9 Panels, 4 3/4 In. 210.00
Sugar Shaker, Cranberry, Wide-Waisted, 4 1/2 In. 240.00
Tumbler, Shaded Amber To Clear, 3 3/4 In. 80.00

COIN-OPERATED MACHINES of all types are collected. The vending machine is an ancient invention dating back to 200 B.C., when holy water was dispensed in a coin-operated vase. Smokers in seventeenth-century England could buy tobacco from a coin-operated box. It was not until after the Civil War that the technology made modern coin-operated games and vending machines plentiful. Slot machines, arcade games, and dispensers are all collected.

Arcade, Electricity, Metal Case, Figural Coin Slot, 12 In. 635.00
Cigar, Elm City, 5 & 10 Cent, Oak Case, Beveled Mirror, 29 1/2 In. 2860.00
Cigarette, Rowe, Cast Metal, Glass Front, Brass Oval Inset, 31 1/2 In. 358.00
Dispenser, Card, 1 Cent, Men, Women, Metal Case, 17 3/4 In. 165.00
Dispenser, Pencil, 5 Cents, A Pencil With Your Name, Oak Case, 22 In. 1375.00
Dispenser, Postcard, 1 Cent, Painted Metal, Glass Front, 10 In. 385.00
Fortune Teller, Horoscope, 10 Cent, Gypsy Inside, 24 x 79 In. 2255.00
Fortune Teller, Madam X, 1 Cent, Menu, Napkin Holder, 6 1/2 In. ....120.00 to 220.00
Fortune Teller, Mills Wizard, Oak Case, Paper Lithograph, 16 In. 660.00
Fortune Teller, Woman Behind Glass, Yellow, Tent Top, c.1910, 46 In. 3910.00
Gambling, Clown, Wall Mount, Oak, Germany, 1915, 19 x 28 In. 1550.00
Gum, Baseball, 1 Cent, Flock Painted Wood Case, 15 3/4 In. 320.00
Gum, Colgan's, National Vending, 1 Cent, Metal, Glass Dome, 14 1/2 In. 4620.00
Gum, Columbus, Cast Iron A, Embossed Globe, c.1914 .... 363.00
Gum, Columbus, Model M, Hexagonal Globe 330.00

Gum, Columbus, Penny, Painted, Embossed, Metal Case, 7 3/4 In. 3300.00
Gum, Daval Trade, Stimulator, Aluminum, Paper Lithograph, 11 1/2 In. 1760.00
Gum, Mansfield's Choice Pepsin, 5 Cents, Glass, Mirrored Marquee 1100.00
Gum, Pulver, Porcelain Cased, 1 Cent, 9 x 5 x 20 In. 920.00
Gum, Snacks, Trimount Coin, 1 Cent, Metal Case, 19 1/4 In. 410.00
Gum, Victor Vending, 5 Cent, Wood Case, Plastic Inserts, 12 In. 50.00
Gumball, Glass Dome, Metal Base, 15 In. 176.00
Matches, 1 Cent, Metal, Glass Dome 880.00
Matches, 1 Cent, Oak Case, Embossed Case, Iron Front, 14 In. 825.00
Matches, Cleveland National Bank, Embossed Cast Metal, 5 In. 495.00
Matches, Hamilton Manufacturing, Safety, 1 Cent, Oak Case, 15 In. 2530.00
Matches, Krema Co., 1 Cent Matches, Cast Iron, Wooden, 10 x 14 x 9 In. 385.00
Matches, United Machine, Knapsack, Etched Glass, Metal Case, 11 In. 3850.00
Music Box, Kalliope, Walnut Case, 13 Discs, 44 1/2 In. 7370.00
Music Box, Mermod Freres, No. 18749, 11 1/2-In. Cylinder, 40 In. 2468.00
Music Box, Polyphon No. 103, Walnut, 78 Teeth, 3 16-In. Discs, 1900 . . . . 1540.00
Music Box, Regina, Oak, 2 Combs, 15-In. Disc, 10 Discs, 20 In. 4400.00
Nut, Hot Peanuts, Star, Gilt Metal, Glass, Blue & White Enamel, 14 x 16 In. 316.00
Nut, Peanut, Northwestern, No. 33 . . . . 165.00
Nut, Peanut, Northwestern, No. 49 . . . . 55.00
Nut, Tropical Trading Co., Challenger Fresh Hot, Cast Aluminum, 18 In. 690.00
Pachinko, Sanyo, Three Ocean, Wood, Plastic Case, 32 In. 22.00
Pinball, Baffle Ball, Wood Case, Metal Marquee & Gameboard, 24 In. 415.00
Pinball, Coney Island, Electronic, Game Plan U.S.A., 31 x 52 x 64 In. 166.00
Pinball, Fleet, Painted, Wood Case, Gameboard, Metal Cannons, 43 In. 358.00
Pinball, Frisky, Bally & Co., Carved, Painted Wood, 42 1/2 In. 385.00
Pinball, Golden Nugget, Genco, Wood Case, Gameboard, 60 1/2 In. 330.00
Pinball, Pippin, Animated, Chicago Coin Mfg. Co., 1935, 41 x 21 x 51 In. 330.00
Pinball, Rapid Transit, Chicago Coin Mfg. Co., 1935, 39 x 21 x 11 In. 135.00
Pinball, Score-A-Lite, Genco, Wood Case, Gameboard, 51 In. 385.00
Pinball, Skill Score, Caldwell Co., 1 Cent, Wood Case, Gameboard, 39 In. 415.00
Pinball, Twister Ball, Wood Case, Painted, Wood Gameboard, 30 1/2 In. 198.00
Poker, Le Poker D'As, Walnut, Wood & Metal Case, France, 26 1/2 In. 550.00
Skill, Caldwell Novelty Co., 5 Cents, Wood, Rubber Balls, 50 In. 360.00
Skill, Daisy Ball Game, Stenciled Wood Frame, Tin Target, 19 In. 275.00
Skill, Drinker-Tinker, 5 Cent, Wood Case, Plastic Backdrop, 19 1/2 In. 165.00
Skill, Master Target Practice, 1 Cent, Metal, Wood, Glass, 20 1/2 In. 2090.00
Slot, Boop-A-Doop-Ball Flip Game, Cast Metal, Wood Top, Bottom, 17 In. 880.00
Slot, Comet, 5 Cent, Wood Sides & Base, Metal Front, 24 In. 965.00
Slot, Earth Satellite Flip Game, Plastic Backdrop, England, 31 1/2 In. 440.00
Slot, Jack-Pot, Coin, Instruction, Buffalo Toys, 6 In. 116.00
Slot, Jennings Sun Chief, 25 Cent, 18 x 27 x 15 1/4 In. 2250.00
Slot, Jennings, Sun Chief, 1 Dollar 2400.00
Slot, London Ball Flip Game, Automatic Machine Co., Oak Case, 33 1/4 In. 468.00
Slot, Mills High Top, 5 Cent, Side Arm 1375.00
Slot, Mills Sweetheart QT, 5 Cent, 12 x 19 In. 1450.00
Slot, Mills, 5 Cent, Black Cherry, Cast Metal Case 2310.00
Slot, Mills, 5 Cent, Lion Head, Metal Case, Red Enamel, c.1929 . . . . 2500.00
Slot, Mills, Bursting Cherry, 25 Cent, 1938-1942 . . . . 1700.00
Slot, Mills, Mystery, Golden, 5 Cent, Oak Case, Candy Dispenser, 26 In. 2860.00
Slot, Mills, Owl, 5 Cent, Oak Case, Tin Lithograph Wheel, 64 1/2 In. 9350.00
Slot, Mills, Q.T., 5 Cent, Side Candy Dispenser, 18 1/2 In. 1870.00
Slot, Mills, Q.T., 10 Cent, Metal Front, Wood Case, 18 1/2 In. 2200.00
Slot, Nevada, Metal Case, Aluminum Front, 4 Reel, 8 x 7 x 11 In. 58.00
Slot, Official Rock-Ola, Sweepstakes, Metal Horses, Wood Case, 15 1/4 In. 1705.00
Slot, Pace Comet, 5 Cent, Cast Metal Case 1375.00
Slot, Poison The Rat, Groetchen Tool Company, Hitler Caricature, 24 In. 5170.00
Slot, Prize Cup Flip Game, Oak Case, Felt Gameboard, England, 32 1/2 In. 440.00
Slot, Rol-A-Top, 10 Cent, Watling 2530.00
Slot, Skill, Pitchem, Ball Flip, 1 Cent, Speckled, Wood Case, 17 1/2 In. 605.00
Slot, Steeplechase Marble Race Game, Cardboard Lithograph, 18 In. 990.00
Slot, Universal Co., 25 Cent, Electric, Jackpot 7, 46 x 22 x 19 In. 920.00
Stamp, American Postmaster, Metal Case, Embossed Front, 10 3/4 In. 176.00

Stamp, Sanitary Postage, Glass, Metal, Paper Lithograph Insert, 13 1/4 In. 132.00
Stamp, Shipman Manufacturing, Porcelain Case, 16 In. 88.00
Stamp, Shipman, 5 Cents, 10 Cents, Porcelain Front, 3 Slots 35.00
Strength Tester, National Novelty Co., 5 Cent, Lift Grip & Pull, 71 In. 1725.00
Strength Tester, Try Your Strength, 5 Cents, Lift, Grip, Pull, 71 In. . . . . *Illus*   1725.00
Trade Stimulator, High Stakes, Horses, Cast Metal, Wood, 14 In.   825.00
Trade Stimulator, Lucky Strike, Cigar, Gumball, Baker, 7 1/2 x 15 In. 495.00
Trade Stimulator, Puritan Baby Bell, Embossed, Painted, Aluminum, 10 1/2 In. 660.00
Trade Stimulator, Rabbit In Felt Hat, Rabbit Pops Up, Down, 20 In. 908.00
Trade Stimulator, Sure-Winner Candy Game, Zingerline Bros. Label, Wood Case, 15 In. . .   85.00
Vending, Bayer Aspirin, 25 Cent, Lithograph, Sheet Steel Case, 14 1/4 In. 110.00
Vending, Candy, Art Deco, Walnut & Plastic Case, Glass Front, 72 In. 525.00
Vending, Candy, Dean Bros., Metal, Chrome, Panel, England, 33 1/4 In. 80.00
Vending, Candy, Nut, Master, 1 Cent, Painted Metal, Glass Case, 16 In. 415.00
Vending, Candy, Nut, Norris Manuf., 1 Or 5 Cent, Porcelain Case, 16 In. 550.00
Vending, Candy, Try Some, 1 Cent, Glass Dome, Cast Aluminum, 13 1/2 In. 55.00
Vending, Chocolate, Column, Cast Iron, Painted Red, England, 6 x 25 In. 80.00
Vending, Chocolate, Egg-Laying Hen, Germany, c.1935, 17 x 17 x 55 In. 846.00
Vending, Collar Button, 10 Cent, Glass Case, Cast Metal Base, 10 1/4 In. 525.00
Vending, Hershey's, Column, Duplex, 5 Cents, Painted, Metal Case, Decals, 32 In. 165.00
Vending, Kopper King Gum, 1 Cent, Painted Metal, Glass, 18 In.   60.00
Vending, Kotex, 5 Cent, Embossed, Painted, Metal Case, 20 In. 120.00
Vending, Mint & Gum, National, 5 Cent, Metal, Tin Lithograph, 15 1/4 In. 165.00
Vending, National Vending Corp., Claw, Walnut, Chrome Case, 70 In. 2310.00
Vending, Nut, Candy, 1 Cent, Metal Base, Glass Dome, Contents, 10 1/4 In. 1210.00
Vending, Pencil, Vendex Inc., New York, Green & Silver Paint, 54 In. 690.00
Vending, Pepsin Gum & Huyker's Chocolate, L-Shaped, Wooden 17600.00
Vending, Pharmacy, Wood Case, Glass, Celluloid Labels, England, 15 1/2 In. 550.00

COMIC ART, or cartoon art, is a relatively new field of collecting.
Original comic strips, magazine covers, and even printed strips are collected. The first daily comic strip was printed in 1907. The paintings
on celluloid used for movie cartoons are listed in this book under
Animation Art.

Cover, Joe Palooka, Foreign Legionnaire, Oct. 29, 1956, 11 x 12 In. 250.00
Drawing, James Thurber, You May Not Have Charm, 8 1/2 x 11 In. 4182.00
Drawing, Short Suitor, Ink, Wash, Watercolor, Charles Addams, 1938, 11 1/4 x 10 1/4 In. .   4950.00
Drawing, Woman Shops, Man Holds Packages, R. Van Buren, 18 1/4 x 23 In. 1430.00
Strip, Baby Marvin, Shaving, Tom Armstrong, Signed, Feb. 5, 1990, Mat, 6 x 16 In. 35.00

COMMEMORATIVE items have been made to honor members of royalty
and those of great national fame. World's fairs and important historical
events are also remembered with commemorative pieces. Related collectibles are listed in the Coronation and World's Fair categories.

Badge, Queen Victoria, Brass, Longest Reign In England History, 1837-1897, 2 x 3 In. . . .   180.00
Bread Plate, Hindenburg, Portrait, Scalloped, Open Frieze Work, 10 In. 58.00
Jug, Eglington Tournament, Aryshire, Medieval Tournament, Ridgway, 1839, 9 In. 618.00
Mug, Prince William Of Wales, Birth, Canada, 1982, 3 3/4 In. 40.00

Commemorative, Plate,
Queen Victoria, Golden
Jubilee, 1885

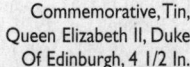

Commemorative, Tin,
Queen Elizabeth II, Duke
Of Edinburgh, 4 1/2 In.

Pin Tray, Queen Elizabeth II, Silver Jubilee, Royal Grafton, 1977, 4 1/2 In. 20.00
Plate, Honor, Modlin, Prussian Soldiers In Field, Meissen, Germany, 10 In. 95.00
Plate, James Dean, Photos, Eulogy On Back, Kettlesprings Kilns, 1955, 10 In. 75.00
Plate, Queen Elizabeth II, Silver Jubilee, Mason's, 1952-1977, 10 3/4 In. 60.00
Plate, Queen Victoria, Golden Jubilee, 1885 . . . . *Illus* 100.00
Tin, Queen Elizabeth II, Duke Of Edinburgh, 4 1/2 In. . . . . *Illus* 38.00

COMPACTS hold face powder. A woman did not powder her face in
public until after World War I. By 1920, the beauty parlor, permanent
waves, and cosmetics had become acceptable. A few companies sold
cake face powder in a box with a mirror and a pad or puff. Soon the
compact was designed by jewelers and made of gold, silver, and precious materials. Cosmetic companies began to sell powder in attractive
compacts of less valuable metal or plastic. Collectors today search for
Art Deco designs, commemorative compacts from world's fairs or
political events, and unusual examples. Many were made with companion lipsticks and other fittings.

18K Gold, Art Deco, Enamel, Mother-Of-Pearl, Castle, Mountain, Parrots, Chaumet 5290.00
Art Deco, Enamel, Hardstone 500.00
Metal, Enamel Cartouche, Scrolling, Filigree, Round, France, 1930s, 3/4 x 2 5/8 In. 115.00
Silver, Gemstone, Engraved Fish Yin-Yang, France, 3 1/8 x 3 1/8 In. 200.00
Silver & Enamel, Japanese Landscape, Mount Fuji, P.H.V., Marked 925, 3 1/2 In. 518.00
Sterling Silver, Enamel, Man, Woman, Under Tree, Dog, Lamb, Beveled Mirror, 5 In. . . . 575.00

CONSOLIDATED LAMP AND GLASS COMPANY of Coraopolis, Pennsylvania, was founded in 1894. The company made lamps, tablewares,
and art glass. Collectors are particularly interested in the wares made
after 1925, including black satin glass, Cosmos (listed in its own category in this book), Martele (which resembled Lalique), and Ruba Rombic
(1928–1932 Art Deco line), and colored glasswares. Some Consolidated
pieces are very similar to those made by the Phoenix Glass Company.
The colors are sometimes different. Consolidated made Martele glass
in blue, crystal, green, pink, white, or custard glass with added fired-on
color or a satin finish. The company closed for the final time in 1967.

Bowl, Love Birds, Orange, Green Leaves On White, Oval, 10 In. 170.00
Cologne Bottle, Bulging Loops, Canary, Hollow Stopper, 7 1/4 x 4 3/4 In. 385.00
Jar, Cover, Flowers, Pink Cased, Silver Plate Rim, Handle, 8 1/2 In. 350.00
Tumbler, Bulging Loops, Pigeon Blood, 3 5/8 In. 55.00
Vase, 3 Geese, Pillow Shape, Brown, 11 x 9 In. 130.00
Vase, Jonquils, Yellow, Pale Green Stem, 7 1/2 In. 125.00
Vase, White, Green, Flowers, Leaves, Rim Feathers, 9 1/2 In. 200.00
Whiskey, Ruba Rombic, Opalescent Green, c.1950, 2 5/8 In. 110.00

CONTEMPORARY GLASS, see Glass-Contemporary.

COOKBOOKS are collected for various reasons. Some are wanted for
the recipes, some for investment, and some as examples of advertising.
Cookbooks and recipe pamphlets are included in this category.

Armour & Co., 36 Ways To Serve Bacon 2.00
Aunt Susan's Recipe Book, Paperback, 1940, 19 Pages 5.00
Betty Crocker Cookbook For Boys & Girls, First Edition 60.00
Carnation Co., Fun To Cook Book, 1967, 8 x 5 1/2 In., 48 Pages . . . . *Illus* 3.00
Complete Cookbook, Plain, Practical Directions, Philadelphia, Sanderson, 1869 . . . . 127.00
Cookbook For Good Nutrition, Carlton Fredericks, 1960 . . . . 12.00
Delicious Quick Desserts, Junkett, 24 Pages, Paperback, 1929 . . . . 4.00
Family Fare, A Guide To Good Nutrition, Dept. Of Agriculture, c.1971, 91 Pages 3.00
Fleischmann Treasury Of Yeast Baking, Paperback, 1962, 51 Pages 8.00
Homemakers Digest, Paperback, 1948, 28 Pages 2.00
Jack & Mary's Jell-O Recipe Book, Jack Benny & Mary Livingston, c.1937, 23 Pages . . . 35.00
Jell-O, America's Most Famous Dessert, Genessee Pure Food Co., 1920, 14 Pages . . . *Illus* 20.00
Lady's Companion Of Cookery, London, 1751, 23 Volume Set 595.00
Mazola Salad Bowl, Corn Products Refining Co., 1939, 9 1/4 x 6 In., 32 Pages . . . . . *Illus* 1.00
Minute Tapioca, Prize Winning Recipes To Vary Your Menus, c.1927, 32 Pages 16.00
Modern Menu Magic Coldspot Reapers, 31 Pages 2.00

Cookbook, Carnation Co., Fun To Cook Book, 1967, 8 x 5 1/2 In., 48 Pages

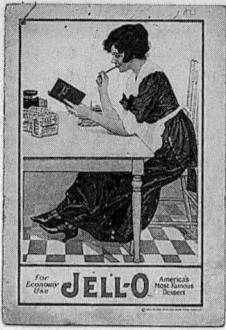

Cookbook, Jell-O, America's Most Famous Dessert, Genessee Pure Food Co., 1920, 14 Pages

Cookbook, Mazola Salad Bowl, Corn Products Refining Co., 1939, 9 1/4 x 6 In., 32 Pages

Pennsylvania Dutch Recipe Book, Paperback, 1966, 62 Pages	2.00
Pillsbury, 100 Delicious Foods From 4 Basic Recipes, c.1927, 30 Pages	20.00
Royal Baking Guide, 1927	8.00
Royal Baking Powder, 24 Easy Baking Recipes Your Family Will Rave About, 1944	6.00
Royal Baking Powder, Making Biscuits, Paperback, 1927, 14 Pages	3.50
Souvenir Recipe Book, Oklahoma Farmer-Stockman, Paperback, 1932, 15 Pages	8.00
Spry, Frying Made Easy, Paperback, 19 Pages	4.00
Treasury Of Meat Recipes, National Live Stock & Meat Board, c.1940, 40 Pages	10.00
Wesson Oil, Glorious Eating For Weight Watchers, c.1961, 96 Pages	8.00

COOKIE JARS with brightly painted designs or amusing figural shapes became popular in the mid-1930s. Many companies made them and collectors search for cookie jars either by design or by maker's name. Listed here are examples by the less common makers. Major factories are listed under their own names in other categories of the book, such as Abingdon, Brush, Hull, McCoy, Red Wing, and Shawnee. See also the Disneyana category.

Baby, Diaper Pin, Regal China	375.00
Bear With Cookie, Avon, 1979	125.00
Black, Chef, Someone's In The Kitchen, White Hat & Coat, 12 In.	201.00
Black, Hand Painted Asters, Randsburg	45.00
Black Woman In Sunday Dress, Hands On Belly, 13 In.	25.00
Clown With Drum, Pfaltzgraff	250.00
Crawling Clown, Black, 2 Knob Handles, 6 1/2 In.	145.00
Dutch Girl, Pink, Pottery Guild, 12 1/4 In.	110.00
Elf, Sitting On Stump, Cookie In Hand, Sack On Back, Twin Winton, 13 In.	75.00
Figural, Large Woman, Blue Tie, 11 1/2 In.	80.00
Fred Flintstone, Family, Friends, Ceramic, Box, 1990, 8 1/2 x 9 x 14 1/2 In.	65.00
Friar Tuck, Thou Shalt Not Steal, Twin Winton, 12 In.	75.00
Goldilocks, Regal China, 12 1/2 In.	150.00
Kitten, On Beehive, American Bisque, 11 3/4 In.	145.00
Lamb, Hands In Pockets, Yellow, Green, Airbrush Glaze, American Bisque, 10 1/2 In.	195.00
Leprechaun, Green Hat, Shirt, Pot Of Gold Base, Doranne Of California	110.00
Noah's Ark, Brown, Twin Winton, 11 In.	40.00
Pennsylvania Dutch Boy, American Bisque, 11 1/2 In.	450.00
Pig, Dancer, Clover, Bow, American Bisque	250.00
Pillsbury Doughboy, Ceramic, White, Blue, c.1970, 5 x 5 1/2 x 10 1/2 In.	15.00
Pinocchio, Head, Hat	150.00
Santa, Winking, American Bisque, 9 3/4 In.	325.00
Squirrel, On Stump, No. 2620-1-2, California Originals, 14 1/2 In.	45.00
Tomato, Stanford Red, Pantry Parade, 8 1/4 In.	65.00
Uncle Sam Bear, Metlox	850.00
Witch, Fitz & Floyd	225.00

COORS ware was made by a pottery in Golden, Colorado, a company founded with the help of the Coors Brewing Company. Its founder, John Herold, started the Herold China and Pottery Company in 1910. The company name was changed in 1920, when Herold left. Dishes and decorative wares were produced from the turn of the century until the pottery was destroyed by fire in the 1930s. The name *Coors* is marked on the back. The company is still in business making industrial porcelain. For more information, see *Kovels' Depression Glass & Dinnerware Price List*.

Pitcher, Yellow, Ivory Interior, Coorsite, c.1929, 52 Oz., 7 1/2 In.	65.00
Tumbler, Rosebud, Blue, Handle, 8 1/2 Oz., 3 1/2 In.	95.00
Tumbler, Rosebud, Rose, Handle, 8 1/2 Oz., 3 1/2 In.	95.00

COPELAND pieces listed here are those that have a mark including the word Copeland used between 1847 and 1976. Marks include Copeland Spode and Copeland & Garrett. See also Copeland Spode and Royal Worcester.

Dinner Set, Imari Pattern, c.1877, 9 3/4 In., 24 Piece	1435.00
Figurine, Mending Net, Woman Seated, Net On Lap, Parian, E.W. Wyon, 1873, 16 1/2 In.	500.00
Figurine, Parian, Napoleon, Seated, Marked, c.1850, 11 1/2 In.	980.00
Jardiniere, Spode Italian Pattern, Blue & White Transfer, 6 x 7 In.	60.00
Pitcher, Applied Relief Vignettes, Tavern Scenes, Cobalt Ground, Rustic Handle, 8 In.	145.00
Plate, Imari Pattern, Fluted Edge, 8 1/2 In., 17 Piece	1495.00
Plate, Luncheon, Flowering Urn, Cobalt Rim, Gilt, 20th Century, 9 In.	290.00
Platter, Tower, Flow Blue, 12 x 15 In.	45.00

COPELAND SPODE appears on some pieces of nineteenth-century English porcelain. Josiah Spode established a pottery at Stoke-on-Trent, England, in 1770. In 1833, the firm was purchased by William Copeland and Thomas Garrett and the mark was changed. In 1847, Copeland became the sole owner and the mark changed again. W.T. Copeland & Sons continued until a 1976 merger when it became Royal Worcester Spode. Pieces are listed in this book under the name that appears in the mark. Copeland Spode, Copeland, and Royal Worcester have separate listings.

Bone Dish, Cabbage Leaf Shape, 10 3/8 x 7 x 1 3/8 In.	20.00
Bowl, Vegetable, Cover, Christopher Wren Pattern, Marked, 9 1/2 In.	160.00
Bowl, Vegetable, Cover, Jasmine Pattern, Green & Brown, Marked, 1930s	60.00
Candlestick, Greek Maidens, Jasperware, Olive Green, Marked, 1891, Pair	295.00
Coffeepot, Cover, Buttercup Pattern, Marked, 1940s	150.00
Creamer, Bouquet Pattern, Pink Transfer, Marked	60.00
Cup & Saucer, Demitasse, Old Salem Pattern, Blue Transfer, Marked	23.00
Figurine, Cupid, Holding Shell-Shaped Bowl, Insects & Leaves, Marked, 6 In.	295.00
Pitcher, Mayflower Pattern, Multicolored Transfer, Marked, 6 1/2 In.	250.00
Plate, Mother Rabbit & Bunnies, Blue Transfer, Marked, 9 In.	225.00
Platter, Fairy Dell Pattern, Multicolored Transfer, Marked, 10 x 13 In.	40.00
Platter, Gainsborough Pattern, Multicolored Transfer, Marked, 11 x 15 In.	50.00
Sugar & Creamer, Chelsea Wicker Pattern, Embossed, Marked	30.00
Tureen, Italian Pattern, Blue Transfer, Marked, 9 x 9 In.	60.00

COPPER has been used to make utilitarian items, such as teakettles and cooking pans, since the days of the early American colonists. Copper became a popular metal with the Arts & Crafts makers of the early 1900s, and decorative pieces, like desk sets, were made. Other pieces of copper may be found in the Arts & Crafts, Bradley & Hubbard, Kitchen, and Roycroft categories.

Ashtray, Hammered, Matchbox Stand, Patina, Stamped, Burton Studio, 5 x 10 In.	750.00
Ashtray, Official Cork Ball Baseball In Center, 8 In.	30.00
Ashtray, Stylized Leaf Shape, Relief Silver Frog & Insect, Gorham, 4 1/2 In.	489.00
Bathtub, Zinc Lined, Panels, Double Lift Rings, England, c.1900, 29 x 31 In.	4370.00
Bed Warmer, Brass & Iron, Pierced, Star Of David, Garden Of Eden, 41 In.	180.00
Bed Warmer, Brass Mounted, Round, Fruitwood Handle, c.1815, 39 In.	375.00
Bed Warmer, Brass Supports, Turned Wood Handle, Signed IB, Early 19th Century	525.00

Don't cook acid foods in copper pots unless they have tin lining. The combination of acid and copper creates a poison.

Copper, Cuspidor, Turtle, Stepping On Head Opens Shell, 14 In.

Bed Warmer, Engraved Leaves, Turned Cherry Handle, 45 In. 90.00
Bed Warmer, Grain Painted Wood Handle, 40 In. 140.00
Bed Warmer, Stamped, Tooled, Bird, Flowers, Beehive, Turned Wood Handle, 45 In. 220.00
Bed Warmer, Tooled, Flower Designs, Turned Wood Handle, 12 x 45 In. 165.00
Bed Warmer, Turned Wood Handle, Black Paint Trace, 43 1/2 In. 220.00
Bowl, Hammered, Flared Shape, Arts & Crafts, 15 In. 230.00
Bowl, Novick, Nickel Plated Interior, Patina, 6 In. 80.00
Box, Hammered, Tooled Designs, Arts & Crafts, 6 1/2 x 3 In. 460.00
Box, Lid, Hinges, Enamel Mounted, Arts & Crafts, c.1900, 2 1/2 x 7 1/2 x 5 1/2 In. 635.00
Box, Stylized Flowers, John Pearson, Initialed, 5 3/4 In. 235.00
Box, Tender, Hinged Cover, Rectangular, 19th Century, 3 x 5 In. 120.00
Box, Tobacco, Geometric Patterns, Round, England, 18th Century 210.00
Bucket, Wrought Iron, Swing Handle, c.1900, 12 x 12 1/2 In. 115.00
Chafing Dish, Cover, Hammered, Scroll Legs, Rabbits, Mushroom Finial, Gorham, 10 In. . 2940.00
Chamberstick, Riveted Strap Handle, Stamped, Jarvie, 3 x 5 3/4 In. 635.00
Charger, Birds, Flower Border, John Pearson, Signed, Arts & Crafts, 1895, 20 In. 2350.00
Charger, Hammered, Round, Rolled Rim, Patina, Arts & Crafts, 29 In. 750.00
Charger, Hammered, Spade Design, Rolled Rim, Dark Patina, Arts & Crafts, 15 In. 2070.00
Cuspidor, Turtle, Stepping On Head Opens Shell, 14 In. .... *Illus* 100.00
Distillation Pot, Tapered Spout, E.H. Sargent & Co., Chicago, 1852, 14 x 12 In. 245.00
Figurine, Elk Head, Embossed, Life Size, 80 In. 5040.00
Frame, Hammered, Flower Design, Patina, Frame, Arts & Crafts, 7 1/2 In. 185.00
Holder, Pretzelman, Chase, Cutout Silhouette, Brass Round, Tray, Lurelle Guild, 16 In. .. 70.00
Jardiniere, Cylindrical, 3 Handles, Paw Feet, Emantee, Art Nouveau, 13 x 12 1/2 In. 295.00
Jardiniere, Hammered, Flared, Riveted Handles, Base, Original Patina, Mark, 13 In. 575.00
Kettle, Candy, Dovetailed, Round Bottom, Iron Handles, Late 19th Century, 8 x 16 In. ... 170.00
Kettle, Dovetailed, Iron Band, Swing Handle, 29 In. 135.00
Kettle, Wrought Iron Mounted, France, c.1900, 14 1/2 x 24 In. 690.00
Mirror, Hammered, Embossed Ship, Arts & Crafts, 30 x 48 In. 1295.00
Molds are listed in the Kitchen category.
Pan, Saute, Wrought Iron Handle, Tin Interior, Late 19th Century, 2 1/2 x 8 1/4 In. 115.00
Picnic Set, Teapot, Burner, Cups, Saucers, 4 Food Boxes, Flatware, Wicker Case, England 375.00
Pitcher, Hammered, Tapered, Charles Stickley, Mark, 17 x 6 In. 605.00
Pitcher, Tin Lining, Falick Novick, Early 20th Century, 9 In. 5500.00
Planter, Hammered, Footed, Stylized Floral Struts, Arts & Crafts, 7 x 24 x 11 In. 290.00
Plaque, His Grace Arthur Duke Of Wellington, KG 375.00
Pot, Wrought Iron Handle, Provincial, Tin Surface, c.1900, 4 x 8 3/4 In. 80.00
Pot, Wrought Iron Handle, Tin Interior, Burnished, c.1900, 4 1/4 x 7 1/2 In. 115.00
Punch Bowl, Hammered, Sea Gulls On Scalloped Rim, Short Reeded Foot, Mauser, 13 In. 5290.00
Sconce, Hammered, Arts & Crafts, Original Patina, 12 1/2 In., Pair 185.00
Scuttle, Coal, Hammered, Rolled Rim, Flower, Arts & Crafts, 15 x 12 In. 635.00
Tankard, Hammered, Iron Handle, Arts & Crafts, Patina, 14 In. 635.00
Tankard, Hand Hammered, Impressed Mark, Patina, Arts & Crafts, 7 1/2 In. 115.00
Teakettle, Bail Handle, Turned Wood Grip, Late 19th Century 90.00
Teakettle, Gooseneck, Dovetailed, Bail Handle, W. Heyser, Chambersburg, 5 Qt. 1240.00
Teakettle, Gooseneck, Dovetailed, Brass Finial, Penn., 6 In. 1650.00
Teakettle, Gooseneck, Finial, Ram's Horn, G. Youse, c.1797 .... 990.00
Teakettle, Removable Lid, Brass Finial, Bail Handle, c.1815, 9 1/2 In. 575.00
Teapot, Hammered, Dovetailed Seam, Swing Handle, Covered Spout, 4 1/4 x 3 3/4 In. ... 110.00
Tray, Hammered, Conjoined Initials OMS, Patina, Onondaga Metal Shop, c.1904, 24 In. ... 2070.00

Tray, Hammered, Gustav Stickley, Impressed Mark, 7 In. 290.00
Tray, Hammered, Peacocks In Corners, Blue Squares, Art & Crafts, 16 1/2 x 11 3/4 In. . . . 345.00
Tray, Onondaga Metalshop, Hammered, Patina, Impressed Mark, 24 In. 2070.00
Tray, Round, Shallow, Shield, Crown, Crossed Arrows, England, c.1910, 13 In. 59.00
Tray, Stickley Bros., Hammered, Lobed Rim, Embossed Dots, Stamped 36, 13 1/2 In. 805.00
Umbrella Stand, Hammered, Jos. Heinrichs, 20th Century, Arts & Crafts, 16 x 10 1/2 In. . 100.00
Umbrella Stand, Stylized Repousse Flowers, Drip Tray, Arts & Crafts, 30 1/4 x 29 1/2 In. 430.00
Vase, Copper Overlay, Green Iridescent Glass, Arts & Crafts, 7 3/4 In. 60.00
Vase, Hammered, 3 Handles, Original Patina, Stickley Brothers, 10 In. 255.00
Vase, Hammered, Broad Form, Patina, Signed, Harry Dixon, 9 In. 1610.00
Vase, Hammered, Cylindrical, A. Hairian, San Francisco, 3 In. 288.00
Vase, Hammered, Footed, Original Patina, Benedict, 6 In. 195.00
Vase, Hammered, Original Dark Patina, Stamped, Hans Jauchens, 7 1/2 x 4 In. 805.00
Vase, Hammered, Stylized Design, Continental, Arts & Crafts, 4 1/2 In. 60.00
Vase, Tapering, Cylindrical Shape, 2 Handles, Flowers, Arts & Crafts, 1895, 8 1/4 In. 590.00
Wall Plaque, Gustav Stickley, c.1905, 15 In. 9560.00

COPPER LUSTER items are listed in the Luster category.

CORALENE glass was made by firing many small colored beads on the outside of glassware. It was made in many patterns in the United States and Europe in the 1880s. Reproductions are made today. Coralene-decorated Japanese pottery is listed in the Japanese Coralene category.

Bottle, Blue Satin, Yellow Seaweed, Stopper, 7 In. 125.00
Vase, Blue & White, 4 1/2 In. 30.00
Vase, Mother-Of-Pearl, Diamond-Quilted, Blue, 19th Century, 9 1/4 In. 430.00
Vase, Pink, Allover Yellow Seaweed, 19th Century, 5 1/2 In. 35.00
Vase, Stick, Pink, Allover Yellow Seaweed, 9 3/4 In. 635.00
Vase, Tan, Over Pink, Mother-Of-Pearl, Fleur-De-Lis, Shouldered, 6 1/2 In. 1345.00
Vase, White & Pink, 4 1/2 In. 30.00
Vase, Yellow Fleur-De-Lis, On Cranberry Mother-Of-Pearl, Bulbous, Ruffled Rim, 5 In. . . 730.00

CORKSCREWS have been needed since the first bottle was sealed with a cork, probably in the seventeenth century. Today collectors search for the early, unusual patented examples or the figural corkscrews of recent years.

Brass & Bone Handle, England, 18th Century 165.00
Butler, Drunk, Ivory Finish, Marked Syroco, 4 1/2 In. 50.00
Monk, Syracuse Ornamental Co., King Sticker, 1940s, 8 1/2 In. 395.00
Waiter, Natural Finish, Marked Syroco, 4 1/2 In. 80.00

CORONATION souvenirs have been made since the 1800s. Pottery, glass, tin, silver, and paper objects with a picture of the monarchs and date have been sold at many coronations. The pieces that mention King Edward VIII, the king who was never crowned, are not rare; collectors should be sure to check values before buying. Related pieces are found in the Commemorative category.

Beaker, Czar Nicholas II, Cup Of Sorrow, Khodinka Cup, Enamel, 1896 . . . . 350.00
Beaker, King Edward VII & Queen Alexandra, 1902 . . . . 195.00
Beaker, Queen Elizabeth II, Brentleigh Ware, 1953, 4 In. 30.00
Bread Plate, Queen Elizabeth II, Falcon Ware, Weatherby, 1953, 7 In. 12.00
Card Tray, Queen Mary, Porcelain, Schmidt & Co., Czechoslovakia, 1911, 6 x 9 In. 60.00
Cup & Saucer, Queen Elizabeth II, Grafton Bone China, 1953 . . . . 16.00
Jug, King Edward VII, Stoneware, Mortlocks, Royal Doulton, 1902 . . . . 295.00
Jug, King William IV & Queen Adelaide, Portrait, Plumed Headpiece, 1831, 5 1/2 In. 795.00
Jug, Queen Victoria, Blue & White, Portrait, Windsor Castle, 1838 . . . . 1200.00
Loving Cup, King Edward VIII, Paragon, Gold Handles, 1936, 7 1/2 x 4 3/8 In. 395.00
Mug, King Edward VIII, Musical, For He's A Jolly Good Fellow, 1937 . . . . 225.00
Mug, King George V & Queen Mary, Bone China, Military Scenes, 1911 . . . . 135.00
Mug, Queen Elizabeth II, Sepia Portrait, Alfred Meakin, 1952, 3 In. 50.00
Pencil, King Edward VIII, Wood, Westminster Abbey, May 12, 1937, 6 1/2 In. . . . . . .12.00 to 15.00
Pin, Queen Elizabeth II, 1953, 2 In. 35.00
Pin Tray, Queen Elizabeth II, Ivy Ground, Royal Crown Derby, 1952, 4 x 3 In. 55.00
Plate, King Edward VII & Queen Alexandra, Flow Blue, 1901, Pair 195.00

Plate, King George V, Royal Worcester, Coat Of Arms, Portraits, 1911, 10 1/2 In. 135.00
Plate, King William IV, Portrait, Daisy Border, 8 Sides, 1831 . . . .   950.00
Plate, Queen Elizabeth II, 40th Anniversary, Royal Doulton, 1992, 7 3/4 In. 350.00
Program, King George VI & Queen Queen Elizabeth, May 12, 1937 . . . .   35.00
Scarf, Queen Elizabeth II, Silk, 1953, 26 In. 35.00
Tankard, Beer, Queen Elizabeth II, Crown Devon, Joshua Tetley & Sons, 5 1/4 In. 75.00
Tankard, King George VI, Elizabeth, Waisted, Portraits, Scalloped Edge, 1937 . . . .   68.00
Tin, Duke Of Edinburgh, Bilsland Bakery, Tea Caddy Shape, 1952, 6 In. 30.00
Tin, Toffee, Queen Elizabeth II & Prince Philip, Blue Boy Assorted, 1953, 5 x 4 x 3 In. . .   45.00
Tray, Queen Elizabeth, Palaces, Metal, 1953, 18 In. 36.00
Tumbler, King Edward VIII, Portrait, Porcelain, Pink Glaze, Johnson Bros., 4 1/2 In. 80.00

COSMOS is a pressed milk glass pattern with colored flowers made from 1894 to 1915 by the Consolidated Lamp and Glass Company. Tablewares and lamps were made in this pattern. A few pieces were also made of clear glass with painted decorations. Other glass patterns are listed under Consolidated Lamp and also in various glass categories. In later years, Cosmos was also made by the Westmoreland Glass Company.

Butter, Cover 135.00
Salt & Pepper, 3 1/2 In. 70.00
Syrup, 7 In. 160.00
Tumbler, Opaque White, Pastel Flowers, Pink Rim, 3 3/4 In. 35.00

COVERLETS were made of linen or wool during the nineteenth century. Most of the coverlets date from 1800 to the 1880s. There was a revival of hand weaving in the 1920s and new coverlets, especially geometric patterns, were made. The earliest coverlets were made on narrow looms, so two woven strips were joined together and a seam can be found. The weave structures of coverlets can include summer and winter, double weave, overshot, and others. Jacquard coverlets have elaborate pictorial patterns that are made on a special loom or with the use of a special attachment. Quilts are listed in this book in their own category.

Double Weave, Geometric, Snow Flake, 2 Panel, 72 x 74 In. 138.00
Double Weave, Snowflakes, Pine Trees, Deep Blue & White, 2 Panel, 74 x 86 In. 150.00
Double Weave, White, Blue, Geometric, 2 Panel, 76 x 84 In. 220.00
Flowers, Leaves, 3 Colors, C. Fehr, 2 Panel, 1842, 74 x 89 In. 176.00
Flowers, Leaves, 4 Colors, Isaac Kepner, Sophia Smith, 2 Panel, 1841, 80 x 95 In. 578.00
Flowers, Leaves, Eagle In Corners, 4 Colors, A. Frey, Mt. Joy, 2 Panel, 1858, 72 x 78 In. . .   138.00
Jacquard, 4 Colors, Acorn & Leaves, Mathias Rudisill, 19th Century, 80 x 90 In. 275.00
Jacquard, 4 Colors, Star & Flowers, H. Stager Mt. Joy, 83 x 85 In. 305.00
Jacquard, Agriculture & Manufactures, Foundation Of Independence, 78 x 79 In. 715.00
Jacquard, Bird Of Paradise In Corners, Red & White, 85 x 76 In.   415.00
Jacquard, Birds, Roses, Tulip Border, Blue Stripes, P. Hartman, 2 Panel, 1838, 70 x 80 In.   655.00
Jacquard, Blue & White, Elizabeth Garrison, 1837, 90 x 70 In. 575.00
Jacquard, Blue, Burgundy, White, Pine Tree Borders, 66 x 76 In.   195.00
Jacquard, Blue, Red, Green Stripes, Delaware, Ohio, 2 Panel, 1854, 58 x 86 In. 440.00
Jacquard, Blue, Red, Green, Yellow Stripes, Knox County, Ohio, 1864, 74 x 88 In. 495.00
Jacquard, Blue, Red, Ivory, Green, Samuel Mansfield, Richland, Ohio, 1850, 70 x 88 In. . .   230.00
Jacquard, Blue, Stripes, Peter Hartman, Wooster, Ohio, 1843, 77 x 90 In. 248.00
Jacquard, Blue, White, 26 Eagles, Shields, Plants, Carolyn Phelps, 1835, 80 x 91 1/2 In. . .   633.00
Jacquard, Centennial, Center Medallion, Red, Green, Blue Stripes, 80 x 87 In. 110.00
Jacquard, Conch Shell Corner, Blue, Salmon, Natural, 2 Panel, 75 x 86 In. 358.00
Jacquard, Eagle Border, Tan, Green, Brown, Red, 2 Panel, 70 x 92 In. 415.00
Jacquard, Eagle Corners, Building, Floral Urns, Mid 19th Century, 86 x 70 In. 125.00
Jacquard, Eagles, Buildings, Blue & White, A.R. Benton, N.Y., 1832, 86 x 93 In. 590.00
Jacquard, Eagles, Masonic Symbols, Blue & White, July 4, 1824, 78 x 98 In. 956.00
Jacquard, Flower Medallions, Hearts, Grape Vine Border, 84 x 87 In. 310.00
Jacquard, Flowers, Blue, Red, Natural, Eagle Border, Ohio, 2 Panel, 70 x 82 In. 550.00
Jacquard, Flowers, Deep Blue & White, Signed TS, 1836, 84 x 84 In. 200.00
Jacquard, Flowers, John Klinhinz, Ohio, 2 Panel, 1854, 70 x 84 In. 495.00
Jacquard, Flowers, Leaves, Bird & Flower Border, M. Will, W.B., 1844, 73 x 90 In. 187.00

Jacquard, Flowers, Stars, Rooster Border, Natural, Blue, 1846, 68 x 86 In. 248.00
Jacquard, Flowers, Thistles, Red, White & Blue, Fringe, 90 x 82 In. 900.00
Jacquard, Fruit & Flowers, Eagle Corners, Fringe, 1 Panel, 74 x 86 In. 375.00
Jacquard, Indigo, Flowers, Eagles, 1850, 84 x 94 In. 1528.00
Jacquard, Leaf Scrolls, Classical Urns, Red, Natural, 77 x 86 In. 305.00
Jacquard, Lilies, Star Medallions, Eagle, Willow Trees, Blue & White, 76 x 86 In. 715.00
Jacquard, Medallions, Natural, Navy Blue, 2 Borders, Daniel Bury, c.1802, 66 x 88 In. . . 330.00
Jacquard, Medallions, Seaweed, Shells, Birds, c.1850, 80 x 88 In. 550.00
Jacquard, Medallions, Urns, Blue & White, Initialed MAD, 1854, 74 x 81 In. 375.00
Jacquard, Medallions, Vine Borders, Natural, Blue, Red, 2 Panel, 1846, 75 x 82 In. 770.00
Jacquard, Memorial Hall, Red, White, Green & Blue, Aug. 17th, 1875, 84 x 78 In. 140.00
Jacquard, Natural, Blue, A. Smith, Lodi, 2 Panel, 1837, 74 x 82 In. 330.00
Jacquard, Natural, Blue, Red, Green, Loudonville Ohio, 1855, 71 x 90 In. 440.00
Jacquard, Natural, Blue, Red, Wayne County, 1845, 72 x 88 In. 605.00
Jacquard, Natural, Red, Blue, Green, Lewis Weichley, 1853, 74 x 82 In. 220.00
Jacquard, Natural, Red, Green, Signed, Columbiana County, Ohio, After 1848, 72 x 76 In. 415.00
Jacquard, Natural, Salmon, Blue, Jacob Snyder, Indiana, 68 x 85 In. 385.00
Jacquard, Overshot, Blue, Red, Natural, F. Yearous, Ohio, 1853, 2 Panel, 90 1/2 x 70 In. . 495.00
Jacquard, Red, Blue, Natural, 2 Panel, 68 x 78 In. 415.00
Jacquard, Rows Of Flower Urns, Grapes, Pinwheels, Leaf Border, 84 x 88 In. 365.00
Jacquard, Rows Of Stars, Red, White & Blue, Wool, Fringe, 78 x 94 In. 255.00
Jacquard, Ship Corner Blocks, Blue & White, 1839, 74 x 80 In. 440.00
Jacquard, Stars, Tulip & Leaf Borders, Blue, White, 77 x 88 In. 413.00
Jacquard, Thistle Medallions, Roses, Vine Borders, 72 x 78 In. 550.00
Jacquard, Tulips, Birds, Canton, Stark County, Ohio, 1840, 70 x 72 In. 415.00
Jacquard, White, Blue, Tulips, Hearts, Stark County, Ohio, 2 Panel, 1848, 68 x 83 In. 248.00
Jacquard, Wide Loom, Stripes, Medallions, Xenia, Ohio, c.1851, 76 x 86 In. 220.00
Jacquard, Yellow, Salmon, Blue Stripes, William & Rachel Guthrie, 84 x 96 In. 385.00
Overshot, Natural, Blue, Red, Tied Fringe, 2 Panel, 80 x 90 In. 220.00
Overshot, Optical, Natural, Red, Blue, Trimmed Fringe, 68 x 78 In. 415.00
Overshot, Red, Black, White, 3 Panel, 96 x 99 In. 175.00
Overshot, Red, Green Blue, Stylized Flying Geese, Fringe, 2 Panel, 64 x 94 In. 325.00
Overshot, Wide Loom, Optical, Natural, Purple, Rust, 74 x 106 In. 495.00
Summer & Winter, Blue, Red, Flowers, Hearts, Grape Vine Border, 84 x 87 In. 310.00
Summer & Winter, Blue, Red, Green, 1842, 76 x 100 In. 385.00
Summer & Winter, Centre County, Penn., 1865, 78 x 81 In. 305.00
Summer & Winter, Checkerboard & Chain, Deep Blue & White, 2 Panel, 76 x 90 In. 150.00
Summer & Winter, Indigo & White, Double Rose & Tile, Tulip Border, 1839, 90 x 75 In. . . 560.00

COWAN POTTERY made art pottery and wares for florists. Guy Cowan
made pottery in Rocky River, Ohio, a suburb of Cleveland, from 1913
to 1931. A stylized mark with the word *Cowan* was used on most
pieces. A commercial, mass-produced line was marked *Lakeware*.
Collectors today search for the Art Deco pieces by Guy Cowan, Viktor
Schreckengost, Waylande Gregory, or Thelma Frazier Winter.

Bookends, Boy & Girl, Kneeling, Ivory Hi-Glaze, Impressed Mark, 6 1/2 In., Pair 80.00
Bookends, Elephant, Blue, Green Mottled Glaze, 7 1/2 x 5 1/4 In. 575.00
Bookends, Sunbonnet, Green Crystalline Glaze, c.1925, 7 1/2 In., Pair 375.00
Bowl, Speckled Turquoise, Yellow Mottled Glaze, 3 1/2 x 13 In. 80.00
Candleholder, Byzantine, Thick Guava Glaze, Shape, No. 746, Marked, 9 In. 105.00
Candleholder, Ming Green Glaze, c.1928, 8 1/2 In., Pair 69.00
Charger, Couple Dancing, Egyptian Blue Glaze, Black Slip, Schreckengost, 1931, 11 In. . . 5750.00
Console, Oriental Red Glaze, Impressed, 5 7/8 In. 175.00
Figurine, Flamingo, Ivory Hi-Glaze, Impressed Mark, 11 In., Pair 345.00
Figurine, Nocturne, Ivory Glaze, Black Details, Circle Mark, 9 x 7 In. 2300.00
Figurine, Russian Peasant Accordion Player, A. Blazys, No. 79, 8 In. 1375.00
Figurine, Woman, Morning, Ivory Crackle Glaze, 9 x 7 In. 1095.00
Trivet, Fish, 4 Seashell Feet, Polychromed, Impressed, 6 3/8 In. 210.00
Vase, Bud, Tapered, Delphinium Luster Glaze, 11 3/8 In. 115.00
Vase, Egyptian Blue, Cap Style Metal Lid, Impressed, 7 In. 185.00
Vase, Feu Rouge Glaze, Shape, No. 932, Impressed, 8 In. 60.00
Vase, Fish, Egyptian Blue Glaze, c.1931, 6 3/8 In. 1380.00
Vase, Guava Glaze, 2 Scroll Handles, Impressed Logo, 6 In. 140.00

Vase, Iridescent Orange Glaze, Shouldered, Slightly Flared Rim, 4 1/2 In. 80.00
Vase, Mottled Green & Brown Crystalline Glaze, Stepped Shape, Impressed Mark, 6 In. . . 230.00
Vase, Turquoise Glaze, Blue Ground, Squirrel, Birds, Flowers, Bulbous, 8 1/2 In. 1095.00
Vase, Waisted Form, Long Neck, Blue Luster Glaze, Marked, 12 In. 50.00

CRACKER JACK, the molasses-flavored popcorn mixture, was first
made in 1896 in Chicago, Illinois. A prize was added to each box in
1912. Collectors search for the old boxes, toys, and advertising materials. Many of the toys are unmarked.

Mirror, White, Blue Lithograph, Jack & Dog, More You Eat More You Want, 2 x 2 In. . . . 300.00
Puzzle, Parrot, Paper, C. Carey Cloud, 1946, 2 1/4 x 3 1/4 In. 15.00
Toy, Circus Wagon, Tin, 1947 . . . . 110.00
Toy, Prairie Whistle, Warbler Bird Call, Japan, 1950s, 1 In. 8.00

CRACKLE GLASS was originally made by the Venetians, but most of the
ware found today dates from the 1800s. The glass was heated, cooled,
and refired so that many small lines appeared inside the glass. It was
made in many factories in the United States and Europe.

Butter, Cover, Underplate, Blue, Applied Amber Finial 75.00
Pitcher, Enameled Butterfly, Dragonfly, Floral, Brown, Blue, Green, Pink, c.1890, 5 In. . . 265.00
Vase, Bud, Heart Shape, Green Stem, Frosted Ball Base, 3 1/2 In. 130.00
Vase, Clear, Cylindrical, Stepped, Ribbed, Footed, Flared Rim, 8 1/2 In. 2250.00

CRANBERRY GLASS is an almost transparent yellow-red glass. It resembles the color of cranberry juice. The glass has been made in Europe
and America since the Civil War. It is still being made, and reproductions can fool the unwary. Related glass items may be listed in other
categories, such as Northwood, Rubena Verde, etc.

Basket, Shaded, Opalescent, Clear Handle, 6 3/4 In. 115.00
Box, Hinged Lid, Applied Clear Leaf, 5 In. 225.00
Card Tray, Mary Gregory, Girl With Basket, 4 In. 275.00
Chalice, Cone Shape, Engraved Fox Hunt, Gold, 6 1/2 In., Pair 325.00
Chalice, Feather & Butterfly, Gold Overlay, Stippled, 10 1/4 In. 275.00
Compote, Iridescent Overlay, Brass, Trefoil Stand, c.1900, 8 1/2 In. 1150.00
Cruet, Amber Handle, 4 1/2 In. 50.00
Cruet, Clear Stopper, Ribbed Handle, 5 1/2 In. 70.00
Decanter, Clear Applied Handle, 3-Petal Top, Clear Ball, Stopper, 11 In. 175.00
Decanter, Wine, Cut Flower Design, Clear Stopper, Applied Foot, 10 3/4 In. 165.00
Decanter, Wine, Pinched Sides, Enameled Gold Flowers, 12 In. 310.00
Decanter, Wine, White Dot Flowers, Gold Bands, Clear, Ball Stopper, 9 1/4 x 3 1/2 In. . . 165.00
Epergne, Tree Style, Ruffled Base, Curled Arm, Basket, Reeded Handle, 9 In. 80.00
Finger Bowl, Reverse Swirl, Gold Trim, 8 Piece 400.00
Pitcher, Applied Clear Handle, 7 1/2 In. 110.00
Pitcher, Inverted Thumbprint, Yellow Enameled Lattice, 8 In. 190.00
Salt, Clear Rigaree, Ribbed, Ruffled Edge, 3-Footed Metal Holder, 6 In. 170.00
Vase, Enameled Lily, Gold Highlights, Handles, 7 1/2 In. 175.00
Vase, Flute, Ruffled Edge, Applied Clear Rigaree, 12 In. 125.00
Vase, Hobnail, Fold-Over Top, 7 5/8 In. 896.00
Vase, Jack-In-The-Pulpit, Cranberry To Pink, 7 1/2 x 4 3/4 In., Pair 295.00
Vase, Ribbon, Enameled, Garland, Tricornered Rim, 12 1/4 In. 145.00
Vase, Tapered Neck, Flared Rim, Black Threading, Spiral Bands, 11 In. 200.00
Vase, Textured Gold Flower, Leaves, White Outline, 10 1/4 x 3 1/4 In. 175.00
Vase, White Enameled Dragonfly & Flowers, 8 In. 68.00

CREAMWARE, or queensware, was developed by Josiah Wedgwood
about 1765. It is a cream-colored earthenware that has been copied by
many factories. Similar wares may be listed under Pearlware and
Wedgwood.

Bowl, Archers, Medallions, Black Transfer, Leafy Border, Ferrybridge, 8 3/4 In. 470.00
Bowl, Black Transfer, British Sailing Ship, Nautical Design, Memory Verse, 7 1/8 In. 295.00
Bowl, Blue, Rust, White, Brown Slip, Mustard Ground, Green Reeded Rim, 7 3/8 In. 415.00
Candlestick, Molded Tree Shape, Applied Bird, Leaves, Shells, 11 3/4 In. 646.00

Candlestick, Molded Tree Shape, Applied Flower Heads, 11 1/4 In. 1175.00
Canister, Tea, Translucent Brown Tortoiseshell Glaze, Rectangular, Cut Corners, 5 In. . . . 500.00
Coffeepot, Cover, Mottled Gray & Brown Enamel, Crabstock Handle, 5 In. 999.00
Figurine, Bagpiper, Glazed Redware Bagpipe & Base, 6 3/8 In. 590.00
Figurine, Neptune, Leg On Dolphin's Head, On Relief Carved Square Plinth, 11 In. 1410.00
Figurine, Parrot, Perched On Branch, Translucent Blue, Green, Brown, 5 1/4 In. 1528.00
Figurine, Sailor, Translucent Green, Brown, Blue & Yellow Underglaze, 5 In. 235.00
Jug, Black Transfer, Tom Trulove Going To Sea, Lovers, Ship, 9 In. 645.00
Pitcher, Basin, Chamber, Painted, Red, Blue, Green, Black, Flowers, 10 In. 499.00
Pitcher, Transfer, Rural English Scenes, Winstone Cottage, 6 In. 205.00
Plate, Black Transfer, Sailing Ship, Green Sea, Birds On Rim, 9 5/8 In., 4 Piece 440.00
Plate, Prince William Of Orange, Enamel, Molded Feather Edge, 9 3/4 In. 1175.00
Platter, Mazarin, Marked Sewell 14, 14 1/2 In. 230.00
Spoon, Underglaze Translucent Enamels, Pierced Oval Bowl, c.1775, 9 1/4 In. 825.00
Tea Set, Flowers, Gilt, 18th Century, 8 1/2 In., 15 Piece 345.00
Teapot, Bullet Shaped, Single Cup Size, c.1780, 2 x 4 In. 875.00
Urn, Flowers, Enamel, 18th Century, 15 1/2 In. 575.00
Vase, Globular Shape, Ridges, Peonies, England, 5 In. 230.00
Vase, Neoclassical Figure, Flowers, Handles, 15 In. 175.00
Wall Pocket, Flower Spray, Translucent Green, Yellow, Gray, Scrolled Cornucopia, 9 In. . . 470.00
Wall Pocket, Satyr Head, Leaves, Translucent Green Underglaze, Blue Splashes, 6 In. . . . 295.00

CREDIT CARDS, credit tokens, metal charge plates, phone cards, and other similar collectibles that replace money are now part of the numismatic collecting hobby.

Bambergers, 1940 . . . . 8.00
Esso, 1972 . . . . 12.00
Gulf, 1950 . . . . 10.00
John Wanamaker, New York, London, Paris, Holder 12.00
Sears, 1970 . . . . 8.00
Standard Oil, Sohio National, Expired December 1960 . . . . 20.00

CROWN DERBY is the name given to porcelain made in Derby, England, from the 1770s to 1935. Pieces are marked with a crown and the letter *D* or the word *Derby*. The earliest pieces were made by the original Derby factory, while later pieces were made by the King Street Partnerships (1848–1935) or the Derby Crown Porcelain Co. (1876–1890). Derby Crown Porcelain Co. became Royal Crown Derby Co. Ltd. in 1890. It is now part of Royal Doulton Tableware Ltd.

Urn, Gilt Decorated, Oval, Reserves Of Birds, Cobalt Blue Ground, 13 1/2 In., Pair 1315.00
Vase, Birds, Insects, Flowers, Handles, Turquoise Ground, c.1880, 6 In. 230.00
Vase, Potpourri, Imari, Squat Urn Shape, Pierced Top, Artichoke Finial, 6 In., Pair 750.00

CROWN DUCAL is the name used on some pieces of porcelain made by A. G. Richardson and Co., Ltd., of Tunstall and Cobridge, England. The name has been used since 1916.

Bowl, Cereal, 6 1/2 In. 18.00
Bowl, Cover, Carved, Fruit, Leaves, Matte Glaze, Staffordshire, 4 1/2 x 5 1/4 In. 35.00
Bowl, Fruit, 5 1/4 In. 12.00
Bowl, Fruit, Athena, Gold, Navy, England, 5 In. 10.00
Bowl, Vegetable, Cover, Vale, 10 x 4 1/2 In. 45.00
Bowl & Server, Salad 70.00
Cake Plate, Primula, Chintz, 8 3/4 In. 125.00
Cup & Saucer, Bristol, Mulberry 40.00
Gravy Boat, Attached Underplate 75.00
Plate, Queen Elizabeth II, Gold Trim, Flowers, Burgundy Band, England, 10 In. 200.00
Platter, Oval, 12 1/4 In. 70.00
Sugar, Cover, Vale, 7 x 4 3/4 In. 40.00
Teapot, Chintz, Rimula, 5 In. 390.00
Vase, Art Deco, 3 In. 70.00
Vase, Chrysanthemums, Multicolored, Cylindrical, Flared Rim, c.1900, 11 In. 90.00
Vase, Poppy, 9 x 4 1/2 In. 165.00

Cruet, Aqua Glass, Swirled
Ribs, 3-Piece Mold, Chevron
Stopper, Polished Pontil, 8 In.

Cruet, Sapphire Blue Glass,
Pattern-Molded, Blown
Stopper, Applied Handle, 5 1/4

CROWN MILANO glass was made by Frederick Shirley at the Mt. Washington Glass Works about 1890. It had a plain biscuit color with a satin finish. It was decorated with flowers and often had large gold scrolls.

Biscuit Jar, Enameled, Flowers, Leaves, Signed Pairpoint Frame, 7 1/2 In.	518.00
Biscuit Jar, Gold Enameled Flowers, Peach Ground, Metal Frame, 8 1/4 In.	345.00
Biscuit Jar, Pansies, Cream Ground, Metal Cover, Embossed Flowers, 7 1/4 In.	300.00
Bride's Basket, Gold, Brown, Salmon Blossoms, Branches, Silver Plated Holder, 10 In. . .	575.00
Jar, Sweetmeat, Blue & Red Enamel, Silver Plated Rim & Cover, 5 1/2 In.	375.00
Jar, Sweetmeat, Cover, Melon Ribbed, Yellow, Leaves, Flowers, Metal Handle, 6 In.	925.00
Jar, Sweetmeat, Yellow, Flowers, Silver Plated Cover, 5 In.	100.00
Jardiniere, Pink, Maroon, Gold Enameled Flowers, Signed, 8 1/4 x 10 In.	400.00
Sugar & Creamer, Burmese Shading, Gold Enameled Flowers, Silver Plated Trim	375.00
Sugar Shaker, Melon Ribbed, Amethyst & Yellow Flowers, Green Leaves, 5 In.	390.00
Vase, Gold Enameled Chrysanthemums, Leafy Stems, Tan Body, Oval, Squat, 4 1/2 In. . .	505.00
Vase, Stick, Pink & Yellow Daisies, Tricornered, 3 Applied Handles, 7 1/2 In.	140.00
Vase, Thistles, Multicolored, Gold Highlights, Scrolling On Rim, 14 1/4 In.	2520.00

CROWN TUSCAN pattern is included in the Cambridge glass category.

CRUETS of glass or porcelain were made to hold vinegar, oil, and other condiments. They were especially popular during Victorian times and have been made in a variety of styles since the eighteenth century. Additional cruets may be found in the Castor Set category and also in various glass categories.

Amber Glass, Enameled Flowers, Ribbed, Sapphire Blue Stopper, Applied Handle, 7 In. . .	127.00
Amberina Glass, Ribbed, Applied Handle, Trefoil Pinched Spout, 5 1/8 In.	2200.00
Amethyst Glass, White Enameled Daisies, Ribbed, Stopper, 6 1/2 In.	104.00
Aqua Glass, Swirled Ribs, 3-Piece Mold, Chevron Stopper, Polished Pontil, 8 In. . . . *Illus*	150.00
Clear Glass, 15 Vertical Ribs, Cylindrical, 8-Panel Stopper, Pittsburgh, 9 1/2 In.	80.00
Clear Glass, 16 Ribs, Air-Trap Rigaree C-Scroll Handle, 8 1/2 In.	180.00
Clear Glass, 21 Ribs, Swirled To Left, Squat, Bulbous, Stopper, 8 1/2 In.	120.00
Cranberry Glass, Diamond-Quilted, Applied Handle, Teardrop Stopper, 6 1/4 In.	138.00
Pink Opaque Glass, Pine Cone, Clear Handle & Stopper, 6 In.	90.00
Sapphire Blue Glass, 16 Ribs, Hollow Handle, Bakewell & Pears, c.1820	3150.00
Sapphire Blue Glass, Pattern-Molded, Blown Stopper, Applied Handle, 5 1/4 In. . . . . *Illus*	40.00

CT GERMANY was first part of a mark used by a company in Altwasser, Germany, in 1845. The initials stand for C. Tielsch, a partner in the firm. The Hutschenreuther firm took over the company in 1918 and continued to use the *CT*.

C.T.

Bowl, Flowers, Handles, 1875, 14 1/2 x 9 In.	75.00
Bowl, Flowers, Leaves, Pink, Yellow, Gold, No. 5295, Victorian, 12 1/2 In.	190.00
Bowl, Flowers, Oval, Scalloped Border, 13 In.	43.00
Plate, Plums, Marked, C. Tielsch, c.1875-1934, 8 1/4 In.	55.00

CUP PLATES are small glass or china plates that held the cup while a diner of the mid-nineteenth century drank coffee or tea from the saucer. The most famous cup plates were made of glass at the Boston and Sandwich factory located in Sandwich, Massachusetts. There have been many new glass cup plates made in recent years for sale to gift shops or limited edition collectors. These are similar to the old plates but can be recognized as new.

Pressed Glass, 8-Plume Rosette, Plum Border, Rope Rim, Opalescent, 3 1/2 In.	125.00
Pressed Glass, Acorn & Maple Leaf, Opalescent, 3 5/8 In.	1880.00
Pressed Glass, American Eagle, Shield, Star & Ray, Cobalt Blue, 3 1/2 In.	150.00
Pressed Glass, Bull's-Eye & Star, Green, Thistle Border, Scalloped Rim, 3 1/4 In.	90.00
Pressed Glass, Eagle & Shield, Bull's-Eye & Point Rim, Opalescent, 3 1/2 In.	470.00
Pressed Glass, Eagle, Palmette, Roman Rosette Border, Scalloped Rim, Blue, 3 1/4 In.	350.00
Pressed Glass, Eagle, Serrated Border, Bull's-Eye & Point Rim, Blue, 3 1/2 In.	645.00
Pressed Glass, Flower, Leaf Border, Scalloped Rim, Opalescent, 3 3/8 In.	135.00
Pressed Glass, Flower, Sheaf Border, Scalloped Rim, Turquoise Blue, 3 1/2 In.	235.00
Pressed Glass, Hearts, Lyre & 6 Scroll, Uneven Scalloped Rim, Cobalt Blue, 3 1/2 In.	175.00
Pressed Glass, Henry Clay, Cornucopias, Scalloped Rim, Sapphire Blue, 3 1/2 In.	235.00 to 300.00
Pressed Glass, Lily, Quatrefoil & Trefoil Border, Scalloped Rim, 3 3/8 In.	411.00 to 500.00
Pressed Glass, Log Cabin, Flower Border, Scalloped Rim, Orange Amber, 3 1/4 In.	475.00
Pressed Glass, Roman Rosette, Rosette Border, Scallop & Point Rim, Teal, 3 1/2 In.	265.00
Pressed Glass, Rosette, Shield & Pine Tree Border, Opalescent, 8 Sides, 3 5/8 In.	90.00
Pressed Glass, Scroll, 13-Heart Border, Uneven Scalloped Rim, 1832-1834, 3 1/2 In.	60.00
Pressed Glass, Sunburst, Plain Border, Bull's-Eye Scalloped Rim, Orange Amber, 3 In.	100.00
Pressed Glass, Sunburst, Serrated Border, Scalloped Rim, Amethyst, 3 1/2 In.	170.00
Pressed Glass, Sunburst, Serrated Border, Scalloped Rim, Yellow Green, 3 5/8 In.	335.00
Pressed Glass, Sunburst, Serrated Border, Scalloped Rim, Yellow, 3 1/4 In.	120.00

CURRIER & IVES made the famous American lithographs marked with their name from 1857 to 1907. The mark used on the print included the street address in New York City, and it is possible to date the year of the original issue from this information. Earlier prints were made by N. Currier and use that name from 1835 to 1847. Many reprints of the Currier or Currier & Ives prints have been made. Some collectors buy the insurance calendars that were based on the old prints. The words *large*, *small*, or *medium folio* refer to size. The original print sizes were very small (up to about 7 x 9 in.), small (8.8 x 12.8 in.), medium (9 x 14 in. to 14 x 20 in.), large (larger than 14 x 20 in.). Other sizes are probably later copies. Other prints by Currier & Ives may be listed in the Card category under Advertising and in the Sheet Music category. Currier & Ives dinnerware patterns may be found in the Adams or Dinnerware categories.

Across The Continent, Frame, 1868, 17 7/8 x 27 3/8 In.	13200.00
American Country Life, Pleasures Of Winter, Frame, 24 x 30 1/4 In.	1100.00
Barefoot Girl, Frame, 18 x 14 In.	140.00
California Scenery, Seal Rocks-Point Lobos, Lithograph, 13 x 17 In.	360.00
Great Fire At Boston, November 9th & 10th 1872, 10 1/2 x 13 3/8 In.	265.00 to 500.00
Home In The Wilderness, c.1870, 11 3/4 x 15 3/4 In.	646.00
Home On The Mississippi, 10 x 14 1/4 In.	220.00
Hunter's Shanty In The Adirondacks, 18 1/16 x 23 3/4 In.	1430.00
Hunting Fishing & Forest Scenes, Shantying On The Lake Shore, 20 x 28 In.	1760.00
Life Of A Sportsman, Camping In Woods, 15 x 18 In.	25.00
Life Of A Sportsman, Camping In Woods, Hunters Cooking Over Fire, 11 x 14 In.	550.00
Life Of A Sportsman, Coming Into Camp, Hunter In Canoe With Dog, 12 x 16 In.	550.00
Little Beau, Frame, 16 x 12 In.	150.00
Magnificent Steamship, City Of Paris, Inman Line, 11 1/2 x 15 3/8 In.	355.00
Mollie McCarthy, Racing Queen Of Pacific Slope, 1878, 11 x 16 In.	355.00
Moonlight On The Lake, Frame, 18 x 24 In.	60.00
New England Homestead, Lithograph, c.1852, 10 1/2 x 13 7/8 In.	90.00
Old Farm House, Lithograph, c.1872, 10 3/4 x 13 7/8 In.	558.00
Old Oaken Bucket, 1864, 16 x 23 1/4 In.	840.00
Old Oaken Bucket, Lithograph, c.1872, 9 3/4 x 13 7/8 In.	90.00
Pioneer's Home, On Western Frontier, Frame, Large Folio, 22 x 30 1/2 In.	1092.00

Roadside Mill, Lithograph, Frame, 14 x 18 In.	220.00
Sinking Of Steamship Oregon Of Cunard Line, 1886, 13 x 18 In.	118.00
Sylvan Lake, Lithograph, Hand Colored, Mahogany Frame, 13 x 17 In.	248.00
Trotting Stallion Dan Rice, 1866, 16 3/4 x 26 1/8 In.	1560.00
Well-Bred Setter, Lithograph, Frame, 17 5/8 x 21 In.	660.00

CUSTARD GLASS is a slightly yellow opaque glass. It was first made in
England in the 1880s and was first made in the United States in the
1890s. It has been reproduced. Additional pieces may be found in the
Cambridge, Fenton, Heisey, and Northwood categories. Custard glass
is called Ivorina Verde by Heisey and other companies.

Argonaut Shell, Tumbler, Gold Trim, Northwood, 3 3/4 In.	60.00
Beaded Circle, Tumbler, Enameled Flowers, Gold Trim, Northwood, 3 7/8 In.	130.00
Beaded Swag, Tumbler, Enameled, Gold Flowers, Heisey, 3 3/4 In., Pair	20.00
Cherry & Scale, Tumbler, Nutmeg Stain, Fenton, 4 In.	35.00
Chrysanthemum Sprig, Cruet, Stopper, 6 3/4 In.	80.00 to 175.00
Chrysanthemum Sprig, Toothpick	60.00 to 85.00
Chrysanthemum Sprig, Tumbler, Blue, Flowers, Gold Trim, Northwood, 3 3/4 In.	110.00
Chrysanthemum Sprig, Tumbler, Green, Pink & Gold Enamel, Northwood, 4 In.	40.00
Delaware, Tumbler, Blue Stained Leaves, U.S. Glass, 3 3/4 In.	70.00
Delaware, Tumbler, Green Stained Leaves, U.S. Glass, 3 3/4 In.	60.00
Everglades, Tumbler, Green & Gold Trim, Northwood, 3 7/8 In.	120.00
Fan, Tumbler, Gold Swags, Dugan, 4 In.	60.00
Geneva, Salt, 3 1/2 In.	20.00
Geneva, Tumbler, Enameled Swag, Northwood, 3 7/8 In.	35.00
Geneva, Tumbler, Green & Gold Decoration, Northwood, 3 7/8 In.	80.00
Grape, Tray, Dresser, Cinnamon Stain, 7 3/4 In.	155.00
Grape & Cable, Hatpin Holder, Footed, 7 In.	90.00
Grape & Cable, Tumbler, Nutmeg Stain, Northwood, 4 In.	15.00
Grape & Gothic Arches, Tumbler, Blue Stain, Northwood, 4 In.	140.00
Grape Arbor, Tumbler, Blue Stain, Satin, Northwood, 4 1/4 In.	90.00
Grape Arbor, Tumbler, Nutmeg Stain, Northwood, 4 1/4 In.	90.00
Grape Arbor, Tumbler, Pink Stain, Satin, Northwood, 4 1/4 In.	120.00
Intaglio, Salt & Pepper, 3 1/4 In.	46.00
Intaglio, Tumbler, Blue & Gold Trim, Northwood, 3 3/4 In.	80.00
Inverted Fan & Feather, Bowl, 9 In.	130.00
Inverted Fan & Feather, Tumbler, Pink & Gold Trim, Northwood, 4 In.	40.00
Maize is its own category in this book.	
Maple Leaf, Tumbler, Green & Gold Leaves, Northwood, 3 7/8 In.	150.00
Nautilus, Pitcher, Water, Custard, 8 1/2 In.	300.00
Ribbed Drape, Tumbler, Enameled Flowers, Jefferson, 4 In.	35.00
Ribbed Thumbprint, Tumbler, Enameled, Gold Flowers, Jefferson, 4 In.	15.00

CUT GLASS has been made since ancient times, but the large majority
of the pieces now for sale date from the brilliant period of glass design,
1880 to 1905. These pieces have elaborate geometric designs with a
deep miter cut. Modern cut glass with a similar appearance is being
made in England, Ireland, and the Czech and Slovak republics. Chips
and scratches are often difficult to notice but lower the value dramati-
cally. A signature on the glass adds significantly to the value. Other cut
glass pieces are listed under factory names.

Bottle, Dresser, Fan, Block, Star Base, Faceted Stopper, 8 In.	75.00
Bottle, Dresser, Ruby Cut To Clear, Scrolled Gold Leaves, c.1900, 11 1/4 In.	85.00
Bottle, Whiskey, Hobstar, Honeycomb Cut Neck, 13 x 3 3/8 In.	425.00
Bottle Cooler, Caned Arch & Buzz Saw, Flared, Handles, 9 x 9 1/2 In.	200.00
Bowl, Allover Canes, Star Cut On Each, 4 x 8 In.	500.00
Bowl, Banana Shape, Hobstar & Flashed Star, 12 x 8 In.	250.00
Bowl, Diamonds Cut With Stars, 8-Sided Stem, Footed, 9 x 11 In., Pair	325.00
Bowl, Expanding Star, Flat Bottom, 9 In.	350.00
Bowl, Fern, Hobstar, 3-Footed, 3 3/4 x 7 1/4 In.	50.00
Bowl, Flowers, Squares, Alternating Crosshatch, Diagonal Lines, 4 1/4 x 8 In.	50.00
Bowl, Hartford, Stars, Button Border, Scalloped Rim, 9 x 4 In.	110.00
Bowl, Hobstar, Fan & Finecut, J. Hoare & Co., 7 In.	50.00

Bowl, Hobstar, Vesica & Fan, 8 In. 30.00
Bowl, Hobstars, Crosshatch & Fans, 4 1/2 x 8 1/4 x 5 1/2 In. 385.00
Bowl, Hobstars, Crosshatch, Leaves & Flowers, 4 1/4 x 9 In. 425.00
Bowl, Hobstars, Fans, Crosshatch, 32-Point Hobstar Base, Faceted Stem 1250.00
Bowl, Hobstars, Pedestal, 5 x 8 1/4 In. 425.00
Bowl, Hobstars, Separated By Panels, Crosshatch, Cane, Reverse Fans, 4 1/2 x 10 In. 100.00
Bowl, Russian, Gem, 9 x 3 1/4 In. 325.00
Bowl, Strawberry-Diamond & Fan, Large Central Star, 2 1/2 x 8 7/8 In. 75.00
Bowl, Strawberry-Diamond & Fan, Panels, Applied Foot, 8 1/4 x 4 1/2 In. 330.00
Bowl, Strawberry-Diamond, France, c.1900, 8 x 13 1/2 In. 975.00
Box, Cover, Hinged, Hobstars, 5 3/4 x 4 1/2 In. 695.00
Butter, Cover, Engraved Deer In Forest, 19th Century, 5 x 6 In. 80.00
Butter, Cover, Hobstars, Fans, Cane, 5 1/2 x 5 1/8 x 8 In. 125.00
Butter Cooler, Cover, Fan & Flute, Gallery Rim, Star Finial, Pedestal, 6 1/4 In. 132.00
Candlestick, Diamond Cut Stem, Center Teardrop, 6 In., Pair 975.00
Candlestick, Inverted Tear Drop, Scalloped Top, St. Louis Diamond, 8 1/2 In., Pair 1150.00
Carafe, Adonis, 7 x 6 1/4 In. 155.00
Carafe, Hobstars, Fans, Strawberry-Diamond, Zipper, 5 Cut Rings, Flat Base, 8 x 6 In. . . . 410.00
Celery Dish, Hobstars, Crosshatch & Fans, Crimped Edges, 11 1/2 x 4 3/4 In. 325.00
Celery Dish, Hobstars, Crosshatch Bars, Reversed Fans, 4 3/4 x 11 3/4 In. 50.00
Celery Dish, Russian, Folded Sides, Mt. Washington, 3 3/4 x 2 1/4 In. 295.00
Celery Vase, Strawberry-Diamond & Fan, Rayed Roundels, Flared, Round Base, 8 In. . . . 300.00
Cheese & Cracker Dish, Daisies, Leaves, Circle Rim, 10 x 3 In. 195.00
Cologne Bottle, Buzz Star, Bulbous, Facetted Stopper, 4 1/2 In. 100.00
Cologne Bottle, Croesus, Cylinder, J. Hoare 1485.00
Cologne Bottle, Ruby To Clear, Leaves, Clear Stopper, 5 1/2 In. 45.00
Compote, Engraved Tiger Lily, Leaves, Vines, Notched Rim, 5 1/2 x 6 In. 590.00
Compote, Floral, Notched 6-Sided Stem, Star Base, 8 x 6 In. 25.00
Compote, Gladys, Faceted Pedestal, Chrysanthemum Base, c.1920, 9 1/4 x 10 1/4 In. 545.00
Compote, Hobstars, Crosshatch, Fans, Teardrop Stem, 6 3/4 x 5 In. 325.00
Compote, Hobstars, Scalloped Bowl, Paneled Stem, 9 1/8 x 6 1/4 In. 385.00
Compote, Ovals, Fans & Prisms, Notched Edge, Button Stem, Pittsburgh, 7 1/4 In. 220.00
Compote, Russian, Scalloped Foot, Rim, Faceted Stem, 8 1/4 x 8 3/4 In. 468.00
Compote, Snowflake, Cut Pedestal, Hobstar Base, 10 In. 275.00
Compote, Stars Within Diamonds, Scalloped Rim, Circular Base, 9 x 10 1/2 In. 440.00
Compote, Strawberry-Diamond & Chain Sawtooth Rim, Pedestal, 7 x 4 1/4 In. 85.00
Compote, Strawberry-Diamond & Fan, Notched Rim, Footed, Pittsburgh, 7 1/2 In. 770.00
Compote, Strawberry-Diamond & Fan, Roundels & Rays, Notched Rim, 6 3/4 In. 175.00
Compote, Teardrop Stem, Hobstar Base, 9 In. 185.00
Compote, Trefoil, Curved Edge, T.B. Clark & Co., Pedestal, 6 3/4 x 5 1/2 In. 385.00
Cordial, Royal, 3 1/2 In. 100.00
Cordial, Star, Dorflinger, 3 1/2 In. 115.00
Cordial Set, Diamonds, Fluted, Star Base, Decanter, Cordials, Tray, 8 Piece 175.00
Cruet, Stars, Paneled Neck, Zipper, Scallop-Cut Handle, Rayed Base, Tuthill, 6 7/8 In. . . . 220.00
Decanter, Amber, Scroll, Flower, Crosshatch, Sterling Overlay, Stopper, 9 1/2 In. 400.00
Decanter, Block Diamond, Teardrop Stopper, Footed, Rayed Star Base, 11 1/2 In. 360.00
Decanter, Bulbous, Applied Neck Rings, Diamond & Fan, Pittsburgh, 10 1/2 In., Pair . . . 385.00
Decanter, Crosshatch, Stars, Fan, 8-Sided Neck, Lines, Faceted Stopper, 12 In. 75.00
Decanter, Diamond, Pineapple, Zipper-Cut Rim, J. Hoare & Co., 1853, 7 7/8 In. 303.00
Decanter, Grape Cluster & Vine Band, 3-Ring Throat, Cut Stopper, 11 In. 275.00
Decanter, Hobstar, Stopper, 6 1/2 x 10 In. 250.00
Decanter, Hobstars, Crosshatch, Strawberry-Diamond, Bell Shape, 12 1/2 x 4 1/4 In. 445.00
Decanter, Red To Clear, Diamond, Stopper, Tooled Flared Lip, 10 1/2 In. 270.00
Decanter, Ruby To Clear, Grape & Vine, Stopper, 8 1/2 In. 160.00
Decanter, Strawberry-Diamond & Fan, 3 Neck Rings, Ball Stopper, Pittsburgh, 7 1/2 In. . . 175.00
Decanter, Strawberry-Diamond & Fan, 3 Neck Rings, Stopper, Pittsburgh, 7 In., Pair 580.00
Decanter, Wine, Cranberry To Clear, Clear Cut Stopper, Cut Loops At Base, 7 x 4 1/2 In. . 185.00
Decanter Set, Ruby To Clear, Hobstar, Vesica & Feather, W. Germany, 13 Piece 275.00
Dish, Napoleon's Hat, Hobstars, Star, 12 1/2 x 9 In. 500.00
Dresser Box, Hinged Cover, Allover Hobstars, 4 x 7 1/2 In. 785.00
Dresser Box, Hinged Cover, Flower, Ribbon, Ormolu Mounted, 2 1/2 x 4 1/2 x 3 1/2 In. . 240.00
Dresser Box, Pinwheel Cane, 8 In. 45.00
Finger Bowl, Cobalt Blue To Clear, 6 Panels, Fans Under Base, 3 1/2 In., Pair 66.00

Goblet, Comet, Button Stem, Paneled, Pittsburgh, 4 In., 4 Piece 155.00
Goblet, Cranberry To Clear, Flattened Knop Stem, 4 7/8 In., 6 Piece 275.00
Goblet, Dandelion Bloom, Paneled Baluster Stem, Star Base, 6 In., 4 Piece 50.00
Goblet, Strawberry-Diamond & Fan, Cone Shape, Square Foot, 4 7/8 In., 8 Piece 175.00
Goblet, Strawberry-Diamond, Stepped Bands, Button Stem, Rayed Foot, 5 In., 6 Piece ... 140.00
Goblet, White To Clear To Ruby, Ovals, Stylized Leaves, Honeycomb Stem, 5 3/4 In. ... 30.00
Goblet, Wine, Hobstar Base, 4 1/4 In. 45.00
Ice Cream Set, Snowflake, Compote, Hobstar Base, 17 Piece 275.00
Jar, Apothecary, Cover, Snowflake & Lancer Arch, Spherical Finial, 15 In., Pair 1380.00
Jar, Cover, Hobstars, Crosshatch, Fans, Lid, 3 3/4 x 4 3/4 In. 245.00
Knife Rest, Hobstars, Notched Shaft, 5 1/2 In. 245.00
Knife Rest, Notched Prisms, Star On Ends, 4 1/2 In. 55.00
Lamp, Sunburst & Floral, 16 1/2 x 10 In. 250.00
Lemonade Set, Wheat, Hobnail, 9 5/8 In., 7 Piece 315.00
Light Globe, Strawberry-Diamond, Cranberry, Amber, 6 x 4 In. 280.00
Loving Cup, Hobstar & Cane, Hobstar Base, 3 Handles, 7 x 5 1/2 In. 1250.00
Loving Cup, Hobstar, 3 Handles, Sterling Silver Collar, Monogram, Dated 1899, 6 In. 690.00
Mustard Jar, Zipper 30.00
Napkin Ring, Buffalo, Sinclaire, Pair 155.00
Nappy, Hobstar & Intaglio, Handle, 6 In. 70.00
Pitcher, Champagne, Vesica, Flashed Hobstars, Deep Cane, Meriden, 14 In. 1250.00
Pitcher, Crosshatch, Hobstars & Fans, 8-Point Star Base, 9 1/2 x 7 1/2 In. 770.00
Pitcher, Flowers, Star & Crosshatch Band, 9 1/2 In. 75.00
Pitcher, Hobstars, Strawberry-Diamond, Triple Notched Handle, 12 x 6 3/4 In. 685.00
Pitcher, Oval Panels, Grapes & Vines, 8 In. 85.00
Pitcher, Primrose, Signed, Tuthill, 8 In. 600.00
Pitcher, Punty, Star & Fan, Large Star On Base, 9 x 5 3/4 In. 300.00
Pitcher, Quatrefoil Flowers, Diamond Point, Hobstar, Fan, Tapered Body, 12 1/2 In. 468.00
Pitcher, Tankard, Buzz Star With Rays, Crosshatch, 11 1/2 In. 100.00
Pitcher, Tankard, Hobstar, Buzz Star, Crosshatch & Fans, 9 1/2 x 5 1/4 In. 125.00
Plate, Allowed, Crosshatch, 7 In. 145.00
Plate, Beverly, Greek Key, Meriden, 9 3/4 x 1 1/4 In. 650.00
Punch Bowl, Base, 24-Point Hobstars, c.1890, 10 x 11 In. 950.00
Ramekin, Hobstars, 2 x 4 3/4 In. 185.00
Rose Bowl, Diamond Point, 3 Applied Feet, 3 In. 145.00
Salt, Strawberry-Diamond, Leaf Shape, 4 7/8 x 2 In. 40.00
Spooner, Alameda, Dorflinger, 5 x 3 In. 175.00
Stringholder, Punty, 4 Rows, Blue To Clear, Applied Ring On Top, 4 1/8 x 4 5/8 In. 525.00
Sugar & Creamer, Hobstar, Oval Cut Handles, 3 1/4 x 3 3/4 In. 215.00
Tazza, Hobstar, Paperweight Base, 5 1/2 x 8 In. 420.00
Tray, Celery, Assyrian, Sinclaire, 4 1/4 x 2 In. 685.00
Tray, Diamond Point Border, Star, Daisies, Leaves, Sawtooth Rim, 16 x 1 1/4 In. 305.00
Tray, Pointed Loops Of Russian, Hobstars, Flashed, Straus, 9 x 2 In. 1050.00
Tumbler, Diamond Point & Rays, Panels Below Pattern, 3 1/4 In., 4 Piece 66.00
Tumbler, Strawberry-Diamond & Roundels With Rays, Ribbed Base, Pittsburgh, 3 1/4 In. .. 187.00
Urn, Cover, Diamond Cut, 6-Sided Base, Neoclassical Style, Ormolu, 16 In. 374.00
Urn, Whiskey, Diamonds, Stepped Foot, Chromium Spigot, Engraved Oval Stopper, 12 In. .. 489.00
Vase, 12 Flutes On Lower Bowl, Knop Stem, Footed, Flared Rim, 8 3/4 In., Pair 255.00
Vase, Amethyst To Clear, Allover Swirled Ribs, Notched Foot, 8 In., Pair 90.00
Vase, Bud, Cranberry, Crisscross, Clear Notched Foot, 9 In. 170.00
Vase, Butterfly, Zipper, Intaglio, 10 In. 149.00
Vase, Cane & Snowflake Reserves, Pyriform, 17 x 8 In., Pair 316.00
Vase, Cranberry To Clear, Flared, Sawtooth Rim Waist, Triangular Panels, 7 1/4 In. 336.00
Vase, Diamond & Leaf Band, 6 In. 50.00
Vase, Fan, Sawtooth Rim, Hobstar Base, 8 1/2 x 8 3/4 In. 700.00
Vase, Hearts, Fans, Flared, Scalloped Rim, Footed, 16 In. 4600.00
Vase, Hobstar, Flower Center, 3 x 4 In. 240.00
Vase, Hobstars & Vesica, 3 In. 250.00
Vase, Hobstars, Rayed Stars, Caning, Strawberry-Diamond & Fan, Handles, 8 x 7 In. 685.00
Vase, Hobstars, Vertical Bars, Crosshatch, Buttons, Notched Prism, 8 1/4 In. 50.00
Vase, Intaglio, Grape, Flower Base, Flared, Tooled 6-Panel Rim, 6 3/4 In. 50.00
Vase, Leaf Band, Silver Mounted, Waisted, 10 1/2 In. 390.00
Vase, Mandorla & Hobstar Reserves, Pinwheel Cut Base, Pinched Waist, 13 In. 145.00

Vase, Russian Gold Bands, Leaves, Swirled Ribs, Flared, 20 In. 200.00
Vase, Stars, Crosshatch, Engraved Flowers, Waisted, 11 3/4 x 5 In. 50.00
Vase, Strawberry-Diamond & Fan, Shells, Scalloped Rim, Footed, Pittsburgh, 9 1/2 In. 90.00
Vase, Trumpet, Hobstar, Paneled Ring, Diamond Faceted Ball, 23 1/4 In. 1350.00
Water Set, Engraved, Daisy, Prism Highlights, 7 In., 6 Piece 90.00
Water Set, Floral Central, Stars, Crosshatch, 8 3/4 In., 5 Piece 50.00
Wine, Emerald Cut, Urn Shape, Anglo-Irish, 5 1/4 x 2 3/4 In., 4 Piece 290.00
Wine, Emerald, Panel Cut, Faceted Stem, Round Foot, Anglo-Irish, c.1835, 5 1/2 In., Pair   105.00

CUT VELVET is a special type of art glass, made with two layers of
blown glass, which shows a raised pattern. It usually had an acid finish or a texture like velvet. It was made by many glass factories during
the late Victorian years.

Ewer, Pink, Diamond-Quilted, 7 1/2 In. 160.00
Vase, Blue, 5 1/4 In. 85.00
Vase, Blue, 8 1/2 In. 60.00
Vase, Blue, Satin, 6 In. 80.00

CYBIS porcelain is a twentieth-century product. Boleslaw Cybis came to
the United States from Poland in 1939. He started making porcelains in
Long Island, New York, in 1940. He moved to Trenton, New Jersey, in
1942 as one of the founders of Cordey China Co. and started his own
Cybis Porcelains about 1950. The firm is still working. See also Cordey.

CYBIS

Figurine, Great Horned Owl, On Branch, Oyster Mushrooms, Signed, 1975, 19 In. 2300.00
Figurine, Madonna, Garland Headdress, Roses, Blue Leaves, 9 In. 135.00
Figurine, Whale, Emerging From Water, 13 In. 345.00
Vase, Raspberry & Grape, 9 In. 160.00

CZECHOSLOVAKIA is a popular term with collectors. The name, first
used as a mark after the country was formed in 1918, appears on glass
and porcelain and other decorative items. Although Czechoslovakia
split into Slovakia and the Czech Republic on January 1, 1993, the
name continues to be used in some trademarks.

CZECHOSLOVAKIA GLASS, Lamp, Amber, Cone Shade, Brass Figural Leaf, Engraved, 20 In. ...400.00
Perfume Bottle, Fan Shape, Jeweled, Lily-Of-The-Valley Cutting, Tiara Stopper 770.00
Perfume Bottle, Violet Cutting, Filigree, Jewels, Pearls, Spider Web Stopper 2430.00
Tray, Salt, 2 Wells, Blue, Grape Cutting, Jeweled Holder, 4 1/4 In. 107.00
Vase, Aqua Opalescent, Hobnail & Rib, Marked, 12 In. 115.00
Vase, Clear, Fine Cobalt Threading, Oval, Signed, 5 x 7 In. 200.00
Vase, Gold Iridescent, Purple Highlights, Pedestal, Signed, 7 1/2 In. 230.00
Vase, Malachite, Green, Molded Female Nudes, Curt Schlevogt, 1930s, 5 In. 353.00
Vase, Orange, Spatter Finish, Ruffled Edge, Signed, 12 In. 195.00
Vase, Orange, Yellow, Amethyst, Spatter, 6 1/2 x 5 In. 70.00
Vase, Tulips, Quatrefoil Rim, Opalescent, Molded, 9 1/4 In. 260.00
CZECHOSLOVAKIA POTTERY, Plate, Hand Painted Scene, 7 1/2 In. 65.00
Vase, Amphora, Bird In Flight, Checkerboard At Top, 11 In. 375.00
Vase, Art Deco Design, White, Handles, 8 1/4 In. 65.00
Vase, Orange, Gray, Ivory Glaze, Gunmetal Ribs, 11 In. 115.00
Wall Mask, Blond Hair Girl, Blue Scarf, Terra-Cotta, Marked, Keramic 400.00
Wall Pocket, Bird, Birdhouse, 5 1/2 In. 35.00

D'ARGENTAL is a mark used in France by the Compagnie des
Cristalleries de St. Louis. The firm made multilayered, acid-cut cameo
glass in the late nineteenth and twentieth centuries. D'Argental is the
French name for the city of Munzthal, home of the glassworks. Later
they made enameled etched glass.

Box, Cover, Stylized Flowers & Leaves, c.1910, 3 x 3 5/8 In. 881.00
Lamp, Flowers, Red, Green Leaves, Yellow Ground, Cameo, Signed, 22 In. 4140.00
Vase, 2 Men In Rowboat, Trees, Brown, Amber, Signed, 13 3/4 In. 1495.00
Vase, Cameo, Pod Branches, Amber, Plum Over Burgundy, c.1910, 11 3/4 In. 1610.00
Vase, Cherries, Branches, Leaves, Cameo, 12 In. 1495.00
Vase, Geese In Flight, Red, Yellow Ground, Cameo, Signed, 6 1/4 In. 690.00
Vase, Tropical Island Scene, Shades Of Purple, Signed, 11 1/2 In. 1840.00

DANIEL BOONE, a pre–Revolutionary War folk hero, was a surveyor, trapper, and frontiersman. A television series, which ran from 1964 to 1970, was based on his life and starred Fess Parker. All types of Daniel Boone memorabilia are collected.

Action Figure, 1965, 12 In.	68.00
Book, Wilderness Scout, Illustrated, 1922, 274 Pages	11.00
Lunch Box, Thermos, Aladdin	158.00
Marionette, Talking, Plastic, Hazelles, No. 316, Box, 1950s	95.00
Photograph, Fess Parker As Daniel Boone On TV, Signed, 8 x 10 In.	10.00
Pocket Knife	3.00

DAUM, a glassworks in Nancy, France, was started by Jean Daum in 1875. The company, now called *Cristalleries de Nancy*, is still working. The *Daum Nancy* mark has been used in many variations. The name of the city and the artist are usually both included.

Bottle, Flowers, Leaves, Gilded, Green Ground, Stopper, Signed, 11 1/4 In.	480.00
Bowl, Brown, Etched, Chipped Ice V Design, Art Deco, Signed, 4 3/4 x 6 3/4 In.	175.00
Bowl, Brown, Green, Silver Foil, Round, Bulbous Rim, Footed, Signed, 6 3/4 In.	410.00
Bowl, Console, Gray, Lavender, Amethyst, Blue, Silver Foil, c.1935, 10 1/2 In.	635.00
Bowl, Cornflowers, Cameo, Signed, 1910, 3 In.	2630.00
Bowl, Geometric Design, Golds, Orange & Clear, 1925, 9 In.	2100.00 to 2115.00
Bowl, Handles, Boat Shape, Mountain Lake Landscape, Cameo, 14 In.	4000.00
Bowl, Poppies, Mottled Yellow Ground, Enameled, 4-Fold Rim, Signed, 6 In.	2470.00
Bowl, Reddish Gold Enamel, Leafy Seed Pods, Trifold Top, Cut Ribbon, c.1895, 10 In.	1610.00
Bowl, Round, Fruit Branches, Matte Ground, Footed Base, Marked, 1920, 6 In.	435.00
Creamer, Trees, Lake, Applied Amber Handle, Cameo, Signed, 3 3/4 In.	180.00
Ewer, Cranberry, Gold Overlay, Purple, Grapevine, Metal Mount Handle, 7 1/2 In.	1380.00
Ewer, Silver, Gold Highlights, Flowers, Embossed Collar, Handle, Cameo, c.1895, 11 In.	1955.00
Figurine, Pate-De-Verre, Macaw, Sapphire Hyacinth, Green Pedestal, 12 In.	1150.00
Inkwell, Mottled Green, Purple, Falling Oak Leaves, Cameo, c.1900, 3 1/2 x 4 1/4 In.	1265.00
Jar, Cover, Gray, Mottled With Pink, Yellow, Leafy Seed Pods, Cameo, c.1915, 6 In.	1265.00
Jug, Whiskey, Grapevine, Enameled, Cameo, Metal Lid, Handle, c.1895, 10 1/2 In.	800.00
Lamp, Enameled Winter Scene, Baluster, Round Base, c.1910, 8 3/8 In.	325.00
Lamp, Etched Glass, c.1930, 17 1/2 In.	5380.00
Perfume Bottle, Cameo Glass, Enameled, Amethyst Flowers, Leaves, Signed, 4 1/2 In.	2358.00
Plaque, Trees, Brown, Ducks, Yellow Ground, Rust, Enameled, Cameo, Signed, 9 x 12 In.	2700.00
Salt, Bucket Shape, Flowers, Yellow & Purple, Cameo, 1 1/4 x 1 3/4 In.	1320.00
Salt, Sailing Ships, Yellow & Orange, Cameo, Enameled, 1 x 2 In.	1440.00
Salt, Snowy Woodland, Gold Ground, Cameo, Signed, 2 1/8 In.	1050.00
Shade, Ceiling, Domed, Mottled Orange, Yellow, 1900s, 15 1/2 In.	2115.00
Shade, Dome, Mottled Orange, Brown, Shading To Clear Frosted, Signed, 17 1/2 In.	315.00
Sugar, Enameled Flower, Bee, Spider Web, Yellow Amber, Cameo, Silver Collar, 7 x 4 In.	720.00
Toothpick, Frosted Lavender, Gold Trim, Cameo, Enameled, 2 In.	175.00
Tumbler, Clear, Cranberry, Stylized Flowers, Cameo, Signed, 3 1/2 In.	518.00
Tumbler, Gray, Mottled Yellow, Amethyst, Enameled Flowers, Cameo, 3 1/4 In.	1035.00
Tumbler, Green, Alternating Intaglio Cut Rosettes, Gold Enameled, Cameo, c.1900, 5 In.	460.00
Tumbler, Red & Purple Fuchsia, Square, Enameled, Cameo, Signed, 4 3/4 In.	865.00
Vase, 2 Coiled Snakes, Leaves, Green, Purple, Yellow, Pate De Verre, c.1965, 6 7/8 In.	500.00
Vase, Autumnal River Landscape, Shouldered, Oval, Cameo, Enameled, 8 In.	7170.00
Vase, Barren Forest, Spring Rain, Grayish Frosted Sky, Pink Clouds, Signed, 6 1/2 In.	4715.00
Vase, Berries, Cameo, Signed, 1910, 4 1/4 In.	840.00
Vase, Bleeding Heart Blossoms, Cameo, Signed, 1910, 7 3/4 In.	2390.00
Vase, Blue, Pale Green, Frosted, Marked, 9 3/4 In.	400.00
Vase, Blue, Yellow, Carved, Hand Cut Daisies, Cameo, 15 In.	13225.00
Vase, Brown Forest, Umber Meadow, Amber Sky, Footed, Cameo, Signed, 24 In.	3585.00
Vase, Bumble Bees & Flowers, Enameled, Cameo, 8 3/4 In.	8625.00
Vase, Butterfly, Flower On Leafy Stem, Frosted, Purple, Gold Enameled, Signed, 7 1/4 In.	470.00
Vase, Cameo, Berried Branches, Mottled Green, Yellow, Rust, Tapered Oval, 17 1/2 In.	4185.00
Vase, Cameo, Gray Over Amethyst, Enameled, Buds, Flowers, Stems, c.1900, 8 1/4 In.	3335.00
Vase, Carved, Purple Wisteria, Mottled Ground, Cameo, 7 In.	4025.00
Vase, Cornflowers, Cameo, Signed, 1910, 8 3/4 In.	1435.00
Vase, Day Lilies, Orange & Yellow, Diamond Shape, Cameo, 4 1/2 In.	1840.00

Vase, Enameled Berries, Leaves, Vines, Cameo, Enameled Signature, 5 In. 1265.00
Vase, Enameled Boats, Birds, Windmills, 3 In. 550.00
Vase, Fern, Leaves, Martele Ground, Gold Enamel Signature, 1910, 8 1/4 In. 3100.00
Vase, Flowering Vines, Gray, Waisted, Cameo, c.1910, 13 3/4 In. 1265.00
Vase, Flowers, Cranberry, Orange Ground, Shouldered, Oval, Cameo, 6 1/2 In. 1675.00
Vase, Forest, Snow, Orange Sky, Signed, 3 1/2 In. 1725.00
Vase, Frosted Gray Over Green, Yellow Dandelions, Cameo, c.1910, 10 In. 2070.00
Vase, Fuchsia Flowers, Tricornered, Enameled, c.1905, 15 1/8 In. 3000.00
Vase, Gold Flowers, Waisted Lozenge, Cameo, Signed, 4 1/2 In. 440.00
Vase, Gray, Bands Of Yellow, Cranberry To Brown Shades, Thistle, c.1900, 5 In. 840.00
Vase, Gray, Shaded Amber, Green, Enameled, Burgundy Thistle, Cameo, c.1910, 6 1/2 In. 550.00
Vase, Gray, Yellow, Amethyst, Red Flowers, Stems, Cameo, Enameled, c.1900, 4 3/4 In. . . 1495.00
Vase, Green Leaves, Yellow, Orange Ground, Cameo, Signed, 6 In. 635.00
Vase, Green Thistles, Pink Ground, Martele, Mark On Base, c.1900, 8 3/4 In. 1645.00
Vase, Green To Rose, Stemmed Flowers, Cameo, c.1900, 8 In. 3000.00
Vase, Lake, Pine Trees, Cameo, Signed, 1910, 19 3/4 In. 5375.00
Vase, Landscape, Boats At Sea, Flying Birds, Mottled Ground, Flared, 19 1/2 In. 3000.00
Vase, Landscape, Brown, Gold Ground, Cameo, Signed, 19 1/4 In. 2160.00
Vase, Marigolds, Enameled, Signed, 1910, 16 1/2 In. 5975.00
Vase, Mottled Blue, Amethyst, Overlay, Blue Day Lilies, Cameo, c.1900, 3 3/4 In. 1265.00
Vase, Orchids Varicosum, Handles, Cameo, Signed, 12 3/4 In. 2270.00
Vase, Peony, Yellow, Peach, Brown Ground, Flared, Shouldered, 12 In. 4025.00
Vase, Pillow, Mottled Yellow, Orange Frosted Glass, Etched, c.1920, 4 1/2 In. 290.00
Vase, Pink, Gold Daisies, Butterflies, Bee, Slender, Cameo, Signed, 13 3/4 In. 690.00
Vase, Poppies, Lavender, Coral, Carved, Martele Ground, 9 3/4 In. 14400.00
Vase, Purple, Gold Enameled, Stemmed Flower, Cameo, Signed, c.1895, 5 3/4 In. 490.00
Vase, Rain, Windswept Trees, Cameo, Signed, 1 1/2 In. 1955.00
Vase, Red Berries, Shouldered, Oval, Cameo, Enameled, 5 In. 1555.00
Vase, Red Flowers, Enameled, Yellow Ground, Baluster, 4 Openings, Cameo, 5 1/2 In. . . . 1685.00
Vase, Red, Purple Flowers, Cameo, 5 In. 920.00
Vase, Rose Buds, Yellow, Pink, Mottled Yellow Ground, Cameo, Signed, 4 3/4 In. 835.00
Vase, Rose Yellow, Gray, Green Overlay, Red Stemmed Flowers, Cameo, c.1920, 21 In. . . 5520.00
Vase, Seascape, Yellow, Orange Ground, Enamel, Oval, c.1905, 1 3/4 In. 1115.00
Vase, Small Circles, Turquoise, Cylindrical, Flared Rim, Footed, 14 1/2 In. 900.00
Vase, Spring Landscape, Baluster, Cameo, c.1890, 20 1/8 In. 4830.00
Vase, Stemmed Bleeding Hearts, Martele, Burgundy, c.1900, 7 3/4 In. 3000.00
Vase, Stick, Blackbirds, Snow, Mottled, Opal, Enameled, Cameo, 2 7/8 In. 2645.00
Vase, Stick, Cranberry Orchids, Leaves, Orange & Amethyst Mottled Ground, 5 1/2 In. . . 2690.00
Vase, Stick, Pink & Purple, Swung, 16 In. 515.00
Vase, Stylized Floral, Ormolu Mount At Rim, Gilt, Enameled Signature, c.1890, 5 In. 380.00
Vase, Summer Scene, Green Trees, Orange Ground, 7 In. 540.00
Vase, Sunflower, Textured Green, Gold Highlights, Signed, Cameo, c.1910, 3 1/2 In. 460.00
Vase, Thistle, Opalescent, Burgundy, Gold Enameled, Cameo, c.1910, 4 3/4 In. 550.00
Vase, Thistle, Red, Yellow Ground, Stripes, Gold Enameled, Cameo, Signed, 5 In. 420.00
Vase, Tree, Pink Blossoms, Enameled, Cameo, Signed, 6 3/4 In. 2415.00
Vase, Trees In Front Of Lake, Sailboats, Brown, Yellow, Orange, Pedestal Foot, 6 1/2 In. . 1100.00
Vase, Trees, Lake, Orange, Yellow, Green, Cameo, 7 In. 345.00
Vase, Trees, Mountain, Water, Mottled Orange Ground, Yellow, Red Ground, Cameo, 5 In. 1325.00
Vase, Trumpet, Pink Campanula, Grasses, Pink Ground, Cameo, 17 1/2 In. 6740.00
Vase, Vines & Leaves, Enameled, Applied Red Berries, Cameo, 21 3/4 In. 17250.00
Vase, Vines, Cabochon & Enameled Berries, Orange Mottled Ground, 4 Sides, 4 1/2 In. . . 2800.00
Vase, White Opalescent, Martele Flowers, Pink & Green, Signed, 2 1/2 In. 2800.00
Vase, Winter Scene, Enameled, Yellow Mottling, Cameo, 3-Footed, c.1915, 5 1/2 In. 4025.00
Vase, Yellow & Green Mimosa, Orange, Enameled, Cylindrical, Cameo, 10 In. 2470.00
Vase, Yellow, Aqua, Purple Ground, 2 Martele Insects, Green, Orange, 7 1/2 In. 1325.00
Vase, Yellow, Orange Flowers, Leaves, Mottled Ground, Cameo, 10 In. 2015.00

DAVENPORT pottery and porcelain were made at the Davenport factory
in Longport, Staffordshire, England, from 1793 to 1887. Earthenwares,
creamwares, porcelains, ironstone, and other ceramics were made.
Most of the pieces are marked with a form of the word *Davenport*.

DAVENPORT
LONGPORT
STAFFORDSHIRE

Jug, Relief Scene, Fox Hunt, Brown Glazed Neck, Pewter Rim, Stoneware, 8 In. 200.00

Plate, Dinner, Imari Style Flowers, Enamel, Gilt, 10 1/4 In., 12 Piece 765.00
Sugar & Creamer, Large Pink Roses, Gold Trim, Bulbous, Marked 30.00
Tureen, Sauce, Cover, Undertray, Polychrome, Marked 6 1/2 In. 138.00
Urn, Cover, Creamware, Chinoiserie Figures, Silver Spigot, c.1810, 22 1/2 In. 4780.00

DAVY CROCKETT, the American frontiersman, was born in 1786 and
died in 1836. The historical character gained new fame in 1954 when
the Walt Disney television show ran a series of episodes featuring Fess
Parker as Davy Crockett. Coonskin caps and buckskins became popu-
lar and hundreds of different Davy Crockett items were made.

Beverage Set, Water Pitcher, 8 Glasses 150.00
Button, Indian Fighter, Red, Yellow, Black, Lithograph, 1 1/2 In. 30.00
Cap, Coonskin, Indian Fighter, Fess Parker As Davy, Plastic, 1950s, 9 x 13 In. 255.00
Clock, Electric, Animated, Davy On Horse, Charging Bear, Haddon Product 1000.00
Clock, Pendulum, Child's, Box 150.00
Cookie Jar, Marked USA, Brush, c.1956, 10 In. 325.00
Costume, Pioneer Scout, Walt Disney Productions Eddy, Box, 1955, 10 x 10 In. 220.00
Doll, Celluloid Face, 25 In. 70.00
Doll, Celluloid Face, Shoe Straps To Walk With Child, 38 In. 80.00
Game, Davy Crockett Adventures 35.00
Guitar, Yellow, Wood, Paperboard, 31 In. 60.00
Hat, Indian Fighting, Box 140.00
Indian Scout Set, Kilgore 90.00
Lamp, Cowboy Boot Base, Davy Crockett Shade 60.00
Lunch Box 50.00
Mug, Brush 95.00
Pin, Silver Horseshoe, Ribbon, Celluloid 35.00
Plate, Brown, White, Universal Potteries, 10 In. 65.00
Puzzle Set, Defending The Fort, Indian Fighter & Indian Attack, 3 Piece 40.00
Sheet Music, Ballad Of Davy Crockett, Fess Parker, 1954 .... 9.00
Toy, Frontier Wagon, 2 Horses, Friction, Linemar, 5 In. 95.00
Toy, Horse, Box 200.00
Tumbler, Indian Fighter, Hero Of Alamo, Indian, Bear, 5 In. 3.00
Wastebasket, Lithographed Tin 90.00

DE VEZ was a signature used on cameo glass after 1910. E. S. Monot
founded the glass company near Paris in 1851. The company changed
names many times. Mt. Joye, another glass by this factory, is listed in
its own category.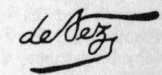

Bowl, Castle, 3 Ships, Brown, Green, 4 Sides, Cameo, Signed, 12 x 6 1/2 In. 1840.00
Lamp, San Marco Square, Gondolas, Bulbous Shade, Tree Trunk Stem, Leaves, 18 In. 3640.00
Lamp Base, Mountain Lake Scene, Metal Fittings, Gray, Cameo, 10 In. 290.00
Vase, Amethyst, Pink, Lake, Trees, Signed, Cameo, 8 In. 460.00
Vase, Burgundy Over Amber, Rose, Blooming Flowers, Cameo, c.1910, 2 In. 2400.00
Vase, Geese On Lake, Through Tall Trees, Turquoise & Chartreuse Ground, 17 In. 2130.00
Vase, Maiden & Child, Country Farmhouse, Mountains, Amber Sky, Cameo, 6 In. 840.00
Vase, Sailing Ships, Mountains, Water, Sky, Cameo, 10 In. 810.00
Vase, Trees, Lake, Castle, Blue, Green, Pink Sky, Cameo, Signed, 8 In. 1200.00

DECORATED TUMBLERS have been made by Anchor Hocking, Federal,
Hazel Atlas, Libbey, and other companies since the 1930s, when the
pyroglaze process of printing was introduced. The barware and other
glasses feature drinking jokes, characters, or decorative geometric patterns. Swankyswigs are listed in their own category. Decorated tumblers may also be listed in Coca-Cola, Pepsi-Cola, and many other
categories.

7-Eleven, Incredible Hulk, Marvel Comics, 1977 .... 14.00
7-Eleven, Scooby Doo, Hanna Barbera, Wrap Around, 1976 .... 176.00
7-Eleven, Thor, Marvel Comics, 1977 .... 14.00
7-Up, Ziggy, Here's To Good Friends 3.00
Actor, Peep Window, Theater, Gary Cooper, 3 1/2 In. 4.00
Al Capp, Lonesome Polecat, Maroon, 1949, 4 3/4 In. 20.00

Al Capp, Sadie Hawkins, Light Blue, 1949, 4 3/4 In.	7.00
Animal, Elephant, York, 4 3/4 In.	10.00
Animal, Kicky Kangaroo Kicking Field Goal, Yellow, Black, 1940s, 4 3/4 In.	20.00
Animal, Tricky Tiger Doing Magic, Orange, Black, Federal, 1940s, 4 3/4 In.	20.00
Arby's, Bugs Bunny, Head In Star, Warner Bros.	4.00
Arby's, Daffy Duck In Jungle Jitters, Looney Tunes Adventures	10.00 to 20.00
Arby's, Mae West, Actor's Series, No. 4	3.00
Arby's, Yosemite Sam, Head In Star, Warner Bros.	8.00
Bama Jelly, Adventures Of Rocky & Bullwinkle, 6 Piece	40.00
Battlestar Galactica, Apollo, 1979	5.00
Bicycle Built For Two, Forest Green, Anchor Hocking, 6 1/4 In.	16.00
Care Bear, Friend Bear, Canada, 5 5/8 In.	3.00
Carnation Malted Milk, Soda Fountain	300.00
Civil War Centennial, Iced Tea, Crossed Confederate Flags	5.00
Colorado Centennial, Iced Tea, Discovery Of Gold At Little Dry Creek	3.00
Currier & Ives, White Milk Glass, Blue, Hazel Atlas, 12 Oz., 5 In.	12.00
Dr Pepper, Happy Days, The Fonz, Pizza Hut Logo	8.00
Elsie In Sunflower, Borden, Yellow & Brown, 5 1/2 In.	14.00
Flintstones, Canada's Wonderland, Wilma & Pebbles, 1980, 5 1/8 In.	25.00
Flintstones, Fred With Bedrock Sign, Bedrock City, 1977	17.00
Game Of Croquet, Forest Green, Anchor Hocking, 5 In.	16.00
Gold Leaf, Hi-Ball Set, Metal Holder, 7 Piece	25.00
Goonies, Data On Waterslide, 1979	3.00 to 7.00
Goonies, Sloth & The Goonies, 1979	20.00
Hamm's Beer, New Patio, Aluminum, Box, 6 Piece	72.00
Harvey Cartoons, Casper, Button Bottom, 6 1/8 In.	11.00
Horse Car, Iced Tea, Royal Ruby, Anchor Hocking, 13 Oz., 5 In.	12.00
Kansas, Iced Tea, Chisholm Trail, 6 1/2 In.	5.00
Kansas, Iced Tea, Dodge City Marshal, 3 3/4 In.	4.00
Kellogg's, Snap, Crackle, Pop, 1977	5.00
Kellogg's, Tony The Tiger, 1977	18.00
McDonald's, Big Mac, Embossed Arches On Base & Bottom, 1983	26.00
McDonald's, Peter Pan, Canadian Movie Series	14.00
Michigan, Traverse City, Famous Sugar Sand Miracle Mile, Frosted, 6 In.	3.00
Miss Dairylea, Drive Slow, c.1950, 3 1/4 x 3 1/2 In.	8.00
Missouri, Iced Tea, Capitol, Jefferson City, 6 1/2 In.	5.00
Missouri, Iced Tea, Tom Sawyer, 3 3/4 In.	4.00
Moby Dick, Libbey Classics, 3 1/4 In.	10.00
New Years, Baby New Year, Federal Glass Co., 1950s, 4 3/4 In.	15.00
New Years, Clock At Midnight, Federal Glass Co., 1950s, 4 3/4 In.	15.00
Nursery Rhymes, Hickety Pickety, Ribbed, Yellow, Hazel Atlas, 4 1/8 In.	24.00
Nursery Rhymes, Little Boy Blue, Dark Blue, Federal, 5 In.	6.00
Nursery Rhymes, Little Miss Muffet, Libbey, Red, 4 5/8 In.	8.00
Nursery Rhymes, Mary Had A Little Lamb, Ribbed, White, Hazel Atlas, 4 1/8 In.	20.00
Nursery Rhymes, Queen Of Hearts, Ribbed, Yellow, Hazel Atlas, 4 1/8 In.	14.00
Nursery Rhymes, Tom, Tom, Piper's Son, Ribbed, White, Hazel Atlas, 4 1/8 In.	20.00
Ohio Indians, Iced Tea, Pontiac The Red Napoleon	5.00
Ohio Indians, Iced Tea, Tecumseh, Shawnee	4.00
Sportsman, Wild Birds, Federal Glass, Frosted, 1956	25.00
Sunday Funnies, Little Orphan Annie	5.00
Sunday Funnies, Terry & The Pirates	5.00 to 7.00
Surrey, Forest Green, Anchor Hocking, 5 In.	16.00
Thanksgiving, Campfire, Brown, Green, Yellow, Federal, 1950s, 4 3/4 In.	15.00
Thanksgiving, Hat & Turkey, Brown, Yellow, Green, Federal, 1950, 4 3/4 In.	15.00
Thanksgiving, Pilgrim, Brown, Green, Yellow, Federal, 1950s, 4 3/4 In.	15.00
Universal Movie Monsters, Mummy, 1960, 6 1/2 In.	44.00
Welch's, Archie, Jughead, Wins Pie Eating Contest, 1973	3.00
Welch's, Elmer Fudd, Warner Bros., 1976	3.00
Welch's, Flintstones, Fred, Playing Golf, 1962	5.00
Wizard Of Oz, Cowardly Lion, Yellow, Fluted, 5 In	5.00
Wizard Of Oz, Dorothy, Pink, Wavy, Swift & Co., 5 In.	6.00
Wizard Of Oz, Wizard, Red, Fluted, Baum, Swift & Co., 5 In.	8.00

DECOYS are carved or turned wooden copies of birds, fish, or animals. The decoy was placed in the water or propped on the shore to lure flying birds to the pond for hunters. Some decoys are handmade; some are commercial products. Today there is a group of artists making modern decoys for display, not for use in a pond.

Black Duck, Captain Harry Jones	196.00
Black Duck, Carved, Painted, Crowell, East Harwich, Mass., 2 1/2 x 5 1/2 In.	2016.00
Black Duck, Chesapeake Bay, 1950	202.00
Black Duck, Don Parker, 16 1/2 In.	172.00
Black Duck, Glass Eyes, Mounted On Lamp, Crowell, East Harwich, Mass., Oversize	2300.00
Black Duck, Hollow, Reg Culver, Stratford, Connecticut, c.1935	1076.00
Black Duck, Mounted, Robert McGaw, Havre De Grace, Mass., Miniature	575.00
Black Duck, Preening, Ward Brothers, Crisfield, Maryland, 1960	11950.00
Black Duck, William Breitt, Stratford, Connecticut, c.1965	1434.00
Blackhead Drake, Gray, Black, White, Ned Burgess, 8 1/2 x 15 In.	550.00
Blue Heron, 3-D, Gray Paint, Primitive, Nailed Construction, 28 x 25 x 2 In.	140.00
Blue Jay, A. Elmer Crowel, East Harwich, Mass, Miniature	1208.00
Blue-Winged Teal Drake, Preening, A. Elmer Crowell, Massachusetts	3680.00
Bluebill, Carved, Glass Eyes, Keel Weight, Mason, 14 1/2 In.	328.00
Bluebill, Carved, Painted, Crowell, East Harwich, Mass., 2 1/2 x 3 1/4 In.	1568.00
Bluebill Drake, New Jersey	104.00
Brant, Carved, Painted, Crowell, East Harwich, Mass., 2 1/2 x 5 1/2 In.	2912.00
Brant, H.V. Shourds, 1975	104.00
Bufflehead, Carved, Painted, Crowell, East Harwich, Mass., 2 1/2 x 5 1/2 In.	1680.00
Bufflehead Drake, Corbin Reed, Chincoteague, Virginia, c.1965	717.00
Canada Goose, A. Elmer Crowel, Massachusetts	3105.00
Canada Goose, Glass Eyes, Lead Weight, Initialed RLW, 19 In.	440.00
Canada Goose, Hollow Carved, Nova Scotia	288.00
Canada Goose, Hollow, Glass Eyes, Dodge Factory, Detroit, Mich, c.1884-1894	9250.00
Canada Goose, Painted Black & White, A. Elmer Crowell, 23 In.	2990.00
Canada Goose, Painted Feathers, Madison Mitchell, 1930, 12 3/4 x 24 1/2 In.	360.00
Canada Goose, Painted, Black & White, Horizontal Slats, Joe Lincoln, 39 In., Pair	5462.00
Canada Goose, Preening, Painted, L.C. Hornick, Jr., Stoney Point Plaque, 23 In.	290.00
Canada Goose, Seated, A. Elmer Crowell, East Harwich, Mass., Signed	2530.00
Canada Goose, Southeastern Mass, 27 In.	259.00
Canada Goose, Swimming, Mounted, Dr. Hill, Signed, Miniature	865.00
Canvasback, Carved, Painted, M. Mitchell, Md., 8 1/2 x 14 1/2 In.	468.00
Canvasback, Carved, Painted, Wood, Crowell, East Harwich, Mass., 2 1/2 x 5 In.	2575.00
Canvasback, Glass Eyes, Lead Keel, Stamped Blair's, 14 In.	440.00
Canvasback, John Heffner, High Rock, Pa., 1940	95.00
Canvasback, Sleeping, Charles Jobes, 1998, 13 1/2 In.	50.00
Canvasback Drake, Carved, Painted, Glass Eyes, Early 20th Century, 8 x 16 In.	235.00
Canvasback Drake, Glass Eyes, Original Paint, 11 x 18 1/2 In.	4180.00
Canvasback Drake, Susquehanna River Bird, 15 1/2 In.	205.00
Canvasback Hen, Ben Schmidt, 16 3/4 In.	259.00
Coot, Whimsical, Neck In Knot, Open Mouth, Glass Eyes, 9 In.	281.00
Curlew, Cork, France, c.1890	2800.00
Curlew, Feeding, Carved, Painted, Brown & White, Glass Eyes, 16 In.	172.00
Duck, Carved, Applied Glass Eyes, Alvirah Wright, N.C., 8 x 14 x 5 1/2 In.	1980.00
Duck, Carved, Painted Black, Brown Textured Head, Green Bill, Benjamin Holmes, 16 In.	2185.00
Duck, Carved, Painted Black, Glass Eyes, Cassius Smith, 14 In.	575.00
Duck, Carved, Painted, Brown, Gray, Alvirah Wright, N.C., 9 1/4 x 12 1/2 In.	880.00
Fish, Perch, 6 1/2 In.	575.00
Fish, Sunfish, 5 1/2 In.	230.00
Fish, Wood & Metal, Applied Fins, 19 1/2 In.	220.00
Golden Crowned Kinglet, Mounted, A. Elmer Crowell, East Harwich, Mass, Life Size	5980.00
Goose, Slat, New England	145.00
Green-Winged Teal Drake, Lloyd Johnson, Bay Head, New Jersey, c.1955	1435.00
Green-Winged Teal Drake & Hen, Lloyd Johnson, Bay Head, New Jersey, c.1955	3110.00
Green-Winged Teal Hen, Ward Brothers, Crisfield, Maryland, 1967	5975.00
Herring Gull, Hurley Conklin, Manahawkin, New Jersey	1795.00
Herring Gull, Spread Wings, Mounted, 25 In.	605.00

Decoy, Mallard Drake, Stamped, Roswell Bliss,
Stratford, Conn., 1950-1975

Decoy, Red-Breasted Merganser Drake,
Signed, Jon Floyd, Jr., Gilm, Del., 1977

Highland Grouse, Pair, Painted, Wood Base, A.J. King, N. Scituate, R.I.	1434.00
Hooded Merganser Drake, James Lapham, Dennisport, Mass., Quarter Size	505.00
King Eider, Flying, A.J. Dando, No. 1972	350.00
Long Island Shorebird, Carved, Painted, Brown, White, Black, Bronze, 11 In.	1440.00
Louisiana Mallard, Carved, Painted, Nick Trahon, Lake Charles, La., 13 In.	520.00
Mallard, Canvas, Glass Eyes, Factory Made, Hand Stitched Seam Support, 15 In., Pair	145.00
Mallard, Carved Madison Mitchell, Md., 7 1/2 x 15 1/2 In.	305.00
Mallard, Carved, Painted, Wood, Crowell, East Harwich, Mass., 4 x 4 1/2 In.	1790.00
Mallard Drake, Ben Schmidt, 15 1/2 In.	546.00
Mallard Drake, Corbin Reed, Chincoteague, Virginia, c.1965	1076.00
Mallard Drake, Stamped, Roswell Bliss, Stratford, Conn., 1950-1975 ....*Illus*	837.00
Mallard Drake & Hen, Ben Schmidt, 17 1/4 & 17 In.	1955.00
Mallard Hen, Brown Over Black, Green On Wings, Glass Eyes, 16 1/2 x 7 In.	385.00
Merganser, Carved, Painted, Crowell, East Harwich, Mass., 2 x 4 3/4 In.	2016.00
Merganser, Wood, Carved, Painted, 6 1/2 x 15 1/2 In.	440.00
Oldsquaw Drake, William Cranmer, Beach Haven, New Jersey, 1968	837.00
Owl, Carved, Painted, White, Inset Eyes, Wooden Base, 16 In.	4025.00
Pike, Gray, Metal Fins, Paul McNair, Brooklyn, N.Y., 10 In.	55.00
Pintail, Carved, Painted, Crowell, East Harwich, Mass., 3 1/4 x 5 1/4 In.	2128.00
Pintail, Hollow Body, c.1900, 15 1/2 In.	546.00
Pintail Drake, Balsa Wood, Don Briddell, Crisfield, Maryland, c.1985	1912.00
Pintail Drake, Madison Mitchell, 17 In.	880.00
Pintail Drake, Original Paint, R. Madison Mitchell, 7 1/2 x 18 In.	522.00
Pintail Hen, John McLoughlin, Bordentown, New Jersey, c.1985	3346.00
Red Knot, Glass Eyes, Spring Plumage, A. Elmer Crowell, East Harwich, Mass.	40250.00
Red-Breasted Merganser Drake, Signed, Jon Floyd, Jr., Gilm, Del., 1977 ....*Illus*	956.00
Red-Breasted Merganser Hen, Painted, Cape Cod	150.00
Redhead, Carved, Painted, Wood, Crowell, East Harwich, Mass., 3 1/2 x 4 1/4 In.	1680.00
Ring-Necked Pheasant, Pair, Carved, Painted, Wood Base, A.J. King, N. Scituate, R.I.	2988.00
Sea Gull, Frank Finney, 1960, 10 1/2 x 19 1/2 In.	140.00
Sea Gull, Turned Head, Carved Feathers, DD Hawthorne, 10 x 16 1/2 In.	495.00
Sea Gull, Ward Brothers, Crisfield, Maryland, 1965	6575.00
Shell Drake, Carved, Painted, Crowell, East Harwich, Mass., 3 x 6 In.	2350.00
Shorebird, Applied Eyes, Beak, Gray & Black, 1900s, N.C., 10 1/2 x 11 1/2 In.	195.00
Shorebird, Call, Leather, Tin, 5 In.	40.00
Shorebird, Carved, Painted, Early 20th Century, Mounted, 11 In.	530.00
Shorebird, Carved, Painted, Mahogany Base, Willard C. Baldwin, 8 3/8 In.	646.00
Shorebird, Glass Eyes, Cedar Base, Cape Cod, Mass., 1880s, 10 3/4 x 11 In.	330.00
Shorebird, Outstretched Wings, Curved Tail, Brown, White, Black, Tin, 9 x 12 In.	275.00
Shorebird, Red, Brown, Black, Iron Stand, Virginia, 19th Century, 4 1/2 x 11 1/2 In.	470.00
Sucker, Metal Fins, Paul McNair, Brooklyn, N.Y., 9 In.	55.00
Sucker, Spearing, Carved, Painted, Metal Fins, Wood Base, Ian McNair, 11 In.	193.00
Turtle, Carved, Painted, 7 1/2 x 30 x 17 1/2 In.	264.00
Tuveson Duck, Flying, Brass Plaque, 24 In.	633.00
White-Winged Scoter Drake, Roswell Bliss, Stratford, Connecticut, c.1965	1793.00
Widgeon Drake, Raised Wing Feathers, Turned Head, Patrick R. Godin, 16 In.	1093.00
Widgeon Drake, William Baldwin, Stratford, Connecticut, c.1965	1912.00
Willet, Glass Eyes, Recessed Sockets, Black, Brown Paint, William Bowman	34500.00
Wood Duck, Carved, Painted, Crowell, East Harwich, Mass., 2 3/4 x 4 In.	2912.00
Wood Duck Drake, Ken Harris, Woodville, N.Y.	575.00
Yellowlegs, Black, White, Gray, R. Snow, Wood Base, 12 In.	230.00
Yellowlegs, Full-Bodied, Glass Eyes, A.E. Crowell, c.1905, 14 In.	10000.00

Yellowlegs, Outstretched Wings, Head, Ward Brothers, Crisfield, Maryland, 1965 . . . . 3585.00
Yellowlegs, Preening, Driftwood Base, Ward Brothers, Crisfield, Maryland, 1964 . . . . 9560.00

DEDHAM Pottery was started in 1895. Chelsea Keramic Art Works was established in 1872 in Chelsea, Massachusetts, by members of the Robertson family. The factory closed in 1889 and was reorganized as the Chelsea Pottery U.S. in 1891. The firm used the marks *CKAW* and *CPUS*. It became the Dedham Pottery of Dedham, Massachusetts. The factory closed in 1943. It was famous for its crackleware dishes, which picture blue outlines of animals, flowers, and other natural motifs.

Azalea, Bowl, No. 2, Stamped, 2 1/4 x 9 1/2 In.	165.00
Azalea, Cup & Saucer, Blue Rabbit Mark	115.00
Azalea, Plate, Blue Rabbit Mark, 10 In.	288.00
Azalea, Plate, Impressed Blue Rabbit Mark, 6 In. . . . . .150.00 to 195.00
Azalea, Plate, Impressed Blue Rabbit Mark, 8 1/4 In.	259.00
Azalea, Plate, Leaves, Stamped, 6 1/4 In.	385.00
Bird, Vase, Ocher Tan Glaze, Flower & Bee On Clover, Marked CKAW, 7 x 3 1/2 In.	468.00
Bird In Potted Orange Tree, Plate, Impressed Rabbit, 20th Century, 8 5/8 In.	470.00
Bird In Potted Orange Tree, Plate, White Ground, Doves Carousing, 8 1/2 In.	358.00
Butterfly, Plate, Deep Blue, Flowers, Blue Ink Stamp, 8 1/2 In.	303.00
Crab, Plate, Blue Ink Stamp, 1 Impressed Rabbit, c.1910, 8 1/2 In. . . . . .235.00 to 558.00
Crab, Plate, White Background, 8 1/2 In.	695.00
Day Lily, Plate, Signed, Hugh Robertson, 8 1/2 In.	935.00
Dolphin, Plate, Dolphins & Babies, Marked CPUS, 8 1/2 In.	950.00
Dolphin, Plate, Waves, Stamped, 8 1/2 In.	1760.00
Duck, Plate, Deep Blue, Ducks In Pond & Water Lilies, Maude Davenport, 8 1/2 In.	375.00
Duck, Plate, Deep Blue, Tufted Head Feathers, Swirling Water, Pond Lilies, 10 In.	1210.00
Duck, Plate, Pond Lily, Stamped, 8 1/2 In.	248.00
Duck, Tile, Duck Wading In Water, Stamped, 5 1/2 In.	715.00
Elephant, Bowl, Rice, Deep Blue, Midnight Blue Ground, Blue Ink Stamp, 2 x 3 In.	660.00
Elephant, Creamer, Deep Blue, Blue Ink Stamp, 3 x 3 In.	550.00
Elephant, Cup & Saucer, Impressed Blue Rabbit Mark . . . . .690.00 to 880.00
Elephant, Eggcup, Deep Blue, 3 1/2 In.	880.00
Elephant, Pitcher, Stamped, 4 1/2 x 5 In.	1100.00
Elephant, Plate, 8 1/2 In.	1380.00
Elephant, Plate, Baby Elephant, Stamped, 10 In.	1320.00
Elephant, Plate, Deep Blue, Cobalt Blue Ground, Blue Ink Stamp, Registered, 7 1/2 In. . .	880.00
Elephant, Plate, Impressed Blue Rabbit Mark, 6 In.	920.00
Elephant, Plate, Impressed Blue Rabbit Mark, 8 1/2 In.	1380.00
Elephant, Plate, Impressed Rabbit Mark, 9 7/8 In.	1553.00
Flower, Plate, Deep Blue, Stems, Buds, Blue Ink Stamp, 10 In.	1650.00
Flower, Vase, Khaki Green, High Glaze, Marked CKAW, 6 1/4 x 3 1/2 In.	605.00
Grape, Plate, Blue Ink Stamp, 20th Century, 9 3/4 In.	147.00
Grape, Plate, Deep Blue, Blue Ink Stamp, 6 In.	220.00
Grape, Plate, Deep Blue, Blue Ink Stamp, 8 1/2 In. .165.00 to 195.00
Grape, Plate, Overlapping Grapes To Center, Stamped, 6 In. . . . . .195.00 to 275.00
Horse Chestnut, Plate, Deep Blue, Flowers, Blue Ink Stamp, 6 In.	193.00
Horse Chestnut, Plate, Deep Blue, White Glaze, Marked CPUS, 10 In.	275.00
Horse Chestnut, Plate, Impressed Rabbit, 20th Century, 8 3/8 In.	147.00
Iris, Plate, Blue Leaves, Stamped, 10 In.	330.00
Iris, Plate, Blue Rabbit Mark, 8 1/2 In.	230.00
Iris, Plate, Deep Blue, Leaves, Blue Ink Stamp, 6 In.	193.00
Landscape & Boat, Plate, Hills, Sailboats, Lake, Sky, Blue Ink Stamp, 6 In.	1650.00
Lobster, Bacon Rasher, White Ground, Waves, 10 In.	990.00
Lobster, Charger, Deep Blue, Swirling Waves, Blue Ink Stamp, Registered, 12 1/4 In. . . .	1320.00
Lobster, Charger, Swirling Waves	1320.00
Lobster, Plate, Bread & Butter, Blue Ink Stamp, 6 1/8 In. . . . . .176.00 to 590.00
Lobster, Plate, Seaweed Tendrils, Blue Ink Stamp, 8 1/4 In. . . . . .695.00 to 990.00
Lotus, Bowl, Embossed Panels As Lotus Petals, Blue Ink Stamp, 2 x 5 In.	825.00
Magnolia, Cup & Saucer, Blue Rabbit Mark	115.00
Magnolia, Plate, Impressed Rabbit, 6 1/4 In. . . . . .144.00 to 220.00
Magnolia, Plate, Impressed Rabbit, 8 1/2 In.	230.00

Magnolia, Plate, Impressed Rabbit, 10 In. 431.00
Magnolia & Vine, Tile, Vine & Leaf, Blue Ink Stamp, 3 3/4 x 3 3/4 In. 1870.00
Match & Cigarette Holder, Man's Head, Gray, Glazed, Marked CKAW, c.1800, 6 In. 1210.00
Moth, Plate, Butterfly & Fan Border, Stamped, 10 In. 385.00
Moth, Plate, Luna, Broad Winged Moths At Night, Moon, 8 1/2 In. 950.00
Moth, Plate, Stripes, Dots, Swirls, Flowers, Stamped, 6 In. 385.00
Mushroom, Plate, Blue Ink Stamp, 2 Impressed Rabbits, c.1910, 10 1/8 In. 353.00
Mushroom, Plate, Deep Blue, White Ground, Blue Ink Stamp, 8 1/2 In. 715.00
Night & Morning, Pitcher, Rooster, Hen, Sun, Owl, Moon, Blue Ink Stamp, 5 x 5 1/4 In. . . 605.00
Owl, Plate, Moon, Stars, Stamped, 9 3/4 In. 4950.00
Pansy, Butter Pat, 5 Raised Overlapping Petals, Blue Ink Stamp, 3 1/2 In. . . . . .295.00 to 385.00
Peony, Vase, 8 In. 1610.00
Pineapple, Plate, Alternating Pineapple & Flowers, 8 1/2 In. 475.00
Polar Bear, Plate, Blue, Bear On Icebergs, Blue Ink Stamp, 9 3/4 In. 1100.00
Polar Bear, Plate, Bread & Butter, Blue Ink Stamp, 2 Impressed Rabbits, 1900s, 6 1/4 In. . 235.00
Polar Bear, Plate, Icebergs, Stamped, 10 1/4 In. 1100.00
Pond Lily, Plate, Deep Blue, Blue Ink Stamp, 6 In. 248.00
Pond Lily, Plate, Deep Blue, Blue Ink Stamp, 10 In. . . . . .295.00 to 413.00
Pond Lily, Sauce, Swirled Points, Blue Ink Stamp, Registered, 1 1/2 x 5 1/2 In. 715.00
Poppy, Bowl, Reticulated Edge, Stamped, 5 3/4 x 10 1/2 In. 1100.00
Poppy, Bread Plate, 6 In. 1955.00
Poppy, Plate, Arched Stem, Poppy Border, 8 1/2 In. . . . . .220.00 to 395.00
Rabbit, Ashtray, Deep Blue, Circular, Blue Ink Stamp, Registered, 6 1/2 In. 358.00
Rabbit, Ashtray, Deep Blue, Circular, Rabbits On Flared Rim, 3 1/4 In. 165.00
Rabbit, Bowl, Deep Blue, Blue Ink Stamp, Registered, 2 x 4 1/2 In. 165.00
Rabbit, Bowl, Deep Blue, Blue Ink Stamp, Registered, 3 3/4 x 9 In. 303.00
Rabbit, Bowl, Rice, Deep Blue, Rabbits Along Midsection, 2 x 3 1/4 In. 193.00
Rabbit, Candlesnuffer, Bell Shape, Rounded Finial, 2 In. 1430.00
Rabbit, Candlestick, Flat Rim, Blue Bands, Stamped, 1 1/3 x 3 3/4 In. 385.00
Rabbit, Card Holder, Slot Along Ears, Blue Ink Stamp, 2 1/4 In. 1430.00
Rabbit, Charger, Blue Ink Stamp, 20th Century, 12 In. 294.00
Rabbit, Coffeepot, Flared, Cylindrical, Angled Handle, 1931, 10 In. 558.00
Rabbit, Creamer, Bulbous, No. 8, Stamped, 3 1/2 In. 715.00
Rabbit, Cup & Saucer, 4 O'Clock, 1 3/4 x 5 In. 220.00
Rabbit, Cup & Saucer, White Ground, Blue Ink Stamp, 2 x 4 In., 5 1/4 In. . . . . . . .110.00 to 220.00
Rabbit, Dish, 5-Point Star, Deep Blue, Blue Ink Stamp, 6 x 6 In. 1210.00
Rabbit, Dish, Deep Blue, Flared Rim With Rabbits, Blue Glaze, Blue Ink Stamp, 7 3/4 In. 1100.00
Rabbit, Dish, Pickle, Deep Blue, Canoe Shape, Blue Ink Stamp, 2 1/4 x 9 1/2 In. 248.00
Rabbit, Flower Frog, Rabbit On Dome Shape Holder, Blue Ink Stamp, 6 x 4 In. .1200.00 to 1430.00
Rabbit, Jar, Cover, Border At Base, Stamped, 4 1/4 x 3 1/2 In. . . . . .440.00 to 660.00
Rabbit, Knife Rest, Stamped, 2 3/4 x 3 3/4 In. 660.00
Rabbit, Nappy, Cover, Deep Blue, No. 4, Stamped, 10 In. 605.00
Rabbit, Nappy, Deep Blue, 1 1/2 x 6 In. 175.00
Rabbit, Pitcher, Deep Blue, Bulbous, Blue Ink Stamp, 5 x 6 In. 660.00
Rabbit, Plate, Deep Blue, Blue Ink Stamp, 10 In. 193.00
Rabbit, Plate, Deep Blue, Blue, Black Ground, Blue Ink Stamp, 6 In. 193.00
Rabbit, Plate, Deep Blue, Marked CPUS, 8 1/2 In. 140.00
Rabbit, Plate, Deep Blue, Stamped, 6 In. 220.00
Rabbit, Plate, Medium Blue, Stamped, 8 1/2 In. 220.00
Rabbit, Plate, White Glaze, Rabbits In Relief, Marked CPUS, 8 1/2 In. 175.00
Rabbit, Plate, White Glaze, Rabbits In Relief, Maude Davenport, 8 1/2 In. 195.00
Rabbit, Platter, Rounded Corners, 17 1/2 x 10 In. 550.00
Rabbit, Salt & Pepper, Flower Band, 3 1/2 In. . . . . .305.00 to 358.00
Rabbit, Soup, Dish, Deep Blue, Blue Ink Stamp, 1 1/2 x 8 1/2 In. 138.00
Rabbit, Spoon, Baby's, Ladle Style, 4 1/2 In. 880.00
Rabbit, Stein, Deep Blue, Rabbit Border At Base, Stamped, 5 x 5 1/2 In. 330.00
Rabbit, Sugar & Creamer, Deep Blue, Bulbous, Blue Ink Stamp, 4 x 4 & 3 1/4 x 5 In. . . . 715.00
Rabbit, Sugar, Cover, 1931, 4 7/8 In. 411.00
Rabbit, Tea Set, Blue Rabbit Mark, 5 3/4-In. Teapot, 3 Piece 1610.00
Rabbit, Tea Stand, Round, Stamped, 7 1/2 In. 220.00
Rabbit, Teapot, Blue Band, White Ground, 5 1/4 In. 546.00
Rabbit, Teapot, Deep Blue, Final, Bulbous, Blue Ink Stamp, Registered, 5 1/2 x 7 In. 1320.00
Rabbit, Teapot, Midsection Band, Bulbous, Cover, Stamped, 6 1/2 x 8 1/2 In. 550.00

Snowtree, Plate, Bread & Butter, Blue Ink Stamp, 2 Impressed Rabbits, 1900s, 6 1/8 In. . . . 118.00
Snowtree, Plate, Deep Blue, Blue Glaze, 10 1/4 In. . . . . .220.00 to 358.00
Snowtree, Plate, Trees, Snow, Stamped, 8 1/2 In. 248.00
Swan, Bowl, Cattails, Stamped, 3 1/4 x 7 In. 440.00
Swan, Bowl, Swans & Cattails, Blue Rabbit Mark, 3 3/4 x 9 In. 201.00
Swan, Cup Plate, Deep Blue, Swans & Cattails, Blue Ink Stamp, Registered, 4 1/4 In. . . . 385.00
Swan, Pitcher, Deep Blue, Bulbous, Blue Ink Stamp, 5 x 6 In. 715.00
Swan, Plate, Blue, Swans & Cattails, Blue Ink Stamp, Registered, 7 1/2 In. . . . . .300.00 to 440.00
Swan, Plate, Deep Blue, Swans & Cattails, Blue Ink Stamp, Registered, 6 In. 413.00
Swan, Plate, Deep Blue, White Glaze, 8 1/2 In. 395.00
Swan, Plate, Swans & Cattails, Impressed Rabbit Mark, 8 1/2 In. 345.00
Swan, Plate, Swans & Cattails, Impressed Rabbit Mark, 10 In. 518.00
Swan, Saucer, Swans & Cattails, Blue Rabbit Mark, 6 In. 92.00
Swan, Vase, Spherical, Center Band, Blue Ink Stamp, c.1910, 3 7/8 In. 529.00
Tapestry Lion, Plate, Deep Blue, Lions, Shrubbery, Blue Ink Stamp, Registered, 9 3/4 In. 990.00
Tapestry Lion, Plate, Moon Over Lion, Shrubs, Stamped, 8 1/2 In. 825.00
Turkey, Plate, Alternating Turkeys & Stalks, 8 1/2 In. . . . . .395.00 to 550.00
Turkey, Plate, Deep Blue, Feathers, Corn Stalks, Blue Ink Stamp, Registered, 7 1/2 In. . . . 385.00
Turkey, Plate, Luncheon, Blue Ink Stamp, 7 5/8 In. 353.00
Turtle, Flower Holder, 4 Legs, Tail, Head, Rounded Back, 1 1/2 x 5 In. 1210.00
Turtle, Plate, Double Turtle, Stamped, 8 1/2 In. 1430.00
Vase, 6 Rabbits, Blue & Ivory Crackle Glaze, 4 1/2 In. 405.00
Vase, Bulbous, Beige, Ivory, Blue Luster Glaze, 8 x 4 1/2 In. 1840.00
Vase, Bulbous, Crackled Green, Brown, Red Glaze, Hugh Robertson, 6 1/2 x 7 In. 1725.00
Vase, Bulbous, Ivory, Blue, Hugh Robertson, 8 x 4 1/2 In. 1840.00
Vase, Bulbous, Oxblood Glaze, 7 x 5 3/4 In. 1265.00
Vase, Bulbous, Oxblood Glaze, 10 x 7 In. 6325.00
Vase, Green, Brown, Gray, Streaked, Signed, B.W., 8 x 6 1/4 In. 1760.00
Vase, Oxblood, Glaze Streaked, Marked CKAW, c.1800, 8 3/4 x 4 1/4 In. 3080.00
Vase, Pillow, Blue Violets, Green Ground, Scrolled Feet, Marked CKAW, 3 3/4 x 4 1/4 In. 880.00
Vase, Slender Shape, Oxblood Glaze, Iridescent Highlights, 7 1/2 In. 1045.00

DEGUE is a signature acid-etched on pieces of French glass made in the
early 1900s. Cameo, mold blown, and smooth glass with contrasting
colored rims are the types most often found.

Bowl, Rose Glass, 11 Pieces Of Glass Fruit, Wrought Iron Frame & Handle, 14 1/2 In. . . . 978.00
Vase, Burgundy Bull Thistles, Silhouetted On Verde Green, Signed, 14 1/2 In. 750.00
Vase, Grapes, Leaves, Yellow, Brown, Orange, Cameo, 10 In. 633.00
Vase, Leafy Branches, Red, Orange Yellow, Bulbous, Swollen, Etched, 15 In. 1909.00
Vase, Ray, Mottled Yellow, Orange Overlay, Leaves, Buds, Cameo, c.1925, 10 3/4 In. 750.00

DELATTE glass is a French cameo glass made by Andre Delatte. It was
first made in Nancy, France, in 1921. Lighting fixtures and opaque
glassware in imitation of Bohemian opaline were made. There were
many French cameo glass makers, so be sure to look in other appropriate categories.

Vase, Blue, Jelly Fish, Enameled, Art Deco, Signed, 4 1/2 x 3 In. 490.00
Vase, Brown Trees, Turquoise Ground, Cylindrical, Signed, 3 3/4 In. 300.00
Vase, Dragonfly, Red Iris, Red Ground, Baluster, Footed, Engraved Mark, 14 1/4 In. 1350.00
Vase, Flowers, Maroon, Mottled Mauve, White Ground, Cameo, Signed, 13 1/2 In. 975.00
Vase, Garden Flowers, Frosted Amethyst To Sky Blue Ground, Oval, Signed, 12 In. 2300.00
Vase, Gray Satin, Mottled Orange, Amethyst, c.1915, 18 In. 490.00
Vase, Gray Satin, Mottled Orange, Cobalt Blue, Signed, c.1920, 11 3/4 In. 200.00
Vase, Winter Scene, Frosted Blue Ground, Signed, 8 In. 115.00

DELDARE, see Buffalo Pottery Deldare.

DELFT is a tin-glazed pottery that has been made since the seventeenth
century. It is decorated with blue on white or with colored decorations.
Most of the pieces sold today were made after 1891, and the name
Holland appears with the Delft factory marks. The word *delft* also
appears on pottery from other countries. Delft was made in England in
the eighteenth century.

Blotter, Windmill & Sailboat Scene, Blue, 4 In. 70.00

Bottle, Blue & White Bouquet In Oriental Bowl, Bulbous, Elongated Neck, 10 In. 950.00
Bowl, Blue, White, Flowers, Leaves, c.1740, 6 In. 495.00
Bowl, Elaborate Flowers, Blue Chain Band & Medallion On Interior, 9 In. 940.00
Bowl, Flowers, Blue, White, c.1740, 6 1/2 In. 495.00
Bowl, House & Garden Landscape, Blue Banded Interior Border, Leaves, 9 1/4 In. 1175.00
Bowl, Polychrome, Flared Edge, Flowers, Leaves, 4 1/2 x 10 In. 360.00
Bowl, Polychrome, White Ground, Cobalt Blue Borders, Footed Base, 10 x 5 1/2 In. 2200.00
Candelabrum, 7-Light, Blue & White, Central Floral Aperture, 18th Century, 12 In. 4180.00
Charger, Blue Flowers, Tin Glaze, 13 1/2 In. 100.00
Charger, Blue, Allover Geometric Design Front & Back, Signed, 13 In. 225.00
Charger, Chinese Man Holding Spear, Banded Lattice & Flower Border, 14 In. 645.00
Charger, Courtyard Scenes, Asian Figures, 18th Century, 15 3/8 In. 411.00
Charger, Floral Landscape, Flower & Insect Border, 12 1/4 In. 353.00
Charger, Oriental-Style Landscape, Floral Border, Blue, Red, Yellow, 1600s, 13 1/4 In. . . . 1808.00
Charger, Oriental-Style Landscape, Polychrome, Red, Blue, Green, 1600s, 12 1/2 In. 1920.00
Charger, Seated Figure In Landscape, Blue, White, 12 In. 518.00
Clock, Boat & Windmill Scene, Figural Boy & Girl On Top, Blue & White, 7 x 4 In. 20.00
Creamer, Figural, Cow, Windmill & Sailboat Scene, Blue & White, 9 1/2 In. 75.00
Figurine, Cat, On Pillow, Blue Sponge, Dark Blue Pillow, White Flowers, Holland, 7 In. . 525.00
Flower Brick, Blue & White Flowers, Rectangular, Pierced Top, c.1760, 5 5/8 In. 440.00
Jar, Cover, Blue & White, Octagonal, Panels, Kylin Knop, Late 19th Century, 13 9/16 In. . 1076.00
Letter Holder, Windmill, Sailboat, Blue, White, 4 In. 44.00
Luncheon Set, Flowers, Blue & White, Plates, Cups, Saucers, Serving Items, 27 Piece . . . 805.00
Mug, Polychrome, In Memory Of Lord Nelson, 19th Century 850.00
Plaque, Embossed Scrolled Acanthus, Dutch Windmill, Canal, c.1900, 19 x 14 In. 546.00
Plate, Blue & White, King William III Of England, c.1690, 10 In. 1250.00
Plate, Flowers, Oriental Style, Red, Blue, Green, Yellow, White Ground, 13 3/4 In. 765.00
Posset Pot, 3 Boss Rows, 2 Scroll Handles, Short Spout, London, c.1670, 4 3/8 In. 4780.00
Salver, Skaters, Village, Square, Canted Corners, Shells On Rim, 4 Trumpet Feet, 8 5/8 In. 176.00
Shoe, Windmill, Blue, White, Hand Painted, 3 3/4 x 2 1/4 In. 15.00
Tankard, Faience, Blue Ground, Flower Panels, Marked PVM, c.1760, Pair 1075.00
Tazza, Flowers, Goddess Of Spring, 9 1/4 In. 33.00
Tile, Baker, Rolling Out Dough, Raised Lines, Multicolored, Incised, 8 x 11 1/2 In. 300.00
Tile, Flying Goose, Carved, Impressed Mark, 12 x 4 In. 200.00
Tile, Framed Goose, White, Burnt Orange, Green Matte Ground, 7 1/4 x 7 1/4 In. 248.00
Tile, Man, Woman, Dutch, Raised Outline, De Porceleyne Fles, Frame, 5 In., Pair 259.00
Tile, Parakeet, Cloisonne, De Porceleyne Fles, 12 x 4 1/2 In. 230.00
Tile, Peacock, Raised Outline, Polychrome, De Porceleyne Fles, Frame, 5 x 17 In. 290.00
Tobacco Jar, Harbor Scene, Varinas, Havana, Oval, Brass Lid, 15 In., Pair 1495.00
Tobacco Jar, Indian Beside Urn, Trade Goods, Ships, Brass Cover, 14 1/2 In. 450.00
Urn, Cover, Blue & White, Conjoined Monogram, 19th Century, 14 1/2 In. 550.00
Vase, Blue & White, Cover, Blue Painted Mark, Holland, 21 3/4 In., Pair 3285.00
Vase, Blue & White, Landscape, Figural Reserve, Baluster Form, 1700s, 8 In. 230.00
Vase, Cover, Blue & White, Landscape, Figures, Foo Dog Finial, 1700s, 13 In. 230.00
Vase, Iridescent Turquoise Glaze, 5 3/4 In. 230.00

DENTAL cabinets, chairs, equipment, and other related items are listed
here. Other objects may be found in the Medical category.

Cabinet, 2 Marble Surfaces, Burled Panels, Cylinder Roll, Pullout, Victorian 3715.00
Cabinet, Art Deco Style, Ebonized Top, Push Button Spring-Action Storage Area 635.00
Cabinet, Lacquered Wood, 24 Metal Lined Drawers, Art Deco, 50 x 38 x 15 In. 200.00
Cabinet, Mahogany, Glass Handles, X-Ray Film Dispenser On Side, c.1910, 34 x 46 In. . . . 960.00
Cabinet, Victorian, Oak, Drawers, Glass Doors, Roll-Up Sections, 45 x 73 x 17 In. 1725.00
Chair, Favorite Columbia, Hydraulic, Velvet Upholstery, Pinstripe, Nickel Trim, 1890 . . . . 39.00
Chair, Oak, Iron, Seat, Back & Footrest Adjustable By Crank, U.S. Army, 1890 . . . . 1307.00
Chair, Wood, Centrifugal Mechanism On Headrest, Reclining Back, Upholstered, 40 In. . . . 120.00
Denture, Carved Bone, Twin Support Holes 560.00
Instruments, Mother Of Pearl Handles, Scalars, Elevators, c.1850, 10 Piece 2350.00
Scalers, 12 Ivory Handles, 4 Replacements, Wm R. Goulding & Co., c.1850, 7 1/2 In. 295.00
Skull, Flexible Lower Jaw, Teeth, Plastic, Square Plastic Base, 1950s, 3 In. 70.00
Sterilizer, Mahogany Case, Paneled, 19th Century, 11 3/4 x 7 x 8 In. 230.00
Waxed Dental Floss Silk, Box, Label, White Dental Mfg. Co., Philadelphia, 5 x 4 In. 70.00

DENVER is part of the mark on an American art pottery. William Long of Steubenville, Ohio, founded the Lonhuda Pottery Company in 1892. In 1900 he moved to Denver, Colorado, and organized the Denver China and Pottery Company. This pottery, which used the mark *Denver*, worked until 1905 when Long moved to New Jersey and founded the Clifton Pottery. Long also worked for Weller Pottery, Roseville Pottery, and American Encaustic Tiling Company.

DENVER
C &
P Co

Vase, Bulbous, Pinecones, Boughs, Natural Ground, Skiff, 5 3/4 x 4 1/2 In.	558.00
Vase, Gold, Green Matte Glaze, 1916, 3 3/4 x 6 1/2 In.	201.00
Vase, Lonhuda, Carnation, Impressed, 9 1/4 In.	230.00

DEPRESSION GLASS was an inexpensive glass manufactured in large quantities during the 1920s and early 1930s. It was made in many colors and patterns by dozens of factories in the United States. Most patterns were also made in clear glass, which the factories called *crystal*. If no color is listed here, it is clear. The name *Depression glass* is a modern one. For more descriptions, history, pictures, and prices of Depression glass, see the book *Kovels' Depression Glass & Dinnerware Price List*.

Adam, Berry Bowl, Green, 4 3/4 In.	28.00
Adam, Bowl, Cover, Pink, 8 3/4 In.	69.00 to 78.00
Adam, Bowl, Dessert, Green, 4 3/4 In.	28.00
Adam, Bowl, Dessert, Pink, 4 3/4 In.	20.00
Adam, Bowl, Green, 5 3/4 In.	57.00 to 66.00
Adam, Bowl, Green, 8 In.	125.00
Adam, Bowl, Green, Oval, 10 In.	52.00
Adam, Bowl, Pink, Oval, 10 In.	35.00
Adam, Butter, Cover, Pink	110.00
Adam, Butter, Green	65.00
Adam, Cake Plate, Green, 10 In.	37.00
Adam, Cake Plate, Pink, 10 In.	28.00
Adam, Cup & Saucer, Pink	31.00
Adam, Pitcher, Pink, 32 Oz.	90.00
Adam, Plate, Dinner, Green, Square, 9 In.	33.00
Adam, Plate, Dinner, Pink, Square, 9 In.	45.00
Adam, Plate, Salad, Pink, Square, 7 3/4 In.	15.00
Adam, Plate, Sherbet, Pink, 6 In.	13.00
Adam, Platter, Green, Oval, 11 3/4 In.	46.00
Adam, Platter, Pink, Oval, 11 3/4 In.	34.00
Adam, Salt & Pepper, Pink, 4 In.	90.00
Adam, Saltshaker, Pink	55.00
Adam, Sherbet, Pink, 3 In.	26.00
Adam, Sugar & Creamer, Pink	46.00
Adam, Tumbler, Pink, 4 1/2 In.	35.00
American Pioneer, Sugar & Creamer	38.00
American Sweetheart, Berry Bowl, Pink, 9 In.	55.00 to 60.00
American Sweetheart, Bowl, Cereal, Cremax, 6 In.	20.00
American Sweetheart, Bowl, Cereal, Pink, 6 In.	18.00 to 20.00
American Sweetheart, Bowl, Vegetable, Oval, Pink, 11 In.	62.00 to 85.00
American Sweetheart, Cup & Saucer, Monax	12.00 to 13.00
American Sweetheart, Cup & Saucer, Pink	24.00
American Sweetheart, Plate, Dinner, Pink, 9 3/4 In.	45.00
American Sweetheart, Plate, Salad, Pink, 8 In.	14.00
American Sweetheart, Platter, Pink, Oval, 13 In.	55.00
Apple Blossom pattern is listed here as Dogwood.	
Aurora, Cup, Pink	15.00
Avocado, Bowl, Green, 3-Footed, 6 In.	35.00
Avocado, Bowl, Green, Oval, Handles, 8 In.	35.00
Avocado, Bowl, Salad, 7 1/2 In.	13.00
Avocado, Sugar, Green	40.00
Avocado, Tumbler, Footed	20.00
Ballerina pattern is listed here as Cameo.	

Banded Rib pattern is listed here as Coronation.
Banded Rings pattern is listed here as Ring.
Basket pattern is listed here as No. 615.
Block pattern is listed here as Block Optic.
Block Optic, Butter, Cover Only 30.00
Block Optic, Console, Pink, Rolled Edge 98.00
Block Optic, Goblet, Pink, 9 Oz., 5 3/4 In. 40.00
Block Optic, Sherbet, Green, 5 1/2 Oz., 3 1/4 In. 13.00
Block Optic, Sugar, Green, Handles, 4 In. . . . . 13.00 to 16.00
Block Optic, Sugar, Yellow, Handles 12.00
Block Optic, Tumbler, Pink, 11 Oz., 5 In. 19.00
Block Optic, Tumbler, Pink, 12 Oz., 4 7/8 In. 30.00
Boopie, Goblet, Forest Green Bowl, 9 Oz., 5 1/2 In. .13.00 to 15.00
Boopie, Sherbet, Forest Green Bowl, 6 Oz., 3 1/2 In. .9.00 to 10.00
Boopie, Tumbler, Iced Tea, 14 Oz., 6 Piece 10.00
Bouquet & Lattice pattern is listed here as Normandie.
Bubble, Berry Bowl, Sapphire Blue, 8 3/8 In. 16.00
Bubble, Berry Bowl, White, 8 3/8 In. 17.00
Bubble, Bowl, Cereal, 5 1/4 In. 10.00
Bubble, Candleholder, 3 In., Pair 11.00
Bubble, Creamer, White 45.00
Bubble, Cup & Saucer, Royal Ruby 13.00
Bubble, Sugar & Creamer, White 13.00
Bubble, Tumbler, 8 Oz. 17.00
Bubble, Tumbler, Iced Tea, Royal Ruby, 12 Oz., 4 1/2 In. . . . . .10.00 to 15.00
Bullseye pattern is listed here as Bubble.
Buttons & Bows pattern is listed here as Holiday.
Cabbage Rose pattern is listed here as Sharon.
Cameo, Bowl, Vegetable, Green, Oval, 10 In. 45.00
Cameo, Compote, Mayonnaise, Green, 5 In. 50.00
Cameo, Cookie Jar, Cover, Green 50.00
Cameo, Cookie Jar, No Cover, Green 25.00
Cameo, Cup, Green 20.00
Cameo, Cup, Yellow 8.00
Cameo, Ice Bowl, Green, Tab Handles, 3 x 5 1/2 In. 330.00
Cameo, Plate, Dinner, Green, 9 1/2 In. 20.00
Cameo, Plate, Dinner, Yellow, 9 1/2 In. 8.00
Cameo, Plate, Sherbet, Green, 6 In. 7.00
Cameo, Platter, Green, Closed Handles, 12 In. 30.00
Cameo, Salt & Pepper, Green, 4 In. 50.00
Cameo, Sugar, Green 33.00
Cameo, Tumbler, Juice, Green, 5 Oz., 3 3/4 In. 39.00
Candlewick pattern is listed in the Imperial Glass category.
Caprice pattern is included in the Cambridge Glass category.
Charm, Bowl, Dessert, Forest Green, 4 3/4 In. 7.00
Charm, Bowl, Salad, Forest Green, 7 3/8 In. 15.00
Cherry Blossom, Berry Bowl, Pink, 4 3/4 In. 21.00
Cherry Blossom, Berry Bowl, Pink, 8 1/2 In. 48.00
Cherry Blossom, Bowl, Cereal, Green, 5 3/4 In. 39.00
Cherry Blossom, Bowl, Cereal, Pink, 5 3/4 In. 40.00
Cherry Blossom, Bowl, Fruit, 3-Footed, Pink, 3 x 10 In. 110.00

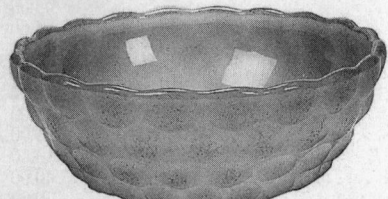

Depression Glass, Bubble

Depression Glass, Cameo

Cherry Blossom, Bowl, Handle, Pink, 9 In. 48.00
Cherry Blossom, Bowl, Pink, 5 3/4 In. 40.00
Cherry Blossom, Bowl, Pink, 10 1/2 In. 56.00
Cherry Blossom, Bowl, Vegetable, Oval, Green, 9 In. ....35.00 to 45.00
Cherry Blossom, Cake Plate, Green, 3-Footed, 10 1/4 In. 45.00
Cherry Blossom, Cake Plate, Pink, 3-Footed, 10 1/4 In. 55.00
Cherry Blossom, Cup & Saucer, Pink ....26.00 to 30.00
Cherry Blossom, Cup & Saucer, Pink, Child's 37.00
Cherry Blossom, Plate, Dinner, Green, 9 In. 40.00
Cherry Blossom, Plate, Dinner, Pink, 9 In. ....30.00 to 40.00
Cherry Blossom, Plate, Salad, Green, 7 In. 28.00
Cherry Blossom, Platter, Green, Oval, 11 In. 50.00
Cherry Blossom, Platter, Pink, Oval, 13 In. 85.00
Cherry Blossom, Sandwich Server, Pink, Handle 45.00
Cherry Blossom, Sugar & Creamer 46.00
Cherry Blossom, Sugar, Cover, Pink 33.00
Cherry Blossom, Sugar, No Cover, Pink 15.00
Cherry Blossom, Tumbler, Footed, 9 Oz., 4 1/2 In. 43.00
Cherry Blossom, Tumbler, Footed, Green, 4 Oz., 3 3/4 In. 22.00
Cherry Blossom, Tumbler, Pink, 12 Oz., 5 In. ....75.00 to 90.00
Christmas Candy, Plate, Luncheon, 8 In. 10.00
Christmas Candy, Sugar & Creamer 20.00
Circle, Cup & Saucer, Green 18.00
Circle, Sherbet, 3 1/8 In. 13.00
Cloverleaf, Cup & Saucer, Black 30.00
Cloverleaf, Sugar & Creamer, Black 45.00
Colonial, Berry Bowl, Green, 9 In. 30.00
Colonial, Butter, Cover 49.00
Colonial, Butter, Cover Only, Green 23.00
Colonial, Platter, Green, Oval, 12 In. 25.00
Colonial, Sherbet, Green, 3 3/8 In. 15.00
Colonial Fluted, Berry Bowl, Green, 7 1/2 In. 22.00
Colonial Fluted, Creamer, Green 13.00
Colonial Fluted, Cup & Saucer, Green 9.00
Colonial Fluted, Plate, Luncheon, Green, 8 In. 10.00
Colonial Fluted, Plate, Sherbet, Green, 6 In. ....4.00 to 6.00
Colonial Fluted, Sugar & Creamer, Green 16.00
Columbia, Bowl, Cereal, 5 In. ....17.00 to 19.00
Columbia, Plate, Luncheon, 9 1/2 In. 12.00
Columbia, Plate, Snack, 6 In. 20.00
Columbia, Soup, Dish, 8 In. 26.00
Constellation, Serving Bowl, Green, Handles, 11 In. 12.00
Coronation, Berry Bowl, Royal Ruby, Handles, 4 1/2 In. 11.00
Cube pattern is listed here as Cubist.
Cubist, Bowl, Deep, Pink, 4 1/2 In. 10.00
Cubist, Bowl, Salad, Pink, 6 1/2 In. 14.00
Cubist, Butter, Cover, Pink 79.00
Cubist, Candy Jar, Cover, Pink, 6 1/2 In. 38.00
Cubist, Coaster, Green, 3 1/4 In. 10.00
Cubist, Coaster, Pink, 3 1/4 In. 10.00
Cubist, Pitcher, Pink, 45 Oz., 8 3/4 In. 350.00
Cubist, Plate, Sherbet, Green, 6 In. 4.00
Cubist, Plate, Sherbet, Pink, 6 In. 4.00
Cubist, Powder Jar, Cover, 3-Footed, Pink 39.00
Cubist, Sherbet, Pink 9.00
Cubist, Tumbler, Green, 9 Oz., 4 In. 80.00
Cubist, Tumbler, Pink, 9 Oz., 4 In. 65.00
Daisy pattern is listed here as No. 620.
Dancing Girl pattern is listed here as Cameo.
Diamond pattern is listed here as Miss America.
Diamond Point, Candlelamp, 5 3/8 In. 12.00
Diamond Point, Candlelamp, Amber, 5 3/8 In. 12.00
Diamond Point, Candy Dish, Ruby Stain 12.00

Depression Glass, Cubist

Depression Glass, Dogwood

Diamond Point, Compote, Ruby Stain, 7 1/4 In.	13.00
Diamond Point, Creamer, Footed, 3 1/2 In.	10.00
Diamond Point, Ice Tub, 5 3/8 In.	8.00
Diana, Bowl, Fruit, Amber, 11 In.	18.00
Diana, Bowl, Soup, Cream, 5 1/2 In.	13.00
Diana, Cup, After Dinner, Pink	30.00
Diana, Plate, Dinner, Pink, 9 1/2 In.	15.00 to 20.00
Diana, Platter, Amber, 12 In.	16.00 to 22.00
Dogwood, Bowl, Cereal, Pink, 5 1/4 In.	34.00
Dogwood, Creamer, Pink, Thin, 2 1/2 In.	20.00
Dogwood, Cup & Saucer, Pink, Thick	24.00
Dogwood, Cup & Saucer, Pink, Thin	18.00 to 30.00
Dogwood, Plate, Bread & Butter, Pink, 6 In.	10.00
Dogwood, Plate, Luncheon, Pink, 8 In.	9.00
Dogwood, Salver, Pink, 12 In.	38.00
Dogwood, Sugar & Creamer, Pink, Thick	45.00
Dogwood, Sugar & Creamer, Pink, Thin	38.00
Dogwood, Sugar, Thick	19.00
Doric, Berry Bowl, Green, 4 1/2 In.	14.00
Doric, Berry Bowl, Green, 8 1/4 In.	36.00
Doric, Berry Set, Pink, 7 Piece	109.00
Doric, Bowl, Vegetable, Pink, Oval, 9 In.	47.00
Doric, Candy Dish, 3 Sections, Pink	13.00
Doric, Candy Dish, Cover, Pink	46.00
Doric, Cup & Saucer, Pink	13.00 to 18.00
Doric, Pitcher, Pink, 32 Oz., 5 1/2 In.	42.00
Doric, Soup, Cream, Green, 5 In.	50.00
Doric, Tray, Pink, Square, Handles, 8 In.	43.00
Doric, Tray, Pink, Square, Handles, 10 In.	32.00
Doric, Tumbler, Pink, 9 Oz., 4 1/2 In.	35.00
Doric & Pansy, Candy Dish, Ultramarine	23.00
Doric & Pansy, Plate, Sherbet, Ultramarine, 6 In.	14.00
Doric & Pansy, Salt & Pepper, Ultramarine	326.00
Doric & Pansy, Sugar & Creamer, Ultramarine	250.00
Doric & Pansy, Tray, Ultramarine, Round, Handles, 10 In.	33.00
Double Shield pattern is listed here as Mt. Pleasant.	
Early American Prescut, Ashtray, 7 3/4 In.	15.00
Early American Prescut, Bowl, Salad, 10 3/4 In.	12.00 to 18.00
Early American Prescut, Bowl, Scalloped, 8 3/4 In.	11.00
Early American Prescut, Butter, Cover, 7 1/4 In.	12.00
Early American Prescut, Candy Dish, Cover, 5 1/4 In.	10.00 to 15.00
Early American Prescut, Candy Dish, Cover, 7 1/2 In.	12.00
Early American Prescut, Lamp, Oil, 17 3/4 In.	300.00
Early American Prescut, Pitcher, 60 Oz., 8 1/2 In.	25.00 to 45.00
Early American Prescut, Pitcher, Square, 40 Oz., 5 1/2 In.	45.00
Early American Prescut, Plate, 11 In.	12.00 to 14.00
Early American Prescut, Plate, 13 1/2 In.	13.00 to 15.00

Early American Prescut, Relish, 2 Sections, 10 In.	10.00
Early American Prescut, Syrup, 12 Oz.	20.00
Early American Prescut, Tray, Scalloped, 12 x 6 1/2 In.	14.00
Early American Prescut, Vase, 10 In.	13.00 to 17.00
Early American Rock Crystal pattern is listed here as Rock Crystal.	
Fine Rib pattern is listed here as Homespun.	
Fire-King, Beverage Set, Hobnail, Milk White, 5 Piece	48.00
Fire-King, Beverage Set, Wrought Iron Decoration, Pink & Black, 7 Piece	69.00
Fire-King, Casserole, 12 x 7 In.	15.00
Fire-King, Casserole, Cover, 11 x 7 In.	18.00
Fire-King, Casserole, Square, 8 In.	22.00
Fire-King, Cookie Jar, Cover, Hobnail, Milk White	25.00
Fire-King, Jardiniere, Hobnail, Scalloped Rim, Milk White, 5 1/2 In.	12.00
Fire-King, Pitcher, Hobnail, Milk White, 72 Oz.	16.00
Fire-King, Refrigerator Jar, Jade-Ite, 4 x 8 In.	50.00
Fire-King, Relish, 3 Sections, Milk White, Gold Trim, 9 3/4 In.	12.00
Fire-King, Relish, 3 Sections, Milk White, Oblong, Gold Trim, 11 1/8 In.	12.00
Fire-King, Vase, Hobnail, Milk White, Flared, 9 1/2 In.	12.00
Floragold, Bowl, Ruffled Edge, 9 1/2 In.	43.00
Floragold, Bowl, Square, 4 1/2 In.	6.00
Floragold, Cup & Saucer	19.00
Floragold, Pitcher, 64 Oz.	35.00
Floragold, Sugar & Creamer	15.00
Floral, Berry Bowl, Green, 4 In.	30.00
Floral, Bowl, Salad, Green, 7 1/2 In.	33.00
Floral, Bowl, Salad, Pink, 7 1/2 In.	24.00
Floral, Bowl, Vegetable, Cover, Green, 8 In.	49.00
Floral, Butter, No Cover, Green	25.00
Floral, Candlestick, Pink, 4 In.	40.00
Floral, Candy Jar, Cover, Green	48.00
Floral, Cup & Saucer, Green	22.00
Floral, Cup & Saucer, Pink	22.00
Floral, Cup, Pink	13.00
Floral, Pitcher, Cone, Green, 32 Oz., 8 In.	45.00
Floral, Plate, Dinner, Pink, 9 In.	28.00
Floral, Plate, Salad, Green, 8 In.	14.00
Floral, Plate, Salad, Pink, 8 In.	17.00
Floral, Plate, Sherbet, 6 In.	9.00
Floral, Platter, Green, Oval, 10 3/4 In.	30.00
Floral, Platter, Pink, Oval, 10 3/4 In.	20.00
Floral, Sugar & Creamer, Green	60.00
Floral, Tumbler, Juice, Footed, Pink, 5 Oz., 4 In.	28.00
Floral, Tumbler, Water, Footed, Pink, 7 Oz., 4 3/4 In.	24.00
Floral & Diamond Band, Compote, Green, 5 1/2 In.	28.00
Florentine No. 1, Cup, Green	8.00
Florentine No. 2, Berry Bowl, Green	17.00
Florentine No. 2, Candy Dish, Cover, Pink	100.00
Florentine No. 2, Pitcher, Yellow, 48 Oz.	296.00
Florentine No. 2, Plate, Dinner, Yellow, 10 In.	16.00
Florentine No. 2, Plate, Sherbet, Yellow, 6 In.	6.00
Florette, Cup & Saucer	15.00
Flower & Leaf Band pattern is listed here as Indiana Custard.	
Forest Green, Bowl, Swirl, Crimped, 7 1/4 In.	12.00
Forest Green, Vase, 8 In.	22.00
Fruits, Cup & Saucer, Green	14.00
Fruits, Cup, Green	8.00
Gay Fad, Bowl, Grape & Vine Design, Milk Glass, Anchor Hocking, 5 3/4 In.	23.00
Georgian, Berry Bowl, Green, 4 1/2 In.	10.00
Georgian, Berry Bowl, Green, 7 1/2 In.	80.00
Georgian, Creamer, Green, 3 In.	11.00 to 12.00
Georgian, Creamer, Green, 4 In.	17.00
Georgian, Plate, Sherbet, Green, 6 In.	7.00
Georgian, Platter, Closed Handles, 11 1/2 In.	54.00

Georgian, Sugar & Creamer, Green 33.00
Georgian, Sugar & Creamer, Green, 4 In. 33.00
Georgian, Sugar, Green, 3 In. 14.00
Georgian, Sugar, Green, 4 In. 18.00
Hairpin pattern is listed here as Newport.
Harp, Cake Stand, 9 In. 25.00
Harp, Cake Stand, Gold Trim, 9 In. 30.00
Harp, Coaster, Gold Trim 3.00
Harp, Plate, Gold Trim, 7 In. 18.00
Harp, Tray, Handles, Gold Trim, 12 3/4 x 9 3/4 In. 37.00
Harp, Vase, Gold Trim, 7 1/2 In. 27.00
Harpo, Pitcher, Cobalt Blue 125.00
Harpo, Tumbler, Cobalt Blue, 4 1/8 In. 19.00
Harpo, Tumbler, Cobalt Blue, 5 1/8 In. 28.00
Heritage, Berry Bowl, 8 In. 45.00
Heritage, Creamer 30.00
Heritage, Cup & Saucer 8.00
Hex Optic pattern is listed here as Hexagon Optic.
Hexagon Optic, Pitcher, Green, 32 Oz., 5 In. 28.00
Hexagon Optic, Pitcher, Green, 70 Oz., 8 In. 295.00
Hexagon Optic, Plate, Luncheon, Green, 8 In. 14.00
Hexagon Optic, Plate, Sherbet, Green, 6 In. 5.00
Hobnail pattern is listed in the Hobnail category.
Holiday, Butter, No Cover, Pink 10.00
Holiday, Candlestick, Pink, 3 In., Pair 145.00
Holiday, Pitcher, 52 Oz., 6 3/4 In. 40.00
Homespun, Berry Bowl, Pink, Handles, 4 1/2 In. 18.00
Homespun, Cup & Saucer, Pink 15.00
Homespun, Plate, Sherbet, Pink, 6 In. 6.00
Honeycomb pattern is listed here as Hexagon Optic.
Horizontal Ribbed pattern is listed here as Manhattan.
Horseshoe pattern is listed here as No. 612.
Indiana Custard, Berry Bowl, 5 1/2 In. 11.00
Iris, Berry Bowl, Beaded Edge, Iridescent, 4 1/2 In. 9.00
Iris, Bowl, Fruits, Ruffled Edge, Iridescent, 11 1/2 In. 14.00
Iris, Bowl, Salad, Ruffled Edge, 5 In. 9.00
Iris, Bowl, Salad, Ruffled Edge, 9 1/2 In. 14.00
Iris, Bowl, Salad, Ruffled Edge, Iridescent, 9 1/2 In. 13.00
Iris, Butter, Cover, Iridescent 45.00
Iris, Butter, No Cover 14.00
Iris, Candlestick, Pair 48.00
Iris, Candy Dish, Cover, Handles, 7 In. . . . . .200.00 to 230.00
Iris, Cover, Butter 70.00
Iris, Creamer 12.00
Iris, Cup & Saucer 26.00
Iris, Cup & Saucer, After Dinner, Iridescent, Rose Tint 350.00
Iris, Goblet, Wine, 3 Oz., 4 1/2 In. . . . . .17.00 to 33.00
Iris, Nut Set, Bowl, Metal Base, 6 Picks, 4 1/2 In. 130.00
Iris, Pitcher, Footed, 9 1/2 In. 65.00
Iris, Plate, Dinner, Iridescent, 9 In. 45.00
Iris, Saucer 13.00
Iris, Sherbet, Iridescent, 2 1/2 In. 15.00
Iris, Vase, 9 In. 33.00
Iris, Vase, Iridescent, 9 In. . . . . .27.00 to 30.00
Iris & Herringbone pattern is listed here as Iris.
Jadite, Bowl, Vertical Rim, 9 In. 53.00
Jane-Ray, Bowl, Vegetable, Jade-Ite, 8 1/4 In. 48.00
Knife & Fork pattern is listed here as Colonial.
Laurel, Candlestick, French Ivory, 4 x 4 In., Pair 46.00
Line 300 pattern is listed in the Paden City category as Peacock & Wild Rose.
Lorain pattern is listed here as No. 615.
Louisa pattern is listed here as Floragold.
Lovebirds pattern is listed here as Georgian.

Madrid, Bowl, Vegetable, Amber, Oval, 10 In. 19.00
Madrid, Candlestick, Amber, 2 1/4 In., Pair 30.00
Madrid, Console, Amber, 11 In. 14.00
Madrid, Cup & Saucer, Amber 9.00
Madrid, Jello Mold, Amber, 2 1/8 In. 16.00
Madrid, Plate, Salad, Amber, 7 1/2 In. 8.00
Madrid, Platter, Amber, Oval, 11 1/2 In. 15.00
Madrid, Salt & Pepper, Amber, 3 1/2 In. 41.00
Madrid, Saucer 18.00
Madrid, Soup, Dish, Amber, 7 In. 17.00
Madrid, Sugar & Creamer 13.00
Madrid, Tumbler, Amber, 5 Oz., 3 7/8 In. 12.00
Madrid, Tumbler, Amber, 12 Oz., 5 1/2 In. 18.00
Manhattan, Candy Dish, 3-Footed, Pink, 6 1/2 In. ....15.00 to 18.00
Manhattan, Sugar & Creamer, Pink 40.00
Many Windows pattern is listed here as Roulette.
Martha Washington pattern is included in the Cambridge Glass category.
Mayfair Open Rose, Bowl, Fruit, Deep, Blue, 12 In. 125.00
Mayfair Open Rose, Bowl, Handled, 10 In. 45.00
Mayfair Open Rose, Candy Dish, Cover, Blue, 8 1/2 x 4 7/8 In. 340.00
Mayfair Open Rose, Cookie Jar, No Cover, Pink, 5 1/2 In. 19.00
Mayfair Open Rose, Cup, Pink 18.00
Mayfair Open Rose, Pitcher, Water, Pink, 80 Oz., 8 1/2 In. 130.00
Mayfair Open Rose, Platter, Pink, Oval, Open Handles, 12 1/2 In. 38.00
Mayfair Open Rose, Tumbler, Iced Tea, Footed, Pink, 15 Oz., 6 1/2 In. 55.00
Mayfair Open Rose, Vase, Sweetpea, Blue 135.00
Mayfair Open Rose, Wine, Pink, 3 Oz., 4 1/2 In. 100.00
Milano, Pitcher, Aqua, 9 x 8 1/4 In. 45.00
Milano, Pitcher, Honey Gold, 9 In. 35.00
Milano, Tumbler, Aqua, 5 1/2 In. 20.00
Miss America, Bowl, Cereal, 6 1/4 In. 10.00
Miss America, Bowl, Cereal, Pink, 6 1/4 In. 34.00
Miss America, Bowl, Vegetable, Pink, Oval, 10 In. ....45.00 to 47.00
Miss America, Celery Dish, Pink, Oval, 10 1/2 In. 36.00
Miss America, Coaster, 5 3/4 In. 20.00
Miss America, Creamer, Pink 25.00
Miss America, Cup & Saucer 16.00
Miss America, Cup & Saucer, Pink ....35.00 to 38.00
Miss America, Goblet, Water, Pink, 10 Oz., 5 1/2 In. 48.00
Miss America, Platter, Pink, Oval, 12 1/4 In. ....43.00 to 47.00
Miss America, Relish, 4 Sections, 8 3/4 In. 15.00
Miss America, Relish, 4 Sections, Pink, 8 3/4 In. 30.00
Miss America, Sherbet 20.00
Miss America, Sherbet, Pink 19.00
Miss America, Sugar 8.00
Miss America, Tumbler, Juice, Footed, 5 Oz., 4 In. 27.00
Moderntone, Cheese Dish, Cobalt Blue, Wood Base 395.00
Moderntone, Cup & Saucer, Amethyst 17.00
Moderntone, Cup & Saucer, Cobalt Blue 17.00
Moderntone, Custard Cup, Cobalt Blue 23.00
Moderntone, Plate, Dinner, Amethyst, 8 7/8 In. 14.00
Moderntone, Plate, Sherbet, Amethyst, 5 3/4 In. 6.00
Moderntone, Saltshaker, Cobalt Blue 23.00
Moderntone, Sherbet, Cobalt Blue 13.00
Moderntone, Sugar & Creamer, Cobalt Blue 30.00
Moderntone, Tumbler, Cobalt Blue, 9 Oz. 39.00
Moderntone Little Hostess Party, Creamer, Rust 13.00
Moderntone Little Hostess Party, Cup & Saucer, Gray 20.00
Moderntone Little Hostess Party, Cup & Saucer, White 50.00
Moderntone Little Hostess Party, Cup, Burgundy 14.00
Moderntone Little Hostess Party, Cup, Pink 30.00
Moderntone Little Hostess Party, Cup, Turquoise 15.00
Moderntone Little Hostess Party, Plate, Burgundy, 5 1/4 In. 13.00

Depression Glass,
Mt. Pleasant

Depression Glass,
No. 620

Depression Glass,
Patrician

Moderntone Little Hostess Party, Plate, Gray, 5 1/4 In.	9.00
Moderntone Little Hostess Party, Sugar & Creamer	25.00
Moderntone Platonite, Cup & Saucer, Gold	20.00
Moderntone Platonite, Cup & Saucer, Turquoise	11.00
Moderntone Platonite, Salt & Pepper, Turquoise	23.00
Moderntone Platonite, Sugar, Turquoise	23.00
Moondrops pattern is listed in the New Martinsville category.	
Moonstone, Bowl, 2 Sections, 7 3/4 In. . . . . .20.00 to	22.00
Moonstone, Bowl, Cloverleaf Shape	22.00
Moonstone, Bowl, Crimped, 9 1/2 In.	28.00
Moonstone, Bowl, Crimped, Handles, 6 1/2 In.	22.00
Moonstone, Bowl, Dessert, Crimped, 5 1/2 In.	13.00
Moonstone, Candleholder, 4 1/2 In.	12.00
Moonstone, Candy Dish, Cover, Handles, 6 In.	40.00
Moonstone, Vase, Bud, 5 1/2 In.	15.00
Moonstone, Vase, Ruffled Edge, 5 1/2 In.	60.00
Moroccan Amethyst, Goblet, Water, 9 Oz., 5 1/2 In.	10.00
Moroccan Amethyst, Punch Cup	6.00
Moroccan Amethyst, Punch Set, White Bowl, Amethyst Cups & Base	110.00
Moroccan Amethyst, Sherbet, 7 1/2 Oz., 4 1/4 In.	8.00
Moroccan Amethyst, Tumbler, Juice, 4 Oz., 2 1/2 In.	9.00
Moroccan Amethyst, Wine, 4 1/2 Oz., 4 In.	10.00
Mt. Pleasant, Cup & Saucer, Black	15.00
Mt. Pleasant, Plate, Handles, Scalloped Edge, Black, 7 In.	13.00
Mt. Pleasant, Sandwich Server, Center Handle, Black	16.00
Mt. Pleasant, Vase, Cobalt Blue, 7 1/4 In.	40.00
Mt. Vernon pattern is included in the Cambridge Glass category.	
New Century, Tumbler, Cobalt Blue, 5 Oz., 3 1/2 In.	17.00
New Century, Tumbler, Cobalt Blue, 10 Oz., 5 In.	30.00
Newport, Berry Bowl, Pink, 4 3/4 In.	13.00
No. 601 pattern is listed here as Avocado.	
No. 612, Berry Bowl, Green, 9 1/2 In.	45.00
No. 612, Creamer, Green	22.00
No. 612, Cup & Saucer, Green	15.00
No. 612, Cup, Green	15.00
No. 612, Saucer, Green . . . . .5.00 to	10.00
No. 612, Sherbet, Yellow	18.00
No. 612, Sugar, Green . . . . .16.00 to	22.00
No. 612, Tumbler, Footed, Green, 9 Oz., 5 In.	45.00
No. 612, Tumbler, Green, 9 Oz., 4 1/4 In.	15.00
No. 615, Berry Bowl, Green, 8 In.	50.00
No. 615, Creamer, Yellow	30.00
No. 615, Cup & Saucer, Green	20.00
No. 615, Plate, Luncheon, Green, 8 3/8 In.	15.00
No. 615, Plate, Salad, Green, 7 3/4 In.	8.00
No. 615, Plate, Salad, Yellow, 7 3/4 In. . . . . .15.00 to	28.00
No. 615, Platter, Green, 11 1/2 In.	20.00

No. 615, Relish, 4 Sections, 7 1/2 In. 12.00
No. 615, Relish, 4 Sections, Yellow, 8 In. 70.00
No. 615, Sugar, Green 13.00
No. 615, Tumbler, Footed, 9 Oz., 4 3/4 In. 40.00
No. 615, Tumbler, Green, 9 Oz., 4 3/4 In. 19.00
No. 615, Tumbler, Yellow, 9 Oz., 4 3/4 In. 35.00
No. 618, Bowl, Salad, 7 In. 10.00
No. 618, Bowl, Salad, Milk Glass, 7 In. 11.00
No. 618, Compote, Milk Glass, 7 In. 7.00
No. 618, Cup & Saucer, Amber 13.00
No. 618, Dish, 4 1/8 x 6 1/2 x 3 In. 18.00
No. 618, Plate, Dinner, 9 3/8 In. 25.00
No. 618, Vase, Pink, 9 In. 25.00
No. 620, Berry Bowl, Amber, 4 1/2 In. 11.00
No. 620, Berry Bowl, Amber, 9 3/8 In. 35.00
No. 620, Berry Bowl, Green, Deep, 7 3/8 In. 8.00
No. 620, Bowl, Vegetable, Oval, 10 In. 20.00
No. 620, Cup & Saucer, Amber . . . . 9.00 to 14.00
No. 620, Cup & Saucer, Indiana 12.00
No. 620, Cup, Amber 8.00
No. 620, Plate, Dinner, Amber, 9 3/8 In. 10.00
No. 620, Plate, Salad, 7 3/8 In. 9.00
No. 620, Plate, Salad, Amber, 7 3/8 In. 9.00
No. 620, Plate, Salad, Green, 7 3/8 In. 7.00
No. 620, Plate, Sherbet, Amber, 6 In. 5.00
No. 620, Platter, Amber, Oval, 10 3/4 In. 16.00
No. 620, Relish, 3 Sections, 3-Footed, 8 3/8 In. 25.00
No. 620, Sandwich Server, 11 3/8 In. 15.00
No. 620, Sandwich Server, Amber, 11 3/8 In. 22.00
No. 620, Saucer, Amber, 6 In. . . . . 4.00 to 6.00
No. 620, Sherbet, Amber 8.00
No. 620, Soup, Cream, Amber, 4 1/2 In. 12.00
No. 620, Sugar, Amber, Footed 10.00
No. 620, Tumbler, Amber, 9 Oz. 30.00
No. 622 pattern is listed here as Pretzel.
Normandie, Berry Bowl, 8 1/2 In. 24.00
Normandie, Cup & Saucer 15.00
Normandie, Cup, Pink 12.00
Normandie, Grill Plate, 11 In. 16.00
Normandie, Plate, Salad, Pink, 7 3/4 In. 14.00
Normandie, Sherbet, Underplate, Pink 13.00
Old Cafe, Candy Dish, Royal Ruby, 8 3/4 In. 25.00
Old Cafe, Vase, 7 1/2 In. 15.00
Old Colony, Bowl, Cereal, Pink, 6 3/8 In. 28.00
Old Colony, Bowl, Pink, 9 1/2 In. 30.00
Old Colony, Bowl, Ribbed, Pink, 9 1/2 In. . . . . 35.00 to 45.00
Old Colony, Compote, Pink, 7 In. 33.00
Old Colony, Creamer, Pink 33.00
Old Colony, Goblet, Amber, 6 1/2 In. 7.00
Old Colony, Plate, Salad, Pink, 7 1/4 In. 30.00
Old Colony, Relish, 3 Sections, 10 1/2 In. 29.00
Old Colony, Relish, 3 Sections, Pink, 7 1/2 In. 90.00
Old Florentine pattern is listed here as Florentine No. 1.
Open Rose pattern is listed here as Mayfair Open Rose.
Oyster & Pearl, Candleholder, 3 1/2 In., Pair 25.00
Oyster & Pearl, Relish, Pink, Oblong Sections, 10 1/4 In. 19.00
Parrot pattern is listed here as Sylvan.
Patrician, Berry Bowl, Amber, 5 In. 12.00
Patrician, Bowl, Sugar, Amber 22.00
Patrician, Bowl, Vegetable, Amber, Oval, 10 In. 31.00
Patrician, Cereal, Amber, 6 In. 18.00
Patrician, Creamer, Amber 15.00
Patrician, Cup & Saucer, Amber 19.00

Patrician, Cup, Green 9.00
Patrician, Plate, Dinner, Amber, 10 1/2 In. 8.00
Patrician, Plate, Luncheon, Amber, 9 In. 10.00
Patrician, Plate, Salad, Amber, 7 1/2 In. 18.00
Patrician, Plate, Sherbet, Amber, 6 In. 9.00
Patrician, Platter, Amber, Oval, 11 1/2 In. ....29.00 to 33.00
Patrician, Salt & Pepper, Amber 58.00
Patrician, Sherbet, Amber ....11.00 to 13.00
Patrician, Soup, Cream, Amber, 4 3/4 In. 13.00
Patrician, Sugar & Creamer, Amber 19.00
Patrician, Tumbler, Amber, 14 Oz., 5 1/2 In. 30.00
Patrician, Tumbler, Juice, 5 Oz., 4 In. 38.00
Patrick, Dish, Mayonnaise, Underplate, Ladle, 3-Toed, Pink 165.00
Peach Lustre, Sugar & Creamer 18.00
Peach Lustre, Vase, 7 1/4 In. 10.00
Peacock & Wild Rose pattern is listed in the Paden City category.
Petal Swirl pattern is listed here as Swirl.
Petalware, Cup & Saucer, Pink 10.00
Petalware, Plate, Salad, Cremax, 8 In. 5.00
Petalware, Sugar, Pink 8.00
Pineapple & Floral pattern is listed here as No. 618.
Pinwheel pattern is listed here as Sierra.
Poinsettia pattern is listed here as Floral.
Poppy No. 1 pattern is listed here as Florentine No. 1.
Poppy No. 2 pattern is listed here as Florentine No. 2.
Pretty Polly Party Dishes, see also the related pattern Doric & Pansy.
Pretzel, Bowl, 9 3/8 In. 20.00
Pretzel, Bowl, Amber, Scorpio, 5 1/2 In. 7.00
Pretzel, Bowl, Fruit, 4 1/2 In. 5.00
Pretzel, Celery Dish, 10 1/4 In. 3.00
Pretzel, Celery Dish, Amber, 10 1/4 In. 6.00
Pretzel, Celery Dish, Green, 10 1/4 In. 6.00
Pretzel, Creamer ....5.00 to 7.00
Pretzel, Cup 5.00
Pretzel, Cup & Saucer 8.00
Pretzel, Plate, Dinner, 9 3/8 In. 11.00
Pretzel, Plate, Salad, 8 3/8 In. 7.00
Pretzel, Plate, Snack, Square, Indent, 7 1/4 In. 8.00
Pretzel, Plate, Tab Handle, 6 In. 3.00
Pretzel, Relish, Square, 3 Sections, Handles, 8 1/2 In. 8.00
Pretzel, Sandwich Server, 11 1/2 In. ....11.00 to 13.00
Pretzel, Saucer 1.00
Pretzel, Soup, Dish, 7 1/2 In. ....8.00 to 10.00
Pretzel, Sugar 7.00
Pretzel, Tumbler, 9 Oz., 4 1/2 In. 50.00
Princess, Butter, Cover, Pink, 7 1/2 In. 130.00
Princess, Cup & Saucer, Green 23.00
Princess, Cup & Saucer, Pink 24.00
Princess, Cup, Green 12.00
Princess, Cup, Pink 13.00
Princess, Pitcher, Water, Pink, 60 Oz., 8 In. 78.00
Princess, Sherbet, Green 20.00
Prismatic Line pattern is listed here as Queen Mary.
Provincial pattern is listed here as Bubble.
Queen Mary, Berry Bowl, Pink, 4 1/2 In. 9.00
Queen Mary, Candlestick, 2-Light, 4 1/2 In., Pair 25.00
Queen Mary, Creamer, Pink 10.00
Queen Mary, Cup & Saucer, Pink, Large 12.00
Queen Mary, Sherbet, Pink 11.00
Queen Mary, Soup, Dish, Lug Handles, Pink, 5 In. 18.00
Queen Mary, Sugar & Creamer 15.00
Queen Mary, Tumbler, Juice, Pink, 5 Oz., 3 1/2 In. ....12.00 to 15.00
Queen Mary, Tumbler, Water, Pink, 9 Oz., 4 In. 18.00

Ring, Pitcher, Green, 80 Oz., 8 1/2 In. 125.00
Ring, Plate, Sherbet, 6 1/4 In. 15.00
Ring, Sugar 15.00
Ring, Vase, Green, 8 In. 35.00
Rock Crystal, Candlestick, 5 1/2 In., Pair 45.00
Rock Crystal, Champagne, 6 Oz. 16.00
Rock Crystal, Cocktail, 3 1/2 Oz. 18.00
Rock Crystal, Console, Footed, 12 1/2 In. 60.00
Rock Crystal, Cordial, 1 Oz. 25.00
Rock Crystal, Dish, Ice 45.00
Rock Crystal, Eggcup 65.00
Rock Crystal, Finger Bowl, Dark Red, 5 In. ....65.00 to 70.00
Rock Crystal, Finger Bowl, Underplate 35.00
Rock Crystal, Goblet, Water, 8 Oz. 23.00
Rock Crystal, Goblet, Water, Red, 8 Oz. 65.00
Rock Crystal, Pitcher, 50 Oz., 9 In. 145.00
Rock Crystal, Plate, Plain Edge, Dark Red, 8 1/2 In. 30.00
Rock Crystal, Plate, Scalloped Edge, Scalloped Edge, Dark Red, 11 1/2 In. ... 175.00
Rock Crystal, Sugar, Red 45.00
Rock Crystal, Sundae, 6 Oz. 12.00
Rock Crystal, Sundae, Dark Red, 6 Oz. 35.00
Rock Crystal, Tumbler, Concave, 12 Oz. 35.00
Rock Crystal, Tumbler, Juice, Concave, 5 Oz. 24.00
Rock Crystal, Water Set, 6 Piece 300.00
Rock Crystal, Whiskey, 2 1/2 Oz. 25.00
Rock Crystal, Whiskey, Dark Red, 2 1/2 Oz. 50.00
Rock Crystal, Wine, 3 Oz. 23.00
Rock Crystal, Wine, Amberina, 3 Oz. 50.00
Rope pattern is listed here as Colonial Fluted.
Roulette, Cup, Green 14.00
Roulette, Sandwich Server, Green, 12 In. 65.00
Roulette, Saucer, Green 11.00
Roulette, Sherbet, Green 10.00
Roulette, Tumbler, Juice, Green, 5 Oz. 89.00
Royal Lace, Cookie Jar, Cover, Pink 40.00
Royal Ruby, Bowl, Vegetable, Oval, 8 1/4 In. 25.00
Royal Ruby, Cup & Saucer 10.00
Royal Ruby, Ivy Ball, Vase, 4 In. 12.00
Royal Ruby, Plate, Dinner, 9 In. 11.00
Royal Ruby, Sherbet 11.00
Royal Ruby, Soup, Dish, 7 3/4 In. 16.00
Royal Ruby, Sugar & Creamer ....16.00 to 18.00
Royal Ruby, Tumbler, 9 Oz. 25.00
Royal Ruby, Tumbler, 10 Oz., 5 1/2 In. 15.00
Royal Ruby, Tumbler, 13 Oz. 13.00
Royal Ruby, Tumbler, Footed, 12 Oz., 4 1/2 In. 15.00
Royal Ruby, Vase, 6 3/8 In. 13.00
Royal Ruby, Vase, Crimped, 9 In. 18.00

Depression Glass, Princess

Depression Glass, Sharon

Depression Glass, Windsor

Royal Ruby, Vase, Hand Painted Scene Of Niagara Falls, 6 3/8 In. 18.00
Royal Ruby, Wine, Footed, 2 1/2 Oz. 13.00
Sandwich Anchor Hocking, Bowl, Crimped, 6 1/2 In. 12.00
Sandwich Anchor Hocking, Bowl, Desert Gold, 6 1/2 In. 15.00
Sandwich Anchor Hocking, Bowl, Salad, Desert Gold, 9 In. 35.00
Sandwich Anchor Hocking, Cookie Jar, Cover, Desert Gold 45.00
Sandwich Anchor Hocking, Cup & Saucer 10.00
Sandwich Anchor Hocking, Punch Bowl, 9 3/4 In. 20.00
Sandwich Anchor Hocking, Sugar 10.00
Sandwich Anchor Hocking, Sugar & Creamer . . . . .12.00 to 15.00
Sandwich Anchor Hocking, Tumbler, Juice, 5 Oz., 3 1/4 In. 15.00
Sandwich Anchor Hocking, Tumbler, Juice, Forest Green, 5 Oz., 3 3/4 In. 15.00
Sandwich Indiana, Ashtray, Heart, Pink 10.00
Sandwich Indiana, Bowl, Amber, 10 In. 23.00
Sandwich Indiana, Plate, Luncheon, 8 3/8 In. 8.00
Sandwich Indiana, Sherbet, 3 1/4 In. 9.00
Sandwich Indiana, Sherbet, Teal, 3 1/4 In. 6.00
Saxon pattern is listed here as Coronation.
Sharon, Berry Bowl, 5 In. 17.00
Sharon, Berry Bowl, Amber, 8 1/2 In. . . . . .6.00 to 8.00
Sharon, Berry Bowl, Green, 5 In. 18.00
Sharon, Berry Bowl, Green, 8 1/2 In. 42.00
Sharon, Berry Bowl, Pink, 5 In. 12.00
Sharon, Berry Bowl, Pink, 8 1/2 In. . . . . .33.00 to 40.00
Sharon, Bowl, Cereal, Pink, 6 In. 31.00
Sharon, Bowl, Fruit, Pink, 10 In. 48.00
Sharon, Candy Jar, Cover, Amber 40.00
Sharon, Candy Jar, Cover, Pink 45.00
Sharon, Creamer, Amber 14.00
Sharon, Cup & Saucer, Amber . . . . .13.00 to 15.00
Sharon, Cup & Saucer, Pink . . . . .20.00 to 26.00
Sharon, Cup, Amber 12.00
Sharon, Plate, Bread & Butter, 6 In. 10.00
Sharon, Plate, Bread & Butter, Pink, 6 In. 9.00
Sharon, Plate, Dinner, 9 1/2 In. 23.00
Sharon, Plate, Dinner, Pink, 9 1/2 In. . . . . .23.00 to 25.00
Sharon, Platter, Pink, Oval, 12 1/2 In. . . . . .30.00 to 35.00
Sharon, Sherbet, Amber 11.00
Sharon, Sugar, Amber 9.00
Sharon, Sugar, Cover, Pink 50.00
Sharon, Sugar, Pink 14.00
Shell Pink, Bowl, Wedding, Cover, 8 In. 23.00
Shell Pink, Sugar & Creamer, Cover, Baltimore Pear 40.00
Sierra, Berry Bowl, Green, 8 1/2 In. 55.00
Sierra, Bowl, Cereal, Pink, 5 1/2 In. 15.00
Sierra, Butter, Cover, Pink 63.00
Sierra, Plate, Dinner, Pink, 9 In. 23.00
Sierra, Platter, Pink, Oval, 11 In. 55.00
Sierra, Tray, 2 Handles, Pink, 10 1/2 In. 22.00
Soreno, Bowl, Salad, Avocado, 8 1/2 In. 15.00
Soreno, Pitcher, Avocado, 64 Oz., 9 1/2 In. 13.00
Spiral Flutes pattern is listed in the Duncan & Miller category as Swirl.
Spoke pattern is listed here as Patrician.
Starburst Aztec, Candy Dish, Cover, Indiana Carnival, 6 x 5 7/8 In. 15.00
Starlight, Creamer 10.00
Strawberry, Sherbet, Green 14.00
Sunburst, Snack Set, 4 Trays, 4 Cups 20.00
Sunflower, Cake Plate, Green, 3-Footed, 10 In. . . . . .15.00 to 17.00
Sunflower, Cup, Pink 14.00
Swirl, Berry Bowl, Ultramarine, 5 1/2 In. 18.00
Swirl, Bowl, Salad, Ultramarine, 9 In. 32.00
Swirl, Butter, Cover, Ultramarine 375.00
Swirl, Candy Dish, Pink, 3-Footed 16.00

Swirl, Console, Footed, Ultramarine, 10 In. 35.00
Swirl, Cup & Saucer, Ultramarine 16.00
Swirl, Plate, Dinner, Ultramarine, 9 1/4 In. 24.00
Swirl, Plate, Sherbet, Ultramarine, 6 1/2 In. . . . . .7.00 to 8.00
Swirl, Sandwich Server, Ultramarine, 12 1/2 In. 30.00
Swirl, Sherbet, Ultramarine 20.00
Swirl, Sugar & Creamer, Ultramarine 25.00
Swirl, Vase, Footed, Ultramarine, 8 1/2 In. 25.00
Sylvan, Bowl, Vegetable, Green, Oval, 10 In. 70.00
Sylvan, Cup & Saucer, Green 46.00
Sylvan, Plate, Salad, Green, 7 1/2 In. 40.00
Tea Room, Ice Bucket, Pink, 6 1/2 x 5 1/2 In. 95.00
Tea Room, Pitcher, Green, 64 Oz., 10 In. 335.00
Tea Room, Sherbet, Green 40.00
Tea Room, Tumbler, Green, 4 1/4 In. 125.00
Tea Room, Vase, Ruffled Edge, Green, 11 In. 175.00
Tulip, Creamer, Green 20.00
Tulip, Ice Tub, Turquoise 95.00
Tulip, Tumbler, Juice, Turquoise, 2 3/4 In. 40.00
Vertical Ribbed pattern is listed here as Queen Mary.
Victory, Cup & Saucer, Cobalt Blue 48.00
Waffle pattern is listed here as Waterford.
Waterford, Butter, No Cover, Pink 95.00
Waterford, Goblet, Water, 5 1/4 In. 17.00
Waterford, Plate, Dinner, 9 1/2 In. 13.00
Waterford, Relish, 5 Sections, 13 3/4 In. 25.00
Waterford, Sandwich Server, 13 3/4 In. 12.00
Waterford, Sugar, Cover, 6 1/4 In. 18.00
Waterford, Sugar, Handles 12.00
Waterford, Tumbler, Footed, 10 Oz., 4 7/8 In. 13.00
Wexford, Bowl, Salad, 6 In. 7.50
Wexford, Bowl, Salad, 9 3/4 In. 10.00
Wexford, Butter, Cover, 1/4 Lb. 11.00
Wexford, Decanter, Stopper, 32 Oz., 15 In. 16.00
Wexford, Sugar & Creamer, Cover 20.00
Wexford, Vase, 10 1/2 In. 15.00
Whirly Twirly, Tumbler, Cobalt Blue, 4 3/4 In. 30.00
Whirly Twirly, Tumbler, Juice, Cobalt Blue, 3 In. 25.00
Wild Rose pattern is listed here as Dogwood.
Windsor, Ashtray, Pink, 5 3/4 In. 45.00
Windsor, Berry Bowl, Pink, 4 3/4 In. 13.00
Windsor, Berry Bowl, Pink, 8 1/2 In. . . . . .22.00 to 28.00
Windsor, Butter, Cover, Pink . . . . .40.00 to 60.00
Windsor, Candy Dish, Cover, Blue, 7 1/2 x 3 In. 12.00
Windsor, Chop Plate, 13 5/8 In. 45.00
Windsor, Compote, Pink, 5 1/2 In. 35.00
Windsor, Plate, Dinner, Pink, 9 In. . . . . .23.00 to 28.00
Windsor, Plate, Sherbet, Pink, 6 In. 6.00
Windsor, Sugar, Cover, Pink 30.00
Windsor, Sugar, Green 33.00
Windsor, Tumbler, Red, 9 Oz., 4 In. 55.00
Windsor, Tumbler, Water, Pink, 9 Oz., 4 In. 20.00
Windsor Diamond pattern is listed here as Windsor.

DERBY has been marked on porcelain made in the city of Derby, England, since about 1748. The original Derby factory closed in 1848, but others opened there and continued to produce quality porcelain. The Crown Derby mark began appearing on Derby wares in the 1770s.

Bust, Matthew, Inscribed Prior, Marble Socle Base, c.1775, 9 1/4 In. 1675.00
Compote, Cobalt Blue, Red, Gold Highlights, 4 Scroll Feet, 10 1/8 In. 345.00
Dish, Sweetmeat, Blue & White, 2 Sections, Scallop Shells, Flowers, Footed, 1765, 14 In. 5378.00
Figure, Allegorical, Feeling, Woman Seated With Parrot, c.1760, 6 1/2 In. 2150.00
Figure, Allegorical, Taste, Woman Seated, Tasting Fruit From Basket, c.1760, 6 1/2 In. 2150.00

Figure Set, Minerva, Jupiter, Standing, Plumed Helmet, Mound Base, c.1765, 6 3/4 In. 1314.00
Mug, Floral, White Ground, Greek Key Border On Orange, Gilt Leaves, c.1795, 3 In. 450.00
Plate, Cobalt Ground, Floral & Fowl Cartouches, c.1830 . . . . 290.00
Tureen, Cover, Partridge, Seated In Nest, Grasses, Feather Edge, c.1765, 6 1/2 In. 1910.00
Urn, Puce, Floral Basket Cartouches, Heavy Gilt, Lamp, Electrified, c.1850, 19 In., Pair . . 748.00

DICK TRACY, the comic strip, started in 1931. Tracy was also the hero
of movies from 1937 to 1947 and again in 1990, and starred in a radio
series in the 1940s and a television series in the 1950s. Memorabilia
from all these activities are collected.

Belt Buckle, Gold Luster Image Dick Tracy, Pyramid Belt Co., 1973, 2 1/2 x 2 3/4 In. . . . 15.00
Book, Pop-Up, Capture Of Boris Arson, Chester Gould, Blue Ribbon, c.1935 . . . . 650.00
Button, Member, Secret Service Patrol, Black, Gold, Lithograph, 1 1/4 In. 17.00
Game, Bagatelle, 8 Color Illustrations Of Characters, Marx, 1967, Box, 24 x 14 In. 225.00
Game, Dick Tracy Detective, Board, Spinner, Famous Artists Syndicate, Box, 1933 . . . . . 70.00
Lunch Box Thermos, Aladdin 30.00
Toy, B.O. Plenty, Walker, Tin Lithograph, Battery Operated, Box, c.1939, 8 1/4 In. 435.00
Toy, Car, Plastic, Green, Siren, Marx, 1950s, 10 In. 425.00
Wrapper, Dick Tracy Caramels, Waxed Paper, Johnson Candy Co., 1941, 4 Piece . . . *Illus* 810.00
Wristwatch, Dick Tracy On Face, New Haven, Chester Gould, Box, 1948 . . . . 798.00
Wristwatch, Dick Tracy, Gun Second Hand 450.00

DICKENS WARE pieces are listed in the Royal Doulton and Weller categories.

DINNERWARE used in the United States from the 1930s through the
1950s is listed here. Most was made in potteries in southern Ohio,
West Virginia, and California. A few patterns were made in Japan,
England, and other countries. Dishes were sold in gift shops and
department stores, or were given away as premiums. Many of these
patterns are listed in this book in their own categories, such as Autumn
Leaf, Azalea, Coors, Fiesta, Franciscan, Hall, Harker, Harlequin, Red
Wing, Riviera, Russel Wright, Vernon Kilns, Watt, and Willow. For
more information, see *Kovels' Depression Glass & Dinnerware Price
List.*

America, Trivet, Bride, Pfaltzgraff, 7 3/4 In. 35.00
American Modern, Bowl, Vegetable, Divided, Chartreuse, Steubenville 85.00
American Modern, Casserole, Cover, Cedar Green, Steubenville 55.00
American Modern, Cup, Black Chutney, Steubenville 10.00
American Modern, Pitcher, Coral 100.00
American Modern, Plate, Black Chutney, Steubenville, 6 In. 8.00
American Modern, Plate, Black Chutney, Steubenville, 10 In. 12.00
American Modern, Plate, Coral, Steubenville, 6 In. 5.00
American Modern, Plate, Coral, Steubenville, 10 In. 10.00
American Modern, Saucer, Coral, Steubenville 3.00
American Modern, Saucer, Gray, Steubenville 3.00

Dick Tracy, Wrapper, Dick Tracy Caramels, Waxed
Paper, Johnson Candy Co., 1941, 4 Piece

> **To remove wrinkles from old
> paper, set a regular iron for
> cotton. Iron out the wrinkles
> from the wrong side of the
> paper. Be sure to iron quickly so
> you do not scorch the paper.**

American Modern, Soup, Dish, Chartreuse, Steubenville	15.00
Americana, Bowl, Homer Laughlin, 5 3/4 In.	8.00
Antique Leaf, Pie Server, Blue Ridge	25.00
Apple Blossom, Cup & Saucer, After Dinner, Homer Laughlin	24.00
Autumn Apple, Creamer, Colonial, Blue Ridge	20.00
Ballerina, Plate, Blue, Universal, 10 In.	18.00
Ballerina, Plate, Chartreuse, Universal, 10 In.	18.00
Ballerina, Plate, Dove Gray, Universal, 10 In.	18.00
Ballerina, Plate, Pink, Universal, 10 In.	18.00
Becky, Bowl, Fruit, Blue Ridge, 5 1/4 In.	8.00
Becky, Cup & Saucer, Blue Ridge	10.00
Becky, Plate, Blue Ridge, 6 In.	4.00
Becky, Plate, Blue Ridge, 10 In.	12.00
Blossom, Sugar, Cover, Gray, Weil Ware	20.00
Bluebird, Casserole, Cover, Oval, Open Handles, Saxon China, 11 1/2 In.	125.00
Boots & Saddle, Plate, Wallace China, 7 In.	70.00
Butterfly, Box, Cigarette, Cover, Square, Blue Ridge, 4 1/4 In.	100.00
Cassandra, Pie Baker, Maroon Border, Blue Ridge	30.00
Celandine, Saucer, After Dinner, Blue Ridge	15.00
Ceramex, Mixing Bowl, Pink, Pfaltzgraff, 8 In.	45.00
Cherry Bounce, Plate, Square, Blue Ridge, 7 In.	25.00
Cherry Tree Glen, Bowl, Blue Ridge, 5 In.	10.00
Cherry Tree Glen, Plate, Blue Ridge, 9 In.	20.00
Chickory, Plate, Blue Ridge, 10 In.	12.00
Chintz, Saucer, Colonial, Blue Ridge	15.00
Cobblestone, Teapot, 8 Cup, Porcelier	40.00
Colonial, Teapot, 4 Cup, Porcelier	40.00
Coralitos, Salt & Pepper, Verdugo Green, Pacific Pottery, 2 3/4 In., Pair	45.00
Corn, Dish, Vallona Starr, 8 1/2 x 4 1/8 In.	30.00
Corn, Platter, Vallona Starr, 13 x 8 3/4 In.	60.00
County Fair, Plate, Peach, Strawberry, Blue Ridge, 8 In.	25.00
County Fair, Plate, Plums, Blue Ridge, 8 In.	25.00
Currier & Ives, Ashtray, Royal China, 5 1/2 In.	15.00
Currier & Ives, Bowl, Blue, Homer Laughlin, 7 In.	10.00
Currier & Ives, Bowl, Cereal, Blue, Royal China, 6 1/2 In.	16.00
Currier & Ives, Butter, Fashionable Turn-Outs In Central Park, Royal China	46.00
Currier & Ives, Cup & Saucer, Royal China	5.00
Currier & Ives, Gravy Boat, Royal China	18.00
Currier & Ives, Mug, Square Handle, Royal China, 2 3/4 In.	35.00
Currier & Ives, Pie Plate, Early Winter, Royal China, 10 In.	24.00
Currier & Ives, Pie Plate, Snowy Morning, Royal China, 10 In.	28.00
Currier & Ives, Plate, Blue, Royal China, 6 1/2 In.	4.00
Currier & Ives, Plate, Blue, Royal China, 10 In.	6.00
Currier & Ives, Plate, Country Life, Blue, Royal China, 10 In.	10.00
Currier & Ives, Plate, Royal China, 10 1/4 In.	12.00
Currier & Ives, Soup, Dish, Blue, Royal China, 8 1/2 In.	14.00
Edgemont, Platter, Blue Ridge, 13 In.	30.00
Empire, Platter, Turkey, Gold Border, Turkeys, Taylor, Smith & Taylor, 15 3/4 In.	175.00
Epicure, Casserole, Cover, Pink, Homer Laughlin, 9 1/2 In.	125.00
French Peasant, Plate, Woman, Blue Ridge, 10 In.	125.00
Geranium, Plate, Winfield, 5 3/4 In.	8.00
Golden Pheasant, Casserole, Cover, Metal Holder, Royal Rochester, 9 In.	150.00
Grandmother's Garden, Sugar, Cover, Blue Ridge	30.00
Grape Harvest, Plate, Round, Blue Ridge, 12 In.	40.00
Green Eyes, Plate, Blue Ridge, 6 In.	5.00
Green Plaid, Cup & Saucer, Blue Ridge	15.00
Grenada, Bowl, Tangerine, French Saxon, 5 1/2 In.	3.00
Grenada, Creamer, Blue, French Saxon	4.00
Grenada, Cup, Blue, French Saxon	4.00
Grenada, Plate, Dark Green, French Saxon, 9 In.	10.00
Grenada, Plate, Tangerine, French Saxon, 9 In.	7.00
Grenada, Plate, Yellow, French Saxon, 6 In.	1.00
Grenada, Soup, Dish, Blue, French Saxon	10.00

Grenada, Sugar, Yellow, French Saxon	5.00
Hearth, Teapot, 6 Cup, Porcelier	35.00
Honolulu, 3 Apples, Plate, Blue Ridge, 8 In.	25.00
Honolulu, Cherries, Plate, Blue Ridge, 8 In.	25.00
Jubilee Pomegranate, Plate, Blue Ridge, 8 In.	25.00
Kraft, Eggcup, Blue, Homer Laughlin	18.00
Liberty Blue, Berry Bowl, 5 In.	5.00
Liberty Blue, Cup & Saucer	7.00
Liberty Blue, Plate, 5 1/2 In.	4.00
Liberty Blue, Plate, 7 In.	10.00
Liberty Blue, Plate, 9 3/4 In.	6.00
Liberty Blue, Platter, 14 In.	95.00
Lighthearted, Platter, Blue Ridge, 13 In.	25.00
Lu-Ray, Bowl, Fruit, Blue, Taylor, Smith & Taylor, 5 In.	6.00
Lu-Ray, Bowl, Fruit, Sharon Pink, Taylor, Smith & Taylor, 5 In.	5.00 to 6.00
Lu-Ray, Bowl, Fruit, Surf Green, Taylor, Smith & Taylor, 5 In.	6.00
Lu-Ray, Bowl, Fruit, Windsor Blue, Taylor, Smith & Taylor, 5 In.	6.00
Lu-Ray, Bowl, Salad, Persian Cream, Taylor, Smith & Taylor, 9 1/2 In.	55.00
Lu-Ray, Bowl, Salad, Surf Green, Taylor, Smith & Taylor, 9 1/2 In.	75.00
Lu-Ray, Bowl, Tab Handle, Windsor Blue, Taylor, Smith & Taylor	20.00
Lu-Ray, Cup & Saucer, Surf Green, Taylor, Smith & Taylor	12.00
Lu-Ray, Plate, Sharon Pink, Taylor, Smith & Taylor, 6 In.	3.00
Lu-Ray, Plate, Surf Green, Taylor, Smith & Taylor, 6 In.	3.00
Lu-Ray, Plate, Windsor Blue, Taylor, Smith & Taylor, 6 In.	3.00
Lu-Ray, Plate, Windsor Blue, Taylor, Smith & Taylor, 9 In.	10.00
Lu-Ray, Platter, Persian Cream, Taylor, Smith & Taylor, 11 1/2 In.	13.00 to 18.00
Lu-Ray, Salt & Pepper, Sharon Pink, Taylor, Smith & Taylor	18.00
Lu-Ray, Salt & Pepper, Windsor Blue, Taylor, Smith & Taylor	18.00
Lu-Ray, Saucer, Sharon Pink, Taylor, Smith & Taylor	3.00
Lu-Ray, Soup, Dish, Surf Green, Taylor, Smith & Taylor, 7 1/4 In.	13.00
Lu-Ray, Soup, Dish, Windsor Blue, Taylor, Smith & Taylor, 7 1/4 In.	13.00 to 18.00
Majestic, Gravy Boat, Aqua, Homer Laughlin	25.00
Muggsy, Mug, Cockeyed Charlie, Pfaltzgraff	35.00
Muggsy, Mug, Pickled Pete, Pfaltzgraff	35.00
Nocturne, Bowl, Blue Ridge, 5 In.	10.00
Nocturne, Platter, Blue Ridge, 11 In.	25.00
Old McDonald's Farm, Creamer, Rooster, Regal China	150.00
Old McDonald's Farm, Sugar, Cover, Hen, Regal China	175.00
Ovenserve, Baker, Oval, Yellow, Oval, Homer Laughlin, 6 In.	10.00
Ovenserve, Plate, Yellow, Embossed, Homer Laughlin, 9 1/2 In.	16.00
Pears, Coffeepot, French Drip, 6 Cup, Porcelier	35.00
Pebbleford, Bowl, Granite, Taylor, Smith & Taylor, 5 In.	6.00
Pebbleford, Cup, Granite, Taylor, Smith & Taylor	8.00
Pebbleford, Cup, Turquoise, Taylor, Smith & Taylor	8.00
Pebbleford, Plate, Granite, Taylor, Smith & Taylor, 6 In.	4.00
Pebbleford, Plate, Granite, Taylor, Smith & Taylor, 10 In.	15.00
Pebbleford, Plate, Turquoise, Taylor, Smith & Taylor, 10 In.	15.00
Peek-A-Boo, Saltshaker, Red Dots, Regal China, 3 3/4 In.	150.00
Peek-A-Boo, Saltshaker, Red Dots, Regal China, 5 1/2 In., Pair	500.00
Petal Point, Bowl, Blue Ridge, 5 1/2 In.	5.00
Poinsettia, Bowl, Tab Handle, Blue Ridge, 7 In.	30.00
Poinsettia, Plate, Blue Ridge, 6 In.	5.00 to 14.00
Poinsettia, Platter, Blue Ridge, 13 In.	75.00
Poppy, Coffee Set, Electric, Sugar, Cover, Creamer, Royal Rochester, 3 Piece	150.00
Poppy, Pie Plate, Royal Rochester, 10 In.	45.00
Red Flower, Bowl, Aluminum Basket, Blue Ridge, 6 In.	35.00
Republic, Creamer, Homer Laughlin, 3 1/2 In.	12.00
Riviera, Plate, Deep, Homer Laughlin, 8 In.	24.00
Romance, Pitcher, Antique, Blue Ridge, 5 In.	125.00
Rose Chintz, Bowl, Johnson Brothers, 5 In.	8.00
Rose Chintz, Bowl, Oval, Johnson Brothers, 9 In.	30.00
Rosemary, Bowl, Salad, Iroquois, 7 In.	15.00
Rosemary, Creamer, Iroquois	25.00

Rosemary, Cup & Saucer, Iroquois 15.00
Rosemary, Plate, Iroquois, 8 In. 10.00
Rosemary, Platter, Iroquois, 11 In. 25.00
Rosemary, Platter, Iroquois, 13 In. 35.00
Sailboat, Teapot, 4 Cup, Porcelier 40.00
Spiderweb, Coffeepot, Ovide, Blue, Gray, Blue Ridge 125.00
Sungold No. 2, Plate, Blue Ridge, 6 In. 5.00
Sweet Clover, Plate, Blue Ridge, 10 In. 15.00
Thorny Mayflower, Bowl, Blue Ridge, 5 In. 5.00
Tom & Jerry, Mug, Ivory, Gold Trim, Homer Laughlin 10.00
Tulip, Bowl, Leigh Potters, 7 5/8 In. 20.00
Tulip, Casserole, Lug, Cover, Blue, Cronin, 7 In. 20.00
Tulip, Casserole, Lug, Cover, Individual, Blue, Cronin, 4 In. 15.00
Tulip, Tureen, Slotted Cover, Taylor, Smith & Taylor, 12 x 8 In. 250.00
Victory Blossom, Casserole, Cover, Royal China 45.00
Waterlily, Soup, Dish, Blue Ridge, 7 1/2 In. 20.00
Wells Art Glaze, Platter, Rust, Oval, Homer Laughlin, 11 1/2 In. 35.00
Wild Rose, Plate, Blue Ridge, 10 In. 30.00
Wrinkled Rose, Plate, Blue Ridge, 9 In. 20.00
Yellowstone, Creamer, Homer Laughlin 15.00

DIONNE QUINTUPLETS were born in Canada on May 28, 1934. The
publicity about their birth and their special status as wards of the
Canadian government made them famous throughout the world.
Visitors could watch the girls play; reporters interviewed the girls and
the staff. Thousands of special dolls and souvenirs were made picturing the quints at different ages. Emilie died in 1954, Marie in 1970,
and Yvonne in 2001. Annette and Cecile still live in Canada.

Banner, Quaker Oats, Today They Had Quaker Oats, 31 x 14 In. 200.00
Doll, Annette, Brown Eyes, Closed Mouth, Madame Alexander, 11 In. 250.00
Doll, Annette, Composition, Brown Sleep Eyes, Madame Alexander, 14 In. 200.00
Doll, Doctor Dafoe, Composition, Madame Alexander, 1935, 14 In. 2000.00
Doll, Madame Alexander, Composition, Painted Curly Hair, 7 In., 5 Piece 1600.00
Doll, Madame Alexander, Composition, Pink Basket, Set Of 5, 7 In. 805.00
Doll, Madame Alexander, Swivel Head, Tagged, 1935, 8 In., 5 Piece 1500.00
Doll, Marie, Brown Eyes, Open Mouth, 4 Teeth, Madame Alexander, 11 In. 425.00
Doll, Yvonne, Composition, Brown Sleep Eyes, Madame Alexander, 14 In. 275.00
Spoon Set, Box, Carlton Silver Plate, Colgate, Palmolive, Peet Co. 61.00

DIRK VAN ERP was born in 1860 and died in 1933. He opened his own
studio in 1908 in Oakland, California. He moved his studio to San
Francisco in 1909 and the studio remained under the direction of his
son until 1977. Van Erp made hammered copper accessories, including
vases, desk sets, bookends, candlesticks, jardinieres, and trays, but he
is best known for his lamps. The hammered copper lamps often had
shades with mica panels.

Basket, Copper, Hammered, Handle, Canoe Shape, 7 x 12 In. 1495.00
Bookends, Sailing Ship, Square, Windmill Mark, 1915, 4 In. 1285.00
Bowl, Hammered Copper, Patina, Marked, 12 In. 400.00
Console, Copper, Hammered, Red Brown Patina, Oblong, After 1940, 19 x 9 In. 1175.00
Desk Set, Hammered, Patina, 2 3/4 x 10 x 6 1/4 In., 5 Piece 1495.00
Humidor, Copper, Hammered, Riveted Handle, Original Patina, 5 1/2 In. 1955.00
Lamp, Copper, Hammered, 3-Light, Bulbous Base, 3 Mica Panels, 21 x 16 In. 6325.00
Lamp, Copper, Hammered, Mica Shade, Original Patina, 15 In.   2990.00
Lamp, Copper, Hammered, Mica, Tapered Shouldered Base, 11 1/2 In. 8050.00
Match Holder, Hammered Copper, Cutout, Dutch Girl, Cat, 6 1/2 In. 430.00
Pitcher, Bulbous, Copper, Hammered, Hinged Lid, 11 3/4 x 9 1/2 In. 4406.00
Planter, Tray, Signed, 5 x 5 1/4 & 6 1/2 x 8 3/4 In., Pair 3740.00
Vase, Copper, Hammered, Bulbous, 7 1/2 x 6 1/2 In. 3450.00
Vase, Copper, Hammered, Classical Shape, Medium Patina, 9 1/2 x 4 In. 2300.00
Vase, Copper, Hammered, Rolled Rim, Medium Patina, 7 1/2 x 6 In. 3450.00
Vase, Hammered, Rolled Rim, Medium Brown Patina, 9 1/2 x 4 In. 2300.00
Vase, Warty Hammered Copper, Bulbous, Brass Collar, 2 Ring Handles, 9 x 8 In. 3525.00

DISNEYANA is a collector's term. Walt Disney and his company introduced many comic characters to the world. Collectors search for examples of the work of the Disney Studios and the many commercial products modeled after his characters, including Mickey Mouse and Donald Duck, and recent films, like *Beauty and the Beast* and *The Little Mermaid*.

Bank, Bookends, Mickey Mouse, Sitting, Cast Iron, 5 In., Pair	88.00
Bank, Donald Duck, Composition, W.D. Enterprises, 1938, 6 In.	248.00
Bank, Donald Duck, Nodder, Donald On Boat, SS Donald Duck, 1938, 6 1/2 In.	1295.00
Bank, Donald Duck, Wooden, 13 In.	143.00
Bank, Mickey Mouse, Hands On Hips, Ceramic, Hand Painted, 6 In.	299.00
Bank, Mickey Mouse, Posing, Cast Aluminum, Depeche Co., France, 8 In.	265.00
Bank, Mickey Mouse, Wooden, 13 In.	110.00
Bank, Pluto, Ceramic, Leeds Pottery, 6 1/2 In.	17.00
Banner, Donald Duck, Sunoco, Canvas	1350.00
Basketball, Goofy, Gardner, Box, 9 In.	95.00
Blotter, Donald Duck, Adding Machine, Sunoco, 1942	26.00
Blotter, Donald Duck, In Jeep, Sunoco, 1943	24.00
Blotter, Goofy, Polar Bear, Sunoco, 1939	26.00
Blotter, Mickey Mouse, With Cannon, Sunoco, 1942	29.00
Book, Activity, Mickey Mouse, Things To Make & Do, Collins, 1937, 63 Pages	350.00
Book, Life Of Donald Duck, Dust Wrapper, Random, 1941, 72 Pages	475.00
Book, Mickey & Minnie March To Macy's, 1935	275.00
Book, Mickey Mouse & His Friends, Dust Wrapper, Whitman, 1936	450.00
Book, Mickey Mouse & His Horse Tanglefoot, Dust Jacket, 1936	2580.00
Book, Mickey Mouse Box Set, Color Covers, 1939, 51/2 x 5 In., 64 Pages	685.00
Book, Mickey Mouse Has A Party, A School Reader, Whitman, 1938, 48 Pages	400.00
Box, Pinocchio Chewing Gum, Dietz Gum Co., Cardboard, 1940	325.00
Box, Pinocchio, Tin Lithograph, 12 x 19 In.	11.00
Calendar, Silly Symphony, 1938, 9 x 16 1/2 In.	500.00
Candy Container, Snow White & Seven Dwarfs, Papier-Mache, Box, 10 In.	310.00
Carousel, Bell, Tin, Celluloid, Windup, Linemar, Walt Disney Production, 7 In.	1430.00
Cel, see Animation Art category.	
Chair, Donald Duck, Wood, Painted, 18 In.	38.00
Chair, Mickey Mouse, Wooden, Side-Arm Desk, Die Cut Mickey Back, 1940s	145.00
Clock, Alarm, Mickey Mouse, Art Deco Style, Molded Case, 1987, 9 In.	25.00
Clock, Alarm, Mickey Mouse, Red, Yellow Bells, Bradley, 1950s, 6 In.	110.00 to 125.00
Clock, Alarm, Mickey Mouse, Talking, Plastic, 9 In.	45.00
Clock, Wall, Mickey Mouse, Figural, Pendulum, Continental, 1930s	450.00
Coloring Book, Walt Disney Enterprise, Saalfield, 1937, 14 x 10 In., 24 Pages	95.00
Creamer, Mickey Mouse, G. Borgfeldt, 1930, 4 1/2 In.	660.00
Cup, Mickey Mouse, Pie-Eyed	150.00
Display, Donald Duck Bread, Die Cut, 1940s, 29 1/2 x 38 1/4 In.	1090.00
Display, Mickey Mouse, Pressed Paper, Old King Cole Inc., 1930s, 43 In.	2350.00
Doll, Donald Duck, Robin Hood, 1950s, 22 In.	625.00
Doll, Dopey, Composition Head, Hinged Mouth, Felt Shoes, Ideal, 1937, 20 In.	750.00
Doll, Dopey, Size 2, Musical, Knickerbocker Toy Co., Box *Illus*	300.00
Doll, Happy Dwarf, Lantern, Original Tag, Ideal, WD Enterprises, 1937	295.00
Doll, Mickey Mouse, Flannel, 1930s, 15 In.	425.00

Disneyana, Doll, Dopey, Size 2, Musical, Knickerbocker Toy Co., Box

Disneyana, Rug, Snow White & Seven Dwarfs, Crossing Log Bridge, Italy, 22 x 40 In.

Doll, Mickey Mouse, Plastic & Cloth, Schuco, Walt Disney Prod., Box, 4 In. 110.00
Doll, Mickey Mouse, Stuffed, Dean's Rag Book Co., 1930s, 9 In. 450.00
Doll, Minnie Mouse, Cloth, Dress, High Heels, 12 In. 290.00
Doll, Pinocchio, Painted Composition Head, Smiling Mouth, Ideal, 1940, 10 In. 350.00
Doll, Pinocchio, Wood, Composition, Ideal, 8 1/2 In. 120.00
Doll, Pinocchio, Wooden Limbs, Composition Head, Cloth Clothes, Crown, 9 In. 235.00
Figurine, 3 Little Pigs, Bisque Set, Walt Disney, Borgfeldt Japan, Box, c.1930, 4 In. 495.00
Figurine, Bashful Dwarf, Composition, Box, 1940s, 8 In. 250.00
Figurine, Disney Characters, Bisque, 1930s, 9 Piece 465.00
Figurine, Disneykin Set, Plastic, Marx, Hong Kong, Box, c.1960, 34 Piece 330.00
Figurine, Donald Duck, Acrobat, Celluloid, Windup, Gym-Toys, Linemar, Box 475.00
Figurine, Donald Duck, Ceramic, Leeds Pottery, 7 In. 28.00
Figurine, Donald Duck, Jointed, Celluloid, 1940s, 3 In. 125.00
Figurine, Donald Duck, Playing Violin, Bisque, 1930s, 4 1/2 In. 475.00
Figurine, Jiminy Cricket Membership, WDCC, Classics Collection, 1993, 4 In. 200.00
Figurine, Mickey Mouse & Minnie Mouse, Pie-Eyed, 2 7/8 In. 45.00
Figurine, Mickey Mouse, Bisque, Hand Painted, Walt E. Disney, Japan, c.1930, 3 3/4 In. . 85.00
Figurine, Mickey Mouse, Black & White, Porcelain, 3 1/4 In. 225.00
Figurine, Mickey Mouse, Jazz Drummer, 1930s 950.00
Figurine, Mickey Mouse, Jointed, Celluloid, 1940s, 6 In. 160.00
Figurine, Mickey Mouse, Lollipop Hands, Wood, 1930s, 9 In. 650.00
Figurine, Mickey Mouse, Playing Mandolin, Bisque, 1930s, 3 1/2 In. 350.00
Figurine, Mickey Mouse, Rubber, Seiberling, 3 1/2 In. 28.00
Figurine, Mickey Mouse, Wood, Metal Arms & Legs, Fun-E-Flex, 6 1/2 In. ....126.00 to 220.00
Figurine, Minnie Mouse, Thumper's Girlfriend, Metlox, 4 In. 85.00
Figurine, Minnie Mouse, Wood, 1930s, 5 In. 195.00
Figurine, Pinocchio, Bisque, 9 In. 300.00
Figurine, Snow White & Seven Dwarfs, Ceramic, Walt Disney Productions, 16, 8 In. 209.00
Fork & Spoon, Mickey & Minnie Mouse, Child's, Silver Plated, Winthrop, England 95.00
Game, Mary Poppins, Puzzle, Let's Go Fly A Kite, Jaymar 12.00
Game, Mickey Mouse, Card, Tellings Ice Cream, Lakewood, Ohio, Box, 1934 .... 220.00
Game, Red Riding Hood, Walt Disney Enterprises, 1938, 13 x 16 In. 22.00
Lunch Box, Snow White, Aladdin 80.00
Marionette, Minnie Mouse, Pelham Puppet, Handmade, Box, England 95.00
Music Box, Sleeping Beauty, Ceramic, Disney Figures, 18 x 9 x 9 1/2 In. 17.00
Night-Light, Mickey Mouse, Glass, Tin, Box, England, 8 In. 15.00
Nodder, Donald Duck, Celluloid, Windup, 1930s 1250.00
Noisemaker, Mickey Mouse, Minnie Mouse, Cardboard, 7 In. 125.00
Pail, Disney Character Heads 245.00
Pencil Box, Mickey Mouse, Red, Cardboard, Dixon, 1937, 8 1/2 In. 55.00
Pencil Sharpener, Donald Duck, Celluloid, 2 1/2 In. 165.00
Pennant, Mickey Mouse Toytown, Christmas, Donald, Pluto, Santa, Singing, 1930s 500.00
Pennant, Sleeping Beauty, Castle, Dark Blue, Gold Letters, Gold Trim, 1955, 26 In. 100.00
Pitcher, Donald Duck, Aqua, Airbrushed, Bisque, American, 6 1/2 In. 165.00
Pitcher, Dumbo, 6 In. 140.00
Pitcher, Mickey Mouse, Porcelain, 4 In. 145.00
Plaque, Mickey Mouse & Pluto, Wooden Inlay, Painted, 1930s, 26 1/2 x 12 In. 345.00
Plate, Mickey Mouse, Bavarian China, 1931, 6 In., Pair 900.00
Poster, Le Chat Qui Vient De L'Espace, Walt Disney Productions, Color, 51 x 46 In. 529.00
Puppet, Mickey & Minnie Mouse, Vinyl, Cloth, Gund Walt Disney, c.1950 .... 55.00
Purse, Mickey Mouse, Beaded, Red, Black, Yellow, On White 75.00
Quilt, Mickey Mouse & Friends, Patchwork, 1930s, 70 x 80 In. 747.00
Rug, Snow White & Seven Dwarfs, Crossing Log Bridge, Italy, 22 x 40 In. .... *Illus* 150.00
Salt & Pepper, Pluto, Ceramic, 3 1/4 In. 17.00
Scissors, Mickey Mouse, Tin, Lithograph Mickey Running On Handle, 3 1/2 In. 200.00
Sign, Donald Duck, RPM Motor Oil, Snowman, Tin, 23 1/2 In. 1100.00
Sign, Mickey Mouse, Standard Gasoline, Round, Tin, 23 1/2 In. 1210.00
Sign, Mickey Mouse, Sunoco Winter Oil, Cardboard, c.1939, 20 x 28 In. 360.00
Song Folio, Mickey Mouse, Silly Symphony, Irving Berlin, c.1930, 12 x 9 In., 32 Pages .. 138.00
Statue, Snow White & Seven Dwarfs, Lawn Statuettes, 9 1/2 In. 230.00
Sugar & Creamer, Mickey & Minnie Mouse, Hand Painted, Made In Japan 125.00
Tea Set, Mickey Mouse, 6 Cups & Saucers, Faiencerie D'Onnaing, c.1935 .... 330.00
Tea Set, Mickey Mouse, China, Box, Japan, 8 x 10 In. 360.00

Tea Set, Mickey Mouse, Lusterware, Sugar, Teapot, Creamer, 1930, 23 Piece 540.00
Tea Set, Mickey Mouse, Teapot, Sugar, Creamer, Lids, Faincerie D'Onnaing, c.1935 . . . .   470.00
Thermometer, Donald Duck, In Policeman Uniform, Ceramic, c.1940, 6 x 6 In. 150.00
Tin, Snow White & Seven Dwarfs, 8 x 13 In. 120.00
Tin, Three Little Pigs, England, 5 1/2 In. 66.00
Toothbrush Holder, Donald Duck, Arms Around Mickey & Minnie, Bisque, 1930s 350.00
Toothbrush Holder, Mickey & Minnie Mouse, Sitting On Sofa, Pluto, Bisque 350.00
Toothbrush Holder, Mickey Mouse, Movable Arm, Bisque, 5 In.   350.00
Toy, Bambi, Walking, Battery Operated, Cloth, Remote Control, 8 In 44.00
Toy, Disneyland Express, Train, Tin, Plastic, Windup, Display Board, Marx, 13 In. 145.00
Toy, Donald Duck & Goofy, Crazy Dancers, Windup, Tin Lithograph, Marx, 10 In. 440.00
Toy, Donald Duck & Goofy, Drums, Tin, Marx 440.00
Toy, Donald Duck & Pluto, Handcar, Windup, 1930s 750.00
Toy, Donald Duck, Acrobat, Celluloid, Windup, Box, Linemar, 12 In. 440.00
Toy, Donald Duck, Acrobat, Celluloid, Clockwork, George Borgefeldt, 1934 . . . .   415.00
Toy, Donald Duck, Beats Drum, Goofy Jigs, Windup, Tin, 1946, 10 1/2 In. 405.00
Toy, Donald Duck, Bubble Blowing, Box, 1940s 225.00
Toy, Donald Duck, Bubble, Soda Jerk, Soda Glass With Bubbles, Squeeze, 1950s, 8 In. . . .   320.00
Toy, Donald Duck, Car, Donald Drives, Mechanical, Box, Linemar 750.00
Toy, Donald Duck, Car, Piston Race, Battery Operated, Tin, Plastic, Japan, Box, 9 1/2 In. .   145.00
Toy, Donald Duck, Car, Tin, Windup, Walt Disney Production, Spain, Box, 5 1/2 In. 110.00
Toy, Donald Duck, Drives Delivery Wagon, Friction, Tin Lithograph, Box, Linemar, 6 In. .   825.00
Toy, Donald Duck, Drummer, Red Coat, Hat, Marx, 11 In. 450.00
Toy, Donald Duck, Drummer, Tin, Windup, Linemar, 6 In. 298.00
Toy, Donald Duck, Duckmobile, Tin, Celluloid, Friction, 6 1/2 In. 149.00
Toy, Donald Duck, Goofy, Platform, Drums, c.1946, 10 In. 200.00
Toy, Donald Duck, Gym, High Bar, Celluloid, Windup, Linemar, 6 In. 140.00
Toy, Donald Duck, Handcar, Windup, Lionel, 1930s 750.00
Toy, Donald Duck, Mickey Mouse, Goofy, Car, TV On Roof, Marx, 8 In. 800.00
Toy, Donald Duck, Nodder, Plastic, Irwin, Box, 5 1/2 In. 180.00
Toy, Donald Duck, Nodder, Windup, Celluloid, 6 In. 385.00
Toy, Donald Duck, On Motorcycle, Tin, Friction, Linemar, 3 1/2 In. 225.00
Toy, Donald Duck, On Skis, Windup, Tin Lithograph, Linemar, 6 In. 990.00
Toy, Donald Duck, Pluto, Train, Track, Tin, Windup, Lionel, Box, 11 In. 525.00
Toy, Donald Duck, Straight Shooter, Waddles, Plastic, Windup, Mavco, Box, 6 In. 195.00
Toy, Donald Duck, Tin, Plastic, Windup, Schuco, 1950s, 6 1/2 In. 425.00
Toy, Donald Duck, Tin, Remote Control, Linemar, 6 In. 165.00
Toy, Donald Duck, Tin, Windup, Box, Schuco, 6 In 330.00
Toy, Donald Duck, Train, No. 450, Fisher-Price, c.1940 . . . .   140.00
Toy, Donald Duck, Vibrates, Tail Spins, Plastic, Windup, Marx, Box, c.1950, 6 1/2 In. 248.00
Toy, Donald Duck, Vibrates, Tin, Plastic, Windup, Schuco WDP, W. Germany, 6 In. 396.00
Toy, Donald Duck, Waddles, Beak Goes Up & Down, German, Schuco, 1930s 650.00
Toy, Donald Duck, Walker, Composition, Windup, Borgfeldt, 1930s, 11 In. 650.00
Toy, Donald Duck, Walker, Windup, Celluloid, Box, Borgfeldt, 3 1/4 In. 750.00
Toy, Donald Duck, Windup, Schylling, 4 1/2 In. 20.00
Toy, Dumbo, Flips, Tin, Windup, Marx Walt Disney Productions, 1941, 4 1/4 In. 193.00
Toy, Goofy, Car, Tin, Windup, Walt Disney Production, Spain, Box, 5 1/2 In. 165.00
Toy, Goofy, Gardener, Legs Move, Tin, Windup, Marx England, 8 In. 440.00
Toy, Goofy, Pushes Windup Crate Over & Over, France, Jouets De Marseille, 1950s . . . . . . • 350.00
Toy, Goofy, Stock Car, Long, Friction 495.00
Toy, Goofy, Sway-Play, Wood, Box, 10 1/2 In. 120.00
Toy, Goofy, Unicycle, Tin, Windup, Box, 6 In. 1250.00
Toy, Goofy, Unicycle, Tin, Windup, Linemar, 6 In. 360.00
Toy, Goofy, Vibrates, Tail Spins, Tin, Windup, Linemar, 5 1/2 In.   715.00
Toy, Mickey & Donald, Railroad, Melody, Handcar, Tin, Plastic, Japan, Box, 9 x 15 In. . . .   285.00
Toy, Mickey & Minnie Mouse, Acrobat, Celluloid, Windup, Box, 13 In. 1210.00
Toy, Mickey & Minnie Mouse, Acrobat, Celluloid, Windup, 12-In. Wire, 1930s 750.00
Toy, Mickey & Minnie Mouse, Handcar, Windup, Lionel, 1930, 8 In. . . . . .495.00 to 850.00
Toy, Mickey & Minnie Mouse, Tin, 1933, 10 x 8 x 7 In. 625.00
Toy, Mickey Mouse & Donald Duck, Xylophone, 6 1/2 In. 126.00
Toy, Mickey Mouse & Pluto, Washing Machine, Tin Lithograph, Ohio Art, 1930s, 9 In. 550.00
Toy, Mickey Mouse, Acrobat, Celluloid, Box, 1930, 5 1/2 In. 2275.00
Toy, Mickey Mouse, Band, Tin, Lithograph, 1930s, 9 In. 495.00

Toy, Mickey Mouse, Black, Rubber, Seiberling, c.1931, 6 1/2 In.   650.00
Toy, Mickey Mouse, Bus, TV Camera, Bell, Tin, 20 In. 715.00
Toy, Mickey Mouse, Car, Travels & Turns, Tin, Windup, Linemar, Box, 7 In. 690.00
Toy, Mickey Mouse, Climbs String, Paperboard, Dolly Toy Co., 1930s, 10 In. 385.00
Toy, Mickey Mouse, Delivery Wagon, Friction, Tin Lithograph, Box, Linemar, 6 In. 880.00
Toy, Mickey Mouse, Drives Dipsy Car, Windup, Linemar, Box . . . . .875.00 to 975.00
Toy, Mickey Mouse, Drummer, Tin, Cloth, Battery Operated, Linemar, 11 1/2 In. 440.00
Toy, Mickey Mouse, Ferris Wheel, Disneyland, Tin, 13 In. 330.00
Toy, Mickey Mouse, Ferris Wheel, Tin, Windup, Chein, Box, 16 1/2 In. 525.00
Toy, Mickey Mouse, Fire Truck, Walt Disney Productions Sun Rubber Canada, 7 In. 286.00
Toy, Mickey Mouse, Gym, High Bar, Celluloid, Windup, Linemar, 6 In. 165.00
Toy, Mickey Mouse, Handcar, Wells, England, 7 1/2 In. 2265.00
Toy, Mickey Mouse, Hi-Wheel Bike, Tin, Windup, Linemar, 7 In. 550.00
Toy, Mickey Mouse, Hobbyhorse, Celluloid, Wood, Prewar Japan, 5 3/4 In. 1075.00
Toy, Mickey Mouse, Horse, Cowboy, Wood, Celluloid, Windup, Prewar Japan, 7 1/2 In. . .   1760.00
Toy, Mickey Mouse, Magician, Tux, Top Hat, Battery Operated, Linemar, 10 In. 690.00
Toy, Mickey Mouse, Nodder, Plastic, Irwin, Box, 6 In. 155.00
Toy, Mickey Mouse, Pluto, Rocking, Tin, Mechanical, Linemar, Japan, Box, 5 1/2 In. 3300.00
Toy, Mickey Mouse, Pull, Steel, 10 In. 99.00
Toy, Mickey Mouse, Race Car, Tin, Windup, Automatic Toy Co., c.1930, 4 In. 385.00
Toy, Mickey Mouse, Rocking Horse, Bounces, Celluloid, Wood, Spring, 4 In. 1250.00
Toy, Mickey Mouse, Rocking Horse, Wood, Celluloid, Windup, Prewar Japan, 7 1/2 In. . .   2860.00
Toy, Mickey Mouse, Roller Skater, Windup, Tin Lithograph, Linemar, 6 1/2 In. 609.00
Toy, Mickey Mouse, Roly Poly, Celluloid, 1940 . . . .   350.00
Toy, Mickey Mouse, Scooter, Rides, Head Nods, Tin, Windup, Linemar, 4 1/2 In. 770.00
Toy, Mickey Mouse, Scooter, Windup, 1940s, 6 In. 90.00
Toy, Mickey Mouse, Slate Dancer, Tin Lithograph, Windup, 6 1/2 In. 14300.00
Toy, Mickey Mouse, Sparkler, Tin, Nifty, Borgfeldt, Walt E. Disney, Box, 5 3/4 In. 855.00
Toy, Mickey Mouse, Tail Spins, Plastic, Marx, Box, 7 In. 250.00
Toy, Mickey Mouse, Train, Circus, Locomotive, Tender, 4 Cars, Tent, Lionel 1980.00
Toy, Mickey Mouse, Train, No. 485, Fisher-Price, c.1949 . . . .   110.00
Toy, Mickey Mouse, Tricycle, Tin, Celluloid, Windup, Linemar, Box, 4 In. 275.00
Toy, Mickey Mouse, Unicyclist, Legs Move, Tin, Windup, Linemar, 6 In. 715.00
Toy, Mickey Mouse, Waddles, Celluloid, Windup, Walt Disney, Japan, c.1934, 8 In. 1265.00
Toy, Mickey Mouse, Walks, Drums, Tin, Battery, Remote, Linemar, Box, 11 In. 1606.00
Toy, Mickey Mouse, Whirligig, Celluloid, Windup, Walt Disney, c.1934, 7 1/2 In. 1128.00
Toy, Mickey Mouse, Xylophone Player, Tin, Windup, WDP Linemar, 7 In. 360.00
Toy, Mickey Mouse, Xylophone, Plastic, Windup, WDP, Marx, Box, c.1950, 11 In. 257.00
Toy, Minnie Mouse, Hobbyhorse, Celluloid, Wood, Japan, Prewar, 5 3/4 In. 1075.00
Toy, Minnie Mouse, Knitting, Rocks, Tin, Windup, Linemar, Box, 7 In. 715.00
Toy, Pinocchio, Acrobat, Swings, Base Rocks, Tin, Windup, Marx, Box, 1939, 16 In. 415.00
Toy, Pinocchio, Pig, In Boat, Celluloid, Japan, Prewar, 5 1/2 In.   165.00
Toy, Pinocchio, Scooter, Tin, Windup, Bell, Italy, c.1930, 6 In. 935.00
Toy, Pinocchio, Walker, Tin, Windup, Linemar, 6 In. 180.00
Toy, Pinocchio, Walker, Tin, Windup, Marx, 6 In. 176.00
Toy, Pinocchio, Walker, Windup, Tin Lithograph, Box, Marx, 8 1/2 In. 330.00
Toy, Pluto & Goofy, Vibrate, Tail Spin, Tin, Windup, Linemar, Box, 5 1/2 In. 1320.00
Toy, Pluto, Acrobat, Celluloid, Tin Lithograph, Battery Operated, Linemar, 9 In. 110.00
Toy, Pluto, Drives Delivery Wagon, Friction, Tin Lithograph, Linemar, Box, 6 In. 580.00
Toy, Pluto, Drum Major, Tin, Windup, 6 1/4 In. 200.00
Toy, Pluto, Pulling Mickey Mouse, Windup, 8 In. 2990.00
Toy, Pluto, Pup, Flexi-Toy, Wooden, George Borgfeldt, Box, 6 In. 470.00
Toy, Pluto, Push Tail, Scoots, Tin, Marx, c.1939, 9 1/2 In. 195.00
Toy, Pluto, Rollover, Tin Lithograph, Windup, Marx, 9 In. 95.00
Toy, Pluto, Rollover, Tin, Windup, Chein, 13 In. 99.00
Toy, Pluto, Rollover, Windup, Marx, Box, 1939 . . . .   460.00
Toy, Pluto, Running, Friction, Yellow, Tin Lithograph, Linemar, Box, 4 1/2 In. 495.00
Toy, Pluto, Sniffing Ground, Tin Lithograph, Spring Powered, 10 1/2 In. 130.00
Toy, Pluto, Twirly Tail, Plastic, Great Britain, Box, 5 1/2 In. 198.00
Toy, Pluto, Unicyclist, Windup, Tin Lithograph, Box, Linemar, 5 1/2 In. 880.00
Toy, Pluto, Vibrates, Tail Spins, Plastic, Windup, Marx, Box, c.1950, 6 In. 248.00
Toy, Pluto, Walks, Felt, Windup, Linemar, Box, 6 In. 275.00
Toy, Snow White & Seven Dwarfs, Roly Poly, Celluloid, Box, Holland, 2-In. Dwarfs 675.00

Tumbler, Colonel Hathi, Jungle Book, Pepsi-Cola 25.00
Tumbler, Goofy, Happy Birthday Mickey, 1978 .... 5.00
Tumbler, Lady & The Tramp, Dachsie, Thick Bottom, 5 1/4 In. 90.00
Tumbler, Mickey Mouse, Hooks Rug, 1984 .... 23.00
Tumbler, Mowgli, Jungle Book, Pepsi-Cola 15.00
Tumbler, Sleeping Beauty, Canada, No. 1 .... 25.00
Tumbler, Snow White & Seven Dwarfs, Sneezy, Black, 3 3/4 In. 9.00
Watch, Pocket, Mickey Mouse, Plastic, 1 7/8 In. 39.00
Wristwatch, Alice In Wonderland, Blue Band, Ceramic Figure, Timex, Box, c.1950 ..... 330.00
Wristwatch, Bambi, Birthday, Green Band, Ingersoll US Time, Box, 1949 .... 140.00
Wristwatch, Cinderella, Pink Band, Plastic Figure, Timex, Box, c.1950 .... 250.00
Wristwatch, Donald Duck, Box, 1950s 125.00
Wristwatch, Mickey Mouse, Convex Sides, Yellow Hands, Ingersoll, 1939 .... 200.00
Wristwatch, Mickey Mouse, Mice On Seconds Bit, Ingersoll, c.1934 .... 375.00
Wristwatch, Mickey Mouse, Red Band, Plastic Figure, Timex, Box, c.1950 .... 220.00
Wristwatch, Mickey Mouse, Tall Stem, Mice On Seconds Bit, Ingersoll, c.1934 .... 375.00
Wristwatch, Mickey Mouse, Timex, Mickey Figure, Plastic, Box, Stand, 1958, 5 In. 175.00
Wristwatch, Minnie Mouse, 2 Extra Bands, 1950s 125.00
Wristwatch, Minnie Mouse, Yellow Band, Celluloid Plaque, Ingersoll WDP, c.1948 ..... 385.00

DOCTOR, see Dental; Medical

DOLL entries are listed by marks printed or incised on the doll, if possible. If there are no marks, the doll is listed by the name of the subject or country or maker. Notice that Barbie is listed under Mattel. G.I.
Joe figures are listed in the Toy section. Eskimo dolls are listed in the
Eskimo section and Indian dolls are listed in the Indian section. Doll
clothes and accessories are listed at the end of this section. The twentieth-century clothes listed here are in mint condition.

A.M., 200, Bisque Head, Googly Eyes, Closed Mouth, Mohair Wig, c.1910, 8 3/4 In. 765.00
A.M., 233, Bisque Socket Head, Sleep Eyes, Blond Mohair, Composition, 14 1/2 In. 425.00
A.M., 241, Bisque Socket Head, Googly Eyes, Closed Mouth, Hair, 10 1/2 In. 2500.00
A.M., 323, Bisque Head, Googly Eyes, Brunette Mohair, Composition, Bent Limb, 9 In. .. 1750.00
A.M., 323, Bisque Head, Googly Eyes, Smiling Mouth, Chunky Body, 1920s, 9 1/4 In. ... 1116.00
A.M., 323, Bisque Socket Head, Blue Googly Eyes, c.1925, 8 In. 800.00
A.M., 323, Bisque Socket Head, Googly Eyes, Blond Hair, c.1925, 10 In. 1100.00
A.M., 324, Bisque Socket Head, Intaglio Eyes, Painted Hair, 6 1/2 In. 400.00
A.M., 327, Bisque Socket Head, Blue Sleep Eyes, 2 Upper Teeth, Blond Curly Hair, 19 In. 449.00
A.M., 327B, Bisque Socket Head, Sleep Eyes, Open Mouth, Bent Limb, 1913, 18 In. 365.00
A.M., 351, Black Bisque, Brown Sleep Eyes, Open Mouth, Painted Hair, 2 Teeth, 20 In. .. 660.00
A.M., 370, Bisque Shoulder Head, Brown Sleep Eyes, Open Mouth, Leather Body, 23 In. . 180.00
A.M., 370, Bisque Shoulder Plate, Brown Sleep Eyes, Kid Body, Bisque Hands, 20 In. ... 145.00
A.M., 390, Bisque Head, Blue Set Eyes, Open Mouth, 4 Teeth, Papier-Mache Body, 14 In. 80.00
A.M., 390, Bisque Head, Sleep Eyes, Human Hair, Composition Body, Carriage, 25 In. ... 235.00
A.M., 390, Bisque Head, Sleep Eyes, Mohair Wig, Composition Body, c.1910, 11 1/2 In. . 205.00
A.M., 390, Bisque Socket Head, Blue Sleep Eyes, Open Mouth, Teeth, Mohair Wig, 22 In. 145.00
A.M., 390N, Blue Set Eyes, Open Mouth, 4 Teeth, Mohair Wig, 20 1/2 In. 175.00
A.M., 401, Bisque Socket Head, Sleep Eyes, Mohair, Jointed, Composition, 14 1/2 In. 2300.00
A.M., 401, Flapper Lady, Bisque Socket Head, Blue Glass Sleep Eyes, c.1920, 14 In. 2700.00
A.M., 550, Bisque Socket Head, Blue Sleep Smiling Eyes, Mohair, Jointed, c.1915, 17 In. . 3900.00
A.M., 590, Character, Toddler, Bisque Head, Blue Sleep Eyes, Auburn Hair, 1916, 17 In. .. 1700.00
A.M., 3200, Bisque Shoulder Plate, Sleep Eyes, Teeth, Leather Body, Amish Outfit, 21 In. 160.00
A.M., Bisque Head, Blue Eyes, Open Mouth, Jointed Composition Body, 26 In. 275.00
A.M., Bisque Shoulder Head, Brown Sleep Eyes, Open Mouth, Brown Human Hair, 27 In. 205.00
A.M., Bisque Shoulder Head, Sleep Eyes, Open Mouth, Mohair Wig, Bride, c.1910, 14 In. 150.00
A.M., Bisque Socket Head, Amber Complexion, Sleep Eyes, Chinese Baby, c.1920, 12 In.. 1000.00
A.M., Bisque Socket Head, Blue Eyes, Open Mouth, Blond Synthetic Wig, 20 1/2 In. 205.00
A.M., Bisque Socket Head, Blue Eyes, Open Mouth, Lower Teeth, 14 In. 316.00
A.M., Bisque Socket Head, Brown Eyes, Open Mouth, 22 In. 189.00
A.M., Bisque Socket Head, Brown Sleep Eyes, Open Mouth, 6 Teeth, Brown Hair, 23 In. . 200.00
A.M., Bisque Socket Head, Painted Hair & Eyes, Open Mouth, 9 In. 230.00
A.M., Bisque Socket Head, Set Eyes, Open Mouth, Wig, c.1900, 20 In. 140.00
A.M., Bisque Socket Head, Sleep Eyes, Open Mouth, 4 Teeth, Human Hair, 1894, 22 In. .. 450.00

A.M., Bisque, Blue Sleep Eyes, Lashes, Open Mouth, Blond Wig, 23 1/2 In.	120.00
A.M., Bisque, Blue Sleep Eyes, Open Mouth, Teeth, Blond Wig, 13 1/2 In.	118.00
A.M., Bisque, Brown Glass Eyes, Open Mouth, Brown Human Hair Wig, 19 In.	176.00
A.M., Fany, Bisque, Pouty, Glass Eyes, Articulated Body, Blue Outfit, Hat, c.1910, 13 In. .	4465.00
A.M., Florodora, Bisque Shoulder Head, Sleep Eyes, Open Mouth, Brown Wig, 21 In.	176.00
A.M., Just Me, Bisque Socket Head, Glass Googly Sleep Eyes, c.1928, 10 In.	2100.00
A.M., Just Me, Bisque, Painted, Googly Sleep Eyes, Composition Body, c.1925, 10 In. . . .	850.00
A.M., Queen Louise, Bisque Head, Sleep Eyes, Mohair Wig, Composition, c.1900, 25 In. .	411.00
A.M., Queen Louise, Bisque Socket Head, Blue Sleep Eyes, 4 Teeth, Hair, 25 1/2 In.	325.00
A.M., Queen Louise, Bisque Socket Head, Blue Sleep Eyes, Teeth, Brown Wig, 24 In. . . .	118.00
Advertising, 7-Up, Fresh Up Freddie, Vinyl, Felt, Painted, c.1950, 16 In.	140.00
Advertising, Buddy Lee, Composition, Jointed Arms, Lee Overalls, 1940s, 12 In.	225.00
Advertising, Buddy Lee, Plastic, Brown Uniform, Phillips 66, 12 In.	285.00
Advertising, Buddy Lee, Plastic, Original Clothes, Hat, 13 In.	160.00
Advertising, Clown, Kellogg's Sugar Smacks, Paul Jung, 1953	50.00
Advertising, Colonel Sanders, Bobbin' Head, Holding Bucket Of Chicken, 1961, 8 In. . . .	275.00
Advertising, Cracker Jack, Vogue, 1979, 16 In.	45.00
Advertising, Dairy Premium Cow, Stuffed, Plush, Bell, c.1960, 7 x 12 In.	15.00
Advertising, Edswan Radios, Wooden, Jointed, Tube Hat, 15 In.	965.00
Advertising, Hamburglar, McDonald's, Cloth, 16 In.	45.00
Advertising, Hostess Munchie, Cloth, Orange, Plush, c.1980, 6 x 9 x 14 In.	10.00
Advertising, Ideal, Uneeda Kid, Composition Head, Painted, Cloth Body, Box, 16 In.	475.00
Advertising, Nestle, Little Hans, Fabric, Stuffed, c.1970, 13 In.	28.00
Advertising, Old Smuggler Scotch Whiskey, Scotsman, Tam, Sash, Kilt, Vinyl, 30 In.	225.00
Advertising, Puppet, Burger Chef, Hand, Flannel, Felt, Vinyl, c.1970, 10 In.	35.00
Advertising, Ralston Purina, Scarecrow, Vinyl Head, Cloth Body	65.00
Advertising, Speedy Alka-Seltzer, 6 In.	165.00
Alexander dolls are listed in this category under Madame Alexander.	
Alexander Girard, Yarn, Textiles & Objects Shop, Marilyn Neuhart, 6 x 7 In.	805.00
Amberg, Bottle Babe, Bisque Head, Sleep Eyes, Baby Bottle, 12 1/2 In., Twins	500.00
Amberg, Charlie Chaplin, Composition Head, Molded Hair & Mustache, 1915, 14 In.	800.00
Amberg, Dolly Drake, Cloth Body, 8 In.	75.00
Amberg, Newborn Babe, Bisque Head, Sleep Eyes, Painted Features, Cloth Body, 16 In. .	275.00
Amberg, Vanta Baby, Composition Head, Sleep Eyes, Open Mouth, Teeth, Jointed, 20 In. .	325.00
American Character, Betsy McCall, Pink Dress, c.1960, 14 In.	175.00
American Character, Betsy McCall, Plaid Flannel Dress, 22 In.	200.00
American Character, Boy & Girl, Felt Swivel Head, Painted Features, Lisa, Scott, 17 In. .	2100.00
American Character, Campbell Kid, Composition, Swivel Head, 12 In.	600.00
American Character, Toni, Vinyl, Blue Sleep Eyes, Pink Dress, Box, 14 In.	300.00
Armand Marseille dolls are listed in this category under A.M.	
Arranbee, Littlest Angel, Plastic, Sleep Eyes, Saran Wig, Walks, Box, 10 1/2 In.	325.00
Arthur Gerling, Bisque Head, Sleep Eyes, Closed Mouth, Protruding Jaw, 1920s, 14 In. . .	200.00
Automaton, 2 Finches, Birdcage, Stepped Marble Base, c.1900, 23 x 12 In.	1265.00
Automaton, Ballerina, Pirouettes, Bisque Head, Long Brunette Curls, A.M., 37 In.	4200.00
Automaton, Bird In Cage, Feathered, Gilt Metal, Key Wind, France, c.1900, 11 In.	550.00
Automaton, Bugler, Shakespearean Figure, Clock Mechanism, 6 Ft. 8 In.	1380.00
Automaton, Clown Balancing On Ball, Balancing 2 Balls, Cloth Clothing, 22 In.	468.00
Automaton, Dolley Madison, Hard Plastic, Electrical, Original Crate, 39 In.	935.00
Automaton, Harlequin, Tumbles, Enamel Inset Eyes, Wood Box, c.1800, 14 x 11 In.	16500.00
Automaton, Lady Playing Guitar, Blue Glass Eyes, Velvet & Wood Base, c.1900, 23 In. .	6000.00
Automaton, Old Woman Knitting, Papier-Mache, Mohair Wig, Wood Base, c.1890, 21 In. .	5000.00
Automaton, Women, Windmill, Spinning Wheel, Bone, Prisoner-Of-War, 5 In.	8365.00
Automaton, Zouave, Walks, Brown Eyes, Mustache, Box, c.1862, 11 In.	1100.00
Averill, Bonnie Babe, Bisque Flange Head, Blue Eyes, 2 Lower Teeth, 15 In.	350.00
Averill, Bonnie Babe, Bisque Flange Head, Blue Eyes, Cloth Body, 12 In.	575.00
Averill, Bonnie Babe, Bisque, Brown Sleep Eyes, Open Mouth, Loop-Jointed, 7 In.	1900.00
Baby Barry Toy Co., Mammy Yokum, Dog Patch Family, Box, 1957, 14 In.	425.00
Bahr & Proschild, 536, Boy, Bisque Head, Brown Intaglio Eyes, Ball-Jointed, 18 In.	3750.00
Bahr & Proschild, 567, Bisque Socket Head, 2-Face, Composition, Wood, c.1911, 18 In. .	2400.00
Bahr & Proschild, 585, Bisque Socket Head, Sleep Eyes, Papier-Mache Body, Boy, 12 In.	350.00
Barbie dolls are listed in this category under Mattel.	
Barrois, Bisque Shoulder Head, Blue Enamel Inset Eyes, Closed Mouth, c.1860, 28 In. . .	3500.00
Barrois, Fashion, Bisque Swivel Head, Shoulders, Cobalt Glass Eyes, Kid Body, 20 In. . .	3100.00

Barrois, Fashion, Blond, Glass Eyes, Gusset Joints, Kid Body, 1890s, 25 In. 2990.00
Barrois, Fashion, Brown Mohair Wig, Kid Body, Joint Gussets, 18 In. 1800.00
Bawo & Dotter, 214, Bisque Socket Head, Glass Sleep Eyes, Composition, c.1917, 14 In.   4800.00
Belton-Type, 106, Bisque Socket Head, Threaded Paperweight Eyes, 15 1/2 In. 600.00
Belton-Type, Bisque Shoulder Head, Closed Mouth, Mohair Wig, Kid Body, 1880s, 16 In.   940.00
Bergmann dolls are also in this category under S & H and Simon & Halbig.
Bergmann, Porcelain Head, c.1900, 20 In. 525.00
Bing, Cloth Swivel Head, Painted, Closed Mouth, Jointed, Germany, 10 1/2 In. 300.00
Bisque, Baby, Painted Brown Eyes, Hair, Boy, 6 In. 550.00
Bisque, Black Complexion, Shoulder Head, Germany, c.1890, 13 In. 1500.00
Bisque, Blue Set Eyes, Painted Features, Cloth, Composition, Boy, 13 In. 325.00
Bisque, Blue Sleep Eyes, 4 Teeth, Brunette Human Hair, Original Wedding Dress, 21 In. .   4200.00
Bisque, Closed Mouth, Composition Body, Clothes, France, 24 In. 4200.00
Bisque, Closed Mouth, Leather Body, France, 21 In. 3800.00
Bisque, Fairy, Stiff Neck, Glass Eyes, 2 Teeth, Mohair, Jointed Shoulders, 4 3/4 In. 190.00
Bisque, Glass Inset Eyes, Box, France, c.1885, 6 In. 1000.00
Bisque, Painted Eyes, Jointed Arms, Mohair Wig, Molded Shoes, Child, 6 In. 300.00
Bisque, Set Eyes, Painted Features, Closed Mouth, Mohair, Jointed Body, 7 1/2 In. 450.00
Bisque, Shoulder Head, Bisque Hands, Molded Hair, Kid Body, 15 In. 430.00
Bisque, Shoulder Head, Blue Eyes, Closed Mouth, Blond Mohair Wig, 19 1/2 In. 499.00
Bisque, Shoulder Head, Blue Eyes, Open Mouth, Cloth & Kid Body, 23 In. 345.00
Bisque, Shoulder Head, Blue Glass Eyes, Open Mouth, Kid Body, 30 In. 430.00
Bisque, Shoulder Head, Blue Painted Eyes, Closed Mouth, Blond Hair, c.1880, 10 In. 175.00
Bisque, Shoulder Head, Blue Painted Eyes, Closed Mouth, Molded Blond Curls, 10 In. . . .   106.00
Bisque, Shoulder Head, Blue Painted Eyes, Closed Painted Mouth, Blond Hair, 13 In. . . .   150.00
Bisque, Shoulder Head, Blue Sleep Eyes, Open Mouth, Teeth, 22 In. 176.00
Bisque, Shoulder Head, Brown Eyes, Open Mouth, Kid Body, 22 In. 345.00
Bisque, Shoulder Head, Brown Sleep Eyes, Open Mouth, Brown Mohair Wig, 15 In. 410.00
Bisque, Shoulder Head, Glass Eyes, Closed Mouth, Molded Blond Hair, 22 In. 600.00
Bisque, Shoulder Head, Painted Blond Hair, Skirt, Blouse, 24 In. 1300.00
Bisque, Socket Head, Blue Eyes, Open Mouth, Blond Wig, 24 1/2 In. 175.00
Bisque, Socket Head, Blue Eyes, Open Mouth, Pierced Ears, 18 In. 400.00
Bisque, Socket Head, Blue Paperweight Eyes, Blond Mohair Ringlets, Bebe, 22 In. 4750.00
Bisque, Socket Head, Blue Paperweight Eyes, Pierced Ears, 17 In. 575.00
Bisque, Socket Head, Brown Eyes, Open Mouth, Pierced Ears, Wig, 27 In. 170.00
Bisque, Socket Head, Closed Mouth, Blue Paperweight Eyes, Kid Body, 21 In. 460.00
Bisque, Socket Head, Glass Eyes, Open Mouth, Fur Bunny Suit, Germany, c.1898, 11 In. . .   850.00
Bisque, Socket Head, Paperweight Eyes, Pouty Mouth, Composition Body, c.1880, 10 In. .   880.00
Bisque, Swivel Head, Painted Face, Brunette Wig, Migonette, France, 2 1/2 In. 350.00
Black dolls are included in the Black category.
Blampoix, Fashion, Bisque Swivel Head, Glass Enamel Inset Eyes, c.1860, 14 In. 3100.00
Blossom Doll Co., Wedding Party, Painted Features, Cloth, c.1925, 18-29 In., 10 Piece . . .   1300.00
Borgfeldt, 253, Bisque Socket Head, Glass Googly Sleep Eyes, c.1920, 7 In. 850.00
Boudoir, Mohair Wig, Painted Features, Cloth Top, Satin & Lace, 1920s, 28 In. 75.00
Bru Jne, 1, Bisque Socket Head, Glass Enamel Inset Eyes, Blue Silk Dress, c.1887, 12 In. 14500.00
Bru Jne, 1, Bisque Swivel Head, Amber Brown Eyes, Kid Body, Bebe, c.1885, 11 In. 20000.00
Bru Jne, 2, Bebe Teteur, Bisque, Swivel Head, Glass Enamel Inset Eyes, c.1880, 12 In. . .   6000.00
Bru Jne, 2, Bebe Teteur, Bisque, Swivel Head, Glass Paperweight Eyes, c.1880, 12 In. . . .   7000.00
Bru Jne, 2, Bisque Swivel Head, Glass Enamel Inset Eyes, Closed Mouth, c.1880, 13 In. .   7000.00
Bru Jne, 4, Bisque Swivel Head, Blue Glass Enamel Eyes, Blond Mohair, c.1883, 16 In. . 22000.00
Bru Jne, 6, Bisque Swivel Head, Glass Paperweight Eyes, Brown Hair, Bebe, 19 In. 1600.00
Bru Jne, 6, Bisque Swivel Head, Kid Body, Silk, Lace Dress, Bebe, 1882, 19 In. . . . *Illus* 16000.00
Bru Jne, 7, Bebe, Bisque Swivel Head, Brown Enamel Inset Eyes, Bebe, c.1880, 21 In. . . 17500.00
Bru Jne, 8, Bisque Swivel Head, Brown Paperweight Inset Eyes, Bebe, c.1888, 18 In. . . .   7000.00
Bru Jne, 8, Bisque Swivel Head, Glass Enamel Inset Eyes, c.1880, 21 In. 27000.00
Bru Jne, 8, Bisque Swivel Head, Glass Paperweight Inset Eyes, c.1882, 22 In. 15000.00
Bru Jne, 9, Bisque Swivel Head, Blue Glass Paperweight Inset Eyes, c.1880, 24 In. 21000.00
Bru Jne, 14, Bisque Swivel Head, Glass Enamel Inset Eyes, Closed Mouth, c.1886, 31 In.   13000.00
Bru Jne, 15, Bisque Socket Head, Paperweight Eyes, Composition, Bebe, c.1885, 38 In. . . . 13000.00
Bru Jne, Bebe Marcheur, Bisque, Blue Glass Paperweight Inset Eyes, Walker, 25 In. 9750.00
Bru Jne, Bebe Teteur, Bisque Swivel Head, Glass Enamel Inset Eyes, c.1886, 17 In. 6500.00
Bru Jne, Bisque Shoulder Head, Blue Paperweight Eyes, Mohair, 17 In. 9500.00
Bru Jne, Bisque Socket Head, Glass Inset Eyes, c.1885, 8 In. 1500.00

Bru Jne, Bisque Socket Head, Paperweight Eyes, Hair, Jewelry, Bebe, 16 In. 8000.00
Bru Jne, Bisque Swivel Head, Blue Glass Enamel Inset Eyes, Kid Body, c.1873, 16 In. .. 3600.00
Bru Jne, Bisque Swivel Head, Glass Eyes, Wooden Body, Dowel-Jointed, 1873, 15 In. 10000.00
Bru Jne, Bisque, Blue Glass Enamel Inset Eyes, Closed Mouth, Bebe, c.1882, 19 In. 27000.00
Bru Jne, Fashion, Bisque Shoulder Head, Wooden Body, Dowel-Jointed, 14 In. 5750.00
Bru Jne, Fashion, Bisque Swivel Head, Glass Enamel Inset Eyes, Kid Body, c.1868, 15 In. 3000.00
Bucherer, Becassine, Composition Head, Painted Features, Metal-Jointed, 1905, 8 In. 120.00
Bucherer, Composition, Ball-Jointed, Molded Shoes, Switzerland, 1921, 8 In. 175.00
Bye-Lo, Bisque Flange Head, Sleep Eyes, Closed Mouth, Painted& Molded Hair, 13 In. .. 140.00
Bye-Lo, Bisque Head, Blue Eyes, Closed Mouth, Cotton Gown, Layette, c.1925, 5 In. 400.00
Bye-Lo, Bisque Head, Blue Eyes, Closed Mouth, Knit Costume, Basket, c.1925, 7 In. 425.00
Bye-Lo, Bisque Head, Blue Eyes, Painted Mouth, Cloth, Celluloid Hands, 1923, 14 In. ... 120.00
Bye-Lo, Bisque Head, Blue Glass Sleep Eyes, White Gown, c.1923, 12-In. Head 525.00
Bye-Lo, Bisque Head, Blue Sleep Eyes, Cloth Body, 11 In. 500.00
Bye-Lo, Bisque Head, Blue Sleep Eyes, Painted Features, Cloth Body, 14 In. 300.00
Bye-Lo, Bisque Head, Sleep Eyes, Cloth Body, Celluloid Hands, 1920s, 18 In. 265.00
Bye-Lo, Bisque, Blue Eyes, Cloth Body, Celluloid Hands, Grace Putman, 11 In. 550.00
Bye-Lo, Bisque, Domed Swivel Head, Blue Glass Sleep Eyes, Closed Mouth, c.1923, 5 In. 750.00
Bye-Lo, Bisque, Domed Swivel Head, Blue Glass Sleep Eyes, Closed Mouth, c.1923, 6 In. 775.00
Bye-Lo, Bisque, Painted Features, Loop-Jointed Arms & Legs, c.1925, 5 In. 225.00
Bye-Lo, Blue Sleep Eyes, Cloth Body, Celluloid Hands, Grace Putnam, 14 In. 200.00
Cameo Doll Co., Margie, Composition, Wood Body, Joseph Kallus, Label, 1929, 10 In. .. 225.00
Catterfelder Puppenfabrick, Bisque Socket Head, Blue Shaded Eyes, c.1910, 15 In. 9000.00
Celluloid, Socket Head, Blue Sleep Eyes, Lashes, Open Mouth, 2 Teeth, Toddler, 15 In. .. 880.00
Chase, Child, Cloth, Painted Features, Blue Eyes, Blond Hair, Sateen Body, c.1910, 16 In. 80.00
Chase, George Washington, Stockinet Head, Oil Painted, Blue Eyes, Box, 27 In. 2300.00
Chase, Hospital Baby, Stockinet Head, Blue Eyes, Oil Painted, Jointed, 20 In. 325.00
China, Shoulder Head, Blue Eyes, Black Molded Hair, Closed Mouth, 15 In. 700.00
China, Shoulder Head, Blue Eyes, Black Painted Hair, Cloth Body, Maroon Suit, 25 In. .. 800.00
China, Shoulder Head, Blue Eyes, Painted Features, Black Hair, Black, Dress, 28 In. 750.00
China, Shoulder Head, Blue Eyes, Painted Features, Blond Mohair Wig, 14 In. 600.00
China, Shoulder Head, Blue Painted Eyes, Black Hair, Center Part, 16 In. 90.00
China, Shoulder Head, Blue Painted Eyes, Long Nose, Center Part, Black Hair, 20 1/2 In. ... 323.00
China, Shoulder Head, Brown Painted Eyes, Lip & Cheek Coloring, c.1860, 18 1/2 In. ... 295.00
China, Shoulder Head, Brown Painted Eyes, Painted Hair, 20 In. 823.00
China, Shoulder Head, Painted Blue Eyes, Molded Black Hair, Cloth Body, 15 1/2 In. ... 425.00
Cloth, Blue Glass Eyes, Fringed Spanish Costume, Mid 20th Century, 11 In. 10.00
Cloth, Boy's Suit, High-Waisted, Double-Breasted Jacket, Fly Front, 1840, 32 In. 80.00
Cloth, Hand-Drawn Facial Features, Black Fabric Hair, 19th Century, 21 1/2 In. 25.00
Cloth, Oil Painted, Blue Eyes, Pink Cheeks, Blond, Cotton Undergarments, c.1890, 33 In. 3400.00
Cloth, Painted Features, Brown Hair, Stuffed, 20th Century, 27 In. 10.00
Cloth, Swivel Head, Pressed & Painted Features, Brunette Mohair, 17 In. 500.00
Composition, Clown, Molded Hair, Painted Features, Straw-Stuffed Body, 1920s, 28 In. . 100.00
Composition, Straw Stuffed, Dark Skin, 15 In. 125.00
Danel, Bisque Socket Head, Paperweight Inset Eyes, Bebe, c.1890, 24 In. 3700.00
Danel, Ebony Bisque Socket Head, Glass Eyes, Closed Mouth, Coral Lips, Jointed, 13 In. 4750.00
Demalcol, Bisque Head, Glass Googly Eyes, Closed Mouth, Molded Shoes, c.1910, 10 In. 355.00
Denamur, Bisque Socket Head, Glass Eyes, Mohair, Composition, Wood, Bebe, 14 In. 4200.00
Door Of Hope, Mourner, Man, Chinese, 11 1/2 In. 1800.00
Door Of Hope, Widow, Chinese, 11 In. 1500.00
Dressel, 1469, Flapper, Bisque Socket Head, Blue Glass Sleep Eyes, c.1920, 14 In. 2000.00
Dressel, Bisque Head, Brown Glass Eyes, Open Mouth, Teeth, 1912, 23 In. 120.00
Effanbee, Anne Shirley, Human Hair, Sleep Eyes, Original Clothes, 1935, 16 In. 300.00
Effanbee, Brown Composition Shoulder Head, Sculpted Hair, Grumpy Features, 14 In. 200.00
Effanbee, Bubbles, Composition Head, Arms & Legs, Cloth Body, c.1930, 16 In. 265.00
Effanbee, Christopher Columbus, Suit, Stockings, Hat, Stand, 16 In. 30.00
Effanbee, Composition, Button Nose, Totally Jointed, 1939, 9 In. 250.00
Effanbee, Jambo The Jiver, Marionette, Purple Coat, Wood, c.1948, 13 In. 55.00
Effanbee, Little Lady, Composition, Blue Sleep Eyes, Hair, Jointed, 17 In. 225.00
Effanbee, Little Lady, Composition, Sleep Eyes, Closed Mouth, Hair, 20 In. 425.00
Effanbee, Nancy, Composition, Jointed At Neck, Original Clothes, 1930, 16 In. 300.00
Effanbee, Patsy Ann, 1930s 285.00
Effanbee, Patsy Ann, Composition, Painted Hair, Sleep Eyes, 1930s, 19 In. 450.00

Doll, Bru Jne, 6, Bisque Swivel
Head, Kid Body, Silk, Lace Dress,
Bebe, 1882, 19 In.

Doll, Japanese,
Emperor,
15 In.

Doll, Jumeau, 9, Bisque Socket
Head, Composition,
Wood-Jointed, c.1884, 20 In.

Effanbee, Patsy, Composition, Brown Sleep Eyes, 14 In. 525.00
Effanbee, Patsy, Molded Hair, Patsy Pin, 1928, 14 In. 400.00
Effanbee, Patsyette, Composition, Brown Googly Eyes, Jointed, 9 In. 325.00
Effanbee, Rosemary, Composition Head, Blue-Green Tin Sleep Eyes, 1926, 11 1/2 In. . . . 885.00
Effanbee, Skippy, Composition, Painted Forelock Curl, White Horse Inn Costume, 14 In. . 550.00
Effanbee, Skippy, Soldier's Uniform, Brown Complexion, c.1940, 14 In. 550.00
Effanbee, Skippy, Soldier's Uniform, Composition, Socket Head, c.1940, 14 In. 1600.00
Effanbee, Tintair, Plastic, Blue Sleep Eyes, Hair Color & Curl, Box, Accessories, 14 In. . . 475.00
Fashion, Bisque Shoulder Head, Enamel Inset Eyes, Closed Mouth, France, c.1865, 16 In. 2400.00
Fashion, Bisque Swivel Head, Blue Glass Inset Eyes, France, c.1860, 22 In. 2000.00
Fashion, Bisque Swivel Head, Brown Glass Enamel Inset Eyes, France, c.1878, 17 In. . . . 3100.00
Fashion, Bisque Swivel Head, Glass Inset Eyes, Kid Body, Jointed, c.1870, 14 In. 4000.00
Fashion, Bisque Swivel Head, Gray Glass Eyes, Articulated Arms, France, c.1865, 13 In. . 1700.00
Fashion, Bisque, Blue Glass Eyes, Original Folk Costume Of Brittany, 14 In. 4000.00
Fashion, Bisque, Man, Painted Features, Hair Wig, Cloth Body, Suit, 22 In. 1400.00
Fashion, Bisque, Swivel Head, Blue Glass Eyes, Blond Mohair Wig, c.1870, 11 In. 705.00
Fashion, Bisque, Swivel Head, Glass Eyes, Normandy Costume, c.1875, 12 In. 2100.00
Fashion, Bisque, Swivel Head, Paperweight Eyes, Closed Mouth, c.1880, 16 In. 560.00
Fashion, Bisque, Swivel Head, Set Eyes, Mohair Wig, Kid Body, c.1870, 16 In. 2350.00
Fashion, Bisque, Swivel Head, Stationary Eyes, Mohair Wig, France, 1880s, 16 In. 1410.00
Fashion, Boy, Blue Paperweight Eyes, Gusseted Kid, 18 In. 2245.00
Franz Schmidt, Bisque Socket Head, Sleep Eyes, Open Mouth, 4 Teeth, Jointed, 22 In. . . 175.00
French, Bisque Socket Head & Shoulder Plate, Blue Glass Eyes, Pierced Ears, 17 In. 1840.00
French, Bisque Socket Head, Blond Wig, Hat & Brown Suit, 5 In. 2645.00
French, Bisque Socket Head, Paperweight Eyes, Hair, Composition, Jointed, 21 1/2 In. . . . 850.00
French, Bisque Socket Head, Sleep Eyes, 4 Teeth, Hair, Jointed Body, Crier, 22 In. 375.00
French, Bisque Swivel Head, Blue Glass Enamel Inset Eyes, Peg-Jointed, c.1882, 5 In. . . . 1000.00
French, Bisque Swivel Head, Blue Glass Inset Eyes, Fortune Teller, c.1885, 13 In. 2300.00
French, Bisque Swivel Head, Blue Glass Inset Eyes, Wood Body, Jester, c.1867, 16 In. . . . 7500.00
French, Bisque Swivel Head, Glass Inset Eyes, Wood Articulated Body, c.1870, 18 In. . . . 6250.00
French, Bisque, Blue Glass Sleep Eyes, 2 Teeth, Peg-Jointed, Mignonette, c.1885, 6 In. . . 2200.00
French, Bisque, Brown Glass Enamel Inset Eyes, Green Dress, Mignonette, c.1885, 5 In. . 950.00
French, Celluloid, Clothes, Early 20th Century, 13 In. 50.00
French, Domed Bisque Swivel Head, Blue Glass Inset Eyes, Mignonette, c.1885, 4 In. . . . 1500.00
French, Leather, Boy, Pouty, Oil-Painted Features, Green Knit Suit, c.1925, 5 In. 1600.00
French, Leather, Girl, Oil-Painted Features, Dotted-Swiss Outfit, c.1925, 5 1/2 In. 1700.00
French, Leather, Girl, Pouty, Oil-Painted Features, White Pique, c.1925, 5 1/2 In. 1300.00
French, Leather, Swivel Head, Blond Sculpted Hair, White Dress, Baby, c.1925, 4 1/2 In. . 1700.00
French, Papier-Mache, Shoulder Head, Enamel Glass Inset Eyes, 8 Teeth, c.1850, 22 In. . . 1300.00
French, Papier-Mache, Socket Head, Painted, Smiling, Guard Uniform, c.1890, 42 In. . . . 2000.00
French, Porcelain Shoulder Head, Painted Hair, Blue Eyes, Kid Body, c.1855, 12 In. 1100.00
French, Porcelain, Painted, Black Hair, Blue Eyes, Shell Costume, c.1860, 4 In. 1000.00
Freundlich, Baby Sandy, Molded Head, Sleep Eyes, Open Mouth, 1940s, 16 In. 250.00

Freundlich, Douglas MacArthur, Composition, Painted Features, 18 In. . . . . .225.00 to 250.00
G.I. Joe figures are listed in the Toy category.
Gaultier, Bebe, Bisque Socket Head, Glass Inset Eyes, Closed Mouth, c.1890, 15 In. 2200.00
Gaultier, Bisque Head, Brown Glass Eyes, Gesland, Composition Body, Bebe, 26 1/2 In. . 2000.00
Gaultier, Bisque Shoulder Head, Blue Glass Enamel Inset Eyes, Blond Mohair, 16 In. . . . 1800.00
Gaultier, Bisque Socket Head, Blue-Glass Spiral Threaded Eyes, Bebe, c.1882, 13 In. . . . 3500.00
Gaultier, Bisque Socket Head, Glass Paperweight Inset Eyes, c.1890, 28 In. 4000.00
Gaultier, Bisque Swivel Head, Blue Glass Eyes, Human Hair, Kid Body, 13 In. 3600.00
Gaultier, Bisque Swivel Head, Glass Inset Eyes, Kid Body, Jointed, Bride, c.1885, 18 In. . 2000.00
Gaultier, Fashion, Bisque, Blue Glass Eyes, Original Folk Costume Of Normandy, 13 In. . 4400.00
Gebruder Heubach dolls are also in this category under Heubach.
Gebruder Heubach, 7102, Bisque Socket Head, Closed Mouth, Sailor, Dog, c.1915, 12 In. 425.00
Gebruder Heubach, 7246, Bisque Socket Head, Sleep Eyes, Scottish Boy, c.1915, 10 In. . 1300.00
Gebruder Heubach, 7603, Bisque Socket Head, Blue Intaglio Eyes, Baby, 14 1/2 In. 600.00
Gebruder Heubach, 7847, Bisque Shoulder Head, Painted, 2 Teeth, Boy, c.1912, 11 In. . . 900.00
Gebruder Heubach, 10532, Bisque Socket Head, Brown Glass Eyes, Teeth, c.1920, 28 In. 1800.00
Gebruder Heubach, 10633, Dainty Dorothy, Bisque Head, Sleep Eyes, Box, 27 In. 675.00
Gebruder Heubach, Coquette, Bisque Socket Head, Googly Eyes, 12 1/2 In. 1000.00
Gebruder Heubach, Dolly Dimple, Bisque Head, Sleep Eyes, Open Smiling Mouth, 21 In. 3400.00
Gebruder Kuhnlenz, 165, Bisque Socket Head, Brown Sleep Eyes, Jointed Body, 23 In. . . 240.00
German, 110, Bisque Socket Head, Green Eyes, Composition, c.1910, 16 In. 1400.00
German, 137, Bisque Socket Head, Blue Glass Inset Eyes, Closed Mouth, c.1888, 15 In. . 2100.00
German, 222, Our Fairy, Bisque, Glass Eyes, Smiling, Mohair Wig, Jointed, c.1910, 5 In. . 382.00
German, 248, Bisque Head, Dimples, Set Eyes, Open Mouth, Pierced Ears, c.1890, 14 In. 470.00
German, Bisque Domed Head, Blue Glass Eyes, Papier-Mache Body, c.1885, 10 In. 600.00
German, Bisque Flange Head, Sleep Eyes, Open Mouth, Teeth, Child, 27 1/2 In. 1150.00
German, Bisque Head, Closed Mouth, Intaglio Eyes, Painted Hair, Baby, c.1910, 15 In. . . 235.00
German, Bisque Head, Sleep Eyes, Pouty Mouth, Cloth Body, c.1925, 13 In. 380.00
German, Bisque Shoulder Head, Brown Sleep Eyes, Painted Features, Hair Wig, 22 In. . . 250.00
German, Bisque Shoulder Head, Painted, Mustache, Military Uniform, c.1890, 7 In. 1500.00
German, Bisque Shoulder Head, Set Eyes, Closed Mouth, Kid Body, 1880s, 19 In. 355.00
German, Bisque Socket Head, Brown Glass Eyes, Composition, Chinese Costume, 11 In. . 1100.00
German, Bisque Socket Head, Brown Glass Sleep Eyes, Alsatian Costume, c.1915 . . . . . . 550.00
German, Bisque Socket Head, Glass Inset Eyes, Papier-Mache Body, c.1890, 7 In., Pair . . 1000.00
German, Bisque Socket Head, Gray Glass Sleep Eyes, Open Mouth, Teeth, c.1920, 20 In. 650.00
German, Bisque Socket Head, Paperweight Eyes, Human Wig, 1880s, 13 In. 1295.00
German, Bisque Socket Head, Sleep Eyes, Mohair Wig, Composition Body, c.1910, 16 In. 235.00
German, Bisque Socket Head, Sleep Eyes, Open Mouth, Mohair Wig, 1920s, 12 In. 140.00
German, Bisque Socket Head, Teeth, Mohair Braids, c.1925, 12 In. 1600.00
German, Bisque, Blond, Molded Hair, Bow, Jointed Arms, Legs, Satin Dress, 7 In. 25.00
German, Bisque, Painted Blue Eyes, Blond Hair, Features, Closed Mouth, c.1920, 6 In. . . 450.00
German, Bisque, Painted Features, Glass Top, Outfits, Baby, 8-Sided Box, c.1915, 7 In. . . 950.00
German, Bisque, Painted Features, Yellow Cap, Chinese Silk Costume, c.1900, 4 In. 250.00
German, Bisque, Socket Head, Sleep Eyes, Open Mouth, Mohair Wig, c.1910, 13 In. 59.00
German, Earthenware Domed Head, Brown Googly Eyes, c.1935, 20 In. 1500.00
German, Fashion, Molded Hair, Painted Eyes, Closed Mouth, Cloth Body, 1870, 13 In. . . 325.00
German, Metal Shoulder Head, Closed Mouth, Molded Hair, Cloth Body, c.1890, 12 In. . . 29.00
German, Moritz, Bisque, Sculpted Brown Hair, Painted Features, c.1915, 5 1/2 In. 1100.00
German, Porcelain Shoulder Head, Black Sculpted Hair, Painted Features, c.1865, 14 In. . 1050.00
German, Porcelain Shoulder Head, Black Sculpted Hair, Painted Features, c.1870, 13 In. . 2900.00
German, Porcelain Shoulder Head, Brown Glass Eyes, Stitch-Jointed Body, c.1865, 17 In. 1400.00
German, Porcelain Shoulder Head, Limbs, Painted Features, Wooden Body, c.1860, 5 In. . 1500.00
German, Porcelain Swivel Head, Blue Shaded Eyes, Stitch-Jointed Body, c.1880, 16 In. . . 850.00
German, Shoulder Head, Turned, Blue Eyes, Leather Body, Late 19th Century, 23 In. 140.00
Giebeler-Falk, Metal Socket Head, Blue Sleep Eyes, Open-Close Mouth, 23 In. 47.00
Giebeler-Falk, Metal Socket Head, Sleep Eyes, Open-Close Mouth, c.1920, 22 In. 82.00
Greiner, Head Only, Papier-Mache, Black Hair, Philadelphia, c.1858 . . . . 390.00
Greiner, Papier-Mache, Black Hair, Blue Eyes, Red Jacket, Dress, 30 In. 750.00
Grodner Tal, Wood, Painted Features, Silk Gown, Base, Box, c.1850, 2 In. 200.00
Half Dolls are listed in the Pinchushion category.
Handwerck, 1, Bisque Head, Sleep Eyes, Open Mouth, Composition Body, c.1910, 18 In. 265.00
Handwerck, 79, Bisque Socket Head, Blue Sleep Eyes, 4 Teeth, Mohair, 17 1/2 In. 375.00
Handwerck, 109, Bisque Socket Head, Blue Set Eyes, Hair, Braided, 35 1/2 In. 800.00

Handwerck, 119, Bisque Head, Sleep Eyes, Inset Teeth, Composition Body, c.1910, 19 In. 259.00
Handwerck, 421, Bisque Socket Head, Blue Sleep Eyes, 4 Teeth, Mohair, 21 In. 700.00
Handwerck, Bebe Cosmopolite, Bisque Socket Head, Blue Glass Sleep Eyes, 1900, 25 In. 1200.00
Handwerck, Bisque Head, Blue Eyes, Open Mouth, Wig, Pierced Ears, 25 In. 805.00
Handwerck, Bisque Head, Blue Sleep Eyes, Open Mouth, Teeth, 22 1/2 In. 265.00
Handwerck, Bisque Head, Brown Sleep Eyes, Open Mouth, 23 In. 265.00
Handwerck, Bisque Head, Brown Sleep Eyes, Open Mouth, Inset Teeth, 16 1/2 In. 529.00
Handwerck, Bisque Head, Wood & Composition Body, Sleep Eyes, Open Mouth, 28 In. . . . 440.00
Handwerck, Bisque Socket Head, Blue Eyes, Open Mouth, 24 In. 316.00
Handwerck, Bisque Socket Head, Blue Glass Sleep Eyes, Pink Dress, c.1915, 24 In. 950.00
Handwerck, Bisque Socket Head, Blue Sleep Eyes, 4 Teeth, Mohair, Pink Dress, 18 In. . . . 350.00
Handwerck, Bisque Socket Head, Blue Sleep Eyes, 4 Teeth, Wig, 23 In. 400.00
Handwerck, Bisque Socket Head, Blue Sleep Eyes, Open Mouth, Teeth, 14 1/2 In. 700.00
Handwerck, Bisque Socket Head, Blue Sleep Eyes, Ball-Jointed, Straw Hat, 40 In. 2075.00
Handwerck, Bisque Socket Head, Brown Glass Eyes, Open Mouth, Teeth, 24 In. 206.00
Handwerck, Bisque Socket Head, Brown Sleep Eyes, 4 Teeth, Curly Mohair, 33 In. 900.00
Handwerck, Bisque Socket Head, Brown Sleep Eyes, 4 Teeth, Hair, Composition, 25 In. . 600.00
Handwerck, Bisque Socket Head, Brown Sleep Eyes, Open Mouth, 4 Teeth, 22 In. 1900.00
Handwerck, Bisque Socket Head, Brown Sleep Eyes, Open Mouth, 32 In. 1090.00
Handwerck, Bisque Socket Head, Helmet, Blue Glass Googly Eyes, c.1916, 12 In. 1500.00
Handwerck, Bisque Socket Head, Sleep Eyes, 4 Teeth, Mohair, Composition, 24 In. 500.00
Handwerck, Bisque Socket Head, Sleep Eyes, 4 Teeth, Pierced Ears, c.1900, 15 In. 265.00
Handwerck, Bisque, Brown Sleep Eyes, Black Mohair Fleecy Wig, 4 Teeth, 18 In. 1000.00
Handwerck, Mohair Wig, Composition Body, Articulated, Lawn Dress, Lace, 1905, 23 In. 382.00
Handwerck, Uncle Sam, Bisque Socket Head, Blue Glass Googly Eyes, c.1916, 12 In. . . . 2900.00
Hertel Schwab, 136, Bisque Socket Head, Brown Sleep Eyes, 20 In. 375.00
Hertel Schwab, 141, Bisque Socket Head, Brown Glass Sleep Eyes, c.1912, 13 In. 2500.00
Hertel Schwab, 151, Blue Glass Sleep Eyes, Composition Body, Baby, 16 In. 230.00
Hertel Schwab, 151, Brown Glass Sleep Eyes, Jointed Composition Body, Boy, 22 In. 259.00
Hertel Schwab, 152, Sleep Eyes, Open Mouth, Teeth, Composition Jointed Body, 16 In. . . 300.00
Hertel Schwab, 152/1, Bisque Head, Blue Sleep Eyes, Open Mouth, Baby, c.1905, 11 In. . 265.00
Hertel Schwab, 165, Jubilee Googly, Bisque, Composition Bent Limb Body, 12 In. 2900.00
Hertel Schwab, 222, Bisque Head, Blue Glass Googly Sleep Eyes, Fairy, c.1912, 11 In. . . . 1700.00
Hertel Schwab, Bisque, Painted Features, Googly Eyes, Closed Mouth, c.1915, 7 In. 550.00
Hertel Schwab, Jubilee Googly, Bisque Socket Head, Glass Eyes, Chubby Body, 17 In. . . 12750.00
Heubach dolls are also in this category under Gebruder Heubach.
Heubach, 302, Bisque, Socket Head, Sleep Eyes, Open Mouth, Brown Wig, c.1910, 26 In. 155.00
Heubach, 320, Bisque Head, Brown Sleep Eyes, Open Mouth, Brown Hair, 14 In. 255.00
Heubach, 320, Bisque Socket Head, Painted Face, Blue Flirty Eyes, 1930, 24 In. 180.00
Heubach, 417, Bisque Head, Sleep Eyes, Open Mouth, 12 In. 975.00
Heubach, 6969, Bisque Head, Sleep Eyes, Closed Mouth, Mohair Braids, c.1912, 12 In. . . 3000.00
Heubach, 6969, Bisque Shoulder Head, Glass Sleep Eyes, White Dress, c.1912, 18 In. . . . 2400.00
Heubach, 6969, Bisque Socket Head, Blue Glass Sleep Eyes, Character, c.1915, 14 In. . . . 3100.00
Heubach, 7926, Bisque Socket Head, Brown Glass Inset Eyes, 1912, 10 In. 1500.00
Heubach, 8191, Bisque Socket Head, Blue Intaglio Eyes, 10 Teeth, 9 In. 300.00
Heubach, 8420, Bisque Socket Head, Blue Glass Sleep Eyes, White Gown, c.1912, 13 In. 950.00
Heubach, Bisque Shoulder Head, Glass Sleep Eyes, Open Mouth, c.1915, 22 In. 1500.00
Heubach, Bisque Socket Head, Blue Intaglio Eyes, Smiling Mouth, Teeth, Dimples, 16 In. 1410.00
Heubach, Bisque Socket Head, Paperweight Eyes, 6 Teeth, 1907, 18 In. 1600.00
Horsman, Baby Bumps, Composition Flange Head, Cloth Body, Label, 1910, 14 In. 145.00
Horsman, Babyland, Rag, Cloth, Brown Eyes, Hand Painted, Stitch-Jointed, 30 In. 300.00
Horsman, Bisque Head, Blue Glass Eyes, Bent-Limb Body, Loop-Jointed, c.1924, 8 In. . . . 1700.00
Horsman, Blink, Gene Carr Character, Composition, Closed Eyes, Teeth, 1916, 8 In. 200.00
Horsman, Emmett Kelly Jr., Original Box, 24 In. 185.00
Horsman, Mama, Composition Head, Mohair Wig, Sleep Tin Eyes, 1920s, 16 In. 165.00
Horsman, Rosebud, Flange Head, Sleep Eyes, Open Mouth, 3 Teeth, Mohair, 24 In. 400.00
Horsman, Tynie Baby, Bisque Flange Head, Sleep Eyes, Painted, Cloth Body, 14 In. . . . 650.00
Huret, Bisque Socket Head, Painted Features, Wood Articulated Body, Flapper, 18 In. . . . 1000.00
Huret, Bisque Socket Head, Painted, Lamb's-Wool Wig, Composition, Bebe, 13 In. 5500.00
Ideal, Bud Abbott & Lou Costello, Who's On First, Baseball Uniforms, 1983, 10 In. 300.00
Ideal, Judy Garland, Dorothy, Wizard Of Oz, Composition, 1939, 16 In. 1350.00
Ideal, Liberty Boy, Composition, Jointed, Doughboy Hat, 1917, 12 In. 145.00
Ideal, Mama, Composition Head, Arms & Legs, Cloth Body, 1920s, 16 In. 225.00

Ideal, Pattie Play Pal, Vinyl Head, Sleep Eyes, Closed Mouth, Curly Rooted Wig, 35 In. . .   675.00
Ideal, Princess Beatrix, Composition Head, Swing Legs, Bonnet, 1939, 16 In. 100.00
Ideal, Saucy Walker, Plastic, Blue Sleep Eyes, Cries, Walks, Box, 16 In. 300.00
Ideal, Soozie Smiles, 2 Heads, Smiling, Crying, Cloth Body, Rompers & Hat, 1923, 15 In.   400.00
Ideal, Toni, Plastic Head, Blue Green Sleep Eyes, Curly Red Wig, Walker, 1956, 16 In. . .   1340.00
Indian dolls are listed in the Indian category.
Izannah Walker, Cloth, Painted Features, Jointed, 18 In. 3400.00
J.D.K. dolls also may be listed in this category under Kestner.
Japanese, Bisque Head, Sleep Eyes, Teeth, Composition Body, Child, Nippon, 16 In. 220.00
Japanese, Bisque, Painted Features, Jointed Arms, Early 20th Century, 7 In. 30.00
Japanese, Emperor, 15 In. . . . . *Illus*   300.00
Jullien, Bisque Socket Head, Blue Glass Inset Eyes, Composition, Wood, c.1895, 23 In. . . .   3200.00
Jumeau, 3, Bisque Head, Paperweight Eyes, Closed Mouth, Mohair Wig, Bebe, 11 In. 7050.00
Jumeau, 3, Closed Mouth, Paperweight Eyes, Human Hair, Bebe, c.1890, 12 In. 1765.00
Jumeau, 4, Bisque Head, Paperweight Eyes, Human Hair, Tete Bebe, c.1890, 13 In. 3290.00
Jumeau, 6, Bisque Socket Head, Glass Paperweight Inset Eyes, c.1885, 15 In. 7500.00
Jumeau, 7, Bisque Head, Paperweight Eyes, Composition, Wood-Jointed, c.1885, 16 In. . . .   4900.00
Jumeau, 7, Bisque Head, Paperweight Eyes, Closed Mouth, Mohair Wig, Bebe, 17 In. 3055.00
Jumeau, 8, Bisque Socket Head, Blue Glass Paperweight Inset Eyes, c.1888, 20 In. 3400.00
Jumeau, 8, Open Mouth, Blue Eyes, Composition, Ball-Jointed, 23 In. 1035.00
Jumeau, 9, Bisque Head, Paperweight Eyes, Open Mouth, Tete Bebe, 1885, 21 In. 2820.00
Jumeau, 9, Bisque Socket Head, Blue Paperweight Eyes, Closed Mouth, c.1885, 20 In. . . .   5000.00
Jumeau, 9, Bisque Socket Head, Composition, Wood-Jointed, c.1884, 20 In. . . . . *Illus* 24500.00
Jumeau, 11, Bisque, Brown Glass Inset Eyes, Mohair Wig, Composition, c.1885, 24 In. . .   9000.00
Jumeau, 14, Triste Bebe, Paperweight Eyes, Closed Mouth, Mohair Wig, 1885, 29 In. . . .   14100.00
Jumeau, 15, Bisque Socket Head, Glass Paperweight Eyes, Closed Mouth, c.1885, 32 In. . .   13500.00
Jumeau, Bisque Head, 4 Teeth, Hair Wig, Jointed, Tete, Box, 19 1/2 In. 850.00
Jumeau, Bisque Head, Blue Paperweight Eyes, Brunette Mohair, Marquis Costume, 22 In.   7700.00
Jumeau, Bisque Head, Brown Glass Eyes, Composition, Jointed, 1878, 12 In. 15000.00
Jumeau, Bisque Head, Sleep Eyes, Open Mouth, Human Hair Wig, Tete, 19 In. 650.00
Jumeau, Bisque Head, Sleep Eyes, Open Mouth, Mohair Wig, Composition, c.1890, 20 In.   1058.00
Jumeau, Bisque Head, Sleep Eyes, Open Mouth, Pierced Ears, Voice, Bebe, 1907, 23 In. .   1800.00
Jumeau, Bisque Head, Sleep Eyes, Open Mouth, Teeth, Pierced Ears, Human Hair, 15 In. .   450.00
Jumeau, Bisque Socket Head, Blue Eyes, Open Mouth, Ball-Jointed, Tete, 24 In. 1550.00
Jumeau, Bisque Socket Head, Blue Glass Paperweight Inset Eyes, Bebe, c.1885, 27 In. . .   7250.00
Jumeau, Bisque Socket Head, Blue Glass Paperweight Inset Eyes, Bebe, c.1892, 26 In. . .   4000.00
Jumeau, Bisque Socket Head, Blue Glass Eyes, Closed Mouth, Blond, 9 In. 4315.00
Jumeau, Bisque Socket Head, Brown Glass Enamel Inset Eyes, Bebe, c.1885, 20 In. 7500.00
Jumeau, Bisque Socket Head, Brown Glass Paperweight Eyes, Bebe, c.1885, 14 In. 4400.00
Jumeau, Bisque Socket Head, Brown Glass Paperweight Eyes, Bebe, c.1885, 18 In. 4700.00
Jumeau, Bisque Socket Head, Cafe-Au-Lait, Amber Glass Eyes, Bebe, 17 In. 11000.00
Jumeau, Bisque Socket Head, Glass Inset Eyes, Closed Mouth, Bebe, c.1878, 13 In. 3500.00
Jumeau, Bisque Socket Head, Glass Paperweight Eyes, Blond Human Hair, c.1885, 18 In.   7000.00
Jumeau, Bisque Socket Head, Glass Paperweight Eyes, Blond Mohair, c.1880, 20 In. 5500.00
Jumeau, Bisque Socket Head, Glass Paperweight Eyes, Closed Mouth, c.1888, 19 In. 10500.00
Jumeau, Bisque Socket Head, Glass Paperweight Eyes, Wood-Jointed, c.1888, 24 In. 4500.00
Jumeau, Bisque Socket Head, Glass Paperweight Inset Eyes, Bebe, c.1890, 24 In. 6000.00
Jumeau, Bisque Socket Head, Glass Paperweight Inset Eyes, Spanish Dancer, 24 In. 3800.00
Jumeau, Bisque Socket Head, Paperweight Eyes, Composition, Wood, Bebe, 12 In. 4750.00
Jumeau, Bisque Socket Head, Paperweight Eyes, Hair, 6 Teeth, 1907, 23 1/2 In. 800.00
Jumeau, Bisque Socket Head, Paperweight Eyes, Blond Mohair Wig, 25 In. 9000.00
Jumeau, Bisque Socket Head, Paperweight Eyes, Closed Mouth, Mohair, Jointed, 26 In. . . .   4750.00
Jumeau, Bisque Socket Head, Sleep Eyes, 6 Teeth, Composition, Pink Dress, 25 In. 650.00
Jumeau, Bisque Socket Head, Threaded Paperweight Eyes, Mohair, Jointed, 14 In. 4100.00
Jumeau, Bisque Swivel Head, Blue Glass Enamel Inset Eyes, Wood Body, c.1870, 20 In. .   6250.00
Jumeau, Fashion, Bisque Head, Blue Glass Eyes, Smiling, Kid Body, 1873, 13 In. 5500.00
Jumeau, Louvre Bebe, Bisque Socket Head, Blue Glass Paperweight Eyes, c.1895, 11 In. .   4700.00
Jumeau, Portrait, Bisque Swivel Head, Glass Eyes, Human Hair, Kid Body, 20 In. 7200.00
Jumeau, Princess Elizabeth, Bisque Socket Head, Blue Glass Inset Eyes, c.1938, 34 In. . .   4800.00
Jumeau, Samaritaine Bebe, Bisque Socket Head, Glass Sleep Eyes, Box, c.1895, 29 In. . .   4400.00
K & K, Bisque Shoulder Head, Brown Sleep Eyes, 2 Teeth, Mohair, White Dress, 20 In. . .   250.00
K & K, Shoulder Plate, Blue Glass Eyes, Open Mouth, 4 Teeth, Cloth Body, 16 In. 450.00
K * R, 34, Bisque Socket Head, Sleep Eyes, Open Mouth, 4 Teeth, Mohair, 13 1/2 In. . . .   475.00

K * R, 68, Bisque, Blue Glass, Flirty Sleep Eyes, Open Mouth, Teeth, 26 In. 295.00
K * R, 100, Bisque Head, Blue Eyes, Open-Closed Mouth, Knit Outfit, Baby, 10 In. 375.00
K * R, 100, Bisque Socket Head, Blue Eyes, Open-Closed Mouth, Baby, 15 In. 275.00
K * R, 100, Bisque Socket Head, Shaded Blue Eyes, Composition Body, c.1909, 20 In. . . 750.00
K * R, 101, Bisque Socket Head, Painted Blue Eyes, Blond Mohair, Jointed, 18 In. 3700.00
K * R, 101, Marie, Bisque Socket Head, Blue Painted Eyes, Closed Mouth, c.1909, 20 In. 4100.00
K * R, 107, Bisque Socket Head, Painted Features, Closed Mouth, c.1910, 12 In. 10000.00
K * R, 112, Bisque Socket Head, Painted Features, Closed Mouth, 2 Teeth, c.1910, 14 In. . 5200.00
K * R, 114, Gretchen, Bisque Socket Head, Blond Mohair Wig, c.1912, 10 In. 1800.00
K * R, 114, Gretchen, Bisque Socket Head, Blue Shaded Eyes, c.1915, 7 1/2 In. 1300.00
K * R, 114, Gretchen, Bisque Socket Head, Brown Painted Eyes, c.1910, 18 In. 2600.00
K * R, 114, Gretchen, Bisque Socket Head, Painted Eyes, Closed Mouth, c.1910, 18 In. . . 3700.00
K * R, 114, Gretchen, Bisque Socket Head, Painted Eyes, Human Hair, c.1910, 25 In. . . . 625.00
K * R, 114, Gretchen, Bisque Socket Head, Blond Mohair, Painted Features, Pouty, 13 In. 2700.00
K * R, 114/49, Gretchen, Bisque Socket Head, Painted, Pouty, Mohair Wig, 19 In. 7500.00
K * R, 115A, Phillip, Bisque Socket Head, Brown Glass Inset Eyes, Closed Mouth, 13 In. 1600.00
K * R, 116, Bisque Socket Head, Blue Glass Sleep Eyes, Upper Teeth, c.1912, 17 In. 2600.00
K * R, 117, Liebling, Bisque Socket Head, Brown Glass Eyes, c.1912, 16 In. 4600.00
K * R, 117, Mein Liebling, Bisque Head, Glass Eyes, Blond Mohair Wig, c.1912, 18 In. . . 5000.00
K * R, 117, Mein Liebling, Bisque Socket Head, Glass Sleep Eyes, Closed Mouth, c.1912, 24 In. 4600.00
K * R, 117A, Bisque Socket Head, Blue Sleep Eyes, Hair, Composition Body, 11 1/2 In. . . 750.00
K * R, 117N, Bisque Head, Blue Sleep Eyes, Open Mouth, Human Hair Wig, 27 In. 1100.00
K * R, 117N, Bisque Socket Head, Flirty Eyes, Lashes, Open Mouth, 4 Teeth, 20 1/2 In. . . 600.00
K * R, 117N, Bisque, Brown Googly Eyes, Mohair Bob, 4 Teeth, c.1914, 24 In. 1800.00
K * R, 121, Bisque Socket Head, Blue Sleep Eyes, 2 Teeth, Blond Mohair, Baby, 11 In. . . 350.00
K * R, 121, Bisque Socket Head, Blue Sleep Eyes, 2 Teeth, Mohair, 13 1/2 In. 425.00
K * R, 121, Bisque Socket Head, Blue Sleep Eyes, 2 Teeth, Mohair, Baby, 14 In. 300.00
K * R, 122, Bisque Socket Head, Glass Sleep Eyes, 2 Upper Teeth, Toddler, c.1915, 17 In. 1050.00
K * R, 122, Bisque Socket Head, Glass Sleep Eyes, Upper Teeth, Tongue, c.1912, 18 In. . 1750.00
K * R, 126, Bisque Head, Sleep Eyes, Open Mouth, Human Hair, Baby, c.1910, 20 In. . . . 225.00
K * R, 126, Bisque Socket Head, Sleep Eyes, 2 Teeth, Hair, Composition, Baby, 16 In. . . . 250.00
K * R, 126, Bisque, Brown Sleep Eyes, Brunette Mohair, Composition, Toddler, 7 In. 725.00
K * R, 127, Bisque Head, Glass Sleep Eyes, Painted Hair, 2 Upper Teeth, c.1918, 23 In. . . 1300.00
K * R, 127, Bisque Socket Head, Sleep Eyes, 2 Teeth, Composition Body, Baby, 17 In. . . 450.00
K * R, 301/1, Bisque Head, Painted Pouty Features, Blond Mohair, Boy, 12 In. 3400.00
K * R, 301/2, Marie, Intaglio Eyes, Mohair Wig, Oilcloth Body, German Costume, 14 In. . 220.00
K * R, 314, Hans, Bisque Socket Head, Brown Hair, Blue Shaded Eyes, c.1912, 14 In. . . . 6250.00
K * R, 403/58, Bisque Head, Sleep Eyes, Open Mouth, Mohair Wig, 1920s, 23 In. 325.00
K * R, 728, Celluloid Socket Head, Open Mouth, 2 Teeth, Mohair, Boy, 14 In. 450.00
K * R, Bisque Head, Blue Eyes, Open Mouth, Blond Wig, Composition Body, 10 In. 565.00
K * R, Bisque Head, Sleep Eyes, Open Mouth, Blond Wig, Composition Body, 14 In. 255.00
K * R, Bisque Socket Head, Blue Glass Eye, Pierced Ears, 25 In. 400.00
K * R, Bisque Socket Head, Blue Sleep Eyes, 4 Teeth, Wig, Composition, 33 In. 900.00
K * R, Bisque Socket Head, Brown Glass Sleep Eyes, Jester Costume, c.1900, 39 In. 6400.00
K * R, Bisque Socket Head, Brown Sleep Eyes, 2 Teeth, Scottish Costume, c.1915, 10 In. 525.00
K * R, Bisque Socket Head, Brown Sleep Eyes, Ball-Jointed, 31 In. 1030.00
K * R, Bisque Socket Head, Glass Sleep Eyes, Toddler, c.1925, 27 In. 1550.00
K * R, Bisque Socket Head, Human Hair, Composition, Ball-Jointed, 27 In. 375.00
K * R, Bisque Socket Head, Painted Hair & Features, Molded Mouth, 11 In. 258.00
K * R, Bisque Socket Head, Sleep Eyes, 4 Teeth, Blond Mohair, Walks, 11 1/2 In. 400.00
K * R, Bisque Socket Head, Sleep Eyes, 4 Teeth, Hair, Composition, 25 1/2 In. 550.00
K * R, Bisque Socket Head, Sleep Eyes, Open Mouth, 4 Teeth, Mohair, 15 1/2 In. 450.00
K * R, Bisque, Blue Eyes, Hair, Features, Closed Mouth, Baby, c.1915, 8 In. 700.00
K * R, Hans, Bisque Head, Painted Features, Pouty, Jointed, Schoolboy Costume, 13 In. . . 2300.00
K * R, Mein Liebling, Bisque Socket Head, Brown Glass Sleep Eyes, c.1912, 31 In. 6000.00
K * R, My Playmate, Bisque Socket Head, Sleep Eyes, 3 Teeth, Mohair, Box, 12 In. 1275.00
Kamkins, Cloth Swivel Head, Blue Eyes, Painted Features, Mohair, Jointed, 18 In. 1600.00
Kamkins, Cloth Swivel Head, Painted Eyes, Mohair, Cloth Body, Jointed, Boy, 18 In. 575.00
Kathe Kruse, Celluloid Socket Head, Human Hair, Painted Features, 15 In 225.00
Kathe Kruse, Cloth Head, Oil Painted, Blue Eyes, Brown Hair, Girl, 16 In. 1500.00
Kathe Kruse, Cloth Head, Threaded Eyes, Closed Mouth, Painted Hair, 16 In 725.00
Kathe Kruse, Cloth, Brown Eyes, Blond Hair, Jointed Body, Boy, c.1935, 14 In. 1600.00
Kathe Kruse, Cloth, Hazel Eyes, Rounded Mouth, Blond, Red Print Dress, 1950s, 20 In. . . 1000.00

Kathe Kruse, Cloth, Painted Face, Brown Hair, Blue Eyes, Froghand, c.1911, 17 In. 1500.00
Kathe Kruse, Cloth, Painted Face, Brown Hair, Green Eyes, c.1915, 17 In. 900.00
Kathe Kruse, Cloth, Painted Features, Brown Shaded Eyes, Pouty, c.1920, 17 In. 1800.00
Kathe Kruse, Cloth, Painted Hair & Features, Dutch Costume, 1915, 17 In. 3200.00
Kathe Kruse, Cloth, Swivel Head, Brown Eyes, Red Floral Dress, c.1935, 21 In. 1500.00
Kathe Kruse, Hampelchen, Cloth Head, Brown Eyes, Painted Features, 16 In. 1300.00
Kathe Kruse, Hampelchen, Cloth, Brown Hair, Green Shaded Eyes, c.1930, 14 In. 2400.00
Kathe Kruse, Leila, Cloth, Pressed Painted Eyes, Closed Mouth, Mohair Braids, 20 In. . . 1900.00
Kathe Kruse, Painted Brown Eyes, Closed Mouth, Human Hair, Girl, 1893, 20 In. 700.00
Kathe Kruse, Plastic Head, Painted Blue Eyes, Hair, Cloth Body, U.S. Zone, 14 In. 350.00
Kathe Kruse, Schlenkerchen, Cloth, Painted Face, Brown Hair, Grey Eyes, c.1922, 13 In. 4000.00
Kathe Kruse, Socket Head, Blue Eyes, Brown Hair, Red Cap, Boy, Box, c.1952, 14 In. . . 800.00
Kayo, Jointed, Wood, c.1930, 4 In. 65.00
Kenner, Blythe, Redhead, Pull String, Changes Eye Color, Turn Waist, 1972, 11 In. 705.00
Kestner dolls are also in this category under J.D.K.
Kestner, 7, Bisque Socket Head, Pouty Mouth, Glass Eyes, Mohair Wig, c.1890, 15 In. . . 764.00
Kestner, 143, Bisque Head, Sleep Eyes, Mohair Wig, Teeth, Composition Body, 14 In. . . . 500.00
Kestner, 143, Bisque Head, Sleep Eyes, Open Mouth, Composition Body, c.1910, 7 In. . . 440.00
Kestner, 143, Bisque Head, Sleep Eyes, Open Mouth, Cut-In Teeth, Mohair Wig, 9 In. . . . 265.00
Kestner, 143, Bisque Socket Head, Glass Sleep Eyes, Composition Body, c.1915, 8 In. . . . 650.00
Kestner, 146, Bisque Socket Head, Brown Sleep Eyes, 4 Teeth, Mohair, 30 In. 525.00
Kestner, 150, Bisque, Blue Sleep Eyes, 4 Teeth, Mohair, 8 1/4 In. 450.00
Kestner, 154, Bisque Shoulder Head, Glass Eyes, Open Mouth, Kid Body, c.1900, 20 In. . 206.00
Kestner, 164, Bisque Socket Head, Brown Sleep Eyes, 4 Teeth, Mohair, 25 In. 500.00
Kestner, 167, Bisque Head, Sleep Eyes, Open Mouth, Mohair Wig, White Dress, 15 In. . . 850.00
Kestner, 167, Bisque Socket Head, Blue Sleep Eyes, 4 Teeth, Wig, 21 In. 475.00
Kestner, 171, Bisque Socket Head, Blue Sleep Eyes, 4 Teeth, Hair, 25 In. 400.00
Kestner, 172, Gibson Girl, Bisque Shoulder Head, Blue Sleep Eyes, Kid Body, 15 In. 3400.00
Kestner, 179, Bisque Socket Head, Painted Features, Googly Eyes, c.1912, 16 In. 3000.00
Kestner, 211, Bisque Socket Head, Blue Glass Sleep Eyes, Closed Mouth, c.1912, 19 In. . 1300.00
Kestner, 215, Bisque Socket Head, Sleep Eyes, 4 Teeth, Hair, Composition, 23 1/2 In. . . . 325.00
Kestner, 220, Bisque Socket Head, Glass Sleep Eyes, 2 Upper Teeth, Baby, c.1915, 24 In. 1650.00
Kestner, 221, Bisque Socket Head, Blue Googly Eyes, c.1912, 16 In. 10750.00
Kestner, 221, Bisque Socket Head, Glass Googly Eyes, 14 In. 2400.00
Kestner, 234, Bisque Shoulder Head, Glass Sleep Eyes, Composition, Baby, c.1915, 13 In. 800.00
Kestner, 237, Hilda, Bisque Socket Head, Brown Sleep Eyes, Two Teeth, Hair, 16 In. 1800.00
Kestner, 241, Bisque, Brown Sleep Eyes, Blond Mohair Curls, 4 Teeth, Jointed, 23 In. . . . 2750.00
Kestner, 243, Bisque Socket Head, Brown Glass Sleep Eyes, Chinese Baby, c.1912, 13 In. 4400.00
Kestner, 243, Bisque Socket Head, Sleep Eyes, 2 Teeth, Chinese Baby, c.1914, 13 In. 5250.00
Kestner, 247, Bisque Socket Head, Sleep Eyes, 2 Teeth, Mohair, Baby, 15 1/2 In. 500.00
Kestner, 257, Bisque Head, Sleep Eyes, Open Mouth, Blond Wool Wig, Baby, 20 In. 900.00
Kestner, 257, Bisque Socket Head, Brown Glass Sleep Eyes, White Gown, c.1915, 22 In. . 1050.00
Kestner, 257, Bisque Socket Head, Sleep Eyes, 2 Teeth, Hair, Composition, 25 In. 900.00

**Do not wash or restyle
the hair on an old doll.
It lowers the value. Never
use your hairbrush on
your doll. Your hair oils
will harm the doll's wig.
Dolls should have their
own brushes.**

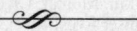

Doll, Kestner, 257, Bisque
Socket Head, Upper Teeth,
Composition Body, Baby, 25 In.

Doll, Kestner, Bisque Head,
Upper Teeth, Blue Sleep Eyes,
Jointed Body, 8 1/4 In.

Kestner, 257, Bisque Socket Head, Sleep Eyes, Open Mouth, 2 Teeth, 17 In. 300.00
Kestner, 257, Bisque Socket Head, Upper Teeth, Composition Body, Baby, 25 In. . . . *Illus* 900.00
Kestner, 260, Bisque Socket Head, Blue Glass Sleep Eyes, Open Mouth, c.1912, 16 In. . . 1100.00
Kestner, 260, Bisque Socket Head, Sleep Eyes, 4 Teeth, Hair, Composition, 24 In. 650.00
Kestner, Baby Jean, Bisque Socket Head, Blue Sleep Eyes, 2 Teeth, Composition, 13 In. . 300.00
Kestner, Bisque Domed Head, Wide Open Mouth, Pouty, Bonnet, c.1921, 13 In. 1300.00
Kestner, Bisque Head, Blue Glass Sleep Eyes, Closed Pouty Mouth, Rose Cheeks, 24 In. . 3175.00
Kestner, Bisque Head, Brown Eyes, Open Mouth, 4 Teeth, Blond Wig, 14 1/2 In. 382.00
Kestner, Bisque Head, Sleep Eyes, Open Mouth, Teeth, Composition Body, c.1890, 10 In. 705.00
Kestner, Bisque Head, Upper Teeth, Blue Sleep Eyes, Jointed Body, 8 1/4 In. . . . . . . *Illus* 450.00
Kestner, Bisque Shoulder Head, Closed Mouth, Set Eyes, Human Hair, c.1890, 20 In. . . . 235.00
Kestner, Bisque Shoulder Head, Sleep Eyes, 4 Teeth, Hair, Pink Dress, 27 1/2 In. 500.00
Kestner, Bisque Shoulder Head, Sleep Eyes, Blond Hair, 2 Teeth, Chemise, 17 In. 500.00
Kestner, Bisque Socket Head, Blue Eyes, Closed Mouth, Wig, 24 In. 520.00
Kestner, Bisque Socket Head, Brown Eyes, Closed Mouth, Jointed Body, 30 In. 950.00
Kestner, Bisque Socket Head, Brown Glass Eyes, Pink Sweater, Germany, 42 In. 4255.00
Kestner, Bisque Socket Head, Brown Sleep Eyes, Open Mouth, Teeth, Blond Wig, 19 In. . 380.00
Kestner, Bisque Socket Head, Googly Eyes, Blond Hair, Jointed Body, 11 In. 7750.00
Kestner, Bisque Socket Head, Painted Blue Eyes, Open-Close Mouth, Baby, 11 In. 225.00
Kestner, Bisque Socket Head, Painted, Blond, Sleep Eyes, 2 Teeth, Baby, c.1915, 24 In. . 1600.00
Kestner, Bisque Socket Head, Set Eyes, 4 Teeth, Mohair, Composition, Child, 17 In. 350.00
Kestner, Bisque Socket Head, Sleep Eyes, Open Mouth, 4 Teeth, Hair Wig, 21 1/2 In. . . . 400.00
Kestner, Bisque Swivel Head, Blue Glass Sleep Eyes, Closed Mouth, c.1915, 10 In. 1050.00
Kestner, Bisque Swivel Head, Brown Glass Eyes, c.1890, 9 In. 2300.00
Kestner, Bisque Swivel Head, Glass Enamel Eyes, 3 Teeth, Peg-Jointed, c.1890, 8 1/2 In. 3800.00
Kestner, Bisque Swivel Head, Glass Inset Eyes, Peg-Jointed Arms, Legs, c.1885, 6 In. . . 4400.00
Kestner, Bisque Swivel Head, Gray Glass Inset Eyes, 3 Teeth, Yellow Boots, c.1885, 8 In. 2300.00
Kestner, Bisque, Brown Glass Inset Eyes, Closed Mouth, Lace Dress, Box, c.1890, 7 In. . 1600.00
Kestner, Bisque, Brown Glass Sleep Eyes, 4 Teeth, Brown Mohair Wig, c.1900, 11 In. . . . 1200.00
Kestner, Bisque, Brown Glass Sleep Eyes, Open Mouth, Teeth, c.1910, 11 In. 1050.00
Kestner, Bisque, Glass Sleep Eyes, Open Mouth, 4 Teeth, c.1910, 11 In. 1550.00
Kestner, Bisque, Gray Glass Sleep Eyes, Auburn Mohair Wig, Yellow Boots, c.1885, 9 In. 2800.00
Kestner, Gibson Girl, Bisque Shoulder Head, Blue Glass Inset Eyes, c.1910, 20 In. 1800.00
Kestner, Gibson Girl, Bisque Shoulder Head, Brown Glass Sleep Eyes, c.1900, 21 In. . . . 1800.00
Kestner, Hilda, Bisque Socket Head, Domed, Blue Glass Sleep Eyes, Teeth, c.1915, 14 In. 1850.00
Kestner, Hilda, Bisque Socket Head, Glass Sleep Eyes, 2 Upper Teeth, c.1914, 16 In. . . . 2600.00
Kestner, Lady, Bisque Swivel Head, Brown Sleep Eyes, Lamb's-Wool Wig, 14 In. 3800.00
Kewpie dolls are listed in the Kewpie category.
Kley & Hahn, 161, Bisque Socket Head, Brown Glass Sleep Eyes, Crier, c.1912, 11 In. . . . 425.00
Kley & Hahn, 548, Bisque Socket Head, Painted Features, Closed Mouth, c.1912, 21 In. . . 1600.00
Kley & Hahn, Bisque Head, Sleep Eyes, Open Mouth, Human Hair Wig, Walkure, 31 In . . 550.00
Klumpe, Felt, Woman Doing Needlepoint, c.1940, 11 In. 375.00
Knickerbocker, Bozo The Clown, Vinyl Head, Yellow Feet, 1973, 11 In. 35.00
Konig & Wernicke, Bisque, Blue Flirty Eyes, Mohair Bob, Bent-Limb Body, Baby, 22 In. 750.00
Krahmer, Boy & Girl, Carved Wood Head, Painted, Tyrolean Costume, c.1970, 14 In. . . . 400.00
Lambert, Bisque Head, Glass Paperweight Inset Eyes, Mechanical, Music, c.1890, 20 In. . 12000.00
Lenci, 109/76, Felt Swivel Head, Painted Features, Black Dress, Box, c.1928, 23 In. 1800.00
Lenci, 300/45, Scottish Boy, Felt Swivel Head, Painted Features, Pipe, c.1928, 17 In. . . . 2300.00
Lenci, 300/45, Scottish Girl, Felt Swivel Head, Painted Features, Cap, c.1928, 17 In. 1800.00
Lenci, 563, Bellhop, Felt Swivel Head, Blue Googly Eyes, Blue Uniform, 22 In. 2500.00
Lenci, Bride, Swivel Head, Googly Eyes, Blond Curls, Ruffled Gown, 17 1/2 In. 4000.00
Lenci, Felt Swivel Head, Brown Googly Eyes, Mohair, Cloth Torso, Black Dress, 19 In. . . 300.00
Lenci, Felt Swivel Head, Googly Eyes, Painted Features, Closed Mouth, c.1930, 27 In. . . . 600.00
Lenci, Girl, Black Felt Swivel Head, Braids, Grass Skirt, Duck, c.1920, 15 In. 2500.00
Lenci, Girl, Black Felt Swivel Head, Googly Eyes, Red Dress, c.1928, 19 In. 1600.00
Lenci, Girl, Felt Swivel Head, Blue Eyes, Closed Mouth, Mohair, Ball, 14 In. 1000.00
Lenci, Girl, Felt Swivel Head, Blue Shaded Eyes, Green Coat, Fur Trim, c.1935, 16 In. . . . 900.00
Lenci, Girl, Felt Swivel Head, Brown Eyes To Side, Mohair, Organdy Dress, 16 In. 600.00
Lenci, Girl, Felt Swivel Head, Brown Googly Eyes, Closed Mouth, Mohair, 18 In. 300.00
Lenci, Girl, Felt Swivel Head, Dark Skin, Mohair, Cloth Body, Jointed, 10 1/2 In. 275.00
Lenci, Girl, Felt Swivel Head, Glass Inset Eyes, Black Gown, Dog, c.1932, 20 In. 3300.00
Lenci, Girl, Felt Swivel Head, Gray Googly Eyes, Organdy Dress, c.1935, 24 In. 2200.00
Lenci, Girl, Felt Swivel Head, Painted Features, Mohair, Cloth Torso, Oriental, 14 In. . . . 1200.00

Lenci, Girl, Felt Swivel Head, Painted Features, Taffeta Dress, Yellow Hat, c.1938, 14 In. . 1400.00
Lenci, Girl, Felt, Swivel Head, Googly Eyes, Pouty, Pink Dress, Shoes, c.1935, 17 In. . . . 1500.00
Lenci, Groom, Felt Swivel Head, Googly Eyes, Closed Mouth, 17 1/2 In. 3800.00
Lenci, Marlene Dietrich, Green Dress, Sitting On Stool, Box, c.1930, 30 In. 10500.00
Lenci, Orphan Annie, Felt Swivel Head, Brown Eyes, Mohair, Cloth Torso, Box, 12 In. . . 500.00
Lenci, Pepito, Felt Swivel Head, Brown Googly Eyes, Green Jacket, c.1927, 17 In. 1800.00
Lenci-Type, Spanish Dancer, Felt Head, Painted Eyes, Floss Hair, Italy, 1930s, 28 In. 325.00
Madame Alexander, Alice In Wonderland, Hard Plastic, Mohair Wig, 1950s, 18 In. 100.00
Madame Alexander, Baby Jane, Composition Head, Brown Eyes, Brown Mohair, 16 In. . . 900.00
Madame Alexander, Bride, Plastic Socket Head, Brown Sleep Eyes, Box, c.1955, 14 In. . . 700.00
Madame Alexander, Bride, Sleep Eyes, Composition, Ivory Gown, Veil, 1935, 21 In. 4300.00
Madame Alexander, Cissy, Hard Plastic, Vinyl Arms, Jointed Knees, c.1959, 20 In. 365.00
Madame Alexander, David Copperfield, Molded Felt Face, Blond, Red Hat, 1930s, 16 In. 310.00
Madame Alexander, Jacqueline, Vinyl Head, Brown Sleep Eyes, 1962, 21 In. 475.00
Madame Alexander, Little Women, Plastic, Boxes, c.1972, 8 In., 5 Piece 230.00
Madame Alexander, Madeline, Composition, Sleep Eyes, Human Hair, 1940, 11 In. 175.00
Madame Alexander, Maggie, Plastic Head, Blue Sleep Eyes, Closed Mouth, 14 In. 2250.00
Madame Alexander, McGuffrey Ana, Composition Head, Sleep Eyes, Human Hair, 13 In. 325.00
Madame Alexander, Miss Scarlett, Black Hair, Blue Eyes, 1937, 21 In. 1200.00
Madame Alexander, Princess Elizabeth, Blond Mohair Wig, Sleep Eyes, 1937, 16 In. 400.00
Madame Alexander, Queen, Composition Socket Head, Tiara, Banner, c.1935, 21 In. 3100.00
Madame Alexander, Romeo & Juliet, Sleep Eyes, Court Dress, 1955, 8 In. 1050.00
Madame Alexander, Sonja Henie, Brown Sleep Eyes, 6 Teeth, Hair, Composition, 17 In. . 500.00
Madame Alexander, Sonja Henie, Composition Head, Brown Sleep Eyes, 6 Teeth, 21 In. . 600.00
Madame Alexander, Sonja Henie, Composition, Dress In Ice Skating Outfit, 1939, 21 In. . 900.00
Madame Alexander, Susie Q & Bobby Q, Cloth Face, c.1940, 15 In. 3000.00
Madame Alexander, Sweet Violet, Plastic Head, 1954, 18 In. 1700.00
Marionette, Composition, Wood, Elderly Woman, Brown Dress, 20 In. 58.00
Mascotte, Bisque Socket Head, Paperweight Inset Eyes, Crier, Bebe, c.1890, 24 In. 3100.00
Mattel, Barbie, American Girl, Blond, Beige Lips, Jumpsuit, Shoes 450.00
Mattel, Barbie, American Girl, Blond, Peach Lips, Swimsuit 350.00
Mattel, Barbie, American Girl, Brunette, Beige Lips, Nostril Paint, Swimsuit 400.00
Mattel, Barbie, American Girl, Brunette, Coral Lips, Cheek Blush, Jumpsuit, Box 1500.00
Mattel, Barbie, American Girl, Brunette, Long, Peach Lips 750.00
Mattel, Barbie, American Girl, Brunette, Pink Lips, Cheek Blush, Swimsuit 875.00
Mattel, Barbie, American Girl, Brunette, Red Flowered Kimono, Gold Obi, Purse . . . *Illus* 2333.00
Mattel, Barbie, American Girl, Brunette, Side Part, Peach Lips, Swimsuit 600.00
Mattel, Barbie, American Girl, Brunette, Tan Lips, Knit Dress, Fringe, Belt 300.00
Mattel, Barbie, American Girl, Light Blond, Beige Lips, Nostril Paint 375.00
Mattel, Barbie, American Girl, Light Blond, Peach Lips, Sleeveless Dress 450.00
Mattel, Barbie, American Girl, Light Blond, Peach Lips, Swimsuit 425.00
Mattel, Barbie, American Girl, Medium Blond, Ribbon, Pink Lips, Nostril Paint, Japan . . 1750.00
Mattel, Barbie, American Girl, Titian Hair, Gold Lips, Dress, Red Bodice, Blue Skirt 475.00
Mattel, Barbie, American Girl, Titian Hair, Pink Lips, White Outline, Nostril Paint, Box . . 375.00
Mattel, Barbie, Bubble Cut, Blond, Coral Lips, Nostril Paint, Sheath With Button Accents 105.00
Mattel, Barbie, Bubble Cut, Brunette, Peach Lips, Black, White Swimsuit 95.00
Mattel, Barbie, Bubble Cut, Brunette, Pink Lips, Red Swimsuit, Shoes, Earrings, Box . . . 325.00

Doll, Mattel, Barbie, American Girl, Brunette,
Red Flowered Kimono, Gold Obi, Purse

Doll, Mattel, Barbie, Bubble Cut, Brunette,
Red & Gold Evening Sheath, Accessories

Doll, Mattel, Francie, Brunette, Blue Kimono,
Gold Lame Obi, Purse, Japan

Doll, Mattel, Francie, Brunette, Red Flowered
Kimono, Gold Lame Obi, Japan

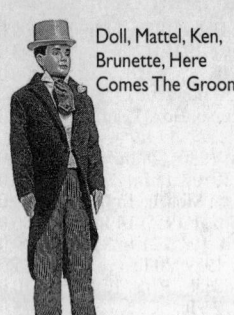

Doll, Mattel, Ken,
Brunette, Here
Comes The Groom

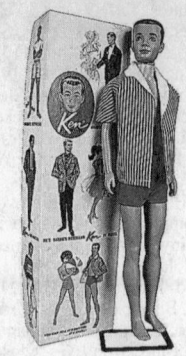

Doll, Mattel, Ken,
Brunette, Painted Hair,
Red & White Striped
Jacket, Red Swim
Trunks, Box

Doll, Mattel, Ken,
Play It Cool,
Brunette, Painted
Hair, Bendable Legs

Mattel, Barbie, Bubble Cut, Brunette, Red & Gold Evening Sheath, Accessories .... *Illus*   3590.00
Mattel, Barbie, Bubble Cut, Brunette, Red Lips, Nostril Paint, Silk Sheath Dress, Shoes ..   350.00
Mattel, Barbie, Bubble Cut, Brunette, Red Lips, Striped Swimsuit, Shoes, Box 30.00
Mattel, Barbie, Bubble Cut, Light Blond, Pink Lips, Red Dress With Bow, Print Skirt ...   125.00
Mattel, Barbie, Bubble Cut, Titian Hair, Red Lips, One-Piece Outfit, Shoes, Stand, Box ..   149.00
Mattel, Barbie, Bubble Cut, Wheat Blond, Coral Lips, Red Playsuit, Gathered Skirt 115.00
Mattel, Barbie, Color Magic, Yellow Hair, Pink Lips, Cheek Blush ....225.00 to 400.00
Mattel, Barbie, Designer, Gold, Bob Mackie, Box, 1990 ....   220.00
Mattel, Barbie, Empress Bride, Bob Mackie, Box, 1992 ....   310.00
Mattel, Barbie, Fashion Queen, Brown Hair, Sunglasses, Black Carrying Case, 1963 ....   340.00
Mattel, Barbie, Gay Parisienne, Porcelain, Box, 1991 ....   150.00
Mattel, Barbie, Happy Holidays, Box, 1988 ....   105.00
Mattel, Barbie, Hiromichi Nakano, Ponytail, Brunette, Pink Lips, Japanese Market, 1985 .   425.00
Mattel, Barbie, Nighty Negligee, Pink Nightgown, Robe, Slippers, Stuffed Dog, 1959 ...   280.00
Mattel, Barbie, Pink Jubilee, Box, 1989 ....   130.00
Mattel, Barbie, Plantation Belle, Porcelain, Box, 1991 ....   125.00
Mattel, Barbie, Platinum, Bob Mackie, Box, 1991 ....   230.00
Mattel, Barbie, Ponytail, Brunette, Blue Eyes, Kimono, Shoes, Gloves, 1962 ....   550.00
Mattel, Barbie, Ponytail, Brunette, Red Lips, Swimsuit, Shoes, Rimmed Glasses, 1960 ...   600.00
Mattel, Barbie, Ponytail, Swirl, Blond, Pink Lips, Shirt, Scarf, Skirt, Shoes, Gloves, Purse   500.00
Mattel, Barbie, Ponytail, Swirl, Titian Hair, Coral Lips, Stand, Booklet, Box 550.00
Mattel, Barbie, Ponytail, Yellow Blond, Pink Lips, Pajamas, Alarm Clock 275.00
Mattel, Barbie, Royal Splendor, Presidential Series, Porcelain, Box, 1993 ....   70.00
Mattel, Barbie, Starlight Splendor, Bob Mackie, Box, 1991 ....   180.00
Mattel, Barbie, Swan Lake, Box, 1991 ....   90.00
Mattel, Barbie, Talking, Brunette, Orange Lips, Cheek Blush, Purple Print Skirt, Shirt ...   155.00
Mattel, Barbie, Talking, Brunette, Pink Lips, Cheek Blush, Swimsuit, Lace Jacket, Box ..   195.00
Mattel, Barbie, Twist 'n Turn, Blond, Pink Lips, Cheek Blush, Swimsuit, Vinyl Top, Box .   285.00
Mattel, Barbie, Twist 'n Turn, Brunette Hair, Pink Lips, Cheek Blush, Swimsuit 75.00
Mattel, Brad, Painted Black Hair, Beige Lips, Shirt, Shorts, Box 325.00
Mattel, Brad, Talking, Painted Black Hair, Brown Lips, Shorts, Print Top, Vinyl Trim 155.00
Mattel, Casey, Baggie, Blond, Peach Lips, Cheek Blush, 2-Piece Swimsuit, Package 115.00
Mattel, Casey, Baggie, Blond, Peach Lips, Cheek Blush, Fuchsia Swimsuit, Package 165.00
Mattel, Chatty Cathy, Vinyl, Blue Sleep Eyes, Rooted Hair, Talks, Box, 1962, 20 In. 350.00
Mattel, Christie, Malibu, Black Hair, Light Beige Lips, Yellow Swimsuit, Box 115.00
Mattel, Francie, Brunette, Blue Kimono, Gold Lame Obi, Purse, Japan ....*Illus*   1528.00
Mattel, Francie, Brunette, Pink Lips, Cheek Blush, Dress, Print Top, Pleated Skirt 75.00
Mattel, Francie, Brunette, Red Flowered Kimono, Gold Lame Obi, Japan ....*Illus*   1469.00
Mattel, Francie, Malibu, Blond, Sunglasses, Head Cover, Peach Lips, Painted Teeth 115.00
Mattel, Francis, Blond, Pink Lips, Cheek Blush, Wrist Tag, Red Pumps, Booklet, Box ...   400.00
Mattel, Ken, Baggie, Talking, Painted Brown Hair, Peach Lips, Painted Teeth, Package ...   90.00
Mattel, Ken, Blond, Flocked Hair, Beige Lips, White Jacket, Pants, Ribbon, Shoes, Socks   320.00
Mattel, Ken, Blond, Peach Lips, Red Football Jersey & Pants, Helmet, Cleats 45.00
Mattel, Ken, Brunette, Flocked Hair, Beige Lips, Red Shorts, Cork Sandals, Towel, Box .   185.00
Mattel, Ken, Brunette, Flocked Hair, Tennis Outfit, Socks, Shoes, Tennis Racquet, Balls .   105.00

Mattel, Ken, Brunette, Here Comes The Groom . . . . *Illus*	863.00
Mattel, Ken, Brunette, Painted Hair, Peach Lips, Molded Teeth, Felt Coat, Sweater, Pants	110.00
Mattel, Ken, Brunette, Painted Hair, Peach Lips, Sleeper Set, Alarm Clock, Glass Of Milk	45.00
Mattel, Ken, Brunette, Painted Hair, Red, White Striped Jacket, Red Swim Trunks, Box *Illus*	85.00
Mattel, Ken, Play It Cool, Brunette, Painted Hair, Bendable Legs . . . . *Illus*	125.00
Mattel, Ken, Prince, Green Cape, Diamond Buttons, Tights, 1964	325.00
Mattel, Ken, Talking, Brunette, Painted Hair, Pink Lips, Painted Teeth, Box	155.00
Mattel, Midge, Blond, Pink Lips, Party Dress, Shoes, Gloves	85.00
Mattel, Midge, Blond, Pink Lips, Sleeveless Shirt, Bolero Jacket, Wrap Skirt, Hat, Bow . .	85.00
Mattel, Midge, Brunette, Painted Hair, Pink Lips, Vinyl Band, Japanese Market	300.00
Mattel, Midge, Brunette, Pink Lips, Dress, Lace Trim, Corset, Knee Socks, Shoes, Basket	130.00
Mattel, Midge, Brunette, Pink Lips, Ribbon Band, Swimsuit	155.00
Mattel, Midge, Titian Hair, Pink Lips, Striped Swimsuit	265.00
Mattel, Mrs. Beasley, Vinyl Head, Blue Eyes, Glasses, Talks, Box, 20 In.	550.00
Mattel, P.J., Baggie, Talking, Blond, Bead Accents, Sunglasses, Pink Lips, Cheek Blush . .	175.00
Mattel, P.J., Blond, Pink Lips, Cheek Blush, Print Dress, Shorts, Head Cover, Shoes, Box	235.00
Mattel, P.J., Talking, Blond, Bead Accents, Head Cover, Sunglasses, Pink Lips, Blush . . .	95.00
Mattel, Ricky, Painted Red Hair, Light Tan Lips, Striped Jacket, Black Pants, Shoes	65.00
Mattel, Ricky, Painted Red Hair, Pink Lips, Striped Jacket, Blue Shorts, Booklet, Box .	70.00
Mattel, Skipper, Blond, Headband, Pink Lips, Clam-Digger Pants, Shoes, Sun Visor	105.00
Mattel, Skipper, Blond, Metal Hairband, Pink Lips, One-Piece Swimsuit, Wrist Tag, Box .	250.00
Mattel, Skipper, Blond, Pink Lips, One-Piece Red Swimsuit, White	65.00
Mattel, Skipper, Drizzle Sizzle, Titian Hair, Knit Dress, Raincoat, Boots	105.00
Mattel, Skipper, School Days, Blond Hair, Sweater, Pleated Skirt	175.00
Mattel, Skipper, Titian Hair, Pink Lips, Bodysuit, Velveteen Skirt, Fur Hat, Pompon, Muff	65.00
Mattel, Skooter, Brunette, Pink Lips, Cheek Blush, Hair Ribbons, Dress, Shoes, Gloves . .	70.00
Mattel, Stacey, Talking, Blond, Pink Lips, Painted Teeth, Hair Ribbons, 2-Piece Knit Suit	175.00
Mattel, Steffie, Walk Lively, Brunette, Light Peach Lips, Cheek Blush, Jumpsuit, Shoes . .	105.00
Mattel, Twiggy, Blond, Pink Lips, Painted Teeth, Striped Knit Dress, Yellow Boots	150.00
Minerva, Metal Head, Blue Painted Eyes, Painted Hair, 23 In.	118.00
Ming Ming Baby, Composition, Painted Facial Features, 20th Century, 10 In.	15.00
Mommy To Be, Blond, Pregnant, Box, 11 In.	66.00
Moon Mullins, Hat, Paint, Wood, Jointed, c.1938, 6 In.	175.00
Moon Mullins, Wood, Jointed, c.1930, 5 1/2 In.	65.00
Morimura, Bisque Head, Blue Sleep Eyes, Composition, Bent Limb, Baby, 9 In.	60.00
Motschmann Baby, Papier-Mache, Black Pupilless Eyes, Closed Smiling Mouth, 11 In. . .	645.00
Nancy Ann Storybook, Polly Put The Kettle On, Bisque, Painted Eyes, 1941, 5 1/2 In. . . .	55.00
Nancy Ann Storybook, Pretty Maid, Where Have You Been, Bisque, 5 In.	110.00
Norah Wellings, Felt Face, Glass Eyes, Mohair Wig, Cloth Body, Child, 1920s, 19 In. . . .	250.00
Orsini, Bisque, Laughing Expression, Brown Glass Sleep Eyes, Girl, c.1919, 5 In.	600.00
Paper dolls are listed in their own category.	
Papier-Mache, Black Painted Hair, Stuffed Body, Leather Arms, Late 1800s, 30 In.	210.00
Papier-Mache, Black, Shoulder Head, Black Painted Eyes, Closed Mouth, c.1870, 24 In. . .	150.00
Papier-Mache, Black, Shoulder Head, Painted Eyes, Closed Mouth, Child, 23 In.	175.00
Papier-Mache, Clown, Socket Head, Glass Eyes, Teeth, France, c.1900, 16 In.	950.00
Papier-Mache, Puss In Boots, Socket Head, Googly, Boots, France, c.1900, 18 In.	1900.00
Papier-Mache, Shoulder Head, Black Molded Hair, Painted Eyes, c.1850, 9 In.	120.00
Papier-Mache, Shoulder Head, Black Painted Eyes, Closed Mouth, Painted Hair, 28 In. . .	1880.00
Papier-Mache, Shoulder Head, Blue Eyes, Closed Mouth, Brown Wig, 28 In.	175.00
Papier-Mache, Shoulder Head, Blue Eyes, Kid Body, Mitten Hands, France, 1845, 15 In. . .	1100.00
Papier-Mache, Shoulder Head, Blue Eyes, Open Mouth, Teeth, Blond Wig, 22 In.	295.00
Papier-Mache, Shoulder Head, Blue Painted Eyes, Black Braided Bun, 22 In.	1058.00
Papier-Mache, Shoulder Head, Blue Painted Eyes, Black Molded Hair, c.1840, 15 In.	411.00
Papier-Mache, Shoulder Head, Blue Painted Eyes, Closed Mouth, Blond, c.1870, 27 In. . .	150.00
Papier-Mache, Shoulder Head, Blue Painted Eyes, Closed Mouth, c.1840, 21 1/2 In.	645.00
Papier-Mache, Shoulder Head, Blue Painted Eyes, Molded Black Hair, c.1825, 11 In.	940.00
Papier-Mache, Shoulder Head, Blue Sleep Eyes, Smiling Mouth, 2 Teeth, 28 In.	176.00
Papier-Mache, Shoulder Head, Brown Eyes, Closed Mouth, Blond Mohair Wig, 32 In. . . .	120.00
Papier-Mache, Shoulder Head, Brown Painted Eyes, Closed Mouth, Black Hair, 25 In. . . .	150.00
Papier-Mache, Shoulder Head, Double Chin, Painted Features, c.1840, 14 In.	1300.00
Papier-Mache, Shoulder Head, Moving Mouth, Cobalt Blue Eyes, Mohair Wig, 19 In. . . .	90.00
Papier-Mache, Shoulder Head, Painted Eyebrows, Closed Mouth, c.1840, 21 In.	705.00
Papier-Mache, Shoulder Head, Painted Eyes, Kid Body, Wood Limbs, c.1850, 9 1/2 In. . .	470.00

Papier-Mache, Shoulder Head, Sculpted Black Hair, Antique Costume, Germany, 11 In. . . . 1100.00
Papier-Mache, St. Nicholas, Painted, Silver Hooded Cape, France, c.1900, 19 In. 650.00
Papier-Mache Head, Applied Mustache, Human Hair, 5 Finger, Chinese, c.1900, 18 In. . . 280.00
Parian, Blond Molded Hair, Blue & Gold Tiara, Dotted-Swiss Dress, 24 In. 1900.00
Parian, Swivel Head, Blond Molded Curls, Pin-Tucked Dress, 14 1/2 In. 3600.00
Petit Et Dumontier, Bisque Socket Head, Blue Glass Threaded Eyes, c.1880, 16 In. 10500.00
Pierotti, Wax Shoulder Head, Glass Eyes, Cloth Body, Wax Arms & Legs, c.1870, 19 In. . 1050.00
Pincushion dolls are listed in their own category.
Poulbot, Boy & Girl, Composition, Painted Features, Smiling, Mechanical, c.1910, 14 In. 1600.00
Punch, Clothes, Stuffed, Skullcap, Velvet Boots, Victorian 385.00
Puppet, Cat, Kater, Black, Missing Tag & Button, Steiff 190.00
Puppet, Hand, Koko The Clown, Vinyl, Cloth, Gund Mfg., 1962, 11 In. 25.00
Puppet, Hand, Smokey The Bear, Vinyl, Cloth, Ideal Toy Corp., c.1960, 9 In. 25.00
Puppet, Katze, Button In Ear, Missing Chest Tag, Steiff 190.00
Puppet, Ronald McDonald, Astronaut Helmet, Vinyl, c.1970, 9 1/2 x 13 1/4 In. 12.00
Puppet, Speedy Gonzalez, Hand, Vinyl, Warner Bros.-Seven Arts, Japan, c.1970, 9 1/2 In. 15.00
Puppet, Wendy, Vinyl, Cloth, Harvey Famous Cartoons, c.1960, 10 1/2 x 10 In. 20.00
Rabery & Delphieu, Bisque Socket Head, Composition, Wood, c.1885, 28 In. 2500.00
Raggedy Ann, Stitched Facial Features, Yarn Hair, Dress, Straw Bonnet, Slippers, 26 In. . 60.00
Raggedy Ann & Andy, Cloth, Bean Bag, Red Mop Hair, Knickerbocker, 1971, 10 In. 510.00
Raynal, Fashion, Felt Swivel Head, Googly Eyes, Alsatian Costume, Box, c.1928, 17 In. . 1300.00
Revalo, Bisque Socket Head, Blue Eyes, Old Sailor Suit, 20 1/2 In. 402.00
Roullet & Decamps, Bisque Socket Head, Closed Mouth, Wind-Up Walker, 14 In. 1000.00
Roullet & Decamps, Bisque, Socket Head, Bebe, Walker, c.1895, 22 In. 2600.00
Rubber, Shoulder Head, Black Pupilless Eyes, Closed Smiling Mouth, 19 In. 2820.00
Rubber, Swivel Head, Blue Eyes, Blond Mohair, Dutch Outfit, 21 In. 425.00
S & H dolls are also listed here as Bergmann and Simon & Halbig.
S & H, 1079, Bisque Head, Sleep Eyes, Open Mouth, Human Hair Wig, 30 In. 600.00
S.F.B.J, Bisque Socket Head, Brown Complexion, Mohair Wig, Bebe, c.1910, 13 In. 1500.00
S.F.B.J., 60, Bisque Head, Sleep Eyes, Open Mouth, Mohair Wig, 13 1/2 In. 325.00
S.F.B.J., 226, Bisque Head, Domed, Brown Eyes, Brown Painted Curls, Baby, 17 In. 1100.00
S.F.B.J., 236, Bisque Head, Sleep Eyes, Open-Closed Mouth, Human Hair, Toddler, 20 In. . 550.00
S.F.B.J., 236, Bisque Socket Head, Blue Sleep Eyes, 2 Teeth, Composition, 27 In. 650.00
S.F.B.J., 237, Bisque Socket Head, Glass Jewel Eyes, Scottish Costume, c.1912, 18 In. . . . 3200.00
S.F.B.J., 245, Bisque Socket Head, Googly Eyes, Mohair Wig, c.1912, 8 In. 4200.00
S.F.B.J., 247, Bisque Socket Head, Blue Glass Sleep Eyes, 2 Upper Teeth, c.1915, 20 In. . . 1800.00
S.F.B.J., 247, Bisque Socket Head, Glass Inset Eyes, 2 Beaded Teeth, c.1915, 7 In. 2900.00
S.F.B.J., 247, Bisque Socket Head, Glass Sleep Eyes, Mohair Wig, Box, c.1912, 13 In. . . . 3000.00
S.F.B.J., 252, Bisque Socket Head, Blue Glass Sleep Eyes, Closed Mouth, c.1912, 12 In. . . 3200.00
S.F.B.J., 301, Bisque Socket Head, Blue Glass Sleep Eyes, Harlequin, Box, c.1920, 16 In. . 2000.00
S.F.B.J., 301, Bisque Socket Head, Sleep Eyes, Open Mouth, 4 Teeth, Mohair, 8 In. 650.00
S.F.B.J., Bisque Head, Brown, Black Eyes, Papier-Mache Body, 16 1/2 In. 500.00
S.F.B.J., Bisque Head, Set Eyes, Open Mouth, Synthetic Hair, 25 In. 750.00
S.F.B.J., Bisque Socket Head, Blue Sleep Eyes, Closed Mouth, Dimples, c.1915, 14 In. . . . 2000.00
S.F.B.J., Bisque Socket Head, Blue Sleep Eyes, Open Mouth, Jointed, Bebe, 9 1/2 In. 825.00
S.F.B.J., Bisque Socket Head, Open Mouth, 4 Teeth, Walker, Bebe, 20 In. 550.00
S.F.B.J., Bisque Socket Head, Pupilless Eyes, 6 Teeth, Hair, Composition, 26 In. 700.00
S.F.B.J., Bisque, Brown Sleep Eyes, Hair, Wool Suit, Leather Boots, 1890s, 14 In. 3885.00
S.F.B.J., Bleuette, Bisque Socket Head, Blue Glass Sleep Eyes, Nurse, c.1935, 11 1/2 In. . . 1900.00
S.F.B.J., Bleuette, Bisque Socket Head, Glass Inset Eyes, Mariner, c.1918, 11 In. 1800.00
S.F.B.J., Bleuette, Bisque Socket Head, Glass Sleep Eyes, Floral Dress, 1921, 11 In. 2300.00
S.F.B.J., Bleuette, Bisque Socket Head, Glass Sleep Eyes, Gingham Dress, 1924, 11 In. . . . 1900.00
S.F.B.J., Bleuette, Bisque Socket Head, Paperweight Eyes, Muslin Dress, c.1905, 11 In. . . . 3900.00
Sascha, Cloth Over Gypsum, Painted Eyes, Braided Human Hair Wig, Swiss Outfit, 20 In. 2000.00
Schmidt, 1285, Bisque Socket Head, Glass Sleep Eyes, 2 Teeth, Tongue, c.1918, 24 In. . . 1800.00
Schmidt, Bisque Head, Sleep Eyes, Pierced Nostrils, Upper Teeth, Toddler, c.1920, 10 In. 764.00
Schmidt, Bisque Socket Head, Baby, Blue Eyes, Open Mouth, 24 In. 2875.00
Schmidt, Bisque Socket Head, Brown Sleep Eyes, Open Mouth, Brown Wig, 62 In. 345.00
Schmitt & Fils, 2, Bisque Socket Head, Composition, Ball-Jointed, c.1882, 19 In. 9250.00
Schmitt & Fils, 4, Bisque Head, Gray Eyes, Spiral Threading, Human Hair, c.1880, 23 In. 19500.00
Schmitt & Fils, Bisque Head, Glass Eyes, Mohair Wig, Jointed, Bebe, 14 In. 9500.00
Schmitt & Fils, Bisque, Brown Glass Enamel Eyes, Blond, Dress, Bebe, c.1884, 16 In. 9000.00
Schoenau & Hoffmeister, Bisque Head, Cloth, Glass Eyes, Mideastern Clothes, 12 In. 115.00

Schoenhut, 101, Wood, Brown Eyes, White Dress, Poodle, c.1915, 14 In. 2800.00
Schoenhut, 301, Wood, Intaglio Eyes, Blond Mohair Wig, Blue Suit, c.1915, 16 In. 1000.00
Schoenhut, 405, Wood, Blue Intaglio Eyes, White Suit, Derby Hat, c.1912, 19 In. 2200.00
Schoenhut, Blue Intaglio Eyes, Closed Somber Mouth, Brown Wig, Child, 15 In. 264.00
Schoenhut, Blue Painted Eyes, Closed Mouth, Ash Blond Wig, Toddler, 11 1/2 In. 382.00
Schoenhut, Blue Painted Eyes, Closed Somber Mouth, Painted Hair, Baby, 17 In. 176.00
Schoenhut, Intaglio Eyes, Serious Mouth, Brown Wig, Child, 19 In. 150.00
Schoenhut, Wood Head, Blue Intaglio Eyes, 6 Teeth, Jointed, 16 In. 3300.00
Schoenhut, Wood Socket Head, Blue Intaglio Eyes, Mohair, Jointed Body, Girl, 22 In. . . . 1400.00
Schoenhut, Wood Socket Head, Blue Sleep Eyes, Mohair, Spring-Jointed, 16 In. 1700.00
Schoenhut, Wood Socket Head, Brown Intaglio Eyes, Mohair, Girl, Sailor Suit, 16 In. . . . 850.00
Schoenhut, Wood Socket Head, Intaglio Eyes, Jointed, Painted Bonnet, Girl, 16 In. 3700.00
Schoenhut, Wood, Carved Hair, Socket Head, Boy, c.1912, 16 In. 1500.00
Schoenhut, Wood, Intaglio Eyes, Mohair Wig, Sailor Suit, Straw Hat, Boy, 1910, 19 In. . . 106.00
Shirley Temple dolls are included in the Shirley Temple category.
Simon & Halbig dolls are also listed here under Bergmann and S & H.
Simon & Halbig, 4, Bisque Socket Head, Sleep Eyes, Open Mouth, Teeth, c.1900, 24 In. . 129.00
Simon & Halbig, 134, Black Composition, Brown Flirty Eyes, Open Mouth, 20 In. 199.00
Simon & Halbig, 540, Bisque Socket Head, Sleep Eyes, 4 Teeth, Mohair, 21 In. 575.00
Simon & Halbig, 719, Bisque Socket Head, Blue Glass Paperweight Inset Eyes, 22 In. 5000.00
Simon & Halbig, 886, Bisque Swivel Head, Brown Sleep Eyes, Open Mouth, c.1890, 9 In. 1300.00
Simon & Halbig, 886, Bisque, Brown Glass Inset Eyes, 2 Teeth, Blond, c.1885, 7 In. 1900.00
Simon & Halbig, 905, Bisque Head, Glass Inset Eyes, Scottish Costume, 1890, 13 In. 2300.00
Simon & Halbig, 949, Bisque Socket Head, Blue Glass Paperweight Inset Eyes, 34 In. 5200.00
Simon & Halbig, 949, Bisque, Brown Glass Paperweight Inset Eyes, 2 Teeth, 17 In. 1410.00
Simon & Halbig, 970, Bisque, Blue Glass Inset Eyes, Blond Mohair Wig, c.1890, 14 In. . . 1300.00
Simon & Halbig, 979, Bisque Socket Head, Blue Glass Paperweight Inset Eyes, 33 In. . . . 4600.00
Simon & Halbig, 1009, Bisque Socket Head, Brown Set Eyes, 4 Teeth, Wig, 25 In. 375.00
Simon & Halbig, 1009, Bisque Socket Head, Sleep Eyes, Open Mouth, Teeth, 11 1/2 In. . . 265.00
Simon & Halbig, 1009, Brown Bisque, Socket Head, Mohair Wig, 4 Teeth, 20 In. 900.00
Simon & Halbig, 1078, Bisque Socket Head, Blue Sleep Eyes, 4 Teeth, Mohair, 8 1/2 In. . 400.00
Simon & Halbig, 1078, Bisque Socket Head, Brown Set Eyes, 4 Teeth, Wig, 25 1/2 In. . . . 500.00
Simon & Halbig, 1078, Bisque Socket Head, Brown Sleep Eyes, 4 Teeth, Hair, 33 1/2 In. . 550.00
Simon & Halbig, 1079, Bisque Head, Blue Sleep Eyes, Open Mouth, Teeth, 26 1/2 In. . . . 410.00
Simon & Halbig, 1079, Bisque Head, Brown Sleep Eyes, 4 Teeth, Composition, 42 In. . . . 3900.00
Simon & Halbig, 1079, Bisque Head, Glass Inset Eyes, Spiral Threading, c.1890, 25 In. . . 1400.00
Simon & Halbig, 1079, Bisque Head, Sleep Eyes, Open Mouth, Mohair Wig, c.1910, 8 In. 235.00
Simon & Halbig, 1079, Bisque Socket Head, Blue Sleep Eyes, 4 Teeth, 21 In. 375.00
Simon & Halbig, 1080, Bisque Shoulder Head, Kid, Composition Body, c.1890, 20 In. . . . 450.00
Simon & Halbig, 1159, Bisque Head, Blue Glass Eyes, Open Mouth, Corset, 22 In. 1450.00
Simon & Halbig, 1159, Bisque Socket Head, Blue Glass Sleep Eyes, Teeth, c.1900, 18 In. 1800.00
Simon & Halbig, 1159, Bisque Socket Head, Glass Sleep Eyes, Trousseau, c.1900, 22 In. . 2100.00
Simon & Halbig, 1159, Bisque Socket Head, Set Eyes, 4 Teeth, Mohair, 18 In. 900.00
Simon & Halbig, 1199, Bisque, Amber, Sleep Eyes, Asian Features & Dress, Child, 12 In. 1200.00
Simon & Halbig, 1249, Bisque Socket Head, Gray Glass Sleep Eyes, Child, c.1895, 24 In. 1700.00
Simon & Halbig, 1249, Bisque Socket Head, Sleep Eyes, Blond, 4 Teeth, 19 1/2 In. 600.00
Simon & Halbig, 1279, Bisque Head, Sleep Eyes, Painted Features, 2 Teeth, 30 In. 2800.00
Simon & Halbig, 1279, Bisque Socket Head, Glass Sleep Eyes, 2 Teeth, c.1912, 26 In. . . . 2200.00
Simon & Halbig, 1279, Bisque Socket Head, Glass Sleep Eyes, 4 Teeth, c.1912, 32 In. . . . 3600.00
Simon & Halbig, 1299, Bisque Socket Head, Blue Sleep Eyes, 2 Teeth, Mohair, 20 In. . . . 1300.00
Simon & Halbig, 1301, Bisque Socket Head, Brown, Brown Glass Eyes, c.1910, 20 In. . . 33000.00
Simon & Halbig, 1303, Bisque Socket Head, Amber, Brown Glass Eyes, c.1900, 15 In. . . . 6750.00
Simon & Halbig, 1329, Bisque Head, Glass Eyes, Human Hair, Asian Child, c.1910, 21 In. 3525.00
Simon & Halbig, 1329, Bisque Socket Head, Sleep Eyes, Asian Child, c.1910, 14 In. 1700.00
Simon & Halbig, 1329, Bisque Socket Head, Sleep Eyes, Asian Child, 12 In. 1800.00
Simon & Halbig, 1358, Bisque Socket Head, Brown, Glass Sleep Eyes, c.1910, 22 In. . . . 9500.00
Simon & Halbig, 1358, Bisque Socket Head, Brown, Glass Sleep Eyes, Girl, 20 In. 9000.00
Simon & Halbig, 1368, Bisque Head, Brown, Glass Eyes, Teeth, Black Fleecy Hair, 14 In. 3800.00
Simon & Halbig, 1488, Bisque Socket Head, Composition, Wood-Jointed, c.1912, 20 In. 3000.00
Simon & Halbig, Bisque Head, Blue Eyes, Jointed Wood & Composition Body, 24 In. . . . 385.00
Simon & Halbig, Bisque Shoulder Head, Blue Glass Inset Eyes, Blond, c.1875, 13 In. . . . 1100.00
Simon & Halbig, Bisque Socket Head, Blue Sleep Eyes, 4 Teeth, Blond Hair, 23 1/2 In. . . 300.00
Simon & Halbig, Bisque Socket Head, Brown Eyes, Open Mouth, 17 In. 1035.00

Simon & Halbig, Bisque Socket Head, Brown Eyes, Open Mouth, 22 In. 402.00
Simon & Halbig, Bisque Socket Head, Brown Sleep Eyes, Open Mouth, 21 In. 605.00
Simon & Halbig, Bisque Socket Head, Brown, Brown Glass Sleep Eyes, c.1900, 15 In. . . . 1050.00
Simon & Halbig, Bisque Socket Head, Glass Sleep Eyes, Open Mouth, c.1914, 18 In. 1300.00
Simon & Halbig, Bisque Socket Head, Sleep Eyes, 4 Teeth, Mohair, Boy, 13 1/2 In. 250.00
Simon & Halbig, Bisque Socket Head, Sleep Eyes, Mohair Wig, Asian Child, c.1900, 5 In. 650.00
Sonneberg, 136, Bisque Swivel Head, Glass Enamel Inset Eyes, Child, c.1886, 13 In. 1200.00
Sonneberg, Bisque Socket Head, Amber, Brown Glass Eyes, Asian Child, 10 In. 1600.00
Sonneberg, Bisque Socket Head, Blue Glass Enamel Inset Eyes, c.1885, 8 In. 2100.00
Sonneberg, Bisque Socket Head, Blue Glass Inset Eyes, Closed Mouth, c.1888, 10 In. . . . 900.00
Steiff, Felt, Fat Policeman, Blue Uniform, c.1910, 14 In. 1470.00
Steiff, Felt, Swivel Head, Face Seam, Button Eyes, Blond Mohair, 14 In. 1500.00
Steiff, Policeman, Felt, Fat, Blue Uniform, c.1910, 14 In. 1470.00
Steiff, Professor, Felt, Pointy Nose, Elongated Limbs, Slender, c.1911, 16 In. 1850.00
Steiner, Bisque Head, Brown Eyes, Pierced Ears, Brown Wig, Bebe, 1890, 14 In. 2000.00
Steiner, Bisque Head, Brown Paperweight Eyes, Pierced Ears, Wig, Bebe, 1890, 14 In. . . 2000.00
Steiner, Bisque Head, Glass Paperweight Eyes, Teeth, Mechanical, Bebe, c.1890, 23 In. . . 4250.00
Steiner, Bisque Head, Sleep Eyes, Open Mouth, Composition, Wood Body, c.1910, 11 In. 206.00
Steiner, Bisque Shoulder Head, Gray Sleep Eyes, Teeth, Leather, Bisque Body, 24 In. . . . 250.00
Steiner, Bisque Socket Head, Blue Glass Inset Eyes, Closed Mouth, c.1890, 9 In. 3200.00
Steiner, Bisque Socket Head, Blue Glass Paperweight Eyes, Walker, Bebe, c.1890, 23 In. . 6250.00
Steiner, Bisque Socket Head, Brown, Amber Glass Inset Eyes, 4 Teeth, c.1890, 15 In. . . . 2900.00
Steiner, Bisque Socket Head, Brown, Brown Paperweight Eyes, Fleecy Wig, 15 In. 3600.00
Steiner, Bisque Socket Head, Glass Eyes, Closed Mouth, Series A, Bebe, c.1882, 24 In. . . 3600.00
Steiner, Bisque Socket Head, Glass Eyes, Closed Mouth, Series C, Bebe, c.1882, 24 In. . . 5750.00
Steiner, Bisque Socket Head, Glass Paperweight Eyes, Closed Mouth, c.1890, 11 In. 4300.00
Steiner, Bisque Socket Head, Glass Paperweight Eyes, Closed Mouth, c.1890, 24 In. 4500.00
Steiner, Bisque Socket Head, Paperweight Eyes, 12 Teeth, Hair, Jointed Body, 16 In. 1900.00
Steiner, Bisque Socket Head, Paperweight Eyes, Composition, Bebe, 19 In. 3250.00
Steiner, Bisque Socket Head, Sleep Eyes, Closed Mouth, Mohair Wig, Bebe, 16 In. 4000.00
Steiner, Bisque Socket Head, Threaded Eyes, Painted Features, Hair Wig, 10 1/4 In. 7500.00
Steiner, Bisque, Blue Glass Enamel Inset Eyes, Blond Mohair, Bebe, c.1870, 18 In. 4750.00
Steiner, Bisque, Blue Glass Paperweight Inset Eyes, Blond Mohair, c.1890, 8 In. 4000.00
Steiner, Bisque, Blue Glass Sleep Eyes, Blond Mohair, Series C, Bebe, c.1885, 21 In. . . . 6000.00
Terri Lee, Bride, Plastic Head, Brown Eyes, Closed Mouth, Blond, 16 In. 425.00
Terri Lee, Plastic Socket Head, Brown Curly Hair, Pouty Lips, Cowboy, c.1955, 16 In. . . . 850.00
Terri Lee, Plastic Socket Head, Brown Eyes, Full Lips, White Dress, Slip, c.1955, 16 In. . . 400.00
Terri Lee, Plastic, Brown Eyes, Wig, Jointed, Frontier Costume, 16 In. 575.00
Terri Lee, Plastic, Brown Eyes, Wig, Jointed, Heart Fund Costume, 16 In. 375.00
Terri Lee, Plastic, Painted Features, Skin Wig, Jointed, Box, 16 In. 600.00
Terri Lee, Plastic, Tea Party, Painted Features, Synthetic Wig, Jointed, Box, 16 In. 700.00
Thuillier, 11, Bisque Socket Head, Glass Paperweight Eyes, Closed Mouth, c.1888, 22 In. 15500.00
Thuillier, Bisque Socket Head, Glass Paperweight Inset Eyes, Bebe, c.1885, 16 In. 18500.00
Thuillier, Bisque Socket Head, Wooden Body, Silk Dress, Bebe, c.1882, 17 In. . . . . . *Illus* 33000.00
Vichy, Bisque Head, Standing On Tinplate, 3-Wheeled Base, Mechanical, c.1865, 11 In. . . 2700.00

**Use acne soap and water to clean a very
dirty bisque doll.**

**Don't clean a cloth doll's body with water:
use cornstarch or talc. Rub it into the fabric,
then gently brush it away after 4 hours.**

Doll, Thuillier, Bisque Socket
Head, Wooden Body, Silk
Dress, Bebe, c.1882, 17 In.

Vichy, Bisque, Wheeled Base, Moves In Circle, Waves Arms, c.1870, 10 In. 2750.00
Vogue, Ginny, Dutch Girl, Painted Lashes, Braids, Straight Leg, Wood Shoes, 1953, 7 In. . . 306.00
Vogue, Ginny, Hard Plastic, Painted Lashes, Elastic Strung, Straight Leg, c.1952, 7 1/2 In. 320.00
Vogue, Ginny, Kindergarten Afternoon Series, Blue Sleep Eyes, 1953, 8 In. 945.00
Vogue, Toodles, Composition, Mohair Wig, Painted Eyes, Original Clothes, 1937, 8 In. . . . 200.00
Walkure, 13, Bisque Head, Sleep Eyes, Open Mouth, Composition, Articulated, 25 In. . . . 212.00
Walkure, Bisque Socket Head, Blue Sleep Eyes, Ball-Jointed, Sailor Dress, 27 In. 575.00
Walkure, Bisque Socket Head, Brown Sleep Eyes, Open Mouth, Teeth, 22 1/2 In. 206.00
Wax, Dome Head, Painted Eyes, Perky Mouth, Composition Legs, c.1860, 6 In. 560.00
Wax, Fashion, Cobalt Glass Eyes, Closed Mouth, Blond Mohair Wig, 31 In. 1295.00
Wax, Over Composition, Cloth Stuffed Body, Leather Lower Arms, 19th Century, 12 In. . . 60.00
Wax, Over Composition, Shoulder Head, Black Pupilless Eyes, Closed Mouth, 28 In. 355.00
Wax, Over Papier-Mache, Black Pupilless Glass Eyes, Closed Mouth, Brown Hair, 27 In. . . 120.00
Wax, Over Papier-Mache, Pink Toned, Brown Glass Eyes, Brown Human Wig, 22 In. 165.00
Wax, Over Papier-Mache, Shoulder Head, Blue Glass Eyes, Closed Mouth, c.1870, 19 In. . . 590.00
Wax, Over Papier-Mache, Shoulder Head, Cobalt Blue Sleep Eyes, Closed Mouth, 21 In. . 129.00
Wax, Over Papier-Mache, Shoulder Head, Sleep Eyes, Mohair Wig, c.1890, 17 In. 82.00
Wax, Over Papier-Mache, Sleep Eyes, Mohair Wig, Cloth Body, Germany, c.1890, 13 In. . . 100.00
Wax, Shoulder Head, Black Pupilless Eyes, Closed Mouth, 26 1/2 In. 590.00
Wax, Shoulder Head, Blue Sleep Eyes, Mohair, Cloth Body, Jointed, 17 1/2 In. 350.00
Wax, Shoulder Head, Brown Eyes, Closed Mouth, Cloth Body, 20 In. 264.00
Wax, Shoulder Head, Glass Eyes, Human Wig, Cloth Body, England, c.1870, 22 In. 182.00
Wooden, Blond Hair, Jointed, Metal Hands & Feet, c.1870, 12 In. 88.00
Wooden, Carved Head, Braids, Gold Brocade Gown, 18th Century, 16 In. 950.00
Wooden, Carved, Center-Part Hair, Corkscrew Curls, 4 In. 382.00
Wooden, Carved, Gingerbread Shape, Amber Glass Inset Eyes, Pin-Jointed, c.1875, 12 In. 350.00
Wooden, Carved, Painted, 2 Sides, Costume, String, c.1800, 17 In. 2300.00
Wooden, Flapper, Painted Features, Jointed Arms, Carved Hands, 20th Century, 12 1/2 In. 375.00
Wooden, Shoulder Head, Painted Features, Cloth Body, Bedpost, c.1950, 21 In. 50.00
DOLL CLOTHES, Barbie, After Five, Black Sleeveless Dress, White Hat, Shoes, No. 934 . . . . 65.00
Barbie, American Airlines Stewardess, Navy Jacket, Skirt, Cap, Wings, Shoes, No. 984 . . 110.00
Barbie, Baby-Sits, Striped Apron, Rimmed Glasses, Phone, Cola, Alarm Clock, No. 953 . . 70.00
Barbie, Black Magic Ensemble, Black Sheath, Cape, Ribbon, Shoes, Gloves, No. 1609 . . 115.00
Barbie, Braniff Airlines, Green Coat, Yellow Cuffs, Green Gloves, Boots 110.00
Barbie, Braniff Airlines, Raspberry Suit, Jacket & Skirt, Velveteen Hat, Pumps 185.00
Barbie, Brunch Time, Print Dress, Rickrack Trim, Orange Shoes, No. 1628 . . . . 75.00
Barbie, Busy Gal, Jacket, Skirt, Body Shirt, Cap, Belt, Shoes, Glasses, No. 981 . . . .85.00 to 130.00
Barbie, Campus Sweetheart, Satin Gown, Tulle Panels, Long Gloves, Pearls, No. 1616 . . . 305.00
Barbie, Career Girl, Tweed Jacket, Skirt, Hat, Body Shirt, Long Gloves, No. 954 . . . . 110.00
Barbie, Cloud 9, Short Nightie, Long Robe, Satin Slippers, No. 1489 . . . . 55.00
Barbie, Commuter Set, Navy Jacket, Skirt, Satin Body Shirt, Shoes, Gloves, No. 916 . . . . 195.00
Barbie, Cruise Stripes, Dress, Navy Skirt, Striped Bodice, Belt, Shoes, No. 918 . . . . 50.00
Barbie, Disc Date, Body Shirt, Ruffles, Lace, Long Skirt, Shoes, Record Player, No. 1633 . 80.00
Barbie, Disco Dater, Satin Dress, Pleated Skirt, Sleeveless Shell, Hanger, No. 1807 . . . . . 95.00
Barbie, Easter Parade, Print Sheath Dress, Black Coat, Short Gloves, Shoes, No. 971 . . . . 355.00
Barbie, Enchanted Evening, Satin Gown, Sequins, Fur Stole, Gloves, No. 983 . . . . 155.00
Barbie, Fashion Editor, Sheath, Skirt, Print Bodice, Jacket, Cap, Shoes, No. 1635 . . . . . . 65.00
Barbie, Fiery Felt, Orange Felt Coat, Fringe Trim, Button Accents, Hat, Boots, No. 1789 . 50.00
Barbie, Friday Night Date, Corduroy Jumper, Appliques, Underdress, Shoes, No. 979 . . . . 80.00
Barbie, Gay Parisienne, Taffeta Dress, Long Gloves, Fur Stole, Clutch Purse, No. 964 . . . 300.00
Barbie, Golden Elegance, Brocade Sheath, Fur Trim Coat & Hat, Gloves, No. 998 . . . . . . 205.00
Barbie, Golden Glory, Long Dress, Chiffon Scarf, Long Coat, Fur Trim, Purse, No. 1645 . 250.00
Barbie, Golden Groove, Lame, Rhinestone Buttons, Jacket, Fur Trim, Skirt, No. 1593 . . . 150.00
Barbie, Great Coat, Yellow Vinyl Coat, Plush Trim, Hat, Shoes, No. 1459 . . . . 25.00
Barbie, International Fair, Red, White Pleated Skirt, Shoes, Plastic Camera, No. 1653 . . . . 45.00
Barbie, Invitation To Tea, Chiffon Jumpsuit, Lame Vest, Belt, Shoes, Glitter, No. 1632 . . . 90.00
Barbie, Jump Into Lace, Hot Pink Jumpsuit, White Lace, Shoes, No. 1823 . . . . 50.00
Barbie, Knit Hit, Knit Shirt, Navy Skirt, Red Shoes, Newspaper, No. 1621 . . . . 65.00
Barbie, Knitting Pretty, Knit Sweater, Skirt, Shell, Shoes, Book, No. 957 . . . . .105.00 to 160.00
Barbie, Learns To Cook, Print Dress, Belt, Turquoise Shoes, Toaster, Pots, No. 1634 . . . . 150.00
Barbie, Let's Dance, Blue, White Print Dress, Satin Sash, Purse, Black Shoes, No. 978 . . . 95.00
Barbie, London Tour, Vinyl Coat, Button, Hat, Handbag, Chiffon Scarf, Shoes, No. 1661 . 140.00
Barbie, Lovely Sleep-Ins, Pink Nightgown, Print Robe, Fur Trim, Slippers, No. 1463 . . . . 30.00

Barbie, Lunch On The Terrace, Gingham Dress, Polka Dot, Brimmed Hat, No. 1649	185.00
Barbie, Midi-Marvelous, Satin Dress, Embroidered Overdress, Hat, Shoes, No. 1870	85.00
Barbie, Open Road, Coat, Toggle Buttons, Sweater, Pants, Wedgies, Straw Hat, No. 985 . .	175.00
Barbie, Outdoor Life, Checked Coat, Print Pants, Shirt, Hat, Tennis Shoes, No. 1637	95.00
Barbie, Pan American Stewardess, Blue Jacket, Skirt, Cap, Gloves, No. 1678	700.00
Barbie, Party Date, Satin Dress, Gold Glitter, Belt, Purse, Shoes, No. 958	95.00
Barbie, Picnic Set, Body Shirt, Denim Pants, Straw Hat, Bamboo Pole, Basket, No. 967 . .	125.00
Barbie, Pink Formal, Satin Halter Dress, Tulle Trim, Pink Boa, Sears, No. 1681	405.00
Barbie, Pink Sheath, Rolled Neckline, Coat, Headband Hat, Gloves, Shoes	575.00
Barbie, Plantation Belle, Dress, Slip, Wide-Brimmed Hat, Purse, Jewelry, No. 966	205.00
Barbie, Purse, Vinyl, Graphics, Zipper, Coin Sections, Comb, Nail File, Pencil	325.00
Barbie, Record Tote, Vinyl, Graphics, Plastic Handle, Record Sleeves, 1961	65.00
Barbie, Roman Holiday, Sheath, Red, White Bodice, Navy Blue Skirt, Coat, No. 968	1250.00
Barbie, See-Worthy, Dress, Yellow Trim, Cap, Pompon, Socks, Tennis Shoes, No. 1872 . .	70.00
Barbie, Senior Prom, Satin Gown, Tulle Overskirt Panels, Shoes, No. 951	100.00
Barbie, Sheath Sensation, Dress, Short Gloves, Shoes, Straw Hat, No. 986	45.00
Barbie, Solo In Spotlight, Black Glitter Gown, Gloves, Scarf, Shoes, No. 982	135.00
Barbie, Suburban Shopper, Dress, Straw Hat, Pearl Necklace, Shoes, Phone, No. 969	150.00
Barbie, Super Scarf, Knit Sweater, Scarf, Fringe, Wool Skirt, Red Boots, No. 3408	30.00
Barbie, Sweet Dreams, Nightie, Panties, Scuffs With Pompons, Diary, Apple, No. 973 . . .	40.00
Barbie, Vacation Time, Knit Sweater, Checked Shorts, Flat Shoes, Camera, No. 1623	95.00
Barbie, Winter Wedding, Brocade Gown, Fur Trim, Cap, Headband, Veil, No. 1880	65.00
Barbie, Zigzag Bag, Zigzag Pants, Sleeveless Shirt, Tennis Shoes, No. 3238	100.00
Bonnet, Silk, Ivory, Twill, Organza, Hat Box, Modes De Paris, 1860-1885	660.00
Bonnet, Straw, Open Weave, Red, Natural Brim, Red Poppies, c.1885, 3 In.	385.00
Bonnet, Velvet, Peach, Rounded Top, Wide Brim, Bow, Feather, Buckle, 1885, 4 In.	245.00
Bonnet, White Cotton, Self Cording, Ruffled Cutwork Brim, 3 In.	110.00
Boots, Leather, Tan, Silver Buckles, Applied Heels, 2 3/4 In.	413.00
Boots, Quilted, Blue, High, Laced, White Kid Leather, Twill Lining, 4 3/4 In.	121.00
Bustle, Rounded, Linen Cover, 5 Covered Busks, Brass Grommets, 1860-1885	700.00
Cape, Wool Soutache Embroidery, Red, Full Length, Undercoat, 1860-1885	248.00
Coronet, Veil, Silk Flowers, Engraved, Lace Tulle, Gilt Trimmed Box, 19th Century	400.00
Corset, Black Silk, Satin, Boned, Shaped Waist, Gussets, Embroidered, 10 In.	198.00
Corset, Ivory Silk, Satin, Embroidered, Shaped Waist, Ribbon Edging, 17 x 7 In.	138.00
Day Gown, Muslin, Empire, White, Drawn Work, 1840-1860, 14 In.	550.00
Dress, Chambray Cotton, Red, Dropped Waist, Fitted Yoke, 18 In.	275.00
Dress, Corduroy, Navy Blue, Full Sleeves, Straw Bonnet, 1860-1885, 11 In.	468.00
Dress, Cotton Batiste, Rose, Cotton Fitted Yoke, Silk Braid, c.1885, 11 In.	413.00
Dress, Cotton, Chemise, Red & White, Accessories, Jumeau Bebe, c.1885, Size 11	650.00
Dress, Pique, Patterned, Detached Belt, Red, Mauve Roses, 1860-1885, 14 In.	688.00
Dress, Rose Flannel, Silk Sash, Basket Of Berries, Box, Jumeau, Bebe Pin, Size 11	1300.00
Dress, Tweed, Brown, Lace Yoke, Cotton & Wool, Ribbon Trim, c.1885, 18 In.	330.00
Francie, Combo, Sleeveless Shirt, Striped Skirt, Checked Coat, Scarf, No. 1215	65.00
Francie, Concert In The Park, Dress, Sleeveless Vest, Hat, Purse, Pumps, No. 1256	75.00
Francie, Dance Party, Crepe Dress, Hat, Stockings, Pumps, Record Player, No. 1257	80.00
Francie, First Formal, Gown, Crepe Bodice, Ruffled Cape, Gloves, Pumps, No. 1260	70.00
Francie, Fur Coat, Suede Trim, Fur Hat, Suede Skirt, Chain, Boots	70.00
Francie, Midi Duet, Print Dress, Long Vest, Hot Pink Shoes, No. 3451	75.00
Francie, Mini-Chex, Sleeveless Dress, Striped Socks, Boots, Shoulder Bag, No. 1209	45.00
Francie, Shopping Spree, Dress, Coat, Clutch Purse, Gloves, Pumps, No. 1261	85.00
Francie, Slacks Suit, Pants, Suede Belt, Buckle, Shirt, Shoes, Vinyl Handbag	45.00
Francie, Snazz, Striped Dress, Satin Waistband, Bow, Teddy, Lace, Shoes, No. 1225	40.00
Francie, Two For The Ball, Velveteen Gown, Satin Skirt, Lace Cover, Coat, No. 1232	155.00
Francie, Victorian Wedding, Satin Lace Gown, Headband, Tulle Veil, Shoes, Bouquet	95.00
Francie, Yellow Dress, Blue Trim, Flower Sleeves, Stockings, Flat Shoes	85.00
Francie Fashion Pak, Western Wild, Felt Vest, Boots, Braid Trim, Purse	50.00
Gown, Cotton, Red & Black Diamonds, Skirt, Pagoda Sleeve Jacket, 1865, For 17-In. Doll	750.00
Gown, Grenadine, Windowpane Print, High Waist, Pleats, 3/4 Sleeves, 14 In.	288.00
Gown, Linen, Bustle Skirt, Low Bodice Jacket, Pearl Buttons, c.1870, For 18-In. Doll . . .	1900.00
Gown, Natural Linen, Mauve Tint, Fitted Jacket, Flounce Skirt, For 17-In. Doll	500.00
Gown, Red Cashmere Flannel, Black & Ivory Soutache Embroidery, Caplet, c.1868	1600.00
Hat, Woven Straw, Rounded Flat Top, Ribbon, Box, c.1890, For 15-In. Doll	500.00
Julia, Brr-Furr, Dress, Satin Bodice, Knit Skirt, Aqua Coat, Fur Trim, No. 1752	85.00

Ken, Chef's Apron, Bandanna, Chef Hat, White Mitt, Spoon, Spatula, Fork 85.00
Ken, Fountain Boy, White Shirt, Hat, Plastic Tray, Napkins, Drinks, No. 1407 . . . .   150.00
Ken, Jazz Concert, Blue, Brown Shirt, Tan Pants, Socks, Tennis Shoes, No. 1420 . . . .   95.00
Ken, Mexico, Shirt, Felt Jacket, Braid Trim, Sombrero, Cowboy Boots, Cummerbund 105.00
Ken, Play Ball, Striped Shirt, Pants, Belt, Socks, Cleats, Mitt, Cap, Baseball, No. 792 . . . .   115.00
Ken, Prince, Brocade Jacket, Gold Trim, Lace Cuffs, Collar, Pantaloons, Cape 300.00
Ken, Ski Champion, Coat, Tie, Knit Pants, Cap, Pompon, Boots, Skis, Poles, No. 798 . . . .   95.00
Ken, Switzerland, White Shirt, Lederhosen, Suspenders, Socks, Boots, Felt Hat, Stein 105.00
Muff, Gray Fur & Wool Leggings, Au Bon Marche, Paris, Box, c.1870, For 18-In. Doll . . .   500.00
Parasol, Bone Handle, Pagoda Shape, Flared Sides, Blue Silk, Lace, 8 In. 578.00
Shoes, Kidskin, White, Ankle Straps, Buttons, Silver Buckle, Bebe Bru, 4 x 3 In. 468.00
Shoes, Leather, Brown, Pearl Button, Bebe, Box, c.1915, 3 In. 200.00
Skipper, Chill Chasers, White Fur Coat, Red Cap, Pompon, Red Shoes, Socks, No. 1926 . .   45.00
Skipper, Flower Jacket, Zipper, Fur Collar, Shirt, Pants, Hat, Socks, Boots, No. 1936 . . . .   85.00
Skipper, Happy Birthday, Skirt, Blue Bodice, Straw Hat, Socks, Gloves, No. 1919 . . . . . .   280.00
Skipper, Learning To Ride, Jacket, Riding Pants, Boots, Cap & Crop, No. 1935 . . . .   125.00
Skipper, Navy Blue Skirt, Belt, Shoes, Cookbook, Spoon, Cookie Mix Box, No. 1912 . . .   70.00
Skipper, Pink & White Checkered Dress, Ribbon Ties, Socks, Shoes, No. 1913 . . . .   75.00
Skipper, School Girl, Jacket, Sleeveless Shirt, Pleated Skirt, Books, No. 1921 . . . .   185.00
Skipper, Sledding Fun, Print Jacket, Zipper, Fur Collar, Shirt, Pants, Hat, Boots, No. 1936   70.00
Slippers, Velvet, Embroidered, Purple, Thick Leather Soles, c.1885, 3 1/2 In. 193.00
Suit, Boy's, Homespun, Double-Breasted Jacket, Fly Front, Flap, 1840-1860 . . . .   550.00

DONALD DUCK items are included in the Disneyana category.

DOORSTOPS have been made in all types of designs. The vast majority
of the doorstops sold today are cast iron and were made from about
1890 to 1930. Most of them are shaped like people, animals, flowers,
or ships. Reproductions and newly designed examples are sold in gift
shops.

3 Puppies, In Basket, Cast Iron, John Wright, 6 1/4 x 7 1/2 In. 345.00
Bird Of Prey, Cast Iron, England 450.00
Bobby Blake, Clutching Teddy Bear, Blue Shirt, Black Pants, Red Socks, Hubley 950.00
Bulldog, Seated, Red Collar, Cast Iron, 7 1/2 In. 84.00
Camel, 2 Humps, Cast Iron, Early 20th Century, 7 x 9 1/2 In. 210.00
Cat, Arched Back, Black, Cast Iron, Hubley, 10 1/2 In. 220.00
Cat, Black, Eyes, Mouth, Cast Iron, Painted, 19th Century, 11 x 8 1/4 In. 881.00
Cat, Brown Paint, White Features, Green Base, Iron, 11 1/2 x 9 1/2 In. 353.00
Cat, Hunchback, Cast Iron, Black Paint, 10 3/4 In. 275.00
Cat, Seated, Painted, Cast Iron, 1920s 495.00
Cat, Sleeping, Hubley, No. 214, 8 1/8 In. 850.00
Christmas Carolers, Painted, Cast Iron, John Wright 425.00
Clipper Ship, Painted, 1930 . . . .   375.00
Clown, Red, White, Blue, Black, Art Deco, Cast Iron, 10 1/2 In. 1300.00
Conch Shell, Bronze, Patinated, 9 x 9 x 12 In. 230.00
Cottage, Cape Cod, Cast Iron, Hubley, 7 3/4 x 1 7/8 x 5 5/8 In.   325.00
Cottage, Flowers Around Door, Cast Iron 132.00
Cottage, In Woods, Cast Iron, 10 1/8 x 2 1/2 x 4 5/8 In. 550.00
Courting Couple, Cast Iron, Signed, Martha Cahoon, 8 In. 69.00
Daylilies, Drooping Heads, Green Leaves, Cast Iron, 8 1/2 In. 275.00
Deco Lady, Holding Up Dress, Judd Manufacturing 950.00
Deer, Black Paint, Cast Iron, 9 In. 440.00
Dog, Airedale, White, Black Paint, Cast Iron, 8 1/2 In. 440.00
Dog, Borzoi, Cast Iron, Early 20th Century, 7 3/4 x 12 In. 350.00
Dog, Boston Terrier, Cast Iron, 8 In. 175.00
Dog, Boston Terrier, Cast Iron, 9 x 10 In. . . . . .115.00 to 138.00
Dog, Boston Terrier, Head Turned Left, Painted, Cast Iron, 1890s 350.00
Dog, Boston Terrier, Head Turned Right, Painted, Cast Iron, 1890s 160.00
Dog, Bulldog, Black & White Paint, Cast Iron, 9 1/2 In. 135.00
Dog, Bulldog, Black, Brown Paint, Cast Iron, 10 In. 107.00
Dog, Bulldog, Black, Cast Iron, 5 3/4 x 8 In. 100.00
Dog, Bulldog, Brown, White, Cast Iron, 8 3/4 In. 193.00
Dog, Bulldog, Cast Iron, Hubley 225.00
Dog, Cocker Spaniel, Dream Boy, Cast Iron, Virginia Metal Crafters, 1949, 9 In. 295.00

Dog, Cocker Spaniel, Hubley 175.00
Dog, English Setter, On Point, Cast Iron, 5 x 8 In. 175.00
Dog, Fox Terrier, Cast Iron, 9 x 8 In. 196.00
Dog, Fox Terrier, Hubley, c.1930s 395.00
Dog, French Bulldog, Sitting, Cast Iron, Hubley, No. 304, 8 In. 300.00
Dog, German Shepherd, Cast Iron, Painted, 10 In. 230.00
Dog, Pointer, Black, White Paint, Cast Iron, 9 In. 180.00
Dog, Scotty, Black Paint, Cast Iron, 8 In. 160.00
Dog, Sealyham Terrier, Cast Iron, 2 Sections 928.00
Dog, Spaniel, Cast Iron, Bronze Finish, 6 3/4 x 4 1/2 In. 85.00
Dog, Spaniel, Dark Blue Paint, Cast Iron, 5 1/2 In. 180.00
Dogs, 2 Scotties, Bronze, 5 x 8 In. 190.00
Dutch Girl, Painted, Cast Iron, 6 1/2 In. 110.00
Eagle, Painted, Black, Wings Spread, Half-Round Bases, Cast Iron, 7 In. 116.00
Eagle, Spread Wings, Cast Iron, 4 x 11 In. 50.00
Elephant, Jumbo, Gray Paint, Cast Iron, 10 In. 46.00
Elephant, Raised Front Leg, Trunk, Green, Gray, Red, Yellow, Cast Iron, 4 1/2 x 6 In. ... 140.00
Elephant & Palm Tree, Cast Iron, 14 1/4 In. 690.00
Fisherman, Yellow Slicker & Sou'wester, Cast Iron, 15 In. ....105.00 to 259.00
Flower Basket, Cast Iron, 7 In. 80.00
Flower Basket, Cast Iron, 9 3/4 In. 85.00
Flower Basket, Chrysanthemum Highlights, Cast Iron, Patented 1926, 9 In. 140.00
Flower Basket, Leaves, White, Hubley, 1920s 425.00
Flower Basket, Multicolored, White Basket, Cast Iron, 10 In. 170.00
Flower Basket, Roses, Cast Iron, 6 3/4 In. 105.00
Flower Door, Hubley, No. 471, 1930s 395.00
Flower Urn, Cast Iron, 10 1/4 In. 105.00
Flower Vase, Ribbon Drapery, Polychrome, Cast Iron 385.00
Flowers, Cast Iron, 7 1/4 In. 145.00
Frog, Green Paint, Cast Iron, 5 1/2 In. ....63.00 to 90.00
Fruit Bowl, Flowers, Leaves, Yellow, Black Base, Hubley, 1930s 395.00
George V, Dolphin, Bronze, Upraised Tail Spiraling Around Trident, 15 x 4 In. 460.00
Gnome Holding Lantern, Cast Iron, 10 In. 325.00
Golfer, Painted, Cast Iron, 10 In. 470.00
Henry VIII, Painted, Order Of The Garter, Wood, 21 In. 300.00
Heron, Resting, Yellow Beak, Cast Iron 155.00
Horse, Hunter, Cast Iron, Virginia Metal Crafters, 1949, 11 3/4 In. 225.00
Horse & Dog At Fence, Cast Iron, 7 In. 50.00
Humpty Dumpty, Sits On Brick Wall Leaning Back, Green Bowtie, Red Suit, 1920s 750.00
Humpty Dumpty, Sitting On Wall, Cast Iron 105.00
Kissing Dutch Boy & Girl, Hubley, No. 332, 1930s 250.00
Kittens, Boy & Girl, Dressed, Cast Iron, 10 In. 350.00
Lilies Of The Valley, Hubley, No. 189, 1930s 395.00
Lion, Reclining, Hollow Body, Black, Cast Iron, 5 x 7 In., Pair 450.00
Mammy, Blue Dress, White Apron, Red Bandanna, Cast Iron, Hubley 1045.00
Mammy, Painted, Cast Iron, 11 1/4 In. 110.00
Nasturtiums, Cast Iron, Hubley, No. 221, 7 1/8 In. ....125.00 to 225.00
Parrot, Red Body, Yellow, Green, Blue Wings, Cast Iron, 12 In. 220.00
Parrot In Ring, Cast Iron, Bradley & Hubbard, 7 1/4 x 4 1/8 x 13 1/2 In. ....525.00 to 535.00
Pirate Ship, Cast Iron, 8 1/2 In. 90.00
Punch, Black Paint, Cast Iron, 12 x 9 In. 250.00
Rabbit, Black Paint, Cast Iron, 21 In. 440.00
Rabbit, Seated, Full Figure, White Paint, Cast Iron, 10 3/4 In. 165.00
Rabbit, Seated, White, Pink, Kramer Bros. Fdy. Co., Dayton, Ohio, 10 7/8 In. 385.00
Ram, Black Paint, Cast Iron 205.00
Ram, Red Paint, Steel, 7 1/2 In. 75.00
Sailor, Cadet, Cast Iron, 13 3/4 In. 315.00
Sheep, Cast Iron, White Paint Traces, 7 1/2 x 10 1/2 In. 275.00
Ship, Clipper, Rising Sun Painted On Sails 750.00
Ship, Constitution Clipper, A.M. Greenblatt Studios, 1924 .... 495.00
Soldier, Colonial, Blue Uniform, Cornered Hat, Cast Iron 375.00
Southern Belle, Polychrome Paint, Cast Iron, 5 1/2 In. 110.00
Squirrel, On Tree Stump, Painted, Cast Iron, 1930s 495.00

Stirrup Cup, Bronze, Patinated, Oblong, Marble Base, 26 x 7 x 11 1/2 In.	230.00
Tree, Fence, Bradley & Hubbard, c.1900	450.00
Tulip Pot, Art Deco, White, Black, Red, Yellow, Green Leaves, Cast Iron, 8 In.	195.00
Tulip Pot, Cast Iron, c.1930s	495.00
Turkey, Black, Red, Silver, & White, Iron, Bradley & Hubbard, 12 In.	1550.00
Turkey, Painted, Black, Red, Silver, White, Cast Iron, Bradley & Hubbard, 12 1/4 In. . . .	1550.00
Victorian Woman, Floral Dress, Shawl, Parasol, Cast Iron, Marked B & H 7796, 2 x 8 In.	1540.00
Wolf's Head, Bronze Tail, Cast Iron, 1880	475.00
Woman, Nude, In Meditation, Cast Iron, Bronze Finish, Art Deco, 5 7/8 x 5 5/8 In.	135.00

DORCHESTER POTTERY was founded by George Henderson in 1895 in Dorchester, Massachusetts. At first, the firm made utilitarian stoneware, but collectors are most interested in the line of decorated blue and white pottery that Dorchester made from 1940 until it went out of business in 1979.

DORCHESTER POTTERY WORKS BOSTON, MASS.

Bowl, Rooster, Incised, Yellow, Green, Rising Sun, Teal Green Ground, 1 3/4 x 6 In.	1540.00
Bowl, Rooster, Yellow, Brown, Sky, Hillside, Yellow Drip Glaze, 1 3/4 x 6 In.	660.00
Casserole, Cover, Colonial Lace, Cobalt Blue Bands, White Glaze, 4 1/2 x 7 1/2 In.	275.00
Cup & Saucer, Pear, Blue, Half Scroll, 3 1/4 & 6 1/4 In., Pair	110.00
Honey Pot, Scenic Landscape, 6 Panels, Cottage On Hillside, S. Gainer, 4 1/2 x 3 In.	5225.00
Jar, Sugar, Polka Dot, R. Brake, Signed, 3 1/2 In.	99.00
Mug, Whale, Deep Blue, Seagulls, 2 3/4 & 3 In., 3 Piece	195.00
Pitcher, Pilgrim, Blue, Striped Handle, R. Trotter, Stamped, 7 1/2 x 7 1/2 In.	220.00
Plate, Ducks In Repeat, Chicory Blue, Ivory, 6 1/4 In.	990.00
Plate, Rooster, Yellow, Brown, Green, L. Shapiro & E. Brown, 6 1/8 In.	660.00
Sugar & Creamer, Strawberry, Deep Blue, Flower, Leaf, 3 1/2 & 3 1/4 In.	80.00

DOULTON pottery and porcelain were made by Doulton and Co. of Burslem, England, after 1882. The name *Royal Doulton* appeared on their wares after 1902. Other pottery by Doulton is listed under Royal Doulton.

Bowl, Rectangular, Burslem, Farm Scene, 1932 Mark, 9 x 7 1/2 In.	105.00
Bowl, Wild Roses, Orange, Yellow, Mottled Blue Ground, 10 In.	260.00
Cracker Jar, Burslem, Flowers, Silver Plate Lid, 6 x 5 In.	115.00
Cracker Jar, Slater's Patent, Silvered Lid, Bail, Collar, Sharkskin Ground, 6 x 5 In.	115.00
Flask, Stoneware, Sharkskin Ground, Flowers, Fruit, Burslem, 8 In.	115.00
Jar, Chinese Jade, Cover, Madonna & Child Finial, Charles Noke, 4 1/4 x 3 1/4 In.	999.00
Jar, Cover, Cameo Style, Vines On Base, Cover, Mark, Lambeth, 5 1/2 x 4 1/2 In.	140.00
Jardiniere, Gloire-De-Dijon, 4 Scenes, Square, Burslem, 9 1/4 x 9 In.	1430.00
Jug, Milk, Stoneware, White Tavern, Hunt Scene, Brown, Silver Rim, 5 1/2 In.	80.00
Pitcher, 2-Tone Brown, Pewter Lid, Raised Design, Lambeth, 8 1/2 In.	80.00
Pitcher, Blue & Gold Flowers, White Ground, Burslem, 19th Century, 9 x 3 In.	80.00
Pitcher, Blue Rosettes, White Dots, Impressed, Lambeth, 1884, 7 3/4 In.	80.00
Pitcher, Burslem, Sharkskin Ground, Cobalt Blue Flowers, Gold Trim, 7 In.	144.00
Pitcher, Cylindrical, Rope Handle, Mark, Lambeth, 4 x 4 1/2 In.	110.00
Pitcher, Flowers, Vertical Panel, White Beads, Mark, Lambeth, 7 x 4 1/2 In.	110.00
Pitcher, Warlords, Blade Shaped Panels, Incised Leaves, Beads, Mark, Lambeth, 8 In. . . .	165.00
Plate, Dr. Johnson At Bootham Bar-York, Burslem, 9 x 7 1/2 In.	81.00
Plate, Egerton, Flow Blue, 8 1/2 In.	65.00
Plate, Egerton, Flow Blue, 9 1/2 In.	90.00
Plate, Egerton, Flow Blue, 10 1/2 In.	100.00
Plate, Melrose, Flow Blue, 9 3/4 In.	90.00
Plate, Turkey, Blue & White Transfer, Staffordshire, 10 In.	250.00
Plate Set, Flow Blue, Gilt Highlights, Flower, Medallion, Platter, 9 1/4 In.	345.00
Platter, Egerton, Flow Blue, 12 In.	165.00
Platter, Egerton, Flow Blue, 16 In.	400.00
Platter, Egerton, Flow Blue, 18 In.	500.00
Platter, Turkey, Blue & White Transfer, Staffordshire, 21 x 17 In.	1100.00
Pottery, Jug, Whiskey, Uncle Sam Smoking Pipe, Glazing, c.1907, 7 3/8 In.	310.00
Punch Bowl, Burslem Pottery, Blue, Flowers, Gilt, 14 In.	150.00
Punch Bowl, Daffodils, Blue & White Transfer, Footed, 19th Century, 9 1/2 x 16 In.	980.00
Tureen, Cover, Underplate, Floral & Scroll, Flow Blue, Burslem, 6 1/2 x 8 1/2 In.	50.00
Tureen, Sauce, Cover, Underplate, Melrose, Flow Blue	105.00

Vase, Fruit & Flower, Purple, Lavender, Cobalt Blue, Oval, Maude Bowder, 10 3/4 In. 300.00
Vase, Fruit & Flower, Yellow, Lavender, Magenta, Winnie Bawstead, 14 1/4 x 5 1/2 In. . . 360.00
Vase, Fruit, Leaves, Yellow, Green, Shaded Blue Ground, Tapered, Mark, 7 1/2 In. 81.00
Vase, Ladies With Flowers, Landscape, Art Nouveau, Lambeth, 12 1/2 In. 825.00
Vase, Lions, Hannah Barlow, 19 In. 7000.00
Vase, Middle Eastern Flower Design, c.1880, 10 In., Pair 316.00
Vase, Mother & Children, Classical Scene, Flower & Scroll Borders, J.P. Hewitt, 11 In. . . 1380.00
Vase, Stoneware, Rough Brown Lace Ground, Flower Sprays, 16 In. 374.00
Vase, Stylized, Enameled, Blue, Gold & White, 10 1/2 In. 259.00
Vase, Women Standing Outdoors, With Bouquet Of Flowers, No. 8096, 12 1/4 In. 550.00
Vase, Wreath Of Pomegranates, Leaves, Earth Tones, 6 7/8 In. 546.00

DRAGONWARE is a form of moriage pottery made since the late 19th
century. Moriage is a type of decoration on Japanese pottery. Raised
white designs are applied to the ware. White dragons are the major
raised decorations on the moriage called *dragonware*. The background
can be one of many different colors. It is still being made.

Creamer, Black, Turquoise, Pink, Gold, Kutani Moriage, 3 3/4 In. 11.00
Cup & Saucer 15.00
Cup & Saucer, Black Matte 25.00
Cup & Saucer, Geisha Girl Lithophane, Blue-Eyed Dragon, c.1937-1950 . . . . 18.00
Cup & Saucer, Yellow, White, Occupied Japan 175.00
Plate, Black, Turquoise, Pink & Gold, Kutani Moriage, 7 3/4 In. 13.00
Sugar & Creamer, Luster, 3 3/8 In. 25.00
Tea Set, Black Matte, Plate, Cup, Teapot, Wooden Holder 40.00
Tea Set, Embossed, Cups, Saucers, Dessert Plates, Sugar, Creamer, 15 Piece 125.00
Tea Set, Florida, Sugar & Creamer, c.1940, 5 x 4 1/4 & 3 1/2 x 3 1/4 In. 30.00
Tea Set, Teapot, Cups, Saucers, Plates, Lithophane, Geisha, Occupied Japan, 13 Piece . . . 225.00
Tea Set, Teapot, Sugar, Creamer, Cups, Saucers, Plates, 15 Piece 490.00
Teapot, Black Matte, Gold Handle, Japan, 5 In. 85.00
Vase, 2 Handles, Gray, Dragon, Blue Eyes, 4 1/8 In. 20.00
Vase, Galveston, Texas, Lavender, Gold Handles, 2 1/2 x 2 In. 5.00
Vase, Moriage Slip Trail, Brown, Blue Enameled Eyes, Maroon Tongue, 3 1/4 In. 45.00
Vase, Orange, 2 3/4 x 2 In. 12.00

DRESDEN china is any china made in the town of Dresden, Germany.
The most famous factory in Dresden is the Meissen factory. Figurines
of eighteenth-century ladies and gentlemen, animal groups, or cherubs
and other mythological subjects were popular. One special type of figurine was made with skirts of porcelain-dipped lace. Do not make the
mistake of thinking that all pieces marked *Dresden* are from the
Meissen factory. The Meissen pieces usually have crossed swords
marks, and are listed under Meissen. Some recent porcelain from
Ireland, called *Irish Dresden*, is not included in this book.

Bowl, Pink Roses, Satin Finish, Shell Handles, 7 1/2 x 8 In. 45.00
Box, Brass Mounted, Gilt Decorated, 18th Century Couple Scenes, 7 1/2 In. 1675.00
Box, Flower Sprays, Gold Borders, Round, Hinged Lid, 3 1/4 In. 105.00
Candelabrum, 5-Light, Polychrome Flowers, Figural, Gilt Decoration, 20 In., Pair 365.00
Charger, Stag & Fawn At River, Signed, Becker, 13 In. 60.00
Compote, Enameled Flowers, Pierced Rim, Gilt Trim, Pedestal Base, c.1900, 12 x 7 In. . . 118.00
Compote, Flutists, Courting Couples, Flowers, Reticulated, 11 x 9 1/4 In., Pair 358.00
Cup & Saucer, Hand Painted, Medallion, Marked GLC Dresden 145.00
Dessert Set, Enameled Flowers, Pierced Border, Scalloped Rim, 7 3/4-In. Plates, 13 Piece 765.00
Figurine, 2 Children Sitting On Rock, Signed, Blue Crown Mark, 6 1/2 In. 115.00
Figurine, 2 Seated Cherubs, Glass Dome, c.1900, 8 x 5 1/4 x 7 In. 230.00
Figurine, Boy & Girl, With Birdcage, Lamb, 5 x 6 In. 110.00
Figurine, Woman Feeding Chickens, 4 1/2 In. 90.00
Figurine, Woman On Settee, c.1950, 5 In. 460.00
Figurine, Young Girls With Flowers, c.1950, 4 In., 3 Piece 575.00
Plaque, Mary & Jesus, Cherubs At Base, T. Lichtenberg, 6 x 4 In. 518.00
Plaque, Oval, Contemplation, Signed, Frame, c.1900, 9 3/4 In. 1890.00
Plaque, Rectangular, Neopolitan Dancer, On Terrace, Frame, c.1880, 8 3/4 x 5 3/4 In. . . . 946.00
Plate, Dessert, Flower Sprays, Shaped Latticework Rim, 9 3/8 In., 12 Piece 1175.00

Serving Dish, Blue & White, Gilt Design, Crossed Swords Mark, 1800s, 7 1/2 x 5 3/4 In. .   17.00
Tray, Asparagus, Flowers, Gilt, 2 Compartments, 2 Reservoirs, Center Loop Handle, 11 In.   120.00
Urn, Cover, Amphora Form, Pedestal, 8 Sides, Flowers, Lion Masks, c.1880, 29 x 15 In. .   4500.00
Vase, Garniture, Meissen Style, Blue Ground, Flowers, c.1885, 12 1/4 In., Pair 430.00
Vase, Oval, Dome Cover, Applied Flowers, 18th Century Lovers Scene, 15 1/2 In., Pair . .   1195.00
Vase, Oval, Swan Shape Handles, Castle Scene, Gold Ground, 13 1/2 In. 1915.00
Vase, Pictorial, Couple, Gilt Floral Border, Long Neck, Long Neck, c.1880, 12 In., Pair . .   575.00
Vase, Portrait, Medallion, Female, With Oil Lamp, Gold & Green Flowers, c.1900, 7 1/2 In.   400.00
Vase, Woman, Plumed Hat, White Gown, Gold Flowers, Blue Ground, Marked, 8 3/4 In. .   575.00
Wall Pocket, Horn Of Plenty Shape, Cherub, Putti, Polychrome, Gilt, 15 1/2 In. 250.00

DUNCAN & MILLER is a term used by collectors when referring to glass
made by the George A. Duncan and Sons Company or the Duncan and
Miller Glass Company. These companies worked from 1893 to 1955,
when the use of the name *Duncan* was discontinued and the firm
became part of the United States Glass Company. Early patterns may
be listed under Pressed Glass.

Adoration, Goblet, 10 Oz., 7 1/2 In. 25.00
Adoration, Sherbet, 6 Oz., 3 1/2 In. 15.00
Adoration, Vase, Cornucopia, 8 In. 60.00
Astaire, Goblet, 10 In. 13.00
Button Arches, Sugar, Cover, 6 1/2 In. 70.00
Canterbury, Basket, 11 x 8 In. 70.00
Canterbury, Bowl, Fruit, 5 1/2 In. 7.50
Canterbury, Candlestick, 6 In., Pair 15.00
Canterbury, Candy Dish, Cover, Chartreuse, 6 1/2 In. 40.00
Canterbury, Centerpiece, Blue Opalescent, 10 In. 100.00
Canterbury, Cocktail, Chartreuse, 3 1/2 Oz., 5 1/4 In. 20.00
Canterbury, Cup & Saucer 15.00
Canterbury, Dish, Mayonnaise, Handles, 7 1/2 In. 9.00
Canterbury, Goblet, 9 Oz., 6 In. 12.50
Canterbury, Marmalade, Underplate, 5 x 3 In. 30.00
Canterbury, Relish, 2 Sections, Handles, 9 In. 30.00
Canterbury, Relish, 3 Sections, Handles, 9 x 4 In. 18.00
Canterbury, Rose Bowl, 5 1/4 In. ....25.00 to 35.00
Canterbury, Sherbet, 6 Oz., 4 1/2 In. 9.00
Canterbury, Tumbler, Chartreuse, 9 Oz., 4 1/2 In. 14.00
Canterbury, Tumbler, Chartreuse, Footed, 9 Oz., 5 1/2 In. 26.00
Canterbury, Vase, 8 1/2 In. 45.00
Canterbury, Vase, Chartreuse, 5 In. 20.00
Canterbury, Vase, Crimped, Blue Opalescent, 4 1/2 In. 45.00
Caribbean, Bowl, Cover, 7 In. 14.00
Caribbean, Cigarette Box, Cover, Cobalt Blue, 3 1/2 In. 125.00
Caribbean, Punch Set, 12 Piece 350.00
Caribbean, Vase, Squat, Flared, Rolled Rim, Blue, 2 1/2 x 7 In. 85.00
Chanticleer, Cocktail, Frosted, 3 Oz. 75.00
Cloverleaf, Vase, Blue Opalescent, 5 In. 50.00
Cornucopia, Chartreuse, 14 In. 85.00
Cornucopia, Rose Opalescent, 14 In. 80.00
Cut Daisy, Compote, 5 1/2 x 7 In. 80.00
Diamond Point, Punch Cup 13.00
Diamond Ridge, Bottle, Water, 8 1/2 x 5 1/2 In. 85.00
Figurine, Fat Goose, 7 1/4 x 5 x 3 1/4 In. 225.00
Figurine, Heron, 7 In. 65.00
First Love, Ashtray, 3 1/2 In. 20.00
First Love, Bowl, Floral, Flared, 12 In. 65.00
First Love, Candlestick, 2-Light, Pair 75.00
First Love, Champagne, 5 Oz., 5 In. 20.00
First Love, Cigarette Box, Cover, 4 3/4 x 3 5/8 In. 130.00
First Love, Cocktail, 3 1/2 Oz., 4 1/2 In. 20.00
First Love, Compote, 6 3/4 In. 35.00
First Love, Cruet 275.00
First Love, Dish, Mayonnaise, 5 1/2 In. 35.00

First Love, Plate, 8 1/2 In.	25.00
First Love, Plate, Handles, 8 In.	15.00
First Love, Plate, Handles, 11 In.	30.00
First Love, Relish, 3 Sections, 7 In.	25.00
First Love, Saucer	8.50
First Love, Sugar	15.00
First Love, Tumbler, Iced Tea, Footed, 12 Oz., 5 1/2 In.	35.00
First Love, Vase, 8 1/2 x 6 In.	90.00
First Love, Wine, 3 Oz., 5 1/4 In.	30.00
Hobnail, Basket, Blue Opalescent, 10 x 4 3/4 In.	115.00
Hobnail, Basket, Pink Opalescent, 12 In.	275.00
Hobnail, Champagne, 5 Oz., 4 1/2 In.	16.00
Hobnail, Goblet, 9 Oz., 6 In.	13.00
Hobnail, Ivy Ball, Blue Opalescent, Footed, 7 x 4 1/2 In.	70.00 to 95.00
Hobnail, Ladle, Blue Opalescent, 10 3/4 x 3 3/8 In.	150.00
Hobnail, Plate, 6 1/8 In.	9.00
Hobnail, Plate, 7 1/4 In.	12.00
Mardi Gras, Vase, Yellow, 8 In.	75.00
Murano, Bowl, Blue Opalescent, 11 1/2 In.	100.00
Murano, Vase, Blue Opalescent, 4 1/2 In.	45.00
Pall Mall, Swan, 7 In.	14.00
Pall Mall, Swan, 9 x 11 3/4 In.	65.00
Pall Mall, Swan, Emerald Green, 12 In.	275.00
Pall Mall, Swan, Green Opalescent, 9 5/8 x 13 In.	250.00
Pall Mall, Swan, Milk Glass, Red Neck, 7 In.	325.00
Sandwich, Banana Boat, Milk Glass	65.00
Sandwich, Basket, Loop Handle, 6 In.	85.00
Sandwich, Bowl, Chartreuse, 5 In.	20.00
Sandwich, Bowl, Grapefruit, Pink, Footed, 5 1/2 In.	25.00
Sandwich, Candlestick, 3-Light, 16 In., Pair	575.00
Sandwich, Champagne, 5 Oz., 5 1/4 In.	12.00
Sandwich, Cocktail, 3 Oz., 4 1/4 In.	12.00 to 15.00
Sandwich, Creamer	9.00
Sandwich, Cup & Saucer	11.00
Sandwich, Dish, Mint, Handle, 7 In.	25.00
Sandwich, Egg Plate, 12 In.	50.00 to 75.00
Sandwich, Goblet, 9 Oz.	15.00
Sandwich, Nappy, 2 Sections, 6 In.	15.00
Sandwich, Nappy, Heart Shape, 6 1/4 x 2 3/4 In.	50.00
Sandwich, Parfait, 4 Oz., 5 1/4 In.	30.00
Sandwich, Plate, 8 In.	10.00
Sandwich, Relish, 3 Sections, 12 In.	15.00
Sandwich, Sugar	9.00
Sandwich, Sundae, Footed, 5 Oz., 3 1/2 In.	12.00
Sandwich, Tray, Oval, 8 In.	20.00
Sandwich, Tumbler, Iced Tea, Footed, 12 Oz., 5 1/2 In.	35.00
Sandwich, Tumbler, Iced Tea, Footed, Pink, 12 Oz., 5 1/2 In.	30.00
Sandwich, Vase, 9 3/4 In.	70.00
Swirl, Candy Dish, Cover, Light Purple, 3 Sections, 4 1/2 x 7 In.	70.00
Swirl, Compote, Green, 6 5/8 In.	25.00
Swirl, Compote, Green, Silver Band On Rim, 6 5/8 x 5 3/4 In.	125.00
Swirl, Plate, Green, 8 1/2 In.	15.00
Swirl, Sherbet, Green, 6 Oz., 4 3/4 In.	20.00
Swirl, Tumbler, Cocktail, Footed, Green, 2 1/2 Oz., 3 3/8 In.	7.50
Tear Drop, Ashtray, 3 In.	6.00
Tear Drop, Bowl, 2 Sections, 6 In.	15.00
Tear Drop, Bowl, Handles, 5 In.	10.00
Tear Drop, Champagne, 5 Oz., 5 In.	9.00
Tear Drop, Dish, Sweetmeat, Center Handle, 6 1/2 In.	35.00 to 55.00
Tear Drop, Nappy, Handles, 5 In.	12.00
Tear Drop, Nappy, Handles, 7 In.	12.00
Tear Drop, Relish, 2 Sections, Heart Shape	20.00
Tear Drop, Sherbet, 5 Oz., 3 3/4 In.	20.00

Tear Drop, Sugar & Creamer	25.00
Tear Drop, Whiskey, 2 Oz., 2 1/4 In.	20.00
Terrace, Plate, 8 1/2 In.	15.00
Terrace, Sugar & Creamer	50.00

DURAND art glass was made from 1924 to 1931. The Vineland Flint Glass Works was established by Victor Durand and Victor Durand, Jr., in 1897. In 1924 Martin Bach, Jr., and other artisans from the Quezal glassworks joined them at the Vineland, New Jersey, plant to make Durand art glass.

Bowl, King Tut, Gold, Iridescent Blue, 10 1/2 In.	700.00
Candle, Lamp, Iridescent Gold, Pulled Green & White Feather, Snuffer, 8 1/2 In., Pair ...	975.00
Compote, Green, Opal Interior, Iridescent Silver, 5 1/4 In.	975.00
Compote, King Tut, Royal Blue, Clear Reeded Stem, 3 1/8 x 7 In.	230.00
Ginger Jar, Cover, Iridescent Blue, Opal Pulled Heart & Vine, Signed, 9 In.	2470.00
Lamp, Moorish Crackle, Red, White Panels, Iridescent Amber, c.1920, 10 3/4 In.	800.00
Lamp, Torchere, Art Nouveau, Bronzed Metal Base, 65 1/2 In.	1095.00
Lamp Base, Ruby, White Pulled Feathers, 2 Sections, Footed, 24 In.	700.00
Luminare, Iridescent Gold, Moorish Crackle, Inverted Shade, Metal Base, 7 In.	375.00
Shade, Green Pulled Heart & Vine, Iridescent Gold, 4 1/2 In., Pair	635.00
Shade, King Tut, Green, Iridescent Gold, Opal Interior, 6 1/4 In.	920.00
Sherbet, Ambergris, Iridescent Gold, 3 1/2 In.	145.00
Sherbet, Cranberry, White Pulled Feather, Ambergris Foot, 3 1/2 In.	560.00
Vase, Amber, Iridescent Gold, Baluster, Signed, 4 1/4 In.	315.00
Vase, Amber, Iridescent Gold, Pulled Feathers, Threading, c.1920, 8 1/2 In.	2185.00
Vase, Amber, Iridescent Gold, White Pulled Feathers, Green Tips, 11 1/2 In.	3565.00
Vase, Beehive, Ambergris, Reddish Iridescent Gold, c.1915, 12 1/2 In.	2300.00
Vase, Bud, Iridescent Blue, Amber Handles, Amber Foot, Baluster, 12 In.	2070.00
Vase, Gold Orange, Iridescent Gold, Gold Threading, Signed, c.1920, 9 3/4 In.	750.00
Vase, Iridescent Blue, 7 In.	575.00
Vase, Iridescent Blue, Applied Threading, 7 1/4 In.	410.00
Vase, Iridescent Blue, Applied Threading, No. 1968, 6 1/8 In.	530.00
Vase, Iridescent Blue, Bulbous, Urn Shape, Collared Neck, Flared Rim, 7 1/2 In.	1065.00
Vase, Iridescent Blue, Cylindrical, No. 1968, Signed, c.1924, 8 1/8 In.	645.00
Vase, Iridescent Blue, Egg Shape, Signed, 4 1/4 In.	500.00
Vase, Iridescent Blue, Opal Pulled Heart & Vine, Urn, Gold Disc Foot, 8 1/4 In.	1570.00
Vase, Iridescent Blue, Pulled Vines & Flowers, Globular, c.1910, 8 1/8 In.	1435.00
Vase, Iridescent Gold, Ambergris, Iridescent Silver, Bulbous, c.1915, 18 1/4 In.	2530.00
Vase, Iridescent Gold, Etched Flower Band, c.1925, 13 1/2 In.	700.00
Vase, Iridescent Gold, Flared Rim, Signed, 8 5/8 In.	440.00
Vase, Iridescent Gold, Gold Threading, Signed, Early 1900s, 7 1/4 In.	575.00
Vase, Iridescent Gold, Green Pulled Feathers, Bulbous, Flared Lip, Signed, 9 1/4 In.	520.00
Vase, Iridescent Gold, Metal Acanthus Leaf Base, 6 In.	400.00
Vase, Iridescent Gold, White Pulled & Hooked Feather, Gold Threading, c.1920, 12 In. ..	1035.00
Vase, King Tut, Ambergris, Green, Iridescent Gold, c.1915, 8 In.	1265.00
Vase, King Tut, Blue, Iridescent Green, Waisted, Ruffled Edge, 4 x 6 In.	840.00
Vase, King Tut, Iridescent Gold, Blue Highlights On Opal, 6 3/4 In.	1320.00
Vase, King Tut, Iridescent Platinum, Green, Orange Ground, Beehive, Signed, 4 In.	1150.00
Vase, King Tut, White, Iridescent Blue, Gold Disc Foot, c.1920, 10 In.	3000.00
Vase, Leaf & Vine, Green Pulled Leaf & Vine, Orange Ground, Gold Lip, 7 In.	1495.00
Vase, Moorish Crackle, Blue & White, Iridescent Ambergris, c.1920, 9 1/4 In.	2300.00
Vase, Opal, Blue Pulled Feathers, Iridescent Gold, Threading, Footed, c.1920, 12 In.	2185.00
Vase, Opal, Green, Gold, Pulled Heart, Vines, Gold Threading, c.1920, 12 In.	750.00
Vase, Opal, Iridescent Green, Gold Pulled Hearts, Allover Gold Threading, c.1920, 13 In. ..	375.00
Vase, Stick, Iridescent Blue, Ribbed, No. 1974, Signed, 1918, 18 1/2 In.	1380.00

DURANT KILNS was founded by Jean Durant Rice in 1910 in Bedford Village, New York. He hired Leon Volkmar to oversee production. The pottery made both tableware and artware. Rice died in 1919, leaving Leon Volkmar to run the business. After 1930 the name Durant Kilns was changed and only the Volkmar mark was used.

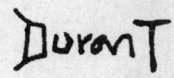

Bowl, Flaring, Ridged Texture, Blue Volcanic Glaze, 1915, 6 x 15 1/2 In.	499.00
Vase, Bulbous, Curdled White Volcanic Glaze, Amber Ground, 1923, 4 1/4 x 5 1/2 In.	529.00

ELFINWARE is a mark found on Dresden-like porcelain that was sold in dime stores and gift shops. Many pieces were decorated with raised flowers. The mark was registered by Breslauer-Underberg, Inc., of New York City in 1947. Pieces marked *Elfinware Made in Germany* had been sold since 1945 by this importer.

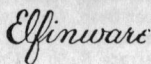

Figurine, Couch With 2 Matching Chairs, Pink & Blue Flowers, Gold Trim, 2 In. 145.00

ELVIS PRESLEY, the well-known singer, lived from 1935 to 1977. He became famous by 1956. Elvis appeared on television, starred in twenty-seven movies, and performed in Las Vegas. Memorabilia from any of the Presley shows, his records, and even memorials made after his death are collected.

Bottle, Wine, Blanco D'Oro, Frontenac, Contents, 1978 . . . . 20.00
Bracelet, Plastic Links With Song Titles, Elastic, 1960s 215.00
Bust, Painted, Ceramic, Statuary Corp., 1977, 19 In. 90.00
Cutout, Life Size, Standing, For Movie Loving You, 1957 . . . . 675.00
Handkerchief, Printed Song Titles, Square, 1956, 13 1/2 In. 290.00
Pin, Best Wishes, Elvis Presley, Copyright Kim Cioffi, Phila., Pa. 50.00
Poster, Jailhouse Rock, W.F. Schey Co., Australia, 40 x 27 In. 400.00
Record, Milkcow Blues Boogie, You're A Heartbreaker, Sun Records, 1955, 45 RPM 1020.00

ENAMELS listed here are made of glass particles and other materials heated and fused to metal. In the eighteenth and nineteenth centuries, workmen from Russia, France, England, and other countries made small boxes and table pieces of enamel on metal. One form of English enamel is called *Battersea* and is listed under that name. There was a revival of interest in enameling in the 1930s and a new style evolved. There is now renewed interest in the artistic enameled plaques, vases, ashtrays, and jewelry. Enamels made since the 1930s are usually on copper or steel, although silver was often used for jewelry. Graniteware is a separate category, and enameled metal kitchen pieces may be included in the Kitchen category.

Blood Cup, Nicholas II, Transfer, Double Headed Eagle, Tsar Cipher, c.1896, 4 In. 690.00
Bowl, Cover, Hammered Copper, Shallow, Finial, Karl Kipp, c.1908, 3 In. 150.00
Bowl, Footed, Owl In Trees, Blue Exterior, Karl Drerup, 1940, 11 1/2 In. . . . . *Illus* 350.00
Bowl Set, Copper, Orange Interior, 1 1/2 x 7 In., 6 Piece 235.00
Box, Fruit Design, Pink, Blue, Purple, Green, Gold, Cover, c.1910, 3 x 4 x 7 In. 940.00
Box, Scrolls, Leaves, Bird Handles, Green, White, Gold Stars, Silver Claw Feet, 2 1/2 In. . 1920.00
Candlestand, Onyx, Flowers, Champleve, 10 In. 355.00
Candlestick, Fretwork, Blue, Purple, Green, Thumb Hold, 3 Legs, Ball Feet, 4 In., Pair . . 3738.00
Casket, Copper, Rectangular Shape, 18th Century Figures In Garden, France, 11 In. 3287.00
Cigarette Case, Silver, Floral, Marked, 84, Kokoshnik, Russia, 1895, 2 1/2 x 4 1/2 In. . . . 1150.00
Cigarette Case, Silver, Red Flower & Scrolls, Blue & White Dots, Russia, 3 x 4 In. 860.00
Compact, Silver, Flowers, Leaves, Man & Woman On Top, 4 1/4 In. 230.00
Crucifix, Brass, Relief Scenes, Saints & Christ, Russia, Late 1800s, 8 3/4 In. 287.00
Cup, Silver, Handleless, Blue, Lavender, White, Red, c.1895, 2 In. 690.00
Figure, Elephant, Indian Gold, White Sapphire, Birds, Flowers, 4 3/8 In. 4180.00
Kovsh, Silver, Flowers, Black Background, Russia, 5 1/2 In. 4200.00

When the weather is bad, the auction will probably be good. Brave storms and cold and attend auctions in bad weather when the crowd is small and the prices low.

Enamel, Bowl, Footed, Owl In Trees, Blue Exterior,
Karl Drerup, 1940, 11 1/2 In.

Enamel, Plate,
Hammered Copper,
Arts & Crafts Design,
Potter Studio, 7 1/2 In.

Enamel, Silent
Butler, Fish, Wood
Handle, Nekrassoff,
12 1/2 In.

Plaque, Copper, Boy Playing Diabolo, Green, Red, Blue, Qing Dynasty, 4 x 3 In.		175.00
Plaque, Copper, Last Supper, Romanesque Style, France, 20th Century, 6 3/4 x 4 3/4 In.		489.00
Plate, Centaur Pulling Chariot, Goddess, Bow, Novembre, Signed, P. Soyer, 8 1/2 In.		635.00
Plate, Hammered Copper, Arts & Crafts Design, Potter Studio, 7 1/2 In.	*Illus*	65.00
Plate, Japanese Woman, Holding Mirror, Bold Colors, C. Erlich, c.1925, 6 3/4 In.		955.00
Silent Butler, Fish, Wood Handle, Nekrassoff, 12 1/2 In.	*Illus*	65.00
Spoon, Demitasse, Green, Lavender, Cream, Red Highlights, Silver, 4 In., 12 Piece		1265.00
Spoon, Red, White & Blue, Crown, Russia, 3 1/4 In., 6 Piece		690.00
Teapot, Yang-Tz'u, Hexagonal Form, Mountain Landscape Panels, Chinese, 8 1/4 In.		124.00
Vase, Bronze, Portrait, Woman In Red Dress, Roses, Silver Foil, c.1900, 7 In.		865.00
Vase, Bronze, Portrait, Woman, Flower Basket, Garden Scene, c.1900, 6 1/2 In.		490.00
Vase, Red & Yellow Flowers, Gilt, Flared Base, Narrow Rim, c.1920, 9 1/2 In.		380.00
Wine Pot, Flowers, Yellow Ground, Pink, Turquoise, Chinese, 18th Century, 6 3/4 In.		590.00

ERPHILA is a mark found on Czechoslovakian and other pottery and
porcelain made after 1920. The mark was used on items imported by
Ebeling & Reuss, Philadelphia, a giftware firm that is still operating in
Pennsylvania. The mark is a combination of the letters *E* and *R*
(Ebeling & Reuss) and the first letters of the city, Phila(delphia). Many
whimsical figural pitchers and creamers, figurines, platters, and other
giftwares carry this mark.

Bookends, Ram's Head, White, Stamped, Hollow, 6 x 7 1/2 In.	140.00
Bowl, Chintz, Rectangular, Gold Rim, 7 1/2 x 6 1/2 In.	80.00
Bowl, Majolica Style, Cabbage Leaves, Bavaria, 9 1/4 x 2 1/2 In.	38.00
Bowl, Square, Spaghetti-Ware Sides, Floral Transfer Bottom, Gold Rim, 9411/3, 8 In.	78.00
Cake Plate, Floral Garlands, Center Bouquet, Gold Rim, Germany, c.1950, 11 1/4 In.	72.00
Cake Plate & Server, Painted Flowers, Marked, Germany, c.1880, 11-In. Plate	130.00
Cigarette Holder, 4 Triangle Ashtrays, Colonial Man, Marked 6594, Germany, 5 3/4 In.	48.00
Creamer, Cat, Majolica, Faience, Pink, Germany, 757/I, 1930s, 5 3/4 In.	80.00
Figurine, Dog, Bloodhound, Paper Label On Side, 5 x 7 In.	75.00
Figurine, Dog, Great Dane, Harlequin, 14018, Germany, 2 x 3 In.	30.00
Figurine, Dog, Terrier, Gray, Marked, Germany, 5 x 5 In.	59.00
Figurine Set, Tiger & Cubs, Germany, Miniature, 1 1/4 In.	19.00
Flower Frog, Scarf Dancer, Bonnie Bull, Germany, 7 x 5 In.	195.00
Napkin Ring, Girl In Sunbonnet, 2 1/2 x 4 In.	70.00
Pitcher, Dog, Orange, Cream Color	1500.00
Pitcher, Lemon, Brown Handle, Green Leaves, c.1920, 4 In.	57.00
Pitcher, Red & White, Gold Stamp, Glazed, 1930s, 2 1/2 x 3 3/4 In.	15.00
Pitcher, Toby, Woman Holding Flowers, Orange Dots, Handle, c.1925, 6 1/4 In.	65.00
Plate, Decal Flowers, Gold Trim, Germany, 7 3/4 In., 4 Piece	10.00
Plate, Sailing Ships, Blue & White, Marked, 10 3/4 In., 4 Piece	200.00
Plate, Viking Ship, Flow Blue, White, Marked, 1930s, 11 In.	45.00
Reamer, Citrus, Orange, Majolica, Handle, c.1915	285.00
Teapot, Cat, Black & White, Pink Neck Bow, Green Eyes, 6700B, Germany, 8 In.	85.00
Teapot, Cat, Incised Copyright 9520, Germany, c.1910, 7 1/2 In.	195.00
Teapot, Dog, Dachshund, Incised 6703B, Stamped Made In US Zone, Germany, 8 In.	175.00
Teapot, Dog, Poodle, Incised 734, Germany, 8 1/4 In.	175.00
Teapot, Dog, Terrier, Black, White, Gray, Pink Neck Bow, 6702B, Germany, c.1940, 8 In.	60.00
Vase, Abstract Design, Yellow, Brown, Blue, Marked, 9 In.	316.00
Vase, Chintz, Green Swirls, Dark Green Rim, Pink Roses, Purple Flowers, 4 1/2 x 2 In.	75.00

Vase, Light Blue Chintz Floral, 2 Handles, Black, No. 2108, Czechoslovakia, 3 3/8 In. 50.00

ES GERMANY porcelain was made at the factory of Erdmann Schlegelmilch from 1861 to 1937 in Suhl, Germany. The porcelain, marked *ES Germany* or *ES Suhl*, was sold decorated or undecorated. Other pieces were made at a factory in Saxony, Prussia, and are marked *ES Prussia*. Reinhold Schlegelmilch made the famous wares marked *RS Germany*.

Cup & Saucer, Allover Gold, White Beading, Band Of Red Flowers	70.00
Plate, 3 Dancing Women & Winged Cherub, ES Royal Saxe, 9 1/4 In.	275.00
Plate, Blond Woman In White & Yellow Dress, Border, Royal Saxe, 8 1/2 In.	300.00
Plate, Diana, Woman & Cupid, Flowers, Prov Saxe, 9 3/4 In.	125.00
Plate, Hibiscus, Gold Rope Border, 8 1/2 In.	25.00
Plate, Mythological Scene, Horses, Chariot, Man, 3 Women, Prov Saxe, 9 7/8 In.	125.00
Plate, Pink Roses, Gold Tracery, Prov Saxe, 8 1/2 In.	65.00
Plate, Woman Holding Roses, Burgundy Band, Beads, Prov Saxe, 9 7/8 In.	475.00
Plate, Woman With Flowers In Blond Hair, Red Ground, Prov Saxe, 10 In.	375.00
Plate, Yellow Roses, Gold Rim, Prov Saxe, 8 1/2 In.	65.00
Tray, Dresser Woman With 2 Roses, Prov Saxe, 1 1/2 x 7 1/2 In.	700.00
Tray, Napoleon, ES Royal Saxe, 10 In.	200.00
Tray, Woman From Napoleon's Court, ES Royal Saxe, 7 1/2 In.	90.00
Vase, Flowers, Iridescent Purple, Handles, ES Royal Saxe, 9 1/2 In.	600.00
Vase, Hand Painted Robin On Branch, Baluster Shape, 8 In.	30.00
Vase, Nude Women, Turquoise Dots, Royal Saxe, 10 In.	800.00
Vase, Portrait, Young Woman With Roses, Art Nouveau Shape, Handles, 12 3/4 In.	425.00
Vase, Woman Smelling Roses, Green Luster, Handles, 10 In.	125.00
Vase, Woman With Holly In Hair, Gold, Yellow, Green Ground, ES Prov Saxe, 9 1/4 In. . . .	475.00

ESKIMO artifacts of all types are collected. Carvings of whale or walrus teeth are listed under Scrimshaw. Baskets are in the Basket category. All other types of Eskimo art are listed here.

Bag, Octopus, Beaded Cloth, Hide, Tlingit, Northwest Coast, 17 1/2 In.	4115.00
Basket, Coiled, Dog, Bird, Geometrics All Around, c.1940, 11 1/2 x 2 In.	100.00
Basket, Cover, Coiled, Multicolored Geometric Design, c.1910, 8 1/2 x 9 1/2 In.	200.00
Basket, Lidded, Bird Design, c.1920, 12 x 10 In.	550.00
Basket, Lidded, Dyed Seal Gut, c.1950, 7 1/2 x 8 In.	330.00
Boat, Model, Accessories, Man, Bowl, Paddles, Early 1900s, 32 In.	605.00
Bow Guard, Bone, Deer Design, 2 1/2 In.	660.00
Bowl, Wood, Carved, Abalone, Pinniped, Northwest Coast, Early 20th Century, 14 In. . . .	705.00
Bowl, Wood, Carved, Avian Shape, Abalone, Northwest Coast, 12 1/2 In.	2350.00
Box, Cover, Ivory Scrimshaw, 40 Figures & Symbols, 7/8 x 2 x 4 In.	550.00
Cane, Ivory Handle, Carved, Etched Ink Circle Designs, 37 In.	250.00
Carved Set, Whales, Seals, Ivory, 1 To 2 In., 5 Piece	360.00
Carving, Whalebone, Man, 6 In.	38.00
Cribbage Board, Ivory Tusk, Scrimshaw, E. Kiminock, 19 In.	250.00
Cribbage Board, Ivory, Scrimshaw, Children, Dogs, Sled, Caribou, Animals, 19 1/2 In. . .	385.00
Cribbage Board, Scrimshaw, Animals, Seals, On Carved Tusk, E. Muktoyuk, 15 In.	660.00
Doll, Leather Face, Fur-Trimmed Parka, Mittens, Hood, Mukluks, 15 1/2 In.	470.00
Effigy, Duck, Fossilized, Prehistoric, 1 1/4 In.	200.00
Effigy, Seal, Fossilized, Prehistoric, 1 1/2 In.	60.00
Figure, Carved Bone, Haida, Northwest Coast, 19th Century, 3 1/2 In.	2585.00
Gaming Sticks, Ivory, Engraved, 4 7/8 In.	90.00
Handle, Carved Bone, Arched, Attachment Perforations, Engraved, Inuit, 8 1/2 In.	560.00
Kayak, Soapstone, Double Seated, 17 In.	540.00
Ladle, Mountain Sheep Horn, Avian Head Handle, Northwest Coast, 19th Century, 23 In. . .	1295.00
Mask, Cedar, White, Carved, Painted, Exaggerated Features, 13 In.	1100.00
Mask, Wood, Painted, Northwest Coast, Early 20th Century, 12 In.	500.00
Model, Kayak, 3-Hole, Wood Framed, Hide Covering, 42 In.	1035.00
Mukluks, Beaded, 15 x 10 In.	145.00
Plate, Argillite, Carved, Stylized Animals, Northwest Coast, 14 In.	1880.00
Rattle, Carved, Painted, Oyster Catcher Shape, Northwest Coast, c.1900, 11 1/2 In.	470.00
Totem Pole, Wood, Polychrome, Northwest Coast, Late 19th Century, 16 3/4 In.	1116.00
Tray, Wood, Carved, Stylized Face, Northwest Coast, c.1892, 14 1/2 In.	650.00

FABERGE was a firm of jewelers and goldsmiths founded in St. Petersburg, Russia, in 1842, by Gustav Faberge. Peter Carl Faberge, his son, was jeweler to the Russian Imperial Court from about 1870 to 1914. The rare Imperial Easter eggs, jewelry, and decorative items are very expensive today.

Bell Push, Gold, Enameled, Diamond-Set, Red, Moonstone, Marked, c.1910, 1 3/4 In.	22705.00
Bowl, Silver, Cut Glass, Marked, c.1910, 8 3/4 In.	6570.00
Bowl, Silver, Nephrite, Cylindrical, Swags, 3-Footed, Marked, c.1900, 4 3/4 In.	9560.00
Box, Cover, Silver, Enameled, Blue, Red, Signed, 3 1/2 x 2 1/4 In.	1380.00
Box, Silver, Enameled, Fluted, Cover, Coin, Catherine II, Red, Marked, c.1900, 2 1/2 In.	7170.00
Buckle, Enameled, Lavender, Rose Cut Diamonds, Seed Pearl Trim, 3 x 2 In.	7475.00
Cane Handle, Bowenite, Green, Gold, Enameled, Carved, Leaves, Marked, c.1890, 5 In.	6570.00
Centerpiece, Silver, Cut Glass, Oval, Water Lilies, 4-Footed, Marked, c.1890, 22 In.	29875.00
Dish, Silver, Enameled, Orange, 3 Sides, Reeded Border, Marked, c.1890, 3 7/8 In.	10755.00
Fan, Gold, Enameled, Jeweled, Man, Woman, Scrolls, Flowers, Marked, c.1900, 8 In.	17925.00
Figurine, Bear, Obsidian, Carved, Diamond Set Eyes, Black, Case, c.1900, 2 In.	6570.00
Frame, Silver, Enameled, Blue, Silver Strut, Marked, c.1910, 4 1/4 In.	10755.00
Frame, Silver, Enameled, Translucent, Pink, Pearls, Bow, Marked, c.1890, 3 1/4 In.	20315.00
Frame, Silver, Wood, Beaded Border, Marked, c.1910, 11 1/2 In.	5975.00
Kovsh, Silver, Enameled, Pan Slavic Style, Moscow Hallmark, c.1908, 3 1/2 In.	2875.00
Letter Opener, Saw, Silver Blade, Gold Handle, Marked, c.1890, 3 1/4 In.	5380.00
Match Holder, Silver, Sandstone, Cylindrical, Floral Garlands, Marked, c.1890, 4 In.	16730.00
Pen Tray, Silver, Gold, Enameled, Translucent, Leaf Border, Marked, c.1900, 6 1/2 In.	9560.00
Pendant, Easter Egg, Gold, Emeralds, Clover Set, Marked, c.1900, 5/8 In.	2150.00
Pin, Spoon, Gold, Jeweled, Ruby, Diamond-Set Mouse, Case, c.1890, 1 1/2 In.	7170.00
Tankard, Cut Glass, Hinged Lid, Marked, c.1900, 5 3/4 In.	1670.00
Wine Cooler, Silver, Swags, Leaves, Scroll Handles, Marked, c.1910, 8 1/4 In.	17925.00

FAIENCE refers to tin-glazed earthenware, especially the wares made in France, Germany, and Scandinavia. It is also correct to say that faience is the same as majolica or Delft, although usually the term refers only to the tin-glazed pottery of the three regions mentioned.

Basket, Polychrome, Handle, 5 3/4 x 7 3/4 In.	60.00
Bowl, Glazed Creamware, Round Base, Flared, Reticulated Sides, 8 1/2 x 3 1/4 In.	55.00
Box, Polychrome, Shaped, Cover, 2 1/2 x 5 1/4 x 5 1/4 In.	45.00
Cachepot, Marseille Style, Striped, Avian Reserve, France, c.1900, 4 1/2 In., Pair	520.00
Charger, Flower Sprays, Kellingheusen, Early 19th Century, 12 1/2 In.	1555.00
Chocolate Pot, Cover, Raised Feet, Nevers	3600.00
Creamer, Polychrome, Decorated, 3 In.	22.00
Cruet, Polychrome, Decorated, 4 In.	11.00
Decanter, Cordial, Parisian Kiosk Form, Art Deco, Lanvin Parfum, Paris, Signed, 11 In.	105.00
Dish, Delft Style, Polychrome, Bird On Branch, Red, Blue, Green, Floral Border, 9 In.	170.00
Figure, Cat, Galle Pottery Style, Seated, Green, Hearts, Glass Eyes, 1900s, 13 In.	646.00
Flower Holder, Polychrome, Turtle Shape, 5 3/4 In.	85.00
Jar, Apothecary, Cover, Polychrome, Man, Dog, Black-Letter Label, Ex Curcum, 5 1/2 In.	735.00
Jardiniere, Marseille Style, Fisherman Reserve, France, c.1900, 5 x 13 1/2 In.	316.00
Lamp, Polychrome, Decorated, Shaped, Handle, 4 1/2 In.	165.00
Menu Holder, Breton Crest, Ermine Taila, Blue Scallop & Dot Border, c.1930	290.00
Plate, Basket Of Flowers, Rooster Mounted, Keller & Guerin, France, 8 1/2 In., Pair	185.00
Platter, Persian-Style Polychrome Design, 23 x 15 1/2 In.	90.00
Relish, Polychrome, 6 In.	5.50
Salt, Master, Polychrome, Double-Shell Shape, Serpent Handle, 2 x 4 1/2 x 3 In.	66.00
Salt, Master, Polychrome, Pig Shape, Double Cellar, 2 1/4 In.	33.00
Shelf, Hanging, Polychrome, Winged Dragon Support, 7 1/4 x 6 x 5 1/2 In.	80.00
Tankard, Castle In Landscape, Pewter Mount, Germany, 9 In.	470.00
Tankard, Coastal Landscape, Fisherman, Polychrome, Baluster Shape, Germany, 9 In.	355.00
Tankard, Landscape, Charging Bull, Pewter Mounts, 6 1/4 In.	380.00
Tankard, Man On Horse, Polychrome, Pewter Mounts, Germany, 5 1/2 In.	295.00
Tankard, Yellow, Green, Manganese, Blue, Fruit, Pewter Mounts, 11 In.	765.00
Vase, Crocus, Oriental Man Smoking, 9 Sockets, France, 7 x 8 In.	299.00
Vase, Lakeside Hill Town, Flowers, Blue, White, Green, 5 Holders, 9 In.	405.00
Vase, Mulberry Glossy Glaze, Impressed, California Faience, 4 3/8 In.	230.00

China can be washed in warm water with mild soapsuds. The addition of ammonia to the water will add that extra sparkle. Don't scrub gilding and gold edges on porcelains.

Fairing, Trinket Box, Boy & Rooster,
Fireplace Base, 4 1/2 In.

FAIRINGS are small souvenir china boxes and figurines that were sold at country fairs during the nineteenth century. Most were made in Germany. Reproductions of fairings are being made, especially of the famous *twelve months of marriage* series.

Figurine, Boy & Girl Reading Book, Victorian, 3 1/4 In.	56.00
Figurine, Boy Putting On Trousers, Canopied Bed, No. 3576, Victorian, 4 In.	84.00
Figurine, Girl Feeding Chicken, No. 3662, Victorian, 4 1/4 In.	60.00
Figurine, Girl, Goat, Victorian, 3 In.	68.00
Figurine, Man & Woman Riding High-Wheeled Bikes, No. 2411, 3 3/4 In.	395.00
Figurine, Seated Woman & Man, Victorian, 1 3/4 In.	56.00
Matchbox, Father, Baby, Mother In Bed, Victorian, 3 1/2 In.	34.00
Matchbox, Man In Rowboat, Gifts, Victorian, 2 3/4 In.	45.00
Matchbox, Man In Rowboat, Gifts, Victorian, 3 1/4 In.	68.00
Matchbox, Man, Woman, Child, Dog, Sofa, No. 216, 3 1/2 In.	75.00
Matchbox, Tureen Form, Rabbit, Blanket, No. 979, Victorian, 2 3/4 In.	79.00
Trinket Box, Altar, Crucifix, Bible, Chalice, Pitcher, No. 484, Victorian, 4 1/4 In.	56.00
Trinket Box, Angel Lying On Cross, Victorian, 2 In.	50.00 to 68.00
Trinket Box, Baby In Bassinet Holding Rattle, Victorian, 3 1/2 In.	248.00
Trinket Box, Boy & Rooster, Fireplace Base, 4 1/2 In.	*Illus* 125.00
Trinket Box, Bureau, 2 Birds On Nest, Victorian, 4 In.	68.00
Trinket Box, Bureau, Baby, Rattle, Highchair, Dog, Victorian, 3 1/4 In.	205.00
Trinket Box, Bureau, Boy, Dog, Conta Shield, No. 3590 162, Victorian, 4 3/4 In.	75.00
Trinket Box, Bureau, Carrier Pigeon, Letter, No. 3518, Victorian, 3 3/4 In.	28.00 to 35.00
Trinket Box, Bureau, Cat, Kitten In Cradle, No. 3907 124, Victorian, 4 3/4 In.	200.00
Trinket Box, Bureau, Dog On Cushion, Paws Crossed, No. 2459, Victorian, 4 1/4 In.	56.00
Trinket Box, Cat Rocking Kitten In Cradle On Lid, Conta & Boehm, 5 x 2 x 3 In.	50.00
Trinket Box, Cherub Emerging From Flower, Victorian, 3 1/2 In.	50.00 to 56.00
Trinket Box, Child, Horn, Jester Doll, Wicker Basket, No. 496 V 42, Victorian, 4 In.	115.00
Trinket Box, Dog Licking Boy's Face, Ball, Stick, Conta Shield Mark No. 3569, 4 1/2 In.	60.00
Trinket Box, Dog Lying On Pillow, Bugle, Ball, Conta Shield Mark, No. 18, 2 1/4 In.	56.00
Trinket Box, Dog On Cushion, Crossed Paws, Victorian, 4 In.	45.00
Trinket Box, Express, Boy, Hat, Lying On Chest, No. 4178, Germany, c.1900, 4 In.	85.00
Trinket Box, Fish Handle, Green, Shiny Glaze, 3 1/4 x 3 3/4 In.	25.00
Trinket Box, Girl Holding Doll, No. 359, Victorian, 4 3/4 In.	60.00
Trinket Box, Girl On Chaise Longue, Doll, Sitting Boy, Victorian, 3 3/4 In.	125.00
Trinket Box, Girl On Pillow, Dog At Feet, Victorian, 3 In.	56.00
Trinket Box, Jester On Drum, 1-Man Band, Conta Shield Mark, 2 3/4 In.	56.00
Trinket Box, Man, Woman Playing Checkers, Woman Standing, Victorian, 4 In.	45.00
Trinket Box, Mantel, Cat Playing With Frog, No. 3524, 4 In.	75.00
Trinket Box, Mantel, Fruit On Top, No. 3534, 4 In.	45.00
Trinket Box, Mantel, Jester On Drum, 1-Man Band, No. 3505, Victorian, 4 1/4 In.	45.00
Trinket Box, Mother At Foot Of Bed, Child Playing With Toes, No. 296, Victorian, 3 In.	215.00
Trinket Box, Painted, Domed Hinged Lid, Tulips, Squiggles, Dots, c.1800, 4 x 8 x 5 In.	1435.00
Trinket Box, Painted, Hinged Lid, Flowers, Tulips, Jacob Weber, Penn., 3 x 4 1/2 x 3 In.	2390.00
Trinket Box, Turk On Pillow, Reading Newspaper, Smoking Water Pipe, Victorian, 4 In.	75.00
Trinket Box, Woman At Vanity, Jewelry, Powder Box, Bottle, No. 2939, Victorian, 4 In.	124.00

Trinket Box, Woman On Horse, Man, Dog, Trough, Victorian, 4 In. 62.00
Trinket Box, Woman Playing Piano, Man Beside Her, No. 306, Victorian, 2 3/4 In. 85.00

FAIRYLAND LUSTER pieces are included in the Wedgwood category.

FAMILLE ROSE, see Chinese Export category.

FANS have been used for cooling since the days of the ancients. By the eighteenth century, the fan was an accessory for the lady of fashion, and very elaborate and expensive fans were made. Sticks were made of ivory or wood, set with jewels or carved. The fans were made of painted silk or paper. Inexpensive paper fans printed with advertising were giveaways in the late nineteenth and early twentieth centuries. Electric fans were introduced in 1882.

Advertising, 666 Laxative Tonic, Child, Birds, Cardboard, Wood, 1936, 7 x 7 1/2 In. 15.00
Advertising, 7-Up, Woman At Beach, Keep Cool, c.1940, 9 x 14 In. 65.00
Advertising, Bradley Knit Wear, Swimsuits, 2 Sides, c.1920, 7 x 8 In. 20.00
Advertising, Endicott-Johnson Shoes, Smiling Worker, 2 Sides, Paper, 1923, 9 x 11 In. . . . 18.00
Advertising, New Home Sewing Machine, Woman, 2 Sides, Paper, c.1900, 8 1/2 x 10 In. . 15.00
Advertising, RC Cola, Shirley Temple 65.00
Advertising, Weaver Pianos, Woman, Piano, 2 Sides, Paper, Wood, c.1920, 8 1/4 x 9 In. . . 15.00
Advertising, Winchester Store, Birch Trees, Stream, John C. Holt, Order Form, 7 x 9 In. . 470.00
Advertising, Winchester, Clark & Son, 9 x 15 In. 80.00
Electric, Emerson, No. 11666, Brass Blades & Cage, Ribbed Base 1500.00
Electric, Emerson, No. 77648-AN, Slide Switch, 16 In. 60.00
Electric, Ezio Pirali Zerowatt, Aluminum, Rubber, Italy, 1954, 10 In. 1840.00
Electric, Hunter, Century, Zephaire-Type Guards, Narrow Paddles, 12 In. 40.00
Electric, Mathas Cooler, Box Type, Wooden, Variable Speed 65.00
Electric, Sears & Roebuck, Metal, Green Plastic 3-Wing Overlapping Blade, 10 In. 25.00
Feather, Ostrich, Box, J.E. Caldwell 118.00
Fly Fan, Cast Iron, Painted, Key Wind, 40 In. 660.00
Ivory, Carved Handle, Interwoven Blade, Silver Strips, India, 19th Century 920.00
Ivory, Carved, Lace, Embroidered, Shadowbox Frame, France, c.1885, 26 1/2 x 37 In. . . . 345.00
Ivory, Hand-Painted Scenes, Couple At Dinner, White & Gold Lace, Frame 294.00
Lace, Faux Mother-Of-Pearl, Lace, White, Silver Spangles, Giltwood Frame, 24 x 16 In. . 235.00
Mother-Of-Pearl, Figures In Palace, Chinese, 19th Century, 9 In. 500.00
Mother-Of-Pearl, Paper, Flowers, Figurine, Landscape, Shadowbox, 24 x 14 In. 230.00
Silk, Bone Frame, Woman, Urn, Butterflies, Hand Painted, 19th Century, 11 x 22 In. 325.00
Tortoiseshell, Lacquer, Birds, Flowering Tree, 19th Century, 9 3/4 In. 633.00

FAST FOOD COLLECTIBLES may be included in several categories, such as Advertising, Coca-Cola, Toy, etc.

FEDERZEICHNUNG is the very strange German name for a pattern of mother-of-pearl satin glass. The pattern had irregularly shaped sections of brown glass covered with a pattern of gold squiggle lines. It was first made in the late nineteenth century.

Vase, Brown, Mother-Of-Pearl Octopus, White Interior, Flared Lip, 6 In. 1610.00

FENTON Art Glass Company, founded in Martins Ferry, Ohio, by Frank L. Fenton, is now located in Williamstown, West Virginia. It is noted for early carnival glass produced between 1907 and 1920. Some of these pieces are listed in the Carnival Glass category. Many other types of glass were also made. Spanish Lace in this section refers to the pattern made by Fenton.

Apple Blossoms & Robins, Bell, Large 125.00
Aqua Crest, Candlestick, Cornucopia, Ribbed, No. 951, Pair 125.00
Aqua Crest, Jug, 60 Oz. 475.00
Aqua Crest, Vase, Hand, 11 In. 295.00
Baroque, Candy Dish, Cover, Lavender, Satin, 3-Footed, 5 In. 80.00
Bicentennial Eagle, Plate, Red Slag 20.00
Black Rose Crest, Compote, 6 1/4 x 8 In. 150.00
Blue Opalescent, Tumble-Up Set, Spiral Optic, 1939, 8 1/2 In., 2 Piece 900.00
Blue Opalescent, Water Set, 8 1/2-In. Cannonball Pitcher, 9 Piece 550.00

Bubble Optic, Vase, Dusty Rose Over Milk Glass, Double Ruffled Edge, 6 In.	115.00
Bubble Optic, Vase, Red Over White, Cased, Ruffled Edge, 10 1/2 x 8 1/2 In.	518.00
Burmese, Basket, Enameled Pink Dogwood, 7 1/2 In.	125.00
Burmese, Basket, Satin, Bird, Signed, Louise Piper, 6 In.	115.00
Burmese, Cruet, Diamond Optic, 7 In.	155.00
Burmese, Cruet, Lotus Mist	100.00
Burmese, Lamp, Diamond Optic, Rose, 20 In.	195.00
Burmese, Pitcher, Enameled Pansies, 5 1/2 In.	95.00
Burmese, Rose Bowl, Poppy, 4 1/2 In.	45.00
Burmese, Toothpick, Daisy & Panel	60.00
Burmese, Vanity Set	350.00
Burmese, Vase, Blue, Ribbed, Pinched & Ruffled Rim, 5 In.	135.00
Burmese, Vase, Wheat, Blue, Serpentine Coil At Center, 8 In.	140.00
Burmese, Water Set, Raspberry, 85th Anniversary, 7 Piece	475.00
Burmese Satin, Basket, Enameled Maple Leaves	115.00
Burmese Satin, Cruet, Stopper, Enameled Roses, 1970s	175.00
Burmese Satin, Relish, Heart Handle, Enameled Rose, Butterfly	110.00
Butterfly, Bonbon, Green Satin	15.00
Butterfly & Berry, Tumbler, Black, Carnival	20.00
Cactus, Basket, Topaz Opalescent, 10 In.	175.00
Cactus, Goblet, Aqua Opalescent	40.00
Cactus, Vase, Fan, Topaz Opalescent	175.00
Cameo Opalescent, Vase, Fan, 8 In.	65.00
Cameo Satin, Vase, Daisies, 3 3/4 In.	38.00
Candleglow Yellow, Vase, Feather, 8 1/2 In.	70.00
Candleglow Yellow, Vase, Spiral, 11 In.	75.00
Clydesdales, Lamp, Hurricane, 11 In.	425.00
Clydesdales, Vase, 6 In.	285.00
Coin Dot, Castor Jar, Cranberry Opalescent, Enameled Birds, Berries, Cameo, 12 In.	145.00
Coin Dot, Lamp, Hurricane, Cranberry, Opalescent, Crimped, 9 1/2 In.	300.00
Coin Dot, Pitcher, Blue Opalescent, 8 3/4 In.	275.00
Coin Dot, Vase, Cranberry Opalescent, Tricornered Rim, 7 In.	135.00
Coin Dot, Vase, Cranberry, Snow Crest Edging, 11 In.	415.00
Coin Dot, Vase, Ivy, Topaz Opalescent, 5 1/2 x 4 1/2 In.	275.00
Coin Dot, Water Set, Cranberry Cut To Clear, Enameled Lily Of The Valley, 7 Piece	600.00
Colonial, Plate, Amber, 8 1/2 In.	12.00
Colonial, Toothpick, Blue, 3 In.	20.00
Colonial Thumbprint, Compote, Cover, Amber	30.00
Curtain, Basket, Aqua Opalescent, Looped Handle, Levay, 1980, 9 In.	130.00
Custard Satin, Basket, Log Cabin, Medium	85.00
Diamond Lace, Cake Plate, Blue Opalescent, Pedestal Base, Smooth Edge	124.00
Diamond Lace, Epergne, Blue Opalescent, 3 Horns, Ruffled & Fluted Rim, 5 In.	265.00
Diamond Lace, Epergne, Green Opalescent, 4 x 13 In.	425.00
Diamond Optic, Basket, Springtime Green, Threaded, 3-Toed, 7 In.	65.00
Diamond Optic, Vase, Fan, Dolphin, Ruby, 6 In.	85.00
Dogwood, Vase, Dusty Rose Overlay, 8 In.	60.00
Dot Optic, Cruet, Topaz Opalescent	139.00
Dot Optic, Pitcher, Blue Opalescent, 9 1/2 x 7 1/2 In.	290.00
Dot Optic, Rose Bowl, Topaz Opalescent, Crimped	79.00
Figurine, Bear Cub, Custard, Pastel Violets	70.00
Figurine, Bear, Custard, Daisies	68.00
Figurine, Bear, Lying, Topaz Opalescent	25.00
Figurine, Bear, Twilight Blue, Pink Apple Blossoms	55.00
Figurine, Bird, White Satin, Winterberry	45.00
Figurine, Cat, Chocolate Roses, Cameo Satin	65.00
Figurine, Cat, Misty Blue Satin, Iridized	25.00
Figurine, Cat, Topaz Opalescent, 5 In.	30.00
Figurine, Donkey, Blue Satin	125.00
Figurine, Duckling, Custard Satin	40.00
Figurine, Duckling, Topaz Opalescent	25.00
Figurine, Frog, Custard Satin	40.00
Figurine, Frog, Topaz Opalescent	30.00
Figurine, Happiness Bird, Custard, Daisies	35.00

Figurine, Kissing Kids, Carnival, Pair	35.00 to 80.00
Figurine, Mallard, Green Carnival, 4 In.	25.00
Figurine, Mouse, Topaz Opalescent	25.00
Figurine, Mouse, White Satin, Red Jacket, Louise Piper	95.00
Figurine, Praying Children, Crystal Velvet, Pair	39.00
Figurine, Praying Children, Shiny Black, Pair	125.00
Figurine, Swan, Blue Custard, Blue Roses	38.00
Geometrics, Bowl, Periwinkle, 8 In.	125.00
Georgian, Bowl, Cereal, Amber, 6 3/4 In.	16.00
Georgian, Plate, Salad, Amber, 8 1/4 In.	16.00
Goldenrod, Vase, Tulip, 7 1/2 In.	39.00
Grape, Bowl, Black, Carnival, 8 3/4 In.	55.00
Grape, Vase, Custard Satin, 3-Toed	40.00
Green Satin, Bonbon, Enameled Butterflies, 2 3/8 x 7 1/2 In.	25.00
Hanging Hearts, Pitcher, Blue, 11 3/8 x 6 1/4 In.	530.00
Heart Optic, Puff Box, Cranberry Opalescent, 4 In.	110.00
Hobnail, Basket, Cranberry Opalescent, 10 In.	165.00
Hobnail, Basket, Lime Green Opalescent, 4 3/4 In.	110.00
Hobnail, Basket, Topaz Opalescent, 10 In.	280.00
Hobnail, Bonbon, Ruby, 8 In.	25.00
Hobnail, Bowl, Blue Opalescent, 11 In.	95.00
Hobnail, Bowl, Milk Glass, Scalloped Edge & Base, 3 1/2 x 8 1/2 In.	25.00
Hobnail, Bowl, Turquoise, 1 1/4 x 4 In.	85.00
Hobnail, Bride's Basket, Cranberry Opalescent, Silver Plated Frame, 11 1/2 In.	300.00
Hobnail, Candy Box, Cover, Milk Glass, White, Footed	25.00
Hobnail, Cigarette Holder, Milk Glass, Top Hat, 3 1/4 x 4 1/2 In.	25.00
Hobnail, Compote, Lime Opalescent, 5 3/4 x 6 1/2 In.	25.00
Hobnail, Compote, Plum Opalescent, 1959-1962	145.00
Hobnail, Cruet, Milk Glass, Stopper, 5 In.	25.00
Hobnail, Epergne, Milk Glass, 3 Lilies	145.00
Hobnail, Fairy Lamp, Green Satin, 4 1/2 In.	45.00
Hobnail, Jug, French Opalescent, 80 Oz.	200.00
Hobnail, Relish, Milk Glass, 3 Sections	15.00
Hobnail, Relish, Milk Glass, Center Handle, 5 x 7 In.	23.00
Hobnail, Slipper, Amber	15.00
Hobnail, Toothpick, Milk Glass	15.00
Hobnail, Tray, Milk Glass, 2 Sections, Center Handle	15.00
Hobnail, Vanity Set, Topaz Opalescent, 3 Piece	275.00
Hobnail, Vase, Blue Satin, 3 In.	75.00
Hobnail, Vase, Bud, Milk Glass, 1940s, 9 1/2 In.	25.00
Hobnail, Vase, Fan, Blue Satin, 4 In.	75.00
Hobnail, Vase, French Opalescent, 8 In.	65.00
Hobnail, Vase, Tulip, Cranberry Opalescent, 7 1/2 In.	70.00
Hobnail, Wedding Bowl, Cover, Milk Glass	35.00
Ivory Crest, Plate, 6 In.	35.00
Ivory Crest, Vase, Tricornered Hat, 1922, 8 In.	125.00
Ivy Overlay, Vase, 6 In.	45.00
Jamestown, Bowl, 6 Sides, Blue, 8 1/2 In.	40.00
Lily Of The Valley, Vase, Bud, Carnival	20.00
Lime Satin, Vase, Beaded Melon, 6 In.	30.00
Maple Leaf, Vase, Burmese Satin, 7 In.	75.00
Moonstone, Egg Plate, 11 1/4 In.	25.00
Moonstone, Vase, 3 1/2 In.	40.00
Mosaic, Vase, Inclusions, Iridescent Black Ground, Threading, 5 1/4 In.	1610.00
Mother's Day, Plate, Cameo Satin, 1980, 9 In.	15.00
New World, Plate, Salad, Lime Opalescent, 9 In.	150.00
New World, Salt & Pepper, Lime Opalescent	195.00
Orange Tree, Loving Cup, Blue Carnival, 5 3/4 In.	58.00
Orange Tree, Loving Cup, Marigold Carnival, 5 3/4 In.	45.00
Orange Tree, Powder Jar, Cover, Black, Carnival	70.00
Orange Tree, Shaving Mug, Mandarin Red	450.00
Paisley, Cake Plate, Footed, Holly & Berries, 12 1/2 In.	250.00
Paneled Daisy, Candleholder, Votive, French Opalescent	15.00

Paneled Daisy, Candy Box, Cover, Blue Satin 75.00
Paneled Diamonds & Bows, Vase, Blue Carnival, 9 1/2 In. 60.00
Paperweight, Apple, Yellow Overlay, c.1980 . . . . 49.00
Patriot, Planter, Lime Satin 75.00
Peach Crest, Bowl, 4 1/2 x 10 In. 125.00
Peach Crest, Jug, Handle, 8 In. 95.00
Peach Crest, Vase, 10 In. 115.00
Peach Crest, Vase, Crimped, 6 In. . . . . .45.00 to 50.00
Periwinkle Blue, Vase, Fan, 1935, 5 1/2 In. 40.00
Pinwheel, Compote, Lime Sherbet 35.00
Plum Opalescent, Basket, 7 In. 200.00
Plum Opalescent, Vase, Bud, 8 In. 65.00
Plum Overlay, Basket, Plum & Sweet Briar, 8 In. 75.00
Poppy, Basket, Lime Sherbet, 7 In. 125.00
Poppy, Lamp, Student, Lime Sherbet, 19 In. 375.00
Regency, Relish, Federal Blue, 8 In. 15.00
Rose Crest, Bonbon, Double Ruffled Edge, 5 1/2 In. 25.00
Rose Satin, Vase, Beaded, Melon, 6 In. 50.00
Silver Crest, Basket, 7 In. 25.00
Silver Crest, Basket, 8 In. 30.00
Silver Crest, Candlestick, Pinecone Extending Down, 10 x 3 3/4 In., Pair 305.00
Silver Crest, Compote, 3 1/4 x 6 In. 25.00
Silver Crest, Compote, Flared, Double Ruffled Edge, Footed, 6 x 8 In. 16.00
Silver Crest, Epergne, 3 Lilies, 14 In. 375.00
Silver Crest, Tray, Metal Center Handle, 8 3/4 In. 20.00
Silver Crest, Vanity Set, Lily Of The Valley, 3 Piece 90.00
Silver Crest, Vase, 10 In. 10.00
Spiral Optic, Basket, Green Opalescent, 12 x 10 In. 530.00
Spiral Optic, Basket, Melon Ribbed, Square Twisted Handle, Burmese Satin, 7 1/2 In. . . . 75.00
Spiral Optic, Pitcher, Cranberry Opalescent, 9 1/2 x 5 1/2 In. 550.00
Stretch, Bowl, Wide Flare, Rolled Rim, Blue, 1920s, 9 1/2 x 5 5/8 In. 45.00
Stretch, Candlestick, Pink, c.1926 . . . . 35.00
Stretch, Compote, Blue, Cupped, 3 3/4 x 5 In. 40.00
Stretch, Dish, Mayonnaise, Pearl, 5 x 4 In. 45.00
Stretch, Vase, Cobalt Blue, Dolphin Handles, Square, Box, 1996, 6 1/4 x 5 1/4 In. 55.00
Swirl, Barber Bottle, Blue Opalescent, Silver Top, Cork, 8 1/4 x 3 1/2 In. 280.00
Tangerine, Vase, Stretch, c.1927, 7 3/4 x 6 3/4 In. 290.00
Topaz Opalescent, Jug, Iridized, Hydrangeas, 7 In. 95.00
Vasa Murrhina, Basket, Blue With Aventurine Green, 11 In. 65.00
Vasa Murrhina, Bowl, Blue With Aventurine Green, 4 In. 30.00
Vasa Murrhina, Vase, Aventurine Green With Blue, 10 In. 140.00
Vasa Murrhina, Vase, Aventurine Green With Rose, 11 In. 130.00
Vasa Murrhina, Vase, Rose With Aventurine Green, 14 In. 85.00
Velva Rose, Basket, 8 1/2 In. 65.00
Water Lily, Basket, Lime Satin, 7 In. . . . . .45.00 to 55.00
Water Lily, Bowl, Blue Satin 45.00
Water Lily, Bowl, Rose, Custard Satin 45.00
Water Lily, Compote, Crystal Velvet 35.00
Water Lily, Vase, Bud, Custard Satin, 9 1/2 In. 23.00
Water Lily, Vase, Bud, Lime Satin, 11 In. 25.00
Wave Crest, Salt & Pepper, White, 2 1/2 In. 25.00
Wisteria, Vase, Threaded Diamond Optic, 7 In. 65.00

FIESTA, the colorful dinnerware, was introduced in 1936 by the Homer
Laughlin China Co., redesigned in 1969, and withdrawn in 1973. It
was reissued again in 1986 in different colors and is still being made.
The simple design was characterized by a band of concentric circles,
beginning at the rim. Cups had full-circle handles until 1969, when
partial-circle handles were made. Harlequin and Riviera were related
wares. For more information about Fiesta, its colors and prices, see the
book *Kovels' Depression Glass & Dinnerware Price List.*

Chartreuse, Plate, 6 In. 9.00

Chartreuse, Platter, 12 In. 58.00
Cobalt Blue, Bowl, Fruit, 4 3/4 In. ....32.00 to 35.00
Cobalt Blue, Bowl, Fruit, 5 1/2 In. 32.00
Cobalt Blue, Carafe 75.00
Cobalt Blue, Cup, After Dinner 60.00
Cobalt Blue, Plate, 6 In. 7.00
Cobalt Blue, Plate, 10 In. 40.00
Cobalt Blue, Saucer, After Dinner ....15.00 to 20.00
Forest Green, Plate, 7 In. 14.00
Forest Green, Plate, Deep, 8 1/4 In. 55.00
Green, Plate, 6 In. 5.00
Ivory, Bowl, Fruit, 5 1/2 In. 32.00
Ivory, Casserole, French, Cover 250.00
Ivory, Plate, 7 In. 10.00
Ivory, Plate, 9 In. 15.00
Ivory, Plate, 10 In. 40.00
Ivory, Soup, Cream 60.00
Kitchen Kraft, Cake Server 265.00
Kitchen Kraft, Spoon 245.00
Light Green, Bowl, Fruit, 5 1/2 In. ....20.00 to 60.00
Light Green, Cup & Saucer 20.00
Light Green, Cup, Tea 25.00
Light Green, Fork, Kitchen Kraft 145.00
Light Green, Soup, Cream 42.00
Lilac, Candleholder, Tripod, Pair 800.00
Lilac, Vase, 8 In. 400.00
Medium Green, Cup & Saucer 45.00
Red, Cup, After Dinner 60.00
Red, Mug 90.00
Red, Pitcher, Water, Ice Lip 135.00
Red, Plate, 9 In. 22.00
Red, Relish, 11 In. 260.00
Red, Saucer 12.00
Red, Soup, Cream 60.00
Red, Spoon, Kitchen Kraft 145.00
Red, Sugar 100.00
Red, Teapot, 6 Cup 175.00
Rose, Bowl, Fruit, 5 1/2 In. 52.00
Rose, Saucer, After Dinner 85.00
Rose, Tumbler, Juice, 5 Oz. 65.00
Turquoise, Bowl, Fruit, 5 1/2 In. 25.00
Turquoise, Casserole, Cover, 7 3/4 In. 75.00
Turquoise, Mug, Tom & Jerry 25.00
Turquoise, Plate, 9 In. 12.00
Turquoise, Plate, 10 In. 25.00
Turquoise, Soup, Cream 42.00
Turquoise, Teapot, 8 Cup 245.00
Yellow, Bowl, Fruit, 5 1/2 In. 25.00
Yellow, Bowl, Salad, 7 1/2 In. 85.00
Yellow, Cake Plate, 11 In. 45.00
Yellow, Cup, After Dinner ....50.00 to 60.00
Yellow, Cup, Tea 25.00
Yellow, Nappy, 8 1/2 In. 40.00
Yellow, Pie Plate, Kitchen Kraft, 10 In. 40.00
Yellow, Plate, 7 In. 8.00
Yellow, Plate, 9 In. 12.00
Yellow, Plate, 10 In. 25.00
Yellow, Sauceboat 45.00
Yellow, Saucer 4.00
Yellow, Soup, Cream 42.00

FINCH, see Kay Finch category.

FINDLAY ONYX AND FLORADINE are two similar types of glass made by Dalzell, Gilmore and Leighton Co. of Findlay, Ohio, about 1889. Onyx is a patented yellowish white opaque glass with raised silver daisy decorations. A few rare pieces were made of rose, amber, orange, or purple glass. Floradine is made of cranberry-colored glass with an opalescent white raised floral pattern and a satin finish. The same molds were used for both types of glass.

Celery Vase, Concentric Rings On Base, 6 1/4 In.	144.00
Creamer, Flowers, Platinium, 4 1/2 In.	173.00
Creamer & Spooner, Platinium, Cream Ground, 4 1/2 & 4 1/8 In.	200.00
Jar, Cover, 5 1/2 In.	81.00
Pitcher, Floradine, White Leaves, Red Satin Ground, Applied Handle, 4 3/4 In.	308.00
Spooner, Floradine, 4 1/2 In.	150.00
Spooner, Raspberry, 4 In.	978.00
Sugar, 5 1/2 In.	58.00
Sugar Shaker, Cover, 5 1/2 In.	405.00
Sugar Shaker, Ivory, 5 1/4 In.	400.00
Syrup, Ivory, 6 3/4 In.	650.00
Syrup, Metal Fittings, Opalescent Handle, 7 1/4 In.	504.00
Tumbler, Ivory, 3 1/2 In.	220.00

FIREFIGHTING equipment of all types is wanted, from fire marks to uniforms to toy fire trucks. It is said that every little boy wanted to be a fireman or a train engineer 75 years ago and the collectors today reflect this interest.

Alarm, Hand Crank, Holtzer Cabot Elec., Chicago, Ill., 10 In.	90.00
Alarm Box, Cast Iron, Gamewell Excelsior, No. 54, 13 In.	325.00
Ax, Dress, Steel Fittings, Black Wooden Handle, 2 Rings, 6 3/4-In. Head	529.00
Ax, Steel Head, Wooden Grip, 9 3/4 In.	80.00
Ax, Viking Style, Wooden Handle	175.00
Ax, Wooden Grip, Leather Frog, Strap, World War II Era, 9 1/4 In.	109.00
Bell, Apparatus, Brass, 8 1/2 In.	225.00
Bell, Gong, Regulator, New York	24000.00
Bell, Muffin, 4 3/4 In.	200.00
Bucket, Leather, Andrew Newman No. 1 Mutual Fire Club, 1802	3410.00
Bucket, Leather, Black, Gold Lettering, C. Goodall No. 1	360.00
Bucket, Leather, E.A. Vickery F.S.S. 1789, Nos. 1 & 2, Pair	690.00
Bucket, Leather, Faded Banner, Early 19th Century, Pair	420.00
Bucket, Leather, Green, Gold Stencil, C.H. Reed, 12 1/2 In.	150.00
Bucket, Leather, Handle, Naumkeag No. 25, B.S. Newhall	2110.00
Bucket, Leather, Painted, 3-Masted Ship, Labeled G. Chase, 1803, 12 1/2 In.	1645.00
Bucket, Leather, Painted, Jesse Smith, 1806, Winged Goddess, Trumpet, 11 In.	1880.00
Bucket, Leather, Painted, Red, Crest, Early 19th Century, 11 x 10 In.	120.00
Bucket, Leather, Painted, T. Moulton, No. 2, 1761, 11 In.	1080.00
Bucket, Leather, Painted, Warren Fire Club, J. Shove Danvers 1929, 12 In.	4406.00
Bucket, Leather, Painted, Yellow Lettering, Black, Handle, c.1826, 15 5/8 In.	1175.00
Bucket, Leather, Painted, Yellow Lettering, Leafy Wreath, Early 1800s, 13 1/2 In.	1530.00
Bucket, Leather, Red & Gilt Coat Of Arms, 11 3/4 In.	275.00
Bucket, Leather, Red, Gold Banner, Handle, Wicasset Fire Society, FP Erskine 1883	775.00
Bucket, Leather, Transfer-Printed Royal Crest, Strap Handle, Mid 1800s, 10 In.	327.00
Bucket, Leather, Yellow, No. 2, Swing Handle, Citizens Fire Society, c.1825, 14 In.	5019.00
Bucket, Red Paint, Iron Bail, Riveted Joints, England, 14 x 7 1/2 In.	150.00
Bucket, Wood, Green & Black Paint, G.D. Cook, 1843, 19 3/4 In.	825.00
Extinguisher, Read & Campbell Ltd., London, 2 Gal., 28 In.	65.00
Figure, Carved, Painted Wood, Blue Uniform, Holding Trumpet, 37 In.	2235.00
Finial, Alarm Box, Cast Iron	20.00
Fire Mark, Fireman's Insurance Co., Baltimore, Md., Iron, c.1835, 15 x 13 In.	690.00
Fire Mark, Mutual Assurance Co. Of Philadelphia, Metal Tree, Wooden Plaque	35.00
Fire Mark, Royal Exchange Assurance, Pine Plaque, Lead, 1700s, 14 In.	175.00
Grenade, Barnums Diamond, Green	370.00
Grenade, Blue Devil CTC	65.00
Grenade, Cobalt Blue, Rib Pattern, Tooled Mouth, 1880-1895, 6 1/4 In.	504.00
Grenade, Fire Extinguisher, Diamond, 4 Panels, Yellow Amber, France, 5 7/8 In.	308.00

Grenade, Harden Star, Turquoise, Contents, Pt. 195.00
Grenade, Harden Star, Turquoise, Contents, Qt. 275.00
Grenade, Harden's Hand, Star, Turquoise, Ground Lip, 1880-1895, 6 3/4 In. 112.00
Grenade, Harden, Turquoise, Quilted, Contents, Partial Label, Pt. 245.00
Grenade, Harkness Fire Destroyer, Blue, Contents, c.1890, 6 1/4 In. 728.00
Grenade, Hayward's Hand Fire, Cobalt Blue, New York, American, c.1890, 6 In. 220.00
Grenade, Hayward's Hand, Fire Extinguisher, Clear, Tooled Mouth, 1880-1895, 6 In. 408.00
Grenade, Hayward's Hand, Turquoise, Tooled Mouth, 1880-1895, 6 1/4 In. 476.00
Grenade, Hayward's Hand, Yellow Olive, Tooled Mouth, August 8, 1971, 6 1/8 In. 336.00
Grenade, Haywards, Aqua, Pleated, Contents, Pt. 375.00
Grenade, Haywards, Cobalt Blue, Round Panel, Pt. 375.00
Grenade, Haywards, Light Amber, Diamond Panel, Contents, Foil Seal, Pt. 395.00
Grenade, Haywards, Olive Green, Diamond Panel, Contents, Pt. 395.00
Grenade, Hazelton High Pressure Chemical Keg 350.00
Grenade, L'Urbaine, Cobalt Blue, Ribbed, Smooth Base, France, c.1890, 6 1/2 In. 420.00
Grenade, Orange Amber, Ribs, Embossed, 1880-1900, 5 3/4 In. 336.00
Grenade, Rack, Hardens, 2-Position, Wall Mount 130.00
Helmet, Copper Eagle, Shield, Leather, Scarborough BFD, 1931 .... 619.00
Helmet, Eagle, Black, Leather 125.00
Helmet, Red Eagle Ornament, Cincinnati 375.00
Helmet, Shield, Leather, Cairns, N.Y., Hope No. 4 Newport 880.00
Helmet, Stamped Aluminum, Black Enameling, Leather Panel, Chopmist F.D. 165.00
Hydrant, Cast Iron, Painted, Black, White, 200 Lbs. 175.00
Key, Gamewell Alarm System, Brass 130.00
Nozzle, Brass, ABC 33.00
Nozzle, Brass, Copper Shield, Ezra Cobb, June 4, 1897, 11 In. 600.00
Nozzle, Underwriters, Cord Wrapping, Powhattan B & I Works 50.00
Photograph, Boston Fire Dept., 2-Horse Wagon 40.00
Rattle, Alarm, Single Reed, Wood 45.00
Sign, Winthrop Fire Dept., Brass 200.00
Trumpet, Brass, Seamed Construction, Red Interior, 10 In. 175.00
Trumpet, Nickel, Brass, 17 In. 300.00
Trumpet, Tin, Painted Panel, To Our President, Dec.11, 1894, 21 In. 450.00

FIREGLOW glass is attributed to the Boston and Sandwich Glass
Company. The light-tan-colored glass appears reddish brown when
held to the light. Most fireglow has an acid finish and enamel decoration, although it was also made with a satin finish.

Pitcher, Water, Enameled Flowers, Melon Ribbed, 8 1/2 In. 60.00
Vase, Pansy Design, 8 1/2 In. 30.00
Vase, Pink Enameled Rose, Birds, 10 3/4 In., Pair 200.00

FIREPLACES were used to cook food and to heat the American home in
past centuries. Many types of tools and equipment were used.
Andirons held the logs in place, firebacks reflected the heat into the
room, and tongs were used to move either fuel or food. Many types of
spits and roasting jacks were made and may be listed in the Kitchen
category.

Andirons, Brass & Iron, Ball Top, Feet, R. Whittingham, N.Y., 18 3/4 x 10 x 22 1/2 In. .. 1410.00
Andirons, Brass & Iron, Baluster Shaft, Ball Finial, Log Guards, 113 x 9 x 15 In. 530.00
Andirons, Brass & Iron, Faceted Ball Finials, Mid 1700s, 22 x 12 3/4 x 16 7/8 In. 2000.00
Andirons, Brass & Iron, Federal, Urn Top, Column, Claw & Ball Feet, 21 x 12 x 19 In. .. 1880.00
Andirons, Brass & Iron, Flame Form, Ribbed Base, Arts & Crafts, 10 In. 259.00
Andirons, Brass & Iron, Hexagonal Base, Beaded Top, Ball Feet, 19 x 9 x 18 In. 560.00
Andirons, Brass & Iron, Philadelphia, c.1790, 27 x 13 1/2 x 20 In. 5975.00
Andirons, Brass & Iron, Queen Anne, Flat Bulbous Shaft, Penny Feet, 15 In. 326.00
Andirons, Brass & Iron, Queen Anne, Twisted Shaft, Brass Finial, Scroll Feet, 18 In. 62.00
Andirons, Brass & Iron, Ring Turned, Baluster Shaft, Ball Feet, c.1840, 14 x 8 x 15 In. .. 558.00
Andirons, Brass & Iron, Stylized Sunflower Top, Pendant Loop Handle, 32 In. 410.00
Andirons, Brass & Iron, Urn Finial, Twisted Stem, Scroll Legs, 23 1/2 In. 405.00
Andirons, Brass, 3 Graduated-Ball Columns, Bull's-Eye Scroll Legs, Ball Feet, 24 In. 300.00
Andirons, Brass, Acorn Top, Ball Feet, Bailey, New York, 22 In. 2070.00
Andirons, Brass, Acorn, Iron Belted, With 2 Tools, John Bailey, 16 3/8 x 9 5/8 In. 2938.00

Andirons, Brass, Ball Top, Iron Belted, Pedestal Shaft, Early 1800s, 11 x 7 x 21 In. 1295.00
Andirons, Brass, Ball Top, John Molineaux, Boston, 18th Century, 16 1/2 In. 518.00
Andirons, Brass, Ball Top, Log Guards, 12 5/8 In. 250.00
Andirons, Brass, Ball Top, Turned Shaft, Spiked Cabriole Legs, Snakehead Feet, 13 In. . . . 219.00
Andirons, Brass, Baluster Shaft, Cabriole Legs, Slipper Feet, Log Guards, 17 x 11 In. 350.00
Andirons, Brass, Baluster Turned Shaft, Arched Legs, Ball Feet, 18th Century, 14 1/2 In. . . 207.00
Andirons, Brass, Double Lemon Drops, Tooled Rings, Ball Feet, 20 1/4 In. 1430.00
Andirons, Brass, Empire Style, Turned Shaft, Ball Finial, Spurred Legs, 14 1/2 In. 75.00
Andirons, Brass, Empire, Octagonal Pedestals, Double Ball Feet, 1820, 19 1/2 In. 990.00
Andirons, Brass, Federal, Banded Ball Finial, Arched Legs, 19th Century, 14 1/2 In. 430.00
Andirons, Brass, Federal, Octagonal Plinth, Tapered Column, 18 1/2 In. 770.00
Andirons, Brass, Federal, Spur Arch, Baluster Turned Posts, Ball Feet, 24 1/2 In. 110.00
Andirons, Brass, George III Style, 1900s, 25 In. 520.00
Andirons, Brass, Iron, Knife Blade, Vertical Wirework, Swag Border, 19 x 8 x 14 In. 765.00
Andirons, Brass, Knife Blade, Urn Finial, Penny Feet, 10 1/2 In. 135.00
Andirons, Brass, Lemon Top, Paneled Finials, Shaft, Scrolled Legs, Spade Feet, 22 In. 675.00
Andirons, Brass, Neoclassical, Heraldic & Scroll Relief, c.1900, 25 In. 405.00
Andirons, Brass, Octagonal Top, Spiral Flame Finial, Claw & Ball Feet, 1900s, 25 In. 1045.00
Andirons, Brass, Polished, Ball Feet, Tops, Scrolled Legs, Early 19th Century, 16 In. 413.00
Andirons, Brass, Renaissance Revival, Baluster Shape, Floral Scroll, 24 1/2 In. 450.00
Andirons, Brass, Ribbed, Faceted Finial, Ball Feet, Late 19th Century, 16 In. 150.00
Andirons, Brass, Riveted Wrought Iron Rod, Scrolled Legs, 2-Part Cast, 14 1/4 In. 190.00
Andirons, Brass, Shaped Ring-Turned Posts, Spurred Cabriole Legs, Ball Feet, 23 In. 605.00
Andirons, Brass, Turned, Spurs, Leg Scrolling, Ball Feet, 16 1/4 In. 195.00
Andirons, Brass, Urn Shape, Turned Finial, Cabriole Legs, 21 1/2 In. 230.00
Andirons, Brass, Urn Top, Ball & Claw Foot, Chippendale, Philadelphia, 35 x 26 In. 952.00
Andirons, Brass, Urn Top, Iron Knife-Blade Shaft, Arched Legs, Penny Feet, 20 x 11 In. . . 590.00
Andirons, Brass, Urn Top, Log Guards, Claw & Ball Feet, 20 In. 230.00
Andirons, Brass, William & Mary Style, c.1880, 36 1/2 In., Pair 1495.00
Andirons, Bronze, Lion, Standing On Crest, c.1890, 22 In. 2240.00
Andirons, Bronze, Lyre, Patera Panels, Flame-Topped Columns, 18 In. 295.00
Andirons, Bronze, Patinated, Louis XVI Style, Gilt, Cupid Warming Hands By Fire, 14 In. 896.00
Andirons, Cast Iron, American Indian, King Philip, Headdress, 1800s, 13 x 7 In. 280.00
Andirons, Cast Iron, Black Paint, Hessian, 19th Century, 20 In. 290.00
Andirons, Cast Iron, George Washington Standing By Tree Stump, 20 In. 175.00
Andirons, Cast Iron, George Washington, Black Paint, 1900s, 20 1/2 In. 430.00
Andirons, Cast Iron, George Washington, Dovetailed Log Holder, 1900s, 20 x 9 In. 224.00
Andirons, Cast Iron, George Washington, Holding Book & Hat, 1800s, 21 x 9 x 14 In. 978.00
Andirons, Cast Iron, Goose Head, Signed R.F.H. Clancey, Needham, Mass., c.1925 . . . . . 725.00
Andirons, Cast Iron, Hessian, 1900s, 19 1/2 In. 288.00
Andirons, Cast Iron, Knife Blade, Ball Finial, Arched Base, Penny Feet, 20 In. 303.00
Andirons, Cast Iron, Owl, Half-Round Figure, Glass Eyes, Twig Base, 14 x 9 x 17 In. 325.00
Andirons, Cast Iron, Pheasant Shape, 14 x 25 In. 1980.00
Andirons, Cast Iron, Turkey, John Burns, c.1870, 18 3/4 x 13 3/8 x 28 In. 1645.00
Andirons, Gilt Bronze, Urn, Swags, Iron Extensions, Early 1800s, 18 x 16 x 25 1/2 In. 550.00
Andirons, Iron, Bradley & Hubbard, Hammered, Crossbar, Scroll, c.1910, 28 x 43 In. 380.00
Andirons, Iron, Comical Black Figures, Trebled Hopes, 16 In. 1469.00
Andirons, Iron, Hammered, Flowers, Original Patina, Arts & Crafts, 10 x 17 In. 58.00
Andirons, Iron, Hammered, Open Rectangular Shape, Arts & Crafts, 10 x 16 x 23 In. 175.00
Andirons, Iron, Man-In-The-Moon, Round Base, 19th Century, 14 x 9 1/2 In. 5175.00
Andirons, Iron, Pyramid Finial, Paneled Post, Diamond, Bradley & Hubbard, 20 In. 235.00
Andirons, Iron, Scrolled, Round Bail, Crane Arm, Arts & Crafts, 24 x 38 In. 150.00
Andirons, Silver Plated Brass, Regency Style, Baluster Shape, Urn Finial, 20 In. 680.00
Andirons, Steel, Knife Blade, Penny Feet, Applied Brass Finial, 20 In. 805.00
Andirons, Wrought Iron, G. Stickley, Curled Finial, Footed, 18 1/2 x 13 1/4 In. 2990.00
Andirons, Wrought Iron, Gooseneck, Ball Top, Penny Feet, 28 x 17 In. 290.00
Andirons, Wrought Iron, Hammered Copper, Scrolling Shield Shape, 15 1/2 In. 355.00
Andirons, Wrought Iron, Horse Head Finial, Early 20th Century, 19 1/2 In. 196.00
Andirons, Wrought Iron, Iberian Style, Turned, Twisted Stretcher, 28 In. 405.00
Bellows, Blacksmith's, On Stand, 1800s, 60 In. 2800.00
Bellows, Brass, Painted, 19th Century, 15 In. 140.00
Bellows, Carved Dragon Heads, Switzerland, Late 19th Century, 19 In. 207.00
Bellows, Carved Tulip Design, Brass & Leather Accents, Arts & Crafts, 21 In. 70.00

Bellows, Leather, Japanned Landscape Scene, Brass Nozzle, Acorn End, 12 1/4 In. 620.00
Bellows, Turtle Back, Leather, Wood, Stenciled Cornucopia, Brass Nozzle, 17 1/2 In. 605.00
Bellows, Turtle Back, Red Paint, Flowers, 17 In., Pair 115.00
Bellows, Turtle Back, Umber Ground, Stenciled, Conch Shell, Brass Nozzle, 18 In. 248.00
Box, Fuel, Tole, Regency, Red & Black Decorated, c.1815, 16 1/2 x 18 x 13 In. 1265.00
Box, Kindling, Brass Covered, Repousse, Tavern Scene, Cover, England, 18 x 24 In. 170.00
Box, Kindling, Repousse Brass, Rural Scenes, England, 1800s, 11 x 16 In. 125.00
Broom, Hardwood Handle, Carved, Painted Bristle Holder, Black Man, 22 In. 440.00
Broom, Ivory, Red Stripes, Stenciling, Smoked, Horsehair Bristles, 29 In. 385.00
Bucket, Kindling, Mahogany, Brass Bound, Handle, Georgian, 13 x 14 3/4 In. 690.00
Chenet, Brass, Louis XVI Style, Sphinx, Belle Epoque, c.1900, 16 x 58 In., Pair 1035.00
Chenet, Bronze, Louis XVI Style, Ormolu, Putto, Garlands, c.1920, 20 In., Pair 2990.00
Chenet, Gilt Brass, Louis XVI Style, Allegorical, c.1910, 16 1/2 In., Pair 978.00
Chenet, Gilt Bronze, Louis XV Style, Leaf Scroll, France, c.1900, 18 x 45 1/2 In., Pair . .   750.00
Coal Bucket, Arts & Crafts, Cylindrical, Applied Shield, Pad Feet, 14 x 25 In. 288.00
Coal Scuttle, Cast Iron, C. Hoefinghoff Co., c.1890, 16 3/4 x 25 1/4 x 15 In. 518.00
Coal Scuttle, Cast Iron, Portrait Medallion, Flowers, Scrolls, Handle, 17 x 12 In. 840.00
Coal Scuttle, Copper, Brass Mounted, Continental, c.1900, 22 In. 230.00
Coal Scuttle, Figured Mahogany, Inlaid, Brass Handle, Regency, 15 x 16 In. 305.00
Coal Scuttle, Shovel, Owl Decoration, Flowers, Cover, Handle, 14 x 16 x 11 In. 60.00
Coal Scuttle, Tin, Slant Lid, Stenciled, Ferns, Scrolls, Iron Handles & Feet, 23 In. 115.00
Fender, Brass & Iron, Bowfront, 6 x 37 In. 120.00
Fender, Brass & Iron, Seated Girl & Boy, 19th Century, 11 x 41 1/2 In. 805.00
Fender, Brass & Steel, George III, 55 x 16 In. 3585.00
Fender, Brass & Wire, Curved Top, Scrolled Ends, 40 x 6 1/2 In. 275.00
Fender, Brass & Wire, Folding, Swag Border, Early 1800s, 23 3/4 x 59 3/4 In. 2940.00
Fender, Brass Spindles, Leather Rail, Club Style, Wooden Base, 30 x 30 In. 460.00
Fender, Brass, Center Ivy Panel, Scrolled Ends, 7 x 63 In. 130.00
Fender, Brass, Curved Front, 11 Finials, For Coal-Fired Hearth, Late 1800s, 17 x 21 In. . .   150.00
Fender, Brass, D-Form Top Rail, Wirework Screen, Swag & Scroll, 24 x 49 x 14 In. 2350.00
Fender, Brass, Federal, Openwork, Scroll Decoration, Medallion Center, 65 1/2 In. 248.00
Fender, Brass, Georgian, Cut, Engraved, D-Form, Dragons, Paw Feet, c.1815, 9 x 31 In. . .   978.00
Fender, Brass, Leaded Glass, Leaf, 42 1/2 In. 144.00
Fender, Brass, Pedestal, Surmounted By Dogs, 42 In. 310.00
Fender, Brass, Pierced Circles, Urns, Column Ends, Urn Finials, 6 1/2 x 46 In. 195.00
Fender, Brass, Pierced Geometrics, Foliage, Paw Feet, 48 3/4 x 13 1/2 x 8 In. 250.00
Fender, Brass, Pierced, England, 19th Century, 36 x 8 In. 115.00
Fender, Brass, Pierced, Gadroon Central Banding, Paw Feet, 19th Century, 9 x 41 In. 259.00
Fender, Brass, Pierced, Victorian, 9 1/2 x 51 1/4 x 15 In. 460.00
Fender, Brass, Rail, Knobs, Mid 19th Century, 11 1/2 x 17 1/2 In. 100.00
Fender, Brass, Reticulated, Paw Feet, England, 19th Century, 9 x 41 x 11 In. 230.00
Fender, Brass, Scrolled Fretwork, 52 In. 415.00
Fender, Brass, Square Wirework Grid, Scroll Design, 36 x 42 3/4 x 14 3/8 In. 1765.00
Fender, Brass, Vertical Wirework, Brass Swag, Late 1700s, 18 x 45 1/2 In. 2233.00
Fender, Brass, Vertical Wirework, Swag Border, Scroll, 24 x 45 In. 1998.00
Fender, Brass, Wire Mesh, Steeple Top, 15 x 47 x 12 In. 920.00
Fender, Bronze, Federal, Bowfront, Fluted Columns, 11 1/2 x 55 In. 645.00
Fender, Gilt Brass, Louis XVI Style, Vase Shape, Serpents, c.1900, 16 x 46 In. 1840.00
Fender, Iron, Brass Top, Wire Grid, Applied Swags, Scrolling, 36 x 14 x 18 In. 1100.00
Fireback, Cast Iron, Decorated, Verse, Figures, Door, Candelabra, 1742, 25 x 24 In. 248.00
Fireback, Cast Iron, Indian Encampment In Relief, 19th Century, 22 x 25 In. 635.00
Footman, Brass, Cabriole Legs, Handles, False Drawers, England, 1900s, 11 x 19 In. 285.00
Footman, Brass, Cabriole Legs, Pierced Bowfront, Handles, England, 12 x 17 In. 395.00
Fork, Forged Iron, 3 Tines, Open Heart Over Center Tine, 1845, 20 3/8 In. 2420.00
Hearth Crane, Iron, Hand Forged, Y-Shape, Late 18th Century, 27 x 40 In. 100.00
Hearth Crane, Wrought Iron, Mountable L-Bracket, Adjustable, 1700s, 34 x 47 In. 2990.00
Hood, Hammered Copper, Riveted Trim, Arts & Crafts, 37 x 25 1/2 In. 690.00
Log Bin, Regency Style, Rectangular, Iron, England, 23 x 48 x 20 In. 200.00
Log Holder, Steel, Leather, Samuel Marx, 1948, 16 x 20 x 16 In. . . . . .6325.00 to 8000.00
Mantel is listed in the Architectural category.
Match Holder, Boot Shape, Cast Iron, Painted, 5 1/2 In. 25.00
Match Holder, Figural, Cherub, Resting On Leaf, Flanked By Urns, Cast Iron, 6 In. 113.00
Screen, Brass, Glass, Stained, Shore, Birds, Victorian, 28 x 24 In.   940.00

Screen, Brass, Tiles, Boy Reading, Animal Feet, J. & J.G. Low, 38 1/4 In. 1610.00
Screen, Brass, Woman, Billowing Dress, England, Late 19th Century, 30 In. 515.00
Screen, Bronze, Hammered Copper, Arts & Crafts, Red Warty, 35 x 60 In. 430.00
Screen, Cartouche Shape, Wildlife Landscape, Floral Garlands, c.1890, 34 x 30 In. 1495.00
Screen, Carved, Needlepoint Panel, Spiral Turned, England, c.1865, 44 x 31 In. 375.00
Screen, Copper, Arts & Crafts, Needlework, Trestle Base, 46 1/2 x 2 In. 175.00
Screen, Copper, Arts & Crafts, Ship, Cobalt Jeweled Finials, England, 19 x 33 In. 345.00
Screen, Copper, Iron, Eagle Standing On Rock Base, 30 x 22 1/2 In. 130.00
Screen, Copper, Mesh, Birds, Butterflies Over Marsh, Curled Feet, 31 1/2 x 41 In. 2415.00
Screen, Ebonized Frame, Fabric, Child In White, Victorian, 33 1/2 x 22 1/2 In. 635.00
Screen, Embroidered Floral Scroll Design, Saber Legs, c.1820, 41 x 28 x 16 In. 748.00
Screen, Fabric, Glass Cover, Columnar Shaft, Bird's-Head Foot, Raised Eye, 60 In. 450.00
Screen, Gilt Brass, Folding Fan, Reticulated Panels, France, 25 1/2 x 19 In. 230.00
Screen, Gilt Brass, Steel Mesh, Louis XV Style, Putto, Lady In Chariot, 31 In. 865.00
Screen, Gilt Bronze, Wire Mesh, Louis XV Style, Cupids, 30 In. 940.00
Screen, Giltwood, Carved, Aubusson Tapestry, France, 1800s, 39 x 28 1/2 In. 275.00
Screen, Hammered Iron, Chiseled Design, France, 1920s, 29 x 13 1/2 x 29 In. 2070.00
Screen, Louis XV Style, Gilt Bronze, Leaves, 30 x 25 In. 2235.00
Screen, Mahogany, Arts & Crafts, Diamonds, Shaped Crest, Beaded Edge, 30 x 22 In. . . . 56.00
Screen, Mahogany, Beadwork Panel, Frame, Trestle Base, 1800s, 57 x 34 In. 365.00
Screen, Mahogany, Needlework, Chenille Silk, c.1810, 54 x 15 In., Pair 3290.00
Screen, Mahogany, Regency, Embroidered, 2 Panels, Folding, Early 1800s, 41 x 36 In. . . . 546.00
Screen, Napoleon III, Scrolling Crest, Oriental Landscape, 1800s, 53 x 25 1/2 In. 1495.00
Screen, Needlepoint, Carved Floral Frame, Late 19th Century, 30 x 12 x 40 In. 460.00
Screen, Papier-Mache, Still Life, Bird, Gilt, Victorian, 48 1/2 x 32 In. 2585.00
Screen, Pediment Top, Padded Slide, Caryatid, Serpents, c.1795, 39 x 26 x 18 In. 4370.00
Screen, Pole, Hepplewhite, Cherry, Painted, Cabriole Legs, Snake Feet, 49 1/2 In. 715.00
Screen, Pole, Mahogany, Green Felt, Tripod Base, 52 In. 765.00
Screen, Pole, Rosewood, Square, Beadwork Inset, 1800s, 60 1/2 In. 400.00
Screen, Rosewood, Adjustable, Turned Pedestal, Platform Base, Paw Feet, 15 In. 880.00
Screen, Rosewood, Needlepoint, Pierced Crest, Barleytwist Columns, 55 x 31 In. 546.00
Screen, Walnut, Napoleon III, Needlework, c.1865, 46 x 27 1/2 In. 405.00
Screen, Walnut, Persian Embroidery, c.1930, 39 x 24 In. 200.00
Screen, Wirework, Serpentine, Brass Finials, Paw Feet, 15 1/2 x 48 1/2 In. 1100.00
Screen, Wrought Iron, Black Paint, T. Molesworth Style, 1940s, 35 1/2 x 49 In. 4480.00
Seat, Forged Iron, Bronze, Spindles, Ships, Velvet Cushion, Oscar Bach, 78 x 20 In. 7475.00
Shovel, Iron, Turned Brass Handle, Early 19th Century, 35 In. 250.00
Spatula, Forged Iron, Cutout Heart In Blade, 2 Heart Cutouts In Handle, 21 In. 2420.00
Surround, Brass, Cast Iron, Victorian, Late 19th Century, 39 1/2 x 48 In. 5378.00
Surround, Cast Iron, Bow & Arrow Design, 32 x 33 In. 58.00
Surround, Inset Delft Tiles, Country Scenes, 38 x 52 In. 295.00
Surround, Walnut, Victorian, c.1870, 42 x 78 1/2 x 15 1/4 In. 748.00
Tongs, Iron, Penny Ends, Brass Finial Handle, Early 19th Century, 31 1/2 In. 300.00
Tool Set, Brass & Iron, Ball Turnings, Tongs, Shovel, Early 19th Century, 35 In. 518.00
Tool Set, Brass & Steel, Poker, Tongs, Shovel, 3 Piece 175.00
Tool Set, Brass, Embossed Fish, Pitcher, Drip Tray, Starter, Cape Cod, May 2, 1916 . . . . . 110.00
Tool Set, Brass, Pierced Designs, Mushroom Finial, 3 Piece 138.00
Tool Set, Brass, Steeple Top, Polished Handle, Tongs, Shovel, 32 In. 1006.00
Tool Set, Brass, Urn Finial, Shovel, Tongs, Early 19th Century, 33 1/2 In. 235.00
Tool Set, Cast Iron, Curved Arms, Shell Shape, Scalloped Edge, Shovel, Poker, 24 In. . . . 55.00
Tool Set, Steel, Poker, Tongs, Shovel, Stand, 19th Century, 4 Piece 316.00
Tool Set, Wrought Iron, Arts & Crafts, Copper Shield On Stems, Scrolls, 5 Piece 385.00
Trammel, Iron, Hand Forged, Bar, Hooked Ends, Holes, 19th Century, 30 To 48 In. 25.00
Trammel, Iron, Hand Forged, Bar, Hooked, 19th Century, 24 1/2 To 32 1/2 In. 50.00
Trammel, Wrought Iron, Adjustable, Chase Decoration, Swing Loop Handle, 32 In. 184.00

FISCHER porcelain was made in Herend, Hungary, by Moritz Fischer. The factory was founded in 1839 and continued working into the twentieth century. The wares are sometimes referred to as *Herend* porcelain.

MF

Dinner Service, Orange, Gilt, Butterflies, Peonies, Herend, 44 Piece 4480.00
Dinner Service, Rothschild Bird, Blue Factory Mark, 60 Piece 3680.00
Dish, Birds, Butterflies, Tricornered, 10 In. 99.00

Figurine, German Shepherd, White, Bisque, 7 x 11 1/2 In. 165.00
Statue, Nude Male, Kneeling, Uplifted Torch, Gondos, Olympiad, 9 1/2 x 5 3/4 In. 193.00
Tureen, Cover, Rothschild Bird, Underplate, 15 In. 1610.00
Vase, Birds, 6 In. 66.00
Vase, Rothschild Bird, 4 3/4 In., Pair 100.00

FISHING reels of brass or nickel were made in the United States by
1810. Bamboo fly rods were sold by 1860, often marked with the
maker's name. Lures made of metal, or metal and wood, were made in
the nineteenth century. Plastic lures were made by the 1930s. All fishing material is collected today and even equipment of the past thirty
years is of interest if in good condition with original box.

Bucket, Minnow, Falls City, Famous Floating Minnow Bucket, Metal, 10 Qt. 55.00
Bucket, Minnow, Tin, Oval, c.1880 . . . .   275.00
Bucket, Minnow, Wade In, No. 1, Made In Falls City, U.S.A., 8 In. 330.00
Canoe Seat, Reed, Adjustable Back, Storage Area, 16 x 16 In. 140.00
Creel, A.B. Nelson, Leather Trim, Split Willow, Front Pocket, Salem, Oregon 1100.00
Creel, Adirondack, Brown, Hinged Lid, Leather Straps, c.1800, 20 x 15 In. 880.00
Creel, Bill Mackowski, Split Ash, Bulbous, Milford, Maine, 6 x 10 x 6 1/2 In. 140.00
Creel, George Lawrence, Split Willow, Leather Trim, Strap, Buckle Latch, Portland, Ore. .   770.00
Creel, George Lawrence, Split Willow, Tooled Leather Trim, Fine Weave, Portland, Ore. .   1650.00
Creel, Reed Over Wood, 8 x 12 x 9 In. 110.00
Creel, Splint, Open Weave, Oblong Hole, 9 x 17 x 8 In. 55.00
Creel, Splint, Wire Frame, Loop & Peg Latch, Bulbous, 6 x 15 x 10 In. 440.00
Creel, Split Willow, Leather Pouch On Front, Leather & Canvas Strap 115.00
Creel, Turtle, Rattan, High Turtle Latch, Rattan Weave, Bulbous, 6 x 13 x 7 In. 990.00
Creel, Turtle, Rattan, Turtle Latch, Brown, Bulbous, 6 x 13 x 7 1/2 In. 1210.00
Creel, Turtle, Whole Willow, Turtle Latch, Twisted Hinges, Harness Loops, Bulbous 660.00
Creel, Turtle, Wicker, Carved-Wood Turtle Latch, Rattan Hinges, Reed-Lashed Lid 550.00
Creel, Whole Willow, Crescent Shape, Twisted Reed Hinges, Belt, Buckle, 6 x 14 x 8 In. .   85.00
Creel, Wood, Rectangular Hole, Brown, 16 x 19 In. 440.00
Float, Blown Glass, Knotted Rope, 14 In., Pair 460.00
Float, Ideal Float Co., Red Finish, White Stripe, Wood Holder, Line, Wire Spreader 220.00
Float, Ideal Float Co., White, Red, 14 1/2 In. 605.00
Float, Ideal Float Co., Yellow Finish, Red Stripe, Wood Winder, Wire Spreader, 8 In. 55.00
Float, Ideal Float Co., Yellow, Red, 15 In. 440.00
Lure, Al Foss, Little Egypt Wiggler, Spinner Blade, Box 275.00
Lure, Arbogast, Tin Liz Sunfish, 2 Fins, Glass Eyes, Wire Weed Guard, 1 5/8 In. 275.00
Lure, Beaver Bait Co., Old Fighter, Spinners, Red Glass Beads, Box, Ambridge, Pa. 85.00
Lure, Buckskin, No. 40, Box, 4 x 5 1/2 In. 55.00
Lure, Chapman & Son, Minnow Propeller, 2 Metal Sides, 1870 Patent, Size 5, 1 1/2 In. . . .   660.00
Lure, Creek Chub, Bug Wiggler, Black, Red Tail, No. 1413, Box, 7/8 In. 300.00
Lure, Creek Chub, Froggie, Green Meadow Frog, True To Nature, Box, 1 In. 165.00
Lure, Creek Chub, Husky Musky, Box, 4 7/8 In. 440.00
Lure, G.M. Skinner, Fluted Spoon, No. 1, Box, c.1900, 10 Piece 220.00
Lure, Gee Wiz Bait Co., Frog, Rubber Over Wood Core, Flexible Legs, Box 193.00
Lure, Heddon, Dowagiac Musky Minnow, Rainbow, No. 700, 5 5/8 In. . . . . *Illus*   3850.00
Lure, Heddon, Dowagiac, Minnow, No. 100, Box, 2 3/4 In. 660.00
Lure, Heddon, Flaptail Bug, Yellow, Yellow Feather Wings, 1 1/8 In. 85.00
Lure, Heddon, Metal Minnow, 3 Double Hooks, 4 Sides, No. 500, c.1908, 2 1/2 In. 275.00
Lure, Heddon, Minnow, No. 300, 3 3/4 In. 330.00
Lure, Heddon, Punkinseed, Single Hook, Crappie Finish 187.00
Lure, Heddon, Surface Minnow, Green, No. 300, Wood Box, Sliding Lid, Flyer, 3 1/2 In. . .   1980.00
Lure, Jamison, Wiggler, Red Head, White Body, Box, 1 1/4 In. 330.00
Lure, L.C. Woods, Expert Minnow, 5 Hooks, Green Back, Gold Belly, c.1904, 3 5/8 In. . . .   305.00
Lure, Minnow, White, Red Stripes, Glass Eyes, Silver Props, 1910, 3 In. 310.00
Lure, Outing Mfg., Bucky Getum, White Feather Tail, Wire Weed Guards, Ind., 1 1/2 In. .   55.00
Lure, Pepper, Underwater Minnow, 5 Hooks, Glass Eyes, Bellyweight, c.1905 . . . .   110.00
Lure, Pflueger, Frog, Glass Eyes, Surface Hardware, 2 Double Hooks, Marked Propeller .   275.00
Lure, Shakespeare, Silver Paint, Wood Body, 2 Propellers, c.1900, 3 1/2 In. . . . . *Illus*   4235.00
Lure, Winchester, 5 Hook Minnow, No. 9211 . . . .   1155.00
Lure, Wood, 3-Prong Hooks, Revolving Head, White, Box, Hopatcong, 2 3/4 In. 385.00
Lure, Ypsilanti, Minnow, Wood, Painted, Propeller, Hillsdale, Michigan, 4 1/4 In. 110.00

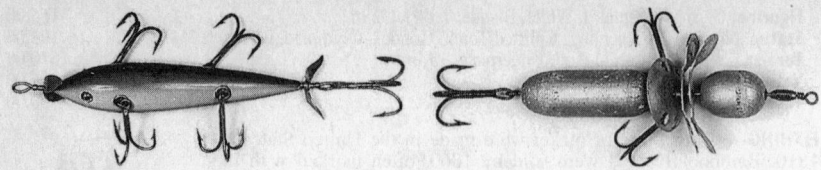

Fishing, Lure, Heddon, Dowagiac Musky
Minnow, Rainbow, No. 700, 5 5/8 In.

Fishing, Lure, Shakespeare, Silver Paint,
Wood Body, 2 Propellers, c.1900, 3 1/2 In.

Net, Anglers Custom, Wooden, Glens Falls, N.Y., 14 In.	55.00
Net, Barnes, Trout, Rattan-Wrapped Handle, Brass Catch, Pat. Nov. 9, 1909	165.00
Net, Hardy Bros., Triangular, Aluminum, Folding, Bag, Alnwick, England, 30 In.	138.00
Net, Hardy Bros., Triangular, Extending, Brass, Aluminum, Belt Clip, 48 In.	165.00
Net, J.S. Sharpe, Triangular, Folding, Brass, Aluminum, Belt Clip, Aberdeen, 16 In.	110.00
Net, Trout, Collapsible, Brass Fixture, Mottled Cane Handle, Belt Clip, 30 In.	110.00
Reel, A.L. Walker, Trout, Case, New York, 2 3/4 x 7/8 In.	1925.00
Reel, Abercrombie & Fitch, Salmon, Model AF300M, Case, 3 5/8 x 1 1/2 In.	1100.00
Reel, B.F. Meek & Sons, Bait Casting, No. 4, Handmade, c.1888, 2 1/4 x 1 5/8 In.	2750.00
Reel, Bill Ballan, Trout, Wide Spool, Box, 2 7/8 x 7/8 In.	275.00
Reel, Billy Pate, Salmon, Saltwater, R12, 3 1/2 x 3/4 In.	275.00
Reel, Bradford & Anthony, Multiplying, Vom Hofe, 1870s, 3 3/8 x 2 1/4 In.	1045.00
Reel, Carter, Brass, Walnut, Slater Latch Star, Nottingham, 4 3/8 In.	303.00
Reel, E.V. Hofe, Bonefish, Top Pillar, No. 800, Size 2, Matecumbe, 2 3/4 x 1 3/4 In.	1045.00
Reel, E.V. Hofe, Salmon, Adjustable Drag Multiplier, Size 4/0	1150.00
Reel, E.V. Hofe, Salmon, Silver, Rubber, Model 504, 1902 Patent, Size 4/0, 4 x 1 1/2 In.	2310.00
Reel, E.V. Hofe, Trout, Perfection Model, 1896 Patent, Size 1/0, 3 1/8 x 1 1/8 In.	3850.00
Reel, E.V. Hofe, Trout, Perfection Model, No. 360, Handmade, Size 32, 1/2 x 7/8 In.	7150.00
Reel, Eliseo, Salmon, Saltwater, No. 10, Leather Case, 3 3/4 x 1 In.	110.00
Reel, F. Godfrey, Salmon, Drag Lever, 3 3/8 x 1 3/8 In.	358.00
Reel, Fin-Nor, Salmon, Saltwater, Wedding Cake, No. 3, Box, Papers, 4 x 1 In.	1045.00
Reel, Garcia, Fly, Landex, Model 1422, Box, 4 In.	83.00
Reel, H.L. Leonard, Fly, Click, Spare Spool, 3 1/2 x 7/8 In.	330.00
Reel, Hardy's Alnwick, Trout, Bougle, Aluminum Finish, Box, 1906, 3 x 7/8 In.	3410.00
Reel, Hardy, Fly, Agate Line Guide, Aluminum Foot, Zippered Case, 3 3/8 x 3/4 In.	303.00
Reel, Hardy, Trout, Agate Line, Case, 3 1/8 In.	385.00
Reel, Heddon, Salmon, No. 300, Box, 3 3/8 x 1 3/8 In.	2090.00
Reel, Horton Meek, Bait Casting, Jeweled German Silver, No. 3, 2 x 1 1/2 In.	440.00
Reel, Lamson, Trout, Box, 3 1/4 x 7/8 In.	220.00
Reel, Leonard Mills, Salmon, Aluminum, Hard Rubber, Model 48N, 3 1/4 x 1 1/8 In.	880.00
Reel, Leonard Mills, Salmon, Raised Pillar, German Silver, Hard Rubber, 4 x 1 1/2 In.	660.00
Reel, Leonard Mills, Trout, Raised Pillar, Crank Handle, Aluminum, Silver, 3 x 7/8 In.	660.00
Reel, Leonard Mills, Trout, Silver Crank, No. 50, 3 x 1 In.	1100.00
Reel, O. Zwarg, Salmon, 2/0 Multiplying, Silver, Rubber, Model 400, 3 3/8 x 1 3/8 In.	1870.00
Reel, Orvis Madison, Fly, Embossed	58.00
Reel, Penn Senator, Big Game, Size 12/0, 5 3/4 x 4 In.	193.00
Reel, Philbrook & Paine, Salmon, Marbleized, Raised Pillar, Line, Size 2/00, 3 3/4 In.	9200.00
Reel, Seamaster, Saltwater, Salmon, Handmade, Anti-Reverse, Mark II, 4 x 1 1/4 In.	605.00
Reel, Simplex, Blue Grass, Silver, No. 25, 1 7/8 x 1 1/2 In.	220.00
Reel, Stan Bogdan, Salmon, No. 2, 3 3/4 x 1 3/8 In.	1210.00
Reel, Talbot, Bait Casting, Star, Handmade, German Silver, Click Switch, 2 x 1 5/8 In.	360.00
Reel, Thomas & Thomas, Trout, Aluminum, Case, 3 x 1 In.	385.00
Reel, Thompson, Fly, 2 Adjustable Drag Controls, Brass Foot, No. 100, 3 1/4 x 3/4 In.	385.00
Reel, Trowbridge, Trout, Click Reel, Raised Pillar, Crank Handle, Boston, 2 7/8 x 1 In.	110.00
Reel, Uniqua, Salmon, Brass Handle Plate, Rubber, Malloch Patent, 3 5/8 x 1 3/8 In.	305.00
Reel, Ustonson, Single Action Winch, London, c.1830, 2 1/2 x 1 In.	3850.00
Reel, Winchester, Double Action, No. 2291, Box	1080.00
Reel, Winchester, Multiplying, 2 1/4 x 3/8 In.	77.00
Reel, Winchester, No. 4252, Box	1029.00
Reel, Winchester, No. 4256, Box	1104.00
Reel, Winchester, Trout, Black Finish, Marked Skeleton, No. 1236, 2 1/2 x 3/4 In.	138.00

Rod, C.C. De France, Palakona, Aluminum Tube, No. H10157, Bag, 6 1/2 Ft., 2 Piece . . .   255.00
Rod, Cortland, Trout, 2 Tips, 6-Weight Line, Labeled Bag, Tube, 8 Ft., 2 Piece 250.00
Rod, E.C. Powell, Trout, 2 Tips, Bag, Tube, Marysville, 1932, 8 1/2 Ft., 2 Piece 2200.00
Rod, E.F. Payne, Trout, Parabolic, 2 Tips, Bag, Tube, 7 Ft. 6 1/2 In., 2 Piece 1320.00
Rod, F.E. Thomas, Fly, Bamboo, Aluminum Case, Label, 8 1/2 Ft. 460.00
Rod, F.E. Thomas, Fly, Bamboo, Cork Handle, Bangor, Maine, 7 Ft. 9 In. 720.00
Rod, F.E. Thomas, Fly, Bamboo, Leather Case, Bangor, Maine, 7 Ft. 10 In. 460.00
Rod, F.E. Thomas, Trout, Dark Cane, Bag, Tube, 8 Ft., 2 Piece 1045.00
Rod, Fenwick, Voyager, Fiberglass, 1950s, 4 1/8 Oz., 7 1/2 Ft., 5 Piece 70.00
Rod, Garrison, Trout, 2 Tips, Ferrule Plug, No. 0-7-1, Model 201, Bag, 7 Ft., 2 Piece 5610.00
Rod, Gene Edwards, Trout, 2 Tips, Bag, Tube, 8 Ft., 2 Piece 550.00
Rod, Goodwin Granger & Co., Denver Special, 2 Tips, Bag, Tube, 9 1/2 Ft., 3 Piece 140.00
Rod, Green River, Mettowee, 2 Tips, No. 6223, Model 704, Bag, Tube, 7 Ft., 2 Piece 880.00
Rod, H.L. Leonard, No. 82117, Bag, Tube, 7 Ft., 2 Piece 3300.00
Rod, H.L. Leonard, Trout, 2 Tips, No. 144, Bag, Tube, 7 1/2 Ft., 2 Piece 3080.00
Rod, H.L. Leonard, Trout, 2 Tips, No. 2576, Bag, Tube, 6 1/2 Ft., 2 Piece 1925.00
Rod, H.L. Leonard, Trout, 2 Tips, No. 3266, Bag, Tube, 6 Ft., 2 Piece 1760.00
Rod, H.L. Leonard, Trout, 2 Tips, No. 8478, Special 49-5, Bag, Tube, 7 1/2 Ft. 3300.00
Rod, H.L. Leonard, Trout, No. 4184, 806 Deluxe, Bag, Tube, 8 Ft. 1320.00
Rod, H.L. Leonard, Trout, Special Tournament, 1 Tip, 9 Ft., 3 Piece 495.00
Rod, H.S. Gillum, Salmon, 2 Tips, No. 1823, Bag, Case, 7 1/4 Oz., 9 1/2 Ft., 3 Piece 2200.00
Rod, Heddon, Bait Casting, 1 Tip, Bag, Tube, 5 Ft., 2 Piece 120.00
Rod, Heddon, Deluxe, 2 Tips, No. 50, Bag, Tube, 7 Ft., 2 Piece 1100.00
Rod, Heddon, Trout, 2 Tips, Model 20, Bag, Tube, 8 Ft., 3 Piece 440.00
Rod, James H. Goss, Fly, Split Bamboo, Cork Handle, Bag, 1931, 8 1/2 Ft., 3 Piece 96.00
Rod, Kingfisher, Fly, Bamboo, Form Case, Canvas Bag, 8 1/2 Ft., 3 Piece 96.00
Rod, Lon Blauvelt, Trout, 2 Tips, Bag, Tube, Maine, 6 1/2 Ft., 2 Piece 550.00
Rod, Lon Blauvelt, Trout, 3 Piece, 2 Tips, Bag, Tube, Maine, 8 Ft., 3 Piece 440.00
Rod, Lt. Paul H. Young, Lt., Trout, 2 Tips, Bag, Tube, June 1943, 8 Ft., 3 Piece 1430.00
Rod, Orvis, Bait Casting, Impregnated, Detachable Handle, Heavy Duty, 6 1/2 Ft. 165.00
Rod, Orvis, Battenkill, Fly, 2 Tips, Bag, Tube, 8 1/2 Ft., 2 Piece 385.00
Rod, Orvis, Battenkill, Trout, 2 Tips, Bag, Tube, 8 Ft., 2 Piece 605.00
Rod, Orvis, Fly, 2 Tips, Bag, Tube, 8 Ft. 9 In., 2 Piece 385.00
Rod, Orvis, Fly, Bamboo, Canvas Bag, 7 1/2 Ft., 3 Piece 400.00
Rod, Orvis, Fly, Bamboo, Impregnated, Deluxe, 6 1/2 Ft., 2 Piece 748.00
Rod, Orvis, Fly, Battinkill Deluxe, Bamboo, Aluminum, No. 18246, 78 In., 2 Piece 422.00
Rod, Orvis, Fly, Battinkill, Bamboo, No. 11012, Bag, Aluminum Tube, 7 1/2 Ft., 2 Piece .   366.00
Rod, Orvis, Fly, Battinkill, Bamboo, No. 13851, Bag, Aluminum Tube, 8 Ft., 2 Piece 450.00
Rod, Orvis, Fly, Graphite, Bag, Aluminum Tube, 8 1/2 Ft., 2 Piece 366.00
Rod, Orvis, Fly, Powerhouse, Graphite, No. 1283, Cloth Bag, 8 1/2 Ft., 2 Piece 115.00
Rod, Orvis, Graphite, Fighting Butt Section, Bag, Aluminum Tube, 9 Ft., 4 Piece 96.00
Rod, Orvis, Salmon, Saltwater, 8 Ft. 9 In., 2 Piece 275.00
Rod, Orvis, Trout, 2 Tips, Double Sliding Ring, Bag, Tube, 2 1/4 Oz., 6 1/2 Ft., 2 Piece . .   605.00
Rod, Orvis, Trout, 2 Tips, No. 9631, Bag, Tube, 6 1/2 Ft., 3 Piece 825.00
Rod, Orvis, Trout, Madison Light, 1 Tip, Bag, Tube, 7 Ft., 2 Piece 468.00
Rod, Orvis, Trout, Rocky Mountain, 2 Tips, 6-Weight Line, Bag, Tube, 6 1/2 Ft., 3 Piece .   605.00
Rod, Orvis, Trout, Wes Jordan, 2 Tips, No. 82294, Bag, Case, 7 1/2 Ft., 2 Piece 1430.00
Rod, Paul H. Young, Fly, Bamboo, Prosperity Rod, Label, Canvas Bag, 8 1/2 Ft., 3 Piece .   304.00
Rod, Paul H. Young, Midge, 2 Tips, 6 Ft. 3 In., 2 Piece 2750.00
Rod, Payne, Trout, 2 Tips, Abercrombie & Fitch, Bag, Tube, 8 Ft., 3 Piece 1980.00
Rod, Payne, Trout, 2 Tips, Bag, Tube, 8 1/2 Ft., 3 Piece 1320.00
Rod, Pezon & Michel, Tournament, Casting, 100 Gram, 7 1/2 Ft., 2 Piece 770.00
Rod, Pezon & Michel, Trout, Midget, Parabolic, 2 Tips, No. A260, 6 Ft., 2 Piece 990.00
Rod, Pezon & Michel, Trout, Parabolic, 2 Tips, No. A261, Bag, Tube, 6 1/2 Ft., 2 Piece . .   770.00
Rod, Pezon & Michel, Trout, Parabolic Supreme, 7-Weight Line, 8 1/2 Ft., 2 Piece 220.00
Rod, Pflueger, Bait Casting, Split Bamboo, 1906 Patent, 5 Ft. 523.00
Rod, Phillipson, Trout, 2 Tips, Bag, Tube, 7 Ft., 2 Piece 660.00
Rod, Poachers, Leather Case, 6 Piece 90.00
Rod, R.L. Winston, Fly, 2 Tips, No. 7343, Bag, Tube, 7 1/2 Ft., 2 Piece 1430.00
Rod, R.L. Winston, Trout, 2 Tips, No. 1709, Bag, Tube, 8 Ft., 2 Piece 1870.00
Rod, Sage, Fly, Graphite, Agate Guides, Bag, Aluminum Tube, 9 Ft., 2 Piece 96.00
Rod, Sam Carlson, Trout, 1 Tip, Bag, Tube, 7 Ft., 2 Piece 2200.00
Rod, Thomas & Thomas, Iliaska Special, Graphite, 9 Ft., 2 Piece 141.00

Rod, Thomas & Thomas, Trout, Amabills, Limited Edition, 1985, 8 Ft.	3850.00
Rod, Thomas & Thomas, Trout, Hendrickson, 2 Tips, 5-Weight, Bag, Tube, 7 Ft., 2 Piece	1760.00
Rod, Thomas & Thomas, Walnut Reel Seat, 2 Tips, Bag, Tube, 6 1/2 Ft., 2 Piece	1210.00
Rod, Tom Maxwell, Prototype, No. 495, 7 Ft., 3 Piece	2200.00
Rod, Tom Maxwell, Trout, 2 Tips, Bag, Tube, 7 1/2 Ft., 2 Piece	3135.00
Rod, Tom Maxwell, Trout, Hunt Pattern, 2 Tips, 5-Weight, Bag, Tube, 7 Ft., 2 Piece	3410.00
Rod, Wright & McGill, Trout, Aristocrat, 2 Tips, Bag, Tube, 7 1/2 In., 3 Piece	1210.00
Rod, Wright & McGill, Trout, Granger Victory, 1 Tip, Bag, Tube, 7 Ft., 2 Piece	550.00
Rod Holder, Wood, Round, 24-Rod Capacity, 31 In.	80.00
Salmon Tailer, Cork Grip, Wrist Strap, 30 In.	39.00
Scaler, Rock-It, Automatic, Iron, Mesh, 10 x 21 In.	71.50
Sign, Fish, Flat, Articulated Fins, Tail, Sheet Iron, 19th Century, 35 In.	6575.00
Sign, Fish, Polychrome, Wood, Metal Hangers, 35 x 11 In.	489.00
Sign, Let's Go Fishing, Fish Shape, Martha's Vineyard, Wood, 2 Sides, 13 x 25 1/2 In.	345.00
Sign, Sea Bass, Carved, Painted, Wood, Mass., Early 20th Century, 8 3/8 x 29 7/8 In.	880.00
Sign, Winchester Split Bamboo Rods, Cardboard, 18 1/2 x 40 In., 3 Piece	1100.00
Sign, Wright & McGill Fishing Tackle, Paper, 54 x 13 In.	540.00
Spear, Eel, Iron, 13 In.	150.00
Tackle Box, E. Vom Hofe, Leather Cover, Brass Latches, 10 x 14 1/2 x 8 1/2 In.	1430.00
Tackle Box, Knickerbocker, Leather Cover, Aluminum Interior, 8 1/2 x 16 x 7 1/2 In.	187.00
Tackle Box, Mahogany, Brass Hardware, 2 Lift-Out Sections, 7 3/4 x 20 x 8 1/4 In.	275.00
Tackle Box, Metal, Black Enamel Finish, W.J. Cummins, 6 1/2 x 2 3/4 In.	220.00
Tackle Box, Metal, Wm. Mills & Son, New York, Metal, 7 x 12 x 6 In.	83.00
Tackle Box, Orvis, Mahogany, 5 Shelves, Finger-Jointed Construction, 14 x 11 In.	75.00
Tackle Box, Sole Leather, Basket Shape, Wm. Mills, N.Y., c.1912, 3 1/4 x 3 1/2 In.	1760.00
Tackle Box, Sole Leather, Brass Hinges, Latch, c.1912, 7 x 2 1/2 x 3 In.	1430.00
Weed Repeller, Aluminum, Steel Wire, Sliding-Lid Box, Brilliant Searchlight, Duluth	110.00

FLAGS are included in the Textile category.

FLASH GORDON appeared in the Sunday comics in 1934. The daily strip started in 1940. The hero was also in comic books from 1930 to 1970, in books from 1936, in movies from 1938, on the radio in the 1930s and 1940s, and on television from 1953 to 1954. All sorts of memorabilia are collected, but the ray guns and rocket ships are the most popular.

Compass, Space, Wrist, Vinyl, Plastic, Card, c.1951, 3 x 8 In.	40.00
Figurine, Chalkware, 15 In.	22.00
Toy, Gun, Click Pistol, Tin, Marx KFS, 10 In.	550.00
Toy, Ray Gun, Siren, 7 In.	700.00
Toy, Rocket, Mars, USAF Planes, Plastic, 1952, 2 1/2 In.	15.00
Toy, Rocket, Moves, Noise, Sparks, Tin, Windup, Marx, Box, 12 In.	1018.00

FLORENCE CERAMICS were made in Pasadena, California, from World War II to 1977. Florence Ward created many colorful figurines, boxes, candleholders, and other items for the gift shop trade. Each piece was marked with an ink stamp that included the name *Florence Ceramics Co.* The company was sold in 1964, and although the name remained the same the products were very different. Mugs, cups, and trays were made.

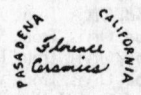

Bust, Pamela, 9 1/2 In.	190.00
Figurine, Abigail, 8 In.	140.00
Figurine, Amelia, 8 1/4 In.	180.00
Figurine, Angels, 7 3/4 In.	85.00
Figurine, Ann, 6 In.	65.00
Figurine, Betsy, 7 1/4 In.	125.00
Figurine, Blynkin, 5 1/2 In.	225.00
Figurine, Catherine, 6 3/4 In.	595.00
Figurine, Choir Boy, 6 In.	110.00
Figurine, Clarrisa, 7 3/4 In.	200.00
Figurine, Claudia, 8 1/4 In.	175.00
Figurine, David, 7 1/2 In.	150.00
Figurine, Dolores, 8 In.	170.00
Figurine, Douglas, 8 In.	195.00

Figurine, Edward, 7 In.	275.00
Figurine, Matilda, 8 1/2 In.	150.00
Figurine, Melanie, 7 1/2 In.	95.00
Figurine, Pheasant, Tail Down, White Matte	195.00
Figurine, Pouter Pigeon, White Matte	275.00
Figurine, Sally, 6 3/4 In.	135.00
Figurine, Sarah, 7 1/2 In.	250.00
Figurine, Sue Ellen, 8 1/4 In.	125.00
Figurine, Victor, 9 1/4 In.	225.00
Figurine, Wynkin, 5 1/2 In.	225.00
Figurine, Yvonne, Blond Hair	120.00
Flower Holder, Ava, 10 1/2 In.	190.00
Flower Holder, Bee, 6 1/4 In.	55.00
Flower Holder, Blossom Girl, 8 3/4 In.	50.00
Flower Holder, Chinese Boy & Girl, 7 3/4 In., Pair	65.00
Flower Holder, Polly, 6 1/2 In.	45.00
Flower Holder, Shen & Yulan, 7 1/2 In., Pair	275.00

FLOW BLUE was made in England and other countries about 1830 to 1900. The dishes were printed with designs using a cobalt blue coloring. The color flowed from the design to the white body so that the finished piece has a smeared blue design. The dishes were usually made of ironstone china. More Flow Blue may be found under the name of the manufacturer.

Berry Bowl, Kenworth, 5 In.	45.00
Biscuit Barrel, Jacobean	66.00
Bowl, Albany, Low, 8 In.	20.00
Bowl, Amoy, 8 In.	595.00
Bowl, Bread, Gondola & Castle, Shell Border, 14 1/2 x 9 In.	175.00
Bowl, Cashmere, 10 3/4 In.	605.00
Bowl, Chapoo, 10 1/2 In.	100.00
Bowl, Chapoo, Rectangular, 8 1/2 x 9 1/2 In.	275.00
Bowl, Cover, Aldine, Footed, Grindley, 12 In.	300.00
Bowl, Cover, Jewel, 6 x 12 In.	60.00
Bowl, Cover, Scinde, Paneled, Alcock, 7 1/2 x 12 1/2 x 10 In.	550.00
Bowl, Harvest, Meakin, 7 1/2 In.	28.00
Bowl, Large Rose Design, Footed, Handles, 5 1/2 x 9 In.	100.00
Bowl, Peacocks In Garden, Rectangular, 12 x 8 In.	275.00
Bowl, Raft In River, 4 1/2 x 8 1/2 In.	70.00
Bowl, Vegetable, Cover, Anemone, Footed	400.00
Bowl, Vegetable, Cover, Arcadia, c.1900	120.00
Bowl, Vegetable, Cover, Baltic, c.1891	180.00
Bowl, Vegetable, Cover, Crumlin, Round	140.00
Bowl, Vegetable, Cover, Hawthorne, c.1891	140.00
Bowl, Vegetable, Cover, Roseville, c.1891	155.00
Bowl, Vegetable, Cover, Venice, c.1908	149.00
Bowl, Vegetable, Kaolin, Chinese, c.1842	120.00
Bowl, Victoria, Round, 10 In.	55.00
Bowl, Waldorf, 9 In.	90.00
Butter Chip, 6 Sides, Grindley	55.00
Butter Chip, Albion, 3 1/4 In.	45.00
Butter Chip, Fairy Villa	40.00
Butter Chip, Flowers, c.1890, 3 1/4 In.	62.00
Butter Chip, Marlborough, 3 1/2 In.	45.00
Butter Chip, Persian, Johnson Bros., England, c.1900, 3 In.	50.00
Cake Stand, Italian Urn, 2 x 8 1/2 In.	28.00
Cake Stand, Oriental Women, Temples, Floral Border, 6 x 9 1/2 In.	70.00
Candlestick, Boy, Coat Against Tree, 7 1/2 In., Pair	160.00
Candy Dish, Flowers, Reticulated, 7 3/4 In.	28.00
Casserole, Cover, Fishing Scene, Castles, 8 Sides, James Edwards, 7 1/2 x 10 In.	190.00
Casserole, Cover, Pheasant, 8 x 12 In.	75.00
Casserole, Cover, Scinde, 7 1/2 x 13 In.	375.00
Casserole, Cover, Watteau, Edge & Malkin, 7 x 9 In.	160.00

Flow Blue, Cheese
Dish, Cover,
Windsor, 7 1/2 x 9 In.

Flow Blue, Pitcher
& Bowl, Albany,
17 x 13 In.

Celery Dish, Baltimore & Ohio, Cheat River Scene, Floral Border, 12 x 6 In.	90.00
Chamber Pot, Cover, Togo, 2 Handles, 9 1/2 In.	75.00
Charger, British Scenery, 13 In.	350.00
Charger, Pendant Group, Open Handles, 15 1/4 x 13 In.	176.00
Charger, Vincennes, Embossed Scale Border, 10 1/2 In.	95.00
Cheese Dish, Cover, Windsor, 7 1/2 x 9 In. *Illus*	150.00
Cheese Keeper, Hawthorne	55.00
Cheese Keeper, Underplate, Egerton, Doulton, 10 In.	325.00
Clock, Sailboat Scene, Delft Style, 9 In.	160.00
Coffeepot, Abbey, George Jones	95.00
Coffeepot, Arabesque, Paneled Spout, 9 1/4 In.	330.00
Coffeepot, Dutch Children	60.00
Coffeepot, Formosa, 13 1/4 In.	4950.00
Coffeepot, King's Rose Variant, Dome Top, 11 1/2 In.	880.00
Coffeepot, Peking, 10 1/2 x 11 In.	150.00
Coffeepot, Temple, Paneled Temple Walker, 8 1/2 In.	770.00
Compote, Amherst, Footed, Japan, 8 In.	187.00
Compote, Amour, Footed, 2 Handles, Societe Ceremique, 10 In.	575.00
Cracker Jar, Cover, La Belle, Wheeling Potteries, 7 1/2 In.	600.00
Creamer, Amoy, 6 1/2 In.	300.00
Creamer, Arabesque, 6 In.	500.00
Creamer, Blue Danube, Johnson Bros., 4 In.	200.00
Cup & Saucer, Albany	80.00
Cup & Saucer, Amoy	195.00
Cup & Saucer, Auld Lang Syne, Farmer's, 8 In.	50.00
Cup & Saucer, Dahlia, Flower Sprays, Wavy Lines, Handleless	50.00
Cup & Saucer, Grosella, Handleless Cup, MV & Co.	55.00
Cup & Saucer, Pelew, Handleless	72.00
Cup & Saucer, Shanghai	11.00
Cup & Saucer, Tea, Albany	115.00
Cup & Saucer, Temple, Handleless, Pair	275.00
Dessert Set, Scinde, 5 Bowls, 5 1/2 In.	300.00
Gravy Boat, Athens	350.00
Gravy Boat, Scinde, 5 x 8 In.	200.00
Jardiniere, 4 Panels, Flowers, Scrolled Relief Border, 10 x 12 In.	45.00
Jardiniere, Flowers, 6 In.	70.00
Mug, Cashmere, 3 1/2 In.	400.00
Mug, Chinese Scenery, Applied Loop Handle, 3 1/4 In.	132.00
Mug, Chocolate, La Belle	400.00
Mug, Watteau, Handles, Edge Malkin, 4 In.	150.00
Pitcher, Amoy, 12 In.	1500.00
Pitcher, Argyle, 1 1/2 Pt.	425.00
Pitcher, Flowers, 6 In.	60.00
Pitcher, La Belle, Wheeling Potteries, 8 In.	66.00
Pitcher, Oregon, 8 1/2 In.	375.00
Pitcher, Paris, 9 In.	138.00
Pitcher, Touraine, Alcock, 8 1/2 In.	190.00
Pitcher, Water, Carlton, 12 3/4 In.	176.00
Pitcher & Bowl, Albany, 17 x 13 In. *Illus*	250.00

Pitcher & Bowl, Cashmere, 13 1/4 x 5 x 14 1/2 In. 1980.00
Pitcher & Bowl, Royal, F. Winkle, 12 x 15 1/2 In. 350.00
Pitcher & Bowl, Scinde, 13 x 13 In. 750.00
Pitcher Set, 7 x 8 x 9 In., 3 Piece 440.00
Plate, Abbey, 9 In. 33.00
Plate, Acme, Scalloped, Sampson Hancock & Sons, 9 In. 125.00
Plate, Alaska, Scalloped, Grindley, 10 In. 115.00
Plate, Amerillia, 7 1/2 In. 70.00
Plate, Amoy, 7 1/2 In. 75.00
Plate, Amoy, 8 1/2 In. 85.00
Plate, Amoy, 9 1/2 In. 120.00
Plate, Amoy, 10 1/2 In. 165.00
Plate, Anemone, 8 1/2 In. 95.00
Plate, Anemone, 9 1/2 In. 125.00
Plate, Argyle, 7 In. 65.00
Plate, Argyle, 8 In. 75.00
Plate, Argyle, 9 In. 85.00
Plate, Argyle, 10 In. 95.00
Plate, Athens, 7 1/2 In. 95.00
Plate, Athens, 10 1/2 In. 125.00
Plate, Banner, 13 State Names, Latin Text, Rayed Center, Henry W. Berry ... 237.00
Plate, Blue Danube, 10 In. 95.00
Plate, Brush Stroke Painted, 6-Petal Flower, Gingham Flower Border, 9 1/4 In. 80.00
Plate, Cabul, Paneled, Ed. Challinor, 9 1/2 In. 40.00
Plate, Canto, 9 1/4 In. 45.00
Plate, Canto, 10 1/4 In. 30.00
Plate, Cashmere, 7 1/2 In. 100.00
Plate, Cashmere, 9 In. 220.00
Plate, Cashmere, 10 1/2 In. 200.00
Plate, Cauldon, Colonial Drummers & Piper, 12 3/4 In. 50.00
Plate, Chapoo, 4 1/4 In. 132.00
Plate, Chapoo, Paneled, 10 3/4 In. 85.00
Plate, English Scenery, Enoch Wood & Sons, 6 In. 40.00
Plate, Florida, Ford & Son, 8 1/2 In. 50.00
Plate, Formosa, 9 3/8 In., Pair 385.00
Plate, Gem, R. Hammersley, 8 1/2 In. 120.00
Plate, Ivanhoe, Podmore Walker, 9 1/2 In. 125.00
Plate, Japan, 9 1/2 In. 39.00
Plate, Leen, Regout, 8 In., 4 Piece 150.00
Plate, Manilla, Border Spills To Underside, Podmore Walker, 10 3/8 In. ... 130.00
Plate, Mikado, 10 In., 4 Piece 140.00
Plate, Mongolia, Johnson Bros., 6 1/2 In. 20.00
Plate, Nonpareil, 7 1/2 In., 8 Piece 325.00
Plate, Nonpareil, Burgess & Leigh, 8 1/2 In. 44.00
Plate, Oriental, 9 3/4 In. 28.00
Plate, Oriental, 10 1/2 In. 50.00
Plate, Pekin, 9 In. 72.00
Plate, Pekin, 12 In. 60.00
Plate, Rhine, 9 3/4 In. 30.00
Plate, Scinde, Alcock, 7 3/8 In., 3 Piece 110.00
Plate, Scinde, Alcock, 10 1/2 In., 8 Piece 920.00
Plate, Shanghai, 9 3/4 In. 40.00
Plate, Sobraon, 9 1/2 In. 40.00
Plate, Tivoli, c.1845, 10 1/2 In. 50.00
Plate, Waldorf, 9 In., Pair 250.00
Platter, Albany, 14 1/2 In. 275.00
Platter, Amerillia, Podmore Walker, 16 In. 600.00
Platter, Amoy, 12 In. 250.00
Platter, Amoy, 18 In. 650.00
Platter, Anemone, Oval, 14 In. 400.00
Platter, Argyle, 14 In. 275.00
Platter, Astral, Grindley, 16 In. 450.00
Platter, Brunswick Evangeline, 9 1/2 x 12 In. 70.00

Flow Blue, Tray, Chapoo, 10 1/2 x 13 3/4 In.

Flow Blue, Tureen, Cover, Burleigh, Ladle, Burgess & Leigh, 7 1/2 x 12 In.

Platter, Cashmere, 15 In.	1430.00
Platter, Cashmere, 15 1/2 x 19 In.	1705.00
Platter, Chatsworth, F. & Sons, Burslem, 14 1/2 In.	47.00
Platter, Chinese, c.1840, 8 x 9 1/2 In.	95.00
Platter, Chinese, c.1840, 14 x 17 In.	300.00
Platter, Heron, c.1840, 13 x 16 In.	187.00
Platter, Hunt Scene, Hill & Henderson, New Orleans, 16 1/2 x 13 In.	750.00
Platter, Leighton, Well & Tree, 14 1/4 x 20 In.	110.00
Platter, Lonsdale, 12 x 15 In.	77.00
Platter, Lorne, Grindley, 12 x 16 1/2 In.	170.00
Platter, Melbourne, Grindley, 10 x 14 In.	110.00
Platter, Scinde, Alcock, 16 In.	630.00
Platter, Tree & Well, Polychrome, Imari Design, Blue Underglaze, 17 x 21 In.	275.00
Rolling Pin, Flowers, 12 In.	150.00
Sauce, Cover, Fulton, Johnson Bros.	116.00
Sauce, Melbourne, Oval, Grindley	72.00
Sauceboat, Oriental	60.00
Soup, Dish, Amoy, Flanged Rim, 10 In.	200.00
Soup, Dish, Blue Danube, 9 In.	80.00
Soup, Dish, Cashmere, Paneled, 10 1/2 In.	440.00
Soup, Dish, Chapoo, 9 1/2 In.	195.00
Sugar, Cover, Amoy	375.00
Sugar, Cover, Formosa, 8 In.	175.00
Sugar, Cover, Peking	115.00
Sugar & Creamer, Corona	55.00
Tankard, Oriental Scenery, 8 Sides, 13 1/2 In.	400.00
Tea Set, Chapoo, 4 Cups & Saucers, 10 Piece	1150.00
Teapot, Indian Jar, Jacobs & Thos. Furnival, 9 x 10 In.	350.00
Teapot, Manilla, Podmore Walker, 9 In.	275.00
Teapot, Nankin, Paneled, 8 1/2 In.	250.00
Toast Rack, Flowers, 7 In.	25.00
Tray, Cattle Scene, 14 1/4 x 10 1/2 In.	20.00
Tray, Chapoo, 10 1/2 x 13 3/4 In. *Illus*	300.00
Tray, Gironde, Oval, Grindley, 15 x 10 1/2 In.	200.00
Tray, Indian Jar, 20 x 16 In.	500.00
Tray, Melbourne, Grindley, 14 In.	125.00
Tray, Oriental Scenery, People, Building, 10 3/4 x 8 3/4 In.	173.00
Tray, Poppy, Gold Highlights, 14 x 10 In.	40.00
Tray, Scinde, 16 1/4 x 12 3/4 In.	325.00 to 400.00
Tray, Waldorf, Oval, 11 x 9 In.	50.00
Tray, Watteau, 10 3/4 x 8 3/4 In.	25.00
Tray, Woodland, Draft Horse Field, Thom. Fell & Co., 12 x 10 In.	25.00
Tureen, Cover, Avon, 8 1/2 In.	50.00
Tureen, Cover, Burleigh, Ladle, Burgess & Leigh, 7 1/2 x 12 In. *Illus*	200.00
Tureen, Cover, Gironde, Ladle, 7 1/2 x 12 In.	200.00
Tureen, Cover, Laurel, Ladle, 7 In.	50.00
Tureen, Cover, Melbourne, Grindley, 9 In.	150.00
Tureen, Cover, Middle Eastern Scene, 8 Sides, Footed, Alexandria, 13 x 14 In.	600.00

Tureen, Cover, Underplate, Carlton, 6 1/2 x 8 In.	225.00
Tureen, Cover, Underplate, Hong Kong, 6 x 8 In.	350.00
Tureen, Sauce, Cover, Underplate, Melbourne, Grindley	180.00
Tureen, Sauce, Cover, Underplate, Watteau	160.00
Tureen, Soup, Cover, Indian Empress	165.00
Tureen, Soup, Monmouth, 7 In.	130.00
Tureen, Soup, Scinde, 9 1/2 In.	255.00
Tureen, Soup, Scinde, Handles, 6 1/2 In.	220.00
Tureen, Underplate, Fulton, Johnson Bros.	105.00
Tureen, Underplate, Scinde, Ladle, 7 x 7 1/2 In.	800.00
Vase, Snowflower, 6 1/2 In.	39.00
Waste Bowl, Amoy, Double Bulge	325.00
Waste Bowl, Knox, New Wharf Pottery	50.00

FLYING PHOENIX, see Phoenix Bird category.

FOLK ART is also listed in many categories of this book under the actual
name of the object. See categories such as Box, Cigar Store Figure,
Paper, Weather Vane, Wooden, etc.

Angel, Holding Star, Scroll Inscription, Relief-Carved Wood, 1800s, 28 x 17 In.	1093.00
Angel, Out-Stretched Wings, Carved, Pine Plank, 19th Century, 41 x 9 In.	863.00
Ashtray, Decorated With Cigar Bands, Felt Back, 9 x 5 In. .... *Illus*	22.00
Banjo, Fretless, Laminated Pine, 5 Strings, Hide Head, Wilkes Co., N.C., 34 In. .... *Illus*	495.00
Barn, Red, White Trim, Roof Lifts Up, Lamb In Window, 21 x 21 x 12 1/2 In.	350.00
Bird, On Perch, Wood, Painted, Glitter, Elijah Pierce, 1983, 9 1/8 In.	990.00
Bird, Wire, Thread, H. Kinsey, Lancaster County, Pa., Late 1800s, Pair	2500.00
Birdhouse, Country Church, Clapboard, Bell Tower, Weathervane, Shingled, 38 x 20 In.	505.00
Black Man, Bust, Wood, Carved, Mounted On Box, 1900s, 13 5/8 In.	529.00
Box, Tin, 13-Star Flag, Gold Color, Wooden Bands, Pat. June 1st, 1887, 10 In.	220.00
Cat, Carved Wood, American School, Early 20th Century, 9 1/2 In.	470.00
Chain, Beer Cap, 7 Colors, 173 Links, 11764 Caps, 45 Ft.	3000.00
Coconut, Carved, Anthropomorphic Face, Gaping Mouth, 19th Century, 6 x 3 1/2 In.	690.00
Cradle, Doll's, Painted, c.1890	270.00
Doll, Wood Carved, Articulated, Mounted Metal, Wooden Stand, Early 1900s, 19 In.	3055.00
Eagle, Wood Carved, Painted, Full Bodied, Flattened, Articulated Feathers, 10 x 7 In.	1410.00
Fiddle, Crystal Peanut Bars Pine Box, Harrisonville, Pa., 20 In. .... *Illus*	660.00
Fiddle, Laminated Spruce, F-Shape Holes, Black Paint, Wyeth County, Va., 23 In. .... *Illus*	715.00
Footstool, Cherry, Splayed Legs, Carved, Compass Star, 19 x 7 1/2 x 10 In.	195.00
Frame, Wooden, Upside-Down Heart Cutouts, Tulip Crest, Painted, 26 In.	85.00
Handbag, Folded Lucky Strike Cigarette Packs, c.1940, 9 x 13 In.	58.00
Horse, Tin, Articulated Features, Movable Joints, 29 In., Pair	259.00
Indian, Bust, Chalk, Hiawatha, Painted, Saloon Figure, c.1900, 27 1/2 In.	495.00
Indian, Frame, Tin, Virgin Mary, New Mexico, c.1890, 15 1/2 x 13 1/2 In.	385.00
Pig, Cement, Molded, Full-Bodied, Standing, Mounted, 20th Century, 24 1/2 x 42 In.	1058.00
Plaque, Cowboy, Indian, On Horseback, Wood, Carved, Elijah Pierce, 1980, 6 1/2 x 9 In.	220.00
Plaque, Rooster, Hen, Wood, Carved, Painted, Elijah Pierce, 1980, 9 x 14 1/2 In.	1045.00
Rattle, Whimsy, Painted, 13 In.	165.00
Retablo, La Sagrada Familia, Tin, Mexico, 19th Century, 9 3/4 x 13 3/4 In.	431.00
Retablo, Madonna & Child, Painted Tin, Frame, 17 x 20 In.	715.00
Retablo, Our Lady Refuge To Sinners, Tin, Mexico, 19th Century, 10 x 14 In.	403.00

Folk Art, Ashtray, Decorated With Cigar Bands,
Felt Back, 9 x 5 In.

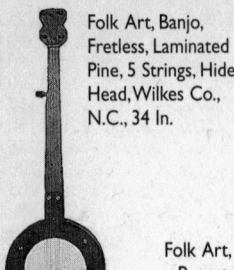

Folk Art, Banjo,
Fretless, Laminated
Pine, 5 Strings, Hide
Head, Wilkes Co.,
N.C., 34 In.

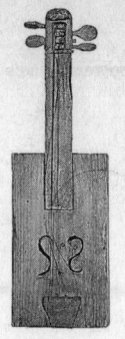

Folk Art, Fiddle,
Laminated Spruce,
F-Shape Holes,
Black Paint, Wyeth
County, Va., 23 In.

Folk Art, Fiddle, Crystal
Peanut Bars Pine Box,
Harrisonville, Pa., 20 In.

Retablo, Powerful Hand Or Five Persons, Tin, Mexico, 19th Century, 10 x 14 In.	316.00
Retablo, San Jeromino, New Mexico, Wood Panel, Painted, 19th Century, 7 x 6 In.	2415.00
Retablo, Sorrowful Mother, Tin, Mexico, 19th Century, 9 3/4 x 13 In.	259.00
Retablo, St. Francis Of Assisi, Tin, Mexico, 19th Century, 10 1/2 x 7 1/2 In.	520.00
Stand, Plant, Green Paint, 3 Legs, Lollipop Plant, 55 x 27 In.	390.00
Stand, Plant, Mustard Yellow Paint, Black Highlights, 2 Tiers, 29 1/2 x 12 In.	140.00
Stand, Twig, Heart, Shamrock, Star, Tripod, Applied Canvas, 29 x 19 x 19 In.	550.00
Table, Inlaid, Turned Legs, D-Shape, 15 3/4 x 11 x 19 1/4 In.	110.00
Whimsy, Cat & Mouse, Articulated, Leather, Painted, 24 In.	1610.00
Whirligig, Black Man Sawing Log, Wood, Early 20th Century, 24 x 31 In.	230.00
Whirligig, Black Man, Jailbird Outfit, Ball & Chain Pedestal, Carved, Painted, 15 In.	3300.00
Whirligig, Happy Jack, Blue Body, 20 1/2 In.	230.00
Whirligig, Hessian Soldier, Blue, Red, White, Paddle Arms 18 x 8 In.	5750.00
Whirligig, Indian In Canoe, Wood, Carved, Painted, 19 1/2 In.	1045.00
Whirligig, Man Sawing Wood, Painted, 19 In.	143.00
Whirligig, Man Sawing, 5 Blades, Painted, Red, White, Blue, 22 In.	230.00
Whirligig, Man With Top Hat, Jointed Legs, Painted, Green, White, Pedestal, c.1850	23000.00
Whirligig, Man, Black Derby, Handlebar Mustache, Orange Jacket, Painted, 15 In.	12100.00
Whirligig, Man, Brimmed Hat, Blue Coat, Vest, Boots, Truncated Paddle Arms, 9 In.	5736.00
Whirligig, Man, Top Hat, Red, White, Blue, Multicolored, Rod, Block, 1850s, 20 In.	7150.00
Whirligig, Rooster, Made From Tin Signs & Model T Ford Hub, c.1920, 55 x 53 In.	5000.00
Whirligig, Sailor, Wood, Carved, Painted, 24 1/4 In.	3819.00
Whirligig, Soldier, Carved, Painted, Red Jacket, Black Belt, Tin Cap, 33 In.	2013.00
Whirligig, Soldier, Wood, Painted Black, Gray, White, 13 In.	353.00
Whirligig, Witch, Cutout Wood, Sheet Iron Paddle Arms, Stand, 22 x 17 In.	4406.00

FOOT WARMERS solved the problem of cold feet in past generations.
Some warmers held charcoal, others held hot water. Pottery, tin, and
soapstone were the favored materials to conduct the heat. The warmer
was kept under the feet, then the legs and feet were tucked into a blanket, providing welcome warmth in a cold carriage or church.

Brass, Oval Box, Hinged, Pierced Lid, Wood & Brass Swing Handle, 5 x 11 In.	60.00
Punched Tin, Mortised & Pegged, Frame, Handle, 19th Century, 5 1/2 x 8 x 9 In.	220.00
Punched Tin, Mortised Wood Frame, Hearts, Bail Handle, Coal Tray, 9 x 8 In.	190.00
Wood, Round, Hinged Door, Tin Insert, Pierced Holes On Sides & Top, 6 x 9 In.	345.00

FOOTBALL collectibles may be found in the Card and the Sports categories.

FOSTORIA glass was made in Fostoria, Ohio, from 1887 to 1891. The
factory was moved to Moundsville, West Virginia, and most of the
glass seen in shops today is a twentieth-century product. The company
was sold in 1983; new items will be easily identifiable, according to
the new owner, Lancaster Colony Corporation. Additional Fostoria
items may be listed in the Milk Glass category.

Alexis, Goblet, Wine, 3 Oz.	12.00
Alexis, Vase, Sweet Pea	85.00
American, Appetizer Set, 10 1/2-In. Tray, 7 Piece	350.00
American, Ashtray, 5 In.	85.00

American, Basket, Reeded Handle	95.00
American, Bonbon, Yellow, 3-Footed, 1 3/4 x 7 1/4 In.	290.00
American, Bowl, 3-Toed, 10 1/2 In.	30.00
American, Bowl, Fruit, 13 In.	85.00
American, Bowl, Oval, 4 1/2 In.	20.00
American, Bowl, Vegetable, Oval, 11 3/4 In.	65.00
American, Cake Plate, Round, Pedestal, 10 In.	125.00
American, Candelabrum, 2-Light, 4 1/2 In.	110.00
American, Candlelamp, Chimney, 4 5/8 In.	75.00
American, Coaster Set, 8 Piece	125.00
American, Cookie Jar, Cover, 8 1/2 x 6 1/2 In.	250.00
American, Cup & Saucer	10.00
American, Decanter, Stopper, 24 Oz.	75.00 to 100.00
American, Dish, Mayonnaise, 2 Sections, Ladle	95.00
American, Goblet, Water, 6-Sided Foot, 10 Oz., 6 7/8 In.	12.00
American, Goblet, Wine, 6-Sided Foot, 2 1/2 Oz., 4 3/8 In.	12.00 to 18.00
American, Ice Tub, 6 1/2 In.	55.00
American, Jam Jar, Cover, 4 3/4 In.	330.00
American, Jelly, Cover	40.00
American, Mug, 12 Oz.	75.00
American, Mug, Tom & Jerry, 5 1/2 Oz., 3 1/4 In.	40.00
American, Pitcher, 1/2 Gal., 8 1/4 In.	195.00
American, Pitcher, Water, Ice Lip, Sunburst Bottom, 1/2 Gal., 8 1/4 In.	120.00
American, Plate, Appetizer, Square	35.00
American, Platter, Oval, 10 1/2 In.	50.00
American, Punch Bowl, Footed, 9 1/2 In.	80.00 to 110.00
American, Punch Bowl, Stand, 14 1/2 x 13 In.	700.00
American, Relish, Oblong, 6 In.	13.00
American, Rose Bowl, 5 In.	30.00 to 38.00
American, Saucer, 6 In.	5.00
American, Shaker, Cheese	75.00
American, Sugar Cuber, Silver Cover With Tongs, Round	300.00 to 450.00
American, Syrup, Bakelite Handle, 5 1/4 In.	225.00
American, Syrup, Drip Cut	95.00
American, Tumbler, Water, 8 Oz., 4 1/8 In.	16.00
American, Vase, Bud, Milk Glass, Blue	100.00
American, Vase, Flared, 10 In.	260.00
American Lady, Sherbet, Regal Blue, 5 1/2 Oz., 4 1/8 In.	85.00
American Lady, Tumbler, Juice, Regal Blue, Footed, 5 Oz., 4 1/8 In.	125.00
Arcady, Cake Plate, Handle, 10 In.	55.00
Arcady, Candelabrum, 3-Light	75.00
Argus, Candy Dish, Cover, Olive Green	45.00
Argus, Goblet, Water, Ruby, 10 1/2 Oz., 6 1/2 In.	24.00
Argus, Sherbet, Olive Green, 8 Oz., 5 In.	10.00
Argus, Tumbler, Iced Tea, Olive Green, Footed, 13 Oz., 6 3/4 In.	16.00
Argus, Tumbler, Old Fashioned, Olive Green, 10 Oz., 3 7/8 In.	16.00
Art Glass, Shade, Opal, Gold Zipper, Green Pulled Decoration, 7 1/4 In.	431.00
Aurora, Goblet, Water, Gold Band, 10 1/2 Oz., 7 In.	20.00
Baroque, Bowl, 7 1/2 In.	45.00
Baroque, Bowl, Flared, Topaz, 12 In.	40.00
Baroque, Bowl, Handle, 10 1/2 In.	35.00
Baroque, Bowl, Nut, Topaz, 3-Toed	45.00
Baroque, Cake Plate, Handle	20.00
Baroque, Candelabrum, 3-Light, Silver Mist, Tiara, 6 In., Pair	165.00
Baroque, Candelabrum, 3-Light, Twilight, Tiara, 6 In., Pair	345.00
Baroque, Candlestick, Topaz, 5 1/2 In., Pair	65.00 to 86.00
Baroque, Compote, 4 3/4 In.	16.00
Baroque, Plate, Topaz, 9 In.	55.00
Baroque, Relish, 3 Sections, 10 In.	20.00
Baroque, Salt & Pepper	135.00
Baroque, Sauce, Topaz	62.00
Baroque, Sherbet, 5 Oz., 3 3/4 In.	11.00
Baroque, Sugar & Creamer	15.00

Baroque, Vase, Azure, 7 In.	140.00
Baroque, Vase, Topaz, 7 In.	120.00
Berry, Berry Bowl, Green	26.00
Berry, Creamer, Green	25.00
Berry, Vase, Bud, Green, 8 In.	44.00
Beverly, Cordial, 3/4 Oz., 3 1/2 In.	45.00
Bouquet, Relish, 2 Sections	28.00
Brazilian, Celery Dish	35.00
Brazilian, Relish	25.00
Buttercup, Bowl, Lily	75.00
Buttercup, Candelabrum, 3-Light, Pair	165.00
Buttercup, Candlestick, 3-Light, 8 In., Pair	140.00
Buttercup, Cordial, 1 Oz., 3 7/8 In.	48.00
Buttercup, Cup	16.00
Buttercup, Plate, 7 1/2 In.	15.00
Buttercup, Relish, 3 Sections	20.00
Buttercup, Relish, 3 Sections, Gold Trim, Handle	95.00
Buttercup, Relish, 3 Sections, Handle	55.00
Camelia, Plate, Salad, 7 Oz.	16.00
Camelia, Tumbler, Iced Tea, Footed, 12 Oz., 6 1/8 In.	28.00
Camellia, Candelabrum, 2-Light, 7 In.	75.00
Cascade, Pickle Castor, Metal Holder, No. 112	165.00
Catalina, Cocktail, Chartreuse	12.00
Catalina, Tumbler, Old Fashioned, Chartreuse	12.00
Century, Bowl, Cereal, 6 In.	23.00
Century, Bowl, Oval, 9 In.	15.00
Century, Butter, Cover	41.00
Century, Creamer	12.00
Century, Cup	13.00
Century, Pitcher, 48 Oz., 7 1/8 In.	85.00
Century, Plate, 8 1/2 In.	14.00
Century, Relish, 3 Sections, Oval, 11 In.	15.00
Century, Relish, 3 Sections, Silver Overlay, Handle, 11 In.	35.00
Century, Salt & Pepper, Tray	18.00 to 24.00
Century, Sugar	12.00
Century, Sugar & Creamer, Underplate	45.00
Century, Torte Plate, 13 In.	25.00
Chalice, Goblet, Water, Ebony Stem, 11 Oz., 5 3/8 In.	24.00
Chalice, Tumbler, Juice, Ebony Stem, Footed, 5 1/2 Oz., 4 1/2 In.	22.00
Chintz, Bowl, Vegetable, Oval, 10 1/2 In.	245.00
Chintz, Candelabrum, 3-Light, Pair	65.00
Chintz, Candlestick, 5 1/2 In.	35.00
Chintz, Cheese & Cracker Plate, Footed	38.00
Chintz, Cocktail, 4 Oz., 5 In.	23.00
Chintz, Cup & Saucer	29.00
Chintz, Sherbet, 6 Oz., 4 3/8 In.	18.00
Chintz, Sugar & Creamer	36.00
Coin, Bowl, Blue, 7 1/2 In.	30.00
Coin, Bowl, Oval, Olive Green, 9 In.	15.00
Coin, Cake Plate, Footed	135.00
Coin, Candlestick, 8 In., Pair	55.00
Coin, Candy Dish, Cover, Amber, 6 In.	50.00
Coin, Candy Dish, Olive Green	28.00
Coin, Cigarette Urn, Olive	23.00
Coin, Punch Cup	45.00
Coin, Punch Set, 11-In. Bowl, 10 Piece	595.00
Coin, Urn, Cover, Olive Green, 12 3/4 In.	40.00
Coin, Vase, Bud, Blue	50.00
Coin, Vase, Bud, Olive Green	28.00
Coin, Wedding Bowl, Cover, Emerald Green	115.00
Colonial Dame, Goblet, Water, 11 Oz., 6 3/8 In.	25.00
Colonial Dame, Tumbler, Iced Tea, Empire Green, Footed, 12 Oz., 6 In.	28.00
Colony, Bowl, Low, Footed, 10 1/2 In.	79.00

Colony, Bowl, Round, Flared, 11 1/4 In. 30.00
Colony, Butter, Cover, White 10.00
Colony, Cake Plate, Footed, 12 In. 95.00
Colony, Candlestick, 9 1/2 In., Pair 110.00
Colony, Candlestick, Prisms, 7 1/2 In. 80.00
Colony, Candy Dish, Blue Cover, White Bowl, 6 1/2 In. 110.00
Colony, Candy Dish, Cover, White . . . . .20.00 to 25.00
Colony, Cheese & Cracker Plate 70.00
Colony, Compote, Cover, Low, 6 3/8 In. 38.00
Colony, Console, Rolled Edge, 9 In. 65.00
Colony, Dish, Mayonnaise, Underplate 38.00
Colony, Pitcher, Ice Lip, 2 Qt. 85.00
Colony, Relish, 2 Sections, 2 Handles, 7 In. 22.00
Colony, Relish, 3 Sections, 2 Handles, 10 1/2 In. . . . . .28.00 to 30.00
Colony, Salt & Pepper, Tray 25.00
Colony, Tray, Muffin, Handles . . . . .32.00 to 35.00
Colony, Tumbler, Juice, 3 5/8 In., 5 Oz. 30.00
Colony, Tumbler, Water, 5 1/4 In., 9 Oz. 28.00
Colony, Urn, Cover, Footed 70.00
Colony, Vase, Cornucopia, 9 In. 150.00
Congo, Tumbler, Iced Tea, Pink, 14 Oz. 12.00
Contour, Celery Dish, Rose Cutting, 9 In. 14.00
Contour, Dish, Mayonnaise, Ebony 45.00
Contour, Pitcher, Pt., 5 1/4 In. 48.00
Contour, Relish, 3 Sections, Rose Cutting 43.00
Contour, Sugar & Creamer 10.00
Coronet, Candlestick, 2-Light, 5 1/8 In. 40.00
Coronet, Cup & Saucer 17.00
Coronet, Ice Bucket, Handles . . . . .20.00 to 25.00
Coronet, Relish, 3 Sections, 10 In. 40.00
Coronet, Sugar & Creamer 30.00
Coronet, Vase, Handles, 6 In. 75.00
Corsage, Cup & Saucer 25.00
Corsage, Oyster Cocktail, 4 Oz., 3 3/4 In. 17.00
Corsage, Plate, 7 1/2 In. 10.00
Corsage, Tumbler, Water, Footed, 9 Oz., 5 1/2 In. 22.00
Crown Collection, Candy Dish, Cover, Hapsburg, Gold 78.00
Crown Collection, Candy Dish, Cover, Luxembourg, Cobalt Blue 155.00
Crown Collection, Candy Dish, Cover, Luxembourg, Topaz 95.00
Crown Collection, Candy Dish, Cover, Windsor, Topaz 75.00
Decorator Collection, Basket, Teal Green, Footed 45.00
Decorator Collection, Vase, Fish, Lavender 55.00
Decorator Collection, Vase, Fish, Teal Green 55.00
Decorator Collection, Vase, Pitcher Shape, Teal Green, 10 In. 57.00
Distinction, Goblet, Water, Cobalt Blue, 11 Oz., 7 3/8 In. 45.00
Distinction, Wine, Cobalt Blue, 6 1/2 Oz., 6 1/4 In. 45.00
Dolly Madison, Champagne, 6 Oz., 4 7/8 In. 18.00
Dolly Madison, Tumbler, Iced Tea, Footed, 12 Oz., 5 3/4 In. 19.00
Dolly Madison, Tumbler, Juice, Footed, 5 Oz., 4 1/2 In. 17.00
Dolly Madison, Wine, 4 Oz., 4 3/4 In. 24.00
Drape, Bowl, Cobalt Blue, Footed, 10 1/2 In. 425.00
Eloquence, Goblet, Water, 14 Oz., 7 In. 25.00
Engagement, Sherbet, 7 Oz., 5 1/8 In. 12.00
Engagement, Tumbler, Iced Tea, Footed, 14 Oz., 6 3/8 In. 25.00
Fairfax, Bouillon, Azure, Footed 22.00
Fairfax, Bowl, Centerpiece, Rolled Edge, Azure, 12 In. 30.00
Fairfax, Bowl, Vegetable, Oval, 9 In. 49.00
Fairfax, Bowl, Whipped Cream, Azure 65.00
Fairfax, Coaster, Azure 9.00
Fairfax, Compote, Azure, 7 In. 65.00
Fairfax, Compote, Green, 7 In. 54.00
Fairfax, Cup & Saucer, Azure 22.00
Fairfax, Cup & Saucer, Topaz, Footed 14.00

Fairfax, Cup, After Dinner, Green ....16.00 to 23.00
Fairfax, Cup, Rose 6.00
Fairfax, Dish, Mayonnaise, Rose 35.00
Fairfax, Icer, Green 15.00
Fairfax, Icer, Liner, Topaz 35.00
Fairfax, Nut Cup, Azure 25.00
Fairfax, Nut Cup, Green 22.00
Fairfax, Pitcher, Rose 235.00
Fairfax, Plate, Azure, 6 In. 5.00
Fairfax, Plate, Canape, Amber 8.00
Fairfax, Relish, 2 Sections, Green 30.00
Fairfax, Relish, Rose, 11 1/2 In. 23.00
Fairfax, Salt & Pepper 50.00
Fairfax, Sauceboat 62.00
Fairfax, Saucer, Amber 3.00
Fairfax, Saucer, Blue 5.00
Fairfax, Saucer, Topaz 4.00
Fairfax, Soup, Cream, Topaz 25.00
Fairfax, Soup, Dish, Azure, 7 In. 66.00
Fairfax, Sugar & Creamer, Ebony 20.00
Fairfax, Sugar & Creamer, Green 85.00
Fairfax, Tumbler, Water, Footed, 9 Oz., 5 1/4 In. 24.00
Fairfax, Tumbler, Whiskey, Footed, 2 1/2 Oz. 26.00
Fascination, Claret, Ruby, 6 Oz., 5 3/4 In. 42.00
Fascination, Goblet, Water, Ruby, 10 Oz., 6 3/4 In. 38.00
Fascination, Sherbet, Ruby, 7 Oz., 4 3/4 In. 28.00
Fascination, Tumbler, Juice, Ruby, Footed, 5 Oz., 4 1/4 In. 22.00
Fascination, Wine, Amethyst, 4 Oz., 5 1/8 In. 25.00
Fern, Bonbon, Handle 25.00
Figurine, Lute & Lotus, Black, Gold Trim, 12 1/2 In., Pair 660.00
Flame, Candleholder, Pair 45.00
Frisco, Candy Dish, Cover 20.00
Gadroon, Goblet, Water, 10 Oz., 7 7/8 In. 16.00
Glacier, Vase, Frosted, 7 In. 15.00
Glamour, Goblet, Water, Green Mist, 12 Oz., 7 1/4 In. 20.00
Glamour, Wine, Green Mist, 7 Oz., 6 3/8 In. 22.00
Gold Lace, Compote, 5 1/2 In. 39.00
Gold Lace, Sauce 35.00
Hartford, Butter, Cover 100.00
Hartford, Creamer & Spooner 55.00
Hartford, Dish, Olive, 5 1/2 In. 35.00
Hawaiian, Basket, Peacock Blue Trim 50.00
Hawaiian, Bowl, Amber, Peacock Blue Trim, Oval, 15 In. 75.00
Hawaiian, Bowl, Deep, Amber, Peacock Blue Trim, 8 In. 55.00
Hawaiian, Bowl, Deep, Amber, Peacock Blue Trim, 11 1/2 In. 65.00
Hawaiian, Bowl, Floral, Amber, Peacock Blue Trim, 8 In. 48.00
Hawaiian, Shrimp & Dip Set, Amber 110.00
Hawaiian, Vase, Amber, Ruffled Edge, 6 3/4 In. 45.00
Heather, Bowl, Lily, 9 In. 48.00
Heather, Goblet, Water, 9 Oz., 7 7/8 In. 26.00
Heather, Tray, Handles 65.00
Heather, Vase, Oval, 8 1/2 In. 85.00
Heirloom, Bowl, Ruby, Crimped Edge, 11 In. 65.00
Heirloom, Bowl, White Opalescent, Oblong, 15 In. 65.00
Heirloom, Candleholder, Opalescent, 3 1/2 In., Pair 67.00
Heirloom, Vase, Bud, Pink 23.00
Heirloom, Vase, Pitcher Shape, Green Opalescent 95.00
Heirloom, Vase, Topaz, 11 In. 75.00
Heirloom, Vase, Winged, White Opalescent, 11 In. 125.00
Heritage, Relish, 2 Sections, 6 In. 10.00
Hermitage, Cocktail, Icer, Amber Liner 20.00
Hermitage, Decanter, Stopper, 28 Oz. 55.00
Hermitage, Goblet, Water, Topaz, 9 Oz. 19.00

Hermitage, Oyster Cocktail, Topaz, 4 Oz., 3 In.	13.00
Hermitage, Tumbler, Whiskey, 2 Oz., 2 1/2 In.	10.00
Holly, Champagne, 6 Oz., 5 5/8 In.	19.00
Holly, Cocktail, 3 1/2 Oz., 5 1/4 In.	15.00
Holly, Sandwich Server, Handles	45.00
Holly, Wine, 3 1/2 Oz., 6 In.	30.00
Homespun, Scotch & Soda, 11 1/2 Oz.	22.00
Homespun, Tumbler, Old Fashioned, Moss Green, 9 Oz.	18.00
Horizon, Bowl, Cereal, Spruce	20.00
Horizon, Console, Spruce Green, 12 In.	48.00
Horizon, Sugar & Creamer, Spruce	28.00
Jamestown, Goblet, Water, 9 1/2 Oz., 5 3/4 In.	25.00
Jamestown, Goblet, Water, Green, 10 Oz., 5 7/8 In.	16.00
Jamestown, Goblet, Water, Pink, 9 1/2 Oz., 5 3/4 In.	24.00
Jamestown, Pitcher, Amber	65.00
Jamestown, Plate, Pink, 8 In.	29.00
Jamestown, Sherbet, Amber	6.00
Jamestown, Sherbet, Green, 8 Oz., 5 In.	13.00
Jamestown, Sherbet, Ruby, 8 Oz., 5 In.	18.00
Jamestown, Tumbler, 12 Oz., 5 1/8 In.	35.00
Jamestown, Tumbler, Iced Tea, Amber, Footed, 13 Oz., 6 3/4 In.	10.00
Jamestown, Tumbler, Juice, Amber, Footed, 5 Oz., 4 3/4 In.	10.00
Jamestown, Tumbler, Juice, Blue, 5 Oz., 4 3/4 In.	26.00
Jamestown, Wine, Amber, 4 Oz., 4 1/4 In.	10.00
Jamestown, Wine, Blue, 4 Oz., 4 1/4 In.	24.00
Jamestown, Wine, Ruby, 4 Oz., 4 1/4 In.	24.00
Jenny Lind, Box, Cover, Milk Glass	70.00
Jenny Lind, Cologne, Milk Glass, 11 In.	70.00
Jewel & Shell, Pitcher, Water	185.00
June, Bowl, Cereal, 6 1/2 In.	30.00
June, Candlestick, Grecian, 5 In., Pair	110.00
June, Cheese & Cracker Plate, Topaz	120.00
June, Claret, Topaz, 4 Oz., 6 In.	75.00
June, Cocktail, Topaz, 3 Oz., 5 1/4 In.	38.00
June, Cup & Saucer	23.00
June, Cup & Saucer, Azure	45.00
June, Cup, After Dinner, Pink	98.00
June, Dish, Mayonnaise, Topaz, Underplate, Ladle	120.00
June, Goblet, Water, 10 Oz., 8 1/4 In.	45.00
June, Plate, Luncheon, 8 1/2 In.	22.00
June, Platter, Topaz, 15 In.	150.00
June, Salt & Pepper, Topaz	200.00
June, Sherbet, 6 Oz., 6 In.	22.00
June, Soup, Cream, Topaz	65.00
June Night, Sherry, 2 Oz.	39.00
Karnak, Tumbler, Cooler, Pink, 21 Oz.	15.00
Karnak, Tumbler, Pink, 14 Oz.	12.00
Kashmir, Sherbet, Green, Stem & Foot, 7 Oz., 4 3/8 In.	20.00
Kashmir, Tumbler, Green Stem & Foot, 13 Oz., 5 1/4 In.	29.00
Lafayette, Bowl, Topaz, 7 In.	40.00
Lafayette, Cup & Saucer, Burgundy	65.00
Lafayette, Torte Plate, Green, 14 In.	45.00
Lamp, Colony, c.1940	130.00
Lido, Candlestick, Pair	32.00
Lido, Compote, 6 1/2 In.	20.00
Lido, Tumbler, Iced Tea, Footed, 14 Oz.	22.00
Loop Optic, Vase, c.1898, 12 In.	45.00
Manor, Plate, Luncheon, Topaz	22.00
Mayfair, Ashtray, Topaz	15.00
Mayfair, Ashtray, Wisteria	35.00
Mayfair, Platter, Topaz, 15 In.	48.00
Mayflower, Tumbler, Juice, Footed, 5 Oz., 4 7/8 In.	18.00
Meadow Rose, Bonbon, 3-Toed, 7 In.	39.00

Meadow Rose, Goblet, Water, 9 Oz., 6 3/4 In.	30.00
Meadow Rose, Sherbet, 5 Oz., 3 3/4 In.	24.00
Meadow Rose, Torte Plate, 14 In.	38.00
Mesa, Goblet, Blue, 13 Oz.	20.00
Mesa, Tumbler, Iced Tea, Blue, 15 Oz.	18.00
Midnight Rose, Bowl, Oblong	175.00
Midnight Rose, Candlestick, Pair	125.00
Midnight Rose, Cup & Saucer	31.00
Midnight Rose, Dish, Sweetmeat, Handles, 4 1/2 In.	18.00
Midnight Rose, Goblet, Water, 9 Oz., 7 5/8 In.	30.00
Midnight Rose, Relish, 5 Sections	75.00
Minuet, Tumbler, Topaz, Footed, 10 Oz.	32.00
Morning Glory, Bowl, Lily, 11 1/2 In.	44.00
Mt. Vernon, Cocktail, 3 1/2 Oz., 5 1/4 In.	13.00
Mt. Vernon, Finger Bowl	13.00
Mt. Vernon, Goblet, 10 Oz., 7 7/8 In.	23.00
Mt. Vernon, Tumbler, Iced Tea, Footed, 12 Oz., 5 7/8 In.	23.00
Navarre, Bonbon, Handles, 4 3/8 In.	20.00
Navarre, Bowl, Crown, Royal Blue, 9 In.	125.00
Navarre, Bowl, Footed, Handles, 10 1/2 x 3 3/8 In.	95.00
Navarre, Candelabrum, 2-Light, Pair	100.00
Navarre, Candelabrum, 3-Light, Pair	135.00
Navarre, Champagne, 6 Oz., 5 5/8 In.	26.00
Navarre, Champagne, Azure, 6 Oz., 5 7/8 In.	70.00
Navarre, Cup & Saucer	34.00
Navarre, Goblet, Water, 10 Oz., 7 5/8 In.	40.00
Navarre, Nappy, 3-Footed, Tricornered, Handle, 4 5/8 In.	17.00
Navarre, Oyster Cocktail, 4 Oz., 3 5/8 In.	34.00
Navarre, Plate, 7 1/2 In.	18.00
Navarre, Plate, Dinner, 9 In.	84.00
Navarre, Saucer	7.00
Navarre, Sugar	19.00
Navarre, Sugar, Individual	26.00
Navarre, Torte Plate, 13 In.	30.00
Navarre, Vase, Footed, 10 In.	275.00
Needlepoint, Tumbler, Water, Teal Blue, 12 1/4 Oz.	30.00
Neo Classic, Champagne, 7 Oz.	25.00
Neo Classic, Goblet, Amethyst, 10 Oz., 6 3/8 In.	24.00 to 32.00
Neo Classic, Tumbler, Iced Tea, Empire Green, Footed, 12 Oz.	35.00
Oakleaf, Dish, Lemon, Green, Handles	38.00
Oakleaf, Ice Bucket	145.00
Oakwood, Ice Bucket, Azure	215.00
Paradise, Sandwich Server, Center Handle, 12 In.	98.00
Pioneer, Relish, 3 Sections, Green	40.00
Plume, Candelabrum, 2-Light, Pair	125.00
Precedence, Goblet, Water, 12 Oz, 7 1/2 In.	42.00
Princess, Wine, Gray Mist Bowl, Onyx Stem & Foot, 5 1/2 Oz., 5 3/4 In.	18.00
Queen Anne, Candlestick, Bobeche, Prisms, Candle Cup, Blue, 14 In., Pair	725.00
Rambler, Bowl, Ruby, 10 1/2 In.	85.00
Rambler, Goblet, Water, 10 Oz., 6 7/8 In.	22.00
Rambler, Vase, Ruby	50.00
Rebecca At The Well, Compote, Avocado Green, Satin, 12 3/4 In.	295.00
Regency, Sauce	40.00
Richmond, Parfait, 5 Oz.	28.00
Robin Hood, Bowl, Footed, No. 603, 7 In.	50.00
Rogene, Jug, No. 4, Footed	95.00
Rogene, Plate, Salad, 7 1/2 In.	15.00
Romance, Candelabrum, 3-Light, Pair	145.00
Romance, Cocktail, 3 1/2 Oz., 4 7/8 In.	23.00
Romance, Cup & Saucer	25.00
Royal, Candy Dish, Blue, 1/2 Lb.	155.00
Royal, Candy Dish, Cover, Green, 3 Sections	135.00
Royal, Cup & Saucer, Green, Footed	16.00

Royal, Plate, Amber, 6 In. 7.00
Royal, Plate, Canape, Blue 59.00
Sakier, Candelabrum, 2-Light, Wisteria, 5 In., Pair 250.00
Sakier, Vase, Ebony, 7 1/2 In. 85.00
Sakier, Vase, Radio, Ebony, Gold Trim 115.00
Sakier, Vase, Tut, Ebony 60.00
Seashell, Vase, Green 45.00
Seville, Console, Rolled Edge, Amber 30.00
Seville, Grapefruit, Liner, Amber, Footed 55.00
Sherwood, Vase, Cobalt Blue, Square, 7 3/4 In. 185.00
Spartan, Wine, 2 1/2 Oz., 4 7/8 In. 26.00
Spartan, Wine, Green, 2 1/2 Oz., 4 7/8 In. 38.00
St. Bernard, Compote, Cover, High Standard, Frosted Dog, 11 1/4 x 8 1/2 In. 475.00
Starflower, Dish, Mayonnaise, Underplate, Etched 45.00
Sun Ray, Bowl, Handles, 9 1/2 x 1 1/4 In. 49.00
Sun Ray, Cruet 42.00
Sun Ray, Nappy, Tricornered 10.00
Sun Ray, Pitcher, Ice Lip, 2 Qt. 118.00
Sun Ray, Relish, 3 Sections 28.00
Sun Ray, Relish, Glacier, 4 Sections 36.00
Sun Ray, Relish, Ruby, 2 Sections 55.00
Sun Ray, Sherbet, 5 1/2 Oz., 3 1/2 In. 10.00
Sun Ray, Tumbler, Footed, 9 Oz., 4 3/4 In. 19.00
Swirl Optic, Jug, Green Foot, No. 7 . . . . 35.00
Trojan, Bowl, Whipped Cream, Topaz 38.00
Trojan, Cup & Saucer, Topaz 24.00
Trojan, Cup, Topaz 18.00
Trojan, Finger Bowl, Topaz 52.00
Trojan, Grapefruit, Liner, Topaz 50.00
Trojan, Saucer, Topaz 6.00
Tut, Vase, Green, Handles 75.00
Vernon, Candy Dish, Cover, 3 Sections, Amber 55.00
Vernon, Candy Dish, Fleur-De-Lis Cover, Green, 3 Sections 110.00
Versailles, Bonbon, Blue, Gold Trim 35.00
Versailles, Bouillon, Underplate, Yellow 45.00
Versailles, Bowl, Whipped Cream, Yellow 45.00
Versailles, Bowl, Yellow, 3-Footed, 12 In. 85.00
Versailles, Celery Dish, Pink, 11 1/2 In. 115.00
Versailles, Compote, Blue, 6 1/2 In. 125.00
Versailles, Compote, Pink, 5 In. 70.00
Versailles, Cruet, Yellow, Footed, Stopper 165.00
Versailles, Cup & Saucer, Yellow 28.00
Versailles, Cup, Green 26.00
Versailles, Cup, Yellow 25.00
Versailles, Dish, Mint, Pink, Footed 35.00
Versailles, Goblet, Water, Pink, 10 Oz., 8 1/4 In. 75.00
Versailles, Plate, Bread & Butter, Pink, 6 In. 12.00
Versailles, Plate, Salad, Pink, 7 In. 15.00
Versailles, Plate, Yellow, 10 1/4 In. 40.00
Versailles, Sugar Pail, Pink 195.00
Versailles, Tumbler, Whiskey, Pink, Footed, 2 1/2 Oz. 47.00
Versailles, Whipped Cream Tub, Pink, Metal Handle, 2 3/4 x 4 3/4 In. 325.00
Versailles, Wine, Pink, 3 Oz., 5 1/2 In. 115.00
Vesper, Ice Bucket, Green 115.00
Vesper, Plate, Amber, 8 In. 10.00
Victoria, Bowl, Frosted Rose, 6 In. 95.00
Victoria, Celery Dish . . . . .35.00 to 65.00
Victoria, Relish, Canoe Shape 25.00
Victorian, Goblet, Water, Empire Green, 10 Oz. 30.00
Victorian, Goblet, Water, Regal Blue, 10 Oz., 5 7/8 In. 85.00
Victorian, Tumbler, Juice, Regal Blue, Footed, 5 Oz., 4 1/4 In. 35.00
Victorian, Wine, Claret, Regal Blue, 3 1/2 Oz., 4 1/2 In. 55.00
Victorian, Wine, Empire Green, 3 1/2 Oz., 4 1/2 In. 26.00

Virginia, Tumbler, Footed, 5 In. 17.00
Vision, Cordial, Midnight Blue, 2 Oz., 3 5/8 In. 26.00
Watercress, Goblet, Water, 10 Oz., 6 7/8 In. 25.00
Wedding Bells, Bowl, Gold Flash, 8 In. 30.00
Wedding Ring, Dish, Mayonnaise, Underplate, Platinum Band 40.00
Wedding Ring, Sugar & Creamer, Platinum Band 35.00
Westchester, Goblet, Water, Ruby, 10 Oz, 7/8 In. 45.00
Westchester, Wine, Regal Blue, 3 Oz., 5 1/4 In. 75.00
Wildflower, Bowl, Fruit Salad, 13 In. 135.00
Wildflower, Bowl, Square, Flared, Footed, Gold Edge, 12 In. 65.00
Wildflower, Dish, Oblong, 10 5/8 In. 29.00
Wildflower, Plate, Handle, Indented Center, Gold Edge, 12 In. 60.00
Willow, Champagne, 6 Oz., 4 7/8 In. ....16.00 to 18.00
Willow, Oyster Cocktail, 4 Oz. 16.00
Willow, Plate, Salad, 8 In. 16.00
Willow, Sherbet, 6 Oz. 14.00
Willowmere, Candelabrum, 2-Light, Pair 145.00
Willowmere, Cocktail, 3 1/2 Oz., 4 3/4 In. 12.00
Willowmere, Jug 345.00
Willowmere, Relish, 4 Sections 75.00
Willowmere, Torte Plate 55.00
Winburn, Cruet 10.00
Wistar, Goblet, Water, Betsy Ross, 9 Oz., 5 7/8 In. 18.00

FOVAL, see Fry category.

FRAMES are included in the Furniture category under Frame.

FRANCISCAN is a trademark that appears on pottery. Gladding, McBean
and Company started in 1875. The company grew and acquired other
potteries. They made sewer pipes, floor tiles, dinnerwares, and art pottery with a variety of trademarks. In 1934, dinnerware and art pottery
were sold under the name Franciscan Ware. They made china and
cream-colored, decorated earthenware. Desert Rose, Apple, El Patio,
and Coronado were best-sellers. The company became Interpace
Corporation and in 1979 was purchased by Josiah Wedgwood & Sons.
The plant was closed in 1984 but a few of the patterns are still being
made. For more information, see *Kovels' Depression Glass &
Dinnerware Price List.*

Apple, Box, Cigarette, Cover 125.00
Apple, Tumbler, 4 5/8 In. 30.00
Cafe Royal, Cup 14.00
Cafe Royal, Mug, 7 Oz., 3 In. 19.00
Coronado, Bowl, Ivory Matte, 7 3/4 In. 45.00
Coronado, Compote, Turquoise Matte 65.00
Coronado, Cup, Turquoise Matte 10.00
Coronado, Platter, Oval, Turquoise Matte, 13 1/8 In. 30.00
Coronado, Soup, Cream, Ivory Matte, 8 1/2 In. 32.00
Coronado, Soup, Cream, Underplate, Coral Matte 50.00
Coronado, Sugar, Cover, Yellow Matte 20.00
Desert Rose, Bell, Danbury Mint, 4 1/4 In. 90.00
Desert Rose, Bowl, Salad, 10 In. 115.00
Desert Rose, Bowl, Vegetable, Oval, Divided, 10 7/8 In. 45.00
Desert Rose, Box, Cigarette 125.00
Desert Rose, Candleholder, 3 1/2 In., Pair 95.00
Desert Rose, Cup & Saucer 10.00
Desert Rose, Cup, Oversized, 4 1/2 In. 30.00
Desert Rose, Dish, Heart Shape, 5 3/4 In. 145.00
Desert Rose, Goblet, 5 In. 18.00
Desert Rose, Gravy Boat, Underplate 50.00
Desert Rose, Mixing Bowl Set, 3 Piece 495.00
Desert Rose, Relish, 10 7/8 In. 45.00
Duotone, Plate, Blue, Ivory, 7 1/2 In. 45.00

El Patio, Creamer 15.00
El Patio, Platter, Oval, 13 In. 30.00
El Patio, Sugar, Cover, Ivory Matte 25.00
Forget-Me-Not, Bowl, Fruit, 5 1/4 In. 14.00
Forget-Me-Not, Cup 7.00
Forget-Me-Not, Cup & Saucer 18.00
Forget-Me-Not, Plate, 6 1/2 In. 10.00
Ivy, Plate, 6 1/4 In. 12.00
Metropolitan, Plate, 10 In. 15.00
Metropolitan, Teapot, Ivory, Mauve 250.00
Rancho, Mustard Jar, Gourd Shape 65.00
Spice, Bowl, 5 1/8 In. 12.00
Spice, Bowl, 9 3/8 In. 40.00
Spice, Creamer 15.00
Spice, Plate, 6 1/2 In. 8.00
Spice, Plate, 8 1/4 In. 10.00
Spice, Plate, 10 1/2 In. 15.00
Spice, Sugar, Open 15.00
Spice, Teapot 75.00
Starburst, Bowl, Vegetable, Oval, 8 3/8 In. 65.00
Starburst, Plate, 6 1/2 In. 6.00
Starburst, Plate, 10 3/4 In. 12.00
Tiempo, Coffeepot, Cover 75.00
Tiempo, Plate, 9 3/4 In. 25.00
Tiempo, Tumbler, 5 In. 25.00

FRANKART, Inc., New York, New York, mass-produced nude *dancing lady* lamps, ashtrays, and other decorative Art Deco items in the 1920s and 1930s. They were made of white lead composition and spray-painted. *Frankart Inc.* and the patent number and year were stamped on the base.

Lamp, 2 Female Nudes, Cylindrical Shade, Black Base, 1 Socket, 11 7/8 In. 2233.00
Lamp, Female Nude, Holding Disk, 1 Socket, Gray Base, 15 In. 1528.00
Lamp, Female Nude, Seated, 3 Frosted Glass Shades, 3 Sockets, Stepped Base, 12 In. ... 2350.00

FRANKOMA POTTERY was originally known as The Frank Potteries when John F. Frank opened shop in 1933. The factory is now working in Sapulpa, Oklahoma. Early wares were made from a light cream-colored clay from Ada, Oklahoma, but in 1956 the company switched to a red burning clay from Sapulpa. The firm makes dinnerwares, utilitarian and decorative kitchenwares, figurines, flowerpots, and limited edition and commemorative pieces. John Frank died in 1973 and his daughter, Joniece, inherited the business. Frankoma went bankrupt in 1990. It was bought by Richard Bernstein in 1991 and is still in business.

Ashtray, Cocker Spaniel, Sleeping, Prairie Green, Ada Clay, No. 460 .... 110.00
Baker, Individual, Mayan Aztec, Desert Gold, Ada Clay, No. 7U 30.00
Baker, Individual, Plainsman, Prairie Gold, No. 5U 30.00
Baker, Individual, Wagon Wheels, Prairie Green, No. 97U 15.00
Bank, Piggy, Prairie Green, Sapulpa Clay, No. 381 .... 25.00
Bookends, Charger Horse, Desert Gold, No. 420 .... 125.00
Bowl, Chili, Mayan Aztec, Prairie Green, No. 7X 5.00
Bowl, Desert Sand, Sapulpa Clay, No. 45 .... 40.00
Bowl, Ivy, Prairie Green, Sapulpa Clay, No. 27 .... 30.00
Bowl, Knobby Cactus, Desert Gold, Sapulpa Clay, No. 203 .... 20.00
Bowl, Leaf, Desert Gold, No. 226, 12 In. 25.00
Bowl, Wedding Ring, Prairie Green, Ada Clay, No. 200 .... 40.00
Butter, Cover, Lazybones, Woodland Moss, No. 4K 15.00
Butter, Lazybones, Desert Gold, Sapulpa Clay, No. 4K 13.00
Candleholder, Oral Roberts, Desert Gold, c.1971 .... 18.00
Canteen, Prairie Green, Sapulpa Clay, No. 59 .... 15.00
Cornucopia, Sapulpa Clay, Flame, No. 56 .... 10.00

Cornucopia, Woodland Moss, No. 222, 12 In.	50.00
Creamer, Wagon Wheels, Prairie Green, c.1948, 2 1/2 In.	70.00
Dish, Corn, Gouda's, Desert Gold, Ada Clay, No. 811	20.00
Dish, Divided, Handles, Plainsman, Brown Satin, Sapulpa Clay, No. 5QD	12.00
Dish, Divided, Plainsman, Desert Gold, Ada Clay, No. 5QD	25.00
Figurine, Flower Girl, Prairie Green, Ada Clay, No.700	125.00
Figurine, Indian Chief, Prairie Gold, Sapulpa Clay, No. 142	50.00
Figurine, Irish Setter, Prairie Gold, Ada Clay, No. 141	225.00
Figurine, Swan, Black, No. 168, 3 In.	85.00
Figurine, Swan, Miniature, White Sand, Ada Clay, No. 168	95.00
Gravy Boat, Plainsman, Woodland Moss, No. 5S	20.00
Honey Jug, Cover, Woodland Moss, No. 833	25.00
Honey Jug, Prairie Green, Sapulpa Clay, No. 8	20.00
Honey Pot, Brown Satin, Sapulpa Clay	20.00
Honey Pot, Prairie Green, Sapulpa Clay	20.00
Jug, Condiment, Prairie Green, Sapulpa Clay	45.00
Mug, Barrel, Prairie Green, No. 97M, 14 Oz.	20.00
Mug, Little White House, Warm Springs, Georgia, No. C7	25.00
Pitcher, Lazybones, Prairie Green, No. 562, Miniature	15.00
Pitcher, Thunderbird, Silver Sage, No. 555, 2 1/2 In.	55.00
Pitcher, Turquoise, Ada Clay, No. 556, Miniature	60.00
Pitcher, Wagon Wheels, Onyx, Ada Clay, No. 560K, Miniature	25.00
Planter, Cactus, Brown, No. 1206	15.00
Planter, Dutch Shoe, Woodland Moss, No. 913	25.00
Planter, Fluted, Desert Gold, Sapulpa Clay, No. F33	10.00
Planter, Owl, Desert Gold, No. 394	5.00
Planter, Swan, Brown Satin, Sapulpa Clay, No. 228	20.00
Plate, Dinner, Lazybones, Desert Gold, Sapulpa Clay, No. 4F	7.00
Plate, Dinner, Mayan Aztec, Prairie Green, Sapulpa Clay, No. 7F	7.00
Plate, Dinner, Westwind, Autumn Yellow, Sapulpa Clay, No. 6F	7.00
Plate, Methodist Bicentennial, White Sand, c.1966, 8 1/4 In.	75.00
Plate, Salad, Lazybones, Desert Gold, Sapulpa Clay, No. 4G	4.00
Plate, Salad, Westwind, Autumn Yellow, Sapulpa Clay, No. 6G	4.00
Plate, Salad, Westwind, Prairie Green, Sapulpa Clay, No. 7G	5.00
Plate, Warm Bread For Your Table, Sapulpa Clay, 2 1/2 x 4 3/4 In.	50.00
Platter, Wagon Wheels, Desert Gold, Ada Clay, No. 94Q	30.00
Platter, Westwind, Autumn Yellow, Sapulpa Clay, 11 In.	6.00
Salt & Pepper, Oil Derrick, Desert Gold, Ada Clay, No. 49H	50.00
Salt & Pepper, Oil Derrick, Prairie Green, Sapulpa Clay	10.00
Salt & Pepper, Prairie Green, Ada Clay, No. 94	20.00
Salt & Pepper, Teepee, Desert Gold, Ada Clay, No. 47H	50.00
Salt & Pepper, Wagon Wheels, Desert Gold, Ada Clay, No. 94H	25.00
Salt & Pepper, Wagon Wheels, Turquoise, Ada Clay	45.00
Salt & Pepper, Westwind, Woodland Moss, No. 6H	15.00
Sugar, Wagon Wheels, Prairie Green, Ada Clay, No. 94B	55.00
Sugar, Westwind, Woodland Moss, No. 6B	10.00
Taco Holder, Red Bud, Brown Satin, No. 249	8.00
Teapot, Wagon Wheels, Desert Gold, 6 Cup	45.00
Tile, Wright Design, Mission Green, Incised, Frame, 6 In.	77.00
Toothbrush Holder, Owl, Robin Egg Blue	5.00
Tray, Dogwood, Desert Gold, Sapulpa Clay, No. 477	5.00
Trivet, American Eagle, Onyx Black	42.00
Vase, Bud, Crocus, Sapulpa Clay, No. 43, 8 In.	10.00
Vase, Bud, Handles, Sapulpa Clay, No. 20, 6 In.	15.00
Vase, Bud, Snail, Prairie Green, Sapulpa Clay, No. 31	15.00
Vase, Bud, Snail, Sapulpa Clay, No. 31	10.00
Vase, Flying Goose, Prairie Green, Ada Clay, No. 60B, 9 In.	45.00
Vase, Free-Form, Prairie Green, Sapulpa Clay, No. 6	25.00
Vase, Leaf Handles, Woodland Moss, No. 71, 10 In.	50.00
Vase, Pillow, Cube, Desert Gold, Ada Clay, No. 68	35.00
Vase, White Sand, Tall, Round, Ada Clay, No. 50	95.00
Wall Pocket, Boot, Sapulpa Clay, No. 133	15.00

FRATERNAL objects that are related to the many different fraternal organizations in the United States are listed in this category. The Elks, Masons, Odd Fellows, and others are included. Also included are service organizations, like the American Legion, Kiwanis, and Lions Club. Furniture is listed in the Furniture category. Shaving mugs decorated with fraternal crests are included in the Shaving Mug category.

Buffaloes, Ceremonial Chain, Royal Antediluvian Order, Bradford Lodge, No. 1512	109.00
Eagle, Doorstop, Marked, 1880s	950.00
Elks, Butter Pat, Moose Lodge, Clock, Hands At 11:55, Gold Trim, 8 1/4 In.	35.00
Elks, Tankard, Insignia, Maddock, Trenton, Tatter Decorating, c.1900, 12 1/2 In.	295.00
Knights Of Columbus, Sword, Ceremonial, Scabbard, 35 1/2 In.	145.00
Knights Of Columbus, Uniform, Marching Regalia, Coat, Accessories, H.L. Lewis	110.00
Knights Of Pythias, Knife, Scabbard, Leather Storage Scabbard	55.00
Knights Of Pythias, Sword, FCB Lodge, Knight, Eagle, McKinney, 37 In.	85.00
Lamp, Elks, Figural Elk, Consolidated Lamp & Glass Co., 13 In.	315.00
Masonic, Column, Lodge, Wood, Composition Globe, Hanging Flowers, 116 In., Pair	908.00
Masonic, Initiation Vehicle, Goat On Wheels, Off-Center Wheels, 1892	5500.00
Masonic, Locket, On Ivory, Trebled Hoops, 2 Views, Early 19th Century	3616.00
Masonic, Medal, Bronze, Triangular Pendant, Blue Ribbon, Red Stripe, 1949	35.00
Masonic, Mug, Knights Templar, Carnival Glass, Ice Blue	400.00
Masonic, Mug, Knights Templar, Carnival Glass, Ice Green	750.00
Masonic, Mug, Knights Templar, Carnival Glass, Marigold	350.00
Masonic, Neck Chain, 21 Badges, Green Cloth Back	180.00
Masonic, Needlework, Wool, All-Seeing Eye, Moon, Star, Compass, 1827, 11 x 13 In. . . .	750.00
Masonic, Shelf, Hanging, Pierced Brass, Masonic Designs, 17 In.	69.00
Masonic, Sword, Ceremonial, Fish Bill, Mahogany Hilt, 1800s, 46 x 7 1/2 In.	448.00
Masonic, Watch Fob, Faceted Cross, 4 Trefoil Clasps, Engraved Symbols, 14K Gold	206.00
Odd Fellows, Doorstop, Cast Iron, 6 x 2 3/4 x 7 1/2 In.	175.00
Odd Fellows, Owl, On Staff, Wood Carving, Painted, Tack Eyes, 67 1/2 In.	330.00
Odd Fellows, Sword, Ivory Grip, Etched Blade, Nickel Scabbard, Lilley & Co., 36 In. . . .	129.00

FRY GLASS was made by the H. C. Fry Glass Company of Rochester, Pennsylvania. The company, founded in 1901, first made cut glass and other types of fine glasswares. In 1922, they patented a heat-resistant glass called *Pearl Ovenglass*. For two years, 1926–1927, the company made Fry Foval, an opal ware decorated with colored trim. Reproductions of this glass have been made. Depression glass patterns made by Fry may be listed in the Depression Glass category. Some pieces of cut glass may also be included in the Cut Glass category.

FRY, Casserole, Cover, Embossed, 1951, 10 1/2 x 8 In.	30.00
Dish, Olive, Zenith Cutting, Flashed Stars, Signed, 9 x 1 3/4 In.	650.00
Platter, Meat, Opalescent, 15 In.	30.00
Salt & Pepper, Diamond Point Cutting, Opalescent, 2 3/4 In.	49.00
Sugar & Creamer, Poppy Cutting	30.00
Tumbler, Poppy Cutting, Ribbed, c.1920, 4 3/4 In.	11.00
FRY FOVAL, Coffeepot, Dome Cover, Straight Sides, White Opalescent, 9 1/2 In.	315.00
Platter, Fish, 12 1/2 x 9 In.	20.00
Tumbler, Lemonade, Jade Handle, No. 9416, 5 1/2 In.	70.00
Bowl, Underplate, Blue Trim, 7 1/2 x 8 1/2 In.	195.00
Bowl, Underplate, Opalescent, Jade Green Base, 2 x 5 3/8 In.	90.00
Cup & Saucer, Blue Handle, 2 1/4 x 5 3/8 In.	90.00

FULPER Pottery Company was incorporated in 1899 in Flemington, New Jersey. They made art pottery from 1910 to 1929. The firm had been making bottles, jugs, and housewares from 1805. Doll heads were made about 1928. The firm became Stangl Pottery in 1929. Fulper art pottery is admired for its attractive glazes and simple shapes.

Bookends, Hearth, Dark Green Matte Glaze, 8 x 6 In.	290.00
Bookends, Stylized Face Shape, Green, Gunmetal Matte Glaze, 5 1/2 x 6 In.	400.00
Bottle, Green, Blue Flambe Glaze, Salamander, 8 x 4 In.	748.00
Bottle, Mahogany Flambe Glaze, Prang Mark, 9 1/4 In.	200.00
Bowl, Black & Ivory To Green Flambe Glaze, Collared Rim, 4 1/2 x 10 1/4 In.	1265.00

Bowl, Blue & Green Flambe Glaze, 3 Griffin Figural Supports, Iridescent, 5 x 10 1/2 In. . . 115.00
Bowl, Blue, Green, Brown Flambe Glaze, Blue, Yellow Interior, Stylized, 3 x 10 1/4 In. . . . 316.00
Bowl, Blue, Green, Ivory Flambe Glaze, Built-In Frog, Shell Shape, 3 3/4 x 11 1/2 In. . . . 230.00
Bowl, Brown Matte Glaze, Green, Brown Drip Glaze, 3 Applied Shields, 1915-1925, 4 In. 375.00
Bowl, Cat's-Eye Flambe Glaze, Handles, Ring Rim, 7 x 9 In. 230.00
Bowl, Chinese Blue Flambe Drip Glaze, Over Mottled Blue Matte Glaze, 13 1/2 In. 115.00
Bowl, Copper Dust, Mahogany, Leopard Skin Crystalline Glaze, Fish, Waves, 11 1/4 In. . . 865.00
Bowl, Flambe Over Mustard Matte Glaze, c.1915, 9 1/2 In. 86.00
Bowl, Gray, Black Glaze, Squat Urn Shape, Applied Scroll Feet, 10 3/4 In. 1295.00
Bowl, Green Flambe Glaze, Carved Leaf Design, Stamped Mark, 8 In. 220.00
Bowl, Green Glaze, Inverted Rim, Footed, Stamped Mark, 3 3/4 x 18 1/4 In. 355.00
Bowl, Ivory, Mustard Matte Glaze, Effigy, 6 1/2 x 10 1/2 In. 980.00
Bowl, Lavender, Cobalt Blue Crystalline Glaze, Impressed Mark, 1920-1925, 11 1/2 In. . . 175.00
Bowl, Turquoise, Green Crystalline Glaze, Handles, Squat, 3 x 8 In. 144.00
Candleholder, Brown, Green, Blue Flambe Glaze, Vertical Mark, 7 In. 299.00
Candlestick, Brown Matte Glaze, Handle, Racetrack Mark, 2 1/4 In. 99.00
Candlestick, Ivory Flambe To Chinese Blue Glaze, Incised Mark, 10 In., Pair 175.00
Cat, Reclining, Dark Brown, Cream Patches, Glossy Glaze, 5 1/4 In. 1295.00
Crock, John Jamison Fine Butter 1650.00
Flask, Amber, Turquoise Crystalline Glaze, Handles, 10 x 7 1/2 In. 1035.00
Flower Frog, Green Flambe Glaze, Froggie, 2 1/2 x 4 1/4 In. 210.00
Flower Frog, Green Mirror Glaze, Ink Stamp, Racetrack Mark, 4 1/8 In. 115.00
Flower Frog, Green Over Blue Flambe Glaze, Scarab, 1 3/8 x 3 1/4 In. 90.00
Jar, Cover, Royal Blue Flambe Glaze, Over Famille Rose Glaze, 4 5/8 In. 160.00
Jug, Black Mirror Glaze Over Green, Silver Overlay, Musical, 8 7/8 In. 150.00
Jug, Blue Slip Inscription, Come Boys, Take A Drink With Me, 9 x 5 1/2 In. 2185.00
Lamp, Cat's-Eye Flambe Glaze, Pinched Body, Stamped Mark, 24 x 11 3/4 In. 90.00
Lamp, Chinese Blue Flambe Glaze, Mushroom Shade, Leaded Slag Glass, 18 x 15 In. . . . 11500.00
Lamp, Green & Brown Glossy Glaze, Oval, Ink Stamp, 10 1/4 In. 235.00
Lamp, Perfume, Perched Parrot, 10 In. . . . . .580.00 to 880.00
Urn, Black Mirror Flambe Glaze, Ivory, Blue, Bulbous, Handles, 6 1/2 x 6 In. 865.00
Urn, Cat's-Eye Flambe Glaze, Buttressed Handles, Squat, 6 1/2 x 8 In. 200.00
Urn, Chinese Blue Flambe Glaze, Over Brown, Handles, 8 x 7 In. 575.00
Urn, Frothy Blue, Light Blue Glaze, Hammered, Racetrack Mark, 11 3/4 In. 1495.00
Urn, Leopard Skin Crystalline Glaze, Bulbous, Handles, Racetrack Mark, 13 1/4 In. 2990.00
Urn, Moss To Rose Flambe Glaze, Bulbous, 8 x 6 In. 259.00
Urn, Mottled Blue, Amber, Mahogany, Caramel Glaze, 11 1/2 x 7 1/4 In. 1610.00
Vase, Aqua Glaze Over Green Crystalline, 7 x 4 In. 220.00
Vase, Bell Pepper, Umber, Green, Cobalt Matte Glaze, 4 x 5 In. 1150.00
Vase, Black Mirror Crystalline Glaze, Faceted, Racetrack Mark, 11 x 5 In. 405.00
Vase, Black Mirror Flambe Glaze, Bottle Shape, 8 x 6 In. 575.00
Vase, Black Mirror Flambe Glaze, Frothy Blue, Ivory, Bulbous, Racetrack Mark, 12 In. . . 1610.00
Vase, Black Mirror Glaze, Chinese Blue Crystalline Flambe Glaze, Bulbous, 7 3/4 In. 1840.00
Vase, Black Mirror Glaze, Famille Rose Flambe, Bulbous, Racetrack Mark, 7 x 8 In. 978.00
Vase, Black Mirror To Copper Crystalline Flambe, Tapered, Racetrack Mark, 12 1/2 In. . . 2990.00
Vase, Black Mirror To Indigo, Ivory Flambe Glaze, Bulbous, Racetrack Mark, 7 x 8 In. . . . 575.00
Vase, Black Mirror, Blue, Ivory Frothy Flambe Glaze, Oval, 9 3/4 In. 405.00
Vase, Black Mirror, Blue, White Flambe Glaze, Round, Buttress Rim, 5 In. 375.00
Vase, Black Mirror, Ivory, Purple Flambe Glaze, Barrel Shape, 7 1/2 In. 175.00
Vase, Black Mirror, Mahogany, Ivory Glaze, Round, Buttressed Rim, 5 In. 290.00
Vase, Black Speckled Blue Glaze, Geometric, Rectangular, 1910-1920, 8 1/4 In. 290.00
Vase, Blue Crystalline Flambe Glaze, Bulbous, 7 3/4 x 6 In. 345.00
Vase, Blue Crystalline Glaze, Olive Green Ground, 1920, 8 x 5 In. 495.00
Vase, Blue Frothy Flambe Glaze, Faceted, Racetrack Mark, 11 x 5 1/2 In. 315.00
Vase, Blue Glaze, Ivory Glaze Neck, Pebble Texture, Classic Shape, 13 1/2 In. 330.00
Vase, Blue Glaze, Zigzag Lines, Flattened Oval, 2 1/2 x 6 1/4 x 3 1/4 In., Pair 138.00
Vase, Blue Mirror, Green Flambe Glaze, Bottle Shape, 15 x 7 In. 575.00
Vase, Blue Snowflake Crystals, Ocher Ground, Handles, Ink Stamp, 6 1/4 In. 575.00
Vase, Blue, Lavender Crystalline Glaze, Bulbous Shape, Handles, 1910-1920, 6 1/4 In. . . . 345.00
Vase, Blue, Light Wisteria Glaze, Handles, 8 In. 415.00
Vase, Brown Drip Glaze Over Caramel, Crystalline, Oval, 6 3/4 In. 305.00
Vase, Brown Flambe, Blue Drip Glaze, Butterscotch Over Mahogany, Handles, 6 3/4 In. . . 525.00
Vase, Brown, Tan Flambe Glaze, 7 Sides, Marked, 8 7/8 In. 115.00

Vase, Butterscotch Flambe Glaze, Bulbous, Handles, 6 3/4 x 7 3/4 In. 290.00
Vase, Butterscotch Flambe Glaze, Round, Handles, Racetrack Mark, 7 In. 345.00
Vase, Caramel, Blue Drip Glaze, Effigy, 3 Gargoyle Supports, 1910-1920, 7 In. 546.00
Vase, Cat's-Eye Flambe Glaze, 16 x 5 1/2 In. 1150.00
Vase, Cat's-Eye Flambe Glaze, Barrel Shape, 7 1/2 x 5 1/4 In. 635.00
Vase, Cat's-Eye Flambe Glaze, Cylindrical, 7 1/2 x 5 1/2 In. 200.00
Vase, Cat's-Eye Flambe Glaze, Faceted, Racetrack Mark, 11 x 5 In. 375.00
Vase, Cat's-Eye Flambe Glaze, Flowers, Paneled, 11 1/2 In. 4025.00
Vase, Cat's-Eye Flambe Glaze, Gray, Green Striated Flambe Glaze, Bulbous, 5 1/4 In. . . . 375.00
Vase, Cat's-Eye Flambe Glaze, Pillow, Racetrack Mark, 6 1/4 In. 175.00
Vase, Cat's-Eye Flambe Glaze, Pinched Waist, 8 x 3 In. 230.00
Vase, Cat's-Eye Flambe Glaze, Salamander, 7 3/4 In. 1265.00
Vase, Cat's-Eye, Blue Flambe Glaze, Bulbous, Ridged, Chinese Shape, 12 1/2 x 8 1/2 In. . 805.00
Vase, Cat's-Eye, Blue Flambe Glaze, Bullet Shape, Racetrack Mark, 9 3/4 x 6 1/2 In. 635.00
Vase, Cat's-Eye, Ivory Matte Drip Glaze, Mustard Ground, Buttressed, 8 1/4 In. 490.00
Vase, Chinese Blue Crystalline Flambe Glaze, Prunts, Bulbous, 7 In. 288.00
Vase, Chinese Blue Crystalline, Over Mustard Flambe, 4 3/8 In. 150.00
Vase, Chinese Blue Crystalline, Over Mustard Flambe, Handles, 3 1/4 In. 140.00
Vase, Chinese Blue Flambe Glaze, Bulbous, Racetrack Mark, 10 1/4 x 10 In. 1495.00
Vase, Chinese Blue Glaze, Over Green & White Ground, Barrel Shape, 8 1/2 In. 575.00
Vase, Chinese Blue, Caramel Flambe Glaze, Tapered, Racetrack Mark, 11 1/2 x 9 In. 1095.00
Vase, Copper Dust Crystalline Glaze, Tapered, Handles, Racetrack Mark, 9 x 6 1/2 In. . . . 1380.00
Vase, Crystalline Mirror Flambe Glaze, Bulbous, Ribbed, 11 1/2 x 8 1/2 In. 2820.00
Vase, Elephant's Breath Flambe Glaze, Green Crystalline, Tapered, 12 3/4 x 7 In. 405.00
Vase, Elephant's Breath, Leopard Skin Crystalline Flambe Glaze, Prang Mark, 8 1/2 In. . . 750.00
Vase, Elephant's Breath, Leopard Skin Crystalline Glaze, Barrel, Prang Mark, 7 x 5 In. . . . 1955.00
Vase, Famille Rose Glaze, Bulbous, 7 x 4 1/2 In. 200.00
Vase, Frothy Blue Crystalline Matte To Chinese Blue Crystalline, 12 x 8 3/4 In. 2115.00
Vase, Frothy Blue Flambe Glaze, Squat, Handles, Racetrack Mark, 5 x 6 In. 200.00
Vase, Frothy Butterscotch Flambe, Ink Stamp, 9 1/2 In. 575.00
Vase, Frothy Ivory, Mahogany, Black Mirror Flambe Glaze, Prunts, 7 x 4 1/2 In. 546.00
Vase, Gray Green Matte Crystalline Glaze, Over Lighter Flambe, Handle, 11 In. 575.00
Vase, Green Flambe Glaze, Buttressed, 13 1/4 x 10 In. 2415.00
Vase, Green Flambe, Blue Midsection, Deep Wisteria Base, Racetrack Mark, 6 3/4 In. . . . 305.00
Vase, Green Glossy Glaze Over Famille Rose, Embossed Collar, 9 7/8 In. 165.00
Vase, Green Matte, Ivory Crystalline Flambe Glaze, Faceted, Racetrack Mark, 9 3/4 In. . . 690.00
Vase, Green Mirror Flambe Glaze, 4 1/4 In. 207.00
Vase, Green Mirror Flambe, Frothy Green Glossy Glaze, Handles, 7 1/8 In. 345.00
Vase, Green, Blue Glaze, 4 Sides, Prang Mark, 8 3/4 x 3 3/4 In. 460.00
Vase, Green, Caramel Crystalline Glaze, Baluster Shape, Impressed Mark, c.1925, 10 In. . 259.00
Vase, Green, Mahogany Flambe Glaze, 7 1/2 x 4 1/2 In. 633.00
Vase, Green, Pink Matte Glaze, Famille Rose Drip Glaze, Racetrack Mark, 12 x 6 3/4 In. . 690.00
Vase, Gunmetal, Chinese Blue Crystalline Flambe Glaze, Bulbous, 12 x 11 1/2 In. 3820.00
Vase, Gunmetal, Green, Blue, Flared, 4 Sides, Prang Mark, 8 1/4 x 3 1/2 In. 635.00
Vase, Gunmetal, Purple, Leopard Skin Crystalline Flambe Glaze, Egg Shape, 8 In. 1265.00
Vase, Ivory To Elephant's Breath Flambe Glaze, Mushrooms, 9 3/4 x 4 1/4 In. 575.00
Vase, Ivory, Blue, Gray, Rose Flambe Glaze, Bullet Shape, 10 In. 635.00
Vase, Ivory, Brown, Blue Flambe Glaze, Baluster, Racetrack Mark, 9 1/2 x 5 3/4 In. 345.00
Vase, Ivory, Brown, Blue, Olive Flambe Glaze, Bullet Shape, 10 x 6 In. 575.00
Vase, Ivory, Mahogany, Blue Crystalline Flambe Glaze, Bullet Shape, 10 x 5 1/2 In. 690.00
Vase, Leopard Skin Crystalline Glaze, Embossed Rectangle Rim, Faceted, 7 1/2 x 7 In. . . 635.00
Vase, Leopard Skin To Amber Flambe Glaze, Round, Closed Rim, 5 1/2 x 7 In. 748.00
Vase, Light Green Drip Glaze, Bulbous Shape, Cylindrical Neck, 1915-1925, 7 3/4 In. . . . 288.00
Vase, Mahogany To Green Flambe Glaze, Bottle Shape, Prang Mark, 8 3/4 In. 805.00
Vase, Mirror, Cat's-Eye Flambe Glaze, Round, Handles, Racetrack Mark, 6 1/4 In. 430.00
Vase, Mottled Green, Blue, Purple Glaze, Egg Shape, Prang Mark, 7 1/2 x 5 In. 1150.00
Vase, Mottled Turquoise Crystalline Glaze, Round, Closed-In Rim, 6 In. 525.00
Vase, Multitone Brown Flambe, Baluster Shape, 11 In. 115.00
Vase, Multitone Green Matte Glaze, Ribbed, Handles, 9 1/2 In. 175.00
Vase, Opaque Crackled White, Brown Matte Glaze Drip, Mustard Ground, Squat, 8 In. . . . 1265.00
Vase, Purple, Raised Rim, 3 Handles, Footed, c.1915, 6 3/8 In. 355.00
Vase, Raspberry Matte Glaze, Hammered, Ear-Shape Handles, 12 In. 345.00
Vase, Red & Purple Matte Glaze, Broad Shape, 9 1/2 In. 518.00

Vase, Rose & Ivory Matte Glaze, Handles, 4 In. 115.00
Vase, Rose Matte Glaze, Buttressed, Squat Base, Racetrack Mark, 8 1/2 x 6 In. 375.00
Vase, Rose, Blue, Green Drip Glaze, Squat, Bulbous, 3 Loop Handles, c.1920, 6 In. 430.00
Vase, Turquoise, Clear Crystalline Flambe Glaze, Bulbous, Handles, 7 1/2 In. 460.00
Vase, Umber To Chinese Blue Crystalline Flambe Glaze, Racetrack Mark, 11 x 5 In. 489.00
Vase, Wisteria, Magenta, Purple Glaze, 1920, 9 1/2 x 6 1/4 In. 525.00
Vase, Yellow, Brown, Blue & Green Drip Glaze, 7 Sides, 10 In. 635.00
Wall Pocket, Green Matte Glaze, Molded Abstract Design, Stamped Mark, 7 1/2 In. 375.00

FURNITURE of all types is listed in this category. Examples dating from the seventeenth century to the 1970s are included. Prices for furniture vary in different parts of the country. Oak furniture is most expensive in the West; large pieces over eight feet high are sold for the most money in the South, where high ceilings are found in the old homes. Condition is very important when determining prices. These are NOT average prices but rather reports of unique sales. If the description includes the word *style*, the piece resembles the old furniture style but was made at a later time. It is not a period piece. Garden furniture is listed in the Garden Furnishings category. Related items may be found in the Architectural, Brass, and Store categories.

Armoire, 2 Paneled Doors, Brass-Mounted Columns, Circular Feet, 84 x 59 x 27 In. 4370.00
Armoire, Art Deco, Fruitwood, Rounded Corners, Door, 2 Drawers, 60 x 58 x 20 In. 118.00
Armoire, Art Deco, Mahogany, Amboyna Wood, Mirror, 2 Doors, 75 x 71 x 18 In. 2390.00
Armoire, Art Deco, Rosewood, 2 Drawers, 3 Doors, Mirror, 78 x 73 x 19 In. 1765.00
Armoire, Biedermeier, Fruitwood, 2 Recessed Paneled Doors Over 2 Drawers, 70 In. 2590.00
Armoire, Continental, Pine, Raised Panel Door Over Drawer, Bracket Base, 48 x 74 In. .. 430.00
Armoire, Empire, Flame Mahogany, 2 Doors, c.1850 .... 1100.00
Armoire, Flemish Provincial, Oak, Carved, Geometric Pattern, 95 x 67 x 25 In. 635.00
Armoire, French Provincial, Fruitwood, 2 Doors, Inset Panels, 93 x 51 x 26 1/2 In. 2990.00
Armoire, French Provincial, Mahogany, Shaped & Arched Panel Doors & Top, 103 In. ... 8338.00
Armoire, French Provincial, Oak, 2 Doors, Carved Panels, Brass, c.1750, 79 x 59 In. ... 2475.00
Armoire, French Provincial, Oak, 2 Doors, Leaf Carving, c.1768, 93 x 62 In. 2070.00
Armoire, French Provincial, Oak, Paneled Doors, Cabriole Feet, 19th Century, 89 x 58 In. 3910.00
Armoire, French Provincial, Walnut, 2 Doors, Angular Panels, Twisted Stiles, 81 In. 880.00
Armoire, French Provincial, Walnut, Kingwood, Mirror Doors, c.1880, 102 x 59 x 20 In. .. 1840.00
Armoire, George III, Mahogany, 2 Doors, Channel Islands, c.1765, 82 x 52 In. 2185.00
Armoire, Herter Bros., Walnut, Ebonized, Inlaid Vines, 2 Paneled Doors, c.1880 .... *Illus* 14100.00
Armoire, Louis Philippe, Burl, Walnut, Door, 19th Century, 80 x 41 x 20 In. 690.00
Armoire, Louis XV Style, Cherry, 2 Doors, 2 Panels, 19th Century, 96 x 58 x 24 In. 3220.00
Armoire, Louis XV Style, Fruitwood, 2 Doors, 19th Century, 85 x 57 x 24 In. 2760.00
Armoire, Louis XV Style, Gilt Bronze Mounted, Fruitwood, Scrolling, 98 x 51 x 23 In. .. 2938.00
Armoire, Louis XV Style, Oak, Leaf Carvings, c.1850, 88 x 65 In. 2760.00
Armoire, Louis XV Style, Pine, Cornice, 2 Doors, 19th Century, 96 1/2 x 54 x 20 In. 2760.00
Armoire, Louis XV Style, Pine, Flower Carved, 2 Doors, 105 x 62 x 25 In. 4370.00
Armoire, Louis XV, Brass Mount, Walnut, Shelves, 18th Century, 88 x 65 x 28 1/2 In. ... 2070.00
Armoire, Louis XV, Fruitwood, 2 Paneled Doors, 104 x 74 x 30 In. 3450.00
Armoire, Louis XV, Oak, 18th Century, 83 1/2 x 58 1/4 x 25 In. 1610.00
Armoire, Louis XV, Oak, 2 Shaped Paneled Doors & Apron, Scrolled Toes, 98 x 59 In. .. 2530.00
Armoire, Louis XV, Walnut, c.1750, 101 1/2 x 59 1/2 x 25 In. 2300.00
Armoire, Louis XV, Walnut, Grille, 1700s, 90 1/2 x 56 x 26 In. 2530.00
Armoire, Louis XVI Style, Kingwood, 2 Coromandel Doors, 81 x 63 x 24 In. 6570.00
Armoire, Mahogany, Inlay, Mirror, Paneled Doors, Copper Floral, c.1900, 83 x 69 x 24 In. 2115.00
Armoire, Neoclassic Style, Step Pediment Top, 2 Doors, 2 Drawers, 49 x 20 x 74 In. 400.00
Armoire, Oak, Carved Crest, 2 Doors, Medieval Figures, 19th Century, 96 x 69 x 27 In. .. 4140.00
Armoire, Rococo Style, Walnut, Foliate Frieze, Mirrored Door, Victorian, 89 x 39 x 17 In. 705.00
Armoire, Victorian, Walnut, Arched Crest, Mirrored Door, 78 x 46 x 22 In. 1880.00
Banquette, Louis XVI Style, Painted, Polychrome, 20 1/2 x 41 In. 2689.00
Banquette, Rampendahl, Horn & Leather, Germany, 1870, 82 In. 1535.00
Bar, Rosewood, Carved, Lift Top, Oriental Battle Scene, Drop Front, 39 x 31 x 17 In. 520.00
Bed, Aesthetic Revival, Inlaid Mahogany, Paneled, Footboard, 67 1/2 In. .... *Illus* 9400.00
Bed, Arts & Crafts, Spindle, Twin, Pyramidal Posts, 44 1/2 x 79 1/4 x 41 1/4 In. 630.00
Bed, Bell Finials, Grain Painted, Rope, Pennsylvania, 19th Century, 3/4 Size 135.00
Bed, Birch, Pine, Red Paint, Turned Legs, Pegged Joints, Rope, 44 x 34 1/2 x 73 In. 220.00

Furniture, Armoire,
Herter Bros., Walnut,
Ebonized, Inlaid Vines,
2 Paneled Doors, c.1880

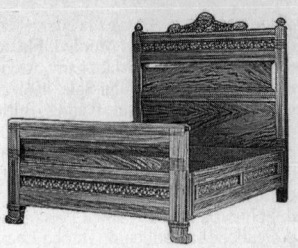

Furniture, Bed, Aesthetic Revival, Inlaid
Mahogany, Paneled, Footboard, 67 1/2 In.

Bed, Bird's-Eye Maple, Turned Posts, Acorn Finials, Rope, 55 x 59 x 76 In. 1100.00
Bed, Brass, Ball Finial, Whitcomb, 60 x 40 x 74 In., Pair 690.00
Bed, Cannonball, Maple, Acanthus Carving, 39 In. 400.00
Bed, Cannonball, Rope, Maple, Posts, Poplar, Cyma Carving, 53 x 51 1/2 x 72 In. 300.00
Bed, Cannonball, Turned Posts, Cutout Headboard, Rope, 19th Century, 56 x 80 In. 950.00
Bed, Cherry, Pine, Wheels, Original Finish, Lebanon, N.Y., c.1850, 34 In. 1495.00
Bed, Curly Maple, Scrolled Headboard & Footboard, Turned Posts, Acorn Finials, 37 In. . . 330.00
Bed, Edwardian, Satinwood, Painted Headboard, Medallions, Cupid, Floral Swags 1135.00
Bed, Federal Style, Mahogany, Twin Size, Rails, Paine Furniture Co., Pair . . . . 118.00 ·
Bed, Federal Style, Maple, Cherry, Tapered, c.1900, 68 x 55 In. 1610.00
Bed, Federal, Mahogany, Arched Canopy Frame, Spiral Carved Posts, 61 x 45 x 72 In. . . . 1760.00
Bed, Federal, Transitional, Birch, Red Stained, Mass., c.1790, 88 x 55 x 76 In. 2689.00
Bed, Field, Sheraton, Birch, Pine, Urn Shape Turnings, Pencil Posts, 55 x 65 x 73 In. 6600.00
Bed, Four-Poster, Cherry & Poplar, Pineapple Finials, 19th Century, 89 x 62 x 75 In. 2760.00
Bed, Four-Poster, Cherry, Acorn, Scrolled Headboard, 19th Century, 57 x 51 x 81 In. 715.00
Bed, Four-Poster, Cherry, Octagon Posts, Top Rail, Raised Panel, c.1830, 90 x 62 x 84 In. 4600.00
Bed, Four-Poster, Federal Style, Carved Eagle Headboard, c.1880, 60 x 57 In. 2800.00
Bed, Four-Poster, Federal, Cherry, Scalloped Headboard, Footboard, c.1810, 83 x 58 In. . . 1380.00
Bed, Four-Poster, George III Style, Mahogany, Reeded Posts, 96 x 60 In. 11950.00
Bed, Four-Poster, Mahogany, Canopy Mounts, Turned, Reeded Columns, 19th Century . . . 1265.00
Bed, Four-Poster, Mahogany, Pineapple Carved, Canopy, c.1830, 94 x 62 x 84 In. 13800.00
Bed, Four-Poster, Mahogany, Reeded Posts, Pierced, Carved Pediment, Victorian, 80 In. . . 1035.00
Bed, Four-Poster, Maple, Rope, Tapered, Reeded Posts, American, 88 x 78 1/2 In. 2200.00
Bed, Four-Poster, Poplar, Rope, 19th Century, 87 x 52 1/2 x 77 In. 1100.00
Bed, Four-Poster, Sheraton, Curly Maple, Pine, Turned Posts, 62 x 76 x 72 In. 3575.00
Bed, Four-Poster, Sheraton, Mahogany, Divided Panels, Swags, Flame Finials, 91 In. 2185.00
Bed, Four-Poster, Sheraton, Mahogany, Urn Form, Turned Posts, c.1800, 51 In. 1150.00
Bed, Four-Poster, Sheraton, Maple, Canopy, C.E. Freeman, Glen Cove, Me., Twin, Pair . . 1265.00
Bed, French Provincial, Purplewood, Floral Carved, c.1880, 63 x 63 x 81 In. 750.00
Bed, G. Nakashima, Walnut, 2 Twin Platforms, King, 76 x 81 x 24 In. 8625.00
Bed, G. Nelson, Birch, Metal, Caned Headboard, Thin Edge, Herman Miller, 34 x 84 In. . 4315.00
Bed, G. Nelson, Twin, Herman Miller, c.1952, 29 x 40 x 78 In., Pair 3230.00
Bed, G. Stickley, Arched Top Rail, Vertical Slats, Red Decal, 44 x 39 In. 1380.00
Bed, G. Stickley, Double Horizontal Rail, Vertical Spindles, 58 x 50 x 80 In. 4315.00
Bed, G. Stickley, No. 923, 3 Wide Slats, Peaked Top Rail, 41 x 79 x 45 In. 2415.00
Bed, G. Stickley, Paneled Headboard, Footboard, Peaked Rail, 59 x 70 x 51 In. 5465.00
Bed, G. Stickley, Pyramidal Posts, 9 Spindles, Side Rails, 49 x 43 3/4 x 79 1/2 In. 1265.00
Bed, L. & J.G. Stickley, Raised Posts, 12 Vertical Slats, Head, Footboard, 50 x 57 In. 2990.00
Bed, Louis XV Style, Gilt Bronze Mounted, Kingwood, Marquetry, Flowers 1530.00
Bed, Louis XVI Style, Beech, Upholstered Headboard, 44 x 42 x 82 In. 1840.00
Bed, Louis XVI Style, Fruitwood, Cane, c.1890, 47 x 43 1/4 In. 460.00
Bed, Louis XVI, Gray Paint, Arched Ends, Padded, Late 18th Century, 50 x 79 x 50 In. . . . 3585.00
Bed, Mahogany, Tapered, Square Head Post, Tapered Feet, Reeded Posts, 80 x 80 In. 3345.00
Bed, Marx, Lacquered Wood, Upholstery, Quigley, 1948, 81 1/2 x 38 x 36 In. 8625.00
Bed, Napoleon III, Polychrome, Metal, Scroll, c.1865, 39 x 50 In. 3450.00
Bed, Neoclassical Revival, Walnut, Carved, Pineapple Finial, Rails 530.00
Bed, Nutting, Hepplewhite Style, No. 848, Double 1870.00
Bed, Nutting, No. 807, Maple, Single, Pair 1045.00

Bed, Oriental Style, Black Lacquer, Pierced Geometric Design, Gold Leaves, 45 In. 220.00
Bed, Plantation, Canopy, Mottled, Flame Mahogany, Gothic Panels, c.1840, 124 In. 14000.00
Bed, Plantation, Flame Mahogany, Arched Rails, Carved, 114 In. 6000.00
Bed, Red Paint, Rope, John Sala, 40 1/2 x 51 1/2 x 79 In. 495.00
Bed, Renaissance Revival, Walnut, Burled, Carved Crest, c.1870, 93 x 61 In. 4480.00
Bed, Renaissance Revival, Walnut, Scroll Crest, Floral Carved, Burl Panel, 88 x 66 In. . . . 1380.00
Bed, Rococo Revival, Rosewood, Tall Arched 2-Panel Headboard, Pierced Crest, 70 In. . . 750.00
Bed, Rococo, Rosewood, Broken Arch Crest, Molded, Paneled Ends, c.1860 . . . . 3575.00
Bed, Rosewood, Carved, 5 Inset Headboard Panels, Urn Finials, 81 x 82 x 90 In. 4315.00
Bed, Salmon, Painted, Turned Posts, Pa., c.1810, 33 x 51 1/2 x 78 In. 715.00
Bed, Scalloped Headboard, Turned Legs, L-Shape Brackets, Rope, 39 x 59 x 74 In. 330.00
Bed, Shaker, Maple, Turned Rails, New Lebanon, c.1850, 42 In. 1610.00
Bed, Sheraton, Curly Maple, Poplar, Turned Legs, Posts, Rope, 52 x 72 x 49 In. 1430.00
Bed, Sheraton, Mahogany, Maple, Carved Posts, Rail, 55 1/2 In. 1380.00
Bed, Sleigh, Burl Walnut, Veneer Panels, Fluted Edge, 36 x 34 x 72 In. 980.00
Bed, Sleigh, Empire, Mahogany, Ormolu Mounts, Turned Columns, 37 x 57 x 78 In. 1725.00
Bed, Sleigh, Mahogany, Scrolled Head & Footboard, Block Feet, c.1835, 82 In. 2200.00
Bed, Sleigh, Neoclassical, Mahogany, Scrolled Head, Footboard, 19th Century, 60 x 90 In. 1725.00
Bed, Sleigh, Restauration, Metal, Putti, Garland Design, c.1835, 46 1/4 x 72 In. 3450.00
Bed, Tiger Maple, Turned Posts, Acorn Finials, Scroder, Lebanon, Ohio, Queen 1430.00
Bed, Trundle, Poplar & Ash, Wood Wheels, 17 x 42 x 63 In. 330.00
Bed, Turned Posts, Stylized Acorn Tops, Red Wash, Rope, Mid 1800s, 43 x 50 x 78 In. . . 100.00
Bed, Turned Posts, Urn Finials, Rope, Mid 19th Century, 52 x 56 x 82 In. 350.00
Bed, Victorian, Burl, Shaped Crest, Scroll, Leaves, 66 1/2 x 60 x 83 In. 1840.00
Bed, Victorian, Walnut, High Back, 3 Arched Raised Panels, Carved, 91 x 63 In. 3150.00
Bed, Victorian, Walnut, Rosewood, Flower Medallion Crest, Double 765.00
Bed, Victorian, Walnut, Rosewood, Stepped-Out Carved Flat Top Over Panels, 73 x 59 In. 675.00
Bed, Walnut & Poplar, Rolling Pin Head & Footboard, Rope, 46 x 51 x 73 3/4 In. 2970.00
Bed, Walnut & Poplar, Turned Legs, Mushroom Top, Rope, 17 x 28 In. 550.00
Bed, Walnut, Arch Crown, Applied Moldings, Carved, c.1900, 83 x 58 In. 690.00
Bed Steps, Cherry, Pine, Painted, 3 Steps, New England, c.1830, 21 x 20 x 18 In. 1530.00
Bed Steps, Mahogany, 3 Tiers, Leather Inset, Middle Slides Out, c.1890, 26 x 16 x 27 In. 1265.00
Bed Steps, Mahogany, George III, Leather, 19th Century, 26 3/4 x 20 x 27 1/2 In. 1495.00
Bed Steps, Regency, Mahogany, Top Stair Compartment, c.1800, 18 x 18 x 26 In. 400.00
Bed Tray, Mahogany, Scrolled Gallery, Turned Legs, 19th Century, 10 x 24 x 15 In. 360.00
Bedroom Set, Aesthetic Revival, Walnut, Marble Tops, 1880, 3 Piece 3740.00
Bedroom Set, Art Deco, Mahogany, Caplan, London, 1930s, 4 Piece 265.00
Bedroom Set, Blond Mahogany, 2 Chests & Nightstands, Reva Lewitt, c.1950, 7 Piece . . 4406.00
Bedroom Set, Donald Deskey, Burled Maple, Black Lacquer, Widdicomb, 1930, 4 Piece . 4000.00
Bedroom Set, Dresser, Marble Top, Mirror, Candleholders, Owl Drawer Pulls 2000.00
Bedroom Set, Eastlake Style, Walnut, Burl, Robert Mitchell, c.1870, 3 Piece 2850.00
Bedroom Set, Herter Bros., Egyptian Revival, Ebonized, Gilt, 1870-1880, 2 Piece . . *Illus* 17625.00
Bedroom Set, Herter Bros., White Onyx, Serpentine Front, Signed, c.1850, 6 Piece 5320.00
Bedroom Set, Louis XV Style, Mother-Of-Pearl Inlay, 5 Piece 5600.00
Bedroom Set, Louis XVI Style, Kingwood, Walnut, France, c.1900, 3 Piece 3680.00
Bedroom Set, Regency Style, Burl, Stiehl, 10 Piece 1175.00
Bedroom Set, Renaissance Revival, Eastlake, Walnut, Bed, Dresser, c.1865, 2 Piece 5750.00

Furniture, Bedroom Set,
Herter Bros., Egyptian
Revival, Ebonized, Gilt, 1870-
1880, 2 Piece

Furniture, Bench, Carved Oak,
Arms, 46 x 60 In.

Bedroom Set, Renaissance Revival, Marble Top, Walnut, c.1870, 4 Piece 9000.00
Bedroom Set, Renaissance Revival, Walnut, White Marble Top, 3 Piece 3850.00
Bedroom Set, Rococo Style, Green Paint, Gold Detail, 8 Piece 2350.00
Bedroom Set, Victorian, Cherry, Carved Panels, Scroll, Ribbon, Bed, Chest, Mirror 575.00
Bedroom Set, Victorian, Walnut, Marble Top, Bradford Onant & Co., c.1886, 4 Piece 1325.00
Bench, Arrow Back, Green Paint, Bamboo Turned Legs & Arms, 9 Spindles, 35 x 35 In. .   275.00
Bench, Art Deco, Giltwood, Upholstered, Fluted Legs, France, c.1925, 20 x 39 x 16 In. . . .   5975.00
Bench, Art Deco, Silvered Wood, Upholstered, Scroll Ends, c.1930, 42 In. 5675.00
Bench, Art Deco, Sycamore, Raised Tapered Round Legs 1060.00
Bench, Ash, Plank Top, Trestle Ends, Shaped Feet, 19 x 71 In. 235.00
Bench, Beech, Scroll Arms, Carved, Pierced Splats, Saber Legs, 1800s, 28 x 28 x 13 In. . . .   290.00
Bench, Biedermeier, Ash, Outscrolled Ends, Padded, Splayed Legs, 22 x 25 x 16 In. 1380.00
Bench, Black Walnut, Carved, 2 Bears Hold Seat, Germany, c.1900, 26 x 34 In. 1670.00
Bench, Bucket, Beaded Splash & Edge, Arched Cutout Ends, Pennsylvania, 37 x 47 In. . . .   1125.00
Bench, Bucket, Blue, 3 Shelves, Half-Moon Cutout Sides, 30 x 48 x 11 In. 1900.00
Bench, Bucket, High Top, Mixed Hardwoods, 3 Drawers, 2 Doors, 42 1/2 x 50 In. 170.00
Bench, Bucket, Pine, Overhanging Top, 3 Shelves, Mid 19th Century, 51 1/2 x 46 In. 850.00
Bench, Bucket, Pine, Shelves, Arched Ends, Gray Paint, Late 1800s, 49 x 38 x 12 In. 125.00
Bench, Bucket, Shaker, Pine, Original Finish, Arched Sides, Enfield, N.H., c.1840, 36 In. .   1725.00
Bench, Bucket, Softwood, Beaded Backboards, Shelves, Cutout Feet, 41 x 31 x 12 In. 1760.00
Bench, Bucket, Softwood, Dovetailed Top, 2 Shelves, Red Wash, 31 x 43 1/2 In. 1015.00
Bench, Bucket, White Pine, Blue, Spoon Holes, Lancaster County, 1700s, 58 x 48 In. 8500.00
Bench, Butternut, 1-Board Seat, Splayed Legs, Hand-Wrought Nails, 18 x 55 In. 170.00
Bench, Carved Oak, Arms, 46 x 60 In. . . . . *Illus*   2420.00
Bench, Deacon's, 13-Spindle Back, 1-Board Seat, Green Paint, Stencils, 34 x 58 In. 800.00
Bench, Deacon's, Pine, Pennsylvania, 120 In. 175.00
Bench, Deacon's, Plank Bottom, Black Paint, Late 19th Century, 32 1/2 x 72 In. 650.00
Bench, Deacon's, Scrolled Arms, 8 Legs, Painted, Late 19th Century, 36 x 80 In. 700.00
Bench, Double Scrolled Skirt, Shaped Legs, Arched Cutouts, Green Paint, 30 1/2 In. 1430.00
Bench, Edwardian, Mahogany, Turned, Carved, Oblong, c.1900, 21 x 38 x 14 In. 750.00
Bench, English Oak, Turned Stretcher Base, Ribbed Leather Seat, 16 x 36 x 14 In. 605.00
Bench, Florence Knoll, Upholstered, c.1954, 17 1/2 x 72 x 18 In. 1116.00
Bench, Frankl, Mahogany, Cork, Johnson Furniture Co., 13 x 71 In. 2185.00
Bench, French Provincial, Fruitwood, 18th Century, 20 1/4 x 61 3/4 x 24 In. 230.00
Bench, G. Nakashima, Black Walnut, American, c.1975, 87 x 14 In. 6900.00
Bench, G. Nakashima, Walnut, Spindle Back, Plank Seat, 28 x 122 x 24 In. 27025.00
Bench, G. Nelson, Birch, Slat, Herman Miller, 1950s, 102 x 14 In. 2070.00
Bench, G. Nelson, Platform, Ebonized Top, Herman Miller, 1950s, 47 x 18 1/2 x 14 In. . . .   750.00
Bench, G. Nelson, Primavera, Slat, Herman Miller, 14 x 56 x 18 1/2 In. 650.00
Bench, G. Nelson, Slat, Black Lacquer, Herman Miller, 14 x 102 x 19 In. 1410.00
Bench, G. Nelson, Slat, Herman Miller, 92 x 18 1/2 x 14 In. 1495.00
Bench, G. Nelson, White Laminate, Black Wool, Herman Miller, 76 x 30 x 16 In. 750.00
Bench, George III, Mahogany, Padded Top, Cabriole Legs, 19th Century, 20 x 24 x 20 In.   1150.00
Bench, Grain Paint, Hinged Cover, Cutout Sides, Pa., 28 3/4 x 51 x 16 In. 2200.00
Bench, Grain Paint, Red Brown, Alligatored, 8 Turned Legs, Plank Seat, 78 x 26 x 35 In. .   880.00
Bench, Greta Grossman, Glen Of California, c.1958, 11 x 65 x 18 In. 1060.00
Bench, H. Bertoia, Knoll, Ash, Steel, 66 x 18 3/4 x 15 1/2 In. 750.00
Bench, H. Bertoia, Knoll, Blond, Wood Slats, Iron Y Joint Legs, 15 x 82 x 18 In. 999.00
Bench, Hall, Gothic Style, Oak, Carved Panels, Tracery Back, Hinged Seat, 79 x 56 In. . . .   880.00
Bench, Hall, McHugh, High Back, V-Board Sides, Back, Tenons, 49 x 29 x 57 In. 420.00
Bench, Hall, Oak, Carved Winged Storks, Northwind Back, Claw Feet, c.1880 . . . .   3080.00
Bench, Hand Decorated, Painted, Peter Ompir, Sheffield, Mass., 34 1/2 x 17 x 23 In. 2860.00
Bench, Jacobean Style, Linenfold, Barley Twist Design, c.1890, 42 x 18 x 40 1/2 In. 518.00
Bench, Kneeling, Black Paint, Gilt Striping, Wooden, 7 x 36 x 6 In. 175.00
Bench, Kneeling, Pine, Cutout Feet, Square Head Nails, 50 x 6 x 7 1/2 In. 165.00
Bench, Kneeling, Shaker, Pine, Brown Wash, 3 Legs, 76 x 7 x 6 In. 415.00
Bench, Limbert, Inglenook, Lift Seat, Leather Seat & Panels, 47 x 48 x 20 In. 1725.00
Bench, Limbert, Oak, Rectangular Seat, Arched Aprons, 1900s, 19 x 20 x 14 In. 205.00
Bench, Long John, E. Wormley, Center Drawer, 1948, 11 x 72 x 19 In. 1175.00
Bench, Long John, E. Wormley, Walnut, Plant Top, Walnut Legs, Dunbar, 11 x 72 x 19 In.   895.00
Bench, Louis XV Style, Painted, Parcel Gilt, Carved, Brown Velvet Upholstery 1765.00
Bench, Louis XVI Style, Suede Upholstery, Silvered, Giltwood, 15 x 38 x 14 In. 598.00
Bench, Mammy's, Painted, Stencil Decoration, c.1850, 47 1/2 x 26 In. 895.00

Bench, Nutting, No. 290, Maple, Rushed, 6 Legs 1320.00
Bench, Oak, Carved Flowers & Scrolls On Back, Paneled Front & Seat, 36 x 44 In. 880.00
Bench, Oak, Carved, Figural, Dolphin Arms, Claw Feet, Red Velvet, 34 x 85 In. 5040.00
Bench, Oak, Relief Carved Panels, Bootjack Ends, Scrolled Flower Finials, 71 In. 825.00
Bench, Oriental, Lacquerware, Flowers, Fern, Black, Gilt, 21 x 20 x 13 1/2 In. 345.00
Bench, Pew, Cypress, Plank Back, Seat, Sides, Shaped Arm Rests, Bootjack Ends, 61 In. . 69.00
Bench, Piano, E. Wormley, Walnut, Leather Button-Tufted Cushion, Dunbar 460.00
Bench, Piano, G. Stickley, Cutout Handles, Plank Sides, 22 x 36 x 12 3/4 In. 4600.00
Bench, Pier, Louis XVI Style, Oblong, Upholstered, France, c.1900, 25 1/2 x 38 In. 690.00
Bench, Pine & Oak, Cast Iron Stretchers, Spain, 19th Century, 19 x 91 x 11 In., Pair 805.00
Bench, Pine, Cutouts, Splayed Legs, Board Top, 1900s, 66 x 17 1/2 In. 85.00
Bench, Pine, Faux Bamboo, Carved Crest, Turned Finials, c.1890, 39 x 52 x 20 In. 1955.00
Bench, Pine, Plank, Skirted Sides, Moon Cutouts, 19 x 72 x 13 In. 345.00
Bench, Pine, Poplar, Trestle Base, Serpentine Shape Legs, 72 x 11 x 17 In. 220.00
Bench, Pine, Scalloped Legs, Cyma Curved Cutouts, 72 x 12 x 19 In. 250.00
Bench, Pine, Slab, Shaven Legs, Mid 19th Century, 19 1/2 x 10 x 47 In. 100.00
Bench, Pine, Walnut, Mortised, Beaded, Stacked 2-Board Top, Splay Leg, 25 x 18 x 26 In. . 140.00
Bench, Plank Seat, Painted, Grapes, Leaves, 8 Turned Legs, Stretcher, 83 x 21 x 33 In. 1320.00
Bench, Poplar, 1-Board, Splayed Maple Legs, Hand Whittled, 45 x 14 1/2 In. 370.00
Bench, Regency Style, Ebonized, Tall Scrolling Sides, Upholstered, 63 In. 1410.00
Bench, Robsjohn-Gibbings, Walnut & Leather, 1962, 15 3/8 x 21 1/2 In., Pair 2629.00
Bench, Rococo Style, Painted, Carved Wood, Exotic Birds, 54 In. 1790.00
Bench, Rosewood, Marble, Scrollwork Apron, Chinese, 19th Century, 19 x 64 In. 430.00
Bench, Roycroft, Oak, Crest Rail, 9 Slats, Open Arms, 1 Drawer, c.1907, 38 x 50 x 20 In. 8225.00
Bench, Shaker, Maple, Original Finish, Splayed Legs, Canterbury, N.H., 43 In. 200.00
Bench, Softwood, Double Skirt, Arched Cutouts, Painted, 14 x 30 1/2 x 14 1/2 In. 1430.00
Bench, Softwood, Mortised & Scalloped Legs, Half-Moon Cutouts, Painted, 70 In. 365.00
Bench, Softwood, Mortised Legs, Arched Cutout Feet, 15 1/2 x 53 x 11 1/2 In. 275.00
Bench, Softwood, Mortised Legs, Arched Cutouts, Painted, 17 x 70 1/2 x 13 In. 250.00
Bench, Softwood, Mortised Legs, Lower Shelf, Painted, Cutouts, 18 x 44 x 12 In. 880.00
Bench, Softwood, Mortised Legs, Single Skirt, Shaped Cutout, Painted, 18 x 69 x 10 In. ... 360.00
Bench, Softwood, Plank Seat, Solid Backboard, Mortised Sides, 29 x 76 x 17 In. 880.00
Bench, Split Log, Butcher Block, Hand-Whittled Tapered Legs, Mortised, 72 x 20 In. 125.00
Bench, Victorian, Papier-Mache, Floral, Crest, Spindle, Gold, Mother-Of-Pearl, 61 In. ... 2115.00
Bench, Wagon, Softwood, Salmon, Red, Yellow, White, 21 1/2 x 33 1/2 x 12 In. 70.00
Bench, Wagon, Woven Rush Seats, Dark Green Paint, Turned Legs, Spindles, 36 In. 1150.00
Bench, Walnut, Framed, Carved, France, 29 In. 320.00
Bench, Water, Pine, Slope Front, 2 Cupboard Doors, Pennsylvania, 44 x 39 x 16 In. 460.00
Bench, William & Mary Style, Upholstered, Tassel Fringe, Late 19th Century, 50 In. 400.00
Bench, William & Mary Style, Walnut, Turned, England, c.1885, 18 x 26 In. 1150.00
Bench, Window, Baroque Style, Beech, Shaped Arms, 24 x 30 x 18 In. 470.00
Bench, Window, Louis XVI Style, Giltwood, Padded, c.1900, 22 x 36 1/2 x 21 In. 405.00
Bench, Window, Louis XVI Style, Polychrome, Padded, c.1900, 30 x 39 1/2 In. 1380.00
Bench, Windsor, Pine, Brown Finish, 19th Century 140.00
Bench, Yellow Pine, Slat Crest, Green Over Blue Paint, Late 19th Century, 32 x 93 In. ... 75.00
Bookcase, Art Deco, Burl, 2 Glazed Doors Over 2 Solid Doors, 67 x 51 x 16 In. 420.00
Bookcase, Arts & Crafts, 3 Doors, Brass Hardware, V-Board Back, 57 x 13 x 61 In. 3450.00
Bookcase, Arts & Crafts, Oak, 2 Doors, Gallery, 6 Shelves, Latticework, 58 1/2 x 58 In. ... 1265.00
Bookcase, Arts & Crafts, Oak, 5 Doors, Beveled Top, 64 x 34 x 15 1/2 In. 2875.00
Bookcase, Arts & Crafts, Rectangular, Stretcher, Plank Sides, 26 1/2 x 24 x 11 In. 290.00
Bookcase, Bamboo, 4 Tiers, Open Back, Sides, Geometric, 51 x 26 x 11 In. 115.00
Bookcase, Barrister, Globe-Wernicke, Oak, 4 Tiers, Label, 1900 .... 440.00
Bookcase, Barrister, Mission Oak, 4 Tiers, Grand Rapids, 54 1/2 x 34 3/4 In. 865.00
Bookcase, Barrister, Mission Oak, 5 Tiers, 86 In. 978.00
Bookcase, Barrister, Oak, 3 Tiers 470.00
Bookcase, Biedermeier Style, Blond Wood, 2 Doors, 95 x 42 x 10 1/4 In., Pair 2300.00
Bookcase, Bowfront, 3 Doors, Carved Acorns & Leaves, c.1890, 78 x 70 x 22 In. 6720.00
Bookcase, Chippendale Style, Mahogany, Pierced, Carved Pediment, 92 x 58 1/2 In. ... 1610.00
Bookcase, Chippendale, Mahogany, Slant Front, Drawers, c.1780, 88 x 40 In. 2990.00
Bookcase, Edwardian, Satinwood, 2 Glazed Doors, 2 Paneled Doors, 86 In. 4400.00
Bookcase, Empire Style, Cream Paint, Gilt, France, 19th Century, 77 In. 2726.00
Bookcase, Federal Style, Mahogany, Glazed Doors, Writing Drawer, 36 x 15 x 81 In. ... 290.00
Bookcase, G. Nakashima, Black Walnut, c.1976, 60 x 50 In. 8050.00

Bookcase, G. Nakashima, Walnut, 4 Shelves, c.1972, 49 3/4 x 60 x 23 In. 7770.00
Bookcase, G. Nelson, Walnut, Steel, Thin Edge, Herman Miller, 1950s, 67 x 32 In. 2875.00
Bookcase, G. Stickley, 1 Door, Leaded Panes, 36 x 14 x 58 In. 18400.00
Bookcase, G. Stickley, Oak, 1 Door, 16 Glass Panes, Mitered Mullions, 32 x 13 x 56 In. . 8050.00
Bookcase, G. Stickley, Oak, 1 Door, 16 Glass Panes, No. 715, Iron Pull, 36 x 13 x 56 In. . 7480.00
Bookcase, G. Stickley, Oak, 2 Doors, 12 Glass Panes, Iron Pulls, 57 x 13 x 56 In. 12650.00
Bookcase, G. Stickley, Oak, 2 Doors, 3 Shelves, 16 Glass Panes, Mortised, 56 x 43 In. . . . 5750.00
Bookcase, G. Stickley, Oak, 2 Doors, 3 Shelves, Gallery Top, 56 x 46 x 13 In. 3450.00
Bookcase, G. Stickley, Oak, 2 Doors, 8 Glass Panes, 3 Shelves, 56 1/4 x 42 3/4 x 13 In. . . 5175.00
Bookcase, George III Style, 2 Astragal Glazed Doors, 83 x 70 In. 1725.00
Bookcase, George III Style, Leather Inset, Chinoiserie, 95 x 84 x 20 1/2 In. 1530.00
Bookcase, George III Style, Mahogany, Astragal Glazed Doors, 86 1/2 x 52 In. 1380.00
Bookcase, George III Style, Mahogany, Astragal Glazed Doors, 90 x 103 In. 2990.00
Bookcase, George III, Mahogany, 4 Glazed Panel Doors, 2 Drawers, 93 x 22 In. 6900.00
Bookcase, George III, Mahogany, Astragal Glazed Doors, 89 1/2 x 51 x 17 1/2 In. 2300.00
Bookcase, George III, Mahogany, Glazed & Paneled Doors, 103 x 116 x 19 In. 5290.00
Bookcase, George III, Mahogany, Glazed Doors, 18th Century, 95 1/2 x 47 x 24 In. 5460.00
Bookcase, George III, Mahogany, Glazed Doors, Slant Front, 18th Century, 92 x 48 In. . . . 7475.00
Bookcase, Georgian, Yew, Carved, 2 Glazed Panel Doors, Splayed Legs, 93 In. 1495.00
Bookcase, Hepplewhite, Mahogany, 2 Doors Over 2 Drawers, 72 x 13 x 45 In. 920.00
Bookcase, Hepplewhite, Mahogany, 3 Doors, Drawers, 82 x 23 x 44 In. 2300.00
Bookcase, Kingwood, Gilt Bronze, Marquetry, 2 Drawers, 1880, 38 x 32 In. 7670.00
Bookcase, L. & J.G. Stickley, Oak, 2 Doors, 12 Panes, Copper Pulls, 55 x 52 x 12 In. 6900.00
Bookcase, Lakeside Craft, Cutouts, 31 x 29 x 10 In. 805.00
Bookcase, Library, 3 Doors, Slide Desk, 19th Century, 59 1/2 x 89 x 14 In. 8250.00
Bookcase, Lifetime, Oak, 1 Door, 10 Squares, Copper Hardware, 28 x 12 x 56 In. 1725.00
Bookcase, Lifetime, Oak, 3 Doors, Gallery Top, Cloud Lift Apron, 57 x 56 1/2 x 13 In. . . 2300.00
Bookcase, Lifetime, Oak, No. 7663, Puritan Line, 2 Doors, 3 Shelves, Signed, 45 x 52 In. 2300.00
Bookcase, Limbert, Glazed Oak, 2 Doors, 4 Glass Panels, 1906, 48 x 47 In. 2350.00
Bookcase, Limbert, Oak, No. 337, Door, Inlaid Copper & Pewter, 37 x 16 x 50 In. 10350.00
Bookcase, Louis XV Style, Fruitwood, Doors, Wire Grills, France, 53 x 35 x 14 In. 1265.00
Bookcase, Mahogany, 4 Glass & 2 Carved Doors, c.1885, 63 x 72 x 15 In. 6160.00
Bookcase, Mahogany, 4 Glass Doors, 2 J-Curved, Full Female Caryatids, 69 x 85 In. 6440.00
Bookcase, Mahogany, Glass Doors, c.1900, 47 x 13 x 57 In. 1295.00
Bookcase, Mahogany, Glazed Paneled Doors, Shelves, 19th Century, 77 x 44 x 12 In. 1645.00
Bookcase, Mahogany, Inlaid Frieze, 2 Shelves, 39 1/2 x 40 1/2 x 12 1/2 In., Pair 920.00
Bookcase, Mahogany, Inlaid Top, Gadrooned Edge, Glazed Panel Doors, 48 x 38 In. 1840.00
Bookcase, Mahogany, Maple, Scroll Top, New England, 18th Century, 84 3/4 In. 7050.00
Bookcase, Mahogany, Molded Cornice, Frieze, 2 Glazed Doors, Pillars, 72 x 16 x 61 In. . 2400.00
Bookcase, Mahogany, Mortised Joints, Dovetailed, Doors, England, 17 1/2 In. 690.00
Bookcase, Mahogany, Step-Down, 3 Doors, Curved Glass, 70 x 63 x 18 In. 2630.00
Bookcase, Napoleon III, Walnut, 3 Sections, Glazed Door, 1800s, 97 x 84 x 25 In. 2990.00
Bookcase, Oak, 2 Doors, Adjustable Shelves, 61 1/2 x 56 x 15 1/2 In. 2070.00
Bookcase, Oak, 2 Mullioned Doors, Acanthus Columns, Claw Feet, 53 x 54 In. 1065.00
Bookcase, Oak, 3 Doors, Beveled Mirrors, Floral Carving, c.1885, 76 x 72 x 18 In. 4480.00
Bookcase, Oak, 3 Doors, Bow Center, Carved, Claw Feet, c.1885, 66 x 74 x 20 In. 7840.00
Bookcase, Oak, Curved Glass, Shaped Curio Gallery, c.1890, 71 x 29 x 13 In. 1960.00
Bookcase, Regency Style, Rosewood, Marble Top, 2 Doors, 1800s, 36 x 42 x 13 In. 2760.00
Bookcase, Regency, Mahogany, 2 Astragal Glazed Doors, Paneled Pilasters, 84 x 44 In. . . 4600.00
Bookcase, Regency, Mahogany, 2 Sides, Casters, Handles, 41 x 30 1/2 x 13 In. 3450.00
Bookcase, Regency, Mahogany, Astragal Glazed Doors, c.1815, 88 x 35 In. 2990.00
Bookcase, Regency, Mahogany, Glazed Doors, Pilasters, Plinth Base, 95 x 50 x 18 In. . . . 2990.00
Bookcase, Regency, Mahogany, Paneled Doors, Pilasters, Cornice, 94 x 48 x 18 In. 6615.00
Bookcase, Renaissance Revival, Walnut, 2 Glazed Doors, Plinth Base, 87 x 49 In., Pair . . 2235.00
Bookcase, Renaissance Revival, Walnut, Burl, Glazed Doors, Panels, 91 x 50 x 19 In. . . . 3910.00
Bookcase, Revolving, Cherry, Square Top, Round Corners, Casters, c.1890, 44 x 20 In. . . 635.00
Bookcase, Revolving, Edwardian, Mahogany, Inlay, Ogee Feet, c.1900, 31 x 20 In. 1265.00
Bookcase, Revolving, John Danner, Oak, Tiers, Cast Iron Legs, c.1880, 51 In. . . . . . *Illus* 575.00
Bookcase, Revolving, Mahogany, Inlaid, Square Top, 3 Tiers, 37 x 18 x 18 In. 460.00
Bookcase, Revolving, Mahogany, Linenfold Inlay Top, England, 34 x 23 1/2 In. 635.00
Bookcase, Revolving, Mahogany, Round, Crossbanded, England, 34 x 23 1/2 In. 520.00
Bookcase, Revolving, Walnut, 3 Shelves, Slated Sides, 44 1/2 x 23 1/2 x 23 1/2 In. 635.00
Bookcase, Roycroft, 1 Door, 16 Glass Panes, c.1910, 40 x 15 x 55 In. 13800.00

Bookcase, Roycroft, Mahogany, 3 Shelves, 20th Century, 50 x 16 x 53 In. 1725.00
Bookcase, Roycroft, Oak, Arch Top & Base, 3 Shelves, c.1907, 37 x 17 x 15 In. 4995.00
Bookcase, Victorian, Mahogany, England, c.1885, 53 3/4 x 48 1/2 x 12 In. 750.00
Bookcase, Victorian, Mahogany, Pedestal Doors, Drawers, 1840, 89 x 65 In. 1620.00
Bookcase, Walnut, 2 Doors, Carved Crest, c.1885, 104 x 50 x 19 In. 2800.00
Bookcase, Walnut, 3 Doors, 2 Carved, 4 Center Shelves, 70 x 66 x 15 1/4 In. 865.00
Bookcase, Walnut, 4 Sections, Glass Door Front, 66 1/2 x 35 1/2 x 11 1/2 In. 1380.00
Bookcase, Walnut, Carved Burled Gallery, 2 Glass Doors Over 2 Drawers, 84 x 53 In. ... 2800.00
Bookcase, Walnut, Marquetry, Crossbanded, 19th Century, 36 x 39 x 11 In. 1410.00
Bookcase, Walnut, Molded Cornice, 2 Glazed Panel Doors, Raised Cabriole Legs, 61 In. . 315.00
Bookcase, William IV, Mahogany, Marble Top, 38 1/2 x 29 x 11 3/4 In. 4180.00
Bookcase, William IV, Rosewood, Breakfront Center, Barley Twist Supports, 44 x 64 In. . 3525.00
Bookcase-Cabinet, George III Style, Inlaid Mahogany, Mid 1800s, 86 x 49 x 14 In. 8050.00
Bookcase-Cabinet, George III, Mahogany, 1 Glazed Door, 1 Drawer, 82 x 25 In. 2040.00
Bookcase-Cabinet, George III, Waxed Pine, 84 1/2 x 48 1/2 x 14 1/2 In. 5975.00
Bookcase-Cabinet, Inlaid Design, Beveled Glass Doors, Mirror, 47 x 18 x 71 In. 2530.00
Bookcase-Cabinet, Regency Style, Mahogany, Leather Top, Brass, 89 x 44 x 21 In. 1150.00
Bookrack, Arts & Crafts, Cutout Handles, Shelf, 29 x 28 x 32 In. 635.00
Bookrack, G. Stickley, No. 74, Oak, V-Top, D-Shape Handles, c.1912, 31 x 30 x 10 In. ... 1410.00
Bookrack, G. Stickley, Oak, 15 3/4 x 5 In. 380.00
Bookrack, G. Stickley, Tabletop, 7 x 12 x 7 In. 1380.00
Bookrack, Lion, Cast Iron, Expands To 23 In., 12 1/4 x 6 1/4 x 5 In. 165.00
Bookrack, Wood, Carved Flowers On Base & Ends, Cincinnati Art, 20 x 7 x 7 In. 290.00
Bookstand, Brass Revolving Gallery, Center Handle, Oak Base, Tripod, 13 x 12 In. 500.00
Bookstand, George III, Mahogany, Hinged, Adjustable Top, 31 x 18 1/2 x 16 In. 32860.00
Bookstand, Napoleon III, Burl, Brass, Malachite, Adjustable, 16 In. 259.00
Bookstand, Revolving, 2 Tiers, Black Lacquer, Gilt, 29 x 21 x 21 In. 690.00
Bookstand, Rococo Revival, Rosewood, Cut-Through Ends & Partitions, 40 x 26 In. 460.00
Bookstand, Roycroft, Little Journeys, 2 Shelves, 26 1/2 x 26 x 14 In. 865.00
Bookstand, Tiger Oak, Carved Eagle, Swivel .... *Illus* 3410.00
Bookstand, Victorian, Walnut, Tabletop, 19th Century, 10 x 12 x 10 In. 635.00
Box, Blanket, Painted Design 325.00
Box, Blanket, Red Over Blue Paint 360.00
Breakfront, E. Wormley, Mahogany, 4 Glazed Doors, Illuminated Panels, Dunbar 1035.00
Breakfront, French Provincial, Fruitwood, 2 Parts, c.1865, 81 x 57 In. 3680.00
Breakfront, George II Style, Walnut, Fluted Pilaster, Hinged, 102 x 81 x 17 In. 8365.00
Breakfront, George III Style, Mahogany, c.1815, 95 1/2 x 85 1/2 In. 6900.00
Breakfront, George III Style, Mahogany, Ebony Inlay, 36 x 66 x 24 In. 3450.00
Breakfront, Hepplewhite Style, Mahogany & Veneer, 2 Sections, 78 x 68 In. 1610.00
Breakfront, Hepplewhite, Mahogany, Wine Drawer, c.1880, 35 x 75 x 28 In. 5865.00
Breakfront, Mahogany, 3 Glass Fretwork Doors Over 3 Flame Veneer Doors, 80 x 59 In. . 1150.00
Breakfront, Mahogany, 4 Top Glass Doors, 4 Base Doors, Long Drawer, 67 x 86 In. 730.00
Breakfront, Mahogany, Foliate Carved, Plinth Base, 64 x 32 x 84 In. 1745.00
Breakfront, Mahogany, Gallery Back, Drawer, c.1850, 84 In. 1090.00
Breakfront, Mahogany, Step Back, 4 Glass Over 4 Paneled Doors, 90 x 72 In. 9200.00
Breakfront, Renaissance Revival, Burl Walnut Panels, Glass Doors, c.1870, 114 In. 5000.00
Breakfront, William IV, Rosewood, Banister Rail, c.1825, 39 x 72 x 20 In. 2990.00
Breakfront-Bookcase, George III Style, Mahogany, 2 Glazed Doors, 72 x 37 In. 259.00
Breakfront-Bookcase, George III Style, Mahogany, 4 Glazed Doors, 85 x 79 x 18 In. 2185.00
Breakfront-Bookcase, Georgian Style, Mahogany, Greek Key Inlay, 85 x 91 x 18 In. 3680.00
Breakfront-Bookcase, Georgian Style, Walnut, 5 Drawers, 101 x 87 x 19 1/2 In. 5290.00
Breakfront-Bookcase, Walnut, 3 Doors, Bonnet Top, Figural Pulls, c.1870, 76 x 69 In. ... 6720.00
Breakfront-Bookcase, Walnut, 3 Doors, Carved Gallery, c.1885, 82 x 62 x 19 In. 3528.00
Breakfront-Bookcase, Walnut, Marquetry, 3 Doors, Shelves, Plinth Base, 42 x 14 x 72 In. 1385.00
Buffet, Art Deco, Burl, Mirror, 4 Small Drawers, Italy, 69 x 70 In. 1765.00
Buffet, Art Deco, Burl, Shaped Marble Top, 5 Drawers, 2 Doors, 35 x 74 x 21 In. 6575.00
Buffet, Art Deco, Mahogany, Inlaid Flowers, Bowed Middle, 38 x 91 x 21 In. 650.00
Buffet, Charles X, Fruitwood, Banded, 4 Drawers, 4 Cupboards, c.1900, 38 x 77 x 22 In. . 5750.00
Buffet, French Provincial, Cherry, 2 Drawers, 2 Doors, c.1865, 39 1/2 x 43 1/4 In. 489.00
Buffet, French Provincial, Fruitwood, Frieze Drawer Over 2 Serpentine Doors, 42 In. 2300.00
Buffet, French Provincial, Oak, Planked Top, 2 Carved Doors, 1800s, 39 x 67 In. 1610.00
Buffet, Louis Philippe Style, Cherry, c.1885, 39 1/2 x 82 In. 4830.00
Buffet, Louis Philippe, Cherry, 2 Drawers, 2 Doors, 19th Century, 41 x 52 x 22 In. 1840.00

Furniture, Bookcase, Revolving, John Danner, Oak, Tiers, Cast Iron Legs, c.1880, 51 In.

Furniture, Bookstand, Tiger Oak, Carved Eagle, Swivel

Furniture, Cabinet, China, Oak, Carved, Leaded Glass Top, 72 x 55 In.

Buffet, Louis Philippe, Fruitwood, Gilt Brass, 3 Doors, c.1835, 36 x 71 In. 4600.00
Buffet, Louis Philippe, Oak, 2 Shelves, Paneled Back, 19th Century, 62 x 51 x 19 In. 1265.00
Buffet, Louis XV, Cherry, Walnut, c.1750, 39 1/4 x 64 1/2 x 16 1/2 In. 1725.00
Buffet, Louis XV, Fruitwood, 2 Drawers, 2 Doors, 19th Century, 44 x 55 x 24 1/2 In. 2990.00
Buffet, Louis XV, Walnut, Basket Carving, c.1790, 49 1/2 x 53 1/2 In. 4140.00
Buffet, Louis XVI Style, Marble Top, 2 Drawers, 2 Doors, c.1900, 41 x 74 x 19 In. 2760.00
Buffet, Louis XVI, Oak, Walnut, Hinges, 18th Century, 43 x 51 1/2 x 20 In. 1469.00
Buffet, Mahogany Veneer, 6 Drawers, 2 Doors, Brass Ring Pulls, 30 x 64 x 20 In. 355.00
Buffet, Mahogany, Blond, 3 Doors, Bracket Base, 31 x 62 In. 410.00
Buffet, McCobb, Planner Group, Winchendon, c.1948, 32 x 60 x 18 3/4 In. 1295.00
Buffet, Oak, 2 Drawers, 2 Doors, Belgium, c.1815, 47 1/2 x 63 1/2 In. 2300.00
Buffet, Oak, 2 Stained Glass Doors, 2 Drawers, 19th Century, 97 x 56 In. 1150.00
Buffet, Oak, 4 Curio Cabinets, Glass Doors, Carved Maiden Head, 76 x 53 In. 3080.00
Buffet, Pollard, Oak, 2 Tiers, Mid 19th Century, 131 1/2 x 61 x 23 1/4 In. 5975.00
Bureau, Boulle & Ebony, Gilt Bronze, Paris, 1890, 31 x 78 x 37 In. 19590.00
Bureau, Cottage, Pine, 3 Drawers, 19th Century, 35 x 39 In. 345.00
Bureau, Dutch Rococo Style, Inlaid Mahogany, Bombe Slant Front, 44 x 38 1/2 x 23 In. . . 1495.00
Bureau, Empire Style, 6 Stepped Drawers, Painted, Elephant Legs, 44 1/2 x 45 x 20 In. . . 145.00
Bureau, Federal, Cherry Inlay, 4 Graduated Drawers, c.1810, 34 x 38 3/4 x 18 1/2 In. 1530.00
Bureau, Federal, Mahogany, Bowfront, 4 Graduated Drawers, 36 3/4 x 40 1/2 x 21 In. . . . 5290.00
Bureau, Federal, Mahogany, c.1810, 49 1/4 x 44 1/2 x 21 1/2 In. 1095.00
Bureau, French Provincial, Oak, Plank Top, Cabriole Legs, c.1885, 29 1/2 x 56 In. 1150.00
Bureau, George I, Walnut, Marquetry, Slant Front, 41 x 37 3/4 x 22 1/4 In. 3680.00
Bureau, George III, Mahogany, Slant Front, c.1800, 40 1/2 x 36 1/2 x 19 In. 980.00
Bureau, Hepplewhite, Mahogany, Bowfront, Inlay, 4 Drawers, c.1700s, 38 x 42 In. 8340.00
Bureau, Louis XV Style, Kingwood, Gilt Metal Mounts, 5 Drawers, 20th Century, 31 In. . . 3060.00
Bureau, Louis XV, Cherry, Kneehole Frieze, Drawer, 19th Century, 37 x 75 x 31 In. 3680.00
Bureau, Louis XV, Gilt Mounts, Leather, Drawers, Cabriole Legs, 42 x 25 x 31 In. 1095.00
Bureau, Louis XVI Style, Oak, Rounded Top, c.1830, 45 x 57 1/2 x 20 In. 805.00
Bureau, Mahogany, Bowfront, 4 Drawers, Rope-Turned Legs, American, 39 x 41 In. 660.00
Bureau, Mahogany, Bowfront, 4 Figured Maple Drawers, Scrolled Splash, 39 In. 2530.00
Bureau, Ralph Cahoon, Painted Flowers, Heart, Hunter, Deer, 4 Drawers, 42 x 26 In. 2530.00
Bureau, Sheraton, Cherry, 4 Drawers, Turned Legs, Oval Brasses, American, 41 x 44 In. . . 575.00
Bureau, Sheraton, Mahogany, 2 Drawers, Backsplash, 4 Drawers Below, 48 x 40 In. 520.00
Bureau, Sheraton, Mahogany, Bowfront, Cookie Corners, Ribbed Legs, 42 x 42 In. 865.00
Bureau, Sheraton, Mahogany, Tiger Maple, 4 Drawers, Carved Legs, 44 x 46 In. 520.00
Bureau-Bookcase, Cherry, Drop Flap, 4 Drawers, 2 Doors, c.1810, 82 x 38 1/2 In. 730.00
Bureau-Bookcase, George I Style, Walnut Inlay, Slant Front, Drawers, 87 x 41 x 21 In. . . 8365.00
Bureau-Bookcase, George II Style, Walnut, Slant Front, 81 x 34 x 20 In. 3680.00
Bureau-Bookcase, George III Style, Mahogany, 2 Doors, c.1885, 90 1/2 x 42 1/2 In. 5060.00
Bureau-Bookcase, George III, Mahogany, 2 Glazed Doors, 4 Drawers, 88 x 48 x 21 In. . . 2990.00
Bureau-Bookcase, George III, Mahogany, Slant Front, c.1775, 94 x 50 x 24 In. 4370.00
Bureau-Bookcase, Gothic Revival, Mahogany, c.1825, 69 x 39 x 21 In. 1610.00
Cabinet, 2 Double Doors, Hidden Compartment, Chinese, c.1890, 28 x 45 In. 635.00

Cabinet, 4 Panels, Crackle Ice, Flowers, 1 Shelf, 3 Drawers, Qing Dynasty, 73 x 45 In. . . 920.00
Cabinet, A. Richard, Walnut, Enameled Metal, 1950, 78 x 41 1/2 In. 4600.00
Cabinet, Aesthetic Revival, Ebonized, Shelves, Doors, Painted, Gilt, 37 x 60 x 16 In. 1195.00
Cabinet, Aesthetic Revival, Mahogany, Carved, Inlaid Sun, 1800, 78 x 46 x 18 In. 5975.00
Cabinet, Art Deco, 4 Drawers, 2 Doors, Germany, 68 x 23 x 33 In. 2530.00
Cabinet, Art Deco, Ivory, Ebony Inlay, 2 Doors, France, c.1930, 47 x 35 In. 2990.00
Cabinet, Art Deco, Mahogany, 3 Parts, France, c.1930, 48 1/2 x 67 1/2 In. 4600.00
Cabinet, Art Deco, Wrought Iron, Rectangular Marble Top, Drawer, 21 x 15 x 12 In. 470.00
Cabinet, Arthur Simpson, Arts & Crafts, Beech, Drawer, 2 Doors, c.1910, 30 x 20 In. . . . 865.00
Cabinet, Arts & Crafts, Oak, Door, Leaf-Carved Panel, 1900s, 35 x 16 x 15 In. 530.00
Cabinet, Baroque, Walnut, Parquetry, Marquetry, Till, Bail Handles, 14 x 23 x 12 3/4 In. . 865.00
Cabinet, Biedermeier, Cherry, 1 Drawer, 2 Doors, 35 x 39 x 21 In. 3680.00
Cabinet, Biedermeier, Mahogany, Glazed Door, Square Feet, c.1815, 68 x 35 In. 3450.00
Cabinet, Birch, Fruitwood, Painted, Continental, 58 1/2 x 23 1/4 x 15 3/8 In., Pair 1495.00
Cabinet, Black Lacquer, Red, Gilt Gardens, Chinese, 33 1/4 x 23 1/2 In. 520.00
Cabinet, Bugatti, Painted, Bone, Metal Inlay, 61 x 39 x 16 In. 14340.00
Cabinet, Burl, Lacquered, Stylized Dragons, Chinese, Qing Dynasty, 72 x 35 x 20 In. 2000.00
Cabinet, Burl, Marquetry, Marble Top, 3 Doors, Panel, c.1900, 44 x 78 x 19 In. 5750.00
Cabinet, China, Arts & Crafts, 3 Shelves, Partial Mirror Back, Glass Doors, 58 x 49 In. . . 865.00
Cabinet, China, Arts & Crafts, Mahogany, Gallery Top, 8 Panel Doors, 65 x 43 x 14 In. . . 1495.00
Cabinet, China, Arts & Crafts, Oak, 2 Doors, 3 Shelves, Overhang Top, 58 x 44 x 15 In. . . 1495.00
Cabinet, China, Arts & Crafts, Oak, 2 Doors, 8 Panes, 3 Shelves, 48 x 35 3/4 x 13 In. . . . 2760.00
Cabinet, China, Arts & Crafts, Oak, 3 Doors, 8 Legs, Latticework, 56 x 62 x 16 1/2 In. . . 3220.00
Cabinet, China, Bowfront, Bellflower Columns, American, 73 1/4 x 53 1/2 x 23 In. 2990.00
Cabinet, China, Chippendale, 3 Glass Doors Over 3 Paneled Doors, 53 x 79 In. 230.00
Cabinet, China, Edwardian, Mahogany, 2 Doors, 2 Drawers, Spade Feet, 72 x 13 x 36 In. . 620.00
Cabinet, China, Federal Style, Mahogany, Doors, Bowfront, 1900s, 40 x 19 x 73 In. 635.00
Cabinet, China, G. Stickley, Door, 12 Glass Panes, No. 820, Red Decal, 36 x 63 In. 4600.00
Cabinet, China, G. Stickley, Oak, 3 Shelves, Paneled Interior, 63 x 42 x 15 In. 6900.00
Cabinet, China, Georgian, Chinoiserie, Glazed Door, Drawer, Bracket Base, 79 x 40 In. . . 575.00
Cabinet, China, L. & J.G. Stickley, Oak, 2 Doors, 62 x 46 x 16 In. 5465.00
Cabinet, China, L. & J.G. Stickley, Oak, 2 Doors, Leaded Panes, Shelves, 66 x 44 x 16 In. 8625.00
Cabinet, China, Limbert, Oak, 1 Door, 3 Shelves, Arched Backsplash, 59 x 44 x 16 In. . . . 6325.00
Cabinet, China, Limbert, Oak, 1 Door, Mullion, Copper Hardware, 32 x 15 x 58 In. 2185.00
Cabinet, China, Limbert, Oak, 2 Doors, 2 Divided Panes, No. 448, 46 x 17 x 62 In. 3335.00
Cabinet, China, Limbert, Oak, 2 Doors, 3 Shelves, No. 1308, 55 3/4 x 30 1/2 x 14 1/4 In. 3740.00
Cabinet, China, Oak, Carved, Leaded Glass Top, 72 x 55 In. . . . . *Illus* 3850.00
Cabinet, China, Step-Down, Beveled Mirror Gallery, Curved Glass, 80 x 56 x 20 In. 2240.00
Cabinet, China, Stickley Bros., Oak, 2 Doors, 3 Shelves, No. 8852, 59 x 47 x 15 In. 1840.00
Cabinet, Chinoiserie, Gold, Red Lacquer, 2 Doors, 29 x 33 In. 200.00
Cabinet, Chinoiserie, Serpentine Front, Drawer, 20th Century, 57 x 16 1/2 x 55 In. 1100.00
Cabinet, Chippendale, Cherry, 2 Glass Panel Doors, Bracket Feet, 72 x 43 In. 935.00
Cabinet, Conrey-Davis, Gallery Top, Pivoting Ashtrays, Door, Shelves, 32 x 18 In. 200.00
Cabinet, Corner, Aesthetic Revival, Cherry, Ebonized, Oval Panel, 1880, 75 x 36 In. 1725.00
Cabinet, Corner, French Provincial, Walnut, Burl, Bowfront, 2 Doors, 37 x 27 x 18 1/2 In. 1150.00
Cabinet, Corner, George III, Green Lacquered, Bowfront, Late 1700s, 42 x 27 x 18 In. . . . 1840.00
Cabinet, Corner, Georgian Style, Mahogany, Glazed Doors, Fret Carving, 61 1/2 In. 865.00
Cabinet, Corner, Hanging, George III, Black Lacquer, Bowfront, 2 Doors, 36 x 23 In. . . . 690.00
Cabinet, Corner, Hanging, George III, Chinoiserie, Scarlet Ground, 41 x 20 x 11 In. 518.00
Cabinet, Corner, Hanging, Mahogany, Arched Panel Door, 43 x 34 In. 1035.00
Cabinet, Corner, Hanging, Pine, Painted, Red Sponging, 1851, 30 x 21 x 37 1/2 In. 880.00
Cabinet, Corner, Mahogany, 2 Panel Doors, Pierced Brackets, c.1910, 56 x 24 x 13 In. . . . 405.00
Cabinet, Corner, Mahogany, Bowfront, 2 Glass Doors Over 1 Drawer & 2 Doors, 73 In. . . 805.00
Cabinet, Corner, Napoleon III, Mahogany, Kingwood, 1 Door, Panel, 34 x 14 x 10 In. . . . 1265.00
Cabinet, Corner, Neoclassical, Rosewood, c.1850, 35 x 42 1/2 In. 1150.00
Cabinet, Corner, Oak, 2 Sections, Bowfront Doors, Frieze Drawer, 60 In. 880.00
Cabinet, Corner, Oak, Carved, Juan Busquets, c.1900, 72 x 33 x 24 In. 7770.00
Cabinet, Corner, Painted, Cat Motif, After Henriette Ronner-Knip, 1900s, 33 In. 2000.00
Cabinet, Corner, Pine, 2 Parts, Molded Cresting, Arched Door, Bracket Feet, 86 x 47 In. . 2300.00
Cabinet, Corner, Pyramid-Carved Crest, Islamic Arch Frieze, 2 Parquetry Doors, 78 In. . . 375.00
Cabinet, Corner, Renaissance Revival, Rosewood Inlay, Marble Top, 1880, 37 x 37 In. . . . 2530.00
Cabinet, Corner, Walnut, Mirror Panel, Divided Door, England, c.1900, 65 x 20 x 10 In. . 460.00
Cabinet, Display, Bowfront Door, Round Glass Shelves, France, 44 x 17 In. 805.00

Cabinet, Display, Bowfront, Serpentine Side Panels, Painted Scenes, Ormolu, 64 In. 660.00
Cabinet, Display, Cast Bronze, 3 Glass Doors, Spiral-Turned Columns, 73 x 84 x 28 In. . . . 5600.00
Cabinet, Display, Eastlake, Walnut, Stepped Shelves, Carved, c.1890, 25 x 15 x 9 In. 405.00
Cabinet, Display, Edwardian, 2 Glass Doors, 2 Drawers, Shelves, Carved, 84 x 48 In. 1456.00
Cabinet, Display, Edwardian, Mahogany, Panel Door, Side Lights, 1900, 58 x 37 x 14 In. . 1150.00
Cabinet, Display, Flowers, Bats, Jade Inlay, 19th Century, 14 x 12 x 6 In. 355.00
Cabinet, Display, Gilt Brass Mounted, France, 45 1/2 x 71 In. 1365.00
Cabinet, Display, Glass Door, Shelves, Late 20th Century, 39 3/4 x 12 x 17 1/2 In. 115.00
Cabinet, Display, Gold Leaf, Cabriole Legs, Ormolu Scroll, 23 x 23 x 43 In. 690.00
Cabinet, Display, Mahogany, 2 Glazed Doors, Mirrored Back, c.1900, 75 x 76 In. 1750.00
Cabinet, Display, Mahogany, 4 Glass Sides, Ormolu Trim On Top & Feet, 39 In. 1570.00
Cabinet, Display, Mahogany, Bronze Ormolu Mounts, Silk Back, 59 x 16 x 24 In. 405.00
Cabinet, Display, Mahogany, Burl & Satinwood Inlay, Beveled Door, 83 1/2 x 47 In. 2070.00
Cabinet, Display, Mahogany, Double Door, Arched Door, Shelves, 82 x 57 x 15 1/2 In. . . . 1610.00
Cabinet, Display, Neoclassical, Mahogany, Parcel Gilt, Early 1800s, 74 x 33 x 19 In. 3825.00
Cabinet, Display, Oak, 4 Glass Door, A.N. Russell & Sons, 5 1/4 x 25 1/2 x 26 3/4 In. . . . 1430.00
Cabinet, Display, Oak, Bowfront & Sides, Claw & Ball Feet, Wheels, 37 x 16 x 67 In. . . . 920.00
Cabinet, Display, Oriental, Rosewood, Late 20th Century, 36 x 3 1/2 In. 200.00
Cabinet, Display, Pierced, Carved Crown & Back Panel, Tiered Shelves, 82 x 30 In. 2300.00
Cabinet, Display, Rococo, Oak, 2 Glass Doors, 2 Carved Paneled Doors, 84 x 49 In. 5050.00
Cabinet, Display, Rosewood, Bamboo, Flowers, Chinese, 1800s, 72 x 41 x 15 In. 1175.00
Cabinet, Display, Rosewood, Dragon, Birds, Flowers, Japan, 1800s, 69 x 42 x 14 In. 1293.00
Cabinet, Display, Rosewood, Flowers, Chinese, 19th Century, 71 x 31 x 14 In. 880.00
Cabinet, Display, Rosewood, Glazed, Carved Dragons, Fabric Back, Chinese, 34 x 20 In. . 290.00
Cabinet, Display, Walnut, Round Case, Curved Glass, Pierced Brass Gallery, 42 In. 250.00
Cabinet, E. Wormley, Walnut, 2 Over 3 Drawers, Birch Pulls, Loop Feet, 33 x 45 In. 1725.00
Cabinet, Edwardian, Mahogany, 2 Glazed Doors, Marquetry, 53 x 54 x 15 In. 765.00
Cabinet, Edwardian, Mahogany, Inlaid, Ogee Top, Spade Feet, 40 1/2 In., Pair 1725.00
Cabinet, Elm, 2 Doors, Rectangular Top, Chinese, c.1850, 16 1/2 x 37 3/8 x 15 3/4 In. . . . 355.00
Cabinet, Elm, 5 Drawers, 2 Doors, Square Legs, Chinese, c.1850, 16 x 43 x 14 In. 645.00
Cabinet, Elm, Black Lacquer, Spindle Gallery, 3 Tiers, 2 Drawers, 2 Doors, 50 In. 489.00
Cabinet, Elm, Burl, 2 Parts, Brass Mounted, Korea, c.1800, 47 x 30 x 16 In. 690.00
Cabinet, Elm, Lacquered, Children At Play, 2 Doors, Chinese, c.1830, 49 x 39 x 19 In. . . . 705.00
Cabinet, Elm, Slat Panel Doors, 2 Drawers, Chinese, c.1880, 74 x 33 x 17 In. 590.00
Cabinet, Empire, Mahogany, Shelves, Drawers, c.1825, 38 x 35 1/2 x 21 1/2 In. 940.00
Cabinet, Federal, Walnut, Tabletop, Pa., c.1820, 20 x 17 x 10 1/2 In. 1435.00
Cabinet, Filing, Globe-Wernicke, Oak, 15 Drawers, Roll-Top Door, 79 x 14 In. 759.00
Cabinet, Filing, Mahogany, Secret Compartment, Philippe, c.1820, 33 x 78 In. 4500.00
Cabinet, Frank Lloyd Wright, Drawer, Open Shelves, Heritage Henredon, 18 x 26 x 26 In. 520.00
Cabinet, Frank Lloyd Wright, Taliesin Design, Heritage Henredon, 21 x 18 x 26 In. 635.00
Cabinet, Frank Lloyd Wright, Taliesin Design, Heritage Henredon, 22 x 20 x 28 In. 1150.00
Cabinet, French Provincial, Fruitwood, 2 Drawers, 2 Doors, Carved, c.1790, 51 In. 3200.00
Cabinet, French Provincial, Mahogany, 2 Paneled Cupboards, 37 x 50 1/2 x 18 In. 1725.00
Cabinet, French Provincial, Walnut, 2 Drawers, 2 Doors, c.1800, 74 x 53 x 17 In. 2300.00
Cabinet, French Provincial, Walnut, 4 Carved Panel Doors, 2 Drawers, 33 x 22 In. 375.00
Cabinet, French Provincial, Walnut, Marble Top, Serpentine, c.1880, 34 x 15 x 15 In. 375.00
Cabinet, Fruitwood, Ormolu Mounted, Jules Leleu, c.1940, 55 x 69 x 18 In. 9560.00
Cabinet, G. Nakashima, Kornblut, English Oak Burl, 22 x 18 x 18 In. 21150.00
Cabinet, G. Nakashima, Walnut, Sliding Doors, Dovetailed, 1960s, 96 x 33 In. 4600.00
Cabinet, G. Nelson, Ebonized Birch, Steel, 5 Drawers, Herman Miller, 1950s, 56 x 39 In. 575.00
Cabinet, G. Nelson, Ebonized, 4 Drawers, Herman Miller, 24 x 18 x 30 In. 405.00
Cabinet, G. Nelson, Lacquered Wood, Steel, Herman Miller, 1950s, 34 x 30 In. 805.00
Cabinet, G. Nelson, Lacquered, Chrome x Pulls, Herman Miller, 39 x 34 x 18 In. 765.00
Cabinet, G. Nelson, Thin Edge, Rosewood, 2 Doors, Aluminum Pulls, 31 x 34 In. 2185.00
Cabinet, G. Nelson, Thin Edge, Rosewood, Aluminum, Herman Miller, 34 x 30 3/4 In. . . . 2070.00
Cabinet, G. Nelson, Walnut Veneer, Sliding Glass, Herman Miller, 24 x 34 x 12 In., Pair . 600.00
Cabinet, G. Nelson, Walnut, 2 Shelves, Herman Miller, 40 x 18 1/2 x 40 In. 2300.00
Cabinet, G. Nelson, Walnut, Aluminum, Herman Miller, 1950s, 40 x 40 In. 865.00
Cabinet, G. Nelson, Walnut, Door, 5 Drawers, Bookmatched, 39 x 40 x 18 In., Pair 3525.00
Cabinet, G. Stickley, Arched Door, Toe Board, 36 x 14 x 60 In. 9200.00
Cabinet, G. Stickley, Gallery Top, 3 Shelves, Door, 47 x 20 x 16 1/2 In. 3220.00
Cabinet, Galle, Walnut, Burl, Fruitwood, Marquetry, c.1900, 42 x 26 x 15 1/2 In. 8960.00
Cabinet, George III, Satinwood Inlay, Bowfront, c.1790, 33 1/2 x 37 In. 8960.00

Cabinet, George III, Satinwood, 3 Shelves, c.1900, 49 x 25 x 12 In. 1495.00
Cabinet, George V, Black Lacquer, Brass Mounted, 18 Drawers, 57 x 21x 21 In. 375.00
Cabinet, Georgian Style, Black Lacquer, Gilt Chinese Scenes, 85 x 68 In. 5290.00
Cabinet, Georgian Style, Mahogany, Pedestal, Paw Feet, c.1885, 45 x 21 In. 2185.00
Cabinet, Georgian, Red Lacquer, 1 Arched Over 2 Small Doors, c.1750, 86 x 36 In. 4140.00
Cabinet, Giltwood, Gesso, Glazed Door, Scroll Feet, Italy, 1800s, 34 x 26 x 14 In. 1495.00
Cabinet, Gio Ponti, Walnut, 8 Drawers, Asymmetrical Handles, 37 x 72 In. 7480.00
Cabinet, Gothic Revival, Oak, 3/4 Gallery, Arch Side, c.1850, 49 1/2 x 24 1/2 In. 1610.00
Cabinet, Gothic Revival, Walnut, Trefoil Piercing, France, c.1850, 93 x 59 In. 5060.00
Cabinet, Gothic Revival, Walnut, Wrought Iron, 19th Century, 71 x 59 x 20 In. 1725.00
Cabinet, Gun, Louis XVI, Mahogany, Arched Crest, 1800s, 105 x 91 x 24 In. 5750.00
Cabinet, Hanging, Baroque Style, Faux Marble, Parcel Gilt, c.1880, 29 x 48 x 15 In. 575.00
Cabinet, Hanging, Dutch Baroque Style, Glazed Door, Domed Top, 39 x 7 x 31 In. 460.00
Cabinet, Hanging, G. Nakashima, Hunter Corp., c.1971, 104 x 18 x 18 1/4 In. 9775.00
Cabinet, Hanging, George III Style, Mahogany, 2 Mullioned Glass Doors, 39 x 27 In. 440.00
Cabinet, Hanging, P. Evans, 2 Doors, Sculpted, Abstract, c.1972, 36 x 24 x 12 In. 1765.00
Cabinet, Hanging, Walnut, Domed Top, Glazed Door, Dutch, 1700s, 33 x 34 In. 2645.00
Cabinet, Hardstone, Black Lacquer, Gilt, Chinese, c.1880, 67 x 34 x 15 In., Pair 1265.00
Cabinet, Harman, Glazed Wood, Glass Doors, Drawers, 69 1/2 x 39 x 17 In., 2 Piece 1530.00
Cabinet, Herter Bros., Mirror, 2 Doors, Inlay Panels, c.1880, 74 x 46 x 20 In. 2240.00
Cabinet, Hinoki Wood, Carved, 6 Half Shelves, Japan, c.1912, 87 1/2 x 48 x 17 In. 1265.00
Cabinet, Italian Rococo, Green Paint, Parcel Gilt, Lower Doors, 88 x 48 x 18 In. 5975.00
Cabinet, Jamestown, Square Top, Open Shelf, Lower Door, 28 x 24 x 24 In. 978.00
Cabinet, Jewelry, McCobb, Birch, Metal, 12 Drawers, 1952, 36 x 12 x 6 In. 1955.00
Cabinet, Jewelry, Papier-Mache, Mother-Of-Pearl, Abalone, 11 1/2 x 11 3/4 x 9 In. 980.00
Cabinet, L. & J.G. Stickley, No. 727, Oak, Door, Arch Aprons, 55 x 34 x 15 In. 4400.00
Cabinet, Lacquer, Black, Gilt, Mother-Of-Pearl, Prunus Trees, Chinese, 29 1/2 x 20 In. . . 375.00
Cabinet, Lacquer, Fowl, Flowers, 7 Drawers, Japan, c.1890, 14 1/2 x 13 In. 545.00
Cabinet, Lacquer, Mother-Of-Pearl, Figures, Birds, Flowers, Korea, c.1900, 57 x 33 In. . . 2350.00
Cabinet, Lacquer, Red Cinnabar Ground, Japan, c.1912, 57 1/2 x 48 1/2 x 19 In. 635.00
Cabinet, Leather Back, Paw Feet, Lion Masques, France, c.1900, 36 x 20 In. 1725.00
Cabinet, Liquor, Napoleon III, Glass, Gilt Bronze, 11 x 13 1/2 x 11 In. 780.00
Cabinet, Liquor, Neoclassical Revival, Mahogany, Fitted Interior 380.00
Cabinet, Loewy, DF2000, Wood, Laminate, Metal, Plastic, France, 1970s, 80 x 20 In. . . . 3450.00
Cabinet, Loewy, Walnut, Steel, 1948, 48 x 30 In. 290.00
Cabinet, Louis XV Style, Fruitwood, Gilt Bronze Mount, 37 x 60 x 19 In. 590.00
Cabinet, Louis XV Style, Fruitwood, Marble Top, Pierced Gallery, 31 x 24 x 16 In. 355.00
Cabinet, Louis XV Style, Oak, Drawer Over Door, 40 x 29 x 18 1/2 In. 705.00
Cabinet, Louis XV Style, Walnut, Mirror, Stand, 1700s, 71 x 55 x 20 In. 1880.00
Cabinet, Louis XV, Green Marble Top, Drawer, Cabriole Legs, 34 x 17 x 14 1/2 In., Pair . 2990.00
Cabinet, Louis XV, Kingwood, Marble Top, 3 Drawers Over 2 Doors, 39 x 60 In. 2300.00
Cabinet, Louis XV, Mahogany, Kingwood, Parquetry, c.1900, 69 x 64 x 20 In. 705.00
Cabinet, Louis XVI Style, Gilt Bronze, Kingwood, Gallery, 23 x 26 x 13 1/2 In. 380.00
Cabinet, Louis XVI Style, Kingwood, Gilt Metal Mounts, Compartments, 52 In. 1230.00
Cabinet, Louis XVI Style, Mahogany, Marble Top, c.1890, 30 1/2 x 39 In., Pair 2390.00
Cabinet, Louis XVI, Walnut, 20th Century, 31 x 21 x 11 In. 235.00
Cabinet, Mahogany, 9 Graduated Drawers Behind Glass Panel Door, 26 x 20 In. 770.00
Cabinet, Mahogany, Bowfront, Mirror Back, 4 Shelves, Paw Feet, 62 x 19 x 42 In. 575.00
Cabinet, Mahogany, Demilune Top, Frieze Drawer, 19th Century, 32 x 31 x 15 In. 2990.00
Cabinet, Mahogany, Marble Top, Mirror, 2 Drawers, Carved Pilasters, c.1850, 79 x 59 In. . 620.00
Cabinet, Mahogany, Rosewood, Spanish Brass, Ebony Veneer, 1830, 46 x 54 In. 5960.00
Cabinet, Mahogany, Step Back, 4 Doors, Carved Columns, Claw Feet, c.1880, 69 x 73 In. 1960.00
Cabinet, Marquetry, Early 20th Century, 33 x 16 1/4 x 42 3/4 In. 3300.00
Cabinet, Marquetry, Lacquer, Brass Mounted, Mother-Of-Pearl, 1800s, 43 x 31 x 15 In. . . 460.00
Cabinet, McCobb, Birch, Nickel, 2 Doors, 1950, 24 x 34 In. 690.00
Cabinet, McCobb, Birch, Nickel, 4 Drawers, 1950, 36 x 66 In. 1035.00
Cabinet, McCobb, Perimeter Group, Birch, 2 Doors, Winchedon, 54 x 15 x 29 In. 1610.00
Cabinet, McCobb, Planner Group, Birch, Chrome, Winchedon, 72 x 18 x 33 1/2 In. 1840.00
Cabinet, McCobb, Walnut, Leather Doors, 42 x 18 x 34 1/4 In. 115.00
Cabinet, Music, Cherry, Carved Panels, Lion's Head Pulls, c.1870, 37 x 22 x 16 In. 3920.00
Cabinet, Music, G. Stickley, Mahogany, Japanese Design Inlay, 20 x 17 x 48 In. 18400.00
Cabinet, Music, Mahogany, Mirror, Lion's Head Crest, c.1890, 61 x 25 x 16 In. 1400.00
Cabinet, Music, Napoleon III, Mahogany, Pierced Gallery, Plaques, 48 x 28 x 13 In. 777.00

Cabinet, Music, Oak, Serpentine Front Door, Scroll Carvings, 1900s, 22 x 16 x 40 In. 230.00
Cabinet, Napoleon III Style, Kingwood, Mahogany, Brass Inlay, c.1900, 33 x 37 x 18 In. . 865.00
Cabinet, Napoleon III, Boulle, Marble, Drawer, 41 1/2 x 44 x 18 In. 1645.00
Cabinet, Napoleon III, Ebonized, Gilt Bronze, Marble Top, Brass Inlay, 39 x 28 x 16 In. . 1075.00
Cabinet, Napoleon III, Ebonized, Velvet Lining, c.1865, 45 x 34 In., Pair 3680.00
Cabinet, Napoleon III, Mahogany, Brass Mounted, c.1890, 98 x 58 x 19 1/2 In. 4600.00
Cabinet, Napoleon III, Mahogany, Parquet, Cornice, 19th Century, 70 x 56 x 19 In. 6040.00
Cabinet, Napoleon III, Rosewood, Ebonized, Carved, Birds, 1800s, 49 x 45 x 20 In. 2300.00
Cabinet, Neoclassical, Mahogany, Rosewood, Demilune, Drawers, 36 x 61 x 25 In. 9200.00
Cabinet, Oak, 2 Drawers, 2 Paneled Doors, Openwork Hinges, Dutch, 1910, 64 x 42 In. ... 3370.00
Cabinet, Oak, 2 Sections, Carved Lions, Heads, 82 x 31 1/2 x 16 In. 1150.00
Cabinet, Oak, 3 Paneled Doors, Interior Shelves, Shaped Feet, Dutch, 1920s, 46 x 63 In. . 1685.00
Cabinet, Oak, Roll-Up Door, 17 Rosewood Drawers, Velvet Lining, 12 1/2 x 15 x 16 In. . 450.00
Cabinet, Oak, Rosewood, 2 Paneled Doors Over Shelf, Shaped Feet, 32 x 26 In. 840.00
Cabinet, P. Evans, Brass, Copper Patchwork, Bifold Door, 41 x 48 x 21 1/2 In. 1645.00
Cabinet, P. Evans, Cityscape, Patchwork Chrome, Directional, 90 x 22 x 32 In. 1725.00
Cabinet, Paine Furniture Co., Mahogany Veneer, Drawer, 32 x 31 In., Pair 1495.00
Cabinet, Painted, 11 Panels, Buddhist Emblems, Tibet, 39 x 41 x 16 In. 2300.00
Cabinet, Piero Fornasetti, Architectura, Painted, 2 Doors, Tapered Brass Legs, 1950 ..... 4885.00
Cabinet, Pine, Painted, Drawer Over Door, 19th Century, 34 x 26 x 13 In. 115.00
Cabinet, Polychrome, 2 Paneled Cupboards, England, 42 x 44 x 25 1/2 In. 1035.00
Cabinet, Polychrome, Lotus-Form Cartouche, Tibet, c.1810, 39 x 49 x 18 In. 1410.00
Cabinet, Prairie School, 2 Doors, Slatted Overlay, Geometric Design, 45 x 62 In. 2070.00
Cabinet, Prayer, Tibet, 21 x 15 x 12 In. 850.00
Cabinet, Print, George Niedecken, Fir, 2 Leaded Glass Doors, 48 x 33 x 77 In. 6325.00
Cabinet, Red Lacquer Front, Black Sides, Butterflies, Chinese, 47 1/2 x 31 In. 750.00
Cabinet, Red, Gilt Lacquer, 2 Doors, 2 Shelves, Flower Vases, Qing Dynasty, 78 x 48 In. . 1035.00
Cabinet, Regency, Black Granite Top, 2 Doors, Bronze Grillwork, Fitted Interior, 48 In. . 520.00
Cabinet, Regency, Mahogany, 2 Tiers, Over Brass Inset Door, 53 x 25 In., Pair 2940.00
Cabinet, Regency, Mahogany, Fabric Panel Insets, 43 1/2 x 44 x 19 In. 2390.00
Cabinet, Renaissance Revival, 2 Drawers, 2 Doors, Shell, Paw Feet, 57 x 20 x 49 In. 6900.00
Cabinet, Renaissance Revival, Marble Top, 2 Recessed-Panel Doors, Plinth Base, 37 In. . 590.00
Cabinet, Renaissance Revival, Walnut, Mid 19th Century, 42 x 46 x 24 In. 460.00
Cabinet, Risom, Primavera, 1950s, 42 x 32 In. ....920.00 to 1265.00
Cabinet, Robsjohn-Gibbings, Fruitwood, Vitrine, Widdicomb, 1950s, 78 x 70 x 17 In. 1435.00
Cabinet, Rohde, Walnut, 3 Drawers, Leatherette Upholstered Fronts, 35 x 44 In. 4315.00
Cabinet, Rosewood, Bone Inlay, 4 Doors, Peacocks, Trees, Anglo-Indian, 72 In. 1880.00
Cabinet, Rosewood, Marquetry, Frieze, 1 Door, Shelves, Ormolu Columns, 16 x 12 x 4 In. 655.00
Cabinet, Saarinen, Birch, 4 Drawers, Aluminum Pulls, 30 x 34 In., Pair 6900.00
Cabinet, Sheraton Style, Burl Walnut, Marquetry, Bowfront, 63 x 41 x 16 In. 1295.00
Cabinet, Sheraton Style, Satinwood, Burl Walnut, Marquetry, 33 x 41 x 18 In. 1060.00
Cabinet, Smoking, Arts & Crafts, Door, Toe Boards, 33 x 20 x 17 1/2 In. 375.00
Cabinet, Smoking, G. Stickley, No. 78, Oak, 1912-1916, 28 3/4 x 20 x 15 In. 5020.00
Cabinet, Smoking, Oak, Royal Ciphers, 3 Drawers, Cigar Cutter, c.1900, 11 x 9 In. 375.00
Cabinet, Spice, Mahogany, Fruitwood, Inlaid Door, 8 Interior Drawers, 18 x 12 In. 635.00
Cabinet, Spice, Polychrome, Bracket Feet, Mediterranean, 24 x 20 x 13 In. 865.00
Cabinet, Stuart Style, Oak, Hinged Top, 17th-Century Design, 34 3/4 x 29 x 16 1/2 In. ... 290.00
Cabinet, Tudor Style, 2 Doors, Turned Legs, Stretcher, 44 x 12 x 44 1/2 In. 320.00
Cabinet, Victorian, Rosewood, Marble, Drawers, 27 x 18 x 17 In. 1645.00
Cabinet, Victorian, Walnut, Burl, Ormolu, Marquetry, c.1875, 42 x 33 x 12 1/4 In. 920.00
Cabinet, Victorian, Walnut, Carved, Glass Door, c.1885, 73 x 50 x 15 In. 1960.00
Cabinet, Victorian, Walnut, Marble, Serpentine Top, 4 Mirrored Doors, 34 In. 530.00
Cabinet, Walnut, Aesthetic Revival, 4 Side Shelves, Decorated Trim, 57 x 48 In. 1850.00
Cabinet, Walnut, Crossbanded, Rectangular Frieze, Brass Door, Ormolu, 41 x 13 x 33 In. . 875.00
Cabinet, Walnut, Floral Marquetry, 2 Panel Doors, Dutch, c.1790, 36 x 41 In. 330.00
Cabinet, Walnut, Parquetry, Continental, 20th Century, 64 x 43 1/2 x 19 1/2 In. 705.00
Cabinet, Wegner, Teak, Brushed Steel, Cube Bar, Tuck, Denmark, 1950s, 19 3/4 In. 6900.00
Cabinet, Wegner, Teak, Hinged Top, Cube, 1950s, 19 3/4 x 19 3/4 In. 3335.00
Cabinet-On-Chest, Baroque, Parquetry, Walnut, 1700s, 80 1/2 x 49 1/2 x 21 1/2 In. 4600.00
Cabinet-On-Stand, Baroque Style, Lacquer, Oriental Design, 68 x 50 x 19 In. 765.00
Cabinet-On-Stand, Corner, Federal, Mahogany, Satinwood, c.1910, 84 x 38 x 20 In., Pair . 2760.00
Cabinet-On-Stand, Corner, George III, Inlaid Oak, 18th Century, 72 x 36 x 20 1/2 In. 460.00
Cabinet-On-Stand, Edwardian, Mahogany, Carved, c.1900, 76 1/2 x 30 1/2 x 17 1/2 In. . 1840.00

Cabinet-On-Stand, George III Style, Mahogany, Dentil Crown, 3 Doors, 79 x 60 x 16 In. . 3050.00
Cabinet-On-Stand, George III, Black Lacquer, Gilt Asian Landscapes, 63 x 38 1/4 In. 575.00
Cabinet-On-Stand, George III, Mahogany, Inlaid, Flowers, 35 x 22 3/4 x 8 7/16 In. 1135.00
Cabinet-On-Stand, Oriental, Bone Carvings, Enamel, Meiji Era, c.1880, 86 x 59 x 15 In. . 3910.00
Cabinet-On-Stand, Queen Anne, Black Lacquer, Domed, 2 Doors, 74 x 36 x 18 In. 3450.00
Candlestand, American Maple, Rustic, Tripod, 19th Century, 28 3/4 x 20 3/4 In. 29.00
Candlestand, Arts & Crafts Style, Iron, Geometric Arms, Twisted Shaft, 42 In., Pair 169.00
Candlestand, Birch, Maple, Urn Pedestal, Snake Feet, 27 3/4 x 14 3/4 x 15 3/8 In. 1870.00
Candlestand, Black Paint, Octagonal Top, Cabriole Legs, New Hampshire 3300.00
Candlestand, Bronze, Hearts, Art Glass Shade, Marked, 20th Century, 21 3/4 In. 120.00
Candlestand, Cherry Shaft, Adjustable Arm, Ring Turned Burl Base, c.1780, 29 In. 9000.00
Candlestand, Cherry, Circular Top, Rhode Island, 18th Century, 27 3/4 In. 1060.00
Candlestand, Cherry, Maple, Cut Corners, Turned Pedestal, Spider Base, 30 In. 375.00
Candlestand, Cherry, Rectangular Top, Curved Corner, c.1820, 27 3/4 In. 1175.00
Candlestand, Cherry, Serpentine Legs, 1-Board Top, 17 x 27 3/4 In. 250.00
Candlestand, Cherry, Square Top, Baluster Post, Tripod Cabriole Leg, 27 x 16 x 17 In. .. 3400.00
Candlestand, Cherry, Square Top, Vase & Ring Turned Post, Cabriole Leg Base, 26 In. .. 1115.00
Candlestand, Cherry, Tripod Cabriole Leg Base, 18th Century, 13 3/4 In. 590.00
Candlestand, Cherry, Turned Column, 3 Tapered Legs, c.1835, 27 x 16 x 18 In. 565.00
Candlestand, Chippendale Style, Beech, Mahogany, c.1800, 27 x 19 x 17 In. 765.00
Candlestand, Chippendale Style, Mahogany, Inlaid, Tilt Top, Tripod Base, 28 1/2 In. ... 195.00
Candlestand, Chippendale, Birch, Maple, Urn Column, New England, 15 x 15 x 26 In. .. 2090.00
Candlestand, Chippendale, Cherry, Cabriole Legs, Beaded Edges, 20 x 27 3/4 In. 470.00
Candlestand, Chippendale, Cherry, Tilt Top, Tripod Base, 1-Board Top, 23 x 17 x 28 In. . 220.00
Candlestand, Chippendale, Mahogany, Birdcage 1410.00
Candlestand, Chippendale, Mahogany, Marble, Pierced Gallery, c.1780, 27 x 18 In. 3825.00
Candlestand, Chippendale, Mahogany, Tilt Top, Cabriole Legs, Snake Feet, 22 x 27 In. .. 330.00
Candlestand, Chippendale, Mahogany, Tilt Top, Tripod Base, c.1780, 27 x 19 In. 635.00
Candlestand, Chippendale, Walnut, Birdcage, 19th Century, 27 x 20 In. 6756.00
Candlestand, Curly Maple, Tilt Top, Ball Feet, Turned Post, 21 x 16 x 28 In. 440.00
Candlestand, Federal, Birch, Octagonal, Tripod Base, c.1795, 27 x 14 3/4 x 14 In. 520.00
Candlestand, Federal, Birch, Tilt Top, Tripod, c.1820, 27 3/4 x 25 1/2 x 16 3/4 In. 430.00
Candlestand, Federal, Blue Paint, Urn Post, Pad Feet, c.1800, 24 x 15 3/4 In. 1060.00
Candlestand, Federal, Cherry Inlay, Bird's-Eye Maple Panel, Tilt Top, 29 x 14 x 18 In. .. 1060.00
Candlestand, Federal, Cherry, Octagonal, Tripod Base, c.1805, 27 x 17 x 16 3/4 In. 259.00
Candlestand, Federal, Cherry, Square Top, 3 Legs, 26 x 15 1/2 x 15 In. 320.00
Candlestand, Federal, Cherry, Turned Baluster, 19th Century, 21 x 17 1/2 x 30 In. 175.00
Candlestand, Federal, Fruitwood, Tilt Top, c.1800, 25 1/2 x 18 1/2 In. 1320.00
Candlestand, Federal, Mahogany, Maple Inlay, Tilt Top, Tripod Stand, c.1800, 29 x 20 In. 2070.00
Candlestand, Federal, Mahogany, Tilt Top, Serpentine Cut Corners, 27 x 23 x 17 In. 495.00
Candlestand, Federal, Mahogany, Tilt Top, Turned Support, c.1800, 29 x 21 x 16 In. 2940.00
Candlestand, Federal, Mahogany, Tilt Top, Turned Support, c.1810, 27 x 14 1/2 x 2 In. .. 3350.00
Candlestand, Federal, Mahogany, Tilt Top, Urn Pedestal, Spider Legs, 29 x 21 x 16 In. .. 440.00
Candlestand, Federal, Mahogany, Tilt Top, Urn Shaft, 28 x 24 x 18 In. 230.00
Candlestand, Federal, Maple, Cherry, Tripod, c.1800, 26 1/2 x 17 1/2 x 18 In. 430.00
Candlestand, Federal, Tiger Maple, Lozenge-Shaped Top, Tripod Base, c.1835, 26 In. ... 460.00
Candlestand, Floral Stencil, Baluster-Turned Post, Curved Legs, c.1820, 22 x 28 In. 480.00
Candlestand, George II, Mahogany, Dish Top, c.1760, 25 x 14 In. 2630.00
Candlestand, George III Style, Mahogany, Tripod, c.1950, 28 x 18 In. 520.00
Candlestand, Hepplewhite, Bird's-Eye Maple, Coffin Top, Pedestal, 27 1/2 x 18 In. 840.00
Candlestand, Hepplewhite, Black Swirls, Red Base, Spider Legs, 27 x 18 1/2 x 18 In. ... 345.00
Candlestand, Hepplewhite, Cherry, Birdcage, Tripod Base, Medallion Feet, 24 1/2 In. ... 1100.00
Candlestand, Hepplewhite, Cherry, Tilt Top, Tripod, Saber Legs, 23 x 16 x 27 1/2 In. ... 306.00
Candlestand, Hepplewhite, Curly Maple, Tripod Base, Spade Feet, 21 x 15 x 28 In. 2750.00
Candlestand, Hepplewhite, Mahogany, Tilt Top, Spider Legs, 22 x 16 x 28 In. 495.00
Candlestand, Hepplewhite, Maple, Birch, Tilt Top, Inlay, Spider Base, 18 x 15 x 29 In. .. 825.00
Candlestand, Hepplewhite, Maple, Spider Legs, Turned Column 330.00
Candlestand, Hepplewhite, Walnut, Tilt Top, Greek Key Inlay, Spider Base, 28 x 20 In. .. 770.00
Candlestand, Jacobean Style, Round Top, Rope-Twist Shaft, Cross-Footed Base, 29 In. .. 115.00
Candlestand, Louis XVI, Mahogany, Lacquered, Hexagon Standard, 27 3/4 x 12 In. 11950.00
Candlestand, Mahogany, Line Inlay, Square Top, Tripod Base, 27 x 20 x 20 1/2 In. 750.00
Candlestand, Mahogany, Tilt Top, Cabriole Legs, Turned Columns, 22 x 17 x 26 In. 330.00
Candlestand, Mahogany, Tilt Top, Curved Legs, 27 3/4 x 22 1/2 x 18 1/2 In. 230.00

Candlestand, Mahogany, Tilt Top, Turtle Top, Pedestal, Paw Feet, 28 1/2 x 27 x 20 In. . . . 1840.00
Candlestand, Mahogany, Tilt Top, Urn Turned Pedestal, Tripod Feet, c.1810 . . . . 635.00
Candlestand, Maple, Molded Edge, Baluster Post, 18th Century, 25 x 16 x 16 In. 1530.00
Candlestand, Maple, Sausage Shaft, Rosehead Nails, New England, 11 1/2 x 12 In. 39.00
Candlestand, Maple, Spider Legs, Urn Shaft, New England, Early 1800s 405.00
Candlestand, Maple, Square Top, Round Corners, Scrolled Legs, c.1815-1825, 17 1/4 In. . . 1060.00
Candlestand, Maple, Tripod Base, Saber Legs, 19th Century, 30 x 20 x 19 In. 825.00
Candlestand, Octagonal Top, Turned Baluster, Scratch Beaded, c.1835, 26 x 20 x 19 In. . . 940.00
Candlestand, Oval Piecrust Top, Cabriole Legs, Pad Feet, 20 1/2 x 15 1/2 x 27 In. 730.00
Candlestand, Queen Anne Style, Mahogany, Cherry, New England, 18 In. 280.00
Candlestand, Queen Anne Style, Mahogany, Dish Top, 27 x 18 In. 200.00
Candlestand, Queen Anne Style, Mahogany, Walnut, Tilt Top, 28 x 22 x 15 In., Pair 485.00
Candlestand, Queen Anne, Cherry, Connecticut, c.1740, 26 1/2 x 20 In. 520.00
Candlestand, Queen Anne, Mahogany, Inlaid, Tilt Top, Early 20th Century, 27 x 22 In. . . 115.00
Candlestand, Queen Anne, Mahogany, Tilt Top, Urn Turned Post, Tripod, 27 x 22 In. 630.00
Candlestand, Queen Anne, Red Paint, Octagonal Top, Urn Pedestal 1100.00
Candlestand, Queen Anne, Round Dish Top, Star Inlay, Turned Post, 28 x 15 In. 920.00
Candlestand, Regency, Lacquerware, Black, Gilt, Octagonal, Tripod Base, 30 x 16 In. . . . 605.00
Candlestand, Regency, Mahogany, Tilt Top, Tripod Base, 24 x 17 1/2 x 28 In. 495.00
Candlestand, Shaker, Butternut, Maple, Round Top, Watervliet, N.Y., c.1845, 24 In. 1495.00
Candlestand, Shaker, Cherry, Square Top, Spider Legs, Hancock, Mass., c.1830, 26 In. . . 1150.00
Candlestand, Shaker, Cherry, Turned Column, Spider Base, South Union, Ky., 16 x 28 In. 770.00
Candlestand, Sheraton, Mixed Wood, Turned Pedestal, Sawn Feet, 26 x 17 In. 545.00
Candlestand, Softwood, Black Paint, Octagonal Top, Tripod, New England, 11 In. 11.00
Candlestand, Tilt Top, Acanthus Carved Base, Paw Feet, American, 27 1/4 x 22 In. 690.00
Candlestand, Tilt Top, Tripod, Round, 3 Snake Feet, 26 x 17 1/2 x 17 3/4 In. 290.00
Candlestand, Transitional To Hepplewhite, Mahogany, Tilt Top, 22 x 16 x 29 In. 550.00
Candlestand, Victorian, Mahogany, Brass Handle, c.1880, 40 x 27 3/4 In. 2030.00
Candlestand, Victorian, Walnut, Dish Top, Stag Head, Eastlake Style Legs, 32 1/2 In. . . . 85.00
Candlestand, Walnut, Rectangular Top, Spider Legs, Pennsylvania 169.00
Candlestand, Walnut, Round, Tilt Top, Birdcage Pedestal, Tripod Base, 30 x 22 In. 2250.00
Candlestand, Walnut, Tilt Top, Oval, Cabriole Legs, Pad Feet, Pennsylvania 900.00
Candlestand, Walnut, Tripod, Turned Pedestal, Saber Legs, 27 1/2 x 21 1/2 x 21 3/4 In. . . 550.00
Candlestand, William & Mary, Maple, Red Paint, c.1750, 43 1/4 In. 3585.00
Candlestand, William & Mary, Oak, Walnut, Octagonal, Barley-Twist Stem, 27 x 14 In. . . 1410.00
Candlestand, Wrought Iron, Swivel Arm, Urn Finial, Tripod Base, Early 1800s, 60 In. . . . 2750.00
Cane Holder, Painted, Sailor, Dolphins, Rope, Anchor, Iron, 27 x 16 In. 750.00
Canterbury, Burled Walnut, Ornately Carved Divider Panels, Drawer Base, 20 In. 670.00
Canterbury, George IV, Mahogany, Curved Splats, Drawer, c.1820, 21 x 21 x 16 In. 4480.00
Canterbury, Mahogany, Brass Mounted, 4 Slots, Drawer, England, 25 x 19 x 15 In. 575.00
Canterbury, Mahogany, Slats, 3 Sections, Brass Caps & Casters, 22 x 14 In. 250.00
Canterbury, Regency Style, Mahogany, 4 Sections, 2 Drawers, 15 1/2 x 19 1/4 In. 375.00
Canterbury, Regency Style, Mahogany, 4 Sections, Handle, 23 1/2 x 18 1/2 In. 316.00
Canterbury, Regency Style, Mahogany, X-Form Sides, 3 Sections, Base Drawer 880.00
Canterbury, Regency, Ebonized Wood, Inlaid Mahogany, c.1810, 21 x 21 x 13 In. 1840.00
Canterbury, Regency, Mahogany, 4 Sections, Drawer, Shaped Feet, 25 x 19 In. 290.00
Canterbury, Rosewood, 4 Dividers, Drawer, Brass Casters, 19 x 20 x 15 In. 1020.00
Canterbury, Sheraton, Mahogany, 4 Sections, Drawer, Mushroom Finials, 20 In. 990.00
Canterbury, Victorian, Mahogany, Base Drawer, c.1885, 20 x 21 x 15 In. 1790.00
Canterbury, Victorian, Turned Supports, 17 1/2 x 17 x 14 In. 705.00
Cart, Serving, Scandinavian, Chrome-Plated Steel, 3 Rosewood Trays, 29 x 18 x 24 In. . . 127.00
Cellarette, Federal, Mahogany, Sarcophagus, Brass Handles, Splayed Feet, 22 x 26 In. . . 6570.00
Cellarette, G. Stickley, Door, Drawer, Pullout Shelf, 39 1/2 x 22 x 16 In. 4315.00
Cellarette, George III Style, Mahogany, Rosewood, Stand, 1800s, 30 x 32 x 21 In. 635.00
Cellarette, George III, Mahogany Inlay, Brass Bail Handles, 26 x 19 x 12 1/2 In. 1910.00
Cellarette, George IV, Mahogany, Hinged Lid, Paw Feet, 21 x 25 x 19 In. 4855.00
Cellarette, Hepplewhite, Mahogany, 4 Sections, Stand, 10 x 10 x 26 In. 468.00
Cellarette, L. & J.G. Stickley, 2 Doors, Arched Backsplash, Shelf, 36 x 32 x 16 In. 13800.00
Cellarette, L. & J.G. Stickley, Drawer, Pullout Copper Shelf, 40 x 22 x 16 In. 2070.00
Cellarette, Lakeside Craft Shop, Oak, Tray, Stained Glass Panel, 29 x 17 x 12 In. 499.00
Cellarette, Lifetime Furniture Co., Slant Front, Copper Tray Inside, 22 x 14 x 43 In. 2400.00
Cellarette, Mahogany, Carved, Brass, Tin Lining, Philadelphia, c.1815, 21 1/2 In. 6570.00
Cellarette, Mahogany, Hinged Lid, Grape Crest, Sections, Bun Feet, 21 x 23 x 28 In. 1675.00

Cellarette, Mahogany, Round, Turned Legs, England, 1800s, 28 x 19 In. 635.00
Cellarette, Satinwood, Inlay, Hinged Lid, Sections, England, 19 x 20 In. 3286.00
Cellarette, Sheraton, Cherry, Inlaid, Hinges, Sections, c.1800, 29 x 18 x 13 1/2 In. 3878.00
Cellarette, Shop Of The Crafters, Painted Door, Monk, Shelf, 23 x 17 x 63 In. 2070.00
Chair, A. Dubreuil, Bent, Welded Steel, France, 1988, 24 1/2 x 33 In. 5175.00
Chair, A. Girard, No. 66307, Aluminum, Wool, Arms, Herman Miller, 24 x 28 In., Pair . . . 4310.00
Chair, A.J. Donahue, Metal Frame, Upholstered, Wooden Ball Feet, 1949, 30 In., Pair . . . 4310.00
Chair, Aalto, Arms, Artek, c.1937, 32 x 24 1/2 x 19 In. 2115.00
Chair, Aalto, Lounge, Artek, c.1937, 32 1/2 x 23 3/4 x 30 In. 1765.00
Chair, Aalto, Molded Birch, Black Webbed Seat, Arms, Artek, 34 x 24 x 26 1/2 In. 530.00
Chair, Aalto, Molded Birch, Webbed Seat, Artek, 23 x 29 x 39 In. 400.00
Chair, Aalto, No. 31, Laminated, Lacquered, Birch, Artek, Finland, 1940s, 24 x 23 In. . . . 3740.00
Chair, Aalto, No. 33, Arms, c.1932 . . . . 6000.00
Chair, Aalto, No. 37, Birch Arms, Putty Fabric, Finland, c.1935, 25 x 34 In. 1880.00
Chair, Aalto, Pension, Birch Frame, Cotton Webbing, ICF, Finland, 24 x 29 x 33 In. 345.00
Chair, Acanthine Crest, Lyre Splat, Saber Legs, Arms, 19th Century, 36 1/2 In., Pair 3680.00
Chair, Adirondack, Twig & Bark, Painted 115.00
Chair, Aesthetic Revival, Maple, Faux Bamboo, Arms, France, c.1885, 39 In. 2300.00
Chair, Allan Gould, Walnut, Vinyl, Herman Miller, 1950s, 20 x 27 1/2 In. 130.00
Chair, Aluminum, Tubular, 3 Horizontal Slats, Leather Seat, 33 1/2 x 18 In., Pair 1645.00
Chair, Arne Jacobsen, Ant, Black Molded Plywood, 3 Steel Legs, Denmark, 30 In., Pair . . 410.00
Chair, Arne Jacobsen, Chrome, Tubular Frame, Upholstered Seat, 28 x 30 In. . . . . . . *Illus* 1115.00
Chair, Arne Jacobsen, Egg, Fritz Hansen, c.1958, 41 x 30 3/4 In. 2350.00
Chair, Arne Jacobsen, Series 7, Fritz Hansen, c.1955, 29 1/2 x 24 1/4 x 17 In., Pair 355.00
Chair, Arne Jacobsen, Swan, Foam, Fiberglass, Fritz Hansen, 30 x 27 x 30 In. 575.00
Chair, Arne Jacobsen, Tubular Chrome, Upholstered, Fritz Hansen, 28 x 28 x 30 In. 1115.00
Chair, Art Deco, Barrel Back, Upholstered, Blond Wood Base, 27 x 29 In., Pair 1530.00
Chair, Art Deco, Bronze, Crackle, Arms, France, c.1935, Pair 4180.00
Chair, Art Deco, Burl, Fluted Exterior, Velvet Upholstery, Arms, Pair 1555.00
Chair, Art Deco, Fruitwood, Arched Back, Gilt Carved Leaf Panel, Upholstered, Pair 3055.00
Chair, Art Deco, Leather, Cushions, Closed Flared Arms, 32 x 40 In., Pair 750.00
Chair, Art Deco, Mahogany, Gilt Bronze, Brass, France, c.1930, 35 1/2 x 24 1/2 In. 2530.00
Chair, Art Deco, Mahogany, Pearl Leather, Swivel, France, c.1930, 34 x 24 In. 2300.00
Chair, Art Deco, Mahogany, Wool, Arms, France, c.1930, 32 1/2 In., Pair . . . . . .5290.00 to 5750.00
Chair, Art Deco, Palissandre, Pearl Leather, Arms, France, c.1930, 33 x 23 In., Pair 4140.00
Chair, Art Deco, Walnut, Leather, Arms, France, c.1930, 31 x 36 In., Pair 4370.00
Chair, Art Deco, Walnut, Pearl Leather, Arms, France, c.1930, 30 x 21 1/2 In., Pair 4830.00
Chair, Art Deco, Walnut, Pearl Leather, Brass Nail Heads, France, c.1930, 28 x 21 In. 1380.00
Chair, Art Deco, Walnut, Upholstered, Arms, France, c.1930, 32 x 32 1/2 In., Pair 5750.00
Chair, Art Deco, Wrought Iron, Parcel Gilt, Leather Seat & Back, c.1925, Pair 6570.00
Chair, Art Nouveau, Mahogany, Floral Carved Back & Legs, Arms, 37 In. 785.00
Chair, Art Nouveau, Mahogany, Upholstered, Slat Back, Arms, 37 x 23 x 23 In. 355.00
Chair, Arts & Crafts, Carved Quatrefoil, Slatted, Paddle Arms, 37 1/2 x 33 x 23 In. 1150.00
Chair, Arts & Crafts, Carved, Reticulated Back, Seat Rail, Upholstered, 19 x 20 x 54 In. . . 865.00
Chair, Arts & Crafts, Chestnut, Posts, Stretchers, Triangular, Arms, 37 x 23 x 19 In. 1150.00
Chair, Arts & Crafts, Mahogany, Semicircular Backrest, Openwork, Inlaid, 31 In. 505.00
Chair, Arts & Crafts, Oak, Arched Crest Rail, 2 Slats, Cushion Seat, Arms, 36 In. 150.00

Furniture, Chair, Arne Jacobsen, Chrome,
Tubular Frame, Upholstered Seat, 28 x 30 In.

Furniture, Chair, Arne
Jacobsen, Swan,
Upholstered, Aluminum,
Swivels, Fritz Hansen,
34 x 29 x 25 In.

Chair, Arts & Crafts, Oak, Arms, Upholstered Pad, England, c.1900, 51 1/2 x 24 In. 1060.00
Chair, Arts & Crafts, Oak, Cane Back, Seat, Arms, England, 29 1/4 x 20 In. 1880.00
Chair, Arts & Crafts, Oak, Crest Rail, 3 Slats, Stretchers, 39 x 27 x 23 3/4 In. 235.00
Chair, Arts & Crafts, Oak, Curved Crest Rail, 5 Slats, Offset Front, 39 x 25 x 19 In. 470.00
Chair, Arts & Crafts, Oak, Curved Crest, 8 Spindles, Leather Seat, c.1910, 41 x 18 In. . . . 765.00
Chair, Arts & Crafts, Oak, Openwork Backrest, Japanese Feudal Design, 42 In., Pair 539.00
Chair, Arts & Crafts, Shield Crest Rail, Leather Seat, Panel, 37 1/2 x 16 x 16 In. 1610.00
Chair, Arts & Crafts, Square Posts, Leather Cushions, 38 x 26 x 27 1/2 In. 145.00
Chair, Ash, Black Paint, Slat Back, Scrolled Arms, Turned Legs, 46 1/2 x 16 In. 2705.00
Chair, Banister Back, Black Paint, 18th Century, 17 1/4 In. 470.00
Chair, Banister Back, Black Paint, Carved, Pierced Crest, Rush Seat, 44 x 17 In. 9400.00
Chair, Banister Back, Black Paint, Double Arched Crest, Paper Rush Seat, 42 In. 275.00
Chair, Banister Back, Painted, Crest Over 4-Split Banister, 18th Century, 47 In. 1295.00
Chair, Banister Back, Painted, Sausage-Turned Legs, Stretcher, 16 1/2 x 39 1/2 In. 880.00
Chair, Banister Back, Red Paint, Shaped Crest, 4 Split Spindles, Double Stretchers, 42 In. 265.00
Chair, Banister Back, Rosette & Scroll Cut Crest, Gold Trim, Rush Seat, 44 In. 920.00
Chair, Banister Back, Shaped Crest, Turned Stiles, American 260.00
Chair, Baroque Style, Beech, Needlepoint Upholstery, Arms 1020.00
Chair, Baroque Style, Fruitwood, Needlepoint Upholstery, Arms, Pair 1530.00
Chair, Baroque Style, Walnut, Carved, Pierced Leaves, Velvet 359.00
Chair, Baroque Style, Walnut, Carved, Upholstered, Italy, Pair 990.00
Chair, Baroque, Walnut, Carved Arms, Stretcher, Upholstered, Italy, Pair 9560.00
Chair, Beech, Cane, Kidney Seat, Barrel Back, France 440.00
Chair, Beech, Coral Velvet, Arms, Venice, c.1865, 31 In., Pair 865.00
Chair, Beech, Gray Linen, Arms, Italy, c.1785, 35 1/2 In. 230.00
Chair, Belter, Henry Clay, Laminated, Carved, Pair 4620.00
Chair, Belter, Rosalie Without Grapes, Rosewood, Open Arms, 43 x 23 x 20 In. 3740.00
Chair, Belter, Rosalie, Rosewood Laminate, Grapes, Low Arms, 44 In. 4140.00
Chair, Belter, Rosalie, Rosewood, Damask Upholstery, c.1850, 38 In., Pair 2800.00
Chair, Belter, Rosewood, Bird Pattern, Open Arms, 46 x 25 1/2 In. 6040.00
Chair, Belter, Rosewood, Carved Fruit, C-Scrolls, Tufted Seat, 45 In. 5465.00
Chair, Belter, Rosewood, Pierced & Carved Grapes, Oak Leaves, 44 In. 8625.00
Chair, Belter, Rosewood, Pierced, Laminated, Arms, 47 1/2 x 26 1/2 In. 6325.00
Chair, Belter, Rosewood, Pierced, Laminated, Carved, 46 1/2 x 25 1/2 In. 2875.00
Chair, Belter, Rosewood, Tuthill King Pattern, 38 x 21 In. . . . . .6900.00 to 7475.00
Chair, Belter, Rosewood, Tuthill King Pattern, Upholstered Arms, 46 1/2 x 24 1/2 In. 8050.00
Chair, Belter, Slipper, Walnut, Oval Upholstered Back, Carved, 40 In. 200.00
Chair, Ben Schulten, Teal Suede, Dowel Legs, Arms, Artek, 30 x 25 x 28 In. 380.00
Chair, Bergere, Art Deco, Tufted Asymmetrical Back, Velvet, Fringe, 36 In., Pair 4370.00
Chair, Bergere, Beech, Carved, Serpentine Front, Fluted Tapered Legs, c.1900 . . . . 315.00
Chair, Bergere, Directoire, Fruitwood, Overscrolled Back, Arms, Early 1800s, 33 In. 2390.00
Chair, Bergere, Empire, Mahogany, Cushion Seat, Closed Arms, Early 1800s, 37 In. 3825.00
Chair, Bergere, Empire, Mahogany, Outscrolled Crest Rail, Closed Arms, c.1810, 30 In. . . 4780.00
Chair, Bergere, French Provincial, Walnut, Closed Arms, Damask Upholstery, Pair 1150.00
Chair, Bergere, Louis XIV Style, Giltwood, Closed Arms, Dolphin Feet, 1800s, 35 In. . . . 1095.00
Chair, Bergere, Louis XIV Style, Giltwood, Scrolled, Closed Arms, 35 1/2 In., Pair 1265.00
Chair, Bergere, Louis XV Style, Fruitwood, Cane, Carved Back & Arms, Cushion 365.00
Chair, Bergere, Louis XV Style, Gilt Frame, Floral Carved, France 290.00
Chair, Bergere, Louis XV Style, Gilt, Carved Wood, Upholstered, Child's 999.00
Chair, Bergere, Louis XV Style, Lacquer, Gilt, Carved, France 365.00
Chair, Bergere, Louis XV Style, Upholstered, Early 20th Century 1035.00
Chair, Bergere, Louis XVI Style, Beech, Carved, Bowfront Seat Rail, c.1910 . . . . 865.00
Chair, Bergere, Louis XVI Style, Giltwood, Padded Back, Arms, 1800, 44 1/2 In. 4600.00
Chair, Bergere, Louis XVI Style, Kingwood, Ormolu Mounted, c.1900 . . . . 865.00
Chair, Bergere, Louis XVI Style, Polychrome, Padded Back, Arms, Fluted Legs, 38 In. . . . 980.00
Chair, Bergere, Louis XVI, Carved, Upholstered, Closed Arms, Late 1700s, 37 x 29 In. . . 17925.00
Chair, Bergere, Louis XVI, Crest, Padded Back, Downswept Arms, 38 1/2 In., Pair 5520.00
Chair, Bergere, Regency, Ebonized, Parcel Gilt, Closed Arms, 19th Century, Pair 14340.00
Chair, Bergere, Restoration, Mahogany, Padded Back, Arms, Cushion, 1800s, 36 1/2 In. . . 1495.00
Chair, Bergere, Russian Neoclassical, Mahogany, Parcel Gilt, Eagle Arms, c.1840, 38 In. . 6575.00
Chair, Bergere, Square Back, Padded Arms, Stuffed Seat, Green, Gilt, 19th Century 545.00
Chair, Biedermeier, Blond Mahogany, Lyre Splat, Square Legs, 19th Century, 35 In. 1955.00
Chair, Biedermeier, Cherry, Padded Back, Arms, Angled Frame, Square Legs, 32 In. 2070.00

Chair, Biedermeier, Walnut, Fan Crest, Inlaid Splat, Padded Seat, 36 1/2 In. 690.00
Chair, Billy Haines, Bamboo, Black Paint, Pair 4830.00
Chair, Bird's-Eye & Tiger Maple, Cane Seat, Lyre Splat, Early 19th Century 90.00
Chair, Black Forest, Pine, Medallion Back, Entwined Twigs, Branch-Post Arms, 45 In. 910.00
Chair, Black Lacquer, Shaped Crest & Arms, Pierced Splat, 46 In., Pair 1495.00
Chair, Black Over Red Paint, Gold Stenciling, Bamboo Turned, 17 1/2 x 33 In. 195.00
Chair, Black Paint, Paper Rush Seat, Urn Splat, Turned Legs, Pad Feet, 40 3/4 In. 330.00
Chair, Black Wood, Dragon, Claw & Ball Feet, Chinese, 41 x 28 1/2 In., Pair 1150.00
Chair, Black, Red, Strap, Plywood Backrest, Arms, Scandinavia, 29 3/4 x 18 3/4 In. 265.00
Chair, Blond Wood, Upholstered, Curved Arms, Saber Legs, 1940s, 29 x 30 x 28 In., Pair 1175.00
Chair, Bugatti, Corner, Walnut, Ebony, Brass, Silk, Italy, c.1895, 17 3/4 x 29 In. 9200.00
Chair, Bugatti, Ebonized Wood, Pewter, Bone, Copper, c.1900 .... 5675.00
Chair, Bugatti, Inlaid & Copper, Arms, 1900, 71 3/4 In. 8365.00
Chair, Bugatti, Walnut, Pewter, Brass, Copper, Parchment, Italy, c.1900, 16 x 63 In. 9200.00
Chair, Burke, Molded Fiberglass, White Shell, Fabric Seat, Aluminum Base, Arms, 32 In. . 70.00
Chair, Burl Walnut, Curved Back, Vase Splat, Cabriole Legs, Claw & Ball Feet, Pair 280.00
Chair, Burl Walnut, Shieldback, Leaf Pattern Upholstery, Casters 126.00
Chair, Burmese, Hardwood, Carved, Reticulated, Pair 235.00
Chair, Butterfly Back, Bamboo Turned, Arms, Painted, 17 x 35 In. 470.00
Chair, C. Pollack, Steel Tubular Frame, Leather Sling Seat, 28 x 26 In., Pair 1725.00
Chair, Camp, Victorian, Walnut, Folding, Child's 46.00
Chair, Carl Westman, Oak, Curved Arms, Slat Back, Carved Apron, Sweden, c.1899 ..... 16730.00
Chair, Carved Oak, Northwind Head, Lion Posts, Claw Feet, c.1890, 39 In. .... *Illus* 336.00
Chair, Carved Oak, Owl, Glass Eyes, c.1890, 41 In. .... *Illus* 1400.00
Chair, Carved Scroll Back, Crest, Upholstered Seat, Twist Turned Legs, Arms, 1850s 240.00
Chair, Carved Walnut, Figural Putti, c.1870, 50 x 37 x 33 In. .... *Illus* 3920.00
Chair, Chan, Steel, Leather, Steiner, Germany, 1970, 33 x 25 1/4 In., Pair 3220.00
Chair, Charles II Style, Walnut, High Back, 19th Century 345.00
Chair, Charles X, Maple, Semicircular, Fan Inlay, Stars, Upholstered, Pair 645.00
Chair, Charles X, Walnut, Padded Back, Seat, Scrolled Arms, 37 1/2 In., Pair 2300.00
Chair, Charlotte Perriand, Oak Rush Seat, Back, Arms, c.1935, 35 x 23 In. 3000.00
Chair, Cherry, Hickory Pencil-Post Legs, Plank Seat, Zoar, Ohio, 38 1/4 In., Pair 495.00
Chair, Chippendale Style, Centennial, Walnut, Molded Seat Frame, 17 1/2 x 37 1/2 In. 140.00
Chair, Chippendale Style, Mahogany, Carved, Pierced Splat, 20th Century, 40 In. 200.00
Chair, Chippendale Style, Mahogany, Carved, Upholstered, Arms, Centennial, Pair 765.00
Chair, Chippendale Style, Mahogany, Claw & Ball Feet, 20th Century, 18 1/2 x 45 In. 495.00
Chair, Chippendale Style, Walnut, Shaped Crest Rail, Curled Ears, 1900, 37 x 21 x 21 In. . 1100.00
Chair, Chippendale Style, Wing, Suede, Cabriole Legs, Scroll Arms, Cocheo Brothers ... 1610.00
Chair, Chippendale, Birch, Shaped Crest, American, 1800s, 36 x 19 1/2 x 15 3/4 In. 660.00
Chair, Chippendale, Birch, Spanish Feet, Stretcher, Rush Seat, 16 1/2 x 38 In. 330.00
Chair, Chippendale, Mahogany, Beaded, Carved, Shaped Crest, Pierced Splat, Slip Seat .. 730.00
Chair, Chippendale, Mahogany, Carved Crest Rail, Pierced Splat, Slip Seat, 38 x 18 In. .. 1058.00

Furniture, Chair, Carved Oak,
Northwind Head, Lion Posts,
Claw Feet, c.1890, 39 In.

Furniture, Chair, Carved
Oak, Owl, Glass Eyes,
c.1890, 41 In.

Furniture, Chair, Carved Walnut,
Figural Putti,
c.1870, 50 x 37 x 33 In.

Chair, Chippendale, Mahogany, Carved Crest, Splat, Stiles, Straight Legs, Stretcher Base . 620.00
Chair, Chippendale, Mahogany, Carved Crest, Upholstered Seat, Arms, American 635.00
Chair, Chippendale, Mahogany, Claw & Ball Feet, Upholstered Seat, Philadelphia, c.1760 1695.00
Chair, Chippendale, Mahogany, Ladder Back, Pierced Serpentine Crest, c.1780 . . . . 920.00
Chair, Chippendale, Mahogany, Pegged Construction, 37 x 22 x 18 In. 280.00
Chair, Chippendale, Mahogany, Pierced Vase-Shape Splat, Upholstered 230.00
Chair, Chippendale, Mahogany, Ribbonback, Rush Seat, 14 x 33 In. 220.00
Chair, Chippendale, Mahogany, Serpentine Pierced Crest, 3 Splats, 38 In., Pair 1175.00
Chair, Chippendale, Mahogany, Shaped Crest, Pierced Splat, Over-Upholstered Seat 395.00
Chair, Chippendale, Mahogany, Slip Seat, Shaped Crest, Pierced Splat, 38 1/2 In. 605.00
Chair, Chippendale, Maple, Birch, Mortise & Peg, Rush Seat, Arms, 40 In. 660.00
Chair, Chippendale, Ribbonback, Square Legs, Needlework Seat, 37 3/4 x 16 1/2 In. 290.00
Chair, Chippendale, Walnut, Roundabout, Shaped Crest, c.1780, 32 3/4 In. 2585.00
Chair, Chrome, Brown Vinyl, Wedge Shape, 28 x 34 x 28 1/2 In., Pair 705.00
Chair, Club, Art Deco, Leather, Brass Nail Heads, France, 36 x 27 1/4 In., Pair 6900.00
Chair, Club, Art Deco, Mahogany, Leather, Square, France, c.1930, 30 x 35 In., Pair 2185.00
Chair, Club, Art Deco, Walnut, Leather, France, 34 1/2 In. 1610.00
Chair, Club, Edwardian, Mahogany, Leather, Square Legs, c.1900, 33 In. 2990.00
Chair, Club, Oak, Leather Upholstered Back, Seat & Armrests, Pair 865.00
Chair, Club, Z-Shape, Upholstered, Mint Green Leather, 28 x 22 x 30 In., Pair 1175.00
Chair, Colombo, Upholstered Foam, Leather, Sormani, Italy, 1970, 24 x 20 In. 5750.00
Chair, Commode, Mahogany, Roundabout, Vase Splat, 16 In. 1265.00
Chair, Continuous Chromium Frame, Jute Seat, Back, Wood Armrests, 1930s, 34 In. 2695.00
Chair, Corner, Chippendale, Back Rail, Claw & Ball Feet, c.1885 . . . . 670.00
Chair, Corner, Chippendale, Oak, Rush Seat, Turned Arm, Back Support, 33 In. 1265.00
Chair, Corner, English Mahogany, Roundabout, Openwork, 18th Century, 31 In. 1150.00
Chair, Corner, George II, Leather Upholstery, c.1725 . . . . 6570.00
Chair, Corner, George III Style, Mahogany, Arms, 2 Lyre Splats, c.1850 . . . . 690.00
Chair, Corner, George III Style, Mahogany, Arms, Late 19th Century 660.00
Chair, Corner, George III Style, Mahogany, Crest, Pierced Splat, c.1900, 32 1/2 In. 800.00
Chair, Corner, George III, Mahogany, Pierced Splats, Square Legs, c.1810, 34 In. 2300.00
Chair, Corner, George III, Walnut, Rush Seat, Arms, c.1760 . . . . 920.00
Chair, Corner, Queen Anne, Shell-Carved Knees, Cabriole Legs, Pad Feet, 32 In. 210.00
Chair, Corner, Renaissance Revival, Oak, Scrolled Carved Crest, Backsplats, Leather Seat 235.00
Chair, Corner, Split Hickory Seat, Late 19th Century, Child's, 12 1/2 In. 70.00
Chair, Corner, Wicker, Ornate, Rolled Arms, c.1875, 37 In. 225.00
Chair, Correction, Beech, Cane Seat, Ring Turned Legs, 19th Century 375.00
Chair, Dark Stain, Cabriole Legs, Massachusetts, 18th Century, 16 1/2 In. 765.00
Chair, Der Colani, Sitzgerat, Orange Polyethylene, c.1972, 25 3/4 In. 980.00
Chair, Desk, G. Stickley, H-Back, Leather Drop-In Cushion, 16 x 16 x 40 In. 400.00
Chair, Desk, G. Stickley, Horizontal Slat, Leather Seat, 16 x 16 x 29 In. 860.00
Chair, Desk, Mahogany, Gilt, Upholstered, Leather, Brass Studs, c.1810 . . . . 1090.00
Chair, Djinn, Steel, Stretch Jersey, Olivier Mourgue, c.1970, 26 3/4 In., Pair 2530.00
Chair, Dressing, Underseat Storage, Trouser Press, Central Mantel Co., 42 x 17 x 18 In. . . 375.00
Chair, Drexel, Chippendale Style, Openwork Splat, Cabriole Legs, Pair 200.00
Chair, Dunbar, Walnut, Wool, Upholstered, 24 x 27 1/2 In., Pair 860.00
Chair, E. Wormley, Lounge, No. 5480, Laminated Ash, Upholstered, 1950s, 24 x 33 In. . . . 1610.00
Chair, E. Wormley, Lounge, Walnut, Upholstered, 1950s, 29 x 26 In., Pair 1610.00
Chair, E. Wormley, Mahogany, Brass, Caning, Upholstered, 1950, 22 x 32 In. 860.00
Chair, E. Wormley, Walnut Base, Upholstered, Dunbar, 25 x 28 x 42 In., Pair 920.00
Chair, E. Wormley, Wing, Upholstered, Tufted, Walnut, Dunbar, 39 x 30 x 31 In. 1295.00
Chair, Eames, Aluminum Group, Herman Miller, Channeled Upholstery 400.00
Chair, Eames, Aniline Dyed Ash, Herman Miller, 1950, 22 x 25 x 26 In. 965.00
Chair, Eames, Armshell, Fiberglass, Wool Upholstery, Herman Miller, 25 x 31 In. 430.00
Chair, Eames, Birch Plywood, Red Aniline, Cutout Heart In Back, 1945, 15 x 13 In. 4900.00
Chair, Eames, Birch, Plastic Coated Steel, Shaped Grid Seat, Dowel Legs, 19 In., Pair . . . 2185.00
Chair, Eames, Birch, Tubular Chrome Legs, Herman Miller, 29 x 19 x 21 In. 206.00
Chair, Eames, DAW, Fiberglass, Walnut, Herman Miller, 25 x 24 x 31 In. 1265.00
Chair, Eames, DCM, Aniline, Red Finish, Chrome, Evans, 29 x 19 x 20 In. 645.00
Chair, Eames, DCM, Rosewood, Chrome Steel, Herman Miller, 1958, 20 x 30 In., Pair . . . 3738.00
Chair, Eames, DCW, Bent Plywood, Herman Miller, 29 x 19 1/2 x 21 In. 1000.00
Chair, Eames, Eiffel Tower, Black Wire, Vinyl, Herman Miller, 19 x 22 x 32 In. 195.00
Chair, Eames, Fiberglass, Armshell, Dark Blue, Molded, Herman Miller, 31 1/2 In. 155.00

Chair, Eames, Fiberglass, Yellow Shell, Aluminum, Wheels, Herman Miller, 32 In. 175.00
Chair, Eames, LAR, Fiberglass, Wire Cage Base, Herman Miller 545.00
Chair, Eames, LAR, White, Herman Miller, c.1950 . . . . 645.00
Chair, Eames, LAX, Light Yellow, Herman Miller, c.1951, 26 x 24 3/4 x 25 1/2 In. 175.00
Chair, Eames, LCW, Molded Plywood, Herman Miller, 27 x 27 1/2 x 22 In. . . . . .805.00 to 1840.00
Chair, Eames, LKR-1, Herman Miller, 1950s, 19 x 23 x 25 In. 805.00
Chair, Eames, Lounge, Ottoman, Rosewood, Leather, Aluminum, 33 x 33 x 33 In. 2990.00
Chair, Eames, Mahogany, Chrome Steel, Rubber, Herman Miller, 22 x 25 x 27 In. 690.00
Chair, Eames, Office, Black Wire, Aluminum, Herman Miller, 19 x 20 x 33 In. 300.00
Chair, Eames, Office, Wire Seat, Hopsack Seat Pad, 19 x 20 x 33 In. 405.00
Chair, Eames, Rocker, Fiberglass, Zinc, Birch, Herman Miller, 1951, 25 x 27 In. 1610.00
Chair, Eames, Secretary, Fiberglass, Herman Miller, 25 x 20 x 33 In. 175.00
Chair, Eames, Walnut Plywood, Herman Miller, 22 x 25 1/2 x 27 1/2 In. 920.00
Chair, Eames, White Fiberglass, Upholstered, Herman Miller, 1964, 25 x 24 1/2 In. 635.00
Chair, Eames, White Fiberglass, Zinc, Upholstered, Herman Miller, 1964, 25 x 24 1/2 In. . . 690.00
Chair, Eames, Wire Seat, Bikini Leatherette, Herman Miller, 31 x 18 x 19 In. 765.00
Chair, Edwardian, Satinwood, Caned Back, Side, Seat, Painted Panel, Arms, Pair 4700.00
Chair, Egon Eiermann, No. SE69, Steel Base, Black Vinyl, 3 Legs, Wilde & Spieth, 29 In. 1840.00
Chair, Egyptian Revival, Walnut, Carved Heads, Medallion Crest, c.1875, 46 In., Pair 5040.00
Chair, Elephant, Gilt Lacquer, Thailand, 20th Century, Pair 645.00
Chair, Elm, Lacquer, Horseshoe, Curved Crest Rail, Chinese, c.1880 . . . . 825.00
Chair, Elm, Lacquer, Ming Style, Yoke Back, Arms, Chinese, c.1860, Pair 1295.00
Chair, Elm, Lacquer, Official, Shaped Crest Rail, Arms, Chinese, c.1850, Pair 765.00
Chair, Elm, Shaped Crest Rail, Pierced Backsplat, Arms, Panel Seat, Chinese, c.1880, Pair 3105.00
Chair, Elm, Upholstered, Scroll Arms, White Muslin, France, c.1930, Pair 8365.00
Chair, Empire Style, Gilt Bronze Mounted, Swan's Head Back, Upholstered, Pair 1910.00
Chair, Empire Style, Gilt Bronze, Mahogany, Eagle Heads, Arms, Upholstered, Pair 3408.00
Chair, Empire Style, Gilt, Ebonized, Scrolling Arms, Lion Paw Feet, Upholstered, Pair . . . 65725.00
Chair, Empire Style, Mahogany, Curled Arms, Upholstered Seat, Kittinger, 35 In., Pair . . . 515.00
Chair, Empire Style, Mahogany, Gilt Bronze Mounted, Sphinxes, Griffin Legs, Pair 2820.00
Chair, Empire Style, Mahogany, Scroll Back To Arms, Winged Figures, Striped, Pair 1115.00
Chair, Empire, Mahogany, Crest, Ionic Column Splat, 19th Century, 34 1/2 In., Pair 1955.00
Chair, Empire, Mahogany, Dolphin Uprights, Downswept Arms, c.1815, 36 1/2 In. 1840.00
Chair, Empire, Mahogany, Tablet Crest Rail, Mask, Paw Feet, Early 19th Century, Pair . . . 3585.00
Chair, Enameled Steel, Birch, Atelier Prouve, 22 x 30 In. 2415.00
Chair, English Mahogany, Ladder Back, Rush Seat, Circular Legs, Arms, 35 1/2 In. 230.00
Chair, English Mahogany, Prince Of Wales Plume, Tapestry, Arms, 20 1/2 In., Pair 1495.00
Chair, English Walnut, Acanthus Crest, Caned Back, Turned Uprights, Padded Seat, 50 In. 315.00
Chair, English Walnut, Bamboo Turned Legs, Stretcher, Rush Seat, 14 x 26 In. 55.00
Chair, Federal, Grain Painted, Stencil Decorated, Rush Seat, Early 19th Century 375.00
Chair, Federal, Mahogany, Carved, Pedestal Back, Pierced Splat, c.1790, 38 In. 4995.00
Chair, Federal, Mahogany, Inlaid, Pedestal Back, Upholstered Seat, c.1800, 39 In. 705.00
Chair, Federal, Mahogany, Serpentine Crest, Upholstered, c.1790, 43 x 27 x 18 In. 7050.00
Chair, Federal, Mahogany, Shieldback, Upholstered, American, c.1800, 36 1/2 In. 1265.00
Chair, Federal, Mahogany, Splat, Urn Swag, Tapered Legs, Spade Feet, 35 In., Pair 825.00
Chair, Fiberglass, White, Original Plaid Seat, Swivel, Expo 67, Ebena Lasalle, 30 In. *Illus* 588.00
Chair, Fin Juhl, Easy Chair, No. 45, Teak, Upholstered, 32 1/2 x 26 3/4 x 27 1/2 In. 1765.00
Chair, Fin Juhl, Teak, Black Leather, France & Sons, 26 1/2 x 29 In., Pair 1150.00
Chair, Fin Juhl, Teak, Brass, Upholstered, Vodder, Denmark, 1953, 28 x 28 In., Pair 2300.00
Chair, Firehouse Windsor, Oak, Arms, c.1890, 31 x 22 1/2 x 18 In. 110.00
Chair, Flemish Style, Mahogany, Scrolled Arms & Legs, Red Velvet Seat, Back, 53 In. . . . 275.00
Chair, Flemish Style, Mahogany, Scrolling, Needlepoint Upholstery, 17 1/2 x 47 In. 1155.00
Chair, Flemish Style, Scroll, Arms, Upholstered, Early 20th Century, 19 x 54 In. 715.00
Chair, Flemish Style, Walnut, Padded Back, Arms, Early 19th Century, 42 1/2 In., Pair . . . 2530.00
Chair, Florence Knoll, Lounge, Gold Orange, c.1952, 29 1/2 x 24 x 28 In. 646.00
Chair, Florence Knoll, Square, Silvery Blue Leather, 23 x 32 In., Pair 2585.00
Chair, Florence Knoll, Steel, Wool, 1954, 24 x 29 1/2 In. 1265.00
Chair, Folding, Walnut, Beadwork, X-Frame, Arms, c.1875 . . . . 4182.00
Chair, Footstool, Windsor, Comb Back, Painted, 5 Spindles, c.1800, 44 In. 6573.00
Chair, Frank Gehry, Edges, Corrugated Cardboard, Masonite, 16 x 21 x 32 In., Pair 1725.00
Chair, Frank Lloyd Wright, Theater, Steel, Laminate, Upholstered, 1953, 21 x 33 In. . . . . . : 1725.00
Chair, French Provincial, Beech, Open Arms, Padded Seat, Carved, Pair 440.00
Chair, French Provincial, Fruitwood, Scalloped Crest, Arms, 19th Century, 37 In., Pair . . . 1495.00

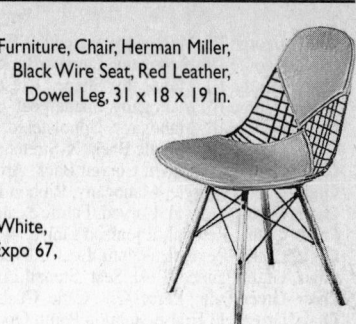

Furniture, Chair, Herman Miller,
Black Wire Seat, Red Leather,
Dowel Leg, 31 x 18 x 19 In.

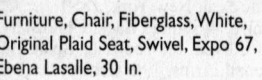

Furniture, Chair, Fiberglass, White,
Original Plaid Seat, Swivel, Expo 67,
Ebena Lasalle, 30 In.

Chair, French Provincial, Fruitwood, Shaped Cane Back Panel & Seat, 37 In., Pair 518.00
Chair, Fruitwood, Louis XIV Style, Upholstered, Arms, France, c.1900, 48 1/2 In. 1150.00
Chair, G. Nakashima, Lounge, Walnut, 12-Spindle Back, Cushions, 30 x 28 In. 3740.00
Chair, G. Nakashima, Walnut, Spindle Back, Single Arm, 1978, 31 x 31 x 26 In. .7050.00 to 8225.00
Chair, G. Nelson, Birch Legs, Arms, Green Wool Upholstery, Herman Miller, 31 x 23 In. . 155.00
Chair, G. Nelson, Birch, Arms, Upholstered, Herman Miller, 23 x 21 x 31 In., Pair 690.00
Chair, G. Nelson, Coconut, Leather, Plastic, Herman Miller, c.1955, 37 x 36 x 40 In. 8625.00
Chair, G. Nelson, Coconut, Triangular Shell, Herman Miller, 41 x 40 x 32 In. 3105.00
Chair, G. Nelson, Lounge, Upholstered, Chromed Steel, Herman Miller, 1962, 28 x 28 In. 3738.00
Chair, G. Nelson, Swag Leg, Charles Pollock, Upholstered, Herman Miller, c.1959, 28 In. 3450.00
Chair, G. Nelson, Thin Edge, Wool, Wood, Foam, Aluminum, Herman Miller, 37 x 31 In. . 1495.00
Chair, G. Stickley, Back Spindles, Corbels, Leather Cushion, 39 1/2 x 27 x 22 In. 4900.00
Chair, G. Stickley, Ladder Back, 37 1/4 x 17 x 16 1/2 In., Pair 805.00
Chair, G. Stickley, Ladder Back, 4 Slats, Molded Arms, 25 x 24 x 38 In. 4025.00
Chair, G. Stickley, Ladder Back, Arms, Scooped Crest Rail, Cane Seat, 39 x 23 x 21 In. .. 2760.00
Chair, G. Stickley, Mahogany, 9 Spindles, Rush Seat, 17 x 15 x 40 In. 980.00
Chair, G. Stickley, Morris, No. 268, Oak, Vinyl Seat, Drop Arms, c.1912, 40 In. 7050.00
Chair, G. Stickley, Morris, No. 332, Slats To Floor, Leather Cushion, 39 x 32 x 36 In. 6325.00
Chair, G. Stickley, Morris, No. 346, Open Arms, 31 x 33 x 40 In. 1955.00
Chair, G. Stickley, Morris, No. 367, 17 Arm Spindles, 30 x 36 x 37 In. 5750.00
Chair, G. Stickley, Morris, No. 369, Slant Arms, 5 Arm Slats, 33 x 38 x 42 In. 12650.00
Chair, G. Stickley, No. 354, V-Back, 5 Slats, Leather Seat, Arms, 26 x 21 x 37 In. 2070.00
Chair, G. Stickley, No. 390, Fixed Back, 24 Arm Spindles, Leather, 29 x 30 x 39 In. 6900.00
Chair, G. Stickley, No. 396, Open Bent Arms, Slat Back, 32 x 36 x 40 In. 2300.00
Chair, G. Stickley, No. 2590, V-Back, 5 Vertical Slats, Rush Seat, Arms, 26 x 22 x 38 In. . 3450.00
Chair, G. Stickley, No. 2632, Inverted V-Top Rail, 2 Horizontal Slats, 28 x 25 x 37 In. ... 2070.00
Chair, G. Stickley, Oak, Drop-In Seat, Arms, Early 20th Century, 39 x 26 1/2 x 33 In. 1115.00
Chair, G. Stickley, Pyramidal Posts, Fabric Seat, Back, Red Decal, 36 3/4 x 27 1/2 In. ... 980.00
Chair, G. Stickley, Slats To Back, Open Arms, Cushion, Red Decal, 37 1/2 x 27 1/4 In. ... 805.00
Chair, G. Stickley, Slipper, Leather Seat, Footrest, 24 1/2 x 15 1/2 x 15 In. 545.00
Chair, George I, Library, Burl Walnut, Shaped Back, Scrolled Arms, 35 1/2 In. 2070.00
Chair, George II Style, Mahogany, Crest, Urn Form, Padded, Cabriole Legs, 39 1/2 In. .. 489.00
Chair, George II Style, Shaped Crest, Padded, Cabriole Legs, Arms, 42 1/2 In., Pair 5750.00
Chair, George II, Mahogany, Scrolled Splat, Arms, Upholstered Seat 4780.00
Chair, George III Mahogany, Domed Crest, Sheaf Splat, Needlepoint Upholstery, 38 In. .. 460.00
Chair, George III Style, Mahogany, Carved Crest & Splat, Padded Seat, Arms, 39 In. 575.00
Chair, George III Style, Mahogany, Leather, Padded Back, Arms, 19th Century, 36 In. 1725.00
Chair, George III Style, Mahogany, Leather, Tufted Barrel Back, 44 1/2 In. 805.00
Chair, George III Style, Mahogany, Scalloped Crest, Padded Seat, Arms, 41 In. 1610.00
Chair, George III Style, Mahogany, Shieldback, Child's, Pair 956.00
Chair, George III Style, Painted, Green, Off White, Arms, Pair 2150.00
Chair, George III Style, Walnut, Carved, Flowers, Shell Carved Knees, Arms 460.00
Chair, George III, Beech, Shieldback, Painted, Arms, c.1790, Pair ....3000.00 to 3585.00
Chair, George III, Gillows Design, Painted, Caned, Catherine Wheel, c.1790, Pair 7170.00
Chair, George III, Gillows Design, Painted, Feather Back, c.1785 .... 5675.00
Chair, George III, Giltwood, Open Arms, Beaded Frame, c.1800, Pair 9560.00
Chair, George III, Mahogany, 3 Shaped Splats, c.1785, 36 In., Pair 375.00
Chair, George III, Mahogany, Oval Back, c.1820, Pair 2150.00

Chair, George III, Mahogany, Pierced & Carved Gothic Splat, Arms, c.1780 .... 170.00
Chair, George III, Mahogany, Pierced Backrest, Carved Stiles, Legs, c.1760 .... 3585.00
Chair, George III, Mahogany, Shaped Crest, Carved, Pierced Splat, 37 In. 750.00
Chair, George III, Mahogany, Spade Feet, c.1800, Pair 1315.00
Chair, George III, Mahogany, Upholstered, Square Back, Stuffed Seats, c.1760, Pair 1380.00
Chair, George III, Spindle Back, X-Stretcher, 33 1/2 x 20 x 20 1/2 In. 8365.00
Chair, George W. Maher, Curved Back, Arched Top Rail, Leather, 19 x 21 x 39 In. 18400.00
Chair, Georgian Style, Mahogany, Ribbon Bow Splat, Upholstered 235.00
Chair, Gothic Revival, Carved, Fabric Seat, New York, 1850 .... 575.00
Chair, Gothic Revival, Ebonized Finish, 4-Spindle Back, Upholstery, 30 x 16 1/2 In. 85.00
Chair, Gothic Revival, Walnut, Leaf Carved, Pierced Back Splat, Bun Feet, c.1890 ...... 115.00
Chair, Grain Painted, Rush Seat, Stencil, Arms, 19th Century 375.00
Chair, Green Paint, Parcel Gilt, Cane, Cushion, Continental, Mid 18th Century 1555.00
Chair, Grosefeld House, Salmon Paint, Open, White Wool Upholstery, 39 In., Pair 5020.00
Chair, H. Bertoia, Bird, Chrome Wire Frame, Upholstered, Knoll, 39 x 37 x 38 In. 645.00
Chair, H. Bertoia, Black Steel Wire, Knoll, 30 In., Pair 410.00
Chair, H. Bertoia, Diamond, Tweed Fabric, 31 x 33 1/2 x 31 In., Pair 705.00
Chair, H. Bertoia, Diamond, White Wire, Black Wire Base, Knoll, 30 x 33 x 27 In. 235.00
Chair, H. Bertoia, White Enameled Steel Seat, Blue Vinyl Cushion, Knoll, 30 In. 765.00
Chair, Harden, 4 Slats Under Horizontal Rail, Spring Cushion, 24 x 26 x 38 In. 690.00
Chair, Harden, Wavy Arms, Slat Back, Sides, Fabric Cushion, 38 1/2 x 29 1/2 x 24 In. ... 980.00
Chair, Harden, Wavy Back, Arched Crest Rail, Slatted, Cushion, 39 x 26 x 21 1/4 In. 375.00
Chair, Henry II Style, Walnut, Padded Back, 2 Finials, 38 In. 1725.00
Chair, Henry IV Style, Walnut, Spindled Arched Crest, c.1890, 42 In., Pair 1955.00
Chair, Hepplewhite, Cushioned Seat & Back, Plaid, Spade Feet, 35 x 27 In., Pair 750.00
Chair, Hepplewhite, Mahogany, Shieldback, Crest, Padded Seat, 37 1/2 In., Pair 865.00
Chair, Hepplewhite, Mahogany, Tapered Legs, Spade Feet, Leaf & Flowers, 35 In. 605.00
Chair, Herman Miller, Black Wire Seat, Red Leather, Dowel Leg, 31 x 18 x 19 In. . . *Illus* 765.00
Chair, Herman Miller, Molded Plastic, Chrome Swivel Base, Upholstered, 28 In. 1060.00
Chair, Herman Miller, Swivel, Molded Plastic, Upholstered, Chrome Base, 28 x 25 In. ... 235.00
Chair, Herter Bros., Ebonized, Gilt Ribbon Crest, Tufted Seat & Back, 32 x 25 In. 865.00
Chair, Hinoki Wood, Japan, c.1912 ....316.00 to 460.00
Chair, Hitchcock Style, Stenciled Gold Fruit Basket, Black Over Red, Cane Seat, 34 In. .. 100.00
Chair, Hitchcock, Stenciled Baskets Of Roses, Green Paint, Rush Seat, 33 In., Pair 110.00
Chair, Horn, Hooves, Upholstered, Fringe, Closed Arms, Western 605.00
Chair, Hove Mobler, Bentwood, 8 Slats, Tubular Chrome Legs, c.1950, 32 x 19 In., Pair .. 265.00
Chair, Hvidt & Neilsen, Lounge, J. Stuart, c.1953, 32 1/4 x 25 x 25 In., Pair 410.00
Chair, Hvidt & Neilsen, Walnut, Bentwood, 29 1/2 x 24 x 27 In., Pair 940.00
Chair, Ice Cream, Bentwire, 1920, Child's, 22 In., Pair 85.00
Chair, Irish Chippendale, Mahogany, Leather, Ribbonback, Bird's Head Arms, c.1890 .... 2300.00
Chair, Italian Neoclassical, Fruitwood, Caned Shieldback, Shaped Arms, Pair 2000.00
Chair, Italian Neoclassical, Fruitwood, Shaped Backrest, Arms, Pair 2235.00
Chair, J. Adnet, Hand Stitched Leather, Brass, Bamboo, c.1950, 17 x 32 In. 5750.00
Chair, J. Adnet, Lounge, Leather Over Steel, Brass, Hermes, 1950, 35 In., Pair 8625.00
Chair, J. Hoffman, Lacquered, Black, Cube, c.1910, 27 1/4 x 25 x 21 1/2 In. 7170.00
Chair, J. Reisling, Black Enamel, Wire, 2 Female Figures, 49 1/2 x 26 x 22 In., Pair 1645.00
Chair, J.M. Young, Morris, Oak, 4 Curved Slats, Flat Arms, c.1912, 39 x 30 x 36 In. 3175.00
Chair, J.M. Young, Morris, Slat Sides, 38 x 30 1/2 x 36 1/2 In. 4600.00
Chair, J.M. Young, Oak, Back & Side Slats, Shaped Arms, 1900s, 39 x 29 x 27 In. 560.00

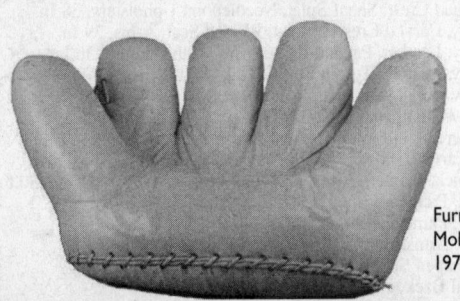

Furniture, Chair, Joe, Baseball Glove,
Molded Urethane, Brown Leather,
1972, 35 x 72 In.

Chair, Jacobean, Oak, Padded Seat & Back, Spotted Horse Hair, Twisted Legs, 35 In. 400.00
Chair, James Mont, Upholstered, Black Enamel Legs, 34 x 19 x 19 1/2 In., Pair 410.00
Chair, Jamestown Furniture, Carved, Cutouts, Round Rivets, Plank Seat, 56 x 16 In. 690.00
Chair, Jean Prouve, Antony, Plywood, Steel, France, 1950, 20 x 34 In. 13800.00
Chair, Jean Rothschild, Fruitwood, Needlepoint Tapestry Seat & Back, c.1934, Pair 9560.00
Chair, Jen Risom, Lounge, Red, Arms, Knoll, c.1941, 29 1/2 x 22 x 25 1/4 In. 645.00
Chair, Joe, Baseball Glove, Molded Urethane, Brown Leather, 1972, 35 x 72 In. . . . . *Illus* 4406.00
Chair, Jules Leleu Style, Oak, Art Deco, Rectangular Back, Tapered Legs, Pair 299.00
Chair, Kaare Klint, Safari, Rasmussen, c.1933, 31 1/2 x 22 1/2 x 22 In. . . . . .410.00 to 470.00
Chair, Kendall School, Arts & Crafts, Back Cutout, c.1910, 23 1/2 x 20 1/2 x 33 In. 805.00
Chair, Kjaerholm, PK22, Brown Leather, Sling Seat, Stainless Steel Base, 28 x 26 In. 940.00
Chair, Klismos, Regency, Mahogany, Scroll Arm, 34 1/2 In. 805.00
Chair, Knoll, Molded Plywood Seat, Back, Label, 31 1/2 x 22 1/4 x 18 In., Pair 235.00
Chair, Krueck & Sexton, Steel, Tesko, Chicago, 1985, 33 1/4 x 29 1/2 In. 6900.00
Chair, L. & J.G. Stickley, 3 Horizontal Slats, Spring Cushion, Arms, 26 x 21 x 37 In. 335.00
Chair, L. & J.G. Stickley, 4 Horizontal Back Slats, Cushion, Arms, 29 x 31 x 40 In. 635.00
Chair, L. & J.G. Stickley, Morris, Long Corbels, Suede Cushions, 37 x 35 x 38 In. 4900.00
Chair, L. & J.G. Stickley, Morris, No. 412, Slats, Open Arms, 40 x 29 x 33 In. 1175.00
Chair, L. & J.G. Stickley, Morris, No. 497, 5 Slats Under Flat Arms, Upholstered, 41 In. . . 5175.00
Chair, L. & J.G. Stickley, Morris, Paddle Arms, Leather Cushion, 35 x 39 x 40 In. 10350.00
Chair, L. & J.G. Stickley, Morris, Slats, Short Corbels, Leather Cushions, 40 x 32 x 35 In. 2990.00
Chair, L. & J.G. Stickley, No. 408, Slats To Floor, Leather Drop Seat, 32 x 26 x 27 In. . . . 5175.00
Chair, L. & J.G. Stickley, Oak, Arch Crest, 5 Slats, Upholstered Seat, c.1912, 38 x 18 In. . 410.00
Chair, L. & J.G. Stickley, Onondaga, 6 Back Slats, Leather Seat, Arms, 37 In. 805.00
Chair, L. & J.G. Stickley, Slat Sides, Arms, Signed, 40 1/2 x 32 x 36 In. 7475.00
Chair, L. & J.G. Stickley, Spindle Back, Leather Seats, 36 1/2 x 16 x 15 In., Pair 2755.00
Chair, L. & J.G. Stickley, Vertical Back Slats, Fabric Seat, Arms, 39 x 27 x 22 In. 605.00
Chair, Ladder Back, 4 Slats, Sausage Turned, Rush Seat, Early 1700s 100.00
Chair, Ladder Back, 5 Arched Slats, Ball Feet, New England, Pair 395.00
Chair, Ladder Back, Arms, Red Paint, Rush Seat, Child's 175.00
Chair, Ladder Back, Black Paint, Turned Posts, Stretchers, Rush Seat, 15 1/2 x 45 In. 1320.00
Chair, Ladder Back, Hardwood, Turned Ball Feet, Posts, Rush Seat, Arms, 46 1/2 In. 275.00
Chair, Ladder Back, Maple & Hickory, Turned Arms & Rounds, 33 In. 415.00
Chair, Ladder Back, Maple, Poplar, Bun Feet, Turned Stretcher, Rush Seat, 16 1/2 x 43 In. 385.00
Chair, Ladder Back, Painted, Rush Seats, Turned Legs, Finials, 17 1/2 x 42 1/2 In., Pair . . 1650.00
Chair, Ladder Back, Pine, Painted, Rush Seat, Turned Front Legs, Stretchers, 15 In. 440.00
Chair, Ladder Back, Rush Seat, Arms, Turned Stretcher, 47 In. 770.00
Chair, Ladder Back, Rush Seat, Bulbous Legs, England, 40 In., Pair 460.00
Chair, Ladder Back, Rush Seat, Turned Stretcher, 43 In. 1210.00
Chair, Ladder Back, Sausage Turned Legs, Rungs, Rush Seat, 3 Slats, 37 In., Pair 360.00
Chair, Ladder Back, Turned Finials, Bulbous Front Stretcher, 41 In. 1210.00
Chair, Ladder Back, Turned Legs, Posts, Paper Rush Seat, 17 x 38 x 38 In., Pair 440.00
Chair, Ladder Back, Virginia, Early 19th Century, 26 x 9 In., Child's 125.00
Chair, Ladder Back, Walnut, Rush Seat, Arms, France, 19th Century, Pair 1265.00
Chair, Ladder Back, William & Mary, Painted, 5 Arched Slats, c.1780, 48 1/2 In. 1910.00
Chair, Ladder Back, Woven Oak Splint Seat, Black Casein Paint, Arms, 1780s 225.00
Chair, Ladder Back, Woven Splint Seat, Red Paint, 15 1/2 In. 165.00
Chair, Laverne, Fiberglass, Metal, Arms, American, 1958, 24 x 24 1/2 In., Pair 2530.00
Chair, Leather Cushion, 5 Slats, Arms, 38 x 27 1/2 x 24 In. 865.00
Chair, Lifetime, Morris, Open Arms, Muslin Drop Seat Cushion, 40 x 29 x 35 In. 345.00
Chair, Lifetime, No. 271, 41 x 16 In. 520.00
Chair, Lifetime, Slatted Back & Arms, Leather Seat, 40 1/2 x 23 1/2 x 21 In. 430.00
Chair, Limbert, Angled Back, Scooped Apron, Paddle Arms, Leather Seat, 32 1/2 x 34 In. 3105.00
Chair, Limbert, Back Slats, Leather Seat, Marked, Child's, 29 x 60 x 32 In. 520.00
Chair, Limbert, H-Back Slat, Leather Seat, Marked, 35 1/4 x 24 1/2 x 20 In. 430.00
Chair, Limbert, Oak Ebony, Inlaid Bell, Leather Drop Seat, 41 x 28 x 25 1/2 In. 5465.00
Chair, Limbert, Vertical, Back Slats, Vinyl Seats, 35 1/2 x 16 1/2 x 16 1/4 In., Pair 920.00
Chair, Lolling, Chinese Chippendale, Ivory Patterned Damask Upholstery 3025.00
Chair, Lolling, Chippendale, Cherry, Connecticut River, 43 x 32 In. 2300.00
Chair, Lolling, Mahogany, Arms, Upholstered, New England, c.1800 . . . . 4480.00
Chair, Lolling, Transitional To Hepplewhite, Mahogany, Birch, 15 1/2 x 43 In. 4510.00
Chair, Louis Philippe, Beech, Padded Seat, Leather, Paterae Head Legs, c.1830, 33 In. . . . 2629.00
Chair, Louis XIII Style, Fruitwood, Bun Feet, Arms, c.1850, 44 In. 2070.00

Chair, Louis XIII Style, Mahogany, Padded, Scrolled Arms, Cabriole Legs, 49 In. 2530.00
Chair, Louis XIII Style, Oak, Upholstered, Rectangular Back, c.1890, 44 1/4 In. 546.00
Chair, Louis XIV Style, Walnut, Gros & Petit Point Upholstery, Arms, 1800s 805.00
Chair, Louis XV Style, Arms, Crest Rail, Skirt, Green, Tufted Upholstery, 34 In. 145.00
Chair, Louis XV Style, Butterfly Wing, Upholstered, Late 19th Century, 19 x 47 In. 660.00
Chair, Louis XV Style, Caned, Arms, Serpentine Rail, Stretcher, Carved 230.00
Chair, Louis XV Style, Carved Wood, Gilt, Shell Crest, Arms, Pair 4780.00
Chair, Louis XV Style, Fruitwood, Shaped Crest, Cushion, Rush Seat, 39 In., Pair 635.00
Chair, Louis XV Style, Gilt Decorated, Leaf Carved Crest, Brocade Upholstered, Pair 4780.00
Chair, Louis XV Style, Gilt, Carved Wood, Arched Crest, Upholstered, Arms 1058.00
Chair, Louis XV Style, Gilt, Carved Wood, Oval Back, Ribbon Crest, Upholstered, Pair . . 355.00
Chair, Louis XV Style, Giltwood, Flower Crest, Cushion, Arms, c.1890, 41 In., Pair 3450.00
Chair, Louis XV Style, Giltwood, Leaf Carved Crest, Damask Upholstery, Pair 2150.00
Chair, Louis XV Style, Mahogany, Upholstered, c.1890, Child's, 42 1/2 x 83 In., Pair 489.00
Chair, Louis XV Style, Padded, Flower Crest, Cabriole Legs, Arms, c.1890, 37 In. 1095.00
Chair, Louis XV Style, Polychrome, Padded, Arms, c.1850, 37 In., Pair 1265.00
Chair, Louis XV Style, Provincial, Padded Back, Flower Crest, Cabriole Legs, 36 1/2 In. . 635.00
Chair, Louis XV Style, Provincial, Scalloped Crest, Carved Basket, Rush Seat, 37 In. 345.00
Chair, Louis XV Style, Serpentine Crest, Rose Carved, Padded Seat & Back, 37 In., Pair . 920.00
Chair, Louis XV Style, Walnut, Cabriole Arms & Legs, Upholstered, 41 In., Pair 1210.00
Chair, Louis XV Style, Walnut, Carved, Swivel Seat, Leather Upholstery 645.00
Chair, Louis XV Style, Walnut, Needlepoint, Arms, 20th Century, Pair 1265.00
Chair, Louis XV Style, Walnut, Tapestry Upholstery, Arms, c.1900, Pair 2415.00
Chair, Louis XV Style, Walnut, Upholstered, Padded, Arms, c.1850, 33 1/2 In., Pair 920.00
Chair, Louis XV To XVI, Giltwood, Upholstered, Padded, Cabriole Legs, c.1790, 42 In. . . 1150.00
Chair, Louis XV, Beech, Carved Back, Leather, c.1750, 35 1/2 In. 4780.00
Chair, Louis XV, Beech, Upholstered, Padded Arms, Peg Feet, c.1750, Pair 5520.00
Chair, Louis XV, Cane Seat & Back, Painted, Arms, c.1750, Pair 920.00
Chair, Louis XV, Curved Back, Blue & Cream Paint, Caned, Carved, c.1750 . . . . 3825.00
Chair, Louis XV, Provincial, Beech, Upholstered, Flat Back, 18th Century, 40 x 20 In. . . . 3885.00
Chair, Louis XVI Style, Beech, Carved, Scroll Arms, Fluted Legs, Casters, c.1900 . . . . . . 345.00
Chair, Louis XVI Style, Beech, Curved Back, Arms, c.1910, Pair 805.00
Chair, Louis XVI Style, Caned, Leaf Carved Crest, Serpentine Seat Rail, Cabriole Legs . . 50.00
Chair, Louis XVI Style, Carved, Giltwood, Damask, Arms, France, c.1900, 44 In., Pair . . . 2760.00
Chair, Louis XVI Style, Fruitwood, Medallion Back, Cushion, Padded Arms, 35 In., Pair . 2990.00
Chair, Louis XVI Style, Fruitwood, Padded Seat, Shamrock Crest, c.1900, 37 In. 200.00
Chair, Louis XVI Style, Gilt, Carved Wood, Oval Back, Ribbon Bow Crest, Yellow, Pair . 825.00
Chair, Louis XVI Style, Giltwood, Floral Upholstery, Arms, Pair 3885.00
Chair, Louis XVI Style, Giltwood, Framed, Carved, Upholstered, Pair 946.00
Chair, Louis XVI Style, Giltwood, Medallion Back, Acanthine Carved Arms, 39 In., Pair . 2760.00
Chair, Louis XVI Style, Giltwood, Padded Seat & Back, Fluted Legs, c.1900, 35 1/2 In. . . 405.00
Chair, Louis XVI Style, Mahogany, Crest, Relief Carved Fruit Basket, Upholstered 460.00
Chair, Louis XVI Style, Salon, Polychromed, Late 19th Century, 34 1/2 In., Pair 1150.00
Chair, Louis XVI Style, Walnut, Parcel Gilt, Open Arms, Upholstered, Carved, Pair 2184.00
Chair, Louis XVI, Caned Medallion Back, Acanthus Carved Arms, Cane Seat, 40 In., Pair 920.00
Chair, Louis XVI, Walnut, Beech, Upholstered, 19th Century, Arms, Pair 1410.00
Chair, Louis XVI, Walnut, Padded Back, Upholstered, 36 1/4 x 18 x 24 In. 1380.00
Chair, Lounge, Barcelona Style, Black Vinyl Tufted Cushions, Chrome, 30 x 31 x 32 In. . 235.00
Chair, Lounge, Colombo, Lacquered Wood, Kartell, Italy, 1964, 25 x 23 In. 5750.00
Chair, Lounge, Colombo, Sella 1001, Plywood, Hide Leather, Italy, 1963, 24 x 28 In. . . . 5750.00
Chair, Lounge, Fiberglass Frame, Leather, Tubular Chrome Base, Italy, 35 x 36 x 38 In. . . 765.00
Chair, Lounge, Leather, Wood, Upholstered, Brass, Italy, 1964, 23 1/2 x 30 1/2 In., Pair . . 8050.00
Chair, Lounge, McCobb, Planner Group, Winchedon, 29 x 25 x 33 In., Pair 115.00
Chair, Lounge, Oliver Mourgue, Wool Upholstered Foam, Steel Frame, 1965, 49 x 26 In. . 2645.00
Chair, Lounge, Tufted Crescent Back, Rolled Arms, Upholstered, 34 In. 140.00
Chair, Lounge, V. Kagan, High Back, Walnut, Upholstered, 30 x 40 x 50 In. 460.00
Chair, Lounge, Warren McArthur, White, Arms, c.1937, 28 1/2 x 25 x 28 1/2 In., Pair 2350.00
Chair, Lounge, Wolfgang Hoffmann, Tubular Chrome Steel, Leather, 1930s, 31 In. 2760.00
Chair, Mahogany, Arms, Upholstered, Early 20th Century, 18 3/4 x 39 1/4 In., Pair 825.00
Chair, Mahogany, Carved, Needlepoint Upholstered Seat & Back, Paw Feet, c.1900 . . . . . . 2645.00
Chair, Mahogany, Leather Back, Seat, Turned Legs, Flat Arms, Spain, c.1890, 56 In. 575.00
Chair, Mahogany, Leather, Deep Cushion Back, Outscrolled Arms, 40 In. 865.00
Chair, Mahogany, Padded, Dome Top, Paw Feet, Arms, Italy, c.1865, 43 In. 1725.00

Chair, Mahogany, Spiral Carved Back Splat, Sloping Arms, c.1820, 17 1/2 In. 2585.00
Chair, Majorelle, Mahogany, Arms, c.1910, 41 3/4 x 21 x 17 3/4 In., Pair 8965.00
Chair, Majorelle, Mahogany, Brocade Upholstery, 38 x 18 x 19 In., Pair 1410.00
Chair, Majorelle, Mahogany, Fruitwood Marquetry, c.1900, 36 5/8 In. 7800.00
Chair, Majorelle, Walnut, Rosewood, Chestnut Leaf Back, c.1900, 40 1/2 In. 6960.00
Chair, Maple, Ash, Banister Back, Arched Crest, Scrolled Arms, Rush Seat, 46 x 16 In. . . 4995.00
Chair, Maple, Ash, Banister Back, Red Paint, 4 Split Spindles, Arms, 44 In. 590.00
Chair, Maple, Roundabout, Crest Shape, Scrolled Arms, 18th Century, 18 1/2 In. 1295.00
Chair, Maple, Shaped Rail, Baluster Back Splat, Rush Seats, Dutch Legs, Pad Feet, Pair . . 1095.00
Chair, Maple, Split Banister Back, Rush Seat 633.00
Chair, Marc Weber, Limed Oak, Back Splat Imitating Swagged Drapery, c.1970, Pair 4780.00
Chair, Marcel Breuer, Lounge, B35, Black Leather Sling, Chrome, Thonet, c.1960, Pair . . 2875.00
Chair, Marx, Burl Walnut, Upholstered, Quigley, 1948, 17 1/2 x 18 1/4 x 33 In. 920.00
Chair, Marx, Lacquered Wood, Nickel Plated Steel, Upholstered, 1948, 20 x 34 In. 2645.00
Chair, Marx, Lounge, Cotton Quilted Upholstery, Quigley, 1948, 28 x 28 In., Pair 4315.00
Chair, Marx, Lounge, Quigley, 1948, 29 x 33 x 32 1/2 In. 635.00
Chair, McCobb, Birch, Iron, 1950s, 18 x 34 In. 1840.00
Chair, McCobb, Directional, No. 1322, Maple Frame, Upholstered, 32 x 25 x 30 In. 825.00
Chair, Meeks, Rosewood, Stanton Hall Pattern, Arms, 44 x 26 x 24 In. 4600.00
Chair, Meeks, Stanton Hall, Rosewood, Upholstered Seat & Back, 41 In., Pair 4200.00
Chair, Michele DeLucchi, Tubular Steel, Wood, Memphis, 25 x 18 x 36 In. 430.00
Chair, Mies Van Der Rohe, Barcelona, Knoll, 1927, 28 x 30 x 27 In., Pair 2820.00
Chair, Mies Van Der Rohe, Lounge, MR, Knoll, c.1931, 29 1/2 x 22 1/2 x 26 1/2 In., Pair . 1175.00
Chair, Mies Van Der Rohe, Lounge, Tugendhat, Knoll, c.1930, 32 x 28 1/2 x 24 In. 3230.00
Chair, Mies Van Der Rohe, No. MR 534, Chrome, Fabric, Arms, Thonet, 1927, 30 In. 9975.00
Chair, Mies Van Der Rohe, Steel, Blue Leather Seat, c.1927, 33 x 29 In., Pair 529.00
Chair, Mixed Hardwoods, Banister Back, Stretchers, Rush Seat, Arms, 17 x 41 In. 990.00
Chair, Monteverdi Young, Brown Seat, Back, Black Legs, Back, 26 x 27 x 28 In., Pair . . . 705.00
Chair, Morris, Shaped Front Seat Rail, Flat Open Arms, c.1912, 30 x 34 In. 499.00
Chair, Morris, Slatted, Panel Under Arms, Cushions, 43 x 32 x 32 In. 690.00
Chair, Music, Victorian, Mixed Woods, Shaped Crest, Spindle Back, Ball Feet, c.1900 . . . 175.00
Chair, Napoleon III, Beech, Upholstered, Arms, c.1865, 36 In., Pair 690.00
Chair, Napoleon III, Carved, Medallion Back, Damask, Arms, c.1865, 40 In., Pair 3450.00
Chair, Napoleon III, Giltwood, Padded Back, Sides, 38 1/4 In. 1955.00
Chair, Napoleon III, Rosewood, Medallion Back, Arms, c.1865, 37 In., Pair 690.00
Chair, Napoleon III, Rosewood, Serpentine Seat, Arms, 41 In., Pair 805.00
Chair, Napoleon III, Walnut, Padded Back, Carved Crest, Cabriole Legs, 41 In., Pair 3910.00
Chair, Native Wood, Marble Inset, Mother-Of-Pearl Accents, Chinese, Pair 460.00
Chair, Nayak Style, Rosewood, Relief Carving, Hindu Symbols, Arms, 34 x 25 x 23 In. . . . 1150.00
Chair, Neoclassical, Burl Walnut, Ebonized, Arms, Austria, 36 x 20 1/2 In. 1915.00
Chair, Neoclassical, Fruitwood, Upholstered Seat & Back, Arms, c.1850, Pair 430.00
Chair, Neoclassical, Mahogany, Square Legs, Slip Seat, 19th Century, 18 x 36 1/2 In. 300.00
Chair, Neoclassical, Polychrome, Arms, Sweden, c.1815, 33 1/2 In., Pair 5520.00
Chair, Neoclassical, Walnut, Open Arms, High Relief Eagle, Lions, Bun Feet 865.00
Chair, Neoclassical, Yellow, Decorated, Bamboo Turned, Arms, c.1835, Pair 575.00
Chair, Neogrecque, Ebonized, Gilt Incised, American, c.1865, 56 In. 1150.00
Chair, Norman Cherner, Ribbon, Plycraft, 31 x 24 1/2 x 21 In. 999.00
Chair, North African, Geometric Mosaic Inlay, Arms, 43 x 27 1/2 In., Pair 2300.00
Chair, North African, Mahogany Inlay, Geometric, Domed Back, 40 In., Pair 460.00
Chair, Nutting, No. 430, Maple, Corner 635.00
Chair, Oak, Arched Back, Padded Headrest, 2 Splats, Art Nouveau Carving, 48 In. 145.00
Chair, Oak, Cabriole Legs, Paw Feet, Stretcher, Griffin Crest, 19 x 51 In., Pair 1210.00
Chair, Oak, Carved Lion, Northwind Heads, Stretcher Base, Arms, c.1885, 50 In. 560.00
Chair, Oak, Curved Crest, Floral Basket Splat, Arms, c.1850, 36 In., Pair 920.00
Chair, Oak, Domed Crest, Carved Couple, Padded, Continental, c.1850, 49 1/2 In. 1150.00
Chair, Oak, Flowers, Scrolled, High Back, Belgium, 19th Century 290.00
Chair, Oak, Ladder Back, Plank Seat, Shaped Legs, Turned Stretchers 405.00
Chair, Oak, Leather, Carved Flowers, Arms, F. Boberg, c.1900 . . . . 7170.00
Chair, Oak, Northwind Head, Lion Posts, Claw Feet, Arms, c.1890, 39 In. 336.00
Chair, Oak, Rush Seat, Curved Crest, Arms, France, c.1890, 35 1/2 In., Pair 405.00
Chair, Oak, Swivel, Slanted Back, Curved Arms, Brass Tacks, 1900s, 37 x 22 x 23 In. 355.00
Chair, Old Hickory Style, Open Arms, Pair 335.00
Chair, Old Hickory, Barrel, Woven, Split-Cane Back, Seat, Marked, 34 1/2 x 30 1/2 In. . . . 635.00

When replacing lost hardware with matching new pieces, put the new handles on the lowest drawers. The difference in patina will be less visible.

Furniture, Chair, Regency Style,
Leather Seat, Opens To Reveal
Steps, 29 x 21 x 41 In.

Furniture, Chair, Renaissance
Revival, Carved Oak, Burled
Panels, Rollers, 54 x 28 In.

Chair, Oliver Mourgue, Steel Frame, Jersey Upholstered Foam, 1965, 24 x 26 In.	920.00
Chair, Oriental, Carved, Black Lacquered, Border Detail, Molded Seat, 17 x 41 3/4 In.	165.00
Chair, Oriental, Carved, Dragon, Bird, Dragon Arms, 34 1/2 x 18 In.	575.00
Chair, Osvaldo Borsani, Steel Frame & Legs, Orange Wool Upholstery, 1956, 31 In.	3335.00
Chair, Ottoman, Jan Ekselius, Polyurethane Foam, Steel Frame, c.1970, 31 1/8 In.	3450.00
Chair, Painted Banister Back, Serpentine Arms, Velvet Seat, England, c.1770, 46 In.	1175.00
Chair, Painted, Red, Mustard, Black, Gold Fruit, Leaves, J. Huey, Zanesville, c.1840	7500.00
Chair, Pascaud, Cherry, Green Leather, Arms, c.1940, 35 1/4 x 21 1/4 In., Pair	5290.00
Chair, Paulin, No. 675, Leather, Metal Rods, c.1964, 25 In.	3450.00
Chair, Paulin, Ribbon, Wood, Foam, Artifort, Dutch, 1965, 37 x 28 In.	1380.00
Chair, Pesce, UP3, Polyurethane Foam, Stretch Jersey, c.1970, 27 1/2 In.	4025.00
Chair, Piero Fornasetti, Transfer Printed Wood, Sunburst Design, 1950s	2350.00
Chair, Pierre Jeanneret, Birch Scissor Frame, Canvas Cushions, 1950s, 28 x 21 In.	920.00
Chair, Pierre Paulin, Tongue, Stretched Jersey Over Tubular Steel, 1967, 25 x 36 In.	4500.00
Chair, Plail Brothers, Barrel Design, Vertical Spindles, Cushion, 25 x 20 x 31 In.	2300.00
Chair, Plank Seat, Arrow Back, Yellow Ground, Scrolled Arms, 16 In.	605.00
Chair, Plank Seat, Bootjack, Scrolled Arms, Bird, Stenciled Crest, Back, 18 1/2 In.	275.00
Chair, Plank Seat, Flowers, Crest Rail, J. Murdick, Pennsylvania, 15 In.	195.00
Chair, Plank Seat, Grain Design, Yellow Trim, 19th Century, Pair	170.00
Chair, Plank Seat, Half Spindle Back, Arms, Grain Painted, 17 1/2 In.	195.00
Chair, Pollack, Knoll, c.1965, 28 x 25 x 26 In., Pair	825.00
Chair, Potty, Chippendale, Walnut, Scrolling Arms, c.1770	545.00
Chair, Potty, Louis XV, Beech, Horseshoe Seat, Lower Cavity, E. Meunier, 1740	4600.00
Chair, Potty, Queen Anne, Walnut, Solid Splat, Deep, Shaped Apron, Cabriole Legs	115.00
Chair, Prairie School, E. E. Roberts, Oak Park Masonic Lodge, 31 x 27 x 39 In.	575.00 to 805.00
Chair, Queen Anne Style, Mahogany, Leaf Carved Top Rail, Slip Seat, c.1880	290.00
Chair, Queen Anne Style, Mahogany, Shaped Back, Padded, Crooked Arms, 37 In., Pair	1725.00
Chair, Queen Anne Style, Maple, Birch, Pine, Red Wash, Arms, Late 19th Century	550.00
Chair, Queen Anne Style, Maple, Spanish Feet, Stretcher, Rush Seat, Arms, 18 x 45 In.	605.00
Chair, Queen Anne Style, Walnut, Figured, Cabriole Legs, Claw & Ball Feet, 19 x 45 In.	1155.00
Chair, Queen Anne Style, Walnut, Upholstered Back, Seat, Molded Armrests, Pair	520.00
Chair, Queen Anne Transitional, Vase Back, Ring Turned Legs, 40 x 16 1/2 In.	375.00
Chair, Queen Anne, Banister Back, Painted, Splint Seat, Shaped Crest, 42 In.	990.00
Chair, Queen Anne, Birch, Front Pad Feet, Ring Collars, Vase Splat, 17 1/2 x 40 In.	1045.00
Chair, Queen Anne, Mahogany, Pierced Splat, Serpentine Slip Seat, Cabriole Legs	135.00
Chair, Queen Anne, Mahogany, Shaped Crest, Over-Upholstered Seat, Cabriole Legs	590.00
Chair, Queen Anne, Mahogany, Shaped Crest, Pierced Splat, Carved Knees, Pad Feet	395.00
Chair, Queen Anne, Maple, Poplar, Front Stretcher, Rush Seat, 16 x 41 In.	165.00
Chair, Queen Anne, Oak, Pad Feet, Rush Seat, 17 x 37 1/2 In.	85.00
Chair, Queen Anne, Painted, Turned Posts, Rush Seat, 15 1/2 x 36 In.	110.00
Chair, Queen Anne, Red Paint, Shaped Crest, Vase Splat Back, Rush Seat	370.00
Chair, Queen Anne, Sausage Turned Legs, Front Ball Feet, Rush Seat, 17 x 42 In.	220.00
Chair, Queen Anne, Shaped Arms, Vase Shape Splat, Rush Seat, 17 x 44 In.	825.00

Chair, Queen Anne, Shaped Crest, Pierced Splat, Rush Seat, Pad Feet, New England 505.00
Chair, Queen Anne, Shell Carved Knees, Arms, Pad Feet, 40 In., Pair 980.00
Chair, Queen Anne, Turned Maple, Ladder Back, Rush Seat, c.1760 . . . .   489.00
Chair, Queen Anne, Walnut, Block Turned Stretchers, Leather, 18 1/2 x 42 In. 935.00
Chair, Queen Anne, Walnut, Vase Splat, Slip Seat, Pa., 1700s, 38 1/2 In., Pair 3450.00
Chair, Queen Anne, Walnut, Yoke Crest, Vase Splat, Scrolled Front Rail, c.1770, 39 In. . . .   4540.00
Chair, Queen Anne, Yoke Crest, Vase Splat, Molded Stiles, Trifid Feet, c.1770, 39 In. 4185.00
Chair, Red Graining, Gold, Black Trim, Ring Turnings, Painted, 33 In., Pair 305.00
Chair, Regency Style, Black Lacquer, Caned Back, Sides, Cushioned, Square Legs, 36 In.   3450.00
Chair, Regency Style, Black Leather Upholstery, Arms, Late 20th Century, 39 In. 750.00
Chair, Regency Style, Black Paint, Parcel Gilt, Open Arms, George Bullock Style, Pair . . .   7170.00
Chair, Regency Style, Ebonized, Padded, Silk Upholstery, Arms, c.1900, Pair 805.00
Chair, Regency Style, Klismos, Oak, Crest, Ribbon Slat, Brass Rosettes, 32 In. 105.00
Chair, Regency Style, Leather Seat, Opens To Reveal Steps, 29 x 21 x 41 In. . . . . . .*Illus*   1265.00
Chair, Regency Style, Tufted Rolled Back & Arms, Cushion, Turned Feet, 32 In., Pair . . .   605.00
Chair, Regency, Black Paint, Parcel Gilt, Cane, Open Arms, c.1810, Pair 8365.00
Chair, Regency, Ebonized, Caned, Open Arms, Cushions, Pair 1435.00
Chair, Regency, Japanned, Black, Parcel Gilt, c.1810, Pair 1910.00
Chair, Regency, Mahogany, 5 Spindle Splats, Cushioned Seat, 38 1/2 In. 1955.00
Chair, Regency, Mahogany, Crest, Wooden Seat, Saber Legs, 33 In. 1955.00
Chair, Regency, Mahogany, Cushioned Back, Brass Caps, Casters, 38 1/2 In. 1840.00
Chair, Regency, Mahogany, Floral Upholstery, c.1800, Pair 430.00
Chair, Regency, Mahogany, Padded Back, Seat, Arms, Finials, Cross Over Base, 35 In. 1380.00
Chair, Regency, Mahogany, Pierced Back Splat, Slip Seat, Carved Rail, c.1880, Pair 259.00
Chair, Regency, Rosewood, Grain Painted, Brass, Inlaid, c.1815, Pair 920.00
Chair, Regency, Rosewood, Leather, Tufted Back, Out-Scrolled Arms, 42 In., Pair 3000.00
Chair, Regency, Walnut, Padded Back, Carved Arms, 19th Century, 45 In. 1150.00
Chair, Renaissance Revival, Bronze, Wrought Iron, Lion's Head Finials, Upholstered, Pair   1435.00
Chair, Renaissance Revival, Carved Oak, Burled Panels, Rollers, 54 x 28 In. . . . .*Illus*   3080.00
Chair, Renaissance Revival, Walnut, Arms, Curved Crest, Burl Panels, Circular Seat 230.00
Chair, Renaissance Revival, Walnut, Banded, Carved Crest, Open Arms, 1800, 43 1/2 In. . .   865.00
Chair, Renaissance Revival, Walnut, Ribbonback, Needlepoint Seat & Back, 42 In. 920.00
Chair, Restauration, Fruitwood, Paneled Crest & Back, Leaf Carved, 36 In., Pair 3680.00
Chair, Richard Schultz, Vinyl, Mesh, Aluminum, Arms, Knoll, Pair 2070.00
Chair, Risom, Leather Webbing, Raking Tapered Legs, Arms, Knoll, 32 x 24 x 26 In. 940.00
Chair, Risom, No. 652W, Birch Frame, Leather Straps, Knoll, 24 x 29 x 30 In. 980.00
Chair, Risom, Scissor, Birch, Webbed Seat, Wool, Knoll, 23 x 28 x 29 1/2 In. 860.00
Chair, Robert Venturi, Queen Anne Style, Plywood, Laminated, Fabric, c.1982, 39 3/8 In. .   5380.00
Chair, Robsjohn-Gibbings, Walnut Frame, Canvas Webbing, Brass Legs, 35 In. 520.00
Chair, Rococo Revival, Rosalie, Rosewood Laminate, Damask, Arms, c.1850, 44 In. 3795.00
Chair, Rococo Revival, Rosalie, Rosewood Laminate, Upholstered, c.1850, 37 In. 1495.00
Chair, Rococo Revival, Rosewood Laminate, Grape, Carved Crest, 37 In., Pair . . . . .*Illus*   5060.00
Chair, Rococo Revival, Rosewood Laminate, Grape, Carved Crest, Arms, 43 In. . . . . .*Illus*   5060.00
Chair, Rococo Revival, Rosewood Laminate, Mid 19th Century, Pair 2390.00
Chair, Rococo Revival, Rosewood Laminate, Serpentine Seat, c.1850, 37 1/4 In. 3910.00
Chair, Rococo Revival, Slipper, Rosewood Laminate, c.1850, 42 1/2 In. 2760.00
Chair, Rococo Revival, Walnut, Raised Claw & Ball Feet, Arms, Cut Velvet Upholstery . .   600.00
Chair, Rococo, Walnut, Elaborately Carved, Upholstered Seat, 42 In., Pair 3000.00

Furniture, Chair, Rococo
Revival, Rosewood
Laminate, Grape, Carved
Crest, Arms, 43 In.

Furniture, Chair, Rococo
Revival, Rosewood
Laminate, Grape, Carved
Crest, 37 In., Pair

Chair, Roger Leib, Flexible Steel, Mesh, Vinyl, 27 x 26 x 47 1/2 In., Pair 60.00
Chair, Rosewood, Apricot Velvet Upholstery, Closed Arms, c.1930, 28 x 22 7/8 In. 1200.00
Chair, Rosewood, Carved Flower, Serpentine Seat, Cabriole Legs, Arms, 44 1/2 In. . . . *Illus* 33350.00
Chair, Rosewood, Circular Stone Panels, Chinese, 19th Century, Pair 325.00
Chair, Rosewood, Laminated, Carved, Open Arms, Upholstered, 38 x 24 x 16 In. 5465.00
Chair, Roycroft, Arms, Signed, 44 x 26 x 26 In. 1550.00
Chair, Rush Seat, Arms, Horizontal Slats, France, 37 1/2 In., Pair 748.00
Chair, Rustic, Root, Burl Detail, Mosaic Seat, Southern, c.1930, Pair 4000.00
Chair, Rustic, Solid Seat, Cutouts, Lower Hudson River Valley, c.1890 . . . .   3500.00
Chair, Saarinen, Bentwood Arms, Tufted Upholstered Back, Blue, 35 x 26 In. . . . . . . *Illus*   765.00
Chair, Saarinen, White Laminate, Pedestal Base, Knoll, 1963, 32 x 19 x 16 In., Pair 410.00
Chair, Saarinen, Womb, Foam, Fabric, Steel Shell, Knoll, 39 x 34 x 36 In. 865.00
Chair, Saarnio Style, Egg Shape, White Enamel, 22 x 35 In., Pair 410.00
Chair, Safari, Leather, Canvas, Rosewood, Khyber, Peshawar, 21 x 21 x 31 In., Pair 690.00
Chair, Sam Maloof, Executive, Oak, Wool Upholstery, c.1960, 28 x 26 x 50 In. 12650.00
Chair, Sam Maloof, Walnut, Arms, Stamped, Dickerman, 1970s, 38 x 26 x 21 In. 5290.00
Chair, Savonarola, Renaissance Revival, Beech, Carved Leaves, Masks, Pair 1000.00
Chair, Savonarola, Renaissance Revival, Walnut, Arms, Heavily Carved, c.1890 . . . .   1150.00
Chair, Scrolled Back, Padded, Ball Feet, Arms, c.1790, 35 In., Pair 5060.00
Chair, Shaker Style, Ladder Back, Red Paint, 41 In. 90.00
Chair, Shaker, Birch, Original Stain, Cane Seat, Enfield, N.H., c.1840, 41 In. 4900.00
Chair, Shaker, Birch, Taped Seats, Tilters, Enfield, N.H., c.1840, 41 In. 2185.00
Chair, Shaker, Ladder Back, Painted, Arched Slats, South Union, Ky., 15 x 39 In. 495.00
Chair, Shaker, Maple, 2 Slats, Mt. Lebanon, N.Y., 28 In. 920.00
Chair, Shaker, Maple, 3 Slats, Rush Seat, New Lebanon, N.Y., c.1840, 39 3/4 In. 520.00
Chair, Shaker, Maple, Cane Seat, Harvard, Mass., c.1850, Child's, 26 In., Pair 2590.00
Chair, Shaker, Maple, Cane Seat, New Lebanon, N.Y., c.1830-1840, 41 In. 5175.00
Chair, Shaker, Maple, Ladder Back, Turned, Shaped Legs, Woven Seat, Youth, 35 In. 440.00
Chair, Shaker, Maple, Original Striped Tape Seat & Back, Mt. Lebanon, N.Y. 980.00
Chair, Shaker, Maple, Rush Seat, 3 Slats, Watervliet, N.Y., 36 1/2 In. 635.00
Chair, Shaker, Maple, Small Round Finial, New Lebanon, N.Y., c.1860, 29 1/4 In. 865.00
Chair, Shaker, Maple, Splint Seat, Watervliet, N.Y., c.1850, 38 1/2 In., Pair 805.00
Chair, Shaker, Maple, Tape Seat, Mt. Lebanon, N.Y., Arms, c.1920, 39 In. 460.00
Chair, Shaker, Maple, Woven Ash Splint Seat, Mt. Lebanon, N.Y., c.1830, 38 In. 920.00
Chair, Shaker, No. 0, Black Paint, Acorn Finials, Late 19th Century, Child's 1045.00
Chair, Shaker, Shaped Pommels, Graduated Splats, 41 In. 400.00
Chair, Shaker, Turned Legs, Double Rungs, Tape Seat, Union Village, Ohio, 15 x 38 In. . .   440.00
Chair, Shaker, Turned Legs, Double Rungs, Woven Seat, South Union, Ky., 16 x 39 In. . .   110.00
Chair, Shaker, Weaver's, Painted, Turned Legs, Splint Seat, Union Village, Ohio, 43 In. . .   415.00
Chair, Sheraton Style, Mahogany, Shieldback, Open Arms, Framed, Trap Seat, Pair 305.00
Chair, Sheraton, Mixed Woods, Slat Back, Rolled Arms, Cane Seat, Reeded Legs, Pair . . .   115.00
Chair, Sheraton, Rosewood, Feathered, Scroll-Carved Crest, Needlepoint Seat 340.00
Chair, Slat Back, Paint Decorated, Turned Crest Rail, Rush Seat, Early 1700s, 43 1/2 In. . .   825.00
Chair, Slipper, Scrolled Carved Back, Balloon Seat 220.00
Chair, Spindle Back, Plank Seat, Kathleen In Brass Head Tacks, 1800s, Child's 450.00
Chair, Stenciled Design, Blue Dove, Yellow, Red Fruit, Pennsylvania, Child's, 23 x 34 In.   1245.00
Chair, Stickley Bros., Bent Arm Shape, Upholstered Back, 27 x 22 x 42 In. 575.00

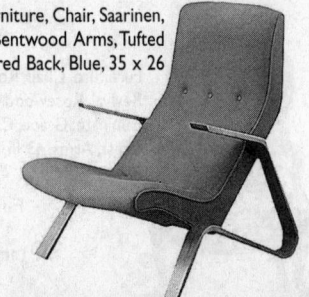

Furniture, Chair, Saarinen,
Bentwood Arms, Tufted
Upholstered Back, Blue, 35 x 26

Furniture, Chair, Rosewood,
Carved Flower, Serpentine Seat,
Cabriole Legs, Arms, 44 1/2 In.

Chair, Stickley Bros., Ladder Back, Leather Seat, Arms, 41 x 27 x 25 In. 635.00
Chair, Stickley Bros., Ladder Back, Slatted, Leather Cushions, 43 3/4 x 28 3/4 x 28 In. . . . 920.00
Chair, Stickley Bros., Morris, Mahogany, Arched Apron, Leather Cushions, 42 x 30 In. . . . 2300.00
Chair, Stickley Bros., Oak, Curved Crest Rail, 4 Slats, Stretchers, 42 3/4 x 27 x 23 1/4 In. 325.00
Chair, Stickley, Oak, Slat Back, Paddle Arms, 39 x 27 In., Pair 765.00
Chair, Sue Et Mare, Mahogany, Upholstered, Beige Velvet, Armless, c.1925, Pair 5676.00
Chair, Teak Frame, Black Leather, Bentwood, Denmark, 33 x 36 In. 190.00
Chair, Thayer Coggin, Egg Shape, Orange, Upholstered, Fiberglass, Swivel, 1962, 45 In. . 530.00
Chair, Thomas Hope Style, Mahogany, Curule, Caned, 19th Century, Pair 4180.00
Chair, Thonet, Bentwood, Birch, Cutout Arms, Trapezoid Back, 33 1/2 x 24 x 20 In. 325.00
Chair, Throne, Rosewood, Carved Dragons, Mountains, Clouds, Chinese, 19th Century . . 470.00
Chair, Tub, George III Style, Mahogany, Leather Upholstery, Early 20th Century, Pair . . 520.00
Chair, Tub, Neoclassical, Birch, Curved Back, Sides, Padded, Splayed Legs, 31 In., Pair . . 3910.00
Chair, Tub, Neoclassical, Polychromed, Giltwood, Sweden, c.1815, 33 1/2 In. 4370.00
Chair, Tub, Restauration, Elm, Curved Back & Sides, Rush Seat, 32 1/2 In. 200.00
Chair, Tub, Restauration, Padded, Flower Upholstery, c.1815, 33 In., Pair 2070.00
Chair, Tub, William IV Style, Mahogany, Dome Back, Downswept Arms, 28 In., Pair 690.00
Chair, Tub, William IV, Mahogany, Upholstered, Arms, c.1850, 33 In., Pair 2185.00
Chair, Tudor, Open Arms, Tooled Leather Upholstery, Heavily Carved Flowers, Pair 520.00
Chair, U-Form Crest, Scroll Carvings On Splat, Arms, Chinese, c.1890, Pair 290.00
Chair, V. Panton, Cone, F. Hansen, c.1958, 33 1/2 x 23 x 18 In., Pair 560.00
Chair, V. Panton, Heart Cone, No. K3, c.1967, 35 1/4 In. 5175.00
Chair, V. Panton, Molded Plastic, Herman Miller, c.1974, 19 x 22 x 33 In., Pair 690.00
Chair, V. Panton, Vitra, Luran S, Plastic, Herman Miller, 32 x 19 x 21 In. 380.00
Chair, V. Panton, Wire Cone, Cushion Seat, Denmark, 1958, 32 x 21 In. 1095.00
Chair, Venetian Rococo Style, Wood, Decorated, 19th Century 1265.00
Chair, Vermont Tubbs, Sno-Shu, Collapsible, Hardwood Frame, Sinew Back, Seat 115.00
Chair, Victorian, Carved, Gilt, Upholstered Back, Arms, 46 x 24 1/2 In. 748.00
Chair, Victorian, Mahogany, Hip Hugger, Corset Back, Needlepoint Upholstery 255.00
Chair, Victorian, Mahogany, Scrolling Arms, Tufted Upholstery 530.00
Chair, Victorian, Mother-Of-Pearl Inlay, Papier-Mache, Gilt Detail, Arms 1000.00
Chair, Victorian, Needlework Upholstery, W. Smee & Sons Style, c.1850 . . . . 1195.00
Chair, Victorian, Oak, Carved, Northwind, X-Form, Arms 590.00
Chair, Victorian, Rosewood Grained, Parcel Gilt, Open Arms, 19th Century, Pair 3585.00
Chair, Victorian, Rosewood, Rose Carved Crest, Shieldback, Arms 200.00
Chair, Victorian, Tufted Barrel Back, Padded, Scrolled Arms, 1800, 35 1/2 In. 1150.00
Chair, Victorian, Upholstered, Floral & Scroll Form Design, 1800s 115.00
Chair, Victorian, Upholstered, Padded, Turned Feet, Casters, 31 In., Pair 1150.00
Chair, Victorian, Walnut, Finger & Scroll Carved Frame, Floral Needlepoint Back 255.00
Chair, Victorian, Walnut, Finger Carved, Arms, Tufted Upholstered, 42 x 24 x 22 In. 175.00
Chair, Victorian, Walnut, Fruit, Nut Crest, Needlepoint Flowers, Back, Seat 340.00
Chair, Victorian, Walnut, Grape Cluster Carved Crest, Flowers, Bird, Upholstered, Arms . 60.00
Chair, Victorian, Walnut, Hip Hugger, Flower Carved Crest, Apron, Legs 280.00
Chair, Victorian, Walnut, Open Arms, Trumpet Legs, Upholstered, Pair 230.00
Chair, Victorian, Walnut, Pierced Crest, Rose, Leaf Carving, Shaped Aprons, Pair 96.00
Chair, W. Katavolos, R. Littell, D. Kelley, Laverne, c.1952, 30 x 23 x 24 1/2 In., Pair 1880.00
Chair, Wagner, Beech, Plywood, Arms, Kohn, Austria, 1902, 20 1/2 x 31 In., Pair 3450.00
Chair, Walnut, Balloon Back, Finger Carved, Hip Rests, Serpentine Rail, c.1865, Pair 230.00
Chair, Walnut, Carved Open Scrollwork, Button Back, Padded Seat, Upholstered 400.00
Chair, Walnut, Carved Putti, Scroll Feet, Upholstered, Arms, 50 x 37 x 33 In. 3920.00
Chair, Walnut, Carved, Upholstered, Pillow Back, 33 1/2 x 17 x 15 In. 200.00
Chair, Walnut, Finger Carved, Balloon Back, Arms, Upholstered, 38 1/2 x 26 In. 335.00
Chair, Walnut, Framed, Padded Seat, Cane Back, Shaped Legs & Stretchers, Pair 220.00
Chair, Walnut, Front Cabriole Legs, Velvet Slip Seat, c.1770, 40 In. 6465.00
Chair, Walnut, Ladder Back, Ring Turned Posts, Bulbous Front, N.C., 45 1/2 In. 715.00
Chair, Walnut, Oak, Padded, Barley Twist & Block Legs, Stretchers, Arms, 45 1/2 In. 2760.00
Chair, Walnut, Parcel Gilt, Portugal, 18th Century, Pair 5975.00
Chair, Walnut, Reticulated Heart-Shaped Back, Upholstered Seat, c.1890, 36 In. 560.00
Chair, Walnut, Stained, Scrolled Carved Leaves, Stretcher, Needlework Seat, 49 In. 805.00
Chair, Warren McArthur, Aluminum, Upholstered Seat, Rubber Feet, 34 In., Pair 2300.00
Chair, Warren McArthur, Deep Seat, Back, c.1937, 32 x 15 1/2 x 15 In., Pair 470.00
Chair, Warren McArthur, Folding, Aluminum, Mayfair Industries, 24 x 24 x 30 1/2 In. . . . 196.00
Chair, Warren Platner, Bronze Wire, Upholstered, Knoll, 36 x 26 x 30 1/2 In. 1840.00

Chair, Webbed Leather Seat, Back, Raking Tapered Legs, 31 1/2 x 16 x 19 In. 235.00
Chair, Wegner, Ash, Teak, Peacock, Woven Twine Seat, Mark, 41 1/2 In., Pair ....!..... 3680.00
Chair, Wegner, Flag Halyard, No. GE225, Getama, Gedsted, 1950s, 41 1/2 In. 6900.00
Chair, Wegner, Peacock Style, Teak, Ash, Papercord, 1947, 30 x 43 In. 2185.00
Chair, Wegner, Stacking, No. 4103, Hansen, c.1955, 28 3/4 x 17 1/4 x 16 1/2 In. 440.00
Chair, Wegner, Swivel, Arms, Hansen, c.1955, 29 x 29 x 20 In. 8815.00
Chair, Wegner, Teak & Oak, Shaped Back, Flip Seat, c.1958, 37 1/4 In. 2468.00
Chair, Wegner, Teak, Panel Back, Curved Top Rail, Doeskin, 32 x 23 x 20 In., Pair 3175.00
Chair, Wegner, The Chair, Woven Cane Seat, Arms, Hansen, 27 1/4 x 25 x 19 In. 590.00
Chair, Wegner, Valet, Teak, Flip-Up Back, Denmark, 1958, 37 In. 4350.00
Chair, Wegner, Wingless Ox, Chromed Steel, Hansen, 35 x 37 x 35 In. 6325.00
Chair, Wegner, Wishbone, C. Hansen, Denmark, c.1950, 28 1/2 x 20 x 16 1/2 In. 265.00
Chair, Wharton Esherick, Hickory, Leather, Hammer Handle, c.1930 .... 5380.00
Chair, Wicker, Scroll Form, c.1900, Child's 170.00
Chair, William & Mary Style, Beech, Scrolled Crest, Open Arms, Caned Trapezoid Seat .. 410.00
Chair, William & Mary Style, Cane Seat & Back, Arms, 19th Century 200.00
Chair, William & Mary Style, Mahogany, Caned Back, Seat, Arms, c.1900, 49 In., Pair .. 1610.00
Chair, William & Mary Style, Walnut, Arch Top, Leaf Carved Arms, Paw Feet, Pair 920.00
Chair, William Birch, Arts & Crafts, Carved, Center Slat, Ebony Inlay, Arms, 51 In. 865.00
Chair, William IV, Mahogany, Barrel Form, Padded, Arms, c.1835, 30 In. 750.00
Chair, William IV, Mahogany, Circular Back, Square Legs, c.1835, 37 1/2 In. 320.00
Chair, William IV, Mahogany, Oval Back, Inset Panel, Saddle Seat, 36 1/2 In. 290.00
Chair, William IV, Oak, Pierced Circular Back, Polychrome Helmet, 34 1/2 In. 1380.00
Chair, Windsor, 5 Spindles, Bamboo, Green Paint, Gold Line Edging, 16 x 32 1/2 In. 165.00
Chair, Windsor, 5 Spindles, Crest, Shaped Seat, Bamboo Legs, Black Paint, Child's 125.00
Chair, Windsor, 7 Spindles, Ash, Concave Crest, Shaped Seat, 26 In. 1530.00
Chair, Windsor, 7 Spindles, Bamboo Turned, D-Shape Seat, 18 x 34 3/4 In. 300.00
Chair, Windsor, 7 Spindles, Continuous Arm, Dark Brown Paint, New England 3100.00
Chair, Windsor, 8 Spindles, Yew, Walnut, Round Handholds, 18 x 45 In. 440.00
Chair, Windsor, 11 Spindles, Hickory, Ash, Maple, Continuous Arm, 16 1/4 x 37 In. 385.00
Chair, Windsor, 4 Spindles, Painted, Bamboo Turned Legs, 12 x 26 In. 220.00
Chair, Windsor, Arms, Elm, Spindles, England, Late 18th Century 1910.00
Chair, Windsor, Ash, Shaped Concave Crest, Turned Legs, 1790, 41 x 26 In. 1530.00
Chair, Windsor, Bamboo Spindles Back, Armrests & Stretcher, Plank Seat, c.1820 ...... 520.00
Chair, Windsor, Bamboo Spindles, Black Paint, 19th Century, 38 1/2 x 18 1/2 In. 550.00
Chair, Windsor, Bamboo Turned Legs, H-Stretcher, Continuous Arm, 14 1/2 x 33 In. 550.00
Chair, Windsor, Birdcage, Bamboo Turnings, Shield-Shape Seat, J.R. Hunt, 34 In. 620.00
Chair, Windsor, Birdcage, Red Wash, Hunt, New England 550.00
Chair, Windsor, Bow Back, 6 Spindles, Brown Paint, Pair 400.00
Chair, Windsor, Bow Back, 7 Spindles, Red Paint, 35 1/4 x 16 In. 230.00
Chair, Windsor, Bow Back, 8 Spindles, Arms, Nichols-Stone, 35 1/2 In. 385.00
Chair, Windsor, Bow Back, 9 Spindles, Bamboo Turned Legs, Painted, 16 x 34 In. 110.00
Chair, Windsor, Bow Back, 9 Spindles, Bamboo Turned, Bulbous, 17 1/2 In. 330.00
Chair, Windsor, Bow Back, 9 Spindles, Green Paint, Incised Shaped Seat, 39 x 19 In. 590.00
Chair, Windsor, Bow Back, 9 Spindles, L.E. Partridge, 18 x 39 1/4 In., Pair 495.00
Chair, Windsor, Bow Back, 9 Spindles, Shaped Seat, Molded Bow, 17 1/2 x 37 In. 825.00
Chair, Windsor, Bow Back, Baluster, Ring Turned Legs, H-Shape Stretcher, 17 x 36 In. .. 330.00
Chair, Windsor, Bow Back, Bamboo Spindles, Splayed Legs, Turned Stretcher, 36 In. 330.00
Chair, Windsor, Bow Back, Bamboo, Old Green Paint, Late 18th Century, 43 x 16 In. 950.00
Chair, Windsor, Bow Back, Knuckle Carved Arms, Bulbous Base, Red, Brown Paint 12500.00
Chair, Windsor, Bow Back, Maple, Hickory, Pine, New England, c.1810 .... 400.00
Chair, Windsor, Bow Back, Split Plank Seat, Child's 2365.00
Chair, Windsor, Bowed Crest Rail, Spindles, Yellow Paint, T.C. Hayward, 37 In., Pair 3825.00
Chair, Windsor, Brace Back, 7 Spindles, Brown Wash, Alligator Varnish, 37 x 17 In. 770.00
Chair, Windsor, Brace Back, 9 Spindles, Molded Bow, Shield Seat, Painted, 35 In. 440.00
Chair, Windsor, Brace Back, 11 Spindles, Saddle Seat, Arms, c.1800, 37 x 17 In. 1555.00
Chair, Windsor, Butterfly, Notched Crest, Bamboo Turnings, Leather Seat, Arms 115.00
Chair, Windsor, Comb Back, 7 Spindles, Painted, Serpentine Crest, c.1790, 37 In. 3820.00
Chair, Windsor, Comb Back, 9 Spindles, Scrolled Ears, 17 1/2 x 23 1/2 x 42 In. 11275.00
Chair, Windsor, Comb Back, Arrow Feet, Scrolled Ears, 43 1/2 In. 2200.00
Chair, Windsor, Continuous Arm, Black Paint, Late 18th Century, 36 1/2 In. 4780.00
Chair, Windsor, Continuous Arm, Bowed Crest, Painted, Late 18th Century, 38 1/2 In. 7050.00
Chair, Windsor, Continuous Arm, Cherry, Black Paint, Pair 495.00

Chair, Windsor, Continuous Arm, E.B. Tracy, 1780 .... 9350.00
Chair, Windsor, Continuous Arm, Painted, H-Stretchers, Conn., c.1790, 37 In. 3110.00
Chair, Windsor, Fanback, 6 Spindles, Saddle Seat, Black Paint, Rhode Island 715.00
Chair, Windsor, Fanback, 7 Spindles, Blue Paint, Shaped Crest, 37 In. 990.00
Chair, Windsor, Fanback, 7 Spindles, Painted, Swelled Crest Rail, c.1790, 36 In., Pair 7170.00
Chair, Windsor, Fanback, 7 Spindles, Shaped Ear Ends & Seat, 36 x 17 In. 630.00
Chair, Windsor, Fanback, 8 Spindles, Painted, Baluster, Ring Turned Legs, Crest 220.00
Chair, Windsor, Fanback, 9 Spindles, Serpentine Crest, Pa., c.1770, 36 In. 3825.00
Chair, Windsor, Fanback, Baluster & Ring Turned Legs, Stretcher Base, 18 1/2 x 39 In. . . 605.00
Chair, Windsor, Fanback, Carved Ears, Brown, Knuckle Carved Arms 5500.00
Chair, Windsor, Fanback, Red Paint, Turned Legs, Shield-Shape Seat, 35 1/2 In. 1815.00
Chair, Windsor, Fanback, Saddle Seat, Vase & Ring Turned Edges, 18th Century 920.00
Chair, Windsor, Fanback, Splayed Vase & Ring Turned Legs, Shield Seat, 35 In. 550.00
Chair, Windsor, Firehouse, American, 19th Century, Child's 90.00
Chair, Windsor, Hoop Back, 7 Spindles, Flared Arms, Shaped Seat, Bulbous Stretchers ... 450.00
Chair, Windsor, Hoop Back, 7 Spindles, Saddle Seat, Bamboo Turnings, Red Paint 110.00
Chair, Windsor, Hoop Back, Pierced & Carved Splat, Scroll Arms, c.1850 .... 546.00
Chair, Windsor, Hoop Back, Turned Spindles, Legs, 1820, 17 In. 305.00
Chair, Windsor, Maple, Pine, Hickory, Arms, CMD Brand, New England, c.1780, 38 In. ... 4480.00
Chair, Windsor, Nutting, Comb Back, 9 Spindles, Scrolled Ears, 45 In. 1155.00
Chair, Windsor, Nutting, Comb Back, Pennsylvania Style, 18 In. 1955.00
Chair, Windsor, Nutting, Comb Back, Writing Arm, 18 x 43 1/2 In. 2750.00
Chair, Windsor, Nutting, No. 326, Fanback 385.00
Chair, Windsor, Nutting, No. 408, Bow Back, Arms 1320.00
Chair, Windsor, Nutting, No. 413, Low Back 850.00
Chair, Windsor, Nutting, No. 420, 9 Spindles, Scrolled Knuckle Arms, 43 In. 1430.00
Chair, Windsor, Nutting, Writing Arm, c.1920 .... 2200.00
Chair, Windsor, Rod Back, Crest, Bamboo, Old Black Paint, 19th Century, 36 x 17 In. ... 350.00
Chair, Windsor, Sack Back, 19th Century, Child's, 23 1/2 In. 460.00
Chair, Windsor, Sack Back, 7 Spindles, Bowed Crest, c.1790, 37 1/2 In. 825.00
Chair, Windsor, Sack Back, 7 Spindles, Poplar, Plank Bottom, 35 In. 360.00
Chair, Windsor, Sack Back, Bamboo Turnings, Carved Seat, 36 x 16 1/2 In. 1090.00
Chair, Windsor, Sack Back, Oval Saddle Seat, Arms, 1780-1790, 37 x 23 x 15 In. 1595.00
Chair, Windsor, Sack Back, Painted, Arched Base, H-Stretcher, 18th Century, 39 In. 3585.00
Chair, Windsor, Sack Back, Painted, Baluster & Ring Legs, 17 x 37 In. 1760.00
Chair, Windsor, Step-Down, Yellow Paint, Stenciled Flowers, American 100.00
Chair, Windsor, Writing, Double Bow Back, Maple, Ash, Pine, Scrolled Arm, 45 1/2 In. .. 3525.00
Chair, Windsor, Writing, Nutting, Comb Back, Left Handed, 43 1/2 In. 2750.00
Chair, Windsor, Writing, Pine, Turned Walnut, Pennsylvania, c.1800, 36 1/2 In. 3825.00
Chair, Wing, Art Deco, Upholstered, Sunburst Pattern, Turned Legs, 35 x 33 In. 90.00
Chair, Wing, Arts & Crafts, Upholstered Seat & Back, c.1900, 45 In. 1265.00
Chair, Wing, Chippendale Style, Green Leather Upholstery, Straight Legs, 40 In., Pair ... 1155.00
Chair, Wing, Chippendale, Arched Back, Rolled Arms, Straight Legs, Stretcher 790.00
Chair, Wing, Chippendale, Claw & Ball Feet, Upholstered, Stretcher Base 345.00
Chair, Wing, Chippendale, Walnut, Upholstered, Rhode Island School, 44 1/2 In. 6600.00
Chair, Wing, George I, Carved, Upholstered Backrest, Cabriole Legs, Arms 7475.00
Chair, Wing, George I, Walnut, Front Rail, Norman Adams Label, c.1715 .... 4780.00
Chair, Wing, George III Style, Padded Domed Back, Cabriole Legs, c.1865, 47 In. 805.00
Chair, Wing, George III, Mahogany, Upholstered, Square Legs, 18th Century, 46 In. 2760.00
Chair, Wing, George III, Oxblood Leather, Brass Tacks, Molded Legs, 40 x 33 In. 920.00
Chair, Wing, George III, Walnut, Velvet Upholstery, c.1885, 46 1/2 In. 2760.00
Chair, Wing, Georgian Style, Carved Flower, Musical Motif, 20th Century, Pair 259.00
Chair, Wing, Hepplewhite, Mahogany, Upholstered 750.00
Chair, Wing, Leather, Brass Casters, Arms, Child's, 23 In. 1006.00
Chair, Wing, Library, George III, Mahogany, U-Shape Barrel Back, Scroll Arms 1410.00
Chair, Wing, Mahogany, Stretcher Base, Bun Feet, Upholstered, 19 x 48 In. 415.00
Chair, Wing, Queen Anne, Painted, Turned Legs, Rungs, Upholstered, 44 1/2 In. 2310.00
Chair, Wing, William & Mary Style, Walnut, 20th Century 460.00
Chair, Wood, Aubusson, Gilt, Floral Upholstery, France, 1870 .... 4260.00
Chair, Woven Upholstery, Chrome Base, Arms, Scandinavia, 27 x 31 x 27 In. 175.00
Chair, Yellow Green Paint, Stenciled Fruit On Crest Rail, Cane Seat, Child's, 21 In. 58.00
Chair, Yoke Back, Carved Kylin In Cloud Splat, Rope Seat, Chinese, 44 In., Pair 805.00
Chair & Ottoman, Arne Jacobsen, Leather, Fiberglass, Aluminum, 1958, 30 x 14 In. 5460.00

Chair & Ottoman, Arne Jacobsen, The Egg, c.1958 . . . . 4000.00
Chair & Ottoman, Art Deco, Giltwood, Silk, France, c.1925 . . . . 4780.00
Chair & Ottoman, Black Leather, Rosewood, Aluminum Base, 1967, 31 x 33 x 33 In. . . . 765.00
Chair & Ottoman, De Sede, Black Leather, Stainless Steel, Pedestal Base 499.00
Chair & Ottoman, Eames, Leather, Rosewood, Herman Miller, c.1956 . . . . .2115.00 to 2350.00
Chair & Ottoman, Eames, Rosewood Shell, Leather Cushions, 33 In. 4025.00
Chair & Ottoman, Ekstrom, Teak, Leather Seat, Sweden, 41 x 27 In. 1530.00
Chair & Ottoman, Fin Juhl, Teak, Upholstered, Arms, France & Sons, 30 x 28 x 24 In. . . . 765.00
Chair & Ottoman, Frankl Style, Skyscraper, Chrome Frame, Vinyl Upholstery 1410.00
Chair & Ottoman, G. Nakashima, Spindle Back, Paddle Arms, Upholstered 4115.00
Chair & Ottoman, H. Bertoia, Bird, Knoll, c.1952, 38 1/4 x 37 1/4 x 29 In. 1530.00
Chair & Ottoman, H. Bertoia, Diamond, Knoll, c.1952, 27 1/4 x 44 x 31 In. 705.00
Chair & Ottoman, Ilmari Tapiovaara, Leather, Aluminum Frame, 32 x 30 x 37 In. 2470.00
Chair & Ottoman, Marc Held, Fiberglass, Wool, Knoll, 1967, 30 x 27 In. 2645.00
Chair & Ottoman, Marc Held, Molded Plastic, High Back, Knoll, 1979, 44 x 30 x 34 In. . . 2115.00
Chair & Ottoman, Paulin, No. 421, Fiberglass, Foam, Artifort, France, 1961, 38 x 36 In. . 3450.00
Chair & Ottoman, Saarinen, Womb, Blue, Knoll, c.1946, 36 x 39 In. 1410.00
Chair & Ottoman, Saarinen, Womb, Brown, Chrome Legs, Cloth Label 1380.00
Chair Set, Aalto, Birch, Upholstered, Finland, 1939, 24 x 31 1/4 In., 4 . . . . 2875.00
Chair Set, Alexander Begge, Red Molded Plastic, Germany, 1973, 14 1/2 x 23 In., 4 . . . . 160.00
Chair Set, Art Deco, Mahogany, Scrolled Back, Upholstered, Cabriole Legs, 6 . . . . 880.00
Chair Set, Art Deco, Oak, Tall Back, Floral Silk, 4 . . . . 330.00
Chair Set, Art Deco, Rosewood, Leather Seat, France, c.1930, 34 3/4 x 18 1/2 In., 6 . . . . . 5750.00
Chair Set, Art Deco, Sycamore, Rectangular Back, 6 . . . . 590.00
Chair Set, Art Deco, Upholstered Seats, Black Lacquer Legs, 2 Armchairs, 33 In., 8 . . . . . 295.00
Chair Set, Audoux Minet, Beech, Raffia Seat, Back, 2 Armchairs, 35 In., 4 . . . . 3600.00
Chair Set, Baroque Revival, Oak, Embossed Leather, Leaves, Vines, Spindle Backrest, 6 . 705.00
Chair Set, Beech, Ladder Back, Carved Crest Over 5 Splats, Rush Seat, 43 In., 12 . . . . 4140.00
Chair Set, Beech, Ladder Back, Rush Seat, Circular Legs, England, 43 In., 10 . . . . 2070.00
Chair Set, Belter, Laminated Oak, Quartersawn, Upholstered, 10 . . . . 9500.00
Chair Set, Bergere, Empire Style, Arched Back, Padded Arms, Paw Feet, 20th Century, 4 . 1725.00
Chair Set, Biedermeier Style, Ebonized, Concave Crest, 3 Shaped Slats, Saber Legs, 4 . . . 235.00
Chair Set, Biedermeier, Elm, Curved Crest, Padded, Square Legs, 36 In., 4 . . . . 3910.00
Chair Set, Biedermeier, Fruitwood, Leather, Saber Legs, 4 . . . . 5080.00
Chair Set, Charles Pollock, Leather, Knoll, 1965, 4 . . . . 115.00
Chair Set, Chinese Chippendale, Mahogany, Carved, Pierced Crest, 39 In., 12 . . . . 2760.00
Chair Set, Chippendale Style, Carved Pierced Back, Carved Knuckles, 2 Armchairs, 10 . . 2585.00
Chair Set, Chippendale Style, Mahogany, Cabriole Legs, 2 Armchairs, 12 . . . . 3680.00
Chair Set, Chippendale Style, Mahogany, Cabriole Legs, Pad Feet, c.1900, 4 . . . . 1150.00
Chair Set, Chippendale Style, Mahogany, Damask, 1 Armchair, c.1876, 40 In., 8 . . . . 7900.00
Chair Set, Chippendale Style, Mahogany, Padded, 2 Armchairs, 39 In., 14 . . . . 4140.00
Chair Set, Chippendale Style, Mahogany, Padded, 2 Armchairs, 41 In., 10 . . . . 2760.00
Chair Set, Chippendale, Mahogany, Cabriole Legs, 2 Armchairs, 38 In., 12 . . . . 2760.00
Chair Set, Chippendale, Mahogany, Ladder Back, 2 Armchairs, 1900s, 6 . . . . 1495.00
Chair Set, Chippendale, Mahogany, Ladder Back, Carved, Pierced, Square Legs, 4 . . . . . . 805.00
Chair Set, Chippendale, Mahogany, Pierced Splat, Leaf Carved Legs, 38 In., 6 . . . . 2300.00
Chair Set, Chippendale, Walnut, Ribbonback, Bowed Seat, 39 1/2 In., 4 . . . . 1323.00
Chair Set, Dorothy Schindele, Green, Modern Color, c.1950, 30 1/2 x 21 In., 4 . . . . 1410.00
Chair Set, Dufrene, Cherry, Bridge, Arms, Aubusson, c.1940, 31 x 20 In., 4 . . . . 9400.00
Chair Set, E. Wormley, Bleached Mahogany, 1940s, 23 1/2 x 37 In., 8 . . . . 3105.00
Chair Set, Eames, La Fonda, Black Seat, Herman Miller, c.1961, 30 x 25 x 21 In., 4 . . . . . 640.00
Chair Set, Edwardian, Oval Cane Back, Painted Panel, 8 . . . . 2940.00
Chair Set, Edwardian, Polychrome, Oval Back, c.1900, 36 1/2 In., 4 . . . . 3910.00
Chair Set, Empire Style, Carved, Lacquered, Gilt, Leather Seat, France, c.1800, 6 . . . . . . 3060.00
Chair Set, Empire Style, Mahogany, Gilt Bronze Mounted, Griffins, 4 . . . . .10575.00
Chair Set, Empire Style, Mahogany, Upholstered, Swan Uprights, c.1890, 38 In., 4 . . . . . . 6615.00
Chair Set, Empire, Mahogany, Saber Legs, Vase-Form Back Splats, Upholstered, 6 . . . . . 460.00
Chair Set, English Beech, Earred Crest, Spindles, Rush Seat, 41 3/4 In., 8 . . . . 2530.00
Chair Set, Federal, Curved Crest, Painted, Medallions, Balloon Seat, 32 In., 5 . . . . 600.00
Chair Set, Federal, Mahogany Veneer, Arches, Reeded, c.1810, 36 1/2 In., 4 . . . . .15275.00
Chair Set, Federal, Mahogany, Shieldback, Carved, 2 Armchairs, 37 1/4 In., 8 . . . . 9200.00
Chair Set, Federal, Mahogany, Shieldback, Reeded Detail, 19 x 38 In., 4 . . . . .11000.00
Chair Set, Federal, Reeded, Crest Rails, Scrolled Splats, Cane, 19th Century, 4 . . . . 460.00

Chair Set, Flame Mahogany, Saber Legs, c.1840, 6 . . . .   900.00
Chair Set, Floral Painted Crest, Rush Seat, Box Stretcher, 32 x 15 In., 8 . . . .   230.00
Chair Set, Frankl, Mahogany, Upholstered, 2 Armchairs, 31 x 20 In., 6 . . . .   1116.00
Chair Set, French Provincial Style, Oak, Carved Crest, Shaped Rails, Rush Seat, 36 In., 6   1265.00
Chair Set, French Provincial, Beech, Ladder Back, Rush Seat, 39 1/2 In., 8 . . . .   1955.00
Chair Set, French Provincial, Fruitwood, 19th Century, 35 In., 8 . . . .   1495.00
Chair Set, French Provincial, Fruitwood, Rush Seat, 19th Century, 38 1/2 In., 12 . . . .   1610.00
Chair Set, French Provincial, Fruitwood, Rush Seat, c.1890, 35 1/2 In., 4 . . . .   1035.00
Chair Set, French Provincial, Fruitwood, Rush Seat, c.1890, 36 3/4 In., 6 . . . .   1265.00
Chair Set, French Provincial, Fruitwood, Serpentine, Shell Carved, Rush Seat, 39 In., 6 . .   690.00
Chair Set, French Provincial, Ladder Back, 4 Shaped & Curved Slats, 43 In., 6 . . . .   865.00
Chair Set, Fruitwood, Rush Seat, Flower Basket Carving, c.1885, 36 In., 6 . . . .   546.00
Chair Set, G. Nakashima, Grass Seat, Barrel Shape, 28 1/2 x 23 x 18 In., 6 . . . .   5300.00
Chair Set, G. Stickley, 3 Vertical Slats, Leather Seat, 17 x 17 x 39 In., 8 . . . .   6325.00
Chair Set, G. Stickley, H-Back, Rush Seat, 17 x 16 x 34 In., 4 . . . .   3740.00
Chair Set, George II, Mahogany, Carved Vase-Form Splat, Saddle Seat, 39 In., 8 . . . . 12075.00
Chair Set, George III Style, Green & Cream Paint, 2 Armchairs, 6 . . . .   2870.00
Chair Set, George III Style, Mahogany, Ladder Back, c.1890, 6 . . . .   980.00
Chair Set, George III Style, Mahogany, Leaf Carved, Needlepoint Seat, c.1890, 4 . . . .   2070.00
Chair Set, George III Style, Mahogany, Pierced Splat, 2 Armchairs, c.1890, 8 . . . .   8625.00
Chair Set, George III Style, Mahogany, Shieldback, 2 Armchairs, 40 In., 10 . . . .   5520.00
Chair Set, George III Style, Mahogany, Shieldback, Carved, Inlaid Fans, 8 . . . .   4400.00
Chair Set, George III Style, Mahogany, Wheat Sheaf Splat, 37 In., 8 . . . .   4140.00
Chair Set, George III, Beech, Painted, Cushions, Cane, Arms, c.1800, 4 . . . .   3000.00
Chair Set, George III, Mahogany, Arched Back, Carved, Pierced Back, 37 In., 12 . . . .   4830.00
Chair Set, George III, Mahogany, Arched Bellflower Crest, Fan Splats, 6 . . . .   2070.00
Chair Set, George III, Mahogany, Pierced Splat, Cabriole Legs, 4 . . . .   920.00
Chair Set, George III, Mahogany, Pierced Splat, Dolphin Feet, Carved, 4 . . . .   4600.00
Chair Set, George III, Mahogany, Satinwood Inlay, Arched Crest, Serpentine Slats, 8 . . . .   4700.00
Chair Set, George III, Mahogany, Shaped Crest, Pierced Splat, c.1785, 38 1/2 In., 4 . . . . .   1100.00
Chair Set, George III, Mahogany, Shieldback, Wheat Sheaves, Spade Feet, 4 . . . .   1880.00
Chair Set, Georgian Style, Ebonized, Shaped Splat, Butterflies, Flowers, 8 . . . .   960.00
Chair Set, Georgian Style, Yew, Parcel Gilt Flutes, Upholstered, 6 . . . .   1410.00
Chair Set, Giltwood, Upholstered Seat & Back, Flower & Leaf Frame, 8 . . . .   920.00
Chair Set, Gio Ponti, Walnut Frame, Leather Seats & Backrests, c.1950, 34 In., 6 . . . .   3105.00
Chair Set, Grotto, Scrolled Feet, Tufted Seat, Back, Italy, 34 In., 6 . . . .   3680.00
Chair Set, Hardwoods, Poplar Seat, Plank Bottom, Arrow Back, 34 In., 4 . . . .   275.00
Chair Set, Hardwoods, Scrolled Crest, 4 Spindles, Rush Seat, Turned Legs, 33 In., 4 . . . .   275.00
Chair Set, Hearts & Leaves On Crest, Red Flame Graining, Plank Seat, 32 In., 6 . . . .   2310.00
Chair Set, Henkel-Harris, Queen Anne, Black Cherry, Upholstered Seat, 10 . . . .   460.00
Chair Set, Hepplewhite, Mahogany, Carved Bellflower, Shaped Crest, Saddle Seat, 6 . . . .   1955.00
Chair Set, Hitchcock Style, Painted, Stenciled, Slat Back, Rush Seat, 34 In., 6 . . . .   470.00
Chair Set, Hitchcock, Painted, Stenciled, Rush Seat, 35 1/2 In., 6 . . . .   575.00
Chair Set, Jacobean Style, Deep Relief Carved Back, Plank Seat, 41 In., 6 . . . .   920.00
Chair Set, Jacobean Style, Oak, Upholstered Seat & Back, c.1900, 42 x 19 x 17 In., 4 . . .   1725.00
Chair Set, Jean Prouve, Birch Seat & Backrest, Enameled Steel Legs, 32 In., 4 . . . .   9200.00
Chair Set, Jen Risom, Black & Red, 1942, 17 1/2 x 31 In., 4 . . . .   1610.00
Chair Set, Joubert & Petit, Art Deco, Rosewood, Mahogany, c.1930, 36 x 24 In., 4 . . . . . .   5060.00
Chair Set, L. & J.G. Stickley, 2 Horizontal Slats, Leather Seat, 1 Armchair, 4 . . . .   3740.00
Chair Set, Lancashire Style, Ashwood, Ladder Back, 2 Armchairs, 12 . . . .   1955.00
Chair Set, Limbert, No. 255, Oak, T-Back, Ebony Inlay, Leather Seat, Branded, 38 In., 6 .   9200.00
Chair Set, Limbert, Single Slat Back, Drop-In Seat, 17 x 18 x 36 In., 6 . . . .   1955.00
Chair Set, Limbert, T-Back, Leather Seat, 17 x 17 x 37 In., 6 . . . .   3220.00
Chair Set, Louis Philippe, Walnut, Padded Back, Seat, c.1830, 34 In., 6 . . . .   7768.00
Chair Set, Louis XV Style, Beech, Cane, Scalloped Shell Carving, France, 38 In., 6 . . . . .   805.00
Chair Set, Louis XV Style, Beech, Serpentine Top Rail & Splats, Rush Seat, 37 In., 6 . . .   1495.00
Chair Set, Louis XV Style, Fruitwood, Carved, Upholstered, 2 Armchairs, 8 . . . .   1058.00
Chair Set, Louis XV Style, Gilt Carved, Pierced Leaf Crest, Upholstered, 6 . . . .   5290.00
Chair Set, Louis XV Style, Leaf Crest, Upholstered, 2 Armchairs, 8 . . . .   1315.00
Chair Set, Louis XV Style, Parcel Gilt, Padded Back, Sprung Seat, 2 Armchairs, 4 . . . . . .   1020.00
Chair Set, Louis XV Style, Provincial, Carved Crest, Cane Back, Seat, 37 In., 6 . . . .   1610.00
Chair Set, Louis XV, Fruitwood, Carved Crest, Cane Back, Cabriole Legs, 38 In., 8 . . . . .   2070.00
Chair Set, Louis XVI Style, Fruitwood, Caned, Arch Back, c.1890, 36 1/2 In., 6 . . . .   1035.00

Chair Set, Louis XVI Style, Painted, Cameo Back, Fluted Legs, Shaped Feet, 12 . . . . 1385.00
Chair Set, Louis XVI Style, Painted, Carved Wood, Silk, 10 . . . . 6575.00
Chair Set, Louis XVI Style, White & Blue Paint, 20th Century, 8 . . . . 5736.00
Chair Set, Louis XVI, White Paint, Padded Back, Scroll Arms, c.1875, 6 . . . . 6575.00
Chair Set, Mahogany, Hepplewhite, Splats, Tapered Legs, 1 Armchair, 35 In., 6 . . . . 1430.00
Chair Set, Mahogany, Lyre Back, Leaf Carved Pediment, Yoke Crest, c.1850, 4 . . . . 863.00
Chair Set, Mahogany, Ormolu Flower, Padded Seat, Saber Legs, c.1900, 34 In., 6 . . . . . . 4600.00
Chair Set, Mahogany, Pierced Splat Backs, Tapered Legs, 2 Armchairs, 38 x 22 In., 8 . . . . 3335.00
Chair Set, Mahogany, Shieldback, Upholstered, Serpentine Arms, 36 In., 6 . . . . 1100.00
Chair Set, Mahogany, Tombstone Back, Blue Leather Seats, 2 Armchairs, c.1920, 8 . . . . . 2800.00
Chair Set, Mahogany, Upholstered Seats, Saber Legs, 1870s, 4 . . . . 1200.00
Chair Set, Mahogany, Vase-Shape Splats, Trap Seats, Claw & Ball Feet, 12 . . . . 2185.00
Chair Set, McCobb, Birch, Perimeter Group, Winchedon, 6 . . . . 489.00
Chair Set, Mies Van Der Rohe, Brno, Knoll, c.1930, 31 x 23 x 18 In., 10 . . . . 7638.00
Chair Set, Napoleon III, Gilt Bronze Mounted, Ebonized, Upholstered, 8 . . . . 6465.00
Chair Set, Neoclassical, Mahogany, Flowers, Leaf Carved Crest, 32 In., 12 . . . . 3220.00
Chair Set, Neoclassical, Mahogany, Gondola, Concave Back, Fabric Seat, 32 1/2 In., 6 . . . 2590.00
Chair Set, Neoclassical, Maple, Figured, Cane Seat, c.1820, 5 . . . . 920.00
Chair Set, Nutting, No. 461, Dutch Arms, 4 . . . . 1870.00
Chair Set, Oak, Square Back, Stuffed Seats, Carved Legs, 2 Armchairs, 6 . . . . 1380.00
Chair Set, Old Hickory, Rush Woven Seat, 2 Chairs, Settee, Stool 1150.00
Chair Set, P. Guariche, Lacquered Plywood, Vinyl, Enameled Steel, 1950s, 20 x 30 In., 6 . 2185.00
Chair Set, Painted, Cornucopia, Fruit Crests, Turned Stiles, Cane, 32 In., 6 . . . . 990.00
Chair Set, Philippe Starck, Mahogany, Barrel Back, 3 Legs, 31 x 19 x 21 In., 6 . . . . 1880.00
Chair Set, Piretti, Plia, Folding, Stainless Steel, Castelli, Italy, c.1969, 29 In. 1530.00
Chair Set, Plank Seat, Bootjack Back, Brown Ground, Fruit Basket, 32 In., 8 . . . . 1650.00
Chair Set, Plank Seat, Red & Black Grain, Fruit, Leaves, 18 In., 6 . . . . 1320.00
Chair Set, Plank Seat, Shaped Seats, Arrow Back, 1900s, 33 1/2 In., 4 . . . . 550.00
Chair Set, Queen Anne Style, Burl Walnut, Shaped Top Rail Splat, Arms, 10 . . . . 2300.00
Chair Set, Queen Anne Style, Mahogany, Shaped Crest, Padded, 1 Armchair, 38 In., 7 . . . 2185.00
Chair Set, Queen Anne Style, Mahogany, Shell-Carved Crest, Vase Splat, 42 In., 10 . . . . . 3910.00
Chair Set, Queen Anne Style, Mahogany, Yoke Crest, 2 Armchairs, c.1890, 5 . . . . 2875.00
Chair Set, Queen Anne Style, Oak, Cabriole Legs, Pad Feet, 2 Armchairs, c.1915, 6 . . . . . 1265.00
Chair Set, Queen Anne Style, Walnut, Baluster Splat, 2 Armchairs, c.1900, 6 . . . . 1955.00
Chair Set, Queen Anne Style, Walnut, Urn Splat, Slip Seat, 2 Armchairs, c.1900, 8 . . . . . . 2300.00
Chair Set, Queen Anne, Mahogany, Pierced Splat, Drake Feet, 10 . . . . 4830.00
Chair Set, Queen Anne, Maple, Cyma Curved Back, Rush Seat, 1700s, 40 1/2 In., 4 . . . . . 7475.00
Chair Set, Queen Anne, Pickled Oak, Carved Acanthus Leaf Wave On Crest, 43 In., 10 . . 2090.00
Chair Set, Queen Anne, Walnut, Serpentine Crest, Carved Splat, 38 1/2 In., 12 . . . . 4370.00
Chair Set, Regency Style, Mahogany, Inlaid Crest, 2 Armchairs, 35 1/2 In., 12 . . . . 3450.00
Chair Set, Regency Style, Mahogany, Late 19th Century, 33 In., 6 . . . . 1840.00
Chair Set, Regency Style, Mahogany, Ribbed Crest, Padded, 1 Armchair, 35 In., 6 . . . . 2300.00
Chair Set, Regency Style, Mahogany, Saber Legs, 2 Armchairs, 20th Century, 6 . . . . 1380.00
Chair Set, Regency Style, Mahogany, Upholstered, 2 Armchairs, 36 1/2 In., 12 . . . . 3910.00
Chair Set, Regency Style, Painted, Brown, Parcel Gilt, Arms, 4 . . . . 5975.00
Chair Set, Regency, Mahogany, Brass Inlaid Crest, 33 In., 12 . . . . 12650.00
Chair Set, Regency, Mahogany, X-Form Backrest, Upholstered Seat, c.1810, 8 . . . . 5875.00
Chair Set, Regency, Oval Central Panel, Upholstered Seat, England, 2 Armchairs, 6 . . . . . 3675.00
Chair Set, Ricchio, Walnut Stain, 6 Back Slats, Knoll Studio, 32 x 23 x 24 In., 4 . . . . 325.00
Chair Set, Rosewood, Dragons, Japan, 19th Century, 4 . . . . 1530.00
Chair Set, Rosewood, Floral, Portrait Carved Crests, 2 Armchairs, c.1885, 48 In., 4 . . . . . 2240.00
Chair Set, Roycroft, No. 25, Mahogany, 38 1/4 x 18 In., 6 . . . . 5975.00
Chair Set, Saarinen, Bent Plywood, Wool, Upholstered, 1950s, 21 x 30 In., 4 . . . . 1495.00
Chair Set, Saarinen, Tulip, Fiberglass, Knoll, 2 Armchairs, c.1956, 32 In., 4 . . . . 560.00
Chair Set, Seignouret Style, Mahogany, Gondola, Carving, 6 . . . . 1290.00
Chair Set, Sheraton Style, English Oak, Stylized Sheaf Splat, 1 Armchair, 34 In., 6 . . . . . . 980.00
Chair Set, Sheraton Style, Polychrome, Cane Seat, Gilt, c.1850, 35 1/2 In., 6 . . . . 2185.00
Chair Set, Sheraton Style, Shield Back, Upholstered, 20th Century, 4 Armchairs, 12 . . . . . 4820.00
Chair Set, Sheraton, Rush Seat, Stenciled Fruit, Ivy, 33 In., 8 . . . . 2350.00
Chair Set, Splayed Back, Rush Seat, France, Mid 19th Century, 6 . . . . 440.00
Chair Set, Stephens, Bent Oak, Turquoise Vinyl, Knoll, 31 x 19 1/2 In., 8 . . . . 355.00
Chair Set, Stickley Bros., 1 Armchair, 37 x 18 x 17 In., 6 . . . . 1725.00
Chair Set, Stickley Bros., No. 479 1/2, Vertical Slats, Upholstered Seat, 37 In., 4 . . . . 1150.00

Chair Set, Thonet, Molded Plywood, Melmac Seat, Back, 16 x 21 x 31 1/2 In., 8 . . . . 690.00
Chair Set, Tudor Style, Leather Seat, Back, Tack Mounts, Twist Legs, 1900s, 6 . . . . 460.00
Chair Set, Victorian, Walnut, Balloon Back, Padded, c.1890, 33 1/2 In., 6 . . . . 1725.00
Chair Set, W. Platner, 2 Armchairs, 1 Lounge, 38 1/2 x 40 x 36 In., 3 . . . . 940.00
Chair Set, Walnut, Applied Burl Panels On Crest, Baluster Splat, Seat Apron, 6 . . . . 200.00
Chair Set, Walnut, Carved, Upholstered, Tapered Legs, 2 Armchairs, 1800s, 8 . . . . 945.00
Chair Set, Walnut, Ladder Back, Rush Seat, Tapered Legs, 2 Armchairs, 8 . . . . 1820.00
Chair Set, Walnut, Open Back, Pierced Foliate, Carved Splat, Sprung Seat, 6 . . . . 1200.00
Chair Set, Walnut, Plank Bottom, 1 Armchair, 1800s, 32 1/2 x 35 In., 3 . . . . 200.00
Chair Set, Walnut, Spindle Back, Rush Seat, Turned Legs, 2 Armchairs, 8 . . . . 728.00
Chair Set, Warren McArthur, Green, c.1937, 29 1/2 x 17 1/4 x 17 In., 6 . . . . 1765.00
Chair Set, Wegner, Teak, Leather, 1960s, 22 1/2 x 29 In., 5 . . . . 1725.00
Chair Set, Wegner, Y-Back, Ebonized, Carl Hansen & Son, 22 x 20 x 29 In., 4 . . . . 978.00
Chair Set, William IV Styl, Mahogany E, Upholstered Seat, Concave Crest Rail, 6 . . . . . . 1840.00
Chair Set, William IV, Saddle Seat, Rounded Concave Back, c.1835, 34 In., 4 . . . . 2990.00
Chair Set, William IV, Upholstered, Fluted Legs, c.1865, 36 1/2 x 20 In., 4 . . . . 980.00
Chair Set, Windsor, Bow Back, Painted, Carved Seat, c.1810, 36 x 17 In., 8 . . . . 9200.00
Chair Set, Windsor, Bow Back, Painted, Incised Crest, Early 1800s, 37 1/2 In., 7 . . . . 2115.00
Chair Set, Windsor, Bow Back, Painted, Incised Crest, Plank Seat, 37 1/2 In., 4 . . . . 1295.00
Chair Set, Windsor, Bow Back, Walnut, Bamboo Turned Legs, c.1980, 38 In., 8 . . . . 4675.00
Chair Set, Windsor, Fanback, Serpentine Crests, c.1800, 36 In., 4 . . . . 1765.00
Chair Set, Windsor, George IV Style, Elm, Scroll-Cut Splat, Open Arms, 40 In., 6 . . . . . . 2415.00
Chair Set, Windsor, Thumb Back, Painted, Fruit, Flowers On Crest, 33 In., 6 . . . . 825.00
Chair Set, Z-Chair, Lucite, 1 Piece Molded, 1970s, 16 x 18 x 33 1/2 In., 4 . . . . 1265.00
Chair-Table, Pine, Walnut, Maple, 3-Board Top, Seat, 19th Century, 27 1/4 In. 3290.00
Chaise Longue, B. Mathsson, Bent Plywood, Original Pad, 35 x 69 x 29 In. 1765.00
Chaise Longue, Charles X, Mahogany, Swan Neck Terminals, c.1835, 36 x 27 In. 2300.00
Chaise Longue, Eames, Aluminum Group, Herman Miller 750.00
Chaise Longue, Eames, Aluminum Group, Sling Seat, 24 1/2 x 28 x 33 In. 375.00
Chaise Longue, Eames, Aluminum, Leather, Herman Miller, c.1975, 17 1/2 x 76 x 29 In. . . 3450.00
Chaise Longue, Eames, Soft Pad, Leather, Aluminum, Herman Miller, 25 x 28 x 34 In. 460.00
Chaise Longue, Fabio Lenci, Glass Sides, Rolled Leather Cushions, 28 x 36 x 30 In., Pair 6900.00
Chaise Longue, G. Nakashima, Walnut, Spindle Back, 1966, 33 x 34 In. 10350.00
Chaise Longue, Hardwood, Bone Inlay, Caned Seat, Back, Spindle Legs, Indo-Portuguese 2115.00
Chaise Longue, Le Corbusier, Black, White, Cassina, 1980s, 32 x 68 x 21 1/2 In. 999.00
Chaise Longue, Louis XV Style, Fruitwood, Carved, Figural Upholstery 420.00
Chaise Longue, Marcel Breuer, Blue Seat, Wood Frame, Knoll, c.1938, 31 3/4 x 54 In. . . . 3525.00
Chaise Longue, Ralph Rapson, Bird, Webbed Seat, Knoll, 21 1/2 x 32 x 30 1/2 In. 1265.00
Chaise Longue, Regency Style, Mahogany, Satinwood, Cushioned Seat, 29 x 72 x 29 In. . . 1035.00
Chaise Longue, Richard Schultz, Vinyl, Mesh, Aluminum, Knoll, 26 x 76 x 16 In. 2300.00
Chaise Longue, Rococo Revival, Dog Head Carved Frame, Upholstered 2950.00
Chaise Longue, Van Keppel & Green, Black Frame, c.1939, 18 1/2 x 80 x 32 In. 3820.00
Chaise Longue, Warren McArthur, White Cushions, c.1937, 29 1/2 x 51 x 25 In. 4115.00
Chaise Longue, Wegner, Padouk Wood, Wool, Iron, 1950s, 23 x 30 In. 2875.00
Chaise Longue, Wicker, Iron, Spring Mounted, Upholstered, c.1900 . . . . 920.00
Chaise Longue & Ottoman, Eames, 670/671, Plywood, Leather 1495.00
Chaise Longue & Ottoman, Eames, Aluminum Group, High Back, Herman Miller 1150.00
Chaise Longue & Ottoman, Saarinen, Womb, Cato Fabric, Knoll, 31 x 40 x 40 In. 999.00
Chest, Adam, Mahogany, 3 Banded Drawers, Bellflower Pilasters, 29 x 20 x 15 In. 1725.00
Chest, Aesthetic Revival, Carved Walnut, Inlaid, Marble, 46 1/2 x 37 1/2 In. . . . . *Illus* 8815.00
Chest, Amish, Cherry, Oak, Decorated Bars On 8 Drawer Fronts, 51 x 43 x 22 In. 1100.00
Chest, Amish, Walnut, Pine, 8 Drawers, Red Wash, Turned Feet, c.1894, 42 x 20 x 50 In. . . 1650.00
Chest, Art Deco, Burl, Cabinet Over 3 Drawers, 1930s, 46 3/4 x 30 In. 210.00
Chest, Arts & Crafts, 2 Short Over 5 Long Drawers, c.1912, 59 x 32 x 19 In. 1295.00
Chest, Arts & Crafts, Carved Panels, Gothic Design, England, 18 x 25 3/4 13 In. 1095.00
Chest, Arts & Crafts, Cedar, Lift Top, Drawers, Copper Fretwork, 40 1/2 x 48 x 24 In. . . . 405.00
Chest, Bachelor's, George I, Walnut Inlay, Hinged Top, Drawer, 29 x 31 x 12 In. 7170.00
Chest, Bachelor's, George II Style, Burl Walnut, 31 1/2 x 30 1/2 x 16 1/4 In. 1840.00
Chest, Bachelor's, Mahogany, Brushing Slide, 2 Short & 3 Long Drawers, c.1750, 30 In. . . 875.00
Chest, Biedermeier, Birch, Plinth Top, 3 Drawers, 34 x 38 1/2 x 30 In. 1725.00
Chest, Biedermeier, Birch, Plinth Top, 3 Drawers, Bracket Feet, 33 x 36 1/4 x 19 In. 1495.00
Chest, Biedermeier, Blond Wood, 4 Drawers, 19th Century 1120.00
Chest, Blanket, 2 Lower Drawers, Blue Gray, Conn., c.1820 . . . . 2800.00

Chest, Blanket, 3-Drawer Base, Pennsylvania, 1700s, 33 1/2 x 46 1/2 In. 1400.00
Chest, Blanket, 6-Board, Red Stain, Square Cutout Ends, 18th Century 565.00
Chest, Blanket, Arts & Crafts, Panel Top, Sides, Butterfly Joints, 18 x 42 x 23 In. 4025.00
Chest, Blanket, Arts & Crafts, Paneled, Cedar Lined, 18 3/4 x 41 x 21 In. 550.00
Chest, Blanket, Baroque, Walnut, Iron Mounted, 18th Century, 27 1/4 x 57 x 27 1/2 In. . . . 550.00
Chest, Blanket, Blue Green, Initials AZ On Lid, 19th Century, 51 1/2 In. 1090.00
Chest, Blanket, Bracket Foot, 2 Drawers, Wooden Knob, 42 1/2 x 39 x 16 1/2 In. 480.00
Chest, Blanket, Brown & Yellow Paint, 17 1/2 x 50 x 20 1/4 In. 960.00
Chest, Blanket, Cherry, 6-Board, Turned Feet, Dovetailed, Midwest, 23 x 37 x 18 In. 900.00
Chest, Blanket, Cherry, Dovetailed, Cutout Walnut Decoration & Molding, 13 In. 675.00
Chest, Blanket, Chestnut, Pine, Black Paint, Drawer, Scalloped Cutouts, 30 x 42 In. 880.00
Chest, Blanket, Chippendale, Walnut & Oak, 2 Drawers, Strap Hinges, 50 x 20 In. 1740.00
Chest, Blanket, Chippendale, Walnut, Dovetailed, Mid 19th Century, 24 x 22 x 48 In. 1100.00
Chest, Blanket, Chippendale, Walnut, Inlaid, 2 Drawers, Pa., 1781, 28 x 48 x 22 In. 10160.00
Chest, Blanket, Chippendale, Walnut, Tiger & Bird's-Eye Maple, Cotter Pin Hinges 3900.00
Chest, Blanket, Curly Maple, Cherry, Raised Panels, Turned Legs, 25 x 43 x 18 In. 1595.00
Chest, Blanket, Dovetailed, Till, Green Paint, Turned Feet, 50 x 32 In. 225.00
Chest, Blanket, Feather & Sponge Paint, Softwood, Dovetailed, 25 x 41 x 21 In. 880.00
Chest, Blanket, Federal, Softwood, 3 Drawers, Striped, Pennsylvania, 35 x 48 In. . . . *Illus* 3575.00
Chest, Blanket, Grain Painted, Gilt, Early 19th Century, 41 1/2 x 37 1/2 x 17 In. 2760.00
Chest, Blanket, Grain Painted, Mortised Turned Feet, Pa., c.1845, 27 x 51 x 22 In. 1695.00
Chest, Blanket, Grain Painted, Nail Construction, Turned Legs, c.1840, 47 x 18 In. 1245.00
Chest, Blanket, Grain Painted, Yellow, Dovetailed, Ball Feet, Wm. Bachman, 42 In. 309.00
Chest, Blanket, Grain Painted, Yellow, Orange, 19th Century, 12 x 20 1/2 x 11 In. 3585.00
Chest, Blanket, Green Vinegar Sponging, Vertical Lines, Bracket Feet, 25 x 49 In. 3300.00
Chest, Blanket, Green, Yellow Ground, Red Trim, Pennsylvania, 1849-1850, 51 In. 1695.00
Chest, Blanket, Hardwood, Brass, Continental, 18th Century, 29 x 53 x 24 1/2 In. 500.00
Chest, Blanket, Lacquer, Border Flowers, Chinese, c.1890, 24 1/2 x 35 In. 490.00
Chest, Blanket, Lift Top, Green Paint, Rope Beckets, American, 16 1/2 x 44 In. 259.00
Chest, Blanket, Molded Lid, Base, Black, Red Flame Graining, York Co., Pa., 1863 . . . . . 340.00
Chest, Blanket, Oak, Panels, Rosewood Feet, Dutch, 1920s, 23 x 38 In. 675.00
Chest, Blanket, Paint Decorated, Unicorns, Flowers, Red, Brown, Pa., c.1780 . . . . 10450.00
Chest, Blanket, Painted, Dovetailed, Lidded Till, Germany, 22 x 47 1/2 x 24 In. 690.00
Chest, Blanket, Pine, 2 Drawers, Green Paint, 19th Century, 41 x 37 x 18 In. 1795.00
Chest, Blanket, Pine, 2 Drawers, Painted, Pennsylvania, c.1890, 25 x 16 x 12 1/2 In. 1950.00
Chest, Blanket, Pine, 3 Drawers, Iron Strap Hinges, Bracket Feet, 52 x 23 x 27 In. 1210.00
Chest, Blanket, Pine, Black Over Red Flame Grain, Bracket Feet, 41 x 17 3/4 In. 1870.00
Chest, Blanket, Pine, Blue, Decorative Panels, Iron Hinges & Lock, c.1790, 19 x 44 In. . . . 995.00
Chest, Blanket, Pine, Dovetailed, Dome Top, Hinges, 19th Century, 11 x 19 x 11 In. 470.00
Chest, Blanket, Pine, Dovetailed, Interior Open Till, Canterbury, N.H., c.1837, 17 In. 1265.00
Chest, Blanket, Pine, Feet, Applied Molding, Arch Cutouts, 24 x 50 x 17 In. 1045.00
Chest, Blanket, Pine, Lift Top, 3 Drawers, Early 19th Century, 50 x 38 1/2 In. 775.00
Chest, Blanket, Pine, Lift Top, Drawer, New England, 19th Century, 35 x 44 x 18 In. 635.00
Chest, Blanket, Pine, Lift Top, Drawers, Skirt, Connecticut, 44 x 37 x 18 1/2 In. 1210.00
Chest, Blanket, Pine, Lift Top, Green Paint, Strap Hinges, 24 x 43 x 22 In. 175.00
Chest, Blanket, Pine, Lift Top, Snipe Hinges, Ditty Box Interior, American, 22 x 37 In. . . 690.00
Chest, Blanket, Pine, Lower Drawer, c.1840, 35 x 39 3/4 x 18 3/4 In. 1095.00
Chest, Blanket, Pine, Molded Lift Top, 2 Drawers, Green Paint, 44 x 43 In. 1438.00

Furniture, Chest,
Aesthetic Revival,
Carved Walnut,
Inlaid, Marble,
46 1/2 x 37 1/2 In.

Furniture, Chest, Blanket, Federal, Softwood,
3 Drawers, Striped, Pennsylvania, 35 x 48 In.

Chest, Blanket, Pine, Molded Lift Top, Drawer, Off-White Paint, Bracket Feet, 35 x 44 In.   1208.00
Chest, Blanket, Pine, Painted Flame Graining, Salmon Ground, 49 x 23 1/2 x 28 1/2 In. . .   550.00
Chest, Blanket, Pine, Painted, 6-Board, Rosehead Nails, 49 1/2 x 15 3/4 x 17 1/2 In. 275.00
Chest, Blanket, Pine, Painted, Flower, Landscapes, c.1890, 5 1/2 x 8 1/2 x 5 In. 2390.00
Chest, Blanket, Pine, Painted, Polychrome, New York, c.1830, 41 1/2 x 19 In. 4200.00
Chest, Blanket, Pine, Painted, Till, Forged Hinges, Lock, 29 x 49 x 25 In. 1875.00
Chest, Blanket, Pine, Polychrome Decoration, Till Inside, 22 x 18 x 40 In. 450.00
Chest, Blanket, Pine, Red Paint, Dovetailed Case, 1-Board Top, 25 x 14 x 17 In. 715.00
Chest, Blanket, Pine, Yellow, Hinges, Scrolled Feet, 25 x 31 x 17 In. 2530.00
Chest, Blanket, Poplar, 3 Tombstone Panels, Tulips, 2 Drawers, Painted, 29 x 48 In. 1100.00
Chest, Blanket, Poplar, Flame Grain, Red, Yellow, Turned Feet, Ohio, 44 x 21 x 25 In. 880.00
Chest, Blanket, Poplar, Grained Red Over Tan, Bracket Feet, c.1860, 39 x 19 x 21 In. 770.00
Chest, Blanket, Poplar, Pine, Grain Painted, Paneled End, 48 x 19 x 25 1/2 In. 660.00
Chest, Blanket, Poplar, Red Paint, High Turned Legs, Child's, 21 x 29 x 15 In. 990.00
Chest, Blanket, Poplar, Smoke Decoration, Painted, Dovetailed, 37 x 17 x 21 In. 660.00
Chest, Blanket, Poplar, Sponged Design, Yellow & Red, Bracket Feet, 19 x 44 In. 2860.00
Chest, Blanket, Poplar, Walnut, Red Grained, Double Arches, Ohio, 37 x 16 x 23 In. 935.00
Chest, Blanket, Queen Anne, Oak, 3 Drawers, Bulbous Feet, 23 1/2 x 12 3/4 x 14 In. 1350.00
Chest, Blanket, Red Paint, Hand Forged Hardware, New York, 22 1/2 x 21 In. 995.00
Chest, Blanket, Sheraton Style, Cherry, Inlaid, c.1810, 26 x 46 1/2 x 21 In. 1810.00
Chest, Blanket, Sheraton, Cherry, Poplar, Turned Legs, Ball Feet, 41 x 18 x 28 In. 1210.00
Chest, Blanket, Sheraton, Walnut, Dovetailed, Bread Board Ends, 27 x 20 x 48 In. 800.00
Chest, Blanket, Softwood, Dovetailed, Iron Jaw Lock, Pa., 36 1/2 x 51 x 23 1/2 In. 1320.00
Chest, Blanket, Softwood, Dovetailed, Snake Head Hinges, 1800s, 25 x 53 x 23 In. 1650.00
Chest, Blanket, Softwood, Feather Grain Painted, Dovetailed, Drawers, 24 x 38 x 21 In. ..   330.00
Chest, Blanket, Softwood, Feather Grained, Stippled, Green, Lancaster County, 50 In. 3630.00
Chest, Blanket, Softwood, Grain Painted, Diamond Border Paint, 24 x 52 x 22 In. 990.00
Chest, Blanket, Softwood, Grain Painted, Stippled, 19th Century, 28 x 50 x 23 In. 3630.00
Chest, Blanket, Softwood, Painted, Dovetailed Drawers, Striped, Pennsylvania, 48 In. 3575.00
Chest, Blanket, Softwood, Painted, Dovetailed, Turned Feet, 23 x 32 x 19 In. 660.00
Chest, Blanket, Softwood, Red Paint, Dovetailed, 18th Century, 22 x 49 x 23 In. 1210.00
Chest, Blanket, Softwood, Red Wash, Dovetailed, Ball Feet, 48 In. 225.00
Chest, Blanket, Softwood, Sponge Decoration, Salmon Ground, 24 1/2 x 44 x 21 In. 495.00
Chest, Blanket, Softwood, Stippled, Dovetailed, Lancaster County, 28 x 50 In. ..... *Illus*   3630.00
Chest, Blanket, Sponge Paint, Green Over Yellow, Wrought Iron, 26 x 50 x 25 In. 2310.00
Chest, Blanket, Strap Hinges, Till Compartment, Bracket Feet, 28 x 53 x 23 In. 3630.00
Chest, Blanket, Walnut, 2 Drawers, Banded Inlay, Bracket Feet, 25 7/8 x 47 x 20 In. 8800.00
Chest, Blanket, Walnut, Dovetailed, 2 Drawers, Ball Feet, 22 x 11 1/2 In. 450.00
Chest, Blanket, Walnut, Dovetailed, 2-Board Top, Breadboard Ends, Reeded Front 650.00
Chest, Blanket, Walnut, Poplar, Hinged Lid, Bracket Feet, 1835, 24 x 43 x 18 1/2 In. 2860.00
Chest, Blanket, William & Mary, Pine, Painted, 18th Century, 40 1/2 x 38 x 18 5/8 In. ..   1175.00
Chest, Blanket, Yellow & Umber Stippled Paint, Center Arch Front, 35 1/2 In. 590.00
Chest, Brass Butterfly Escutcheon, c.1900, Chinese, 21 x 21 x 21 In. 170.00
Chest, Burl Walnut, 3 Drawers, Block Front, Continental, 27 1/2 x 33 x 17 In. 3450.00
Chest, Burl Walnut, Mirror, Marble Top, Ripple Carved, 82 x 48 x 24 In. 635.00
Chest, Butternut, 4 Drawers, Graduated Drawers, 39 1/2 x 3 1/2 x 17 1/4 In. 1610.00
Chest, Butternut, Bonnet, 2 Small & 5 Large Drawers, Shaped Backsplash, 45 In........   900.00
Chest, Butternut, Painted, 3 Drawers, Medallion, Zoar, Ohio, 41 x 19 x 41 In. 605.00
Chest, Butternut, Tiger Maple, 5 Drawers, c.1870, 21 x 17 1/2 In. 2950.00
Chest, Campaign, Camphorwood, Lift Top, Molded Edge, Handles, 19 x 37 x 17 In. 460.00
Chest, Campaign, Teak, Inlaid, Dovetailed, Handles, 16 x 30 1/2 x 14 In. 430.00
Chest, Camphorwood, Brass, Key, Handles, Till, 37 x 17 x 17 In. 550.00
Chest, Camphorwood, Dovetailed, Chinese, 19th Century, 17 1/2 x 36 In. 345.00
Chest, Camphorwood, Green Leather Covered, Chinese, 19th Century, 19 3/4 x 41 In. ...   345.00
Chest, Camphorwood, Ivory, Lift Top, Flower & Vine Inlay, 18 x 36 1/2 x 17 In. 805.00
Chest, Camphorwood, Leather, Painted Flowers, Brass Corners, Hinged, 12 x 29 x 15 In. .   2000.00
Chest, Cedar, Copper Bindings, Lift Out Tray, A.J. Miller, Bellefontaine, Ohio, 22 In. ...   225.00
Chest, Cedar, Lane, Crossbanded Veneer On Front, 46 In. 100.00
Chest, Charles II, Oak, Drawers, 35 x 37 1/2 x 20 3/4 In. 6572.00
Chest, Cherry, 4 Graduated Drawers, Cock-Beaded, Turned Legs, Ball Feet, 40 x 38 In. ..   920.00
Chest, Cherry, 5 Drawers, Bracket Base, 41 x 36 x 20 In. 520.00
Chest, Cherry, 7 Drawers, Flame Cut Veneer, Bobbin Turned Columns, 50 x 49 In. 175.00
Chest, Cherry, Bowfront, 4 Drawers, Brass Hardware, Kentucky, 44 x 42 x 24 In. 1870.00

Chest, Cherry, Curly Maple, 4 Drawers, Full Columns, c.1840, 46 1/2 x 43 In. 1130.00
Chest, Cherry, Line Inlay, 5 Graduated Drawers, Straight Bracket Feet, 40 x 37 1/2 In. . . . 1265.00
Chest, Cherry, Overhanging Top, String Inlay, 4 Scratch-Beaded Drawers, 35 x 38 x 19 In. . 4406.00
Chest, Cherry, Raised Panels, Shaped Bracket Feet, 5 x 11 1/2 x 5 1/2 In. 470.00
Chest, Cherry, Red Stained, 8 Cock-Beaded Drawers, c.1830s, 65 3/4 In. 2940.00
Chest, Chippendale Style, Black Walnut, Mahogany, Pine, 5 Drawers, 42 x 20 x 41 In. . . . 770.00
Chest, Chippendale Style, Mahogany, 7 Drawers, Early 20th Century, 58 x 34 x 21 In. . . . 920.00
Chest, Chippendale, Birch, 4 Graduated Lipped Drawers, Bracket Feet, 38 x 36 In. 1575.00
Chest, Chippendale, Cherry, 2-Board Top, 4 Drawers, Ogee Feet, 43 x 22 x 37 In. 7700.00
Chest, Chippendale, Cherry, 3 Short Drawers, 4 Long, c.1780, 62 x 42 In. 1725.00
Chest, Chippendale, Cherry, 4 Graduated Drawers, Rope Twist Columns, 37 x 42 x 22 In. . 9400.00
Chest, Chippendale, Cherry, Pine, 6 Drawers, Ogee Bracket Base, 57 x 39 x 20 1/2 In. . . . 5750.00
Chest, Chippendale, Cherry, Pine, Reeded Pilasters, 4 Drawers, 40 1/2 x 21 x 38 In. 9900.00
Chest, Chippendale, Cherry, Poplar, 4 Drawers, 2-Board Top, 46 x 19 1/2 x 39 In. 2090.00
Chest, Chippendale, Cherry, Reverse Serpentine, Inlaid, c.1795, 33 x 39 x 20 In. 7640.00
Chest, Chippendale, Cherry, Top Overhangs, Drawers, Claw Feet, 1760, 35 x 38 In. 7050.00
Chest, Chippendale, Curly Maple, 4 Drawers, Scalloped Bracket Feet, 36 x 39 In. 8250.00
Chest, Chippendale, Mahogany, 3 Small Over 5 Graduated Drawers, 56 1/2 x 39 x 21 In. . 4315.00
Chest, Chippendale, Mahogany, 4 Drawers, Cock-Beaded, Bracket Feet, 42 x 20 x 33 In. . 675.00
Chest, Chippendale, Mahogany, Serpentine Front, 4 Graduated Drawers, 36 x 43 In. 1925.00
Chest, Chippendale, Mahogany, Veneer, Pine, Bowfront, Ogee Feet, 40 x 23 x 35 In. 3025.00
Chest, Chippendale, Maple, 5 Drawers, Bracket Base, 47 1/2 x 36 x 18 1/4 In. 2990.00
Chest, Chippendale, Maple, 6 Drawers, Shaped Bracket Feet, 1800, 50 x 18 1/2 In. 9990.00
Chest, Chippendale, Oxbow, 4 Drawers, Ogee Bracket Feet, 33 x 18 1/2 x 40 In. 2645.00
Chest, Chippendale, Pine, 5 Drawers, Dovetailed, Bracket, 44 1/2 x 36 x 18 3/4 In. 1725.00
Chest, Chippendale, Pine, 5 Drawers, Molded Top, Bracket Base, 40 x 40 x 20 In. 920.00
Chest, Chippendale, Red Paint, 5 Drawers, Dovetailed, New England, 45 x 38 In. 9040.00
Chest, Chippendale, Stained, 4 Graduated Drawers, Spain, 40 x 36 1/2 x 18 In. 2350.00
Chest, Chippendale, Tiger Maple, Shaped Top, 4 Drawers, c.1770, 44 x 39 1/2 x 18 In. . . . 2185.00
Chest, Chippendale, Walnut, 2 Short Over 5 Graduated Drawers, 67 x 42 x 24 In. 8365.00
Chest, Chippendale, Walnut, 3 Drawers, Ogee Bracket Feet, 36 x 45 x 24 1/2 In. 825.00
Chest, Chippendale, Walnut, 4 Graduated Drawers, Ogee Feet, 38 x 38 In. 3500.00
Chest, Chippendale, Walnut, Beaded, Dovetailed Doors, 18th Century, 38 x 20 x 36 In. . . . 1600.00
Chest, Chippendale, Walnut, Figured, Philadelphia, c.1780, 28 x 40 x 20 In. 7170.00
Chest, Conant Ball, 5 Long Drawers, 43 x 38 x 18 In., Pair 765.00
Chest, Dower, Lift Top, Grain Painted, Blue Green Paint, 3 Drawers, 1796, 30 x 50 In. . . . 9775.00
Chest, Dower, Painted, Molded Lid, Heart Shapes, Black Grained, 24 x 52 x 23 1/2 In. . . 940.00
Chest, Dower, Sponge Painted, Arched Tulip Panels, Hinged Lid, Pa., 24 x 45 In. 1265.00
Chest, Dower, Yellow Pine, Dovetailed, Lidded Till, Iron Handles, 1700s, 23 x 22 x 52 In. 800.00
Chest, E. Wormley, Mahogany, Bentwood, Dunbar, c.1947, 48 x 22 x 36 In. . . . .4600.00 to 5465.00
Chest, E. Wormley, Walnut, Rosewood, Sliding Doors, Dunbar, 60 1/2 x 18 x 38 1/2 In. . . 3740.00
Chest, Eames, 3 Drawers, Steel Back, Herman Miller, 1950, 24 x 28 In. 5750.00
Chest, Edwardian, Mahogany, Rounded Corners, 20 Leather Drawers, 73 In. 805.00
Chest, Edwardian, Satinwood, Bowfront, Inlaid, 2 Over 3 Drawers, 40 In. 3760.00
Chest, Edwardian, Satinwood, Painted, Medallion, Venus & Cupid, 34 x 40 x 21 In. 1435.00
Chest, Elm, Burl, Brass Mounted, Japan, 19th Century, 11 x 13 x 10 In. 316.00
Chest, Elm, Polychrome, Rectangular Top, 2 Drawers, Chinese, c.1850, 15 x 28 x 14 In. . . 140.00
Chest, Empire Style, Mahogany Veneer, 3 Drawers, c.1865, 9 x 5 In. 550.00
Chest, Empire Style, Mahogany, 5 Dovetailed Drawers, Wood Knobs, 19 x 15 In. 550.00
Chest, Empire, 4 Drawers, Column Supports, Plinth Feet, Continental, 50 x 27 x 35 In. . . . 3450.00
Chest, Empire, Birch, Pine, Bird's-Eye Maple, Mahogany, 6 Drawers, 41 x 21 x 54 In. 1760.00
Chest, Empire, Cherry, 4 Drawers, Flame Graining, Glass Pulls, 43 x 22 5/8 x 46 3/4 In. . . 330.00
Chest, Empire, Curly Maple, 4 Drawers, Turned Feet, Dovetailed, 45 x 24 x 51 In. 715.00
Chest, Empire, Mahogany, 4 Drawers, Frame & Panel, Ogee Borders, 40 x 46 x 20 In. 140.00
Chest, Empire, Mahogany, Carved Posts, Backsplash, Columns, 56 x 20 x 45 In. 980.00
Chest, Empire, Mahogany, Doors, Drawer, c.1840, 12 x 13 1/2 x 8 In. 1450.00
Chest, Empire, Mahogany, Folk Art Carved, 4 Drawers, 19th Century, 46 x 21 x 43 In. . . . 2200.00
Chest, English, Mahogany, 3 Over 3 Dovetailed Drawers, 41 x 40 x 20 1/2 In. 1840.00
Chest, Eugene Schoen, Mahogany Veneer, Ivory Enamel, 4 Drawers, 36 x 48 x 23 In. . . . 2235.00
Chest, Federal Style, Mahogany, 8 Graduated Drawers, c.1875, 45 x 24 x 18 1/2 In. 1150.00
Chest, Federal, 4 Drawers, Turned Feet, Panel Sides, Brown Finish, 33 1/2 x 17 In. 1870.00
Chest, Federal, Bowfront, 4 Drawers, Reeded Columns & Legs, 44 x 43 In. 1150.00
Chest, Federal, Cherry, Bird's-Eye Maple, Split Drawers, 43 x 41 x 21 1/2 In. 1100.00

Chest, Federal, Cherry, Brass, c.1820, 41 x 40 1/2 x 19 In. 575.00
Chest, Federal, Cherry, Cock-Beaded Case, 4 Graduated Drawers, c.1800, 34 x 41 x 19 In.   940.00
Chest, Federal, Cherry, Satinwood Inlay, Bowfront, 1805, 36 1/2 x 39 3/4 x 23 1/2 In. . . .   2990.00
Chest, Federal, Cherry, Serpentine Front, 4 Drawers, Connecticut, 39 1/2 In. 8965.00
Chest, Federal, Feather Grain, Stippled Paint, 4 Drawers, 51 x 43 x 23 In. 1430.00
Chest, Federal, Figured Maple, Bowfront, Inlaid Birch Panels, 36 x 40 In. 5975.00
Chest, Federal, Mahogany, 4 Drawers, Chamfered Corners, G. Rall, 38 x 19 x 36 In. 1690.00
Chest, Federal, Mahogany, 4 Graduated Drawers, c.1805, 38 1/4 x 43 1/2 x 20 In. 1725.00
Chest, Federal, Mahogany, Bowfront, 4 Graduated Drawers, Beehive Turned Legs, 45 In. .   1265.00
Chest, Federal, Mahogany, Crossbanded, Bowfront, c.1800, 35 x 41 1/2 x 22 1/2 In. 7050.00
Chest, Federal, Mahogany, Inlaid Serpentine, Drawers, Brass, 1810, 45 x 22 In. 5580.00
Chest, Federal, Mahogany, Inlay, 2 Drawers Over 3, c.1800, 37 x 32 1/2 x 18 1/2 In. 1116.00
Chest, Federal, Mahogany, Inlay, 3 Drawers Over 5, c.1800, 63 x 44 x 23 In. 4465.00
Chest, Federal, Mahogany, Inlay, Bowfront, c.1800, 37 x 39 x 21 In. 2350.00
Chest, Federal, Mahogany, Tapered Legs, 4 Drawers, 19th Century, 41 x 43 3/4 In. 4400.00
Chest, Federal, Mahogany, Veneer, Bowfront, Early 19th Century, 38 x 43 x 22 In. 1880.00
Chest, Federal, Satinwood, Inlaid Mahogany, Early 19th Century, 41 x 49 x 21 In. 860.00
Chest, Federal, Walnut, Inlay, 3 Over 5 Graduated Drawers, c.1800, 67 x 41 x 21 In. 4700.00
Chest, Flame Birch, 4 Drawers, High Bracket Base, 18th Century, 33 x 38 In. 5290.00
Chest, Furniture, Pine, S. Neilt, Willoughby, Ohio, 39 1/2 x 18 1/4 x 18 1/2 In. 330.00
Chest, G. Nakashima, Cherry, 6 Drawers, Recessed Handles, 48 x 36 x 20 In. 10575.00
Chest, G. Nelson, Thin-Edge, Rosewood, 5 Drawers, Herman Miller, 41 x 56 x 18 In. 6465.00
Chest, G. Nelson, Thin-Edge, Walnut, 4 Drawers, Herman Miller, 31 x 34 x 18 In. 2585.00
Chest, G. Nelson, Thin-Edge, Walnut, 8 Drawers, Herman Miller, 31 x 47 x 18 In. 4700.00
Chest, G. Stickley, 2 Half Over 4 Full Drawers, Iron Pulls, 40 x 20 x 50 In. 8625.00
Chest, G. Stickley, Peaked Mirror, Pegged, Through Tenon, 42 x 22 x 64 In. 7480.00
Chest, George I Style, Walnut, Molded Top, 4 Drawers, 20th Century, 34 x 33 x 19 In. . . .   1380.00
Chest, George I, Walnut, Inlay, 2 Short, 3 Graduated Drawers, c.1715, 36 x 42 x 21 In. . .   4140.00
Chest, George II Style, Walnut Inlay, 2 Short, 3 Long Drawers, c.1880, 40 x 43 x 20 In. . .   3910.00
Chest, George II Style, Walnut, Crossbanded, 5 Drawers, Bracket Feet, 47 x 28 x 21 In. . .   1725.00
Chest, George II, Walnut, 4 Drawers, Burled Panels, 31 x 50 1/2 x 23 In. 2070.00
Chest, George III Style, Burl, Walnut Banded, England, c.1900, 30 x 40 In. 865.00
Chest, George III Style, Mahogany Inlay, c.1850, 47 x 48 3/4 x 20 1/2 In. 1095.00
Chest, George III Style, Mahogany, 2 Short, 3 Long Drawers, c.1860, 41 x 45 x 20 In. . . .   1035.00
Chest, George III Style, Mahogany, Bowfront Top, 5 Drawers, c.1830, 41 x 42 x 20 In. . .   1610.00
Chest, George III Style, Mahogany, Bowfront, c.1850, 44 1/4 x 40 1/2 x 20 3/4 In. 1380.00
Chest, George III Style, Mahogany, Inlay, Bowfront, c.1850, 31 3/4 x 35 x 18 In. 978.00
Chest, George III, Burl Walnut, Sunburst Inlay, 4 Drawers, c.1815, 35 x 42 In. 1840.00
Chest, George III, Mahogany, 2 Drawers, Bracket Feet, 28 1/2 x 45 3/4 x 21 1/4 In. 805.00
Chest, George III, Mahogany, 2 Over 3 Graduated Drawers, Bracket Feet, 39 x 43 In. 1380.00
Chest, George III, Mahogany, 2 Parts, 18th Century, 77 1/2 x 42 x 20 1/2 In. 3880.00
Chest, George III, Mahogany, 3 Short, 3 Long Drawers, c.1800, 41 x 41 x 21 In. 1495.00
Chest, George III, Mahogany, Banded Top, 2 Short & 4 Long Drawers, 49 x 20 x 45 In. . .   690.00
Chest, George III, Mahogany, Bowfront, 2 Over 3 Drawers, 1700s, 40 x 41 x 20 In. 2070.00
Chest, George III, Mahogany, Bowfront, 2 Over 3 Drawers, 37 x 38 x 20 In. 1955.00
Chest, George III, Mahogany, Bowfront, 2 Over 3 Drawers, Splayed Feet, 39 x 41 x 20 In.   1840.00
Chest, George III, Mahogany, Bowfront, 4 Drawers, Bracket Feet, 35 1/2 x 31 x 22 In. 2070.00
Chest, George III, Mahogany, Inlaid Brass, 3 Drawers, 37 x 42 1/2 x 20 1/4 In. 1265.00
Chest, George III, Mahogany, Satinwood, 5 Drawers, c.1800, 40 x 36 x 16 In. 2070.00
Chest, George III, Mahogany, Serpentine, Mid 18th Century, 35 x 37 1/4 In. 7170.00
Chest, George III, Oak, Rosewood, 2 Over 3 Drawers, 18th Century, 35 x 38 x 20 In. 1265.00
Chest, George IV, Mahogany, 5 Drawers, c.1825, 41 1/2 x 42 x 21 1/2 In. 1495.00
Chest, Georgian Style, Bowfront, 5 Drawers, c.1860, 37 x 37 1/2 x 19 3/4 In. 1150.00
Chest, Georgian Style, Inlaid Mahogany, 5 Drawers, c.1860, 42 x 45 x 20 1/2 In. 1610.00
Chest, Georgian Style, Mahogany, 2 Short, 3 Long Drawers, c.1840, 41 x 43 x 18 In. 2070.00
Chest, Georgian Style, Mahogany, Bowfront, 4 Drawers, c.1840, 35 x 35 x 19 In. 1955.00
Chest, Georgian Style, Mahogany, Bowfront, 5 Drawers, c.1850, 44 x 42 x 23 In. 3335.00
Chest, Georgian Style, Mahogany, Inlay, 2 Short, 6 Long Drawers, 76 x 42 x 23 In. 2415.00
Chest, Georgian Style, Mahogany, Inlay, 4 Drawers, c.1860, 46 x 41 x 19 In. 1495.00
Chest, Georgian, Mahogany, Bowfront, 2 Short, 3 Long Drawers, c.1835, 41 x 42 x 21 In.   3335.00
Chest, Georgian, Mahogany, Bowfront, 4 Long Drawers, c.1830, 44 x 40 x 23 In. 2185.00
Chest, Georgian, Walnut, 5 Drawers, Bracket Feet, c.1720, 39 x 35 1/2 In. 2185.00
Chest, Georgian, Walnut, Pine, 2 Over 3 Drawers, c.1800, 32 x 35 1/2 In. 1265.00

Chest, Grain Painted, 4 Drawers, Shaped Skirt, Bracket Feet, 38 x 40 1/2 x 18 In. 5975.00
Chest, Grain Painted, 6-Board, Straight Skirt, Cutout Feet, Brass Pulls, 32 x 41 x 18 In. . . . 2115.00
Chest, Grain Painted, Red, 4 Drawers, New England, 1840s, 38 1/2 x 41 x 19 In. 7170.00
Chest, Hepplewhite Style, Mahogany, Inlaid, Bowfront, Brass, 37 1/2 x 41 x 22 In. 520.00
Chest, Hepplewhite, Cherry, 4 Drawers, Brass, Bracket Base, 36 x 19 x 39 In. 1860.00
Chest, Hepplewhite, Cherry, 4 Drawers, Dovetailed, Late 18th Century, 38 x 19 x 39 In. . . 1600.00
Chest, Hepplewhite, Cherry, 4 Drawers, High Bracket Feet, 38 x 42 In. 1870.00
Chest, Hepplewhite, Cherry, 4 Drawers, Inlaid, 38 1/2 x 37 1/2 x 17 3/4 In. 1670.00
Chest, Hepplewhite, Cherry, Pine, Inlay, 5 Drawers, Beaded Edges, 38 x 20 x 38 In. 2750.00
Chest, Hepplewhite, Cherry, Pine, Poplar, Inlaid, 4 Drawers, 40 x 20 x 41 In. 3300.00
Chest, Hepplewhite, Cherry, Poplar, Band Inlay, Kentucky, 41 3/4 x 18 1/2 x 38 In. 2750.00
Chest, Hepplewhite, Curly Maple, Poplar, Beaded Edges, 4 Drawers, 38 x 20 x 42 In. . . . 9460.00
Chest, Hepplewhite, Figured Mahogany, Inlaid Shell, 2 Over 2 Drawers, 36 x 36 In. 1320.00
Chest, Hepplewhite, Inlaid Mahogany, Bowfront, 4 Drawers, 32 x 26 3/4 x 16 1/4 In. . . . 1325.00
Chest, Hepplewhite, Inlaid Walnut, 4 Drawers, Dovetailed, Late 1700s, 38 x 19 x 40 In. . . 2400.00
Chest, Hepplewhite, Mahogany, Bowfront, Inlaid, 4 Drawers, 36 x 21 x 39 1/2 In. 1380.00
Chest, Hepplewhite, Mahogany, Poplar, Scalloped Base, Fan Inlay, 39 x 20 x 42 5/8 In. . . 1375.00
Chest, Hepplewhite, Mahogany, Scalloped Skirt, Bracket Feet, 38 x 21 x 41 In. 1670.00
Chest, Hepplewhite, Mahogany, Veneer, Pine Inlay, Bowfront, 41 x 22 x 35 In. 3300.00
Chest, Hepplewhite, Tiger Maple, Cherry, 3 Drawers, 40 x 18 1/2 x 40 In. 730.00
Chest, Hepplewhite, Walnut, Inlaid, 5 Dovetailed Drawers, 1700s, 43 x 20 x 40 In. 950.00
Chest, Hepplewhite, Walnut, Inlaid, 5 Drawers, Beading, Late 1700s, 39 x 19 x 38 In. . . . 800.00
Chest, Hepplewhite, Walnut, Inlay, 4 Drawers, Dovetailed, 1700s, 41 x 20 x 40 In. 2100.00
Chest, Hepplewhite, Walnut, Poplar, 4 Drawers, French Feet, 20 x 13 x 23 1/2 In. 3410.00
Chest, Italian Neoclassical, Fruitwood, Portrait & String Inlay, 3 Drawers, 31 x 19 In. 3290.00
Chest, James Mont, Asian Fish Medallion, Mirror, Teal, 4 Drawers, 30 x 78 x 18 In. 2115.00
Chest, Kingwood, Inlaid, 3 Drawers, Chamfered Corners, 1700s, 36 x 49 x 25 In. 4140.00
Chest, L. & J.G. Stickley, 6 Drawers, Arched Backsplash, 50 x 42 x 17 1/2 In. 3740.00
Chest, Lifetime, 5 Drawers, Pivoting Mirror, 77 x 42 x 20 In. 1095.00
Chest, Lingerie, 5 Drawers, Flowers Overall, 41 x 18 In. 1210.00
Chest, Lingerie, Louis XVI Style, Mahogany, Marquetry, Marble Top, 45 x 17 x 15 In. . . . 1495.00
Chest, Louis Philippe, Mahogany, 2 Parts, 7 Drawers, Angled Paw Feet, 40 x 20 In. 1725.00
Chest, Louis XV Style, Kingwood, 7 Drawers, Leaves, c.1890, 58 1/2 x 28 In. 690.00
Chest, Louis XV Style, Marquetry, Ormolu, Marble Top, Serpentine, 38 x 17 x 41 In. 1456.00
Chest, Louis XV, Satinwood, Tulipwood, Ormolu, c.1745, 32 x 35 x 27 In., Pair 23900.00
Chest, Louis XVI Style, Mahogany, Brass Mounts, Mirror, 66 1/2 x 50 In. 1675.00
Chest, Louis XVI Style, Mahogany, Marble Top, 2 Drawers Over 2 Doors, 33 x 46 In. . . . 1175.00
Chest, Mahogany Inlay, 2 Short, 3 Long Drawers, c.1860, 43 x 45 x 20 In. 1610.00
Chest, Mahogany, 3 Drawers, Fluted Columns, Legs, Dutch, 37 x 19 x 33 1/2 In. 2875.00
Chest, Mahogany, 4 Drawers, Carved Leaves, Molded Base, 44 x 15 In. 430.00
Chest, Mahogany, 4 Short, 4 Long Drawers, Scotland, c.1860, 60 x 52 x 23 In. 1840.00
Chest, Mahogany, Bowfront, 2 Short Over 3 Graduated Drawers, Bun Feet, 45 x 49 In. . . 2415.00
Chest, Mahogany, Bowfront, Bracket Base, Beehive Brasses, c.1800, 37 x 40 In. 2530.00
Chest, Mahogany, Bowfront, Inlaid, 2 Over 3 Drawers, Flared Bracket Feet, 43 In. 1120.00
Chest, Mahogany, Breakfront Top, Secret Drawer, Scotland, c.1860, 56 x 51 x 24 In. 1955.00
Chest, Mahogany, Inlaid Top, 2 Short Over 3 Long Drawers, 33 x 37 In. 460.00
Chest, Mahogany, Inlaid, 7 Drawers, Scotland, c.1860, 52 1/2 x 49 x 23 In. 2415.00
Chest, Mahogany, Inlay, 2 Short, 3 Long Drawers, Splay Feet, c.1850, 44 x 45 x 22 In. . . 1925.00
Chest, Mahogany, Mirror, 3 Drawers, Scroll Frame, 24 x 21 x 7 1/2 In. 805.00
Chest, Mahogany, Rope Twist Supports, Scotland, c.1850, 50 1/2 x 44 x 20 1/2 In. 1495.00
Chest, Maple, Cove Molded, 6 Drawers, Bracket Base, Brass Pulls, 49 x 39 x 17 1/2 In. . . 4700.00
Chest, Medicine, Shaker, Key, Brass Hinges, Green Paint, Combination Lock, c.1800 . . . 5995.00
Chest, Mule, George III, Oak, Inlay, Late 18th Century, Hinged Top, 35 x 62 x 21 In. 1195.00
Chest, Mule, Over Drawers, Red Paint, Black Accents, Hinged Top, 28 x 42 x 18 In. 880.00
Chest, Mule, Pine, 3 Drawers, Red Wash, Wooden Knobs, Bracket Feet, 42 x 21 In. 880.00
Chest, Mule, Pine, Blanket Storage At Top, 3 Long Drawers, 1765, 53 x 36 In. 4800.00
Chest, Mule, Pine, Lift Top, Hinges, 2 Drawers, 1700s, 42 1/4 x 39 1/2 x 19 3/4 In. 1210.00
Chest, Mule, Pine, Poplar, Painted, Cyma Curved Cutouts, 39 1/2 x 19 x 36 1/2 In. 1650.00
Chest, Neoclassical, Marble Top, 3 Drawers, France, c.1850, 33 1/4 x 44 1/2 x 19 In. 2185.00
Chest, Neoclassical, Overall Floral Inlay, 6 Graduated Drawers, 38 x 60 In. 2185.00
Chest, Nutting, No. 913, Pine, Block Branded Signature 3410.00
Chest, Oak, 2 Over 3 Drawers, Paneled Fronts, England, 17th Century, 42 x 45 x 24 In. . . 2990.00
Chest, Oak, Bombe, Distressed, 3 Drawers, Paneled Ends, Ball Feet, 34 In., Pair 715.00

Furniture, Chest, Blanket,
Softwood, Stippled, Dovetailed,
Lancaster County, 28 x 50 In.

Furniture, Chest,
Sheraton, Walnut,
8 Dovetailed Drawers,
65 x 43 1/2 x 21 1/2 In.

Chest, Oak, Pilgrim, Carved, Sunflower, 19th Century, 36 x 47 1/2 x 21 In. 1910.00
Chest, Oak, Walnut, Straight Front, 4 Long Drawers, Brass Pulls, c.1710, 36 x 41 In. 765.00
Chest, Oriental, Camphorwood, Brass Bound, 30 3/4 x 16 1/4 x 16 1/2 In. 330.00
Chest, Painted, 2 Fitted Lids, 2 Compartments, Tibet, c.1900, 33 x 60 In. 1725.00
Chest, Pine, 2 Short Over 3 Long Drawers, Molded Top Edge & Base, 38 In. 865.00
Chest, Pine, 5 Drawers, England, Late 19th Century, 41 1/2 x 40 1/2 x 18 1/4 In. 546.00
Chest, Pine, 5 Drawers, Red Paint, Molded Top, Bracket Base, 1700s, 44 x 34 In. 1840.00
Chest, Pine, 6-Board, Grain Painted, Hinged Top, Ochre, 23 x 43 x 17 In. 2940.00
Chest, Pine, 6-Board, Hinged Top, Demilune Cutout Ends, 25 x 39 x 18 In. 325.00
Chest, Pine, 7 Drawers, Applied Molding, Pennsylvania, 48 x 19 1/2 x 63 In. 220.00
Chest, Pine, Black Paint, Red Panels, Yellow Stripes, 3 Drawers, 7 x 5 x 9 1/2 In. 440.00
Chest, Pine, Blue Paint, Dome Top, Hinged Lid, Leather & Iron Hasp, 1900s, 9 x 9 In. . . . 440.00
Chest, Pine, Brown Paint, 3 Drawers, Shaped Skirt, Brass Pulls, 11 x 13 x 6 3/4 In. 235.00
Chest, Pine, Grain Painted, Carved, 3 Drawers, 2 Short Over Long Drawer, 9 1/2 x 9 In. . . 265.00
Chest, Pine, Grain Painted, Red, 5 Drawers, 43 x 18 1/2 x 42 In. 1650.00
Chest, Pine, Original Finish, Dovetailed, Tyringham, Mass., c.1810, 12 3/4 In. 1725.00
Chest, Pine, Painted, 2 Short Over 3 Long Drawers, c.1730, 39 x 38 x 18 1/2 In. 4115.00
Chest, Pine, Painted, Iron Handles, Mid 19th Century, 21 1/2 x 38 1/2 x 21 In. 295.00
Chest, Pine, Red Wash, 3 Drawers, Scalloped Front Apron, 18 x 8 1/8 x 18 1/2 In. 660.00
Chest, Poplar, 6-Board, Blue Paint, Hinged Top, Dovetailed, Late 1700s, 20 x 38 x 16 In. . 2000.00
Chest, Queen Anne Style, Walnut Oyster Veneer, Satinwood, c.1835, 38 x 45 1/2 In. 2760.00
Chest, Queen Anne Style, Walnut, 2 Short, 2 Long Drawers, Bun Feet, 31 1/2 x 42 In. 2530.00
Chest, Queen Anne Style, Walnut, 3 Short Over 3 Long Drawers, 37 x 37 x 21 In. 2070.00
Chest, Queen Anne Style, Walnut, 4 Drawers, Banded, Bun Feet, 36 x 39 1/4 In. 1955.00
Chest, Queen Anne Style, Walnut, 4 Drawers, Mid 19th Century, 37 x 40 x 21 In. 2070.00
Chest, Queen Anne Style, Walnut, 4 Drawers, Scallop Skirt, 1800s, 39 x 33 In. 1035.00
Chest, Queen Anne Style, Walnut, Banded, Veneer, 2 Over 3 Drawers, 34 x 39 x 19 In. . . 1380.00
Chest, Queen Anne Style, Walnut, Block Front, c.1910, 36 1/2 x 38 x 22 In. 2185.00
Chest, Queen Anne Style, Walnut, Starburst, Mid 19th Century, 35 x 42 x 22 In. 1725.00
Chest, Queen Anne Style, Walnut, Veneered, Inlaid, Banded, 4 Drawers, 32 x 41 x 21 In. . 1725.00
Chest, Queen Anne, Birch, Reverse Serpentine Front, 4 Graduated Drawers, 33 x 36 In. . . 8960.00
Chest, Queen Anne, Oak, 5 Graduated Drawers, Early 18th Century, 37 x 41 x 23 In. 1840.00
Chest, Queen Anne, Pine, Old Paint, 3 Drawers, Bracket Feet, 35 x 17 x 32 In. 2530.00
Chest, Queen Anne, Walnut, 2 Over 3 Drawers, c.1720, 38 x 37 1/2 In. 4600.00
Chest, Queen Anne, Walnut, 5 Graduated Drawers, Early 18th Century, 38 x 39 x 22 In. . . 2760.00
Chest, Queen Anne, Walnut, Banded, Veneered, 3 Drawers, 34 1/2 x 40 x 20 1/2 In. 1840.00
Chest, Queen Anne, Walnut, Graduated Drawers, Early 18th Century, 36 x 40 x 22 In. . . . 2760.00
Chest, Queen Anne, Walnut, Veneered, Banded, Bun Feet, 40 x 37 x 21 In. 2990.00
Chest, Queen Anne, Walnut, Veneered, Starburst Inlay, Bun Feet, 38 x 40 x 20 In. 2530.00
Chest, Red Lacquer, 4 Doors, Brass Hardware, Chinese, 77 x 50 1/2 In. 2300.00
Chest, Regency, Bowfront, Mahogany, 2 Over 3 Drawers, Splayed Feet, 41 x 41 x 20 In. . 1610.00
Chest, Regency, Mahogany, 2 Short, 2 Long Drawers, c.1815, 37 x 43 1/2 In. 1495.00
Chest, Regency, Mahogany, Bowfront, 2 Over 3 Drawers, 44 x 45 x 22 1/4 In. 1380.00
Chest, Regency, Mahogany, Bowfront, 2 Over 3 Drawers, 45 1/2 x 40 x 21 In. 1265.00
Chest, Regency, Mahogany, Bowfront, Bamboo Pilasters, c.1810, 36 x 40 x 20 In. 1060.00
Chest, Regency, Mahogany, Bowfront, Sphinx Pulls, c.1815, 41 x 48 1/4 In. 1610.00
Chest, Renaissance Revival, Walnut, Cookie Corners, Drapery Crest, 100 In. 3025.00
Chest, Rococo, Walnut, Serpentine Front, 3 Drawers, Pierced Apron, 30 x 37 In. 2235.00

Chest, Rohde, Exotic Wood, Maple Veneer, Maple Poles, Herman Miller, 36 x 19 In. 2185.00
Chest, Rosewood, Maple, Ebony, Burl Walnut, Inlay, Marble Top, c.1875, 32 x 50 x 25 In. 2800.00
Chest, Rosewood, Shishi Masks, Phoenix, Dragon, Cloud, Japan, 1800s, 54 x 54 x 14 In. . 825.00
Chest, Rustic, Twig Mosaic Work, 3 Drawers, c.1921, 37 x 38 x 19 In. 2100.00
Chest, Rustic, Twig Mosaic, Inscribed, A. Lemay, c.1921, 40 x 45 x 24 In. 2100.00
Chest, Sewing, Walnut, 4 Drawers, Ohio, 17 3/4 x 12 3/4 x 24 1/2 In. 550.00
Chest, Shaker, Seed, Cherry, Pine, 6 Drawers, New Lebanon, N.Y., c.1840, 36 In. 4025.00
Chest, Shaker, Seed, Pine, Rosewood Boxes, New Lebanon, N.Y., c.1880, 17 1/2 In. 980.00
Chest, Shaker, Sewing, Butternut, Pine, Original Finish, New Lebanon, N.Y., 9 1/2 In. ... 1840.00
Chest, Sheraton Style, 4 Drawers, American, c.1810, 44 x 42 1/2 x 21 1/2 In. 1700.00
Chest, Sheraton Style, Mahogany, Bowfront, 4 Drawers, c.1890, 31 x 41 In. 2070.00
Chest, Sheraton, Birch, Mahogany Flame Veneer, 4 Drawers, 44 x 18 3/4 x 40 In. 1760.00
Chest, Sheraton, Bowfront, Walnut, Tiger Maple, 4 Drawers, 44 x 41 x 24 1/2 In. 2970.00
Chest, Sheraton, Cherry, Mahogany Veneer, Bowfront, 4 Drawers, 39 x 41 x 23 In. 1320.00
Chest, Sheraton, Cherry, Reeded Top, 4 Graduated Drawers, 39 1/2 x 20 1/2 x 46 In. 620.00
Chest, Sheraton, Cherry, Tiger Maple, 3 Over 3 Drawers, Paneled Ends, 41 x 46 In. 675.00
Chest, Sheraton, Figured Maple, Graduated Drawers, 42 1/2 x 43 1/2 x 22 1/2 In. 3450.00
Chest, Sheraton, Mahogany, 4 Drawers, Leaf, Pineapple, New England, 39 x 41 In. 1465.00
Chest, Sheraton, Mahogany, 4 Drawers, Ring-Turned 3/4 Column, 38 3/4 x 40 x 20 In. ... 750.00
Chest, Sheraton, Mahogany, 4 Drawers, Scrolled Backsplash, 41 x 44 In. 490.00
Chest, Sheraton, Mahogany, 6 Drawers, Reeded Flat Columns, 49 1/2 x 46 x 20 In. 750.00
Chest, Sheraton, Mahogany, Bowfront, 2 Over 3 Drawers, Paneled Sides, 42 In. 1670.00
Chest, Sheraton, Mahogany, Bowfront, New England, 37 1/2 x 17 1/2 x 39 3/4 In. 730.00
Chest, Sheraton, Mahogany, Lift Top, Oval Mirror, 79 1/2 x 41 1/2 x 19 In. 1035.00
Chest, Sheraton, Mahogany, Veneer, Pine, Bowfront, 4 Drawers, 40 x 19 x 39 In. 1100.00
Chest, Sheraton, Mixed Wood, 4 Drawers, Dovetailed, 29 1/2 x 25 x 12 In. 3630.00
Chest, Sheraton, Pine, Mahogany Veneer, 3 Drawers, Turned Pulls, 13 x 6 x 11 In. . 415.00
Chest, Sheraton, Pine, Turned Legs, Pilasters, 4 Drawers, 44 1/2 x 19 x 38 In. 550.00
Chest, Sheraton, Tiger Maple Inlay, 4 Drawers, Eagle Brasses, 39 x 41 x 18 In. 920.00
Chest, Sheraton, Walnut, 8 Dovetailed Drawers, 65 x 43 1/2 x 21 1/2 In. .... *Illus* 7150.00
Chest, Softwood, Grain Painted, Stylized Tulips, Drawer, Lid, 8 x 15 x 7 1/2 In. 440.00
Chest, Softwood, Lacquered, Floral Panels, Chinese, 28 x 42 x 24 1/2 In. 520.00
Chest, Sowden, Yellow, Red, Turquoise, 2 Glass Doors, Memphis, 1981, 63 x 24 x 16 In. . 2470.00
Chest, Spice, Poplar, 3 Drawers, Paneled Front Door, 14 1/2 x 12 1/4 x 18 3/4 In. 2200.00
Chest, Sugar, Sheraton, Cherry, Poplar, Hinged, Low Drawer, Divided Interior, Kentucky . 4675.00
Chest, Tansu, Rectangular, Drawers, Door, Brass, Handles, Japan, 1800s, 40 x 43 x 17 In. 1725.00
Chest, Tommi Parzinger, Ivory Enamel, 8 Drawers, Brass Pulls, 32 x 84 x 18 In. 4700.00
Chest, Victorian, Burl, Poplar, Marble Top, 3 Drawers, Dovetailed, 39 x 48 x 22 In. 635.00
Chest, Victorian, Faux Bois, 4 Drawers, Bun Feet, 19th Century, 32 1/2 x 37 1/4 x 17 In. .. 290.00
Chest, Victorian, Parcel Gilt, Burl, Marble Top, 3 Drawers, 32 1/2 x 46 x 22 In. 1076.00
Chest, Victorian, Polychrome, 3 Over 3 Drawers, 19th Century, 50 1/2 x 44 x 20 In. 1150.00
Chest, Walnut, 2 Over 3 Drawers, Molded Lips, J. Gheen, N.C., 49 x 44 x 20 In. 6600.00
Chest, Walnut, 3 Over 2 Over 5 Drawers, 1-Board Sides, 63 x 20 In. 6250.00
Chest, Walnut, Carved Eagle On Globe, 6 Drawers, Mirrored Backsplash, 76 In. 2520.00
Chest, Walnut, Carved, Plank Top, Panel Frieze, Stile Feet, Italy, 23 x 22 1/2 x 66 In. 730.00
Chest, Walnut, Cornice, Dovetailed Case, 3 Over 2 Drawers, Ogee, N.C., 66 x 48 x 24 In. 6380.00
Chest, Walnut, Hinges, Paneled, Cupid, Figures, Italy, 1700s, 29 x 64 x 20 In. 2875.00
Chest, Walnut, Marquetry, Mirror, Stepped Top, Drawers, Dutch, 62 x 39 x 20 In. 490.00
Chest, Walnut, Oak, Folk Marquetry, Hinged Top, 15 x 27 x 13 3/4 In. 1060.00
Chest, Walnut, Pine Inlay, Diamond Shaped, 3 Drawers, 15 x 8 x 14 In. 550.00
Chest, Walnut, Pine, Peaked Crest, 10 Drawers, 46 1/2 x 54 In. 1185.00
Chest, Walnut, Red Leather, Hinges, Handles, Italy, 1700s, 14 x 35 x 16 1/2 In. 690.00
Chest, Walnut, William & Mary, Inlaid, Oyster Veneers, Bun Feet, 30 x 41 x 20 In. 2990.00
Chest, William & Mary Style, Walnut, Marquetry, 1800s, 36 x 36 x 20 In. 2300.00
Chest, William & Mary, Maple, Pine, 4 Drawers, Bun Feet, c.1700, 36 x 33 x 17 In. 7475.00
Chest, William & Mary, Pine, 5 Drawers, Turned Ball Feet, Drop Pendant Pulls, 48 In. 3900.00
Chest, William & Mary, Pine, Maple, 5 Drawers, Lift Top, c.1715, 45 x 21 1/2 In. 4180.00
Chest, William & Mary, Seaweed Marquetry, 2 Over 3 Graduated Drawers, 35 x 38 In. ... 4700.00
Chest, William & Mary, Walnut, 2 Over 3 Graduated Drawers, Bun Feet, 36 x 36 In. ... 4585.00
Chest, William & Mary, Walnut, Burl, 4 Drawers, Bun Feet, c.1675, 34 x 44 x 22 In. 5750.00
Chest, William IV, Mahogany, Bowfront, 6 Drawers, c.1835, 42 x 48 1/2 x 22 In. 2415.00
Chest, Wood, Inside Till, Painted Inscription, Norway, 23 1/2 x 37 x 19 In. 450.00
Chest-On-Chest, George I, Black Lacquer, Landscapes, 18th Century, 70 x 36 x 17 In. ... 7480.00

Chest-On-Chest, George II Style, Walnut, Molded Crown, 74 x 42 x 22 1/2 In. 3450.00
Chest-On-Chest, George III Style, Burl, Mahogany, 54 x 24 x 18 In. 1955.00
Chest-On-Chest, George III, Mahogany, 8 Drawers, Bracket Feet, 77 x 44 1/2 In. 2765.00
Chest-On-Chest, George III, Mahogany, Graduated Drawers, c.1770, 74 3/4 x 44 x 21 In. .   4600.00
Chest-On-Chest, George III, Mahogany, Inlaid, 2 Short Over 6 Graduated Drawers, 68 In.   2415.00
Chest-On-Chest, Queen Anne, Maple, Figured, New England, c.1760, 72 x 38 1/2 In. 11950.00
Chest-On-Chest, Walnut, Crossbanded, 8 Drawers, Brushing Slide, c.1750, 67 x 24 In. . . .   1020.00
Chest-On-Frame, William & Mary, Figured Walnut, 2 Inlaid Doors, Drawer, 69 In. 2255.00
Chest-On-Frame, William & Mary, Oak, 2 Over 3 Graduated Drawers, Stretchers, 58 In. . .   825.00
Chiffonier, John Bradstreet, 3 Inlaid Drawers, 2 Cabinet Doors, 54 x 25 x 58 In. 7480.00
Chiffonier, Rosewood, Mirror, Inlay Panels, Ebonized Edges, c.1880, 94 x 60 In. 3450.00
Clothespress, Folk Art Style, Black Paint, Cabinet, 3 Drawers, 69 x 27 x 20 In. 290.00
Clothespress, George II Style, Mahogany, Panel Doors, Ireland, 92 1/2 x 53 x 22 In. 6570.00
Coat Rack, Costumer, Brass, Wrought Iron, Scroll Design, Hooks, Pineapple Finial, 77 In.   375.00
Coat Rack, Costumer, G. Stickley, No. 52, Single, 8 Iron Hooks, c.1904, 26 x 75 In. 3450.00
Coat Rack, Costumer, G. Stickley, Tapered Post, 4 Iron Hooks, Red Decal, 71 x 22 In. . . .   1380.00
Coat Rack, Costumer, L. & J.G. Stickley, Single, 4 Hooks, Cruciform Base, 20 x 71 In. . .   575.00
Coat Rack, Costumer, Stickley Bros., Double, 2 Stretchers, 11 Hooks, 68 1/2 x 17 x 22 In.   1095.00
Coat Rack, Dwarf, On Grass, With Rabbit, Wooden, 5 Hooks, c.1920, 13 1/2 x 30 In. 485.00
Coat Rack, Hanging, Carved Wood, Scalloped Backboard, Scrolled Hooks, 7 x 38 In. 275.00
Coat Rack, Hanging, Hammered Iron, Chiseled, Mirror, France, 1920s, 28 x 7 x 18 In. . . .   545.00
Coat Rack, Hanging, Wrought Iron, 2 Scrolls, Stylized Tulip, 17 x 29 In. 200.00
Coat Rack, Wood, Porcelain, 10 Hooks, Round Shelf, 88 x 31 In. 2300.00
Coffer, Altar, Red Lacquer, 4 Drawers, Flowers, Chinese, c.1890, 34 1/2 x 79 In. 1955.00
Coffer, Baroque, Oak, Dome Top, Carved, Peter Alpers, Anno 1730, 25 x 53 x 25 In. 520.00
Coffer, Black Stained, 4 Legs, Chinese, c.1890, 34 1/2 x 68 In.   405.00
Coffer, Brass Mounted, Inlaid Rosewood, 5 1/4 x 12 3/4 x 9 In. 1725.00
Coffer, George I, Elm, Maple, Part Ebonized, 35 x 53 x 24 In. 4180.00
Coffer, George III Style, Teak, Rectangular, Hinged Lid, 24 x 39 x 24 In. 545.00
Coffer, Jacobean, Oak, 3 Recessed Carved & Arched Panels, Fluted, 23 x 51 In. 645.00
Coffer, Jacobean, Oak, Paneled Lift Top, 2 Drawers, Plank Feet, 33 x 49 In. 470.00
Coffer, Mahogany & Burl, Hinges, 18th Century, 21 1/2 x 45 3/4 x 20 In. 3680.00
Coffer, Oak, 2-Panel Top, Paneled Sides, Block Feet, England, c.1790, 21 x 38 In. 1495.00
Coffer, Oak, Paneled Top, Diamond Designs, England, c.1690, 26 1/2 x 56 1/2 In. 980.00
Coffer, Oak, Veneer Front, Lift Top, Dovetailed Construction, Bracket Base, 8 x 12 In. . . .   200.00
Coffer, Pine, Polychrome, Planked Top, Flowers, Medallions, 1800s, 20 x 46 x 20 In. 1095.00
Coffer, Polychrome, 3 Shaped Panels, Bun Feet, Dutch, 27 x 46 x 25 In. 1035.00
Coffer, Polychrome, Lid, Painted Urns, Bird, Ball Feet, 21 x 37 1/2 x 17 3/4 In. 575.00
Coffer, Wrought Iron, Cover, Handle, Coin Slot, Spain, 1700s, 18 x 27 1/2 x 17 In. 1495.00
Commode, Baroque, Walnut, Serpentine, Italy, 18th Century, 32 x 50 1/2 x 23 In. 6325.00
Commode, Biedermeier Style, Fruitwood, Inlaid, Continental, 38 x 51 x 24 1/2 In. 3450.00
Commode, Biedermeier, Fruitwood, Ebonized, Brass Mounted, 4 Drawers, 38 x 51 In. . . .   2990.00
Commode, Biedermeier, Walnut, 3 Graduated Drawers, 1800s, 32 x 46 x 23 In. 3910.00
Commode, Charles X, Rosewood, Marble Top, Canted Corners, 39 x 47 x 23 In. 1675.00
Commode, Charles X, Walnut, Marble Top, Drawer Over 3 Drawers, 38 x 48 x 21 In. . . .   2185.00
Commode, Chippendale Style, Mahogany, 4 False Drawer Fronts, Lift Top, 29 In. 440.00
Commode, Directoire Style, Mahogany, 20th Century, 29 x 35 1/2 x 17 In. 590.00
Commode, Empire Style, Rosewood, Satinwood Banding, 39 x 48 x 23 In. 1955.00
Commode, Empire, Mahogany, Marble Top, France, c.1820, 35 x 45 x 22 1/2 In. 1175.00
Commode, Empire, Mahogany, Ormolu Mount, c.1810, 34 x 51 x 23 In. 3825.00
Commode, Empire, Mahogany, Ormolu, Marble Top, c.1815, 36 1/2 x 51 x 24 In. 2990.00
Commode, Empire, Mahogany, Ormolu, Marble, Drawer, c.1810, 34 x 50 x 25 In. 4780.00
Commode, Empire, Marble Top, Walnut, 3 Drawers, 32 1/2 x 51 x 24 In. 1955.00
Commode, French Empire, Mahogany, Gilt Bronze, Marble Top, c.1830, 34 x 51 x 23 In.   2415.00
Commode, French Provincial, Walnut, Mahogany, 18th Century, 29 x 23 x 17 In. 1060.00
Commode, Fruitwood, Brass Pulls, Scroll Carved, Bracket Feet, c.1800, 49 In. 1890.00
Commode, Fruitwood, Serpentine Front, Brass Mounted, Germany, 36 x 50 x 22 In. 6610.00
Commode, George III Style, Mahogany, Demilune, Carved Garlands, 36 In., Pair 4110.00
Commode, Georgian, Mahogany, 1 Drawer, 2 Doors, Bracket Feet, 27 x 28 x 17 In. 865.00
Commode, Gilt, Marble Top, 2 Drawers, 2 Cupboards, Scandinavia, 30 x 26 x 13 In. 1610.00
Commode, Gustavian, Satinwood, Parquetry, Sweden, 18th Century, 31 x 37 x 18 In. 2115.00
Commode, Half, Burl Walnut, Marble Top, Continental, 34 x 20 x 16 In. 575.00
Commode, Louis Philippe Style, Burl Oak, Marble Top, c.1865, 38 1/2 x 50 1/2 In. 2530.00

Commode, Louis Philippe, Burl Walnut, Marble Top, c.1850, 40 x 49 1/2 In. 1840.00
Commode, Louis Philippe, Burl, Brass Mounted, 4 Drawers, c.1835, 40 x 51 In. 2070.00
Commode, Louis Philippe, Burl, Fruitwood, Marble Top, c.1835, 40 1/2 x 48 In. 1955.00
Commode, Louis Philippe, Cherry, Marble Top, 4 Drawers, 41 x 47 x 21 In. 1610.00
Commode, Louis Philippe, Fruitwood, Brass Mounted, c.1835, 38 1/4 x 50 1/2 In. 2185.00
Commode, Louis Philippe, Fruitwood, Gilt Brass Mounted, 38 1/2 x 23 1/2 x 51 In. 2530.00
Commode, Louis Philippe, Mahogany, Marble Top, 4 Drawers, 38 x 48 x 21 1/2 In. 2530.00
Commode, Louis Philippe, Maple, Marble Top, 4 Drawers, 19th Century, 39 x 45 x 22 In. 2990.00
Commode, Louis Philippe, Olive Wood, 4 Drawers, Marble Top, c.1835, 39 1/2 x 50 In. . 2185.00
Commode, Louis Philippe, Walnut, Marble Top, 3 Drawers, 39 x 50 1/4 x 22 1/2 In. 2300.00
Commode, Louis Philippe, Walnut, Marble Top, 3 Drawers, Block Feet, 37 x 48 x 21 In. . 2530.00
Commode, Louis Philippe, Walnut, Marble Top, 4 Drawers, 19th Century, 35 x 51 x 23 In. 1495.00
Commode, Louis Philippe, Walnut, Marble Top, 4 Drawers, 19th Century, 37 x 44 x 21 In. 2530.00
Commode, Louis Philippe, Walnut, Marble Top, 4 Drawers, 19th Century, 40 x 49 x 22 In. 2760.00
Commode, Louis Philippe, Walnut, Marble, Drawer Over 3 Drawers, 38 x 51 x 23 In. ... 2070.00
Commode, Louis XIV Style, Brass & Tortoiseshell, 5 Drawers, 1870, 43 x 24 x 15 In. ... 2215.00
Commode, Louis XV Style, Fruitwood, Gilt Bronze, 2 Drawers, 33 x 45 x 18 In. 1115.00
Commode, Louis XV Style, Kingwood, Gilt Bronze Mount, Marble, 38 x 46 x 16 In. 1295.00
Commode, Louis XV Style, Kingwood, Gilt Metal, Serpentine Shaped, 29 x 26 x 15 In. .. 635.00
Commode, Louis XV Style, Kingwood, Marble Top, Serpentine, 1700s, 32 x 31 x 18 In. . 5290.00
Commode, Louis XV Style, Kingwood, Marble Top, Shaped Front, 34 1/2 x 46 In. 1150.00
Commode, Louis XV Style, Kingwood, Parquetry, Gilt Metal, Bombe, 31 x 42 x 21 In. .. 2235.00
Commode, Louis XV Style, Mahogany, Gilt Bronze, Marble Top, 35 x 42 x 22 In. 4780.00
Commode, Louis XV Style, Marquetry, Serpentine, 2 Drawers, 32 x 32 1/2 x 17 1/2 In. .. 880.00
Commode, Louis XV Style, Parquetry, Mixed Woods, 3 Drawers, 38 x 52 In. 1495.00
Commode, Louis XV Style, Rosewood, Marble Top, 20th Century, 39 x 54 x 26 In. 1645.00
Commode, Louis XV Style, Serpentine Front, Burl Inlay, Ormolu Mounts, 36 In. 545.00
Commode, Louis XV Style, Tulipwood, Marble Top, Serpentine, Bronze, 33 x 34 x 19 In. 375.00
Commode, Louis XV Style, Walnut, Serpentine Front, 3 Drawers, 36 x 24 x 16 In. 775.00
Commode, Louis XV Style, Wood, Gilt Bronze, Inlaid, Bombe, 30 x 36 x 16 In. 895.00
Commode, Louis XV Style, Wood, Gilt Bronze, Marble Top, Japanned, 37 x 57 x 27 In. . 1135.00
Commode, Louis XV Style, Wood, Marble Top, Parquetry, Gilt Mounts, 33 x 48 In. 805.00
Commode, Louis XV Style, Wood, Parcel Gilt, Marble Top, Drawers, 34 x 39 x 20 In. ... 2185.00
Commode, Louis XV, Bombe, Molded Top, 2 Drawers, Cabriole Legs, 30 x 25 x 17 In. ... 2070.00
Commode, Louis XV, Mahogany, Marble Top, Parquetry, 3 Drawers, 33 x 51 x 25 In. ... 3220.00
Commode, Louis XV, Pine, Serpentine Top, 3 Drawers, 31 x 38 1/2 x 21 In. 3105.00
Commode, Louis XV, Rosewood, Marble Top, 5 Drawers, 20th Century, 32 x 43 x 19 In. . 5750.00
Commode, Louis XV, Walnut, 3 Drawers, Bowed Edge, c.1790, 41 x 52 In. 4600.00
Commode, Louis XVI Style, Fruitwood, Marble Top, 34 x 44 x 19 In. 2390.00
Commode, Louis XVI Style, Green Marble Top, Bombe, 3 Drawers, 33 x 17 x 33 In. 430.00
Commode, Louis XVI Style, Mahogany, Gilt Bronze, Marble, D-Shape, 33 x 35 x 17 In. . 645.00
Commode, Louis XVI Style, Marble Top, Bombe, 2 Drawers, Inlaid, 49 x 24 x 32 In. ... 405.00
Commode, Louis XVI Style, Marquetry, Marble Top, Bombe, 2 Drawers, 34 x 16 x 30 In. 345.00
Commode, Louis XVI Style, Tulipwood, Kingwood, Parquetry, Marble Top 410.00
Commode, Louis XVI, Mahogany, Marble Top, Frieze Drawer, 34 x 13 x 10 In. 1265.00
Commode, Louis XVI, Mahogany, Parquetry, Marble Top, 34 1/2 x 28 1/2 x 14 In. 2185.00
Commode, Louis XVI, Marble Top, Brass, Mother-Of-Pearl Inlay, 1790, 40 x 34 x 22 In. . 8625.00
Commode, Louis XVI, Tulipwood, Kingwood, Ormolu, 18th Century, 31 x 37 x 22 In. ... 5060.00
Commode, Louis XVI, Walnut, 2 Drawers Over 3 Drawers, 33 1/2 x 51 x 21 1/2 In. 5750.00
Commode, Mahogany, Brass Mounted, Bowfront, Italy, c.1835, 33 1/2 x 47 In. 1095.00
Commode, Mahogany, Drawer, Continental, c.1815, 35 1/2 x 27 In., Pair 4830.00
Commode, Mahogany, Lift Top, False Doors, Bun Feet, 1800s, 25 1/2 In. 475.00
Commode, Marbleized Top, Landscapes, Italy, 18th Century, 36 x 49 In. 9775.00
Commode, Napoleon III, Fruitwood, Brass Mounted, c.1865, 36 1/2 x 47 1/2 In. 3220.00
Commode, Napoleon III, Mahogany, Inlaid, Marble Top, c.1890, 34 1/2 x 14 1/4 In. 1035.00
Commode, Pine, Grain Painted, Faux Tiger Maple, 19th Century, 32 x 30 1/4 In. 259.00
Commode, Regency Style, Beech, Leather Faced, Scarlet, 35 1/2 x 49 In. 3910.00
Commode, Regency Style, Mahogany, 2 Long Drawers, c.1850, 32 x 34 In. 2990.00
Commode, Regency Style, Marquetry, Marble Top, 4 Drawers, 34 x 49 x 24 In. 4995.00
Commode, Regency, Walnut, Rectangular Top, Drawers, Bowed, 37 x 49 x 24 In. 5290.00
Commode, Restauration Style, Walnut, Marble Top, 4 Drawers, 38 x 51 x 23 In. 2530.00
Commode, Restauration, Burl Walnut, Gilt Brass Mounted, 37 x 49 1/2 x 24 In. 3450.00
Commode, Rococo Style, Fruitwood, Serpentine Shape, 5 Drawers, 50 x 37 x 20 In. 705.00

Commode, Rococo, Walnut, Bombe, 3 Drawers, Splayed Feet, 32 x 45 In., Pair 1880.00
Commode, Stained Pine, Yellow Birch, Towel Bar, Old Forge Adirondacks 6000.00
Commode, Victorian, Walnut, Marble Top, Drawer Over Doors, 39 1/4 x 31 x 17 1/2 In. . . 575.00
Commode, Victorian, Walnut, Marble, Carved Pilasters, Scrolling, 36 x 18 x 32 In. 385.00
Commode, Walnut, 3 Bed Steps, Lift-Top Bowl Compartment, Inlaid, 27 x 31 In. 750.00
Commode, Walnut, 3 Drawers, Bun Feet, Italy, c.1820, 32 1/2 x 50 1/4 In. 2070.00
Commode, Walnut, Burl, Brass Mounted, Serpentine, Germany, c.1865, 37 x 43 In. 4830.00
Commode, Walnut, Carpeted, Hidden Cupboard, Porcelain, Thunder Mug, 3 Steps 750.00
Commode, Walnut, Frieze, Drawers, Pilasters, Italy, 34 1/2 x 15 x 13 In............. 1495.00
Commode, Walnut, Marble Top, 2 Drawers, Parquetry, 19th Century, 34 x 26 x 14 In. ... 2875.00
Commode, Walnut, Marble Top, Ormolu, 3 Long Drawers, c.1800, 32 1/4 x 51 x 23 In. . 1380.00
Commode, Widdicomb, Art Deco, Long Drawer, 2 Doors, 44 x 33 1/2 In. 1530.00
Commode, Writing, Neoclassical, Burl Ash, 3 Drawers, Baltic, c.1810, 37 x 50 x 24 In. .. 1265.00
Cradle, Brown Flame Grain, Mustard, Black Line Design, Red & Yellow Scrolling, 24 In. 500.00
Cradle, George II, Bonnet Top, Scalloped Frieze, 18th Century, 24 1/2 x 36 x 14 In. 345.00
Cradle, Hooded, Handcrafted, Ralph Wheeler, Temple, N.H., 1939-1940 .... 350.00
Cradle, Hooded, Painted, White Interior, Rose, Stenciled Roses, 28 x 42 x 19 In. 230.00
Cradle, Mixed Woods, Shaped Stiles, Plank Sides, Molded Rockers, 31 x 41 In. 405.00
Cradle, Pine, Blue Paint, American, 18th Century, 31 x 37 x 19 In. 460.00
Cradle, Pine, Cutout Ends, Red Wash, Early 19th Century, 20 x 34 In. 100.00
Cradle, Platform, Victorian, Mixed Woods, Shaped Slats, Lyre Ends 55.00
Cradle, Poplar, Flame Grain Panels, Painted Cornucopia & Scrolls, 24 x 38 In. 500.00
Cradle, Rattan, Swinging, Removable Round Canopy Frame, 42 x 23 In. 130.00
Cradle, Softwood, Green Paint, Fleur-De-Lis Decoration, Black, Red Striping 310.00
Cradle, Softwood, Red, Green, Black, Cheese-Cutter Rockers, 7 1/4 x 17 x 11 In. 140.00
Cradle, Walnut, Pinned Construction, Heart Cutouts, Turned Posts, Pennsylvania 225.00
Credenza, Eames, ESU 100, Herman Miller, c.1950, 47 x 17 x 20 In. 3738.00
Credenza, Empire, Mahogany, Marble Top, c.1820, 40 3/4 x 74 1/2 In. 3680.00
Credenza, Florence Knoll, Walnut, 4 Sliding Doors, Leather Pulls 430.00
Credenza, G. Nakashima, Walnut, Free Edge, Sliding Panel Doors, 32 x 60 x 22 In. 8815.00
Credenza, Kittinger, Mahogany, Veneer, Oak, 4 Drawers, Cabinet, 81 x 19 1/2 x 30 In. ... 880.00
Credenza, Mahogany, Demilune Top, Jasperware Plaque, Bow Doors, 43 x 17 x 54 In. ... 1090.00
Credenza, Napoleon III, Boulle, Glazed Doors, 45 x 72 x 14 In. 645.00
Credenza, Napoleon III, Porcelain Plaque, 2 Glazed Cupboards, 41 1/2 x 18 x 72 In. 1240.00
Credenza, Renaissance Revival, Rosewood, Marquetry, 42 x 61 x 18 In. 1175.00
Credenza, Walnut, Ormolu, Demilune, Bow Cupboards, Plinth Base, 40 x 18 x 63 In. 2910.00
Crib, Birch, Pine, Red Stain, New England, c.1815, 32 x 30 3/4 In. 1320.00
Crib, Renaissance Revival, Walnut, Canopy Top, Signed, 1875, 50 x 45 In. .... *Illus* 15680.00
Cupboard, 2 Doors, Slant Back, Blue Paint, 70 1/4 x 23 3/4 x 14 In. 1435.00
Cupboard, 2 Doors, Spring Closures, Pegged, Shelves, Original Gray, 79 In. 1150.00
Cupboard, 2 Paneled Doors, Black Paint, 67 3/4 x 78 1/2 x 18 1/4 In. 3585.00
Cupboard, 2 Paneled Doors, Blue Paint, 38 x 29 1/4 x 13 3/4 In. 3110.00
Cupboard, 2 Sections, Step Back, Painted, 4 Raised Panel Doors, Shelf, 1800s, 80 x 66 In. 1800.00
Cupboard, Aesthetic Revival, Burl Veneer, Bowfront, 2 Sections, c.1870 .... 11000.00
Cupboard, Arts & Crafts, 2 Glass Doors & Sides, 2 Shelves, c.1914, 55 x 40 x 14 In. 1410.00
Cupboard, Burl Walnut, 4 Paneled Doors, c.1890, 33 x 78 1/2 In. 1610.00
Cupboard, Butternut, Recessed Panel, 3 Shelves, 19th Century, 18 1/4 In. 3525.00

Furniture, Crib, Renaissance Revival,
Walnut, Canopy Top, Signed, 1875,
50 x 45 In.

Cupboard, Carved Washboard Door Panels, Painted, 19th Century, 44 x 83 x 18 In. 2900.00
Cupboard, Charles I Style, Oak, Marquetry, 19th Century, 65 x 90 x 25 In. 2940.00
Cupboard, Cherry, 4 Shelves, Plate Racks, Plank Door, Tenn., 1800s, 73 x 40 x 15 In. ... 3520.00
Cupboard, Cherry, Arched, Glazed Door, Brass Hinges & Knobs, 19th Century, 13 1/4 In.   765.00
Cupboard, Chimney, Pine, Blue Green Paint, Paneled Door, Latch, 72 In. 880.00
Cupboard, Chimney, Pine, Step Back, 2 Doors, Red, Mid 19th Century, 87 x 32 x 13 In. . 850.00
Cupboard, Corner, 2 Doors, 8 Panels Each, Mortise, Tenon, Philadelphia, c.1800 .... 4675.00
Cupboard, Corner, 2 Shelves, Applied Molding, Hinges, N.C., 75 x 45 x 21 In. 1540.00
Cupboard, Corner, Blind Door, Step Back, Pennsylvania, 18th Century 9995.00
Cupboard, Corner, Blue Paint, 2 Paneled Doors Over 1 Paneled Door, 82 x 27 In. 920.00
Cupboard, Corner, Cherry, 2 Doors, 8 Panes, 3 Shelves, 19th Century, 90 x 54 x 23 In. .. 2760.00
Cupboard, Corner, Cherry, 2 Glass Paned Over 2 Paneled Doors, Shaped Feet, 83 In. 2860.00
Cupboard, Corner, Cherry, 2 Glazed Doors, 8 Panes, 89 x 42 x 17 1/2 In. 805.00
Cupboard, Corner, Cherry, 2 Over 2 Paneled Doors, Drawer, Beveled Cornice, 83 x 47 In. 2640.00
Cupboard, Corner, Cherry, 2 Paneled Doors, Reeded Columns, Shelves, 86 x 31 x 15 In. . 2645.00
Cupboard, Corner, Cherry, Cathedral Door Over 2 Panel Doors, c.1820, 86 In. 2760.00
Cupboard, Corner, Chippendale, Cherry, 2 8-Pane Glass Doors, 2 Paneled Doors, 89 In. .. 4500.00
Cupboard, Corner, Chippendale, Cherry, Glass Top Door, Paneled Bottom Door, 85 In. .. 3300.00
Cupboard, Corner, Chippendale, Green Paint, Late 18th Century, 39 x 30 x 15 In. 8000.00
Cupboard, Corner, Chippendale, Walnut, 2 Glass Doors, 18th Century, 79 x 53 x 24 In. .. 5500.00
Cupboard, Corner, Chippendale, Walnut, 4 Doors, Shelves, Late 1700s, 89 x 56 x 24 In. .. 2700.00
Cupboard, Corner, Federal, 12-Pane Door Over 2 Doors, Grain Painted, 88 x 47 In. 7150.00
Cupboard, Corner, Federal, Cherry, Molded Cornice, Paneled Doors, 73 x 46 x 23 In. ... 969.00
Cupboard, Corner, Federal, Painted, Paneled Doors, c.1810, 81 x 43 x 22 In. 10160.00
Cupboard, Corner, Federal, Walnut, Beaded Doors, Early 1800s, 86 x 54 x 25 In. 2900.00
Cupboard, Corner, George III Style, Satinwood, Ebonized, 2 Parts, c.1875, 94 x 44 In. ... 6900.00
Cupboard, Corner, Louis XV Style, Kingwood, Marquetry, 34 x 26 x 18 1/2 In. 590.00
Cupboard, Corner, Mahogany, 2 Sections, Carved, American, 95 x 40 x 22 In. 4125.00
Cupboard, Corner, Mahogany, Mullioned Glass Door, 3 Drawers, Raised Legs, 88 In. ... 880.00
Cupboard, Corner, Pine, 12 Panes In Upper Door, Painted, Pennsylvania, 1820, 84 In. ... 15000.00
Cupboard, Corner, Pine, 4 Doors, Scalloped Skirt, 19th Century, 84 x 46 x 21 1/2 In. 1400.00
Cupboard, Corner, Pine, Blue Paint, Paneled, Shelf, 19th Century, 85 x 55 x 30 In. 1265.00
Cupboard, Corner, Pine, Stained, Shelves, Early 19th Century, 80 1/2 x 47 x 27 In. 1150.00
Cupboard, Corner, Polychrome, Carved Door, Drawers, 44 1/2 x 27 x 16 In. 805.00
Cupboard, Corner, Poplar, Pine, Raised Panel Door, Shelves, 34 x 13 x 78 3/4 In. 495.00
Cupboard, Corner, Scrolled Backboard, Hinged Door, 19th Century, 31 In. 2470.00
Cupboard, Corner, Stained Pine, 2 Sections, 19th Century, 91 x 44 x 22 In. 2300.00
Cupboard, Corner, Walnut, 2 8-Pane Doors, Drawer, N.C., 1700s, 89 x 51 x 23 In. 7040.00
Cupboard, Corner, Walnut, 2 Double, 2 Single Panel Framed Doors, Central Drawer 2310.00
Cupboard, Corner, Walnut, 3 Sections, Bottom Doors, Pilasters, England, 97 x 46 In. 12500.00
Cupboard, Corner, Walnut, 6 Panes, 2 Upper Doors, Drawers, 84 In. 4200.00
Cupboard, Corner, Walnut, Panel Door, Shelf, American, 19th Century, 79 x 45 x 23 In. .. 3680.00
Cupboard, Corner, Walnut, Paneled, American, Early 19th Century, 80 x 47 x 22 In. 2530.00
Cupboard, Corner, Yellow Pine, Cornice, Panel Doors, Hinges, N.C., 88 x 44 x 22 In. 2200.00
Cupboard, Court, Oak, 2 Pieces, Butterfly Hinges, Continental, 49 1/2 x 20 1/8 x 67 In. .. 990.00
Cupboard, Court, Oak, Carved Knights, France, c.1885, 65 3/4 x 41 1/2 In. 1725.00
Cupboard, Court, Walnut, Molded Cornice, Continental, c.1885, 33 1/2 x 21 In. 1150.00
Cupboard, Desk Top, Pine, Grain Painted Decoration, 2 Doors, Carved, 29 1/2 x 27 In. .. 1650.00
Cupboard, Edwardian, Oak, Leaf Carved, 2 Doors, Mirrored Panels, 38 1/2 x 36 x 16 In. . 750.00
Cupboard, Edwardian, Polychrome, Classical Bust Inset, c.1900, 37 x 18 x 10 In. 490.00
Cupboard, Hanging, Cherry, Blind Door, Molded Cornice, Shelf, 24 x 20 x 12 1/2 In. ... 630.00
Cupboard, Hanging, Cherry, Poplar, Central Ohio, 27 x 12 x 36 1/2 In. 605.00
Cupboard, Hanging, Chippendale, Mixed Wood, Rat Tail Hinges, 37 x 28 x 13 In. 6600.00
Cupboard, Hanging, Corner, Dark Walnut, Late 18th Century, 39 1/2 x 27 1/2 In. 4600.00
Cupboard, Hanging, Corner, Mixed Wood, Cornice, 29 3/4 x 27 x 13 In. 470.00
Cupboard, Hanging, Corner, Pine, Shelf Over Door, Medallion Crest, 39 x 24 In. 550.00
Cupboard, Hanging, Corner, Walnut, Early 19th Century, 44 x 22 x 14 In. 500.00
Cupboard, Hanging, Federal, Grain Painted, Carved, New Jersey, c.1810, 35 x 38 x 12 In. 1076.00
Cupboard, Hanging, Mixed Wood, Cornice, Paneled Door, 28 1/2 x 28 1/2 x 14 In. 990.00
Cupboard, Hanging, Mixed Wood, Triple Panel, Scalloped 39 x 22 1/2 x 10 1/2 In. 415.00
Cupboard, Hanging, Molded Cornice, 6-Pane Glazed Door, 40 1/2 x 31 x 13 In. 3190.00
Cupboard, Hanging, Oak, Barrel Shape, 2 Carved Doors, Scrolled Apron, 39 In. 310.00
Cupboard, Hanging, Painted, Heart Shaped Escutcheon, 31 x 27 x 13 In. 6575.00

Furniture, Cupboard,
Hanging, Softwood,
Original Red Paint,
Door, 29 x 21 x 10 In.

Furniture, Cupboard, Jelly,
Softwood, Red Paint, 2 Drawers
Over 2 Doors, 49 x 41 x 19 In.

Cupboard, Hanging, Pine, Painted, Cornice, Interior Shelves, 1806, 28 x 17 x 36 In. 1870.00
Cupboard, Hanging, Pine, Painted, Leaves, Red, Green, Yellow, Cornice, 12 x 8 x 18 In. . . 715.00
Cupboard, Hanging, Pine, Paneled, American, c.1900, 78 x 45 x 12 1/2 In. 1910.00
Cupboard, Hanging, Pine, Red Stained, 2 Shelves, Beveled Base, 30 1/2 x 24 x 10 In. . . . 765.00
Cupboard, Hanging, Pine, Red Wash, Raised Panel Door, 16 x 6 1/2 x 25 In. 330.00
Cupboard, Hanging, Poplar, Painted, 4 Doors, Shelves, Ohio, 40 1/2 x 17 x 76 In. 1980.00
Cupboard, Hanging, Softwood, Cornice, Raised Panels, 33 1/4 x 22 1/2 x 13 1/4 In. 14300.00
Cupboard, Hanging, Softwood, Original Red Paint, Door, 29 x 21 x 10 In. . . . . *Illus* 2750.00
Cupboard, Hanging, Walnut, Pediment Top, 2 Doors, Drawers, 30 1/2 x 15 1/4 x 8 In. . . . 365.00
Cupboard, Jelly, 2 Drawers Over 2 Sunken-Panel Doors, Scalloped Splash, 45 In. 510.00
Cupboard, Jelly, Grain Design, Panel Door, Bracket Base, 37 x 16 x 59 In. 290.00
Cupboard, Jelly, Pennsylvania Dutch, Butterfly Hinges, Painted, 63 x 40 x 16 In. 1100.00
Cupboard, Jelly, Pine, 2 Doors, Shelves, Painted, Removable Top, 51 x 22 x 72 In. 1100.00
Cupboard, Jelly, Pine, 2-Paneled Door, Molded Cornice, 75 x 39 x 11 In. 1150.00
Cupboard, Jelly, Pine, Yellow Paint, 19th Century, 62 1/2 x 36 x 14 In. 520.00
Cupboard, Jelly, Softwood, 2 Drawers Over 2 Panel Doors, Turned Feet, 46 In. 480.00
Cupboard, Jelly, Softwood, Red Paint, 2 Drawers Over 2 Doors, 49 x 41 x 19 In. . . . *Illus* 1760.00
Cupboard, Jelly, Softwood, Yellow Graining, 2 Drawers, Doors, 43 1/2 x 51 1/2 In. 365.00
Cupboard, Livery, Bleached Mahogany, Iron Grillwork, Anglo-Indian, 55 x 19 In. 175.00
Cupboard, Louis Philippe, Ash, Marble Top, 19th Century, 32 x 16 x 13 In. 690.00
Cupboard, Louis XV, Walnut, Drawer, Paneled, Cabriole Legs, 51 1/2 x 29 x 16 1/2 In. . . 805.00
Cupboard, Mediterranean, Hardwood, Late 1800s, 32 x 37 x 20 1/4 In. 315.00
Cupboard, Mixed Woods, Molded Stiles, Dovetailed, 29 1/2 x 32 x 10 1/2 In. 220.00
Cupboard, Paneled Door, Blue Paint, 19th Century, 68 x 43 1/4 x 17 1/2 In. 2390.00
Cupboard, Pewter, 2 Drawers, Doors & Shelves, Red, Yellow Interior, 49 x 81 In. 115.00
Cupboard, Pewter, Pine, Cornice, 3 Shelves, 2 Plank Doors, N.C., 70 x 36 x 16 In. 2090.00
Cupboard, Pine, 2 Sections, 3 Shelves, Painted Bun Feet, 80 x 25 1/2 x 14 In. 1150.00
Cupboard, Pine, 2 Shelves, Spoon Rack, 2 Plant Doors, N.C., 76 x 57 x 22 In. 660.00
Cupboard, Pine, 4 Shelves, Battened Door, Iron Hinges, N.C., 79 x 38 x 18 In. 770.00
Cupboard, Pine, Gold Striping, Red Ground, Drawer In Base, 13 x 8 x 20 In. 468.00
Cupboard, Pine, Green Paint, 2 Doors, 3 Shelves, 43 1/2 x 43 x 13 In. 605.00
Cupboard, Pine, Old Paint, Reeded Door, Arched Cutouts, Shelves, 49 x 16 x 71 In. 1870.00
Cupboard, Pine, Painted, Paneled, Flaring Cornice, 2 Shelves, c.1850, 77 x 41 x 19 In. . . . 4700.00
Cupboard, Pine, Painted, Step Back, 2 Shelves, 79 1/2 x 39 1/2 x 13 1/2 In. 3525.00
Cupboard, Pine, Planked Top, 2 Paneled Doors, Block Feet, 38 x 28 x 21 In. 200.00
Cupboard, Pine, Poplar, 2 Sections, 4 Over 4 Paneled Doors, Bracket Feet, 84 x 116 In. . . 5225.00
Cupboard, Pine, Poplar, Step Back, Grain Painted, 2 Sections, 54 x 20 x 88 In. 3025.00
Cupboard, Pine, Red Paint, Molded Top, 2 Doors, 3 Shelves, 69 x 38 x 16 In. 575.00
Cupboard, Pine, Red Paint, Single Door, Shelves, c.1850, 40 x 26 x 13 In. 2938.00
Cupboard, Pine, Set Back, Blue, Gray, c.1880, 73 x 42 x 20 In. 1850.00
Cupboard, Pine, Yellow, 2 Frame & Panel Doors, Bracket Feet, 94 1/2 x 56 x 16 In. 3300.00
Cupboard, Poplar, 3 Shelves, 2 Spoon Racks, 66 1/2 x 40 1/2 x 12 1/2 In. 275.00
Cupboard, Poplar, 4 Frame & Panel Doors, Drawer, Punched Tin, 79 x 43 x 18 In. 2860.00
Cupboard, Queen Anne, Pine, 2 Doors, Molding, New England, c.1700, 80 x 42 x 24 In. . . 478.00
Cupboard, Regency, Mahogany, Paneled, Pilasters, 1800s, 38 x 41 3/4 x 15 1/2 In. 2785.00
Cupboard, Shaker, Hanging, Butternut, 5-Shelf Interior, Enfield, Conn., c.1850, 37 1/4 In. 1380.00

Cupboard, Shaker, Hanging, Pine, Inset Panel Door, Sabbathday Lake, Me., 21 In. 1440.00
Cupboard, Shaker, Pine, Painted, Bracket Base, Doors, 3 Drawers, 28 x 83 In. 1650.00
Cupboard, Softwood, 1 Door, Red Paint, Scalloped Skirt, 39 1/2 x 60 x 15 In. 790.00
Cupboard, Softwood, 2 Sections, 2 Over 2 Raised Panel Doors, Brown Paint, 83 In. 1690.00
Cupboard, Softwood, Painted, Yellow, Brown, York Co., Pa., 36 x 17 x 53 In. 1238.00
Cupboard, Step Back, 2 Doors, Shelves, 2 Drawers, Bracket Base, 50 x 19 x 85 In. 1090.00
Cupboard, Step Back, 2 Parts, Glass Doors, Pa., 18th Century, 84 x 47 x 17 In. 2470.00
Cupboard, Step Back, Blue, Double Peg Construction, Pa., 19th Century 3700.00
Cupboard, Step Back, Cherry, 2 Doors Top, 2 Drawers Over 2 Doors, c.1850, 86 x 56 In. . 1840.00
Cupboard, Step Back, Cherry, 2 Parts, c.1850, 77 1/4 x 43 3/4 x 19 1/2 In. 2760.00
Cupboard, Step Back, Oak, 2 Arched Doors, 2 Drawers Over 2 Paneled Doors, 82 In. . . . 1460.00
Cupboard, Step Back, Paneled Door, Blue, Green Paint, 74 x 23 3/4 x 14 1/2 In. 2868.00
Cupboard, Step Back, Pine, Poplar, Mustard, Brown Paint, 2 Parts, 88 x 54 In. 6600.00
Cupboard, Step Back, Red Wash, Ebonized Trim, 1869, 89 x 47 In., 2 Piece 3995.00
Cupboard, Step Back, Shelves, Plate Stands, Hinges, Paneled Doors, 69 x 73 x 17 In. . . . 3825.00
Cupboard, Step Back, Walnut, 2 Parts, 2 Drawers, 2 Doors, 6 Panes, Ohio, 84 x 45 In. . . . 2035.00
Cupboard, Tudor Style, Rectangular Top, 3 Doors, 2 Paneled Doors, 63 x 24 x 72 In. 860.00
Cupboard, Walnut, 2 Doors, 3 Drawers, Over Double Panel Doors, 86 x 20 x 58 In. 3680.00
Cupboard, Walnut, 2 Paneled Doors Over 5 Drawers, Pa., 1770, 89 x 84 x 30 In. 5750.00
Cupboard, Walnut, 28-Pane Doors, 2 Frame & 2 Panel Doors, N.C., 94 x 46 x 20 In. 4180.00
Cupboard, Walnut, Miter Molded Doors, Germany, 18th Century, 59 x 99 x 24 In. 1293.00
Cupboard, Walnut, Molded Cornice, Paneled Door, 22 1/2 x 15 x 9 In. 3410.00
Cupboard, Walnut, Oak, 2 Sections, Christian Shiveley Jr., Ohio, c.1845, 64 x 23 x 98 In. . 9900.00
Cupboard, Welsh, Oak, Scalloped Sides, 30 x 53 1/2 In. 2760.00
Cupboard, William IV, Mahogany, 1 Door, c.1835, 37 x 25 1/2 In., Pair 1725.00
Cupboard, Yellow Pine & Poplar, Drawer, 2 Frame & Panel Doors, 42 x 41 x 16 In. 1320.00
Cupboard, Yellow Pine, 2 Doors, Drawer, Scalloped Skirt, 70 1/2 x 45 1/2 x 24 In. 2310.00
Cupboard, Yellow Pine, Frame & Panel Doors, Applied Molding, 58 x 38 x 31 In. 880.00
Cupboard, Yellow Pine, Molded Cornice, 2 6-Pane Doors, Va., 76 x 47 x 26 1/2 In. 7700.00
Cupboard, Yellow Pine, Plank Door, Backboard, Strap Hinges, N.C., 66 x 40 x 12 In. . . . 715.00
Daybed, Arts & Crafts, 4 Slats To Head, Footboard, Cushions, 24 1/2 x 72 1/2 In. 865.00
Daybed, Arts & Crafts, Oak, Headrest, Rail Stretchers, Slats, Spring Cushion, 24 x 75 In. . 765.00
Daybed, Arts & Crafts, Single Slat On Sides, Vinyl Cushion, 28 x 28 x 78 In. 978.00
Daybed, Arts & Crafts, Square Posts, Slatted, Cushion, 27 1/2 x 57 x 25 1/2 In. 1035.00
Daybed, Biedermeier, Fruitwood, Scrolled Ends, Swan's Neck Supports, 82 In. 2585.00
Daybed, Carved Frame, Lacquered, Upholstered Cushion, Square Supports, 77 x 67 In. . . 580.00
Daybed, Directoire Style, Painted, Green, Off White, 38 7/16 x 31 x 77 1/4 In. 2030.00
Daybed, French Provincial, Beech, 19th Century, 35 1/2 x 63 x 27 1/2 In. 1265.00
Daybed, G. Nakashima, Black Walnut, 1960s, 72 1/2 x 10 In. 3738.00
Daybed, G. Nakashima, Walnut, Plank Back, Cushions, 30 x 80 x 33 In. 8225.00
Daybed, G. Nelson, Upholstered, Chrome, Herman Miller, 90 x 31 x 16 In. 1495.00
Daybed, George III Style, Mahogany, Upholstered, 3 Cushions, 38 1/2 x 56 x 37 In. 1910.00
Daybed, George III, Mahogany, Figured, England, c.1885, 35 x 77 In. 3600.00
Daybed, L. & J.G. Stickley, No. 739, Slanted Headrest, 5 Slats, Leather, Signed, 76 In. . . . 1380.00
Daybed, Louis Philippe, Mahogany, Outscrolled Head & Footboard, 34 x 79 x 31 In. 1840.00
Daybed, Louis XVI Style, Mahogany, Cane Back, Cushion, c.1890, 43 x 81 1/2 In. 3680.00
Daybed, Louis XVI, Walnut, Padded, Reeded Frame, 19th Century, 39 x 77 x 39 In. 1150.00
Daybed, Maple, Scrolled Rolling Pin Ends & Back, Turned Legs, Cushions, 72 In. 420.00
Daybed, Poul Kjaerholm, E. Kold Christensen, Herman Miller, c.1976, 75 x 32 x 12 In. . . 7480.00
Daybed, Prairie School, Slanted Headrest, Paneled Sides, Upholstered, 76 x 30 x 24 In. . . 518.00
Daybed, Rounded Top, Free-Standing Columns, Turret-Shaped Feet, c.1830, 70 In. 1210.00
Daybed, Stickley Bros., Slanted Headrest, Slatted Sides, Cushion, 76 x 29 x 25 In. 805.00
Daybed, Tiger & Bird's-Eye Maple, Turned Legs, Upholstered Slip Seat, 71 In. 860.00
Daybed, William & Mary Style, Oak, Carved, Cane, Adjustable Backrest, 65 In. 470.00
Desk, Aesthetic Revival, Ebonized, Fitted Interior, 43 x 27 1/2 x 21 In. 1058.00
Desk, Aesthetic Revival, Slant Front, Parcel Gilt, Leather, Ebonized, c.1880, 38 x 27 In. . . 865.00
Desk, American Maple, Slant Front, Bracket Feet, 7 Drawers, Prospect Door, 36 In. 4200.00
Desk, Art Deco, Apple Wood, Parquetry, 2 Pedestals, France, c.1930, 30 x 55 1/2 In. 3680.00
Desk, Art Deco, Burl, Drop Front, 3 Drawers, Brass Bar Pulls, 40 3/4 x 16 3/4 In. 940.00
Desk, Art Deco, Rosewood, Mahogany, 2 Pedestals, France, c.1930, 30 x 74 In. 4370.00
Desk, Arts & Crafts, Double Pedestal, 3 Drawers, Side Bookshelves, 30 x 44 3/4 In. 635.00
Desk, Arts & Crafts, Drop Front, 3 Drawers, Lower Shelf, 47 x 28 x 13 1/2 In. 1725.00
Desk, Arts & Crafts, Drop Front, Interior Gallery, Keyhole Cutout, 41 1/2 x 28 x 15 In. . . . 315.00

Desk, Arts & Crafts, Drop Front, Oak, 1 Drawer, Low Shelf, c.1916, 43 x 29 x 16 In. 410.00
Desk, Arts & Crafts, Square Posts, 3 Drawers, 29 1/2 x 48 x 28 In. 175.00
Desk, Biedermeier Style, Ash, Rectangular Top, Banded, Drawers, 29 x 48 x 26 In. 2530.00
Desk, Biedermeier, Walnut, Leather, Gilt, Pedestal, Scroll Feet, c.1850, 30 x 49 x 31 In. . . 2360.00
Desk, Bonheur Du Jour, Louis XV Style, Kingwood, c.1925, 51 x 32 In. 575.00
Desk, Bonheur Du Jour, Louis XVI Style, Mahogany, c.1900, 46 x 31 x 19 In. 490.00
Desk, Bonheur Du Jour, Tulipwood, Boxwood, c.1780, 36 x 28 x 16 In. 5750.00
Desk, Boulle Style, Kneehole, 2 Banks Of 3 Drawers, 34 x 49 x 26 In. 2690.00
Desk, Butler's, Empire, Mahogany, Cylinder Roll, 9 Drawers, Scroll Feet, 42 In. 900.00
Desk, Butler's, Federal, Mahogany, Veneer, Poplar, 43 x 23 1/2 x 50 In. 1210.00
Desk, Butler's, Flamed Cherry, Tiger Maple Drawer Fronts, Cubby Holes, 52 x 43 In. . . . 506.00
Desk, Butler's, Neoclassical, Mahogany, c.1840, 43 x 43 x 22 In. 460.00
Desk, Butler's, Sheraton, Mahogany Veneer, 4 Drawers, 1800s, 46 x 22 x 42 In. 1400.00
Desk, Butler's, Thomas Nisbet, Mahogany, Bird's-Eye Maple 11500.00
Desk, Campaign, Regency Style, Brass Mounted, Tooled Writing Surface, 30 x 66 In. 5676.00
Desk, Carlton House, Mahogany, Leather, Fretwork Carving, c.1910, 36 x 41 x 19 In. 2875.00
Desk, Carlton House, Painted Satinwood, Gilt Tooled Leather Inset, 39 x 52 x 26 In. 5580.00
Desk, Cherry, 2 Frame & Panel Doors, Shelves, 72 x 44 x 21 In. 5060.00
Desk, Cherry, Poplar, Inlay, Slant Front, French Feet, Pigeonholes, 44 1/2 x 20 x 46 In. . . 2200.00
Desk, Chippendale Style, Mahogany, Kneehole, 31 x 72 x 34 In. 646.00
Desk, Chippendale, Cherry, Reverse Serpentine, 4 Drawers, 18th Century, 44 x 42 In. 4600.00
Desk, Chippendale, Curly Maple, Slant Front, 3 Drawers, 40 1/2 x 35 x 19 3/4 In. 920.00
Desk, Chippendale, Mahogany, Claw & Ball Foot, North Shore, c.1760 . . . . 4125.00
Desk, Chippendale, Mahogany, Kidney Shape, Double Pedestal, 45 x 21 x 30 In. 460.00
Desk, Chippendale, Mahogany, Kneehole, 9 Drawers, Leather Top, 30 x 46 In. 127.00
Desk, Chippendale, Mahogany, Kneehole, Reeded Columns, Gadrooned Edge, 32 In. 1625.00
Desk, Chippendale, Slant Front, Fan Carving, 24 Drawers, 45 x 42 1/2 x 21 1/2 In. 2300.00
Desk, Chippendale, Slant Front, Mahogany, 4 Drawers, 38 x 32 In. 1069.00
Desk, Chippendale, Slant Front, Mahogany, 4 Drawers, 39 1/4 x 38 3/4 x 19 1/4 In. 748.00
Desk, Chippendale, Slant Front, Mahogany, Boston, c.1770, 42 1/2 x 39 x 20 In. 5975.00
Desk, Chippendale, Slant Front, Mahogany, Oxbow, c.1780, 44 x 42 x 23 In. 4255.00
Desk, Chippendale, Slant Front, Mahogany, Rhode Island, c.1780, 42 x 39 x 22 In. 13145.00
Desk, Chippendale, Slant Front, Maple, 4 Drawers, Pigeonholes, 39 In. 3885.00
Desk, Chippendale, Slant Front, Pigeonholes, Drawers, c.1780, 39 x 35 x 20 In. 1528.00
Desk, Chippendale, Slant Front, Tiger Maple, 4 Drawers, 40 3/4 x 36 x 18 In. 5225.00
Desk, Chippendale, Slant Front, Walnut, 4 Drawers, Compartments, 43 x 40 In. . . . . *Illus* 4290.00
Desk, Chippendale, Slant Front, Walnut, Brass, c.1780, 41 x 38 x 22 In. 1955.00
Desk, Chippendale, Slant Front, Walnut, c.1790, 35 x 36 x 24 In. 1150.00
Desk, Chippendale, Slant Front, Walnut, Line Inlay, 4 Drawers, 43 x 40 x 20 1/2 In. 4290.00
Desk, Chippendale, Slant Front, Walnut, Paneled Door, Drawers, 40 x 20 x 36 In. 2645.00
Desk, Chippendale, Walnut, Flat Interior, Drawers, Ogee Feet, 41 x 33 In. 4500.00
Desk, Davenport, Regency, Rosewood, Slanted Flip Top, Inset Leather, 34 x 27 In. 2750.00
Desk, Davenport, Walnut, Storage, Hinges, Drawers, Casters, 1800s, 32 x 21 x 21 1/2 In. . . 805.00
Desk, Directoire Style, Slant Front, Mahogany, Gilt Mounted, 40 x 35 x 18 In. 880.00
Desk, Drop Front, Bowfront, Cabriole Legs, Marquetry, Mid 1800s, 34 x 33 x 13 In. 1395.00
Desk, Drop Front, Mahogany, Pigeonhole Separators, Drawer, 60 x 37 x 32 In. 1000.00
Desk, Drop Front, Walnut, Burl, Bombe Base, Shaped Apron, 4 Drawers, c.1790, 51 In. . . 3348.00
Desk, E. Wormley, Blond Mahogany, 7 Drawers, Brass Swag Pulls, Dunbar 978.00
Desk, E. Wormley, Rosewood, Leather Top, 2 Pedestals, Dunbar, 1950s, 29 In. 920.00
Desk, Eastlake, Ebonized, Tooled Leather Top, 2 Drawers, Casters, 30 x 35 In. 575.00
Desk, Edwardian, Mahogany, Leather Lined Surface, c.1900, 43 x 33 In. 2390.00
Desk, Edwardian, Mahogany, Reeded Edge, Tapered Legs, c.1900, 33 1/4 x 35 1/2 In. 865.00
Desk, Edwardian, Satinwood, Cupboard, Drawers, Leather Inset, 38 x 52 x 25 In. 2300.00
Desk, Edwardian, Slant Front, Rosewood, Leather Inset, c.1900, 43 1/2 x 42 In. 1725.00
Desk, Empire Style, Slant Front, Mahogany, 20th Century, 42 x 40 1/2 x 20 In. 705.00
Desk, Empire, Mahogany, Ratcheted Writing Board, 2 Inks, Drawers 565.00
Desk, Escritoire, Louis XV Style, Kingwood, Tambour Construction, 30 x 11 x 8 In. 1076.00
Desk, Federal, Drop Front, Lady's, Mahogany, Inlaid, c.1810, 48 3/4 x 38 x 21 1/4 In. . . . 1295.00
Desk, Federal, Mahogany Inlay, Glazed, Shelves, Gallery, 78 3/4 x 40 1/2 x 20 In. 17625.00
Desk, Federal, Mahogany Veneer, Frieze, Tambour Doors, c.1790, 46 1/4 x 42 x 21 In. . . . 3820.00
Desk, Federal, Maple, Mahogany, Tambour, Massachusetts, c.1810, 49 x 38 1/2 In. 9000.00
Desk, Federal, Slant Front, Mahogany, Fold-Out Surface Over 2 Drawers, 42 In. 1035.00
Desk, Federal, Slant Front, Mahogany, Inlay, c.1805, 42 1/4 x 40 3/4 x 20 1/4 In. 2530.00

Desk, Federal, Slant Front, Tiger Maple, Sections, Drawers, 42 x 20 x 43 In. 1840.00
Desk, Field, Folding Top, Fitted Red Leather Interior, Folding File, Ink Blotter, 2 Boxes . . 865.00
Desk, Flap Front Over Open Shelf Over 2 Drawers, 33 x 31 x 15 In. 290.00
Desk, Florence Knoll, Blond Wood, 3 Blind Drawers, Walnut Legs, 29 x 50 x 28 In. 1645.00
Desk, Florence Knoll, Wood Grain Laminate Top, 66 x 32 x 29 1/4 In. 460.00
Desk, Frank Lloyd Wright, Taliesin Design, Heritage Henredon, 52 x 20 x 28 In. 1840.00
Desk, G. Nelson & Bob Probst, Action Office, Roll Top, Herman Miller, 54 x 30 x 34 In. . . 460.00
Desk, G. Nelson, Drop Front, Walnut, 3 Drawers, Herman Miller, 1950s, 40 x 40 In. 865.00
Desk, G. Nelson, Drop Leaf, Walnut, 3 Drawers, Herman Miller, 40 x 24 x 29 1/2 In. 1380.00
Desk, G. Nelson, Executive L Unit, Laminate, Walnut, Herman Miller 2415.00
Desk, G. Nelson, Home Office, Birch, Leather, Herman Miller, 54 x 28 x 41 In. 8050.00
Desk, G. Nelson, Lacquered Wood, Walnut, Laminate, Herman Miller, 1958, 39 x 34 In. . . 9200.00
Desk, G. Nelson, Modern Management Group, Walnut, Metal, Herman Miller 430.00
Desk, G. Nelson, Swag Leg, Herman Miller, c.1956, 34 1/2 x 39 x 28 3/4 In. 2938.00
Desk, G. Stickley, Drop Front, Backsplash, Drawer, Lower Shelf, 44 x 30 x 13 In. 805.00
Desk, G. Stickley, Drop Front, Drawer, Lower Shelf, Red Decal, 43 x 30 x 13 3/4 In. 920.00
Desk, G. Stickley, Drop Front, Paneled, Drawer, Red Decal, 47 1/4 x 25 3/4 In. 4025.00
Desk, G. Stickley, Letter Holders, Drawer, Tapered Legs, 35 x 28 x 18 In. 1035.00
Desk, G. Stickley, No. 720, 2 Drawers, Gallery, Branded, 38 x 37 In. 2530.00
Desk, G. Stickley, No. 732, Slant Front, 4 Drawers, Slab Sides, 32 x 13 x 34 In. 1380.00
Desk, G. Stickley, Roll Top, No. 619, Interior Gallery, 5 Drawers, 46 x 48 x 32 In. 3680.00
Desk, G. Stickley, Slant Front, 2 Drawers, 2 Cabinet Doors, 48 x 33 x 14 In. 4315.00
Desk, George I, Slant Front, Walnut, Burl, 4 Drawers, c.1710, 40 1/2 x 35 x 20 In. 4600.00
Desk, George II Style, Slant Front, Oak, Pigeonholes, Drawers, 1900, 37 x 27 x 18 In. . . . 765.00
Desk, George II Style, Slant Front, Walnut, 3 Graduated Drawers, 1800s, 37 x 28 x 19 In. 1095.00
Desk, George II Style, Walnut, 2 Pedestals, Late 19th Century, 30 x 60 x 35 1/2 In. 2530.00
Desk, George III Style, Mahogany, Kneehole, 20th Century, 28 1/4 x 30 x 15 3/4 In. 690.00
Desk, George III Style, Mahogany, Leather Top, Pedestal, c.1875, 29 x 68 In. 2150.00
Desk, George III Style, Mahogany, Pedestal, 19th Century, 30 x 41 1/2 x 24 In. 4780.00
Desk, George III Style, Slant Front, Mahogany, 19th Century, 43 1/2 x 42 x 21 In. 1725.00
Desk, George III, Mahogany, Kneehole, Bracket Feet, 33 x 22 x 30 In. 1530.00
Desk, George III, Mahogany, Pedestal, 9 Drawers, 31 1/2 x 73 1/2 x 37 1/2 In. 1725.00
Desk, George III, Slant Front, Mahogany, 18th Century, 39 1/4 x 35 3/4 x 18 1/4 In. 805.00
Desk, George III, Slant Front, Mahogany, Drawers, Pigeonholes, c.1800, 40 x 34 x 19 In. . . 920.00
Desk, George IV, Slant Front, Mahogany, Oak, 44 x 44 x 21 In. 1840.00
Desk, George IV, Slant Front, Mahogany, Serpentine, c.1820, 45 x 51 1/2 x 24 1/2 In. 980.00
Desk, Georgian Style, Mahogany, Kneehole, Early 1900s, 34 1/2 x 30 x 17 1/2 In. 865.00
Desk, Georgian Style, Pedestal, Drawers, Cabriole Legs, 1900s, 48 x 27 x 32 In. 1265.00
Desk, Georgian Style, Slant Front, Mahogany, 5 Drawers, 42 1/2 x 42 x 20 In. 1555.00
Desk, Georgian, Mahogany, Pedestal, Swags, Bellflower Carvings, 4 Doors, 32 x 78 In. . . 5750.00
Desk, Gothic Style, Cherry, Figural Stork Panels, Drawer, 31 x 43 In. 3080.00
Desk, Hepplewhite, Mahogany Inlay, Slant Front, Centennial, 41 x 35 1/2 x 18 In. 345.00
Desk, Hepplewhite, Mahogany, Flip Top, Tapered Legs, 35 x 18 x 36 In. 980.00
Desk, Hepplewhite, Mahogany, Fold-Out, Inlaid, 3 Drawers, 1700s, 34 x 19 x 34 In. 1200.00
Desk, Hepplewhite, Slant Front, Cherry, 4 Graduated Drawers, French Feet, 44 In. 2200.00
Desk, Hepplewhite, Tambour, Burl Veneer, Mahogany Doors, 2 Parts, c.1800 . . . . 5600.00
Desk, Heywood-Wakefield Co., Birch, Wheat Finish, c.1955, 40 x 20 x 30 In. 315.00
Desk, Heywood-Wakefield Co., Pedestal, Birch, Wheat Finish, c.1955, 50 x 24 x 30 In. . . 660.00

Furniture, Desk,
Chippendale,
Slant Front,
Walnut,
4 Drawers,
Compartments,
43 x 40 In.

Furniture, Desk, Partners, Tiger Oak, Oval, 6
Claw Feet, Drawers, 32 x 60 x 38 In.

Desk, Ico Parisi, Mahogany, Rosewood, Metal, MIM, Italy, 1958 .... 7475.00
Desk, Joubert & Petit, Walnut, Ivory, France, c.1925, 32 x 43 1/2 In. 8365.00
Desk, Kittinger, Chippendale Style, Mahogany, Veneer, Oak, 72 x 36 1/4 x 30 1/2 In. 1595.00
Desk, L. & J.G. Stickley, 5 Drawers, Paneled Sides, Tapered Legs, 29 1/4 x 42 x 26 In. 920.00
Desk, L. & J.G. Stickley, Drop Front, 6 Drawers, Bookshelf On Sides, 41 x 45 x 21 In. .. 2070.00
Desk, L. & J.G. Stickley, Kneehole, 5 Drawers, Hidden Bookshelf, 29 x 48 x 30 In. 1095.00
Desk, Larkin Style, Oak, 56 1/2 x 29 In. 275.00
Desk, Lifetime, Drop Front, 2 Drawers, Copper Hardware, 42 x 19 x 43 In. 2875.00
Desk, Lifetime, No. 8555, Drawer, Copper Hardware, Letter Organizer, 36 x 37 In. 1380.00
Desk, Limbert, Cutout Shade, Turned Posts, Letter Divider, 66 x 36 x 40 In. 9200.00
Desk, Limbert, Drawer, Rectangular Top, Stretcher, 29 x 36 x 24 In. 1150.00
Desk, Limbert, Lift Top Compartment, Writing Surface, Drawer, 29 x 24 x 18 In. 1035.00
Desk, Limbert, Oak, No. 141, c.1905, Child's, 29 1/4 x 24 x 20 In. 2630.00
Desk, Louis XV Style, Blond Mahogany, Early 20th Century, 30 x 18 In. 460.00
Desk, Louis XV Style, Gilt Bronze Mounted, Parquetry Inlay, 28 x 21 x 15 1/2 In. 540.00
Desk, Louis XV Style, Kingwood, Gilt Brass, France, c.1900, 38 x 28 In. 1035.00
Desk, Louis XV Style, Mahogany, 3 Frieze Drawers, Cabriole Legs, 39 x 48 x 29 In. 940.00
Desk, Louis XV Style, Mahogany, Satinwood, 3 Drawers, Fold-Out, 41 x 26 x 18 In. 2115.00
Desk, Louis XV Style, Marquetry, 3 Drawers, Flower Designs, 31 x 37 x 21 In. 1315.00
Desk, Louis XV Style, Slant Front, Fruitwood, 2 Drawers, 36 x 39 x 19 In. 1765.00
Desk, Louis XV Style, Tulipwood, Parquetry, Gilt Bronze, 1900, 38 x 31 1/2 x 18 In. 7768.00
Desk, Louis XV Style, Walnut, Gilt Bronze Mounted, 3 Drawers, 29 x 45 x 22 In. 1315.00
Desk, Louis XV, Walnut, Inlaid, Kidney Shape, Pierced Brass Gallery, 38 x 20 In. 2015.00
Desk, Louis XVI Style, Mahogany, Brass Mounted, c.1890, 46 x 31 1/2 In. 2760.00
Desk, Louis XVI Style, Mahogany, Bronze, Parquetry, c.1900, 60 x 48 x 28 In. 6325.00
Desk, Louis XVI, Mahogany, Brass, Leather, 7 Drawers, Tapered Legs, 31 x 71 x 34 In. ... 6325.00
Desk, Louis XVI, Roll Top, Mahogany, Ormolu, Brass Mount, 48 x 57 x 29 In. 5378.00
Desk, Mahogany, 2 Pedestals, 4 Drawers Each, Center Drawer, Ogee Feet, 30 x 70 In. 890.00
Desk, Mahogany, 2 Pedestals, False Drawer, Plinth Bases, Casters, 43 x 26 x 48 In. 765.00
Desk, Mahogany, 7 Drawers, Leather Surface, c.1915, 30 1/4 x 48 x 22 In. 575.00
Desk, Mahogany, Carved Backsplash, 2 Drawers, 19th Century, 34 x 35 1/2 x 20 In. 1150.00
Desk, Mahogany, Leather, 3 Drawers, Tapered Legs, 19th Century, 31 x 58 1/2 x 31 In. ... 748.00
Desk, Mahogany, Molded Top, Valanced Compartments, 19th Century, 18 3/4 In. 2705.00
Desk, Mahogany, Scroll Carved Sides, Cutout Bracket Base, 29 x 74 x 56 In. 1120.00
Desk, McCobb, Windsor Style Chair, Winchendon Planner Group, 29 x 48 x 24 In. 880.00
Desk, Napoleon III, Black Lacquered, 4 Upper Drawers, Frieze Drawer, 34 x 31 x 17 In. . 1725.00
Desk, Napoleon III, Slant Front, Rosewood, Kingwood, Pierced Gallery, 36 x 27 In. 1840.00
Desk, Oak, Figural Standing Eagles, Carved Skirt, 2 Drawers, 31 x 71 In. 3920.00
Desk, Office, Bruce Burdick, U-Shape, Accessories, Herman Miller 7480.00
Desk, Old Hickory, Oak, Drawer, Letter Holders, Signed, Martinsville, 36 In. 3300.00
Desk, Painted Scenes After Salvator Rosa, Parcel Gilt, 1850, 31 x 14 x 28 In. 7670.00
Desk, Partners, Art Deco, Rosewood, France, c.1930, 29 3/4 x 53 1/2 In. 3680.00
Desk, Partners, Campaign, Leather Top, France, 19th Century 2910.00
Desk, Partners, Chippendale Style, Mahogany, Carved, 5 Drawers, 31 x 62 In. 860.00
Desk, Partners, Chippendale, Mahogany, Gadroon Border, 31 1/2 x 71 x 27 In. 1725.00
Desk, Partners, George III Style, Mahogany, 2 Pedestals, Mid 1800s, 31 x 60 x 36 In. ... 2300.00
Desk, Partners, George III Style, Mahogany, Pedestal, Leather Top, 30 x 66 x 53 In. 2990.00
Desk, Partners, Georgian Style, Mahogany, Leather Inset, 9 Drawers, 29 1/2 x 60 In. 2070.00
Desk, Partners, Mahogany, Carved Figures, Claw Feet, c.1885, 31 x 54 x 34 In. 1345.00
Desk, Partners, Mahogany, Carved Pedestals, Lion-Mask Pilasters, 32 x 79 In. 8050.00
Desk, Partners, Mahogany, Leather Top, 4 Short Drawers, Brass Casters, 72 x 48 In. 1600.00
Desk, Partners, Oak, Open-Mouth Lion Heads, Serpentine Carved Skirt, 31 x 48 In. 2800.00
Desk, Partners, R.J. Horner, Mahogany, Standing Winged Griffin Supports, 30 x 58 In. 5710.00
Desk, Partners, Renaissance Revival, Walnut, Burled Panels, Claw Feet, 28 x 56 In. 5320.00
Desk, Partners, Tiger Oak, Oval, 6 Claw Feet, Drawers, 32 x 60 x 38 In. .... *Illus* 2200.00
Desk, Partners, Walnut, Red Leather, Inset, Burl Drawer Fronts, 30 1/2 x 50 x 28 In. 2243.00
Desk, Pine, Red Paint, Convex Drawers, New England, 19th Century, 22 1/2 In. 1115.00
Desk, Pop Art, White Laminate Top, 3 Yellow Plastic Drawers, 30 x 47 1/4 In. 380.00
Desk, Queen Anne Style, Slant Front, Walnut, Hinged Lid, Pigeonholes, 40 x 32 x 19 In. .. 1095.00
Desk, Queen Anne, Walnut, Slant Front, Bracket Feet, 4 Drawers, 40 x 21 x 42 In. 6600.00
Desk, Regency, Rosewood, Rectangular Top, Leather Inlay, 2 Drawers, 28 x 47 x 27 In. .. 3220.00
Desk, Renaissance Revival, Roll Top, Walnut, Cylinder, c.1870 .... 1045.00
Desk, Renaissance Revival, Walnut, Raised Burl Panels, Cylinder, Kneehole, 54 In. 3360.00

Desk, Restauration, Mahogany, 2 Storage Wells, 19th Century, 29 x 26 1/4 x 15 3/4 In. 1725.00
Desk, Riesener, Louis XVI, Mahogany, 2 Pedestals, France, c.1770, 31 1/4 x 57 In. 4600.00
Desk, Rococo, Rosewood, Carved, Floral Pierced, c.1850, 42 1/2 x 28 x 19 In. 2800.00
Desk, Roll Top, Mahogany, Burl Cedar Veneers, Tooled Leather Pullout, 31 x 36 In. 1995.00
Desk, Roll Top, Pullout Surface, 2 Paneled Doors, 3 Drawers, Bun Feet, 58 x 58 In. 920.00
Desk, Roll Top, Walnut, C Roll, Cubby Holes, Paneled Doors & Drawers On Base, 86 In. . . 675.00
Desk, Roll Top, Walnut, Single Bank, 4 Drawers, Spindle Gallery, 16 Pigeonholes, 47 In. . . 1150.00
Desk, Rosewood Veneers, Cylinder, Bombe Form, 3 Drawers, Continental, 44 x 45 In. 2990.00
Desk, Schoolmaster's, Slant Front, Cherry, Pine, 4 Interior Drawers, Tall Legs 340.00
Desk, Schoolmaster's, Slant Front, Walnut, Drawers, Pegged, 38 1/2 x 31 x 24 In. 1155.00
Desk, Shaker, Pine, Poplar, 2 Small Drawers, Step-Out Surface, 32 1/2 x 27 x 20 1/2 In. . . 1410.00
Desk, Sheraton, Drop Front, Mahogany Flame Veneer, Drawer, Rope Twist Legs, 36 In. . . . 1540.00
Desk, Sheraton, Mahogany, 3 Doors, 3 Lower Drawers, c.1810, 52 x 40 In. 9200.00
Desk, Sheraton, Slant Front, Walnut, 4-Drawer Top, 2 Drawers Over 2 Doors, 36 In. 565.00
Desk, Slant Front, Birch, Door, 6 Drawers, 4 Drawers, Dust Panels, 43 x 40 x 20 In. 3190.00
Desk, Slant Front, Carved, Paw Feet, Pigeonholes, 4 Drawers, c.1880, 42 x 37 In. 546.00
Desk, Slant Front, Cherry, 7 Drawers, Door, Astragal Molding, 1900s, 42 x 38 x 23 In. . . . 5720.00
Desk, Slant Front, Cherry, Poplar, Drawers, Sliding Panel, Child's, 27 x 23 x 14 In. 4115.00
Desk, Slant Front, Gilding, Flowers, Cabriole Legs, France, 28 1/2 x 18 1/4 x 37 In. 305.00
Desk, Slant Front, Grain Painted, Signed, Wm. Bentzel, 1872, 29 1/2 x 42 1/2 In. 450.00
Desk, Slant Front, Mahogany, 4 Drawers, 8 Pigeonholes, Center Door, 43 In. 3850.00
Desk, Slant Front, Mahogany, 5 Short Drawers, Compartments, 18th Century, 20 In. 4115.00
Desk, Slant Front, Mahogany, Brass, Rope-Twist Columns, c.1940, 35 x 24 x 22 In. 805.00
Desk, Slant Front, Mahogany, Reverse Serpentine Inlay, Small Drawers, c.1800, 43 In. . . . 5290.00
Desk, Slant Front, Poplar, Bread-Board Top, 2 Shelves, Drawer, 35 x 34 x 19 In. 715.00
Desk, Slant Front, Sections, 2 Drawers, Red Paint, 41 3/4 x 35 3/4 x 19 In. 1076.00
Desk, Slant Front, Walnut, Crossbanded, Italy, 18th Century, 36 x 33 x 18 In. 940.00
Desk, Slant Front, Walnut, Gerard Cartsens, 1869, 87 x 44 In. 385.00
Desk, Slant Front, Walnut, Open Interior, 2 Drawers, c.1850, 32 x 35 x 21 In. 598.00
Desk, Slant Front, Walnut, Pierced Gallery, 5 Side Drawers, Round Feet, 32 x 21 In. 1265.00
Desk, Slant Front, White Pine, Hinged, c.1805, 28 1/2 x 24 x 19 In. 4200.00
Desk, Stickley Bros., Caned Panel, 3 Drawers, Cubbies, 35 3/4 x 36 x 22 In. 805.00
Desk, Stickley Bros., No. 6526, Central Drawer, Copper Hardware, 50 x 27 x 29 In. 2900.00
Desk, Teak, 2 Pedestals, Chinese, Early 20th Century, 34 In. 225.00
Desk, Victorian, Burl, Tooled Writing Surface, 3 Drawers, 31 1/2 x 25 x 50 In. 840.00
Desk, Victorian, Painted, Black, White, Gold Decoration, 2 Doors, 50 x 28 x 30 In. 460.00
Desk, Victorian, Slant Front, American, c.1890, 62 1/2 x 35 1/2 In. 345.00
Desk, Victorian, Walnut, 2 Pedestals, Rectangular Top, 3 Drawers, 28 x 47 x 23 In. 2940.00
Desk, Victorian, Walnut, Pedestal, Leather Top, 3 Frieze Drawers, 30 x 42 In. 1000.00
Desk, Victorian, Walnut, Pedestal, Serpentine, 19th Century, 31 x 53 1/2 x 26 1/2 In. 1725.00
Desk, Walnut, Carved, Hindu Scenes, Indo-Tibetan, c.1900, 84 x 59 x 37 In. 1150.00
Desk, Walnut, Parquetry, 9 Drawers, Italy, 18th Century, 50 x 44 1/2 x 23 In. 4115.00
Desk, Wegner, Steel Banded Drawers, Carved Bevels, 1950s, 77 x 36 x 29 In. 7475.00
Desk, Wooton Style, Grain Painted, Carved Gallery Top, 58 x 35 1/2 x 21 In. 3740.00
Desk, Wooton, Arched Burl Panels, Ornate Gallery, 72 x 42 x 29 In. 9520.00
Desk, Wooton, Drop Front, Oak, Roll Top, Carved Gallery, c.1885, 42 x 70 x 20 In. 4760.00
Desk, Wooton, Oak, 2 Rotary Side Units, Flat Leather Top, 31 x 60 x 33 In. 2240.00
Desk, Wooton, Roll Top, Oak, 2 Rotary Side Units, 52 x 60 x 34 In. 5320.00
Desk, Wooton, Walnut Case, Veneers, Wells Fargo, Carved Gallery, c.1874 . . . . 27500.00
Desk, Wooton, Walnut, Burl Panels, 69 x 39 1/2 x 27 In. 13145.00
Dining Set, Berkey & Gay, Burl Walnut, Inlay, Carved Scenic Panels, c.1910, 12 Piece . . 20720.00
Dining Set, Chippendale Style, Mahogany, Cabinet, Sideboard, 9 Piece 1800.00
Dining Set, Chippendale Style, Mahogany, Carved, Upholstered, 8 Piece 3220.00
Dining Set, G. Nakashima, Walnut, Round Table, Grass Rope Seats, 1955, 4 Piece 5175.00
Dining Set, G. Nelson, Walnut Top, Upholstered, Herman Miller 1035.00
Dining Set, Heywood-Wakefield Co., Folding Table, 4 Chairs, 64 x 32 In. 575.00
Dining Set, Jacobean, Oak, Walnut, Open Leaves, 4 Spindle Chairs, 30 x 80 x 32 In. 230.00
Dining Set, John Widdicomb, Elm Burl Veneer, Wicker-Back Chairs, 5 Piece 405.00
Dining Set, Oak, Bentwood, Trestle Base, Brass Tacks, Davis Co., 9 Piece 290.00
Dining Set, Oak, Table, 6 Chairs, Sideboard, Cupboard, 1920s 2495.00
Dining Set, Saarinen, Tulip Table, 4 Swivel Pedestal Chairs, Knoll, 31 1/2 x 16 In. 1058.00
Dining Set, Trestle Table, Server, Hutch, 12 Ladder-Back Chairs, 1920s, 67 x 66 In. 1900.00
Dining Set, Wegner, C. Hansen, Denmark, c.1958, 59-In. Table, 11 Piece 1410.00

Furniture, Dresser, Aesthetic
Revival, Inlaid Mahogany,
Mirror, 74 x 48 1/2 In.

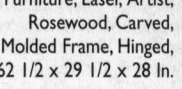

Furniture, Easel, Artist,
Rosewood, Carved,
Molded Frame, Hinged,
62 1/2 x 29 1/2 x 28 In.

Dining Set, Wegner, Stacking Chairs, F. Hansen, c.1958, 47-In. Table, 7 Piece 1765.00
Dresser, Aesthetic Revival, Inlaid Mahogany, Mirror, 74 x 48 1/2 In. . . . . *Illus* 11160.00
Dresser, Chippendale Style, Mahogany, Bowed Ends, Lift Top, Late 1880s 1800.00
Dresser, Danish, Teak Veneer, 6 Drawers, Recessed Pulls, Post Legs, 37 x 39 x 17 1/2 In. . . 825.00
Dresser, Eastlake, Walnut, Arched Crown, Pediment, Mirror, Candle Brackets, 84 In. 750.00
Dresser, English Oak, 3 Shelves, 4 Drawers, Cupboard, 81 x 71 x 17 In. 5520.00
Dresser, Federal, Mahogany, 2 Drawers, Beveled Mirror, Bun Feet, 32 x 18 In. 450.00
Dresser, G. Nelson, Walnut, 5 Drawers, Herman Miller, 24 x 18 1/2 x 40 In. 2300.00
Dresser, G. Stickley, 4 Drawers, Pivoting Mirror, Red Decal, 65 x 48 x 22 In. 5465.00
Dresser, G. Stickley, No. 911, 2 Half Over 2 Full Drawers, Iron Pulls, 48 x 22 x 67 In. . . . 3220.00
Dresser, G. Stickley, No. 913, 9 Drawers, Branded Signature, 36 x 51 In. . . . . . .6900.00 to 8625.00
Dresser, George II, Oak, Rectangular Top, Molded Edge, 3 Drawers, Cabriole Legs, 67 In. 2040.00
Dresser, George III, Mahogany, Serpentine, Late 18th Century, 43 x 71 x 26 In. 4370.00
Dresser, George III, Oak, Inlay, Wales, Early 19th Century, 84 x 80 x 18 In. 7170.00
Dresser, Georgian, Pewter, 3 Shelves, 4 Drawers, 2 Doors, 20 x 72 x 85 In. 520.00
Dresser, Herter Bros., Burl, Bird's-Eye Maple, Gilt, Marble, 84 x 72 x 22 In. 1495.00
Dresser, Loewy, DF2000, Lift Top, Red, Orange Plastic, France, 20 x 20 x 42 In. 2415.00
Dresser, Mahogany, Bowfront, Carved, Lion's Heads, 7 Drawers, 73 In. 2240.00
Dresser, Mahogany, Drawers, Mirror, Brass Pulls, 23 x 21 x 9 In. 495.00
Dresser, Oak, 3 Drawers, Shelf Back, Carved, c.1750, 77 x 67 In. 1020.00
Dresser, Oak, Serpentine, Drop Center, 4 Drawers, 3 Shaped Mirrors, 81 x 51 In. 1790.00
Dresser, Pine, 2 Shelves Over 2 Drawers & 2 Doors, England, 78 In. 2470.00
Dresser, Queen Anne, Walnut, Crossbanded Top, 3 Frieze Drawers, Cabriole Legs, 29 In. . 560.00
Dresser, Renaissance Revival, Walnut, Marble Top, Carved Caryatids, Mirror, 101 In. . . . 1610.00
Dresser, Rococo Revival, Overall Floral Inlay, 3 Short Over 2 Long Drawers, 53 x 74 In. . . 1380.00
Dresser, Rococo Revival, Rosewood, 2 Cupboards, Wig, Marble Top, 8 x 42 x 19 In. 1265.00
Dresser, Rosewood, Marble Top, Domed Caskets, Mirror, c.1870, 74 x 51 x 22 In. 3080.00
Dresser, Rosewood, Marble Top, Maple Interior, Carved Crest, 1870, 108 In. 6050.00
Dresser, Stickley Bros., Inlaid Mirror, 67 x 45 x 22 In. 575.00
Dresser, Tobey Furniture Co., 2 Half Over 2 Full Drawers, Brass, 48 x 24 x 70 In. 1725.00
Dresser, Victorian, Oak, Beveled Mirror, Serpentine Front, 1900s, 44 x 20 x 64 In. 175.00
Dresser, Victorian, Walnut, Marble Top, Burled Panels, Step-Down Base, 107 In. 960.00
Dresser, Walnut, 4 Dovetail Drawers, Astragal Panel, 30 1/2 x 34 In. 605.00
Dresser, Walnut, Drop Front Desk, Grape Pulls, Mirror, c.1870, 77 x 45 x 20 In. 1460.00
Dresser, Walnut, Marble Insert, Shell Carvings, Fruit-Carved Pulls, c.1870, 102 In. 2500.00
Dresser, Walnut, Marble Top, Crest, Mirror, Burl Panels, Candle Shelves, 48 x 20 x 82 In. 460.00
Dresser, Welsh, Oak, Mahogany Crossband, Plate Racks, c.1900, 82 x 72 x 19 1/4 In. 3105.00
Dresser, William & Mary Style, Oak, Dovetailed Drawers, 28 x 30 In. 605.00
Dry Sink, Amish, White, Black, Square Legs, Ohio, 20th Century, 30 x 20 x 32 In. 85.00
Dry Sink, Lacquered, Hardstone, Figural & Landscape Design, c.1950, 32 x 17 x 38 In. . . 345.00
Dry Sink, Pine, 2 Paneled Doors, Zinc Lined, Ochre Paint, Mid 1800s, 34 x 21 x 42 In. . . . 450.00
Dry Sink, Poplar, Red Wash, Bracket Feet, 2 Doors, 4 1/2 x 17 x 35 3/4 In. 1980.00
Dry Sink, Shaker, Walnut, Poplar, Pine, 2 Doors, Union Village, Ohio, 38 x 21 x 32 In. . . 935.00
Dry Sink, Softwood, 2 Drawers Over 2 Shaped Panel Doors, Zinc Well, Brown Paint 675.00
Dry Sink, Softwood, 2 Paneled Doors, Dovetailed Well, Notched Corner, 46 In. 480.00
Dry Sink, Softwood, Copper Lined Well, 2 Drawers, Paneled Doors, Bracket Base 310.00
Dry Sink, Softwood, Overhanging Drawer, 2 Shaped Sunken-Panel Doors, 49 In. 370.00

Dry Sink, Walnut, Poplar, 2 Paneled Doors, 50 1/2 x 21 1/2 x 30 In. 1375.00
Dry Sink, Yellow Paint, Square Tapered Legs, 30 x 34 x 21 In. 1095.00
Dumbwaiter, George III, Mahogany, 3 Tiers, 42 x 23 In. 2390.00
Dumbwaiter, Mahogany, Shaped Backsplash, Drawer, Cabriole Legs, 37 x 39 x 18 In. ... 460.00
Easel, Artist, Rosewood, Carved, Molded Frame, Hinged, 62 1/2 x 29 1/2 x 28 In. .. *Illus* 978.00
Easel, Walnut, Carved Flowers, Storage Panel, Cincinnati Art Carved, 77 x 23 In. 4315.00
Embroidery Frame On Stand, Beech, France, c.1835, 61 3/4 x 35 1/2 In. 2530.00
Empire Style, Burl, 7 Drawers, c.1890, 72 x 45 1/2 In. 1955.00
Etagere, Hardwood, 3 Tiers, Anglo-Indian, Mid 19th Century, 48 x 36 x 12 In., Pair 8065.00
Etagere, Louis XVI, Amboyna, Parcel Gilt, 3 Tiers, 3/4 Gallery, 30 x 13 x 18 In. 985.00
Etagere, Mahogany, 3 Beveled Mirrors, Pierced Carvings, Drop Center, 81 x 49 In. 575.00
Etagere, Regency, Mahogany, 2 Shelves, Door, Turned Supports, 54 x 18 x 18 In. 1380.00
Etagere, Regency, Rosewood, 4 Shelves, Tuned Standards, 43 x 19 x 15 In. 645.00
Etagere, Renaissance Revival, Rosewood, Bonnet Top, 2 Inlaid Paneled Doors, 109 In. .. 6720.00
Etagere, Rococo Revival, Rosewood, Marble, 3 Tiers, 83 x 62 x 18 In. .... *Illus* 11500.00
Etagere, Stick & Ball, Mirror Back, Northwind Gallery, c.1890, 64 x 43 x 13 In. 1456.00
Etagere, Thomas Brooks, Rococo, Rosewood, Mirror Back Shelves, 102 x 71 x 22 In. ... 56350.00
Etagere, Victorian, Carved, Turned, Drawer, George Croone & Co., 51 x 30 x 14 In. 230.00
Etagere, Victorian, Mahogany, 5 Shelves, Scrolling, Turned Standards, 51 x 36 x 10 In. .. 590.00
Etagere, Victorian, Walnut, Burled Panels, Pierced Crest, Drawer Base, Marble, 92 In. .. 3640.00
Etagere, Victorian, Walnut, Marquetry, Ebonized, c.1880, 33 1/2 x 20 1/4 x 13 3/4 In. ... 635.00
Etagere, Victorian, Walnut, Shaped Marble Top, Open Mirrored Back, 72 x 41 In. 2465.00
Etagere, Walnut, Marble Top, Curved Console, Open Carved Back, Mirror, 94 In. 2630.00
Etagere, William IV, Mahogany, 3 Tiers, Drawer, 51 x 17 1/2 x 15 1/4 In. 4180.00
Footstool, Arts & Crafts, Oak, Cut Corner Top, 2 Stretchers, 15 x 18 x 14 In. 470.00
Footstool, Arts & Crafts, Oak, Rush Top, Early 20th Century, 6 x 13 x 11 1/2 In. 70.00
Footstool, Arts & Crafts, Oak, Square Posts, H-Stretcher, Leather, 15 x 17 x 12 In. 265.00
Footstool, Cutout Legs, Mortised Through Top, Old Paint, 8 x 14 x 6 3/4 In. 110.00
Footstool, Ebonized, Fluted Frame, Gilt Metal Mounts, 21 In. 250.00
Footstool, G. Stickley, Mahogany, Arched Sides, Leather, Red Decal, 15 x 20 1/4 In. 1725.00
Footstool, G. Stickley, No. 300, Leather Seat, Red Decal, 15 1/2 x 20 x 16 In. 2070.00
Footstool, G. Stickley, No. 389, X-Shape Frame, Curled Foot, Leather, 21 x 14 x 13 In. .. 5175.00
Footstool, G. Stickley, Rush Seat, Tapered Legs, 20 x 16 x 17 In. 750.00
Footstool, Georgian, Mahogany, Cabriole Legs, Claw & Ball Feet 565.00
Footstool, Harden, Arched Apron, Slatted Sides, Drop Leather Seat, 16 x 20 x 24 In. 920.00
Footstool, L. & J.G. Stickley, Leather Top, Arched Sides, Tacks, 16 x 19 1/4 x 15 1/4 In. .. 865.00
Footstool, L. & J.G. Stickley, Square Posts, Arched Apron, Leather Top, 16 x 20 x 15 In. .. 520.00
Footstool, Limbert, Canvas Top, Drawer, Arched Apron, Marked, 12 3/4 x 18 x 12 In. ... 1265.00
Footstool, Limbert, Cricket, No. 200, Center Cutout, Flared Sides, c.1906, 7 x 18 x 10 In. 355.00
Footstool, Limbert, Cricket, No. 205 1/2, Cutout Heart Sides, 17 3/4 x 20 x 15 In. 920.00
Footstool, Limbert, Leather Seat, Tacked, Stretchers, Marked, 15 1/4 x 18 In. 320.00
Footstool, Louis XV Style, Beech, Needlepoint Upholstery, 12 x 15 x 11 In. 105.00
Footstool, Louis XVI Style, Giltwood, Upholstered, c.1900, 10 1/4 x 10 1/4 In. 1265.00
Footstool, Painted, Turned Finials, Single Rungs, Woven Cord Seat, 14 x 14 x 11 1/2 In. . 195.00
Footstool, Queen Anne Style, Walnut, Needlepoint Upholstery, 13 1/2 In. 645.00
Footstool, Regency Style, Mahogany, Cushioned, Carved Feet, 12 x 27 x 18 In., Pair 545.00
Footstool, Risom, Webbed Seat, Knoll, 17 x 16 x 15 In. 350.00

Furniture, Etagere,
Rococo Revival,
Rosewood, Marble,
3 Tiers,
83 x 62 x 18 In.

Furniture, Hall
Tree, Rococo
Revival, Walnut,
Marble, Mid
19th Century,
107 x 55 x 17 In.

**Be sure the big
furniture you buy
is small enough
to go through
the door into
your room.**

Footstool, Shaker, Maple, Dark Walnut Stain, Mt. Lebanon, N.Y., 8 In. 805.00
Footstool, Shaker, Maple, Dark Walnut Stain, Splint Seat, Mt. Lebanon, N.Y., 9 1/2 In. . .   805.00
Footstool, Shaker, Maple, Hickory, Ocher, Striped Tape Seat, Ky., 13 x 15 x 15 In. 330.00
Footstool, Shaker, Slant, Pine, S-Curved Cutouts, Cove Molding, 14 x 9 1/2 x 8 1/2 In. . .   165.00
Footstool, Turned Leg, Hand Painted Fruit, Basket Top, 1700s, 5 1/2 x 11 In. 390.00
Footstool, Victorian, Metal, Painted, Legs Cast As Standing Women, 15 In. 210.00
Footstool, Victorian, Walnut, Carved, Upholstered, Caster Feet, 14 1/2 x 21 x 17 In. 290.00
Footstool, Walnut, Pine, Cyma-Curved Cutouts On Legs, 18 x 5 1/2 x 7 3/4 In. 100.00
Footstool, Walnut, Round, Carved Trumpet Legs, Brass Caster Feet, 15 x 16 In. 290.00
Footstool, William IV, Mahogany, Leather Upholstery, 7 1/4 x 11 1/2 x 11 1/2 In. 259.00
Footstool, William IV, Mahogany, Ocelet Fur Upholstery, 11 x 20 1/2 x 16 In. 1095.00
Footstool, Wood, Repousse Silver Overlay, India, 19th Century, 19 x 19 x 6 1/2 In. 175.00
Frame, Arts & Crafts, Hand Carved, Gilt, Signed Walfred Thulin, 1920, 33 x 46 x 3 In. . .   2185.00
Frame, Barbizon Style, Gilt, Applied Ornament, Continental, 1800s, 5 x 12 x 4 In. 200.00
Frame, Cassetta Style, Gilt, Hand Carved, Italy, 18th Century, 28 x 44 x 10 In. 2645.00
Frame, Cove, Gilt, Rope Twist Rail, Continental, 19th Century, 28 x 37 x 5 In. 660.00
Frame, Fluted Cove, Foster Bros. Label, 20th Century, 22 x 38 x 6 1/2 In. 570.00
Frame, Gilt, Hand Carved, Continental, 18th Century, 29 x 38 x 6 In. 900.00
Frame, Rococo Style, Gilt Brass, Stones, Flowers, 14 x 11 In. 1530.00
Frame, Tabernacle, Gilt, Polychrome, Hand Carved, Italy, 1700s, 35 x 48 x 12 In. 3450.00
Frame, Twig Mosaic, Rustic, c.1920, 18 x 20 In. 800.00
Frame, Twig, Burl Detail, Lower Hudson River Valley, c.1890, 36 x 24 In. 2800.00
Frame, Walnut, Carved Flowers, Cincinnati Art Carved, 14 1/2 x 12 1/2 In. 35.00
Frame, Wood, Carved, Lotus Flower, Chinese, c.1890, 12 1/4 In. 90.00
Hall Stand, Art Deco, Hammered Iron, Mirror, Rack, Geometric, 27 x 8 1/2 x 79 In. 3740.00
Hall Stand, Art Deco, Wrought Iron, Mirror, Marble Shelf, France, 73 x 35 In. 1410.00
Hall Stand, Art Nouveau, Walnut, Beveled Mirror, Bronze Dragonflies, 33 x 83 In. 4890.00
Hall Stand, Arts & Crafts, Mahogany, Copper Leaf Panel, Drawer, 43 x 36 x 12 In. 2115.00
Hall Stand, Arts & Crafts, Mirror Back, c.1920, 36 x 12 x 79 In.   345.00
Hall Stand, Eastlake, Burl Walnut, Marble Top, Mirror, 95 x 47 x 13 In. 1725.00
Hall Stand, Oak, Winged Griffin Crest, Beveled Horseshoe Mirror, 102 x 61 In. 6720.00
Hall Stand, Victorian, Mahogany, Corinthian Supports, Mirror, Lift Seat, 81 x 42 In. 1070.00
Hall Stand, Victorian, Oak, Molded Frame, 4 Sets Of Coat Hooks, Lift Seat, 78 In. 1015.00
Hall Stand, Victorian, Rococo Detail, Cast Iron, Beveled Mirror, 78 In. 1960.00
Hall Stand, Victorian, Walnut, Arched Crown, Marble Top, Drawer, Bun Feet, 95 In. 1840.00
Hall Tree, Arts & Crafts, Copper Hooks, Drip Pan, Umbrella Support, 14 x 14 x 74 In. . . .   345.00
Hall Tree, Arts & Crafts, Oak, Rectangular, Double Drip Pan, 67 x 16 In. 499.00
Hall Tree, Bentwood, 8 Curved Arms, 4 Arched Legs, Lower Ring, 1800s, 81 In. 530.00
Hall Tree, Black Forest, Carved, 2 Climbing Bears, 87 In. 10575.00
Hall Tree, G. Stickley, Tapered Post, 4 Iron Hooks, 23 x 23 x 72 In. 978.00
Hall Tree, Renaissance Revival, Umbrella Holders, Cast Iron Drip Trays, c.1870 . . . .   440.00
Hall Tree, Renaissance Revival, Walnut, Carved Crest, Incised Burled Trim, 123 In. 7840.00
Hall Tree, Rococo Revival, Walnut, Marble, Mid 19th Century, 107 x 55 x 17 In. . . . . *Illus*   21850.00
Hamper, Wood, Wicker, Lacquered Body, Chinese, 19 x 41 x 24 In. 345.00
Hat Rack, Nutting, No. 40, Maple, Spinning Wheel 798.00
Hat Rack, Squirrels Hold Moon, Red, Yellow Paint, 19th Century, 12 x 24 In. 115.00
Headboard, Baker, Rococo Style, Column Shape Finials, 83 x 80 In. 86.00
Headboard, E. Wormley, Mahogany, Cane, 2 Sliding Doors, 1950s, 57 1/2 x 36 In. 290.00
High Chair, Black Over Red Grained Paint, Gold, Red Crest Stenciling, 35 In. 440.00
High Chair, Cane Seat, Mixed Hardwoods, Shaped Crest, Carved Rosette, Turned Legs . .   225.00
High Chair, Maple, Converts To Stroller, c.1880 . . . .   230.00
High Chair, Maple, Hickory, Walnut, 2-Slat Back, Woven Splint Seat, 34 In. 220.00
High Chair, Oak, Wicker Seat, Pressed Back, Collapsible 425.00
High Chair, Plank Bottom, Curved Back, 8 Turned Spindles, Legs, Black Paint 200.00
High Chair, Salmon Paint, Apple, Cherry, Crest Rail, 19th Century, 21 In. 990.00
High Chair, Windsor Style, Bow Back, Red Paint, MacCormick, Ohio, c.1820, 36 1/2 In. . .   115.00
High Chair, Windsor Style, Maple, Birch, Mahogany, Baluster Turnings, 24 x 35 In. 110.00
High Chair, Windsor, Grain Painted, Rosewood, Stenciling, Maine, 36 x 22 In. 575.00
High Chair, Windsor, Painted, Bamboo Turnings, Arms, 5 Spindles, 22 x 34 1/2 In. 385.00
High Chair, Wood, Green Paint, Slanted Stiles, Early 19th Century, 36 In. 230.00
High Chair, Yew, Rolled Crest, 8 Turned Spindles, Shaped Arms & Seat, 37 In. 635.00
Highboy, Chippendale Style, Mahogany, Early 20th Century, 48 1/2 x 24 1/4 x 81 In. 1100.00
Highboy, Chippendale, Mahogany, Bonnet Top, Fan Carving, 7 Over 4 Drawers, 78 In. . . .   1725.00

Furniture, Highboy, Queen Anne, Birch, Double-Arch, Cutout Skirt, New England, 68 x 38 In.

Furniture, Highboy, Queen Anne, Cherry, Connecticut, Carved Fan, 72 x 38 x 19 In.

Furniture, Highboy, Queen Anne, Inlaid Burl Walnut, Bonnet Top, American, 87 x 38 In.

Highboy, Chippendale, Shell Drawers, Flame Finials, Signed Horner, 90 x 40 x 23 In. 4200.00
Highboy, George II, Oak, Greek Key Cut, 5 Drawers, 18th Century, 66 x 39 x 19 In. 3335.00
Highboy, Kindel, Mahogany, Fluted Columns, Shaped Apron, Cabriole Legs, 58 In. 480.00
Highboy, Philadelphia Style, Mahogany, 2 Sections, 7 Drawers, 81 x 36 x 37 In. 1035.00
Highboy, Queen Anne Style, Cherry, Pine, Cabriole Legs, c.1970, 17 x 9 3/4 x 39 In. ... 2970.00
Highboy, Queen Anne Style, Curly Maple, Pine, Cabriole Legs, c.1980, 35 x 19 x 70 In. ... 3685.00
Highboy, Queen Anne, Birch, Double-Arch, Cutout Skirt, New England, 68 x 38 In. . *Illus* 11500.00
Highboy, Queen Anne, Birch, Pine, Red Wash, Batwing Brass, 71 x 40 In., 2 Piece 33000.00
Highboy, Queen Anne, Cherry, Connecticut, Carved Fan, 72 x 38 x 19 In. .... *Illus* 23000.00
Highboy, Queen Anne, Inlaid Burl Walnut, Bonnet Top, American, 87 x 38 In. ..... *Illus* 18400.00
Highboy, Queen Anne, Mahogany, Center Fan Carving, American, 18th Century 9000.00
Highboy, Queen Anne, Maple, Poplar, Red Finish, Cabriole Legs, 42 x 20 1/2 x 76 In. ... 9350.00
Highboy, Queen Anne, Oak, Burl Veneer, 10 Drawers, Cabriole Legs, 62 x 39 In. 1870.00
Hoosier Cabinet, 2 Parts, 3 Shelves, 2 Doors, 73 x 43 In. 920.00
Hoosier Cabinet, White Enameled Steel Pullout Work Shelf, Flour Bin, Hand Crank 1295.00
Huntboard, Hepplewhite, Elm, 3 Drawers, Bail Handles, 33 x 72 In. 4830.00
Huntboard, Walnut, 3 Sections, Carved, Adjustable Shelves, 109 x 56 x 24 1/2 In. 1380.00
Huntboard, Yellow Pine, 2-Board Top, Applied Molding, 2 Doors, 45 x 53 x 22 In. 5940.00
Hutch, Cupboard Base, Cherry, 3 Drawers, Paneled Doors, 42 1/4 x 56 1/4 x 19 1/2 In. .. 980.00
Hutch, David Smith & Co., Grain Painted, Glazed Doors, Morrow, Ohio, 84 x 19 x 50 In. 2760.00
Hutch, French Provincial, Fruitwood, 3 Shelves, Galleries, 2 Drawers, 2 Doors, 90 In. ... 4370.00
Hutch, McCobb, Perimeter Group, Birch, 2-Door Cabinet, 38 x 18 x 67 In. 978.00
Hutch, Painted, 2-Board Top, Round Corners, Half-Moon Cutout, 54 x 36 x 27 In. 3450.00
Hutch, Painted, Half Lid, Shoe Foot, 18th Century, 29 1/2 x 47 x 30 In. 2300.00
Hutch, Pine, 3-Board Top, Box Stretcher, American, 28 x 35 In. 635.00
Hutch, Pine, Dovetailed, Red Wash, Converts To Bench, c.1890, 59 x 33 In. 2400.00
Hutch, Pine, Hickory, Worn Paint, 3-Board Top, 49 x 39 x 27 1/2 In. 2475.00
Hutch, Sycamore, Pine, Brown Paint, American, 29 x 40 1/2 In. 3585.00
Kas, Baroque Style, 2 2-Panel Doors, Carved Figure Heads & Leaves, 69 x 58 In. 315.00
Kas, Baroque, Walnut, Fruitwood, 2 Shaped Panel Doors, Ball Feet, 77 x 24 In. 3290.00
Kas, Chippendale, Walnut, c.1770, 88 3/4 x 84 1/4 x 30 3/4 In. 5750.00
Kas, Gumwood, Paneled, Ball Feet, Hudson River Valley, 76 1/2 x 68 x 23 1/2 In. 18800.00
Kas, Paint Decorated, Germany, 1806, 62 In. 1320.00
Kas, Pine, Red Brown Grain Painted, 4 Panels, Urns Of Flowers, 1806, 61 x 47 In. 1320.00
Kas, Rosewood, Oak, 19th Century, 74 1/2 x 74 x 26 1/2 In. 3200.00
Kneeling Bench, Prie Dieu, Napoleon III, Ebonized, Armrest, Kneeler, c.1865, 34 In. 980.00
Ladder, Library, Brass-Studded Red Leather, Pole Shape, Fruitwood Rungs, 91 In. 1295.00
Ladder, Library, Edwardian, Pine, Mahogany, Folding, c.1900, 70 1/2 In. 805.00
Ladder, Library, Georgian Style, Mahogany, 4 Steps, Brass Trimmed, 48 x 18 x 28 In. ... 575.00
Ladder, Library, Oak, Hand Rail, 12 Steps, c.1900, 138 x 14 In., Pair 400.00
Ladder, Library, Pine, Waxed, Tapered, 19th Century, 103 1/2 In. 430.00
Ladder, Library, Pine, Waxed, Tapered, c.1885, 120 In. 315.00
Ladder, Library, Wooden, Folding, Brass Mounted, Cuffs, Tack, 92 In. 1610.00

Lap Desk, Brass Inlay, Drawer, Handles, 7 x 20 x 11 In. 55.00
Lap Desk, Burl Walnut, Brass Inlay, Folding, England, 4 x 13 x 10 In. 400.00
Lap Desk, Edwardian, Walnut, Slant, Storage, Square Legs, 25 1/4 x 18 1/2 x 11 In. 920.00
Lap Desk, Edwardian, Walnut, Slant, Storage, Stand, Square Legs, 24 x 16 x 10 In. 575.00
Lap Desk, Federal, Mahogany, Bird's-Eye Maple, Tambour Roll Top, 9 x 16 x 12 In. 1840.00
Lap Desk, George IV, Mahogany, Slant Front, Ball Foot, c.1835, 10 1/4 x 21 In. 1035.00
Lap Desk, Georgian, Satinwood, Brass Mounted, London, c.1815, 6 1/2 x 15 1/2 In. 520.00
Lap Desk, Mahogany, Brass, Felt Lining, Fitted Interior, Key Lock, 7 x 20 x 11 In. 460.00
Lap Desk, Regency, Rosewood, Brass Inlay, Tooled Leather, 5 1/2 x 16 x 10 1/2 In. 635.00
Lap Desk, Regency, Walnut, Lid, Hinges, Slant Leather Front, 24 x 18 x 10 1/2 In. 920.00
Lap Desk, Rosewood, Brass Inset Handles, 7 x 18 x 10 In. 750.00
Lap Desk, Rosewood, Inlaid Mother-Of-Pearl, Interior Compartments, 13 7/8 In. 380.00
Lap Desk, Rosewood, Painted, Scenic View, West Point, Mother-Of-Pearl, 5 x 14 x 5 In. . 1760.00
Lap Desk, Walnut, Brass Bound, Campaign Style, 19th Century, 6 1/2 x 13 x 9 1/2 In. . . . 290.00
Lectern, Carved Wood, Eagle, Spread Wings, Gothic Base, 68 1/2 x 20 In. 6900.00
Lectern, Oak, Eagle, Carved, Feathers, Rocky Plinth, Book Rail, 23 x 24 x 21 In. 3825.00
Lectern, Walnut, Ratcheted Lift Top, Book Rest, Tripod Base, Victorian, 33 In. 410.00
Library Steps, Elm, Spiral Form, Salesman Sample, England, 24 In. 980.00
Library Steps, George II, Mahogany, Pierced Handholds, 21 x 42 x 21 In. 7770.00
Library Steps, George III Style, Mahogany, 6 Steps, Gallery, 69 1/2 x 23 1/2 x 39 In. 1840.00
Library Steps, Mahogany, 5 Steps, Leather Inset, 38 x 20 x 27 In. . . . . *Illus* 575.00
Library Steps, Oak, 4 Steps, Spiral, Round Tapered Lamp Column On Side, 72 In. 770.00
Library Steps, Victorian, Mahogany, Carpeting, Storage, 25 1/4 x 21 1/4 x 35 In. 690.00
Library Steps, Walnut, Folding, Book Rest On Top, Bronze Mounts, 102 In. 1150.00
Library Steps, Wooden, Spiral, Turned Supports, England, 40 In. 1380.00
Library Steps-Chair, Regency Style, Mahogany, Leather Cushion, 34 1/2 In. 1150.00
Library Steps-Chair, Regency Style, Mahogany, Leather, Scroll Arms, 29 x 21 x 41 In. . . 1265.00
Linen Press, Arts & Crafts, 2 Doors, Glass Inserts, Pagoda Top, c.1900, 58 x 83 In. 2645.00
Linen Press, Birch, Walnut, Mahogany, Ivory, 2 Doors, 3 Drawers, c.1925, 65 x 51 In. . . . 6570.00
Linen Press, Cherry, Poplar, 2 Doors, 2 Drawers, Panel Doors, Bracket Feet, 52 x 18 x 90 In. 2090.00
Linen Press, Federal, Cherry, Doors, Sliding Trays, c.1800, 82 x 46 x 22 3/4 In. 4115.00
Linen Press, Federal, Walnut, 2 Paneled Doors, Shelves, c.1810, 91 x 50 x 18 1/2 In. 8050.00
Linen Press, George II Style, Burl Walnut, Inlay, 2 Doors, 4 Drawers, 84 x 47 x 25 In. . . . 1840.00
Linen Press, George III Style, Mahogany, Oval Doors, Dentil, c.1890, 87 x 44 x 24 In. . . . 1610.00
Linen Press, George III, Mahogany, 2 Doors, Bracket Feet, c.1885, 82 x 48 In. 2990.00
Linen Press, George III, Mahogany, 2 Paneled Doors, 3 Drawers, 85 x 42 x 22 In. 2300.00
Linen Press, George IV, Brass Mounted, Mahogany, 84 x 51 x 23 1/2 In. 3335.00
Linen Press, Mahogany, 4 Doors, Carved, Anglo-Indian, c.1835, 76 1/2 x 48 In. .1725.00 to 1840.00
Linen Press, Queen Anne, Walnut, 2 Arched Panel Doors Over 4 Drawers, 80 x 32 In. . . . 1150.00
Linen Press, Queen Anne, Walnut, Cornice, Star Inlaid Frieze, 2 Doors, 96 x 46 x 25 In. . 6325.00
Linen Press, Regency, Mahogany, 2 Parts, Brass, Panel Doors, c.1815, 83 x 49 x 23 In. . . 2990.00
Linen Press, Regency, Mahogany, Domed Cornice, Doors, Drawers, 87 x 48 x 22 In. 2530.00
Linen Press, Shaker, Walnut, Poplar, Union Village, Ohio, 44 x 45 1/2 x 21 In. 3850.00
Linen Press, Sheraton, Cherry, Flame Veneer, Poplar, 3 Shelves, 43 x 21 x 89 In. 4950.00
Linen Press, William IV, Mahogany, 2 Doors Over 2 Drawers, Scroll Carved, 85 x 54 In. . 1645.00
Linen Press, William IV, Mahogany, 2 Doors, Drawers, Bun Feet, 1800s, 89 x 52 x 22 In. . 4370.00
Love Seat, Empire, Scroll Back, Acanthus Leaf Carved, Upholstered 990.00
Love Seat, Le Corbusier LC2, Steel Frame, Leather, Cassina, Italy, 25 x 66 In. 2235.00
Love Seat, Meeks, Rosewood, Laminated, Carved, Henry Ford Pattern 9075.00
Lowboy, Beech, Ball, 3 Drawers, Scalloped Skirt, Claw Feet, 26 x 27 x 18 In. 3490.00
Lowboy, George I, Walnut, Drawers, Cabriole Legs, 27 1/2 x 31 1/2 x 19 3/4 In. 1335.00
Lowboy, George I, Walnut, Inlay, 3 Drawers, Shaped Apron, 27 x 30 x 20 In. 1530.00
Lowboy, Queen Anne Style, Mahogany, Cabriole Legs, c.1885, 28 1/2 x 33 In. 1150.00
Lowboy, Queen Anne Style, Satinwood, Brass, Inlay, c.1780, 30 1/2 x 32 x 18 1/2 In. 3910.00
Lowboy, Queen Anne, Cherry, 1 Long Over 3 Short Drawers, 35 x 37 1/2 x 20 In. 2360.00
Lowboy, Queen Anne, Elm, 3 Drawers, Circular Turned Legs, Pad Feet, 27 x 30 In. 825.00
Lowboy, Queen Anne, Oak, Scalloped Apron, 3 Drawers, Cabriole Legs, 27 x 29 In. 990.00
Lowboy, Shell Carved, 1 Long Over 3 Drawers, Claw & Ball Feet, 30 x 37 x 19 1/2 In. . . 460.00
Lowboy, Walnut, 2 Over 3 Drawers, Notched Corners, Drop Pendants, Trifid Feet, 33 In. . 790.00
Lowboy, Walnut, 3 Drawers, Fretwork Apron, Carved Supports, England, c.1750, 39 In. . . 2185.00
Lowboy, William & Mary Style, Walnut, 1 Drawer, Arcaded Apron, Flat Stretchers, 24 In. 1165.00
Lowboy, William & Mary, Mahogany, Long Drawer, Turned Block Legs, 32 x 28 In. 290.00
Lowboy, William & Mary, Walnut, Pine, Serpentine Cross Stretchers, 34 x 21 x 30 In. . . . 5225.00

Mirror, A. Girard, Wood, Wool Upholstery, 1968, 14 x 14 In. 1610.00
Mirror, Adam Style, Giltwood, Plaster, Oval, England, c.1865, 50 x 28 In. 2990.00
Mirror, Adam Style, Giltwood, Urn & Scroll Pediment, c.1900, 55 x 29 In. 575.00
Mirror, Adam Style, Mahogany, Gilt Design, Bonnet Top, 52 In. 430.00
Mirror, Art Deco, Beveled, Reverse Painted Floral Panels, 36 x 27 In., Pair 1060.00
Mirror, Art Deco, Etched Flower Frame, Rectangular, 28 x 20 In. 359.00
Mirror, Art Deco, Mahogany, Carved, Giltwood, Stylized Flowers, 52 x 38 In. 420.00
Mirror, Art Deco, Parcel Gilt, France, c.1925, 52 3/4 x 30 3/8 In. 5079.00
Mirror, Art Deco, Patinated Bronze, Gazelle, Rectangular, 24 x 30 In. 1195.00
Mirror, Art Deco, Silvered Wood, Stylized Leaf Crest, Rectangular, 24 x 18 In., Pair 600.00
Mirror, Art Deco, Wrought Iron, Scrolling, Triangular, 18 x 18 In. 355.00
Mirror, Art Nouveau, Brass, 4 Candle Supports, Original Patina, 18 In. 1610.00
Mirror, Arts & Crafts, Ceramic, Copper-Like Matte Glaze, Pinecones, 24 In. 175.00
Mirror, Arts & Crafts, Copper, Flowers, Ruskin Roundels, Rectangular, 19 x 25 In. 1058.00
Mirror, Arts & Crafts, Copper, Repousse, Stylized Flowers, Rectangular, 19 x 16 In. 1000.00
Mirror, Arts & Crafts, Mahogany, Marquetry, Stylized Leaves, 33 x 24 In. 1175.00
Mirror, Arts & Crafts, Oak, 3 Wrought Iron Hooks, Iron Chain Suspension, 33 x 50 In. .. 470.00
Mirror, Arts & Crafts, Peaked Top Rail, Splayed Supports, 31 x 23 In. 430.00
Mirror, Baroque Style, Ebonized Wood, Parcel Gilt, 20th Century, 58 1/2 x 37 1/2 In. 575.00
Mirror, Baroque Style, Gesso, Carved, Interlocking Leafy Scrolls, 48 x 30 In. 690.00
Mirror, Baroque Style, Gilt Metal, Pierced Leaves, 68 x 39 In. 2235.00
Mirror, Baroque Style, Giltwood, Cartouche, Pierced Frame, Italy, 1900s, 32 x 17 In., Pair 520.00
Mirror, Baroque Style, Reverse Etched, Leaf Scrolls, Flower Heads, 36 x 15 In., Pair 2390.00
Mirror, Beech, Spiral Ribbon Carved, Rounded Upper Corners, 84 x 55 In. 460.00
Mirror, Beveled, Metallic Embroidery, On Silk Inset Border, Gilt Dividers, 22 x 17 In. 750.00
Mirror, Black Forest, Oak, Carved Foxes, Leaves, Vines, Snail, Fly, 45 x 31 In. 840.00
Mirror, Brass, Copper, Stylized Leaves, Round, W.A.S. Benson, 12 1/2 In. 825.00
Mirror, Bull's-Eye, Carved Wood, Eagle Pediment, Carved Leaf, 27 x 18 1/4 In., Pair 575.00
Mirror, Bull's-Eye, Mahogany, 12 Giltwood Spheres, 13 In., Pair 980.00
Mirror, Bull's-Eye, Regency, Giltwood, Carved Leaves, Berries, 30 1/2 In. 1955.00
Mirror, Bull's-Eye, Regency, Giltwood, Ribbed Ebonized, 31 x 25 x 8 1/2 In. 1840.00
Mirror, Bull's-Eye, Regency, Giltwood, Wood Border, c.1815, 22 In. 980.00
Mirror, Burl Veneer, Inlaid Floral Cartouches At Corners, Birds On Sides, 33 In. 1880.00
Mirror, Carved Shell, Leaf Tip, Flowerhead Surround, Oval, 1800s, France, 38 x 33 In. .. 1380.00
Mirror, Carved Wood, Gilt Gesso, Deer On Rocky Mound, 32 In. 5875.00
Mirror, Cast Iron, Relief Grapevine, Footed Base, Swing Frame 135.00
Mirror, Charles II, Beaded Stumpwork, Figures, Castle, Ebonized Frame, 19 x 6 In. 2115.00
Mirror, Charles X, Giltwood, Rosette & Scroll Leaf Molded Frame, 24 1/2 x 20 1/2 In. .. 635.00
Mirror, Cheval, Arts & Crafts, Oak, Rectangular, c.1910, 63 x 24 In. 1000.00
Mirror, Cheval, Empire Style, Mahogany, Gilt Bronze, Eagle Mounts, 88 x 36 In. 2990.00
Mirror, Cheval, Empire, Gilt Bronze Mounted, Round Top, Columns, 79 x 46 x 22 In. ... 1530.00
Mirror, Cheval, Empire, Mahogany, Brass Mounts, 18 x 15 x 38 In. 1035.00
Mirror, Cheval, Empire, Mahogany, Gilt Bronze, 19th Century, 75 x 44 In. 3750.00
Mirror, Cheval, Faux Bamboo, Maple, c.1885, 77 x 35 x 19 1/2 In. 5600.00
Mirror, Cheval, Faux Bamboo, Trestle Frame, France, 19th Century, 64 x 35 x 24 In. 2185.00
Mirror, Cheval, Mahogany, Birch, Ormolu, Mutton Legs, Brass Paw Caps, 80 In. 770.00
Mirror, Cheval, Mahogany, Carved Legs, Claw & Ball Feet, c.1880, 71 x 39 x 27 In. 2800.00
Mirror, Cheval, Rococo Style, Gilt, Carved, c.1890, 76 x 33 In. 3080.00
Mirror, Cheval, Rococo, Giltwood, Fluted Columns, Scrolled Legs, Crest 2250.00
Mirror, Cheval, Walnut, Burl, Foliate Carved, Trestle Base, 64 x 33 In. 1310.00
Mirror, Chippendale Style, Mahogany, Gilt Bezel, Pierced Phoenix Feet, 41 x 23 In. 315.00
Mirror, Chippendale Style, Mahogany, Scrolling, Urn Finials, Late 20th Century, 52 In. .. 210.00
Mirror, Chippendale Style, Maple, Parcel Gilt, 30 1/2 x 18 In. 240.00
Mirror, Chippendale Style, Walnut, Gilt, 20th Century, 51 x 24 In. 705.00
Mirror, Chippendale, Mahogany Veneer, Pine, Arched Crest, 33 3/4 x 17 3/4 In. 1760.00
Mirror, Chippendale, Mahogany Veneer, Pine, Carved & Gilt Inner Liner, 42 x 23 In. 1100.00
Mirror, Chippendale, Mahogany Veneer, Pine, Gold Liner, 30 x 17 1/2 In. 560.00
Mirror, Chippendale, Mahogany Veneer, Pine, Phoenix Crest, Scroll Ears, 36 x 20 In. 2310.00
Mirror, Chippendale, Mahogany Veneer, Pine, Pierced Carved Leaf Crest, 17 x 29 In. 1045.00
Mirror, Chippendale, Mahogany Veneer, Pine, Scallops, Eagle Crest, 30 1/2 x 21 In. 1210.00
Mirror, Chippendale, Mahogany Veneer, Pine, Scroll, Arched Crest, 30 x 15 1/2 In. 250.00
Mirror, Chippendale, Mahogany Veneer, Pine, Scroll, Incised Carving, 32 x 18 In. 495.00
Mirror, Chippendale, Mahogany, Carved Phoenix, Scrollwork, 42 x 21 In. 1150.00

Mirror, Chippendale, Mahogany, Parcel Gilt, Late 18th Century, 29 In. 1675.00
Mirror, Chippendale, Mahogany, Pine, Scalloped Crest, Ears, 19 3/4 x 11 1/2 In. 330.00
Mirror, Chippendale, Parcel Gilt, Swan Neck Pediment, c.1780, 51 1/2 x 25 In. 5380.00
Mirror, Chippendale, Walnut, Parcel Gilt, c.1780, 26 3/4 x 15 In. 1910.00
Mirror, Chippendale, Walnut, Parcel Gilt, Carved Phoenix, Beveled Glass, 44 x 20 In. . . .   6465.00
Mirror, Convex, Black Lion Over Acanthus Leaf Mount & Apron Surround, 54 x 26 In. . . .   6670.00
Mirror, Convex, Gilt Gesso, American Flag & Sail Ship Design, 21 1/2 In. 1530.00
Mirror, Convex, Giltwood, Carved, Ebonized, Eagle Finial, 19th Century, 46 In. 6575.00
Mirror, Convex, Giltwood, Eagle Top, Reeded Ebonized Frame, Spherules, 42 In. 1765.00
Mirror, Courting, Wood, Rectangular, 18th Century, 18 1/4 In. 1410.00
Mirror, Curly Maple, Beaded Edge, Beveled, 28 1/2 x 34 1/2 In.   275.00
Mirror, Dressing, Empire, Mahogany, 6 Drawers, 6-Footed, 1800s, 31 x 9 x 27 In. 325.00
Mirror, Dressing, Georgian, Walnut, Molded Drawer, Mid 19th Century, 27 1/2 x 20 In. . .   500.00
Mirror, Dressing, Heart Shape, Sterling Silver, W. Comyns & Sons, 1892, 11 x 13 In. 805.00
Mirror, Dressing, Mahogany Veneer, Ivory Inlay, Early 1800s, 23 x 20 3/8 x 8 1/2 In. 560.00
Mirror, Dressing, Rococo, Cast Iron, Bun Feet, Oblong, England, 20 x 15 x 11 In. 635.00
Mirror, Dressing, Stephen Badlam, Jr., c.1815, 17 3/4 x 15 3/4 x 7 1/4 In. 480.00
Mirror, Eastlake, Mahogany, Grooved Lines, Scallops, Victorian, 52 x 22 In. 145.00
Mirror, Ebonized Pine, Brass Mounted, Continental, c.1865, 29 1/2 x 27 1/2 In. 105.00
Mirror, Empire, Mahogany, Ogee, Mid 19th Century, 28 1/2 x 20 1/2 In. 100.00
Mirror, Enamel, Asian Designs, 3 Panes, Folding, Ball Feet, c.1915, 28 x 40 In. 250.00
Mirror, Federal Style, Convex, Eagle Over Scroll, Gilt, 33 x 20 In. 635.00
Mirror, Federal Style, Mahogany, Eagle Crest, c.1910, 30 x 18 1/2 In. 335.00
Mirror, Federal, Black, Gilt Paint, Turned Stiles, Reverse Painted, 18 x 9 3/4 In. 210.00
Mirror, Federal, Convex, Eagle Crest, Gold Paint, Ball Decoration, Round, 25 x 36 In. . . .   140.00
Mirror, Federal, Giltwood, Composition, New York, Early 19th Century, 36 x 14 1/2 In. . . .   1095.00
Mirror, Federal, Giltwood, Eglomise, Eagle, Ship, Grinell & Sons, R.I., 38 x 22 1/2 In. . .   3110.00
Mirror, Federal, Giltwood, Reverse Painted Panel, Fisherman, 28 x 13 In. 1045.00
Mirror, Federal, Giltwood, Wooden Lion On Leaf Decorated Support, c.1820, 54 In. 6670.00
Mirror, Federal, Inlaid Walnut, Scrolled, Early 19th Century, 29 x 16 In. 175.00
Mirror, Federal, Mahogany Inlay, Scrolled Frame, Conch Shell, 31 3/4 x 17 In. 470.00
Mirror, Federal, Mahogany Inlay, Scrolled Frame, New England, c.1800, 31 In. 1530.00
Mirror, Federal, Mahogany Veneer, 2 Sections, Twist Pilasters, 32 x 16 In. 360.00
Mirror, Federal, Reverse Painted Panel, Cermenati & Bernarda, c.1827, 45 1/2 In. 5465.00
Mirror, Federal, Reverse Painted, Church Scene, Turned Stiles, 29 x 14 In. 250.00
Mirror, Florentine, Giltwood, Carved, 19th Century, 42 x 36 In.   1875.00
Mirror, French Baroque, Giltwood, Cast Gesso, Scrolling, Early 1800s, 40 x 28 In., Pair . .   1610.00
Mirror, Fruitwood, Ebonized, Mother-Of-Pearl, Bone, c.1900, 52 x 34 x 3 In. 3220.00
Mirror, G. Stickley, Peaked Top Rail, 4 Iron Hooks, 36 x 28 In.   2415.00
Mirror, G. Stickley, Peaked Top Rail, Iron Hooks, c.1904, 29 x 23 In. 2070.00
Mirror, George II Style, Giltwood, Bellflower & Scroll Frame, 1900s, 50 x 28 In. 490.00
Mirror, George II Style, Giltwood, Late 19th Century, 33 1/2 x 18 1/2 In. 345.00
Mirror, George II Style, Pine, Parcel Gilt, 20th Century, 58 x 35 In. 980.00
Mirror, George II, Mahogany Veneer, Giltwood Eagle, Fruit, Floral Drops, 53 x 26 In. . . .   3820.00
Mirror, George III Style, Giltwood, 20th Century, 49 1/2 x 26 1/2 In. 865.00
Mirror, George III Style, Giltwood, Bamboo, 20th Century, 61 x 46 In. 1035.00
Mirror, George III Style, Giltwood, Chinoiserie, Openwork Frame, 1900s, 56 x 29 In. . . .   980.00
Mirror, George III Style, Giltwood, Fluted Frame, Crest, 60 x 43 In. 9560.00
Mirror, George III Style, Giltwood, Pierced Crest, Serpentine, 41 x 22 In. 3680.00

Furniture, Library Steps,
Mahogany, 5 Steps, Leather
Inset, 38 x 20 x 27 In.

Furniture, Parlor Set,
Rococo Revival,
Rosewood Laminate,
c.1850, 4 Piece

Mirror, George III, Giltwood, Fluted, Beaded Frame, Oval, 30 x 26 In. 1955.00
Mirror, George III, Giltwood, Scrolling Leaves, 46 1/2 x 27 1/4 In. 1035.00
Mirror, George III, Walnut, Parcel Gilt, Leaf Crest, Bird, 18th Century, 34 1/4 x 19 In. 620.00
Mirror, George III, Walnut, Parcel Gilt, Phoenix, c.1790, 26 x 14 1/2 In. 635.00
Mirror, George IV, Carved, Giltwood, Beveled, Vase Form, 65 x 22 In. 1095.00
Mirror, George V, Giltwood, Plaster, Prince Of Wales Feather Crest, c.1900, 48 x 26 In. ... 1035.00
Mirror, Gesso, Arched, Lobed Crest, Rose Garlands, Shells & Scrolls, 54 x 36 In. 1210.00
Mirror, Gilt Gesso, Split Baluster Frame, Raised Mold Panel, c.1825, 18 3/4 In. 940.00
Mirror, Giltwood, 3 Sections, Rosettes, Westing, Evans & Egmore, 27 1/2 x 42 In. 250.00
Mirror, Giltwood, Acanthus Carving, Eagle On Crest, Spread Wings, 23 In. 1760.00
Mirror, Giltwood, Cartouche Crest, Fruit Clusters, Beaded Bellflower Edge, 69 x 45 In. .. 1840.00
Mirror, Giltwood, Carved Crest, Scrolling Acanthus, Swan, 33 x 20 In. 75.00
Mirror, Giltwood, Carved, Carved Bow Knot, Oval, 1800s, 32 x 23 In. 1750.00
Mirror, Giltwood, Chain & Floral Carved, Cartouche, c.1910, 49 1/2 x 43 1/2 In. 865.00
Mirror, Giltwood, Crest, Acanthus Leaf, Rosette, Late 19th Century, 47 x 30 In. 550.00
Mirror, Giltwood, Dome Plate, Openwork Fruit & Vines, c.1850, 79 x 54 In. 580.00
Mirror, Giltwood, Gesso, Flower, Shell Decoration, 32 In. 1265.00
Mirror, Giltwood, Gesso, Flowering Urn, Ram Mask, 19th Century, 65 1/4 x 38 In. 1840.00
Mirror, Giltwood, Incised, Burnished, Floral Design, France, c.1880, 36 x 27 In. 655.00
Mirror, Giltwood, Leaf & Shell Carved, 3 Panels, c.1835, 37 x 64 x 4 In. 2875.00
Mirror, Giltwood, Leaf & Shell Carved, Tiered Design, c.1890, 42 x 31 In. 690.00
Mirror, Giltwood, Leaf Carved, Shield Pediment, c.1880, 76 x 50 In. 2185.00
Mirror, Giltwood, Open Scrollwork, Leaf Carved, 36 x 22 In., Pair 620.00
Mirror, Giltwood, Open Scrollwork, Leaf Tip, 1800s, 29 x 20 In. 189.00
Mirror, Giltwood, Openwork Crest, Winged Angel Head, Beveled, Oval, 37 x 37 In. 480.00
Mirror, Giltwood, Petal, Dart Borders, Oval, 48 x 33 In. 1035.00
Mirror, Giltwood, Plaster, Barbizon, Sewell & Sons, 36 x 31 In. 345.00
Mirror, Giltwood, Plaster, Oval, Carved, Late 19th Century, 14 1/4 x 12 In., Pair 635.00
Mirror, Giltwood, Polychrome, Flower, Shell Crest, Late 1800s, 50 1/2 x 16 In., Pair 2185.00
Mirror, Giltwood, Reverse Painted, Half Columns, 2 Sections, 15 1/2 x 34 In. 145.00
Mirror, Giltwood, Ribbon Crown, Egg & Dart Molding, c.1920, 39 x 44 1/2 In. 575.00
Mirror, Giltwood, Shaped Top, Scrolling Leaves & Flowers Around Shell, 72 In. 2415.00
Mirror, Giltwood, Sunburst, Italy, c.1900, 22 In. 1035.00
Mirror, Girandole, George III Style, Giltwood, Gesso, 3 Lights, c.1875, 38 x 22 1/2 In. 750.00
Mirror, Girandole, Giltwood, Carved, England, c.1800, 38 x 22 1/2 In. 10925.00
Mirror, Girandole, Neoclassical, Gilt Gesso, Eagle, Convex Glass, 29 1/2 x 17 3/4 In. 3525.00
Mirror, Girandole, Rococo Style, Painted, Parcel Giltwood, Venice, 29 1/2 x 15 3/4 In. 840.00
Mirror, Hagenauer, Brass, Female Head, Mounted, Signed, 26 In. 4405.00
Mirror, Hepplewhite, Mahogany, Scrolling, Flame Urn Decoration, 28 x 14 1/4 In. 1045.00
Mirror, Hunzinger, Faceted Jewels, Square, 30 In. 3000.00
Mirror, Italian Baroque Style, Cartouche Shape, Beveled, 20th Century, 46 x 38 In. 2030.00
Mirror, Italian Baroque Style, Giltwood, Pierced Foliate Scrolled Frame, 36 x 31 In. 1910.00
Mirror, Italian Baroque Style, Giltwood, Scroll, Strapwork, 1800s, 30 x 19 In., Pair 1555.00
Mirror, Italian Neoclassical, Mahogany, Giltwood, Ebonized, Ormolu Mount, 79 x 42 In. .. 6575.00
Mirror, Italian Rococo Style, Giltwood, Pierced Scrolled Crest, 20th Century, 62 x 39 In. . 3825.00
Mirror, J. Adnet, Leather Over Steel, Brass, Buckle Detail, 28 x 16 In., c.1950 .... 3450.00
Mirror, J. Hoffman, Ebonized, 6 Balls At 2 Corners, Austria, c.1905, 17 x 9 In. 2150.00
Mirror, Laminated Wood, Octagonal Mirror, Rectangular Base, 66 x 37 x 16 In. 2350.00
Mirror, Louis XIV Style, Beveled, Dutch, 19th Century, 23 1/4 x 13 In. 340.00
Mirror, Louis XV Style, Giltwood, C-Scrolls, Floral Cartouche Crest, 39 x 50 In. 375.00
Mirror, Louis XV Style, Giltwood, Carved, Floral Swags, 90 x 66 In. 3585.00
Mirror, Louis XV Style, Giltwood, Carved, Pierced Foliate Crest, 70 x 44 In. 4780.00
Mirror, Louis XV Style, Giltwood, Carved, Pierced Scroll & Leaf Frame, 54 x 28 In. 765.00
Mirror, Louis XV, Giltwood, Leaves, Pierced Crest, 19th Century, 70 x 33 1/2 In. 1265.00
Mirror, Louis XV, Parcel Gilt, Gray Paint, 63 x 38 In. 2726.00
Mirror, Louis XVI Style, Giltwood, Beaded Edge, Laurel Wreath, 1800s, 89 x 57 In. 8280.00
Mirror, Louis XVI Style, Giltwood, Carved, Wreath Top, France, c.1885, 52 x 31 In. 1495.00
Mirror, Mahogany, Carved Pedestal, Platform, Round, c.1810, 27 x 22 1/2 In. 400.00
Mirror, Mahogany, Eagle, Broken Arch Top, Gilt, 24 1/4 x 14 1/4 In. 300.00
Mirror, Mahogany, Marquetry, Cheval, Dutch, c.1850, 79 1/2 x 37 1/2 In. 1725.00
Mirror, Mahogany, Phoenix, Applied Leaves, Berries, 27 x 54 In. 575.00
Mirror, Mahogany, Scrolled Top, Bottom & Ears, 21 x 11 1/4 In. 350.00
Mirror, Mahogany, Veneer, Pine Inlay, Scroll, 21 1/2 x 11 1/2 In. 330.00

Mirror, Metal, Saw Tooth Inside Edge, Original Patina, 21 x 17 In. 290.00
Mirror, Napoleon III, Brass, Oval, c.1865, 22 1/2 x 19 3/4 In. 460.00
Mirror, Napoleon III, Fruitwood, Carved, Polychrome, Oval, c.1865, 18 x 28 In. 315.00
Mirror, Napoleon III, Giltwood, Arched Plate, Molded Frame, 1800s, 21 1/4 x 18 In. 345.00
Mirror, Napoleon III, Giltwood, Arched Plate, Molded Frame, 57 x 39 In. 1150.00
Mirror, Napoleon III, Giltwood, Arched Plate, Molded Frame, 62 1/2 x 45 1/2 In. 2185.00
Mirror, Napoleon III, Giltwood, Carved, Flower Heads, Leaves, 21 x 18 In. 490.00
Mirror, Napoleon III, Giltwood, Carved, Oval, Flower Sprays, c.1865, 22 x 15 In. 460.00
Mirror, Napoleon III, Giltwood, Carved, Oval, Flowers, c.1865, 24 1/2 x 21 1/2 In. 375.00
Mirror, Napoleon III, Giltwood, Carved, White Pickled, 61 1/4 x 42 In. 1150.00
Mirror, Napoleon III, Giltwood, Egg & Dart Molded Frame, c.1865, 72 x 47 In. 3220.00
Mirror, Napoleon III, Giltwood, Garlands In Corners, Slightly Arched, 69 x 50 In. 1495.00
Mirror, Napoleon III, Giltwood, Ribbon Crest, Oval, 19th Century, 20 x 16 In. 805.00
Mirror, Napoleon III, Giltwood, Shell & Garland Crest, Carved Frieze, 76 1/2 x 46 In. . . . 6615.00
Mirror, Neoclassical Style, Walnut, Copper Mounted, Beveled, 1900s, 46 x 30 In. 980.00
Mirror, Neoclassical, Ebonized, Marble, 20th Century, 47 x 35 In., Pair 5740.00
Mirror, Neoclassical, Giltwood, 2 Parts, 2 Columns, Applied Leaves, c.1800, 41 x 23 In. . 690.00
Mirror, Neoclassical, Giltwood, Rectangular, 18th Century, Italy, 25 x 24 In. 805.00
Mirror, Neoclassical, Paint Decorated, Parcel Gilt, Eglomise, c.1820, 22 x 12 In. 1435.00
Mirror, Nutting, No. 751, Walnut 690.00
Mirror, Nutting, No. 764, Mahogany 2035.00
Mirror, P. Evans, Directional, City Scape, Patchwork Chrome, 20 x 70 x 3 In. 288.00
Mirror, Painted, Silvered, Glass Mounted, Oval, Ireland, 19th Century, 29 x 23 In. 9560.00
Mirror, Pier Rococo Style, Giltwood, Continental, 19th Century, 55 x 47 In., Pair 16753.00
Mirror, Pier, Federal, Mahogany, Inlay, c.1820, 46 1/2 x 25 In. 405.00
Mirror, Pier, George III Style, Carved Giltwood, 19th Century, 93 x 39 In., Pair 21510.00
Mirror, Pier, Giltwood, Composition, Pierced, Scrolled Crests, 132 x 40 In., Pair 19120.00
Mirror, Pier, Louis XVI Style, Carved Giltwood, France, c.1900, 65 3/4 x 35 1/2 In. 2760.00
Mirror, Pier, Napoleon III, Carved Giltwood, Beveled, c.1865, 71 x 38 In. 4830.00
Mirror, Pier, Neoclassical, Fruitwood, Italy, 20th Century, 75 1/2 x 38 In., Pair 4600.00
Mirror, Pier, Neoclassical, Giltwood, Grapevine Relief, 58 x 72 In. 230.00
Mirror, Pier, Parcel Gilt, Polychrome, Scandinavian, c.1815, 30 1/2 x 30 In. 5290.00
Mirror, Pier, Regency, Giltwood, Carved Female Mask, Feathers, Strapwork, 59 x 29 In. . 1410.00
Mirror, Pier, Renaissance Revival, Marble Top, Gold Incised Panels, 129 In. 1400.00
Mirror, Pier, Rococo, Open Floral & Leaf Crest, 1850s, 103 x 16 In. 1200.00
Mirror, Pier, Victorian, Giltwood, Pierced Shell & Scroll Crown, Marble Base, 95 In. 1265.00
Mirror, Pier, Victorian, Incised & Relief Flowers, 92 x 32 In. 405.00
Mirror, Piero Fornasetti Style, Transfer, Ribbon Frame, Mid 20th Century, 51 x 38 In. . . . 8365.00
Mirror, Pine, Brass, Embossed Rococo Design, Beveled, 23 x 12 In. 275.00
Mirror, Pine, Carved, Acanthus Leaf Scrolls, 22 1/4 x 14 In. 275.00
Mirror, Plaster, Gold Leaf, Tombstone Shape, c.1865, 42 x 28 In. 785.00
Mirror, Queen Anne Style, Domed, Beveled, Chinoiserie Lacquer, 36 x 17 In. 400.00
Mirror, Queen Anne Style, Painted, Parcel Gilt, Eglomise Mounted, 42 x 19 In. 2630.00
Mirror, Queen Anne Style, Walnut, Gilt Shell Crest, England, 42 1/2 x 16 In. 235.00
Mirror, Queen Anne, Cut Glass Detail, Arched Top, Beaded Edges, Gilding, 16 x 20 In. . . 220.00
Mirror, Queen Anne, Mahogany Veneer, Scrolled Pediment, Pierced Flower, 32 x 17 In. . . 545.00
Mirror, Queen Anne, Mahogany, 2 Sections, Cutout Top Crest, Bird Silhouettes, 28 In. . . . 5750.00
Mirror, Queen Anne, Mahogany, Pine, Gilt Gesso, Beveled, 48 x 17 In. 1100.00
Mirror, Queen Anne, Painted, Stepped Side Moldings, Beaded Edge, 19 x 15 1/2 In. . . . : . 360.00
Mirror, Queen Anne, Pine, Painted, Tall Crest, Molded Frame, 24 x 11 In. 1870.00
Mirror, Queen Anne, Walnut, Crossbanded, Ogee Crest, Engraved Crown, 33 In. 3175.00
Mirror, Regency Style, Giltwood, Ebonized, Convex, Late 19th Century, 48 1/2 In. 3220.00
Mirror, Regency, Giltwood, Ebonized, Eagle & Leaf Scrolls, 20th Century, 57 x 30 In. . . . 2530.00
Mirror, Regency, Giltwood, Rosette Molding, 2 Pilasters, c.1815, 35 1/2 In. 1380.00
Mirror, Renaissance Revival, Giltwood, Ebonized, Michigan, 15 1/2 x 13 3/4 In. 430.00
Mirror, Renaissance Revival, Walnut, Carved, Italy, c.1835, 45 1/2 x 35 1/4 In. 345.00
Mirror, Rococo Revival, Arched Shape, Mirrored Glass Frame, c.1900, 59 x 36 In. 2760.00
Mirror, Rococo Revival, Giltwood, Carved,, Pierced Leaf Design, 66 x 42 In. 1315.00
Mirror, Rococo Revival, Giltwood, Carved, Flower Basket Shape Crest, 52 x 31 In. 1315.00
Mirror, Rococo Revival, Giltwood, Carved, Flowers, Scrolls, 55 x 44 In. 2940.00
Mirror, Rococo Revival, Giltwood, Carved, Fruit, Leaves, 61 x 53 In. 1880.00
Mirror, Rococo Revival, Giltwood, Carved, Leaf Designs, 29 x 20 In. 598.00
Mirror, Rococo Revival, Giltwood, Carved, Pierced Leaf Decoration, 69 x 39 In. 5290.00

Mirror, Rococo Revival, Giltwood, Carved, Pierced Leaf Decoration, Oval, 11 In. 480.00
Mirror, Rococo Revival, Giltwood, Carved, Pierced Leaf Designs, 57 x 36 In. 900.00
Mirror, Rococo Revival, Giltwood, Carved, Set With Flowers, 17 x 14 In. 540.00
Mirror, Rococo Revival, Giltwood, Carved, Urn, Dragons, 60 x 35 In. 1880.00
Mirror, Rococo Style, Giltwood, Carved, Inset Onyx Top, 102 x 52 x 19 In. 2150.00
Mirror, Rococo Style, Pierced, Cartouche Crest, Continental, 19th Century, 49 x 30 In. ... 1725.00
Mirror, Rococo, Scrolled Leaves, Flowers, 20th Century, 49 1/2 x 30 In. 495.00
Mirror, Roman Style, Giltwood, Italy, Late 19th Century, 68 1/2 x 36 1/2 In. 2760.00
Mirror, Rosewood, Dragons, Clouds, Inlaid Eyes, Japan, 19th Century, 86 x 45 In. 355.00
Mirror, Shaving, Edwardian, Mahogany, Curved Supports, 4 Mushroom Feet, 20 In. 200.00
Mirror, Shaving, George IV, Serpentine Front, Stand, Swing, 24 1/2 x 24 3/4 In. 430.00
Mirror, Shaving, Georgian, Mahogany, Bowfront, Ivory Foot, c.1815, 30 In. 430.00
Mirror, Shaving, Hepplewhite, Mahogany, Shield Shape, Serpentine Front, 33 In. 250.00
Mirror, Shaving, Mahogany, Acanthus Carved, Telescope, Swivel, c.1890, 68 x 16 x 16 In. 1625.00
Mirror, Shaving, Regency, Mahogany, Serpentine Front, Rosettes, 3 Drawers, 23 In. 225.00
Mirror, Shaving, Sheraton, Mahogany, Bowfront, 2 Drawers, 20 x 21 In. 105.00
Mirror, Shell Crest, Cherubs, Oval, 19th Century, 64 x 32 In. 800.00
Mirror, Sheraton, Tiger Maple, Polychrome House, Trees, 29 x 16 In. 2700.00
Mirror, Tabernacle, Giltwood, Carved, Plaster, Italy, c.1865, 56 x 24 3/4 In. 520.00
Mirror, Tabernacle, Sheraton Style, Giltwood, 41 x 25 1/2 In. 200.00
Mirror, Tabernacle, Sheraton, Giltwood, Acorn Drops, Turned Pilasters, 45 x 26 In. 235.00
Mirror, Tiger Maple, Painted Panel, Landscape, Molded Cornice, Reeded, 33 x 21 In. 1095.00
Mirror, Tortoiseshell, Ebonized Wood, Dutch, 37 3/4 x 33 1/2 In. 1035.00
Mirror, Trumeau, Louis XVI Style, Giltwood, Composition, c.1900, 79 1/2 x 49 In. 1095.00
Mirror, Trumeau, Louis XVI Style, Parcel Gilt, c.1900, 84 x 44 In. 2300.00
Mirror, Trumeau, Louis XVI, Beech, Giltwood, 1700s, 68 1/2 x 47 3/4 In. 2760.00
Mirror, Trumeau, Neoclassical, Painted, Parcel Gilt, Frieze Panel, 68 x 33 In. 4780.00
Mirror, Trumeau, Regency Style, Painted, Parcel Gilt, France, 60 x 28 In. 1725.00
Mirror, Venetian, Etched, Applied Flowers, 37 x 22 In. 720.00
Mirror, Venetian, Pierced Foliate Crest, Octagonal, 50 x 45 In. 3290.00
Mirror, Venetian, Rococo Style, Etched, Applied Glass, Mid 20th Century, 20 1/2 In. 405.00
Mirror, Venini, Rope Edge, Brass, Glass, Italy, 1940, 24 x 16 In. 2300.00
Mirror, Victorian, Giltwood, Gesso, Convex, Oval, 19th Century, 35 x 22 In. 880.00
Mirror, Walnut, Brass, Mythological Scene, Floral, c.1890, 51 x 41 In. 2415.00
Mirror, Walnut, Gesso Eagle, Shadowbox Frame, Oval, 27 x 36 In. 330.00
Mirror, Walnut, Gilt Gesso, Scrolled, England, 18th Century, 36 3/4 In. 880.00
Mirror, White, Gold & Black Eglomise Panels, England, 43 x 21 In., Pair 3800.00
Mirror, William & Mary Style, Walnut, Oyster Veneer, Early 20th Century, 45 1/2 In. 520.00
Ottoman, Carved Flower, Leaf Apron, Red Velvet Upholstery, 16 x 42 1/2 x 17 In. 320.00
Ottoman, Empire, Mahogany, Molded Frame, Velvet Upholstery, Ogee Feet, 14 x 20 In. .. 550.00
Ottoman, Robsjohn-Gibbings, Walnut, Canvas Webbing, Brass Legs, 16 x 36 In. 1095.00
Ottoman, Victorian, Mahogany, Needlework, Removable Cushioned Top, 22 x 31 In. 1725.00
Ottoman, Victorian, Walnut, Leather Upholstery, c.1850, 19 x 48 1/2 In. 2070.00
Ottoman, William IV, Mahogany, Padded Top, Zebra Skin, 17 x 25 x 20 In. 5060.00
Ottoman, William IV, Mahogany, Upholstered, Mid 19th Century, 21 x 29 x 24 In. 2530.00
Parlor Set, Art Deco, Burl, Cloud, Back, Cream Leather Upholstery, 3 Piece 3055.00
Parlor Set, Fruitwood, Red Velour, Sofa, 2 Chairs, 1800s, 19 x 14 x 28 In. 1400.00
Parlor Set, Hinoki Wood, Settee, 2 Armchairs, c.1912, 47 1/2 x 48 In. 920.00
Parlor Set, Horn, Elk, Ram Antlers, Sofa, 6 Chairs, Sofa, 60 1/2 x 67 x 26 In. 9200.00
Parlor Set, Ice Cream, Metal, Heart Back, Wood Seat, Top, Child's, 21 x 16 In., 5 Piece . 210.00
Parlor Set, Ice Cream, Milk Glass Top, 4 Twisted Wire Chairs, 30 In., 5 Piece 695.00
Parlor Set, Louis XV Style, Carved Crest, Caned Back, Sides, Upholstered, 3 Piece 4185.00
Parlor Set, Louis XVI Style, Giltwood, Ribbon Crest, Brocade Upholstery, 3 Piece 7170.00
Parlor Set, Louis XVI Style, Wood, Carved, Leaf Crest, Upholstery, Settee, 2 Chairs 3285.00
Parlor Set, Mahogany, Dolphin Back, Lions Heads, Claw Feet, Upholstered, 3 Piece 4200.00
Parlor Set, Napoleon III, Beech, Carved, Ebonized, c.1865, 5 Piece 5520.00
Parlor Set, R.J. Horner, Carved, Female-Head Arms, 3 Piece 6615.00
Parlor Set, Renaissance Revival, Rosewood, Carved, Upholstered, 8 Piece 1295.00
Parlor Set, Renaissance Revival, Walnut, Burl Panels, c.1875, 46 x 71 x 30 In., 5 Piece .. 1400.00
Parlor Set, Rococo Revival, Rosewood Laminate, c.1850, 4 Piece .... *Illus* 13800.00
Parlor Set, Rococo, Rosewood, Carved, Medallion Back, Velvet, Settee, Chairs, 7 Piece . 2800.00
Parlor Set, Rustic Hickory Co., Chair, Settee, Rocker, c.1925 .... 4400.00
Parlor Set, Rustic, Bent Pine Construction, 2 Armchairs & Settee, 3 Piece 575.00

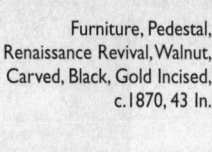

Furniture, Pedestal, Renaissance Revival, Walnut, Carved, Black, Gold Incised, c.1870, 43 In.

Furniture, Pedestal, Adams Style, Mahogany, Fluted, Drawer, Door, Carved, 39 x 21 In., Pair

Patio Set, Heywood-Wakefield Co., Rattan, Brown, Orange Cushions, 6 Piece	650.00
Patio Set, Richard Schultz, Knoll, c.1967, 7 Piece	4700.00
Pedestal, Adams Style, Mahogany, Fluted, Drawer, Door, Carved, 39 x 21 In., Pair . *Illus*	3335.00
Pedestal, Aesthetic Style, Mahogany, Swivel Top, Brass Claw Feet, c.1885, 42 In.	1120.00
Pedestal, Art Deco, Wooden, Painted, Floral Design, Mirrored Panels, 52 In.	2940.00
Pedestal, Arts & Crafts, Square Top, 4-Sided Base, 36 x 12 In.	750.00
Pedestal, Carved Wood, Mephistopheles, Flowers, Leaves, Wings, Round Base, 41 In.	4025.00
Pedestal, Carved, Ebonized, Seated Winged Griffin, c.1885, 46 In.	2240.00
Pedestal, Carved, Putti Climbing Tree, Toed Base, c.1885, 46 In.	3640.00
Pedestal, De Wolfe, Neoclassical, Painted, Octagonal, c.1930, 40 x 13 x 12 In.	2870.00
Pedestal, Edward VII, Mahogany, Polychrome, c.1900, 49 x 14 x 11 In., Pair	2990.00
Pedestal, Empire Style, Mahogany, Gilt Bronze, Classical Busts, 49 In.	880.00
Pedestal, Empire Style, Mahogany, Gray Marble Top, 41 x 17 In.	1955.00
Pedestal, Empire Style, Mahogany, Ormolu Mounted, 20th Century, 33 x 14 In., Pair	4780.00
Pedestal, Empire Style, Marble Top, Bronze Mounted, Reeded Columns, 44 x 17 In.	1120.00
Pedestal, Empire, Mahogany, Marble Top, Ormolu Applied Frieze, 37 1/2 x 14 1/4 In.	2530.00
Pedestal, Faux Marble, Columnar, 20th Century, 38 x 13 1/2 x 13 1/2 In., Pair	956.00
Pedestal, George III, Waxed Pine, Gilt, Painted, c.1790, 38 1/2 x 10 1/2 x 8 1/2 In.	1910.00
Pedestal, Hardwood, Heavily Carved, Marble Top, Chinese, c.1900, 32 x 13 1/2 In.	230.00
Pedestal, Hardwood, Marble Top, Beaded Edge, Chinese, c.1890, 18 x 17 1/2 In.	320.00
Pedestal, Hardwood, Marble Top, Floral Pierced, Chinese, c.1880, 27 1/2 x 12 In.	230.00
Pedestal, Hardwood, Mottled Marble Top, Pierced Skirt, Chinese, 15 x 12 In.	290.00
Pedestal, Hardwood, Octagonal Top, Cabriole Legs, Chinese, 20th Century, 36 x 15 In.	550.00
Pedestal, J. Hoffmann, Beech, 3 Round Standards, 43 In.	1725.00
Pedestal, Kimbel & Cabus, Egyptian Style, Ebonized, Gilt, Female Bust, 42 In.	4995.00
Pedestal, L. & J.G. Stickley, Square Top, 4 Sided Tapered Post, Shoe Feet, 42 x 18 In.	4025.00
Pedestal, Limbert, Octagonal Top, Tapered Base, Cutouts, 18 x 18 x 28 In.	2415.00
Pedestal, Limbert, Round Top, 2 Shelves, Arched Legs, 14 x 14 x 42 In.	4900.00
Pedestal, Louis XV Style, Mahogany, Gilt Bronze, Marble Top, Bombe Case, 50 In.	235.00
Pedestal, Louis XVI Style, Square Top, Flaming Urn On Ribbon Bow, 54 In., Pair	1530.00
Pedestal, Mahogany, Carved, Acanthus Columns, 4 Claw Feet, c.1880, 41 In.	2240.00
Pedestal, Mahogany, Drapery Carved Column, Claw Feet, c.1885, 15 x 37 In.	1790.00
Pedestal, Mahogany, Recessed Panels, Ormolu Cherubs, Square Tapered Legs, 47 In.	305.00
Pedestal, Marble, Bronze, Square Top, Stepped Base, France, c.1890, 41 x 13 x 13 In.	1265.00
Pedestal, Marble, Hunter Green, Circular, Ring-Carved Base, Stepped Plinth, 29 In.	145.00
Pedestal, Marble, Lavender, White & Gray Vein, 20th Century, 43 x 13 In.	1265.00
Pedestal, Neoclassical, Gilt, White Paint, Eagle Heads, 53 3/4 x 14 In.	1295.00
Pedestal, Neoclassical, Mahogany, Carved Ram's Heads, Plinth Base, 30 In., Pair	1295.00
Pedestal, Oak, Marble Top, Carved Columns, Putti, c.1880, 26 x 26 x 57 In., Pair	4760.00
Pedestal, Onyx, Champleve Mounted, Columns, Stylized Flowers, 42 In.	3820.00
Pedestal, Onyx, Cream Color, Brown Striations, Block Base, 11 x 11 x 38 1/4 In.	415.00
Pedestal, Onyx, Embossed, Reticulated Bronze Mounts, c.1880, 39 x 12 x 12 In.	785.00
Pedestal, Onyx, Mottled Gold & White, 39 1/2 x 12 1/2 x 12 1/2 In., Pair	635.00
Pedestal, Onyx, Round Swivel Top, Reeded Bronze Pillars, 4 Claw Feet, 16 x 31 In.	3080.00
Pedestal, Regency, Mahogany, Line Inlay, c.1805, 39 x 23 x 23 In.	7170.00
Pedestal, Renaissance Revival, Walnut, Carved, Black, Gold Incised, c.1870, 43 In. . *Illus*	5320.00
Pedestal, Renaissance Revival, Walnut, Female Busts, Turtle, Hoof Feet, 36 In.	6465.00
Pedestal, Renaissance Revival, Walnut, Incised Panels, c.1875, 18 x 18 x 45 In.	3080.00

Furniture, Recamier, Herter
Bros., Aesthetic Revival, Inlaid
Mahogany, c.1890, 76 In.

Pedestal, Renaissance Revival, Walnut, Marble Top, Incised Ebony, Gold, 36 In., Pair . . . 5040.00
Pedestal, Roycroft, Oak, Stepped Base, Square, c.1907, 39 1/8 x 15 x 15 In. 4115.00
Pedestal, Stepped Rectangular Top, Portrait Medallion, Iron Rings, 1790, 34 x 24 x 15 In. 6440.00
Pedestal, Stork On Dolphin, Shaped Domed Base, c.1920, 27 x 11 In., Pair 950.00
Pedestal, Victorian, Mahogany, Gilt Bronze, Round Marble Top, Hoof Feet, 34 In. 645.00
Pedestal, Walnut, Ebonized Trim, Bronze Mounts, Gold Inlay, c.1870, 16 x 44 In. 1680.00
Pedestal, Walnut, Marble Top, Carved Dog Heads, Claw Feet, c.1875, 21 x 32 In. 2185.00
Pedestal, White Onyx, Ormolu, Square Top, Ram's Head Feet, 12 x 12 x 40 In. 1320.00
Pedestal, Wood, Black Marble Top, Faux Marble Base, 21 x 28 x 14 In., Pair 1435.00
Pedestal, Wood, Silver Leaf, Round Top, Apron, Brass Spheres, c.1980, 36 x 15 In. 150.00
Pew, Church, Pine, Red, Black Paint, Reeded Panels, 56 x 22 1/2 x 32 1/2 In. 330.00
Pie Safe, Cherry, Drawers, Tin Doors, Masonic Emblems, Stars, Hearts, 50 x 54 x 17 In. . . 715.00
Pie Safe, Cherry, Long Drawer Over 2 Doors, 3 Punched Tin Panels, 56 x 40 In. 1015.00
Pie Safe, Green Paint, Pierced Tin Panels, Drawers, 54 x 39 x 17 In. 1725.00
Pie Safe, Hanging, Pine, Brown Finish, Punched Urn, Flowers, Scallops, 35 x 28 In. 1100.00
Pie Safe, Hanging, Punched Compass Star, Circles, Red Brown Paint, 30 x 20 x 43 In. . . . 1650.00
Pie Safe, Pine, Painted, Plank Door, Punched Tin Panels, c.1850, 72 x 37 x 25 In. 920.00
Pie Safe, Pine, Painted, Plank Top, Wire Mesh Door, Drawer, c.1900, 60 x 33 x 15 In. . . . 230.00
Pie Safe, Poplar, 2 Doors, Tin, Circle, Star, Crescent, 19th Century, 60 x 22 x 50 In. 2900.00
Pie Safe, Poplar, Pine, Blue Paint, Punched Tin, Arches, Georgia State Seal, 66 x 40 In. . . 2200.00
Pie Safe, Putty Color, 12 Tin Panels, Pinwheels, 2 Dovetailed Drawers, 39 x 17 x 49 In. . . 1180.00
Pie Safe, Single Door, 4 Shelves, Screen, New Hampshire, 31 x 18 1/2 x 51 1/2 In. 875.00
Pie Safe, Walnut, Horse, Rider, Punched Tin Panels, Scalloped, Ohio, 53 x 20 x 65 In. . . . 3750.00
Planter, Arts & Crafts, Hammered Copper Bowl, 13 x 30 In., Pair 1265.00
Planter, Louis XV Style, Fruitwood, Removable Liner, Flowers, 17 x 47 x 14 1/2 In. 865.00
Podium, Victorian, Walnut, Drop Leaf, Adjustable Height, Turned Shaft, Drawer 56.00
Porch Set, Ficks Reed, Bamboo, Floral Cushions, Early 1950s, 13 Piece 795.00
Porch Set, Wicker, Green Paint, 2 Rockers, Bench, Ottoman, 4 Piece 805.00
Rack, Baker's, Aart Deco, Cast Iron, Brass, 2 Divided Shelves, 1930s, 60 x 48 x 18 In. . . . 4000.00
Rack, Basket, Wood, Square Nails, Cabriole Legs, Iron Supports, 58 x 18 x 20 In. 165.00
Rack, Drying, Shaker, Hickory, Fruitwood, 10 Turned Crosspieces, Crossed Legs, 53 In. . . 413.00
Rack, Game, Pine, 13 Wrought Iron Hooks, Switzerland, c.1800, 65 In. 235.00
Rack, Luggage, L. & J.G. Stickley, Signed, 14 x 40 x 20 In. 1150.00
Rack, Magazine, Arts & Crafts, 5 Shelves, 54 x 23 x 13 In. 1265.00
Rack, Magazine, Crackle Paint, Monkey In 18th-Century Dress, Fruit, 17 x 18 In. 145.00
Rack, Magazine, Hanging, Folding, Shakespeare Medallion, Gold Incised, 34 In. 950.00
Rack, Magazine, Hanging, Walnut, God Bless Our Home, 30 In. 120.00
Rack, Magazine, J. Adnet, Leather Over Steel, Brass, c.1950, 17 x 21 In. 3105.00
Rack, Magazine, Stickley Bros., Mahogany, Slatted, 5 Shelves, 46 x 15 x 12 1/2 In. 1150.00
Rack, Plate, Hanging, Arts & Crafts, Carved Flowers, Vines, 18 x 36 In. 320.00
Rack, Plate, Hanging, Oak, 2 Shelves, Stylized Lion Finials, 35 x 3 3/4 x 29 3/4 In. 140.00
Rack, Plate, Hanging, Oak, 3 Shelves, Spain, 37 1/2 x 3 1/2 x 42 1/2 In. 85.00
Rack, Plate, Pine, Blue Paint, 4 Molded Crosspieces, Scalloped, 36 x 4 x 45 1/2 In. 605.00
Rack, Quilt, Folding, Mortised Crosspieces, Painted, Cast Iron Hinges, 108 x 66 In. 99.00
Rack, Quilt, Fruitwood, Faux Bamboo, Turned Posts, Trestle Supports, 33 x 23 In. 235.00
Rack, Quilt, Pine, Folding, Mortised Construction, 2 Parts, 64 x 34 3/4 In. 83.00
Rack, Quilt, Pine, Hickory, Tapered Uprights, Shoe Feet, 42 1/2 x 67 In. 55.00
Rack, Quilt, Pine, Mortised Joints, Shoe Feet, 48 x 72 In. 149.00
Rack, Quilt, Pine, Painted, Plain Rails, Tapered Posts, Trestle Feet, 48 x 48 In. 530.00
Rack, Quilt, Walnut, Vase-Shaped Posts, 2 Turned Rungs, Scroll Feet, 45 1/2 In. 315.00

Rack, Towel, Chestnut, Needlework Panel, Gilt Liner, Incised Carving, Rosette Crest 550.00
Rack, Towel, Fruitwood, Faux Bamboo, 5 Bars, Late 19th Century, 33 x 22 x 10 1/2 In. ..   173.00
Rack, Towel, Satinwood, Folding, 2 Panels, England, c.1890, 35 1/2 x 25 In. 130.00
Rack, Towel, Walnut, Burl Panels, Incised Carving, Spire, Finials, 2 Bars 385.00
Recamier, Anglo-Colonial Style, Oak, Cane Seat, Back, c.1900, 36 1/2 x 74 In. 1725.00
Recamier, Edwardian, Mahogany, Bellflower, Ribbon Inlay, 30 x 49 x 21 1/2 In. 635.00
Recamier, Flame Mahogany, Pillow-Foot End, c.1830 ....   2500.00
Recamier, Herter Bros., Aesthetic Revival, Inlaid Mahogany, c.1890, 76 In. .... *Illus* 10575.00
Recamier, Meeks, Rosewood, Stanton Hall Pattern, Pierced, 40 1/2 x 54 x 21 In. 6615.00
Recamier, Rococo, Beech, Shaped Backrest, Carved Apron, Cabriole Legs, 71 In. 1295.00
Rocker, Arts & Crafts, 5 Vertical Back & Arm Slats, 28 x 29 x 36 In. 635.00
Rocker, Arts & Crafts, Bentwood, Wicker, Arched Cattail Back Splat, Reeded Rockers ...   740.00
Rocker, Arts & Crafts, Cutout Apron, Double Supports, Cushions, 37 1/2 x 31 1/2 In. 460.00
Rocker, Arts & Crafts, Oak, 3 Vertical Slats, Open Arms, Cushion 220.00
Rocker, Arts & Crafts, Oak, Crest Rail, 4 Slats, Flat Open Arms, 1900s, 30 x 29 x 27 In. .   380.00
Rocker, Arts & Crafts, Oak, Crest Rail, Cutouts, Open Arms, Spring Seat, 34 x 30 x 29 In.   1115.00
Rocker, Bench, Mammy's, Spindle Back, Removable Gate, Early 1800s, 72 x 30 In. 620.00
Rocker, Bentwood, Hickory Branches, Slats, 42 1/2 In. 110.00
Rocker, Bentwood, Twig, Hickory, Intertwined Arms, Oval Back, 44 In. 138.00
Rocker, Birch, Original Brown Varnish, Cane Seat, Enfield, N.H., c.1830, 16 In. 4312.50
Rocker, Boston, Spindle Back, Shaped Headrest, Planked Saddle Seat, Black Paint, 41 In.   69.00
Rocker, Boston, Stenciled Crest Rail, Poplar Seat, J.W. McCrary, 26 In. 330.00
Rocker, Carved Mahogany, Pierced Back, Figural Lions, c.1890, 37 In. .... *Illus*   785.00
Rocker, Curly Maple, Ladder Back, Turned Posts, Scrolled Handholds, 14 x 42 In. 495.00
Rocker, Eames, Fiberglass, Birch, Herman Miller, 1950s, 25 x 27 x 26 In. 1095.00
Rocker, Eames, Fiberglass, Cat Cradle Base, Herman Miller, 27 x 25 x 27 In. 1410.00
Rocker, Eames, Soft Pad, Swivel, Aluminum, Leather, Herman Miller, 31 In., Pair 880.00
Rocker, Eames, Yellow Fiberglass, Birch, Nickel, Herman Miller, 1950s, 25 x 26 In. 1150.00
Rocker, Empire, Tiger Maple, Upholstered Seat, Saber Legs, Scrolled Partial Arms 169.00
Rocker, G. Nakashima, Walnut, Spindle Back, c.1979, 35 1/2 x 25 x 26 In. 3820.00
Rocker, G. Stickley, No. 311 1/2, V-Back, 5 Back Slats, Leather Seat, 26 x 29 x 35 In. ...   748.00
Rocker, G. Stickley, No. 397, Curved Crest, Open Arms, Spring Cushion Seat, 43 x 28 In.   765.00
Rocker, G. Stickley, Oak, 3 Splats, Slip Seat, Arched Skirt, Square Legs 1150.00
Rocker, G. Stickley, Willow, Curved Back, Arms, 28 x 36 x 35 In. 375.00
Rocker, Grain Painted, Spindle Back, Writing Arm, Stretcher Support, 33 3/4 In. 385.00
Rocker, Harden, Vertical Slats, Back, Arms, Drop-In Seat, 36 x 28 x 32 In. 635.00
Rocker, Herman Miller, Orange Fiberglass, Wire Base, Birch Runners, 27 x 25 In. .. *Illus*   1410.00
Rocker, Hickory, Weathered, 6 Vertical Slats, Loop Around Crest, 16 1/2 x 40 In. 248.00
Rocker, Hunzinger, Oak, Lollipop, High Back, Twisted Stretcher, 1890, 42 x 24 In. 896.00
Rocker, Hunzinger, Oak, Spring, Upholstered, Rope Turned Spindles, 34 In. 200.00
Rocker, L. & J.G. Stickley, No. 409, Slats To Floor, Leather Seat, 32 x 26 x 30 In. 5465.00
Rocker, L. & J.G. Stickley, Oak, 6 Back Slats, Open Arms, Fabric Seat, 35 x 27 x 29 In. .   1095.00
Rocker, L. & J.G. Stickley, Slats & Corbels, Flat Arms, Leather Cushion, 37 x 31 x 35 In.   2300.00
Rocker, Ladder Back, 2 Arms, 4 Rungs, Split Hickory Seat, c.1800, 44 In. 750.00
Rocker, Ladder Back, Arms, Black Paint, Twine Seat, 18th Century, Child's 405.00
Rocker, Ladder Back, Hardwood, Painted, Spindle Arms, Splint Seat, 9 1/2 x 25 1/2 In. ..   220.00
Rocker, Ladder Back, Maple, Hickory, Scrolled Arms, Splint Seat, 15 x 43 1/2 In. 360.00
Rocker, Ladder Back, Mixed Hardwoods, Scrolled Fronts, 5 Arched Slats, 44 In. 635.00
Rocker, Ladder Back, Pine, Solid Arms, Cutout, Scrolled Handrests, Va., 42 In. 330.00

Furniture, Rocker,
Carved Mahogany,
Pierced Back,
Figural Lions,
c.1890, 37 In.

Furniture, Rocker,
Herman Miller,
Orange Fiberglass,
Wire Base, Birch
Runners, 27 x 25 In.

Rocker, Ladder Back, Red Paint, Pegged Legs, Splint Seat, 16 x 35 In. 85.00
Rocker, Ladder Back, Scrolled Arms, 3 Splats, 42 x 24 x 24 In. 330.00
Rocker, Lifetime, Wing, Leather Cushions, 36 x 30 1/2 x 30 In. 865.00
Rocker, Liftime, Oak, Upholstered, Curved Back, 34 In. 115.00
Rocker, Limbert, Morris, Oak, Corbels, Flat Arms, Arched Aprons, 32 x 31 x 40 In. 3450.00
Rocker, Limbert, No. 982, Crest Rail, Slats, Open Arms, Marked, 1900s, 33 x 27 x 29 In. . . 325.00
Rocker, Lincoln Form, Walnut, Cane Seat & Back, Painted, Mid 1800s, Child's 215.00
Rocker, Maple, Curvilinear Pegged Arms, Rush Seat, 48 In. 5175.00
Rocker, Maple, Scrolling Arms, Campechy Form, Curule Base, 36 In. 2300.00
Rocker, Oak & Hickory, Slat Back, Rush Seat, Arms, Child's, 9 1/2-In. Seat Height 85.00
Rocker, Onondaga Shops, Crest Rail, Inverted V, Slatted, Cushions, 38 x 28 x 33 In. 440.00
Rocker, Platform, Wicker, Rolled Arms & Headrest, Victorian, 42 x 26 In. 390.00
Rocker, Queen Anne, Spooned Crest Rail, Vase Form Splat, 37 In. 590.00
Rocker, Root, Burl Detail, Mosaic Seat, c.1930, Pair 4000.00
Rocker, Rosewood, Dragons, Masks, Rococo Scroll, Japan, 19th Century, 43 x 46 In. 1295.00
Rocker, Salem, Grain Painted, Yellow, Stenciled, 19th Century 200.00
Rocker, Salem, Mahogany, Paneled Top Rail, Bamboo Spindles, c.1820 . . . . 145.00
Rocker, Sam Maloof, Metal Label, c.1969, 46 x 28 1/4 x 21 In. 17625.00
Rocker, Sewing, 2 Back Planks, Rush Seat, 30 1/2 x 18 x 16 In. 405.00
Rocker, Sewing, Limbert, No. 592, 32 x 18 x 16 In. 460.00
Rocker, Sewing, Victorian, Walnut, Finger Roll, Scroll Crest, Sleigh Runner, 1900s 290.00
Rocker, Shaker Style, Brown Paint, Rush Seat, Scrolled Arms, 4 Slats, 42 1/2 In. 360.00
Rocker, Shaker, 4 Arched Slats, Shaped Arms, Tape Seat, Mt. Lebanon, N.Y., 41 In. 523.00
Rocker, Shaker, Double Rungs, Arms, 4 Slats, Union Village, Ohio, 15 x 43 In. 358.00
Rocker, Shaker, Ladder Back, Hickory, Maple, Arms, Tape Seat, South Union, Ky., 45 In. . 303.00
Rocker, Shaker, Maple, Original Finish, Splint Seat, Mt. Lebanon, N.Y., c.1860, 30 In. . . . 1090.00
Rocker, Shaker, Maple, Scrolled Arms, Rush Seat, Mt. Lebanon, N.Y., c.1830, 45 1/2 In. . . 2300.00
Rocker, Shaker, Maple, Shaped Arms, Blue & White Tape Seat, 20th Century, 37 In. 385.00
Rocker, Shaker, Maple, Splint Seat, Mt. Lebanon, N.Y., 15 1/2 In. 515.00
Rocker, Shaker, Maple, Taped Seat, Covered Seat, Mt. Lebanon, c.1870, 15 1/2 In., Pair . . 690.00
Rocker, Shaker, No. 2.Maple, Original Varnish, Mt. Lebanon, N.Y., 33 1/2 In. 1035.00
Rocker, Shaker, No. 4, Maple, Original Varnish, Tape Seat, Mt. Lebanon, N.Y., 35 In. 690.00
Rocker, Shaker, No. 7, 4 Slats, Rush Seat, Arms, Mt. Lebanon 865.00
Rocker, Shaker, No. 7, Maple, Arms, 4 Slats, Mt. Lebanon, N.Y., 41 In. 1380.00
Rocker, Shaker, Sewing, Maple, Varnished, 3 Arched Slats, Pleasant Hill, Ky., 34 In. 715.00
Rocker, Snowshoe, Wicker, Rolled Arm, Victorian, 41 In. 420.00
Rocker, Steel Frame, Tufted Leather, Woodard & Sons Tag, 37 x 27 x 39 In., Pair 1115.00
Rocker, T.B. Warren, Cast Iron Frame, Spring Metal, Platform Base, 37 In. 690.00
Rocker, Thonet, Bentwood, Pressed Seat & Back, Austria, c.1880, 39 x 17 1/2 In. 590.00
Rocker, V. Panton, Relaxer 2, Walnut Demilune, Leather Cushion, 32 x 38 x 25 In. 4315.00
Rocker, Victorian, Rosewood, Carved Rose & Leaf, Upholstered, c.1860, 21 In. 8050.00
Rocker, Windsor, Painted Design, Thumb Back, c.1830, 30 In. 470.00
Rocker, Windsor, Painted, Rod Back, Tapered Spindles, c.1830, 31 3/4 In. 380.00
Rocker, Windsor, Pine, 4 Spindles, Shaped Seat, Child's, 27 In. 330.00
Rocker, Windsor, Plank Seat, 5 Spindles, Fruit Crest, Yellow, 34 1/2 x 19 1/2 In. 560.00
Screen, 2-Panel, Edgar Brandt, Gilt Bronze, Au Bon Marche, c.1923, 77 x 23 In. 6570.00
Screen, 2-Panel, Mahogany, Carved, Raised Book Spine Design, Gilt 1380.00
Screen, 2-Panel, Oriental, Mahogany Frame, Pierced Fretwork, 41 x 27 1/2 In. 55.00
Screen, 2-Panel, Rosewood, Mirror, Dragon, Cloud, Japan, 19th Century, 73 x 36 In. 1060.00
Screen, 2-Panel, Tale Of Genji, Gold Speckle, Silk Mount, Japan, c.1890, 27 x 42 In. 460.00
Screen, 3-Panel, Aesthetic Revival, Fairy Scenes, Walnut Frame, 1800s, 72 In. 4700.00
Screen, 3-Panel, Art Deco, Zodiac Signs, Feet, 76 x 64 1/2 In. 21510.00
Screen, 3-Panel, Arts & Crafts, Celtic Designs, Bronze Inlay, c.1910, 71 x 73 In. 1115.00
Screen, 3-Panel, Arts & Crafts, Poppies, Red, Green On Top Panel, 68 In. 2530.00
Screen, 3-Panel, Edwardian, Satinwood, Inlaid, Beveled Glass, 72 x 16 1/2 In. 475.00
Screen, 3-Panel, Eugene Schoen, Brown & Tan, Cutouts, Brass, 75 x 18 In. 2940.00
Screen, 3-Panel, Giltwood, Carved, Oil-Painted Figures, Upholstered, France, 73 x 69 In. . 2040.00
Screen, 3-Panel, Louis XVI Style, Gilt, Painted, Figural, 96 x 73 1/2 In. 2530.00
Screen, 3-Panel, P. Evans, Directional, Bright Brass, Chrome, 80 x 36 In., Pair 3820.00
Screen, 3-Panel, Rococo Style, Carved Wood, Leaves, Crest, 72 x 51 In. 1175.00
Screen, 3-Panel, Rosewood, Mirror, Dragon, Cloud, Japan, 19th Century, 71 x 24 In. 765.00
Screen, 3-Panel, Viennese Secessionist, Leaded Glass, Copper Border, 64 x 48 In. 5465.00
Screen, 3-Panel, Walnut, Hammered Copper, Buckeye & Palm Leaves, 72 x 66 In. 6900.00

Screen, 4 Panel, Piero Fornasetti, Farfalle, Transfer-Printed Wood, 78 1/2 x 19 5/8 In. 4600.00
Screen, 4-Panel, Art Deco, Wood, Black Lacquer, Enameled, Richard Haas, 76 In. 2990.00
Screen, 4-Panel, Black Lacquer, Applied Relief Carved Hardstone Figures, 72 In. 175.00
Screen, 4-Panel, Carved, Mother-Of-Pearl Inlay, Flowers, Figures, Parasols, 38 x 44 In. . . .   290.00
Screen, 4-Panel, Coromandel Style, Figures, Birds, Chinese, 20th Century, 72 In. 1315.00
Screen, 4-Panel, Marquetry, Floral Basket & Bow, Brass Hinges, c.1810, 82 x 92 In. 4600.00
Screen, 4-Panel, Needlepoint, Arched Panels, Figures, Animals, Flowers, 71 x 100 In. . . .   2070.00
Screen, 4-Panel, Oriental, Rosewood, Carved, Blossoms, Leaves, c.1900, 72 x 80 In. 575.00
Screen, 4-Panel, Painted Lilies, Insects, Black Ground, Silvered Border, 70 x 88 In. 865.00
Screen, 4-Panel, Rococo, Leather, Embossed, Dutch, c.1850, 77 1/2 x 88 In. 4600.00
Screen, 5-Panel, Louis Philippe, Wallpaper, Landscape, c.1830, 65 x 19 In. 2390.00
Screen, 6-Panel, Art Deco, Lacquered, Flowers, Leaves, Fountain, 102 x 120 In. 8225.00
Screen, 6-Panel, Black Lacquer, Parcel Gilt, Chinese, 19th Century, 78 In. 15535.00
Screen, 6-Panel, Silk, Pictorial, Buddhist, Taoist, Japan, 18th Century, 94 x 18 In. 1440.00
Screen, 6-Panel, Straw Marquetry, Sunburst Pattern, Jean-Michel Frank, 1930s 29900.00
Screen, 8-Panel, Yellow & Green Floral, Leaf Border, Griffins, c.1825, 76 x 164 In. 8280.00
Screen, 12-Panel, Coromandel, Lacquer, Chinese, 73 x 16 In. 4480.00
Screen, 12-Panel, Kano School, Pavilion Scene, Gold Leaf, 19th Century, 44 x 145 In. . . .   805.00
Screen, Arts & Crafts, Copper, Ruffled Edges, Repousse, Tree, 24 x 38 1/4 In. 495.00
Screen, Arts & Crafts, Oak, Slag Glass, 20th Century, 68 1/4 x 80 In. 235.00
Screen, Birch, Fabric Panel, Triangular Crest, Russia, c.1820, 74 x 112 In. 4370.00
Screen, Coromandel, People In Garden, Birds, Flowers, Chinese, 19th Century, 72 x 62 In.   295.00
Screen, Eames, FSW-6, Molded Ash, Folding, Herman Miller, c.1950, 60 x 68 In. 2530.00
Screen, Eames, Molded Ash Plywood, Herman Miller, 1950s, 60 x 68 In. 3450.00
Screen, Frank Lloyd Wright, Painted, Gold & Green Leaves, c.1956, 93 x 150 In. 29900.00
Screen, M. & F. Higgins, Glass, Brass Clips, c.1955, 40 5 1/2-In. Discs 4115.00
Screen, Mahogany Frame, Gate Leg Base, Needlepoint Stag, Hounds, 18 x 23 In. 165.00
Screen, Modernist, Folding, Ebonized Oak Frames, Canework Body, 16 x 80 In., Pair . . .   1000.00
Screen, Needlepoint, Embroidery, Flowers, Cast Iron Stand, 1800s, 21 x 8 1/2 In., Pair . . .   290.00
Screen, Pole, Beech, Needlepoint, Tripod, Urn Pedestal, England, 1900, 55 1/2 In. 385.00
Screen, Pole, George III Style, Mahogany, Needlework Panel, 18th Century, 59 1/2 In. . . .   3585.00
Screen, Pole, George IV, Rosewood, Mother-Of-Pearl, Papier-Mache, c.1820, 55 In. 520.00
Screen, Pole, Huntsman Sharing Meal With Dog, Needlework, Tripod, 56 1/2 In. 345.00
Screen, Pole, Needlework, Children At Ruins, Mahogany, Tripod Base, 60 In. 715.00
Screen, Pole, Petit Point, Sacrifice Of Abraham, Mahogany, 57 In. 470.00
Screen, Pole, Shield Shape, Needlework, Mahogany, String Inlay, 19th Century, 61 In. . . .   315.00
Screen, Pole, Victorian, Needlework Panel, Woman, Horse, Tripod Base, 59 In. 120.00
Screen, Renaissance Revival, Ebonized Wood, Carved Shells, Shore Scene Panel, 42 In. . . .   1765.00
Screen, Table, Ivory, Carved, Deer Design, Continental, 17 In. 2350.00
Screen, Table, Needlework, Woman With Mask Carrying Basket, 28 In. 330.00
Screen, Table, Sandalwood, Figures Under Pine Tree, 10 In. 60.00
Secretary, Baroque Style, Walnut, Marquetry, 2 Glazed Doors, 3 Drawers, Dutch, 35 In. . .   6465.00
Secretary, Burl Walnut, Carved, Commode Base, Divided Cylinder, 103 x 48 In. 3640.00
Secretary, Burl Walnut, Floral Rolling-Pin Crest, Arched Doors, 105 x 46 In. 3920.00
Secretary, Butler's, Georgian, Mahogany, 2 Doors, 4-Drawer Chest, 85 x 20 In. 1955.00
Secretary, Charles X, Walnut, Marble Top, Leather Surface, c.1815, 60 x 39 1/2 In. 3220.00
Secretary, Chippendale Style, Walnut, Dentil Molded Cornice, 39 x 11 3/4 x 47 In. 2475.00
Secretary, Chippendale Style, Walnut, Mullioned Doors, 37 1/2 x 41 In. 489.00
Secretary, Chippendale, Mahogany, Slant Front, 2-Door Top, 82 1/2 x 38 1/4 x 23 In. 3450.00
Secretary, Drop Front, Arts & Crafts, Glass Doors, 31 x 16 x 59 In. 1265.00
Secretary, Drop Front, Biedermeier, Birch, Marquetry, Ebonized, c.1840, 54 x 43 x 18 In.   805.00
Secretary, Drop Front, Burl Walnut, Flame Veneer, 20 Drawers, 50 x 46 x 18 1/2 In. 2070.00
Secretary, Drop Front, McCobb, Multiple Drawers, Birch, Iron, 1950, 72 x 46 In. 1725.00
Secretary, Drop Front, Neoclassical, Walnut, Marquetry, c.1860, 65 x 38 x 19 In. 3680.00
Secretary, Drop Front, Renaissance Revival, Walnut, Bird's-Eye Maple, American, 58 In.   8000.00
Secretary, Drop Front, Sheraton, Mahogany, 2 Drawers, c.1810, 55 x 31 x 23 In. 805.00
Secretary, Drop Front, Sheraton, Mahogany, 2 Mullioned Cathedral Doors, 73 x 40 In. . . .   1790.00
Secretary, Drop Front, Wegner, Mobel, c.1958, 72 x 39 1/2 x 19 1/4 In. 1175.00
Secretary, Eastlake, Burl Walnut, Cylinder, Paneled Doors, 95 x 35 1/2 x 20 1/2 In. 2015.00
Secretary, Eastlake, Divided Cylinder, Carved Crest, c.1880, 102 x 43 x 24 In. 3360.00
Secretary, Empire Style, Mahogany, c.1850, 57 1/2 x 37 1/2 In. 5520.00
Secretary, Empire, Mahogany Veneer, American, 78 1/2 x 40 In. 1035.00
Secretary, Empire, Mahogany Veneer, Blind Front, Elephant Trunk Legs, 75 In. 1380.00

Secretary, Federal, Cherry, Tambour Doors, Flat Front, 48 x 39 x 20 In. 1035.00
Secretary, Federal, Mahogany, Inlaid, Hinged Front, Side Panels, 38 x 65 In. 4780.00
Secretary, George III, Walnut, 2 Doors, Mirrored Panels, Cubbyholes, 85 x 36 x 20 In. . . . 4830.00
Secretary, Georgian Style, Mahogany, Breakfront, Glazed Doors, 82 x 90 x 19 In. 4995.00
Secretary, Hepplewhite, Mahogany, Veneer, Pine, Inlay, Cornice, 41 x 19 x 52 In. 2475.00
Secretary, Louis XV Style, Beech, 2 Doors, 2 Drawers, Fitted Interior, 49 x 22 In. 560.00
Secretary, Mahogany, Breakfront Top, Drawer, Carved, c.1890, 30 x 50 x 24 In. 690.00
Secretary, Mahogany, Fold Front, 4 Drawers, Pigeonholes, 1800, 54 x 32 x 15 In. 1645.00
Secretary, Marquetry, Solid Sides, Marble Top, France, 43 x 36 x 21 In. 1540.00
Secretary, Mixed Woods, Chip Carved, Cutouts, Bracket Feet, 36 x 15 x 81 In. 880.00
Secretary, Napoleon III, Gilt Bronze Mounted, Ebonized, Inlay, 49 x 24 x 14 In. 940.00
Secretary, Neoclassical, Mahogany, 3 Drawers, Pigeonholes, American, 49 x 49 x 21 In. . 2300.00
Secretary, Queen Anne Style, Burl Walnut, Slant Front, 40 1/4 x 32 3/4 x 20 In. 1610.00
Secretary, Queen Anne, Tiger Maple, 3 Drawers, 18th Century, 64 x 36 x 28 In. 27825.00
Secretary, Queen Anne, Walnut, 2 Mirrored Doors, Claw & Ball Feet, 69 x 28 x 16 In. . . . 2990.00
Secretary, Regency, Rosewood, 3 Drawers, Cubbyholes, 44 x 45 x 23 In. 4025.00
Secretary, Restauration, Mahogany, Leather Writing Surface, 55 x 32 x 16 In. 2530.00
Secretary, Rococo Revival, Rosewood, Mechanical Cylinder, 2 Parts, 96 x 47 x 24 In. . . . 6615.00
Secretary, Rococo, Mahogany, Germany, Mid 19th Century, 62 1/4 x 39 x 21 In. 980.00
Secretary, Rococo, Walnut, 2 Shaped Glass Doors, William Tell Head Crest, 107 In. 8960.00
Secretary, Sheraton Style, Mahogany, Satinwood Inlay, 36 x 66 x 16 In. 1530.00
Secretary, Sheraton, Mahogany, Tambour, 2 Sections, 50 x 37 3/4 x 17 In. 575.00
Secretary, Sheraton, Walnut, Slant Front, 2 Parts, American, 19th Century, 33 1/2 x 72 In. 430.00
Secretary-Bookcase, Chippendale Style, Mahogany, Glass Door Panes, Claw Feet 2750.00
Secretary-Bookcase, Chippendale, Burl, 2 Glazed Doors, 4 Drawers, 86 x 43 In. 2300.00
Secretary-Bookcase, Drop Front, Mahogany Veneer, Pine, 3 Drawers, 80 x 38 In. 6800.00
Secretary-Bookcase, Drop Front, Mirror, Panel Doors, Raised Plinth, 66 x 16 x 72 In. . . . 1380.00
Secretary-Bookcase, Empire, Glazed Doors, Flat Front, American, 90 x 43 In. 920.00
Secretary-Bookcase, Empire, Mahogany, Glass Panel Doors, c.1840, 72 x 42 x 20 In. . . . 1150.00
Secretary-Bookcase, Federal, Mahogany, 2 Doors, Shelves, c.1800, 65 x 36 x 22 In. 2940.00
Secretary-Bookcase, George III, Mahogany, 2 Astragal Glazed Doors, 82 x 45 x 20 In. . . . 4370.00
Secretary-Bookcase, George III, Mahogany, 2 Glazed Doors, Drawers, 81 x 49 In. 5290.00
Secretary-Bookcase, George III, Mahogany, Astragal Glazed Doors, 95 x 94 In. 6040.00
Secretary-Bookcase, George III, Mahogany, Ebony Inlay, 2 Glazed Doors, 90 In. 3525.00
Secretary-Bookcase, George III, Mahogany, Glazed Doors, Leather Inset, 91 x 45 In. 5060.00
Secretary-Bookcase, George III, Mahogany, Panel Doors, Inlaid Ivory, 87 x 42 x 22 In. . . . 5060.00
Secretary-Bookcase, George III, Mahogany, Satinwood, Inlaid, 97 x 42 x 21 3/4 In. 4140.00
Secretary-Bookcase, George IV, Mahogany, 2 Upper Glazed Doors, 5 Drawers, 42 In. . . . 5750.00
Secretary-Bookcase, Hepplewhite, Mahogany, Veneer, 4 Drawers, 40 x 19 x 78 In. 12650.00
Secretary-Bookcase, Mahogany, Crossbanded, 2 Doors, Pigeonholes, 86 x 46 x 20 In. . . . 2840.00
Secretary-Bookcase, Mahogany, Parcel Gilt, Brass, 2 Parts, c.1820, 91 x 47 x 24 In. 5060.00
Secretary-Bookcase, Neoclassical, Mahogany, Doors, Drawers, c.1835, 82 x 41 In. 4800.00
Secretary-Bookcase, Neoclassical, Mullioned Doors, Glazed Panels, 98 x 74 x 21 In. 8915.00
Secretary-Bookcase, Schoolmaster's, Softwood, Slant Front, 3 Shelves, 3 Drawers, 62 In. 1180.00
Secretary-Bookcase, Slant Front, 2 Glazed Doors Over 2 Paneled Doors, 91 In. 1035.00
Secretary-Bookcase, William IV, Rosewood, Pigeonholes, c.1830, 52 x 35 x 19 In. 3175.00
Server, Art Deco, Mahogany, Burl, Marble Top, 2 Drawers, 2 Doors, 43 x 44 x 16 In. 5875.00
Server, Art Deco, Oak, Rectangular Top, 2 Drawers, Doors, Dutch, 34 x 58 x 16 In. 999.00
Server, Arts & Crafts, Drawer, Lower Shelf, Rockford National Co., 36 x 18 x 38 In. 635.00
Server, Baroque Style, Walnut, D-Shape Marble Top, Doors, Shelves, 41 x 112 x 24 In. . . 2705.00
Server, Baroque Style, Walnut, Demilune Top, Drawer, Cupboards, 37 x 50 x 22 In. 470.00
Server, Cocktail, Art Deco, Vellum, Chromium, 3 Tiers, France, c.1930, 28 1/2 In. 1725.00
Server, Empire, Mahogany Flame Veneer, Acanthus Pilasters, Base Shelf, 41 In. 770.00
Server, Federal, Marble Columns, Splashboard Mirror, c.1830, 53 x 22 In. 7000.00
Server, Ford & Johnson, Drawer, Open Shelf, Cutouts, 36 x 18 x 32 In. 1095.00
Server, G. Stickley, 2 Drawers, Backsplash, Iron Pulls, Apron, Shelf, 40 x 42 In. 4315.00
Server, G. Stickley, 4 Drawers, Backsplash, Copper Pulls, Shelf, 39 1/4 x 48 x 19 3/4 In. . 2990.00
Server, H. Probber, Ebonized Wood Case, Black Laminate Surface, 30 x 36 In. 200.00
Server, Hepplewhite Style, Mahogany, Inlaid, Serpentine Front, 34 x 37 x 18 In. 920.00
Server, Hepplewhite, Mahogany, 4 Drawers, 4 Doors, Scalloped Skirt, 41 x 21 x 48 In. . . . 3680.00
Server, Hepplewhite, Mahogany, Bowfront, 3 Drawers, Tapered Legs, 30 x 48 In. 860.00
Server, Jacobean, Oak, Drawers, Scalloped Apron, 6 Turned Legs, Onion Feet, 28 x 61 In. 825.00
Server, Limbert, Angled Top, 5 Drawers, Brass Hardware, 45 x 21 x 41 In. 4315.00

Server, Mahogany, Bowfront, Carved Backsplash, 2 Drawers, Square Legs, 30 x 48 In. ... 550.00
Server, Mahogany, Carved, Pierced, Scrolled, Anglo-Indian, 43 x 49 x 22 In. 5520.00
Server, Mahogany, Raised Panel Door, c.1910, 42 x 21 x 16 In., Pair 1120.00
Server, Oak, Marble Top, 2 Drawers Over 2 Paneled Doors, Bun Feet, 43 x 21 x 32 In. .. 460.00
Server, Red Lacquer, D-Form Top, Drawer, 19th Century, Chinese, 39 x 43 x 14 In. 805.00
Server, Sheraton Style, Yew, Bowfront, 2 Doors, Short Drawer, 35 x 42 In. 980.00
Server, Sheraton, Pine, 1 Drawer, Spool Turned Legs, American, 32 x 32 In. 175.00
Server, Sheraton, Tiger Maple, 2 Drawers, Turned Legs, c.1835, 28 x 38 x 24 In. 3390.00
Server, Stickley Bros., No. 8733, Drawer, Lower Shelf, 34 x 21 x 36 In. 1495.00
Server, Stickley Bros., No. 8735, Drawer, Backsplash, Shelf, 37 x 36 x 19 In. 2185.00
Server, Stickley Bros., No. 8902, 2 Over 1 Drawers, Lower Shelf, 48 x 20 x 38 In. 1725.00
Server, Tiger Oak, Beveled Mirror, Gallery Shelf, 59 x 51 In. .... *Illus* 1550.00
Server, Victorian, Mahogany, Single Drawer, Stretcher Base, c.1870, 39 x 43 x 20 In. ... 805.00
Server, Victorian, Walnut, 3 Over 2 Drawers, Side Doors, 19th Century, 50 x 21 x 33 In. .. 345.00
Server, Walnut, Dropn Front Desk, Spindle Gallery, Minton Tiles, c.1875, 59 x 44 x 18 In. 560.00
Server, Walnut, Veneer, Oak, Scrolled Feet, Scalloped Base, France, 48 x 23 x 37 In. 1760.00
Server, William IV, 3 Shelves, Pierced Brass Gallery, c.1835, 56 1/2 x 48 In. 6325.00
Settee, Arts & Crafts, Oak, Backrest, Carved Motto, 43 x 42 x 18 In. 950.00
Settee, Belter, Rococo Revival, Double Back, Child's, 32 x 51 In. 1840.00
Settee, Charles II Style, Oak, Stained, Late 19th Century, 61 In. 1315.00
Settee, Chippendale Style, Mahogany, Upholstered, Camelback, 20th Century, 85 In. ... 825.00
Settee, Chippendale, Mahogany, Carved Double Back, Padded Seat, 41 x 43 In., Pair 520.00
Settee, Cream Yellow Paint, Stencils, Lancaster County, c.1830, 72 In. 4400.00
Settee, Directoire Style, Padded, Dolphin Uprights, Polychrome, c.1810, 33 x 80 In. 1265.00
Settee, Eastlake, Ebonized Finish, Bamboo Design, c.1900, 68 In. 175.00
Settee, Edwardian, Mahogany, Inlaid, Carved & Pierced Chairback, Open Arms, 36 In. .. 550.00
Settee, Edwardian, Mahogany, Open Arms, Padded Seat & Back, Tapered Legs, 42 1/2 In. 440.00
Settee, Empire, Mahogany, Carved Back, Roll Arms, Brass Paw Feet, c.1810, 88 In. 1020.00
Settee, Federal, Mahogany, Double Back, Needlepoint Seat, c.1890, 36 x 43 In. 805.00
Settee, Fin Juhl, Teak, Brass, Upholstered, N. Vodder, Denmark, 1953, 50 x 28 1/2 In. .. 1725.00
Settee, French Provincial Style, Giltwood Frame, Carved, Upholstered, 46 In. 728.00
Settee, French Provincial Style, Upholstered, Floral Tapestry, High Back, 82 In. 1600.00
Settee, French Provincial, Open Arms, Triple Back, Waved Splats, 1800s, 75 In. 1090.00
Settee, French Provincial, Walnut, Domed, Padded Back, c.1850, 42 x 92 In. 2760.00
Settee, G. Nakashima, Walnut, Solid Seat, 16 Vertical Slats, Cushions, 30 x 48 In. 6325.00
Settee, G. Nakashima, Wood, 2 Cushions, c.1950, 30 x 47 1/2 x 26 In. 4700.00
Settee, G. Nelson, Wool, Wood, Foam, Aluminum, Herman Miller, 1954, 62 x 31 In. 2185.00
Settee, George II Style, Mahogany, Camelback, 38 1/2 x 86 1/2 In. 7770.00
Settee, George II Style, Mahogany, Scroll Arm, Upholstered, 41 1/2 x 52 1/2 x 29 In. ... 3680.00
Settee, George III Style, Mahogany, Acanthus Carved, 41 x 46 x 19 In. 460.00
Settee, George III, Mahogany, 4-Chair Back, Arms, c.1800, 33 x 66 In. 2300.00
Settee, Georgian, Mahogany, Framed, Carved Supports, 78 In. 510.00
Settee, Gothic Revival, Cast Iron, Black Paint, Carron, Stirlingshire, 1846, 38 In. 1040.00
Settee, Hinoki Wood, Arms, Japan, c.1912, 45 In. 635.00
Settee, L. & J.G. Stickley, 13 Vertical Slats, Notched Top Rail, 53 x 23 x 36 In. 1610.00
Settee, Louis XV Style, Gilt Carved Wood, Shell, Foliate Crest, 58 In. 1880.00
Settee, Louis XV/XVI Style, Padded, Upholstered, c.1890, 38 x 79 In. 2300.00
Settee, Louis XVI Style, Fruitwood, Upholstered, Box Shape, c.1900, 33 1/2 x 46 1/2 In. 2530.00
Settee, Louis XVI Style, Giltwood, Carved, Crest With Flowers, Upholstered, 72 In. 5975.00
Settee, Louis XVI Style, Giltwood, Framed, Carved, Open Arms, Upholstered, 52 In. 365.00
Settee, Louis XVI Style, Giltwood, Upholstered, 8 Legs, c.1890, 38 x 72 In. 3220.00
Settee, Louis XVI, Oval Back, Padded Arms, Stuffed Seat, Green, 19th Century, 55 In. ... 1610.00
Settee, Mahogany, Carved Birds & Fruit, Scroll Arms, Paw Feet, Casters, 1800s, 63 In. .. 2530.00
Settee, Majorelle, Mahogany, Carved, Clematis, c.1900, 52 In. 8960.00
Settee, Meeks, Rosewood, Carved, Pierced, Hawkins Pattern, c.1850, 48 x 68 x 22 In. .. 9200.00
Settee, Molded Crest Rail, 5-Panel Back, Plank Seat, Red Paint, 43 x 71 x 18 In. 2390.00
Settee, Neoclassical, Mahogany, Acanthus Carved, Russia, 37 x 21 x 22 In. 7770.00
Settee, Neoclassical, Mahogany, Giltwood, Russia, c.1815, 47 x 30 In. 5290.00
Settee, Paul Laszlo, Teak Frame, Cane Seat & Back, c.1950, 32 x 60 In. 4025.00
Settee, Regency Style, Giltwood, Padded, Sphinx Uprights, c.1890, 37 x 61 In. 1840.00
Settee, Regency, Wood, Ebonized, Swags, Flowers, 19th Century, 31 x 70 3/4 In. 2530.00
Settee, Rococo Revival, Walnut, Finger Roll, Scroll Crest, Velvet, 1900s, 61 In. 315.00
Settee, Rococo Style, Giltwood, Carved, Oval Back, Upholstered, 72 In. 2000.00

Settee, Rococo Style, Giltwood, Carved, Scrolling Cabriole Legs, 70 In. 4185.00
Settee, Rococo Style, Painted Wood, Scrolling Arms, Upholstered, 72 In. 440.00
Settee, Rococo, Walnut, Serpentine Carved Double Crest, 6 Cabriole Legs, 39 In. 990.00
Settee, Rush Seat, Triple Back, Painted, Stenciled, 45 1/2 x 57 1/2 In. 690.00
Settee, Stickley Bros., No. 3861, 3 Slats Over Upholstered Back, 62 x 39 In. 1265.00
Settee, Teak Frame, Bentwood, Black Vinyl Cushions, Denmark, 33 x 62 In. 235.00
Settee, Victorian, Mahogany, Triple Back, Leaf Crest, Upholstered, 63 In. 1410.00
Settee, Victorian, Rosewood, Upholstered, Serpentine Back, c.1860, 64 In., Pair 1295.00
Settee, Wakefield Bros., Photographer's, Natural Finish, 40 x 17 1/2 x 30 In. 2160.00
Settee, Wendell Castle, Molded Fiberglass Form, White, Beylerian, 48 x 33 x 26 In. 805.00
Settee, Windsor, 2 Seats, Comb Back, Turned Legs, Stretcher, American, 38 x 36 In. 2875.00
Settee, Windsor, Bamboo, Birdcage Back, Turned Spindles, Plank Seat, 1820s, 77 In. . . . 3900.00
Settee, Windsor, Bow Back, Spindles, Plank Seat, 20th Century, 36 x 72 x 17 1/2 In. 1795.00
Settle, Arts & Crafts, Mahogany, 12 Vertical Slats, Shaped Arms, c.1910, 38 x 72 x 20 In. 645.00
Settle, Arts & Crafts, Oak, 9 Vertical Slats, Square Posts, c.1910, 29 1/2 x 90 x 26 In. . . . 2000.00
Settle, Arts & Crafts, Oak, Drop Arm, 11 Slats, Stretchers, 1900s, 38 x 59 x 25 In. 355.00
Settle, Arts & Crafts, Oak, Drop Arm, Crest Rail, Slats, Shaped Arms, 36 x 85 x 32 In. . . 1765.00
Settle, Arts & Crafts, Oak, Even Arm, 13 Vertical Slats, c.1910, 36 x 77 1/2 x 27 1/4 In. . 645.00
Settle, Birch, Poplar, H-Stretcher, Plank Seat, 12 Spindles, 78 x 22 x 33 In. 220.00
Settle, Birch, Poplar, Turned Legs, 12 Spindles, 78 x 21 x 34 In. 385.00
Settle, Brooks, Even Arm, Slatted, Fabric Cushion, 33 x 82 x 29 In. 2300.00
Settle, G. Stickley, No. 219, 17 Vertical Slats, Oilcloth Cushion, 72 x 29 x 38 In. 2530.00
Settle, G. Stickley, No. 222, Tapered Posts, Canted Slats, Leather Seat, 36 x 80 x 32 In. . . 11500.00
Settle, G. Stickley, Square Posts, Vertical Slats, Rope Seat, 39 x 68 1/2 x 33 In. 5465.00
Settle, George II, Oak, Hinged Seat, c.1750, 46 3/4 x 49 3/4 x 20 In. 980.00
Settle, J.M. Young, Even Arm, Pyramid Posts, Leather Tacked Seat, 34 x 78 In. 2420.00
Settle, J.M. Young, Oak, Drop Arm, Crest Rail, Slats, c.1912, 34 x 82 x 31 In. 2470.00
Settle, Karpen, Slats To Back & Arms, Fabric Cushion, 36 x 76 x 25 In. 2875.00
Settle, L. & J.G Stickley, Oak, Slats, Even Arm, Trundle Bed, 1900s, 33 3/4 x 79 x 27 In. 4406.00
Settle, L. & J.G. Stickley, No. 225, Crest Rail, Slats, Open Arms, c.1914, 36 x 52 x 23 In. 1058.00
Settle, L. & J.G. Stickley, No. 232, 4-Slat Back, Leather Seat, 72 x 28 x 29 In. 2415.00
Settle, L. & J.G. Stickley, No. 281, 16-Slat Back, Even Arm, Cushion, 76 x 34 In. 6900.00
Settle, Lifetime, No. 712 3/4, 6 Wide Back Slats, 3 Arm Slats, Leather, 82 x 33 x 31 In. . . 4315.00
Settle, Lifetime, Puritan, Slatted, Leather Cushions, 32 x 77 x 31 In. 2415.00
Settle, Pine, Curved Back, 12 Panels, 4 Doors, Iron Hinges, 71 x 71 1/2 x 28 In. 5500.00
Settle, Plank Seat, 1-Board, Urn-Shaped Triple Splat, c.1840, 81 x 35 In. 735.00
Settle, Prairie School, E. E. Roberts, Oak Park Masonic Lodge, 100 x 27 x 34 In. 575.00
Settle, Spindle Back, Plank Seat, Scrolled Arms, Blue Paint, c.1840, 108 In. 1470.00
Settle, Stickley & Brandt Co., Slat Back, Sides, Rounded Rail, Leather Seat, 31 x 76 In. . . 5175.00
Settle, Stickley Bros., Square Posts, Vertical Slats, Fabric Cushions, 33 x 67 x 30 In. 1610.00
Settle, Stickley Bros., Trapezoid Shape Slats, Beveled Knobs, 72 x 32 x 35 In. 2875.00
Settle, Warren Platner, Chrome Wire Frame, Wool Upholstery, Knoll, 68 x 28 x 31 In. . . . 2185.00
Shelf, Corner, Bamboo, 4 Lacquered Shelves, Oriental Motif, 63 In. 365.00
Shelf, Corner, Empire Style, Mahogany, Ebonized Top, Brass Caps, c.1885, 57 x 37 In. . . 2185.00
Shelf, Corner, Hanging, Pine, Cove-Molded Cornice, 2 Shelves, 28 x 16 x 36 In. 1430.00

Furniture, Server, Tiger Oak,
Beveled Mirror, Gallery
Shelf, 59 x 51 In.

**Do not use soap
on the bottom of
sticking drawers.
Eventually it will
become sticky.
Use silicone or
paraffin wax.**

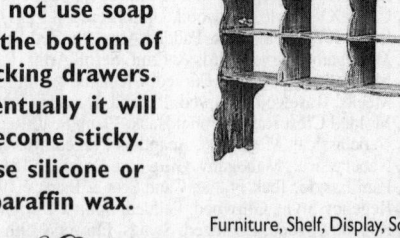

Furniture, Shelf, Display, Softwood,
Scalloped, Vertical Shelves,
59 1/2 x 57 x 16 In.

Shelf, Corner, Hanging, Pine, Poplar, Hickory Twig Design, Door, Shelf, 17 x 31 In. 275.00
Shelf, Display, Softwood, Scalloped, Vertical Shelves, 59 1/2 x 57 x 16 In. . . . . *Illus* 2200.00
Shelf, Eames, 4 Open Tiers, Drawers, Herman Miller, 58 x 47 x 17 In. 10575.00
Shelf, Eames, ESU 200, Wood, Metal, 6 Shelves, Herman Miller, 1952, 16 x 32 In. 4315.00
Shelf, G. Nakashima, Walnut, Free-Edge, 2 Drawers, c.1978, 109 x 23 In. 22325.00
Shelf, Grain Painted, 3 Shelves, Vase & Ring-Turned Posts, Cutout Ends, 39 x 48 x 12 In. 3175.00
Shelf, Hanging, 5 Graduated Shelves, D-Form Ends, Comb Painted, 61 x 31 1/2 x 10 In. . 1528.00
Shelf, Hanging, Cutout, Bracket, Round, Bentwood Gallery, Red Over Brown, 17 1/2 In. . 360.00
Shelf, Hanging, Giltwood, Carved, Trumpet, Tassel, Fruit, Bracket, c.1900, 13 In., Pair . . . 3200.00
Shelf, Hanging, Grain Painted, Scalloped Supports, 45 x 25 x 5 1/2 In. 605.00
Shelf, Hanging, Louis XV Style, Gilt, Carved, Scrolling Motif, Bracket, 15 In. 1435.00
Shelf, Hanging, Louis XV Style, Demilune Form, Bracket, 16 3/4 x 15 In., Pair 490.00
Shelf, Hanging, Louis XVI Style, Mahogany, Bracket, France, c.1900, 28 x 13 In. 635.00
Shelf, Hanging, Mahogany, Canted Ends, Serpentine Corners, 48 x 42 3/4 In. 880.00
Shelf, Hanging, Mahogany, Scrolled Crest, Beaded Edges, 23 x 10 x 37 In. 990.00
Shelf, Hanging, Masonic, Walnut, Compass, Hourglass, J.H. Bellamy, 20 x 11 In. 1008.00
Shelf, Hanging, Neoclassical, Giltwood, Mirror, c.1890, 36 In., Pair 805.00
Shelf, Hanging, Oak, Carved Owl Supports, c.1890, 15 x 41 x 12 In. 2350.00
Shelf, Hanging, Painted, Scrolled Crest, 4 Shelves, 4 Drawers, Early 1900s, 28 x 21 In. . . 480.00
Shelf, Hanging, Pine, Red Wash, Dovetailed, 2 Drawers, 32 x 10 x 27 1/2 In. 385.00
Shelf, Hanging, Regency, Mahogany, Scrolling Crest, 3 Shelves, 27 x 45 x 10 In. 545.00
Shelf, Hanging, Rococo Revival, Walnut, Corner, Marble Top, Bracket, Pair 323.00
Shelf, Hanging, Rococo Style, Gilt, Bracket, Demilune, Pierced Leaves, 21 x 20 In., Pair . 2644.00
Shelf, Hanging, Walnut, 4 Graduated & Turned Supports, 30 x 10 x 37 3/4 In. 550.00
Shelf, Hanging, Walnut, 4 Shelves, Scrolled, Pierced Sides, c.1780, 33 x 19 1/2 In. 2030.00
Shelf, Hanging, Walnut, Carved Deer Head, Black Paint, Victorian 190.00
Shelf, Hanging, Walnut, Dovetailed Corners, Scalloped Sides, 4 Shelves, 25 x 23 x 6 In. . . 495.00
Shelf, Hanging, Walnut, Fir, Rooster Heads At Top, England 2750.00
Shelf, Hanging, Walnut, Shaped Crest, Pa., 19th Century, 32 x 21 1/2 x 8 In. 380.00
Shelf, Hanging, Wood, Carved, Leaf & Scroll, Bracket, 1900s, 15 1/4 In., Pair 510.00
Shelf, Hanging, Yellow Paint, American, Early 19th Century, 10 x 24 x 8 In. 2030.00
Shelf, James Mont, 3 Tiers, Upswept Top, Black Lacquer, 21 x 36 x 13 In. 825.00
Shelf, Linden, Oak, Stained, Bowfront, Eagle, Germany, c.1885, 40 x 22 1/2 In. 750.00
Shelf, Louis XV Style, Oak, Scalloped Frieze, Rosettes, Cabriole Legs, 48 x 58 In. 1035.00
Shelf, Magazine, Limbert, Oak, c.1905, 36 5/8 x 19 1/2 x 13 3/4 In. 600.00
Shelf, Majorelle, Fruitwood, Marquetry, Carved Flowers, c.1904, 23 x 38 x 7 In. 8960.00
Shelf, McCobb, Lacquered Birch, Masonite, Zinc, Sliding Door, 60 x 74 In. 2185.00
Shelf, Michael Coffey, White Oak, Mozambique, 4 x 36 x 12 In. 705.00
Shelf, Oak, Grape Cluster, Leaf Support, England, c.1890, 13 x 12 x 7 In., Pair 1725.00
Shelf, Pine, Pewter, 5 Shelves, Blue Paint, Late 19th Century, 69 1/2 x 40 1/2 x 7 In. 450.00
Shelf, Pine, Poplar, Cutout Ends, Leaf, Fleur-De-Lis, 17 x 9 x 16 1/2 In. 105.00
Shelf, Victorian, Walnut, Spool Turned Supports, 5 Shelves, Pierced Back, 42 In. 85.00
Shelf, Walnut, Tiger Head Carving, Late 19th Century, 11 x 11 1/2 In. 230.00
Shelf, Wrought Iron, Openwork, 4 Tiers, Glass Shelves, 63 x 14 x 14 In. 175.00
Shrine, Gold, Red, Brown, Black Lacquer, Shishi, Dragons, Flowers, Japan, 86 In. 1116.00
Shrine, Kshitagarba, Black, Gold Lacquer, Inlaid Eyes, Japan, 18th Century, 27 In. 2940.00
Sideboard, 2 Drawers, Door, Chinese, 19th Century, 34 x 50 x 39 1/2 In. 1265.00
Sideboard, Art Deco, Burl, Rosewood, Drawers, Sections, 38 1/2 x 86 In. 1410.00
Sideboard, Art Deco, Oak, Silver Gilt, Bowfront, 2 Doors, Glass Top, France, 39 x 78 In. 520.00
Sideboard, Art Deco, Rosewood, Marble Top, 2 Drawers, 2 Doors, 36 In. 230.00
Sideboard, Arts & Crafts, Beveled Mirror, 4 Drawers, 2 Doors, 55 1/2 x 61 1/2 In. 1150.00
Sideboard, Arts & Crafts, Mirror Backsplash, 3 Drawers, 3 Doors, 58 x 50 In. 690.00
Sideboard, Arts & Crafts, Mirror Backsplash, 4 Drawers, 2 Doors, 58 x 54 x 22 In. 230.00
Sideboard, Audoux Minet, Ash, 3 Raffia Panels, France, 36 3/10 x 78 3/4 In. 1080.00
Sideboard, C. Rohlfs, Mahogany, 7 Drawers, 2 Doors, 41 1/4 x 68 3/4 In. 5175.00
Sideboard, E. Wormley, Bleached Mahogany, Brass, 2 Doors, 1940s, 70 x 28 In. 2990.00
Sideboard, Eastlake, Marble Top, Beveled Curio Cabinets, Carved Crest, 85 In. 2070.00
Sideboard, Eastlake, Walnut, Marble Top, Relief-Carved Crest, Mirror Back, 79 x 47 In. . 750.00
Sideboard, Elizabethan Style, Oak, Carved, 19th Century, 90 x 98 x 22 In. 4830.00
Sideboard, Empire, Mahogany, 3 Drawers, 4 Doors, Claw Feet, 65 1/2 x 23 x 44 In. 790.00
Sideboard, Empire, Mahogany, 3 Drawers, 4 Paneled Doors, Paw Feet, 50 x 66 In. 1180.00
Sideboard, Empire, Mahogany, Doors, Shelves, c.1820, 47 x 61 x 22 In. 705.00
Sideboard, Federal, Carved, Inlaid Ivory Escutcheons, Paw Feet, c.1830 . . . . 2250.00

Sideboard, Federal, Cherry Inlay, Crossbanded, 3 Drawers, 38 3/8 x 71 x 23 1/2 In. 7640.00
Sideboard, Federal, Mahogany, Convex Doors, Shelf, c.1810, 42 x 73 1/2 x 24 In. 2300.00
Sideboard, Federal, Mahogany, Maple Inlay, Serpentine, c.1805, 39 x 72 x 29 In. 7475.00
Sideboard, Federal, Satinwood, Mahogany Inlay, Serpentine, c.1800, 37 x 66 x 30 In. 4830.00
Sideboard, Federal, Walnut, Tulipwood & Mahogany Inlay, c.1800, 65 3/4 x 23 In. 19120.00
Sideboard, G. Nelson, Thin Edge, Rosewood Veneer, Herman Miller, 80 x 18 x 32 In. 4025.00
Sideboard, G. Stickley, No. 814 1/2, 4 Drawers, 2 Doors, 56 x 22 x 48 In. 5175.00
Sideboard, G. Stickley, No. 816, Oak, Copper Pulls, Plate Rail, 45 x 48 x 18 In. 2350.00
Sideboard, G. Stickley, Plate Rail, Arched Top, 2 Doors, Copper Hinges, 48 x 56 x 22 In. .. 4025.00
Sideboard, G. Stickley, Plate Rail, Paneled Back, 4 Drawers, Shelves, 50 x 70 x 25 1/2 In. . 6900.00
Sideboard, George II, Mahogany, Drawers, Door, Inlaid Panels, 36 x 59 x 23 In. 4830.00
Sideboard, George III Style, Mahogany, Marquetry, 19th Century, 34 x 60 x 24 In. 2990.00
Sideboard, George III Style, Mahogany, Serpentine, Tapered Legs, 36 x 54 x 22 In. 1495.00
Sideboard, George III Style, Mahogany, Shaped Top, Banded, c.1890, 35 x 52 1/2 In. 2070.00
Sideboard, George III Style, Yew, Inlaid Oval Panels, 4 Doors, 2 Drawers, 72 In. 1060.00
Sideboard, George III, Mahogany, Bowfront, Drawers, Door, 36 x 53 1/2 x 24 In. 1645.00
Sideboard, George III, Mahogany, Inlaid Flowers & Leaves, Serpentine Top, 72 In. 2115.00
Sideboard, George III, Mahogany, Inlaid, Bowfront, Banding, Spade Feet, 35 In. 6325.00
Sideboard, George III, Mahogany, Inlaid, Bowfront, Leaves, Beasts, 35 x 60 x 25 In. 4115.00
Sideboard, George III, Mahogany, Satinwood, Bowfront, 5 Drawers, 38 x 50 In. 6465.00
Sideboard, George IV, Carved, Beaded, Bowfront, Tapered Sides, c.1835, 37 x 52 In. 1380.00
Sideboard, Georgian Style, Mahogany, Inlaid, Serpentine, c.1900, 36 x 66 x 21 In. 2875.00
Sideboard, Hepplewhite Style, Mahogany, Banded, England, c.1900, 36 x 59 1/2 In. 2070.00
Sideboard, Hepplewhite Style, Mahogany, Inlaid, Serpentine Front, 39 x 62 x 23 In. 1440.00
Sideboard, Hepplewhite, Mahogany, 3 Sections, Serpentine Center, 57 x 88 In. 825.00
Sideboard, Hepplewhite, Mahogany, Inlaid, Demilune, 3 Drawers, 4 Doors, 41 x 72 In. 4485.00
Sideboard, Hepplewhite, Mahogany, Satinwood Inlay, Bowfront, Spade Feet, 38 In. 1760.00
Sideboard, Koloman Moser, Mahogany, 2 Sections, 1901, 73 x 47 x 26 In. 5975.00
Sideboard, L. & J.G. Stickley, 5 Drawers, 2 Doors, 48 x 66 x 22 In. 3220.00
Sideboard, L. & J.G. Stickley, Mirror Back, 2 Doors, 4 Drawers, 62 x 54 x 24 In. 5175.00
Sideboard, L. & J.G. Stickley, Mirror Back, Column Supports, 72 x 25 x 61 In. 10350.00
Sideboard, Limbert, No. 457 3/4, Mirrored Back, Cabinet, Base, 45 x 19 x 50 In. 2990.00
Sideboard, Limbert, Oak, 2 Doors, 2 Shelves, c.1905, 56 5/8 x 60 x 19 1/4 In. 4185.00
Sideboard, Louis XVI Style, Marble Top, Gilt Bronze, 35 1/2 x 50 x 20 In. 1315.00
Sideboard, Mahogany, 3 Drawers, 4 Paneled Doors, c.1835, 58 x 78 1/2 x 25 In. 1725.00
Sideboard, Mahogany, Bowed Center, Squared Ends, Splayed Feet, 35 x 66 In. 805.00
Sideboard, Mahogany, Carved, Winged-Griffin Supports, Columns, Claw Feet, 76 In. 2800.00
Sideboard, Mahogany, Curved Front, String Inlay, Lion's-Head Pulls, 19th Century 1760.00
Sideboard, Mahogany, Ebonized, Backsplash, 2 Pedestals, c.1810, 45 x 28 x 94 In. 1240.00
Sideboard, Mahogany, Serpentine Front, 4 Drawers Over Drawer, 4 Doors, 36 x 57 In. 575.00
Sideboard, Mahogany, Serpentine Front, Reeded Edge, c.1940, 37 x 66 x 23 In. 1035.00
Sideboard, Neoclassical, Mahogany, Paneled, c.1820, 48 1/2 x 66 x 21 1/4 In. 1840.00
Sideboard, Oak, Black Lacquer, Bronze Banding, c.1940, 35 1/2 x 82 2/3 In. 9600.00
Sideboard, Oak, Carved Lions, Columns, Crest, Mirror Back, 93 x 72 In. 3640.00
Sideboard, Oak, Carved, Marble Top, Continental, 19th Century, 42 x 59 x 19 In. 880.00
Sideboard, Oak, Copper, Brass, Mirror Back, 2 Drawers, c.1900, 82 x 48 x 22 In. 1175.00
Sideboard, Oak, Griffin-Carved Panels, 83 x 72 In. .... *Illus* 3850.00
Sideboard, Oak, Marble Top, Backsplash, 2 Drawers, 2 Paneled Doors, 43 x 32 In. 460.00
Sideboard, Regency, Mahogany, 4 Drawers, 2 Pedestals, Plinth, 37 x 72 x 23 In. 2185.00
Sideboard, Regency, Mahogany, Backsplash, 2 Doors, c.1830, 37 x 78 x 26 In. 2300.00
Sideboard, Regency, Mahogany, Inlay, Cellaret Drawers, c.1815, 37 x 93 x 30 In. 19120.00
Sideboard, Regency, Mahogany, String Inlay, 7 Drawers, 2 Sliding Doors, 40 x 89 In. 3290.00
Sideboard, Renaissance Revival, Mahogany, Burl Maple, c.1885, 56 x 67 x 24 In. 1265.00
Sideboard, Rustic, Yellow Birch, Pine, Doors, Drawers, Old Forge, N.Y., c.1910, 86 In. .. 13500.00
Sideboard, Sheraton Style, Burl Walnut, Marquetry, 36 1/2 x 75 x 22 In. 1175.00
Sideboard, Sheraton, Cherry, Bird's-Eye Maple, Mahogany, 45 1/2 x 21 x 47 In. 3025.00
Sideboard, Sheraton, Flame-Grain Cherry Veneer, Inlaid, 78 1/2 x 23 1/2 x 44 In. 2200.00
Sideboard, Sheraton, Mahogany, Bowfront, Inlaid, 6 Drawers, 2 Doors, 46 x 71 In. 3395.00
Sideboard, Sheraton, Mahogany, Satinwood Inlay, Biscuit Corners, 70 1/2 In. 8475.00
Sideboard, Sheraton, Walnut, Cutout Scrolls, Beaded Drawers, 1800s, 43 x 68 x 21 In. ... 5250.00
Sideboard, Shop Of The Crafters, Mirror Backsplash, 4 Drawers, 2 Doors, 58 x 54 In. ... 4890.00
Sideboard, Stickley & Brandt Co., 3 Drawers, 2 Doors, Copper Pulls, 53 x 56 In. 2875.00
Sideboard, Stickley Bros., 3 Drawers, 2 Doors, Paneled Plate Rail, 46 x 50 x 22 In. 2415.00

Furniture, Sideboard,
Oak, Griffin-Carved
Panels, 83 x 72 In.

Furniture, Sofa, Rococo Revival, Rosewood,
Laminated, Pierced, 49 1/2 x 76 x 34 In.

Sideboard, Stickley Bros., Mirror Backsplash, 4 Drawers, 2 Doors, 48 x 54 x 21 In. 2300.00
Sideboard, Stickley Bros., No. 8216, 4 Drawers, 2 Doors, 44 1/4 x 54 1/4 x 21 In. 2410.00
Sideboard, Stickley Bros., No. 8604, 4 Drawers, 2 Doors, Gallery, 70 x 64 In. 4315.00
Sideboard, Stickley Bros., No. 8833, 4 Drawers, 3 Doors, Plate Rail, 45 x 56 x 22 In. . . . 4025.00
Sideboard, Victorian, Walnut, Marble Top, Arched Backsplash, Mirror, 91 In. 1495.00
Sideboard, Walnut, Carved Atlas Supports, c.1870, 102 x 73 x 26 In. 8400.00
Sideboard, Walnut, Carved Front Drawers, Brass Bail Handles, 46 x 56 x 16 1/2 In. 345.00
Sideboard, Walnut, Carved, Lion's-Head Drawer Front, 38 x 68 1/2 x 19 In. 750.00
Sideboard, Walnut, Drawers, Doors, Tin Safe, Leaf Scroll, Mid 1800s, 53 x 18 x 47 In. . . . 1000.00
Sideboard, Walnut, Parquetry, Marble Top, Continental, 20th Century, 34 x 83 x 23 In. . . . 560.00
Sideboard, William IV Style, Mahogany, Cutlery Drawer, Pedestals, 39 x 70 x 28 In. 980.00
Sideboard, William IV, Mahogany, Carved Crest, Flowers, c.1835, 68 x 75 1/2 In. 6615.00
Silver Chest, Georgian Style, 4 Drawers, Cabriole Legs, 42 x 21 x 31 1/2 In. 920.00
Silver Chest, Oak, 2 Drawers, Lift Top, Shreve Crump & Low, c.1906, 19 x 24 x 19 In. . . 600.00
Sofa, Alexander Girard, Herman Miller, 1965-1967, 26 x 82 x 21 In. 6325.00
Sofa, Alexander Lawrence, Mahogany, New Brunswick, Canada 500.00
Sofa, Arne Jacobsen, Upholstered, Tubular Chrome, Fritz Hansen, 28 x 50 x 30 In. 1295.00
Sofa, Art Deco, Silver Gilt, White Linen, Down Cushions, 84 In. 200.00
Sofa, Belter, Rosewood, Laminated, Rosalie Pattern, 84 In. 6350.00
Sofa, Belter, Rosewood, Tuthill King Pattern, 47 1/4 x 77 x 33 In. 63000.00
Sofa, Biedermeier, Mahogany, Scroll Arms, Shell Pediment, c.1830, 42 x 73 1/2 In. 1150.00
Sofa, Biedermeier, Walnut, Padded Seat & Back, Scrolled Arms, 36 x 80 x 26 1/2 In. 2300.00
Sofa, Camelback, Chippendale Style, Mahogany, 6 Cabriole Legs, 77 x 37 In. 1495.00
Sofa, Camelback, George II, Mahogany, Carved Acanthus, 1800s, 38 x 21 x 82 In. 850.00
Sofa, Camelback, Georgian Style, Needlepoint, Claw & Ball Feet, 78 In. 4780.00
Sofa, Camelback, Victorian, Walnut, Serpentine Front, Upholstered, 39 x 93 x 30 In. 230.00
Sofa, Chippendale, Yellow Brocade, 6 Straight Legs, Marlborough Feet, 72 In. 956.00
Sofa, Contemporary, Button Tufted, 2 Silk Cushions, 73 1/2 In. 1075.00
Sofa, Contemporary, Green Velvet, 3 Cushions, 103 In. 8960.00
Sofa, Distressed Leather, 3-Cushion Seat, Overstuffed, 33 x 87 In. 200.00
Sofa, E. Sottsass Jr., Eastside, Dark Gray, Light Gray, Red, Knoll, 33 x 86 x 28 In. 3230.00
Sofa, E. Wormley, Mahogany, Wool, Cushions, 96 x 28 In. 3450.00
Sofa, E. Wormley, No. 4907B, Wool Over Wood Frame, 1950s, 97 x 29 In. 3740.00
Sofa, E. Wormley, Oasis, Rosewood, Upholstered, Dunbar, c.1952, 10 x 36 x 31 In. 2990.00
Sofa, E. Wormley, Tufted Seat, 4 Cushions, Dunbar, 89 x 33 x 27 1/2 In. 545.00
Sofa, Eames, Chrome, Wool, Foam, Herman Miller, 1950s, 72 x 29 In. 10925.00
Sofa, Eames, Compact, Girard Fabric, Herman Miller 2185.00
Sofa, Eames, Compact, Slab Seat, Girard Fabric, Herman Miller, 72 x 30 x 36 In. 2990.00
Sofa, Eames, No. 3473, Green, Herman Miller, c.1964, 31 1/2 x 60 x 20 In. 1760.00
Sofa, Eames, Steel & Chrome, Wool Checkered Pads, 34 x 72 In. 3740.00
Sofa, Empire Revival, Mahogany, Carved Phoenix Pediment, Scrolling Arms, 46 x 89 In. . . 1150.00
Sofa, Empire Revival, Mahogany, Rolled Back & Arms, Carved, Paw Feet, 35 x 87 In. 1380.00
Sofa, Federal, Mahogany, Red, 3-Panel Back, Scrolled Arms, 88 In. 1265.00
Sofa, Flame Mahogany, C-Scrolls, Dolphins, Leaf, Rose, Leaf & Paw Feet, c.1830 . . . . . . 3300.00
Sofa, Florence Knoll, Gold Orange, c.1952, 29 1/2 x 48 x 28 In. 825.00
Sofa, Florence Knoll, Tubular Chrome, Upholstered, 72 x 27 x 29 In. 805.00
Sofa, French Provincial, Walnut, Cock-Beaded, Serpentine Back, Padded Arms, 73 In. . . . 365.00

Sofa, G. Nelson, Girard Fabric, Herman Miller, 94 x 31 x 27 In. 2185.00
Sofa, G. Nelson, Sling, Chrome, Black Leather, Herman Miller, 29 x 87 x 36 In. 2705.00
Sofa, G. Nelson, Sling, Chromed Steel, Leather, Herman Miller, 31 x 87 In. 2415.00
Sofa, George III Style, Walnut, Upholstered, 20th Century, 36 x 80 In. 690.00
Sofa, Georgian Style, Satinwood, Floral & Figural, Cane Back, Casters, 71 In. 3680.00
Sofa, Italian Rococo Style, Walnut, Early 20th Century, 36 x 89 In. 1150.00
Sofa, Jansen, Louis XVI Style, White Paint, Cut Velvet, 20th Century, 31 x 67 In. 9560.00
Sofa, Louis XV Style, Beech, Carved, Undulating Crest, Upholstered, 55 In. 4185.00
Sofa, Louis XV Style, Beech, Flowers, Leaves, Upholstered, c.1910, 36 x 70 In. 1980.00
Sofa, Louis XV Style, Walnut, Parcel Gilt, c.1900, 39 x 50 In. 520.00
Sofa, Louis XVI Style, Fruitwood, Padded Back, Carved Crest, 36 x 54 1/2 x 25 In. 750.00
Sofa, Louis XVI Style, Gold Detail, Carved, Upholstered, 20th Century, 18 x 44 In. 2750.00
Sofa, Louis XVI Style, Mahogany, Rectangular Back, Arms, Fluted Legs, 77 In. 950.00
Sofa, Mahogany, Acanthus-Carved Crest, Front Rail, Paw Feet, c.1830, 90 In. 2990.00
Sofa, Mahogany, Leather, Button-Tufted, Serpentine Back, Cabriole Legs, Casters 580.00
Sofa, Mahogany, Pierced & Carved Triple Back, c.1890, 48 x 59 x 32 In. 2070.00
Sofa, Mahogany, Upholstered, Stripes, Scroll Arm, New York, c.1835, 37 1/2 x 86 In. 1610.00
Sofa, Meeks, Rococo, Rosewood, Laminated, Stanton Hall Pattern, c.1850, 65 In. 5750.00
Sofa, Meridienne, Neoclassical, Mahogany, Ormolu, c.1810, 33 x 72 x 27 In. 4780.00
Sofa, Metal Frame, Tubular, Enamel Finish, Jacquard Woven, 27 x 68 x 33 In. 590.00
Sofa, Napoleon III, Floral Spray, Yellow Damask Upholstery, c.1865, 42 x 70 In. 1380.00
Sofa, Neoclassical, Mahogany, Brass Mounted, Damask Upholstery, 34 x 81 In. 865.00
Sofa, Neoclassical, Overall Floral Inlay, Relief Floral, Swan Shape, 90 In. 1210.00
Sofa, Queen Anne, Upholstered, Urns, Doves, Flowers, 8 Legs, 40 x 66 In. 1955.00
Sofa, Renaissance Revival, Mahogany, Scroll Arms, Claw Feet, c.1875, 34 x 85 In. 575.00
Sofa, Robsjohn-Gibbings, 3 Sections, Upholstered, Widdicomb 1725.00
Sofa, Rococo Revival, Rosewood, Laminated, Pierced, 49 1/2 x 76 x 34 In. .... *Illus* 7763.00
Sofa, Rococo Revival, Walnut, Leaves In High Relief, Velvet, Tufted, 70 In. 355.00
Sofa, Rococo Revival, Walnut, Serpentine Back, Velvet, c.1865, 40 1/2 x 80 In. 805.00
Sofa, Rococo, Double Corseted Back, Ebonized Carved Cartouches & Roses, 47 In. 1485.00
Sofa, Rosewood, Open Carved Medallion Back, Velvet, Cabriole Legs, 45 x 72 In. 3585.00
Sofa, Samuel Marx, Dorothy Liebes Fabric, Trundle Bed, Quigley, 1948, 85 x 32 In. 3740.00
Sofa, Studio 65, Marilyn, Upholstered Foam, Red, Gufram, Italy, 1972, 82 x 33 In. 3220.00
Sofa, Tobia Scarpa, Bastiano, Rosewood Frame, Wool, Knoll, 83 x 30 In. 825.00
Sofa, V. Kagan Style, Upholstered, Brocade, Foam Cushions, 32 x 82 x 30 In. 470.00
Sofa, Van Keppel & Green, Orange, Brown Saltman, c.1956, 28 x 90 x 34 3/4 In. 1765.00
Sofa, Victorian, Carved Walnut, Medallion Back, Upholstered, 38 x 58 x 16 In. 345.00
Sofa, Victorian, Walnut, 3-Arch Back, Serpentine Apron, Upholstered, 76 In. 505.00
Sofa, Victorian, Walnut, Serpentine Frame, Rose, Scroll Crest, Upholstered, 73 In. 675.00
Stand, Adirondack, Twig Heart Decoration, 3 Legs, 13 x 11 x 11 In. 60.00
Stand, Arne Jacobsen, Wenge Wood, Steel, Laminated, 1957, 19 1/2 x 6 In. 3450.00
Stand, Art Deco, Chrome Base, Ebonized Wood Surface, 30 1/4 x 12 1/2 In. 235.00
Stand, Art Deco, Chrome, High Gloss Lacquer, France, c.1925, 16 x 14 x 23 In., Pair ... 1840.00
Stand, Arts & Crafts, Daffodils, Hammered Copper Pulls, 35 x 16 1/2 x 15 In. 920.00
Stand, Arts & Crafts, Paneled Door, Shelf, Arched Apron, 28 x 13 x 15 1/2 In. 575.00
Stand, Arts & Crafts, Square Top, Lower Shelf, Arched Cabinet Door, 10 x 10 x 28 In. 545.00
Stand, Birch, Bird's-Eye Maple Veneer, Biscuit Corners, Drawer, Turned Legs, 27 In. 1375.00
Stand, Birch, Bird's-Eye Maple, Drawer, Tapered Legs, Mortised, Early 1800s, 25 In. 1095.00
Stand, Birch, Drawer, Tapered Legs, Chamfered Top, Brass Pull, 29 x 35 1/2 x 24 In. 1045.00
Stand, Black Marble Top, Angel Figural Legs, Stretcher, 17 x 25 1/2 x 19 1/2 In. 750.00
Stand, Bronze, Marble Top, Lion's-Head Capitals, 3 Legs, Paw Feet, 43 x 16 In. 860.00
Stand, Cherry, Batwing Joined, Inlaid Medallions, Drawer, 1790s 750.00
Stand, Cherry, Bird's-Eye Maple, 2 Drawers, Ring & Spiral Legs, Mid 19th Century 600.00
Stand, Cherry, Brass Drawer Pulls, Bamboo-Turned Legs, c.1820, 27 x 18 x 18 3/4 In. ... 660.00
Stand, Cherry, Bulbous, Ball-Turned Shaft, Cabriole Legs, New England, 17 x 27 In. 340.00
Stand, Cherry, Curly Maple, Red Paint, Dovetailed Drawer, 17 x 17 x 30 In. 770.00
Stand, Cherry, Mahogany Veneer, 2 Drawers, Turned Legs, 25 1/2 x 19 x 29 1/2 In. 1100.00
Stand, Cherry, Tiger Maple Veneer, 2 Drawers, Glass Pulls, 28 x 18 x 18 In. 550.00
Stand, Cherry, Tiger Maple, Bowfront, 2 Drawers, Sandwich Glass Pulls, Turned Legs ... 690.00
Stand, Chippendale Style, Mahogany Veneer, 2 Drawers, 19 3/4 x 13 x 27 1/2 In. 165.00
Stand, Chippendale, Pine, Poplar, Painted, Splayed Legs, 24 x 18 x 30 In. 660.00
Stand, Drink, Stickley Bros., Square Inset Top, Rounded Slats, 24 1/2 x 15 In. 1380.00

Stand, E. Wormley, Walnut, Round Composition Top, Tripod Base, 1957, 15 x 15 In. 980.00
Stand, Eastlake, Softwood, Oval, White Marble Top, Carved Apron 140.00
Stand, Eastlake, Walnut, Marble Top, Incised Apron, 4 Carved Legs, Center Support 365.00
Stand, Eastlake, Walnut, Red Marble Top, Caster Feet, 29 x 26 x 18 In. 230.00
Stand, Edwardian, Mahogany, Brass, 2 Tiers Over Panel Door, Casters, 48 x 19 In. 1150.00
Stand, Edwardian, Mahogany, Tambour Front, c.1900, 31 x 19 In., Pair 2185.00
Stand, Egyptian Style, Ebonized Wood, Square, Lower Shelf, c.1870, 27 x 16 In. 2250.00
Stand, Elm, Beaded Apron, Lower Shelf, Chinese, c.1880, 32 In. 530.00
Stand, Empire, Mahogany, Carved, Drop Leaf, Paw Feet, 16 3/4 x 16 1/2 x 32 1/2 In. . . .   605.00
Stand, English, Pine, Drawer, Backsplash, Turned Legs, 19th Century, 36 x 39 x 18 In. . .   300.00
Stand, Federal, Birch, Red Paint, Scratch-Beaded Edge, Drawer, 27 x 18 1/2 x 17 In. 2115.00
Stand, Federal, Mahogany, Inlaid, c.1810, 29 1/4 x 16 1/2 x 16 1/4 In. 575.00
Stand, Federal, Maple, Red Paint, Overhang Top, c.1800, 25 1/2 x 18 1/2 x 17 1/2 In. . . .   1645.00
Stand, Federal, Painted, Serpentine Top, Mount Vernon, Washington's Tomb 6900.00
Stand, Federal, Satinwood, Inlaid, Mahogany, 2 Drawers, 28 x 18 1/4 x 16 In. 3450.00
Stand, Fern, Hardwood, Ebonized, Rouge Marble Insert, Chinese, 16 x 12 x 32 In. 200.00
Stand, Fern, Mahogany, Reeded Columns, Claw Feet, 72 In., Pair 935.00
Stand, Figural, Bathing Beauty, Painted, 35 1/2 In. 240.00
Stand, Figural, Bellboy, Painted, 1920s, 40 1/2 In. 1350.00
Stand, Figural, Ibis, Cherry, Carved, Ebonized, Trefoil Base, 29 In. 2875.00
Stand, Fruitwood, Oak, Flower Inlay, Drawer, Dovetailed, France, 26 x 9 x 13 In. 405.00
Stand, G. Nelson, Drawer, Hairpin Leg, Herman Miller, 18 x 18 1/2 x 24 In., Pair 2185.00
Stand, G. Nelson, Primavera, Wood, Ebonized, Drawer, Door, Herman Miller, 18 x 24 In.   575.00
Stand, G. Stickley, 2 Drawers, Backsplash, Wooden Pulls, 30 1/4 x 20 x 18 In. 2185.00
Stand, George III, Mahogany, Leather Inset, Doors, Drawer, 32 x 22 x 19 In. 4480.00
Stand, George III, Satinwood, Painted, Late 18th Century, 29 1/2 x 18 x 15 In., Pair 23900.00
Stand, Grain Painted, Mustard Yellow, Drawer, Shaped Apron, c.1820, 34 x 31 x 17 In. . .   460.00
Stand, Green Onyx, Bronze, Ormolu, Gadrooned, France, 19th Century, 31 x 20 In. 2415.00
Stand, Hardwood, Inset Marble Top, Chinese, 10 1/2 x 16 1/2 In., Pair 960.00
Stand, Hepplewhite Style, Black Walnut, Poplar, 13 x 13 x 22 In., Pair 550.00
Stand, Hepplewhite, Cherry, Butternut Inlay, Drawer, Brass Pulls, 23 x 17 1/2 x 29 In. . . .   360.00
Stand, Hepplewhite, Cherry, Pine Top, Drawer, Square Tapered Legs, American 345.00
Stand, Hepplewhite, Cherry, Poplar, Pine, Dovetailed Drawer, 22 x 18 x 29 1/4 In. 415.00
Stand, Hepplewhite, Cherry, Tiger Maple, Drawer, American, 28 1/2 x 15 1/4 In. 575.00
Stand, Hepplewhite, Curly Maple, 2 Dovetailed Drawers, 28 x 16 In., Pair 1210.00
Stand, Hepplewhite, Oval, Urn Post, Spider Legs, 27 1/2 In. 375.00
Stand, Hepplewhite, Pine, Demilune, Salmon, Red, c.1800 . . . .   10000.00
Stand, Hepplewhite, Poplar, Walnut, Red Paint, Drawer, Incised Beading, 29 x 22 In. 660.00
Stand, Hepplewhite, Tiger Maple, Drawer, Splayed Legs, 28 x 19 x 19 3/4 In. 400.00
Stand, Herter Bros., Walnut, Floral Inlay, Marble Top, c.1885, 32 x 18 x 18 In. 6720.00
Stand, Hispano-Moresque, Tile Top, Wooden Curved-Leg Base, 20 x 14 In. 115.00
Stand, Jules Leleu, Rosewood, Gilt Bronze, 2 Shelves, c.1930, 37 x 20 x 15 3/4 In. 5736.00
Stand, Kingwood, Gilt Bronze, Veneered Top, 1890, 8 1/2 x 29 In. 1700.00
Stand, L. & J.G. Stickley, No. 583, Round, 39 x 39 In. 1955.00
Stand, Louis Philippe, Mahogany, Marble Top, 29 x 16 3/4 x 14 In., Pair 2070.00
Stand, Louis XV, Marble Top, Mottled Gray, Cane Stretcher Base, 30 x 18 x 13 In. 520.00
Stand, Luggage, Trevor Page & Co., Oak, c.1865, 18 x 17 In. 345.00
Stand, Magazine Tree, E. Wormley, Birch & Walnut, 24 x 28 x 16 In. . . . . *Illus*   3740.00
Stand, Magazine, Arts & Crafts, Poppy Design, 4 Shelves, Leather, 44 x 20 x 10 In. 805.00
Stand, Magazine, Byrdcliffe, Carved Hollyhock, 2 Shelves, 1904, 36 x 14 In. 14900.00
Stand, Magazine, Byrdcliffe, Cherry, 2 Shelves, White Lilies, 1904, 30 x 13 In. 13800.00
Stand, Magazine, Ford & Johnson, Cut-Corner Top, 3 Shelves, 17 x 13 x 41 In. 635.00
Stand, Magazine, G. Stickley, 3 Open Shelves, Rectangular Top, 22 x 13 x 42 In. 3220.00
Stand, Magazine, G. Stickley, 4 Shelves, Arched Toe Board, 14 x 10 x 40 In. 1955.00
Stand, Magazine, G. Stickley, 4 Shelves, Paneled Sides, 35 1/4 x 15 x 14 In. 2415.00
Stand, Magazine, G. Stickley, 4 Shelves, Square Beveled Top, 15 x 15 x 44 In. 6325.00
Stand, Magazine, G. Stickley, 4 Shelves, Tree Of Life, Carved Sides, 43 1/2 x 14 In. 1610.00
Stand, Magazine, G. Stickley, 5 Shelves, Wide Side Slats, 30 x 12 x 47 In. 2645.00
Stand, Magazine, Iron, Divided, Lower Shelf, Square Cutouts, Austria, 37 x 12 In. 345.00
Stand, Magazine, J. Adnet, Leather Over Steel, Brass, 1950, 30 x 23 In. 2760.00
Stand, Magazine, L. & J.G. Stickley, 42 x 21 x 12 In. 1840.00
Stand, Magazine, Lifetime, 4 Shelves, Slatted Sides, 40 x 15 x 12 In. 920.00

Furniture, Stand, Magazine Tree,
E. Wormley, Birch & Walnut,
24 x 28 x 16 In.

Don't store dining table leaves on end. They may warp. Flat under the bed is an ideal storage method.

Stand, Magazine, Limbert, 3 Shelves, Wide Side Slats, 28 x 11 x 28 In. 1035.00
Stand, Magazine, Michigan Chair Co., 3 Graduated Compartments, 38 x 14 In. 750.00
Stand, Magazine, Michigan Chair Co., Mahogany, 4 Shelves, Slats, 33 x 16 1/2 In. 1035.00
Stand, Magazine, Stickley Bros., 3 Shelves, Vertical Slats, 19 x 12 x 32 In. 1095.00
Stand, Magazine, Stickley Bros., 4 Shelves, Slats, 36 x 19 x 15 In. 1955.00
Stand, Magazine, Victorian, Walnut, Shaped Top, Scrolled, Pierced Dividers, Drawer 255.00
Stand, Mahogany, 3 Tiers, Posts, Ball Finials, Turned Legs, Casters, 20 x 18 x 30 In. 330.00
Stand, Mahogany, 3/4 Gallery, Door, Victorian, 32 x 13 In. 470.00
Stand, Mahogany, Marble Top, Drawer Over Shelf, Raised Panel Door, 30 x 16 In. 230.00
Stand, Mahogany, Mottled Slate, Marble Top, Drawer, 2 Doors, 31 x 16 x 13 In. 460.00
Stand, Mahogany, Pine, Cedar, String Inlay, Drawer, 29 x 22 x 17 In. 1980.00
Stand, Mahogany, Tiger Maple, Drawer, Pedestal, 3 Scrolled Spider Legs 170.00
Stand, Marble Top, Bronze Mounts, Columns, 18 x 16 x 29 In. 1265.00
Stand, Marquetry, Gilt Brass, Round, Tripod, 20th Century, 16 x 31 In. 220.00
Stand, McCobb, Walnut, Lacquered Drop Front, Brass Legs, 22 In., Pair 1840.00
Stand, Mixed Wood, Red Paint, 2-Board Top, Drawer, 28 1/2 x 22 1/2 x 26 3/4 In. 360.00
Stand, Music, Mahogany, Spoon Carved, Burl Panels, Inlaid Music Symbols, 32 In. 290.00
Stand, Music, Regency, Rosewood, Grain Painted, Double, c.1815, 47 In. 865.00
Stand, Music, William IV, Rosewood, Cast Iron, Gilt Bronze, Paw Feet, 47 x 14 In. 405.00
Stand, Neoclassical, Fruitwood, Drawer Over Door, Square Legs, Italy, 31 In., Pair 4700.00
Stand, Neoclassical, Mahogany Veneer, Leather Insert, 30 x 18 1/2 In. 575.00
Stand, Neoclassical, Onyx, Gilt, Scroll, Leaf, Finial, 17 3/4 x 12 x 27 In. 290.00
Stand, P. Evans, Directional, Cityscape, Chrome Squares, 20 x 20 x 20 In., Pair 1150.00
Stand, Painted, Stretcher Supports, Splayed Legs, 27 x 15 x 12 In. 300.00
Stand, Parcel Gilt, Lacquer, Chinese, 19th Century, 32 x 15 3/4 In., Pair 5380.00
Stand, Pine, Yellow, Octagonal Top, Drawer, 3 Shaped Legs, 31 x 19 1/2 x 19 In. 495.00
Stand, Plant, Bentwood, Mahogany, Circular, Fence, Lower Tier, Arches, 1905, 32 In. ... 395.00
Stand, Plant, Black Lacquer, Ormolu Decoration, 19 1/2 x 14 1/2 x 30 In. 275.00
Stand, Plant, Cherry, Round Basket, Vertical Slats, Triangular Platform, 24 In. 100.00
Stand, Plant, Elm, Carved, Arches, Square, Side Rails, England, 17 1/2 x 14 x 14 In. 175.00
Stand, Plant, G. Stickley, No. 660, Cut Corner Top, 18 x 18 x 20 In. ....1265.00 to 1380.00
Stand, Plant, G. Stickley, Square Top, Arched Apron, Stretcher, 25 1/2 x 14 In. 2070.00
Stand, Plant, G. Stickley, Square Top, Cloud-Lift Apron, Tenon, Key, 27 x 14 In. 3450.00
Stand, Plant, George III, Mahogany, Oak, Square Top, Lotus Carved, 58 In., Pair 1265.00
Stand, Plant, Hunzinger, Spiral Turned, Carved Apron, c.1885, 36 x 20 x 16 In. 895.00
Stand, Plant, L. & J.G. Stickley, No. 25, 22 x 13 1/2 x 13 1/2 In. 1265.00
Stand, Plant, Lakeside Craftshop, Mahogany, Slats, Tapered, 13 x 24 In. 405.00
Stand, Plant, Limbert, Square Top, Quarter-Round Corbels, Oval Cutouts, 29 x 20 In. ... 6900.00
Stand, Plant, Mahogany, Round Top, Spiral-Twist Column, 4 Ball Feet, 37 x 14 In. 260.00
Stand, Plant, Mahogany, Standing Male Figure, Loincloth, 37 In. 900.00
Stand, Plant, Poplar, Dark Finish, Quatrefoil Shelves, Spool Turned, 35 In. 110.00
Stand, Plant, Round Top, Cutout, Flared, Plank Legs, Shelf, 27 x 14 In. 550.00
Stand, Plant, Roycroft, Tapered Posts, Panel Sides, Cross Mark, 28 x 13 1/2 In. 2875.00
Stand, Plant, Sheraton, Mahogany, Carved Acanthus Leaves, High Tripod Base, 40 In. ... 165.00
Stand, Plant, Stickley Bros., Square Top, Pedestal Base, Feet, 34 x 13 In. 1955.00
Stand, Plant, Victorian, Bamboo, Pottery, Landscape Panels, 34 x 26 x 10 In. 1295.00
Stand, Plant, Victorian, Oak Top, Round, Wicker Legs, 32 x 16 In. 115.00
Stand, Plant, Walnut, Carved Flowers, Round, 3 Legs, Cincinnati Art, 29 x 12 In. 1725.00
Stand, Plant, Wire, Scrolled, Curved, 3 Tiers, 42 In. 175.00

Stand, Queen Anne Style, Tiger Maple, Drawer, Round Legs, 27 x 16 x 29 1/4 In. 300.00
Stand, Red Paint, Round Splayed Legs, Pa., 18th Century, 28 x 14 1/2 In. 7700.00
Stand, Red Wash, Overhanging Top, 2 Drawers, Tapered Legs, 28 x 22 In. 630.00
Stand, Regency, Mahogany, Line & Banded Inlay, Long Drawer, Spade Legs, 28 In. 1460.00
Stand, Renaissance Revival, Onyx, Brass, Square, 2 Tiers, Leaf-Carved Legs, 31 x 14 In. . 295.00
Stand, Renaissance Revival, Walnut, Marble Top, Canted Corners, Oval Door, 31 In. 1495.00
Stand, Renaissance Revival, Walnut, White Marble Top, c.1865, 28 x 21 In. 1380.00
Stand, Rosewood, Carved, Marble Top, Claw & Ball Feet, Chinese, 26 x 19 In. 635.00
Stand, Rosewood, Rouge Marble Top, Pierced Apron, Chinese, 18 x 14 In. 290.00
Stand, Roycroft, Little Journey, Signed, 26 x 26 x 14 In. .690.00 to 805.00
Stand, Shaving, Mahogany, Bowfront, 2 Drawers, Reeded Columns, 21 In. 230.00
Stand, Shaving, Mahogany, Revolving Mirror, 5 Drawers, Turned Feet, c.1820 . . . . 315.00
Stand, Shaving, Mahogany, Swing Mirror, Acorn Finials, 3 Drawers, 19 x 19 In. 240.00
Stand, Sheraton Style, Mahogany, Inlaid, 2 Drawers, 29 1/2 x 16 1/2 In. 805.00
Stand, Sheraton, Birch, Bird's-Eye Maple Drawer, Mouse-Ear Corners 2200.00
Stand, Sheraton, Black, Brown Paint, Drawer, American, 31 x 24 In. 175.00
Stand, Sheraton, Cherry, Curly Maple Band On Drawer, 29 x 17 x 17 In. 250.00
Stand, Sheraton, Cherry, Curly Maple, Drawer, Ring Turned Legs, 16 x 17 x 30 In. 770.00
Stand, Sheraton, Cherry, Figured Mahogany Veneer, 2 Drawers, 16 x 23 x 29 In. 880.00
Stand, Sheraton, Cherry, Poplar, 2 Dovetailed Drawers, Ball Feet, 21 x 20 x 29 In. 440.00
Stand, Sheraton, Cherry, Poplar, 2 Drawers, Ring Turned Legs, 19 x 17 x 29 In. 740.00
Stand, Sheraton, Cherry, Poplar, Inlaid Bands, 2 Drawers, Turned Legs, 28 x 20 In. 440.00
Stand, Sheraton, Cherry, Tiger Maple, 2 Drawers, 19th Century, 29 x 17 1/2 x 19 In. 700.00
Stand, Sheraton, Cherry, Walnut, Bird's-Eye Maple, Drawer, 20 x 17 x 28 In. 495.00
Stand, Sheraton, Curly Maple Veneer, 2 Drawers, Beaded Edges, 29 x 24 x 17 In. 2090.00
Stand, Sheraton, Mahogany, 2 Drawers, 4 Turned & Reeded Legs, 29 x 29 In. 520.00
Stand, Sheraton, Mahogany, 2 Drawers, Sandwich Glass Knobs, Turned Legs 365.00
Stand, Sheraton, Mahogany, Veneer, 2 Drawers, c.1820, 29 1/2 x 17 1/2 x 15 3/4 In. 920.00
Stand, Sheraton, Painted, Red Brown, Drawer, 29 x 18 x 18 In. 315.00
Stand, Sheraton, Poplar, Grain Painted, Drawer, c.1840, 29 x 19 In. 680.00
Stand, Sheraton, Scalloped Top, 2 Drawers, Replaced Brass Knobs, 28 In. 1540.00
Stand, Sheraton, Walnut, Dovetailed Drawer, 19th Century, 29 x 21 x 22 In. 550.00
Stand, Sheraton, Walnut, Dovetailed Drawer, Late 19th Century, 29 x 18 x 23 In. 400.00
Stand, Sheraton, Walnut, Pegged, 1-Board Top, Turned Legs, 24 x 21 x 30 In. 330.00
Stand, Smoking, Arts & Crafts, Iron, Hammered Copper Tray, Snake Feet, 33 1/2 In. 470.00
Stand, Smoking, Carved Wood, Woman, Classical Pose, Plinth, Bronze Insert, 29 In. 375.00
Stand, Smoking, Drawer, Open Shelf, Cabinet Door, Ashtray Inset, 26 x 12 x 10 In. 315.00
Stand, Smoking, Walnut, Carved, Turned Base & Horns, 48 In. 1000.00
Stand, Softwood, 2-Board Top, Dovetailed Drawer, 29 1/2 x 32 x 23 3/4 In. 525.00
Stand, Softwood, Octagonal, Painted Flags, Horses, 22 x 28 In. 450.00
Stand, Softwood, Overhanging Top, Beaded Drawer, Splayed Legs, 31 x 24 In. 730.00
Stand, Telephone, Arts & Crafts, Drawer, Shelf, Stool, 30 x 18 x 14 In. 230.00
Stand, Telephone, Limbert, Oak, Shelf, Chair, 1906, 30-In. Table, 28-In. Chair 765.00
Stand, Telephone, Teak, Black Formica Top, 2 Slide Trays, Drawers, 1958, 22 x 29 In. . . . 510.00
Stand, Tiger Maple, 3 Drawers, Floral Stenciling, Rebecca C. Small, 1820 . . . . 3105.00
Stand, Tommi Parzinger, Ivory Enamel, Drop Front, Brass Pulls, 20 x 20 x 16 In., Pair . . . 4405.00
Stand, V. Kagan, Cherry, Whalebone Legs, 22 x 28 x 16 In., Pair 3820.00
Stand, Victorian, Walnut, Oval, Marble Top, Urn Finial, Scrolled Legs, 40 x 30 In. 1690.00
Stand, Victorian, Walnut, Round Top, Scrolling Tripod Base, 30 x 19 In. 530.00
Stand, Walnut Veneer, Figured, Red Marble Top, Demilune, 2 Drawers, 30 In. 495.00
Stand, Walnut, 2 Drawers, Tapered Legs, Continental, 30 x 26 In. 1840.00
Stand, Walnut, 2-Board Top, Drawer, Turned Legs, N.C., 28 x 30 x 20 In. 495.00
Stand, Walnut, Drawer, Sections, Tapered Legs, Tennessee, 28 x 29 1/2 x 18 1/2 In. 880.00
Stand, Walnut, Marble Top, Ormolu, Early 20th Century, 20 3/4 x 14 3/4 x 28 1/2 In. 330.00
Stand, Walnut, Scalloped, Chamfered-Lip Drawer, 19th Century, 29 x 17 1/2 x 28 In. 1500.00
Stand, Wood, Carved, Painted, Parrot, Urn Base, 11 3/4 In. 900.00
Stand, Yellow Pine, Drawer, Chamfered Lips, 3-Board Top, 30 x 32 1/2 x 25 1/2 In. 715.00
Stand, Yellow Pine, Poplar, 2 Drawers, Turned Legs, N.C., 28 1/2 x 25 1/2 x 20 In. 495.00
Stool, Arne Jacobsen, Teak, Chrome, Stacking, Fritz Hansen, 18 x 13 In., 4 Piece 2820.00
Stool, Arts & Crafts, Black Oilcloth, Slab Sides, Keyed Tenon, 15 x 14 x 16 In. 220.00
Stool, Arts & Crafts, Leather, Webbed Seat, Cutouts, 17 1/2 x 16 In. 315.00
Stool, Arts & Crafts, Rocker, Slab Sides, Cutout Base, Upholstered, 16 x 13 x 17 In. 489.00
Stool, Arts & Crafts, Rush Seat, Cross Stretcher, Through Tenon, 1900s, 16 x 15 In. 200.00

Stool, Bone, Mother-Of-Pearl, Mosaic, Octagonal, Morocco, 17 1/2 x 16 In., Pair 520.00
Stool, C. Perriand, Ebonized Wood, France, 1960s, 13 x 18 In., Pair 7475.00
Stool, Chippendale, Mahogany, Upholstered, Arched Crest, c.1780, 38 In., Pair 8365.00
Stool, Eames, Time Life, Walnut, Herman Miller, c.1960, 15 x 13 In. . . . . .1295.00 to 1725.00
Stool, Eero Aarnio, Wicker, Bamboo Frame, Round, Corset Waist, 14 x 21 In. 865.00
Stool, Empire Style, Mahogany, Parcel Gilt, 17 1/2 x 17 1/2 x 14 In., Pair 880.00
Stool, English Oak, Cane Top, Shaped Stretchers, Block Legs, 16 x 24 x 17 In. 520.00
Stool, Federal, Mahogany, Dolphin Seat, Swivels, Claw Feet, 24 x 15 In. 1455.00
Stool, Frank Gehry, Wiggle, Laminated Cardboard, Masonite, 1972, 16 x 15 In. 5465.00
Stool, G. Nakashima, Triangular Top, 3 Dowel Legs, c.1970, 12 x 20 x 15 In. 1530.00
Stool, G. Nelson, Metal, Upholstered, Herman Miller, 1948, 20 x 20 In. 1035.00
Stool, G. Stickley, No. 395, Leather Seat, 7 Side Spindles, 20 x 16 x 16 In. 4315.00
Stool, George II Style, Mahogany, Carved, Cabriole Legs, 19th Century, Pair 17925.00
Stool, George II Style, Mahogany, Padded Top, c.1850, 18 x 19 1/2 x 14 In. . . . . *Illus* 690.00
Stool, George II, Mahogany, Padded Seat, Cabriole Legs, c.1750, 18 x 28 x 21 In. 3335.00
Stool, George III Style, Mahogany, Carved Frieze, Padded, Cabriole Legs, 19 x 22 In. . . . 200.00
Stool, George III Style, Mahogany, Green Leather, 6 Legs, c.1890, 19 x 41 1/2 In. 920.00
Stool, George III, Mahogany, Leather, Square Legs, 18th Century, 21 x 58 x 29 In. 1840.00
Stool, George III, Mahogany, Padded Seat, Cabriole Legs, 1800s, 20 x 25 x 19 In. 1095.00
Stool, George III, Mahogany, Padded Seat, Square Legs, c.1815, 18 1/2 x 41 1/2 In. 865.00
Stool, J. Adnet, Leather Seat, Brass Legs, Hermes, 1950s, 18 x 15 In. 1725.00
Stool, Jacobean Style, Oak, Plank Seat, Stretchers, Turned Legs, 20 x 13 In. 150.00
Stool, Jacobean, Oak, Chip-Carved Frieze, Stretchers, Turned Legs, 20 x 16 In. 1530.00
Stool, Jacobean, Oak, Rectangular, Stretchers, Turned Legs, 24 x 18 In. 1295.00
Stool, Louis XV Style, Giltwood, Padded Top, 1850-1875, 21 x 21 In. . . . . *Illus* 1840.00
Stool, Louis XV Style, Walnut, Carved, Padded, Cabriole Legs, 16 x 26 x 24 In. 635.00
Stool, Louis XVI Style, Carved Wood, Gilt, Velvet, Fluted Legs 2115.00
Stool, Mahogany, Leather, Padded Top, Cabriole Legs, 1875-1900, 21 x 16 In. . . . . . *Illus* 805.00
Stool, Mahogany, Scalloped Skirt, Splayed Legs, 3 1/4 x 7 In., Pair 105.00
Stool, Maple, Pine, Pegged, Stretcher Base, Turned Feet, 16 x 14 x 16 1/2 In. 1760.00
Stool, Maple, Round Chamfered Seat, 3 Turned & Splayed Legs, 10 In. 920.00
Stool, Maple, Round Concave Top, Turned Legs, Whitewater Village, Ohio, 16 1/2 In. . . . 290.00
Stool, Marcel Breuer, Square, Thonet, c.1926, 19 x 17 1/2 x 14 1/2 In. 1060.00
Stool, Napoleon III, Faux Bamboo, Ebonized, Late 19th Century, 19 x 19 In. 1380.00
Stool, Napoleon III, Giltwood, Padded, Square Legs, 1800s, 17 x 15 x 15 In., Pair 5060.00
Stool, Napoleon III, Mahogany, Padded, Cabriole Legs, c.1865, 18 x 18 In., Pair 1495.00
Stool, Nutting, No. 102, Windsor, Oval . . . . .360.00 to 415.00
Stool, Nutting, No. 164, 3 Legs 660.00
Stool, Nutting, No. 165, Maple 825.00
Stool, Old Hickory, Indiana, Late 1800s 55.00
Stool, P. Evans, Directional, Lucite, 15 1/2 x 13 x 9 In. 380.00
Stool, Perriand, Oak, Round Seat, 3 Dowel Legs, 1960, 18 x 14 In. 920.00
Stool, Piano, Louis Philippe, Mahogany, Vase Splat, Swivels, 19 1/4 x 14 In. 575.00
Stool, Piano, Mahogany, Laminated, Pierced Back, 7 Spindles, 37 x 17 In. 2245.00
Stool, Piano, Mahogany, Rotating Shell-Form Seat, 3 Cabriole Legs, Italy, 23 In. 690.00

Furniture, Stool, George II Style,
Mahogany, Padded Top,
c.1850, 18 x 19 1/2 x 14 In.

Furniture, Stool, Louis XV
Style, Giltwood, Padded Top,
1850-1875, 21 x 21 In.

Furniture, Stool, Mahogany,
Leather, Padded Top, Cabriole
Legs, 1875-1900, 21 x 16 In.

Furniture, Stool, Regency,
Mahogany, Carved,
Flower Upholstered,
c.1825-1850, 19 x 15 In.

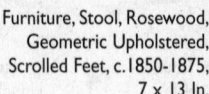

Furniture, Stool, Rosewood,
Geometric Upholstered,
Scrolled Feet, c.1850-1875,
7 x 13 In.

Stool, Piano, Mahogany, Upholstered, Hinged Top, Cabriole Legs, 22 x 21 In. 260.00
Stool, Piano, Napoleon III, Ebonized, Round, Adjustable, c.1865, 19 1/2 In. 230.00
Stool, Piano, Napoleon III, Giltwood, Padded Top, 19 1/2 x 18 x 18 In. 315.00
Stool, Piano, Regency Style, Mahogany, Upholstered, 4 Reeded Legs, 18 1/2 x 15 In. 230.00
Stool, Piano, Victorian, Bronze, Lady's-Boot Legs, c.1865, 20 x 15 In. 2300.00
Stool, Piano, Victorian, Walnut, Folding, Rosette Handles, 1871, 20 x 16 x 16 In. 400.00
Stool, Piano, Walnut, Carved, Upholstered, France, 19th Century, 22 1/2 In. 470.00
Stool, Piano, Walnut, Glass Ball & Talon Feet, 1920s 230.00
Stool, Plattner, Wool, Chrome, Wire, Knoll, 17 x 20 In., Pair 1035.00
Stool, Queen Anne Style, Mahogany, Padded Needlework, 19 x 18 x 14 1/2 In. 750.00
Stool, Queen Anne Style, Mahogany, Padded Top, Cabriole Legs, 18 x 19 x 13 In. 400.00
Stool, Queen Anne Style, Mahogany, Padded Top, Carved Legs, 17 x 23 x 16 In. 520.00
Stool, Queen Anne Style, Walnut, Carved, Oval, Needlepoint Seat, c.1900 . . . .   375.00
Stool, Queen Anne Style, Walnut, Round, Upholstered, England, c.1900, 18 x 50 In. 1840.00
Stool, Queen Anne, Maple, Stretchers, Splayed Legs, Turned Feet, 15 x 9 x 18 In. 1650.00
Stool, Queen Anne, Shell-Carved Knees, Oval, Drop-In Seat, 19 x 21 x 15 In. 575.00
Stool, Queen Anne, Walnut, Drop-In Seat, c.1715, 18 1/2 x 22 x 17 In., Pair 16730.00
Stool, Queen Anne, Walnut, Padded Seat, Cabriole Legs, 17 x 21 1/4 x 17 In. 1725.00
Stool, Regency Style, Mahogany, Zebra Skin, 23 x 42 x 26 In. 1955.00
Stool, Regency Style, Parcel Gilt, Polychrome, Padded Top, c.1900, 20 x 20 In., Pair 2185.00
Stool, Regency Style, Polychrome, Padded, Curule Form, c.1900, 18 x 17 1/2 In. 489.00
Stool, Regency, Mahogany, Carved, Flower Upholstered, c.1825-1850, 19 x 15 In. . . *Illus*   489.00
Stool, Regency, Mahogany, Parcel Gilt, Brass Mounted, c.1810, 17 x 21 1/4 In. 4780.00
Stool, Regency, Rosewood, Green Leather Top, Stretcher, Curule Feet, 16 x 22 In. 1150.00
Stool, Regency, Rosewood, Padded Top, Curule Base, 18 x 20 x 18 1/2 In. 1035.00
Stool, Rosewood, Geometric Upholstered, Scrolled Feet, c.1850-1875, 7 x 13 In. . . . *Illus*   460.00
Stool, Rosewood, Serpentine Top, Scalloped Skirt, c.1840, 20 x 14 1/2 x 14 1/2 In. 259.00
Stool, Rosewood, Square, Upholstered, Carved Pedestal, c.1825, 21 x 11 x 11 In. 315.00
Stool, Saarinen, Swivels, Knoll, c.1956, 16 x 14 1/2 In. 1000.00
Stool, Saarinen, Vinyl, Pedestal Base, Knoll, 16 x 15 In., 3 Piece 1060.00
Stool, Shaker, Maple, Brown Stain, Splint Seat, Sabbathday Lake, Me., c.1850, 30 In. 490.00
Stool, Shaker, Maple, Worn Paint, Mt. Lebanon, N.Y., 10 In. 430.00
Stool, Shaker, No. 5, Cloth Cover, Mt. Lebanon, 7 x 12 In. 150.00
Stool, Softwood, Mortised Leg, Hand-Hold Cutout, 15 x 22 1/2 x 13 1/2 In. 550.00
Stool, Softwood, Skirt Drawer, Arched Cutouts, Mortised Leg, 19 x 14 x 10 1/4 In. 605.00
Stool, Softwood, Yellow Trim, Cutout Legs, 19th Century, 7 1/4 x 14 1/2 x 8 In. 165.00
Stool, Sori Yanagi, Butterfly, Rosewood, Brass, Japan, 1956, 15 In. 1380.00
Stool, V. Panton, Cone, Leather, Metal Base, Gebruder Nehl, c.1967, 18 1/2 In. 4025.00
Stool, V. Panton, Cone, Steel, Upholstered, Cruciform Leg, 1960, 19 x 20 In. 1380.00
Stool, V. Panton, Pantonova, F. Hansen, c.1971, 15 x 20 1/2 x 20 3/4 In., Pair 705.00
Stool, Vanity, Samuel Marx, Lacquered Wood, Upholstered, Quigley, 1948, 17 x 18 In. . . .   2300.00
Stool, Vanity, William & Mary, Walnut, Upholstered Seat, Stretcher Base, 16 x 17 In. 120.00
Stool, Victorian, Mahogany, Leather Top, Cabriole Legs, 21 1/2 x 21 1/2 x 16 In. 805.00
Stool, Victorian, Mahogany, Leopard Print, c.1865, 18 x 36 In.   2185.00
Stool, Victorian, Mahogany, Needlework, Circular Top, Fabric Support, 18 1/2 x 16 In. . .   635.00
Stool, Victorian, Walnut, Needlework Upholstery, c.1875 . . . .   956.00
Stool, W. Constantine & Co., Round, Upholstered, Ogee Feet, Leeds, 5 x 14 In. . . . . *Illus*   75.00
Stool, Walnut, Shell-Carved Seat, Cabriole Legs, Continental, 24 In. 1495.00

Furniture, Stool, W. Constantine & Co., Round,
Upholstered, Ogee Feet, Leeds, 5 x 14 In.

Furniture, Stool, William IV, Mahogany,
Upholstered, Concave Body, 21 x 29 x 24 In.

Stool, Warren McArthur, White Leather, 1937, 30 In., Pair . . . . .1410.00 to 1750.00
Stool, Warren McArthur, White Seat, c.1937, 21 1/2 x 11 1/2 In., Pair 1410.00
Stool, Whale Vertebrae, 3 Carved Tapered Legs, 19th Century, 24 In. 4780.00
Stool, William & Mary, Walnut, Needlepoint Upholstered, 18 x 18 x 18 In. 835.00
Stool, William IV, Mahogany, Linen, Square, c.1835, 8 x 13 In., Pair 430.00
Stool, William IV, Mahogany, Padded, Zebra Skin, Carved Legs, 23 x 42 In. 2770.00
Stool, William IV, Mahogany, Upholstered, Concave Body, 21 x 29 x 24 In. . . . . . . *Illus* 2530.00
Stool, Windsor, Circular Top, Tapered Legs, New England, c.1810, 18 In., Pair 1295.00
Stool, Windsor, Red Paint, Bamboo-Turned Tripod Legs, 16 In. 880.00
Stool, Wood, Red Stain, 3 Sides, Panels, 2 Drawers On End, Oriental Writing, 10 In. 140.00
Table, Aalto, Birch Frame, Glass Top, Artek, 27 1/2 x 18 In. . . . . .69.00 to 127.00
Table, Aalto, Birch, Molded Legs, Artek, 20 1/2 x 26 x 16 1/2 In. 235.00
Table, Aalto, Square Top, Fan Leg, Artek, 35 3/4 In. 645.00
Table, Aalto, Square, Birch Top, Molded Legs, Artek, 24 1/4 x 24 x 24 In. 440.00
Table, Adirondack, Square Oak Top, Twig & Bark Legs, Stretcher, c.1900, 30 x 30 In. . . . 230.00
Table, Altar, Dragon Apron, Square Legs, Chinese, 19th Century, 31 1/2 x 85 In. 1380.00
Table, Altar, Elm, Beaded Apron, Scroll Panel, Square Legs, Chinese, 31 1/2 x 31 3/4 In. . . 575.00
Table, Altar, Elm, Carved, Stained, Bat-Wing Legs, Chinese, c.1885 . . . . 430.00
Table, Altar, Polychrome, Brown Lacquer, Chinese, 31 x 47 x 21 In. 2990.00
Table, Altar, Red Lacquer, 5 Drawers, Hoof Feet, Chinese, 35 x 81 x 26 In. 865.00
Table, Altar, Reeded Legs, Cloud Legs, Chinese, 33 1/2 x 80 x 21 In. 1150.00
Table, Altar, Softwood, Dragon, Hoof Feet, Chinese, 34 1/2 x 51 In. 920.00
Table, Altar, Walnut, 2 Drawers, Beaded Apron, Cabriole Legs, Chinese, 44 x 89 In. 920.00
Table, Andre Arbus, Round Top, Oak, Square Legs, c.1945, 28 3/8 x 27 1/2 In. 7050.00
Table, Art Deco, Amboyna, Marble, Round Top, Columnar Brass Legs, 23 1/2 x 25 In. . . . 1060.00
Table, Art Deco, Beech, Stained, Round Top, Scrolling Flat Legs, France, 19 x 23 1/2 In. . . 500.00
Table, Art Deco, Blond Wood, Cabriole Legs, 19 x 19 1/2 x 20 In., Pair 470.00
Table, Art Deco, Burl, Rectangular Mirrored Top, Scrolling Base, 20 x 39 x 21 In. 1530.00
Table, Art Deco, Ebony, Circular, Spider Legs, France, c.1930, 21 x 28 In. 3680.00
Table, Art Deco, Elm, Mahogany, France, c.1930, 25 1/2 x 32 In. 2760.00
Table, Art Deco, Faux Ivory, Bone Mount, France, c.1930, 29 x 31 1/2 In. 2760.00
Table, Art Deco, Formica Top, Chrome Supports, Circular Base, 27 1/4 x 22 In. 150.00
Table, Art Deco, Fruitwood, Octagonal Top, Bone Geometric Insets, 24 x 20 In. 470.00
Table, Art Deco, Fruitwood, Round Top, Scrolling Stretcher, 20 x 35 In. 940.00
Table, Art Deco, Jules Leleu, Rosewood, Silver, Round, Low Shelf, c.1925, 17 x 31 In. . . 7170.00
Table, Art Deco, Mahogany, Amboyana, France, c.1930, 26 1/2 x 27 3/4 In. 2990.00
Table, Art Deco, Mahogany, Mirror Top, Rectangular, Scroll Legs, 22 x 36 x 20 In. 590.00
Table, Art Deco, Mahogany, Round Mirrored Top, Peach, Round Shelf, 26 x 27 1/2 In. . . . 355.00
Table, Art Deco, Marble, Wrought Iron, Rectangular, Frieze, 29 1/2 x 45 x 27 1/2 In. 3945.00
Table, Art Deco, Marble, Wrought Iron, Stepped Shape, 25 x 19 x 9 In. 780.00
Table, Art Deco, Palissandre, Round Top, Metal Inlay, Flared Legs, 21 x 31 In. 2000.00
Table, Art Deco, Walnut Veneer, Inset Red Glass Top, Chevroned Struts, 26 x 18 In., Pair . 1060.00
Table, Art Nouveau, Floral Marquetry, Shelf Stretcher, England, 28 x 21 1/2 x 22 In. 2645.00
Table, Arts & Crafts, Rectangular, Pierced Skirt, Tapered Legs, England, 28 x 27 x 17 In. . 590.00
Table, Arts & Crafts, Walnut, Square, Cutout Skirt, Shelf Stretcher, 27 x 22 x 22 In. 590.00
Table, B. Mathsson, Birch, Bird's-Eye Maple Veneer, Round, Tapered Legs, 17 x 25 In. . . 520.00
Table, Bagues Style, Gilt Metal, Acrylic, Inset Top, Acanthus Frame, 21 x 40 x 20 In. 3585.00
Table, Bamboo, Sea Grass, Rectangular Top & Shelf, Circular Legs, 28 x 22 In. 145.00

Table, Bamboo, Square Top, Decoupage Fish & Leaves, Canted Corners, 19 x 18 In. 315.00
Table, Baroque Style, 3 Baluster-Form Supports, Blue Paint, 28 x 123 x 36 In. 3110.00
Table, Baroque Style, Leaf-Carved Frieze, Twist Legs, Continental, 33 x 43 x 17 In. 660.00
Table, Baroque Style, Pine, Stained, Parcel Gilt, Italy, c.1885, 13 1/4 x 11 In. 175.00
Table, Baroque Style, Walnut, Marble Top, Turned Pedestals, Pad Feet, 31 x 69 x 31 In. ... 690.00
Table, Baroque Style, White Stone, Oval Top, Putti Legs, Italy, 32 x 53 In. 1955.00
Table, Belter, Marble Turtle Top, Pierced, 29 x 41 3/4 x 29 In. 48300.00
Table, Biedermeier Style, Mahogany, Burl, 20th Century, 25 x 17 x 12 In., Pair 3825.00
Table, Biedermeier Style, Mahogany, Oval Top, Frieze, Stretchers, 28 x 13 x 9 In. 475.00
Table, Biedermeier, Maple, Inlaid Panel Top, Frieze Drawer, Angular Legs, 30 x 21 In. ... 1060.00
Table, Biedermeier, Maple, Round, Dolphin Standard, Paw Feet, 29 x 24 In., Pair 5875.00
Table, Biedermeier, Walnut, 4 Drawers, Block Feet, 19th Century, 30 1/4 x 20 1/4 In. 3680.00
Table, Black Lacquer, D-Form, Wrap-Around Stretchers, Chinese, 34 x 37 In. 805.00
Table, Black Lacquer, Gilt Figural Scenes, Chinese, 28 x 25 1/2 x 17 1/2 In. 805.00
Table, Black Lacquer, Ormolu, Gilding, Cabriole Legs, Shelf, Paw Feet, 34 x 16 x 38 In. . 525.00
Table, Black Paint, Boulle Insert, Ormolu, Gilding, 41 x 27 x 30 In. 3410.00
Table, Bone Inlay, North Africa, 22 1/2 x 17 1/2 In., Pair 490.00
Table, Bugatti, Inlaid Wood, Brass Accents, 16 1/2 In. 2875.00
Table, Burl Walnut, Marble Top, Round, 20th Century, 27 In. 2350.00
Table, Burl, Band Inlay, Oval, Reeded-Edge Base, Casters, 28 1/2 x 59 x 43 In. 2875.00
Table, C. Perriand, White Oak, Beveled Edges, 1950s, 60 x 13 In. 6325.00
Table, Card, Biedermeier, Walnut, Parcel Gilt, Flip Top, Mid 1800s, 30 x 34 x 20 In. 3110.00
Table, Card, Birch, Frieze Drawer, Square Tapered Legs, 29 x 36 In. 940.00
Table, Card, Chippendale, Mahogany, Hinged Top, Cock-Beaded Drawer, 30 x 39 In. 2235.00
Table, Card, Chippendale, Mahogany, Serpentine Molded Top, c.1780, 33 1/2 In. 6800.00
Table, Card, Empire, Mahogany, Ribbed Apron, Turned Legs, Scrolled Feet, 32 In. 575.00
Table, Card, Empire, Mahogany, Scrolled Support, 30 3/4 x 33 x 16 1/4 In. 180.00
Table, Card, Empire, Mahogany, Serpentine, Hinged Top, c.1840, 28 x 33 x 17 In. 1095.00
Table, Card, Federal Style, Flip Top, Carved Pedestal 800.00
Table, Card, Federal, Inlaid Mahogany, Bowed Front, c.1790, 29 x 34 x 16 In. 10575.00
Table, Card, Federal, Inlaid Mahogany, Demilune, c.1790, 29 1/2 x 35 x 16 1/2 In. 880.00
Table, Card, Federal, Inlaid Mahogany, Flip Top, c.1810, 29 1/2 x 35 1/2 x 17 In. 1265.00
Table, Card, Federal, Mahogany, Banded Top, Carved Pedestal, 31 x 36 x 18 In. 1065.00
Table, Card, Federal, Mahogany, Figured Maple, Serpentine, c.1810, 28 x 35 x 18 In. 1380.00
Table, Card, Federal, Mahogany, Flame Birch Veneer, Bowed Front, 29 x 37 x 18 In. 19975.00
Table, Card, Federal, Mahogany, Inlaid, Elliptical Flip Top, c.1805, 30 x 36 x 17 1/2 In. .. 8815.00
Table, Card, Federal, Mahogany, Rosewood Banded Top, Claw Feet, 28 x 36 x 18 In. 1345.00
Table, Card, Federal, Mahogany, Satinwood, Flip Top, c.1800, 29 1/4 x 35 3/4 In. 1095.00
Table, Card, Federal, Mahogany, Satinwood, Inlaid Skirt, 1800, 29 3/4 x 36 In. 5580.00
Table, Card, Federal, Mahogany, Satinwood, Serpentine, c.1800, 28 3/4 x 36 x 17 In. 3450.00
Table, Card, Federal, Mahogany, Veneer, String Inlay, c.1790, 30 x 36 x 17 5/8 In. 4700.00
Table, Card, Federal, Satinwood, Inlaid Mahogany, Flip Top, c.1800, 29 x 36 x 17 In. 1095.00
Table, Card, George II, Walnut, Counter Wells, Ireland, c.1750, 29 x 41 1/2 In. 7170.00
Table, Card, George III, Inlaid Mahogany, Demilune Top, c.1815, 30 x 38 In. 1150.00
Table, Card, George III, Mahogany, Rectangular Top, c.1800, 29 x 32 x 16 In. 2300.00
Table, Card, George III, Mahogany, Serpentine Form, c.1770, 27 1/2 x 38 x 19 In. 16730.00
Table, Card, Hepplewhite, Figured Walnut, Inlaid Bands, Flip Top, Drawer, 29 x 35 In. 1760.00
Table, Card, Hepplewhite, Mahogany & Veneers, Inlaid Eagle, Square Legs, 29 x 35 In. ... 1035.00
Table, Card, Hepplewhite, Mahogany, Birch, Pine, Inlay, 35 x 17 1/2 x 29 In. 1760.00
Table, Card, Hepplewhite, Mahogany, Inlaid, Demilune, Centennial, 31 x 36 x 18 In. 920.00
Table, Card, Hepplewhite, Mahogany, Inlaid, Serpentine Front, 29 1/2 x 35 3/4 x 17 In. .. 405.00
Table, Card, Hepplewhite, Mahogany, Line Inlay, c.1800, 29 1/2 x 36 x 17 1/2 In. 1955.00
Table, Card, Hepplewhite, Mahogany, Satinwood Flame Veneer, 36 x 17 1/2 In. 5500.00
Table, Card, Hepplewhite, Mahogany, Urn & Checkered Inlay, Shaped Top, 32 x 36 In. 750.00
Table, Card, Hunzinger, Mahogany, Shelf, Rope-Twist Legs, c.1885, 36 x 18 x 29 In. 1175.00
Table, Card, Karl Springer, Chromed Metal, Faux Shagreen, 30 x 32 In. 3825.00
Table, Card, Lyre Base, Acanthus-Carved Knees, Claw Feet, 29 x 35 In. 1095.00
Table, Card, Mahogany, Acanthus-Carved Pedestal & Legs, Paw Feet, 30 x 37 In. 805.00
Table, Card, Mahogany, Barber-Pole Inlay On Apron, Square Tapered Legs, 29 x 36 In. ... 235.00
Table, Card, Mahogany, Brass Inlay, Continental, Late 1800s, 29 x 27 In. .... *Illus* 2070.00
Table, Card, Mahogany, Gilt Bronze, Signed P. Somani, 1880, 30 x 23 x 23 In. 9370.00
Table, Card, Mahogany, Hinged Top, Birch Panel, Square Tapered Legs, 29 x 36 x 17 In. . 2115.00
Table, Card, Mahogany, Rounded Corners, Reeded Legs, c.1800, 17 3/4 In. 1175.00

Table, Card, Mahogany, Rounded Corners, Tapered Legs, c.1810-1815, 18 In. 2940.00
Table, Card, Mahogany, Veneers, Ribbed Snake Legs, Brass Feet, Casters, 29 x 36 In. . . . 690.00
Table, Card, Neoclassical, Crossbanded Mahogany, Flip Top, c.1830, 29 x 36 x 18 In. . . . 635.00
Table, Card, Neoclassical, Mahogany, Ebonized, Lyre Base, New York, 29 x 36 In. 8050.00
Table, Card, Neoclassical, Mahogany, Veneer, Carved, Mass., c.1830, 29 x 36 x 17 In. . . . 1645.00
Table, Card, Neoclassical, Rosewood, Mirror Back, New York, 28 1/4 x 35 1/2 In. 8050.00
Table, Card, Regency Style, Mahogany, Flip Top, 29 1/2 x 36 x 18 In. 1115.00
Table, Card, Regency, Mahogany, Lift Top, Carved Frieze, 28 1/2 x 36 x 17 1/2 In. 1495.00
Table, Card, Rosewood, Flip Top, Fluted Pedestal Base, Ball Feet, 36 x 30 In. 690.00
Table, Card, Samuel Field McIntire, Sheraton, Mahogany, Mass., 30 x 37 x 17 In. 1800.00
Table, Card, Sheraton, Flame Birch Inlay, Contoured Corners, Tapered Legs 4125.00
Table, Card, Sheraton, Mahogany, Cookie-Corner Top, Bowed Front, 30 x 37 x 17 In. . . . 805.00
Table, Card, Sheraton, Mahogany, D-Shape Top, Twist-Carved Leg, 30 x 36 1/4 x 18 In. . . 345.00
Table, Card, Stephen Badlam, Hepplewhite, Inlaid Mahogany, Demilune, 29 x 37 x 18 In. 7400.00
Table, Card, Victorian, Elm, Shell-Carved Frieze, Pedestal, Scroll Legs, 29 x 36 In. 705.00
Table, Carl Aubock, Maple, Brass, Austria, 1950s, 32 x 17 In. 980.00
Table, Carved Wood, Polychromed Blackamoor, Pedestal, c.1915, 31 1/4 x 15 In. 635.00
Table, Center, Baltic, Mahogany, Marble Top, 4 Shaped Legs, Fluted Acorn, 30 x 28 In. . . 1380.00
Table, Center, Edwardian, Mahogany, Inlaid Top, Tapered Legs, Spade Feet, 29 x 37 In. . . 865.00
Table, Center, Edwardian, Satinwood, Marble, Floral Marquetry, Oval, 30 x 34 In. 1410.00
Table, Center, Kingwood, Giltwood, Marquetry, Drawer, 1860, 31 1/2 x 54 In. 6815.00
Table, Center, Kingwood, Marquetry, Gilt Bronze, 1890, 30 x 32 1/2 In. 4260.00
Table, Center, Leather Writing Surface, Germany, c.1815, 31 x 40 In. 1380.00
Table, Center, Louis XV, Mahogany, Marble Top, Turreted Corners, 31 x 33 x 19 In. . . . 13225.00
Table, Center, Louis XVI Style, Marble Top, Carved Giltwood, 32 x 56 In. 11075.00
Table, Center, Louis XVI Style, Marble, Triangular, Lion-Paw Base, 28 x 28 In. 530.00
Table, Center, Louis XVI, Mahogany, Marble Top, 29 1/2 x 43 1/2 In. 3450.00
Table, Center, Mahogany, Gray Marble Top, Reeded Vase Splat, 3 Legs, 29 1/2 x 37 In. . . 980.00
Table, Center, Marble Top, Trefoil Base, Paw Feet, France, c.1810, 40 In. 2910.40
Table, Center, Napoleon III, Kingwood, Oval, Floral, Gilt, Scroll Legs, 31 x 57 x 35 In. . . 4995.00
Table, Center, Regency, Mahogany, Pedestal, Plinth Base, Bun Feet, 29 x 44 In. 2185.00
Table, Center, Regency, Rosewood, Circular Top, Scrolled Feet, 30 x 50 1/2 In. 4140.00
Table, Center, Renaissance Revival, Floral & Scroll Carving, Column Legs, 42 x 32 In. . . 750.00
Table, Center, Renaissance Revival, Marquetry, Bronze, c.1865, 48 x 27 x 29 In. 6160.00
Table, Center, Renaissance Revival, Walnut, 3 Carved Caryatids, Trefoil Base, 31 In. 1380.00
Table, Center, Renaissance Revival, Walnut, Marble Top, c.1870, 38 x 29 x 30 In. 2800.00
Table, Center, Restauration, Mahogany, Marble Top, c.1815, 27 x 38 1/4 In. 2070.00
Table, Center, Rococo Revival, Mahogany, Tortoise Top, Flower Frieze, 28 x 39 x 27 In. . . 980.00
Table, Center, Rococo Revival, Rosewood, Marble Top, Cabriole Legs, 27 x 40 x 24 In. . . 1610.00
Table, Center, Rococo Revival, Rosewood, Tortoise Top, Cabriole Legs, 30 x 41 x 27 In. . 1955.00
Table, Center, Rococo Revival, Walnut, Marble Tortoise Top, c.1865, 29 x 46 In. 3220.00
Table, Center, Rococo, Gilt, Wood, Venus, Cupid, Porcelain, Scroll Feet, 32 x 20 In. 3525.00
Table, Center, Rope-Carved Top, Flower-Carved Pedestal, Claw-Carved Feet, 41 In. 1610.00
Table, Center, Victorian, Burl Walnut, Round, Elaborately Carved Base, 30 x 52 In. 2350.00
Table, Center, Victorian, Walnut, Etched Glass, Carved Apron, c.1885, 27 x 27 x 30 In. . . 1175.00
Table, Center, Walnut, Molded Oval Top, Turned Spindle, Scroll Legs, 28 x 32 x 24 In. . . 805.00
Table, Center, Walnut, Oval Top, Scroll Legs, Center Support, 28 x 32 x 23 In. 259.00
Table, Cherry, 5-Board, Turned Legs, Dovetailed Drawer, 42 x 33 x 29 In. 2035.00

Furniture,
Table, Card,
Mahogany,
Brass Inlay,
Continental,
Late 1800s,
29 x 27 In.

Try not to put wooden furniture in direct sunlight. It will fade.

Use a credit card to scrape hardened candle wax from a table.

Table, Cherry, Cock-Beaded Edges, Massachusetts, c.1800, 27 3/4 In. 6465.00
Table, Cherry, Poplar, Walnut, Pegged Joints, 2-Board Top, 84 x 34 x 24 In. 4070.00
Table, Cherry, Square, Tapered Supports, c.1800, 23 x 18 In. 690.00
Table, Chinese Chippendale, Mahogany, Pierced Fretwork Apron, 28 x 38 In. 330.00
Table, Coffee, A. Girard, Aluminum, Marble, Herman Miller, 1967, 38 x 16 In. 5750.00
Table, Coffee, A. Girard, Aluminum, Plastic, Laminated, Herman Miller, 1967, 38 x 16 In. 1300.00
Table, Coffee, Aalto, Birch, Molded Legs, Artek, 18 x 47 x 29 1/2 In. 470.00
Table, Coffee, Art Deco, Gilt Wrought Iron, Green Marble Top, 18 x 43 x 20 In. 2700.00
Table, Coffee, Art Deco, Rosewood, Plate Glass, France, c.1930, 20 3/4 x 55 In. 4140.00
Table, Coffee, Art Deco, Wrought Iron, Painted, Black Marble Top, 19 x 39 In. 1175.00
Table, Coffee, Cast Iron, Brass, Rectangular Glass Top, S-Curve Supports, 17 x 54 In. 200.00
Table, Coffee, Du Plantier, Glass, Steel, Silvered Bronze, c.1950, 15 x 47 1/2 In. 8810.00
Table, Coffee, E. Wormley, Cube Sandalwood Base, Round Glass Top, 42 x 15 1/4 In. . . . 1150.00
Table, Coffee, E. Wormley, Glass, Rosewood, Biomorphic, Dunbar, 57 x 31 x 16 In. 3335.00
Table, Coffee, E. Wormley, Janus Collection, Tiffany Tiles, 5 Sides, Dunbar, 38 x 19 In. . . 2875.00
Table, Coffee, E. Wormley, Mahogany, Walnut, Brass, 1950s, 56 x 15 In. 520.00
Table, Coffee, E. Wormley, No. 5214, Bird's-Eye Maple, Mahogany, Brass, 33 x 15 In. . . . 2300.00
Table, Coffee, E. Wormley, No. 5307, Bleached Mahogany, Rosewood, Brass, 57 x 17 In. 3105.00
Table, Coffee, E. Wormley, Walnut, Ceramic Tiles, 1950s, 38 x 20 In. 2415.00
Table, Coffee, Eames, Laminate, Round, Rubber Edge, Herman Miller, 36 x 16 In. 150.00
Table, Coffee, Fin Juhl, Teak, Tray Top, Rib Stretchers, Slatted Shelf, 18 x 27 x 20 In. . . . 410.00
Table, Coffee, Florence Knoll, Rosewood, Chrome Legs, Square, 1950s, 16 x 40 In. 748.00
Table, Coffee, Frank Lloyd Wright, Taliesin Design, Heritage Henredon, 26 x 26 x 13 In. . 1610.00
Table, Coffee, G. Nakashima, Walnut, Free-Form Top On Slab, Splayed Leg, 12 In. 9200.00
Table, Coffee, G. Nakashima, Walnut, Free-Form Top, Canted-Leg Base, 70 x 30 In. 8225.00
Table, Coffee, G. Nelson, Birch, Leather, Copper, Herman Miller, 1948, 50 x 16 In. 1380.00
Table, Coffee, George III Style, Round Top, Cabriole Legs, c.1920, 19 1/2 x 23 1/2 In. . . . 316.00
Table, Coffee, Georgian, Rectangular, Shaped Frieze, Cabriole Legs, 32 x 23 In. 145.00
Table, Coffee, Gio Ponti, Brass, Onyx, Italy, c.1953, 47 1/2 x 17 In. 3335.00
Table, Coffee, Gio Ponti, Italian Walnut, Travertine, Singer & Sons, 60 x 15 In. 1495.00
Table, Coffee, Grete Jalk, Dowel Legs, 9 Slats, Rectangular, Denmark, 20 x 63 1/2 In. . . . 380.00
Table, Coffee, I. Noguchi, IN-50, Herman Miller, c.1970, 15 x 46 x 36 In. 1295.00
Table, Coffee, I. Noguchi, Walnut Base, Glass Top, Biomorphic, 16 x 51 In. 2115.00
Table, Coffee, I. Noguchi, Walnut, Glass, Biomorphic, Herman Miller, 43 x 26 x 16 In. . . 1840.00
Table, Coffee, James Mont, Glass Top, Gilt, Bronze Finish, 15 1/4 x 54 x 26 1/2 In. 645.00
Table, Coffee, Kittinger, Chippendale Style, Mahogany, 40 x 20 1/4 x 25 In. 660.00
Table, Coffee, Knoll, Black Slate Top, Bright Chrome Base, 17 x 45 x 23 In. 265.00
Table, Coffee, Krueck & Sexton, Fiberglass, Glass, Tesko, 1985, 65 x 15 In. 1725.00
Table, Coffee, Louis Sognot, Oak, Metal, Glass, c.1950, 35 1/2 x 17 1/2 In. 4310.00
Table, Coffee, Luther Conover, Mahogany Slab, Black Iron Legs, c.1948, 14 In. 2300.00
Table, Coffee, Mayen, Glass Top, Aluminum Base, c.1968, 12 3/4 x 31 In. 129.00
Table, Coffee, McCobb, Birch Top, 3 Drawers, Brass Legs, Calvin, 16 1/2 x 66 In. 880.00
Table, Coffee, Mies Van Der Rohe, Barcelona, Knoll, c.1929, 17 x 40 x 40 In. . . . .530.00 to 880.00
Table, Coffee, Oriental, Lacquer, Open Fretwork, Chanteau, London, 15 x 24 x 51 In. 1840.00
Table, Coffee, P. Evans, Directional, Patchwork Square Base, Slate Top, 30 x 30 x 24 In. . 375.00
Table, Coffee, P. Evans, Patchwork, Burled Wood Veneer, Glass, 42 x 16 In. 690.00
Table, Coffee, Paul Laszlo, Teak, 3 Splayed Tapered Legs, c.1950, 16 x 48 In. 1725.00
Table, Coffee, Philip Laverne, Oval, Celestial Mythological Scene, 17 x 60 x 31 In. 2390.00
Table, Coffee, Regency, Lacquer, Gallery, Gilt Stencils, Faux Bamboo Legs, 22 x 30 In. . . . 345.00
Table, Coffee, Richard Schultz, Aluminum, Metal, Knoll, 28 x 28 x 15 1/2 In. 1095.00
Table, Coffee, Risom, Walnut, Round Top, Tray Sides, Tapered Legs, 20 x 45 In. 705.00
Table, Coffee, Robsjohn-Gibbings, Walnut, Free Form, Brass Legs, Widdicomb, 16 In. . . . 2300.00
Table, Coffee, Saarinen, Round, White, Knoll, c.1956, 14 3/4 x 35 3/4 In. 295.00
Table, Coffee, Square, Parallel Grooves, Turned Legs, Shelf, 24 x 32 In. 315.00
Table, Coffee, Tapio Wirkkala, Asko, Finland, c.1958, 18 1/2 x 49 x 24 In. 4115.00
Table, Coffee, V. Kagan, Cherry, Glass Top, Curved Legs, 18 x 42 In. 880.00
Table, Coffee, V. Kagan, Walnut, Onyx, 1950s, 36 x 15 3/4 In. 1150.00
Table, Coffee, Walnut, Floral Marquetry, Oval Glass Top, 2 Handles, 20 In. 405.00
Table, Coffee, Walnut, Oval Marble Top, Scroll Legs, 25 x 34 In. 140.00
Table, Coffee, Warren Platner, Bronze Wire, Glass Top, Knoll, 36 x 14 3/4 In. 575.00
Table, Coffee, Warren Platner, Chrome Wire, Glass Top, Knoll, 1970s, 42 x 15 In. 1410.00
Table, Coffee, Wood, Painted, Black, Green, Brass, Glass Top, 1950s, 53 x 28 x 13 In. 805.00
Table, Composition, Faux Granite, Brown, Ivory, Dish Top, Scalloped, 20 x 14 In. 175.00

Table, Composition, Lacquered, Green, Curved, Leather Top, c.1975, 16 x 32 x 46 In. . . .   325.00
Table, Conference, Florence Knoll, Elliptical, Green Marble Top, 78 x 48 x 28 In. 2185.00
Table, Conference, Florence Knoll, Walnut Veneer, Chrome, 78 x 48 x 29 In. 1175.00
Table, Conference, G. Nakashima, Walnut, Butterfly Joints, Hunter, 84 x 29 In. 20700.00
Table, Conservatory, Wrought Iron Base, Bamboo Form, Rustic Pine Top, 37 x 61 In. 805.00
Table, Console, Adam Style, Satinwood, Gilt, Urn, Garland Top, 35 x 55 x 25 In. 3910.00
Table, Console, Art Deco, Burl, Scrolling Legs, Carved Leaves, 30 x 50 x 12 1/2 In. 1765.00
Table, Console, Art Deco, Gilt Metal, Glass Top, Palm Leaves, 32 x 26 x 10 In. 1880.00
Table, Console, Art Deco, Mahogany, Rectangular Top, Oval Base, 29 1/4 x 42 In. 1060.00
Table, Console, Art Deco, Wrought Iron, Parcel Gilt, Marble, France, c.1925, 33 x 56 In. . . 2390.00
Table, Console, Baroque Style, Marble, Gilt Carved, Skirt, 35 x 53 x 24 1/2 In. 4700.00
Table, Console, Beech, Marble Top, Leaf Carved, Shell Stretcher, c.1800, 33 x 38 In. 1150.00
Table, Console, Biedermeier Style, Blond Wood, Demilune, 30 x 27 x 15 In., Pair 3450.00
Table, Console, Biedermeier, Fruitwood, Gilt, 19th Century, 30 x 46 x 22 In., Pair 10065.00
Table, Console, Biedermeier, Walnut, Demilune, Drawer, Mirrored Back, 39 x 21 In. 3910.00
Table, Console, Charles X, Kingwood, Marble, 1800s, 33 1/2 x 45 x 17 1/2 In. 1495.00
Table, Console, Corner, George III, Mahogany, String Inlay, 2 Frieze Drawers, 26 In. 295.00
Table, Console, Corner, Louis XVI Style, Beech, France, c.1885, 35 1/2 x 22 In. 635.00
Table, Console, Demilune, Polychrome, Marble Top, Italy, c.1900, 32 x 46 1/2 In. 1955.00
Table, Console, Empire Style, Mahogany, Marble Top, Column Supports, 1800s, 48 In. 1750.00
Table, Console, Empire Style, Marble, Carved End Supports, Huge Paw Feet, 56 1/2 In. . . . 1530.00
Table, Console, Empire, Giltwood, Marble Top, Polychrome, c.1820, 33 x 30 1/2 In. 6900.00
Table, Console, Empire, Mahogany, Marble Top, Drawer, Stretcher, c.1840, 32 x 33 In. . . 690.00
Table, Console, Empire, Mahogany, Marble Top, Ormolu Mount Supports, 36 x 48 In. 4140.00
Table, Console, Empire, Walnut, Ebony, Gilt, Mirror, 19th Century, 103 x 36 x 18 In. 5750.00
Table, Console, Federal, Cherry, D-Shape, Drawer, Turned Legs, c.1820, 29 x 37 In. 575.00
Table, Console, G. Poillerat, Marble, Wrought Iron, c.1940, 27 1/2 x 37 3/4 In. 9990.00
Table, Console, George III Style, Mahogany, Bowed Front, 35 x 56 x 26 3/4 In. 460.00
Table, Console, George III Style, Mahogany, Inlaid, 33 x 44 1/2 x 19 In., Pair 1840.00
Table, Console, George III Style, Yew, Inlaid, Demilune, 33 x 44 x 19 In., Pair 2300.00
Table, Console, George III, Mahogany, Demilune Top, c.1885, 29 x 50 In., Pair 3450.00
Table, Console, George III, Mahogany, Serpentine Top, Spade Feet, 34 x 56 x 26 In. 865.00
Table, Console, George III, Yew, Paneled Frieze, Square Legs, 32 x 45 x 18 In. 1380.00
Table, Console, Georgian Style, Mahogany, Inlaid, D-Shape, 29 x 29 x 15 In., Pair 805.00
Table, Console, Georgian Style, Mahogany, Sloped Top, Leaf Carved Panel, 35 x 52 In. . . 375.00
Table, Console, Girard, Plywood, Aluminum, Painted, Herman Miller, 1960s, 48 x 29 In. . . 2070.00
Table, Console, Gothic Revival, Marble Top, 19th Century, 34 x 39 1/2 x 17 1/2 In. 1610.00
Table, Console, Hepplewhite, Mahogany, D-Shape Inlaid Top, 2 Doors, 28 In. 575.00
Table, Console, Hepplewhite, Mahogany, Marquetry, 2 Drawers, 29 x 30 In. 3105.00
Table, Console, Herter Bros., Rosewood, Inlay, 1 Drawer, 2 Doors, c.1875, 42 x 66 In. . . . 14560.00
Table, Console, Jules Leleu, Sycamore, Steel, Gilt Bronze, c.1950, 32 x 35 1/2 In. 5640.00
Table, Console, Louis XV Style, Bronze, Marble, Allegorical Figures, 29 x 28 x 11 In. . . . 956.00
Table, Console, Louis XV Style, Parcel Gilt, Marble Top, Serpentine, c.1925, 33 x 33 In. . 460.00
Table, Console, Louis XVI Style, Gilt, Foliate Carved Frieze, Stretcher, 36 x 47 In. 1555.00
Table, Console, Louis XVI Style, Giltwood, France, c.1900, 33 1/4 x 24 1/4 In. 1380.00
Table, Console, Louis XVI Style, Giltwood, Marble Top, Carved, 1800s, 32 x 15 x 30 In. . . 1890.00
Table, Console, Louis XVI Style, Giltwood, Marble Top, Framed, Carved, 19 In. 655.00
Table, Console, Louis XVI Style, Mahogany, Polychrome, c.1900, 33 x 49 x 18 In. 1725.00
Table, Console, Mahogany, Gilt Brass Inlay, Mahogany Pier Mirror, c.1900, 88 x 37 In. . . . 4140.00
Table, Console, Mahogany, Marble Top, Drawer, Mirrored Back, 37 x 38 x 16 In. 2300.00
Table, Console, Marble Top, Painted, Continental, 18th Century, 34 x 47 x 20 In. 15535.00
Table, Console, Napoleon III, Boulle, Ebonized, Cabriole Legs, 38 x 51 x 17 In. 1645.00
Table, Console, Napoleon III, Mahogany, Marble Top, Drawer, 1800s, 27 x 14 In., Pair . . . 2070.00
Table, Console, Neoclassical Style, Fruitwood, Marble Top, Italy, 34 x 43 x 23 In., Pair . . 3220.00
Table, Console, Neoclassical, Burl, Demilune, Figure, Flowers, 30 x 45 x 21 In. 1115.00
Table, Console, Padouk, Carved, Pierced Skirt, Chinese, c.1900, 34 x 37 x 25 In. 575.00
Table, Console, Queen Anne, Rectangular Top, Frieze, Cabriole Legs, 58 x 27 In. 460.00
Table, Console, Regency Style, Giltwood, Serpentine Front, Italy, 29 1/2 x 29 In. 635.00
Table, Console, Regency Style, Rosewood, Brass Inlay, Parcel Gilt, 35 x 61 x 22 In. 14340.00
Table, Console, Regency, Mahogany, Giltwood, Marble Top, c.1820, 36 x 37 In. 1380.00
Table, Console, Renaissance Revival, Marble Top, Wrought Iron, 1800s, 37 x 27 In., Pair . . 1725.00
Table, Console, Rococo Revival, Giltwood, Marble Top, Pierced Leaves, 31 x 13 x 24 In. . . 510.00
Table, Console, Rococo Style, Giltwood, Carved, Pierced Frieze, Italy, 32 x 40 In. 3000.00

Table, Console, Rococo Style, Painted, Gilt, Carved Wood, Shelf, 41 x 50 x 20 In. 3820.00
Table, Console, Rococo, Walnut, Shaped Marble Top, Flower-Basket Skirt, 37 x 59 In. ... 840.00
Table, Console, Sheraton Style, Mahogany, Chevron Bands, Demilune Top, 30 x 45 In. .   580.00
Table, Console, Subes, Wrought Iron, Marble Top, c.1925, 35 x 37 1/2 x 21 In. 6570.00
Table, Console, Ulrich, Mahogany, Brass, Glass, Italy, c.1942, 59 x 34 1/4 In. 10925.00
Table, Console, Victorian, Serpentine Form, Carved, Marble, Painted, 1860, 36 x 87 In. .. 3320.00
Table, Console, Walnut, 2 Doors, Metal Handles, 32 5/8 x 21 x 29 In. 110.00
Table, Contortionist, Cast Aluminum, Crossed Legs In Front, 16 x 16 In. 770.00
Table, Cricket, Pine, 3-Board Round Top, 3-Sided Scalloped Apron, 3 Legs, 28 x 32 In. .. 460.00
Table, Cricket, Pumpkin Pine, Triangular Shelf, New England, 28 In. 1095.00
Table, Cricket, Tilt Top, Oak, 3-Board Top, Gateleg, Turned Legs, Ball Feet, 23 x 24 In. . 880.00
Table, Cypress, Rectangular Top, Straight Apron, Turned Legs, 30 x 72 In. 980.00
Table, Daver Kossen, John Stuart, c.1960, 25 x 30 x 30 In. 210.00
Table, Dining, American Machine Age, Lloyd Chrome, c.1939, 29 3/4 x 36 1/2 In. 590.00
Table, Dining, Art Deco, Burl, Draw Leaf, U-Shape Supports, 29 x 94 x 39 In. 1175.00
Table, Dining, Art Deco, Burl, Harp-Shape Standard, 29 x 60 x 39 In. 3820.00
Table, Dining, Art Deco, Mahogany, Burl, Lacquer Base, 2 Leaves, 30 x 72 In. 470.00
Table, Dining, Arts & Crafts, Circular Top, 8-Sided Pedestal Base, 28 3/4 x 48 In. 575.00
Table, Dining, Arts & Crafts, Circular, Split Pedestal, Mortised Stretcher, 29 x 48 In. 1610.00
Table, Dining, Arts & Crafts, Oak, Post Legs, Stretchers, 1900s, 29 1/2 x 48 x 30 In. 825.00
Table, Dining, Arts & Crafts, Trestle, Keyed-Through Stretcher, 29 1/2 x 90 x 32 In. 1725.00
Table, Dining, B. Mathsson, Ebonized Oak Veneer, Chrome Legs, 27 x 59 x 39 In. 880.00
Table, Dining, Bubinga Wood, Oval, String Inlay, Lobed Legs, 2 Leaves, 28 x 50 x 46 In. 1175.00
Table, Dining, Cessna, Birch Plywood Top, Metal Legs, 1950s, 64 x 40 x 29 3/4 In. 275.00
Table, Dining, Cherry, Round, Lazy Susan, Shaped Skirt, Cabriole Legs, 30 x 57 In. ... 1495.00
Table, Dining, Chippendale, Mahogany, Triple Pedestal, Reeded Saber Legs, 151 x 53 In. . 7030.00
Table, Dining, Chippendale, Walnut, c.1780, 28 1/2 x 42 x 104 1/2 In., Pair 13145.00
Table, Dining, Directoire Style, Mahogany, Brass Mount, 1900s, 31 x 94 x 46 In. 3345.00
Table, Dining, Drop Leaf, Cherry, Scalloped Skirt, Cabriole Legs, Gateleg, 28 x 52 In. ... 805.00
Table, Dining, Drop Leaf, Chippendale, Mahogany, Claw & Ball Feet, 28 x 50 x 42 In. .. 2070.00
Table, Dining, Drop Leaf, Federal, Cherry, New England, c.1800, 28 x 68 x 43 In. 470.00
Table, Dining, Drop Leaf, G. Nelson, Herman Miller, c.1947, 29 3/4 x 40 x 18 1/2 In. ... 1060.00
Table, Dining, Drop Leaf, Georgian, Mahogany, Claw & Ball Feet, 1760, 28 x 46 In. 1840.00
Table, Dining, Drop Leaf, Hepplewhite, Mahogany, Tapered Legs, 2 Leaves, 27 x 49 In. ... 400.00
Table, Dining, Drop Leaf, Hepplewhite, Splayed Legs, 11 3/8-In. Leaves, 39 x 19 In. 470.00
Table, Dining, Drop Leaf, Neoclassical, Mahogany, American, 30 1/2 x 45 3/4 x 46 In. ... 2300.00
Table, Dining, Drop Leaf, Oak, 2 Leaves, 2 Drawers, Cabriole Legs, 30 x 93 1/2 In. 2760.00
Table, Dining, Drop Leaf, Queen Anne, Mahogany, c.1750, 28 1/2 x 42 x 15 1/2 In. 17925.00
Table, Dining, Drop Leaf, Sheraton, Cherry, 6 Legs, Late 19th Century, 28 x 44 x 20 In. ... 300.00
Table, Dining, Drop Leaf, Sheraton, Walnut, 1-Board Top, 6 Legs, 20 1/2 x 48 In. 275.00
Table, Dining, Drop Leaf, Victorian, Painted, Mid 19th Century, 28 x 42 x 26 In. 315.00
Table, Dining, E. Wormley, Walnut, Round Top, Hexagonal Legs, Brass Feet, Dunbar ... 240.00
Table, Dining, Empire, Circular Top, Tripod Base, 2 Leaves, Continental, 40 x 31 In. 3450.00
Table, Dining, Federal, Cherry, 1 Leaf, c.1825, 27 3/4 x 69 3/4 x 47 3/4 In. 345.00
Table, Dining, French Provincial, Pine, Planked Top, Leaves, 1800s, 30 x 45 x 24 In. 1380.00
Table, Dining, G. Nelson, Oval Soft Edge, Herman Miller, 1950s, 78 x 42 x 29 In. 489.00
Table, Dining, G. Nelson, Rosewood, Walnut, Herman Miller, 1950s, 72 x 29 In. 3740.00
Table, Dining, G. Nelson, Square Legs, Extension, Herman Miller, 30 x 72 x 40 In. 1530.00
Table, Dining, G. Nelson, Walnut Veneer, 2 Leaves, Herman Miller, 29 x 54 x 36 In. 590.00
Table, Dining, G. Stickley, No. 627, Round, Notched Cross-Stretcher Base, 48 x 31 In. 2300.00
Table, Dining, G. Stickley, Round, Pedestal Base, Extended Feet, 54 x 29 In. 3450.00
Table, Dining, George III Style, Mahogany, 2 Pedestals, 2 Leaves, 29 1/2 x 88 In. 2760.00
Table, Dining, George IV, Mahogany, 2 Pedestals, 2 Leaves, c.1825, 29 x 64 x 104 In. ... 5290.00
Table, Dining, Georgian Style, Mahogany, 2 Pedestals, 2 Leaves, 30 x 48 x 120 In. 2645.00
Table, Dining, Girard, Lacquered Wood, Aluminum, Herman Miller, 1965, 44 x 29 In. ... 2990.00
Table, Dining, Girard, Rosewood, Aluminum, Herman Miller, 1965, 38 x 30 In. 4600.00
Table, Dining, I. Noguchi, Iron, Laminated Wood, Knoll, 35 x 28 In. 1150.00
Table, Dining, Jacobean Style, Oak, Oval Top, 2 Leaves, 30 1/2 x 48 x 107 In. 2415.00
Table, Dining, Jacobean Style, Walnut, Gothic-Style Stretchers, Pullout Ends 365.00
Table, Dining, Jean Royere, White Enamel Wire Column, Glass Top, 50 x 29 In. 5875.00
Table, Dining, Johannes Hansen, Oak, Chrome, Teak Legs, c.1958, 28 x 35 x 82 In. 1645.00
Table, Dining, Karl Springer, Demilune Pedestals, Leather Finish, 29 x 96 x 42 In. 2235.00
Table, Dining, Kittinger, Chippendale Style, Mahogany, 96 x 42 x 31 In. 770.00

Table, Dining, L. & J.G. Stickley, Circular Top, Pedestal Base, 4 Leaves, 30 x 48 In. 1380.00
Table, Dining, Limbert, Circular, Pedestal Base, Shoe Feet, Casters, 29 1/2 x 54 In. 2530.00
Table, Dining, Limbert, No. 441, Cruciform Base, Central Leg, 4 Leaves, 54 In. Diam. 2875.00
Table, Dining, Limbert, No. 1480, Round, Double Legs, Arched Tenons, 54 x 30 In. 4600.00
Table, Dining, Louis XV Style, Mahogany, Parquetry, Leaves, Carved, 30 x 39 x 64 In. . . 980.00
Table, Dining, Louis XVI Style, Mahogany, Gilt Metal Mounted, 2 Leaves, 84 In. 3000.00
Table, Dining, Louis XVI, Mahogany, Gilt Bronze, Fluted Legs, 1 Leaf, 31 x 80 x 40 In. . 880.00
Table, Dining, Louis XVI, Mahogany, Ormolu Mount, Extension, 1800s, 28 x 38 x 27 In. . 6575.00
Table, Dining, Mahogany, 3 Pedestals, Mid 19th Century, 29 1/2 x 46 x 35 1/2 In. 8625.00
Table, Dining, Mahogany, Carved Apron, 3 Leaves, Brass Casters, 60 x 48 In. 2620.00
Table, Dining, Mahogany, Crank Extension, Turned Supports, Casters, 54 x 54 In. 800.00
Table, Dining, Mahogany, D-Shape, Ebony Icicle Inlay, Bellflowers, 47 x 84 In. 5740.00
Table, Dining, Mahogany, Wide Inlaid Border, 2 Pedestals, 48 x 119 In. 1380.00
Table, Dining, McCobb, Perimeter Group, Birch, Winchedon, 44 x 29 In. 1380.00
Table, Dining, Napoleon III, Walnut, Brass, Oval, Banded, 2 Leaves, 30 x 63 x 49 In. 805.00
Table, Dining, Neoclassical, Mahogany, Veneer, Pedestal, c.1825, 30 x 48 x 23 In. 19975.00
Table, Dining, Oak, Carved Iron Base, Round, Leaves, 30 x 54 In. 2800.00
Table, Dining, Oak, Rosewood, Supports, Block Feet, 19th Century, 29 x 78 x 41 In. 1150.00
Table, Dining, P. Frankel, Cork, Johnson Furniture, c.1938, 27 x 40 In. 1530.00
Table, Dining, Philippe Starck, For Royalton Hotel, Aleph, 53 x 29 In. 2875.00
Table, Dining, Piero Fornasetti, Wood, Metal, Transfer Printed, c.1955, 29 x 45 In. 4780.00
Table, Dining, Queen Anne Style, Black Cherry, Leaves, Henkel-Harris, 29 x 51 In. 315.00
Table, Dining, Regency Style, Burl, 2 Pedestals, 2 Leaves, 29 x 94 In. 10065.00
Table, Dining, Regency Style, Mahogany, Parcel Gilt, 20th Century, 29 x 46 In. 4780.00
Table, Dining, Regency, Mahogany, 2 Sections, Pedestal, Turned Legs, 66 x 28 x 47 In. . . 10350.00
Table, Dining, Regency, Mahogany, 3 Pedestals, 2 Leaves, 28 x 90 x 54 In. 17925.00
Table, Dining, Regency, Mahogany, Satinwood Inlay, 2 Pedestals, 29 x 126 x 47 In. 3680.00
Table, Dining, Regency, Yew, Mahogany, Circular, Fluted Supports, 30 x 64 In. 1530.00
Table, Dining, Richard Schultz, Aluminum, Metal, Knoll, 38 x 38 x 26 In. 2070.00
Table, Dining, Rococo Style, Walnut, Pedestal, Late 19th Century, 29 x 64 x 87 In. 2185.00
Table, Dining, Rosewood, Round, Claw Feet, Diagonal Carved Edge, 6 Leaves, 144 In. . . 2200.00
Table, Dining, Samuel Marx, Burl, Lucite, Ebonized, c.1940, 28 x 61 x 36 In. 3585.00
Table, Dining, Sheraton Style, Satinwood, Burl Walnut, Marquetry, 29 x 44 x 68 In. 1410.00
Table, Dining, Sheraton, Mahogany, Carved Baskets, Eagles, 48 x 93 In. 5625.00
Table, Dining, Sheraton, Mahogany, Inlay, 2 Pedestals, Reeded Legs, 48 x 129 In. 4600.00
Table, Dining, Stickley Bros., Circular Top, 8-Sided Pedestal, Scroll Feet, 29 x 54 In. 2875.00
Table, Dining, Stickley Bros., No. 2424, Circular Top, 30 x 48 In. 2990.00
Table, Dining, Stickley Bros., Oak, Round Top, 5 Leaves, c.1918, 30 x 60 In. 6465.00
Table, Dining, Stickley Bros., Oak, Round Top, Apron, c.1918, 31 x 48 In. 1295.00
Table, Dining, Victorian, Mahogany, Demilune Top, Turned Legs, c.1865, 30 x 44 In. 1725.00
Table, Dining, Walnut, Tapered 8-Sided Legs, 3 Leaves, 50 x 56 x 29 In. 920.00
Table, Dining, Wegner, Teak, Dowel Legs, Johannes Hansen, 29 x 76 x 41 In. 2235.00
Table, Dining, William IV, Mahogany, 3 Pedestals, 19th Century, 27 x 56 x 116 In. 6325.00
Table, Drafting, Renaissance Revival, Oak, Carved Drawers, Hinged Top, 31 x 52 In. 175.00
Table, Dressing, Arts & Crafts, Swivel Mirror, 2 Candlestands, England, 42 x 20 x 61 In. . 1380.00
Table, Dressing, Charles X, Satinwood, 2 Drawers, c.1840, 58 x 42 1/2 x 20 1/2 In. 4485.00
Table, Dressing, Directoire, Brass Mount, Mahogany, Late 1700s, 28 x 36 x 19 In. 8365.00
Table, Dressing, Edwardian, Crossbanded, Mirror, Bowed Drawers, 45 x 38 x 21 In. 1035.00
Table, Dressing, Edwardian, Satinwood, Frieze Medallion, Cupids, 31 x 44 x 23 In. 895.00
Table, Dressing, Empire, Mahogany, Stepback, Swivel Mirror, 74 x 38 In. 1905.00
Table, Dressing, Fruitwood, Marquetry, Marble Top, Ormolu Mounts, Acorn Finials 1465.00
Table, Dressing, G. Stickley, Oak, Drawers, Copper Pulls, c.1912, 30 x 48 x 22 In. 1175.00
Table, Dressing, George III Style, Mahogany, Brass, c.1900, 27 x 32 1/2 x 17 1/2 In. 865.00
Table, Dressing, George III, Mahogany Inlay, Bowfront, 1800s, 31 x 21 x 42 In. 475.00
Table, Dressing, George III, Mahogany, Fruitwood, Ebony Inlay, Bowfront, 22 x 27 In. . . . 1580.00
Table, Dressing, Herter Bros., Chestnut, 4 Drawers, Mirror, c.1875, 71 x 48 x 22 In. 1510.00
Table, Dressing, Louis XVI Style, Gilt Bronze Mount, Tapered Legs 3525.00
Table, Dressing, Louis XVI Style, Kingwood, Rosewood, Marquetry, 1800s, 29 x 32 In. . . 1790.00
Table, Dressing, Louis XVI, Mahogany, Marble, Fluted Legs, 1700s, 29 x 39 x 24 In. 2300.00
Table, Dressing, Mahogany, 2 Parts, Mirror, Maryland, 1810-1830, 76 x 41 x 23 In. 3110.00
Table, Dressing, Mahogany, D-Shape, Barley-Twist Legs, Bun Feet, 48 x 20 x 74 In. 635.00
Table, Dressing, Mahogany, Mirror, 2 Drawers, American, c.1890, 74 1/2 x 34 In. 460.00
Table, Dressing, Mahogany, Stretcher Shelf, Mirror, c.1825, 76 1/2 x 38 1/2 x 24 In. 1610.00

Table, Dressing, Majorelle, Fruitwood, Rosewood, Marquetry, c.1900, 32 x 19 In. 8960.00
Table, Dressing, Napoleon III, Ebonized, Marquetry, 30 x 25 x 18 In. 1295.00
Table, Dressing, Painted, Drawer, Stenciling, 34 x 31 1/2 x 15 1/2 In. 420.00
Table, Dressing, Queen Anne, Cherry, Carved, Molded Edge, 36 x 29 x 20 In. 5875.00
Table, Dressing, Queen Anne, Oak, 3 Drawers, Bracket & Scallop-Cut Apron, 29 In. 525.00
Table, Dressing, Queen Anne, Walnut, 3 Drawers, Pa., 1740-1760, 29 x 34 x 18 In. 2390.00
Table, Dressing, Rosewood Veneer, 3-Hinged Mirror, Bronze Mounts, 5 x 23 5/8 In. 3360.00
Table, Dressing, Satinwood, Mirror, Gilt Bronze Mounts, 6 Drawers, 43 1/2 In. 1455.00
Table, Dressing, Sheraton Style, Cherry, Pine, Poplar, Ring Turnings, 38 x 17 x 28 In. ... 660.00
Table, Dressing, Sheraton, Mahogany, Veneer, Drawer, c.1820, 29 x 34 x 16 3/4 In. 750.00
Table, Dressing, Victorian Style, 1 Drawer, Shaped Mirror, 64 x 37 x 25 1/2 In. 690.00
Table, Dressing, Victorian, Burl Walnut, Bowfront, Adjustable Mirror, 7 Drawers, 69 In. ... 1410.00
Table, Dressing, Victorian, Tole, Basin Well, Mirror Inside, c.1865, 34 x 21 In. 1150.00
Table, Dressing, Walnut, Arched Carved Kneehole, Turned Legs, 31 x 37 In. 345.00
Table, Dressing, Walnut, Kneehole, 2 Drawers, Tapered Legs, Continental, 30 x 26 In. ... 345.00
Table, Dressing, Yellow, Green Pinstripes, Scroll Back, Tapered Legs, 38 x 36 x 17 In. ... 1765.00
Table, Drop Leaf, Arts & Crafts, Octagonal, Gateleg, Cutouts, 27 x 10 x 31 In. 750.00
Table, Drop Leaf, Arts & Crafts, Stretchers, Posts, 38 x 36 x 24 In. 805.00
Table, Drop Leaf, Blond Wood, Side Cabinet, 4 Drawers, Scandinavia, 30 x 14 x 33 In. ... 1060.00
Table, Drop Leaf, Chippendale, Cherry, Cutout Apron, Cabriole Legs, 27 x 44 1/2 In. 4406.00
Table, Drop Leaf, Chippendale, Walnut, Cabriole Legs, c.1780, 29 1/4 x 47 x 51 In. 4780.00
Table, Drop Leaf, Empire, Acorn Drops, Paw Feet, c.1800, 24 x 39 x 30 In. 805.00
Table, Drop Leaf, Empire, Mahogany, Cylindrical Pedestal, Scrolled Feet, 30 x 18 In. .'... 260.00
Table, Drop Leaf, Federal Style, Cherry, Early 20th Century, 30 x 57 x 42 In., Pair 1380.00
Table, Drop Leaf, Federal Style, Mahogany, Late 19th Century, 29 x 60 1/2 x 40 In. 490.00
Table, Drop Leaf, Federal, Curly Maple, New England, c.1810, 27 1/2 x 43 x 40 In. 1495.00
Table, Drop Leaf, Federal, Mahogany, 8 Legs, Early 19th Century, 29 x 66 x 48 In. 690.00
Table, Drop Leaf, Federal, Mahogany, New York, c.1810, 29 x 36 In. 2990.00
Table, Drop Leaf, Federal, Mahogany, Oval, Stringing, 1815, 29 x 35 In. 8225.00
Table, Drop Leaf, Federal, Mahogany, Spade Feet, c.1800, 30 x 49 1/2 x 30 In. 490.00
Table, Drop Leaf, Federal, Satinwood, Walnut Inlay, c.1800, 28 1/2 x 50 x 39 In. 2300.00
Table, Drop Leaf, Federal, Walnut, 6 Legs, c.1825, 28 3/4 x 20 1/4 x 46 1/2 In. 545.00
Table, Drop Leaf, G. Nakashima, Walnut, Dowel Stretchers, 28 x 36 x 36 In. 2350.00
Table, Drop Leaf, George II, Mahogany, 3 Sections, Gateleg, 1700s, 28 x 48 x 69 In. 2900.00
Table, Drop Leaf, George III Style, Mahogany, Serpentine Flaps, 17 x 41 1/2 In. 955.00
Table, Drop Leaf, George III, Frieze Drawer, Turned Legs, Casters, 29 x 38 In. 920.00
Table, Drop Leaf, George III, Mahogany, Brass, 1 Drawer, Lion-Paw Casters, 20 x 37 In. .. 655.00
Table, Drop Leaf, George III, Mahogany, Drawer, Square Legs, 35 x 16 x 55 In. 865.00
Table, Drop Leaf, George III, Mahogany, Hinged Center, Book Rest, 29 x 22 In. 2115.00
Table, Drop Leaf, George III, Mahogany, Oval Top, Pad Feet, c.1790, 29 x 40 3/4 In. 1265.00
Table, Drop Leaf, George IV, Mahogany, Gateleg, Round Tapered Legs, 21 x 35 In. 550.00
Table, Drop Leaf, George IV, Mahogany, Square Chamfered Legs, c.1820, 27 x 34 In. 1035.00
Table, Drop Leaf, George IV, Mahogany, Tapered Legs, Spade Feet, c.1820, 29 x 24 In. ... 805.00
Table, Drop Leaf, Georgian Style, Oak, Gateleg, 2 Drawers, c.1890, 29 x 36 In. 230.00
Table, Drop Leaf, Handkerchief, Mahogany, Walnut, Diamond Top, 29 x 41 x 26 1/2 In. ... 920.00
Table, Drop Leaf, Hepplewhite Style, Curly Maple, Beaded Edges, 15 x 17 x 30 In. 275.00
Table, Drop Leaf, Hepplewhite, Cherry, Square Tapered Legs, 29 x 48 x 17 In. 259.00
Table, Drop Leaf, Hepplewhite, Mahogany, Tapered Legs, Casters, 29 x 41 In. 440.00
Table, Drop Leaf, Hepplewhite, Walnut, Blue Graining, 42 x 17 1/2 x 11 1/2 In. 110.00
Table, Drop Leaf, Jacobean Style, Oak, Oval Top, Stretchers, 1930, 28 x 42 x 55 1/2 In. .. 460.00
Table, Drop Leaf, Jacobean, Oak, Gateleg, Barley Twist Legs, 29 x 41 x 52 In. 210.00
Table, Drop Leaf, L. & J.G. Stickley, Circular Top, Cross Stretchers, 29 x 35 1/2 In. 1035.00
Table, Drop Leaf, L. & J.G. Stickley, Gateleg, Shoe Feet, 30 x 40 1/2 In. 2070.00
Table, Drop Leaf, Limbert, No. 1148, Gateleg, Arched Corbels, 45 x 25 x 30 In. 2070.00
Table, Drop Leaf, Louis XVI Style, Marquetry, Ebonized, Gilt, Square, 29 x 34 x 34 In. ... 1020.00
Table, Drop Leaf, Mahogany, Convex Drawers, Column Supports, c.1835, 27 x 41 In. 750.00
Table, Drop Leaf, Mahogany, Convex Frieze Drawer, c.1820, 29 x 51 x 39 3/4 In. 1150.00
Table, Drop Leaf, Mahogany, Leaf Inlay, Frieze Drawer, 29 x 35 x 13 In. 5290.00
Table, Drop Leaf, Mahogany, Round Corners, Casters, England, c.1860, 28 x 35 x 57 In. .. 375.00
Table, Drop Leaf, Mahogany, Turned & Carved Pedestal, 2 Paw Feet, 30 x 42 In. 8340.00
Table, Drop Leaf, Maple, Gateleg, Turned Base, 18th Century, 43 x 19 x 27 In. 1210.00
Table, Drop Leaf, Maple, Sycamore, Butterfly, Turned Splayed Legs, 27 x 34 In. 3585.00
Table, Drop Leaf, Oak, Gateleg, Bulbous Feet, England, c.1720, 27 1/2 x 13 In. 920.00

Table, Drop Leaf, Oak, Gateleg, Oval, Early 19th Century, 43 x 15 1/2 x 27 In. 690.00
Table, Drop Leaf, Pine, Flame Graining, 2-Board Top, Drawer, 16 x 17 x 29 In. 550.00
Table, Drop Leaf, Pine, Red Wash, Maine, c.1865, Opens To 36 1/2-In. Square 650.00
Table, Drop Leaf, Queen Anne Style, Double Swing Leg, 26 1/2 x 30 1/2 x 31 In. 520.00
Table, Drop Leaf, Queen Anne Style, Maple, Ring Turned Legs, 27 x 13 x 27 In. 1870.00
Table, Drop Leaf, Queen Anne, Cherry, Hudson Valley, c.1740 . . . . 1650.00
Table, Drop Leaf, Queen Anne, Cherry, Shaped Apron, c.1760, 28 1/2 x 48 1/2 x 49 In. . . . 3290.00
Table, Drop Leaf, Queen Anne, Curly Maple, Pine, Cabriole Legs, Pad Feet, 29 x 45 In. . . 880.00
Table, Drop Leaf, Queen Anne, Mahogany, Cyma-Curved Ends, c.1760, 28 x 48 x 49 In. . . 5020.00
Table, Drop Leaf, Queen Anne, Mahogany, Gateleg, New England, 1700s, 27 x 46 In. . . 4890.00
Table, Drop Leaf, Queen Anne, Mahogany, Gateleg, Pad Feet, 28 x 38 1/2 x 12 In. 990.00
Table, Drop Leaf, Queen Anne, Oak, Walnut, Drawer, c.1740, 28 x 42 x 49 In. 590.00
Table, Drop Leaf, Queen Anne, Round, Gateleg, New England, 1700s, 27 x 48 In. 5460.00
Table, Drop Leaf, Queen Anne, Walnut, c.1770, 28 1/2 x 15 1/2 x 46 3/4 In. 920.00
Table, Drop Leaf, Queen Anne, Walnut, Maple, Pine, Cabriole Legs, 48 x 15 x 28 In. 7150.00
Table, Drop Leaf, Queen Anne, Walnut, Oak, Gateleg, Round Legs, Pad Feet, 29 x 48 In. . 935.00
Table, Drop Leaf, Regency Style, Mahogany, 2 Drawers, 28 1/2 x 38 x 24 In. 895.00
Table, Drop Leaf, Regency Style, Mahogany, Pedestal, 29 x 58 1/2 x 36 1/4 In. 290.00
Table, Drop Leaf, Regency, Mahogany Inlay, Brass Casters, c.1815, 30 x 20 x 35 In. 1955.00
Table, Drop Leaf, Regency, Mahogany, 2 Drawers, Circular Legs, 25 x 20 In. 645.00
Table, Drop Leaf, Regency, Mahogany, Drawers, Trestle Base, 29 x 35 x 25 In. 3910.00
Table, Drop Leaf, Regency, Mahogany, Reeded, Tapered Legs, c.1835, 29 x 20 In. 1265.00
Table, Drop Leaf, Regency, Satinwood, Crossbanded Mahogany, 1800s, 28 x 15 x 27 In. . . 1840.00
Table, Drop Leaf, Rosewood, Fruit Finial, c.1860, 30 x 29 x 26 In. 1960.00
Table, Drop Leaf, Sheraton Style, Mahogany, Gateleg, c.1870, 28 x 35 x 47 In. 290.00
Table, Drop Leaf, Sheraton Style, Mahogany, Reeded Turned Legs, 26 x 60 In. 750.00
Table, Drop Leaf, Sheraton, Cherry, 1-Board Top, 39 x 17 x 29 In. 305.00
Table, Drop Leaf, Sheraton, Cherry, Bird's-Eye Maple Drawers, 30 x 20 1/2 x 16 3/4 In. . . 635.00
Table, Drop Leaf, Sheraton, Cherry, Turned Legs, Kentucky, 29 x 55 3/4 In. 545.00
Table, Drop Leaf, Sheraton, False Drawers, Acanthus Carved, Turned Legs, Rollers 1200.00
Table, Drop Leaf, Sheraton, Mahogany, 6 Rope-Carved Legs, 29 x 47 x 19 In. 550.00
Table, Drop Leaf, Sheraton, Mahogany, Birch, Poplar, Turned Legs, 36 x 20 x 28 1/2 In. . 330.00
Table, Drop Leaf, Sheraton, Mahogany, Cherry, 2 Drawers, 1800s, 29 x 17 x 20 In. 450.00
Table, Drop Leaf, Sheraton, Mahogany, Spiral-Carved Legs, 30 x 44 1/4 x 17 1/4 In. 290.00
Table, Drop Leaf, Sheraton, Maple, Cherry, Dovetailed Drawer, Ball Feet, 40 x 19 In. . . . 935.00
Table, Drop Leaf, Sheraton, Tiger Maple, Turned Cherry Legs, c.1840, 35 x 18 x 41 In. . . 1750.00
Table, Drop Leaf, Tiger Maple, Massachusetts, 28 x 48 In. 1450.00
Table, Drop Leaf, Turned, Fluted Legs, Porcelain Wheel Casters, Oval, 44 x 54 In. 225.00
Table, Drop Leaf, Victorian, Rosewood, Serpentine Top, Drawer, C-Scrolls, 28 x 43 In. . . 1175.00
Table, Drop Leaf, Walnut, 2 Tiger Maple Drawers, Turned Legs, 29 x 17 In. 345.00
Table, Drop Leaf, Walnut, Cut Corners, Rope-Turned Legs, 29 x 38 x 20 1/2 In. 520.00
Table, Drop Leaf, Walnut, Saber Legs, Skirt, N.C., 28 x 47 1/2 x 25 In. 1870.00
Table, Drop Leaf, Wavy Birch, Ring Turned Swelled Legs, c.1825-1835, 41 3/4 In. 705.00
Table, Drop Leaf, William & Mary Style, D-Shape Leaves, Gateleg, 19 x 23 In. 350.00
Table, Drop Leaf, William & Mary Style, Oak, Ebonized, 19th Century, 19 x 31 In. 360.00
Table, Drop Leaf, William & Mary, Mahogany, Gateleg, c.1700, 28 x 15 x 34 1/2 In. 1725.00
Table, Drum, Federal Style, Leather Inset, Urn Standard, 32 x 29 In. 175.00
Table, Drum, Fruitwood, Inlaid, Continental, 27 3/4 x 21 3/4 In. 2030.00
Table, Drum, George II Style, Satinwood, Yew Inlay, Revolving Top, 27 x 25 In. 750.00
Table, Drum, George III Style, Mahogany, Leather Top, 4 Drawers, Pedestal, 33 In. 1600.00
Table, Drum, Georgian Style, Mahogany, Leather, Brass Casters, 29 x 36 In. 2070.00
Table, Drum, Mahogany, 3 Drawers, Shelves, Revolving, England, 30 x 19 3/4 In. 290.00
Table, Drum, Mahogany, Round, 3 Fitted Frieze Drawers, Tripod Base, Paw Feet, 29 In. . 405.00
Table, Drum, Neoclassical, Mahogany, Veneer, Hexagonal Top, c.1830s, 29 x 23 x 24 In. . 1530.00
Table, Drum, Walnut, Black Leather, Conforming Drawer Over Door, 30 x 24 In. 400.00
Table, Dunbar, Mahogany, Brass Step, c.1950, 25 x 25 In., Pair . . . . *Illus* 1150.00
Table, Duncan Phyfe, Mahogany, c.1815, 34 1/2 x 36 1/4 x 18 In. 5750.00
Table, E. Wormley, Ebonized, Leather Top, Horse-Hoof Feet, Dunbar, 13 x 27 x 23 In. . . 530.00
Table, E. Wormley, Mahogany, 3 Tiers, Glass Top, Dunbar, 1940s, 23 x 23 x 23 1/2 In. . . . 750.00
Table, E. Wormley, Mahogany, Folding Top, 1950s, 32 x 29 In. 1725.00
Table, E. Wormley, Mahogany, Inset Red Tiles, Tripod Base, 16 x 15 In., Pair 4025.00
Table, E. Wormley, Round Top, Hand Painted, Dunbar, 26 1/2 x 39 1/2 In. 590.00
Table, E. Wormley, Walnut, Inset With Blue Natzler Tiles, Square Legs, 22 x 30 In. 3450.00

Table, Eames, Action Office, White Top, Herman Miller, c.1954, 28 3/4 x 35 3/4 In.	325.00
Table, Eames, Ash Plywood, c.1950, 20 x 34 1/4 In. . . . . *Illus*	805.00
Table, Eames, CTW, Ash Plywood, Herman Miller, 34 x 16 In.	1035.00
Table, Eames, CTW, Plywood, Dish Top, Herman Miller, 34 x 15 1/2 In.	635.00
Table, Eames, DCWS, Birch Plywood, Herman Miller, 19 1/4 x 21 x 29 In., Pair	690.00
Table, Eames, IT, White Top, Herman Miller, c.1946, 16 3/4 x 21 1/2 x 18 In.	880.00
Table, Eames, Laminate Top, Cat's-Cradle Base, Herman Miller, 10 x 15 x 13 In., Pair . . .	999.00
Table, Eames, LTR, Herman Miller, c.1951, 10 x 15 1/2 x 13 1/2 In., 4 Piece	1765.00
Table, Eames, Rosewood Laminate, Aluminum Base, Herman Miller, 28 x 95 In.	590.00
Table, Eames, Surfboard, 80 In.	1320.00
Table, Eastlake, Walnut, Marble Top, Pierced Floral, Scroll Base, 30 x 33 x 24 In.	345.00
Table, Edwardian, Elm, Satinwood, Banded Top, Shaped Front, 35 x 60 x 20 In.	1725.00
Table, Edwardian, Satinwood, Polychrome, Drawer, Figural Scene, 28 x 30 x 19 In.	4600.00
Table, Edwardian, Satinwood, Rectangular Top, Flower Basket, 31 x 22 x 16 In.	3220.00
Table, Eileen Gray, Chrome Plate, Tubular Steel, Glass Top, 1990s, 20 x 24 In., Pair	520.00
Table, Elizabethan Style, Cherry, Draw-Leaf Ends, Pedestals, 30 x 42 x 132 In.	3335.00
Table, Elm, Lacquered, Black, Chinese, c.1810, 35 1/2 x 64 1/8 x 24 1/2 In.	880.00
Table, Elm, Lacquered, Red, 4 Drawers, Chinese, c.1890, 32 1/4 x 17 1/4 In.	705.00
Table, Elm, Ruji-Head Spandrels, Chinese, c.1830, 19 3/4 x 39 3/8 x 13 In.	380.00
Table, Empire Revival, Mahogany, Circular Top, Pedestal, Platform Base, 28 In.	260.00
Table, Empire Revival, Mahogany, Round, Pedestal, 10-In. Leaves, 60 In.	3500.00
Table, Empire Style, Gilt Bronze, Marble Top, 3 Legs, 26 1/2 x 17 In., Pair	5290.00
Table, Empire Style, Mahogany, Rounded Corners, X-Form Base, 29 x 46 x 30 In.	1295.00
Table, Empire Style, Marble Top, Gilt Bronze, Shelf, Paw Feet, 28 x 31 In.	3220.00
Table, Empire Style, Wood, Round Marble Top, Egyptian Heads, Hoof Feet, 30 x 22 In. . .	650.00
Table, Empire, Mahogany, 2 Parts, Rounded Corners, Scrolled Feet, 46 x 85 In.	395.00
Table, Empire, Mahogany, Marble Top, Concave Shelf, 19th Century, 28 x 24 In.	1495.00
Table, Empire, Mahogany, Ormolu Mounts, Marble Top, Paw Feet, c.1815, 28 x 36 In. . . .	4830.00
Table, Empire, Mahogany, Shaped Top, Tapered Post, Paw Feet, 29 x 34 1/2 In.	805.00
Table, Federal Style, Satinwood, Inlaid Mahogany, Early 1900s, 30 x 150 x 45 In.	2530.00
Table, Federal, Cherry, Inlaid, Tray Top, Stringing, Early 1800s, 28 x 18 1/2 x 18 In.	28200.00
Table, Federal, Cherry, Mahogany Veneer, Drawer, Lower Shelf, c.1825, 29 x 22 x 16 In. . .	490.00
Table, Federal, Figured Maple, Mahogany, c.1820, 29 x 20 x 19 In.	690.00
Table, Federal, Mahogany, 3 Parts, Ribbed Edge & Legs, Brass Paw Feet, 28 In.	2875.00
Table, Federal, Mahogany, Demilune Top, Massachusetts, c.1790, 29 x 35 x 17 In.	8225.00
Table, Federal, Maple, Cherry, Single Drawer, c.1820, 30 x 21 1/2 x 20 3/4 In.	375.00
Table, Federal, Pine, Mustard Yellow, Decorated, c.1820, 30 x 21 1/2 x 17 1/4 In.	1150.00
Table, Federal, Tiger Maple, Painted, Ovolo Corners, 29 1/2 x 21 x 17 In.	12925.00
Table, Folding, Bruno Mathsson, Cherry, Birch, c.1935, 28 1/2 In.	1765.00
Table, Folding, Bruno Mathsson, Teak, 110 x 43 x 28 1/2 In.	1150.00
Table, Folding, Coach, Mahogany, Crossed Serpentine Legs, Center Hinge, 28 x 34 In. . . .	468.00
Table, Folding, J. Adnet, Brass Legs & Stretcher, Leather Frame, Glass Top, 18 x 24 In. . .	4315.00
Table, Francis McCarthy, Tiled, Nudes, Octagonal, Signed, 22 In.	1645.00
Table, Frank Lloyd Wright, Slate Top, Round, Cruciform Base, 22 x 17 In.	2300.00
Table, Frank Lloyd Wright, Taliesin Design, Heritage Henredon, 26 x 27 x 23 In.	1380.00
Table, Frankl, Cork, Biomorphic Top, 4 Mahogany Legs, Johnson, 14 In.	1115.00
Table, French Provincial, Fruitwood, Breadboard Ends, 2 Drawers, 31 x 29 In.	1265.00
Table, French Provincial, Fruitwood, Planked Top, c.1850, 29 x 74 In.	1840.00

Furniture, Table, Dunbar, Mahogany,
Brass Step, c.1950, 25 x 25 In., Pair

Furniture, Table, Eames, Ash Plywood,
c.1950, 20 x 34 1/4 In.

Table, French Provincial, Oak, Fruitwood, Raised Edge, c.1890, 28 x 33 In. 1495.00
Table, French Provincial, Oak, Planked Top, Oval, Square Tapered Legs, 30 x 91 x 56 In. . 1380.00
Table, French Provincial, Rectangular Top, Drawer, Square Legs, 28 x 27 1/2 x 20 In. . . . 920.00
Table, Fruitwood, Geometric Marquetry, Tripod Base, Continental, 29 x 43 In. 560.00
Table, G. Nakashima, Walnut, Cross-Legged, 1966, 21 x 26 x 26 In. . . . . *Illus* 13800.00
Table, G. Nakashima, Walnut, Flaring Legs, 2 Mira Chairs, c.1987, Child's 3055.00
Table, G. Nelson, Cube, Hairpin Legs, Herman Miller, 22 x 34 x 34 In. 590.00
Table, G. Nelson, Enameled Aluminum, Plywood, Herman Miller, 1960s 805.00
Table, G. Nelson, Primavera, Chrome, Glass, Herman Miller, 22 x 18 x 34 In. . . . .545.00 to 705.00
Table, G. Poillerat, Gilt Bronze, Marble, Round Top, c.1940, 21 x 36 In. 3525.00
Table, G. Stickley, Circular Top, Keyhole, Apron, 24 1/2 x 24 In. 1725.00
Table, G. Stickley, No. 612, Cut-Corner Top, Lower Shelf, Stretchers, 24 x 24 x 29 In. . . . 2185.00
Table, G. Stickley, No. 637, Oak, Rectangular Top, Shelf, 28 1/2 x 48 x 30 In. 1880.00
Table, G. Stickley, No. 645, Round, Apron, Arched Cross Stretchers, 36 x 29 In. 1610.00
Table, G. Stickley, No. 647, Trestle Base, Median Shelf, c.1912, 29 x 30 x 48 In. 6110.00
Table, G. Stickley, Round Top, Apron, Stacked Stretcher Base, 30 x 28 In. 5465.00
Table, G. Stickley, Round Top, Spindle Base, Lower Shelf, c.1905, 30 x 29 In. 12650.00
Table, Galle Style, Walnut, Inlay, Flip Top, Late 20th Century, 30 x 41 x 22 In. 520.00
Table, Galle, Fruitwood, Marquetry, 2 Tiers, Reeded Legs, 31 x 23 1/2 x 16 1/2 In. 765.00
Table, Game, Arts & Crafts, Circular Leather Top, Cross Stretchers, 28 3/4 x 41 In. 865.00
Table, Game, Arts & Crafts, Flip Top, Checkerboard, Converts To Chair, 28 3/4 x 25 In. . . 635.00
Table, Game, Chippendale, Mahogany, Drawer, England, 28 x 33 1/2 In. 1335.00
Table, Game, Chippendale, Mahogany, Flip Top, c.1780, 35 x 33 x 16 In. 1645.00
Table, Game, Edwardian, Mahogany, Inlaid, Serpentine Top, Handkerchief, 28 In. 750.00
Table, Game, Edwardian, Mahogany, Leather Surface, Octagonal, c.1900, 28 x 35 In. 805.00
Table, Game, Empire, Mahogany, Ormolu Mounted, Late 19th Century, 28 x 21 In. 960.00
Table, Game, Federal, Mahogany, Bellflower Inlay, Drawer, J. Mack, 1790, 18 x 28 In. . . 6500.00
Table, Game, Federal, Mahogany, Demilune, Eagle, c.1800, 29 x 37 x 18 1/4 In. 5975.00
Table, Game, Federal, Maple, Birch Inlay, c.1810, 29 x 35 x 17 1/4 In. 6570.00
Table, Game, George III Style, Mahogany, Floral Carved, c.1810, 29 x 35 x 17 In. 4140.00
Table, Game, George III, Mahogany, Banded Edge, 18th Century, 29 x 36 x 17 In. 1725.00
Table, Game, George III, Mahogany, Handkerchief, 1 Drawer, Casters, 31 x 21 x 21 In. . . 655.00
Table, Game, George III, Mahogany, Hinged Top, c.1810, 28 1/2 x 36 x 18 In. 1380.00
Table, Game, Georgian, 3-Fold, Serpentine Top, 2 Drawers, 29 x 14 1/2 x 30 In. 2365.00
Table, Game, Georgian, Mahogany, Demilune Top, Carved Edges, Ireland, 28 x 27 In. . . . 2250.00
Table, Game, Georgian, Mahogany, Flip Top, Leather Inset, Trefoil Base, 36 In. 690.00
Table, Game, Hepplewhite, Serpentine Top, Oval Floral Frieze, Inlaid Legs, 31 In. 460.00
Table, Game, Hepplewhite, Walnut, 2 Drawers, Tapered Legs, 32 x 16 x 30 In. 420.00
Table, Game, Indian Ivory, Sandalwood, Chess, 19th Century, 8 x 10 In. 1365.00
Table, Game, J. Adnet, Red, Black Leather, Folding, c.1950, 29 x 30 In. 8965.00
Table, Game, Jansen, Giltwood, Verre Eglomise, Cabriole Legs, c.1945, 28 x 27 In. 4780.00
Table, Game, Jules Leleu, Fruitwood, Mahogany, Flip Top, c.1930, 29 x 31 x 31 In. 4780.00
Table, Game, Karl Springer, Lacquered Vellum, Brass Corners, Inset Board, Cover 1380.00
Table, Game, Louis Philippe, Mahogany, Flip Top, Demilune, 1850s, 29 x 44 x 22 In. . . . 5736.00
Table, Game, Louis XV Style, Faux Tortoiseshell, Boulle, c.1890, 29 x 34 x 17 In. 2415.00
Table, Game, Louis XV Style, Kingwood, Flip Top, Parquetry, 31 x 32 x 23 In. 1060.00
Table, Game, Louis XV Style, Oak, Kingwood Banded, Hinges, 29 x 31 x 15 In. 1120.00
Table, Game, Louis XV Style, Rosewood, Flip Top, Parquet, Ormolu, 29 x 15 x 22 In. . . . 1130.00
Table, Game, Louis XVI Style, Kingwood, Marquetry, Round, France, 30 x 32 In. 2760.00
Table, Game, Mahogany, Burl Inlay, Flip Top, Rotates, Paw Feet, 28 x 18 x 36 In. 440.00
Table, Game, Mahogany, Flip Top, Carved Legs, 19th Century, 29 x 36 x 18 In. 6615.00
Table, Game, Mahogany, Inlaid, Flip Top, Turned Pedestal, 1800s, 29 x 18 x 36 In. 600.00
Table, Game, Mahogany, Ripple Front, Serpentine, 1800s, 28 1/2 x 17 1/2 In. 500.00
Table, Game, McHugh, Circular Top, 2 Drawers, Arched Cross Stretcher, 31 x 44 In. 1955.00
Table, Game, Napoleon III, Rosewood, Leather Surface, c.1865, 30 3/4 x 39 1/2 In. 1840.00
Table, Game, Neoclassical, Mahogany, Swivel Top, Paw Feet, c.1830 . . . . 4400.00
Table, Game, Parquetry Chessboard Top, Drawer, Tapered Legs, 1800s, 27 x 18 In. 450.00
Table, Game, Queen Anne Style, Walnut, Felt Playing Surface, Drawer, 30 x 30 In. 590.00
Table, Game, Queen Anne Style, Walnut, Flip Top, Serpentine Front, 32 x 21 In. 2390.00
Table, Game, Queen Anne, Mahogany, Accordion Action, Chip Wells, 29 x 34 In. 1530.00
Table, Game, Queen Anne, Mahogany, Gateleg, Skirt Drawer, 28 x 13 1/2 x 27 In. 2200.00
Table, Game, Regency, Mahogany, Demilune, Spider-Web Inlay, 29 3/4 x 48 x 21 In. 675.00
Table, Game, Regency, Mahogany, Ebony Inlay, Pedestal, Casters, c.1820, 29 x 36 In. 1035.00

Table, Game, Regency, Mahogany, Urn Pedestal, Brass Casters, c.1815, 30 x 36 x 18 In. . . 1265.00
Table, Game, Regency, Rosewood, 4 Paw Feet, c.1815, 28 x 36 In. 2530.00
Table, Game, Rosewood, Marquetry, Handkerchief, 4 Hinged Leaves, 28 x 19 In. 940.00
Table, Game, Sheraton, Mahogany, Serpentine Front, Twist Legs, 30 x 36 In. 1610.00
Table, Game, Sheraton, Mahogany, Swell Front, Reeded Edge, Turned Legs, 29 x 36 In. . . . 1380.00
Table, Game, Victorian, Flip Top, Mother-Of-Pearl Inlay, 29 x 23 In. 590.00
Table, Game, Victorian, Walnut, Marquetry, Round Top, Tripod Base, 29 x 19 In. 590.00
Table, Game, Victorian, Walnut, Swivel Top, Cathedral-Shaped Frame 170.00
Table, Game, Walnut, Flip Top, Carved Pedestal Base, 1800s, 35 In. 690.00
Table, Game, Walnut, Flip Top, Carved Trestle Base, 1800s, 38 In. 1240.00
Table, Game, William IV, Rosewood, Rectangular Top, 30 1/2 x 36 x 18 In. 920.00
Table, Gateleg, English Oak, 2 Oval Leaves, Turned & Block Legs, 29 x 78 x 24 In. 1610.00
Table, Gateleg, George III Style, Mahogany, Spider, 25 1/2 x 30 1/2 x 9 In. 1435.00
Table, Gateleg, Maple, Single Drawer, Baluster Legs, 18th Century, 42 In. 5290.00
Table, Gateleg, Oak, 1 Drawer, England, c.1780, 27 x 31 x 38 In. 1995.00
Table, Gateleg, Oak, Egg-Shape Leaves, England, 28 x 40 1/2 In. 805.00
Table, Gateleg, Oak, End Drawer, Rope Twist Legs, Block & Ball Feet, 29 In. 880.00
Table, Gateleg, Oak, End Drawer, Vase Turned Legs, Block & Ball Feet, 29 x 43 In. 330.00
Table, Gateleg, Regency, Mahogany, Block & Ring Turned Spider Supports, 22 x 18 In. . . . 530.00
Table, Gateleg, William & Mary Style, Maple, Turned, 27 x 33 3/4 x 14 3/4 In. 5680.00
Table, George II Style, Giltwood Marble Top, 34 x 75 x 28 In. 23900.00
Table, George II Style, Walnut, Marble Top, 20th Century, 34 x 72 x 25 In., Pair 4780.00
Table, George II, Mahogany, Octagonal, Tripod, 23 1/2 x 11 In. 16730.00
Table, George II, Red Japanned, Parcel Gilt, 33 1/2 x 39 x 19 1/2 In. 2690.00
Table, George III Style, Mahogany Inlay, Demilune, 33 x 45 1/2 x 19 In., Pair 2530.00
Table, George III Style, Mahogany, 3 Pedestals, c.1875, 28 x 99 x 42 In. 4830.00
Table, George III Style, Mahogany, Carved, Piecrust, Tripod, c.1900, 27 x 20 In. 660.00
Table, George III Style, Mahogany, Crossbanded, 1800s, 32 x 69 1/2 x 22 3/4 In. 1725.00
Table, George III Style, Mahogany, Oval Top, Box Stretcher, Splayed Legs, 27 x 24 In. . . 765.00
Table, George III Style, Mahogany, Pedestal, Cabriole Legs, Pad Feet, 30 In. 1165.00
Table, George III Style, Mahogany, Reeded Edge, Frieze Drawer, 35 1/2 x 33 x 17 In. . . . 635.00
Table, George III Style, Mahogany, Rosewood, Satinwood, 28 x 22 x 17 In., Pair 1095.00
Table, George III Style, Mahogany, Twin Pillar, S-Extension, 20th Century, 28 x 45 In. . . . 1410.00
Table, George III Style, Satinwood, Crossbanded, Octagonal Top, Casters, 28 x 42 x 42 In. 1385.00
Table, George III, Circular Top, Splayed Legs, Scrolled Feet, Casters, Ireland, 30 x 72 In. . 5750.00
Table, George III, Mahogany, 2 Drawers, Center Door, c.1810, 32 x 16 x 17 1/2 In. 980.00
Table, George III, Mahogany, 5 Leaves, Horseshoe, 30 x 58 1/2 In. 7765.00
Table, George III, Mahogany, Circular Top, 3 Splayed Legs, Pad Feet, 29 x 34 1/2 In. 1955.00
Table, George III, Mahogany, Demilune, Frieze, Tapered Legs, 28 x 45 x 21 In. 1380.00
Table, George III, Mahogany, Drawer, Tapered Legs, Spade Feet, 30 x 34 x 18 In. 920.00
Table, George III, Mahogany, Inlaid, Drawers, Candle Slides, 29 x 21 x 14 In. 1195.00
Table, George III, Mahogany, Parquetry Top, Storage, 3 Legs, 1700s, 29 x 12 1/2 In. 2185.00
Table, George III, Mahogany, Rectangular Top, Drawer, Square Legs, 29 x 33 In. 1060.00
Table, George III, Mahogany, Tripod, Splayed Cabriole Legs, 28 x 33 In. 1380.00
Table, George III, Oak, Rectangular Top, 2 Drawers, Square Legs, 28 1/4 x 38 x 19 In. . . . 920.00
Table, George III, Rectangular, Canted Corners, Square Tapered Splayed Legs, 29 In. 2350.00
Table, George III, Satinwood Inlay, Ebony, 2 Drawers, Flaps, c.1800, 27 x 37 x 24 In. . . . 8960.00
Table, George IV, Mahogany, Parcel Gilt, Marble Inset, Round, 29 1/2 x 26 1/2 In. 3000.00
Table, Georgian, Mahogany Inlay, D-Shape, c.1850, 30 x 46 x 23 In., Pair 1840.00
Table, Georgian, Rosewood, 2 Drawers, Platform Base, Splayed Legs, 37 In. 1750.00
Table, Gilt Onyx, Turtle Top, Carved Apron, Figural Cabriole Legs, 29 x 38 In. 1680.00
Table, Gilt Scroll Carved & Wrought Iron Bracket Base, Glass Top, 30 x 42 In. 405.00
Table, Gio Ponti, Mahogany, Bi-Level, Angled Legs, Ball Feet, 24 x 26 x 18 In. 1060.00
Table, Glass, Mirror, White Paint, Scrolled Leaves, c.1940, 19 x 47 x 24 In. 1910.00
Table, Gold Lacquer, Dragon, Flowers, 19th Century, 13 3/4 x 32 1/2 In. 8960.00
Table, Gothic Revival, Rosewood, Ogee-Molded Frieze, Finials, 20 x 33 x 18 In. 920.00
Table, Gothic, Rosewood, Inset Marble Turtle Top, Rippled Moldings, 28 x 44 In. 2240.00
Table, Grain Painted, Scrub Top, Black, Red, Square Tapered Legs, 29 x 66 x 27 In. 1265.00
Table, Green, Red Lacquer, Parcel Gilt, Hinged Top, Chinese, 27 1/2 x 22 x 22 In. 7170.00
Table, Gueridon, Empire Style, Bronze, Incised Flowers, Continental, 35 x 36 In. 2760.00
Table, Gueridon, Louis XV Style, Giltwood, Marble Top, Rococo Apron, 29 x 24 x 24 In. . 1165.00
Table, Gueridon, Louis XV, Gilt Metal, Marble, Molded Legs, 20th Century, 28 x 19 In. . . . 1670.00
Table, Gueridon, Louis XVI Style, Fruitwood, Parquet, 2 Drawers, Shelf, 29 x 14 x 21 In. . 580.00

Furniture, Table, G. Nakashima,
Walnut, Cross-Legged, 1966,
21 x 26 x 26 In.

Furniture, Table, Hans Wegner,
Knock-Down, Branded Marks,
Denmark, c.1950, 19 x 24 In.

Furniture, Table, I. Noguchi,
Laminated Plywood, Steel, Iron,
Knoll, c.1950, 20 x 24 In.

Table, Gueridon, Mahogany, Marble Top, Scroll Brackets, 3 Paw Feet, c.1820, 32 x 47 In.	9200.00
Table, Hans Wegner, Chromed Steel, Teak, Laminate, 1960s, 25 1/2 x 13 In.	335.00
Table, Hans Wegner, Knock-Down, Branded Marks, Denmark, c.1950, 19 x 24 In. . . *Illus*	805.00
Table, Hardwood, 3 Tiers, Bats, Chinese, 19th Century, 7 1/2 x 16 x 16 In., Pair	545.00
Table, Hardwood, 3-Board Top, Turned Legs, 30 1/2 x 84 x 36 1/2 In.	1100.00
Table, Hardwood, Bird, Flower-Filled Vase, Mother-Of-Pearl, Chinese, 14 x 46 x 22 In.	600.00
Table, Hardwood, Pierced Apron, 2-Board Top, Anglo-Indian, c.1850, 31 x 52 In.	920.00
Table, Harvest, George III Style, Oak, Drop Leaf, Gateleg, 30 1/2 x 59 x 95 In.	1495.00
Table, Harvest, Poplar, Pine, 2 Drawers, Turned Legs, 108 x 45 x 31 In.	1320.00
Table, Harvest, Sheraton, Drop Leaf, Yellow Paint, 2 9-In. Leaves, 29 x 60 x 21 In.	1265.00
Table, Harvest, Yew, Oak, 5-Board Top, Stretcher Base, Turned Legs, 71 x 28 x 29 In.	1430.00
Table, Hepplewhite Style, Mahogany, Band Inlay, Drawer, 28 x 30 x 20 In.	575.00
Table, Hepplewhite, Birch, Scrubbed, 2-Board Top, 36 1/2 x 17 1/4 In.	605.00
Table, Hepplewhite, Pine, Red Wash, Drawer, 2-Board Top, 39 x 24 x 11 In.	660.00
Table, Hepplewhite, Walnut, 2-Board Top, Dovetailed, Late 1700s, 29 x 27 x 35 In.	4500.00
Table, Higgins, Walnut Frame, Glass Tile, Blue, Green, 18 x 15 In.	460.00
Table, Hongmu, Marble Inset, Tripod, Chinese, c.1900, 30 In.	490.00
Table, Horn, Round Wood Top, 3 Intertwined Horn Legs, Brass Feet, 17 In.	115.00
Table, Howell, Chrome, Red Laminate, 2 Tiers, 22 x 23 3/4 x 12 1/2 In.	295.00
Table, Hunzinger, Ornate Stretcher Base, Lion's-Head Supports, 29 x 36 In.	1790.00
Table, Hunzinger, Pedestal, Brass Claw & Ball Feet, c.1890, 24 x 24 x 30 In.	1456.00
Table, I. Noguchi, Laminated Plywood, Steel, Iron, Knoll, c.1950, 20 x 24 In. . . . . . *Illus*	2070.00
Table, Impala, Laminated Wood, Cast Aluminum Legs, Modernica, 29 x 70 In.	140.00
Table, Inset Plank Top, Squared Legs, Cloud Finials, Chinese, 29 x 82 x 30 In.	520.00
Table, Irish Georgian Style, Mahogany, Carved, Scalloped Shell, 34 x 66 x 24 1/2 In.	1840.00
Table, Iron Base, Hammered, Bakelite Top, France, 1920s, 19 1/2 x 29 In.	1495.00
Table, Italian Baroque Style, Marble Top, Gilt, Baluster Scroll Base, 30 x 41 In.	955.00
Table, Italian Rococo Style, Giltwood, Mirror, c.1940, 17 x 49 x 28 In.	1910.00
Table, Jacobean, Oak, Plank Top, Paneled Frieze Drawer, Sausage-Turned Legs, 28 In.	1175.00
Table, Jansen, Limed Oak, Parchment, Square, Cabriole Legs, c.1930, 28 1/2 x 30 In.	4780.00
Table, Jean Prouve, Compass, Oak Top, Bent & Enameled Steel Legs, 28 x 47 In.	5465.00
Table, Jean Prouve, Wood, Enameled Metal, France, c.1950, 26 x 21 1/2 In.	3740.00
Table, Jules Leleu, Rosewood, Verre Eglomise, Pedestal, c.1925, 20 x 35 In.	6570.00
Table, Karl Springer, Chinese Style, Faux Cinnabar, Brass Mounted, c.1970, 19 x 42 In.	1434.00
Table, Karl Springer, Ivory Inlay, Shagreen, Telescopic Round, c.1970, 29 x 41 In.	9560.00
Table, Katavalos, Littell & Kelley, Laverne Originals, Maple, Iron, 62 x 17 x 15 In.	1095.00
Table, Kingwood, Marquetry, Tiered, Brass Mount, France, c.1900, 30 x 25 In.	980.00
Table, Kittinger, George III Style, Mahogany, 4 Drawers, Pedestal Cabinet, 48 x 30 In.	1760.00
Table, Kittinger, Mahogany, Oak, Drawer, Apron, Cabriole Legs, 23 x 15 x 27 In.	110.00
Table, L. & J.G. Stickley, Arched Apron, Horizontal Stretcher, 36 x 28 x 29 In.	750.00
Table, L. & J.G. Stickley, Circular Top, Arched Stretchers, c.1910, 29 x 42 In.	1210.00
Table, L. & J.G. Stickley, Hexagonal Top, Tenon Stretchers, 6 Legs, 48 x 48 x 29 In.	8625.00
Table, L. & J.G. Stickley, Round Top, Lower Shelf, Stretchers, 24 x 29 In.	1150.00
Table, Lacquer, Red, Flowers, Butterflies, Chinese, c.1820, 10 x 29 x 14 In.	380.00
Table, Liberty & Co., Hexagonal Top, 6 Spindle Legs, Cutouts, Shelf, 22 x 22 x 28 In.	240.00

Table, Library, Aesthetic Revival, Rosewood, Burled Walnut, 29 x 45 x 29 In. . . . . . . *Illus* 10575.00
Table, Library, Aesthetic Revival, Walnut, 4 Drawers, N.Y., c.1800s, 29 x 58 x 32 In. 5975.00
Table, Library, Arts & Crafts, 2 Blind Drawers, Lower Stretcher, 48 x 30 x 29 In. 345.00
Table, Library, Arts & Crafts, Blind Drawer, Slatted Sides, Shelf, 27 x 30 x 24 In. 375.00
Table, Library, Arts & Crafts, Oak, 2 Drawers, Through-Tenon Construction, 30 x 44 In. . 715.00
Table, Library, Arts & Crafts, Trestle, Corbel Supports, Shelf, Mortised, 29 x 50 In. 1035.00
Table, Library, Edwardian, Oak, Carved Frieze, Fluted Columns, c.1900, 77 x 34 x 32 In. . 460.00
Table, Library, French Provincial, Walnut, Beaded Serpentine Top, Leather Inset, 1880 . . . 440.00
Table, Library, G. Stickley, 2 Drawers, Long Corbels, Lower Shelf, 30 x 36 x 24 In. 3740.00
Table, Library, G. Stickley, 2 Drawers, Lower Shelf, Mortised Stretcher, 29 x 42 In. 1380.00
Table, Library, G. Stickley, Leather Top, 2 Drawers, Red Decal, 29 x 48 x 30 In. 980.00
Table, Library, G. Stickley, Oak, Rectangular Top, Drawer, Shelf, 28 x 48 x 29 In. 1530.00
Table, Library, G. Stickley, Rectangular, Drawers, Iron Pulls, 42 x 30 x 30 In. 3335.00
Table, Library, G. Stickley, Trestle, Lower Shelf, Keyed-Through Legs, 48 x 29 x 28 In. . . 1035.00
Table, Library, George III, Mahogany, Round, c.1800, 29 x 43 3/4 In. 4180.00
Table, Library, Jules Leleu, Rosewood, Gilt Bronze, c.1925, 28 1/2 x 62 1/2 x 35 In. 5380.00
Table, Library, L. & J.G. Stickley, Drawer, Shelf, Keyed-Through Stretchers, 28 x 36 In. . 1380.00
Table, Library, L. & J.G. Stickley, No. 520, Drawer, Lower Shelf, 30 x 42 x 28 In. 1528.00
Table, Library, L. & J.G. Stickley, No. 531, Drawer, Lower Shelf, 48 x 30 x 29 In. 1955.00
Table, Library, Lifetime, 2 Drawers, Hammered Copper Hardware, 54 x 32 x 30 In. 1095.00
Table, Library, Limbert, 2 Drawers, Copper Pulls, Apron, Corbels, 29 x 48 x 32 In. 5175.00
Table, Library, Limbert, 3 Drawers, Overhanging Top, Lower Shelf, 29 x 60 x 32 In. 1840.00
Table, Library, Limbert, Leather Top, Shelf, 29 x 42 x 26 In. 1095.00
Table, Library, Limbert, Oval, Cutout Sides, Angled Corbels, 29 1/2 x 45 x 30 In. 2530.00
Table, Library, Mahogany, Carved Apron, Serpentine X-Stretcher 420.00
Table, Library, Mahogany, Marble, Rectangular, N.Y., 1820-1840, 30 x 61 x 27 In. 6575.00
Table, Library, Oak, Granite Top, Barley-Twist Legs, England, c.1850, 29 x 45 In. 980.00
Table, Library, Regency Style, Mahogany, Blond Inlay, Medallion, 31 x 47 x 23 In. 3680.00
Table, Library, Regency Style, Mahogany, Frieze Drawers, 31 1/4 x 66 x 36 In. 8960.00
Table, Library, Regency, Rosewood, Leather Writing Surface, c.1815, 28 x 44 In. 2530.00
Table, Library, Renaissance Revival, Carved Borders, Frieze & Trestle Supports 2705.00
Table, Library, Rosewood, Mahogany, Carved, England, c.1865, 30 x 54 In. 1725.00
Table, Library, Stickley Bros., 1 Drawer, 2-Slat Sides, Shelf, 29 x 40 x 26 In. 1095.00
Table, Library, Stickley Bros., 2 Drawers, Slatted Sides, Double Stretcher, 29 1/2 x 46 In. . 920.00
Table, Library, Stickley Bros., Copper Pulls, Hammered, 2 Drawers, 30 x 54 x 32 In. 2185.00
Table, Library, Stickley Bros., Drawer, Pulls, Backplates, Shelf, 29 3/4 x 48 x 35 In. 805.00
Table, Library, Tiger Oak, Drawer, Claw Feet, 30 x 48 In. . . . . *Illus* 500.00
Table, Library, Umphrey Mfg. Co., Drawer, Lower Shelf, Cubbies, 29 x 48 In. 1265.00
Table, Library, Victorian, Mahogany, Mid 19th Century, 29 x 48 x 39 In. 3585.00
Table, Library, Walnut, Carved Griffins, c.1890, 60 x 31 x 31 In. 3920.00
Table, Library, William IV, Burl Walnut, Leather Inset, Drawers, 29 x 67 x 46 In. 3220.00
Table, Library, William IV, Mahogany, Gilt Tooled-Leather Top, 2 Drawers, 31 x 84 In. . . 2350.00
Table, Library, Winged Griffins Support, c.1900, 40 x 26 In. 1400.00
Table, Lifetime, Circular, Lower Shelf On Cross Stretchers, 29 x 24 In. 1035.00
Table, Limbert, No. 146, Oval Top, Splayed Legs, Cutout Slab Sides, 45 x 30 x 29 In. . . . 2530.00
Table, Limbert, No. 202, Oak, Circular, Decal, 22 x 18 In. 410.00
Table, Limbert, No. 2430, Oak, Ebony Inlay, Round, 3 Leaves, Splayed Leg Base, 46 In. . 7480.00

Furniture, Table, Library, Aesthetic Revival, Rosewood,
Burled Walnut, 29 x 45 x 29 In.

Furniture, Table, Library, Tiger Oak, Drawer,
Claw Feet, 30 x 48 In.

Table, Louis Philippe, Mahogany, Marble Top, Triangular Base, c.1835, 29 x 19 In. 2070.00
Table, Louis XV Style, Burl, Bronze Mount, Pierced Gallery, 31 x 33 1/2 x 17 In. 1435.00
Table, Louis XV Style, Fruitwood, Bronze, Marquetry, Drawers, Leather, 30 x 50 In. 7770.00
Table, Louis XV Style, Gilt Bronze Mount, Gilt Tooling, Drawers, 30 x 55 x 30 In. 10000.00
Table, Louis XV Style, Gilt Bronze, Tooled Surface, Drawers, 30 x 58 x 32 In. 3525.00
Table, Louis XV Style, Giltwood, Carved, Onyx Inset Top, Round, 33 In. 1385.00
Table, Louis XV Style, Kingwood, Marble Inset Top, France, 31 x 12 In. 460.00
Table, Louis XV Style, Kingwood, Tooled Surface, 3 Drawers, 30 x 38 x 25 In. 1175.00
Table, Louis XV Style, Mahogany Top, Wrought Iron, Bowfront, Scrolled, 36 x 49 In. 315.00
Table, Louis XV Style, Mahogany, Gilt Bronze, Marble, Square Legs, 21 x 43 x 24 In. ... 3230.00
Table, Louis XV Style, Mahogany, Parquetry, Marble Top, Shelf, 28 x 23 x 14 In. 1195.00
Table, Louis XV Style, Oak, Parquetry, Serpentine Banded Top, Scroll Feet, 29 x 51 In. .. 805.00
Table, Louis XV Style, Walnut, Marquetry, Serpentine, Drawers, 31 x 71 1/2 x 34 In. 705.00
Table, Louis XV, Gilt Bronze Mounted, Marquetry, 29 1/2 x 25 3/4 x 17 1/2 In. 865.00
Table, Louis XV, Kingwood, Oval Marble Top, 3 Drawers, 1800s, 29 x 18 x 13 In. 1035.00
Table, Louis XV, Marble Top, Inlay, Shelf, Ormolu Mounts, 21 1/2 In. 865.00
Table, Louis XVI Style, Black Marble Top, Pierced Frieze, Round, 27 x 24 In., Pair 315.00
Table, Louis XVI Style, Burl, Marquetry, Gilt Bronze, Flip Top, 29 x 36 x 18 In. 1555.00
Table, Louis XVI Style, Gilt Bronze, Parquetry, Flip Top, 29 x 33 x 17 In. 2390.00
Table, Louis XVI Style, Gilt Bronze, Wedgwood Frieze, 23 1/2 x 29 1/2 x 18 1/2 In. 2390.00
Table, Louis XVI Style, Giltwood, Marble Top, Caned Shelf Stretcher, 29 x 17 x 13 In. .. 690.00
Table, Louis XVI Style, Giltwood, Marble Top, Carved, Hoof Feet, 31 x 21 1/2 x 16 In. .. 575.00
Table, Louis XVI Style, Giltwood, Marble Top, Leaf Swag Frieze, 30 x 31 x 21 1/2 In. .. 956.00
Table, Louis XVI Style, Mahogany, Gilt Bronze, Pierced Gallery, 31 x 21 In., Pair 540.00
Table, Louis XVI Style, Mahogany, Leather Surface, France, c.1900, 29 3/4 x 49 1/2 In. .. 3680.00
Table, Louis XVI Style, Mahogany, Marble Top, 2 Drawers, Candle Slides, 20 x 18 In. ... 1495.00
Table, Louis XVI Style, Marble Top, Polychrome, c.1900, 27 1/2 x 27 14 In. 4140.00
Table, Louis XVI Style, Marquetry, Marble, Oval, 1 Drawer, Shelf, 28 x 20 x 15 In. 1765.00
Table, Louis XVI Style, Painted, Parcel Gilt, Rectangular Marble Top, 29 x 34 x 20 In. .. 705.00
Table, Louis XVI Style, Rosewood, Ormolu, Leather Inset, 2 Drawers, 30 x 28 x 54 In. .. 3420.00
Table, Louis XVI Style, Walnut, 1 Drawer, Square, Fluted Leg, 28 x 31 x 31 In. 823.00
Table, Louis XVI, Green, Marble Top, Paneled, 20th Century, 37 x 30 x 17 In., Pair 3220.00
Table, Louis XVI, Tulipwood, Crossbanded, Frieze Drawer, Ormolu Mounts, 29 x 44 In. . 2350.00
Table, Lucca Style, Beech, Antiqued, Shaped Black Marble Top, Italy, 30 x 28 In. 575.00
Table, Mahogany, 3 Tiers, Gallery, 2 Drawers, Brass-Cap Casters, 46 x 45 x 17 In. 1020.00
Table, Mahogany, Ebonized, Gilt, Scrolled, Continental, 29 1/2 x 55 x 25 In. 940.00
Table, Mahogany, Giltwood, Polychrome, c.1890, 20 x 20 In. 575.00
Table, Mahogany, Hinged Top, Round Corners, Paneled Drawer, c.1835, 29 x 23 x 16 In. . 2070.00
Table, Mahogany, Inlaid, Early 20th Century, 25 x 18 1/2 x 30 1/2 In. 550.00
Table, Mahogany, Maple, Drawer, Sections, c.1820, 31 x 21 1/2 x 16 1/2 In. 4680.00
Table, Mahogany, Marble Top, 6 Fluted Tapered Legs, c.1920, 23 x 53 x 19 In. 230.00
Table, Mahogany, Marble Top, Baluster Pedestal, Trefoil Base, Paw Feet, 30 x 39 In. 2620.00
Table, Mahogany, Marble Top, Brass Gallery, Square Column, 29 1/2 x 16 In. 865.00
Table, Mahogany, Marquetry, Floral, Fluted Legs, c.1910, 30 x 32 x 24 In. 545.00
Table, Mahogany, Parcel Gilt, Marble, Continental, 1800s, 35 x 27 1/2 x 16 In. 2150.00
Table, Majorelle, 2 Tiers, Marquetry, Flowers, Butterflies, 31 x 32 x 20 In. 895.00
Table, Majorelle, Mahogany, Clematis, c.1900, 32 x 24 1/4 In. 7170.00
Table, Maple, Skirt, Tapered Legs, Button Feet, 18th Century, 26 1/2 x 21 x 15 In. 1760.00
Table, Marble Inlay, Round, Wrought Iron Base, Bun Feet, Italy, 29 x 41 1/2 In. 1725.00
Table, Marble Top, Pierced, Double Cross-Stretcher, 30 1/4 x 48 x 24 1/2 In. 21275.00
Table, Marquetry, Black Ebonized Finish, Drawer, 29 1/2 x 34 x 23 1/2 In. 3280.00
Table, Max Kuehne, Silvered, Gilt, Floral, Signed, 17 x 36 x 18 In. 3820.00
Table, McCobb, Connoisseur, Mahogany, Brass Stretchers, 24 x 30 x 22 In. 690.00
Table, Memphis, Enamel, 3 Tiers, Geometric Shelves, Rolling, c.1980, 20 x 28 x 18 In. .. 705.00
Table, Michele DeLucchi, Kristall, Yellow, Black & White, Memphis, 20 x 16 x 24 In. ... 1380.00
Table, Mies Van Der Rohe, Tubular Metal, Glass, c.1929, 24 x 27 3/4 x 27 3/4 In. 4780.00
Table, Moravian Tile, Green & Ivory, Seasons, Animals, Twisted Iron Base, 19 x 29 In. .. 750.00
Table, Moresque Design, 4 Tiles, c.1930, 17 1/2 x 18 In. .... *Illus* 750.00
Table, Moresque, Blue, Yellow, Orange, Green, c.1920, 20 x 12 In. .... *Illus* 115.00
Table, Napoleon III Style, Kingwood, Oblong, Drawer, France, 30 x 22 In., Pair 980.00
Table, Napoleon III, Ebonized, Marquetry, 3 Tiers, Pierced Gallery, 32 x 17 x 13 In. 380.00
Table, Napoleon III, Ebonized, Pierced Gallery, 19th Century, 30 x 22 1/2 In., Pair 6040.00
Table, Napoleon III, Gilt Bronze, Porcelain, 19th Century, 34 1/2 x 23 In. 8365.00

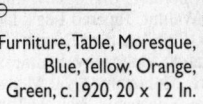

To remove white marks from table tops, rub with olive oil, then a rag dipped in alcohol.

Furniture, Table, Moresque
Design, 4 Tiles, c.1930,
17 1/2 x 18 In.

Furniture, Table, Moresque,
Blue, Yellow, Orange,
Green, c.1920, 20 x 12 In.

Table, Napoleon III, Mahogany, Kingwood, Marble Top, 30 x 17 x 13 1/2 In. 920.00
Table, Napoleon III, Oriental, Bamboo, Lacquered, 19th Century, 30 x 13 x 13 In. 490.00
Table, Napoleon III, Walnut, Carved, Octagonal Top, 19th Century, 21 x 17 1/2 In. 920.00
Table, Neoclassical, Elm, Burl, Sweden, c.1885, 24 1/4 x 29 In. 2070.00
Table, Neoclassical, Mahogany, Round Top, Continental, 29 x 48 1/2 In. 5060.00
Table, Neoclassical, Walnut, Figured Top, Drawer, 30 x 35 x 23 In. 1840.00
Table, Nesting, Edwardian, Mahogany, Foliate Carving, c.1900, 22 x 23 1/2 x 17 In. 550.00
Table, Nesting, Fruitwood, Rectangular, c.1900, 28 1/2 x 21 1/2 x 14 3/4 In., 4 Piece 490.00
Table, Nesting, George III Style, Mahogany, 26 x 28 In., 4 Piece 600.00
Table, Nesting, Grete Jalk, Teak, Tapered Legs, P. Jeppesen, 22 x 14 x 19 In., 3 Piece 6325.00
Table, Nesting, J. Adnet, Leather Over Steel, Glass, c.1950, 22 x 18 In. 5750.00
Table, Nesting, Mahogany Top, Steel Base, 20 1/2 x 14 In., 3 Piece 765.00
Table, Nesting, Regency Style, Burl, 29 1/2 To 23 x 15 In., 4 Piece 2585.00
Table, Nesting, Rosewood, Mother-Of-Pearl, Brass, Copper Inlay, Early 1900s, 4 Piece . . 7170.00
Table, Nesting, Teak, Pierced Grapevines On Apron, 4 Piece 170.00
Table, Nesting, Victorian, Lacquered, Dragons, 28 1/2 x 21 In., 3 Piece 920.00
Table, Oak, 2-Board Top, Vase, Ring & Ball-Turned Legs, Block Feet, 24 x 30 In. 550.00
Table, Oak, Rectangular Top, Rounded Corners, Beaded Edge, Painted, 26 x 42 In. 115.00
Table, Oak, Red Marble Top, Panels On Apron, Carved Scrolls, 21 x 63 x 39 In. 1210.00
Table, Oak, Turned Legs & Stretcher, Continental, 19 x 27 In. 75.00
Table, Old Hickory Chair Co., Octagonal Top, c.1915, 30 In. 2100.00
Table, Oriental, Carved, Dragon, Black Finish, Pierced Skirt, 30 x 47 x 32 In. 920.00
Table, Oriental, Carved, Inlaid, Tiered, Late 20th Century, 40 x 31 x 21 In. 145.00
Table, Oyster Burled Walnut, Oval, Turned Pedestal, 4 Scrolled Feet, 27 x 60 x 42 In. . . . 2185.00
Table, Pander & Zonen, Walnut, Dutch, c.1890, 28 x 30 1/2 In. 2990.00
Table, Parquetry, Herringbone & Diamond, Ebonized Piecrust Edge, 28 x 41 In. 990.00
Table, Pembroke, Chippendale, Mahogany, Reeded Legs, 1-Board Top, 32 x 17 1/2 In. . . . 7975.00
Table, Pembroke, Federal, Cherry Inlay, c.1810, 27 1/2 x 19 3/4 x 35 In. 705.00
Table, Pembroke, Federal, Cherry, Serpentine Leaves, c.1810, 27 x 33 x 31 In. 4185.00
Table, Pembroke, Federal, Mahogany, Inlaid, c.1800, 28 x 38 1/2 x 33 In. 20700.00
Table, Pembroke, Federal, Mahogany, Inlaid, Faux Drawer, c.1795, 28 x 21 x 32 In. 4700.00
Table, Pembroke, Federal, Tiger Maple, Inlaid, Faux Drawers, c.1810, 28 3/8 x 23 In. 3175.00
Table, Pembroke, Federal, Walnut, Acanthus-Carved Legs, 29 x 38 x 24 In. 1380.00
Table, Pembroke, George II, Mahogany, Tapered Legs, Pad Feet, 1700s, 37 In. 620.00
Table, Pembroke, George III Style, Mahogany, Pierced Stretcher, 27 1/2 x 27 In. 1555.00
Table, Pembroke, George III, Mahogany Inlay, Quarter Veneer, 28 3/4 x 19 x 28 In. 5975.00
Table, Pembroke, George III, Mahogany, Band & Shell Inlays, c.1810, 27 x 19 x 24 In. . . . 1095.00
Table, Pembroke, George III, Mahogany, Drawer, Casters, c.1780, 28 x 19 x 28 In. 5080.00
Table, Pembroke, George III, Mahogany, Square Fluted Legs, Casters, 28 In. 1175.00
Table, Pembroke, George III, Satinwood Inlay, c.1780, 27 3/4 x 26 3/4 x 40 1/2 In. 7770.00
Table, Pembroke, George III, Satinwood, Ebonized, c.1775, 28 x 41 1/2 x 27 In. 23900.00
Table, Pembroke, George IV, Mahogany, Tapered Legs, c.1830, 28 x 21 x 30 In. 865.00
Table, Pembroke, Georgian Style, Mahogany, Drawer, 26 x 33 x 13 In. 355.00
Table, Pembroke, Hepplewhite Style, Mahogany, 28 x 29 3/4 x 18 In. 520.00
Table, Pembroke, Hepplewhite Style, Satinwood, c.1890, 26 x 17 3/4 x 29 1/2 In. 2300.00
Table, Pembroke, Hepplewhite, Avodire, Figured, Ebony Line Inlay, 28 x 36 In. 2860.00
Table, Pembroke, Hepplewhite, Cherry, Tapered Legs, X-Stretchers, 34 x 16 x 28 In. 3960.00
Table, Pembroke, Hepplewhite, Mahogany, Figured Veneer, 29 1/4 x 18 1/2 In. 1485.00

Table, Pembroke, Hepplewhite, Mahogany, Poplar, Pine, Inlay, 32 x 20 x 10 In. 2035.00
Table, Pembroke, Hepplewhite, Mahogany, Shell Inlay, c.1820, 28 x 17 x 33 In. 1035.00
Table, Pembroke, Kittinger Co., Sheraton Style, Mahogany, 28 3/4 x 34 x 23 In. 460.00
Table, Pembroke, Mahogany, 1-Board Top, Drawer, Turned & Reeded Legs, 30 x 45 In. . . .   1035.00
Table, Pembroke, Regency, Mahogany, Crossbanded, Drawers, c.1815, 29 x 42 x 43 In. . . .   1175.00
Table, Pembroke, Regency, Mahogany, Drawer, 29 1/4 x 32 1/2 x 22 In. 1955.00
Table, Pembroke, Regency, Mahogany, Reeded Edge, Leaves, Drawers, 27 x 48 x 49 In. . . .   1610.00
Table, Pembroke, Satinwood, Inlaid, Tapered Legs, c.1830, 27 x 21 x 30 In. 1095.00
Table, Pembroke, Sheraton, Mahogany, Inlaid, Curved Corners, Drawer, 29 x 33 In. 1955.00
Table, Pembroke, Walnut, Tapered Legs, Drawer, 1700s, 28 1/2 x 17 x 36 1/2 In. 1320.00
Table, Peter Glass, Floral & Bird Design, Inlay, Lift Top, Inscribed, 22 x 28 In. 3450.00
Table, Philippe Starck, Mahogany, Stainless Steel, Aleph, 16 1/4 x 20 In., Pair 1840.00
Table, Pier, Empire, Mahogany, Oval Medallions, Scroll Legs, c.1840, 35 x 39 x 19 In. . . .   1345.00
Table, Pier, Empire, Rosewood, Marble Top, Tapered Columns, Acanthus Leaf Scroll 5500.00
Table, Pier, Flame Mahogany, White Pine, Marble Top, Mirror, Bronze, c.1820 . . . .   6500.00
Table, Pier, George III Style, Satinwood, Giltwood, Painted, 33 x 39 x 17 In., Pair 6570.00
Table, Pier, Mahogany, Marble Top, 2 Drawers, Bronze Mounts, Gallery, 45 x 32 In. 950.00
Table, Pier, Neoclassical, Mahogany, Veneer, Marble, c.1840, 32 x 36 x 18 In. 1765.00
Table, Pier, Restauration, Rosewood, Carved, Marble Top, c.1835, 39 x 52 1/2 In. 2990.00
Table, Piero Fornasetti, Lacquered Wood, Italy, 19 x 16 In. 630.00
Table, Pine, 2-Board, Tapered Legs, Cut Nails, N.C., 28 1/2 x 115 x 32 In. 3520.00
Table, Pine, Black Paint, Drawer, Tuned Leg, 30 x 64 x 26 1/2 In.   115.00
Table, Pine, Painted, 1-Board Top, Sawbuck Base, Shoe Feet, 24 x 22 x 28 In. 770.00
Table, Pine, Painted, 2-Board Top, Tapered Legs, Mid 19th Century, 30 x 66 x 36 In. 2235.00
Table, Polychrome, Blackamoor Figure, Italy, c.1850, 27 x 19 1/2 In. 2530.00
Table, Polychrome, Marble Top, Demilune, Italy, c.1850, 31 x 32 In., Pair 3220.00
Table, Poplar, Pine, Painted, Drawer, 3-Board Top, 60 x 29 1/2 x 32 1/2 In. 440.00
Table, Queen Anne Style, Mahogany, 3 Parts, Triangle Section, Tripod, 27 x 96 x 40 In. . . .   765.00
Table, Queen Anne, Inset Marble Top, Round, Scalloped, 6 Cabriole Legs, 23 x 25 In. 415.00
Table, Queen Anne, Mahogany, Porringer Top, Rounded Corners, 26 x 32 x 22 In. 6575.00
Table, Queen Anne, Maple, Oval Top, Skirt, Padded Feet, 1700, 26 x 31 x 23 In. 5020.00
Table, Red Paint, Rectangular Top, Skirt, 19th Century, 29 1/2 x 25 x 22 1/2 In. 850.00
Table, Red, Black Lacquer, Gilt Decoration, Chinese, 23 1/2 x 16 In., Pair 345.00
Table, Refectory, Elizabethan, Oak, Plank Top, Carved Grapevines, 32 x 96 In. 2000.00
Table, Refectory, French Provincial, Cherry, End Drawer, 30 1/2 x 71 x 33 1/4 In. 2070.00
Table, Refectory, French Provincial, Walnut, Square Legs, 1800s, 29 x 59 x 29 In. 920.00
Table, Refectory, Nutting, No. 601, Oak 1705.00
Table, Refectory, Oak, Plank Top, Scrolling Iron Stretcher, Square Legs, 30 x 84 In. 1495.00
Table, Refectory, Oak, Stretcher Base, Shoe Feet, Early 20th Century, 71 x 27 x 30 In. . . .   1540.00
Table, Refectory, Pine, Walnut, 6 Turned Supports, Stretcher, France, c.1850, 31 x 78 In. . .   2040.00
Table, Refectory, Teak, Metal, Studs, Portugal, 18th Century, 31 x 79 x 43 In. 1150.00
Table, Refectory, Walnut, Plank Top, Drawer, 19th Century, 30 x 84 x 35 1/2 In. 1840.00
Table, Regency Style, Burl Walnut, Parcel Gilt, c.1812, 28 1/2 x 48 In. 3885.00
Table, Regency Style, Mahogany, Inlaid, 2 Drawers, Brass Paw Casters, 29 x 36 x 21 In. .   575.00
Table, Regency Style, Mahogany, Rounded Rectangular Top, Drawer, 28 x 15 x 12 In. . . .   315.00
Table, Regency, Ebonized, Octagonal Top, Pastoral Scene, Flowers, Stretcher, 30 In. 520.00
Table, Regency, Iron, Marble Top, X-Shape Supports, Mid 1800s, 35 x 46 x 14 In. 4830.00
Table, Regency, Mahogany, Baluster, Saber Legs, England, c.1820, 30 x 53 x 56 In. 2940.00
Table, Regency, Rosewood, Circular Top, Curved Legs, 29 x 13 3/4 In. 1955.00
Table, Regency, Rosewood, Frieze, Triangular Pedestal, Bun Feet, 29 x 52 In. 2750.00
Table, Regency, Rosewood, Painted, Parcel Gilt, c.1810, 27 1/2 x 52 In. 9560.00
Table, Regency, Rosewood, Round, Ribbed Columnar Standard, 29 x 51 In. 4830.00
Table, Renaissance Revival, Bronze, Relief Of Pandora, Griffins, 32 In. 1115.00
Table, Renaissance Revival, Gilt Bronze, Onyx Top, Openwork Frieze, 32 In. 705.00
Table, Renaissance Revival, Mahogany, Gadroon Top, Drawers, 72 x 26 x 30 In. 635.00
Table, Renaissance Revival, Oak, Flip Top, Carved Masks, Trelliswork, Paw Feet, 31 In. .   440.00
Table, Renaissance Revival, Rosewood, Inlaid Marble Turtle Top, 30 x 40 In. 5600.00
Table, Renaissance Revival, Walnut, Marble Top, Carved Skirt, Claw Feet, 30 In. 1120.00
Table, Renaissance Revival, Walnut, Marble, Gold Incised, 28 x 72 x 18 In. . . . . *Illus*   3080.00
Table, Renaissance Revival, Walnut, Marquetry, Gold, Ebony, c.1875, 27 x 44 x 26 In. 7840.00
Table, Risom, Teak, Shelf, Tapered Dowel Legs, 24 x 21 x 27 In., Pair 440.00
Table, Robsjohn-Gibbings, Walnut, Patinated Bronze, 1962, 19 3/4 x 26 In. . . . .6575.00 to 7170.00
Table, Robsjohn-Gibbings, Walnut, Widdicomb, 1950s, 89 x 15 In. 6900.00

Table, Rococo Revival, Giltwood, Marble Top, Foliate Carved, 30 x 20 x 20 In.	545.00
Table, Rococo Revival, Marble Top, Serpentine Sides, Canted Corners, Scroll, 29 x 48 In.	550.00
Table, Rococo Revival, Rosewood, Marble Top, New York, c.1850, 30 x 42 1/2 In.	5520.00
Table, Rococo Revival, Silver Gilt, Marble Top, Acanthus Carved, 20 x 16 x 16 In.	620.00
Table, Rococo, Mahogany, Marble Turtle Top, Shaped Skirt, c.1860, 29 x 39 x 22 In.	1120.00
Table, Rococo, Mahogany, Round, 2-Board Top, c.1855, 28 x 46 1/2 In.	1035.00
Table, Rococo, Mahogany, Round, Pedestal, 4 Legs, c.1850, 28 1/2 x 40 In.	750.00
Table, Rococo, Marble Turtle Top, Stretcher Base, c.1865, 30 x 40 x 26 In.	3360.00
Table, Rococo, Walnut, 3/4-Gallery, Open Shelf, Drawer, Cabriole Legs, 27 x 18 In.	590.00
Table, Rococo, Walnut, Accordion Extension, Double Pedestals, 108 In.	2250.00
Table, Rohde, Burled Veneer, Leatherette, Herman Miller, 15 x 44 x 22 In.	590.00
Table, Rohde, Walnut, Drawer, Leatherette, Herman Miller, 34 x 18 x 12 In., Pair	705.00
Table, Rosewood Veneer Top, Chrome Base Pedestal, Scandinavia, 21 1/2 x 31 1/2 In. . . .	500.00
Table, Rosewood Veneer, Inlaid, Cabriole Legs, Scalloped Aprons, 19 x 13 x 28 In.	385.00
Table, Rosewood, Inlaid Cross Designs, Folding Base, Dunbar, c.1965, 23 x 21 x 25 In. . .	1295.00
Table, Rosewood, Marble Top, Grapevines & Flowers On Apron, Chinese, 19 x 35 In. . . .	690.00
Table, Rosewood, Marble Turtle Top, Rose-Carved Apron, Shaped Stretchers, 29 In.	3360.00
Table, Saarinen, Gray, White Marble, Round Top, Pedestal, Knoll, 24 x 18 In., Pair	940.00
Table, Sawbuck, Grain Painted, Center Stretcher, 29 x 72 x 21 In.	805.00
Table, Sawbuck, Pine, 18th Century, 72 x 22 In.	4200.00
Table, Sawbuck, Walnut, Poplar, Painted, 27 x 42 x 23 In.	660.00
Table, Sewing, 2 Drawers, Milk Glass Pulls, Rope-Twist Legs, 23 x 18 x 29 1/2 In.	430.00
Table, Sewing, 2 Drawers, Pottery Pulls, Square Tapered Legs, 22 x 19 x 29 In.	115.00
Table, Sewing, Ash, Pine, Painted, H-Stretcher, Apron Drawer, 54 x 37 x 27 1/2 In.	385.00
Table, Sewing, Biedermeier Style, Fruitwood, Lift Top, 3 Supports, c.1810, 19 In.	655.00
Table, Sewing, Biedermeier, Birch, Turned Feet, 33 x 12 1/2 x 12 1/2 In.	590.00
Table, Sewing, Birch, Pine, Red Wash, Turned Legs, 2-Board Top, 25 x 16 x 17 In.	330.00
Table, Sewing, Burl, Veneer Panels, Drawer, Key Lock, Continental, 29 x 15 x 19 In.	290.00
Table, Sewing, Carpenter Co., Mirror, Fitted Interior, Jackson, Mississippi	825.00
Table, Sewing, Cherry, Drawer, Hinged Leaves, Tripod Base, c.1830, 29 x 18 x 18 In. . . .	353.00
Table, Sewing, Cherry, Maple, American, c.1790, 28 3/8 x 22 3/4 x 18 3/4 In.	1380.00
Table, Sewing, Cherry, Stepped, Backsplash, 2 Short Over 1 Long Drawer, 38 x 35 In. . . .	920.00
Table, Sewing, Curly Maple, Pine, Tapered Feet, Sliding Shelf, Ohio, 17 x 14 x 29 In. . . .	880.00
Table, Sewing, Empire, Mahogany, Drop Leaf, Pedestal, 19th Century, 28 x 14 x 18 In. . .	275.00
Table, Sewing, Federal, Mahogany, Drop Leaf, Drawer, c.1825, 29 x 18 x 18 In.	560.00
Table, Sewing, Federal, Mahogany, Upper Drawer, Dividers, c.1810, 31 x 22 In.	5375.00
Table, Sewing, G. Stickley, No. 630, Drop Leaf, 3 Drawers, 18 x 18 x 28 In.	5465.00
Table, Sewing, Grain Painted, 1-Board, X-Stretcher Base, 29 x 69 x 24 1/2 In.	4950.00
Table, Sewing, Grain Painted, 3 Drawers, Drop Leaf, 27 3/4 x 16 x 17 1/2 In.	2300.00
Table, Sewing, Mahogany Veneer, Serpentine Front, 3 Drawers, Pedestal, 29 x 23 In.	375.00
Table, Sewing, Mahogany, 2 Drawers, Rounded Corners, Column Supports, 4 Claw Feet .	225.00
Table, Sewing, Mahogany, Canted Corners, Fitted Interior, Raised Base, 30 x 19 In.	635.00
Table, Sewing, Mahogany, Lift Top, Compartments, Spool Legs, 1800s, 23 x 15 x 28 In. . .	200.00
Table, Sewing, Maple, Birch, Square Top, 2 Drawers, c.1825-1835, 17 1/8 In.	1060.00
Table, Sewing, Neoclassical, Mahogany, 2 Drawers, Claw Feet, 28 1/2 x 17 x 14 In.	1265.00
Table, Sewing, Pine Top, 2 Drawers, Pennsylvania, c.1820, 58 1/2 x 34 3/4 In.	2260.00
Table, Sewing, Pine, Rectangular Top Over Case, 3 Drawers, 87 x 23 x 27 In.	635.00
Table, Sewing, Regency, Inlaid, Lift Top, Tapered Legs, Oval, 30 1/2 x 16 x 11 In.	2415.00
Table, Sewing, Renaissance Revival, Walnut, Sliding Basket, c.1870, 33 x 22 x 16 In.	785.00
Table, Sewing, Restauration, Mahogany, Ormolu, Mirror Inside, c.1815, 30 x 20 In.	2070.00
Table, Sewing, Sawbuck, Grain Painted, 1-Board, Scrubbed Top, Drawers, 69 1/2 In.	4950.00

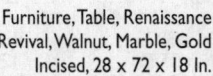

Furniture, Table, Renaissance
Revival, Walnut, Marble, Gold
Incised, 28 x 72 x 18 In.

Table, Sewing, Shaker, 4-Board Top, High Turned Legs, Deep Drawer, 54 x 32 x 30 In. . . . 1100.00
Table, Sewing, Shaker, Pine Top, Birch Legs, Sabbathday Lake, Me., 29 In. 690.00
Table, Sewing, Shaker, Pine, 3-Board Top, Union Village, Ohio, c.1850, 28 3/4 In. 1265.00
Table, Sewing, Shaker, Pine, Red Stain, Rectangular, Mt. Lebanon, N.Y., c.1830, 27 In. . . 1035.00
Table, Sewing, Shaker, Pine, Stain, Dovetailed Drawer, Mt. Lebanon, c.1830, 26 In. 2300.00
Table, Sewing, Sheraton Style, Drop Leaf, Drawers, Metal Pulls, 20 x 9 x 9 1/2 In., Pair . . 575.00
Table, Sewing, Sheraton, Cherry, Drop Leaf, 2 Drawers, Turned Legs, 28 1/2 x 18 In. 575.00
Table, Sewing, Sheraton, Cherry, Tiger Maple, 2 Drawers, American, 27 x 19 1/2 In. 490.00
Table, Sewing, Sheraton, Mahogany, Drop Leaf, 1 Drawer, 2 Leaves, 26 3/4 x 19 In. 460.00
Table, Sewing, Sheraton, Mahogany, Drop Leaf, 2 Drawers, Turned Legs, 29 1/2 x 18 In. . . 430.00
Table, Sewing, Sheraton, Walnut, Sliding Top, Drawer, Ohio, 36 x 21 1/2 In. 2750.00
Table, Sewing, Softwood, Polychrome, Revolving Spool Holder, 1800s, 13 x 9 x 6 In. . . . 3630.00
Table, Sewing, Walnut, 2 Drawers, Canted, Early 20th Century, 29 1/2 x 14 1/2 x 21 In. . . 275.00
Table, Sewing, William IV, Walnut, Oval Top, 3 Splayed Legs, c.1835, 28 x 18 In. 2300.00
Table, Sewing, Wood, Painted, Thread Caddy, Lobed Pincushion, Carved Legs, 10 x 11 In. 220.00
Table, Shaker, Birch, Drop Leaf, Scrubbed Top, Leaves, Red Wash, 41 x 15 x 11 3/4 In. . . 495.00
Table, Sheraton Style, Mahogany, Serpentine Front, Fluted, c.1875, 33 x 54 x 24 In. 2185.00
Table, Sheraton, Birch, Butternut, Drawer, Turned Legs, 30 x 18 x 29 In. 385.00
Table, Sheraton, Mahogany, Greek Key Inlay, Reeded Legs, Silk Basket, 29 x 19 1/2 In. . . 460.00
Table, Sheraton, Mahogany, Poplar, 2 Drawers, Shelf, Rope-Twist Legs, 29 In. 935.00
Table, Sheraton, Walnut, Flip Top, Turned-Wood Pins, Drawers, Pa., c.1820, 29 x 58 In. . . 2260.00
Table, Side, Art Deco, Oak, Rectangular, Flat & Curved Sides, 20 x 32 x 20 In. 410.00
Table, Side, Art Deco, Walnut, Chrome, Marble, France, c.1930, 30 1/2 x 62 In. 8050.00
Table, Side, Arts & Crafts, Rectangular Top, Shelf, Supports, 30 x 30 x 16 1/2 In. 575.00
Table, Side, Chippendale, Mahogany, Rhode Island, c.1780, 27 1/4 x 29 3/4 In. 4780.00
Table, Side, Chippendale, Mahogany, Walnut, 27 1/2 x 36 1/2 x 20 In. 1530.00
Table, Side, Demilune Top, Round Legs, Chinese, 34 x 43 x 21 1/2 In. 980.00
Table, Side, E. Wormley, Janus, Tiffany Tile, Dunbar, c.1956, 13 x 23 1/2 In. 8050.00
Table, Side, E. Wormley, Walnut, Mahogany, Dunbar, 1957, 13 x 18 1/2 In. 6325.00
Table, Side, Eileen Gray, Round Top, Silver Colored, Cassina, c.1927, 22 x 20 In. 295.00
Table, Side, French Provincial, Cherry, 1 Drawer, c.1890, 30 x 31 1/2 In. 375.00
Table, Side, Gabriel Viardot Style, Beech, Gilt Bronze, 1880, 29 x 26 In. 6475.00
Table, Side, George II, Walnut, Rectangular, Cabriole Legs, 28 x 31 x 19 In. 2350.00
Table, Side, George III, Mahogany, Carved Edge, Frieze, 33 x 50 1/2 x 23 In. 6040.00
Table, Side, George III, Mahogany, D-Shape Top, Tapered Legs, c.1785, 31 x 42 1/2 In. . . 635.00
Table, Side, Hepplewhite, Cherry, Mixed Wood, 1 Drawer, American, 25 x 20 In. 150.00
Table, Side, Hepplewhite, Mahogany, Inlaid, Demilune, 1700s, 28 x 21 x 43 In. 1400.00
Table, Side, Limbert, Rectangular Top, Arched Apron, Mortised To Posts, 29 x 30 x 22 In. 1035.00
Table, Side, Louis XV Style, Carved Wood, Gilt, Flower Skirt, 27 x 18 1/2 x 14 In. 355.00
Table, Side, Louis XV Style, Mahogany, Marquetry, Marble, Oval, 31 x 32 x 22 In. 3055.00
Table, Side, Louis XV, Marble Top, Parquetry, Serpentine Frieze, 29 x 14 x 11 In. 1150.00
Table, Side, Louis XVI Style, Mahogany, Gilt Bronze, Marble Top, 29 x 29 x 18 In. 295.00
Table, Side, Louis XVI, Giltwood, Marble Top, Oval, Fluted Tapered Legs, 31 x 36 In. . . . 980.00
Table, Side, Mahogany, Brass Inlay, Demilune, 19th Century, 29 x 28 x 14 In. 1175.00
Table, Side, Mangiarotti, Black Marble, Skipper, Italy, 1971, 26 1/4 x 28 In. 2990.00
Table, Side, Marquetry, Gilt Bronze, Shaped Top, 3 Drawers, 1880, 30 x 22 1/2 In. 7670.00
Table, Side, Neoclassical, Mahogany, Inlaid, Brass Band, 29 x 33 x 16 1/2 In. 2185.00
Table, Side, Oak, Planked Top, England, c.1835, 29 1/2 x 33 1/2 In. 980.00
Table, Side, Red Lacquer, Incised, Dragons & Bats, Chinese, c.1900, 53 x 16 x 36 In. 345.00
Table, Side, Rococo Style, Marble Top, Painted, Door, 27 x 19 x 12 In., Pair 1765.00
Table, Side, Saarinen, Marble Top, Oval, Knoll, c.1956, 20 3/4 x 22 1/2 x 15 In. 940.00
Table, Side, Sheraton Style, Bird's-Eye Maple, c.1850, 28 1/2 x 20 x 16 1/4 In. 575.00
Table, Side, Walnut, Marble Panel, Pedestal, Cabriole Legs, Italy, 29 x 20 x 16 In. 1380.00
Table, Softwood, Grain Painted, Chamfered Stretcher, Pa., 29 x 118 x 32 1/2 In. 335.00
Table, Softwood, Hinged Lid, Old Red Paint, Pa., 29 1/2 x 60 x 41 In. . . . . *Illus* 2035.00
Table, Softwood, Stained, 2 Drawers, Chinese, c.1900, 36 x 33 In., Pair 2070.00
Table, Stickley Bros., No. 2501, Cross Stretcher, Through Tenon, Round, 24 x 30 In. 750.00
Table, Stickley Bros., No. 2674, Square Top, Cross Stretchers, 36 x 36 x 30 In. 1610.00
Table, Stickley Bros., Oak, Round Top, Splayed Legs, X-Stretcher, 26 x 25 In. 1295.00
Table, Stickley Bros., Rectangular, Low Stretcher, Keyed Tenons, 46 x 27 30 In. 1495.00
Table, Stylized Chrome Pedestal Base, Glass Top, 28 x 18 1/2 x 20 In., Pair 1645.00
Table, Sutherland, Mixed Wood, Oval Top, England, c.1880, 26 x 32 x 36 1/2 In. 489.00
Table, Tavern, Cherry, Red Paint, Breadboard Ends, Block Legs, 26 x 31 x 23 In. 2940.00

Furniture, Table, Taylor, 6 Tiles,
Spanish Dancers,
19 x 25 1/2 x 18 In.

Furniture, Table, Softwood, Hinged Lid,
Old Red Paint, Pa., 29 1/2 x 60 x 41 In.

Table, Tavern, Gray Green Paint, Square Tapered Legs, 23 1/2 x 36 x 23 In. 90.00
Table, Tavern, Hepplewhite, Red Scrub Top, 2-Board, Overhanging Top, 47 x 31 x 27 In. . .   980.00
Table, Tavern, Maple, Oval, 4 Blocks, Vase & Ring Turned Legs, 23 x 29 x 20 In. 4995.00
Table, Tavern, Nutting, No. 613, Maple 1375.00
Table, Tavern, Painted, Oval Top, Splayed Legs, c.1810, 28 1/2 x 25 1/2 x 20 In. 1295.00
Table, Tavern, Pine, 2-Board, Oval Top, Stretcher, Pegged Shoe Feet, 30 x 22 x 25 In. . . .   440.00
Table, Tavern, Pine, Breadboard Top, Box Stretcher, Turned Legs, 24 x 32 In. 865.00
Table, Tavern, Pine, Maple, Breadboard Top, Ball Feet, Painted, 1700s, 25 x 20 x 30 In. . .   4310.00
Table, Tavern, Pine, Maple, Rectangular Top, Turned Legs, 18th Century, 23 In. 1880.00
Table, Tavern, Pine, Oval, Dovetailed Drawer, Maple Legs, c.1700, 26 x 32 x 24 In. 3105.00
Table, Tavern, Queen Anne, Butternut, Maple, 2-Board Round Top, 28 x 26 7/8 In. 1320.00
Table, Tavern, Queen Anne, Cherry, Pine, Stretcher, 39 x 30 x 28 In. 2200.00
Table, Tavern, Queen Anne, Maple, Pine, Stretcher Base, 26 x 18 x 26 In. 2200.00
Table, Tavern, Queen Anne, Maple, Scalloped Skirt, 27 1/2 x 26 1/2 x 35 1/2 In. 7170.00
Table, Tavern, Sheraton, Red Paint, Scrub Top, Reeded Legs, 42 1/2 x 27 3/4 In. 980.00
Table, Tavern, Softwood, 3-Board Scrubbed Top, Round, Tripod Base, 28 x 28 In. 3850.00
Table, Tavern, Walnut, 3 Drawers, Removable Top, 1740-1780, 29 x 54 x 29 In. 2115.00
Table, Tavern, William & Mary, Maple, Oval Top, c.1735, 26 1/2 x 33 x 27 1/2 In. 4540.00
Table, Tavern, William & Mary, Walnut, Inlaid Star, Drawer, Bun Feet, 30 x 40 In. 3055.00
Table, Taylor, 6 Tiles, Spanish Dancers, 19 x 25 1/2 x 18 In. *Illus*   865.00
Table, Tea, Arts & Crafts, Pine, Hexagonal, Leather Top, 30 x 49 1/2 x 42 1/2 In. 3740.00
Table, Tea, Chippendale, Mahogany, Flip Top, 19th Century, 29 1/2 x 44 x 17 In. 1380.00
Table, Tea, Chippendale, Mahogany, Tray Top, Chinese, Early 1900s, 26 x 16 x 23 In. 750.00
Table, Tea, Edwardian, Satinwood, Polychrome, Hinges, Floral Swag, 30 x 36 x 18 In. . . .   2760.00
Table, Tea, Empire Style, Mahogany, Round, Square Tapered Post, Scrolled Footed Base .   340.00
Table, Tea, Fruitwood, Gilt Bronze, Tray Top, 2 Tiers, c.1900, 32 x 30 x 18 In. 7170.00
Table, Tea, G. Stickley, Round Top, Notched Cross Stretcher, 20 x 26 In. 1725.00
Table, Tea, George II Style, Walnut, Flip Top, Demilune, c.1900, 28 x 30 x 15 In. 575.00
Table, Tea, George II, Mahogany, Carved, Round, Dish Top, 28 x 33 In. 6570.00
Table, Tea, George II, Walnut, Flip Top, Drawer, c.1745, 28 x 29 x 14 In. 920.00
Table, Tea, George III Style, Ebonized, Hinged D-Shape Top, 29 x 36 x 17 In., Pair 2530.00
Table, Tea, George III, Mahogany, Banded Frieze, Hinges, 29 x 35 1/2 x 17 1/2 In. 2760.00
Table, Tea, L. & J.G. Stickley, No. 539, Circular Top, c.1910, 29 x 42 In. 430.00
Table, Tea, Limbert, Circular Top, Mortised, 29 x 42 In. 1495.00
Table, Tea, Mahogany, Brass Mounts, Oval Tray, 4 Legs, England, c.1900, 20 x 25 1/2 In.   920.00
Table, Tea, Mahogany, Dish Top, Drawer, Dutch, c.1785, 28 1/2 x 31 1/2 In. 2300.00
Table, Tea, Majorelle, Fruitwood, Chestnut Inlay, Marquetry, c.1900, 30 x 32 x 24 In. 8365.00
Table, Tea, Maple, Black Paint, Oval Top, Scalloped Skirt, Rhode Island, c.1750 . . . .   2310.00
Table, Tea, Maple, Overhanging Top, Valanced Skirt, Splayed Legs, 25 x 28 In. 4700.00
Table, Tea, Queen Anne Style, Mahogany, Drawer, 26 1/2 x 29 x 18 In. 230.00
Table, Tea, Queen Anne, Cherry, Dish Top, Birdcage, Philadelphia, c.1750, 29 x 35 In. . . .   7200.00
Table, Tea, Queen Anne, Curly Maple, Scalloped Apron, Shaped Legs, 29 x 20 In. 1180.00
Table, Tea, Queen Anne, Mahogany, Cannon Barrel Shaft, Cabriole Legs, 36 In. 730.00
Table, Tea, Queen Anne, Mahogany, Dovetailed Birdcage, Bulbous, 34 1/2 In. 1070.00
Table, Tea, Queen Anne, Maple, Porringer Top, Pad Feet, c.1760, 26 x 32 x 25 In. 3055.00
Table, Tea, Queen Anne, Oval Top, Round Tapered Legs, Pad Feet, 27 In. 5750.00
Table, Tea, Queen Anne, Tapered Legs, Pad Feet, Molded Skirt, Oval Top 9200.00
Table, Tea, Regency Style, Mahogany, Drawer, 3 Legs, c.1830, 28 x 20 x 16 1/4 In. 315.00
Table, Tea, Regency, Mahogany, Hinges, Drawer, Square Legs, 31 x 37 1/2 x 18 In. 1495.00

Table, Tea, Rosewood, Flip Top, D-Shape, Carved & Turned Pedestal Base, 40 In. 875.00
Table, Tea, Spider, Tiger Maple, Dish Top, Legs, 28 1/2 x 17 x 16 3/4 In. 300.00
Table, Tea, Stickley Bros., Square Top, Shelf, Tapered Legs, 29 1/2 x 24 In. 1150.00
Table, Tea, Tilt Top, Cherry, Walnut, Birdcage Support, Cabriole Legs, 26 1/2 x 28 In. ... 310.00
Table, Tea, Tilt Top, Chippendale, Mahogany, c.1790, 27 1/4 x 24 In. 635.00
Table, Tea, Tilt Top, Chippendale, Maple, Walnut, Tripod, c.1790, 27 1/2 x 26 1/2 In. 575.00
Table, Tea, Tilt Top, Federal, Maple, 3-Board Top, c.1775, 27 1/2 x 31 In. 430.00
Table, Tea, Tilt Top, George II, Walnut, Mahogany, c.1730, 27 1/2 x 29 1/2 In. 635.00
Table, Tea, Tilt Top, George III, Mahogany, Piecrust Edge, c.1770, 27 1/2 x 33 3/4 In. ... 1840.00
Table, Tea, Tilt Top, George III, Mahogany, Tripod, c.1780, 27 1/2 x 30 3/4 In. 1610.00
Table, Tea, Tilt Top, Mahogany, Birdcage, Dish Top, American, 28 1/2 x 22 1/2 In. 690.00
Table, Tea, Tilt Top, Mahogany, Dovetailed Box Support, Cabriole Legs, 34 x 26 In. 565.00
Table, Tea, Tilt Top, Maple, Square Top, Tripod Base, Early 1800s, 27 x 33 x 34 In. 750.00
Table, Tea, Tilt Top, Piecrust, Carved, Claw & Ball Feet, c.1790, 28 x 28 x 43 In. 1175.00
Table, Tea, Tilt Top, Queen Anne, Mahogany, Round, 1750-1780, 28 x 32 In. 3345.00
Table, Tea, Tilt Top, Queen Anne, Mahogany, Urn Column, 36 x 27 x 26 In. 880.00
Table, Tea, Tilt Top, Queen Anne, Walnut, Tripod, c.1760, 26 3/4 In. 920.00
Table, Tea, Tilt Top, Tiger Maple, Birdcage Platform, Tripod Base, 23 x 35 In. 2350.00
Table, Tea, William IV, Rosewood, 2 Round Wells, c.1835, 28 1/2 x 19 1/2 In. 1910.00
Table, Teak, Relief Edge Moldings, Scrolling, Raised Panel, 46 x 16 3/4 x 33 1/2 In. 440.00
Table, Tilt Top, Birch, Bullnose Edge, Turned Pedestal, Tripod Cabriole Legs, 27 x 34 In. 6465.00
Table, Tilt Top, Black Lacquer, Tripod, Chinese, 30 x 36 x 24 In. 1840.00
Table, Tilt Top, Burl Walnut, Circular, Turned Standard, Tripod Base, 27 x 21 In. 825.00
Table, Tilt Top, Burl Walnut, Oval Top, 4 Floral-Carved Cabriole Legs, 29 x 44 x 56 In. ... 1675.00
Table, Tilt Top, Chippendale Style, Mahogany, Cabriole Legs, 32 x 27 1/2 In. 440.00
Table, Tilt Top, Chippendale Style, Mahogany, Tripod, 19th Century, 27 x 29 In. 880.00
Table, Tilt Top, Chippendale, Cherry, Ball & Ring Turned Post, Tripod Leg, 29 x 27 In. .. 3820.00
Table, Tilt Top, Chippendale, Mahogany, Birdcage, c.1780, 29 1/2 x 32 In. 4115.00
Table, Tilt Top, Chippendale, Mahogany, Gadroon Carved, Paw Feet, 29 x 48 In. 800.00
Table, Tilt Top, Chippendale, Walnut, Round Top, Tripod Base, 1700s, 27 x 27 In. 2200.00
Table, Tilt Top, Empire Style, Mahogany, Giltwood, c.1890, 29 1/2 x 37 1/2 In. 3450.00
Table, Tilt Top, Federal, Cherry, Oval, Cabriole Legs, 1790, 26 3/4 x 19 1/2 In. 9400.00
Table, Tilt Top, Federal, Mahogany, Octagonal, Tripod Base, c.1810, 29 x 22 x 18 In. 645.00
Table, Tilt Top, French Provincial, Oak, Planked, Swing Support, 29 x 77 1/2 x 48 In. 1495.00
Table, Tilt Top, George II, Mahogany, Circular Birdcage, 18th Century, 28 x 31 In. 1150.00
Table, Tilt Top, George II, Mahogany, Figured, Carved, Piecrust Top, 28 In. 3290.00
Table, Tilt Top, George II, Mahogany, Tripod, c.1740, 27 1/2 x 36 In. 1790.00
Table, Tilt Top, George III Style, Birdcage, 3 Saber Legs, 28 x 28 In. 635.00
Table, Tilt Top, George III Style, Black Lacquer, Polychrome, Landscape, 30 x 31 In. 1150.00
Table, Tilt Top, George III, Mahogany, Octagonal Top, Birdcage, Tripod Feet, 29 In. 1295.00
Table, Tilt Top, George III, Mahogany, Pedestal, Snake Feet, c.1790, 28 x 29 In. 805.00
Table, Tilt Top, George III, Mahogany, Piecrust, Tripod, Ireland, c.1760, 29 x 32 In. 3290.00
Table, Tilt Top, George III, Mahogany, Round Top, 2 Drawers, Snake Feet, 28 In. 690.00
Table, Tilt Top, George III, Mahogany, Round, Twist-Reeded Stem, Pad Feet, 28 x 36 In. . 940.00
Table, Tilt Top, George IV, Burr Elm, Oak-Branch Border, c.1825, 29 x 30 In. 3585.00
Table, Tilt Top, Green Paint, Open Box Base, Drawer, Child's, 24 x 43 1/2 In. 1195.00
Table, Tilt Top, Mahogany, 3 Downswept Legs, Early 19th Century, 29 x 41 x 52 In. 800.00
Table, Tilt Top, Mahogany, 3 Splayed Reeded Legs, c.1785, 29 x 55 In. 2185.00
Table, Tilt Top, Mahogany, Birdcage, Carved, Slipper Feet, 1800s, 27 x 32 In. 230.00
Table, Tilt Top, Mahogany, Line & Ribbon Inlay, Birdcage, Tripod Base, 28 x 35 In. 865.00
Table, Tilt Top, Mahogany, Molded Edge, Notched Corners, Tripod, 31 x 33 x 27 In. 520.00
Table, Tilt Top, Mahogany, Pierced & Shell-Carved Top, Fluted Column, 28 In. 805.00
Table, Tilt Top, Mahogany, Shell-Carved Edge, Fluted Column, Claw & Ball Feet, 27 In. . 690.00
Table, Tilt Top, Mahogany, Trefoil Base, Scroll & Leaf-Carved Feet, 29 1/4 x 42 In. 575.00
Table, Tilt Top, Painted, Inlaid Mother-Of-Pearl Cottage, Oval, Scalloped Edge, 26 In. ... 530.00
Table, Tilt Top, Papier-Mache, Scalloped, Polychrome Flowers, 28 x 27 x 22 1/2 In. 750.00
Table, Tilt Top, Regency, Black Lacquered, Flowers, Scroll, 26 1/2 x 28 In. 144.00
Table, Tilt Top, Regency, Gilt Metal Mounted, Black Japanned, 24 x 18 1/2 x 13 In. 960.00
Table, Tilt Top, Regency, Mahogany, 3 Downswept Legs, Casters, 29 x 42 In. 1175.00
Table, Tilt Top, Regency, Mahogany, Curved Corners, Pedestal, 30 x 59 x 54 In. 2760.00
Table, Tilt Top, Regency, Mahogany, Lotus-Carved Feet, 29 1/2 x 51 1/2 In. 2185.00
Table, Tilt Top, Regency, Rosewood, 3-Part Base, Early 19th Century, 29 1/2 x 48 In. 2530.00
Table, Tilt Top, Walnut, Burl, Birdcage, Tripod Base, 21 x 29 In. 605.00

Table, Tilt Top, Walnut, Marquetry, Gadroon Baluster Pedestal, Rosettes, 30 x 55 In. 2985.00
Table, Tilt Top, Walnut, Piecrust Edge, Round Top, Carved Legs, Child's 600.00
Table, Tilt Top, Walnut, Round, Scratch Beaded, 18th Century, 17 In. 590.00
Table, Tray, Chippendale, Cherry, Concave Edges, 29 x 33 1/2 x 19 In. 1435.00
Table, Tray, G. Nelson, Ebonized Wood Top, Chrome, Herman Miller, 15 x 15 In. 529.00
Table, Tray, Georgian Style, Mahogany, Marquetry, 18 1/2 x 26 x 17 In. 550.00
Table, Tray, Mahogany, Bowfront Gallery, Cutout Handles, 33 x 30 In. 880.00
Table, Tray, Regency, Papier-Mache, Lacquered, Parcel Gilt, 19 x 22 1/4 x 12 1/2 In. 865.00
Table, Tray, Victorian, Papier-Mache, Black Lacquered, Mother-Of-Pearl, 21 x 27 x 21 In. 1150.00
Table, Trestle, G. Stickley, No. 637, Lower Shelf, Shoe-Foot Base, 48 x 30 x 28 In. 3450.00
Table, Trestle, L. & J.G. Stickley, Double Column Sides, Overhang Top, 29 x 72 x 45 In. . 4900.00
Table, Trestle, L. & J.G. Stickley, Rectangular Top, 29 x 48 x 32 In. 2300.00
Table, Trestle, Louis XV Style, Walnut, Inlaid, 19th Century, 28 x 21 1/2 x 16 In. 345.00
Table, Trestle, Oak, Planked Top, England, c.1890, 32 1/2 x 30 1/2 In. 1725.00
Table, Trestle, Regency, Oak, Serpentine Legs, Iron Stretcher, 29 x 76 x 30 In. 1840.00
Table, Trestle, Spanish, End Supports, 30 1/2 x 79 1/2 x 36 In. 1150.00
Table, Trestle, Spanish, Mahogany, Scalloped Supports, 1800s, 29 x 63 x 27 In. 2185.00
Table, Trestle, Spanish, Walnut, Oak, Carved Bases, Iron Stretcher, 31 x 81 x 28 In. 3220.00
Table, Trestle, Stickley & Brandt Co., Double Planks, 28 1/2 x 48 x 30 In. 920.00
Table, Trestle, Stickley Bros., No. 2570, Lower Shelf, Corbelled Legs, 40 x 26 x 30 In. .. 1265.00
Table, Trestle, Walnut, 3-Board Top, Block & Thread-Turned Legs, 30 x 77 In. 770.00
Table, V. Kagan, Walnut, Glass, American, 1950s, 24 x 22 1/2 In. 4025.00
Table, Victorian, Black Lacquer, Rectangular Top, Landscape, 28 1/2 x 18 x 15 In. 1035.00
Table, Victorian, Burl Walnut, Turtle Top, Carved 4-Leg Base, 22 x 69 In. 999.00
Table, Victorian, Fruitwood, Burl Walnut Inlay, Oval Top, Carved Lappets, 26 x 36 In. 590.00
Table, Victorian, Mahogany, Carved, Turned, Octagonal, c.1875, 28 1/2 x 32 In. 7770.00
Table, Victorian, Marble Turtle Top, Pierced Legs, Stretcher, c.1870, 30 x 30 x 41 In. 2240.00
Table, Victorian, Walnut, Serpentine Top, Urn Pedestal, 26 x 45 In. 375.00
Table, Walnut Veneer, Royal Copenhagen Tiles, Denmark, 17 x 18 x 15 In. 295.00
Table, Walnut, 2 Drawers, 3-Board Top, Stretcher Base, 56 1/2 x 29 x 28 1/2 In. 605.00
Table, Walnut, Carved Flowers & Leaves, Trestle Legs, Cincinnati, 34 x 30 In. 2300.00
Table, Walnut, Ebony Inlay, Saber Legs, Platform Base, Continental, 30 1/4 x 47 In. 2070.00
Table, Walnut, High Tapered Legs, Scalloped Apron, 29 x 16 x 29 In. 415.00
Table, Walnut, Hinged Top, Pullout Cubbyhole Desk, c.1930 .... 695.00
Table, Walnut, Inlaid Mercury In Chariot, Geometric Bands, Splayed Legs, 29 x 28 In. ... 545.00
Table, Walnut, Oval, Crossbanded, Stretcher, Shelf, Tapered Legs, 24 x 18 x 15 In. 230.00
Table, Walnut, Parcel Gilt, Round, Bookend Spines, 3 Doors, Pedestal, 42 x 16 In., Pair .. 690.00
Table, Walnut, Pine Top, 3-Drawer Base, Spool-Turned Legs, 73 x 36 x 30 In. 1070.00
Table, Walnut, Shell-Carved Apron, Leaf-Carved Cabriole Legs, Scroll Feet, 19 x 26 In. ... 260.00
Table, Walnut, Thumb-Molded Top, Drawer, Shaped Apron, H-Stretcher, 29 x 41 In. 1115.00
Table, Walnut, Winged Swan Supports, 6-Sided Marble Top, 23 x 25 In. 785.00
Table, Walter Lamb, Glass Top, Textured, Metal Base, Verdigris, c.1950, 26 x 38 In. 1175.00
Table, Widdicomb, Walnut, Hexagonal Legs, 1959, 30 x 23 In. 230.00
Table, William & Mary, Barley-Twist Legs, Bun Feet, 1700s, 32 x 40 x 26 In. 9775.00
Table, William & Mary, Fruitwood, Elm, Frieze Drawer, Block-Turned Legs, 29 In. 1115.00
Table, William IV Style, Mahogany, Rounded Corners, 3 Leaves, Casters, 31 x 55 In. 3220.00
Table, William IV, Mahogany, D-Shape, Turned Tapered Legs, 29 x 42 In., Pair 1725.00
Table, William IV, Mahogany, Hinged Top, Frieze Drawer, X-Stretcher, 31 In. 2585.00
Table, William IV, Mahogany, Rosewood, Hinged Top, Carved Tripod Base, 25 In. 315.00
Table, Wine Tasting, French Provincial, Burl, Elm, Plank Top, 1800s, 30 x 52 x 42 In. 1610.00
Table, Wine Tasting, French Provincial, Fruitwood, Oval Top, 1900s, 28 x 60 x 43 In. ... 1265.00
Table, Wine Tasting, French Provincial, Fruitwood, Swing Base, 1800s, 29 x 54 x 40 In. . 920.00
Table, Wine Tasting, French Provincial, Fruitwood, Tilt Top, c.1850, 29 1/2 x 78 In. 805.00
Table, Wine Tasting, French Provincial, Fruitwood, Tilt Top, c.1890, 29 1/2 x 47 1/4 In. .. 1035.00
Table, Wine Tasting, George III Style, Demilune, c.1910, 29 x 41 x 22 In., Pair 1265.00
Table, Wine Tasting, Queen Anne, Cherry, Round Top, Turned Legs, 27 x 30 In. 400.00
Table, Wine Tasting, Yellow Rosewood, Rectangular Top, Chinese, 1700s, 32 x 35 In. ... 2070.00
Table, Wood & Bone Geometric Inlay, Octagonal, North Africa, 23 x 14 In. 175.00
Table, Writing, Biedermeier, Burl Ash, Rectangular Top, Drawer, 31 x 19 x 24 In. 1840.00
Table, Writing, Biedermeier, Cherry, Tooled Leather, Drawers, 31 x 39 x 27 In. 1495.00
Table, Writing, Biedermeier, Walnut, Satinwood, Serpentine Top, Drawer, 30 x 50 In. 2990.00
Table, Writing, Burl, Ebonized Banding, Apron Drawer, 2 Pedestals, Lady's, 43 In. 1310.00
Table, Writing, Ebonized, Brass Mounts, Strap Hinges, c.1875, 58 x 35 x 20 1/2 In. 6720.00

Table, Writing, French Provincial, Oak, 1 Drawer, Turned Legs, 1800s, 27 x 37 x 25 In. . . . 1495.00
Table, Writing, George II, Mahogany, Leather Inset, Drawers, 31 x 51 x 30 1/2 In. 23900.00
Table, Writing, George III, Mahogany, Frieze, Dummy Drawers, 31 x 72 x 37 3/4 In. 5975.00
Table, Writing, George III, Mahogany, Square, Leather Inset, Drawers, 30 x 42 x 35 In. . . 920.00
Table, Writing, Jacobean Style, Oak, Heavily Carved, Drawer, c.1900, 30 x 42 x 28 In. . . . 1095.00
Table, Writing, Louis XV Style, Japanned, Red, Leather Top, 3 Frieze Drawers, 30 In. . . . 380.00
Table, Writing, Louis XV, Parquetry, Ormolu, Marble Top, 28 x 17 x 12 1/2 In. 1035.00
Table, Writing, Louis XVI Style, Tulipwood, Gilt Bronze Mounts, Drawer, 29 x 27 In. . . . 3750.00
Table, Writing, Lucien Rollin, Beech, Exotic Wood, Drawer, c.1940, 29 3/4 x 39 In. 8225.00
Table, Writing, Mahogany, Hinged Top, Bowfront, 2 Drawers, c.1825, 32 x 25 x 17 In. . . . 5060.00
Table, Writing, Mahogany, Leather, Gilt, 6 Drawers, England, c.1880, 31 x 53 x 96 In. . . . 2070.00
Table, Writing, Mahogany, Marquetry, Ebony, Flemish, 30 x 44 1/2 x 29 1/2 In. 3910.00
Table, Writing, Mahogany, Rope-Turned Legs, Drawer, Fold-Top Niche, c.1810 . . . . 4800.00
Table, Writing, Plum Mahogany, Brass Inlay, Sliding Top, c.1890, 29 x 27 x 17 In. 2070.00
Table, Writing, Regency, Burl, Oak, Leather Writing Surface, c.1815, 29 3/4 x 60 In. 2990.00
Table, Writing, Regency, Rosewood, Leather Inset, 2 Drawers, 29 x 48 1/2 x 23 1/2 In. . . 2070.00
Table, Writing, Satinwood, Ebonized, Drawer, Bronze Mounts, c.1870, 30 x 54 x 28 In. . . 2240.00
Table, Writing, Victorian, Molded Skirt, Long Drawer, Fluted Legs, 1890, 30 x 50 In. 690.00
Table, Writing, Victorian, Satinwood, Tulipwood, Brass, c.1868, 36 x 50 x 32 In. 15535.00
Table, Writing, Walnut, Marquetry, Oval, Leather Top, Lift-Top Niche, 1800s, 42 In. 1820.00
Table, Writing, Yew, Satinwood, Drawers, Casters, c.1810, 28 1/2 x 38 x 25 In. 8960.00
Table, Wrought Iron, Floral Apron, Basket, Shaped Marble Top, 31 x 40 In. 1150.00
Table, Yellow Pine, 3-Board Top, Tapered Legs, Cut Nails, La., 29 x 53 x 34 In. 660.00
Table Set, Bistro, Wood, Folding Iron Base, 4 Chairs, France, 28 x 35 x 24 In. 265.00
Table Set, S. Watanabe, Walnut, Free-Edge Top, Dowel Legs, 16 In., 3 Piece 1175.00
Tabouret, Arts & Crafts, Circular Top, Inset, Cross Stretchers, 21 1/2 x 16 1/4 In. 545.00
Tabouret, Arts & Crafts, Copper Clad, Stretchers, Turned Legs, Bun Feet, 16 x 22 In. . . . 345.00
Tabouret, Arts & Crafts, Octagonal, Quatrefoil Cutouts, 17 1/4 x 15 1/2 In. 545.00
Tabouret, Arts & Crafts, Square Top & Legs, Cut Corners, 1900s, 22 x 20 x 20 In. 999.00
Tabouret, G. Stickley, Circular Top, Cloud-Lift Cross Stretchers, 17 3/4 x 16 In. 1610.00
Tabouret, G. Stickley, Circular, Cross Stretchers, 17 3/4 x 16 In. 690.00
Tabouret, G. Stickley, Mahogany, 5 Legs, Star Stretcher, 20 x 19 In. 2760.00
Tabouret, L. & J.G. Stickley, Clip-Corner Top, Arched Cross Stretchers, 20 x 17 In. 575.00
Tabouret, L. & J.G. Stickley, No. 558, Octagonal, Cross Stretcher, 17 In. 1150.00
Tabouret, L. & J.G. Stickley, Square, Lower Shelf, 28 x 15 In. 635.00
Tabouret, Limbert, Circular Top, Tapered Posts, Square Lower Shelf, 22 x 18 1/2 In. 1095.00
Tabouret, Limbert, Square Top, Splayed-Leg Base, 12 x 12 x 16 In. 575.00
Tabouret, Limbert, Square Top, Stretchers, Flared Legs, 16 x 12 In. 1265.00
Tabouret, Stickley Bros., No. 138, Square Posts, Macmurdo Feet, 18 x 13 3/4 In. 635.00
Tabouret, Stickley Bros., Square Top, Quaint Tag, 12 x 18 In. 265.00
Tea Cart, Aldo Tura, Goatskin Over Wood, Glass, Brass Casters, 1950s, 26 x 33 In. 1265.00
Tea Cart, Modernist, Birch, 3 Retractable Top Surfaces, 31 1/2 x 42 1/2 In. 499.00
Tea Cart, Oak, Tray Top, Spoke Wheels, 20th Century, 31 x 18 x 30 In. 290.00
Tea Cart, Stickley Bros., Glass Top, Turned Posts, Shelf, 29 1/2 x 28 In. 575.00
Tray On Stand, George III, Mahogany, Pierced Handles, c.1810, 31 x 28 x 18 In. 1265.00
Tray On Stand, Gilt Greek Key Designs, Bamboo Stand, 22 x 30 1/4 x 21 1/2 In. 460.00
Tray On Stand, Mahogany, Gallery, Side Handles, X-Form Stand, 36 x 29 x 17 In. 765.00
Tray On Stand, Papier-Mache, Gilt, Enamel, Mother-Of-Pearl Stand, 18 x 22 x 28 In. . . . 875.00
Tray On Stand, Papier-Mache, Scalloped Edge, Gilt, Lacquer Cabriole Legs, 18 In. 575.00
Tray On Stand, Parcel Gilt, Grape & Vine Design, Bamboo Stand, 22 x 30 x 21 1/2 In. . . . 520.00
Trolley, Mahogany, 3 Tiers, Molded Galleries, Turned Legs, 45 In. 1035.00
Trolley, William IV, Mahogany, 3 Tiers, Porcelain Casters, 43 x 42 In. 2070.00
Umbrella Stand, Arts & Crafts, Mahogany, Copper Tray 225.00
Umbrella Stand, Arts & Crafts, Oak, Square Posts, Sikes Co., c.1915, 28 x 14 x 10 In. 429.00
Umbrella Stand, Edwardian, Brass, Cast Iron, Tole, Tubular, 1900s, 24 x 24 x 15 In. 750.00
Umbrella Stand, Iron, Brown Matte Surface, Terrier, Canes, J.W. Fiske, N.Y., 14 x 8 In. . . 880.00
Umbrella Stand, Iron, Figural Backplate, Admiral Nelson, Shell, Drip Pan, 31 In. 705.00
Umbrella Stand, Oak, Copper, Drip Pan, American, c.1910, 29 In. 840.00
Umbrella Stand, Tapered Posts, Drip Pan, Paper Label, 12 x 12 x 33 In. 2330.00
Vanity, Empire Style, Mahogany, Oval Mirror, Lyre Frame, Pilaster Legs, 65 In. 1200.00
Vanity, Figured Marble Top, Gray & White, 2 Cherubs, Metal Base, 20 x 35 In. 1375.00
Vanity, G. Nelson, Walnut, 4 Drawers, Herman Miller, 29 x 34 x 18 In. 999.00
Vanity, G. Nelson, Walnut, Lift Top, Mirror, Herman Miller, 17 x 30 x 18 In. 470.00

Vanity, Louis Philippe, Walnut, Mirror, Marble Lift Top, 4 Drawers, c.1850, 36 x 31 In. . . . 1150.00
Vanity, Mahogany, Mirror, 3 Drawers Each Side, Supports, England, 1890 . . . . 440.00
Vanity, Walnut, 3-Fold Mirror, 4 Drawers, Depression Era 185.00
Vitrine, Aesthetic Revival, Cherry, Mother-Of-Pearl, Gallery, Mirror, Shelves 4900.00
Vitrine, Art Deco, Patinated Metal, Mirror Back, 3 Glass Shelves, 76 x 27 x 10 In. 2585.00
Vitrine, Chippendale Style, Mahogany, Glazed Doors, 3 Drawers, 78 x 43 x 20 In. 2185.00
Vitrine, Edwardian, Mahogany, Marquetry, 2 Parts, c.1900, 86 x 37 1/2 x 16 In. 1095.00
Vitrine, Edwardian, Satinwood, Painted, Figures, Flowers, 62 x 26 1/2 x 13 In. 3285.00
Vitrine, Empire Revival, Mahogany, Ormolu Mounted, c.1890, 36 x 39 In. 895.00
Vitrine, Empire Style, Kingwood, Marble, Ormolu, 1900s, 63 1/2 x 35 x 20 1/2 In. 865.00
Vitrine, French Provincial, Fruitwood, 2 Doors, Wire Mesh Panels, 92 x 66 x 23 In. 2530.00
Vitrine, Galle, Fruitwood, Marquetry, c.1910, 51 x 34 3/4 x 13 In., Pair 9560.00
Vitrine, George III Style, Mahogany, Molded Cornice, 4 Doors, 87 x 98 x 16 In. 2990.00
Vitrine, George III, Mahogany, Glazed Doors, Ionic Pilaster, 83 1/2 x 53 x 19 In. 1610.00
Vitrine, George III, Mahogany, Molded Cornice, 3 Glazed Doors, 85 x 93 x 20 In. 2760.00
Vitrine, Georgian Style, Mahogany, 2 Doors, Mirrored Back, 74 1/2 x 33 x 16 In. 470.00
Vitrine, Giltwood, Carved, 2-Headed Eagle, Austria, 45 1/2 x 16 1/2 In. 920.00
Vitrine, Louis Philippe, Elm, 2 Doors, c.1850, 90 x 53 In. 2760.00
Vitrine, Louis XV Style, Kingwood, Marble Top, Gilt Metal Mounted, 1890, 52 In. 7670.00
Vitrine, Louis XV Style, Mahogany, Gilt Metal Mount, 20th Century, 55 x 26 x 13 In. . . . 1470.00
Vitrine, Louis XV Style, Marble, Gallery, Gilt Bronze Mount, 52 x 43 x 16 1/2 In. 2000.00
Vitrine, Louis XV Style, Polychrome, Beveled Glass, c.1865, 31 1/4 x 28 In. 2760.00
Vitrine, Louis XV Style, Rosewood, Parquetry, Ormolu, Hinge Top, 30 x 18 x 31 In. 1310.00
Vitrine, Louis XV Style, Vernis Martin, Ormolu Mount, c.1900, 46 x 19 In. 920.00
Vitrine, Louis XV, Walnut, Dome, Carved Frieze, 2 Doors, 1800s, 68 x 27 x 12 In. 1610.00
Vitrine, Louis XVI Style, Giltwood, Lobed, Relief, 57 x 28 x 15 In. 1175.00
Vitrine, Louis XVI Style, Mahogany, Brass, Door, Shelf, c.1910, 29 x 22 x 10 In. 460.00
Vitrine, Mahogany, Gilt Metal, Cabriole Legs, 21 x 29 In. 650.00
Vitrine, Mahogany, Inlaid, Satinwood Panel, Line Border, Drop Front, 21 x 16 x 28 In. . . . 550.00
Vitrine, Mahogany, Molded Cornice, 2 Doors, Glazed Panels, 1800s, 78 x 57 x 18 In. . . . 1610.00
Vitrine, Neoclassical, Mahogany, Mirror, Panel Doors, Dutch, c.1900, 60 x 38 In. 2070.00
Vitrine, Regency, Mahogany, Breakfront, Cabriole Legs, c.1815, 95 x 54 In. 3450.00
Vitrine, Renaissance Revival, Walnut, Marble Top, Leaf Carving, 63 x 41 x 19 In. 1175.00
Vitrine, Rococo Revival, 2 Sections, Italy, c.1910, 77 1/2 x 33 x 16 In. 1150.00
Vitrine, Rococo Revival, Walnut, Glazed Doors, Shelves, 20th Century, 91 x 70 In. 2760.00
Vitrine, Vernis Martin, Giltwood, Figural Panel Door, 60 x 31 x 15 In. 1315.00
Vitrine, Victorian, Mahogany, Ogee Cornice, 2 Doors, 19th Century, 84 x 46 x 13 In. 1380.00
Wall Unit, G. Nelson, Walnut Veneer, 3 Drawers, Cupcake Pulls, 29 x 24 x 18 In. 2115.00
Wardrobe, Cherry, 2 Paneled Doors, Cove-Molded, Lancaster County, 84 x 53 In. . . *Illus* 5610.00
Wardrobe, Cherry, Molded Cornice, Raised Panel Doors, 84 x 53 x 21 1/2 In. 5610.00
Wardrobe, Edwardian, Rosewood, Mahogany, Crossbanded, 1900s, 86 x 55 In. 2990.00
Wardrobe, Frank Lloyd Wright, Oak, Doors, Shelves, Rack, 61 x 66 x 22 In. 3585.00
Wardrobe, George III Style, Mahogany, 2 Oval Panel Doors, Bracket Feet, 78 In. 2070.00
Wardrobe, George III Style, Mahogany, Panel Doors, Mirrored, 80 x 62 x 21 In. 980.00
Wardrobe, Georgian Style, Inlay, Molding, Mirror Door, 1 Drawer, 50 x 17 x 77 In. 830.00
Wardrobe, Mahogany, Line Inlay Panels, Incised Crest, 3 Sliding Drawers, 10 3/4 In. 440.00

Look at the pegs on old furniture when you
can. Old pegs are usually straight and
sometimes have a small notch at the top
to let excess glue escape. Modern machine-
made pegs usually have spiral grooves.

Furniture, Wardrobe, Cherry,
2 Paneled Doors, Cove-Molded,
Lancaster County, 84 x 53 In.

Wardrobe, Neoclassical, Mahogany, c.1830, 87 x 76 1/2 x 30 3/4 In. 1380.00
Wardrobe, Pine, Fruitwood, Door Over 1 Drawer, 1800s, France, 83 x 40 In. 1090.00
Wardrobe, Poplar, Linenfold, Panel Door, c.1830, 78 x 51 x 18 1/4 In. 1725.00
Wardrobe, Poplar, Painted, Double Paneled Door, Drawer, Ohio, 42 x 17 x 80 In. 1870.00
Wardrobe, Poplar, Red Wash, Molded Cornice, Door, c.1820, 79 x 42 x 14 In. 825.00
Wardrobe, Regency, Flame Mahogany, 3 Bipanel Doors, c.1815, 81 x 82 In. 2185.00
Wardrobe, Regency, Mahogany, 6 Drawers, 2 Side Doors, c.1835, 77 x 91 In. 2185.00
Wardrobe, Regency, Walnut, Early 19th Century, 85 x 58 x 23 1/2 In. 5060.00
Wardrobe, Stickley & Brandt Co., Drawers, 71 1/2 x 35 x 27 In. 8056.00
Wardrobe, William IV, Mahogany, 6 Drawers, 2 Doors, 1800s, 81 x 94 x 23 In. 3220.00
Washstand, Cherry, Pine, Mahogany, Serpentine Front, c.1810, 34 x 32 1/2 x 16 In. 690.00
Washstand, Corner, George III, Mahogany, Drawer, Shelf, 25 In. 1020.00
Washstand, Corner, Sheraton, Curly Maple, Mahogany, 23 x 17 x 38 1/2 In. 1870.00
Washstand, Curly Maple, Lower Shelf, Ring Turned Legs, Drawer, 19 x 17 x 31 In. 660.00
Washstand, Empire, Faux Tiger Maple Paint, 2 Drawers, Turned Legs, 33 x 18 x 16 In. ... 575.00
Washstand, Federal, Satinwood, Mahogany Inlay, Ebonized, 29 x 23 x 16 In. 865.00
Washstand, George IV, Walnut, Marble Gallery Top, c.1825, 31 x 33 1/2 x 15 In. 520.00
Washstand, Grain Painted, Marble Top, 2 Drawers, Mid 19th Century 635.00
Washstand, Grain Painted, Shaped Backsplash, Cutout Top, Shelf, Drawer, 18 x 36 In. 115.00
Washstand, Hepplewhite, Mahogany, Dovetailed, Step-Back Gallery, Tapered Legs 425.00
Washstand, Hepplewhite, Painted, Flowers, Cutouts, Square Legs, Tapered, c.1830 ..... 2100.00
Washstand, Hepplewhite, Painted, Stencil, 2 Corner Shelves, c.1820, 37 x 18 In. 790.00
Washstand, Maple, Peaked Backsplash, Drawer, Shelf, Pencil-Post Turned Legs 310.00
Washstand, Maple, Poplar, Drawer, Scalloped Gallery, 17 3/4 x 16 x 39 In. 165.00
Washstand, Marble Top, 4 Drawers, Plinth Base, Bun Feet, 1800s, 38 x 39 x 26 In. 690.00
Washstand, Marble Top, Carved, Tiled Backsplash, Turned Legs, c.1900, 49 x 30 x 18 In. 230.00
Washstand, Neoclassical, Stained Pine, c.1820, 29 1/4 x 47 x 38 In. 230.00
Washstand, Pine, Marbleized, Scroll-Cut Backsplash, Shelf, Drawer, 1960s, 37 x 19 In. .. 56.00
Washstand, Rococo, Walnut, Marble Top, Drawer, 2 Scalloped Panel Doors, 31 In. 145.00
Washstand, Shaker, Pine, Paneled Cupboard, Enfield, Conn., 40 1/2 In. 3160.00
Washstand, Sheraton, Mahogany, Backsplash, Spool Legs, c.1840 .... 495.00
Washstand, Sheraton, Mahogany, Pine, Front Apron, Gallery, 19 1/4 x 15 1/4 In. 1430.00
Washstand, Sheraton, Softwood, Yellow Wash, Dovetailed Splash, Drawer, 2 Doors 280.00
Washstand, Softwood, Painted, Scrolled Ear Terminals, Drawer, Scalloped Shelf 280.00
Washstand, Swing Mirror, Oval Top, Incised Scene, Drawer 170.00
Washstand, Victorian, Marble Top, c.1880, 29 x 16 x 28 1/2 In. 115.00
Washstand, Walnut, Applied Fruit-Form Handles, 1800s, 30 x 17 1/2 x 36 In. 290.00
Washstand, Walnut, Marble Top, Shaped Backsplash, Base Drawer Over 2 Doors 450.00
Wastebasket, Arts & Crafts, Oak, Square Panel, 20th Century, 17 x 12 x 12 In. 90.00
Wastebasket, Frank Lloyd Wright, Mahogany Plywood, Cutout Handle, 19 x 14 In. 3110.00
Wastebasket, Frank Lloyd Wright, Sheet Copper, 1953, 16 x 14 In. 4900.00
Wastebasket, G. Stickley, Slats, Iron Hoops, Red Decal, 14 x 12 In. 3450.00
Wastebasket, Samuel Marx, Parchment, Tin, 1948, 10 x 11 In. 1610.00
Wastebasket, Stickley Bros., Slats, Cutout Handles, Flared, 17 1/2 x 14 1/4 In. 1265.00
Wastebasket, Stickley Co., Oak Slats, Copper, Craftsman Label 1035.00
Whatnot Shelf, Corner, Regency Style, Marquetry, 68 x 25 x 16 In. 660.00
Whatnot Shelf, George III, Mahogany, 4 Shelves, 2 Drawers, Footed, 49 x 26 x 16 In. ... 1955.00
Whatnot Shelf, Regency, Mahogany, 3 Tiers, Block & Ring Turned Stiles, 30 x 20 In. ... 765.00
Whatnot Shelf, Victorian, Mahogany, Foliate Crest, Mirrored Back, 60 x 38 x 15 In. 1765.00
Whatnot Shelf, Victorian, Rosewood, 3 Graduated Shelves, Fretwork, 41 In. 355.00
Whatnot Shelf, William IV, 4 Tiers, Block & Ring Turned Stiles, c.1830, 52 x 18 In. 1645.00
Window Seat, Arts & Crafts, Cutout Sides, Spindles, Rush Seat, 23 x 14 x 28 In. 865.00
Window Seat, Edwardian, Satinwood, Cushion, Padded Arms, c.1900 .... 1095.00
Window Seat, Michigan Chair Co., Oak, Arched Rails, Cutouts, Tapered Legs 4500.00
Wine Cooler, George III, Mahogany, Brass Bound, c.1800, 22 1/2 x 17 1/2 In. 5675.00
Wine Cooler, Georgian, Mahogany, Medallion Inlay, Brass Bound, 8 Sides, 29 In. 2140.00
Wine Cooler, Regency, Mahogany, Sarcophagus, Hinges, c.1820, 24 x 29 x 20 In. 3335.00

G. ARGY-ROUSSEAU is the impressed mark used on a variety of objects
in the Art Deco style. Gabriel Argy-Rousseau, born in 1885, was a
French glass artist. In 1921, he formed a partnership that made pate-
de-verre and other glass. He worked until 1952 and died in 1953.

G-ARGY-
ROUSSEAU

Coupe, Danseuses, Pate-De-Verre Cameo, c.1920, 2 3/8 In. 8365.00

Coupe, Feuilles Larges, Pate-De-Verre, c.1914, 1 5/8 In. 2030.00
Coupe, Sorbier, Pate-De-Verre, c.1915, 2 5/8 In. 4180.00
Lamp, Art Deco, Cone Shape Shade, Burgundy, Cream, 12 1/4 In. 6465.00
Paperweight, Amber, 2 Butterflies, Pate-De-Verre, Signed, 1 3/4 x 2 1/2 In. 3000.00
Pendant, Parakeet's Head, Purple, Yellow, Green, Blue, Pate-De-Verre, 2 1/2 In. 1350.00
Pendant, Red Peony, Petals, Trapezium Shape, Pate-De-Verre, Pink Silk Cord, 2 In. 1575.00
Vase, Flowered Medallions, Pate-De-Verre, Bleuets, c.1922, 9 In. 8065.00
Vase, Masques, Pate-De-Verre, c.1914, 4 In. 4180.00
Vase, Red Roses, Stems, Purple Ground, Cylindrical, Flared, Pate-De-Verre, 2 3/4 In. 3930.00

GALLE was a designer who made glass, pottery, furniture, and other Art
Nouveau items. Emile Galle founded his factory in France in 1874.
After Galle's death in 1904, the firm continued to make glass and furniture until 1931. The name *Galle* was used as a mark, but it was often
hidden in the design of the object. Galle glass is listed here. Pottery is
in the next section. His furniture is listed in the Furniture category.

Bottle, Berries, Leaves, Spider Web, Stopper, Cameo, Fire Polished, Signed, 4 1/2 In. . . . 980.00
Bottle, Gold Enameled, Dragonfly, Flowers, Rim, Signed, 6 1/2 In. 2300.00
Bottle, Scent, Flowers, Pink, Translucent Green Ground, Cameo, Silver Cover, Foot, 5 In. 2588.00
Bowl, Amber, Dragonfly, Flowers, Gold Enameled, Semi-Globular, 3-Footed, 3 x 5 In. . . . 2470.00
Bowl, Canoe Shape, Yellow Ground, Red Leaves, Flowers, Cameo, 2 3/4 x 9 1/2 In. 1920.00
Bowl, Cover, Cranberry Flowers, Mottled Orange Ground, Cameo, 7 In. 3465.00
Bowl, Flowers, Leaves, Brown, On Yellow Ground, Cameo, Signed, 3 1/4 x 9 1/2 In. 1440.00
Bowl, Lotus Flowers, Opaque Green, Round Fruitwood Stand, Cameo, 4 In. 3145.00
Bowl, Octopus, Marine Life, c.1895, 3 1/8 In. 8365.00
Bowl, Rose, Red Flowers, Leaves, Cameo, 4 x 8 1/4 In. 2160.00
Chandelier, Cameo Glass, Dome Shade, Red Cut To Yellow, Flowers, 15 3/4 In. 2940.00
Chandelier, Green To Cream To Green, Red Flowers, Cameo, 3 Brass Chains, 12 In. 3740.00
Ewer, Enameled, Man Playing Bagpipe, Peasants, Round Handle, Signed, 8 x 6 In. 900.00
Jar, Cover, Egg Shape, Eagle, Flowers, Amber To Frosted Ground, Cameo, Signed, 4 In. . . 1200.00
Jar, Cover, Egg Shape, Green Butterflies, Lilac Meadow, Green Leaves, Signed, 3 3/4 In. . 1035.00
Jar, Enameled, Le Coq Du Village, Fire Polished, Cover, Signed, c.1900, 4 In. 2990.00
Lamp, Butterflies, Aqua, Green, Iron Stand, Signed, 4 3/8 In. 1035.00
Lamp, Deer & Trees, Cameo, Bronze, F. Gornik, 1906, 23 In. 4600.00
Lamp, Domed Shade, Purple Flowers, Yellow, Spreading Base, Cameo, 19 x 12 In. 9560.00
Lamp Base, Blue, Orange Over Gray, Cascading Stemmed Fruit, c.1915, 16 3/4 In. 1380.00
Perfume Bottle, Cameo Glass, Butterflies, Lime, Frosted Ground, Disk Stopper, 4 In. . . . 2465.00
Perfume Bottle, Cameo Glass, Purple Flowers, White, Metal Top, Atomizer, 3 1/2 In. . . . 690.00
Pitcher, Cover, Enameled Pansies, Gold Foil, Swirled, Signed, 10 1/2 In. 540.00
Plate, Tulips & Leaves, Peach & Blue, Gold Enameled, Signed, 9 In. 588.00
Salt, Blue & White Enameled, Signed, 2 1/2 In. 210.00
Tray, Poppies, Marquetry, Signed, 15 3/4 x 10 1/4 In. 1210.00
Tray, Rosewood, Tiger Maple, Elephant Family, Sun, 2 Handles, 15 x 23 In. 1736.00
Urn, Orange Nasturtiums, Leaves, Frosty Ground, Signed, 3 In. 260.00
Vase, Bell Flowers, Yellow Ground, Cameo, Signed, 6 3/4 In. 1530.00
Vase, Berried Branches, Pink Shaded Ground, Flat, Egg Shape, Cameo, Signed, 10 In. . . . 1880.00
Vase, Berries, Pink, Leaves, Peach To Frosted Ground, Banjo Shape, Cameo, Signed, 6 In. 1035.00
Vase, Blue Flowers, Pink Ground, Globular Shape, Cylindrical Neck, Cameo, 7 3/4 In. . . . 1435.00
Vase, Blue Flowers, Yellow Ground, Flattened Sphere, Cameo, 9 1/4 In. 3465.00
Vase, Blue, Purple Flowers, White Opalescent Ground, Cameo, 3 1/2 In. 360.00
Vase, Blueberries, Snail, Green Over Brown, Oval, Stepped Rim, Signed, c.1925, 7 In. . . . 4115.00
Vase, Bud, Amethyst Flowers, Cylindrical, Pinched Ruffled Edge, Cameo, 11 In. 730.00
Vase, Bud, Butterflies, Gentian Flowers, Cameo, c.1904, 29 1/2 In. 3360.00
Vase, Bud, Ferns, Green Ground, Frosted, Cameo, c.1904, 6 3/4 In. 360.00
Vase, Bud, Hydrangea, Rounded Purple Base, Frosted, Cameo, 8 1/4 In. 1080.00
Vase, Bud, Orchids, Orange Ground, Frosted, Cameo, 7 7/8 In. 720.00
Vase, Bud, Red Leafy Branches, Berries On Frosted Citron Ground, Signed, 4 5/8 In. 490.00
Vase, Budding Floral, Pink, White, Purple, Flattened Oval, Signed, c.1904, 5 3/4 In. 500.00
Vase, Burgundy Leafy Branches, Rosy Flowers, Citron Ground, Signed, 3 1/4 In. 575.00
Vase, Burnt Orange Over Oyster White, Leaves, Cameo, Signed, 4 3/4 In. 865.00
Vase, Butterflies, Grass, Blue, Green, Gold Enameled, Cream Ground, Cylindrical, 9 In. . . . 3595.00
Vase, Church On Lake In Cityscape, Frosted Orange Sky, Footed, Signed, 12 In. 2745.00
Vase, Citron, Royal Blue Thistles, Footed, Cameo, c.1915, 6 In. 805.00

Vase, Clematis, Flowers & Vines, Blown-Out, Frosted, Cameo, c.1924, 9 1/2 In. 9320.00
Vase, Cranberry Colored Flowers, Yellow, Flattened Sphere, Cameo, 10 In. 4480.00
Vase, Cranberry Flowers, Yellow Ground, Globular Shape, Flared Neck, Cameo, 5 3/4 In. . 1195.00
Vase, Ferns, Leaves, Green Ground, Banjo Shape, Cameo, Signed, 6 1/2 In. 1100.00
Vase, Fire Polished, Red Berried Branch, White Ground, Sphere, Cameo, 4 1/4 In. 660.00
Vase, Fish, Pearlized Lavender, Yellow, Applied Black & White Eyes, Signed, 5 1/2 In. . . 3160.00
Vase, Floral Branches, Pink, White, Purple, Round, Footed, Signed, c.1904, 3 7/8 In. 300.00
Vase, Flowers, Amber, Yellow Ground, Bulbous, Tall Flared Neck, Cameo, 8 In. 1435.00
Vase, Flowers, Amethyst, Leaves, Green, Pink Ground, Signed, 2 In. 360.00
Vase, Flowers, Blue, Green & Blue Over Frosted Pink, Cameo, Signed, 6 In. 900.00
Vase, Flowers, Blue, Leaves, Citron Ground, Bulbous, Cameo, Signed, 7 In. 1200.00
Vase, Flowers, Leaves, Orange, Frosted Ground, Cameo, Signed, 7 1/4 In. 2360.00
Vase, Flowers, Red On Frosted & Yellow Ground, Cameo, 11 In. 3335.00
Vase, Fuchsia Blossoms, Enameled, Silver Mount, 1910, 8 1/4 In. 1015.00
Vase, Ginger Mums, Leafy Stems, Citron Ground, Cameo, Signed, 6 1/2 In. 1035.00
Vase, Grapevine, Light Gray Shaded To Reddish Brown, Signed, 27 In. 5750.00
Vase, Gray, Blue Over Green, Leafy Stemmed Hyacinths, Cameo, c.1915, 16 In. 2415.00
Vase, Gray, Chartreuse, White, Leaves, Seed Pods, Cameo, c.1900, 7 1/2 In. 1035.00
Vase, Gray, Olive, Pink Over Lemon, Pillow Shape, Cameo, c.1915, 13 In. 5750.00
Vase, Green & Brown Gingko, Elongated Stems, Cylindrical, Footed, Signed, 16 In. 900.00
Vase, Green Seed Pods, Leafy Vines, Green, Coral Ground, Banjo Shape, Signed, 6 1/2 In. 575.00
Vase, Hibiscus, Yellow Ground, Blown-Out, Cameo, Signed, c.1925, 9 1/2 In. 9560.00
Vase, Hydrangea, Green, Lavender, Banjo Shape, Cameo, Signed, 8 In. 980.00
Vase, Internal Sea Kelp Design, Etched, Fire Polished, c.1895, 9 1/2 In. 8365.00
Vase, Landscape, Blue, Green, Frosted Ground, Cameo, 7 In. 1150.00
Vase, Landscape, Blue, Green, Frosted, Pedestal, Cameo, 6 In. 980.00
Vase, Landscape, Brown Over Mottled Pink, Footed, Oval, Cameo, 10 1/4 In. 2390.00
Vase, Landscape, Brown, Green, Water, Frosted To Green Ground, Cameo, Signed, 11 In. . 1035.00
Vase, Leaves & Blossoms, Brown, Flared, Banjo Shape, Cameo, Signed, 5 1/2 x 2 1/2 In. . 850.00
Vase, Leaves & Vines, Brown Over Amber, Bulbous, Foot, Signed, c.1900, 11 1/2 In. 3885.00
Vase, Leaves, Acorns, Peach, Frosted Ground, Cameo, Signed, 10 1/4 In. 635.00
Vase, Leaves, Branches, Flower Pods, Seeds, Frosty Green, Brown Ground, 11 1/2 In. . . . 690.00
Vase, Lilies, Blue, Violet, Rose, Frosted, Cameo, 19 5/8 In. 4200.00
Vase, Lily Pads, Frosted Amber Sky, Tapered Neck, Footed, Signed, 9 1/4 In. 1850.00
Vase, Lily Pads, Leaves, Frosted Yellow Ground, Cylindrical, Cameo, Signed, 6 1/4 In. . . 1175.00
Vase, Magnolia Blossoms, Crimson Over Mottled Amber, Cameo, Signed, c.1900, 10 In. . 6500.00
Vase, Maple Pods, Leaves, Green, Peach, Frosted Ground, Cameo, 9 1/2 In. 1150.00
Vase, Mountain Landscape, Purple On Yellow, Cameo, Signed, c.1900, 15 3/8 In. 5975.00
Vase, Mountain Laurel, Flowers, Vines, Berries, Frosted, Cameo, c.1924, 11 1/4 In. 7770.00
Vase, Octopus & Sea Kelp, Cameo, c.1895, 5 3/8 In. 6575.00
Vase, Olives, Leaves, Green, Brown, Amber To Peach Ground, Cameo, Signed, 6 1/4 In. . 1955.00
Vase, Orange Leafy Stems, Frosted Ground, Squat, Flared Neck, Cameo, Signed, 7 3/4 In. 400.00
Vase, Orchids, Yellow Ground, Tapered, Cameo, 6 1/2 In. 575.00
Vase, Pink Frosted, Amethyst Stemmed Flowers, Signed, Cameo, c.1920, 5 1/4 In. 575.00
Vase, Pink Over Gray, Chartreuse, Stemmed Thistles, Cameo, c.1915, 16 1/4 In. 1380.00
Vase, Plums, Blown-Out, Cameo, 15 1/2 In. 14500.00
Vase, Purple Flowers, On Yellow Ground, Teardrop, Cameo, Signed, 11 In. 1880.00
Vase, Purple Veronica, Yellow To White Ground, Cylindrical, Footed, Cameo, 13 1/2 In. . . 1070.00
Vase, Purple Vines, Fruit, Spider & Web, Fire Polished, Lozenge, 6 In. 7055.00
Vase, Red Berry Pods, Leafy Branches, Frost & Tangerine Ground, Barrel, 5 In. 375.00
Vase, Red Flowers, Leaves, Yellow, Frosted Ground, Cameo, 3 1/2 In. 575.00
Vase, Red Over Amber, Maroon, Leafy Stemmed Flowers, Cameo, c.1900, 14 In. 4830.00
Vase, Red Over Yellow, Stemmed Leafy Branches, Cameo, c.1910, 5 1/2 In. 1150.00
Vase, Red Overlay, Berries, Leaves, Pillow Shape, Cameo, c.1900, 5 3/4 In. 805.00
Vase, Rooster, Parrot, Footed, Cameo, Signed, 1915, 12 In. 8365.00
Vase, Rose, Milky White Ground, Leaves, Buds, Umbellate, Cameo, 27 3/4 In. 6600.00
Vase, Ruby Flowers, Green Ground, Flattened Sphere, Cameo, 7 In. 2390.00
Vase, Snail Among Mushrooms & Spider Webs, Cameo, Signed, 1915, 12 1/4 In. 3585.00
Vase, Stick, Landscape, Trees, Lake In Background, Green, Rose, Cameo, 7 In. 1000.00
Vase, Stick, Purple Columbine, Green Leaves, Cameo, Signed, 11 In. 1035.00
Vase, Tall Flared Neck, Red Berries, Flattened Sphere, Frosted, Cameo, 7 In. 900.00
Vase, Thistle, Chartreuse, Peach Ground, Cameo, Signed, 12 In. 1035.00
Vase, Thorny Berry Branches, Blue, Purple, Yellow Ground, Flared, Cylinder, 8 In. 4500.00

Vase, Trees, Mountain, Lake, Amethyst, Blue, Yellow, Green, Signed, 10 In. 2990.00
Vase, Water Lilies, Blue, Green, Cameo, 5 1/2 In. 545.00
Vase, Wisteria, Orange Ground, Frosted, Cameo, 10 5/8 In. 660.00
Vase, Wooded Lake Scene, Bridge, Cameo, Signed, 1910, 20 3/4 In. 6575.00

GALLE POTTERY was made by Emile Galle, the famous French
designer, after 1874. The pieces were marked with the initials *E. G.*
impressed, *Em. Galle Faiencerie de Nancy*, or a version of his signature. Galle is best known for his glass, listed above.

Figurine, Heraldic Lion, White, Blue Highlights, Tin Glaze, 1 5/8 In., Pair 3000.00
Figurine, Lion, Shield, Helmet & Castle Tower, Blue Over White, Signed, 16 1/2 In. 1175.00
Figurine, Pug Dog, Floral On White, Glass Eyes, Faience, Signed Nancy, c.1890, 12 In. . . 5080.00
Vase, Shell Raised On Fish, Frog On Rim, Harbor Scene, Signed, 10 In. 2000.00

GAME collectors like all types of games. Of special interest are any
board games or card games. Transogram and other company names are
included in the description when known. Other games may be found
listed under Card, Toy, or the name of the character or celebrity featured in the game.

Adler Luftwaffenspiel, German Artillery Downs British Bomber, 12 1/4 x 9 1/4 In. 85.00
American Way, Liberty & Justice For All, Balance The Scales Of Justice, 3 1/2 x 5 In. . . . 85.00
Animal Ten Pins, 10 Different Animal Characters, Milton Bradley, c.1910 . . . . 500.00
Aunt Sally Parlour, Cloth Doll, Wooden Head & Legs, Pipe In Mouth, Ring Pipe, 1910 . . 525.00
Authors, Parker Brothers, 5 x 6 1/2 In. 39.00
Babe Ruth's Baseball Game, Board, Playing Pieces, Milton Bradley, Box, 1936 . .385.00 to 395.00
Ball Toss, Lion-Head Target, c.1890, 38 In. 7500.00
Barney Google & Spark Plug, Milton Bradley, Board, 1923, 9 x 17 In. 330.00
Baseball, Field, Pegs, Spinner, Cards, Instructions, Case, Philadelphia, 19 1/2 In. 235.00
Beetle Bailey, Hilarious New Army, Jaymar, No. 930, Board, c.1950, 15 3/4 x 16 In. 25.00
Blow Football, Board, Box, 1912, 6 1/2 x 10 In. 44.00
Board, Checkers & Backgammon, 2 Sides, Blue, Black, White, Mustard, 17 x 17 In. 5060.00
Board, Checkers & Backgammon, Blue, Black, White Squares, 16 x 16 In. 7770.00
Board, Checkers & Parcheesi, 2 Sides, Orange, Black, Canada, 19th Century, 16 x 27 In. . 115.00
Board, Checkers & Parcheesi, 2 Sides, Painted, 22 x 28 3/4 In. 1880.00
Board, Checkers & Parcheesi, Red, Lime Green, Yellow, Black, Under Glass, 21 x 18 In. . 646.00
Board, Checkers & Parcheesi, White, Red, Black Boxes, 1900s, 18 x 18 In. 3585.00
Board, Checkers, 2 Sides, Wooden, Red, Yellow, Black, 20 1/4 x 16 3/4 In x 1 In. 600.00
Board, Checkers, Mustard, Ocher, Brown & Black, New England, c.1870, 18 1/2 In. 1595.00
Board, Checkers, Pine, Leather, Baseball Drawing On Reverse, 19 1/8 In. 85.00
Board, Checkers, Pine, Slat Ends, Green Ground, Red & Black Squares, 14 3/8 x 20 In. . . . 195.00
Board, Emulation, Cloth Mounted, 66 Figures, J. Harris, 1805, 18 x 23 In. 900.00
Board, Green Ghost, Transogram, 1965 . . . . 85.00
Board, Painted, 2 Sides, Black, Red Squares, Scrolling Leaves, Verso, c.1870, 16 x 16 In. . 2890.00
Board, Painted, Red Ground, Red, Black Squares, Early 20th Century, 22 3/4 x 14 In. 2630.00
Board, Painted, Yellow Ground, Yellow, Black Squares, Early 1900s, 21 x 17 1/2 In. 3105.00
Board, Parcheesi, Pine, 3 Panels, Red, Green, Yellow, Blue Field, 33 x 36 In. 825.00
Board, Slate, Hand Painted, Incised Geometric Design, Green, Red, Yellow, Black, 19 In. 1645.00
Board, Solitaire, Turned Wood, 400 Clay Marbles 303.00
Bop The Beetle, Ideal, Plastic, 1963 . . . . 85.00
Bozo The Clown, Circus, Transogram, No. 3841, Board, 1960, 17 In. 20.00
Bozo The World's Most Famous Clown, Parker Bros., 1967 . . . . 20.00
Bullwinkle & Rocky, Ideal, No. 2216-0-200, 1963, 18 1/2 x 19 In. 50.00
Calvin & The Colonel High Spirits, Milton Bradley, Board, c.1962, 9 1/4 x 15 3/4 In. 25.00
Card, Panko, Suffrage, 48 Cards 1350.00
Carl Hubbell Strike Out King Of The Major League, Mechanical, 1930s 325.00
Centennial Presidential Game, McLoughlin, Board, 1876, 4 1/2 x 7 1/2 In. 700.00
Chess, Box, Ebony, Brass, Dome Top, Hinged, Lift-Out Tray, Pieces, c.1900, 7 x 9 x 5 In. . 690.00
Chess Set, Chinese Figures, Ivory, 16 Stained Crimson, Lacquered Case, 20th Century . . . 1095.00
Chess Set, Chinese Figures, Ivory, 16 Tea Stained, Wood Case, 20th Century 920.00
Chess Set, Howdahs On Elephants, Horseback & Camels, Polychrome Ivory, 7-In. Kings . 6815.00
Chess Set, Israeli Silver, Metal, 20th Century, 2 1/2-In. Kings 5450.00
Chess Set, Ivory, Carved, Opposing Armies, Chinese, 19th Century, 4 1/2-In. King 2215.00
Chess Set, Ivory, Carved, Oriental, Mystery Ball Bases, Late 20th Century, 3 To 7 In. 690.00

Chess Set, Ivory, Light Brown & White, Case, Chinese 430.00
Chess Set, Ivory, Macao, 19th Century, 4-In. Kings 2555.00
Chess Set, Medieval Courtly Figures, Composition, Painted, 6 In. 470.00
Chess Set, Medieval Knights, Lead, Painted, 3 In. 176.00
Chess Set, Napoleonic Wars, Inlaid Board, 32 Painted Figures, Wooden Base, 15 x 15 In. . 215.00
Circus, Magnetic, Red, Yellow, Metal Board, Metal Figures, Smethport Co., 1920s 110.00
Cribbage, Buffalo Brewing Co., Bohemian New Brew, 13 x 4 1/4 x 3/4 In. 120.00
Cribbage, Ivory, Carved, Fish Shape, Inuit, 16 In. 295.00
Cribbage, Ivory, Walrus, Eskimo, Ship, Reindeer, Seal Hunting Scenes, 13 1/2 In. 259.00
Croquet, Table, Wooden, Bliss, 4 1/2 x 11 1/2 In. 45.00
Croquet, Wood, Metal Wickets, Box, Tabletop, Late 19th Century, 11 1/2 In. 150.00
Croquet Set, Parlor, Bliss, J. Pressman, Wooden, N.Y., 8 x 14 In. 100.00
Croquet Set, Parlor, J. Pressman, 4 Mallets, Balls, Wickets, Wood, N.Y., Box, 5 x 20 In. . 35.00
Cross Up, Lucille Ball, Milton Bradley, Board, Box, 1974 .... 25.00
Darkey Ten Pins, Wooden, Cardboard, Box, Milton Bradley, 7 1/4 x 10 1/4 x 1 1/2 In. ... 220.00
Dating Game, Hasbro, Cards, Money, Board, 1968 .... 30.00
Deputy Dawg, Milton Bradley No. 4105, Board, 1960, 15 3/4 x 18 1/2 In. 50.00
Dexterity Puzzle, Bear & Barrel, 1930s 75.00
Dexterity Puzzle, Children & Monkey On 1 Side, Clown On Other, 1930s 75.00
Do You Speak English, Board, Germany, c.1900, 12 x 13 In. 300.00
Dominoes, Bone, Ebonized Wood, 28 Dominoes, Dovetailed Box, Slide Lid, 7 In. 127.00
Dominoes, Bone, Hardwood Dovetailed Case, Cribbage Lid, 29 Dominos, 5 x 1 1/4 In. ... 440.00
Donkey, Linen, 14 Tails, C. Zimmerling, 34 x 24 1/2 In. 29.00
Dr. Busbey S.B. Ives, Card, 3 x 4 In. 20.00
Dragnet, Transogram, Sherry TV, Jack Webb On Cover, Board, 1955 .... 85.00
E.T., Parker Bros., Card, 1982 .... 8.00
Electric Target, Ball Blowing, Target, Tin, 2 Guns, 8 Darts, Box, c.1950, 17 x 16 In. 250.00
Elsie & Her Family, Board, c.1940, 9 1/2 x 19 In. 35.00
Excuse Me, Game Of Manners, Parker Brothers, Box, 4 1/2 x 7 1/2 In. 50.00
Famous Men, Parker Bros., Box, 4 x 6 In. 85.00
Fangface, Parker Brothers, No. 152, Board, 1979, 16 In. 45.00
Fantasy Island, View Of Island, Columbia Pictures, Ideal, Board, 1978 .... 15.00
Fibber McGee & Wistful Vista Mystery, Milton Bradley, Board, 1940, 5 1/2 x 7 1/2 In. .. 55.00
Fine Arts, Question & Answer, Milton Bradley, Box, 5 1/2 x 8 1/2 In. 11.00
Fish Pond, McLoughlin Bros., Magnetic, Poles, Fish, c.1891 .... 715.00
Fish Pond, Poles, Fish, Paper, Milton Bradley, Board, Box, c.1910, 10 1/2 x 20 In. 35.00
Flintstones, Stone Age, Transogram, Board, 1961, 9 x 17 In. 25.00
Football, Figures, Instructions, Tudor, 16 In. 60.00
Football, Tudor Tru Action, Electric, Plastic Pieces, Tin Field, 1962 .... 25.00
Fun With Bubbles, 6 Pipes, Lead Figures, J.W. Spears, J.W. Bavaria, London, c.1900 ... 850.00
Gambling Chip, Ivory, 5-Point Texas Star .... .69.00 to 75.00
Gambling Chip, Ivory, Golden, Round, 25 Dollars 119.00
Gambling Chip, Ivory, Iron Cross, Circle 55.00
Gambling Chip, Pearl, Green, Round, 10 Dollars, 1 1/2 In. 45.00
Gambling Chip, Pearl, Light Blue, Oval, 500 Dollars, 2 1/2 x 1 1/2 In. 85.00
Gambling Chip, Pearl, Red, Octagonal, 20 Dollars, Monogram, 1 1/3 In. 54.00
Gambling Wheel, Mason, Counter Model, 2 Sides, 34 In. 745.00
Game Of Cops & Robbers, Policeman, Selchow & Righter Co., Board, 1957 .... 35.00
Game Of Flags, McLoughlin Bros., Card, Box, 5 x 6 1/2 In. 90.00
Game Of Rich Uncle, Parker Bros., Board, 1946 .... 35.00
Game Of The Day At The Circus, McLoughlin Bros, Board., 1898 .... 900.00
Gee-Wiz Horse Race, Wolverine, Board, Box, 1940s, 6 x 16 In. .... .88.00 to 165.00
Golf, Tin Lithograph, Domo Game Co., N.Y., 1935, 17 x 22 In. 121.00
Grandmama's Sunday Game, New Testament, McLoughlin Bros., Card, 4 1/2 x 6 In. 11.00
Gulliver, Board, c.1930, 18 1/4 x 18 1/2 In. 15.00
Hersheyland, CBS Toys & Hershey Foods, Box, 1983, 2 x 10 x 19 In. 15.00
Indian Clubs, Painted, Wood, Raised Ring Turnings, 15 1/4 In., Pair 220.00
Jack & Jill, Spinner, Pieces, Milton Bradley, Box, Board, 8 x 16 In. 187.00
James Bond 007, Goldfinger, Milton Bradley, Board, 1966 .... 150.00
Jerome Park Steeple Chase, McLoughlin, Board, 1875 .... 495.00
Jeu Des Cyclistes, French Cyclist, Figures, Cycles, Metal, Box, Board, 12 x 17 In. 605.00
Jeu Des Mots Historiques, Cards, Booklet, Brevete, 1896, 14 x 10 1/2 In. 1750.00
Jigsaw Puzzle, Alien, Space Jockey, 1979, 10 x 14 In. 12.00

Jigsaw Puzzle, Battlestar Gallactica, Under Attack, Parker Bros., 140 Piece 17.00
Jigsaw Puzzle, Beverly Hillbillies, Slide Tray, Plastic, c.1960, 2 1/2 In. 40.00
Jigsaw Puzzle, Big Boy, Cheeseburger, 2 Sides, Envelope, c.1960, 6 1/4 x 9 1/4 In. 45.00
Jigsaw Puzzle, Bringing Up Father, Paper Lithograph, 4, Box, 8 1/2 x 10 1/2 In. 35.00
Jigsaw Puzzle, Bugs Bunny, Bugs Licking Lollipop, Box, 1960, 11 1/2 x 15 In. 10.00
Jigsaw Puzzle, Captain Huffenpuff, Playskool, Frame, Tray, Wood, 11 1/4 x 13 1/2 In. . . . 25.00
Jigsaw Puzzle, Centennial Exposition, Wood, Box, Chinnock, N.Y., 1875, 22 x 12 In. 700.00
Jigsaw Puzzle, Dudley Do Right, Dudley Steals Dick Dastardly Clothes, 100 Pieces, 1975 10.00
Jigsaw Puzzle, Exposition Universelle Paris 1878, Boxed Set Of 6, 8 x 11 In. 550.00
Jigsaw Puzzle, Fire Engine, Blown-Up Steamer, Milton Bradley, Box, 20 Pieces, 6 1/2 In. 380.00
Jigsaw Puzzle, Gumby & Pokey, Frame, Tray, c.1980, 11 1/2 x 14 In. 8.00
Jigsaw Puzzle, Jeremy Fisher, Wood, Box, B. Potter, Warne & Co., 50 Pieces, 1930 . . . . . 450.00
Jigsaw Puzzle, Linus The Lionhearted, Tray, Frame, No. 4514, 11 1/2 x 14 1/2 In. 8.00
Jigsaw Puzzle, Peep At The Circus, Dissected, McLoughlin, Box, 1887, 10 x 12 In. 176.00
Jigsaw Puzzle, Perils Of Penelope Pitstop, Frame, Tray, 1969 . . . . 15.00
Jigsaw Puzzle, Quick Draw McGraw & Baba Looey, Frame, Tray, Wooden, 1960 . . . . 20.00
Jigsaw Puzzle, Rusty Riley, Dog, Girl, Frame, Tray, King Features, 1949, 8 3/4 x 12 In. . . 12.00
Jigsaw Puzzle, Smokey The Bear, c.1950, 14 1/2 x 10 1/4 In. 110.00
Jigsaw Puzzle, Space Travel, Milton Bradley, 1959, 10 x 18 In. 25.00
Jigsaw Puzzle, Steamboat, Blown Up, Peter Thompson, Cincinnati, Box, 5 1/2 x 6 1/2 In. 525.00
Jigsaw Puzzle, United States, Map, McLoughlin Bros., Dissected, Paper, 7 1/2 x 10 1/2 In. 20.00
Katze Und Maus, Chromolithograph, Board, Germany, Early 1900s, 11 1/2 x 13 1/2 In. . . 382.00
Keno, Movie Land, Photos Of Actors & Actresses, Box, 8 x 9 In. 66.00
Knockout, James Braddock, Board, Pieces, Instructions, 20 x 20 In. 200.00
Le Jeu Des Fables, L'Auteur, 15 Fables, 27 Game Pieces, Board, 1815, 5 1/4 x 6 1/2 In. . . 1650.00
Learning In Sport, William Darton, Board, Linen Mounted, 44 Pictures, 1822, 18 x 15 In. 1500.00
Les Departments De La France, Aussine, Magnetic 5 Discs, Instructions, 1840 . . . . 2500.00
Life's Mishaps, Domino Rex, Bookshelf, 14 In. . . . . *Illus* 150.00
Lindy Flying, Parker Brothers, Card, Box, 1927, 6 1/2 x 10 In. 20.00
Little Red Riding Hood, Board, Box, 10 x 14 In. 50.00
Lotto, Casper & Company, Card, Built Rite Toys, c.1970, 7 1/2 x 14 x 1 In. 10.00
Mad Magazine, Parker Brothers, Board, 1979, 18 In. 12.00
Maiou-Maiou, Chromolithograph, Board, France, 19th Century, 14 1/2 x 19 3/4 In. 590.00
Marble, Wood, Painted, 417 Colored Clay Marbles, 7 3/8 In. 305.00
Mighty Mouse, Rescue Dinky Duck, Transogram, No. 3846, Board, 1961, 17 In. 25.00
Moving Picture, Milton Bradley, Board, c.1920, 9 x 15 In. 175.00
Mr. Ed The Talking Horse, Parker Brothers, Board, 1962 . . . . 50.00
Mr. Magoo, Standard Toycraft No. 95, Board 2, 1964, 18 x 18 In. 20.00
Mr. Magoo, Visits Zoo, Lowell No. 50-198, Board, 1961, 17 In. 45.00
New Game Of The Jew, Passmore, Board, 12 Sections, 1860 . . . . 3000.00
Obstacle Race, Spears, Board, Box, 8 1/2 x 12 In. 28.00
Our Country, Patriotic Theme, Red, White, Blue Graphics, 1884 . . . . 550.00
Paddle Board, Lollipop Paddles, Wooden, 1928, 9 & 10 1/2 In., Pair 155.00
Pigs In Clover, Clay Marbles, Round, 1890s 175.00
Pinball, Poosh-M-Up Baseball, 23 x 14 In. 69.00
Pinhead, Hide & Seek, Remco, Board, 1959 . . . . 9.00

Game, Life's Mishaps, Domino Rex,
Bookshelf, 14 In.

Game, Puzzle, Auto Scenes, Lithographed
Paper On Wood Blocks, 7 x 8 In.

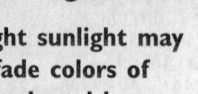

**Bright sunlight may
fade colors of
gameboard boxes.**

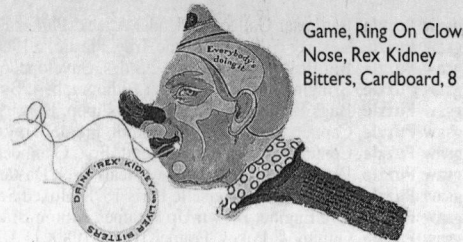

Game, Ring On Clown's
Nose, Rex Kidney
Bitters, Cardboard, 8 In.

Playset, Noah's Ark, Paper, Wood, Box, 10 1/2 x 20 In.	220.00
Pocket, Pinball, Marx, 5 1/2 x 3 In.	30.00
Pocket, Skee-Skill, Marx, 7 x 2 In.	30.00
Poker, Chip Holder, Wooden, Cylindrical, Hunting & Fishing Scenes, 9 1/2 x 4 In.	220.00
Poker Chips, Wood, Slots For Chips & Decks Of Cards, Cover, 5 x 14 x 9 In.	145.00
Puzzle, Auto Scenes, Lithographed Paper On Wood Blocks, 7 x 8 In. . . . . *Illus*	60.00
Puzzle, Block Set, Chromolithographed, Farm Animals, 7 3/4 x 9 1/4 In., 20 Piece	195.00
Puzzle, Block, Children At Play, Paper On Wood, Box, 4 x 5 1/2 In.	80.00
Puzzle, Blocks, Cat & Kittens, Photo Sheets, Wood, Paper Lithograph, Box, 7 x 8 1/2 In.	28.00
Puzzle, Blown-Up Steamboat, Paper, Peter Thompson, Cincinnati, Ohio, Box	495.00
Puzzle, Edison Mazda Lamps, Celluloid, 2 In.	150.00
Puzzle, Engman-Matthews Range Co., South Bend, Twisted Nail	50.00
Puzzle, National Baseball, Keep Matty In Box, Evers Makes Homerun, Steel Balls	550.00
Puzzle, Proverbs Lotto, Germany, Box, 12 3/4 In.	225.00
Puzzle, Revolution, Cut-Up History, Parker Bros., Box, 7 1/2 x 9 1/2 In.	40.00
Puzzle, Slide, Casper The Friendly Ghost, TV Pals, c.1960, 4 3/4 x 6 In.	28.00
Quick Change, Spears, Box, 9 x 10 In.	65.00
Ring On Clown's Nose, Rex Kidney Bitters, Cardboard, 8 In. . . . . *Illus*	30.00
Ring Toss, Quoits, Milton Bradley, Box, 7 x 13 1/2 In.	99.00
Ring Toss, Underdog, Larami, 1975, 6 x 12 In.	18.00
Rummy, Yogi Bear, Card, 1961	10.00
Shooting Gallery, Tabletop, Pinball, Manufactured By Challenger Co., 1925	175.00
Space Strike, Ideal, 1980	150.00
Spelling Bee, Paul Wing, Box, 7 1/2 x 11 1/2 In.	11.00
Star Soap, Woman, Schultz & Co., Zanesville, 1 3/4 In.	113.00
Steeple Chase, Jerome Park, McLoughlin Bros., Board, 12 1/2 x 14 In.	495.00
Steeple Chase, Spinner, 6 Horses, Metal, McLoughlin Bros., Board, Box, 16 1/2 In.	204.00
Stratego, Milton Bradley, Board, 1962	20.00
Target, Beanbag, Carnival, Polychrome Wood, Swashbuckler, 30 x 16 In.	1595.00
Target, Red Ryder, Game Pieces, Board, Box, 10 x 13 In.	176.00
Target, Satellite, Tin Gun, Battery Operated, Japan, Box, 10 In.	85.00
Target, Young America, Parker Bros., 9 1/2 x 12 In.	275.00
Target Shooting, Quick Draw McGraw, 1960s	60.00
Tiddlywinks, Cat, McLoughlin, 12 1/4 In.	295.00
Tobruk, War Simulation, Tank Battle, North Africa, Avalon Hill Bookcase, 1975	46.00
Tom Barker Baseball, 50 Cards, 1913	350.00
Tom Sawyer & Huck Finn, Stoll & Edwards, Board, 1925, 9 1/2 x 18 In.	230.00
Touchdown Football, Wilder, Box, Board, c.1920, 7 1/2 x 12 In.	176.00
Touring, Parker Bros., Card, Box, 1958	10.00
Trolley, Snyder Bros., Elmira, New York, Card, 1904, 3 x 4 In.	39.00
Turn Over, Milton Bradley, 1908, 5 x 12 In.	95.00
Uncle Wiggily, Milton Bradley, Board, c.1950, 8 1/2 x 17 In.	45.00
United States, Across The Continent, Parker Bros., Board, Box, 11 1/2 x 18 In.	22.00
Wheel, Dice Emblems, Painted, Red, Yellow, Hardin County, Ohio, 20 In.	415.00
Wheel, Gambling, Cast Iron, Red, White & Blue, H.C Evans & Co., Late 1900s, 5 In.	1800.00
Wheel, Roulette, 6-Panel Lithophane, Elephant, Car, Dog, Mounted, France, 9 1/2 In.	115.00
Wheel, Roulette, Portable, Wooden Case, Cigar Payoffs, Cast Iron, 13 x 13 x 4 1/2 In.	900.00
Who's Afraid Of The Big Bad Wolf, Board, Parker Brothers, 1933	175.00
Wilder Football, Game Pieces, Board, Box, c.1930, 12 1/2 x 20 1/2 In.	66.00
Wizard Of Oz, First Edition, Parker Brothers, Copyright 1922	1645.00
Woody Woodpecker Knot Hole, Marx, Box, c.1950, 24 x 6 In.	195.00

Yertle, Dr. Seuss, Balancing, 1960 . . . .   70.00
Young Folks Historical Game, 35 Cards, Cardboard Box, Directions, McLoughlin Bros. . . .   132.00

GAME PLATES are plates of any make decorated with pictures of birds, animals, or fish. The game plates usually came in sets consisting of twelve dishes and a serving platter. These sets were most popular during the 1880s.

2 Ducks, Raly, Limoges, c.1910, 11 In. 410.00
Bird, Lanny, Legran, Lazeyras, Rosenfeld, Lehman, Limoges, 1920s, 11 In. 175.00
Bird, White, Hand Painted, Transfer Holly Decoration, Gold Trim, Limoges, 9 1/4 In. 185.00
Birds, 4 Scenes, E. Offner, New Orleans, 8 3/8 In., 8 Piece 310.00
Birds, Rim Gilding, Holes For Hanging, S. Barbus, Limoges, 11 In. 450.00
Common Snipe, Transfer Print, R.K. Beck, Taylor, Smith & Taylor, c.1915, 9 1/2 In. 65.00
Game Birds, Green Border, Gold Edge, Limoges, c.1880, 9 In., 6 Piece 675.00
Geese, Hand Painted, Scalloped Rim, Muville, Limoges, c.1905, 9 1/2 In. 150.00
Mallard, Hand Painted, Scalloped Rim, Muville, Limoges, c.1905, 9 1/2 In. 150.00
Pheasant, Hand Painted, Limoges, 9 In. 45.00
Pheasant, Lace Look Rim, Gold Gilding, Hand Painted, Schumann, Dresden, 7 1/2 In. 75.00
Pheasant, Transfer Print, R.K. Beck, Taylor, Smith & Taylor, c.1915, 9 1/2 In. 65.00
Pheasant & Quail, Gold, Scalloped Rim, Bayreuth, 11 1/2 In. 37.50
Pheasants, Hand Painted, Scalloped Rim, Muville, Limoges, c.1905, 9 1/2 In. 150.00
Quail, Hand Painted, Scalloped Rim, Muville, Limoges, c.1905, 9 1/2 In. 150.00
Quail, Transfer Print, Gold Rim, Bavaria, 9 3/4 In. 49.00
Ring Neck Pheasant, Hamilton Collection, 1989 . . . .   20.00
Sandpipers, Hand Painted, Scalloped Rim, Muville, Limoges, c.1905, 9 1/2 In. 150.00

GARDEN FURNISHINGS have been popular for centuries. The stone or metal statues, wire, iron, or rustic furniture, urns and fountains, sundials, and small figurines are included in this category. Many of the metal pieces have been made continuously for years.

Basket, Cherry Branch Sprays, Scroll Ends, Wrought Iron, 2 Handles, 16 x 16 In. 200.00
Basket, Napoleon III Style, Cast Stone, Oval, Handle, France, 18 x 22 In. 200.00
Basket, Wirework, Pear Shape, Victoria, France, 22 In., Pair 430.00
Bench, 3 Arches, Entwined Fans, Leaves, Buds, White, Cast Iron, 30 x 68 In. 770.00
Bench, 3-Chair Back, Cupids, Lyre, Ram's Head Arms, Cast Iron, 32 x 70 x 19 In. 2530.00
Bench, 3-Chair Back, Open Scrolled, Geometric Seat, Cast Iron, 46 In. 1015.00
Bench, Carved Rabbits, Molded Arms, Wood, Double Plank Seat, Shaped Legs, 58 In. . . .   750.00
Bench, Ferns, Cast Iron, Barbee Iron & Wire Works, Chicago, Ill., 1900s, 45 x 29 In. 220.00
Bench, Laurel Pattern, Concave Seat, Cast Iron, c.1900, 28 1/2 x 43 1/2 In. 3450.00
Bench, Lion Head Medallions, Scrolled Arms, Cast Iron, Slatted Wood Seat, 50 In. 85.00
Bench, Neoclassical Style, H-Stretcher, Wrought Iron, Provincial, 26 1/2 x 70 In. 690.00
Bench, Openwork, Scrolls, Rosettes, Geometric, 3-Panel Back, Cast Iron, 36 x 44 In. 380.00
Bench, Renaissance Revival, Scrollwork, Rosettes, Lattice, Cast Iron, 38 x 46 In. 1808.00
Bench, Serpentine Crest, Shell Molding, Cast Iron, Edwardian, c.1900, 24 1/2 x 73 In. . . .   635.00
Bench, Teakwood, Green Paint, Cast Iron Frame, Bench Mfg., Co., 16 x 62 In. 200.00
Bench, Vines & Flowers, Cabriole Legs, White Paint, Cast Iron, 31 In. 338.00
Birdbath, Figural, 2 Putti, Flower Shape, Cornucopia Stem, Lead, 26 x 15 In. 400.00
Birdbath, Fluted Basin, Seahorse On Top, 3-Seahorse Base, Concrete, 34 x 27 In. 750.00
Birdbath, Shell Shape, Lovebirds, Dolphin Shape Base, Concrete, 25 In. 145.00
Birdhouse, Barn Shape, 2 Tiers, Painted, Green Shingles, 26 x 24 x 40 In. 633.00
Birdhouse, Octagonal, 6 Tiers, Raised Cap, White Paint, 22 x 48 1/2 In. 275.00
Boot Scraper, Cast Iron, Beaded, Rosettes, Paw Feet, 10 1/2 x 10 x 8 1/2 In. 200.00
Boot Scraper, Cast Iron, Bronze Horses, Tombstone Shape, 8 x 17 1/2 x 7 1/2 In. 880.00
Boot Scraper, Iron, Cat Shape, Cast, Mounted, Shallow Pan, 19th Century, 7 3/4 x 11 In. .   1058.00
Chair, Arms, Green Paint, Wrought Iron, England, 18th Century, 40 1/2 In., Pair 805.00
Chair, Basket Weave Seat, X-Stretcher Back, Curved Arms, Cast Iron, Pair 790.00
Chair, Curved Back, Fern, Flower, Griffins, Blue, Iron, 1860, 30 x 44 x 34 In. 550.00
Chair, Regency Style, Pierced Arched Back, Wrought Iron, Plank Seats, 39 In., Pair 259.00
Chair, Victorian, Crosshatch Back, Wire, Green Paint, 37 In., 4 Piece 375.00
Cistern, Georgian, Relief Flowers, Cast Iron, 20 x 41 In. 1840.00
Cross, Log Shape, Grapevines, Leaves, Cattails, Cast Iron, White Paint, 51 x 26 In. 400.00
Fence, Iron, Rounded Spike Terminals, 6 Posts, 42 In. x 31 Ft. 6 In. 2640.00
Figure, Blackamoor, Wearing Hat, Holding Ring, Cast Cement, 32 In. 405.00

Figure, Boy, Holding Bowl Above His Head, Cast Lead, 32 In. 290.00
Figure, Dalmatian, Black, White, Cast Iron, 48 In. 4830.00
Figure, Doe, Reclining, Red Marble Eyes, Cement, 10 x 17 In. 366.00
Figure, Dog, Retriever, Cast Concrete, Life-Size, Pair 275.00
Figure, Frog, Clay, Glazed, 7 1/2 In. . . . . *Illus* 45.00
Figure, Lion, Sitting, Plinth Base, Cast Stone, 26 x 31 In., Pair 575.00
Figure, Rabbit, Seated, Cast Iron, White Paint, 11 x 11 In., Pair 360.00
Figure, Sphere, Hercules Resting, Fluted Column, Arrow, Cement, Iron, 59 In. 310.00
Figure, Sphinx, Cast Stone, Molded Platform, Greek Key Edge, 21 In., Pair 750.00
Finial, Gatepost, Beaux Arts Style, Lion, Cast Stone, France, 16 In., Pair 290.00
Font, Marble, Round, Molded, Carved Putti Pedestal, 43 x 16 In., Pair 2185.00
Fountain, 3 Tiers, Victorian, 3-Dolphin Base, Cast Iron, 66 x 43 1/2 In. 3450.00
Fountain, Figural, Fish, Spouting, Marble, Wave-Shaped Base, 50 In., Pair 920.00
Fountain, Figure, Goose, Spread Wings, Lead, Early 20th Century, 25 In. 489.00
Fountain, Half-Round Bowl, Shell Shape, Rolled Lip, Arched Back, Marble, 59 x 38 In. . . 635.00
Fountain, Renaissance Revival, Shell Shape Bowl, Grotesque, Italy, 61 In. 2350.00
Frog, Cement, Red Marble Eyes, Open Mouth, 7 In. 255.00
Gate, Cast & Wrought Iron, Scrolled Lyre, Pointed Spikes, 51 x 37 In. 605.00
Gate, Lattice Design, Flower Finial, Iron, 48 x 32 In. 230.00
Gnome, Pushing Wooden Wheelbarrow, Plaster, Painted, 16 In. 35.00
Hitching Post, Black Jockey, Brick Red Pants & Hat, Green Vest, Cast Iron, 23 1/2 In. 248.00
Hitching Post, Dog Head, Cast Iron, 14 1/2 In. 1925.00
Hitching Post, Horse, Cast Iron, Shaped Wooden Standard, 53 In. 200.00
Hitching Post, Jockey, Black, Iron, Polychrome, 38 In. 230.00
Hitching Post, Reeded Columns, Horse Head Finials, Cast Iron, 45 In., Pair 2200.00
Hose Reel, Oak, Iron, Bentwood, Victorian 69.00
Jardiniere, Amorini, Oval, Flower Baskets, Iron, France, 40 1/2 x 17 1/2 In., Pair 1035.00
Jardiniere, Basket, Curled Ends, Oval, Arched Handle, Wire, 19 x 24 In. 92.00
Jardiniere, Louis XVI Style, Mahogany, Gilt Brass Mounts, c.1900, 16 x 15 x 14 In. 1265.00
Jardiniere, Neoclassical Style, Iron, France, 1900s, 14 1/2 x 19 x 14 3/4 In., Pair 750.00
Jardiniere, Regency Style, Tole, Oval, Pierced Gallery, 28 1/2 x 18 In. 1035.00
Jardiniere, Rococo, Gesso, Winged Children, Acanthus Leaves, Tripod Base, 45 In. 330.00
Pedestal, Neoclassical Style, Variegated Stone, Circular Plinth, c.1900, 34 x 17 In. 575.00
Plant Stand, Glass Top, Pierced Rim & Lower Shelf, Iron, Victorian, 28 x 13 In. 50.00
Planter, Garlands, Round, Cast Lead, 17th Century, 10 x 12 1/2 In., Pair 2032.00
Planter, Gothic Revival, Tole, Iron, Metal Liner, c.1815, 20 1/2 x 20 1/2 In., Pair 4600.00
Planter, Obelisk, Square, Regency Style, Cast Iron, 84 1/2 x 20 x 20 In. 1265.00
Planter, Pedestal, Footed, Cast Iron, Distressed Green Paint, 24 x 18 1/2 x 18 1/2 In. 3450.00
Planter, Swan Shape, Cement, Red Marble Eyes, 16 In., Pair 280.00
Planter, Urn Shape, 2 Ram's Head Handles, Black Paint, Cast Iron, 21 In., Pair 219.00
Seat, Blackamoor Child Among Bulrushes, Majolica, England, c.1870, 17 1/2 In. 1435.00
Seat, Blue & White, Hexagonal, Continuous Pagoda, Lake, Chinese Export, 18 In., Pair . . 1495.00
Seat, Egyptian Woman, Sitting, Holding Tray, Owl, Cobras, Pottery, Yellow, 1870, 30 In. . 2020.00
Seat, Elephant Shape, Terra-Cotta, Green, Multicolored Glazes, 24 In. 690.00
Seat, Famille Rose, Baluster Shape, Flowers, Chinese Export, 19th Century, 26 In., Pair . . 1495.00
Seat, Famille Rose, Barrel Form, Canton, 1800s, 18 3/4 In., Pair 8400.00
Seat, Frieze, Figures On Terrace, Hexagonal, Chinese Export, 19th Century, 18 3/4 In. . . . 896.00
Seat, Majolica, Bamboo Stalks, Ribbon, Minton, 18 1/2 In. 4994.00
Seat, Octagonal, People In Garden Scene, Famille Verte, Chinese Export, 18 x 14 In. 259.00
Seat, Rose Medallion, Barrel, Money Cartouches, Chinese Export, 1875-1908, 17 1/2 In. . 1610.00

Garden, Figure, Frog,
Clay, Glazed, 7 1/2 In.

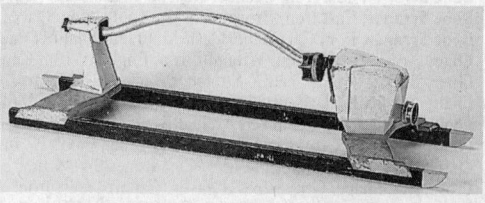

Garden, Sprinkler, Oscillating, Aluminum, Melnor, Model

Set, Bench, Chair, Table, Gothic Style, Urns, Medallions, Cast Iron, c.1890 . . . .   55.00
Set, Regency Style, Patinated, Cast Aluminum, Upholstered, Settee, 2 Chairs 805.00
Settee, Woman's Head In High Relief, Scrolls, Cabriole Legs, Wrought Iron 825.00
Settee Set, Openwork, Geometric Seats, Wraparound Arms, Cast Iron, 3 Piece 415.00
Sprinkler, Oscillating, Aluminum, Melnor, Model No. 800, USA, 25 1/2 In. . . . . *Illus*   20.00
Sundial, Man, Scythe, Engraved Time Ring, Octagonal Base, Bronze, c.1760, 6 x 3 In. . . .   336.00
Sundial, Roman Numerals, Wedge Time Keeper, Iron, Signed Mauch Chunk, 1832, 10 In.   750.00
Sundial, Rose, I'll Only Count Your Sunny Hours, Cast Brass, 1800s, 10 x 5 In. 420.00
Table, Neoclassical Style, Verde Antico, Marble Top, Cast Iron, 26 1/2 x 31 In. 978.00
Table, Picnic, Teakwood, Cast Iron Frame, Green Paint, Bench Mfg. Co., 28 x 61 In. 316.00
Table, Wicker, White Paint, Early 1900s, 30 x 41 x 27 In. 400.00
Trellis, Spiral Shapes, Iron, Weathered White Paint, 36 In. 150.00
Trough, Georgian, Hewn, Square, Limestone, 19th Century, 11 1/2 x 20 x 20 In. 980.00
Trough, Georgian, Oval, Limestone, 19th Century, 8 x 26 x 16 1/2 In. 230.00
Urn, Campana Shape, Black Paint, Cast Iron, 19th Century, 16 x 13 In. 1035.00
Urn, Carved, Leaf-Molded, Everted Lip, Reeded Column, Marble, 35 x 10 In., Pair 316.00
Urn, Inverted Teardrop Shape, Round Turned Base, Granite, 31 x 18 In. 403.00
Urn, Molded Lip, Scrolling Leaf, Reeded Body, Handles, Cast Stone, 47 1/2 x 24 In., Pair   1495.00
Urn, Molded, Palmetto & Wreath, Plinth Base, Cast Iron, 11 x 23 In., Pair 175.00
Urn, Plinth Base, Limestone, 19th Century, 18 1/2 x 23 In., Pair 1150.00
Urn, Regency Style, Neoclassical Warrior Relief, 2 Handles, Terra-Cotta, 20 1/4 In., Pair .   460.00
Urn, Relief Flowers, Cast Iron, 1800s, 28 x 34 In., Pair 1150.00
Urn, Round, Flared, Open Handle, Cast Iron, 19th Century, 34 x 20 In. 345.00
Urn, Square, Geometric, Leaf Design, Stone, 23 x 19 1/2 In., 4 Piece 1175.00
Vase, Louis XVI Style, Bacchanalian, Terra-Cotta, 27 x 25 In., Pair 1265.00
Watering Can, Iron, Brass, Black Paint, c.1900, 16 In., 2 1/2 Gal. 90.00
Watering Can, Iron, Green Paint, Brass Nozzle, c.1900, 16 In., 2 Gal. 127.00

GAUDY DUTCH pottery was made in England for America from about
1810 to 1820. It is a white earthenware with Imari-style decorations of
red, blue, green, yellow, and black. Only sixteen patterns of Gaudy
Dutch were made: Butterfly, Carnation, Dahlia, Double Rose, Dove,
Grape, Leaf, Oyster, Primrose, Single Rose, Strawflower, Sunflower,
Urn, War Bonnet, Zinnia, and No Name. Other similar wares are called
Gaudy Ironstone and *Gaudy Welsh.*

Cup & Saucer, Diamond, Handless, Pearlware 367.00
Cup & Saucer, Double Rose, Handleless 231.00
Cup & Saucer, Oyster 75.00
Cup & Saucer, Oyster, Handleless 330.00
Cup & Saucer, Single Rose, Orange, Green, Yellow, Blue, Handleless 550.00
Cup & Saucer, Sunflower, 5 1/2 In. 276.00
Cup & Saucer, War Bonnet, Orange, Green, Blue, Yellow, Handleless . . . . .495.00 to 510.00
Mug, Grape, Pearlware, Applied Handle, Child's, 2 In. 249.00
Plate, Carnation, 7 1/2 In. . . . . .200.00 to 330.00
Plate, Double Rose, 7 1/2 In., Pair 288.00
Plate, Single Rose, 8 1/4 In. 413.00
Plate, Sunflower, 8 In. 173.00
Plate, War Bonnet, 7 In. 375.00
Saucer, Oyster, 5 1/2 In. 52.00
Sugar, Footed, Flowers, 6 In. 75.00
Sugar, Grape Variant, Double Handles, Molded Finial, 7 3/4 x 5 1/4 In. 935.00
Teapot, Leaf, 6 In. 880.00
Toddy Plate, Grape, 6 In. 58.00
Toddy Plate, Single Rose, 6 In. 275.00

GAUDY IRONSTONE is the collector's name for the ironstone wares
with the bright patterns similar to Gaudy Dutch. It was made in
England for the American market after 1850. There may be other
examples found in the listing for Ironstone or under the name of the
ceramic factory.

Compote, Floral, 5 1/2 x 10 In. 220.00
Creamer, Strawberry, Pearlware 124.00
Cup & Saucer, Black Berry, Handleless 143.00

Cup & Saucer, Feather, Handleless	165.00
Cup & Saucer, Lyre, Handleless, Pair	193.00
Cup & Saucer, Pinwheel	50.00
Cup & Saucer, Plate, Wagon Wheel, Child's Set, 6 3/4 In.	210.00
Cup & Saucer, Seeing Eye, Handleless, Pair	60.00
Cup & Saucer, Strawberry, Pearlware, Handleless	180.00
Pitcher, Floral, Cobalt Blue, Red Orange, Paneled, Creature Handle, 6 5/8 In.	248.00
Pitcher, Milk, Seeing Eye, 7 3/4 In.	1320.00
Plate, Blackberry, 8 1/2 In.	132.00
Plate, Feather, Paneled, 8 1/2 In.	198.00
Plate, Feather, Paneled, 9 1/2 In.	187.00
Plate, Morning Glory, Paneled, 8 1/4 In.	60.00
Plate, Seaweed, Paneled, 9 1/2 In.	110.00
Plate, Seeing Eye, Paneled, 8 1/2 In., 3 Piece	132.00
Plate, Soup, Pinwheel, Paneled, 10 1/4 In.	308.00
Plate, Soup, Strawberry, Paneled, 9 1/2 In.	358.00
Plate, Strawberry, Paneled, 8 3/4 In.	165.00
Platter, Strawberry, 13 1/4 In.	50.00
Waste Bowl, Fern, 3 1/2 x 5 1/2 In.	120.00
Waste Bowl, Pinwheel, Large Flared Top, 4 x 6 1/2 In.	176.00
Waste Bowl, Seeing Eye, 3 3/4 x 5 1/4 In., Pair	145.00

GAUDY WELSH is an Imari-decorated earthenware with red, blue, green, and gold decorations. Most Gaudy Welsh was made in England for the American market. It was made from 1820 to about 1860.

Creamer, Flowers & Leaves Pattern, 3 1/2 In.	132.00
Pitcher, Bellflower, 7 1/2 In.	110.00
Plate, Blackberry, Yellow, Orange, Black, Flow Blue, Luster, E. Walley, 8 1/2 In.	110.00
Plate, Urn Pattern, Pink, Orange, Green, Blue, Paneled Rim, 8 1/2 In., 6 Piece	715.00

GEISHA GIRL porcelain was made for export in the late nineteenth century in Japan. It was an inexpensive porcelain often sold in dime stores or used as free premiums. Pieces are sometimes marked with the name of a store. Japanese ladies in kimonos are pictured on the dishes. There are over 125 recorded patterns. Borders of red, blue, green, gold, brown, or several of these colors were used. Modern reproductions are being made.

Bowl, Hand Decorated, Scalloped, Blue Trim, Red Mark, 1940s, 10 In.	65.00
Bowl, Oriental Scene, Scalloped Edge, Torii Nippon, 5 x 1 1/4 In.	7.50 to 12.50
Creamer, Garden Scene, Silk Screen & Hand Painted, Red Trim, Handle, 4 In.	12.00
Cup & Saucer, Garden Scene, c.1920, 3 7/8 In.	20.00
Dish, Footed, Hand Painted, Scalloped Edge, 7 1/4 x 2 In.	32.00
Hair Receiver, Blue Borders, Gold Trim	25.00
Pin Tray, Garden Scene, Red Trim, 1800s, 4 1/4 x 3 x 1 In.	5.00
Pitcher, Garden Scene, Red Trim, c.1895, 3 1/4 In.	5.00
Plate, Garden Scene, Tree, Boat On Water, Hand Painted, 7 1/4 In.	9.00
Saucer, Garden Scene, Red Trim, Silk Screen & Hand Painted, 5 1/2 In.	3.00
Toothpick Holder, Garden Scene, Red Trim, c.1895, 2 1/4 In.	10.00
Vase, Baluster Shape, Garden Scene, Red Trim, 1800s, 4 1/4 In.	5.00
Vase, Shouldered, Garden Scene, Red Trim, 1800s, 5 In.	5.00

GENE AUTRY was born in 1907. He began his career as the *Singing Cowboy* in 1928. His first movie appearance was in 1934, his last in 1958. His likeness and that of the Wonder Horse, Champion, were used on toys, books, lunch boxes, and advertisements.

Book, Ghost Riders, 1955	35.00
Cap Gun, Pearl Handles, Cast Iron, Nickel Plated, Kenton, Box, 6 1/2 In.	347.00
Cap Gun Set, Ivory Grips, Holster & Belt, Kenton C.I., 8 x 12 In.	605.00
Guitar, Plastic, Emenee, Box, 32 In.	230.00
Pin, Black, White, 1 3/4 In.	28.00
Wristwatch, Champion, Gene On Face, Leather Band, Wilane, Box, 1948	305.00
Wristwatch, Gene On Face, 6-Shooter, New Haven, Box, 1951	715.00
Wristwatch, Wilane, Box, 1948	385.00

GIBSON GIRL black-and-blue decorated plates were made in the early 1900s. Twenty-four different 10 1/2-inch plates were made by the Royal Doulton pottery at Lambeth, England. These pictured scenes from the book *A Widow and Her Friends* by Charles Dana Gibson. Another set of twelve 9-inch plates featuring pictures of the heads of Gibson Girls had all-blue decoration. Many other items also pictured the famous Gibson Girl.

Drawing, Butterfly Man, Flower Women, Pen, Ink, C.D. Gibson, 1902, 18 x 28 In.	11000.00
Plate, Mr. Waddles Arrives Late, Finds Card Filled, c.1900, 10 1/2 In.	265.00
Plate, Quiet Dinner With Dr. Bottles, Marked, c.1900, 10 1/2 In.	265.00
Plate, Some Think She Has Remained In Retirement Too Long, c.1900, 10 1/2 In.	265.00
Postcard, Leap Year 1908, Now Is Your Chance, Get Busy	6.00
Vase, Portrait In Blue Hat, Cream Ground, 2 Apple Handles, Austria, 12 In.	120.00

GIRL SCOUT collectors search for anything pertaining to the Girl Scouts, including uniforms, publications, and old cookie boxes. The Girl Scout movement started in 1912, two years after the Boy Scouts. It began under Juliette Gordon Low of Savannah, Georgia. The first Girl Scout cookies were sold in 1928.

Badge, 60 Yards Freestyle, 1922	100.00
Beret, Patch Metal Insignia, Green Felt, Red Lining, Box, 1940s, Size Medium	29.00
Bicentennial Patch, 1776-1976	3.00
Bracelet, White Metal, Logo, 2 1/2 In.	15.00
Calendar, 1958	24.00
Calendar, 1961	18.00
Calendar, 1964	15.00
Catalog, Uniform & Equipment, 1930, 40 Pages	81.00
Charm Bracelet, Brass, Eagle, Turtle, Seashell	38.00
Compass, Taylor Instrument, Box	21.00
Equipment Book, 1947	52.00
Handbook, Brownie Scout, Illustrated, Hard Bound, New York, 1959, 95 Pages	8.00
Handbook, Girl Scout, Illustrated, Hard Bound, New York, 1951, 527 Pages	11.00
Key Case, 6 Hooks, Pocket, Identification Card, Insignia, 3 3/4 In.	111.00
Pail, Cover, Active Girl Scouts, Tin Lithograph, 3 x 6 x 3 3/4 In.	150.00
Pennant, Camp Kaufmann, Penn.	14.00
Pin, Brownie, 1 3/4 In.	9.00
Tin, Cookies, Burry Biscuit Corp.	16.00
Whistle, Brass, Round, 1920s, 2 1/2 In.	11.00

GLASS-ART. Art glass means any of the many forms of glassware made during the late nineteenth or early twentieth century. These wares were expensive and production was limited. Art glass is not the typical commercial glass that was made in large quantities, and most of the art glass was produced by hand methods. Later twentieth-century glass is listed under Glass-Contemporary, Glass-Midcentury, or Glass-Venetian. Even more art glass may be found in categories such as Burmese, Cameo Glass, Tiffany, and other factory names.

Banana Bowl, Apricot, Tricornered, Silver Plated Frame, 13 1/2 In.	470.00
Bowl, Blue, Frosted, Molded Mermaids, Art Deco Style, 15 1/2 In.	360.00
Bowl, Cobalt Blue, Ram's Head, Louis XVI Style, Gilt Bronze Mount, 9 1/2 In., Pair	1175.00
Bowl, Cover, Satin, Mottled Yellow, Orange, 6 In.	1445.00
Bowl, Green, Red, Pink, Translucent, Applied Pear On Vine, 8 1/4 In.	355.00
Box, Belle Ware, Heart Shape, Opaque Tan, Red, Yellow Mums, Victorian, 6 In.	460.00
Box, Cover, Stylized Flowers, Blue, Orange, White, Globular, Wiener Werkstatte, 5 In.	1010.00
Charger, Opalescent, Molded Fish In Swirl Pattern, Art Nouveau, 12 In.	345.00
Cup, Gold Iridescent, Green Zigzag Design, Handle, Polished Pontil, 2 1/2 In.	175.00
Dish, Sweetmeat, Blue Bowl, Enameled Butterflies, Ruffled, Silver Plated Holder, 10 In.	250.00
Finger Bowl, Pink Interior, White Exterior, Ruffled Edge, 5 In.	30.00
Goblet, Amber, Blue Rim, Applied Prunts, Polished Pontil, c.1910, 7 1/2 In.	60.00
Goblet, Geometric Panels, Yellow Overlay, Flared, Wiener Werkstatte, 8 In.	840.00
Jam Jar, Turquoise, Enameled Stork & Branch, Silver Plated Cover & Bail, 5 In.	75.00
Jar, Sweetmeat, Cover, Etched Grapevines, Ovoid, Bronze Art Nouveau Stand, 16 In.	380.00
Jug, Enameled Leaves, Insects, Handle, Oval, Diamond Rim, c.1880, 7 7/8 In.	735.00

 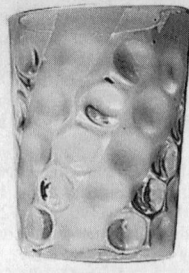 

Glass-Art, Tumbler, Blue Opaque, Embossed School Scene, Marked, Sowerby, 4 In.

Glass-Art, Tumbler, Polka Dot, Swirled Frances Decoration, Hobbs, Brockunier & Co., 4 In.

Glass-Art, Tumbler, Stone Glass, Mottled Green, Purple, Draped, Mustard Interior, 3 1/2 In.

Shade, Green Pulled Feathers, Gold Tipped, Early 20th Century, 6 1/4 In.	260.00
Shade, Opal, Green Tipped, Gold Pulled Feathers, 20th Century, c.1920, 6 In.	145.00
Shade, Translucent, Iridescent Gold Pulled Feathers, Green Tipped, Early 1900s, 6 In.	545.00
Tankard, Cobalt, Gold Enameled, 15 In.	100.00
Tumbler, Blue Opaque, Embossed School Scene, Marked, Sowerby, 4 In. *Illus*	90.00
Tumbler, Florentine Cameo, Amber, White Enameled Iris, Satin, 3 3/4 In.	100.00
Tumbler, Polka Dot, Swirled Frances Decoration, Hobbs, Brockunier & Co., 4 In. *Illus*	20.00
Tumbler, Stone Glass, Mottled Green, Purple, Draped, Mustard Interior, 3 1/2 In. *Illus*	20.00
Vase, Allover Amberina Swirl, Thumbprint Design, Lutz-Style, 10 In.	80.00
Vase, Amber To Crimson, Gold Spot, Tricornered, Rindskopf, c.1900, 5 In.	145.00
Vase, Amber, Gold Iridescent, Allover Gold Threading, 7 1/2 In.	345.00
Vase, Austrian, Organic Shape, Handles, Iridescent Blue, Green Glaze, 11 1/2 In.	575.00
Vase, Blue, Enameled Cherry Branches, Book Of Japanese Characters, Gold Trim, 10 In.	4720.00
Vase, Blue, Oval, Shouldered, Flared Rim, A.D. Copier, Leerdam, c.1926, 6 1/2 In.	900.00
Vase, Cased, Flowers, Vines, Applied, Pink, White, Amber, Green, 11 In.	90.00
Vase, Cobalt Blue, Silver Iridescence, Blue Threading, 9 1/2 In.	430.00
Vase, Enameled Purple Flowers, Falling Seeds, Clear Satin, Holland, 1900, 11 In.	280.00
Vase, Flaring, Amethyst Stripes, Arne Jon Jutrem, Hadeland, Norway, 1953, 8 1/2 In.	165.00
Vase, Floral & Linear Relief, Satin, Blue Wash, Andre Hunebelle, Paris, 1920s, 8 In.	470.00
Vase, Frosted, Mottled Blue, Wrought Iron Reeded Armature, c.1920, 8 3/4 In.	1610.00
Vase, Glass, Enamel Horse, Rider, Hunting Dog, Emerald Green, M. Goupy, 8 x 5 1/2 In.	2800.00
Vase, Gold Iridescent, Opal Interior, Early 20th Century, 9 1/4 In.	345.00
Vase, Green Satin, Amber Applied Stem, Cherries, Pink Flower, Amber Feet, 9 3/4 In.	260.00
Vase, Iridescent Gold, Blue King Tut Decoration, Late 20th Century, 10 1/4 In.	260.00
Vase, Iridescent Green, Applied Cherries, Rolled Rim, Bulbous Base, Pontil, c.1910, 9 In.	700.00
Vase, Opaque, Enameled Underwater Scene, Amber Applied Feet, 6 1/2 x 7 In.	860.00
Vase, Orange, Mounted In Floral Shaped Wrought Iron, c.1890, 10 1/4 In.	960.00
Vase, Pan Playing Flute, Sand Blasted, Flared, A.D. Copier, Leerdam, 1936, 7 In.	1010.00
Vase, Shaded Cream To Pink, Amber, Enameled Child In Tree, 19th Century, 7 1/2 In.	260.00
Vase, Stork, Imperial Glass Mfg., St. Petersburg, Russia, 1894, 12 In.	10158.00
Vase, Stylized Peony Buds, Yellow, Purple, Blue Iridescent Ground, Baluster, 10 3/4 In.	3370.00
Vase, Yellow, Globular, Short Flared Rim, Marked, Leerdam Unica, 1929, 9 3/4 In.	1900.00
Water Set, Dew Drop, Frances Decoration, Hobbs, Brockunier & Co., Child's, 6 Piece	475.00
Water Set, Pigeon Blood, Enameled Daisies, 11-In. Pitcher, 7 Piece	300.00
Water Set, Windows, Frances Decoration, Satin, Hobbs, Brockunier & Co., 7 Piece	450.00

GLASS-BLOWN was formed by forcing air through a rod into molten glass. Early glass and some forms of art glass were hand blown. Other types of glass were molded or pressed.

Bell, Clear, White Looping, Tooled Rim, Swirled Handle, 11 1/4 In.	225.00
Bird Fountain, Green, Shaped Body, Applied Spout & Flat Finial, 6 In.	230.00
Bottle, Bride's, Enameled Lady & Man, Colonial Garb, Pewter Collar, Cap, 5 In., Pair	275.00
Bowl, 14 Ribbed Panels, Footed, Folded Rim, c.1800, 10 1/2 x 11 In.	2100.00
Bowl, Amber, Folded Rim, Footed, 5 1/2 x 2 In.	3740.00
Bowl, Applied Cobalt Blue Rim, 2 5/8 x 5 5/8 In.	300.00
Bowl, Blue, Ribbed, Circular, Flared, Applied Foot, Polished Pontil, Blue, 9 3/8 In.	330.00

Bowl, Clear, Red & White Looping, Clear Stem, Footed, 1840-1860, 6 1/8 In. 730.00
Bowl, Cobalt Blue, Slanted Sides, Outward Rolled Rim, Midwestern, 2 In. 470.00
Bowl, Diamond Diaper Band & Sunburst, 3-Piece Mold, Pontil, 3 x 5 3/8 In. 1900.00
Bowl, Fruit, Clear, Engraved Berry & Vine, Baluster Stem, Flat Foot, 10 x 10 1/4 In. 672.00
Bowl, Olive Green, Folded Rim, Pontil, 5 1/2 x 10 1/4 In. 1570.00
Bowl, Urn Shape, Green, Footed, Pittsburgh Type, 4 1/4 x 4 1/4 In. 20.00
Bowl, White Opalescent, Pink, Beaded Scale, Footed, 8 In. 30.00
Candleholder, Cobalt Blue, Expanded Diamond, Folded Rim, 3 1/2 x 2 1/2 In. 165.00
Candleholder, Emerald Green, Expanded, Diamond Folded Rim, 3 1/4 In. 110.00
Candlestick, Air Twist Stem, Double Stepped Foot, 11 x 4 1/4 In. 4100.00
Candlestick, Ring Turnings, Hollow Baluster Stem, Domed Foot, 10 1/2 In., Pair 2825.00
Candy Jar, Cover, Paneled, Graduated Base, 9 In. 70.00
Canister, Cover, Applied 4 Cobalt Blue Rings & Tall Finial, Pittsburgh, 17 3/4 In. 1650.00
Canister, Cover, Cobalt Blue Rings & Wafer Finial, 10 1/4 x 5 1/4 In. 660.00
Chalice, Clambroth, Slightly Flared Bowl, Knop Stem, Domed Foot, 11 1/2 In. 40.00
Compote, 12 Panels, Baluster Stem, Folded Rim, Pontil, 7 3/8 In. 530.00
Compote, Amethyst, Solid Stem, Medial Ring, Domed Foot, 8 3/4 In. 40.00
Compote, Engraved Love Knots, Swags, Leaves, Knop Stem, Pittsburgh, 7 In. 275.00
Compote, Half-Pillar Bowl, Folded Rim, Baluster Stem, Round Base, 8 3/4 x 7 7/8 In. 715.00
Compote, Pillar-Molded, Footed, Snap Pontil, Pittsburgh, c.1840, 9 1/2 In. 680.00
Creamer, 16 Ribs, Swirled Left, Feather Crimped Handle, Pittsburgh, 4 5/8 In. 240.00
Creamer, 24 Ribs, Swirled Right, Aqua Tint, Olive Striations, Pittsburgh, 6 In. 175.00
Creamer, Amber, Bulbous, Applied Loop Handle, 4 1/2 In. 330.00
Creamer, Amethyst, Bulbous, Applied Handle & Foot, 4 1/2 In. 220.00
Creamer, Bulbous, Applied Scrolled, Loop Handle, Pinched Spout, 3 In. 300.00
Creamer, Cobalt Blue, Tooled Rim & Spout, Handle, Pontil, 4 1/8 In. 500.00
Creamer, Fiery Opalescent, Amethyst Spatter, Bulbous, Tapered, Aqua Handle, 5 1/2 In. . . 120.00
Creamer, Ribbed, Air-Trap C-Scroll Handle, Pontil, 5 3/4 In. 145.00
Creamer, Sunburst Band, Sunburst & Diamonds, 3-Piece Mold, Handle, Rigaree, 4 In. . . . 580.00
Cruet, 8-Pillar Mold, Applied Foot, Neck Bank, Handle, Stopper, Pontil, 8 3/8 In. 785.00
Cruet, Ribs, Swirled Right, Tam-O-Shanter Stopper, Deep Cobalt Blue, 6 1/2 In. 300.00
Cuspidor, Amber, Compressed Bulbous Base, Wide Flared Rim, 4 In. 230.00
Decanter, Diamond Diaper Band & Sunburst, Olive Green, 3-Piece Mold, 9 1/2 x 4 In. . . . 1045.00
Decanter, Waffle, 3-Piece Mold, 3 Neck Rings, Stopper, 8 1/2 In. 290.00
Decanter, White Marbrie Loopings, 2 Neck Rings, Tooled Lip, Circular Foot, 9 3/4 In. 45.00
Decanter, Yellow Green, 10-Panel Side, 6-Panel Stopper, 10 1/4 In. 380.00
Dish, Fiery Opalescent, Round, Flared Sides, 2 7/8 In. 358.00
Dish, Waffle Sunburst & Diamond Diaper Band, Ribbed, Folded Rim, 1 1/4 In. 165.00
Finger Bowl, Emerald Green, Applied Triple Ring, Flared Rim, 3 1/4 x 5 In. 110.00
Fish Bowl, Rolled Outward Rim, Raised Trumpet Foot, 19th Century, 9 3/4 In. 206.00
Fly Catcher, Clear, Ground Lip, Neck Ring & Feet, 7 1/4 In. 62.00
Fly Catcher, Green, Applied Flattened Penny Feet, 6 x 8 In. 143.00
Fly Catcher, Turquoise, Coin Spot, Applied Neck Ring, 3-Footed, c.1910, 6 3/8 In. 952.00
Goblet, Engraved Masonic Decoration, Wreath, Trumpet Bowl, Teardrop Stem, 4 In. 440.00
Goblet, Overshot, Applied Double Knop Stem, Frosted, 7 1/2 In. 140.00
Goblet, Overshot, White Interior, Gold Decoration, Lattice Bowl, 8 In. 190.00
Goblet, Terraced Bull's-Eye, Amethyst, Rough Pontil, 6 1/4 In. 275.00
Hat, Diamond Diaper Band, Ribbed, 3-Piece Mold, Cobalt Blue, Pontil, Tooled, 2 3/8 In. . . 615.00
Inkwell, Sapphire Blue, 8 Sides, Original Hinged Brass Closure, 1850-1870, 2 1/2 In. 165.00
Jar, Storage, Cover, Cobalt Blue Rings & Wafer Finial, 12 In. 690.00
Jug, Blue, Engraved, Floral Swags, Love Knots, Vine, c.1800 . . . . 1760.00
Mug, Aqua, Applied Double Ribbed Handle, 4 1/4 x 3 5/8 In. 220.00
Mug, Enameled Figures, Flared Base, Straight Sides, Strap Handle, 4 5/8 In. 45.00
Mug, Enameled Forget-Me-Not, Remember Me, Handle, 3 1/2 In., Pair 55.00
Mug, Opaque Blue, Bulbous, Flared, Enameled Remember Me, Loop Handle, 3 1/4 In. 40.00
Pan, Diamond Diaper Band, Double Ribbed, 3-Piece Mold, Pontil, 5 3/4 In. 215.00
Pan, Gold Amber, Swirled Ribs, Folded Rim, Kent, Ohio, 10 x 2 1/2 In. 110.00
Pan, Sunburst & Diamond Band, Double Ribbed, 3-Piece Mold, Pontil, 4 In. 145.00
Pan, Waffle Sunburst & Diamond Diaper, Ribbed, 3-Piece Mold, Pontil, 5 1/2 In. 225.00
Pan, Yellow, Folded Rim, Sloped Sides, Kent, Ohio, 4 5/8 x 1 1/2 In. 690.00
Pitcher, 8-Pillar Mold, Tooled Rim & Spout, Pontil, 10 1/8 In. 420.00
Pitcher, Cobalt Blue, High Relief Enameling, Ruffled Edge, c.1875, 7 1/2 In. 150.00
Pitcher, Pillar Mold, Applied Circular Foot, Scrolled Ear Handle, Pittsburgh, 11 In. 990.00

Pitcher, Straight Sides, Corseted Waisted Shoulder, 6 Threaded Rings, 8 In. 535.00
Plate, Diamond Diaper Band, Double Ribbed, 3-Piece Mold, Folded Rim, Pontil, 6 In. 145.00
Plate, Sunburst & Diamond Diaper Band, Ribbed, 3-Piece Mold, Pontil, 6 x 1 3/8 In. 190.00
Plate, Waffle Sunburst & Diamond, 4 Bands Of Ribbed, 3-Piece Mold, 5 3/4 x 1 In. 190.00
Punch Bowl, Footed, Tooled Lip & Foot, Pittsburgh, 7 1/4 x 8 In. 850.00
Rolling Pin, Pink & White Marbrie Looping, Open End, 14 1/2 In. 55.00
Rummer, Cobalt Blue, Button Knop Stem, Circular Foot, 4 1/2 In. 90.00
Salt, Expanded Diamond, Cobalt Blue, Footed, 3 x 2 1/2 In. ....400.00 to 550.00
Salt, Expanded, Diamond, Petal Base, 3 In. 110.00
Salt, Fluted, Flared Rim, Applied Round Foot, 3 x 1 3/4 In. 330.00
Smoke Bell, Clambroth, Blue, Scalloped Rim, Wafered Ring, 8 3/4 In. 336.00
Smoke Bell, Olive Green, Folded Rim, Applied Knob Finial, 9 1/2 x 7 3/4 In. 1232.00
Smoke Bell, Opalescent Milk Glass, Ruby Edge, Metal Cap & Ring, 3 7/8 x 4 1/2 In. 179.00
Spill Holder, Octagonal Paneled, Scalloped Top, Footed, 10 1/4 In. 124.00
Sugar, Cover, Folded Rim On Cover, Gallery Rim, Circular Foot, 3 1/2 In. 660.00
Sugar, Cover, Sheared Finial Tip, Cobalt Blue, Gallery Rim, Applied Low Foot, 6 In. 330.00
Sugar, Domed Cover, Tab Finial, Cobalt Blue, Bulbous, Footed, Pittsburgh, 7 In. 2200.00
Sugar, Mottled Red & White, Yellow, Green & White Swirled Interior, Footed, 6 In. 145.00
Sugar, Pagoda Cover, Flat Finial, Band Of Grapes, Acorns, Leaves, Footed, 7 1/2 In. 440.00
Sugar & Creamer, Satin Pigeon Blood, Silver Plated Rim, Handles, 3 3/4 x 5 In. 140.00
Syrup, White Spots, 19th Century 100.00
Tumbler, Ale, Colonial Style, Pontil, 6 3/8 In. 240.00
Tumbler, Brown, Enameled, Masonic Symbol, Flared, 3 1/4 In. 30.00
Tumbler, Diamond Diaper Band, Double Ribbed, 3-Piece Mold, Pontil, Tooled Rim, 4 In. 110.00
Tumbler, Enameled Flowers, Drape, Flared, 3 3/4 In. 330.00
Tumbler, Flip, Fluted, Engraved, 4 1/2 x 3 3/4 In. 143.00
Tumbler, Sunburst & Diamond Diaper Band, 3 Bands Of Ribs, 3-Piece Mold, 2 7/8 In. 193.00
Urn, Cover, Clear, Red, White Looping, Tooled Rim, Pontil, 12 5/8 In. 400.00
Urn, Cover, Gray Tint, Corseted Waist, Baluster Stem, Footed, 13 In., Pair 330.00
Vase, 8-Pillar Mold, Baluster, Oversized Round Foot, Pittsburgh, 10 In. 320.00
Vase, 8-Pillar Mold, Swirled Right, Cobalt Blue, Footed, Pittsburgh, 8 7/8 In. 2970.00
Vase, Aqua, Silver Resist, Globular, 3 1/2 x 4 1/2 In. 90.00
Vase, Cobalt Blue, Enameled Woman In Dress, Clear Handles, Clear Base, 8 1/2 In. 50.00
Vase, Dark Amber, 22 Ribs, Globular, Elongated Neck, Flared Lip, 10 In. 1320.00
Vase, Etched Ferns, Footed Spill, Tooled Lip, 9 3/4 In. 290.00
Vase, Festoons, Flowers, 20-Rib Gadrooning, Flared Rim, Circular Foot, 8 1/4 In. 145.00
Vase, Hyacinth, Amethyst, Tooled Rim, Pontil, 7 1/4 In. 145.00
Vase, Hyacinth, Grape Amethyst, Tooled Rim, Pontil, 6 3/4 In. 85.00
Vase, Hyacinth, Teal Green, Ribbed, Swirled To Left, Tooled Rim, Pontil, 8 3/8 In. 500.00
Vase, Opaque White, Blue, Green Oxide, Applied Handles, 6 1/4 In. 35.00
Vase, Pillar Mold, Cobalt Blue, Scalloped Rim, Double Neck Rings, Pontil, 11 1/2 In. ... 3360.00
Vase, Swirl, Blue Opaque, White Opaque Base, 8 In. 100.00
Vase, Trumpet, 8 Ribs, Twisted, Cobalt Blue, Footed, 11 1/4 x 5 1/2 In. 1980.00
Vase, Trumpet, Amethyst, 2-Piece Mold, Rim Folded Inward, Footed, 7 1/2 In. 880.00
Vase, Tulip, Amethyst, 6-Sided Base, Paneled Stem, Scalloped Rim, 10 In. 3300.00
Waste Bowl, Waffle, Cobalt Blue, Ground Pontil, American, 3 1/5 x 4 In. 575.00
Whimsy, Bellows, Cobalt Blue, Rigaree, Handles, Neck & Mouth Ring, 7 1/4 In. 180.00
Whimsy, Cane, Tobacco Amber, Twist, Tooled Ends, 32 1/4 In. 190.00
Whimsy, Darner, Clear, Blue Marbrie Loopings, Cased White, 3 1/8 x 6 3/4 In. 470.00
Whimsy, Dog, Clear, Applied Amber Tail, Ears, Legs, Rigaree, 7 1/2 In. 35.00
Whimsy, Powder Horn, Translucent White Looping, Red Stripes, Circular Foot, 10 3/4 In. 175.00
Whimsy, Swan, Canary, Pulled Neck & Tail, Ribbed, Lemon Squeezer Base, 4 5/8 In. ... 165.00
Wine, Blue, Applied Base, 4 1/2 In. 20.00
Wine, Bulbous Shape, Teardrop Stem, Folded Base Rim, 5 In. 55.00
Wine, Fluted Bowl, Button Knop Stem, 4 1/8 In. 60.00
Wine, Stepped Bowl, Flared Rim, Applied Button Stem, Circular Foot, 4 1/4 In. 40.00
Wine, Trumpet Shape, Teardrop Stem, 6 5/8 In. 55.00
Witch's Ball, Blue, White Swirled Swag, 19th Century, 6 1/2 In. 1035.00
Witch's Ball, Clear, White Looping, Tooled, Pontil, Stand, 1840-1895 .... 900.00
Witch's Ball, Clear, White Swirled Swag, 8 1/2 In. 750.00
Witch's Ball, Cobalt Blue, Sheared Mouth, 3 3/4 In. 125.00
Witch's Ball, Cranberry, White Swags, 5 In. 460.00
Witch's Ball, Oilspot, Pink, Blue, Yellow, 3 3/4 In. 160.00

Witch's Ball, Opaque White, Rose Marbrie Loopings, 5 1/2 In. 440.00
Witch's Ball, Pink, Blue, Green, Gold Oil Spot, White Ground, 6 In. 145.00

GLASS-BOHEMIAN Bohemian glass is an ornate overlay or flashed
glass made during the Victorian era. It has been reproduced in
Bohemia, which is now a part of the Czech Republic. Glass made from
1875 to 1900 is preferred by collectors.

Basket, Threaded, Iridescent, Stag Antler Handle, Art Nouveau, 7 In. 230.00
Bonbon, Bundt Rococo, Enameled, Lobmeyr, c.1885, 3 x 6 1/4 In. 920.00
Bottle, Dresser, Cut Panel, Enameled, c.1890, 8 1/4 In. 85.00
Bottle, Water, Cobalt To Cranberry, Acid Frosted Leaves, Ovals, Vines, Gold, 8 1/2 In. ... 55.00
Bottle, Wine, Ruby Flashed, Engraved, c.1890, 10 In. 70.00
Bowl, Iridescent Green, Random Ruby Threading, c.1910, 6 In. 175.00
Box, Ruby Flashed, Engraved, Stag, 7 x 11 x 8 In. 3885.00
Candlestick, Amethyst Cut To Clear, Wide Flanged Rims, 10 1/2 In., Pair 490.00
Chalice, Cranberry Flashed, White Cased, Gold Enameled Vines, Trumpet Foot, 10 In. 765.00
Chalice, Maidens Dancing, Playing Instruments, Amber Flashed, Enameled, 10 In. 161.00
Compote, Blue Cut To Clear, Trumpet Foot, Ogee Crenellated Rim, 8 In., Pair 1300.00
Compote, Gadrooned Rim, Diamond Cut Band, Circular Foot, 5 x 9 1/2 In. 260.00
Compote, Iridescent, Crimson Threading, Pallme Koenig, c.1900, 3 1/2 In. 315.00
Decanter, Cranberry Flashed, 8 Ribs, Swirled To Right, Ribbed Stopper, 15 1/2 In. 110.00
Decanter, Red Bands & Reserve, Birds, Flowers, White & Gold Highlights, 11 1/2 In. ... 85.00
Decanter, Rococo Style, Engraved, Silver Collar & Base, Germany, c.1910, 9 In., Pair ... 230.00
Decanter, Ruby Flashed, Engraved, Stag In Woodland Setting, 11 In. 175.00
Decanter Set, Enameled Children, Cranberry, Vaseline, 10 3/4 In., 11 Piece 400.00
Decanter Set, Ruby Cut To Clear Flowers, Double Cut Clear Panels, 10 x 2 1/2 In. 25.00
Finger Bowl, Cranberry, Gold Border, 5 In. 40.00
Goblet, Amethyst, Panels, Gold Colonial Style Decoration, 5 7/8 In. 187.00
Goblet, Cobalt Blue Cut To Clear, Stag & Fowl Design, Gold Rim, 6 1/2 In. 175.00
Goblet, Enameled Multicolor Floral Panel, Oval, Punty & Panel Stem, Gold, 5 1/2 In. ... 28.00
Goblet, Green Stained Panels, Gold Trim, 6-Sided Stem, Listovane, 4 3/4 In. 22.00
Goblet, Ruby Cut To Clear, 4 Panels, Buildings, Scalloped Foot, 6 3/4 In. 385.00
Humidor, Ruby Cut To Clear, Grapes, 6 In. 92.00
Jar, Cover, Ruby Cut To Clear, Grapes, Faceted Body, 19th Century, 8 In. 81.00
Jar, Mantel, Cover, Ruby Flashed, Engraved Stag, Forest, Cone Shape, 15 1/2 In., Pair ... 940.00
Jug, Claret, Stag, Doe In Forest, Loop Handle, Stopper, 15 In. 403.00
Pitcher, Ruby Cut To Clear, Deer In Woods, Grape & Leaf, Handles, 11 In. 460.00
Pokal, Amber Cut To Clear, Deer In Forest, 9 1/2 In. 165.00
Pokal, Cover, Ruby Stain, Engraved Dogs Attacking Deer, 19 1/2 In. 1955.00
Pokal, Enameled Knight On Horseback, Green, Acanthus, Austria, c.1890, 18 1/2 In. 400.00
Rose Bowl, Topaz, Enameled Man Drinking, c.1900, 4 In. 115.00
Sauceboat, Underplate, Bundt Rococo, Oval, Enamel, Lobmeyr, c.1885, 3 x 7 In. 1093.00
Shade, Green Pulled Stripes, Orange Oil Spot Body, 6 In., Pair 489.00
Shade, Green Zigzags, Oil Spot, 5 In. 173.00
Tumble-Up Set, Ruby Cut To Clear, Block & Puntie, Stopper, 8 1/4 In., 2 Piece 253.00
Tumble-Up Set, Sapphire Blue Cut To Clear, Paneled, Finger Flutes, Rays, 7 In., 2 Piece . 253.00
Tumbler, Ruby Cut To Clear, Deer, 5 In. 10.00
Tumbler, Ruby Cut To Clear, Stag & Woodland, Faceted Base, 5 x 3 In., Pair 201.00
Tumbler, Stags In Woodland, Ruby Cut To Clear, Engraved, 6 1/2 In. 175.00
Urn, Cover, Enameled Flowers, Leaves, 17 In. 374.00
Urn, Ruby Cut To Clear, Lid Scroll, Building, 16 In. 165.00
Vase, Amber Translucent, Applied Blue Stemmed Red Flowers, Footed, Harrach, 11 In. .. 200.00
Vase, Amber, Floral, Scroll Leaves, Handles, Henrik Giergl, c.1930, 12 In. 218.00
Vase, Blue, Iridized Gold, Silver Oil Spot, 10 1/2 In. 145.00
Vase, Cranberry, Gold Enameled Flowers, Bowling Pin Shape, 8 1/2 In. 70.00
Vase, Enameled Design, Satin, Signed, Fritz Hocker, 8 In. 440.00
Vase, Enameled Woman Portrait, Green, Gold Accents, Handles, c.1855, 13 In. 1295.00
Vase, Engraved, Figures, Vines, Leaves, Lobmeyr, c.1920, 6 1/2 In. 7170.00
Vase, Green Swirl, Metal Collar, Austria, c.1900, 5 x 7 1/2 In. 155.00
Vase, Green Translucent, Enameled Daffodil, Handles, Pohl, c.1895, 8 In. 374.00
Vase, Grenada, Ruby, Purple, Green Iridescent, Rindscopf, c.1900, 6 1/2 In. 135.00
Vase, Iridescent Green, Crimson Threading, Pallme Koenig, c.1910, 3 3/4 In. 290.00
Vase, Iridescent, Textured Amber, Art Nouveau Flowers, Silver, c.1920, 5 In. 115.00

Vase, Jack-In-The-Pulpit, Cranberry, Gold Feathered Highlights, 20 1/2 In.	400.00
Vase, Pink Satin, Ruffled Edge, Applied Snake, 12 In.	45.00
Vase, Prussian Blue, Amber Applied Stemmed Flowers, Scrolled Feet, 10 In.	144.00
Vase, Purple, Iridescent Blue, Allover Heavy Threading, Pallme Koenig, 10 In.	200.00
Vase, Red, Opaline & Turquoise Beads, Quatrefoil Neck, Bulbous Base, 10 In.	120.00
Vase, Sculptured Drape, Clear Satin, Green Oil Spot, c.1920, 5 3/4 In.	200.00
Vase, Stick, Yellow Satin, Enameled, Gold Vines, Cased, Harrach, 10 1/2 In.	115.00
Vase, White Cut To Cranberry, Gold Enameled Design, Islamic Design, 11 In.	460.00
Wine, Blue, Green, Cranberry, Amber, 8 In., 4 Piece	70.00
Wine, Green, Enameled Floral, Gold Trim, 7 1/2 In.	40.00

GLASS-CONTEMPORARY includes pieces by glass artists working after 1975. Many of these pieces are free-form, one-of-a-kind sculptures. Paperweights by contemporary artists are listed in the Paperweight category. Earlier studio glass may be found in Glass-Venetian.

Bowl, Handkerchief, Ruby, Enameled, 5 In.	40.00
Bowl, Sandblasted, Airbrush Oil Paint, Fused, Jay Musler, 1986, 18 In.	9560.00
Sculpture, Amber, Blue, Gray, Signed, Harvey Littleton, 1972, 5 In.	590.00
Sculpture, Macchia, Pink Mottled, Cadmium Yellow Lip Wrap, Signed, Chihuly, 1985 ...	9560.00
Sculpture, Navajo, Basket With Apple Green Lip, Chihuly, Signed, 1991	7770.00
Sculpture, Persian, Opaline & Cadmium, Chihuly, Signed, 1987, 7 Piece	9000.00
Sculpture, Spirits Encased, John Kuhn, 1993, 18 In.	15535.00
Sculpture, Venetian, No. 1258, Gold, Dale Chihuly, 1989, 16 1/2 In.	8960.00
Vase, Black Iridescence Over Yellow Glass, Opal Blue Rim, Labino, 1969, 8 3/4 In.	575.00
Vase, Cobalt, Applied Thick Rings, Nuutajarvi-Notsjo, Finland, 1973, 19 1/2 In.	380.00
Vase, Dark Amber, Flared & Ruffled Edge, Dominick Labino, 6 3/4 In.	400.00
Vase, Fish, Blue Over White, Applied Frosted Foot, Hiroshi Yamano, 21 In.	8050.00
Vase, Green Opal, Encased Multicolors, Globular, Signed, Labino, 1968, 4 In.	630.00
Vase, Lime Green, Cobalt Blue Pulled Design, Charles Lotton, 1974, 8 In.	375.00
Vase, Multicolored, Ocean Wave, Teal Interior, Signed, Ridabock, 1994, 9 In.	550.00
Vase, Opalescent, Blue, Yellow, Green, Pink, Bulbous, Pillared Sides, Labino, 8 In.	165.00
Vase, Opaque Orange Glass, Black Detail, Nuutajarvi-Notsjo, 1960s, 4 x 11 In.	230.00
Vase, Paperweight, Clear, Floral & Vine Design, 5 In.	40.00
Vase, Red, Spindle Neck, Applied Black Foot, Signed, Carlson, 12 1/2 In.	259.00
Vase, Satin, Iridescent, Blue Prunties, Labino, 1968, 4 1/2 In.	100.00

GLASS-CUT, see Cut Glass category.

GLASS-DEPRESSION, see Depression Glass category.

GLASS-MIDCENTURY refers to art glass made from the 1950s to the 1980s. Some glass factories, such as Baccarat or Orrefors, are listed under their own categories. Earlier glass may be listed in the Glass-Art and Glass-Contemporary categories. Italian glass may be found in Glass-Venetian.

Bottle, Orange, Hexagonal, Blue, White, Murines, c.1960, 10 1/4 In.	525.00
Bowl, Flared, Random Pattern, Violet, Aqua, Gold, Higgins, 4 1/2 x 17 In.	200.00
Bowl, Regalia, Gold Crown Transfer, Georges Briard, 5 1/4 In. .... *Illus*	15.00
Bowl, Smoke Gray, Flared, Per Luken, Holmegaard, 2 x 9 1/2 In.	150.00
Candy Jar, Cover, Duck Finial, Orange, Viking, 8 In.	40.00

Glass-Midcentury, Figurine, Alice, King, Queen, Edris Eckhardt, 1977, 5 1/2 In.

Glass-Midcentury, Bowl, Regalia, Gold Crown Transfer, Georges Briard, 5 1/4 In.

Decanter Set, Figural, Face Stopper, Green, Blue, Amber, Erik Hoglund, 3 Piece 355.00
Figurine, Alice, King, Queen, Edris Eckhardt, 1977, 5 1/2 In. . . . . *Illus* 950.00
Mobile, Circles, Half-Moon Shapes, Fused, Wire, Michael & Francis Higgins, 32 In. 3220.00
Platter, Yellow, Green Coral Squares, Fused, Higgins Studio, 20 In. 400.00
Sculpture, Fused, Gas Expanded, Tom Patti, 1976, 4 In. 7770.00
Snack Set, Southern Belle, 4 Trays, 4 Cups 22.00
Vase, Blue Green Design, Floris Meydam, Holland, 1950s, 7 In. 400.00
Vase, Controlled Bubbles, Abstract, Orange Black Gold, Flared, Leerdam, 6 In. 249.00
Vase, Orange, Fluted Edge, Blenko, 8 In. 95.00
Vase, Paperweight, Flowers, Leaves, Iridescent Amber, C. Lotton, 1974, 8 In. 805.00
Vase, Paperweight, Flowers, Yellow, Red, Green, Blue, C. Lotton, 1974, 9 In. . . . .980.00 to 1150.00

GLASS-VENETIAN. Venetian glass has been made near Venice, Italy, since the thirteenth century. Thin, colored glass with applied decoration is favored, although many other types have been made. Collectors have recently become interested in the Art Deco and 1950s designs. Glass was made on the Venetian island of Murano from 1291. The output dwindled in the late seventeenth century but began to flourish again in the 1850s. Some of the old techniques of glassmaking were revived, and firms today make traditional designs and original modern glass. Since 1981, the name *Murano* may only be used on glass made on Murano Island. Other pieces of Italian glass may be found in the Glass-Contemporary and Glass-Midcentury categories of this book.

Bookends, Aquarium Series, Fish & Seahorse, Quarter Circle Shape, Cenedese, 6 In. 1035.00
Bottle, Amber, Red Ribbing, Red Knob Stopper, Signed, Venini Italia, 9 1/2 In. 1800.00
Bottle, Cane Glass, Vertical Stripes, Teal, Red, Stopper, Venini, 18 x 3 3/4 In. 530.00
Bottle, Crimson, White Interior, Black Rim, Fratelli E Toso, 23 x 10 In. 590.00
Bottle, Sommerso, Purple Interior, Cenedese, 14 x 7 In. 325.00
Bottle, Tapered, Conical, Green Bubbles, Gold, Barovier, c.1950, 13 In. 925.00
Bowl, Medusa, Blue, Purple Spiraling Lines, Cylindrical Stem, Footed, Venini, 4 x 10 In. . 2135.00
Bowl, Merletto, A. Seguso, Italy, 1952, 6 1/2 x 2 1/2 In. 460.00
Bowl, Murrhina, Yellow & Black, R. Licata, Italy, 1957, 8 1/2 x 2 1/4 In. 3450.00
Bowl, Nautilus Shell, Iridescent, E. Barovier, Italy, 1942, 5 1/2 In. 460.00
Box, Green Domed Lid, Finial, Yellow, Cylindrical, Black Border, E. Sottsass, 10 In. 900.00
Candlestick, Christmas Angel, Millefiori, Aventurine Gown, 8 In. 81.00
Charger, Red, Green, Blue Concentric Rings, Venini, 13 1/2 x 12 x 2 3/4 In. 690.00
Dish, Cover, Gold Swirl Finial, Oil Spot, Lavender, Italy, 4 1/2 In. 155.00
Figurine, Angel, Kneeling, Lavender Gown, Gold Wings, Halo, 6 1/2 In. 60.00
Figurine, Bird, Pulcini, Turquoise, Brass Legs, Feet, A. Painon, Vistosi, 12 In. 1840.00
Figurine, Buffalo, Sommerso, Yellow, Orange, Cenedese, 8 1/2 x 9 In. 700.00
Figurine, Turtle, Amber, Blue Marquetry Inlay, Signed, Venini Italia, 5 In. 690.00
Figurine, Victorian Courtly Lady, Opal, Clear Mica, Seguso, 1955, 15 In. 290.00
Goblet, Green, Gold Enameled Cherubs, Speckled Stem, Murano, c.1910, 7 In., 6 Piece . . 430.00
Goblet, Ruby, Baluster Stem, Applied Amberina Rigaree, 6 1/2 In., 9 Piece 220.00
Hourglass, Cobalt Blue, Teal Lobes, Venini, 5 1/2 x 2 In. 500.00
Sculpture, Aquarium Block, Interior Fish, Orange, Yellow, Green, Cenedese, 7 x 9 In. . . . 500.00
Sculpture, Embryo, Signed, Livio Seguso, 1976, 14 3/8 In. 4780.00
Sculpture, Obelisk, Dark Base, Clear Striped Top, Venini, Murano, c.1960, 10 In., Pair . . 705.00
Sculpture, Stylized Elliptical Head, Seguso, 14 1/2 x 6 In. 530.00
Sculpture, Turkey, Applied Murrhina Lattimo, Bronze, Venini, c.1964, 17 In. 7170.00
Tray, Leaf Shape, Spirals, White, Green, Blue, Venini, 16 1/2 In. 865.00
Vase, Aqua, Applied Black Foot, M.V.M. Cappellin, Italy, 1930, 5 In. 375.00
Vase, Barrel, Mushroom Top, Peacock, Green, Blue, Vetreria Vistosi, 14 In. 600.00
Vase, Blue, Globular, Clear Flared Rim, 8 Colored Applied Handles, E. Sottsass, 13 In. . . 1800.00
Vase, Conical, Pod, Orange, Blue, Gray, Pedestal, Favio Poli, c.1950, 15 In. 625.00
Vase, Lattimo, Flaring, Cane Spiral Stripes, Dino Martens, 13 x 7 In. 940.00
Vase, Millefiori, Blue, White, Purple Canes, Gold, Silver Inclusions, Flattened, 13 In. 4720.00
Vase, Pinched, Black, Fulvio Bianconi, Italy, 1950s, 8 1/2 In. 2070.00
Vase, Red & Green Stripe, Fulvio Bianconi, Italy, 1955, 13 1/2 In. 4600.00
Vase, Red Basin, Cut Exterior, A. Barbini, Italy, 1962, 8 3/4 x 7 In. 3450.00
Vase, Red, Applied Black Handles, M.V.M Cappellin, Italy, 1930, 5 In. 430.00
Vase, Sommerso E Battuto, Clear Satin, Dark Gray Heart, Cylindrical, Flattened, 10 In. . . 340.00
Vase, Sommerso Sassi, Clear Cover Pink, Yellow Teardrop Heart, Square, Flattened, 9 In. 1900.00

Vase, Sommerso Sassi, Red Opal Over Blue, Square Top, Tapers To 3-Sided Base, 9 In. ... 1125.00
Vase, Sommerso, Clear, Yellow Interior, Heart Shape, Flared Rim, Seguso, 9 In. 1800.00
Vase, Spicchi, Mauve, Turquoise, Yellow Bands, Bulbous, Fulvio Bianconi, 7 3/4 In. 3450.00
Vase, Stacked Forms, Applied Orange & Blue Ornaments, E. Sottsass, 1983, 18 In. 2250.00
Vase, Striate, Barovier & Toso, c.1950, 12 1/2 In. 1500.00
Vase, Stripes, Red, Blue & Green, Luigi Scarpa Croce, Italy, 1960, 13 3/4 In. 2300.00
Vase, Teatrino, Applied Design, F. Bianconi, Italy, 1954, 13 1/2 In. 3450.00
Vase, Vetro A Fenicio, Frosted Loopings, Squared Mouth, T. Lundgren, Venini, 10 1/2 In. . 3220.00
Vase, Yellow, Domed, Black Base Ring, Black Disc Neck, E. Sottsass, 1980, 8 In. 900.00
Water Set, Striped, Venini, Gio Ponti, Murano, c.1954, 6 3/4-In. Pitcher, 4 Piece 765.00

GLASSES for the eyes, or spectacles, were mentioned in a manuscript in
1289 and have been used ever since. The first eyeglasses with rigid
side pieces were made in London in 1727. Bifocals were invented by
Benjamin Franklin in 1785. Lorgnettes were popular in late Victorian
times. Opera Glasses are listed in their own category.

Lorgnette, Black, Red Enamel, 14K Gold Case, Platinum Bail, Onyx, Tiffany & Co. 1410.00
Lorgnette, Platinum, 14K White Gold, Diamond Chain, Art Deco, c.1920, 28 In. 6325.00
Lorgnette, Platinum, Diamond, Hinged Opera Glasses, Onyx, Art Deco, c.1920 .... 2070.00
Lorgnette, Scroll & Leaf Design, Monogram, 10K Gold, c.1890, 3 In. 196.00
Spectacles, Cat's-Eye Mask Frame, Rhinestones, American, 1950s 150.00
Spectacles, Maria, Cat's-Eye Mask, Rhinestones, Hand Etching, France 350.00
Spectacles, Martin's Margins, Iron Frame, Horn Insets, England, c.1750 .... 395.00
Sun, Cat's-Eye Mask, Cobalt Blue Glass Lens, Pink Satin, Handmade, France, c.1958 ... 150.00
Sun, Cat's-Eye Mask, Cobalt Blue Glass Lens, White, Black Laminate, France, c.1958 ... 450.00
Sun, Laminated, Fabric, Multicolor, Large Round Lenses, Pucci Style, France, c.1958 ... 350.00
Sun, Laminated, Fabric, Plaid, c.1958 .... 175.00

GLIDDEN Pottery worked in Alfred, New York, from 1940 to 1957. The
pottery made stoneware, dinnerware, and art objects.

Ashtray, Gulfstream, 10 x 10 In. 65.00
Baker, Turquoise Matrix, 8 x 8 In. 25.00
Bowl, Feather, Beige, White, Oval, 7 In. 35.00
Casserole, Cover, Turquoise Matrix, 8 1/2 x 5 1/2 In. 45.00
Plate, Incised Hippo, Unglazed Back, Square, 5 1/2 In. .... *Illus* 10.00
Plate, Turquoise Matrix, Square, 7 In. 20.00
Vase, Light Blue, Mottled Dark Blue, No. 12, 5 x 4 1/2 In. 50.00
Vase, Pink, Blue, No. 89, 4 In. 40.00

GOEBEL is the mark used by W. Goebel Porzellanfabrik of Oeslau,
Germany, now Rodental, Germany. Many types of figurines and dishes
have been made. The firm is still working. The pieces marked *Goebel
Hummel* are listed under Hummel in this book.

Cigarette Holder, Camel, Wide Crown Mark, c.1936, 5 x 2 3/4 In. 250.00
Creamer, Cow, Bee Mark, c.1960, 6 3/4 x 4 In. 95.00
Cup, Yellow Chicks, Child's, Wide Crown Mark, c.1935, 2 3/4 In. 65.00
Figurine, Baby Jesus, Glass, Signed, 1978, 3 3/4 In. 18.00
Figurine, Dog, Polka Dot, Comical, Wide Crown Mark, c.1936, 1 3/4 In. 175.00
Figurine, Quail, c.1985, 2 3/4 In. 25.00

**Need a quick measurement at an
antiques show? A penny is ¾ inch
in diameter; a dollar bill is almost
6 inches long.**

Glidden, Plate, Incised Hippo,
Unglazed Back, Square, 5 1/2 In.

Figurine, Rabbit Jumping Over Eggshell, Wide Bee Mark, c.1975, 3 x 3 1/4 In. 25.00
Mug, Friar Tuck, Bee Mark, c.1955, 4 1/4 In. 35.00
Reamer, Baby's Orange Juice, Figural Orange, Spout, Ring Handle, Wide Crown, c.1927 .   95.00
Salt & Pepper Shakers, Squirrels, c.1985, 3 1/4 In., Pair 40.00

GOLDSCHEIDER has made porcelains in three places. The family left
Vienna in 1938 and started factories in England and in Trenton, New
Jersey. The New Jersey factory started in 1940 as Goldscheider-U.S.A.
In 1941 it became Goldscheider-Everlast Corporation. From 1947 to
1953 it was Goldcrest Ceramics Corporation. In 1950 the Vienna plant
was returned to Mr. Goldscheider, and the company continues in busi-
ness. The Trenton, New Jersey, business, now called *Goldscheider of
Vienna,* imports all of the pieces.

Bust, Young Woman, Period Dress, Holding Hat, 6 1/2 In. 23.00
Figurine, Dancing Woman Holding Dress, Art Deco, England, 12 In. 380.00
Figurine, German Shepherd Dog, 17 In. 115.00
Figurine, Hunting Dog, Gray, White, Signed, 10 x 6 In. 95.00
Figurine, Madonna, Crown, USA, 9 In. 135.00
Figurine, Madonna, Yellow Shawl, 4 1/2 In. 75.00
Figurine, Pierrot Draping Shawl On Lady, Floral Dress, Blue, Green, 1920, 15 In. 325.00
Figurine, Rendezvous Man, Yellow, Green, Porcher, USA, 9 In.   95.00
Figurine, Victorian Woman, Umbrella, Coat, Muff, Cape, Dress, 11 3/4 x 7 In. 40.00
Figurine, Woman In Harem Outfit, Austria, 18 In. 2800.00
Figurine, Woman, Gold Decorated, Kathi Urbach, 1940s, 12 1/2 In. 100.00

GOLF, see Sports category.

GOSS china has been made since 1858. English potter William Henry
Goss first made it at the Falcon Pottery in Stoke-on-Trent. The factory
name was changed to Goss China Company in 1934 when it was taken
over by Cauldon Potteries. Production ceased in 1940. Goss china resembles Irish Belleek in both body and glaze. The company also made
popular souvenir china, usually marked with local crests and names.

Bust, Ann Hathaway, Inscribed, England 100.00
Teapot, Lid, Liverpool Crest, c.1897, 2 x 3 1/2 In. 45.00
Tumbler, Concilio & Labor Manchester, 1 5/8 In. 35.00

GOUDA, Holland, has been a pottery center since the seventeenth century. Two firms, the Zenith pottery, established in the eighteenth century,
and the Zuid-Hollandsche pottery made the brightly colored art pottery
marked *Gouda* from 1898 to about 1964. Other factories followed.
Many pieces featured Art Nouveau or Art Deco designs. Pattern names
in Dutch, listed here, seem strange to English speaking collectors.

Basket, Flower, Fuchsia, Stylized Green Leaves, Signed, Van Der Huist, 4 x 8 1/2 In. 248.00
Bowl, Abstracts, Rust, Green, Cobalt Blue, 1923, 3 x 10 1/4 In. 195.00
Bowl, Dahlia, Orange Floral, Blue, Brown, Leaves, Green Rim, c.1925, 11 1/2 x 2 In. 145.00
Bowl, Fan Abstracts, Cobalt Blue, Rust, 1924, 3 x 8 1/4 In. 110.00
Bowl, Flowers, Abstracts, Yellow, Peach, Green, 1925, 3 x 10 In.   195.00
Bowl, Flowers, Buds, Magenta, Lavender, Brown, 2 1/2 x 9 1/4 In. 140.00
Bowl, Peacock Feathers, Arches, Cobalt Blue, Green, 1825, 3 3/4 x 7 3/4 In. 248.00
Bowl, Unica, Mottled Ivory Glaze, Yellow, Blue Flowers, Brown Leaves, c.1940, 2 x 9 In.   138.00
Bowl, White Feathers, Ocher Glaze, Flared, Footed, Amstelhoek, c.1900, 7 1/2 In. 3145.00
Candlestick, Candia, 4 In., Pair 295.00
Candlestick, Candia, Rope Design, Rain Drops, Floral On Base, 1923, 10 x 6 In., Pair . . .   275.00
Candlestick, Chrysanthemum, Brown, Blue, Yellow Dots, Buttressed, Blocmen, 8 1/4 In. .   385.00
Candlestick, Double Gourd Neck, Signed, GSS, 1931, 12 x 5 1/2 In., Pair 295.00
Candlestick, Flowers, Blue, Yellow, Bottle Shape, 6 Sides, 1921, 7 x 3 1/4 In., Pair 355.00
Charger, Breetvelt, Red, Blue, Gold Swirls, Purple Mottled Glaze, Gray Ground, 20 In. . .   2310.00
Clock, 3 Pansies, Purple, Stylized Leaves, Signed, F.C., 1800, 14 x 7 1/2 In. 1540.00
Clock, Tulip, Violet, Magenta, Beveled Glass, 1900-1910, 20 x 7 In. 2420.00
Colander, Fruit, Peaches, Red, Ochre, Leaves, Aqua, Green, Amp Smit, c.1920, 4 1/4 In. .   99.00
Decanter, Peacock Band, Orange, Brown Flowers, Green Ground, Polo, 1910, 11 1/2 In. .   275.00
Dish, Tulip, Leaves, Yellow, Green, White Ground, 5 Sides, 2 x 9 In. 185.00
Ewer, Flowers, Leaves, Indigo Blue, Rust, Green, Yellow, 1918, 15 3/4 x 8 In. 825.00

Ginger Jar, Cover, Flowers, Stylized, Multicolored Abstracts, Oval, Signed, H., 1921, 10 In.   550.00
Incense Burner, Jar, Cover, Man Playing Banjo, Girl, Light Blue Glaze, 9 1/4 In. 80.00
Inkwell, Abstract Design, Stylized Tulips, Purple, Brown, Tan, 1921, 2 1/4 x 9 1/4 In. . . .   165.00
Inkwell, Cover, Ivora, Pansies, Purple, Green Leaves, Insert, 3 x 5 1/2 In. 80.00
Inkwell, Pen Tray, Pansies, Tulip, Purple, Pink, Green, Signed, J., 2 1/2 x 12 In. 110.00
Jar, Broad 7 Petal Flowers, Crisscross Pierced Metal Cover, c.1925, 4 x 4 1/2 In. 95.00
Jar, Cover, Flowers, Square, Recessed Panels, Marked, Renee, c.1930, 3 3/4 x 3 1/4 In. . .   45.00
Jar, Flowers, Leaves, Yellow, Maroon, Turquoise, Lavender, 1927, 6 x 4 1/2 In. 165.00
Jardiniere, Daffodils, Yellow, Multicolored Abstracts, Signed, M.W., 1931, 6 1/2 x 8 In. . .   110.00
Jardiniere, Goedwaagen, Orange, Green, Yellow, Blue Abstracts, Brown Ground, 10 In. . .   305.00
Jardiniere, Lydia, Flowers, Multicolored, Deep Brown Ground, Signed, 5 3/4 x 7 In. 77.00
Lantern, Cover, 4 Vents, Loop Handle, Cobalt Blue, Yellow, Rust, 10 1/2 x 6 1/2 In. 66.00
Lantern, Massa, Open Chimney, Pierced Flowers, Green, Blue, White, 10 x 6 In. . . . *Illus*   250.00
Matchbox Holder, Flower, Abstracts, Sea Green Glaze, 1919, 3 1/2 x 5 In. 220.00
Pitcher, Abstract Design, Flowers, Ocher, Peach, Gold, Ivory, 1927, 8 x 6 In. 140.00
Pitcher, Abstract Design, Yellow, Rust, Matte Glaze, 1906-1917, 9 3/4 x 5 In. 275.00
Pitcher, Ajour, Rust Leaves, Blue Spiral Ground, Marked, c.1920, 6 3/4 x 4 In. 165.00
Pitcher, Cyprus, Yellow, Blue, Green, Abstract, Marked, 1906-1917, 9 3/4 x 5 In. . . . *Illus*   248.00
Pitcher, Fan Abstracts, Brown, Yellow, Blue, Sage Ground, Signed, V.V., 8 1/2 x 4 1/2 In.   248.00
Pitcher, Favorite, Bulbous, Bulging Neck, Multicolor Abstract Design, 1925, 8 x 5 In. . . .   125.00
Pitcher, Flowers, Yellow, Brown, Blue, Sea Green, Cobalt Blue, 13 1/2 x 7 In. 360.00
Pitcher, Orchids, Flowers, Multicolored, Black Ground, Marked, 1920, 7 1/4 x 5 In. 110.00
Pitcher, Rhodian, Yellow, Rust, Blue, Abstract, Marked, 1906-1917, 9 3/4 x 5 In. . . . *Illus*   275.00
Pitcher, Shira, Gourd Style, Yellow, Pink, White Bouquet, 9 x 6 In. 100.00
Pitcher, Swirls, White, Gold, Brown Matte Ground, Bulbous, 5 1/2 x 4 In. 140.00
Planter, Abstract Design, Lavender, Yellow, Blue, Blue Ground, 1923, 3 1/2 x 11 In. 165.00
Planter, Hanging, Abstract Design, Scrolls, Round, Aspasir, 5 1/4 x 7 1/2 In. 140.00
Planter, Hanging, Areo, Geometric Band, Flowers, Red, Black, Round, 4 1/2 x 10 1/2 In.. .   90.00
Planter, Hanging, Arnhem, Fan Abstracts, Blue, Brown, 1925, 5 x 7 In. 140.00
Planter, Hanging, Lydia, Flowers, Abstracts, Multicolored, 6 1/4 x 7 1/2 In. 77.00
Planter, Tulips, Stylized, Purple, Fuchsia, Yellow, Blue Swirls, Handles, 3 1/2 x 12 In. . . .   250.00
Plaque, Arnhem, Flowers, Lavender, White, Multicolored Leaves, Roza, 1925, 8 1/4 In. . .   110.00
Plaque, Bird, Multicolored, Stylized Flowers, Trees, Goldenete, A.D.K., 1918, 8 1/2 In. . .   440.00
Plaque, Brigette, Flowers, Green, Orange, Brown, Lavender, 1940s, 14 In. 220.00
Plaque, Duck, Cerulean To Sea Green Matte Ground, Raindrop Border, Incised, 10 1/4 In.   360.00
Plaque, Eyes, Abstracts, Multicolored, Signed, Amp Smit, 1929, 10 1/4 In. 330.00
Plaque, Irises, Orange, Brown, Yellow, Signed, Lakerveld, 8 1/4 In. 220.00
Plaque, Peacock On Branch, Flowers, Feathers, Gold, Brown, Ivory, 1920s, 17 In. 715.00
Plaque, Raindrop, Cobalt Blue, Brown, Green, Yellow, Signed, c.1918, 17 1/2 In. 605.00
Plate, Lovebirds, Stylized Feathers, Green, Green, Cobalt Blue, Ivory Ground, 8 In. 66.00
Tazza, Cover, Stylized Mushroom, Yellow, Rust, 1924, 5 x 6 In. 195.00
Tazza, Snowflake Flowers, White, Red Raindrops, Tristan, c.1920, 7 1/4 x 9 1/2 In. 220.00

Gouda, Lantern, Massa,
Open Chimney, Pierced Flowers,
Green, Blue, White,
10 x 6 In.

Gouda, Pitcher, Cyprus,
Yellow, Blue, Green
Abstract Design, Marked,
1906-1917, 9 3/4 x 5 In.

Gouda, Pitcher, Rhodian,
Yellow, Rust, Blue Abstract,
Marked, 1906-1917,
9 3/4 x 5 In.

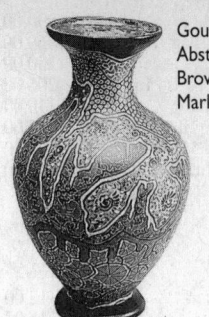

Gouda, Vase, Breetvelt,
Abstract Pathway, Yellow,
Brown, Rust, Blue,
Marked, 17 x 10 In.

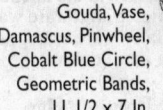

Gouda, Vase,
Damascus, Pinwheel,
Cobalt Blue Circle,
Geometric Bands,
11 1/2 x 7 In.

To remove sediment
in the bottom of a
vase or pitcher, put
salt and crushed ice
into the vase and
stir. The friction will
remove the stain.

Teapot, Pensec, Pansies, Leaves, Blue, Purple, Green, Yellow, Mark, 1921, 5 3/4 x 9 In. . . .	250.00
Tobacco Jar, Cover, Pansies, Blue, Purple, Green Field, Cylindrical, Footed, 1920, 7 In. . . .	165.00
Tobacco Jar, Cover, Stylized Tulips, Yellow, Ivory, 1910-1915, 7 1/2 x 6 1/4 In.	140.00
Tray, Butterfly, Blue, Green, Orange, Sea Green, Brown, 12 1/2 In.	165.00
Tray, Pen, Bird On Branch, Green, Yellow, Brown, Lavender, Orange, 1919, 9 3/4 In.	385.00
Tray, Yselstroom, Diamond Shape, Jade, Ochre, Blue, Lavender, 1923, 18 x 12 1/2 In. . . .	525.00
Urn, Flowers, Leaves, Brown, Rust, Turquoise, Lavender, Signed, 1926, 17 1/2 x 9 In.	1540.00
Vase, 4-Petal Flowers, Leaf, Green, Brown, Pink, Yellow, 1928, 8 1/4 x 5 In.	138.00
Vase, Abstract Design, Green, Rust, Gold, Cobalt Blue, Yellow, 1926, 10 3/4 x 6 In.	495.00
Vase, Abstract Design, Heart, Yellow, Blue, Green, Rust, Spherical, 1903, 12 x 5 In.	360.00
Vase, Abstract Design, Snowflake, Gray, Gold, Cobalt Blue, 1920s, 6 1/2 x 5 In.	275.00
Vase, Abstract, Cobalt Blue, Gray, Brown Ground, 1923, 7 x 5 In.	250.00
Vase, Advertising, Holland America Line, 5 1/4 x 3 1/4 In.	195.00
Vase, Aqua, Blue, Gray Abstracts, Black Base, Bulbous, A.A., 1926, 5 3/4 x 2 1/2 In.	165.00
Vase, Astra, Stars, Orange, Blue, Red, Brown Accents, Handle, 4 1/4 x 4 In.	80.00
Vase, Breetvelt, Abstract Pathway, Yellow, Brown, Rust, Blue, Marked, 17 x 10 In. . . . *Illus*	2200.00
Vase, Butterfly, Flowers, Brown, Yellow, Blue, Mauve, 1925, 5 1/8 x 3 1/2 In.	220.00
Vase, Butterfly, Flying To Flower, Brown, Blue, Gray Ground, 1920s, 4 3/4 x 3 1/2 In. . . .	138.00
Vase, Daisy, Rust, Maroon, Cobalt Blue, 1902, 12 1/4 x 6 In.	140.00
Vase, Damascus, Pinwheel, Cobalt Blue Circle, Geometric Bands, 11 1/2 x 7 In. . . . . *Illus*	525.00
Vase, Engraved Carduus Pattern, Green, Brown, Black, Cylindrical, Distel, 1915, 13 In. . .	3370.00
Vase, Eskaf, Flowers, Yellow, Abstracts, Deep Brown Ground, 10 1/4 x 8 3/4 In.	495.00
Vase, Feathers, Abstract Design, Green, Blue, 1926, 10 1/2 x 6 In.	305.00
Vase, Flower Band, Multicolored, Black Body, Bulbous, Incised, 1920, 4 1/2 x 6 In.	1650.00
Vase, Flower, Petals, Ivory, Green, Peach, 1924, 10 1/2 x 7 1/2 In.	550.00
Vase, Flowers, Blue, Purple, Pink Dots On Ivory Ground, Santurza, 1925, 12 x 6 3/4 In. . .	415.00
Vase, Flowers, Leaf, Abstract, Yellow, Cobalt Blue, Handles, 1928, 14 x 5 1/2 In.	305.00
Vase, Flowers, Magenta, Violet, Green, Turquoise, 6 1/2 x 3 In.	220.00
Vase, Flowers, Purple, Green Stems, Bulbous, 11 1/2 x 4 In.	605.00
Vase, Flowers, Purple, Red, Blue, Green, Black Ground, Shouldered, 16 1/2 In.	230.00
Vase, Flowers, Stylized Leaves, Yellow, Green, Rust, Turquoise, 1929, 12 1/2 x 8 1/2 In. . .	385.00
Vase, Flowers, Swirls, Green, Gold, Rust, 1910-1915, 8 1/4 x 5 In.	470.00
Vase, Flowers, U-Shape Panels, Abstracts, Brown, 6 x 4 1/4 In.	165.00
Vase, Flowers, Yellow, Brown, Purple, Collier Iris, Signed, F.Y., 9 1/2 x 6 1/2 In.	195.00
Vase, Gourd, Purple Pansies, Green Panel, Leaves, c.1900, 6 1/4 x 4 In.	140.00
Vase, High Glaze, Loop Handles, Mauve, Purple, Green, Signed, CB, 7 1/2 x 6 In.	335.00
Vase, Irises, Burgundy, Black Accents, Round, Abuca, 1931, 7 1/2 x 8 In.	305.00
Vase, Irises, Polychrome, Cream Ground, Baluster Shape, Dutch, 1907, 22 1/2 In.	3145.00
Vase, Ivora, Bird, Brown, Green Branch, Stylized Leaves, Lavender, 7 x 5 In.	770.00
Vase, Leaf, Abstract Design, Rust, Mahogany, Gray, Green, Signed, 9 1/4 x 4 3/4 In.	305.00
Vase, Massa, Teardrop, Green, Rust, Blue, 1920s, 4 3/4 x 5 1/2 In.	110.00
Vase, Oval Shape Bands, Cobalt Blue, Turquoise, Brown, Yellow, 1928, 6 3/4 x 4 In.	140.00
Vase, Pansies, Purple, Green Leaves, Dot Accents, 3 1/4 In.	33.00
Vase, Papaver, 3 Orange Tulips, Multicolored Abstracts, c.1915, 9 3/4 x 5 In.	175.00
Vase, Pheasant Walking On Trail, Blue, Lavender, Hillside, 1920-1922, 6 x 5 In.	440.00
Vase, Pink, Purple Flowers, Green Leaves, Tall Neck, Handles, 9 1/2 x 7 1/2 In.	529.00
Vase, Pinwheel, Blades, Flowers, Cobalt Blue, Green Ground, 1910-1915, 11 1/2 x 7 In. . . .	525.00

Vase, Poppies, Orange, Blue, Aqua Stems, De Jong, 1928, 8 1/4 x 7 1/2 In.	90.00
Vase, Red, Blue, Green, Linear Design, Globular, Neck, Holland, 5 1/2 In., Pair	1460.00
Vase, Regina, Flowers, Abstracts, Multicolored, Signed, T., 8 x 5 In.	250.00
Vase, Stylized Birds, Purple, Black, Green Leaves, Distal, Holland, 1900s, 10 1/4 In.	206.00
Vase, Symbol, Yellow, Brown, Blue, 1923, 7 3/4 x 4 3/4 In.	140.00
Vase, Tulips Over Pansies, Multicolored Abstract Design, Signed, E., 1924, 10 x 5 In. . . .	275.00
Vase, Tulips, Pansies, Purple, Magenta, Green, Orange, Yellow, 1924, 4 x 5 1/2 In.	220.00
Vase, Upside Down Hearts, Orange, Lavender, Turquoise, 1902, 7 x 4 1/4 In.	140.00

GRANITEWARE is an enameled tinware that has been used in the kitchen from the late nineteenth century to the present. Earlier graniteware was green or turquoise blue, with white spatters. The later ware was gray with white spatters. Reproductions are being made in all colors.

Basin, Gray, 11 x 2 1/2 In.	12.00
Bowl, Cobalt Blue Marbleized, Label, Peermahomed, Japan, 6 1/4 In. . . . . *Illus*	15.00
Bowl, Emerald Green Swirl, 8 1/4 x 3 3/4 In.	141.00
Breadbox, England, 14 x 15 x 10 In.	195.00
Butter, Cover, Blue, White, Geometric Design, France, 4 x 6 3/4 In.	125.00
Candleholder, Blue, White Swirl, 5 3/4 x 2 1/2 In.	75.00
Candleholder, Yellow, 6 1/2 x 2 1/2 In.	30.00
Canister, Yellow, White Marbling, 6 Piece	425.00
Chamber Pot, Flowers, Red, Orange, Green, White Ground, 9 1/4 x 5 1/4 In.	125.00
Coffeepot, Blue, Brown, White, Duchess Ware, 11 x 7 In.	745.00
Coffeepot, Dutch Scene, c.1890, 9 1/4 x 8 1/4 In.	125.00
Colander, White, Black Trim, Loop Handles, 10 1/2 x 4 1/2 In.	40.00
Cup, Red, Blue Stripes, Label, Labowsky & Co., Czechoslovakia, 2 7/8 In. . . . . *Illus*	10.00
Diaper Pail, Cover, Red, White, Redwood Handle, 8 x 9 3/4 In.	45.00
Flask, Cobalt Blue, Tin, On Cork, Cord, 9 1/2 In.	95.00
Funnel, Mottled Gray, 7 3/4 x 9 In.	85.00
Lunch Pail, Blue, White	35.00
Lunch Pail, Brown, White Speckled, Aluminum Insert, 5 1/2 x 6 1/4 In.	95.00
Lunch Pail, Octagonal, Dark Blue, White, Mottled, France	55.00
Milk Can, Blue, White Swirl, 8 1/2 In.	375.00
Pan, Muffin, 8 Cup, Blue	50.00
Pan, Muffin, Mottled Gray, 9 Compartments, Square, 11 1/2 In.	65.00
Pan, Utility, Cream, Black Trim, 9 x 2 3/4 In.	12.00
Pie Plate, Blue Swirl, Light Blue Interior, 9 1/4 x 1 In.	40.00
Pitcher, Green & Red Graphic Design, White Ground, c.1940, 14 In.	185.00
Pitcher, Marbleized, Blue & White Inside & Out, c.1940, 14 5/8 In.	165.00
Pitcher, Red, White, c.1930, 14 In.	145.00
Plate, Cream, Green, Flat Rim, 9 In.	35.00
Platter, Blue, White Speckled, Oval, 16 In.	55.00
Platter, Turkey, Hong Kong, 18 x 14 In.	40.00
Pot, Double Boiler, Steamed Clams, Clam Broth Bottom, Spigot	39.00
Rack, Utensil, Orange, Yellow, Bowl, Brown, Gray, Scalloped, 22 x 15 In.	595.00
Soap Dish, Dark Blue, White Speckled, 6 x 4 In.	18.00
Spoon, Sky Blue, 12 In.	38.00
Sugar, Cover, Flowers, Gold Accents, Handles, 5 1/4 x 6 3/4 In.	195.00
Tea Steeper, 4 1/2 x 4 1/4 In.	145.00
Teapot, Gooseneck, Green, Chrysolite	130.00
Teapot, Red, Enameled Design, 4 3/4 In. . . . . *Illus*	35.00

Graniteware, Cup, Red, Blue Stripes, Label, Labowsky & Co., Czechoslovakia, 2 7/8

Graniteware, Bowl, Cobalt Blue Marbleized, Label, Peermahomed, Japan, 6 1/4 In.

**Clean the inside of a
graniteware pot by adding
a teaspoon of baking soda,
and bringing it to a boil.**

Graniteware, Teapot,
Red, Enameled
Design, 4 3/4 In.

Tray, Oblong, Blue, White Interior, Cobalt Trim, 9 1/2 x 13 1/2 In.	28.00
Tray, Red, White, Blue, End Of The Day, 12 In.	150.00

GRUEBY Faience Company of Boston, Massachusetts, was incorporated in 1897 by William H. Grueby. Garden statuary, art pottery, and architectural tiles were made until 1920. The company developed a matte green glaze that was so popular it was copied by many other factories making a less expensive type of pottery. This eventually led to the financial problems of the pottery.

Bowl, Blue, Gray Curdled Glaze, Applied Square Leaves, Erickson, 1907, 2 x 6 1/2 In. . . .	1725.00
Bowl, Leathery Green Matte Glaze, Closed Rim, Circle Mark, 1 1/2 x 4 In.	805.00
Bowl, Sculpted, Applied Overlapping Leaves, Green Matte Glaze, 9 1/2 In.	1610.00
Bowl, Swirled, Curdled Cucumber Green Matte Glaze, Marked, 2 3/4 x 8 In.	770.00
Jardiniere, Flared, Embossed Ribs, Feathered Green Matte Glaze, Stamped, 4 1/2 In.	865.00
Paperweight, Scarab, Brown, Caramel Matte Glaze, 3/4 x 2 1/4 In.	525.00
Paperweight, Scarab, Mottled Green Glaze, Oval, c.1915, 1 1/4 x 3 3/4 In.	560.00
Tile, Candle, Yellow, Brown Candlestick, Green Ground, Cuenca, Stamped, 6 x 6 In.	11500.00
Tile, Duck, Yellow, Brown Frog, Alice In Wonderland, Signed, M.K., Frame, 4 In.	1540.00
Tile, Geometric, White Moorish Star, Blue Ground, Red Clay, 3 x 3 In., 6 Piece	230.00
Tile, Green Oak Tree, Oatmeal Glaze, Raised Outline, Addison Leboutiller, 12 1/4 In.	44063.00
Tile, Landscape & Lake, Green, Blue, Ivory, River, Trees, Cloud, Frame, 4 x 4 In.	4125.00
Tile, Monk Playing Cello, Mustard Glaze, Stamped, Frame, 6 x 6 In.	518.00
Tile, Oak Tree, Puffy Clouds, Green, Brown, Raised Outline, Signed, M.H., 6 x 6 3/4 In. . .	5465.00
Tile, Pines, Landscape, Green, Blue, Raised Outline, Signed, H.H., Square, 6 x 6 In.	4025.00
Tile, Putto Holding Cornucopia, Red Clay, Mustard Matte Ground, 6 x 6 In.	405.00
Tile, Tree, Blue, Green Matte Glaze Landscape, Arts & Crafts Frame, 8 1/4 In.	7480.00
Tile, Tulip, Yellow, Green Matte Ground, Silver Trivet, Karl Leinonen, 6 1/4 In.	6900.00
Tile, Viking Ship, Polychrome, 12 x 12 In.	59400.00
Tile, Water Lilies, White, Yellow, Green, Raised Outline, 6 In.	4888.00
Vase, 2 Colors, Wilhelmina Post, 9 In.	26450.00
Vase, Applied Buds, Alternating Buds, Feathered Green Matte Glaze, 10 1/2 x 3 3/4 In. . .	5520.00
Vase, Applied Buds, Leaves, Green Matte Glaze, Circle Stamp, 7 1/2 x 4 3/4 In.	2760.00
Vase, Applied Leaf & Flower, Green Matte Glaze, Impressed Mark, 13 In.	4600.00
Vase, Applied Leaves, Buds, Leathery Green Matte Glaze, Round, Circle Mark, 6 x 8 In. . .	6325.00
Vase, Applied Leaves, Green Matte Glaze, Bulbous, Post, Circle Mark, 12 3/4 x 8 In.	3740.00
Vase, Applied Leaves, Green Matte Glaze, Flared, Squat, 7 x 4 1/2 In.	2415.00
Vase, Applied Leaves, Green Matte Glaze, Bulbous Shouldered Shape, 8 x 6 In.	3335.00
Vase, Applied Leaves, Yellow Flowers, Green Matte Glaze, Ovoid, Marked, 6 1/2 In.	7480.00
Vase, Applied Pods, Leaves, Green Matte Glaze, Cylindrical, Stamped, 6 3/4 x 3 In. . .	5175.00
Vase, Broad Leaves, Buds, Flower Form Rim, Green Matte Glaze, G. Priest, 7 x 4 1/2 In. .	2000.00
Vase, Bulbous Bottom, Applied Leaves, Carved Panels, Green Matte Glaze, 7 1/4 In.	1840.00
Vase, Bulbous Bottom, Flaring Neck, 3 Carved Panels, Green Matte Glaze, 7 1/2 In.	1955.00
Vase, Bulbous, Tooled Panels, Leathery, Brown Matte Glaze, Marked, 8 x 5 In.	4025.00
Vase, Carved, Abstract Leaf & Crocus Design, Yellow Matte Glaze, 8 1/2 In.	3450.00
Vase, Cylindrical, Cucumber Green Matte Glaze, Veined, Brown Interior, 8 x 3 1/2 In. . . .	1540.00
Vase, Egg Shape, 3 Tooled, Applied Leaves, Leathery Matte Green, 7 1/2 x 3 3/4 In.	2940.00
Vase, Feathered Green Matte Glaze, Circle Stamp, 4 1/2 In.	863.00
Vase, Flaring Shape, Mottled Stems, Applied Leaves, Green Matte Glaze, 8 In.	3450.00
Vase, Flaring Shape, Sculpted, Applied Leaved, Green Matte Glaze, Signed, 5 1/2 In.	2300.00

Vase, Green Curdled Matte Glaze, Bulbous, Circle Mark, 5 1/4 x 6 1/2 In. 1150.00
Vase, Green Matte Glaze, 3 Leaves, Carved, Yellow Buds, Slender Stems, 6 1/2 In. 2300.00
Vase, Green Matte Glaze, Sculpted, Applied Leaves, Impressed Mark, W. Post, 7 1/2 In. . . . 4900.00
Vase, Green Matte Glaze, Yellow Tipped Buds, Hand Thrown, 10 In. 8000.00
Vase, Leathery Green Matte Glaze, Ribbed Band, Squat, Circle Stamp, 3 1/2 x 6 In. 1495.00
Vase, Leaves, Green Frothy Matte Glaze, Round, Circle Stamp, 4 x 4 In. 1095.00
Vase, Leaves, Yellow Buds, Green Matte Glaze, Trefoil Rim, Circle Mark, 6 1/2 x 4 In. . . . 2875.00
Vase, Oval, Applied Daffodils, Yellow, Blue, Red, Leaves, Green Matte Glaze, 11 x 5 In. . . 12650.00
Vase, Paneled, Cucumber Green Glaze, Oblong Panels, Marked, D.S., 1902, 9 x 7 In. 4400.00
Vase, Pinched Top, Applied Leaves, Buds, Multitone Green Matte Glaze, Mark, 4 1/2 In. . . 920.00
Vase, Sculpted, Applied Overlapping Leaves, Green Matte Glaze, 8 1/2 In. 4025.00
Vase, Shouldered, Textured Green Matte Glaze, Impressed Mark, 13 In. 2185.00
Vase, Swollen Bottom, Textured Green Matte Glaze, 7 In. 805.00
Vase, Tear Shape, Triangular Leaves, Frothy Green Matte Glaze, 6 3/4 x 3 3/4 In. 4700.00
Vase, Tooled Panels, Leathery Blue Glaze, Stamped, 6 3/4 x 4 1/4 In. 1840.00
Vase, Tooled, Applied Leaves, Buds, Green Matte Glaze, Pear Shape, 7 1/2 x 4 1/2 In. . . . 3450.00
Vase, Tooled, Applied Leaves, Green Matte Glaze, Wilhelmina Post, 12 3/4 x 8 In. 4315.00
Vase, Waisted Shape, Sculpted, Applied Leaves, Stem, Buds, Green Matte Glaze, 8 In. . . . 1840.00

GUNS that may be classed as toys, such as BB guns, air rifles, and cap guns, are
listed in the Toy category.

GUSTAVSBERG ceramics factory was founded in 1827 near Stockholm,
Sweden. It is best known to collectors for its twentieth-century art- **Gustafsberg**
wares, especially a green stoneware with silver inlay called *Argenta.*

Plate, Carved Stylized Fish, Brown Matte Glaze, Signed, Kage, 7 In. 144.00
Vase, Nudes, Green Glaze, Silver Inlay, Footed, Argenta, c.1940, 7 1/2 In. 705.00
Vase, Silver, Standing Cupid, Cylindrical, Argenta, Signed, 9 In. 999.00
Vase, Surrea, Ceramic, Wilhelm Kage, c.1940, 9 In. 470.00
Vase, Swordfish, Bubbles, Ultramarine Ground, Stamped Mark, 7 1/4 In. 290.00
Vase, Turquoise, Applied Silver Flowers, Flared Shape, 6 In. 69.00
Vase, White, Impressed Factory Mark, Stig Lindberg, 3 x 14 In. 1265.00

GUTTA-PERCHA was one of the first plastic materials. It was made from
a mixture of resins from Malaysian trees. It was molded and used for
daguerreotype cases, toilet articles, and picture frames in the nineteenth century.

Bracelet, Hinged 45.00
Case, Cartouche, Pineapple, Daguerreotype Of Man & Child, 3 1/4 x 4 1/4 In. 775.00
Case, Oval, Flowers, Littlefield, Parsons, c.1857, 2 5/8 x 2 1/4 In. 225.00
Case, Union, Embossed Design, Littlefield, Parsons, c.1857, 3 3/4 x 3 1/4 In. 250.00
Case, Union, Rounded Corners, Velvet Interior, Tintype, Scovill, 3 x 2 1/2 In. 245.00
Case, Union, Stars, Banners, Velvet, Littlefield, Parsons, c.1857, 3 3/4 x 3 1/2 In. 335.00
Case, Union, Velvet Interior, Ambrotype, Holmes, Booth & Hayden, 3 x 2 1/2 In. 245.00
Case, Velvet Liner, Young Girl Daguerreotype, 2 1/2 x 1 1/2 In. 290.00
Comb, 4 x 4 1/2 In. 55.00
Corn Razor, Handle, Beehive, D. Perts, Solingen, Germany, 3 13/16 In. 55.00
Frame, Embossed Design, Oval, c.1870 . . . . 280.00
Frame, Embossed Design, Square, c.1870 . . . . 295.00
Locket & Chain, Oval, Sterling 4 Leaf Clover, 25-In. Chain 185.00
Matchbox, King Edward VII Coronation, Flowers, 2 x 1 1/2 In. 179.00
Mirror, Hand, Elk, Antlers, Roses, Hand Painted Accents, c.1880, 10 x 4 In. 80.00
Mirror, Hand, Patent 1878, 5 3/8 x 12 In. 185.00
Pin, Corn, Stalks, C-Clasp, 3/4 x 1 3/4 In. 50.00
Pin, Mourning, Jet, Black, Victorian, 1 x 1 3/4 In. 195.00
Shuttle Tatting, Brass Rivets, Victorian, 2 3/4 In. 35.00

HAEGER Potteries, Inc., Dundee, Illinois, started making commercial
artwares in 1914. Early pieces were marked with the name *Haeger* written over an *H.* About 1938, the mark *Royal Haeger* was used in honor
of Royal Hickman, a designer at the factory. The firm is still making
florist wares and lamp bases. See also the Royal Hickman category.

Ashtray, Free-Form, Turquoise Interior, Black Exterior, Matte, 104, 12 1/4 x 9 In. 45.00

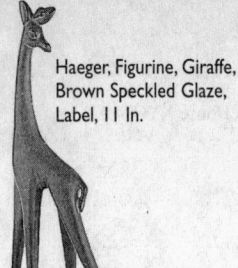

Haeger, Figurine, Giraffe,
Brown Speckled Glaze,
Label, 11 In.

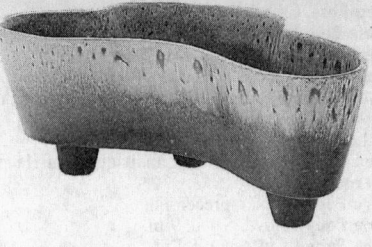

Haeger, Planter, Biomorphic, 3-Footed,
Mottled Pink Glaze, Marked, 4 x 10 In.

Bank, Cat, Orange, 9 5/8 x 4 1/4 In.	95.00
Bowl, Burnt Orange, 15 x 6 1/4 In.	35.00
Bowl, Celadon Green, 1985, 13 3/4 In.	60.00
Bowl, Green Granite Finish, 101, 8 x 4 In.	55.00
Bowl, Sponge Basket, Yellow, Angled Handle, 13 1/2 x 4 In.	45.00
Candlestick, Double, White Matte Glaze, 129, c.1940, 4 1/2 x 5 3/4 In.	25.00
Coffeepot, Green, Brown Speckle, R-1585-S, 1957, 10 1/2 In.	55.00
Console Set, Pink Blue Glaze, 9 & 4 3/4 x 14 3/4 In., 3 Piece	75.00
Dish, 3 Candle Holes, Yellow, 12 1/2 In.	45.00
Dish, Violin, Mauve Agate, Pink, Blue Splotches, R-293, 16 1/4 x 5 3/4 In.	55.00
Figurine, Cat, Orange, R-1792, 21 x 10 In.	189.00
Figurine, Giraffe, Brown Speckled Glaze, Label, 11 In. ....*Illus*	25.00
Figurine, Mother & Child, 6053, 1990, 14 x 12 In.	45.00
Figurine, Panther, Black, Gold Jewel Eyes, Multicolored Collar, 19 x 5 x 8 1/2 In.	115.00
Figurine, Ram, Rearing, 19 x 16 In.	85.00
Fountain, Faux, R-1691, 19 In.	75.00
Lamp Base, Earth Wrap, Olive Green, Textured Brown, Yellow Over Glaze, 13 In.	115.00
Pitcher, Earth Wrap, Chocolate Brown, Textured Band, Marked, 8 5/8 In.	35.00
Pitcher, Earth Wrap, Orange, Yellow, Brown Ground, Handle, 10 7/8 In.	230.00
Pitcher & Bowl, White, Ornate Rim Design, 3055, 7 & 9 1/2 In.	50.00
Planter, Biomorphic, 3-Footed, Mottled Pink Glaze, Marked, 4 x 10 In. ....*Illus*	10.00
Planter, Boy & Teddy Bear, Green, J. Koenig, c.1940	45.00
Planter, Madonna, Praying, Off-White Matte, 17 x 6 In.	60.00
Planter, Palm Trees, White, c.1946, 7 1/2 x 2 1/2 In.	58.00
Planter, Swan	35.00 to 60.00
Vase, Bennington Brown Foam Glaze, 6 x 7 x 4 1/2 In.	35.00
Vase, Blue Abstract Design, Green Speckled Ground, 2 Handles, 15 1/2 In.	259.00
Vase, Deer, Amber Crystal, 15 1/4 In., Pair	80.00
Vase, Lily, Blue, Green, Pink, R-446, c.1940, 14 In.	100.00
Vase, Lime Peel, Rolled Rim, Ink Stamp In Gold, 5 3/8 In.	23.00
Vase, Pedestal, Matte Green, 6 x 8 In.	35.00
Vase, Yellow Matte, J. Koenig, 1930s, 9 x 5 1/4 In.	95.00

HALF-DOLL, see Pincushion Doll category.

HALL CHINA Company started in East Liverpool, Ohio, in 1903. The firm made many types of wares. Collectors search for the Hall teapots made from the 1920s to the 1950s. The dinnerwares of the same period, especially Autumn Leaf pattern, are also popular. The Hall China Company is still working. For more information, see *Kovels' Depression Glass & Dinnerware Price List.* Autumn Leaf pattern dishes are listed in their own category in this book.

HALL'S
SUPERIOR
QUALITY
KITCHENWARE

Blue Garden, Casserole, Lid, Sundial, No. 4	75.00
Brown Eyed Susan, Bowl, Fruit, 5 1/4 In.	9.00
Brown Eyed Susan, Cup & Saucer	14.00
Brown Eyed Susan, Plate, 9 1/4 In.	14.00
Brown Eyed Susan, Platter, 13 1/2 In.	25.00
Buffet Service, Salt & Pepper, Red Dot, Handles	65.00

Cameo Rose, Creamer 18.00
Chinese Red, Jug, Ball, No. 3, 2 Qt. 85.00
Chinese Red, Jug, Doughnut, 1930s 285.00
Chinese Red, Saltshaker, Handle, Raised Letters 40.00
Christmas & Holly, Bowl, Plum Pudding, Keen's English Chop House NYC, 4 1/2 In. ... 24.00
Flare-Ware, Cookie Jar, Ivory, Gold Lace, 3 Qt. ....65.00 to 75.00
G.E., Leftover, Lid, Round, 6 3/4 In. 15.00
Golden Glo, Creamer, Sundial, Individual, Saf-Handle 35.00
Mt. Vernon, Creamer 18.00
Orange Poppy, Baker, French Flute 35.00
Orange Poppy, Bowl, Salad, 9 In. 45.00
Orange Poppy, Coffeepot, S Lid 100.00
Orange Poppy, Drip Jar 45.00
Orange Poppy, Pretzel Jar 170.00
Pert, Sani-Grid, Casserole, Lid, Chinese Red 45.00
Pert, Sani-Grid, Jug, Chinese Red, 7 1/2 In. 50.00
Poppy & Wheat, Bowl, No. 4, 7 1/2 In. 50.00
Red Poppy, Coffeepot, Daniel 65.00
Rose Parade, Bean Pot, Tab Handle 90.00
Springtime, Cake Plate 20.00
Springtime, Cup 8.00
Springtime, Plate, 9 In. 10.00
Springtime, Soup, Dish, Flat, 8 1/2 In. 14.00
Sunshine, Bowl, No. 3, 6 1/8 In. 8.00
Teapot, Aladdin, Turquoise, Standard, Gold, Infuser 110.00
Teapot, Boston, Orange Poppy 425.00
Teapot, New York, Chartreuse, Standard Gold, 8 Cup 150.00
Teapot, Pert, Sani-Grid, Chinese Red, 6 Cup 80.00
Tom & Jerry, Mug, Black, 5 Oz. 10.00
Tomorrow's Classic, Bowl, Cereal, Arizona, 6 In. 14.00
Tomorrow's Classic, Bowl, Fruit, Arizona, 5 3/4 In. 8.00
Tomorrow's Classic, Cup & Saucer, Arizona 12.00
Tomorrow's Classic, Plate, Arizona, 11 In. 16.00
Tomorrow's Classic, Plate, Bread & Butter, Arizona, 6 In. 5.00
Tomorrow's Classic, Plate, Salad, Arizona, 8 In. 8.00
Tulip, Bowl, Fruit, 5 1/2 In. 8.00
Wildfire, Creamer, Pert 25.00

HALLOWEEN is an ancient holiday that has changed in the last 200 years. The jack-o'-lantern, witches on broomsticks, and orange decorations seem to be twentieth-century creations. Collectors started to become serious about collecting Halloween-related items in the late 1970s. The papier-mache decorations, now replaced by plastic, and old costumes are in demand.

Border, Crepe Paper, Orange, Black, On White Ground, 1920s, 20 x 29 In. 70.00
Candle Light, Jack-O'-Lantern, Original Paint, Patented 1904, 7 1/2 In. 1540.00
Candy Container, Black Cat, Cardboard, West Germany, 7 In. 33.00
Candy Container, Black Cat, Papier-Mache, Francie Schmidt, Goodie Sakes, 8 In. 17.00
Candy Container, Cat, Cardboard, West Germany, 4 1/2 In. 22.00

Halloween, Paper Napkin, Cat & Pumpkins, Square, 6 3/4 In.

Halloween, Wall Decoration, Dancing Witch, Beistle Co., U.S.A., 15 In.

Keep insecticides away from old papers. The sprays may kill the bugs but may also damage the paper.

Candy Container, Devil, Cardboard, West Germany, 7 In. 33.00
Candy Container, Jack-O'-Lantern, Open Top, Wire Bail, No Closure 385.00
Candy Container, Jack-O'-Lantern, Orange, Black Cat, 2 3/4 In. 17.00
Candy Container, Jack-O'-Lantern, Pop-Eyed, No Bail, Original Closure 880.00
Candy Container, Jack-O'-Lantern, White, Black Cat, Plastic, 2 3/4 In. 17.00
Candy Container, Jack-O'-Lantern, Wire Bail, Tin Plug, No Closure 550.00
Candy Container, Jack-O'-Lantern, With Cat & Witch, Plastic, 3 In. 25.00
Candy Container, Owl, Hand-Pressed Papier-Mache, Glass Eyes, Germany, 4 In. 695.00
Candy Container, Pumpkin Head Witch, No Bail, Original Closure 1540.00
Candy Container, Pumpkin Man, Cardboard, West Germany, 7 In. 35.00
Candy Container, Witch, Cardboard, West Germany, 7 In. 38.00
Cat, Paper Lithograph, Honeycomb, Tissue Paper Arms, Legs, Torso, 1930s, 28 In. 44.00
Cat On Pumpkin, Papier-Mache, 4 In. 17.00
Costume, Counterspy, Man From U.N.C.L.E., Bullet Lighter, Marx, 1966 . . . .   1090.00
Costume, Evel Knievel, Ben Cooper, Box, 1973, Small 160.00
Costume, Spiderman, Mask, Ben Cooper, Box, 1976 . . . .   85.00
Costume, Wonder Woman, Mask, Red, Blue, Yellow, Box, Ben Cooper, c.1987 . . . .   20.00
Figure, Witch, Holding Broom, Germany, c.1925, 8 1/4 In. 495.00
Jack-O'-Lantern, Bowtie, Celluloid, Germany, c.1925, 7 In. 535.00
Jack-O'-Lantern, Die Cut Sheet, Germany, c.1920 . . . .   78.00
Jack-O'-Lantern, Double Face, Papier-Mache, c.1925, 6 In. 695.00
Jack-O'-Lantern, Face, Papier-Mache, Insert, 4 1/2 In. 80.00
Jack-O'-Lantern, Open Mouth, Papier-Mache, 4 In. 50.00
Jack-O'-Lantern, Papier-Mache, Germany, c.1925, 4 In. 375.00
Jack-O'-Lantern, Papier-Mache, Germany, c.1930, 4 In. 135.00
Jack-O'-Lantern, Smiling, Papier-Mache, 4 1/2 In. 70.00
Jack-O'-Lantern, Tin, 7 In. 965.00
Mask, Cat, Paper, Full Face 25.00
Mask, Froggy The Gremlin, 1948, 10 In. 70.00
Noisemaker, Cat, Tin 25.00
Noisemaker, Cat, Witch, Owl, Metal, Plastic Handle 30.00
Noisemaker, Clown, Sitting, On Drum, Wood, Germany, 11 In. 260.00
Noisemaker, Jack-O'-Lantern, Tin 27.00
Noisemaker, Witch, Metal, Wood Handle 25.00
Paper Napkin, Cat & Pumpkins, Square, 6 3/4 In. . . . . *Illus*   1.00
Pen, Float About, Floatilla Halloween Hair-Do 3.75
Postcard, Boy, Peering Pumpkin Heads, Verse, John Winsch, 1913 . . . .   45.00
Postcard, Girl, Pumpkin & Owl, Verse, 75 Cents, John Winsch, 1913 . . . .   70.00
Postcard, Laughing Moon, Witches Dancing, Jack-O'-Lantern, Verse, c.1910 . . . .   80.00
Postcard, Witch & Owl, Perched On Crescent Moon, Red Outfit, Verse, 1910 . . . .   75.00
Skeleton, Cardboard, Jointed, Copr. H.E. Luhrs, 27 In. 30.00
Skeleton, Paper Lithograph, Honeycomb, Tissue Paper Arms, Legs, Torso, 1930s, 18 In. .   34.00
Straw, Crazy, Shattered Eye, Purple, Taco Bell, 1996, 13 1/2 In.   11.00
Wall Decoration, Dancing Witch, Beistle Co., U.S.A., 15 In. . . . . *Illus*   7.00
Witch, Paper Lithograph, Honeycomb, Tissue Paper Arms, Legs, Torso, 1930s, 28 In. 44.00
Witch's Hat, Cone, Black, 1940s 15.00

HAMPSHIRE pottery was made in Keene, New Hampshire, between 1871 and 1923. Hampshire developed a line of colored glazed wares as early as 1883, including a Royal Worcester-type pink, olive green, blue, and mahogany. Pieces are marked with the printed mark or the impressed name *Hampshire Pottery* or *J.S.T. & Co., Keene, N.H.* Many pieces were marked with city names and sold as souvenirs.

Bowl, Artichoke, Rust Streaking Glaze, Leaves Repeat, 2 3/4 x 4 1/2 In. 440.00
Bowl, Landscape, Green Matte Glaze, Raised Shrub Border, Round, 2 3/4 x 5 1/2 In. 220.00
Bowl, Lotus Blossom, Green Matte Glaze, Embossed Petals, 2 1/3 x 4 1/2 In. 220.00
Candlestick, Crystalline Green Matte Glaze, Impressed, 5 1/2 In.   185.00
Ewer, Green Matte Glaze, Reticulated Mouth, 6 1/2 x 6 In. 195.00
Lamp, Buds, Leaves On Base, Green Matte Glaze, Wicker Shade, Stamped, 11 In. 1265.00
Lamp, Embossed Leaves & Vines, Crystalline Green Matte Glaze, Marked, 16 1/4 In. 1840.00
Lamp, Water Lilies, Green Matte Glaze, Floral Metal Shade, Marked, 16 In. 990.00
Pitcher, Green Matte Glaze, Deco, Bulbous, Looped Handle, 4 x 5 In. 350.00
Tankard, Embossed Rings, Green Matte Glaze, Scrolled Handle, 9 x 5 In. 120.00

Vase, Bag, Green Matte Glaze, Crimped Mouth, Ribbon Tied Neck, 11 x 6 1/2 In. 895.00
Vase, Black Matte, Red, Brown Mottling, Black Veining, 7 x 4 1/2 In. 385.00
Vase, Blue Matte Glaze, Mottled, Molded Lappets, c.1905, 4 1/4 In. 500.00
Vase, Blue Matte Glaze, Tan Veining, Mottled Indigo Blue, 5 1/2 x 3 1/4 In. 660.00
Vase, Blue, Embossed Leaves, Rose Matte Glaze, Tall Neck, Stamped, 10 In. 690.00
Vase, Blue, Rose Mottled Matte Glaze, Bulbous, Stamped, 7 x 4 1/2 In. 748.00
Vase, Buds Around Neck, Long Leaves, Blue Matte Glaze, White Mottled, 6 3/4 x 4 In. ... 770.00
Vase, Bulbous, Leathery Green, Blue Matte Glaze, 8 3/4 x 9 3/4 In. 2705.00
Vase, Cattails, Leaves, Embossed, Blue, Green Mottled, Dark Blue Veins, 4 x 6 1/2 In. 1100.00
Vase, Cerulean Blue Mottled Glaze, Textured Finish, 5 1/4 x 3 1/4 In. 360.00
Vase, Cucumber Green Glaze, Deep Green Veining, Bulbous, 8 3/4 x 7 In. 770.00
Vase, Dandelion, Flowers, Leaves, Stem, Green Matte Glaze, 6 x 5 1/4 In. 605.00
Vase, Ears Of Corn & Husks, Green Matte Glaze, James Scollay Taft, 1900s, 5 3/4 In. ... 650.00
Vase, Embossed Scrolls, Green Matte Glaze, Handles, 4 3/4 x 4 In. 220.00
Vase, Embossed, Mocha Brown, White Mottled Matte Glaze, 3 1/3 x 5 1/2 In. 250.00
Vase, Feathers, Pink Glaze, Mottled, Cerulean Blue Glaze, 9 1/2 x 8 In. 1760.00
Vase, Floor, Tulips, Stems, Leaves, Green Matte Glaze, 15 1/4 x 8 1/2 In. 1760.00
Vase, Green Matte Glaze, Oval, Panels, Speckled, 4 1/2 x 3 1/2 In. 330.00
Vase, Green Matte Glaze, Ribbed Neck, Recessed Panels, 7 x 5 1/2 In. 605.00
Vase, Green Matte Glaze, Tapered, Impressed Mark, 7 1/4 In. 175.00
Vase, Green Mottled & Blue Glaze, 3 Feathers, Square, 6 3/4 x 3 3/4 In. 1045.00
Vase, Leaves, Fringed Edges, Brown, Green, Tan Glaze, 3 3/4 x 3 1/2 In. 990.00
Vase, Lightning Bolt, Green Matte Glaze, Gray Veining, Handles, 7 1/2 x 4 1/2 In. 605.00
Vase, Lilly Pad, Vines, Blue Matte Glaze, 8 1/4 x 6 In. 715.00
Vase, Midnight Black, Light Luster Glaze, Bulbous, 8 1/2 x 6 1/4 In. 440.00
Vase, Pink, Mottled, Drip Style Cerulean Blue Glaze, 9 1/2 x 8 In. 1760.00
Vase, Raspberries, Green Matte Glaze, 3 3/4 x 3 1/4 In. 495.00
Vase, Red, Brown Glaze, Mottled Over Midnight Blue Glaze, 4 1/2 x 3 1/4 In. 715.00
Vase, Stylized Leaves, Green Frothy Matte Glaze, Oval, Stamped, 6 3/4 In. 405.00
Vase, Tulips Repeating, Leaves, Mottled Green Matte Glaze, 7 x 3 1/4 In. 825.00
Vase, Water Lily, Incised, Water, Green Matte Glaze, W. King, 2 1/4 x 5 1/2 In. 770.00

HANDEL glass was made by Philip Handel working in Meriden,
Connecticut, from 1885 and in New York City from 1893 to 1933. The
firm made art glass and other types of lamps. Handel shades were
made not only of leaded glass in a style reminiscent of Tiffany but also
of reverse painted glass. Handel also made vases and other glass
objects.

Ashtray, Golfing Scene, Bronze Mounts, 5-In. Diameter 1552.00
Candlestick, Hammered Brass, 2 Handles, Signed, 9 1/2 In., Pair 230.00
Chandelier, Chipped Ice Shade, Tropical Scene, Palm Trees, 12 In. 3795.00
Humidor, Hunter & Companion, Lid, Signed, 6 1/2 x 3 In. 1150.00
Humidor, Hunting Dog, On Point, Silver Plated Cover, Removable Pipe, 7 x 5 1/2 In. ... 805.00
Humidor, Setter At Point, Metal Lid, Removable Pipe, Signed 5 x 5 1/2 In. 805.00
Humidor, Woman Golfer, Hinged Lid, Decorated By P.J. Hanal, 7 x 5 In. 3450.00
Lamp, 6 Panels, Alternating Green & Blue Stripes, Stylized Flower Border, 13 In. 1064.00
Lamp, 6 Panels, Metal Overlay, Palm Trees, Sunset Ground, Signed, 25 In. 5750.00
Lamp, 6 Panels, Metal Overlay, Sunset, Pine Trees, Twined Base, Signed, 14 1/2 In. 805.00
Lamp, 7 Panels, Metal Overlay Landscape, Bronzed Metal Base, 23 x 17 In. 4600.00
Lamp, 8 Panels, Latticed Metal Overlay, 3 Falcons Under Orb, Round Base, 22 In. 1960.00
Lamp, 8 Panels, Metal Overlay, Leaves & Vines, Slag Glass, Signed, 24 In. 3640.00
Lamp, 8 Panels, Metal Overlay, Swags, Yellow Slag Glass, Stylized Leaf Base, 24 In. 1008.00
Lamp, 16 Ribs, 6 Sides, Berries, Leaves, Textured Base, Signed, 23 In. 4424.00
Lamp, Autumn Leaves, Brown, Red, Reverse Painted, Yellow, 18 x 25 In. 5175.00
Lamp, Baskets Of Flowers, Brown Border, Basket Weave On Foot, 13 1/2 In. 1344.00
Lamp, Butterflies On Flowers, Reverse Painted, Tripod Base, Signed, 24 1/2 x 18 In. 11163.00
Lamp, Butterflies, Poppies, Red, Pink, Orange, Rolled Handles, 18 x 19 1/2 In. ...... *Illus* 56000.00
Lamp, Cameo Berries, Le Verre Francais Shade, Bronzed Metal, Signed, 56 In. 1380.00
Lamp, Chipped Ice Shade, Leaves, Vines, Black Base, Pierced Foot, 23 In. 4760.00
Lamp, Chipped Ice Shade, Ribbed, Trees In Sunset, Copper Base, 23 x 18 In. 5600.00
Lamp, Chipped Ice Shade, Stylized Leaf & Scroll Border, Blues, Greens, Yellows, 21 In. .. 6440.00
Lamp, Desk, Metal Overlay, Grapevine, Carmel Slag Glass, Harp, 5 1/2 x 18 In. 1955.00
Lamp, Desk, Moserine Glass Shade, Bronze, Double Stem Base, Marked, 12 x 9 1/2 In. ... 2070.00

Handel, Lamp,
Butterflies, Poppies,
Red, Pink, Orange,
Rolled Handles,
18 x 19 1/2 In.

To remove the remains of sticky glue and tape from antiques, try rubbing peanut butter on the sticky area. Don't use this method on porous materials, the oil from the peanut butter could leave a stain.

Lamp, Desk, Pine Needle, Adjustable Arm, Weighted Foot, Swivels, Signed, 11 In.	2576.00
Lamp, Dogwood, Pink, Yellow, White, Reverse Painted, 16-In. Shade, 23 In.	3105.00
Lamp, Domed Shade, Cased Green & White, Swivels, Bronzed Harp Base, 57 x 13 1/2 In.	1265.00
Lamp, Domed Shades, Landscape, Bronze Base, No. 6534, c.1917, 26 In.	7638.00
Lamp, Figural, Ribbed Shade, Water Bearer Base, Entwined Leaf Border, 24 In.	7840.00
Lamp, Flared Shade, Yellow, Green Slag Glass, Bronze, Stamped, 26 x 20 In.	1265.00
Lamp, Floral, Brass Base, Pull Chain, Signed Handel 6704, 7 In.	1960.00
Lamp, Flowers, Butterflies, Domed Shade, Patinated Metal, 21 x 15 1/4 In.	8365.00
Lamp, Flowers, Reverse Painted, Domed Shade, Bronze Base, No. 6295, Marked, 20 In.	1000.00
Lamp, Forest Scene, Reverse & Obverse Painted, Gourd Base, Signed, 22 In.	8960.00
Lamp, Green & Brown, Bell Shape Shade, Adjustable Arm, Weighted Base, 12 In.	700.00
Lamp, Hanging, Globe, Junglebird, Parrots, Flowers, 9 x 10 In.	7475.00
Lamp, Hanging, Metal Overlay, Palm Tree, Red, Orange, Green, Slag Glass, 24 In.	6325.00
Lamp, Hanging, Swallows In Flight, Iridized Amber, Bronze Ceiling Mount, 31 In.	3565.00
Lamp, Lake Scene, Reverse Painted, Oval Base, Signed, 13 In.	2800.00
Lamp, Landscape, Reverse Painted Shade, Bronzed Metal, No. 6734, Signed, 21 1/2 In.	4025.00
Lamp, Leaded Glass, Striated Green, Red Triangles, Pierced Cap, Acorn Pulls, 15 In.	6720.00
Lamp, Leaded, Diamond Border, Red, Green, Caramel, Slag Glass, Bronze Base, 64 In.	11500.00
Lamp, Leaded, Flower Border, Green, Pink, Bronzed Metal Base, c.1910, 16 x 21 In.	1725.00
Lamp, Leaded, Grape, Vines, Leaves, Green, Brown, Blue, 24 x 65 1/2 In.	5750.00
Lamp, Leaded, Lotus, Flower & Bud, Caramel & White Slag Glass Petals, 12 In.	1008.00
Lamp, Lions, Shields, Textured Green, Apricot Ground, Signed, 24 In.	1495.00
Lamp, Metal Overlay, Bamboo Leaves, 24 x 61 In.	7475.00
Lamp, Metal Overlay, Cattail, Green, Red, Slag Glass, 24 x 17 In.	3738.00
Lamp, Metal Overlay, Geometric, Domed Shade, Caramel Slag Glass, Brass, 56 x 13 In.	1725.00
Lamp, Metal Overlay, Hawaiian Sunset, 20 In.	14950.00
Lamp, Metal Overlay, Palm Trees, Sunset, Basket Weave Base, Signed, 25 1/4 In.	6900.00
Lamp, Metal Overlay, Sunset, Pine Needles, Footed Base, 24 x 30 In.	9775.00
Lamp, Mountain & Lake Scenes, Wide Apron, Ribbed, Textured, 6-Sided Base, 23 In.	4480.00
Lamp, Piano, Leaded, Mixed Slag Glass, Ribbed Arm, Round Foot, 6 In.	1848.00
Lamp, Piano, Metal Overlay, Scenic, Evergreen Tree, Red, Green, Slag Glass, 14 1/2 In.	1323.00
Lamp, Piano, Metal Overlay, Scenic, Palm Trees, Sunset, Signed, 14 1/4 In.	1093.00
Lamp, Pine Needle Design, Green, Ivory, Cylindrical Shade, 16 In.	1380.00
Lamp, Pink Flowers, Leaves, Yellow Butterflies, 3-Leg Base, 23 In.	7840.00
Lamp, Poppies, Red, Striated Green, White Ground, Rippled Leaves, Signed, 22 In.	2760.00
Lamp, Red Poppies, Black Bands, Round Base, Acorn Pulls, 20 1/2 In.	2800.00
Lamp, Red Roses, Yellow Pine Needles, Basket Weave Base, Signed, 14 In.	690.00
Lamp, Scenic, Trees, Clouds, Reverse Painted, Signed, No. 7111, 18 x 23 1/5 In.	5462.00
Lamp, Ship, Moon, Palm Trees, Reverse Painted, Bronze Base, Signed, 57 In.	7475.00
Lamp, Teal, Blue, Yellow, Enameled, Art Deco, 18 x 26 1/2 In.	3450.00
Lamp, Trees In Mountain Landscape, Gourd Shape Base, Pierced Foot, Signed, 24 In.	5040.00
Lamp, Trees, Seascape, Reverse Painted, Gourd Base, Oriental Foot, Signed, 23 In.	9800.00
Lamp, Windmill, Water, Brown, Orange, Yellow, Reverse Painted, 6 3/4 x 13 3/4 In.	2587.00
Lamp, Wreath & Pansy Shade, Bronze Verdigris Stick Base, Hibbell, 23 In.	2185.00
Lamp Base, 3 Winged Lions, On Circular Foot, Fluted Column, Signed, 25 In.	3640.00
Lamp Base, Fluted Column Stem, Round Base, Acorn Pulls, 25 1/2 In.	1680.00
Lamp Base, Lobed, Tapered Stem, Round Base, Acorn Pulls, 23 In.	1120.00

Shade, 16 Panels, Domed, Slag Glass, Metal Tag, 1900s, 5 3/4 x 7 3/4 In. 764.00
Shade, Globe, Parrot, Reverse Painted, Signed, 10 In. 2300.00
Vase, Amber Iridescent, Enameled, Brown Trees, Flared, Fluted Rim, 7 In. 420.00
Vase, Teroma, Mountain Scene, Signed, Bedigie, No. 4221, Early 20th Century, 10 In. . . . 1610.00
Vase, Teroma, Trees, Mountain, Pond, Green, Blue Lavender, Signed, 10 In. 1725.00
Vase, Teroma, Woodland Scene, Bulbous, Enamel, Signed, Peter Broggi, c.1910, 11 In. . . 1410.00
Vase, Yellow On Clear, Florets, Scrolls, Frosted Ground, Cameo, Signed, Gubisch, 10 In. .   920.00

HARDWARE, see Architectural category.

HARKER Pottery Company was incorporated in 1890 in East Liverpool, Ohio. The Harker family had been making pottery in the area since 1840. The company made many types of pottery but by the Civil War was making quantities of yellowware from native clays. They also made Rockingham-type brown-glazed pottery and whiteware. The plant was moved to Chester, West Virginia, in 1931. Dinnerwares were made and sold nationally. In 1971 the company was sold to Jeannette Glass Company and all operations ceased in 1972. For more information, see *Kovels' Depression Glass & Dinnerware Price List.*

Bridal Rose, Fork 30.00
Cameo, Cup, Jumbo, Blue 18.00
Chesterton, Salt & Pepper, Gray 20.00
Mallow, Bowl, Fruit, 5 1/2 In. 12.00
Mallow, Custard Cup, 8 Oz., 2 1/2 In. 15.00
Mallow, Plate, 6 In. 6.00
Mallow, Salt & Pepper, Skyscraper 60.00
Modern Tulip, Rolling Pin 110.00
Olympic, Coffeepot, Lid, Pink, Beige 35.00
Olympic, Creamer 6.00
Pine Cone, Bowl, Cereal, 5 1/4 In. 10.00
Souvenir, Plate, Adirondack Mountains, Stag, Bow & Arrow Mark, 6 3/4 In. 30.00

HARLEQUIN dinnerware was produced by the Homer Laughlin Company from 1938 to 1964, and sold without trademark by the F. W. Woolworth Co. It has a concentric ring design like Fiesta, but the rings are separated from the rim by a plain margin. Cup handles are triangular in shape. Seven different novelty animal figurines were introduced in 1939. For more information on Harlequin dinnerware, see *Kovels' Depression Glass & Dinnerware Price List.*

Chartreuse, Casserole, Cover, 9 1/2 In. 75.00
Chartreuse, Teapot, Cover 160.00
Gray, Pitcher, Ball, 22 Oz. 130.00
Maroon, Pitcher, 22 Oz. 110.00
Maroon, Soup, Cream, Handles 20.00
Mauve Blue, Bowl, 36s, 6 1/2 In. 40.00
Medium Green, Creamer 30.00
Medium Green, Plate, Luncheon, 9 In. 16.00
Medium Green, Platter, Oval, 11 In. 20.00
Medium Green, Soup, Cream, Handles 35.00
Red, Nut Dish 20.00
Rose, Plate, 6 In. 7.00
Rose, Platter, 11 In. 14.00
Rose, Teapot, Cover 65.00
Spruce Green, Bowl, Oatmeal, 36s 20.00
Tangerine, Bowl, Salad, 7 1/2 In. 18.00
Tangerine, Cup & Saucer, After Dinner 60.00
Tangerine, Plate, Luncheon, 9 In. 16.00
Turquoise, Bowl, Fruit, 5 1/2 In. 7.00
Turquoise, Figurine, Fish 150.00
Turquoise, Plate, 6 In. 4.00
Turquoise, Relish Set, Tray, 4 Inserts, Mauve Blue, Tangerine, Yellow, 11 7/8 In. 380.00
Turquoise, Sugar, Cover 20.00
Yellow, Bowl, Oatmeal, 36s 17.00
Yellow, Bowl, Oatmeal, 6 1/4 In. 18.00

Yellow, Creamer	10.00
Yellow, Cup & Saucer	8.00
Yellow, Cup & Saucer, After Dinner	30.00
Yellow, Figurine, Duck	175.00
Yellow, Mustard, Cover, Glasss Spoon, 3 In.	175.00
Yellow, Pitcher, Straight Sides, 22 Oz.	30.00
Yellow, Reamer	25.00

HATPIN collectors search for pins popular from 1860 to 1920. The long pin, often over four inches, was used to hold the hat in place on the hair. The tops of the pins were made of all materials, from solid gold and real gemstones to ceramics and glass. Be careful to buy original hatpins and not recent pieces made by altering old buttons.

Amethyst, Seed Pearl, 5 Graduated Gems, Openwork Frames, Rose Cut Diamonds	499.00
Black, Ebonized Wood, Metal Separator, 11 1/2 In.	100.00
Carnival Glass, Black Amethyst, Belle	165.00
Carnival Glass, Dark Waves	115.00
Carnival Glass, Dimples & Brilliants, Black Amethyst	85.00
Carnival Glass, Fly On Net, Marigold	120.00
Carnival Glass, Flying Bat, Black Amethyst	175.00
Carnival Glass, Owl, Blue	1600.00
Diamond, Rock Crystal, Platinum, Elliptical Form, Frame, Signed Cartier, Box	3760.00
Enamel, Elkington & Co., Box, 10 Piece	748.00

HAVILAND china has been made in Limoges, France, since 1842. The factory was started by the Haviland Brothers of New York City. Pieces are marked *H & Co.*, *Haviland & Co.*, or *Theodore Haviland*. It is possible to match existing sets of dishes through dealers who specialize in Haviland china. Other factories worked in the town of Limoges making a similar chinaware. These porcelains are listed in this book under Limoges.

HAVILAND & CO.

Bouillon, Gold Bands, Green Underglaze Mark, c.1915	20.00
Butter Chip, Blue & Gold Flowers, 3 In.	24.00
Butter Chip, Marseille, 4 1/4 In.	18.00
Butter Chip, Pink Flowers, 1925, 3 In.	12.00
Butter Chip, Sweetheart Rose, Coupe Shape	18.00
Charger, Pink Drop Rose, 11 3/4 In.	110.00
Charger, Roses, Gold, Charles Field	61.00
Cup & Saucer, Bouillon, Gold Bands, Green Underglaze Mark, c.1915	35.00
Cup & Saucer, Bouillon, Pink Roses, Blue Flowers, Gold Trim, c.1915	45.00
Fish Set, Gilt Rocaille Roundel, Cobalt Blue Border, Gilt Rim, 12 Piece	353.00
Oyster Plate Set, Floral Swags, Gilt Details, 8 1/2 In., 10 Piece	780.00
Saucer, Green Loops, Gold Potted Plants, Green Underglaze Mark, c.1915	15.00
Tray, Hand Painted, Signed, 1891	140.00
Vase, Demilune, Handles, Brown, Grouse, Pottery, 7 3/4 x 10 1/2 In. .... *Illus*	650.00
Wash Set, Multicolored Flower Sprays, Pitcher, Chamber Pot, 13-In. Basin, 7 Piece	176.00

Haviland, Vase, Demilune, Handles, Brown, Grouse, 7 3/4 x 10 1/2 In.

HAWKES cut glass was made by T. G. Hawkes & Company of Corning, New York, founded in 1880. The firm cut glass blanks made at other glassworks until 1962. Many pieces are marked with the trademark, a trefoil ring enclosing a fleur-de-lis and two hawks. Cut glass by other manufacturers is listed under either the factory name or in the general Cut Glass category.

Ashtray, Copper Wheel Cut, Flowers, 2 1/2 x 7 In.	495.00
Bowl, Carnation Engraved, Signed, Gravic Glass 8 x 3 In.	775.00
Bowl, Centauri Pattern, 2 Handles, 3 1/2 x 13 x 7 In.	1115.00
Bowl, Cobweb Design, 4 x 9 1/4 In.	1495.00
Cake Stand, Cut Star In Center, Signed, Curved Feet, 9 1/2 x 2 In.	550.00
Candlestick, Clear, Engraved C., c.1920, 12 1/4 In., Pair	375.00
Carafe, Navarre Cutting, Hobstar Base, 8 1/4 x 5 3/4 In.	235.00
Celery Dish, Signed, 12 1/2 In.	105.00
Cocktail Shaker, Etched Rooster, Cylindrical, Silver Rim, Spout, 1901, 9 In.	110.00
Cocktail Shaker, Etched Rooster, Silver Rim, Spout, c.1930, 9 In.	106.00
Compote, Star & Fan Form, Etched Mark On Base, c.1900, 8 In.	86.00
Compote, Starburst Panels, Scalloped Rim, 8 1/2 In.	125.00
Console Set, Bowl, Candlestick, Cut Line Design, Amber, Star, Signed, 12 1/4 x 2 1/4 In.	300.00
Dish, Ice Cream, Chrysanthemum, 6 1/4 In.	150.00
Dish, Mayonnaise, Underplate, Paneled, Signed	55.00
Goblet, Strawberry-Diamond & Fan, Notched Hexagonal Stem, Signed, 6 In.	50.00
Pitcher, Brunswick Cutting, Triple Notched Handle, Rayed Star Base, 7 1/2 In.	755.00
Relish, Canoe Shape, Hobstars, Fans, Squares, Stars, Fern, 12 x 3 x 4 3/4 In.	495.00
Rose Bowl, Priscilla, Pedestal, 18-Point Hobstar, 6 x 5 In.	625.00
Vase, Iris Pattern, Gravic, Signed, 11 In.	400.00
Vase, Millicent Variation, Engraved Birds, Signed, 12 x 4 In.	660.00
Vase, Servia Pattern, 4 Rows Of Bull's-Eyes, Hobstars, Fans, 12 x 5 1/2 In.	590.00
Vase, Square Feet, Pedestal Base, Blown, Signed, 10 x 7 In.	375.00
Vase, Trumpet, Teutonic, 13 3/4 x 5 1/4 In.	825.00
Vase, Vertical, Strawberry Cut, 3 Medallions, Cornucopia, Signed, 12 In.	460.00

HEAD VASES, generally showing a woman from the shoulders up, were used by florists primarily in the 1950s and 1960s. Made in a variety of sizes and often decorated with imitation jewelry and other lifelike accessories, the vases were manufactured in Japan and the U.S.A. Less elaborate examples were made as early as the 1930s. Religious themes, babies, and animals are also common subjects. Other head vases are listed under manufacturers' names and can be located through the index at the back of this book.

Blond Woman, Pearl Necklace, Earring, Lavender Dress, No. 911, 5 1/2 In.	175.00
Deco Woman, Broad Brimmed Hat, White, No. 836, 5 1/4 In.	45.00
Madonna & Child, No. 4150, Shafford, 6 1/2 In.	20.00
Marilyn Monroe, Earrings, Relpo, Box & Label, 6 3/4 In.	3000.00
Wall Pocket, Deco Woman, Broad Brim Hat, White, U.S.A., 5 1/4 In.	45.00

HEDI SCHOOP Art Creations, North Hollywood, California, started about 1945 and was working until 1954. Schoop made ceramic figurines, lamps, planters, and tablewares.

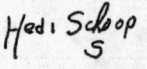

Box, 2 White Cats, Gray Ground, Irregular Shape, Marked, 7 1/2 In.	145.00
Figurine, Cocker Spaniel, Dog Plate, 7 1/2 x 7 1/2 In.	35.00
Figurine, Nude Bathing Beauty, Double Leaf Dish, 11 1/2 In.	40.00
Planter, Cat, Flower Bells, Baskets Holding Flowers, 7 1/2 x 4 1/2 x 5 1/2 In.	127.00
Planter, Woman Carrying Basket On Head, Applied Flowers & Leaves, 12 1/2 In.	66.00
Vase, Tropical Flowers, Cranberry, 11 In.	25.00
Wall Pocket, Black Boy & Girl Angels, 8 In., Pair	200.00

HEINTZ ART Metal Shop made used the letters *HAMS* in a diamond as a mark. Otto Heintz took over the Arts & Crafts Company in Buffalo, New York, in 1903. By 1906 it had become the Heintz Art Metal Shop. It remained in business until 1930. The company made ashtrays, bookends, boxes, bowls, desk sets, vases, trophies, and smoking sets. The best-known pieces are made of patinated bronze with silver overlay.

Similar pieces were made by Smith Metal Arts and were marked *Silver Crest*. Some pieces by both companies are unmarked.

Bowl, Applied Geometric Designs, Bronze, Silver, c.1915, 4 In.	35.00
Bowl, Geometric Design, Silver On Bronze, Marked, 7/8 x 4 In.	25.00
Bowl, Overlaid Branches On Green Finish, Silver On Bronze, Stamped, 8 In.	490.00
Candlestick, Jonquils, Silver On Bronze, 4 1/2 x 5 3/4 In., Pair	520.00
Compote, Birds On Branch, Silver On Bronze, 5 x 6 1/2 In.	259.00
Desk Set, Geometric Design, Sterling Silver, Bronze Body, Blotter, Inkwell, Calendar	175.00
Desk Set, Poppy Design, Blotter, Inkwell, Letter Holder & Opener, Brass, 19 x 11 In.	375.00
Humidor, Abstract Cover, Silver On Bronze, Bronze Patina, Stamped, 5 1/2 x 6 1/4 In.	431.00
Humidor, Fox Hunting Scene, Silver On Bronze, Verdigris Patina, 3 x 8 1/2 x 4 In.	575.00
Lamp, Berries, Leaves, Silver On Bronze, Mushroom Shape, Stamped, 17 x 15 In.	1095.00
Lamp, Desk, Helmet Shade, Berries, Leaves, Silver On Bronze, 11 x 7 3/4 In.	750.00
Lamp, Desk, Helmet Shade, Verdigris Patina, 10 x 8 In.	865.00
Lamp, Flowers, Sterling Silver, 11 In.	980.00
Lamp, Geometric Design, Sterling Silver, Green Verdigris Patina, Paper Label, 11 In.	920.00
Lamp, Poppy Design, Brass, Paper Label, 10 1/2 In.	1265.00
Lamp, Sterling On Bronze, Verdigris Patina, Signed, 12 x 15 In.	1725.00
Trophy, Bowling, Bowler, Stylized Border, Silver On Bronze, 7 1/2 x 7 1/4 In.	430.00
Trophy, Golf, Silver On Bronze, Geometric Overlay, Stamped, 9 1/4 x 8 In.	315.00
Vase, Birds On Branch, Silver On Bronze, 8 1/2 x 3 1/2 In.	145.00
Vase, Cornflower, Silver On Bronze, Original Patina, 7 1/2 x 3 1/4 In.	375.00
Vase, Mottled Green Patina, Applied Silver Flowers, Bronze, Impressed, 10 5/8 In.	259.00
Vase, Rose, Verdigris Ground, Silver On Bronze, Stamped, 12 1/4 x 5 In.	805.00
Vase, Sterling Silver Geometric Design, Bronze Body, Silvercrest, 7 1/2 In.	345.00
Vase, Stylized Iris, Sterling On Bronze, Cylindrical, 8 x 3 1/2 In.	290.00

HEISEY glass was made from 1896 to 1957 in Newark, Ohio, by A. H. Heisey and Co., Inc. The Imperial Glass Company of Bellaire, Ohio, bought some of the molds and the rights to the trademark. Some Heisey patterns have been made by Imperial since 1960. After 1968, they stopped using the *H* trademark. Heisey used romantic names for colors, such as *Sahara*. Do not confuse color and pattern names. The Custard Glass and Ruby Glass categories may also include some Heisey pieces.

Albemarle, Cordial, Chateau Cutting, 1 Oz.	30.00
Angel Fish, Bookends	345.00
Animal, Bull	3500.00
Animal, Clydesdale	550.00 to 600.00
Animal, Colt, Standing	950.00
Animal, Colt, Standing, Amber	675.00
Animal, Elephant, Mama	395.00
Animal, Gazelle	1525.00 to 2800.00
Animal, Giraffe, Head To Side	285.00
Animal, Goose, Wings Down	535.00
Animal, Goose, Wings Half	110.00
Animal, Mallard, Wings Down	375.00 to 495.00
Animal, Poulter Pigeon	700.00 to 1200.00
Animal, Rabbit, Mama	3500.00
Animal, Ring-Necked Pheasant	125.00
Animal, Rooster, Fighting	1200.00
Animal, Sparrow	165.00
Banded Flute, Chamberstick, 4 In.	30.00
Banded Flute, Claret, 5 Oz.	40.00
Banded Flute, Cocktail, Footed	20.00
Banded Flute, Custard, 4 Oz.	10.00
Banded Flute, Punch Bowl, Base	105.00
Banded Flute, Salt & Pepper	60.00
Carcassone, Cordial, Alexandrite, 1 Oz.	195.00
Carcassone, Pilsner, Moongleam, Footed, 12 Oz.	149.00
Carolina, Wine, Osage Etch, 2 Oz.	25.00
Centennial, Candlestick, 6 In.	60.00
Charter Oak, Bowl, Shallow, 4 1/4 x 3/4 In.	20.00

Cheshire, Salt & Pepper, Footed, Flamingo 75.00
Coleport, Ice Bucket 125.00
Colonial, Goblet, 8 Oz., 3 3/4 In. ....10.00 to 20.00
Colonial, Oyster Cocktail, 3 Oz., 4 1/2 In. 40.00
Colonial, Punch Bowl, Base 20.00
Colonial Panel, Pitcher, 6 1/2 In. 45.00
Coronation, Cocktail, 3 Oz. 25.00
Criss Cross, Nappy, 4 1/2 In. 40.00
Crystolite, Bowl, Oval, Footed, 13 In. 80.00
Crystolite, Box, 4 x 3 1/2 x 2 1/4 In. 35.00
Crystolite, Box, Cigarette, Cover, 4 1/2 In. ....30.00 to 40.00
Crystolite, Candy Box, Cover, Round 7 In. 60.00
Crystolite, Candy Dish, Cover, 3 Sections, 6 3/4 In. 40.00
Crystolite, Candy Dish, Cover, Shell 40.00
Crystolite, Celery Dish, Oval, 13 In. 50.00
Crystolite, Celery Dish, Oval, Handle, 7 In. 35.00
Crystolite, Cocktail, 3 1/2 Oz. 20.00
Crystolite, Cruet, Stopper, 2 Oz. 25.00
Crystolite, Cruet, Stopper, 3 Oz. 40.00
Crystolite, Cup & Saucer ....20.00 to 30.00
Crystolite, Dish, Jelly, Footed, 5 In. 20.00
Crystolite, Mustard, Cover, 2 1/2 In. 40.00
Crystolite, Plate, 7 In. 10.00
Crystolite, Plate, Coupe, 7 1/2 In. 25.00
Crystolite, Plate, Star Bottom, 8 In. 20.00
Crystolite, Platter, 13 In. 40.00
Crystolite, Punch Cup 10.00
Crystolite, Relish, 5 Sections, 10 In. 40.00
Crystolite, Relish, Cloverleaf Shape 20.00
Crystolite, Relish, Oval, 3 Sections, 9 In. 25.00
Crystolite, Salt & Pepper 35.00
Crystolite, Sherbet, 6 Oz., 3 7/8 In. 18.00
Crystolite, Sugar & Creamer, Tray ....35.00 to 40.00
Crystolite, Tray, Oval, Handles, 9 1/2 x 7 In. 25.00
Crystolite, Tumbler, 10 Oz. 40.00
Crystolite, Tumbler, Barrel, 10 Oz. 95.00
Daisy & Leaves, Nappy, 4 1/2 In. 35.00
Elephant, Mug, Amber, Trunk Handle 700.00
Empress, Bowl, Alexandrite, Flower Cutting, 11 In. 625.00
Empress, Bowl, Flamingo, 4 1/2 In. 25.00
Empress, Bowl, Flamingo, 6 In. 40.00
Empress, Bowl, Sahara, Deep, 8 In. 60.00
Empress, Bowl, Sahara, Dolphin Footed, 3 x 8 1/2 In. 50.00
Empress, Candlestick, Dolphin, Footed, Flamingo, 6 In. 75.00
Empress, Candlestick, Sahara, Dolphin Footed, 6 In. 120.00
Empress, Compote, Oval, Flamingo, 7 In. 90.00
Empress, Creamer 10.00
Empress, Cup & Saucer 45.00
Empress, Dish, Mayonnaise, Barcelona Cutting 45.00
Empress, Ice Bucket, Handle, Sahara 125.00
Empress, Ice Bucket, Tongs, Antarctica Etch 100.00
Empress, Jug, Flamingo, Dolphin, Footed, 3 Pt. 175.00
Empress, Jug, Sahara, Dolphin, Footed, 3 Pt. 185.00
Empress, Mustard, Cover, Sahara 150.00
Empress, Plate, 8 In. 25.00
Empress, Plate, Flamingo, Square, 7 In. 20.00
Empress, Plate, Sahara, Square, 8 In. 20.00
Empress, Plate, Salad, Sahara, 8 1/8 In. 45.00
Empress, Platter, Flamingo, Oval, 14 In. 65.00
Empress, Platter, Sahara, Oval, 14 In. 70.00
Empress, Sherbet, Flamingo, 4 Oz. 40.00
Empress, Sugar & Creamer, Flamingo 110.00

Empress, Sugar & Creamer, Sahara, Individual 75.00
Empress, Sugar, Sahara, Dolphin Footed 50.00
Empress, Tumbler, Flamingo, 8 Oz. 60.00
Empress Etch, Cup & Saucer, Yeoman, Moongleam 35.00
Fancy Loop, Salt 24.00
Fandango, Bowl, Crimped Edge, 8 In. 25.00
Fandango, Creamer, 3 In. 35.00
Fandango, Sugar, 2 1/2 In. 30.00
Fern, Candlestick, 7 1/4 In., Pair 75.00
Fern, Cheese Tray, Zircon, Handle, 6 In. 150.00
Fern, Dish, Jelly, Zircon, 12 In. 125.00
Fifth Avenue, Cordial, 1 Oz. 25.00
Flat Panel, Toothpick 55.00
Gascony, Sauceboat 45.00
Gascony, Tumbler, Iced Tea, Tangerine, 10 Oz. 250.00
Greek Key, Celery Dish, 9 In. 65.00
Greek Key, Cruet, Stopper 80.00
Greek Key, Sugar, Oval, Hotel 60.00
Grid & Square, Jug, 1/2 Gal. 400.00
Half Circle, Sugar & Creamer, Moongleam 250.00
Hobstar & Cane, Punch Bowl, Base 110.00
Horsehead, Bookends 365.00
Ipswich, Candlestick Vase, Moongleam, Pair 200.00
Ipswich, Candlestick Vase, Sahara, Pair 175.00
Ipswich, Candy Jar, Cover, Moongleam, 1/2 Lb. 695.00
Ipswich, Plate, Sahara, 7 In. 60.00
Ipswich, Sherbet, Moongleam, 4 Oz. 45.00
Ispwich, Plate, Sahara, 8 In. 60.00
Jamestown, Tumbler, Juice, Barcelona Cutting, Footed, 5 Oz. 14.00
Kalonyal, Celery Dish, Flat, 12 In. 95.00
Kohinoor, Candlestick, 2-Light, Zircon Prisms 650.00
Lariat, Bowl, Moonglo Cutting, 7 In. 50.00
Lariat, Candlestick, 4 1/8 In., Pair ....20.00 to 30.00
Lariat, Candy Dish, Cover, 5 In. 60.00
Lariat, Cocktail, Moonglo Cutting, 3 1/2 Oz. 26.00
Lariat, Dish, Mayonnaise, 2 Sections, 7 In. ....25.00 to 30.00
Lariat, Nappy, Silver Overlay Flowers, 7 In. 35.00
Lariat, Oyster Cocktail, 4 1/4 Oz. 20.00
Lariat, Plate, 6 In. 7.50
Lariat, Plate, 7 In. 12.50
Lariat, Punch Cup 8.00
Lariat, Vase, Fan 50.00
Mars, Candleholder, Moongleam, Pair 110.00
Mayflower Etch, Cocktail, Wabash, Moongleam Stem, 3 Oz., 5 7/8 In. 35.00
Mayflower Etch, Sherbet, Wabash, Green Stem, 6 Oz., 3 3/4 In. 35.00
Minuet Etch, Champagne, 6 3/8 In. 25.00
Minuet Etch, Cordial, Symphone, 1 Oz. 125.00
Minuet Etch, Plate, 8 In. 30.00
Minuet Etch, Tumbler, Iced Tea, Footed, 12 Oz. 60.00
Octagonal Square, Plate, Dessert, Flamingo 20.00
Old Sandwich, Ashtray, Cobalt Blue, Square, 2 1/4 In. 50.00
Old Sandwich, Mug, 12 Oz. 60.00
Old Sandwich, Oyster Cocktail, 4 Oz. 15.00
Old Sandwich, Plate, Moongleam, 8 In. 30.00
Old Sandwich, Plate, Square, 8 In. 50.00
Old Sandwich, Salt 10.00
Old Sandwich, Sundae, Flamingo, Footed, 6 Oz. 30.00
Old Sandwich, Tumbler, 8 Oz. 20.00
Old Williamsburg, Candlestick, 9 In. 75.00
Old Williamsburg, Goblet, 8 Oz., 5 1/2 In. 30.00
Old Williamsburg, Sherbet, Tall, 5 Oz. 10.00
Old Williamsburg, Sugar & Creamer, Amber Stain 35.00

Orchid, Ashtray, Etch, 3 In.	30.00
Orchid Etch, Bowl, Oval, 7 In.	45.00
Orchid Etch, Butter, Cover, Waverly, 1/4 Lb.	165.00
Orchid Etch, Candy Dish, Cover, Wave, Finial, 5 In.	210.00
Orchid Etch, Champagne, 6 Oz.	40.00
Orchid Etch, Cigarette Holder, Footed	165.00
Orchid Etch, Cup & Saucer, Waverly	75.00
Orchid Etch, Decanter, Sherry, Oval, Silver Plated, Stopper, Pt.	335.00
Orchid Etch, Dish, Mayonnaise, Flared, Footed, 5 1/2 In.	70.00
Orchid Etch, Goblet, 10 Oz., 8 1/4 In.	50.00
Orchid Etch, Pitcher, Donna, 1/2 Gal.	625.00
Orchid Etch, Plate, 7 1/4 In.	20.00
Orchid Etch, Plate, Salad, 8 In.	40.00
Orchid Etch, Relish, 3 Sections, 11 In.	70.00
Orchid Etch, Saucer	15.00
Orchid Etch, Sherbet, 6 Oz.	40.00
Orchid Etch, Tumbler, Iced Tea, 12 Oz., 6 1/2 In.	75.00
Orchid Etch, Wine, Tyrolean, 3 Oz.	85.00
Park Avenue, Cordial, 2 Oz.	60.00
Patrician, Candlestick, 9 1/4 In., Pair	65.00
Peerless, Cocktail, 2 Oz.	25.00
Peerless, Compote, 8 In.	20.00
Peerless, Goblet, Water, 8 Oz.	20.00
Pinwheel & Fan, Bowl, 8 In.	45.00
Plantation, Card Box, Cover, 6 In.	495.00
Plantation, Claret, 4 Oz., 5 1/8 In.	50.00
Plantation, Cocktail, Ivy Etch, 3 1/2 Oz.	70.00
Plantation, Cup & Saucer	70.00
Plantation, Goblet, Pressed, 10 Oz.	45.00
Plantation, Relish, 3 Sections, 11 In.	75.00
Plantation, Snack Tray, Cup, 7 In.	425.00
Plantation, Syrup, Cover	160.00
Plantation, Wine, 3 Oz., 5 1/4 In.	50.00
Pleat & Panel, Cup, Flamingo	27.00
Priscilla, Cordial, Oz.	40.00
Priscilla, Punch Set, Bowl, Base, 10 Cup	220.00
Priscilla, Toothpick	35.00
Provincial, Goblet, 9 Oz.	15.00
Provincial, Sherbet, 5 Oz.	12.00
Provincial, Tumbler, Iced Tea, Zircon, 12 Oz.	95.00
Provincial, Tumbler, Juice, Footed, 5 Oz.	11.00
Puritan, Celery Dish, 11 3/4 In.	15.00
Puritan, Dish, Jelly, Footed, 5 In.	25.00
Puritan, Ice Tub, Tab Handles, 6 1/2 In.	60.00
Puritan, Jug, Squat, Qt.	95.00
Puritan, Sherbet, 4 Oz., 3 1/2 In.	15.00
Quator, Bowl, Square, 9 In.	40.00
Quator, Creamer, Paneled	40.00
Queen Anne, Bowl, Dolphin Footed, 2 1/2 x 6 3/4 In.	25.00
Queen Anne, Candlestick, 8 In., Pair	175.00
Ridgeleigh, Ashtray Set, Bridge, Diamond, Heart, Spade, Club	125.00
Ridgeleigh, Bonbon, 2 Handles	25.00
Ridgeleigh, Candlestick, 2-Light, Boboches, Prisms, Pair	140.00
Ridgeleigh, Champagne, Blown, 5 Oz.	25.00
Ridgeleigh, Creamer, 4 In.	17.00
Ridgeleigh, Plate, 8 In.	15.00 to 18.00
Ridgeleigh, Plate, 12 1/2 In.	45.00
Ridgeleigh, Sherbet, Pressed, 5 Oz.	15.00
Ridgeleigh, Sugar & Creamer	50.00
Ridgeleigh, Sugar, 4 1/2 In.	15.00
Ridgeleigh, Tumbler, Whiskey, 2 1/2 Oz.	40.00
Ridgeleigh, Vase, 9 In.	90.00

Rococo, Creamer, Sahara 80.00
Rose Etch, Ashtray, 3 In. 50.00
Rose Etch, Butter, Cabochon, 1/4 Lb. 325.00
Rose Etch, Cake Plate, Footed, 14 In. 310.00
Rose Etch, Champagne, 6 Oz., 4 1/2 In. . . . . .30.00 to 40.00
Rose Etch, Cocktail, 4 Oz. 35.00
Rose Etch, Compote, Oval, 5 3/8 x 7 1/4 In. 50.00
Rose Etch, Cordial, 1 Oz. 150.00
Rose Etch, Goblet, 9 Oz. 45.00
Rose Etch, Plate, 8 1/2 In. 30.00
Rose Etch, Relish, 3 Sections, 8 In. 50.00
Rose Etch, Salt & Pepper, Footed 80.00
Rose Etch, Sandwich Tray, Waverly, 11 In. 65.00
Rose Etch, Torte Plate, 10 1/2 In. 50.00
Rose Etch, Torte Plate, 14 In. 100.00
Rose Etch, Tumbler, Iced Tea, Footed, 12 Oz. 68.00
Rose Etch, Tumbler, Juice, Footed, 5 Oz. 58.00
Rose Etch, Vase, Violet, 4 x 3 1/4 In. 50.00
Round Colonial, No. 459, Basket, Butterfly & Daisy, Etch, 13 3/4 In. 200.00
Saturn, Vase, Violet, Zircon 200.00
Sawtooth Band, Syrup 10.00
Spanish, Champagne, Cobalt Blue, 5 1/2 Oz. 65.00
Spanish, Tumbler, Juice, Footed, Cobalt Blue, 4 Oz., 4 3/8 In. 50.00
Stanhope, Champagne, Saturn Optic, Zircon, 5 1/2 Oz. 100.00
Stanhope, Goblet, 9 Oz., 6 In. 30.00
Stanhope, Relish, 4 Sections, Red Bakelite Knobs, 12 In. 65.00
Stanhope, Sugar & Creamer, Art Deco, Black Bakelite Knob, 3 1/4 & 4 In. 150.00
Sunburst, Bowl, 8 In. 95.00
Sunburst, Dish, Jelly, Footed, 5 1/2 In. 65.00
Sunburst, Relish, Oval, 9 In. 25.00
Sunburst, Toothpick 160.00
Sunburst, Tray, 13 In. 70.00
Swirl, Dish, Baked Apple, Underplate, Moongleam, 6 In. 50.00
Town & Country, Platter, Dawn, 14 In. 30.00
Trident, Candlestick, Sahara, 5 In., Pair 165.00
Tudor, Box, Cigarette, Cover, Hawthorne 130.00
Twist, Cruet, Flamingo, 4 Oz. 140.00
Twist, Cruet, Sahara, 4 Oz. 185.00
Twist, Plate, 8 In. 8.00
Twist, Salt & Pepper, Flamingo 150.00
Universal, Cordial, 1 Oz. 22.00
Victorian, Champagne, 5 Oz. 19.00
Victorian, Goblet, 9 Oz. 30.00
Victorian, Plate, 8 In. 35.00
Victorian, Sherbet, 5 Oz. . . . . .20.00 to 25.00
Victorian, Sugar 30.00
Wabash, Champagne, Moongleam Stem, 5 Oz., 5 1/2 In. 40.00
Wabash, Goblet, Moongleam Stem, Green, 10 Oz., 7 In. 48.00
Warwick, Vase, Horn Of Plenty, Sahara, 7 In. 188.00
Waverly, Bowl, 4 1/4 x 12 In. 50.00
Waverly, Celery Dish, 12 In. 25.00
Waverly, Chocolate Dish, Cover, 5 In. 45.00
Waverly, Dish, Mayonnaise, 2 Sections, Footed, 6 1/2 In. 40.00
Waverly, Plate, Salad, 8 1/2 In. 25.00
Waverly, Sugar & Creamer 55.00
Waverly, Torte Plate, 13 In. 25.00
Yeoman, Candy Dish, Moongleam, Handles, 6 1/2 In. 75.00
Yeoman, Compote, Gold Trim, 5 In. 40.00
Yeoman, Goblet, Sahara, 8 Oz., 5 3/8 In. 35.00
Yeoman, Sugar & Creamer, Engraved Flowers, Oval 55.00

HEREND, see Fischer category.

HEUBACH is the collector's name for Gebruder Heubach, a firm working in Lichten, Germany, from 1840 to 1925. It is best known for bisque dolls and doll heads, their principal products. They also manufactured bisque figurines, including piano babies, beginning in the 1880s, and glazed figurines in the 1900s. Piano Babies are listed in their own category. Dolls are included in the Doll category under *Gebruder Heubach* and *Heubach*. Another factory, Ernst Heubach, working in Koppelsdorf, Germany, also made porcelain and dolls. These will also be found in the Doll category under Heubach Koppelsdorf.

Figurine, Dutch Boy & Girl, 5 In., Pair	210.00
Figurine, Dutch Girl, Orange Skirt, White Top, Green Scarf, White Cap, 3 1/2 In.	95.00

HISTORIC BLUE, see factory names, such as Adams, Clews, Ridgway, and Staffordshire.

HOBNAIL glass is a style of glass with bumps all over. Dozens of hobnail patterns and variants have been made. Clear, colored, and opalescent hobnail have been made and are being reproduced. Other pieces of hobnail may also be listed in the Duncan & Miller, Fenton, and Francisware categories.

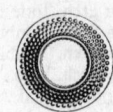

Decanter, Stopper, Hocking Glass Co., 11 In.	35.00
Egg Plate, Indiana Glass Co., 11 In.	15.00
Pitcher, Shaded Pink To White, Satin, Applied Reeded Handles, 7 In.	127.00
Tumbler, 10 Oz., 3 3/4 In.	12.00
Vase, Shaded Pink, Applied Reeded Handles, 5 In.	58.00

HOLLY AMBER, or golden agate, glass was made by the Indiana Tumbler and Goblet Company of Greentown, Indiana, from January 1, 1903, to June 13, 1903. It is a pressed glass pattern featuring holly leaves in the amber-shaded glass. The glass was made with shadings that range from creamy opalescent to brown-amber.

Butter, Cover Only	475.00
Mug	650.00
Spooner	510.00
Toothpick	220.00

HOLT-HOWARD was an importer who started working in 1949 in Stamford, Connecticut. The company sold many types of table accessories, such as condiment jars, decanters, spoon holders, and saltshakers. The figures shown on some of his pieces had a cartoon-like quality. The company was bought out by General Housewares Corporation in 1969. Holt-Howard pieces are often marked with the name and the year or *HH* and the year stamped in black. The HH mark was used until 1974. There was also a black and silver label.

Ashtray, Kozy Kitty	61.00
Bell, Elf, Label	20.00
Butter Chip, Reindeer, Frolicking, White, Gold Bands, 1960s, 3 7/8 In., 6 Piece	45.00
Candle Climber, Elf, White, 1958, Pair	40.00

Holt-Howard, Salt & Pepper, Coq
Rouge, Red Rooster, 1960, 4 1/2 In.

The material used to make repairs is warmer to the touch than the porcelain. Feel the surface of a figurine to see if there are unseen repairs.

Candleholder, Santa With Bags, Label, 1958, Pair 30.00
Candlestick, Bride & Groom, 1959, 4 1/2 In. 20.00
Candlestick, Camel, No. 6416, Japan, 1960 .... 10.00
Candlestick, Deer Peeking Out, Gold Trim, 1961, 4 x 3 1/4 In. 8.00
Candlestick, SS Noel Tugboat, Santa, Red, Green, White, Label, 1959 ....15.00 to 20.00
Dish, Cottage Cheese, Kozy Kitten, 4 In. 150.00
Figurine, Li'l Girl, Green Outfit, Glued Red Wig 20.00
Jar, Condiment, Cherry, Pixieware, Cherry For Nose, 5 1/2 In. 200.00
Jar, Condiment, Cocktail Onions, Pixieware 155.00
Jar, Condiment, Olive, Pixieware, Winking, 5 1/2 In. 200.00
Jar, Decanter, Devil Brew, Pixieware, 1958 .... 15.00
Match Holder, Merry Mouse, Partial Label 85.00
Salt & Pepper, Coq Rouge, Red Rooster, 1960, 4 1/2 In. .... *Illus* 36.00
Salt & Pepper, Goose & Golden Egg 20.00
Salt & Pepper, Santa, Winking 35.00
Spoon Holder, Li'l Boy 95.00
Tape Dispenser, Pelican Pete, 8 3/4 x 4 In. 8.00

HOPALONG CASSIDY was a character in a series of twenty-eight books
written by Clarence E. Milford, first published in 1907. Movies and
television shows were made based on the character. The best-known
actor playing Hopalong Cassidy was William Lawrence Boyd. His
first movie appearance was in 1919, but the first Hopalong Cassidy
film was not until 1934. Sixty-six films were made. In 1948, William
Boyd purchased the television rights to the movies, then later made
fifty-two new programs. In the 1950s, Hopalong Cassidy and his
horse, named *Topper*, were seen in comics, records, toys, and other
products. Boyd died in 1972.

Autograph Book, Hoppy On Topper, Leather, Zipper, Embossed, 5 x 6 In. 100.00
Badge, Chicago Tribune, Sheriff 83.00
Badge, Jaeger's Bread, Polk Dairy 44.00
Bag, Carry, Portrait, Paper, Dairyleas Ice Cream, c.1950, 5 1/2 x 12 In. 25.00
Bag, Freezer, Dairylea Ice Cream 45.00
Bicycle, Girl's, Double-Barreled Highlight, Rollfast, 1940s, 20 In. 1800.00
Binoculars, Hoppy & Topper In Desert, Black, Plastic, Glass, c.1950, 4 x 5 In. 50.00
Book Cover, Hoppy, Bond Bread, 12 x 8 In. 18.00
Bottle, Hair Trainer, Hoppy Image, Milky White Liquid, 4 Oz., 6 In. 14.00
Bottle, Milk, Hoppy On 2 Sides, Red Art Work, Dairylea, c.1950, Qt., 8 1/2 In. 35.00
Calendar, 1952 .... 143.00
Card, Cereal, 18 Piece 72.00
Card, Membership, Savings Club, c.1950, 2 1/2 x 4 In. 25.00
Coloring Book, Story, Doubleday, 1950, 11 x 15 In. 40.00
Comic Book, Fawcett, Vol. 5, No. 28, Feb. 1949 .... 38.00
Decal, Sheet, 1950s, 30 x 22 In. 115.00
Ear Muffs, Tin, Plush, Bailey, Box, c.1950 .... 116.00
Figurine, Hopalong Cassidy & Topper, Metal, Timpo 143.00
Fishing Rod 286.00
Game, Canasta, Hoppy, Guns Drawn, Pacific Playing Card, 1950 .... 65.00
Game, Dominoes, Box, Milton Bradley, c.1950, 9 1/2 x 12 x 1 1/4 In. 145.00
Game, Target, Tin, W. Boyd, Marx, Box, c.1950, 16 x 27 In. 138.00
Gum Packs, 1 Cent, Green, 2 Packs 132.00
Gun, Zoomerang, Plastic, Tigrett, Box, 9 In. 220.00
Handkerchief, Hoppy Topper, c.1950, 11 x 11 3/4 In. 20.00
Hat, Bar 20, Wool, Silk, Saks Fifth Ave., 1950, 12 1/2 x 14 x 5 1/2 In. 225.00
Knife, Pocket, Hoppy On Topper, 2 Blades, Can Opener, 3 3/8 In. 60.00
Label, Bond Bread 33.00
Label, Sunbeam Bread, 6 Piece 50.00
Lamp, Gun & Holster Shape, Caramel Slag Glass, Aladdin 310.00
Packet, Drink, Hopalong Aid, 1950, 3 1/2 x 5 In. 90.00
Pencil Case, Figure, Die Cut, c.1950, 2 3/4 x 9 1/2 In. 70.00
Pencil Case, Smiling Hoppy, Red, Pencils, Crayons, Protractor, 1950s, 8 1/2 In. 70.00
Pennant, Black Ground, Pink Letters, Grauman's Chinese Theatre, 1950 .... 125.00
Pennant, Black Ground, White Lettering, Rope Script, Late 1940s, 28 In. 125.00

Place Mat, Hoppy On Topper, Paper, c.1950, 10 1/2 x 13 1/4 In. 20.00
Plate, Hopalong On Topper, Ceramic, 9 1/4 In. 18.00
Plate, Party, White, Green, Cardboard, Hoppy On Topper, 1950s, 8 1/2 In. 15.00
Poster, Creed For American Boys & Girls, c.1950, 10 1/2 x 13 1/2 In. 90.00
Poster, Helten Fra, Nevada, K. Wenzel, c.1950, 24 x 33 In. 35.00
Press Book, Mystery Man, Movie, 11 1/2 x 14 3/4 In. 18.00
Radio, Antenna, Metal, Plug, Arvin, 8 x 5 x 4 In. 506.00
Roller Skates, Copper Hubs, Spurs, Jeweled Leather, Rollfast, Box, c.1950 .... 1238.00
Sheet Music, Meadow Gold Song, Hopalong & Butch Atcher, 8 x 10 In. 72.00
Sign, Bond Bread, Hoppy's Favorite, Day-Glo, Cardboard, 21 x 27 In. 65.00
Sign, Park Your Shooting Irons Here, Come & Get It, Chuck Wagon, 6 x 10 In. 95.00
Slippers, Hoppy & Name, Felt, Vinyl, c.1950, 5 1/2 x 5 1/2 In. 145.00
Target Set, 2 Sides, Tin, Toy Enterprises, 1950, 14 x 17 In. 149.00
Thermos, Hoppy & Topper, Plastic, Aladdin, 6 3/8 In. 65.00
Toy, Rocker, Tin Lithograph, Lariat Spins, c.1946, 11 x 11 In. 895.00
Toy, Twirls Lasso On Horse, Rocking Platform, Windup, Marx, 1940s 375.00
Toy, View-Master, Hopalong & Topper, No. 955, c.1950 .... 10.00
Toy, View-Master, The Cattle Rustler, 1953 .... 12.00
Wallpaper, Hoppy On Topper, Twirling Rope Spells Name, 1950, 18 x 19 In. 50.00
Window Shade, Rollup, Hopalong On Horseback, Stagecoaches, 40 In. 144.00
Woodburning Set, American Toy & Furniture Co., Chicago, 2 x 13 x 17 In. 55.00
Wristwatch, Hoppy On Face, U.S. Time, Box, c.1950 ....220.00 to 330.00
Wristwatch, Saddle Watch Holder, Display, U.S. Time, Original Box, 1950 .... 855.00
Wristwatch, Silvertone 40.00

HORN was used to make many types of boxes, furniture inlays, jewelry, and whimsies.

Beaker, Blond & Gray, England, 5 In. 115.00
Beaker, Blond & Gray, England, Late 19th Century, 4 1/2 x 3 In. 173.00
Beaker, Polished, England, Late 19th Century, 4 1/2 In. 115.00
Beaker, Sterling Silver Mounted, Blond, Shield Form Monogram, 1878, 3 1/4 x 2 1/4 In. . 173.00
Cup, Bovine, Engraved, Hunting Scene, Scotland, c.1900, 6 In. 388.00
Salad Servers, Sterling Mounted, Spoon, Fork, American, c.1900 .... 173.00

HOWARD PIERCE has been working in Southern California since 1936. In 1945, he opened a pottery in Claremont. His contemporary-looking figurines are popular with collectors. Pieces are marked with his name. He stopped making pottery in 1991.

Howard Pierce

Figurine, Cat, White Satin Matte, Brown, 10 x 3 1/2 & 8 x 3 In., Pair 66.00
Figurine, Girl Reading, 7 x 4 In. 75.00
Figurine, Hippopotamus, Blue Glaze, Ink Stamp, 3 x 6 1/2 In. 278.00
Figurine, Horse, Deco, 8 In. 160.00
Figurine, Madonna & Child, Crystalline Glaze, 9 1/2 In. 41.00
Figurine, Quail Set, Stamped, 6 x 3 & 3 x 2 In., 3 Piece 38.00

HOWDY DOODY and Buffalo Bob were the main characters in a children's series televised from 1947 to 1960. Howdy was a redheaded puppet. The series became popular with college students in the late 1970s when Buffalo Bob began to lecture on campuses.

Book, Howdy Doody's Circus, Little Golden Book, 1950 .... 25.00
Clock, Alarm, Talking, Plastic, 1974, 7 In. 143.00
Cookie Jar, Purinton, 9 3/4 In. 275.00
Key Chain, Plastic, Puzzle Figure, 1950s 15.00
Marionette, Bisque Head, Cloth Body, Chief Thunderbird, 13 In. 110.00
Marionette, Plastic, Air Brushed, Pelham, 16 In. 170.00
Puzzle, Set Of 3, Kagran, c.1950 .... 138.00
String Puppet, Princess Summerfall-Winterspring Composition, Charm Necklace 275.00
Toy, Band, Dances, Man Plays Piano, Tin, Windup, Unique Art, 7 In. ....630.00 to 715.00
Toy, Clarabell The Clown Jumps With Cable Squeeze, Linemar, 1950s 275.00
Toy, Paint Set, Plaster Figures, Bob Smith Hadley Corp., c.1950, 7 In. 143.00
Toy, Trapeze, Jointed, Celluloid, Box, 9 1/2 In. 1320.00
Tumbler, Clarabell, Kick Out Of Circus Mule, Pink, Kagran, Welch's, 1950s 11.00
Tumbler, On Land Or Sea We All Agree, Princess, Yellow, Welch's, 1953 .... 14.00

HULL pottery was made in Crooksville, Ohio, from 1905. Addis E. Hull bought the Acme Pottery Company and started making ceramic wares. In 1917, A. E. Hull Pottery began making art pottery as well as the commercial wares. For a short time, 1921 to 1929, the firm also sold pottery imported from Europe. The dinnerwares of the 1940s, including the Little Red Riding Hood line, the high gloss artwares of the 1950s, and the matte wares of the 1940s, are all popular with collectors. The firm officially closed in March 1986.

Bow Knot, Vase, 6 In.	70.00
Early Utility, Stein, Embossed Scene, Yellow, Brown Wash, 6 1/2 In.	80.00
Early Utility, Stein, Happy Days Are Here Again, 4 1/2 In.	30.00
House & Garden, Mixing Bowl, Pour Spout, Brown, 8 In.	12.00
Imperial, Vase, Urn, Green, 5 In.	25.00
Little Red Riding Hood, Salt & Pepper, Small	75.00
Magnolia, Ewer, Pink, Blue, 4 3/4 In.	50.00
Magnolia, Vase, Yellow, Brown, 2 Handles, 9 In.	65.00
Planter, Kitten, Gold Trim, 8 In.	75.00
Planter, Siamese Cats, Pink, Aqua, 12 In.	95.00
Water Lily, Vase, 8 3/4 In.	106.00
Wildflower, Vase, 8 1/2 In.	195.00
Woodland, Basket, 8 3/4 In.	145.00

HUMMEL figurines, based on the drawings of the nun M.I. Hummel (Berta Hummel), are made by the W. Goebel Porzellanfabrik of Oeslau, Germany, now Rodenthal, Germany. They were first made in 1935. The *Crown* mark was used from 1935 to 1949. The company added the *bee* marks in 1950. The *full bee* with variations, was used from 1950 to 1959; *stylized bee,* 1957 to 1972; *three line mark,* 1964 to 1972; *last bee,* sometimes called *vee over gee,* 1972 to 1979. In 1979 the V bee symbol was removed from the mark. *U.S. Zone* was part of the mark from 1946 to 1948; *W. Germany,* was part of the mark from 1960 to 1990; The *Goebel, W. Germany* mark, called the *missing bee* mark, was used from 1979 to 1990; *Goebel, Germany* with the crown and WG, originally called the *new mark,* was used from 1991 through part of 1999. The newest version of the bee mark with the word *Goebel,* the *current mark* or *Goebel with full bee,* was adopted in 2000. A special *Year 2000* backstamp was also introduced. Porcelain figures inspired by Berta Hummel's drawings were introduced in 1997. These are marked BH followed by a number. They are made in the Far East, not Germany. Other decorative items and plates that feature Hummel drawings have been made by Schmid Brothers, Inc., since 1971.

Ashtray, No. 62, Happy Pastime, Full Bee	90.00
Ashtray, No. 114, Let's Sing, Full Bee	340.00
Figurine, No 2/11, Little Fiddler, Crown Mark	1840.00
Figurine, No. 2/0, Little Fiddler, Three Line Mark	120.00
Figurine, No. 7/1, Merry Wanderer, Stylized Bee	575.00
Figurine, No. 7/111, Merry Wanderer, Full Bee	2530.00
Figurine, No. 8, Bookworm, Missing Bee	80.00
Figurine, No. 10/1 Flower Madonna, Full Bee	160.00
Figurine, No. 10/1, Flower Madonna, Missing Bee	115.00
Figurine, No. 11/2/0, Merry Wanderer, Full Bee	96.00
Figurine, No. 12, Chimney Sweep, Crown Mark	402.00
Figurine, No. 12/1, Chimney Sweep, Full Bee	110.00 to 270.00
Figurine, No. 16/1, Little Hiker, Stylized Bee	105.00
Figurine, No. 23/1, Adoration, Stylized Bee	104.00
Figurine, No. 47/0, Goose Girl, Stylized Bee	225.00
Figurine, No. 49/0, To Market, Stylized Bee	128.00
Figurine, No. 51/0, Village Boy, Vee Over Bee	158.00
Figurine, No. 51/3/0, Village Boy, Three Line Mark	65.00
Figurine, No. 56/A, Culprits, Full Bee	385.00
Figurine, No. 57/0, Chick Girl, Three Line Mark	85.00
Figurine, No. 59, Missing Bee	178.00
Figurine, No. 65, Farewell, Full Bee	230.00

Figurine, No. 67, Doll Mother, Stylized Bee ....105.00 to 160.00
Figurine, No. 69, Happy Pastime, Vee Over Gee ....90.00 to 100.00
Figurine, No. 71, Stormy Weather, Crown Mark 215.00
Figurine, No. 81/2/0, School Girl, Missing Bee 80.00
Figurine, No. 84/V, Worship, Crown Mark 675.00
Figurine, No. 87, For Father, Missing Bee 79.00
Figurine, No. 87, For Father, Three Line Mark 295.00
Figurine, No. 89/1, Little Cellist, Crown Mark 518.00
Figurine, No. 98, Sister, Stylized Bee. 325.00
Figurine, No. 99, Eventide, Last Bee 69.00
Figurine, No. 111/1, Wayside Harmony, Last Bee 225.00
Figurine, No. 124/1, Hello, Missing Bee 130.00
Figurine, No. 127, Doctor, Stylized Bee 225.00
Figurine, No. 129, Band Leader, Missing Bee 87.00
Figurine, No. 141/3/0, Apple Tree Girl, Full Bee 300.00
Figurine, No. 141/3/0, Apple Tree Girl, Three Line Mark 288.00
Figurine, No. 142, Apple Tree Boy, Three Line Mark 230.00
Figurine, No. 142/X, Apple Tree Boy, Vee Over Gee, 32 In. 11500.00
Figurine, No. 143/1, Boots, Vee Over Gee 195.00
Figurine, No. 153, Auf Wiedersehen, Full Bee 295.00
Figurine, No. 154/1, Waiter, Vee Over Gee 140.00
Figurine, No. 171, Little Sweeper, Stylized Bee 70.00
Figurine, No. 176/0, Happy Birthday, Stylized Bee 98.00
Figurine, No. 184, Latest News, Vee Over Gee 135.00
Figurine, No. 185, Accordion Boy, Crown Mark 303.00
Figurine, No. 185, Accordion Boy, Full Bee 75.00
Figurine, No. 195/1, Barnyard Hero, Stylized Bee 143.00
Figurine, No. 197/2/0, Be Patient, Full Bee 400.00
Figurine, No. 198/2/0, Home From Market, Three Line Mark 200.00
Figurine, No. 198/2/0, Home From Market, Vee Over Gee 70.00
Figurine, No. 218/2/0, Birthday Serenade, Vee Over Gee 80.00
Figurine, No. 238/A, Angel With Flute, Three Line Mark 50.00
Figurine, No. 238/B, Angel With Accordion, Stylized Bee 55.00
Figurine, No. 238/C, Angel With Horn, Stylized Bee 55.00
Figurine, No. 258, Which Hand, Stylized Bee. 35.00
Figurine, No. 308, Little Tailor, Vee Over Gee 120.00
Figurine, No. 314, Confidentially, Missing Bee 95.00
Figurine, No. 328, Carnival, Three Line Mark 280.00
Figurine, No. 331, Crossroads Halt Down, New Mark 350.00
Figurine, No. 334, Homeward Bound, Missing Bee 170.00
Figurine, No. 340, Letter To Santa, Clause, Vee Over Gee 200.00
Figurine, No. 342, Mischief Maker, Vee Over Gee 119.00
Figurine, No. 346, Smart Little Sister, Missing Bee 115.00
Figurine, No. 361, Favorite Pet, Vee Over Gee 119.00
Figurine, No. 374, Lost Stocking, Missing Bee 55.00
Figurine, No. 377, Bashful, Vee Over Gee 75.00
Figurine, No. 386, On Secret Path, Vee Over Gee 120.00
Figurine, No. 548, Flower Girl, Missing Bee 80.00
Plaque, No. 30/0/B, Ba-Bee Ring, Missing Bee 60.00
Plaque, No. 140, Mail Is Here, Last Mark 100.00
Plaque, No. 180, Tuneful Goodnight, Last Mark 115.00
Plaque, No. 310, Searching Angel, Last Mark 150.00
Plaque, No. 323, Merry Christmas, Last Mark 150.00
Plate, Annual, 1971, Heavenly Angel, First Edition 150.00

HUTSCHENREUTHER Porcelain Company of Selb, Germany, was established in 1814 and is still working. The company makes fine quality
porcelain dinnerwares and figurines. The mark has changed through
the years, but the name and the lion insignia appear in most versions.

LORENZ
HUTSCHEN REUTER

GERMANY

Group, 2 Eagles, Printed Marks, 24 In. 448.00
Plate, Faces, Black & White, P. Fornasetti, Tema Variazioni, 10 1/2 In., 7 Piece 920.00
Plate Set, Gilt Decorated Blue Border, Etched Gilt Rim, 10 3/4 In. 328.00
Sculpture, Sea Frolic, No. 73 Of 500, Oak Base, 14 x 24 1/2 In. 250.00

ICONS, special, revered pictures of Jesus, Mary, or a saint, are usually Russian or Byzantine. The small icons collected today are made of wood and tin or precious metals. Many modern copies have been made in the old style and are being sold to tourists in Russia and Europe and at shops in the United States. Rare, old icons have sold for over $50,000.

Apostle Mark, Seated, Writing Gospel, Russia, 18th Century, 15 1/2 x 19 1/4 In.	3740.00
Archangel Michael, On Winged Red Horse, Russia, 19th Century, 10 3/4 x 8 3/4 In.	1150.00
Archangel Michael, Wearing Armor, Red Cape, Shield, Sword, c.1890, 6 1/2 x 8 1/2 In. ..	690.00
Birth Of The Mother Of God, Russia, 19th Century, 12 1/4 x 10 1/2 In.	1495.00
Blessing Of The Children, Russia, c.1890, 10 1/2 x 12 1/2 In.	980.00
Bogoliubskaya Mother Of God, Gathering Of Saints, Russia, c.1800, 8 1/2 x 10 1/2 In. ..	805.00
Christ Immanuel, Gilded Repousse Riza, Russia, 18th Century, 10 1/4 x 12 1/2 In.	2760.00
Christ Pantocrator, Embossed Brass Riza, Parcel Gilt, Enameled, Russia, 7 x 6 In.	490.00
Crucifixion, 4 Registers, Russia, 19th Century, 18 3/8 x 15 1/4 In.	750.00
Deisis With Selected Saints, Palekh School, Russia, 19th Century, 12 1/4 x 14 In.	1900.00
Dormition Of The Mother Of God, Gold Leaf, Russia, c.1890, 8 1/2 x 10 1/2 In.	575.00
Entry Into Jerusalem, Each Apostle Identified, Russia, 1890-1910, 12 1/2 x 10 3/4 In. ..	3680.00
Fiery Ascension Of Elijah, Life Scenes, Russia, c.1890, 12 1/4 x 14 1/4 In.	865.00
Georgian Mother Of God, Silver Gilt Repousse Riza, Russia, 19th Century, 7 x 8 3/4 In. .	805.00
Iverskaya Mother Of God, Life Scenes, Bleeding Cheek, 19th Century, 12 x 14 In.	4025.00
Kazan Mother Of God, Decorated Haloes, Borders, Russia, 1890-1900, 14 x 12 In.	460.00
Kazan Mother Of God, Repousse Overlay, Silver Gilt Riza, Cloisonne, c.1908, 12 x 14 In.	2300.00
Last Supper, Round, Signed M. Gololobov, Russia, 19th Century, 14 In.	2760.00
Lord Almighty, Partial Gilt Silver Repousse Riza, Cloisonne Halo, c.1900, 7 x 8 1/2 In. ..	920.00
Lord Almighty, Silver Riza, Filigree Borders, Cloisonne, Russia, c.1900, 9 x 10 1/2 In. ...	1495.00
Lord Immanuel, Lengthy Inscription, Russia, 18th Century, 10 1/4 x 12 1/4 In.	920.00
Madonna & Child, Silver Mounted, Shadowbox Frame, Russia, 10 x 8 1/2 In.	345.00
Mary Magdalene & The Apostle Saint James The Less, Russia, c.1890, 9 x 7 In.	805.00
Mother Of God Of The Sign, Custom Fitted Kiot, c.1890, 7 x 8 In.	980.00
New Testament Trinity, Gold Leaf Incised Field, Dove, Russia, c.1890, 7 x 8 3/4 In.	805.00
New Testament Trinity, Signed, Eliya Yakovlev, Russia, c.1843, 23 x 28 In.	2875.00
Not Made By Hands Image Of Christ, Face Imprinted On Cloth, 1700s, 11 x 12 1/2 In. ..	1725.00
Old Testament Trinity, Abraham, Sarah, Angels, Russia, c.1900, 11 x 12 1/2 In.	1440.00
Pokrov Mother Of God, Incised Borders, Russia, c.1890, 12 1/4 x 14 In.	1380.00
Prayer Of The Cup, Based On Matthew 26:36-39, c.1890, 10 1/2 x 12 1/4 In.	575.00
Pre-Annunciation, Protoevangelion Of James, Mary At Well, 18th Century, 11 x 13 In. ...	2185.00
Resurrection, Jesus Reaching Down To Adam & Eve, Russia, 19th Century, 12 x 14 In. ..	865.00
Resurrection Of Christ, Christ Above Empty Tomb, Angels, c.1890, 7 x 8 3/4 In.	575.00
Saints Zosim & Savvatiy, Holding Monastery, Russia, 18th Century, 11 x 12 1/2 In.	1725.00
Shrine, Spanish Colonial, Heavily Carved, Painted Wood, 1800s, 23 x 15 1/2 x 8 In.	1035.00
Shui-Smolensk Odigitria Mother Of God, Mother-Of-Pearl Beads, c.1800, 11 x 13 In. ...	2760.00
Simeon The God Receiver, Engraved Silver Riza, c.1900, 9 x 10 1/2 In.	920.00
Smolensk Mother Of God, Border Saints, Palekh, Russia, c.1800, 10 1/2 x 12 1/2 In.	1150.00
Sophia Wisdom Of God, Russia, c.1825, 8 x 9 In.	520.00
St. Barbara, Christ, Haloed, Silver, Hammered, Engraved, Russia, 1864, 9 x 10 1/2 In. ..	2537.00
St. Jacob, Holding Bible, Greece, 19th Century, 10 1/2 x 7 1/2 In.	235.00
St. Rose, Lima Patron Saint, Painted, Gesso, Peru, Early 20th Century, 32 x 25 1/4 In. ...	605.00
Triptych, Virgin De Guadeloupe, Wooden, 2 Doors, Mexico, 1950s, 29 x 21 In.	1850.00
Virgin & Child, John The Baptist, 3 Saints, Greece, c.1880, 10 3/4 x 7 In.	690.00
Virgin Mary, Holy Family Medallions, Wood, Repousse Silver Frame, Russia, 23 x 18 In.	4315.00
Vladimir Mother Of God, Silver Gilt, Repousse Riza, Russia, 20th Century, 9 x 10 1/2 In.	1265.00
Wedding, Lord Almighty, Champleve Enamel, c.1900, 7 x 9 In.	1495.00
Year, 12 Panels, Saints, Events, Faux Enameling, c.1890, 17 1/2 x 21 In.	7475.00

IMARI porcelain was made in Japan and China beginning in the 17th century. In the 18th century and later, it was copied by porcelain factories in Germany, France, England, and the United States. It was especially popular in the 19th century and is still being made. Imari is characteristically decorated with stylized bamboo, floral, and geometric designs in orange, red, green, and blue. The name comes from the Japanese port of Imari, which exported the ware made nearby in a factory at Arita. *Imari* is now a general term for any pattern of this type.

Bowl, Brocade Pattern Around Minogame Center, c.1870, 8 1/2 In.	375.00

Bowl, Center, Anton Scene, Blue, Red, Green, Footed, 19th Century, 4 x 9 1/2 In. 335.00
Bowl, Chrysanthemum, Polychrome, c.1912, 11 3/4 In., 3 Piece 460.00
Bowl, Crane, Marsh Medallion, Dragon, Phoenix, Flower Border, c.1860, 11 In. 690.00
Bowl, Figure Of Dragon, Shallow, Scalloped Rim, 1800s, 9 In. 69.00
Bowl, Flower Medallion, Garden Scenes, Scalloped Rim, 19th Century, 11 In. 920.00
Bowl, Flowers, Fan-Shaped Reserves, Meiji, 10 In. 265.00
Bowl, Landscape, Karako Landscape, 19th Century, 8 3/4 In. 230.00
Bowl, Lion & Brocade Border, Kirin Center, 11 1/4 In. 776.00
Bowl, Melon Shape, Scalloped Rim, c.1890, 9 1/2 In. 200.00
Bowl, Phoenix Center, Red & Blue, 19th Century, 7 1/4 In. 160.00
Bowl, Ribbed, Scalloped Rim, Red Ground, Blue Underglaze, 19th Century, 12 In. 1095.00
Bowl, Ribs, Scalloped Rim, Enamels, 19th Century, Japan, 8 1/2 In. 230.00
Bowl, Serving, Phoenix Medallion, c.1975, 8 1/2 In. 316.00
Bowl, Ship & Pine Tree Center, Flowers, 8 Sides, 19th Century, 12 In. 290.00
Charger, Bamboo, Children At Play, Meiji Period, Japan 430.00
Charger, Basket With Flowers In Center, 2 Boats, Scrolling Leaves, Japan, 20 In. 805.00
Charger, Bird On Blooming Branch, Late 19th Century, 17 3/4 In. . . . . *Illus*   112.00
Charger, Blue, White, Chrysanthemum, Prunus Reserves, 12 In. 85.00
Charger, Butterflies, Cranes, Flowers, Medallions, 19th Century, 13 In. 499.00
Charger, Central Flowers, Grape & Brocade Borders, Japan, 19th Century, 14 1/2 In. 206.00
Charger, Central Medallion, 3 Friends, Blue & White, Aster Border, 16 1/2 In. 175.00
Charger, Flowers & Figural, Meiji, 18 5/8 In. 415.00
Charger, Flowers, Crane & Minogame Border, Late 19th Century, 13 1/2 In. 230.00
Charger, Ladies, Birds, Flowers, Fans, c.1880, 15 1/2 In. . . . . *Illus*   215.00
Charger, Landscape, Floral Cartouches, Women, Scroll, 19th Century, 18 1/4 In. 604.00
Charger, Octagonal, Flower, Brocade, Meiji Period, Japan, 11 1/2 In. 316.00
Charger, Polychrome, Gilt Edge, c.1912, 21 1/2 In. 690.00
Charger, Red, Blue, Green, Orange, Gold, Family At Table Under Tree, 23 1/2 In. 550.00
Charger, Scalloped, Reeded Rim, Body, Alternate Panels, 1880, 12 In. . . . . *Illus*   190.00
Charger, Scenic Cartouches, Mount Fuji, Birds, c.1870, 22 In. 518.00
Dish, Birds, Feathers, Flowers, 1 1/2 x 8 1/2 In. 100.00
Dish, Flower Sprays, 18th Century, 11 In. 288.00
Dish, Lozenge Form, Peacock, Swallow, Floral, 19th Century, 11 1/2 In. 430.00
Dish, Seashell Design, Flower Shape Rim, Mid 19th Century, 8 3/4 In., Pair 138.00
Dish Set, Boat Shape, Polychrome, 20th Century, 12 1/4 In., 5 Piece 1725.00
Figure, Gama Sennin, Seated, Holding Frog, White Glaze, 7 1/2 In. 316.00
Figure, Kwannon, Woman Holding Scroll, Phoenix & Cloud Robe, 19 3/4 In. 719.00
Jar, Cover, Ribbed, Shishi Finials, Japan, 19th Century, 26 In., Pair 1998.00
Jardiniere, Polychrome, Lobed, c.1926, 15 1/4 In., Pair 1840.00
Plate, Blue, Red Flowers Triangular Cartouches, 19th Century, 8 1/2 In., 9 Piece 460.00
Plate, Central Stylized Tree, Landscape Panels, 8 Sides, 10 1/4 In. 195.00
Plate, Flower, Butterfly, Rising Sun, Flower Form, 11 In. 315.00
Plate, Flowers, Cobalt Blue, Gilt Petal Borders, c.1900, 8 1/2 In., Pair 259.00
Plate, Landscape, Flowers, 18th Century, 9 In., Pair 520.00
Plate, Phoenix Center, Flower Transfer Border, 7 1/2 In., 6 Piece 316.00
Plate, Scalloped Rim, Flower Design, Japan, 8 1/2 In., 12 Piece 750.00

Imari, Charger, Bird On Blooming
Branch, Late 19th Century,
17 3/4 In.

Imari, Charger, Ladies, Birds,
Flowers, Fans, c.1880,
15 1/2 In.

Imari, Charger, Scalloped, Reeded
Rim, Body, Alternate Panels,
1880, 12 In.

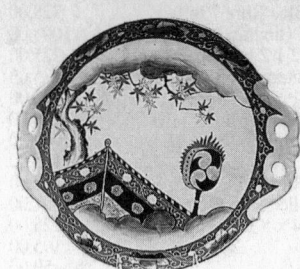  

Imari, Tray, Upturned Rim,   Imari, Urn, Cover, Domed   Imari, Vase, Cobalt Blue & Rust,
Double Handles, c.1920,   Cover, Foo Dog Finial, Oval   On White Ground, c.1860,
13 1/4 In.   Body, c.1900, 20 1/2 In.   14 7/8 In., Pair

Plate, Serving, Scalloped Rim, Morning Glories, 11 In. 259.00
Plate, Square, Cobalt Decoration, Scalloped Corners, Central Medallion, 12 x 12 In. 1100.00
Punch Bowl, Chrysanthemum, Polychrome, c.1926, 6 3/4 In. 805.00
Sake Bottle, Figural Landscape, Pine Branch Finial, Rectangular, 18th Century, 9 1/4 In. .   3565.00
Sauce, Floral Rondels, 5 1/2 In., 4 Piece 175.00
Tea Service, Painted, Flowering Branches, c.1815, 26 Piece 1315.00
Tray, 2 Birds On Rocks, Flowers, Round, 13 In. 50.00
Tray, Upturned Rim, Double Handles, c.1920, 13 1/4 In. . . . . Illus   157.00
Umbrella Holder, Blue & White, Deer, Woods, Cylindrical, 24 x 8 1/2 In. 230.00
Umbrella Stand, Hexagonal Panels, Gold Pheasants, Dragons, Flowers, Plants, 25 In. 550.00
Umbrella Stand, Ribbed, Blue, Red, Gilt, Japan, 19th Century, 23 In. 705.00
Urn, Cover, Domed Cover, Foo Dog Finial, Oval Body, c.1900, 20 1/2 In. . . . . Illus   896.00
Urn, Red, Green, Mauve, Cobalt Blue, Gold, Flower Panels, Birds, 36 1/2 In. 2090.00
Vase, Bottle, Lobed, Red, Green, Aubergine Enamels, 19th Century, 11 In., Pair 705.00
Vase, Cobalt Blue & Rust, On White Ground, c.1860, 14 7/8 In., Pair . . . . Illus   2912.00
Vase, Cover, Shaped Cartouches, Bird & Flower Design, Oval, Japan, 8 1/2 In. 690.00
Vase, Double Gourd, Floral, Brocade, Insect, Meiji, 8 3/4 In. 205.00
Vase, Dragons, Birds, Baluster, 18 1/2 x 9 In. 175.00
Vase, Flower Panel, Cylindrical Neck, Faceted Body 19th Century, 14 1/2 In. 920.00
Vase, Flying Storks, 15 In. 200.00
Vase, Foo Dog, Finial Lids, 18 In., Pair 430.00
Vase, Landscape, Lion's Head Handles, Cylindrical, 11 3/4 In. 160.00
Vase, Mei Phing Shape, Chrysanthemums, Reserve Panels, Japan, 6 In., Pair 690.00
Vase, Ribbed Body, Traditional Enamels, Flower Panels, Buddhist Books, 9 1/2 In., Pair . .   1095.00
Vase, Tear Shaped, Flowers, 19th Century, 12 1/2 In., Pair 1380.00

IMPERIAL GLASS Corporation was founded in Bellaire, Ohio, in 1901.
It became a subsidiary of Lenox, Inc., in 1973 and was sold to Arthur
R. Lorch in 1981. It was sold again in 1982, and went bankrupt in
1984. In 1985, the molds and some assets were sold. The Imperial
glass preferred by the collector is freehand art glass, carnival glass,
slag glass, stretch glass, and other top-quality tablewares. Tablewares
and animals are listed here. The others may be found in the appropriate sections.

Animal, Colt, Kicking, On Bustoff, Amber, 5 1/4 In. 125.00
Animal, Elephant, Caramel Slag, 6 3/4 x 4 In. 40.00
Animal, Hen, Sunshine Yellow, 4 1/4 In. 100.00
Animal, Horse, Clydesdale, Verde Green, 7 1/2 In. 125.00
Animal, Owl, Ice Blue, 6 1/2 x 3 1/4 In. 75.00
Animal, Rabbit, Mother, Ultra Blue, 5 1/2 x 5 In. 250.00
Animal, Scolding Bird, Blue Jay, Verde, 5 x 7 In. 50.00
Animal, Scotty Dog, Brown, White, Caramel Slag, 3 1/2 x 4 1/2 In. 315.00
Art Glass, Bowl, Alternating Draped Loops, Blue & Orange, Bulbous, 6 In. 1120.00
Art Glass, Candlestick, Green, Gold Iridescent Pulled Hearts & Vines, Blue Cup, 12 In. . .   600.00
Art Glass, Compote, Amethyst Heart & Vine, Green Ground, Blue Foot, 2 1/2 x 3 1/2 In. .   500.00

Art Glass, Urn, Iridescent Orange, Blue Disk Foot & Handles, Blue Rim, 7 In.	728.00
Art Glass, Vase, Blue Pulled Heart & Vine, Iridescent Orange, Cylindrical, 12 In.	1008.00
Art Glass, Vase, Bud, Lead Lustre, Flared Base & Rim, 8 1/2 x 2 1/2 In.	275.00
Art Glass, Vase, Cobalt Blue Over White, Iridescent Marigold Interior, 9 3/4 In.	185.00
Art Glass, Vase, Iridescent Blue, Tricorner Rim, 8 In.	896.00
Art Glass, Vase, Iridescent Orange, Blue Pulled Zigzags, Flared Rim, 8 In.	336.00
Art Glass, Vase, Jack-In-The-Pulpit, Blue & Orange Pulled Loops, Disk Foot, 11 In.	1904.00
Art Glass, Vase, Opal, Glossy Orange Iridized Finish, c.1920, 6 In.	145.00
Art Glass, Vase, Orange, White Interior, Pinched Waist, Flared Rim, 6 1/2 In.	275.00
Art Glass, Vase, Threading, Alabaster, Blue Hanging Hearts, Rolled Rim, Bulbous, 9 In.	1064.00
Aurora Jewels, Vase, 3 Swan's Head Handles, Cobalt Blue, 8 3/4 x 8 In.	225.00
Aurora Jewels, Vase, Corn, Cobalt Blue, 9 1/2 In.	195.00
Beaded Block, Pitcher, Pt., 5 1/4 In.	50.00
Beaded Block, Tumbler, Juice, Pink, 5 1/4 In.	35.00
Candlewick, Ashtray, Matchbook Holder Center, 6 In.	165.00
Candlewick, Basket, Beaded Handle, 5 In.	350.00
Candlewick, Basket, Scroll, Handle, Blue, 6 1/4 x 5 In.	22.00
Candlewick, Bonbon, Black, Handles, 10 1/8 In.	200.00
Candlewick, Bowl, 3-Footed, 10 In.	175.00
Candlewick, Bowl, Bell Shape, 10 1/2 In.	60.00
Candlewick, Bowl, Float, 11 In.	60.00
Candlewick, Bowl, Handle, 8 In.	40.00
Candlewick, Bowl, Heart Shape, Handle, 9 In.	200.00
Candlewick, Bowl, Vegetable, Cover, 8 In.	300.00
Candlewick, Cake Plate, Birthday, 72 Candleholders, 14 In.	325.00
Candlewick, Candle Holder, Mushroom, Pair	90.00
Candlewick, Candlestick, 2-Light, 5 x 6 3/4 In.	35.00
Candlewick, Candlestick, 2-Light, Lace Edge, 4 1/2 In., Pair	180.00
Candlewick, Candlestick, 3-Toed, 4 1/4 x 3 In., Pair	225.00
Candlewick, Candy Box, Cover, 3 Sections	175.00
Candlewick, Candy Box, Cover, Round, Square Beaded Rim, 6 1/2 In.	450.00
Candlewick, Celery Dish, 13 1/2 In.	45.00
Candlewick, Celery Dish, Oval, 8 1/2 In.	28.00
Candlewick, Centerpiece, Flower, Candle, 5 x 9 In.	150.00
Candlewick, Chip & Dip Plate, 14 In.	650.00
Candlewick, Cocktail, Red, 4 Oz., 3 1/2 x 2 5/8 In.	90.00
Candlewick, Compote, 3-Bead Stem, 5 x 5 3/4 In.	230.00
Candlewick, Compote, Beaded Stem, 4 1/2 In.	30.00
Candlewick, Compote, Beaded Stem, 8 x 7 In.	125.00
Candlewick, Cordial, 1 Oz.	210.00
Candlewick, Cup & Saucer	11.00
Candlewick, Cup & Saucer, After Dinner	25.00
Candlewick, Cup, Tea	8.00
Candlewick, Goblet, 10 Oz., 7 1/4 In.	150.00
Candlewick, Goblet, Amber Ball Stem & Foot, 4 3/4 In.	10.00
Candlewick, Gravy Boat, Underplate, 8 In.	175.00
Candlewick, Ice Tub, 5 1/2 x 7 3/4 In.	125.00
Candlewick, Parfait, 6 Oz.	80.00
Candlewick, Pitcher, Lilliputian, 16 Oz., 6 1/2 In.	285.00
Candlewick, Pitcher, Manhattan, 40 Oz., 9 1/2 In.	275.00
Candlewick, Plate, 4 1/2 In.	10.00
Candlewick, Plate, 7 In.	7.50
Candlewick, Plate, Handles, 7 In.	45.00
Candlewick, Platter, Oval, 16 1/2 x 13 In.	220.00
Candlewick, Punch Bowl, Cover	270.00
Candlewick, Punch Bowl, Ladle, 11 1/2 x 7 In.	150.00
Candlewick, Relish, 2 Sections, Tab Handles, 6 1/2 In.	23.00
Candlewick, Relish, 3 Sections, Beaded Rim, 3-Toed, 10 In.	125.00
Candlewick, Relish, 3 Sections, Rectangular, 12 In.	45.00
Candlewick, Relish, 5 Sections, 10 1/2 In.	40.00
Candlewick, Salad Set, Mallard Etch, 10 1/4 x 3 3/8 In., 4 Piece	250.00
Candlewick, Sherbet, 6 Oz., 4 In.	24.00

Candlewick, Soup, Cream, Handles, 5 1/2 In.	55.00
Candlewick, Spoon, Mayonnaise, 6 3/8 In.	40.00
Candlewick, Tray, Fruit, 7 1/2 In.	250.00
Candlewick, Tray, Handles, Black, 8 1/2 In.	290.00
Candlewick, Tray, Round, 10 In.	80.00
Candlewick, Tumbler, Flared Rim, 12 Oz.	50.00
Candlewick, Tumbler, Juice, 5 Oz.	11.00
Candlewick, Vase, 7 x 3 In.	375.00
Candlewick, Wine, 4 Oz., 3 In.	40.00
Cape Cod, Bowl, Salad, Fork, Spoon	70.00
Cape Cod, Butter, Cover, 1/4 Lb.	110.00
Cape Cod, Cake Plate	110.00
Cape Cod, Cake Plate, Square, Footed, 10 In.	165.00
Cape Cod, Console, 13 In.	60.00
Cape Cod, Eggcup	55.00
Cape Cod, Goblet, Antique Blue, 11 Oz.	40.00
Cape Cod, Goblet, Ruby, 9 Oz.	25.00
Cape Cod, Goblet, Wine, 4 1/2 In.	12.00
Cape Cod, Lamp, Oil, Milk Glass, 8 3/4 x 4 1/2 In.	230.00
Cape Cod, Plate, Dinner, 10 In.	45.00
Cape Cod, Punch Cup, 2 3/4 In.	6.00
Cape Cod, Relish, 3 Sections, Oval, 9 1/2 In.	15.00
Cape Cod, Relish, 5 Sections, 11 In.	70.00
Cape Cod, Saltshaker, Footed, Chrome Top, 4 In.	8.00
Cape Cod, Saltshaker, Pepper Mill	40.00
Cape Cod, Sherbet, 6 Oz., 5 In.	7.00
Cape Cod, Sugar, 2 Handles, 3 1/2 In.	4.00
Cape Cod, Sugar, 4 1/8 x 5 In.	35.00
Cape Cod, Tumbler, Water, Footed, 5 1/2 In.	23.00
Caramel Slag, Candy Box, Dog, Cover, Finial, 6 1/2 In.	100.00
Caramel Slag, Compote, Flared, Crimped, 8-Sided Base, 4 1/2 In.	45.00
Caramel Slag, Pitcher, 3 1/4 In.	45.00
Cathay, Candy Dish, Cover, Verde Satin, 8 x 5 1/2 In.	45.00
Cathay, Paperweight, Tiger, Jade, 8 In.	100.00
Colonial Lady, Vase, Milk Glass	60.00
Corinthian, Candlestick, 2-Light, 4 1/2 x 6 3/4 In.	45.00
Double Scroll, Console, Amberina	300.00
Grape, Bowl, Custard, Scalloped Edges, Handle, 2 1/2 x 6 1/2 In.	30.00
Grape, Pitcher, Water, Green Carnival, 8 1/2 In.	60.00
Grape, Saucer, Milk Glass	6.00
Hobnail, Vase, Blue, Crimped Top, 6 In.	40.00
Hoffman House, Goblet, Water, Nut Brown, 6 In.	22.00
Loganberry, Vase, Milk Glass, 10 1/4 x 6 In.	35.00
Milk Glass, Knife Rest, 4 1/4 In.	45.00
Mums, Vase, Bud, Stippled Background, 6 1/2 In.	22.00
Pie Crust, Bowl, Painted Flowers, 3-Toed, 1 3/4 x 6 1/2 In.	22.00
Star Medallion, Pitcher, Milk, Smoke Iridescent, 6 In.	24.00
Stippled Rays, Creamer, Marigold, 4 In.	22.00
Suzanne, Bell, Carnival Glass, Cobalt Blue, 6 In.	50.00

INDIAN art from North America has attracted the collector for many years. Each tribe has its own distinctive designs and techniques. Baskets, jewelry, pottery, and leatherwork are of greatest collector interest. Eskimo art is listed in another category in this book.

Adze, Inca, Jade Blade, Original Handle, Early 1800s, 8 1/2 In.	415.00
Armband, Blackfoot, Deer Hide & Hoof, Beaded Trim, Moon Shells, 14 x 5 In.	120.00
Armband, Sioux, Quilled, 14 1/2 In.	560.00
Awl Case, Apache, Mescalero, Beaded, Hide, Tapered Body, c.1900, 17 In.	765.00
Awl Case, Plains, Beaded, Feather & Cone Drops, Early 1900s, 13 In.	145.00
Awl Case, Plains, Beaded, Hide, Cone Danglers, Late 19th Century, 18 In.	765.00
Awl Case, Sioux, Lakota, Plains, 8 5/8 In.	165.00
Ax, Huron, French Trade, 1 Cross Cartouche Mark, c.1600, 7 In.	300.00

Bag, Apache, Beaded, Hide, Beaded Fringe, c.1940, 8 1/2 x 7 In. 275.00
Bag, Central Plains, Beaded, Hide, Box, Border Design, Late 19th Century, 18 In. 4115.00
Bag, Cheyenne, Beaded, Painted, Leather, Bow Tie, Stripe Pattern, c.1870, 10 1/2 In. 3055.00
Bag, Chippewa, Great Lakes, Felt, Beaded Fringe, Design, Northwest Wisconsin, c.1885 . 110.00
Bag, Crow, Pipe, Beaded, Tube Beads, Fringe, 1940s, 37 x 6 In. 825.00
Bag, Nez Perce, Corn Husk, Geometric Designs, Green, Red, Yellow, 1880s, 7 1/2 x 7 In.. 385.00
Bag, Northwest, Hide, Beaded, U-Shape, Abstract Flowers, Ribbon, c.1900, 7 In. 175.00
Bag, Ojibwa, Bandolier, Beaded, Geometric Designs, Late 19th Century, 42 In. 2820.00
Bag, Plains, Beaded Sides, Fringe, Beaded Drop, 1870s, 10 In. 468.00
Bag, Plateau, Beaded, 2 Bears Fighting, Bald Eagle, Trees, 14 x 11 In. 330.00
Bag, Plateau, Beaded, Geometric, Flowers, Beaded Fringe, 1920s, 10 x 6 In. 300.00
Bag, Plateau, Beaded, Indian On Horse, c.1920, 15 x 13 In....................... 825.00
Bag, Plateau, Bull Elk, Trees, Beaded, c.1940, 13 x 12 In. 415.00
Bag, Sioux, Hide, Fringed Horseshoe Shape, Beaded, c.1900, 11 In. 705.00
Bag, Sioux, Rawhide, Quilled Purple Horse, Geometric Designs, 10 x 7 1/2 In. 1540.00
Bag, Sioux, Strike-A-Light, White, Red, Brown & Black Design, c.1870, 6 x 2 In. 595.00
Bag, Sioux, Tobacco, Quilted Hide, Thread Sewn Beads, Fringe, c.1880, 35 In. 4600.00
Bag, Tobacco, Animal Hide, Beaded, Fringe, 22 x 6 1/2 In. 2530.00
Bandolier, Chippewa, Beaded, Flowers, Cotton Lined, Fringes, 18 x 14 1/4 In. 1725.00
Bandolier, Ojibwa, Flowers, c.1900, 37 x 12 In. 1540.00
Basket, Apache, Alternating Triangles, c.1900, 16 In. 2200.00
Basket, Apache, Bowl Shape, Pictorial, Figures, Animals, Geometric, 15 3/8 In. 3850.00
Basket, Apache, Bowl, Coiled, Stacked Triangles, c.1920, 17 In. 1645.00
Basket, Apache, Bowl, Coiled, Whirlwind Pattern, Stylized Dogs, c.1900, 16 1/2 In. 4700.00
Basket, Apache, Burden, Hide Trim, Tin Cones, 1970, 7 x 5 In. 75.00
Basket, Apache, Coiled, Devil Claw, Radiating Star Center, Dogs, People, 14 3/4 In. 4025.00
Basket, Apache, Coiled, Polychrome, Radiating Lines, 9 1/2 x 3 In. 190.00
Basket, Apache, Dish Shape, 3 Figures, 19th Century, 4 1/2 In. 865.00
Basket, Apache, Miscalero, c.1920, 19 5/8 x 13 1/4 In. 2200.00
Basket, Apache, Tray, Figure In Maze, 7 1/4 In. 805.00
Basket, Apache, Twined, Fringe, Color Design, c.1900, 14 1/2 x 11 In. 500.00
Basket, Apache, Twined, Fringe, Tin Cone Suspension, c.1970, 14 1/2 x 11 In. 110.00
Basket, Apache, Willow & Devil's Claw, People & Animals, 1886, 17 3/4 In. 4830.00
Basket, Apache, Woven, Dogs, Central Star Design, c.1940, 11 1/2 x 2 In. 300.00
Basket, Bowl, Pima, Flared, Lizard Patterns, c.1900, 9 1/2 In. 235.00
Basket, Chippewa, Storage, c.1970, 14 1/2 x 10 In. 39.00
Basket, Cover, Geometric Design, Cone Shaped, Zigzag Pattern, 9 x 4 1/2 In. 575.00
Basket, Cover, Pima, Oval, Squares Forming Diamonds, 1 7/8 x 1 7/8 In. 834.00
Basket, Cowlitz, Twined, Fringe, Tin Cone Suspensions, 20 x 12 In. 187.00
Basket, Eastern Woodland, Splint, Potato Stamp, 19th Century, 5 x 13 x 19 In. 470.00
Basket, Fraser River, Coiled, Imbricated, Geometric, Lid, Late 19th Century, 30 In. 940.00
Basket, Great Lakes, Lid, 8 x 5 1/2 In. 40.00
Basket, Havasupai, Star & Arrowhead, c.1920, 2 1/2 x 11 1/2 In. 470.00
Basket, Hopi, Plaited, Spirit Release Line, c.1920, 15 x 12 In. 575.00
Basket, Hupa, Northern California, 1890s, 7 In. 825.00
Basket, Iroquois, Birch & Elm, Sweet Grass Lacings, Panels, 9 1/2 In. 400.00
Basket, Klickitat, Woven, Imbricated Geometric, c.1880, 14 x 14 In. 750.00
Basket, Klickitat, Woven, Rim Loops, Radiating Snake Design, c.1920, 7 x 8 In. 550.00
Basket, Lid, Green, Brown, Red Duck Designs, 2 1/2 x 4 In. 110.00
Basket, Lilooet, Imbricated Step Design, Rectangular, 7 x 9 x 11 In. 440.00
Basket, Maidu, Bowl, Coiled, Wishbone Pattern, Natural Ground, 6 1/4 In. 646.00
Basket, Maidu, Coiled, Round, Red Triangles, Star On Bottom, c.1920, 5 1/2 x 3 In. 250.00
Basket, Makah, Polychrome, Twined, Lid, Eagle, Arrows, 3 In. 558.00
Basket, Mission, Bowl, Coiled, Interlocking Box Pattern, 19th Century, 5 1/2 In. 294.00
Basket, Mission, Coiled, Black, Design, c.1930, 10 x 12 In. 200.00
Basket, Mission, Polychrome, Gap Stitch, c.1930, 4 1/2 x 6 In. 65.00
Basket, Mono, Bowl, Coiled, Floating Diamond Bands, Late 19th Century, 18 In. 4113.00
Basket, Navajo, Coiled, Black & Brown Crosses, c.1980, 14 In. .... *Illus* 198.00
Basket, Northern Californian, Lid, Twined, Polychrome, c.1900, 6 In. 4994.00
Basket, Ojibway, Birch Bark, Incised Birds & Flowers, Lid, Loop Handle, Straps, 26 In. . 360.00
Basket, Paiute, Coiled, Brown Stepped Design, c.1920, 7 x 4 In. 325.00
Basket, Paiute, Jar, Water, Pinnon Pitch, Globe Shape, Shell Around Neck, 7 x 8 In. 275.00
Basket, Panamint, Coiled, Black Geometrics, Star On Bottom, 3 x 8 3/4 In. 3300.00

Basket, Panamint, Coiled, Negative Cross, c.1930, 10 x 4 1/4 In. 880.00
Basket, Papago, Coiled, Geometric Design, Handles, Round, c.1950, 12 x 1 1/2 In. 60.00
Basket, Papago, Coiled, Row Of Friendship Figures, c.1960, 10 x 8 In. 170.00
Basket, Papago, Overall Geometric Design, 15 x 23 In. 2588.00
Basket, Pima, Black & White Geometric, 5 In. 345.00
Basket, Pima, Bowl, Coiled, Stepped Geometric Pattern, Early 20th Century, 9 1/4 In. . . .   264.00
Basket, Pima, Chicken Design, 7 1/8 In. 275.00
Basket, Pima, Coiled, Fret Design, c.1920, 14 x 2 1/2 In. 300.00
Basket, Pima, Geometric Design, Turquoise & White Beads, Cylindrical, 3 In. 201.00
Basket, Pima, Maricopa, Coiled, Round, c.1920, 10 x 3 1/2 In.   450.00
Basket, Pima, Southwest, Inverted Triangle Design, 9 In. 358.00
Basket, Pima, Swan Design, 3 1/4 In., Miniature 165.00
Basket, Pit River, c.1920, 8 x 13 In. . . . . *Illus*   990.00
Basket, Pit River, Twined, Redbud, Flying Geese & Stepped Designs, c.1910, 7 x 12 In. .   825.00
Basket, Pomo, Bowl, Coiled, Compressed Oval, Lightning Pattern, c.1900, 6 3/4 In. 353.00
Basket, Pomo, Bowl, Coiled, Round, Interlocking Stepped Diamond Pattern, 5 1/2 In. 705.00
Basket, Pomo, Bowl, Twined, Bulbous, Geometric Bands, Late 19th Century, 7 In. 411.00
Basket, Pomo, Coiled, Feathered, Quail Top Knot, Shell Bead Trim, M. McKay, 4 1/2 In. .   1980.00
Basket, Pomo, Shallow Bowl, Cover, Yellow & Black Feathers, 7/8 x 7/8 In. 248.00
Basket, Rawhide, Painted, Handle, Lid, 19th Century, 4 x 9 3/4 In. 288.00
Basket, Salish, Trunk, Lid, Pink & Yellow Geometrics, 11 x 6 1/2 x 6 In. 305.00
Basket, Salish, Urn Shape, c.1900, 13 1/2 x 13 In. 5175.00
Basket, Southwest, Cone Shape, Brown & White, 11 3/4 In. 145.00
Basket, Thompson River, Coiled, Flared, Imbricated Bands, 19th Century, 9 1/2 In. 295.00
Basket, Tlingit, Orange, Brown, Tan, Natural, c.1920, 4 x 3 1/2 In. 660.00
Basket, Tlingit, Rattle Top, Twined, Polychrome, Lid, Branded Fret Pattern, 3 1/4 In. 705.00
Basket, Tlingit, Twined, Polychrome, Rattle Top, Lid, Trellis Weave, 5 1/4 In. 1060.00
Basket, Washo, Bead Covered, Coiled, Spider Design, c.1920, 3 1/2 x 5 In. . . . . *Illus*   770.00
Basket, Washo, Coiled, Arrows, Butterflies, Sarah Jim Mayo, c.1920, 7 x 3 3/4 In. 1210.00
Basket, Winnebago, Canada, 3 1/4 x 3 5/8 In. 110.00
Basket, Yauapai, Stained, Line Design, 10 x 6 In. 145.00
Basket, Yokuts, Bowl, Coiled, Flared, Stepped Pattern, Late 19th Century, 7 In. 2820.00
Basket, Yokuts, Bowl, Coiled, Interlocking Diamonds, Late 19th Century, 6 3/4 In. 3290.00
Basket, Yokuts, Bowl, Coiled, Interlocking Diamonds, Late 19th Century, 16 1/4 In. 1645.00
Basket, Yokuts, Bowl, Polychrome, c.1920, 3 1/2 x 1 1/2 In. 935.00
Basket, Yokuts, Jar, Coiled, Diagonal Stepped Geometric Pattern, c.1900, 6 In. 880.00
Basket, Yokuts, Rows Of Rattlesnakes, Round, 11 x 5 In. 2750.00
Basket, Yurok, Twined Bowl, Open Edge, Stair Step Design, c.1890, 10 1/2 x 5 In. 1400.00
Basket, Yurok, Twined, Open Edge, Stair Step, 10 1/2 x 5 In. 1540.00
Bean Pot, Taos, Pottery, Loop Handle, Lid, c.1940, 9 1/2 x 7 In.   165.00
Belt, Beaded, Alternating Triangles & Crosses, Blue, Red, White, 1890s, 30 1/2 In. 440.00
Belt, Beaded, Arrowheads, Crosses, Tack Borders, Men's, 1900s 105.00
Belt, Beaded, Heart Design, Red, Blue, White, Woman's, 33 x 1 3/8 In. 120.00
Belt, Beaded, Porcupine Quills, Bells, c.1900, 39 In. 460.00
Belt, Crow, Panel, Beaded & Tacked, Split Tail, c.1900, 1 1/2 x 65 In. 440.00
Belt, Navajo, 5 Oval Silver Conchas, 6 Silver Butterflies, Square Buckle, c.1950, 36 In. . .   305.00

Indian, Basket, Navajo, Coiled,
Black & Brown Crosses,
c.1980, 14 In.

Indian, Basket,
Pit River, c.1920,
8 x 13 In.

Indian, Basket, Washo, Bead
Covered, Coiled, Spider Design,
c.1920, 3 1/2 x 5 In.

Belt, Navajo, 6 Conchas, Sterling Buckle, Turquoise Hinge Plates, M. Begay, 38 In.	1840.00
Belt, Navajo, 8 Conchas, Buckle, 39 In.	190.00
Belt, Navajo, Concha, Silver, Turquoise, 12 Conchas, Buckle, J.W. Tom, 40 1/2 In.	215.00
Belt, Navajo, Concha, Silver, Turquoise, Scalloped, Repousse, c.1930, 42 1/2 In.	1765.00
Belt, Navajo, Silver, 5 Conchas, 1 Stone In Each, Butterflies In Buckle, 3 x 39 In.	825.00
Belt, Northern Calif. Coast, Dance, Leather, Carved Dew Claw Rattles, 35 In.	440.00
Belt, Plains, German Silver, Leather, 19th Century, 26 In.	175.00
Belt Buckle, Hopi, Silver, Turquoise, Eagle Dancer, Kachina Form, 2 3/4 x 3 1/2 In.	330.00
Blanket, Chimayo, Red, Central Lozenge Pattern, 82 x 52 In.	154.00
Blanket, Navajo, Cream Field, Geometric, Brown, Red, 40 x 62 In.	460.00
Blanket, Navajo, Crystal, Hand Loomed, 46 x 66 In.	470.00
Blanket, Navajo, Saddle, Diamond, Zigzag Design, c.1920, Single	950.00
Blanket, Navajo, Transitional, Repeating Geometrics, 1920s, 48 x 91 In.	550.00
Blanket, Navajo, Yei, Wool, Ivory, Brown, Standing Woman, 20th Century, 16 x 30 In. . .	315.00
Blanket, Pawnee, Saddle, Beaded, Brass Bells, c.1900, 35 x 35 In.	190.00
Blanket, Rio Grande, Purple, Yellow & White Lines, c.1920, 79 x 45 In.	360.00
Blanket, Rio Grande, Red & Yellow Lines, c.1900, 54 x 84 In.	470.00
Bolo Tie, Hopi, Silver Overlay, Kachina Mudhead, Laurence Saufkie, 3 In.	200.00
Bolo Tie, Zuni, Inlaid, Red Cardinal, Dennis Edaakie, 2 1/4 In.	190.00
Bolo Tie, Zuni, Large Jet Stone, Surrounded By Turquoise Cabochons, 18 In.	145.00
Bonnet, Apache, Horned, Ermine Drops, Brass Tacks, Cloth Drop, 1870s, 23 x 14 In. . . .	1100.00
Bonnet, Sioux, Turkey Feathers, Wig & Braid, 1920s, Full Size	605.00
Bottle, Apache Southwest, Water, Pitch Covered, 15 1/2 In.	580.00
Bottle, Apache Southwest, Water, Pitch, Leather Straps, 13 1/4 In.	415.00
Bottle, Klamath, Basket Cover, Geometrics, Dark Brown, 7 In.	415.00
Bottle, Paiute, Beaded, Stopper, Hide Bottom, c.1930, 7 1/2 x 2 1/2 In.	825.00
Bottle, San Ildefonso, Wedding, c.1910, 8 x 6 1/2 In.	800.00
Bottle, Wasco, Whiskey, Beaded, Stopper, Bottom, c.1930, 6 x 2 1/2 In.	385.00
Bottle, Washo, Basket Cover, Brown Lines, 9 1/2 In.	300.00
Bow, Plains, Wood, Sinew, c.1870, 40 In.	1100.00
Bow, Wood, Painted, Yellow, Green, 41 3/4 In.	550.00
Bowl, Anaszi, Pottery, Black On White, Geometric Painted Design, 7 x 3 In.	160.00
Bowl, Apache, Basketry, Coiled, Crosses & Triangles, 18 x 5 In.	1430.00
Bowl, Great Lakes, Effigy, Turtle, Stylized Head, Tail, Early 1800, 13 1/2 In.	1530.00
Bowl, Hopi, Polychrome, Stylized Butterflies, Abstract Feather, Contemporary, 4 In.	1060.00
Bowl, Hopi, Polychrome, Stylized Feather Pattern, 20th Century, 4 1/2 In.	600.00
Bowl, Hupa Mush, Negative Design, c.1915, 3 1/2 x 7 1/2 In.	360.00
Bowl, Hupa, Arrowpoint & Hourglass Designs, c.1900, 5 x 7 In.	300.00
Bowl, Hupa, Twined Basketry, Geometric Bands, Early 20th Century, 6 1/2 In.	380.00
Bowl, Karok, Twined, Black Geometric, c.1910, 3 x 4 1/2 In.	358.00
Bowl, Klamath, Twined Basketry, Arrow Designs, Early 20th Century, 9 1/2 In.	175.00
Bowl, Klickitat Basketry, Scalloped Rim, Human Life, c.1920, 7 x 13 In.	440.00
Bowl, Maricopa, Effigy, Polychrome, 3 Frogs On Outside, c.1920, 7 x 5 1/2 In.	990.00
Bowl, Mission, Coiled, Fret Band, Multicolored Ground, Late 19th Century, 18 1/2 In. . . .	294.00
Bowl, Northern Californian, Twined, Globe Shape, Geometric Pattern, 3 In.	823.00
Bowl, Northwest Coast, Effigy, Inlaid Wood, Mother-Of-Pearl, 20th Century, 18 In.	978.00
Bowl, Olla, Red, Dark Brown, Red Field, Marked El Concho, 9 1/4 x 12 In.	715.00
Bowl, Pima, Basketry, Fine Weave, Geometric Cross, Beadwork, 19th Century, 7 1/8 In. . .	750.00
Bowl, San Ildefonso, Shallow, Polished, Marie & Julian, 8 3/4 In.	1538.00
Bowl, Santa Clara, Blackware, Polished, Signed, P. Naranjo, c.1940, 2 1/2 x 11 1/2 In. . . .	305.00
Bowl, Santa Clara, Blackware, Swirls, Terasita Naranjo, 6 1/4 In.	520.00
Bowl, Santa Clara, Melon Design, Signed, Camelo Tafoya, c.1960, 4 1/2 x 7 1/2 In.	193.00
Bowl, Santo Domingo, Black On Cream, Signed Paulita Pacherco, 4 x 13 1/2 In.	275.00
Bowl, Santo Domingo, Flaring, Black On Cream, Early 20th Century, 14 In.	2233.00
Bowl, Santo Domingo, Pottery, Black On Cream, c.1950, 5 x 8 1/2 In.	165.00
Bowl, Tlingit, Twined, Polychrome, Basketry, Fret Stacked Diamonds, 6 1/4 In.	1000.00
Bowl, Washo, Coiled Basketry, Zigzag Pattern, c.1900, 6 1/4 In.	295.00
Bowl, Yokuts, Coiled, Tulare, Red & Black Rattlesnake Band, c.1920, 3 x 7 1/2 In.	525.00
Bowl, Yokuts, Polychrome, Coiled Basketry, 19th Century, 9 1/2 In.	1295.00
Bowl, Yurok, Twined, Reddish Split Parallelogram Designs, c.1910, 4 1/4 x 4 1/2 In.	440.00
Bowl, Zuni, Fetish, Polychrome, Dragonflies, c.1955, 3 1/2 x 6 1/2 In.	195.00
Box, Birch Bark, Quill, Lid, c.1900, 3 1/2 x 5 1/2 x 8 3/4 In.	230.00
Box, Birch Bark, Quill, Zigzag Design, c.1940, 4 1/2 x 5 x 9 In.	460.00

Box, Eastern, Birch Bark, Lid, 19th Century, 6 x 4 In. 175.00
Box, Micmac, Quilled, Bark, Dome Lid, Chevron & Lattice, Mid 19th Century, 10 In. 5580.00
Box, Woodlands, Birch Bark, Moose Hair, Embroidered, Flowers, 3 1/4 In. 235.00
Bracelet, Laloma, Cuff, Silver, Carved Coral Bird, Square-Cut Side Stones, 3 x 4 In. 415.00
Bracelet, Navajo, 3 Spider Webs, Turquoise Stones, Stamped, c.1960, 2 1/2 In. 1210.00
Bracelet, Navajo, 9 Turquoise Stones, E-Wire Shank, c.1930-40 .... 250.00
Bracelet, Navajo, Cluster, 19 Turquoise Stones, c.1940, 1 1/2 In. 275.00
Bracelet, Navajo, Cuff, Silver, Hammered, Stamped, c.1940, 7 In. 209.00
Bracelet, Navajo, Cuff, Turquoise Stones, Stamped Design, c.1950, 2 In. 99.00
Bracelet, Navajo, Green Turquoise Cluster, Ingot Silver, c.1940, 1 3/4 In. 660.00
Bracelet, Navajo, Row, 4 Shanks, Square Turquoise Stones, c.1950, 2 In. 250.00
Bracelet, Navajo, Silver, 1 Blue Gem Turquoise Stone, Signed, M.P., c.1950, 9 In. 525.00
Bracelet, Navajo, Silver, Hammered, 27 Nevada Green Turquoise Stones, c.1940, 8 In. .. 550.00
Bracelet, Navajo, Silver, Turquoise, Cluster, 76 Stones, c.1940, 6 1/4 x 2 1/2 In. 120.00
Bracelet, Navajo, Split Shank, Ingot Silver, Turquoise, c.1930, 1 In. 660.00
Bracelet, Navajo, Sterling Silver, Square Turquoise Stones, c.1950, 1 1/4 x 2 1/2 In. 360.00
Bracelet, Navajo, Sterling Silver, Turquoise Stone, c.1960, 2 1/2 x 2 1/2 In. 140.00
Bracelet, Northwest Coast, Silver, Hook & Eye Clasp, 1 1/2-In. Wide 2645.00
Bracelet, Zuni, Silver & Turquoise, Petit Point, Woman's, 2 3/4 In. 150.00
Bracelet, Zuni, Silver, Turquoise, Coral, Jet Channel Inlay, 8 In. 360.00
Bridle, Cheyenne, Beaded, Reins, c.1900, 104 In. 220.00
Bridle, Navajo, Silver Mounted, Silver Bit, c.1930 .... 935.00
Buckle, Zuni, Silver, Inlaid Thunderbird, Bobby & Corraine Schock, 3 x 2 In. 220.00
Canoe, Birch Bark, Quill Decorated, 19th Century, 34 In. 920.00
Canoe, Ojibwa, Birch Bark, Ely, Minnesota, Early To Mid 1900s, 74 In. 300.00
Canteen, Acoma, Parrot Design, Flattened Bulbous, 2 Twist Handles, 11 In. 410.00
Canteen, Acoma, Polychrome Bird Design, c.1950, 10 1/2 x 10 x 8 In. 605.00
Canteen, Hopi, Black On Red, c.1910, 7 x 7 1/2 In. 715.00
Canteen, Navajo, Silver, 2 Incised Steer Heads, 3 1/4 In. 330.00
Canteen, Navajo, Silver, Engraved, Turquoise Nugget On Each Side, 4 In. 195.00
Canteen, Navajo, Silver, Star, Crescent Design, 3 3/4 In. 385.00
Canteen, Zuni, Geometric Designs, All Red Reverse, Polychrome, Woven Strap, 8 In. ... 5175.00
Charm Bag, Great Lakes, Beaded, Thunderbirds, Late 19th Century, 2 1/2 x 2 1/2 In. 1295.00
Charm Bag, Great Lakes, Finger Woven, Panther, Late 19th Century, 2 3/4 x 3 3/4 In. 1765.00
Charm Bag, Great Lakes, Wool, Beaded, Otter Tail Pattern, Late 19th Century, 6 1/2 In. ... 1528.00
Cigarette Case, Navajo, Silver, Thunderbird, Bisbee Stone, Coral, c.1940, 3 x 2 x 5/8 In. .. 190.00
Club, Beaded, Animal Hide, Horsetail, 2 Feathers, 1900s, 56 In. 250.00
Club, Central Plains, Skull Cracker, Stone, Quilled, Late 19th Century, 26 1/2 In. 2585.00
Club, Cheyenne, Great Head Effigy Ceremonial War, Parfleche Handle, 15 In. 1540.00
Club, Iroquois, Wood, Metal, Ball Head, Tack Decoration, Mid 19th Century, 13 1/2 In. ... 3525.00
Club, Penobscot, Ball Headed Root, Anthropomorphic, Human Face, Tack Eyes, 21 In. 195.00
Club, Penobscot, Face, Large Nose, Furrowed Brow, Notch Carved Handle, 29 In. 1670.00
Club, Penobscot, Root, Carved, Painted, Indian Profile, Chief Wolf, 33 In. 764.00
Club, Plains, Ball, Horsehair Drop, 1880s, 36 In. 275.00
Club, War, Double Pointed, Beaded Handle, c.1890, 18 1/2 In. 410.00
Club, War, Northern Plains, Catlinite, Beaded Rawhide Handle, Fringed Drop, 35 In. 1210.00
Coat, Chief's, Mooshide, Floral Beadwork, Shawl Collar, c.1930 .... 415.00
Collar, Red Velvet Field, Flowers, Bugle Beads, 20 x 26 1/2 In. 220.00
Comb, Bone, 7 1/4 In. 190.00
Cradle, Doll, Hupa, Twined, 22 x 9 x 5 In. 175.00
Cradleboard, Apache, Pine, Bentwood Frame, Wicker Visor, c.1920, 36 x 13 1/2 x 10 In. .. 495.00
Cradleboard, Cheyenne, Stylized Flowers & Geometric Beadwork, 18 x 6 In. 715.00
Cradleboard, Plains, Doll Carrier, 23 1/2 In. 605.00
Cradleboard, Plateau, Floral Beadwork, Beaded Trim, Fringe, 10 x 4 In. 305.00
Cradleboard, Sioux, Geometric Beadwork, 44 1/2 x 11 x 10 In. 990.00
Cradleboard, Ute, Yellow Ocher, c.1900, 42 x 20 In. 3850.00
Cup, Pima, Basketry, Fine Weave, Bead Trim, Footed, 2 1/2 In. 290.00
Doll, Central Plains, Warrior, Headdress, Fringed Outfit, Beaded Bag, 15 In. 1100.00
Doll, Comanche, Beaded, Hide, Fringed Buckskin Shirt, Leggings, c.1900, 8 In. 2000.00
Doll, Crow, Muslin Body, Beaded Dress, Moccasins & Bag, Human Hair, 11 In. 1320.00
Doll, Iroquois, Carved Wood, Polychrome, Cloth & Hide, Beaded, Cradle, 1800s, 13 In. ... 8225.00
Doll, Lakota, Beaded Cloth, Hide, Buckskin Dress, Late 19th Century, 12 In. 1880.00
Doll, Paper Face, Black Bead Eyes, Mohair Wig, Wood Feet, M.F. Woods, 15 In. 1300.00

Doll, Plains, Hide, Beaded Cloth Dress & Moccasins, Beaded Cradleboard, 12 x 8 In. 770.00
Doll, Plains, Rawhide, Beaded Shirt, Pants, Moccasins, 19th Century, 12 In. 900.00
Doll, Seminole, Traditional Dress, c.1950, 18 In. 85.00
Doll, Skookum, Display, Chief, Beaded Clothes, Woven Blanket, 36 In. 1400.00
Doll, Skookum, Traditional Dress, c.1930, 36 In. 1320.00
Doll, Skookum, Wearing Blanket, c.1920, 9 1/4 In. 90.00
Dress, Cheyenne, Hide, Beaded, Hawks, Bells, Child's, c.1930, 37 x 16 In. 275.00
Dress, Lakota, Trade Cloth, Ribbonwork, Cowrie Shells, Late 19th Century, 52 In. 940.00
Dress, Northern Plains, Deerskin, Scalloped Neck, Fringe, Woman's, 1884 .... 9775.00
Dress, Plateau, Brain-Tanned Buckskin, Beaded, c.1920, 30 x 29 In. 1430.00
Dress, Plateau, Crow, Trade Cloth, Carved Bone, Elk Teeth, c.1920, 47 x 34 In. 415.00
Dress, Plateau, Red, 7-Row Cowrie Shell Yoke, c.1920 .... 470.00
Dress, Sioux, Wool, Cowrie Shell, c.1910, 9 In. 60.00
Drum, Animal Hide, Painted Wood, 11 1/4 x 11 In. 290.00
Drum, Hopi, Face, Orange, Green, Yellow, Turquoise, Pink, c.1960, 11 x 11 1/2 In. 360.00
Drum, Northern Plains, Hide, Polychrome, Wood Hoop, Buffalo Center, Leather Handle . 2590.00
Drum, Plains, Warrior, Wooden, Rawhide, Round Hoop, Early 20th Century, 13 In. 560.00
Drum, Pueblo, Dance, Blue, White, Black, c.1960, 18 x 8 In. 220.00
Drum, Pueblo, Hide Cover, c.1950, 18 x 17 In. 190.00
Drum, Pueblo, Yellow, Red, Natural, c.1950, 13 x 11 In. 330.00
Earrings, Navajo, Coral & Silver, Drop, Silver Bead Suspensions, 1 1/2 x 3/4 In. 90.00
Earrings, Navajo, Turquoise, Single Stone, Silver, 1 1/2 x 3/4 In. 70.00
Effigy, Haida, Northwest, Wooden, Carved, Totem, c.1890, 8 3/4 In. 120.00
Effigy, Totem, Northwest Coast, Early 1900s, 11 1/2 In. 330.00
Fetish, Plains, Beaded, Cone Dangles, 1890s, 5 1/4 In. 330.00
Fetish, Sioux, Lizard, Beaded, 1890s, 7 5/8 In. 265.00
Fork, Navajo, Serving, Silver, Stamped Design, c.1940, 8 1/2 x 2 1/2 In. 110.00
Gloves, Animal Hide, Beaded Floral, Leaves, Fringe, Cuffs, c.1900, 12 In. 230.00
Hairpin, Iroquois, Bone, 4 1/2 In. 440.00
Hat, Iroquois, Beaded Flower, Large Beads, c.1890, 5 x 11 x 5 1/2 In. 220.00
Hat, Northern California, Twined Basketry, Geometric Designs, 6 3/4 In. 590.00
Hat, Northwest California, Twined Basketry, Polychrome, Parallelograms, 7 In. 470.00
Hat Band, Navajo, Link Concha, Thunderbirds, Arrows, Buckle, c.1940, 21 In. 195.00
Headdress, Blackfoot, Split Horn Bonnet, Ermine Crown, Beaded Brow Band, 27 x 13 In. 3025.00
Headdress, Ceremonial, Porcupine Quill, c.1900, 8 In. 315.00
Jacket, Blackfoot, Buckskin, Beaded, Fringe, 31 x 40 In. 1870.00
Jacket, Chimaya, Gray Wool, Diamond, Men's, Size 44 .... *Illus* 150.00
Jacket, Scout, Santee Sioux, Beaded, Child's 11500.00
Jar, Acoma, Black, White, c.1920, 5 1/2 x 6 1/2 In. 330.00
Jar, Acoma, Globe Shape, Tapered Neck, Polychrome Early 20th Century, 12 In. 880.00
Jar, Acoma, Orange & Brown Slip, Diamonds, Zigzags, 1920s, 7 x 9 In. 495.00
Jar, Acoma, Parrot & Leaves, Orange & Black, Buff Slip, Signed, 6 x 6 In. 250.00
Jar, Black & Red, Feathers, Beige Slip Field, Marked Tavo Siveira, 14 3/4 In. 185.00
Jar, Black Matte, Flared Rim, Geometric, Marked Lety Lopez, 4 3/4 x 7 In. 825.00
Jar, Blackware, Feathers, Marked, Alonso Sandoval, 7 1/2 In. 470.00
Jar, Hohokam, Corrugated, N.E. Arizona, 1100 A.D., 8 1/4 x 7 1/2 In. 550.00
Jar, Hopi, Frog Woman, Geometric Design, Buff Ground, 4 1/2 x 6 1/2 In. 580.00
Jar, Hopi, Swirled Geometric, Brown & Red, Buff Ground, F. Nampeyo, 3 1/2 In. 770.00
Jar, Iroquois, Incised, Face, 4 1/2 x 4 In. 2860.00
Jar, Oval, Blackware, Geometric, Fish, Snakes, Birds, 6 3/4 In. 165.00
Jar, Polished & Matte Blackware, Checkerboard, Signed, Chela Ortiz, 8 In. 1320.00
Jar, San Ildefonso, Black On Red, Flowers, Triangles, c.1920, 9 1/4 x 11 In. 6325.00
Jar, San Ildefonso, Blackware, Matte, Signed, Anna, c.1930, 5 1/2 x 5 1/2 In. 495.00
Jar, Santa Clara, Blackware, Polished, c.1890, 12 x 11 1/2 In. 5175.00
Jar, Santa Clara, Double Spout, Wedding, 12 In. 4115.00
Jar, Santa Clara, Globe Shape, Paw Prints, Polished, 20th Century, 9 In. 500.00
Jar, Santa Domingo, Red Flowers, White Ground, Globe Shape, Flared Lip, 7 x 6 In. 115.00
Jar, Zia, Polychrome, Painted, Cream Ground, Stylized Bird, Flowers, 15 In. 705.00
Jar, Zuni, Polychrome, Black Designs On Cream, Red Interior, 9 x 11 In. 11500.00
Kachina, Hopi, Buli Mana, Cloud Symbols, Sunflowers, 13 In. 780.00
Kachina, Hopi, Mountain Sheep, Black Kilt, Bill Sewemaenewa, 15 1/4 In. 250.00
Kachina, Hopi, Polychrome, Wooden, Carved, Early 20th Century, 9 1/2 In. 1293.00
Kachina, Hopi, Polychrome, Wooden, Carved, Mid 20th Century, 11 In. 650.00

Kachina, Hopi, White Buffalo Dancer Of Kocha Mosairv, Earl Yowytewa, 9 3/4 In. 240.00
Kachina, Hopi, Zuni Kachina's Uncle, Squash Shape Mask, 9 3/4 In. 920.00
Knife, Athabascan, Northwest Coast, Bone, Wrapped Handle, 10 In. 250.00
Knife, Iroquois, Wooden, Steel, Crooked, Carved, Hand, Pointing Finger, Heart, 8 1/2 In. . 470.00
Knife, Penobscot, Crooked, Chip Carving In Handle, 8 3/8 In. 195.00
Knife Sheath, Cree, Beaded, Hide, Tin Cone Danglers, Late 19th Century, 9 In. 4115.00
Knife Sheath, Lakota, Beaded, Hide, Rawhide Lined, Late 19th Century, 16 In. 3760.00
Knife Sheath, Plains, Beaded, Yellow On Back, 1880s, 7 1/4 In. 550.00
Knife Sheath, Plains, Beadwork, Blue, White, Red, Tan, Painted On Reverse, 15 In. 430.00
Knife Sheath, Sioux, Cone Drops, Knife, 10 3/4 In. 1430.00
Ladle, Great Lakes, Effigy, Carved Wood, Bear's Head, Brass Eyes, 9 1/4 In. 4113.00
Ladle, Hopi, Frog Motif, 1920s, 11 1/2 x 5 In. 1265.00
Ladle, Hopi, Koshari Clown, c.1930, 4 x 3 1/2 In. 330.00
Ladle, Mesa Verde, Pottery, Black On White, 2 1/2 x 5 x 11 In. 165.00
Ladle, Sac-Fox, Wooden, Carved, Hooked Handle, 19th Century, 8 In. 1530.00
Leggings, Beaded, Leather, Blue, Red, Green, Arrow, White Field, 18 In., Pair 1210.00
Leggings, Comanche, Fringed, Painted, Bead, Brass Buttons, Late 1800s 3300.00
Leggings, Crow, Women's, Beaded Panels, Wool Cloth Extensions, c.1900, 16 3/4 In. 506.00
Leggings, Ojibwa, Black, Flowers, c.1900, 29 In. 605.00
Leggings, Oto, Beaded Strips Front & Back, Wool Trade Cloth, Boy's, 25 In. 220.00
Leggings, Plains, Beaded, Trade Blanket Cloth, c.1900, 34 In. 355.00
Leggings, Shoshone, Hide, Beaded, Multicolored, Geometric, c.1940, 15 In. 330.00
Leggings, Ute, Beaded, Hide, White Ground, Side Fringe, c.1900, 36 In. 1880.00
Leggings, Winnebago, Cloth, Beaded Strip Of Black, Teepee Design, White Ground 1725.00
Leggings, Woman's, Beaded, Hide, Geometric, Hearts, Early 20th Century, 23 1/2 In. 805.00
Mask, Iroquois, False Face Society, Corn Husk, 14 In. 275.00
Mask, Northwest Coast, Carved Cedar, c.1950, 9 x 7 x 6 In. 385.00
Medicine Bag, Crow, Mountain Sheep, Sinew Sewn, Beaded, Contents, 12 x 15 In. 2475.00
Medicine Bag, Sioux, Buckskin, Quilled, Beaded, Fringe, Tin Cones, c.1920, 12 x 13 In. . 1760.00
Medicine Rattle, Northern Plains, Buffalo Hide & Hair, Dew Claws, Red Ocher, 16 In. ... 880.00
Mirror, Lakota, Dreamer's, Black-Tailed Deer, 19th Century 7500.00
Moccasins, Apache, Beaded, Hide, Hard Sole, c.1900, 10 In. 645.00
Moccasins, Arapaho, Beaded, Hide, U-Shape Vamp, Late 19th Century, 7 In. 940.00
Moccasins, Assiniboin, Rawhide, Sinew Sewn, Beaded, Diamonds & Triangles, 10 3/4 In. . 385.00
Moccasins, Athabascan, Pucker Toed, 1880s, 9 3/4 In. 550.00
Moccasins, Beaded, Blue, Red, Green, Black, White, c.1900, 10 In. 1150.00
Moccasins, Beaded, Flowers, Wool Sides, Cotton Ankle Covers, 10 In. 250.00
Moccasins, Beaded, Split Tongues, Parfleche Soles, c.1880, 3 1/2 x 10 1/2 In. 990.00
Moccasins, Blackfoot, Assiniboin, Beaded Toe Panel, c.1890, 10 1/2 In. 440.00
Moccasins, Blackfoot, Child's, Beaded, 1870s, 7 1/2 In. 825.00
Moccasins, Cayuse, Soft Sole, Beaded, Stylized Star On Toe, 9 In. 360.00
Moccasins, Central Plains, Beaded, Hide, Hard Sole, Late 19th Century, 10 In. 940.00
Moccasins, Cheyenne, Woman's, Beaded, Hide, Hard Sole, Early 20th Century, 9 In. 1495.00
Moccasins, Cheyenne, Woman's, Beaded, Hide, Hard Sole, Early 20th Century, 20 In. ... 3680.00
Moccasins, Cree, Beaded, Parfleche Soles, c.1920, 3 1/2 x 9 1/2 In. 195.00
Moccasins, Dakota, Beaded, Hide, Flowers, Hard Sole, 1860s, 10 1/2 In. 1765.00
Moccasins, Iroquois, Beaded Toes, Cloth Trim, c.1900, 1 1/2 x 4 In. 115.00
Moccasins, Kickapoo, Front Seam, Loom Beaded Panel, 9 1/2 In. 120.00
Moccasins, Kiowa, Apache, Beaded, Red, White, Blue, Yellow, c.1920, 3 x 10 In. 660.00
Moccasins, Kiowa, Hide, Glass Beads, Geometric Designs, c.1890, 9 In., Pair 695.00
Moccasins, Kiowa, High Tops, Beaded, Metal Studs, Yellow Ocher, c.1900, 19 x 9 In. ... 1540.00
Moccasins, Lakota, Beaded, Hide, Buffalo Track Design, Late 19th Century, 10 In. 4700.00
Moccasins, Lakota, Beaded, Hide, Checkered Diamond, c.1900, 9 1/2 In. 355.00
Moccasins, Northeast Woodlands, Beaded, Hide, Velvet, Early 20th Century, 9 1/4 In. 200.00
Moccasins, Ojibwa, Beaded, Cuffs & Toes, 9 1/2 In. 1100.00
Moccasins, Ojibwa, Beaded, Hide, Late 19th Century, 9 1/2 In. 382.00
Moccasins, Ojibwa, Beaded, Pink, Green, Blue, Black Flowers, 1890s, 10 In. 275.00
Moccasins, Plains, Beaded, Green, Red, White, 10 In. 715.00
Moccasins, Plains, Ceremonial, Fully Beaded, 1870s, 10 In. 2530.00
Moccasins, Plateau, Flower Beaded, Buttons, Parfleche Soles, c.1930, 8 x 9 1/2 In. 525.00
Moccasins, Quilled, Painted Parfleche Bottom, 11 1/2 In. 360.00
Moccasins, Sioux, Beaded, Blue, Red, Green, White, Crosses, c.1890, 4 x 10 In. 440.00
Moccasins, Sioux, Beaded, Dyed Quill Design, Ribbon Edged, 1880s, 9 In. 550.00

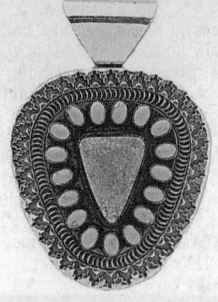

Indian, Jacket, Chimaya, Gray Wool,
Diamond, Men's, Size 44

Indian, Pendant, Navajo, Green
Turquoise, Sterling Silver,
Q. Martinez, 1950s, 3 1/2 In.

Indian, Pin, Zuni, Pendant,
Coral, Sterling Silver, Stamped,
Alvina Q., 1950s, 1 3/4 In.

Moccasins, Sioux, Buffalo Hide, High Top, Seed Beaded, Dragonflies, c.1880 . . . . 4950.00
Moccasins, Sioux, Buffalo Hide, Sinew Sewn, Buffalo Tracks, c.1880, 10 1/2 In. 825.00
Moccasins, Sioux, Child's, Quilled Beading, c.1930, 2 x 4 1/2 In. 470.00
Moccasins, Sioux, Child's, Red & Pin Quilled Design, c.1900, 2 x 5 1/2 In. 275.00
Moccasins, Sioux, Quills & Beads, 1920s 1760.00
Moccasins, Woodlands, High Top, Flower Beaded Toes, c.1940, 8 x 9 In. 85.00
Model, Canoe, Ojibway, Birch Bark, Ribbed, Incised Chieftain On Bow, 10 1/2 x 40 In. . . . 1430.00
Necklace, 6 Strands Hubbell, Coral, Turquoise Glass Beads, c.1930, 25 In. 85.00
Necklace, Crow, Beaded, Venetian Polychrome, Snake River Drainage Area, 29 In. 250.00
Necklace, Elk's Teeth, Rawhide, c.1880 . . . . 1265.00
Necklace, French Trade Beads, Cobalt, c.1790, 20 In. 410.00
Necklace, Hopi, Silver, Rainbow Man, Squash Blossom, 2 Strands, 30 In. 305.00
Necklace, Navajo, Graduated Silver Beads, Leaf Design, Turquoise Pendant, 29 In. 120.00
Necklace, Navajo, Silver & Turquoise, 6 Squash Blossoms, Open Wreath, Navajo 3450.00
Necklace, Navajo, Silver, Squash Blossom, 23 Oxblood Red Coral Stones, 27 In. 660.00
Necklace, Navajo, Squash Blossom, Silver, Turquoise Stones In Naja, c.1930, 25 In. 385.00
Necklace, Northern Plains, 67 Elk Teeth, Brass Beads, Turtle Leg Bones, 40 In. 5463.00
Necklace, Plains, Shell Disks, Blue Trade Beads, Late 19th Century, 26 In. 264.00
Necklace, Pueblo, Nugget, 3 Strands, Turquoise, Squaw Wrapped, c.1930, 27 In. 340.00
Necklace, Pueblo, Silver, Isletta Cross, 27 Small Crosses, Silver Beads, 30 In. 825.00
Necklace, Pueblo, Turquoise Nuggets, Shell Heshi, 3 Strands, c.1940, 30 In. 220.00
Necklace, Trade Beads, Blue Padre, c.1800, Oregon, 38 In. 275.00
Necklace, Trade Beads, Yellow, 1800s, 25 In. 165.00
Necklace, Turquoise, Silver, Squash Blossom, 30 In. 220.00
Necklace, Zuni, Silver, Turquoise, Needlepoint Squash Blossoms, 29 In. 440.00
Noisemaker, Navajo, Wooden, 1880s, 18 In. 85.00
Olla, Acoma, Black, White, Red, Geometric, 11 x 12 In. 4600.00
Olla, Acoma, Gila Monster Designs, Wide Shoulder, Scalloped Rim, 11 x 13 In. 248.00
Olla, Acoma, Painted, Rounded, Hatched Diamond, Geometric, c.1900, 10 In. 2235.00
Olla, Apache, Basket, Coiled, Flared, Lightning, Kite Tail Patterns, 10 1/2 In. 1410.00
Olla, Apache, Basket, Coiled, Stepped Interlocking Diamonds, c.1900, 14 In. 5290.00
Olla, Apache, Basket, Woven, Checkered Diamond, c.1920, 6 1/2 x 5 1/2 In. 1210.00
Olla, Pima, Basket, Gap Stitch, c.1930-40, 8 x 15 In. 210.00
Olla, Santa Clara, Globe Shape, Flared Neck, Abstract Arms, 16 In. 3645.00
Olla, Santo Domingo, Blackware, Flared Rim, 16 x 18 In. 525.00
Paddle, Canoe, Kwakiutl, Hand Carved, Painted, Alert Bay, 7 x 47 In. 275.00
Paddle, Northwest Coast, Wooden, Painted, 31 1/2 In. 415.00
Painting, Kiowa, Oil On Canvas, Woody Big Bow, c.1930, 17 x 14 In. 440.00
Painting, Kiowa, Warrior & Horse, Signed Al Momaday, 22 x 27 In. 1100.00
Painting, San Ildefonso, Deer, Skunk, Bird, Signed John, c.1950, 9 x 12 1/2 In. 385.00
Painting, San Ildefonso, Pen & Ink, Watercolor, Turkey, Awatsoreh, c.1920, 10 x 13 In. . . 415.00
Pendant, Navajo, Green Turquoise, Sterling Silver, Q. Martinez, 1950s, 3 1/2 In. . . . *Illus* 150.00
Pendant, Navajo, Silver, Leaf Work Edges, 16 Contour Turquoise Stones, 2 Sides, 3 In. . . 358.00
Pendant, Zuni, Turquoise, Figural, Butterfly, c.1970, 3 1/4 In. 155.00
Pin, Navajo, Silver, 1 Oval Turquoise, Surrounded By 23 Coral Stones, 1950, 3 x 2 In. . . . 250.00

Pin, Zuni, 3 Turquoise Stones, Branch Coral, Dan Simalicio, c.1950, 3 x 2 1/2 In. 605.00
Pin, Zuni, Pendant, Coral, Sterling Silver, Stamped, Alvina Q., 1950s, 1 3/4 In. . . . . . *Illus*   100.00
Pincushion, Great Lakes, Beaded, Fringed, Early 1900s, 10 In. 70.00
Pincushion, Iroquois, Great Lakes, 9 x 7 1/2 In. 95.00
Pincushion, Ojibwa, c.1900, 5 1/2 x 5 1/4 In. 40.00
Pipe, Cherokee, Effigy, Bear, Steatite, Tennessee, 3 3/8 In. 440.00
Pipe, Plains, Wood, Stone, Elbow Type Bowl, Late 19th Century, 20 In. 825.00
Pipe, Raven, Northwest Coast, Coarse Sandstone, 3 3/4 In. 2990.00
Pipe, Sandstone, Fort Ancient, Brown Co., Ohio, 1 1/2 In. 170.00
Pipe, Sioux, T Bowl & Stem, c.1900, 7 x 42 In. 715.00
Pipe, Steatite, Cloud Blower, Incised, 5 5/8 In. 880.00
Pipe, Stone, Contact Period, Washington Co., Ohio, 2 3/4 In. 70.00
Pipe Bag, Cree, Beaded, Hide, Stepped Diamond Designs, Late 19th Century, 30 In. 2235.00
Pipe Bag, Hide, Quilled Geometric Design, Quill & Hide Fringe, 6 x 32 In. 470.00
Pipe Bag, Kootenai, Beaded Flowers, Quill Wrapped Fringe, 40 x 7 In. 990.00
Pipe Bag, Lakota, Beaded, Quilled Hide, Geometric Designs, Late 19th Century, 38 In. . .   2470.00
Pipe Bag, Quilled, Beaded, 23 1/2 In. 250.00
Pipe Bag, Sioux, Beaded, Fringed, 1880s, 25 In. 2695.00
Pipe Bowl, Dakota, Effigy, Hooked Shape, Incised, Late 19th Century, 5 In. 150.00
Pipe Bowl, Ojibwa, Lead, Inlaid, Canoe Prow Shape, 19th Century, 8 1/2 In. 3820.00
Pipe Bowl, Ojibwa, Lead, Inlaid, Spider Web Design, 19th Century, 6 3/4 In. 3290.00
Pipe Bowl, Plains, Red, Elbow Shape, 19th Century, 5 In. 1880.00
Pipe Stem, Great Lakes, Puzzle, Carved, Cutouts, Tempera Paint, Inscription, 24 1/2 In. . .   4025.00
Pipe Stem, Sioux, Beaded On Entire Length, 19 In. 165.00
Pitcher, Anasazi, Pottery, Black On White, 3 1/2 x 3 1/2 In. 225.00
Pitcher, Anasazi, Pottery, Black On White, Geometric Design, 7 x 6 1/2 In. 500.00
Pitcher, Anasazi, Whiteware, Corrugated, 4 1/2 x 5 In. 150.00
Pitcher, Santo Domingo, Black On Cream, c.1940, 4 1/2 x 8 x 11 In. 415.00
Plate, San Ildefonso, Feather Design, Blackware, Marie & Santana, 14 3/4 In. 4950.00
Poncho, Navajo, Serape, Wool, Ivory, Black, Brown, 20th Century, 34 3/4 x 65 In. 259.00
Pot, Acoma, Geometric Design, White, Brown, Orange, 1920, 10 x 9 In. 1800.00
Pouch, Apache, Beaded, Hide, Drawstring, Fringe, c.1900, 11 In. 206.00
Pouch, Beaded, Animal Hide, Tassels, c.1900, 4 x 6 In. 200.00
Pouch, Beaded, Black Velvet, Floral, Vines, Fishbone Border, c.1910, 3 3/4 x 3 3/4 In. . . .   58.00
Pouch, Beaded, Crosses, Zigzags, Yellow, Black, Red, Green, c.1900, 9 x 9 In. 575.00
Pouch, Beaded, Eagle, 2 American Flags, Stars, Floral, c.1900, 10 x 8 1/2 In. 865.00
Pouch, Beaded, Floral, Blue, Red, Orange, Yellow, Green, c.1900, 11 x 9 In. 920.00
Pouch, Crow, Beaded, Leather, c.1870, 4 1/2 x 6 In. 1725.00
Pouch, Ojibwa, Plains, Charm, Beaded, 1880s, 3 1/2 In. 105.00
Pouch, Plains, Beaded, Early 1900s, 7 1/2 In. 220.00
Pouch, Plains, Beaded, Quilted Hide, Bison Head, Quillwork Flap, 6 1/2 x 5 In. 5465.00
Pouch, Shawnee, Beaded, Cloth, U-Shape, Mid 19th Century, 6 In. 825.00
Pouch, Southern Plains, Strike-A-Lite, Beaded, Leather, Trapezoid, 19th Century, 6 In. . . .   3055.00
Pouch, Ute, Beaded, Hide, Geometric Designs, Trapezoid, Late 19th Century, 7 3/4 In. . . .   645.00
Pouch, Velvet, Beaded, c.1900, 37 1/2 In. 1150.00
Powder Horn, Buffalo, Wooden Top, Beaded Tag, 1880s, 6 1/2 In. 130.00
Purse, Ojibwa, Brain Tanned, Beaded, 1880s, 11 1/2 x 6 5/8 In.   385.00
Purse, Woodlands, Beaded, 1920s, 8 x 7 1/2 In. 30.00
Rattle, Iroquois, Turtle Shell, 15 In. 145.00
Rattle, Northwest Coast, Dance, Red, Blue 575.00
Rattle, Plains, Hide, Horse Hair, Bead Drops, c.1920, 8 x 3 In. 140.00
Ring, Zuni, Knife Wing God, Stone-To-Stone, c.1940, 1 1/2 In. 250.00
Ring, Zuni, Silver, Thunderbird, 1 1/2 In. 65.00
Robe, Crow, Ceremonial, Buckskin, Beaded, c.1930, 49 x 60 In.   3300.00
Robe, Tanned Horse Hide, Painted Indian Marks, 20th Century 385.00
Rug, Diamonds, Terraced, Rolling Log, Red, Orange, Black, White, c.1900, 45 x 69 In. . .   1760.00
Rug, Navajo, 2 Gray Hills, Brown, Gray, Cream, 20th Century, 65 1/2 x 36 In. 345.00
Rug, Navajo, Banded, Browns, White, Red, 20th Century, 77 1/2 x 55 In. 520.00
Rug, Navajo, Brown, Gray Geometric Design, Cream Field, 43 x 63 In. 489.00
Rug, Navajo, Buffalo Hunt, J. Begar, c.1970, 33 x 32 In. 470.00
Rug, Navajo, Central Diamond, Black, White, Gray, Tan, Wool, c.1940, 34 x 50 In. 605.00
Rug, Navajo, Cream, Brown, Gray, Black & Gold, 1930s, 41 x 71 In. 600.00
Rug, Navajo, Crystal, Burntwater, Zigzag, Camel, Tan, Brown, Cream, 59 x 42 In. 350.00

Rug, Navajo, Crystal, Cream, Vegetable Dyed, c.1920, 82 x 56 In. 605.00
Rug, Navajo, Crystal, Ganado, Black, Gray, Cream, Zigzags, 59 1/2 x 31 3/4 In. 546.00
Rug, Navajo, Crystal, Ganado, Diamonds, Brown, Cream, Red, Camel, 62 x 37 In. 865.00
Rug, Navajo, Crystal, Whirling Logs & Feathers, 1920s, 39 x 55 In. 1155.00
Rug, Navajo, Diamonds, Stripes, Cream, Mustard, Taupe, Wool, 64 1/2 x 39 1/2 In. 460.00
Rug, Navajo, Diamonds, Swastikas, 1920s, 115 x 62 In. 1925.00
Rug, Navajo, Double Weave Ganado, Diamonds, c.1950, 24 x 36 In. 550.00
Rug, Navajo, Eye Dazzler, Orange, Red, Black & Gray Crosses, c.1910, 48 x 72 In. 825.00
Rug, Navajo, Ganado, Red, Gray, Cream, Figures, Gray Ground, 33 x 34 1/4 In. 1150.00
Rug, Navajo, Geometric Design, Initials, F.Z.R., 88 x 48 In. 635.00
Rug, Navajo, Geometric, 2 Crosses, Red, Black, Cream, 60 x 30 In. 605.00
Rug, Navajo, Geometric, Brown, Tan, Rust, 40 x 64 In. 865.00
Rug, Navajo, Geometric, Diamond, Sawtooth Border, Gray, Brown, Red, 91 x 43 In. 440.00
Rug, Navajo, Handwoven, Pictorial, Aniline Dyed Wool, 1880s, 36 x 20 In. 1500.00
Rug, Navajo, Pictorial Weaving, Feather, Arrow Point, 38 x 68 In. 1045.00
Rug, Navajo, Pictorial, Truck, Horses & Cattle, c.1970, 46 x 63 In. 660.00
Rug, Navajo, Red, Brown, White, Tan Ground, c.1900, 80 x 57 In. 550.00
Rug, Navajo, Red, Brown, Yellow, Tan, White, c.1890, 62 x 50 In. 275.00
Rug, Navajo, Repeating Descending Pattern Of Cowboys, Horses, Cattle, 82 x 56 In. 880.00
Rug, Navajo, Tan, Brown, Gray, Yellow & Green, White Ground, 1960s, 52 x 32 In. 495.00
Rug, Navajo, Tan, Brown, Gray, Yellow, Green, c.1960, 52 x 32 In. 495.00
Rug, Navajo, Two Gray Hills, Storm Pattern, Cornstalks On Ends, c.1960, 36 x 60 In. . . . 495.00
Rug, Navajo, Yei, Rainbow Colors, White Field, c.1950, 36 x 47 In. 250.00
Rug, Round, Horsehide, Quilled, Hand Sewn Seams, Scalloped Edges, 80 In. 220.00
Rug, Yei, Multicolored, c.1950, 36 x 47 In. 250.00
Sash, Loom Beaded, Geometrics, Crosses, Thunderbirds, 30 In. 66.00
Scabbard, Rifle & Bow, Buffalo Hide, Beaded, Fringe, c.1870, 46 In. 385.00
Seed Jar, Hopi, Polychrome, Stylized Feather, Geometric, 20th Century, 8 In. 1295.00
Seed Jar, Hopi, Sikyatki Revival, Black & Rust, Cream Ground, c.1895, 7 x 14 1/4 In. . . . 10925.00
Serape, Saltillo, Mexico, 2 Panel, Diamond, Zigzag Ground, Fret Border, 75 x 45 In. 1115.00
Sheath, Knife, Plains, Beaded, Brass Tacks, Knife, Painted, 1 1/8 In. 360.00
Sheath, Knife, Sioux, Pink Background, 1890s, 9 In. 550.00
Shield, Plains, War, Leather, Beaded Drops, 18 In. 220.00
Shield, War, Blackfoot, Rawhide, Painted Buffalo Design, 20th Century, 19 In. 550.00
Shirt, Blackfoot, Beaded, Cloth, Muslin, Painted, Fringe, Early 20th Century, 38 In. 3525.00
Shirt, Crow, War, Beaded, Green Stained Hide, c.1950 . . . . 900.00
Shirt, Iroquois, Flower Beaded, c.1880, 3 x 10 1/2 In. 85.00
Shirt, Sioux, Child's, Beaded On Hide, Cloth Lined, c.1930, 20 x 24 In. 85.00
Shirt, War, Lakota Sioux, Hide, Beaded Strips & Bib, Hair Trim, c.1910 . . . . 2750.00
Shirt, Winnebago, Cloth, Beaded Panels, Tassels, Ribbon Work, c.1900, 35 In. 2235.00
Snowshoes, Cree, Moose Hide, Rawhide Laces, Red Wool Tassels, 33 x 9 1/2 In. 415.00
Snowshoes, Cree, Wooden Frame, Hide Webbing, Germantown Yarn, c.1900, 42 x 11 In. . 140.00
Snowshoes, Penobscot, Child's, 1880s, 30 In. 300.00
Spoon, Northeast, Effigy, Carved Wood, Beaver Shape, 8 In. 705.00
Spoon, Northwest Coast, Sheep Horn 690.00
Spoon, Tiger Maple, Flattened Bowl, c.1860, 10 1/2 In. 165.00
Spoon Set, Iced Tea, Navajo, Silver, Kachina Design On Handle, 7 1/4 In., 6 Piece 176.00
Tapestry, Navajo, Pictorial, Skin Walker, Animals, Stars, Figures, 52 x 32 In. 495.00
Tepee, Blackfoot, Painted Hide, Buffalo, Beaded Trim, Tine Cones, Miniature Model 550.00
Tomahawk, Northeast, Pipe, Forged Head, 4 Pierced Holes, 18 1/2 In. 940.00
Tomahawk, Plains, Pipe, Cast Steel Head, File Branded & Pierced Handle, 24 In. 11500.00
Tomahawk, Sioux, Pipe, Iron Pipe, Ax, Fire Burned Handle, Horsehair Drop, 8 x 37 In. . . 1430.00
Totem Pole, Northwest Coast, Cedar, Carved, Painted, Removable Wings, 14 1/2 x 10 In. 140.00
Trade Beads, Chevron, 19th Century, 36 In. 825.00
Trade Beads, Crow, Late 1800s, 29 In. 305.00
Trade Beads, Iroquois, 17th Century, 28 In. 110.00
Trade Beads, Silver, Black, White, 3 Strands, 15 In. 190.00
Tray, Apache, Basketry, Woven, Star Design, c.1920, 10 x 2 1/2 In. 715.00
Tray, Apache, Coiled, Basket, Pinwheel Pattern, c.1900, 15 In. 1880.00
Tray, Apache, Geometric, 1920s, 13 1/2 In. 990.00
Tray, Maidu, Basketry, Coiled, Radiating Lightning Pattern, 8 1/2 In. 1530.00
Tray, Pima, Coiled, Basketry, 4-Point Central Star, Whirling Log Pattern, 13 In. 880.00
Tray, Pima, Coiled, Basketry, Radiating Block & Cross, Early 20th Century, 12 1/2 In. . . . 825.00

A MENAGERIE *of* COLLECTIBLES

Cats, poodles, and horses have all been singled out for special one-subject auctions in the past year. Dogs, ducks, elephants, Scotties, and cows have been featured in other auctions. Many online dealers have added animal-themed categories to their Internet shops. Sales have been brisk because of the interest shown by animal lovers.

Cats outsell dogs two to one, whether at auctions, gift shops, or antiques shows. After cats and dogs, horses are next in popularity, followed by elephants, cows, and pigs, but other four-footed or winged creatures are popular collectibles, too. Some, like poodles, are in fashion now and have increased in price. Others, like sheep, are out-of-fashion and can be bargains. Trademarked animals, like Nipper (the RCA dog), Mickey Mouse, and Felix the Cat, have their own followings.

The book cat is seated on a pile of books that form an umbrella stand. The 28-inch-high embossed tin stand is decorated with a transfer-printed design and hand coloring. It auctioned for $2,115.

This cow was an advertising figure in the window of a dairy store in the 1920s. The 28-inch-long cow is made of papier-mâché covered with the hide of an unborn calf. It is worth $795. Cows have been an important part of life in America since 1624, when the first few were brought to Jamestown from England.

Before the invention of photography, stories of strange places and unknown animals fascinated the public. In ancient times, mythical beasts were often featured on ceramics, mosaics, or jewelry. By the Middle Ages, dragons were shown in paintings and tapestries. Asians made figurines and statues representing a stylized lion that is now often called a foo dog or foo lion, a symbol of prestige.

Once European explorers started wandering the globe, the public wanted to "see" a camel or an elephant or a dodo bird to believe it really existed. Every new expedition or war introduced an interesting mix of animal and bird representations from far-away lands. Arms of chairs were swan-shaped in the Empire period. Lions, tigers, monkeys, and elephants were exotic reminders of military campaigns in India and Africa. Shopkeepers knew that paintings, drawings, prints, and figurines showing the unfamiliar flora and fauna of faraway countries were easy to sell.

Horses of all sizes are popular collectibles, especially among teenage girls. These tiny 1 3/4- to 2 1/4-inch-high horses were made by Britains, the well-known English firm that made lead soldiers beginning in 1893. These horses are part of various Britains farm sets manufactured since 1918. Value: $15 each.

By the nineteenth century, the most popular animal pictures and prints showed farm animals, cows, chickens, sheep, and horses. Well-to-do landowners often commissioned portraits of favorite animals. Potters depicted famous racehorses or prize-winning hens. During the last half of the century, potters in Staffordshire, England, made thousands of figurines of spaniels and of a spaniel-like breed of dog known as the "comforter." On this side of the Atlantic, the eagle as a symbol of the United States was pictured on crocks, fabrics, or woven coverlets. It was also the subject of furniture inlay, folk art paintings, figurines, and many other objects that proclaimed national pride.

Although animals of many kinds, including rabbits, skunks, and even whales, have been popular as decorative objects, some animals remain outcasts. Few collectors have ever wanted porcupines, camels, or turkeys.

Nature was more a part of life and the habits of animals were better understood in Victorian times. So while it may not seem strange today to see a pair of candlesticks that show baby birds in a nest, look again. A rat is hanging over the nest on one candlestick, probably waiting to eat the baby birds. These bronze-colored metal candlesticks were made by Auguste-Nicolas Cain, a famous French sculptor working in the late 1800s. The 20-inch candlesticks are worth $600.

DOMESTIC ANIMALS

Hard-working farm animals and loyal household pets have often been part of a household's decor. These animals are still favored by collectors.

Fantasy cat figures have been popular since the nineteenth century. Emile Gallé, a famous French glass and furniture maker, also made pottery cat figures. The smiling cats were usually decorated with colorful designs. This twentieth-century 13 1/2-inch Gallé-style cat has glass eyes. Even with some restoration it sold for $646.

Philip Handel's company is best known for lamps with reverse-painted glass shades. But the company also made other painted glass accessories. This combination tobacco jar and pipe holder is decorated with a setter at point. The jar has a metal lid with a removable pipe on top just waiting to be smoked. It sold for $805.

Folk art is hard to explain to those who like traditional art. This early 1900s table was made by a carver with a sense of humor. Each leg is carved to look like a hound dog chasing a squirrel up a tree. The oak tabletop has a scalloped edge. It is 26 inches square with the original finish. At auction it brought $69,000.

Howard Pierce opened a pottery in Claremont, California, in 1945. He made stylized figurines, including many birds. This 8-inch-high goose is signed with his name and numbered 250P. It was found at a flea market for a reasonable $20.

Holt-Howard was an import company that marked each of its clever products with the company name and the date it was made. Most pieces were figural and useful, such as cat-shaped string-holders, mouse-topped cheese boxes, pixie-handled mustard jars, and saltshakers shaped like cow's heads that moo when turned over. These rooster-shaped salt and pepper shakers are part of a kitchen line called "Coq Rouge" that included a spoon-holder, napkin holder, snack sets, and other dishes. The 1960 shakers, 4 1/2 inches high, sell for $36 a pair.

SYMBOLIC

Symbols of nations, like the American eagle, political and military insignia, and animals that represent particular products, are all featured in collectibles from the past.

The English painting His Master's Voice, *featuring a white terrier with black ears listening to a phonograph, was so popular it was purchased as a trademark for the Victor Talking Machine in 1906. RCA bought both Victor and rights to the trademark in 1929. This tin box, showing Nipper and a gramophone, held phonograph needles. The 1 1/2-inch tin sold for a bargain $10.*

Exotic animals were often woven or embroidered on mandarin textile squares, symbols of rank in China from about 1280 to 1911. This pair, picturing a panther and Buddhist symbols on a metallic ground, was made about 1800. It indicated that the wearer was female, the wife of a military officer of the fourth rank. A pair of the squares sold for $1,208.

The lion was a perfect symbol of power for Lion gasoline. The glass globe sat at the top of a gas pump. It has two lenses and a metal base. The 13 1/2-inch-diameter globe is rare and auctioned for $1,430.

These eagles are really flasks. The heads can be removed and used as shot glasses. The American salt-glazed stoneware flasks are marked MW, perhaps for Morris & Willmore, potters working in Trenton, New Jersey. These flasks may have been made for the World's Columbian Exposition, held in Chicago in 1893. They sold for $5,750.

The 2-foot-tall papier-mâché stork figure is part of an ad for cigars, not baby products. Castle Hall Cigar Company ads from the early 1900s featured a stork. This stork with a sign auctioned for $600.

PRACTICAL

Sometimes designers of serving dishes think not only about how the dishes look, but what is to be served on them. Collectors can find fish plates that look like fish and cheese dishes with heads shaped like dairy cows.

At a formal dinner a century or more ago, there was always a fish course. The fish was usually served whole and each diner had to remove dozens of tiny fish bones. This kidney-shaped fish dish was kept next to the dinner plate for unwanted fish bones. Fish dishes were small, only about 7 inches long, and many were hand-painted. Some unusual fish dishes were actually shaped like a fish with a head, a raised tail, and a center section made to hold small bones. These dishes are inexpensive, $15 to $35.

It is was not uncommon to have to look your food in the eye at a Victorian dinner party. Fish and fowl were often served with head and tail still attached. An entire suckling pig would be presented on a platter at the table. Serving dishes were made to resemble the life-sized heads of large animals like cows or buils. This Staffordshire cheese plate was made between 1860 and 1870. The decorated cow's head is about 10 inches high. Lift it and find a large block of cheese. It is worth $1,000 to $1,500.

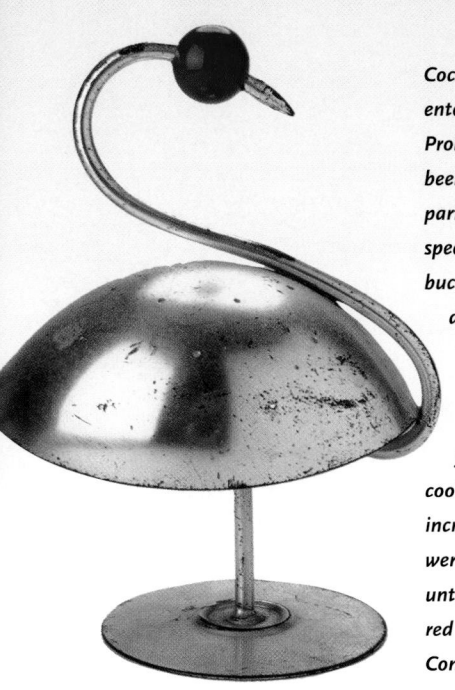

Cocktail parties were a new form of entertainment in the Roaring Twenties. Prohibition (1920 to 1933) seems to have been the spark that led to home cocktail parties. With the parties came a need for special glasses, cocktail shakers, trays, ice buckets, and other barware. A guest held a drink in one hand while walking around and talking to friends. Food was served in bite-sized pieces that did not require plates, knives, or forks. Hors d'oeuvres, first noted in cookbooks in the United States in 1896, increased in popularity. However, they were not the subject of a major cookbook until 1940. This chrome swan with a red Catalin head, made by the Napier Company, held toothpicks used for cocktail snacks or canapés. It was patented in 1935. You can find one online for $15.

Another cocktail party requirement was an ice bucket. This penguin ice bucket was made by West Bend Aluminum Company of West Bend, Wisconsin. Although it features an Antarctic bird, it could be used to serve hot food, too. It was patented in 1941 and manufactured until the 1950s. Many survive, so it sells for under $10 at any garage sale.

CUTE

Cute cartoon-like toys, dishes, and kitchen items came into style in the twentieth century. In the nineteenth century, few comic figures were made for anything that was not alcohol-related or a toy.

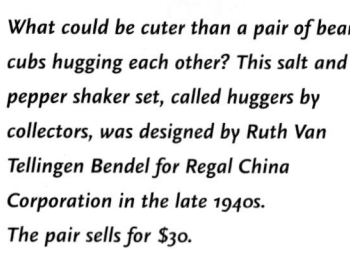

It's a monkey, it's a clown, it's a bank. This 5 1/8-inch tin roly-poly bank auctioned for $310.

What could be cuter than a pair of bear cubs hugging each other? This salt and pepper shaker set, called huggers by collectors, was designed by Ruth Van Tellingen Bendel for Regal China Corporation in the late 1940s. The pair sells for $30.

Felix the Cat was a popular cartoon character. The Schoenhut Company made this 4-inch wooden toy in 1925. The jointed toy has a long tail and black leather ears. In mint condition, this toy brings $300. Alas, this toy cat is dog-eared and worth only about $100.

Old purses have become so popular that almost every style made since the 1880s has been copied. Many of these copies are sold in modern department stores. Wooden purses with decoupage poodle decorations were fashionable in the 1970s. This octagonal box purse has a white plastic handle. It brought $325 at an auction devoted to poodle collectibles.

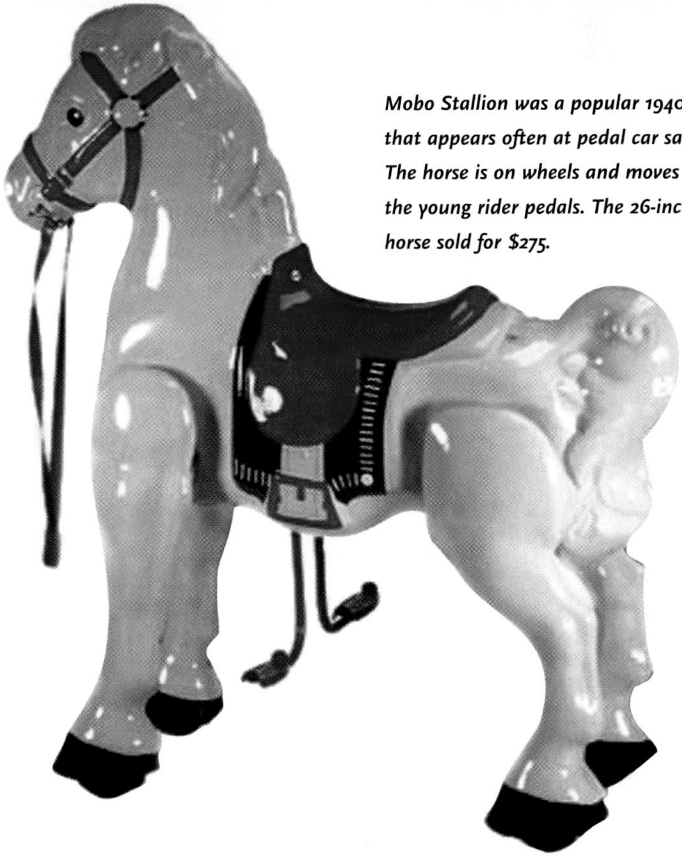

Mobo Stallion was a popular 1940s toy that appears often at pedal car sales. The horse is on wheels and moves when the young rider pedals. The 26-inch-long horse sold for $275.

The most famous mouse in the world, Mickey Mouse, has appeared on millions of toys, watches, textiles, and books. This toy Mickey is a windup walker that was made in Japan for George Borgfeldt & Co. The 7 1/2-inch-high celluloid figure sold for $2,750 at auction.

Snoopy Sniffer is a Fisher-Price toy made of wood covered with lithographed paper. The toy, with jointed legs, a spring tail, and a woof-woof noisemaker, was manufactured from 1938 to 1955. In this condition, it is worth $45.

Bakelite jewelry sells for high prices today and cute animal pins are very popular with collectors. This pin by Martha Sleeper is a carved burro with a quizzical look. The body is dyed and painted. The 2 3/4-inch-long pin sold for $788.

Bookends are going up in price. Painted iron bookends like these cost $15 a few years ago and are $75 today. These bronze-colored iron bookends each show a begging spaniel finished in gold. They are signed "Nuart Creations, NYC."

Animal lovers can find hundreds of different animal-shaped candy containers. This glass dog is wearing a fancy top hat, but the 4-inch-high container cost only $23. The candy inside does not add to the value.

WILDLIFE

Commune with nature and fill the house with wildlife figures from all over the world.

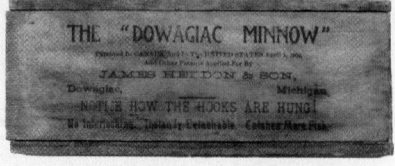

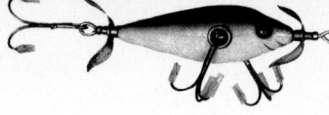

Fish are easily fooled by carved wooden lures that resemble minnows or frogs. This Heddon No. 100 underwater minnow has a crackled green finish and glass eyes. It is 2 3/4 inches long. The lure sold with its box for $660.

Weller Pottery of Roseville, Ohio, made a line of pottery called Coppertone that included vases and figures. Lifelike frogs in several sizes were part of the line. This frog, 4 1/2 inches long, is worth $250. Larger frogs sell for up to $800. A Weller frog sprinkler for the garden can bring $3,000.

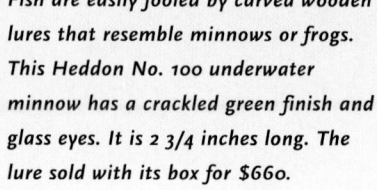

Why a bottle opener would be shaped like a seahorse is a mystery. This iron seahorse with a small hook at the side of the base was made by John Wright Company. It brought $231 at a sale a few years ago.

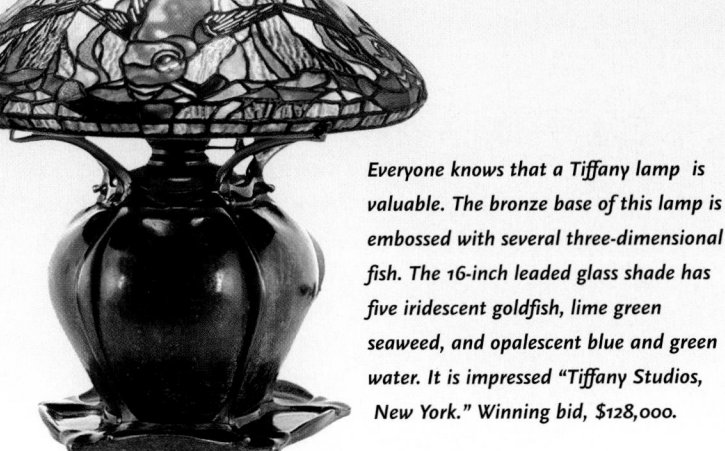

Everyone knows that a Tiffany lamp is valuable. The bronze base of this lamp is embossed with several three-dimensional fish. The 16-inch leaded glass shade has five iridescent goldfish, lime green seaweed, and opalescent blue and green water. It is impressed "Tiffany Studios, New York." Winning bid, $128,000.

Water buffalo are not often made into decorative objects like jewelry. These 14K gold cufflinks shaped like water buffalo heads have diamond eyes. They were made as a special order in the 1960s. Value, $450.

Insects and snakes were popular as jewelry in Victorian times. This pair of earrings shaped like beetles was made of gold, enamel, and semiprecious stones. The Victorian set is worth $350.

Stangl Pottery made dishes, but it is the company's birds that are prized by collectors. This flying blue jay with a leaf, marked "No. 3716," is 10 1/4 inches high. It sold for $460.

FAR OUT

Creativity sometimes finds an outlet in odd inventions or outlandish designs. Here are a few that feature creatures.

Cigarette smoke bothersome? In the 1950s, there was a partial solution. This cat's head is really an ashtray. Rest a lit cigarette in the cat's mouth and the smoke escapes through its ears. The 3-inch-wide piece was made in Japan. Buy it for about $38.

Carnival glass was often referred to as "The poor man's Tiffany." In addition to imitating the expensive iridescent glass, carnival glass makers used exotic animals on some of their pressed patterns. Peacock at the Fountain is one of many patterns featuring the fancy bird. This aqua opalescent footed orange bowl sold for $11,000 because the color is rare.

Weird, bizarre, amusing, and unique are words used to describe the pottery of the Martin Brothers of England. Each piece is different, and each is hand-potted, signed, and dated. This 6-inch pottery creature was made to hold spoons on the dinner table. The Martin Brothers, who worked from 1873 to 1915, made relatively few pieces. Because every piece is rare and a work of art, this spoon holder is worth over $2,000.

Trunk, Klickitat Basketry, Lid, c.1900, 8 x 13 1/2 x 7 1/2 In. 358.00
Urn, Silver, Hammered, Feather Design, Signed, White Buffalo, 1 3/4 x 2 1/4 In. 300.00
Vase, Hopi, Birds, Red To Umber, Creamy Slip, B. Polacca, 3 3/4 x 12 In. 220.00
Vase, San Ildefonso, Black Senna Rim, Signed, Anita Martinez, 4 1/2 x 4 In. 550.00
Vase, San Ildefonso, Wedding, Blackware, Polished, c.1950, 7 x 5 1/2 In. 470.00
Vase, Santa Clara, Wedding, Blackware, Polished, c.1950, 10 1/2 x 7 In. 140.00
Vase, Wedding, Acoma, Painted, Geometric Design, Early 20th Century, 13 1/2 In. 3525.00
Vase, Wedding, Acoma, Polychrome Parrot Design, c.1950s, 9 x 7 In. 1010.00
Vest, Beaded, Cotton, Eagles, Red, White, Blue Shields, 22 x 17 1/2 In. 770.00
Vest, Beaded, Lined, Red, White, Blue Flowers, Child's, 9 x 10 1/2 In. 495.00
Vest, Blackfoot, Beaded, Cotton, Geometric, Shoulder Bands, Flags, 19 x 19 In. 1760.00
Vest, Lakota Sioux, Beaded, Buckskin, Upside-Down American Flags, c.1875, Child's ... 5750.00
Vest, Lakota, Beaded, Hide, Thunderbird, Cotton Liner, c.1900, 20 In. 1880.00
Vest, Lakota, Cloth, Hide, Beaded, Geometric Design, Late 19th Century, 15 In. 940.00
Vest, Plateau, Beaded On Hide, Cloth Lined, c.1930, 22 x 18 In. 193.00
Vest, Sioux, Hide, Beaded, Flowers, c.1930, 26 x 19 In. 195.00
Wall Pocket, Iroquois, White & Blue Beaded, Red Ground, Flat Design, 1875 .... 5225.00
Watch Holder, Plains, Beaded, Fringe, Wrapped Around Belt, 1880s, 9 In. 130.00
Weaving, Navajo, Diamond Pattern, Serrated Edge, Dyed Homespun Wool, 98 x 59 In. ... 705.00
Weaving, Navajo, Dyed Homespun Wool, Banded Pattern, 69 x 45 In. 940.00
Weaving, Navajo, Dyed Homespun Wool, Chief's Blanket, 67 x 46 In. 1060.00
Weaving, Navajo, Dyed Wool, Pictorial, Yei Figure, Arrows, 71 1/2 x 38 1/2 In. 3820.00
Weaving, Navajo, Germantown, Chief's, Late 19th Century, 69 x 54 In. 4995.00
Weaving, Navajo, Homespun Wool, Geometric, Red Ground, 88 x 56 In. 825.00
Weaving, Navajo, Homespun Wool, Natural Dyes, 8-Point Star, 67 x 38 In. 590.00
Weaving, Navajo, Homespun Wool, Natural Dyes, Banded Pattern, Zigzag, 73 x 45 In. ... 645.00
Weaving, Navajo, Homespun Wool, Natural Dyes, Stepped Diamond, Cross, 78 x 39 In. .. 560.00
Weaving, Navajo, Homespun Wool, Natural Dyes, Zigzag, 83 x 58 In. 470.00
Weaving, Navajo, Homespun Wool, Pictorial, Bilateral Feather Design, 75 x 40 In. 2350.00
Weaving, Navajo, Homespun Wool, Serrated Diamond Center, Fret Border, 108 x 48 In. .. 645.00
Weaving, Navajo, Serrated Border, Geometric Design, 36 x 26 In. 705.00
Weaving, Navajo, Stepped, Serrated Edge Diamonds, Cream Ground, 85 x 53 In. 880.00
Whistle, Cherokee, Rooster, 1930s, 3 1/2 In. 116.00
Wrist Cuffs, Ojibwa, Child's, Late 1880s, 5 1/2 In. 195.00

INKSTANDS were made to be placed on a desk. They held some type of container for ink, and possibly a sander, a pen tray, a pen, a holder for pounce, and even a candle to melt the sealing wax. Inkstands date to the eighteenth century and have been made of silver, copper, ceramics, and glass. Additional inkstands may be found in these and other related categories.

Bronze, Dogs, Airedale, 2 Stump Form, Impressed, Austria, c.1900, 6 x 14 1/4 In. 489.00
Bronze, Elephants, Water Hole Pen Well, Rocky Outcrop Inkwell, 17 In. 940.00
Bronze, Mermaid Seated, Amphora Form, Signed, G. Gurschner, c.1900, 6 1/2 x 12 In. .. 2760.00
Bronzed, Elk, Dogs Leap Over Fence, 2 Ribbed Inkwells, 4 x 8 In. 300.00
Cast Bronze Dore, 2 Wells, Applied Champleve Enamels, France, c.1880, 13 x 9 In. 725.00
Leather Over Wood, 2 Crystal Inkwells, Pen Rest, J. Adnet For Hermes, 11 x 7 x 4 In. .. 865.00
Marble, Gilt Brass, Pantheon, 2 Brass Capped Glass Ink Bottles, 4 1/2 x 8 1/2 In. 430.00
Mixed Metal, Figural Design, Japanese Style, Gold On Copper, c.1920, 3 x 13 x 11 In. .. 690.00
Pottery, Tile, Swans, Towers, Ivory, Blue Ground, Cube, Domed Lid, Moravian, 4 x 4 In. . 460.00
Silver, Copper, Bull & Bear, Cartouche Shape, Black Starr & Frost, 13 1/2 In. 4500.00
Silver, Figurine, Hunting Scene, Mayrhofer, 9 x 6 3/4 x 7 1/2 In. 1325.00
Silver, Reticulated Gallery Rim, Beaded, 4 Paw Feet, T. Bradbury & Son, 1917, 11 In. ... 495.00
Silver Plate, Chased Leaves On Rim & Feet, Cut Glass Bottles, 1855, 9 1/4 In. 2200.00
Silver Plated Mount, Victorian, Square, Molded Glass, c.1885, 6 x 6 1/2 In. 2185.00
Statue Of Liberty, 2 Bottles, Green Glass Pen, Brass Base 110.00

INKWELLS, of course, held ink. Ready-made ink was first made about 1836 and was sold in bottles. The desk inkwell had a narrow hole so the pen would not slip inside. Inkwells were made of many materials, such as pottery, glass, pewter, and silver. Look in these categories for more listings of inkwells.

Applied Swag, Flowers, Russia, c.1900 .... 935.00

Bisque, Ma & Pa Carter, Stopper Heads, Carter's Ink c.1915, 3 3/4 In., Pair ......176.00 to 230.00
Black Glass, Chrome, Lucite Top, Pen Holder, Esterbrook, 3 x 3 x 2 In. 78.00
Black Glass, Pen, Well Removable From Base, 4 x 4 x 5 In. 68.00
Blown Glass, Ruby Red, Square, Brass Neck Ring & Hinged Lid, c.1910, 1 7/8 In. 392.00
Blue Crystal Deer, Enamel Design 60.00
Brass, 5 Inset Plaques, Blue & White Jasperware 92.00
Brass, Bird & Roses, Cobalt Blue & White Insert 88.00
Brass, Set, Galleried, Oval, Ball-Footed Tray, Candleholder, 3 1/2 x 9 1/2 x 8 1/4 In. 495.00
Bronze, Cupid, Gilt, Patinated, Late 19th Century, 8 1/2 In. 538.00
Bronze, Gothic Style, Arches, 4 Wells, Pen & Watch Rests, c.1835, 12 x 11 x 5 In. 863.00
Bronzed Gilt, Rococo Style, Lion's Head Pen Rest Support, 19th Century, 14 In. 460.00
Cast Bronze, Figural, Greyhound, Chained To Fencepost, 2 Wells, Victorian, 12 In. 805.00
Ceramic, Book Form, Flowers, Gilt, France, Late 19th Century, 2 1/4 x 3 1/2 x 5 1/2 In. ... 75.00
Clear Crystal, 3 3/4 x 3 3/4 In. 50.00
Copper, Brass, WMF, Stylized Flowers, Mark, 9 In. 353.00
Crystal, Clear, Pyramid, Hinged Lid 50.00
Crystal, Silver Plate, Square, Beveled Edge, Hinged Lid, England, 1800s, 3 x 3 x 3 In. 60.00
Cut Glass, Deep Turquoise Blue, Glass Lid On Brass Hinges, 3 In. 135.00
Cut Glass, Diamond Shape, Turquoise Blue, Brass Ring, American, c.1880, 2 1/8 In. 125.00
Cut Glass, Silver, Openwork, Chased, Scrolled Leaves, 1906, 2 x 4 In. 305.00
Cut Glass, Swirled Ribs, Silver Band & Knob Lid, Repousse, Gorham, 1908, 2 x 2 1/2 In. .. 825.00
Desk Set, Brass, Pot, Sander, Water Reservoir, Candleholder, Tray, England, 1700s 1017.00
Desk Set, Master Pen, Black Glass, Butterscotch Bakelite, Sinclair & Company 225.00
Double, Blue, Cut Crystal, 2 3/4 In. 88.00
Enamel, 2 Wells, Candlestand, Boy, Figural Scenes, Austria, 5 1/2 In. 1410.00
Faience, Decorated, France, c.1910 .... 190.00
Faience, Polychrome, Boat Shape, Double Receptacle, Footed, 4 1/2 x 7 x 3 1/4 In. 105.00
Faience, Polychrome, Clover Shape, Cover, 3 1/2 In. 80.00
Faience, Polychrome, Hinge Top, Cover, 2 1/2 x 4 5/8 In. 90.00
Faience, Polychrome, Mustard Pot, Cover, 4 In. 110.00
Faience, Polychrome, Round, 1 3/4 x 3 1/2 In. 35.00
Faience, Polychrome, Round, Cover, 4 3/4 In. 105.00
Faience, Spade Shape, France, c.1900 .... 70.00
Glass, 4 Lobes, Inset Pen Rest, Porcelain Lid, Cat On Lid, 3 1/2 In. 145.00
Glass, 6 Sides, Blue, Frosted Lid, Spaniel On Lid, 3 3/4 In. 205.00
Glass, 8 Sides, Blue, Flip Lid, 3 1/2 In. 175.00
Glass, 12 Sides, Green, Rolled Lip, Pontil, Whittle Marks, 9 1/2 In. 209.00
Glass, Benjamin Franklin's Head, 4 1/2 In. 358.00
Glass, Blackwood & Co., London, Cobalt Blue, Ground Lip 385.00
Glass, Blue Aqua, Funnel Type, Circles & Dots, Rough Pontil, 1 3/4 In. 1320.00
Glass, Blue, Pyramid, Hinged Lid, Square Base 250.00
Glass, Chrome, Lucite Top, Pen Holder, Pen, 3 1/4 x 3 In. 115.00
Glass, Faceted Lid, Brass Fittings, Block Base, Late 19th Century, 2 3/4 x 1 3/4 In. 75.00
Glass, Gemstones, Gold Bearing Ore, Westove, Santa Monica, Victorian, 4 x 3 x 3 In. ... 56.00
Glass, Geometric, Yellowish Olive Green, Pontil, American, c.1825, 1 1/2 x 2 1/4 In. 246.00
Glass, German Helmet, Puce, Removable Spike, Gold, Embossed Eagle, 3 1/2 In. 165.00
Glass, Green Aqua, Bears Holding Placards, Funnel Type, Rough Pontil, 2 In. 1760.00
Glass, Holder, Cobalt Blue Tray, France, c.1880 .... 170.00
Glass, Lavender & Yellow, Porcelain Insert, Tiffany Type, 4 x 4 In. 360.00
Glass, Loetz Green, Copper Lid, Czechoslovakia, c.1880 .... 350.00
Glass, Pitkin, 36 Ribs, Swirled Left, Emerald Green, Pontil, 3 In. 880.00
Glass, Scented, Blue, Enamel Flowers, Original Stopper, Polished Pontil, 3 1/4 In. 495.00
Glass, Scottie Dog, Czechoslovakia, c.1920 .... 170.00
Glass, Spiral Ribbing, Cut Ovals, Crosses Applied Finger Loop, Pressed Lid, 4 1/2 In. ... 110.00
Glass, Square, Citron Olive, 4 Pen Rests, 2 1/4 In. 90.00
Glass, Stoddard Umbrella, Olive Green, Sheared Lip, Pontil, 1840-1860, 2 1/2 In. 240.00
Glass, Stoddard Umbrella, Red Amber, Flared Sheared Lip, Pontil, 1840-1860, 2 1/2 In. .. 275.00
Glass, Stoddard Umbrella, Yellow, Sheared Lip, Pontil, 2 1/2 In., 1840-1860 .... 275.00
Glass, Tapered, 6 Lobes, Gorham Silver Lid, Chased, Embossed Scrolls, Beadwork, 5 In. . 765.00
Glass, Umbrella, Puce, Flared, Rolled Lip, Tubular Pontil, 2 1/2 In. 825.00
Glass, Umbrella, Red, Sheared, Rolled Lip, Tubular Pontil, 2 1/2 In. 305.00
Glass, Waffle Diamond In Waffle Band, 3-Piece Mold, Olive Amber, 2 1/4 x 1 1/2 In. 140.00
Hammered Copper, Carved Coral Jewel On Lid, Patina, Potter Studio, 3 In. 230.00

Iridescent Green Glass, Embossed Floral Metal Lid, c.1910, 2 3/8 In. 175.00
Lucite, Penholder, Boomerang Shape, Red, Green, 6 1/2 x 5 1/2 x 3 In. 95.00
Lucite, Penholder, Pen, Red, Clear, 3 x 3 x 3 In. 145.00
Metal, Bronze Color, Flowers, Angels Head, Scrolls, Enamel Lid, 8 x 4 1/2 In. 230.00
Metal, Camel, Cold Painted, Glass Insert, 5 In. 265.00
Metal, Camel, Glass Insert, 5 In. 265.00
Metal, Kitten, Tree Stump, White, Hand Painted, Austria, c.1900 .... 140.00
Metal, Shoe, 4 In. 125.00
Molded Glass, 22 Vertical Ribs, Opalescent, 1825-1840, 2 x 1 5/8 In. 410.00
Molded Glass, Teakettle, Sapphire Blue, Paneled, c.1840, 2 x 3 5/8 x 2 1/8 In. 440.00
Paperweight, Cutting, Cobalt Blue, Silver Finial, Cover, 1840-1860, 3 In. 165.00
Patent Glass, Iron, Double, Hinged Lid, American, c.1880 .... 90.00
Pewter, Porcelain Insert, 5 Pen Holes, Round Hinged Lid, Disc Base, 3 1/4 x 7 In. 109.00
Pewter, Stylized Vegetal, 2 Hinged Covers, Impressed, Tudric, 2 x 6 5/8 In. 288.00
Porcelain, Bird & Hatchlings, Blue, Yellow, White, Staffordshire, 2 5/8 In. 165.00
Porcelain, Bronze, Pump, Shell, Leaf, France, c.1860 .... 220.00
Porcelain, Cherub, Holding Bouquet, Pink, Yellow, Red Heart, Scrolled Base, 4 In. 220.00
Porcelain, Cover, Mythological Scene, Flowers, Gold Tracery, RS Prussia 375.00
Porcelain, Dog, On Pillow, Red, White, Cobalt Blue, Staffordshire, 3 3/4 In. 275.00
Porcelain, Double, Leaves, Flower Shape, Bumblebees, 10 1/2 In. 235.00
Porcelain, Floral Applique, Germany, c.1910 .... 170.00
Porcelain, Flowers, Gilding, Germany, c.1890 .... 45.00
Porcelain, Revolving Snail On Tray, France, c.1870 .... 200.00
Porcelain, Sailboat, Signed, Germany, c.1925 .... 280.00
Porcelain, Swan, Lying On Nest, Pink, Yellow, Orange, Staffordshire, 3 1/4 In. 204.00
Pottery, Bird & Hatchlings In Nest, White, Blue, Yellow, Pink, Staffordshire 2 5/8 In. ... 165.00
Pottery, Clown, Head & Collar Lift, France, c.1920 .... 210.00
Pottery, Figures, Depicting Penn's Treaty With Indians, Brown Glaze, Harker, 12 In. 8960.00
Pottery, Revolving Snail, Tatum, American, c.1880 .... 200.00
Pottery, Teakettle, Flowers, France, c.1890 .... 210.00
Sandwich Type, Glass, White, Pink Looping, Pewter Lid, American, c.1860, 2 1/2 In. 1980.00
Silver, Blotter, Cox, c.1900, 6 In. 220.00
Silver, Water Lilies, Stippled Ground, Glass Insert, Art Nouveau, 2 3/4 In. 440.00
Silver Plate, Figural, Devil-Head Bust, Stand, Pen Tray, Round Base, Meriden, 5 1/2 In. . 169.00
Stoneware, Blue Glaze, Red, Impressed, Jugtown Ware, 3 In. 360.00
Stoneware, S.C. & C.R., 4 Holes, 4 3/4 In. 130.00
Teakettle, Beehive, Aqua, Ground Lip, c.1885, 1 In. 420.00
Teakettle, Double Font, Milk Glass, 8 Sides, Mother-Of-Pearl, c.1885, 2 1/4 In. 880.00
Teakettle, Jade Green, Marble Pedestal, Brass Flowers, 3 In. 1540.00
Teakettle, Opalescent, Lime Green, Brass Neck Ring, Flower Shape, c.1880, 2 3/4 In. ... 715.00
Walnut, Carved, Figural, Dog's Head On Shell, 4 3/4 x 6 3/4 In. 520.00
Wooden, Black Forest, Perched Owl, Reading Book, 8 1/2 In. 616.00

INSULATORS of glass or pottery have been made for use on telegraph
or telephone poles since 1844. Thousands of different styles of insulators have been made. Most common are those of clear or aqua glass;
most desirable are the threadless types made from 1850 to 1870.

Am. Tel. & Tel. Co., No. 121, Dome Emb, Strong Amber Swirl 20.00
Am. Tel. & Tel. Co., No. 121, Green 20.00
Am. Tel. & Tel. Co., No. 121, Purple 45.00
Armstrong, No. 217, Root Beer Amber 11.00
Armstrong, No. 272, Dark Red Amber 17.00
B, No. 103, Deep Blue Aqua 20.00
B, No. 145, Deep Yellow Green, Slag & Bubbles 25.00
B & O, No. 136, Light Blue, Embossed 30.00
B.T. Co., No. 102, Royal Purple, Canada 30.00
Brookfield, Cauvets, No. 131, Light Aqua 25.00
Brookfield, No. 121, Aqua, Amber 30.00
Brookfield, No. 164, Dark Yellow Green 30.00
Cable, No. 3, Blue Aqua, Small Rocks 48.00
California, No. 152, Sage Green 5.00
California, No. 161, Light Yellow, Purple, Amber, Dome 30.00
California, No. 161, Plum, Dome Glass 28.00

California, No. 161, Plum, Streaky, Dome 48.00
California, No. 166, Sage Green 8.00
Canada, No. 121, Pleated Skirt, Light Blue, Dome, 1899 .... 40.00
Cauvet's, No. 131, Pat July 225, 1865, Light Aqua 40.00
Chicago Insulating Co., No. 135, Blue .... 70.00 to 75.00
Duquesne, No. 121, Ice Blue, 4 Ribs 9.00
Dwight Pattern, No. 143, Light Aqua 10.00
E.C. & M. Co., S.F., No. 123, Deep Teal, Original Metal Stand 440.00
H.B.R., No. 145, Aqua 30.00
Hemingray, No. 9, 7-Up Green 15.00
Hemingray, No. 9, Light Blue Milk 35.00
Hemingray, No. 12, Jade Green Milk 25.00
Hemingray, No. 40, Deep Olive Green 15.00
Hemingray, No. 43, Deep Blue Aqua 20.00
Hemingray, No. 61, Cable, Hemingray Blue 30.00
Hemingray, No. 660, Honey Amber, Bubbles 42.00
Hemingray, No. 660, Lowex, Honey Amber 35.00
Lynchburg, No. 38-20, Yellow Green 30.00
Maydwell, No. 19, U.S.A., Pink 16.00
Maydwell, No. 20, U.S.A., Light Yellow 10.00
Maydwell, No. 20, U.S.A., Straw 8.00
Maydwell, No. 20, U.S.A., White Milk 12.00
Maydwell, No. 20, U.S.A., White Milk With Blue Tint 20.00
Maydwell, No. 42, U.S.A., Pink 14.00
Maydwell, No. 42, U.S.A., Straw 8.00
McLaughlin, No. 16, Apple Green 50.00
McLaughlin, No. 16, Dark Teal Green 20.00
McLaughlin, No. 19, Blue 20.00
McLaughlin, No. 19, Dark Forest Green 30.00
McLaughlin, No. 19, Steel Gray 50.00
McLaughlin, No. 19, Yellow Green, Bubbles 60.00
McLaughlin, No. 20, Emerald Green .... 20.00 to 30.00
McLaughlin, No. 20, Emerald Green, Small Bubbles 32.00
McLaughlin, No. 20, Lime Green 12.00
N.E.G.M. Co., No. 145, Emerald Green, Bubbles 55.00
No. 20, SB, Narrow Dome, Light Lime Green 25.00
No. 134, Oakman Style, Green 45.00
No. 141, Cross Top, Blue Aqua 27.00
No. 145, Grand Canyon Style, Mica Beehive, Gray 14.00
Postal, SB, No. 210, Dark Aqua, Amber Streaks 28.00
Pyrex, No. 662, Orange Carnival 35.00
S.F., No. 152, Yellow Green, Dome 15.00
T.C.R., No. 145, Aqua 12.00
W.G.M. Co., Denver, Colo, No. 121, Royal Purple 30.00
Whitall Tatum, No. 9, Light Olive Green 30.00
Whitall Tatum, No. 154, Purple 27.00
Whitall Tatum, No. 216, 512U, Dark Red Amber 13.00

IRISH BELLEEK, see Belleek category.

IRON is a metal that has been used by man since prehistoric times. It is
a popular metal for tools and decorative items like doorstops that need
as much weight as possible. Items are listed here or under other appropriate headings, such as Bookends, Doorstop, Kitchen, Match Holder,
or Tool. The tool that is used for ironing clothes, an iron, is listed in the
Kitchen category under Iron and Sadiron.

Ax Holder, Ax, Keeper Ring Handle, Conestoga Wagon 110.00
Bulldog, Standing, Painted, Black, 15 1/2 x 26 In. 430.00
Bust, Lady Of Fashion, France, 19 1/2 In., Pair 405.00
Bust, Young Girl, Smelling Flower, 19th Century Style, 21 1/2 In., Pair 430.00
Cannon, Monarch, 32 Rimfire Blank, Black, Red, Silver, 10 In. 450.00
Cannon, Scale Model, Touch Hole, Wood Carriage, 7 x 16 In. 165.00
Chain, Stay, Wrought, Double Twisted Link, 29 In. 80.00
Chain Hook, Wrought, Spiral, Snake Head End, Threaded Bolt Ends, 11 x 14 In., Pair ... 1265.00

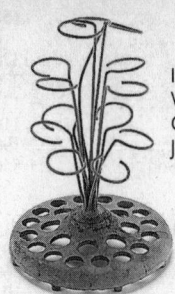

Iron, Flower Frog,
Wire Holders,
Green Paint, Patd.,
J.P.O., 4 3/4 In.

Ironstone, Platter, Decorator's Sample,
Baker Knowlton & Co., 20 In.

Crucifix, Immortelle, French Provincial Style, Splayed Ends, Scrolled Wreath	375.00
Cuspidor, Cast, Stovepipe Hat Shape, White Enamel Inside, Standard Mfg. Co.	1500.00
Figure, Children Playing Leap Frog, Bronze Patina, c.1900, 10 In.	105.00
Figure, Crusader, Forged Steel, Nickel Plating, Wood Mounting, Wilson, c.1938, 13 In.	575.00
Figure, Foo Dog, Parcel Gilt, Burgundy Paint, Wood Plinth, 20th Century, 11 In., Pair	750.00
Figure, George Washington, Holding Papers, In Long Robe, Cast, 1800s, 46 1/2 In.	6050.00
Figure, Happy Hooligan, c.1900, 3 7/8 In.	35.00
Figure, Hound, Recumbent, Cast, 21 In.	260.00
Figure, Rooster, Cast, Painted, Black, 35 In.	635.00
Figure, Stag, Standing, Brown, 19th Century	3630.00
Figure, Venus, Nude, Beside Tree Trunk, Cast, Classical, Early 20th Century, 35 In.	1150.00
Flower Frog, Wire Holders, Green Paint, Patd., J.P.O., 4 3/4 In. ....*Illus*	18.00
Foot Warmer, Charcoal Fuel, Filigree Decoration, Handle, c.1880, 11 In.	395.00
Game Hook, Tulip Ends, Scrolled & Twisted Crest, 5 Hooks, Black Paint, 17 x 18 In.	430.00
Heater, Scrolled, Bellflowers, Shell Feet, Black, Marked, Ralc, 22 1/2 In.	127.00
Jagging Wheel, Crimping Disk, Steel Shaft, Pierced Eye Bird, 8 In.	920.00
Lavabo, Lion's Head, Cast, 30 In.	80.00
Lock Chain, Hand Wrought, Conestoga Wagon, 33 In.	45.00
Mailbox, Cross Pierced, Griswold	105.00
Plaque, Surrender Of 1820, Berlin, 1800-1820, 3 x 5 1/4 In.	750.00
Porringer, Pierced Tab Handle, Signed, Kenrick 1 Pt. No. 1, Early 1800s, 5 1/2 x 2 In.	23.00
Pot Tree, 4 Scroll Hooks, Tapered Stem, Splayed Legs, Penny Feet, c.1790, 46 x 24 In.	489.00
Rack, Bottle, Drying, 4 Scroll Feet, 6 Tiers, 38 x 16 In.	152.00
Safe, Black Paint, Handle, Cook's Patent, 12 In.	465.00
Safe, External Hinges, Portrait Panels, Sharts Patent 1858, 15 x 12 1/2 In.	280.00
Safe, Painted Flowers, Gilt, Pedestal Base, Herring & Co., 43 x 15 In.	4200.00
Spur, Rounded Roped Sides, American Southwest, Spanish Colonial, 1700s	375.00
Stamp, Cast, Oval, Bird On Branch, 3 1/4 x 5 In.	130.00
Stove Plate, Stiegel, Cast, c.1758, 23 1/2 x 25 1/2 In.	6325.00
Stringholder, Cutter, Embossed, Herman Gunther, 10 In.	190.00
Stringholder, Revolves, Patented 1890, 10 In.	250.00
Top Hat, Painted, Black, White Interior, Late 19th Century, 7 x 8 1/2 x 10 1/2 In.	325.00
Vase, Bird, Peonies, Black Lacquer, Meiji Period, Japan, 12 In.	290.00
Vase, Maritime Theme, Relief, Dragon Handle, Oval, Stepped Foot, 26 In., Pair	560.00
Windmill Weight, Rooster, White Paint, Relief Lettering, 17 x 17 1/4 In.	1485.00

IRONSTONE china was first made in 1813. It gained its greatest popularity during the mid-nineteenth century. The heavy, durable, off-white pottery was made in white or was decorated with any of hundreds of patterns. Much flow blue pottery was made of ironstone. Some of the decorations were raised. Many pieces of ironstone are unmarked, but some English and American factories included the word *Ironstone* in their marks. Additional pieces may be listed in other categories, such as Chelsea Grape, Chelsea Sprig, Flow Blue, Gaudy Ironstone, Mason's Ironstone, Moss Rose, Staffordshire, and Tea Leaf Ironstone.

Bowl, Vegetable, Cover, Flowers, Cobalt Blue, Gold Accents, 12 x 9 In.	115.00
Bowl, Vegetable, Cover, Forget-Me-Not, E. & C. Challinor, 6 3/4 x 8 x 12 In.	55.00
Bowl, Vegetable, Cover, Sydenham Shape, White, T. & R. Boote & Co., 9 x 9 In.	230.00

Bowl, Vegetable, Cover, Wheat, Elsmore & Foster, 13 1/4 In. 158.00
Butter Chip, Green Bands, White Ground, 3 1/4 In. 6.00
Charger, Adam's Rose, Rabbits, Frog Transfer, 12 1/2 In. 1375.00
Charger, Anemone Pattern, Blue On White, Newstone, 14 1/2 In. 230.00
Charger, Sea Flower Pattern, Gold Accents, 15 In. 173.00
Coffeepot, Blue Brushstroke Leaves, Paneled, 9 1/4 In. 110.00
Coffeepot, Wheat Pattern, Elsmore & Foster, 11 1/8 In. 190.00
Creamer, Commodore McDonough's Victory, Dark Blue, Enoch Wood & Son 850.00
Cup & Saucer, Blue Brushstroke Leaves 55.00
Cup & Saucer, Queen's Rose, Vine Border 28.00
Footbath, Water Jug, Painted, Flower Sprays, C.J. Mason & Co., c.1845, 14 1/2 In. 1315.00
Jug, Commedia Del Arte, Actors, Posing, Ellsmere & Forster, 1853-1871, 8 1/2 In. 2395.00
Mug, Blue Brush Stroke Leaves, Flared, 3 1/4 In. 60.00
Pitcher, Blue Poppy Design, Silver Plated Pouring Spout, 10 1/2 In. 104.00
Pitcher, George Washington Transfer, Wreath, Stars, Elsmore & Forster, 12 In. 1035.00
Pitcher & Bowl, Brown Transfer, Japonaise Pattern, 6 Piece 450.00
Pitcher & Bowl, Sydenham Shape, White, T. & R. Boote & Co., 12 x 13 In. 165.00
Plate, Blue Brushstroke Leaves, 9 1/4 In., Pair 55.00
Plate, Blue Brushstroke Leaves, Paneled, 8 1/4 In., Pair 154.00
Plate, Purple Transfer, Union Pattern, 8 3/4 In. 39.00
Plate, Purple, Landscape Transfer, Paneled, Castle, 5 In. 80.00
Plate, Red Roses, Blue Bell Flowers, Green Leaves, 10 In. 39.00
Plate, Toddy, Transfer Scene, Verse, Plough Deep While Sluggards Sleep, 5 1/4 In. 145.00
Plate Set, Blue Brushstroke Leaves, Paneled, 4 1/2 In., 5 Piece 140.00
Plate Set, Blue Brushstroke Leaves, Paneled, 6 1/4 In., 7 Piece 250.00
Plate Set, Blue Brushstroke Leaves, Paneled, 7 1/4 In., 4 Piece 250.00
Platter, Blossom, Oval, Polychrome, F. Morley & Co., 19th Century, 21 In. 144.00
Platter, Blue Brushstroke Leaves, 13 3/8 In. 220.00
Platter, Blue Brushstroke Leaves, 15 1/2 In., Pair 385.00
Platter, Decorator's Sample, Baker Knowlton & Co., 20 In. .... *Illus* 85.00
Platter, Oriental Scene, Blue & White, Combed Back, 22 x 16 In. 795.00
Platter, Strawberry, Hand Painted, Clementson, c.1830, 12 x 16 In. 185.00
Platter, Wild Rose, Fishermen In Village, Blue Transfer, England, 15 1/2 In., Pair 635.00
Punch Bowl, Stone China, J. W. Pankhurst & Co., 6 1/2 x 10 In. 300.00
Teapot, Ceres, Shape, Elsmore & Forester, Mid 19th Century, 9 1/2 In. 200.00
Tureen, Cover, Berry Cluster, Jacob Furnival, 9 1/2 x 9 In. 209.00
Tureen, Cover, Blue Brushstroke Leaves, Paneled, Footed, 7 1/2 In. 195.00
Tureen, Cover, Underplate, Blue Brushstroke Leaves, Paneled, Footed, 8 1/2 In. 440.00
Tureen, Sauce, Cover, Sydenham Shape, White, Footed, T. & R. Boote, 8 In. 88.00
Tureen, Sauce, Wheat & Hops, White, 6 3/4 x 8 3/4 In. 99.00
Tureen, Soup, Dome Lid, Floral Finial, Twig Handles, Pedestal, 1890, 10 x 13 In., Pair .. 2185.00
Tureen, Underplate, Ladle, Wheat, Elsmore & Foster, 14 1/2 In. 675.00
Tureen, Undertray, Ladle, White, Sydenham Shape, c.1850, 8 1/2 In. 290.00
Urn, Japan Pattern, Dragon Head Handles, Foo Dog Finial, Gilt, 1800s, 19 1/2 In. 1150.00
Vase, Cover, Oriental Flowers, Blue Ground, Gilt, c.1825, 21 1/2 In. 1554.00

IVORY from the tusk of an elephant is thought by many to be the only
true ivory. To most collectors, the term *ivory* also includes such natural
materials as walrus, hippopotamus, or whale teeth or tusks, and some
of the vegetable materials that are of similar texture and density. Other
ivory items may be found in the Scrimshaw and Netsuke categories.
Collectors should be aware of the recent laws limiting the buying and
selling of elephant ivory and scrimshaw.

Box, Carved Angel, Man, Nude Woman, 2 Malachite Borders, Silver Back, 3 x 2 1/2 In. ... 550.00
Box, Cover, Comic Masks, Carved, Cylindrical, 4 1/2 In. 2415.00
Box, Overall Flowers, Japan, 19th Century, 4 1/2 In. 560.00
Brushpot, Figures In Palace Garden, Chinese, 19th Century, 7 1/2 In. 705.00
Brushpot, Hollowed Tusk, Carved Figures, Woman, Man On Horse, 1800s, 4 x 3 1/2 In. .. 259.00
Card Case, Carved, Lily Of The Valley, France, c.1865, 2 1/2 x 3 7/8 In. 316.00
Card Case, Engraved Italian Cathedral, Hinged Lid, Gold Mounts, 3 1/4 x 1 3/4 In. 620.00
Cheroot Holder, Carved Talons, Holding Amber & Ivory Bowl, Amber Stem, 6 In. 39.00
Corkscrew, Carved, Wolf's Head, Glass Eyes, Red Tongue, Teeth, 4 1/4 In. 287.00
Cup, Engraved, Figural Landscape, 4 Characters, Marked, Chi Ien Lung, 1 1/2 In. 105.00

Etui, Carved, Velvet Case, Victorian, 19th Century, 4 1/2 In. 865.00
Figurine, 3 Men, Entangled In Octopus, 2 5/8 In. 750.00
Figurine, Basket Of Flowers, Chinese, 11 x 20 In. 2350.00
Figurine, Basket Vendor With Stock In Trade, Japan, 10 In. 940.00
Figurine, Birds Perched On Pine Branch, Chinese, 19th Century, 7 3/4 In. 645.00
Figurine, Bodhisattva & Elephant, Robes, Jewelry, Chinese, 18 3/4 In., Pair 80.00
Figurine, Buddhist Lions, Chinese, 19th Century, 5 1/2 In., Pair 646.00
Figurine, Child Holding Basket Of Grapes, Signed, Japan, 19th Century 940.00
Figurine, Corpus, Gold Leaf Wooden Cross, Gilded Frame, 19th Century, 1 1/2 x 8 In. 805.00
Figurine, Courtier, India, 19th Century, 5 1/2 In. 380.00
Figurine, Elephant, Carved, 18K Gold, Precious Stones, Hong Kong, 3 1/2 x 3 1/2 In. 2875.00
Figurine, Elephant, Running, Wooden Stand, 3 1/4 In. 105.00
Figurine, Erotic Couple, Engraved, Japan, 4 In., 4 Piece 430.00
Figurine, Fruit Seller & Helper, Japan, 3 1/2 In. 4404.00
Figurine, Geisha, Holding Origami Crane, 20th Century, 8 1/2 In. 835.00
Figurine, Goddess Standing On Lotus Throne, Signed, Japan, 19th Century, 6 1/4 In. 560.00
Figurine, Krishna Playing Flute, 12 In. 588.00
Figurine, Kuan Yin Holding Scroll, Rosary, Chinese, 18th Century, 7 In. 765.00
Figurine, Kwan Yin, Carved, Woman Holding Roses, Bird Headdress, 12 In. 440.00
Figurine, Madonna & Child, Oval Plinth, 20th Century, 9 3/4 In.   635.00
Figurine, Man, Holding Wisteria Branch, Signed, Harukazu, 14 1/2 In. 4025.00
Figurine, Man, Sparrows, Landscape, 19th Century, 2 5/8 In. 575.00
Figurine, Meirin Standing With Long Robes, Chinese, 10 In. 288.00
Figurine, Monkey Trainer, 11 1/2 In. 1410.00
Figurine, Okimono, Rats Eating Turnips, Japan, 5 In. * 1095.00
Figurine, Okimono, Tengu On Mat, Japan, 19th Century, 4 In. 295.00
Figurine, Oriental, Persimmon, Scrimshaw Lovebirds, Erotic, 1 3/4 In. 140.00
Figurine, Polar Bear, Seal In Mouth, 1 1/2 x 3 3/4 In. 575.00
Figurine, Pu Tai Seated Surrounded By Children, Chinese, 19th Century, 4 In. 235.00
Figurine, Scheherazade, Gilt Bronze Costume, Green Marble Trapezoid Base, 21 In. 8985.00
Figurine, Virgin & Child, 19th Century, 7 1/4 In. 1600.00
Figurine, Wise Man, Book Of Proverbs, Carved, Wooden Plinth, 20th Century, 11 1/2 In. . .   518.00
Figurine, Woman & Child Playing With Marionette, Signed, Japan, 19th Century 823.00
Figurine, Woman Holding Baby & Fan, Chinese, 19th Century, 8 In. 1175.00
Figurine, Woman Holding Lute, Chinese, 19th Century, 10 In. 295.00
Figurine, Woman Reclining On Side, Holding Head, Bracelets, Chinese, 8 1/2 In. 880.00
Figurine, Woman With 2 Children & Basket Of Flowers, Japan, 19th Century, 10 In. 3878.00
Figurine, Woman, Oriental, Hooded Wrap, Bamboo Branch, Signed, 11 In. 1356.00
Figurine, Woman, Renaissance Costume, Wooden Base, Continental, 8 In. 1645.00
Figurine, Zeus Capturing Maiden, Entwined Figures, Stylized Shell, Oval Base, 8 5/8 In. .   7050.00
Frame, Carved, Bird & Flowers, Oval, 4 1/2 In., Pair 230.00
Gambling Chip, 3 Leaf Sprigs, 2 Circles 35.00
Gavel, Crouching Bear Handle, Early 20th Century, 10 1/2 In. 500.00
Group, 2 Soldiers Vanquished By Third, Continental, 4 1/2 In. 765.00
Group, Ariadne Riding Lioness, Continental, After Von Dannecken, 4 1/2 In. 765.00
Group, Carved, Chinese, Men, Women, 10 To 12 In., 8 Piece 2151.00
Jar, Cover, Figural Landscape, Cylindrical, Masks & Ring Handles, c.1800, 11 In. 865.00
Knife, Paper, Hounds Chasing Stag Through Wooded Landscape, Openwork, 11 5/8 In. . .   295.00
Letter Holder, Country Scenes, Foo Dog, Claw Feet, Chinese, c.1900, 5 x 8 1/4 In. 980.00
Miniature, Military Officer, Wife In Lace Shawl & Bonnet, Blue Ground, 3 1/2 In., Pair . .   440.00
Miniature, Portrait, John Ellis Mace, Frame, 1831, America, 2 7/8 x 2 1/8 In. 325.00
Miniature, Portrait, Woman, Lace Headdress, Continental, c.1940, 2 x 2 In. 469.00
Miniature, Portrait, Young Woman, White Dress, Upswept Hair, Mahogany Frame, 3 In. . .   825.00
Mirror, Dresser, Silver Mounted, Tusk Shaped, Ball Feet, 7 1/2 In. 825.00
Okimono, Farmer With Hoe, Sparrows, Signed, 19th Century, 6 1/8 In. 185.00
Okimono, Juggler Standing, Signed, Japan, Box, c.1890, 10 In. 805.00
Okimono, Lady With Sewing Basket, Signed, c.1912, 8 1/2 In. 690.00
Pendant, Stylized Face, Flowers, Carved, H. Krop, 1920s, 3 1/2 In. 2020.00
Perfume Holder, Crane & Children, Landscape, Cylindrical, 18th Century, 4 3/4 In. 518.00
Plaque, Ape, Sitting, Child In Lap, Relief, Rectangular, J.C. Altorf, 1920s, 3 1/4 x 2 In. . .   1800.00
Portrait, Woman Wearing Lace Shawl, America, 19th Century, 3 1/2 x 2 5/8 In. 118.00
Portrait, Woman, Frances Dehon, Blue Dress, Fur Collar, Pearl Brooch, 4 1/4 x 4 In. 110.00
Potpourri, Leaves & Vines, Gourd Form, 19th Century, 4 1/4 In. 775.00

Puzzle Ball, Ornately Carved, Thin Figural Shaft Pedestal, 9 3/4 In. 85.00
Shoehorn, Horse Hoof Handle, Brass Shoe Nails, Leather Loop, 21 In. 300.00
Stand, Lotus Pond, Ducks, Crabs, Fish, Frogs, Chinese, 19th Century. 295.00
Tankard, Silver Gilt, Oval Barrel, Cavalier Carvings, German, Late 19th Century, 7 In. .. 2988.00
Thimble Case, Egg Shape, Polychrome, Flower Basket, Silver Thimble, 1851, 2 1/2 In. .. 1265.00
Triptych, Queen Elizabeth, c.1800, 6 In. 3740.00
Tube, Carved Cherubs Playing Among Clouds, Braided Trim, Threaded Lid, 7 In. 250.00
Tusk, 20 Human Figures, Spiral, c.1900, 10 In. 375.00
Tusk, Parade Of Gods & Satyrs, Leaf Tip Trim, Gadrooned Base, 6 3/8 x 4 5/8 In. 1530.00
Tusk, Walrus, Engraved, Goddess Of Liberty, Monrovia Coast Of Africa, c.1850, 12 In. .. 2350.00
Urn, Onyx, Brass Foot, Neck, Enamel Ground, Polychrome, 6 3/8 In. 85.00
Urn, Relief, Bear Hunt, Domed Cover, Pedestal Base, Leaf Scroll, Germany, 1800s, 14 In. 2910.00
Vase, 4 Bands, Men, Women, Drums, c.1930, 11 x 4 1/2 x 3 3/4 In. 1200.00
Vase, Goddess In Chariot, Carved, Silver Mounted, Ball Feet, 11 In. 5290.00
Vase, Grove Of Peonies, Baluster Shape, Gold Lacquer Rims, Chinese, 4 1/2 In. 460.00

JACK-IN-THE-PULPIT vases, oddly shaped like trumpets, resemble the wild plant called jack-in-the-pulpit. The design originated in the late Victorian years. Vases in the jack-in-the-pulpit shape were made of ceramic or glass, and the complete list of page references can be found in the index.

Vase, Green Over White, Hobnail, 6 In. 134.00
Vase, Light Blue, Dark Red Trim, Hobnail, 7 In. 280.00
Vase, Opalescent, Green, Swirl, Applied Red Flower, Crystal Stem, 6 In. 115.00

JADE is the name for two different minerals, nephrite and jadeite. Nephrite is the mineral used for most early Oriental carvings. Jade is a very tough stone that is found in many colors from dark green to pale lavender. Jade carvings are still being made in the old styles, so collectors must be careful not to be fooled by recent pieces. Jade jewelry is found in this book under Jewelry.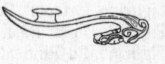

Bowl, Translucent, Black, White, Wooden Stand, 18th Century, 2 1/2 x 5 1/2 In. 750.00
Box, Panels, Engraved Copper, Chinese, 19th Century, 4 1/4 x 3 1/2 In. 120.00
Brush Rest, Celadon, Chih Lung On Rockery Base, 18th Century, 4 In. 290.00
Brush Rest, Celadon, Ducks, Sitting, Lotus Vines, 18th Century, 3 In. 490.00
Cup Stand, Dragons & Pearls, Green, Chinese, 18th Century, 7 x 5 In. 4700.00
Figurine, 2 Children, Lying On Pumpkins, Spinach Green, 6 1/2 In. 1095.00
Figurine, 3 Monkeys In Peach Tree, Green, Chinese, 20th Century, 6 In. 295.00
Figurine, Camel, Celadon Green, Russet, 19th Century, 5 In. 645.00
Figurine, Cat With Kitten, Celadon, Chinese, 2 1/4 In. 590.00
Figurine, Chinese Princess, Attendants, Garden, Wooden Base, 20th Century, 24 In. 1150.00
Figurine, Cranes, Spinach Jade, 13 In., Pair 345.00
Figurine, Gray, Birdman With Carved Feathers, 2 1/2 In. 345.00
Figurine, Guanyin, Boulder, Green, Amber Exterior, 20th Century, 13 In. 805.00
Figurine, Horse, Tang Style, Mottled Green, Lavender, Wooden Base, 20th Century, 19 In. 430.00
Figurine, Kuan Yin, On Cloud, Holding Scepter, Hardwood Stand, 27 1/2 In. 2300.00
Figurine, Nephrite, Female Immortal In Garden, 20th Century, 7 In. 115.00
Figurine, Phoenix Pair, Curved Rocks, Nephrite, Oriental, 20th Century, 12 In. 690.00
Figurine, Qilin, Seated With Cat, Head Upright, Celadon, Ming Dynasty, 3 1/4 In. 575.00
Figurine, Quan Yin, Carved, Chinese, 7 3/4 In. 1035.00
Figurine, Water Buffalo, Carved Wood Base, Japan, 19th Century 750.00
Figurine, Wise Man, Scroll, White, Lavender, Green, Oriental, 20th Century, 18 In. 1495.00
Inkstand, Carved, Chinese, c.1920, 4 x 6 1/8 x 4 1/4 In. 230.00
Lamp, Floral Form, Wood Base, Brass Pedestal, Chinese, c.1890, 24 In. 230.00
Letter Opener, Eagle Finial, Diamond, Enamel, Ormolu, Russia, 11 1/2 In. 420.00
Plaque, Dragon Surrounded By Leaves, Yellow, 18th Century, 5 In. 2235.00
Ring, Scholar's, Dark Brown, Mask, T'ang Dynasty 230.00
Ring, Scholar's, White, Raised Brown & White Chih Lung Carving, 19th Century 127.00
Seal, Chih Lung Dragon On Platform, 1 1/2 In. 460.00
Urn, Buddhist, Cover, Open Work Foliage, Lavender, Green, 20th Century, 11 In. 1095.00
Vase, Flattened Baluster Body, Duck Shape, Duck Finial, Light Gray, Chinese, 6 3/4 In. .. 345.00

JAPANESE WOODBLOCK PRINTS are listed in this book in the Print category under Japanese.

JASPERWARE can be made in different ways. Some pieces are made from a solid colored clay with applied raised designs of a contrasting colored clay. Other pieces are made entirely of one color clay with raised decorations that are glazed with a contrasting color. Additional pieces of jasperware may also be listed in the Wedgwood category or under various art potteries.

Cheese Dish, Cover, White Classical Relief, Oak Leaf Border, Dark Blue, 10 In.	380.00
Jardiniere, White Classical Relief, Flower Band Border, Light Blue, c.1880, 7 1/2 In.	235.00
Pitcher, Applied Design, Panels, Angels, Oak Leaf Band, Pewter Lift Lid, 8 1/2 In.	115.00
Plaque, Neoclassic Scene, Green, White, Late 19th Century, 5 1/2 x 9 3/4 In.	25.00

JEWELRY, whether made from gold and precious gems or plastic and colored glass, is popular with collectors. Values are determined by the intrinsic value of the stones and metal and by the skill of the craftsmen and designers. Victorian and older jewelry have been collected since the 1950s. More recent interests are Art Deco and Edwardian styles, Mexican and Danish silver jewelry, and beads of all kinds. Copies of almost all styles are being made. American Indian jewelry is listed in the Indian category. Tiffany jewelry is listed here.

Barrette, Leaf Chased, Engraved, Clip Corners, Lattice, Seed Pearls, 14K Gold, c.1900	1295.00
Barrette, Rhinestone, Celluloid, Chocolate Brown, Art Deco, 3 3/4 x 1 1/2 In.	30.00
Barrette, Yellow Gold, Platinum, Old Mine Cut Diamonds, Edwardian, c.1910, 3 1/4 In.	550.00
Belt Buckle, Laminated Wood, Cut To Layered Colors, 1930s, 2 1/2 In. ....*Illus*	3.00
Bracelet, Amethyst & Pearl, Yellow Gold, Art Nouveau, Signed, Krementz	935.00
Bracelet, Bakelite, Black, Carved, 1/2 x 3 1/4 In.	175.00
Bracelet, Bakelite, Butterscotch, Carved, 1 1/2 x 3 In. ....325.00 to 450.00	
Bracelet, Bakelite, Butterscotch, Red, Carved, 3/4 x 3 In.	275.00
Bracelet, Bakelite, Green, Carved, Made In USA, 1/2 x 3 In.	135.00
Bracelet, Bakelite, Red Beads On Electric String, 1 In.	570.00
Bracelet, Bakelite, Red, Carved, 1/2 x 3 In.	175.00
Bracelet, Bakelite, Yellow, Twisted, 1/4 x 3 1/4 In.	125.00
Bracelet, Bangle, 13 Mine Cut Diamonds, 15K Yellow Gold, Victorian, c.1885	2070.00
Bracelet, Bangle, 15 Diamonds, Bypass, 18K Yellow Gold, Double Lock, 1970s	5300.00
Bracelet, Bangle, Diamond, Golf Club, Flexible, 18K Gold, Garrard	881.00
Bracelet, Bangle, Dragon Head, Sphere Terminals, 15K Gold, Victorian, c.1880	1840.00
Bracelet, Bangle, Floral & Leaf Chased, Engraved, 10K Gold & Diamond, Edwardian	881.00
Bracelet, Bangle, Panther Head, Sapphire Eyes, Onyx Nose, 18K Gold, Signed, Cartier	3055.00
Bracelet, Bangle, Rock Crystal, 14K Gold, Seaman Schepps	1469.00
Bracelet, Bangle, Silver, Cut Back Design, Applied Balls, Modernist, 2 1/2 In.	58.00
Bracelet, Bangle, Silver, Flowers, 25 Mixed Cut Diamonds, 18K Gold, c.1890	3220.00
Bracelet, Bangle, Silver, Oval Lapis, Turkmenistan, 19th Century	92.00
Bracelet, Bangle, Sterling Silver, Hexagonal, Navette Apertures, Los Ballesteros	323.00
Bracelet, Blue Stones, Seed Pearls, 9K Yellow Gold, c.1900, 7 In.	176.00
Bracelet, Cabochon Moonstone Flowers, Sapphire Center, 14K Gold Links, Tiffany	948.00
Bracelet, Charm, 15, Edwardian, 14K Gold	1410.00
Bracelet, Charm, 22 Charms, 14K Gold, Gemstones, 1966, 7 In.	2070.00
Bracelet, Charm, 7 Gold Coin Charms, 14K Yellow Gold	1380.00
Bracelet, Charm, Double Curb Links, Puppy, Sailboat, Crown, Bell, 14K Gold, 7 In.	646.00
Bracelet, Charm, Puppy, Slipper, Mandolin, Heart, Monkeys, Diamond, 14K Gold, 7 In.	999.00
Bracelet, Chased, Engraved Flowers, 14K Gold, Allsopp & Allsopp, Victorian	323.00
Bracelet, Cocktail, Diamonds, Emeralds, Platinum Art Deco, c.1950, 7 In.	5750.00

Don't store sterling jewelry in cotton-filled boxes. The cotton makes it tarnish faster.

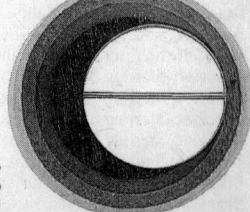

Jewelry, Belt Buckle,
Laminated Wood, Cut To
Layered Colors, 1930s, 2 1/2

Bracelet, Coins, 1852, 1989, 1901, 1902, 1907, 1911, 1913, 14K Gold, 7 1/2 In. 2115.00
Bracelet, Coral, Button Pearls, Victorian, 7 In. 500.00
Bracelet, Cuff, Ancient Roman Coin, European, 14K Yellow Gold 460.00
Bracelet, Cuff, Gold Colored Nugget, Pave Centerpiece, Kenneth Jay Lane 150.00
Bracelet, Cuff, Sterling Silver, Signed Pierre Cardin 147.00
Bracelet, Cuff, White Enamel, Multicolor Stones, Kenneth Jay Lane 150.00
Bracelet, Diamond, 14K White Gold, Art Deco 1293.00
Bracelet, Diamond, Filigree, Platinum, Art Deco, 6 1/2 In. 1763.00
Bracelet, Diamond, Sapphire, 18K White Gold, Center Medallion, Art Deco 805.00
Bracelet, Diamond, Sapphire, Platinum, Straight Line, Art Deco 3960.00
Bracelet, Diamond, Sapphires, Garnet, Platinum, Art Deco 5500.00
Bracelet, Diamonds, Sapphires, Platinum, 18K Yellow Gold, Art Deco, c.1920, 7 1/4 In. . 3450.00
Bracelet, Double Link, Free Form, 18K Gold, Early 20th Century, 8 In. 225.00
Bracelet, Enamel, Black, White, Kenneth Jay Lane 98.00
Bracelet, Enamel, Figural Design, Goldtone Edges, Hermes 195.00
Bracelet, Extension, Gold Color, Rhinestones, Paste Stones, 1940s 165.00
Bracelet, Flexible, Rubies, Diamonds, 18K Gold, Paris, No. 7535, Signed, Boucheron . . . 8225.00
Bracelet, Flowers, Paste, Geometric, Art Deco 1175.00
Bracelet, Geometric Clasp, 3 Pearl Strands, Chrysoprase, Art Deco, c.1920, 7 1/2 In. 1725.00
Bracelet, Gold Links, White & Rose Gold Geometric Design, A.J. Hedges & Co., c.1880 . 2115.00
Bracelet, Gold Over Brass, Red Stone, Rhinestones, Victorian, c.1900 . . . . 185.00
Bracelet, Gold Tone, Orange Cabochon Stones, Kenneth Jay Lane 165.00
Bracelet, Gold, 6 Aquamarines, Leather Fitted Presentation Box, Victorian, 7 In. 805.00
Bracelet, Gold, Fan, Flowers, Green Stones, Czechoslovakia, c.1940, 7 3/4 In. 235.00
Bracelet, Green Jadeite, Jui-Style, 14K Gold Mounts, c.1900 . . . . 920.00
Bracelet, Green Onyx Bead, Diamond, Platinum Clasp, Art Deco 825.00
Bracelet, Hinged Bangle, Garnet, Gemstones, Turquoise, Georgian, 14K Gold, 7 In. 940.00
Bracelet, Hinged Bangle, Ram's Head, Pearl, Revival Period, 18K Gold, 7 1/2 In. 295.00
Bracelet, Hinged Bangle, Wolf's Head & Ball, Victorian, 14K Gold, 8 In. 380.00
Bracelet, Lava Snake, Spiral, Griffin Head, Open Jaws, Garnet Eyes, Victorian 646.00
Bracelet, Link, 18K Gold & Enamel Leaf Form, Signed, Tiffany, 7 In. 2115.00
Bracelet, Link, Crescent Shaped, Fruit, Leaves, Monogram, Inscribed, 1858, 7 In. 380.00
Bracelet, Link, Diamond, European Cut, Openwork, Platinum, Art Deco, 7 1/4 In. 1880.00
Bracelet, Link, Garnet, Art Nouveau, Shiman Mfg. Co., 10K Gold, 7 1/4 In. 150.00
Bracelet, Link, Garnets, Pearls, Victorian, 6 1/4 In. 529.00
Bracelet, Link, Heart Shaped Lock, Victorian, 7 In. 206.00
Bracelet, Link, Peasants Bezel Set Field, Wire Work, Mid Victorian, 14K Gold, 7 x 3/4 In. 2115.00
Bracelet, Link, Platinum, Diamond, Square Synthetic Sapphires, Art Deco, c.1920, 7 In. . 3220.00
Bracelet, Link, Sapphires, French Cut, Platinum, Art Deco, 6 3/4 In. 3645.00
Bracelet, Link, Sterling Silver, Cornucopia, Modernist, 7 In. 58.00
Bracelet, Oval Faux Topaz, Rhinestones, Gold-Tone Frame, Benedict Of N.Y., 7 1/2 In. . . 120.00
Bracelet, Platinum, 15 Box Set Diamonds, Expandable Link, Art Deco 880.00
Bracelet, Platinum, 20 Diamonds, 18 Blue Sapphires, c.1930, Art Deco, 7 In. 1725.00
Bracelet, Platinum, Diamond, Chased & Engraved, 14K Gold Mount, Allsopp, 7 In. 1293.00
Bracelet, Platinum, Diamond, Sapphire, Art Deco, c.1920 . . . . 5520.00
Bracelet, Platinum, Filigree, 2 Strands, 42 Cultured Pearls, 11 Diamonds, Art Deco, 7 In. . 230.00
Bracelet, Platinum, Sapphire, Diamond, Waslikoff & Sons, c.1950, 7 In. 4700.00
Bracelet, Ring & Earrings Set, Gold, Emerald, White Sapphire, Art Deco, c.1935 . . . . 750.00
Bracelet, Rope Design, Silver, Modernist, 8 In. 58.00
Bracelet, Rose Diamonds, Silver Topped Mounts, Buckle, Mesh, Victorian, 7 1/2 x 3/4 In. 558.00
Bracelet, Ruby & Pearl, Central Medallion, Triangular Settings, Burmese, c.1875 . . . . 950.00
Bracelet, Sapphire, Diamond, Straight Line, 14K White Gold, c.1930 . . . . 1955.00
Bracelet, Silver, Multicolor Enamel, Geometric Links, MacKinstry, 7 1/2 In. 765.00
Bracelet, Silver, Triple Band Diamond Design, Modernist, 7 In. 60.00
Bracelet, Slide, Victorian, 14K Yellow Gold, 11 In. 690.00
Bracelet, Sterling Silver, 6 Links, Flowers, Danecraft, 7 1/4 x 5/8 In. 115.00
Bracelet, Sterling Silver, 8 Oval Flying Birds, Links, Leonore Doskow, 7 1/2 In. 225.00
Bracelet, Sterling Silver, Abstract, Coral, Signed, Georg Jensen, 7 In. 1645.00
Bracelet, Sterling Silver, Classical Figure Profile, Art Nouveau, Shiebler, 7 In. 646.00
Bracelet, Sterling Silver, Gold Wash, Rectangular Links, Flower Heads, Jensen, 7 1/4 In . 600.00
Bracelet, Sterling Silver, Link, Denmark, Georg Jensen, No. 89 . . . . 1380.00
Bracelet, Sterling Silver, Linked Form, Stylized Leaves, Georg Jensen, 7 3/4 In. 403.00
Bracelet, Sterling Silver, Navette Links, Signed, Georg Jensen, No. 86, 6 3/4 In. 1295.00

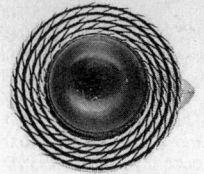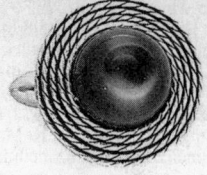

Jewelry, Cuff Links,
Blue Cabochon,

Jewelry, Cuff Links, Zebra, Black Enamel,
Judith Leiber, Winston, 18K Gold, 1 1/4 In.

Chain, Slide, Gold, Box Link, Cameo, Seed Pearls, Victorian, 23 1/2 In. 1035.00
Charm, American Flag, Kenneth Jay Lane 22.00
Cigarette Case, 14K Gold, 14 Inlaid Platinum Lines, Engraved, 5 1/4 x 3 1/4 In. 647.00
Cigarette Case, Gilt Metal, Landscape Scenes, Japan, c.1915, 3 1/2 x 2 1/2 In. 230.00
Cigarette Case, Vermeil, Basket Weave, Lighter, Tiffany & Co., 3 3/8 x 5 In. 323.00
Clip, Fur, Sterling Silver, Lady's Face, Pink Rhinestone Crown, Corocraft, 1 1/2 In. 250.00
Clip, Scallop, Enamel, Crystal, Cobalt Blue Enamel, Art Deco, Cartier, 18K White Gold . . 2350.00
Comb, Tortoiseshell, 5 Teeth, Silver Frame, Oval Amazonite Cabochon, 1912, 4 In. 1800.00
Compact, Rectangular, Ribbed, Diamond Thumbpiece, 9K Gold, Cartier, 1 7/8 x 2 5/8 In. . . 410.00
Cuff Links, Bear & Bull, 14K Yellow Gold, Lindsay, 1 In. 315.00
Cuff Links, Blue Cabochon, Silver Metal, Swank, 5/8 In. . . . . *Illus* 25.00
Cuff Links, Blue Enamel, Gold Wire Twist Spiral, Schlumberger, Tiffany & Co. 1880.00
Cuff Links, Double Disk, Platinum & Diamond, 14K Yellow Gold, c.1930 . . . . 430.00
Cuff Links, Horse & Jockey, Reverse Painted, 14K Gold, 1881 . . . . 1295.00
Cuff Links, Malachite Bead, Cartier, 18K Yellow Gold, 1 1/4 In. 750.00
Cuff Links, Nude Female, Breaking Wave, Oval, 14K Gold, Art Nouveau 500.00
Cuff Links, Oval, Crosshatched, Full-Cut Diamond Center, Tiffany, 14K Gold 940.00
Cuff Links, Zebra, Black Enamel, Judith Leiber, Winston, 18K Gold, 1 1/4 In. . . . . . . *Illus* 125.00
Earrings, 3 Drops, Heart Shape Sapphires, Diamonds, Platinum, 14K Gold, c.1930 . . . . . . 2760.00
Earrings, 3 Freshwater Pearls, 18K Bicolor Gold, Clip-On, Signed Janiye, Box 880.00
Earrings, 18 Rose Cut Diamonds, Honeycomb Frame, Victorian, 14K Gold 2940.00
Earrings, Amethyst Top, Suspended Seed Pearl, Rock Crystal, Smith Patterson Co. 1410.00
Earrings, Aquamarine, Ruby, Diamond Melee, 14K Gold Mount, Clip-On, Hallmark 470.00
Earrings, Bands Of Onyx, Pave Round Diamonds, 18K Gold, Van Cleef & Arpels 5170.00
Earrings, Black Enamel, Wirework, Revival Style, Victorian, 15K Gold 323.00
Earrings, Coral, Tear Shape, Applied Flower, Gold, Late 19th Century, 1 1/2 In. 150.00
Earrings, Cultured Pearl, 11 Diamonds, 18K Gold Mounts, Mikimoto, Box 1645.00
Earrings, Diamond, Floret, Full Cut, Platinum Mount, Cathy Carmendy 558.00
Earrings, Diamond, Hoop, 18K Gold, Signed, C De Cartier, No. 763607 . . . . 8225.00
Earrings, Diamond, Ruby, 18K Gold, Art Deco 518.00
Earrings, Emerald, Diamond, 18K Gold, Suede Pouch, Clip-On, David Webb 2703.00
Earrings, Gold Tassels, 18K Gold Filigree, c.1870 . . . . 375.00
Earrings, Half Sphere Shape, Ribbed, 14K Gold, Clip-On, Signed, Cartier 764.00
Earrings, Hoop, 24 Round Diamonds, Signed, Bulgari 2350.00
Earrings, Hoop, Panther, Emerald Eyes, Onyx Nose, 18K Gold, Cartier, No. 686305 . . . . . 2110.00
Earrings, Lapis, Coiled Shell, Seaman Scheppes, 18K Yellow Gold, 1 3/4 In. 2350.00
Earrings, Oval Jadeite, 3 Diamonds, 18K Gold, Signed, Cartier 705.00
Earrings, Oval Peridot, Quatrefoil Prongs, 20K Gold Mounts, Cathy Waterman 353.00
Earrings, Pearl, Each With 2 Pearls, 14K Yellow Gold, Screwback, Mid 20th Century 125.00
Earrings, Pearl, Full Cut Diamonds, 18K Gold, Platinum Mount, Clip-On, Webb 1998.00
Earrings, Pearl, Shell, Iridescent Brown, 14K Gold Mounts, Clip-On, Seaman Scheppes . . . 1000.00
Earrings, Pendant, 25 Mine Cut Diamonds, Jadeite, Platinum, Art Deco, c.1920, 2 In. 690.00
Earrings, Prong Set Emeralds, 18K Gold Flowers, Signed, Cartier 1116.00
Earrings, Round, 8 Apertures, 18K Gold, Signed, JM 355.00
Earrings, Rounded Form, Central Dome, 18K Gold, Clip-On, Jean Mahie 355.00
Earrings, Shell, Sapphire, Emerald, Signed Patricia S. Vail, c.1970 . . . . 1028.00
Earrings, Snake Charmer, Kenneth Jay Lane 65.00
Earrings, South Sea Tahitian Pearls, 2 Emerald Cut Diamonds, Signed, Sabbadini 9400.00
Earrings, Spiral, Lion's Head, 18K Gold, Signed Zolotas 1175.00
Earrings, Star Shape, Rhinestone, Clip-On, Kenneth Jay Lane, 2 In. 80.00
Earrings, Sterling Silver, Abstract, Clip-On, Sam Kramer, 1 3/4 In. 175.00

Earrings, Sterling Silver, Abstract, Pierced Shape, Modernist, 3 1/2 In. 80.00
Earrings, Sterling Silver, Eggshell Lacquer, Jean Dunand, c.1925, 2 5/8 In. 6570.00
Earrings, Sterling Silver, Lily Of The Valley, Pierced & Chased, Screwback, Kalo, 1 In. . . 225.00
Earrings, Sterling Silver, Sam Kramer, Abstract, Dangling Elements, Clip-On, 1 1/4 In. . . 115.00
Earrings, Sterling Silver, Wood, Abstract, Screwback, Spratling, 3 In. 65.00
Earrings, Sterling, Copper, Green Hardstone, Screwback, Sam Kramer, 1 1/2 x 3/4 In. 380.00
Earrings, Tourmaline, Diamond, 18K Gold Mount, Abstract Mount, K. Mattei 1116.00
Earrings, Tourmaline, Green, Emerald-Cut, Hammered Finish, Elizabeth Locke 2938.00
Earrings, Trefoil Loops, 22K Gold, Amy Moss 120.00
Earrings, Venetian Glass, Blue Intaglio, Classical Figure With Lyre, Elizabeth Locke 1765.00
Hatpins are listed in this book in the Hatpin category.
Lavaliere, 5 Mine Cut Diamonds, Pearls, Platinum, Chain, Edwardian, c.1910, 2 1/2 In. . . 1725.00
Lavaliere, Aquamarine, Platinum, Pearl, Heart Shape, Diamonds, Edwardian, 14K Gold . . 1410.00
Lavaliere, Diamond, Arabesque Design, Edwardian Style, 18K White Gold 881.00
Lavaliere, Pearl, Diamond, Pearls, Openwork, Edwardian, 17 1/2 In. 1528.00
Lavaliere, Plique A Jour Lozenges, Bow, 2 Pear Cut Crystals, Art Nouveau, France, 16 In. 1998.00
Lipstick Case, Enameled Black, Platinum Bands, Diamonds, France, 18K Yellow Gold . . . 382.00
Locket, 2 Gold U.S. Dollar Coins, Hinged, Photo Compartment, 1857 . . . . 115.00
Locket, Gem Set Rubies & Diamonds, Oval, Chased, Engraved, Hallmark, 18K Gold 558.00
Locket, Silver, Enamel, Round, Abstract Blue Enamel, Silver Mount 118.00
Minaudere, Back Diamante Crystals, Gilt Chain, Clasp, Demi-Shaped, Judith Leiber 1265.00
Minaudere, Swan, Black, Gray, White Diamante Crystals, Gilt Chain, Judith Leiber 1370.00
Necessaire, Vermeil, 800 Silver, Mirror, Pad, Card Holder, c.1885, 3 1/2 x 2 1/2 In. 115.00
Necklace, 11 Oval Cut Citrines, Fleur-De-Lis Prong, Floral Links, Victorian, 14K Gold . . 1725.00
Necklace, 18 Concave Disks, Coral Beads In Center, 18K Gold, Victorian, 16 In. 1645.00
Necklace, 50 Amber Nuggets, 18K Gold Serpent Clasp, Signed W.B.E., 22 In. 230.00
Necklace, 50 Pearls, 18K Gold Clasp, Signed, Mikimoto, 17 3/4 In. 4115.00
Necklace, 57 White Cultured Pearls, 14K Gold Box Clasp, Mikimoto, 19 3/4 In. 2585.00
Necklace, 74 Cultured Pearls, 18K Gold Clasp, Mikimoto, Box 3525.00
Necklace, Amethyst, Carved Amulet, 16 Beads, Seed Pearls, Early 20th Century, 32 In. . . . 170.00
Necklace, Amphora Shaped Pendants, Cube Links, Beaded, Fontenay, c.1867, 17 In. 7865.00
Necklace, Bakelite, Colored Beads, Red, Amber, Green, Brown, Brass Spacers, 26 1/2 In. 110.00
Necklace, Bib, Black, White Stones, Drop Pearls, Kenneth Jay Lane 200.00
Necklace, Bib, Clear Rhinestones, Kenneth Jay Lane 300.00
Necklace, Black Faceted Beads, Black Spacers, On Fine Link Chain, Hobe, 17 In. 16.00
Necklace, Chain, 5 Faberge Style Enameled Eggs, Wire Links, c.1870 . . . . 635.00
Necklace, Chain, Jet Links, Seed Pearls, Victorian, 15 1/2 In. 265.00
Necklace, Chain, Spiral Link, 14K Yellow Gold, Late 20th Century, 16 In. 75.00
Necklace, Choker, Overlapping Leaves, Ribbed Design, 18K Gold, Adlers 2530.00
Necklace, Choker, Rectangular Links, Bellflowers, 15K Gold, Victorian, c.1870 . . . . 1890.00
Necklace, Choker, Silver, Orange, Coral, Oscar De La Renta, Simon Alcanthara, 16 In. . . . 575.00
Necklace, Choker, Urn, Precious Stones, 2 Pearl Strands, Art Deco, c.1920, 13 In. 2300.00
Necklace, Coin, 20-Dollar Gold Piece, 1925, Twisted Frame, 14K & 22K Yellow Gold . . . 1150.00
Necklace, Collar, Duchess Of Windsor, Blue, Green Rhinestone, Kenneth Jay Lane 600.00
Necklace, Conch Shell, Kenneth Jay Lane 55.00
Necklace, Coral Bead, 16 Strand, Jade Carved Clasp, Kenneth Jay Lane 90.00
Necklace, Coral Bead, Faceted, Barrel Shaped, Yellow Gold & Cameo Clasp, 62 In. 999.00
Necklace, Coral, Reddish Orange, Leaf Pendants, Box, 18K Gold, Buccellati, 15 1/2 In. . . 8225.00
Necklace, Diamond, Bar Clasp, 20K Gold, Marked Cathy Carmendy, Box, 18 1/2 In. 3290.00
Necklace, Diamond, Freshwater Pearl, Platinum Chain, 14K Gold, Edwardian, 14 In. 999.00
Necklace, Diamond, Sapphire, Center Medallion, 18K White Gold, Art Deco 1095.00
Necklace, Etruscan Revival, Bead, 18K Gold, Applied Wirework, Hoop Clasp, 16 In. 2705.00
Necklace, Festoon, Amethyst, Freshwater Pearls, Art Nouveau Style, 14K Gold, c.1895 . . . 1495.00
Necklace, Galalith Plastic, Blue, Black, Signed, G. l'Hoir, France, c.1970, 23 3/4 In. 294.00
Necklace, Galalith Plastic, Geometric, Signed G. l'Hoir, France, c.1970, 18 In. 325.00
Necklace, Graduated Oval Amber Beads, Russia, c.1870, 28 In. 225.00
Necklace, Hand Hammered, 22K Gold, Harry Bertoia, c.1960s, 14 In. 14950.00
Necklace, Ivory, 8 Round Diamonds, 18K Gold, Signed, Van Cleef & Arpels, 17 In. 355.00
Necklace, Ivy Leaf, Berry Design, 18K Gold, Etruscan Revival 2820.00
Necklace, Jade, Pearl, 14K White Gold, Art Deco, 16 In. 625.00
Necklace, Lacy Bezel, 18K Gold Rope Chain, Krugerrand, 1975 . . . . 588.00
Necklace, Lucite Center Flower, Leaves, Bellflowers, Miriam Haskell, 16 In. 295.00
Necklace, Mesh Links, 58 Diamonds, 18K Gold, Signed, Cartier, No. 738316, 16 1/2 In. . 9999.00

Necklace, Negligee, 14K Gold, Garnet, c.1915, 15 3/4 In. 1410.00
Necklace, Patterned Pink, Blue Patinated, Metal Beads, Flapper Era, c.1930, 28 In. 205.00
Necklace, Pearl, 18K Gold Clasp, Mine Cut Diamonds, T.B. Starr 705.00
Necklace, Pearl, Diamond, 2 Pendants, 14K Gold, Art Nouveau, Krementz, 14 In. 2115.00
Necklace, Pearl, Freshwater, Hammered Silver, Paperclip Chain, 28 In. 206.00
Necklace, Pearl, Pearl Cross Pendant, 3 Strand, Kenneth Jay Lane 150.00
Necklace, Pearl, Rose, 14K Clasp, 14 Diamonds, 7.5 mm, 20th Century, 28 In. 1900.00
Necklace, Pendant, Blue, Green Enamel, Art Nouveau, C.H., 1911 . . . .   325.00
Necklace, Pendant, Coral, Jade, Light Blue Rhinestones, Kenneth Jay Lane 150.00
Necklace, Pendant, Sterling Silver, Green Agate, Jugendstil, Stamped 1528.00
Necklace, Platinum Curb Link Chain, 18K Gold, Freshwater Pearls, Art Nouveau, 49 In. . .   7050.00
Necklace, Platinum, Diamond, 68 Graduated Diamonds, Art Deco, 15 In. 12925.00
Necklace, Rubies, Seed Pearls, Starburst Pendant, Burma, c.1900 . . . .   1035.00
Necklace, Sapphire Center, Diamonds, Double Strand Of Pearls, Edwardian 14100.00
Necklace, Sliding Diamond Pendant, Snake Chain, 18K Gold, 18 In. 3400.00
Necklace, Snake Chain, Box Clasp, 14K Gold, Signed, Forstner, 14 1/2 In. 1058.00
Necklace, Spiked Beads Strand, Sterling Silver, Modernist, 15 In. 105.00
Necklace, Sterling Silver Rope, Modernist, 15 1/4 In. 105.00
Necklace, Sterling Silver, 14K Yellow Gold Collar, Last Quarter Of 20th Century 805.00
Necklace, Sterling Silver, Abstract Flowers, Leaves, No. 25, Georg Jensen, 16 1/2 In. . . .   1998.00
Necklace, Sterling Silver, Flower, Leaf Links, Ball Spacers, No. 1, Georg Jensen, 14 In. . . .   1765.00
Necklace, Thick Linked Chain, Sculpted, Dangling Elements, Modernist, 14 In. 115.00
Necklace, Turquoise, Sterling Silver, Signed, Ray Bennett, 14 1/2 In. . . . . *Illus*   100.00
Necklace, Victorian Silver, Tiger's Tooth, Cased 881.00
Necklace, Yellow Faux Moonstones, Citrine, Amber Rhinestones, Leo Glass, 16 In. 145.00
Necklace & Earring, Choker, Rhinestones, Roxanne Assoulin 80.00
Necklace & Earring Set, Metal Stones, Silver, Gold, Bronze, Kenneth Jay Lane 475.00
Necklace & Pendant, Mourning, Black Onyx Bead, Diamond, Victorian, 17 In. 1195.00
Necklace & Tiara, Silver Topped Diamond & Pearl, 14K Gold, c.1875, 12 x 5 In. 4830.00
Pendant, Bellflower Form, Silver, Blue Enamel, Oval Cartouche, Arts & Crafts, 3/4 In. . . .   118.00
Pendant, Black Onyx Cabochon, Pearl, 14K Gold, E.E. Oakes, 1 3/4 In., 16-In. Chain . . .   3000.00
Pendant, Bow & Vines, Amethyst, Diamond, Edwardian, 18K Gold 2115.00
Pendant, Cameo, 2 Hanging Bells, Foxtail Fringe, Applied Leaf & Bead, 14K Gold 323.00
Pendant, Cameo, Carved, Oval, Profile, Classical Woman, 14K Gold 1058.00
Pendant, Cameo, Cupid Playing Flute Standing On Clam Shell, Victorian, 18K Gold 499.00
Pendant, Cameo, Hardstone, Suspending Cones, Chain Fringe, 14K Gold . . . . *Illus*   325.00
Pendant, Cameo, Pearl, Diamond, Snake Chain, 18K Yellow Gold, 24 In. 1265.00
Pendant, Cameo, Shell, Angel, Frame, Fringe, Applied Bead & Wirework, 14K Gold 1175.00
Pendant, Diamond, Emerald, Lapis, 18K Yellow Gold, Wander, France 550.00
Pendant, Diamond, Panther, 18K Gold, Cartier 1175.00
Pendant, Diamond, Silver Wash, Ribbon Form, Open Floral, 14K Gold, c.1860 . . . .   1265.00
Pendant, Gilt, Sundial, Compass, Scaphie, Japan, 19th Century, 1 1/4 In. 176.00
Pendant, Harry Bertoia, 14K Gold, 1960s, 2 1/4 x 2 In. 3450.00
Pendant, Jadeite, Insect & Flower, 14K Yellow Gold, 19th Century, 2 1/4 In. 1495.00
Pendant, Knot Entwined Blossoms, Mesh, Seed Pearls, Mid Victorian, 18K Gold 235.00
Pendant, Leaves & Tendrils, Bellflowers, Silver, Ivory, Coral, Wiener Werkstatte 3525.00
Pendant, Locket, Woman's Profile, Enamel & Diamond, Art Nouveau, 18K Gold 1540.00

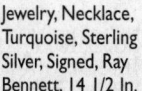

Jewelry, Pendant,
Cameo, Hardstone,
Suspending Cones,
Chain Fringe, 14K Gold

Jewelry, Necklace,
Turquoise, Sterling
Silver, Signed, Ray
Bennett, 14 1/2 In.

Jewelry, Pin, Bee, Turquoise Body,
18K Gold, Stamped Italy,
19th Century, 1 3/4 In.

Pendant, Mourning, Rubies, Diamonds, Emeralds, Locket, Victorian, 14K Gold, 2 1/4 In. 1765.00
Pendant, Pansy, Gold, Old Mine Cut Diamonds, Enamel, Edwardian, c.1910, 1 1/4 x 1 In. 2760.00
Pendant, Pate De Verre, Square, Flowers, Purple, Green, Knotted Cord, G.A. Rousseau . . 1295.00
Pendant, Pearl, Diamond, Leaf Frame, Bead Set, Platinum Top, Edwardian, 15 In. 705.00
Pendant, Pietra Dura, Rose Branch, Flower, Buds, 14K Rose Gold, Victorian 360.00
Pendant, Portrait, Blond, Blue-Eyed Baby, Ivory, 18K Gold, Leather Box, T.B. Starr 470.00
Pendant, Portrait, Man, Ivory, Glaze Oval Frame, 19th Century, 2 1/2 x 3 1/16 In. 645.00
Pendant, Rubies, Pearls, Flower Shape, c.1900, 2 1/4 In. 835.00
Pendant, Silver, 3 Flowers, Red Coral Centers & Drop, Chain, G. Jensen, 2 3/4 In. 1910.00
Pendant, Silver, Cabochon, Tourmaline, Garnets, Scrolled, Hobe 205.00
Pendant, Sterling Silver, Abstract, Guitar, Signed, Lobel 325.00
Pendant, Sterling Silver, Heart Form, No. 126, Georg Jensen, Box, 32 In. 355.00
Pendant, Sterling Silver, Oval, 2-Part Torsade, Georg Jensen, 17 In. 646.00
Pendant, Sterling Silver, Shield Shape, Blister Pearl, Kalo, 1 1/2 In., 17-In. Chain 1900.00
Pendant, Sterling Silver, St. George Slaying A Dragon, c.1950, 1 1/2 In. 115.00
Pendant, Strawberry, Leaf, 14K Gold, D. Pollard, Lead Crystal, Steuben Glass 500.00
Pendant, Teardrop Shape Citrine, Hammered Finish, 18K Gold, Elizabeth Locke 1175.00
Pendant, Teardrop Shape, Oval Citrine, 59 Diamonds, Marcus & Co., 17 1/2 In. 8815.00
Pin, 4 Half Pearls, Mine Cut Diamond, Circle, Arts & Crafts, 14K Yellow Gold 176.00
Pin, 4-Leaf Clover, Crescent Moon, Gold Nuggets, Rose & Green Gold, c.1950, 1 5/8 In. . 485.00
Pin, 5 Old Mine Cut Diamonds, Cultured Pearl, 18K Gold, c.1910 . . . . 750.00
Pin, 5-Blossom Cluster, Rubies, 18K Gold, Signed, Cartier 764.00
Pin, Abstract, Gold, Enamel, 14 Diamonds, J. Rossi, Signed 235.00
Pin, Amethyst & Pearl, Oval Faceted, 18K Gold, Victorian, 1 1/2 x 1 1/4 In. 646.00
Pin, Amethyst Cabochon, Ornate Metalwork Frame, Sarah Coventry, 1 3/4 In. 30.00
Pin, Amethyst, Rose Cut Diamond, Victorian, 14K Gold 382.00
Pin, Arrow Shape, Emerald, Diamond, Art Deco, 18K Gold, No. 10031, Cartier, Box 823.00
Pin, Baguette & Emerald Cut Rhinestones, White Tone Metal Frame, Weiss 92.00
Pin, Baguette Cut Rhinestones, 2 Circles, White Tone Metal Frame, Ledo 115.00
Pin, Bakelite, Hanging Red Cherries, 1940s 475.00
Pin, Bar, 14 Mine Cut Diamonds, Pearl, Platinum, Arabesque Set, 18K Gold, c.1900 . . . . 176.00
Pin, Bar, 15 Graduated Square Rubies, 84 Diamond Surround, Platinum, Art Deco 2350.00
Pin, Bar, 19 Single Cut Diamonds, Platinum, Art Deco 940.00
Pin, Bar, Diamonds, Cultured Pearl, 14K White Gold, c.1930, Art Deco, 2 In. 431.00
Pin, Bar, Diamonds, Filigree Platinum, Art Deco, c.1920, 2 In. 805.00
Pin, Bar, Diamonds, Pearls, Platinum, Mappin & Webb, Art Deco, c.1920, 2 1/2 In. 1150.00
Pin, Bar, Green Center Stone, 10K White Gold, Early 20th Century, 2 1/4 In. 25.00
Pin, Bar, Jade, Enamel, Nephrite, 14K Gold Mount, Leaves, c.1915 . . . . 118.00
Pin, Bar, Jadeite Plaques, 6 Mine Cut Diamonds, Platinum Top, 14K Gold, Walton, c.1920 558.00
Pin, Bar, Old Mine Cut Diamond, 14K Gold, Victorian, 1 3/4 In. 980.00
Pin, Bar, Platinum, 13 Diamonds, Framed By 28 Garnets, Scallop Design, Edwardian 6756.00
Pin, Bar, Prong Set Round Ruby, Flanked By Pearls & Diamonds, Tiffany & Co. 1880.00
Pin, Bar, Sterling Silver, Pierced, Chased Flower, Leaf, Rectangular, Panis, 1/2 x 2 1/2 In. 135.00
Pin, Bar, Violet Glass, Brass Bar Back, Barrette Birds, Stamped, Lalique, 2 1/2 In. 690.00
Pin, Bee, Turquoise Body, 18K Gold, Stamped Italy, 19th Century, 1 3/4 In. . . . . *Illus* 75.00
Pin, Birds On Branch, Onyx, Micro Mosaic, 18K Gold Frame, c.1870, 2 In. 430.00
Pin, Black Opal, Pear Shaped, 14K Gold Mount, Marcus & Co. 1763.00
Pin, Bow Shaped, Gold Tone, Metal Frame, Citrines, Topaz, Weiss 69.00
Pin, Bow, Diamond, Bead Set, Platinum, Art Deco 3290.00
Pin, Bow, Sapphire, Diamonds, European Cut, Openwork, Art Deco 1763.00
Pin, Bowknot, Filigree, Platinum, Diamonds, Synthetic Sapphires, Art Deco, c.1920 . . . . . 1955.00
Pin, Branch & Leaves, Textured, 18K Gold, Buccellati 646.00
Pin, Branch Design, 9 Green Tourmalines, 14 Diamond Melee, 18K Gold, c.1965 . . . . 1528.00
Pin, Brass, Oval, Green Cabochon, Acid Etched, George W. Frost, 2 1/4 x 2 1/2 In. 350.00
Pin, Butterfly, Enamel, Diamond, Art Nouveau, 18K Gold, Whiteside & Blank, c.1908 . . . 6756.00
Pin, Butterfly, Rhinestone, Kenneth Jay Lane 27.00
Pin, Cabbage Rose, Sterling Silver, Guglielmo Cini 76.00
Pin, Cameo, 2 Diamonds, Art Deco, 2 1/2 In. 1165.00
Pin, Cameo, Coral, Seed Pearl, Hinged, Victorian, 1 3/8 x 1 1/8 In. 353.00
Pin, Cameo, Gold Filled Shell, First Quarter 20th Century, 2 1/2 In. 345.00
Pin, Cameo, Hardstone, Female Profile, Pearls, Black Enamel, 1800s . . . . *Illus* 1293.00
Pin, Cameo, Hardstone, Woman, Elaborate Coiffure, Seed Pearl, 14K Gold, Victorian 382.00
Pin, Cameo, Lady, Flowers In Hair, Diamond, Filigree, Oval, Late 1800s, 1 3/4 x 1 3/8 In. 300.00

Pin, Cameo, Oval, Rose Gold Frame, Late 19th Century, 1 7/8 x 1 5/8 In. 200.00
Pin, Cameo, Shell, Female Bacchante, Goldtone Frame, Inscribed, Arturo . . . . *Illus*   499.00
Pin, Circle, 8 Diamonds, 8 Button Pearls, 14K Gold, Edwardian 940.00
Pin, Circle, Cultured Pearl, Diamond, Emerald, 14K Gold, Cartier 529.00
Pin, Circle, Peridot, Oval Gems, Prong Set, 18K Gold, Signed, Cartier 999.00
Pin, Copper, Coronet, Renoir, 3 x 1 3/8 In. 35.00
Pin, Coral Branch & Berries, Victorian, Leaves, 14K Gold 765.00
Pin, Coral Rose, Textured Gold Leaves, 18K Gold, Signed Buccellati, Original Pouch . . .   1998.00
Pin, Curled Cat, Emerald, Diamond, Donald Chaflin, Tiffany, 18K Gold 2820.00
Pin, Diamond, Emerald, Circular Openwork, Ribbon Form, 18K White Gold, c.1880 . . . .   1150.00
Pin, Diamond, Emerald, Diamonds, European Cut, Platinum, Art Deco 2938.00
Pin, Diamond, Flowers, Leaves, Swags, 14K Gold, c.1890, 1 1/2 x 1 In. 4700.00
Pin, Diamond, Platinum, Arrow Shape, 81 European & Mine Cut Gems, Art Deco 3995.00
Pin, Diamond, Platinum, Openwork, Art Deco 2000.00
Pin, Diamond, Ruby, White Gold, Openwork, Art Deco, c.1930 . . . .   980.00
Pin, Diamonds, European Cut, Bow Design, Platinum, Art Deco, c.1930 . . . .   2160.00
Pin, Dove & Roses, Mosaic Frame & Bail, Applied Wirework & Beads, 15K Chain 2703.00
Pin, Ebony, Carved, Melted Silver Wire, H. Bertoia, 1943, 2 1/2 In. 2875.00
Pin, Enamel Portrait, Turquoise, Pearls, France, 18K Yellow Gold, c.1870 . . . .   920.00
Pin, Enamel, Flowers, Leaf Tendril, Seed Pearls, Art Nouveau, 14K Yellow Gold, 1 1/4 In.   295.00
Pin, Father Christmas, Applied Figures, Victorian, 18K Yellow Gold 470.00
Pin, Faux Ivory, Branch Coral, Abstract Design, Signed, Miriam Haskell, 3 In. 80.00
Pin, Femmes Dans Les Fleurs, Blue Glass, Metal, Gray Patina, Lalique, 2 In. 2645.00
Pin, Fish, Black Enamel, Pave Stones, Drop Pearl, Kenneth Jay Lane 235.00
Pin, Flag, Pole, Tassels, Rhinestones, 1940s, 1 3/4 In. 35.00
Pin, Flower Shape, 14K Gold Filigree, Rose Cut Diamond, c.1880, 1 1/8 In. 430.00
Pin, Flower Spray, Diamonds, Pearls, Retro, 14K White Gold, 3 In. 441.00
Pin, Flower, 6 Brilliant Cut Diamonds, Tiffany & Co., 18K Yellow Gold 1880.00
Pin, Flower, Purple & Yellow Aurora Borealis Stones, Purple Chatons, Weiss, 1 In. 35.00
Pin, Flower, Rubies, Emeralds, Diamond, J. Parmentier, 18K Gold 705.00
Pin, Flowerhead, Textured Pearls, 18K Gold, Signed, Cartier 588.00
Pin, Flowers, Prong Set Emeralds, 18K Gold, Signed, Cartier 881.00
Pin, Flowers, Sapphire, Emerald, Diamond Melee, 18K Gold, Signed, Cartier 1058.00
Pin, Frog, Emerald, 1 Extended Leg, Emerald Eyes, Kurt Wayne, 18K Gold 880.00
Pin, Gift Basket, Kenneth Jay Lane 60.00
Pin, Gold Circle, 16 Pale Blue Sapphires, c.1950 . . . .   170.00
Pin, Gold, European Cut Diamonds, Pearl, Flower Form, c.1920 . . . .   1150.00
Pin, Golf, Sterling Silver, Lenore Doskow 90.00
Pin, Griffin, Garnet Eye, Riker Bros., 1890-1900, 1 3/4 x 3/4 In. 325.00
Pin, Guitar Form, 14K Gold, c.1920, 2 In. 225.00
Pin, Hair, Carved, Jade, Coral, Chinese, Qing Dynasty, 6 In., Pair 690.00
Pin, Horse Head, Wood, Glass Eye, Raffia Reins, c.1940, 3 x 4 In. 30.00
Pin, Horseshoe, Sapphire, Diamond, 14K Gold, c.1915 . . . .   529.00
Pin, Hugs & Kisses, Paloma Picasso, Tiffany & Co., 18K Yellow Gold, 2 3/4 In. 205.00
Pin, Ice Floral, Flower With Ribbons, Faux Citrines, Quartz, Rhinestones, Eisenberg 104.00

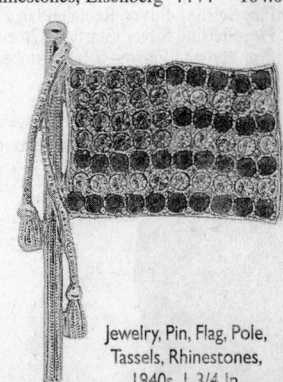

Jewelry, Pin, Cameo, Hardstone,
Female Profile, Pearls, Black
Enamel, 18K Gold, 1800s

Jewelry, Pin, Cameo, Shell,
Female Bacchante, Goldtone
Frame, Inscribed, Arturo

Jewelry, Pin, Flag, Pole,
Tassels, Rhinestones,
1940s, 1 3/4 In.

Pin, Jabot, Spiral Handle, Oval Amethysts, Pearl, Mermod & Jaccard, Victorian, 6 In. 355.00
Pin, Krazy Kat, Brass, Black Enamel, Cat Playing Banjo, Red Rhinestone Eyes, 1 3/8 In. .   125.00
Pin, Leaf & Berry Design, Sterling Silver, Modernist, 1 1/4 In.   60.00
Pin, Maltese Cross, Ornate Gold, Rhinestones, Green Cabochons, Florenza, 2 In. 145.00
Pin, Maple Leaf & Seeds Within Twig, 14K Gold, Arts & Crafts, Potter Studio 1293.00
Pin, Mushrooms, Goldtone, Multicolored Jewel Caps, Trifari, 1 1/2 In. 235.00
Pin, Navette Form, Leaf & Vine, Chased, Engraved, 3 Opals, 14K Gold, Arts & Crafts . . .   323.00
Pin, Octagonal Shape, Folded Center, Diamonds, Onyx In Corners, Scrolled, Art Deco . . .   8225.00
Pin, Open Octagon, Platinum, Diamond, Emerald, Art Deco, Marcus 7050.00
Pin, Openwork Trefoil, Applied Bead & Rope Twist, Etruscan Revival, 15K Gold 265.00
Pin, Orient, Gilt Metal Bird, Enameled Red, Rhinestones, Faux Lapis, Marked Trifari 4995.00
Pin, Orion Star, Kenneth Jay Lane 70.00
Pin, Oval, Leaf & Scroll, 14K Gold, c.1890, 2 In. 80.00
Pin, Owl, Perched On Crescent Moon, Diamond Beak, Emerald Eyes, 18K Gold, Cartier .   705.00
Pin, Panther, Lacquer Spots, Emerald Eyes, Signed Cartier, 18K Gold 3880.00
Pin, Pearl, 14K Gold Wreath, 4 mm Pink Lustre Pearls, c.1950, 1 1/4 In. 168.00
Pin, Pearl, Garnet, 7 Shell Shapes, 14K Gold, c.1930, 1 3/4 In. 460.00
Pin, Pearl, Sapphire, Flower, 18K Gold, c.1930, 1 3/4 In. 748.00
Pin, Pearls, Amethysts, Edwardian, 9K Gold, England 175.00
Pin, Pelican, Sapphire Eye, Paris, Hermes, 18K Gold 940.00
Pin, Pendant, Hinged Bail, Diamond, Onyx, Victorian, 19K Gold, 1 1/2 x 1 1/8 In. 705.00
Pin, Penguin, Terra-Cotta, Glazed, Signed, Edris Eckhardt, 3 In. . . . . *Illus*   25.00
Pin, Pink Spinel, Diamond, Seed Pearl, T.B. Starr, 18K Gold 3175.00
Pin, Platinum, 57 Round Diamonds, 1 Pearl, Art Deco, c.1920-1930, 2 3/4 x 1 In. 2300.00
Pin, Platinum, Diamond, Oval Openwork, Signed, Tiffany 9106.00
Pin, Platinum, Diamond, Rectangular, Openwork, Clipped Corners, c.1920 . . . .   1410.00
Pin, Platinum, Diamonds, Emeralds, Art Deco, c.1920-1930, 2 3/4 In. 1840.00
Pin, Platinum, Filigree, Old European Cut Diamonds, Art Deco, c.1920, 2 x 1 In. 3220.00
Pin, Ribbon Shape, Cultured Pearl, Mikimoto, 18K Gold, 1 1/2 x 3/4 In. 260.00
Pin, Rock Crystal, Box, 24K & 18K Layered Gold Mount, Signed, Nancy Michel 825.00
Pin, Rows Of Clear Pave Stones, Carved Gold Leaves, Eisenberg, 3 1/2 In. 225.00
Pin, Ruby, Amethyst, 14K Gold Mount, Abstract Scrolling Pattern, Retro, Tiffany & Co. .   1765.00
Pin, Ruskin Pottery, Oval, Hammered Brass, Stamped, Forest Craft Guild, 3 3/4 In. . *Illus*   250.00
Pin, Sapphire, Pearl, Crescent Shape, Victorian, 14K Yellow Gold, 3 In. 205.00
Pin, Scotty Dog, Kenneth Jay Lane 35.00
Pin, Seed Pearls, Openwork Lattice Mount, Flower Design, 14K Gold, Edwardian 500.00
Pin, Silver Wire & Ebony Frame, Strung With Green & Black Thread, H. Bertoia, 3 In. . .   8624.00
Pin, Sterling Silver, 2 Butterflies, Flower Stems, No. 283, Georg Jensen 470.00
Pin, Sterling Silver, 2 Tulips, Buds, No. 100B, Signed, Georg Jensen 176.00
Pin, Sterling Silver, Blue Agate Cabochon, Carence Crafters, 1 1/8 x 1 1/2 In. 995.00
Pin, Sterling Silver, Butterflies On Flowers, Circular Frame, Signed, Georg Jensen 470.00
Pin, Sterling Silver, Cat, Green Agate Eye, Whiskers, Signed Jopol, Georg Jensen, Inc. . . .   825.00
Pin, Sterling Silver, Flower Bouquet, Pierced & Chased Details, Panis, 1 1/2 x 2 3/4 In. . .   165.00
Pin, Sterling Silver, Leaf, Blue Turquoise Cabochon, Gilbert Oakes, 1 1/2 x 1 3/4 In. 1800.00
Pin, Sterling Silver, Oval Frame, Green Glass Cabochon, W.N. Brooks, 5/8 x 1 5/8 In. . . .   285.00
Pin, Sterling Silver, Rectangular, Pierced, Chased Flowers, Leaves, Panis, 1 1/2 x 2 In. . . .   150.00
Pin, Sterling Silver, Starfish, Green Glass Cabochon In Center, Hazel B. French, 3 In. 975.00
Pin, Stylized Flower, Silver, Amber, Chrysoprase Cabochons, G. Jensen, 1 x 1 3/4 In. 2022.00

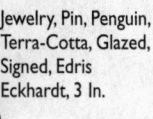

Jewelry, Pin, Penguin,
Terra-Cotta, Glazed,
Signed, Edris
Eckhardt, 3 In.

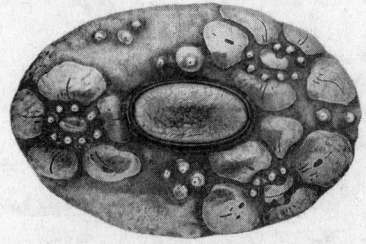

Jewelry, Pin, Ruskin Pottery, Oval, Hammered Brass,
Stamped, Forest Craft Guild, 3 3/4 In.

Jewelry, Pin, Sunburst,
Green & Blue
Cabochons, Clear
Rhinestones, Stamped,
Jomaz, 2 In.

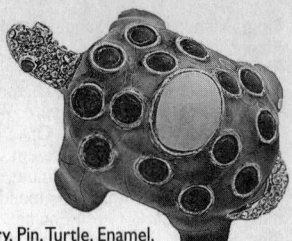

Jewelry, Pin, Turtle, Enamel,
Green & Blue Cabochons,
Clear Rhinestones, K.J.L., 2 1/2

Pin, Sunburst, Diamond, Seed Pearl, Necklace, Victorian, 14K Yellow Gold, 1 1/2 In.	294.00
Pin, Sunburst, Green & Blue Cabochons, Clear Rhinestones, Stamped, Jomaz, 2 In. . *Illus*	30.00
Pin, Sword Form, 3 Diamonds, 2 Rubies, 2 Garnets, 10K Gold, c.1900, 2 1/2 In.	168.00
Pin, Turquoise, Silver, Flower, c.1900, 1 5/8 In.	80.00
Pin, Turtle, Enamel, Green & Blue Cabochons, Clear Rhinestones, K.J.L., 2 1/2 In. . *Illus*	35.00
Pin, Watch, Eagle, Diamonds, Platinum, Pospisil, France, 18K Gold	705.00
Pin, Watch, Leaves, Platinum, Diamonds, c.1910	235.00
Pin, Winged Dragon, Full Cut Diamond, Bezel Set, 14K Gold, Art Nouveau	705.00
Pin, Winged Victory, Diamond, Nobis Maxima Victoria, 18K Gold, Platinum Top	765.00
Pin, Woman Holding Monstrance, Baroque, Porcelain Painted, 19th Century, 2 3/8 In. . . .	115.00
Pin, World War II Mother's, USN Anchor Chained To Enameled Heart, Diamonds, Box . .	36.00
Pin, Wrought Brass, Free-Form, Harry Bertoia, c.1943, 4 In.	4995.00
Pin & Earrings, Cabochon, Emerald Cut Stones, H. Carnegie	230.00
Pin & Earrings, Flowers, Pearls, Cornflower Sapphires, Retro, 14K Yellow Gold	235.00
Pin & Earrings, Metal, Hammered, Red, Orange Plastic, Signed, Fabrice, France	235.00
Pin & Earrings, Sterling Silver, Abstract, Signed, M. Turner	265.00
Pin & Earrings, Turquoise, Bead & Scrolling Frame, Bezel Set, Turquoise Fringe	1116.00
Pin & Earrings, White Onyx, Rhinestones, Star & Cluster Shape, Kramer Of New York . .	145.00
Pin & Earrings, White, Smokey Rhinestones, White Tone Frames, Warner	175.00
Ring, 2 Diamonds, Blue Sapphire, 18K White Gold, Art Deco, c.1930, Size 7 1/4	920.00
Ring, 3 Diamonds, European Cut, Platinum, Edwardian	4585.00
Ring, 3 Garnets, Leaves, Beads, Scrolls, Blossoms, 14K Gold, S.O. Peabody, Size 8	2000.00
Ring, 3 Pearls, Engraved Leaf Design, 14K Gold, c.1950	200.00
Ring, 5 Graduated Oval Diamonds, Prong Set, Platinum Mount, Signed Cartier, Size 4 . . .	2350.00
Ring, 9 Mine Cut Diamonds, Navette Mount, Victorian, Size 7	765.00
Ring, Band, Diamond, Eternity, Platinum, c.1920, Size 5 1/2	430.00
Ring, Band, Eternity, Sapphires, Platinum, Tiffany & Co., Size 7 1/2	880.00
Ring, Blue Zircon, Bead, Leaf, Scroll, 14K Green Gold, E.E. Oakes, Size 7	3200.00
Ring, Bombe Shape, Honeycomb, Diamonds, Rubies, Signed Tiffany & Co.	1528.00
Ring, Cabochon Sapphire, Diamond, Scrolled Platinum, Edwardian, 18K Gold	3055.00
Ring, Cameo, Elongated Oval, 14K Yellow Gold, Mid 20th Century	50.00
Ring, Cat's Eye Chrysoberyl, 18K Gold, Gypsy Mount, Size 4 1/4	529.00
Ring, Coral, Pearls, 14K Gold, Mid 20th Century	50.00
Ring, Crouching Frog, Diamond, Emerald, 18K Gold, Kurt Wayne, Size 5 1/2	825.00
Ring, Diamond Center, Geometric Mount, Diamond Accents, Platinum, Art Deco	2235.00
Ring, Diamond Pave, Dome Top, 18K Gold Florets, Signed, Tiffany, Size 6 3/4	1000.00
Ring, Diamond Solitaire, 18K Gold Mount, Cartier, Size 7 1/4	5875.00
Ring, Diamond, European Cut, Open Work Scroll, Edwardian, 18K Gold	2115.00
Ring, Diamond, European Cut, Platinum, Art Deco	1000.00
Ring, Diamond, European Cut, Platinum, Openwork Scroll, Art Deco	2468.00
Ring, Diamond, Graduated, Bead Set, Platinum Mount, Signed, Tiffany, Size 4 1/4	1765.00
Ring, Diamond, Open Flower, 18K Gold, 18K White Gold, Art Deco, c.1920	400.00
Ring, Diamond, Platinum Filigree, Flowers, c.1920, Size 5 1/2	2585.00
Ring, Diamond, Platinum, Bezel Set, Openwork, Signed, Tiffany, Size 6 3/4	3175.00
Ring, Diamond, Platinum, Blue Green Zircon, Art Deco, Size 6 3/4	1058.00
Ring, Diamond, Platinum, Oval Openwork, Bow & Leaf, Edwardian, Size 8	1175.00
Ring, Diamond, Sapphire, Platinum, Quatrefoil, Art Deco, 18K Gold, Size 7	560.00
Ring, Diamond, Soaring Eagle Shape, Gold Feathers, Mayor's, Carrera Y Carrera	1175.00
Ring, Diamonds, Aquamarine, 14K White Gold, Openwork, Art Deco, Size 7	460.00

Ring, Diamonds, Blue Sapphires, Platinum, Art Deco, c.1920, Size 6 1/2 . . . .   1840.00
Ring, Diamonds, French Cut Sapphires, Platinum & 14K Gold Mount, c.1940, Size 7 . . . .   1175.00
Ring, Dinner, 14 Mine Cut Diamonds, Platinum, 14K Gold, Art Deco, c.1920, Size 6 1/4 .   805.00
Ring, Dinner, Blue Sapphire, Diamonds, Platinum, Art Deco, c.1920, Size 7 1/4 . . . .   1495.00
Ring, Dinner, Blue Star Sapphire, White Sapphire, Platinum, Art Deco, c.1920, Size 3/4 . .   375.00
Ring, Dinner, Carved Flower Opal, Diamond, Platinum, Art Deco, c.1920, Size 6 1/2 . . . .   1380.00
Ring, Dinner, Diamonds, Platinum, Art Deco, c.1920, Size 5 1/4 . . . .   1955.00
Ring, Dinner, Diamonds, Platinum, Retro, c.1940, Size 8 . . . .   920.00
Ring, Dinner, Emerald, 34 Diamonds, Platinum, Art Deco, c.1920, Size 6 1/2 . . . .   920.00
Ring, Dome, Black, Green Enamel, 18K Yellow Gold, Cartier, c.1950, Size 6 1/4 In. 460.00
Ring, Emerald, Diamond, Platinum Mount, Rectangular, Maurice Tishman, Size 7 3/4 . . .   1645.00
Ring, Emerald, Oval, 2 Side Diamonds, Open Scrollwork, Gold, Mid 20th Century 125.00
Ring, Enamel, Black, Alternating Pattern, 18K Gold, Cartier, London, 1974 . . . .   325.00
Ring, Eternity Band, 10 Diamonds, Platinum Bezels, Etoile, Signed, Tiffany & Co. 530.00
Ring, Eternity Band, Square Cut Rubies, Platinum, Art Deco, c.1920, Size 5 1/2 . . . .   490.00
Ring, Filigree, Platinum, Old European & Single Cut Diamonds, Art Deco, Size 6 . . . .   9200.00
Ring, Filigree, Rectangular, Smoky Stone, 14K Gold, G.C.C., Early 20th Century 75.00
Ring, Fire Opal, 4 Peridots, Handmade Mount, 14K Gold, Mexico, Arts & Crafts 2235.00
Ring, Frog, Gold, Emerald, Kurt Wayne 470.00
Ring, Gold, Citrine, Art Deco 205.00
Ring, Gold, White Opal, Rose Cut Diamonds, c.1900, Size 5 . . . .   805.00
Ring, Heart Shape Cabochon, Diamond, Platinum, Marina B., 18K Gold, Size 6 1/2 . . . . .   940.00
Ring, High Crown Setting, Various Stones, 14K Gold, Mid 20th Century 100.00
Ring, Lapis Lazuli Cabochon, Ribbed, 18K Gold Knot, Signed, Van Cleef, Size 5 3/4 . . . .   880.00
Ring, Mabe Pearl, 18K Gold Wings, Encircling Pearl, Signed, David Webb, Size 5 1/4 . . .   825.00
Ring, Memorial, Chased, Engraved, Navette, 14K Gold, Dated 1870, Size 7 1/2 . . . .   235.00
Ring, Memorial, Gold, Ivory, Urn, Willow Tree, Inscribed, Wm Telfair, 18 Mo., c.1793 . . .   440.00
Ring, Mine Cut & Rose Cut Diamonds, Platinum, Edwardian, c.1910 . . . .   1035.00
Ring, Opal, Diamond, Oval, 14K Gold Mount, Maurice Tishman 410.00
Ring, Opal, Pear Shape, 2 Diamonds On Either Side, Mid 20th Century 150.00
Ring, Oval Citrine, 2 Green Tourmalines, Gemstones, 14K Gold, E.E. Oakes, Size 5 1/2 . .   3600.00
Ring, Oval Diamond, Blue Sapphire, Mine Cut Diamonds, 14K 2-Color Gold, c.1925 . . . .   2185.00
Ring, Pearl, 4 Mine Cut Diamonds, Platinum Mount, Signed, Marcus, c.1915, Size 7 . . . .   645.00
Ring, Peridot, Diamond, Platinum & 18K Yellow Gold Mount, Signed, Cartier, Size 4 . . .   1645.00
Ring, Pink Sapphire, Platinum, Art Deco 3525.00
Ring, Platinum & Diamond Mount, Art Deco, Size 5 . . . .   1528.00
Ring, Platinum, 1 Emerald Cut & 2 Baguette Diamonds, Art Deco, c.1930, Size 5 1/4 . . . .   2185.00
Ring, Platinum, 3 Old Mine Cut Diamonds, 18K Gold, J.E. Caldwell, Size 4 1/2 . . . .   9775.00
Ring, Platinum, 7 Diamonds, Blue Velvet Box, Tiffany & Co., Size 5 1/2 . . . .   635.00
Ring, Platinum, 22 Rose Cut & 3 Mine Cut Diamonds, Sapphire, c.1930 . . . .   1150.00
Ring, Platinum, Arched Rows Of Diamonds, 45 Full Cut, 14 Baguettes, Art Deco 1575.00
Ring, Platinum, Emerald, Diamond Bypass, Signed, Cartier, Size 4 1/2 . . . .   3525.00
Ring, Platinum, Golden Sapphire, Diamond, Art Deco, c.1930 . . . .   2760.00
Ring, Platinum, Yellow Brown Diamond, Diamond Set Shank, Platinum, Art Deco 2350.00
Ring, Round Ruby Center, 12 Diamonds, 6 Rubies, Platinum, Art Deco 2585.00
Ring, Rubellite, Tourmaline, Diamond, Platinum Mount, Box, H. Stern, Size 9 1/4 . . . .   1880.00
Ring, Ruby, Diamond, 18K Yellow Gold, Edward E. Ayre, 9 1/2 In. 545.00
Ring, Sapphire Center, 2 Diamonds, Art Deco 646.00
Ring, Sapphire, Diamond, European Cut, Engraved Platinum, Art Deco, Tiffany & Co. 8225.00
Ring, Sapphire, Diamond, European Cut, Platinum, Art Deco 2585.00
Ring, Sapphire, Diamond, Platinum Topped, 14K Gold Mount, c.1915 . . . .   590.00
Ring, Sapphire, Synthetic, Diamond, Platinum, Art Deco 440.00
Ring, Silver, Bezel Set, Opal Cabochons, Silver Balls, Arts & Crafts, Size 3 3/4 . . . .   205.00
Ring, Snake Form, Diamond, 14K Gold, Mid 20th Century 100.00
Ring, Square Cut Synthetic Ruby Center, S-Scroll Design, Diamonds, Art Deco 1060.00
Ring, Sterling Silver, Asymmetric Shield, Carnelian Cabochon, Brandt, Size 4 1/2 . . . .   475.00
Ring, Sterling Silver, Baroque Pearl, Oval Black Onyx, W.N. Brooks, Size 5 . . . .   285.00
Ring, Sterling Silver, Copper, Abstract, Modernist, 15 1/4 In. 60.00
Ring, Sterling Silver, Opal, Square, Silver Bars, Open Shoulders, Signed, Antonio Pineda .   470.00
Ring, Sterling Silver, Oval Green Onyx Cabochon, Art Deco Style, Bjarne, Size 7 . . . .   350.00
Ring, Sterling Silver, Square Green Nephrite Intaglio, Initials ELB, Georg Jensen 205.00
Ring, Tanzanite, Diamond, Prong Set, Platinum Mount, Signed, Tiffany, Size 2 1/4 . . . . . .   880.00
Ring, Tourmaline, Green, Rectangular, Split Shank, 18K Gold, Elizabeth Locke 1410.00

Ring, Turquoise, Diamond, Bezel Set, Cabochon, 14K Gold Mount, c.1915, Size 3 1/2 ... 645.00
Ring, Turquoise, Diamond, Platinum, Oval, Edwardian, Size 7 .... 380.00
Ring, Turquoise, Enamel, Bamboo Design, 18K Gold, Tiffany & Co. 355.00
Ring, Yellow Sapphire, Diamond, Prong Set, 18K Gold Mount, Signed Tiffany 2115.00
Stickpin, 9 Diamonds, Pearl Center, Flower Design, 14K Gold, Edwardian 765.00
Stickpin, Natural Gold Nugget, Late 19th Century 190.00
Stickpin, Platinum, Oval Blue Sapphire, c.1920 .... 575.00
Stickpin, Sterling Silver, Trillium Blossoms, Bloodstone Cabochon, Matthias Hanck 225.00
Tiara, Countess, Rhinestones, Silvertone Setting, Side Combs, Weiss, 1950s, 2 1/4 In. ... 110.00
Tie Bar, 14K Yellow Gold, Diamonds, Early 20th Century, 2 1/2 In. 500.00
Watches are listed in their own category.
Watch Chain, Foxtail, Spherical Slides, 14K Gold, Victorian, 15 In. 355.00
Wristwatches are listed in their own category.

JOSEF ORIGINALS ceramics were designed by Muriel Joseph George. The first pieces were made in California from 1945 to 1962. They were then manufactured in Japan. The company was sold to George Good in 1982 and he continued to make Josef Originals until 1985. The company was then sold to Southland Corporation. The name is now owned by Applause, and the Birthday Girl series is still being made.

Figurine, 4 Season Series, Spring, Yellow Dress, Parasol, 9 In. 190.00
Figurine, At Home, Colonial Woman, Embroidery Work, 6 1/2 In. 115.00
Figurine, Birthday Angel, 7 Year, Green Dress, Holding Baby, 4 1/2 In. 29.00
Figurine, Colonial Days, Louise, White Floral Gown, Gold Trim, 9 1/2 In. 115.00
Figurine, Doll Of The Month, January, Rose Winter Outfit, Muff, Girl, 3 1/2 In. 60.00
Figurine, Doll Of The Month, June, Holding Flowers, Girl, 3 1/2 In. 60.00
Figurine, Doll Of The Month, September, Green Dress, Bouquet, Girl, 3 1/2 In. 60.00
Figurine, Donkey, Oval Foil Label, 6 x 6 1/2 In. 55.00
Figurine, Greetings Series, Bon Voyage, Girl, Purple Dress, 4 In. 60.00
Figurine, Little International Series, American Indian, 3 1/2 In. 78.00
Figurine, Love Makes The World Go Round Series, Love Locket, Girl, 8 1/2 In. ..165.00 to 225.00
Figurine, Memories Music Box Series, Oh What A Beautiful Morning, 5 3/4 In. 80.00
Figurine, Memories Music Box Series, Woman, Peach Gown, Holding Picture, 6 1/2 In. .. 90.00
Figurine, Peanuts The Mouse, Standing In Peanut Shell, 2 1/8 In. 25.00
Figurine, Sweet Sixteen Series, Woman, With Daisy, Inscription, 8 In. 110.00
Figurine, Wee Ching, Boy, M.J. George Copyright, 5 In. 65.00
Music Box, Fascination, Girl Playing Violin, 6 1/2 In. 75.00
Music Box, Love Theme, Impossible Dream, 6 In. 78.00

JUDAICA is any memorabilia that refers to the Jews or the Jewish religion. Interests range from newspaper clippings that mention eighteenth- and nineteenth-century Jewish Americans to religious objects, such as menorahs or spice boxes. Age, condition, and the intrinsic value of the material, as well as the historic and artistic importance, determine the value.

Cup, Kiddush, Silver Gilt, Johann Samuel Beckensteiner, Germany, c.1760, 5 3/4 In. 2390.00
Flagon, Silver, George II, Guerney & Cook, London, c.1751, 9 3/4 x 6 1/4 In. 8850.00
Lamp, Hanukkah, Parcel Gilt, Griffon, Lion, M. Puritz, Russia, c.1870, 10 1/4 In. 29875.00
Plaque, Entebbe, July 4, 1976, Menorah & Sword, Bronze, Paul Vincze 285.00
Stuffing Spoon, Hook End, George III, Irish, John Craig, Dublin, 1774, 12 3/4 In. 3950.00
Yad, Silver, Gold, Baleen, Inscribed, Spain, 1765-1790, 14 1/2 x 2 1/4 In. 85000.00

JUGTOWN Pottery refers to pottery made in North Carolina as far back as the 1750s. In 1915, Juliana and Jacques Busbee set up a training and sales organization for what they named *Jugtown Pottery*. In 1921, they built a shop at Jugtown, North Carolina, and hired Ben Owen as a potter in 1923. The Busbees moved the village store where the pottery was sold to New York City. Juliana Busbee sold the New York store in 1926 and moved into a log cabin near the Jugtown Pottery. The pottery closed in 1959. It reopened in 1960 and is still working near Seagrove, North Carolina.

Bowl, Chinese Style, Green, Blue Exterior, Red, Blue Interior, 4 x 11 1/2 In. .... *Illus* 1430.00
Bowl, Chinese Style, Red, Turquoise Field, Impressed, 4 1/4 x 7 In. 715.00

Jugtown, Bowl, Chinese Style, Green, Blue Exterior, Red, Blue Interior, 4 x 11 1/2 In.

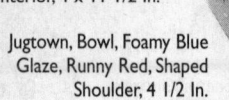

Jugtown, Bowl, Foamy Blue Glaze, Runny Red, Shaped Shoulder, 4 1/2 In.

Jugtown, Vase, Han, 2 Applied Lugs, Runny Blue Glaze, Red Highlights, 9 1/4 In.

Bowl, Chinese Style, Turquoise Glaze, Impressed, 3 1/2 In.		468.00
Bowl, Flared, Flattened Rim, Black, Impressed, 4 3/4 x 11 1/2 In.		495.00
Bowl, Flared, Korean Style, Red Glaze, Turquoise Field, Impressed, 3 1/4 x 8 1/4 In.		990.00
Bowl, Foamy Blue Glaze, Runny Red, Shaped Shoulder, 4 1/2 In.	*Illus*	550.00
Bowl, Footed, Chinese Style, Red, Turquoise Field, Impressed, 2 x 4 3/4 In.		248.00
Bowl, Orange Glaze, Gourds & Leaves, Impressed, 2 x 10 In.		220.00
Bowl, Red Glaze Over Blue Field, Impressed, 3 x 9 In.		660.00
Bowl, Shaped Shoulder, Chinese Glaze, Impressed, 4 1/2 In.		550.00
Charger, Orange Glaze, Stamped, 15 In.		230.00
Jar, 3 Applied Loop Handles, Yellow, Green Glaze, Impressed, 7 1/4 In.		330.00
Jar, 4 Applied Handles, Frogskin Green Glaze, Impressed, 8 1/4 In.		220.00
Jar, Chinese Style, 4 Applied Loop Handles, Frogskin Glaze, Impressed, 8 1/4 In.		550.00
Jar, Chinese Style, 4 Handles, Yellow, Orange Glaze, Impressed, 11 1/4 In.		1100.00
Punch Bowl, Tapered Sides, Turquoise Glaze, Mottled Purple, 7 1/4 x 11 1/2 In.		4400.00
Vase, 4 Applied Handles, White Glaze, Impressed, 6 3/4 In.		580.00
Vase, Blue Glaze, Impressed, 3 1/4 x 4 3/4 In.		330.00
Vase, Bulbous, Dripping Blue Glaze, Stamped Mark, 5 1/4 In.		375.00
Vase, Chinese Blue Frothy Matte Glaze, 6 x 7 In.		705.00
Vase, Chinese Style, 2 Knobs, Turquoise Glaze, Red & White Field, Impressed, 7 1/2 In.		1320.00
Vase, Chinese Style, Red Glaze, Turquoise Field, Strap Handles, Impressed, 7 3/4 In.		1760.00
Vase, Chinese Style, Red, Turquoise Field, 2 Applied Lugs, Impressed, 8 1/2 In.		1540.00
Vase, Chinese Style, Red, Turquoise, Jade Green Field, Impressed, Oval, 7 In.		2310.00
Vase, Chinese Style, Yellow Glaze, Orange Base, Loop Handles, Impressed, 7 In.		525.00
Vase, Egg, Blue, Red, Impressed, Ben Owen, 3 3/4 In.		360.00
Vase, Egg, Mirror Black Glaze, Impressed, 6 1/2 In.		440.00
Vase, Egg, Red Glaze Over Turquoise, Impressed, 5 1/2 In.		525.00
Vase, Egg, Red Glaze, Blue Field, Impressed, 4 1/2 In.		660.00
Vase, Egg, Speckled Red, Turquoise Field, Impressed, 4 1/4 In.		495.00
Vase, Egg, Turquoise Blue Glaze, Impressed, 4 3/4 In.		165.00
Vase, Flared & Collared Rim, Chinese Glaze, Turquoise Field, Impressed, 9 1/2 In.		880.00
Vase, Flared Rim, Applied Knobs, White, Chinese Blue Glaze, Marked, 7 1/2 In.		495.00
Vase, Flat Shoulder, White Semimatte Glaze, 3 3/4 x 5 In.		176.00
Vase, Han, 2 Applied Lugs, Runny Blue Glaze, Red Highlights, 9 1/4 In.	*Illus*	1210.00

JUKEBOXES play records. The first coin-operated phonograph was demonstrated in 1889. In 1906 the *Automatic Entertainer* appeared, the first coin-operated phonograph to offer several different selections of music. The first electrically powered jukebox was introduced in 1927. Collectors search for jukeboxes of all ages, especially those with flashing lights and unusual design and graphics.

AMI, Model JEK 200, 45 RPM, 1960		330.00
Rock-Ola, Model 1000, Nostalgia, Arched Form, 45 RPM, 1987		1705.00
Rock-Ola, Model 449, 450 Single Records, 1971		1990.00
Rock-Ola, Model A, Walnut Case, Wurlitzer Amplifier, 12 Records, 1935, 49 1/2 In.		1320.00
Seeburg, Model 147, Barrel, Trashcan, Metal Cabinet, 78 RPM, 1948		2860.00

Seeburg, Model DS 160, 45 RPM, 1962	495.00
Seeburg, Model V-200, 45 RPM, 1955	2970.00
Seeburg, Royal, Wooden, 1930s	195.00
Seeburg, Symphonola 1-47, Wooden, Lighted Plastic, Blue Mirror Panels, 36 x 57 In. . . .	2925.00
Wurlitzer, Model 312, Simplex, Wood Case, 50 1/2 x 30 x 22 In.	1440.00
Wurlitzer, Model 1015, 24 Selections, 78 RPM, 1947	10450.00
Wurlitzer, Model 1015, No. 1019422, 24 Selections, Walnut Case, 78 RPM, 60 In.	7640.00
Wurlitzer, Model 1050, 50 Records, 45 RPM, 1973	5500.00
Wurlitzer, Model 1100, 78 RPM, 1948	4400.00
Wurlitzer, Model 1500, Wurlimagic Brain, 1952	770.00
Wurlitzer, Model 1650, 48 Selections, 1954	440.00

KATE GREENAWAY, who was a famous illustrator of children's books, drew pictures of children in high-waisted Empire dresses. She lived from 1846 to 1901. Her designs appear on china, glass, and other pieces. Figural napkin rings depicting the Greenaway children may also be found in the Napkin Ring category under Figural.

Book, Mother Goose, Milkmaid On Cover, 1900s	19.00
Napkin Ring, Figural, c.1840, 2 3/4 x 2 3/4 In.	250.00
Thimble Holder, Boy, 2 x 2 In.	13.00

KAY FINCH Ceramics were made in Corona Del Mar, California, from 1935 to 1963. The hand-decorated pieces often depicted whimsical animals and people. Pastel colors were used.

Kay Finch
CALIFORNIA

Figurine, Bunny, Baby Cottontail, Blue Eyes, 2 1/2 In.	110.00
Figurine, Cat, Ambrosia Persian, 10 In.	595.00
Figurine, Cat, Jezebel, 6 In.	325.00
Figurine, Cat, Muff, 3 1/4 In.	75.00
Figurine, Cherub Head, Black Hair, 2 1/4 In.	85.00
Figurine, Elephant, 4 1/2 In.	290.00
Figurine, Godey Lady, 7 1/2 In.	45.00
Figurine, Lamb, Rearing, Blue Eyes, 5 1/2 In.	99.00
Figurine, Lamb, Standing, Pink, 5 3/4 In.	230.00
Figurine, Owl, Hoot, Brown, Gold, 8 3/4 In. . . . . 75.00 to 100.00
Figurine, Owl, Toot, Pink, Green Pastel, 5 3/4 In.	110.00
Figurine, Owl, Tootsie, Pearl Gray, Brown Eyes, Tail, Black Trim, 3 3/4 In.	75.00
Figurine, Peasant Boy, 6 In.	35.00
Figurine, Peasant Girl, Blond, Green Apron, 6 3/4 In. . . . . 49.00 to 95.00
Figurine, Penguin, Pee Wee, Black, White, Green Under Wings, 3 1/4 In.	145.00
Figurine, Pig, Sassy, Brown Ears, Yellow Flowers, 3 1/2 In.	150.00
Figurine, Pig, Smiley, 6 3/4 In.	350.00
Figurine, Swan, 3 1/2 x 3 1/2 In., Pair	180.00
Lamp, Lady Godey, Pink Dress, 15 1/2 In.	195.00
Planter, Cat, Jezzy Kitten On Front, 6 1/2 In.	185.00
Planter, Teddy Bear, 7 1/2 In.	230.00
Vase, Moon, 8 In.	250.00

KAYSERZINN, see Pewter category.

KELVA glassware was made by the C. F. Monroe Company of Meriden, Connecticut, about 1904. It is a pale, pastel-painted glass decorated with flowers, designs, or scenes. Kelva resembles Nakara and Wave Crest, two other glasswares made by the same company.

KELVA

Biscuit Jar, Orange Poppies, Blue Mottled Ground, Silver Plated Lid, Bail Handle	700.00
Box, 6 Sides, Mottled Green, Brown & Tan Flowers, White Enameled Dots, 3 1/2 In.	345.00
Box, Mottled Green, Pink Flowers, Signed, 3 1/2 In.	230.00
Dresser Box, Mottled Red Opaque, Earth Tone, Enameled Flowers, Victorian, 5 1/2 In. . .	690.00
Humidor, Blue Mottled Ground, Pink Flowers, Gold Enameled Cigars, Signed, 5 3/4 In. . .	805.00
Jewelry Box, Pink Poppies, Mottled Blue Ground, 6 Sides, 3 1/2 In.	460.00
Pin Dish, Pink Flowers, Mottled Green Ground, 4 1/2 In.	40.00
Vase, Daisies, Red Mottled Ground, Silver Plated Base, 13 1/2 In.	2200.00
Vase, Mottled, Cobalt Blue Design, Pink Roses, Metal Base, 8 In.	400.00

KEMPLE glass was made by John Kemple of East Palestine, Ohio, and Kenova, West Virginia, from 1945 to 1970. The glass was made from old molds. Many designs and colors were made. Kemple pieces are usually marked with a *K* on the bottom. Many milk glass pieces were made with or without the mark.

Banana Split, Ivy In Snow, Milk Glass, 8 1/4 In.	18.00
Bowl, Milk Glass, Uneven Scalloped Edge, 5 3/4 x 6 1/4 In.	13.00
Dish, Fox On Lacy Base Cover, Milk Glass, 7 x 6 1/4 In.	100.00
Dish, Lacy Heart, Milk Glass, 3 Sections, 13 In.	35.00
Goblet, Lace & Dewdrop, Amber, 5 7/8 In.	15.00
Pin Tray, Roses & Bows, Milk Glass, 6 x 8 In.	75.00
Plate, Lacy Edge, Peach, Acanthus Border, 8 In.	18.00
Toothpick, Pony & Cart, 2 x 4 3/4 In.	25.00

KENTON HILLS Pottery in Erlanger, Kentucky, made artwares, including vases and figurines that resembled Rookwood, probably because so many of the original artists and workmen had worked at the Rookwood plant. Kenton Hills opened in 1939 and closed during World War II.

Vase, Mirror Umber Glaze, White Prunts, Cylindrical, William Hentschel, 7 3/4 In.	805.00

KEW BLAS is the name used by the Union Glass Company of Somerville, Massachusetts. The name refers to an iridescent golden glass made from the 1890s to 1924. The iridescent glass was reminiscent of the Tiffany glass of the period.

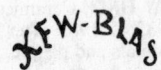

Bowl, Underplate, Iridescent Gold, Ribbed, Scalloped, Magenta, Signed, 2 x 6 1/2 In.	288.00
Candlestick, Blue Gold, Spiral Stem, 8 In., Pair	865.00
Vase, Gold Iridescent, Pulled Feather, White Ground, 10 1/2 In.	518.00
Vase, Rainbow, Magenta Hues, Speckled, Satin Stem, Marked, 8 3/8 In.	405.00
Vase, Stick, Gold Iridescent, Damascene Design, Flared Base, 5 1/2 In.	980.00

KEWPIES, designed by Rose O'Neill, were first pictured in the *Ladies' Home Journal.* The figures, which are similar to pixies, were a success, and Kewpie dolls and figurines started appearing in 1911. Kewpie pictures and other items soon followed. Collectors search for all items that picture the little winged people.

Bisque, Blue Wings, Black Side-Glancing Eyes, Jointed Arms, Legs, c.1915, 5 In.	900.00
Bisque, Jointed, Painted Eyes, Lashes, Single Dot Brows, 5 1/4 In.	425.00
Bisque, Side-Glancing Eyes, Sitting, Hammock, Book, Rose O'Neill, c.1920, 2 1/2 In.	5600.00
Bisque, Side-Glancing Eyes, Standing, Holding Spoon, Rose O'Neill, c.1915, 9 In.	2450.00
Bisque Head, Stiff Neck, Side-Glancing Eyes, Dash Brows, Jointed Shoulders, 9 In.	675.00
Bride, Bisque, Side-Glancing Eyes, Closed Mouth, c.1912, 12 In.	2900.00
Candy Container, Kewpie By Barrel, No Closure	149.00
Composition, Molded Hair, Starfish Hands, Blue Wings, Cameo, 1930s, 11 In.	60.00
Figurine, Girl, Long Brown Hair, Chalkware, 18 In.	105.00
Plate, Pictures, Trees, Rose O'Neill, Rudolstadt, 6 1/4 In.	80.00
Scootles, Bisque, Blue Side-Glancing Eyes, Blond Sculpted Hair, c.1915, 6 1/2 In.	900.00
Tray, Doll Holding Ice Cream Sundae, Tin Lithograph, c.1920, 17 1/2 x 11 1/2 In.	221.00

KIMBALL, see Cluthra category.

KING'S ROSE, see Soft Paste category.

KITCHEN utensils of all types, from eggbeaters to bowls, are collected today. Handmade wooden and metal items, like ladles and apple peelers, were made in the early nineteenth century. Mass-produced pieces, like iron apple peelers and graniteware, were made in the nineteenth century. Also included in this category are utensils used for other household chores, such as laundry and cleaning. Other kitchen wares are listed under manufacturers' names or under Advertising, Iron, Tool, or Wooden.

Apple Corer, Tin & Wood, Vantage, R.M.S. Co., 6 1/2 In.	50.00
Ashtray, Griswold, No. 00	30.00
Basin, Pewter, Compton & Townsend, 8 In.	45.00

Basket, Onion, Wire, Reticulated Folding Top, Loop Handles, Early 1900s, 10 x 8 1/2 In. . . 440.00
Basket, Wire, Fixed Handle, Loop Feet, Early 20th Century, 15 x 8 1/2 In. 435.00
Basket, Wire, Fixed Handle, Loop Feet, Early 20th Century, 16 x 12 In. 275.00
Blender, Excelsior, Electric, Plastic Housing, Dial, Removable Container, 1955, 19 In. . . . 110.00
Board, Cutting, Wood, Pig Shape, Painted Man & Woman, Peter Hunt, 1939, 18 x 12 In. . . 175.00
Bowl, Burl, Round, Turned, 2 Carved Handles, Early 19th Century, 8 1/2 x 20 In. 210.00
Bowl, Carved Wood, c.1880, 20 x 8 1/2 In. 375.00
Bowl, Chopping, Wooden, Trencher-Type, Notched Handles, c.1825, 32 x 11 x 4 In. 255.00
Bowl, Patty, Griswold, No. 72, Bail Handle 60.00
Bowl, Scotch, Wagner Ware, No. 2, Sidney, O. 25.00
Bowl, Wood, Burl, 30 x 13 In. 115.00
Bowl Set, Black Exterior, Bright Colors Inside, Herbert Krenchel, c.1953, 11 Piece 645.00
Box, Pantry, Bentwood, Pinwheel Cover, Relief Carved, Green Wash, Round, 6 x 10 In. . . 935.00
Box, Pantry, Oval, Painted, Bentwood Finger, Late 19th Century, 2 1/4 x 4 x 5 3/4 In. 300.00
Box, Salt, Decorated, 1843, 5 3/4 In. 300.00
Box, Salt, Stoneware, Waffle Weave, Hanging, Wooden Cover 35.00
Box, Spice, Saffron, Turned Wood, Salmon Ground, Painted Flowers, 4 1/2 x 2 1/2 In. . . . 1100.00
Box, Sugar, Pyramid Shape Lid, Brass Knob, Amish, 7 In. 12650.00
Bread Board, Bird's-Eye Maple, 13 x 6 In. 95.00
Bread Board, Hand Painted, Reid Perez Kolman, 20th Century, 18 x 26 In. 46.00
Bread Box, Tin, Rolling Lid, Heart, Flowers, Birds, Painted, Ralph Cahoon, 12 x 16 In. . . 546.00
Butter, Cover, Jadite, 1 Lb. 100.00
Butter Bowl, Burl, Molded Lip Edge, Pennsylvania, 6 x 18 In. 1650.00
Butter Drain, Walnut, 21 1/2 In. 115.00
Butter Mold, look under Mold, Butter in this category.
Butter Paddle, Burl, 9 5/8 In. 935.00
Butter Paddle, Burl, Bird-Head Hooked Handle, Pennsylvania, 10 1/4 x 6 In. 525.00
Butter Paddle, Carved Pinwheel, Tulip, Leaves, Lollipop Handle 3900.00
Butter Paddle, Dipper, Maple, Handle, Open Heart, 10 1/2 In. 2750.00
Butter Paddle, Hooked Handle, 9 1/2 In. 20.00
Butter Paddle, Lollipop, 2 Sides, Carved Pinwheel, Tulip, Leaves On Reverse, 11 5/8 In. . 4290.00
Butter Paddle, Maple, Figured, Open Heart At Handle 2500.00
Butter Stamp, 3 Fish, Poplar, Chip Carved, Pennsylvania, 19th Century, 4 1/4 In. 1910.00
Butter Stamp, 6-Petal Flower, Dots, Tab Handle, 3 1/8 In. 110.00
Butter Stamp, Acorn & Leaves, 1 Piece, Wood, 2 3/4 x 2 1/4 In. 305.00
Butter Stamp, Acorns & Leaves, In Bell, 4 3/4 x 5 1/2 In. 95.00
Butter Stamp, Bear, Collared, Flower, Cylindrical, 1 7/8 x 1 3/4 In. 110.00
Butter Stamp, Beaver, Rope Twist Border, Case, 3 1/4 In. 110.00
Butter Stamp, Bird On Branch, 1 Piece, Wood, 4 x 2 3/4 In. 305.00
Butter Stamp, Bird On Branch, 2 Piece, Turned, 5 x 4 In. 275.00
Butter Stamp, Bird, Disc, Marked, E.S., 4 In. 440.00
Butter Stamp, Blue Jay, Calling, Handle, 3 3/8 In. 1265.00
Butter Stamp, Corn, Ear, Glazed, 4 1/4 x 3 In. 1540.00
Butter Stamp, Cow, Double Border, 4 1/4 In. 660.00
Butter Stamp, Cow, Facing Left, In Bell, Glass, Turned Oak Handle, 4 3/4 x 6 In. 28.00
Butter Stamp, Cow, Facing Left, Maple, 1 5/8 x 2 1/2 In. 165.00
Butter Stamp, Cow, Fence, Threaded Handle, 4 In. 990.00
Butter Stamp, Cow, Fence, Tree, Case, 3 1/4 In. 110.00
Butter Stamp, Cow, Fence, Tree, Case, 4 3/4 In. 165.00
Butter Stamp, Cow, Half Moonshape, 2 Piece, Turned Handle, 7 x 4 1/4 In. 495.00
Butter Stamp, Cow, Redware, 3 5/8 In. 1430.00
Butter Stamp, Cow, Wood, 1 3/4 In. 295.00
Butter Stamp, Cross, Maltese, Cow, House, Flowers, 4 In. 250.00
Butter Stamp, Daisy, Cased, 3 3/4 In. 55.00
Butter Stamp, Double, Hearts, Leaves, Threaded Handle, 3 1/4 x 6 In. 770.00
Butter Stamp, Duck, Flying, Landing On Water, 4 1/2 In. 740.00
Butter Stamp, Duke Of Wellington, Turned Handle, 2 In. 150.00
Butter Stamp, Eagle & Star, Coggled Edge, 3 1/2 x 5 In. 525.00
Butter Stamp, Eagle, Facing Over Left Shoulder, 1 Piece, Wood, 3 1/2 x 2 1/4 In. 330.00
Butter Stamp, Eagle, Facing Over Right Shoulder, 1 Piece, Wood, 5 1/2 In. 250.00
Butter Stamp, Eagle, Half Moon Shape, 2 Piece, Wood, Turned Handle, 7 x 4 In. 415.00
Butter Stamp, Eagle, Laurel Branch, Star, Wavy Feather, 1-Piece Handle, 4 1/2 In. 385.00
Butter Stamp, Eagle, Shield, Eye, 3 3/4 In. 85.00

Butter Stamp, Eagle, Shield, Handle, 3 1/2 In. 110.00
Butter Stamp, Eagle, Star, 4 1/4 In. 605.00
Butter Stamp, Eagle, Wood, Handle, 3 x 4 1/2 In. 395.00
Butter Stamp, Fern, 2 Piece, 3 1/2 x 6 In. 95.00
Butter Stamp, Fern, Initial W, 1 Piece, Wood, 4 3/8 x 3 In. 240.00
Butter Stamp, Fish, 1 Piece, Wood, 4 3/4 In. 360.00
Butter Stamp, Flower Basket, Handle, 3 1/2 In. 880.00
Butter Stamp, Flowers, Buds, Rope Twist Borders, Handle, 5 In. 55.00
Butter Stamp, Flowers, Leaves, 1-Piece Handle, 4 1/2 x 2 3/4 In. 90.00
Butter Stamp, Flowers, Swan, House, Tree, 5 Sections, Hinged, Canted Sides, 7 x 7 In. ... 110.00
Butter Stamp, Flowers, Wood, 5 5/8 x 3 3/8 x 3 1/2 In. 150.00
Butter Stamp, Geometric, Disc, Wood, 4 1/4 In. 220.00
Butter Stamp, Heart Shape, 2 Sides, Pine Tree, Person, Fish, Ladder, 4 1/4 In. .. 495.00
Butter Stamp, Heart, Notched Border, Maple, 19th Century, 3 1/4 In. 415.00
Butter Stamp, Horseshoe, Star, 2 Piece, Turned, 4 1/2 x 5 In. 305.00
Butter Stamp, Ladle, Combination, Maple, Cockscomb Finial, 19th Century, 11 In. 440.00
Butter Stamp, Leaf, Cow, Crimped Edges, Wood, 5 1/4 In. 330.00
Butter Stamp, Leaves, Branch, Cylindrical, 2 1/2 x 3 In. 110.00
Butter Stamp, Lollipop, Carved Eagle & Shield, Wm. Redmon 1820, 9 7/8 In. 3300.00
Butter Stamp, Lollipop, Carved, Pennsylvania German 650.00
Butter Stamp, Lollipop, Cow, Geometric, 2 Sides, F. McD, 3 1/2 x 7 1/2 In. ... 800.00
Butter Stamp, Lollipop, Daisy, Zigzag Border, 8 In. 85.00
Butter Stamp, Lollipop, Star, Geometric, 2 Sides, Wood, 4 x 7 1/4 In. 990.00
Butter Stamp, Lollipop, Stylized Eagle, Spread Wings, Crest, 9 3/4 In. 275.00
Butter Stamp, Pine Boughs, Wrapped In Ribbon, 3 In. 77.00
Butter Stamp, Pineapple, Handle, 4 1/8 In. 220.00
Butter Stamp, Pineapple, Leaf, Wood, M.C., 3 x 4 1/2 In. 140.00
Butter Stamp, Pineapple, Leaves, Handle, 4 7/8 In. 55.00
Butter Stamp, Pomegranate, Concentric Ring Border, 1-Piece Handle, 4 1/4 In. .. 85.00
Butter Stamp, Rolling, 4 Designs, Wood, G.M.T. Co., Germany, 8 In. 110.00
Butter Stamp, Rooster, Speckled, Leaves, 1-Piece Handle, 3 In. 275.00
Butter Stamp, Rooster, Tree, Case, 3 3/4 In. 220.00
Butter Stamp, Rose, 2 Buds, Threaded Handle, 4 1/8 In. 55.00
Butter Stamp, Rose, Yellow Butternut, Handle, 4 In. 110.00
Butter Stamp, Sheaf Of Wheat, Double, Oval, Signed, J.H., 1859, 3 3/4 x 6 In. 935.00
Butter Stamp, Sheaf Of Wheat, Handle, 4 1/2 In. 305.00
Butter Stamp, Sheaf Of Wheat, Handle, Wood, 3 x 5 1/8 In. 225.00
Butter Stamp, Sheaf Of Wheat, In Bell, 5 1/4 x 6 1/2 In. 110.00
Butter Stamp, Sheaf Of Wheat, In Bell, Wood, 3 1/4 x 3 3/4 In. 50.00
Butter Stamp, Sheep, Handle, 2 7/8 In. 990.00
Butter Stamp, Strawberries, Threaded Handle, 4 In. 220.00
Butter Stamp, Strawberry, In Bell, 3 x 5 In. 50.00
Butter Stamp, Stylized Eagle, Shield, Concentric Ring Border, 3 7/8 In. 110.00
Butter Stamp, Swan, Extended Wings, Cased, 1 3/4 In. 330.00
Butter Stamp, Swan, Feathered, 4 1/4 In. 165.00
Butter Stamp, Swan, In Bell, 1 3/4 x 3 1/4 In. 66.00
Butter Stamp, Swan, Leaves, Thistle, Handle, 4 In. 1760.00
Butter Stamp, Thistles, Double Border, 4 In. 110.00
Butter Stamp, Tulip, Flower, Leaves, Oval, Handle, 8 1/2 In. 660.00
Butter Stamp, Tulip, Flowers, Ferns, Handle, 5 1/4 In. 165.00
Butter Box, Tulip, Flowers, Handle, 3 1/3 In. 165.00
Butter Stamp, Tulip, Star, Handle, 3 3/4 In. 220.00
Butter Stamp, Tulip, Star, Moon, Crescent, 1 Piece, Turned, Wood, 5 In. 550.00
Butter Tub, Pine, Green Paint, Hand-Wrought Nails, Carved Handles, 1700s, 8 x 9 In. ... 1150.00
Cabbage Cutter, Hickory, Shaped Finial, Heart Cutout, 7 3/4 x 23 1/4 In. 275.00
Cabbage Cutter, Walnut, Heart Cutout, 19th Century, 16 x 7 In. 35.00
Cake Board, Woman Wearing Top Coat, Man On Reverse, 33 x 10 In. 575.00
Cake Board, Wood, Carved, 2 Sides, Man, Woman, Detailed Costume, 33 x 10 In. 575.00
Cake Box, Tin, Round, Inscribed, 11 x 8 1/2 In. 80.00
Can Opener, Adjustable, Crank Handle, Edlund, Pat. Apr. 21, 1925 .... 25.00
Can Opener, Cast Iron, Duket Mfg. Co., Toledo, Ohio, 1925, 6 1/4 In. 20.00
Can Opener, Steel, Sieger, 5 1/2 In. 15.00
Can Opener & Jar Opener, Tin, C.S. Ripley & Co., Cleveland, Oh., 8 1/4 In. 25.00

Canister, Cover, Jadite, Round, 5 3/4 In. 50.00
Canister, Cover, Sugar, Jadite, Square, 4 1/4 x 5 In. 295.00
Canister, Cover, Tea, Jadite, Square, 4 1/4 x 5 In. 265.00
Canister, Tea, Coffee, Tole, Black, Boardman & Sons, Conn., 19th Century, 20 x 14 In. . . . 92.00
Canister, Tea, Tin, Red, Gold Leaf Stenciling, 10 In. 56.00
Carving Set, Flint, Knife, Fork, Box 25.00
Cauldron, Brass, Hammered, Patinated, 11 In., Pair 175.00
Cheese Cutter, Cast Iron, Self Gauging, Revolving Wood Platform, Enterprise, 26 In. . . . 440.00
Cheese Cutter, Cast Iron, Steel, Wooden, Revolving Platform, 16 In. Diam. 225.00
Cherry Pitter, Cast Iron, Boss Raisin Seeder, Pat. Pdg., 11 3/4 In. 150.00
Cherry Pitter, Cast Iron, Cherry Stoner, Enterprise Pat Appl'd For, No. 12, 13 In. 125.00
Cherry Pitter, Cast Iron, Mechanical, Painted Wheel & Feet, 7 In. 1430.00
Cherry Pitter, Glass & Tin, Krasco, Pat. App For, Chicago Ill., 9 In. 30.00
Chestnut Roaster, Wrought Iron, Sheet Metal, Handle, Cylindrical, 15 x 18 x 9 1/2 In. . . 308.00
Chocolate Pot, Cover, Poppies, Austrian 170.00
Churn, Base, 4 Wood Staves, Painted, Tapered Sides, Steel Band, 23 In. 305.00
Churn, Cylindrical, Hand Crank, Early 20th Century, 15 In. 160.00
Churn, Dazey, No. 40, Glass, Embossed, Iron Crank, Wooden Paddles, Tin Lid 70.00
Churn, Pine, Green Paint, Original Dash, New England, 18th Century, 40 In. 920.00
Churn, Stave Construction, Red Wash, Piggin-Type Handle, 36 In. 385.00
Churn, Stave Construction, Turned Wooden Top, Piggin-Type Handle, 20 1/2 x 35 1/2 In. . 385.00
Churn, Tabletop, Glass, Whip, Beater Blades, Dazey, Churn Co., 11 In. 950.00
Churn, Tin, Cast Iron, Home Butter Merger, Patd Sept. 14, 1909 . . . . 300.00
Churn, Tin, Sloped Sides, Lid, Dasher, Green Paint, 21 In. 1760.00
Churn, White Cedar, No. 1, Cylinder Type, Wood, Crank, 3 Gal. 198.00
Churn, White Cedar, No. 2, Cylinder Type, Stenciled, 3 Gal. 75.00
Coffee Grinders are listed in their own category.
Coffee Mill, Cast Iron, Double Wheel, Drawer, Wooden Base, Enterprise 12 1/2 In. 478.00
Coffee Mill, Cast Iron, Single Wheel, Wooden Drawers, Base, Blue Paint, Spain, 10 In. . . . 180.00
Coffee Mill, King, No. 630 . . . . 30.00
Coffee Mill, Red Paint, Decal, Enterprise No. 5, Philadelphia 1200.00
Coffee Roaster, Cast Iron, 9 3/4 In. 575.00
Coffee Roaster, Crank Handle, Charcoal Fired, 4 Legs, 10 x 6 In. 525.00
Coffee Server, Lid, Thermo Proof, Orange Flowers, Silver Trim, Fraunfelter, 6 Cup 50.00
Coffeepot, Brown, White Flowers, Gooseneck Spout, Enamelware, c.1910, 10 In. 185.00
Coffeepot, Flowers, Blue Ground, Enamel, Nickel Plated, Late 19th Century, 12 x 5 In. . . 130.00
Coffeepot, Flowers, Pink, Blue & White, Enamelware, c.1910, 10 In. 495.00
Coffeepot, Perculator, Brass Base & Fittings, 2 Porcelain Handles, Wmf, 1920, 16 In. . . . 278.00
Coffeepot, Teal Blue & White Swirl, White Interior, Enamelware, c.1930, 9 1/2 In. 245.00
Coffeepot, Tin, Punched, Tulip, Flower Vase, Impressed J. Ketterer On Handle, 11 In. . . . 4050.00
Coffeepot, Wagner Mfg. Co., Sidney, O., Cast Iron, 5 In. 60.00
Colander, Tinware, Flared Edge, Riveted Handles, Collar Foot, 19th Century, 7 x 13 In. . . 80.00
Colander, Tinware, Shaker Style, Conical, 2 Ribbed Handles, 11 x 5 3/4 In. 110.00
Condiment Set, Donkey, Pulling Cart, Barrel Shape, Japan, 7 3/4 In., 4 Piece 30.00
Cooker, Campbell's Soup, Can Form, Chrome Legs, Kercher Electric, 23 In. 259.00
Cooker, Hot French Fried Popcorn, Art Deco Style, Black & White, 56 In. 1150.00
Cookie Board, Baby, Swaddled, Ruffled Bonnet, Wood, Tin Edge, 12 x 4 1/4 In. 305.00
Cookie Board, Flower Urn, Fruit, Indian, Tomahawk, Wood, 2 Sides, 4 x 6 In. 578.00
Cookie Board, Hand-Carved Images, Buildings, Figures, Wood, 4 x 19 3/4 In. 66.00
Cookie Board, Heart, Vine, 2 Flowers, Wood, Beveled Corners, 7 1/4 x 9 In. 415.00
Cookie Board, Incised Hearts, Stars, Wood, Penna., 2 3/4 x 4 3/4 In. 165.00
Cookie Board, King, Queen, Carved, 9 x 1 3/4 x 39 1/2 In. 440.00
Cookie Board, Man Carrying Baby In Backpack, Walnut, Carved, 10 x 26 1/2 In. 305.00
Cookie Board, Man Wearing Vest, Leggings, Coat, Hat, Walnut, Carved, 5 1/2 x 15 In. . . . 165.00
Cookie Board, Man, Woman, Victorian Clothes 3000.00
Cookie Board, Medieval Rider, Armored Horse, Carved, 13 1/4 x 10 In. 165.00
Cookie Board, Monkey, Insects, Bear, Swan, Cast Iron, 6 Sections, 4 1/4 x 6 In. 85.00
Cookie Board, Ovals, Eagle, Shield, Lion, Wood, 2 Sides, 4 1/2 x 7 In. 330.00
Cookie Board, Soldier, Holding Sword, Tent, Flag, Drum, Walnut, 10 x 12 In. 3750.00
Cookie Board, Woman In Long Dress, Man In Waistcoat, Hat, Carved, 20 x 8 In. 220.00
Cookie Cutter, Bear, Facing Left, Backplate, Rolled Edge Handle, 3 x 4 In. 22.00
Cookie Cutter, Bird, Applied Handle, Tin, 4 In., Pair 22.00
Cookie Cutter, Bird, Backplate, Tin, 4 & 5 In., Pair 105.00

Cookie Cutter, Bird, Tin, Loop Handle, 5 1/4 In. 165.00
Cookie Cutter, Bird, Tin, Wood, 4 1/2 In. 130.00
Cookie Cutter, Chalice, Tin, Backplate, Rectangular, Mounted, 3 3/4 In. 22.00
Cookie Cutter, Chalice, Tin, Backplate, Square, Mounted, 2 In. 6.00
Cookie Cutter, Dachshund, Backplate, 6 1/4 In. 72.00
Cookie Cutter, Deer, Leaping, Facing Right, Backplate, Handle, 4 1/4 x 5 1/4 In. 85.00
Cookie Cutter, Dog, Raised Tail, Facing Left, Facing Right, 3 3/4 In., Pair 70.00
Cookie Cutter, Elephant Facing Left, Backplate, 3 1/4 x 4 3/4 In. 95.00
Cookie Cutter, Elephant, Tin, Ear Detail, 5 1/4 In. 85.00
Cookie Cutter, Fish, Backplate, Handle, 4 1/2 & 6 In., 2 Piece 28.00
Cookie Cutter, Fish, Facing Left, Backplate, 2 1/4 x 6 In. 70.00
Cookie Cutter, Flowers, Geometric, Scalloped Edge, Tin, 3 Piece 39.00
Cookie Cutter, Heart, Spade, Club, Diamond, Tin, 3 In., 4 Piece 22.00
Cookie Cutter, Horse, Facing Left, Backplate, Finger Holes, 4 1/4 x 5 3/4 In. 110.00
Cookie Cutter, Horse, Facing Left, Backplate, Tin, 5 In. 39.00
Cookie Cutter, Horse, Tulip, Women, Cat, Bird, Duck, 3 1/4 To 6 1/2 In., 5 Piece 110.00
Cookie Cutter, Horse, With Rider, Tin, Spot Soldered, Handmade, 5 x 6 In. 275.00
Cookie Cutter, Indian, With Tomahawk, Tin, 8 1/2 In. 990.00
Cookie Cutter, Lion, Facing Left, Tin, Backplate, Handle, 3 x 4 In. 35.00
Cookie Cutter, Lovebirds, Shield, Bell, Tin, Folded Edge Handle, 1900s, 3 x 5 In. 240.00
Cookie Cutter, Man & Woman, Dancing, Tin, 8 In. 4290.00
Cookie Cutter, Man, Facing Forward, Top Hat, Backplate, 4 1/2 x 2 1/4 In. 60.00
Cookie Cutter, Man, Facing Right, Top Hat, Coattails, 11 1/4 x 3 3/4 In. 1155.00
Cookie Cutter, Man, On Horseback, Tin, 7 1/4 x 9 In. 1430.00
Cookie Cutter, Men, Standing, Tin, Early 20th Century, 12 In., 3 Piece 480.00
Cookie Cutter, Pioneer, Protesting, Tin, 8 1/2 In. 440.00
Cookie Cutter, Rabbit, Tin, 5 3/4 In. 80.00
Cookie Cutter, Revolver, Tin, 5 1/2 In. 110.00
Cookie Cutter, Rocking Horse, Handle, Tin, 10 x 14 1/4 In. 495.00
Cookie Cutter, Rocking Horse, Oval Backplate, Handle, 4 1/4 x 5 3/4 In. 50.00
Cookie Cutter, Roller, 6 Designs, Tin & Wood, 9 In. 65.00
Cookie Cutter, Saw, Carpenter, Tin, 6 In. 165.00
Cookie Cutter, Scissors, Tin, 5 1/4 In. 165.00
Cookie Cutter, Swan, Wood, Tin, 5 1/4 In. 250.00
Cookie Cutter, Uncle Sam, Tin, G.M.T. Co., Germany, 12 5/8 In. 825.00
Cookie Cutter, Woman, Facing Left, Hair Bun, Rectangular Backplate, 5 1/4 In. 61.00
Cookie Cutter, Woman, In Dress, Tin, 6 In. 105.00
Cookie Cutter, Woman, With Bonnet, Backplate, 4 1/2 x 5 In., Pair 61.00
Cookie Cutter, Woman, With Bonnet, Feet Facing Right, 5 1/4 In. 105.00
Cookie Press, Shortbread, Geometric Design, Maple, 15 In. 55.00
Corn Holders, Bakelite, Yellow, 3 In., 4 Piece 50.00
Cracker Jar, Flower Garlands, German, Signed, 1919 . . . . 66.00
Cream Separator, DeLaval, Model No. 7, Cast Iron, 24 In. 470.00
Cutlery Tray, Cover, Heart Shape Handle, Wood, 15 x 13 In. 1100.00
Cutlery Tray, Whalebone Handle, 6 x 14 x 10 In. 1150.00
Dipper, Brass, Iron, Star Chase Sign, Pierced Holes, 21 In., Pair 375.00
Dipper, Coconut Shell, Pewter Mounts, Wood Handle, 19th Century, 15 In. 115.00
Dish, Chicken Pie, Orange Glaze, Earthenware, Signed, 1970s, 3 1/2 x 12 1/2 In. 275.00
Dispenser, Kleanser Kate, No. K2356, Holes In Head, 6 3/8 In. . . . . *Illus* 28.00
Double Broiler, Griswold, Gridiron 195.00
Dough Box, Cover, Painted, Red, Dovetailed, Applied Handles, 32 x 19 x 11 In. 275.00
Dough Box, Cover, Poplar, Curved Ends, 13 x 34 x 15 In. 165.00
Dough Box, Painted, Orange, Dovetailed, Stenciled Cover, M Kroul 1846, 30 In. 56.00
Dough Box, Pine, Poplar, Red Wash, Canted Sides, Turned Legs, 26 x 37 In. 330.00
Dough Box, Poplar, Dovetailed, Red Wash, Cutout Handles, 1800s, 31 x 16 x 13 In. 395.00
Dough Box, Tuned Legs, Stretchers 2090.00
Dough Scraper, Wrought Iron, Single Piece, 3 In. 16.50
Dough Scraper, Wrought Iron, Triangular Blade, Marked AG, 1900, 3 1/4 x 4 1/2 In. 275.00
Doughnut Cutter, Cloverleaf Shape, Cast Iron, Metal Handles, 13 1/2 In. 110.00
Doughnut Cutter, Wood, 4 1/8 x 2 1/2 In. 65.00
Doughnut Lifter, 15 In. 85.00
Dry Measure, Wood, Red Paint, Peck, 1/2 Peck, 2 Piece 50.00
Dustpan, Sheet Iron, Oak Handle, New England, Late 18th Century, Large 285.00

Kitchen, Dispenser,
Kleanser Kate, No. K2356,
Holes In Head, 6 3/8 In.

Kitchen, Egg Plate, Ceramic,
Blue & Rust Flowers, Gold Trim,
12 Wells, 9 1/4 In.

Kitchen, Egg Plate, Pressed Glass,
Diamond Point, 12 Wells,
4 Sections, 12 In.

Dutch Oven, Cover, Griswold, Nickel Plated		85.00
Dutch Oven, Griswold, No. 6, Tite Top		115.00
Dutch Oven Set, Tin Cover, Marietta, Cast Iron, 2 Qt. & 1 Gal. & 2 Gal.		175.00
Egg Basket, Wire, Swing Handles, Arched Base, Early 20th Century, 11 x 11 In.		209.00
Egg Plate, Ceramic, Blue & Rust Flowers, Gold Trim, 12 Wells, 9 1/4 In.	*Illus*	15.00
Egg Plate, Pressed Glass, Diamond Point, 12 Wells, 4 Sections, 12 In.	*Illus*	40.00
Egg Timer, Little Red Riding Hood, Holding Timer, Wolf Sitting At Feet, 3 1/2 In.		185.00
Eggbeater, Betty Aplin, Tin, Red Plastic Cup, 6 Oz., 6 In.		50.00
Eggbeater, Cast Iron, Cyclone, Pat. 6-25-1901, 11 1/2 In.		85.00
Eggbeater, Cast Iron, Holts Patented Flared Dasher Egg Beater, N.Y., U.S.A., 10 1/2 In. . .		45.00
Eggbeater, Cast Iron, R.P. Scott & Co., Newark N.J., Patented, 10 1/2 In.		1250.00
Eggbeater, Christy Knife, Patented, Fremont, 11 1/2 In.		325.00
Eggbeater, Cyclone, Iron, Tin, Patented 1902, 11 1/2 In.		20.00
Eggbeater, Dover, Patented May 31, 1870, 10 In.		65.00
Eggbeater, H.L. Co., Side Handle, 8 1/2 In.		325.00
Eggbeater, Holt's, Patented, Flared Dasher, Side Handle, 8 1/2 In.		265.00
Eggbeater, Holt-Lyon, Rotary, 12 1/2 In.		45.00
Eggbeater, Maynard, Plastic Gear, Housing, Gold Plated, Handle, Roses, 11 1/2 In.		25.00
Eggbeater, Steel, Ladd Beater, July 7, 1908, Oct. 18, 1921, 11 1/2 In.		25.00
Eggbeater, Taplin, Light Running, Rotary, 11 1/2 In.		95.00
Eggbeater, Tin, Full Vision, A&j, Made In U.S.A., 7 In.		40.00
Eggcup, Wood, Flowers, Blue Ground, Yellow Interior, Pedestal Base, 2 5/8 x 2 In.		4180.00
Eggcup, Wood, Sprays Of Flowers, Salmon Ground, Polychrome, Lehnware, 3 1/2 In.		425.00
Food Chopper, Figural, Bird's Head, Steel Ferrule, Iron Blade, Wood Handle, 11 1/2 In. . . .		180.00
Fork, Toasting, Brass, Queen Anne Style		850.00
Fryer, Deep Fat, Wagner Ware, Basket		40.00
Funnel, Blown Glass, Ground Spout, Fluted, 6 1/4 x 4 1/2 In.		100.00
Grater, Nutmeg, Carved Coquilla Nut, Acorn Shape, 1800s, 2 1/2 In.		247.00
Grater, Nutmeg, Cast Iron, Bellows Shape, J.M. Smith, Patented June 7, 1870, 4 In.		259.00
Grater, Nutmeg, Egg Shape, Floral Sprays, Gilt Scrollwork, Enamel, France, c.1800, 2 In. .		320.00
Grater, Nutmeg, Japanned Tin, Paper Label, Rapid Nutmeg Grater, 6 In.		250.00
Grater, Nutmeg, Melon Shape, Whiting, c.1890		1265.00
Grater, Nutmeg, Silver, Screw Top, Egg Shape, Engraved WS, c.1790, 1 3/4 x 1 In.		1250.00
Grater, Nutmeg, Tin, Wood, Mechanical, Null, 8 In.		850.00
Grater, Tin, Punctured, Cast Iron Frame, Wood Plungers, Painted, 13 In.		468.00
Griddle, New England, Griswold, No. 12		245.00
Griddle, Wrought Iron, Slats, Hinged, Penny Feet, Handle, Early 1800s, 24 In.		56.00
Grill, Griswold, Box		45.00
Grinder, Nutmeg, Cowrie Shell, Silver Mounted, 3 In.		1090.00
Grinder, Nutmeg, Silver, Swinging Arm, W. McDonald, Scotland, 1864, 5 In.		1840.00
Grinder, Spice, Walnut, Brass, Iron, Top Crank Handle, 8 In.		240.00
Hourglass, 13 Seconds, Worn Label, 18th Century, 4 3/4 In.		405.00
Ice Cream Freezer, Wood, Cast Iron & Tin Crank, Triple Motion, White Mountain, 8 In. . .		113.00
Ice Cream Scoop, Brass, Chrome Plated, Gilcrest Co., 1920s		165.00

Ice Cream Scoop, Round, Hamilton Beach, 1950s 35.00
Ice Shaver, Nickel Plated, Cylindrical Shaving Catcher, 10 In. 99.00
Ice Tongs, Iron, Patented Mar 2 1869, 12 3/4 x 5 1/4 In. 85.00
Iron, Alcohol, Cast Iron, Nickel Plated, Fabrik Marke, 3 1/2 In. 615.00
Iron, Cast Iron, Turned Wood Handle, Trivet, Germany, c.1860, 7 1/2 In. 230.00
Iron, Charcoal Burning, Brass, Geometric Cutouts, Wood Handle, Holland, 8 1/2 In. 180.00
Iron, Charcoal, Cast Iron, Dragon, Wood Handle, Trivet, 6 In. 185.00
Iron, Crimper, Painted Design, American, 10 In. 155.00
Iron, Fluter, Cast Iron, Brass Rollers, Hand Crank, c.1866 .... 185.00
Iron, Gasoline, Cast Iron, Brass Tank, Fire Devil Chimney, Wood Handle, 9 1/2 In. 4999.00
Iron, Gasoline, Cast Iron, Brass Tank, Raropyr-Patent, 9 3/4 In. 3690.00
Iron, Gasoline, Cast Iron, Nickel Plated Tank, Rex-Patent, Trivet, 10 In. 3384.00
Iron, Polished Brass, Pierced Gallery, Turned Wood Handle, Trivet, Germany, 7 In. 269.00
Iron, Sadiron, Wapak, No. 5 .... 20.00
Iron, Slug, Bronze, Oak Leaves On Top, Wood Handle, Germany, 1870, 8 In. 77.00
Iron, Slug, Cast Iron, Nickel Plated, Heat Shield, Trivet, Brass, Pierced, c.1920, 7 1/2 In. .. 77.00
Iron, Slug, Nuremburg Box-Type, Brass, Wrought Iron Posts, Germany, 5 In. 215.00
Iron, Slug, Polished Brass, Etched Flowers, Germany, c.1780, 6 In. 215.00
Iron, Slug, Steel, Turned Wood Handle, 6 In. 140.00
Iron, Slug, Westphalian, Wrought Iron, Trivet, Germany, c.1840, 7 In. 255.00
Iron, Westphalian Ox-Tongue, Cast Iron, Porcelain Handle, Flowers, Germany, 8 In. 185.00
Jar, Cover, Bisque, Figural, Child's Head, Polychrome, Late 19th Century, 3 1/2 In. 15.00
Jar, Spice, Cover, Gray, Green Glaze, Stoneware, 1684 .... 495.00
Jar Opener, Tin, Turney Mfg. Co., Detroit, Mich, Pat Oct 31, 1905 .... 30.00
Kettle, Gypsy, Cast Iron, Wrought Swing Handle, Attached Tripod Feet, 12 x 13 1/2 In. .. 250.00
Kettle, Iron, Swing Bail Handle, Name On Lid, W. Resor & Co. Cincinnati, 6 1/2 In. 70.00
Knife Cleaner, Cast Iron Frame, Wood Drum Cylinder, Crank, Kents, England, 17 In. 320.00
Ladle, Deep Bowl, Singe Piece, Shaped Handle, 12 In. 95.00
Ladle, Maple, Oval Bowl, Hooked Handle, 18 In. 72.00
Ladle, Maple, Round Bowl, Hooked Handle, 15 1/2 In. 110.00
Ladle, Rat-Tail Support, Scrolled Handle, Wrought Iron, Brass Bowl, 12 1/2 In. 303.00
Ladle, Steel, Brass, Copper, Hanging Hook, 18th Century, 5 1/2 In. 441.00
Lemon Squeezer, Griswold, No. 250, Japanned, Aluminum Insert, 9 1/2 In. 80.00
Lemon Squeezer, Wood, 2 Arms Hinged, 10 1/2 In. 35.00
Match Holders can be found in their own category.
Match Safes can be found in their own category.
Mayonnaise Mixer, Wesson Oil, Glass, Metal, Screw Lid, Recipe On Jar, 12 1/2 In. . *Illus* 39.00
Measure Set, Straight Sides, Rectangular Handle, France, Liter To Centiliter, 7 Piece 575.00
Meat Grinder, Winchester, No. W12, Metal, Steel, Clamp, Wooden Handle, 6 x 11 In. ... 45.00
Meat Hook, 4 3-Prong Hooks, Center Ring Brace, Cross Straps, Iron, 10 x 13 In. 220.00
Mixer, Malt, Hamilton Beach, No. 18, Porcelain, Black, 2 Speeds, 1940s 120.00
Mixer, Milk Shake, Hamilton Beach, 3 Beaters, Porcelain, Green, 14 x 20 In. 248.00
Mixer, Milk Shake, Hamilton Beach, Steel, Enameled, 3 Speeds, 3 Beaters, 20 In. 90.00
Mixer, Milk Shake, Handy Hannah, No. 504, Cast Iron Base, Whitman, Mass., 13 In. 90.00
Mixer, Milk Shake, Mix 'n Whip Master, Green Porcelain, Racine Electric Prod., 20 In. .. 120.00
Mixer, Milk Shake, White Flash, Hamilton Beach, Brass Label, 17 In. 55.00
Molds may also be found in the Pewter and Tinware categories.
Mold, Butter, Beaver, Maple, New York, Early 19th Century, 10 3/4 In. 49.00
Mold, Butter, Flowers, Cow, Farmers, Sickle, Rake, 5-Part, Hinged, 20 1/2 x 20 1/2 In. 330.00

Kitchen, Mayonnaise Mixer,
Wesson Oil, Glass, Metal
Screw Lid, Recipe On Jar,
12 1/2 In.

Kitchen, Mold,
Chocolate, Shells,
Matfer-Inoxydable,
7 1/2 x 4 3/4 In.

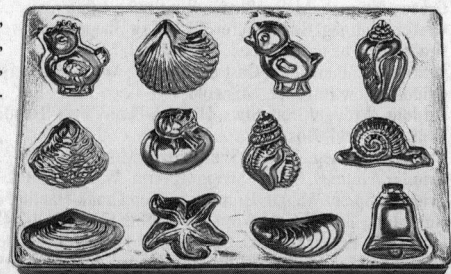

Mold, Butter, Flowers, House, Shield, 5-Part, Hinged, Primitive Style, 13 x 13 In. 55.00
Mold, Butter, Flowers, Swan, House, Deer, 5 Sections, Hinged, Canted Sides, 7 x 7 In. . . . 110.00
Mold, Butter, Fruit, Thistles, 8 Squares, Cased, Footed Frame, 5 x 11 x 3 In. 165.00
Mold, Butter, Geometric Hearts, Herringbone, Carved, 2 Panels, 4 3/4 x 8 In. 165.00
Mold, Butter, Pomegranate, Round, Pat. April 17, 1866 . . . . 120.00
Mold, Butter, Swan, Square, Wood, 4 1/4 x 8 In. 125.00
Mold, Butter, Wheat Sheaf, Round, Late 19th Century 50.00
Mold, Butter, Wheat Stalk, Wood 80.00
Mold, Cake, Rabbit, Cast Iron, Griswold, 11 In. . . . . .230.00 to 285.00
Mold, Cake, Santa, Hello Kiddies On Front, Griswold, c.1940, 12 x 6 3/4 In. 575.00
Mold, Cake, Swirls, Manganese Glaze, Earthenware, John Bell, 6 1/2 x 9 1/2 In. 4900.00
Mold, Candle, see Tinware category.
Mold, Cheese, Stave Construction, Bentwood Bands, Wooden Pegs, Painted, 14 x 8 In. . . . 195.00
Mold, Chocolate, Bonzo The Dog, 1930s 95.00
Mold, Chocolate, Lamb, Cast Iron, 12 1/2 In. 88.00
Mold, Chocolate, Santa Claus, Brass, 2 Parts 59.00
Mold, Chocolate, Santa Claus, Hiking, Tin, No. 221 . . . . 450.00
Mold, Chocolate, Shells, Matfer-Inoxydable, 7 1/2 x 4 3/4 In. . . . . *Illus* 60.00
Mold, Cookie, Cow, Round, 19th Century 345.00
Mold, Flower & Leaf, Cherry, A. Collard, New England, 10 1/8 x 1 3/8 x 8 1/8 In. 625.00
Mold, Food, Bear, On Sled, Wood, 14 x 16 In. 80.00
Mold, Food, Bear, Oval, Ceramic, Tan Glaze, England, 9 1/4 In. 138.00
Mold, Food, Circular, Ribbed, Tin Lined, France, c.1900, 4 x 10 1/2 In. 145.00
Mold, Food, Sheaf Of Wheat, Brown Glaze, Redware, Maine, 3 1/4 x 4 3/4 x 6 1/4 In. . . . 112.00
Mold, Food, Swirl Shape, Redware, 19th Century, 7 1/2 In. 69.00
Mold, Food, Thistle, Flowers, Ironstone 62.00
Mold, Food, Turk's Head, Copper, Rim Mounted Ring, 10 1/2 In. 290.00
Mold, Gingerbread, Man On 1 Side, Woman On Other, 15 x 4 In. 144.00
Mold, Ice Cream, see Pewter category.
Mold, Jelly, Ear Of Corn, Tin Sides, Copper Top, 5 3/4 x 4 x 4 In. 125.00
Mold, Jelly, Flower, Butternut, 4 1/2 In. 110.00
Mold, Jelly, Grape Bunch, Tin Sides, Copper Top, 5 3/4 x 4 1/4 x 3 3/4 In. 125.00
Mold, Jelly, Lion, Tin Sides, Copper Top, 19th Century, 7 In. 205.00
Mold, Lamb Shape, 2 Parts, Redware, 19th Century, 6 x 8 In. 200.00
Mold, Maple Sugar, Cutout Heart, New England, 18th Century, 9 In. 250.00
Mold, Maple Sugar, Mermaid, Monkey, Ship, Figures Working, Carved Wood, 3 x 20 In. . . 248.00
Mold, Pastry, Cornucopia, Cast Iron, Oval, 4 1/4 x 5 3/4 In. 72.00
Mold, Patty, Griswold, No. 1, Box 30.00
Mold, Patty, Griswold, No. 2, Round & Heart Shaped 55.00
Mold, Pudding, Glaze, Scalloped Edge, Redware, Pa., 19th Century, 1 1/2 x 5 1/2 In. 154.00
Mold, Pudding, Mottled, Glazed, Embossed Flower Urn, Redware, 2 x 5 1/2 In. 110.00
Mold, Santa Claus, Black, Iron, Griswold 455.00
Mold, Squirrel Eating Nut, Wood, Scratch Carved, 5 3/4 x 5 1/4 In. 440.00
Mold, Turk's Head, Glazed, Scalloped Sides, Redware, 2 1/4 x 6 1/4 In. 44.00
Mold, Turk's Head, Glazed, Spiral, Embossed Interior, Redware, 3 x 8 In. 22.00
Mold, Turk's Head, Orange Glaze, Brown Sponged Rim, Redware, Pa., 8 3/4 x 2 1/4 In. . . 55.00
Mortar & Pestle, Burl, Turned Bands, Ceramic Head On Pestle, 5 3/4 x 5 In. 110.00
Mortar & Pestle, Burl, Vertical Figure In Bowl, Turned Pestle, 5 1/2 x 5 1/4 In. 220.00
Mortar & Pestle, Cast Iron, 7 1/2 In. 45.00
Mortar & Pestle, Cast, Flared, Molded Rim, Iron, W.B. & Co., No. 2, 3 3/4 x 4 In. 60.00
Mortar & Pestle, Ceramic, T.M. & S. Acid Proof, 14 In. 190.00
Mortar & Pestle, Hardwood, Blue Paint On Mortar, 5 1/2 x 7 1/4 In. 605.00
Mortar & Pestle, Iron, c.1900, 7 In. 80.00
Mortar & Pestle, Turned Hardwood, 1700s, 8 1/2 x 6 In. 364.00
Mortar & Pestle, Walnut Burl, 7 1/2 In. 125.00
Mortar & Pestle, Wood, Turned Maple, Incised Rings, 6 5/8 In. 110.00
Muffineer, Silver Plated, Geometric Engraving, Footed, Baluster Shape, 7 5/8 In. 190.00
Napkin Holder, Bakelite, Bird, Red, 2 1/5 In. 80.00
Napkin Holder, Bakelite, Dog, Green, Painted Eyes & Nose, 2 3/4 In. 70.00
Oyster Cooler, Countertop, Tin, Insulated, Hinged Glass Center, Spigot, Lid, 17 1/2 In. . . 75.00
Pan, Corn Stick, Griswold, No. 262, Crispy Corn Or Wheat 75.00
Pan, Corn Stick, Griswold, No. 273 . . . . 35.00
Pan, Loaf, Griswold, No. 877, 9 5/8 x 5 3/16 In. 325.00

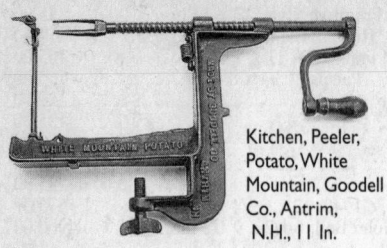

Kitchen, Peeler,
Potato, White
Mountain, Goodell
Co., Antrim,
N.H., 11 In.

Kitchen, Planning Kit,
Con Edison, Modern
Kitchen, Plastic
Appliances, Box, 10 1/2 In.

Pan, Muffin, Gem, Favorite, Piqua Ware, No. 3	275.00
Pan, Muffin, Gem, Griswold, No. 3	45.00
Pan, Muffin, Gem, Griswold, No. 11, Erie, Pa., U.S.A., 950	50.00
Pan, Muffin, Gem, Griswold, No. 12	410.00
Pan, Muffin, Gem, Griswold, No. 17	125.00 to 145.00
Pan, Muffin, Gem, Griswold, No. 17, Wide Center	310.00
Pan, Muffin, Gem, Wagner Ware L	265.00
Pan, Muffin, Golf Ball, Griswold, No. 19	100.00
Pan, Muffin, Griswold, No. 14	290.00
Pan, Muffin, Griswold, No. 16	325.00 to 385.00
Pan, Popover, Griswold, No. 10, Erie	60.00
Pan, Popover, Wagner Ware, No. 1323	30.00
Pan, Wagner Ware, Sidney, O., No. 4, Center Logo, Heat Ring	150.00
Pan, Wagner Ware, Sidney, O., No. 7, Center Logo, Heat Ring	85.00
Pan Set, Brass, Copper Rivets, Tubular Iron Handles, 4 1/2 x 10 To 9 1/2 x 20 In.	660.00
Pastry Blender, Tin, 6 Wires In Round Hoop, Lambert, Patent No. 148655	20.00
Pastry Wheel, Iron Shaft, Brass Handle, New England, 18th Century	285.00
Pastry Wheel, Wood, 4-Tine Biscuit Prick On End, Punched BC, 1842	310.00
Peel, Ram's Horn Finial, Wrought Iron, 46 1/4 In.	99.00
Peel, Wrought Iron, Ram's-Head End, Branded, S. Dill, 40 In.	290.00
Peeler, Apple, Cast Iron, Ax Head, Keen Kutter, E.C. Simmons Hardware Co., 1898	60.00
Peeler, Apple, Hand Crank, R.P. Scott & Co., Baltimore, 1880, 10 x 8 x 14 In.	85.00
Peeler, Apple, Hudson, Leominster, Mass.	110.00
Peeler, Apple, Nonpareil, J.L. Haven & Co., Cin., O., Patented May 6, 1856	1000.00
Peeler, Potato, White Mountain, Goodell Co., Antrim, N.H., 11 In. .... *Illus*	59.00
Pie Bird, Duck, Blue, Yellow, 5 1/4 In.	75.00
Pie Bird, Duck, Yellow, Brown, 5 1/4 In.	75.00
Pie Bird, Morton's, Yellow, Green, Pink, Patch, 5 In.	35.00
Pie Board, Pine, Round, Hanging Hole, Cutout Handle, 33 x 38 In.	330.00
Pie Board, Wooden, Lollipop Handle, Late 18th Century, 27 x 19 In.	350.00
Pie Crimper, Iron, 5 1/2 In.	35.00
Pie Crimper, Whalebone, Figural, Unicorn, 7 In.	1100.00
Pie Lifter, Wire Prongs, Wood Handle, 15 In.	55.00
Pie-Alamoder, Triangular Flat Bowl, Push Plunger, Aluminum, Wood Handle, 9 In.	5500.00
Planning Kit, Con Edison, Modern Kitchen, Plastic Appliances, Box, 10 1/2 In. ..... *Illus*	30.00
Pot, Copper, Tin Interior, Wrought Iron Mount, Cylindrical, 5 3/4 x 10 1/2 In.	69.00
Pot, Water, Wooden, Turned Incised Rings, Bulbous Base, Flared Rim, 16 x 10 In.	140.00
Pot, Wrought Iron Mounted, Tin Interior, Cylindrical, France, c.1885, 6 x 10 1/2 In.	90.00
Pot, Wrought Iron, Copper Cover, France, c.1900, 5 x 10 In.	105.00
Pot Set, Enamel, White, Red Handle, Rim, Covers, 6 1/4 To 8 1/2 In., 3 Piece	45.00
Rack, Drying, Candle, Maple & Ash, X-Shaped Base, 4 Arms, Ohio, 20 In.	374.00
Rack, Roasting, Wrought Iron, Bell Shaped Spits, Tripod Base, 29 In.	3740.00
Reamers are listed in their own category.	
Recipe Box, Cover, Copper, Brass Plaque, Old Dutch International, 3 1/4 x 5 1/4 In.	10.00
Roaster, Chestnut, Tin, Pierced Lid, Curved Raising Lever, Turned Wood Handle, 33 In.	165.00
Roaster, Oval, Wagner Ware, Magnalite, Large	55.00
Roasting Jack, Brass Clockwork Drive Mechanism, 2 Speeds, Lion Paw Feet, Iron, 13 In.	245.00
Rolling Pin, Glass Blown, Aqua, Cobalt Blue Looping, 13 1/4 In.	110.00
Rolling Pin, Springerle, Animals, Buildings, Flowers, Birds, Turned Handles, 17 In.	435.00
Rolling Pin, Springerle, Boat, House, Fish, Bird, Castle, Flowers, Berry, Germany, 16 In.	165.00

Rolling Pin, Stoneware, Blue & White Flower Border, Compliments Of W.M. Holbert ... 358.00
Rolling Pin, Stoneware, Blue & White, 2 Wood Handles, 14 In. 120.00
Rolling Pin, Whale Bone & Lignum Vitae 840.00
Salamander, Shaped Handle, Hole, Iron, 18th Century, 18 In. 210.00
Salt, Master, Flowers, Leaves, Pink Ground, Red, Green, Footed, 3 In. . . . . .2310.00 to 3360.00
Salt & Pepper Shakers are listed in their own category.
Sausage Stuffer, Cherry, Walnut, Screw-On Filler Cap, Chip Carved Edge, J.E. John, 9 In. 395.00
Sausage Stuffer, Enterprise, No. 15, Cast Iron, Crank, 2 Qt. 99.00
Sausage Stuffer, Enterprise, No. 31, Cast Iron, Crank, Drake Hardware, 6 Qt. 396.00
Scoop, Ice Cream, Block Cutter, Standard Industrial, Patented 1903, 19 In. 525.00
Scoop, Ice Cream, Clipper Cone Disher, Nickel Plated, Wood Handle, Geer Co., 9 1/2 In. . 90.00
Scoop, Ice Cream, Cone Shape, Nickel Plated, Wooden Handle, c.1935 . . . . 4200.00
Scoop, Ice Cream, Gilchrist, No. 31, Brass, Wood Handle, Thumb Trigger, 11 In. 145.00
Scoop, Ice Cream, Gilchrist, No. 31, Polished Brass, Box 140.00
Scoop, Ice Cream, Heart Shape, Nickel-Plated Brass, Wooden Handle, 1925 . . . . 8000.00
Scoop, Ice Cream, Nickel-Plated Brass, Square Bowl, Thumb Push Plunger, 7 1/2 In. 245.00
Sharpener, Knife, Sharpeit, Cast Iron, Dazey Churn Co., St. Louis, 5 1/2 In. 25.00
Shaver, Snow Cone, Brass, Nickel Plated, Cone Shape Bowl, Cast Iron Handle, 7 1/2 In. . 358.00
Shirt Ruffler, Cast Iron, Marked North Bros. Mfg. Co., Philadelphia, 19th Century, 9 In. . 58.00
Sifter, Flour, Pine & Tin, Wood Handle, Label, Blood's, Ptd. Sept. 17, 1861 . . . . 1265.00
Sifter, Flour, Tin & Wood, Duplex Brand, Ullrich Tinware Co., Pat. Nov. 1917, 5 Cup. . . . 30.00
Sifter, Flour, Tin, Wood, Duplex, Ullrich Tinware, Patent 1917 & 1922, 5 Cup 30.00
Skillet, Cover, Glass, Wagner Ware, 11 In. 25.00
Skillet, Griswold, Breakfast, Best Made, Square, 3 Sections 50.00
Skillet, Griswold, Breakfast, Cliff Cornell, Square . . . . .125.00 to 135.00
Skillet, Griswold, No. 3, Small Logo 15.00
Skillet, Griswold, No. 4, Large Logo 60.00
Skillet, Griswold, No. 5, Small Logo, Hinge 55.00
Skillet, Griswold, No. 5, Small Logo, Small Bottom 25.00
Skillet, Griswold, No. 8, Good Health 40.00
Skillet, Griswold, No. 8, Slant Logo, Smooth Bottom 25.00
Skillet, Griswold, No. 9, Large Emblem 40.00
Skillet, Griswold, No. 10, Block, Heat Ring 55.00
Skillet, Griswold, No. 11, Erie 95.00
Skillet, Griswold, Victor, No. 8 . . . . 35.00
Skillet, Griswold, Victor, No. 9 . . . . 45.00
Skillet, Piqua Ware, No. 3, Favorite 20.00
Skillet, Sidney, No. 10 . . . . 45.00
Skillet, Vollrath Ware, No. 4 . . . . 45.00
Skillet, Wagner Ware, Aluminum, Hammered, Stylized Logo 35.00
Skillet, Wagner Ware, No. 2 . . . . 120.00
Skillet, Wagner Ware, No. 4, Heat Ring, Stylized Logo 35.00
Skillet, Wagner Ware, No. 7, Center Heat Ring 75.00
Skillet, Wagner Ware, No. 7, Raised Letters, Cover, Nickel Plated 25.00
Skillet, Wagner Ware, No. 9, Cover, Drip Drop 65.00
Skillet, Wagner Ware, No. 9, Heat Ring, Sidney, O. 65.00
Skillet, Wagner Ware, No. 11, Heat Ring, Sidney, O. 100.00
Skillet, Wapak, No. 3, Indian Chief, Hollow Ware High Grade, Iron, Marked, 6 1/2 In. . . . 220.00
Skillet, Wapak, No. 11 . . . . 60.00
Skillet Set, Griswold, Nos. 0, 3, 14 & 20, Rack 4500.00
Skimmer, Brass Bowl, Ring Turned, Scrolled Hook, Wrought Iron Handle, 18 In. 49.00
Skimmer, Brass, England, c.1880, 18 x 6 In. 295.00
Slicer, Bread, Cast Iron, Rotating Knife, Pe. De., Germany 111.00
Slicer, Stalk, Rhubarb, Heart Cutout Base & Sides, Dated 1853 . . . . 395.00
Smoothing Board, Painted, Blue, Red Tulip, Carved, Horse Handle, 5 x 27 In. 193.00
Smoothing Board, Painted, Initials, Carved Horse Handle, Incised Bridle, 4 x 26 1/2 In. . 160.00
Smoothing Board, Wood, Chip Carved, Compass Star, Painted, Horse Handle, 5 x 21 In. . 248.00
Soap Dish, Carved Wood, 1 Piece, 1 1/2 x 4 3/4 x 2 1/2 In. 130.00
Spatula, Forged Iron, Cutout Heart In Handle, Marked BL, 1818, 18 3/8 In. 4180.00
Spatula, Handle Punched P.E. Will, Iron, c.1800 . . . . 450.00
Spatula, Punched Engraved With Initials, Iron, Pennsylvania, 1820, 16 1/2 In. 495.00
Spatula Fork, Combination, Blacksmith, Iron, Pennsylvania, Early 19th Century 165.00
Spice Box, 7 Drawers, Almond Label, 10 In. 325.00

Spice Box, Pewter, Flowers, Cherubs, Hinged Covers, German, 1708 .... 695.00
Spice Box, Slide Lid, Dovetailed, Blue Ground, White, Salmon, Tulips, c.1780, 9 x 5 In. . 36300.00
Spice Box, Softwood, 3 Drawers, Scrolled, Pegged, 19th Century, 12 1/2 x 12 1/2 x 7 In. . . 440.00
Spice Box, Tin, Oriental Design, 13 x 9 In. 200.00
Spice Box, Walnut, c.1860 .... 1450.00
Spice Box, Wooden, Round, 8 Containers Inside, Contents 350.00
Spice Chest, Burlwood, 8 Small & 2 Large Drawers 715.00
Spice Chest, Dovetailed, 12 Drawers, Green Paint, 19 x 12 1/4 x 8 1/2 In. 2588.00
Spit, Cased Clockwork Mechanism, Forged Iron, Brass Bail Handle, Paw Feet 450.00
Spit Jack, Round, Cast Iron Hanger, Brass Crane, Key, 12 1/2 In. 165.00
Spoon Rest, Black-Eyed Susan, Cardinal China 10.00
Spoon Rest, Fish Shape, Blue, White, Porcelain, 5 3/4 In. 39.00
Sprinkler Bottle, Flat Iron, Ivy Decoration, Cardinal China 50.00
Sprinkler Bottle, Iron, Green Ivy, Cardinal China Co., 5 1/4 In. 50.00
Sprinkler Bottle, Merry Maid, Plastic, Yellow, 6 2/3 In. 75.00
Sprinkler Bottle, Siamese Cat, Ceramic, 8 3/4 In. 225.00
Stand, Kettle, Brass, Iron, Scalloped Apron, 2-Headed Eagle, 9 1/2 x 9 1/2 In. 135.00
Stand, Kettle, Brass, Pierced Top, Wrought Iron Base, Hinged Handles, 12 1/2 x 14 In. ... 275.00
Stand, Kettle, Brass, Wrought Iron, Openwork, Leaves, Scroll, Cabriole Legs, 15 x 11 In. 205.00
Stand, Kettle, George III Style, Mahogany, Late 19th Century, 28 1/2 x 17 In. 405.00
Stand, Kettle, George III, Mahogany, Inlaid, Oval Scalloped Gallery, 26 x 15 In. 530.00
Stand, Kettle, Iron, Brass, Heart, Scrolled Supports, Cabriole Legs, 11 x 11 In. 39.00
Stove, Tall Belly, Flat Top, Square Base, Iron, Tin Ash Drawer, Zoar, 24 x 23 x 36 In. 275.00
Stove Plate, Horatio Seymour Bust, Cast Iron, Blue, Silver, 16 x 17 In. 650.00
Strawholder, Glass, Metal Insert, 11 In. 145.00
Stringholder, Beehive, Cast Iron, 1855 Patented, 7 x 7 1/2 In. 225.00
Stringholder, Beehive, Cast Iron, 5 x 6 1/2 In. 45.00
Stringholder, Dutch Girl, Red Hat, Chalkware 60.00
Sugar, Cover, Wooden, Molded Base, Yellow Paint, 4 3/4 x 4 1/4 In. 358.00
Sugar, Wooden, Sponge Painted, 6 x 5 In. 495.00
Sugar, Wooden, Wire Bail Handle, 2 1/2 x 2 1/4 In. 175.00
Sugar Nippers, Cast Iron, 9 1/2 In. 195.00
Sugar Nippers, Cast Iron, Tooled Flower, 10 In. 635.00
Sugar Nippers, Engraved Feathers, Wrought Steel, Brass, 10 In. 150.00
Sugar Nippers, Forged Iron, Mid 1800s, 7 1/2 In. 280.00
Sugar Nippers, Stamped, Star & Scallop, Iron, J. Nibb, 9 1/4 In. 360.00
Table, Dough, French Provincial, Fruitwood, Planked Top, Square Legs, 19 x 48 x 24 In. . 1090.00
Table, Dough, Softwood, 1-Board Top, Tapered Legs, Painted, 28 1/2 x 39 x 19 In. 660.00
Table, Dough, Softwood, 2-Board Top, Dovetailed, Pa., 28 1/2 x 48 x 27 1/2 In. 798.00
Table, Dough, Softwood, 2-Board Top, Pine Top, Dovetailed, Stretchers, 28 x 46 x 26 In. . 2090.00
Table, Dough, Walnut, Plank Top, End Drawer, Trough, 31 x 31 x 71 In. 1380.00
Tea Strainer, Boy, Kneeling, Ruffled Collar, Yellow & Green, Screw Top, Germany, 4 In. 175.00
Teakettle, Cast Iron, Gooseneck Spout, Hinged, I.A. Sheppard & Co., Baltimore, 9 1/2 In. 110.00
Teakettle, Copper, Dovetailed, Gooseneck Spout, Cast Brass Handle, Acorn Finial 125.00
Teakettle, Copper, Dovetailed, Gooseneck Spout, J.H. Blondel, 6 Qt. 200.00
Teakettle, Cover, Cast Iron, Gooseneck Spout, Swing Handle, 7 In. 29.00
Teakettle, Donut, Copper, 2 Iron Handles, 20 x 10 In. 145.00
Teakettle, Electric, Copper, Silver Plated, Hammered, 8 Sides, Peter Behrens, 1909 ..... 650.00
Teakettle, Gooseneck Spout, Cast Iron, Swing Handle, 7 1/4 In. 145.00
Teakettle, Griswold, No. 6, Slant Logo, Erie, Flat Bottom 85.00
Teakettle, Wagner Ware, Wire Bail Handle, Wood Grip, Aluminum, 6 Qt. 90.00
Teapot, Cover, Oval, Raised Rice Design, Cast Iron, Signed, 19th Century, 8 In. 345.00
Toaster, Flip-Flop, Chrome, Emergex, Patented July 28, 1914 .... 55.00
Toaster, Wrought Iron, 8 U-Shaped Holders, Open Spike, Swing Handle, 7 x 15 In. 290.00
Toaster, Wrought Iron, Arched Racks, Hinged, Handle, 31 x 13 x 26 In. 2420.00
Toaster, Wrought Iron, Christmas Tree Dividers, Ring Top, 18th Century, 20 In. 290.00
Toaster, Wrought Iron, Ram's-Horn Supports, Swivel Rack, Tripod Base, Penny Feet 160.00
Trammel, Keyhole, Bird, Flowers, Leaves, Wrought Iron, Brass Urn Finial, 1846, 21 In. . . 2310.00
Trivet, see Trivet category.
Utensil Rack, Black, Stepped Crest, 2 Birds, Scrolling, 5 Hooks, Iron, 9 1/2 x 14 In. 248.00
Utensil Set, Brass & Iron, Pennsylvania, 18th Century, 4 Piece 495.00
Utensil Set, Oval, Scrolled Ends, Wrought Iron, 19th Century, 3 Piece 195.00
Vacuum Bottle, Balloon Brand, Tin, Lithograph, H.H. Vacuum Bottle Works, 11 In. 365.00

Wafer Iron, Flowers, Round, Long Handles, Cast Iron, 28 x 6 In.   160.00
Wafer Iron, Scissors, Handle, Rectangle Terminals, Heart, Monogram, 1763, 32 1/2 In. . .   978.00
Wafer Iron, Scissors, Loop Handle, Eagle, Shield, Inscribed, Penna., c.1800, 29 1/4 In. . .   1610.00
Waffle Iron, 5 Hearts, Cast Iron, Handles, Late 19th Century, 14 In. 160.00
Waffle Iron, C.H. Phillips, Cast Iron, 16 In. 130.00
Waffle Iron, Griswold, Heart & Star, Ball Hinge, 8 1/2 In. 230.00
Waffle Iron, Griswold, No. 7, Finger Slot Hinge 70.00
Waffle Iron, Griswold, No. 8, Finger Slot Hinge, Wood Handles 125.00
Waffle Iron, Griswold, No. 8, Hammered, 8-Sided Base 135.00
Waffle Iron, Griswold, No. 8, The American . . . . .40.00 to 75.00
Waffle Iron, Griswold, No. 8, Victor, Ball Hinge 85.00
Waffle Iron, O.M.S., No. 8, Cross Shape, 5 Small Rectangular Waffles, 10 In. 110.00
Waffle Iron, Wagner Ware, Cast Iron, 8 In. 88.00
Warming Dome, Iron, Tin, Shaped Handle, 19th Century, 9 1/2 x 19 1/2 x 14 1/2 In. 110.00
Wash Tub, Wooden, Shaker Type, Iron Band Around Bottom, 21 x 18 In. 140.00
Washing Machine, Rocket, c.1870, 25 x 28 In. 425.00
Washing Machine, Steam, Paramount, Copper, Cast Metal, Crank, Patented 1916, 19 In. .   176.00
Washing Machine, Wood, Side Handle, Iron Gears, Success, S.M. Smith, 39 In. 565.00
Whip, Dream Cream, Mechanical, Kohler Die & Specialty Co., 9 In. 95.00
Whisk, Twisted Wire, c.1890, 8 In. 15.00
Wine Measure, Painted, France, c.1900 . . . .   750.00
Wringer, Household No. 20, Wood, Cast Iron Marquee, American, 29 In. 154.00
Wringer, Salesman's Sample, Lovell, Pat.1896, 7 x 7 In. 220.00

KNIFE collectors usually specialize in a single type. In the 1960s, the
United States government passed a law that required knife manufacturers to mark their knives with the country of origin. This seemed to
encourage the collectors, and knife collecting became an interest of a
large group of people. All types of knives are collected, from top quality twentieth-century examples to old bone- or pearl-handled knives in
excellent condition.

Anglers, Stainless Steel, Serrated Edge, Disgorger, Retractable Ruler, Luna, Italy 55.00
Army, 1P1888, Second Type, Wood Grip, Leather Scabbard, England, 1899, 11 3/4 In. . . .   86.00
Belt Buckler, Touche, Stainless Handle, Folding Blade, Gerber, Box, 1 3/4 x 2 5/8 In. . . .   120.00
Berber Belt, Leather Grip, Fiber Bands, Leather Scabbard, Tassel, North Africa, 8 In. . . .   43.00
Blubber, Mincing, Wood Scabbard, 2 Handles, 19th Century, 36 In. 470.00
Blubber, Wrought Iron, Wood, T-Style Handle, 1800s, 40 x 22 In. 78.00
Bolo, US, Scabbard, 1910, 10 In. 58.00
Bolo, Wood Grip, Jute Scabbard, American, 1917, 10 1/4-In. Blade 125.00
Bowie, Collins No. 18, 9 1/2 In. 230.00
Bowie, D-Handle, Confederate, Wood, Scabbard, 20 In. 1380.00
Bowie, Double X, Sheath, 9 1/2 In. 69.00
Bowie, Wood Handle, c.1850, 14 1/8 In. 425.00
Bowie, Wood Handle, S Brass Crossguard, Leather Scabbard, Modern, 15 In. 69.00
Bowie, Wrought Iron Blade, D-Shape Guard, Carved Wood Grip, 20 1/2 In. 588.00
Bullet, Lockback, Remington No. R1306, 8 In. 489.00
Dagger, Armor Piercing, Gold Damascene Inlaid, Watered Blade, Leaves, 9 7/8 In. 1555.00
Dagger, Herder, Solingen Wood Handle, c.1930 . . . .   575.00
Dagger, Hitler Youth, Scabbard, 5 In. . . . . .58.00 to 92.00
Dagger, Horse Head, Gold Damascene Inlaid, Watered Blade, Leaves, 1800s, 15 1/2 In. . .   1725.00
Dagger, Nazi Red Cross, Scabbard, 10 1/2 In. 374.00
Dagger, Nazi, S.A., Black Scabbard, 9 In. 259.00
Diving, Steel Blade, Aluminum Grip, Plastic Sheath, East Germany, 6 7/8-In. Blade 190.00
Facine, Revolutionary War, Iron 185.00
Fighting, Western, Leather Handle, 8 In. 80.00
Fighting, Wilkinson, 1st Model, Fairborn-Sykes, Scabbard 450.00
Gaucho, Pierced Leather Covered Scabbard, Argentina, c.1850, 10 1/8 In. 185.00
Hunting, Arkansas Toothpick, Antler Handle, Brass Guard, 13 In. 220.00
Hunting, Bone Handle, Sid Bell, 3 1/2 In. 69.00
Hunting, Sheath, Henckel, 5 1/2 In. 35.00
Lucite Washer Handle, Aluminum Pommel, Gray Scabbard, World War II, 9 In. 40.00
Machete, Canvas Case, Truetemper, American, 1945, 22 3/4 In., 18-In. Blade 70.00
Paratrooper, Gravity, Black Grip, Eickhorn Rosterie, 1960, 9 In.   190.00

Pesh Kabz, Bone Grip, Leather Covered Scabbard, Persia, 7 3/4-In. Blade	335.00
Pocket, Folding, Hammerhead, Etched Blade, Sheath, Box, Paperwork, Case, 1978	61.00
Pocket, Stainless Handle, Opener, Screwdriver, Camillus, American, 1992, 3 3/4 In.	40.00
Royal Flush, Case, 5 Piece	330.00
Schrade, Model SC 509, Synthetic Ivory, Scrimshaw Design, Leather Sheath, 2 1/2 In. . . .	40.00
Single Blade, Sheath, Bone Handle, Engraved, Hunter & Bird Dog, Parker, 3 In.	46.00
Spring Blade, US, Camouflage, Gelcote Handle, Belt Clip, 3 1/2 In.	45.00
Survival, U.S. Navy Pilot, 5 In.	35.00
Sword, Emerson, Silver, Brass Hilt, Metal Scabbard, Stamped US 1863, 28 In.	290.00
Trench, U.S., World War I, 12 In.	35.00
Union Cutlery, Oleany, Sheath, New York, 1928 Patent, 4 1/2 x 1 3/8-In. Blade	220.00
US Army Combat, Plastic Washer Grip, Leather Sheath, World War II, 4 3/4 In.	55.00

KNOWLES, TAYLOR & KNOWLES items may be found in the KTK and Lotus Ware categories.

KOREAN WARE, see Sumida.

KOSTA, the oldest Swedish glass factory, was founded in 1742. During the 1920s through the 1950s, many pieces of original design were made at the factory. The firm is still working.

Figurine, Cactus, 2-Arm, Green, Circular Purple Base, Signed, 4 In.	98.00
Vase, Amethyst, Cobalt, Flat Sides, Signed, Warff, No. 47267, 7 In.	288.00
Vase, Pink, Blue & Green Spirals, Controlled Bubbles, Shaped Neck, Signed, Warff, 11 In.	786.00
Vase, Ruby Core, Encased Crystal, Controlled Bubbles, Signed, 7 In.	150.00

KPM refers to Berlin porcelain, but the same initials were used alone and in combination with other symbols by several German porcelain makers. They include the Konigliche Porzellan Manufaktur of Berlin, initials used in mark, 1823–1847; Meissen, 1723–1724 only; Krister Porzellan Manufaktur in Waldenburg, after 1831; Kranichfelder Porzellan Manufaktur in Kranichfeld, after 1903; and the Kister Porzellan Manufaktur in Scheibe, after 1838.

Cup & Saucer, Iron Cross, 1st Class, Gold Wreath, Blue Border, 1914, 5-In. Cup	385.00
Dessert Service, Reticulated Rim, Swag, Leaf Design, Late 19th Century, 12 Piece	635.00
Figurine, Cupid, Holding Flowers, Cup, Ewer, Mark, 6 In., Pair	558.00
Lithophane, see also Lithophane category.	
Lithophane, Grandmother Helping Child With Knitting, Marked, Frame, 9 x 7 In.	290.00
Lithophane, Soldier, Rifle, Walking Dog, 2 Ladies, Impressed, 5 x 4 1/2 In.	115.00
Lithophane, Victorian Girl Cuddling Puppy, Dog, Impressed, 5 3/4 x 4 1/2 In.	185.00
Plaque, Aurora, Hand Painted, Bierschneider, Beehive Mark, 9 3/4 In.	3450.00
Plaque, Christopher Columbus, Oval, Scepter Mark, c.1890, 9 x 6 5/8 In.	1150.00
Plaque, Empress Marie Louise, Walking Stairs, Gilt Wood Frame, Marks	3525.00
Plaque, First Snowfall, Grandfather, 2 Children, Wood Frame, 18 x 21 In.	4370.00
Plaque, Hunt Scene, Hounds Bringing Down Stag, White Painted Frame, 6 7/8 In.	765.00
Plaque, King Meeting Farmer, Hand Painted, Modern Wood Frame, 9 1/2 x 7 1/2 In.	805.00
Plaque, Madonna & Child, St. John, Gilt Frame, After Raphael, 13 3/8 x 11 3/8 In.	2940.00
Plaque, Mary Magdalene, Oval, Verso, Scepter Markpierced Frame, c.1875, 7 x 5 In.	690.00
Plaque, Mother Feeding Child, Gilt & Gesso Frame, 19th Century, 9 In.	2645.00
Plaque, Sibyl, Classical, Gray Robe & Veil, Holding Lamp, Oval, Gilt Frame, 8 In.	1410.00
Plaque, Sistine Madonna, After Raphael, Gilt Wood Scrolled Frame, 30 x 24 1/2 In.	4025.00
Plaque, Sistine Madonna, After Raphael, Period Gilt Frame, 10 x 12 In.	1955.00
Plaque, Woman In Pearls, Oval, Oak Frame, Beaded, Gilt, 10 3/4 x 8 3/4 In.	1295.00
Plaque, Young Woman, Garden, Holding Amphora, Frame, Impressed, c.1875, 16 x 10 In.	7130.00
Plate, Oval Relief Figural Plaque, Art Deco, 8 In., 4 Piece	69.00
Plate, River Scene, Gilt, Pink Border, Inscribed, Mark, 9 3/4 In.	999.00
Vase, Baluster Form, Floral Reserves, Gilt Rim, 8 In.	545.00

KTK are the initials of the Knowles, Taylor & Knowles Company of East Liverpool, Ohio, founded by Isaac W. Knowles in 1853. The company made many types of utilitarian wares, hotel china, and dinnerwares. They made the fine bone china known as Lotus Ware from 1891 to 1896. The company merged with American Ceramic Corporation in 1928. It closed in 1934. Lotus Ware is listed in its own category in this book.

Cigarette & Match Holder Set, Watering Can, Wheelbarrow, Blue, 3 In., 2 Piece	60.00

Pitcher, White, Ironstone, 9 1/2 In. 100.00
Plate, Old Glory & Her Allies, 9 1/2 In. 35.00
Teapot, Black, Gold Trim, Marked, 4 3/4 In. 25.00
Vase, Berries & Leaves, Hand Painted, Fired On Gold, Footed, Marked, Signed, 3 3/4 In. . 80.00

KU KLUX KLAN items are now collected because of their historic importance. Literature, robes, and memorabilia are available. The Klan
was outlawed in 1869 and reemerged in 1915. It is still in existence, so
new material is found.

Booklet, Women Of The Ku Klux Klan, Constitution, June 2, 1923, 4 x 6 In., 83 Pages .. 35.00
Button, Fiery Cross Souvenir, Celluloid, Grand Klan Jubilee, No. 37, 1 3/4 In. 1010.00
Circular, Movie, Promo, The Face At Your Window, 9 x 12 In. 150.00
Figurine, Klansman, Plaster, Glazed, 1923, 8 In. 150.00
Greeting Card, Christmas, Klansman On Horse, For God & Country 100.00
Knife, Folding, Schoolhouse, Klansman, Flag, Burning Cross 325.00
Knife, Folding, Washington, Lincoln, Klansman, Marbleized 275.00
Mirror, Robed Klansmen, Celluloid, 1800s, 2 1/4 In. 757.00
Pamphlet, Practice Of Klanishness, c.1924, 3 3/4 x 8 3/4 In., 8 Pages 30.00
Plate, Stone Mountain, Cross, Burning, Red, White, Blue, Gold, 6 In. 75.00
Plate, Women Of KKK, Blue Rim, Gold Letters, 7 In. 150.00
Poster, Tri-State Klonkave, Sioux City, Red, White, Blue, 12 x 18 In. 325.00

KUTANI ware is a Japanese porcelain made after the mid-seventeenth
century. Most of the pieces found today are nineteenth-century.
Collectors often use the term *kutani* to refer to just the later, colorful
pieces decorated with red, gold, and black pictures of warriors, animals, and birds.

Bowl, Landscape Center, Flowers On Exterior, Early 19th Century, 10 1/4 In. 489.00
Cup, Sake, Poets Of Japan, Calligraphy Interior, 19th Century, 2 In. 58.00
Figurine, Buffalo With Seated Child On Back, Showa Period, Japan 805.00
Figurine, Duck, Feathers, Purple, Blue, Green, Yellow, Japan, 19th Century, 7 In. 999.00
Vase, 2 White Figures, Black Ground, Square Tapered Body, c.1900, 5 1/8 In. 80.00
Vase, Birds, Flowering Branches, 19th Century, 7 In. 205.00
Vase, Rabbits & Waves In Repeated Rows, Baluster Shape, 12 In. 545.00
Vase, Women, Birds, In Reverse, Mask & Ring Handles, 10 1/2 In. 150.00

L.G. WRIGHT Glass Company of New Martinsville, West Virginia,
started selling glassware in 1937. Founder "Si" Wright contracted with
Ohio and West Virginia glass factories to reproduce popular pressed
glass patterns, like Rose & Snow, Baltimore Pear, and Three Face, and
opalescent patterns, like Daisy & Fern and Swirl. Collectors can tell
the difference between the original glasswares and L.G. Wright reproductions because of colors and differences in production techniques.
Some L.G. Wright items are marked with an underlined W in a circle.
Items that were made from old Northwood molds have an altered
Northwood mark--an angled line was added to the N to make it look
like a W. Collectors refer to this mark as "the wobbly W."

Amethyst Crest, Epergne, 5 Lilies, Crimped, Fluted, 10 3/4 In. 825.00
Coin Dot, Lamp, Oil, Cranberry Opalescent, 11 In. 600.00
Daisy & Button, Plate, Salad, Cranberry, Raised Edge, 7 1/2 In. 35.00
Daisy & Button, Spooner, Amberina, 5 In. 32.00
Daisy & Fern, Castor, Cranberry Opalescent, Birds, Berries, Cameo, 12 In. 145.00
Daisy & Fern, Cruet, Cranberry Opalescent, 7 x 4 In. 250.00
Daisy & Fern, Hat, Vaseline, White & Blue Ruffled Edge, 9 x 8 In. 265.00
Daisy & Fern, Lemonade Set, Cranberry Opalescent, 7 Piece 2000.00
Daisy & Fern, Pitcher, Blue Opalescent, Ribbed Clear Handle, Ruffled Edge, 11 In. 250.00
Dot Optic, Sugar Shaker, Cranberry Opalescent, 4 5/8 x 3 1/2 In. 290.00
Eye Winker, Butter, Cover, Green Opalescent, 5 1/2 x 5 1/2 In. 50.00
Eye Winker, Jam Jar, Red, 5 In. 55.00
Eye Winker, Spooner, Red, 5 3/4 In. 65.00
Eye Winker, Sugar & Creamer, Green Opalescent 60.00
Moon & Stars, Ashtray, 6 Sides, 5 1/2 In. 75.00
Moon & Stars, Compote, Cover, Amber Satin, 10 x 6 In. 80.00

Moon & Stars, Goblet, Vaseline, 6 In. 75.00
Moss Rose, Creamer, Peach Blow, Cased, Applied Handle, 5 1/2 In. 125.00
Moss Rose, Pitcher, Peach Blow, Cased, Ruffled Edge, Applied Handle, 6 1/2 In. 135.00
Three Face, Pitcher, Pedestal Base, 7 In. 25.00
Westward Ho, Pitcher, Pedestal Base, 6 3/4 In. 100.00

LACQUER is a type of varnish. Collectors are most interested in the
Chinese and Japanese lacquer wares made from the Japanese varnish
tree. Lacquer wares are made from wood with many coats of lacquer.
Sometimes the piece is carved or decorated with ivory or metal inlay.

Album, Priest Blessing Warrior, Maid Serving Wine, Russia, 19th Century, 13 x 10 In. ... 805.00
Altar Stand, Carved & Gilt Peonies, Black, Gold, Drawer, Edo Period, Japan, 12 x 20 In. 460.00
Box, Black & Red, Cherry Blossom, Black Ground, c.1900, 13 1/4 x 9 3/4 In. 29.00
Box, Black, Mother-Of-Pearl Inlay, Pavilion, Foliage, Korea, 12 x 24 x 12 1/2 In. 460.00
Box, Cinnabar, Carved, Square, Flower Design, 18th Century, 8 In. 690.00
Box, Decanter, Inlaid, Serpentine Front, Lift Lid, Fold-Out Sides, 4 Decanters, 11 In. 2220.00
Box, Glove, Black, Gold, Figures Boating In Garden Pond, Red Interior, 2 x 12 In. 35.00
Box, Gold, Brown, Black, Boat Shape With Dove, Marsh Grass, 5 1/2 In. 80.00
Box, Landscape Decoration, Signed, Russia, 2 x 7 x 5 In. 86.00
Box, Mother-Of-Pearl, Phoenix, Korea, 20th Century, 7 In. 29.00
Box, Obi, Brown, Gilt Mon Decoration, Gilt Chased Mounts, Japan, 12 1/2 In. 575.00
Cabinet, Black, 2 Doors, 3 Drawers, Feather Decoration, Japan, 8 1/2 x 10 1/8 x 7 In. ... 405.00
Chest, Marriage, Lift Top, Black, Gray-Green & Red 3-Leaf Mon Design, Japan, 59 In. .. 575.00
Cigarette Case, Metal, Eggshell Lacquer, Jean Dunand, c.1925, 3 3/4 In. 3286.00
Cup, Sake, Red, Gold, Calligraphic, Kiriwood Box, 20th Century, 3 1/2 In. 50.00
Cup, Sake, Red, Gold, Rising Sun, 3 Piece 29.00
Cup, Sake, Red, Silver, Sword, Anchor, Star, 20th Century, 3 Piece 29.00
Figurine, Immortal, Hardwood Stand, Wood Plinth, Japan, 1800s, 13 In. 490.00
Figurine, Temple Guardian Lion, Open Mouth, Glass Eyes, 1700s, 10 In., Pair 1265.00
Humidor, Sleigh Scene, Black, Hand Painted, Russia, c.1900 .... 105.00
Jardiniere, Mother-Of-Pearl Inlay, Bronze Mounts, Serpentine, c.1970, 8 x 16 x 10 In. ... 980.00
Jardiniere, On Stand, Carved, Trestle End Supports, Pierced Floral Urn, 38 x 29 In. 1200.00
Screen, 4-Panel, Black, Relief Carved, Bone On Top, Wood On Bottom, Gilt, 70 x 95 In. . 1380.00
Shrine, Black, Gilt Wood, Standing Buddha On Lotus Throne, 12 1/2 In 405.00
Shrine, Buddha, Seated On Lotus Throne, Gold, Stand, Japan, 19th Century, 15 3/4 In. ... 1668.00
Shrine, Buddha, Standing, On Lotus Throne, Black, 9 In. 259.00
Table, Sewing, Black, Chinoiserie, 2 Basket Compartments, Shaped Foot Base, 28 In. ... 865.00
Tea Caddy, Black, Gilt Pavilion Scene, Birds, 2 Compartments 550.00
Tray, Shaped Border, Warriors Battling, 12 1/2 x 8 1/2 In., Pair 290.00

LADY HEAD VASE, see Head Vase.

LALIQUE glass was made by Rene Lalique in Paris, France, between
the 1890s and his death in 1945. The glass was molded, pressed, and
engraved in Art Nouveau and Art Deco styles. Pieces were marked   **R.LALIQUE**
with the signature *R. Lalique.* Lalique glass is still being made. Pieces
made after 1945 bear the mark *Lalique.* Jewelry made by Rene Lalique
is listed in the Jewelry category.

Ashtray, Alice, Gray Patina, Molded & Stenciled R. Lalique, c.1924, 4 1/2 In. 545.00
Ashtray, Archers, Clear & Frosted, Molded R. Lalique, c.1922, 4 1/2 In. 805.00
Ashtray, Canard, Duck, Opalescent Green, Engraved, R. Lalique, c.1925, 3 In. 865.00
Ashtray, Chien, Dog, Topaz, Engraved, R. Lalique, c.1926, 3 3/4 In. 400.00
Ashtray, Dindon, Turkey, Amber, Engraved, R. Lalique, c.1925, 3 In. 460.00
Ashtray, Double, Chevre, Goat, Clear, Frosted, R. Lalique, c.1936, 5 In. 575.00
Ashtray, Martinique, Amber, Stenciled R. Lalique France, c.1928, 6 In. 1090.00
Ashtray, Vezelay, Deep Amber, Molded R. Lalique, c.1928, 4 1/2 In. 400.00
Atomizer, Epines, Thorns, Sepia Stain, Gold Wash, Marked, 5 3/4 In. 220.00
Blotter, Rocker, Deux Sirenes Couche Face A Face, Gray Patina, R. Lalique, c.1920, 6 In. 2415.00
Blotter, Rocker, Faune Et Nymphe, Sepia Patina, Molded R. Lalique, c.1920, 6 In. 2070.00
Bowl, Bulbes, Opalescent, Stenciled R. Lalique, c.1935, 8 1/4 In. 518.00
Bowl, Chene, Oak Leaves, Molded, Frosted, 17 3/4 In. 980.00
Bowl, Chieoree, Molded Leaves, Frosted, c.1932, 9 1/4 In. 540.00
Bowl, Dauphins, Opalescent, Sepia Patina, R. Lalique, c.1932, 11 1/2 In. 1150.00
Bowl, Dauphins, Waves, Opalescent, Stenciled, R. Lalique, c.1932, 9 1/2 In. ...... .657.00 to 863.00

Lalique, Box, Cover, Georgette, Dragonflies,
Blue Opalescent, Satin, R. Lalique, c.1922, 8 In.

Lalique, Box, Cover, Quatre Scarabees, 4 Beetles,
Black, White R. Lalique, c.1911, 3 In.

Bowl, Floride, Leaves, Clear & Green, Black Enamel Details, Engraved, c.1960, 7 1/2 In. . .	375.00
Bowl, Lys, Lilies, Molded Flowers, Frosted, c.1924, 9 In.	1076.00
Bowl, Marguerites, Daisies, Molded, Frosted, c.1941, 13 In.	520.00
Bowl, Mesanges, Band Of Birds, Molded, Frosted, c.1931, 9 1/2 In.	660.00
Bowl, Muguet, Opalescent, Stenciled, R. Lalique, c.1931, 12 In.	2185.00
Bowl, Nemours, Rosettes, Enamel Centers, 1/2 Round Form, c.1930, 10 In.	646.00
Bowl, Nemours, Rosettes, Sepia, Brown Enamel Highlights, R. Lalique, 10 In.	865.00
Bowl, Ondes, Waves, Opalescent, Stenciled R. Lalique, c.1935, 8 1/4 In.	460.00
Bowl, Ondines, Water Nymphs, Pressed Opalescent & Clear, Inscribed France, 8 x 3 In. . .	575.00
Bowl, Ondines, Water Nymphs, Swirls, Blue Patina, Engraved R. Lalique, 8 1/2 In.	865.00
Bowl, Perruches, Parakeets, Opalescent, Blue Patina, R. Lalique, c.1931, 9 3/4 In.	4888.00
Bowl, Pinsons, Birds On Leaves, Frosted, 3 5/8 x 9 1/4 In.	175.00
Bowl, Poissons, Fish, Blue Opalescent, c.1921, 9 1/2 In.	920.00
Bowl, Volubilis, 3 Morning Glories, Molded, Opalescent, c.1921, 8 1/2 In.	315.00
Bowl, Volubilis, 3 Morning Glories, Molded, Opalescent, Yellow, c.1921, 8 1/2 In.	400.00
Box, Cover, Cerises, Red Celluloid, Square, Molded R. Lalique, c.1923, 2 In.	1095.00
Box, Cover, Cigales, Cicadas, Molded, Opalescent, 10 In.	1434.00
Box, Cover, Cleones, Amber, Molded R. Lalique, c.1921, 6 3/4 In.	1150.00
Box, Cover, Coppelia, Gilt Metal Mounts, Engraved, Lalique, c.1960, 6 3/4 In.	489.00
Box, Cover, Georgette, Dragonflies, Blue Opalescent, R. Lalique, c.1922, 8 In. . . . . . *Illus*	2070.00
Box, Cover, Mesanges, Birds, Opalescent Amber, Molded R. Lalique, c.1921, 6 3/4 In. . . .	1150.00
Box, Cover, Quatre Scarabees, 4 Beetles, Black, White, R. Lalique, c.1911, 3 In. . . . . *Illus*	2990.00
Box, Cover, Saint-Marc, Doves, Opalescent, R. Lalique, c.1922, 9 3/4 In. . . . . *Illus*	1955.00
Box, Cover, Trois Figurines, D'Orsay, Clear, Frosted, R. Lalique, c.1912, 3 3/4 In.	316.00
Box, Cover, Vallauris, Leaves, Clear & Frosted, Engraved, R. Lalique, c.1928, 5 1/2 In. . .	375.00
Carafe, Masques, Sepia Face Medallion, Engraved, R. Lalique, c.1913, 10 In.	2185.00
Ceiling Light, Dahlias, Molded Bowl, Floral Relief, Ceiling Mount, c.1921, 12 In.	3055.00
Chandelier, Dahlias, Stylized Flower, Frosted Glass, Molded, Signed, c.1934, 12 In.	3231.00
Cocktail, William, Rooster Stem, Blue Enamel Stem Design, Engraved, R. Lalique	518.00
Decanter, Stopper, Selestat, Black Glass Neck Ring, R. Lalique, c.1925, 10 3/4 In.	863.00

**Lalique glass made before 1945 will
fluoresce yellow under a black light.
Glass made after 1945 does not.**

Lalique, Box, Cover, Saint-Marc, Doves,
Opalescent, Molded, R. Lalique, c.1922, 9 3/4 In.

Figurine, Suzanne, Opalescent, Blue Patina, Engraved, R. Lalique, 9 1/4 In. 16100.00
Figurine, Tete D'aigle, Eagle Head, Frosted, Inscribed, France, 4 3/8 In. 235.00
Goblet, Ange, Frosted, Angel's Head Stem, Engraved Wings, 1948, 4 Piece 460.00
Goblet, Cannes, Stenciled R. Lalique, c.1938, 8 In., 6 Piece 978.00
Goblet, White Wine, Hagueneau, Stenciled R. Lalique, c.1924, 4 Piece 375.00
Hood Ornament, Coq Nain, Rooster, Clear & Frosted, Molded R. Lalique, c.1928, 8 In. . . 1035.00
Hood Ornament, Faucon, Falcon, Clear & Frosted, Molded R. Lalique, c.1925, 6 In. 3565.00
Hood Ornament, St. Christophe, Amethyst Tone, Molded R. Lalique, c.1928, 5 1/4 In. 805.00
Hood Ornament, Tete D'Aigle, Eagle Head, Clear & Frosted, Engraved, Lalique, 4 In. . . . 259.00
Hood Ornament, Victoire, Clear, Frosted, R. Lalique, c.1928, 10 1/2 In. 28750.00
Knife Rest, Nippon, Deco Hobnails, Stenciled R. Lalique, 3 1/2 In., 6 Piece 2875.00
Lamp, Perles, Vertical Lines, Ball Trim, Cone Shape, Black Base, 8 x 18 In. 2022.00
Lamp, Six Danseuses, 6 Dancers, Clear, Frosted, Sepia Patina, R. Lalique, 10 In. 18400.00
Liqueur, Enfants, Children, Clear, Frosted, Sepia, Stenciled, c.1932, 1 1/2 In., 6 Piece . . . 978.00
Menu Holder, Pinsons, Finches, Engraved R. Lalique, c.1924, 1 3/4 In., Pair 690.00
Mirror, Muguet, Lilies Of The Valley, Clear, Frosted, Tassel, R. Lalique, c.1921, 6 1/2 In. . . 865.00
Mirror, Narcisse Couche, Clear, Frosted, c.1912, 11 3/4 In. 2629.00
Paperweight, Antilope, Antelope, Clear & Frosted, R. Lalique, c.1929, 3 1/2 In. 805.00
Paperweight, Moineau Moqueur, Sparrow, Clear & Frosted, R. Lalique, c.1930, 3 1/2 In. . 430.00
Paperweight, Toby, Elephant, Clear & Frosted, Stenciled, R. Lalique, c.1931, 3 1/2 In. . . . 2070.00
Paperweight, Turtle, Caroline, Frosted Amber & Crystal, Inscribed Mark, 5 1/2 In. 92.00
Pendant, Guepes, Wasps, Amber, Sepia Patina, Black Cord, R. Lalique, c.1920, 2 1/4 In. . 863.00
Pendant, Panier De Fruits, Basket, Frosted, Blue Patina, R. Lalique, c.1922, 1 1/2 In. 400.00
Perfume Bottle, Amphitrite, Shell, Clear, Frosted, Blue, R. Lalique, c.1920, 3 3/4 In. 2300.00
Perfume Bottle, Bouquet De Faunes, Guerlain, Frosted, c.1925, 4 In. 980.00
Perfume Bottle, Cyclamen, Coty, Stopper, 1920, 5 1/2 In. 956.00
Perfume Bottle, Dans La Nuit, Worth, Frosted, Blue Enamel, Stars, R. Lalique, 9 1/2 In. . 1495.00
Perfume Bottle, Guerlain, Bouquet De Faunes, 4 Faces, Women & Satyrs, Frosted, 4 In. . 1870.00
Perfume Bottle, Helene, Lotus, Clear, Frosted, Stenciled, R. Lalique, c.1928, 2 3/4 In. . . . 2185.00
Perfume Bottle, La Violette, Gabilla, Clear, Violet Enamel, c.1925, 3 1/2 In. 3680.00
Perfume Bottle, Le Jade, Roger Et Gallet, Jade Green, R. Lalique, c.1926, 3 1/4 In. 3335.00
Perfume Bottle, Marquila, Artichoke Leaves, Blue, Frosted, c.1927, 3 1/4 In. 1675.00
Perfume Bottle, Niobe, Violet, Clear, Stopper, c.1919, 4 1/4 In. 1195.00
Perfume Bottle, Oree Claire, Clear, Frosted, Stopper, 1930, 3 1/4 In. 1910.00
Perfume Bottle, Perles, Opalescent, R. Lalique, c.1926, 5 1/2 In. 748.00
Perfume Bottle, Quatres Cigales, Molded Insects, Frosted, c.1910, 5 1/2 In. 1554.00
Perfume Bottle, Requete, Worth, Clear, Blue Enamel Trim, Box, 1949, 6 1/2 In. 1150.00
Plate, Coquilles, Shells, Opalescent, c.1924, 10 1/2 In. 920.00
Plate, Ecailles, Scales, Clear, Stenciled R. Lalique, c.1928, 12 3/4 In. 230.00
Plate, Laure, Black Glass, Wave Pattern, Scalloped Border, Engraved, c.1970, 11 In. 460.00
Plate, Marienthal, Grape Clusters, Frosted Glass, Molded, 1927, 9 1/4 In., 8 Piece 805.00
Plate, Volutes, Bubbles, Opalescent, Stenciled, R. Lalique, c.1934, 10 3/4 In. 865.00
Seal, Lapin, Rabbit, Topaz, Engraved, R. Lalique, c.1925, 2 1/4 In. 635.00
Seal, Rapace, Owl, Frosted, Inscribed, 2 7/8 In. 106.00
Seal, Tete D'aigle, Eagle Head, Black Glass, Engraved, R. Lalique, c.1911, 3 In. 2070.00
Seal, Tete D'aigle, Eagle Head, Gray Patina, Engraved, Lalique, c.1911, 3 1/4 In. 1725.00
Tray, Epines, Thorns, Clear & Frosted, R. Lalique, c.1920, 12 In. Diam. 430.00
Tumbler, Juice, Blidah, Oranges, Sepia Patina, R. Lalique, c.1931, 5 1/4 In., Pair 316.00
Vase, Acacia, Panels Of Leaves, Topaz, R. Lalique, c.1921, 8 In. 1150.00
Vase, Acanthes, Relief Thistles, Oval, Frosted, c.1921, 11 In. 2468.00
Vase, Archers, Butterscotch Yellow, Engraved, Lalique, c.1921, 10 1/2 In. 21850.00
Vase, Archers, Clear, Frosted, Blue Patina, Bulbous, R. Lalique, 10 1/2 In. 5750.00
Vase, Archers, Frosted Amber, 10 Arches, 10 Birds, c.1921, 10 1/2 In. 12650.00
Vase, Avallon, Birds & Berries, Topaz, R. Lalique, c.1927, 5 3/4 In. 2070.00
Vase, Bacchantes, 10 Nude Figures, Molded, Signed, c.1927, 9 3/4 In. 3220.00
Vase, Bagatelle, Birds In Branches, Blue Stain, Egg Shape, Signed, c.1939, 7 In. 2940.00
Vase, Bagatelle, Relief Birds & Foliage, Inscribed On Base, c.1975, 6 3/4 In. . . . . . .196.00 to 264.00
Vase, Beautreillis, Cabachons, Topaz, R. Lalique, c.1927, 5 3/4 In. 1840.00
Vase, Beliers, Ram Shaped Handles, Molded, Opalescent, 7 3/4 In. 2390.00
Vase, Camargue, Horse Medallions, Clear, Frosted, Engraved, c.1942, 11 3/4 In. 2415.00
Vase, Caudebec, Frosted Leaves, Flowers, Dome Handles, Oval, c.1929, 5 3/4 In. 646.00
Vase, Ceylan, 8 Parakeets, Frosted, Blue Patina, c.1924, 9 1/2 In. . . . . .2530.00 to 2585.00
Vase, Ceylan, 8 Parakeets, Opalescent, Blue Patina, R. Lalique, c.1924, 10 In. 8338.00

Vase, Chamois, Clear, Frosted, Blue Patina, Stenciled, R. Lalique, c.1931, 5 In. 980.00
Vase, Courges, Molded Gourds, Electric Blue, White Patina, R. Lalique, c.1914, 8 In. 12075.00
Vase, Courges, Molded Gourds, Mauve, 1914, 7 1/2 In. 8965.00
Vase, Courlis, Curlews, Emerald Green, White Patina, Signed, 1931, 6 5/8 In. 8963.00
Vase, Cyrus, Clear, Turquoise Twisted Band At Neck, Squat, Engraved, 6 In. 1485.00
Vase, Dahlias, Gray Patina, Black Enamel, Silver Rim, R. Lalique, c.1923, 5 1/2 In. 2185.00
Vase, Dentele, Clear, Frosted, Gray Patina, Stenciled, R. Lalique, c.1912, 6 3/4 In. 865.00
Vase, Domremy, Thistle, Amber, Engraved, R. Lalique, c.1926, 8 3/4 In. 2875.00
Vase, Eglantines, Wild Roses, Opalescent, Bulbous, R. Lalique, c.1921, 5 1/4 In. 750.00
Vase, Espalion, Ferns, Opalescent, Blue Patina, R. Lalique, c.1927, 7 1/4 In. 1495.00
Vase, Esterel, Oleander, Amber, R. Lalique, c.1923, 6 In. 2185.00
Vase, Feuilles, Leaves, Opalescent, Engraved, R. Lalique, c.1934, 7 In. 345.00
Vase, Font-Romeu, Ridged Ferns, Clear, Frosted, R. Lalique, c.1936, 8 3/4 In. 1840.00
Vase, Fontainebleau, Molded Grape Vines, Blue, c.1930, 6 In. 777.00
Vase, Formose, Fish, Emerald Green, Engraved, R. Lalique, c.1924, 7 1/4 In. 4900.00
Vase, Fougeres, Ferns, Mauve, Frosted, c.1912, 6 1/4 In. 7170.00
Vase, Grenade, Black Glass, White Patina, Stenciled R. Lalique, c.1930, 4 3/4 In. 2530.00
Vase, Gui, Mistletoe, Frosted, Molded, Signed, c.1920, 7 In. 1000.00
Vase, Gui, Mistletoe, Opalescent, Blue Patina, Engraved, R. Lalique, c.1920, 6 3/4 In. . . . 1380.00
Vase, Hedera, Inscribed Signature, 6 7/8 In. 230.00
Vase, Lagamar, Geometric Bands, Enameled, Frosted, 1926, 7 3/8 In. 8365.00
Vase, Le Mans, Amber, White Patina, Bulbous, R. Lalique, c.1931, 4 1/4 In. 2300.00
Vase, Malesherbes, Medlar Leaves, Amber, White, Engraved, R. Lalique, c.1927, 9 In. . . . 3220.00
Vase, Marisa, Molded Fish, Opalescent, c.1927, 9 1/4 In. 3885.00
Vase, Monnaie Du Pape, Money Plant, Brown Patinated, Cylindrical, c.1914, 9 1/4 In. . . . 2135.00
Vase, Muquet, Lily Of The Valley, Molded, Frosted, c.1920, 6 1/4 In. 460.00
Vase, Oleron, Molded Fish, Cased Opalescent, Green Patina, R. Lalique, 1927, 3 1/2 In. . . 1093.00
Vase, Orly, Bubbles, Clear, Stenciled, R. Lalique, c.1935, 5 1/2 In. 2070.00
Vase, Ormeaux, Overlapping Elm Leaves, Frosted, Round, Signed, c.1926, 6 1/2 In. 850.00
Vase, Ornis, 2 Applied Bird Handles, Clear, Signed, c.1926, 7 1/2 In. 4025.00
Vase, Ornis, 2 Bird Handles, Opalescent, R. Lalique, c.1926, 8 3/4 In. 6900.00
Vase, Palissy, Molded Shells, Opalescent, Engraved, R. Lalique, c.1926, 6 1/2 In. 1265.00
Vase, Piriac, Medial Band Of Fish & Waves, Blue, c.1930, 7 1/2 In. 5175.00
Vase, Poissons, Fish, Blue Gray Patina, Frosted, R. Lalique, c.1921, 9 1/4 In. 2530.00
Vase, Raisins, Grapes & Vines, Clear, Frosted, Blue Patina, R. Lalique, c.1928, 6 1/4 In. . . . 520.00
Vase, Rampillon, Relief Cabachons, Opalescent, Stenciled, R. Lalique, c.1927, 5 In. 1115.00
Vase, Renoncules, Raised Ranuculus Flowers, Blue Wash, Flared, c.1930, 5 3/4 In. 1500.00
Vase, Ronces, Molded Thorny Vines, Cased Yellow Glass, R. Lalique, c.1921, 9 1/2 In. . . . 5980.00
Vase, Ronces, Molded Thorny Vines, Opalescent, c.1921, 9 1/4 In. . . . . .2705.00 to 2820.00
Vase, Ronces, Molded Thorny Vines, Yellow Opalescent, c.1921, 9 In. 2703.00
Vase, Sophora, Vines, Amber, Rene Lalique, 1926, 10 1/8 In. 8963.00
Vase, St. Francois, Birds, Branches, Cased Opalescent, Blue, R. Lalique, c.1930, 7 In. 2990.00
Vase, St. Tropez, Leaves, Berries, Opalescent, Cylindrical, c.1937, 7 3/8 In. . . . . .558.00 to 1495.00
Vase, Tournai, Leaf Panels, Frosted, Gray Patina, Marked, R. Lalique, c.1924, 4 3/4 In. . . 489.00
Vase, Tournesols, Yellow Patina, Engraved, R. Lalique, c.1927, 4 3/4 In. 1380.00
Vase, Tristan, Leaf Handles, Frosted, Molded, c.1928, 8 1/8 x 13 In. 835.00
Vase, Violettes, Clear, Frosted, Blue Patina, Engraved, R. Lalique, c.1921, 6 1/2 In. 1495.00
Wine Cooler, Epernay, Clear, Frosted, Grape Leaf, Handles, R. Lalique, c.1938, 7 1/2 In. . . 1495.00

LAMPS of every type, from the early oil-burning Betty and Phoebe
lamps to the recent electric lamps with glass or beaded shades, interest
collectors. Fuels used in lamps changed through the years; whale oil
(1800–1840), camphene (1828), Argand (1830), lard (1833–1863), turpentine and alcohol (1840s), gas (1850–1879), kerosene (1860), and
electricity (1879) are the most common. Other lamps are listed by
manufacturer or type of material.

Aladdin, B-26, Decalcomania, Burner . . . . .170.00 to 275.00
Aladdin, B-39, Washington Drape, Clear, Round Base, Burner .50.00 to 70.00
Aladdin, B-40, Washington Drape, Green, Round Base, Burner 100.00
Aladdin, B-47, Washington Drape, Clear, Bell Stem, Burner . . . . .100.00 to 110.00
Aladdin, B-53, Washington Drape, Clear, Plain Stem, Burner 50.00
Aladdin, B-55, Washington Drape, Amber, Burner 90.00
Aladdin, B-55, Washington Drape, Amber, Plain Stem, Burner 120.00

Aladdin, B-60, Alacite, Short Lincoln Drape 500.00
Aladdin, B-76, Tall Lincoln Drape, Cobalt, Plain Foot ....650.00 to 1400.00
Aladdin, B-76, Tall Lincoln Drape, Cobalt, Scallop, Burner 1600.00
Aladdin, B-77, Tall Lincoln Drape, Ruby 450.00
Aladdin, B-77, Tall Lincoln Drape, Ruby, Some Amberina At Base 350.00
Aladdin, B-81, Beehive, Green, Burner 110.00
Aladdin, B-82, Beehive, Amber 110.00
Aladdin, B-82D, Beehive, Dark Amber 145.00
Aladdin, B-83, Beehive, Ruby 500.00
Aladdin, B-85, Quilt, White Moonstone, Burner 325.00
Aladdin, B-86, Quilt, Green Moonstone 275.00
Aladdin, B-87, Vertique, Rose Moonstone 475.00
Aladdin, B-92, Vertique, Green Moonstone 375.00
Aladdin, B-95, Queen, White Moonstone 200.00
Aladdin, B-97, Queen, Green Moonstone, Fluted Shade 250.00
Aladdin, B-101, Corinthian, Amber, Burner 90.00
Aladdin, B-102, Corinthian, Green 90.00
Aladdin, B-104, Colonial, Clear 90.00
Aladdin, B-104, Colonial, Green 160.00
Aladdin, B-105, Colonial, Green, Burner, Table 170.00
Aladdin, B-105, Corinthian, Clear, Green, Burner ....90.00 to 120.00
Aladdin, B-110, Cathedral, White Moonstone 210.00
Aladdin, B-122, Majestic, Green Moonstone 250.00
Aladdin, B-126, Corinthian, White Moonstone, Rose Moonstone 210.00
Aladdin, B-130, Oriental, Ivory 110.00
Aladdin, B-131, Oriental, Green 100.00
Aladdin, B-134, Oriental, Bronze 180.00
Aladdin, Caboose Lamp, Model B, Union Pacific 250.00
Aladdin, Coach & Four Shade, 14 In. 130.00
Aladdin, E-303, Vogue Vase, Orange 210.00
Aladdin, G-15, Floral Base, Crystal, Pair 575.00
Aladdin, G-16, Etched Crystal 800.00
Aladdin, G-36, Pear Finial 160.00
Aladdin, G-44, Chartreuse, No. 804 Shade 45.00
Aladdin, G-44, Mantle Lamp, Amber, Gracette 250.00
Aladdin, G-44, Switch In Base 30.00
Aladdin, G-77, Susie, Green Moonstone 3100.00
Aladdin, G-130, Lady With Cape, Frosted, Wreath 3700.00
Aladdin, G-163, Double Nudes, Clear Wreath 2000.00
Aladdin, G-165, Metal Base 70.00
Aladdin, G-190, Switch In Base 50.00
Aladdin, G-191, Opalique 150.00
Aladdin, G-227, Prince's Feather 200.00
Aladdin, G-239, Floral ....45.00 to 55.00
Aladdin, G-267, Alacite, Pair 55.00
Aladdin, G-268, Wheat Staff, No. 1534 Shade 130.00
Aladdin, G-278, Alacite 30.00
Aladdin, G-282, Alacite Tag, Anglia Finial 75.00
Aladdin, G-284, Tan, Bouquet Finial, No. 909H Shade 70.00
Aladdin, G-307, Coral, Bouquet Finial, No. 2309 .... 100.00
Aladdin, G-311, No. 500 Shade & Plume 50.00
Aladdin, G-312, Ivory, Green, Turn Key, No. 500 Shade 50.00
Aladdin, G-333, Bride & Groom, Green 125.00
Aladdin, G-375, Dancing Ladies Urn 1200.00
Aladdin, Kerosene, Nickel Finish, Mantle, Box 675.00
Aladdin, M-143, Classic Figurines 40.00
Aladdin, Model B, Hanging 150.00
Aladdin, Model No. 1, Ceiling Extension 170.00
Aladdin, Model No. 6, Hanging, Tube 225.00
Aladdin, Model No. 12, Florentine Vase, White Moonstone 2000.00
Aladdin, Model No. 1231A, Tan, Vase 160.00
Aladdin, Model No. 1241, Vase, Variegated Tan 85.00
Aladdin, Model No. 1242, Bengal Red Vase, Tripod 475.00

Aladdin, Model No. 1243, Vase, Green, Venetian, Art-Craft, 12 In. 440.00
Aladdin, No. 1258, Model B, Log Cabin Shade 300.00
Aladdin, No. 3685, Mogul, 3-Way, Ivory, Brass, 1947, Floor 275.00
Aladdin, Student, Harvard, Brass, Blue Green Shade, White Interior, Stepped Base, 21 In. 1232.00
Argand, 2-Light, Gilt Brass, Glass Shade, Electrified, Anglo-American, c.1835, 21 1/2 In. 1265.00
Argand, Bronze, Engraved Frosted Glass Shades, Covered Urn Shape, 11 7/8 In., Pair . . . 3820.00
Argand, Gilt Bronze, Clark, Coit, Cargill, New York, 19th Century 7475.00
Astral, Banquet, George Washington, Bronze, Prisms, Frosted Leaded Glass Shade, 28 In. 960.00
Astral, Brass, Corinthian Column Support, Electrified, Cornelius & Co., c.1843, 23 In. . . . 440.00
Astral, Brass, Gilding, Sinumbra Font, Marble, 27 Cut Prisms, Frosted Shade, 29 1/2 In. . 2310.00
Astral, Brass, Matte, Cut Glass Prisms, Black Marble Base, 20 In., Pair 550.00
Astral, Brass, Square Marble Base, Etched Shade, Drop Prisms, Pair 405.00
Astral, Cut Glass, Victorian Ormolu, Electrified, 19th Century, 26 1/4 In. 635.00
Astral, Frosted & Cut Shade, Prisms, Opalescent Swirled Column, Marble Base, 25 In. . . 360.00
Astral, Frosted, Cut Glass, Shade, Marble Base, Prisms, Scrolls, Flowers, 22 In. 220.00
Astral, Gilded Brass, Double Marble Base, Electrified, 19th Century, 19 In. 600.00
Astral, Gilded Brass, Square Base, Reeded Column, Cornelius & Co., Phila., 22 1/2 In. . . 880.00
Astral, Glass Prisms, Cornelius & Co., 1843 Patent, 23 1/2 In. 200.00
Astral, Stepped White Marble Base, Cast Ormolu, 27 Cut Prisms, Frosted Shade, 29 In. . . 1650.00
Betty, Tin, Hinged Reservoir Door, Chain Wick-Pick, 6 In. 140.00
Betty, Tin, Tidy Stand, Early 19th Century, 14 1/4 In. 294.00
Bouillotte, 2-Arm, Brass, Birds, Oval Metal Shade, Orange, Gold Paint, 19 In. 405.00
Bouillotte, 3-Light, Bronze, France, 19th Century, Pair 2016.00
Camphene, Pratt's Buggy Lamp & Feeder Co., Tin, c.1858, 8 In. 880.00
Candle, Hanging, Brass, 3 Candlestick Sockets, Swan Heads, c.1920, 12 x 9 1/2 In., Pair . 1680.00
Chandelier, 3-Light, Art Nouveau, Shell-Form Shades, Gilt Bronze, c.1900, 39 x 23 In. . . 5676.00
Chandelier, 3-Light, Brass Scroll Rods, 4-Panel Mottled Glass Shades, 42 x 66 In. 750.00
Chandelier, 3-Light, George III Style, Brass, Frosted Glass, 24 In., Pair 805.00
Chandelier, 3-Light, Gilt Bronze, Louis XVI Style, Electrified, c.1900, 26 1/2 In. 1725.00
Chandelier, 3-Light, Green Venetian Glass, Ribbed, c.1930, 57 x 22 In. 9560.00
Chandelier, 3-Light, Regency Style, Gilt Brass, England, c.1885, 24 x 22 In., Pair 2300.00
Chandelier, 3-Light, Star Fellows, Figure On Orb, Scroll Arms, Etched Bulbous Shades . . 4760.00
Chandelier, 3-Light, Wrought Iron, Suspended Shades, Lavender Bowl, c.1925, 20 In. 805.00
Chandelier, 4-Arm, Tin, Diamond Shape Body, Candle Sockets, 1800s, 29 x 14 1/2 In. . . . 1210.00
Chandelier, 4-Arm, Wrought Iron, Mottled Shades, c.1925, 32 In. 805.00
Chandelier, 4-Light, Art Deco, Wrought Iron, Glass, Octagonal, Stylized Flowers, 23 In. . 896.00
Chandelier, 4-Light, Art Nouveau, Gilt Metal, Quezal Glass, Pulled Feather 1998.00
Chandelier, 4-Light, Cast, Rolled Brass, 4 Chains, Electric, Mid 19th Century, 43 In. 750.00
Chandelier, 4-Light, Empire Style, Gilt Bronze, Malachite, Winged Dragons, 21 In. 2390.00
Chandelier, 4-Light, Gilt Bronze, Louis XVI, Prisms, France, 27 1/2 x 18 In. 3220.00
Chandelier, 4-Light, Gilt Bronze, Prisms, Drops, Chains, Electrified, 27 1/2 x 18 In. 3220.00
Chandelier, 4-Light, Neoclassical, Flowers, Scroll, Shell Design, Glass Shades, 37 In. . . . 375.00
Chandelier, 4-Light, Pendant Lantern, Ceiling Plate, 36 x 20 In. 805.00
Chandelier, 4-Light, Pendant, Verdigris, Gold Iridescent Shades, 34 1/2 x 16 In. 1150.00
Chandelier, 4-Light, Riveted Iron Shades, Caramel Slag Glass, Arts & Crafts, 35 In. 635.00
Chandelier, 4-Light, Victorian, Brass, Square, 56 x 33 In. 705.00
Chandelier, 5-Arm, Chrome Collar, Bulbous, Candlestick Sockets, 13 1/4 x 15 1/2 In. . . . 60.00
Chandelier, 5-Light, Appliques, Chains, Flowers, 29 1/2 x 18 In., Pair 2300.00
Chandelier, 5-Light, Art Deco, Carved Wood, Scrolling Arms, France, 29 In. 600.00
Chandelier, 5-Light, Art Deco, Gilt Metal, White Iridescent Shades, 6 In. 705.00
Chandelier, 5-Light, Beaded Crystal, Teardrop Prisms, Italy, c.1900, 25 In. 1150.00
Chandelier, 5-Light, Cast Brass, Crystal, Prisms, Bobeche, Mid 20th Century, 46 x 19 In. . 275.00
Chandelier, 5-Light, Copper, Wrought Iron, Glass Globes, W.A.S. Benson, 29 In. 2937.00
Chandelier, 5-Light, Louis XIV Style, Giltwood, France, c.1900, 26 In. 805.00
Chandelier, 6-Light, Antler, Circular, Brass Shade Rings, Continental, 25 x 31 In. 980.00
Chandelier, 6-Light, Art Deco, Chrome, Frosted Glass, Cylindrical To Star-Shape, 30 In. . 1175.00
Chandelier, 6-Light, Art Deco, Chrome, Frosted Glass, Foliage, Round, 35 In. 2940.00
Chandelier, 6-Light, Arts & Crafts, Brass, Pierced Rail, Chain Link Upper Rail, 29 In. . . . 280.00
Chandelier, 6-Light, Brass, Framed, Button & Pendant Chains, 36 x 28 In. 655.00
Chandelier, 6-Light, Bronze, Figural, Classical Winged Woman, Gold Dore, 6 1/2 In. 2825.00
Chandelier, 6-Light, Candle, Brass, Crystal, Prisms, Sweden, c.1885, 28 In. 1840.00
Chandelier, 6-Light, Cast Brass, Flowers, Electric, 22 x 24 In. 29.00
Chandelier, 6-Light, Cast Iron, Kerosene Font Holder, 48 In. 1035.00

Chandelier, 6-Light, Cut Glass, Ireland, 1900s, 36 x 32 In. 750.00
Chandelier, 6-Light, Empire Style, Gilt, Patinated Bronze, Foliate Cast Arms, 21 In. 825.00
Chandelier, 6-Light, Faceted Bead Chains, Cut Glass Drops, Electrified, 14 x 15 In. 515.00
Chandelier, 6-Light, Gilt Bronze, Facet-Cut Drop, Trapezoid Pendants, 28 In. 805.00
Chandelier, 6-Light, Gooseneck Arms, Drip Plates, Diamond, Prisms, 35 x 26 In. 605.00
Chandelier, 6-Light, Louis XV Style, Brass, Cut Glass, c.1900, 30 x 20 In. 1035.00
Chandelier, 6-Light, Louis XVI Style, Gilt Bronze, Cut Glass, Bead Chains, 35 x 19 In. ... 3220.00
Chandelier, 6-Light, Louis XVI Style, Gilt, Wrought Iron, Frame, 25 x 16 3/4 In. ... 1955.00
Chandelier, 6-Light, Louis XVI, Gilt Bronze, Glass Bead Chains, Amethyst, 28 x 21 In. ... 2185.00
Chandelier, 6-Light, Rococo Style, Gilt Bronze, Leaf Decoration, 30 In. 470.00
Chandelier, 6-Light, Silvered, Hammered, 3 Tiers Of Rectangular Prisms, 36 In. 1065.00
Chandelier, 6-Light, Tole, Porcelain, Flower Set Frame, 32 In. 1135.00
Chandelier, 6-Light, Wrought Iron, Jewel Chains, Drops, Pheasant Feather Shades, 37 In. . 690.00
Chandelier, 7-Light, Neoclassical, Crystal, Inverted Dome, 32 x 24 In. 1095.00
Chandelier, 8-Arm, Brass, Cast, Torch Shape Ends, 20th Century, 25 x 20 In. 250.00
Chandelier, 8-Light, Brass, Opalescent Glass Panels, Electric, 20th Century, 15 In. 275.00
Chandelier, 8-Light, Cut Glass Baluster, Drip Pans, Scrolls, Glass Prisms, 20 In. 475.00
Chandelier, 8-Light, Empire, Gilt, Circular, Scroll Arms, Cast Chains, 26 In. 1165.00
Chandelier, 8-Light, George III Style, Brass, Glass, 20th Century, 36 x 32 In. ..... 575.00 to 690.00
Chandelier, 8-Light, Gilt Brass, Oval Pendants, Electrified, France, c.1900, 36 x 26 In. ... 2990.00
Chandelier, 8-Light, Giltwood, Wrought Iron, Crystal, Italy, c.1900, 48 x 36 In. 2300.00
Chandelier, 8-Light, Iron, Bronze, Glass, Electrified, France, c.1900, 33 In. 2530.00
Chandelier, 8-Light, Louis XV Style, Brass, Cage Form, 4 Double Arms, Prisms, 38 In. ... 1530.00
Chandelier, 8-Light, Louis XVI Style, Gilt Bronze, Arrow-Filled Quiver Standard, 35 In. . 2645.00
Chandelier, 8-Light, Maria Theresa Style, Ribbed Glass, Amethyst Drops, 19 In. 1725.00
Chandelier, 8-Light, Neoclassical, Electrified, Italy, 20th Century, 31 x 31 In. 1675.00
Chandelier, 8-Light, Neoclassical, Glass Standard, Bobeches, Prisms, 26 x 24 In. 690.00
Chandelier, 8-Light, Regency Style, Gilt Brass, Cut Glass, Electrified, 42 x 28 In. 1840.00
Chandelier, 8-Light, Wrought Iron, Parcel Gilt, Bowl Center, 31 In. 200.00
Chandelier, 9-Light, Art Nouveau, Copper, Brass, Pink Ruffled Glass Shades, 38 In. 600.00
Chandelier, 9-Light, Brass, Wirework, c.1966, 6 x 18 x 36 In. 176.00
Chandelier, 9-Light, Louis XV Style, Gilt Bronze, Leaf Cast Shades, 32 In. 1793.00
Chandelier, 9-Light, Louis XVI Style, Gilt Bronze, Cut Glass, France, 35 x 23 1/2 In. ... 1725.00
Chandelier, 9-Light, Porcelain, Slip-In Branches, Cherubs, Fronds, 20th Century, 40 In. ... 6475.00
Chandelier, 9-Light, Victorian, Gilt Bronze, Cut Glass Shades, Bowl, 38 x 19 In. 590.00
Chandelier, 10-Light, Gilt Bronze, 5 Double Arms, Glass Drip Pans, Prisms, 51 In. 1895.00
Chandelier, 10-Light, Louis XVI Style, Gilt Bronze, Skeleton, Beaded Pendants, 27 In. ... 1765.00
Chandelier, 10-Light, Rococo Style, Glass, Knopped, Twisted Arms, 34 In. 1645.00
Chandelier, 12-Light, Baroque Style, Brass, Dutch 1295.00
Chandelier, 12-Light, Gilt Bronze, Cut Glass, Mardi Gras Beads, Continental, 36 x 29 In. 1095.00
Chandelier, 12-Light, Louis XV Style, Ormolu, Cut Glass, 19th Century, 66 x 32 In. 14950.00
Chandelier, 12-Light, Neoclassical, Austria, 20th Century, 24 In. 375.00
Chandelier, 12-Light, Plumed Corona, Coupe, Scrolled Branches, 36 x 27 In. 3450.00
Chandelier, 15-Light, Louis XV Style, Brass, Scroll Arms, Pendants, Spire Finials, 37 In. . 1455.70
Chandelier, 16-Light, Gilt Bronze, Cut Glass, Russia, c.1815, 57 x 36 In. 8340.00
Chandelier, 16-Light, Louis XV Style, Brass, Cut Glass, c.1940, 37 x 30 1/2 In. 1725.00
Chandelier, 16-Light, Neoclassical Giltwood, 2 Tiers, 4 Arms, Ram's Heads, 29 x 37 In. . 6900.00
Chandelier, 18-Light, Rococo Style, Gilt Brass, Continental, c.1900, 39 x 28 In. 5750.00
Chandelier, 20-Arm, Radiating, Bright Chrome, Black Enamel, Mid 1900s, 31 x 23 In. .. 380.00
Chandelier, 24-Light, Napoleon III, Beaded Cut Glass, Drops, Pendants, 33 x 35 In. 1150.00
Chandelier, 25-Light, Rococo Style, Bronze, Foliate Scrolling Arms, 38 In. 3768.00
Chandelier, 35-Light, Cut Crystal, Blown Glass Balusters, Lustre Ropes, 48 In. 5290.00
Chandelier, Alabaster, Dish Form, 3 Cords, Italy, c.1900, 16 In. 690.00
Chandelier, Alabaster, Ribbed Dish, 3 Brass Chains, Italy, c.1900, 14 In. 1035.00
Chandelier, Alabaster, Tangerine, Bronze Mounted, Gilt Brass, c.1900, 18 In. 1150.00
Chandelier, Art Deco, Alabaster, Lotus Form, 3 Gilt Brass Chains, France, c.1900, 13 In. . 920.00
Chandelier, Art Deco, Bronze, Frosted Glass, Stylized Fruit, Flowers, Gilt, 36 In. 6820.00
Chandelier, Art Deco, Gilt Bronze Mounted, Alabaster, Dome Shape, 13 In. 840.00
Chandelier, Art Deco, Glass, Chrome, Turned Shape, Rose Glass Panels, 24 In. 600.00
Chandelier, Art Deco, Metal, Glass, Painted, Skyscraper Shape, 51 In. 235.00
Chandelier, Art Deco, Stained Glass, Pierced Landscape Border, 18 In. 590.00
Chandelier, Arts & Crafts, Brass, Bronze, Leaded Glass, Hammered, c.1910, 27 In. 999.00
Chandelier, Arts & Crafts, Bronze, Hammered, Suspended Sockets, c.1910, 14 x 18 In. ... 1380.00

Chandelier, Arts & Crafts, Hammered Brass, Slag Glass Panels, Octagonal, 16 x 34 In. . . . 690.00
Chandelier, Brass Mounted, Gilt, Cut Glass, Bead Chain, Prisms, 29 1/2 x 12 In. 2185.00
Chandelier, Brass, Glass Shades, Ribbed, Gold Aurene, Contemporary, 18 In. 715.00
Chandelier, Bronze, Baccarat Crystal Pendants, Nickeled Bronze Dome, 1960s, 16 In. 2820.00
Chandelier, Cast Metal Frame, Orange, Yellow Slag Glass, Chain, 55 1/2 x 24 In. 805.00
Chandelier, Charder Le Verre, Cameo Glass, Berry & Floral, Signed, c.1920, 22 x 24 In. . . 5975.00
Chandelier, Cut Glass, Button Chain, 4 Rows Of Spears, 26 x 14 In., Pair 655.00
Chandelier, Cut Glass, Gilt Brass, 20th Century, 20 1/2 In. 1705.00
Chandelier, Cut Glass, Gilt Brass, 4 Tiers, 20th Century, 31 x 22 1/2 In. 3410.00
Chandelier, Glass Palmettes, Bead Chains, Electrified, 25 In. 2530.00
Chandelier, Lightolier, Frosted Glass Fixture, 3 Globes, 5 Spherical Pendants, 20 x 16 In. 235.00
Chandelier, Louis XVI Style, Cut Glass Beads, Corbeille Shape, c.1900, 23 1/2 x 8 In. . . . 978.00
Chandelier, Mauer, Bamboo, Paper, Brass, Germany, 1980s, 17 1/4 x 16 3/4 In. 4315.00
Chandelier, Murano, Metal Rings, Murano Glass Discs, Italy, 1960s, 20 x 34 In. 1265.00
Chandelier, Neoclassical, Rope Twist Glass, Bead Chains, Stars, Pendants, 48 x 33 In. . . . 4600.00
Chandelier, Painted Tole, Porcelain Flowers, Gilt Green Leaves, Continental, 39 In. 4995.00
Chandelier, Panton, Fun 10, Shell, Metal, Luber, Switzerland, 1964, 19 1/2 x 14 1/4 In. . . 2300.00
Chandelier, Panton, Fun 13, Shell, Metal, Luber, Switzerland, 1964, 19 3/4 x 19 In. 8855.00
Chandelier, Vico Magistretti, Pianeta, Venini, 1987, 41 x 35 1/4 In. 2645.00
Electric, 2 Light, Greta Grossman, White Shades, Ralph O. Smith, c.1949, 15 In. 705.00
Electric, 2-Light, Gothic Style, Cast Brass, Gilding, Engraved, Triangular Base, 36 In. 935.00
Electric, 3-Light, Art Nouveau Woman, Flower Bulbs, White Metal, Gold Wash, 34 In. . . . 3080.00
Electric, 2-Light, Beaded, Antiqued Brass, Lace Shade, American, c.1900, 57 x 24 In. . . . 978.00
Electric, 3 Circular Plastic Shades, Chrome Base, Shaft, Brackets, Mid 1900s, 55 In. 225.00
Electric, 3-Light, Aluminum, Enamel, Yellow, Red, Black, Swivel Arms, c.1957, 60 In. . . . 225.00
Electric, 3-Light, Art Nouveau, Nude Woman Leaning Against Vine, Lily Shades, 25 In. . . 1000.00
Electric, 3-Light, Arts & Crafts, Copper, Hammered, Mushroom Shape, 19 1/2 In. 978.00
Electric, 3-Light, Black Forest, Carved, Squirrels Sitting On Log, Grapevine, 60 In. 2185.00
Electric, 3-Light, Lightolier, Brass, Lacquered, Walnut, Tripod, American, 1950s, 48 In. . . 920.00
Electric, 3-Light, Poppy, Leaded & Slag Glass, Bronze Base, 1900s, 26 3/4 In. 2585.00
Electric, 3-Light, Robsjohn-Gibbings, Metal Tripod, Hansen, 22 In. 646.00
Electric, 3-Light, Slag Glass, 8-Panel Shade, Metal Leaf Overlay, c.1925, 23 In. 205.00
Electric, 3-Tier, Arts & Crafts, Square, 4-Panel Shade, Green Slag Glass Inserts, 26 In. . . . 865.00
Electric, 4-Light, Bronze, Roman God Mercury, Pirouetting, Marble Base, 35 In. 450.00
Electric, 6-Light, Bronze, Leaded Glass, Red Poppy, Tiffany Style, 76 x 27 In. 4025.00
Electric, 7-Light, Bronze, Patinated, Art Glass Flower-Form Shades, c.1900, 71 In. 1265.00
Electric, Achille & Pier Giacomo Castiglioni, Arco, Marble Base, c.1962, 104 In. 1175.00
Electric, Achille & Pier Giacomo Castiglioni, Gatto, Plastic, Flos, 7 1/2 x 12 In., Pair 1380.00
Electric, Aquamarine Glass, Twisted Column, Murano, Wrought Iron Stand, 67 In. 575.00
Electric, Arab Riding Elephant Under Palm Tree, Bronze, Painted, Vienna, 20 In. 1410.00
Electric, Arens, Copper, Goosenecks, Bell Shades, American, 1930s, 30 x 24 In. 1725.00
Electric, Arne Jacobsen, Visor, Zinc Plate, Lacquer, Louis Poulsen, c.1956, 21 1/2 In. 265.00
Electric, Arredoluce, Brass, Enameled Metal, Blue, Red, Yellow, Italy, 1950s, 68 In. 3740.00
Electric, Arredoluce, Brass, Enameled, Leather, c.1954, 61 1/4 x 46 1/2 In. 5750.00
Electric, Arredoluce, Easel, Brass, Chrome, Italy, 85 1/2 In. 4600.00
Electric, Arredoluce, Easel, Brass, Italy, 82 1/2 In. 4900.00
Electric, Art Deco, Brass, Striking Serpent, Holding Hat-Shape Shade In Jaws, 27 In. 2070.00
Electric, Art Deco, Bronze, Rearing Cobra, Bowl-Shaped Rose & Blue Shade, 60 In. 978.00
Electric, Art Deco, Female, Spelter, Brass Plated, White Glass Shade, 22 In. 200.00
Electric, Art Deco, Fringed Shade, Adjustable, 1930 . . . . 330.00
Electric, Art Deco, Gilt Decorated, Sphere Shape, 20 In. 500.00
Electric, Art Deco, Silvered Metal, Glass Paneled Shade, 16 In. 219.00
Electric, Art Nouveau, Bronze, Stone, Glass, 6-Petal Shade, Leaf & Pod, 8 x 14 x 7 In. . . 1410.00
Electric, Artemide, Megaron, Red Enameled Shaft, Gianfranco Frattini, Italy, 71 1/4 In. . . 410.00
Electric, Artichoke, Matte Copper, Poul Henningsen, Louis Poulsen, 23 1/2 x 18 1/2 In. . . 2415.00
Electric, Arts & Crafts Style, Copper, Mica 206.00
Electric, Arts & Crafts, Bronze, Harp Mount, Spherical Shade, 46 In. 69.00
Electric, Arts & Crafts, Bronzed Metal, Green Glass Insert Shade, 13 x 12 In. 1035.00
Electric, Arts & Crafts, Copper, Rectangular Shade, Wood Pedestals, 24 x 16 x 18 In. . . . 3740.00
Electric, Arts & Crafts, Hammered Copper, Mica, Patina, 14 In. 2070.00
Electric, Arts & Crafts, Hammered, Leaded Glass, Caramel, Green, Bronze Base, 22 In. . . . 975.00
Electric, Arts & Crafts, Leaded Glass, Bird, Flowers, Metal Base, 25 x 19 In. 575.00
Electric, Arts & Crafts, Metal & Slag Glass Shade, Hammered Metal, 16 1/2 In. 499.00

Electric, Arts & Crafts, Oak Tree Form, Wrought Iron, 10 1/2 In. 2875.00
Electric, Arts & Crafts, Wicker, Woven Base, Domed Shade, Silk Liner, 16 x 22 In. 90.00
Electric, Arts & Crafts, Wrought Iron, Twisted Stem, Cylindrical Shade, 15 x 69 In. 1495.00
Electric, Austrian Secessionist, Brass, 3 Cutout Buttresses, 6 Jewels In Shade, 17 x 11 In. 978.00
Electric, Baroque Style, Giltwood, Velvet, Gadroon, Italy, c.1900, 67 1/2 In. 805.00
Electric, Bed, Reading, Leaded Glass, Blue, Butterflies, 2 Headboard Hooks 560.00
Electric, Bellova, Reverse Painted, Stylized Flowers, Leaves, 8 x 14 In. 1265.00
Electric, Benedict, Hammered Copper, Mica, 6-Sided Shade, 6-Sided Base, 26 x 20 In. . . 5465.00
Electric, Bent Panel, Gilt Panel Base, Floral & Scroll, c.1900, 24 In. 750.00
Electric, Bent Panel, Spelter Shade, Floral Accents, Brass Plate, Iron Base, 23 In. 230.00
Electric, Bill Curry, White, Egg Shape Dome, Design Line, c.1968, 21 1/2 In. 380.00
Electric, Black Enamel Metal Shade, Steel Shaft, Tripod Base, Denmark, 64 1/2 In. 440.00
Electric, Blue Hobnail Glass Shade, Brass Hanging Hardware, Pull-Down Frame, 11 In. . . 315.00
Electric, Brass, Candlearm, Quatrefoil Bobeche, Quilted Stem, Scrolled Legs, 19 In., Pair 160.00
Electric, Brass, Enameled Metal, Glass, Italy, 1950, 81 In. 950.00
Electric, Brass, Leaf Molding, 63 In. 120.00
Electric, Bridge, Wrought Iron, Brass, Tripod Base, Penny Feet, 20th Century 220.00
Electric, Bright Chrome, 5 Adjustable Jointed Spheres, Square Base 206.00
Electric, Bronze Base, Frosted Glass Shade, Cut Cherry & Flower Design, 28 In. 1765.00
Electric, Bronze, Gilt, Bacchus, Seated, Shell & Scroll Base, c.1880, 30 In., Pair 2329.00
Electric, Bronze, Leaded Glass Shade, Stylized Tree, 21 x 18 In. 1035.00
Electric, Bronze, Pine Needle Relief Design, Disk Base, 4-Footed, 1900s, 20 In. 4115.00
Electric, Bronze, Urn Shape, Mythical Heads, Cherubs, France, 20th Century, 33 In. 275.00
Electric, Bruno Gecchelin, Messaluna, Marble Base, Chrome, Enamel, Italy, 70 In. 470.00
Electric, Cast Iron, Cage, Painted Flower Vines, Early 20th Century, 71 x 7 In. 300.00
Electric, Cast Iron, Smoking Stand, Butler Shape, 54 In. 330.00
Electric, Cast Metal, Marble, Gilt, Urn Shape, Paw Feet, France, 20 1/2 In., Pair 460.00
Electric, Ceiling, Art Deco, Faceted Frosted Shade, 14 x 15 x 13 In. 355.00
Electric, Ceiling, Bronze, Glass, Turtleback, 20 In. 5040.00
Electric, Ceiling, George III Style, Brass, Blown Glass, 3-Light, 1900s, 20 x 8 1/2 In., Pair 805.00
Electric, Ceiling, George III Style, Brass, Glass, 20th Century, 22 1/2 In. 405.00
Electric, Ceiling, George Nelson, Bubble, 3 Saucer Shades, Howard Miller, c.1950 . . . . . . 4115.00
Electric, Ceiling, George Nelson, Bubble, Howard Miller, c.1950, 27 x 12 In. 295.00
Electric, Ceiling, Green, Multicolor Flowers, Murano, c.1960, 39 In. 5400.00
Electric, Ceramic, Acid Green, Red Squiggles, Turquoise Ground, 38 3/4 x 8 In. 150.00
Electric, Charles X Style, Brass, Columnar, Early 20th Century, 19 In. 460.00
Electric, Cherry Blossom, Leaded Glass, Bronze, 22 1/2 x 24 1/4 In. 5278.00
Electric, Chrome Stem, Lucite Leaves, Spherical Bulbs, 1950s, 38 In. 165.00
Electric, Chrysanthemum, Orange Band, Reverse Painted, Silver, Brass, 1900s, 24 In. . . . 300.00
Electric, Cinnabar, Figural Scenes, Chinese, 17 In. 720.00
Electric, Classique 1604, Reverse Painted, Floral, Gold Base, Ribbed Stem, 14 In. 900.00
Electric, Cloud, Guy De Rougemont, Plastic, Eric Germaine, c.1971, 20 In. 3450.00
Electric, Coach, Brass, Tin, Iron, Beveled Window, 2 Iron Wall Brackets, 16 1/2 In., Pair . 325.00
Electric, Colonial Kitchen, Ivory, Maroon, Gold Trim, Homer Laughlin, 15 3/4 In. 150.00
Electric, Copper, Hammered, Mica Panel Shade, Spherical Base, Arts & Crafts, 20 In. . . . 1645.00
Electric, Cork, Chrome, Bulbous Base, Parchment Drum Shade, 27 x 20 In., Pair 206.00
Electric, Cranberry, Coin Dot Shade, 25 In. 1100.00
Electric, Cut Glass, Mushroom Style Shade, Pendant Prisms, 2 Parts, 21 1/2 In. 750.00
Electric, Desk, Bell Shape, Leaded, Tapered & Ribbed Arm, Round Stepped Base, 15 In. . 784.00
Electric, Desk, Bronze, Pyramid Shade, Angle Arm, Footed Base, c.1910, 11 In. 235.00
Electric, Desk, J. Adnet, Leather, Wood, c.1950, 20 In. 2875.00
Electric, Desk, Landscape, Reverse Painted, Gilt Metal Base, 13 In. 750.00
Electric, Desk, Metal, Dome Shade, Stepped Base, Green Patina, 9 1/2 In. 120.00
Electric, Desk, Reverse Painted, Flowers, Shields, 5 3/4 x 15 In. 690.00
Electric, Duffner & Kimberly, Hanging, Leaded Shade, Cone Shape, Geometrics, 20 In. . . 3080.00
Electric, Duffner & Kimberly, Hanging, Leaded Shade, Pink & Orange Flowers, 24 In. . . . 7840.00
Electric, Duffner & Kimberly, Leaded, Geometric, Circular Base, 20 x 24 In. 3450.00
Electric, Duffner & Kimberly, Leaded, Scrolls, Shells, Purple, Green, Tan, 22 In. . . . *Illus* 12320.00
Electric, Edwardian, Black Lacquer, Gilt, Octagonal Base, c.1900, 69 In. 1035.00
Electric, Egyptian Revival, Standing Woman, Gilt, Patinated Bronze, 26 In. 8225.00
Electric, Emeralite, Cased Green Glass Shade, Brass Base 255.00
Electric, Ernst Bohne, Nude Women, Fawn, Rudolstadt, Germany, 1920, 9 1/2 x 5 1/2 In. . 450.00
Electric, Famille Rose, Oriental Scenes, Gilt, Jar Shape, Porcelain, 28 In., Pair 290.00

Lamp, Electric, Duffner &
Kimberly, Leaded, Scrolls, Shells,
Purple, Green, Tan, 22 In.

Lamp, Electric, Jefferson, Reverse
Painted, Hollyhocks, Red, Yellow,
Signed, 1884, 18 In.

Lamp, Electric, Miller, Palms,
Walkways, Red, Green Slag
Glass, 6-Panel, Overlay, 26 In.

Electric, Filigree, Bent Slag Panel, Bronzed Base, Water Lily, Bamboo, c.1920, 25 In. . . .   575.00
Electric, Filigree, Bent Slag Panel, Embossed Iron Base, 6-Panel Shade, c.1920, 22 In. . . .   400.00
Electric, Filigree, Bent Slag, Flower Cast Base, 7-Panel Shade, c.1920, 25 x 22 In. 575.00
Electric, Flambeau, Glazed Pottery, Gilt Metal Mounts, 1900s, 15 1/2 In., Pair 2215.00
Electric, Frederick Weinberg, Ceramic Male & Female, Black Shades, 12 x 39 In. 690.00
Electric, G. Stickley, Copper, Heart Shade, Ruby Slag 11300.00
Electric, G. Stickley, Hammered Copper, Wicker Shade, 14 x 7 In. 2070.00
Electric, G. Stickley, Japanese Wicker & Silk Shade, Wood Base, Copper Bands, 17 In. . . .   1725.00
Electric, G. Stickley, Lantern, Hammered Iron, Frosted Glass Shade, Patina, 17 1/2 In. . . .   1725.00
Electric, Galle, Cameo Cut Flowers, Red, Yellow Ground, 4 1/4 In. 1725.00
Electric, George Nelson, Bubble, Howard Miller, 1960s, 27 x 10 In. 460.00
Electric, George Nelson, Lantern Series, Howard Miller, Walnut & Plastic, c.1958 . . . . . .   805.00
Electric, Gherpe, Plastic, Metal, Superstudio, Polronova, c.1970, 16 7/8 In. 2875.00
Electric, Gilt Bronze, Pendant Shade, Bird's Beak Top, Claw Support, c.1900, 17 1/4 In. .   1020.00
Electric, Gio Ponti, Porcelain, Painted Pineapples, Black Ground, Globular Base, 21 In. .   3930.00
Electric, Glass, Patinated Metal, Compote Shape, France, 20th Century, 9 x 12 x 9 In. . . .   978.00
Electric, Gone With The Wind, Glass, Red, Puffy, Flowers, Brass Base, Electrified 450.00
Electric, Green Slag Glass Shade, Pyramid Shape, Bronze Frame, & Base, 25 In. 390.00
Electric, Green To White Slag Glass Overall, 10 Panels, Grapevine, 6 Paw Feet, 25 In. . . .   2800.00
Electric, Grueby Base, 2 Colors, Tiffany Shade, 20 In. 44800.00
Electric, Hanging, 8 Sides, Palm Trees, Large Apron, Metal Overlay, 21 In. 1065.00
Electric, Hanging, Ansolo Fuga, Bulbous, Lattimo, Transparent Murrine, 17 x 8 In. 880.00
Electric, Hanging, Art Deco Moon, Leaded Glass, Red, Green, Caramel, 27 In., Pair 950.00
Electric, Hanging, Arts & Crafts, Hammered Copper, Yellow Slag Glass, 4-Light, 30 In. . . .   3220.00
Electric, Hanging, Arts & Crafts, Lantern, 4 Panels, Metal Frame, 13 x 9 1/2 In. 575.00
Electric, Hanging, Brass Stem & Chains, Scrolls, 4-Panel Pink Glass Shade, 61 x 30 In. . . .   635.00
Electric, Hanging, Cast Iron, Prisms, Openwork, 9 3/4 x 22 In. 305.00
Electric, Hanging, Cranberry Glass, Bell Shape, Adjustable Chain, 11 In., Pair 315.00
Electric, Hanging, Frederick Ramond, Atomic, Bentwood, Lucite, 9 1/2 x 21 In. 200.00
Electric, Hanging, Frosted Blue Shade, Iris Flowers, 11 In. 275.00
Electric, Hanging, G. Ulrich, Brass, Glass, Italy, 1961, 16 1/2 x 45 In. 4900.00
Electric, Hanging, Gaetano Scolari, Brass, Steel, Aluminum, c.1960, 23 x 30 In. 1765.00
Electric, Hanging, George Nelson, Bubble, Drum Shape, Howard Miller, 17 In. 405.00
Electric, Hanging, George Nelson, Bubble, Egg Shape, Howard Miller, 18 In. 345.00
Electric, Hanging, Hart, Dome, Stained Glass, 4 Butterflies, Greens, Rust, Ivory, 22 In. . . .   3190.00
Electric, Hanging, Jeweled, Multicolored, 14 1/2 In. 175.00
Electric, Hanging, Leaded Glass, Flowers, Red, Pink, White Striated Glass, 23 1/2 In. . . .   2240.00
Electric, Hanging, Leaded Glass, Gilt, Embossed Iron Frame, c.1925, 20 x 20 In. 1095.00
Electric, Hanging, Leaded Glass, Wide Apron, Flowers, Reds, Pinks, Greens, 24 In. 2465.00
Electric, Hanging, Marigold, Iridized Glass, Enameled Winter Scene, Brass, c.1920, 19 In.   345.00
Electric, Hanging, Panton, Circular Chrome Frame, Hanging Shell Discs 2875.00
Electric, Hanging, Panton, Flowerpot, No. 16562, Poulsen, c.1968, 49 In., Pair 2185.00
Electric, Hanging, Panton, Fun 4 DM, J. Luber, c.1964, 40 x 22 1/2 In. 4406.00

Electric, Hanging, Poul Henningsen PH5, L. Poulsen, Denmark, c.1958, 19 x 9 1/2 In. 529.00
Electric, Hanging, Poul Henningsen, Copper, Denmark, 1920, 34 1/2 x 18 1/2 In. 5175.00
Electric, Hanging, Poul Henningsen, PH, Blue Enamel, Box, Label, 16-In. Shade 705.00
Electric, Hanging, Stained Glass, Wisteria, Irregular Rim, 27 In. 1120.00
Electric, Hanging, Teak, Adjustable, Plastic Cone Shade, Luxus, Sweden 175.00
Electric, Hanging, Tubular, Chrome, Adjustable, Spheres, Globe Bulb, 60 x 14 In., Pair . . 646.00
Electric, Hanging, Vignelli, Orange, Gray, Tan, White, Glass, Venini, Italy, 1960s, 20 In. . 1035.00
Electric, Hanging, White To Yellow Slag Glass, Rope Twist Metal Work, Fringe 2520.00
Electric, Harlequin & Ballerina, 6 1/4 In., Pair 45.00
Electric, Heron, Pottery, Glazed, c.1950, 33 In., Pair 1554.00
Electric, Hula Girl, Copper Plated, Circular Base, 23 1/2 In. 460.00
Electric, I. Noguchi, Cherry, Fiberglass, Polyvinyl, Knoll, c.1945, 7 x 15 3/4 In. 1150.00
Electric, J. Adnet, Bronze, Leather, Pierced Metal Shades, c.1948, 21 3/4 In. 7170.00
Electric, J. Adnet, Green Glass Standard, Chromium Plated Mounts, 1930s, 59 In. 3000.00
Electric, J. Adnet, Leather Bound, Metal, Faux Bamboo, Hermes, c.1950, 24 In. 3450.00
Electric, J. Adnet, Leather, Metal Frame, Pivoting Shade, France, 1950, 63 In. 10925.00
Electric, J. Hollings & Co., Brass, Ornate, American, 1888 Patent, Floor 495.00
Electric, Jade, Mythical Figure, Wood Base, Brass Mechanism, Chinese, c.1900, 26 In. . . 690.00
Electric, Jansen, Neoclassical, Urn Shape, Pine, Partially Painted, 40 x 9 In., Pair 1075.00
Electric, Jefferson, Reverse Painted, Drum Shade, Faux Marble Design, Marked, 22 In. . . 1495.00
Electric, Jefferson, Reverse Painted, Field Of Poppies In Bloom, 23 In. 3700.00
Electric, Jefferson, Reverse Painted, Hollyhocks, Red, Yellow, Signed, 1884, 18 In. . *Illus* 3360.00
Electric, Jefferson, Reverse Painted, Landscape, Patinated Spelter Base, Signed, 20 In. . . . 865.00
Electric, Joe Columbo, Coupe, Chrome, Enameled Metal, Shade, O-Luce, Italy, Floor . . . 750.00
Electric, Joe Columbo, Opaque White, Chromed Plastic, 12 x 9 In. 145.00
Electric, Kurt Versen, Aluminum, Adjustable Flip-Top Shade, 1940s, 16 1/2 x 62 In. 489.00
Electric, Kutani, Scene, People, Flowers, Vase Shape, 22 1/2 In. 145.00
Electric, L. Alliot, Art Nouveau Woman, Spelter, 3 Beaded Bulb Covers 3080.00
Electric, Laurel, Blue Fused Glass, Chromed Metal Base, Signed, 12 x 9 In. 85.00
Electric, Laurel, Enameled White Shaft, Flaring Base, Linen Shade, 60 In. 265.00
Electric, Laurel, Mushroom, White Frosted Glass Shade, Black Tulip Base, 56 1/2 In. . . . 650.00
Electric, Laurel, Wooden Shaft, Mushroom Frosted Glass Shade, 55 x 12 In. 705.00
Electric, Leaded Glass, Flowers, Pink, Yellow, American, 18 x 24 In. 2300.00
Electric, Leaded Glass, Flowers, Slag Glass, Trumpet Base, 3 Acorn Pulls, 23 In. 2240.00
Electric, Lightolier, 3 Metal Shades, Red, White, Blue, 60 x 48 In. 690.00
Electric, Lightolier, Brass, Walnut Tripod, Enamel Disk Shades, 1950s, 48 In. 920.00
Electric, Lightolier, Plastic Shade, Enameled Metal Shaft, Base, 1950s, 19 In. 380.00
Electric, Limbert, Floral Cutout Shade, Red Slag Glass, Copper, 22 1/2 x 23 In. 4315.00
Electric, Louis Baldwin, Ceramic, Rectangles, Speckled Glaze, Green, Gold, 20 In. 235.00
Electric, Louis XV Style, Gilt Bronze, Rock Crystal, Shaped Oval, Handles, 20 In. 5378.00
Electric, Louis XVI Style, Gilt Bronze, Sevres Style, Porcelain, Urn Shape, 17 In., Pair . . 1435.00
Electric, Louis XVI Style, Gilt Metal, Marble, Medallion, 1900s, 13 5/8 In., Pair 520.00
Electric, M. Arnaboldi, Mira, Adjustable, Black, Labels, Progammaluce, c.1980, 58 In. . . . 380.00
Electric, Mahogany, Turned Column, Silk & Lace Shade, Fringe, Tassels, 68 In. 575.00
Electric, Malachite, Carved, Figural Relief, Vase Shape, Chinese, 7 In. 720.00
Electric, Marbro, American, c.1950, 57 x 24 In. 440.00
Electric, Marx, Brushed Steel, Leatherette, 1948, 16 1/2 x 69 In., Pair 4025.00
Electric, Maurice Dufrene, Enamel, Brass, Pedestal, c.1902, 25 3/4 In. 8365.00
Electric, Metal & Slag Glass, Multicolor, 7 Panel, Dome Shade, 23 3/4 x 17 In. 765.00
Electric, Metal Base, Lily Pad, Flowers, Leaves, Urn Shape, 23 1/2 In. 440.00
Electric, Metal Overlay, 8 Panels, Flower Borders, Green, Yellow, Red Slag Glass, 25 In. . 1008.00
Electric, Milk Glass, Painted Flowers, Leaves, Stems, Brass Filigree, 3-Footed, 23 In. . . . 240.00
Electric, Miller, Leaded Glass Shade, Oranges, Lattice, Slag Glass, 6 Sections, 26 In. 1960.00
Electric, Miller, Palms, Walkways, Red, Green Slag Glass, 6-Panel, Overlay, 26 In. . *Illus* 2296.00
Electric, Mission Oak, Green Slag, 4 Panels 775.00
Electric, Modern, Black Enamel Dome Shade, Adjustable Chrome Shaft, 55 In. 440.00
Electric, Moe-Bridges, Greek Ruins, Painted Shade, Urn Shape Base, 18 In. . . . . *Illus* 3080.00
Electric, Moe-Bridges, Landscape, Windmills, Reverse Painted, Yellow Shade, 14 1/4 In. . 405.00
Electric, Murano, Crystal, Early 20th Century, Pair 2910.00
Electric, Neoclassical, Gilt, Patinated Bronze, Marble Base, 13 1/2 In., Pair 5975.00
Electric, Nessen, Brass, Cylindrical Shade, Swiveling Arm, 13 1/4 In. 105.00
Electric, Nessen, Chrome Column, Metal Base, Metal Diffuser, 15 1/2 x 27 In. 299.00
Electric, Nessen, Chrome, Spun Aluminum Shade, Pivoting Arm, 49 In. 650.00

Electric, Nessen, Swing Arm, c.1927, 48 3/4 x 13 1/4 In. 165.00
Electric, Oak, Pyramidal Shade, Yellow, Green Slag Glass, 23 3/4 x 13 1/2 In. 575.00
Electric, Oak, Trapezoid Shade, Green Slag Glass, Buttressed Shaft, 22 1/2 x 14 1/2 In. ... 635.00
Electric, Onyx, Ormolu, Satyr Mask Handles, Italy, c.1910, 16 In., Pair 430.00
Electric, Oriental, Bronze Casting, Turtles, Foo Dogs, Dragons, Butterflies, 59 In. 605.00
Electric, Outdoor Scene, Embossed Bronzed Base, Opal Shade, c.1920, 22 x 16 In. 635.00
Electric, P. Guariche, Iron, Enameled Metal, Plastic, 1950, 54 In. 2645.00
Electric, Painted Fruit, Flowers, Landscape, Vase Shape, 29 In., Pair 230.00
Electric, Palm Tree Overlay, 6-Sided Shade, Slag Glass, Round Foot, 24 In. 900.00
Electric, Palshus, Ribbed Form, Textured, Blue, Green High Glaze, 16 In. 175.00
Electric, Panton, Flowerpot, Red, Orange, Louis Poulsen, Denmark, c.1970, 20 In. 1380.00
Electric, Panton, Fun 2 TM, Luber, Switzerland, 1964, 11 x 17 In. 1610.00
Electric, Panton, Panthella, Chrome Plate, Plastic Diffuser, 1970s, 12 1/2 In. 290.00
Electric, Panton, SP3 Spiral, Plastic, Luber, Switzerland, 1969, 18 x 72 In. 8625.00
Electric, Panton, VP Globe, Louis Poulsen & Co., c.1969, 22 x 19 In. 2115.00
Electric, Panton, Wonderlamp, Plastic, Luber, Switzerland, 1964, 19 x 44 In. 11500.00
Electric, Passiflora, Superstudio, Plastic, Poltronova, c.1969, 11 In. 2990.00
Electric, Patinated Brass, Cast Iron, Rose Silk Shade, Fringe, Faceted Garnets, 60 In. 1095.00
Electric, Perzel, Model 41E, White Paint, Polished Brass, Glass, 1930, 67 3/4 In. 7050.00
Electric, Phillip Semmer, Green Granite Glass, Red Border, Tree-Trunk Base, 15 In. 670.00
Electric, Pierced Brass Overlay, 9 Panels, Amber Slag Glass, Acorn Pulls, c.1910, 70 In. . 823.00
Electric, Pierre Paulin, Brass Frame, Weighted Base, Phillips, 1950s, 12 1/2 x 17 In. 430.00
Electric, Pipistrello, Gae Aulenti, Martinelli Luce, Italy, c.1967, 36 In. 1530.00
Electric, Pittsburgh, Autumn Leaf, Dome Shade, Painted, Red, Gold, 18 In. 3080.00
Electric, Pittsburgh, Reverse Painted, Butterflies, Rose Border, Square Foot, 20 In. 1230.00
Electric, Pittsburgh, Reverse Painted, Forest Scene, Purple Sky, Gold Shaped Base, 11 In. 1345.00
Electric, Pittsburgh, Reverse Painted, Swan, Pond, Trees, Black Base, Incised Foot, 20 In. 3305.00
Electric, Porcelain, Adult, Child Playing, Urn, Handles, Chinese, 20th Century, 13 In. ... 125.00
Electric, Porcelain, Bronze, Urn Shape, Ram's Head, Hoof Feet, 32 In. 690.00
Electric, Porcelain, Gilt, Brass Mounted, Biscuit, Neoclassical Figures, 23 1/2 In., Pair ... 980.00
Electric, Porcelain, Half Doll, Seated Colonial Lady, Silk Shade, Germany, 14 In. 115.00
Electric, Puffy Glass Shade, Trellis, Grapes, Vines, No. 40712, c.1910, 24 In. 275.00
Electric, Quartz, Carved Lid, Pierced Brass Band, Carnelian Cabochon, Chinese, c.1850 . 1955.00
Electric, Red Plastic, Mushroom Shape, Red Shade, White Column Base 70.00
Electric, Reverse Painted Panels On Stem & Shade, Scenic Roads, Field, Trees, 22 In. ... 1460.00
Electric, Reverse Painted, Strawberries, Domed, Bronze Base, 12 In., Pair 785.00
Electric, Reverse Painted, 8 Panels, Mountainscape, Round Stem, 3-Footed, 22 In. 1230.00
Electric, Reverse Painted, Windmill, 4-Footed, Pull Chain, 14 In. 1000.00
Electric, Reverse Painted, Winter Scene, Brass Candlestick, c.1915, 17 x 12 In. 460.00
Electric, Riviere, Grapevine, Metal Overlay, Green, White Slag Glass, 21 x 25 In. . . *Illus* 2800.00
Electric, Ruby Glass Shade, Black Metal Arms, 10 In. 150.00
Electric, Serge Roche, Plaster, Stylized Acanthus Leaves, c.1937, 32 1/2 In., Pair 1915.00
Electric, Seville Studios, Art Deco, Iron, Circular, Relief Grape Clusters, 21 x 20 In. 430.00

Lamp, Electric, Moe-Bridges,
Greek Ruins, Painted Shade, Urn
Shape Base, 18 In.

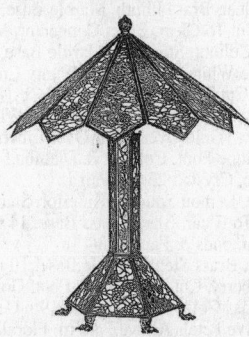

Lamp, Electric, Riviere, Grapevine,
Metal Overlay, Green, White Slag
Glass, 21 x 25 In.

Lamp, Electric, Wilkinson, Leaded
Glass, Pink, Red, Orange, Green
Flowers, Signed, 26 In.

Electric, Sevres Style, Gilt Bronze Mounted, Landscape, Cobalt Ground, 21 In. 450.00
Electric, Sevres Style, Oval, Venus & Cupids, Porcelain, 24 In. 646.00
Electric, Sierakowski, Delta, Weighted Base, Koch & Kowy, c.1983, 22 x 18 In. 23.00
Electric, Silver Plate, Slag Glass, Paneled Shade, Conical Base, 5 Sockets, 20 1/2 In. 1100.00
Electric, Silvered Spelter, Reverse Painted, Landscape, Paneled Base, 21 In. 575.00
Electric, Skyscraper, Shelf Unit, Chrome, Black Laminate, Intersecting Cubes, 62 In. 470.00
Electric, Spelter, Cast Metal, Bronze Patina, Man Lighting Pipe, Red Bulb, c.1900, 21 In.   635.00
Electric, Stemlite, Mushroom, Black Enameled Tulip Base, 11 3/4 In. 440.00
Electric, Student, Brass, Double, Shaped Green & White Cased Glass Shades, 21 x 26 In.   1380.00
Electric, Student, Brass, Double, Yellow Cased Ribbed Shades, 20 x 27 In. 575.00
Electric, Student, Brass, Spiral Ribbing, Milk Glass Shade, Pat. May 27, 1922 . . . .   330.00
Electric, Student, Cleveland Safety, Brass, White Milk Glass Shade, 18 3/4 In. 330.00
Electric, Student, Vertical Post, Glass Shade, Electrified, 21 In. 395.00
Electric, Tillman, Oak, Slag Glass, Prairie School Style 382.00
Electric, Triennale, Koch & Lowy, Italy, c.1957, 70 x 11 1/2 In. 1645.00
Electric, Turtleback Shade, Illuminated Turtleback Base, 16 In. 34720.00
Electric, Vistosi, Glass, Yellow, Green, 2-Piece, Mushroom Top, Donut Base, 12 x 15 In. .   450.00
Electric, Walnut & Brass Pole, 22 Adjustable Cone Shades, Marble Base, 84 In. 4900.00
Electric, White, Pod Shape, Wood, Plastic Panel, 41 1/2 x 7 x 7 In., Pair 175.00
Electric, Wilkenson, Leaded Glass 4500.00
Electric, Wilkinson, Leaded Glass, Bronze Base, 18 In. 3450.00
Electric, Wilkinson, Leaded Glass, Pink, Red, Orange, Green Flowers, Signed, 26 In. *Illus*   2800.00
Electric, Wilkinson, Leaded Glass, Yin Yang Symbols, Swirl Base, Ball Pull, 24 In. 2465.00
Electric, Wilkinson, No. 23, Leaded Glass, Floral, Leaves, Splay Feet, 30 In. 5600.00
Electric, Williamson, Leaded Glass, Geometric, Irregular Border, Ornate Base, 27 In. 5040.00
Electric, Woman, Tree, Fruit, Spelter, Gilt, Signed Hippolyte Moreau, 25 In. 890.00
Fairy, Burmese, Egg Shape, Crystal Insert, Porcelain Bowl, 19th Century, 6 1/2 x 8 In. . . .   1380.00
Fairy, Florentine Cameo, Cranberry, White Enameled Floral & Branch, 4 1/2 In. 75.00
Fairy, Millefiori, 4 1/4 In. 210.00
Fairy, S. Clarke, 3 3/4 In. 59.00
Fluid, 6-Light, Restauration Style, Gilt Brass Mount, Tole Peinte, France, 37 1/2 x 32 In. .   3450.00
Fluid, Amber Font, Milk Glass Base, Ribbed Loop, Brass, c.1875, 8 In. 140.00
Fluid, Amber, Frosted, Chimney, Brass Neck Ring, Smooth Base, c.1885, 11 In. 179.00
Fluid, Barrie, Clear Font, Chimney, Milk Glass Base, c.1870, 8 1/4 In. 100.00
Fluid, Blown Glass, Clear Font, Base, Red Stem, Brass Neck, Burner, c.1875, 7 3/4 In. . . .   670.00
Fluid, Blown Glass, Hollow Stem, Tooled Opening, Applied Foot, Font, c.1830, 7 In. 125.00
Fluid, Blown Glass, Paw Foot Base, Stand, 11 1/4 In. 358.00
Fluid, Brass, Etched Chimney, Persian Script, Scalloped Flared Rim, 19 In., Pair 90.00
Fluid, Bronze Patinated, Cast Iron, Brass Paw Feet, England, c.1863, 18 In., Pair 920.00
Fluid, Central Glass Co., Clear Glass Font, Cobalt Blue Base, c.1875, 7 1/2 In. 157.00
Fluid, Clambroth Glass, Tulip, Columns, Beaded Square Base, 12 1/4 In. 175.00
Fluid, Clear, Cobalt Blue Base, Brass Neck Ring, Double Wick Burner, 6 1/4 In. 896.00
Fluid, Clear, Smooth Base, Brass Neck Ring, c.1855, 6 3/4 In. 70.00
Fluid, Cranberry Glass Cut To Clear, Brass Plinth, Marble Base, Bohemia, 14 1/2 In. 401.00
Fluid, Cut Glass Overlay, Blue Cut To Clear, Brass Connector, Mid 1800s, 13 1/4 In. 470.00
Fluid, Cut Glass Overlay, Brass Column Standard, Marble Base, c.1870, 8 1/8 In. 140.00
Fluid, Cut Glass Overlay, Opaque White Cut To Clear, Punty Cuts, 19th Century, 9 In. . . .   176.00
Fluid, Cut Glass Overlay, White Cut To Clear, Marble Base, c.1880, 15 7/8 In. 3525.00
Fluid, Cut Glass, Double Overlay, Opaque Raspberry Cut To White, Mid 1800s, 12 1/4 In.   880.00
Fluid, Cut Glass, Double Overlay, White Over Clear Over Emerald 2750.00
Fluid, Cut Glass, Free Blown, Globe Font, Cut Fan & Diamond Designs, 9 1/2 In., Pair . .   355.00
Fluid, Cut Glass, Knopped Shape, Crystal, 23 In., Pair 705.00
Fluid, Cut Glass, Octagonal Font, Lemon Squeezer Interior, Stand, 9 1/2 In. 305.00
Fluid, Cut Glass, Red To White To Clear, Black Glass Base, 14 1/4 In. 1560.00
Fluid, Cut Glass, Strawberry Diamonds & Fans, 3 3/4 In. 550.00
Fluid, Cut Glass, White To Clear, Brass Stem, Marble Base, 10 In. 345.00
Fluid, Cut Glass, White To Cranberry, Cut Flowers On Font, Gold Trim, 16 1/2 In. 633.00
Fluid, Daisy & Cube, Amber, Brass Collar, Burner, Late 19th Century, 5 In. 50.00
Fluid, Diamond Point Font, Twelve Petals Above Pattern, Floral Flange Top, Marble Base   28.00
Fluid, Directoire Style, Columnar, Patinated, Parcel Gilt, 37 In., Pair 2390.00
Fluid, Ellipse Band & Rib, Clear Font, Opalescent Base, c.1860, 8 3/4 In. 70.00
Fluid, Empire Style, Brass, 4 Corinthian Column Standard, 14 In.   540.00
Fluid, Free Blown Bulb Font, Engraved Grapes, Stand, 10 1/4 In.   120.00

Fluid, Free Blown, Flattened Globular Font, Circular Foot, 4 1/4 x 2 15/16 In. 99.00
Fluid, Free Blown, Striped Glass, Transparent Blue, Opaque White, 1800s, 9 3/8 In. 1765.00
Fluid, French Style, Amber Glass, Cut Panels, Round Brass Base, 21 1/2 In., Pair 690.00
Fluid, Gardon, Brass, Bulbous Pedestal Base, Wick Adjuster, Continental, 9 In. 27.00
Fluid, Gilt Bronze, Figural, Red Frosted Flambeau Shade, 1860, 31 1/2 In., Pair 4260.00
Fluid, Gilt Bronze, Onyx, Bird Shape, Iridescent Glass Oil Font, 19 In. 470.00
Fluid, Green Font, 16 Rids, Swirl, Brass Standard, Marble Base, c.1860, 9 1/4 In. 150.00
Fluid, Hanging, Cranberry Swirl, Deep, Crystal Font & Prisms 1550.00
Fluid, Organ, Brass, Onyx, Green, Yellow Flowers, Painted Shade, Scrolled Feet 1069.00
Fluid, Organ, Brass, Onyx, White Shade, Flowers, Torches, S-Curved Paw Feet 1295.00
Fluid, Organ, Brass, Spiral Turned Shaft, Marble Shelf, Font Cap Marked S.A.W. 1240.00
Fluid, Paneled Glass, Hexagonal Base, Dark Amethyst, 7 1/2 x 3 1/4 In. 6465.00
Fluid, Pattern Molded, Circle & Ellipse, Hexagonal Base, Pewter Collar, 8 In. 50.00
Fluid, Pressed Glass, Acanthus Leaf Font, Clambroth, Jade Green, 13 3/4 In. 1410.00
Fluid, Pressed Glass, Acanthus Leaf Font, White, Brass, c.1855, 10 3/8 In. 765.00
Fluid, Pressed Glass, Acanthus Leaf, Blue, Clambroth, Mid 1800s, 11 In., Pair 1998.00
Fluid, Pressed Glass, Acanthus Leaf, Clambroth Font, Wafer, Blue Step Base, 11 1/4 In. . . .   616.00
Fluid, Pressed Glass, Amethyst, Black Bull's-Eye Font, c.1850, 8 1/4 In. 825.00
Fluid, Pressed Glass, Beehive, Pontil, Pewter Neck Band, Double Wick Burner, 8 In. 448.00
Fluid, Pressed Glass, Bulb Font, Sheaf Of Wheat Border, 6 1/2 In. 1058.00
Fluid, Pressed Glass, Canary Yellow, Octagonal Font, Mid 19th Century, 10 1/8 In. 380.00
Fluid, Pressed Glass, Circle & Ellipse Font, Emerald Green, 7 1/2 In. 1880.00
Fluid, Pressed Glass, Clear, Globular Font, Wafered, Circular Base, Pontil, 3 5/8 In. 269.00
Fluid, Pressed Glass, Clear, Loop, Wafered To Octagonal, Neck Ring, Burner, 9 7/8 In. 125.00
Fluid, Pressed Glass, Clear, Octagonal Font, Brass Standard, Marble Base, 9 3/4 In. 100.00
Fluid, Pressed Glass, Clear, Pontil, Sheared, Tooled Mouth, Sparking, 3 1/4 In. 196.00
Fluid, Pressed Glass, Clear, Pontil, Tooled Mouth, Folded Rim, Sausage Stem, 8 1/8 In. . . .   3360.00
Fluid, Pressed Glass, Clear, Stepped Pontil, Tin Double Font Burner, 4 In. 112.00
Fluid, Pressed Glass, Drapery & Step, Sheared Lip, Neck Band, Cobalt Blue, 9 1/4 In. 365.00
Fluid, Pressed Glass, Ellipse, Hexagonal Font, 10 3/8 In., Pair 235.00
Fluid, Pressed Glass, Elongated Loop Pattern, Hexagonal Font, Yellow, 9 5/8 In., Pair 1058.00
Fluid, Pressed Glass, Elongated Loop, Amethyst, Finger, c.1850, 3 1/8 In. 590.00
Fluid, Pressed Glass, Elongated Loop, Hexagonal Base, Cobalt Blue, 9 5/8 In. 470.00
Fluid, Pressed Glass, Elongated Loop, Peacock Green, Finger, c.1850, 3 1/4 In. 441.00
Fluid, Pressed Glass, Free Blown, Conical Font, Bulbous Knop, c.1835, 11 1/4 In., Pair . .   175.00
Fluid, Pressed Glass, Gilt, Heart Pattern, Hexagonal Font, Base, c.1850, 10 1/8 In. 176.00
Fluid, Pressed Glass, Globular Font, Wafered, Pontil, Tin Burner, 4 3/8 In. 269.00
Fluid, Pressed Glass, Gothic Revival, Hexagonal Base, 1840-1860, 10 3/4 In., Pair 590.00
Fluid, Pressed Glass, Green, 3 Bull's-Eye Block Font, Mid 19th Century, 7 3/4 In. 1645.00
Fluid, Pressed Glass, Green, Clambroth, Acanthus, Mid 19th Century, 11 3/8 In., 2 Piece .   1175.00
Fluid, Pressed Glass, Hexagonal Standards & Base, 10 1/2 In., Pair 2470.00
Fluid, Pressed Glass, Lacy Acanthus Base, Clear, Bulbous Font, 7 In. 235.00
Fluid, Pressed Glass, Loop Font, Amethyst, c.1850, 7 7/8 In. 825.00
Fluid, Pressed Glass, Loop, 1 Piece, Hexagonal Base, Pewter Collar, 8 1/2 In. 50.00
Fluid, Pressed Glass, Loop, Blue, Octagonal Standard, Mid 19th Century, 9 7/8 In., Pair . .   2350.00
Fluid, Pressed Glass, Loop, Conical Font, Hexagonal, Marble Base, Amethyst, 12 3/8 In. . .   940.00
Fluid, Pressed Glass, Loop, Octagonal Standards, Square Base, Burners, Green, 8 1/8 In. .   8815.00
Fluid, Pressed Glass, Octagonal Font & Standard, Square Base, 1840-1860, 9 x 3 In. 1410.00
Fluid, Pressed Glass, Octagonal Font & Standard, Square Base, Amethyst, 9 x 3 In. 1880.00
Fluid, Pressed Glass, Paneled Bull's-Eye, Pear Shape Font, White, Squared Base, 13 In. . . .   100.00
Fluid, Pressed Glass, Paneled Waffle Pattern, Brass, Marble, Canary Yellow, 12 1/4 In. . . .   265.00
Fluid, Pressed Glass, Petticoat, Clear, Wafered To Lacy Base, Pontil, 4 3/4 In. 150.00
Fluid, Pressed Glass, Pink Tint, Reeded Font, Mid 19th Century, 9 1/8 In. 380.00
Fluid, Pressed Glass, Star & Cable, Brass, Marble, Blue Font, c.1860, 12 1/4 In. 2700.00
Fluid, Pressed Glass, Star & Punty, Brass Collar, 1840-1865, 9 3/4 In., Pair 235.00
Fluid, Pressed Glass, Star & Punty, Paneled, Gilt Foliate, Mid 1800s, 11 1/4 In., Pair 1115.00
Fluid, Pressed Glass, Triple Flute & Bar, Hexagonal Base, 8 5/8 In., Pair 650.00
Fluid, Pressed Glass, Tulip, Clambroth, Mid 19th Century, 11 1/8 In. 295.00
Fluid, Pressed Glass, Turquoise, Brass, Marble Base, Mid 19th Century, 8 1/4 In., Pair . . .   235.00
Fluid, Pressed Glass, Waisted Loop Font, Canary Yellow, Mid 1800s, 11 5/8 In. 176.00
Fluid, Pressed Glass, Yellow Green Font, Glass Base, Brass Neck Ring, 9 3/8 In. 420.00
Fluid, Pressed Glass, Yellow, Octagonal Font, Wafered, Brass Neck Ring, 11 In. 785.00
Fluid, Ring & Oval, Hexagonal Base, Pewter Cap, 1850-1865, 8 3/4 In., Pair 410.00

Fluid, Ruby To Crystal Chimney, Brass Base, 19 1/2 In., Pair 125.00
Fluid, Sinumbra, Brass, Prisms, Star & Flower, Frosted Shade, Square Base, 26 In. 2860.00
Fluid, Skater's, Molded Globe, Brass, Tin, Gold Paint, 6 1/2 In., Pair 85.00
Fluid, Starburst Font, Purple Amethyst Stem, Metal Foot, c.1880, 11 1/8 In. 505.00
Fluid, Tavern, Free Blown, Globe Font, Mid Drip Dish, Double Bulb Shaft, 6 7/8 In. 323.00
Gas, Leaded Glass, Bronze, Square, Wavy Glass Tiles, Red, Amber, Electrified, 24 x 9 In. 635.00
Gas, Wrought Iron, Square, Scrollwork, 4 Side Lights, Victorian, Electrified, 24 In. 315.00
Gasolier, 2-Light, Brass, Pres-Cut Notched Glass Shades, Bowl Shape, 32 1/2 In. 145.00
Gasolier, 6-Arm, Napoleon III, Neogrecque, Frosted Glass Globes, c.1865, 38 x 42 In. ... 6900.00
Grease, Wrought Iron, 4 Spouts, Pedestal Base, Rivet Construction, 14 3/4 In. 136.00
Kerosene, Atterbury, Shelley, Brass Socket, Opaque White Base, Stand, c.1868, 9 1/4 In. . 30.00
Kerosene, Banquet, Pansies, White Ground, Albertine, Crown Milano, 16 1/2 In. 300.00
Kerosene, Basket Weave, Medallions, Footed Finger, Amber, Handle, Burner, 5 In. 230.00
Kerosene, Beaded Medallion & Daisy, Finger, Burner, Chimney, 3 In. 90.00
Kerosene, Blue Cased, Satin Glass, Melon Ribbed Base, Pansy Ball Shade, 7 In. 1150.00
Kerosene, Blue Opaque Glass, Raised Flowers, Garland, Filigree Brass Foot, 19 In. 345.00
Kerosene, Brass, 8 Sides, Etched Glass Panels, Hinged Door, 18 1/2 In. 90.00
Kerosene, Bronze, Arab Under Tent With Water Pot, Austria, c.1900, 13 In. 1495.00
Kerosene, Bull's-Eye Safety Handle, Finger, Footed, 5 3/8 In. 30.00
Kerosene, Cathedral, Amber Shade, Font, Blue Base, Brass Connector, Stand, 13 In. 325.00
Kerosene, Cleveland Safety, Library, Nickel Plated, Milk Glass Shade, 20 In. 358.00
Kerosene, Cup & Saucer, Finger, Amber, Molded Handle, Late 19th Century, 3 1/4 In. ... 275.00
Kerosene, Cut Glass, Hobstar & Box Band, Mushroom Shade, Engraved, 11 In. 46.00
Kerosene, Cut Glass, Lacquered, Brass Mounted, 19th Century, 30 1/4 In. 2300.00
Kerosene, Dorothy, Finger, Footed, 4 3/4 In. 70.00
Kerosene, Emblem, Stand, Round Stem, Prism Pattern, 6 1/4 In. 160.00
Kerosene, Finger, Amber, Brass Neck, Burner, White Flame Light, c.1885, 3 1/2 In. 60.00
Kerosene, Finger, Cobalt Blue, 8 Sides, Burner, Chimney, c.1895, 6 3/4 In. 190.00
Kerosene, Finger, G.H. Lomax, Burner, c.1875, 4 In. 60.00
Kerosene, Finger, Green, Molded Handle, Burner, Chimney, Footed, 5 3/8 In. 160.00
Kerosene, Finger, Match Holder, Amber, Molded Basket Weave, 2 7/8 In. 190.00
Kerosene, Finger, Molded Body, Applied Handle, Late 19th Century, 2 1/8 In. 75.00
Kerosene, Flowers, White Porcelain, Embossed Basket, 7 7/8 In. 175.00
Kerosene, Gone With The Wind, Brown, Cupid & Garland, 23 In. 175.00
Kerosene, Gone With The Wind, Checkered Ground, Fruit & Vegetable Bands, 22 In. 2130.00
Kerosene, Gone With The Wind, Desert Scene, Pierced Metal Base, 4-Footed, 22 In. 785.00
Kerosene, Gone With The Wind, Light Green, White Flowers, Squat, 19 In. 275.00
Kerosene, Gone With The Wind, Pink, Brown, Pink Jonquils, 25 In. 300.00
Kerosene, Gone With The Wind, Pink, Pink Floral, 24 In. 125.00
Kerosene, Gone With The Wind, Red Satin, Drapery, 8 Panels, 25 In. 575.00
Kerosene, Gone With The Wind, White, Embossed Pink & Green Flowers, 22 In. 250.00
Kerosene, Gone With The Wind, Yellow, Green, Pink Roses, 28 In. 375.00
Kerosene, Green Font, Green Enameled Shade, Brass & Marble Base, 16 In. 200.00
Kerosene, Hanging, Cast Iron Frame, Opaque White Glass Shade, Leaf, Vine, 43 In. 160.00
Kerosene, Hanging, Cranberry Ribbed Optic Shade, Brass Frame, Glass Font, 24 In. 200.00
Kerosene, Hanging, Hobnail, Cranberry, Diamond Embossed Glass Font, 14 In. 290.00
Kerosene, Hanging, Tin, Raised Leaf & Egg, 20 In. 275.00
Kerosene, Hobbs, Brockunier, Plain Band, Stand, Blackberry Base, 9 5/8 In. 50.00
Kerosene, Light Blue Glass, Pink Flowers, Green Leaves, 15 In. 200.00
Kerosene, Little Harry's Night, Opalescent Shade, Brass Burner, Collar, N.Y., 3 3/4 In. ... 90.00
Kerosene, Little Jewel, Finger, Footed, Apple Green, Galleried Burner, 3 1/4 In. 140.00
Kerosene, Milk Glass, Flowers, Red, Green, Pink Ground, 8 1/2 In. 345.00
Kerosene, Milk Glass, Flowers, Red, Yellow, Green, Green Ground, 23 1/2 In. 605.00
Kerosene, Milk Glass, White, Painted Owl, Black, Gray, Yellow Eyes, 7 3/4 In. 748.00
Kerosene, Miller, Copper, Spherical Glass Shade, Sunflower, Frosted, 25 In. 1265.00
Kerosene, Napoleon III, Gilt Bronze Mount, Pink Over Opalescent, 35 In. 1495.00
Kerosene, Opaline Glass, Neogrecque, Electrified, 19th Century, 18 In. 403.00
Kerosene, Pink Cased, Satin Glass, Melon Ribbed Base, Pansy Ball Shade, 7 In. 489.00
Kerosene, Pink Ribbed Glass Shade, Brass Hanging Hardware, 11 In. 170.00
Kerosene, Pressed Glass, Beaded Drape, Blue, 8 In. 75.00
Kerosene, Pressed Glass, Beaded Swirl, Brown, Red, Yellow, Stellar Burner, 8 In. 425.00
Kerosene, Pressed Glass, Blackberry, Clambroth, Opaque Blue, 1850-1860, 11 x 5 1/4 In. 2000.00
Kerosene, Pressed Glass, Britannia, Finger, Footed, 4 3/4 In. 35.00

Kerosene, Pressed Glass, Bull's-Eye, Finger, 3 1/8 In. 40.00
Kerosene, Pressed Glass, Cable, Finger, Footed, 6 3/8 In. 40.00
Kerosene, Pressed Glass, Chilton, Molded Handle, Finger, 3 1/2 In. 10.00
Kerosene, Pressed Glass, Columbian Coin, c.1892, 11 x 5 1/2 In. 978.00
Kerosene, Pressed Glass, Columbian Coin, Stand, 9 1/2 In. 210.00
Kerosene, Pressed Glass, Concord Grape, Finger, 2 3/4 In. 70.00
Kerosene, Pressed Glass, Convex Window, Finger, 5 3/8 In. 50.00
Kerosene, Pressed Glass, Coolidge Drape, Burner, Chimney, Stand, 9 1/4 In. 80.00
Kerosene, Pressed Glass, Coolidge Drape, Finger, Applied Handle, 3 3/8 In. 60.00
Kerosene, Pressed Glass, Coolidge Drape, Finger, Footed, 5 7/8 In. 80.00
Kerosene, Pressed Glass, Corn, Finger, Applied Handle, La Belle Glass Co., 3 1/4 In. 190.00
Kerosene, Pressed Glass, Crown, Finger, 3 3/4 In. 25.00
Kerosene, Pressed Glass, Cup & Saucer, Finger, Burner, Chimney, 3 1/8 In. 140.00
Kerosene, Pressed Glass, Cup & Saucer, Finger, Taplin Brown Collar, 3 1/8 In. 120.00
Kerosene, Pressed Glass, Daisy & Cube, Stand, Amber, Shade, Chimney, 7 1/2 In. 325.00
Kerosene, Pressed Glass, Daisy, Green, Galleried Collar, Stand, 4 3/4 In. 140.00
Kerosene, Pressed Glass, Dart, Finger, Footed, 4 3/8 In. 130.00
Kerosene, Pressed Glass, Dart, Finger, Footed, Burner, Chimney, 4 1/4 In. 100.00
Kerosene, Pressed Glass, Diamond Sawtooth & Sheath, Finger, 3 3/8 In. 70.00
Kerosene, Pressed Glass, Diamonds Reversed, Finger, 3 1/8 In. 10.00
Kerosene, Pressed Glass, Dogtooth, Finger, 3 1/4 In. 25.00
Kerosene, Pressed Glass, Ellipse With Thumbprint, Finger, Footed, 4 3/4 In. 45.00
Kerosene, Pressed Glass, Erin Fan, Finger, Footed, 5 In. 35.00
Kerosene, Pressed Glass, Feather Duster, Finger, Amber, Burner, 5 1/2 In. 150.00
Kerosene, Pressed Glass, Feather Duster, Finger, Light Blue, Burner, 3 1/2 In. 240.00
Kerosene, Pressed Glass, Fickle Block, Finger, Burner, Chimney, 3 1/2 In. 45.00
Kerosene, Pressed Glass, Filley, Finger, 1868, 3 3/16 In. 10.00
Kerosene, Pressed Glass, Fishscale, Burner, Chimney, Stand, 9 In. 50.00
Kerosene, Pressed Glass, Heart, Finger, Burner, Chimney, 3 In. 90.00
Kerosene, Pressed Glass, Heart, Finger, Footed, 4 3/4 In. 50.00
Kerosene, Pressed Glass, Herringbone Band, Finger, Footed, 4 3/8 In. . . . . .20.00 to 50.00
Kerosene, Pressed Glass, Icicle, Finger, 3 1/2 In. 25.00
Kerosene, Pressed Glass, Icicle, Finger, Star Pattern, Burner, Chimney, 1868, 3 In. 60.00
Kerosene, Pressed Glass, King Comet, Stand, 9 1/4 In. 25.00
Kerosene, Pressed Glass, King Melon, Finger, 3 3/8 In. 25.00
Kerosene, Pressed Glass, Lomax, Finger, Footed, Burner, Chimney, c.1870, 4 In. 35.00
Kerosene, Pressed Glass, Lomax, Finger, Footed, c.1870, 4 3/16 In. 25.00
Kerosene, Pressed Glass, Melon, Finger, Applied Handle, Burner, Chimney, 2 7/8 In. 40.00
Kerosene, Pressed Glass, Nosegay, Finger, Applied Handle, Burner, Chimney, 3 In. 30.00
Kerosene, Pressed Glass, Oak Leaf Bubble, Finger, Footed, 5 3/8 In. 90.00
Kerosene, Pressed Glass, Onion, Dove Gray, 1865-1880, 12 In. 2468.00
Kerosene, Pressed Glass, Onion, Opaque Blue, 1865-1880, 23 1/2 In. 5290.00
Kerosene, Pressed Glass, Onion, Turquoise, 1865-1880, 13 In.   1765.00
Kerosene, Pressed Glass, Onion, White, 1865-1880, 21 In. 7050.00
Kerosene, Pressed Glass, Paneled Variant, Finger, 1868, 3 3/8 In. 50.00
Kerosene, Pressed Glass, Peacock Feather, Amber, Iridescent, Stand, 8 1/4 In. 300.00
Kerosene, Pressed Glass, Peanut, Finger, Burner, 3 1/4 In. 60.00
Kerosene, Pressed Glass, Pioneer's Victoria, Finger, 3 1/2 In.   25.00
Kerosene, Pressed Glass, Prince Edward, Finger, Footed, 5 In.   70.00
Kerosene, Pressed Glass, Princess Feather, Sewing, Burner, Bulbous Chimney, 9 1/4 In. . . .   90.00
Kerosene, Pressed Glass, Prisms & Ribbed Bands, Finger, Footed, 5 1/8 In. 150.00
Kerosene, Pressed Glass, Quartered Block, Finger, Footed, 6 In. 70.00
Kerosene, Pressed Glass, Scroll, Cartouche, Diamond, Cobalt Blue, 10 1/4 In. 176.00
Kerosene, Pressed Glass, Skedden, Stand, Amber, 8 3/4 In. 80.00
Kerosene, Pressed Glass, Snail, Frosted Glass, 8 In. 635.00
Kerosene, Pressed Glass, Teardrop & Eyewinker, Plume Font, Moss Green, Stand, 10 In. . .   110.00
Kerosene, Pressed Glass, Torch & Wreath, Finger, 3 1/2 In. 30.00
Kerosene, Pressed Glass, Turkey Foot, Finger, Burner, Chimney, 3 1/2 In. 100.00
Kerosene, Pressed Glass, Wild Rose & Bowknot, Finger, Burner, 3 In. 200.00
Kerosene, Pressed Glass, Wild Rose & Bowknot, Stand, Burner, Chimney, 7 1/2 In. 110.00
Kerosene, Pressed Glass, Zipper Loop, Finger, Burner, Chimney, Footed, 5 In. 70.00
Kerosene, Pressed Glass, Zipper Loop, Stand, Burner, Bulbous Chimney, 10 3/4 In. 80.00
Kerosene, Ripley Patent, Finger, Stippled Web Stem, Footed, c.1868, 5 5/8 In. 110.00

Kerosene, Riverside, No. 515, Finger, Molded Handle, Footed, 5 1/4 In. 30.00
Kerosene, Rogers, Silver Plate, Bronze, Stand, Flowers, Acanthus Leaf Stem, 9 5/16 In. . . .   30.00
Kerosene, Ship, Gimbaled, Brass Bracket, Bulbous, Double Burner, 17 In. 1409.00
Kerosene, Solar, Brass, Frosted & Etched Shade, Plaque, Marble Base, Electrified, c.1850   575.00
Kerosene, Student, Perfection, Patented Nov. 22, 1881 . . . .   350.00
Kerosene, White Glass, 1870-1880, 13 1/2 In. 120.00
Kerosene, Yellow Cased, Gold Flowers On Base, Stand, 8 1/2 In. 575.00
Lard, Redware, Slip Glazed, Round Saucer Base, Pa., 19th Century, 6 5/8 In. 235.00
Oil, Blown Glass, Cobalt Cut To Clear Column, Engraved Font, Marble Base, 13 1/2 In. . . .   470.00
Oil, Blue Swan, Clear Swan Scene Font, 11 In. 1400.00
Oil, Brass, Enamel, Elephant Support, Electrified, Middle Eastern, c.1900, 72 In. 805.00
Oil, Bronze, Relief Dragons, 2 Elephant-Head Handles, Opalescent Shade, 34 In. 460.00
Oil, Bronze, Russet, Green, Brown Patina, Electrified, Japan, 1912, 24 In. 315.00
Oil, Empire Style, Bronze, Marble, Cut Glass, Electrified, Late 19th Century, 15 1/2 In. . . .   430.00
Oil, Empire, Pendant, Gilt, Dark Verdigris, Swan, Tripod Stand, c.1815, 7 3/4 In. 865.00
Oil, Etched Frosted Shade & Body, Brass & Metal, Electrified, c.1880, 24 In. 345.00
Oil, Fiery Opalescent Font, Cobalt Overlay, Clambroth Base, Fluted Column, 12 In. 1155.00
Oil, Flowers On Pedestal, Clear Glass Font, Amethyst Shade, Iron Base, 22 In. 96.00
Oil, Glass, Hexagonal Base, Concave Edges, Paneled Baluster Stem, Loop Font, 8 3/4 In. . .   55.00
Oil, Juno, Brass, Applied Cast Metal Fruit, c.1890, 26 1/2 In. 145.00
Oil, Lion & Baboon, No. 2 Burner, Bulge Chimney, Late 19th Century, 9 1/2 In. 200.00
Oil, Onion, Opaque Apple Green, Ribbed Base & Font, Brass Fittings, 13 1/4 In. 1980.00
Oil, P & A Mfg. Co, Satin Glass, Blister Design, c.1890, 10 In.   175.00
Oil, Peg, Kosmos-Brenner, Cranberry Glass, Enamel Scroll Design, c.1880, 9 In., Pair . . .   259.00
Oil, Pink Quilted Font, Clear Quilted Base, 11 In. 700.00
Oil, Pressed Glass, Bull's-Eye, Fleur-De-Lis Font, Hexagonal Base, Concave Sides, 9 In. .   920.00
Oil, Pressed Glass, Camphored Chimney, Brass Plinth, Marble, 17 1/2 In. 115.00
Oil, Pressed Glass, Cobalt To Clear Font, Opaque White Base, Stepped, Reeded, 12 In. . . .   525.00
Oil, Pressed Glass, Hollow Base, 22 In. . . . . *Illus*   600.00
Oil, Sanctuary, Bronze, Cast, Cherub Chain, 17th Century, 39 In. 1035.00
Oil, Sanctuary, Bronze, Gilt, France, 19th Century, 49 In. 750.00
Oil, Sinumbra, Brass, Frosted Floral Cut Glass, Prisms, Marble Base, 24 In. 175.00
Oil, Sinumbra, Cornelius & Co., Patinated Bronze, Spherical Shade, Lancet Arch, 30 In. . . .   805.00
Oil, T. Webb, Amber Satin Glass, Red & White Swirls, 2-Wick Burner, Brass Feet, 20 In. .   2300.00
Oil, Ufford, Tin, Oblong, Ring Handle, Saucer Base, Boston, 11 In. 495.00
Perfume, Jacob Petit, Porcelain, Flowers, Stopper, Dove, 19th Century, 8 In. 1610.00
Perfume, Little Girl, Holding Flower, Spaghetti 38.00
Perfume, Parrot, Hollyhocks, Black Tassel, DeVilbiss, 12 In. . . . . *Illus*   2310.00
Perfume, Semi-Nude Lady, Painted Shade, Dimmer Switch, DeVilbiss, 10 In. . . . . . . *Illus*   4675.00
Rush, Hand-Forged Iron Clamp, Wood Stand, Turned Feet, 56 In. 3080.00
Rush, Iron, Candle Counterbalance 675.00
Rush, Iron, Candleholder, Tripod Base, Rose-Head Finial, 35 1/4 In. 495.00
Rush, Wrought Iron, Carved Wood Base, Early 19th Century, 10 3/4 In. 560.00
Rush, Wrought Iron, Holder, Spring Clamp, Wood Pole, Base, 23 1/2 In. 468.00
Rush, Wrought Iron, Holder, Spring Clamp, Wood Post, Base, 21 In. 275.00
Rush, Wrought Iron, Holder, Twisted Stem Detail, Tripod Feet, 15 3/4 In. 330.00

Lamp, Oil, Pressed
Glass, Hollow
Base, 22 In.

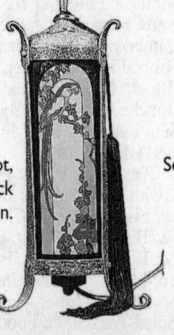

Lamp, Perfume, Parrot,
Hollyhocks, Black
Tassel, DeVilbiss, 12 In.

Lamp, Perfume,
Semi-Nude Lady, Painted
Shade, Dimmer Switch,
DeVilbiss, 10 In.

Sconce, 2-Arm, Gilt Bronze, Lion, Faces, Belgium, 20th Century, 23 x 10 In., Pair 350.00
Sconce, 2-Arm, Rococo Revival, Bronze, Brass, Electrified, c.1850, 22 x 20 In., Pair 2530.00
Sconce, 2-Light, Bronze, Gilt, Porcelain, Flowers, 19th Century, 15 In. 1610.00
Sconce, 2-Light, Bronze, Ram's Head, 2 Scroll Arms, France, 1900s, 11 3/4 In., Pair 510.00
Sconce, 2-Light, Cartouche, Floral Spray, Scroll Arms, Polychrome, c.1890, 16 In., Pair .. 315.00
Sconce, 2-Light, G. Stickley, Hammered, Bracket, Lanterns, Heart Cutout, 16 x 11 In. .. 4890.00
Sconce, 2-Light, George V, Carved Giltwood, Gilt Wrought Iron, 36 1/2 x 14 In., Pair ... 2185.00
Sconce, 2-Light, Giltwood, 46 x 18 In., 4 Piece 11350.00
Sconce, 2-Light, Giltwood, Carved Anthemion, 9 x 12 In., Pair 920.00
Sconce, 2-Light, Giltwood, Lozenge Form, Scroll Arms, Urn Finial, c.1910, 36 In., Pair .. 635.00
Sconce, 2-Light, Giltwood, Wrought Iron, Mirrored, Electrified, Italy, c.1900, 25 In. 489.00
Sconce, 2-Light, Louis XV Style, Gilt Bronze, Foliate Cast Arms, 15 In., 4 Piece 775.00
Sconce, 2-Light, Louis XV Style, Gilt Bronze, France, 1860, 18 1/2 In., Pair 1705.00
Sconce, 2-Light, Louis XVI Style, Bronze, Gilt, Cartouche, Feathers, 17 In., 3 Piece ... 1880.00
Sconce, 2-Light, Patinated Bronze, Intertwined Snakes, Continental, 9 1/4 x 19 1/2 In. ... 805.00
Sconce, 2-Light, Regency Style, France, c.1885, 16 x 9 1/2 In., Pair 1840.00
Sconce, 2-Light, Silvered Bronze, Porcelain, Renaissance Man, Woman, 23 x 10 In. 2350.00
Sconce, 3-Arm, Hammered Metal, Sunflower Heads, Electrified, 28 x 25 In. 420.00
Sconce, 3-Light, Art Nouveau, Leaves, Glass Shade, Ruffled Trim, Brass, 23 In. 1568.00
Sconce, 3-Light, Brass, Scroll Arms, Handle Top, Ball Bottom, 13 x 14 In., Pair 185.00
Sconce, 3-Light, Eastlake, Pierced Brass, Electrified, 18 x 12 In. 690.00
Sconce, 3-Light, Gilt Bronze, France, 1900, 21 In., Pair 2726.00
Sconce, 3-Light, Louis XV Style, Cut Glass, Ormolu, Prisms, c.1925, 13 3/4 In., Pair 980.00
Sconce, 3-Light, Regency Style, Patinated Bronze, Eagle Holds Snake, 4 1/4 x 9 In., Pair . 805.00
Sconce, 3-Light, Restauration, Gilt Bronze, Flower Sprays, c.1815, 10 x 10 1/2 In., Pair .. 1380.00
Sconce, 3-Light, Venetian, Beaded Glass, Gilt Metal, Early 20th Century, 22 In., Pair 1610.00
Sconce, 3-Light, Wrought Iron, Hanging Plate, Heart Design, 1800s, 22 x 11 x 6 In. 635.00
Sconce, 4-Light, Gilt Brass, Electrified, 21 1/4 x 18 x 16 In. 1265.00
Sconce, 4-Light, Gilt Brass, Vintage Decor, 21 1/4 x 18 x 16 In., Pair 1725.00
Sconce, 4-Light, Louis Philippe, Bronze, Gilt, Patinated, 10 x 9 In., Pair 2300.00
Sconce, 5 Light, Brass, Baroque, Shell-Form Drip Pan, Continental, 24 x 15 In., Pair 4180.00
Sconce, 5-Arm, Art Deco, Gilt Metal, Urn, Lily Bobeche, c.1925, 46 x 3 x 7 1/2 In. 7270.00
Sconce, 5-Light, Louis XV Style, Faceted Drops, Late 1800s, 29 x 18 In., Pair 2530.00
Sconce, 5-Light, Louis XV Style, Foliate Scrolling Arms, 18 In., Pair 825.00
Sconce, 6-Light, Louis XVI Style, Bronze, Cut Glass, c.1885, 28 x 16 In., Pair 1725.00
Sconce, 9-Light, Ges. Gesch No. 93, Scroll & Leaf Design Arm, 28 x 16 In. 960.00
Sconce, Art Deco Style, Pendant, Metal, Enameled, Glass, 33 1/2 x 6 In., Pair 520.00
Sconce, Art Deco, Lucite, Brass, Flared Petal Rim, France, 1950s, 15 In. 3465.00
Sconce, Art Deco, Patinated, Stepped Square, 12 In., Pair 1075.00
Sconce, Blackamoor, Turbaned, Holding Cornucopia, Gilt, Patinated Bronze, 17 1/2 In. ... 2990.00
Sconce, Brass Plate, Molded Glass Bubbles, 1960s, 6 x 8 In., Pair 635.00
Sconce, Brass, Openwork Leaves, Dolphins, Mirrored, Cut Glass Prisms, 21 In., Pair 110.00
Sconce, Frosted Egg-Shape Shade, Italy, 10 x 5 In. 120.00
Sconce, George III Style, Brass, Glass, 20th Century, 21 1/2 In., Pair 460.00
Sconce, Giltwood, Wrought Iron, Scallop Shell, Electrified, 20 1/4 x 7 In., Pair 520.00
Sconce, Iron, Flower Bobeche, Spiraled Center, Claw Feet, 16 x 6 In., Pair 323.00
Sconce, Neoclassical, Gilt, Gesso, Carved, Early 19th Century, 44 x 36 x 15 1/2 In. 1645.00
Sconce, Panton, Fun 2 WM, J. Luber, c.1964, 19 x 11 x 6 1/2 In. 3230.00
Sconce, Rococo Style, Bronze, Winged Cupid Holding Goblet, 28 In., Pair 2235.00
Sconce, Semi-Cylindrical White Plastic Shade, France, 31 x 10 1/2 In., Pair 500.00
Sconce, Tin, Crimped Shell Crest, Mirrored Back, 14 3/4 In., Pair 535.00
Sconce, Visa Lighting, Aluminum, Half Cylinder, American, 16 In., 3 Piece 560.00
Sconce, Wrought Iron, Heart Shape, Dished Bobeche, 19th Century, 12 x 10 In., Pair 478.00
Torchere, 5-Light, Arts & Crafts, Curled Wrought Iron, 3-Footed Base, 78 In. 402.00
Torchere, 5-Light, Iron, Arched Arms, Tripod Base, 60 In., Pair 558.00
Torchere, 6-Light, Wood, Bronzed, Parcel Gilt, Fit For Electricity, Italy, c.1900, 73 In. ... 500.00
Torchere, Art Deco, Chinese Pagoda, Metal, 74 In. 1315.00
Torchere, Art Deco, Polished Metal, Fluted Shade, 77 In. 480.00
Torchere, Art Deco, Pressed Glass Opalescent Shade, Brass Washed Shaft, 63 x 16 In. ... 150.00
Torchere, Classique, Birds, Silvered Trees, Cylindrical Stem, Round Base, 14 In., Pair ... 785.00
Torchere, Empire Style, Gilt, Ebonized Metal, 3 Crossed Arrows, 56 In., Pair 3450.00
Torchere, Giltwood, Continental, 19th Century, 77 1/2 x 24 In., Pair 14340.00
Torchere, Giltwood, Shaft Leaves, 3-Part Base, Italy, c.1850, 60 In. 1610.00

Torchere, Louis XIV Style, Carved Beech, 19th Century, 52 In. 1675.00
Torchere, Louis XVI Style, Gilt Carved Wood, Ram's Heads, Tripod Base, 60 In. 1795.00
Torchere, Parcel Silvered Bronze, Glass, France, c.1930, 74 1/2 x 16 x 11 In., Pair 11950.00
Torchere, Regency, Painted, Parcel Gilt, c.1810, 55 x 19 In. 5380.00
Torchere, William IV, Mahogany, Twist Standard, 3-Footed, c.1835, 58 x 11 In. 375.00
Whale Oil, Blown Glass, Bulbous, Petal Base, 3 1/4 In. 105.00
Whale Oil, Blown Glass, Font, Low Foot, 1825-1835, 7 3/8 In. 1175.00
Whale Oil, Blown Glass, Opalescent, S-Curve Spout, Acanthus, Early 19th Century, 10 In. · . 380.00
Whale Oil, Brass, Lemon Shape, Portland, Maine, 8 1/2 In., Pair 635.00
Whale Oil, Bulbous Fonts, Acanthus Leaf, 1828-1835, 6 In. 529.00
Whale Oil, Bulbous, Knopped Standards, Tin Burners, Square Base, 6 x 2 1/4 In., Pair . . . 765.00
Whale Oil, Cast Brass Fluted Column, Cut Leaded Glass, Marble Base, 12 In. 215.00
Whale Oil, Clambroth Molded Base, Blown Ribbon Glass, 10 1/2 In. 565.00
Whale Oil, Emerald Green, Pewter, Marble Feet, 9 1/2 In. 805.00
Whale Oil, Flint Stick, Hexagonal, Dome Base, Peg-Type Font, 9 1/2 In. 160.00
Whale Oil, Free Blown, Pressed Glass, Bulb Font, Acanthus Leaf, c.1830, 7 7/8 In. 235.00
Whale Oil, Free Blown, Purple Blue, Bulb Font, Early 19th Century, 5 In. 2235.00
Whale Oil, Globe Font, Fluted Square Base, 4 7/8 x 5 x 2 1/2 In., Pair 325.00
Whale Oil, Loop, Flint, Opaque White Base, Gilt, 13 1/2 In. 138.00
Whale Oil, Milk Glass Cut To Red, Quatrefoil Pattern, Brass Ring, c.1865, 10 1/2 In. 280.00
Whale Oil, Molded Glass, Bulbous Font, Quatrefoil Base, 1830-1840, 11 3/4 In., Pair 705.00
Whale Oil, Pattern Molded, Petticoat, 12 Flute Font, Folded Rim, c.1828, 8 1/4 In. 2000.00
Whale Oil, Pedestal, Trumpet Shape Base, c.1810 . . . . 470.00
Whale Oil, Petticoat, Globe Font, 3-Knop Shaft, Dome Base, c.1828, 8 3/4 In. 1528.00
Whale Oil, Pewter, Double Burner, Acorn Shape Font, Round Stepped Base, 9 In. 205.00
Whale Oil, Pewter, Sparking, Ring-Turned Lemon-Shape Font, Dome Base, 4 In., Pair . . . 380.00
Whale Oil, Pressed Glass, Acanthus Leaf, 11 In. 205.00
Whale Oil, Pressed Glass, Basket Of Flowers, Opalescent, 1830-1855, 7 3 1/8 In. 880.00
Whale Oil, Pressed Glass, Bulb Font, Knopped Standard, 7 1/4 x 3 3/8 In. 382.00
Whale Oil, Pressed Glass, Chamfered Octagonal Fonts, Amethyst, 1840-1860, 9 In., Pair . 5875.00
Whale Oil, Pressed Glass, Flutes, Punties, 1828-1835, 11 1/4 In. 295.00
Whale Oil, Pressed Glass, Free Blown, Opalescent, c.1855, 8 3/8 In., Pair 2350.00
Whale Oil, Pressed Glass, Horn Of Plenty, Pewter Collar, c.1845, 11 In., Pair 765.00
Whale Oil, Pressed Glass, Lion's Head, Paw Foot Base, 1827-1835, 8 1/4 In., Pair 1528.00
Whale Oil, Pressed Glass, Lyre, Flint Glass, Paneled, 10 In. 85.00
Whale Oil, Pressed Glass, Pattern Molded, Hexagonal Font, 2-Tube Burner, 7 1/4 In. 28.00
Whale Oil, Pressed Glass, Sandwich Star Pattern, Mid 19th Century, 11 7/8 In. 200.00
Whale Oil, Pressed Glass, Smocking, Feather Crimped Applied Handle, 3 7/8 In. 140.00
Whale Oil, Pressed Glass, Star & Sheaf Of Wheat, 1828, 6 In. 1060.00
Whale Oil, Ram's Head, Gadrooned Base, 8 x 3 1/2 In. 529.00
Whale Oil, Sandwich Type, Amethyst, 8 1/2 In. 520.00
Whale Oil, Warren's Hard Metal, Pewter, Egg Shape Fonts, 9 In. 180.00
LAMPSHADE, Amber, Gold, Yellow, Overall Iridized Finish, Early 20th Century, 6 3/4 In. . . . 115.00
Art Deco, Amber, Black Pattern, Colorful Fruit Accents, 3 3/4 x 4 In., 3 Piece 80.00
Art Glass, Crimson Pulled Feathers, Opal Body, Early 20th Century, 5 1/4 In. 230.00
Art Glass, Opal, Gold Interior, 5 In. 69.00
Art Glass, Opal, Green, Gold Hearts, Overall Threading, c.1925, 5 1/4 In. 460.00
Arts & Crafts, Riveted Iron, Hammered, Slag Glass Panels, Wire Cage, 23 x 25 In. 863.00
Cameo, Stylized Flowers, Ferns, Amber, Green Gray Stain, 10 1/2 In. 633.00
Candle, Pigeon Blood, 3 1/4 x 7 In. 604.00
Glass, Green, Bubbles, 12 x 5 In. 44.00
Green, Molded Lines, Fleur-De-Lis Design, Textured Ground, Dentil Rim, 7 3/4 In. 374.00
Green Pulled Feathers, Gold Iridescent Diamond Quilted Body, c.1920, 4 In. 288.00
Green Pulled Feathers, Tipped Gold, Opal Body, c.1920, 5 In., Pair 144.00
Hanging, Bent Slag, Filigree, Cast Foliage, c.1920, 15 In. 259.00
Iridescent, Gold, White Pulled Feathers, Tipped Blue, Gold Threading, 6 1/2 In., Pair . . . 575.00
Leaded Glass, Green & White Slag, Stylized Acorn Border, 16 In. 489.00
Pink & Vaseline Opalescent Swirl, 6 1/2 In. 325.00

LANTERNS are a special type of lighting device. They have a light
source, usually a candle, totally hidden inside the walls of the lantern.
Light is seen through holes or glass sections.

Barn, Half-Round, Painted, Pierced Tin, Hinged Glass Panel, Ring Handle, 14 3/4 In. 265.00

Barn, Pine, Natural Finish, Pegged, Old Glass, 15 1/2 In. 220.00
Barn, Tin, Triangular, Ring Handle, Pierced Air Vent, Hinged Tin Back Panel, 15 1/2 In. . 265.00
Barn, Wooden, 3 Glass Panes, Tin Candle Socket, Wire Latch, Bail Handle, 6 x 11 In. ... 385.00
Brass, Blue, Clear, Red Lenses, 11 In. 295.00
Brass Mounted, Copper, Glass, Electric Fitted, Restauration Style, France, 18 x 12 In. .. 200.00
Bronze, Openwork, Man & Scrolling Leaves, Dragon, Meiji Period, Japan, 9 1/2 In 345.00
Bronze, Ruby Overlay, Etched Glass Panels, Russia, 35 In. 4780.00
Bull's-Eye, Tin, Brass, Retractable Chimney, Walton Bro's N.Y., 1872, 4 1/6 In. 110.00
Candle, Cylindrical, Punched Tin, Cone Top, Hang Ring, 19th Century, 16 x 5 1/2 In. 412.00
Candle, Tin, Bull's-Eye, Red, Green Glass, Late 19th Century, 4 1/2 In. 90.00
Coach, Candle, Dome Top, Folding Handle, Hinged Door, Tin, 6 1/4 In. 300.00
Coleman, Model 220A, Red, 1957, 30 In. 58.00
Coleman, Model 228E, Green, 1952, 15 1/2 In. 58.00
Copper, Candle, Peaked Top, 4 Glass Panes, Ring Handle, 7 x 7 x 13 1/4 In. 85.00
Fireman's, Brass, Universal Spinning & Stamping Co., New York, Clear Globe, 12 In. ... 281.00
Folding, Galvanized Steel, 3 Clear Plastic Lens, Bail Handle, 10 1/4 x 4 x 4 In. 69.00
G. Stickley, Copper, Hammered, Latticework Over Amber Slag Glass, 8 x 6 In., Pair 2990.00
G. Stickley, Copper, Hammered, Latticework Over Yellow Glass, 11 x 6 In., Pair 2300.00
G. Stickley, Hammered Iron, Cutout Design, Frosted Shade, 17 1/2 In. 1725.00
Gate Post, Patinated Brass, Wrought Iron, Late Gothic Style, Continental, c.1900, 47 In. . 1725.00
Gilt Bronze, Glazed Sides & Door, France, 1870, 36 In. 4089.00
Globe, Fixed, Configured, Black Painted Pierced Tin Frame, Mid 19th Century, 15 In. ... 880.00
Globe, Fixed, Onion, Pierced Tin Frame, Ring Handle, Mid 19th Century, 11 1/4 In. 380.00
Hall, Glass, Colonial, Blown, Molded, Emerald, Spherule Globe, c.1885, 18 x 7 1/2 In. .. 405.00
Hanging, Blown Glass, Amethyst, Inverted Bell Jar Shape, 3 Lights, Electrified, 15 In. ... 646.00
Hanging, Bronzed Metal, Mica Inserts, Ceiling Cap, Arts & Crafts, 14 In. 175.00
Hanging, Gilt Brass, Glazed Door, Winged Dragons, France, 1810, 44 In. 5111.00
Iron, Arts & Crafts, Yellow Hammered Glass, 20 In. 345.00
Iron, Hexagonal, Glass Panels, Multicolored, Mediterranean, 19 In. 127.00
Leaded Glass Sides, Brass Frame, Chain, Arts & Crafts, 19 x 11 In. 1380.00
Miner, Iron, Brass, Threaded Font, Hasp, Thomas & Williams, Cambria Type, 9 3/4 In. .. 105.00
Onion Globe, Cranberry Glass, Pierced Tin Frame, Ring Handle, Mid 1800s, 18 1/4 In. .. 1295.00
Onion Globe, Tin Mounted, Round, Diamond Shaped Pieces, Hanging Loop, 14 1/2 In. .. 880.00
Portico, Wrought Iron, Renaissance Style, c.1900, 26 x 10 x 10 In. 805.00
Regency, Hanging, Gilt, Glass Panels, Flower Decoration, 37 7/16 x 17 In. 5676.00
Ship's, 360 Degree, Copper Seahorse Label, Ribbed Glass Lens, 21 x 11 In. 290.00
Skater's, Brass, Clear Globe, Carrying Chain, 9 In. 305.00
Tin, 3 Panes, Wire Guards, Starburst Design, Ring Handle, Bohrmann's Universal, 10 In. . 220.00
Tin, Glass Front Bays, Punched Slits, Cone Shape Top, Loop Handle, 10 1/2 In. 280.00
Tin, Glass Panels, Wire Handle, 11 1/4 In. 110.00
Tin, Paul Revere Style, Extensive Punchwork, 12 In. 96.00
Tin, Punched, Blown Glass Globe, Pear Shape, Painted, Wire Guards, 20 In. 330.00
Tin, Punched, Herringbone, Round Designs, Conical Top, 9 1/2 In. 240.00
Tin, Punched, Protruding Glass Panes, Candle Socket, Conical Top, Ring Handle, 14 In. .. 220.00
Tin, White Paint, Glass Front, Half-Round Back, Door, Wire Handle, 12 In. 135.00
Victorian, Brass, Glass, Flaring Shape, Frosted, 12 In. 470.00
Wall, Baroque Style, Brass, Frosted Glass, Electrified, c.1900, 32 In., 4 Piece 2030.00
Whale Oil, Tin, Glass, 19th Century, 17 In. 630.00
Whale Oil, Tin, Glass, Shade Engraved Lyman Mills, 19th Century, 17 In. 635.00
Wrought Iron, Etched Glass, 3 Curved Legs, Pierced Base, 37 1/2 In., Pair 4180.00

LE VERRE FRANCAIS is one of the many types of cameo glass made in France. The glass was made by the C. Schneider factory in Epinay-sur-Seine from 1920 to 1933. It is a mottled glass, usually decorated with floral designs, and bears the incised signature *Le Verre Francais*.

Chandelier, Flowers, Leaves, Red, Green, Signed, 18 In. 1998.00
Ewer, Black Ruby, Fruit, Satin Ox Blood Ground, Pulled Spout, Signed, 12 In. 1610.00
Lamp, Cased, Frosted Exterior, Swirled End Of Day Colors, 19 In. 1320.00
Lamp, Hanging, Mushroom Shape, Orange Over Gray, Yellow, c.1925, 11 In. 2300.00
Vase, Birds, Brown, Yellow, Blue, Signed, 12 In. 1265.00
Vase, Dahlias, Lavender, Mottled Pink Ground, Footed, Signed, 12 1/2 In. 2130.00
Vase, Dragonfly, Millefiori Cane, Red, Mauve, c.1922, 18 1/3 In. 3360.00
Vase, Flower Bud, Citron, Red & Burgundy, Marked, 13 3/4 In. 1265.00

Vase, Geese In Flight, Brown, Blue, Yellow Mottled Ground, Signed, 13 3/4 In. 4313.00
Vase, Gray, Yellow, Amber, Amethyst, Blue, Leaves, c.1925, 12 1/2 In. 2990.00
Vase, Mirette, Gray, Yellow, Blue, Flowers, c.1926, 14 1/2 In. 2070.00
Vase, Mottled Blue Over Yellow, Oval, Birds, Footed, 14 In. 3000.00
Vase, Orange, Yellow, Grapes, Arched Border, Signed, 11 In. 750.00
Vase, Orchids, Orange, Brown On Mottled Yellow Ground, Signed, 22 In. 3450.00
Vase, Papillons, Butterflies, Gray, Turquoise, Crimson, c.1924, 17 1/2 In. 6670.00
Vase, Pavot, Gray, Yellow, Red, Brown Flowers, c.1925, 10 In. 1610.00
Vase, Peach, Green, Yellow Ground, Art Deco, Signed, 10 1/2 In. 1035.00
Vase, Pendant Berries, Orange To Brown, Yellow Ground, Signed, 14 3/4 In. 1955.00
Vase, Red Orchids, Yellow Ground, Footed, Tall Oval, 22 In. 2035.00
Vase, Roses, Green, 1925, 9 5/8 In. 4541.00
Vase, Rosettes, Flowers, Pink Ground, Etched, Cameo, 1920s, 7 7/8 In. 1200.00
Vase, Rubanier, Orange, Amethyst Cut, Bead & Spiral, c.1926, 10 3/4 In. 800.00
Vase, Snail, Buds, Wine, Sage Green, Leaves, Custard Ground, Signed, 3 1/8 In. 633.00
Vase, Stylized Abstract, Etched, Orange Red, Flared Rim, Footed, 19 1/2 In. 3370.00
Vase, Stylized Flowers, Yellow Overlay, Blue, Orange, Signed, 16 In. 1528.00
Vase, Waisted Shape, Cameo Cut Design, 14 In. 1150.00
Vase, Yucca A'droite, Gray, Yellow, Orange, c.1927, 15 1/2 In. 4370.00

LEATHER is tanned animal hide and it has been used to make decorative and useful objects for centuries. Leather objects must be carefully
preserved with proper humidity and oiling or the leather will deterio-
rate and crack. This damage cannot be repaired.

Bag, Metal Snap, 2 Straps, 8 1/2 x 6 In. 45.00
Basket, Black Paint, Punch Decorated, Tooled, Virginia, 19th Century, 6 x 7 3/4 x 5 In. .. 5640.00
Basket, Oval, Star Piercing, 5 x 7 In. 115.00
Belt, Cowboy On Horse, Roping Steer, 3 Buckles, Mahogany 295.00
Billfold, Beadwork, Eagle With Shield, Stars, American Flags, Va., c.1758, 7 1/2 In. 950.00
Bosal, Braided, Color, Luis B. Ortega 4700.00
Bridle, Quirt, Horsehair, Multicolored, Braided, Prison Made, Western, 29 In. 2235.00
Bull Whip, Bone, Silver, 19th Century 60.00
Chaps, Cowboy, Batwing Style, Heiser, Denver, 37 In. 770.00
Chaps, Red & White, Initialed WRB Inside Pink Hearts 69.00
Folio, Bound, Painted Image Of Madonna & Child, 19th Century, 14 3/4 x 9 1/4 In. 430.00
Holster, Flower Tooling, Hold Down Strap, Colorado Saddlery Denver, 4 3/4 In. 175.00
Holster, Loop, Brass Button, Strap, Shelton-Payne Arms Co., El Paso, Texas, 5 1/2 In. ... 490.00
Holster, Single Action, Loop, Whip Stitched, Eubanks Leather, Boise, Holds 7 1/2 In. ... 75.00
Pipe Case, Umimatsu, Tobakoire With Shibuichi Snail, 19th Century 130.00
Quill Case, Inscribed I.G. 1737 .... 395.00
Saddle, Half-Seat, Square Skirt, Cheyenne, F.A. Meanea Pattern No. 10 .... 4620.00
Saddle, McClelland, U.S. Cavalry, Marked U.S., c.1880, 35 x 13 x 20 In. 250.00
Saddle, Riata, Rawhide, Western, Floral Carving, Texas, c.1930, 26 In. 355.00
Saddle, Side, J.S. Collins, Re-Wooled Seat 578.00
Saddle, Square Skirt, Hf Bar Ranch, Collins & Morrison, Wy., Stamped, 1900s, 16 In. ... 770.00
Scabbard, Buckskin, Whip Stitched, H.H. Heiser, Denver, Colorado 325.00
Scabbard, Folding Shotgun, Buckles, Straps, Whip Stitch, 10 1/2 x 15 1/2 In. 95.00
Stool, Stuffed Animal, Bull, Hand Sewn Seams, 1930s, 16 x 25 In. 150.00
Wastebasket, Leather Over Wood 8-Sided, J. Adnet For Hermes, 1950s, 14 x 12 In. 2415.00

LEEDS pottery was made at Leeds, Yorkshire, England, from 1774 to
1878. Most Leeds ware was not marked. Early Leeds pieces had distinctive twisted handles with a greenish glaze on part of the creamy
ware. Later ware often had blue borders on the creamy pottery. A   **LEEDS POTTERY.**
Chicago company named Leeds made many Disney-inspired figurines.
They are listed in the Disneyana category.

Bowl, Blue & White, Oriental Design, 8 x 3 1/4 In. 275.00
Bowl, Blue & Yellow Roses, Gold Buds, Green & Brown Leaves, 7 x 3 1/4 In. 550.00
Bowl, Flower, Leaves, Brown Bands, Soft Paste, Polychrome, 3 1/4 x 7 3/8 In. 165.00
Bowl, Flowers, Leaves, Yellow Border, Polychrome, 4 1/2 x 9 1/2 In. 330.00
Bowl, Vegetable, Blue Feather Edge, Rectangular, Canted Corners, 7 1/2 In. 95.00
Bowl Set, Graduated, Chinese Pattern, 6 1/4 & 7 1/2 & 9 In. 520.00

Charger, Feather, Blue, Scalloped Edge, Floral, Sprig, 13 1/4 In. 1870.00
Coffeepot, Flowers, Leaves, Dome Top, Bulbous, 11 In. 880.00
Creamer, Flower Scroll, Bulbous, Soft Base, 4 1/4 In. 70.00
Cup & Saucer, 3 Colors, Dot & Line Design, Child's 550.00
Cup & Saucer, Berry, Tan, Blue, Brown Band, Soft Past, Handleless 120.00
Cup & Saucer, Blue, Yellow, Green, Buds, Leaves, Chain Link Border, Handleless 468.00
Cup & Saucer, Brown Band, Blue Zigzag, Brown, Green, Sprig, Soft Paste, Handleless .. 22.00
Cup & Saucer, Handleless, Blue Flowers, Tan, Green Leaves, Child's 120.00
Cup & Saucer, Handleless, Blue, Tan, Green, Flowers, Leaves, Blue Band Border 275.00
Cup & Saucer, Handleless, Flowers, Buds, Leaves, 4 Colors 195.00
Cup & Saucer, Handleless, Flowers, Leaves 105.00
Cup & Saucer, Handleless, Sunflower, Leaves, Blue Band Border 220.00
Cup & Saucer, Oriental, Blue On White Oriental Design, Pagoda 66.00
Cup & Saucer, Peafowl, 5 Colors, Blue & Gold Bands, Handleless 1815.00
Cup & Saucer, Pomegranate, Sun, Blue, Soft Paste, Handleless 195.00
Mustard, Cover, Pagoda, Polychrome, Soft Paste, 2 1/2 In. 85.00
Pepper Pot, Pineapples, Yellow & Green, Brown Outlining, 4 1/2 In. 55.00
Pitcher, Blue On White Oriental Design, Bulbous, Cottage, Landscape, 3 1/4 In. 55.00
Pitcher, Blue, Blue, Brown Bands, Brown Flowers, Leaves, Bulbous, Soft Paste, 8 In. ... 385.00
Pitcher, Bulbous, Salmon Spatter Ground, Polychrome, Gentleman With Cane, 4 3/4 In. . 635.00
Pitcher, Cream, Bulbous, Blue, Tan, Green Flowers, Leaves, 3 3/4 In. 265.00
Pitcher, Cream, Peafowl, 5 Colors, 2 3/8 In. 605.00
Pitcher, Cream, Queen's Rose, Bulbous, Flowers, Sprig Design, 4 In. 305.00
Pitcher, Flowers, Leaves, 4 Colors, Banding, Highlights, 3 In. 330.00
Pitcher, Flowers, Leaves, Chain Link, Bulbous, Soft Paste, Applied Handle, 7 In. 275.00
Plaque, Wall, Prattware, Oval, Woman Portrait, 7 1/4 x 9 In. 220.00
Plate, 5 Colors, Tree Green Feather Edge, 8 In. 1870.00
Plate, Blue Feather Edge, Blue Pagoda, Landscape, 9 3/4 In. 195.00
Plate, Blue, Feather, Scalloped Edge, Embossed Flowers, Leaf Border, 10 In., Pair 360.00
Plate, Blue, Mustard Flowers, Leaves, Impressed Spode, 9 1/2 In. 440.00
Plate, Brown, Green, Mustard Bud & Leaf, Dot & Line Border, 7 1/4 In. 55.00
Plate, Chinese Pattern, Scalloped Edge, 9 3/4 In. 250.00
Plate, Feather, Blue, Pomegranate, Leaf, Blue, Floral Border, Soft Paste, 10 1/4 In. 880.00
Plate, Feather, Blue, Toddy, Flower, Acorns, Leaves, Scale Edge, 5 1/4 In. 85.00
Plate, Feather, Flowers, Leaves, Scale Border, Blue, 7 3/4 In. 165.00
Plate, Feather, Green, Flowers, Leaves, Scale Border, Polychrome, Soft Paste, 7 3/4 In. .. 360.00
Plate, Grape & Leaf Design, Blue, Green, Blue Striped Border, 7 1/4 In. 165.00
Plate, Leaf & Vine Border, Green, Tan, Sprig Center, 8 1/4 In. 17.00
Plate, Soup, 3 Colors, Tan, Yellow, Green, Roses, Buds, Leaves, 9 3/4 In. 250.00
Plate, Toddy, Peafowl, 5 Colors, Brown Stripe Border, 7 In. 330.00
Plate, Toddy, Pineapple Pattern, Yellow, Green, Blue, Tan, Leaf Vine, 6 3/8 In. 825.00
Plate, Vine Border, Peafowl In Tree, 8 1/4 In. 209.00
Platter, Blue Feather Edge, 15 1/2 x 19 3/4 In. 145.00
Platter, Blue Feather Edge, Rectangular, Canted Corner, 12 1/4 In. 66.00
Platter, Blue Feather Edge, Rectangular, Canted Corners, 14 1/4 In. 95.00
Platter, Gaudy, Green Edge, Molded Leaves, Fish Scales, Flowers, 9 1/4 x 12 In. 550.00
Sugar, Cover, Blue Chain Link, Blue, Green, Brown Sprig, Leaf, Acorn Finial, 7 In. 468.00
Sugar, Cover, Lattice, Leaves, Blue, Brown, Green, Acorn Finial, Shell Handles, 6 In. ... 230.00
Sugar, George Washington Portrait, U.S. Seal On Reverse, 18th Century 450.00
Teabowl, Saucer, Blue, White Stag, Landscape 50.00
Teabowl, Sprig, Leaf, 4 Colors, 2 3/8 x 4 In. 95.00
Teapot, Diamond Shape, Blue & White, Pineapple Finial, 18th Century 315.00
Teapot, Embossed, Blue, White, 11 In. 345.00

LEFTON is a mark found on pottery, porcelain, glass, and other wares
imported by the Geo. Zoltan Lefton Company. The company began in
1941 and is still in business. It was restructured in 2002 and is now
called the Lefton Company. The company mark has changed through
the years; but because marks have been used for long periods of time,
they are of little help in dating an object.

Ashtray, Blue Paisley, Round, No. 2344, 5 In. 18.00
Bank, Retirement Fund, No. 00135 .... 6.00

Bank, Retirement, Old Man In Rocker, No. 4266, 7 In. 12.00
Dish, Lemon, Blue Paisley, Handle, No. 2141, 6 In. 35.00
Figurine, Baby Blue Bird, No. 1637, 3 1/2 In. 17.00
Figurine, Baby Robin, No. 1637, 3 1/2 In. 22.00
Figurine, Bird, Painted Bunting, No. 1184, 5 In. 22.00
Figurine, Blue Bird, 7 In. 33.00
Figurine, Canary 22.00
Figurine, Chickadee 17.00
Figurine, Cocker Spaniel 6.00
Figurine, Elf, Shelf Sitter, No. 1904, 3 1/4 In. 25.00
Figurine, June Bride Angel, No. 808B, 4 In. 45.00
Figurine, Little Girl, Striped Cat, Patched Pants, Squirrel In Pocket, 2 3/8 In. 17.00
Figurine, Little Treasures, Boy With Dogs, 5 In. 23.00
Head Vase, Woman, Hat & Dress, Raised Flower On Collar, Label, 6 In. 17.00
Head Vase, Woman, Pearlized Hat & Dress, Bow, Pearl Necklace, Paper Label, 4 In. 11.00
Holder, Lipstick & Ring, Will Hold 4 Lipsticks, Pink Roses, Foil Label 18.00
Pin Box, Blue Paisley, Cover, 3 Legs, No. 2154, 1 3/4 In. 35.00
Plaque Set, Bird, No. 4047, 4 In., 4 Piece 75.00
Plaque Set, Kitchen Objects, Diamond Shape, Brown, Gold, Blue, 8 x 6 In., 4 Piece 33.00
Plate, Apple, 8 In. 11.00
Plate, Chickadee, 8 In. 6.00
Salt & Pepper, Blue Paisley, No. 2346, 3 In. 10.00
Sugar & Creamer, Blue Paisley, No. 2358, Cover 30.00
Sugar & Creamer, Violet Chintz 8.00
Urn & Ashtray Set, Blue Paisley, No. 2350, 3 Piece 65.00
Vase, Bud, White Bisque, Applied Pink Flowers, No. 1847, 4 In. 20.00

LEGRAS was founded in 1864 by Auguste Legras at St. Denis, France. It is best known for cameo glass and enamel-decorated glass with Art Nouveau designs. Legras merged with Pantin in 1920 and became the Verreries et Cristalleries de St. Denis et de Pantin Reunies.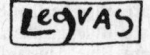

Bowl, Enameled Burgundy, Vines, Berries, Textured Ground, Cameo, Signed, 6 In. 460.00
Bowl, Frosted Rose, Rust Leaves, Buds, Crimped Rim, Signed, 7 In. 374.00
Vase, Bellflowers, Amethyst, Textured Ground, Signed, 15 1/2 In. 748.00
Vase, Blossoms, Leaves, Branches, Cameo, Textured Ground, 8 1/2 In. 805.00
Vase, Blue Stylized Waves, Textured Ground, Shouldered, Oval, 10 In. 720.00
Vase, Crimson, Leafy Branches Enameled In Burgundy, Cameo, c.1920, 11 In. 518.00
Vase, Deer, Bird, Brick Red On Blue-Gray Ground, Signed, 8 1/2 In., Pair 1670.00
Vase, Enameled Landscape, Cylindrical, Flaring Edge, Cameo, 3 1/2 In. 270.00
Vase, Enameled Purple Flowers, Oval, Cameo, Signed, 5 In. 475.00
Vase, Enameled River Landscape, Goblet Shape, Cameo, 7 1/4 In. 720.00
Vase, Enameled Ruby Leaves, Tapered Cylinder, Cameo, 18 In. 720.00
Vase, Enameled, Art Deco Flowers, Citrine, Signed, 8 1/2 In. 175.00
Vase, Enameled, Light Green, Peacock, Leaves, Cylinder, 16 In., Pair 590.00
Vase, Enameled, Purple Violets, Signed, c.1920, 4 In., Pair 430.00
Vase, Flowers, Purple, Enameled, Chipped Ice Ground, Signed, 8 In. 8000.00
Vase, Gray, Enameled Winter Scene, c.1900, 13 3/4 In. 230.00
Vase, Gray, Green Over Pink, Enameled, Lake Scene, Cameo, c.1915, 7 3/4 In. 490.00
Vase, Gray, Mauve, Underwater Scene, Cameo, c.1915, 14 In. ....575.00 to 805.00
Vase, Green Over Rose Amber, Trees, Lake Scene, Cameo, c.1910, 24 In., Pair 4025.00
Vase, Kelp, Green, Burgundy, Cream Ground, Cameo, Early 20th Century, 14 1/2 In. 635.00
Vase, Leaves, Flowers, Mottled Brown, Black Ground, Gold Enameled, Flared, 14 1/2 In. ... 1010.00
Vase, Panoramic View, Enameled Trees, Orange, Yellow, Cameo, Signed, 9 1/4 In. 1840.00
Vase, Pink Ground, White Spatter, Purple Geometric, Cameo, 14 In. 495.00
Vase, Rose Over Yellow, Trailing Fruit & Leaves, Cameo, c.1910, 23 1/2 In. 2645.00
Vase, Seaweed, Sea Life, Brown, Green, Ivory Ground, Cameo Signed, 23 In. 1150.00
Vase, Shaded Crimson, Art Deco Motif, Textured, Cameo, c.1920, 11 In. 545.00
Vase, Stick, Green Leaves & Vines, Textured Ground, Cameo, 14 3/4 In. 1100.00
Vase, Stick, Virginia Creeper, Enameled, Red, Orange, Yellow, 12 1/4 In. 375.00
Vase, Undersea Shells, Rustic Brown, Green, Ivory Ground, Cameo, 22 In. 1035.00
Vase, White Rose Branches, Blue Green Ground, Tapered, Swollen Rim, Gilt, 12 In., Pair ... 2470.00
Vase, Woman With Basket, In Snow, Brown Trees, Cabins, Enameled, 13 1/4 In. 230.00
Vase, Yellow, Orange, Enameled Berries, Tapering Square Section, Cameo, 7 1/4 In. 420.00

Letter Opener, Dubuque,
Iowa, Marbleized Plastic,
Lithographed Insert,
Ruler, 7 In.

Lenox, Vase, Roses,
Pink, Gilt, Green
Stamp, 18 3/4 x 8 In.

Letter Opener,
Minneapolis
Vocational, Composite
Plastic, 8 1/4 In.

LENOX is the name of a porcelain maker. Walter Scott Lenox and Jonathan Cox founded the Ceramic Art Company in Trenton, New Jersey, in 1889. In 1906, Lenox left and started his own company called *Lenox*. The company makes a porcelain that is similar to Irish Belleek. The marks used by the firm have changed through the years and collectors prefer the earlier examples. Related pieces may also be listed in the Ceramic Art Co. category.

Ashtray, Shell Shape, Ivory, Gold Trim, c.1978, 5 1/2 In.	25.00
Bookends, Bust, Man & Woman, Green Ink Stamp, 9 x 3 1/4 In.	259.00
Bowl, Shell, Oval, Ivory, Gold Trim, Green Wreath Mark, c.1930, 6 1/4 x 4 In.	75.00
Bust, Head, Man, Woman, Art Deco, White, 8 3/4 x 4 In., Pair	315.00
Coaster, Dartmouth University, Crest, White China, Sterling Rim	40.00
Coffee Set, Swags Of Roses, Ivory Ground, Classical Style, 10 3/4-In. Pot, 8 Piece	635.00
Figurine, Ballerina, White Tutu, Roses, Green Stamp, 6 In.	805.00
Figurine, Reader, 18th Century Lady With Book, 5 1/2 x 5 In.	545.00
Figurine, Woman, Standing, Head Turned, White Glaze, Art Deco, c.1937, 13 1/2 x 6 In. . .	295.00
Plate, Game Bird Design, Gilt Rim, W.H. Morley, 9 In., 10 Piece	920.00
Plate Set, Fountain, Center Medallion, Turquoise & Gilt Border, 10 1/2 In., 12 Piece	920.00
Stein, Green & White, Monk Drinking, Sterling Lid, 2/6/1901, 6 1/2 In.	120.00
Tea Set, Green & Gold Bands, Ivory Ground, Gold Handles, 6 x 9-In. Teapot, 3 Piece . . .	460.00
Tea Set, Mount Vernon, Green Stamp Mark, 12 Piece	520.00
Vase, Belleek, Painted, Urn Shape, Scrolled Handles, 14 1/2 In.	865.00
Vase, Cabbage Leaf, Yellow Glaze, White Branch Base, 6 x 7 In.	259.00
Vase, Iris, B. Ciggs, c.1900, 16 1/2 x 5 1/4 In.	765.00
Vase, Roses, Pink, Gilt, Green Stamp, 18 3/4 x 8 In. . . . . *Illus*	2415.00

LETTER OPENERS have been used since the eighteenth century. Ivory and silver were favored by the well-to-do. In the late nineteenth century, the letter opener was popular as an advertising giveaway and many were made of metal or celluloid. Brass openers with figural handles were also popular.

Black Forest, Ebony & Horn Handle, Stanhope Window, Views Of Germany, 9 In.	95.00
Boston Terrier, Ruby Set, Silver Gilt, Amethyst Quartz, Continental, 6 1/2 In.	1035.00
Cook Oil Company, Brass, Railroad Tank Car, 9 In.	20.00
Crucifix, Sterling, George W. Shiebler & Co., Monogram, c.1900, 12 3/4 In.	1725.00
Dogs On Handle, Celluloid, Germany	40.00
Dubuque, Iowa, Marbleized Plastic, Lithographed Insert, Ruler, 7 In. . . . . *Illus*	2.00
English Coronation, Sword Shape, Sterling Silver, Leather Case, 1952, 10 1/2 In.	69.00
Fish, Bronze, Hurley, 6 3/8 In.	690.00
Magnifier, Cabochon Carnelian, Diamond Set, Silver Gilt, 8 3/4 In.	431.00
Minneapolis Vocational, Composite Plastic, 8 1/4 In. . . . . *Illus*	2.00
Shrapnel Handle, Iron Cross Design, 4 1/4 In.	63.00

LIBBEY Glass Company has made many types of glass since 1888, including the cut glass and tablewares that are collected today. The stemwares of the 1930s and 1940s are once again in style. The Toledo, Ohio, firm was purchased by Owens-Illinois in 1935 and is still working under the name *Libbey Incorporated*. Additional pieces may be listed under Amberina, Cut Glass, and Maize.

Bowl, Amberina, 6 Crimps, Signed, 7 1/4 In.	518.00

Bowl, Cross Bars, Flowers, Scalloped Rim, 8 x 2 In. 165.00
Bowl, Cut, Rayed Base, Diamond Point Border, 8 x 1 1/2 In. 140.00
Bowl, Thistle Cutting, Center Flower, Scalloped Rim, 4 x 8 In., Pair 385.00
Champagne, Figural, Squirrel, Opalescent, Signed, 4 In. 175.00
Compote, Amberina, Applied Amber Foot, 6 1/4 In. 920.00
Punch Bowl, Hobstar & Fan, Signed, 12 In. 575.00
Relish, Glenda, Signed 195.00
Tray, Comet, Signed 2425.00
Tumbler, Whiskey, Fuchsia, Amberina, Diamond-Quilted, 2 5/8 In. 260.00
Vase, Amberina, Ground Pontil, Signed, 10 3/4 In. 575.00
Vase, Amberina, Ribbed, Flared Shape, Ruffled Edge, 6 1/2 In. 520.00
Vase, Amberina, Ribbed, Wide Ruffled Edge, Polished Pontil, 6 In. 460.00

LIGHTERS for cigarettes and cigars are collectible. Cigarettes became
popular in the late nineteenth century, and with the cigarette came
matches and cigarette lighters. All types of lighters are collected, from
solid gold to the first of the recent disposable lighters. Most examples
found were made after 1940. Some lighters may be found in the
Jewelry category in this book.

7-Up, Dark Green Ground, Logo In Center, Park Aluminum, Box 25.00
Alba Art Studios, Timelite, Telephone, Clock, Cast Metal, Enamel Finish, Table, 5 x 6 In.   67.00
Cigar, Art Nouveau Lady With Torch, Cranberry Globe, Metal, 21 In. 1375.00
Cigar, Bulbous, Red Globe, Oil Tank, Black Glass, 2 Wicks, Metal Base, 15 In. 770.00
Cigar, Cherub, Blue Globe, Cast Iron, Copper Finish, 6 x 16 In. 1210.00
Cigar, Cherub, Red Globe, Embossed Base, Cast Iron, 6 x 17 In. 660.00
Cigar, Duralectric, Push-Button Operation, Metal, 10 In. 303.00
Cigar, Elephant, Milk Glass Globe, Cast Iron, 11 x 10 In. 1210.00
Cigar, Gas, Gargoyle, Green Glass Globe, Metal, 20 In. 1320.00
Cigar, Gas, Victorian Lady, Embossed Base, 8 x 19 In. 1100.00
Cigar, Indian, Yellow Globe, Cast Iron, 6 x 19 In. 990.00
Cigar, Knight, Blue Globe, Cast Iron, 6 x 19 In. 880.00
Cigar, Omar, Oak Case, Eldred No. 28 .... 330.00
Cigar, Wireless No. 12, Eldred Mfg., Oak Case, Jump Spark, c.1910 .... 440.00
Cigar Form, Negbaur, N.Y., 2 1/2 In. 35.00
Cutter, Piedmont, Red Globe, 8 1/2 x 10 In. 1320.00
Ideal Adliter, Metal, Japan, Box, 1/2 x 2 x 2 1/4 In. 10.00
Kool, Penguin, Figural, Cast Metal, c.1940, 4 1/8 x 1 3/4 In. 410.00
Kool Cigarettes, Mr. Kool Penguin, Figural, Plastic, Electric, 9 x 4 In. 325.00
Lektrolite, Embossed Design, Fluid Can, Box, 1940s 45.00
Man, Lamppost, Metal, Marble Base, 4 x 9 In. 330.00
Marathon, Ladylite, Cigarette Case & Lighter, Brass Toned Case, Enamel, Box, 3 x 3 In. .. 58.00
Monoplane, Devine Garment Co., Stainless Steel, Prop, 6 x 5 x 4 In. 35.00
Pres-A-Lite, Car, Brown Bakelite, Mounts To Steering Column, 4 x 4 In. 90.00
RCA Victor, Peacock, Chrome, Enamel, 2 3/4 x 2 1/8 x 3/8 In. 55.00
Weltzunder, Knight, Chrome Plated, Germany, Table, 6 1/2 In. 29.00
Wind Master, Pioneer Parachute Company, Inc., Brushed Gray, Engraved, Box, 1950s ... 35.00
Windsor Omnia Watch, Gold Finish, Fifth Avenue, Box, Bag, 2 1/2 In. 49.00
Zippo, Easton Metal Powder Co., Brushed Metal, Red Flame Box, 1968 .... 58.00
Zippo, Marathon Advertising, Enamel Logo, Brushed Finish, Box, 1967 .... 50.00
Zippo, Sports Series, Out Of The Sandtrap, Golfer, 1979 .... 35.00

LIGHTNING ROD and lightning rod balls are collected. The glass balls
were at the center of the rod that was attached to the roof of a house or
barn to avoid lightning damage.

LIGHTNING ROD BALL, Amethyst, Diamond Shape, 4 3/4 In. 53.00
  Challine Blue, Ribbed 70.00
  Delphite Blue, Chestnut 70.00
  Milk Glass, Blue Moon & Star, 5 In. 36.00
  Red, Globe 110.00

LIMOGES porcelain has been made in Limoges, France, since the mid-
nineteenth century. Fine porcelains were made by many factories,
including Haviland, Ahrenfeldt, Guerin, Pouyat, Elite, and others.
Modern porcelains are being made at Limoges and the word *Limoges*

as part of the mark is not an indication of age. Haviland, one of the
Limoges factories, is listed as a separate category in this book.

Bowl, Celery, Molded, Zinnias, Gold Highlights, 13 x 5 1/2 x 2 In.	30.00
Bowl, Cover, Morning Glory, Gilt, Marked, Elite Limoges France, 5 x 9 1/4 In.	275.00
Box, Enameled, Hand Painted, Napoleon By Fire, Battle Names, Cut Corners, 2 In.	205.00
Box, Gilt Brass Mounted, Walnut Shell Shape, 18th Century Style, 2 1/4 In.	60.00
Cake Plate, Blue Flowers, Gold Trim, 10 1/2 In.	125.00
Charger, 2 Women Looking Into Creek, Signed, 13 In.	750.00
Charger, Cherries, Hand Painted, 13 3/4 In.	88.00
Charger, Girl Pulling Calf, Signed, Blakeman & Henderson, 12 1/2 In.	450.00
Charger, Pheasant Scene, Signed, Rene, 14 In.	190.00
Charger, Roses, Hand Painted, 13 1/2 In.	60.00
Charger, Roses, Hand Painted, Gold Designs, 12 In.	77.00
Chocolate Pot, Flowers, Off-White Ground, Polychrome, Gilt, 10 1/4 In.	144.00
Chop Plate, Pansies, White & Gold Border, 3 Lavender & Yellow Flowers, 12 3/4 In.	265.00
Cruet, Stopper, Red Roses, 5 1/2 In.	250.00
Cup & Saucer, Bouillon, White, Gold Greek Key Design, Gold Band, c.1920	45.00
Cup & Saucer, Violets, White Ground, Gold Trim, Coiffe Star Mark, c.1900	75.00
Cuspidor, Pink, Painted Flowers Around Inside Lid, Gold Feet	504.00
Dresser Box, Enamel, Signed, Landscape, 4 3/4 x 2 1/2 In.	660.00
Dresser Set, Violets, Tan, Green Ground, Gold Trim, Finials, 5 Piece	295.00
Fish Set, Gilt Border, Printed Mark, 8 1/2 In., 8 Piece	420.00
Fish Set, Gold Trim, Painted Fish, Flowers, Signed, 15 In.	1265.00
Mug, Cider, Corn Cob Design, Hand Painted, A. Klingenberg, c.1900	85.00
Mug, Pinecone Design, Hand Painted, J. Pouyet, Signed Whitridge, c.1910, 5 1/2 In.	105.00
Oyster Plate, 5 Wells, Center Sauce, White, Gilt Design, 8 1/2 In., 8 Piece	375.00
Oyster Plate, 6 Wells, Gold Accents, Trim, c.1930	75.00
Pitcher, Cider, Corn Cob Design, Hand Painted, Guerin Co., Signed B. Vaelpell, c.1900	245.00
Pitcher, Milk, Birds & Blueberries, Signed, 6 1/2 In.	275.00
Plaque, Cavalier & Footman, Enamel, Signed, T. Soyer, c.1875, 10 3/4 x 8 3/4 In.	3220.00
Plaque, Portrait, Greek Maiden, Column, Gold Gilt Scalloped Rim, Dubois, 12 1/4 In.	180.00
Plaque, Stream, Hill, Castle, Laurcy, Gold Gilt Rim, Comte Barton, 10 1/2 In.	75.00
Plaque, Virgin & Child, Enamel, Gold Highlights, 19th Century, 3 1/2 x 2 1/4 In.	2875.00
Plaque, Virgin Mary, Enamel, Signed Marchaison, c.1900, 7 x 5 In.	375.00
Plate, 2 Cherubs, Flowers, Tambourine, Gold Gilt Rim, Scrolled Handles, 15 In.	360.00
Plate, Bernardaud, Broad Gold Matte Border, 11/12 In., 8 Piece	575.00
Plate, Blue & Gold, Rose Border Design, 10 3/4 In., 12 Piece	490.00
Plate, Brown Leaves, Flowers, Berries, T & V Mark, Purple Overglaze, c.1913, 8 1/2 In.	35.00
Plate, Cobalt Blue Rim, Gilt Edge, 19th Century, 8 1/2 In., 8 Piece	185.00
Plate, Coronet, Monk Scene, 10 In., Pair	70.00
Plate, Fireman Holding Child, Hand Painted, Signed, T & V Limoges, 9 In.	385.00
Plate, Fish, In Reeds, Gilt Scalloped Border, Signed Valentine, 1920s, 10 3/4 In.	230.00
Plate, Flying Duck, Hand Painted, 10 In.	50.00
Plate, Game, Pheasant Scene, Intricate Border, 9 1/2 In., Pair	160.00
Plate, Game, Pheasants In Flight, Coronet, Signed, Fredy, 10 In., Pair	245.00
Plate, Hunting Dogs Chasing Stag Across Moors, Gilded Border, c.1893, 9 1/2 In.	285.00
Plate, Pheasants, Hand Painted, 10 In.	60.00
Plate, Resting Duck, Hand Painted, Signed, 9 1/2 In.	70.00
Plate, Standing Bird, Hand Painted, 10 In.	50.00
Plate Set, Transfer, Peacocks, Flowers, Hand Painted Border, 8 In., 6 Piece	290.00
Punch Bowl, Hand Painted, Grapes, Marked T & V Limoges France Depose, 6 1/2 In.	315.00
Punch Bowl, Raised Gold, Enamel Decoration, Footed, 14 In.	300.00
Punch Set, Grape & Leaf Decoration, Gilt Trim, 8 5/8-In. Footed Bowl, 8 Piece	575.00
Service Plate Set, Cobalt Border, Gold Embossed Border, 10 3/4 In., 11 Piece	375.00
Serving Plate Set, Gilt, Marked, c.1925, 10 3/4 In., 12 Piece	805.00
Spit Cup, Crushed Bag Shape, Pink Roses, T & V, France, 4 3/4 In. Diam. .... *Illus*	120.00
Tankard, Grapevines, Gold Dragon Handle, Signed, M. Farson, 15 In.	500.00
Teapot, Underhill, Relief Gothic Arches, Gilded Ivy, Pear Finial, 9 In.	80.00
Tile, Color Lithograph, 19th Century Tennis Match, 10 x 9 In.	175.00
Tile, Pate-Sure-Pate, Sword Wielding Warrior, On Horseback, Frame, 7 x 5 In.	220.00
Tray, Flowers, Gold, Scalloped, 11 1/2 In.	176.00
Tureen, Soup, Cover, Under Tray, Double Handles, Painted, Haviland Marks, 14 In.	69.00
Vase, Enameled Bronze, Portrait, Young Man, Silver Foil, 20th Century, 7 1/2 In.	750.00

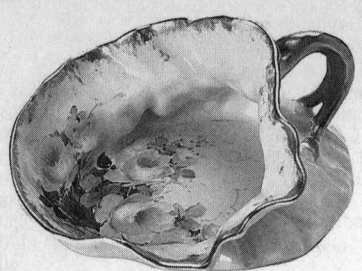

Limoges, Spit Cup,
Crushed Bag Shape,
Pink Roses, T & V,
France, 4 3/4 In. Diam.

Lladro, Figurine, Fisher
Boy, No. 4809, 1972

Vase, Figural Landscape, Baluster Form, Enamel, Late 1800s, 3 3/4 In.	105.00
Vase, Hand Painted, Blue Jay, K.T. Jack, 10 In.	130.00
Vase, Roses, Corset Shape, 13 1/2 In.	275.00
Vase, Woman, Mirror, Forest, Enamel, c.1900, 6 1/4 In.	260.00
Waste Basket, Hand Painted Roses, Oval, 8 In.	375.00

LINDBERGH was a national hero. In 1927, Charles Lindbergh, the aviator, became the first man to make a nonstop solo flight across the Atlantic Ocean. In 1932, his son was kidnapped and murdered, and Lindbergh was again the center of public interest. He died in 1974. All types of Lindbergh memorabilia are collected.

Button, Lindy Pride Of U.S.A, Black, White, 1 1/4 In.	150.00
Button, Our Hero, Red, White, Blue, Black, Celluloid	85.00
Button, Universal Lindbergh Day, May 21, Red, White, Black	150.00
Button, Welcome Home Cpt. Chas. Lindbergh, Red, White, Blue, Celluloid, 7/8 In.	100.00
Mirror, Captain Charles A. Lindbergh, Photo, Sepia, White	385.00
Pillowcase, Photo, Fringe, Acetate, 20 In.	200.00
Plaque, Waving In Front Of Plane, Geo. Gray Barnard Studio, Plaster, 11 x 15 In.	350.00
Plate, New York, Paris May 20 1927, Brown, Green Line Border, 8 1/2 In.	125.00
Postcard, Offers Bronze Prudhomme Medal	175.00
Sheet Music, Eagle Of U.S.A., Spirit Of St. Louis, 1927	10.00
Sheet Music, Lindbergh En Panama, Panamanian	55.00
Tapestry, N.Y. To Paris, Spirit Of St. Louis, Statue Of Liberty, 19 x 54 In.	200.00
Tapestry, New York & Mexico, 19 x 54 In.	300.00
Tapestry, New York To Paris Flight, 20 x 54 In.	77.00
Tumbler, Spirit Of St. Louis, Statue Of Liberty, Eiffel Tower, Milk Glass, 4 In.	125.00

LITHOPHANES are porcelain pictures made by casting clay in layers of various thicknesses. When a piece is held to the light, a picture of light and shadow is seen through it. Most lithophanes date from the 1825–1875 period. A few are still being made. Many lithophanes sold today were originally panels for lampshades.

Box, Cover, Flowers, White Ground, Child, Rooster, Duck, 1 x 3 1/4 In.	175.00
Candlestick, Votive, Scenes Of Paris, 4 In.	40.00
Lamp, 5-Sided Shade, Double Inkstand Base, 16 In.	1035.00
Panel, Children Collecting Eggs Attacked By Hen, No. 1329, 1800s, 4 3/4 x 4 In.	130.00
Panel, Courting Couple, No. 1521, 4 3/4 x 4 In.	90.00
Panel, Woman Coming Across Deer In Forest, No. 1399, 4 3/4 x 4 In.	260.00

LIVERPOOL, England, was the site of several pottery and porcelain factories from 1716 to 1785. Some earthenware was made with transfer decorations. Sadler and Green made print-decorated wares from 1756. Many of the pieces were made for the American market and feature patriotic emblems, such as eagles, flags, and other special-interest motifs. Liverpool pitchers are always called Liverpool jugs by collectors.

Bowl, Sailing Ship Apollo, Military & Nautical Themes, 11 3/8 In.	5875.00
Bowl, Ship, Apollo, Transfer	5875.00
Jug, A Point Of Honour, Dueling Scene, Creamware, 1810, 8 x 11 In.	1600.00
Jug, American Eagle, Chain Of States	2468.00

Jug, American Eagle, Ring Chain, 15 States, Ship, 8 In. 2468.00
Jug, American Militia, Jefferson Quote, Success To Trade, 8 3/4 In. 3525.00
Jug, E Pluribus Unum 1116.00
Jug, George Washington, Indian, Soldier, Flag, Stars, 13 State Border, 8 1/4 In. 1650.00
Jug, George Washington, Justice, Liberty, Victory, 10 1/2 In. 3055.00
Jug, Masonic, 3 Panels, Symbols, 11 1/4 In. 1840.00
Jug, Militia & Success To Trade 3525.00
Jug, Olive Leaf Wreath, O Liberty Thou Goddess, 15 States, 8 1/8 In. 1060.00
Jug, Tom Truelove Going To Sea 645.00
Jug, Washington, Transfer Print 3055.00
Jug, Wounded Officer, Aides, Sharpshooter Waving Gun, 10 1/2 In. 1645.00
Punch Bowl, Marine Decoration, Transfer, Ship On Ocean, 5 1/2 x 12 In. 1900.00

LLADRO is a Spanish porcelain. Juan, Jose, and Vicente Lladro opened
a ceramics workshop in Almacera in 1951. They soon began making
figurines in a distinctive, elongated style. In 1958 the factory moved to
Tabernes Blanques, Spain. The company makes stoneware and porcelain figurines and vases in limited and unlimited editions. Dates given
are first and last years of production.

LLADRÓ®

Ball, Christmas, No. 1603, 1988 .... 80.00
Ball, Christmas, No. 5730, 1990 .... 100.00
Ball, Christmas, No. 5829, 1991 .... 75.00
Bell, Christmas, No. 5525, 1988 .... 40.00
Bell, Christmas, No. 5616, 1989 .... 80.00
Bell, Spring, No. 7613, 1991 .... 50.00
Bell, Summer, No. 7614, 1992 .... 35.00
Bell, Winter, No. 7616 .... 100.00
Figurine, Admiration, No. 4907, 1974-1985 .... 295.00
Figurine, All Aboard, No. 7619, 1992-1993 .... 315.00
Figurine, At Attention, No. 5407, 1987-1990 .... 400.00
Figurine, At The Stroke Of Twelve, No. 1396/1500, 25 In. 4675.00
Figurine, Billy Football Player, Soccer Player, No. 5135, 1982-1983 .... 600.00
Figurine, Boy With Double Bass, No. 4615, 1969-1979 .... 475.00
Figurine, Boy With Guitar, No. 4614, 1969-1979 .... 375.00
Figurine, Bugler, No. 5406, 1987-1990 .... 400.00
Figurine, Cadet Captain, No. 5404, 1889-1990 .... 400.00
Figurine, Can I Play, No. 7610, 1990-1991 .... 475.00
Figurine, Cat Girl, No. 5164, 1982-1985 .... 500.00
Figurine, Christmas Carols, 3 Kids Singing, No. 1239, 1973-1981 .... 800.00
Figurine, Circus Sam, No. 5472, 1988, 8 In. 99.00
Figurine, Clown, No. 4618, 1969, 6 1/2 x 15 In. 173.00
Figurine, Curious Angel, No. 4960, 1977, 9 1/2 In. 125.00
Figurine, Death Of The Swan, No. 4855, 1973, 5 In. 150.00
Figurine, Doctor, No. 4602-3, 1969 .... 220.00
Figurine, Dreamer, No. 5008, 1978 ....77.00 to 195.00
Figurine, Drummer Boy, No. 5403, 1987-1990 .... 450.00
Figurine, Dutch Boy, No. 4811, 1972-1988 .... 110.00
Figurine, Eskimo, Polar Bear, No. 5238, 1984, 5 1/2 In. 110.00
Figurine, Fish A' Plenty, No. 5172, 1982-1994 .... 575.00
Figurine, Fisher Boy, No. 4809, 1972 ....*Illus* 160.00
Figurine, Flapper, No. 5175, 1982-1995, 15 1/4 In. 230.00
Figurine, Flower Curtsey, No. 5027, 1979, 10 In. 165.00
Figurine, Flower Song, No. 7607, 1988-1989 .... 550.00
Figurine, Flowers In Pot, Girl Kneeling, No. 5028, 1980-1985 .... 600.00
Figurine, Garden Classic, No. 7617, 1991 .... 800.00
Figurine, Girl Gathering Flowers, No. 1172, 1971-1993 .... 210.00
Figurine, Girl Holding Lamb, No. 1010, 1969-1983 .... 240.00
Figurine, Girl Putting On Slippers, No. 0000 .... 450.00
Figurine, Girl Tennis Player, No. 4798, 1972-1981 ....220.00 to 400.00
Figurine, Girl With Dice, No. 1176, 1971-1981 .... 300.00
Figurine, Girl With Doll, No. 1083, 1969-1985 .... 300.00
Figurine, Girl With Lamb, No. 4584, 1969-1993 .... 250.00
Figurine, Girl With Milk Pail, No. 4682, 1970-1991 .... 325.00

Figurine, Good Bear, Seated, No. 1205, 1972-1989 .... 150.00
Figurine, Gossips, No. 4984, 1978-1985 .... 850.00
Figurine, Goya Lady, No. 5125, 1982-1990 .... 300.00
Figurine, Hamlet, Holding Skull, No. 4729, 1970-1980 .... 700.00
Figurine, He Loves Me, No. 4599, 1969-1972, 12 1/2 In. 110.00
Figurine, Holy Shepherds, No. 5809, 1991, 3 1/4 In., 3 Piece 175.00
Figurine, Isabel, No. 5412, 1987-1990, 6 In. 195.00
Figurine, Josefa Feeding Her Duck, No. 5201, 1984, 10 1/4 In. 85.00
Figurine, Lamplighter, No. 5205, 1984, 18 1/2 In. 275.00
Figurine, Lilly Soccer Player, No. 5134, 1982-1983 .... 500.00
Figurine, Little Riders, No. 7623, 1994 .... 350.00
Figurine, Little Shepherd & Goat, No. 4817, 1972-1981 .... 400.00
Figurine, Love Letter, Norman Rockwell Series, No. 1406, 1982 .... 1000.00
Figurine, My Buddy, Collectors Club, No. 7609, 1989-1990 .... 415.00 to 450.00
Figurine, Nippon Lady, Oriental With Fan, No. 5327, 1985-Present 595.00
Figurine, Pekingese, Sitting, No. 4641, 1969-1985 .... 450.00
Figurine, Pelusa, No. 1125, 1971-1978 .... 770.00
Figurine, Pick Of The Litter, No. 7621, 1993 .... 450.00
Figurine, Picture Perfect, Collectors Club, No. 7612, 1991 .... 525.00
Figurine, Pondering, Girl Leaning On Basket, No. 5173, 1982-1993 .... 300.00
Figurine, Pottery Seller, No. 5079, 1980-1985 .... 700.00
Figurine, Prayerful Stitch, No. 2205, 1990-1994 .... 185.00
Figurine, Pretty Pickings, No. 5222, 1984 .... 55.00
Figurine, Quest, No. 5224, 1984, 11 In. 275.00
Figurine, Rabbit's Food, No. 4826, 1972-1993 .... 130.00
Figurine, School Days, Club Piece, No. 7604, 1988-1989 .... 450.00
Figurine, Summer Stroll, Collectors Club, No. 7611, 1991-1992 .... 245.00 to 600.00
Figurine, Sweet Harvest, Boys Eating Watermelon, No. 5380, 1986-1990 .... 900.00
Figurine, Valencia Girl, No. 1304, 1974 .... 305.00
Figurine, Wedding, No. 4808, 1972 .... 185.00
Figurine, Young Lady In Trouble, No. 4912, 1974-1985 .... 245.00
Josefa Feeding Her Duck, No. 5201, 1984-1991 .... 85.00
Ornament, Three Kings, No. 5729, 1990, 3 Piece 145.00
Plate, Miniature, No. 7501, 1990, 3 1/4 In. 55.00

LOETZ glass was made in many varieties. Johann Loetz bought a glassworks in Austria in 1840. He died in 1848 and his widow ran the company; then in 1879, his grandson took over. Most collectors recognize
the iridescent gold glass similar to Tiffany, but many other types were
made. The firm closed during World War II.

*Loetz
Austria*

Bowl, Centerpiece, Iridescent Gold, Dimpled, Squat, Fold Over Top, 7 x 14 In. 950.00
Bowl, Diaspora, Iridescent Green, Box Pleated Rim, 4 1/4 x 8 1/2 In. 115.00
Bowl, Iridescent White, Oblong, Pinched Rim, Green Threading, 3 5/8 x 6 x 3 1/2 In. 250.00
Bowl, Oil Spot, Purple, Iridescent Green & Purple Interior, Star Shape, 9 1/2 In. 100.00
Bowl, Peach Shading To Raspberry, Entirely Threaded, Fluted Rim, 6 1/2 x 10 In. 630.00
Bowl, Satin Iridescent, Metal Holder, Leaves, Branches, 10 1/4 In. 1265.00
Candlestick, Iridescent Gold, Double Collar, Large Bobeche, Footed, 14 1/2 In. 1680.00
Compote, Art Nouveau, Brass, 20th Century, 8 1/2 In. 1150.00
Compote, Variegated Red & Yellow, Scarlet Red Interior, 9 In. 105.00
Humidor, Green, Silver Plated Cover, Pipe Finial, 7 1/2 In. 200.00
Inkwell, Green, Seaweed Pattern, Brass, Hinged Cover, 1920s, 5 1/4 In. 550.00
Lamp, 3 Nude Men On Bronze Base, Globe Shade, Oscar Bach, 17 x 7 In. 3450.00
Lamp, 4-Arms, Bronze Base, 22 1/2 x 16 1/2 In. 4025.00
Lamp, Green Opalescent, Green Trailing, Bronze Harp Base, 20 1/2 In. 3640.00
Lamp, Harp, Dore, Stylized Flower Buds, Yellow 3160.00
Lamp, Iridescent Ball Shade, Orange Trailings, Bronze Curved Branch Stem, Leaf Base .. 4480.00
Letter Holder, Diamond Shaped, Applied Tadpoles & Coins, 5 x 9 In. 900.00
Pitcher, Iridescent Green, Ground Pontil, c.1910, 6 In. 65.00
Shade, Blue Pulled Chain, Mottled Ground, 6 1/2 In. 375.00
Shade, Dome, Oil Spot, Green Peacock Feathers, Blue Eyes, 6 In. 635.00
Shade, Dome, Oil Spot, Green, Amber 14 3/4 In. 865.00
Shade, Iridescent Red, Craquelle, Onion Skin, 6 1/2 In. 345.00
Shade, Oil Spot, Allover Blue Gold, Green Horizontal Chain, On Opal, 4 1/4 In., Pair ... 635.00

Tumbler, Marmorierte Carneol, Rose & Brown Marble, Enameled Moorish Design, 4 In. . . 175.00
Vase, 3 Indentations, Green, Hooked, Pulled Blue Drape, Tapered, 7 1/2 In. 635.00
Vase, Amethyst Pulled Hearts, Iridescent Blue Threading, 4 1/2 In. 4600.00
Vase, Blue, White Ribs, White Bell Shape Base, Cylindrical, Flared, Powolny, 6 In. 955.00
Vase, Brown, Air Trapped Scrolls, Gold Enameled, Pink Interior, 10 In. 2300.00
Vase, Candia Papillion, Nautilus Shell, 1898, 4 1/2 x 7 1/2 In. 646.00
Vase, Cobalt Blue, Iridescent Silvery Blue, c.1915, 4 In. 430.00
Vase, Diaspora, Gold, Ruffled Edge, Pinched Shoulder, 7 In. 175.00
Vase, Green To Maroon, Pinched Bottom, Folded At Top, Bulbous, 8 In. 405.00
Vase, Green Twisted Shape, Applied Snake, Purple, 6 In. 175.00
Vase, Green, Pulled Blue & Purple Drape, Fluted Rim, 10 In. 575.00
Vase, Green, Red Rim, 3 Red Ball Feet, Flared, 5 In. 345.00
Vase, Iridescent Blue Green, Green, 10 1/4 In. 575.00
Vase, Iridescent Blue, Brown, Silver Overlay Cyclamens, c.1900, 5 1/4 In. 2040.00
Vase, Iridescent Blue, Goblet Shape, Engraved Mark, 10 In. 999.00
Vase, Iridescent Gold, Blue, Globular, Long Neck, 10 In. 389.00
Vase, Iridescent Gold, Blue Highlights, Applied Silver Flowers, 4 In. 420.00
Vase, Iridescent Gold, Green, Double Gourd, c.1900, 7 1/2 In. 720.00
Vase, Iridescent Gold, Tapered, Cylindrical, Flared Neck, 14 In. 1555.00
Vase, Iridescent Green Metallic, Clear Cased, Ribbed, Bulbous, 7 1/2 In. 336.00
Vase, Iridescent Green, Baluster, Ruffled & Rolled Edge, 13 In., Pair 2185.00
Vase, Iridescent Green, Crimped, 3 1/2 In. 115.00
Vase, Iridescent Green, Tricornered Rim, Early 20th Century, 6 1/8 In. 315.00
Vase, Iridescent Green, Vine Handles, Ruffled Edge, 8 1/4 In. 205.00
Vase, Iridescent Pink, Oval Thumbprints, Oval, 8 1/2 In. 299.00
Vase, Iridescent White, Applied Green Tadpoles, Ground Pontil, 5 In. 90.00
Vase, King Tut, Gold Iridescent, Blue Swirls, 4 In. 780.00
Vase, Lavender, White & Blue Speckles, 10 In. 180.00
Vase, Marmoriete Carneol, Pink Marbled, Enameled, Cased, 4 Concave Panels, 6 In. 2250.00
Vase, Mottled Green, Flared & Ruffled Rim, Art Deco, 6 1/2 In. 225.00
Vase, Mottled Green, White Pulled Trailings, Flared, 5 In. 460.00
Vase, Mottled Yellow, Red Spots, Black 3-Footed Base, 7 1/2 In. 92.00
Vase, Oceanic, 4 Pinched Sides, Metallic Wave Pattern, Squat, c.1902 . . . . 350.00
Vase, Oil Spot, Allover Gold, Iridescent Amber, Cranberry Draped Loops, 8 In. 635.00
Vase, Oil Spot, Blue, Applied Drips, Polished Pontil, 5 1/4 In. 2760.00
Vase, Oil Spot, Blue, Gray, Amethyst Iridized Finish, c.1910, 3 3/4 In. 865.00
Vase, Oil Spot, Brown & Blue, Silver Overlay, Snap Dragons, 8 3/4 In. 635.00
Vase, Oil Spot, Green, Amber To Rose, Blue Leaves, Trailings, c.1910, 2 3/4 In. 2070.00
Vase, Oil Spot, Green, Blue, Red Ground, 4 1/2 In. 750.00
Vase, Oil Spot, Green, Chalice Shape, 6 1/2 In. 75.00
Vase, Oil Spot, Green, Flower Form, Stem, Footed, 9 1/2 In. 520.00
Vase, Oil Spot, Iridescent Gold, Trefoil Rim, 6 1/2 In. 550.00
Vase, Oil Spot, Iridescent Green, Pinched Sides, Bulbous, 7 In. 265.00
Vase, Oil Spot, Iridescent Purple, Goblet Shape, Folded Edge, 5 1/2 In. 359.00
Vase, Oil Spot, Iridescent Purple, Oval Shape, Dimpled Sides, 6 In 705.00
Vase, Oil Spot, Red, Green, Amber, Green Body, Crimped Top, 13 1/2 In. 430.00
Vase, Oil Spots, 3 Necks, Iridescent Gold, Freeform Shape, 6 In. 1265.00
Vase, Pampas, Iridescent Green, Vines, 6 5/8 In. 345.00
Vase, Paperweight, Sapphire To Emerald Green, Silver Overlay & Scalloped Rim, 7 In. . . . 2530.00
Vase, Papillion, Indigo Blue, Footed, 6 In. 196.00
Vase, Phanomen, 3 Twists, Amethyst, Iridescent Blue Threading, c.1900, 9 1/2 In. 12650.00
Vase, Phanomen, Gold, Classical Shape, Signed, 5 1/4 In. 1645.00
Vase, Phanomen, Yellow, Iridescent Blue, Gold, Pulled, Signed, 9 In. 1495.00
Vase, Pumpkin Orange, Spiraling Cobalt Blue Serpent, Ruffled Edge, 9 1/2 In. 80.00
Vase, Purple Highlights, Shouldered, Textured, 6 1/2 In. 375.00
Vase, Purple Over Green, Stemmed Tulip, Cameo, c.1900, 8 In. 605.00
Vase, Red, Iridescent Silver, Pinched Body, Ribbed Shoulder, Bulbous Mouth, 5 1/2 In. . . 175.00
Vase, Rose, Orange, Blue, Lion's Head Ornaments, Bulbous, 6 3/4 In. 299.00
Vase, Stick, Oil Spot, Aqua, Applied Gold Flowers, 11 3/4 In. 230.00
Vase, Translucent White, Pale, Iridescent Green, Swirled Ribs, Cased, 8 1/4 In. 110.00
Vase, Triangular, 3 Elongated Drops, Pulled, Iridescent Blue, Tapered, Signed, 10 1/2 In. . . 5750.00
Vase, Twisted Shape, Red, Textured Iridescent Design, 12 1/2 In. 400.00
Vase, Twisted Shape, Textured Green, Iridescent Blue Highlights, 7 In. 520.00

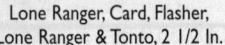

Lone Ranger, Card, Flasher,
Lone Ranger & Tonto, 2 1/2 In.

Lone Ranger, Toy, Rocking, Gun In Hand,
Lasso Spins, Windup, 1938, 11 In.

Vase, Yellow, Horizontal Panels, Pulled Iridescent Gold Design, c.1910, 7 1/2 In. 1035.00

LONE RANGER, a fictional character, was introduced on the radio in 1932. Over three thousand shows were produced before the series ended in 1954. In 1938, the first Lone Ranger movie was made. Television shows were started in 1949 and are still seen on some stations. The Lone Ranger appears on many products and was even the name of a restaurant chain for several years.

Bank, A Cache For Coins, Brass, Leather, Zell Products, N.Y., c.1938, 1 x 3 x 4 In.	160.00
Belt, Head Portraits, Brown, Vinyl, Metal, c.1950, 1 x 31 In.	95.00
Belt, Photograph, Scenes, Plastic, Brass, Esquire Novelty Co., c.1940, 7/8 x 33 1/2 In. . . .	60.00
Bracelet, Picture, Gold, Plastic, c.1950, 1/2 x 8 In.	25.00
Card, Flasher, Lone Ranger & Tonto, 2 1/2 In. . . . . *Illus*	1.00
Costume, Mask, Star, Vinyl, Box, Ben Cooper, No. 261, 1977	15.00
Eggcup, Ceramic, England, 1961, 2 x 2 3/8 In.	35.00
Eyeglass Case, Holster Shape, Tan Leather, Snap Fastener Flap, 1950s, 6 1/2 In.	30.00
Figurine, Chalkware, 15 In.	115.00
Figurine, Plaster, Hand On Holster, Carnival, c.1940, 15 1/4 In.	60.00
Football, Rubber, White, Sun Rubber Co., c.1950, 9 In.	60.00
Gun, Clicker, Tin, Marx, c.1930, 8 In.	250.00
Gun, Pistol, Clicker, Steel, Black, Marx, c.1940, 8 In.	55.00
Gun, Rifle, Cap Shooting, Plastic, Marx, Box, 26 In.	195.00
Holster & Belt, Rubber, Black, CBS Toys, 1978, 1 3/4 x 28 In.	15.00
Pen, Fountain, Hi-Yo Silver, Lone Ranger, Plastic, Marbelized, c.1938, 5 1/4 In.	145.00
Pencil Case, Illustrations, Cardboard, American Lead Pencil Co., 1938, 1 x 5 x 8 In.	60.00
Photograph, Good Luck Always, Lone Ranger & Tonto, Glossy, c.1950, 8 x 10 In.	10.00
Pin, Riding Horse, Multicolor, Celluloid, 1 1/4 In.	40.00
Poster, Wants You, Restaurant, Franchise, c.1970, 17 1/2 x 21 1/2 In.	45.00
Radio, Lights, Antenna, Plastic, Plug, Airline, c.1940, 6 x 5 In.	1680.00
Record, Legend Of The Lone Ranger, MCA Records, No. 5212, c.1981, 12 x 12 In.	12.00
Safety Club, Letter, Pledge, Membership, Code, Merita Bread, c.1938, 4 x 9 1/2 In.	225.00
Sign, 6 Shooter Ring, Shoots Sparks, Kix Cereal Premium, 1940s, 17 x 22 In.	175.00
Toy, Bop, Inflatable, Vinyl, Weighted, Plinno Toys, c.1950, 14 1/2 In.	70.00
Toy, Picture Printing Set, Stamper Kraft, No. 4092, Superior Type Co., 5 x 6 1/2 In.	75.00
Toy, Range Rider, Tin Lithograph, Windup, Marx, 10 In.	300.00
Toy, Rocking Horse, Wooden, 40 In.	650.00
Toy, Rocking, Gun In Hand, Lasso Spins, Windup, 1938, 11 In. . . . . *Illus*	286.00
Wrist Cuffs, Leather, Snap, Metal, c.1930	35.00
Wristwatch, Movable Hands, Disk, Pictures, Vinyl, Case, Tonto, c.1950, 1 1/2 In.	15.00

LONGWY Workshop of Longwy, France, first made ceramic wares in 1798. The workshop is still in business. Most of the ceramic pieces found today are glazed with many colors to resemble cloisonne or other enameled metal. Many pieces were made with stylized figures and Art Deco designs. The factory used a variety of marks.

Bowl, Flowers, Almond Shape, Green Ink Stamp, 2 1/4 x 11 In.	115.00
Box, Flower Panels, Geometric Border, Blue, White, Red, Cream, Crackle Glaze, 3 x 3 In.	325.00
Candlestick, Flowers, Dolphin Shaft, Unmarked, 9 1/4 x 4 In.	140.00

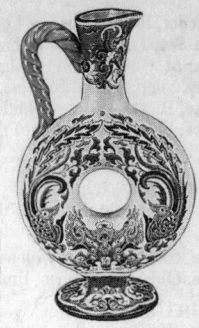

Longwy, Charger, 3 Storks By
Water, Flowers, Green Ink
Stamp, 14 1/2 In.

Longwy, Flask, Stylized
Birds, Flowers, Rope
Handle, Stamped,
11 1/2 x 6 1/2 In.

Charger, 3 Storks By Water, Flowers, Green Ink Stamp, 14 1/2 In. . . . . *Illus*   690.00
Charger, Allover Flowers, Embossed, Black Ink Stamp, 11 1/8 In. 260.00
Charger, Flowers, Storks, Green Ink Stamps, 14 1/4 In. 690.00
Charger, Phoenix & Flower Decoration, Scrolling Border, Marked, 13 3/4 In. 460.00
Compote, Flowers, Vines, Maroon Ground, Impressed Mark, 9 1/4 In. 260.00
Flask, Stylized Birds, Flowers, Rope Handle, Stamped, 11 1/2 x 6 1/2 In. . . . . *Illus*   259.00
Flask, Wine, Handle, Bird & Flower Decorations, Stamped, 11 1/2 x 6 1/2 In. 260.00
Inkstand, Birds, Flowers, 2 Ink Pots, Pen Tray, Stamp Box, 3 3/4 x 10 x 6 1/2 In. . . . . *Illus*   230.00
Jardiniere, Multicolored Flowers, Straight Sides, Green Ink Stamp, 7 1/2 In. 230.00
Lamp, Brass Burner, Etched Shade, Hinks & Sons, 19th Century, 25 In. 1955.00
Nut Dish, Incised Design, Mocha, Yellow, Magenta, Cobalt, 2 1/2 In., 4 Piece 200.00
Tray, Handles, Boating Scene, Flowers, Rectangular, Stamped, 15 x 7 In. 260.00
Vase, Flowers, Goblet Form, Green Ink Stamp, 9 3/4 x 5 1/2 In. 400.00
Vase, Roses & Violets, Turquoise Crackled Ground, Stamped Mark, 10 1/2 In. 175.00

LONHUDA Pottery Company of Steubenville, Ohio, was organized in
1892 by William Long, W. H. Hunter, and Alfred Day. Brown underglaze slip-decorated pottery was made. The firm closed in 1896. The
company used many marks; the earliest included the letters *LPCO*.

LONHUDA

Ewer, Carnations, Silver Overlay, Impressed, L.P. 66, 1892 . . . .   920.00
Vase, 2 Handles, Daisies, Celadon, Orange Ground, 3 1/4 x 5 1/2 In. 175.00

LOSANTI was made by Mary Louise McLaughlin in Cincinnati, Ohio,
about 1899. It was a hard paste decorative porcelain. She stopped making it in 1906.

Losanti

Vase, Bulbous, Blossoms, White, Oxblood Flashes, McLaughlin, 4 3/4 x 3 1/2 In. 26438.00
Vase, Peacock Feathers, Swirled, Beige, Red Crackle Glaze, 4 1/4 In. 2645.00
Vase, Squat, Scrolled White Wreath, Blue Ground, McLaughlin, 2 3/4 x 4 1/4 In. 1175.00

LOTUS WARE was made by the Knowles, Taylor & Knowles Company
of East Liverpool, Ohio, from 1890 to 1900. Lotus Ware, a thin porcelain which resembles Belleek, was sometimes decorated outside the
factory. Other types of ceramics that were made by the Knowles,
Taylor & Knowles Company are listed under KTK.

Bowl, Columbia, Flowers, Blue Jeweling, Beaded, Oval, Scalloped Rim, 4 In. 235.00

Longwy, Inkstand, Birds, Flowers, 2 Ink Pots,
Pen Tray, Stamp Box, 3 3/4 x 10 x 6 1/2 In.

Lotus Ware, Vase,
Flowering Branch,
Filigree Handles,
Ivory Glaze, 4 In.

Pitcher, Roses, Transfer Logo, Gold Signed, 4 1/4 In. 175.00
Tea Set, Triangles Of Fishnet Work In Relief, 4-In. Teapot, 3 Piece 440.00
Teapot, Cover, Netting, Marked, KTK, 6 3/4 In. 255.00
Tray, Shell, Raised Flowers, Gilt Trim, Yellow Ground, Leaf Shape, 3 Twig Feet, 8 In. 235.00
Vase, Bugs, Leaves, Cylinder, Marked, KTK, 7 3/4 In......................... 255.00
Vase, Flowering Branch, Filigree Handles, Ivory Glaze, 4 In. .... *Illus* 650.00

LOW art tiles were made by the J. and J. G. Low Art Tile Works of
Chelsea, Massachusetts, from 1877 to 1902. A variety of art and other
tiles were made. Some of the tiles were made by a process called *nat-*
ural, some were hand modeled, and some were made mechanically.

J.&J.G.LOW

Tile, Classical Man, Woman Profiles, Olive Green Glaze, J. & J.G. Low, 6 In., Pair 206.00
Tile, Old Man, Woman, Embossed, Amber High Glaze, Frame, Marked, J. & J.G., 6 1/8 In.   160.00

LOY-NEL-ART, see McCoy category.

LUNCH BOXES and lunch pails have been used to carry lunches to
school or work since the nineteenth century. Today, most collectors
want either early tobacco advertising boxes or children's lunch boxes
made since the 1930s. These boxes are made of metal or plastic. Boxes
listed here include the original Thermos bottle inside the box unless
otherwise indicated. Movie, television, and cartoon characters may be
found in their own categories. Tobacco tin pails and lunch boxes are
listed in the Advertising category.

LUNCH BOX, American Flag, Day Time, Night Time, Metal, Ohio Art, c.1970 .... 28.00
Barbie, Black Vinyl, Graphics, Handle, Metal Closure, 1962 .... 205.00
Battlestar Galactica, Aladdin 90.00
Beany & Cecil, Picnic, Vinyl, Tan 125.00
Big Boy, Red Plastic, Image & Logo Of Manners Restaurant, 1970, 5 x 7 x 11 In. ..100.00 to 110.00
Dark Crystal, Metal, Plastic, 1982 .... 15.00
Dawn, Vinyl, Topper Corp., c.1970 .... 115.00
Donny & Marie, White Vinyl, Aladdin, 1978 .... 160.00
Fall Guy, Aladdin ....55.00 to 90.00
Flintstones, Bedrock Festival, Metal, Aladdin, 1971 .... 35.00
Flintstones, Day At The Zoo, Dennys, Plastic, 1989 .... 20.00
Heathcliff, Video Game, Metal, Aladdin, 1982 .... 20.00
Jetsons, Space, Plastic, 1987 .... 50.00
Knight Rider, Universal City Studios, Thermos Co., c.1982 .... 30.00
Marvin The Martian, Frito-Lay, Plastic, 1998 .... 50.00
Masters Of The Universe, Metal, Plastic Thermos, Aladdin, 1983 .... 10.00
Munsters, Sitting In Munstermobile, King Seeley Thermos, 1960s 525.00
Pac-Man, Metal, Aladdin 70.00
Pink Panther & Sons, Metal, King Seeley Thermos, 1984 .... 60.00
Popples, Metal, Aladdin, 1986 .... 40.00
Pussycats, Brunch Bag, Vinyl, Red, Black Handle, Aladdin, c.1968 .... 115.00
Red Barn, Thermos Co., c.1958 .... 125.00
Teenage Mutant Ninja Turtle, Turtles In Street, Vinyl, 1990, 5 x 9 x 8 In. ... 10.00
LUNCH BOX THERMOS, Campus Queen, King Seeley Thermos Co., c.1967 .... 60.00
Donny & Marie, Aladdin, Late 1970s 28.00
Dukes Of Hazard, Red Cup, Early 1980s 18.00
GI Joe, Aladdin 30.00

LUNEVILLE, a French faience factory, was established about 1730 by
Jacques Chambrette. It is best known for its fine biscuit figures and
groups and for large faience dogs and lions. The early pieces were
unmarked. The firm was acquired by Keller and Guerin and is still
working.

K 👑 G
Luneville

Basket, White & Gold, Reticulated, Circular, 4 x 9 In............................ 35.00
Bowl, Flowers, Leaf Shaped, Scalloped, Impressed Veining, Handle, 7 3/8 x 6 11/16 In. ... 40.00
Bowl, Stenciled, Red Flowers, Marked, 3 1/4 x 6 1/8 In. 10.00
Creamer, Roses, Flower Spray, Faience, 4 3/4 In. 80.00
Knife Rest, Roses, Majolica, 3 1/4 In. 15.00
Sugar Shaker, Roses, 9 1/4 In.. 28.00
Vase, White Flowers, Lavender Shaded To Green, Gilt, Footed, Marked, 10 In. ...... *Illus* 300.00

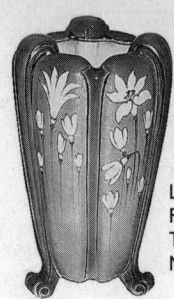

Luneville, Vase, White
Flowers, Lavender Shaded
To Green, Gilt, Footed,
Marked, 10 In.

Luster, Pink, Figurine, Set, 4 Seasons, Dixon,
Austin & Co., c.1800s, 8 In., 4 Piece

LUSTER glaze was meant to resemble copper, silver, or gold. The term *luster* includes any piece with some luster trim. It has been used since the sixteenth century. Some of the luster found today was made during the nineteenth century. The metallic glazes are applied on pottery. The finished color depends on the combination of the clay color and the glaze. Blue, orange, gold, and pearlized luster decorations were used by Japanese and German firms in the early 1900s. Tea Leaf pieces have their own category.

Blue, Creamer, Band At Top, White Ground, Red & Purple Fruit & Leaves, Trim	20.00
Blue, Vase, Dragon, Oriental Village Scenes, Gold Trim, Wedgwood, 8 1/2 In.	805.00
Copper, Bowl, Blue Transfer, Polychrome, Marked, Footed, 6 1/4 x 11 In.	500.00
Copper, Creamer, Blue Band, Black Transfer, Gen. Jackson, Hero, New Orleans, 5 3/4 In.	2200.00
Copper, Creamer, Canary Yellow, Transfer Print, Andrew Jackson, Staffordshire	4700.00
Copper, Figurine, 4 Seasons, Polychrome Decoration, 4 Piece	5290.00
Copper, Figurine, Dog, White, Black Nose, Yellow Eyes, 8 In., Pair	358.00
Copper, Jug, Circular Panels, Clock Face, Oriental Figures In Garden, 7 5/8 In.	646.00
Copper, Jug, Cornwallis At Yorktown, Oval Cartouches, Black Transfer, 6 3/8 In.	1410.00
Copper, Mustard Pot, Cover, Yellow Glaze, 2 x 2 3/4 In.	175.00
Copper, Pitcher, Copper Luster, Gold Luster Ocher Bands, c.1815, 7 1/4 In.	230.00
Copper, Pitcher, Embossed, Floral, Blue Band, C-Scroll Handle, England, 5 1/2 In.	135.00
Copper, Pitcher, Painted, Schoolhouse, Blue Band, England, Mid 1800s, 5 1/2 In.	85.00
Copper, Salt, Pink & Green Stylized Flowers, Footed, 1 7/8 In.	28.00
Copper, Teapot, Underplate, Flowers, Cobalt Blue Trim, 7 1/2 In.	50.00
Cup, Pink, Leaves, Branches, Green Flowers, Red Twigs, Hand Painted, Handleless	35.00
Fairyland luster is included in the Wedgwood category.	
Pink, Chamber Pot, Wedding Gift, Verses, Frog Inside, England, c.1815, 6 1/4 In.	6600.00
Pink, Cup & Saucer Set, Flowers & Leaves, Wide Pink Band, 2 3/4-In. Cup, 6 Piece	90.00
Pink, Dish, God & Warriors, Greek Key Border, Gilt Edge, 8 1/2 In., Pair	470.00
Pink, Figurine, Set, 4 Seasons, Dixon, Austin & Co., c.1800s, 8 In., 4 Piece .... *Illus*	3850.00
Pink, Lamp, White Rose Design, Large Prisms, 22 In., Pair	125.00
Pink, Punch Bowl, Shipwright's Arms, 10 In.	118.00
Pink, Tea Set, Teapot, Cup & Saucer, Sugar & Creamer, Waste Bowl, Undertray	360.00
Pink, Tea Set, Teapot, Sugar & Creamer, Plate	1060.00
Pink, Tea Set, Woman With Child	1320.00
Pink, Teapot, Cattle, Pasture, Scalloped Rim, Green Dots, Rose Finial, 6 In.	165.00
Silver, Jug, Pineapple, Burnt Orange Flower, Leaf Decoration, Thumb Tab Handle, 6 In.	110.00
Silver, Sugar, Cover, Ribbed Medial Band, Curved Handles, Flanged Cover, 7 In.	80.00
Sunderland luster pieces are listed in the Sunderland category.	
Tea Leaf luster pieces are listed in the Tea Leaf Ironstone category.	

LUSTRE ART GLASS Company was founded in Long Island, New York, in 1920 by Conrad Vahlsing and Paul Frank. The company made lampshades and globes that are almost indistinguishable from those made by Quezal. Most of the shades made by the company were unmarked.

Shade, Art Glass, Yellow Bands On Opal, Gold Interior, 5 1/4 In.	69.00
Shade, Blue Feather, Double Hooked Gold Border, Opal, 5 1/4 In., Pair	633.00
Shade, Iridescent Gold Band, Opal, Gold Interior, 5 In.	60.00
Shade, Lily, Opal, Iridescent Gold Pulled Feathers, Signed, 4 1/2 In.	260.00

If you are the victim of a theft, be sure to give the police complete information about your antiques. You should have a good description, a photograph, and any known identifying marks. You might want to send information about the stolen antiques to the antique papers.

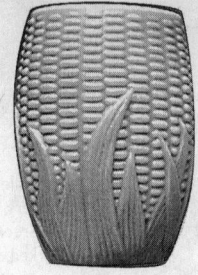

Maize, Tumbler, Unpainted, 4 In.

Shade, Opal, Iridescent Gold Pulled Feathers, Tipped Green, Etched, 5 In.	115.00
Shade, Pulled & Hooked Gold Feather, White Ground, 5 1/2 In., 5 Piece	920.00
Shade, Pulled Feather, Purple, Ivory, Iridescent, 5 x 4 7/8 x 2 1/8 In.	315.00
Shade, White, Green & Gold Pulled Leaves, Signed, 5 1/2 x 2 1/4 In.	160.00
Vase, White Pulled Hearts, Blue Ground, Platinum Threading, Iridescent, 5 3/4 In.	325.00

LUSTRES are mantel decorations or pedestal vases with many hanging glass prisms. The name really refers to the prisms, and it is proper to refer to a single glass prism as a lustre. Either spelling, luster or lustre, is correct.

Cobalt Blue, Enameled Flowers, Gilt Ground, Pendants, Bohemian, 3 1/2 In.	144.00
Cranberry, 10 Prisms, 1880s, 13 & 6 1/2 x 5 In.	710.00
Green Glass, White, Gilt Highlights, Polychrome Flowers, Late 1800s, 12 In., Pair	865.00
Green Opaline, Black, Gold Enameled Flowers, Back-Cut Prisms, Crenellated Lip, 13 In.	145.00
Milk Glass Cut To Cranberry, Gold Highlights, Moorish Window Cut, 13 x 7 1/2 In.	173.00
Opal Cut To Cobalt Blue, Flower Garlands, 11 In., Pair	290.00
Ruby, Hand Cut, 1920s, 17 1/2 In., Pair	225.00
Satin Glass, Gilt Baluster, Scalloped Rim, Prisms, c.1900, 14 1/2 In., Pair	430.00
Star Cut, Scalloped Rim, Baluster Stem, Molded Pedestal, c.1870, 14 In., Pair	978.00
White, Green Opaline, Flower Form, Gilt & Green Opaline Serpent Around Stem, 12 In.	144.00

MAASTRICHT, Holland, was the city where Petrus Regout established the De Sphinx pottery in 1836. The firm was noted for its transfer-printed earthenware. Many factories in Maastricht are still making ceramics.

Petrus.Regout&C.º
MAASTRICHT

Bowl, Chinoiserie Design, Flat Rim, Mid 19th Century, 9 In.	36.00
Bowl, Polychrome, Stamped, 1900s, 4 1/4 x 2 1/2 In.	15.00
Gravy Boat, Willow	75.00
Pitcher, Milk, Red, Green, Blue, 5 x 6 1/2 In.	50.00
Plate, Willow, Petrus Regout & Co., Holland, 9 In.	25.00 to 65.00
Saucer, Oriental Scene, Green, Rust, Marked, 5 3/4 In.	10.00

MAIZE glass was made by W.L. Libbey & Son Company of Toledo, Ohio, after 1889. The glass resembled an ear of corn. The leaves were usually green, but some pieces were made with blue or red leaves. The kernels of corn were light yellow, white, or light green.

Celery Vase, Green Corn Husks, 6 1/2 In.	90.00
Tumbler, Blue & Gold Leaves, Gold Rim, 4 In.	140.00
Tumbler, Green & Brown Leaves, 4 In.	88.00
Tumbler, Unpainted, 4 In. *Illus*	39.00

MAJOLICA is a general term for any pottery glazed with an opaque tin enamel that conceals the color of the clay body. It has been made since the fourteenth century. Today's collector is most likely to find Victorian majolica. The heavy, colorful ware is rarely marked. Some famous makers include Wedgwood; Minton; Griffen, Smith and Hill (marked *Etruscan*); and Chesapeake Pottery (marked *Avalon* or *Clifton*). Majolica made by Wedgwood is listed in the Wedgwood category.

Basket, Fruit, Oval Green Marbled Base, Late 19th Century, 15 1/8 In.	2689.00

Basket, Hanging Flowers, 11 In. 396.00
Basket, Leaf Form, Flowers, Pale Blue Ground, Pink Interior, 2-Strap Handle, 13 In. 690.00
Basket, Leaves & Blossoms, Yellow, Lavender Interior, Handle, 11 x 8 In. 395.00
Berry Bowl, Underplate, Branches, Blue Ground, Pink Interior, Registry Mark, 4 1/2 In. . . 85.00
Bowl, Dolphin, Flanked By 2 Shell Dishes, Green & Brown Mottled Glaze, 13 In. 359.00
Bowl, Fruits, Cream, Lattice Ground, Turquoise Interior, Footed, 4 3/4 x 8 3/4 In. 250.00
Bowl, Morning Glories & Leaves, Twisted Twig Handles, 4 x 11 x 9 1/2 In. 165.00
Bowl, Multicolored Flowers & Scroll Design, Gilt, Oval, c.1900, 13 x 8 In. 170.00
Bowl, Pond Lily, Dark Green, Light Blue Interior, Holdcroft, Footed, 4 x 10 1/2 In. 250.00
Bowl, Shell Shape, Raised Seahorse Base, Continental, 17 In. 325.00
Bowl Set, Cover, Basket Weave Sides, Mushroom, Cauliflower Knops, 5 & 9 & 12 In. . . . 210.00
Bread Plate, Banana Leaves, Basket Weave Ground, Yellow Rope Border, 12 In. 175.00
Bread Tray, Pond Lilies, Shaped Edges, Impressed J. Holdcroft, 12 3/4 In. 316.00
Bust, Woman, Feathered Hat, Ruffled Collar & Sleeves, Square Base, 24 1/2 In. 1210.00
Bust, Young Boy, French Colonial Garb, Marked BU 677, 19 In. 865.00
Butter Chip, Begonia Leaf, Figural, c.1920s, 3 In. 145.00
Butter Chip, Green & Yellow Leaf, Pink Ground, Etruscan, c.1875, 3 In. 90.00
Butter Chip, Leaves On Basket Weave, 1920s, 3 1/2 x 2 3/4 In. 135.00
Butter Chip, Water Lily Pad, 1920s, 3 1/4 In. 125.00
Cachepot, Leaves, Raised On Molded Elephant, 13 3/4 In. 540.00
Centerpiece, Figure Grasping Garlands, Oval, 19th Century, 9 x 20 x 9 1/2 In. 575.00
Charger, Applied Serpent, Frogs, Lobsters, Pond Flowers, Naturalistic, Palissy, 16 In. . . . 860.00
Charger, Lobster, Oyster Shells, Seaweed, Palissy Ware, Angelico, Portugal, 14 In. 1093.00
Charger, Naturalistic Shells & Seaweed, Brown Streaked Ground, Palissy, 7 1/2 In. 690.00
Cheese Stand, Cover, Leaves, Cow, George Jones, c.1875, 10 1/2 In. 2990.00
Coffeepot, Cabbage-Leaf Form, Serpent Handle & Spout, Palissy, Portugal, 9 In. 3740.00
Coffeepot, Rustic Tree-Stump Form, Lizard Handle & Spout, Palissy, 10 In. 2070.00
Compote, Lily-Pad Shape, Cranes, 3 Legs, 3 x 9 In. 115.00
Compote, Molded Lily, Leaves, 3 Shorebirds, Raised Base, 13 In. 660.00
Compote Set, Molded Lily, Leaves, 9 To 12 In., 14 Piece 660.00
Cup & Saucer, Japanese Fan, Blue Pebbled Ground, Registry Mark, c.1875, 6 In. 145.00
Dish, Banana-Leaf Form, Impressed J. Holdcroft, c.1875, 13 1/2 In. 86.00
Dish, Game, Cover, Basket Weave Pattern, Leaves, Ducks, Rabbit, 7 1/2 x 13 In. 115.00
Dolphin, Raised Head & Tail, Stylized Water Base, Mottled Green, Brown, 33 In. 3055.00
Ewer, Flowers, Long Stems, Baluster Shape, Art Nouveau, Delphin Massier, 21 In. 1335.00
Frieze, Tile, Ivory Water Lilies, Lily Pads, Water, Germany, 6 x 36 In., 4 Piece 290.00
Frieze, Tile, Ivory Water Lilies, Teal Grasses & Water, Germany, 6 x 18 In., 3 Piece 200.00
Humidor, Begging Dog, 9 In. 440.00
Humidor, Black Man, Green Jacket, Smoking, 11 In. 650.00
Humidor, Clown's Head, Multicolored Cap, Green Collar, 6 In. 305.00
Humidor, Dog's Head, Word Fox On Collar, Signed St. Clement, 6 In. 305.00
Humidor, Drum, Organ Grinder Monkey Finial, Cobalt Blue, England, 6 1/2 In. 358.00
Humidor, Eagle, Perched On Cliff, 5 1/2 x 9 In. 22.00
Humidor, Frog, Red Smoking Jacket, Pipe, Continental, 6 1/2 In. 470.00
Humidor, Jockey's Head, Green, White Helmet, 7 In. 140.00
Humidor, Man, Green Hat, Brown Trench Coat, 7 1/2 In. 360.00
Humidor, Monkey Smoking Pipe, Sitting On Floral Base, 5 1/2 In. 140.00
Humidor, Monkey, Green Cap, Green Vest, Red Bowtie, 6 1/2 In. 28.00
Humidor, Sailor, Drinking From Mug, Seated On Coiled Rope, Minton, No. 716, 9 In. 2200.00
Jardiniere, Melon Form, Wardle & Co., c.1900, 6 In. 85.00
Jardiniere, Polychrome, Rectangular, Footed, Italy, 9 3/4 x 13 3/4 x 9 3/4 In. 865.00
Jardiniere, Water Lilies, Turquoise Ground, Impressed, Minton, 1882, 14 1/2 In. 2030.00
Jug, 2 Faces, Inverted & Conjoined, Happy & Sad, Red Scarf, France, 9 In. 290.00
Jug, Frog With Open Mouth, On Melon, c.1880, 6 1/2 In. 865.00
Jug, Gurgling Fish Form, Green & Yellow Seaweed & Rock Base, Palissy, 14 In. 775.00
Jug, Lily Of The Valley, White Ground, Yellow Rope Handle, S. Lear, 1880, 9 In. 90.00
Jug, Monkey, Seated, Holding Bamboo Stalk On Back, Pink Interior, 9 In. 805.00
Jug, Seated Spaniel Shape, Yellow Hat, c.1880, 6 3/4 In. 375.00
Jug, Strawberries, Cream Ground, Choisy-Le-Roi, 1910, 7 1/2 In. 259.00
Jug, U.S. Grant In Uniform & Civilian Clothes, Green, Pink, Brown, Yellow, 10 In. 1150.00
Lamp, Flattened Oval, Grotesque Mask Handles, Renaissance, Battle Scenes, 22 In. 420.00
Mirror, Branches, Ivy, 3 Birds, Nest, Eggs, Lizard, Easel Back, Hugo Lonitz, 22 In. 8340.00
Mug, Child's, Organ Grinder With Monkey, 4 1/2 In. 230.00

An old Majolica or Staffordshire pitcher has a small hole inside where the handle meets the body. A new pitcher will not have this hole but will often have a large hole in the base.

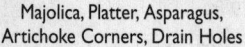

Majolica, Platter, Asparagus,
Artichoke Corners, Drain Holes

Oyster Plate, Seashells, Coral, c.1873, 11 Piece	9430.00
Pitcher, Basket Weave, Cherry Branch, Leaves, Blossoms, Twig Handle, 7 In.	90.00
Pitcher, Brown, Twig Border & Handle, Pink Flowers, 7 1/2 In.	145.00
Pitcher, Corn, Naturalistic Colors, 9 In.	345.00
Pitcher, Owl, Green, Brown, Pink Glaze, 11 In.	269.00
Pitcher, Portrait Of Man, Embossed, Eagle Spout, 7 In.	80.00
Pitcher, Raised Scroll Design, Flowers, Cobalt Blue, Handles, 12 1/4 In.	200.00
Pitcher, Smiling Mailman, France, 7 1/2 In.	70.00
Pitcher, Syrup, Sunflowers, Blue Ground, Pewter Top, 8 In.	450.00
Pitcher, Tree Trunk, Chocolate Glaze, Vine & Flower Handle, c.1900, 10 In.	410.00
Pitcher, Yellow Blossoms, Cobalt Blue, Butterfly Molded Lip, Etruscan, 6 3/4 In.	200.00
Plate, Asparagus, Luneville, 8 3/4 In.	60.00
Plate, Beer Hall Scene, Man, Stein, Pitcher, Keg, 10 1/2 In.	250.00
Plate, Cauliflower Star, Leaves, Etruscan, c.1875, 9 1/4 In.	145.00
Plate, Dessert, Dogwood, Pale Blue Ground, George Jones, 8 In.	405.00
Plate, Dessert, Flower Head, Green, Yellow & Brown Glazes, Basket Weave Rim, 8 In.	115.00
Plate, Dessert, Flying Crane On Cobalt Blue, Prunus, Branch Handle, 8 1/2 In.	175.00
Plate, Grape Leaf, Cobalt Blue Ground, Vine Rim, J. Holdcroft, 8 1/4 In.	259.00
Plate, Lily Pad, Zell, Baden, 8 In.	355.00
Plate, Luncheon, Leaf Pattern, Stamped Copeland, 7 3/4 In., 6 Piece	230.00
Plate, Maple Leaves, Rustic Stemmed Foot, Etruscan, 1875, 9 1/4 In.	200.00
Plate, Pond Lily, Lily Pads, Naturalistic Colors, George Jones, c.1869, 8 3/4 In.	660.00
Platter, Asparagus, Artichoke Corners, Drain Holes *Illus*	850.00
Platter, Round, Edge Molded Leaves, Mottled Green, Brown Glaze, 19 In.	269.00
Platter, Shell Design, Scalloped, Oval, Etruscan, 13 1/2 x 9 1/4 In.	605.00
Stool, 6 Panels, Prunus Blossoms, Cobalt Blue Ground, Yellow Rope Borders, 18 In.	1610.00
Sugar, Cover, Flowers, Ferns, Brown Rustic Ground, Pink Interior, 5 In.	80.00
Sugar & Creamer, Wild Rose, Blue Green Borders, Butterfly, Etruscan	65.00
Teapot & Jug, Green, Brown Mottled Glaze, 8 1/2 & 9 In.	300.00
Vase, Applied Flowers, Child, Baker's Dress, 3-Footed, 9 1/2 In.	115.00
Vase, Applied Toads, Lizards, Mossy Ground, 2 Serpent Handles, Palissy, 7 In., Pair	920.00
Vase, Bust Of Military Officer, Blue Hat, Pink Interior, France, 6 3/4 In.	260.00
Vase, Cobalt Blue, White, Yellow, Bacchic Satyr Masque Handles, Italy, 14 x 15 In.	1035.00
Vase, Double, Renaissance Style, Figural Reserves, Serpent Handles, 22 1/2 In., Pair	2300.00
Vase, Man, Wearing Turban, Stealing Bear Cub From Mother, 24 In.	920.00

MAPS of all types have been collected for centuries. The earliest known printed maps were made in 1478. The first printed street map showed London in 1559. The first road maps for use by drivers of automobiles were made in 1901. Collectors buy maps that were pages of old books, as well as the multifolded road maps popular in this century.

19th Corps In Action D-Day To Germany, Frame, 1944, 23 x 28 In.	50.00
Acapulco, Fort, Bay, Bellin, Paris, c.1754, 6 x 7 1/2 In.	110.00
Algeria, Mountains, Color, J. Perthes, Gotha, 1877, 14 1/4 x 12 In.	100.00
America, Hand Colored, Engraved, 2 Pages, Frame, 1626, 16 x 20 5/8 In.	6050.00

Americas, Totius Americae, Hand Colored, Johannes Baptista Homann, 1735, 23 x 20 In. . 260.00
Asia, East Indies, Burmese Empire, Longman Co., London, 1808, 15 1/2 x 13 1/4 In. 70.00
Austria, Parts Of Italy, Croatia, Tirion, Amsterdam, c.1734, 13 x 11 In. 110.00
Britain, Ireland, Scotland, Hand Colored, Abraham Ortelius, c.1590, 16 x 20 In. 400.00
Bull & Combahee Rivers, S.C., U.S. Coastal Survey, Frame, 1871, 16 1/2 x 23 1/8 In. . . . 660.00
California, Hand Colored, Diderot's Encyclopedia, Paris, 1777, 18 3/4 x 15 In. 900.00
Canada, Southern, Rivers, Mountains, Houbert Jaillot, 17th Century, 19 3/4 x 24 In. 720.00
Caribbean, Color, Outline, Duval, Paris, c.1660, 4 3/4 x 4 In. 150.00
Colorado, Railroads, Forts, Harry King, Washington, D.C., 1902, 34 1/3 x 29 In. 200.00
Connecticut, Drawn & Engraved, Amos Doolittle, 1795, 12 3/8 x 15 1/4 In. 350.00
Currituck Sound, Outer Banks, N.C., Frame, 1933, 40 3/4 x 30 1/2 In. 88.00
Delaware, From The Best Authorities, Matthew Carey, Philadelphia, 16 1/2 x 9 1/4 In. . . . 146.00
Denmarke, Kingdome Of, John Speede, G. Humble, Dated 1626, 16 x 21 In. 230.00
England, Monmouth, Gloucester, T. Bowen, London, 1775, 11 x 6 1/2 In. 15.00
France, Loire River Valley, Antwerp, c.1595, 4 x 3 1/2 In. 60.00
Gettysburg, Antietam, Bonneauville, Topographical, Army Training, Sheet, 1925 . . . . 10.00
Globe, Celestial, 24 Gores, Brass Meridian, Stand, 4 Legs, J. Doppelmayer, 13 In. 7050.00
Globe, Library, Rosewood Frame, Crossbar, Globe Casters, 1900s, 38 In. 235.00
Globe, Mahogany Stand, Brass Meridian Arc, Signed, c.1900, 24 1/2 In. 325.00
Globe, Paper, Plaster, Wood, Cast Iron Base, G. Joslin, c.1870, 16 x 24 x 23 In. 2240.00
Globe, Terrestrial, Carved Oak Base, Figural, Dolphin, W. & A.K. Johnston, 46 x 24 In. . . 5040.00
Globe, Terrestrial, Eastlake, Carved Oak Base, Andrews, Chicago, c.1885, 18 x 44 In. . . . 9520.00
Globe, Terrestrial, Electrical, Magnet, Albert Lotz, E. Schotte, c.1900, 2 x 7 In. 1116.00
Globe, Terrestrial, Joseph Schedler, On Cardboard Storage-Carton Lid, 3 x 7 In. 2820.00
Globe, Terrestrial, Lithograph, Ebonized Wood Stand, J. Forest, Paris, c.1900, 17 1/2 In. . . 750.00
Globe, Terrestrial, Russian Empire, Mahogany Base, C. Smith & Sons, 1800s, 13 1/2 In. . 1035.00
Globe, Terrestrial, Stand, F.G. Haan, Dresden, Germany, 1823, 28 In. 1610.00
Globe, Terrestrial, Walnut & Brass Tripod Stand, Edward Wormley, 1962, 32 x 20 In. 2300.00
Indiana, Hand Coloring, French Text, Facts, Frame, 25 1/2 x 32 In. 275.00
Ireland, Color, Giants Causeway, Bank, J. Thomson, Edinburgh, 1817, 23 x 19 1/2 In. . . . 190.00
Italy, John Blaeu, Frame, 17th Century, 19 1/4 x 23 3/4 In. 175.00
Massachusetts, Engraved, Steel, City Plans, Sduk, c.1845, 12 x 14 1/2 In. 160.00
Michigan, Railway, Lakes, Colton, New York, 1855, 12 1/2 x 15 1/2 In. 30.00
Mississippi & Ohio Rivers, Indian Nations, 2 Pages, c.1784, 14 1/2 x 20 1/4 In. 1760.00
Netherlands, Friesland, Ships, Ortelius, Galle, Antwerp, c.1595, 4 1/2 x 3 In. 85.00
North America, Arctic, Asia, Coastal, Engraved, C.V. Monin, Paris, 1835, 18 x 12 1/2 In. . 90.00
North America, Chesapeake Bay To California, Bonne, 1771, 16 x 11 1/2 In. 300.00
North America, Diffusion Of Useful Knowledge, Baldwin & Cradock, 1834, 16 x 14 In. . . 138.00
North America, French-Owned Territory, Hand Colored, Frame, c.1687, 19 x 23 In. 978.00
Ohio, Northeastern U.S., Paper, 1928, 9 x 4 In. 11.00
Omi Province, Japanese, Dunsei 7th, Frame, Late 19th Century, 53 1/2 x 32 1/2 In. 358.00
Planetarium, Trippensee, Sun, Earth, Moon, Planet, Case, Detroit, c.1920, 20 In. 1763.00
Poland, 5 Regions, Engraved, Copper, Phillipe De Pretot, Paris, c.1787, 12 x 10 In. 140.00
Portugal, Kingdom, J. Gibson, London, c.1762, 7 1/2 x 12 1/2 In. 40.00
Quebec, River, Lake Saint Charles, Bellin, Paris, 1744, 11 x 8 In. 50.00
Road, California, Standard Oil, Paper, 2 Panels, 1938, 8 7/8 x 4 In. 22.00
Road, Delaware, Maryland, Virginia, West Virginia, Amoco, 2 Panels, 1920, 9 x 4 In. 50.00
Road, Delaware, Maryland, Virginia, West Virginia, Texaco, 1931, 7 x 3 3/4 In. 35.00
Road, Ohio, Shell, Paper, 1931, 9 x 4 In. 17.00
Road, Ohio, Sohio, 3 Panels, Paper, 1931, 7 x 3 3/4 In. 11.00
San Francisco, Crocker's Guide Map, National Brewing Co., 1896, 28 x 23 In. 110.00
San Francisco, Decorative Border, Colton, New York, 1855, 13 x 15 1/2 In. 130.00
Solar System, Cartouches, Glazed, Mattio Gio, Frame, 18th Century, 28 x 23 In. 499.00
South America, Engraved, T. Kitchin, London, 1783, 13 x 17 1/2 In. 80.00
Street, New York, Manhattan, 1960 . . . . 8.00
United States, Des Provinces Septies, Etats-Unis, Maine Through Delaware, 20 x 13 In. . . 170.00
United States, Engraved, Color, Longman Co., London, 1808, 15 1/2 x 13 1/2 In. 325.00
United States, Southern Dominions, Laurie & Whittle, London, 1794, 20 1/2 x 28 1/2 In. 1035.00
United States, Southern, County Development, Sduk, London, 1833, 12 x 15 1/2 In. 190.00
Utah, Color, General Land Office, 1902, 13 x 16 3/4 In. 100.00
Western Hemisphere, Engraved, Phillip Cluver, c.1711, 10 x 7 1/2 In. 325.00
World, Oval View, Hand Colored, Emanuel Bowen, London, 1744, 22 x 15 In. 850.00

MARBLE collectors pay highest prices for glass and sulphide marbles. The game of marbles has been popular since the days of the ancient Romans. American children were able to buy marbles by the mid-eighteenth century. Dutch glazed clay marbles were least expensive. Glazed pottery marbles, attributed to the Bennington potteries in Vermont, were of a better quality. Marbles made of pink marble were also available by the 1830s. Glass marbles seem to have been made later. By 1880, Samuel C. Dyke of South Akron, Ohio, was making clay marbles and The National Onyx Marble Company was making marbles of onyx. The Navarre Glass Marble Company of Navarre, Ohio, and M. B. Mishler of Ravenna, Ohio, made the glass marbles. Ohio remained the center of the marble industry, and the Akron-made Akro Agate brand became nationally known. Other pieces made by Akro Agate are listed in this book in the Akro Agate category. Sulphides are glass marbles with frosted white figures in the center.

Candy Stripe, 1 3/4 In.	88.00
Candy Stripe, 2 In.	195.00
Candy Stripe, Red & White Center, 2 1/8 In.	250.00
Candy Stripe, White Swirl, 2 1/4 In.	360.00
Glass, Green Galaxy, Peltier Glass Company, 1920s, 7/8 In.	1065.00
Glass, Mica, Turquoise Blue, American, c.1890, 1 5/8 In.	280.00
Goldstone, Blue, Goldstone Bands, 1 5/8 In.	530.00
Indian, Cloud Type, Germany, 1800s, 15/16 In.	1750.00
Latticinio Core Swirl, White Center, 4 Ribbons, 3-Color Stripes, 1 3/4 In.	110.00
Latticinio Core Swirl, White Center, Multicolored Ribbons, Early 20th Century, 2 In.	110.00
Lutz, Green, Onionskin, 2 In.	100.00
Onionskin, Blue, White, Red, Yellow, Orange Bands, 2 In.	235.00
Onionskin, Stripped, Wooden Chinese Checker Box, 25 Piece	650.00
Onionskin, Stripped, Wooden Chinese Checker Box, 8 In., 15 Piece	300.00
Onionskin, Swirl, 1 1/4 In.	90.00
Slag, Amber, 2 In.	200.00
Sulphide, Cat, 1 3/8 In.	85.00
Sulphide, Cow, Grazing, Early 20th Century, 1 3/4 In.	140.00
Sulphide, Dog, 1 5/8 In.	95.00
Sulphide, Dog, Lying Down, Clear, 1 3/8 In.	200.00
Sulphide, Dog, Standing, Clear, 2 In.	560.00
Sulphide, Duck, 1 1/2 In.	420.00
Sulphide, Eagle, 1 In.	70.00
Sulphide, Eagle, Spread Wings, Clear, 1880-1920, 1 3/4 In.	310.00
Sulphide, Elephant, 1 3/8 In.	130.00
Sulphide, Fish, 2 In.	145.00
Sulphide, Goat, 1 3/4 In.	95.00
Sulphide, Rooster, 1 1/2 In.	110.00
Sulphide, Sheep, Lying Down, Early 20th Century, 1 1/2 In.	90.00
Transparent Swirl, Multicolored Ribbons, Yellow Outer Ribbons, 1 3/4 In.	60.00

MARBLE CARVINGS, such as large or small figurines, groups of people or animals, and architectural decorations, have been a special art form since the time of the ancient Greeks. Reproductions, especially of large Victorian groups, are being made of a mixture using marble dust. These are very difficult to detect and collectors should be careful. Other carvings are listed under Alabaster.

Bust, Child, Classical, Renard, 16 x 10 In.	1905.00
Bust, Girl, Veiled, Giovanni Battista Lombardi, Italy, 1823-1880, 26 1/2 In.	5975.00
Bust, Helen Of Troy, Diademed, Bonded, White, England, 26 1/2 In.	750.00
Bust, Madame Du Barry, White, Signed, 28 In.	1265.00
Bust, Man, Laurel Wreath, Cylindrical, Green Base, 6 1/2 In.	290.00
Bust, Marie Antoinette, Variegated Green Bodice, Salmon Socle, 26 In.	765.00
Bust, Mark Antony, Draped, Bonded, White, 30 1/2 In.	690.00
Bust, Woman & Baby, 13 3/4 In.	670.00
Bust, Woman, Bare Neck, Hair Back, Socle Base, Italy, 19th Century, 23 In.	1725.00
Bust, Woman, Flowers, Vines, Art Nouveau, c.1880, 27 1/2 In.	6720.00
Bust, Woman, Pietro Magni, Italy, c.1871, 29 1/2 In.	3885.00

Bust, Woman, Raised On Socle, Continental, Early 19th Century, 8 1/2 In. 896.00
Bust, Woman, Waisted Socle, Signed, Korbel, 19 1/2 In. 1880.00
Bust, Woman, White, Jean A. Barre, France, 1856, 18 1/2 In. 1705.00
Column, George III, Spar, Mounted As Lamp, Derbyshire, 20 In., Pair 7170.00
Column, Ionic, Grand Tour, Circular Well, 12 1/4 In., Pair 230.00
Garniture, Louis Philippe, Bronze, Psyche, Cupid, 23 x 14 x 6 In. 5520.00
Jardiniere, Carrara Marble, 19th Century, 9 1/2 x 21 1/2 x 9 1/8 In. 1035.00
Jardiniere, Louis XVI Style, Putti, Brass Ball Feet, 5 1/2 x 8 1/2 In., Pair 200.00
Obelisk, Italian Neoclassical, Red, 20th Century, 78 x 15 x 15 In. 4780.00
Obelisk, Louis XVI Style, Violette De Villette, France, 19 In., Pair 230.00
Obelisk, Purple & White Mottled, Stepped Base, 1900s, 19 x 4 1/2 In. 1910.00
Pedestal, Basal Collar, Square Base, Black Slate, France, 19th Century, 46 In. 1610.00
Pedestal, Beaux Arts, Gilt Bronze, Verone Marble, White Onyx, c.1900, 44 In. 1495.00
Pedestal, Column, Molded Top, Ribbed, Octagonal Base, Pink, 39 1/2 In. 490.00
Pedestal, Louis XVI, Fluted Column, Square Base, France, 40 In. 1035.00
Pedestal, Louis XVI, Fluted Columns, Square Base, c.1900, 51 1/2 In. 1150.00
Pedestal, Renaissance Revival, Mixed Marble, France, c.1885, 45 x 10 In., Pair 1725.00
Pedestal, Travertine, Circular Top, Molded Standard, Base, 27 1/2 x 14 In., Pair 635.00
Pedestal, White, Spiral, Leaf-Shape Top, 8-Sided Base, 3 Sections, 38 x 12 In. 520.00
Pen Tray, Elliptical Trough, Italy, 19th Century, 2 1/2 x 9 3/4 x 3 In. 230.00
Plaque, Virgin Mary Relief, Tabernacle Frame, 29 x 14 1/2 In. 646.00
Sculpture, Buddha, Seated On Lotus Throne, Nepal, 19th Century, 22 1/2 In. 920.00
Shelf, Bracket, Goddess Diana, Garland, White, Bonded, 10 x 7 x 5 In., Pair 489.00
Shelf, Bracket, Renaissance Revival, Flowers, Ivy, 6 1/4 x 6 1/4 x 6 In., Pair 345.00
Statue, 2 Girls, Holding Basket Of Flowers, c.1900, 21 1/2 In. 1960.00
Statue, Blackamoor, Relief Profiles, Continental, 12 In., Pair 5378.00
Statue, Diaphanously Clad Maiden Looking Down, Allegorical, 28 In. 1765.00
Statue, Eros, Helmeted, Nude, Baroque Style, 13 In. 290.00
Statue, Female Devotee, India, 19th Century, 23 1/2 In. 600.00
Statue, Indian Maiden, Seated In Canoe, After Duchoiselle, 18 In. 3525.00
Statue, Persephone, Classically Dressed, Holding Wreath, Carrara, 42 In. 5875.00
Statue, Rebecca At The Well, Neoclassical, Mottled Green Pedestal, 76 In. 4600.00
Statue, Saint Patrick, As Bishop, Crosier, Issuing Blessing, 1800s, 48 In. 1610.00
Statue, Spring Dream, Atilio Piccirilli, 29 In. 4400.00
Statue, Venus At The Bath, After Christophe Gabriel Allegrain, 36 In. 2350.00
Statue, Venus At The Bath, Signed, Allegrain, 18th Century, 27 1/2 In. 1265.00
Statue, Woman & Child, Modernist, White, Late 20th Century, 31 In. 115.00
Statue, Woman, Modernist, Black, Late 20th Century, 28 In. 230.00
Statue, Woman, Poised To Dive, Signed, Barzanti, 39 In. 5675.00
Statue, Woman, Seated In Savonarola Armchair, Art Nouveau, 26 In. 3205.00
Statue, Young Girl, Flirtatious Pose, Victorian, 21 1/2 In. 460.00
Urn, Louis XVI Style, Ormolu, Putto, Gilt, Scroll Handles, c.1925, 17 In., Pair 1265.00
Urn, Louis XVI Style, White, Gilt Bronze, 1870, 20 In. 3070.00
Urn, Turned, Campana Shape, Square Paneled Plinth, 34 In., Pair 1600.00
Vase, Navette Shape, Gilt Bronze Mounts, France, 19th Century, 7 1/2 x 24 In. 2725.00

MARBLEHEAD Pottery was founded in 1905 by Dr. J. Hall as a rehabilitative program for the patients of a Marblehead, Massachusetts, sanitarium. Two years later it was separated from the sanitarium and it
continued operations until 1936. Many of the pieces were decorated
with marine motifs.

Bowl, Blue Matte Glaze, Aqua Interior, 3 1/8 x 5 1/2 In. 475.00
Bowl, Caramel Glaze, Wheat Glaze Interior, 3 x 5 1/2 In. 635.00
Bowl, Caramel Matte Glaze, Semi-Closed, Spherical, 3 1/4 x 5 1/2 In. 550.00
Bowl, Green Glaze, Brown Interior, Ship Mark, 4 1/8 x 8 1/2 In. 415.00
Bowl, Lavender Glaze, Frothy Lavender Interior, 2 1/8 x 7 1/4 In. 275.00
Bowl, Lotus Pattern, Dark Blue Matte Glaze, Blue, Gray Interior, Flared, 8 In. 290.00
Bowl, Purple Matte Glaze, Light Purple Interior, Flared, Ship Mark, 3 3/4 x 7 In. 65.00
Bowl, Rose Matte Glaze, Spherical, 2 1/4 x 6 1/2 In. 330.00
Bowl, Yellow Glaze, Mustard, Ship Logo, 3 x 7 3/4 In. 440.00
Candleholder, Rose Matte Glaze, 4 x 4 1/2 In. 305.00
Flowerpot, Speckled Mustard Glaze, Rigid Texture, Flared, 7 In. 345.00
Tile, Pink Flowers, Indigo Vase, Dust Pressed, Wax Resist, Frame, 6 In. 520.00

Tile, Potted Topiaries, Green, Brown, Blue, Gray Ground, Square, 6 1/4 In. 2760.00
Tile, Sailboat, Blue, Speckled Gray Matte Ground, Square, 6 In. 3220.00
Tile, Ship, White Glaze, Sky Blue Glaze Ground, Frame, 6 1/2 In. 330.00
Trivet, 3-Masted Ship, Stormy Sea, Ivory Matte Glaze, Blue Ground, 6 1/4 In. 520.00
Vase, Band Of Incised Grapevines, Blue & Gray, Impressed, 3 1/2 In. 1725.00
Vase, Beaker Shape, Brown Leaves, Black Branches, Blue Ground, 6 x 5 In. 1955.00
Vase, Blue Matte Glaze, Berry & Leaves Relief, Aqua Interior, 3 x 5 In. 1900.00
Vase, Blue Matte Glaze, Bulbous, 7 1/2 In. 345.00
Vase, Blue Matte Glaze, Bulbous, Impressed Mark, 9 In. 1035.00
Vase, Blue Matte Glaze, Shouldered, Paper Label, 9 In. 1035.00
Vase, Blue Matte Glaze, Speckled, Arthur Baggs, 8 3/4 x 4 In. 880.00
Vase, Blue Matte Glaze, Tapered, Impressed Mark, 9 In. 865.00
Vase, Blue Matte Glaze, Vessel, Tapered, Ship Mark, 3 3/4 x 4 1/2 In. 415.00
Vase, Brown Matte Glaze, Cylindrical, 10 x 5 In. 1998.00
Vase, Bud, Deep Green Matte Glaze, Tapered, Spherical, 4 1/2 x 2 3/4 In. 550.00
Vase, Caramel Matte Glaze, Speckled, 3 1/2 x 2 1/4 In. 303.00
Vase, Caramel Matte Glaze, Speckled, Oval, 3 5/8 x 3 In. 440.00
Vase, Cobalt Blue Matte Glaze, Flowers, Gray Ground, A. Baggs, 8 3/4 x 4 In. 9900.00
Vase, Deep Blue Matte Glaze, 3 1/4 x 5 1/2 In. 410.00
Vase, Flying Geese, Blue, Gray, Speckled Gray Ground, Barrel Shape, 6 1/4 x 6 In. 4025.00
Vase, Geese, Black Glaze, Speckled, Tan Interior, Ship Mark, 6 x 5 In. 1320.00
Vase, Golden Caramel Glaze, Speckled, Frothy Interior, Broad, 4 3/4 x 5 3/4 In. 445.00
Vase, Gray Blue Matte Glaze, Impressed Ship Mark, 2 In. 145.00
Vase, Gray Matte Glaze, Blue Interior, Speckled, Oval, 7 1/4 x 4 In. 520.00
Vase, Gray Matte Glaze, Carved & Painted Geometric Design, 6 1/4 In. 1150.00
Vase, Gray Matte Glaze, Flared, 5 1/4 In. 200.00
Vase, Gray Matte Ground, Painted 3-Color Design, Carved, Round, 3 1/2 In. 2875.00
Vase, Gray, Blue Mottled Glaze, Blue Interior, Ship Mark, 4 1/8 x 8 1/2 In. 525.00
Vase, Green Matte Glaze, Speckled, Bulbous, Flared Lip, 5 x 3 1/4 In. 715.00
Vase, Green Matte Glaze, Squat, 3 1/2 x 5 In. 295.00
Vase, Green Matte Glaze, Tapered, 3 1/2 In. . . . . .430.00 to 575.00
Vase, Landscape, Blue Matte Glaze, Stylized Trees, White Berries, Ship Mark, 7 In. 3850.00
Vase, Lavender Matte Glaze, 1 3/4 x 3 1/4 In. 330.00
Vase, Lavender, Curved Rim, Impressed Mark, c.1915, 6 In. 645.00
Vase, Mottled Purple Over Green Matte Glaze, Flared Rim, 4 1/2 In. 575.00
Vase, Rose Matte Glaze, Oval, 5 1/2 x 3 1/4 In. 360.00
Vase, Rose Matte Glaze, Tapered, Flared Mouth, 7 1/4 x 3 3/4 In. 415.00
Vase, Stylized Flowers, Indigo, Speckled Gray Ground, Hannah Tutt, 4 1/2 x 4 In. 4025.00
Vase, Stylized Fruit Trees, Hannah Tutt, 4 In. 20700.00
Vase, Stylized Trees, Arts & Crafts Style, 7 In. 2650.00
Wall Pocket, Beehive, Yellow Glaze, Ribbed Body, Ship Mark, 4 1/2 x 5 1/4 In. 275.00

MARTIN BROTHERS of Middlesex, England, made Martinware, a salt-
glazed stoneware, between 1873 and 1915. Many figural jugs and
vases were made by the three brothers. Of special interest are the fanciful birds, usually made with removable heads.

Martin Bro
London

    Jug, 2-Sided Face, Semigloss Glaze, Orange, Brown Hair, Smile, 1902, 7 In. 4715.00
    Vase, Incised Leaves, Berries, Lines, Cylindrical, Signed, 6 3/4 In. 546.00

MARY GREGORY is the name used for a type of glass that is easily identified. White figures were painted on clear or colored glass as the decoration. The figures chosen were usually children at play. The first
glass known as Mary Gregory was made about 1870. Similar glass is
made even today. The traditional story has been that the glass was
made at the Sandwich Glass works in Boston by a woman named Mary
Gregory. Recent research suggests that it is possible that none was
made at Sandwich. In general, all-white figures were used in the
United States, tinted faces were probably used in Bohemia, France,
Italy, Germany, Switzerland, and England. Children standing, not playing, were pictured after the 1950s.

    Decanter, Girl, Looking At Flowers, Green, 10 In. 55.00
    Tumbler, Boy & Girl, Green Opaque, Pair 60.00
    Vase, Blue, Boy Holding Flower, 10 1/2 In. 170.00

Vase, Boy & Girl, Telescopes, Green, Clear Applied Ridges, 10 1/2 In., Pair 130.00
Vase, Girl, Chasing Birds, Cobalt Blue, Ruffled Rim, 12 In. 385.00
Vase, Girls, Playing Badminton, Blue Over White, 6 1/4 x 2 4/2 In., Pair 150.00
Vase, Woman, Holding Pitcher, Black Amethyst, Meridian & Co., 8 3/4 In. 150.00

MASON'S IRONSTONE was made by the English pottery of Charles J. Mason after 1813. Mason, of Lane Delph, was given a patent for this improved earthenware. He usually called it "Mason's Patent Ironstone China." It resisted chipping and breaking so it became popular for dinnerwares and other table service dishes. Vases and other decorative pieces were also made. The ironstone was decorated with orange, blue, gold, and other colors, often in Japanese inspired designs. The firm had financial difficulties but the molds and the name Mason were used by many owners through the years, including Francis Morley, Taylor Ashworth, George L. Ashworth, and John Shaw. Mason's joined the Wedgwood group in 1973 and the name is still found on dinnerwares.

Bowl, Fruit, Mandalay, 10 1/2 In. 149.00
Bowl & Pitcher, Bird, Flowers, Polychrome 250.00
Dinner Service, Nabob, c.1900, 72 Piece 750.00
Inkstand, Imari Pattern, 2 Ink Pots, Covers, c.1835, 13 1/4 In. 480.00
Jug, Japan Pattern, 6 1/2 In. 285.00
Pitcher, Basin, Hoho Birds, Flowers, Stylized Clouds, 8 Sides, 11 3/8 In. 150.00
Pitcher, Water, 11 In. 120.00
Plate, Heraldic Crest, Oriental Design Border, Early 1800s, 9 In., 6 Piece 630.00
Platter, Chinese Pattern, Blue, White, 19th Century, 19 1/2 In. 230.00
Platter, Chinese Pattern, Blue, White, 19th Century, 21 In. 315.00
Platter, Chinese Pattern, Blue, White, Octagonal, 19th Century, 17 1/2 In. 175.00
Platter, Chinese Pattern, Blue, White, Well, Tree, 19th Century, 17 1/2 In. 230.00
Platter, Flowers, Birds, Blue, White, 19 x 16 In. 675.00
Tumbler, Flowers, Branches, Pink, White 10.00

MASONIC, see Fraternal category.

MASSIER, a French art pottery, was made by brothers Jerome, Delphin, and Clement Massier in Vallauris and Golfe-Juan, France, in the late nineteenth and early twentieth centuries. It has an iridescent metallic luster glaze that resembles the Weller Sicardo pottery glaze. Most pieces are marked *J. Massier*.

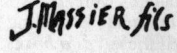

Bottle, Swallows Flying, Yellow Ground, Gold Sponge, Signed, 12 x 5 In., Pair 316.00
Cachepot, Molded Nude Catching Wave, Iridescent, Glazed, 13 In. 780.00
Ewer, Iridescent, Shouldered, Maiden-Shape Handle, 24 In. 2749.99
Pitcher, Iridescent Glaze, Pink, Green, Gold, 7 1/2 In. 230.00
Pitcher, Neptune, Mermaid Handle, Mottled Turquoise Crystalline Glaze, 10 x 8 In. 650.00
Vase, Fall Scene, Birch Trees, Creek, Bulbous, 2 Handles, Delphin, 5 1/4 x 4 1/2 In. 529.00
Vase, Ferns, Berries, Gold, Burgundy Luster Glaze, Egg Shape, 5 3/4 x 3 1/2 In. 590.00
Vase, Medallion Of Woman, Purple Iridescent, 14 In. 400.00
Vase, Portrait Of Young Woman, Iridescent Glaze, 9 1/4 In. 400.00
Vase, Stylized Flowers, Gold, Green, Purple Glaze, Bottle Shape, 11 1/2 x 4 3/4 In. 575.00

MATCH HOLDERS were made to hold the large wooden matches that were used in the nineteenth and twentieth centuries for a variety of purposes. The kitchen stove and the fireplace or furnace had to be lit regularly. One type of match holder was made to hang on the wall, another was designed to be kept on a tabletop. Of special interest today are match holders that have advertisements as part of the design.

Bailey The Dentist, Tin Lithograph, 5 x 3 x 1 1/2 In. 169.00
Basket, Milk Glass, Chicken, Rabbit, Pink, Gold Highlights, Wall, 4 1/4 In. 50.00
Bellhop, Black, Open Cap For Matches, Painted, Copper, 3 1/2 In. 167.00
Black, Scalloped Crest, Starburst, Blue, Yellow, Red, Tole, 7 1/2 In. 660.00
Bliss Herbs, Tin Lithograph, 6 1/2 In. 250.00
Boot, Nickel Plated, Bootjack Striker, Weighted Base, 3 1/4 In. 16.50
Bull Dog Tobacco, Red Bulldog, Die Cut, Tin Lithograph, 6 3/4 x 3 In. 590.00
Bulldog, Silver Plate 90.00
Bullock, Ward & Co., Chicago, Tin Lithograph, 4 7/8 x 3 3/8 In. 330.00
Cast Iron, Game Hanging On Trout Creel, Gold Paint Finish, Wall 50.00

Cast Iron, Hunting, Nickel Plated, 9 1/4 In. 120.00
Cast Iron, Painted Oval, Patented 1867, 6 In. 110.00
Cat & Kettle, Metal, Painted, Signed, Cornelius & Baker, 7 1/2 In. 165.00
Ceresota, Boy, In Straw Hat, Die Cut, Tin, 5 3/8 x 2 1/4 In. 220.00
Ceresota, Prize Bread Flour Of Minnesota, Tin Lithograph, 4 7/8 x 3 3/8 In. 169.00
Ceresota Bread, 3-D Barrel, Tin Lithograph, Embossed, Die Cut, 5 1/2 In. 305.00
Ceresota Bread Flour, Embossed, Tin Lithograph, 5 3/8 x 2 1/4 In. 285.00
DeLaval, Separator Shape, Tin Lithograph, Die Cut, 6 1/4 x 3 3/4 In. 230.00
Devil's Head, Cast Iron, Painted, 6 In. 110.00
Dr. Shoops Health Coffee, Tin Lithograph, 3 1/2 x 5 x 1 In. 250.00
Dr. Shoops Health Coffee, Tin Lithograph, 4 7/8 x 3 3/8 In. 276.00
E.O. Webber, Lumber & Building Material, Marysville, Kansas, Metal, 6 1/2 In. 110.00
Eagle Brand Lye, Tin Lithograph, 4 7/8 x 3 3/8 In. 460.00
Garland Stoves & Ranges, Yellow, Tin Lithograph, 7 x 3 7/8 In. 359.00
Garland Stoves Co., Green, Wall, 7 x 4 7/8 In. 365.00
Hanging, Orange, Lithograph, Flowers, Checkerboard, Tin, 1940s, 6 x 3 x 3 In. 40.00
Lady Liberty, Shield, Cap, Eagle On Cannon, Porcelain, c.1860, 7 In. 700.00
Laurel Stoves & Ranges, Tin Lithograph, 4 7/8 x 3 3/8 In. 290.00
Lax-Ets, Tin Lithograph, 4 3/4 In. 85.00
Merry War Powdered Lye, Girl Who Can Tell The Best Lye, 5 x 3 3/4 In. 795.00
Michigan Stoves, Are The Best, Cast Iron, 7 In. 105.00
Milk Glass, Gondola Shape, Wall, 5 In. 35.00
Milwaukee Binders & Mowers, Always Reliable, Tin, 4 7/8 x 3 3/8 x 1 1/4 In. 250.00
Milwaukee Harvesting Machines, Always Reliable, Tin, 5 x 3 3/4 In. 275.00
Old Judson Whiskey, Tin Lithograph, J.C. Stevens, 4 7/8 x 3 3/8 In. 195.00
Pan Dandy Bread, Red & Blue, Tin Lithograph, 4 7/8 x 3 3/8 In. 235.00
Puppy & Chicken, At Chimney, Porcelain, Conta & Boehm, 2 1/2 x 2 x 3 1/2 In. 50.00
Rex Flintkote Roofing, Horse, Barn, Tin Lithograph, 4 7/8 x 3 3/8 In. 435.00
Sharples, Tubular Cream Separator, Mother, Daughter, Tin, 6 3/4 x 2 1/8 In. 500.00
Siegles Department Store, Everything For Everybody, 4 x 3 5/8 x 1 3/8 In. 150.00
Vulcan Plow Co., Man, Hammer, Evansville, Ind., 7 7/8 x 21 3/4 In. 335.00

MATCH SAFES were designed to be carried in the pocket. Early matches were made with phosphorus and could ignite unexpectedly. The matches were safely stored in the tightly closed container. Match safes were made in sterling silver, plated silver, or other metals. The English call these *vesta boxes.*

Bottle, Bass Pale Ale Co., Brass 250.00
DeLaval, Separator Shape, Die Cut, Tin Lithograph, 6 1/4 x 3 3/4 In. 210.00
Green & Red Berries, Copper Swag, Cutout & Crimped Crest, Tole, 7 3/8 In. 275.00
Moose, Stars, Inlaid, Matchstick Exterior, Drawer, 13 x 10 x 10 In. 400.00
Prizer Stoves, Henderson Water Heaters, Reading, Pa., Brass 100.00
Sex-Ine Pills, 2 Men, Tin Lithograph, 8 x 5 In. 880.00

MATSU-NO-KE was a type of applied decoration for glass patented by Frederick Carder in 1922. There is clear evidence that pieces were made before that date at the Steuben glassworks. Stevens & Williams of England also made an applied decoration by the same name.

Bowl, Peachblow, Knurled Branches, No. 4293, 4 1/2 In. 750.00
Candlestick, Peachblow, Stem, Ruffled Foot, 6 3/4 In. 670.00
Vase, Blue Opaque, Applied Flowers, Leaves, Flared, Ruffled Top, Oval, c.1800, 7 In. ... 750.00
Vase, Peachblow, Clear, Thorn Base, Vines Up Side, Webb Style, 4 1/2 In. 70.00

MCCOY pottery was made in Roseville, Ohio. Nelson McCoy and J.W. McCoy established the Nelson McCoy Sanitary and Stoneware Company in Roseville, Ohio, in 1910. The firm made art pottery after 1926. In 1933 it became the Nelson McCoy Pottery Company. Pieces marked *McCoy* were made by the Nelson McCoy Pottery Company. Cookie jars were made from about 1940 until December 1990, when the McCoy factory closed. In 1990 the McCoy mark was put back on pottery by a firm unrelated to the original company. Because there was a company named Brush-McCoy, there is great confusion between Brush and Nelson McCoy pieces. See Brush category for more information.

Bank, Figural, Seaman, 5 1/2 In. 54.00

Bowl, Pasta Corner, 12 1/2 In. 30.00
Bowl, Suburbia, Brown, 5 In. 10.00
Bowl, Suburbia, Yellow, 5 In. 10.00
Candy Dish, Sunburst Gold, Gondola Shape, 10 In. 65.00
Canister Set, Lancaster Colony, Stamped, 4 Piece 179.00
Canister Set, Strawberry Country, 8 & 10 In., 2 Piece 65.00
Casserole, Cover, Brown Drip Glaze, 8 In. 20.00
Casserole, Cover, Krugs, Eagle, Stars, Cobalt Blue, 9 1/2 In. 95.00
Console, Embossed Pond Lilies, Pink Glaze, 8 1/2 In. 60.00
Console, Leaves & Berries, Aqua Matte, 9 1/2 In. 65.00
Cookie Jar, Apple, Red, Green Leaf Cover 50.00
Cookie Jar, Apple, Yellow, Touches Of Red 65.00
Cookie Jar, Bear, Honey, Tree Trunk 115.00
Cookie Jar, Bobby Baker . . . . .70.00 to 100.00
Cookie Jar, Bronze Teakettle 58.00
Cookie Jar, Brown Drip 40.00
Cookie Jar, Chef Head 110.00
Cookie Jar, Chipmunk 210.00
Cookie Jar, Cookie House . . . . .125.00 to 200.00
Cookie Jar, Corn 225.00
Cookie Jar, Covered Wagon 55.00
Cookie Jar, Friendship 7 . . . . 200.00
Cookie Jar, Goodie, Goose 50.00
Cookie Jar, Green Pepper . . . . .55.00 to 78.00
Cookie Jar, Hamm's Bear 250.00
Cookie Jar, Happy Face, Have A Good Day . . . . .30.00 to 94.00
Cookie Jar, Hot Air Balloon, Box 90.00
Cookie Jar, Ice Cream Cone, Box 125.00
Cookie Jar, Indian & Teepee 250.00
Cookie Jar, Keebler Cookie House, Box 160.00
Cookie Jar, Kitten On Basketweave 60.00
Cookie Jar, Kitten, Black, On Coal Bucket 250.00
Cookie Jar, Liberty Bell, Bronze Finish 100.00
Cookie Jar, Log Cabin 99.00
Cookie Jar, Lunch Box, Yellow, Orange 75.00
Cookie Jar, Mammy 300.00
Cookie Jar, Mammy With Cauliflower Jar 475.00
Cookie Jar, Market Lady, Original Box 450.00
Cookie Jar, Nabisco 50.00
Cookie Jar, Picnic Basket 75.00
Cookie Jar, Pig, Winking 350.00
Cookie Jar, Sack Of Cookies 80.00
Cookie Jar, Snoopy On Doghouse 200.00
Cookie Jar, Spirit Of 76, Milk Can, Box 125.00
Cookie Jar, Strawberry 100.00
Cookie Jar, Touring Car 100.00
Cookie Jar, W.C. Fields 250.00
Cookie Jar, Woodsy Owl 275.00
Ewer, Grapes & Leaves, Brown, Green, Cream, Ornate Handle, 9 1/2 In. 65.00
Ewer, Olympia, Flower, 4 1/2 In. 35.00
Flower Box, Green Matte, Brown, 4 1/2 In. 35.00
Flower Holder, Basketweave, Dark Green, Attached Saucer, 6 1/4 In. 45.00
Flowerpot, Basketweave, Dark Green, Attached Saucer, 3 1/2 In. . . . . .30.00 to 45.00
Flowerpot, Greek Key & Hobnail, Green, Attached Saucer, 6 x 4 In. 40.00
Iced Tea Server, El Rancho, 11 1/2 x 7 1/2 In. 360.00
Jardiniere, Lattice Design, Aqua, Pinched & Flared Rim, 8 3/4 In. 55.00
Lamp, Figural, Cowboy Boot, Brown & Ivory Glaze, Marked, 6 In., Pair 92.00
Mug, Happy Face, Yellow, Black Eyes, Smile 15.00
Pitcher, Tankard, Green Glaze, 8 3/8 In. 100.00
Pitcher, Tankard, Yellow, Green Glaze, 8 1/4 In. 70.00
Planter, Bird, Green, Yellow Bowl, 7 In. 50.00
Planter, Car, Roadster, Green, Gold Trim, 8 x 4 In. 16.00
Planter, Duckling, Green, Orange Bill 45.00

McCoy, Planter,
Pelican, Yellow, Black
& Red Paint, 5 In.

McCoy, Vase, Floraline,
Green, Handle, Embossed
Mark, 3 3/4 In.

Planter, Gondola Shape, Black Glaze, 11 1/2 In. 49.00
Planter, Panther, Sunburst Gold, 16 x 5 1/2 In. 70.00
Planter, Pelican, Yellow, Black & Red Paint, 5 In. .... *Illus* 12.00
Planter, Pheasant, Double, Green, Brown, 7 1/2 In. 60.00
Planter, Rooster, 7 1/2 In. 50.00
Planter, Twin Shoes, Pink, Bows 30.00
Stein, American Flag, Eagle, White, 5 1/2 In. 25.00
Teapot, Daisy, Green & Brown Matte, 6 In. 65.00
Vase, Arcature, Birds, Burgundy, Gray 50.00
Vase, Arcature, Green, Yellow & Black Bird, 6 3/4 In. 50.00
Vase, Berry & Leaf, Green, Ocher Ground, Matte, 8 1/4 x 5 In. 22.00
Vase, Bird, Leaves & Berries, Pink Glossy Glaze, 8 1/2 In. 75.00
Vase, Birds, Cherries, Yellow, 8 In. 50.00
Vase, Blossomtime, Flowers, White Matte, 4 Flat & Flared Sides, 6 In. 55.00
Vase, Chrysanthemum, Label, 8 In. 135.00
Vase, Cornucopia, Leaves & Berries, Brown, Green, Matte Glaze, 6 In. 40.00
Vase, Dark Blue Semi-Matte Drip Glaze, Stoneware, 2 Handles, 8 In. 59.00
Vase, Dogwood Flowers, Springwood Line, 7 1/2 In. 65.00
Vase, Embossed Wheat Sheaves, Yellow Ground, 6 Sides, 2 Handles, 8 1/4 In. 60.00
Vase, Floraline, Avocado, 6 1/2 In. 12.00
Vase, Floraline, Green, Handle, Embossed Mark, 3 3/4 In. .... *Illus* 10.00
Vase, Heart, Green, Glossy Glaze, 7 1/2 In. 85.00
Vase, Loy-Nel-Art, Daffodils, Green Glaze, Tapered, 11 In. 115.00
Vase, Loy-Nel-Art, Poppies, Brown Glaze, 13 1/2 In. 69.00
Vase, Pillow, Green Matte, Garden Club Line, 4 1/2 In. 55.00
Vase, Pink Matte Glaze, Embossed Flowers, Flared, Handles, 8 In. 60.00
Vase, Planter, Pink Flowers, Yellow Ground, Square, 4 In. 120.00
Vase, Rustic, Matte Green, Brown, 8 In. 40.00
Vase, Urn Shape, Green, 6 In. 30.00
Vase, Vines, Turquoise Blue Glossy Glaze, 2 Handles, 9 In. 75.00
Vase, White, Art Deco Style, 9 1/2 In. 60.00
Wall Pocket, Apple, Red, 6 1/2 In. 75.00
Wall Pocket, Grapes, Dark Purple, Green Leaves, 7 In. 175.00
Wall Pocket, Leaves & Berries, Green Matte, 6 1/2 In. 55.00
Wall Pocket, Leaves & Berries, White Matte, 6 1/2 In. 55.00

MCKEE is a name associated with various glass enterprises in the United States since 1836, including J. & F. McKee (1850), Bryce, McKee & Co. (1850 to 1854), McKee and Brothers (1865), and National Glass Co. (1899). In 1903, the McKee Glass Company was formed in Jeannette, Pennsylvania. It became McKee Division of the Thatcher Glass Co. in 1951 and was bought out by the Jeannette Corporation in 1961. Pressed glass, kitchenwares, and tablewares were produced. Jeannette Corporation closed in the early 1980s. Additional pieces may be included in the Custard Glass category.

Bowl, Milk Glass, 3-Footed, 3 x 7 In. 20.00
Carafe, Milk Glass, Black Plastic Lacing On Neck, Cork Cover, Glass Stopper, 6 3/4 In. ... 25.00
Casserole, Cover, Round, Tab Handles, 5 In. 7.00
Mixing Bowl, Horizontal Ribs, Delphite, 9 3/4 In. 250.00
Mug, Tom & Jerry, Clambroth, 3 1/2 x 4 In. 18.00
Pepper Shaker, Roman Arches, Black, Enameled P, 4 In. 20.00

Refrigerator Dish, Cover, Custard, Rectangular, 2 1/2 x 8 x 5 In. 40.00
Tumbler, Bottoms-Up, Jade, Legs Open 250.00

MECHANICAL BANKS are listed in the Bank category.

MEDICAL office furniture, operating tools, microscopes, thermometers, and other paraphernalia used by doctors are included in this category. Veterinary collectibles are also included here. Medicine bottles are listed in the Bottle category. There are related collectibles listed under Dental.

Amputation Set, 3 Liston Knives, Finger Saw, Mahogany Case, 17 1/2 In. 1880.00
Amputation Set, Signed, Chapman, Mahogany Case, Mid 19th Century, 15 In. 1880.00
Belt, Electric, Addison's Galvanic, Box, 9 x 2 1/2 In. 198.00
Belt, Electric, Mioxrls, No. 3, Label, Box, 9 3/4 x 2 3/4 In. 165.00
Bleeder, Bone Handle, Sheffield, c.1861, 5 1/2 In. 90.00
Bleeding Bowl, Brass, Polished, Hole For Hanging, Child's, 5 In. 385.00
Bleeding Cup, Glass, Clear, 2 In., 5 Piece 55.00
Cabinet, Apothecary, 4 Over 3 Over 2 Drawers, Pine, Bracket Feet, 30 x 29 In. 660.00
Cabinet, Apothecary, 21 Drawers, Pine, Hanging, c.1890, 10 3/4 x 25 1/2 In. 365.00
Cabinet, Apothecary, 36 Drawers, White, Chinese Characters, 45 x 36 x 20 In. 468.00
Cabinet, Apothecary, 38 Drawers, Red Paint, Signed S. Root, Lancaster Co., Pa., c.1850 . 8800.00
Cabinet, Apothecary, 60 Drawers, Curved Cutout Base, Wood Knobs 4125.00
Cabinet, Apothecary, Ash, Chestnut, Curly Maple, 20 Drawers, 38 1/2 x 16 1/2 x 33 In. . 550.00
Cabinet, Apothecary, Mahogany, Pine, 8 Drawers, Scalloped Apron, 24 x 11 x 29 1/2 In. . 910.00
Cabinet, Apothecary, Oak, Beveled Glass Mirror, 21 x 24 x 7 1/4 In. 395.00
Cabinet, Apothecary, Pine, 16 Drawers Over 2 Doors, 54 x 40 In. 715.00
Cabinet, Apothecary, Pine, Green Paint, 19th Century, 21 x 29 x 12 In. 545.00
Case, Doctor's, 13 Glass Bottles, Corks, Labels, Civil War, 3 1/2 x 6 In. 415.00
Chair, Invalid, Wicker, Closed Arms, Oak Armrests, Iron Wheels, c.1900, 50 In. 460.00
Chest, Apothecary, Mahogany Veneer, 6 Bottles, Early 1800s, 9 1/2 x 12 x 8 In. 230.00
Chest, Apothecary, Mahogany, 26 Bottle Sections, Drop Handles, c.1850, 15 In. 881.00
Chest, Apothecary, Mahogany, Brass Bail Handle, Hinge Lid, Drawer, c.1880, 10 3/4 In. . 400.00
Corset, Dr. Warner Coraline Health, White Linen, Lace, Clasp Front, c.1881, Size Large . 510.00
Cupping Set, Brass Scarificator & Pump, Signed, L.B. White, N.Y., c.1850, 6 In. 764.00
Doctor's Field Bag, Leather, Glass Bottles, C.S. Arsenal, Baton Rouge, 1862 . . . . 2200.00
Dose Glass, A.M. Cole Druggist, Virginia City Nev., Table Dessert Tea, 1 7/8 In. 358.00
Ear Trumpet, Early 1900s 175.00
Earphone, Glass Vial, Directions, Label, Morley Co., Philadelphia, Box, 3 1/4 In. 143.00
Examining Table, Mahogany, W.D. Allison & Co., Indianapolis, c.1890, 75 In. 95.00
Eye, Artificial, Brass, Cylindrical Body, American, Early 20th Century, 3 1/2 In. 59.00
Eye Chart, Celluloid On Linen, F.A. Hardy & Co., Chicago, 36 x 10 In. 70.00
Eyecup, Cobalt Blue, Footed, Pontiled Base, 2 3/4 In. 99.00
Eyecup, Green, Bulbous Base, Oval, Box, 2 1/4 In. 187.00
Eyecup, Green, Footed, 2 3/4 In. 65.00
Eyecup, Vaseline, B In Diamond 35.00
Inhaler, Dr. Nelson's Improved, Black & White, Boots Chemists, England, 1920 . . . . 110.00
Inhaler, G. & R. Moorcrom, Stoneware, Bulbous, 19th Century 95.00
Inhaler, Stoneware, Shell Crest Logo, Shield Transfer Decoration, Bulbous 125.00
Kit, Brain Surgeon's, Traveling Case, Red Velvet Lining, 19th Century 660.00
Kit, Field Surgeon's, Canvas Roll Bag, S. Rampling Surgical Instruments, c.1915, 13 In. . 65.00
Kit, Minor Surgery, Case, W.F. Ford, Caswell, Hazard & Co., New York, 8 3/4 In. 705.00
Kit, Surgeon's, Ebony Handles, Case, Shepard & Dudley, New York, 18 In. 1116.00
Kit, Surgeon's, Mahogany Case, Tiemann & Co., New York, 9 1/2 In. 1295.00
Lamp, Surgeon's, Brass, Glass Chimney, Scott Lamp Co., San Francisco, c.1890, 30 In. . . 646.00
Lancet, Spring, Brass, Depth Guide, Wiegand & Snowden, Philadelphia, 4 1/2 In. 235.00
Machine, Suppository, Cast Iron, Wheel, Gold Stencil, W.T. Co. No. 3, c.1895, 13 x 8 In. . 525.00
Medication Dispenser, Brass Spigot, Cut Design To Font, 30 In. 575.00
Mold, Suppository, Tin, Oval, Brass & Copper Cone-Shape Inserts, 5 1/2 In. 145.00
Pill Case, Leather, Charles T. Hulbert's Homeopathic Pharmacy, N.Y., 6 x 4 In. 165.00
Pill Roller, Wood, Brass, 2 Handles, 14 x 7-In. Base, 3 x 14-In. Roll Bar 110.00
Pill Rounder, Finisher, Wood Turned, 2 Pill Sizes, Reversible, 3 In. 70.00
Quack Box, Electro-Medical, Oak Hinged Top, 19th Century, 6 x 8 x 10 In. 225.00
Saw & Knife, Amputation, Wood Handle, c.1861, 17 1/2 In. 220.00
Sitz Bath, Metal, Green Paint, Yellow Interior, Flowers, Victorian 175.00

Speaking Trumpet, Brass, 19th Century, 18 In. 335.00
Surgeon's Set, Brass Shield, Engraved, Ja Shepard & Ga Janes, c.1861 .... 7000.00
Surgeon's Set, Field, Leather Case, c.1861 .... 240.00
Surgeon's Set, Madieras Of Philadelphia, Ivory Handles, Leather Case, c.1861, 5 Piece .. 250.00
Surgical Instruments, Ebony Handles, Mahogany Tray, Evans, London, c.1825, 17 In. 1175.00
Syringe, Metal, Wooden Case, Tiemann & Co., c.1861. .... 110.00
Tooth Extractor, F. Arnold, Baltimore, c.1861 .... 60.00
Training Dummy, Red Cross, Case, Instructions On Lid, 1960s 58.00
Vaporizer, Simplex Lamp Co., Tin, Early 20th Century, 7 1/4 In. 100.00

MEERSCHAUM is a soft white, gray, or cream-colored mineral named
magnesium silicate. The name comes from the German word for
seafoam, because it was sometimes found floating in the Black Sea and
people thought it was petrified seafoam. Pipes and other pieces of
carved meerschaum listed here date from the nineteenth century to the
present.

Cheroot Holder, Bust, Black Man, Top Hat, 4 1/2 In. 590.00
Pipe, 2 Bulldogs, Case 55.00
Pipe, 3 Bears, Prowling Around Tree Trunk, Fitted Case, 6 1/2 In. 355.00
Pipe, Bearded Sultan, Silver Collar, Case, 1879 .... 305.00
Pipe, Black Man's Head, Straw Hat, Case, 5 In. 350.00
Pipe, Brothel Scene, 2 Drinking Men, Dancing Women, 8 In. 765.00
Pipe, Buffalo Bill, Windswept Hat Brim, Mustache, G. Fischer, 1915, 7 In. 1060.00
Pipe, Bust, Arabian Chieftain, Bearded, Turban, Bearing Knife, 2-Tone, 8 In. 1880.00
Pipe, Bust, Edwardian Lady, Straw Hat, Rose Band, G. Fischer, Sr., 6 1/2 In. 825.00
Pipe, Bust, Florentine Gentleman, Beard, Feathered Cap, Amber Stem, 7 1/2 In. 470.00
Pipe, Bust, Indian Chief, Feathered Headdress, Amber Stem, 7 In. 705.00
Pipe, Bust, Mephistopheles, Hood, Tongue Out, Oxblood, Amber Stem, 6 In. 235.00
Pipe, Claw Holding Bowl, Case .... .28.00 to 60.00
Pipe, Dog, Bird In Mouth, Case 250.00
Pipe, Fox Attacking Rooster, Amber Stem, 5 7/8 In. 205.00
Pipe, Game Hunters, Stalking Lion, Amber Stem, 5 7/8 In. 150.00
Pipe, Lion's Head, Case 105.00
Pipe, Mariner, Leaning On Anchor, Holding Oar, Amber Stem, 7 1/2 In. 380.00
Pipe, Mastiff, Brass Mounted Lid, Flexible Stem 50.00
Pipe, Metal Lid, Collar, Stained Birch Stem 50.00
Pipe, Mother Dog, Puppy 70.00
Pipe, Nathan The Wise, Tasseled Cap, Cloak Buttons, Cherry Amber Stem, 10 In. 355.00
Pipe, Nude Woman, Art Nouveau, Flower-Form Bowl, Case 145.00
Pipe, Prancing Horse, Trees, Case 80.00
Pipe, Skull & Crossbones, Amber Stem, 6 In. 175.00
Pipe, St. Stephen Fighting Ottoman Turks, Suspended Silver Rope, 8 In. 470.00
Pipe, Wind In The Willows Scene, Ratty Mole, Carrying Valises, Amber Stem, 7 In. 235.00
Pipe, Winged Fairy, Wraparound Wings 230.00
Plaque, 2 Girls, Classically Dressed, Oval, Ebonized Frame, E.W. Wyon, 1848, 7 In. 295.00
Smoking Set, 2 Pipes, 2 Cigarette Holders, Match Holder, Fitted Box, 5 Piece 165.00
Smoking Set, Carved Skull Bowls, Graduated Sizes, Largest 5 In., 3 Piece 1295.00

MEISSEN is a town in Germany where porcelain has been made since
1710. Any china made in the town can be called Meissen, although the
famous Meissen factory made the finest porcelains of the area. The
crossed swords mark of the great Meissen factory has been copied by
many other firms in Germany and other parts of the world. Pieces of
Meissen dinnerware in the Onion pattern are listed in their own category in this book.

Basket, Floral Sprays, Pierced Basket Weave, Oval, Branch Feet, 10 1/2 In. 355.00
Basket, Pierced, Children Of 4 Seasons Support, 1800s, 21 1/4 In. 5975.00
Bottle, Cover, Schneeballen, Yellow Bird Perched On Branch, Late 1800s, 13 In. 2030.00
Bowl, Grape & Leaf, Blue & White Glaze, Victorian, 19th Century, 11 In. 80.00
Box, Lid With Landscape, Round, Flowers, Cobalt Blue, 3 In. 1116.00
Candelabrum, 3-Light, Bearded Man, On Scrolled Base, Molded Leaves, 12 3/4 In. 500.00
Candelabrum, 3-Light, Green Enameled Leaves, Flowers, Scrolled Base, Gilt, 9 In., Pair . 765.00
Candelabrum, 3-Light, Shepherds, Recorder, Bagpipes, Curved Arms, 16 In., Pair 3290.00

Candlestick, Classical Woman, Seated, Holding Child, Oval Base, 12 3/4 In., Pair 1175.00
Candlestick, Surmounted Eagle, 19th Century, 11 5/8 In., Pair 2150.00
Candlestick, Swords, Relief Gilt, Pedestal Base, Hard Paste, Star Mark, c.1775, 12 In. 4830.00
Clock, Mantel, Ornamental Flowers, Putti, Late 19th Century, 22 1/2 x 16 In. 4600.00
Coffee Set, Polychrome Flowers, Cobalt Blue & Gilt Trim, White Ground, 16 Piece 175.00
Compote, Alternating Gilt Cartouches & Latticework, Twisted Stem, 2 Sections, 9 In. ... 230.00
Compote, Cartouches Of Children At Play, Scalloped Rim, Pedestal Base, 6 In. 175.00
Dish, Flowers, Leaf Shape, Crossed Swords Mark, c.1765, 10 5/6 In., Pair 2690.00
Dish, Fruit & Leaves, Gilt, Deep Blue Ground, 19th Century, 10 3/4 In. 145.00
Figurine, Blackamoor With Parrot, Painted, Mark, 11 In. 3820.00
Figurine, Boy Gathering Fish From Trap, Blue Crossed Swords Mark, 4 1/2 In. 600.00
Figurine, Boy On Ice Skates, Signed, Blue Crossed Swords Mark, 5 In. 635.00
Figurine, Boy Playing Flute, Girl With Flower Basket, 5 3/4 In., Pair 450.00
Figurine, Boy With Flower Basket, Boy With Wreath, 5 In., Pair 540.00
Figurine, Buffalo, Reclining, Stoneware, Wooden Base, E. Oehme, 1937, 16 In. 1410.00
Figurine, Cherub, Beggar, On Crutches, Torn Jacket, Crossed Swords Mark, 8 1/2 In. 1116.00
Figurine, Cherub, Holding Hammer, Heart On Anvil, Crossed Swords Mark, 7 1/4 In. 1060.00
Figurine, Chickadee, Walnut Shell, Blue, Green, Yellow, Impressed Mark, 3 1/4 In. 230.00
Figurine, Child With Flower Basket, Blue Crossed Swords Mark, 5 In. 635.00
Figurine, Child With Sheaf Of Wheat, Blue Crossed Swords Mark, 5 1/4 In. 660.00
Figurine, Cupid Perched On Stump Feeding Birds, 19th Century, 16 3/4 In. 2150.00
Figurine, Cupid, Bow & Arrow, Pedestal, Lovebirds, Crossed Swords Mark, 7 1/4 In. 940.00
Figurine, Cupid, Holding Bird, Burning Heart, Crossed Swords Mark, 11 3/4 In. 2115.00
Figurine, Dancing Girl, Striped Bodice, Floral Skirt, Gilt Scroll Base, c.1880, 4 1/2 In. 580.00
Figurine, Female, Nude, White Glaze, R. Ullman, c.1940, 12 1/4 In. 880.00
Figurine, Flower Seller, Woman & Basket, Man, Crossed Swords Mark, 7 In., Pair 2235.00
Figurine, Girl, Seated, Holding Dog & Mirror, Oval Base, Pink Lappet Rim, 6 In. 1175.00
Figurine, Hermes, In Fur-Trimmed Robe, Playing Flute, Oval Rocaille Base, 9 1/2 In. 880.00
Figurine, Lottery Of Love, Cherubs Drawing, Inscribing Names, 19th Century, 8 In. 1790.00
Figurine, Monkey, Seated, Painted Mark, 9 In. 2390.00
Figurine, Moor & Cockatoo, Lady Playing Flute, Paul Scheurich, c.1926, 8 In., Pair 5290.00
Figurine, Musicians & Putti, Scroll Edged Base, Crossed Swords Mark, 1800, 14 In. 2990.00
Figurine, Night & Day, Flowers, Bird, 19th Century, 20 In. 9490.00
Figurine, Nude Male Resting On Tree Stump, Painted, 14 In. 1528.00
Figurine, Parrot, Perched On Branch, Freeform Base, Enamel Decoration, 10 3/4 In. 940.00
Figurine, Playful Cat, Blue Ribbon On Neck, Crossed Swords Mark, 6 1/2 In. 500.00
Figurine, Swan, Grassy Base, Applied Reeds, 19th Century, 8 5/8 In., Pair 10755.00
Figurine, Violinist, Man Playing Violin, Friedrich Elias Meyer, c.1755, 5 In. 720.00
Group, 2 Cherubs, Holding Torch, Polishing Helmet, Oval Base, 5 1/2 In. 645.00
Group, 2 Seated Women, Cupid, Pigeons, 19th Century, 14 In. 6325.00
Group, Boy, Girl In 18th Century Costume, 3 1/2 In. 480.00
Group, Cherubs Gathered Around Easel, 19th Century, 7 5/8 In. 2990.00
Group, Children On Tree Stumps, Crossed Swords Mark, 5 5/8 In. 1530.00
Group, Children, With Sheep & Flowers, Circular Base, 7 In. 2585.00
Group, Crinoline, Man & Woman, Formally Dressed, Oval Base, Flowers, 8 1/4 In. 825.00
Group, Equestrian Couple, Detachable Hounds, c.1910, 15 x 15 In., Pair 16100.00
Group, Gallant & Companion, Boy Carrying Doves, Late 19th Century, 13 In. 3286.00
Group, Lady Reading Letter, With Her Beau, 6 In. 540.00
Group, Little People, On Pedestal, Fruits & Flowers, 18th Century, 10 x 6 In. 9500.00
Group, Milkmaid, Pulling Goats, Pale Underglaze Enamels, Oval Base, 9 1/4 In. 410.00
Group, Monkey Band, Organ, Bassoon, Cello, Singer, Pipe & Tabor, 6 In. 8365.00
Group, Monkey Band, Sitting Atop Other Monkey, Playing Piano, 5 1/2 In. 1610.00
Group, Putto, Artists, 3 Cherubs, 1 Sketching, c.1850-1900, 7 5/8 In. .... *Illus* 2998.00
Group, Venus Placing Hearts On Flame, Cupid, Flower, 19th Century, 14 In. ..... *Illus* 2689.00
Group, Vine Dressers, Boys, Girls, Around Wine Barrel, Early 1900s, 11 1/2 In. 5750.00
Group, Woman, Scantily Clad, On Bull, 2 Attendants, Oval Base, 1910, 8 1/2 In. 2115.00
Plate, Autumn Being Carried Off By Centaur, Cobalt Blue Ground, 9 In. 1880.00
Plate, Courting Couple, Blue, Gilt, Pierced Trellis Rim, c.1875, 10 In. 2330.00
Plate, Dessert, India Tree, Reticulated Border, Blue, White, c.1885, 9 1/2 In., 6 Piece 1095.00
Plate, Dinner, Flower Spray, Basket Weave Border, 10 In., 12 Piece 1195.00
Plate, Goat & Cattle Herders, Blue, Gilt, Molded & Pierced Rim, c.1875, 9 1/2 In. 1675.00
Plate, Leaf, Molded, Rose, White, Gilt, Impressed Mark, 8 1/2 In. 75.00
Plate, Luftwaffe Fliegerhorst Grossehnain, Blue Eagle, Leaves, 1914-1939, 9 1/2 In. 230.00

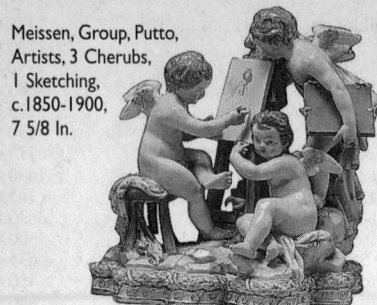

Meissen, Group, Putto,
Artists, 3 Cherubs,
1 Sketching,
c.1850-1900,
7 5/8 In.

Meissen, Group,
Venus Placing Hearts
On Flame, Cupid,
Flower, 19th
Century, 14 In.

Platter, Pheasants In Landscape, Scalloped, Gilt Design, 16 x 11 In. 1250.00
Platter, Roasted Meat, Oval, Blue Underglaze, 18th Century, 18 1/2 In. 405.00
Stein, Crossed Swords With Shield, Sculpted Pewter Lid, Shell Thumb Lift, 1/2 Liter 680.00
Tea & Coffee Service, Yellow Lion Pattern, Plates, Cups, Saucers, 43 Piece 2689.00
Teapot, Ball Shape, Summer Flowers, Gold Loop Handle, Spout, Flower Finial, 4 1/2 In. . 345.00
Teapot, Bamboo Cluster, Enamel Flowers, Faux Bamboo Ear Handle & Spout, 3 1/2 In. . 470.00
Tray, Village, Dancing Man, Mill, Purple Border Scenes, 4-Footed, 2 x 10 x 7 1/2 In. 660.00
Tureen, Cover, Bird & Flowers, Putti Finial, Undertray, Oval, c.1800, 14 1/2 In. 805.00
Urn, Bronze Dore, Scroll Band, Crossed Swords Mark, c.1890, 8 1/2 In. 1150.00
Urn, Panel Of Woman, Applied Porcelain Flowers, Marked, 12 In. 345.00
Vase, Cover, Cupid Holding Garlands, Mark, 17 1/2 In. 1175.00
Vase, Flower Spray, Cobalt Blue Ground, Flared, 6 1/2 In. 295.00
Vase, Spill, Botanical Decoration, Gilt Banding, Baluster Shape, 4 1/4 In. 85.00
Wine Cooler, Strawberry, Flowers, Landscape, Figures, 9 1/2 x 7 3/4 In., Pair 1495.00

MERCURY GLASS, or silvered glass, was first made in the 1850s. It lost
favor for a while but became popular again about 1910. It looks like a
piece of silver.

    Reflecting Ball, Silvered, Mercury Stand, Circular Foot, Cork Plug, 13 1/2 In. 550.00

MERRIMAC POTTERY Company was founded by Thomas Nickerson in
Newburyport, Massachusetts, in 1902. The company made art pottery,
garden pottery, and reproductions of Roman pottery. The pottery
burned to the ground in 1908.

MERRIMAC
CERAMIC
COMPANY

Bowl, Deep Green Glaze, Ruffled Rim, 3 x 7 In. 770.00
Jardiniere, Green Matte Glaze, Melon Shape, Stamped, 8 1/4 x 12 In. 1725.00
Urn, Cover, Green, Orange Mottled Matte Glaze, Squat, 4 1/4 x 4 1/4 In. 690.00
Vase, Blue Matte Glaze, Turquoise Ground, Barrel Shape, 4 x 3 1/2 In. 1380.00
Vase, Brown Matte Glaze, Mustard Ground, Squat, 3 Handles, Stamped, 3 1/4 x 5 In. 1840.00
Vase, Cucumber Green, Charcoaling, Ribbed, Mark, 15 x 11 In. 3300.00
Vase, Forest Green Glaze, Brown Mottled Ground, Baluster, 11 x 5 In. 920.00
Vase, Green & Yellow Matte Glaze, Waisted Gourd Shape, 7 3/4 In. 1725.00
Vase, Green Glaze, Applied Plants, Tooled, Cylindrical, 5 1/4 x 3 1/2 In. 1095.00
Vase, Green Matte Glaze, Feathered, Baluster, 4 1/4 x 3 1/2 In. 375.00
Vase, Green Matte Glaze, Yellow Matte Ground, Squat, Handles, 4 3/4 x 8 In. 1265.00
Vase, Green Matte Glaze, Yellow Matte Ground, Squat, 2 Handles, 5 x 8 In. 2185.00
Vase, Green Semimatte Glaze, Mottled, Squat, Stamped, 3 x 3 3/4 In. 1150.00
Vase, Mottled Blue Matte Glaze, Classic Shape, c.1915, 5 1/2 In. 90.00
Vase, Textured Green Glaze, Green Matte Ground, 13 x 6 1/2 In. 1980.00

METLOX POTTERIES was founded in 1927 in Manhattan Beach, California. Dinnerware was made beginning in 1931. Evan K. Shaw purchased the company in 1946 and expanded the number of patterns.
Poppytrail (1946-1989) and Vernonware (1958-1980) were divisions
of Metlox under E.K. Shaw's direction. The factory closed in 1989.

Butterscotch, Saucer, Vernonware, 6 3/8 In. 6.00
California Aztec, Twin Vegetable, No. 3465 .... 250.00
California Fruit, Teapot 75.00

California Ivy, Bowl, Vegetable, Round, 9 1/4 In.	40.00
California Ivy, Butter, Cover, 1/4 Lb.	50.00
California Ivy, Plate, 6 1/2 In.	5.00
California Ivy, Salt & Pepper	28.00
California Provincial, Creamer, Green Rooster	28.00
California Strawberry, Bowl, Cereal, 5 5/8 In.	14.00
California Strawberry, Bowl, Vegetable, Round, 9 In.	40.00
California Strawberry, Canister Set, Cover, 4 Piece	60.00
California Strawberry, Mug	20.00
Camellia, Cup, Prouty	10.00
Camellia, Saucer, Prouty	4.00
Della Robbia, Platter, 11 1/8 In.	20.00
La Mancha White, Platter, 14 1/2 In.	25.00
Pintoria, Plate, Dinner, Prouty, 10 In.	60.00
Provincial Blue, Canister, Coffee, Cover	95.00
Provincial Blue, Canister, Sugar, Cover	45.00
Provincial Blue, Canister, Tea, Cover	85.00
Provincial Blue, Cruet Set, 5 Piece	150.00
Red Rooster, Canister, Coffee, Cover, Red	60.00
Red Rooster, Canister, Flour, Cover, Red	75.00
Red Rooster, Canister, Sugar, Cover	35.00
Red Rooster, Canister, Tea, Cover, Red	50.00
Red Rooster, Creamer, Red	25.00
Red Rooster, Plate, 10 In.	15.00
Red Rooster, Platter	40.00
Red Rooster, Salt & Pepper	30.00
Red Rooster, Soup, Dish, 8 In.	20.00
Red Rooster, Sugar & Creamer, Cover, Red	60.00
Sculptured Daisy, Plate, 6 In.	6.00
Sculptured Grape, Gravy, Attached Underplate	35.00
Sculptured Grape, Platter, 14 In.	50.00
Sculptured Zinnia, Plate, 10 1/4 In.	12.50
Vernon Rose, Plate, Vernonware, 6 5/8 In.	6.00
Woodland Gold, Butter, Round	45.00
Yorkshire, Bowl, Cereal, Lug Handle, Prouty	20.00
Yorkshire, Chop Plate, Prouty	50.00
Yorkshire, Plate, Prouty, 6 In.	6.00
Yorkshire, Salt & Pepper, Prouty	25.00

METTLACH, Germany, is a city where the Villeroy and Boch factories worked. Steins from the firm are marked with the word *Mettlach* or the castle mark. They date from about 1842. Pieces marked *Mettlach* are still being made. *PUG* means painted under glaze. The steins can be dated from the marks on the bottom, which include a date-number code. Other pieces may be listed in the Villeroy & Boch category.

Ashtray, Polar Bear, 4 x 7 1/2 In.	170.00
Basket, No. 1211, Etched, Glazed, Silver Plated Lid, 4 In.	185.00
Beaker, 1/4 Liter, Lions Holding Shield, 1874-1909, 5 In.	99.00
Beaker, No. 2327-425, 1/4 Liter, Ratskeller Bremen	145.00
Beaker, No. 2327-426, 1/4 Liter, Hamburg Jungfernstieg	140.00
Beaker, No. 2327-427, 1/4 Liter, Brandenburger Tor, PUG	219.00
Beaker, No. 2327-429, 1/4 Liter, Burg Nurnberg	140.00
Beaker, No. 2327-430, 1/4 Liter, Hofbrauhaus Munchen	180.00
Beaker, No. 2327-1290, 1/4 Liter, State Crest	105.00
Beaker, No. 2327-1302, 1/4 Liter, American Eagle, Flag, Monuments, PUG	345.00
Beaker, No. 3327, 1/3 Liter, Cavalier Serenading Woman, Etched	375.00
Beaker, Old Brownie Smoking Pipe, 5 In.	175.00
Beaker, Souvenir Of Boston, Old North Church, Black Transfer, 5 In.	105.00
Beaker, Suum-Cuique, Eagle, Spread Wings, Marked, 5 In.	90.00
Bowl, Cover, No. 3452, Repeating Design, Etched, Glazed, Brown Interior, 4 x 3 1/2 In.	130.00
Creamer, No. 3321, Art Nouveau, Clovers, Etched, 4 In.	129.00
Gravy Boat, No. 3341, Art Nouveau, Etched, 6 In.	360.00
Pitcher, No. 2486, Swans, Art Nouveau, Etched, Otto Eckman, 7 1/2 In.	1380.00

Planter, No. 3075, Art Deco, Etched, 10 x 3 1/4 In. 460.00
Planter, No. 7015, Children Playing, 4 Stoneware Feet, 2 1/2 x 9 1/2 In. 169.00
Plaque, No. 1044, Munich, Bavaria, PUG, 12 In. 335.00
Plaque, No. 1044-1014, Munich Child, Steins Walking, H. Schlitt, PUG, 17 1/2 In. 635.00
Plaque, No. 1044-130, Heidelberg, Schloss, PUG, 12 In. 195.00
Plaque, No. 1044-148, Neuschwanstein, PUG, 14 In. 360.00
Plaque, No. 1044-157, Koln, PUG, 14 In. 360.00
Plaque, No. 1044-169, Dresden, Altstadt, PUG, 12 In. 360.00
Plaque, No. 1044-411 & 412, Barmaid & Postman Drinking, PUG, 12 In., Pair 575.00
Plaque, No. 1044-527, Wirtschaft Zur Treib Am Vierwaldstatter, PUG, 12 In. 210.00
Plaque, No. 1044-528, Tellskapelle, PUG, 12 In. 240.00
Plaque, No. 1044-9031, Pheasants, PUG, 14 In. 120.00
Plaque, No. 1044-92, Stadthaus In Berncastel, PUG, 14 In. 290.00
Plaque, No. 1044-93, Burghaus Kurbisch, PUG, 14 In. ....290.00 to 300.00
Plaque, No. 2078, Military Ulanen, Etched, Stocke, 15 In. 1150.00
Plaque, No. 2195, Castle On Cliff, Rheinstein, Etched, 17 1/2 In. 430.00
Plaque, No. 2196, Castle On Cliff, Stolzenfels, Etched, 17 1/2 In. 290.00
Plaque, No. 2362, Heidelberg Castle, Etched, 17 1/2 In. 690.00
Plaque, No. 2518, Town Scene Of Meissen, 17 1/2 In. 935.00
Plaque, No. 2622, Cavalier Holding Glass, Etched, Quidenus, 7 1/2 In. 235.00
Punch Bowl, No. 2234, 6 Liter, Birds Eating Grapes From Vines, Figural Dwarf Lid 478.00
Relish Tray, No. 3363, Art Nouveau, 7 In. 330.00
Stein, No. 24, 1 Liter, Figures, 4 Panels, Inlaid Lid 175.00
Stein, No. 24, 1/2 Liter, Figures, 4 Panels, Inlaid Lid 265.00
Stein, No. 171, 1/4 Liter, Five People, Dog, Inlaid Lid 156.00
Stein, No. 385, 1/2 Liter, Student Society, Hand Painted, Pewter Lid, 1891 .... 375.00
Stein, No. 485, 1/2 Liter, Musical Scene, Relief, Inlaid Lid 375.00
Stein, No. 675, 1/2 Liter, Barrel Form, Marble Finish, Inlaid Lid 135.00
Stein, No. 812, 1 Liter, Hunting Scene, Eagle Thumblift, Inlaid Lid 400.00
Stein, No. 812, 1 Liter, Hunting Scene, Serpent Thumblift, Inlaid Lid 380.00
Stein, No. 812, 1/2 Liter, Hunting Scenes, Inlaid Lid 305.00
Stein, No. 1005, 1 Liter, Tavern Scene, Inlaid Lid 435.00
Stein, No. 1028, 1/2 Liter, Couple Carrying Harvest, Inlaid Lid. 90.00
Stein, No. 1028, 4 Liter, Couple Carrying Harvest, Inlaid Lid 515.00
Stein, No. 1053, 1 Liter, Dwarfs Drinking, Inlaid Lid 375.00
Stein, No. 1100, 1/3 Liter, Season's Activities, Pedestal Base, Inlaid Lid 120.00
Stein, No. 1148, 1/2 Liter, Geometric Design, Inlaid Lid 185.00
Stein, No. 1180, 1/2 Liter, Drinking Verse, Inlaid Lid 127.00
Stein, No. 1221, 1 1/2 Liter, Mosaic, Geometric, Inlaid Lid 865.00
Stein, No. 1266, 1/2 Liter, 3 Panels, Drinking Scene, Glazed Relief, Inlaid Lid 110.00
Stein, No. 1266, 1/4 Liter, 3 Panels, Drinking Scene, Inlaid Lid ....100.00 to 130.00
Stein, No. 1300, 1/2 Liter, Medallions Around Stein, Relief, Inlaid Lid 285.00
Stein, No. 1390, 2 Liter, Hunter At Table, Verse, Pewter Lid, Shell Thumblift 180.00
Stein, No. 1395, 1/2 Liter, French Card, Etched, Inlaid Lid ....430.00 to 520.00
Stein, No. 1403, 1/2 Liter, Man Bowling In Tavern, C. Warth, Etched, Inlaid Lid 375.00
Stein, No. 1455, 1 2/5 Liter, Geometric Design, Glazed Relief, Pewter Lid 460.00
Stein, No. 1471, 1/2 Liter, Musicians, C. Warth, Inlaid Lid 145.00
Stein, No. 1494, 5 1/2 Liter, Men Sitting On Barrel, Drinking Beer, Etched, Pewter Lid .. 1150.00
Stein, No. 1519, 1/2 Liter, Rowing Scenes, Etched, Inlaid Anchor Lid 605.00
Stein, No. 1526, 1/2 Liter, Bavaria, Pro Fide, Hand Painted, Pewter Lid 290.00
Stein, No. 1526, 1/2 Liter, Isenbecker Munchener, Transfer, Pewter Lid 300.00
Stein, No. 1526, 1/2 Liter, Munich Child, Lions, Verse, Hand Painted, Pewter Lid 430.00
Stein, No. 1526, 1/2 Liter, Munich Child, With Hops & Malt, Hand Painted, Inlaid Lid .. 235.00
Stein, No. 1526, 1/2 Liter, Post Telegraph, Hand Painted, Pewter Lid 230.00
Stein, No. 1526, 1/2 Liter, Student Society, Transfer, Enameled, Pewter Lid, 1911 .... 360.00
Stein, No. 1526, 2 Liter, Student Society, Pewter Lid, Eagle Thumblift, 1912 .... 660.00
Stein, No. 1526-1078, 1/2 Liter, Cavalier, PUG, Pewter Lid, H. Schlitt 220.00
Stein, No. 1526-1272, 1/2 Liter, Nightwatchman, PUG, Pewter Lid 185.00
Stein, No. 1526-599, 1 Liter, Soldier Blowing Trumpet, PUG, Pewter Lid 185.00
Stein, No. 1526-601, 1/2 Liter, Dwarfs, PUG, Pewter Lid 195.00
Stein, No. 1527, 1/2 Liter, Cavaliers Drinking, Etched, Inlaid Lid, C. Warth 357.00
Stein, No. 1530-581, 1/2 Liter, Student Smoking Pipe, PUG, Inlaid Lid 390.00
Stein, No. 1540, 4 Liter, Geometric Design, Mosaic, Inlaid Lid 978.00

Stein, No. 1566, 1/2 Liter, Man, On High-Wheel Bicycle, Etched, Inlaid Lid, Gorig 720.00
Stein, No. 1655, 1/2 Liter, Young People Dancing, Etched, Inlaid Lid ....345.00 to 440.00
Stein, No. 1675, 1/2 Liter, Heidelberg, 1386-1886, Etched, Inlaid Lid 255.00
Stein, No. 1695, 1/2 Liter, Hunters, 4 Panels, Etched, Inlaid Lid ....530.00 to 802.00
Stein, No. 1724, 1/2 Liter, Fireman, Fireman's Hat Inlay, Etched, Inlaid Lid, C.Warth 1957.00
Stein, No. 1725, 1/4 Liter, Man & Woman, Etched, Inlaid Lid 340.00
Stein, No. 1733, 1/2 Liter, Jockey, Jockey's Cap Inlay, Etched, Inlaid Lid, C. Warth 845.00
Stein, No. 1734, 1 1/2 Liter, Lovers, Jeweled Base, Etched, Inlaid Lid, C. Warth 950.00
Stein, No. 1736, 3 Liter, 4 Panels, Man In Each, Inlaid Lid, C. Warth 275.00
Stein, No. 1737, 2 Liter, Hops & Wheat, Relief, Inlaid Lid 290.00
Stein, No. 1742, 1/2 Liter, Gottingen, Etched, Inlaid Lid 660.00
Stein, No. 1745, 1/4 Liter, Leaves & Scroll, Relief, Inlaid Lid 130.00
Stein, No. 1796, 1/2 Liter, Cavalier Drinking, Etched, Inlaid Lid, C. Warth 560.00
Stein, No. 1802, 1/2 Liter, Floral Design, Mosaic, Inlaid Lid 225.00
Stein, No. 1856, 1 Liter, Postman, Eagle On Blue Body, Etched & Glazed, Inlaid Lid 1175.00
Stein, No. 1861, 1/2 Liter, Frederick III, Etched, PUG, Inlaid Lid ....275.00 to 360.00
Stein, No. 1861, 1/2 Liter, Wilhelm I, Etched, PUG, Inlaid Lid 489.00
Stein, No. 1861, 1/2 Liter, Wilhelm II, Etched, PUG, Inlaid Lid 460.00
Stein, No. 1890, 1/2 Liter, Wilhelm I, Wilhelm II, Frederick III, Etched, PUG, Inlaid Lid . 660.00
Stein, No. 1909-1038, 1/2 Liter, Frogs Drinking, PUG, Pewter Lid, Schlitt 575.00
Stein, No. 1909-726, 1/2 Liter, Steins With Legs, Filling At Tap, PUG, Pewter Lid, Schlitt 430.00
Stein, No. 1915, 1/2 Liter, Cologne Cathedral, Etched, PUG, Inlaid Lid, Warth 1955.00
Stein, No. 1932, 1/2 Liter, Cavaliers Drinking, Etched, Inlaid Lid, C. Warth .....403.00 to 605.00
Stein, No. 1934, 1/2 Liter, Military Scenes, Evolution Of Uniform, Etched, Inlaid Lid ... 600.00
Stein, No. 1940, 3 Liter, Keeper Of Wine Cellar, Etched, Inlaid Lid, C. Warth 1086.00
Stein, No. 1947, 1/2 Liter, Man Seated In Vines, Verse, Etched, Inlaid Lid 380.00
Stein, No. 1976, 1/2 Liter, Verse, Etched, Inlaid Lid 270.00
Stein, No. 1998, 1/2 Liter, Trumpeter Of Sackingen, Etched, PUG, Inlaid Lid 460.00
Stein, No. 2001B, 1/2 Liter, Medicine 385.00
Stein, No. 2001C, 1/2 Liter, Scholars, Glazed & Hand Painted, Inlaid Lid 760.00
Stein, No. 2001K, 1/2 Liter, Banking, Glazed & Hand Painted, Inlaid Lid 605.00
Stein, No. 2002, 1 Liter, Munich, Etched, Inlaid Lid ....281.00 to 575.00
Stein, No. 2005, 1/2 Liter, People Having Dinner, Etched, Inlaid Lid, H.D. 440.00
Stein, No. 2015, 5 1/2 Liter, St. George, Slaying Dragon, Glazed Relief, Pewter Lid 805.00
Stein, No. 2018, 1/2 Liter, Pug Dog, Character, Inlaid Lid 740.00
Stein, No. 2024, 1/2 Liter, Berlin, Etched, Glazed, Inlaid Lid ....695.00 to 835.00
Stein, No. 2025, 1/2 Liter, Cherubs Carousing, Etched, Inlaid Lid ....130.00 to 462.00
Stein, No. 2035, 1/3 Liter, Bacchus Carousing, Etched, Inlaid Lid 220.00
Stein, No. 2038, 3 3/4 Liter, Town Of Rodenstein, House & Tower Inlay, Inlaid Lid 3080.00
Stein, No. 2077, 1/2 Liter, Coat Of Arms, Relief, Inlaid Lid 175.00
Stein, No. 2082, 1/2 Liter, William Tell Shoots Apple, Etched, Inlaid Lid 1006.00
Stein, No. 2082, 1/3 Liter, William Tell Shoots Apple, Etched, Inlaid Lid 490.00
Stein, No. 2086, Festive Scene, Relief, Inlaid Lid 155.00
Stein, No. 2089, 1/2 Liter, Winged Barmaid Serving Man, Etched, Inlaid Lid, Schlitt 635.00
Stein, No. 2091, 1/2 Liter, St. Florian Pouring Water On Head, Etched, Inlaid Lid, Schlitt . 460.00
Stein, No. 2093, 1/2 Liter, Cards, Etched, Glazed, Inlaid Lid 920.00
Stein, No. 2095, 2 1/2 Liter, Germans & Romans Drinking, Etched, Inlaid Lid, Schlitt ... 4025.00
Stein, No. 2123, 1/2 Liter, Knight Drinking, Etched, Inlaid Lid, H. Schlitt 750.00
Stein, No. 2126, 5 1/2 Liter, Composers, Pewter Lid, Schultz 3565.00
Stein, No. 2130, 1/2 Liter, Man Drinking, Relief, Inlaid Lid 240.00
Stein, No. 2131, 1/2 Liter, Barroom Characters, Cameo, Inlaid Lid 290.00
Stein, No. 2140-1068, 1/2 Liter, Infantrie Regiment No. 85, PUG, Pewter Lid 690.00
Stein, No. 2140-761, 1/2 Liter, Infantrie Regiment No. 48, PUG, Pewter Lid 750.00
Stein, No. 2140-769, 1/2 Liter, Infantrie Regiment No. 36, PUG, Pewter Lid 748.00
Stein, No. 2140-952, 1/2 Liter, Bicycle Rider, PUG, Pewter Lid 560.00
Stein, No. 2176-1055, 2 Liter, Drunken Man In Beer Cellar, PUG, Pewter Lid 200.00
Stein, No. 2176-954, 2 Liter, Knight Drinking, PUG, Pewter Lid, Schlitt 460.00
Stein, No. 2192, 1/2 Liter, Greek Figures, Party Scene, Etched, Inlaid Lid 345.00
Stein, No. 2204, 1/2 Liter, Prussian Eagle, Decorated, Relief, Inlaid Lid 520.00
Stein, No. 2231, 1/2 Liter, Tavern Scene, Etched, Inlaid Lid 415.00
Stein, No. 2255, 1 Liter, Wedding Scene, Etruscan Style, Etched, Inlaid Lid 880.00
Stein, No. 2277, 1/2 Liter, Nurnberg, Etched, Inlaid Lid 430.00
Stein, No. 2277, 1/3 Liter, Heidelberg, Etched, Inlaid Lid. 275.00

Stein, No. 2278, 1/2 Liter, Sport Scene, Relief, Inlaid Lid. 605.00
Stein, No. 2285, 1/2 Liter, Guitar Player & Young Couple, Etched, Inlaid Lid 330.00
Stein, No. 2373, 1/2 Liter, St. Augustine, Florida, Alligator Handle, Etched, Inlaid Lid . . .   485.00
Stein, No. 2382, 1/2 Liter, Thirsty Rider, Etched, Inlaid Lid, Schlitt 820.00
Stein, No. 2388, 1/2 Liter, Stacked Pretzels, Pretzel Handle, Character, Inlaid Lid 345.00
Stein, No. 2391, 1 Liter, Lohengrin Wedding, Etched, Inlaid Lid 2415.00
Stein, No. 2394, 1/2 Liter, Scenes From Siegfried's Youth, Etched, Inlaid Lid . . . . .550.00 to 880.00
Stein, No. 2402, 1/2 Liter, Courting Of Siegfried, Etched, Inlaid Lid 720.00
Stein, No. 2441, 1/2 Liter, Gamblers Playing Dice, Etched, Inlaid Lid, F. Quidenus 490.00
Stein, No. 2479, 1/2 Liter, Hildebrand, 3 Panels, Cameo, Inlaid Lid, Stahl 750.00
Stein, No. 2488-1106, 4 3/4 Liter, 7 Swabians, PUG, Pewter Lid, H. Schlitt 750.00
Stein, No. 2530, 1 Liter, Boar Hunt Scene, Cameo, Inlaid Lid, Stahl 605.00
Stein, No. 2531, 1/2 Liter, Monk With Jug Of Beer, Etched, Inlaid Lid, F. Quidenus 575.00
Stein, No. 2580, 1/2 Liter, Knight In Castle, Etched, Inlaid Lid, H. Schlitt 805.00
Stein, No. 2581, 1/2 Liter, Musical Scene With Women, Etched, Inlaid Lid, F. Quidenus . .   525.00
Stein, No. 2599, 1 Liter, Shooting Festival Scenes, Inlaid Lid, F. Quidenus 750.00
Stein, No. 2652, 1/2 Liter, Rodenstein, 3 Panels, Cameo, Inlaid Lid 690.00
Stein, No. 2692, 3 Liter, Tavern Scene, Etched, Inlaid Lid 980.00
Stein, No. 2693, 1/2 Liter, Tavern Scene, Etched, Inlaid Lid 575.00
Stein, No. 2701-180, 1/2 Liter, Apple Form, Brown Glaze, Pewter Lid 690.00
Stein, No. 2757, 2 1/3 Liter, Drinking Scenes, Cameo, Inlaid Lid 645.00
Stein, No. 2765, 1/2 Liter, Knight On White Horse, Etched, Inlaid Lid 2185.00
Stein, No. 2776, 1/2 Liter, Keeper Of Wine Cellar, Etched, Inlaid Lid 660.00
Stein, No. 2785-6130, 2 1/5 Liter, Man Playing Bagpipe, Rookwood, Pewter Lid 690.00
Stein, No. 2787-6132, 2 Liter, Man Smoking, Rookwood, Pewter Lid 385.00
Stein, No. 2808, 1/2 Liter, Girl Bowling, Etched, Inlaid Lid 575.00
Stein, No. 2829, 1/2 Liter, Rodenstein, Decorated Relief, Inlaid Lid 2185.00
Stein, No. 2830, 1/2 Liter, Tyrolean Girl, Etched, Inlaid Pewter Lid 1449.00
Stein, No. 2832, 1/2 Liter, Woman Watering Flowers, Etched, Inlaid Lid 425.00
Stein, No. 2833B, 1/2 Liter, Men Sitting Under Tree, Etched, Inlaid Lid 425.00
Stein, No. 2880, 1/2 Liter, Men Eating At Table, Etched, Inlaid Lid 230.00
Stein, No. 2893-1302, 3 1/4 Liter, American Eagle, Flag, PUG, Pewter Lid 605.00
Stein, No. 2921, 1/2 Liter, Hunter Drinking In Front Of Campfire, Etched, Inlaid Lid 523.00
Stein, No. 2957, 1/2 Liter, Bowling Scene, Etched, Inlaid Lid 375.00
Stein, No. 2994, 1/2 Liter, Art Nouveau, Etched, Inlaid Lid 405.00
Stein, No. 3005, 1/2 Liter, Man With Drink, Etched, Pewter Lid 489.00
Stein, No. 3043, 1/2 Liter, Sheild Of Munich, Etched, Glazed, Inlaid Lid . . . . . .1265.00 to 1725.00
Stein, No. 3091, 1/2 Liter, Drinking Knight, Etched, Inlaid Lid, Schlitt 825.00
Stein, No. 3142, 1/2 Liter, Bavarian Scene, Etched, Inlaid Lid, F. Quidenus 460.00
Stein, No. 3143, 1/2 Liter, Tyrolean Scene, Etched, Inlaid Lid, F. Quidenus 865.00
Stein, No. 3144, 1/2 Liter, Black Forest Scene, Etched, Inlaid Lid, F. Quidenus 949.00
Stein, No. 3156, 1/2 Liter, Chicago, 3 Buildings, Etched, Inlaid Lid 5060.00
Stein, No. 3173, 1/2 Liter, Man, Woman, Etched, Inlaid Lid, L. Hohlwein 920.00
Stein, No. 3177, 2 1/5 Liter, Hunting Scenes, Cameo, Inlaid Lid, Stahl 2185.00
Stein, No. 3188, 1/2 Liter, Man In Checkered Coat, Etched, Glazed, F. Ringer 485.00
Stein, No. 3249, 1/2 Liter, Hikers At Table, Etched, Inlaid Lid 430.00
Stein, No. 3250, 1/2 Liter, People Eating, Etched, Inlaid Lid 520.00
Stein, No. 3252, 1/2 Liter, Couple Drinking, Etched, Inlaid Lid 605.00
Stein, No. 3507, 1/2 Liter, Munich Child, Relief, Pewter Lid, Wekara 690.00
Stein, No. 5001, 4 1/2 Liter, Coat Of Arms, Faience, Pewter Lid 865.00
Stein, No. 5005, 1/2 Liter, Man Smoking At Table, Faience, Pewter Lid 432.00
Stein, No. 5014, 1/4 Liter, Flowers, Faience, Pewter Lid 305.00
Stein, No. 5393, 1 Liter, Diana The Huntress, Faience, Pewter Lid 679.00
Tea Set, Stylized Tree Design, Marked, 8 1/2-In. Teapot, 3 Piece 460.00
Teapot, No. 2946, Art Nouveau, Etched, 6 In. 145.00
Tray, No. 2960, Art Nouveau, Etched, 15 In. 362.00
Vase, No. 1462, Women, 4 Panels, 13 In. 485.00
Vase, No. 1591, Boy, 4 Scenes, Etched, 13 In. 485.00
Vase, No. 2253, People Dancing, Musicians, Etruscan, Etched, 12 1/2 In. 430.00
Vase, No. 2299, Children, 4 Panels, Etched, Relief, 11 1/2 In. 460.00
Vase, No. 2328, Women & Cherub, Etruscan, Etched, 13 1/2 In. 489.00
Vase, No. 2422, Art Nouveau, Flowers, 13 In. 1430.00
Vase, No. 2435, Art Nouveau, Flowers, Etched, 4 In. 635.00

Vase, No. 2462, Art Nouveau, Flowers, Etched, 4 1/2 In. 805.00
Vase, No. 2605, Art Nouveau, Clovers, Etched, 3 Handles, 4 3/4 In. 375.00
Vase, No. 2706-6113, Man Smoking While Reading, Rookwood, 12 In. 600.00
Vase, No. 2706-6114, Woman Playing Violin, Rookwood, 12 1/2 In. 1090.00
Vase, No. 2868, Geometric Design, Mosaic, 9 In. 485.00
Vase, No. 2976, Art Nouveau, Flowers, Etched, 14 1/2 In. 835.00
Vase, No. 3060, Repeating Flowers, Transfer, Enameled, 9 1/2 In. 259.00
Vase, No. 3264, Woman, Cameo, Stahl, 7 1/2 In. 290.00

MILK GLASS was named for its milky white color. It was first made in
England during the 1700s. The height of its popularity in the United
States was from 1870 to 1880. It is now correct to refer to some colored glass as blue milk glass, black milk glass, etc. Reproductions of
milk glass are being made and sold in many stores. Related pieces may
be listed in the Cosmos and Westmoreland categories.

Bowl, Tree Of Life, Yellow & Red Blossoms, 3 Panels, Footed, 6 x 5 In. 325.00
Compote, Raised Diamond, Yellow, Wafered Stem, 6 1/8 In. 180.00
Cracker Jar, Roses, Silver Plated Mountings, Canada, Mid 1900s, 6 3/4 x 6 In. 25.00
Cracker Jar, Roses, Silver Plated Rim, Handle, Fig Finial, 10 x 5 1/4 In. 100.00
Dish, Swan Cover, Basket Base, Lattice Edge, 19 In. 56.00
Pitcher, Milk, Hobnail, 18 Oz. 12.00
Plate, Looped Edge, c.1890, 8 3/8 In. 25.00
Vase, Swirl Pattern, Footed, 3-Piece Mold, 9 1/4 x 5 In. 15.00
Vase, Yellow Enameled Ducks In Flight, Cattails, 4 Sides, 8 In. 30.00

MILLEFIORI means, literally, a thousand flowers. Many small pieces of
glass resembling flowers are grouped together to form a design. It is a
type of glasswork popular in paperweights and some are listed in that
category.

Cruet, Satin Handle & Stopper, 7 1/2 In. 100.00
Ink Bottle, Rose, White, Blue, Mushroom Stopper, England, 5 1/2 In. 490.00
Lampshade, Acorn Shape, Pink, Ruby & White Florets, Cobalt Blue Ground, 6 1/2 In. . . . 140.00

MINTON china has been made in the Staffordshire region of England
from 1793 to the present. The firm became part of the Royal Doulton
Tableware Group in 1968, but the wares continued to be marked
Minton. The word *England* was added in 1891. Minton majolica is
listed in this book in the Majolica category.

Basket, 3 Putti Holding Turquoise & White Basket, Footed, c.1860, 11 1/2 In., Pair 3885.00
Butter Chip, Lorraine 38.00
Canteen, Black, White Figures, 3 Children, Gold Enamel, Pate-Sur-Pate, Signed, 6 In. . . . 1785.00
Cup & Saucer, Gilt Flower Sprays, Twisted, Fluted, 8 Piece 145.00
Cup & Saucer, Vine Pattern, Blue & White 29.00
Dessert Set, Centerpiece, Tazza Pair, Celadon Ground, Orchids, c.1875, 14 Piece 6870.00
Dinner Set, Armorial, Louis XVI Style, Blue Border, Boy Carrying Yoke, 22 Piece 1610.00
Figurine, Ariadne & Panther, c.1865, 14 1/4 x 11 1/2 In. 1150.00
Figurine, Babes In The Woods, 2 Children Sleeping, Bird Looks On, Parian, 1849, 12 In. . . 765.00
Figurine, Solitude, Seminude Woman, Seated On Rocky Base, Parian, c.1852, 19 3/4 In. . . 705.00
Figurine, Una & Lion, Nude Woman, Seated On Lion, Parian, 1851, 13 3/4 In. 2468.00
Flask, Stylized Flowers, Leaves, Turquoise Ground, 7 3/4 In. 9560.00
Plate, African Man & Leopard, Signed, c.1860, 9 In. 325.00
Plate, Birds, Tulip Border, Pierced, Gold Beading, Aqua Border, Mark, 1855, 9 1/2 In. . . . 165.00
Plate, Cobalt Blue, Gilt Border, 10 1/2 In., 12 Piece 1725.00
Plate, Dessert, Diamond, 9 1/2 In. 720.00
Plate, Ripon, Pink, Turquoise, 7 3/4 In. 30.00
Plate, Yellow Daisies, Brown Butterfly, White, Gold Accents, Pink Border, 1870, 9 In. . . . 145.00
Plate Set, Portraits, Names On Reverse, Signed, 9 In., 4 Piece 345.00
Saucer, Ripon, Pink, Turquoise 10.00
Tile, Aestas, Goddess Figure, Classical Bands, Corner Urns, Turquoise Glaze, 8 In. 230.00
Tile, Cupids, Studio, Marked, 8 x 8 In., 5 Piece 598.00
Tile, Flowers In Vase, Vines, Black, Cream, Marked, Hollins & Co., 5 7/8 In. 215.00
Tureen, Soup, Flow Blue 880.00
Urn, Blue Ground, Parcel Gilt, Pate-Sur-Pate, Handled, Signed L. Solon 9000.00

Urn, Cover, Blue Ground, Parcel Gilt, Handled, Bulbous, M.L. Solon, c.1900, 14 1/2 In. . 8500.00
Vase, Basket, Gilt Dots, Circles, Cobalt Ground, 2 Scrolled Leaf Handles, 8 In., Pair 2703.00
Vase, Bird, Irises, Painted, Japanese Style, Flattened Sphere, Sheave Handles, 13 1/2 In. .. 4269.00
Vase, Flask, Cloisonne Flowers, Dragonheads, Turquoise, Gilt, Loop Handles, 10 1/2 In. . 4269.00
Vase, Pinecones, Yellow Stylized Leaves, Green & Blue Vines, 9 1/2 In. 173.00

MIRRORS are listed in the Furniture category under Mirror.

MOCHA pottery is an English-made product that was sold in America during the early 1800s. It is a heavy pottery with pale coffee-and-cream coloring. Designs of blue, brown, green, orange, black, or white were added to the pottery and given fanciful names, such as *Tree*, *Snail Trail*, or *Moss*. Mocha designs are sometimes found in pearlware. A few pieces of mocha ware were made in France, the United States, and other countries.

Bowl, Balloon, Burnt Orange, Brown Rim, White, 2-Tone Brown, 6 3/8 x 3 In. 7040.00
Bowl, Cat's-Eye, Wide Band, 3 Narrow Blue Bands, London Shape, Pearlware, 9 x 4 In. . 536.00
Bowl, Diaper, Green, Olive, Rust Bands, Creamware, 10 In. .... *Illus* 1150.00
Bowl, Earthworm, Glazed Bands, Looping, London Shape, 5 3/8 x 7 3/8 In. 410.00
Bowl, Earthworm, Hemispherical, Bands, Looping Design, 4 1/2 x 10 1/4 In. 940.00
Bowl, Earthworm, Wide Taupe Band, London Shape, c.1830, 3 1/4 x 6 5/8 In. 410.00
Bowl, Mottled Brown, Gold & Green Rim, Circular Foot, 7 1/4 In. 1265.00
Bowl, Seaweed, Mustard Ground, 3 1/2 In. 175.00
Bowl, Zigzag, Brown, Opaque White & Blue, Blue Band, Flared Edge, 4 1/4 x 8 1/4 In. ... 525.00
Creamer, Balloons, Pink, Black, White, Green & Blue Bands, Black Stripes, 5 In. 440.00
Creamer, Cat's-Eye, Gray Bands, White, Tan, Tooled Stripes, Leaf Handle, 4 1/2 In. 990.00
Creamer, Tooled Stripes, Dark Brown, Burnt Orange, Molded Leaf Handle, 4 In. 1540.00
Cup, Feather, Light, Dark Brown, 2 1/2 In. 4830.00
Cup & Saucer, Marbled Ocher, Green, Brown, France, c.1820 .... *Illus* 405.00
Jug, Bands, Barrel Shape, Black Slip, c.1830, 6 3/4 In. 355.00
Jug, Blue Rim Band, Marbled Slip, Tan Field, Handle, Pearlware, Early 1800s, 6 In. 3290.00
Jug, Dendritic Design, Barrel Shape, Bands, Mustard Field, 6 3/4 In. 1116.00
Jug, Earthworm, Bands, Barrel Form, Blue, Black, White, Ocher Field, 7 1/2 In. 1880.00
Jug, Earthworm, Bands, Looping Earthworm Pattern, Baluster Shape, c.1820, 7 In. 4115.00
Jug, Earthworm, Barrel Shape, Bands, Looping, Handle, c.1835, 8 In. 3055.00
Jug, Earthworm, Barrel Shape, Bands, White Looping, c.1835, 9 In. 880.00
Jug, Geometrics, Reeded Rim Band, Extruded Handle, Early 1800s, 3 5/8 In. 999.00
Jug, Looped Cable, 3 Bands, Orange Ground, Brown & Green Raised Borders, 8 In. 5280.00
Mixing Bowl, Seaweed, Blue, 6 1/4 x 13 1/4 In. 330.00
Mug, Bands, Black, Ocher, Blue, White Slip Circles, Pearlware, c.1820, 4 3/4 In. ... *Illus* 2990.00
Mug, Bands, Black, Rust, Blue, Vertical Diamonds, c.1800, 5 7/8 In. .... *Illus* 3450.00
Mug, Bands, Brown, Green Ribbing, Handle, 5 In. 230.00
Mug, Bands, Glazed Rouletted 4-Bead Pattern, Extruded Handle, c.1830, 4 3/4 In. 235.00
Mug, Brown, Light Blue Rim Band, Cream Marbled Slip Field, Pearlware, 5 3/8 In. 765.00
Mug, Cat's-Eye, Bands, Earthworm, Handle, c.1830, Qt., 5 3/4 In. 3525.00
Mug, Cat's-Eye, Bands, White Diamond Dots, Extruded Handle, Qt., 5 7/8 In. 2820.00
Mug, Cat's-Eye, Blue, Tan Bands 5750.00
Mug, Combed, Marbled Slip, White Field, Pearlware, Early 19th Century, 5 7/8 In. 206.00
Mug, Dendritic Bands, Extruded Handle, 19th Century, 4 7/8 In. 176.00
Mug, Earthworm, Bands, Looping Pattern, Extruded Handle, 4 3/8 In. 3408.00
Mug, Earthworm, Tan, Black, Brown, White, Blue Ground, 6 1/4 In. 4125.00
Mug, Marbled, Pink, Blue, Black, Footed, Pearlware, 3 1/2 In. 355.00
Mug, Marbleized, Brown & Green, Tapered Sides, 3 3/4 In. 85.00
Mug, Seaweed, Beige Ground, c.1870, Qt., 6 In. 300.00
Mug, Seaweed, Black, Brown Ground, 3 3/4 In. 535.00
Mug, Seaweed, Blue Band, 2 Black Bands Top & Bottom, Tavern Measure Mark, 4 In. 190.00
Mug, Seaweed, Blue Black, Gray Band, Blue Roulette Band At Top, 5 In. 345.00
Mug, Seaweed, Dark Brown Stripes, Blue Band, Gray Band, Leaf Molded Handle, 6 In. .. 440.00
Mug, Seaweed, White Band, Blue Stripes, 3 1/4 In. 468.00
Mug, Vertical Combing, Brown & Black Slip, Pearlware, c.1790, 6 1/4 In. .... *Illus* 3335.00
Mug, White Wavy Lines, Black Stripes, Tan Bands, Leaf-Molded Handle, 4 5/8 In. 550.00
Mustard, Cover, Seaweed, Orange, Black, Green, Barrel, Pearlware, c.1810, 4 In. .... *Illus* 575.00
Pepper Pot, Bands, Burnt Orange, Tooled Design, Brown, Green, 4 1/8 In. 1430.00
Pepper Pot, Cat's-Eye, Black & Gray Bands, Rust, White, Pearlware, c.1830, 5 In. . *Illus* 1380.00

Mocha, Mustard, Cover, Seaweed, Orange, Black, Green, Barrel, Pearlware, c.1810, 4 In.
Mocha, Bowl, Diaper, Green, Olive, Rust Bands, Creamware, 10 In.
Mocha, Cup & Saucer, Marbled Ocher, Green, Brown, France, c.1820
Mocha, Mug, Vertical Combing, Brown & Black Slip, Pearlware, c.1790, 6 1/4 In.
Mocha, Mug, Bands, Black, Ocher, Blue, White Slip Circles, Pearlware, c.1820, 4 3/4 In.
Mocha, Mug, Bands, Black, Rust, Blue, Vertical Diamonds, c.1800, 5 7/8 In.
Mocha, Pepper Pot, Cat's-Eye, Black & Gray Bands, Rust, White, Pearlware, c.1830, 5 In.

Pepper Pot, Cat's-Eye, Blue Bands, Burnt Orange Stripes, Bulbous, 4 3/4 In.	1045.00
Pepper Pot, Cat's-Eye, Blue, Orange & Brown Stripes, Footed, 4 1/2 In.	995.00
Pepper Pot, Cat's-Eye, Tan, Slate Blue Band, Brown Stripes, White, Brown, 5 1/4 In. . . .	1320.00
Pepper Pot, Seaweed, Brown Band, Slate Blue Stripes, Blue, White, Orange, 4 1/2 In. . . .	1650.00
Pepper Pot, Seaweed, Brown, Blue, Shading To Yellow Bands, 4 1/4 In.	1430.00
Pitcher, Bands, Blue & Black, White Ground, 3 1/2 In.	45.00
Pitcher, Bands, White & Cinnamon, Black Herringbone, Blue Stripes, 4 1/2 In.	575.00
Pitcher, Cat's-Eye, Earthworm, Brown Bands, Thin Blue & Black Bands, 1800s, 6 In. . . .	1095.00
Pitcher, Cat's-Eye, Earthworm, White Band, Blue Band, White Band, 7 1/2 In.	1150.00
Pitcher, Cat's-Eye, Rust, Blue Bands, 2 Engine-Turned Bands, 9 In.	1265.00
Pitcher, Checkered Band, Blue Ground, Bulbous, 2 1/2 In.	523.00
Pitcher, Earthworm, Blue Ground, Gray Bands, Black Stripes, Leaf Handle, 5 In.	330.00
Pitcher, Earthworm, Tan Band, Brown Stripes, Blue, White, Brown, 4 3/4 In.	495.00
Pitcher, Looped Cable, Double, Brown, Opaque White, Blue, Bulbous, 6 1/2 In.	580.00
Pitcher, Seaweed, Black, Aqua, Black & Brown Bands, 10 5/8 In.	5775.00
Pitcher, Seaweed, Blue, Black, Moss Green, C-Shaped Handle, 6 In.	370.00
Pitcher, Variegated Dot, Blue, Black & Cream, Orange Ground, 6 3/4 In.	2760.00
Pitcher, Wide Green Band, White Tulips, Stripe, Wavy Lines, Dots, Leaf Handle, 8 In. . . .	3355.00
Pitcher, Zigzag, Blue, Brown, Clay, Barrel Shape, 4 3/4 In.	990.00
Platter, Combware, Harwood, England, c.1860, 16 x 14 In.	495.00
Salt, Footed, Burnt Orange Band, Brown Stripes, Slate Blue, 3 x 2 In.	1925.00
Salt, Seaweed, Blue, White Band, Footed, East Liverpool, Ohio, 3 x 2 1/4 In.	550.00
Shaker, Pepper, Seaweed, Blue & White Bands, East Liverpool, Ohio, 5 In.	1400.00
Sugar, Cover, Seaweed, Black, Green Band, Yellow Ground, 5 In.	2420.00
Sugar, Cover, Seaweed, Blue, Yellowware, 4 In.	470.00
Tankard, Bands, 2 Narrow Blue, 1 Wide Brown, c.1810, 6 1/4 In.	230.00
Urn, Seaweed, Blue, Wide Tan & Thin Brown Horizontal Bands, 2 Handles, 7 In.	805.00
Waste Bowl, Earthworm, Brown, White, Ocher, Gray Band, 4 1/2 x 2 3/4 In.	605.00
Waste Bowl, Earthworm, White & Brown, Blue Ground, 5 x 2 1/2 In.	330.00

MONT JOYE, see Mt. Joye category.

MOORCROFT pottery was first made in Burslem, England, in 1913.
William Moorcroft had managed the art pottery department for James
Macintyre & Company of England from 1898 to 1913. The Moorcroft
pottery continues today, although William Moorcroft died in 1945. The
earlier wares are similar to the modern ones, but color and marking
will help indicate the age.

Bowl, Anemone, Flowers, Leaves, Cobalt Blue, Magenta, 1920, 2 1/4 x 9 3/4 In.	303.00
Bowl, Cover, Clematis, Green & Blue Glazes, Mark, 1928-1949, 4 1/2 x 6 1/2 In.	201.00
Bowl, Hibiscus, Red, Green Ground, 5 3/4 In.	144.00
Bowl, Pomegranate, Blue Ground, Mark, 1918-1926, 3 1/4 x 8 1/4 In.	575.00

Box, Flowers, Leaves, Fuchsia, Sage Green, Blue Glaze Ground, Signed, 4 x 1 1/2 In. . . . 100.00
Compote, Pansies, Tudric Pedestal, Pewter Base, Hammered, 5 1/4 In. 230.00
Jar, Cover, Spring Flower, Yellow, Magenta, Gray Ground, 4 3/4 x 3 1/2 In. 360.00
Pitcher, Anemone, Flowers, Leaves, Magenta, Cobalt Blue Ground, 1945, 5 3/4 x 7 In. . . 330.00
Pitcher, Spring Flowers, Yellow, Magenta, Teal Green Ground, 1920, 6 x 6 In. 360.00
Tazza, Flowers, Round, Pewter Base, c.1910, 3 1/4 x 6 7/8 In. 206.00
Vase, Anemone, Flowers Repeating, Leaves, Violet, Cobalt Blue, 7 1/4 x 4 3/4 In. 495.00
Vase, Anemone, Flowers, Leaves, Magenta, Cobalt Blue Ground, 5 1/4 x 5 1/4 In. 415.00
Vase, Anemone, Flowers, Leaves, Magenta, Cobalt Blue Ground, 5 x 4 1/2 In. 385.00
Vase, Birds & Fruit, Multicolored High Glaze, Shoulder Handles, Signed, 13 In. 865.00
Vase, Blackberry, Leaves, Magenta, Cobalt Blue Glaze, c.1930, 4 1/2 x 3 1/2 In. 415.00
Vase, Cattails, Yellow, Blue, Brown, 9 1/2 In. 175.00
Vase, Clematis, Flowers, Leaves, Magenta, Cobalt Blue Glaze, Spherical, 8 1/4 x 5 In. . . . 525.00
Vase, Finches, Fruit, Stamped Mark, 8 In. 635.00
Vase, Grapes, Leaves, Multicolored, Blue, Green Ground, 1928, 4 1/4 In. 265.00
Vase, Hibiscus, Blue Ground, 12 In. 546.00
Vase, Hibiscus, Green, c.1960, 4 1/4 In. 235.00
Vase, Leaf & Fruit, Green Ground, Coupe Shape, Mark, 1928-1949, 7 1/2 In. 635.00
Vase, Leaves & Berries, Multicolored, Blue Ground, 12 1/2 In. 635.00
Vase, Lemons, Bird, Ivory Ground, 10 In. 23.00
Vase, Orchid, Flowers, Magenta, Green, Cobalt Blue Ground, 5 x 4 1/2 In. 495.00
Vase, Orchid, Hand Decorated Flowers, Cobalt Blue Ground, 4 In. 355.00
Vase, Orchid, Leaves, Multicolored, Blue, Green Ground, Bulbous, c.1949, 6 3/4 In. 264.00
Vase, Oxblood Glaze, Ring Neck, Bottle Shape, B. Moore, 18 1/2 x 6 1/2 In. 1116.00
Vase, Pansy, Leaves, Multicolored, Oval, 10 In. 590.00
Vase, Peacock Feathers, Blue, Tan, 8 1/2 In. 175.00
Vase, Pomegranate, Flared Rim, Impressed Mark, c.1916, 10 1/2 In. . . . . .890.00 to 1035.00
Vase, Pomegranate, Hand Decorated, Soft Tones, Cobalt Blue Interior, 3 1/3 In. 410.00
Vase, Poppy, Red, Flambe Glaze, Bulbous, 1928-1949, 12 1/2 x 6 3/4 In. 2530.00
Vase, Raised Flowers, Blue Drip Glaze, Impressed Mark, 7 In., Pair 200.00

MORGANTOWN GLASS WORKS operated in Morgantown, West Virginia, from 1900 to 1974. Some of their wares are marked with an adhesive label that says *Old Morgantown Glass.*

Adam, Goblet, 6 In. 17.00
Adam, Sherbet, 4 1/2 In. 13.00
Bramble Rose, Goblet, 6 In. 20.00
Crinkle, Finger Bowl, Topaz 16.00
Crinkle, Tumbler, Iced Tea, Amethyst, Footed, 13 Oz. 16.00
Crinkle, Tumbler, Water, Amethyst, 10 Oz. 11.00
El Mexicano, Jug, Ice LMX Line 185.00
Filament, Cocktail, Red, 3 1/2 Oz. 50.00
Filament, Goblet, Red, 10 Oz. 70.00
Golf Ball, Cocktail, Blue, 3 1/2 Oz., 4 1/2 In. 45.00
Golf Ball, Compote, Celeste Cover, Spanish Red, 9 In. 425.00
Mayfair, Cordial, 1 Oz. 35.00
Mayfair, Tumbler, Footed, 5 Oz. . . . . .18.00 to 25.00
Patriat, Goblet, Ruby, 7 Oz. 13.00
Patriat, Tumbler, Iced Tea, Ruby, 14 Oz. 14.00
Priscilla, Tumbler, Footed, Gold Band, 5 1/2 In. 20.00
Queen Anne, Cordial 60.00
Queen Anne, Wine 40.00
Rooster, Cocktail, Light Brown, 3 1/2 In. 33.00
Spanish Red, Wine, 3 Oz., 4 3/4 In. 55.00

MORIAGE is a special type of raised decoration used on some Japanese pottery. Sometimes pieces of clay were shaped by hand and applied to the item; sometimes the clay was squeezed from a tube in the way we apply cake frosting. One type of moriage is called *Dragonware* and is listed under that name.

Bowl, Deer Scene Interior, Maple Leaves Exterior, 3 Trim Handles, Mark, Nippon, 7 In. . . 70.00
Bowl, Purple Violets, Melon Shape, Nippon Mark, 4 1/2 x 6 In. 180.00
Coffeepot, Orchids, Leaves, Light Green Ground, Nippon, 8 1/2 In. 195.00

Dish, Nile Scene, Trim, Scalloped, Green Mark, Nippon 95.00
Ewer, Flowers, Overall Blue Enamel Beading, Green Ground, Nippon 138.00
Ewer, Man & Cane, Woman With Fan, Burgundy Ground, Trim, Leaf Mark, Nippon, 6 In. 275.00
Ewer, Orchids, Lime Green Ground, Lip, Handle, Trim, 5 In. 85.00
Mug, Landscape, Mission, Blue Leaf Mark, Nippon 248.00
Tea Set, Flowers, Purple, Light Green Ground, Nippon, 3 Piece 165.00
Tray, Flower Ovals, Green, White, Handle, 9 1/4 x 5 1/4 In. 95.00
Vase, 4 Painted Flower Panels, 2 Handles, Nippon, 7 In. 430.00
Vase, Eagle, Tapestry Ground, Enameled Swags, 3 Handles, Footed, Nippon, 12 1/2 In. ... 248.00
Vase, Magenta Ground, Nippon, 8 1/2 In. 750.00
Vase, Poppies, Nippon, 7 3/4 In. 440.00
Vase, Roses, Bamboo, Blue Maple Leaf Mark, Nippon, 7 In. 250.00
Vase, Roses, Leaves, Green Ground, Blue Maple-Leaf Mark, Nippon, 6 1/4 In. 360.00
Vase, Sunflower, Cobalt At Top, Nippon, 7 In. 195.00
Vase, Sunflowers, Cobalt Trim, Handles, Nippon, 7 In. 330.00

MOSAIC TILE COMPANY of Zanesville, Ohio, was started by Karl
Langerbeck and Herman Mueller in 1894. Many types of plain and
ornamental tiles were made until 1959. The company closed in 1967.
The company also made some ashtrays, bookends, and related giftwares. Most pieces are marked with the entwined *MTC* monogram.

Box, Turtle Shape, Cover, White, Impressed, 1 1/2 x 4 1/2 In. 80.00
Figurine, Bear, Dark Green Matte Glaze, White Accents, 10 In. 115.00
Figurine, Dog, Reclining, Tan Matte Glaze, White Accents, 11 In. 45.00
Paperweight, Globe, Green, Logo On Base, 4 1/4 In. 35.00
Tile, Artist & Easel, Pink, Brown, Tan, Gray Ground, Marked, Frame, 4 In. 195.00
Tile, Bird With Worm, Black, Turquoise Ground, Raised, Frame, 4 In. 195.00
Tile, Flower, Hearts, Yellow, Green, Aqua Border, Marked, Frame, 6 In. 55.00
Tile, Frog, White, Teal Ground, Ocher Band, Frame, 4 In. 138.00
Tile, Little Bo Peep, Marked, 6 In. 250.00
Tile, Lobster, Gray, Red Ground, Ocher Band, Frame, 4 In. 99.00
Tile, Turkey, Red, Gray, Black, Beige Ground, Frame, 4 In. 140.00
Tile, Viking Ship, White Sail, Blue Green Ground, Frame, 6 In. 345.00

MOSER glass is made by Ludwig Moser und Sohne, a Bohemian
(Czech) glasshouse founded in 1857. Art Nouveau-type glassware and
iridescent glassware were made. The most famous Moser glass is dec-
orated with heavy enameling in gold and bright colors. The firm,
Moser Glassworks, is still working in Karlsbad, West Czech Republic.
Few pieces of Moser glass are marked.

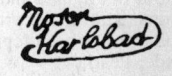

Basket, Brown, Opaline, Butterfly, Pink & Blue Flowers, Gold Trim, Handle 280.00
Bowl, Amber, Applied Blue Button Prunts, White Enameled Flowers, Dentil Edge, 9 In. ... 40.00
Box, Bird In Oval Medallion On Cover, Cobalt Blue, Snow Branches, 4 In. 756.00
Card Holder, Dark Cranberry, Gold Border, Pedestal, 4 In. 200.00
Cup, Cranberry, Gold Coralene Flowers, Blue & White Highlights, Applied Handle, 3 In. .. 280.00
Cup, Emerald Green Shading To Clear, Applied Fluted Gold Handle, 6 Piece 210.00
Decanter, Green, 6 Panels, Gold Design On Top & Bottom, Elongated, 12 In. 280.00
Dresser Box, Green Amber, Enameled Flowers, White Trim, 2 1/4 x 4 In. 115.00
Flagon, Lavender To Crystal, Engraved Poppies, Silver Plated Cap & Handle, 11 In. 225.00
Match Holder, Amethyst To Clear, Engraved Jonquils, 2 3/4 In. 60.00
Perfume Bottle, Cranberry, Gold & White Scrolls, Gold Handles, 3 Ball Feet, 4 1/2 In. ... 365.00
Plate, Light Blue, Gold Enameled Flowers, 8 3/4 In. 50.00
Rose Bowl, Enameled, Cranberry, Flowers, Butterfly, Acorns, c.1900, 3 1/2 In. 750.00
Tankard, Enameled, Emerald To Clear, Silvered, Gold Scrolled Flowers, c.1910, 12 In. .. 403.00
Tumbler, Cranberry, Enameled Oak Leaves, Gold Branches, 4 Acorn Prunts, 4 In. 392.00
Vase, Amber, Applied Blue Rim & Drips, Enameled Flowers, Metal Base, 6 In., Pair 325.00
Vase, Amethyst Ribs, Enameled Pansies, Sponged Gold Rim, 14 In. 748.00
Vase, Amethyst To Clear, Bow & Flowers, Signed, 7 1/2 In. 80.00
Vase, Amethyst, Gold Cameo Band, Engraved, Roman Warrior, 11 1/4 In. 575.00
Vase, Blue Alexandrite, Horizontal Waves, Pedestal Foot, Signed, 10 1/2 In. 690.00
Vase, Bud, Amethyst To Clear, Enameled Bow & Flowers, Signed, 9 In. 225.00
Vase, Citrine Cut To Clear, Engraved Flowers, Signed, 14 In. 420.00
Vase, Cranberry, Enameled Flowers, Rolled Rim, Clear Applied Feet, 4 Tassels, 7 In. 112.00

Vase, Cranberry, Enameled White, Blue, Amber & Lavender, Ferns, Insects, Acorns, 9 In. . .	2240.00
Vase, Cranberry, White Enameled Cupid, Gold, Pillow Shape, Footed, 8 In.	900.00
Vase, Enameled, Cranberry, Ferns, Cornucopia Shape, Pedestal Foot, c.1900, 12 1/4 In. . . .	1495.00
Vase, Gemel, Light Amethyst, Gold, 5 In.	250.00
Vase, Gold Enameled, 4 Columns, 5 1/2 In.	25.00
Vase, Green, Cut With Flowers, Flared, Cameo, Signed, 8 In.	529.00
Vase, Pigeon Blood, Applied Fish & Drips, Enameled Flowers, 6 3/4 In.	375.00
Vase, Ruby, Enameled Pink & Blue Flowers, Gold Highlights, 8 Panels, 8 1/4 In.	160.00
Vase, Shaded Purple To Clear, Flowers, Cylindrical, Signed, 15 In.	411.00
Vase, Stick, Intaglio Jonquils, Green Cut To Clear, 14 In.	350.00
Wine, Dark Cranberry, Gold Flowers, 8 In.	170.00
Wine, Green To Clear, Enameled Feather Design, Cone Foot, 6 1/2 In.	100.00
Wine, Marigold Color, Enameled Daisy, 7 3/4 In.	50.00
Wine, Olive Green, Gold Enameled, Leaf & Grapevine, 5 3/4 In.	30.00

MOSS ROSE china was made by many firms from 1808 to 1900. It has a typical moss rose pictured as the design. The plant is not as popular now as it was in Victorian gardens, so the fuzz-covered bud is unfamiliar to most collectors. The dishes were usually decorated with pink and green flowers.

Bowl, Vegetable, Cover, Gold Trim, Ironstone	85.00
Bowl, Vegetable, Pompadour Shape, Johann Haviland, Germany, 8 1/2 x 3 In.	32.00
Coffee Set, Haviland, 10 3/4-In. Coffeepot, 3 Piece	120.00
Cup, Luster Ware, Gold Trim, 2 1/2 x 3 3/4 In.	3.00
Cup & Saucer, Demitasse, 1 3/4 x 2 1/8 & 4 1/4 In.	6.50
Cup & Saucer, Gold Trim, Large Rose Front, Small Rose Back, 2 1/4 x 3 1/2 & 5 1/2 In. . .	6.50
Cup & Saucer, Luster Ware, Pearlized, Gold Trim, Japan, 2 1/2 x 3 3/4 & 5 3/4 In.	5.50
Cup & Saucer, Pompadour Shape, Johann Haviland, Germany, 3 x 3 & 6 1/4 In.	25.00
Plate, Luster Ware, Pearlized Finish, Gold Trim, Japan, 10 1/2 In.	7.50
Platter, Transfer Pattern, Hand Tinted, Ironstone, 1890s, 13 1/2 In.	35.00
Serving Set, 2 Platters, 2 Bowls, Haviland	120.00
Sugar, Cover, Luster Ware, Pearlized, Gold Trim, Japan, 3 1/2 x 6 In.	9.50
Tureen, Homer Laughlin, 11 x 7 1/8 In.	59.00

MOTHER-OF-PEARL GLASS, or pearl satin glass, was first made in the 1850s in England and in Massachusetts. It was a special type of mold-blown satin glass with air bubbles in the glass, giving it a pearlized color. It has been reproduced. Mother-of-pearl shell objects are listed under Pearl.

Basket, Herringbone, Blue Satin, Satin Handle, Wishbone Feet, 5 1/4 In.	35.00
Basket, Herringbone, Pink, Ruffled Edge, Applied Handle, 7 3/4 In.	405.00
Bonbon, Diamond-Quilted, Rainbow, Triangular, Ruffled, 3-Footed, 4 1/2 In.	896.00
Bowl, Coin Spot, Blue, Cased, 2 3/4 x 4 1/2 In.	69.00
Bowl, Diamond-Quilted, Caramel, Satin Ruffled Edge, 3 3/4 x 9 In.	336.00
Bowl, Diamond-Quilted, Rose Satin, Rainbow, 3 3/4 x 4 In.	1095.00
Bowl, Herringbone, Rose, Cased, Pink Satin, 3 1/2 In.	65.00
Bowl, Inverted Thumbprint, Red Satin, Ruffled Edge, 4 x 8 1/2 In.	259.00
Celery Vase, Herringbone, Blue, Cased, 19th Century, 5 In.	175.00
Cruet, Diamond-Quilted, Blue, Squat, Satin Handle & Stopper, 6 In.	500.00
Cruet, Diamond-Quilted, Pink, Satin Handle, Thorn Stopper, 7 1/2 In.	785.00
Finger Bowl, Underplate, Diamond-Quilted, 3 x 6 1/2 In.	980.00
Pitcher, Coin Spot, Shaded Rose To Pink, Applied Handle, 8 1/2 In.	400.00
Pitcher, Diamond-Quilted, Yellow, Satin, Clear Satin Reeded Handle, 7 1/4 In.	375.00
Pitcher & Tumbler Set, Diamond-Quilted, 5 Piece	600.00
Rose Bowl, Herringbone, Shaded Blue, 6-Crimp Edge, 3 1/2 x 4 3/4 In.	150.00
Salad Set, Gold Bowl, Gold Utensil Handles, 4 1/2 x 9 1/2 In., 3 Piece	545.00
Shade, Diamond-Quilted, Pink Satin, 6 In.	1800.00
Shade, Drape, Apricot Satin, 6 In.	300.00
Sugar & Creamer, Diamond-Quilted, Pink, 4 1/2 x 4 1/2 In.	345.00
Tumbler, Diamond-Quilted, Yellow, Satin, 3 7/8 In.	120.00
Vase, Coin Spot, Amber To White, Gold, Bird, Flowering Branches, 6 In.	80.00
Vase, Diamond-Quilted, Blue Satin, Satin Snakes Entwined At Neck, 7 In., Pair	250.00
Vase, Diamond-Quilted, Blue, Applied Enameled Stems, 19th Century, 7 In.	490.00

Vase, Diamond-Quilted, Yellow Satin, White Lining, 7 In., Pair 90.00
Vase, Diamond-Quilted, Yellow, Cased, 9 1/2 In. 70.00
Vase, Diamond-Quilted, Yellow, Cased, Handles, 19th Century, 9 1/2 In. 290.00
Vase, Diamond-Quilted, Yellow, Satin, Double Gourd, Applied Rustic Handles, 7 In. 90.00
Vase, Fleur-De-Lis, Yellow, Cased, Beaded Insect, Leaves, 5 In. 520.00
Vase, Herringbone, Apricot Satin, 8 1/2 In., Pair 150.00
Vase, Herringbone, Pink, Cased, 4 1/4 In. 70.00
Vase, Herringbone, Pink, Crimped Fan Rim, 4 3/4 In. 115.00
Vase, Herringbone, Pink, Ribbed, Pinched Neck, 9 In., Pair 365.00
Vase, Herringbone, Rose Shaded To Pink, Cased, 9 1/4 In. 490.00
Vase, Herringbone, Shaded Pink, 10 3/4 In., Pair 295.00
Vase, Raindrop, Green Satin, Ruffled Edge, 5 1/2 In. 120.00
Vase, Stick, Coin Spot, Yellow Shaded To Caramel, Cased, 9 In. 145.00
Vase, Swirl & Pink Satin, Slender Neck, Entwined Snakes, 10 1/2 In. 450.00

MOTORCYCLES and motorcycle accessories of all types are being collected today. Examples can be found that date back to the early years
of the twentieth century. Toy motorcycles are listed in the Toy category.

Boots, Harley-Davidson, Leather, Embroidered Patch On Sides, Buckles, Size 11 .... 29.00
Jacket, Harley-Davidson, Black Leather, Zipper, Belt, Size 36 .... 115.00
Oil Can, C.A.M. Motorcycle Oil, Speeding Motorcycle, Text, Qt. 175.00
Scooter, Cushman Eagle, Passenger Seat, Red Paint, 1958 .... 3575.00
Sign, Harley-Davidson Motorcycles, Sales & Service, Tin, 29 1/2 x 23 1/2 In. 1980.00
Sign, Raleigh Motorcycles, Record Breaker, Porcelain, 16 x 20 In. 4370.00

MOUNT WASHINGTON, see Mt. Washington category.

MOVIE memorabilia of all types is collected. Animation Art, Games,
Sheet Music, Toys, and some celebrity items are listed in their own
sections. Listed here are costumes and paper collectibles. A lobby card
is 11 by 14 inches. A set of lobby cards includes seven scene cards and
one title card. A one sheet, the standard movie poster, is 27 by 41
inches. A three sheet is 81 by 40 inches. A half sheet is 22 by 28 inches.
A window card, made of cardboard, is 14 by 22 inches. An insert is 14
by 36 inches. A herald is a promotional item handed out to patrons. A
press book was sent to newspapers and magazines to promote a picture. Press books and/or press kits (with photos) were sent to the media
to promote a movie.

Advertising Display, The Haunting, Video Release, Mansion Shape, 24 1/2 x 21 In. 30.00
Autograph, Dick Powell, June Allison, Personal Message, Autograph Book Page 35.00
Button, Sunrise At Campobello, Ralph Bellamy As FDR, Celluloid, 1960, 1 1/4 In. 20.00
Check, Greta Garbo, Dated July 10, 1942, Amount $10.80, Signed, 6 x 2 3/4 In. 2750.00
Herald, All The President's Men, Robert Redford, 1976 .... 7.00
Herald, Clockwork Orange, Tabloid Newspaper, 1972 .... 11.00
Lobby Card, Hitchcock, Lifeboat, 1944 .... 80.00
Lobby Card, John Ford, Wagonmaster, Title Card, 1950 .... 75.00
Lobby Card, The Professionals, Lee Marvin, 1970 .... 19.00
Photograph, Angel Tompkins, Signed 30.00
Photograph, Fred MacMurray, Signed 30.00
Photograph, George Peppard, Signed 30.00
Photograph, Glenn Ford, Signed 39.00
Photograph, James Cagney, Signed 55.00
Photograph, Olivia De Haviland, Exotic Medieval Costume, Signed, 8 x 10 In. 37.00
Photograph, Robert Young & Dorothy McGuire, Signed 50.00
Photograph, The Man Without A Face, Silent Film, 1927, 8 x 10 In. 45.00
Photograph, Walter Pidgeon, Signed 35.00
Poster, All Through The Night, Humphrey Bogart, 1942, 1 Sheet 805.00
Poster, Boots Of Destiny, Ken Maynard, 1937, 1 Sheet 259.00
Poster, Call Of The Wild, Clark Gable, 1935, Insert 175.00
Poster, Cowboy & The Lady, Gary Cooper, 1938, 1 Sheet 290.00
Poster, Day The Earth Stood Still, Michael Rennie, Patricia Neal, 1951, 6 Sheet 5969.00
Poster, East Of Eden, James Dean, 1955, 1 Sheet 259.00
Poster, Edge Of Darkness, Errol Flynn, 1943, 1 Sheet 230.00

Poster, Goldfinger, Sean Connery, 1964, 1 Sheet 610.00
Poster, Hard Day's Night, Beatles, 1964, 1 Sheet 1095.00
Poster, Home Town Story, Marilyn Monroe, 1951, 1 Sheet 290.00
Poster, House On Haunted Hill, Vincent Price, Linen Backing, 1958, 1 Sheet 2340.00
Poster, It Came From Outer Space, Richard Carlson, Barbara Rush, 1953, 1 Sheet 805.00
Poster, Lifeboat, Alfred Hitchcock, 1944, 1 Sheet 1380.00
Poster, Mr. Lucky, Cary Grant, 1943, 1 Sheet 805.00
Poster, Night Of The Hunter, United Artists, 1955, 1/2 Sheet 150.00
Poster, Return Of Captain America, Dick Purcell, Lorna Gray, 1953, 1 Sheet 340.00
Poster, Sands Of Iwo Jima, John Wayne, 1950, Insert 320.00
Poster, Small Town Idol, Lithograph, c.1920, 1 Sheet. 690.00
Poster, Stranger From Ponca City, Durango Kid, Frame, 24 x 36 In. 250.00
Poster, The Champ, Wallace Beery, Jackie Cooper, 1931, 19 1/2 x 30 In. 400.00
Poster, To Kill A Mockingbird, Gregory Peck, 1962, 1 Sheet 740.00
Poster, Treasure Of The Sierra Madre, Humphrey Bogart, 1948, 1/2 Sheet 635.00
Poster, Wake Island, Robert Preston, 1942, Insert 86.00
Poster, Wizard Of Oz, Judy Garland, Insert 690.00
Poster, Yellow Submarine, 1968, 6 Sheet 1090.00
Press Book, Cabaret, Liza Minnelli, 1972 .... 13.00
Press Book, Petulia, Julie Christie, 1968 .... 11.00
Press Kit, Eye Of The Needle, Donald Sutherland, 1981 .... 15.00
Program, Gone With The Wind, Color, 9 x 12 In., 20 Pages 51.00
Prop, Flying Saucer, Forbidden Planet, 1956 .... 165.00
Schedule, Silent Movie, Betty Compson, Eden Theater, N.Y., 1926, 3 1/2 x 6 In., 4 Pages . 18.00
Schedule, Silent Movie, Tom Mix, Sanders Globe, N.Y., 1926, 3 1/2 x 5 3/4 In., 4 Pages . 20.00
Sheet Music, To Catch A Thief, Cary Grant, Grace Kelly, 1955 .... 40.00

MT. JOYE is an enameled cameo glass made in the late nineteenth and twentieth centuries by Saint-Hilaire Touvier de Varraux and Co. of Pantin, France. This same company made De Vez glass. Pieces were usually decorated with enameling. Most pieces are not marked.

Bowl, Enameled Irises, Gilt Leaves, Frosty Texture, Sponged Gold Rim, Marked, 8 In. 460.00
Vase, Chipped Ice, Enameled Flowers, Gold Leaves & Stems, 6 1/2 In. 518.00
Vase, Dimpled, Sycamore Branches, Seed Pods, Applied Raindrops, Signed, 27 1/2 In. ... 1150.00
Vase, Enameled Carnations, Leaves, Frosty Green Satin, Cone Shape, Gold Mark, 12 In. . 490.00
Vase, Enameled Flowers, Amethyst Shading To Clear, Ribbed, 15 3/4 In. 1035.00
Vase, Enameled Flowers, Lavender To Clear, 7 1/2 In. 325.00
Vase, Enameled Flowers, Spider Web, Spider, 9 1/2 In. 431.00
Vase, Enameled Irises, Cristallerie De Pantin, No. 20, c.1900, 9 1/4 In. 635.00
Vase, Enameled Pansies, Lavender To Clear, Cylindrical, 16 In. 800.00
Vase, Enameled Pink Poppies, Art Nouveau, Gold Wash, Satin, 15 1/4 In. 750.00
Vase, Enameled, Platinum Teasel Pods, Gold Stems, Green Body, Signed, 26 In. 1380.00
Vase, Flowering Iris, Cameo, Signed In Gold, c.1900, 15 1/4 In. 127.00
Vase, Flowers, Leaves, Bronze, Yellow, Green, 15 1/2 In. 1008.00
Vase, Flowers, Leaves, Gilt, Platinum, Marked, 9 1/4 In. 400.00
Vase, Green, Gold Flowers, Signed, 12 1/2 In. 360.00
Vase, Green, Gold Flowers, Stems, Gold Rim, Signed, 5 1/2 In. 345.00
Vase, Stick, Enameled Violet Bouquet, Gold Leaves, Irregular Flared Rim, 13 1/2 In. 345.00
Vase, White & Pink Poppies, Gold Stems, Icicle Rim, Twist, 7 3/4 In. 375.00

MT. WASHINGTON Glass Works started in 1837 in South Boston, Massachusetts. In 1870 the company moved to New Bedford, Massachusetts. Many types of art glass were made there until 1894, when the company merged with Pairpoint Manufacturing Co. Amberina, Burmese, Crown Milano, Cut Glass, Peachblow, and Royal Flemish are each listed in their own category.

Biscuit Jar, Cover, Dancing Man & Woman, No. 4419, Signed, 6 In. 320.00
Biscuit Jar, Cover, Enameled Camels, Pyramid, Mosque, Opal, 8 In. 2760.00
Biscuit Jar, Cover, Enameled Forget-Me-Nots, Melon Ribbed, Opal, 5 1/2 In. 175.00
Biscuit Jar, Cover, Flowers, Leaves, Gold Enamel, No. 4404, Signed, 7 In. 690.00
Biscuit Jar, Cover, Pink Flowers, Yellow Ground, No. 4436, Signed, 5 3/4 In. 345.00
Bowl, Amberina, Tricornered Rim, 5 In. 40.00
Box, Cover, Cabbage Head Shape, Scroll Designs, Brown & Green, 8 In. 1325.00

Mt. Washington, Tumbler,
Albertine, Opaque White,
Gold Ribbon, Flower
Swag, Signed, 4 In.

**Wash art glass in lukewarm water
with a little softening agent and
some mild dishwashing soap.**

Condiment Set, Enameled Flowers & Berries, Blue Ground, Metal, 4 Piece	400.00
Finger Bowl, Amberina, Ruffled Edge, 5 1/4 In.	75.00
Jar, Mayonnaise, Flowers, Ribbed, Metal Cover, Spoon Cutout, No. 4158, Signed	400.00
Jar, Sweetmeat, Cream Ground, Lavender Enamel, Melon Shape, Bail, 4 In.	190.00
Jar, Sweetmeat, Rose To Yellow, Gold Enameled, Cabochons, Handle, 5 1/2 In.	805.00
Jar, Temple, Blue Flowers, Green Leaves & Vines, Gold Beads, 8 In.	635.00
Perfume Bottle, Egg Shape, Irises, Blue, Amethyst, Beige Ground, 4 In.	1440.00
Pitcher, Applied Blue Handle, Wishbone Feet, 4 5/8 In.	3470.00
Pitcher, Mother-Of-Pearl, Rainbow, Diamond-Quilted, Clear Handle, 5 In.	1456.00
Plate, Enameled Portrait Of Thomas Jefferson, Paper Label, 6 1/4 In.	50.00
Rose Bowl, Blue, Pink, White, Spatter, 4 In.	120.00
Rose Bowl, Burmese, Triple Siamese, 3 x 8 In.	100.00
Salt & Pepper, Blue To White Satin, Red Enameled Flowers, 3 In., Pair	125.00
Salt & Pepper, Flowers, Melon Ribbed, Silver Plated Holder	140.00
Salt & Pepper, Green On Blue, Enameled Daisies, Tomato Shape, 2 1/4 In.	90.00
Salt & Pepper, White Ground, Enameled Flowers, Silver Plated Holder	225.00
Sugar Shaker, Blue To Yellow, Pink Flowers, Leaves, Egg Shape, 4 In., Pair	460.00
Sugar Shaker, Blue, Pink Enameled Flowers, Egg Shape, 4 In.	175.00
Sugar Shaker, Cream Ground, Gold Enameled Flowers, Silver Plate, 5 In.	225.00
Sugar Shaker, Cream Ground, Lavender Flowers, Egg Shape, 4 1/2 In.	200.00
Sugar Shaker, Cream Ground, Pansies, Egg Shape, 4 In.	150.00
Sugar Shaker, Enameled Autumn Leaves, Sapphire Berries, Melon Ribbed	400.00
Sugar Shaker, Enameled Holly, Red Berries, Egg Shape, 4 1/4 In.	144.00
Sugar Shaker, White Ground, Enameled Fall Leaves, Tomato Shape, 2 1/2 In.	200.00
Syrup, Enameled Pink Daisies, Opaline, Hinged Lid, c.1890, 8 1/4 In.	65.00
Toothpick, Satin, White, Hand Painted, Roman Column Shape, 2 3/4 In.	85.00
Tumbler, Albertine, Opaque White, Gold Ribbon, Flower Swag, Signed, 4 In. ...... *Illus*	230.00
Vase, Butterscotch Satin, Herringbone, 9 In.	60.00
Vase, Stick, Beaded Flowers, Cream Yellow, Bulbous Base, Handles, 11 1/2 In.	335.00

MULBERRY ware was made in the Staffordshire district of England from
about 1850 to 1860. The dishes were decorated with a reddish brown
transfer design, now called *mulberry*. Many of the patterns are similar
to those used for flow blue and other Staffordshire transfer wares.

Creamer, Tyrol, Ironstone, 6 In.	30.00
Mug, Tyrol, Ironstone, 3 1/2 In.	60.00
Pitcher, Nonpariel Pattern, T.J. & J. Mayer, 1836-1838, 7 1/2 In.	600.00
Pitcher, Tyrol, Ironstone, 10 In.	145.00
Pitcher & Bowl, Tyrol, Ironstone, 12 1/4 x 13 1/4 In.	360.00
Plate, Castle Scenery Pattern, Jacob Furnival, 1845-1870, 7 In.	90.00
Plate, Corean Pattern, Podmore Walker, Marked, 9 3/4 In.	65.00
Plate, Grecian Pattern, Ridgway, Marked, 10 1/2 In.	80.00
Plate, Indian Bridge, 12 Sides, S.A. & Co., 10 1/4 In.	75.00
Plate, Washington Vase Pattern, Podmore Walker, c.1850, 10 1/4 In.	110.00
Platter, Blantyre Pattern, Charles Meigh & Son, 1845-1949, 21 1/2 In.	450.00
Platter, Foliage Pattern, Canted Corners, A. Walley, Marked, 15 1/4 In.	275.00
Platter, Syria, R. Cochran, 15 1/2 In.	200.00
Saucer, Rhone Scenery Pattern, T.J. & J. Mayer, 6 In.	24.00
Tureen, Sauce, Cover, Undertray, 19th Century, 6 1/2 In.	150.00

MULLER FRERES, French for Muller Brothers, made cameo and other glass from about 1895 to 1933. Their factory was first located in Luneville, then in nearby Croismare, France. Pieces were usually marked with the company name.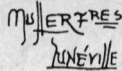

Basket, Gray, Yellow, Orange, Amethyst, Chapelle, Iron Openwork Handle, 18 In.	1495.00
Basket, Yellow, Brown, Blue, Chapelle, Wrought Iron Frame, c.1920, 9 In.	750.00
Chandelier, Frosted Dome, Iron, Hand Hammered, Art Deco, c.1926, 42 x 28 In.	1880.00
Chandelier, Mottled Shades, Wrought Iron, Scrolled Arms, c.1920, 21 x 11 In.	2415.00
Dish, Boat Shape, Orange, Brown Overlay, Ships, Lake, Cameo, c.1910, 5 In.	635.00
Lamp, Forest, Lake, Red On Yellow, Cameo, Signed, 15 1/2 In.	2600.00
Lamp, Trees, Water, Cameo, Hammered Iron Base, 15 1/2 In.	2530.00
Vase, 3 Vignettes, Geisha, Cranes, Mt. Fuji, Yellow Ground, Signed, 10 3/4 In.	3450.00
Vase, Amethyst, Brown, Yellow, White, Cameo, 5 1/2 In.	865.00
Vase, Blue Green Trees, Mountainous Shoreline, Amber & Blue Sky, Oval, 15 In.	3475.00
Vase, Boat, Fisherman, Gray Forested Shoreline, Cylindrical, 14 1/4 In.	2350.00
Vase, Brown Stylized Flowers, Orange Ground, Iron Holder, Signed, 12 1/4 In.	920.00
Vase, Crimson Over White Flowers, Mottled Yellow, Turquoise, Bulbous, 8 In.	1625.00
Vase, Dark Blue Trees, Mountain Landscape, Yellow Orange Sky, Footed, 12 In.	1510.00
Vase, Evening Sun, Clouds, Brown, Orange, Signed, 4 In.	175.00
Vase, Flowers, Blue Opalescent, Burgundy, Signed, Croismare, 10 In.	1035.00
Vase, Flowers, Wheel Carved, Amethyst, c.1910, 3 1/4 In.	144.00
Vase, Green, Rose Over Crimson, Mottled Gray, Cameo, 7 3/4 In.	2990.00
Vase, Mountains, Trees, Brown, Beige, Signed, 5 3/4 In.	865.00
Vase, Orange Streaks, Blue, Chapelle, Iron Holder, c.1910, 21 In.	1095.00
Vase, Orange, Pumpkinseed Shape, Applied Handles, Signed, 5 x 4 1/2 In.	172.00
Vase, Purple Trees, Mottled Orange Ground, Signed, 9 3/4 In., Pair	2300.00
Vase, Roses, Red, Orange, Yellow, Peach Ground, Cameo, Signed, 10 In.	3625.00
Vase, Trees, Lake, Green, Beige, Cameo, Signed, 5 3/4 In.	865.00
Vase, Village, Trees, Harbor, Boats, Cameo, Signed, 5 In.	690.00

MUNCIE Clay Products Company was established by Charles Benham in Muncie, Indiana, in 1922. The company made pottery for the florist and giftshop trade. The company closed by 1939. Pieces are marked with the name *Muncie* or just with a system of numbers and letters, like *1A*.

Vase, Blue Frothy Glaze, Medium Blue Ground, Squat, Stamped, 5 1/2 In.	145.00
Vase, Ruba Rombic, Triangular Panels, Green Drip Glaze Over Purple, c.1930, 4 x 5 In.	300.00

MURANO, see Glass-Venetian category.

MUSIC boxes and musical instruments are listed here. Phonograph records, jukeboxes, phonographs, and sheet music are listed in other categories in this book.

Accordion, Mouth, Weiss Harmonikafabrik, Fluto, Nickel Mouthpiece, 1907	275.00
Accordion, Otto, Miner, Model OA 1C, No. 1018, 6 Instruments, Oak Cabinet, 47 In.	5580.00
Automaton, Singing Bird, 2 Birds, Paper Branches, Brass Wire Cage, Germany, 10 1/2 In.	1320.00
Banjo, 5 Strings, Bay State, No. 301, 19 In.	115.00
Banjo, 5 Strings, Celluloid Inlaid Fingerboard, 20th Century, 3 x 34 x 11 1/2 In.	605.00
Banjo, 5 Strings, Cherry Neck & Pot, Octagonal Head, N.C., 3 1/2 x 35 x 9 1/2 In.	2310.00
Banjo, 5 Strings, Fretless, Hide Head, Laminated, N.C., 3 x 34 1/2 x 11 In.	495.00
Banjo, 5 Strings, Fretless, Maple & Cherry, N.C., 2 3/4 x 33 x 9 In.	825.00
Banjo, Cheese Box, Square, Fretless, Pine, Chestnut Neck, 3 1/2 x 33 x 10 In.	468.00
Banjo, Tenor, Vega, Fairbanks, Style N, Silver Lynn & Healey Pick Guard, Case	175.00
Banjo, Tenor, Vega, Fairbanks, Whyte Laydie, Ebony Fingerboard, Mother-Of-Pearl Dots	546.00
Banjo, Tenor, Vega, Soloist, Resonator, Case	635.00
Banjo Frame, Pine, Oak, Carved, Virginia, Late 19th Century, 33 In.	350.00
Bow, Contrabass, Pierre Molyneux Paris, Ebony Frog & Adjuster, Parisian Eye, Nickel	765.00
Bow, Viola, Francois Lotte, Silver, Ebony Frog & Adjuster, Pearl Eye, Silver	1645.00
Bow, Violin, Edwin Herrmann, Ebony Frog, Silver Adjuster	470.00
Bow, Violin, Jean Dominique Adam, Ivory Frog, Silver Adjuster, Pearl Eye, c.1839	3820.00
Bow, Violin, Nurnberger, Ebony Frog & Adjuster, Pearl Eye, Silver	600.00
Bow, Violin, Otto Hoyer, Ebony Frog & Adjuster, Pearl Eye, Silver	825.00
Bow, Violin, Richard Weichold, Ebony Frog & Adjuster, Pearl Eye, Nickel	600.00
Bow, Violin, Silver, J.B. Vuillaume, Ebony Frog & Adjuster, Pearl Eye, Silver	2468.00

Music, Box, Chalet, Clock, Walnut Case, 18 In.   Music, Box, Polyphon, No. 20303, 22 1/2 In.

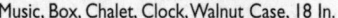

Bow, Violin, W.E. Hill & Sons, Ebony Frog, Silver Adjuster 1530.00
Bow, Violin, W.E. Hill & Sons, Faux Tortoiseshell Frog, Parisian Eye, Gold Adjuster 5405.00
Bow, Violincello, Roger Lotte, Ebony Frog, Parisian Eye, Silver Adjuster 1410.00
Box, 3 Dancing Figures, Grained Case, 9 Bells, 8 Tunes, 13-In. Cylinder, 23 In. 3525.00
Box, American Music Box Co., Triumph, Mahogany Case, 15 1/2-In. Disc, 22 In. 7050.00
Box, Bird, Gilt Silver, Enamel 6325.00
Box, Boy & Sheep, Tin Can, Hand Crank 70.00
Box, Bremond, Cylinder, Orchestral, Organ, Drum, Bells, Veneered Case, 8 Tunes, 28 In. . 4700.00
Box, Bremond, Lid, Grained Case, 10 Tunes, 24 In. 1998.00
Box, Bremond, Lid, Veneered Case, 8 Tunes, 20 In. 646.00
Box, Chalet, Clock, Walnut Case, 18 In. .... *Illus* 940.00
Box, Church, Belltower, Trinity Chimes, Wood, Paper, 10 x 18 1/2 In. 248.00
Box, Clock, 2-Piece Comb, Serpentine Case, 8 Tunes, 11-In. Cylinder, 27 In. 2115.00
Box, Cylinder, Burl Veneer, Sliding Panels, Bail Handle, Germany, 1822, 4 x 9 x 5 In. ... 3740.00
Box, Cylinder, Inlaid Kingwood, Rosewood Case, Swiss, 6 3/4 x 25 1/2 x 9 1/2 In. 2990.00
Box, Cylinder, Lid, Tune Indicator, Tune Card, Grained Case, 8 Tunes, 16 1/2 In. 353.00
Box, Cylinder, Mandarin, Lid, 6 Bells, Strikers, Veneered Case, 8 Tunes, 25 1/2 In. 999.00
Box, Cylinder, Piccolo, Lid, Comb, Zither Attachments, Flowers, 8 Tunes, 31 In. 1528.00
Box, Cylinder, Rosewood Painted Case, 12 Tunes, Swiss, 6 3/4 x 20 3/4 x 9 1/4 In. 980.00
Box, Cylinder, Rosewood, 8 Discs, Swiss, Patented 1894, 20 x 9 1/2 x 6 1/2 In. 1040.00
Box, Gilt, Enamel, Continental, 1 3/4 x 4 In. 3450.00
Box, Glass Dome, Boat, Castle, Watermill, Germany, c.1880, 9 x 18 In. 3400.00
Box, Griesbaum, Black Forest, Model R, Sterling Silver, Bird Sings & Flaps Wings, 4 In. . 1879.00
Box, Gutta-Percha, Death Of Socrates, Brass Cylinder, Key Wind, 2 1/2 x 4 In. 715.00
Box, Gutta-Percha, Fishing Scene On Lake, Castle, Brass Works, 2 x 4 In. 990.00
Box, Hausleighter, Cylinder, Burl Walnut, Signed, Germany, 1822 .... 3740.00
Box, Heubach, Bisque Doll, Dutch Bonnet, Pink Silk Petaled Flower, c.1915, 11 In. 1150.00
Box, Kalliope, No. 172321, Walnut Case, Bells, 13 1/2-In. Disc, 16 In. 2585.00
Box, Lecoultre, Brass Cylinder, Tortoiseshell, Relief-Carved Figures, Key, 3 1/2 x 2 In. .. 1980.00
Box, Lecoultre, Mandarin, Zither, Veneered Case, 6 Tunes, c.1900, 16 x 2 3/4 In. 1175.00
Box, Mermod Freres, No. 24726, Grained Case, Veneer, 17-In. Cylinder, 34 In. 3525.00
Box, Mira, Oak Case, 12 Discs, 10 x 8 1/2 x 7 In. 1380.00
Box, Nicole Freres, Brass Cylinder, Tortoiseshell, Inlaid Copper Stars, Key, 2 x 3 1/2 In. . 990.00
Box, Nicole Freres, Tortoiseshell, Inlaid Mother-Of-Pearl, Key Wind, 3 1/4 x 2 In. 1760.00
Box, Olympia, Mahogany Case, Style 5, Stand, 2 Drawers, 15 3/4-In. Disc, 23 In. 4406.00
Box, Olympia, Oak Case, Embossed, 16 Discs, 15 x 14 1/2 x 8 1/2 In. 960.00
Box, Paillard, Brass Cylinder, Wooden Inlaid Case, 12 Tunes, 1880, 23 x 9 x 6 In. 610.00
Box, Paillard, Interchangeable, Walnut Veneer Case, 4 11-In. Cylinders, 38 In. 7050.00
Box, Photo Album, Battleship Maine At Sea, 10 x 12 In. 523.00
Box, Piccolo, Cylinder, Double Spring Movement, Grained Case, 8 Tunes, 22 In. 1175.00
Box, Polyphon, No. 20303, 22 1/2 In. .... *Illus* 2468.00
Box, Polyphon, Table, Disc, Cherubs Dancing, 11 1/4 In. 1610.00
Box, Regina, Mahogany Case, Dome Lid, 15 1/2-In. Disc, 12 Discs, 12 x 21 x 19 In. 3360.00
Box, Regina, Mahogany Case, Dome Lid, Single Comb, 12 Discs, 8 In. 590.00
Box, Regina, Mahogany Case, Paneled Lid, Single Comb, 11 Discs, 15 1/2 In. 1998.00
Box, Regina, Mahogany Disc, Lithograph Lid, 2 Combs, c.1900, 13 x 22 x 20 In. 3450.00
Box, Regina, No. 7927, Bird's-Eye Maple Case, 15 1/2-In. Disc, 12 Discs, 21 In. 3410.00
Box, Regina, No. 8172, Mahogany Case, Print Lid, 8 1/8-In. Disc, 14 Discs 1410.00
Box, Regina, No. 31964, Style 26, 20 3/4-In. Folding-Top Disc, 1899, 29 In. 4700.00

Box, Regina, No. 64483, Vernis Martin Oak, Case, 15 1/2-In. Disc, 50 Discs, 21 In. 3525.00
Box, Regina, No. 70575, Mahogany Case, Domed Lid, 15 1/2-In. Disc, 21 Discs, 22 In. .. 4585.00
Box, Regina, Oak Case, Dome Lid, Disc, Double Comb, Paneled Sides, 15 1/2 In. 3525.00
Box, Regina, Oak Case, Paneled Lid, Rope Twist, 15 1/4-In. Disc, 12 Discs, 22 x 19 In. .. 3305.00
Box, Regina, Oak Case, Single Comb, 8-In. Disc, 12 In. 770.00
Box, Regina, Upright Disc, No. 1501278, Single Comb, 3 Dancers, 44 In. 2820.00
Box, Reuge, Interchangeable, Grand Piano Form, 2 1/2-In. Cylinders, 5 Cylinders, 16 In. . 560.00
Box, Rosewood Veneer Case, Crossband, Interchangeable, 6 Tunes, 42 In. .... *Illus* 10575.00
Box, Scrappy, Wooden, Windup, c.1930, 3 1/2 x 8 x 5 In. 35.00
Box, Silver, Gilt, Shipwreck In Storm Scene, Floral Scrolls, Key, France, 3 1/2 x 2 In. ... 2970.00
Box, Silver, Tooled, Gold Wash, Key Wind, London, 1816, 2 1/8 x 3 1/8 In. 1430.00
Box, Singing Bird, Black Horn, Tortoiseshell, Enamel Mountain Lake Scene, 3 x 4 In. ... 3300.00
Box, Singing Bird, Cage, Moving Head, Beak, Tail, Gilt Gesso Base, 11 In. 1058.00
Box, Singing Bird, Cage, Yellow, Green Bird, Animated, Germany, c.1935, 12 In. 838.00
Box, Singing Bird, Engraved Oval Lid, Tortoiseshell, Gilt Metal Bezel & Grille, 3 3/4 In. . 2820.00
Box, Singing Bird, Germany, 10 1/2 In. 1320.00
Box, Singing Bird, Pop-Up, Sterling Silver, Enamel, 2 x 4 x 2 1/2 In. 2300.00
Box, Singing Bird, Silver, Chased Scrollwork, Enamel Landscape & Flowers, 3 x 4 In. ... 9900.00
Box, Singing Bird, Sterling Silver, Repose, Feathered, 4 x 2 3/4 In. 3740.00
Box, Stella, No. 53381, Mahogany Case, Domed Lid, 15 1/2-In. Disc, 31 In. 3820.00
Box, Symphonion, Style 28, Black Case, Hand Crank, 40-Teeth Comb, 19 Discs 365.00
Box, Symphonion, Walnut Case, 84 Teeth, 12 Discs, 18 x 14 x 10 In. 885.00
Box, Symphonion, Walnut Case, Brass Handles, 13 5/8-In. Disc, 13 Discs, 22 In. 3645.00
Box, Talbot Toys, Smurf, Vinyl, Plastic, Mirror, Windup, 1982 .... 15.00
Box, Upright Banjo, Iridescent Patinated Brass, Round Base, Plays Oh, Susannah, 10 In. . 58.00
Box, Wood, Chimney Sweep, Hand Crank, Marcheta, Paper Lithograph Scene 95.00
Box, Wood, Painted, Cylinder, Chinoiserie Decoration, 12 Songs, Victorian, 22 In. 2350.00
Bugle, Brass, 12 In. 46.00
Calliaphone, Tangley, CA-43, Roll Operated, Brass Pipes, Red, Metal Cabinet, 32 In. 4115.00
Calliope, National, Model B, Manual Play, 53 Notes 4500.00
Cittern, Maple, Ebony Neck, Curved Pegbox, Ebony Fingerboard, c.1800, 13 9/16 In. ... 646.00
Cittern, Rausch, 1-Piece Back, Curved Pegbox, Ebony Fingerboard, 1758, 12 7/16 In. ... 470.00
Clarinet, Boxwood, Ivory Fittings, Brass Keys, Mouthpiece, 19th Century 265.00
Clarinet, Premier, Marked On Bell, The Peddler, Elkhart, Ind. 22.00
Clock, Wall, Gilt Frame, Tune Card, Bruder Stern, Vienna, 26 x 23 In. .... *Illus* 823.00
Contrabass, Plain Back, Scroll, Medium Grain, Brown, Case, 44 In. 2585.00
Cornet, A. Hileron, Silver, Lyre, Key Change Slides, 3 Mouthpiece Mounts, Case, Paris .. 863.00
Cornet, Boosey & Hawkes, Brass, King Mouthpiece, England 69.00
Cornet, C.H. Missenharter, Mute, Silver Plate, 2 Mouthpieces, Lyre, Case, c.1890 ...... 345.00
Cornet, Walberg & Auge, Silver Plate, Mother-Of-Pearl Valve, Worcester, Mass., c.1910 . 200.00
Drum, Cylinder Form, Leather & Tin, Africa, Early 1900s, 12 x 16 In. 150.00
Drum, Log, Primitive, 7-In. Diameter 47.00
Dulcimer, George F. Brewer, Appalachia, 1966, 25 1/2 In. 35.00
Dulcimer, Oak, Double Triangle, Flowers, Scrolled Peg Head, Tenn., 1933, 4 x 32 x 7 In. . 825.00
Dulcimer, Walnut & Poplar, 3 Strings, Teardrop Shape, Snowflake, 38 x 7 In. 2090.00
Dulcimer, Walnut, Hammer, Mid 1800s, 41 x 19 In. 245.00
Fife, Rosewood, Brass Fittings 40.00
Flute, Clementi & Co., Rosewood, Silver Fittings, Multiple Keys, Case, 19th Century ... 646.00

Music, Clock, Wall, Gilt
Frame, Tune Card,
Bruder Stern, Vienna,
26 x 23 In.

Music, Box, Rosewood Veneer Case,
Crossband, Interchangeable, 6 Tunes, 42 In.

Flute, E.G. Williams, Ivory Fittings, Square Key, 19th Century 355.00
Flute, Gunter Korser, Rosewood, Ivory Fittings, Square Key 235.00
Flute, Ivory, Hen Above Crown, Silver Keys, Fittings, Case 825.00
Flute, Potter, Rosewood, 4 Round Keys 59.00
Flute, Whiteley, Boxwood, Ivory Fittings, Brass Key, 19th Century 380.00
Flute, Wm. F. Seefeldt, Rosewood, Nickel Keys, Case, 19th Century 470.00
French Horn, Ed Kruspe, Double Horn, Brass Valves, Tubing, Case 2235.00
Gramophone, Nirona-Werke, Nier & Elmer, Patent No. 300, Tin, Wooden Box, Miniature 775.00
Gramophone, Polyphon Concert, Wooden Body, Inlaid Front, Green Horn, 16 3/4 In. 509.00
Guitar, C.F. Martin & Co., 2-Piece Back, Rosewood, Ebony, Pearl Inlay, 15 3/4 In. 2350.00
Guitar, C.F. Martin & Co., 2-Piece Rosewood, Mahogany, Ebony Fingerboard, 15 In. 3645.00
Guitar, Fender, Jazzmaster, Maple Neck, Rosewood Fingerboard, 1965, 17 3/8 In. 1998.00
Guitar, Fender, Stratocaster, Maple Neck, Rosewood Fingerboard, 15 11/16 In. 4115.00
Guitar, Gibson, Acoustic Archtop, Case, 1910 . . . . 770.00
Guitar, Lyre, France, c.1820, 16 3/4 In. 355.00
Guitar, Manoel De Medeiros, Parlor, Mahogany, Fruitwood Neck, Spruce, 17 7/16 In. . . . 530.00
Guitar, Manuel Rodriguez, No. 239, Classical, Case, 1965 . . . . 770.00
Harmonica, M. Hohner, Very Best Tremolo Concert Harp, Box, 7 In. 25.00
Harp, Erard, Parcel Gilt, Metal Mount, Maple, 72 x 6 In. 7170.00
Harp, Francis Serouet, Giltwood, Brass, Maple, London, c.1815, 68 x 30 In. 5290.00
Harp, Sebastian Eraro, Corinthian Post, Painted Gold, London, Pat. 2023 . . . . 3080.00
Harp Piano, Andersson, Wooden, Crank, 16 Tunes, 18 Notes, 1840, 37 x 20 x 31 In. 690.00
Horn, Baritone, Holton, B-Flat, No. 135, Polished Brass, Swivel Bell, Case 405.00
Hurdy-Gurdy, Painted Wood, Push Cart, 6 Tunes, Spain, Child Size, 48 In. 715.00
Lyre, Silhouette, Sheet Metal, Gilt, Painted, Germany, c.1842, 22 x 15 In. 1210.00
Mando Cello, Gibson, 2-Piece Back, Cedar Neck, Ebony Fingerboard, Case, 1915, 18 In. . . 7050.00
Mandola, Gibson, 2-Piece Back, Cedar Neck, Ebony Fingerboard, 1923, Case, 14 3/4 In. . . 6345.00
Melodeon, Rosewood, Lyre Form, Pierced Ends, Ribbon Moldings, 29 x 37 In. 175.00
Organ, Barrel, Spanish Barrel Piano, 6 Airs, Red, Painted Case, 16 In. 295.00
Organ, Barrel, Wooden Case, Pinned Wooden Cylinder, 10 Tunes, 1900, 22 x 12 x 21 In. . 2415.00
Organ, Roller, Gem, Table, Wood Cabinet, 15 Music Rolls, 1885, 8 x 11 1/2 x 14 1/2 In. . . 500.00
Organette, Celestina, 20 Notes, Gilt Stenciled, Walnut Case, 7 Rolls, 16 In. 940.00
Phonolamp, Burus-Pollick Elect. Mfg. Co., Capitol Model L, Hinged Lid, 1919, 29 In. . . 3095.00
Piano, Baby Grand, Chickering, Mahogany, c.1935, 37 3/4 x 63 1/2 In. 4600.00
Piano, Baby Grand, Knabe & Co., Mahogany, Cabriole Legs, Scroll Feet, 39 x 54 x 62 In. 4025.00
Piano, Grand, Broadwood, Rosewood, London, c.1890, 37 x 54 In. 2530.00
Piano, Grand, Player, Weber, Duo-Art, No. 76996, Louis XV Case, Bench, 68 In. 5875.00
Piano, Grand, Steinway & Sons, Figured Mahogany, No. A100691, 75 In. 23900.00
Piano, Kuhse, Burl Walnut, Toupie Feet, Germany, Late 1800s, 38 x 59 1/2 x 70 In. 1955.00
Piano, Mahogany, Gilt Stencil, 2 Pedestals, String Cover, c.1835, 36 x 70 x 26 In. 1380.00
Piano, Player, Aeolian, Metrostyle, Black Case, 65 Keys, 60 Rolls 105.00
Piano, Player, Aeolian, Pianola, Push-Up, Mahogany Case, 100 Roles 1000.00
Piano, Player, Behr Brothers, Oak, 1890 . . . . 550.00
Piano, Player, Chickering, Ampico, Model B, 95 Rolls, 37 x 54 x 67 In. 4480.00
Piano, Player, Chickering, Ampico, Passage Repeat, Mahogany Stool, 1916, 50 Rolls 7900.00
Piano, Player, Seeburg, Oak Case, Stained Glass Door Panels, Paper Roll, 53 1/2 In. 3410.00
Piano, Steinway, No. 91611, Renaissance Style, White, Parcel Gilt, Bench, 41 x 73 In. 6570.00
Piano, Trainquart, Coin-Operated, Wood Case, 8 Tunes On Paper Card, 46 In. 1265.00
Piano, Upright, Pacific-Pasadena, Arts & Crafts, Paneled Top, Tenon, 65 x 28 x 57 In. . . . 2300.00
Piano, Wetzels, Walnut, Ivory Inlay, Carved, France, c.1810, 48 x 23 x 41 In. 3220.00
Saxophone, Alto, Vito, Brass, Case 145.00
Saxophone, Soprano, Martin Band Co., Case, c.1930 . . . . 999.00
Stereo Console, Clairtone, 7000 Project G, Speakers, c.1967, 27 1/2 x 75 x 17 In. 2235.00
Theremin, RCA, Model AR 1264, No. 200085, Loudspeaker No. 106, c.1930, 46 In. 9988.00
Trumpet, Boston Musical Instrument Co., No. 24058, Silver Plate, Case, c.1919 . . . . 316.00
Ukulele, C.F. Martin & Co., Mahogany, Rosewood, Dot Inlay, Case, c.1940, 9 1/2 In. 529.00
Viola, Giovanni Batta Morassi, 1-Piece Back, Orange, Case, 1975, 16 3/8 In. 5580.00
Violin, 1-Piece Back, Red, Brown, 2 Bows, Case, c.1790, 13 7/8 In. 4700.00
Violin, 2-Piece Back, Bow, Case, Child's, 13 3/8 In. 1645.00
Violin, 2-Piece Back, Germany, Child's, 10 1/4 In. 295.00
Violin, 2-Piece Back, Medium Grain Top, Golden Brown, 2 Bows, Case, 1916, 14 In. 3820.00
Violin, Archibald Morrison, 2-Piece Back, Case, 1847, 14 In. 590.00
Violin, Arthur Nelson, 1-Piece Back, Case, 13 3/4 In. 175.00

Violin, August Gemunder, 2-Piece Back, Medium Grain, Amber, Bow, Case, 1870, 14 In. .   2938.00
Violin, Caressa & Francais, 2-Piece Back, Fine Grain, Golden Brown, Case, 14 1/8 In. . . .   1295.00
Violin, Carlo Guiseppe Oddone, 2-Piece Back, Golden Red, Case, 14 1/16 In. 4995.00
Violin, Caussin School, 1-Piece Back, Fine To Wide Grain, Brown, 14 1/16 In. 560.00
Violin, Caussin School, 1-Piece Back, Golden Red, Case, Bow, c.1880, 13 13/16 In. 3995.00
Violin, Cigar Box, Pine Neck, Walnut Fingerboard, Oak Pegs, Paper, 4 x 19 x 5 1/4 In. . . .   660.00
Violin, Ernest Heinrich Roth, 2-Piece Back, Fine Grain, Orange, 1971, 14 In. 880.00
Violin, Gabriele Magniere, 2-Piece Back, Brown, Case, 1921, 14 1/8 In. 705.00
Violin, Gaetano Gadda Dimantova, 2-Piece Back, Fine Grain, Brown, Case, 1937, 14 In. .   1765.00
Violin, George Gemunder, 2-Piece Back, Medium Grain, Orange, Case, c.1880, 14 In. . . .   7050.00
Violin, Georges Apparut, 2-Piece Back, Fine To Medium Grain, Red, Case, 1779, 14 In. . .   2585.00
Violin, Giovanni Grancino, 1-Piece Back, Fine Grain, Yellow, Case, 1716, 13 13/16 In. . . .   2468.00
Violin, Grandjon Fils, 1-Piece Back, Fine Grain, Gold, Case, c.1890, 14 1/16 In. 940.00
Violin, Heinrich Heberlein, 1-Piece Back, Golden Brown, Case, 14 In. 1765.00
Violin, J. Guarnerius, Figured Maple, Inlaid Mother-Of-Pearl Inlaid, Label, 1736 . . . .   115.00
Violin, J. Jorgenson, Case, 1-Piece Back, 1897, 13 15/16 In. 50.00
Violin, Joseph Rocca Fecit, 1-Piece Back, Medium Grain, Amber, Case, c.1900, 14 In. . . .   6756.00
Violin, Mittenwald, 1-Piece Back, Case, c.1880, 14 1/8 In. 470.00
Violin, Nazzareno Ciarma, 2-Piece Back, Red, Brown, Case, 1903, 14 In. 7640.00
Violin, Phillip Injean, 1-Piece Back, Fine Grain Top, Orange, Case, 1990, 13 15/16 In. . . .   1765.00
Violin, Pine Box, S-Holes, Oak Tuners, Tin Tailpiece, Pa., 3 1/2 x 20 1/2 x 6 In. 660.00
Violin, Rudolfo Camacho, 2-Piece Back, Fine Grain, Brown, 1943, 14 In. 940.00
Violin, Santino Lavazza, 2-Piece Back, Germany, 14 5/16 In. 175.00
Violin, Simon Voigt, 1-Piece Back, Fine Grain, Orange, Brown, Case, 1767, 13 15/16 In. .   1175.00
Violin, Spruce, Laminated Bottom, Tailpiece, Fingerboard, Va., 3 1/2 x 23 x 7 1/2 In. . . .   715.00
Violin, Thomas D. Paine, 1-Piece Back, Fine Grain Top, Red, Bow, Case, 1856, 14 1/4 In. .   355.00
Violin, William Gilks, 2-Piece Back, Brown, Case, 1846, 14 In. 1765.00
Violoncello, 2-Piece Back, Fine To Wide Grain, Amber, Soft Cover, c.1930, 30 In. 2000.00
Violoncello, 2-Piece Back, Fine To Wide Grain, Golden Brown, 29 3/4 In. 4406.00
Violoncello, 2-Piece Back, Germany, 29 3/4 In. 1015.00
Violoncello, 2-Piece Back, Irregular Curl, Ribs, Scroll Curl, Orange, 1976, 29 5/8 In. 1880.00
Violoncello, Gastone, Bargelli Di Giuseppe, 2-Piece Back, 29 5/8 In. 2115.00
Violoncello, Joseph Cilecek, 2-Piece Back, Medium To Wide Grain, Orange, 29 1/2 In. . . .   1293.00
Violoncello, Karl Mueller, 2-Piece Back, Bow, Case, 29 5/8 In. 705.00
Violoncello, Ton-Klar, 2-Piece Back, Bow, Case, Germany, 27 3/16 In. 120.00
Xylophone, Degan, Rosewood, 37 Notes 1200.00

MUSTACHE CUPS were popular from 1850 to 1900 when the large,
flowing mustache was in style. A ledge of china or silver held the hair
out of the liquid in the cup. This kept the mustache tidy and also kept
the mustache wax from melting. Left-handed mustache cups are rare
but are being reproduced.

Face, St. Pierre & Patterson, 1956 . . . .   20.00
Floral Spray, Smaller Spray Inside 75.00
Flowers, Gold Trim, 3 x 2 1/2 In. 35.00
Flowers, Leaves, Embossed, Yellow Luster Ground, Saucer, Painted, Germany 50.00
Men, Drinking Ale, Running Stag On Back, Embossed, Japan, 3 1/2 x 5 In. 40.00
Old-Style Man, So's Your Father's Mustache, Double-Ring Handle, Japan, 4 1/2 In. 13.00
Roosevelt, Grant, Lincoln, Names Inside Wreath, Gold Trim, Porcelain, 4 In. 65.00
Roses, Painted, RM Bavaria, c.1920 . . . .   60.00
Scroll, Scalloped Mustache Insert, Gold Trim 8.00

NAILSEA glass was made in the Bristol district in England from 1788
to 1873. It was made by many different factories, not just the Nailsea
Glass House. Many pieces were made with loopings of either white or
colored glass as decoration.

Bride's Bowl, Blue, Folded, Simpson, Hall & Miller Silver Plated Holder, 10 In. 725.00
Decanter, Sapphire Blue & White Looping, Clear Handle, Stopper, 11 x 3 1/2 In. 175.00
Fairy Lamp, Clear, Cranberry, Looping, Clarke Burner 800.00
Flask, Blue & White Looping, Sheared Lip, Pontil 275.00
Flask, Clear, Cranberry, Looping, Applied Clear Rigaree, Sheared Tooled Lip, Pontil 165.00
Flask, Clear, Pink & White Looping, 8 1/2 In. 160.00
Flask, Clear, White & Navy Looping, 8 1/2 In. 400.00

Flask, Clear, White, Cobalt Blue, Powder Blue Looping, Pontil, Rolled Lip, 8 In. 187.00
Flask, Gemel, Clear, Cranberry & White Looping, Pontil, Tooled Mouth, 9 3/4 In. 310.00
Flask, Gemel, Clear, Cranberry & White Looping, Sheared Lips, Pontil 220.00
Flask, Gemel, Clear, White & Pink Looping, Pontil, Tooled Mouths, 10 1/2 In. 260.00
Flask, Gemel, Clear, White Spiral Looping, Pontil, Rigaree, Bands, Tooled Mouth, 10 In. . . 235.00
Flask, Opal, Cranberry Looping, Pontil, Tooled Mouth, 7 1/4 In. 246.00
Flask, Red & Clear Looping, Oval, Flattened, 1800s, 7 In. 175.00
Flask, Red, White & Blue Looping, Sheared Lip, Pontil, 9 In. 358.00
Flask, White, Red & Blue Looping, Pontil, Tooled Mouth, 4 5/8 In. 336.00
Pitcher, Olive Green, Opalescent Swirls, White Bands, Rolled Rim, 8 In. 785.00
Pitcher, Olive Green, White Swirls Splotches, Pontil, Handle, 5 3/4 x 2 5/8 In. 235.00
Rolling Pin, Clear, Powder Blue & White Looping, 16 In. 330.00
Vase, Blue Satin, Applied Satin Handles, 11 In. 60.00

NAKARA is a trade name for a white glassware made about 1900 by the
C. F. Monroe Company of Meriden, Connecticut. It was decorated in
pastel colors. The glass was very similar to another glass made by the
company called *Wave Crest*. The company closed in 1916. Boxes for
use on a dressing table are the most commonly found Nakara pieces.
The mark is not found on every piece.

NAKARA

Box, Red Flowers, White Enamel Dots, Blue Ground, Signed, 3 1/2 In. 290.00
Dresser Box, Hinged Cover, Woman, Purple Plume Hat, Lavender, Flowers, 7 1/2 In. 5500.00
Humidor, Cigar, Indian Portrait, Green, Signed, 6 In. 1900.00
Humidor, Hinged Cover, Owl In Tree, Cigars, Dark Green Ground, Sponge, 5 1/2 In. 1500.00
Jewelry Box, Applied Yellow Daisies, Brown Ground, 6 Sides, 5 In. 1200.00
Jewelry Box, Pink Petals, Green Ground, Open, Brass Rim & Handles, Signed, 5 In. 275.00
Jewelry Box, Sailboat Scene, Cameo Cut, 8 Sides, Signed, Kuttonia, 3 3/4 In. 2600.00
Match Holder, Elk Scene, Light Brown & Green, 3-Footed, 3 In. 525.00
Match Holder, Pink Flowers, Green Ground, Gilt Metal Handles, 1 3/4 In. 375.00
Tobacco Jar, White Daisies, Script Tobacco, Brown Ground, Brass Cover, 6 1/2 In. 425.00
Whiskbroom Holder, Flowers, Pink, White, Green Ground, 9 1/2 x 7 In. 1955.00

NANKING is a type of blue-and-white porcelain made in Canton, China,
since the late eighteenth century. It is very similar to Canton, which is
listed under its own name in this book. Both Nanking and Canton are
part of a larger group now called *Chinese export* porcelain. Nanking
has a spear-and-post border and may have gold decoration.

Bowl, Riverscape, Oval, 12 3/8 x 9 1/2 In. 470.00
Dish, Trees & Pagoda Center, Leaf Shape, 7 1/2 x 5 3/4 In. 70.00
Loving Cup, Cover, Pomegranate Finial 6800.00
Plate, China, 9 In., 12 Piece 705.00
Plate, Riverscape, 9 3/4 In., 6 Piece 275.00
Platter, Orange Highlights, Flowers, Octagonal, 19th Century, 16 5/8 In. 705.00
Platter, Riverscape, Oval, 13 x 10 1/4 In. 470.00
Platter, Roast, Blue & White, 19th Century, 14 1/2 In., Pair 635.00
Platter, Tree, Well, Oval, 17 5/8 x 13 1/2 In. 415.00
Salt, Riverscape, Oval, Canted Base, 4 1/4 x 3 7/8 In., 4 Piece 990.00
Sauceboat, Exterior Scenic Design, Blue & White, 2 Handles, 8 In. 345.00
Strainer, Pagodas, Trees, Bridge, Blue & White, Geometric Border, Oval, 14 x 11 In. 110.00
Syllabub Cup, Landscapes, Strap Handle, Cover, 3 1/2 In., 6 Piece 470.00
Teapot, Blue & White, Molded Leaf End Handle, Gilt Trim, 5 7/8 In. 275.00
Teapot, Insulated, Rice Grain Decoration, Shape Feet, China, 19th Century 825.00
Tureen, Cover, Oval, Double Strap Handles, Gold Finial, 3 3/8 In. 1495.00
Tureen, Sauce, Cover, Underplate, 3 Piece 2200.00

NAPKIN RINGS were in fashion from 1869 to about 1900. They were
made of silver, porcelain, wood, and other materials. They are still
being made today. The most popular rings with collectors are the silver plated figural examples. Small, realistic figures were made to hold
the ring. Good and poor reproductions of the more expensive rings are
now being made and collectors must be very careful.

Band, Flowers, Hollow Ware, Victorian 25.00
Figural, Birds At End, Engraved Flowers, Barrel, Silver Plate, Meriden, Pair 500.00

Figural, Birds Holding Ring, Silver Plate, 2 1/2 In.	70.00
Figural, Boy, Lying On Stomach, Openwork Ring, Kate Greenaway, Victorian	995.00
Figural, Boy, Stealing Bird Eggs, Silver Plate, Meriden, No. 274, 2 1/2 In.	895.00
Figural, Bulldog, Silver Plate, 1 3/4 In.	420.00
Figural, Bunny, Silver Plate, Pairpoint, No. 69, 2 In.	470.00
Figural, Cat, Ring On Body, Glass Eyes, Silver Plate, 3 1/2 In.	475.00
Figural, Cherub, Grasping Bud Vase, Silver Plate, Reed & Barton, c.1880, 3 x 5 In.	950.00
Figural, Cherub, Swan, Engraved Mother, Silver Plate, Marked, Aurora	1800.00
Figural, Conquistador, Marked, Toronto, No. 1137	1500.00
Figural, Dogs, In Doghouse, Silver Plate, Meriden B. Co., 1 3/4 x 2 In.	250.00
Figural, Girl Carrying Basket, Silver Plate, Victorian	795.00
Figural, Girl Pushing Napkin Ring, Silver Plate, Kate Greenaway, 2 x 2 In.	525.00
Figural, Girl, Rifle On Shoulder, Silver Plate, William J. Miller & Co., No. 205, 3 In.	1300.00
Figural, Goat Pulls Holder, Silver Plate, No. 212, Meriden, c.1880, 4 x 3 In.	700.00
Figural, Heron Holding Leaf, Standing, Reed & Barton	850.00
Figural, Miner, Holding Pick, Inscription, Death Valley, Ca.	475.00
Figural, Owl, Stands On Open Book, Silver Plate, Marked Meriden, No. 282	1100.00
Figural, Peacock, Oval Base, Silver Plate, Stamped, Schade	650.00
Figural, Rabbits, Sitting, Mound Of Earth, Silver Plate, Pairpoint	950.00
Figural, Turtles, Peering Around Ring, Ferns, Silver Plate	550.00
Floral Trumpet Vase, Silver Plate, E.G. Webs, 4 In.	75.00
Pewter, Hand Hammered, Concave Band, 6 Ribs, Flower Design, 1 1/2 In.	29.00
Porcelain, Hand Painted, Shafford, Original Box, 6 Piece	18.00
Pressed Glass, Bird With Berry, Salt Cellar, Pepper Shaker, Blue, 5 1/4 x 4 In.	425.00

NASH glass was made in Corona, New York, from about 1928 to 1931.
A. Douglas Nash bought the Corona glassworks from Louis C. Tiffany
in 1928 and founded the A. Douglas Nash Corporation with support
from his father, Arthur J. Nash. Arthur had worked at the Webb factory
in England and for the Tiffany Glassworks in Corona.

NASH

Bowl, Iridescent Gold, Magenta Highlights, Footed, Signed, 1 1/4 x 4 In.	316.00
Vase, Chintz, Yellow-Green To Teal, Olive Stripes, Pulled Design, Inscribed, 12 In.	575.00

NAUTICAL antiques are listed in this category. Any of the many objects
that were made or used by the seafaring trade, including ship parts,
models, and tools, are included. Other pieces may be found listed
under Scrimshaw.

Apron, Mariner Star, 3 Boats, Fringe	475.00
Backstaff, Signed, William Hart, Portsmouth, N.E., 1763, 24 In.	10925.00
Barigraph, Copper Cased, Cargo Care, 8 1/2 x 12 x 5 In.	145.00
Bell, Ship's, Bronze, Raised Linear Bands, 19th Century, 17 x 14 In.	560.00
Bell, Ship's, Chelsea Clock Co., Key, Brass Case, Boston, 7 1/2 In.	700.00
Bell, Ship's, J. Warner & Sons, Bronze, London, 1855, 13 1/2 x 13 In.	1175.00
Bell, Ship's, McKay, Louisville, Kentucky, 21 In.	950.00
Bell, U.S. Navy, Iron, 10 In.	35.00
Binnacle, Conn Ltd., Brass, Liquid Compass, Elkhart, Ind., 9 In.	300.00
Binnacle, W. Rudolph, Lifeboat, Brass, Gimbaled Compass, 9 x 8 In.	200.00
Box, Sailor's, Carved, England, c.1820	4500.00
Candelabrum, Globe Ironworks, 6-Light, Great Lakes Steamship, Iron, Oh., 18 In., Pair	1580.00
Cannon, Signal, Cast Iron, Wood Base, 15 In.	290.00
Canoe, Birchbark, Bentwood Staves, Round Nail, 13 Ft. 3 In.	825.00
Canoe, Birchbark, Northern Maine, 1860s, 16 Ft.	5800.00
Canoe, Old Town Canoe, Canvas Covered, Green, Gold Lettering, 8 Ft.	11000.00
Canoe, Wood Frame, Canvas Cover, Cane Seats, E.M. White, Maine, c.1920, 16 Ft.	1456.00
Chest, Blue Paint, Molded Edge Lift Lid, Lidded Till, Iron Hinges, 15 x 36 x 17 1/2 In.	345.00
Chest, Medicine, 12 Amber Bottles, 2 Spoons, American, 1860s, 14 3/4 In.	3525.00
Chest, Pine, 6-Board, Painted, Blue, Hinged Top, Early 1800s, 16 x 36 x 17 1/2 In.	380.00
Chest, Sea, Lift Top, Molded Top, Base, Snipe Hinges, Blue, American, 17 x 42 In.	345.00
Chest, Sea, Pine, Green, Grain Painted, Canted, Beckets, Dovetail, 17 x 36 In.	200.00
Chest, Sea, Pine, Red Paint, Canted, American, 14 x 42 x 14 In.	145.00
Chronometer, Litherland, Davies & Co., Marine, 8-Day, Liverpool, c.1830, 7 1/4 In.	5875.00
Chronometer, T. Mercer, 8-Day, Fusee, Mahogany Case, England, c.1950, 9 1/4 In.	1595.00
Chronometer, Thomas Mercer, Marine, 2-Day, London, 1917, 6 3/4 In.	940.00

Chronometer, Ulysse Nardin, Marine, 2-Day, Switzerland, 1941, 7 1/2 In. 1295.00
Chronometer, Waltham Watch Co., Deck, Day, Case 700.00
Clinometer, Wall, Brass Arc, Weighter Indicator, Oak, 11 In. 176.00
Clock, Ship's Bell, Chelsea, U.S. Maritime Commission, Brass, Silvered Dial, 6 In. 340.00
Clock, Ship's, Chelsea, Brass Case, Single Train Movement, 7 In. 355.00
Clock, Ship's, Chelsea, Time & Strike, Mahogany Stand, 4 1/2 In. 635.00
Clock, Ship's, Seth Thomas, Brass Case, Silvered Dial, Cub-Second Hand, 7 1/4 In. 115.00
Clock, Ship's, Seth Thomas, Nickel Plate, 1-Day, Outside Bell, c.1930, 10 1/2 In. 485.00
Clock, Ship's, Waterbury, Circular Brass Case, Wood Stand, 5 1/2 In. 150.00
Clock & Barometer, Seth Thomas, Chrome, Wood Base, 19 x 7 1/2 In. 150.00
Compass, Liquid, Light Metal, Silva, Sweden, 1940, 5 1/4 x 5 1/4 In. 66.00
Compass, Ship's, Danforth-White, Gimbal Mounted, Brass Sac, Mahogany Box, 6 In. . . . 145.00
Compass, Ship's, H. Browne & Son, Sestrel, Brass Gimbal, Case, c.1940, 10 In. 295.00
Compass, Ship's, Ritchie & Son, Black Bowl, Wood Case 176.00
Compass, U.S. Navy, No. 3264, Gimbal-Mounted, Mahogany Box, 1917 . . . . 275.00
Compass, Union Instrument Corp., Cover, 4 1/2 x 5 In. 70.00
Compass & Binnacle, J. Bliss & Co., Brass, Lamp Housings, Case, Panels, 38 In. 590.00
Deck Watch, Elgin, 40-Hour, U.S.S.B., No. 1508, 5 In. 705.00
Deck Watch, Hamilton, Model 22, No. 5446, 2-Day, Pennsylvania, 1942, 6 In. 765.00
Deck Watch, Waltham, No. 16629507, 8-Day, Mahogany Case, Square, 5 In. 560.00
Desk, Captain, Traveling, Mahogany, Brass, Candle Holders 450.00
Dial, Langlois Paris Aux Galleries Du Louvre, Equinoctial, Case, 3 5/8 x 3 1/2 In. 1200.00
Diorama, Glass Cased Ship, Essex, Conn. Scene Back, 30 x 42 1/2 In. 805.00
Diorama, Shadowbox Frame, 3-Masted Schooner At Sea, Mass., 12 x 14 In. 175.00
Dipper, Coconut Shell, Carved Rosewood Handle, Abalone Nautilus Inlay, 15 In. 345.00
Drinking Fountain, From River Boat Pilot House, Brass, Porcelain 1155.00
Figurehead, Woman, Holding Torch, Hand On Hip, 54 In. 3850.00
Foghorn, Faraday Electric Corp., Brass, Hand Pump, 24 In. 175.00
Foghorn, Norwegian Pattern Rotary, Cased, Copper Trumpet, 23 1/4 x 15 x 8 In. 230.00
Gauges, Brass, Salvage, Island Queen Riverboat, Early 1900s 1035.00
Half-Model, Defender, America's Cup, Planked Deck, Mounted, 8 x 28 In. 219.00
Half-Model, Maxi Boat, Sorcery, Mounted, Teak Backboard, 11 x 45 In. 200.00
Half-Model, Yacht, Enterprise, America's Cup, Planked Deck, 8 x 28 In. 175.00
Harpoon, Orange, Iron, 34 In. 650.00
Harpoon, Toggle, Iron, Cole, 37 In. 750.00
Inclinometer, Moeller Inst. Co., Brass, Richmond Hill, N.Y., 10 In. 300.00
Lamp, J.H. Peters Hamburg, Brass, Copper, Red Insert Lens, 20 In. 325.00
Lantern, Bulpitt & Sons, Brass, 3 Glass Panes, Birmingham, 1941, 18 In., Pair 495.00
Lantern, Ship's, Anchor, Copper, Brass, Electrified, 24 In. 200.00
Lantern, Ship's, Brass, 3 Beveled Panes, Arched Top, Handle, 14 3/4 In. 358.00
Lantern, Signal, Ships, USS Maine, Brass, Iron Bail 345.00
Life Preserver, Nutmeg Marine Saybrook, 25 In. 105.00
Lights, Port & Starboard, Brass, Scandinavia, 25 In. 345.00
Looking Glass, Leather Covered Barrel, 19th Century, 23 In. 104.00
Model, 2-Masted, Gunboat, Wood, Oars, Bow, Stern Guns, Tools, 19th Century, 20 In. . . . 410.00
Model, 2-Masted, Trawler, North Sea, Ann, England, 20th Century, 31 In. 588.00
Model, 3-Masted, Chinese Junk, Sau Kee Shipyard, 20th Century, 75 In. 470.00
Model, 3-Masted, Prisoner Of War, Minerve, Carved Bone, 9 In. 1645.00
Model, Admiral's Gig, Sloop Rigged, Planked Model, Skylight, Lifeboat, Case 1035.00
Model, Benjamin W. Latham, Fishing, Schooner, Cased, 33 x 39 x 12 In. 1840.00
Model, Boat, 3 Masts, Solid Hull, Fully Rigged, Copper Clad, c.1910, 26 x 35 In. 670.00
Model, Canoe, Red Painted Interior, Rice Lake, c.1890, 48 In. 6000.00
Model, Chris Craft, Cabin Cruiser, Wood, Metal, Battery, 31 x 8 In. 25.00
Model, Clipper Ship, Flying Cloud, Standing, Running Rigging, 24 x 34 x 10 In. 748.00
Model, Destroyer, USS Preston, America, Carved Wood, 1920, 31 1/2 In. 355.00
Model, Lifeboat, Titanic, White, Black, Wood, Oars, Mast, Sail, Rudder, 31 In. 200.00
Model, Maude E. Briggs, Schooner, 4-Masted, Fully Rigged, 28 x 42 In. 345.00
Model, Meteor, Schooner Yacht, Sails, Planked Deck, Skylights, Details, 53 x 59 In. 2300.00
Model, Ocean Liner, 2 Funnels, Lifeboats, Folk Art, American, c.1930, 34 In. 470.00
Model, Raymond Carter, Tugboat, Carved Wood, 1 Stack, Lifeboat, Diorama, 13 1/2 In. . . 588.00
Model, Sailboat, Victoria, U.S. 77, Blue & Yellow, White Sail, Electric, 53 In. 86.00
Model, Ship, Screw Sloop, Display Case, Hartford, c.1859, 63 x 49 x 16 1/2 In. 2300.00
Model, Ship, United States, Carved, Painted, Wood Base, 1800s, 33 x 37 In. 120.00

Model, Sneak Boat, Wood, 12 In.	69.00
Model, Tugboat, Salutation, Painted, Case, Early 20th Century, 7 1/2 x 12 3/4 x 4 In.	1955.00
Model, USS Constitution, Cased, Plank On Frame, 32 x 44 x 16 In.	2300.00
Model, W. Hitchcock, Blackfish, Gloucester Fishing Schooner, Case, 29 x 34 In.	3450.00
Model, Whale Ship, Cased, Plank On Frame, 27 x 32 x 10 In.	1840.00
Model, Yacht, Cloth Sails, Brass Fitting, Wood Block, Cradle, 48 x 46 In.	125.00
Octant, Berge, London, Ebony, Ivory, Case, c.1800, 12 In.	558.00
Octant, Ebony, Brass, Ivory Scales, Marked, Original Box, 19th Century	575.00
Octant, England, Silver, Sea Creature, Flowers, Index Arm, Shade, Mirror, 5 In.	118.00
Octant, F. Walker, Ebony, Ivory, Brass Hardware, Cased, London, 12 In.	633.00
Oil Can, Duplex Outboard Special Motor Oil, Metal, Qt.	30.00
Paddle, Canoe, Wooden, Voyageur Steinsman, c.1880, 90 In.	220.00
Paddle, Raised Rattlesnake, Wood, Geometric Carved Handle, 45 1/2 In.	360.00
Pelorus, Sperry Gyroscope Co., Ring, Case, Negus, New York, 9 1/2 In.	225.00
Pilot Wheel, Stand, Steamship, U.S. General Chartiers	1380.00
Porthole, Oval, Brass, Hinged Door, 2 Dogs, 14 x 10 In., Pair	230.00
Pump, Bilge, Hand Operated, Wood	50.00
Quadrant, Spencer Barrett & Co., Ebony, Ivory, Brass, Wood Case, London, 13 In.	575.00
Rule, Hughes Owen Co. Ltd., Rolling, Nickel, Brass, Dovetail Case, 9 In.	25.00
Safe, Iron, Enclosed In Dovetailed Pine Box, Key, Stencil Inside Lid, c.1820	2000.00
Sailor's Valentine, Ever Thine, 9 In.	5079.00
Sailor's Valentine, Shells, Geometric, Home Again, Heart, Octagonal, Mahogany Box	3960.00
Sextant, Brass, Rosewood, 4 Lens, Mahogany Case, England, 10 In.	518.00
Sextant, Francis Barker & Son Ltd., Pocket, Leather Case, Strap	60.00
Sextant, Nicent Capmay, Brass, Ebony, Oak Case, Accessories, 5 x 11 1/4 x 11 1/2 In.	550.00
Sextant, W. Gerrard, Brass, Silver, Case, Signed, Liverpool, 10 In.	410.00
Sextant, Watkins & Hill, London, Lattice, Accessories, Case, 10 In.	353.00
Ship In Bottle, 3-Masted, 2 Lighthouses, Village, 12 In.	100.00
Ship Model, see Nautical, Model.	
Sink, Stateroom, R.M.S. Mauretania, China, Gold Trim, Brass, Mahogany, c.1912	2200.00
Spade, Blubber, Iron, Wood Pole, 17 In.	150.00
Spear, Eel, Iron, 13 In., Pair	58.00
Sternboard, Eagle, Wooden, Carved, Island Of Nantucket, 34 In.	489.00
Sword, F.J. Heilberger, Naval Officer's, Etched Blade, Anchor, Shield, USN Banner	236.00
Telegraph, Brass, Double Face, Chas Corey New York Patentees, 13 In.	425.00
Telescope, Ashmore Imperial, Wood Barrel, Brass Tubes, Mounts, London, 20 In.	259.00
Telescope, Bardou, Brass, Wood Tri Pod, Floor Standing, France	1900.00
Telescope, Bradford, Glass, Sail Cloth Covered, Wood Box, London, 36 In.	225.00
Telescope, Brass, Collapsible Tripod, Gear Driven Focus, Box, 19th Century, 3 x 36 In.	1380.00
Thermometer, U-Boat, Cardboard Container, 14 In.	70.00
Timer, Glass, Red Sand, Wood, 4 Turned Columns, Tin Container, 6 In.	375.00
Wheel, Ship's, Brass, Copper, Maple, 6 Handle, 35 1/2 In.	225.00
Wheel, Ship's, Wood, 8 Turned Spokes, Steel Hub, 48 In.	750.00
Wheel, Ship's, Mahogany, Brass Band, Iron Hub, 54 In.	600.00 to 690.00
Wheel, Ship's, Various Hardwoods, Spokes, Iron Center Hub, 48 In.	330.00
Wheel, Ship's, Walnut, 8 Turned Spokes, Handles, 44 In.	600.00
Wheel, Ship's, Wooden, 8 Turned Spokes, Handles, Central Hub, 37 In.	46.00
Whistle, M.B. Sands & Son Co., N.Y., Brass, Hand Pump, Handled Plunger, 16 In.	259.00
Whistle, Sweet Bread Steamboat, 29 In.	989.00

NETSUKES are small ivory, wood, metal, or porcelain pieces used as toggles on the end of the cord that held a Japanese money pouch or inro. The earliest date from the sixteenth century. Many are miniature, carved works of art. This category also includes the ojime, the slide or string fastener that was used on the inro cord.

Bone, Dutchman With Walking Stick, 19th Century	60.00
Bone, Karako In Treasure Sack, 19th Century	30.00
Bone, Sennin With Tree Branch Staff, 19th Century	35.00
Boxwood, Storyteller Holding Fan, Inlaid Eyes	470.00
Ebony, Seated Monkey, 19th Century	265.00
Gold Lacquered Body, 5 Compartment, Shibayama, 3 1/4 In.	690.00
Inro, 4 Compartments, Cylindrical, Crab, Foliage, Lacquer, Japan, 19th Century, 3 1/2 In.	750.00
Ivory, 2 Apsara In Clouds, Holding Blossom, Playing Drum, Signed, Meiji	2530.00

Ivory, 2 Monkeys Riding Deer, Bull, 18th Century, 2 1/2 In. 175.00
Ivory, 2 Samurai Hauling 2 Giant Vegetables, Signed, 19th Century 500.00
Ivory, 2 Shishi Cubs Playing, Late 18th Century 2250.00
Ivory, 4 Gods Struggling To Subdue An Octopus, Signed, 19th Century 430.00
Ivory, 7 Lohans With Dragon, 19th Century 60.00
Ivory, Benkei Fighting Demons, Animal Warriors, Signed, 19th Century 1058.00
Ivory, Blind Man With Walking Stick & Umbrella, 20th Century 90.00
Ivory, Boy Playing Flute Seated On Ox, Signed 940.00
Ivory, Child Resting On Badger Teapot, Signed, Suke, 20th Century 127.00
Ivory, Coiled Serpent, c.1800, 1 x 1 1/2 In. 175.00
Ivory, Daikoku As Rat Catcher, 19th Century 60.00
Ivory, Daruma Doll Coming To Life By Carver, Signed, 19th Century 470.00
Ivory, Daruma Seated In Grotto, 18th Century 1380.00
Ivory, Daruma With Pop Eyes, Signed, Tanichi, 20th Century 130.00
Ivory, Demon Containing Shukei In Basket, 19th Century 440.00
Ivory, Demon With Bell Around Neck, Inlay Lacquer, Signed, 19th Century 1410.00
Ivory, Ear Of Corn, Signed, Masatsugu, 20th Century 145.00
Ivory, Farmer Discovering Boy In Bamboo Stalk, 20th Century 90.00
Ivory, Frog & Crab On Lotus Leaf, Signed 440.00
Ivory, Frog Resting On Roof, Signed, Masano, 20th Century 80.00
Ivory, Gama Sennin & Frog, Signed Ichiyusai, 19th Century 1380.00
Ivory, Hare With Inlaid Coral Eyes, Signed, 19th Century 440.00
Ivory, Hotei Carrying Small Child Through Stream, Signed 295.00
Ivory, Karako Pulling At Beard Of Jurojin, 19th Century 46.00
Ivory, Kintaro With Giant Carp, Signed, 20th Century 90.00
Ivory, Lion & Cub, Curled Manes & Tails, Signed, 18th Century 1380.00
Ivory, Man Holding Paper Lantern, Signed, 20th Century 60.00
Ivory, Manju, Chrysanthemums, 2 1/4 In. 500.00
Ivory, Monkey With Basket Of Peaches, Signed, 19th Century 558.00
Ivory, Okame With Demon In Front Of Screen, Signed, 19th Century 355.00
Ivory, Oni Polishing Bell, Signed, 19th Century 825.00
Ivory, Oni With Large Drum, 19th Century 355.00
Ivory, Puppy With Bow Playing With Ball, 19th Century 1295.00
Ivory, Samurai On Horseback, 20th Century 127.00
Ivory, Sennin Encased In Peach, Signed Chokosai, 19th Century 776.00
Ivory, Sennin Screaming, Double Gourd Bottle, 19th Century 105.00
Ivory, Sennin Seated By Rockery, 19th Century 50.00
Ivory, Shishi On Table, Yellow, 18th Century 440.00
Ivory, Shoki With 2 Demons, 19th Century 940.00
Ivory, Shukei Riding & Drinking Saki, 19th Century 500.00
Ivory, Tengu Emerging From Broom, Signed, 19th Century 265.00
Ivory, Traveling Monk Accosted By Demons, 19th Century 355.00
Ivory, Woman & 2 Children Riding Horse, c.1900 . . . . 196.00
Ivory, Woman Seated Beside Tiger Claw Covered Table, Signed Rantei, c.1800 . . . . 1840.00
Ivory, Woodcutter In Bamboo Grove, 18th Century 430.00
Lacquer, Cat, Silver, Black, Vermilion, Gold, 19th Century 470.00
Lacquer, Woman Holding Staff, Base, Bird, 19th Century 605.00
Ojime, Ivory, Carved Ball In Box, Meiji 140.00
Ojime, Ivory, Peony & Chrysanthemum, 20th Century 90.00
Ojime, Ivory, Seed Form, Squirrel & Grapevine, 19th Century 230.00
Ojime, Lacquer, Carp & Wave, Gold, 19th Century 4650.00
Ojime, Metal, Staghorn, Leaves, 19th Century 230.00
Ojime, Staghorn, Shishi Seated On Platform, 19th Century 430.00
Ojime, Wood, Seated Rabbit, Inlaid Eyes, Signed Shugyoku, 20th Century 80.00
Oni Beating Drum, Signed, 19th Century 325.00
Sashi, Deerhorn, Scepter, 19th Century 138.00
Sennin With Large Head, 19th Century 325.00
Wood, 2 Seated Puppies With Inlaid Eyes, 19th Century 115.00
Wood, 2 Shishi With Ball, Signed, 19th Century 440.00
Wood, Cicada Perched On Shitake Mushroom, 19th Century 345.00
Wood, Frog On Water Bucket, Signed 645.00
Wood, Ivory, Okimono, Monkey Examining Painting, 3 1/4 In. 2075.00
Wood, Man Falling Asleep, 19th Century 380.00

Wood, Man Scratching Shoulder, Signed, 19th Century 765.00
Wood, Monkeys, Examining Monkeys, Amber & Horn Inlaid Eyes, 19th Century 1092.00
Wood, Mother-Of-Pearl, Cluster Of Shells, Signed, 19th Century 690.00
Wood, Mother-Of-Pearl, Ivory, Metal Inlay, Kappa Caught In Clamshell, 1800s 805.00
Wood, Oni Dragging Drum Through Clouds, 19th Century 1955.00
Wood, Penitent Man Carving Large Gourd, 19th Century 230.00
Wood, Porter Waking From Nap, Open Mouth Yawn, Signed Sari, 19th Century 690.00
Wood, Rooster Seated On Drum, 19th Century 1410.00
Wood, Skeleton With Bell, Signed, 19th Century 1410.00
Wood, Tenaga & Ashinaga Holding Fish, Signed, Edo Period 635.00
Wood, Woman Bathing Small Child, Signed, 19th Century 530.00
Wood, Woman With Small Child & Octopus Escaping From Trap, Signed 500.00

NEW HALL Porcelain Manufactory was started at Newhall, Shelton,
Staffordshire, England, in 1782. Simple decorated wares were made.
Between 1810 and 1825, the factory made a glassy bone porcelain
sometimes marked with the factory name. Do not confuse New Hall
porcelain with the pieces made by the New Hall Pottery Company,
Ltd., a twentieth-century firm.

New Hall

Bowl, Oriental Decoration, 6 In. 175.00
Dish, Junket, Lady In The Window Pattern, c.1800, 8 In. 345.00
Tea Set, Enameled Floral Sprays & Baskets, Red Dot Borders, c.1825, 7 Piece 230.00
Teapot, Stand, House In Landscape, Blue Transfer Print, Oval, 9 3/4 In. 410.00

NEW MARTINSVILLE Glass Manufacturing Company was established
in 1901 in New Martinsville, West Virginia. It was bought and
renamed the Viking Glass Company in 1944. In 1987 Kenneth Dalzell,
former president of Fostoria Glass Company, purchased the factory
and renamed it Dalzell-Viking. Production ceased in 1998.

Addie, Creamer, Amber 14.00
Addie, Cup & Saucer, Green 12.00
Addie, Cup & Saucer, Ruby 24.00
Addie, Cup, Amber 8.50
Addie, Plate, Amethyst, 8 1/4 In. 12.00
Addie, Plate, Amethyst, 10 3/4 In. 40.00
Addie, Plate, Green, 10 3/4 In. 22.00
Addie, Plate, Ruby, c.1930, 8 1/4 In. 20.00
Addie, Sherbet, Amber, 2 In. 12.00
Addie, Sugar & Creamer, Ruby 65.00
Addie, Sugar, Amber. 14.00
Addie, Sugar, Black 18.00
Cornucopia, Bookends, 5 3/4 In. 45.00
Cornucopia, Candlestick, 3 1/2 In., Pair 60.00
Fancy Square, Plate, Amber, Handle, 10 In. 22.00
Fancy Square, Sugar & Creamer, Amber 20.00
Figurine, Baby Bear, 4 1/4 x 3 1/2 In. 65.00
Figurine, Polar Bear, 6 x 4 In. 95.00
Figurine, Seal, Ball On Nose, 7 1/4 In. 75.00
Figurine, Squirrel, c.1930, 5 x 6 In. 55.00
Figurine, Swan, Hand Painted Roses, Roses, 4 In. 40.00
Figurine, Woodsman, 7 1/4 x 4 In. 115.00
Georgian, Sugar, Cover, Ruby 45.00
Janice, Basket, 4-Footed, Handle, 3 1/2 In. 65.00
Janice, Basket, Black, 12 In. 190.00
Janice, Bonbon, Upturned Handle, Blue, 7 In. 18.00
Janice, Bowl, Centerpiece, 3-Footed, 11 x 3 3/4 In. 45.00
Janice, Bowl, Crimped, 12 In. 50.00
Janice, Candlestick, 6 In., Pair 35.00
Janice, Cruet, Stopper, 5 Oz. 40.00
Janice, Plate, Handle, 25th Anniversary, Silver Trim, 12 In. 25.00
Janice, Plate, Handles, Blue, 7 In. 18.00
Janice, Relish, 2 Sections, 22K Gold Rose Overlay, 6 In. 25.00
Janice, Relish, 2 Sections, Handles, 6 In. 15.00

Lazy Susan, Plate, 3-Footed, Silver Metal Base, Revolving, 13 In.		150.00
Leaf & Star, Hair Receiver, Metal Cover, 3 In.		65.00
Moondrops, Butter, Cover, Cobalt Blue, 6 x 3 1/2 In.	165.00 to	250.00
Moondrops, Candlestick, Amethyst, 2 x 2 1/2 x 4 3/4 In.		45.00
Moondrops, Candy Dish, Cobalt Blue, Metal Cover, Bird Finial, 5 x 8 1/8 In.		150.00
Moondrops, Celery Dish, Ruby, 11 1/2 In.		17.00
Moondrops, Creamer, Amethyst, 3 7/8 In.		15.00
Moondrops, Creamer, Ruby, 3 7/8 In.		17.00
Moondrops, Cup & Saucer, Amethyst		14.00
Moondrops, Cup, Emerald Green		9.00
Moondrops, Cup, Ruby		16.00
Moondrops, Decanter Set, Ruby, 5 Piece		240.00
Moondrops, Decanter, Emerald Green, Beehive Stopper, 10 1/2 In.		150.00
Moondrops, Goblet, Water, Ruby, 8 Oz.		21.00
Moondrops, Plate, Amethyst, 9 1/2 In.		16.00
Moondrops, Plate, Ruby, 9 1/2 In.		25.00
Moondrops, Salt & Pepper, Emerald Green, 3 1/2 In.		45.00
Moondrops, Sherbet, Ruby		18.00
Moondrops, Soup, Dish, Ruby, 1 7/8 x 6 3/4 In.		80.00
Moondrops, Sugar & Creamer, Ruby		40.00
Moondrops, Tumbler, Amethyst, 4 3/4 In.		11.00
Moondrops, Wine, Ruby, 4 Oz.		22.00
Mt. Vernon, Sherbet, Ruby, 4 1/8 In.		12.00
Mt. Vernon, Tumbler, 5 1/4 In.		14.00
Muranese, Bowl, Salmon, Crimped Rim, Fluted Lower Body, 10 In.		125.00
Muranese, Bride's Bowl, Salmon, 4 x 11 In.		175.00
Newport, Creamer, Ruby,		18.00
No. 10, Decanter Set, Evergreen, Clear Stopper, 7 Piece		165.00
No. 15, Decanter Set, Amber, Clear Fan Stopper, Footed Goblets, 7 Piece		165.00
No. 18, Candlestick, Saucer Foot, Ring Handle, Pair		60.00
No. 38, Ice Bucket, Host Master, Ruby, 6 1/4 In.		350.00
No. 728, Guest Set, Pink, Pitcher, Cover, Tray, Tumbler		190.00
Paperweight, Apple, Red, Frosted, 3 x 4 In.		20.00
Paperweight, Mushroom, Orange, 3 1/4 x 2 1/4 In.		15.00
Prelude, Bowl, Ruffled, 12 In.		55.00
Prelude, Candlestick, 2-Light, 5 In., Pair		65.00
Prelude, Candy Dish, Cover, 5 5/16 x 6 3/4 In.		90.00
Prelude, Creamer		15.00
Prelude, Tumbler, Iced Tea, Footed, Ball Stem, 13 Oz.		23.00
Princess, Cake Stand, 11 In.		45.00
Princess, Punch Bowl, 3-Toed, Ladle		95.00
Radiance, Bowl, Scalloped Edge, Pedestal Base, 6 In.		20.00
Radiance, Butter, Cover, Cutting, 4 x 6 In.		100.00
Radiance, Cheese & Cracker Set, Enameled, Flowers, Ice Blue		195.00
Radiance, Cordial, Cobalt Blue		55.00
Radiance, Relish, Gold, Wild Rose Overlay, 3 Sections & Handles, 7 In.		20.00
Radiance, Sugar & Creamer, Tray, Etched Flowers, 10 1/4 x 5 3/4 In.		95.00
Radiance, Vase, Ruby, 10 1/8 x 5 1/2 In.		170.00
Swans, Bowl, Yellow, 5 In.		35.00
Teardrop, Bowl, 3-Footed, 4 x 11 In.		45.00
Teardrop, Candlestick, 2-Light, Light Blue		65.00
Teardrop, Relish, 3 Sections, Flower Etch		25.00

NEWCOMB Pottery was founded by Ellsworth and William Woodward at Sophie Newcomb College, New Orleans, Louisiana, in 1895. The work continued through the 1940s. Pieces of this art pottery are marked with the printed letters *NC* and often have the incised initials of the artist as well. Most pieces have a matte glaze and incised decoration.

Bowl, Carved Irises & Leaves, Blue Matte Ground, Irvine, 1923, 3 1/4 x 9 1/4 In.	1610.00
Bowl, Carved, Pink Blossoms, Purple, Blue Matte Ground, Irvine, 1927, 2 1/2 x 5 In.	1955.00
Bowl, Center, Wreath, Narcissus, Blue Ground, Anna Simpson, 1928, 4 1/2 x 10 1/4 In.	1035.00
Bowl, Spherical, Flowers, Ivory, White, Green, Anna Frances Simpson, 3 1/4 x 5 In.	2090.00
Bowl, White Jonquils, Green Leaves, Henrietta Bailey, Joseph Meyer, c.1920, 11 In.	1610.00

Chamberstick, Applied Slip, Flowers At Base, Signed, Sadie Irvine, 3 1/2 In. 1265.00
Chamberstick, Blue-Green, Vellum-Glazed, J.F. Meyer & A.F. Mason, 5 In. 1265.00
Chocolate Pot, Landscape, Blue, Green, Lucia Jordan, 1907, 11 x 6 In. 21150.00
Creamer, Flowers, Ribbon Style, Blue, White Glaze, Signed, 2 1/2 x 4 1/2 In. 1100.00
Lamp, 3 Lights, Ocher, Green Crystalline, Green Matte Glaze, 16 1/2 x 8 1/2 In. 1610.00
Pitcher, Stylized Berries, Blue, Green, Raised Rim, Alice Rosalie Urquhart, 5 1/8 In. 3175.00
Plate, Mistletoe, 4 Colors, High Glaze, M. Morel, 9 1/2 In. 4315.00
Pot, Sailboats, Reflections, High Glaze, 6 In. 12650.00
Trivet, Blossoms, White Swirl, Waxy Green Ground, Bailey, 1912, 3 3/4 In. 1265.00
Urn, Ribbed, Turquoise Over Ivory Glossy Glaze, Stamped, 12 x 5 1/4 In. 750.00
Vase, Bud, Cicada, Ochre, Green, Blue Ground, Tapered, 1906, 6 1/4 x 32 1/2 In. 13800.00
Vase, Carved Dogwood Branches, Bulbous, Sadie Irvine, 1915, 8 1/4 x 6 In. 8815.00
Vase, Carved Pine Trees, Full Moon, Egg Shape, A.F. Simpson, 1930, 9 x 4 In. 14100.00
Vase, Carved Roses, Painted, Sadie Irvine, 1918, 6 In. 3565.00
Vase, Carved Wreath, Flowers, White, Green, Blue Matte Ground, Bulbous, 1910, 4 In. . . 1840.00
Vase, Carved, Flowers, Yellow, Rose, Green, Rose To Blue Ground, Handles, 6 In. 4025.00
Vase, Carved, Moonlit Landscape, Multitone Blue Matte Glaze, Sadie Irvine, 7 1/2 In. . . . 4900.00
Vase, Carved, Oak Trees, Moss Laden, Yellow Moon, Sadie Irvine, 8 1/2 In. 6325.00
Vase, Carved, Painted Flowers, Blue, White, Green, Yellow Matte Glaze, 5 1/2 In. 1495.00
Vase, Carved, Painted, Daffodils, Pink & Yellow, Blue Ground, Sadie Irvine, 6 In. 3165.00
Vase, Carved, Painted, Mossy Oak Tree, Yellow Moon, Sadie Irvine, 5 1/2 In. 2300.00
Vase, Daffodils, Carved, Painted, Yellow, Blue, Green, Blue Ground, Bulbous, 5 In. 2415.00
Vase, Flowers, Green, Blue Matte Glaze, A. Simpson, J. Meyer, 4 3/4 x 3 1/2 In. 2310.00
Vase, Flowers, Lavender, Pink, Green, Blue Glaze, Oval, Sadie Irvine, 4 x 3 1/2 In. 1870.00
Vase, Flowers, Pink, Blue, Blue Leaves, Matte Glaze, Oval, Sadie Irvine, 1906, 6 In. 3175.00
Vase, Incised Stylized Flowers, Pink, Green, Oval, Henrietta Bailey, 1900s, 6 In. 3055.00
Vase, Painted Landscape, Moss Laden Trees, Carved, Squat, Sadie Irvine, 5 1/2 In. 4025.00
Vase, Painted Trees, Spanish Moss, Moon, Marked, Bailey, c.1935, 4 7/8 In. 2300.00
Vase, Pink, Yellow Flowers, Leaves, Blue Ground, Anna Simpson, c.1917, 6 In. 1840.00
Vase, Spanish Moss On Trees, Oval, Henrietta Bailey, 1915, 11 1/2 x 5 1/2 In. 8625.00
Vase, Spanish Moss, Moon, Blue, Green Matte Glaze, A.F. Simpson, c.1908, 8 In. 2115.00
Vase, Spanish Moss, Moon, Impressed, Oval, Sadie Irvine, c.1908-1929, 5 1/4 In. 880.00

NILOAK Pottery (Kaolin spelled backward) was made at the Hyten
Brothers Pottery in Benton, Arkansas, between 1909 and 1947. Although the factory did make cast and molded wares, collectors are most
interested in the marbleized art pottery line made of colored swirls of
clay. It was called *Mission Ware*. By 1931 the company made cast-
ware, and many of these pieces were marked with the name *Hywood*.

ℕᎥℒᎾᗩᏦ

Candlestick, Marbleized, Blue, Gray, 8 In., Pair 345.00
Ewer, Pink, Hywood, 7 1/2 In. 35.00
Pitcher, Marbleized, Blue, Rust, Tan, 8 3/4 In. 575.00
Punch Bowl, Marbleized, Brown, Tan, Blue, Impressed Mark, 11 x 13 1/2 In. 3738.00
Vase, Marbleized, 1910-1924, 8 1/2 In. 230.00
Vase, Marbleized, Blue, Brown, Rust, Tan, Hourglass Shape, Impressed Mark, 6 In. 58.00
Vase, Marbleized, Blue, Brown, Tan, Impressed Mark, 13 In. 288.00
Vase, Marbleized, Blue, Tan, Gray, Rust, Marked, 5 In. 115.00
Vase, Marbleized, Brown, Blue, Cream, 8 In. 200.00
Vase, Marbleized, Brown, Blue, Red, Cream, Rolled Rim, Impressed, 6 3/8 In. 115.00
Vase, Marbleized, Brown, Green, Cream, Bulbous Bottom, Knob Top, 10 In. 259.00
Vase, Marbleized, Brown, Tan, Ivory, Shouldered, Marked, 6 In. 104.00
Vase, Marbleized, Brown, Terra-Cotta, Cylindrical, 10 In. 489.00
Vase, Marbleized, Cream, Rust, Blue, Gray, Agate, 1930s, 3 1/2 In. 44.00
Vase, Marbleized, Red, Blue, Brown & Tan, Squat, Marked, 4 In. 265.00
Vase, Marbleized, Swirl Design, Shouldered, Impressed Mark, 8 In. 175.00
Vase, Marbleized, Swirling Blue, Red, Ivory, Brown, 10 In. 635.00
Vase, Tan, Incised Birds, Impressed Mark, Hywood, 5 In. 175.00

NIPPON porcelain was made in Japan from 1891 to 1921. *Nippon* is the
Japanese word for *Japan*. A few firms continued to use the word *Nippon*
on ceramics after 1921 as a part of the company name more than as an
identification of the country of origin. More pieces marked Nippon
will be found in the Dragonware, Moriage, and Noritake categories.

Hand Painted
NIPPON

Ashtray, Dog, Black, Wreath Mark, 7 In. 523.00

Berry Bowl Set, Floral, Cobalt Border, 5 1/2 & 6 In. 60.00
Biscuit Jar, Desert Arabian Scene, Blue Border, Silver Plated Handle, 6 In. 125.00
Bowl, Black Man Fishing In Boat, Green Wreath Mark, 6 1/4 In. 55.00
Bowl, Indian In Canoe, Pointing Gun At Deer, Geometric, Gold Handles, 6 1/4 In. 105.00
Bowl, Roses, Raised Gold, Blue Maple Leaf Mark, 11 In. 149.00
Bowl, Roses, Red, Gold Swag Beading, Aqua Enameled Beads, Scalloped, 11 1/4 In. 165.00
Bowl, Sailing Ship, Palm Tree, Ruins, 3 Handles, Green Wreath Mark, 8 1/2 In. 145.00
Bowl, Sailing Ship, Palm Trees, 3 Handles, Hand Painted, Green Wreath Mark, 8 1/2 In. . . . 144.00
Cake Plate, Plushy Roses, Gold Beading, Jewels, Royal Kinran Mark 140.00
Chocolate Pot, Cottage & Lake, Cylindrical, Green Wreath Mark, 7 1/2 In. 259.00
Chocolate Pot, Landscape, Flowers, Jeweled Design, Green Wreath Mark, 9 1/2 In. 175.00
Chocolate Set, Blue Poppy, Pink Flowers, Trees, 9 1/2-In. Pot, 13 Piece 225.00
Compote, Hand Painted, Green Mark, 9 1/2 x 5 1/2 In. 395.00
Condiment Set, Blue Tree Crest, Flowers, Salt, Pepper, Mustard Jar, Spoon, Tray 70.00
Dish, Indian, Silhouetted On Cliff, Flowers, Geometric Border, Gold, Footed, Square, 5 In. 60.00
Ewer, 3 Floral Medallions, Hand Painted, Gold Outline, 13 1/2 In. 375.00
Honey Pot, Underplate, Cover, Multi-Color Roses 130.00
Humidor, Cover, Camel, Rider, Pyramids, Signed, 7 1/4 In. 900.00
Inkwell, 2 Geese, Black Outline 140.00
Jam Jar, Underplate, Cover, Pink Flowers 90.00
Jam Jar, Underplate, Cover, Pink Roses, Gold 140.00
Jar, Cover, Galle Pattern, Leaf Mark, 4 In. 525.00
Jug, Whiskey, Painted, Enamel Border, Blue Maple Leaf Mark, 8 In. 460.00
Pitcher, Roses, Pink, Leaves, Outlined In Black, Brown Ground, Leaf Mark, 6 1/2 In. . . . 195.00
Pitcher, Roses, Raised Gold, Green Maple Leaf Mark, 7 In. 165.00
Plaque, 2 Pheasants, Gold Embossed Border, 6 Burgundy Medallions, Leaf Mark, 11 In. . 165.00
Plaque, Bluebirds, On Sky, Gold Geometric Border, Marked, Shofu Nagoya, 8 In. 55.00
Plaque, Mountain Scene, Black Trees, Raised Gold Border, Outline, Green Mark 90.00
Plate, Dessert, Woodland Scene, CGN China Co., 6 In., 6 Piece 60.00
Salt & Pepper, Grape Clusters, Blue, Green Leaves, Beige Ground, Gold Trim, 3 1/2 In. . 45.00
Tankard, Roses, Red, Pink, White, Cobalt Trim, Raised Gold Overlay, 10 1/4 In. 495.00
Tankard, Roses, Yellow, Green, Red, Gold Highlights, Royal Mark, 12 1/2 In. 275.00
Tea Set, Swans, Powder Blue Ground, Paulownia Flower Mark, 3 Piece 315.00
Tea Strainer, White, Gold Roses, Leaves, Gold Trim, 1 3/4 x 6 1/8 In., 2 Piece 60.00
Tile, Tea, House, Road, Trees, Birds, Gold Branch Of Roses, Green Wreath Mark, 6 In. . . 85.00
Tobacco Jar, House, Trees, Mountains, c.1921, 6 In. 380.00
Toothpick Holder, Purple Violets, Green Bands, White Dots, Cream & Gold Bands, 3 In. . 85.00
Tray, 2 Portrait Medallions, Scalloped Border, 12 x 9 In. 65.00
Tray, Dresser, Jeweled, Green, Raised Gold, Blue Maple Leaf Mark, 8 x 10 In. 80.00
Tray, Oblong, Rose Medallions, Hand Painted, Green Wreath Mark, 8 x 6 1/4 In. 145.00
Trivet, Buildings, Flowers, Hand Painted, Rising Sun Mark 30.00
Urn, 4 Scenic Panels, Gold, Cobalt, Greek Key Handles, Green Wreath Mark, 17 In. 1095.00
Urn, Cover, Flowers, Gold Bead, 15 1/4 In. 3300.00
Urn, Landscape, Hand Painted, Handles, Gold, Square Foot, 12 In. 430.00
Vase, Art Deco, Lotus Leaves, Pink Flowers, Cylindrical, Kinran, Feb. 9, 1909, 9 In. 660.00
Vase, Birds, Dogwood Blossoms, 4 Handles, Blue & White Grapes, 7 3/4 In. 1920.00
Vase, Black, Gold Silhouette, Trees, Green Leaf Mark, 11 In. 430.00
Vase, Bluebells, Purple, Jewels, Green Marbleized Border, Gold, White, 9 In. 240.00
Vase, Boats, Flowers, Panels, Hand Painted Trim, Marked, China E-Oh, 12 In. 110.00
Vase, Chrysanthemums, Pink, Burgundy, Light Green Ground, Marked, EE, 9 1/2 In. 66.00
Vase, Coralene, Art Deco, Lotus Leaves, Flowers, Kinan, c.1909, 9 In. 660.00
Vase, Dutch Girl On Scene, 10 In. 215.00
Vase, Flower Design, Hand Painted, Handles, 9 1/2 In. 60.00
Vase, Flowers & Grapes, Tapered, Handles, Sharkskin, Royal Kinjo Japan, 11 In. 489.00
Vase, Flowers On Magenta, Oval Shape, Handles, 8 1/2 In. 750.00
Vase, Flowers, Hand Painted, Landscape, Etched Gold, Handles, Green M Wreath, 13 In. . 489.00
Vase, Flowers, Pink, White, Satin Finish, Blue Maple Leaf Mark, 7 3/4 In. 190.00
Vase, Flowers, Pink, Yellow, Tapered, Handles, Magenta Maple Leaf Mark, 12 In. 400.00
Vase, Gold Ferns, Jeweled Designs, Magenta Leaf Mark, 12 In. 400.00
Vase, Grapes, Purple, Yellow, Gold Beaded, Leaf Mark, 10 1/2 In. 170.00
Vase, Indian Silhouette On Cliff, Sunset, Rams Head Handles, Marked, 9 In. 176.00
Vase, Indians, On Shore, Sailing Ship, Handles, Imperial Mark, 9 In. 165.00
Vase, Lake, House, Trees, Outlined In Black, Handles, Art Deco, Wreath Mark, 7 In. 215.00

Vase, Lilac & Peonies, 10 3/4 In. 695.00
Vase, Peonies, Raised Gold Overlay Trim, Dark Green Ground, 9 1/2 In. 110.00
Vase, Pinecone, Polychrome, Gilt, Handles, Signed, c.1900, 10 In. 46.00
Vase, Pink Peonies, Brown Ground, Gold Dots, Small Circles, Handles, 14 In. 580.00
Vase, Pink Roses, On Gold Ground, Handles, Blue Leaf Mark, 8 In. 250.00
Vase, Pirate Ships, Royal Nishiki, 10 In. 195.00
Vase, Portrait Of Woman, Floral, Cobalt Trim, 3 Handles, 7 In. 125.00
Vase, Prunus, Blue & White, Gilt, Egg Shape, Handles, 7 1/2 In. 50.00
Vase, Red Roses, Mountain Ground, Green Maple Leaf Mark, 8 1/2 In. 275.00
Vase, Red, White Roses, Relief Molded, Basket Weave Body, 9 In. 748.00
Vase, Roses, Hand Painted, Parcel Gilt, Urn Shape, Handles, Signed, 13 x 8 In. 230.00
Vase, Roses, Yellow, Gold, 3 Handles, Gold, Oval, Green M Wreath, 11 1/2 In. 315.00
Vase, Ruins Scene, Geometric, Enameled Designs, Handles At Top, 8 1/2 In. 80.00
Vase, Sailboats, Cobalt & Gold Overlay, Wreath Mark, 9 1/4 In. 440.00
Vase, Sailing Ships, Flower Border, Handles, Green Mark, 6 In. 77.00
Vase, Swans On Water, Wreath Mark, 9 1/4 In. 580.00
Vase, Tapestry, Gold, Violet, Handles, Blue Maple Leaf Mark, 6 In. 550.00
Vase, Trees & Lake, Gold Flared Rim, Handles, Foot, 9 1/2 In. 290.00
Vase, Trees, Black & Gold Silhouette, Cylindrical, Green Leaf Mark, 11 In. 430.00
Vase, Yellow, Gold Roses, 3 Handles, Gold, Rings, 11 1/2 In. 316.00

NODDERS, also called nodding figures or pagods, are figures with heads and hands that are attached to wires. Any slight movement causes the parts to move up and down. They were made in many countries during the eighteenth, nineteenth, and twentieth centuries. A few Art Deco designs are also known. Copies are being made. A more recent type of nodder is made of papier-mache or plastic. These often represent sports figures or comic characters. Sports nodders are listed in the Sports category.

Alligator, Bluebird In Mouth, Bisque, Japan, Takito Patent, 5 In. 150.00
Baby Pulling Sock, Pink Nightgown, Bisque, Germany, 1890s, 4 In. 175.00
Cat In Chair, Handpainted, Staffordshire, 6 In., Pair 200.00
Colonial Man & Woman, Vase, Parrot Rocks, Conta & Boehme, 9 In., Pair 300.00
Mandarin, Seated, Cross Legged, Porcelain, Polychrome, 4 3/4 x 4 1/2 In. 1150.00
Salt & Pepper shakers are listed in the Salt & Pepper category.
Skunk, Freeman McFarlan Original, Calif., 1940s, 3 In. 15.00
Woman On Sofa, Legs In Air, Porcelain, 3 x 6 In. 25.00

NORITAKE porcelain was made in Japan after 1904 by Nippon Toki Kaisha. The best-known Noritake pieces are marked with the M in a wreath for the Morimura Brothers, a New York City distributing company. This mark was used until the early 1950s. There may be some helpful price information in the Nippon category, since prices are comparable. Noritake Azalea is listed in the Azalea category in this book.

Bowl, Vegetable, Cover, Ho Wo Bird, c.1921 .... 28.00
Coffeepot, Tree In The Meadow, 6 1/2 In. 350.00
Cup, Demitasse, Phoenix Bird, c.1908 .... 15.00
Nut Dish, Clover Shape, Pastoral Scene, Cow, 3 In. 20.00
Nut Dish, Diamond Shape, Sailboats, 3 1/4 In. 20.00
Salt & Pepper, Holder, Parrots, No. 27, c.1918, 2 1/2 In. 45.00
Salt & Pepper, Pink, Blue Flowers, Gold, 2 3/4 In. 35.00
Shrimp Bowl, Tree In The Meadow 225.00

NORTH DAKOTA SCHOOL OF MINES was established in 1892 at the University of North Dakota. A ceramic course was included and pieces were made from the clays found in the region. Students at the university made pieces from 1909 to 1949. Although very early pieces were marked *U.N.D.*, most pieces were stamped with the full name of the university.

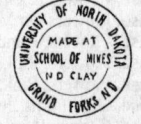

Bowl, Birds, Cornflowers, Blue, Ivory, Green, Mark, 4 1/4 In. 1725.00
Bowl, Flowers, Brown Glaze, Faceted, Van Kamp, 3 x 7 In. 380.00

Bowl, Green Matte Glaze, Black Band, Round, 1 Flat Side, 3 1/2 In. 105.00
Cookie Jar, Mammy, Brown Matte Glaze, Cable, 10 1/2 x 6 3/4 In. 1610.00
Figurine, Rabbit, Tan High Glaze, Signed Billy & M.C. 105, 4 In. 405.00
Trivet, Band Of Rabbits, Blue, Circular, J. Mattson, 6 1/2 In. 1265.00
Trivet, Pears, Grapes, Blue, Green, Brown, Round, Dyyaen, 4 3/4 In. 230.00
Vase, Carved Acorns, Green, Brown Matte Glaze, Mattson, 3 In. 690.00
Vase, Carved Designs, Blue High Glaze, Signed, 7 1/4 In. 316.00
Vase, Carved Designs, Red High Glaze, Signed, 6 1/2 In. 145.00
Vase, Covered Wagon, Pioneer, Brown Ground, 4 1/2 In. 1840.00
Vase, Covered Wagons, Squat Shape, Green Matte Glaze, 3 1/4 In. 375.00
Vase, Cowboys, Brown Matte Glaze, Mark, 3 1/2 x 5 In. 978.00
Vase, Raspberry To Black Glaze, 8 x 4 1/2 In. 290.00
Vase, Tapered, Ribbed, Aqua Glaze, Marked, 10 In. 255.00

NORTHWOOD Glass Company was founded by Harry Northwood, a glassmaker who worked for Hobbs, Brockunier and Company, La Belle Glass Company, and Buckeye Glass Company before founding his own firm. He opened one factory in Indiana, Pennsylvania, in 1896, and another in Wheeling, West Virginia, in 1902. Northwood closed when Mr. Northwood died in 1923. Many types of glass were made, including carnival, custard, goofus, and pressed. The underlined N mark was used on some pieces.

Apple Blossom, Tumbler, 3 3/4 In. 35.00
Chrysanthemum Sprig, Banana Bowl, Blue Custard, 5 x 10 1/2 In. 175.00
Chrysanthemum Sprig, Berry Bowl, Blue, Opaque, Gold Trim, 4 3/4 In. 120.00
Chrysanthemum Sprig, Tumbler, Rays In Base, 3 3/4 In., 6 Piece 115.00
Leaf Umbrella, Tumbler, Blue Over White, 3 3/4 In. 120.00
Netted Oak, Tumbler, Opaque White, Pink & Green Paint, 3 3/4 In. 50.00
Pillar & Drape, Lamp, Double Arm, 17 In. 161.00
Royal Ivy, Syrup, Rubina, 6 1/4 In. 150.00
Royal Ivy, Syrup, Spatter, Cased, 6 1/4 In. 325.00
Royal Ivy, Toothpick, Rainbow, Spatter, Craquelle, 2 1/4 In. 495.00
Royal Oak, Tumbler, Rubina, Satin, 3 3/4 In. 88.00
Strawberries, Bowl, Blue-Black, Ruffled, Signed, c.1900, 10 In. 58.00
Stretch, Bowl, Blue, Flared, 9 1/2 In. 55.00
Stretch, Bowl, Blue, Footed, 10 1/2 In. 25.00
Stretch, Bowl, Celeste Blue, 8 In. 55.00
Stretch, Cheese Dish, Blue, 4 5/8 In. 25.00
Stretch, Console, Blue, No. 648, Flared, 12 3/4 x 3 In. 65.00
Stretch, Sandwich Server, Marigold, Footed, 11 In. 60.00
Stretch, Tumbler, Diamond, Blue, c.1920, 3 1/4 x 4 5/8 In. 30.00
Stretch, Vase, Pearl, Pulled Spirals, Shell Handles, 8 3/4 In. 863.00

NU-ART see Imperial category.

NUTCRACKERS of many types have been used through the centuries. At first the nutcracker was probably strong teeth or a hammer. But by the nineteenth century, many elaborate and ingenious types were made. Levers, screws, and hammer adaptations were the most popular. Because nutcrackers are still useful, they are still being made, some in the old styles.

Bear, Glass Eyes, Wooden, Switzerland, 1910, 9 1/2 In. 180.00
Chimney Sweep, Painted Wood, Steinbach, Germany, 8 In. 130.00
Dog, Brass, 9 In. 35.00
Elephant, 2 Parts, Cast Iron, Painted, Art Deco, 9 1/2 x 4 3/4 In. 248.00
Elephant, Cast Iron, Red & Black Paint, 9 1/2 In. 80.00
Kangaroo, Cast Iron, Bronzed, England, 1930s, 5 1/2 In. 180.00
Man, In Hat & Lederhosen, Painted Wood, Anri, Italy, 7 In. 75.00
Man's Head, Yarn Hair, Painted Wood, Japan, 5 In. 25.00
Soldier, Painted Wood, France, 6 In. 35.00
Squirrel, On Branch, Mounted To Bowl, Bronze, Acorn & Leaf Handle, 8 In. 90.00

NYMPHENBURG, see Royal Nymphenburg.

OCCUPIED JAPAN was printed on pottery, porcelain, toys, and other goods made during the American occupation of Japan after World War II, from 1945 to 1952. Collectors now search for these pieces. The items were made for export.

Box, Cigarette, Lid, Hand Painted, Pink Lotus Blossoms, 3 1/2 x 4 1/2 In.	30.00
Cup & Saucer, Demitasse, Fuchsia Flowers, Pink, Orange, Gold Trim	14.00
Cup & Saucer, Demitasse, White China, Violets	14.00
Figurine, Asian Girl Carrying Water Jut, 6 In.	30.00
Figurine, Ballerina, Lace Skirt, Rosebuds, Kouwa, 5 1/2 In.	55.00
Figurine, Bird Of Paradise, Blue Head, 3 x 3 1/2 In.	12.00
Figurine, Colonial Man Plays Violin, Woman Plays Cello, 3 1/4 In., Pair	20.00
Figurine, Colonial Woman Carrying Basket, Gold Trim, 4 In.	10.00
Figurine, Colonial Woman, Pink, Green Pannier Gown, Gold Trim, 6 3/8 In.	40.00
Figurine, Historically Dressed Man, Blue Coat, Powdered Wig, 6 In.	33.00
Figurine, Pheasant, Green Head, 2 1/4 x 4 In.	12.00
Planter, Duckling, Broken Eggshell, Horseshoe Mark, 6 1/2 x 5 In.	18.00

OFFICE TECHNOLOGY includes office equipment and related products, such as adding machines, calculators, and check-writing machines. Typewriters are in their own category in this book.

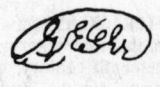

Adder, Engraved, Brass, 2 Dials, Wooden Base, C.H. Webb, New York, 6 3/4 In.	411.00
Adding Machine, Addac, 8-Column, Direct Result Reading, 1925	420.00
Arithmometer, Burkhardt, 9-Column, Wood Case, Germany, 1878	2764.00
Arithmometer, Graber, Serial No. 143, J. Graber, Vienna, Austria, 1902	3617.00
Bank Punch, Cast Iron, Automatic Bank Punch Co., N.Y.C., 7 1/2 In.	270.00
Calculator, Archimedes Junior, Step Drum, 1925	2211.00
Calculator, Curta, Type I, Step Drum, Cylindrical Metal Box, Top Crank, 1948	420.00
Calculator, Hans Sabielny, Computator, 9-Column, Germany, 1908	243.00
Calculator, Hewlett Packard, HP 9820 A, Electronic, Programmable, 1972	354.00
Calculator, Rapid, No. 9618, S.W. Allen Co., Philadelphia, 1920s, 12 In.	153.00
Calculator, Thales Geo, Spoke Wheel, Geodetic & Surveying Operations, Germany, 1930	1216.00
Calculator, Thatcher, Magnifier, Original Box, Instruction Book	575.00
Check Writer, Mars, Serial No. 1448, Pressing Roller, Mahogany Box	184.00
Check Writer, Wesley, New York, 1890	243.00
File Cabinet, Architect's, Oak, 10 Drawers, 2 Doors, Glass Knobs, 61 x 27 x 26 In.	1945.00
Hole Punch, Unimatic No. 2, Cast Iron, 11 In.	66.00
Printing Press, Manual, Cast Iron, Marked Baltimore, 19th Century	150.00
Stenographic Machine, Universal Stenotype Co., Stenotype, Owensboro, Ky., 1911	155.00
Telegraph, Stock Ticker, T.A. Edison, Inc., No. 10539, Iron Stand, 1920, 15 In.	2985.00
Teletype Machine, U.S. Navy, 3-Row Keyboard, Case, Teletype Corp., Chicago, 10 In.	59.00
Ticket Printer, British Or Jenner Marking Machine	299.00

OHR pottery was made in Biloxi, Mississippi, from 1883 to 1906 by George E. Ohr, a true eccentric. The pottery was made of very thin clay that was twisted, folded, and dented into odd, graceful shapes. Some pieces were lifelike models of hats, animal heads, or even a potato. Others were decorated with folded clay *snakes*. Reproductions and reworked pieces are appearing on the market. These have been reglazed, or snakes and other embellishments have been added.

Ashtray, Pipe Knocker In Center, Moss Green & Brown, Marked Biloxi, Miss., 2 x 4 In.	515.00
Bowl, High Glaze, Russet, Green Interior, Biloxi, c.1896, 3 7/8 In.	2300.00
Chamber Pot, Brown, Green, Yellow, Sponge, Handles, 2 x 3 3/4 In.	2860.00
Inkwell, Artist's Palette, 2 Paint Tubes, 2 Brushes, 1 1/2 x 6 1/4 x 5 1/2 In.	3820.00
Mug, Ear Shape Handle, Rose Matte Glaze Exterior, Brown Interior, 3 3/4 x 5 In.	2938.00
Mug, Incised Here's To Your Good Health & Your Family, Dated 3-18-96, 4 In.	315.00
Mug, Puzzle, Brown, Glaze, Incised, 3 3/8 In.	920.00
Pitcher, Bird, Landscape, Mottled Brown & Amber Glaze, Handle, Stamped, 7 1/2 x 7 In.	6325.00
Pitcher, Pinched, Folded, Bisque Clay, Signed, 3 3/4 x 5 1/4 In.	5175.00
Pitcher, Pinched, Folded, Bisque, Terra-Cotta, Buff Clays, Signed, 4 1/4 x 5 1/4 In.	3738.00
Teapot, Red Sponge Glaze, Amber Ground, Snake Like Spout, 5 1/2 x 12 1/2 In.	55815.00
Vase, 2 Tiers, Cupped, Folded Rim, Gunmetal, Green Amber Glaze, 4 1/4 x 4 1/2 In.	8625.00
Vase, 3 Gourd, Pebbly Black, Green Glaze, Signed, 4 3/4 x 2 3/4 In.	2750.00

Vase, Baluster, Blue, Raspberry, Green Sponge Glaze, 5 x 2 In. 4995.00
Vase, Brown, Green, Gunmetal High Glaze, Crimped, Folded, 3 1/2 In. 1600.00
Vase, Bulbous, Dimpled Base, Folded Rim, Gray, Lavender, Sponge Glaze, 5 x 5 1/2 In. . 16450.00
Vase, Bulbous, Pinched Rim, Body Twist, Red, Amber Mottled Glaze, 5 x 3 3/4 In. 19975.00
Vase, Cabinet, Marbled, High Glaze, Ivory, Russet, Biloxi, c.1896, 2 3/4 In. 2300.00
Vase, Collared Rim, Bulbous, Mottled Dark Brown, Gunmetal Glaze, Biloxi, 4 1/2 x 3 In. 2300.00
Vase, Corseted, Cupped Rim, Gunmetal Glaze, Stamped, 3 3/4 x 2 1/4 In. 865.00
Vase, Crimped, Tapered Base, Aventurine Glaze, Marked, 4 x 4 1/2 In. 4600.00
Vase, Flared, Black Glossy Glaze, Black Matte Dots, Brown, Pedestal Base, 4 x 3 1/3 In. . 2200.00
Vase, Folded Rim, Cinched Middle, Speckled Brown & Amber Glaze, 3 1/4 x 4 In. 3220.00
Vase, Futuristic, Brown Bisque, Flared Mouth On Vessel Body, Signed, 4 x 3 In. 1045.00
Vase, Gunmetal, Speckled Brown Glaze, Green, Amber, Totemic Shape, 7 1/2 x 3 1/2 In. . 3740.00
Vase, Pedestal, Hunter Green, Yellow, Signed, 3 1/3 x 2 1/2 In. 1320.00
Vase, Pedestal, Raised Rim, Green, Brown High Glaze, 4 1/4 x 2 1/2 In. 1210.00
Vase, Ruffled, Bending, Green Gloss Glaze, Ash, 3 x 4 In. 825.00
Vase, Speckled Ocher Semimatte Glaze, Dimple, Asymmetrical, 2 3/4 x 4 In. 3450.00
Vase, Spherical, 3-Footed, Black, Green Drip Glaze, 2 3/4 x 3 3/4 In. 1540.00
Vase, Squat, Bisque, Closed-In Rim, In-Body Twist, 2 1/4 x 3 3/4 In. 2415.00
Vase, Squat, Dimpled, Floriform Rim, Black Mirror Glaze, Amber Ground, 3 x 4 1/2 In. ... 4025.00
Vase, Tiger Striped, Green, Black Stripes, Brown, Yellow Interior, 2 3/4 x 3 In. 1540.00

OLD PARIS, see Paris category.

OLD SLEEPY EYE, see Sleepy Eye category.

OLYMPIC, see Souvenir category.

ONION PATTERN, originally named *bulb pattern*, is a white ware decorated with cobalt blue or pink. Although it is commonly associated
with Meissen, other companies made the pattern in the late nineteenth
and the twentieth centuries. A rare type is called *red bud* because there
are added red accents on the blue-and-white dishes.

Bell, Blue, Wood Ringer, Meissen, 4 1/2 In. 150.00
Bowl, Crossed Swords Mark, Meissen, 1814-1860, 15 3/4 In. 470.00
Butter, Blue, Cover, Attached Underplate, Meissen, 7 In. 250.00
Coaster Set, Blue, Staffordshire Ironstone, England, 4 In., 4 Piece 24.00
Cruet Set, Vinegar, Oil, Underplate, Meissen, 20th Century, 3 Piece 160.00
Invalid Feeder, Blue Designs, White Ground, Gold Accents, 3 x 6 1/2 In. 202.00
Plate, Blue, Reticulated Edge, Meissen, 9 3/4 In. 150.00
Plate, Dessert, Crossed Swords Mark, Meissen, c.1885, 8 1/4 In., 6 Piece 375.00
Plate, Salad, Meissen, c.1930, 8 1/2 In., Pair 40.00
Platter, Blue, Circular, Meissen, 1900s, 12 In. 650.00
Platter, Circular, Meissen, 14 1/4 In. 200.00
Platter, Shaped Gilt Rim, Oval, Meissen, 20 3/8 In. 175.00
Relish, Oval, Meissen, 9 1/2 In. 175.00
Soup, Dish, Blue, Meissen, England, 9 1/2 In. 95.00
Soup, Dish, Underplate, Blue, Scalloped Borders, Meissen, 6 3/4 & 7 In., 10 Piece 300.00
Stein, Crossed Swords, Porcelain Lid, Meissen, 1 Liter 600.00
Teapot, Blue, Rosebud Finial Handle, Hand Painted, Meissen, 7 3/4 In. 125.00
Tureen, Soup, Stand, Bittersweet, Meissen, 14 x 18 1/2 In. 805.00
Vase, Cover, Baluster Shape, Meissen, 14 1/2 In., Pair 645.00

OPALESCENT GLASS is translucent glass that has the tones of the opal
gemstone. It originated in England in the 1870s and is often found in
pressed glassware made in Victorian times. Opalescent glass was first
made in America in 1897 at the Northwood glassworks in Indiana,
Pennsylvania. Some dealers use the terms *opaline* and *opalescent* for
any of these translucent wares. More opalescent pieces may be listed
in Hobnail, Northwood, Pressed Glass, Spanish Lace, and other glass
categories.

Admiral, Tumbler, Straight Sides, Vaseline, 3 5/8 In. 80.00
Alaska, Table Set, Vaseline, 3 Piece 104.00
Alhambra, Tumbler, Blue, 3 7/8 In. 250.00
Arabian Nights, Pitcher, Clear, Ruffled Edge, 9 In. 650.00
Arabian Nights, Pitcher, Cranberry, 9 1/2 In. ....1800.00 to 3000.00

Arabian Nights, Tumbler, Blue, 3 3/4 In. 140.00
Argonaut Shell, Tumbler, Blue, 3 3/4 In. 60.00
Basketweave, Plate, Open Edge, Blackberry, White 1050.00
Beatty Honeycomb, Celery Vase, Blue, 6 1/4 In. 60.00
Beatty Honeycomb, Tumbler, Blue, 3 3/4 In. 70.00
Beatty Rib, Celery Vase, Blue, 6 1/4 In. 45.00
Beatty Rib, Tumbler, Blue, 3 3/4 In. 40.00
Beatty Swirl, Celery Vase, Blue, 5 1/2 In. 90.00
Beatty Swirl, Pitcher, Vaseline, 7 3/4 In. 240.00
Big Windows, Pitcher, Blue, Translucent Blue Handle, 9 In. 475.00
Buttons & Braids, Tumbler, Green, 4 In. 60.00
Buttons & Braids, Water Set, Blue, 5 Piece 550.00
Chrysanthemum Swirl, Pitcher, Blue, 8 7/8 In. 1000.00
Chrysanthemum Swirl, Tumbler, Cranberry, 3 3/4 In. 170.00
Circled Scroll, Tumbler, Clear, 3 3/4 In. 35.00
Circled Scroll, Tumbler, Green, 3 7/8 In. 40.00
Coinspot & Swirl, Syrup, Blue, 6 In. 140.00
Coral Reef, Barber Bottle, Cranberry, Round, Tapered, 6 3/4 In. 800.00
Criss-Cross, Tumbler, Cranberry, Satin, 3 1/2 In. 200.00
Criss-Cross, Tumbler, Rubina, 3 1/2 In. 210.00
Daffodil, Tumbler, Blue, 3 3/4 In. 200.00
Daffodil, Tumbler, Green, 4 In. 190.00
Daisy & Fern, Pitcher, Blue, Applied Translucent Blue Handle, 8 5/8 In. .. 230.00
Daisy & Fern, Water Set, Cranberry, 6 Piece 900.00
Daisy In Criss-Cross, Pitcher, Green, Applied Translucent Green Handle, 9 In. .. 550.00
Daisy In Criss-Cross, Tumber, Blue, 3 5/8 In. 100.00
Daisy In Criss-Cross, Tumbler, Cranberry, 3 5/8 In. 250.00
Diadem, Tumbler, Blue, 4 In. 100.00
Diamond Point, Vase, Aqua Opalescent, 10 In. 1700.00
Diamond Point, Vase, Blue Opalescent, 10 1/2 In. 450.00
Diamond Spearhead, Tumbler, Cobalt Blue, 3 3/4 In. 160.00
Diamond Spearhead, Tumbler, Vaseline, 3 3/4 In. 90.00
Diamonds, Tumbler, Blue Crackle, 3 3/4 In. 80.00
Diamonds, Tumbler, Reverse Rubina, 3 1/2 In. 90.00
Dolly Madison, Tumbler, Green, 3 3/4 In. 45.00
Double Greek Key, Tumbler, Clear, 3 3/4 In. 80.00
Drapery, Pitcher, Blue, Blown, Applied Translucent Blue Handle, 9 3/8 In. . 425.00
Drapery, Tumbler, Cranberry, Blown, 3 1/2 In. 170.00
Duchess, Tumbler, Clear, 3 3/4 In. 30.00
Ellipse & Diamond, Pitcher, Ball, Blue, Squat, Applied Translucent Handle, 7 In. .. 160.00
Encore, Tumbler, Blue, Gold, 4 In. 80.00
Encore, Tumbler, Vaseline, Gold, 4 In. 100.00
Everglades, Pitcher, Water, Blue, 7 3/4 In. 58.00
Herringbone, Pitcher, Blue, Translucent Blue Handle, 8 3/4 In. 1150.00
Herringbone, Pitcher, Cranberry, Clear Handle, 9 In. 5000.00
Hobnail, Pitcher, Water, Cranberry To Clear, Opalescent Handle, 8 In. .. 180.00
Honeycomb, Pitcher, Ball, Blue, Ruffled Edge, Clear Handle, 7 1/2 In. .. 210.00
Honeycomb, Tumbler, Vaseline, Enameled Flowers, 3 3/4 In. 140.00
Intaglio, Tumbler, Blue, Gold Trim, 3 3/4 In. 50.00
Inverted Fan & Feather, Tumbler, Blue, Gold Trim, 3 7/8 In. 60.00
Inverted Fan & Feather, Tumbler, Clear, Gold Trim, 3 7/8 In. 25.00
Iris With Meander, Tumbler, Vaseline, 3 3/4 In. 60.00
Lattice, Spooner, Blue, 4 x 3 1/4 In. 70.00
Lattice, Tumbler, Cranberry, 4 In. 190.00
Lattice, Water Set, Amber, 7 1/2-In. Pitcher, 5 Piece 220.00
Lustre Flute, Tumbler, Clear, 4 In. 45.00
Manila, Tumbler, Vaseline, 4-Footed, 3 3/4 In. 150.00
Manila, Tumbler, Vaseline, Collar Foot, 3 3/4 In. 50.00
National, Tumbler, Blue, 3 3/4 In. 45.00
New York, Tumbler, Blue, 3 3/4 In. 45.00
Opalescent Fern, Creamer, Clear, Clear Handle, 3 3/4 In. 150.00
Opalescent Fern, Pitcher, Cranberry, Clear Handle, Square Top, 8 1/2 In. .. 2100.00
Opalescent Fern, Tumbler, Blue, 3 7/8 In. 140.00

Opaline Brocade, Barber Bottle, Cranberry, Corset Waist, 7 1/2 In.	1900.00
Opaline Brocade, Butter, Clear, Cranberry Cover, Dome Shape, 5 1/2 In.	1000.00
Opaline Brocade, Celery Vase, Vaseline, 6 In.	180.00
Opaline Brocade, Finger Bowl, Blue, 2 3/4 x 4 1/2 In.	90.00
Opaline Brocade, Tumbler, Blue, 3 1/2 In.	60.00
Opaline Brocade, Tumbler, Green, 4 In.	60.00
Opaline Brocade, Water Set, Cranberry, 9 1/2-In. Pitcher, Clear Handle, 6 Piece	950.00
Over-All Hob, Tumbler, Amethyst, 3 3/4 In.	100.00
Palm Beach, Tumbler, Blue, 3 3/4 In.	40.00
Palm Beach, Tumbler, Vaseline, 3 3/4 In.	160.00
Paneled Holly, Tumbler, Blue, Gold Trim, Marked, 4 In. . . . . *Illus*	65.00
Paneled Holly, Tumbler, White, Green & Red Enamel, Marked, 4 In. . . . . *Illus*	65.00
Poinsettia, Tumbler, Cranberry, 3 3/4 In.	240.00
Poinsettia, Tumbler, Green, 3 3/4 In.	130.00
Poinsettia, Water Set, Blue, 13 In., 7 Piece	1350.00
Polka Dot, Tumbler, Clear, 3 3/4 In.	140.00
Regal, Tumbler, Green, 4 In.	40.00
Reverse Swirl, Celery Vase, Blue, 6 In.	110.00
Reverse Swirl, Creamer, Blue, Transparent Blue Handle, 5 1/2 In.	100.00
Reverse Swirl, Sugar, Cover, Blue, Transparent Blue Finial, 6 1/4 In.	300.00
Reverse Swirl, Tumbler, Cranberry, 3 3/4 In.	150.00
Reverse Swirl, Tumbler, Vaseline, 3 3/4 In.	100.00
Ribbed Opal Lattice, Pitcher, Blue, Straight Sides, Translucent Handle, 10 In.	550.00
Ribbed Opal Lattice, Pitcher, Cranberry, Straight Sides, Clear Handle, 10 In.	1700.00
Ribbed Opal Rings, Tumbler, Blue, 3 3/4 In.	130.00
Ribbed Opal Rings, Tumbler, Cranberry, 3 3/4 In.	200.00
Ribbed Spiral, Tumbler, Blue, 3 3/4 In.	70.00
Ribbed Spiral, Tumbler, Vaseline, 3 3/4 In.	70.00
Scottish Moor, Pitcher, Water, Cranberry, Corset Waist, Reeded Handle, 8 1/4 In.	5300.00
Scottish Moor, Tumbler, Cranberry, 3 3/4 In.	220.00
Seaweed, Pitcher, Blue, 3-Sided Crimped Rim, Translucent Blue Handle, 9 In.	500.00
Seaweed, Pitcher, Cranberry, 3-Sided Crimped Rim, Clear Handle, 9 In.	850.00
Seaweed, Tumbler, Blue, 3 3/4 In.	100.00
Stars & Stripes, Barber Bottle, Blue, 7 In.	275.00
Stars & Stripes, Pitcher, Cranberry, Straight Sides, Clear Handle, 8 1/4 In.	4700.00
Stripe, Pitcher, Cranberry, Ring Neck, Clear Handle, 9 1/4 In.	1600.00
Stripe, Pitcher, Light Blue, Ruffled Edge, Translucent Blue Handle, 9 1/2 In.	600.00
Stripe, Tumbler, Blue, 3 3/4 In.	50.00
Stripe, Tumbler, Cranberry, 3 3/4 In.	90.00
Swag With Brackets, Tumbler, Blue, 4 In.	40.00
Swag With Brackets, Tumbler, Green, 3 7/8 In.	90.00
Swastika, Tumbler, Clear, 3 3/4 In.	325.00
Swastika, Tumbler, Green, 3 3/4 In.	350.00
Swirl, Barber Bottle, Blue, 7 1/4 In.	180.00
Swirl, Pitcher, Cranberry, Square Top, Clear Handle, 8 1/2 In.	600.00
Swirl, Straw Jar, Cover, Blue, 11 1/4 In.	4100.00
Swirl, Tumbler, Cranberry, 3 3/4 In.	110.00

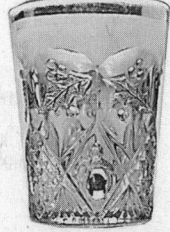

If you live in an old house and the locks are old, check the new types. There have been many improvements, and new locks provide much better security. Never leave the key under the door mat.

Opalescent, Paneled Holly, Tumbler, Blue, Gold Trim, Marked, 4 In.

Opalescent, Paneled Holly, Tumbler, White, Green & Red Enamel, Marked, 4 In.

Swirl, Vase, Clear, Bulbous, Rolled Rim, 7 3/4 In.	130.00
Swirl, Water Set, Blue, Square Top, 6 Piece	400.00
Swirling Maze, Bowl, Cranberry, Ruffled Edge, 3 3/4 In.	150.00
Swirling Maze, Tumbler, Blue, 4 In.	80.00
Swirling Maze, Tumbler, Cranberry, 4 In.	230.00
Toothpicks are listed in the Toothpick category.	
Twist, Tumbler, Cranberry, 3 7/8 In.	275.00
Twist, Tumbler, Green, 4 In.	210.00
Victor, Tumbler, Apple Green, 3 1/2 In.	40.00
Waterlily With Cattails, Tumbler, Amethyst, 3 3/4 In.	60.00
Waterlily With Cattails, Tumbler, Green, 4 In.	30.00
Wide Stripe, Tumbler, Cranberry, 3 3/4 In.	110.00
Wild Bouquet, Tumbler, Blue, 3 3/4 In.	60.00
Wild Bouquet, Tumbler, Green, 3 3/4 In.	70.00
Windows, Celery Vase, Blue, Swirl, 3 1/2 x 4 In.	100.00
Windows, Pitcher, Blue, Tricornered Rim, 8 5/8 In.	350.00
Windows, Sugar, Cover, Cranberry, Swirl, Facetted Finial, 5 1/2 In.	60.00
Windows, Tumbler, Blue, Swirl, 3 5/8 In.	110.00
Windows, Tumbler, Cranberry, 3 3/4 In.	100.00
Windows Reverse Swirl, Celery Vase, Blue, 6 In.	140.00

OPALINE, or opal glass, was made in white, green, and other colors. The glass had a matte surface and a lack of transparency. It was often gilded or painted. It was a popular mid-nineteenth-century European glassware.

Barber Bottle, Red Flowers, Green Leaves, Blue Windowpanes At Collar, Stopper, 12 In.	78.00
Basket, Opaque, Applied Amber Stemmed Pink Flowers, Amber Twist Handle, 7 1/4 In.	69.00
Bowl, Sweetmeat, Napoleon III, Blue, Gilt Bronze Mount, c.1865, 2 1/4 x 5 In., Pair	1035.00
Bowl, Sweetmeat, Napoleon III, Rose, Gilt Bronze Mount, 5 3/8 x 6 3/4 In.	1725.00
Goblet, Napoleon III, Rose, Gilt Bronze Mount, Dolphin, c.1865, 6 x 3 1/4 In.	1265.00
Jam Jar, Pink, Painted Flowers, Leaf Shaped Dish, Cover, c.1820, 6 In.	3100.00
Shade, Yellow, Ribbed, Flared, Ruffled Rim, 4 In.	118.00
Vase, Birds & Flowers, Pink Ground, Baluster Shape, Trumpet Base, 30 3/4 In.	823.00
Vase, Bristol Blue, Shouldered, Oval, Flaring Neck, Mounted As Lamp, 14 In., Pair	896.00
Vase, Cased Pink, Enameled Flower Spray, 6 1/4 In.	23.00
Vase, Gilt, Enamel, Shouldered, Oval, Leaf Decoration, Yellow Ground, 12 1/2 In.	646.00
Vase, Gray, Homogenized, Enameled, Perching Birds, 19th Century, 10 In., Pair	115.00
Vase, Pink, Enameled Gold Day Lilies, Rolled Rim, Cased, Victorian, 9 1/2 In.	85.00

OPERA GLASSES are needed because the stage is a long way from some of the seats at a play or an opera. Mother-of-pearl was a popular decoration on many French glasses.

Mother-Of-Pearl, Brass Fittings, Swivel Handle, Marked, Badere, Paris, Pouch, 4 In.	110.00
Mother-Of-Pearl, Enamel, Ribbon & Floral Swag, Signed Lemaire, Paris	264.00
Mother-Of-Pearl, Gilt Brass Frame, Lemaire, Paris, Velvet Bag, 7 In.	575.00
Mother-Of-Pearl, Gilt Brass, Fitted Leather Case, Lemarie, c.1900, 2 x 3 3/4 In.	210.00
Mother-Of-Pearl, Original Case, 19th Century	46.00

ORPHAN ANNIE first appeared in the comics in 1924. The redheaded girl and her friends have been on the radio and are still on the comic pages. A Broadway musical show and a movie in the 1980s made Annie popular again and many toys, dishes, and other memorabilia are being made.

Game, Board, Figures, Box, 9 x 17 In.	66.00
Toy, Circus, 6-10 x 14 Cards, Ovaltine Premium, c.1930	249.00
Toy, Skips Rope, Sandy, Briefcase, Windup	475.00
Wristwatch, Annie On Face, New Haven, Harold Gray, Box, 1948	495.00

ORREFORS Glassworks, located in the Swedish province of Smaaland, was established in 1898. The company is still making glass for use on the table or as decorations. There is renewed interest in the glass made in the modern styles of the 1940s and 1950s. Most vases and decorative pieces are signed with the etched name.

Orrefors

Vase, Cased, Bulbous, Internal Bubbles, Cobalt Blue, Ariel No. 487F, 4 x 6 1/2 In.	999.00

Vase, Clear Over Olive Green, 4 Sides, Tear Shape, Sommerso, 10 x 5 In. 253.00
Vase, Cylindrical, Geometric Tapped Bubbles, Cobalt Blue, Inscribed, 6 x 4 In. 860.00
Vase, Horizontal Bands Of Translucent Blue & Green, Signed, Nils Landberg, 6 In. 336.00

OTT & BREWER Company operated the Etruria Pottery at Trenton, New Jersey, from 1863 to 1893. They started making belleek in 1882. The firm used a variety of marks that incorporated the initials *O & B.*

Bottle, Bird Flying To Nest, Gilt Painted, Brown, Elongated Neck, 9 3/4 x 5 1/2 In. 2990.00
Bottle, Morning Glories, Gilt, Olive-Green Ground, Crown Stamp, 10 x 7 In. ...... *Illus* 17250.00
Bowl, Cherry Blossoms, Scalloped Rim, 3 Lion Feet, Red Crown Stamp, 3 1/2 x 9 In. ... 690.00
Bowl, Water Lily, Gilt Painted, Thistles, Applied Leaves, Bud, 4 x 10 In. 690.00
Jar, Cover, Daisies, Clouds, Gilt, Ivory Ground, Tapered, Marked, 11 x 5 In. .... *Illus* 1840.00
Jar, Gilt Daisies, Clouds, Ivory Ground, 2 Pierced Gilt Handles, Tapered Cover, 11 x 5 In. 1840.00
Pitcher, Pink Lilies, Gilt, Ivory Ground, Branch Handle, Red Crown Stamp, 9 x 6 In. 750.00
Vase, Belleek, Gilded Nasturtium, Cobalt Ground, Filigree Handles, 10 x 7 1/2 In. 5290.00

OVERBECK pottery was made by four sisters named Overbeck at a pottery in Cambridge City, Indiana. They started in 1911. They made all types of vases, each one-of-a-kind. Small, hand-modeled figurines are the most popular pieces with today's collectors. The factory continued until 1955, when the last of the four sisters died.

Bowl, Hunter Green Earthen Glaze, Mahogany Flambe Glaze, 3 x 5 3/4 In. 770.00
Candleholder, Bluebirds, 3 In., Pair 1100.00
Figurine, Billy Goat, 4 In. 575.00
Figurine, Colonial Lady, Walking Dog, 4 1/2 In. 450.00
Figurine, Colonial Mother & Child, 4 1/2 In. 2900.00
Figurine, Frog, Green, Pink & Blue Back, 2 In. 468.00
Figurine, George Washington, 5 In. 1800.00
Figurine, Goose, Blue Feet & Wings, Impressed, 3 In. 750.00
Figurine, Insect, Flying, 1 In. 175.00
Figurine, Martha Washington, 5 In. 1800.00
Figurine, Mother & Daughter, Floral Dresses, Bonnets, 4 1/2 In. 2900.00
Figurine, Paul Revere & Horse, 3 1/2 In. 2200.00
Figurine, Pirate, Yellow, Red, Blue, Impressed, 3 3/4 In. 1035.00
Figurine, Quaker Man, 5 1/4 In. 2000.00
Figurine, Quaker Woman, 6 In. 1200.00
Figurine, Rabbit, Pink, 1 1/2 x 1 1/2 In. 415.00
Figurine, Southern Belle, Holding Umbrella, 7 1/2 In. 5300.00
Figurine, Southern Belle, Large Hoop Dress, 7 1/2 In. 3750.00
Figurine, Southern Belle, Parasol, 7 1/2 In. 5300.00
Figurine, Southern Woman, Seated, Victorian Chair, 3 In. 1600.00
Figurine, Turtle, 2 x 1 In. 525.00
Flower Frog, 5 Petal Flowers, Yellow, Purple, Blue, 5 In. 206.00
Invalid Feeder, Flowers, 3 1/4 In. 575.00
Paperweight, Chickadee Pair On Top 400.00
Paperweight, Dog, Irish Setter, 3 In. 500.00
Powder Box, Cover, Hand Painted, Signed Mary Frances & Elizabeth 650.00
Tea Set, Red Glaze, Teapot, Cup & Saucer, 31 Piece 4500.00

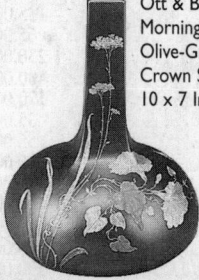

Ott & Brewer, Bottle, Morning Glories, Gilt, Olive-Green Ground, Crown Stamp, 10 x 7 In.

Ott & Brewer, Jar, Cover, Daisies, Clouds, Gilt, Ivory Ground, Tapered, Marked, 11 x 5 In.

To dry a small-necked bottle, give it a last rinse with alcohol.

Vase, Aqua Blue, Square Double-Handles, Incised School Girls, c.1918, 12 In. 7750.00

OWENS Pottery was made in Zanesville, Ohio, from 1891 to 1928. The
first art pottery was made after 1896. Utopian Ware, Cyrano, Navarre,
Feroza, and Henri Deux were made. Pieces were usually marked with
a form of the name *Owens*. About 1907, the firm began to make tile
and discontinued the art pottery wares.

Chamberstick, Organic, Twisted Body, Moat Pedestal, Antique Green Glaze, 6 x 6 1/4 In.	358.00
Jardiniere, Etched Sunflowers, Orange, Ivory, Celadon, F. Ferrell, 10 x 13 1/2 In.	500.00
Plaque, Stylized Flowers, Green Matte Ground, Frame, 11 3/4 x 5 3/4 In.	1910.00
Tankard, Leathery Green Glaze, Brown Trim, Stamped, 6 1/2 x 5 In.	345.00
Tile, Purple Grapes, Leaves, Mustard Ground, Bullnose, Matte, Raised Outline, 6 In.	259.00
Vase, Bottle Shape, Autumn Leaves, 10 1/2 x 5 In.	545.00
Vase, Flowers, Ocher, Yellow, Leaves, Sage Green, 3 1/2 x 4 In.	55.00
Vase, Green Matte Glaze, Mottled, 2 Lizards, 3 Handles, Impressed Mark, 5 In.	60.00
Vase, Leaves, Gourd, Incised, J.B.O., 5 1/8 In.	160.00
Vase, Lotus, Blackberries, Handles, Penny, Marked, 8 1/8 In.	185.00
Vase, Nudes Among Poppies, Molded Leaves, Handles, Henri Deux, 13 1/2 In.	375.00
Vase, Parchment, Poppies, Pink, Yellow, Painted In Heavy Slip, Marked, 15 1/2 In.	690.00
Vase, Utopian, Cat, Mae Timberlake, 10 1/2 In.	3450.00
Vase, Utopian, Horse Head, Marked, 16 3/8 In.	920.00
Vase, Utopian, Jack Russell Terrier, Marked, Claude Leffler, 8 3/8 In.	1955.00
Vase, Utopian, Orange Rose, Owenzart Stamp, 13 1/4 x 6 In.	118.00
Vase, Utopian, Pansies, Bottle Shape, Impressed, 3 7/8 In.	35.00
Vase, Utopian, Pansies, Impressed, 12 1/4 In.	115.00
Vase, Utopian, Pansies, Signed A.J., 8 1/2 In.	265.00
Vase, Utopian, Virginia Creeper, Incised, Harry Robinson, 5 1/2 In.	140.00
Vase, Utopian, Wild Rose, Matte, Impressed, 14 In.	185.00
Vase, White Chrysanthemums, Gray Ground, 12 1/4 In.	300.00

OYSTER PLATES were popular from the 1880s. Each course at dinner
was served in a special dish. The oyster plate had indentations shaped
like oysters. Usually six oysters were held on a plate. There is no
greater value to a plate with more oysters, although that myth continues to haunt antiques dealers. There are other plates for shellfish,
including cockle plates and whelk plates. The appropriately shaped
indentations are part of the design of these dishes.

5 Wells, Blue, Rust Brown Flowers, Victoria Pottery Mark, Austria	115.00
5 Wells, Haviland Limoges, 8 1/2 In.	225.00
5 Wells, Seashells, Shell Ridges, Gold & Blue Border, Limoges, c.1895, 8 1/2 In.	279.00
6 Wells, Majolica, Sarreguemines, France, 9 1/4 In.	165.00
8 Wells, Pink & Gold Decoration, Porcelain, Oval, Marked, Germany, 9 1/2 In.	175.00
Pink & Yellow Floral, Porcelain, Germany, 8 1/2 In.	30.00
Porcelain, Gilt Details, 8 1/2 In., 12 Piece	896.00

PADEN CITY Glass Manufacturing Company was established in 1916
at Paden City, West Virginia. The company made more than seventy
different colors of glass. The firm closed in 1951. Paden City Pottery
is not listed here.

Ardith, Bowl, Handles, 11 1/4 In.	45.00
Black Forest, Cake Plate, Green, Handles	135.00
Black Forest, Candleholder, Green, Mushroom, 2 1/2 In.	65.00
Black Forest, Plate, 10 3/8 In.	230.00
Black Forest, Sandwich Server, Round, Center Handle, Green, 10 1/4 In.	80.00
Bunny, Cotton Holder, Cheriglo, Satin, 5 x 4 1/2 In.	170.00
Crow's Foot, Bowl, Green, 10 In.	35.00
Crow's Foot, Bowl, Oval, 10 3/4 x 7 In.	55.00
Crow's Foot, Bowl, Square, Red, 9 In.	10.00
Crow's Foot, Candlestick, Mushroom, Black, 2 1/2 In., Pair	80.00
Crow's Foot, Candlestick, Mushroom, Cobalt Blue, 2 1/2 In., Pair	90.00
Crow's Foot, Creamer, Red	20.00
Crow's Foot, Cup, Red	5.00
Crow's Foot, Ice Bucket, Black, Wicker Handle, 6 3/4 x 7 In.	290.00

Crow's Foot, Plate, Black, 8 5/8 In. 15.00
Crow's Foot, Sandwich Server, Mulberry, Center Handle, 10 1/4 In. 300.00
Crow's Foot, Vase, Red, 9 3/4 x 6 5/8 x 4 1/2 In. 150.00
Eleanor, Candy Jar, Gold Trim, 1930s 30.00
Figurine, Chinese Pheasant, Blue, c.1930, 13 1/2 In. 185.00
Figurine, Pheasant, Blue, 6 1/2 x 13 In. 125.00
Figurine, Pony, Blue, 12 In. 175.00
Figurine, Rooster, Drilled For Lamp, 11 1/8 x 6 1/2 In. 230.00
Gadroon, Cup, Royal Blue 20.00
Gadroon, Saucer, Royal Blue 8.00
Gazebo, Bowl, Salad, Etched Flowers, c.1930, 12 x 3 3/4 In. 80.00
Gothic Garden, Platter, Oval, 14 1/2 In. 30.00
Lela Bird, Vase, Green, 10 In. 160.00
Maya, Candlestick, Double, 6 1/4 In., Pair 25.00
Paden Garden, Platter, Oval, 14 1/2 In. 30.00
Party Line, Console, 4 x 12 In. 15.00
Peacock & Wild Rose, Cake Plate, 10 1/4 x 1 1/4 In. 130.00
Peacock & Wild Rose, Vase, 10 1/8 x 6 1/4 In. 290.00
Pheasant Hunt, Compote, Gadroon Shape, 3 3/8 x 5 5/8 In. 50.00
Regina, Candlestick, Mushroom, Black, 2 1/2 In., Pair 125.00
Spring Orchard, Candy Dish, Red, Crow's Foot Shape 225.00
Spring Orchard, Cocktail, Glades Shape 50.00
Spring Orchard, Decanter Set, 5 Piece 195.00
Top Hat, Vase, Red, 4 3/4 In. 245.00

PAINTINGS listed in this book are not works by major artists but rather decorative paintings on ivory, board, or glass that would be of interest to the average collector. Watercolors on paper are listed under Picture. To learn the value of an oil painting by a listed artist you must contact an expert in that area.

Gouache On Paper, Gold Around Enthroned Rajah Rajasthan, 1800s, 5 1/2 x 5 In. 375.00
Gouache On Paper, Kangra, Goddess, Durga, Multi-Armed, 19th Century, 6 x 4 In. 145.00
Gouache On Paper, Kotah, 2 Attendant Figures In Respectful Pose, India, 7 x 4 In. 400.00
Ink On Paper, Jazz Musicians At Preservation Hall, Noel Rockmore, 20 x 30 In. 575.00
Oil On Board, Couple, European Street Scene, Coby Whitmore, c.1960, 21 x 17 In. 3080.00
Oil On Board, Misty Morning On Hudson River, Bayard Henry Tyler, c.1900, 20 x 24 In. ... 1495.00
Oil On Board, Mountainscape, Birch Trees, Cullen Yates, c.1940, 12 x 16 In. 865.00
Oil On Board, Portrait Of Nathan Hale, Edward Percy Moran, c.1915, 20 x 15 1/2 In. 1150.00
Oil On Board, Still Life, Flowers, George Ames Aldrich, c.1920, 20 x 16 In. 345.00
Oil On Board, Still Life, Peaches, Pears, Grapes, Clear Compote, Red Basket, 24 x 30 In. ... 550.00
Oil On Board, Woman Escapes Jail, Norman Saunders, 1950, 20 x 15 In. 15400.00
Oil On Canvas, 3 Young Ladies, English School, 19th Century, 18 x 18 In. 920.00
Oil On Canvas, Baby With Rattle, American School, 19th Century, 20 x 25 In. 748.00
Oil On Canvas, Bedoin Portrait, Continental, 1880, 16 x 12 In. 193.00
Oil On Canvas, Chicks In Basket, Gold Frame, Signed, Ben Austrian, c.1907, 15 x 17 In. . 21450.00
Oil On Canvas, Encampment, Peasant Woman & Child, E. Fanfani, 1800s, 32 x 21 In. ... 2070.00
Oil On Canvas, Flower Girl, George Kugelman Benda, Frame, c.1900, 31 1/2 x 19 In. ... 1430.00
Oil On Canvas, Folk Art, Black Boy, c.1875, 16 x 24 In. 11220.00
Oil On Canvas, Fruit Seller, American, c.1860, 26 x 20 In. 1800.00
Oil On Canvas, George Washington, Life Size, 72 1/4 x 33 In. 3818.00
Oil On Canvas, Gray Day, Alexander H. Wyant, 1836-1892, 14 x 21 In. 9200.00
Oil On Canvas, Henry Ford, John C. Johansen, 44 x 34 In. 3500.00
Oil On Canvas, House, Saltbox, Barn, Stone Wall, Dirt Path, 20th Century, 16 x 21 In. .. 110.00
Oil On Canvas, Masted Junk In Calm Waters, Chinese, 19th Century, 20 1/2 x 26 In. 2689.00
Oil On Canvas, Memorial To George & Martha Washington, 18 x 25 In. 6462.00
Oil On Canvas, Military Officer, Post-Civil War, 34 x 29 In. 700.00
Oil On Canvas, Moroccan Pottery Seller, Margaret Murray Cookesley, c.1900, 12 x 8 In. . 3165.00
Oil On Canvas, Mountainous Landscape, Ann Hill, Fl., c.1820, 13 x 19 In. 2689.00
Oil On Canvas, Musicale, J. Gontard, 1800s, 18 3/4 x 23 3/4 In. 2588.00
Oil On Canvas, Neoclassical Female, 19th Century, 40 x 19 In. 1495.00
Oil On Canvas, Portrait Of Lady, 19th Century, 50 x 40 In. 1265.00
Oil On Canvas, Portrait Of Mrs. Wright, 20th Century, 33 x 25 In. 288.00
Oil On Canvas, Portrait Of Young Boy, c.1850, 40 x 30 In. 2300.00

Painting, On Ivory, Woman,
Brenda Francklyn, Cleveland,
Gold Potter Studio Frame, 5 In.

A miniature painting should not be washed. Most miniatures are painted on ivory and the paint will wash off.

Pairpoint, Lamp,
Puffy, Butterflies,
Lilacs, Pink, Red,
Green, Signed,
10 In.

Oil On Canvas, Portrait, Woman Holding Daguerreotype, Giltwood, 29 3/8 x 24 3/8 In.	1998.00
Oil On Canvas, Reluctance, Edmund Henry Wuerpel, Arts & Crafts Frame, 39 x 50 In.	2900.00
Oil On Canvas, River Landscape, People, 1800s, 18 x 16 In.	172.00
Oil On Canvas, Rural Landscape, Log Cabin, People, 1800s, 19 1/4 x 35 1/4 In.	200.00
Oil On Canvas, Seascape, Sailboats, Wesley Elbridge Webber, c.1890, 36 x 26 In.	2012.00
Oil On Canvas, Seated Dog, H. Eisenbach, 1900s, 18 1/2 x 15 In.	86.00
Oil On Canvas, Tavern Scene, Barmaid, 2 Seated Men, 1900s, 31 x 27 In.	230.00
Oil On Canvas, Winter's Twilight Shadows, Svend Svendson, Arts & Crafts, 29 x 21 In.	978.00
Oil On Canvas, Winterscape, Horses Towing People, Juliusz Slabiak, 1900s, 19 x 27 In.	316.00
Oil On Canvas, Woman With Children In Bedroom, Frederick Cohen, 1853, 28 x 36 In.	3450.00
Oil On Linen, Table Set, Robert Oliver, 39 x 39 In.	145.00
Oil On Masonite, Red & Gray Barns, Bertram Bruestle, Born 1902, 15 1/2 x 19 1/2 In.	2090.00
Oil On Oak Panel, Kettle Arrangement, Ferdinand Brutt, 20 3/4 x 27 3/4 In.	6875.00
Oil On Panel, Farm Scene, Chickens, Birds, Francois Van Severdonck, c.1880, 7 x 10 In.	2588.00
Oil On Panel, Landscape, Annotated On Verso, Dated June 1872, 8 x 12 3/4 In.	200.00
Oil On Panel, Woman With Shawl, Frame, American, 19th Century, 22 3/4 x 18 In.	1765.00
Oil On Tin, Primitive, English Landscape, Farm, River, Frame, 23 1/2 x 29 1/2 In.	440.00
Oil On Tin, Stigmata Of Christ, 5 Saint Figures, 13 3/4 x 9 3/4 In.	260.00
On Ivory, George Washington, Portrait, Brass Frame, 4 x 3 In.	425.00
On Ivory, Marie Louise, Portrait, Round, Frame, Signed, 3 In.	260.00
On Ivory, Woman, Brenda Francklyn, Cleveland, Gold Potter Studio Frame, 5 In. .... *Illus*	450.00
Reverse On Glass, 2 Dancing Girls, Calf, Mother-Of-Pearl, c.1900, 26 x 20 In.	288.00
Reverse On Glass, Admiral Perry, American, 19th Century, Frame, 4 1/2 x 3 1/2 In.	1175.00
Reverse On Glass, Floral Still Life, Frame, 9 1/2 x 7 1/2 In.	80.00
Reverse On Glass, M. Van Buren, Blue Coat, Brown Ground, Frame, 9 x 12 In.	1350.00
Reverse On Glass, St. Dominic, Receiving Rosary From Virgin, 12 3/4 x 17 In.	175.00
Reverse On Glass, Woman Admiring Miniature Portrait, Chinese, c.1800, 11 x 8 In.	3300.00

PAIRPOINT Manufacturing Company started in 1880 in New Bedford, Massachusetts. It soon joined with the glassworks nearby and made glass, silver-plated pieces, and lamps. Reverse-painted glass shades and molded shades known as *puffies* were part of the production until the 1930s. The company reorganized and changed its name several times but is still working today. Items listed here are glass or glass and metal. Silver-plated pieces are listed under Silver Plate.

Biscuit Jar, Cover, Pansies, Gold Scrolls, No. 3930, Signed, 6 In.	490.00
Bowl, Amberina, Polished Pontil, Silver Plated Base, 9 In.	330.00
Bowl, Rosaria, Bubble Ball Connector, Clear Foot, 12 In.	175.00
Box, Russian Cutting, Silver Overlay, Signed, 7 1/4 In.	460.00
Candlestick, Cobalt Blue, Grapes Cutting, 11 In., Pair	1440.00
Candlestick, Emerald Green, Ribbed, Bubble Connector, 4 In., Pair	70.00
Candlestick, Green, Grapes Cutting, 16 In., Pair	1080.00
Compote, Canaria, Grapes Cutting, 8 In.	260.00
Compote, Canaria, Grapes Cutting, Flared Rim, Bubble Ball Connector, 12 1/8 In.	330.00
Compote, Cobalt Blue Twist, Ruffled Edge, Clear Stem, Foot, 8 In.	780.00
Lamp, Berkeley Shade, Poppies, Roses, Pansies, Urn Base, Signed, 21 1/2 In.	1680.00
Lamp, Bombay Shade, New Bedford Harbor, Silver Plated Base	3525.00
Lamp, Directore Shade, Fisherman, Large Fish, Rough Seas, 6 Sides, 27 In.	5320.00

Lamp, Florence Shade, Reverse Painted, Chrysanthemums, Red, Lavender, White, 21 In. .	6900.00
Lamp, Metal Overlay, Basketweave, Swags, Blue, Purple, Puffed Slag, 8 Sides, 31 In. . . .	980.00
Lamp, Pierced Brass Shade, Prisms, 2 Pulls, Circular Base, 4-Footed, 17 In.	1000.00
Lamp, Prism Stem, Marble Base, Fluted Shade, Signed, 4 1/2 x 5 In., Pair	1800.00
Lamp, Puffy, Butterflies, Lilacs, Pink, Red, Green, Signed, 10 In. . . . . *Illus*	21280.00
Lamp, Puffy, Flowers, Butterflies, Leaves, Silver Metal Base, 7 x 10 1/2 In.	3450.00
Lamp, Puffy, Flowers, Pink, Red, Yellow, Orange, Silver Metal Base, 6 1/2 x 6 1/2 In. . . .	4025.00
Lamp, Puffy, Orange Tree, Tree Trunk Base, 24 In.	51750.00
Lamp, Puffy, Red, Blue Flowers, Green Leaves, Yellow Lattice, Signed, 14 1/2 In.	1150.00
Lamp, Puffy, Reverse Painted, Tulip, Floral, Urn Base, Square Foot, Signed, 24 In.	4200.00
Lamp, Puffy, Rose Bonnet, Roses, Pink & Yellow, Silver Tree Trunk Base, 10 1/2 In.	5750.00
Lamp, Puffy, Stratford, Hummingbirds, Flowers, Gold Metal Base, 13 x 21 1/2 In.	9200.00
Lamp, Puffy, Stratford, Roses, Butterflies, Tree Trunk Base, Signed, 14 1/2 In.	3080.00
Lamp, Puffy, Stratford, Yellow Lattice, Floral Border, Brass Base, Signed, 8 1/2 In.	2200.00
Lamp, Puffy, Torino, Pink Blossoms, Vine & Flower Base, c.1915, 15 1/2 In.	4600.00
Lamp, Puffy, Tulip, Closed Top, Gold Accents, Square, Legs, Paw Feet, No. B3025, 15 In.	7280.00
Lamp, Reverse Painted, Band Of Peacocks, Urns, Multicolored Scrolling, 15 In.	1175.00
Lamp, Reverse Painted, City, Sailing Ships, Brass Base, 2 Handles, 19 x 25 In.	2875.00
Lamp, Reverse Painted, Floral, Embossed Floral Base, Pull Chain, Signed, 15 In.	3640.00
Lamp, Reverse Painted, Flowers, Blue, Yellow, Pink Ground, Signed, 22 1/2 In.	2600.00
Lamp, Reverse Painted, Italian Garden Scene, Baluster Base, 2 Sockets, 22 In.	2235.00
Lamp, Reverse Painted, Parrots, Branches, Fronds, 3-Footed, Urn On Stem, 22 In.	4480.00
Lamp, Reverse Painted, Pink Flowers, Handled Urn Base, Scalloped Foot, 22 In.	2130.00
Lamp, Reverse Painted, Red & Purple Flowers, Yellow Lattice, Signed, 14 In.	2800.00
Lamp, Reverse Painted, Red, Yellow, Flowers, Turquoise Ground, Signed, 19 1/2 In.	3163.00
Lamp, Reverse Painted, Ships, Ocean, Dolphin Footed Base, Signed, 22 In.	3850.00
Lamp, Reverse Painted, Triangular Shade, Poppies, Waisted 8-Sided Base, 23 x 16 In. . . .	2645.00
Lamp, Reverse Painted, Vases Of Stylized Flowers, 3-Leg Base, 21 In.	2800.00
Lamp, Reverse Painted, Venetian Harbor, Flower Stem, Square Foot, 16 x 22 In.	7475.00
Lamp, Reverse Painted, Venetian Scene, 6-Sided Base, Signed, 22 In.	3360.00
Lamp, Reverse Painted, Wind, Landscape, Tripod Base, No. 427, 22 3/4 In.	1300.00
Lamp, Reverse Painted, Yellow & Pink Roses, Green Leaves, Flared Bottom, 16 In.	2800.00
Lamp, Seville Shade, Reverse Painted, Garden Scene, Metal Base, c.1920, 16 x 21 In. . . .	3335.00
Lamp, Springfield Shade, Purple Flowers, Exterior Outlined Leaves, Signed, 16 In.	3165.00
Lamp, Touraine Shade, Painted Parrots, Floral, Foliage, Gold, 3-Leg Base, 22 1/2 In.	800.00
Lamp Base, Planter, Ring Handles, Tree Trunk Supports, 14 1/2 In.	2015.00
Shade, Puffy, Butterflies, Flowers, Blue & Green Ground, Signed, 3 3/4 x 5 1/2 In.	2072.00
Vase, Rosaria Cut To Clear, Bubble Ball Connector, Square Clear Base, 13 1/4 In.	978.00
Vase, Ruby, Urn Shape, Clear Handles, Bubble Ball Connector, 12 In.	336.00

PALMER COX, BROWNIES, see Brownies category.

PAPER collectibles, including almanacs, catalogs, children's books, some greeting cards, stock certificates, and other paper ephemera, are listed here. Paper calendars are listed separately in the Calendar category. Paper items may be found in many other sections, such as Christmas and Movie.

Birth, Baptismal Record, Catharina Ritter, 1808, Ink, Watercolor, Frame, 10 x 16 In.	413.00
Birth, Baptismal Record, Daniel Arner, 1816, Ink, Watercolor, Frame, 11 x 16 In.	440.00
Birth, Baptismal Record, Elizabeth Weitnechtin, 1799, Ink, Color, Frame, 16 x 19 In.	1650.00
Birth, Baptismal Record, Ink, Watercolor, Frame, c.1818, 15 x 18 In.	3300.00
Birth, Baptismal Record, Ink, Watercolor, York County, Penn., Frame, c.1823, 16 x 19 In.	8250.00
Birth, Baptismal Record, Johan Scherider, Ink, Watercolor, 19th Century, 12 x 15 In.	1434.00
Birth, Baptismal Record, Johonnus Heller, Watercolor, Gold Leaf, c.1816, 7 x 12 In.	7170.00
Birth, Baptismal Record, Owen Krauss, 1811, Ink, Watercolor, Frame, 19 x 21 1/2 In. . . .	5500.00
Birth, Baptismal Record, Printed, Illuminated, George Dietrich, Berks Co., 16 x 13 In. . . .	132.00
Birth, Baptismal Record, Printed, Illuminated, John Long, Lebanon, Penn., 16 x 20 In. . . .	550.00
Birth, Baptismal Record, Sam Reinschmitt, Ink & Watercolor, Penn., c.1810, 11 x 15 In. .	1760.00
Birth, Baptismal Record, Suwsettaguthard, Berks Co., Frame, c.1841, 18 x 15 1/2 In.	302.00
Birth, Baptismal Record, Watercolor, Ink. Pinprick Design, c.1820, 7 3/8 x 12 In.	3585.00
Birth Record, Eliza Dunn, 1810, Ink & Watercolor, Frame, 10 1/4 x 12 1/2 In.	3300.00
Birth Record, Watercolor, Flowers, Leaves, German Text, c.1786, 15 1/2 x 11 In.	2200.00
Blotter, Baby In Officer's Hat Saluting New Year, Leyendecker, 1942	18.00

Book, Big Little Book, Secret Agent, 1938 . . . . 20.00
Book, Little Golden Book, Bozo The Hide & Seek Elephant, 1968 . . . . 5.00
Book, Little Golden Book, Bugs Bunny, Simon & Schuster, Third Printing, 1949 . . . . 5.00
Book, Little Golden Book, Madeline, 1954 . . . . 10.00
Book, Little Golden Book, Woody Woodpecker, Simon & Schuster, 1952 . . . . 4.00
Booklet, Art Of Bait Casting, William Shakespeare Jr., c.1902, 3 1/2 x 6 In., 16 Pages . . . 495.00
Booklet, Winchester, How Many Birds Get Through, 1918, 5 1/2 x 3 1/4 In., 14 Pages . . . 265.00
Bookplate, Ink & Watercolor, Debit & Credit Book For Jacob Opp, 1785, 14 x 9 1/4 In. . . 1650.00
Bookplate, Optics, Cyclopedia, Arts & Sciences, Frame, London, 1785, 21 x 17 In. 353.00
Bookplate, Watercolor, Ink, Barbara Eby, American School, Dated 1827, 4 x 6 5/8 In. . . . 478.00
Bookplate, Watercolor, Ink, Susana Stauffer, Cherry Mitered Frame, c.1791, 9 x 6 1/2 In. . . 660.00
Broadside, Public Vendu, Phila., April 9, 1880, D. Humphreys, Frame, 17 x 14 1/2 In. . . 195.00
Brochure, Winchester, Close Out Special, 1932, 8 1/2 x 11 In. 55.00
Calligraphy, Stag, Ink On Paper, M. E. Blackman, c.1883, 45 1/2 x 31 In. 1610.00
Catalog, Bristol, Horton Mfg., 1916, Fishing Camp Scene Cover, 40 Pages 170.00
Catalog, Edward Vom Hofe, 1929, Fishing Tackle, New York, 9 x 6 In., 173 Pages 440.00
Catalog, F.E. Chester, 1922, Manufacturer Of Floats, Providence, 10 x 7 1/2 In., 32 Pages 688.00
Catalog, Huck Manufacturing Company, 1905, Illinois, 10 1/4 x 6 1/2 In., 32 Pages 44.00
Catalog, King Folding Canvas Boat Co., 1922, Kalamazoo, Michigan, 32 Pages 110.00
Catalog, New Ithaca Gun, 1932, Shotguns, 13 1/2 x 8 1/2 In., 20 Pages 90.00
Catalog, Park, Davis & Co., 1889, Soft Cover, 4 x 9 1/4 In., 124 Pages 50.00
Catalog, Pflueger Trade, 1940, No. 61, Supplements, 9 x 6 In., 244 Pages 120.00
Catalog, Pilling Cattle Instrument, 5 3/4 x 3 1/4 In., 48 Pages 50.00
Catalog, Superior Stoves & Range, 1913, 7 1/2 x 10 1/2 x 3/4 In., 168 Pages 66.00
Coloring Book, Calvin & The Colonel, Artcraft No. 1669, 1962 . . . . 20.00
Coloring Book, Mr. Magoo, Shakespearian Dress, Whitman, No. 1137, 1965 . . . . 20.00
Coloring Book, Pink Panther Painting Self Portrait, Whitman, No. 1051, 1975 . . . . 12.00
Coloring Book, Underdog, Whitman, No. 1010, 1972 . . . . 18.00
Coloring Book, Yogi Bear Playing Tuba, Whitman, 1963 . . . . 8.00
Comic Book, The Shadow, Who Is The Freak Show Killer, The Shadow Knows, 1973 . . . 15.00
Deed, Land Indenture, Henry Stiegel, Manheim, Penn., 1762, 15 x 21 3/4 In. 990.00
Document, Marriage, Quaker, Reay King & Anna Wilson, Philadelphia, 1795, 16 x 26 In. 120.00
Document, Ship's Passage, Signed, Andrew Jackson, c.1831, 14 1/2 x 10 In. 1840.00
Fraktur, Birds, Blue, Tulip, Flowers, Bucks Co., Frame, 6 3/4 x 5 5/8 In. 5500.00
Fraktur, Eagle, Double Head, Snakes In Talons, Frame, 1812, 10 3/4 x 9 3/4 In. 8800.00
Fraktur, Hand Drawn, Watercolor, Washington County, Md., c.1786, 9 x 14 In. 3575.00
Fraktur, Medallion, Peacocks, Flowers, Names, Dates, 1794, 13 1/4 x 15 3/4 In. 2310.00
Fraktur, Parrots, Tulips, Flowers, Lancaster Co., Pa., 4 x 6 1/2 In. 2475.00
Fraktur, Psalm, Watercolor, Ink, Flowers, Curly Maple Frame, 17 x 20 1/4 In. 495.00
Fraktur, Taufschein, Angels, Cherubs, Fruit, Red, Gold, Penn., Frame, c.1814, 17 x 19 In. 660.00
Fraktur, Taufschein, Illuminated, Anna Maria Ledig, Penn., c.1824, 15 3/4 x 12 3/4 In. . . 165.00
Fraktur, Watercolor, Ink, Flowers, Musical Notations, 1803, 8 x 12 1/2 In. 1925.00
Fraktur, Watercolor, Tulip & Heart, Sam Ensminger, Lancaster Co., c.1839, 6 x 5 In. 580.00
Handout, Keen Kutter, Pan Pacific Expo, Made Of 10,000 Tools, 1915, 10 1/2 x 7 In. . . . 55.00
House Blessing, German, Birds, Flowers, J. Bauman, c.1803, 8 1/2 x 8 1/2 In. 470.00
House Blessing, German, Printed, Illuminated, Henrich Otto, Lancaster Co., 19 x 15 In. . . 3850.00
House Blessing, Illuminated, Johann Ritter & Co., Reading, Penn., 15 x 10 In. 195.00
Letterhead, Wells Fargo, Office General Agent, Red, White, Blue, c.1900, 8 x 5 In. 35.00
Logbook, Whaling, Henry Worth, Leather Binder, Pictures, c.1789, 12 1/2 x 8 In. 7475.00

Paper, Napkin, Valentine's Day,
Heart, Square, 6 1/2 In.

Paper, Napkin, Thanksgiving,
Turkey & Vegetables, Square, 6

Lottery Ticket, University Of Maryland, $250,000.00, 1818, 9 1/2 x 4 In. 115.00
Manuscript, Illuminated, Watercolor, Gilt, Gouache, Arabic, Early 19th Century, Pair 835.00
Map, United States, J.B. Holmes, July 1876, States & Territory In Color, 30 x 42 In. 350.00
Memorial, Cut, 2 Doves, Heart, Open Hand, Lock Of Hair, Frame, 19th Century, 5 x 3 In. 1410.00
Napkin, Thanksgiving, Turkey & Vegetables, Square, 6 3/4 In. . . . . *Illus* 1.00
Napkin, Valentine's Day, Heart, Square, 6 1/2 In. . . . . *Illus* 1.00
Plate, Let's Have A Pat Boone Party, Orange Rim, Heart, Music Notes, 1950s, 6 Piece . . . 15.00
Presentation Drawing, Watercolor, Ink, Penn. School, Late 18th Century, 8 x 4 In. 837.00
Program, Ringling Bros. & Barnum & Bailey Circus, Gunther Gebel-Williams, 1974 . . . . 40.00
Receipt, Edw. Hardy Mfr. Of Fancy Flowerpots, Penn., 1900, 10 x 11 1/2 In. 130.00
Reward Of Merit, Watercolor, Ink, Mary E. Long, Lancaster, c.1820, 7 x 7 In. 690.00
Reward Of Merit, Watercolor, Lancaster Seminary, Jacob M. Long, c.1827, 9 x 6 1/2 In. . 580.00
Scrapbook, Elbert Hubbard, 228 Pages, Embossed Leather Cover, c.1923, 7 x 10 In. 69.00
Stock Certificate, American Express, Wells & Fargo, Dated Oct. 18, 1865, 27 x 41 In. . . . 1005.00
Stock Certificate, Barnum & Bailey, England, 1902 . . . . 1500.00
Stock Certificate, Nevada Territory, Bowery Gold & Silver Mining Co., 1863 . . . . 700.00
Stock Certificate, Tonopah Nevada Mining, Signed By Jim Butler, c.1903 . . . . 220.00
Stock Certificate, United Artists Studio Corp., California, March 2, 1928 . . . . 4500.00
Ticket, Lady, Jackson Fishing Club, December 11, 1872, Frame, 5 1/2 x 8 1/2 In. 44.00
Ticket, Military Ball In Honor Of The Creek Indians, New Orleans, Jan. 1824, 4 1/2 In. . . 250.00
Ticket, Yellow Cab Co., Chicago, Good For One Ride 20.00
Tourist Guide, Yosemite, Ansel Adams Photo, 1936 . . . . 35.00

PAPER DOLLS were probably inspired by the pantins, or jumping jacks, made in eighteenth-century Europe. By the 1880s, sheets of printed paper dolls and clothes were being made. The first paper doll books were made in the 1920s. Collectors prefer uncut sheets or books or boxed sets of paper dolls. Prices are about half as much if the pages have been cut.

Baby Snooks, Dancing, Lewis Howe Co., 1950, 16 In. 35.00
Barbie, Design-A-Fashion, Doll, Patterns, Tissue Paper, Colored Pencils, Box, 1979 . . . . . 20.00
Betsy McCall, Easter, 1 Doll, 2 Dresses, 1958, Uncut 20.00
Buffy & Jody, Family Affair, 2 Dolls, 32 Clothing Pieces, Box, 1970 . . . . 35.00
Colonial Williamsburg, 8 Dolls, 8 Costumes, Box, 1967, Uncut 40.00
Dame Trot, 3 Dresses Accordion Fold, 1880s, Uncut 600.00
Dinah Shore, 2 Dolls, Outfits, Whitman 55.00
Judy Garland, 3 Dolls, 30 Outifts, Tom Tierney, 1982, Uncut 10.00
Let's Play House, 16 Dolls, Outfits, Furniture, Lowe, Box, 1949, Uncut 80.00
Miss Minnie Warren, 3 Dresses, 2 Hats, 1860s, Uncut, Wrappers, 2 x 3 In. 400.00
Peter Rabbit, 5 Dolls, 6 Clothing Pages, Color, A. Stanley, New York, Dell, 1939 . . . . . . 325.00
Raggedy Ann & Andy, Saalfield, Folio, Die Cut, Uncut, c.1944 . . . . 250.00
Real Life, Dolly Land, Painting, Cutting, Dressing, Charles Thompson, Chicago, 1913 . . . 750.00
Ruby Rose, McLoughlin Bros., N.Y., c.1850 . . . . 600.00
Stella, McLoughlin Bros., N.Y., c.1865 . . . . 400.00
Sturbridge Village, Box, 1950s, Partially Cut 80.00
Texas Rose, Cowgirl, Doll, 6 Sheets, Saalfield, 1959, Uncut 35.00
Twiggy, Carrying Pocket, Whitman, 1967, Uncut 110.00
Woody Woodpecker & Miranda, No. 1344, 1963, 10 1/2 x 4 In. 18.00

PAPERWEIGHTS must have first appeared along with paper in ancient Egypt. Today's collectors search for every type, from the very expensive French weights of the nineteenth century to the modern artist weights or advertising pieces. The glass tops of the paperweights sometimes have been nicked or scratched, and this type of damage can be removed by polishing. Some serious collectors think this type of repair is an alteration and will not buy a repolished weight; others think it is an acceptable technique of restoration that does not change the value. Baccarat paperweights are listed separately under Baccarat.

Advertising, Anderson Concrete, Skyline, Trucks, Glass, Dome, c.1950, 3 In. 24.00
Advertising, Archies Lobster House, Boat, Fish, Glass, c.1950, 3 In. 60.00
Advertising, Ballards Obelisk Flour, Louisville, Mirror, Metal Rim, 3 1/2 In. 200.00
Advertising, Boyertown Casket, Figural Casket, Cast Metal, 5 1/8 x 2 1/4 In. 160.00
Advertising, Consolidated Ice Co., Figural, Glass, Pittsburgh, Pa., 2 1/4 x 4 In. 150.00

Advertising, Exide Battery, Factory Scene, Glass, 4 1/2 x 2 3/4 x 3/4 In. 84.00
Advertising, Henry J. Weilersbacher, Beer, Carbonated Beverages, Glass, 4 x 2 In. 126.00
Advertising, Husky Refining Company, Figural Dog, Husky, Bronze, 4 x 4 In. 143.00
Advertising, Imperial Glass, 3 In. 100.00
Advertising, John Stetson, Domed Glass, Bust, c.1910, 3 In. 195.00
Advertising, Lawrence Cement Co., Strongest Of American Cements, Glass, 3 In. 18.00
Advertising, Lion, Monarch Fire Insurance Co., Cleveland, Ohio, 5 1/2 In. 140.00
Advertising, Precision Die Casting, Horseshoe, Metal, c.1930, 2 3/4 x 3 In. 18.00
Advertising, Smith & Wesson, Model 29.44 Magnum, Lucite, Blue Base, 3 x 5 In. 100.00
Advertising, Smith Brothers Cough Drops, S.B., Round, Cast Iron, 2 1/4 x 3/4 In. 80.00
Advertising, Sun Vapor Street Light Co., Sun Gas Arc, Glass, 2 1/2 x 4 x 3/4 In. 75.00
Advertising, Tuff Guy, Westinghouse, Plaster, Gold, c.1950, 5 In. 45.00
Bear, Standing, Cast Iron 176.00
Caldwell & Co., Gilt Bronze, Chinese Girl, Seated, Blue Lazuli Base, Signed, 4 In. 2115.00
Cannon Projectile, Oak Leaves, Acorns, Komorau, Iron, 1914, 2 3/4 x 5 In. 85.00
Cartlidge, Charles, Spaniel, Seated, Porcelain, White Glaze, Rectangular Base, 2 In. 295.00
Clasped Hands, Stone, Carved, Sailor's Sleeve, Lady's Hand, 1800s, 2 x 5 In. 1295.00
Clichy, Concentric, Scattered Millefiori, France, c.1850, 2 5/8 In. 705.00
Clichy, Concentric, Scattered Millefiori, France, c.1960, 2 1/2 In. 765.00
Clichy, Millefiori, Concentric, Multicolored Rings, Blue & White Swirl, 1 x 2 In. 425.00
Clichy, Millefiori, Concentric, Rose Canes, Turquoise Ground, 1 1/2 x 2 1/4 In. 1500.00
Clichy, Millefiori, Concentric, Star, White Cane, 2 Rings, 1 x 2 In. 300.00
Clichy, Millefiori, Green, White Center Cane, 26 Cane Outer Ring, 1 1/2 x 2 1/8 In. 400.00
Clichy, Millefiori, Multicolored Canes, Twists, Eagles, Rabbit, 1 7/8 x 2 3/4 In. 350.00
Clichy, Millefiori, Star Center, 2 Outer Rings, 5 Sides, 1 1/4 x 1 3/4 In. 325.00
CM & StP, Milwaukee Road Bi-Polar, Electric, Metal, No. 10250, 6 x 1 3/4 In. 75.00
Cobalt Blue Dahlia, White Cane Center, Speckled Red & White Ground, 3 In. 470.00
Corrina, Silver Crescent Moon, Silver Waves, Iridescent Blue, Signed, 2 1/2 In. 46.00
Dog, Scottish Terrier, Painted, Black, Red Collar, Cast Iron, 20th Century, 3 x 3 1/2 In. . . . 60.00
Dog, Springer Spaniel, Standing, Cast Iron 50.00
Dog, Wolfhound, Reclining, Cast Iron 127.00
Figural, Man, Woman, Colonial Dress, Cast Iron, Pair 28.00
Figural, Tractor, Cast Metal 55.00
Figurine, Reclining Dog, Rockingham Glaze, Lyman Fenton & Co., 1849, 4 1/2 In. 848.00
Flower, Red Poinsettia, White Latticinio, 1870-1887 . . . . 120.00
Frog, Pressed Glass, Dark Teal, Head Up, Mouth Open, 2 1/8 x 2 7/8 x 4 In. 110.00
Fruit On Swirled Latticinio, Fruit, Green Leaves, Late 19th Century, 2 x 2 1/2 In. 275.00
Glass, Multicolored Swirl, Metallic Accents, 3 3/4 In. 25.00
Glass, Pear Shape, Pale Yellow To Blush, Clear Base, 2 1/2 In. 1155.00
Labino, Free Form, Flower-Like Center, White, Amber, Iridescent Gold, 1969, 2 1/2 In. . . . 209.00
Labino, Mottled Polychrome Flower, Bold Ruby Swirled Base, 1976, 2 3/4 In. 220.00
Locomotive, Car, Budd Co., Rail Diesel, 8 1/8 In. 50.00
Lotton, Crystal Magnum, Leaves, Vines, Iridized Tips, 15 Lbs., Signed, 6 x 7 1/2 In. 978.00
Lotton, Pink Flowers, Blue Leaves, Frosted Crystal, Signed, 1976, 2 1/2 In. 46.00
Lucite, Dried Flowers, Chenille Bumblebee, Dome Shape, 2 5/8 x 2 3/8 In. 28.00
Mammy, Standing, Hands On Hips, White Apron, Cast Iron 99.00
Marinot, Glass, Bubbles, Blue Inside Clear, c.1930, 2 3/8 In. 7800.00
McKinley, Roosevelt, Terry Of Columbus, Line Drawn Pictures 330.00
Memorial Hall, Oval, Frosted, Intaglio Building, 1 1/4 x 3 1/8 x 5 In. 110.00
Metal, Felix The Cat, Figural, c.1920, 2 1/4 In. 125.00
Millefiori, Red Ground, Lavender, Celadon Canes, Spoked, Scotland, 2 x 3 In. 29.00
New England Glass Co., Bouquet, Double Swirled Latticinio, Multicolored, 2 x 3 In. 1600.00
Pairpoint, Rose Canes & Facet 69.00
Pansies, Purple & Yellow, Red & White Cane Center, 3 In. 550.00
Photo, Railroad, Car & Pavilion On Summit, Mt. Tom, Glass, 4 1/4 In. 20.00
Poinsettia, 2 Tiers, Red, White Stripes, Green Leaves, Late 1800s, 1 1/2 x 2 1/2 In. 600.00
Red Poinsettia, White & Blue Cane Center, White Latticinio Ground, 3 1/4 In. 358.00
Red Shaded To White Rose, Green Petals, Round Base, 3 1/2 In. 110.00
Rose, 13 Red Petals, 4 Green Leaves, Applied Foot, 20th Century, 3 1/2 x 3 In. 175.00
Rubber, Figural, Fred Flintstone, Hear, See, Speak, No Evil, 1973, 2 x 4 x 3 In. 50.00
Sandwich, Fruit, Alternating Pears & Leaves, White Latticinio Ground, 2 x 2 In. 210.00
Sandwich, Poinsettia, 12 Pink Petals, Green, White & Pink Cane, 2 x 3 In. 330.00
Sandwich, Poinsettia, Red Petals, Pink, White Canes, White Latticinio Ground, 2 In. 360.00

Sandwich, Red Poinsettia, Center Cane, Dewdrops, 5 Green Leaves, 2 x 3 In. 350.00
Scarab, Blue Glaze, Marked, 1 x 2 7/8 In. 259.00
Shackamaxon Worsted Co., Factory, Milk Glass Bottom, 3 1/2 x 2 In. 85.00
Snookums, Crawling, Chalk, c.1910, 3 1/2 x 4 In. 60.00
Squirrel, Painted, Cast Iron, Base, c.1930, 2 In. 25.00
St. Clair, Clear Glass, Blue Rose, Pedestal 5500.00
St. Clair, Hand Bell Form, Rose, Dark Pink 3025.00
St. Louis, Faceted Nosegay, 4 Millefiori, 5 Leaves, Strawberry Base, c.1960, 3 In. 705.00
St. Louis, Mushroom, Double Overlay, Millefiori, 6 Oval Facets, 1900s, 2 7/8 In. 380.00
St. Louis, Nosegay, Millefiori, Leaves, Stems, Strawberry Cut Base, c.1870, 2 5/8 In. 235.00
St. Louis, Red Berries, Leafy Stem, Latticinio Ground, Signature Cane, c.1952, 3 In. 175.00
St. Louis, Sulphide, Cameo Of Queen Elizabeth, Millefiori, Faceted, 1953, 3 In. 110.00
Stahl, Redware, Slab, Canted Corners, Incised Decoration, 8/18/41, 3 x 4 In. 110.00
Steer For Iron Mountain Route, Domed, Round, Longhorn's Head, c.1900 . . . .   190.00
Stetson, Glass, White Ground, 3 1/4 In. 150.00
Taft, Sherman, Octagon 357.00
Yellow Crescent Moon, Stars, Ocean, Signed, Lundberg, 1987, 3 1/4 In. 58.00
Yellow Flowers, Burgundy Vines, Iridescent Blue, Lilac, Signed, Lundberg, 3 In. 86.00

PAPIER-MACHE is made from paper mixed with glue, chalk, and other ingredients, then molded and baked. It becomes very hard and can be painted. Boxes, trays, and furniture were made of papier-mache. Some of the nineteenth-century pieces were decorated with mother-of-pearl. Papier-mache is still being used to make small toys, figures, candy containers, boxes, and other giftwares. Furniture made of papier-mache is listed in the Furniture category.

Box, Cat Face, Early 20th Century 355.00
Box, Foil Back Transfers, Russian Scenes, Lock, c.1890, 6 1/2 x 4 1/2 In., Pair 460.00
Candlestick, Polychrome Design, Art Nouveau-Style, England, 1800s, Pair 430.00
Cat, Recumbent, Painted, Glass Eyes, 19th Century, 9 1/2 & 10 5/8 In., Pair 1880.00
Charger, Tabbies On Oak Branch, American, c.1880, 16 In. 265.00
Crumbs Collect, Shell Shape, Asian Scene, Pont A Mousson, c.1870, 12 x 10 In. 100.00
Fan, Birds & Flowers, 13 In. 60.00
Game, Clown Face, Carnival Pitching Game, c.1930 . . . .   2200.00
Goat, Mechanical, Fur, White, Nodding Head, Brown Glass Eyes, c.1920, 21 In. 1750.00
Hat, Party, Monkey, Side-Glancing Green Eyes, Cigar, France, c.1910, 20 In. 375.00
Hat Stand, Woman's Head, Straw Bonnet, Danjard, Paris, 19th Century 1430.00
Horse Head, 11 1/2 In. 115.00
Jewelry Box, Scroll Edge, Hinge Lid, Gilt, Mother-Of-Pearl Inlay, c.1850, 10 In. 306.00
Letter Rack, Gold Chinoiserie Scene, Samurai Battle, Wall Mount, c.1880, 8 In. 160.00
Letter Sorter, Naturalist Relief Pattern, France, c.1860, 12 1/2 x 9 1/2 In. 380.00
Mannequin Head, Female, France, 15 In. 835.00
Matchbox, Gold Chinoiserie Scene, Black Lacquered Ground, c.1880, 3 x 3 In. 80.00
Milliner's Model, Lithographed Eyebrows, Eyes, Mouth, Bodice, France, 15 In. 764.00
Milliner's Model, Painted Hair, Facial Features, Lithographed Bodice, Paris, 15 In. 235.00
Milliner's Model, Striped Cap, Delphine Painted In Script, Early 1800s, 15 In. 1645.00
Pencil Box, 4 Men Racing, High Wheel Bikes, 8 In. 275.00
Roly Poly, Boy Soldier, 4 In. 200.00
Roly Poly, Happy Hooligan, 4 In. 250.00
Roly Poly, Schoenhut Drummer Boy, 4 In. 200.00
Snuffbox, Brass Shell Medallion Under Glass, William Pitt, 3 3/4 In. 450.00
Statue, Nipper, Painted, 36 In. 633.00
Tray, 2 Hunting Dogs, Flowers, Black Lacquer, Painted, Wood Base, 25 x 19 In. 1650.00
Tray, Black Lacquer, Oriental Country Estate, 19th Century, 19 x 26 x 21 In. 978.00
Tray, Painted Scene, Serpentine Edge, Stenciled Scroll Gilding, 24 1/2 x 31 In. 3819.00
Tray, Rectangular, Painted Birds, Floral, Gilt, Ebonized, Stand, c.1850, 30 1/2 In. 946.00
Tray, Regency, Black Lacquer, Polychrome, Gilt, Oval, Bamboo Stand, 19 x 20 In. 748.00
Tray, Regency, Lacquered, Rounded Rectangle, Ships, c.1815, 22 x 24 1/2 In. 1610.00
Tray, Scenic, Court House At Pittsburgh, Penn., Gold Design, 1856, 10 x 14 In. 495.00
Tray, Stand, Regency, Polychrome Painted, Early 19th Century, 19 x 30 x 22 In. 6572.00
Tray, Stand, Victorian, Nymph, Satyr, 29 1/2 x 21 1/2 In. 705.00
Tray, Victorian, Scalloped, Oval, Acanthine Border, Stand, Gilt, 21 x 31 1/2 x 26 In. 1093.00
Tray, William IV, Parcel Gilt, Brown Lacquer, c.1835, 21 1/2 x 30 In. 1495.00

PARASOL, see Umbrella category.

PARIAN is a fine-grained, hard-paste porcelain named for the marble it resembles. It was first made in England in 1846 and gained in favor in the United States about 1860. Figures, tea sets, vases, and other items were made of Parian at many English and American factories.

Bust, Marie Antoinette, Draped Shawl, Ribbon Tied Hair, Gilt Brass Base, c.1880, 11 In. . .	218.00
Figurine, Dante, Ariosto, 20 In., Pair	717.00
Figurine, Discobolo, Man Poised With Discus, Black & White Marble Base, 15 1/2 In. . . .	104.00
Figurine, Seaman, Standing, Arm Resting On Obelisk, White, Round Base, 12 1/2 In.	28.00
Figurine, Sunshine, Scantily Clad Woman, Holding Wheat, Titled Circular Base, 18 In. . .	410.00
Figurine, Woman Standing, Arms Crossed, Gilt-Trimmed Base, England, 14 In.	175.00
Group, Innocence Protected, Centurion Protecting Woman & Child, 20 In.	2350.00
Group, Wrestlers, Black & White Egyptian Marble Base, 11 x 12 In.	201.00
Tea Set, Donegal, 6-In. Teapot, 15 Piece . . . . , ...	115.00

PARIS, Vieux Paris, or Old Paris, is porcelain ware that is known to have been made in Paris in the eighteenth or early nineteenth century. These porcelains have no identifying mark but can be recognized by the whiteness of the porcelain and the lines and decorations. Gold decoration is often used.

Basket, Anneau D'Or, Reticulated, Paw Feet, c.1835, 4 1/2 x 9 In.	405.00
Basket, Applied Flowers, Polychrome, Enamel, Gilt Trim, Oval, Bail Handle, 9 x 16 In. . .	235.00
Basket, Gilded, Reticulated, Footed, c.1835, 8 1/2 x 8 7/8 In., Pair	1380.00
Bulb Pot, Alternating Floral Panels, 8 Sides, Lion's Head Feet, Square Base, 7 1/2 In. . . .	405.00
Bulb Vase, Cover, Imari Style, Paw Feet On Square Base, 6 x 4 1/2 In., Pair	1150.00
Coffee Service, Clauss Shape, White, Gold Striped, Child's, c.1835, 5 Piece	489.00
Coffee Set, Anneau D'Or, Faceted Pot, Fluted Cups & Saucers, 9-In. Pot, 28 Piece	144.00
Compote, Pierced Basket, Reeded Stem, Aqua, Gilt Bands, Ribbon Handles, 7 In., Pair . .	374.00
Compote, Tripodal, Gilded Melon Ground, Paw Feet, Mid 19th Century, 6 x 9 1/4 In. . . .	546.00
Cup & Saucer, Cylindrical Form, Gilded, Classical Designs, c.1835, 3 x 5 In.	230.00
Dish, Pierced Leaf Form, Cobalt & White Floral Panels, Flowers, c.1890, 10 In., Pair	430.00
Garniture Vase, Paul & Virginia, Flared, Late 19th Century, 16 x 11 In., Pair	3680.00
Plate, Dessert, Anneau D'Or, 5 Piece	40.00
Plate, Major General Brown, U.S. Army, Black, Gold Trim, 9 In.	950.00
Sauceboat, Scrolling Rope Twist Handle, Gilt, Oval Underplate, c.1910, 8 x 11 1/4 In. . . .	230.00
Tureen, Cover, White, Gilt Scrolling Leaves, Pink Ground, 1840s, 13 x 11 1/2 In.	495.00
Tureen, Raised Leaf Design, Rose, White, Gilt Accents, Cover, c.1880, 7 x 13 x 6 In., Pair	259.00
Urn, Campana Shape, Courting Couples, 2 Satyr Handles, Square Base, 16 In., Pair	1175.00
Urn, Goat Head Handles, Applied Flowers, c.1890, 17 1/4 In.	748.00
Vase, Egg Shape, Rustic Lovers, Masks, Red Ground, Gilt, Flare Neck, 17 In., Pair	1528.00
Vase, Enamel Flowers, Gray Ground, Black Rim & Foot, 11 5/8 In., Pair	440.00
Vase, Garniture, Swan Rhyton Shape, Gilt, Teal Green, Flowers, 10 x 7 x 5 In., Pair	1265.00
Vase, Gold Ground, Oval Panel, Classical Cameo Portraits, 19th Century, 10 3/4 In., Pair .	6570.00
Vase, Horse Head Handles, Middle Eastern Couple Panels, Flowers, Gilt, 21 In., Pair	1554.00
Vase, Hunting Figures, Acanthus Leaf Form, Biscuit, Gilt, 14 In., Pair	2070.00
Vase, Oval Floral Reserve, Gilt Scroll Spray, Rococo, Gilt Trim, 13 In.	430.00
Vase, Oval, Scroll Twig Handle, Acorn Design, Pedestal Base, Cartouche, c.1910, 7 In. . .	345.00
Vase, Painted Landscape, River, Butterfly, Birds, Gargoyle Handles, c.1875, 11 In., Pair . .	345.00
Vase, Polychrome, Floral Spray, Satyr Handles, c.1875, 18 In., Pair	605.00
Vase, Raised Gilt Scrollwork, Red & Blue Ground, Cartouches, Fruit, Flowers, 13 In., Pair	4700.00
Vase, White, Floral, Gold Highlights, 17 In., Pair	150.00

PATE-DE-VERRE is an ancient technique in which glass is made by blending and refining powdered glass of different colors into molds. The process was revived by French glassmakers, especially Galle, around the end of the nineteenth century.

Bowl, Green, Variegated Ebony, Silver Base, Art Deco, Initials, 5 1/4 In.	2300.00
Figurine, Sculpture, Dancer, Jean Descomps, c.1921, 7 1/2 x 11 3/8 In.	5975.00
Paperweight, Lobster, Charcoal, Red Spots, Yellow Ground, Impressed, 3 In.	805.00
Paperweight, Mouse, Signed, Decorchemont, c.1920, 2 1/4 x 4 In.	1554.00
Pendant, Blue Lizard, Rust Berries, Green, Frosted Ground, 2 1/4 In.	1275.00

PATE-SUR-PATE means paste on paste. The design was made by painting layers of slip on the ceramic piece until a relief decoration was formed. The method was developed at the Sevres factory in France about 1850. It became even more famous at the English Minton factory about 1870. It has since been used by many potters to make both pottery and porcelain wares.

Box, Cover, Victorian Courting Scene, Blue Ground, Transfer Mark, 6 x 2 3/4 In.	175.00
Vase, Flask Form, Cupids, Gold Wreath, Fruit, Flowers & Handles, 10 5/8 In., Pair	6900.00
Vase, Roman Woman, Laurel Wreath, Green, G. Heubach, c.1912, 4 In.	200.00
Vase, Simulated Tortoiseshell Ground, Cased, Girl Feeding Birds, 8 x 4 In., Pair	375.00

PAUL REVERE POTTERY was made at several locations in and around Boston, Massachusetts, between 1906 and 1942. The pottery was operated as a settlement house program for teenage girls. Many pieces were signed *S.E.G.* for Saturday Evening Girls. The artists concentrated on children's dishes and tiles. Decorations were outlined in black and filled with color.

Bookends, Landscape, Gray Matte Glaze, 1926, 4 x 5 1/4 In.	1035.00
Bookends, Owls On Tree Branch, Pink, Paper Label, Black Slip, c.1923, 3 3/4 In.	1265.00
Bowl, Daffodil, Curved Rim, Green Grass, Blue Ground, S.E.G., 1900s, 8 1/2 In.	3995.00
Bowl, Flared Rim, Teal Glaze, Eva Geneco, 1922, 3 x 7 1/2 In.	195.00
Bowl, Green Band, Gray On Ivory Ground, S.E.G., Mark, 6 In.	405.00
Bowl, Lotus Blossom, Cream & Yellow Ground, Impressed, 8 1/2 In.	410.00
Bowl, Lotus, Underplate, S.E.G., c.1910, 2 1/8 In.	1058.00
Bowl, Squirrel On Branch, Blue Ground, Motto, Sylvia Lois Kay, 1934, 1 1/2 x 5 In.	550.00
Cup, Goose Walking, Blue, Green, S.E.G., Sylvia Lois Kay, 3 1/2 x 4 1/4 In.	470.00
Cup, Hare & Cabbage, Green, Blue Band, S.E.G., Lillie Shapiro, 1920, 3 x 4 In.	495.00
Cup, Hen & Chick, Cream Ground, Black, Yellow Bands, S.E.G., 1900s, 1 1/2 In.	645.00
Cup & Saucer, Landscape, Motto	575.00
Cup & Saucer, Yellow, White Band, Black Band, c.1920	125.00
Honey Pot, Landscape, 6 Panels, Saturday Evening Girls, c.1914	5225.00
Paperweight, Ship, Blue, Brown, 8 Sides, Frame, S.E.G., 2 1/2 In.	470.00
Pitcher, Greek Key Border, White, Green, Blue, S.E.G., 4 1/4 In.	765.00
Pitcher, White Ducks, Blue Band, 1915, 3 In.	825.00
Planter, White Flowers, Green Leaves, Yellow, Blue, S.E.G., 1917, 4 x 8 In.	2530.00
Plate, 3 Chicks, Blue, Green, Sylvia Lois Kay, Marked, 8 1/4 In.	825.00
Plate, Cuerda Seca, White Lotus Blossoms, Blue, Gray Ground, S.E.G., 10 In.	650.00
Plate, Incised Trees, Houses, Beige, Cream, Yellow, S.E.G., c.1914, 6 1/4 In.	940.00
Plate, Lotus Blossom, Incised Border, Cream, Yellow Ground, S.E.G., c.1914, 8 In.	590.00
Plate, Stylized Flowers, Yellow, Cream, White Bands, S.E.G., c.1920, 7 1/2 In.	235.00
Plate, Swan, Ivory, Blue Border, S.E.G., Frannie Levine, 1919, 8 In. . . . . .660.00 to 875.00
Plate, Viking Ships, Green, Yellow, Blue, Brown, 8 3/4 In.	1650.00
Plate, Yellow, White Band, Black Band, 1919, 10 In.	95.00
Plate, You Must Still Be Bright, Ivory, Blue, Signed A.M., 1911, 6 1/4 In.	1430.00
Tile, Badger House, Corner Prince & Thacher St., Green, Blue, 3 3/4 In.	935.00
Trivet, Tile, Green Square In Gray, Semimatte Glaze, S.E.G., Frame, 6 In.	575.00
Vase, Blue, Gray Semimatte Glaze, Oval, Marked, 1927, 10 In.	200.00
Vase, Brown Glaze, Tapered, S.E.G., Eva Geneco, 1922, 5 1/2 x 4 1/2 In.	195.00
Vase, Midnight Black Glaze, S.E.G., 1920, 7 x 5 1/2 In.	250.00
Vase, Oval, Trees, Blue Sky, Blue, Green Semimatte Glaze, 1924, 4 1/4 In.	978.00
Vase, Scenic Border, Trees, S.E.G., 4 1/8 In.	720.00

PEACHBLOW glass was made by several factories beginning in the 1880s. New England peachblow is a one-layer glass shading from red to white. Mt. Washington peachblow shades from pink to bluish-white. Hobbs, Brockunier and Company of Wheeling, West Virginia, made coral glass that they marketed as Peach Blow. It shades from yellow to peach and is lined with white glass. Reproductions of all types of peachblow have been made. Related pieces may be listed under Gunderson and Webb Peachblow.

Bowl, Rose To Amber, Cased Blue, Enameled Trailings, 19th Century, 2 1/2 x 5 In.	865.00
Creamer, Cream To Deep Crimson, Glossy, Amber Handle, Wheeling, 3 In.	1120.00

Don't store ceramic dishes or figurines for long periods of time in old newspaper wrappings. The ink can make indelible stains on china.

Peachblow, Tumbler, White Interior,
Pontil, Hobbs, Brockunier & Co., 3 3/4 In.

Cruet, Glossy, Applied Reeded Handle, Amber Faceted Stopper, Wheeling, 6 3/4 In.	2240.00
Fairy Lamp, Enameled Ivy & Branch Pattern, Clarke Base	550.00
Jug, Shaded Red To Yellow, Oval, Flattened, Slender Neck, Twisted Handle, 1900s, 7 In.	645.00
Paperweight, Pear, Full Stem, Mt. Washington	75.00
Paperweight, Pear, Translucent, Shaded White To Pink, New England, 4 1/2 In.	90.00
Pitcher, Amber Thorn Handle, 7 1/2 In.	175.00
Punch Cup	30.00
Rose Bowl, Blue Shaded To Pink, Ribbed, Rolled Ruffled Rim, Mt. Washingon, 5 In.	2240.00
Rose Bowl, Enameled Flowers, Yellow Leaves	100.00
Rose Bowl, Satin, Bulbous, Exaggerated Rolled Rim, 6 In.	2520.00
Salt & Pepper, Bulbous, White Lining, Metal Tops, Wheeling, 2 3/4 In.	690.00
Toothpick, Shaded White To Pink, Spreading Rim, New England	95.00
Toothpick, White To Deep Rose, Glossy, Squared Top, 2 1/4 In.	450.00
Tumbler, White Interior, Pontil, Hobbs, Brockunier & Co., 3 3/4 In. *Illus*	200.00
Vase, Blue Shaded To Pink, Vertical Ribs, Bulbous, Mt. Washington, 4 1/2 x 5 In.	4480.00
Vase, Double Gourd, 8 1/2 In.	1610.00
Vase, Enameled, Bird Flying Among Branches, Multicolored, 20th Century, 5 In.	380.00
Vase, Flowering Vine, Gold Enamel, White Interior, Bulbous, Round Neck, 9 1/2 In.	205.00
Vase, Gold Enameled Cascading Fern, Ginkgo Decoration, 6 3/4 In.	69.00
Vase, Jack-In-The-Pulpit, World's Fair, 1893, 7 1/2 In.	750.00
Vase, Lily, White To Pink, Glossy, Tricornered Tim, 6 In.	365.00
Vase, Morgan, Glossy, Red Shading To Yellow, 8 x 8 In., Pair	500.00
Vase, Pink To Yellow, Ruffled Rim, 20th Century, 8 1/2 In.	120.00
Vase, Shaded Amber To Rose, Cased, Wheeling, 9 In.	965.00

PEANUTS is the title of a comic strip created by cartoonist Charles M. Schulz (1922-2000). The strip, drawn by Schulz from 1950 to 2000, features a group of children, including Charlie Brown and his sister Sally, Lucy Van Pelt and her brother Linus, Peppermint Patty, and Pig Pen, and an imaginative and independent beagle named Snoopy. The Peanuts gang has also been featured in books, television shows, and a Broadway musical.

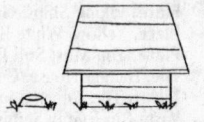

Bank, Snoopy, Anchor Hocking Glass, 6 In.	15.00
Bank, Snoopy, Composition, Doghouse, 1970, 7 In.	25.00
Book, Snoopy, Suppertime, Determined Productions, 1968	4.00
Button, Charlie Brown, Vote October 29, CBS TV, c.1970, 3 In.	30.00
Jigsaw Puzzle, Lucy Foils Charlie's Kicking Attempt, 100 Pieces, 1978, 11 x 16 In.	5.00
Lunch Box, Charlie Brown & Baseball Team, Thermos, Vinyl, c.1971	40.00
Lunch Box, Orange Color Rim, Metal, King Seeley Thermos, c.1966	38.00
Music Box, Snoopy, World War I, Aviator, Windup, Wood, Composition, 1968, 4 x 4 In.	120.00
Pencil Case, Snoopy On Doghouse, Vinyl, White, Zipper, c.1970, 5 x 8 In.	8.00
Scissors, Snoopy, Battery Operated, Plastic, c.1970, 2 x 2 x 6 In.	8.00
Snoopy, Flight Helmet, Goggles, Scarf, Vinyl, Plastic, Movable Head, Legs, 1966, 7 In.	58.00
Strip, Snoopy Imagines Golf To Sleep, Pen, Ink, Signed, 1964, 5 1/2 x 27 In.	9350.00
Toy, Space Patrol, Snoopy, Tin, Plastic, Battery Operated, Japan, Box, 11 In.	415.00
Toy, Telephone, Snoopy & Woodstock, American, 1976, 8 1/4 x 8 1/4 x 2 1/2 In.	50.00
Toy, View-Master, Baseball, 3 Reels, c.1966	18.00

PEARL items listed here are made of the natural mother-of-pearl from shells. Such natural pearl has been used to decorate furniture and small utilitarian objects for centuries. The glassware known as mother-of-pearl is listed by that name. Opera glasses made with natural pearl shell are listed under Opera Glasses.

Card Case, Inlaid Diamond Pattern, Etched Branch & Berry, 3 3/4 x 2 1/2 In.	68.00
Oyster Set, Shell, Sterling Ball Feet, Knife, Fork, c.1896, 18 Piece	1410.00
Paper Holder, Ormolu, Carved Figure, Continental, 2 3/4 x 3 7/8 In., Pair	7800.00

PEARLWARE is an earthenware made by Josiah Wedgwood in 1779. It was copied by other potters in England. Pearlware is only slightly different in color from creamware and for many years collectors have confused the terms. Wedgwood pieces are listed in the Wedgwood category in this book. Most pearlware with mocha designs is listed under Mocha.

Pearl

Beaker, Green, Reeded Rim Band, Marbling, Early 19th Century, 2 5/8 In.	118.00
Bowl, Blue, Brown Slip, White Band, God Save The King, Wood & Caldwell, 9 In.	7050.00
Bowl, Hemispherical, Rouletted Circle Band, Rust Field, c.1820, 2 3/4 x 5 5/8 In.	4995.00
Bowl, Vine Pattern Rim Band, Wavy Design, London Shape, c.1830, 5 x 10 In.	880.00
Coffeepot, Blue & White Transfer Printed	175.00
Coffeepot, Pear Shape, Flowers, Leaves, Green, Blue, Red, Scroll Handle, 10 1/2 In.	405.00
Creamer, Cow, Blue & Dark Red Splotch, England, 19th Century, 2 1/2 x 7 In.	235.00
Cup & Saucer, Sprig, Blue, Red, Green, Impressed Star At Base, 1 1/2 x 2 1/2 x 4 In.	75.00
Cup Plate, Evening Song, Lay My Body Down, Flange Edge, Brown Transfer, 4 1/2 In.	140.00
Cup Plate, Green Tall Ships Transfer, Alcock, 3 7/8 In.	79.00
Cup Plate, Present For A Good Boy, Molded Flange, Flowers, Dogs, Child's, 3 3/4 In.	169.00
Dessert Set, Leaf Border, Peach, Rust, White, Tureens, 10 1/2-In. Dishes, 5 Piece	1380.00
Dish, Leaf Shape, White, Blue Veining, 6 1/2 x 5 In.	90.00
Figurine, Boy In Red Coat, Yellow Knickers, Holding Bird Nest, Green Stump Base, 7 In.	275.00
Figurine, Cradle, Hooded, Sleeping Child, Polychrome Enamel, Oval, Pratt Type, 8 In.	590.00
Figurine, Figure Of Peace, Holding Torch To Helmet & Battle Gear, Plinth Base, 8 In.	176.00
Figurine, Setters, Black Spotted, Recumbent, Oval Base, c.1810, 5 5/8 In., Pair	2390.00
Figurine, Woman, Wide Brim Hat, Atop Tapering Plinth, 5 3/4 In.	295.00
Flask, Shell Form, Polychrome Enamel, Pratt Type, 4 1/8 In.	765.00
Group, Sheep, Shepherd, Recumbent Dog, Yorkshire, c.1820, 6 1/4 In.	1435.00
Group, Traveling Performers, c.1825, 6 1/4 In.	5975.00
Jug, Black Transfer, Eagle, Ribbon In Beak, Enamel Highlights, 6 1/4 In.	1116.00
Jug, Cream, Brown Field, Green Glazed Bands, Leaves, Handles, c.1820, 4 1/4 In.	5290.00
Jug, Face, Head Of Bacchus, Fruiting Grape Leaves, Monkey Handle, 7 1/2 In.	235.00
Jug, Relief Design, Old Mother Slipper Slopper, Banded Leaf Borders, Pratt Type, 5 In.	881.00
Mug, Blue, Black Bands, Extruded Handles, 19th Century, 8 In.	765.00
Mug, Britannia Looking To Sea, Sailor's Return, Frog Interior, Pratt Type, 4 In.	880.00
Mug, Child's, Present For A Good Boy, Blue Transfer, Mill Scene, 2 1/2 In.	85.00
Mug, Silver, Black Transfer, Hope Figure, Landscape Scene, 3 3/4 In.	59.00
Pitcher, Acanthus Leaves, Ribbons, Oak Leaves, Military Bust, Pink, Brown, 6 5/8 In.	495.00
Pitcher, Farmer's Wife Going To Market, Purple Transfer, 6 1/2 In.	135.00
Plate, Eagle On Limb, Flowers Rim, Red, Blue, Green, c.1820, 7 1/4 In.	600.00
Plate, Eagle, Enamel, Polychrome, Earthtone Colors, Early 19th Century, 5 3/4 In.	705.00
Plate, Pheasant, Multicolored, Green Sponged Tree Limbs, Blue Feather Edge, 9 In.	450.00
Plate, Polychrome Enamel Peafowl, Leaves, Blue Feather Edge, 9 5/8 In.	825.00
Punch Bowl, Enameled, Flowers, Red, Rose, Purple, Green, Yellow, 5 x 10 1/4 In.	940.00
Punch Pot, Cover, Blue & White, Lao Tzu On Water Buffalo, c.1794, 7 3/4 In.	1315.00
Soup, Dish, Strawberry, Pair	3250.00
Sugar, Cover, Blue Slip, White Fluted Bands, Gilt, Acorn Knop, c.1795, 5 1/4 In.	176.00
Sugar, Cover, Mustard, Blue & Green Fuchsia, Rounded Rectangular, 5 1/4 In.	303.00
Teapot, Blue Slip, Checked Roulette, Fluted Bands, E & Co., 3 1/2 In.	295.00
Teapot, Cover, Classical Reliefs, Oval, Fluted Sides, Swan Finial, 8 3/4 In.	118.00
Teapot, Cover, Oriental Figures, Leafy Scrolls, Polychrome Enamel, 7 3/8 In.	590.00
Teapot, Enamel, Multicolored, Wavy Fluting, Painted, Vines, Early 19th Century, 5 In.	120.00
Teapot, Gaudy, Blue Flowers, Soft Paste, Applied Handle, 7 1/2 In.	305.00
Tureen, Swan Shape, Sponged Enamel, Neck Tucked Under Wing, 11 In.	100.00
Wall Pocket, Molded Mask, Urns, Stag Head, Lion Head, Underglaze, 3 Sides, 6 1/2 In.	355.00

PEKING GLASS is a Chinese cameo glass first made popular in the eighteenth century. The Chinese have continued to make this layered glass in the old manner, and many new pieces are now available that could confuse the average buyer.

Bowl, Cover, Pink, Pair, 3 3/4 In.	403.00
Bowl, Floral, Tapered, Carved Wooden Base, c.1800, 2 1/2 x 6 In., Pair	518.00
Brush Pot, Imperial Yellow, 4 Clawed Dragons, Pearl Of Wisdom, Waves, 6 In.	1840.00
Cup, Pale Lemon Yellow, Dragon Handles, Carved, Footed, Geometric, c.1750, 3 In.	735.00
Snuff Bottle, Gilt Bronze, Cover, Vase, Carved Flower	529.00
Vase, Cover, Double Gourd Shape, Mustard Green, Carved, Gourds, Vines, 10 1/2 In.	403.00
Vase, Emerald Green, Oval, Cylindrical, c.1800, 8 In.	403.00
Vase, Green Over White, Carved, Man Riding Tiger Scene, 10 1/4 In.	340.00
Vase, Ku Shape, Imperial Yellow, Demon Masques, 8 1/4 In., Pair	2530.00

PELOTON glass is a European glass with small threads of colored glass rolled onto the surface of clear or colored glass. It is sometimes called spaghetti, or shredded coconut, glass. Most pieces found today were made in the nineteenth century.

Tumbler, Light Amber, Multicolored Threads, 3 3/4 In.	154.00

PENS replaced hand-cut quills as writing instruments in 1780 when the first steel pen point was made in England. But it was 100 years before the commercial pen was a common item. The fountain pen was invented in the 1830s but was not made in quantity until the 1880s. All types of old pens are collected.

PEN, Bakelite, Victorian, Metal Nib, Mount, 6 1/2 In.	20.00
Ballpoint, Gold & Black, 14K Filigree, Arpege, Channel No. 5, Pair	23.00
Ballpoint, Guy M. Grove Co. Plumbing & Heating, Funkstown, M.D., Black, Orange	8.00
Box, Nibs, Pelikan Graphos, Wood, Leather, Velvet Lined, 6 1/4 x 3 1/2 In.	99.00
Ceramic, Green, Black Marble, 5 1/4 In.	10.00
Christmas, Red, Silver, Christmas Tree On Clip	5.00
Cobalt Glass, Silver, Oliver Hotel, Blarney Inn & Emerald Room, Indiana, 3 3/4 In.	55.00
Cross, Black, Leaf Design	12.00
Cross, Operation Team 1997, CRM, Red	10.00
Cross, Silver, Brass Clip, Joy Imprinted	8.00
Float About, Amtrak, Train Moves In & Out Of Station	3.25
Float About, Beatles, 4 Lads Float Across Abbey Road	6.00
Float About, Black Ants, Carrying Picnic Food, Bon Appetit	3.75
Float About, Boston Tea Party, Tea Crates Fall From Ship	3.25
Float About, Elvis, Performs Blue Suede Shoes	3.75
Float About, Green Tree Frog, Leaps Across Stream	3.25
Float About, Jantzen Swimsuit, Woman, Diving Position	40.00
Float About, Java Joe, Emerges From Coffee Shop Perky	3.75
Float About, Moon Landing, Neil Armstrong Carries Flag	3.75
Float About, Mr. Rogers, Neighborhood Trolley & Props	3.50
Float About, New York City, Central Park, Horse Drawn Carriage	3.25
Float About, Smithsonian, Hot Air Balloon, 1783 Flight	3.25
Float About, Woody Woodpecker, Takes A Dive	4.50
Fountain, Esterbrook, Emerald Green, Marbled, 26S Nib	35.00
Fountain, Eye Dropper Style, Herringbone Cap, Black Base, Gold Design, 14K Gold Nib	150.00
Fountain, Mighty Prince, Platinum Ultra Tip, Gold	18.00
Fountain, Parker, Striped, 4 3/4 In.	30.00
Garland, Westinghouse Emblem In Window, Maroon, Silver	12.00
Gospel Rescue Mission, 40th Anniversary, 1953-1993, U.S.A.	5.00
Holder, Bakelite, Black Glass Base, Red Plastic Pen, 3 1/4 x 5 In.	145.00
Holder, Esterbrook, Silver Neck, Felt Bottom, Made In U.S.A.	18.00
Holder, Paperweight, Acrylic, Dried Flowers, Day Zee Line, Plastic Penholder	15.00
Linton, Gray, Esterbrook Top No. 2556	10.00
Mars Staedtler Ink Pen, Tin, 1920s, 6 In.	18.00
Montblanc Meisterstuck, Gold, Gold Filled, Resin, Fountain, No. 146, 5 1/2 In., Set	345.00
New York Gulf Air Style, Maroon, 5 1/4 In.	8.00
Onoto, Fountain, Engraved R. D. Charman, 6 In.	190.00
Parker, Fountain, Blue, Silver, Arrow Clip, 5 In.	15.00

Parker, Insignia, Black, Gold Accent, Box 25.00
Parker, Sterling Silver, Vintage, 5 In. 125.00
Pebble Beach Resort, Black 6.00
Phillip Morris, Chrome, Smokers Have Rights, Too!, U.S.A. 10.00
Quill, Pearl Handle, 14K Gold Tip, 6 In. 95.00
Quill, Sterling, 19th Century, 7 1/2 In. 325.00
Reflections, Black, Gold Accent, 5 1/2 In. 8.00
Ricci, Gold Ripple, Ricci On Clip 6.00
Risperdal, Green Marble Look, Gold Accent, 5 1/2 In. 10.00
Roswell, Red, New Mexico Military Institute 8.00
Sanford, Black, Soft Rubber Grip, PhD Trademark, Japan, 5 1/2 In. 8.00
Sanford, Soft Rubber Grip, Success Is A Journey Not A Destination, 5 1/2 In. 5.00
Scotchguard, Anso Crushresister, Stain Release Victory Parade, June 10, 1991, 5 1/4 In. . 6.00
Sheaffer, Fountain, Italic F, Green, Silver, 5 In. 20.00
Sheaffer, Gold, Silver, Ballpoint 30.00
Silver, Ring & Scroll Decoration, 5 1/2 In. 175.00
Splash, Aqua Top, Purple Bottom Hot Pink Clip, When You're Serious About Color 6.00
Trovan, Black, Gold Accent, 5 1/4 In. 8.00
Union Pacific Railroad, Black, Operation Red Black Union Pacific Railroad 6.00
Vital, Gold, Diamond-Like Stones On Clip 8.00
Voltaren Declofenac Sodium, Wood, Gold Trim 6.00
W, Black, Brown Rings, W On Clip, 5 In. 6.00
Waterford, Ballpoint, Marquis, Black, Gift Box 50.00
Wood, Old South Peterbilt Inc. 10.00
Wood, POS Professional Office Service Co. Inc., 5 1/4 In. 8.00
Wood, Red, Gold Accent Trim, 5 1/2 In. 6.00
Zebra, Silver, Black Rubber Grip, F-402, Japan 8.00
PEN & PENCIL, Cross, Ertl Employee 10 Year Service, 12K Gold 75.00
Mechanical, Chain Loop, Fogel, Victorian, Box 8 x 2 In., 7-In. Pen, 2 1/2-In. Pencil 150.00
Paper Mate, My Buddy Falls City, Stratton & Tersegge, Louisville, Ky., c.1950 ...... 25.00
Plastic, Yellow, Amber Crystal, Plastic Case, Embroidered Flower, 1950s, 4 1/4 In. 5.00

PENCILS were invented, so it is said, in 1565. The eraser was not added
to the pencil until 1858. The automatic pencil was invented in 1863.
Collectors today want advertising pencils or automatic pencils of
unusual design. Boxes and sharpeners for pencils are also collected.
Advertising pencils are listed in the Advertising category. Pencil boxes
are listed in the Box category.

PENCIL, Elephant, Cast Metal, Pencil Tied To Feet, Engraved Barrel, Desktop 20.00
Faber Castell, TK Matic, Black, Textured Metal, West Germany, Box 125.00
Girl In Ball Gown, Pink, Porcelain, Torso Is Pencil, Desktop, 3 1/2 In. 45.00
Lapel Pin, Pullout Chain, Satin Pearlized Lucite 20.00
Norma, Chrome, 4 Lead Colors 30.00
Parker, Duofold, Jade Green Marbleized Plastic 40.00
Schaeffer, Lady, Gold Filled 25.00
Torpedo, Chrome Plated, Newport, R.I., 1940s-1950s 35.00
Wahl, Gold Filled, Box 30.00
Waterman, Sterling Silver, Floral Overlay, Ring Top, 3 1/2 In. 30.00
Wearever, Red, Pearlized Plastic 4.00
PENCIL SHARPENER, Bakelite, Clock, 1 In. 75.00
Globe, On Stand, Cast Metal, Tin Lithograph, 3 In. .... *Illus* 4.00
Perfect Pencil Pointer, E.S. Drake, Goodell Co., Antrim, N.H., 1890 .... 499.00
U.S. Automatic, 5 In. 195.00

PENNSBURY Pottery worked in Morrisville, Pennsylvania, from 1950
to 1971. Full sets of dinnerware as well as many decorative items were
made. Pieces are marked with the name of the factory.

Amish, Creamer, Man, Heart Flower, Brown Glaze, 2 1/2 x 1 3/4 In. 40.00
Amish, Creamer, Woman, Heart Flower, Brown Glaze, 2 1/2 x 1 3/4 In. 40.00
Amish, Jug, Man, 2 1/2 In. 25.00
Amish, Jug, Man, 5 In. 35.00
Amish, Pitcher, Milk, Farm Scene, 6 1/2 In. 175.00
Amish, Plaque, 4 In. 25.00

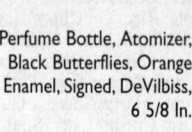

Pencil Sharpener,
Globe, On Stand,
Cast Metal, Tin
Lithograph, 3 In.

Perfume Bottle, Atomizer,
Black Butterflies, Orange
Enamel, Signed, DeVilbiss,
6 5/8 In.

Ashtray, Don't Be So Doppish, Man Tripping Over Feet, 5 In.	20.00
Ashtray, What Giffs? What Ouches You?, 5 In.	25.00
Barbershop Quartet, Beer Mug	35.00
Hex, Mug, Coffee, Store Label	22.00
Hex, Plate, Pennsylvania Dutch, 10 In.	30.00
Plaque, Baltimore & Ohio R.R., 1837, Green Trim, 8 x 5 3/4 In.	49.00
Plaque, Baltimore & Ohio R.R., Inscribed Railroad Veterans, c.1955, 5 3/4 x 8 In.	65.00
Plaque, Pennsylvania R.R., Tiger 1856, 1960s, 8 x 5 3/4 In.	60.00
Plaque, Pop's Half Et Already, 4 In.	25.00
Plaque, Such Smootzers, 4 In.	25.00
Plate, Mother's Day, 1971, Mother In Flower Garden, Stumar, Glen View, 8 1/2 In.	50.00
Yellow Rooster, Creamer, White Ground, Yellow, Green, 4 1/2 In.	45.00
Yellow Rooster, Pitcher, Milk, 7 1/2 In.	150.00
Yellow Rooster, Tip Tray, Painted, 6 x 8 In.	49.00

PEPSI-COLA, the drink and the name, was invented in 1898 but was not trademarked until 1903. The logo was changed from an elaborate script to the modern block letters in 1963. Several different logos have been used. Until 1951, the words *Pepsi* and *Cola* were separated by 2 dashes. These bottles are called *double dash*. In 1951 the modern logo with a single hyphen was introduced. All types of advertising memorabilia are collected, and reproductions are being made.

Blackboard, Special Of The Day, 1950s, 19 x 30 In.	32.00
Clock, Drink Ice Cold, Double Bubble, Red, White, Blue	550.00
Cooler, Logo, Can Shape, Wheels, 48 x 24 In.	40.00
Dispenser, Plastic, Box, 9 1/2 x 4 3/4 x 10 In.	72.00
Door Push, Drink Pepsi-Cola, 5 Cents, Yellow Ground, 3 1/2 x 13 1/2 In.	495.00
Menu Board, Light-Up, Plastic, 21 x 53 1/2 x 8 In.	28.00
Pen, Brass Pepsi Bottle Clasp	85.00
Radio, Bottle Shape, Plastic, Cap Is Tuner, Tube, 23 1/4 x 8 In.	300.00
Radio, Portable, Leather Strap, Speakers, Dials, 7 x 3 1/2 x 6 1/2 In.	165.00
Sign, Enjoy Pepsi, Five Cents, Bottle Cap, Tin, 1940s, 26 x 10 In.	440.00
Sign, Enjoy Pepsi-Cola, Hits The Spot, 5 Cents, Red, White, Blue, Tin, 55 x 31 In.	880.00
Sign, Pepsi Please, Yellow Ground, Tin, 16 3/4 x 46 3/4 In.	220.00
Sign, Pepsi's Got A Lot To Give, Girls On Beach, Cardboard, Frame, 1960s, 38 x 26 In.	70.00
Sign, Refresh Without Filling, Woman, Oval, Paper Lithograph Under Celluloid, 12 In.	66.00
Sign, Say Pepsi, Please, Bottle, Celluloid Over Cardboard, 8 x 12 In.	15.00
Sign, So Up-To-Date, So Slim, So Smart, Summer Scene, Board, 1950s, 16 x 22 In.	800.00
Thermometer, Say Pepsi Please, Enamel Over Tin, Glass Cover, 9 x 9 In.	66.00
Thermometer, Say Pepsi Please, Tin Lithograph, Embossed, Stick, 27 In.	66.00
Toy, Truck, Plastic, Marx, 1950s, 7 1/8 In.	150.00
Tumbler, Batgirl, Super Series, 1976	46.00
Tumbler, Disney, Donald & Daisy, Happy Birthday Mickey Series, 1978	14.00
Tumbler, Disney, Goofy, Single Character, Round Bottom	11.00
Tumbler, Disney, Pluto, Picnic Series, Round Bottom	42.00
Tumbler, Harvey Cartoons, Big Baby Huey, Action, 5 In.	3.00
Tumbler, Superman The Movie, Superman Saves The Day	8.00
Tumbler, Warner Bros, Foghorn Leghorn, Brockway, Black Letters, 16 Oz.	6.00

Tumbler, Wonder Woman, Super Series, 1978 .... 7.00

PERFUME BOTTLES are made of cut glass, pressed glass, art glass, silver, metal, enamel, and even plastic or porcelain. Although the small bottle to hold perfume was first made before the time of ancient Egypt, it is the nineteenth- and twentieth-century examples that interest today's collector. DeVilbiss Company has made atomizers of all types since 1888 but no longer makes the perfume bottle tops so popular with collectors. These were made from 1920 to 1968. The glass bottle may be by any of many manufacturers even if the atomizer is marked *DeVilbiss*. The word *factice*, which often appears in ads, refers to store display bottles. Glass or porcelain examples may be found under the appropriate name such as Lalique, Czechoslovakia, Glass-Bohemian, etc.

3-Mold, Cobalt Blue, Glass Blown, Stopper, 6 1/2 In. 330.00
Atomizer, Amber, Gold Iridized Finish, Steuben, c.1910, 6 In. 400.00
Atomizer, Base, Green, Pink, Cameo, Signed, Galle, 7 1/2 In. 230.00
Atomizer, Black Butterflies, Orange Enamel, Signed, DeVilbiss, 6 5/8 In. .... *Illus* 110.00
Atomizer, Blue Over Yellow, Cockle Shell Flowers, Cameo, Loetz, c.1910, 7 In. 430.00
Atomizer, Brown Leaves, Flowers, Yellow Ground, Cameo, Galle, 9 1/4 In. 480.00
Atomizer, Cloud Shape, Blue, Gold Iridescent, DeVilbiss, Steuben, 10 In. 2880.00
Atomizer, Crystal, Band Of Grapes, 3 Bands, 6 1/2 In. 110.00
Atomizer, Glass, Iridescent Gold, Brass Base With Music Box, 8 In. 165.00
Atomizer, Iridescent, Glass, Gilt Metal Mounted, American, 6 1/2 In. 94.00
Atomizer, Pink, Satin, Blue Flowers, Gold Scrolls, Melon Ribbed, 3 1/2 In. 168.00
Atomizer, White, Blue Flowers, Ball Shape, Wave Crest, 5 In. 400.00
Aurene, Gold, Blue Highlights, Stopper, 6 In. 635.00
Aurene, Lobed Body, Blue Stopper, Steuben, 4 1/2 In. 1287.00
Aurene, Lobed, Gold Iridescence, Flower Shape Stopper, Steuben, 5 1/2 In. 1075.00
Bergdorf Goodman, Number 9, Apothecary, Ball Stopper, Box, 3 1/2 In. 44.00
Black Amethyst, Art Deco, Black Ground, Gold Dots, Ball Stopper, 5 1/2 x 3 In. 145.00
Black Amethyst, Intaglio Cut, Floral, Stopper, 7 In. 40.00
Bohemian Glass, Cranberry Stain, Gilt Flowers, Silver Overlay Animals, 6 x 3 In. 50.00
Bourjois, Evening In Paris, Miniature, 1/2 x 2 In. 45.00
Brajan, Azaello, Black Glass, Stopper, Metal Cap, Pearls, Box, 2 1/4 In. 145.00
Cameo Glass, Blue Body, Stalactite Neck, Bulbous, Stick, Silver Cap, 2 3/4 In. 2400.00
Cameo Glass, Branches, Blue Body, Teardrop, Lay Down, Flip Lid, Stopper, 4 In. 1428.00
Cameo Glass, Flowering Branch, Orange, Lay Down, Screw Cap, 4 3/4 In. 670.00
Cameo Glass, Flowers On Leafy Stems, Butterfly, Silver Mounted Lid, 3 1/8 In. 825.00
Cameo Glass, Round, Carved Petals, Yellow, Applied Leaf, Webb, 2 1/2 In. 3585.00
Cameo Glass, Silver Mount, Sampson Mordan & Co., London, 1883 .... 295.00
Cameo Glass, Teardrop, Lay Down, Blue, Branches, Grasses, Flip Lid, Stopper, 4 In. 1430.00
Cara Nome, White Mink, Clear Glass, Stopper, Triangular Shape, Box 300.00
Carmel Myers, Gamin, Gold Stopper, Urn Shape, 3 3/4 In. 20.00
Caron, Bellodgia, Faceted, Rectangular, Box, 2 1/2 In. 20.00
Caron, Le Tabac Blond, Square, Stopper, Tassel, Box, 3 1/4 In. 121.00
Clamy, Femmes Ailees, Frosted, Clear, Stopper, Woman Against Wings, 2 1/2 In. 77.00
Clear Iridescent, Light Blue Threading, Loetz, 7 In. 115.00
Cologne, Bird & Leaves, Polychrome Enamel, 5 3/4 In. 110.00
Cologne, Black Amethyst, Gold Dots, Ball Stopper, Gold Trim, 5 1/2 In. 165.00
Cologne, Citron To Clear Glass, Poppy, Leaves, Engraved, Stopper, Moser, 6 In. 288.00
Cologne, Cobalt Blue, Rows Of Beads, Smooth Base, Tooled Lip, 9 1/4 In. 875.00
Cologne, Cobalt Blue, Vertical Ribs, Wafer Stopper, Ball Finial, Sandwich, 6 In. 305.00
Cologne, Corseted Shape, Teal Blue, Paneled, Tooled Mouth, 1860-1880, 4 5/8 In. 560.00
Cologne, Cut Glass, White To Opaque Starch Blue, Hourglass Panels, Stopper, 5 In. 80.00
Cologne, Daisies, Blue & White, Wave Crest, 6 In. 500.00
Cologne, Double Overlay, Salmon To White To Clear, Sandwich, 7 In., Pair 805.00
Cologne, Etched Horse, Birds, Tri-Con Shape, Spear Stopper, 3 Knob Feet, 14 1/2 In. 336.00
Cologne, Milk Glass, Tooled Mouth, Stopper, Label, 1885-1910, 6 1/4 In. 530.00
Cologne, Monument, Tooled Mouth, Embossed, Pontil, 1840-1855, 5 1/4 In. 112.00
Cologne, Pressed Glass, Bulging Loops, Canary, Pointed Finial, 7 In. 385.00
Cologne, Pressed Star & Punty, 8-Sided, Canary, Stopper, Sandwich, 5 In., Pair 550.00
Cologne, White Enamel, Tulip, Flowers, Leaves, Squiggle Line, 4 1/2 In. 220.00
Cologne, Wrisley Co., Hobnail, French Opalescent, Bulbous, Fenton 25.00

Corday, Jet Parfume, Clear, Frosted Stopper, Fountain Shaped, c.1924, 5 3/4 In. 3575.00
Corday, Toujours Moi, Clear Glass, Brown Patina, Flat Round Shape, Box, 3 In. 240.00
Coty, La Jacee, Clear Crystal, Frosted Stopper, Square Base, Signed, 2 1/4 In. 90.00
Cranberry Glass, Applied Fish, Enameled Leaves, Clear Stopper, Moser, 3 In. 104.00
Cranberry Glass, Brass Chain, Glass Stopper, Leaves, Flowers, Bird, 3 1/2 In. 310.00
Cut Glass, Bell Shape, Fan Stopper, 20th Century, 6 In. 35.00
Cut Glass, Crystal, Heart Shape, Stopper, Silver Enameled Cap, 1 3/4 In. 220.00
Cut Glass, Flower, Stopper, Abstract Leaves, 6 In. 35.00
Cut Glass, Hinged, Melon Shape, Silver, Birmingham, 1891, 5 1/2 x 4 In., Pair 520.00
Cut Glass, Intaglio, Pink To White, Windowpane, Flip Lid, Stopper, 4 1/2 In. 1290.00
Cut Glass, Melon Form, Sterling, J.G & S., Birmingham, 1891, 5 1/2 x 4 In., Pair 520.00
Cut Glass, Silver Cap, Rose Medallion, 7 1/2 In. 35.00
Cyrita, Suggestion, Frosted, Zeppelin Shaped, Propeller Stopper, 7 In. 1980.00
D'Orsay, Duo D'Orsay, Clear Glass, Stopper, Man In Top Hat, Box, 1 3/4 In. 55.00
D'Orsay, Toujours Fidele, Crystal, Stopper, Pillow Shape, 3 1/2 In. 120.00
DeVilbiss, Abstract Gold, Metal Atomizer, Signed, 7 1/2 In. 470.00
DeVilbiss, Atomizer, Orange Poppies, Money Plant, Green Interior, 10 In. 1980.00
DeVilbiss, Blue, Gold, 6-Sided, Signed, 4 In. 45.00
DeVilbiss, Cranberry Glass, Swirled, Stopper Dabber, 6 1/4 In. 415.00
DeVilbiss, Orange, Gold Enamel, Signed, 5 1/2 In. 110.00
DeVilbiss, Pink Glass, Metal Atomizer, 6 1/2 In. 45.00
DeVilbiss, Songbird, Enamel, Glass Dropper, Signed 6 3/4 In. 825.00
Elizabeth Arden, Cyclamen, Crystal, Stopper, Fan Shape, 6 1/2 In. 1760.00
Eroy, Adoree, Clear, Stopper, Cushion Shaped, Kneeling Nude Woman, 4 1/2 In. 200.00
Figural, Hand Of Cards, Enamel, France 9350.00
Frances Denney, Night Life, Clear, Figurine, Stage, Stopper, Box, 3 1/2 In. 275.00
Francis Whittemore, Rose, Leaves, Teardrop Stopper, W On Base, 1900s, 4 1/2 In. 295.00
Fuchsia Blossoms, Silver Mount, Gold Enameled, Signed, Galle, 1910, 6 7/8 In. 2868.00
Gelle Freres, Seduction, Crystal, Stopper, Box, 5 1/2 In. 440.00
Gold Aurene, Signed, Steuben, c.1915, 6 In. 690.00
Gold Iridescent, Stopper, Steuben, Signed, Aurene, 7 1/2 In. 1150.00
Gourielli, 5 O' Clock, Clear, Stopper, Brass Overcap, Cocktail Shaker, Box, 3 In. 130.00
Guerlain, Fleur De Feu, Clear Glass, Stopper, Ribbed, 8-Sided, Box, 5 1/2 In. 330.00
Guerlain, Jicky, Crystal, Quadrilobe Stopper, Box, 3 3/4 In. 120.00
Harrison's Columbian Perfumery, Sheared Lip, Applied Pewter Top, 2 1/2 In. 99.00
Hattie Carnegie, Gold Enamel, Stopper, Woman's Head & Shoulders, 3 1/4 In. 300.00
House Of Tre-Jur, Frosted Stopper, Woman In Skirt, Symbols, Dabber, 2 1/2 In. 275.00
Iridescent Gold, Teardrop, Stopper, Quezal, Signed, 7 1/2 In. 475.00
Jean Baptiste, Vol A Voile, Rectangular, Stopper, Ball Shaped Overcap, Box, 4 In. 360.00
Jean Patou, Vacances, Clear Glass, Stopper, Signed, Box, 3 3/4 In. 330.00
Jonteel, Clear, Frosted Glass, Stopper, Bird & Long Tail, Box, 3 3/4 In. 145.00
L.T. Piver, Astris, Crystal, Stopper, Signed 468.00
Lancome, Cuir, Clear, Frosted Stopper, Rectangular, 3 3/4 In. 360.00
Lancome, Magie, Clear, Gold Cap, Columnar, Abstract Clouds, Box, 4 1/4 In. 660.00
Lancome, Nativite, Frosted, Stopper, Overcap, Winged Angel, Gold Rays, 4 In. 2310.00
Lancome, Qui Sait, Semi Rectangular, Stopper, Box, 4 In. 55.00
Lanselle, Valenciennes, Clear, Stopper, Flags, Waves, Scallops, Box, 3 1/2 In. 605.00
Lay-Down, Enameled, 8 Paneled, Brass Cylinder, Inlaid, Hinged, 3 1/2 In. 1438.00
Lenzhei, Eau De Cologne, Molded Leaves, Frosted, 13 In. 120.00
Lionceau, Parfum Pour Blondes, Green Glass, Stopper, Beige, Box, 2 1/2 In. 935.00
Lubin, Rose Lilliputian, Crystal, Stopper Silver Overcap, Box, 2 1/2 In. 935.00
Lucien Lelong, Impromptu, Clear, Frosted, Stopper, Futuristic Tower, 5 1/2 In. 110.00
Lucien Lelong, Tailspin, Clear Glass, Stopper, Ribs, Box, 2 3/4 In. 99.00
Lydes, Arabian Passion, Black Glass, 6-Sided, Stopper, 2 3/4 In. 660.00
Marcy, L'Heure Est Venue, The Hour Has Arrived, Cobalt Blue, 3 In. 2500.00
Mary Chess, Souvenir D'Un Soir, Clear, Frosted, Fountain, 3 1/2 In. 470.00
Molinard, Habanita, Clear, Stopper, Cube, Raised Facet, Signed, Box, 2 1/2 In. 110.00
Monkey, Schuco, Green Mohair 785.00
Ota, Bouquet, Figural, String Of Pearls, 10 Individual Bottles, Box 4125.00
Oudinet, Jolira, Clear Glass, Frosted Stopper, Stylized Bow, Box, 2 1/4 In. 440.00
Poiret, Moment Supreme, Black, Stopper, Flowers, 5 1/2 In. 80.00
Porcelain, Figural Heart, Flowers, Gold Neck, c.1830, 1 1/2 In. 633.00
Pressed Glass, Cornucopia, Flower, Leaves, Stopper, 8 1/2 In., Pair 110.00

Pressed Glass, Paneled Diamond Point, Opalescent, Gilt, Stopper, 5 In., Pair 175.00
Prince Matchabelli, Added Attraction, Red, Red Velvet Box 198.00
Richard Hudnut, Le Debut Vert, Green Glass, Gilded Stopper, Octagonal, 2 1/2 In. 220.00
Rosine, Nuit De Chine, Clear, Green Stopper, Flask Shape, Symbols, Box, 3 1/2 In. 220.00
Ruby, Silver Overlay, Stopper, Marked, Steuben, 4 3/4 In. 1035.00
Ruby Glass, Double Vial, 2 Brass Stoppers At Each End, Continental, 1800s, 5 In. 115.00
Ruby Red, Lay Down, Double, 2 Silver Caps, 4 1/2 In. 200.00
Sabino, Opalescent, Pearlized, Stopper, 5 1/2 In. 80.00
Schiaparelli, Shocking, Heart Shape, Pink Rhinestones, Box 255.00
Schiaparelli, Sleeping, Blue Candlestick, Gold Flame, Lettering, Box, 1938, 7 In. 175.00
Scrolled End, Opalescent Swirls, Applied Rigaree, 2 7/8 In. 55.00
Shell Shape, Amethyst, 2 3/8 In. 195.00
Sterling Silver, Blue Enamel, Rose & Flowers, c.1930, 1 3/4 In. 115.00
Suzy, Ecarlate De Suzy, Stopper, Woman's Head & Hat, Red Enamel, 4 1/4 In. 155.00
Tosca, Clear Glass, Stopper, Square, Roses, Box, 3 In. 110.00
Venetian Glass, Murrine, Gilt Brass, Portraits, Gondola, 1800s, 2 3/4 In. 655.00
Verre De Soie, Amethyst Teardrop Dauber, Steuben, 8 In. 545.00
Verre De Soie, Rosaline Over Alabaster Button Stopper, Steuben, 4 1/4 In. 400.00
Violet, Contes Des Fees, Clear Glass, Gold Cap, Box, 1 3/4 In. 470.00
Weill, Bambou, Clear, Stopper, Pagoda Shape, Red Enameled Stopper, 3 1/2 In. 275.00
Woodworth, Tous Les Bouquets, Frosted, Stopper, Gray Patina, J. Viard, 5 In. 1210.00
Worth, Requete, Clear, Stopper, Flat Shape, Scalloped, Blue Enamel, 6 1/4 In. 1540.00

PETERS & REED Pottery Company of Zanesville, Ohio, was founded
by John D. Peters and Adam Reed in 1897. Chromal, Landsun,
Montene, Pereco, and Persian are some of the art lines that were made.
The company, which became Zane Pottery in 1920 and Gonder Pottery
in 1941, closed in 1957. Peters & Reed pottery was unmarked.

Bowl, Chromal, 3 x 9 1/4 In. 59.00
Figurine, Frog, Marbleized, 4 7/8 In. 185.00
Flower Frog, Frog, Green Matte Over Red Clay, 2 5/8 In. 115.00
Jardiniere, Brown & Green, Brown High Glaze Interior, 6 In. 315.00
Jardiniere, Moss Aztec, 7 1/2 In. 175.00
Vase, Camouflage Design, Brown, Green, Yellow, 2 Handles, 13 1/2 In. 46.00
Vase, Chromal, Clouds, Hillside, Landscape, Brown Matte, Speckled, 8 x 3 3/4 In. 250.00
Vase, Chromal, Multicolored Drip Glaze, Mocha Ground, 8 x 5 1/2 In. 220.00
Vase, Flowers, Brown Hi-Glaze, Aladdin Shape, 2 Handles, 4 1/2 In. 80.00
Vase, Ivy, Brown & Green, 12 In. 255.00
Vase, Landsun, Brown, Cobalt Blue, 9 3/4 In. 430.00
Vase, Landsun, Moonlit Scene, Green, Brown, Blue, 7 3/8 In. 405.00
Vase, Leaf & Berry Design, Brown & Green, 7 3/4 In. 200.00
Vase, Moss Aztec, Corseted, Embossed Tulips, 12 In. 440.00
Vase, Moss Aztec, Embossed Blackberries, 7 3/4 In. 115.00
Vase, Moss Aztec, Raised Grape Design, Signed Ferrell, 17 In. 575.00
Vase, Moss Aztec, Tree Stump, 3 1/8 In. 45.00
Vase, Multicolored Drip Glaze, 9 1/2 x 5 1/4 In. 140.00
Vase, Olive Green, Black, Marbleized, 8 3/4 In. 90.00
Vase, Pinecone Design, Brown & Green, 9 1/2 In. 405.00
Vase, Shadow Ware, Green, Black, Mirror Finish, 8 In. 115.00
Vase, Shadow Ware, Russet, Dark Blue, Green, 3 In. 80.00
Vase, Standard Ware, Garland & Cherub Design, 2 Handles, 13 1/2 In. 80.00
Vase, Swirl, Ivory, Brown, Blue Gray, Tan, Matte, 11 x 4 1/2 In. 165.00
Wall Pocket, Molded Silhouette, Ivory High Glaze, 9 In. 80.00
Wall Pocket, Moss Aztec, Grapevine Design, Signed, Frank Ferrell, 7 7/8 In. 220.00
Wall Pocket, Moss Aztec, Tree Branch Design, 8 In. 115.00

PETRUS REGOUT, see Maastricht category.

PEWABIC POTTERY was founded by Mary Chase Perry Stratton in 1903
in Detroit, Michigan. The company made many types of art pottery,
including pieces with matte green glaze and an iridescent crystalline
glaze. The company continued working until the death of Mary Stratton
in 1961. It was reactivated by Michigan State University in 1968.

Bookends, Animal, Blue, Green Lustered Glaze, Stamped, 4 3/4 x 4 In. 405.00

Bowl, Broad Shape, Metallic Black, Blue, Green Glaze, 7 1/2 In. 230.00
Figurine, Deer, Snowflake, Brown, Aqua Ground, Frame, 2 3/4 In. 165.00
Plate, White Crackleware, Yellow, Red Roosters, Green Field, Stamped, 9 1/4 In. 920.00
Tile, Ali Baba & 40 Thieves, Carved, Bisque Fired, Marked, 10 3/4 x 9 In. 460.00
Tile, Black Dog, Turquoise Ground, Frame, 2 3/4 In. 195.00
Tile, Flying Fish, Brown, Orange, Aqua Ground, Frame, 2 3/4 In. 165.00
Tile, Ship, Stylized, Round Border, Iridescent Maroon Glaze, Frame, 3 1/2 In. 140.00
Tile, Turtle, Brown, Aqua Ground, Impressed, 2 7/8 In. 250.00
Vase, Blue Luster Glaze, Rose & Gold Highlights, Impressed, 9 1/4 In. 1265.00
Vase, Blue Mottled High Glaze, Bisque Clay Body, 3 1/2 In. 300.00
Vase, Cobalt Blue, Green Glaze, Bulbous, Stamped, 5 3/4 x 6 1/4 In. 1380.00
Vase, Copper, Purple Iridescent Glaze, Squat Bulbous, 3 1/2 x 4 In. 635.00
Vase, Flared Shaped, Incised Design, Metallic Green, Yellow & Caramel Glaze, 4 In. 230.00
Vase, Iridescent Blue, Blue, Blue Green, Gunmetal Glaze, c.1910-1967, 20 1/2 In. 5750.00
Vase, Iridescent Sapphire Blue Glaze, Turquoise Over Copper Luster, 6 1/8 In. 575.00
Vase, Mauve, Copper, Turquoise Glaze Dripping, Round, Circle Mark, 3 1/2 In. 1725.00
Vase, Mottled Copper Red, Over Green Luster Glaze, 5 5/8 In. 230.00
Vase, Ribbed, Lavender, Green, Gold, Bulbous, 8 x 6 In. 2530.00
Vase, Teal Glaze, Ribbed, Bulbous, Stamped, 5 1/2 x 5 1/4 In. 520.00
Vase, Turquoise Crackle Glaze, Blue Plumes, Stamped, 2 In. 259.00

PEWTER is a metal alloy of tin and lead. Some of the pewter made after
1840 has a slightly different composition and is called *Britannia metal*.
This later type of pewter was worked by machine; the earlier pieces
were made by hand. In the 1920s pewter came back into fashion and
pieces were often marked *Genuine Pewter*. Eighteenth-, nineteenth-,
and twentieth-century examples are listed here.

Baluster, Hinged Cover, Hammerhead, England, 1680-1700 . . . .   850.00
Basin, Eagle Mark, c.1790s, 7 3/4 In. 495.00
Basin, Gershom Jones, Touchmark, 1774-1809, 2 x 7 3/4 In. 290.00
Basin, Townsend & Compton, Hammered Bouge, Tooled Rim, Touchmark, 8 x 2 In. 165.00
Basin, Townsend & Compton, Hammered, Molded Rim, Signed, London, 3 1/4 x 12 In. . .   495.00
Beaker, Boardman & Hart, Flared Rim, Incised Rings, c.1830s, 5 1/8 In. 415.00
Beaker, Munden & Grove, London, 1760-1773 . . . .   275.00
Beaker, Thomas Danforth II, Mark, Middletown, Connecticut, 1755-1782, 5 1/4 In. 2950.00
Biscuit Box, Liberty & Co., Removable Lid, Stylized Leaves, c.1900, 4 1/2 In. 920.00
Bleeding Bowl, Barber's, Scalloped Border, Rolled Rim, England, 1700s, 10 1/2 x 9 In. . .   250.00
Bowl, Boardman & Hart, Wide Rim, New York, 1830s, 9 5/8 In.   195.00
Bowl, Footed, Shaped Base, Flared Rim, 5 x 8 In. 55.00
Bowl, Molded Edge, American Eagle & Stars Stamp, 2 x 8 In. 770.00
Bowl, Thomas Danforth II, 2 1/2 x 9 In. 345.00
Bowl, Townsend & Compton, Molded Rim, Signed, London, 12 In. 165.00
Bowl, Urania, Oval, Embossed, Jugendstil Design, 4 x 13 1/2 In. 60.00
Box, Tobacco, Round, Dolphin Finial On Lid, Dutch, 1784 . . . .   575.00
Candlestick, Flaff & Homan, c.1840s, 9 7/8 In., Pair 635.00
Candlestick, Flared, Molded Edge, Continental, 9 1/2 In., Pair 1925.00
Candlestick, Pushup, 19th Century, 10 In., Pair 210.00
Candlestick, Round Domed Base, Exaggerated Baluster Stem, 7 In., Pair 1495.00
Castor Set, 4 Bottles, Frame, Cathedral Decoration, Israel Trask, Mass., c.1856, 8 In. . . .   145.00
Charger, Bush & Co., Bristol, 18th Century, 14 1/2 In. 345.00
Charger, Continental, Cherubim, Monogram, 1789, 13 3/4 In. 118.00
Charger, David Melville, Newport, Rhode Island, c.1875, 14 In.   1955.00
Charger, Deep, Continental, Triple-Angle Touchmarks, 13 In. 68.00
Charger, England, Early 19th Century, 4 1/2 In. 145.00
Charger, England, Early 19th Century, 13 1/2 In. 105.00
Charger, Good Love, Molded Edge, 13 In. 3850.00
Charger, John Skinner, Boston, Semper Eadem Mark, c.1790 . . . .   1955.00
Charger, London, 2-In. Rim, 16 1/2 In. 115.00
Charger, Love, Molded Edge, 13 In. 3850.00
Charger, Rose Mark, England, 18 In. 127.00
Charger, Samuel Duncombe, Birmingham, England, c.1750, 18 In. 290.00
Charger, Samuel Ellis, England, 15 In. 175.00
Charger, Signed A.R.H., Continental, 18th Century, 11 1/2 In. 145.00

Charger, Stamped, Initials IWE, Crowned Rose Touchmark, 14 3/4 In. 580.00
Charger, Townsend & Compton, Hammered Bouge, Raised Rim, Touchmarks, 16 In. 440.00
Claret Jug, French Pewter Lid, Handle, Collar, Amber Swirl Glass Body, 8 5/8 x 5 In. . . .   235.00
Coffee Set, Reed & Barton, J. Pripp, Denmark, Looping Handles, V-Wing Finial, 3 Piece .   295.00
Coffeepot, A. Porter, Scroll Handle, Westbrook, Maine, 1835, 11 1/2 In. 316.00
Coffeepot, Allen Porter, Elongated Pear Shape, Westbrook, Maine, 1830-1840 . . . .   725.00
Coffeepot, Daniel Curtiss, Albany, New York, Painted Handle, 1822-1840, 11 In. 750.00
Coffeepot, Dome Lid, Fluted Band, Scroll Handle, Wooden Wafer Finial, 10 3/4 In. 525.00
Coffeepot, Freeman Porter, Urn Form, Inscription, Westbrook, Me., c.1850 . . . .   725.00
Coffeepot, J.H. Hopkins, Lighthouse, Wooden Scroll Handle, 10 3/4 In. 90.00
Coffeepot, Leonard, Reed & Barton, 8 Sides, Shaped Spout, Wooden Handle, 12 1/2 In. . .   145.00
Coffeepot, Lighthouse, Dome Lid, Flare Base, Engraved Band, c.1856, 13 1/4 In. 660.00
Coffeepot, Lighthouse, Unmarked, Wooden Handle, Finial, Engraved Bands, 10 3/8 In. . .   875.00
Coffeepot, Palethorp & Connell, Dome Lid, Scroll Handle, Philadelphia, 1820, 10 In. 525.00
Coffeepot, Roswell Gleason, 8 Sides, Wooden Handle, Finial, Dorchester, Mass., 13 In. . .   80.00
Coffeepot, S. Simpson, Pear Shape, Raised Bands, Scroll Handle, Dome Lid, 11 1/4 In. . .   165.00
Coffeepot, Sellew & Co. Cincinnati, C-Scroll Handle, 9 1/2 In. 205.00
Coffeepot, Shaped Spout, Scroll Handle, Flared Base, 9 In. 165.00
Coffeepot, Wm. McQuilkin, Bulbous, Ringed Body, Gooseneck, Scroll Handle, 10 In. . . .   130.00
Compote, Hammered, Narrow Bowl, Cherubs Support, Marked Denmark, 11 x 7 In. 105.00
Compote, James Couper & Sons, Cluthra Glass Liner, c.1904, 6 3/4 x 7 7/8 In. 7170.00
Compote, Liberty & Co., Leaves, Tripartite Standard, Vegetable Design, 10 1/2 In. 805.00
Decanter, Green Glass, Silvered, Figural Foot, Lily Pad Feet, Stylized Blossoms, 14 In. . .   405.00
Dish, Deep, Thomas D. Boardman, Hartford, Connecticut, 11 1/8 In. 725.00
Dish, Deep, Townsend & Compton, Hammered Bouge, Stamped Letters, 14 1/2 In. 385.00
Dish, Samuel Danforth, Marked Hartford, 13 1/2 In. 605.00
Ewer, Armorial Relief Crest, Crown, 18th Century, 23 In. 230.00
Flagon, Figural, Knight, Boar's Head, Engraved, 3-Cherub Base, Eagle Finial, 20 In. 400.00
Flagon, Hinged Lid, Double Acorn Thumb Latch, Stamped JLM, 12 1/2 In. 145.00
Flagon, Sheldon & Feltman, Flared Molded Base, Banding, Scroll Handle, 10 3/4 In. 690.00
Flagon, Thomas Danforth Boardman, Dome Lid, Scroll Handle, 11 1/8 In. . . . . . ● 1210.00
Flask, 8 Sides, Chased Vines, Flowers, Screw Lid, Swing Handle, 1865, 10 In. 98.00
Flask, Book Shape, Screw-Off Lid, c.1850, 6 1/2 x 4 1/4 In. 230.00
Funnel, Decorative Turnings, Hanging Ring, 4 1/2 x 3 1/2 In. 44.00
Inkstand, Palmer & Co., Flared Rim, Banding, Glass Well, Signed, 2 1/2 x 3 3/4 In. 247.00
Inkwell, Liberty & Co., Glass Insert, c.1902, 3 1/4 In. 3585.00
Inkwell, Tapered Round, Hinged Round Lid, 5 Quill Holes, 2 x 3 In. 90.00
Ladle, Marked EC, Wooden Handle, c.1850 . . . .   220.00
Ladle, Unmarked, Wooden Handle, American, c.1850, 15 1/8 In. 165.00
Lamp, Acorn Font, Round Base, Fluid Burners, Snuffer Caps, 9 5/8 In. 165.00
Lamp, Cylindrical, Font, American, c.1850, 7 3/4 In. 275.00
Lamp, Gimbal, 8-Sided Base, Ringed Dome, Wrought Iron Tab Handle, Frame, 9 1/2 In. .   85.00
Lamp, Saucer Base, Baluster Stem, Whale Oil Burner, 7 In. 195.00
Lamp, Sparking, Capen & Molineux, New York City, 1848-1854, 4 1/2 In. . . . . .92.00 to 175.00
Measure, Double Volute, CM Base Stamp, FC Lid Stamp, 1770-1800, Qt., 8 In. 1300.00
Measure, J. Moyes, Edinburgh, c.1850, 1/2 Pt., 4 3/8 In. 345.00
Measure, J. Moyes, Edinburgh, Gill, c.1850, 3 1/2 In. 275.00
Measure Set, 5 Graduated Sizes, Square Handle, France, 5 Piece 150.00
Mold, Candle, 18 Tubes, Poplar Frame, Bootjack Ends, 21 x 7 x 13 1/2 In. 990.00
Mold, Candle, 32 Tubes, Arch Cutout Feet, 19th Century, 12 1/2 x 23 x 8 In. 1540.00
Mold, Chocolate, Basket, Hinged, 3 Sections, Late 19th Century, 1 3/4 x 3 x 4 1/2 In. 15.00
Mold, Ice Cream, Brownie, Marked E & Co., 1894, 5 In. 165.00
Mold, Ice Cream, Father Christmas, 4 1/4 In. 1155.00
Mold, Ice Cream, Yum Yum, No. 201, 3 3/4 In. 50.00
Mold, Spoon, Decorative Relief Cast, 18th Century, 8 1/2 In. 465.00
Mold, Spoon, Rattail, 18th Century, 7 7/8 In. 325.00
Mug, Bassetts, Unmarked, 2-Level Fillet, Qt., 6 In. 2650.00
Mug, Boardman & Hart, New York, Ball Terminal Handle, 1828-1853, 3 1/16 In. 425.00
Mug, Bulbous Shape, Scroll Handle, Signed W.B. Under Crown, Pt., 4 3/4 In. 120.00
Mug, Ingram & Hunt, Straight-Sided, Inverted Heart Handle, Bewdley, c.1790, 4 3/8 In. . .   325.00
Mug, Thomas Danforth III, Philadelphia, Ball Terminal, 1806-1812, 3 15/16 In. 2400.00
Pitcher, Kayserzinn, Iris & Satyr, 12 3/4 In. 360.00
Pitcher, R. Dunham, Bulbous, Flared Foot & Rim, 6 3/4 In. 495.00

Pitcher, Raoul Larche, Man & Woman Handle, Vines, Leaves, c.1890, 14 1/4 In. 2400.00
Pitcher, Water, Sheffield, Round Baluster Form, Curved Handle, 6 1/2 x 7 1/4 In. 150.00
Plate, Baby In Cradle, Shelf Of Pots, Clock, Germany, 1793 . . . . 295.00
Plate, David Melville, Newport, Rhode Island, 8 1/4 In. 550.00
Plate, Frederick Bassett, c.1770, 8 1/2 In. 863.00
Plate, George Lightner, Baltimore, Md., Deep, 1806-1815, 8 3/4 In. . . . . .330.00 to 650.00
Plate, Luftwaffe Service, Presentation, Applied Swastika, c.1937, 14 In. 160.00
Plate, Nuremberg, Decorated Panels, 17th Century, 10 In. 495.00
Plate, Richard Yates, London, Flat Rim, Lawrence Yates' Marks, 1775-1824, 9 3/8 In. . . . 175.00
Plate, Townsend & Compton, Molded Rim, London, 8 In., Pair 55.00
Plate, William Billings, Providence, R.I., 1791-1806, 8 5/16 In. 775.00
Plate, William Danforth, Middletown, Conn., 1790-1820, 7 15/16 In. 545.00
Plate, Wm. Boddeker, Flared Rim, Signed, 9 In. 220.00
Porringer, Boardman, Bossed Basin Bowl, Old English Handle, Unmarked, 4 1/2 In. 345.00
Porringer, Gershom Jones, Providence, R.I., Flower Handle, 1774-1809, 5 3/8 In. 725.00
Porringer, Hamlin, Flowered Handle, Providence, R.I., c.1856, 5 1/4 In. 660.00
Porringer, Heart & Crescent Handle, Inscription, Plymouth, 3 1/2 In. 248.00
Porringer, Plain Handle, Center Hole, Stamped H.S., Cast Initials IAR, 5 1/4 In. 65.00
Porringer, Round, Tab Handle, Hanging Hole, 5 1/2 In. 375.00
Porringer, Samuel Hamlin Sr., Modified Old English Handle, c.1885, 4 3/8 In. 975.00
Porringer, SG Crown Handle, 1780-1820, 5 1/2 In. 465.00
Porringer, T. Samuel Boardman, 18th Century, 5 In. 460.00
Porringer, Thomas & Sherman Boardman, Bossed, Old English Handle, c.1825, 4 1/2 In. . 695.00
Porringer, William Billings, Flowered Handle, c.1790s, 5 In. 1100.00
Porringer, William Calder, Providence, R.I., Flowered Handle, 1817-1856, 5 1/4 In. 1100.00
Pot, F. Porter, Tooled Lines, Wooden Wafer Finial, Touchmark, c.1860, 11 3/4 In. 440.00
Pot, I.C. Lewis, Scroll Handle, Touchmark, c.1852, 11 In. 330.00
Pot, Infusion, c.1820-1840, 5 1/4 In. 508.00
Salt Cellar, Flared Molded Pedestal Base, 3 1/2 x 4 In. 220.00
Salt Cellar, Footed, Continental, 3 1/4 x 3 1/4 In. 93.00
Snuff Canister, A.F. Pears, Oval, Signed, London, 2 x 3 x 2 1/2 In. 70.00
Stein, Blue Shaded To Clear, Hinged Top, Applied Handle, 8 In. 165.00
Sugar, Tapered Body, Decorative Bands, Acorn Finial, Cover, 6 x 3 7/8 In. 412.00
Sugar Castor, James Dixon & Son, Sheffield, England, 19th Century, 4 1/4 In. 65.00
Sugar Castor, James Dixon & Son, Sheffield, England, 19th Century, 5 1/8 In. 70.00
Sundial, Nathaniel Miller, Massachusetts, Early To Mid 1800s, 3 In. 365.00
Tankard, Dome Lid, Scroll Handle, Tapered Body, 10 1/2 In. 175.00
Tankard, Dome Lid, Tulip Form, England, 19th Century, 6 1/4 In., Pair 1525.00
Tankard, Flat Dome Lid, Scroll Handle, Rib & Stepped Round Base, 10 1/2 In. 145.00
Tankard, Hugo Leven, Kayserzinn, Jugendstill, Germany, c.1905, 11 In. 400.00
Tankard, Lid, Communion, Boardman & Hart N. York, 11 1/8 In. 3410.00
Tankard, Richard Pitt, London, 1747-1781, Qt., 6 7/8 In. 3850.00
Tankard, Townsend & Compton, London, Inscription, 1779-1806, Qt., 7 1/2 In. 2250.00
Tankard, Tulip Shape, Dome Lid, Tubbs, 19th Century, Pt., 6 1/4 In., Pair 1525.00
Tankard, Tulip Shape, Signed, c.1841, 6 1/4 In. 535.00
Tea Set, Liberty, Tudric, Hammered, Teapot, Sugar, Creamer, England, 1900s, 2 & 5 In. . . 118.00
Teapot, A. Porter, Squat, Ear Handle, Horn Wafer Finial, 6 1/4 In. 330.00

Pewter, Teapot, Reed &
Barton, 4-Footed,
Engraved, Britannia Metal,
No. 2589, 10 In.

Phonograph, Cylinder, U.S.
Phonograph Co.,
4-Min. Everlasting Record,
Box, 4 1/2 In.

Teapot, Boardman & Hart, Inverted Mold, Design No. 9, 1828-1853 .... 425.00
Teapot, Daniel Curtiss, Inverted Mold, Albany, New York, 1822-1840, 7 3/4 In. 425.00
Teapot, Edwin & Lemuel J. Curtis, Meriden, Conn., Inverted Mold, c.1839, 9 3/4 In. 425.00
Teapot, Freeman Porter, Westbrook, Me., 1835-1860s, 7 1/2 In. 405.00
Teapot, Gooseneck Spout, Ear Handle, Sellew & Co., c.1850, 7 1/2 In. ....155.00 to 370.00
Teapot, H.B. Ward & Co., Black Handle, Impressed Mark, 11 1/2 In. 345.00
Teapot, I. Trask, Incised Lines, Dome Lid, Pewter Handle, Early 1800s, 6 3/4 In. 495.00
Teapot, James Dixon & Sons, 8 Sides, Scroll Handle, Wooden Finial, 8 3/4 In. 115.00
Teapot, R. Gleason, Scroll Handle, Touchmark, Mass., 9 1/8 In. 275.00
Teapot, Reed & Barton, 4-Footed, Engraved, Britannia Metal, No. 2589, 10 In. ..... *Illus* 100.00
Teapot, Rufus Dunham, Scroll Handle, Footed Base, Stepped Lid, 1837-1861, 7 1/4 In. .. 290.00
Teapot, S. Ellis, Pear Shape, Dome Lid, Incised Lines, Wooden Handle, 5 1/2 In. 605.00
Teapot, Sellew & Co., Urn Shape, Scroll Handle, Cincinnati, 1830-1860, 7 1/2 In. 275.00
Tray, Osiris, Round, Art Nouveau, 10 1/2 In. 115.00
Tureen, Cover, Paneled Base, Ball Feet, 2 Putti Handles, Ball Finial, 8 x 14 In. 220.00
Tureen, Soup, Hallmark, Germany, 19th Century, 14 In. 600.00
Vase, Kayserzinn, Bleeding Heart Design, 3 Pierced Openings, Signed, 9 In. 230.00
Vase, Liberty, Tudric, Blue, Green Cabochons, 2 Whiplash Handles, 9 3/4 x 6 In. 1175.00
Vase, Liberty, Tudric, Faceted, Band Of Ovals, 4 Claw Feet, Circular Base, 8 x 3 3/4 In. ... 1528.00

PHOENIX BIRD, or Flying Phoenix, is the name given to a blue-and-white kitchenware popular between 1900 and World War II. A variant is known as Flying Turkey. Most of this dinnerware was made in Japan for sale in the dime stores in America. It is still being made.

Bowl, Hoho Bird Theme, Beaded Rim, Feet, 7 1/4 x 2 3/4 In. 215.00
Casserole, Round, Cover, Blue & White Transfer, 10 x 5 In. 45.00
Creamer, Sugar, Lid, Japan 40.00
Cup & Saucer, Japan, 3 3/4 In. 8.00
Plate, 6 In. 6.00
Plate, Japan, 7 1/4 In. 7.00
Shaker, Japan, 3 1/4 In., Pair 35.00

PHOENIX GLASS Company was founded in 1880 in Pennsylvania. The firm made commercial products, such as lampshades, bottles, and glassware. Collectors today are interested in the "Sculptured Artware" made by the company from the 1930s until the mid-1950s. Some pieces of Phoenix glass are very similar to those made by the Consolidated Lamp and Glass Company. Phoenix made Reuben Blue, lavender, and yellow pieces. These colors were not used by Consolidated. In 1970 Phoenix became a division of Anchor Hocking, then was sold to the Newell Group in 1987. The company is still working.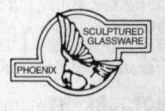

Cake Stand, Jewel & Dewdrop, Blue On White, 11 1/2 In. 200.00
Vase, Dancing Nymphs, Tan On White, c.1925, 13 In. 750.00
Vase, Lovebirds, Opalescent Pink, Oval, 10 1/4 In. 315.00
Vase, Screech Owls, Green Satin, 6 In. 155.00

PHONOGRAPHS, invented by Thomas Edison in 1877, have been made by many firms. This category also includes other items associated with the phonograph. Jukeboxes and Records are listed in their own categories.

Columbia, Graphophone, Oak Case, Needles, Sizers, Envelope 165.00
Cylinder, U.S. Phonograph Co., 4-Min. Everlasting Record, Box, 4 1/2 In. .... *Illus* 6.00
Edison, Amberola 50, Mahogany, 16 In. 330.00
Edison, Amberola, Oak Case, 24 Cylinders, Cardboard Sleeves, 14 In. 635.00
Edison, Chippendale Console, Model Cc-22, No. 1583, Mahogany Cabinet, 40 In. 159.00
Edison, Cylinder, Morning Glory Horn 495.00
Edison, Fireside, Model A, 7 Cylinders 1725.00
Edison, Fireside, Model A, Oak Case, Brass Bell Horn, 6 Cylinders, 12 x 12 x 9 In. 635.00
Edison, Gem, Cylinder Player, Oak Case, Decal, External Horn, Stand, 9 1/2 In. 578.00
Edison, Gem, Model K, Combination, Oak Case, 10 In. 963.00
Edison, Home, Combination Attachment, H Reproducer, Oak Case, 31-In. Horn 655.00
Edison, Home, Model A, Brass Bell, Black Horn, 18 x 12 x 9 In. 460.00
Edison, Opera, Cylinder, Mahogany Case, Mahogany Horn, 1911 .... 7500.00

Edison, Standard, Combination Attachment, H Reproducer, Oak Case, 28 In. 355.00
Edison, Standard, Cylinder Player, Morning Glory Horn, Japanned Stand, 12 In. 1045.00
Edison, Standard, Cylinder, Double Reproducer & Horn Adapter 4300.00
Edison, Standard, Model C, Oak Case, Tin Horn, 13 In. 825.00
Edison Type, Tinfoil, c.1880 . . . .   2430.00
Odeon, Disc Machine, With Horn, Mahogany Case, Red Label 400.00
Pathephone, No. 4, Morning Glory Horn, Hardwood, 14 x 30 x 26 In. 660.00
Victor, Monarch Special, Rigid Arm, Oak Case, Nickeled Brass Horn, 1902 . . . .   2690.00
Victor, Schoolhouse, Disk, Oak Case, Oak Horn, Floor Model 5000.00
Victor E, Front Mount, Turntable, Oak, Brass Bell, Black Horn, 11 x 16 x 23 In. 1150.00
Victor IV, Disc, Red Metal Horn 2000.00
Victrola, Sonora Upright, Mahogany Bombe Case, 47 In. 670.00
Victrola 4-3, Orthophonic Soundbox, Mahogany Cabinet, 37 In. 150.00
Victrola X, Exhibition Soundbox, Mahogany Cabinet, 44 In. 59.00

PHONOGRAPH NEEDLE CASES of tin are collected today by music and phonograph enthusiasts and advertising addicts. The tins are very small, about 2 inches across, and often have attractive graphic designs lithographed on the top and sides.

Ashco, 1 5/8 x 1 1/4 In. 40.00
Decca Loud, 2 1/4 x 1 1/8 In. 55.00
Embassy Gramophone, 1/2 x 1 5/8 x 1 1/4 In. 40.00
Gold Medal Brand, Medium Tone, Vancouver Drug, Canada, 1 1/2 x 1 In. 35.00
Gramophone, Paper Label, Never Opened 35.00
Lux Original, 3/8 x 1 7/8 x 1 3/8 In. 25.00
Marschall, 1 5/8 x 1 1/2 In. 44.00
Marschall, 1/2 x 1 5/8 x 1 5/8 In. 36.00
Marschall, Dog & Baby, 1 5/8 x 1 1/2 In. 36.00
Marschall Zukunft, Square, 1 5/8 In. 38.00
Montgomery Ward, Slide Top, Contents 35.00
Natural Voice, 3/8 x 1 3/4 x 1 3/8 In. 38.00
Pegasus Original, 1 7/8 x 1 1/4 In. 38.00
Rojar, 1 7/8 x 1 3/8 In. 40.00
Songster, Blue, 1 7/8 x 1 1/4 In. 38.00
Songster, Gold, 1 7/8 x 1 1/4 In. 35.00
Taj Mahal, 3/8 x 1 7/8 x 1 3/8 In. 38.00
Verona Needles, Nude Woman, 1 3/4 In. 80.00

PHOTOGRAPHY items are listed here. The first photograph was a view from a window in France taken in 1826. The commercially successful photograph started with the daguerreotype introduced in 1839. Today all sorts of photographs and photographic equipment are collected. Albums were popular in Victorian times. Cartes de visite, popular after 1854, were mounted on 2 1/2-by-4-inch cardboard. Cabinet cards were introduced in 1866. These were mounted on 4 1/4-by-6 1/2-inch cards. Stereo views are listed under Stereo Card. The cases for daguerreotypes are listed in the Gutta-Percha category. Stereoscopes are listed in their own section.

Album, Admiral George Dewey, Flag, Fleet, 8 1/2 x 11 In. 470.00
Album, Box, Cover, Rack, Flowers, Brass, Late 1800s, 12 1/2 x 4 3/4 x 9 1/2 In. 300.00
Album, Lacquer, Leather Bound, Painted, Lukutin Factory, c.1880, 13 x 10 1/2 In. 1380.00
Album, Music Box, Winter Scene, Stand, Drawer, Late 1800s, 13 x 9 x 12 In. 110.00
Albumen, Abraham Lincoln's Great Uncle, A.D. Clifford, Frame, 22 x 19 In. 1000.00
Albumen, American Indian, War Club & Gun 1350.00
Albumen, Chinese Justice, 8 1/2 x 10 7/8 In. 275.00
Albumen, Church In Brooklyn, St. Marys, S. Spitzer, 13 1/4 x 9 In. 250.00
Albumen, Custer, Family, Friends, On Sleigh Ride, c.1875 . . . .   8625.00
Albumen, Harvard Crew, Sophomore, Mounted On Board, c.1887, 7 x 9 In. 70.00
Albumen, Heidelberg University Confinement Cell, 7 5/8 x 10 In. 1000.00
Albumen, Indian Medicine Man & Wife, Haynes, 1883, 4 x 6 1/2 In. 600.00
Albumen, Men In Spa, Aix Les Bains, 6 x 4 In. 700.00
Albumen, Petersburg, Va., After Capture, 6 1/2 x 9 In. 450.00
Albumen, Ruins Of Gaines Mills, Reekie & Gardner, 9 x 7 In. 460.00

Albumen, Stagecoaches On Train, Abbot, Downing Shipping, 1868, 10 x 17 1/2 In. 4600.00
Albumen, Telegraph Shelter, Hass & Peale, Labeled No. 9 Bombproof, 4 x 7 In. 265.00
Albumen, U.S. Navy Civil War Class, 1863, 8 3/4 x 6 1/4 In. 460.00
Ambrotype, Black Woman, Scroll Design Union Case, 1/6 Plate 265.00
Ambrotype, Civil War Captain & Friend, Composition Case, 1/4 Plate 1095.00
Ambrotype, Civil War Naval Officer, Composition Case, 1/2 Plate 2300.00
Ambrotype, Family Group, Father Playing Violin, Hanging Half Case, 1/6 Plate 850.00
Ambrotype, Girl Holds Box, 1/6 Plate 40.00
Ambrotype, Hammer Dulcimer Player, 1/6 Plate 490.00
Ambrotype, Horse Drawn Wagon, Man, Dog, House, 4 3/4 In. 395.00
Ambrotype, Man Posing With Violin, Maroon Leather Case, 11 x 8 In. 650.00
Ambrotype, Massachusetts Officer, Alone At Rendezvous, Union Case, 1/4 Plate 765.00
Ambrotype, Monument, Washington On Horseback, Thermoplastic Case, 5 x 4 In. 275.00
Ambrotype, Occupational, Cab Driver, Whip, 1/2 Plate 450.00
Ambrotype, Post Mortem Girl, White Dress, In Bed, Brass Frame, 1/6 Plate 405.00
Ambrotype, Post Mortem, Baby, Leather Case, 1/6 Plate 206.00
Ambrotype, Rugby Players, Outside Public House, England, 1/4 Plate 300.00
Ambrotype, Soldier, Elegantly Dressed For The Cold, Holding Sword, 1/4 Plate 730.00
Ambrotype, Soldier, Leather Case, Inscribed Fredericksburg, Va., 1863 .... 380.00
Ambrotype, Street Corner, Businesses & Patrons, Carriages, 1/2 Plate 1500.00
Ambrotype, Young British Naval Apprentice, July, 1857, 1/2 Plate 2750.00
Autochrome, French Church Interior, Labeled Lumiere, 5 x 7 In. 130.00
Autochrome, Mother & Daughter, Dressed For Church, France, 5 x 7 In. 200.00
Autochrome, Seminude Dancer, Veil, Goldschmidt & Mantes, c.1905, 5 x 7 In. 1500.00
Autochrome, Sunset Over French City, Labeled Lumiere, France, 5 x 7 In. 90.00
Autochrome, Trees, Wild Flowers, Woman & Dog, France, 1925, 4 x 6 In. 140.00
Backdrop, Cowgirl, Painted Board, 56 In. 198.00
Cabinet Card, 2 Equipped Miners, Tombstone, Ariz., C.S. Fly, 7 1/2 x 4 1/2 In. 2705.00
Cabinet Card, 4 Men Roughing It, Berg's Cabin, Alaska, Dall Deweese 150.00
Cabinet Card, Advertising Lady, Scissors, Keys, Arnold's, Jefferson, Iowa 405.00
Cabinet Card, Annie Oakley, Lace Dress, Bow, Signed, Gray Of Boston 8750.00
Cabinet Card, Bearded Lady, Eisenmann, 6 1/2 x 4 1/2 In. 125.00
Cabinet Card, Boy Rolls Dough, Merker, Belleville, Illinois, 6 1/2 x 4 1/4 In. 100.00
Cabinet Card, Cactus In Desert, Imperial, C.S. Fly, 7 1/4 x 4 3/4 In. 295.00
Cabinet Card, Captive White Boy In Geronimo's Camp, C.S. Fly, 7 1/2 x 4 1/2 In. 6465.00
Cabinet Card, Carlisle Indian School, 28 Students, Name, Tribe Label, Choate 175.00
Cabinet Card, Figures Atop Mt. Monadnock, J.A. French, Keene, N.H., June, 1902 ..... 140.00
Cabinet Card, Freight Teams Hauling Ore, Imperial, C.S. Fly, 7 1/2 x 4 1/2 In. 590.00
Cabinet Card, Geronimo's Surrender, No. 176, C.S. Fly, 7 3/8 x 4 In. 7050.00
Cabinet Card, Gila Monster, Imperial, C.S. Fly, 7 1/4 x 4 3/4 In. 470.00
Cabinet Card, Girl, White Dress, Sitting, Dog, W.H. Fulton, Kingston, N.Y. 39.00
Cabinet Card, Indians, Custer Massacre Survivors, Inscription, Taken At State Fair 500.00
Cabinet Card, Jeff Davis, Washburn, New Orleans, Signed 3250.00
Cabinet Card, Little Girl With Camera, Atelier Schubert Bad Wildingen, c.1900 .... 170.00
Cabinet Card, Lord Roberts, Field Marshall, Uniform, Medals, Signed 225.00
Cabinet Card, Man Painting Sign For W.H. Silk Bakery, Stadler Busser, York, Pa. 275.00
Cabinet Card, Men Holding Money, Weber, Lancaster, Pa., July 12, 1892 .... 135.00
Cabinet Card, Miners, Cart Rails, Building, Inscription, Copper Mines, Arizona 150.00
Cabinet Card, Music Teacher, H. Ramshaw, Ontario, Canada, 6 1/2 x 4 1/4 In. 100.00
Cabinet Card, Samoset Hotel, Fishermen, Rockport, Me., Early 1900s, 9 1/2 x 8 In. 400.00
Cabinet Card, Set, Champion Roller Skater, In Velvet Suit, Medals, Feeley, N.Y., Set Of 4 .... 500.00
Cabinet Card, Set, Santa Barbara Earthquake Damage, 1925, Set Of 10 .... 150.00
Cabinet Card, Siamese Twins, Valley Forge, Tennessee 35.00
Cabinet Card, Snaffle's Bridge, Ungapahgre Canon, Ouray, Colo., Vertical Boudoir 45.00
Cabinet Card, Tigers Pulling Chariot, Sarony, c.1893 .... 150.00
Cabinet Card, University Singers Of News Orleans, For Black Orphans, Sayer, Pa. 285.00
Cabinet Card, Woman With Camera, Fowlds, Frostburg, & Lonaconing, Maryland 175.00
Cabinet Card, Woman With Performing Birds, Dempsie, Minneapolis 400.00
Camera, Aerial, Fairchild, Type K20, Red A Lens Filter, USN43, 1940s, 4 x 5 In. 375.00
Camera, Argus, 50 mm, 3.35 Lens, Case, Chrome, Telephoto Lens, Germany, 1950s 80.00
Camera, Asahiflex II A, Takumar 2.4 Lens, Japan, 1955 .... 325.00
Camera, Century, Model 39, Leather Covered Wood, Bausch & Lomb Lens, 1900 ...... 235.00
Camera, Cocarette IV Luxus, Tessar 4.5 Lens, 1920 .... 260.00

Camera, Eastman Kodak, No. 1 Panoram-Kodak, Goerz Lens, 1900 .... 324.00
Camera, Ernemann Stereo, Ernoflex, F3 Ernon Lenses, Germany, c.1925 .... 1300.00
Camera, FED, Single Lens Reflex, 35mm, F-50 mm 1:35 Lens, Brown Case, Soviet 112.00
Camera, Field, Mahogany, 1/2 Plate, Stamped F. Lammang's Pat. Oct. 20, 1885 .... 155.00
Camera, Hasselblad 500 C, Chrome, S-Planar 5.6/120 Lens, Film Magazine 1165.00
Camera, Keystone, Movie, 8 mm, Metal, Leather Strap, Case, Original Box, 6 In. 66.00
Camera, Kodak, Brownie, Folding, No. 3A, Bellows, Adjustment Knobs, c.1910 .... 90.00
Camera, Kodak, Girl Guide, Blue, Girl Guide Logo, Case, England, 1929 .... 209.00
Camera, Kodak, Key, String, Shutter, Case 175.00
Camera, Kodak, Mahogany, Wollensak Pneumatic Shutter, 70 In. 295.00
Camera, Kodak, Panoram No. 3A, c.1927 .... 350.00
Camera, Kodak, Reflex II, Look-Down Viewer, Anastar Lens, Leather Case 75.00
Camera, Kodak, Retina III C, Lens, Case, 1958 .... 345.00
Camera, Lancaster, Lady's Handbag Case, c.1897, 1/4 Plate 2750.00
Camera, Lancaster, Stereo Instantograph, c.1891 .... 1800.00
Camera, Leica IA, Nickel Surface, Elmar 3.5 Lens, Lizard Skin, 1930 .... 1465.00
Camera, Leica IIIA, Collapsible Summar 2.5 Lens, 1934 .... 1200.00
Camera, Military, Aerial, Aero-Xenar 3.5 Lens, Isco, Gottingen, Germany, 1942 ..... 160.00
Camera, Movie, Bolex 16 mm, Viewfinder, Manual, Case, Switzerland, 1940 .... 105.00
Camera, Movie, Bolex Model B, 16 mm, Switzerland, 1929 .... 209.00
Camera, Movie, De Vry, 35 mm, Hand Crank, 1932 .... 525.00
Camera, Nikkorex Zoom 35, SLR, Zoom-Nikkor 3.5 Lens, 1963 .... 146.00
Camera, Pentax Auto 110 Slr System, Lenses, Winder, Flash, Box 190.00
Camera, Perken, Son & Rayment, Mahogany, Brass, Half Plate, c.1890 .... 600.00
Camera, Polaroid, SX-70, Brushed Finish, Brown Leatherette Panels, Original Case 100.00
Camera, Presto, E.B. Koopman, New York, Holds 4 Plates, c.1896 .... 950.00
Camera, Revere, Model No. 50, 8 mm, Brown Metal Case, Carton 40.00
Camera, Robot Star, Spring Motorized, Xenon 1.9 Lens, Red Filter, 1952 .... 270.00
Camera, Rollei 35, Germany, 1967 .... 270.00
Camera, Rolleicord V, Leather Case, Germany, 1954 .... 209.00
Camera, Rolleiflex-Baby 3.5, Green Leather Case, 1931 .... 160.00
Camera, Seneca, No. 9, Double Extension, Folding Plate, c.1915 .... 275.00
Camera, Stylophot, Pen Style, Case, Instructions, France, c.1955 .... 150.00
Camera, Voigtlander, Bergheil, Heliar 3.5 Lens, Green, 1933 .... 150.00
Camera, Voigtlander, Prominent, 2 Braunschweig Lenses, 1932 .... 730.00
Camera, Yogi Bear, Box, 1970s 150.00
Camera, Zeiss Ikon Contax IIIA, Zeiss Sonnar 3.5 Lens 315.00
Camera, Zeiss Ikon, Baldur, Box Style, Look-Down Viewer, 120 mm Film, Case 85.00
Camera, Zeiss Ikon, Contax IIIA, Lens, Case, 1949 .... 575.00
Carte De Visite, 7 Ute Indians, Carter, Salt Lake City 375.00
Carte De Visite, Abe Lincoln, Mount, Embossed, Salisbury Bro. & Co. 55.00
Carte De Visite, Adj. Gen. Lorenzo Thomas, Fredricks 125.00
Carte De Visite, Admiral George Hollins, CSN, Anthony, Brady 250.00
Carte De Visite, Admiral WB Shubrick, Anthony, Brady 125.00
Carte De Visite, Black Girl From Jackson, Miss., Star Gallery, 4 1/4 x 6 1/2 In. 125.00
Carte De Visite, Black Man From Florida, Fire Department Badge No. 54 .... 100.00
Carte De Visite, Brigadier General H Marshall, CSA, Anthony, Brady 200.00
Carte De Visite, Cheyenne Chief Big Horse, Family, Bliss, Fort Sill 500.00
Carte De Visite, Colonel Theodore Roosevelt, 6 1/2 x 4 1/2 In. 400.00
Carte De Visite, Commander Thoedorous Bailey, US Navy, Gurney 125.00
Carte De Visite, Fort Fisher Fundraiser, Wounded Soldier, Boy, Wagon, c.1866 .... 345.00
Carte De Visite, General Tom Thumb & Bride, E & H.T. Anthony, N.Y., Signed 25.00
Carte De Visite, Hon. W.F. Cody, Buffalo Bill 950.00
Carte De Visite, Hunter, Sitting At Table, Smoking Pipe, With Dog, 1866 .... 80.00
Carte De Visite, Lovers, Alexandre Dumas & Ada Isaacs Menken, Liebert, Paris 300.00
Carte De Visite, Mail Box, A.E. Deuble, Rochester, New York 150.00
Carte De Visite, Major General I McDowell, Fredricks 100.00
Carte De Visite, Man In Military Attire, Grand Duke Michel, Levitsky 275.00
Carte De Visite, Man Pruning Tree, Charles H. Shively, Millersburg, Pa. 85.00
Carte De Visite, Melvin Beal, Colonel, 6th Mass., Potter, Lawrence, Mass. 150.00
Carte De Visite, Parakeet On Stand, Halseys Gallery, Brooklyn 90.00
Carte De Visite, Pigs, Uncle Tom & Belle, Drawing, I.M. Baker, 4 1/4 x 6 1/2 In. 100.00
Carte De Visite, Poor Wolf, Hidatsa Head Chief, In Feathered Bustle, c.1870 .... 1500.00

Carte De Visite, Rome, Illinois, Main Street, Cadman Gallery Imprint 260.00
Carte De Visite, Slave Children, Isaac & Rosa, Kimball, N.Y., 1863 . . . .   240.00
Carte De Visite, Slave Girl From New Orleans, Tackaberry, 1864 . . . .   150.00
Carte De Visite, Union Soldier, Holding 2 Swords, Frame, 5 x 4 In. 115.00
Carte De Visite, Washington's Lantern, Fork, Knife, T. Meehan, Boston 100.00
Carte De Visite, Wild Bill Hickok, Philadelphia, Early 1870s, 2 1/2 x 4 In. 4995.00
Carte De Visite, Woman, In Moth Costume, V. Buel, Norwalk, Conn. 300.00
Daguerreotype, 2 Girls With Matching Dresses & Handbags, R.N. Keely, 1/6 Plate 325.00
Daguerreotype, 2 Men Posing By Pillar, Leather Case, 1/2 Plate 650.00
Daguerreotype, 2 Men, 1 With Hand On Other's Leg, Brass Frame, 1/6 Plate 345.00
Daguerreotype, 3 Girls, Beaded Purse, Rings, 1/6 Plate 175.00
Daguerreotype, 9 Miners, Picks & Shovels, 1/2 Plate 7500.00
Daguerreotype, Baby In Highchair, Ribbons In Hair, 1/6 Plate 160.00
Daguerreotype, Baby, Postmortem, Push-Button Case, 1/6 Plate 475.00
Daguerreotype, Bernini's Pieta, Leather Case, 1/6 Plate 380.00
Daguerreotype, Big Sister Loves Small Sister, AM Allen, Pottsville, 1/6 Plate 65.00
Daguerreotype, Black Woman, Bonnet, White Girl 1600.00
Daguerreotype, Boy In Military Uniform & Sister, Full Case, 1/4 Plate 850.00
Daguerreotype, Boy On Red Sofa, Blue Sky, Leather Case 300.00
Daguerreotype, Boy With Riding Crop, Full Case, 1/6 Plate 250.00
Daguerreotype, Boy, Sitting, 2 Different Poses, Same Plate 300.00
Daguerreotype, Child In Checkered Outfit, 1/6 Plate 225.00
Daguerreotype, Child With Dog, Full Case, 1/6 Plate 850.00
Daguerreotype, Couple, Gilt Highlights, Leather Case, 1/2 Plate 325.00
Daguerreotype, Elderly Gentleman, Leather Case, 1/2 Plate 206.00
Daguerreotype, Family Of 5, Full Case, 1/6 Plate 230.00
Daguerreotype, Family, Anson, 589 Broadway, Full Case 3000.00
Daguerreotype, Gentleman, Vignette, Full Case 225.00
Daguerreotype, George Warner Jr., Last Bennington Battle Veteran, 1/4 Plate 560.00
Daguerreotype, Girl Holds Book, Red Dress, Full Case, Flowers, 1/6 Plate 250.00
Daguerreotype, Girl In Chair, Black Pushbutton Case, 1/6 Plate 250.00
Daguerreotype, Girl, Gothic Chair, Green Tint Dress, 1/9 Plate 70.00
Daguerreotype, Little Boy Pouting, 1/6 Plate 40.00
Daguerreotype, Little Girl With Dog On Her Lap, Leather Case, 1/6 Plate 950.00
Daguerreotype, Man & Wife, Push-Button Case, 1/4 Plate 350.00
Daguerreotype, Man Holding Sears Book, Full Case, c.1840, 1/6 Plate 150.00
Daguerreotype, Man In Sulky, Full Case, 1/6 Plate 1200.00
Daguerreotype, Man, Ivory Mounted Instrument, Leather Case, 1/6 Plate 700.00
Daguerreotype, Man, Long Side Whiskers, Top Hat, 1/6 Plate 100.00
Daguerreotype, Man, Phrenology Book, Leather Case, 1/6 Plate 380.00
Daguerreotype, Man, Shotgun, Blue Eyes, Leather Case, 1/2 Plate 7000.00
Daguerreotype, Mary Sinclair Williams, George Sinclair, c.1840, 1/4 Plate 600.00
Daguerreotype, Miner, Robert Vance, Leather Case, Labeled Liner, 1/6 Plate 1295.00
Daguerreotype, Minister, Leather Case, Ecclesiastic Gilt Tooling, 1/6 Plate 355.00
Daguerreotype, Niagara Falls Viewed By People, Full Case, c.1850, 1/6 Plate 1200.00
Daguerreotype, Nobleman Painting, c.1840s, 1/4 Plate 500.00
Daguerreotype, Profile Of Man On Horse, Half Case, 1/4 Plate 1750.00
Daguerreotype, Smiling Mom & Baby, Black Push-Button Case, 1/6 Plate 1200.00
Daguerreotype, St. Matthias Church, Barbados, Case, Jan. 1853, 1/2 Plate 7500.00
Daguerreotype, Woman In Bonnet, O.C. Schoonmaker, Full Case 1/6 Plate 250.00
Daguerreotype, Woman In Lace Cap, Cameo Pin, Full Case, 1/6 Plate 350.00
Daguerreotype, Woman Wearing Fur Stole & Bonnet, Leather Case, 1/4 Plate 850.00
Daguerreotype, Woman, Earrings, Fruit & Vegetable Display, 1/6 Plate 45.00
Daguerreotype, Young Girl With Book, Snake & Bird's Nest Case, 1/6 Plate 270.00
Daguerreotype, Young Girl, Dog, Leather Case, 1/6 Plate 1750.00
Daguerreotype, Young Man, Pocket Watch Around Neck, William Shew, 1/6 Plate 65.00
Film, 8 mm, Heckle & Jeckle, Box, 1950s-1960s 15.00
Funnygraph, Ed. N Son, 6 1/2 x 4 1/2 In. 600.00
Gelatin Silver Print, Mr. & Mrs. Woodman, Man Ray, 1970, 6 1/2 x 5 In. 2235.00
Hudson River At The Highlands, Signed Sawyer, Frame, 9 x 23 In. 69.00
Magic Lantern, 2 Glass Slides, 19th Century 275.00
Magic Lantern, Ernst Plank, Child's, Black, 1/2 Cylinder Body, Brass Lens, Slides 94.00
Magic Lantern Slides, Wood Mounted, American History, 38 Piece 355.00

Photograph, Admiral Chester Nimitz, Autograph, Treaty Signing, 9 x 11 In. 460.00
Photograph, Albert Einstein, 70th Birthday, Princeton, 1949, 8 x 10 In. 90.00
Photograph, American Indian, Fast Horse, No. 123, Heyn, c.1899, 8 3/4 x 6 3/4 In. 600.00
Photograph, Babe Ruth, Choosing Bat, 1926, 10 x 8 In. 260.00
Photograph, Bert Elliott, Strong Man, 11 1/2 x 11 In. 200.00
Photograph, Chief Hollow Horn Bear, Rinehart, 1898, 9 1/4 x 7 3/4 In. 750.00
Photograph, Colonel Cody's Sheridan Inn, Wyoming, Coach, 6 1/4 x 10 1/2 In. 1375.00
Photograph, Devil Mask & Woman, Decamp, N.Y., 10 x 8 In. 250.00
Photograph, Family By Tent After Earthquake, July 22, 1906, 4 7/8 x 6 7/8 In. 100.00
Photograph, Helen Keller, On Horse, Autographed, 9 1/2 x 7 1/2 In. 1750.00
Photograph, Hemingway & Kid Tunero In Cuba, July 11, 1954, 5 x 10 In. 150.00
Photograph, Indian Man, Heltick Black Bird, Heyn & Co., Omaha, 1899, 9 x 7 In. 1500.00
Photograph, Indian, In Blanket, Blue Toned, Framed, Edward Curtis, 7 x 5 1/2 In. 120.00
Photograph, Irish Peasants, At Earthen Hovel, County Cork, 8 In., Pair 695.00
Photograph, John Grimek, Mr. Universe, London, 1948, 6 1/4 x 4 1/2 In. 200.00
Photograph, Log Rafts, Lee Passmore, September 19, 1908, 4 7/8 x 6 7/8 In. 125.00
Photograph, Margaret Bourke-White, U.S. Airship Akron, Duraluminum Frame 2400.00
Photograph, Marilyn Monroe, East Of Eden Premiere, 1955, 10 x 8 In. 90.00
Photograph, Mary McCarthy, Halsman, Gelatin Silver Print, c.1943, 10 x 8 In. 750.00
Photograph, Mediation, Roland W. Reed, 13 x 9 In. 173.00
Photograph, Ohio River Scene & Steamboat, Paul Briol, c.1920, 7 3/8 x 9 5/8 In. 225.00
Photograph, Peaches, Betrayer Of Geronimo, Indian Scout, A. Frank Randall 1075.00
Photograph, Street Performer, Georgii Zelma, 1925, 4 1/2 x 5 1/2 In. 2500.00
Photograph, The Moose Call, Roland W. Reed, 9 x 13 In. 633.00
Photograph, The Pottery Maker, Roland W. Reed, 9 x 13 In. 520.00
Photograph, Tlingit Indians, Dance Costume, Winter & Pond Co., c.1890, 7 x 5 In. 323.00
Photograph, U.S. Navy Destroyer Wreck, September, 1925, 8 x 10 In. 50.00
Photograph, Western Landscape, Mountains, Arts & Crafts Frame, 9 x 5 In. 310.00
Photograph, Woman Balloonist, Allen Photo, San Francisco, c.1940, 10 x 8 In. 100.00
Photograph, Women, 4 Nudes, No. 90, 1925, Dritikol, 5 1/4 x 3 3/8 In. 850.00
Photograph, Wounded Knee Survivors Scene, Grabill, c.1891, 12 1/2 x 9 1/2 In. 1295.00
Photograph, Yuma Girl, Tattooed Face, In Victorian Chair, 7 x 4 1/4 In. 205.00
Projector, Acme, Portable, Chicago, c.1920s, 35 mm, 18 In. 59.00
Projector, Bolex, G3, 3-Format, For 8, 9.5 & 16 mm, Switzerland, 1960 . . . . 250.00
Projector, Hand Cranked, Electric Light, Eastman Kodak, c.1931 . . . . 125.00
Stanhope, Binoculars, Stanhope, Niagara Falls, Ivory, Celluloid 23.00
Stereo Card, Chinese Embassy Crossing Cable Bridge, Niagara, C. Bierstadt, No. 676 . . . 75.00
Stereo Card, Log Cabins, Corral, Horses, Men, Justus Fey 430.00
Stereo-Graphoscope, Mahogany, Folding Holder, Magnifier, Stereo Lenses, c.1890, 12 In. 323.00
Stereo-Graphoscope, Rowsell-Pattern, Walnut, England, c.1875, 23 In. 382.00
Tintype, 2 Civil War Soldiers, Tinted, Wooden Frame, Carved Crosses, 1/4 Plate 175.00
Tintype, 2 Firemen, Wearing Caps & Long Coats, Leather Case, 1/6 Plate 150.00
Tintype, 2 Male Sock Makers, Socks, Forms, Leather Case, 1/6 Plate 325.00
Tintype, 2 Soldiers, Holding Swords Down, U.S. Flag, 1/4 Plate 490.00
Tintype, Armed Union Calvaryman, Private, Civil War, Case, 1/9 Plate 520.00
Tintype, Black Girl From Selma, H.T. McCormicks Gallery, 4 1/4 x 6 1/2 In. 150.00
Tintype, Butcher, Carving Meat, Leather Case, 1/6 Plate 175.00
Tintype, Camp Willard, 22 Men, Tent, U.S. Flag, Matted, Frame, 1/2 Plate 355.00
Tintype, Captain Francis Bedell, Seated, Holding Sword, Leather Case, 1/4 Plate 325.00
Tintype, Carpenter, Hammer, Saw, Ruler, Leather Case, 1/6 Plate 175.00
Tintype, Cavalry Soldier, Gilt Highlights, Leather Case, 1/4 Plate 470.00
Tintype, Child In High Chair, Case, Gutta-Percha, 4 1/4 x 3 1/4 In. 80.00
Tintype, Civil War, Man Holding Horn In Band Uniform, Case, 2 x 2 1/2 In. 275.00
Tintype, Civil War, Man In Uniform Sitting, Ft. Sumter Case 300.00
Tintype, Civil War, Man In Uniform Sitting, Holding Cap, Case, 2 3/4 x 3 1/4 In. 110.00
Tintype, Delivery Wagon, Tea, Coffee & Spices, Horse, Leather Case, 1/4 Plate 205.00
Tintype, Fort, Cannon, Plants, Tree, Grass, 1/4 Plate 200.00
Tintype, Girl With Finger In Mouth, 4 1/4 x 6 1/2 In. 75.00
Tintype, Hunter With Gear, 4 1/4 x 6 1/2 In. 150.00
Tintype, James Cobb, 7th Michigan Cavalry, Patriotic Union Case, 1/6 Plate 470.00
Tintype, Little Boy Beside Boat, Frame, 10 x 8 In. 225.00
Tintype, Logger, Post Mortem, By Taber & Howland, Union Case, 1/9 Plate 200.00
Tintype, Man & Woman In Wagon, 2 1/4 x 3 1/4 In. 25.00

Tintype, Man Sews Button For Another Man, 1/2 Plate 450.00
Tintype, Man, Baby In Carriage, 2 1/2 x 4 In. 17.00
Tintype, Medical Man, Holding Bottle, Table, Bottle Case, Leather, 1/4 Plate 325.00
Tintype, Officer, Gilbert E. Winters, Mexican & Civil Wars Veteran, 1/4 Plate 295.00
Tintype, Soldiers Wearing Medals, Flag, Bugle, 2 3/4 x 3 1/2 In. 50.00
Tintype, Stone Mason, Maul, Chisel, Union Case, 1/6 Plate 265.00
Tintype, Union Private, Standing, Musket, Bayonet, Case, 1/4 Plate 575.00
Tintype, Violinist, With Instrument & Dog, Pink Tint, Full Plate 405.00

PIANO BABY is a collector's term. About 1880, the well-decorated home had a shawl on the piano. Bisque figures of babies were designed to help hold the shawl in place. They range in size from 6 to 18 inches. Most of the figures were made in Germany. Reproductions are being made. Other piano babies may be listed under manufacturers' names.

Bisque, Child Reading Book, 8 In. 56.00
Bisque, Heubach, Laying On Back, No. 3102, 8 3/4 In. 270.00
Lying On Back, Touching Toes, Molded Bonnet, Heubach, c.1890, 10 In. 70.00

PICKARD China Company was started in 1898 by Wilder Pickard. Hand-painted designs were used on china purchased from other sources. In the 1930s, the company began to make its own china wares in Chicago, Illinois. The company now makes many types of porcelains, including a successful line of limited edition collector plates.

Bowl, Fruit, Berry, Leaf, Vine, O. Goess, Limoges, France, c.1905, 3 x 9 3/4 In. 805.00
Bowl, Red & White Tulips, Limoges Blank, 10 x 3 In. 230.00
Candy Dish, Footed, Reury, J & C Malmaico In Green, c.1905, 7 In. 495.00
Charger, Daisies, Cobalt, Green, Gold Etching, 12 3/4 In. 205.00
Pitcher, Poppy, Signed, 7 1/2 In. 305.00
Plate, Cabinet, Decorated, Gold Enamel Border, Limoges Blank, 8 1/2 In. 175.00
Plate, Cabinet, Lilies, Gold Background, Signed, Yeschek, 9 In. 92.00
Plate, Violet, Vine, Leaf, Signed, A.W., AKD France, 8 3/4 In. 295.00
Sugar, Cover, Fruit Basket, Flowers, Scroll, Gilt 140.00
Sugar & Creamer, Cover, Flowers, Gilt 85.00
Sugar & Creamer, Violets, Signed, T & V Limoges, France, 4 1/4 In. 450.00
Tankard, Poppy, Daisy, Gasper, Limoges, J.P.L. France, 1909, 11 In. 1350.00
Tea Service, Gilt & Turquoise Bands, Scrolling Vines, Floral, c.1900, 5 Piece 460.00
Teapot, Fruit Basket, Flowers, Scroll Design, Gilt 220.00
Vase, Bird Of Paradise Medallion, Stippled Gold Ground, 17 In. 865.00
Vase, Flower, Leaf, Rean, W.A. Pickard, c.1900, 8 In. 675.00
Vase, Vobor, Marked In Gold, 5 In. 195.00

PICTURE FRAMES are listed in this book in the Furniture category under Frame.

PICTURES, silhouettes, and other small decorative objects framed to hang on the wall are listed here. Sandpaper pictures are black and white charcoal drawings done on a special sanded paper. Some other types of pictures are listed in the Print and Painting categories.

Beadwork, Woman Reading Outdoors, Black & Gilt Painted, Giltwood Frame, 8 1/2 In. ... 294.00
Calligraphy, Bird, Frame, 11 1/2 x 14 In. 66.00
Calligraphy, Birds, Ribbon, Frame, A.J.S. Williard, Millerville, Penn., c.1918, 11 x 15 In. . 83.00
Cat Caged In Wooden Crate, Citizens Clothing House, Boston, 13 x 16 x 11 In. 2310.00
Chalk On Sandpaper En Grisaille, Rural Winterscape, Horse, Buggy, People, 11 x 16 In. . 402.00
Charcoal, Young Man, Bambro, Frame, American, 19th Century, 1841, 15 x 11 In. 353.00
Charcoal & Chalk, On Sandpaper, Brigantine, Icebergs, Moonlit Night, 17 x 21 1/2 In. ... 1645.00
Chromolithograph, White Headed Eagle, J. Bein, c.1860, 25 1/4 x 38 3/8 In. 2300.00
Collage, Grapevine, Alphabet, Luther Bell, Sparkill, N.Y., Frame, 1877, 13 1/2 x 20 In. .. 288.00
Compass, Watercolor, Ink, Directional, Degrees, Painted Frame, 8 1/2 x 8 1/2 In. 962.00
Diorama, Cutwork, Fox Hunting Scene, In Layers, Matted, Frame, 29 x 22 In. 323.00
Diorama, Sailing Ship, 3-Mast, American Flag, Relief Carved, Frame, 23 1/2 x 36 In. 1430.00
Drawing, Clock, Spread-Wing Eagle Crest, Flowers, Watercolor, Frame, 10 x 7 In. 7700.00
Drawing, Don't Start Anything, Dogs In Uniform, Tom Patten, 1919, 14 x 23 In. 540.00
Drawing, Dove, Spencerian, H. Hendrickson, W. Manchester, Oh., 1906-1907, 17 x 17 In. . 55.00
Embroidered, Circle Of Gopis, Krishna, India, c.1900, 25 x 26 In. 690.00
Embroidered, Courtesan, Flower Basket, Chinese, 19th Century, 28 x 20 In. 345.00

Embroidered, Felt, Blue, Cat, Birds, Chain Stitched, White, Yellow, Tan, 29 x 35 In. 870.00
Embroidered, Silk, Bird, Tree, Glass Beads, Metallic Thread, c.1900, 20 x 32 In. 85.00
Embroidered, Silk, Crane, Flowering Tree, Japan, 1867-1912, 17 x 13 In. 320.00
Embroidered, Silk, Parade, Attendant Figures, Chinese, c.1900, 19 x 16 In., Pair 1840.00
Embroidered, Silk, Peacock, In Tree, Metallic Thread, c.1900, 51 x 25 In., Pair 200.00
Embroidered, Silk, Peacock, Metallic Threads, India, c.1900, 30 x 21 In. 175.00
Embroidered, Silk, Tiger Hunt, India, c.1900, 39 x 50 In. 259.00
Embroidered, Silk, Velvet, Dancing Figure, Panels, Glass, Metallic, 14 x 66 In. 290.00
Embroidered, Silk, Velvet, Scrolling Leaves, Metallic Threads, India, c.1900, 32 x 31 In. . 86.00
Embroidered, Stars, Ferns, Flowers, Dated May 10, 1889, Frame, 18 x 18 1/2 In. 316.00
Embroidered, Velvet, Abstract, Star, Brocade, Sequins, Beads, Late 19th Century 175.00
Engraving, Sailor's Farewell, Colored, P. Robert, Gilt Oval Frame, 6 1/4 x 5 1/2 In. 145.00
Engraving, Steel Plate, William Penn's Treaty With Indians, c.1775, 18 1/2 x 23 In. 275.00
Gouache On Cotton, Tara, On Lotus Throne, Brocade, Early 19th Century, 30 x 21 In. . . . 750.00
Gouache On Paper, Farm Landscape, Ruth Wolff, Signed, Frame, 8 x 10 1/2 In. 489.00
Gouache On Paper, Topeka Railroad Depot, Steam Engine, c.1950, 13 3/4 x 19 In. 345.00
Hair Wreath, Shadow Box, Flowers, Leaves, Beige Fabric, Victorian, 27 1/2 x 23 1/2 In. . 175.00
Ink & Watercolor, Potted Tree, Tiger Maple Frame, c.1840, 10 1/2 x 8 1/2 In. 7700.00
Ink & Watercolor, Rooster, Worm In Beak, D.Y. Ellinger, Frame, 5 3/4 x 6 In. 1210.00
Ink On Kesi Silk, Shouloa, Mounted, Chinese, 19th Century, 23 1/4 x 13 In. 7170.00
Ink On Paper, Brocade Mount, River Scene, Boatman, Chinese, 1900s, 19 1/2 x 20 In. . . . 259.00
Ink On Paper, Hand Scroll, Landscape, Dignitaries On Horses, c.1912, 97 1/2 x 10 In. . . . 3220.00
Ink On Silk, Washing The Elephant, Chinese, Early 20th Century, 47 x 23 In. 1790.00
Lithograph, Animals, Royal Agricultural Society's Show, Battersea Park, 24 x 19 1/2 In. . 198.00
Lithograph, Revd., M. Sambo's Sarmont, At Lectern, Hands In Air, 24 1/2 x 18 In. 415.00
Needlepoint, Girl With Parrot Perched On Hand, Dog, Matted, Gilt Frame, 24 x 26 In. . . . 825.00
Needlework, Chenille, Bouquet Of Flowers, Stumpwork, Giltwood Frame, 12 x 12 In. . . . 235.00
Needlework, Eagle, Flags, Shield, Arrows, Banner, E Pluribus Unum, 30 x 34 In. 825.00
Needlework, Embroidered, Maid, Holding Horn, Dog, Oval, Frame, 9 3/4 x 7 1/4 In. 185.00
Needlework, Embroidery, Patriotic, Eagle, Flags, E Pluribus Unum, 24 3/4 x 30 1/2 In. . . . 330.00
Needlework, Flower Urn, Butterfly, Verse, Silk, France, Frame, 17 1/2 x 14 1/2 In. 470.00
Needlework, Lady, Garden, Flowers, Animals, Tent Stitch, Frame, 1600s, 14 x 17 In. 1100.00
Needlework, Landscape, Man In Boat, Frame, 19th Century, 9 1/2 x 9 1/2 In. 200.00
Needlework, Landscape, Silk, Watercolor, Woman, Child, c.1800, 9 x 6 In. 175.00
Needlework, Madonna & Child, Silk Ground, Color & Metallic Thread, 12 1/2 x 9 In. . . . 405.00
Needlework, Maiden Carrying Grain Bundle, Embroidered, Painted, Silk, 12 x 14 In. 880.00
Needlework, Map, England, Signed Ann Turton, Aged 7, 1835, Frame, 17 1/2 x 13 1/2 In. 518.00
Needlework, Memorial, Mourning Woman, Urn Topped Monument, Willow, 17 x 15 In. . . 2235.00
Needlework, Memorial, Silk, Sarah Goodridge, 14 Yrs., Willow, Monuments, 19 x 22 In. . 3055.00
Needlework, Mourning, Woman, Cross, Goblet, Chenille, Watercolor, c.1820, 12 x 10 In. . 230.00
Needlework, Paper, Silk, Shepherdess, Sleeping Sheep, Cottage, Oval, Frame, 19 x 14 In. 275.00
Needlework, Patriotic, Spread-Wing Eagle, Flags, Shield, Wood Frame, 23 1/2 x 27 In. . . 460.00
Needlework, Petit Point, Pug, Green & Rose Rickrack Border, Frame, 18 x 16 In. 165.00
Needlework, Queen Of Sheba, Charles II Style, Late 17th Century, 15 x 20 In. 4480.00
Needlework, Sally Clar, Aged 8, 1801, Verse, Flowers, Birds, Cottages, 21 x 17 In. 880.00
Needlework, Shepherd, Playing Horn To Shepherdess, Sheep, Dog, Frame, 9 x 10 In. 660.00
Needlework, Silk & Chenille, Caroline, Heroine Of Litchfield, Frame, 18 x 17 1/2 In. . . . 940.00
Needlework, Silk, Britannia, Minerva, Flower Border, George III, 18 x 14 1/2 In. 7170.00
Needlework, Silk, Fruit Basket, Bird, Butterflies, Frame, 12 x 14 In. 575.00
Needlework, Silk, Memorial, Monument, Willow, Sarah Eliza Cook, 1815, 30 x 25 In. . . . 5390.00
Needlework, Silk, Memorial, Woman In Mourning, Church, Cemetery, 1870, 17 x 15 In. . 2235.00
Needlework, Silk, Shepherdess, Feeding Sheep, Vines, Oval Frame, 16 x 17 In. 355.00
Needlework, Silk, Watercolor, Woman, Anchor, Brig, Sail, Early 1800s, 11 1/2 x 10 In. . . 518.00
Needlework, Spaniel, With Puppies On Pillow, Glass Eyes, Frame, 22 1/2 x 18 In. 935.00
Needlework, Woman, Boy Selling Flowers, Coach, Petit Point, Black Border, 22 x 18 In. . 55.00
Panel, Gold Brocade, Persia, Frame, c.1600, 41 1/2 x 10 In. 880.00
Pastel, House Portrait, Kittery, Maine, On Sandpaper, Harry Remick, 1868, 15 x 21 In. . . 2115.00
Pastel, Naughty Puppy Chewing Piece Of Lace, Frame, 13 1/4 x 17 1/4 In. 1295.00
Pastel, Puppy Sleeping On Green Cushion, 12 1/2 x 17 1/4 In. 1175.00
Pastel On Paper, Wind Blown Maiden With Suitor, 19th Century, 14 x 17 In. 345.00
Pastel On Paper, Woman In White Bonnet, American, Frame, 1800s, 8 1/4 x 6 1/4 In. . . . 380.00
Pastel On Paper, Woman In White Dress, America, 19th Century, 7 7/8 x 6 1/8 In. 999.00
Pen & Ink, Buffalo Bill's Wild West & Exhibition, Signed J.P. Newton, 10 x 14 In. 350.00

Pen & Ink, Geometric Equations, The Rule Of A Trapezoid, 19th Century, 12 3/4 x 16 In. 55.00
Pen & Ink, Needlework Design, Verse, Signed, Mary Pryton, 1758, 5 1/2 x 3 3/4 In. 290.00
Pen & Ink, Universalist Church, Leesburg, Ohio, 10 3/4 x 15 In. 525.00
Presentation Drawing, Watercolor, Ink, On Paper, Penn. School, 1816, 4 x 7 In. 6573.00
Sandpaper, Castle, Water, People, Black & White, Oak Frame, 17 1/2 x 22 1/2 In. 240.00
Sandpaper, Looking Down On Hudson River From Balcony, 9 x 11 In. 400.00
Scherenschnitte, Watercolor, Sun, Flowers, Sarah Kets, Frame, Early 1800s, 13 x 10 In. . 880.00
Scroll, Ink On Brocade Silk, Ducks & Reeds, 19th Century, 52 x 14 1/2 In. 430.00
Scroll, Ink On Paper, Flowers, Rocks, Brocade Mount, Chinese, 20th Century, 27 x 18 In. 405.00
Scroll, Ink On Paper, Hanging, Orchid & Wisteria, 19th Century, 46 1/2 x 11 In. 635.00
Scroll, Ink On Paper, Silk Mount, Fisherman Talking To Crab, Chinese, 40 1/2 x 21 In. . . . 259.00
Scroll, Ink On Parchment, Traveler With Attendants, 19th Century, 18 1/2 x 11 3/8 In. . . . 259.00
Scroll On Silk, Mountain Huts With Figure, Signed, Watanabe Kazan, c.1820, 41 x 12 In. . 490.00
Silhouette, Boy, Carrying Book, Cap, White Ink Detail, Frame, c.1845, 9 7/8 x 8 1/4 In. . . 990.00
Silhouette, Boy, In Cap, With Dog, Homer Mongering, c.1840, 11 3/8 x 9 3/8 In. 3080.00
Silhouette, Dapper Gentleman, Telescope, Walking Stick, c.1834, 8 5/8 x 6 1/4 In. 1430.00
Silhouette, Drummer Boy, Tasseled Cap, Sam Loomis, Gilt Frame, c.1840, 9 x 7 1/2 In. . . 2200.00
Silhouette, Full-Length, Gentleman, Signed, Monsieur Deodar, c.1830, 12 x 9 1/2 In. . . . 2640.00
Silhouette, Full-Length, Hon. Cassius M. Clay, Seated, Reading, c.1845, 12 x 11 1/2 In. . 11000.00
Silhouette, Gentleman, Hollow Cut Head, Jacket, Inked Hair, Oval Frame, 6 x 4 1/2 In. . . 220.00
Silhouette, Gentleman, Portrait, Waist-Length, Wood Frame, 5 1/4 x 4 1/2 In. 79.00
Silhouette, Gentleman, Seated, Reading Book, Frame, c.1840, 14 x 10 1/4 In. 1100.00
Silhouette, Gentleman, Waistcoat, Drawn Details, Frame, 18 x 10 In. 220.00
Silhouette, Gentlemen, Hollow Cut, Inked Hair, Walnut Frame, 8 x 6 3/4 In. 330.00
Silhouette, Husband & Wife, Inked Details, Framed Together, 9 1/4 x 11 In. 415.00
Silhouette, Husband & Wife, Seated, Double Reverse Glass, Gilt Frame, 8 1/4 x 10 In. . . 825.00
Silhouette, Ink, English Woman, Mrs. Jane Blencove Cheltonham, 1829, 6 x 12 In. 226.00
Silhouette, Man & Woman Portrait, Watercolor, Oval Matte, Frame, 6 x 5 In., Pair 950.00
Silhouette, Man & Woman, Paper Cut, British School, 1800s, 4 1/4 x 3 In., Pair 200.00
Silhouette, Olive Agusta Bailey, 3 Years, Inked Hair, Hollow Cut, Frame, 5 x 4 1/2 In. . . . 360.00
Silhouette, Portrait, Family Activities, American School, 19th Century, 15 1/2 x 21 In. . . . 4400.00
Silhouette, Rev. D. Panting, John Miers, Reverse Glass Painted, 1805, 6 1/2 x 5 1/2 In. . . 220.00
Silhouette, Woman, Lace Collar, Hair Comb, Gilt Frame, 7 1/4 x 6 1/4 In. 165.00
Silhouette, Woman, Madme. Ve. Touville, Calais, c.1851, 14 x 12 In. 195.00
Silhouette, Young Woman, Hair Up, Embossed, Todd's Patent, Hollow Cut, 6 3/4 x 5 In. . . 305.00
Silk, Portrait, Victor Hugo, 1885, 8 x 10 1/2 In. 125.00
Silkscreen, Fallen Man Series, Ernest Tino Trova, c.1969, 26 1/2 x 25 1/2 In. 147.00
Silkwork, Young Woman, Mourning Sweetheart's Departure, Frame, 1800s, 11 In. 365.00
Sketch, Robber Squirrel, Seated On Table, Stealing Nut From Bowl, Frame, 9 x 12 In. . . . 285.00
Straw, Cottage, Sailboats On Lake, Frame, 10 x 12 In. . . . . *Illus* 35.00
Theorem, Clipper Ship, Signed, Bill Rank, Sponge Decorated Frame, 21 1/2 x 23 3/4 In. . 2145.00
Theorem, Cornucopia, Flowers, Toning, Frame, 19th Century, 10 x 13 In. 575.00
Theorem, Flower Basket, Oil, Watercolor, Signed Julia P. Paine, c.1840, 12 3/8 x 15 In. . . 13200.00
Theorem, Fruit Basket, Signed, M. Ruhl, Molded Frame, c.1829, 13 x 17 In. 2860.00
Theorem, On Velvet, Compote Of Fruit, Butterfly, Hummingbird, Frame, 14 x 28 1/2 In. . 690.00
Theorem, On Velvet, Flower Urn, Polychrome, Greta C. Kidner, Frame, 21 x 17 In. 165.00
Theorem, Owl On Branch, Frame, Bill Rank, 13 3/4 x 11 1/2 In. 470.00

Picture, Straw, Cottage, Sailboats On Lake, Frame, 10 x 12 In.

Picture, Tinsel, Flowers, Gilt Frame, 15 x 18 1/2 In.

Theorem, Paper Quill, Mica, Flowers Vase, Fruitwood Frame, c.1793, 18 x 26 In. 2200.00
Theorem, Rooster, Red, Black, Frame, Jessie N. Boyer, 15 7/8 x 12 1/4 In. 385.00
Theorem, Spray Of Flowers, Frame, Softwood, Molded, 20 x 16 In. 220.00
Theorem, Watercolor On Paper, Still Life, Fruit Basket, Giltwood Frame, 11 x 14 In. 880.00
Theorem, Watercolor On Velvet, Peaches, Grapes, Cherries, 11 x 13 1/2 In. 440.00
Theorem, Watercolor On Velvet, Still Life, Fruit In Bowl, Frame, 14 1/4 x 17 5/8 In. 825.00
Tinsel, Flowers, Gilt Frame, 15 x 18 1/2 In. . . . . *Illus* 120.00
Tinsel, Reverse Glass, Flower Urn, Silver, Red Stool, Black Ground, Frame, 19 x 23 In. . . 385.00
Watercolor, Bird, On Thistle, Red Head, Yellow Wings, Mahogany Frame, 8 x 7 In. 300.00
Watercolor, Clapboard House, Picket Fence, Dirt Road, Signed, McCombs, 17 x 20 In. . . 250.00
Watercolor, Eagle, Spread Wings, Shield, E Pluribus Unum, c.1850, 6 1/4 x 7 5/8 In. 5225.00
Watercolor, Flower Spray, Polychrome, To Miss Mary Hyde, 11 1/4 x 10 1/4 In. 305.00
Watercolor, Flowers, Leaves, Folk Art, Frame, 8 3/4 x 9 1/2 In. 70.00
Watercolor, Ink, Profile, Man, Black Waistcoat, Penn. School, 6 x 3 3/4 In. 5378.00
Watercolor, Interior Tavern Scene, Frame, M. Schuibbeo, Folk Art, 22 3/4 x 25 3/4 In. . . . 195.00
Watercolor, May Queen, Currier & Ives Style, Painted Frame, 15 x 12 In. 175.00
Watercolor, Mourning, John Gilmore, Silk, Chenille, Gold Thread, 26 1/2 x 21 In. 1550.00
Watercolor, Paddle Streamer, Frame, America, 19th Century, 5 1/8 x 9 1/8 In. 470.00
Watercolor, Peafowl, Urn & Flowers, Leaves, Tulip Frame, 9 3/4 x 8 1/4 In. 2640.00
Watercolor, Portrait, Full-Length, Charles White, 3 Years Old, 1825, 7 x 5 1/2 In. 1210.00
Watercolor, Praying Girl, Angel, Religious Text, Frame, 12 x 9 In. 3300.00
Watercolor, Seascape, Blue, Purple, Brown, Frame, William Rice, Signed, 14 x 10 In. . . . 750.00
Watercolor, Velvet, Mourning, Women In Black, Urn Under Willow, 1825, 20 x 26 In. . . . 2090.00
Watercolor, Woman In Lace Bonnet, Frame, American, 19th Century, 8 1/2 x 6 1/2 In. . . . 765.00
Watercolor On Paper, Cathedral Interior, Charles Wilde, England, c.1800, 15 x 11 In. . . . 575.00
Watercolor On Paper, Gentleman, Frame, Oval, America, 19th Century, 3 x 2 1/4 In. 205.00
Watercolor On Paper, Girl, With Cat, Holding Flower, Frame, 10 x 9 1/2 In. 2420.00
Watercolor On Paper, Hudson River View, Frame, American, 1800s, 8 5/8 x 13 1/2 In. . . 1058.00
Watercolor On Paper, Sailboats, Roiling Sea, Robert Hopkin, c.1900, 13 1/2 x 9 1/2 In. . 460.00
Watercolor On Paper, Venetian Canal Scene, A. Minotto, 11 1/2 x 23 1/4 In. 575.00
Wax, Portrait, John Paul Jones, Lace Collar, Blue Waistcoat, Shadowbox Frame, 6 x 7 In. . 1582.00
Woolwork, Sailor's, 3-Masted Bark, Steam & Sail Powered, 12 x 22 In. 1595.00
Woolwork, Scenic, Hunters, Dead Fox, Gate, Giltwood Frame, c.1841, 19 x 25 In. 1792.00

PIERCE, see Howard Pierce category.

PIGEON FORGE Pottery was started in Pigeon Forge, Tennessee, in 1946. Red clay found near the pottery was used to make the pieces. Molded or thrown pottery with matte glaze and slip decoration was made. The pottery closed in 2000.

    Cup, Handleless, Gray Clay, Horizontal Ridges, Blue Interior Glaze 10.00
    Cup, Souvenir, Pigeon Forge, Tennessee, 3 Oz. 3.50
    Dish, Yellow Glaze Interior, Carved Exterior, Rectangular 32.00
    Mug, Fox, Animal Series, 3 1/2 In. 10.00
    Pitcher, Dogwood Blossoms, Blue Interior, 1958, 5 1/2 In. 45.00
    Pitcher, Dogwood, Flowers, c.1955, 3 3/4 In. 25.00

PILKINGTON Tile and Pottery Company was established in 1892 in England. The company made small pottery wares, like buttons and hatpins, but soon started decorating vases purchased from other potteries. By 1903, the company had discovered an opalescent glaze that became popular on the Lancastrian pottery line. The manufacture of pottery ended in 1937. Pilkington's Tiles Ltd. has worked from 1938 to the present.

    Vase, Bulbous, Golden Dragon, Amber, Red Ground, 10 1/2 x 6 1/2 In. 2235.00
    Vase, Bulbous, Green, Amber Matte Glaze, 12 x 7 In. 385.00

PINCUSHION DOLLS are not really dolls and often were not even pincushions. Some collectors use the term *half-doll*. The top half of each doll was made of porcelain. The edge of the half-doll was made with several small holes for thread, and the doll was stitched to a fabric body with a voluminous skirt. The finished figure was used to cover a hot pot of tea, powder box, pincushion, whisk broom, or lamp. They were made in sizes from less than an inch to over 9 inches high. Most

date from the early 1900s to the 1950s. Collectors often find just the porcelain doll without the fabric skirt.

Baby, Bisque, Movable Arms, Rosey Cheeks, Blond, Blue Eyes, 1 3/4 In.	125.00
Celluloid, American Flag Dress Front, French Flag Dress Back, 1920s	180.00
Celluloid Head, Arms, Feet, Satin Body, Human Hair, 4 In.	49.00
China Top, Brush Bottom, Numbered, Marked, Germany, c.1900, 8 In.	58.00
Cupid, Bisque, Peach Costume, Hat, Base, Box, c.1920, 5 In.	450.00
Painted Face, Bonnet, Pockets, Hanging Bag, 18 In.	28.00
Senorita Half-Doll, Arms Away Pose, No. 5063, Germany, 3 In.	40.00
Woman, Gold Skirt, Hair Bow, Box, 2 In.	95.00
Woman, Hand On Hip, Porcelain, No. 2348, Germany, c.1930, 3 1/2 In.	50.00
Woman, Holds Hands In Front, Glazed Bisque, No. 1489, Germany, 2 1/4 In.	35.00
Woman, Plaster, Silk Skirt, 6 x 5 In.	18.00
Woman, Porcelain Half-Doll, Crocheted Skirt Pincushion, 5 3/4 x 4 7/8 In.	130.00
Woman, Sits On Pincushion, Ceramic, Hat, Lace Necklace, 10 In.	125.00

PINK SLAG pieces are listed in this book in the Slag Glass category.

PIPES have been popular since tobacco was introduced to Europe by Sir Walter Raleigh. Carved wooden, porcelain, ivory, and glass pipes may be listed here. Meerschaum pipes are listed under Meerschaum.

Bowl, Character, Barmaid Sits On Barrel, Porcelain, Lid, 4 1/2 In.	345.00
Burl, Sterling Silver, Overlay Golfer, Football Player, Silversmith Sterling	77.00
Ceramic, Figural, Beer All Girl, Regional Costume, Beer Barrel, Tankards, Germany, 5 In.	323.00
Ivory, Sterling Silver Collar, Asian Man	39.00
Meerschaum, Blue Velvet Box, Kitchen Scene, Cigarette Holders, Match Safe	1150.00
Opium, Bamboo Shaft, Embossed Silver Band, Bone Bowl, 20th Century, 21 In.	175.00
Porcelain, Deer, Forest Decoration	28.00
Porcelain, German Hunter, Dogs	50.00
Wood, Head Of Civil War Soldier	61.00
Wood, Powder Horn Shape, Eagle, Shield, 1st RI Lt Arty, Baty B, 6 In.	675.00
Wood, Revolver, Bowl, 5 In.	95.00

PISGAH FOREST pottery was made in North Carolina beginning in 1926. The pottery was started by Walter B. Stephen, who had been making pottery in that location since 1914. The pottery continued in operation after his death in 1961. The most famous kinds of Pisgah Forest ware are the cameo type with designs made of raised glaze and the turquoise crackle glaze wares.

Mottled Green, Turquoise Glossy Glaze, Pink Interior, Marked, 1939, 9 In.	138.00
Mug, Horse & Covered Wagon, Green, Cameo, Marked, 3 3/4 In.	184.00
Pitcher, Wine & Turquoise, Crackle, Feldspathic Glaze, Signed, c.1942, 8 In.	88.00
Sugar & Creamer, Green, Blue High Glaze, Signed, 1948	205.00
Sugar & Creamer, Sea Green, Cord Handle, Feldspathic Glaze, 1980s, 3 1/4 In.	22.00
Teapot, Cameo, Wagon Scene, Dark Teal, Glossy White, Marked, 5 1/2 In. *Illus*	633.00
Vase, Blue Glaze, Raised Mark, 28 In.	1100.00

Pisgah Forest, Teapot, Cameo, Wagon Scene, Dark Teal, Glossy White, Marked, 5 1/2 In.

Pisgah Forest, Vase, Cameo, Wagon Scene, Dark Teal, Glossy Turquoise, Marked, 9 In.

Pisgah Forest, Vase, Cameo, Wagon, Oxen, Green Matte, Mottled Turquoise, Marked, 7 In.

Vase, Cameo, Wagon Scene, Dark Teal, Glossy Turquoise, Marked, 9 In. . . . . *Illus*		978.00
Vase, Cameo, Wagon, Oxen, Green Matte, Mottled Turquoise, Marked, 7 In. . . . . *Illus*		863.00
Vase, Covered Wagon Scene, Green Matte Band, Blue Ground, 1924, 12 In.		2185.00
Vase, Covered Wagon Scene, Green Matte, Blue, Green Ground, 1930, 8 x 6 In.		865.00
Vase, Covered Wagon Scene, Wedgwood Blue Ground, Bulbous, 1951, 5 1/2 In.		460.00
Vase, Covered Wagon Scene, Wedgwood Blue Matte Ground, 4 x 6 In.		430.00
Vase, Crystalline Glaze, Gray & White, Raised Mark, 6 In.		210.00
Vase, Green Glaze, Aqua Blue Ground, 9 3/4 x 5 1/2 In.		330.00
Vase, Indian Camp Scene, Green Matte Collar, Green Crackle Glaze, 1940, 8 In.		1725.00
Vase, Mottled Green, Turquoise Glossy Glaze, Pink Interior, c.1940, 5 5/8 In.		58.00
Vase, Oyster, White Crystals, White Over Buff Glazes, Pink Interior, 1946, 4 1/4 In.		230.00
Vase, Sea Green, Feldspathic Glaze, Small Neck, c.1983, 4 7/8 In.		45.00
Vase, Turquoise, Wine Crackle Glaze, Marked, 1942, 5 1/2 In.		35.00
Vase, Turquoise, Wine Crackle Glaze, Pink Interior, Handles, 1941, 6 1/4 In.		92.00

PLANTERS PEANUTS memorabilia is collected. Planters Nut and Chocolate Company was started in Wilkes-Barre, Pennsylvania, in 1906.
The Mr. Peanut figure was adopted as a trademark in 1916. National
advertising for Planters Peanuts started in 1918. The company was
acquired by Standard Brands, Inc., in 1961. Standard Brands merged
with Nabisco in 1981. Some of the Mr. Peanut jars and other memorabilia have been reproduced and, of course, new items are being made.

Advertisement, Fall Fiesta, Paper, 1954, 9 x 13 In.		12.00
Advertisement, Jerry Lewis, Nutty Professor, Eating Peanuts, 10 x 13 In.		20.00
Badge, Celluloid, Plant Workers Name, Brass Clip, 1920s, 2 1/4 In.		605.00
Bag, Burlap, Mr. Peanut, 15 x 8 In.		12.00
Bag, Mr. Peanut Logo, 3 Lb.		5.00
Bank, Mr. Peanut, Plastic, 8 1/2 In.		20.00
Blotter, Nickel Lunch, 6 1/4 x 3 3/8 In.		60.00
Blotter, Truck, Snow, Pennant Brand, c.1930, 3 1/2 x 6 1/4 In.		15.00
Bookmark, 1940 New York World's Fair, 6 1/2 x 3 1/4 In.		19.00
Canister, Planters, On Front, Peanuts, On Back, 9 1/2 x 7 1/4 In.		15.00
Coaster Set, Mr. Peanut, Tin, Round, 4 Piece		18.00
Coloring Book, Mr. Peanut & U.S. Presidents From Washington On, 1953		40.00
Dispenser, Wood, Glass, c.1970, 13 1/2 In.		25.00
Figure, Mr. Peanut, Top Floats On Spring, Body Nods, 7 x 2 1/2 In.		84.00
Jar, Cover, Glass, Counter Display, Square, Peanut Finial		99.00
Jar, Cover, Glass, Embossed, Peanut Finial, 12 In.		77.00
Jar, Glass, Counter Display, Tin Lithograph Lid		72.00
Jar, Mr. Peanut, Glass, 1982, 9 In.		6.00
Jar, Peanut Butter, Glass, Paper Label, 1940, 1 Lb., 5 1/4 x 2 3/4 In.		78.00
Jar, Peanut Finial, Glass Lid, 9 1/4 In.		56.00
Jar, Peanut Pattern, On Bottom, 8 x 11 In.		4.00
Key Chain, Mr. Peanut, Figural, 3 1/2 In.		10.00
Printing Block, Mr. Peanut With Cane, Metal, On Wood, 5 1/2 x 2 5/8 x 1 In.		110.00
Puppet, Hand, Figural Mr. Peanut, Yellow, Rubber, 6 1/2 x 6 In.		685.00
Salt & Pepper, Mr. Peanut, c.1950, 4 In.		45.00
Salt & Pepper, Mr. Peanut, Green, Plastic, 3 In.		12.00
Tin, Black Walnuts, Planters Peanut Co., 2 7/8 x 2 5/8 In.		60.00
Tin, Boscul Butter Coated Party Peanuts, Key Wind, 3 x 3 3/8 In.		45.00
Tin, Cocktail Peanuts, Canada, 3 x 3 3/8 In.		45.00
Tin, Mr. Peanut, Planters Nut & Chocolate Co., 4 Oz. . . :		20.00
Tin, Nickel Lunch, Planters Lifesavers Co., Winston Salem, N.C., 5 x 6 3/8 In.		6.00
Tin, Planter Hi-Hat Peanut Oil, Unopened, Qt., 7 1/4 x 3 3/4 x 2 5/8 In.		51.00
Tin, Redskin Spanish Peanuts, Suffolk, Va., 4 1/4 x 4 In.		68.00
Tray, Pennant Brand Fresh, Mr. Peanut, 15 5/8 x 11 1/8 In.		18.00
Trivet, Pennant Brand Fresh, Mr. Peanut, 8 3/8 x 6 1/2 In.		9.00
Wristwatch, Mr. Peanut, Date Window, Reorder Form, 1971		100.00

PLASTIC objects of all types are being collected. Some pieces are listed
in other categories; gutta-percha cases are listed in photography, celluloid in its own category.

Baby Bath, Alligator, Thermometer Insert, Bakelite, Germany, 6 1/2 In.		165.00

Plastic, Dish, Soup, Underplate, Arrowhead,
Brookpark, Everware, Chartreuse

Plastic, Figurine,
Elephant, Lucite, Pink
Ears & Feet, 2 3/4 In.

Basket, Fruit, Cast & Applied Resin, Red, Brown, Purple, Gaetano Pesche, 6 x 14 In.	635.00
Box, Cigarette, Lucite, Roses, Red, Orange, Green Leaves, 6 1/2 x 4 1/8 x 2 1/2 In.	40.00
Dish, Soup, Underplate, Arrowhead, Brookpark, Everware, Chartreuse . . . . *Illus*	5.00
Figurine, Elephant, Lucite, Pink Ears & Feet, 2 3/4 In. . . . . *Illus*	5.00
Knife, Paper, Art Nouveau, Openwork Handle, Molded & Painted Violets, 10 In.	450.00
Salt & Pepper, Aunt Jemima	30.00
Tissue Holder, Reverse Carved Design, Clear, Rectangular	12.00

PLATED AMBERINA was patented June 15, 1886, by Joseph Locke and made by the New England Glass Company. It is similar in color to amberina, but is characterized by a cream colored or chartreuse lining (never white) and small ridges or ribs on the outside.

Bowl, 7 In.	8300.00
Bowl, Ruffled, Applied Handle, 7 3/4 In.	8050.00
Cruet, Ribbed, Applied Amber Handle, Stopper, 6 3/4 In.	5465.00
Cruet, Ribbed, Lapidary Cut Stopper, Applied Amber Handle, 5 1/4 In.	2130.00
Pitcher, Lemonade, Applied Amber Handle, 5 In.	3640.00
Punch Cup, Applied Handle, 2 1/2 In.	2875.00
Spooner, Ribbed, 4 1/4 In.	3910.00

PLIQUE-A-JOUR is an enameling process. The enamel is laid between thin raised metal lines and heated. The finished piece has transparent enamel held between the thin metal wires. It is different from cloisonne because it is translucent.

Bowl, 6 Alternating Flower Panels, Mushroom Rim, Wood Stand, Box, 7 x 3 In.	179.00
Bowl, 16 Lotus Leaves, Pink, Wood Stand, Gift Box, 5 x 2 1/2 In.	249.00
Bowl, Dragon Boat, Marked, 9505, 3 3/8 x 7 In.	715.00
Snuff Bottle, Pink & Blue Flowers, Pink, Transparent Cloisonne, 2 1/2 x 1 3/4 In.	79.00
Snuff Bottle, Red & Yellow Flowers, Transparent Cloisonne, Blue Ground, 3 In.	79.00

POLITICAL memorabilia of all types, from buttons to banners, is collected. Items related to presidential candidates are the most popular, but collectors also search for material related to state and local offices. Memorabilia related to social causes, minor political parties, and protest movements are also included here. Many reproductions have been made. A jugate is a button with photographs of both the presidential and vice presidential candidates. In this list a button is round, usually with a straight pin or metal tab to secure it to a shirt. A pin is brass, often figural, sometimes attached to a ribbon.

Almanac, Democratic Almanac, Van Buren Biography, 1841	50.00
Apron, Housewives For Johnson, Red, White, Blue, 1964, 17 x 21 In.	70.00
Ashtray, JFK, When A Great Man Dies, Eternal Flame, Smoked Glass, 1960s, 5 x 7 In. . .	27.00
Badge, Democratic National Convention, Delegate, 1964	32.00
Badge, Democratic National Convention, Missouri Delegate, 1900	261.00
Badge, Franklin D. Roosevelt, Okay America, You Bet I'm With You, 1933	323.00
Badge, Harrison, Protection, Red, White, Blue, 1892	342.00
Badge, Herbert C. Hoover, Inauguration, Celluloid At Top, 1929, 2 1/2 In.	565.00
Badge, Peoples Party, National Convention, Omaha Neb., 1892	150.00
Badge, Republican National Convention, Alternate, Red, White, Blue Enamel, 1916	70.00

Badge, Republican National Convention, Kansas City, Delegate, 1928 .... 55.00
Badge, Republican National Convention, Miami Beach, Alternate, August, 1972 .... 30.00
Badge, Republican National Convention, Press, 1968 .... 45.00
Badge, Teddy Roosevelt, Color Portrait, Bond Co. Illinois, Ribbon, 1904 .... 276.00
Bag, Ballot, St. Louis, 1956 .... 47.00
Bag, Canvas, Campaign, Dewey, Red, White, Blue, 1948, 18 In. 131.00
Ballot, California, Lincoln & Garfield, 1880, 3 3/4 In. 35.00
Ballot Box, Red, White & Blue, Word Colored On Front 850.00
Bandanna, Carter, Peanut Dancing, Silk, c.1976 .... 155.00
Bandanna, Cleveland, Thurman, Linen 168.00
Bandanna, McKinley, Hobart, Sound Money, Crossed Flags, Eagle, Protection, 1896 .... 150.00
Bandanna, Our President, Hoover, Cotton, States' Seals, Eagle, 16 1/2 x 18 In. 135.00
Bandanna, Teddy Roosevelt, Progressive Battle Flag, 1912 .... 250.00
Banner, Dallas Grand National Banner, 1844, 10 x 14 In. 146.00
Banner, Garfield & Arthur, Black, White, Painted, 1800, 31 x 34 In. 1600.00
Banner, Vote For Eisenhower & Nixon, Red, White, Blue, 34 x 40 In. 1750.00
Banner, Vote For Stevenson & Sparkman, Red, White, Blue, 34 x 40 In. 2500.00
Baseball Jersey, Wallace '68 On Back & Breast Pocket, Terry Cloth, 1968 .... 40.00
Beanie, Harding & Coolidge, Orange, Brown, Felt, 1920, 9 In. 136.00
Belt Buckle, Abraham Lincoln, Circular, Tintype, Embossed, 1900s, 1 3/8 x 1 1/2 In. 374.00
Blotter, For Gov. Vote For Louis, 4 x 9 In. 25.00
Book, Campaign, That Man, 1944, 8 1/2 x 11 In., 78 Pages 71.00
Book, Democratic National Convention, Capitol, FDR Portrait, 1936 .... 40.00
Book, Inaugural, FDR, 1933, 8 1/2 x 11 In., 64 Pages 74.00
Bookend, Bryan, Democratic Donkey, Metal, Celluloid, 8 In. 770.00
Bookend, Taft, Republican Elephant, Metal, Celluloid, 7 In. 250.00
Booklet, Case Against Franklin D. Roosevelt, 20 Pages 12.50
Booklet, Communist Election Platform, 1932, 16 Pages 39.00
Booklet, Harrison Inaugural Ball, 1889, 7 1/2 x 9 1/2 In. 2218.00
Bumper Sticker, America Needs Nixon Now 4.00
Bumper Sticker, Reagan, For Governor, 1966 .... 6.00
Button, Adlai Stevenson, Campaign, Photo, 1950, 6 In. 96.00
Button, Al Smith For President, 7/8 In. 32.00
Button, Alfred E. Smith For President, Red, White, Blue, Black, Celluloid, 1 1/4 In. 109.00
Button, All The Way With Adlai, Red, White & Blue, 1952, 1 1/4 In. 8.00
Button, Anti Smith, White, Blue, 1928, 3/4 In. 43.00
Button, Arizonans For Ducactus, Multicolored, Celluloid, 2 1/4 In. 225.00
Button, Bike For Peace, Blue, White, Celluloid, 4 Languages, 2 1/4 In. 67.00
Button, Br(a)y On & Sewell, Donkey, 7/8 In. 255.00
Button, Bryan, Alschuler, Coattail, Illinois, 7/8 In. 754.00
Button, Bryan, Bohmrich, President, Governor, Coattail, 1 1/4 In. 1380.00
Button, Bryan, Color Tinted Portrait, Red, White, Blue, Silver Background, 1 1/2 In. 276.00
Button, Bryan, Defenders Of The Constitution, Celluloid, 1 3/4 In. 4800.00
Button, Bryan, Me For, Red, Blue, 1908, 5/8 In. 117.00
Button, Bryan, Red, White, Blue, Black, Silver, Celluloid, Jugate, 1900, 1 1/4 In. 61.00
Button, Bryan, Sewall, Silver Background, Victory 1896, 1 1/2 In. 613.00
Button, Bury Goldwater In 64, Black, White, Celluloid, 1 3/4 In. 22.00
Button, California Republicans For Reagan, June 3 Primary, Elephant, 1980, 3 In. 31.00
Button, Carter, Illinois, Richard J. Daley Chairman, Black, Green, 3 In. 152.00
Button, Carter, Photo, Green, Black, White, Celluloid, 1 3/4 In. 30.00
Button, Charles Evans Hughes, My First Vote For President, 1916, 1 1/4 In. 759.00
Button, Chelsea Clinton, Vote For My Daddy, 2 1/4 In. 385.00
Button, Citizens For Eisenhower, Let's Back Ike, Vote Republican, 7/8 In. 40.00
Button, Cleveland Needs Ness For Mayor, Celluloid, Red, White, 1947, 7/8 In. 130.00
Button, Clinton Blues Brothers, Gore, Waymon Burke, Purple Background, 2 In. 310.00
Button, Clothing, G. Washington Inaugural, Long Live The President, States, 1789 ..... 2450.00
Button, Coloradans For Goldwater, Black, Gold & White, Celluloid, 1 3/4 In. 303.00
Button, Committee To Liberate Black Voters, Carter Head On Donkey Kicking, 3 In. 43.00
Button, Coolidge & Dawes, Brown Background, 7/8 In. 75.00
Button, Coolidge Keep Square Deal, Celluloid, 7/8 In. 1049.00
Button, Coolidge, Dawes, Full Dinner Pail, 7/8 In. 61.00
Button, Coolidge, Deeds Not Words, Sepia Portrait, Easel Back, 4 In. 5264.00
Button, Davis & Bryan Campaign Fund, Red, White, Blue, Paper, 1 1/4 In. 106.00

Button, Davis, Red, White, Blue, 7/8 In. 175.00
Button, Deadheads For Dukakis, Red, White, Blue & Black, Celluloid, 1988, 2 1/4 In. . . . 352.00
Button, Debs, Hanford, Socialist Party, 1904, 1 1/4 In. 795.00
Button, Democracy Stands For, People, Republic, 3-Leaf Clover, 1900, 1 1/4 In. 284.00
Button, Dewey For Governor, 1950, 3 1/2 In. 180.00
Button, Dewey Is Due In 48, Blue, Black, White, Celluloid, 7/8 In. 62.00
Button, Dewey, Eagle, Red, White, Blue, Lithograph, Tab, 7/8 In. 16.00
Button, Dewey, Warren, Bright Blue Background, 7/8 In. 42.00
Button, Dicky Poo For 72, Caricature, 1972, 3 In. 35.00
Button, Dole Heartland Tour, McConnell, Kentucky, Coattail, 1996, 2 In. 127.00
Button, Dole, Kemp, Zimmer Corodemus, Volunteer, New Jersey Coattail, 2 In. 38.00
Button, Don't Change The Pilot, Re-Elect F.D. Roosevelt, Fortis Non Timet, 7/8 In. 55.00
Button, Donkey, Brown & Black Plastic, I'm So Wild About Harry, 2 1/4 In. 265.00
Button, Dukakis, Attorney General, Blue, Green, 2 In. 421.00
Button, Dukakis, Bentsen, Issued By Chicago Steelworkers, 3 In. 45.00
Button, Eisenhower & Nixon, Inauguration Day, Wyoming, 1953 . . . . 1238.00
Button, Eisenhower Headquarter Working Staff, Orange, Black, Celluloid, 1952, 2 In. . . . 288.00
Button, Eisenhower, Gwinn, Nixon, Blue & White, Celluloid, 1952, 3 1/2 In. 1650.00
Button, Eisenhower, Now Do You Like Ike, 1 3/4 In. 20.00
Button, Eugene Debs, For President, Convict No. 9653 . . . . 802.00
Button, FDR For A New Deal, Blue, Black, White Celluloid, 3 1/2 In. 457.00
Button, FDR, Red, White, Blue, Young Democrats Of Wake County, Victory, 1936, 1 In. . . 1227.00
Button, FDR, Stars & Stripes, Red, White, Blue Celluloid, Photo, 3 1/2 In. 726.00
Button, Fight With Dwight, Blue Printing, 2 In. 123.00
Button, Ford & Dole, Peace & Prosperity, Michigan, Celluloid, 2 3/4 In. 23.00
Button, Ford & Reagan 76, Black, White, Celluloid, 1 1/2 In. 50.00
Button, Franklin D. Roosevelt, Our Leader, 2 In. 86.00
Button, Free Miss., All The Way With LBJ, Red, White, 3 In. 38.00
Button, Free The Scottsboro Boys, Lithograph, Blue, White, 7/8 In. 116.00
Button, General Douglas MacArthur, Red, White, Blue, Celluloid, 1 1/4 In. 13.00
Button, General Dwight D. Eisenhower, Gold Crest, Red Border, World War II, 1 In. 245.00
Button, George McGovern, Black, White, 1972, 6 In. 99.00
Button, Goldwater, Gold Flecks In Raised Center, 3 In. 36.00
Button, Happy Days Are Here Again, Beer Glass, Plastic, 1933, 1 1/4 In. 550.00
Button, Harding & Coolidge Smile, Celluloid, 1920, 7/8 In. 25.00
Button, Harding & Coolidge, Coattail, First Women Vote, 1 3/4 In. 494.00
Button, Harding, The People's Choice For President, Ribbon, 1 1/4 In. 215.00
Button, Harding, Think Of America First, 1 1/4 In. 242.00
Button, Harry S. Truman For President, Celluloid, 3 1/2 In. 130.00
Button, Harry S. Truman, Sepia Tone, 1 1/4 In. 139.00
Button, Hayes, Wheeler Centennial Candidates, Brass & Cardboard Inserts, 1 1/2 In. 1759.00
Button, Henry G. Davis For Vice President, Celluloid, 1904, 1 1/4 In. 713.00
Button, Herbert Hoover, Charles Curtis, Jugate, Windham County, 1928 . . . . 5700.00
Button, Herbert Hoover, For President, Black & White, 7/8 In. 45.00
Button, Honor America, Leave Vietnam, American Flag, 1 3/4 In. 2.00
Button, Hoover For President, 7/8 In. 45.00
Button, Hoover, Curtis, For All Of U.S., 1 1/4 In. 595.00
Button, Hoover, Curtis, Jugate, Black & White Portraits, Eagle Below, 1 1/4 In. 3920.00
Button, Hoover, Curtis, Jugate, Red, White, Blue & Black, 1 1/4 In. 1375.00
Button, Hoover, Jugate, Red, White, Blue, Black, 1 1/4 In. 1375.00
Button, Hoover, Play Safe With Hoover, Celluloid, 1 1/4 In. 3195.00
Button, Hubert Humphrey, Wobble Eye, Donkey, 3 1/2 In. 219.00
Button, Huckleberry Hound For President, Tin Lithograph, c.1960, 7/8 In. 8.00
Button, Hughes, San Diego Exposition, Hughes Day, 1 In. 500.00
Button, Humphrey & Muskie In 68, 3 1/2 In. 1210.00
Button, Humphrey, Muskie, 1968, 7/8 In. 32.00
Button, I Don't Want Nixon Or Kennedy, Green & White, Celluloid, 1960, 1 3/4 In. 315.00
Button, I Like Ike, Red, Blue & Cream, Celluloid, 1952, 2 1/8 In. 932.00
Button, I'm A Truman Democrat, Blue, 1 1/2 In. 276.00
Button, I'm For Harding, Black, White, Celluloid, 7/8 In. 37.00
Button, I'm For Ike, Red, White, Blue, Celluloid, 7/8 In. 19.00
Button, I'm Just Wild About Harry, Inaugural, Blue, White, Celluloid, 1949, 2 1/8 In. 738.00
Button, Ike For President, Celluloid, 9 In. 71.00

Button, Ike's Working Man's Club, Red, Blue, Cream Celluloid, 1950s, 3 1/2 In. 605.00
Button, Ike, Dick, Full Color Lithograph, 3 In. 32.00
Button, It's The 60s For Kennedy, Red, White, Celluloid, 3 In. 170.00
Button, Jackie Robinson, Nelson Rockefeller, Celluloid, 3 In. 517.00
Button, Jimmy Carter, Indiana Labor Coalition, New York, July 1976, 3 In. 36.00
Button, John Kennedy For Vice President Convention, Profile In Courage, 1956, 2 In. 805.00
Button, Johnson & Civil Rights, Red, White & Blue, 3 In. 3322.00
Button, Keep Carter In The White House, 1980, 3 In. 35.00
Button, Keep Coolidge, Black, White, Lithograph, 7/8 In. 28.00
Button, Keep Coolidge, Red, White, Blue, 7/8 In. 123.00
Button, Kennedy & Johnson, Jugate, Red, Black, White, Celluloid, 1960, 7/8 In. 182.00
Button, Kennedy For President, Red, White, Blue, Black, Celluloid, 1 1/4 In. 19.00
Button, Kennedy, Johnson, America's Men For The 60s, 4 In. 116.00
Button, Kennedy, Johnson, Vote Straight, Democratic Ticket, 3 In. .... .300.00 to 400.00
Button, Kennedy, On The Right Track With Jack, 1 3/4 In. 40.00
Button, Labor For Dukakis, 1 1/4 In. 5.00
Button, Ladies For Johnson, Humphrey, Blue & White Celluloid, 1964, 3 In. 484.00
Button, Lafollette & Wheeler, 1924, 7/8 In. 159.00
Button, Lafollette & Wheeler, Peoples Choice, Jugate, 7/8 In. 392.00
Button, Land On Washington, Red, White, Blue, Celluloid, 1 1/4 In. 889.00
Button, Landon Knox Out Roosevelt, Brown, Yellow & White, Celluloid, 1936, 7/8 In. ... 5050.00
Button, Landon, Knox, Cannon, Missouri, 7/8 In. 320.00
Button, Landon, Let Landon Lead U.S., 7/8 In. 297.00
Button, Landon, Lithograph, Dark Brown Background, Elephant In Sunflower, 13/16 In. .. 69.00
Button, LBJ Wants McGrath, Vote Democrat, Coattail, Celluloid, 3 In. 1079.00
Button, Lyndon Tree, Gold & Black, Celluloid, 1964, 3 1/2 In. 457.00
Button, Malcolm X, By Any Means Possible, 1 1/4 In. 7.50
Button, Map Of United States, Nixon, Metal, Light Blue Paint 7.00
Button, March On Washington For Jobs & Freedom, Black, White Handshake, 3 1/2 In. .. 91.00
Button, Martin Luther King, Benjamin Spock, Peace & Freedom, Celluloid, 1968, 1 In. ... 40.00
Button, McCarthy For America, Red, White, Blue, 7/8 In. 43.00
Button, McCarthy For Fuehrer, But Not In My Country, Celluloid, Blue, White, 2 1/4 In. .. 438.00
Button, McGovern & Eagleton, Red, Black, White, Celluloid, 1972, 1 1/2 In. 12.00
Button, McKinley & Prosperity, Factory & Farming Scenes, 1 1/4 In. 304.00
Button, McKinley & Roosevelt American Flag, Celluloid, 1900, 1 1/2 In. 1771.00
Button, McKinley, Red, White, Blue, Black, Celluloid, Ribbon, 1896, 1 1/4 In. 40.00
Button, McKinley, Red, White, Blue, Gold Trim, 2 1/4 In. 114.00
Button, McKinley, Roosevelt, Dinner Bucket, Blue, Gold, Tan, Celluloid, 1 1/4 In. 165.00
Button, McKinley, Roosevelt, First Voters League, Reddish Orange Border, 7/8 In. 56.00
Button, McKinley, Roosevelt, Jugate, Red, White, Blue, Gold Trim, 2 1/4 In. 920.00
Button, McLevy, Vote Socialist, Orange, White, Celluloid, 1942, 7/8 In. 73.00
Button, Mike Dukakis For President, Photo, Multicolored, Celluloid, 2 1/2 In. 36.00
Button, Minnesota Women For Humphrey 54, Celluloid, 2 1/4 In. 254.00
Button, Mondale, Ferraro, '84, 7/8 In. 5.00
Button, Mondale, Ferraro, Elmore, Minnesota, Jugate, 1984, 3 In. 63.00
Button, Mondale, Ferraro, Pavich, Iowa Coattail, Red, Green Celluloid, 2 In. 115.00
Button, Mondale, Ferraro, Red, White, Blue, Black, 1984, 6 In. 85.00
Button, More Than Ever I Like Ike, 1 1/4 In. 69.00
Button, Mt. St. Helens, Reagan, Snohomish Cty. Republican. Women's Club, 2 In. 670.00
Button, Nebraskans For Kennedy, 1 In. 260.00
Button, Newer Heights With Al Smith, Blue & White Celluloid, 1928, 1 In. 1099.00
Button, Nixon Again, Red, White, Blue Thumb, Pocket Mirror Reverse, 3 In. 51.00
Button, Nixon In November, Red, White, Blue, Black, Celluloid, 1960, 6 In. 97.00
Button, Nixon Lodge, Vote Republican, 1 1/4 In. 82.00
Button, Nixon, Votes Preference Slate, 3 In. 150.00
Button, No More Fireside Chats, Red, White, Celluloid, 1 1/4 In. 11.00
Button, Parker, Davis, Portraits & Flag, 1 1/4 In. 125.00
Button, Parker, Red, White, Blue, Gold, 1 1/4 In. 604.00
Button, Penna Hughes Alliance, Celluloid, 5/8 In. 12.00
Button, Play Safe With Hoover, Red, White, Blue & Black, Celluloid, 1 1/4 In. 3195.00
Button, Re-Elect Eisenhower, Nixon, Progress & Prosperity, Celluloid, 1956, 3 1/2 In. ... 435.00
Button, Reagan & O'Neal, Play In Peoria, Coattail, Illinois, 2 In. 32.00
Button, Reagan Bayou State, Yellow, Black, White, Celluloid, 1980, 4 In. 445.00

Button, Reagan's Angels, Red, White, Celluloid, 2 In. 60.00
Button, Reagan, The Working Man Candidate, Red, White, Blue, 1980, 3 In. 35.00
Button, Richard Nixon, Man Of Steel, Red, White, Blue, Black, Celluloid, 3 In. 352.00
Button, Right Men In The Right Place At The Right Time, Celluloid, 1 1/4 In. 1634.00
Button, Robert F. Kennedy For President, Red, White, Blue, Black, Celluloid, 1 1/4 In. . . .   20.00
Button, Robert Kennedy & Fulbright, Photo, Blue, Gold, Celluloid, 6 In. 413.00
Button, Robin McGovern, He Takes From Rich, Gives To Poor, 4 In. 480.00
Button, Ronald Reagan, Celluloid, Blue, Black, White, 6 In. 55.00
Button, Ronald Reagan, Vanna White, Yellow, Black, White, Celluloid, 6 In. 174.00
Button, Roosevelt & Garner, Jugate, Bastian Bros., 7/8 In. 175.00
Button, Roosevelt & Truman, All For One, One For All, Lithograph, 1944, 1 1/4 In. 341.00
Button, Roosevelt, Blood, Economic Security, Coattail, 1 In. 314.00
Button, Roosevelt, Fairbanks, Miss Liberty, 1 1/4 In. 382.00
Button, Ross Perot, American Dream, Celluloid, 1996, 6 In. 22.00
Button, Seattle Sheriff's Convention, Celluloid, 1909, 1 1/4 In. 254.00
Button, Shirley For President, Black, Green, Celluloid, 7/8 In.   31.00
Button, Shoeworkers For Kennedy, Celluloid, 1960, 3 1/2 In. 633.00
Button, Sign For Stevenson, Red, White, Blue, 6 In. 232.00
Button, Sign Language For Clinton, Gore, Celluloid, 1996, 2 1/4 In. 107.00
Button, Skinny Cat For McGovern, Orange, Black, White, Celluloid, 2 In. 198.00
Button, Smith & Robinson, Red, White, Blue, Celluloid, 7/8 In. 20.00
Button, Sock It To 'Em Spiro, Day Glow Orange, Black, 1 1/4 In. 2.00
Button, Speak Up Elect Jimmy Carter, 1970, 1 1/2 In. 32.00
Button, Stalin, Churchill, FDR Victory Pin, Multicolored Celluloid, 7/8 In. 880.00
Button, Stevenson Press, Black, White, Celluloid, 1 3/4 In. 181.00
Button, Stevenson, Don't Let Them Take It Away, Celluloid, 1950, 2 1/4 In. 799.00
Button, Stevenson, Humphrey, Will Sweep The Country, 3 In. 175.00
Button, Stop The War Now, Peace Sign, Octagonal, Red, White, Blue, 3 1/2 In. 3.00
Button, Support Johnson & Civil Rights, Flag, Donkey, 3 In. 2090.00
Button, Support Roosevelt, Vote Democratic, Gold Background, Blue Border, 7/8 In. 66.00
Button, Taft & Sherman, Sepia, Celluloid, 1 1/4 In. 145.00
Button, Taft, Hadley Club, Black, White, Celluloid, 7/8 In. 44.00
Button, Taft, Red, White, Blue, 1912, 7/8 In. 77.00
Button, Taft, Red, White, Blue, Green, 1912, 1 1/4 In. 278.00
Button, Taft, Sherman Elephant Ears, Celluloid, 1908, 1 1/4 In. 8250.00
Button, Taft, Sherman, Red, White, Blue, 7/8 In. 414.00
Button, Team 70, Governor Reagan, Flournoy Secretary Of State, Coattail, 1970, 3 In. . . .   43.00
Button, Teddy Roosevelt & Fairbanks Holding Hand, 1904, 1 3/4 In. 11000.00
Button, Teddy Roosevelt, Bear, Walking, Berryman, Celluloid, 1902, 1 3/4 In. 11000.00
Button, Teddy Roosevelt, Black, White, Gold, Celluloid, 1 1/4 In. 214.00
Button, Teddy Roosevelt, Capital, Multicolored, 1904, 7/8 In. 224.00
Button, Texas, For Personal Liberty, Against Prohibition, Red, White, Blue, 3/4 In. 40.00
Button, Theodore Roosevelt, Fairbanks Lady Liberty, Celluloid, 1904, 2 1/8 In. 2027.00
Button, Theodore Roosevelt, Fairbanks, Dinner Pail, Let Well Enough Alone, 1 1/2 In. . . .   7018.00
Button, Theodore Roosevelt, Fairbanks, Eagle Flag Jugate, Celluloid, 1 1/4 In. 3997.00
Button, Theodore Roosevelt, For President, Flag, Horse, San Juan, 1904, 1 1/4 In. 811.00
Button, Theodore Roosevelt, Hugging Uncle Sam, Celluloid, 1 3/4 In. 6000.00
Button, Theodore Roosevelt, Let Well Enough Alone, Celluloid, 1904, 1 1/4 In. 757.00
Button, Theodore Roosevelt, Memorial, Black & White, 7/8 In.   30.00
Button, Theodore Roosevelt, Sepia Portrait, 1 3/4 In. 80.00
Button, Theodore Roosevelt, Sunrise, 1 3/4 In. 4695.00
Button, Truman Was Screwy To Build A Porch For Dewey, 1 In. 31.00
Button, Uncle Sam Welcomes Theodore Roosevelt, 1 1/4 In. 2662.00
Button, Utah For Reagan, Republican Convention, 1980, 3 In. 94.00
Button, Vote Communist, W.Z. Foster, J.W. Ford, 7/8 In. 36.00
Button, Vote Dewey For President, Picture, Attached Banner & Elephant, 1 3/4 In. 484.00
Button, Vote For Wallace, To Repeal The Draft, Row C, 1948, 7/8 In. 50.00
Button, Vote Hoover For President, Red, White, Blue, Celluloid, 1 In. 20.00
Button, Vote LaGuardia American Labor Party, 7/8 In. 47.00
Button, Vote Republican, For Dewey, Warren, 9 In. 235.00
Button, Vote Truman For President, Red & Blue Stripes, White Ground, 3 1/2 In. 4054.00
Button, Vote Truman For President, Red, White, Blue, Celluloid, 1948, 7/8 In. 560.00
Button, Vote Truman For President, Red, White, Blue, Phila. Badge, 1 3/4 In. 675.00

Button, W.J. Bryan, Peoples Air Line, Bicycle On Tightwire, 1900, 1 1/4 In. 5750.00
Button, Wallace For President S.C. Party, Liberty Bell, 1 1/2 In. 125.00
Button, Wallace, Taylor, Young Progressives Of America, 1948, 7/8 In. 154.00
Button, War Is Not Healthy For Children & Other Living Things, Flower, 3 1/2 In. 3.00
Button, Warren G. Harding For President, Black, White, Celluloid, 1 In. 92.00
Button, Warren G. Harding, For President, 7/8 In. 100.00
Button, Warren Harding, Best Ever, Celluloid, Mirror Back, 1920, 1 3/4 In. 1452.00
Button, We Want Wallace, Black & White, 1948, 1 In. 443.00
Button, Welcome Jerry Ford, Red & Black Celluloid, 1973, 2 1/4 In. 301.00
Button, Welcome Truman 42nd Ward, Red & White, Celluloid, 1948, 3 1/2 In. 1395.00
Button, Wendall Lewis Willkie, Our Next President, Celluloid, 1 1/4 In. 33.00
Button, Wendell Lewis Willkie, Our Next President, Black & White, Celluloid, 1 3/4 In. . 315.00
Button, William J. Bryan, For President, In Victorian Chair, 1 1/4 In. 213.00
Button, William J. Bryan, For President, Sepia, 1 1/4 In. 150.00
Button, William J. Bryan, Let The People Rule, 1908, 1 1/4 In. 144.00
Button, Willkie McNary & Chemurgy, 1940, 1 1/4 In. 935.00
Button, Willkie, Key, Black, Gold, Enamel, 7/8 In. 49.00
Button, Willkie, Red, White, Blue, 7/8 In. 55.00
Button, Wilson I've Paid My $1, Celluloid, 1 1/4 In. 1513.00
Button, Woodrow Wilson, American Red Cross, Celluloid, 1 1/4 In. 505.00
Button, Woodrow Wilson, Celluloid, Red, White, Black, 6 In. 146.00
Button, Woodrow Wilson, Multicolored, Celluloid, 1 1/4 In. 78.00
Button, Woodrow Wilson, Peace With Honor, Celluloid, 7/8 In. 21.00
Button, Woodrow Wilson, Wilson Will Win, 7/8 In. 175.00
Button, Yonkers Citizens For Eisenhower & Nixon, 3 In. 1017.00
Button, Yonkers For Eisenhower, Nixon, Celluloid, 3 1/2 In. 1017.00
Calendar, Franklin Delano Roosevelt, 1933 .... 50.00
Campaign Kit, RFK, Photograph, 2 Buttons, Pennant, Key Chain, 1968 .... 40.00
Candle, Presidential Seal, Wax, Gold Sales Label, LBJ, Nixon Era, 4 1/2 x 6 In. 14.75
Cane, Alf Landon Campaign, Wood, 1936, 34 1/2 In. 248.00
Cane, Benjamin Harrison, 33 1/2 In. 188.00
Cane, Franklin Roosevelt, 1932, 35 In. 82.00
Cane, Gerald Ford, Campaign, Stamped, S.B. Outlaw, 35 In. 50.00
Cane, Jimmy Carter, Campaign, Stamped, S.B. Outlaw, 34 1/2 In. 15.00
Cane, McKinley, 1896, 35 1/2 In. 183.00
Cap, All The Way With Adlai, Blue, White Cloth, Brimmed 40.00
Card, Campaign, Hiram W. Johnson For Gov., 3 1/4 x 5 1/2 In. 30.00
Card, Cleveland, Sepia, Heisel's Nominee Gum, c.1880 .... 36.00
Card, Democratic Primary, Make Your Vote Count, Kennedy, 3 x 5 1/2 In. 25.00
Card, Election, Lincoln At White House Door, Salt River Steamboat, 1864 .... 282.00
Card, Garfield, Arthur, Fitchburg Photo Adv., Sepia 185.00
Card, Shirley Temple Black For Congress, 1970s, 3 1/2 x 6 In. 12.00
Card, Truman, Barkley Club Membership, Blue 61.00
Card, Union Labor, Stevenson, Dever, Kennedy, 3 x 5 In. 58.00
Card, Wallace For Governor, Black, White, 1958, 2 1/2 x 4 In. 190.00
Cards, Playing, Baby, Political Sayings, 56 Cards 45.00
Cartoon, Beating A Dead Horse To The Finish, Bob Dole, March 22, 1988, 11 x 14 In. .. 225.00
Cartoon, By Way Of Helping You, Carter Leaving, Reagan Arriving, 1980, 11 x 14 In. 250.00
Charm, Teddy Roosevelt, Red, White, Blue, Brass, 1904, 1 1/2 In. 45.00
Cigar Band, I'm The Watergate Bug, Red, White, Blue, 5 1/8 In. 1.00
Comic Book, Barry Goldwater, Color Cover, Comic Type Text, Story, Dell Issued, 1964 .. 16.00
Coverlet, Harry Truman, White House, Capitol, Washington Monument, 21 x 21 In. 174.00
Cup, Arkansas, The President Is A Resident, Flag Draped Portrait, 1992 .... 14.75
Cup, Jimmy Peanut, Plains, Ga. Home Of Jimmy Carter Country, Plastic, 1976 .... 16.75
Cup, John F. Kennedy, President, Robert F. Kennedy, Senator, Color Portraits, 1960s 19.75
Decal, Harding, Coolidge, Multicolored, 1920, 6 x 7 In. 121.00
Envelope, Roosevelt For President, FDR, Blue Shades, Unused 25.00
Fabric, Zachary Taylor, Horseback, Troops, 15 1/2 x 13 1/2 In. 445.00
Fan, Hoover & Meyers Cooper, Blue, White 40.00
Figurine, Elephant, Nixon, GOP, Gray, Ceramic, 3-Dimensional 132.00
Flag, Blaine, Picture, Red, White, Blue, Brown, 1884, 26 x 17 In. 1694.00
Flag, Campaign, Bell, Everett, Cloth, 1860 .... 1530.00
Flag, Cleveland, Hendricks, Silk, 17 x 10 In. 2218.00

Flag, Henry Clay Campaign, Clay & Frelinchuysen, 1844, 27 x 49 In. 6038.00
Flag, Lincoln, Hamlin, 33 Stars On Light Blue Field 8250.00
Flag, Presented By President Of U.S., Theodore Roosevelt, May, 1903, 4 1/2 x 7 In. 770.00
Flag, President Cleveland & Vice President Hendricks, 1884, 17 x 11 In. 2218.00
Flag, Theodore Roosevelt, Red, White, Blue, Gold, May 13, 1903, 4 1/2 x 7 In. 770.00
Flasher, John F. Kennedy, Men For The 60's, 2 1/2 In. 38.00
Flasher, Kennedy For President, He Will Win, 2 1/2 In. 47.00
Flyer, California's First Choice For Nation's First Family, Nixons' Photographs 8.00
Flyer, Child Painting Sign, Everybody Vote Dry, c.1915, 5 x 7 In. 19.75
Flyer, Draft Eisenhower For President, 1948, 8 1/2 x 11 In. 30.00
Flyer, Jimmy Carter For Pres, Democratic Primary, Civil Rights Record, 8 1/2 x 11 In. . . . 7.00
Goblet, Grant & Wilson, 6 1/4 In. 1050.00
Handkerchief, Louisiana Purchase Expo, Silk, Theodore Roosevelt, 1904, 10 1/2 In. 133.00
Handkerchief, Post War Edition, Webster Memorial Constitution, 1936-1940, 12 In. 100.00
Handkerchief, Teddy Roosevelt, National Progressive, Bears, Red, Silk, 17 x 26 In. 250.00
Hat, Cox, Roosevelt, Felt, Beanie Style 406.00
Hat, Paper, Die Cut Images Of McKinley, Roosevelt, Paper Band Attaches At Back 605.00
Hat, Paper, Goldwater, Miller 43.00
Hat, Win With Dewey & Warren, Wide Brim, Gray Cloth 70.00
Invitation, Entertainment Stars For McCarthy, Blue & White, 1968, 14 In. 99.00
Invitation, Inaugural, Woodrow Wilson, Thomas Marshall, 1913, 6 1/2 x 10 In. 49.00
Invitation, McKinley White House, February 16, 1898, 4 3/4 x 5 1/2 In. 524.00
Letter Opener, James Garfield Memorial, Copper, Curved Blade, Lion Handle, 9 1/2 In. . . 138.00
License Plate, Al Smith, Green, White Embossed 50.00
License Plate, America Needs Wallace, Red, White, Blue 28.00
License Plate Attachment, America First, Last, Always, 5 In. 135.00
License Plate Attachment, Barry Goldwater, Hit The Rose With Barry, 1964, 12 In. 334.00
License Plate Attachment, Dewey, Republican Elephant, Red, White, Blue, 6 In. 162.00
License Plate Attachment, George Wallace, Staff, Blue, White, 1971, 1975, 12 In. 40.00
License Plate Attachment, Goldwater In 64, Gold, Blue Embossed 45.00
License Plate Attachment, Landon, Knox, Brown, Yellow, Metal 62.00
License Plate Attachment, Landon, Leave It To Landon, 4 3/4 In. 606.00
License Plate Attachment, LBJ For The USA 35.00
License Plate Attachment, National Defense Worker, Red, White, Blue 58.00
License Plate Attachment, Nixon, Agnew, Blue, White, Embossed 32.00
License Plate Attachment, Press On With Hoover, Red, White 100.00
License Plate Attachment, Reflecting, 4 Dewey, State Of Pennsylvania 95.00
License Plate Attachment, Victory In 64, Goldwater, Blue, Golden, Embossed 35.00
License Plate Attachment, Vote Republican, c.1960 . . . . 18.00
License Plate Attachment, Wallace Country, Confederate Flag, Red, White, Blue 58.00
License Plate Attachment, We Want Willkie, Red, White, Blue 50.00
License Plate Attachment, Willkie, Red, White, Blue, Black, 1940, 6 1/4 In. 213.00
License Plate Attachment, Win With Willkie, 4 3/4 x 10 In. 44.00
License Plate Attachment, World War II Victory With Morse Code 62.00
License Reflector, Franklin Roosevelt, Thank God For Roosevelt, Red, White, 5 1/2 In. . . 633.00
Litter Bag, Clean Up California, Elect Nixon Governor, 6 x 9 In. 50.00
Match Holder, Teddy & The Bear, China, Germany 385.00
Match Safe, Grant Profile 594.00
Match Safe, McKinley Profile 267.00
Matchbook, Truman, Barkley, Inaugural Dinner Souvenir 61.00
Mirror, Pocket, Wm. H. Murray, He Wins Our Battles, Bread & Butter, Bacon & Bean . . . 285.00
Mirror, Robert E. Lee Gettysburg, Celluloid, 1900s, 2 1/4 In. 1102.00
Mug, Taft Picture, Our Choice, Tankard Shape, Weller 632.00
Mug, Teddy Roosevelt, Gun, Book, Elephant Trunk Handle, Toby, 1909, 8 In. 2118.00
Pen, Ballpoint, Bush, Quayle, Red, White, Blue, '92, Bald Eagle, Stars, Stripes 7.50
Pen, Ballpoint, COPB, Central Intelligence Agency, White, Black, Logo 10.00
Pen, Ballpoint, Mike Dukakis For President In '88, Donkey Emblem, Blue, White 8.00
Pen, Float About, John F. Kennedy In The Oval Office 3.50
Pen, Float About, President Eisenhower, Golfs On Estate 3.75
Pencil, Adlai Stevenson, Sparkman 39.00
Pencil, Compliments Of Senator Lyndon Johnson, Mechanical 94.00
Pencil, For President Wm. H. Taft Of Ohio, Black & White, Portrait Of Taft, 10 In. 150.00
Pencil, Franklin Delano Roosevelt, Mechanical, Red, White, Blue 59.00

Pencil, I Like Ike, Unused 5.00
Pencil Clip, Wilson, Red, White, Blue, Gold Decoration 168.00
Pennant, Cape Kennedy, Man On The Moon, July, 1969 .... 27.00
Pennant, I Like Ike, Felt, Red, White, Blue, 1950s, 26 In. 77.00
Pennant, Inaugural, LBJ, Red, White, Blue, Felt, 1965, 30 In. 85.00
Pennant, Repeal The 18th Amendment, Purple, Gold, Felt, 26 In. 121.00
Pennant, The Man Of The Hour, FDR, 1937 .... 95.00
Pennant, Wallace, Taylor, 48, Brown, White, 18 In. 325.00
Picture Frame, Star Shape, Bronze Finish, FDR, MacArthur, Ike, Others 84.00
Pillow, Overstuffed, V Crossed British & U.S. Flags, British Bulldog 65.00
Pin, Andrew Johnson, Brass, 1 3/4 In. 1644.00
Pin, Cleveland, Hendricks, C&H, Purity, Patriotism, Red, White, Blue Enamel, Brass 80.00
Pin, Derby Hat, Al Smith, Metal 22.00
Pin, Elephant, Eisenhower, Mechanical, Opens To Reveal Photo, Original Card 68.00
Pin, Elephant, McKinley, Mechanical, 1896, 1 1/4 In. 182.00
Pin, Gold Bug, McKinley, 1 5/8 In. 91.00
Pin, Gun, Harrison, Brass 87.00
Pin, Hatchet, Carry A Nation, Mother-Of-Pearl Head, 1 3/4 In. 73.00
Pin, Henry Clay, Hand Colored Lithograph, Beveled Glass, Gilt Frame, Hinged Pin 4592.00
Pin, I Like Ike, Red, White, Blue, Flag, Cloth, 7/8 In. 19.00
Pin, Mechanical, Taft, Sherman, Red, White, Blue, Lithograph, Pictures Pop Out 790.00
Pin, PT Boat, Kennedy 60, Gold, Black .... 25.00 to 35.00
Pin & Earrings, Plastic, Caricature Of Agnew 4.00
Pipe, Harrison, Protection For American Labor, Eagle & Shield, Clay 136.00
Plaque, Thermometer, F. Roosevelt, Albany Furniture Company, Original Frame 45.00
Plate, Alf Landon, Etched, Glass, 1936, 8 In. 85.00
Plate, FDR In Car, Waving, Warm Springs, Georgia, Ceramic, 1940s, 11 In. 30.00
Plate, Garfield Campaign, China, 1880, 7 3/4 In. 56.00
Plate, Lincoln, Kennedy, Assassination Facts, JFK Museum Souvenir, 1960s, 10 In. 30.00
Plate, McKinley, Protection & Plenty, Frosted Bust In Shield, 9 In. 55.00
Popgun, Franklin Roosevelt, Red, Blue, Yellow, Black, Paper, 12 In. 606.00
Popgun, Landon, Red, Blue, Yellow, Black, Paper, 12 In. 935.00
Postcard, Adlai, 1952 .... 31.00
Postcard, Ballot Is Denied To Woman, No. 109 In Series, Unused 22.50
Postcard, Bill Taft & His Brother Charley 8.00
Postcard, Boy On Porch, Girl Carries Buckets, What Vote Has Done For Women, 1921 .. 45.00
Postcard, Do We Want Dewey? We Do!, 2 Elephants, Unused, 1940 .... 11.00
Postcard, Donkey Wearing Bryan Portrait Around His Neck 36.00
Postcard, FDR, Garner, Capitol Between Pictures, Brown, White, Unused 28.00
Postcard, Harding, America First, Red, White, Blue, Black 140.00
Postcard, Hon. Wm. Jennings Bryan's Home, Lincoln, Neb., Color, Canceled, 1907 ..... 12.50
Postcard, Mr. & Mrs. George C. Wallace, Govs. Of Alabama, Unused 7.00
Postcard, NY Democratic Club, Parker & Davis Flag, 1904 .... 45.00
Postcard, President Harding Silhouette, 1921 .... 10.00
Postcard, T. Roosevelt Returns From Africa, Uncle Sam, Elephant, Taft Welcome Him ... 35.00
Postcard, Taft, Bryan, All The Prophets Quite Agree, Which Willie Will It Be?, Unused .. 14.00
Postcard, Taft, Oval Sepia Photograph, Facsimile Signature Below Photograph, Unused .. 11.00
Postcard, Teddy Roosevelt In Hunting Gear, Crossed Rifles, Teddy Giraffe Rubber, 1914 . 30.00
Postcard, Teddy Roosevelt, Cartoon, Statue Of Liberty Welcomes, Dee-Lighted, Sepia ... 38.00
Postcard, Teddy Roosevelt, Lincoln, George Washington, Flag Background, Mailed 17.50
Postcard, Teddy Roosevelt, Rough Rider Hat, Leather 27.00
Postcard, Willkie, No A 1000 Times No, 1941 .... 17.00
Postcard, World War II, Anti-Axis, WAC Kicking Hitler, Big Kick In This Outfit, 1943 .. 19.00
Poster, Cleveland, Thurman, Black, White, 1888, 21 x 28 In. 1600.00
Poster, Economy, Uncle Sam Lectures, Coolidge In Mirror On Table, 20 x 30 In. 1500.00
Poster, FDR, Churchill Democracy, United For Victory, 15 x 21 1/2 In. 1209.00
Poster, Franklin Roosevelt, Re-Elect As Governor, 1930, 14 x 22 In. 1209.00
Poster, George Wallace, 16 3/4 x 22 3/4 In. 47.00
Poster, Harrison, Morton, Black, White, Song Lyrics, 1888, 18 1/2 x 24 In. 330.00
Poster, Hubert Humphrey, Frame, 1954, 11 x 14 3/4 In. 413.00
Poster, Humphrey, Muskie Campaign, Red, White, Blue, Plastic, 1968, 18 x 24 In. 29.00
Poster, James A. Blaine, Plumed Knight, 1884, 10 3/4 x 15 1/2 In. 59.00
Poster, James Meredith Civil Rights, Red, White, Blue, Black, 1966, 10 x 13 1/2 In. 127.00

Political, Ribbon,
Benjamin Harrison,
Campaign, Printed
Silk, Black, 1888,
9 In.

Political, Ribbon,
Stephen Douglas,
Campaign, Printed
Silk, Black,
6 1/4 In.

Political, Ribbon, William
Henry Harrison, Campaign,
Tippecanoe Club, 5 7/8 In.

Political, Ring, Flicker,
John F. Kennedy, Silver Plastic

Poster, John F. Kennedy, Red, White, Blue, Black, 1960, 13 1/2 x 21 1/2 In. 85.00
Poster, Kennedy & Johnson, The Democrats Care About You, 24 x 36 In. 350.00
Poster, Landon & Knox, Deeds Not Deficits, 14 x 22 In. 131.00
Poster, Lincoln Memorial, He Being Dead Yet Speaketh, 1865, 15 1/2 x 20 In. 92.00
Poster, Lyndon Johnson, United States Senator, 1948, 14 x 22 In. 2057.00
Poster, McGovern Concert, Carole King, Streisand, J. Taylor, Black, Cream, 36 x 24 In. . 3812.00
Poster, Miss Liberty Leads Mother, Child, League Of Women Voters, 1920, 15 x 25 In. . . 8100.00
Poster, Nixon For Senator, Red, Black, White, 1950, 11 x 14 In. 2057.00
Poster, Richard Nixon, Watergate, 10 Most Wanted List, 11 x 14 In. 40.00
Poster, Teddy Roosevelt Rough Rider, 14 x 20 In. 31.00
Poster, Vote Communist, 1934, 14 x 22 In. 28.00
Poster, Wooley, Metcalf, Prohibition Standard Bearers, Campaign 1900, 28 x 42 In. 1500.00
Poster, You Win, When You Vote For Ike & Dick, 10 x 14 In. 39.00
Print, James Buchanan, Black & White, Ambrotype, 8 1/2 x 11 In. 146.00
Print, James Monroe, 10 x 14 In. 48.00
Print, John Tyler Silhouette, E.B. Kellogg Co., Frame, 13 1/2 x 19 In. 133.00
Print, President Taylor, Currier, 1849, 14 x 18 In. 130.00
Print, Presidents Through President-Elect Polk, Currier, 1844 . . . . 106.00
Program, Inaugural, Truman, Barkley, Original Mailer, 1949 . . . . 70.00
Puzzle, Race Between McKinley's Gold, Bryan's Silver Issue 467.00
Razor, Straight, Zachary Taylor, Original Box, Engraved, Taylor On Horse 259.00
Recording Cylinder, Recording Of Theodore Roosevelt On Rights Of People, 4 1/2 In. . . . 1694.00
Ribbon, Benjamin Harrison, Campaign, Printed Silk, Black, 1888, 9 In. . . . . *Illus* 489.00
Ribbon, Bryan & Sewall, Jacksonville, Illinois, Black, Cream, 1896, 9 In. 545.00
Ribbon, Buchanan, Breckenridge, Portrait 2420.00
Ribbon, Buchanan, Breckinridge, The Constitution, Eagle, Liberty Temple, Ships 565.00
Ribbon, Camden Cox Club, 8 3/4 In. 250.00
Ribbon, Cleveland, Hendricks, Paper Photographs, 1884 . . . . 78.00
Ribbon, Cleveland, Multicolored, 1888, 7 In. 289.00
Ribbon, Cleveland, Woven, Red, White, Blue 83.00
Ribbon, Democratic National Convention, Alternate, Multicolored, 9 In. 133.00
Ribbon, G.O.P. Vote Ford, President, Republican, Liberty Bell, Blue On White, 1976 . . . . 10.00
Ribbon, Goldwater, Cloth 50.00
Ribbon, Harding For State Senator, Gold, Black, 6 1/2 In. 605.00
Ribbon, Harrison, Woven, Red, White, Blue 92.00
Ribbon, Henry Clay, 1844 . . . . 720.00
Ribbon, Millard Fillmore, Photo, Black, White, 1856 . . . . 239.00
Ribbon, Our Next President, Grant, Woven 154.00
Ribbon, Polk Portrait 1210.00
Ribbon, Republican G.O.P Convention, Baltimore Club, 1896, 10 In. 133.00
Ribbon, Stephen Douglas, Campaign, Printed Silk, Black, 6 1/4 In. . . . . *Illus* 1380.00
Ribbon, Taft, Ohio, Red, White, Blue, 6 In. 47.00
Ribbon, Votes For Women, Black, Gold, Paper 92.00
Ribbon, William Henry Harrison, Campaign, Tippecanoe Club, 5 7/8 In. . . . . *Illus* 345.00
Ribbon, Z. Taylor, The Peoples Choice, Inaugurated March 5th, 1849 . . . . 1140.00
Ring, FDR, Roosevelt & Garner On Band, Black, Silver, 1932 & 1940 On Band 68.00
Ring, Flicker, John F. Kennedy, Silver Plastic . . . . *Illus* 6.00

Sack, Gold For Goldwater, Canvas 45.00
Sash, McKinley, Black, Gold, Yellow, Silk, 1896, 36 1/2 In. 182.00
Scarf, Jimmy Carter, With Peanuts, Cloth, 1976 . . . .   40.00
Sheet Music, Coolidge & Dawe For The Nation's Cause 31.00
Sheet Music, Elliott, I Wanna Be A Cap'n Too, 1940 . . . .   50.00
Sheet Music, Everyone's Gone To The Moon, London, 1965 . . . .   35.00
Sheet Music, Follies Of 1908, Pictures Of Roosevelt, Taft, Bryan, Hughes 36.00
Sheet Music, General Grant's March, Morris Music Co., 6 Pages 20.00
Sheet Music, Happy Democrats Are We, 1964 . . . .   8.00
Sheet Music, Harding's The Man For Me, 1920, 10 1/2 x 14 In. 28.00
Sheet Music, In The Summer Of His Years, John Fitzgerald Kennedy, 1963 . . . .   28.00
Sheet Music, Let's Give Franklin D. A Helping Hand, 1942 . . . .   18.00
Sheet Music, Our Cue For 52, Republican Campaign 35.00
Sheet Music, President Roosevelt March, 1965 . . . .   12.00
Sheet Music, Prohibition You Have Lost Your Sting, 1919 . . . .   20.00
Sheet Music, Roosevelt NRA March Song, Eagle, FDR 35.00
Sheet Music, Save Our Liberty, Author Ira J. Kunze In Cowboy Garb, 1941 . . . .   29.00
Sheet Music, The Great Know Nothing Song, I Don't Know, Frances Eastlack 40.00
Socks, Nixon, Agnew, Red, White, Blue Logo 28.00
Stein, Ronald W. Reagan 40th President, Color Portrait, 1981 . . . .   19.75
Stereo Card, McKinley's Funeral, Sept. 17, 1901, Underwood 12.00
Sticker, Window, I Like Ike 52, Red, White, Blue 15.00
Sticker, Window, We Want Willkie, Red, White, Blue 9.00
Stickpin, Bryan, Flag, Enamel, 7/8 In. 184.00
Stickpin, Harrison, Cloth Hat 88.00
Stickpin, Harrison, Gold Color 23.00
Stickpin, Harrison, Morton 21.00
Stickpin, Smith, Robinson, Sepia Celluloid Portraits 915.00
Stickpin, Socialist Party, Workers Of The World Unite, Enamel, Brass 45.00
Stickpin, Teddy Roosevelt, Moose, Pewter 22.00
Stud, Cox & Roosevelt, Donkey, Gold, White, Enamel, 1/2 In.   220.00
Stud, Franklin Roosevelt, 100 Club, Black, Gold, Enamel, 7/8 In. 66.00
Stud, Franklin Roosevelt, Brass, 7/8 In. 14.00
Stud, Franklin Roosevelt, Churchill, World War II, Red, Blue, Yellow, Silver, 7/8 In. 114.00
Stud, Harrison, Flag, 1888 . . . .   27.00
Stud, Ike, Star, Black, Gold, Enamel, Screwback, 7/8 In. 25.00
Stud, O'Hara, Porcelain, Gold, Bug, Gilt Decoration, White Background 165.00
Sunglasses, Eisenhower, White, Red, Blue, Peace & Prosperity 127.00
Sunglasses, I Like Ike, Peace, Prosperity, Red, White, Blue, Plastic 60.00
Suspenders, Reagan, Red, White, Blue, 7 In. 20.00
Suspenders, Support Ike, Red, Brass 117.00
Tab, Suffrage, Votes For Women, Tan, Black, Paper, 1 1/2 In. 61.00
Tape Measure, Bob Dole For President, Control With Dole, Steel, Square, 1980, 2 In. . . .   25.00
Textile, Blaine, Logan, Printed Cotton Bunting, Red, White, Blue, 24 In. . . . . Illus   150.00
Textile, Cleveland, Thurman, Campaign, Printed Cotton, Black, Red, 1888, 21 In. . . . . Illus   288.00

Political, Textile, Blaine, Logan, Printed Cotton Bunting, Red, White, Blue, 24 In.

Political, Textile, Cleveland, Thurman, Campaign, Printed Cotton, Black, Red, 1888, 21 In.

Political, Textile, Harrison, Morton, Campaign, Printed Linen, Flags Border, 19 In.

Textile, Harrison, Morton, Campaign, Printed Linen, Flags Border, 19 In. . . . . *Illus* 259.00
Textile, Roosevelt Bears, Carrying Lynx On Pole, Cloth, 1907, 22 x 23 In. 1855.00
Textile, Washington, Franklin, Miss Liberty, Tree, England, c.1785, 29 1/2 x 38 1/4 In. . . . 1725.00
Thimble, Nixon For Congress 212.00
Thimble, Richard Nixon, Senate Campaign, Plastic, 1946 . . . . 81.00
Ticket, Andrew Johnson Impeachment Trial, April 8, 1868, Cardboard, 4 7/8 In. 1160.00
Ticket, Bill Clinton Impeachment Trial, Red, Black, February 12, 1999, 5 1/2 x 2 1/2 In. . . 560.00
Ticket, Democratic National Convention, Chicago, Guest, First Balcony, 1940 . . . . 22.50
Ticket, Democratic National Convention, Philadelphia, Guest, Grandstand, 1936 . . . . 25.00
Ticket, Democratic National Convention, Press Issue, Punched, 1948, 2 3/4 x 4 3/4 In. . . . 15.00
Ticket, Electoral, Blaine, Logan, A Free Ballot For The Whole Country, 1884 . . . . 36.00
Ticket, Grant, Colfax, Electoral, Grant Portrait 55.20
Ticket, Republican G.O.P. Convention, Minneapolis, Red, Black, White, 1892 . . . . 22.00
Ticket, Republican National Convention, Chicago, Third Session, TV Lounge, July, 1960 . 15.00
Ticket, Republican National Convention, San Francisco, Delegate, 1956 . . . . 25.00
Tie, Campaign, Alf Landon, Brown, White, Red, Black 935.00
Tie, Hoo! Hoo! Hoover, Embroidered Owl, Red, White 96.00
Tie Clasp, FDR, Donkey, Enameled 27.00
Tie Clasp, Flasher, I Like Rocky's, Rockefeller 15.00
Tie Clasp, Flasher, Man For The 60's, J.F. Kennedy 18.00
Tie Clasp, N.R.A., Eagle, Ed, White, Blue, Silver, 2 3/4 In. 61.00
Toy, J.F.K., Rocking Chair, Plays Happy Days Are Here, Windup, Box, Japan 475.00
Tray, W. Bryan, Red, Green Leaf Border, Tin, 12 x 17 In. 175.00
Tray, Wm. McKinley, Red, Green Leaf Border, Tin, 12 x 17 In. 200.00
Tumbler, Campaign, Pressed Glass, 13-Star Flag, Eagle On Shield, Paneled Base, 3 In. . . . 275.00
Tumbler, Campaign, Pressed Glass, 13-Star Flag, Stars & Bars Shield, 4 In. 358.00
Umbrella, Bryan, Stevenson, Flag, Cloth, Wood, 33 In. 726.00
Umbrella, McKinley, Roosevelt, Flag, Cloth, Wood, c.1900, 33 In. 611.00
Vehicle Pass, Inauguration, Through All Lanes, Over Any Thoroughfare, 1969 . . . . 15.00
Viewer, Cleveland Pig, Anti Item, For President Grover Cleveland 278.00
Viewer, Stanhope, Lucy Stone, National American Woman Suffrage Association 460.00
Viewer, Stanhope, Susan B. Anthony, National American Woman Suffrage Association . . . 675.00
Watch Fob, Harding, Coolidge, Brass, High Relief 95.00
Watch Fob, Taft Holds The Key, White House Lock, Padlock Shape, 1908 . . . . 32.00
Watch Fob, Taft, Multicolored, Celluloid, Leather, 1 1/4 In. 139.00
Window Sticker, Johnson, Eat American Beef Not LBJ Baloney, 2 3/4 x 8 1/2 In. 8.00
Window Sticker, Landon, Knox, 2 1/2 x 9 1/4 In. 17.50

POMONA glass is a clear glass with a soft amber border decorated with pale blue or rose-colored flowers and leaves. The colors are very, very pale. The background of the glass is covered with a network of fine lines. It was made from 1885 to 1888 by the New England Glass Company. First grind was made from April 1885 to June 1886. It was made by cutting a wax surface on the glass, then dipping it in acid. Second grind was a less expensive method of acid etching that was developed later.

Bowl, Underplate, Inverted Thumbprint, Ruffled Edges, 2 1/2 x 6 1/2 In. 175.00
Bowl, Wreath Of Gold Leaves, Berries, Red Vine, 2 1/2 x 5 1/4 In. 219.00
Creamer, Diamond-Quilted, Wishbone Feet, 4 1/2 In. 80.00
Cruet, Cornflower, 8 1/2 In. 390.00
Finger Bowl, Diamond-Quilted, Midwestern, 2 1/8 x 4 1/2 In. 35.00
Lamp, Burgundy Flowers, Satin, Inverted Thumbprint, 17 In. 230.00
Pitcher, Blue Cornflowers, Amber Leaves, Satin, Clear Handle, 4 1/4 In. 950.00
Pitcher, Cornflower, Bulbous, Amber Rim, 2nd Grind, 5 3/4 In. 1300.00
Sugar & Creamer, Lavender Blue Cornflowers, Ruffled Edge, Scalloped Base, 3 In. 489.00
Tankard, Diamond-Quilted, Amber Handle, Scalloped Rim, 12 In. 546.00
Toothpick 75.00
Tumbler, Champagne, Inverted Thumbprint, 1st Grind, 4 3/4 In. 66.00
Tumbler, Cornflower, Amber Rim, 3 5/8 In. 180.00
Tumbler, Cornflower, Diamond-Quilted, 1st Grind, 3 3/4 In. 55.00
Tumbler, Diamond-Quilted, 2nd Grind, 3 3/4 In., Pair 66.00
Tumbler, No Decoration, Amber Rim, 2nd Grind, 3 5/8 In. 30.00

PONTYPOOL, see Tole category.

POOLE POTTERY was started by Jesse Carter in 1873 in Poole, England. The company specialized in architectural ceramics. In 1908 the company was incorporated as Carter and Company. In 1920 it became Carter & Co. The name Poole Pottery Ltd. was taken in 1963. The company is still in business.

Charger, Portrait, Olive Bourne, 1950, 10 3/4 In.	2040.00
Platter, Antelope, Fruit Tree, Art Deco, R. Sommerfelt, 16 In.	499.00
Vase, Abstract Design, 2 Handles, Truda Carter, c.1932, 10 1/2 In.	3713.00

POPEYE was introduced to the Thimble Theatre comic strip in 1929. The character became a favorite of readers. In 1932, an animated cartoon featuring Popeye was made by Paramount Studios. The cartoon series continued and became even more popular when it was shown on television starting in the 1950s. The full-length movie with Robin Williams as Popeye was made in 1980.

Badge, I'm Keepin' Fit With Popeye, Lithograph Of Popeye Making Muscle, 1950s, 3 In.	25.00
Bank, Dime, Register, Square, Tin Lithograph, KFS, 1929, 2 1/2 In.	140.00
Bank, Turns, Knocks Down Man, Tin, Raitts, U.S.A, c.1930	770.00
Book, Wimpy Tricks Popeye & Rough House, Segar, Racine, Whitman, 1937	150.00
Christmas Tree Set, 7 Shades, Box, Mazda, c.1930, 16 In.	440.00
Cover, Pillow, Popeye & Olive Oyl, White, With Swee'pea, 1930s, 16 x 16 In.	50.00
Cover, Table, Paper, Popeye & Friends, Character, Balloons, 1936, 9 1/2 x 9 1/2 In.	30.00
Doll, Cloth, Straw Stuffed, Velveteen Cap & Outfit, 1930s, 9 In.	145.00
Doll, Cloth, Velveteen Cap & Outfit, 9 In.	140.00
Doorstop, Hubley	4000.00
Figure, Chalkware, 9 In.	27.00
Figure, Olive Oyl, Movable Legs, Arms, Head, Dakin, 1960s, 9 In.	30.00
Figure, Popeye, Smoking, Sitting On Spinach Can, Box, 1950s, 9 In.	4140.00
Figure, Popeye, Smoking Pipe, Composition, 1930s, 12 In.	225.00
Game, Card, Box, 5 x 6 1/2 In.	30.00
Game, Popeye Bubble Target, Tin, King Features, 1935, 14 x 23 In.	65.00
Game, Ring Toss, Stand-Up Figure, Plastic Rings, Box, 14 x 15 In.	165.00
Glass, Milk, Popeye & Swee'pea, Yellow, Vinyl, Blue Balloons, 1950s, 3 1/2 In.	20.00
Lunch Box, Squabbling With Brutus Over Olive Oyl, Other Characters, Metal, Aladdin	50.00
Napkin Ring, Green, Bakelite, 1930s	100.00
Pencil, Popeye, Oversized, Mechanical, 1930s, 10 1/2 In.	24.00
Pencil Box, Hazle-Maid Bread Co., Premium, 1934, 7 1/2 x 17 In.	18.00
Pencil Sharpener, Bakelite, Orange, Decal, 1 3/4 In.	95.00
Ring, Flicker, Popeye & Swee'pea, Silver Plastic .... *Illus*	10.00
Sand Set, Red Sand Pail, Blue Cartoon Panel, Shovel, Peer Products Co., 1960	12.00
Sign, Westinghouse Mazda Lamps, 2 Sides, 1934, 31 x 21 In.	3500.00
Toy, Airplane, Eccentric, Back & Forth Action, Tin, Windup, Marx, KFS, Box, 1940, 7 In.	935.00
Toy, Boxer, Punching Bag, Tin, Celluloid, Windup, Chein, 7 1/2 In.	633.00
Toy, Gun Set, 2 Guns, Holster, Halco, Box, 1961, 12 1/2 In.	187.00
Toy, Handcar, Popeye, Olive Oyl, Tin, Pull Toy, Linemar, 6 In.	990.00
Toy, Head Bobs, Wood, Linemar, Box, 4 In.	965.00
Toy, Head Goes Up & Down, Windup, Celluloid, King Features Syndicate, 1929, 8 In.	1250.00
Toy, Heavy Hitter, Popeye With Mallet Trying To Ring Bell, Tin, Windup, 12 In.	4180.00
Toy, Jack-In-The-Box, Tin, Mattel, 1953	175.00
Toy, Motorcycle, Patrol, Cast Iron, Hubley	2750.00
Toy, Olive Oyl, Ballerina, Tin, Gyro Motor, Box, Linemar, 5 1/2 In.	880.00
Toy, Pilot, Plane Travels, Tin, Windup, 9 In.	965.00
Toy, Popeye & Olive Oyl, Windup, Tin Lithograph, Marx, 9 1/2 In.	575.00
Toy, Popeye & Wimpy Walk Away, Plastic, Marx, Hong Kong, Box, 5 In.	150.00
Toy, Popeye Dances On Roof, Windup, Marx, 1930s	750.00
Toy, Popeye Express, Tin Lithograph, Windup, Walker, Parrot In Wheelbarrow, 8 1/2 In.	742.00
Toy, Popeye On Patrol Motorcycle, Cast Iron, Movable Arms, Hubley	3200.00
Toy, Popeye On Tricycle, Bell, Tin Lithograph, Celluloid, Linemar, Box, c.1950, 4 In.	2500.00
Toy, Popeye The Pilot, Windup, Marx, 1940	675.00
Toy, Popeye, Champ, Boxing Ring, Celluloid, Tin Base, Marx, Box, 7 1/2 x 7 In.	1650.00
Toy, Popeye, Drummer, Tin Lithograph, Spring, 7 1/2 In.	1320.00

Popeye, Ring,
Flicker, Popeye
& Swee'pea,
Silver Plastic

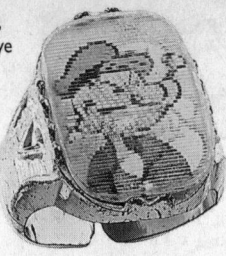

Battery-operated toys should be run regularly to keep the parts working. Remove batteries before storing the toy.

Toy, Popeye, Handcar, Olive Oyl, Tin Lithograph, Linemar, Japan, 7 In. 1210.00
Toy, Popeye, Lantern, Tin Lithograph, Battery Operated, Linemar, Box, 7 1/2 In. 578.00
Toy, Popeye, Olive Oyl Plays Accordion, Roof Top, Windup, Tin Lithograph, Marx, 10 In.   660.00
Toy, Popeye, Olive Oyl, Play Ball, Tin Lithograph, Windup, Linemar, Box, 19 In. 2310.00
Toy, Popeye, Parrot Cages, Walker, Windup, Tin Lithograph, Box, Marx, 8 In. . . . .385.00 to 523.00
Toy, Popeye, Parrot Cages, Windup, Tin, Chein, 8 1/2 In. 270.00
Toy, Popeye, Pop-Up, Squeaker, Cloth, Felt, Box, Linemar, 7 1/2 In. 550.00
Toy, Popeye, Puncher, Overhead, Windup, Tin Lithograph, Chein, 9 1/2 In. 1210.00
Toy, Popeye, Punching Bag, Windup, Tin Lithograph, Chein, 7 In. . . . . .850.00 to 1100.00
Toy, Popeye, Roller Skater, Holds Can, Windup, Tin Lithograph, Box, Chein, 6 1/2 In. . . . 1210.00
Toy, Popeye, Rowboat, Tin Lithograph, Battery Operated, Linemar, Japan, 10 In. 2420.00
Toy, Popeye, Tumbling, Pipe In Mouth, Tin, Windup, Linemar, Box, 5 In. 1540.00
Toy, Popeye, Walking, Celluloid, Box, 9 In. 880.00
Toy, Popeye, Wooden Tumbler, Red & Blue, 1930s 35.00
Toy, Shooting Basketball, Windup, Linemar 1250.00
Toy, Spinach Patrol, Cast Iron, Rubber Tires, Hubley 825.00
Toy, Truck, Popeye Transport Co., Long Distance Local Moving, Friction, Linemar, 12 In.   750.00
Toy, Wimpy, Waddles, Sways, Swings Cane, Nods, Celluloid, Windup, Japan, 7 1/2 In. . . . 360.00
Trinket Box, Popeye & Wimpy, Wood, 1930s 125.00
Wristwatch, Popeye, Wimpy, Olive Oyl, Swee'pea, Box, c.1948 . . . . 633.00

PORCELAIN factories that are well known are listed in this book under the factory name. This category and the two following list pieces made by the less well-known factories. Porcelain-Contemporary lists pieces made by artists working after 1975. Porcelain-Midcentury includes pieces made from the 1940s to the 1980s.

Basket, Centerpiece, Reticulated, Kneeling Cherubs, 10 1/2 x 12 1/2 x 7 In. 3450.00
Basket, Eros Kneeling With Gilded Quiver, White, Gold, 10 x 9 In., Pair 2760.00
Basket, Leaf Form, RPM, Germany, Late 19th Century, 7 x 13 1/4 x 10 In. 145.00
Bottle, Buddhist Lion Dogs, Blue, White, Square, Chinese, c.1630, 11 1/2 In. 2115.00
Bottle Stopper, Lady, Gay Nineties, Buttocks Exposed, 5 In. 400.00
Bowl, Beaded Rim, Landscape, House, Lavender, Green, Yellow, Brown, 8 Sides, 7 In. . . . 15.00
Bowl, Bird On Twig, Landscape, Tao Te-Head Feet, Fuku Mark, 1800s, 1 1/2 x 5 3/4 In. . . 405.00
Bowl, Black Floral, Gilt, Inverted Rim, Footed, Sidney Callowhill, c.1910, 10 In. 325.00
Bowl, Blue & White, 2 Fishermen Under Tree, K'ang Hsi, 11 In. 575.00
Bowl, Blue & White, 3 5-Claw Dragons Chasing Flaming Pearls, 1700s, 2 x 11 In. 230.00
Bowl, Blue & White, Dragon Chasing Flaming Pearl, 11 In. 405.00
Bowl, Blue & White, Flowers, Scroll Work, Sanskrit, 2 x 7 1/4 In. 978.00
Bowl, Blue & White, Imperial, 9 Dragons, 18th Century, 2 x 3 1/2 In. 575.00
Bowl, Blue & White, Mongolian Invasion, c.1800, 4 x 7 In. 60.00
Bowl, Chrysanthemum, Coral, Bell Form, Yellow Ground, Chia Ch'ing, 3 1/2 x 5 In. 690.00
Bowl, Cover, Stupa Shape, Chinese, 19th Century, 5 1/2 In. 235.00
Bowl, Dragon & Pearl, Bell Form, Yellow, Green Glaze, Kuang Hsu Mark, 6 In. 375.00
Bowl, Floral Spray, Cobalt Rim, Sevres Style, c.1900, 5 1/2 x 13 In. 316.00
Bowl, Lavender, Yellow, Brown, Royal Blue, 19th Century, 6 In. 69.00
Bowl, Oriental Carnations, Flowers, Leaves, Buds, 15 1/2 x 5 1/2 In. 138.00
Bowl, White, Pink, Yellow, Germany, 11 In. 20.00
Bowl, Woman In Garden Interior, Floral Spray Exterior, Japan, c.1900, 9 3/8 In. 230.00
Box, Basket Of Flowers, Signed, Jacob Petit, France, 19th Century, 8 x 10 1/2 x 5 In. 3450.00
Box, Cigarette, White Ground, Gold Trim, Flowers, Footed, Inverted Lid Is Ashtray 33.00
Box, Cover, Chinese Man, Head, Hirado, 4 1/2 In. 259.00

Box, Cover, Flowers, Gold Highlights, Musicians, Signed, P. Roche, 8 x 6 In.	575.00
Box, Cover, Light Green, Red & Green Rose, Limoges Type, 7 1/2 In.	15.00
Box, Cranberries, Gold Flowers, Moser Style, 4 In.	170.00
Box, Hirado, Tango's Head, Blue, Brown, 2 1/4 In.	140.00
Bread Bowl, Winter Scene, Pink & White, Germany, 13 In.	20.00
Brush Pot, 2 Brushes, Zitan, Celadon Green Hardstone, 20th Century, 7 In.	200.00
Brush Rest, Mountain Form, Flowers, Blue Glaze, 19th Century, 4 In.	115.00
Brush Washer, Beehive Form, Dragon, Cloud, Wang Bing Rong, 2 3/4 In.	374.00
Brush Washer, Blue & White, Beehive, Carp, 19th Century, 2 x 3 In.	400.00
Brush Washer, Robin's-Egg Blue, Square, Tien Lung Dragon, Tao Kuang, 2 1/2 In.	201.00
Brush Washer, Squat, Oval, Imperial Blue Glaze, Kuang Hsu, 1 x 4 In.	690.00
Cachepot, Alexander II, Putti, Mauve Ground, Imperial Russia, c.1865, 6 In.	345.00
Cachepot, Bow Type, Reticulated, Ormolu Mount, Early 20th Century, 4 x 7 1/4 In.	200.00
Cachepot, Figural Scene, Gilt On Cobalt Blue, Sevres Style, 4 1/2 In., Pair	1528.00
Cachepot, Gilt Bronze, c.1900, 10 3/4 In.	3286.00
Censer, Blanc De Chine, Branch Handles, 5 3/4 In.	230.00
Centerpiece, Flared, Loop Handles, Flowers, Cattails, Continental, 1800s, 10 x 7 x 9 In.	865.00
Centerpiece, Gilt Edge, Moore Bros., England, c.1890, 4 x 9 In.	115.00
Charger, Blue, White, Double Center Circle, Mountains, Riverscape, Chinese, 10 1/2 In.	290.00
Charger, Orange Floral, Tan, Black Border, Oriental Style, 14 In.	20.00
Charger, Oriental, Blue Flowers, Leaves, Bird, 11 In.	11.00
Charger, Overall Multicolored Flowers, Center Armorial Medallion, Japan, 18 In.	230.00
Chocolate Set, 10-In. Pot, Cover, 4 Cups & Saucers, Germany, 19th Century	316.00
Chocolate Set, Tray, Enameled Cherubs, Silver Overlay, Blue Ground, 8 Piece	2820.00
Compote, 4 Children, Roses, Floral Sprays, Von Shierholz Mfg., c.1900, 14 In.	400.00
Compote, Basket Form, Off-White, Gilt Trim, Applied Flowers & Cherub, 12 x 12 In.	200.00
Compote, Peach, Peacock Feather Ground, Chinese, 19th Century, 3 x 8 3/4 In.	520.00
Cup, Blue & White, Dragon, Stem, Ming Period, 4 In.	690.00
Cup, Carp, Bell, Cheng Style, 20th Century, 3 In., Pair	35.00
Cup, Eggshell, Erotic Figures, Calligraphy, Signed, Japan, c.1900, 3 1/2 x 2 In., Pair	290.00
Cup, Libation, Deer, Pine Tree, Blanc De Chine, 4 In., Pair	58.00
Cup, Saki, Imperial Guard Infantry Regiment, White, Gilt, Star, Wreath, 2 1/4 x 1 In.	33.00
Cup, Saki, Military Service Design, Crossed Flags, Gilt, Japan, 3 1/4 In.	40.00
Cup & Saucer, First Empire Style, Turquoise, Military Objects, J. Nast, Paris, c.1815	1725.00
Cup & Saucer, Pink, Lavender Flowers, Gold Trim, C. Tielsch, Germany, c.1900	20.00
Dial Tray, Wreck Of The Maine	250.00
Dish, Blue & Red, Enameled, Dragon, Brocade, K'ang Hsi, 6 1/4 In.	345.00
Dish, Blue & White, Imperial, Dragon, K'ang Hsi, 7 3/4 In.	1208.00
Dish, Blue & White, Lotus Form, Flower Basket, K'ang Hsi, 4 1/2 In., Pair	345.00
Dish, Deer, Pine Tree, Water, Flowers, Blue, White, Marked, 18th Century, 8 3/4 In.	1380.00
Dish, Flower Form, Flowers, Kakiemon, 19th Century, 5 1/2 In.	230.00
Dish, Fukagawa, Bird, Flower, Oval, 19th Century, 7 3/4 In.	160.00
Dish, Round, Embossed Basket Weave, Rose Finial, 4 1/2 x 6 In.	45.00
Egg, Easter, Imperial, Claret Ground, Gilded, Monogram, Russia, Late 1800s, 3 3/4 In.	2390.00
Ewer, 2 Women In Garden, Flowers, Gold, Signed, Wagner, Germany, 19 7/9 In.	2300.00
Ewer, Landscape, Pear Shape, Ao Kutani, c.1900, 9 In.	230.00
Ewer, Painted, Portrait, Urn Shape, Dragon Handle, Austria, 20 In.	405.00
Figurine, 2 Freemasons Studying Globe, Continental, 19th Century, 9 1/8 In.	1792.00
Figurine, Actor, Long Robes, Cape, Polychrome, Showa, Japan, 10 1/2 In.	140.00
Figurine, Art Deco, Woman In Profile, Flowing Hair, Dress, White Glaze, 5 x 4 1/2 In.	765.00
Figurine, Athlete, White Biscuit, Denmark, 19th Century, 8 1/2 x 5 3/4 x 7 In.	518.00
Figurine, Bird, Pedestal Base, Chinese, 18 1/2 In.	115.00
Figurine, Boy With Bundle Of Sticks, Girl Carrying Wheat, c.1800, 8 1/2 In.	345.00
Figurine, Buddha Seated On Lotus Throne, Bisque Face, Holding Pearl, 1800s, 8 In.	520.00
Figurine, Children In Grown-Up Clothes, Continental, 20th Century, 10 In., Pair	345.00
Figurine, Cow, Black & White, 4 1/2 x 6 In.	12.00
Figurine, Dog, Hirado, Japan, 19th Century, 7 In.	470.00
Figurine, Dog, No. 27260, Germany, c.1902, 7 1/2 In.	350.00
Figurine, Dog, Seated, S-Form Ears, Open Mouth, Teeth, Tongue, 1900s, Pair, 20 1/2 In.	2760.00
Figurine, Dragon, Blue & White, 4 Claws, 19th Century, 6 1/4 In.	127.00
Figurine, Duck, Yellow Beak, Black Eyes, Chinese, Pair, 5 1/4 In.	259.00
Figurine, Empress, Seated, Elaborate Dress, White Glaze, Cartouche, 20th Century, 12 In.	69.00
Figurine, Equestrian, Man, Colonial Garb, Late 20th Century, 20 x 18 In.	290.00

Figurine, Equestrian, Uniformed Royal Figure, Germany, 11 1/2 & 13 1/2 In. 2350.00
Figurine, Equestrian, Woman, Colonial Dress, Late 20th Century, 20 x 18 In. 660.00
Figurine, Figure Standing On Wave, Blanc De Chine, 19th Century, 17 In. 290.00
Figurine, Foo Dog, Male & Female Standing On Base, Glazed, Chinese, 12 1/2 In., Pair . .   345.00
Figurine, Geese, Celadon Glaze, Brown Glaze Base, 20th Century, 14 In., Pair 2390.00
Figurine, German Soldier, World War II, Throwing Hand Grenade, 13 In. 679.00
Figurine, Greyhound, Dead Rabbit, Gilt Details, Oval Naturalistic Base, 9 5/8 In. 380.00
Figurine, Hi Hi Brothers Standing On Base, Blanc De Chine, 19th Century, 6 In. 290.00
Figurine, Kuan Yin On Elephant, Blanc De Chine, c.1800, 5 1/2 In. 175.00
Figurine, Kuan Yin Reclining On Foo Dog, Blanc De Chine, 18th Century, 8 1/2 x 8 In. . . .   690.00
Figurine, Kuan Yin, Holds Vase, Branch, Japanese Style, Chinese, 15 1/2 In. 230.00
Figurine, Lady, Gentleman, 18th-Century Costume, Gilt Details, 16 In. 825.00
Figurine, Lion, Peach Luster Body, Blue Luster Base, 3 3/4 x 5 1/4 In. 65.00
Figurine, Lion, Shamrock Mark, Japan 15.00
Figurine, Lohan Seated Wearing Prayer Beads, Holding Leaf Fan, 1800s, 6 1/2 In. 375.00
Figurine, Man Riding Elephant With Servant, Germany, 20th Century 2530.00
Figurine, Man Standing With Staff, Chinese, 15 In. 81.00
Figurine, Ming Figure Seated, Holding Scepter, T'ung Chih, 10 1/4 In. 460.00
Figurine, Miniature Black Shoe, 2 White Mice, 2 1/2 x 3 1/2 In.   17.00
Figurine, Napoleon Bonaparte Au Passage Des Alpes, 20th Century, 16 1/2 In. 1356.00
Figurine, Rebecca At The Well, Young Woman, Fancy Dress, White, Gold, 18 1/2 In. 200.00
Figurine, Satyr, Seated, Eating Apple, White, Biscuit, Napoleon III, c.1865, 18 1/4 In. . . .   405.00
Figurine, Swan, White, Pink & Black Wings, 1 1/8 x 1/4 In. 10.00
Figurine, Woman On Chair, Mark, Crossed Arrows, France, 7 1/2 In., Pair 403.00
Garniture Set, Teardrop Shape, Applied Flowers, Gilt Foot, 21 In., 3 Piece 2235.00
Garniture Vase, Classical Maidens, Landscapes, Handles, c.1815, 11 1/4 In., Pair 2300.00
Garniture Vase, Figures, Flowers, Apple Green Ground, France, 10 1/2 In., Pair 520.00
Garniture Vase, Rococo, Courting Couple, Flared, Handles, France, 31 x 16 1/2 x 8 In. . . .   3450.00
Ginger Jar, Cover, Celadon, Flowers, Chinese, 6 In. 2300.00
Ginger Jar, Wood Cover, Figural Landscape, Blue & White, c.1800, 4 1/2 In. 144.00
Gravy Boat, Shell Shape, Wheel Lock, White, Green, Pink Rose, Austria, 6 In. 15.00
Group, Man & Woman, Playing Chess, Meissen Style, 12 x 9 x 10 In. 290.00
Group, Man, Woman, Cherub, Goat, Flower Basket, 7 1/2 x 7 1/2 In. 290.00
Humidor, 5 Mermaids, Yellow, Pink, Silver Plated Lid, Pipe Finial, 8 In. 400.00
Humidor, Pennants, Harvard, Yale, Princeton, Cornell, Imperial Cube, 1914, 6 In. 125.00
Incense Burner, Elephant Heads, Ivory Glaze, Rosewood, Japan, 19th Century, 6 In. 295.00
Jar, Blue & White, Calligraphy & Fret, Oval, Korea, 9 1/2 x 9 In.   978.00
Jar, Blue & White, Flowers, Bulbous, 4 Handles, 19th Century, 11 In. 345.00
Jar, Blue, Oval, Crane & Lotus, c.1900, 2 3/4 In. 90.00
Jar, Buddhist Lion Dogs On Cloud, Handles, Chinese, 19th Century, 32 In. 2938.00
Jar, Cover, Baluster, Flowers, Butterflies, Blue Ground, 26 In. 940.00
Jar, Cover, Blue & White Hawthorn, England, 19th Century, 13 In., Pair 489.00
Jar, Cover, Blue & White, Bulbous, Children, Horses, Flags, Wood Stand, 1700s, 9 In. 748.00
Jar, Cover, Flowers, Ivory Ground, Chinese, 19th Century, 11 1/2 In. 88.00
Jar, Cover, Flowers, Scrolling Branches, Calligraphy, Qing Dynasty, Kangxi, 7 1/2 In. . . .   546.00
Jar, Cover, Rose Petal, Pink Swirl, Birds In Flight, France, 6 In. 25.00
Jar, Flower, Oval, Korea, Yi Dynasty, 9 In. 978.00
Jar, Phoenix, Peony, Blue, White, 18th Century, 13 1/4 In. 575.00
Jar, Potpourri, Bronze, Leaves, Pinecone, Cherubs, Handles, 20th Century, 10 1/2 In. 980.00
Jar, Prunus On Cracked Ice, Blue & White, Oval, 5 In., 3 Piece 230.00
Jardiniere, Blue, White, Iron Brown Glaze, Japan, c.1890, 14 In. 460.00
Jardiniere, Flowers, Ming Dynasty, 11 1/2 x 7 1/4 In. 1725.00
Jug, Cover, Low Relief, Leaf Scrollwork Band, Horodnica, Poland, c.1851, 9 1/8 In. 956.00
Jug, Peach Luster Ground, Flowers, Bulbous, Narrow Mouth, 3 3/4 x 3 In. 12.00
Lamp Base, Blue, Ormolu, Crackle Glazed, Garlic Mouth, 19th Century, 14 3/4 In. 2988.00
Lamp Base, Crackle Glazed, Dragon-Head Handles, 19th Century, 11 In., Pair 4180.00
Lid, Cupids In Clouds Design, Cobalt Border, Sevres Type, 3 1/2 In. 30.00
Match Holder, Cover, Ben Butler, Contraband Of War, Set Them At Work 700.00
Medallion, Hand Painted, Angels, Madonna By Rafael, Brass Frame, Florence, 2 In. 115.00
Medallion, Young Woman, Framed, 3 x 2 1/2 In. 105.00
Mug, 3-Masted Ship, Sebastian Cabot, Gold Trim, Germany, 3 1/2 x 4 1/2 In. 950.00
Pitcher, Cover, Saki, Phoenix Bird, Blue, Makuzu Kozan, Japan, c.1900, 7 In. . . . . . *Illus*   195.00
Pitcher, Gold Trim, Tucker, 9 1/2 In. 350.00

Pitcher, Scalloped Rim, Oval, Loop Handle, Flowers, Franco-Bohemian, 6 1/2 In. 46.00
Planter, Armorial Crest, Gold Phoenix, Leaves, Shield Of Diamonds, 14 1/2 In. 1725.00
Planter, Man On Bridge, Ox, Landscape Scene, Cobalt Blue, Chinese, 8 x 10 In. 230.00
Plaque, Children Whispering, Signed, Walther, Germany, 13 1/8 x 8 In. 8050.00
Plaque, Children, In Garden, Germany, 7 7/8 x 13 3/8 In. 6900.00
Plaque, Eagle, Pine Tree, Mt. Fuji, Rectangular, Frame, Japan, 13 x 18 In. 805.00
Plaque, Fruit & Floral Bouquet, Cartouche Form, Rococo, Gilt, c.1910, 10 x 15 In. 290.00
Plaque, Madonna & Child, Painted, Gilded Frame, Water Font, 19th Century, 4 In. 85.00
Plaque, Maiden Wearing Head Scarf, Impressed, Frame, 4 x 5 1/2 In. 150.00
Plaque, Mary With Halo, Oval, 5 3/4 x 4 1/2 In. 80.00
Plaque, Middle Eastern Woman, Jug, Continental, Frame, 7 1/2 x 10 In., Pair 1645.00
Plaque, Monkeys Looking At Reflections, Japan, Frame, c.1900, 24 x 37 In. 1050.00
Plaque, Nude Spinning Thread, Giltwood Frame, Continental, 7 1/2 x 5 In. 1795.00
Plaque, Nymph Kneeling At Pool, 1907, 11 x 8 1/2 In. 720.00
Plaque, Painted, After Rembrandt, Carved Giltwood Frame, Germany, 14 x 10 In. 518.00
Plaque, Samurai Searching Riverbed, Japan, Meiji, 21 x 16 1/2 In. 500.00
Plaque, Vienna Type, Arab Woman At Well, Wagner, Signed, 22 In. 5875.00
Plaque, Virgin & Child, Painted, Bronze Frame, Paste Stones, 19th Century, 9 x 7 In. 635.00
Plaque, Virgin, Hand Painted, After Murillo's Immaculate Conception, 6 3/4 In. 405.00
Plaque, Warriors, Landscape, c.1900, Chinese, 16 1/2 In. 865.00
Plaque, Woman & Gypsy, Brass Mounted, Continental, 6 1/2 In., Pair 470.00
Plate, 2 Dragons On Bat, Blue & White, Cloud-Filled Ground, 13 1/2 In. 805.00
Plate, 2 Soldiers, Painted, Underglaze Mark, Russia, 19th Century, 8 3/4 In. 748.00
Plate, Bamboo & Crockery, 6 Figures, K'sang Hsi, 8 In. 316.00
Plate, Bamboo, Brocade Border, Koransha, c.1900, 9 1/2 In. 127.00
Plate, Buddha Symbols, Blue & White, 16th Century, 6 1/2 In. 635.00
Plate, Butterfly, Peony, Hirado, 8 3/4 In. 255.00
Plate, Catherine II, Imperial Porcelain Manufactory, Marked, 1762-1796, 9 1/2 In. 495.00
Plate, Charioteer, Parcel Gilt Monochrome, Greek Key Frame, 18th Century, 9 1/4 In. 805.00
Plate, Crane & Dragon, Korea, Yi Dynasty, 6 5/8 In. 405.00
Plate, Dessert, Flowers, Gilt Border, Scalloped Edge, 19th Century, 8 3/4 In., 10 Piece ... 1035.00
Plate, Dragon, Blue & White, Imperial, K'ang Hsi, 8 In. 546.00
Plate, Figure Surrounded By Butterflies, Blue & White, 18th Century, 9 In. 175.00
Plate, Plums, Naturalistic, Reticulated, Andrews, Schumann, Germany, c.1918, 7 3/4 In. . . 35.00
Plate, Portrait, French Kings, Blue Borders, Sevres Type, 10 In. 3819.00
Plate, Portrait, Young Woman, Wreath Of Flowers, Royal Munich, 10 In. 104.00
Plate, Shells, Seaweed, Butterflies, Leaves, England, 19th Century, 9 1/4 In. 173.00
Plate Set, Flowers, Shaped Rim, Blue Border, Ivory Ground, 10 1/2 In., 12 Piece 600.00
Plate Set, Sevres Style, Cupids, Cobalt Blue Border, 8 3/4 In., 9 Piece 530.00
Plateau, 2 Young Women At Dressing Table, Gilt, Muller, 14 x 10 x 15 1/2 In. 460.00
Portrait, Woman In Sheer Dress, Gold Gilt, Erblicht, Frame, 4 1/4 In. 395.00
Portrait, Woman Plays Harp, Gold Gilt Acanthus Leaf, Ferdi, Frame, 4 1/4 In. 366.00
Powder Jar, Cover, Lady, Footed, Compliments Of Republic Mfg., Chicago, 5 x 3 1/2 In. . 165.00
Punch Bowl, Yellow & Gold Vine Band, Gold Rim, Footed, 19th Century, 11 x 5 3/4 In. . 345.00
Ring Holder, White, Painted Flowers, Gold Rim, Figural Hand From Center, c.1900, 4 In. 225.00
Scepter, Dragon, Figural, Blue, White, Box, 15 In. 1000.00
Screen, 3 Gods, Attendant Talking With Farmer, Frame, Stand, Chinese, 44 x 51 In. 920.00
Seal, Blue & White, Ax Form, Calligraphy, Warriors, 18th Century, 3 In. 230.00

Porcelain, Pitcher,
Cover, Saki,
Phoenix Bird,
Blue, Makuzu Kozan,
Japan, c.1900, 7 In.

Porcelain, Watch Stand, Columbia
With Shield, Wreath Holds Watch,
6 In.

Shaving Bowl, Oriental, Blue Flowers, Leaves, 12 1/2 In. 605.00
Shelf, Applied Flowers, Cupid, Meissen Type, 8 x 7 1/2 x 6 1/2 In. 175.00
Sugar & Creamer, Figural Tomatoes, Cover, 6 1/2 In. 48.00
Tankard, Rose, Landscape, Enamel, Chinese, 18th Century, 4 In. 355.00
Tea Caddy, Blue & White, Landscape, Scrolled Border, Rectangular, K'ang Hsi, 5 In. 290.00
Tea Caddy, Wood Cover, Blue & White, 5-Claw Dragon, Hexagonal, 1800s, 6 1/2 In. 230.00
Tea Set, Yellow Ground, Flowers, Scroll, Colonial Couples, 20th Century, 14 Piece 175.00
Teapot, Cover, Blue & White, Buildings, Figures, Chinese, c.1820, 6 1/4 In. 380.00
Tete-A-Tete, Flowers, Royal Blue, Gold Trim, France, c.1860, 2 1/2 In. 225.00
Tureen, Birds, 2 Handled, Cover, England, c.1850, 11 1/2 x 14 1/2 x 10 1/2 In. 690.00
Urn, Cover, Pedestal, Meissen Style Design, Potschappel, 42 1/2 In., Pair 3450.00
Urn, Cover, Stand, Lovers, Floral, Putti, Crown, Potschappel, 1900s, 27 1/2 In. 1265.00
Urn, Faux Malachite, 20 In., Pair 7768.00
Urn, Gilt Bronze, Bisque, Louis XVI Style, c.1900, 16 In. 3000.00
Urn, Raised Lyres, Grapevines, Peach Ground, Gilt Rim, Scroll Handles, 8 3/8 In., Pair . . 195.00
Urn, Sevres Style, Gilt Bronze, Oval, Lion Ring Handle, Pink, 12 In., Pair 1528.00
Urn, Sevres Style, Painted, Ormolu Mount, Brass Base, 17 1/2 In. 345.00
Vase, 4-Claw Dragon In Sky, Blue & White, Korea, Yi Dynasty, 11 x 10 1/2 In. 4600.00
Vase, Birds On Branches, Schneeballen, Continental, Lamp Mounted, 14 1/2 In., Pair 5676.00
Vase, Blue, White, Globular, Blue Underglaze, Medallions, Chinese, 1700s, 11 In. 230.00
Vase, Children In Forest, Blue, Imperial Porcelain Mfg., St. Petersburg, 16 1/2 In. 16730.00
Vase, Club Shape, Birds, Flowering Lotus Tree, Black Ground, Qing Dynasty, 20 In., Pair 2300.00
Vase, Cobalt Blue Glaze, Bulbous Shape, Flared Neck, Chinese, 16 In. 575.00
Vase, Cobalt Blue Glaze, Flared, Bamboo, Bronze Base, Chinese, 10 1/2 In. 230.00
Vase, Cornucopia, 1 Large, 2 Small, Rococo Style, Polychrome Flowers, 15 x 8 In. 58.00
Vase, Courtiers & Peasants, Handles, Cylindrical, Japan, 19th Century, 11 In. 410.00
Vase, Courting Couple, Baluster Shape, Reeded Neck, 2 Handles, Bohemia, 26 In., Pair . . 1175.00
Vase, Cover, Birds, Branches, Schneeballen, Continental, Mid 1800s, 17 In., Pair 4180.00
Vase, Cover, Meiji Style, Geisha Reserves, Floral Panels, Baluster Shape, 25 In., Pair 175.00
Vase, Cover, Sevres Style, Gilt Bronze Leaf Handles, Woman, Cupids, Oval, 34 In. 4700.00
Vase, Cover, Sevres Style, Oval, Reserves, Rustic Lovers, Cobalt Ground, 25 In. 956.00
Vase, Crackle Glaze, Baluster, 19th Century, 5 In. 29.00
Vase, Dragon In Branches On Crackle Ice, Blue & White, Oval, Japan, 22 1/2 In., Pair . . . 2035.00
Vase, Flower, Trumpet Mouth, Sometsuke, Japan, 19th Century, 12 1/2 In. 560.00
Vase, Flowers, Blue, White, Scroll, Pear Shape, Chinese, 16 1/4 In., Pair 1210.00
Vase, Flowers, Leaves, Green Ground, Gilt, 19th Century, 4 In. 345.00
Vase, Flowers, Scroll Mold Base, Continental, Mid 19th Century, 17 In., Pair 8960.00
Vase, Hyacinth, Blue & White, 5 Jars Around Stem, 19th Century, 9 1/2 In. 520.00
Vase, Landscape, Blue & White, Bottle Form, Leaf Mark, 18th Century, 3 In. 290.00
Vase, Landscape, Flowers, Hung Hsien, Oval, 6 In. 345.00
Vase, Landscapes, Maebyong Shape, Korea, 18th Century, 8 3/4 In. 2000.00
Vase, Magpies, Prunus Branch, Pear Shape, Flared Mouth, Tao Kuang, 11 In. 1265.00
Vase, Mountain Landscape, Blue & White, Foo Dog Finial, Japan, Oval, 6 In., Pair 175.00
Vase, Ormolu Mounted, Courting Scene, Landscape, Cobalt Blue Ground, 12 In., Pair . . . 200.00
Vase, Painted, Figures, Landscape, Ruins, 2 Dolphin Handles, c.1825, 14 In. 1795.00
Vase, Polychrome, Celadon Ground, Japan, c.1890, 32 In. 1610.00
Vase, Polychrome, Gilt, Fukagawa, c.1890, 36 In. 575.00
Vase, Portrait, Young Girl, Gold Enamel, Violet Luster Ground, Germany, 8 In. 374.00
Vase, Rectangular, Medallions, Dragon, Blue, Copper Red, Qing Dynasty, 14 1/2 In. 175.00
Vase, Red Poppies, Overall Gold Enamel, Bavaria Mark, 12 In. 259.00
Vase, Renaissance Style, Classical Figures, Gilt Bronze Mounted, 21 In., Pair 1880.00
Vase, Royal Blue Ground, Courting Shepherd, Resting, 19th Century, 13 1/2 In., Pair 1093.00
Vase, Sevres Style, Amorous Couple, Bronze Mounted, Ram's-Head Handles, 25 In. 2235.00
Vase, Sevres Style, Jewel, Shell Shape, Creature & Shell Horn, Blue, Gilt, 12 In., Pair 2820.00
Vase, Sevres Style, Painted, Venus, Cupid, Landscape, Gilt, Oval, 21 1/2 In., Pair 3820.00
Vase, Sevres Style, Shield Shape, Gilt Intertwined Snake Handles, 18 In. 1765.00
Vase, Sevres Style, Venus & Cupid, Bronze Mount, Egg Shape, 19 1/2 In. 355.00
Vase, Stand, Vienna Style, Allegorical Scene, Gilt, Cobalt Blue, Oval, 21 In. 3885.00
Vase, Tiger & Bamboo, Blue & White, Korea, 12 In. 110.00
Vase, Vienna Type, Cleopatra, Gilt Decorated Iridescent Blue Ground, 5 In. 1000.00
Vase, Vienna Type, Depicting Joy, Ivy Hair, Blue Ground, 10 In. 1765.00
Vase, Vienna Type, Gypsy Portrait, Gilt, Cobalt Blue Ground, Oval, 11 1/4 In. 1175.00
Vase, Woman In Kimono, Landscape On Reverse, 2 Snake Handles, Germany, 20 In. 4700.00

Porcelain-Midcentury, Toast Rack, Painted
Orange, Black Flowers, Scrolls, 4 1/4 x 5 In.

Postcard, Observation Automobile,
March 23, 1904, 9 1/2 x 8 In.

Watch Stand, Columbia With Shield, Wreath Holds Watch, 6 In. . . . . *Illus*   250.00
Water Dropper, Blue & White, Mountain Landscape, Korea, 2 1/2 In. 230.00
Water Dropper, Blue Glaze, Bracketed Feet, Korea, Yi Dynasty, 2 3/4 In. 575.00
Water Font, Figural, Angel, Painted, Germany, 19th Century, 11 In. 489.00
Wine Cup, Blue & White, Figural, K'ang Hsi, 2 x 2 In. 115.00
Wine Cup, Blue & White, Phoenix & Dragon, Ming Dynasty, 2 In., Pair 175.00

PORCELAIN-CONTEMPORARY lists pieces made by artists working after
1975.

    Ashtray, Scottish Terrier, Hounds, Rabbits, Hermes 50.00
    Vase, Glazed, Painted Design, Signed, B. Wiinblad, 1981, 25 1/2 In. 575.00
    Vase, Rust, Silver Crystalline Glaze, Phil Morgan, c.1981, 7 In. 99.00

PORCELAIN-MIDCENTURY includes pieces made from the 1940s to the
1980s.

    Bowl, Sea Scene, Turquoise Ground, Waylande Gregory, c.1935, 4 x 7 In. 520.00
    Toast Rack, Painted Orange, Black Flowers, Scrolls, 4 1/4 x 5 In. . . . . *Illus*   65.00
    Vase, Bulbous, Bottle Neck, Purple Crystalline, Harding, Black, 8 In. 235.00
    Vase, Cornucopia, Luster Band, Floral Spray, White Ground, 1940-1950 . . . .   27.00

POSTCARDS were first legally permitted in Austria on October 1, 1869.
The United States passed postal regulations allowing the card in 1872.
Most of the picture postcards collected today date after 1910. The
amount of postage can help to date a card. The rates are: 1872 (1 cent),
1917 (2 cents), 1919 (1 cent), 1925 (2 cents), 1928 (1 cent), 1952 (2
cents), 1959 (3 cents), 1963 (4 cents), 1968 (5 cents), 1973 (8 cents),
1975 (7 cents), 1976 (9 cents), 1978 (10 cents), 1981 (12 cents), 1981
(13 cents), 1985 (14 cents), 1988 (15 cents), 1991 (19 cents), 1995 (20
cents).

    7 Men & Pig, Sitting On Porch, Photograph, Azo, 1904-1918 . . . .   11.00
    58 Bleriot Sur Son Monoplane 16, October, 1909 . . . .   10.00
    Alaska Gold, 12 Million In Gold, Alaska Cleanup, Gold Ingots, Coins 60.00
    Army Air Forces Gunnery School, Tyndall Field Florida, Linen 6.00
    Cable Car, Die Cut, John D. Anderson, San Francisco, Signed, c.1950, 9 x 4 In. 16.00
    Camp Lee, Virginia, 5 Photographs, Black & White, Thompson Illustragraph, 1918 . . . . .   2.50
    Dog On Stool, Photograph 24.00
    Eclipse Machine Co. Brakes, Raymond Seymour, 1910 . . . .   28.00
    Ed Mirado Hotel, Palm Springs, Ca., View Of Hotel, 1950, 3 x 9 In. 12.00
    Grand St. Bernard, Trois Heros, Photograph, Geneva 11.00
    Mob Attacking Strike-Breakers On Car, Keystone Views, Philadelphia, 1910 . . . .   27.00
    Observation Automobile, March 23, 1904, 9 1/2 x 8 In. . . . . *Illus*   50.00
    Ostrich-Drawn Wagon, Photograph, Azo 13.00
    Owl In Tree, Photograph, Azo, 1910-1930 . . . .   14.00
    Parker Gun, Bird, Rifle, 5 1/2 x 3 1/2 In. 440.00
    Peters Cartridge Co., Canoeing For Ducks, 3 1/2 x 5 1/2 In. 110.00
    Snowmen, 4 Snowmen In Shape Of 1908, Hold-To-Light, 1908 . . . .   20.00

Thanksgiving, Cherub Holding Corn Ear, Ribbon Around Body, Postmarked 1910 ..... 10.00
Times Square At Night, N.Y., Linen 6.00
Toasting Ovens, Kellogg Co., Battle Creek, Michigan, Black, White, 3 x 5 In. 1.00
Tris Speaker, Bat, Boston American Series, 1912 .... 500.00
Valentine's Day, Little Nemo, Tuck, 1907 .... 40.00
Valentine's Day, Man Standing In Black Suit, Seated Woman Holds Hearts, Verse, 1910 .. 12.00
Valentine's Day, Mechanical, Cupid, Wheel To Change Color Of Flame, Verse 20.00
Winchester, Men, Dog, Getting Skunked, 1908, 5 1/2 x 3 1/2 In. 413.00

POSTERS have informed the public about news and entertainment events since ancient times. Nineteenth-century advertising or theatrical posters and twentieth-century movie and war posters are of special interest today. The price is determined by the artist, the condition, and the rarity. Other posters may be listed under Movie, Political, and World War I and II.

Aero Espresso Italiana, Sea Plane, Aegean Sea Air Routes, Lithograph, 1932, 24 x 39 In. 1092.00
Air France, Airplane Over African Jungle, Lithograph, Signed, 1946, 24 x 39 In. 1106.00
Alexander, The Man Who Knows, Man In Turban, Red Ground, Frame, 28 x 42 In. 55.00
BEA, British European Airways, Elegant Lady On Runway, Lithograph, 1948, 26 x 41 In. . 635.00
Brotherhood Of Painters, Decorators & Paperhangers, Frame, 1918, 22 x 28 In. 190.00
But Will He Get Them Under Tariff Reform, Frame, 20th Century, 29 1/2 x 19 1/2 In. ... 45.00
Carter The Great, Carter Beats The Devil, Magician, Devil, Cardboard, 14 x 22 In. 200.00
Catalina, Cruise Ship On River, c.1930, 50 x 39 In. 2468.00
Circus, G.C. Quick & Co., Mammoth Menagerie, Astor Place, 1850, 24 x 12 1/2 In. 635.00
Circus, Tom Mix Circus & Wild West Show, Tom, Tony, Clowns, 1938, 20 x 40 In. 800.00
Clairborne County Fair, Boy, Corn Stalks, Port Gibson, Mississippi, 1918, 20 x 30 In. ... 330.00
Clementine Hunter, Centennial Salute, New Orleans Museum Of Art, 1985, 26 x 18 In. ... 115.00
Cleveland Bicycles, Lucien Lesna, Bicyclist, Paris-Bordeaux Race 1901, 49 x 35 In. 1150.00
Clyde-Beatty-Cole Circus, Clown, 1950s, 14 x 21 In. 60.00
Fak Hongs Magic, 29 x 36 In. 55.00
Famous Cole 3 Ring Circus, 4 Color, Captain Robert Grubb, Horses, 1958 .... 110.00
Germany Wants To See You, c.1930, 37 x 24 In. 225.00
Gigantic Railroad Circus, Clyde Beatty In Ring, With Lions, 26 x 39 In. 120.00
Gilmore Traveling Circus, California, Clowns, Caged Lions, 1930s 900.00
Great Kar-Mi Troupe, Different Acts, c.1900, 42 x 28 In. 325.00
Hamburg-Amerika Line, Graf Zeppelin, Map, Lithograph, Germany, 1931, 24 x 32 In. ... 2070.00
Imperial Airways, Fly Between Cairo Bagdad & Basra, Lithograph, 1927, 24 x 38 In. ... 2185.00
Italian Line, Lido All The Way, 1937, 36 x 24 In. 705.00
Jamaica Calling You, c.1930, 27 x 18 In. 265.00
Joe Louis In Person At Kingston, N.Y., Photo, 1946, 22 x 27 In. 350.00
KLM, London, Paris, Hamburg En Kopenhagen, Airplane, Lithograph, 1924, 24 x 33 In. .. 370.00
KLM Royal Dutch Air Lines, Amsterdam-Batavia, Map, Lithograph, 1925, 39 x 28 In. ... 440.00
Krazy Kat, Mandolin, Textured, Bob McLaughlin, c.1980, 17 x 22 In. 30.00
L'Estampe Moderne, Mucha, Frame, 11 1/4 x 15 1/2 In. 115.00
Lake Districts For The Holidays, c.1930, 40 x 25 In. 175.00
Mexican Travel, Eruption Of Mt. Paricutin, c.1940, 37 x 27 In. 590.00
Money In This Bank Takes No Vacation, Men Camping, 1924, 15 x 22 In. 155.00
New York State Fair, Syracuse, September 13-18, 1909, Roll Down, 17 x 33 1/2 In. 385.00
New York Sunday World, Dancing Gypsy, F.H. Ising, c.1995, 12 x 19 In. 95.00
Old Colony Railroad, Concert, 1888, 20 1/2 x 14 1/2 In. 46.00
Old Colony Railroad, Stockholders Meeting, November 22, 1881, 28 3/4 x 20 1/2 In. 265.00
Paris Travel, Arche De Triomphe By Falcucci, c.1930, 39 x 24 In. 294.00
Parmigiano-Reggiano Bertozzi, 3 Faces, Big Noses, Cheese, 1930, 54 1/4 x 38 1/4 In. ... 5750.00
Polo Player, Lady Golfer, Brion, 1937, 39 x 27 In. 295.00
Prisonnieres Des Martiens, 48 x 64 In. 330.00
Racing, Bright Colors, Italian, Milano, Red Contemporary Frame, 1960, 55 x 38 1/2 In. ... 275.00
Ramonite, Your Chimney Sweep Awaits You, Polychrome, Belgium, c.1920, 63 x 47 In. . 295.00
Remington UMC, Hunter & Dogs, Frame, 12 1/2 x 27 1/2 In. 230.00
Robbins Brothers Circus, Elephant Pyramid, London Bridge In Back, 28 In. 125.00
Savon, Le Chat, Color Lithographic, France, 20th Century, 62 1/2 x 47 In. 470.00
Scottish Defence, Lend To Defend The Right To Be Free, Stafford & Co., 15 x 24 In. 28.00
Shrewsbury, England, No. 198, c.1930, 40 x 25 In. 441.00

South Devon, Coastal View, c.1930, 40 x 50 In.	1175.00
T-Men, Reliance, Insert, 1948, 14 x 36 In.	118.00
Tom Mix Circus & Wild West Show, Bucking Broncos, Clown, 1938, 20 x 40 In.	800.00
Union Label Bulletin, 64 Labels, Frame, Samuel Gompers, 1906, 17 1/4 x 26 1/2 In.	314.00
We French Workers Warn You, Ben Shahn, 1942, 38 3/4 x 28 In.	473.00
Wells Fargo, Look Out For The Stage Robber, $600 Reward, c.1900, 5 1/4 x 8 1/4 In. . . .	385.00
Wild West Rodeo, Camel, Horses, Indians, Lithograph, 3 Sheet, 21 x 55 1/2 In.	420.00
Yankee Clippers Sail Again 1838-1939, Pan American Airways, 25 x 20 In.	294.00
Yuma County, Buildings, Town, Commentary On Crops, Churches, 1890, 28 x 42 In.	1150.00

POTLIDS are just that, lids for pots. Transfer-printed potlids had their heyday from the 1840s to the early 1900s. The English Staffordshire potteries made ceramic containers with decorative lids for bear's grease, shrimp or meat paste, cold cream, and toothpaste. Printed advertising and pictures of historical events, portraits of famous people, or scenic views were designed in black and white or color. Reproductions have been made.

Almond Shaving Cream, Green Print, Army & Navy Co-Operative, 3 1/4 In.	225.00
Bears On Rock, Pratt, c.1860	350.00
C.R. Coffin D.D.S., American Dentifrice, Black Print, Late 19th Century, 3 1/2 In.	145.00
Cherry Toothpaste, Bowl Of Cherries, c.1880, 2 1/2 In.	125.00
Dog Saving Sheep, Snow Scene, Pratt, Mid 19th Century, 4 1/4 In.	325.00
Feeding The Chickens, Children, Victorian Scene, 5 Colors, Pratt, c.1870, 4 1/4 In.	275.00
Fortnum & Mason, Chicken & Ham, 4 In.	110.00
Fox, Rocks, Grass, Multicolored Transfer Print, 4 1/4 In.	225.00
Hand Painted Artist Signed MKS, 6 1/4 In.	35.00
Henry Peck Wakelee, Cold Cream, San Francisco, 3 Colors, Gold Trim, 1880s, 3 In.	375.00
Kettle Of Fish, Dogs Fighting Spilling Kettle Of Fish, Victorian, c.1860	350.00
Morris's Eye Ointment, Lid & Base, 19th Century, 1 1/2 In.	125.00
Osborne Garrett & Co., Cherry Toothpaste, c.1900	145.00
Otto Of Rose Cold Cream, W. Owen & Son, Roses & Scrolls, c.1880, 2 1/2 In.	175.00
Uncle Toby, Pratt, Mid 19th Century, 4 1/8 In.	375.00

POTTERY and porcelain are different. Pottery is opaque; you can't see through it. Porcelain is translucent. If you hold a porcelain dish in front of a strong light, you will see the light through the dish. Porcelain is colder to the touch. Pottery is softer and easier to break and will stain more easily because it is porous. Porcelain is thinner, lighter, and more durable. Majolica, faience, and stoneware are all pottery. Additional pieces of pottery are listed in this book in the categories Pottery-Art, Pottery-Contemporary, Pottery-Midcentury, and under the factory name. For information about pottery makers and marks, see *Kovels' Dictionary of Marks—Pottery & Porcelain: 1650–1850* and *Kovels' New Dictionary of Marks—Pottery & Porcelain: 1850 to the Present.*

Air Freshener, Pink, Prayer Lady, Enesco	195.00
Basin, Leaf Designs, Bird, Hispano-Moresque, 5 x 15 In.	1610.00
Bottle, Cylindrical, Handles, Brown Glaze, 19th Century, 3 1/2 In.	230.00
Bowl, Brown, Green, Yellow, Deer, Continental, 1818, 3 1/4 x 15 1/2 In.	1210.00
Bowl, Cover, Pierced Geometric Design, Green Ground, Weiner Werkstatte, 4 1/2 In.	646.00
Bowl, Earthenware, Mottled Lead, Manganese Glaze, Footed, 3 1/2 x 11 In.	150.00
Bowl, Floral, Brown, Green, 4 3/4 In.	259.00
Bowl, Green Interior, Quail Exterior, 2-Footed, France, 5 In.	20.00
Bowl, Handles, Lead Glaze, Cobalt Blue, Yellow, Earthenware, 1920s, 4 1/2 x 6 In.	195.00
Bowl, Hearts, Birds, Redware, Applied Openwork Handle, 3 x 9 1/4 In.	1540.00
Bowl, Matador, Bull, Band Rim, Painted, Footed, Hunt Diedrich, c.1925, 4 x 13 In.	940.00
Bowl, Redware, Coggled Edge, Dots, Lines, 12 1/2 In.	550.00
Bust, Eagle, Brown, Yellow Salt Glaze, 11 In., 2 Piece	550.00
Bust, Man, Applied Collar, Tie, Unglazed, Pedestal Base, 5 In.	950.00
Butter, Cover, Keele Street Pottery Co., England	65.00
Candlestick, Butter Buff Glaze, Earthenware, 1978, 12 In.	250.00
Candlestick, Orange Glaze, Earthenware, 1920s, 11 7/8 & 12 1/4 In., Pair	305.00
Candy Basket, Handle, White, Red Stripes, Candies Printed, 7 In.	25.00
Charger, Covered Wagon, 2 Figures, Cobalt Blue Ground, San Jose, 16 In.	315.00

Charger, Flowers, Fish, Sea Grass, 13 1/4 In. 375.00
Churn, Dark Brown Glaze, Handles, 17 In. 75.00
Coffeepot & Cover, Palissy, Cabbage Leaf, Snake Handle, Spout, Portuguese, 1880, 9 In. . . 3738.00
Console Set, Fluted Bowl, Semimatte White Glaze, Jalanovich, 1926, 15 1/2 & 10 In. 2233.00
Crock, Lead Glaze, Shenandoah Valley, 1/2 Pt., 3 1/2 x 3 1/2 x 2 1/2 In. 650.00
Dish, Earthenware, French Glaze, Molded, Zeus & Callisto, Fluted Border, 10 1/2 In. 718.00
Dish, Elephant, Landscape, Grapevine Border, 19th Century, 14 1/2 In. 575.00
Dish, Fan Form, Landscape Design, Marked, Karatsu, 19th Century, 11 1/2 x 9 1/4 In. 185.00
Dish, Lobster, 3 Parts, Green, Lobster Center Handle, Victoria Crown Mark, 7 1/2 In. 85.00
Figurine, Bull, Turquoise Matte Spots, White Ground, Marianna Van Allesch, 8 x 12 In. ... 176.00
Figurine, Dog, Seated, Reddish Brown Glaze, Peter Bell, Pa., 7 1/2 x 8 In. 22000.00
Figurine, Dog, White Clay, Brown Shiny Glaze, 7 1/4 In. 95.00
Figurine, Dutch Girl Holding Toddler's Hand, Marked Haga, c.1905, 14 In. 2247.00
Figurine, Elephant, Blue & White, Ming Dynasty, 7 1/4 In. 5175.00
Figurine, Foo Dog, Yellow, Green, Brown Glaze, Chinese, Late 1800s, 21 x 13 x 18 In. ... 1495.00
Figurine, Goose, Stanford, 7 1/4 In. 20.00
Figurine, Goose, Stanford, 8 1/2 In. 25.00
Figurine, Guardian Standing In Militant Pose, 13 1/2 In. 430.00
Figurine, Hound, Yellow Glazed, Brown Ears, Tail, 5 In. 9900.00
Figurine, Lion, White, Reclining, Scalloped Base, Dark Patina, Ohio, 10 1/2 x 5 x 7 In. ... 250.00
Figurine, Monkey Mother, Baby, Art Deco, Glazed, Square Base, Signed M. Marx, 28 In. . . 1175.00
Figurine, Parrot, Blue Eyes, Green Glaze, Ming Dynasty, 7 1/2 In. 115.00
Figurine, Schoolgirl With Books, Anzengruber, Austria, 8 3/4 In. .... *Illus* 160.00
Figurine, Squirrel, Cream, Rust, Incised Tail, Claws, Earthenware, 1980s, 3 x 4 1/2 In. 22.00
Figurine, Turquoise, Lotus Platform, 12 In., Pair 345.00
Flower Frog, Pink Lotus Blossom, Japan, 2 1/2 x 1 3/4 In. 20.00
Ginger Jar, Blue, White, Cover, Squat Baluster Shape, Double Happiness, Chinese, 16 In. 633.00
Jar, Brown Glaze, Tan Ground, Egg Shape, Marked, 20th Century, Hirotami, 10 1/4 In. . . 115.00
Jar, Cover, Green & Orange Spotted Glaze, Rolled Rim, Egg Shape, Galena, 7 1/2 In. 1072.00
Jar, Cover, Red Tomato, Stanford, 4 In. 35.00
Jar, Green Glaze, Chinese, 6 3/4 In. 265.00
Jar, Green Paulownia Design, Cream Crackle Ground, Japan, Edo Period, 6 1/4 In. 605.00
Jar, Handles, Cobalt Blue, North State Pottery, Sanford, N.C., 7 1/2 In. 300.00
Jar, Standing Woman, Long Dress, Tulips, Circled V 9000.00
Jardiniere, Memory Lane, Abstract Trees, Landscape, Wilkinson, 7 1/2 x 8 1/2 In. 235.00
Jardiniere, Stand, Sponge Decorated, Yellow Ground, Green, Gold, 28 x 12 In. 405.00
Jug, Devil Face, Applied Horns, Teeth, Red, Black, Inscribed, 13 1/4 In. 525.00
Jug, Earthenware, Mottled Lead & Manganese Glaze, Isaac Good, 1/2 Gal., 9 In. 3250.00
Jug, Face, Applied Features, Feldspathic Glaze, Flat Handle, R.E. Albright, c.1991, 8 In. ... 248.00
Jug, Face, Chocolate, Frogskin, Otto Brown, Early 1920s, 6 In. 4070.00
Jug, Face, Green Running Glaze, Stone Eyes, Teeth, Ears, Lanier Meaders, 9 1/2 In. 2090.00
Jug, Face, Monkey, Orange, Lead Glaze, M.L. Owens, c.1976, 10 1/2 In. 770.00
Lemonade Set, Japanese Style, Fruit & Flowers, Painted, Gilt, England, 1880, 4 Piece ... 675.00
Pitcher, Bird, Yellow With Mauve, 7 In. .... *Illus* 45.00
Pitcher, Blue Chinese Glaze, Red, Blue, North State Pottery, Sanford, N.C., 1939, 7 In. .. 385.00
Pitcher, Cobalt Blue Transferware, Mark, 7 1/2 In. 935.00

Pottery, Figurine,
Schoolgirl With
Books, Anzengruber,
Austria, 8 3/4 In.

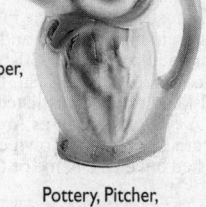

Pottery, Pitcher,
Bird, Yellow With Mauve,
7 In.

Pottery, Plaque, Arco Di
Costantino, Roma, Bas Relief, Johann
Maresh 5149, 12 1/2 In.

Pitcher, Cream, Pumpkin, Leaves, Hand Painted, Cash Family, Clinchfield Artware, 4 In. .	25.00
Pitcher, Glossy Cobalt Blue Edge Over Gray Glaze, Earthenware, Signed, 1920, 3 3/4 In.	550.00
Pitcher, Mottled Yellow, Brown Glaze, Octagonal Base, Paneled Sides, England, 9 In. ...	99.00
Pitcher, Olive, Gray Glaze, North State Pottery, Sanford, N.C., 1926-1938, 8 3/4 In.	110.00
Pitcher, Smiling Face, Redware, 6 1/2 In.	99.00
Pitcher, Swirl Clear Glaze, Earthenware, 1920, 8 1/2 In.	120.00
Planter, Figural, Chinese Girl, Double, Signed, Kaye Of Hollywood, 9 In.	75.00
Plaque, Arco Di Costantino, Roma, Bas Relief, Johann Maresh 5149, 12 1/2 In. .... *Illus*	50.00
Pot, Cobalt Blue, Green Glaze, North State Pottery, Sanford, N.C., 1926-1938, 6 1/2 In. ..	110.00
Roof Tile, Dragon, Yellow Glaze, Pierced Head, Chinese, Qing Dynasty, 17 1/2 In.	358.00
Salt, Yellow Glaze, Pedestal, Scalloped, Dutch, Mid 1800s	495.00
Sugar, Cover, Blue Flowers, Kutani, Silver Paint Accents, 3 In.	33.00
Tray, Round, Blue Flowers, Teal Ground, Metal Frame, WMF, Germany, c.1930, 12 In. ..	176.00
Tub, Tree, Beaker Form, Yellow, Green, Drip Glaze, France, 31 x 26 In., Pair	1265.00
Urn, Blue Glaze, 2 Handles, W. Owen, North State Pottery, Sanford, N.C., 10 In.	525.00
Vase, American Indian, War Dancer, Yellow, Brown, Signed, J. Lavender, 10 1/2 In.	138.00
Vase, Art Nouveau, 4 Handles, Austria, c.1900, 10 1/2 In.	230.00
Vase, Baluster Form, White Body, Black Rim, Emile Decoeur, c.1930, 10 1/4 In.	7637.00
Vase, Bottle, Flowers, Celadon, Teardrop Shape, Korea, Yi Dynasty, 12 In.	2070.00
Vase, Bulbous, Rolled Rim, Tortoiseshell Brown Glaze, 19th Century, 28 In.	865.00
Vase, Butter Over Orange Glaze, 3 Double Cord Handles, Earthenware, 1930s, 6 1/8 In. ..	468.00
Vase, Cadinen, Brown, Gold Painted Lip, Gold, Blue Pattern, Handmalere Mark, 4 1/2 In.	253.00
Vase, Chalice, Green, Cobalt Blue, Turquoise, Italy, 13 x 3 1/2 In.	71.00
Vase, Chrome Red Glaze, Saddle Rim, Earthenware, Handles, Footed, 1926, 4 3/4 x 9 In. .	440.00
Vase, Chrysanthemum, Birds, Brown Ground, Ryosui Studios, 12 1/2 In.	299.00
Vase, Cover, Brown Glaze, Polygon Shape, 6 1/2 In.	60.00
Vase, Double Gourd, Horse, Cloud, Marked, Shimazu, 19th Century, 14 1/2 In.	374.00
Vase, Earthenware, Figural, Face, Hair, Signed, Claude Coquerel, c.1940, 17 In.	3286.00
Vase, Flowers, Grapes, Sharkskin Glaze, 2 Handles, Royal Kinjo, c.1910, 11 In.	489.00
Vase, Gallelio Chini, Daffodils, Art Nouveau Maidens, Arte Della Ceramica, 4 x 3 In.	940.00
Vase, Glossy Chinese White Glaze, 1930s, Signed, 5 1/2 In.	275.00
Vase, Glossy Green, Blue, Buff, Speckled, Dripping, Earthenware, 1926-1927, 7 1/2 In. ..	358.00
Vase, Glossy Royal Blue Glaze, Oval, Double Ring Handle, Earthenware, 1930s, 9 x 9 In.	193.00
Vase, Glossy Turquoise, Flambe Glaze, Earthenware, 3 Handles, Signed, 1930s, 15 In. ...	660.00
Vase, Han Dynasty, Chinese Blue Glaze, Earthenware, 1940s, 8 1/2 In.	3960.00
Vase, Han Dynasty, Glossy Chinese White Glaze, Earthenware, 1930s-1940s, 9 In.	2420.00
Vase, J. Doris, Rene Buthaud, c.1930, 11 3/4 In.	7050.00
Vase, Lead Glaze, Blue, White Speckled, Earthenware, 3 Handles, 1930s, 5 x 7 1/4 In. ...	80.00
Vase, Lead Glaze, Chrome Red, Earthenware, 2 Handles, 1930s, 5 3/4 In.	220.00
Vase, Lead Glaze, Chrome Red, Earthenware, 2 Handles, 1930s, 10 In.	305.00
Vase, Lily, Glossy Chinese White Glaze, Earthenware, Signed, 1930s, 9 1/2 In.	1045.00
Vase, Maroon, Leather, Glaze, Swirl Side, Collar, Earthenware, Handles, 1930s, 10 7/8 In.	66.00
Vase, Mottled Green, Ring Handles, 7 In.	85.00
Vase, Mottled Tan, Dark Rim, Emile Decoeur, c.1930, 5 3/4 In.	8225.00
Vase, Pinched Rim, Runny Green Glaze, Stamped, N.C., 9 In.	195.00
Vase, Red Glaze, Turquoise, 8 Handles, Billy Ray Hussey, 10 1/4 In.	935.00
Vase, Songbird Perched On Branches, Blossoms, Oval, A. Humphreys, 1883, 7 1/2 In. ...	295.00
Vase, Tang Dynasty, Glossy Chinese White Glaze, Signed, 1930s-1940s, 6 7/8 In.	525.00
Vase, White, Dogwood, Green Ground, Gourd Shape, Nonconnah, Arden, N.C., 6 1/2 In. .	1035.00
Vase, Yellow Flowers, Green Medallion, Bulbous, Cylindrical Neck, Handle, 12 In.	69.00
Wash Bowl, Pitcher, Fruit, Banded Gilt, 10 1/2 & 15 1/2 In.	173.00

POTTERY-ART Art pottery was first made in America in Cincinnati, Ohio, during the 1870s. The pieces were hand thrown and hand decorated. The art pottery tradition continued until the 1930s when studio potters began making the more artistic wares. American, English, and Continental art pottery by less well-known makers is listed here. Most makers listed in *Kovels' American Art Pottery,* such as Arequipa, Ohr, Rookwood, Roseville, and Weller, are listed in their own categories in this book. More recent pottery is listed under the name of the maker or in the Pottery category.

Bowl, Dinanderie, Claudius Linossier, Inscribed, c.1929, 9 In.	4182.00

Bowl, Figural, Couple Running, Earthenware, Jean Mayodon, c.1925, 8 In. 6570.00
Bowl, Figural, Musical Nudes, Gold, Green, Edouard Cazaux, c.1930, 12 1/2 In. 2988.00
Bowl, Fruit, White Vertical Lines, Black, Flared, Footed, Germany, 1920, 6 x 10 In. 315.00
Candlestick, Dark Matte Green, Flared, Handle, Zigzag Base, 7 1/2 x 6 In. 160.00
Candlestick, Medium Matte Green, 4 Lobes, Open Base, 7 1/2 x 4 1/4 In. 160.00
Jar, Cover, Footed, Apple Blossoms, Burgundy Ground, J. Bennet, 12 1/2 x 6 In. 3220.00
Jar, Cover, Peonies, Yellow, White, Burgundy Ground, J. Bennet, 12 1/2 x 6 In. 9200.00
Jar, Swimming Sharks, Terra-Cotta, Green Glaze, Cover, Redlands, 4 x 5 1/2 In. 15275.00
Jardiniere, Stand, Large Flower Mold, Base, Continental, 51 In. 3525.00
Jug, Glossy Blue Glaze, Handle, Earthenware, 1920s-1930s, 2 3/4 In. 45.00
Jug, Purple Plaiting, Blue Bands, White Ground, Globular, Footed, Spout, Handle, 8 In. ... 390.00
Pitcher, Green Glossy Glaze, Marked, Clara Poillon, 4 1/2 x 5 In. 316.00
Planter, Seals & Hunters, Relief Design, Oval, 1900s, 6 1/2 In. 176.00
Plaque, Art Nouveau, Lilies Surround Woman's Head, E. Wahliss, c.1900, 15 In. 499.00
Plate, Multitoned Brown Glaze, Drip Glaze Center, 10 In. 58.00
Vase, Bamboo Design, Slip, Faience Mfg. Co., c.1900, 8 In. 230.00
Vase, Bretby, Woodgrain, Brown, Gunmetal Glaze, Mock Hardware, 8 1/2 x 8 3/4 In. 235.00
Vase, Brown Speckled Glaze, Green Ground, Paneled, Gourd, W.J. Walley, 8 1/4 In. 413.00
Vase, Brown, Black Mottled Matte Glaze, 11 Various Stized Holes, Round, 5 1/2 In. 60.00
Vase, Bulbous, Birds, Branches, 3 Handles, Lauder, Royal Barum, 1910, 9 x 4 1/2 In. 470.00
Vase, Bulbous, Blue, Brass Braids, Baudin, 1915, 4 3/4 x 4 In. 558.00
Vase, Carved Design, Blue Matte Glaze, Cylindrical, 6 1/4 In. 185.00
Vase, Centaur With Lyre, Earthenware, Edouard Cazaux, c.1925, 32 1/2 In. 3585.00
Vase, Dead-Matte Volcanic Glaze, No. 6187, Markham, 4 1/4 x 2 3/4 In. 705.00
Vase, Earthenware, Etruscan, Battle Scenes, Greek Key Border, c.1880, 36 In., Pair 1165.00
Vase, Egg Shape, Blue Crystalline Glaze, Pierrefonds, 5 3/4 x 4 1/2 In. 235.00
Vase, Egg Shape, Blue, Green, 5 1/2 x 4 1/4 In. 206.00
Vase, Egg Shape, Periwinkle Blue, Green Flambe Glaze, 9 x 6 1/2 In. 206.00
Vase, Green Mottled Matte Glaze, Swirling Rib, Chicago Crucible, 8 In. 60.00
Vase, Green, Brown Mottled Matte Glaze, Twisted Shape, 8 In. 242.00
Vase, Green, Charcoaling, Spirals, Globular, Incised, Jervis, 4 3/4 In. 330.00
Vase, Leaf Design, Iridescent, Flared Rim, Bulb Base, c.1880, 19 1/2 In. 1175.00
Vase, Leda & The Swan, Blue, Green, Eduard Cazau, 10 x 8 In. 1645.00
Vase, Molded, Applied Trees, Pinecones, Paul Daschel, Marked Terex, Austria, 11 In. 633.00
Vase, Owls, Ocher, Yellow, Black, Cream, Baluster Shape, Haga, c.1905, 13 1/2 In. 6740.00
Vase, Purple Mottled Matte Glaze, New Orleans Pottery, 2 3/4 x 4 1/4 In. 176.00
Vase, Stylized Lilacs, Gray, Blue, Corseted, Handles, Footed, Utrecht, 18 1/2 In. 2120.00
Vase, Swimming Sharks, Redlands, Squat 31625.00
Vase, Turquoise Glaze, Star Design, Spherical, Tall Neck, Burmanstoff, England, 12 In. ... 389.00

POTTERY-CONTEMPORARY lists pieces made by artists working after
1975.

Basket, Rust Brown, Earthenware, Cream Handle, Brown, 1980s, 10 In. 35.00
Biscuit Jar, Caned Wood Handle, Lid, Painted, Japan, 1958, 7 x 11 x 13 In. 175.00
Bowl, Blue, Oxblood, Glaze, Beatrice Wood, Signed Beato, 2 3/4 x 7 In. 1295.00
Bowl, Folded Form, Yellow Glaze, Signed, B. Wood, 1960, 6 x 2 In. 1150.00
Bowl, Oval, Shallow, Dark Brown Matte Glaze, Stoneware, Lucie Rie, England, 5 7/8 In. .. 880.00
Bowl, Purple, Gold, Verdigris, Beatrice Wood, Signed Beato, 6 x 10 In. 3408.00
Chalice, Luster Oxblood, Cobalt, Volcanic Glaze, Beatrice Wood, 9 x 6 In. 3408.00
Charger, Abstract, Red, Gray, Brown, Douglas Cornett, 21 3/4 In. 235.00
Face, Plaque, Chocolate, Feldspathic Glaze, Cole, c.1982, 3 1/2 x 3 1/2 In. 99.00
Figurine, 3 Boys, Derby Hats, Each Holding Something, c.1983, 4 In. 24.00
Figurine, Anteater, Fur, Glass Eyes, Striped Face, W. Germany, 2 1/2 x 4 In. 20.00
Figurine, Cat, Multicolored, Whiskers, Claws, Earthenware, 3 x 4 1/2 In. 22.00
Figurine, Catfish, Green, Incised Fins, Tail, Horn, Earthenware, 2 x 6 In. 44.00
Figurine, Giraffe, White Glaze, Earthenware, 1980s, Signed, 6 x 2 1/2 In. 66.00
Figurine, Lion, Orange, Butter, Glaze, Signed BH, c.1986, 5 x 4 1/2 In. 525.00
Figurine, Owl, On Stump, Colonial Cream, Feldspathic Glaze, c.1980, 3 In. 5.50
Figurine, Salvatore Fiume, Italy, 1970s, 3 1/2 x 8 x 15 In. 805.00
Figurine, Spaniel, Turquoise, Incised, Signed BH, c.1987, 6 1/2 x 7 In. 605.00
Jar, Storage, Cobalt Blue Decorated, Salt Glaze, R. E. Albright, c.1986, 12 In. 77.00
Jug, Face, Rock-Tooth, Pierced Ears, Lancer Meaders, c.1970, 9 1/2 In. 2300.00

Jug, Picasso, White Glaze, Handles, Black Devil Face, Madoura, 5 1/2 In. 1140.00
Pie Plate, Flowers, Coggle Wheel, Brown, Camp David, 1978, 8 In. 468.00
Pitcher, Mottled White, Green, Feldspathic Glaze, C.B. Craven, 1980s, 4 In. 22.00
Pitcher, Pillow, Elizabeth Abrahams Woodman, c.1980, 17 x 22 x 15 In. 7170.00
Pitcher, Pinched Spout, Brown, Swirled Ocher, Southern, GKE, 13 In. 85.00
Plate, Feldspathic Glaze, Slip, Oakland Pottery, c.1983, 1 1/2 x 7 In. 121.00
Plate, Lions, Birds, Flowers, Tan Ground, 10 7/8 In. 770.00
Vase, 3 Equestrian Figures, Blue & Brown Ground, P. Pillin, 9 x 10 In. 2530.00
Vase, Blue, Green Mottled Glaze, Brown Body, Flowers, W. Germany, 7 In. 110.00
Vase, Cover, Domed, Clown, Dove, Blue, Yellow, Round, A. Mendini, 15 In. 505.00
Vase, Euphrates, Round, Globular Shapes, Yellow, Black, Sottsass, 16 In. 1123.00
Vase, Flaring, Resist, Amber, White, Gray, Black, Stoneware, Maija Grotell, 9 x 6 In. 7640.00
Vase, Flaring, Teal, Cobalt Mottled Matte Glaze, Stoneware, Maija Grotell, 9 x 10 1/2 In. . 2000.00
Vase, Flattened, Woman, Kitten, Polychrome, Avocado, Pillin, 6 x 4 x 3 In. 764.00
Vase, Glossy Red Drip Over Aqua Glaze, Earthenware, 1938, 21 1/2 In. 468.00
Vase, Green, Brown, Blue Matte Glaze, Round, Rounded Top, Telerski, 7 In. 60.00
Vase, Kirchmann, Cover, Round, Broad Base, Red Crystalline Glaze, 8 In. 230.00
Vase, Light Blue Crater Glaze, James Lovera, 5 In. 290.00
Vase, Modernist Design, Multitone Brown, Finger Ridges, Heino, 2 1/2 In. 58.00
Vase, Multitone Blue Glaze, Red Body, Beatrice Wood, 7 1/2 In. 978.00
Vase, Oval, Gold, Green, Lavender Luster, Beato, Beatrice Wood, 5 x 5 In. 2235.00
Vase, Purple, Green, Gold Glaze, Footed, Beatrice Wood, Beato, 9 x 9 In. 7050.00
Vase, Red, Turquoise, Glazed, Footed, Beatrice Wood, Beato, 6 x 5 1/2 In. 2700.00
Vase, Sand Color, Orange & Green Swirl, Nemadji, American, 4 In. 25.00
Vase, White, Blue Lines, Round, Flattened, Disc Neck, M. Bedin, 12 1/2 In. 279.00

POTTERY-MIDCENTURY includes pieces made from the 1940s to the 1980s.

Air Freshener, Shmoo, Figural, c.1940, 3 x 4 x 5 1/2 In. 70.00
Airwick Cat, Green, Morton Pottery, 4 In. 25.00
Armature, Piero Fornasetti, c.1955, 10 In., 6 Piece 411.00
Ashtray, Round, Yellow, Gold Rim, English Setter, Leaf Decal, Pearl China, 6 In. 10.00
Ashtray, Santa Monica, Winfield, 2 3/4 x 3 3/4 In. 15.00
Basket, Rust Over Green Glaze, Groove Handle, Earthenware, 1960s, 5 x 6 In. 165.00
Bowl, Brown Glaze, Mocha, Tan, Mahogany, Circles, Scheier, 3 1/2 In. 523.00
Bowl, Brown, Tooled Lines, Incised, Scheier, 3 1/2 In. 440.00
Bowl, Ceramic, Black, Volcanic Glaze, G. & O. Natzler c.1956, 4 x 8 In. 4994.00
Bowl, Ceramic, Yellow, Volcanic Glaze, G. & O. Natzler, c.1956, 10 In. 4400.00
Bowl, Flambe, Taupe Glaze, Ivory, Incised, Scheier, 4 x 5 In. 248.00
Bowl, Flaring Form, Bluish Glossy Glaze, Scheier Studio, 3 x 8 1/2 In. 500.00
Bowl, Folded Form, Gray Glaze, Natzler, Ink Signature, 6 3/4 x 2 1/2 In. 1495.00
Bowl, Footed, Arms, Cutout Windows, Werkstatte, Austria, 4 1/2 x 8 1/2 In. 2115.00
Bowl, Footed, Green Crackle Glaze, G. & O. Natzler, 1950s, 9 x 2 1/2 In. 1495.00
Bowl, Glazed, Rust, Yellow, Gunmetal, E. Deutsch, 1942, 7 3/4 x 3 In. 575.00
Bowl, Glossy Chinese White Glaze, Earthenware, c.1940, Signed, 4 x 7 In. 165.00
Bowl, Thumbprint, Blue, Feldspathic Glaze, Signed Teagues, c.1970, Pair 78.00
Bowl, Turquoise Over Flambe Glaze, Handle, Earthenware, 1940s, 2 x 5 In. 99.00
Charger, Exotic Bird, Black, Silver, Gold, W.S. Gregory, 10 1/2 In. 150.00

Pottery-Midcentury, Cruet, Chinese Soy Sauce, 7 In.

Pottery-Midcentury, Cruet, Italian Dressing, Figural, 7 In.

Pottery-Midcentury, Dish, Dresser, Cover, Black, Chartreuse, Marked, California, 4 1/2 In.

Pottery-Midcentury, Eggcup,	Pottery-Midcentury,	Pottery-Midcentury, Jug,
Clown, Hat Is Cover, Italy,	Figurine, Bird, Thelma	Volcanic Glaze, Red, Piped Lines,
3 1/2 In.	Frazier Winter, 6 In.	Carstens, W. Germany, 5 In.

Crock, Galena, Thick Rim, Incised Line, Green Glaze, 2 Handles, 13 x 13 In. 880.00
Cruet, Chinese Soy Sauce, 7 In. . . . . *Illus* 20.00
Cruet, Italian Dressing, Figural, 7 In. . . . . *Illus* 20.00
Demitasse Pot, Lid, Keele Street Pottery Co., England, 6 1/4 In. 110.00
Dish, Dresser, Cover, Black, Chartreuse, Marked, California, 4 1/2 In. . . . . *Illus* 30.00
Eggcup, Clown, Hat Is Cover, Italy, 3 1/2 In. . . . . *Illus* 35.00
Ewer, Pablo Picasso, Abstract Face, Signed, Madoura, 12 1/4 x 5 1/2 In. 1880.00
Figurine, Bird, Thelma Frazier Winter, 6 In. . . . . *Illus* 150.00
Figurine, Black Jazz Band, Drummer, Bass Player, Guitarist, Brayton Laguna, 3 Piece . . . 750.00
Figurine, Clown, With Goat On Leash, Kreiss, Japan, 7 x 2 1/2 In. 29.00
Figurine, Cow, Bull, Calf, Blue, Original Sticker, Brayton Laguna, 3 Piece 450.00
Figurine, Cow, Purple, Original Sticker, Brayton Laguna 150.00
Figurine, Giraffe, Robert Simmons Ceramics, 1950, 6 3/4 In., Pair 60.00
Figurine, Pink Flamingo, Head Down, 6 In. 22.00
Figurine, Poodle, Gray, Spaghetti, Jane Calendar, 3 In. 75.00
Figurine, Rooster, On Post, Brown Matte Ground, W.S. Gregory, 13 3/4 In. 295.00
Figurine, Salvatore Fiume, Italy, 1970s, 4 1/4 x 13 1/2 x 33 3/4 In. 2530.00
Figurine, Siamese Cat, Sparkler, Blue Rhinestone Eyes, Roselane, 4 1/2 In. 25.00
Figurine, Siamese Cat, Sparkler, Blue Rhinestone Eyes, Roselane, 9 1/4 In. 45.00
Figurine, Singing Accordion Player, W. Werkstatte, Austria, 4 In. 646.00
Figurine, Vase, Mexican Boy, Guitar, Delee, 7 1/2 In. 45.00
Figurine, We Welcome Suggestions, Rhinestones, Fur, Kreiss Psycho, 5 In. 75.00
Figurine, Whimsy Girl & Boy, Marked N Within Circle, 5 1/2 In., Pair 29.00
Jardiniere, Tapering Cylindrical Form, Embossed Leaf, Green, Morton, 7 In. 50.00
Jug, Face, Monkey, Earthenware, Brown Pottery, 1950s, 9 5/8 In. 825.00
Jug, Handle, Rust Brown, Feldspathic Glaze, Earthenware, 1970s, 8 In. 33.00
Jug, Matte Gold Glaze, Earthenware, 1970s, Impressed Granny's XXX, 4 In. 55.00
Jug, Volcanic Glaze, Red, Piped Lines, Carstens, W. Germany, 5 In. . . . . *Illus* 25.00
Lamp Base, G. Gambone, Signed, Italy, 1950s, 18 1/2 In. 2070.00
Pie Bird, Yellow, Green Pink, Morton Pottery, 5 In. 35.00
Pitcher, Gooseneck, Mustard, Handle, Ridges, Earthenware, 1940s, 16 In. 145.00
Pitcher, Green, Feldspathic Glaze, Straw, Aqua, Gold, Handle, c.1970, 7 In. 80.00
Pitcher, Owl, Ceramic, Bulbous, Stamped, Madoura, Edition Picasso, 5 1/2 In. 200.00
Pitcher, Rebekah, Glossy Turquoise, Flambe Glaze, Earthenware, 1940s, 9 In. 165.00
Pitcher, Rebekah, Green Streaked Glaze, Earthenware, Signed, 1970s, 19 In. 99.00
Planter, Attached Bambi Figurine, Green, Bisque, American, 6 1/2 x 8 1/2 In. 95.00
Planter, Bugs Bunny, Figural, Warner Bros., 1977, 4 x 6 x 5 In. 30.00
Planter, Bulldog, Pastel Blue, No. 386, Morton Pottery 18.00
Planter, Chinese Girl, Double, Signed 3129 Kaye, Kaye Of Hollywood, 9 In. 75.00
Planter, Dog, Large Blue Eyes, Block Pottery, 4 In. 30.00
Planter, Dutch Boy, Pink Wooden Shoe, Bisque, American, 6 1/4 In. 28.00
Planter, Easter Rabbit, Baby, Pulling Egg Cart, Daisy Wheel, 7 x 6 In. 19.00
Planter, Elephant, Trunk Up, Chartreuse, Green, 4 x 5 1/2 In. 30.00
Planter, Figural, Homer Pigeon, Walter Lanz, 1958, 2 x 5 x 6 In. 25.00
Planter, Mountain Boy, Paul Webb, 4 1/4 x 6 1/2 In. . . . . *Illus* 30.00
Planter, Parrot, White, Multicolored Glaze, Morton Pottery 30.00

Pottery-Midcentury,
Planter, Mountain
Boy, Paul Webb,
4 1/4 x 6 1/2 In.

"Cold-painted" items like some glass and porcelain, especially cookie jars, should never be put in a dishwasher. Just wipe them with a damp cloth.

Planter, Porky Pig, Figural, 1951, 4 1/2 In.		15.00
Planter, Turkey, No. 619, Morton Pottery, 4 1/2 In.		35.00
Planter, Victorian Girl, Parasol, Chartreuse, No. 6447, Relpo, 9 In.	*Illus*	30.00
Planter, Woman, Skirt, Sunbonnet, Chartreuse, Green, 5 In.		24.00
Plaque, Oh Tell Me Pretty Maid, Heart Shape, Cleminson, 6 1/4 In.		30.00
Plaque, Your Obedient Lucifer, Dutifully Yours Lucinda, Cleminson, 7 In., Pair		45.00
Plate, Ceramic, Donkey, Guido Gambone, Italy, c.1955, 11 x 8 1/4 In.		499.00
Plate, Gray, Flowing Yellow Matte Glaze, Maija Grotell, 1 1/2 x 9 1/2 In.		530.00
Plate, Wax-Resist Feather, Raspberry, Green, Blue Ground, Maija Grotell, 6 In.		470.00
Vase, Accordion, Scalloped Rim, Amber, Brown Glaze, J.B. Cole, 7 1/4 In.		275.00
Vase, Applied Figures, Standing, Reclining, Round, Footed, H. Krop, 1948, 8 In.		5617.00
Vase, Aqua Glaze, Taupe, Raised Metallic Black, Stamped, Shearwater, 6 In.		413.00
Vase, Aqua Matte, Cobalt Blue Overglaze, Closed Rim, Maija Grotell, 4 x 3 In.		410.00
Vase, Aqua, Brown Glaze Streaking, Gold, Oval, Incised, Cabat, 3 1/3 In.		303.00
Vase, Art Deco, Butterscotch Flambe Glaze, Carillon China, c.1940, 7 3/4 In.		75.00
Vase, Art Nouveau, Polychrome, Sunflower, Women, Salviati, 13 x 5 In.		764.00
Vase, Birds, Geometric, Blue Matte Ground, Luxembourg, c.1935, 11 In.		206.00
Vase, Black, Red Lines, Signed, Donkey Mark, Guido Gambone, Italy, 1950s, 21 In.		1725.00
Vase, Blue Glaze, Specks, Flared, Natzler, 7 In.		1265.00
Vase, Blue To Brown Harefurs Glaze, Berndt Friberg, Sweden, 13 1/2 In.		2645.00
Vase, Bottle Shape, Yellow Drip, Brown, Blue Matte Glaze, Italy, 8 x 8 x 5 In.		441.00
Vase, Bugs Bunny, Figural, Tree Design, Warner Bros., c.1940, 2 x 5 x 7 In.		35.00
Vase, Cubist, Blue Glaze, Signed, Fantoni, Italy, 1950s, 4 1/2 x 18 1/2 In.		1150.00
Vase, Dinanderie, Inscribed Claudius Linossier, c.1953, 7 1/4 In.		5019.00
Vase, Donkey, Guido Gambone, Italy, c.1957, 12 3/4 x 4 In.		588.00
Vase, Double-Tailed Mermaids, Fish, Leaves, W.S. Gregory, 15 In., Pair		3819.00
Vase, Figural Chinese Man & Baskets, Weil Donkey Mark, 10 3/4 In.	*Illus*	65.00
Vase, Fish, Scrolled Handles, Ruffled Rim, Lauder, Royal Barum, 9 x 4 In.		235.00
Vase, Geometric Panels, Signed, Donkey Mark, Guido Gambone, Italy, 1950s, 4 x 21 In.		1093.00
Vase, Glazed Earthenware, Clyde Burt, 1950s, 4 1/4 x 33 In.		4600.00
Vase, Globular, Lime Green Glaze, Black Speckled, Incised, Cabat, 3 1/2 In.		358.00
Vase, Green Blue Glaze, Brown Body, Flared, Natzler, 5 In.		1495.00
Vase, Green Lead Glaze, Earthenware, 3 Handles, 1940s, 9 5/8 In.		77.00

Pottery-Midcentury,
Planter, Victorian
Girl, Parasol,
Chartreuse, No.
6447, Relpo, 9 In.

Pottery-Midcentury,
Vase, Figural Chinese
Man & Baskets, Weil
Donkey Mark, 10 3/4 In

Pottery-Midcentury, Vase,
Millefiori, Valleris, France, 5 1/2

Vase, Green, Pierced, Signed, Donkey Mark, Guido Gambone, Italy, 1950s, 5 x 16 In. . . .	2530.00
Vase, Green, Taupe, Black, Emerald Green Drip, Oval, Incised, Cabat, 6 In.	935.00
Vase, Leather, Marcello Fantoni, c.1958, 11 3/4 In.	264.00
Vase, Millefiori, Valleris, France, 5 1/2 In. . . . . *Illus*	85.00
Vase, Onion Shape, Sky Blue Glaze, White, Green Streaks, Incised, Cabat, 3 1/3 In.	220.00
Vase, Onion Shape, Yellow, Green, Peach Drip Glaze, Cabat, 2 1/2 In.	193.00
Vase, Onion, Black Matte, Luster, Lavender Swirl Glaze, Cabat, 2 3/4 In.	275.00
Vase, Pedestal Shape, Painted Geometric Design, Gambone, 12 In.	750.00
Vase, Red Lines, Signed, Donkey Mark, Guido Gambone, Italy, 1950s, 7 3/4 x 17 In.	1725.00
Vase, Rose Shading To Cream, Speckled, Oval, Footed, Marked, Scheier, 6 In.	265.00
Vase, Stonelain, Rooster, Red, Black, Ivory Ground, Carl Walters, 11 x 8 In.	235.00
Vase, Tapered, Green Glaze, M. Fantoni, Italy, 1950s, 5 x 17 1/2 In. . . . . `.	310.00

POWDER FLASKS AND POWDER HORNS were made to hold the gunpowder used in antique firearms. The early examples were made of horn or wood; later ones were of copper or brass.

POWDER FLASK, Copper, Acanthus Leaf, 4 1/2 In.	115.00
Copper, Dog's Head, 9 In.	185.00
Copper, Drapery, 9 In.	46.00
Copper, Hounds, Hunter, Treed Bear, 8 In.	81.00
Copper, Indian, Game, 8 In.	259.00
Copper, Violin Shape, Grape, Leaf, 8 In.	46.00
Cow Horn, Flat Side, Brass Top, Cylindrical Banded Spout, 1747, 7 1/2 In.	245.00
Cow Horn, Flat, Round, Geometric Design, Brass Tack, Scotland, c.1670, 10 1/2 In.	1250.00
Engraved, Coat Of Arms, House, Hunter, Deer, Dog, Banner, 12 In.	1540.00
Monster Head, 2 Beasts Holding Flower, Wooden Base, 1762, 12 1/2 In.	550.00
POWDER HORN, Brass Nozzle, 12 1/2 In.	205.00
Carved, Engraved, Nichols Armistead, Raised Rings, Panels, 1804, 17 In.	646.00
Cow Horn, Beaded Edges, Turn Stepped Baluster, Wooden Base, c.1700-1750, 14 In.	275.00
Cow's, Carved, Warrior Wearing Roman Skirt, Other Side Man, Horse, 9 x 2 5/8 In.	630.00
Egg & Dart Carved, Brass Rings, Chains, Leather Strap, 18th Century, 14 In.	650.00
Engraved, Adam & Eve, Village, Lion, Initialed G.S.M., 13 In.	1760.00
Engraved, Heart & Flower, Initials	90.00
Engraved, New York Scene, Men, Animals, c.1800, 7 In.	1155.00
Engraved, Soldier, Horse, Lion, Cannon, Snake, Dogs, James Fitch, 1775, 12 1/4 In.	290.00
Engraved, Town Harbor, Ships, Benjamin Hill Horn, c.1760, 11 In.	1760.00
Flat, Brass Measure, Viewing Window, 12 In.	176.00
Flowers, Scrolls, Flat, Engraved Plate, Jacob Ernst, 1799, 10 In.	4275.00
Hounds, Acorn Carved Mouthpiece, Snake In Relief, Marked, Arkansas, 1877	3520.00
Hudson Bay Seal, Engraved, Trading Posts Banner, 19th Century, 8 1/2 In.	4406.00
Inscribed, Admiral Dewey, USS Olympia, Flag, Sailor, T.W. Corkhill, 17 1/2 In.	353.00
Inscribed, Engraved Lioness, Timothy Willey, 1848, 9 1/2 In.	120.00
Mythological Beast, Faceted Edge Body, Wooden Base, c.1700-1750, 9 1/2 In.	275.00
Painted, Carved, Heraldic Eagle, Trees, Geometric Designs, 19 In.	295.00
Presentation, Carved Edinburgh Landmarks, C. Plumber, Scotland, 1853, 14 In.	1380.00
Ship, Engraved, 14 In.	80.00
Steer's Horn, Carved, Artichoke Form, Plug, Continental, 15 In.	345.00

PRATT ware means two different things. It was an early Staffordshire pottery, cream-colored with colored decorations, made by Felix Pratt during the late eighteenth century. There was also Pratt ware made with transfer designs during the mid-nineteenth century in Fenton, England. Reproductions of the transfer-printed Pratt are being made.

PRATT
FENTON

Bank, Cottage, Man On Each Side, Polychrome Enamel, 5 In.	30.00
Figurine, Winter, Orange Fur Robe, Flaming Brazier, Green, Yellow, Brown, 8 3/4 In. . . .	110.00
Jug, Bear, Seated, Collar, Muzzle, Spout Between Paws, Cover, c.1810, 6 5/8 In.	1790.00
Pitcher, Acanthus Leaves, Sailor Farewell & Arrival Scenes, Molded, 6 In.	525.00
Pitcher, Fluted Neck, Molded Leaves, Man Drinking, Smoking, Horse, 6 In.	495.00
Plate, Independence Hall Interior, Centennial, Kerrs China Hall, 9 In.	100.00
Pomade Jar, Cover, Room Where Shakespeare Was Born, 1564 Stratford On Avon, 4 In. . .	80.00
Pomade Jar, Cover, That No Jealous Rival Shall Laugh Me To Scorn, 4 In.	125.00
Stirrup Cup, Figural, Ram's Head, Sprig Band Around Rim, 4 1/2 In.	1045.00

PRESSED GLASS was first made in the United States in the 1820s after the invention of glass pressing machines. Hundreds of patterns of pressed glass were made in complete table settings. Although the Boston and Sandwich Works was the most famous of the pressed glass factories, there were about sixteen other factories making pressed glass from 1830 to 1850, and still more from 1850 to 1900, when pressed glass reached its greatest popularity. It is now being widely reproduced. The pattern names used in this listing are based on the information in the book *Pressed Glass in America* by John and Elizabeth Welker. There may be pieces of pressed glass listed in this book in other categories, such as Lamp, Ruby, Sandwich, and Souvenir.

Actress, Cake Stand, Frosted Rim, Border, 6 3/4 x 9 3/4 In.	170.00
Actress, Champagne, Frosted Stem, Foot, 5 In.	450.00
Actress, Goblet, 6 1/4 In.	75.00 to 90.00
Alligator, Goblet, Etched, 6 1/4 In.	30.00
Arch & Checkerboard, Plate, Medium Green, 72 Scallops, Beaded Row, 6 In.	100.00
Argosy, Wine, 3 3/4 In.	15.00
Argus, Goblet, Faceted Knop Stem, Goblet, Polished Pontil, 6 1/2 In.	240.00
Ashburton, Bottle, Bitters	65.00
Ashburton, Goblet, Double Knop Stem, 6 1/2 In.	80.00
Ashburton, Goblet, Emerald Green, 16-Point Star Base, 4 3/4 In.	670.00
Ashburton, Goblet, Semi-Squared Foot, 6 In.	35.00
Ashburton, Goblet, Squared Foot, 6 5/8 In.	50.00
Ashburton, Tumbler, Ale, Footed, 6 1/2 In.	90.00
Ashburton, Vase, Baluster Stem, Scalloped Rim, Round Foot, 10 In., Pair	440.00
Atlanta, Compote, 8 3/4 x 7 1/8 In.	130.00
Atlanta, Goblet, Engraved Leaves, 6 In.	90.00
Baby Face, Compote, Cover, Frosted Finial, Stem, Foot, 12 1/2 x 8 3/4 In.	325.00
Baby Thumbprint pattern is listed here as Dakota.	
Bakewell Block, Goblet, 6 3/8 In.	150.00
Banded Crystal, Goblet, Bulb Stem, Gold Trim, 6-Sided Foot, 6 1/2 In.	120.00
Barberry, Syrup, Applied Handle, Britannia Cover, 7 In.	130.00
Barley, Pitcher, Applied Handle, 9 1/2 In.	140.00
Barred Oval, Pitcher, Ruby Stain, 8 3/4 In.	400.00
Barrel Honeycomb, see the related pattern Honeycomb.	
Battleship Maine, Dish, Cover, Green, Remember The Maine, 3 1/2 x 7 In.	120.00
Beaded Acorn Leaf Band, Goblet, 5 3/4 In.	160.00
Bear Climber, Goblet, Etched, 6 1/4 In.	30.00
Beehive & Thistle, Plate, Octagonal, Scalloped Edge, Lacy, 9 1/4 In.	55.00
Bellflower, Decanter, Ribbed, Cut Ovals On Shoulders, 12 3/4 In.	550.00
Bellflower, Pitcher, Double Ribbed, Applied Handle, 9 In.	385.00
Bird & Strawberry, Goblet, Flared Rim, 6 1/2 In.	800.00
Birds In Swamp, Goblet, 5 1/8 In.	45.00
Blackberry, Pitcher, Applied Handle, 8 1/4 In.	120.00
Bleeding Heart, Egg Tray, 4 Eggcups, 1 1/4 x 7 In.	350.00
Bleeding Heart, Goblet, Knop Stem, 6 1/4 In., 6 Piece	350.00
Bleeding Heart, Pitcher, Applied Handle, 8 3/4 In.	185.00

Pressed Glass,
Barberry

Pressed Glass, Strawberry

Pressed Glass,
Cable

Pressed Glass,
Dakota

Bleeding Heart, Wine, 4 In. 70.00
Block & Fine Cut pattern is listed here as Fine Cut & Block.
Block Band, Goblet, Ruby Stain, 6 1/8 In. 60.00
Bluebird pattern is listed here as Bird & Strawberry.
Bowtie, Orange Bowl, Footed, 10 1/8 x 10 1/4 In. 160.00
Bradford Blackberry, Goblet, 5 7/8 In. 90.00
Bradford Grape pattern is listed here as Bradford Blackberry.
Branches, Pitcher, 8 5/8 In. 40.00
Brilliant, Goblet, Amber Stain 185.00
Buck & Doe, Goblet, Etched, 6 3/8 In. 40.00
Bull's-Eye & Broken Column, Goblet, 5 1/2 In. 75.00
Bull's-Eye & Fleur-De-Lis, Pitcher, Applied Handle, 9 In. 275.00
Bull's-Eye & Fleur-De-Lis, Pitcher, Rigaree Handle, 7 1/8 In. 330.00
Cabbage Leaf, Table Set, Light Amber, 4 To 6 3/4 In., 4 Piece 3400.00
Cable, Goblet, 6 1/2 In. 90.00
Canadian, Compote, Cover, 8 3/4 x 6 In. 100.00
Candlewick as a pressed glass pattern is properly named *Banded Raindrop*. There is also a pattern called *Candlewick*, which has been made by Imperial Glass Corporation since 1936. It is listed in this book in the Imperial Glass category.
Centennial, see the related pattern Liberty Bell
Circle & Ellipse, Vase, Plain Rim, Double Knop Stem, 6-Sided Foot, 9 In. 30.00
Cleat, Pitcher, Milk, Applied Handle, Polished Pontil, 8 1/2 In. 200.00
Cleat, Pitcher, Water, 9 In. 75.00
Coin Spot pattern is listed in this book in its own category.
Cord & Tassel, Pitcher, Applied Handle, 8 3/4 In. 170.00
Corona, Bowl, Ruby Stain, Engraved Leaf, Tendril, Footed, 2 3/4 x 7 In. 110.00
Corona, Cake Stand, Ruby Stain, 5 1/4 x 8 1/2 In. 275.00
Corona, Compote, Cover, Ruby Stain, 11 x 7 1/8 In. 1450.00
Corona, Cruet, Enameled Leaf, Flowers, Stopper, Ruby Stain, 6 1/2 In. 120.00
Corona, Decanter, Stopper, Ruby Stain, 13 5/8 In. 120.00
Cosmos pattern is listed in this book as its own category.
Croesus, Creamer, Green, 4 1/4 In. 20.00
Croesus, Pitcher, Amethyst, 11 1/2 In. 225.00
Crystal Wedding, Goblet, Amber Stain, 5 3/4 In. 200.00
Cupid & Venus, Bread Plate, Amber, Round, Tab Handles, 10 1/2 In. 60.00
Currant, Pitcher, Milk, Applied Handle, 7 1/4 In. 100.00
Daisy & Button, Sitz Bath Tub, Oval, 4 3/4 x 9 1/4 In. 120.00
Dakota, Cake Stand, Cover, Engraved, Fern & Berry, 12 1/2 x 8 1/4 In. 1900.00
Dakota, Compote, Cover, Engraved, Fern & Berry, 13 1/2 x 9 In. 160.00
Dakota, Goblet, Engraved, Leaf, Ruby Stain, 6 1/2 In. 70.00
Dakota, Pitcher, Milk, Engraved, Fern & Berry, Qt., 9 1/8 x 4 1/4 In. 40.00
Dakota, Tumbler, Ruby Stain, 3 1/2 In. 50.00
Deer & Dog, Goblet, 6 1/4 In. 55.00
Deer & Dog, Pitcher, Milk, Straight Sides, Applied Handle, 7 1/4 x 3 1/4 In. 750.00
Deer & Oak Tree, Pitcher, 8 3/4 In. 180.00
Deer & Pine Tree, Bread Tray, Apple Green, 7 7/8 x 13 In. 100.00
Deer & Pine Tree, Bread Tray, Blue, 7 7/8 x 13 In. 70.00
Dewey, Cruet, Amber, Stopper, 5 1/2 In. 70.00
Dewey, Pitcher, 9 1/4 In. 110.00
Diamond, Compote, 9 x 9 In. 60.00
Diamond Point With Leaf, Compote, 5 7/8 x 8 1/2 In. 55.00
Diamond Thumbprint, Celery Vase, Lobed Stem, Scalloped Edge, 9 1/4 In., Pair 715.00
Diamond Thumbprint, Compote, Lobed Stem, Scalloped Edge, 7 x 9 1/2 In. 440.00
Dolphin, Compote, Flattened Starch Blue, Opalescent Base, Stepped Foot, 6 In. 415.00
Dolphin, Creamer, Frosted Stem, Foot, 6 3/4 In. 90.00
Dolphin, Pitcher, Water, Frosted Stem, Foot, 10 In. 375.00
Doric pattern is listed here as Feather.
Double Disced Prism, Goblet, Apple Green, 5 7/8 In. 120.00
Double Wedding Ring pattern is listed here as Wedding Ring.
Dragon, Goblet, McKee & Brothers, 5 5/8 In. 1900.00
Drape, Tumbler, Orange Shaded To Vaseline, 9 Vertical Drape Columns, 3 3/4 In. 65.00
Early Thumbprint, Tumbler, Ale, Footed, 6 3/4 In. 155.00
Egyptian, Compote, Covered, 11 1/2 x 8 1/4 In. 50.00

Elk & Doe, Goblet, 6 1/8 In.	250.00
Empress, Pitcher, Green, 9 1/4 In.	90.00
Etched Dakota pattern is listed here as Dakota.	
Excelsior, Goblet, Barrel, 5 7/8 In.	20.00
Feather, Cake Stand, Amber Stain, 5 x 9 3/4 In.	400.00
Feather, Cake Stand, Green, 5 1/4 x 9 1/2 In.	190.00
Feather, Goblet, 5 3/4 In.	50.00
Findlay, Dish, Dog, Cat, Beaded Edge, Columbia Glass, 5 3/4 In., Pair	275.00
Fine Cut & Block, Compote, Amber Stain, 4 3/4 x 4 3/4 In.	90.00
Fine Cut & Block, Pitcher, Amber Stain, 8 5/8 In.	140.00
Fine Cut & Feather pattern is listed here as Feather.	
Fine Diamond Point, Goblet, Engraved, 5 7/8 In.	45.00
Fine Rib, Compote, Scallop & Point Rim, 8-Sided Hollow Stem, 8 x 9 3/4 In.	325.00
Fleur-De-Lis & Drape, Sugar & Creamer, Emerald Green	60.00
Flower Band, Pitcher, Frosted, 9 1/4 In.	110.00
Flower Flange pattern is listed here as Dewey.	
Flute, Goblet, Opaque Starch Blue, Sand Finish, Circular Foot, 7 1/2 In.	55.00
Flute & Spear, Tumbler, Apple Green, Rayed Base, 3 1/2 In.	145.00
Flying Robin pattern is listed here as Hummingbird.	
Four Printie Block, Vase, Emerald Green, 11 1/2 x 4 1/4 In.	3850.00
Four Printie Block, Vase, Tulip, Canary, Scalloped Rim, 6-Sided Foot, 10 1/4 In.	990.00
Framed Ovals, Goblet, Emerald Green, Gold Trim, 6 1/4 In.	375.00
Frosted patterns may also be listed under name of main pattern.	
Gargoyle, Goblet, 6 1/4 In.	330.00
George Washington, Plate, Acorns, Leaves, Star & Scroll, Scallop & Point Rim, 6 In. ...	110.00
Giant Honeycomb, Goblet, 6 3/8 In.	230.00
Gonterman Swirl, Goblet, Frosted, Amber Stain, 6 1/4 In.	1550.00
Gonterman Swirl, Spooner, Frosted, Amber Stain, 6 In.	325.00
Good Luck pattern is listed here as Horseshoe.	
Goosegirl, Cake Stand, Frosted Stem, Foot, 7 3/4 x 8 1/2 In.	190.00
Gothic Arch, Sugar, Cover, Canary, 8 Sides, Round Foot, 5 1/4 In.	660.00
Gothic Arch, Sugar, Cover, Sapphire Blue, 8 Sides, Scalloped Foot, 5 1/2 In.	1650.00
Grape, see the related pattern Magnet & Grape patterns.	
Harp, Toddy Plate, Peacock Blue, Rope & Grapes, Scroll & Star Border, 4 3/8 In.	275.00
Hawaiian Pineapple, Goblet, 6 1/2 In.	165.00
Hexagon Block, Pitcher, Water, Tankard, Etched Flower, Bird, Ruby Stain, 11 7/8 In.	375.00
Hexagon Block, Pitcher, Water, Tankard, Ruby Stain, 12 In.	150.00
Hexagon Block, Tankard, Etched Leaf, Flower, Amber Stain, 11 1/8 In.	150.00
Historical, Goblet, Grant & Wilson, 6 1/4 In.	660.00
Historical, Tumbler, Civil War, Cannon, 34-Star Flag, Eagle, Sword, Footed, 6 1/4 In. ...	935.00
Historical, Tumbler, Civil War, Cannon, Eagle, Flag, 4 3/4 In.	495.00
Historical, Tumbler, Civil War, Footed, Polished Pontil, 6 1/4 In.	935.00
Historical, Tumbler, Civil War, Union For Ever, Constitution On Scroll, 3 1/8 In.	330.00
Historical, Tumbler, Union, Ashburton, Polished Pontil, 3 3/8 In.	770.00
Hobnail pattern is in this book as its own category.	
Holland, Goblet, 5 7/8 In.	250.00

Pressed Glass,
Deer & Dog

Pressed Glass, Dewey

Pressed Glass, Hexagonal Block

Holly, Syrup, Applied Handle, Tin Cover, 6 3/4 In.................................. 180.00
Honeycomb, Tumbler, Variant, Blue, Fiery Opalescent, Scalloped Foot, 4 1/2 In. 210.00
Horn Of Plenty, Bowl, Footed, Pattern Under Foot, 3 3/4 x 7 In..................... 100.00
Horn Of Plenty, Celery Vase, Footed, Wafer Stem, 8 3/4 In......................... 240.00
Horn Of Plenty, Decanter Set, Scalloped Foot, Stopper, Silver Plated Holder, 3 Piece 440.00
Horn Of Plenty, Decanter, Scalloped Foot, Gilt Rim, 13 5/8 In., Pair 275.00
Horn Of Plenty, Sugar & Creamer, Cover, Scalloped Foot, Paneled Finial 440.00
Horse, Cat & Rabbit, Goblet, 6 1/2 In.................................935.00 to 1100.00
Horseshoe, Cake Stand, 6 1/2 x 8 In.. 60.00
Horseshoe, Dish, Oval, Cover, 3-Horseshoe Finial, 5 x 5 1/8 x 8 1/8 In............... 300.00
Hummingbird, Pitcher, Blue, 9 1/4 In.. 180.00
Hummingbird, Pitcher, Milk, 8 In... 100.00
Icicle, Celery Vase, 8 1/2 x 3 5/8 In.. 45.00
Icicle With Chain Band, Goblet, Frosted, 6 1/2 In................................. 100.00
Idyll, Tumbler, Blue, Gold Trim, 4 In... 55.00
Indian Tree, Vase, 8 1/2 x 5 3/4 In... 70.00
Indiana Swirl pattern is listed here as Feather.
Jacob's Ladder, Relish, Amber, 1 3/8 x 5 1/2 x 9 7/8 In............................. 45.00
Jeweled Heart, Cruet, Blue, Gold Trim, Stopper, 7 1/4 In........................... 260.00
Jumbo, Compote, Cover, 12 1/2 In... 1000.00
Jumbo, Mug, 3 5/8 x 3 1/8 In... 250.00
Jumbo, Spoon Rack, 11 1/2 In.. 350.00
Jumbo, Spooner, Ribbed, 5 x 3 3/4 In.. 650.00
Lacy, Bowl, Panel & Sunburst, Cobalt Blue, Scalloped Rim, Oval, 9 In............... 275.00
Lacy, Bowl, Thistle & Rose, Vining Thistle Border, 8 1/8 In......................... 55.00
Lacy, Dish, Openwork, Low Foot, Milky Amethyst 1265.00
Lacy, Nappy, Heart & Shield, Rope Rim, Circular Foot, 4 1/2 In..................... 1320.00
Lacy, Plate, Shell & Circle, Yellow Green, Scallop & Point Rim, 5 3/4 In. 220.00
Lacy, Salt, Flowers, Opaque White, N.E. Glass Co., Boston, 1 3/4 x 3 x 2 1/8 In. 235.00
Lacy, Sugar & Creamer, Cover, Octagonal, Cobalt Blue, Scalloped Rim 715.00
Lacy, Sugar, Cover, Octagon, Cobalt Blue, Scalloped Rim, Base, 3-Step Cover, 7 In. 715.00
Lacy, Sugar, Cover, Octagonal, Sapphire Blue, Stand-Up Scalloped Rim, Footed, 8 In. ... 2200.00
Lacy, Sugar, Cover, Shell & Thistle, Clear, Oval, 1830-1850, 4 1/8 In................ 2700.00
Lattice With Ovals, Cake Stand, Vaseline, 3 1/2 x 8 3/8 In.......................... 160.00
Lattice With Ovals, Syrup, Amber, Britannia Cover, 6 3/4 In......................... 50.00
Liberty Bell, Creamer, Applied Handle, 6 3/4 In.................................... 50.00
Lily-Of-The-Valley, Pitcher, Applied Handle, 8 3/4 x 4 In.......................... 210.00
Lion, Cheese Dish, Frosted, Lion & Tree Trunk Finial, 5 3/4 x 7 5/8 In............... 700.00
Lion, Compote, Cover, Frosted, Lion & Tree Trunk Finial, 10 1/4 x 6 In.............. 400.00
Lion, Cup & Saucer, 2 In. 160.00
Lion, Table Set, 2 1/2 To 4 1/4 In., 4 Piece 280.00
Lion In The Jungle, Goblet, Etched, 6 1/4 In..............................70.00 to 80.00
Lion With Cable, Compote, Cover, Frosted Bowl, Cut, 12 1/2 x 8 In................. 90.00
Loop & Chain Band, Goblet, 6 1/4 In.. 65.00
Magnet & Grape With American Shield & Frosted Leaf, Wine, 3 7/8 In. 100.00
Mario, Pitcher, Hobbs No. 341, Tankard, Amber, 11 5/8 In......................... 140.00
Mario, Pitcher, Hobbs No. 341, Tankard, Etched Leaves, Amber Stain, 11 1/2 In. 190.00
Master Argus, Goblet, Flattened Ball Stem, 5 3/4 In............................... 30.00
Michigan, Goblet 210.00
Michigan, Goblet, Maiden's Blush, Rim & Loops, 5 3/4 In.......................... 70.00
Michigan, Sugar & Creamer, Maiden's Blush, Gold Trim, 3 x 2 5/8 In. 140.00
Monkey, Mug, Deep Amethyst, 3 Balls On Handle, 3 3/8 x 3 In..................... 200.00
Monkey, Mug, Light Blue, 3 Balls On Handle, 3 3/8 x 3 In......................... 275.00
New England Centennial, Goblet, 6 3/4 In... 200.00
New England Pineapple, Compote, 8 1/2 x 10 In................................... 375.00
New England Pineapple, Goblet, 6 In., 6 Piece 315.00
New England Pineapple, Sugar & Creamer, 7 1/2 & 7 In............................ 290.00
New York Honeycomb, Goblet, Fiery Powder Blue, 6 1/4 In......................... 605.00
Paneled Swan, Goblet, 5 5/8 In... 450.00
Pavonia, Celery Vase, Engraved Leaves, Ruby Stain, 7 1/2 x 3 5/8 In................ 70.00
Pheasant, Casserole, Cover, Oval, Frosted, 8 In.................................... 125.00
Pigs In Corn, Goblet, Unbent Husks, 6 In.. 1050.00
Pinafore pattern is listed here as Actress.

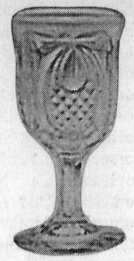

Pressed Glass, Horn of Plenty

Pressed Glass,
Idyll

Pressed Glass,
New England Pineapple

Prayer Rug pattern is listed here as Horseshoe.
Prism & Thumbprint, Vase, Lobed Baluster Stem, Scalloped Edge, Footed, 9 In. 470.00
Roman Key, Goblet, 5 3/4 In. 40.00
Roman Key, Salt, Frosted, Footed, 3 x 2 1/2 In. 70.00
Rosette, Puff Box, Beaded Cover, Opaque Yellow Green, Clambroth Bud Finial, 5 In. . . .   55.00
Sandwich Ivy, Celery Vase, 8 1/2 x 4 1/2 In. 50.00
Sandwich Star, Wine, 4 1/2 In. 265.00
Scalloped Swirl, Compote, Ruby Stain, 7 1/4 x 7 1/2 In. 240.00
Scalloped Swirl, Pitcher, Milk, Ruby Stain, 9 7/8 In. 160.00
Scarab, Goblet, Plain Foot, 6 1/4 In. 180.00
Scroll & Flower, Eggcup, Cobalt Blue, Pleated Rim, Rayed Foot, 2 1/4 In. 75.00
Scroll With Acanthus, Tumbler, Pale Blue Opalescent, 4 In. 55.00
Sheaf & Diamond, Pitcher, Milk, Ruby Stain, 7 1/4 In. . . . . .90.00 to 100.00
Shell & Tassel, Berry Bowl, Amber, Oval, Scalloped Rim, 5 1/2 x 10 In. 40.00
Shell & Tassel, Berry Bowl, Blue, Oval, Scalloped Rim, 5 1/2 x 10 In. . . . . .80.00 to 100.00
Shell & Tassel, Berry Bowl, Vaseline, Oval, Scalloped Rim, 5 1/2 x 10 In. 180.00
Shell & Tassel, Salver, 3 3/4 x 5 3/4 In. 250.00
Shell & Tassel, Salver, 4 1/2 x 7 In. 130.00
Shield, Goblet, 5 7/8 In. 75.00
Shoshone, Goblet, Ruby Stain, 6 1/4 In. 190.00
Shoshone, Tumbler, Amber Stain, Diamonds, 3 5/8 In., Pair 150.00
Singing Birds, Tumbler, Blue & Green Enameled Birds, 4 1/8 In.   75.00
Squirrel, Goblet, 6 In. 600.00
Stars & Bars, Spice Tray, Variant, Clear, Blue, 7 1/4 x 5 5/8 In.   190.00
Stippled Diamonds, Butter, Bell Cover, Metal Clapper, 6 3/4 x 5 7/8 In. 140.00
Sunburst, Bowl, Amber, Rectangular 4 1/2 x 6 1/4 In. 65.00
Sunburst & Diamond, Cruet, Variant, Stopper, Handle 145.00
Swan, Goblet, 5 7/8 In. 495.00
Swan, Goblet, Vaseline, 5 7/8 In. 240.00
Swirl, Ice Cream Set, Frances Decoration, Hobbs No. 326, 7 Piece 230.00
Swirled Rib, Wash Set, Bowl, Pitcher 220.00
Ten Panels, Tumbler, Cobalt Blue, 3 1/2 In. 100.00
Texas, Tumbler, Maiden's Blush Stained Loops, 3 3/4 In. 415.00
Three Face, Champagne, Engraved Fern, Berry, 5 1/2 x 2 7/8 In. 375.00
Three Face, Champagne, Saucer, 4 1/2 x 3 5/8 In. 200.00
Three Face, Claret, 4 3/4 In. 90.00
Three Face, Compote, Covered, 13 x 8 3/8 In. 250.00
Three Face, Goblet, Engraved Fern, 6 3/8 In. 110.00
Three Face, Wine, Engraved Decoration, 4 In. 150.00
Three Graces, see the related pattern Three Face.
Three Presidents, Goblet, Etched, 5 3/4 In. 220.00
Three Printie Block, Vase, Yellow, Gauffered Rim, 9 In., Pair 880.00
Three Sisters pattern is listed here as Three Face.
Tiger, Goblet, Etched, 6 1/4 In. 35.00
Tree Of Life, Cake Stand, Hand Stem, 8 1/4 x 10 1/4 In. 90.00
Tree Of Life, Compote, Sapphire Blue, Hand Stem, 9 x 8 3/4 In.   280.00
Trilby, Goblet, 5 3/4 In. 230.00

Turkey, Candy Dish, Cover, Figural, 7 1/2 In.	135.00
Twist, Goblet, Enameled White Twists, Stepped Foot, 3 1/2 In.	375.00
Two Owls, Compote, Cover, Frosted Owls, Engraved Leaves, Berries, 13 x 8 1/2 In.	325.00
Two Panel, Compote, Cover, Vaseline, 12 3/4 x 7 1/2 x 9 1/8 In.	190.00
U.S. Coin, Butter, Cover, Frosted Coins, c.1892, 6 1/2 In.	520.00
U.S. Coin, Cake Stand, Frosted Coins, c.1892, 6 1/2 x 10 In.	520.00
U.S. Coin, Compote, Cover, Dollar Finial, c.1892, 11 1/2 x 7 In.	750.00
U.S. Coin, Compote, Cover, Dollar Finial, Frosted Coins, c.1892, 9 1/4 x 6 In.	750.00
U.S. Coin, Compote, Cover, Dollar Finial, Frosted Coins, c.1892, 10 1/2 x 7 In.	635.00
U.S. Coin, Compote, Straight Sides, Frosted Coins, c.1892, 6 1/2 x 8 1/4 In.	520.00
U.S. Coin, Dish, Pickle, Frosted Coins, c.1892, 3 3/4 In.	230.00
U.S. Coin, Pitcher, Cranberry, Square Mouth, Rope-Twist Handle, 8 1/2 In.	175.00
U.S. Coin, Pitcher, Milk, Frosted Coins, c.1892, 8 1/2 x 4 In.	978.00
U.S. Coin, Pitcher, Water, Blue Satin, 8 1/2 In.	375.00
U.S. Coin, Sugar, Cover, Dollar Finial, Frosted Coins, c.1892, 7 x 4 In.	315.00
U.S. Coin, Syrup, Pewter Lid, Frosted Coins, c.1884, 7 x 3 1/4 In.	1035.00
U.S. Coin, Toothpick, Frosted Coins, c.1892, 3 In.	290.00
U.S. Coin, Tumbler, Frosted Coins, 10 x 7 In.	750.00
Union Frigate, Plate, 8 Sides, Scallop & Point Rim, 6 1/8 In.	440.00
Valentine pattern is listed here as Trilby.	
Victoria, Pitcher, Water, Engraved Fern, Berry, Ruby Stain, 12 3/8 In.	375.00
Waffle, Compote, Frosted Blocks, Dolphin Stem, 7 1/4 x 8 1/4 In.	160.00
Waffle, Compote, Paneled & Faceted Knop Stem, Scalloped Rim, 9 x 5 In., Pair	250.00
Waffle, Pitcher, Frosted Blocks, Rattlesnake, 10 In.	1250.00
Washington, Celery Vase, 8 1/2 In.	65.00
Wedding Ring, Goblet, 6 In.	90.00
Wedding Ring, Goblet, Facetted Knop Stem, 6 1/4 In.	130.00
Wedding Ring, Wine, Ruby Flashed, 8 In., 6 Piece	115.00
Westward Ho, Champagne, 5 In.	400.00
Westward Ho, Compote, Cover, 8 1/2 In.	815.00
Westward Ho, Compote, Cover, 14 1/2 In.	225.00
Westward Ho, Compote, Cover, Oval, 4 x 6 3/4 In.	170.00
Westward Ho, Goblet, 6 1/2 In.	110.00
Wild Bouquet, Cracker Jar, Teal, Frosted, 8 x 5 In.	325.00
Wolf, Mug, Amber, Tree Branch Handle, 3 3/4 x 3 5/8 In.	30.00

PRINT, in this listing, means any of many printed images produced on paper by one of the more common methods, such as lithography. The prints listed here are of interest primarily to the antiques collector, not the fine arts collector. Many of these prints were originally part of books. Other prints will be found in the Advertising, Currier & Ives, Movie, and Poster categories.

Audubon bird prints were originally issued as part of books printed from 1826 to 1854. They were issued in two sizes, 26 1/2 inches by 39 1/2 inches and 11 inches by 7 inches. The quadrupeds were issued in 28-by-22-inch prints. Later editions of the Audubon books were done in many sizes, and reprints of the books in the original size were also made. The bird pictures have been so popular they have been copied in myriad sizes by both old and new printing methods. This list includes originals and later copies because Audubon prints of all ages are sold in antiques shops.

Audubon, Bird Of Washington Or American Sea Eagle, R. Havell, Jr., 25 3/4 x 38 In.	6038.00
Audubon, Cock Of The Plains, After R. Havell, Frame, c.1837, 11 3/4 x 16 In.	120.00
Audubon, Mallard, Drakes & Hens, 12 x 15 In.	110.00
Audubon, Passenger Pigeon, Columba Migratoria, R. Havell, 29 3/4 x 24 In.	1610.00
Audubon, Passenger Pigeon, R. Havell, 1829, 37 1/2 x 24 1/2 In.	160.00
Audubon, Republican Cliff Swallow, R. Havell, 1829, 19 1/4 x 11 5/8 In.	1069.00
Audubon, Say's Squirrel, Lithograph, J.T. Bowen, Frame, c.1846, 24 1/2 x 30 1/2 In.	770.00
Audubon, Scaup Duck, After R. Havell, Frame, c.1837, 12 x 16 In.	240.00
Audubon, Sharp-Tailed Grouse, After R. Havell, Frame, c.1837, 12 x 16 In.	240.00
Audubon, Swallow-Tailed Hawk, Bien, 25 1/2 x 35 1/2 In.	805.00
Audubon, White-Fronted Goose, R. Havell, 1836, 25 x 39 In.	978.00

Borne, Mortimer, Fishing Boat At Harbor, Etching, Signed, 1928, 16 x 12 In. 115.00
Bufford's, Abraham Quary, Last Indian Of Nantucket Tribe, 19th Century, 10 x 7 In. 355.00
Currier, N., Camping Out, Some Of The Right Sort, Frame, 1836, 18 3/4 x 27 1/4 In. 2400.00
Currier, N., Prairie Hunter, One Rubbed Out, Frame, 1852, 14 1/4 x 21 In. 2280.00
Currier, N., Tacony & Mac, Frame, 1853, 17 1/4 x 26 3/8 In. 960.00
Dali, Salvador, Les Chants De Maldoror, Numbered 6/30, 13 x 10 In. 403.00
Elliot, Daniel, Birds, Lithograph, Hand Colored, New York, 1896, 21 x 13 In., 4 Piece . . . 2185.00
Fox, R. Atkinson, In The Heart Of The Sierra Nevadas 165.00
Gamy, Excelsior On Banked Speedway, Lithograph, Frame, France, 17 1/2 x 34 1/2 In. . . 1495.00
Greenough, Sioux Chief Waa-Pa-Shaw, Color, 1838, 13 1/2 x 19 In. 495.00
Gutmann, Bessie Pease, My Darling 255.00
Gutmann, Bessie Pease, The Newcomer 495.00

Icart prints were made by Louis Icart, who worked in Paris from 1907
as an employee of a postcard company. He then started printing magazines and fashion brochures. About 1910 he created a series of etchings of fashionably dressed women and he continued to make similar
etchings until he died in 1950. He is well known as a printmaker,
painter, and illustrator. Original etchings are much more expensive
than the later photographic copies.

Icart, Devil & Girl, Pastel, Crayon, Matted, Frame, 17 x 10 3/4 In. 1440.00
Icart, La Lettre, Woman In Fancy Dress, Oval, Frame, 19 1/2 x 15 1/2 In. 780.00
Icart, Sleeping Beauty, Oval Matting, 23 1/2 x 27 1/4 In. 1320.00

Jacoulet prints were designed by Paul Jacoulet (1902-1960), a
Frenchman who spent most of his life in Japan. He was a master of
Japanese woodblock print technique. Subjects included life in Japan,
the South Seas, Korea, and China. His prints were sold by subscription
and issued in series. Each series had a distinctive seal, such as a sparrow or butterfly. Most Jacoulet prints are approximately 15 x 10
inches.

Jacoulet, Ancestral Hommage, Shinto Priest, Japan, Peony Seal, c.1956 . . . . 403.00
Jacoulet, Camellia Seeds, Peony Seal, c.1957 . . . . 1150.00
Jacoulet, Chinese Gamblers, Sparrow Seal, c.1941 . . . . 805.00
Jacoulet, December, Peony Seal, c.1953 . . . . 1035.00
Jacoulet, First Love, Yap, West Carolina Islands, c.1937 . . . . 3910.00
Jacoulet, Flowers Of The Distant Islands, South Seas, c.1940 . . . . 5175.00
Jacoulet, Geisha Kiyoka, Tokyo, c.1935 . . . . 1610.00
Jacoulet, God Of Wealth, Courtesan Of The Shimabara, Coin Seal, c.1952 . . . . 1265.00
Jacoulet, Hong Kong, Peony Seal, c.1958 . . . . 2013.00
Jacoulet, Hunchback, Ivy Seal, c.1952 . . . . 518.00
Jacoulet, Indian Poetess, c.1941 . . . . 1095.00
Jacoulet, Joaquina & Her Mother At Sermon By Father Pons, Owl Seal, c.1947 . . . . 300.00
Jacoulet, Kiyoshi, Tokyo, c.1939 . . . . 1035.00
Jacoulet, Korean Baby In Ceremonial Costume, c.1934 . . . . 920.00
Jacoulet, Laundress, Coree, Peony Seal, c.1955 . . . . 1095.00
Jacoulet, Little Robbers, Left View, Peony Seal, c.1959 . . . . 1035.00
Jacoulet, Living God, Owl Seal, c.1952 . . . . 805.00
Jacoulet, Longevity, Peach Seal, c.1948 . . . . 345.00
Jacoulet, Man Of Yap, West Carolina Islands, c.1935 . . . . 1150.00
Jacoulet, Master Potter, c.1940 . . . . 1725.00
Jacoulet, Mr. Chikabumi, An Old Ainu Man, Hokkaido, Owl Seal, c.1950 . . . . 1380.00
Jacoulet, Mysterious Pacific, Peach Seal, c.1951 . . . . 8165.00
Jacoulet, Nautilus Shell, Yap, Peony Seal, c.1958 . . . . 2760.00
Jacoulet, On Tinian Island, Marianes, Peony Seal, c.1960 . . . . 4370.00
Jacoulet, Paul, Man Yap, West Carolina Islands, Signed 15 x 18 In. 1120.00
Jacoulet, Paul, Shimabara Koyto Japan, 14 x 19 In. 748.00
Jacoulet, Red Lacquer Mirror, Tokyo, c.1938 . . . . 1610.00
Jacoulet, Returning From The Jungle, Sparrow Seal, c.1948 . . . . 1095.00
Jacoulet, Rock Of Jokadj, Ponape, East Carolinas, c.1936 . . . . 1265.00
Jacoulet, Son Who Mourns His Father, Ivy Seal, c.1948 . . . . 690.00
Jacoulet, Two Brothers, Izu, Japan, c.1936 . . . . 690.00
Jacoulet, Watermelons, c.1939 . . . . 1150.00

Jacoulet, Yagourough & Mio, Yap, West Carolina Islands, c.1938 .... 4370.00
Jacoulet, Young Girl Of Fiji, Oceania, c.1935 .... 1150.00

Japanese woodblock prints are listed as follows: Print, Japanese, name
of artist, title or description, type, and size. Dealers use the following
terms: Tate-e is a vertical composition. Yoko-e is a horizontal composition. The words Aiban (13 by 9 inches), Chuban (10 by 7 1/2 inches),
Hosoban (13 by 6 inches), Oban (15 by 10 inches), and Koban (7 by 4
inches) denote approximate size. Modern versions of some of these
prints have been made. Other woodblock prints that are not Japanese
are listed under Print, Woodblock.

Japanese, Distant View Of Mio From Ejiri, Harbor Scene, Green Sea, 10 x 15 In. 405.00
Japanese, Eisen, 2 Ladies With Child Flying Kite, 15 x 10 In. 835.00
Japanese, Eisen, Lady Arranging Flowers Beneath Temple Cartouche, 15 x 10 In. 259.00
Japanese, Eisen, Lady With Puppy On Shoulder, 15 x 10 In. 1095.00
Japanese, Eisen, Woman In Dragon Kimono Beneath Cherry Tree, 15 x 10 In. 127.00
Japanese, Eishi, Lady Adjusting Hair, Sitting On A Go Board, 15 x 10 In. 1555.00
Japanese, Eishi, Lady In Green Kimono Holding Fan, 29 x 5 In. 980.00
Japanese, Fireworks At Rygyoku Bridge, 15 x 10 In. 2300.00
Japanese, Hasui Kawase, Canal Scene, House, Figures, Rain, Tate-e 345.00
Japanese, Hasui Kawase, Child With Ball, Tate-e 316.00
Japanese, Hasui Kawase, Moon Over Matsue, Buildings, Tate-e, 1924 .... 1440.00
Japanese, Hasui Kawase, Moonrise At Futago Island, Frame, Yoko-e 259.00
Japanese, Hasui Kawase, Night Scene, Riverside Buildings, Tate-e, 1936 .... 1150.00
Japanese, Hasui Kawase, Night Scene, Temple Stairway, Tate-e, 1935 .... 865.00
Japanese, Hasui Kawase, River View, Cherry, Pine Trees, Tate-e, 1934 .... 920.00
Japanese, Hasui Kawase, Snow At Mukojima, Tate-e 375.00
Japanese, Hasui Kawase, Snow At Temple, Tate-e 405.00
Japanese, Hasui Kawase, Sunset At Morigasaki, Frame, c.1930, 14 x 9 1/4 In. 863.00
Japanese, Hasui Kawase, Sunset, Figures, Cottage At Lakeside, Tate-e, 1936 .... 1380.00
Japanese, Hasui Kawase, Temple In Snow, Figure, Tate-e, 1925 .... 1610.00
Japanese, Hasui Kawase, Temple, Fall Foliage, Watanabe Publishing, Tate-e 546.00
Japanese, Hasui Kawase, Zaimoku Island At Matsushima, Signed, 14 1/4 x 9 In. 920.00
Japanese, Hiroshige II, Boats & Swimmers In River, 15 x 10 In. 276.00
Japanese, Hiroshige II, Snow Scene With Boats In Harbor, 15 x 10 In. 949.00
Japanese, Hiroshige II, View Of Nagasaki & Woman With Telescope, 15 x 10 In. 259.00
Japanese, Hiroshige, Bird On Prunus Branch, 13 x 9 In. 1065.00
Japanese, Hiroshige, Bridge & Fireworks, 10 x 15 In. 316.00
Japanese, Hiroshige, Bridge, Willow, 36 Views Of Mount Fuji, Tate-e 370.00
Japanese, Hiroshige, City View From Temple, 10 x 15 In. 200.00
Japanese, Hiroshige, Clear Weather After Snow At Kameyama, Travelers, 10 x 15 In. 403.00
Japanese, Hiroshige, Clear Weather After Snow, Kanda Myojin Shrine, Tate-e 127.00
Japanese, Hiroshige, Figures Enjoying Cherry Blossoms, 10 x 15 In. 210.00
Japanese, Hiroshige, Fishermen On Canal, 10 x 15 In. 210.00
Japanese, Hiroshige, From Famous Teahouses In Edo, Signed, 9 x 14 In. 690.00
Japanese, Hiroshige, Futami Bay In Ise Province, View Of Mt. Fuji, 15 x 10 In. 460.00
Japanese, Hiroshige, Goyu On Tokaido Road, Figures, Willow Trees, Tate-e 230.00
Japanese, Hiroshige, Iki Island, Frame, 13 x 8 1/2 In. 920.00
Japanese, Hiroshige, Kanasugi Bridge At Shibaura, Poles, Banners, Tate-e 380.00
Japanese, Hiroshige, Mount Fuji, Figures, Tate-e 375.00
Japanese, Hiroshige, Ocean View Slope Near Shirasuka, 10 x 15 In. 489.00
Japanese, Hiroshige, Province Of Hizen, Frame, 13x 8 1/2 In. 690.00
Japanese, Hiroshige, Province Of Kai, 13 x 9 In. 865.00
Japanese, Hiroshige, Shops Selling Arimatsu Cloth, Narumi, Tate-e 1065.00
Japanese, Hiroshige, Snow Scene Along River, Tate-e 230.00
Japanese, Hiroshige, Toji, Kyoto, Signed, 14 x 10 In. 545.00
Japanese, Hokuba Teisai, Geisha & Immortal, Signed, 38 1/4 x 12 In. 1955.00
Japanese, Koitsu, Akiba Shrine, Tate-e 290.00
Japanese, Koitsu, Cherry Tree Bridge, Signed, Tate-e 605.00
Japanese, Koitsu, Eagle Owl, Tate-e 405.00
Japanese, Koitsu, Fishing Boats Leaving Shore, Frame, Yoko-e 144.00
Japanese, Koitsu, Mill In Snow, Sunset, Tate-e, 1935 .... 540.00
Japanese, Koitsu, Pine Tree, Lake, Moonlight, Frame, Tate-e 150.00

Japanese, Koitsu, Plum Tree In Farmyard, Tate-e 460.00
Japanese, Koitsu, Temple Scene, Moonlight, Tate-e 518.00
Japanese, Koitsu, Temple Scene, Rain, Yoko-e 255.00
Japanese, Koitsu, Ukimido Temple, Snow, Frame, Tate-e 345.00
Japanese, Kunisada II, From Tale Of Genji, Frame, 13 x 9 In., Pair 196.00
Japanese, Kunisada, 2 Samurai Practice Fencing, c.1850, 9 3/4 x 13 3/4 In. 165.00
Japanese, Kunisada, Night Attack Of Samurai Group, c.1850, 9 3/4 x 13 3/4 In. 165.00
Japanese, Kunisada, Old Samurai Reaches For Sword, c.1850, 9 3/4 x 13 3/4 In. 175.00
Japanese, Kunisada, Samurai At Court, Removes Helmet, c.1850, 9 3/4 x 13 3/4 In. 160.00
Japanese, Kunisada, Samurai Clutching Long Sword & Fan, c.1850, 9 3/4 x 13 3/4 In. 170.00
Japanese, Kunisada, Samurai On Garden Wall, c.1850, 9 3/4 x 13 3/4 In. 165.00
Japanese, Kunisada, Samurai On Porch Drawing Sword, c.1850, 9 3/4 x 13 3/4 In. 165.00
Japanese, Kunisada, Woman & Child, Tate-e 185.00
Japanese, Kunisada, Woman On Water Buffalo, Snow Scene Background, 10 x 7 1/2 In. . 425.00
Japanese, Kunisada, Woman Washing Clothes, Tate-e 219.00
Japanese, Kunisato, Gods Of Good Fortune, Mount Fuji, Tate-e 115.00
Japanese, Kuniyoshi, Pearl Diver, Woman Silhouetted Against Full Moon, 15 x 10 In. ... 173.00
Japanese, Kuniyoshi, Woman Grasping Koto, Cartouche, Tate-e 575.00
Japanese, Kuniyoshi, Woman Holding Leaf Crown, Cartouche, Tate-e 405.00
Japanese, Kuniyoshi, Woman In Checked Kimono, Holding Sake Cup, 15 x 10 In. 405.00
Japanese, Kuniyoshi, Woman On Waves, Tate-e 200.00
Japanese, Kuniyoshi, Woman With Doll, Tate-e 230.00
Japanese, Kuniyoshi, Woman With Water Buckets, Birds Flying, Tate-e 545.00
Japanese, Kuniyoshi, Woman With Writing Box, Tate-e 275.00
Japanese, Sadanobu, Woman In Peony-Decorated Kimono Under Cherry Tree, 15 x 10 In. 275.00
Japanese, Shigenobu, Figures On Balcony Overlooking Nihonbashi At Night, 15 x 10 In. . 219.00
Japanese, Shiro Kasamatsu, Boathouse Scene, Blue, Tate-e, 1956 .... 175.00
Japanese, Shiro Kasamatsu, Temple Scene, Tate-e 175.00
Japanese, Shiro Kasamatsu, Temple, Snow Covered, Tate-e 345.00
Japanese, Shoson Ohara, Birds & Water Landscape, Frame, 14 x 9 In., Pair 460.00
Japanese, Shotei, Watanabe, Autumn Moon With Geese, Signed, 17 1/4 x 19 1/2 In. 1150.00
Japanese, Shuncho, 2 Warriors, Horse, Tate-e 145.00
Japanese, Shuncho, Figures Viewing Bonsai, Tate-e 635.00
Japanese, Sumiyoshi Hironao, Mount Fuji, Signed, 14 x 22 In. 345.00
Japanese, Toyokuni I, 4 Ladies In Tea House, Tate-e, c.1840 .... 690.00
Japanese, Toyokuni I, Woman In Kimono, Walking In Garden, Pink, Black, Leaf, Tate-e . 949.00
Japanese, Toyokuni II, Lady In Chrysanthemum-Decorated Robe, Tate-e 405.00
Japanese, Toyokuni II, Lady In Dragon & Leaf Kimono, Tate-e 230.00
Japanese, Toyokuni II, Lady In Lavender & Pink Kimono, 15 x 10 In. 604.00
Japanese, Toyokuni II, Woman With Sword Views Man In Boat, 15 x 10 In. 316.00
Japanese, Toyokuni III, Figures On Road Beneath Mt. Fuji, 10 x 15 In. 230.00
Japanese, Toyokuni III, Man In Costume, Horse Design, Tate-e 290.00
Japanese, Toyokuni III, Warrior With Sword, Mirror Print, Tate-e 460.00
Japanese, Toyokuni III, Woman Looking At Cloth, Mount Fuji Cartouche, Tate-e 150.00
Japanese, Toyokuni III, Woman, Red & Black Checked Kimono, At Seashore, 15 x 10 In. 219.00
Japanese, Utamaro, 2 Geisha, Seated, Standing, Tate-e 632.00
Japanese, Utamaro, Lady Serving Sake, 15 x 10 In. 2300.00
Japanese, Utamaro, Lady, Bonsai Blooming, Tate-e 230.00
Japanese, Utamaro, Man, 2 Women, Falcon, Tate-e 259.00
Japanese, Yokohama, Triptych, Fireworks On River, Signed, 19th Century, 13 1/2 x 9 In. . 259.00
Japanese, Yoshida Hiroshi, Caravan From Afghanistan, Moonlight, Frame, 9 1/2 x 15 In. . 489.00
Japanese, Yoshida Hiroshi, Eboshidake, Signed 1035.00
Japanese, Yoshida Hiroshi, Gate To The Stupa Of Sanchi, Signed, 14 1/2 x 10 In. 546.00
Japanese, Yoshida Hiroshi, Himeiji Castle, Frame, Tate-e 105.00
Japanese, Yoshida Hiroshi, Otenjo, Signed, 9 1/2 x 14 In. 1955.00
Japanese, Yoshida Hiroshi, River, Bridge, House, Trees, Signed, Yoko-e 978.00
Japanese, Yoshida Hiroshi, Shinobazu Pond, Signed, 14 1/2 x 9 1/2 In. 575.00
Japanese, Yoshida Hiroshi, The Horse Turnback At Umagaeshi, Signed, 14 x 9 1/2 In. .. 1495.00
Japanese, Yoshida Hiroshi, Yasaka Shrine, Signed, Frame, 14 1/2 x 9 1/2 In. 489.00
Japanese, Yoshida Hiroshi, Yatsugatake, Signed, 9 1/2 x 14 In. 2185.00
Japanese, Yoshiiku, Man With Sword & Woman Kneeling At His Feet, 15 x 10 In. 230.00
John Lennon Portrait, International Print Society, Etching, On Paper, c.1983, 25 x 22 In. 380.00
Kelly, Thomas, Midnight Race On Mississippi, Lithograph, Frame, 23 1/2 x 29 In. 470.00

Linocut, Whittemore, Margaret, Twin Buttes, Colored, Oak Frame, 7 1/4 x 10 In. 403.00
Lithograph, Bachman, Bird's-Eye View, Niagara Falls, 1851, 21 3/8 x 31 1/8 In. 1800.00
Lithograph, North American Indian Portfolio Plate 25, c.1844, 17 1/4 x 12 In. 1920.00

Nutting prints are now popular with collectors. Wallace Nutting is
known for his pictures, furniture, and books. Nutting *prints* are actually hand-colored photographs issued from 1900 to 1941. There are   *Wallace Nutting*
over 10,000 different titles. Wallace Nutting furniture is listed in the
Furniture category.

Nutting, A Basket Full, Floral 2200.00
Nutting, A Colonial Window ...'..................................... 965.00
Nutting, A Knight Errant Vase, Floral 2255.00
Nutting, An Eventful Journey, Signed, 9 3/8 x 7 1/2 In. 290.00
Nutting, April In Sheep Pastures, Sheep 800.00
Nutting, Distinction, Floral 965.00
Nutting, First Proposal 770.00
Nutting, Going For The Doctor, Child 1375.00
Nutting, Good Bye 1815.00
Nutting, Italian Arches 798.00
Nutting, Little Washerwoman, Amalfi 770.00
Nutting, Milford Water, New England Church Reflecting In River, 14 x 16 In. 160.00
Nutting, Spring In The Dell, 6 1/2 x 4 3/4 In. 55.00

Parrish prints are wanted by collectors. Maxfield Frederick Parrish
was an illustrator who lived from 1870 to 1966. He is best known as a   *Maxfield Parrish*
designer of magazine covers, posters, calendars, and advertisements.

Parrish, 2 Cooks With Spoons, 13 3/4 x 11 1/2 In. 46.00
Parrish, Canyon, 15 x 12 In. 440.00
Parrish, Chef Carrying Cauldron, 13 3/4 x 11 1/2 In. 28.00
Parrish, Dawn, Bronze-Finish Frame, 17 1/2 x 29 1/2 In. 295.00
Parrish, Daybreak, 1922, 30 x 18 In. 225.00
Parrish, Evening, 1922, 16 1/2 x 13 1/2 In. 300.00
Parrish, Misty Morn, 1956, 10 1/4 x 8 3/4 In. 260.00
Parrish, Modern Magic Shoes, 10 3/4 x 8 7/8 In. 90.00
Parrish, New Moon, 1958, 10 1/4 x 8 3/4 In. 172.00
Parrish, Page, 1928, 13 x 10 1/2 In. 85.00
Parrish, Potato Peelers, 13 3/4 x 11 1/2 In. 55.00
Parrish, Stars, 18 x 30 In. 528.00
Parrish, With Trumpet & Drum, Giltwood Swiveling Desktop Frame, c.1904, 7 x 5 In. 350.00
Pescheret, Leon, Mountainous Desert Scene, Woods, Etching, Frame, Matted, 17 x 13 In. 575.00
Stowell, M. Louise, Lithograph, Imprimerie-Chaix, Man Signing Books, c.1897, 9 x 13 In. 115.00
Terpning, Offerings To Sun, Western Scene, Indian On Horseback, 25 3/4 x 34 In. 635.00

Woodblock prints that are not in the Japanese tradition are listed here.
Most were made in England and the United States during the Arts and
Crafts period. Japanese woodblock prints are listed under Print,
Japanese.

Woodblock, Arts & Crafts Lamp, Tile, Stickley Table, Oak Frame, 10 x 12 In. 240.00
Woodblock, Baumann, Gustave, Eagle Ceremony At Tesque Pueblo, 6 1/2 x 6 1/2 In. 865.00
Woodblock, Baumann, Gustave, Martha's Alley, Signed, Matted, Frame, 13 1/2 x 10 In. ... 1955.00
Woodblock, Baumann, Gustave, Men Cleaning Fish, Frame, c.1917, 10 x 11 In. 3450.00
Woodblock, Baumann, Gustave, Summer Breeze, Arts & Crafts, 1916, 11 x 10 In. 3750.00
Woodblock, Bixler, David, Prodigal Son, Hand Colored, Lancaster Co., Penn., 4 x 3 In. ... 2475.00
Woodblock, Bixler, David, Seated Woman, Hand Colored, 3 3/4 x 2 3/4 In. 2200.00
Woodblock, Chase, Waldo, Nomad, Boat, Sunset, Signed, Frame, 1932, 12 x 7 In. 1265.00
Woodblock, Dow, Arthur Wesley, Flower Designs, Signed, Oak Frame, 7 x 7 1/2 In. 865.00
Woodblock, Dow, Arthur Wesley, Houses, Trees, Arts & Crafts Oak Frame, 5 1/2 x 4 In. . 1265.00
Woodblock, Droege, Oscar, Lake & Mountain In Snow, Colored, Frame, 8 x 13 3/4 In. .. 460.00
Woodblock, Gearhart, Frances, Low Tide, Coast Scene, 11 x 10 In. 3740.00
Woodblock, Gerhardt, Frances, Mountains & Trees, Matted, Frame, 5 1/2 x 9 In. 2530.00
Woodblock, Hoffines, Vera, Trees, Colored, Oak Frame, 6 x 10 3/4 In. 403.00
Woodblock, Hyde, Helen, Asian Mother Bathing Child, Signed, Dated 1905, 10 x 16 In. . 405.00
Woodblock, Hyde, Helen, Mother & Children, Colored, Frame, Signed, 5 x 21 1/2 In. ... 635.00

Woodblock, Hyde, Helen, The Greeting, 2 Children Bowing, Ming Trees, 1910, 6 x 6 In. .	650.00
Woodblock, Hyde, Helen, Three Friends Of Winter, 1913, 5 x 8 In.	430.00
Woodblock, Keith, Elizabeth, Asian House, At Shore, Palm Trees, Frame, 10 x 14 1/2 In. .	175.00
Woodblock, Keith, Elizabeth, Forbidden City, Peking, Signed, Yoko-e, 1935	518.00
Woodblock, Keith, Elizabeth, Lama Temple, Peking, Signed, Yoko-e, 1922	750.00
Woodblock, Keith, Elizabeth, Moro Vintas, Sulu, Signed, Yoko-e, 1924	375.00
Woodblock, Keith, Elizabeth, Shigiyama, Actor, Tate-e	1322.00
Woodblock, Keith, Elizabeth, Te-Sheng-Men, Peking, Signed, Tate-e, 1921	635.00
Woodblock, Keith, Elizabeth, Ying Lin Monastery, Figures, Signed, Tate-e, 1925	1295.00
Woodblock, Lum, Bertha, 2 Asian Women, Colored, Bamboo Frame, 14 1/2 x 5 In.	690.00
Woodblock, Lum, Bertha, 3 Men On Camels In Desert, Dated 1921, 9 1/2 x 16 1/2 In. . . .	489.00
Woodblock, Lum, Bertha, House, Garden, Chufu, Signed, 1924	430.00
Woodblock, Lum, Bertha, Japanese Children Flying Kites, Frame, 1913, 8 x 14 In.	805.00
Woodblock, Lum, Bertha, Landscape, Flowers, Bird Flock, 10 1/2 x 12 1/2 In.	405.00
Woodblock, Lum, Bertha, Pine Trees By Sea, Signed, Yoko-e, 1912	375.00
Woodblock, Lum, Bertha, Sailboats, Paths, Trees, Colored, 12 1/2 x 8 1/2 In.	920.00
Woodblock, Lum, Bertha, Shrine, Figure With Umbrella, Signed, Tate-e, 1936	230.00
Woodblock, Lum, Bertha, Wave, Signed, Frame, 1932, 36 x 23 In.	1955.00
Woodblock, Lum, Bertha, Wedding Banners, Figures, Signed, 20 x 25 In.	575.00
Woodblock, Lum, Bertha, Woman In Waves, Signed, 1918, 29 x 17 In.	1095.00
Woodblock, Miller, Lilian May, Cathedral Cliffs, Diamond Mountains, Tate-e	374.00
Woodblock, Miller, Lilian May, Dwarf Plum Tree, Tate-e	375.00
Woodblock, Miller, Lilian May, Snow On Temple Roofs, Signed, Yoko-e	259.00
Woodblock, Rice, William S., Glacial Lake Sierras, Black & White, Frame, 6 x 8 In.	748.00
Woodblock, Rice, William S., Buoy, Sailboat, Green, Blue, Gold, Frame, c.1936, 6 x 4 In.	2185.00
Woodblock, Schmidt-Wolfratshausen, Karl, Mountain Lake, Frame, c.1925, 12 x 15 In. . .	345.00
Woodblock, Seiler, Willie, Heartbroken, Signed, 12 1/4 x 8 1/2 In.	175.00
Woodblock, Summer, Young Girl Picking Flowers, Hand Colored, Frame, 9 x 7 In.	120.00
Woodblock, Tyson, Dorothy, Procession, Colored, Frame, 6 1/2 x 8 1/4 In.	259.00
Woodblock, Falilecft, W., Landscape Scene, Signed, Frame 10 1/2 x 7 1/2 In.	460.00

PURINTON POTTERY COMPANY was incorporated in Wellsville, Ohio, in 1936. The company moved to Shippenville, Pennsylvania, in 1941 and made a variety of hand-painted ceramic wares. By the 1950s Purinton was making dinnerware, souvenirs, cookie jars, and florist wares. The pottery closed in 1959.

Apple, Chop Plate, 12 In.	70.00
Apple, Teapot, 6 Cup, Domed Cover, 6 1/2 In.	75.00
Daisy, Canister, Coffee, Cobalt Blue Trim	160.00
Daisy, Canister, Flour, Cobalt Blue Trim	160.00
Daisy, Canister, Sugar, Cobalt Blue Trim	160.00
Daisy, Canister, Tea, Cobalt Blue Trim	160.00
Fruit, Jug, 2 Qt.	35.00
Fruit, Oil & Vinegar, Square, 5 In.	50.00
Fruit, Relish, 3 Sections, Wooden Center Handle, Apple, Grapes, 10 In.	45.00
Fruit, Salt & Pepper, 4 In.	30.00
Fruit, Teapot, Individual, 2 Cup, 4 In.	50.00
Intaglio, Baker, Ivory, Brown Slip, 7 In.	22.00
Intaglio, Bowl, 8 In.	5.00
Intaglio, Casserole, Cover, Brown, Oval, Handles, 7 In.	55.00
Intaglio, Cookie Jar, Brown, Square, Wooden Lid, 9 1/2 x 6 In.	75.00
Intaglio, Jam Jar, Cover, Brown	50.00
Intaglio, Mug, Ivory, Brown Slip, 4 In.	18.00
Intaglio, Plate, 6 3/4 In.	6.50
Intaglio, Plate, 8 1/2 In.	10.00
Intaglio, Plate, 9 3/4 In.	13.00
Intaglio, Plate, Divided	12.00
Intaglio, Platter, 12 In.	25.00
Intaglio, Relish, 2 Sections, 10 In.	30.00
Intaglio, Saucer	4.00
Intaglio, Sugar, Cover, Ivory, Brown Slip	20.00
Mountain Rose, Planter, Basket, 6 1/4 In.	60.00
Mountain Rose, Teapot, Cover, 2 Cup	50.00

Normandy Plaid, Canister Set, Lazy Susan, 4 Sections, 10 x 10 In. 190.00
Normandy Plaid, Jug, 2 Qt., 7 1/2 In. 110.00
Open Apple, Chop Plate, 12 In. 70.00
Open Apple, Teapot, 6 1/2 In. . . . . .75.00 to 90.00
Red Ivy, Creamer, 3 1/2 In. 15.00
Red Ivy, Jug, Honey, 6 1/4 In. 35.00
Red Ivy, Teapot, 4 Cup, 5 In. 25.00

PURSES have been recognizable since the eighteenth century, when
leather and needlework purses were preferred. Beaded purses became
popular in the nineteenth century, went out of style, but are again in
use. Mesh purses date from the 1880s and are still being made. How to
carry a handkerchief and lipstick is a problem today for every woman,
including the Queen of England.

Alligator, Leather, Black, Rectangular, Front Flap Closure, 2 Compartments, Hermes 764.00
Basket, Nantucket-Style, Lidded 129.00
Basket, Oval, Scrimshaw On Lid, B. O'Neill, Swing Hoop Handle, Nantucket, 7 x 8 In. . .   1840.00
Basket, Wooden Base, Lid Disks, Bentwood Swing Handle, Nantucket, 1982, 10 x 7 In. . .   220.00
Beaded, Black, Faceted, Gold Braid, Lining, Simon, 1960s, 11 x 7 1/2 x 2 1/2 In. 100.00
Beaded, Blue, Rounded Box Shape, Rope Handle, Josef, 3 1/4 x 6 3/4 x 4 1/2 In. 100.00
Beaded, Flower Design, Beaded Tassels, Victorian 200.00
Beaded, Geometric Design, Blue Beads, Gold, Silver, Metal Frame, c.1875, 9 In. 58.00
Beaded, Glasses Case, Flowers, White & Gold Ground, Silk Lining, France, 1950s 95.00
Beaded, Hearts & Diamonds, 2 Beaded Handles, Gold Link Chain, 7 x 6 1/2 x 4 In. 95.00
Beaded, Ivory, Pearl, 7 x 5 1/4 In. 45.00
Beaded, Metal Closure, Chain Handle, Walborg, 7 1/4 x 4 1/2 x 1 3/8 In. 48.00
Beaded, Seed Pearls, Pastel Blue, Pink, Turquoise, Green, Violet, Gold, Handle, 6 x 8 In. .   100.00
Beaded, Tambour Stitch, Satin Lining, 8 x 5 In. 100.00
Beaded, White, Pink, Yellow, Clear, Light Blue, Walborg, Japan, 6 x 4 x 3 In. 95.00
Beaded, White, Whiting & Davis 100.00
Celluloid, Evening, Black & Brass, Dark Lilac, Velvet Lined 100.00
Cloth, Black, Matching Wallet, Attached Coin Purse 18.00
Cloth, Half Circle Shape, Navy, Handle, 1940s, 7 x 5 In. 30.00
Coin, Tweed, Brown, Gold Tone Coin Motif, Leather Trim, Snap Closure, 13 x 9 In. 95.00
Flamestitch, Multicolored, New England, 18th Century 695.00
Knit, Clutch, Rhinestone Circle Flap Pin, 7 1/2 x 4 In. 10.00
Leather, Black, Tan, Sac De Voyage Airport, Stitch Handles, Hermes, 151/2 x 17 1/2 In. .   4585.00
Leather, Embossed, Goldenrod Color, 10 x 8 x 3 1/2 In. 95.00
Leather, Herbag, Black, Canvas, Silver Tone, Interchangeable Bags, Hermes, 15 1/4 In. . .   590.00
Leather, Kelly, Black, Gold Tone Fittings, Padlock Closure, Hermes, 12 1/2 In. 2235.00
Leather, Painted, House, Mt. Fuji, Carved Ivory Clasp & Netsuke, Japan, 19th Century . .   210.00
Leather, Pink, Straps, Fred Hayman, Beverly Hills 99.00
Leather, Silk, Gold Chain, Buttons, Emilio Pucci 265.00
Leather, Sport Kelly, Black, Brown, Gold Tone Fittings, Hermes, 11 3/8 In. 1645.00
Leather, Tooled, Red Strips, Celluloid Latch, Stamped, Meeker, 1920s, 7 1/2 In. . . . . *Illus*   650.00
Linen, Hand Embroidered, Arts & Crafts Design, 10 1/2 In. 115.00
Lucite, Amber, Marbleized, Signed, Wilardy 348.00
Lucite, Cigarette Case, Sterling Overlay, Floral, c.1950, 5 x 3 In. 95.00
Lucite, Evening, White & Gold, Leather Lined, Neiman Marcus 100.00
Lucite, White, Clear, Texture 210.00
Mesh, 14K Gold, 2 Sugarloaf Sapphires, Floral & Scroll Frame, Link Chain, Edwardian . .   1116.00
Mesh, 14K Gold, Blue Cabochon Stones, Edwardian, Inscribed L.S. Scoville 880.00
Mesh, 14K Gold, Engraved Flowers & Leaves Clasp, Curb Link Chain, Edwardian 880.00
Mesh, 14K Gold, Interior Coin Purse 705.00
Mesh, Chain, Bullet Trim, 1920s, 3 3/4 x 3 1/2 In. 95.00
Mesh, Dresden, Pink, Green, Blue Flowers, Yellow Ground, Whiting & Davis, 8 1/2 In. . .   280.00
Mesh, Gold Tone, White Enamel, Diagonal Stripe, Etched Frame 185.00
Mesh, Gold Tone, Whiting & Davis 145.00
Mesh, Ivory, Hot Pink, Lime Green, Silver Frame, Whiting & Davis, 7 x 4 In. 310.00
Mesh, Mandalian, Enameled White, Turquoise, Gold Flowers, Scroll, Bird Clasp, 7 1/4 In.   96.00
Mesh, Sterling, Blackinton Art Nouveau, Lady Flows Into Flowers, Relief Frame, 6 In. . . .   295.00
Mesh, Taffeta Lining, Knob Clasp, Snake Handle, Whiting & Davis, 8 x 6 In. 180.00
Molded Plastic, Silver Cat, Applied Rosettes, Gray, Lucite Handle . . . . *Illus*   353.00

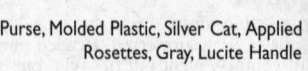

Purse, Leather, Tooled, Red Strips,
Celluloid Latch, Stamped, Meeker,
1920s, 7 1/2 In.

Purse, Molded Plastic, Silver Cat, Applied
Rosettes, Gray, Lucite Handle

Needlework, Flame Stitch, Clutch, Cream Colored Seed Beads, Art Deco Style, France	95.00
Needlework, Flame Stitch, Wool, Green, Yellow, Pink, Purple, 2 Pockets, 1772, 8 x 8 In.	2645.00
Needlework, Silk, Wool Yarn, Irish Stitch, Diamond, Zigzag, c.1818, 2 1/2 x 3 In.	440.00
Pearl, Strap, Zipper Across Top	35.00
Pigskin, Kelly, Hermes, 1998, 11 In.	1998.00
Plastic, Clear, Rhinestones, Silver Tone Closure, Chain, 9 x 5 1/2 In.	48.00
Plastic, Molded, Brass Chain Strap, Italy	125.00
Plastic, Transparent, Kelly, Muy Pronto, Barcelona Fashion Show, Hermes, 1999	235.00
Pouchette, Black Suede, Gold Tone, Peham Bit, Curb Chain, Velvet Pouch, Hermes	499.00
Rhinestones, Enamel Clasp, Hand Painted, Chain, France	265.00
Satin, Black, Embroidered, Swarovski Crystals, Clutch, Judith Leiber, 6 x 9 In.	920.00
Silver, Rhinestone Clasp, Whiting & Davis	85.00
Silver Threads, Clutch, Light Blue	35.00
Sterling, Clutch, Rectangular, Banded, Vermeil	325.00
Sterling Silver, 2 Compartments, Mirror, Initials, Chain, Bellis, 3 1/2 x 2 1/2 In.	850.00
Straw, Interior Zippered Compartment, Cloth Lining, Lucite Handles, 6 1/2 x 3 1/2 x 6 In.	18.00
Suede, Black, Telephone Shape, Gold Dial, Receiver Is Frame, Anne Marie	850.00
Velvet, Black, Rhinestone Clasp	24.00
Vinyl, Half Circle Shape, Leather, Tan, Beige, Cloth Lining, Noray	30.00
Wicker, Red, Wooden Handle, Metal Fitting, Zippered Pocket, c.1960, 12 1/2 x 4 x 7 In.	11.00
Wooden, Box, Hand Painted Flowers, Decoupage Gold Foil, Felt Lining, 5 1/8 x 8 1/8 In.	20.00
Wooden, Original Box Bag, Whimsical Decoration, Enid Collins, 1965	45.00
Wooden, Oval, Marine Ivory Carved Shell, Hinged Lid, Swing Handle, 10 1/2 In.	1095.00
Woven Metal, 6 Sides, Gold, Faux Tortoise Shell, Dorset Rex, 5 1/8 x 6 11/16 In.	145.00

QUEZAL glass was made from 1901 to 1924 by Martin Bach, Sr., in
Queens, New York. Other glassware by other firms, such as Loetz,
Steuben, and Tiffany, resembles this gold-colored iridescent glass.
Martin Bach died in 1921. His son-in-law, Conrad Vahlsing, Jr., went
to work at the Lustre Art Company about 1920 and his son, Martin
Bach, Jr., worked at the Durand Art Glass division of the Vineland
Flint Glass Works after 1924.

Quezal

Bowl, Iridescent Green, Ribbed, Shaped Rim, 6 7/8 In.	200.00
Chandelier, 6-Light, Hanging Arms, Pulled Feathers, Shades, Brass, 1900s	1600.00
Compote, Iridescent Blue-Green, Amber Stem, Signed, 6 1/4 In.	805.00
Compote, Iridescent Gold, Waisted Bowl, Blue-Gold Knopped Stem, Signed, 4 1/2 In.	1035.00
Compote, Iridescent Green Rim, Shaded To Blue, Gold Center, 9 1/2 In.	750.00
Compote, Yellow, Iridescent Gold, White Pulled Feathers, Ruffled Rim, 5 1/2 x 7 In.	2530.00
Lamp, Hanging, Pulled Feathers, Green Band, Flared Mouth, Art Nouveau Links, 16 In.	2800.00
Nightlight, Green Pulled Feathers On Stem, Cap & Foot, Ivory Ground, 13 In.	2575.00
Salt, Iridescent Red Gold, Green Interior, Ribbed, 1 1/8 x 2 5/8 In.	160.00
Saucer, Iridescent Gold, Ruffled Edge, 6 In.	490.00
Sconce, 2-Light, Black Satin, Iridescent Gold Shades, Purple Highlights, 5 In., Pair	2520.00
Sconce, Gold Iridescent Shade, Brass, S-Shaped Arms, Signed, 7 1/4 In., Pair	360.00
Shade, Blue Pulled Feathers, Double Hooked Iridescent Gold Borders, Opal, 5 1/2 In.	230.00
Shade, Gold Pulled Zipper, Opal, Signed, 3 1/2 x 3 1/2 In.	175.00
Shade, Gold Spider Webbing, Green & Gold Leaves, Opal, Signed In Silver, 6 In.	175.00
Shade, Gold Tipped Blue Pulled Feathers, Opal, 6 In.	430.00
Shade, Gold Vine, Green Pulled Feathers, Signed, 5 1/2 x 6 1/2 In.	400.00
Shade, Gold, White, Gold Pulled Loops, Signed, 6 1/2 x 5 3/4 In., Pair	835.00

Shade, Green & Gold Pulled Leaves, Cream Ground, Threading, 5 3/8 x 2 1/4 In., Pair . . . 470.00
Shade, Green, Gold Pulled Hearts, Allover Gold Threading, 4 3/4 In. 145.00
Shade, Iridescent Gold Broken Chain, Opal, Signed, 4 In., Pair 230.00
Shade, Iridescent Gold Pulled Feathers, Green Tips, Opal, 5 In. 145.00
Shade, Iridescent Gold, Diamond-Quilted, 4 1/2 In. 115.00
Shade, Iridescent Gold, Ribbed, 4 1/2 x 4 1/2 In. 150.00
Shade, Iridescent Gold, White Pulled Feathers, Green Tips, 5 1/2 In. 175.00
Shade, Iridescent, Silver & Gold Pulled Feathers, Green Tips, 5 1/4 In. 290.00
Shade, Lily, Opal, Green Pulled Feathers, Gold Tips, 5 In. 315.00
Shade, Morning Glory, Iridescent Red Gold, Ribbed, Signed, 6 1/4 In. 70.00
Shade, Opal, Green, Gold Pulled Feathers, Green Swags, 4 1/2 In. 175.00
Shade, Pulled Feathers, Blue, Bell Shape, 5 1/2 In. 250.00
Shade, White & Platinum Pulled Zipper, On Green Bordered Gold, Signed, 5 1/4 In. 375.00
Shade, White, Green Pulls, On Iridescent Gold, Bubbles, 5 1/4 In. 115.00
Shade, Yellow Pulled Zipper, King Tut, On Opal, Signed, 3 x 4 In. 230.00
Torchere, Orange & Gold Iridescent Shade, Rope Twist Stem, 55 In., Pair 2350.00
Urn, Cover, King Tut, Royal Blue, Purple, Applied Ambergris Base, Signed, 14 In. 4945.00
Vase, Alabaster, Emerald Green, Iridescent Gold Pulled Loops, Inscribed, 4 1/4 In. 3680.00
Vase, Alabaster, Green Pulled Feathers, Iridescent Gold Trim, Pinched Waist, 9 In. 700.00
Vase, Amber, Allover Gold Iridescent, Ruffled Edge, c.1910, 12 1/2 In. 2300.00
Vase, Blue, Silver Iridescent Blue, Signed, 7 In. 575.00
Vase, Flower Form, Green, Iridescent Gold, Pulled Vines, c.1905, 13 1/2 In. 2870.00
Vase, Iridescent Blue & Gold Pulled Feathers, Green, Gold Striations, 8 1/4 In. 4830.00
Vase, Iridescent Blue, Egg Shape, Flared Rim, Early 20th Century, 8 1/4 In. 920.00
Vase, Iridescent Blue, Flared Rim, Oval, Signed, 7 In. 645.00
Vase, Iridescent Gold & Orange, Bulbous, Flared Neck, Signed, 7 1/2 In. 1035.00
Vase, Iridescent Gold, Purple Highlights, Pinched Sides, Signed, 3 In. 200.00
Vase, Iridescent, Teardrop, Flared Mouth, Silver Poppy Overlay, Signed, 15 1/2 In. 1150.00
Vase, Jack-In-The-Pulpit, Gold, Pink Highlights, Signed, 8 1/2 In. 865.00
Vase, Opalescent, Pulled Feathers, Gold Interior, Ruffled Rim, Tapered, c.1920, 5 3/8 In. . . 1175.00
Vase, Opaque White, Iridescent Gold Vines, Green Padded Flowers, c.1910, 7 x 5 In. 3500.00
Vase, Stick, Iridescent Gold, Green, Silver, Cream, Waves, Bubbles Base, 8 In. 3700.00
Vase, Stick, Wave Design, Iridescent Gold, Green, Silver, Bulbous Base, c.1910, 8 In. 3760.00
Vase, Trumpet, Gold Pulled Hearts, Vines, Opal Ground, Gold Iridescent Interior, 10 In. . . 4310.00
Vase, Trumpet, Iridescent White, Green Pulled Feathers, Ruffled Edge, 8 3/4 In. 2300.00
Vase, Trumpet, Pulled Green Feathers, Gold, White Tips, Scalloped Rim, Ribbed, 4 3/8 In. 1495.00

QUILTS have been made since the seventeenth century. Early textiles were very precious and every scrap was saved to be reused. A quilt is a combination of fabrics joined to a filler and a backing by small stitched designs known as quilting. An appliqued quilt has pieces stitched to the top of a large piece of background fabric. A patchwork, or pieced, quilt is made of many small pieces stitched together. Embroidery can be added to either type.

Amish, Log Cabin, Pineapple, Red, Navy, Wool, Brown Thread, 66 x 66 In. 935.00
Amish, Patchwork, Fans, Multicolored, Various Fabrics, Ohio, 68 x 78 In. 415.00
Appliqued, 9 Blocks, Laurel Leaves, Geometric Borders, M. Wright, N.C. 65 x 82 In. . . . 1045.00
Appliqued, 9 Floral Medallions, Red Calico, Green, Red Border, 79 x 79 In. 413.00
Appliqued, 9 Panels, Whig Rose, Floral Vine Border, Red, Green, Yellow, 86 x 92 In. 500.00
Appliqued, 18 Blocks, Wreaths, Vine Border, Virginia Mayapple, 84 x 88 In. 425.00
Appliqued, 30 Panels, Embroidered, Knightstown, Indiana, c.1899 . . . . 1100.00
Appliqued, Baskets, Calico, Red & White Stripes, Sawtooth Border, 71 x 72 In. 440.00
Appliqued, Bud, Rose Wreath, Green, Red Calico, Princess Feather Stitches, 88 x 91 In. . . 770.00
Appliqued, Diamonds Forming Stars, Red & Orange Calico, 89 x 96 In. 460.00
Appliqued, Embroidered, Morning Glory, White Ground, Blue Border, 80 x 101 In. 315.00
Appliqued, Flowers, Meandering Feather Borders, 82 x 74 In. 305.00
Appliqued, Friendship, Red & White, Maine, 1869, 70 x 60 In. 11500.00
Appliqued, Gold Eagles, White Ground, 9 Block Border, Cotton, 83 x 77 In. 2350.00
Appliqued, Grandmother's Flower Garden, Multicolored, 1930, 88 x 100 In. 300.00
Appliqued, Green, Purple, Grapevines, 66 x 82 In. 770.00
Appliqued, Harriet Powers Bible, Biblical Events, 87 x 84 In. 468.00
Appliqued, Lilies, Red, Green, Triangle Border, Shenandoah Valley, Carolina, 72 x 86 In. . 850.00
Appliqued, Orange, Green Snowflakes, 20th Century, 100 x 70 In. 394.00

Appliqued, Red & White Triangles, Blue Stripes, Crib 58.00
Appliqued, Red Pots, Yellow, Red Flowers, Leaves, White, Double Border, 86 x 88 In. . . .   195.00
Appliqued, Rose Of Sharon, Multicolored Calico, Scalloped Border, Cotton, 88 x 90 In. . .   1528.00
Appliqued, Rows Of Green Wreaths, Red Buds, Serpentine Vine Border, 90 x 86 In. 190.00
Appliqued, Signature, Red, White, Masonic, Victory Council No. 122, 1896, 78 x 81 In. . .   275.00
Appliqued, Squares, Red Calico, Gray Leaves, Feather Quilting, 100 x 100 In. 495.00
Appliqued, Sunflower, Oak Leaf Medallions, Princess Feather Quilting, 86 x 88 In. 605.00
Appliqued, Trapunto Fish, Green, Red Flowers, Vines Border, 82 x 90 In. 550.00
Appliqued, Trapunto, 4 Panels, Flower Baskets, Leaf Border, Birds, 1880, 80 x 80 In. . . .   1490.00
Appliqued, Tulips, Navy Blue Calico, White, Green Border, Gold Binding, 67 x 82 In. . . .   825.00
Appliqued, Turkey Tracks, Green, Blue, Yellow, Brown, Purple, Virginia, 72 x 90 In. 175.00
Counterpane, White, Sunburst Quilting, Diamonds, Oak Leaves, Feathers, 76 x 84 In. . . .   275.00
Crazy, Animal, Human, Flowers, Fruit, Embroidered, K.W. 1886, 80 x 76 In. 3300.00
Crazy, Appliqued & Embroidered, Squares, Velvet, Silk, Minnie Lada, 68 x 68 In. .   440.00
Crazy, Dresden Plate, 9 Multicolored Panels, Black Ground, 1905, 76 x 82 In. 275.00
Crazy, Figures, Symbols, Frame, 45 x 60 In. 305.00
Crazy, Hearts, Flowers, Insignias, Names, Dates, Cherokee, N.C., 72 x 69 In. 360.00
Crazy, Honeycomb, Multicolored, Silk, 20th Century, 83 x 93 In.   385.00
Crazy, Red, White, Wide Stripes, c.1890 . . . .   160.00
Crazy, Shams, Flowers, Fish, Cat, Bird, Brown, Yellow, Red, 1878, 60 x 61 In. 1765.00
Mennonite, Dark Blocks, Wool, Crepe, Striped Shirt Fabric Backing, Crib, 36 1/2 x 37 In.   225.00
Patchwork, 4-Patch, Multicolored, Cotton, Floral Binding, Backing, c.1885, 74 x 72 In. . . .   1058.00
Patchwork, 4-Point Star, Pink, Green, White Ground, Pennsylvania, c.1900, 84 x 84 In. . .   750.00
Patchwork, 4-Point Star, White, Red, Yellow, 73 x 70 In. 330.00
Patchwork, 6-Point Stars, Navy, Blue, Red, White Ground, Ohio, 66 1/2 x 84 In. 660.00
Patchwork, 8-Point Star, Red Center, Multicolor, Lattice Border, 73 x 80 In. 250.00
Patchwork, 9-Patch Variation, Inset Diamonds, Vintage Prints, 1894, 80 x 83 In. 300.00
Patchwork, 9-Patch Variation, White, Calico, Sawtooth Border, Band Border, 82 x 82 In. .   550.00
Patchwork, 9-Patch, Alternating Prints, Sawtooth Border, Cotton, c.1875, 70 x 80 In. 499.00
Patchwork, 12 Blocks Feathered Star, Rose Sashing, 81 x 64 In. 440.00
Patchwork, 12 Stars, Orange, Maroon, Green, Brown Print Backing, 96 x 85 1/2 In. 690.00
Patchwork, Animals, Birds, Children, White Field, 63 x 42 In. 275.00
Patchwork, Appliqued, Compass Star, 12 Blocks, Cotton, 1800s, 90 1/2 x 70 In. 2868.00
Patchwork, Bars & Blocks, 36 Blocks, Multicolored, Brown Calico Border, 68 x 66 In. . .   60.00
Patchwork, Baskets, 40 1/2 x 57 1/2 In. 105.00
Patchwork, Birds In Flight, Paisley Backing, 19th Century, 67 x 74 In. 468.00
Patchwork, Block, Initials, Swicegood & Sink Families, 20th Century, 64 x 77 In. 358.00
Patchwork, Blocks, Geometric Star, Red, Green, Pale, Cotton Backing, 66 x 84 In. 415.00
Patchwork, Blocks, Pink Print Border, Brown Backing, 71 x 73 In. 358.00
Patchwork, Blue & White, Flower Cross-Stitch, 83 x 84 In. 110.00
Patchwork, Blue, Pink Lattice, Brown Print Backing, 84 x 91 In.   105.00
Patchwork, Bow Tie, Navy Blue Calico & White, 50 x 68 In. 140.00
Patchwork, Brick Work, Multicolored Rectangles Alternating With White, 82 x 116 In. . .   990.00
Patchwork, Bull's-Eye, Burgundy, White, Calico, Green & Yellow Borders, 85 x 72 In. . .   450.00
Patchwork, Calico, Central Medallion, Pineapple Corner, Yellow, Red, Green, 92 x 92 In.   690.00
Patchwork, Carolina Lily, Baskets, Feathers, 71 x 67 In. 195.00
Patchwork, Carpenter's Wheel, 8-Point Center Star, Diamonds, 83 x 80 In. 500.00
Patchwork, Cathedral, Multicolored, White Circles, 92 x 110 In. 303.00
Patchwork, Checkerboard, Green, White, Princess Feather Quilting, 86 x 87 In. 550.00
Patchwork, Circles, Postage Stamp, Pickle Dish, 20th Century, 64 x 85 In. 385.00
Patchwork, Cross Variation, Pink, Salmon, Green Calico, 74 x 76 In. 248.00
Patchwork, Diamond 9-Patch, Blocks, Pink, Green, Red, Brown Border, 90 x 92 In. 353.00
Patchwork, Diamond In The Square, Birds, Feathers, Stars, Red, Purple, Tan, 72 x 72 In. . .   2988.00
Patchwork, Diamonds, Wavy Double Line Border, White, 76 x 84 In. 360.00
Patchwork, Double Irish Chain, Triple Border, Red, Green Print, Wreath, 80 x 82 In. 475.00
Patchwork, Double Irish Chain, Yellow & Green Squares, Shaped Border, 84 x 84 In. . . .   450.00
Patchwork, Drunkard's Path, Calico, White, Princess Feather Quilting, 70 x 90 In. 440.00
Patchwork, Feathered Star, Red Centers, Circular, Flowers, 87 x 67 In. 1430.00
Patchwork, Flying Geese Variation, Triple Border, Red & White, 76 x 76 In. 255.00
Patchwork, Flying Geese, Multicolored Triangles, White Ground, 65 x 85 In. 220.00
Patchwork, Friendship Star, 56 Stars, Vermont, New York Locations, c.1847, 85 x 76 In. . .   316.00
Patchwork, Geometric, Sawtooth Border, Checker Backing, 77 x 78 In. 175.00
Patchwork, Goose Track Variation, Chain, Calico, Cotton, 77 x 77 In. 590.00

Patchwork, Hawaiian, 9 Pineapple Medallions, Floral Vines, 64 x 64 In. 550.00
Patchwork, Hole In The Barn Door, White, Red, Triple Border, 68 x 84 In. 200.00
Patchwork, Indigo, Olive, Feather, Grapevine, Wool, Tabby Backing, c.1800, 82 x 83 In. . . 2115.00
Patchwork, Irish Chain, Calico, Blue, Gray, Red, Brown, Green Ground, 84 x 84 In. 225.00
Patchwork, Irish Chain, Red, White Ground, Grid, 78 x 60 In. 360.00
Patchwork, Irish Chain, White, Orange, Cotton, 1800s, 69 x 77 In. 598.00
Patchwork, Log Cabin, Assorted Fabrics, c.1880, 75 x 75 In. 625.00
Patchwork, Log Cabin, Purple Bands, Red, Black Borders, Silk, 78 x 85 In. 550.00
Patchwork, Log Cabin, Red, Brown, Blue, 71 x 80 In. 368.00
Patchwork, Lone Star, Corner Stars, Yellow Calico Ground, 86 x 86 In. 330.00
Patchwork, Lone Star, Crossed Feather Blocks, Intertwining Band Borders, 63 x 70 In. . . 495.00
Patchwork, Lone Star, Red, Green, White, Yellow, Flower Baskets In Corners, 82 x 82 In. . 565.00
Patchwork, Mariner's Compass, Red, Pink, Orange, Green, White Ground, 87 x 78 In. . . . 550.00
Patchwork, Mennonite, Log Cabin, Pineapple, Calico, Cotton, Border, c.1880, 96 x 84 In. 1175.00
Patchwork, Moon & Stars, Rust, Green, Tan, Wool Backing, Twill Binding, 83 x 96 In. . . 765.00
Patchwork, Ohio Star, White, Brown Calico, Sawtooth Border, 94 x 68 In. 135.00
Patchwork, Old Maid's Puzzle, Calico, Green Border, Red, White, 1909, 73 x 73 In. 610.00
Patchwork, Orange Ground, Blocks, Initials M.S., 70 x 84 In. 175.00
Patchwork, Pine Tree, Blue, Green, 83 x 69 In. 770.00
Patchwork, Postage Stamp, Pinks, Blues, Browns, Blue Binding, 70 x 86 In. 305.00
Patchwork, Red Calico Fleur-De-Lis Medallions, Black & Yellow, 85 x 85 In. 220.00
Patchwork, Red, Blue, Orange, Green Border, Geometric, Initials, 1899, 70 x 70 In. 195.00
Patchwork, Robbing Peter To Pay Paul, Blue & White, 76 x 80 In. 460.00
Patchwork, Robbing Peter To Pay Paul, Paisley Border, 81 x 87 In. 440.00
Patchwork, Sawtooth Diamond, Early 1800s, 98 x 76 In. 260.00
Patchwork, Sawtooth Diamond, Red, White, Blue, Red Plaid Backing, 76 x 76 In. 480.00
Patchwork, Sawtooth Stars, Blue, Green Calico, Yellow Calico Ground, 79 x 83 In. 220.00
Patchwork, Schoolhouse, 30 Blocks, White Ground, Cotton, Early 1900s, 80 x 63 In. 470.00
Patchwork, Star Blocks, Multicolored Calicos, White Ground, 68 x 80 In. 165.00
Patchwork, Star Flower Blocks, Green & Red, Double Border, 80 x 80 In. 160.00
Patchwork, Star Of Bethlehem, 8-Point Star Center, Flowering Vine Border, c.1850 . . . . . 1895.00
Patchwork, Star Of Bethlehem, 8-Point Star, Compass Stars, Calico, 92 x 92 In. 450.00
Patchwork, Star Of Hope, Red & White Calico, Grapevine Quilting, Initials, 102 x 95 In. . 175.00
Patchwork, Star Variation, 16 Stitches To Inch, Pennsylvania, c.1830, 102 x 104 In. 2195.00
Patchwork, Stars, Multicolored Calicos, White Trapunto Blocks, 78 x 92 In. 1980.00
Patchwork, Stars, Stripes, Red, White, Blue, Brown, 80 x 88 In. 275.00
Patchwork, State Of Ohio, Shows Counties, Stitched Names, Feather Border, 72 x 76 In. . 2750.00
Patchwork, Triangle, Block, Blue, Red, 1880, 38 x 38 1/2 In. 176.00
Patchwork, Trip Around The World, Pumpkin, Purple, Maroon, 1890s, 40 x 40 In. 1455.00
Patchwork, Tulip Medallions, Zigzag, Tulip, Star Borders, 88 x 88 In. 770.00
Patchwork, Tulip, Multicolored, 3 Gold Borders, 101 x 68 In. 863.00
Patchwork, Variable Star, Navy Blue Calicos, White, 56 x 66 In. 605.00
Patchwork, Wedding, White, Feather Quilting, Medallions, Diamond Ground, 68 x 68 In. . 413.00
Patchwork, Zachary Taylor, Sword Raised, Eagle, Flag, Trumpets, Chintz, 65 x 74 In. . . . 7250.00
Patchwork & Appliqued, 20 Blocks, Bear Paw, Pumpkin, Brown, 63 x 77 In. 415.00
Patchwork & Appliqued, Carolina Lily, Red, Blue, Printed Ground, 70 x 74 In. 550.00
Patchwork & Appliqued, Central Flower, Red, Green Border, Crib, 42 x 42 In. 2750.00
Patchwork & Appliqued, Eagle, Shield, 8 Stars, Red, White, Blue, c.1940, 74 x 66 In. . . . 529.00
Patchwork & Appliqued, Flag, Eagle, Shield, Red, Blue, Cotton, c.1915, 68 x 75 In. 9988.00
Patchwork & Appliqued, Flower Wreath, Vines, Poppy Border, 90 x 73 In. 220.00
Patchwork & Appliqued, Flowers, Feathers, Diamond Border, 91 x 85 In. 1540.00
Patchwork & Appliqued, Lone Star, Tulips, Green, Yellow, Pink, Red, White, 74 x 74 In. . 825.00
Patchwork & Appliqued, Red & Yellow Star, Flowers, Diamond Borders, 80 x 80 In. 660.00
Patchwork & Appliqued, Red Thistle Squares, Red & White, Cotton, 72 x 80 In. 460.00
Patchwork & Appliqued, Stars & Waves, Block, Wreath, Feather, 94 x 92 In. 1045.00
Patchwork & Appliqued, Wedding Rings, Multicolored, 70 x 78 In. 75.00

QUIMPER pottery has a long history. Tin-glazed, hand-painted pottery
has been made in Quimper, France, since the late seventeenth century.
The earliest firm, founded in 1685 by Jean Baptiste Bousquet, was
known as HB Quimper. Another firm, founded in 1772 by Francois
Eloury, was known as Porquier. The third firm, founded by Guillaume
Dumaine in 1778, was known as HR or Henriot Quimper. All three

firms made similar pottery decorated with designs of Breton peasants
and sea and flower motifs. The Eloury (Porquier) and Dumaine
(Henriot) firms merged in 1913. Bousquet (HB) merged with the oth-
ers in 1968. The group was sold to a United States family in 1984. The
American holding company is Quimper Faience Inc., located in
Stonington, Connecticut. The French firm has been called Societe
Nouvelle des Faienceries de Quimper HB Henriot since March 1984.

Basket, Swan Handle, Woman, Floral, Henriot Quimper, c.1930, 7 In.	435.00
Clock, Morbier, Repousse Brass Dial Mask, Pendulum, c.1860	1500.00
Fish, Poised With Open Mouth, Atop Shell, De La Hubaudiere, HB Quimper	1995.00
Frame, Man & Woman, 19th Century, 6 1/2 x 8 1/4 In.	1305.00
Plate, Profile Of Man, Ruffled, France, Henriot Quimper, c.1950, 10 1/4 In.	175.00
Tray, Man With Dog, Les Chansons De Botrel, Recessed, Henriot Quimper, 1 1/4 x 9 In.	615.00
Tray, Men Playing Instruments, Recessed, Henriot Quimper, 1 1/4 x 9 2/3 In.	350.00
Tray, Round, Croisille, Peasant Smoking Pipe, Milk Pail On Woman's Head, 9 1/2 In.	425.00
Vase, Quintal, 5 Openings, Peasant Man Seated On Rock, France, Henriot, 4 In.	135.00
Vase, Swan, Polychrome Enamels, H.R. Quimper, c.1930, 11 1/2 x 5 x 8 1/4 In.	595.00

RADIO broadcast receiving sets were first sold in New York City in
1910. They were used to pick up the experimental broadcasts of the
day. The first commercial radios were made by Westinghouse
Company for listeners of the experimental shows on KDKA Pittsburgh
in 1920. Collectors today are interested in all early radios, especially
those made of Bakelite plastic or decorated with blue mirrors. Figural
advertising radios and transistor radios are also collected.

Addison, Model 2A, Yellow & Burgundy Bakelite, Art Deco Design	2000.00
Admiral, Clock, Model 5A32, White & Brown	30.00
Admiral, Model 4X11, Plastic, Portable, 1950s	40.00
Admiral, Model 5Y22, Phonograph, Brown Bakelite	30.00
Admiral, Model 34F5, Decorative Grill, Portable, 1940s	25.00
Air Chief, Model 4-A-24, AM/FM, Wooden, Tabletop, 1940s	30.00
Air King, Model 52, Skyscraper Style, White Bakelite, 1933	3500.00
Air King, Model A-510, Leatherette Case, Portable	25.00
Arborphone, 5 Valves, 3 Dials, Wooden Case, Machine Specialty Co., Ann Arbor, 1920s	355.00
Arvin, Model 302A, Phonograph, Streamlined Painted Bakelite, 1940s	45.00
Atwater Kent, Model 10, Controls & Tubes Exposed, Breadboard Style	1250.00
Colonial Globe, Figural, Globe, Metal Equator, Shaped Stand, 1930	577.00
Dahlberg Co., Model D 413-S, Pillow Speaker, Minneapolis, Minn., 1955	177.00
Fada, Bullet, Catalin, Maroon, Orange Trim	605.00
Fada, Catalin, Orange, Red Trim	825.00
Gecophone Crystal Detector Set D I, Wooden Case, Hinged Lid, 1922	442.00
Ingellen-Radio, Model Geographic 438, 5 Tubes, Lighted Dial, 1938	829.00
Minerva, Model DKE 38, Bakelite Case, Round Speaker Opening, 1938	127.00
Mork & Mindy, Space Ship, Egg Shape, White Plastic, Box	40.00
Motorola, S Grille, Model 51X, Black Catalin, Red Grille & Handle, 1941, 10 x 6 In.	6325.00
Philco, Model 71, c.1932	395.00
RCA, Radiola 18, Circular Atwater Speaker On Top, 27 x 27 In.	80.00
RCA, Victor, Model R-71, c.1931	345.00
Saba, Type 311 W, Bakelite Case, 1933	210.00
Spartan, Bakelite, Cloisonne, 5 x 8 In.	17600.00
Stewart Warner, Catalin, No. 62T36, Yellow, Table Model, 1946	780.00
Tonfunk, Model W 332, Violetta, Lyra, 1954	175.00
Tropicana, Orange, Straw, Plastic, Battery, AM/FM, c.1970, 3 1/2 In.	12.00

RAILROAD enthusiasts collect any train memorabilia. Everything is
wanted, from oilcans to whole train cars. The Chessie system has
a store that sells many reproductions of their old dinnerware and
uniforms.

Badge, B & M RR, Police, Round, Nickel Finish	115.00
Badge, Boston & Maine, Nickel Over Brass, Wire Pin, Circle, 1 3/4 In.	240.00
Badge, Cap, Boston & Maine, Trainman, Nickel Finish	45.00
Badge, Cap, PRR, Police, Eagle, Screwback, Nickel Finish	75.00
Badge, Cap, United Electric Railways, No. 880, Heeren Bros.	30.00

Badge, CPRY, Constable, Wire Pin, 1 3/4 x 2 1/8 In. 245.00
Badge, Delaware & Hudson Co., Police Patrolman 39, Nickel Finish 95.00
Badge, GW & F, Railway Police, 14, Nickel Finish 175.00
Badge, KCTRY Co., Police, Kansas City, Allen Stamp & Seal Co., 1917, 2 1/4 In. 230.00
Badge, Middlesex & Boston Railway Co., Motorman, Case 25.00
Badge, N Mass St Ry Co., Street Railway Police, Nickel Finish 120.00
Badge, Railroad Police, Eagle, Spring Pin, C-Catch, 2 1/8 x 3 In. 230.00
Booklet, Tourist, North Pacific, Through Wonderland, Yellowstone, 1910 .... 20.00
Bowl, Fruit, Great Northern Railway, Glacier, Syracuse, 5 1/4 In. 98.00
Broadside, Old Colony RR, May 1883, 20 x 28 In. 35.00
Broadside, Old Colony RR, Sept 1885, To Newport, R.I., 20 x 28 In. 45.00
Cap, Conductor, Black, Gold, Straw, Cloth 132.00
Cap, Conductor, Pennsylvania RR, Black, Yellow Name Plate 165.00
Chair, Parlor Car, Wicker, Michigan Central Railroad, c.1810, Pair 400.00
Cup & Saucer, After Dinner, Baltimore & Ohio Centenary, Lamberton, Scammell 55.00
Cup & Saucer, Atchison, Topeka & Santa Fe, California Poppy, Syracuse 45.00
Cup & Saucer, Great Northern Railway, Empire, Syracuse, 1951 .... 20.00
Finger Bowl, Canadian Pacific, Bird, Blue Flowers, Blue Band, Vine, Spode, 3 In. 96.00
Glass, Pennsylvania Railroad, Train Passing Through Cities, 4 1/2 In. 4.00
Gravy Boat, Denver & Rio Grande Western, Prospector, Old Ivory, Syracuse, 1948 ..... 235.00
Headlight, No. 469, Brass, Cast Iron, Glass, 15 In. 2900.00
Jacket, Conductor, B & M, Blue, Buttons, Patches 40.00
Lantern, Adams & Westlake, Nickel Plated, Bell Bottom, Jr. Jones, Floral Band, 1864 ... 521.00
Lantern, Adams & Westlake, Nickel Plated, Twist-Off Base, 1864 .... 172.00
Lantern, Adlake C & O, Kero, Short Red Globe, Early 20th Century, 9 In. .... 50.00 to 80.00
Lantern, B & M RR, Tin, Round, Chimney, Burner, 9 In. 75.00
Lantern, Burlington Route, Handlan, Flat Top, Wire Guard, Red Globe, 3 1/4 In. 50.00
Lantern, C & NWRY, Adams & Westlake, Double Wire Guards, 1909 .... 149.00
Lantern, C & SRY, Adams & Westlake, Bell Bottom, Double, Corning Style Globe, 1895 . 550.00
Lantern, Caboose, Cast Iron, Wall Mount, Chimney, Burner, 20 In. 65.00
Lantern, Canadian National Railroad, Hiram L. Piper Co., Embossed Adlake Kero 225.00
Lantern, Colorado Midland, Single Wire Guard, Twist-Off Pot, CMRR In Panel, 5 1/2 In. . 800.00
Lantern, Delaware Lackawanna & Western, Drop-In Pot, Red Base Globe, 1913, 5 1/2 In. . 250.00
Lantern, Denver & Rio Grande Western, Flat Top, Handlan, Kopp Glass, 3 1/4 In. 86.00
Lantern, Denver & Rio Grande Western, Tin Flat Top, Handlan, Etched Safety First 1265.00
Lantern, Dietz D 1, 16 In. 130.00
Lantern, Dietz N.Y., Tin, Blue Glass Chimney, Etched MCRR, 15 In. 259.00
Lantern, Dietz, Tin, Kerosene Burner, 19th Century, 14 1/2 In. 87.00
Lantern, DL & RGW, Deitz Vesta 35.00
Lantern, Erie Railroad, Adams Westlake, Adlake Reliable, c.1911 .... 275.00
Lantern, Kansas City Terminal, Bell Bottom, Drop-In Pot, 1913, 5 In. 580.00
Lantern, MM Buck, Nickel Plated, Bell Bottom, Gothic Letter MHM, Wreath Design ... 1735.00
Lantern, New York Central, Reflectors, Star Headlight & Lantern, Rochester, Kerosene .. 165.00
Lantern, Pullman, Nickel Plated, Wire Guard, 3 In. 276.00
Lantern, South Pacific, Adlake Kero 3-52 Frame, SPCO On Shoulder, 3 1/4 In. 40.00
Lantern, Wabash, Reflectors, Kerosene 165.00
Lock, Key, CPPR, Brass, 1993 .... 350.00
Padlock, I C RR On Front, Miller On Back, Brass, Push Key, 2 1/2 In. 130.00
Plate, Chicago Milwaukee & Puget Sound, Logo, Warwick, 7 In. 70.00
Plate, Denver & Rio Grande Western, Prospector, Syracuse China, 1948, 5 1/2 In. 85.00
Plate, Great Northern Railways, Wild Flowers, Glacier Nat'l. Park, Syracuse, 10 In. 1295.00
Plate, Lunch, Great Northern Railway, O.P. Co., Syracuse, 1925, 7 In. 110.00
Sauce, Chicago, Milwaukee, St. Paul & Pacific, Ye Olde Ivory, Buffalo China, 4 1/2 In. .. 345.00
Sign, Great Western Line, Smith Mfg. Co., Tin Over Cardboard, 19 x 27 In. 1850.00
Sign, MCRR, Destination, Eastwind, Casco, Hardboard, Painted, 60 x 36 In. 800.00
Sign, MCRR, Destination, Forget Your Travel Problems, Hardboard, Painted, 32 x 54 In. . 900.00
Sign, MCRR, Destination, Katahdin, Depart Time, Stops, Hardboard, Painted, 36 x 60 In. . 1700.00
Sign, MCRR, Destination, Pine Tree, Depart Time, Stops, Hardboard, Painted, 36 x 60 In. 1000.00
Sign, Railway Express Agency, Red, White, Porcelain, 11 x 11 In. 150.00
Sign, Railway Express, Century Of Service, 1839-1939, Tin, Celluloid, 28 x 12 In. 495.00
Soup, Dish, Denver & Rio Grande, Curecanti, O.P. Co., Syracuse, Logo, 1916, 8 In. 280.00
Tray, Soo Line Railroad, Michigan, Wisconsin, Dakotas, Map, Metal, 15 x 10 In. 175.00
Whistle, Northwestern, Logging Train, Etched Rim, Acorn Finial, Brass, 12 In. 400.00

RAZORS were used in ancient Egypt and subsequently wherever shaving was in fashion. The metal razor used in America until about 1870 was made in Sheffield, England. After 1870, machine-made hollow-ground razors were made in Germany or America. Plastic or bone handles were popular. The razor was often sold in a set of seven, one for each day of the week. The set was often kept by the barber who shaved the well-to-do man each day in the shop.

A.S. Daas Co., Horseman & Dog Chasing Steer, Celluloid Handle, Silver Inlay, Germany .	150.00
Easy Cutter, Black Celluloid Handles, Flowers, Owl	175.00
Eneva Cutlery Co., Flying Eagle, Celluloid Handle, Improved Eagle Razor	95.00
Folding, Dewey, Portrait, Defeated Spanish Fleet Off Manila	125.00
Folding, Tortoise, Celluloid Handle, Gold Wash Panel, German	60.00
George Washington, Black Celluloid Handle, Sheffield, England	150.00
George Wostenholm & Son, Spotted Handle, Sheffield, England	125.00
Hibbard, Spencer, Bartlett Co, Celluloid Handle, Twisted Rope, Partial Nude, Germany . .	120.00
Horn, Silver Inlay, Bird, Vines, Leaves, Cupid, Germany	150.00
Ivory Celluloid Handle, Wading Heron, Fish, Germany	135.00
John Sellers, Ivory Handle, Engraved Scroll, Sheffield, England	275.00
Joseph Rodgers & Sons, Folding, Pearl Handle, Beveled Back, England	275.00
Joseph Rodgers & Sons, Ivory Handle, Shell, Beveled, Sheffield, England	175.00
Oxford Co., Standing Nude, Grapes, Leaves, Celluloid Handles, Germany	125.00
Oxford Razor, Stag In Forest, Celluloid Handle, Flower Border, Oval, Germany	125.00
Peacock, Green, Celluloid Handle	85.00
Straight, Celluloid Handles, Silver Inlay, Flowers, Stems, Leaves, Germany	120.00
W.H. Morley & Sons, Straight, Peacock, Cellulite Handle, Germany, 1800-1830	45.00
Wade & Butcher, Horn Handle, You Shave Well, I'll Shave Well	135.00

REAMERS, or juice squeezers, have been known since 1767, although most of those collected today date from the twentieth century. Figural reamers are among the most prized.

Aluminum, 3 1/2 In.	9.00
Ceramic, Clown, Sitting, Cross Leg, Orange, White Ruffle, 2 Piece, Germany, 5 In.	300.00
Ceramic, Pig, California Classics, 2 Piece, 1989, 3 1/4 In.	25.00
Ceramic, Pitcher, White, Yellow Plaid, Marked Japan, 7 In.	65.00
Child's Face, Figural, Japan, 3 In.	235.00
Citrus, Goebel, c.1927, 3 1/2 In.	98.00
Clear, Square Loop Handle, Embossed Balencia, On Front, 6 In.	225.00
Clown, Japan, c.1940, 7 3/4 In.	295.00
Clown, Lustroware Face, Napco, Japan, 5 1/4 In.	210.00
Clown, Lustroware, Japan, c.1940, 4 3/4 In.	285.00
Clown, Lustroware, Mikori Ware, c.1940, 7 1/4 In.	295.00
Clown, Yellow Body, Maroon Buttons, Cone Hat, 2 Piece, 6 In.	100.00
Crystal, Jenny, Loop Handle, 5 1/2 In.	135.00
Crystal, Lemon, 2 1/2 x 6 In.	15.00
Depression Glass, Green, 4 1/2 In.	18.00
Duck, Lustroware, c.1940, 3 1/2 In.	195.00
Flat, Green, 5 1/2 x 3 In.	14.00
Flowers, Japan, c.1940, 5 1/4 In.	120.00
Glass, Blue & White Opalescent Hobnail, Saucer Type, Tab Handle, 4 In.	165.00
Glass, Frosted Crystal, Decorated With Baby's Orange, 4 1/4 In.	75.00
Glass, Green, Opaque, Long Pointed Cone, Embossed Saunders, 6 In.	1600.00
Glass, Green, Ribbed, Loop Handle, Anchor Hocking, 6 In.	25.00
Glass, Saucer Type, Small Loop Handle, Cambridge, 4 1/8 In.	20.00
Glass & Metal, Hinged Black Metal, Clear Glass Insert, Marked Williams, 4 3/4 In.	75.00
Ivory, Saucer Type, Loop Handle, McKee, 5 1/2 In.	35.00
Majolica, Orange, Figural, Erphila Art Pottery, 6 In.	285.00
Milk Glass, Sunkist, Thatcher Glass, Elmira, New York, 8 1/2 x 3 1/2 In.	22.00
Milk Glass, Vitrock, 8 3/4 In.	22.00
Pink, Flowers, Paden City, 8 1/4 x 7 1/2 In.	170.00
Pink, Glass, 2-Cup Measure, Hazel Atlas, 2 Piece, 5 3/8 In.	160.00
Plastic, Turquoise, Lustroware, U.S.A.	10.00
Sunkist, Opalescent White, Marked Pat. No. 18764, U.S.A., 6 In.	150.00
Sunkist, Opaque Pink, Marked Pat. No. 18764, Made In U.S.A., 6 In.	225.00

Vaseline Glass, Edna Barnes, 2 Piece, c.1980 .... 250.00
Vaseline Glass, Fry, 3 1/8 x 7 1/4 In. 130.00

RECORDS have changed size and shape through the years. The cylinder-shaped phonograph record for use with the early Edison models was made about 1889. Disc records were first made by 1894, the double-sided disc by 1904. High-fidelity records were first issued in 1944, the first vinyl disc in 1946, the first stereo record in 1958. The 78 RPM became the standard in 1926 but was discontinued in 1957. In 1932, the first 33 1/3 RPM was made but was not sold commercially until 1948. In 1949, the 45 RPM was introduced. Compact discs became available in the U.S. in 1982 and many companies began phasing out the production of phonograph records.

Al Capp On Campus, Jubilee, c.1970 .... 18.00
Bob Dylan, Greatest Hits, Vol. II, LP, 1971 .... 30.00
Brenda Lee, 10 Golden Years, Decca, No. DL 74757, LP, 1966 .... 22.00
Dee Clark, Hey Little Girl, Abner, No. 1029, 45 RPM, 1959 .... 6.00
Doris Day, Listen To Day, Columbia Records, No. DD1, LP, 1960 .... 12.00
Dorothy Moore, Funny How Time Slips Away, Malaco Records, No, 1033, 45 RPM 6.00
Francis Sinatra & Edward Ellington, Reprise Records, No. RS1024, LP, 1967 ... 25.00
Frank Sinatra, Only The Lonely, Monophonic, Capital, No. ST1053, LP, 1958 .... 15.00
Henry Mancini, Warm Shade Of Ivory, RCA, No, LSP-4140, LP 7.00
Hey There It's Yogi Bear, Mailer, Kellogg's, 33 1/3 RPM, c.1962, 7 x 7 In. 20.00
Huckleberry Hound, Stories & Songs Of Uncle Remus, CBS Records, 33 1/3 RPM, 1977 ... 12.00
Ronald McDonald, Night Before Christmas, 2 Sides, Vinyl, 45 RPM, c.1960 .... 8.00
Sgt. Barry Sadler, Ballad Of The Green Berets, Stereo, RCA Victor, 33 1/3 RPM, 1966 .. 12.00
Strawberry Shortcake, Picture Disc, Cardboard, American Greetings, 45 RPM, 1982 .... 10.00
Yogi Bear & Boo Boo, Colpix, 33 1/3 RPM, c.1960, 12 x 12 In. 10.00
Yogi Bear & Huckleberry Hound, Fairy Tale, 33 1/3 RPM, 1977, 12 x 12 In. 5.00

RED WING Pottery of Red Wing, Minnesota, was a firm started in 1878. The company first made utilitarian pottery, including stoneware jugs and canning jars. In the 1920s art pottery was made. Many dinner sets and vases were made before the company closed in 1967. Rumrill pottery was made for George Rumrill by the Red Wing Pottery and other firms. It was sold in the 1930s. For more information, see *Kovels' Depression Glass & Dinnerware Price List.*

Advertising, Bean Pot, Cover, Peterson 200.00
Advertising, Bowl, Midwest Malt Products Co., Davenport, Spongeware, 7 1/2 In. 220.00
Advertising, Bowl, Rock Island Lumber Co., Spongeware, 9 In. 100.00
Art Pottery, Planter, Violin, No. 1484, Yellow Fleck 51.00
Art Pottery, Vase, No. 734, Butterscotch, Green Interior, 2 Handles, 9 1/2 In. 79.00
Blossom Time, Egg Dish 225.00
Blue Indian Head, Churn, Handles, Lid With Wood Dasher, 3 Gal., 14 In. 158.00
Bob White, Cup 15.00
Bob White, Teapot 63.00
Bob White, Tray 51.00
Cobalt Blue, Vase, No. 154, Paneled Sides, 2 Handles 83.00
Drummer Boy, Cookie Jar 550.00
Lions, Vase, Leaves, Egg Shape, Raised Rim, Green, Blue, Semigloss Glaze, 7 5/8 In. ... 120.00
Lotus, Cup 12.00
Lotus, Cup & Saucer 16.00
Lotus, Soup, Dish 12.00
Magnolia, Creamer 20.00
Magnolia, Planter, Eggshell Ivory, Antiqued Brown, 3 7/8 x 14 1/8 In. 75.00
Magnolia, Teapot, Cover 125.00
Midnight Rose, Creamer 25.00
Nassau, Plate, Dinner, 10 1/2 In. 140.00
Nokomis, Vase, Marked, 10 3/8 In. 345.00
Poultry Feeder, Ko-Rec, Base Tray 110.00
Random Harvest, Tidbit Tray, 3 Tiers, 10 1/2, 8 1/2 & 5 In. Plates 55.00
Saffron, Bowl, No. 6 .... 80.00
Spongeware, Jug, White Clay, Cream Glaze & Blue, Shoulder Ring, 6 1/2 In. 275.00

Stoneware, Bowl, Salt Glaze, Albany Slip Interior, 11 In. 28.00
Stoneware, Bowl, Yellowware, Shouldered, Blue Bands, 11 In. 125.00
Stoneware, Butter Jar, No. 3, Corner's New Store, Owatonna, Mn., Zinc Glaze 3200.00
Stoneware, Butter Jar, No. 3, Stieren-Jerman Co. General Merchandise, West Point 4000.00
Stoneware, Butter Jar, No. 20, Blue Print 1250.00
Stoneware, Crock, Birch Leaf, 2 Elephant Ear Handles, 4 Gal. 72.00
Stoneware, Crock, Butterfly, Salt Glaze, 20 Gal. 1250.00
Stoneware, Crock, Butterfly, Side Stamp, 15 Gal. 2500.00
Stoneware, Crock, Large Wing, 60 Gal. 3800.00
Stoneware, Crock, Leaf, 6 Gal. 50.00
Stoneware, Jar, Canning, Brown, Qt. 55.00
Stoneware, Jar, Lid, Stone Mason Fruit Jar, Union Stoneware Co., Jan. 24, 1899, 8 In. ... 124.00
Stoneware, Jug, Beehive, 5 Gal. 275.00
Stoneware, Jug, Beehive, Birch Leaf, Oval, 4 Gal. 200.00
Stoneware, Jug, Salt Glaze, Signed RWSW, 1 Gal. 1300.00
Stoneware, Jug, Shoulder, 3 Gal. 39.00
Stoneware, Jug, Shoulder, Whiskey, Medicinal Use, Zinc Glaze, Creston, Ia., 1/4 Gal. ... 2000.00
Tampico, Cup 12.00
Tampico, Plate, 6 1/2 In. 7.00
Village Green, Tray, Casserole, Handles, 12 In. 35.00

REDWARE is a hard, red stoneware that originated in the late 1600s and
continues to be made. The term is also used to describe any common
clay pottery that is reddish in color.

Bank, Bird Shape Finial, Coin Slot Shoulder, Red, Yellow Glaze, c.1880, 6 3/4 In. 1435.00
Bank, Birdhouse, Bird, Yellow, Green & Black Splotches, Breininger, 1970, 11 1/2 In. ... 600.00
Bank, Bulbous, White Slip, Brown Mottled Glaze, 3 1/4 x 2 1/2 In. 340.00
Bank, Cat, Reclining, Yellow, Brown, Green Glaze, 6 x 7 In. 745.00
Bank, Dog Head, Initial J.H.G., Manheim, Pennsylvania, 2 3/4 In. 1485.00
Bank, Dog, Coleslaw Mane, 6 1/2 In. 4315.00
Bank, Face, Wheel Thrown, Applied Features, Brown Glaze, 19th Century, 4 3/4 In. 330.00
Bank, Schoolhouse, Roof Peak Coin Slot, Glazed, Mid 1800s, 3 1/2 x 3 1/4 x 4 In. 1195.00
Bank, Sgraffito, Initialed J.H., 1895 .... 1250.00
Bank, Stepped Rim, Coin Slot Shoulder, Red, Yellow Glaze, 19th Century, 5 1/4 In. 720.00
Bank, Still, Jug Shape, Red Paint, Unglazed, 4 1/4 In. 50.00
Bank, Still, Spherical, Flared Base, Yellow Slip Polka Dot, Glazed, 3 3/8 In. 330.00
Bean Pot, Brown, Slip Trailed Flowers, Black, White, Green, Yellow, Handles, 7 In. ... 140.00
Bottle, Water, Applied Leaves, Grapes, Narrow Throat, Green & Yellow Glazes, 9 In. ... 28.00
Bowl, 2-Line Cream Slip Scallops On Rim, Flared, 2 1/2 x 13 1/4 In. 365.00
Bowl, Flat Rim, Incised Line, Burnt Orange Glaze, Black Flecks, 8 1/2 x 3 1/2 In. 99.00
Bowl, Green, Orange Glaze, Brown Line, Stahl, 1953, 7 3/4 In. 70.00
Bowl, Green, Yellow Slip, Molded Rim, Glazed, Shenandoah Valley Pottery, 3 x 9 1/2 In. . 3520.00
Bowl, Incised Band, Green Glaze, Handle, Thomas Stahl, 12/23/38, 3 x 5 1/2 In. 70.00
Bowl, Interior Glaze, Stuart Mossoms, Schofield Pottery, c.1941, 3 1/2 x 7 3/4 In. 110.00
Bowl, Leaves, Multicolored, Pinched Sides, Opaque White Glaze, 2 1/4 x 6 3/4 In. 16.00
Bowl, Moravian, Flared Rim, Molded Rim, Brown Glaze, Squiggle, 3 1/2 x 12 In. 2750.00
Bowl, Moravian, Molded Rim, White, Green, Brown Glaze, Squiggle, 3 x 11 In. 3025.00
Bowl, Mottled, Green, Orange Glaze, Stahl, 1953, 8 In. 110.00
Bowl, Slanted Side, Black Flecks, Wavy Concentric Liness, Glazed Interior, 15 x 5 In. ... 325.00
Bowl, Slanted Sides, Brown, Gold Flecks, Streaks, Glazed Interior, 11 x 3 1/2 In. 120.00
Bowl, Vegetable, Oval, Beaded Edge, Orange, Glazed, 19th Century, 1 3/4 x 6 x 8 In. 176.00
Bowl, Wheel Thrown, Flared Edge, Glazed Interior, 4 1/2 x 16 In. 220.00
Bowl, Yellow Slip, Orange Glaze, 2 1/2 x 7 In. 22.00
Charger, Bird, Round, Squiggle Brim, Glazed, c.1822, 12 1/4 In. 3107.00
Charger, Coggled Rim, Yellow Slip Looping, 19th Century, 12 In. 580.00
Charger, Coggled Rim, Yellow Triple Quill Squiggle Work, c.1870, 13 1/2 In. 2150.00
Charger, Coggled Rim, Yellow, 4-Line Slip, 13 3/8 x 2 1/2 In. 1210.00
Charger, Stylized Branch, Round, Concentric Bands, Squiggles, Glazed, 11 5/8 In. 1195.00
Creamer, 2-Tone, Applied Loop Handle, Schofield Pottery, 3 1/2 In. 145.00
Creamer, Applied Doves, Rose, Paneled, High Curving Rosette Handle, 4 3/4 In. 330.00
Creamer, Bulbous, Blue, Yellow Rainbow Spatter 690.00
Creamer, Bulbous, Glazed, Applied Strap Handle, Schofield Pottery, 4 In. 165.00
Creamer, Bulbous, Red Spatter Cluster Of Buds, 4 In. 140.00

Creamer, Flower, Bulbous, Brown, Orange Glaze, Handle, R.R. Stahl, 4/28/53, 3 1/4 In. . .   95.00
Creamer, Flowers, Green, Brown Glaze, R.R. Stahl, 10/19/48, 5 1/4 In. 200.00
Creamer, Paneled, Mottled Glaze, Applied Loop Handle, 3 1/4 In. 550.00
Crock, Bulbous, Manganese, Glazed, 19th Century, 1 5/8 In. 330.00
Crock, Manganese Polka Dots, Yellow, Orange Glaze, Ear Handles, 4 3/4 x 8 1/4 In. 28.00
Crock, Oval, Brown Vertical Rows, Flared Rim, Incised Lines, Ear Handles, 8 5/8 In. 660.00
Crock, Oval, Thick Rim, Orange, Brown, Rope-Twist Applied Handles, 4 3/8 In. 660.00
Crock, Storage, Molded Rim, Incised Line, Green, Orange Glaze, 6 1/4 In. 440.00
Crock, Straight Sides, Molded Rim, Manganese, Glazed, 9 3/4 In. 35.00
Cup, 4-Color Rainbow, Loop Pattern, Green, Purple, Yellow, Black, Handleless 690.00
Cup, Rainbow Thistle, Red, Green, Yellow, Handleless, Pair 385.00
Cup & Saucer, Holly Berry, Purple Spatter 440.00
Cup & Saucer, Peafowl, Green Spatter, Blue, Yellow, Red, Handleless 220.00
Cup & Saucer, Red & Yellow Rainbow Spatter, Handleless, Child's Size 745.00
Dish, George Washington, Sgraffito Border, Green Glaze, Stahl, Germany, 10 In. 1430.00
Dish, Loaf, Coggled Rim, 4-Quill Slip, 19th Century, 3 1/2 x 16 x 12 In. 3585.00
Dish, Loaf, Coggled Rim, Yellow Slip, 19th Century, 3 x 11 1/2 x 17 In. 4400.00
Dish, Loaf, Oval, Double Crisscross Lines, Yellow Slip, Brown Glaze, 12 x 15 x 3 In. 825.00
Dish, Loaf, Slip Design, 7 Trails, Signed, Breininger, Robesonia, Pa., Aug 1982, 17 1/2 In.   120.00
Dish, Loaf, Yellow Slip, Squiggle Line & Dot Slip, Early 19th Century, 10 3/4 x 11 In. . . .   880.00
Figurine, Dog Carrying Basket, Continental, 19th Century, 8 x 8 x 4 In. 248.00
Figurine, Dog, Seated, Basket, John Bell, Waynesboro, Pa., c.1880, 4 3/4 x 5 1/2 In. 770.00
Figurine, Dog, Seated, Collar, Face, Brown Semimatte Glaze, Inscribed FK, 6 1/2 In. 130.00
Figurine, Dog, Seated, Detailed Face, Brown Glaze, 6 In. 165.00
Figurine, Dog, Standing, Basket, Manganese Glaze, Tooled Details, 4 1/4 x 5 1/2 In. 4950.00
Figurine, Lion, Crouching, 4 x 4 In. 230.00
Figurine, Lion, Reclining, Open Mouth, Copper Oxide, Lead Glaze, 4 x 7 1/4 In. 5775.00
Figurine, Lion, Seated, Hollow, Black Mica, Painted Mouth & Eyes, 6 3/4 x 11 x 14 In. . .   1210.00
Figurine, Man, Straddling Barrel, Smoking Cigar, Manganese Splotches, 9 In. 395.00
Flask, Pretzel Shape, 3 1/2 x 5 1/2 In. 85.00
Flowerpot, Coggled Rim, Mottled, Tan, Brown, Attached Base, Stamped V. Rudolph, 6 In.   330.00
Flowerpot, Pinched Top, Mottled Glaze, Incised Band, 6 x 7 In. 50.00
Flowerpot, Tulip Design, Rope Handle, John Bell 3520.00
Hotplate, Round, Manganese Splotches, 7 1/2 In. 293.00
Hotplate, Round, Molded Rim, Mottled Glaze, 19th Century, 6 3/4 In. 105.00
Jar, Black Vertical Brush Marks, Incised Rings, Raised Ring Bottom, 8 1/2 In. 280.00
Jar, Bulbous, Brown Glaze, Applied Ear Handle, 7 3/4 x 9 1/2 In. 176.00
Jar, Bulbous, Flared Rim, Base, Green Glaze, Orange Splotches, 5 In. 165.00
Jar, Bulbous, Incised Rings, 3-Tone Glaze, Signed, Henry Schofield, 7 3/4 In. 770.00
Jar, Bulbous, Manganese Glaze, 19th Century, 2 In. 440.00
Jar, Bulbous, Manganese Glaze, Molded Rim, Penn., 19th Century, 6 3/4 In. 70.00
Jar, Canning, Yellow, Green Glaze, John Bell, 7 1/2 In. 900.00
Jar, Flared Raised Rim, Incised Line, Oval, Olive Green Glaze, Lug Handles, 10 3/4 In. . . .   558.00
Jar, Oval, Wide Mouth, Yellow, Brown Glazed Exterior, Lug Handles, 1800s, 7 1/4 In. . . .   2705.00
Jar, Slanted Shoulders, Incised Rings, Green Glaze, Orange Spots, Galena Pottery, 8 In. . .   248.00
Jar, Storage, Bulbous, Molded Lip, Glazed, 19th Century, 5 In.   11.00
Jar, Storage, Bulbous, Mottled Glaze, 19th Century, 5 In. 250.00
Jar, Storage, Mottled Glaze, Applied Loop Handle, Incised Band, 5 3/4 In. 140.00
Jar, Storage, Mottled Glaze, Coggled Rim, 7 1/4 In. 440.00
Jar, Storage, Mottled Glaze, Molded Rims, 5 3/4 In., Pair 145.00
Jar, Storage, Mottled Glaze, Straight Sides, Incised Line, 8 In. 110.00
Jar, Straight Sides, Flared Rim, Green & Brown Mottled Glaze, 6 5/8 In. 300.00
Jar, Straight Sides, Flared, Molded Rim, Orange Glaze, 6 3/4 In. 220.00
Jar, Tapered Shoulder, Black, Sponged Decoration, 13 1/4 In. 220.00
Jar, Tobacco, Glaze, Oval, Footed, Everted Rim, Yellow, Green, Brown Slip, 9 1/4 In. . . .   3825.00
Jar Set, Storage, Graduated, Manganese Glaze, 19th Century, 4 3/4 To 9 3/4 In., 4 Piece . .   250.00
Jar Set, Storage, Graduated, Molded Rim, 4 1/4, 5 1/4, & 5 3/4 In., 3 Piece 195.00
Jug, Black Glaze, Strap Handle, 5 In. 115.00
Jug, Brown Glaze, Thumbprint Handle, 8 1/2 In. 58.00
Jug, Bulbous, Brown, Yellow, 2-Tone, Glazed, Applied Handle, 19th Century, 6 1/2 In. . . .   910.00
Jug, Bulbous, Copper Oxide Glaze, Applied Loop Handle, 19th Century, 8 3/4 In. 578.00
Jug, Bulbous, Glazed, Applied Ribbed Handle, 8 1/2 In. 155.00
Jug, Bulbous, Incised Rings, Manganese Glaze, Applied Handle, 19th Century, 8 In. 155.00

Jug, Bulbous, Manganese Glaze, Applied Loop Handle, 6 3/4 In. 94.00
Jug, Bulbous, Manganese Glaze, Applied Ribbed Handle, 9 1/2 In. 50.00
Jug, Bulbous, Opaque White Crescent, Orange Glaze, Applied Strap Handle, 9 In. 85.00
Jug, Bulbous, Orange Glaze, Applied Handle, Scholfield Pottery, 4 1/4 In. 220.00
Jug, Cider, Cover, Bulbous, Side Spout, Manganese Glaze, Applied Handle, 6 1/2 In. 110.00
Jug, Cider, Side Spout, Mottled Glaze, Applied Loop Handle, 19th Century, 5 1/2 In. 275.00
Jug, Egg Shape, Dark Brown Slip Glaze, Handle, c.1850, 7 1/4 In. 170.00
Jug, Egg Shape, Manganese Glaze, Incised Line, Ribbed Strap Handle, 6 1/2 In. 165.00
Jug, Grotesque, 4 Stone Teeth, Eyes, Green Ash Glaze, Lanier Meaders, 8 1/2 In. 935.00
Jug, Grotesque, Double Face, Horns, Clay Teeth, Eyes, Handles, Lanier Meaders, 9 In. . .   3740.00
Jug, Grotesque, White Eyes, Teeth, Brown To Green Ash Glaze, Lanier Meaders, 9 In. . . .   1925.00
Jug, Impressed Line, Manganese Glaze, Applied Loop Handle, Schofield, 4 In. 165.00
Jug, Manganese Glaze, Applied Ribbed Loop Handle, 6 In. 28.00
Jug, Manganese Glaze, Applied Ribbed Loop Handle, Penn., 19th Century, 6 1/2 In. 140.00
Jug, Orange Glaze, Rice, Draper & Co., Providence, R.I., 2 Gal.   395.00
Jug, Orange, Brown Glaze, Applied Loop Handle, Schofield Pottery, 5 1/2 In. 190.00
Jug, Oval, Incised Shoulder Lines, Mottled Yellow, Brown, Olive, 7 1/2 x 6 5/8 In. 2235.00
Jug, Oval, Mottled Green, Brown Alkaline Glaze, c.1810, 1/2 Gal., 9 1/2 In. 358.00
Jug, Puzzle, Bulbous, Green, Yellow Glaze, Bucks County, Pa., c.1833, 6 1/4 In. 5225.00
Mug, Bulbous, Flared Top, Manganese Glaze, Applied Loop Handle, 4 1/4 In. 275.00
Mug, Bulbous, Opaque White, Glazed, Applied Loop Handle, 6 In. 30.00
Mug, Flared Top, Glazed, Applied Loop Handle, Schofield Pottery, 4 In. 110.00
Mug, Flared Top, Manganese Glaze, Applied Strap Handle, 3 1/2 In. 130.00
Mug, Flared Top, Mottled Glaze, Applied Loop Handle, 3 In. 155.00
Mug, Mottled Glaze, Applied Loop Handle, Pa., 19th Century, 3 In. 165.00
Mug, Stoneware, Manganese Glaze, Applied Loop Handle, 3 3/4 In. 39.00
Pail, Milk, Molded Rim, Interior Glaze, Ear Handles, 6 1/2 x 18 1/2 In. 550.00
Pail, Milk, Pouring Spout, Interior Glaze, 6 x 13 In. 190.00
Pan, Milk, Cover, Flared Sides, Scalloped Green Band, Brown Band, 11 x 3 In. 90.00
Pie Plate, Coggled Rim, Yellow Line & Dot Slip, 10 1/4 In. 220.00
Pie Plate, Pinched Side, Bright Yellow Glaze, 10 1/4 In. 22.00
Pie Plate, Wavy Lines, Yellow Slip, 7 1/4 In. 305.00
Pie Plate, Yellow Slip, Stylized Tulip Slip Decoration, Pa., c.1790, 9 7/8 In. 1765.00
Pitcher, 3-Color Rainbow, Paneled, Green, Yellow, Red, 6 1/4 In. 2970.00
Pitcher, Blue Spatter Cockscomb Pattern, Paneled, Red, Green, 8 In. 990.00
Pitcher, Bulbous, Mottled Glaze, Applied Ribbed Handle, 19th Century, 9 In. 275.00
Pitcher, Bulbous, Mottled, Green Glaze, Loop Handle, Thomas Stahl, 1938, 7 In. 275.00
Pitcher, Bulbous, Spoutless, Glazed, Applied Loop Handle, Yellow Slip, 5 In. 95.00
Pitcher, Cover, Black Sponge, Orange Glaze, Applied Handle, 19th Century, 7 1/2 In. 250.00
Pitcher, Cylindrical, Pulled Lip, Green Washed, Green, Brown, 19th Century, 9 3/4 In. . . .   1195.00
Pitcher, Double Bulbous, Red, Brown, Gray Sponge, Applied Loop, Handles, 3 1/2 In. . . .   55.00
Pitcher, Incised Bow, Handleless, Schofield Pottery, 5 3/4 In. 130.00
Pitcher, Incised Lines, Green, Orange Spotted Glaze, Applied Handle, 10 In. 440.00
Pitcher, Madonna, Birds, Flowers, Mottled Glaze, 19th Century, 10 In. 195.00
Pitcher, Orange, Brown Glaze, Handleless, Impressed Bow, Schofield Pottery, 6 1/4 In. . .   410.00
Pitcher, Sgraffito, Eagle & Bird, Mottled Glaze, Strap Handle, 7 3/4 In. 2420.00
Pitcher, Spoutless, Manganese Glaze, Opaque Glaze Interior, Loop Handle, 7 1/4 In. 60.00
Pitcher, Squat, Gallery Rim, Red Glaze, Dark Splotches, Applied Handle, 5 3/4 In. 165.00
Pitcher, Wheel Thrown, Bulbous, Pinched Spout, Applied Handle, c.1840, 8 1/4 In. 440.00
Pitcher, Wide Rim, Yellow, Green, Applied Handle, 7 In. 660.00
Pitcher, Yellow Spatter Tulip, Paneled, Red, Green, 9 3/4 In. 3740.00
Planter, Saucer Base, Molded Rim, Green Mottled, Opaque Glaze, 5 1/4 In. 330.00
Planter, Saucer Base, Mottled Glaze, 4 3/4 In. 140.00
Plate, 3-Color Rainbow, Open Field Center, Alternating Bands, 9 In. 745.00
Plate, Brown, Yellow Slip, Glazed, 8 1/2 In. 305.00
Plate, Coggled Rim, ABC, Yellow Slip, New England, Early 19th Century, 10 1/4 In. 2233.00
Plate, Coggled Rim, Manganese Glaze, 7 1/2 In. 72.00
Plate, Coggled Rim, Round, Slip Decoration, Stylized Tulip, 19th Century, 8 In. 2150.00
Plate, Coggled Rim, Sgraffito, Fish, Fowl, Stylized Tulips, Leaves, 1800s, 11 In. 1795.00
Plate, Coggled Rim, Sgraffito, Perched Bird, Yellow, Green Glaze, c.1920, 8 3/4 In. 3410.00
Plate, Coggled Rim, Slip Decorated, Yellow, Green Squiggle, 1800s, 13 5/8 In. 1435.00
Plate, Coggled Rim, Stylized Tulip, Yellow Slip, Green Daubs, 19th Century, 7 In. 1315.00
Plate, Coggled Rim, Yellow 4-Quill Glaze, Green Daubs, Pa., 1800s, 10 In. 960.00

Plate, Coggled Rim, Yellow Slip Line, Orange Glaze, 6 1/2 In. 605.00
Plate, Coggled Rim, Yellow Slip, 3 Triple Wavy Lines, Early 19th Century, 10 3/8 In. ... 940.00
Plate, Coggled Rim, Yellow Slip, 4 Wavy Line Bands, Early 19th Century, 11 1/2 In. 440.00
Plate, Coggled Rim, Yellow Slip, Glazed, 19th Century, 7 1/4 In. 365.00
Plate, Coggled Rim, Yellow Slip, Glazed, 7 3/4 In. 195.00
Plate, Coggled Rim, Yellow Slip, Green Glaze Daubs, 19th Century, 12 1/2 In. 4540.00
Plate, Coggled Rim, Yellow Slip, Inscription, Plump, c.1840, 12 In. 2868.00
Plate, Coggled Rim, Yellow Slip, Orange Glaze, Initials L. B., 10 In. 1870.00
Plate, Coggled Rim, Yellow Slip, Orange, Brown Glaze, 10 In. 410.00
Plate, Coggled Rim, Yellow Slip, Orange, Brown Ground, 7 3/4 In. 165.00
Plate, Coggled Rim, Yellow Slip, Pa., 19th Century, 10 3/4 In. 145.00
Plate, Coggled Rim, Yellow Slip, Wavy Line, Leaf Motif, Early 19th Century, 8 In. 410.00
Plate, Coggled Rim, Yellow Slip, Wavy Line, Stylized Leaf, 19th Century, 9 3/4 In. 705.00
Plate, Coggled Rim, Yellow Slip, Wavy Lines, Early 19th Century, 11 In. 380.00
Plate, Coggled Rim, Yellow Squiggle Slip, Green Daubs, Pa., 1800s, 6 In. 3825.00
Plate, Cut Edge, Green, Yellow Hexes, Dots, Willoughby Smith, c.1880, 8 In. 4540.00
Plate, Green, Brown Slip, Orange Glaze, 7 3/4 In. 635.00
Plate, Mary's Dish, Dots, Squiggly Lines, Slip Decorated, 11 3/4 In. 5280.00
Plate, Mottled Glaze, Pa., 19th Century, 8 3/4 In. 330.00
Plate, Orange Glaze, Mid 19th Century, Signed John W. Bell, Pa., 8 In. 360.00
Plate, Purple Spatter Tulip, Paneled, Blue, Red Tulip, Green Leaves, 8 1/4 In. 415.00
Plate, Red & Green Flower, Tapering Sides, Yellow Glaze Interior, c.1880, 6 In. 1435.00
Plate, Sgraffito, Bird, Flowers, Yellow, Green Glaze, 12 In. 1035.00
Plate, Sgraffito, Militia Men, Shoulder Firelock, Mottled Glaze, 8 1/4 In. 358.00
Plate, Sgraffito, Pig & Tulip, Yellow & Green, Seagreaves, 11 x 8 3/4 In. 248.00
Plate, Sgraffito, Tree, Tulips, Flowers, Yellow, Green Glaze, 1 3/4 x 11 In. 11000.00
Plate, Slip, Squiggle, Green, 19th Century, 8 3/4 In. 72.00
Plate, Tulip, Green Sponge, Paneled, Red, Green, 10 In. 635.00
Plate, Tulip, Red Flower, Blue Sponge, Yellow Highlights, Leaves, 8 3/4 In. 165.00
Plate, Yellow Slip Zigzag, 19th Century, 7 1/4 In. 330.00
Plate, Zigzag, Crisscross, Glazed, Pa., 19th Century, 8 1/4 In. 105.00
Saucer, Blue, Red, Green Spatter Festoon 220.00
Sugar, Bulbous, Red, Yellow Spatter Drape Pattern, Corn Flower, 4 1/2 In. 2640.00
Sugar, Cover, Bulbous, Red, Blue Spatter Drape, 4 3/4 In. 415.00
Sugar, Cover, Manganese Glaze, 19th Century, Applied Ribbed Handles, 3 1/4 x 5 In. ... 94.00
Teapot, Yellow Spatter Tulip, Red, Green, 5 In. 4400.00
Vase, Coggled Rim, Applied Strap Handles, Bulbous, Mottled Glaze, 11 In. 1210.00
Vase, Cylindrical, Relief Dragon Design, Japan, 12 In. 58.00
Wash Bowl, Paneled, Black House, Teal Trees, Blue Sponge, Green, 4 1/2 x 14 In. 1760.00
Waste Bowl, Blue Spatter, Blue Interior Transfer, Eagle, Shield, 3 x 5 1/2 In. 220.00
Waste Bowl, Flared Edge, Bull's-Eye, Red, Green Rainbow Spatter, 3 x 5 1/2 In. 110.00

REGOUT, see Maastricht category.

RICHARD was the mark used on acid-etched cameo glass vases, bowls, night-lights, and lamps made by the Austrian company Loetz after 1918. The pieces were very similar to the French cameo glasswares made by Daum, Galle, and others.

Bottle, Boats In Water, Brown, Citron, Signed, 4 3/4 In. 290.00
Vase, Cameo, Gray, Amethyst Overlay, Mountain Lake Scene, Castle, c.1915, 21 1/2 In. ... 635.00
Vase, Cameo, Lemon Yellow, Cut With Royal Blue Thistles, c.1915, 6 In. 315.00
Vase, Crimson Palm Trees, Mosque, Mountains, Yellow Orange Sky, Signed, 16 In. 2800.00
Vase, Purple Berries, Leaves, Mottled Orange Ground, Cameo, 4 In. 290.00

RIDGWAY pottery has been made in the Staffordshire district in England since 1808 by a series of companies with the name Ridgway. The transfer-design dinner sets are the most widely known product. They are still being made. Other pieces of Ridgway are listed under Flow Blue.

Butter, Cover, Heritage Pattern, Green Transfer, Marked, 7 1/2 In. 50.00
Pitcher, Embossed Floral Band, Painted Flowers, Shaped Handles, Stoneware, 5 In. 70.00
Pitcher, Indus Pattern, Registry Mark, 1877, 11 1/4 In. 230.00
Plate, Turkey Scene, Flow Blue, 10 In. 150.00

Plate, Tyrolean Pattern, Brown Transfer, Marked, 10 1/4 In.	135.00
Platter, Classic Pattern, Black Transfer, Hand Painted Yellow Trim, Oval, 17 In.	70.00
Teapot, Black Cover, Homemaker Pattern, 1950s, 5 In.	570.00
Teapot, English Garden Pattern, Marked, 8 3/4 In.	40.00
Tureen, Cover, Burlington Pattern, Cobalt Blue Flowers, Gold Trim, Handles, 7 1/2 In.	75.00
Tureen, Cover, Stand, Imari Pattern, Imperial Stone, c.1835, 15 In.	1016.00

RIFLES that are firearms are not listed in this book. BB guns and air rifles are listed in the Toy category.

RIVIERA dinnerware was made by the Homer Laughlin Co. of Newell, West Virginia, from 1938 to 1950. The pattern was similar in coloring and in mood to Fiesta and Harlequin. The Riviera plates and cup handles were square. For more information, see *Kovels' Depression Glass & Dinnerware Price List.*

Ivory, Cup	13.00
Ivory, Plate, Dinner, 9 3/4 In.	16.00
Ivory, Platter, Oval, 11 In.	20.00
Light Green, Cup	10.00
Light Green, Plate, Salad, 7 In.	15.00
Light Green, Plate, Soup, 8 In.	25.00
Light Green, Saltshaker	12.00
Mauve Blue, Casserole, Cover	140.00
Mauve Blue, Pitcher, Juice, 5 3/4 In.	55.00
Mauve Blue, Plate, Bread & Butter, 6 1/4 In.	9.00
Mauve Blue, Tumbler, Handle	75.00
Red, Bowl, Vegetable, 8 1/4 In.	30.00
Red, Casserole, Cover	90.00
Red, Sugar	12.00
Yellow, Bowl, Fruit, 5 1/2 In.	14.00
Yellow, Pitcher, Juice, 5 3/4 In.	195.00
Yellow, Platter, Oval, 11 In.	25.00
Yellow, Teapot, Cover	185.00

ROCKINGHAM, in the United States, is a pottery with a brown glaze that resembles tortoiseshell. It was made from 1840 to 1900 by many American potteries. Mottled brown Rockingham wares were first made in England at the Rockingham factory. Other types of ceramics were also made by the English firm. Related pieces may be listed in the Bennington category.

Baking Dish, Cloud Glaze, Elongated, Octagonal, Molded Rim, 9 1/2 x 11 3/4 In.	50.00
Bowl, Rolled Rim, Late 19th Century, 4 1/2 x 10 1/2 In.	75.00
Bust, John Wesley, Glazed, Redware, Early 19th Century, 10 3/4 In.	315.00
Candlestick, Dark Flint Glaze, Round, Tapered, Flared Base, Mid 19th Century, 9 1/4 In.	200.00
Creamer, Toby-Type, Mottled Brown, C-Scroll Handle, 6 In.	34.00
Croup Kettle, Mottle Brown Glaze, 7 In.	104.00
Cuspidor, Glazed, Yellowware, 5 x 9 In.	28.00
Figurine, Cat, Seated, Brown, Glaze, 12 1/4 x 6 1/2 In.	360.00
Figurine, Dog, Poodle, Seated, White, Fur, Gilt Collar, Lock, 19th Century, 4 3/4 In.	290.00
Figurine, Dog, Spaniel, Seated, 11 In.	425.00
Figurine, Dog, Spaniel, Seated, Staffordshire Style, Lock On Collar With Chain, 9 In.	99.00
Flask, Boot, Lacing On Left, Unglazed Sole, Mid 19th Century, 6 x 7 In.	50.00
Flask, Dark Glaze, Molded Cherubs, Man Resting, Floral Wreaths, Round, 7 3/4 In.	425.00
Flask, Figural, Mermaid, Brown Glaze, 7 x 4 In.	90.00
Flask, Fish, 10 3/4 In.	385.00
Jar, Cover, Glazed, Brown, Circular, Squat, Flattened Handle On Cover, 6 x 7 1/2 In.	99.00
Mug, Frog, Fling Glaze, Frog On Interior Base, Coggled, Ribbed Strap Handle, 3 3/8 In.	330.00
Pie Plate, Mottled, Glazed, Brown, Yellow, Curled Rim, 10 1/2 In.	66.00
Pitcher, 6 Sides, Mottled Brown Glaze, W. Bromley, Yellowware, 8 In.	1920.00
Pitcher, Flint Glaze, Paneled, 8 Sides, Bands At Rim, Neck & Base, 7 1/2 In.	300.00
Pitcher, Glazed, Hound Handle, Embossed Eagle, Stag, Rabbit, Yellowware, 8 1/2 In.	39.00
Pitcher, Glazed, Revolutionary War Battle Scene, George Washington, 12 In.	3050.00
Pitcher, Hound Handled, Grapevines, Hunt Scenes, East Liverpool, Ohio, 7 1/8 In.	1760.00
Pitcher, Hunter, Dog, Molded, Late 19th Century, 7 1/2 In.	25.00

Pitcher, Light Glaze, Flowers Under Spout, Paneled, Mid 19th Century, 9 In.	50.00
Pitcher, Oval Base, Paneled Sides, Flaring Rim, 11 In.	95.00
Pitcher, Peacock Pattern, 8 In.	56.00
Pitcher, Sydenham, Brown, Scrolled Rim, 9 3/4 In.	99.00
Pitcher, Water, Jolly Face, Figural, Brown Glaze, 8 In.	60.00
Pitcher, Water, Slip Case, Embossed Daniel Boone & Dog, Yellowware, 9 1/2 In.	226.00
Soap Dish, Signed Harker, 1840	195.00
Tureen, Glazed, Yellowware, 6 1/2 x 15 x 9 3/4 In.	165.00

ROGERS, see John Rogers category.

ROOKWOOD pottery was made in Cincinnati, Ohio, from 1880 to 1960. All of this art pottery is marked, most with the famous flame mark. The R is reversed and placed back to back with the letter P. Flames surround the letters. After 1900, a Roman numeral was added to the mark to indicate the year. The name and some of the molds were purchased in 1984. A few new pieces were made, but these were glazed in colors not used by the original company.

Ashtray, Buff High Glaze, Lions Club, 1950, 6 3/8 In.	58.00
Ashtray, Butterfly, Green Matte Glaze, 3 Sides, No. 2890, 1935, 5 1/2 In.	196.00
Ashtray, Fish, Celadon Green High Glaze, 1945, 7 In.	100.00
Ashtray, Fish, Green High Glaze, Kay Ley, 1947, 5 5/8 In.	80.00
Ashtray, Grotesque Face, Ivory Matte Glaze, No. 2457, 1945, 5 In.	200.00
Ashtray, Owl, Crystalline Matte Glaze, 1930, 4 In.	345.00
Ashtray, Rook, Black Matte Glaze, No. 1139, W. McDonald, 7 In.	520.00
Ashtray, Rook, Blue Matte Glaze, No. 1139, 1946, 7 1/2 x 4 In.	140.00
Basket, Yellow Pansies, Standard Glaze, Handles, Anna Bookprinter, 1886, 4 1/4 In.	200.00
Bookends, Bear, Nubian Black Glaze, 1948, 4 3/8 In.	748.00
Bookends, Blackbirds, Black Crystalline Matte Glaze, 1922, 5 3/8 In.	1265.00
Bookends, Colonial Women Standing, Polychrome, High Glaze, 1922, 5 7/8 In.	1265.00
Bookends, Cornucopia, Red, Green, Brown, Polychrome, 1921, 4 7/8 In.	1093.00
Bookends, Eagle, Wine Madder Glaze, 1945, 6 In.	230.00
Bookends, Flower Basket, Multicolored, Shirayamadani, 1927, 6 1/8 In.	345.00
Bookends, Girl, Sitting On Bench, Blue Matte Glaze, 1929, 6 1/4 In.	920.00
Bookends, Horse, Kneeling, Black Crystalline Matte Glaze, 1922, 5 1/2 In.	1955.00
Bookends, Kingfisher, Gray Matte Glaze, William McDonald, 1924, 5 3/4 In.	575.00
Bookends, Owl, Beige, Blue Speckled Matte Glaze, 1929, 6 3/4 In.	499.00
Bookends, Peacock, Yellow Matte Glaze, 1922, 5 In.	115.00
Bookends, Planter, Violet, Gray Glaze, 1952, 5 In.	173.00
Bookends, Rook, Blue Crystalline Matte Glaze, 1922, 5 1/8 In.	405.00
Bookends, Rook, Green & Red Matte Glaze, McDonald, 1930, 5 In.	635.00
Bookends, Rook, Mottled Blue Matte Glaze, McDonald, 1919, 6 1/4 In.	546.00
Bookends, Rook, Wine Madder Glaze, McDonald, 1943, 5 3/8 In.	230.00
Bookends, Sphinx, 7 1/2 In.	1350.00
Bookends, St. Francis, Ivory Matte, 1949, 7 1/4 In.	115.00
Bookends, Sunflower & Ladybug, Nursery Rhyme, Vellum, 1937, 3 3/4 In.	3450.00
Bookends, Water Lilies, Blue Matte Glaze, 1946, 3 1/2 In.	175.00
Bookends, Woman Holding Fan, Ivory, 1943, 6 5/8 In.	260.00
Bookends, Woman With Fan, Pink Matte Glaze, McDonald, 6 1/2 In.	92.00
Bowl, Animals, Embossed, Black Crystalline, Orange Interior, 1921, 2 7/8 In.	460.00
Bowl, Arts & Crafts, Blue Matte Glaze, No. 2133, 1916, 4 1/2 In.	175.00
Bowl, Blue, Teal Abstracts, Brown Bands, Turquoise Ground, Hentschel, 1921, 3 1/4 In. . . .	468.00
Bowl, Brown Matte Exterior, Blue Matte Interior, Scalloped, 1924, 4 3/4 x 10 In.	115.00
Bowl, Brown, Yellow, Rope Handle, Standard Glaze, 1886, 3 1/2 x 5 In.	248.00
Bowl, Butterflies, Green, Charcoal Drip Glaze, Aqua Interior, 1915, 3 In.	330.00
Bowl, Cherry Blossoms, Blue Tinted High Glaze, Charles McLaughlin, 1919, 5 1/2 In.	635.00
Bowl, Cobalt Blue Matte Glaze, 1915, 3 x 6 In.	195.00
Bowl, Diamonds & Leaves, Embossed Yellow Matte Glaze, Footed, 1922, 6 1/4 In.	140.00
Bowl, Greek Key, Blue, Green Vellum, Epply, 1909, 1 1/8 x 6 3/8 In.	750.00
Bowl, Lotus Blossom, Blue, Green, Red, Polychrome, Coyne, 1924, 4 1/2 In.	750.00
Bowl, Lotus Blossom, Green Matte Glaze, 1936, 3 x 7 3/4 In.	90.00
Bowl, Lotus Blossom, Petal, Embossed, Blue Matte Crystalline Glaze, 1928, 4 1/2 In.	185.00
Bowl, Stylized Peacock Feathers, Blue Matte Glaze, No. 2133, Hentschel, 8 1/2 In.	1380.00

Bowl, Underplate, Blue Ship, 1 1/2 x 6 3/8 In. 127.00
Box, Cigarette, Cover, Legionnaire, Green, 1934, 3 1/2 In. 127.00
Box, Cigarette, Cover, Pink Matte Glaze, Flower Finial, 1935, 4 3/8 In. 69.00
Box, Cover, Flowers, Faceted Corners, Lenore Asbury, 1924, 2 1/8 x 4 1/4 In. 750.00
Box, Cover, Pink Matte Glaze, 4 3/4 In. 115.00
Candlestick, Black Glossy Glaze, Flared Bobeche & Base, 1922, 10 1/2 In., Pair 175.00
Candlestick, Elephant, Ivory Matte Glaze, 1928, 4 In., Pair 290.00
Candlestick, Green Matte Glaze, Fluted, 1936, 5 1/8 In., Pair 127.00
Candlestick, Holly Leaf & Berry, Brown Ground, 1901, 3 In. 275.00
Candlestick, Mottled Blue Matte Glaze, 1917, 6 1/2 In., Pair 230.00
Candlestick, Pink, Green, Butterfly Matte Glaze, 1916, 1 1/2 In. 115.00
Candlestick, Relief Scroll, Red Matte Glaze, 1917, 9 In., Pair 290.00
Candlestick, Tulips, Embossed, Pink Matte Glaze, 1922, 10 1/2 In., Pair 405.00
Candlestick, Webbed, Mottled Black & Pink, 1937, 3 5/8 In., Pair 127.00
Chalice, Cincinnatus, Bust, Berries & Leaves, Green Matte Glaze, 1906, 5 3/4 In. 385.00
Chamberstick, Violets, Yellow, Standard Glaze, Jeannette, Swing, 1894, 3 In. 345.00
Coffeepot, Frogs, Crickets, Glossy Glaze, Gold Highlights, Nichols, 1882, 9 5/8 In. 1035.00
Coffeepot, Sparrow, Yellow, Brown, Matt Daly, 1884, 9 In. 115.00
Creamer, White, Ribbed, Sara Sax, 1912, 3 In. 230.00
Dish, Cover, Blue Ship, 3 3/8 x 7 3/8 In. 375.00
Dish, Powder Blue, Summit Country Day School, 1965, 7 1/2 In. 115.00
Ewer, Autumn Leaves, 3 Lips, Rose Fechheimer, 1898, 8 3/4 In. 635.00
Ewer, Autumn Leaves, Edith Felton, 1899, 4 3/4 In. 345.00
Ewer, Blackberries, Emma Foertmeyer, 1891, 9 3/4 In. 1095.00
Ewer, Cherries, No. 3874, 14 1/2 In. 1335.00
Ewer, Clovers, Helen Stuntz, 1892, 5 In. 865.00
Ewer, Daffodils, Standard Glaze, Silver Overlay, Mary Nourse, 1897, 10 7/8 In. 1495.00
Ewer, Flowers Marian Hastings Smalley, c.1901, 7 1/4 In. 440.00
Ewer, Flowers, Leaves, Peach, Yellow, A.R. Valentien, 1893, 9 3/4 x 9 In. 660.00
Ewer, Flowers, Molded Trefoil Lip, 1895, 6 In. 325.00
Ewer, Leaves & Berries, Pink & Blue Matte Glaze, No. 6008E, Coyne, 10 1/4 In. 978.00
Ewer, Leaves, Green, Standard Glaze, Jeannette Swing, 1900, 6 1/8 In. 520.00
Ewer, Maple Leaves, Standard Glaze, Caroline Steinle, 1899, 7 In. 489.00
Ewer, Nasturtiums, Kataro Shirayamadani, 1890, 8 1/2 In. 1955.00
Ewer, Nasturtiums, Standard Glaze, Trefoil Spout, Hickman, 1897, 7 1/4 In. 440.00
Ewer, Orange Clover Blossoms, Standard Glaze, Wm. McDonald, 1891, 10 x 6 1/4 In. . . . 750.00
Ewer, Pansies, Artus Van Briggle, 1890, 10 1/4 In. 1035.00
Ewer, Red Maple Leaves, Standard Glaze, No. 584C, R. Fechheimer, 5 1/2 In. 405.00
Ewer, Water Lilies, L.N. Lincoln, No. 611B, 1902, 10 In. 978.00
Ewer, Wild Rose, Standard Glaze, Valentien, 1890, 9 1/2 In. 920.00
Ewer, Yellow Apple Blossoms, Standard Glaze, William P. McDonald, 7 1/4 In. 520.00
Figurine, Cat, Brown High Glaze, 4 In. 460.00
Figurine, Elephant, Green & Ivory Matte Glaze, No. 6124, W. McDonald, 1931, 7 In. 405.00
Figurine, Kingfisher, Green, 1925, 5 1/8 In. 210.00
Figurine, Radio Singers, Trio, Pink High Glaze, No. 6683, 4 1/2 In. 635.00
Flower Frog, Nude Woman, Mushrooms, Green High Glaze, No. 2281, 1921, 6 1/2 In. . . . 375.00
Ginger Jar, Cover, Birds Perched On Branches, Edward Hurley, c.1922, 14 1/2 In. 4780.00
Humidor, Orange Nicotana Blossoms, Standard Glaze, Robert Horsfall, 1893, 6 1/4 In. . . . 575.00
Humidor, Pueblo Indian, Standard Glaze, Grace Young, 1901, 6 In. 4315.00
Humidor, Spiders, Bats, Brown Ground, Maria Nichols, 1882, 6 x 6 In. 2185.00
Humidor, Tobacco Flowers, Standard Glaze, Silver Overlay, Pipes, S. Toohey, 5 1/2 In. . . 920.00
Inkwell, Chinese Medallions, Standard Glaze, Round, No. 418, Van Briggle, 5 1/4 In. 490.00
Inkwell, Maple Leaf, Embossed, Mottled Sea Green Over Blue, 1921, 2 3/4 In. 360.00
Inkwell, Oak Leaf, Olive Green, Cobalt Blue, 4 Panels, 1912, 2 1/2 x 2 1/4 In. 330.00
Inkwell, Sphinx, Blue Green Glaze, 1921, 8 x 10 In. 1600.00
Jar, Chartreuse High Glaze, 1948, 3 5/8 In. 45.00
Jar, Cover, Birds, Flowers, Vines, Turquoise, Tan Interior, Epply, 1923, 10 1/4 In. 2875.00
Jar, Cover, Dome, Thistle, Yellow Ground, 6 Sides, No. 2750, L.N. Lincoln, 8 In. 1265.00
Jar, Cover, Flowers, Black Opal Glaze, 4 Sides, No. 2249, S. Sax, 4 1/2 In. 1265.00
Jar, Cover, Flowers, Red, Orange, Mauve, Blue, Green Matte Ground, Sax, 4 1/2 In. 6900.00
Jar, Cover, Nuts, Green, Peanut Finial, 1949, 5 1/4 In. 115.00
Jar, Cover, Oak Leaves, Ombroso Glaze, 1911, 4 1/4 In. 1035.00
Jar, Potpourri, Pink Matte Glaze, 4 1/8 In. 140.00

Jardiniere, Pinecone, Cream, Green, Brown Glaze, 1931, 8 In. 470.00
Jug, Beagle Head, Standard Glaze, Edward T. Hurley, 1900, 8 In. 1430.00
Jug, Butterflies, Bamboo, Brown, Green, Tan Ground, Valentien, 1884, 8 1/4 In. 805.00
Jug, Butterfly, Bamboo, Brown, Ivory, Blue, Green Ground, Hirschfeld, 1883, 4 1/2 In. . . 405.00
Jug, Geometric Pattern, Charcoal Green Matte Glaze, 1906, 7 1/2 In. 660.00
Jug, Grapes, Standard Glaze, Fechheimer, 1898, 5 1/2 In. 520.00
Jug, Stopper, Brown Berries, Standard Glaze, E.T. Hurley, 1900, 7 3/4 In. 635.00
Jug, Whiskey, Greek Key, Matte Glaze, Earl Menzel, 1901, 7 5/8 In. 690.00
Lamp, Flowers, Yellow, Green, Brass Fittings, K. Shirayamadani, 1903, 13 x 5 In. 6900.00
Lamp, Roses, 2 Handles, Foil Label, 1949, 10 1/4 In. 290.00
Letter Holder, Ben Franklin Postage Stamp, Blue High Glaze, 3 In. . . . . 175.00 to 290.00
Loving Cup, Portrait Of Man, Sturgis Laurence, 1898, 6 1/4 In. 1725.00
Match Holder, Lion, Embossed, Mottled Rose Over Brown, 1911, 4 7/8 In. 635.00
Match Holder, Owl, Acorn, Leaf Base, Ivory Matte Glaze, 1933, 4 1/2 In. 345.00
Mug, Corn, Cornflowers, Light Standard Glaze, E. Nourse, 1896, 4 5/8 In. 690.00
Mug, Corn, Kernels On Cob, Husk Leaves, Brown Matte, 1902, 5 1/2 x 5 1/2 In. 440.00
Mug, Flowers, Carrie Steinle, 1898, 5 3/4 In. 750.00
Mug, Gooseberries, Standard Glaze, 3 Handles, Lenore Asbury, 1899, 4 1/2 In. 520.00
Mug, Leaves, Sea Green, Silver Overlay, Sallie Coyne, 1905, 5 1/4 In. 920.00
Mug, Monkey Hanging From Tree, Matthew Daly, 1891, 4 1/2 x 4 1/2 In. 635.00
Mug, Owl, Acorns, Oak Leaves, Gray Vellum Glaze, Sara Sax, 1906, 5 1/4 In. 546.00
Paperweight, 2 Geese, Green Matte Glaze, Mottled Rust, 1935, 4 In. 115.00
Paperweight, Canary, Ivory Matte, 1946, 4 In. 150.00
Paperweight, Cat, Blue High Glaze, 1965, 4 1/2 In. 920.00
Paperweight, Cat, Gray, Box, 1964, 4 1/2 In. 805.00
Paperweight, Cat, Ivory Matte Glaze, 1929, 2 3/4 In. 400.00
Paperweight, Cocker Spaniel, Turquoise Matte Crystalline Glaze, 1965, 4 1/4 In. 345.00
Paperweight, Cocker Spaniel, Wine Madder Glaze, 1954, 4 1/4 In. 520.00
Paperweight, Crab, Bronze, Green Over Brown Patina, Hurley, 5/8 x 3 1/2 In. 1095.00
Paperweight, Deer, Ivory Matte Glaze, Louise Abel, 1935, 4 3/8 In. 260.00
Paperweight, Dog, Raised Paw, Feathery Blue Matte Glaze, 1927, 4 3/4 In. 375.00
Paperweight, Donkey, White Matte Glaze, Louise Abel, 1935, 6 In. 490.00
Paperweight, Duck, Yellow Porcelain Glaze, 1950, 4 3/8 In. 575.00
Paperweight, Elephant, Seated, Ivory Matte Glaze, 1937, 3 3/4 In. 290.00
Paperweight, Elephant, White Matte Glaze, 1934, 3 3/4 In. 575.00
Paperweight, Goat, Ivory Matte Glaze, 1931, 6 1/4 In. 140.00
Paperweight, Kitten, Black Matte Glaze, Louise Abel, 1931, 6 3/4 In. 1150.00
Paperweight, Pelican, Mottled Burnt Orange Matte Glaze, 1925, 6 1/4 In. 520.00
Paperweight, Penguin, Ivory Matte Glaze, 1934, 5 1/8 In. 1265.00
Paperweight, Potter At Wheel, Green Matte Glaze, 1940, 3 5/8 In. 196.00
Paperweight, Rabbit, Blue, White Base, 1946, 3 1/4 In. 430.00
Paperweight, Rabbit, Ivory Matte Glaze, 1949, 3 1/4 In. . . . . 260.00 to 490.00
Paperweight, Rook, Blue Matte Glaze, 1918, 2 3/4 In. 430.00
Paperweight, Rook, Tile, Advertising, Brown Matte Glaze, 1919, 2 5/8 In. 1035.00
Paperweight, Rooster, Polychrome, McDonald, 1943, 5 In. 690.00
Paperweight, Rooster, White, No. 6030, 1928, 5 In. 70.00
Paperweight, Squirrel, Blue Glaze Over Brown, Sallie Toohey, 1937, 4 1/8 In. 635.00
Paperweight, Squirrel, Buff, Green Matte Glaze, 1928, 4 1/4 In. 220.00
Paperweight, Woman, Nude, Glossy Teal Glaze, 4 1/2 In. 145.00
Pencil Holder, Dark Blue Crystalline Matte Glaze, 1925, 4 3/4 In. 545.00
Pencil Holder, Rook, Green Matte Frogskin Glaze, 1934, 4 5/8 In. 490.00
Pie Plate, Bamboo Trees, Landscape, Matt Daly, 1883, 6 1/2 In. 230.00
Pitcher, Cherries, Ed Diers, 1901, 3 1/2 In. 430.00
Pitcher, Cherries, Elizabeth Lincoln, 1900, 4 In. 475.00
Pitcher, Cottonwood Seeds, Ivory Jewel, Harriet Elizabeth Wilcox, c.1888, 7 1/2 In. 460.00
Pitcher, Daisies, Leaf Handle, Standard Glaze, Constance Baker, 1890, 3 3/4 In. 259.00
Pitcher, Mottled Green Matte Glaze, 1932, 8 3/4 In. 175.00
Pitcher, Orchids, Yellow, Green Leaves, Brown, Yellow Ground, 1899, 11 3/4 In. 885.00
Pitcher, Poppies, Petals, Albert Robert Valentien, 1891, 20 1/2 x 11 In. 2310.00
Pitcher, Roses, Silver Overlay, 1886, 5 3/8 In. 3795.00
Pitcher, Woman, Trees & Grasses, Aerial Blue Glaze, No 769, Horsfall, 1895, 3 In. 1725.00
Planter, Fruit & Flower Swags, Faience, Pastel, Gray Crackle Ground, 10 1/4 In 460.00
Planter, Papyrus Leaves, Turquoise Matte Glaze, Art Deco, 1921, 4 x 8 3/4 x 5 In. 115.00

Plaque, Cockatoo, Red, Green, Polychrome, Shirayamadani, 1943, 9 3/8 x 7 In. 1610.00
Plaque, Landscape, Framed, E.T. Hurley, 1914, 8 1/2 x 10 1/2 In. 6575.00
Plaque, Landscape, Gray, Blue, Tan, Vellum Glaze, Sax, 1914, 9 x 14 1/4 In. 5750.00
Plaque, Landscape, River, Kate Van Horne, 1915, 8 3/4 x 11 In. 5750.00
Plaque, Landscape, Tall Pine Tree, Vellum Glaze, Hurley, 1912, 6 x 8 In. 4900.00
Plaque, Landscape, Winter Twilight, Vellum, E. Mcdermott, 1910, 9 x 11 1/2 In. 8625.00
Plaque, Waterfall, F. Rothenbusch, 1927, 9 x 7 In. 10350.00
Plate, White Lotus, Brown Ground, Matt Daly, 1886, 10 In. 520.00
Rose Bowl, Carved Roses, Turquoise Matte Glaze, No. 6031, 1928, 7 In. 460.00
Stein, American Indian, No. 656, Pewter Lid, Horsfall, c.1895, 1/2 Liter, 6 1/2 In. 4025.00
Stein, Corn, Asbury, 1899, 7 1/4 x 4 5/8 In. 475.00
Stein, Cucumber Green Matte Glaze, Art Deco, 1904, 5 1/2 In. 300.00
Stein, Eagle, Green Matte Glaze, 1965, 5 In. 140.00
Stein, Eagle, Wine Madder Glaze, Pewter Lid, 1948, 5 1/2 In. 460.00
Stein, Frogs, Water Lilies, Brown, Green Ground, Lid, Shirayamadani, 1896, 8 3/4 In. . . . 2990.00
Stein, Owl, Oak Branch & Acorns, 1907, 5 3/8 In. 635.00
Sugar, Cover, Holly, Standard Glaze, Carl Schmidt, 1899, 3 3/4 In. 578.00
Sugar & Creamer, Sunny Yellow High Glaze 90.00
Tea Set, Blue Ship, 1887, 14 Piece 920.00
Tea Set, Blue Ship, 8 Sides, 6-In. Pot, 3 Piece 430.00
Teapot, Cover, Blue Ship, 1925, 4 3/8 In. 260.00
Tile, Carved Poppy, Brown, Blue, Orange & Green Matte Glaze, Frame, 6 x 12 In. 1840.00
Tile, Flower, Green, Gray, Tan Matte Glaze, Faience, 1976, 5 7/8 In. 690.00
Tile, Glasgow Rose Tree, Blue & Red Matte Glaze, Faience, Arts & Crafts, 4 In. 290.00
Tile, Mountains, Lake, Trees, Faience, Polychrome Raised Outline, 17 1/2 In. 3105.00
Tile, Pink Flowers, Green Leaves, Blue Ground, 1930, 6 In. 115.00
Tile, Pink Grapes, Green Leaves, Blue Ground, 1925, 6 In. 145.00
Tile, Sea Dragon, Tan, Green Seaweed, Red Glaze, Faience, Frame, 5 3/4 In. 525.00
Tile, Seagulls In Flight, Green & Blue Ground, 1925, 5 3/4 In. 175.00
Tile, Seagulls, Embossed, Green Over Mottled Red, Brown, Round, 1930, 5 3/4 In. 375.00
Tile, Ship, Green, Yellow, Blue, Brown, Round, Faience, 12 In. 2760.00
Tile, Ships At Sea, Green, Yellow, Blue, Brown, Round, Faience, 12 In. 2760.00
Tile, Stylized Birds In Paradise, Blue & Green Leaves, 1921, 6 In. 290.00
Tile, Stylized Fruit, Yellow, Green Ground, Black, Faience, Matte Raised Outline, 6 In. . . 345.00
Tile, Trees Along Riverbank, Green, Brown, Blue, Faience, Oak Frame, 12 In. 2875.00
Tile, Woman With Parasol, Blue Ground, Amber, Pink Matte Glaze, Faience, Frame, 6 In. 175.00
Tray, Blue & Green Matte Glaze, No. 1048D, 1905, 5 In. 230.00
Tray, Card, Grapes, Turquoise Crystalline Matte Glaze, 1943, 7 In. 175.00
Tray, Duck, Maroon Matte Glaze, 1929, 2 5/8 In. 115.00
Tray, Nude, Blue High Glaze, 1945, 1 1/4 In x 4 1/4 In. 185.00
Tray, Peach Bloom, Iris Glaze, Irregularly Shaped Rim, S. Toohey, 5 1/2 In. 155.00
Trivet, Basket Of Flowers, Butterflies, Matte Glaze, 1940, 5 5/8 In. 345.00
Trivet, Bluebird, On Branch, Blue Ground, Round, 1922, 6 In. 316.00
Trivet, Bull, Brown High Glaze, Round, 1949, 3 1/4 In. 175.00
Trivet, Dove, No. 3124, Pink, Purple, Pink Lattice, Blue Ground, 1924, 5 3/4 In. 230.00
Trivet, Dutch Family, No. 3205, 1940, 5 1/2 In. 175.00
Trivet, Dutch Landscape, Green, Purple, Blue, Ivory, 1927, 5 3/4 In. 345.00
Trivet, Golden Grapes, Leaves, Blue Ground, Arts & Crafts Frame, 1929, 6 In. 375.00
Trivet, Parrot, No. 3077, 1921, 5 1/2 In. 259.00
Trivet, Pigeon, 1924, 5 3/4 In. 635.00
Trivet, Pink Poppies, No. 1631, 1921, 5 1/2 In. 345.00
Trivet, Rook, No. 1794, 1943, 5 1/2 In. 520.00
Trivet, Seagulls, No. 2350, Round, 1925, 6 In. 345.00
Trivet, Seagulls, No. 2351, Round, 1930, 5 3/4 In. 316.00
Trivet, Vines, No. 3091, 6 Sides, 1930, 6 In. 345.00
Trivet, Yellow Bird, No. 2349, Round, 1930, 6 In. 200.00
Urn, Deer, Leaves, Maroon, Mauve Ground, Handles, Jens Jensen, 1930, 8 In. 805.00
Urn, Orange Clover Blossoms, Green Leaves, Standard Glaze, Valentien, c.1889, 7 In. . . . 920.00
Vase, Abstract Leaves, Matte Glaze, Wilhelmine Rehm, 1934, 5 5/8 In. 980.00
Vase, Amaryllis, Rose Matte Glaze, Shirayamadani, 1933, 6 1/8 In. 865.00
Vase, American Indian, Artus Van Briggle, 1898, 6 5/8 In. 6615.00
Vase, American Indian, Standard Glaze, Baker, 1900, 9 7/8 In. 5750.00
Vase, Apple Blossoms At Neck, Vellum, No. 1655F, K. Van Horne, 6 1/2 In. 635.00

Vase, Bamboo, Embossed, On Shoulder, Mottled Green & Brown Glaze, 1911, 6 7/8 In. ... 765.00
Vase, Berries & Leaves, Embossed, Green Matte Glaze, Round, 1939, 4 In. 290.00
Vase, Berries, Branches, Green, Brown, Oval, 1903, 6 1/4 In. 440.00
Vase, Berries, Leaves, Underglaze Slip, c.1890, 6 In. 345.00
Vase, Berries, Vellum, Lenore Asbury, 1924, 7 In. 1495.00
Vase, Birch Trees, Gray, White Ground, Vellum, L. Epply, 1914, 9 x 3 1/2 In. 2090.00
Vase, Birch Trees, Pink, Blue Sky, Oval, E.T. Hurley, 1916, 11 x 4 1/2 In. 3740.00
Vase, Bird Perched On Branch, Oriental Grasses, M. Andrew Daly, 1882, 7 In. 440.00
Vase, Birds, Flowers, Red, Purple, Green, Purple Ground, Blue Interior, Oval, 7 3/4 In. 1495.00
Vase, Birds, Leaves, Blossoms, Teal Ground, High Glaze, Jens Jensen, 1948, 6 In. 2990.00
Vase, Black Man, Incised, Teal, Cobalt, French Red, Orange Interior, Sax, 1921, 13 3/4 In. 1725.00
Vase, Blossoms, Embossed, Turquoise Crackle Glaze, 1947, 12 In. 259.00
Vase, Blossoms, Leaves, Yellow Ground, Porcelain, Sara Sax, 1923, 10 x 3 1/4 In. 3335.00
Vase, Blossoms, On Shoulder, Blue, Gold, White, Shirayamadani, 1887, 6 In. 1840.00
Vase, Blue Matte Glaze, Embossed, Swirled Band, Handles, 1919, 8 1/2 In. 400.00
Vase, Blue Matte Glaze, Embossed, Swirled Panels, Tapered, 1925, 6 In. 375.00
Vase, Blue Semimatte Glaze, Faceted, Flared Rim, 1924, 5 1/2 In. 259.00
Vase, Blue, Green Butterfat Matte Glaze, Bottle Shape, Handles, 1921, 7 1/2 In. 400.00
Vase, Blue, Terra-Cotta, Mauve, Impressed, 1913, 10 3/4 In. 1528.00
Vase, Blueberries, Leaves, Jewel Porcelain, Pink, Blue, No. 5194F, L. Epply, 5 In. 550.00
Vase, Blueberries, Leaves, Shaded Pink To Green Ground, Tapered, Jones, 1927, 7 In. 980.00
Vase, Bluebirds Flying, Mauve Ground, Spherical, Sara Sax, 1917, 4 1/2 x 8 1/2 In. 1840.00
Vase, Boats, Vellum Glaze, Sara Sax, 1913, 9 1/4 In. 1840.00
Vase, Boomerang, On Shoulder, Wave Panels, Mocha Brown Glaze, 1925, 9 1/8 In. 358.00
Vase, Branches, Flowering, Pink, Iris Glaze, Edward T. Hurley, 1901, 9 1/4 In. 2760.00
Vase, Branches, Incised, Brown Ground, Matte, Rose Fechheimer, 1905, 10 x 4 In. 3220.00
Vase, Brown Coromandel Glaze, Flared Rim, No. 6308C, 1932, 7 In. 575.00
Vase, Brown Glaze, Earl Menzel, 1954, 6 In. 260.00
Vase, Buckeyes, Leaves, Standard Glaze, Silver Overlay, 1892, 9 1/2 In. 2300.00
Vase, Bud, Calla Lily, Turquoise Blue Matte Glaze, 1958, 5 In. 104.00
Vase, Bud, Fruit Over Lattice Ground, Ivory, Square, 1935, 5 1/2 In. 90.00
Vase, Bud, Turquoise, 1949, 6 3/4 In. 105.00
Vase, Butterflies, Embossed, Green Matte Glaze, 1935, 4 3/4 In. 195.00
Vase, Butterflies, Embossed, Turquoise Matte Crystalline Glaze, 1948, 4 3/8 In. 196.00
Vase, Butterflies, Green High Glaze, Round, Tapered, No. 6509, 4 1/2 In. 185.00
Vase, Butterfly, Grasses, Limoges Style, Bottle Shape, A.R. Valentien, c.1884, 12 In. 400.00
Vase, Butterfly, Grasses, Mahogany Glaze, Low, Wide Mouth, M. Rettig, 1885, 3 In. 490.00
Vase, Butterfly, Ocher, Indigo Blue, Ivory Tan, 1946, 4 3/4 x 5 In. 715.00
Vase, Cardinals On Bowl, Brown Matte, Magenta Interior, 6 Sides, 1918, 4 3/4 In. 385.00
Vase, Carnations, White, Blue, Green Ground, Vellum Glaze, Diers, 1926, 8 1/8 In. 1725.00
Vase, Checkerboard, Purple Matte Glaze, 1930, 5 1/8 In. 230.00
Vase, Cherries, Standard Glaze, Flared, Mary Nourse, 1892, 7 3/8 In. 460.00
Vase, Cherry Blossoms, Black Branches, Iris Glaze, No. 951C, Shirayamadani, 10 In. 8625.00
Vase, Cherry Blossoms, Blue Matte Ground, Pink Interior, McLaughlin, 1925, 8 1/4 In. .. 660.00
Vase, Cherry Blossoms, Ivory Panel, Mint Green Body, Vellum, Lincoln, 1909, 6 In. 660.00
Vase, Cherry Blossoms, Stylized, Gray, Brown, Lenore Asbury, 1925, 5 5/8 In. 430.00
Vase, Cherry Blossoms, Stylized, On Shoulder, Blue, Mauve, Wilcox, 1925, 4 1/8 In. 635.00
Vase, Cherry Blossoms, Stylized, On Shoulder, Blue, Rose, Ed Diers, 1929, 4 1/8 In. 805.00
Vase, Chrysanthemums, Iris Glaze, Edward Diers, 1900, 8 1/2 In. 2300.00
Vase, Chrysanthemums, Multicolored, Black, Red To Cream Base, Lincoln, 14 In. 2875.00
Vase, Clover, Black, Brown, Iris Glaze, Ed Diers, 1902, 7 1/4 x 3 3/4 In. 2090.00
Vase, Clover, Brown To Gold Ground, Iris Glaze, Rothenbusch, 1903, 6 5/8 In. 1095.00
Vase, Clover, Orange, White, Gray To Peach Ground, Iris Glaze, Oval, 1903, 7 3/4 In. ... 1150.00
Vase, Clover, Standard Glaze, Cutout Top, No. 452, A.M. Valentien, 1892, 7 1/2 In. 1035.00
Vase, Clover, Standard Glaze, Lindeman, 1900, 8 3/4 In. 259.00
Vase, Cobalt Blue Porcelain Glaze, Citron Interior, 1921, 8 7/8 In. 115.00
Vase, Columns, Lake, Poplars, Vellum, No. 1663D, Ed Diers, 1910, 9 In. 3740.00
Vase, Cornflowers, Yellow, Orange, Standard Glaze, Oval, Lincoln, 1902, 6 1/2 In. 92.00
Vase, Crocuses, Blue Ground, Vellum, Bulbous, Ed Diers, 1930, 6 1/2 x 3 1/2 In. 2530.00
Vase, Crocuses, Blue, Gold, Iris Glaze, Carl Schmidt, 1908, 9 In. 3105.00
Vase, Currents, Red, Vellum, Lenore Asbury, 1922, 9 In. 2300.00
Vase, Daffodils, Yellow, Green, Standard Glaze, Sallie E. Coyne, 1898, 7 3/4 In. 865.00
Vase, Daisies, Blue High Glaze, 1946, 5 1/2 In. 105.00

Vase, Daisies, Caroline Steinle, 1909, 4 3/4 In. 500.00
Vase, Daisies, White, Black Shaded To Cream Ground, Olga Reed, 1903, 10 1/4 In. 2300.00
Vase, Daisies, White, Tan Ground, Valentien, 1885, 10 In. 173.00
Vase, Daisies, White, Yellow, Green, Vellum, Elizabeth Lincoln, 1912, 7 1/2 x 3 In. 1210.00
Vase, Daisy, Golden Yellow, Standard Glaze, Anna Bookprinter, 1885, 9 1/2 x 3 In. 385.00
Vase, Dandelions, Leaves, 1897, 13 In. 1380.00
Vase, Deer, Jens Jensen, 1943, 9 In. 1850.00
Vase, Deer, Leaves, Wine Madder Glaze, Barrett, 1948, 12 In. 920.00
Vase, Diamonds, Yellow, Blue Ground, Chartreuse Mouth, Mark, 1904, 5 In. 275.00
Vase, Dogwood Blossoms, Leaves, Blue, Yellow, Wax Matte, K. Jones, 1928, 6 x 4 In. ... 880.00
Vase, Dogwood Blossoms, Pink, Gray To White Ground, Bulbous, 1905, 10 1/2 In. 1265.00
Vase, Dogwood Branches, Vellum Glaze, Lorinda Epply, 1920, 7 In. 805.00
Vase, Dogwood, Maroon Glaze, Blue Feathering, Black Opal, Footed, Sax, 1925, 15 In. ... 3680.00
Vase, Dogwood, Pink Slip, Iris Glaze, Sara Sax, 1904, 6 1/8 In. 750.00
Vase, Dogwood, Pink, Cream, Margaret McDonald, 1938, 6 In. 750.00
Vase, Dogwood, Stylized, Rectangular, Shirayamadani, 1940, 7 1/2 In. 750.00
Vase, Dogwood, Vellum, Sallie Coyne, 1905, 8 In. 1035.00
Vase, Dogwood, White, Blue Ground, Flat, Footed, 1881, 8 In. 520.00
Vase, Dragon, Catfish, White, Green, Red, Blue, Gold, 1882, 31 5/8 In. 8050.00
Vase, Dragonflies, Gray, White, Shaded Yellow, Blue Ground, Bulbous, 1907, 9 In. ... 2415.00
Vase, Dragonflies, Red & Green Matte Glaze, No. 942d, S.E. Coyne, 1905, 5 1/4 In. 1380.00
Vase, Dragonfly, Pink Matte Glaze, No. 1894, 6 1/2 In. 200.00
Vase, Embossed Dots, Blue Crystalline Matte Glaze, 2 Handles, 5 3/8 In. 185.00
Vase, Exotic Bird, Tiger Eye Glaze, W. McDonald, 1898, 8 1/4 In. 2760.00
Vase, Feathered Blue, Green Glossy Glaze, R. Menzel, 1957, 7 3/4 In. 405.00
Vase, Fern Leaves, Tan Berries, Green Glaze, Yellow, Brown Ground, 1893, 5 1/4 In. 880.00
Vase, Fish, Blue Crystalline Matte Glaze, Hentschel, 1931, 6 7/8 In. 690.00
Vase, Fish, Blue, Green, Vellum, E.T. Hurley, 1909, 11 1/2 In. 1610.00
Vase, Fish, Captured In Gold Net, Green, Nichols, 1882, 12 1/2 In. 690.00
Vase, Fish, Embossed, Black Glaze, Green Interior, Oval, Shirayamadani, 1928, 6 In. ... 635.00
Vase, Fish, Incised, Blue, Purple, Blue Matte Ground, Green Glaze, Pons, 1907, 8 In. 2530.00
Vase, Fish, Iris Glaze, No. 917C, Hurley, 1904, 7 1/4 In. 2185.00
Vase, Fish, White Slip On Rust Ground, Wax Matte, Jens Jensen, 1944, 5 5/8 In. 635.00
Vase, Flower Garland, Yellow Matte, Green, Pink, Inlay, Fechheimer, 1903, 3 7/8 In. 430.00
Vase, Flower Garlands, Green Matte Ground, No. 1870, C. Todd, 1911, 6 1/4 In. 1035.00
Vase, Flower Petals, Embossed, Blue Matte Glaze, 4 7/8 In. 315.00
Vase, Flower Sprays, Ivory Limoges Style, L.M. McLaughlin, 1882, 10 x 7 In. 1345.00
Vase, Flower Stems, Embossed, Blue Gray Matte, 1928, 9 In. 350.00
Vase, Flowering Vine, Yellow Matte Glaze, 6 3/8 In. 260.00
Vase, Flowers, Applied, Leaves, Buds, Brown & Tan, 23 1/2 In. 2358.00
Vase, Flowers, Applied, Wax Matte, Heavy Slip, Jens Jensen, 1943, 6 1/8 In. 920.00
Vase, Flowers, Basket Weave, Blue Matte Glaze, Bulbous, 1942, 6 1/2 In. 230.00
Vase, Flowers, Berries, Maroon, Blue Leaves, Matte Ground, McLaughlin, 1925, 10 In. ... 1100.00
Vase, Flowers, Blue Crystalline Matte Glaze Over Tan, 1929, 7 5/8 In. 635.00
Vase, Flowers, Blue, Green Leaves, Rose Matte, Tapered, Barrett, 1924, 7 1/2 In. 715.00
Vase, Flowers, Blue, Green, Cream Ground, Barrett, 1948, 5 1/2 In. 375.00
Vase, Flowers, Blue, Green, Vellum Glaze, Schmidt, 1914, 11 In. 1150.00
Vase, Flowers, Branches, Turquoise Ground, Lorinda Epply, 1919, 7 3/4 In. 235.00
Vase, Flowers, Buds, Leaves, Yellow, Pink, Green, Vellum, L. Asbury, 1913, 9 x 4 In. 1320.00
Vase, Flowers, Buds, Peach, Standard Glaze, Josephine Zettel, 1894, 4 1/2 x 3 1/2 In. 495.00
Vase, Flowers, Burgundy, Black Drip, Caramel Matte Glaze, V. Tischler, 1923, 8 x 4 In. ... 825.00
Vase, Flowers, Burgundy, Brown Leaves, Matte, Elizabeth Lincoln, 1925, 7 x 3 1/2 In. ... 1430.00
Vase, Flowers, Burgundy, Green Glaze, Orange Ground, Shirayamadani, 1935, 6 3/4 In. ... 1045.00
Vase, Flowers, Celadon High Glaze, No. 6830, 6 3/4 In. 200.00
Vase, Flowers, Circles At Bottom, Blue, Wax Matte, Wilhelmine Rehm, 1944, 6 3/8 In. ... 1150.00
Vase, Flowers, Embossed On Shoulder, Purple Matte Glaze, 1931, 6 In. 259.00
Vase, Flowers, Embossed Turquoise Matte Glaze, 1919, 4 3/8 In. 150.00
Vase, Flowers, Embossed, Blue, No. 2854, 1928, 4 1/2 In. 175.00
Vase, Flowers, Embossed, Ivory Matte, Bulbous, Flared, 4 In. 75.00
Vase, Flowers, Embossed, Olive Brown Matte Glaze, W.E. Hentschel, 7 3/8 In. 1760.00
Vase, Flowers, Embossed, Red Matte Glaze, 1927, 5 1/2 In. 175.00
Vase, Flowers, Embossed, Stippled Button, Multicolored, Gold, Handles, 1885, 8 In. 161.00
Vase, Flowers, Embossed, Tan Glaze, No. 2179, 1921, 3 3/4 In. 172.00

Vase, Flowers, Embossed, Teal, Ohio Home Builders Convention, Marked, 1956, 4 1/4 In.   58.00
Vase, Flowers, Green, White, Blue, 1942, 6 1/3 In. 430.00
Vase, Flowers, Incised Branches, Sage Green High Glaze, 1884, 13 In. 715.00
Vase, Flowers, Incised, Aventurine, Sara Sax, 1920, 8 1/2 In. 1725.00
Vase, Flowers, Incised, Blue, Red Drip Glaze, Charcoal Gray Matte, 1918, 9 1/3 In. 1210.00
Vase, Flowers, Incised, Red, Yellow, Leaves, Chartreuse To Green Glaze, 1918, 13 In. . . .   1870.00
Vase, Flowers, Incised, Yellow, Green, Blue, On Mottled Maroon, Todd, 1914, 13 In. 2070.00
Vase, Flowers, Ivory, Jewel Porcelain, Loretta Holtkamp, c.1951, 12 In. 400.00
Vase, Flowers, Ivory, Jewel Porcelain, Margaret McDonald, c.1943, 6 1/2 In. 460.00
Vase, Flowers, Leaves Band, Brown, Green Matte Glaze, Bulbous, 1925, 9 1/4 In. 489.00
Vase, Flowers, Leaves, Blue, Green, Brown Ground, Jensen, 1935, 4 x 4 1/2 In. 1150.00
Vase, Flowers, Leaves, Blue, Yellow Ground, Elizabeth Barrett, 1924, 8 1/2 x 4 1/2 In. . . .   990.00
Vase, Flowers, Leaves, Bulbous, Flared Rim, Elizabeth Lingenfelter Lincoln, 1901, 9 In. .   530.00
Vase, Flowers, Leaves, Pink, Sallie Coyne, 1923, 6 1/2 x 3 3/4 In.   825.00
Vase, Flowers, Magenta, Yellow, White, Vellum, C. Klinger, 1917, 6 1/2 x 4 1/2 In. 825.00
Vase, Flowers, Mottled Blue & Pink Matte Ground, No. 939C, C.S. Todd, 9 1/2 In. 550.00
Vase, Flowers, Orange High Glaze, No. 6870, 12 1/2 In. 259.00
Vase, Flowers, Pink, Gray To Pink Ground, Vellum Glaze, Ed Diers, c.1913, 8 3/4 In. 1315.00
Vase, Flowers, Pink, Green, Blue, Turquoise Ground, No. 890E, R. Rothenbusch, 4 In. . . .   630.00
Vase, Flowers, Pink, Green, Vellum Glaze, Bulbous, No. 2100, L. Abel, 5 In. 748.00
Vase, Flowers, Pink, Vellum, Margaret McDonald, 1937, 7 1/8 In.   1035.00
Vase, Flowers, Purple, Blue, No. 999C, C. McLaughlin, 1919, 9 1/2 In. 3165.00
Vase, Flowers, Red, Brown Branches, Leaves, Yellow Ground, Handles, 1924, 10 In. 2860.00
Vase, Flowers, Red, Green Vine Border, Mottled Brown Lip, Yellow Glaze, 1925, 6 In. . . .   825.00
Vase, Flowers, Red, Standard Glaze, Bruce Horsfall, 1892, 5 1/8 In. 520.00
Vase, Flowers, Stylized, Embossed, Blue Crystalline Matte Glaze, 1931, 4 In. 196.00
Vase, Flowers, Stylized, Geometric, Celadon Green Glaze, 1940, 4 3/4 In. . . . . .80.00 to 105.00
Vase, Flowers, Stylized, On Shoulder, Turquoise Matte Glaze, 1925, 6 1/4 In. 207.00
Vase, Flowers, Stylized, On Shoulder, Vellum Glaze, Kate Curry, 1917, 7 1/4 In. 375.00
Vase, Flowers, Stylized, On Shoulder, Vellum Glaze, Steinle, 1919, 6 5/8 In. 430.00
Vase, Flowers, Stylized, Pink Matte Glaze, Cone Shape, 1929, 6 1/4 In. 138.00
Vase, Flowers, Stylized, Pink Tinted High Glaze, Blue Striations, McDonald, 1938, 6 In. .   405.00
Vase, Flowers, Stylized, Puffy, Pink, Porcelain, Shirayamadani, 1923, 6 1/4 In. 3105.00
Vase, Flowers, Stylized, White, Black Opal Glaze, Harriet Wilcox, 1926, 6 1/2 In. 750.00
Vase, Flowers, Stylized, Yellow Matte Glaze, Oval, 1918, 7 1/2 In. 375.00
Vase, Flowers, Teardrops, Green, Arts & Crafts, McDonald, 1901, 25 In. 5940.00
Vase, Flowers, Vellum Glaze, Lenore Asbury, 1922, 8 1/4 In. 1150.00
Vase, Flowers, Vellum, Elizabeth Lincoln, 1923, 5 7/8 In. 3105.00
Vase, Flowers, White Star, Iris Glaze, Corset Shape, Lincoln, 1911, 7 1/8 In. 1035.00
Vase, Flowers, White, Blue, Black, Orange Glaze, Jens Jensen, 1931, 9 1/2 x 5 3/4 In. . . .   1540.00
Vase, Flowers, White, Branches, Edith Noonan, 1905, 5 5/8 In. 1150.00
Vase, Flowers, White, Gray Ground, Iris Glaze, Carl Schmidt, 1911, 7 1/2 In. 2875.00
Vase, Flowers, Yellow Matte, Shirayamadani, 5 In. 920.00
Vase, Flowers, Yellow, Green Ground, Bulbous, Harriet E. Wilcox, 1902, 4 3/4 x 3 In. . . .   805.00
Vase, Flowers, Yellow, Green, Blue, Brown Ground, Bulbous, Todd, 1914, 5 In. 635.00
Vase, Flowers, Yellow, Maroon, Turquoise Leaves, Katherine Jones, 1929, 5 x 5 In. 825.00
Vase, Fruit, Leaves, Purple, Umber Ground, Matte, Oval, E. Lincoln, 1918, 10 1/2 x 5 In. .   3450.00
Vase, Geese, Bamboo, Vellum, K. Shirayamadani, 1911, 7 1/2 x 3 1/2 In. 8625.00
Vase, Geese, Embossed, Blue, Ivory Ground, 1945, 6 1/8 In. 259.00
Vase, Geese, Flying, Bands, Vellum, Shirayamadani, 1911, 7 1/2 In. 8625.00
Vase, Geometric Pattern, Arrows, 3 Handles, Green Matte, 1921, 5 1/3 x 6 1/2 In. 165.00
Vase, Geometric Pattern, Blue Matte Crystalline Glaze, Marked, 1927, 9 1/8 In. 405.00
Vase, Geometric Pattern, Blue Matte Glaze, 1927, 9 In. 545.00
Vase, Geometric Pattern, Brown Matte Glaze, 1909, 17 In. 2530.00
Vase, Geometric Pattern, Brown, Green, Yellow, Barrett, 1930, 9 1/2 In. 1495.00
Vase, Geometric Pattern, Browns, Mat Moderne, No. 6201D, E. Barrett, 6 3/4 In. 1095.00
Vase, Geometric Pattern, Embossed, Green Butterfat Matte Glaze, 1930, 7 3/4 In. 316.00
Vase, Geometric Pattern, Green Matte Glaze, 1910, 7 1/4 In. 575.00
Vase, Geometric Pattern, Incised, Green & Maroon Matte Glaze, 4 1/2 In. 489.00
Vase, Geometric Pattern, Mottled, Green, Deep Rose Matte, 1909, 4 5/8 In. 375.00
Vase, Goose, Green Matte Glaze, Bulbous, Sallie Toohey, 1905, 3 1/2 In. 550.00
Vase, Grapes, French Red Glaze, Flared Rim, No. 2721, H. Wilcox, 6 In. 1610.00
Vase, Grapes, Leaves, Matte Glaze, Jens Jensen, 1930, 13 3/4 In.   2530.00

Vase, Grapes, Matte Glaze, Elizabeth Lincoln, 1930, 7 7/8 In. 2185.00
Vase, Grapes, Matte Glaze, Louise Abel, 1928, 8 3/8 In. 1265.00
Vase, Grapevine, Deep Brown Ground, Amelia Browne Sprague, 1897, 9 x 5 1/2 In. 550.00
Vase, Grapevine, Fruit, Purple, Blue, Charles Stewart Todd, c.1915, 17 3/4 In. 3335.00
Vase, Grasses, Incised, Black Ground, Black Iris Glaze, Shirayamadani, 9 1/2 In. 5750.00
Vase, Greek Key, Mottled Mauve Matte Glaze, c.1900, 3 1/2 In. 230.00
Vase, Greek Key, Pink Matte Glaze, 6 In. 210.00
Vase, Green High Glaze, Square, No. 7084, 10 In. 150.00
Vase, Green To Red Butterfat Matte Glaze, Handles, 1916, 5 In. 290.00
Vase, Half-Moon, Incised, On Shoulder, Speckled Rose Glaze, 1926, 6 1/2 In. 193.00
Vase, Harbor Scene, Venice, High Glaze, Carl Schmidt, 1923, 5 7/8 In. 2415.00
Vase, Harbor Scene, Venice, Vellum Glaze, 1908, 8 3/4 In. 2820.00
Vase, Hawthorne Branches, Iris Glaze, No. 9265, L.E. Lindeman, 6 In. 978.00
Vase, Hercules Parsnip, Sea Green, A.R. Valentien, 1895, 14 1/2 In. 6325.00
Vase, Holly, Standard Glaze, 1897, 5 1/8 In. 288.00
Vase, Honeysuckle, Standard Glaze, No. 844, E.R. Felton, 5 1/2 In. 405.00
Vase, Horse & Carriage, Bridge, Blue, Green, Brown, Rectangular, 6 In. 175.00
Vase, Incised Grapes, Green & Blue Matte Glaze, No. 218B, C. Todd, 1915, 10 1/2 In. ... 2185.00
Vase, Iris Thistle, Purple, Pink, Gray Glaze, Carl Schmidt, 1900, 5 1/4 In. 1100.00
Vase, Iris, Blue, Gray, Green, Lenore Asbury, 1905, 11 1/4 In. 4700.00
Vase, Iris, Blue, Green Leaves, Ivory, Yellow Ground, Iris Glaze, Oval, Steinle, 7 In. 1610.00
Vase, Iris, Cherry Blossoms & Branches, Kataro Shirayamadani, 1906, 10 In. 8625.00
Vase, Irises, Blue, Green, Brown & Green Ground, Standard Glaze, Oval, 1901, 7 1/2 In. . 750.00
Vase, Irises, Blue, Standard Glaze, Harriet Wilcox, 1898, 10 3/4 In. 2070.00
Vase, Irises, Blue, Yellow, Green Leaves, Matte, L. Hanscom, 1929, 9 3/4 x 4 1/2 In. 1210.00
Vase, Irises, Purple, Pink Ground, Vellum, Carl Schmidt, 1906, 10 1/4 x 4 1/2 In. 1725.00
Vase, Irises, Stylized, Purple, Blue, Green Matte, Abel, 1921, 9 1/2 In. 460.00
Vase, Irises, Yellow, Standard Glaze, Marianne Mitchell, 1904, 6 3/4 In. 260.00
Vase, Japanese Quince, Standard Glaze, No. 905D, L. Asbury, 1903, 7 1/2 In. 865.00
Vase, Japanese Quince, Standard Glaze, Squat, F. Zettle, 1894, 6 In. 635.00
Vase, Jonquils, Carved, White, Brown, Green, Footed, Shirayamadani, 1903, 9 1/8 In. ... 2760.00
Vase, Jonquils, Yellow, Elizabeth Lincoln, 1903, 9 In. 1725.00
Vase, Lake At Sunset, Vellum, No. 977, C. Schmidt, 1917, 11 In. 5465.00
Vase, Lake, No. 951E, Hurley, 1940, 7 1/2 In. 4025.00
Vase, Lake, Snow, Vellum, Charles McLaughlin, 1915, 8 3/4 x 3 3/4 In. 1495.00
Vase, Lake, Vellum, Fred Rothenbusch, 1920, 9 1/2 In. 2415.00
Vase, Landscape, Blue, Green, Brown, Ivory Ground, Oval, 1938, 14 1/2 In. 1955.00
Vase, Landscape, Blue, Green, Yellow, Vellum Glaze, Rothenbusch, 1917, 12 5/8 In. 1095.00
Vase, Landscape, Bulbous, 1922, 17 3/4 x 8 In. 5175.00
Vase, Landscape, Cerulean & Aqua Sky, Sage, Green Charcoal, Ivory, Oval, 1922, 5 In. ... 1100.00
Vase, Landscape, Cherry Trees, Porcelain, Conant, 1919, 7 1/8 In. 2185.00
Vase, Landscape, Gray, Peach, Blue, Vellum Glaze, No. 2039D, 9 1/2 In. 1998.00
Vase, Landscape, Vellum Glaze, Alice Craven, 1917, 8 In. 805.00
Vase, Landscape, Vellum Glaze, E.T. Hurley, 1912, 16 In. 9200.00
Vase, Landscape, Vellum Glaze, Slightly Tapered, Sallie Coyne, 8 In. 3165.00
Vase, Landscape, Vellum, No. 950F, F. Rothenbusch, 6 In. 2185.00
Vase, Landscape, Vellum, Oval, Ed Diers, 1916, 9 1/4 x 4 3/4 In. 3450.00
Vase, Leaves & Berries, Blue, Green, Sky Blue Ground, Barrett, 1929, 8 5/8 In. 980.00
Vase, Leaves & Berries, Blue, Standard Glaze, Howard Altman, 1904, 4 3/4 In. 316.00
Vase, Leaves & Berries, Crystalline Glaze, C.S. Todd, 1920, 11 3/4 In. 1495.00
Vase, Leaves & Berries, Elizabeth Lincoln, 1893, 5 5/8 In. 865.00
Vase, Leaves & Berries, Embossed, Purple Matte Glaze, Oval, 1923, 5 1/4 In. 550.00
Vase, Leaves & Berries, Emerald Matte Glaze, 4 3/4 In. 125.00
Vase, Leaves & Berries, Green Matte Glaze, Round, No. 6545, 1938, 4 In. 200.00
Vase, Leaves & Berries, Green Matte Ground, Barrett, 1927, 6 1/2 x 5 In. 690.00
Vase, Leaves & Berries, Shaded Green To Umber Matte Ground, Oval, 1916, 7 1/2 In. ... 575.00
Vase, Leaves & Berries, Stylized, Ocher Glaze, 1921, 6 In. 375.00
Vase, Leaves & Berries, Turquoise Crystalline Matte Glaze, 1925, 6 3/4 In. 220.00
Vase, Leaves, Berries, Salmon, Green, Iris Glaze, Brown, Sara Sax, 1905, 6 x 3 1/2 In. ... 1980.00
Vase, Leaves, Black & Russet, Matte Glaze, Jens Jensen, 1931, 4 3/4 In. 1035.00
Vase, Leaves, Blue Matte Glaze, Arts & Crafts, No. 2095, 1909, 5 In. 290.00
Vase, Leaves, Edith Felton, 1903, 7 1/4 In. 1150.00
Vase, Leaves, Embossed, Pink Matte Glaze, Green Highlights, 1928, 10 In. 245.00

Vase, Leaves, Embossed, Turquoise Matte Glaze, 1927, 5 1/4 In. 140.00
Vase, Leaves, Embossed, White Matte Glaze, 1934, 5 In. 105.00
Vase, Leaves, Footed, C.S. Todd, 1911, 7 1/2 In. 635.00
Vase, Leaves, Green, Wax Matte, William Hentschel, 1929, 7 In. 2185.00
Vase, Leaves, Overlapping, Blue Matte Glaze, Bulbous, c.1928, 3 1/4 In. 195.00
Vase, Leaves, Standard Glaze, Ed Diers, 1897, 6 In. 690.00
Vase, Leaves, Yellow Ground, Squeezebag, Elizabeth Barrett, c.1927, 16 1/2 In. 2585.00
Vase, Leaves, Yellow Matte Glaze, c.1919, 5 In. 345.00
Vase, Leaves, Yellow Matte Glaze, No. 1824, 1925, 6 1/4 In. 205.00
Vase, Lily Of The Valley, Gray To Pink Ground, Iris Glaze, Oval, Schmidt, 8 1/2 In. 2530.00
Vase, Lily Of The Valley, Yellow, Green Leaves, Brown Ground, 1906, 8 1/2 In. 770.00
Vase, Lotus Blossoms, E.T. Hurley, 1900, 8 3/8 In. 3910.00
Vase, Magnolia Blossoms, Branches, Blue, Brown, Beige, 1889, 5 3/4 In. 990.00
Vase, Magnolia Blossoms, Purple, White, Blue Ground, No. 900A, L. Asbury, 13 In. 9775.00
Vase, Magnolia Blossoms, Yellow, Wine Madder Glaze, Elizabeth Barrett, 1944, 6 In. 805.00
Vase, Magnolias, Orange, Green, Blue, Yellow Ground, Holtkamp, 1951, 13 In. 520.00
Vase, Magnolias, Pink, Green Matte Glaze, 1925, 6 1/4 In. 865.00
Vase, Magnolias, Vellum Glaze, Marianne Mitchell, 1905, 6 3/4 In. 805.00
Vase, Magnolias, White, Blue, Yellow, Shirayamadani, 1946, 7 3/8 In. 920.00
Vase, Maple Leaves, Carrie Steinle, 1899, 5 1/4 In. 460.00
Vase, Maple Leaves, Embossed, Emerald Matte Glaze, 5 3/8 In. 315.00
Vase, Maple Leaves, Standard Glaze, 2 Handles, Lenore Asbury, 1902, 8 3/4 In. 825.00
Vase, Maple Leaves, Yellow Tinted, Porcelain, Shirayamadani, 1925, 6 In. 1725.00
Vase, Mariposa Lilies At Shoulder, Shirayamadani, No. 2831, 5 1/2 In. 1725.00
Vase, Maroon, Green Matte Glaze, Arts & Crafts, Flared, c.1914, 6 In. 230.00
Vase, Mistletoe, Standard Glaze, Carrie Steinle, 1909, 3 7/8 In. 405.00
Vase, Mistletoe, Turquoise Butterfat Matte Glaze, Embossed, 1929, 7 1/2 In. 259.00
Vase, Mistletoe, Vellum, Helen Lyons, No. 918E, 1913, 6 In. 805.00
Vase, Molded Southwestern Figures, Blue High Glaze, No. 6762, 1941, 6 In. 140.00
Vase, Nasturtium, Orange, Standard Glaze, Bulbous, Asbury, 1899, 7 1/2 In. 489.00
Vase, Nasturtiums, Standard Glaze, Silver Overlay Flowers, No. 565, Lincoln, 8 In. 6615.00
Vase, Nocturnal Scene, Sailboats, No. 938D, E.T. Hurley, 1912, 7 In. 4025.00
Vase, Nude Diving, Fish, Celadon High Glaze, Louise Abel, 1945, 9 1/2 In. 518.00
Vase, Oak Leaf & Acorn, E.T. Hurley, 1901, 8 In. 865.00
Vase, Oak Leaves, Leona Van Briggle, 1899, 6 7/8 In. 520.00
Vase, Orange Blossoms, Standard Glaze, Bulbous, Grace Hall, 1903, 5 3/4 In. 200.00
Vase, Orchids, Turquoise, Blue, Shirayamadani, 1927, 4 3/4 In. 1495.00
Vase, Palm Trees, Birds, Vellum, K. Shirayamadani, 1910, 10 1/2 x 4 In. 2530.00
Vase, Panels, Turquoise Matte Glaze, 1923, 6 1/8 In. 160.00
Vase, Pansies, Carrie Steinle, 1898, 6 1/2 In. 635.00
Vase, Pansies, Lavender To Gray, Iris Glaze, Diers, 1901, 9 1/4 In. 605.00
Vase, Pansies, Violet, Spherical, No. 6133F, E.T. Hurley, 1944, 4 3/4 In. 575.00
Vase, Pansies, Yellow, Orange, Standard Glaze, Squat, Hurley, 1899, 4 3/4 In. 635.00
Vase, Peacock Feathers, Black Iris, Carl Schmidt, 1908, 9 1/2 In. 5750.00
Vase, Peacock Feathers, Blue Matte Glaze, Tapered, No. 2121, 7 In. 175.00
Vase, Peacock Feathers, Carrie Steinle, 1905, 5 5/8 In. 1725.00
Vase, Peacock Feathers, Geometric, Blue, Green, Orange, Brown Ground, 1914, 11 In. . . . 1380.00
Vase, Peacock Feathers, Green, Shaded Blue Ground, Schmidt, 1910, 7 1/2 x 3 In. 1840.00
Vase, Peacock Feathers, Pink Matte Glaze, 1922, 9 1/4 In. 259.00
Vase, Peacock Feathers, Pink Matte Glaze, 6 3/8 In. 220.00
Vase, Peacock Feathers, Pink Matte Glaze, No. 1905, 7 7/8 In. 175.00
Vase, Peacock Feathers, Teal Matte Glaze, Green Ground, Oval, Sax, 1908, 9 In. 3220.00
Vase, Pebble Texture, Burgundy Matte Glaze, 2 Handles, 5 In. 290.00
Vase, Peonies, Magenta, Green Leaves, Margaret McDonald, 1936, 5 3/4 x 4 In. 990.00
Vase, Peonies, Yellow, Standard Glaze, Shirayamadani, 1898, 12 7/8 In. 2185.00
Vase, Pillow, Flowers, Peach, Yellow, Leaves, Josephine Zettel, 1894, 5 x 5 1/2 In. 413.00
Vase, Pinecone, Green Matte Glaze, No 1889, 1924, 6 3/4 In. 575.00
Vase, Pinecone, Incised, Blue, Cerulean Blue Glaze To Navy, 1917, 6 1/2 In. 415.00
Vase, Pinecones, Arts & Crafts, No. 1096, M. Mitchell, 4 3/4 In. 920.00
Vase, Pinecones, Blue, Green Matte Glaze, 1928, 6 3/4 In. 345.00
Vase, Pinecones, On Shoulder, Carved, Vellum, Epply, 1909, 5 5/8 In. 1380.00
Vase, Pink Matte Glaze, Footed, 1928, 3 1/8 In. 150.00
Vase, Pink Matte Glaze, Mottled Green, Handles, 1928, 4 1/2 In. 196.00

Vase, Pomegranate Glaze, Rolled Rim, 1949, 7 5/8 In. 196.00
Vase, Pomegranate Glaze, Tapered, 1950, 3 3/4 In. 140.00
Vase, Poppies, Burnt Orange, Green, Deep Brown Ground, Sara Toohey, 1898, 11 x 5 In. . 1430.00
Vase, Poppies, E.N. Lingenfelter, 1903, 9 In. 500.00
Vase, Poppies, Embossed, Burnt Orange Matte Glaze, 1931, 11 3/4 In. 575.00
Vase, Poppies, Howard Altman, 1902, 7 1/2 In. 980.00
Vase, Poppies, Matte Glaze, Oval, c.1904, 9 In. 2840.00
Vase, Poppies, Red, Delphinium, Blue, 1943, 5 3/4 In. 315.00
Vase, Poppies, Red, Green Ground, Elizabeth Lincoln, 1922, 11 x 5 1/4 In. 4025.00
Vase, Poppies, Red, Green Leaves, Mary Luella Perkins, c.1896, 5 In. 345.00
Vase, Poppies, Red, Matte Glaze, C.S. Todd, 1913, 10 In. 3335.00
Vase, Poppies, Red, Pink, Yellow, Green, Deep Violet, Pale Green Ground, 1939, 6 In. . . . 3520.00
Vase, Poppies, Red, Purple Into Burgundy Ground, Green Base, Lincoln, 1926, 9 In. 1210.00
Vase, Poppies, Red, Silver Overlay, 1894, 7 1/8 In. 4715.00
Vase, Poppies, Red, Wheat, Porcelain, Shirayamadani, 1925, 9 1/4 In. 1725.00
Vase, Poppies, Seed Pods, Incised, Red, Blue, Green Matte Glaze, Hentschel, 1911, 16 In. 1265.00
Vase, Poppies, Vellum Glaze, No. 6578, Shirayamadani, 8 1/2 In. 1955.00
Vase, Poppies, White, Mauve, Double Vellum, Shirayamadani, 1930, 5 1/8 In. 1150.00
Vase, Red Quatrefoils, Blue, Green Ground, Hentschel, 1913, 7 3/4 In. 546.00
Vase, River, Cobalt Blue, Vellum, Sara Sax, 1911, 7 x 3 In. 6900.00
Vase, Roadrunners, Clouds, Grass, Berries, Nichols, 1881, 13 3/4 In. 2300.00
Vase, Rooks, Molded, Purple Matte Glaze, No. 1795, 1922, 4 3/4 In. 690.00
Vase, Rooks, Turquoise Matte Glaze, No. 1795, 5 Sides, 4 1/2 In. 69.00
Vase, Rooks, Yellow Matte Glaze, 5 Straight Sides, No. 1795, 1928, 4 3/4 In. 460.00
Vase, Rose Thistle, Celadon, Peach Ground, Iris Glaze, c.1898, 3 1/4 In. 550.00
Vase, Roses, Green Ground, Yellow Tinted High Glaze, Ed Diers, 1924, 10 In. 2875.00
Vase, Roses, Yellow, Brown Ground, Crimped Mouth, Handle, 1899, 8 3/4 In. 880.00
Vase, Roses, Yellow, Standard Glaze, Bottle Shape, Anna Bookprinter, 1889, 9 1/2 In. . . . 805.00
Vase, Rust, Tan, Black, Mottled Yellow Ground, Todd, 1918, 7 1/2 In. 1495.00
Vase, Sailboats On Stormy Sea, Full Moon, Grenadiers, Blue, 1909, 9 In. 1265.00
Vase, Scroll, Blue Tinted High Glaze, Lorinda Epply, 1921, 8 5/8 In. 575.00
Vase, Seagulls Over Turbulent Sea, Vellum, No. 1126C, E.T. Hurley, 9 In. 4025.00
Vase, Seahorses, Embossed, Turquoise Matte Crystalline, 1921, 5 7/8 In. 260.00
Vase, Seahorses, Incised, Tiger Eye Empire Green Glaze, E.T. Hurley, 1923, 9 1/4 In. 4025.00
Vase, Seahorses, Incised, Turquoise, Mauve Lines, No. 531, Wareham, 1901, 5 7/8 In. . . . 10350.00
Vase, Sharks, Embossed, Blue Matte Glaze, Tapered, 1920, 7 3/4 In. 440.00
Vase, Ship, Embossed, Wine Madder Glaze, 1944, 4 1/2 In. 140.00
Vase, Ships, Embossed, Green Matte Glaze, 1945, 4 1/2 In. 69.00
Vase, Snowdrops, White, Pink, Blue Shaded Ground, 1928, 5 x 3 In. 2300.00
Vase, Snowy Landscape, Vellum, Sallie Coyne, 1917, 7 5/8 In. 2530.00
Vase, Snowy Landscape, Yellow, Green, Blue, Peach, Shirayamadani, 1911, 8 5/8 In. 1725.00
Vase, Sparrows, Iris Glaze, 7 In. 2000.00
Vase, Spiderworts, Band, Iris Glaze, Wildman, 1912, 7 3/8 In. 520.00
Vase, Spiderworts, Blue, Band, Asbury, 1925, 9 3/8 In. 2645.00
Vase, Spiderworts, Double Vellum, Shirayamadani, 1940, 7 In. 2070.00
Vase, Spiderworts, Purple, Yellow, Butterfat Ground, Shirayamadani, 1935, 7 3/8 In. 2300.00
Vase, Spotted Deer, High Glaze, Jens Jensen, 1945, 6 1/8 In. 2875.00
Vase, Storks, Incised, Black, Green Ground, Wareham, 1899, 9 7/8 In. 2875.00
Vase, Swallows In Flight, Impressed, 1905, 7 1/8 In. 2000.00
Vase, Sweet Peas, White, Shaded Green To Pink Ground, Iris Glaze, 1910, 6 1/4 In. 750.00
Vase, Tan Matte Glaze, Blue Crystals, Handles, 1927, 4 1/8 In. 290.00
Vase, Tapestry, Blue Matte Glaze, 6 7/8 In. 160.00
Vase, Tiger, Maroon, Orange, Gray, Mauve Ground, Heavy Slip, Wax Matte, 1946, 7 In. . . 1093.00
Vase, Tree By Pond, Vellum, Elizabeth McDermott, 1916, 8 1/2 x 3 3/4 In. 4600.00
Vase, Tree, Green, Handles, William Hentschel, 1910, 5 1/4 In. 1265.00
Vase, Trees, Brown, Green, Yellow, Brown Ground, Ed Diers, 1911, 6 x 3 In. 3335.00
Vase, Trees, Cobalt Blue, Plum, Green, Ed Diers, 9 1/4 In. 635.00
Vase, Trees, Hillside, Sky, Gray, Peach, Lenore Asbury, 1914, 7 x 3 1/2 In. 2090.00
Vase, Trees, Orange Sky, Vellum, Cora Crofton, 1917, 9 x 3 1/4 In. 1840.00
Vase, Trees, Riverbank, Blue, Green, Brown, Yellow, Tapered, Coyne, 1910, 7 1/4 In. 1725.00
Vase, Trees, Stylized, Green Matte Glaze, Swollen Shoulder, C. Duell, 8 In. 1610.00
Vase, Trumpet Flowers, Orange, Vine, Rust, Brown Glossy Glaze, 1906, 6 1/2 In. 355.00
Vase, Trumpet Vines, Ivory Ground, Porcelain, K. Shirayamadani, 1945, 8 3/4 x 4 In. 920.00

Vase, Tulip, Embossed, Violet Matte Glaze, Arts & Crafts, 1914, 5 1/8 In. 430.00
Vase, Tulips, Incised, Sara Sax, 1921, 4 3/4 In. 11500.00
Vase, Tulips, Inset Panels, Pink Matte Glaze, No. 1907, 1929, 5 1/4 In. 575.00
Vase, Turquoise Blue Matte Glaze, Handles, 1927, 5 In. 150.00
Vase, Turquoise Matte Glaze, Flared Rim, 1937, 3 7/8 In. 130.00
Vase, Turquoise Matte Glaze, Impressed, 1923, 7 In. 431.00
Vase, Umber, White Drip Glaze, Menzel, 1951, 8 3/4 In. 345.00
Vase, Vines, Star Flowers, Blue, 2 Handles, K. Shirayamadani, 1936, 10 1/4 In. 2645.00
Vase, Violets, Green Glaze, 1959, 6 5/8 In. 175.00
Vase, Violets, Sea Green Glaze, No. 921, M. Mitchell, 6 1/2 In. 575.00
Vase, Virginia Creeper, Standard Glaze, Dibowski, 1895, 9 3/4 In. 920.00
Vase, Wheat, Molded, Yellow Matte Glaze, No. 2136, 1921, 6 1/4 In. 460.00
Vase, White Matte, Glossy Turquoise Interior, 1929, 4 3/4 In. 105.00
Vase, Wild Roses, Blue Ground, No. 363, Harriet Wilcox, 1926, 6 In. 1265.00
Vase, Wild Roses, Coral, Iris Glaze, Sallie Coyne, 1906, 6 3/8 In. 750.00
Vase, Wild Roses, Handles, Ed Diers, 1900, 6 In. 920.00
Vase, Wild Roses, Iris Glaze, Ed Diers, 1903, 5 In. 1095.00
Vase, Wild Roses, Light Standard Glaze, Shirayamadani, 7 1/4 In. 805.00
Vase, Wild Roses, Pink, White, Yellow, Vellum, Edward Diers, 1911, 7 1/2 x 4 In. 1045.00
Vase, Wild Roses, Standard Glaze, Sallie Coyne, 1895, 6 1/4 In. 460.00
Vase, Wisteria, Matte Glaze, Margaret McDonald, 1933, 10 1/4 In. 805.00
Vase, Wisteria, Vellum, Flared Rim, Oval, E.T. Hurley, 1946, 8 In. 646.00
Vase, Wisteria, Vellum, Matte Glaze, Oval, M.H. McDonald, 1924, 11 1/8 In. 470.00
Vase, Women & Stars, Ivory Matte Glaze, Handles, 1935, 8 7/8 In. 160.00
Vase, Yellow Porcelain Glaze, 1950, 3 1/2 In. 69.00
Vase, Yellow, Green Matte Glaze, Flared Panels, Tapered, 1915, 7 1/4 In. 520.00
Wall Pocket, Blue Matte Glaze, Handles, 1926, 7 In. 316.00
Wall Pocket, Cicada, Wings, Cerulean Blue Matte Ground, 1922, 2 3/4 x 9 In. 1100.00
Wall Pocket, Leaves, Embossed, Gray Blue, Shield Shape, 1915, 8 In. 489.00
Wall Pocket, Peacock Feather, Blue Matte Glaze, No. 1395, 1919, 11 1/2 In. 520.00

RORSTRAND

RORSTRAND was established near Stockholm, Sweden, in 1726. By the nineteenth century they were making English-style earthenware, bone china, porcelain, ironstone china, and majolica. The company is still working. The three crown mark has been used since 1884.

Candlestick, Linear Design, Gunmetal Glaze, Carl Harry Stalhane, 6 1/2 In. 58.00
Pitcher, Green, Semimatte Glaze, Gunnar Nylund, 13 1/2 In. 440.00
Vase, Geometric Design, Hand Thrown, Gunnar Nylund, 7 1/2 In. 290.00
Vase, Mottled Deep Purple To Umber Glaze, Bottle Shape, 10 3/4 In., Pair 144.00

ROSALINE, see Steuben category.

ROSE BOWLS

ROSE BOWLS were popular during the 1880s. Rose petals were kept in the open bowl to add fragrance to a room, a popular idea in a time of limited personal hygiene. The glass bowls were made with crimped tops, which kept the petals inside. Many types of Victorian art glass were made into rose bowls.

Block & Lattice, Ruby Stain, 2 1/2 x 2 1/4 In. 100.00
Blue Satin, Glass Seashell Relief, Seaweed, Hand Painted, Ruffled Rim, 5 In. 135.00
Green Opalescent, Ribbed, Applied Pink Flowers, Clear Glass Stems, 5 x 6 In. 58.00
Millefiori, 4 In. 40.00
Pink, Orange, Black, Gold Mica Inclusions, 4 In. 100.00

ROSE CANTON

ROSE CANTON china is similar to Rose Mandarin and Rose Medallion, except no people or birds are pictured in the decoration. It was made in China during the nineteenth and twentieth centuries in greens, pinks, and other colors.

Cachepot, Flowers, Scrolls, c.1840, 9 1/2 x 12 In. 1150.00
Charger, Cabbage Leaf, Border, 19th Century, 14 3/4 In. 5690.00
Dish, Domed Cover, Fruit Finial, 5 1/2 x 14 x 9 3/4 In. 765.00
Punch Bowl, Flowers, Scrolls, 6 x 14 In. 1840.00
Tray, Ice Cream, Design, Flange Handles, 7 x 13 3/4 In. 590.00
Tureen, Cover, Undertray, Oval, Gilt Handles & Finial, 8 In. 865.00

ROSE MANDARIN china is similar to Rose Canton and Rose Medallion. If the panels in the design picture only people and not birds, it is called Rose Mandarin.

Bowl, c.1879, 7 1/4 In.	230.00
Bowl, Gilt Bronze Mount, c.1785, 6 3/4 x 12 1/2 In.	1035.00
Candlestick, Chinese Women, Flowers, Cylindrical, Circular Flared Base, 8 In., Pair	1035.00
Canister, Cover, Chinese Women, Flowers, Cylindrical, 3 1/2 In.	375.00
Dish, Hot Water, Figures Outside Of Pagoda, Circular, Tab Handles, c.1840, 9 1/4 In.	1955.00
Dish, Kidney Shape, Warriors, Butterfly & Flower Border, 8 x 11 In.	295.00
Jar, Cover, Bulbous, Fluted Sides, Gilt Finial, c.1840, 7 1/2 In.	460.00
Plate, Soup, Center Figural Reserve, 19th Century, 10 In., 3 Piece	690.00
Soup, Dish, Figural Center, 9 3/4 In., 8 Piece	1150.00
Tankard, Figures, Landscape, Dragon Handle, 5 3/4 In.	415.00
Teapot, Figures, Seated At Table, Prunt Finial, Strap Handle, 4 3/4 In.	468.00
Tray, Court Figures, Oval, c.1840, 16 1/2 In.	1840.00
Tray, Dresser, 19th Century, 10 x 5 In.	518.00
Vase, Butterfly Band, c.1825, 11 1/2 In., Pair	1265.00

ROSE MEDALLION china was made in China during the nineteenth and twentieth centuries. It is a distinctive design with four or more panels of decoration around a central medallion that includes a bird or a peony. The panels show birds and people. The background is a design of tree peonies and leaves. Pieces are colored in greens, pinks, and other colors. It is similar to Rose Canton and Rose Mandarin.

Bowl, Alternating Panels, Mandarin Scenes, Flowers, Butterflies, 14 In.	1210.00
Bowl, Bronze, Mounted, 19th Century, 12 3/4 x 15 In.	2000.00
Bowl, Fruit, Louis XVI Style, c.1865, 10 x 17 In.	2185.00
Bowl, Nested, 20th Century, 4 x 10 In.	805.00
Bowl, Scalloped Rim, Gilt Trim, c.1840, 10 1/2 In.	635.00
Bowl, Undertray, Oval, Pierced Sides, 9 In.	460.00
Box, Cover, Round, 19th Century, 3 1/2 In.	259.00
Box, Oval, Figural Design, c.1830, 2 7/8 In.	140.00
Brushpot, Mandarins, Flowers, Cylindrical, 5 x 3 In.	230.00
Candlestick, Cylindrical Stem, Circular Flared Base, 6 1/2 In.	290.00
Canister, Cover, c.1840, 4 1/4 In.	316.00
Chamberstick, Snuffer, c.1840, 5 1/2 In.	430.00
Charger, Court Scene In Medallion, Famille Rose Border, 19th Century, 13 1/2 In.	705.00
Charger, Mandarin Scene, Pink, Green, Blue, Orange, 13 1/2 In.	110.00
Compote, Scalloped & Shaped Border, Pedestal Base, 3 1/2 x 13 In.	575.00
Creamer, Mandarin Scene, Polychrome Enamel, Gilt, Bullnose Spout, 4 In.	80.00
Creamer, Marked China, 4 In.	115.00
Cuspidor, Hardwood Stand, 1851-1861, 6 1/2 x 8 In.	405.00
Dish, Scalloped Edge, 9 1/2 In.	375.00
Ewer, Wine, Bottle Form, 5 In.	200.00
Hair Receiver, Cover, 19th Century, 8 3/4 In.	345.00
Jardiniere, 20th Century, 4 Piece, 9 1/2 x 12 In.	690.00
Jardiniere, 4 Panels, Figures, Birds, 20th Century, 13 In.	345.00
Lamp Base, Flared Rim, Baluster, Kylin Figures, Foo Dog Handles, 22 1/2 In.	440.00
Mug, c.1840, 5 In.	405.00
Pitcher, Bird Scenes, Courtyards, c.1885, 6 1/2 In.	375.00
Pitcher, Cream, Domestic Scenes, Flowers, c.1890, 5 3/4 In.	259.00
Plate, 10 1/2 In.	95.00
Plate, Hot Water, Spouts, Figures, Flowers, Famille Rose Enamel, 2 x 11 x 9 In.	460.00
Plate, Melon Panels, c.1840, 9 1/2 In.	195.00
Platter, Figural Panels, Oval, Mid 19th Century, 13 1/4 In.	290.00
Platter, Fish, 18 1/2 In.	1265.00
Platter, Oval, 19th Century, 17 1/2 In.	380.00
Platter, Oval, Nest, Late 19th Century, 14 1/2 In., 5 Piece	865.00
Platter, Scalloped Edge, Modified Oval, On Stand, 12 1/2 In.	230.00
Pomade Jar, Cover, Cylindrical, 2 x 2 In.	145.00
Punch Bowl, 19th Century, 6 5/8 x 15 3/8 In.	1645.00
Punch Bowl, Footed, Mandarin Scenes, Pink, Green, Blue, Gilt, 15 3/4 x 6 1/4 In.	605.00

Punch Bowl, Hardwood Stand, 1851-1861, 5 3/4 x 13 1/2 In. 805.00
Sauceboat, Double Spout, Attached Tray, Handle, 19th Century, 9 1/2 In. 150.00
Serving Bowl, Flowers, Insects, Famille Rose Enamel, c.1920, 4 x 10 x 10 In. 375.00
Serving Dish, Flowers, Musicians, 19th Century, 15 In. 290.00
Soap Dish, Cover, Garden, Figures, Border, 5 1/4 In., 3 Piece 265.00
Soap Dish, Cover, Pierced Interior Tray, 5 1/2 In. 550.00
Soup, Dish, Wide Rim, Mandarin Scene, Gilding, 8 1/4 In., Pair 110.00
Sugar, Twisted Branch Handles, Cover, Lychee Fruit Finial, 5 In. 259.00
Teapot, 19th Century, 4 1/2 In. 265.00
Teapot, Domed Cover, Gold Flowers On Handle & Spout, 19th Century, 8 In. 765.00
Teapot, Drum Form, 6 In. 175.00
Teapot, Straight Sides, 19th Century, 6 In. 345.00
Teapot & Cup, Insulated Traveling Basket 200.00
Tray, Square, Landscapes, Orange Peel Glaze, 9 1/8 x 9 1/8 In. 220.00
Tureen, Cover, Oval, Floral Gilt Finial, 13 In. 1150.00
Tureen, Cover, Oval, Pedestal Base, Gilt Braid Handle & Finial, c.1840, 8 In. 489.00
Tureen, Plate, 19th Century, 8 x 9 3/4 In. 400.00
Urn, Cover, 1875-1908, 16 1/4 In. 690.00
Vase, Alternating Panels, Birds, Mandarin Scenes, Flared Top & Bottom, 16 In. 305.00
Vase, Baluster Form, Applied Kylins, Foo Dog Handles, 10 In., Pair 380.00
Vase, Baluster Form, Mid 19th Century, 8 In. 155.00
Vase, Baluster Shape, Figural & Floral Reserves, Gilt Serpents, 1800s, 24 In. 2070.00
Vase, Cartouche Decorated, Flared Rim, c.1860, 24 In., Pair 3450.00
Vase, Cylindrical, Court Life, Birds, Flowers, 1875, 10 1/2 In., 6 Piece 748.00
Vase, Domestic Scenes, Elephant Head, Ring Handles, c.1890, 9 1/2 In. 145.00
Vase, Figures, Applied Gilt Salamanders, 9 1/2 In., Pair 805.00
Vase, Flower Ground, Baluster Shape, Famille Rose Enamel, c.1880, 18 x 9 In. 1725.00
Vase, Flowers, Domestic Scenes, Foo Dog Handles, Cover, c.1900, 25 In. 1150.00
Vase, Gold Dragons, Foo Dogs, 19th Century, 17 1/4 In. 1116.00

ROSE O'NEILL, see Kewpie category.

ROSE TAPESTRY porcelain was made by the Royal Bayreuth factory of
Tettau, Germany, during the late nineteenth century. The surface of the
porcelain was pressed against a coarse fabric while it was still damp,
and the impressions remained on the finished porcelain. It looks and
feels like a textured cloth. Very skillful reproductions are being made
that even include a variation of the Royal Bayreuth mark, so be careful when buying.

Basket, 4 In. 175.00
Chocolate Set, Pot, 4 Cups & Saucers, Chocolate Pot, 9 Piece 3950.00
Creamer, Pinched Front Spout, 3 3/8 In. 236.00
Creamer, Pinched Spout, Flared Base, 4 In. 160.00
Creamer, Pink, Yellow, White Roses, Gold Rim, 3 1/4 In. 425.00
Hair Receiver, Swans On Lake, 4 In. 120.00
Pitcher, Cavalier Design, Unmarked, 2 1/2 In. 125.00
Pitcher, Pinch Spout, 6 In. 325.00
Plate, 6 In. 175.00
Sugar & Creamer . . . . .289.00 to 335.00
Tray, Dresser, Roses, Yellow, White, 11 x 8 In. 288.00
Tray, Dresser, Violets, Marked, 7 1/4 x 10 In. 200.00
Vase, Scenic, Cottage, Lake, Windmill, Trees, 5 x 3 In. 335.00
Vase, Women Bathing At River Scene, Castle, Barrel Shape, 5 In. 500.00

ROSEMEADE Pottery of Wahpeton, North Dakota, worked from 1940 to
1961. The pottery was operated by Laura A. Taylor and her husband,
R.I. Hughes. The company was also known as the Wahpeton Pottery
Company. Art pottery and commercial wares were made.

Indian Moccasin, Clear, Maroon, Black Glaze, 1 1/2 x 3 1/2 In. . . . . .44.00 to 65.00
Pitcher, Pink, 3 1/2 In. 34.00
Planter, Swan, Blue, 5 1/4 In. 49.00
Salt & Pepper, Bear, 3 In. 77.00
Salt & Pepper, Bobwhite, Corks, 2 1/2 In. 65.00

Salt & Pepper, Dog, Fox Terrier, Original Stickers, 2 In. 56.00
Salt & Pepper, Dog, Original Stoppers, Stickers, 3 In. 81.00
Salt & Pepper, Dog, Russet Chow Chow, 2 In. 70.00
Salt & Pepper, Pheasants, 2 1/2 x 3 In. ....36.00 to 75.00
Salt & Pepper, Skunks, 3 x 3 3/4 In. 69.00
Sugar & Creamer, Blue Tulip Shape, 2 In. 85.00
Sugar & Creamer, Light Blue Glaze, Miniature 100.00

ROSENTHAL porcelain was made at the factory established in Selb, Bavaria, in 1880. The factory is still making fine-quality tablewares and figurines. A series of Christmas plates was made from 1910. Other limited edition plates have been made since 1971.

MARKE

Bowl, Studio Line, Geometric Black Rectangles, Blue, White, c.1960, 6 1/2 x 19 In. 150.00
Box, Tapio Wirkkala, Lid, Black Porcelain, High Glaze, 3 3/4 In. 290.00
Butter Chip, Rendezvous, 4 3/8 In. 20.00
Butter Chip, Studio Line 15.00
Candlestick, Columnar, 3 Dancing Girls, Hurricane Shade, 1900s, 24 1/2 In., Pair 580.00
Cup & Saucer, Cobalt Blue Leaves, Art Nouveau, c.1915, 8 Piece 360.00
Figurine, Nude Female, Seated, Parian, Signed, 8 1/2 In. 775.00
Figurine, Soaring Seagull, F. Heidenreich, 11 1/2 In. 500.00
Plate, Orange Blossoms, Mark, 10 1/4 In. 15.00
Tea Set, Studio Line, Matte Black Body, Glossy Black Handles, Spouts, Teapot 5 x 10 In. 264.00
Teapot, Sailboat & Windmill Scene, Blue Delft, 4 x 7 In. 30.00
Tray, Birds, Gold Accents, Hand Painted, 15 In. 299.00
Vase, Chicken, White, Tapio Wirkkala, c.1970, 3 3/4 x 5 In. 75.00
Vase, Cover, Silver Overlay, Flowers, 12 3/4 In. 1437.00
Vase, Frosted, Cylindrical Shape, Geometric, Studio Line, 5 1/2 In. 58.00

ROSEVILLE Pottery Company was organized in Roseville, Ohio, in 1890. Another plant was opened in Zanesville, Ohio, in 1898. Many types of pottery were made until 1954. Early wares include Sgraffito, Olympic, and Rozane. Later lines were often made with molded decorations, especially flowers and fruit. Most pieces are marked *Roseville*. Many reproductions made in China have been offered for sale the past few years.

Roseville
U.S.A.

Apple Blossom, Basket, Green, 10 In. 259.00
Apple Blossom, Candlestick, Green, 2 Low Handles, 2 In. 58.00
Apple Blossom, Jardiniere, Pedestal, Green, 10 In. 150.00
Apple Blossom, Vase, Blue, Footed, c.1948, 9 In. 206.00
Apple Blossom, Vase, Pink, 12 In. ....75.00 to 175.00
Apple Blossom, Wall Pocket, Blue, 8 1/4 In. 264.00
Apple Blossom, Wall Pocket, Green, 8 1/4 In. 230.00
Apple Blossom, Wall Pocket, Pink, 8 1/4 In. ....195.00 to 400.00
Apple Blossom, Window Box, Blue, 2 1/2 x 10 1/2 In. 259.00
Artcraft, Planter, Brown, Foil Label, 5 x 7 1/2 In. 264.00
Aztec, Vase, Blue, 10 1/2 In. ....525.00 to 690.00
Aztec, Vase, Blue, White, 4 Triangular Sides, 10 3/4 In. 523.00
Aztec, Vase, Brown, 4 Tapered Sides, 10 1/2 In. 290.00
Azurean, Vase, Blue, White, Handles, Anthony Dunlevy, 8 3/4 In. 1495.00
Baneda, Bowl, Green, 6 Sides, 3 1/2 x 11 In. 690.00
Baneda, Bowl, Green, 7 1/2 In. 441.00
Baneda, Bowl, Pink, 8 5/8 In. 315.00
Baneda, Jardiniere, Green, 8 x 11 1/2 In. 2875.00
Baneda, Vase, Green, 9 In. 990.00
Baneda, Vase, Green, Blue Drip Glaze, 9 1/4 x 8 In. 1320.00
Baneda, Vase, Green, Foil Label, 7 In. 499.00
Baneda, Vase, Green, Foil Label, 9 In. 1265.00
Baneda, Vase, Green, Handles, 4 In. 415.00
Baneda, Vase, Green, Handles, 5 In. 345.00
Baneda, Vase, Green, Handles, 8 In. 1430.00
Baneda, Vase, Pink, 4 In. ....290.00 to 375.00
Baneda, Vase, Pink, 6 In. 595.00
Baneda, Vase, Pink, 7 In. ....230.00 to 635.00

Baneda, Vase, Pink, 10 In. 770.00
Baneda, Vase, Pink, 2 Handles, 4 In. 230.00
Baneda, Wall Pocket, Pink, 8 In. 265.00
Bittersweet, Bookends, Pink, 5 1/2 In. ....115.00 to 145.00
Bittersweet, Console, Blue, 12 In. 28.00
Bittersweet, Ewer, Pink, 8 In. 175.00
Bittersweet, Vase, Blue, 10 In. 173.00
Bittersweet, Vase, Bud, Double, Green, Connecting Handle, Footed, 6 In. 86.00
Bittersweet, Wall Pocket, Brown, 7 In. 299.00
Bittersweet, Wall Pocket, Gray, 7 In. 235.00
Bittersweet, Wall Pocket, Green, 7 1/4 In. 285.00
Blackberry, Console, Handles, 13 x 3 In. 460.00
Blackberry, Jardiniere, Handles, 6 In. ....445.00 to 690.00
Blackberry, Vase, Handles, 5 In. 460.00
Blackberry, Vase, Handles, 8 In. 770.00
Blackberry, Vase, Handles, 10 In. 715.00
Blackberry, Vase, Handles, Wide Mouth, 4 In. 460.00
Blackberry, Vase, Squat, 6 In. 380.00
Blackberry, Wall Pocket, 8 1/2 In. 1650.00
Bleeding Heart, Basket, Blue, 10 In. 430.00
Bleeding Heart, Bowl, Pink, Angular Handles, 4 In. 115.00
Bleeding Heart, Ewer, Blue, 6 In. 175.00
Bleeding Heart, Ewer, Green, 6 In. 115.00
Bleeding Heart, Vase, Green, 6-Sided Rim, 4 In. 145.00
Bleeding Heart, Wall Pocket, Blue, 8 In. 523.00
Bleeding Heart, Wall Pocket, Pink, 8 In. 323.00
Bushberry, Basket, Blue, 8 In. 259.00
Bushberry, Basket, Blue, 10 In. 345.00
Bushberry, Basket, Orange, 8 In. 175.00
Bushberry, Ewer, c.1941, 15 In. 518.00
Bushberry, Jardiniere, Pedestal, Orange, 31 In. 880.00
Bushberry, Sugar & Creamer, Green 118.00
Bushberry, Vase, Blue, Handles, 14 In. 460.00
Bushberry, Vase, Bud, Orange, Branch Handles, 7 1/2 In., Pair 375.00
Bushberry, Vase, Canoe, Green, Handles, 12 1/4 x 10 In. 330.00
Bushberry, Vase, Orange, 6 In. 110.00
Carnelian, Vase, Green, Mustard Yellow Drip, Marked, 10 In. 115.00
Carnelian I, Bowl, Green To Rose Glaze, 3 x 6 In. 315.00
Carnelian I, Ewer, Green, 15 In. 400.00
Carnelian I, Vase, 18 In. 3819.00
Carnelian II, Candlestick, Rose, 3 1/2 In. 115.00
Carnelian II, Ewer, Pink Glaze, Purple Drip, 15 In. 690.00
Carnelian II, Urn, Green, Pink Matte Glaze, 9 1/2 x 10 In. 499.00
Carnelian II, Vase, Bulbous, Green, Purple, Pink Glaze, 8 In. 1765.00
Carnelian II, Vase, Candlestick, Green, Aqua Drip Glaze, 4 In. 220.00
Carnelian II, Vase, Green, Purple, Rose Glaze, 7 x 5 In. 353.00
Carnelian II, Vase, Mauve Glaze, Aqua, Purple, Handles, 8 In. 470.00
Carnelian II, Vase, Pillow, Orange, 5 In. 175.00
Carnelian II, Vase, Pink, Green Glaze, 9 In. 380.00
Carnelian II, Wall Pocket, Pink, Ocher Glaze, Paper Label, 7 In. 410.00
Carnelian II, Wall Pocket, Red Mottled Glaze, 8 In. 440.00
Cherry Blossom, Jardiniere, Brown, 2 Handles, 4 In. 288.00
Cherry Blossom, Vase, Brown, 5 In. 325.00
Cherry Blossom, Vase, Brown, 8 In. 375.00
Cherry Blossom, Vase, Brown, Foil Label, 9 In. 825.00
Cherry Blossom, Vase, Brown, Handles, 4 In. 325.00
Cherry Blossom, Vase, Brown, Handles, 5 In. 345.00
Cherry Blossom, Vase, Brown, Oval, 10 In. 750.00
Cherry Blossom, Vase, Brown, Oval, 12 In. 978.00
Cherry Blossom, Vase, Pink, Handles, 4 In. 450.00
Cherry Blossom, Vase, Pink, Handles, 5 In. 215.00
Cherry Blossom, Vase, Pink, Incised, 8 In. 1210.00
Cherry Blossom, Vase, Urn Shape, Brown, Handles, Striped Bottom, 15 1/2 In. 1495.00

Chloron, Vase, Green, Raised Grapes, 9 In. 1380.00
Clemana, Vase, Blue, Handles, 8 In. 230.00
Clemana, Vase, Blue, Handles, Ball Shape, 6 In. 200.00
Clemana, Vase, Green, Handles, Footed, 6 In. 375.00
Clemana, Vase, Tan Matte, White, Purple, 9 In. 275.00
Clematis, Cookie Jar, Brown, 8 In. 259.00
Clematis, Ewer, Blue, Flared Handles, 15 In. 200.00
Clematis, Vase, Blue, Handles, 6 In. 17.00
Clematis, Vase, Blue, Shoulder Handles, 7 In. 35.00
Columbine, Basket, Blue, 10 In. 29.00
Columbine, Basket, Blue, 12 In. 290.00
Columbine, Bowl, Brown, Handles, 7 In. 115.00
Columbine, Candlestick, Brown, 2 In., Pair 118.00
Columbine, Jardiniere, Blue, Handles, 5 In. 175.00
Columbine, Vase, Blue, Handles, 8 In. 225.00
Corinthian, Wall Pocket, Green, 8 In. 145.00
Corinthian, Wall Pocket, Green, 10 In. 545.00
Cosmos, Basket, Blue, 12 In. 489.00
Cosmos, Ewer, Blue, 10 In. 345.00
Cosmos, Vase, Blue, 4 In. 70.00
Cosmos, Vase, Blue, Handles, 7 In. 235.00
Cosmos, Vase, Bud, Double, Tan, Arched Connection, 5 In. 115.00
Cosmos, Wall Pocket, Tan, 6 In. 460.00
Creamware, Candlestick, Good Night, 7 In. 750.00
Creamware, Juvenile, Plate Set, Sunbonnet Girl, Cup, Saucer, 8-In. Plate, 3 Piece 35.00
Creamware, Mug, Dutch Scene, 5 In. 35.00
Cremo, Vase, 6 1/2 In. 2875.00
Cremo, Vase, Glaze, 6 In. 2300.00
Cremona, Vase, Green, Baluster, 12 1/4 In. 410.00
Cremona, Vase, Pink, Buttressed Rim Handles, 12 In. 315.00
Cremona, Vase, Pink, Lavender Freesia, 12 In. 230.00
Crocus, Vase, Brown, Bulbous, 9 1/2 In. 375.00
Crystalis, Vase, Tan & Orange Glaze, Squat, 3 3/4 In. 630.00
Dahlrose, Basket, Hanging, Ocher, Flared, 6 In. 325.00
Dahlrose, Candlestick, Handles, Footed, 3 In., Pair 175.00
Dahlrose, Chamberstick, Shaped Handle, 7 1/2 In. 315.00
Dahlrose, Jardiniere, Ocher, Handles, 6 In. 225.00
Dahlrose, Vase, 10 1/4 x 7 1/2 In. 330.00
Dahlrose, Vase, Bud, Triple, 6 In. 105.00
Dahlrose, Vase, Bulbous, Handles, 8 In. 489.00
Dahlrose, Vase, Flattened, Angular Handles, 8 x 6 In. 405.00
Dahlrose, Vase, Pillow, Handles, 5 x 7 In. 165.00
Dahlrose, Wall Pocket, 10 In. 575.00
Dawn, Vase, Pink, Bulbous, Footed, 6 In. 230.00
Dawn, Vase, Pink, Tab Handles, Footed, 8 In. 230.00
Dawn, Vase, Yellow, Tab Handles, Footed, 4 In. 230.00
Della Robbia, Vase, Carved Dandelions, 6 1/2 In. 3105.00
Della Robbia, Vase, Carved Grape Panels, 11 In. 2750.00
Della Robbia, Vase, Cypress Tree, Triangular Panels, Etched, Taupe, 10 1/2 In. 2860.00
Della Robbia, Vase, White Daisies, Green Stems, Leaves, 8 In. 9200.00
Dogwood, Vase, 10 In. 390.00
Dogwood, Wall Pocket, Branch Handles, 9 In. 92.00
Dogwood I, Wall Pocket, Flowers, 9 In. 400.00
Dogwood II, Jardiniere, 8 In. 230.00
Dogwood II, Jardiniere, Handles, 8 In. 259.00
Dogwood II, Jardiniere, Pedestal, 35 In. 1980.00
Dogwood II, Vase, 8 In. 230.00
Donatello, Compote, 7 In. 145.00
Donatello, Jardiniere, Green, 8 In. 100.00
Donatello, Jardiniere, Pedestal, Green, 23 In. 520.00
Donatello, Wall Pocket, Green, 10 In. 175.00
Earlam, Vase, Green Glaze, 8 In. 550.00
Earlam, Vase, Green Handle, Mottled Turquoise Glaze, 7 In. 440.00

Earlam, Vase, Pink, Handles, 4-Sided Rim, 8 In. 440.00
Egypto, Pitcher, 5 1/4 In. 690.00
Egypto, Vase, Bud, 5 1/2 In. 545.00
Egypto, Wall Pocket, 8 1/4 In. 3565.00
Falline, Urn, Brown, Flared, 6 1/2 In. 470.00
Falline, Vase, Blue, Handles, Oval, 7 In. 1295.00
Falline, Vase, Brown, Bulbous, Handles, 6 In. 690.00
Falline, Vase, Brown, Green Pea Pods, 2 Handles, 8 In. 605.00
Falline, Vase, Brown, Green, Handles, 7 1/2 In. 690.00
Falline, Vase, Brown, Handles, 12 In. 1035.00
Ferella, Bowl, Flower Frog, Brown, 9 1/2 In. 410.00
Ferella, Compote, Brown, Yellow Flowers, Spattered White, Oval, 7 x 12 In. 880.00
Ferella, Rose Bowl, 6 x 8 1/2 In. 1035.00
Ferella, Vase, Brown, Cutout Rim & Foot, Handles, 5 1/2 In. 290.00
Ferella, Vase, Brown, Cutout Rim & Foot, Handles, 9 In. 405.00
Ferella, Vase, Brown, Flowers, Handles, Ocher, Matte, Globular, 6 In. ... 715.00
Ferella, Vase, Brown, Yellow Flowers, Blue Base, Handles, 9 x 5 In. .... 545.00 to 935.00
Ferella, Vase, Brown, Yellow Flowers, Spattered White, Globular, 8 x 7 1/2 In. 770.00
Ferella, Vase, Bud, Rose, 4 In. 545.00
Ferella, Vase, Bud, Rose, 6 In. ....690.00 to 920.00
Ferella, Vase, Pink, Green, 2 Handles, 9 In. 1035.00
Ferella, Vase, Rose Cutout Green Rim, 8 In. 1650.00
Ferella, Vase, Rose, 6 In. 600.00
Ferella, Vase, Rose, 9 In. 1380.00
Ferella, Vase, Rose, Cutouts, 4 x 6 In. 715.00
Ferella, Vase, Rose, Handles, Windows, Mottled Teal Green, 5 In. .. 615.00
Ferella, Wall Pocket, Rose, Black Label, 6 1/2 In. 1725.00
Florane, Window Box, Green, Flared, Ink Mark, 9 x 8 In. 150.00
Florentine, Jardiniere, Brown, 10 In. 175.00
Florentine, Jardiniere, Cream, Green, Brown Design, 7 In. 110.00
Florentine, Vase, Brown, Handles, 12 In. 200.00
Florentine, Wall Pocket, Brown, 12 In. 405.00
Foxglove, Basket, Pink, 8 In. ....175.00 to 201.00
Foxglove, Basket, Pink, 10 In. 230.00
Foxglove, Ewer, Pink, 15 In. 489.00
Foxglove, Vase, Green, 16 In. 405.00
Foxglove, Vase, Pink, Handles, 7 In. 230.00
Foxglove, Wall Pocket, Blue, 8 In. 460.00
Foxglove, Wall Pocket, Pink, 8 In. 295.00
Freesia, Cookie Jar, Green, Handles, 10 In. 546.00
Freesia, Ewer, Brown, 6 In. 105.00
Freesia, Ewer, Green, Squat, 6 In. 80.00
Freesia, Jardiniere, Pedestal, Blue, Molded Flowers, c.1935, 24 In. 865.00
Freesia, Tea Set, Green, 8-In. Teapot, 3 Piece 230.00
Freesia, Wall Pocket, Brown, 8 In. 175.00
Fuchsia, Basket, Attached Flower Frog, Green, 8 In. 345.00
Fuchsia, Bowl, Blue, 14 In. 294.00
Fuchsia, Bowl, Brown, Embossed Leaves, 12 In. 165.00
Fuchsia, Bowl, Flower Frog, Green, 8 1/2 In. 345.00
Fuchsia, Compote, Brown, Marked, 4 In. 125.00
Fuchsia, Ewer, Blue, 10 In. 345.00
Fuchsia, Flower Frog, Brown, 3 In. 105.00
Fuchsia, Jardiniere, Blue, 6 In. 315.00
Fuchsia, Vase, Blue, 6 In. ....201.00 to 285.00
Fuchsia, Vase, Blue, Impressed Mark, 18 In. 1175.00
Fuchsia, Vase, Blue, Salmon, Flowers, Leaves, Deep Blue, 5 x 7 In. .. 470.00
Fuchsia, Vase, Brown, 6 In. 175.00
Fuchsia, Vase, Brown, 12 In. 195.00
Fuchsia, Vase, Brown, 5 x 8 In. 230.00
Fuchsia, Vase, Green, 8 In. 150.00
Fuchsia, Vase, Green, Handles, 7 In. 176.00
Fuchsia, Vase, Green, Handles, 8 In. 176.00
Futura, Jardiniere, Pink & Purple Leaves, Green Body, Handles, 8 In. 200.00

❦

Light your yard so that some of the lights face the garage door and light up the entrances to the house. Put the lights high enough to be out of easy reach.

❦

Roseville, Futura,
Vase, Blue, Triangular,
c.1924, 9 In.

Futura, Jardiniere, Tan, 9 In.	415.00
Futura, Jardiniere, Tan, 10 In.	330.00
Futura, Jardiniere, Tan, Stylized Leaves, 8 In.	770.00
Futura, Vase, Blue & Green, Geometric, 4 Flaring Sides, 10 In.	635.00
Futura, Vase, Blue & Green, Green, Ivory, Balloon Shape, 7 In.	1095.00
Futura, Vase, Blue, Triangular, c.1924, 9 In. *Illus*	700.00
Futura, Vase, Brown, 3 Small Blue Flowers, Linear Design, Flattened Shape, 6 In.	405.00
Futura, Vase, Brown, 4 Buttressed Feet, 4 In.	1265.00
Futura, Vase, Bud, 2-Pole, Pink, 4 In.	315.00
Futura, Vase, Double V, Embossed, 7 x 4 In.	770.00
Futura, Vase, Four Ball, Blue, Green Leaves, 8 In.	765.00
Futura, Vase, Green Twist, 7 In.	210.00
Futura, Vase, Green, 4 Sides, Buttresses, Blue To Beige Ground, 8 x 3 3/4 In.	635.00
Futura, Vase, Green, 6 Sides, Twisted, Blue Triangles, Matte Pink Base, 8 x 4 In.	765.00
Futura, Vase, Green, Pink Glaze, Geometric, Straight Handles, 8 In.	748.00
Futura, Vase, Leaf Design, 3 Sides, Conical, Blue, 9 x 4 In.	460.00
Futura, Vase, Ostrich Egg, Tan, 7 In.	805.00
Futura, Vase, Pink, Green, 7 In.	230.00
Futura, Wall Pocket, Purple, Yellow, Green, Blue, 8 In.	375.00
Gardenia, Basket, Green, Round Handle, 10 In.	17.00
Gardenia, Bookends, Green, 5 1/2 In.	175.00
Gardenia, Ewer, Brown, Tan, 6 In.	25.00
Gardenia, Ewer, Green, 10 In.	115.00
Hexagon, Rose Bowl, Brown, Emblem, Incised, Burnt Orange Glaze, 4 In.	440.00
Imperial I, Basket, 10 x 6 In.	205.00
Imperial I, Wall Pocket, Green, 10 In.	144.00
Imperial II, Candlestick, Orange & Green, 2 3/4 In., Pair	345.00
Imperial II, Vase, Blue & White, Collar Rim, 10 In.	805.00
Imperial II, Vase, Frothy Turquoise, Yellow Rim Band, 8 In.	355.00
Imperial II, Vase, Turquoise Glaze, Yellow Stylized Design, 8 In.	288.00
Iris, Bookends, Blue, 5 In.	175.00
Iris, Ewer, Tan, Handles, 10 In.	345.00
Iris, Vase, Blue, Bulbous, 15 In.	920.00
Iris, Vase, Blue, Handles, 5 In.	145.00
Iris, Vase, Green, Handles, 4 In.	110.00
Iris, Vase, Pink, 6 In.	115.00 to 150.00
Iris, Vase, Pink, Handles, 4 In.	115.00
Ixia, Vase, Green, 6 In.	115.00
Ixia, Vase, Green, Handles, 7 In., Pair	173.00
Jonquil, Basket, Brown, Flowers, Leaves, Paper Label, 8 In.	470.00
Jonquil, Bowl, Built-In Flower Frog, Flare, 10 In.	765.00
Jonquil, Candlestick, Brown, White Flowers, Green Leaves, 4 In., Pair	825.00
Jonquil, Jardiniere, Handles, 7 In.	230.00
Jonquil, Vase, Brown, Handles, 8 In.	315.00
Jonquil, Vase, Green & Ocher, 12 x 9 In.	1100.00
Jonquil, Vase, Handles, 4 In.	230.00
Juvenile, see Roseville, Creamware	
Landscape, Sugar & Creamer, Ships & Windmills, Blue & White	115.00
Laurel, Vase, Brown, Buttressed Handle, 6 In.	635.00
Laurel, Vase, Red, Buttressed Handles, Foil Label, 7 In.	295.00

Laurel, Vase, Red, Green Leaves, Branches, Berries, Red Orange Glaze, 9 1/4 In.	525.00
Laurel, Vase, Red, Handles, 7 1/4 In.	290.00
Laurel, Vase, Yellow, Egg Shape, 6 In.	265.00
Laurel, Vase, Yellow, Flared, 10 In.	545.00
Laurel, Vase, Yellow, Marked, 7 1/4 In.	460.00
Lotus, Vase, Brown, Vertical Overlapping Leaves, 10 In.	145.00
Luffa, Bowl, Brown, 5 x 7 In.	206.00
Magnolia, Ashtray, Brown, 7 In.	46.00
Magnolia, Basket, Green, 8 In.	50.00
Magnolia, Cookie Jar, Green, 11 In.	375.00
Magnolia, Vase, Blue, Bulbous, Raised Mark, 12 In.	155.00
Magnolia, Vase, Green, 2 Handles, 14 In.	375.00
Magnolia, Wall Pocket, Blue, Marked, 8 In.	259.00
Mayfair, Planter, Green, Chartreuse Interior, 5 In.	85.00
Ming Tree, Ewer, Ivory, Shaped Branch Handle, 10 In.	46.00
Ming Tree, Planter, Green, 11 In.	69.00
Ming Tree, Vase, Green, 15 In.	885.00
Ming Tree, Wall Pocket, Blue, 8 In.	175.00
Mock Orange, Basket, Pink, 8 In.	173.00
Monticello, Urn, Green, Fleur-De-Lis, 9 x 8 In.	999.00
Monticello, Vase, Blue, 2 Low Handles, Flared, Footed, 10 In.	520.00
Monticello, Vase, Brown, 2 Handles, White Fleur-De-Lis, 5 In.	295.00
Monticello, Vase, Brown, Squat, 5 In.	175.00
Monticello, Vase, Green, Black, Yellow, Orange Abstracts, Handles, 7 In.	550.00
Monticello, Vase, Green, Handles, 7 In.	460.00
Monticello, Vase, Mottled Blue Glaze, Bulbous, 7 In.	765.00
Morning Glory, Bowl, Green, 6 In.	1150.00
Morning Glory, Vase, Green, Flared Rim, 2 Angular Handles At Base, 8 In.	635.00
Morning Glory, Vase, Pillow, Cream, Foil Label, 7 In.	380.00
Moss, Bowl, Flower Frog, Pink, 2 Low Handles, 3 x 12 In.	225.00
Moss, Jardiniere, Blue, Ivory, Branches, Leaves, 10 In.	385.00
Moss, Jardiniere, Pedestal, Green, 29 In.	3738.00
Moss, Vase, Blue, 2 Angular Handles, Flattened Shape, 7 In.	200.00
Moss, Vase, Blue, 2 Angular Handles, Footed, Bulbous, 6 In.	345.00
Moss, Vase, Pink, 7 In.	316.00
Mostique, Vase, Gray, 6 In., Pair	310.00
Mostique, Vase, Gray, 10 In.	1355.00
Mostique, Wall Pocket, Gray, 10 In.	288.00
Mostique, Wall Pocket, Gray, 12 In.	405.00
Orian, Bowl, Peach, Turquoise Interior, 10 In.	230.00
Orian, Vase, Green, 2 Handles, Footed, 10 In.	345.00
Orian, Vase, Ocher Glaze, White, Handles, Aqua Glaze, 9 1/2 x 6 In.	165.00
Orian, Vase, Pink, 2 Long Low Handles, Footed, 10 In.	259.00
Orian, Vase, Squat Base, Stovepipe Neck, 6 1/2 x 8 1/2 In.	175.00
Panel, Bowl, Green, Purple Blossoms, 9 In.	200.00
Panel, Vase, Brown, Nude, Flattened, 8 In.	430.00
Panel, Vase, Double, Brown Matte, Vine, Berry, Stamped, 8 In.	248.00
Panel, Vase, Green, Embossed Dandelions, Marked, 9 In.	518.00
Pauleo, Lamp Base, Pink Crackle Glaze, 19 In.	1645.00
Pauleo, Vase, Purple, Life Size Bunches Of Grapes, Green Leaves, 15 In.	1035.00
Peony, Jardiniere, Green, White Flowers, 6 In.	39.00
Peony, Jardiniere, Yellow, Handles, 4 In.	55.00
Peony, Jug, Yellow, 7 1/2 In.	144.00
Peony, Tea Set, Pink, 3 Piece	58.00
Peony, Vase, Conch Shell, Footed, 9 1/2 In.	173.00
Peony, Vase, Green, Flared, 15 In.	345.00
Peony, Vase, Pink, 18 In.	489.00
Peony, Vase, Yellow, 2 Handles, 8 In.	92.00
Peony, Wall Pocket, Green, 8 In.	230.00
Peony, Wall Pocket, Yellow, 8 In.	375.00
Petite White Rose, Vase, Blue, Raised Mark, 4 1/4 In.	35.00
Pine Cone, Ashtray, Blue, Leaf Shape, 4 In.	259.00
Pine Cone, Basket, Blue, 10 In.	529.00
Pine Cone, Basket, Brown, Hanging, 5 In.	323.00

Pine Cone, Basket, Built In Flower Frog, Blue, 8 In. 1035.00
Pine Cone, Basket, Green, Hanging, Offset Handles, 5 In. 195.00
Pine Cone, Basket, Hanging, Brown, 5 In. 230.00
Pine Cone, Basket, Impressed Mark, 11 In. 529.00
Pine Cone, Bowl, Blue, 9 In. ....316.00 to 382.00
Pine Cone, Bowl, Blue, Oval, 10 In. 411.00
Pine Cone, Bowl, Brown, Oval, 10 In. 230.00
Pine Cone, Console, Blue, 12 1/2 In. 345.00
Pine Cone, Cornucopia, Blue, 6 In. 259.00
Pine Cone, Cornucopia, Brown, 6 In. 219.00
Pine Cone, Ewer, Green, 15 In. 863.00
Pine Cone, Jardiniere, Blue, 3 In. ....127.00 to 285.00
Pine Cone, Jardiniere, Brown, 5 In. 195.00
Pine Cone, Pitcher, Brown, 8 In. 518.00
Pine Cone, Pitcher, Brown, Bulbous, Branch Handle, 10 In. 460.00
Pine Cone, Pitcher, Green, Branch Handle, 2 Qt., 7 In. 770.00
Pine Cone, Pitcher, Green, Ice Lip, 2 Qt., 7 In. 345.00
Pine Cone, Planter, Green, 5 In. 118.00
Pine Cone, Urn, Brown, Raised Mark, 10 In. 588.00
Pine Cone, Vase, Blue, 10 In. 920.00
Pine Cone, Vase, Blue, 2 Branch Handles, 8 In. 259.00
Pine Cone, Vase, Blue, Brown, Pine Needles, Handles, Glaze, Ivory, 12 In. 1210.00
Pine Cone, Vase, Blue, Bulbous, 6 In. 265.00
Pine Cone, Vase, Blue, Bulbous, Buttressed Base, 10 In. 345.00
Pine Cone, Vase, Blue, Flared, Basket Handle, 10 In. 489.00
Pine Cone, Vase, Blue, Squat Base, Impressed Mark, 8 In. 470.00
Pine Cone, Vase, Brown, 7 In. 315.00
Pine Cone, Vase, Brown, Pine Needles, 2 Handles, Black Glaze, 12 In. 470.00
Pine Cone, Vase, Bud, Triple, Blue, 8 In. 518.00
Pine Cone, Vase, Fan, Blue, 6 In. 470.00
Pine Cone, Vase, Pillow, Blue, 8 In. 635.00
Pine Cone, Vase, Pillow, Brown, Foil Label, 8 In. 355.00
Pine Cone, Vase, Pillow, Green, 8 In. 200.00
Pine Cone, Vase, Pillow, Green, Foil Label, 8 In. 355.00
Pine Cone, Vase, Trumpet Shape, Blue Glaze, Branch Handles, 7 1/2 x 6 1/4 In. 375.00
Pine Cone II, Ashtray, Brown, 5 In. 288.00
Pine Cone II, Bowl, Brown, 12 In. 294.00
Pine Cone II, Jardiniere, Blue, 4 In. 345.00
Pine Cone II, Jardiniere, Green, 4 In. 132.00
Pine Cone II, Jardiniere, Green, 6 In. 260.00
Pine Cone II, Planter, Blue, Round, 5 In. 290.00
Pine Cone II, Planter, Brown, Rectangular, 8 In. 290.00
Pine Cone II, Tray, Brown, Rectangular, 13 In. 144.00
Pine Cone II, Tumbler, Brown, 5 In., Pair 144.00
Pine Cone II, Vase, Bud, Blue, 7 In. 405.00
Pine Cone II, Wall Pocket, Brown, Bucket, Triple, 8 3/4 In. 805.00
Pine Cone II, Window Box, Green, 8 3/4 In. 175.00
Pine Cone II, Window Box, Green, Marked, 8 In. 180.00
Poppy, Ewer, Green, 18 In. 635.00
Poppy, Jardiniere, Pink, Handles, 4 In. 175.00
Poppy, Vase, Green, 10 In. 200.00
Primrose, Jardiniere, Orange, Blossoms, Leaves, Impressed, 1932, 9 In. 265.00
Primrose, Vase, Pink, 2 Handles, 6 In. 175.00
Primrose, Vase, Tan, 6 In. 175.00
Rosecraft Black, Vase, Glaze, 2 Scrolled Handles, 12 In. 69.00
Rosecraft Hexagon, Wall Pocket, Brown, Stamped, 8 In. 805.00
Rosecraft Panel, Bowl, Brown, Freesia Design, 4 In. 130.00
Rosecraft Panel, Vase, Brown Matte, Daffodils, Orange Glaze, Stamped, 8 In. 330.00
Rosecraft Panel, Vase, Brown, Dandelion Design, Footed, 7 In. 260.00
Rosecraft Panel, Vase, Brown, Red Roses, Stamped, 7 In. 150.00
Rosecraft Panel, Vase, Fan, Brown, Nudes, Marked, 6 In. 690.00
Rosecraft Panel, Wall Pocket, Brown, Standing Nude, Stamped, 7 In. 920.00
Rosecraft Vintage, Bowl, Brown, 7 In. 290.00
Rosecraft Vintage, Bowl, Green, 9 In. 260.00

Rosecraft Vintage, Bowl, Green, Marked, 6 In. 210.00
Rosecraft Vintage, Vase, Brown, 10 In. 690.00
Rosecraft Vintage, Vase, Brown, Barrel Shape, 6 In. 230.00
Rosecraft Vintage, Vase, Brown, Oval, 12 In. 980.00
Rosecraft Vintage, Vase, Bud, Double, 5 In. 490.00
Rosecraft Vintage, Wall Pocket, Dark Brown, Stamped, 9 In. 460.00
Rozane, Vase, Brown Glaze, Leaves & Berries, 3 Handles, 3-Footed, 7 In. 259.00
Rozane, Vase, Green, Marked, 10 In. 316.00
Rozane Egypto, Vase, Green Matte, Lotus Leaves, Blossoms, Smooth, Vellum, 8 In. 4406.00
Rozane Royal, Ewer, Clover, Leaves, 1904, 7 1/2 In. 410.00
Rozane Royal, Vase, Brown, Man In Profile, Teardrop, Anthony Donlevy, 8 In. 920.00
Rozane Royal, Vase, Lilies, 4 x 4 In. 115.00
Rozane Royal, Vase, Virginia Creeper, Timberlake, 18 In. 1380.00
Russco, Vase, Gold Matte, Silver Metallic Crystalline Glaze, Handles, 7 In. ......138.00 to 170.00
Russco, Vase, Green, Semigloss, Yellow Glaze, Footed, Marked, 7 In. 138.00
Savona, Bowl, Blue, Volpato Shape, 10 In. 250.00
Savona, Vase, Blue, 12 In. 265.00
Silhouette, Basket, Blue, Tropical Blossoms, Raised Mark, 10 In. 95.00
Silhouette, Box, Cigarette, Cover, Brown, 3 x 4 1/2 In. 230.00
Silhouette, Vase, Aqua, 14 In. 650.00
Silhouette, Vase, Brown, 6 In. 518.00
Silhouette, Vase, Fan, Brown, 7 In. 290.00
Silhouette, Wall Pocket, Brown, 8 In. 115.00
Snowberry, Bowl, Pink, 7 In. 35.00
Snowberry, Bowl, Pink, 10 In. 60.00
Snowberry, Candlestick, Blue, 4 1/2 In., Pair 200.00
Snowberry, Ewer, Blue, Cutout Design At Neck, 10 In. 145.00
Snowberry, Ewer, Pink, 10 In. 175.00
Snowberry, Jardiniere, Pedestal, Blue, Glaze, Branches, 1946, 24 In. 560.00
Snowberry, Tea Set, Blue, Teapot, Creamer, Open Sugar, 3 Piece 430.00
Snowberry, Vase, Pink, 7 In. 195.00
Sunflower, Basket, Hanging, 10 In. 1595.00
Sunflower, Bowl, 4 Sides, Flower Frog, 2 Handles, 12 In. 230.00
Sunflower, Bowl, Bulbous, 2 Handles, 5 In. 575.00
Sunflower, Jardiniere, 16 In. 3105.00
Sunflower, Vase, 10 In. ....1870.00 to 2090.00
Sunflower, Vase, 2 Handles, 5 In. ....470.00 to 715.00
Sunflower, Vase, 2 Handles, 6 In. 865.00
Sunflower, Vase, 2 Handles, Bulbous Base, Cylindrical Neck, 9 In. 1495.00
Sunflower, Vase, 2 Handles, Mottled Yellow, Green, Orange, 1930, 9 In. 1645.00
Sunflower, Vase, 6 In. 490.00
Sunflower, Vase, Bulbous, 5 In. 470.00
Sunflower, Vase, Bulbous, 7 In. 990.00
Sunflower, Vase, Golden Yellow, Leaves, Stems, 7 In. 1430.00
Sunflower, Wall Pocket, 7 In. ....1380.00 to 1430.00
Teasel, Vase, Blue, 8 In. 175.00
Teasel, Vase, Peach, Buttress Shape, 7 In. 230.00
Teasel, Vase, Tan High Glaze, 6 In. 145.00
Thorn Apple, Jardiniere, Pedestal, Brown, White Flowers, Matte, 29 In. 1650.00
Thorn Apple, Pedestal, Pink, 17 In. 345.00
Thorn Apple, Urn, Pink, 6 In. 90.00
Thorn Apple, Vase, Brown, 2 Handles, 4 In. 90.00
Thorn Apple, Vase, Pink, 2 Handles, 8 In. 175.00
Topeo, Bowl, Blue, 9 1/4 In. 259.00
Topeo, Vase, Blue, 8 1/2 In. 590.00
Topeo, Vase, Red, Foil Label, 9 In. 316.00
Tourist, Bowl, Creamware, Cars, Geese, 3 x 5 1/2 In. 1265.00
Tourmaline, Bowl, Blue Matte Crystalline, Over Glossy Ocher Flambe, Footed, 6 In. 92.00
Tourmaline, Vase, Blue Matte Crystalline Glaze, Over Ocher Flambe, Handles, 6 In. 115.00
Tourmaline, Vase, Blue Matte Glossy Ocher, Gold Label, 7 In. 140.00
Tourmaline, Vase, Blue, Beaded Neck, Flambe Drip Glaze, 7 In. 145.00
Tourmaline, Vase, Blue, Blue Drip Glaze, 2 Handles, 6 In. ....115.00 to 144.00
Tourmaline, Vase, Blue, Round, 5 In. 69.00
Tourmaline, Vase, Green Mottled Matte, Over Turquoise Glaze, Footed, 8 In. 161.00

Tourmaline, Vase, Pillow, Blue, 6 In. 115.00
Tourmaline, Vase, Pink & Aqua, Mottled, Twist, 8 In. 195.00
Tourmaline, Vase, Pink & Aqua, Square, 9 In. 260.00
Tourmaline, Vase, Yellow, 6 Sides, 10 In. 460.00
Tourmaline, Window Box, Salmon Mottled, Over Gold Glaze, 6 In. 90.00
Tuscany, Vase, Green, 2 Handles, 4 In. 90.00
Tuscany, Wall Pocket, Pink, 8 In. 230.00
Velmoss, Vase, Green, Bulbous, 6 In. 650.00
Velmoss, Vase, Seafoam Glaze, Foil Label, 8 In. 175.00
Vista, Bowl, 4 x 8 In. 290.00
Vista, Bowl, 7 In. 235.00
Vista, Jardiniere, 9 In. 405.00
Vista, Planter, 6 x 11 In. 1610.00
Vista, Vase, 14 In. 805.00
Vista, Vase, Footed, 10 In. 750.00
Vista, Vase, Tapering, 15 In. 1093.00
Water Lily, Basket, Hanging, Pink, 2 Handles, Chains, 5 1/2 In. 200.00
Water Lily, Basket, Pink, 8 In. 145.00
Water Lily, Cookie Jar, Pink, Green, 10 In. 405.00
Water Lily, Jardiniere, Pedestal, Brown, Marked, 24 In. 805.00
Water Lily, Vase, Blue, 2 Handles, 8 In. 45.00
Water Lily, Vase, Brown, 2 Handles, 4 1/2 In., Pair 69.00
White Rose, Bowl, Pink, Green, Notched Rim, Marked, 6 In. 105.00
White Rose, Ewer, Pink, 6 In. 115.00
White Rose, Jardiniere, Blue, 4 In. 240.00
White Rose, Jardiniere, Pink, 2 Handles, 10 In. 175.00
White Rose, Teapot, Pink, 6 1/2 In. 115.00
White Rose, Wall Pocket, Brown, Marked, 6 1/2 In. 195.00
Wincraft, Tea Set, Tan, 7-In. Pot, 3 Piece 200.00
Wincraft, Vase, Blue, Flared, Squat Base, Pine Cone, 8 In. 118.00
Wincraft, Vase, Brown, Blowing Wind Panels, 7 In. 145.00
Wincraft, Vase, Tan, Pine Cone, 6 In. 80.00
Wincraft, Wall Pocket, Blue, Ivy, Raised Mark, 5 In. 206.00
Wincraft, Wall Pocket, Green, 8 In. 175.00
Wincraft, Wall Pocket, Tan Glaze, 5 In. . . . . .105.00 to 150.00
Windsor, Bowl, Blue, Black Label, 10 In. 325.00
Windsor, Vase, Blue Matte, Yellow, Green, Bulbous, 6 In. 605.00
Windsor, Vase, Blue Speckled Glaze, Looped Handles, Incised, 7 In. 825.00
Wisteria, Bowl, Flower Frog, Brown, 6 In. 375.00
Wisteria, Candlestick, Brown, Gold Label, 4 In., Pair 340.00
Wisteria, Jardiniere, Brown, Yellow, Green, Lavender Flowers, 9 In. 450.00
Wisteria, Jardiniere, Pedestal, Blue, Marked, 24 In. 3565.00
Wisteria, Vase, Blue Glaze, 2 Handles, Pumpkin Shape, 6 1/2 x 8 1/2 In. 1045.00
Wisteria, Vase, Blue, 2 Angular Handles, Cylindrical, Tapered, 10 In. 2300.00
Wisteria, Vase, Blue, 2 Handles, Bulbous, 8 In. 1035.00
Wisteria, Vase, Blue, 2 Handles, Leaves, 4 1/3 x 6 In. 495.00
Wisteria, Vase, Blue, Flared, 8 In. 880.00
Wisteria, Vase, Blue, Handles, Marked, 12 In. 219.00
Wisteria, Vase, Bottle Shape, 15 In. 1955.00
Wisteria, Vase, Brown, 2 Angular Handles, Squat, 4 In. 345.00
Wisteria, Vase, Brown, Foil Label, 6 In. 430.00
Wisteria, Vase, Brown, Gourd, 9 In. 605.00
Wisteria, Vase, Brown, Gourd, Foil Label, 7 x 6 In. 500.00
Wisteria, Vase, Brown, Jug, 2 Handles, 8 1/2 In. 635.00
Wisteria, Vase, Brown, Lavender Floral, Green Leaves, 2 Handles, 6 1/2 In. 575.00
Wisteria, Vase, Brown, Purple Glaze, Leaves, Ocher, Green, 7 In. 525.00
Wisteria, Vase, Trumpet, Brown, 2 Handles, Leaves, Ocher, Green Glaze, 10 In. 1045.00
Woodland, Vase, Mistletoe, 4 Sides, 9 In. 999.00
Zephyr Lily, Basket, Blue, Vase Shape, Irregular Shaped Rim, 10 In. 230.00
Zephyr Lily, Basket, Hanging, 7 In. 176.00
Zephyr Lily, Basket, Hanging, Blue, 5 In. 310.00
Zephyr Lily, Bookends, Brown, 5 1/2 In. 105.00
Zephyr Lily, Candlestick, Brown, 2 Handles, 2 In., Pair 35.00

Zephyr Lily, Cookie Jar, Marked, 10 In. 405.00
Zephyr Lily, Ewer, Brown, 6 In. 46.00

ROWLAND & MARSELLUS Company is part of a mark that appears on
historical Staffordshire dating from the late nineteenth and early twentieth centuries. Rowland & Marsellus is the mark used by an American
importing company in New York City. The company worked from
1893 to about 1937. Some of the pieces may have been made by the
British Anchor Pottery Co. of Longton, England, for export to a New
York firm. Many American views were made. Of special interest to
collectors are the plates with rolled edges, usually blue and white.

Plate, American, Poets, Blue Transfer, 10 In. 25.00
Plate, Chicago, State Street, Blue Transfer, Rolled Edge, 10 In. 65.00
Plate, Cleveland, Blue Transfer, Rolled Edge, 10 In. 95.00
Plate, Cornell College, Sage Walk, Blue Transfer, Rolled Edge, 10 In. 300.00
Plate, Myles Standish Monument, Blue Transfer, 10 In. 45.00
Plate, Theodore Roosevelt, Blue Transfer, Rolled Edge, 10 In. ....150.00 to 195.00
Tumbler, Views Of Plymouth, Blue Transfer, 4 In. 70.00

ROY ROGERS was born in 1911 in Cincinnati, Ohio. In the 1930s, he
made a living as a singer; in 1935, his group started work at a Los
Angeles radio station. He appeared in his first movie in 1937. From
1952 to 1957, he made 101 television shows. The other stars in the
show were his wife, Dale Evans, his horse, Trigger, and his dog,
Bullet. Roy Rogers memorabilia is collected, including items from the
Roy Rogers restaurants.

Book, Enchanted Canyon, 1954 .... 35.00
Book, My Favorite Western Stories, Box, D. Snow, Whitman, 1956, 252 Pages 225.00
Boot-Sters, Leather, Roy, Trigger, Boot-Ster Mfg., Box, c.1950, Pair 275.00
Cereal Container, Figural Cap, Quaker Oats Premium 275.00
Clay, Molds, Instructions, Std Toykraft Prod.Box, c.1950, 11 x 19 In. 220.00
Clock, Alarm, With Trigger, Brown Frame, Roy On Moving House, Ingraham 225.00
Cup, Figural, Quaker Oats Premium 350.00
Double Holster Rig, Cap Guns & Bullets 575.00
Game, Ring Toss & Horseshoe, Tin Lithograph Of Roy & Trigger, Ohio Art, 1950s 85.00
Hat, Cowboy, Red, Chinstrap, Hat Band, Silk Screened Inside 99.00
Holster & Gun Set, Jeweled, Gold & Black, Bakers Instant Chocolate Contest, 1957 .... 5100.00
Holster Set, Copper Handle, Schmidt Guns, 10 In. 1200.00
Holster Set, Double, Leather, 88 Studs, RR Brand, 16 Bullets 385.00
Holster Set, Leather, Bullets, Guns, Box, c.1955, 10 1/2 In. 855.00
Lamp, Figural, Roy Rogers & Dale Evans, Cincinnati Savings & Loan Co., 18 In. 305.00
Lunch Box, Dale Evans, Double R Chow Wagon, American Thermos, 1950s 600.00
Pennant, Thrill Circus, Roy On Bucking Bronco, 1940s, 28 In. 110.00
Poster, Rainbow Over Texas, Frame, 16 x 38 In. 55.00
Record Player, Portable, Detachable Speakers, Speartone 430.00
Scarf & Slide, Silk, Roy & Trigger, Double R Bar Ranch, Yellow, Cream & Red, Box 195.00
Stagecoach, 3 Wagons, Tin, Plastic, Marx, Box, 14 In. 239.00
Tie, Roy On Trigger, Child's 95.00
Toy, Hauler & Van Trailer, Battery Operated, Remote Control, Linemar, Box 2000.00
Toy, Telephone, Bunkhouse, Plastic, Crank-Type, Sears, 1950s 180.00
Turntable, 45 RPM, RCA Victor 325.00
Wristwatch, Dale Evans, Buttermilk, Pop-Up Box, Bradley, c.1950 ....275.00 to 495.00
Wristwatch, Roy & Trigger, Bradley, Box, c.1950 .... 275.00

ROYAL BAYREUTH is the name of a factory that was founded in Tettau,
Bavaria, in 1794. It has continued to modern times. The marks have
changed through the years. A stylized crest, the name *Royal Bayreuth*,
and the word *Bavaria* appear in slightly different forms from 1870 to
about 1919. Later dishes may include the words *U.S. Zone*, the year of
the issue, or the word *Germany* instead of *Bavaria*. Related pieces may
be found listed in the Rose Tapestry, Sand Babies, Snow Babies, and
Sunbonnet Babies categories.

Bowl, Bathers' Scene, Scalloped Rim, 2-Tone Green Sides, Blue Mark, 3 x 11 In. 146.00

Bowl, Girl With Dog, Marked, 3 x 4 In. 125.00
Bowl, Portrait, Woman Leaning Against Horse, 6 Lobes, Gilt Rim, 3 1/2 x 10 In. 281.00
Bowl, Radish, 2 1/2 x 5 In. 56.00
Box, Cover, Tomato, 4 In. 40.00
Box, Ring, Cover, Farmer & Chicken Scene, Round, 2 1/2 In. 70.00
Candleholder, Corinthian, Black, Male & Female Figures, 5 3/4 In. 23.00
Chocolate Pot, Cover, Boy, 3 Donkeys, 8 1/2 In. 230.00
Chocolate Pot, Farmer, 2 Draft Horses, 8 1/2 In. 275.00
Cracker Jar, Tomato, 6 1/2 In. 175.00
Creamer, Apple, 4 In. 80.00
Creamer, Corinthian, Grecian Figure, Orange, 5 In. 60.00
Creamer, Cow Scene Border, 5 In. 140.00
Creamer, Crow, 4 3/4 In. 200.00
Creamer, Milk Maiden, Blue Dress, 4 In. 375.00
Creamer, Red Clown, 3 1/2 In. 150.00
Creamer, Spiky Shell, Pastel Ground, Iron Red Accents, 4 In. 75.00
Creamer, Tomato, 3 3/4 In. 50.00
Cup & Saucer, Arabs With Camels, Green Matte Handle & Rim, 3-In. Cup 50.00
Dish, Light Green, Swans, 2 Handles, 5 1/2 In. 90.00
Flowerpot, Roses, Pink, Yellow, Handles, 2 3/4 In. 115.00
Hatpin Holder, Stork, Yellow, Square Base, Blue Mark, 4 1/2 In. 40.00
Nappy, Rose Leaves, Pink Blossoms, Stem Handle, 7 In. 28.00
Pitcher, Classical Design, Black Ground, Wedgwood Style, 3 1/2 In. 40.00
Pitcher, Corinthian, Green, Orange Interior, Pinched Spout, 4 1/2 In. 35.00
Pitcher, Pelican, 6 1/2 In. 375.00
Pitcher, Santa, With Pack Handle, 7 1/4 In. 4380.00
Pitcher, Sunset Band, Fighting Roosters, Wide Round, Tapered Base, 5 In. 75.00
Plate, Anheuser Busch, 6 Wreaths, 8 In. 700.00
Plate, Boy With Turkeys, Marked, 7 1/2 In. 100.00
Plate, Luncheon, Floral, Square, 9 In. 160.00
Toothpick, 2 1/2 In. 425.00
Vase, Farmer & Chicken Scene, 2 Handles, 3 1/2 In. 60.00

ROYAL BONN is the nineteenth- and twentieth-century trade name for
the Bonn China Manufactory. It was established in 1755 in Bonn,
Germany. A general line of porcelain was made. Many marks were
used, most including the name *Bonn*, the initials *FM*, and a crown.

Clock, Ansonia, La Bretagne, 8-Day, Time & Strike, Green, Flowers, c.1915, 15 In. 1005.00
Clock, Ansonia, La Flandre, 8-Day, Blue, Pink, Yellow, c.1914, 14 3/4 In. 2669.00
Clock, Ansonia, La Manche, Green, Yellow, Porcelain, c.1904, 13 3/4 In. 1570.00
Clock, Ansonia, La Nord, 8-Day, Blue, Porcelain, c.1900, 11 3/4 In. 1020.00
Clock, Ansonia, La Tosca, Pink Top, Yellow Bottom, c.1904, 14 1/2 In. 2065.00
Clock, Ansonia, La Vergne, Blue, Yellow, Green, c.1904, 11 3/4 In. 1485.00
Clock, Ansonia, La Vogue, Porcelain, Cream Case, 8-Day, c.1901, 12 3/4 In. 1265.00
Clock, Mantel, White, Light Green, Pink Flowers, No. 413, 10 x 8 1/2 In. 300.00
Ewer, Gold Highlights, Painted Flower Band, F. H. Mehlem Factory, 7 In. 98.00
Pitcher, Ivory Matte, Flowers & Leaves, Gilt Trim, Rim, Rustic Handle & Spout, 8 In. 60.00
Vase, Art Nouveau Style, Slip Trimmed, Stylized Flowers & Leaves, 12 In. 118.00
Vase, Irises, Cerulean Blue, Black, Orange, Green On Ivory Ground, Mark, 7 1/4 In. 413.00
Vase, Old Dutch, Flowers, Blue, Green, Marked, 4 3/4 In. 196.00
Vase, Old Dutch, Stylized Violets, Glossy Finish, Marked, 5 1/8 In. 138.00
Vase, Painted, Flower, Classical Courtyard Setting, Tapestry, 12 1/4 In. 109.00
Vase, Pillow Shape, Portrait Of Woman, Green, Brown, Pink, 8 1/2 x 8 1/2 In. 150.00
Vase, Pink Roses, Flowers, Blue Lattice Ground, Bulbous, Signed, W. Enstirchen, 9 In. .. 375.00
Vase, Tokio Pattern, G.F. Schultz, No. 2834, 8 In. 350.00

ROYAL COPENHAGEN porcelain and pottery have been made in Denmark since 1775. The Christmas plate series started in 1908. The figurines with pale blue and gray glazes have remained popular in this
century and are still being made. Many other old and new style porcelains are made today.

Butter Chip, Den Gamle, Aarhus, No. 23-2010, 3 1/4 In. 12.00
Butter Chip, Frederisksborg Slot, No. 42-2010, 3 1/4 In. 12.00

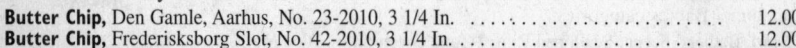

Butter Chip, Hans Christian Andersen, 3 1/4 In. 17.00
Butter Chip, Kobenhavns Radhus, 3 1/4 In. 17.00
Butter Chip, Lillebaelts, 3 1/4 In. 17.00
Butter Chip, Marmorkirken, 3 1/4 In. 17.00
Butter Chip, Mindesmaerket Nyhavn, 3 1/4 In. 17.00
Butter Chip, Pigen Med Guldhorn, 3 1/4 In. 17.00
Butter Chip, Svendborg Havn, No. 39-2010, 3 1/4 In. 12.00
Figurine, Dachshund, Blue Wave Mark, No. 856, 7 1/2 x 11 In. 374.00
Figurine, Farm Laborer, 8 3/4 In. 161.00
Figurine, Ganymede & Eagle, White Biscuit, 7 1/2 x 10 3/4 In. 865.00
Figurine, Ganymede & Eagle, White Biscuit, Marked, 19th Century, 8 x 10 1/4 In. 1495.00
Figurine, Pan Seated On Pedestal With Lizard, 8 3/4 In. 138.00
Group, Middle Eastern Man, Nude Female, 9 In. 645.00
Group, Nude Couple Kissing On Rocks, Waves, 1897, 18 1/2 In. 990.00
Mug, 1967, 2 3/4 In. 375.00
Mug, 1967, 4 3/4 In. 400.00
Mug, 1968, 2 3/4 In. 60.00
Mug, 1968, 4 3/4 In. 42.00
Mug, 1981, 2 3/4 In. 60.00
Plaquette, Christmas, 1984 . . . . 18.00
Plate, Christmas, 1908, Madonna & Child 6000.00
Plate, Christmas, 1909, Danish Landscape, St. Ussing 175.00
Plate, Christmas, 1910, Magi 285.00
Plate, Christmas, 1911, Danish Landscape, Oluf Jensen 175.00
Plate, Christmas, 1912, Elderly Couple By Christmas Tree 175.00
Plate, Christmas, 1913, Spire Of Frederick's Church 125.00
Plate, Christmas, 1914, Sparrows In A Tree 110.00
Plate, Christmas, 1915, Danish Landscape, A. Krog 243.00
Plate, Christmas, 1916, Shepherds In Field On Christmas 110.00
Plate, Christmas, 1917, Tower Of Our Savior's Church 110.00
Plate, Christmas, 1918, Shepherds, Oluf Jensen 110.00
Plate, Christmas, 1920, Mary With Child 95.00
Plate, Christmas, 1921, Market Place In Aabenraa 95.00
Plate, Christmas, 1922, 3 Singing Angels 95.00
Plate, Christmas, 1923, Danish Landscape, Oluf Jensen 95.00
Plate, Christmas, 1924, Christmas Star Over The Sea .95.00 to 180.00
Plate, Christmas, 1925, Street Scene 95.00
Plate, Christmas, 1926, View Of Christianshaun 85.00
Plate, Christmas, 1927, Ship's Boy At Tiller . . . . .95.00 to 175.00
Plate, Christmas, 1928, Vicar Family On Way To Church 95.00
Plate, Christmas, 1929, Grundtvig Church, Copenhagen 95.00
Plate, Christmas, 1930, Fishing Boats 95.00
Plate, Christmas, 1931, Mother & Child . . . . .95.00 to 186.00
Plate, Christmas, 1932, Ferry & Great Belt 95.00
Plate, Christmas, 1935, Fishing Boat Off Kronborg Castle 150.00
Plate, Christmas, 1938, Round Church In Osterlars 150.00
Plate, Christmas, 1945, Peaceful Motif 400.00
Plate, Christmas, 1946, Zealand Village Church 250.00
Plate, Christmas, 1947, Good Shepherd 250.00
Plate, Christmas, 1949, Church Of Our Lady 150.00
Plate, Christmas, 1950, Boeslunde Church, Zealand 150.00
Plate, Christmas, 1951, Christmas Angel 325.00
Plate, Christmas, 1952, Christmas In The Forest . . . . .125.00 to 170.00
Plate, Christmas, 1953, Frederiksborg Castle 125.00
Plate, Christmas, 1954, Amalienborg Palace 110.00
Plate, Christmas, 1955, Fano Girl . . . . .150.00 to 225.00
Plate, Christmas, 1956, Rosenborg Castle, Copenhagen . . . . .110.00 to 180.00
Plate, Christmas, 1957, Good Shepherd 95.00
Plate, Christmas, 1958, Sunshine Over Greenland . . . . .95.00 to 170.00
Plate, Christmas, 1959, Christmas Night 95.00
Plate, Christmas, 1960, Stag 95.00
Plate, Christmas, 1961, Training Ship Danmark 75.00
Plate, Christmas, 1962, Little Mermaid At Wintertime .150.00 to 240.00

Plate, Christmas, 1965, Little Skaters 75.00
Plate, Christmas, 1979, Choosing The Christmas Tree 96.00
Plate, Christmas, 1985, Snowman 129.00
Plate, Christmas, 1988, Christmas Eve In Copenhagen 120.00
Plate, Dinner, Flora Danica, Botanical, Painted, 10 3/4 In...................... 705.00
Plate, Flora Danica, Quatrefoil Shape, Gilt Rim, 1900s, 9 1/2 In. 619.00
Platter, Floral Danica, Round, 11 1/4 In. 660.00
Tureen, Cover, Flora Danica, Black, Green & Blue, 12 In. 3910.00
Vase, 4 Sides, Black Calligraphic Painted Design, 12 1/2 x 8 x 8 In. 206.00
Vase, Blue, Fluted, Applied Figural Snails, Lace Edging On Top Rim, c.1894, 11 In. 1450.00
Vase, Fluted, Ringed With Flared Rim, White With Gilt, 10 1/2 x 7 In. 50.00
Vase, Nils Thorrson, Tapered, Purple, Light Blue Crackle, 6 1/2 x 5 1/2 In. 175.00
Vase, Stylized Gray-Blue Flowers, Matte Ivory Round, 10 x 4 3/4 In. 120.00
Vase, Trumpet, Roses, Leaves, Fluted, White, Gold, 10 3/4 x 7 1/4 In. 405.00
Vase, White Cattleya Orchid, Gray Ground, 12 1/2 x 6 1/4 In. 705.00
Vase, Windmill, Landscape, Signed, 13 In. 345.00

ROYAL COPLEY china was made by the Spaulding China Company of
Sebring, Ohio, from 1939 to 1960. The figural planters and the small
figurines, especially those with Art Deco designs, are of great collector interest.

Ashtray, Mallard Duck, Paper Label, 2 1/2 x 4 1/4 In. 20.00
Figurine, Cat, Brown, Leans To Left, 8 In. 55.00
Figurine, Kitten, Yellow Yarn Ball, Head Tilted Left, 6 1/2 In. 40.00
Figurine, Mallard Drake, Erect Head, 6 In..................................... 20.00
Figurine, Mallard Drake, Head Bent, 5 1/2 In. 20.00
Figurine, Parrot, 8 x 6 In. ....45.00 to 55.00
Figurine, Rooster, Hen, Green, Brown, Pink, Yellow, Black, 8 1/8 & 7 1/4 In., Pair 95.00
Figurine, Swallow, Yellow Body, Black Highlights, Green Base, 6 In. 25.00
Figurine, Thrush, Blue Head, Green Back, Brown Wings, Pink Chest, 6 1/4 In. 30.00
Figurine, Vase, Warbler, 5 In. 30.00
Figurine, Vireo, Pink, Blue Tail, 4 3/8 In. 10.00
Figurine, Wren, Pink Head, Brown Back, Blue Tail, Wings, 6 In. 30.00
Pin Dish, Leaf, Flower 11.00
Planter, Bamboo, 1940s, 7 1/2 x 3 1/4 In. 15.00
Planter, Big Apple, Finch, 6 1/4 In. 25.00
Planter, Bird, 4 In. 17.00
Planter, Boy, Bucket, 6 1/4 In. 25.00
Planter, Deer & Fawn Head, 9 1/4 In. ....40.00 to 50.00
Planter, Dog, At Mailbox, 8 In. 25.00
Planter, Dog, Cocker Spaniel, 7 3/4 In. 40.00
Planter, Duck Starting Flight, Maroon Body, Green Base, 5 1/4 x 5 In. 20.00
Planter, Duck, c.1950, 8 In. 38.00
Planter, Duckling, 5 5/8 x 7 1/2 In. 28.00
Planter, Horse, Yellow Mane, 8 In. 40.00
Planter, Kitten, c.1950, 8 1/4 In. 42.00
Planter, Kitten, Yellow, Green Eyes, Yellow Ball, 5 In. 20.00
Planter, Peter Rabbit, 6 1/4 x 6 1/4 In. 25.00
Planter, Puppy & Mailbox, 8 1/2 x 4 3/4 x 8 In. 35.00
Vase, Art Deco, Leaf Design, Pink On Beige, Purple Handles, 1940s, 5 x 5 1/2 In. ... 40.00
Vase, Bird, Black, Yellow, Gold Trim, 5 In. 6.00
Vase, Bud, Parrot, Yellow, Blue Face, Wing Tips, Tail, 5 In. 25.00
Vase, Bud, Warbler, 5 In. 30.00
Vase, Relief Flowers, Blue, 7 3/4 x 5 In. 35.00
Wall Pocket, Big Apple, 5 3/4 x 5 3/4 In. ....25.00 to 30.00
Wall Pocket, Granny, 7 1/2 x 7 In. 84.00

ROYAL CROWN DERBY Company, Ltd., was established in England in
1890. There is a complex family tree that includes the Derby, Crown
Derby, and Royal Crown Derby porcelains. The Royal Crown Derby
mark includes the name and a crown. The words *Made in England*
were used after 1921. The company is now a part of Royal Doulton
Tableware Ltd.

Bottle, Stopper, Molded, Handles, Hand Painted Flowers, Gold Accents, 6 In. 145.00

Compote, Imari, Ruffled Rim, Pedestal Base, 1900, 2 3/4 x 8 3/4 In., 3 Piece 430.00
Cup & Saucer, Bouillon, Gold Trim, Pattern D 8855, c.1912 . . . .   65.00
Ewer, Flowers, Bulbous, Gilt, Peach Ground, c.1890, 6 In. 175.00
Ewer, Handled, Oriental Style, Gold Enameling, Coral Ground, 6 In. 200.00
Ewer, Raised Gilt Persian Style Design, Red Ground, Pierced Handle, 13 In. 380.00
Jug, Figural, Owl, White, Gilt Trim, Oak Leaves Around Rim & Base, 10 1/2 In. 190.00
Plate, Luncheon, Pattern 8450, c.1912, 9 In., 12 Piece 490.00
Plate, Mikado, Cobalt, White Ruffle, 8 7/8 In. 40.00
Vase, Elizabeth II, Imari, Cover, 2 Handles, 18 1/2 In. 3450.00
Vase, Flowers, Gold Encrusted Lip, 7 1/2 In. 315.00

ROYAL DOULTON is the name used on Doulton and Company pottery made from 1902 to the present. Doulton and Company of England was founded in 1853. Pieces made before 1902 are listed in this book under Doulton. Royal Doulton collectors search for the out-of-production figurines, character jugs, vases, and series wares. Some vases and animal figurines were made with a special red glaze called flambe. Sung and Chang glazed pieces are rare. The multicolored glaze is very thick and looks as if it were dropped on the clay.

Animal, Cat, Lucky Black, Cat, K 12 . . . .   150.00
Animal, Dog, Airedale Terrier, HN 1024 . . . .   350.00
Animal, Dog, Alsatian, HN 1116 . . . .   250.00
Animal, Dog, Alsatian, Seated, K 13 . . . .   125.00
Animal, Dog, Boxer Champion, Warlord Of Mazelaine, HN 2643 . . . .   225.00
Animal, Dog, Bulldog, Brindle, HN 1043 . . . .   700.00
Animal, Dog, Bulldog, Brown, White, HN 1047 . . . .   250.00
Animal, Dog, Bulldog, Draped In Union Jack, D 5913 . . . .   1000.00
Animal, Dog, Bulldog, Standing, White, Brown Collar, HN 1074 . . . .   250.00
Animal, Dog, Bulldog, Union Jack, Small, D 5913C 350.00
Animal, Dog, Bulldog, White With Fawn Around Eyes, DA 222 . . . .   75.00
Animal, Dog, Chow, Shibuino, K 15, 1940-1977 . . . .   175.00
Animal, Dog, Cocker Spaniel With Pheasant, HN 1001 . . . .   750.00
Animal, Dog, Cocker Spaniel With Pheasant, HN 1029 . . . .   275.00
Animal, Dog, Cocker Spaniel, Golden Brown, HN 1186 . . . .   625.00
Animal, Dog, Cocker Spaniel, HN 1002 . . . .   450.00
Animal, Dog, Dalmatian, Ch. Goworth Victor, HN 1114 . . . .   500.00
Animal, Dog, Fox Terrier, Seated, K 8 . . . .   135.00
Animal, Dog, Foxhound, Seated, K 7 . . . .   150.00
Animal, Dog, Irish Setter, HN 1056 . . . .   300.00
Animal, Dog, Pekingese, K 6 . . . .   100.00
Animal, Dog, Rough-Haired Terrier, HN 1014 . . . .   220.00
Animal, Dog, Scottish Terrier, Seated, K 18 . . . .   175.00
Animal, Dog, Sealyham Terrier, HN 1032 . . . .   450.00
Animal, Dog, Sealyham, Begging, K 3 . . . .   125.00
Animal, Dog, Springer Spaniel, HN 2517 . . . .   250.00
Animal, Dog, St. Bernard, K 19 . . . .   125.00
Animal, Dog, Terrier Puppies In Basket, HN 2588 . . . .   150.00
Animal, Dog, Terrier Sitting In Basket, White, Brown, HN 2587 . . . .   125.00
Ashtray, Parson Brown, No. 5600, 1936-1960 . . . .   175.00
Butter Chip, Hampton Court 75.00

Royal Doulton character jugs depict the head and shoulders of the subject. They are made in four sizes: large, 5 1/4 to 7 inches; small, 3 1/4 to 4 inches; miniature, 2 1/4 to 2 1/2 inches; and tiny, 1 1/4 inches. Toby jugs portray a seated, full figure.

Character Jug, 'Arriet, D 6256, Tiny 200.00
Character Jug, 'Arriet, Green Hat, D 6208, Large 195.00
Character Jug, 'Arriet, Green Hat, D 6236, Small 100.00
Character Jug, 'Arriet, Green Hat, D 6250, Miniature 85.00
Character Jug, 'Arry, D 6207, Large 225.00
Character Jug, 'Arry, D 6235, Small 100.00
Character Jug, 'Arry, D 6249, Miniature 85.00
Character Jug, Amy, D 6255, Tiny 200.00

Character Jug, Anne Boleyn, D 6644, Large 150.00
Character Jug, Annie Oakley, Wild West Series, D 6732, Large 125.00
Character Jug, Apothecary, D 6567, Large 150.00
Character Jug, Apothecary, D 6574, Small 85.00
Character Jug, Apothecary, D 6581, Miniature 85.00
Character Jug, Aramis, D 6508, Miniature 65.00
Character Jug, Aramis, Three Musketeers, D 6454, Small 75.00
Character Jug, Artful Dodger, Dickens, D 6678, Tiny 45.00
Character Jug, Athos, Three Musketeers, D 6439, Large 85.00
Character Jug, Athos, Three Musketeers, D 6452, Small 60.00
Character Jug, Athos, Three Musketeers, D 6509, Miniature 45.00
Character Jug, Auctioneer, D 6838, Large 225.00
Character Jug, Auld Mac, D 6253, Miniature 50.00
Character Jug, Auld Mac, D 6257, Tiny 175.00
Character Jug, Bacchus, D 6499, Large 100.00
Character Jug, Bacchus, D 6505, Small 55.00
Character Jug, Bacchus, D 6521, Miniature 60.00
Character Jug, Baseball Player, D 6878, Small 100.00
Character Jug, Beefeater, Collectors Club, D 6806, Tiny 150.00
Character Jug, Benjamin Franklin, D 6695, Small 125.00
Character Jug, Betsy Trotwood, D 6685, Tiny 45.00
Character Jug, Bill Sykes, D 6684, Tiny 45.00
Character Jug, Blacksmith, Williamsburg Collection, D 6585, Miniature 65.00
Character Jug, Bootmaker, D 6586, Miniature 70.00
Character Jug, Bootmaker, Williamsburg Collection, D 6579, Small 70.00
Character Jug, Bowls Player, D 6896, Small 100.00
Character Jug, Buzfuz, Bust, D 6048 .... 100.00
Character Jug, Buzfuz, D 5838, Small 115.00
Character Jug, Cap'n Cuttle, D 5842, Small 100.00
Character Jug, Capt Ahab, D 6500, Large 125.00
Character Jug, Capt Ahab, D 6506, Small ....65.00 to 85.00
Character Jug, Capt Ahab, D 6522, Miniature 75.00
Character Jug, Capt Henry Morgan, D 6409, Small 50.00
Character Jug, Capt Henry Morgan, D 6467, Large 125.00
Character Jug, Capt Henry Morgan, D 6510, Miniature 65.00
Character Jug, Capt Hook, D 6597, Large ....235.00 to 650.00
Character Jug, Capt Hook, D 6605, Miniature 525.00
Character Jug, Cardinal, D 5614, Large 150.00
Character Jug, Cardinal, D 6033, Small 75.00
Character Jug, Cardinal, D 6129, Miniature 65.00
Character Jug, Cardinal, D 6258, Tiny 250.00
Character Jug, Catherine Howard, D 6645, Large 225.00
Character Jug, Catherine Howard, D 6693, Miniature 225.00
Character Jug, Catherine Of Aragon, D 6643, Large 150.00
Character Jug, Catherine Of Aragon, D 6657, Small 165.00
Character Jug, Catherine Of Aragon, D 6658, Miniature 150.00
Character Jug, Cavalier, D 6114, Large 135.00
Character Jug, Cavalier, D 6173, Small 65.00
Character Jug, Charles Dickens, D 6901, Small 160.00
Character Jug, Chelsea Pensioner, D 6833, Large 225.00
Character Jug, Chief Sitting Bull & George Armstrong Custer, D 6712, Large 225.00
Character Jug, Clown, D 6322, Large 1500.00
Character Jug, D'Artagnan, D 6691, Large .... *Illus* 150.00
Character Jug, David Copperfield, D 6680, Tiny 75.00
Character Jug, Davy Crockett & Santa Ana, D 6729, Large 150.00
Character Jug, Dick Turpin, D 535, Small 80.00
Character Jug, Dick Turpin, D 5485, Large 175.00
Character Jug, Dick Turpin, D 5618, Small 70.00
Character Jug, Dick Turpin, D 6128, Miniature 50.00
Character Jug, Dick Turpin, D 6542, Miniature 75.00
Character Jug, Dick Whittington, D 6375, Large 550.00
Character Jug, Dick Whittington, Lord Mayor Of London, D 6846, Large 200.00
Character Jug, Don Quixote, D 6455, Large 125.00

If a capital letter A is printed next
to the usual Royal Doulton mark, it
means the piece was made between
about 1939 and 1955.

Royal Doulton,
Character Jug,
D'Artagnan,
D 6691, Large

Character Jug, Don Quixote, D 6460, Small	70.00
Character Jug, Don Quixote, D 6511, Miniature	65.00
Character Jug, Fagin, D 6679, Tiny	75.00
Character Jug, Falconer, D 6533, Large	100.00
Character Jug, Falconer, D 6540, Small	70.00
Character Jug, Falconer, D 6547, Miniature	60.00
Character Jug, Falstaff, D 6385, Small	55.00
Character Jug, Falstaff, D 6519, Miniature	65.00
Character Jug, Falstaff, Smoked Rim, D 6287, Large	150.00
Character Jug, Farmer John, D 5788, Large	150.00
Character Jug, Farmer John, D 5789, Small	75.00
Character Jug, Fat Boy, D 6139, Miniature	85.00
Character Jug, Fat Boy, D 6142, Tiny	85.00
Character Jug, Fortune Teller, D 6497, Large	650.00
Character Jug, Friar Tuck, D 6321, Large	550.00
Character Jug, Gaoler, D 6570, Large	150.00
Character Jug, Gaoler, Williamsburg Series, D 6584, Miniature	85.00
Character Jug, Gardener, D 6630, Large	175.00
Character Jug, Gardener, D 6638, Miniature	110.00
Character Jug, Gardener, Red Flowering Potted Plant Handle, D 6868, Small	100.00
Character Jug, Gardener, Spade & Vegetables Handle, D 6634, Small	95.00
Character Jug, Geoffrey Chaucer, D 7029, Large	800.00
Character Jug, George Harrison, D 6727, Mid	275.00
Character Jug, George Washington, D 6669B, Large	200.00
Character Jug, George Washington, George III, D 6749, Large	175.00
Character Jug, Geronimo, Wild West Series, D 6733, Mid	200.00
Character Jug, Gladiator, D 6553, Small	450.00
Character Jug, Golfer, D 6623, Large	100.00
Character Jug, Golfer, D 6757, Miniature	80.00
Character Jug, Golfer, Modern, D 6865, Small	100.00
Character Jug, Gone Away, D 6538, Small	75.00
Character Jug, Gone Away, D 6545, Miniature	75.00
Character Jug, Gone Away, Fox Handle, D 6531, Large	125.00
Character Jug, Graduate, D 6916, Small	100.00
Character Jug, Granny Toothless, D 5521, Large	950.00
Character Jug, Granny, One Tooth Showing, D 6520, Miniature	85.00
Character Jug, Grant & Lee, D 6698, Large	400.00
Character Jug, Groucho Marx, D 6710, Large	175.00
Character Jug, Guardsman, D 6771, Small	80.00
Character Jug, Guardsman, D 6772, Miniature	100.00
Character Jug, Guardsman, Williamsburg, D 6568, Large	150.00
Character Jug, Guardsman, Williamsburg, D 6582, Miniature	100.00
Character Jug, Gulliver, D 6560, Large	900.00
Character Jug, Gulliver, D 6566, Miniature	475.00
Character Jug, Gunsmith, Williamsburg, D 6573, Large	125.00
Character Jug, Gunsmith, Williamsburg, D 6587, Miniature	80.00
Character Jug, Guy Fawkes, Lantern & Barrel Handle, D 6861, Large	150.00
Character Jug, Hamlet, Shakespeare Series, D 6672, Large	150.00
Character Jug, Henry VIII, D 6642, Large	150.00
Character Jug, Henry VIII, D 6647, Small	80.00

Character Jug, Henry VIII, D 6648, Miniature 110.00
Character Jug, Jane Seymour, Mandolin Handle, D 6646, Large 175.00
Character Jug, Jarge, D 6295, Small 250.00
Character Jug, Jimmy Durante, D 6708, Large 200.00
Character Jug, Jockey, D 6625, Large 425.00
Character Jug, John Doulton, Two O'Clock, D 6656-2, Small 75.00
Character Jug, John Lennon, D 6725, Mid 300.00
Character Jug, John Peel, Gray Handle, D 5612, Large 175.00
Character Jug, John Peel, Gray Handle, D 5731, Small 70.00
Character Jug, John Peel, Gray Handle, D 6130, Miniature .... .65.00 to 75.00
Character Jug, Johnny Appleseed, D 6372, Large .... 135.00 to 425.00
Character Jug, Juggler, Circus Collection, D 6835, Large 200.00
Character Jug, King Charles I, D 6917, Large 400.00
Character Jug, Lawyer, D 6498, Large 100.00
Character Jug, Lawyer, D 6504, Small 65.00
Character Jug, Lawyer, D 6524, Miniature 70.00
Character Jug, Lobster Man, D 6620, Small 70.00
Character Jug, Lobster Man, White Fisherman's Jersey, D 6617, Large 85.00
Character Jug, Lobsterman, D 6652, Miniature 50.00
Character Jug, Long John Silver, D 6335, Large 150.00
Character Jug, Long John Silver, D 6386, Small 75.00
Character Jug, Long John Silver, D 6512, Miniature 55.00
Character Jug, Louis Armstrong, Celebrity Collection, D 6707, Large 300.00
Character Jug, Mad Hatter, D 6606, Miniature 125.00
Character Jug, Mark Twain, D 6654, Large 150.00
Character Jug, Merlin, D 6536, Small 75.00
Character Jug, Merlin, D 6543, Miniature 60.00
Character Jug, Michael Doulton, D 6808, Small 50.00
Character Jug, Mikado, D 6501, Large 800.00
Character Jug, Mikado, D 6507, Small 400.00
Character Jug, Mine Host, D 6468, Large 150.00
Character Jug, Mine Host, D 6470, Small 80.00
Character Jug, Mine Host, D 6513, Miniature 90.00
Character Jug, Mr. Bumble, Dickens, D 6686, Tiny 50.00
Character Jug, Mr. Micawber, D 5843, Small 100.00
Character Jug, Mr. Micawber, D 6138, Miniature 55.00
Character Jug, Mr. Micawber, D 6143, Tiny 80.00
Character Jug, Mr. Pickwick, D 5839, Small 190.00
Character Jug, Mr. Pickwick, D 6254, Miniature 80.00
Character Jug, Mr. Pickwick, D 6260, Tiny 225.00
Character Jug, Mr. Quaker, D 6738, Large 1000.00
Character Jug, Napoleon & Josephine, D 6750, Large 150.00
Character Jug, Neptune, D 6552, Small 75.00
Character Jug, Neptune, D 6555, Miniature 60.00
Character Jug, Neptune, Trident Handle, D 6548, Large 110.00
Character Jug, Night Watchman, D 6569, Large 150.00
Character Jug, Night Watchman, D 6583, Miniature 85.00
Character Jug, North American Indian, D 6611C, Large 250.00
Character Jug, Old Charley, Brown Hat, Green Coat, D 5420, Large 100.00
Character Jug, Old Charley, D 6046, Miniature 55.00
Character Jug, Old Charley, D 6144, Tiny 90.00
Character Jug, Old King Cole, D 6871, Tiny 150.00
Character Jug, Old Salt, D 6554, Small 85.00
Character Jug, Oliver Twist, Dickens, D 6677, Tiny 50.00
Character Jug, Othello, D 6673, Large 150.00
Character Jug, Paddy, D 5753, Large 100.00
Character Jug, Paddy, D 5768, Small 65.00
Character Jug, Paddy, D 6042, Miniature 55.00
Character Jug, Paddy, D 6145, Tiny 85.00
Character Jug, Parson Brown, D 5486, Large 175.00
Character Jug, Pearly King, D 6760, Large 175.00
Character Jug, Pearly Queen, D 6759, Large 175.00
Character Jug, Pied Piper, 3 Rats Handle, D 6403, Large 125.00

Character Jug, Pied Piper, D 6462, Small 85.00
Character Jug, Pied Piper, D 6514, Miniature 80.00
Character Jug, Poacher, Fish Handle, D 6515, Miniature 50.00
Character Jug, Punch & Judy Man, D 6590, Large 775.00
Character Jug, Punch & Judy Man, D 6596, Miniature 475.00
Character Jug, Queen Victoria, Dark Blue & Yellow Crown, D 6816, Large 200.00
Character Jug, Queen Victoria, Dark Blue & Yellow Crown, D 6913, Small 150.00
Character Jug, Red Queen, D 6777, Large 175.00
Character Jug, Ringo Starr, D 6726, Mid 275.00
Character Jug, Rip Van Winkle, D 6463, Small 65.00
Character Jug, Rip Van Winkle, D 6517, Miniature 50.00
Character Jug, Rip Van Winkle, Gray Blue Cap, D 6438, Large 100.00
Character Jug, Robin Hood, Hat With Feather, D 6527, Large 100.00
Character Jug, Robin Hood, Hat With Feather, D 6541, Miniature 60.00
Character Jug, Robin Hood, Hat With No Feathers, D 6205, Large 175.00
Character Jug, Robin Hood, Hat With No Feathers, D 6234, Small 80.00
Character Jug, Robin Hood, Hat With No Feathers, D 6252, Miniature 75.00
Character Jug, Robinson Crusoe, D 6532, Large 150.00
Character Jug, Robinson Crusoe, D 6539, Small 85.00
Character Jug, Robinson Crusoe, D 6546, Miniature 60.00
Character Jug, Romeo, D 6670, Large 100.00
Character Jug, Sairey Gamp, D 5451, Large 90.00
Character Jug, Sairey Gamp, D 6045, Miniature 50.00
Character Jug, Sairey Gamp, D 6146, Tiny 80.00
Character Jug, Sam Johnson, D 6289, Large 350.00
Character Jug, Sam Weller, D 6064, Large 125.00
Character Jug, Sam Weller, D 6140, Miniature 70.00
Character Jug, Sam Weller, D 6147, Tiny 90.00
Character Jug, Samson & Delilah, D 6787, Large 150.00
Character Jug, Santa Claus, Doll Handle, D 6668, Large 250.00
Character Jug, Santa Claus, Plain Handle, D 6705, Small 100.00
Character Jug, Santa Claus, Plain Handle, D 6950, Tiny 85.00
Character Jug, Santa Claus, Reindeer Handle, D 6675, Large 350.00
Character Jug, Santa Claus, Sack Of Toys Handle, D 6690, Large 375.00
Character Jug, Scaramouche, Guitar Handle, D 6564, Miniature 500.00
Character Jug, Simon The Cellarer, D 5504, Large 150.00
Character Jug, Sir Francis Drake, D 6174, Small 80.00
Character Jug, Sir Henry Doulton, D 6703, Small 150.00
Character Jug, Sleuth, D 6631, Large 110.00
Character Jug, Sleuth, D 6635, Small 65.00
Character Jug, Sleuth, D 6639, Miniature 75.00
Character Jug, Smuggler, D 6616, Large 200.00
Character Jug, Smuggler, D 6619, Small 90.00
Character Jug, Snooker Player, D 6879, Small 100.00
Character Jug, Soldier, Desert Rat Patch, D 6876, Small 100.00
Character Jug, St. George, D 6618, Large 350.00
Character Jug, St. George, D 6621, Small 275.00
Character Jug, Tam O'Shanter, D 6632, Large 150.00
Character Jug, Tam O'Shanter, D 6636, Small 100.00
Character Jug, Tony Weller, D 5531, Large 200.00
Character Jug, Tony Weller, D 6044, Miniature 60.00
Character Jug, Touchstone, D 5613, Large 325.00
Character Jug, Town Crier, D 6530, Large 250.00
Character Jug, Town Crier, D 6544, 1960-1973, Miniature 200.00
Character Jug, Town Crier, D 6895, Large 200.00
Character Jug, Trapper, D 6612, Small 70.00
Character Jug, Ugly Duchess, D 6599, Large 700.00
Character Jug, Ugly Duchess, D 6603, Small 475.00
Character Jug, Ugly Duchess, Flamingo Handle, D 6607, Miniature 450.00
Character Jug, Uncle Tom Cobbleigh, D 6337 .... 500.00
Character Jug, Uriah Heep, D 6682, Tiny 45.00
Character Jug, Veteran Motorist, D 6633, Large 175.00
Character Jug, Veteran Motorist, D 6637, Small 125.00

Character Jug, Veteran Motorist, D 6641, Miniature 125.00
Character Jug, Vicar Of Bray, D 5615, Large 275.00
Character Jug, Vice-Admiral Lord Nelson, D 6932, Large 300.00
Character Jug, Viking, D 6496, Large 275.00
Character Jug, Viking, D 6502, Small 175.00
Character Jug, Viking, D 6526, Miniature 200.00
Character Jug, Walrus & Carpenter, D 6604, Small 150.00
Character Jug, Walrus & Carpenter, D 6608, Miniature 150.00
Character Jug, Witch, D 6893, Large 300.00
Character Jug, Yachtsman, D 6626, Large 200.00
Coffee Set, Slip Decorated Pied Piper, Tapered Cylindrical Pot, 1905, 14 Piece 295.00
Dish Set, Breakfast, Bunnykins, Postman, Artist, Ice Cream Man, Child's, 3 Piece 60.00
Figurine, Across The Miles, HN 3934, 1997-1999 .... 100.00
Figurine, Amy, Blue, Rose, HN 3316, 1991 .... 575.00
Figurine, Annabella, Green, Blue, HN 1872, 1938-1949 .... 1400.00
Figurine, As Good As New, Childhood Days, HN 2971, 1982-1985 .... 200.00
Figurine, Ascot, Reclining Woman, Green, HN 2356, 1968-1995 .... 250.00
Figurine, Autumn Breezes, Black, White, HN 2147, 1955-1971 .... 475.00
Figurine, Autumn Breezes, Blue, Yellow, HN 3736, 1997-1998 .... 400.00
Figurine, Autumn Breezes, Green, Pink, HN 1911, 1939-1976 .... 300.00
Figurine, Autumntime, Turquoise, Brown, HN 3621, 1994-1996 .... 350.00
Figurine, Babie, Green, HN 1679, 1935-1992 .... 110.00
Figurine, Bachelor, Man Sewing Socks, HN 2319, 1964-1975 .... 475.00
Figurine, Balloon Girl, HN 2818, 1982-1997, 6 1/2 In. 115.00
Figurine, Bedtime Story, Harradine, HN 2059, 1950-1996 .... 475.00
Figurine, Belle, Red, Gold, HN 3703, 1996 .... 300.00
Figurine, Bess, Pink Dress, Purple Cloak, HN 2003, 1947-1950 .... 900.00
Figurine, Bess, Red Cloak, HN 2002, 1947-1969 .... 425.00
Figurine, Biddy, Pink Dress With Mauve, HN 513, 1932-1937 .... 325.00
Figurine, Biddy, Yellow, Green, HN 1445, 1931-1937 .... 475.00
Figurine, Blithe Morning, Bone China, HN 2065, 1950-1973 .... 325.00
Figurine, Blithe Morning, Mauve, Pink, HN 2021, 1949-1971 .... 315.00
Figurine, Bluebeard, Purple, Green, Brown, HN 2105, 1953-1992 .... 675.00
Figurine, Bo-Peep, Pink, M 82, 1939-1949 .... 620.00
Figurine, Bon Appetit, Matte, Cooking Fish, HN 2444, 1972-1976 .... 250.00
Figurine, Bride, Pink Dress, HN 2166, 1956-1976 .... 275.00
Figurine, Bride, White, Gold, HN 2873, 1980-1989 .... 200.00
Figurine, Bridesmaid, Style 4, 5 1/4 In., HN 2196, 1960-1976 .... 150.00
Figurine, Bridesmaid, White, HN 2874, 1980-1989 .... 90.00
Figurine, Bridget, Older Woman Standing, HN 2070, 1951-1973 .... 425.00
Figurine, Broken Lance, Knight On Horse, HN 2041, 1949-1975 .... 725.00
Figurine, Bunnykins, 60th Anniversary Bunnykins, DB 137, 1994 .... 85.00
Figurine, Bunnykins, Astro Bunnykins Rocket Man, DB 20, 1983-1988 ...... 200.00
Figurine, Bunnykins, Aussie Surfer Bunnykins, DB 133, 1994 .... 150.00
Figurine, Bunnykins, Boy Skater Bunnykins, DB 152, 1995-1988 .... 50.00
Figurine, Bunnykins, Buntie Bunnykins Helping Mother, DB 2, 1972-1993 ... 85.00
Figurine, Bunnykins, Family Photograph Bunnykins, DB 1, 1972-1988 ...... 165.00
Figurine, Bunnykins, Father Bunnykins, DB 154, 1996 .... 78.00
Figurine, Bunnykins, Gardener Bunnykins, DB 156, 1996-1998 .... 60.00
Figurine, Bunnykins, Harry The Herald, Ellow, Green, DB 115, 1991 ...... 552.00
Figurine, Bunnykins, Homerun Bunnykins, DB 43 .... 125.00
Figurine, Bunnykins, Jogging Bunnykins, Yellow, Blue, White, DB 22, 1983-1989 ...... 150.00
Figurine, Bunnykins, Mr. Bunnykins Autumn Days, DB 5, 1972-1982 .... 475.00
Figurine, Bunnykins, Sleepytime Bunnykins, 2 Bunnies In Bed, DB 15 ..... 85.00
Figurine, Bunnykins, Tom Bunnykins, DB 072, 1988-1993 .... 100.00
Figurine, Caroline, Pink, Yellow, HN 3694, 1995-1998 .... 325.00
Figurine, Celeste, Blue, HN 2237, 1959-1971, 6 3/4 In. 350.00
Figurine, Cherie, Blue Dress, HN 2341, 1966-1992 .... 165.00
Figurine, Chief, HN 2892, 1979-1988 .... 275.00
Figurine, China Repairer, HN 2943, 1982-1988 .... 300.00
Figurine, Chinese Dancer, HN 2840, 1980 .... 1000.00
Figurine, Chitarrone, HN 2700, 1974 .... 975.00
Figurine, Christine, Pink, White, HN 3172, 1987 .... 325.00

Figurine, Cissie, Pink, HN 1809, 1937-1993 . . . . 165.00
Figurine, Clare, Lavender Dress With Flowers, HN 2793, 1980-1984 . . . . 275.00
Figurine, Clown, HN 2890, 1979-1988 . . . . 300.00
Figurine, Cobbler, Green & Brown, HN 1706, 1935-1969 . . . . 425.00
Figurine, Collinette, Blue Cloak, HN 1998, 1947-1949 . . . . 1000.00
Figurine, Collinette, Red Cloak, HN 1999, 1947-1949 . . . . 1000.00
Figurine, Curtsey, HN 518 . . . . 4600.00
Figurine, Cymbals, HN 2699, 1974 . . . . 345.00
Figurine, Daddy's Girl, Vanity Fair Children, HN 3435, 1993-1998 . . . . 100.00
Figurine, Dancing Years, HN 2235, 1965-1971 . . . . 550.00
Figurine, Danielle, Vanity Fair Ladies, Pink, HN 3001, 1990-1995 . . . . 200.00
Figurine, Darby, Old Man In Chair, HN 2024, 1949-1959 . . . . 275.00
Figurine, Darling, Style 2, White, HN 1985, 1944-1997 . . . . 100.00
Figurine, David Copperfield, M 88, 1949-1983 . . . . 125.00
Figurine, Dawn, Vanity Fair Ladies, HN 3600, 1993-1998 . . . . 300.00
Figurine, Daydreams, Pink, Girl Standing With Flowers, HN 1731, 1935-1996 . . . . 350.00
Figurine, Debbie, Blue, HN 2385, 1969-1982 . . . . 150.00
Figurine, Debbie, Peach, HN 2400, 1983-1995 . . . . 135.00
Figurine, Deborah, Yellow, HN 3644, 1995 . . . . 300.00
Figurine, Delight, Red, HN 1772, 1936-1967 . . . . 275.00
Figurine, Diana, Red, HN 1986, 1946-1975, 5 3/4 In. 225.00
Figurine, Dinky Doo, Lavender, HN 1678, 1934-1996 . . . . 110.00
Figurine, Dorcas, Purple, HN 1558, 1933-1952, 6 3/4 In. 450.00
Figurine, Dulcimer, Lady Musicians, HN 2798, 1975 . . . . 1100.00
Figurine, Elaine, Blue, HN 3214, 1988-1998 . . . . 115.00
Figurine, Eleanor Of Provence, HN 2009, 1948-1953 . . . . 950.00
Figurine, Elegance, HN 2264, 1961-1985 . . . . 225.00
Figurine, Eliza Farren, Countess Of Derby, HN 3442, 1993 . . . . 375.00
Figurine, Eliza, Gold, HN 2543, 1974-1979, 11 3/4 In. 300.00
Figurine, Ellen, Blue, HN 3816, 1997, 8 3/4 In. 175.00
Figurine, Elyse, Blue, With White Hat, HN 2429, 1972-1995 . . . . 300.00
Figurine, Enchantment, HN 2178, 1957-1982 . . . . 260.00
Figurine, Fagin, M 49, 1932-1983, 4 In. 125.00
Figurine, Fair Lady, Green, HN 2193, 1963-1996 . . . . 225.00
Figurine, Fair Lady, Red, White, HN 2832, 1977-1996, 7 1/4 In. 75.00
Figurine, Fair Maiden, Green, HN 2211, 1967-1994 . . . . 150.00
Figurine, Falstaff, Brown & Pink, HN 2054, 1950-1992 . . . . 200.00
Figurine, Favorite, HN 2249, 1960-1990 . . . . 70.00
Figurine, Fiona, Red, White, HN 2694, 1974-1981 . . . . 225.00
Figurine, First Recital, HN 3652, 1994-1996 . . . . 100.00
Figurine, Fleur, Green Gown, HN 2368, 1968-1995 . . . . 225.00
Figurine, Flora, Old Woman With Flowers, HN 2349, 1966-1973 . . . . 450.00
Figurine, Flowers For Mother, Pink, HN 3454, 1994-1997 . . . . 100.00
Figurine, Foaming Quart, Seated Drinker, HN 2162, 1955-1992 . . . . .88.00 to 200.00
Figurine, Forty Winks, HN 1974, 1945-1973 . . . . 400.00
Figurine, Fragrance, Gold, HN 3220, 1988-1992 . . . . 110.00
Figurine, Gay Morning, Pink, HN 2135, 1954-1967, 7 In. 450.00
Figurine, Genie, Blue, HN 2989, 1983-1990 . . . . 300.00
Figurine, Good Catch, Man With Fish, HN 2258, 1966-1986 . . . . 275.00
Figurine, Good Day Sir, HN 2896, 1986-1989, 8 1/4 In. 52.00
Figurine, Gossips, Red, Cream, HN 1429, 1930-1949 . . . . 1500.00
Figurine, Gossips, Red, Cream, HN 2025, 1949-1967 . . . . 700.00
Figurine, Grace, HN 2318, 1966-1981 . . . . 120.00
Figurine, Guy Fawkes, Red Cape, HN 3271, 1989-1991 . . . . 115.00
Figurine, Gwynneth, HN 1980, 1945-1952 . . . . 525.00
Figurine, Gypsy Dance, HN 2157, 1955-1957 . . . . 1400.00
Figurine, Gypsy Dance, HN 2230, 1959-1971 . . . . 500.00
Figurine, Hannah, Blue, HN 3655, 1995 . . . . 300.00
Figurine, Happy Birthday 2000, HN 4215, 2000 . . . . 195.00
Figurine, Harmony, Woman With Dove, HN 2824, 1978-1984 . . . . 325.00
Figurine, Helen, White, HN 2994, 1985-1987, 5 In. 35.00
Figurine, Hilary, Blue, HN 2335, 1967-1981 . . . . 220.00
Figurine, Hinged Parasol, Red, Purple, HN 1579, 1933-1949 . . . . 380.00

Figurine, Home Again, HN 2167, 1956-1995 ....58.00 to 70.00
Figurine, Home At Last, Child With Dog, HN 3697, 1995-1999 .... 150.00
Figurine, Hometime, HN 3685, 1995-1997 .... 140.00
Figurine, Honey, Pink, HN 1909, 1939-1949 .... 650.00
Figurine, Innocence, On Knees Praying With Dog, Pink, White, HN 3730, 1996-2000 ... 90.00
Figurine, Innocence, Red, HN 2842, 1979-1983 .... 200.00
Figurine, Invitation, Girl With Fan, Pink, HN 2170, 1956-1975 .... 200.00
Figurine, Isabella, Countess Of Sefton, HN 3010, 1991 .... 310.00
Figurine, Jack, HN 2060, 1950-1971 .... 2225.00
Figurine, Jacqueline, Pink, HN 2001, 1947-1951, 7 1/4 In. 800.00
Figurine, Jane, HN 3711, 1997 .... 300.00
Figurine, Jasmine, Green, Blue, Orange, HN 1862, 1938-1949 .... 1500.00
Figurine, Jean, Green, Red, HN 2032, 1949-1959 .... 550.00
Figurine, Jean, Pink, Purple, HN 1877, 1938-1949 .... 950.00
Figurine, Jennifer, Blue, HN 2392, 1982-1992 .... 300.00
Figurine, Jennifer, Pink, HN 3447, 1994 .... 450.00
Figurine, Jennifer, Yellow, Cream, HN 1484, 1931-1949 .... 600.00
Figurine, Jill, Nursery Rhyme, HN 2061, 1950-1971 .... 225.00
Figurine, Jovial Monk, Brown, HN 2144, 1954-1976 .... 350.00
Figurine, Julia, Gold, HN 2705 .... 225.00
Figurine, June, Mauve, Pink, M 65, 1935-1949 .... 1100.00
Figurine, June, Pale Green, Pink, HN 1690, 1935-1949 .... 1200.00
Figurine, Katrina, Red, HN 2327, 1965-1969, 7 1/2 In. 500.00
Figurine, Kirsty, Red, HN 3213, 1988-1997 .... 115.00
Figurine, La Sylphide, White, Blue, HN 2138, 1954-1965 .... 550.00
Figurine, Lady Betty, Red, HN 1967, 1941-1951 .... 650.00
Figurine, Lady Charmain, Red Dress, Green Shawl, HN 1949, 1940-1975, 8 In. 160.00
Figurine, Lady Charmian, Green Dress, Red Shawl, HN 1948, 1940-1973 .... 350.00
Figurine, Lambing Time, Shepherd With 2 Lambs, HN 1890, 1938-1981 .... 325.00
Figurine, Laurianne, Seated, Dark Blue, White, HN 2719, 1974-1979 .... 250.00
Figurine, Lavina, Girl With Red Dress & Basket, HN 1955, 1940-1979 .... 150.00
Figurine, Lights Out, Boy With Pillow, HN 2262, 1965-1969 .... 350.00
Figurine, Lily, Flowered Shawl Over Pink, HN 1798, 1936-1971 .... 175.00
Figurine, Lindsay, White, Blue, Cream, HN 3645, 1994-1998 .... 175.00
Figurine, Lisa, Blue, White, HN 2310, 1969-1982 .... 225.00
Figurine, Little Boy Blue, Nursery Rhymes, HN 2062, 1950-1973 .... 225.00
Figurine, Little Bridesmaid, Yellow, Green, HN 1434, 1930-1949 .... 500.00
Figurine, Lobster Man, Blue, Sea Characters, HN 2317, 1964-1994 .... 250.00
Figurine, Love Letter, HN 2149, 1958-1976 .... 625.00
Figurine, Lunchtime, Man Feeding Squirrel, HN 2485, 1973-1981 .... 275.00
Figurine, Margaret, Red, Green, HN 1989, 1947-1959 .... 575.00
Figurine, Margaret, White, Green, HN 3496, 1993-1999 .... 200.00
Figurine, Marguerite, HN 1928, 1940-1959 .... 600.00
Figurine, Marie, Purple, HN 1370, 1930-1988 .... 100.00
Figurine, Mary Had A Little Lamb, HN 2048, 1948-1988 .... 200.00
Figurine, Mary Queen Of Scots, Blue, Purple, HN 3142, 1989 .... 368.00
Figurine, Mary, White, HN 2374, 1984-1986 .... 400.00
Figurine, Mask Seller, Street Vender, Green, Yellow, HN 2103, 1953-1995 .... 300.00
Figurine, Masquerade, Blue, White, HN 2251, 1960-1965 .... 425.00
Figurine, Masquerade, Red, Cream, HN 2259, 1960-1965 .... 425.00
Figurine, Master, HN 2325, 1967-1992 .... 77.00
Figurine, Maureen, Pink, M 84, 1939-1949 .... 713.00
Figurine, May, White, Green, HN 2711, 1987 .... 200.00
Figurine, Maytime, Pink Dress, Blue Scarf, HN 2113, 1953-1969 .... 425.00
Figurine, Medicant, Brown, HN 1365, 1929-1969 .... 400.00
Figurine, Melanie, Holding Flowers, Blue, HN 2271, 1965-1981 .... 275.00
Figurine, Memories, Pink, Green, HN 2030, 1949-1959 .... 600.00
Figurine, Midinette, Blue, Grey, HN 2090, 1952-1965, 7 1/4 In. 425.00
Figurine, Milkmaid, Green, Brown, White, HN 2057A, 1975-1981 .... 200.00
Figurine, Mirabel, Pink, Green, M 68, 1936-1949 .... 620.00
Figurine, Miss Muffet, Red., HN 1936, 1940-1947, 5 1/2 In. 225.00
Figurine, Monica, Girl Seated Holding Flowers, Purple, HN 1467, 1931-1995 .... 150.00
Figurine, Mr. Micawber, Dickens, M 42, 1932-1983, 4 In. 125.00

Figurine, Nina, Blue, HN 2347, 1969-1976	185.00
Figurine, October, White, Blue, HN 2693, 1987	200.00
Figurine, Off To School, Boy With Book Bag, HN 3768, 1996-1998	200.00
Figurine, Old Balloon Seller, HN 3737, 1999	375.00
Figurine, Omar Khayyam, Brown, HN 2247, 1963-1983	250.00
Figurine, Orange Lady, Green, HN 1953, 1940-1975	110.00
Figurine, Orange Lady, Pink Dress, HN 1759, 1936-1975	425.00
Figurine, Owd Willum, Old Man With Hand To Ear, HN 2042, 1949-1973	375.00
Figurine, Paisley Shawl, Green, Red, HN 1914, 1939-1949	375.00
Figurine, Paisley Shawl, M 4	265.00 to 500.00
Figurine, Paisley Shawl, Red, Pink, HN 1988, 1946-1975, 6 1/2 In.	250.00
Figurine, Pantalettes, Blue, Green Dress, 1929-1942, HN 1362	850.00
Figurine, Patricia, Lavender, M 28, 1932-1945	700.00
Figurine, Patricia, Yellow, Green, HN 1414, 1930-1949	1250.00
Figurine, Pearly Boy, HN 2767A, 1989-1992	275.00
Figurine, Pearly Girl, HN 2036, 1949-1959	225.00
Figurine, Pearly Girl, HN 2769A, 1989-1992	275.00
Figurine, Pecksniff, Dickens, Third Series, HN 2098, 1952-1967	395.00
Figurine, Peggy, Red, White, HN 2038, 1949-1979	160.00
Figurine, Penny, Green, White, HN 2338, 1968-1995	100.00
Figurine, Phyllis, Purple, Green, HN 1420, 1930-1949	966.00
Figurine, Pied Piper, Man Playing Flute With Rats, HN 2102, 1953-1976	400.00
Figurine, Pierrette, Black & White Suit, Black Base, HN 644, 1924-1938, 7in.	294.00
Figurine, Pillow Fight, HN 2270, 1965-1969	288.00
Figurine, Poacher, Kneeling On 1 Leg, HN 2043, 1949-1959	450.00
Figurine, Polka, HN 2156, 1955-1969	450.00
Figurine, Potter, Brown, HN 1493, 1932-1992	310.00 to 650.00
Figurine, Priscilla, Red, M 24, 1932-1945	650.00
Figurine, Priscilla, Red, Purple, HN 1340, 1929-1949, 8 In.	600.00
Figurine, Prized Possessions, HN 2942, 1982	700.00
Figurine, Professor, Man Reading Book, HN 2281, 1965-1981	250.00
Figurine, Queen Victoria, HN 3125, 1987-1988	760.00
Figurine, Rag Doll Seller, HN 2944, 1983-1995, 7 1/2 In.	138.00
Figurine, Rag Doll, HN 2142, 1954-1986	140.00
Figurine, Rebecca, Pale Blue, Lavender, HN 2805, 1980-1996	625.00
Figurine, Repose, Reclining Lady, Pink, Green, HN 2272, 1972-1979	350.00
Figurine, Reverie, HN 2306, 1964-1981, 7 In.	175.00
Figurine, Ritz Bellboy, HN 2772, 1989-1993	250.00
Figurine, River Boy, Boy Frying Fish, HN 2128, 1962-1975	275.00
Figurine, Rose, Lavender, HN 2123, 1983-1995	100.00
Figurine, Rose, Pink, HN 1368, 1930-1995	50.00
Figurine, Roseanna, Pink, HN 1926, 1940-1959, 8 In.	650.00
Figurine, Rosemary, HN 3143, 1988-1991	275.00
Figurine, Sabbath Morn, Red, HN 1982, 1945-1959, 7 1/4 In.	400.00
Figurine, Samantha, HN 2954, 1982-1984	225.00
Figurine, Sarah, Red, Pink, HN 3384, 1995-2000	285.00
Figurine, Sea Harvest, HN 2257, 1969-1976	100.00
Figurine, Secret Thoughts, Green, HN 2382, 1971-1988	275.00
Figurine, Sharon, HN 3603, 1994	250.00
Figurine, She Loves Me Not, Blue, Nursery Rhymes, HN 2045, 1949-1962	325.00
Figurine, Shore Leave, HN 2254, 1965-1979	90.00
Figurine, Silversmith Of Williamsburg, HN 2208, 1960-1983	250.00
Figurine, Simone, Waving Fan, Green, HN 2378, 1971-1981	200.00
Figurine, Single Red Rose, HN 3376, 1992-1995	275.00
Figurine, Sir Walter Raleigh, HN 2015, 1948-1955	1000.00
Figurine, Skater, Red, White, Brown, HN 2117, 1953-1971	575.00
Figurine, Sleepy Darling, HN 2953, 1981	275.00
Figurine, Sleepy Head, Child With Teddy Bear, HN 3761, 1996-1998	125.00
Figurine, Sonia, Pink, White, Green, HN 1692, 1935-1949	2000.00
Figurine, Sophia Charlotte, Lady Sheffield, HN 3008, 1990	290.00
Figurine, Sophie, HN 2833, 1977-1987	44.00
Figurine, Southern Belle, Pale Blue, Pink, HN 2425, 1983-1994	275.00
Figurine, Special Friend, Boy With Blue Shorts, HN 3607, 1994-1998	120.00

Figurine, Spring Morning, Green, Cream, HN 1923, 1940-1949 . . . . 685.00
Figurine, Spring Morning, Pink, Blue, HN 1922, 1940-1973 . . . . 400.00
Figurine, Springtime, The Seasons, HN 3033, 1983 . . . . 350.00
Figurine, St. George, HN 2051, 1950-1985 . . . . 650.00
Figurine, Stiggins, Dickens, M 50, 1932-1981 . . . . 125.00
Figurine, Strolling, Red, Yellow, HN 3755, 1996-1999 . . . . 250.00
Figurine, Summer Rose, White, Pink, HN 3309, 1991-1997 . . . . 250.00
Figurine, Summertime, Lilac, Green, HN 3478, 1994-1996 . . . . 350.00
Figurine, Summertime, White, Blue, HN 3137, 1987 . . . . 250.00
Figurine, Sunday Best, Pink, White, HN 2698, 1985-1995 . . . . 225.00
Figurine, Sunday Best, Yellow, HN 2206, 1979-1984 . . . . 250.00
Figurine, Sunday Morning, Red, Brown, HN 2184, 1963-1969 . . . . 495.00
Figurine, Susan, Blue, Black, Pink, HN 2952, 1982-1993, 8 1/2 In. 146.00
Figurine, Sweet & Twenty, Red Dress, HN 1589, 1933-1949 . . . . 550.00
Figurine, Sweet Anne, Blue, M 6, 1932-1945 . . . . 276.00
Figurine, Sweet Anne, Lavender, Green, M 5, 1932-1945 . . . . 345.00
Figurine, Sweet Anne, Purple, HN 1496, 1932-1967 . . . . 360.00
Figurine, Sweet Anne, Red, Blue, Yellow, HN 1331, 1929-1949 . . . . 550.00
Figurine, Sweet Seventeen, White, Gold, HN 2734, 1975-1993 . . . . 325.00
Figurine, Sweet Sixteen, Blue, White, HN 2231, 1958-1965, 7 1/4 In. 450.00
Figurine, Swimmer, HN 4246, 2000 . . . . 440.00
Figurine, Take Me Home, Girl With Puppies, HN 3662, 1995-1990 . . . . 250.00
Figurine, Tall Story, HN 2248, 1968-1975 . . . . 90.00
Figurine, Teatime, Old Woman Pouring Tea, HN 2255, 1972-1995 . . . . 325.00
Figurine, Time For Bed, Girl With Lantern, HN 3762, 1996-1998 . . . . 125.00
Figurine, Tinkle Bell, HN 1677, 1935-1988 . . . . 55.00
Figurine, Toinette, HN 1940, 1940-1949 . . . . 1700.00
Figurine, Tony Weller, Dickens, M 47, 1932-1981, 4 In. 125.00
Figurine, Top O' The Hill, Green, Blue, HN 1833, 1937-1971, 7 In. 350.00
Figurine, Town Crier, HN 2119, 1953-1976, 8 In. 86.00
Figurine, Town Crier, HN 3261, 1989-1991, 4 In. 150.00
Figurine, Tuppence A Bag, HN 2320, 1968-1995 . . . . 88.00
Figurine, Twilight, HN 2256, 1971-1976 . . . . 66.00
Figurine, Uriah Heep, Dickens, HN 2101, 1952-1967, 8 In. 425.00
Figurine, Valerie, Red, Pink, White, HN 2107, 1953-1995 . . . . 160.00
Figurine, Vanity, Red, HN 2475, 1973-1992 . . . . 185.00
Figurine, Veronica, Red, Cream, HN 1517, 1932-1951 . . . . 525.00
Figurine, Veronica, White, Pink, HN 3205, 1989-1992 . . . . 250.00
Figurine, Victoria, HN 2471, 1973-2000 . . . . 400.00
Figurine, Victorian Lady, Pink, Purple, HN 728, 1925-1952 . . . . 700.00
Figurine, Vivienne, Red, HN 2073, 1951-1967, 7 3/4 In. 400.00
Figurine, Wayfarer, HN 2362, 1970-1976 . . . . 295.00
Figurine, Wendy, Little Girl In Blue, HN 2109, 1953-1995 . . . . 100.00
Figurine, What's The Matter, Girl Holding Teddy, HN 3684, 1995-1998 . . . . 140.00
Figurine, Winsome, HN 2220, 1960-1985 . . . . 250.00
Figurine, Wistful, Blue, White, HN 2472, 1985 . . . . 350.00
Figurine, Young Miss Nightingale, HN 2010, 9 1/4 In. 575.00
Humidor, Spring-Loaded Brass Handle Cover, Scenes, Impressed Alfred Dunhill, 5 1/4 In. 300.00
Inkwell, Girl, Head & Shoulders On Brass Hinge, 3 5/8 In. 467.00
Jug, Proverb, Twixt The Cup & The Lip, Buff Ground, Flower, Brown, Handle, 7 In. 160.00
Mother Goose Panel, 88 Tiles, Girl, Geese, Brown Tile Border, 71 x 47 In. 11500.00
Pitcher, Columbus Portrait, Spanish Armada Border, 7 1/2 In. 325.00
Pitcher, Dickens Dream, 10 1/2 In. 2013.00
Pitcher, Motto, Be Always As Merry As You Ever Can, 7 1/2 In. 92.00
Pitcher, Old English Scenes, The Gleaners, 6 In. 127.00
Pitcher, Owl, Mice, Tapered, Pattern D 3607, 5 1/2 In. 81.00
Pitcher, Shakespeare Series, Wolsey, 9 In. 585.00
Pitcher, Silhouette Series, Stoneware, Green, Brown, 7 1/2 In. 150.00
Pitcher, Vignettes Of Dogs, Cats, Cobalt Blue Ground, Hannah Barlow, 9 3/4 In. 1315.00
Plate, Christmas, 1977 . . . . 85.00
Plate, Commemorative, Robert Burns, Blue & White, 10 1/2 In. 46.00
Plate, English Garden Series, 8 1/2 In. 104.00

Plate, Fisherwoman 125.00
Plate, Niagara Falls 50.00
Plate, Old Balloon Seller 150.00
Plate, Pierrette 125.00
Plate, Roger De Coverley, 8 1/2 In. 125.00
Plate, Series Ware, African Waterbuck, African Game Reserve, 10 1/4 In. 45.00
Plate, Series Ware, Game At Drinking Pool, African Game Reserve, 10 1/4 In. 45.00
Plate, Valentines Day, 1976 .... 50.00
Plate, Valentines Day, 1977 .... 50.00
Plate, Valentines Day, 1978 .... 50.00
Plate, Valentines Day, 1979 .... 50.00
Plate, Valentines Day, 1980 .... 50.00
Plate, Valentines Day, 1981 .... 50.00
Plate, Valentines Day, 1982 .... 50.00
Plate, Valentines Day, 1983 .... 50.00
Plate, William Shakespeare 125.00
Teapot, Hamlet, Shakespeare Series, Pale Yellow Ground 110.00
Toby Jug, Best Is Not Too Good, D 6107, 4 1/4 In. 75.00
Toby Jug, Betty Bitters, D 6716, Small 85.00
Toby Jug, Charlie Cheer, D 6768, Small 110.00
Toby Jug, Cliff Cornell, Black Hat, Coat, Suit 300.00
Toby Jug, Cliff Cornell, Large 300.00
Toby Jug, Clown, D 6935, Small 150.00
Toby Jug, Dr. Pulse The Physician, D 6723, Small 80.00
Toby Jug, Falstaff, Seated, Small, D 6063 ....60.00 to 90.00
Toby Jug, Father Christmas, D 6940, Medium 150.00
Toby Jug, Happy John, 5 1/2 In. 58.00
Toby Jug, Happy John, Seated, D 6070, Small ....60.00 to 90.00
Toby Jug, Honest Measure, Holding Pipe & Stein, D 6108, Small 110.00
Toby Jug, Madame Crystal, Clairvoyant, D 6714, Small 90.00
Toby Jug, Miss Nostrum, D 6700, Small 75.00
Toby Jug, Miss Studious, Schoolmistress, D 6722, Small 110.00
Toby Jug, Mr. Furrow, D 6701, Small 85.00
Toby Jug, Mr. Tonsil, Town Crier, D 6713, Small 90.00
Toby Jug, Reverend Cassock, Clergyman, D 6702, Small 85.00
Toby Jug, Sir Francis Drake, D 6660, Large 150.00
Toby Jug, Winston Churchill, D 6172, Medium 90.00
Toby Jug, Winston Churchill, D 6175, Small 80.00
Toby Jug, Winston Churchill, Seated, D 6171, Large 125.00
Toothpick Holder, Sairey Gamp, D 6150 .... 450.00
Vase, Huntsmen & Hounds, Yellow Ground, 8 1/2 In., Pair 230.00
Vase, Lily Pattern, Flow Blue, 6 In. 60.00

ROYAL DUX is the more common name for the Duxer Porzellan-
manufaktur, which was founded by E. Eichler in Dux, Bohemia, in
1860. By the turn of the century, the firm specialized in porcelain
statuary and busts of Art Nouveau–style maidens, large porcelain figures, and ornate vases with three-dimensional figures climbing on the
sides. The firm is still in business.

Bowl, Shell Shape, Maidens, Instrument, Waves, Signed, 15 x 12 In. 1495.00
Bowl, Women Climbing Conch Shell, Art Nouveau, 18 In. 1120.00
Figurine, Dancer, Female, Enamel, Gilt Decoration, Raised Oval Base, 22 3/4 In. 940.00
Figurine, Dog, Game Bird In Mouth, c.1920, 18 x 9 1/4 In. 1450.00
Figurine, Female Nude, White, Bohemia, 9 x 5 In. 78.00
Figurine, Girl Holding Cat, Pink Triangle Mark, No. 421, 20 In. 1150.00
Figurine, Girl Sitting Next To Large Basket, Cat Looking Down At Her, 8 x 7 In. 375.00
Figurine, Harlequin, 20 In., Pair 310.00
Figurine, Maiden In Flowing Gown, Grecian Pot, Signed, 24 In. 1035.00
Figurine, Partially Nude Woman, Cobalt Blue Skirt, 11 In. 440.00
Vase, Floor, Palm Shape, Middle Eastern Women, Gilt, 36 1/2 x 37 1/4 In., Pair 525.00
Vase, Woman Hanging Pink Bowtie Garland, 18 In. 600.00
Vase, Woman, Sitting, Holding Urn, Trailing Iris On Vase, No. 417, 17 In. 1345.00

ROYAL FLEMISH glass was made during the late 1880s in New Bedford, Massachusetts, by the Mt. Washington Glass Works. It is a colored satin glass decorated with dark colors and raised gold designs. The glass was patented in 1894. It was supposed to resemble stained glass windows.

Biscuit Jar, Cover, Earth Tones, Raised Gold Grid, 4 Medallions, Bail Handle, 10 In.	1735.00
Castor Jar, Pickle, Daisies, Gold Trim, Bulbous, Gold-Plated Frame, 10 In.	2100.00
Castor Jar, Pickle, Pansies, Gold Trim, Bulbous, Silver-Plated Frame, 10 1/2 In.	2900.00
Ewer, 8 Keyhole-Shape Panels, Rose & Blue, Enameled, Gold Flowers, 11 1/2 In.	9200.00
Lamp, Flying Ducks, Night Sky, Frank Guba, Medallion. Shade, 9 x 20 In.	28112.00
Lamp Base, Blue & Green Panels, Enameled, Gold Griffin, Filigree Brass Foot, 19 In.	920.00

ROYAL HAEGER, see Haeger category.

ROYAL IVY, see Northwood, Royal Ivy

ROYAL OAK pieces are listed in the Pressed Glass category by that pattern name.

ROYAL RUDOLSTADT, see Rudolstadt category.

ROYAL VIENNA, see Beehive category.

ROYAL WORCESTER is a name used by collectors. Worcester porcelains were made in Worcester, England, from about 1751. The firm went through many different periods and name changes. It became the Worcester Royal Porcelain Company, Ltd., in 1862. Today collectors call the porcelains made after 1862 *Royal Worcester*. In 1976, the firm merged with W. T. Copeland to become Royal Worcester Spode. Some early products of the factory are listed under Worcester.

Ashtray, Pink, Bell Shape Flowers, 4 In.	12.00
Biscuit Jar, Cover, Purple Blossom On Branch, 6 1/2 In.	240.00
Cigarette Holder & Ashtray, Arden, Fruit Pattern, c.1974, 2 1/2 x 4 In., 2 Piece	35.00
Cup & Saucer, Floral, Pink Ground, Demitasse	40.00
Cup & Saucer, Grazing Long Horn Steer, Signed, Marked, Demitasse, 2 In.	431.00
Cup & Saucer, Japanese Style Design, Tiffany & Co.	29.00
Figurine, Canyon Wren, Fitted Case, Doughty, c.1957, 9 In., Pair	2875.00
Figurine, Grandmother's Dress, No. 3081, 6 1/4 In.	195.00
Figurine, Johnnie, 6 1/2 In.	130.00
Figurine, Man & Woman, Japanese, 16 In., Pair	8050.00
Figurine, Mockingbird, No. 3326, Fitted Case, Doughty, c.1964, 10 1/2 In.	1035.00
Figurine, Parakeet, No. 3087, 7 In.	225.00
Figurine, Redstart, Fitted Case, Doughty, c.1965, 8 1/2 In.	2070.00
Figurine, Wagtail, Fitted Case, Doughty, c.1968, 6 In.	750.00
Figurine, Woodpecker, Fitted Case, Doughty, c.1967, 11 1/4 In., Pair	3220.00
Jar, Sweetmeat, Thistles, Swirl Base, Silver Plate Lid, Bail Handle, 6 In.	200.00
Pitcher, Butterfly & Daisy, 5 1/2 In.	130.00
Pitcher, Cream, Gold Enameling, 5 3/4 In.	145.00
Pitcher, Flowers, Gold Handles, 6 x 5 In.	230.00
Pitcher, Flowers, Ivoryware, Late 19th Century, 8 In.	200.00
Pitcher, Indian Elephant Head Handle, 5 3/4 In.	175.00
Pitcher, Powder Horn, Gold Stag Horn Handle, 9 In.	145.00
Pitcher, Tricornered, Blue & White Circles, Gold Enamel, c.1860, 7 1/4 In.	259.00
Plaque, Pheasants In Landscape, Polychrome Enamel, Frame, Stinton, 1920, 12 3/4 In. ..	3055.00
Plate, Blue & Red Flower & Vine Pattern Edge, Tiffany Mark, 8 In.	60.00
Plate, Classical Ruins, Gilt & Cobalt Blue Border, 1800s, 10 1/2 In., 8 Piece	1150.00
Plate, Floral Still Life, Green Ground, Gold Leafy Border, 10 5/8 In., 12 Piece	1295.00
Plate, Imari Style, Blues, Oranges, Greens, Gilt Trim, 9 3/4 In., 12 Piece	165.00
Plate, Painted Fishing Flies, Shaped Cobalt Rim, 8 5/8 In., 12 Piece	4115.00
Ramekin Set, Palmyra, Case, Recipe Booklet, Shape 48, Size 00, c.1970, 6 Piece	60.00
Teapot, Gold Lily Pads, Cream Ground, 6 In.	450.00
Toothpick Holder, Pink Flowers, Gold Trim, 2 1/2 In.	60.00
Vase, 3 Dolphin Stem, 3 Paw Feet, Leaves, c.1897, 8 3/4 In.	290.00
Vase, Bramble Branches, Red Enamel, Gilt, Yellow, Aesthetic Revival, c.1883, 9 In.	1195.00
Vase, Double Arm, Flower Shape Top, Painted Flowers, 8 In.	290.00
Vase, Floral Reticulated Reserves, Vertical Gold Bands, Oval, 4 In.	115.00

Vase, Flowers, Hand Painted, Gilt Details, Pitcher Form, 1885-1891, 5 In. 195.00
Vase, Gold Dragon Handles, Aesthetic Movement Scene, 16 In. 405.00
Vase, Majolica, Shore Bird, Bamboo Stalk, Mark, 27 In. 2350.00
Vase, Oil Lamp, 3 Dolphin Flower Holders, Green Ground, c.1893, 11 3/4 In. 375.00

ROYCROFT products were made by the Roycrofter community of East
Aurora, New York, in the late nineteenth and early twentieth centuries.
The community was founded by Elbert Hubbard, famous philosopher,
writer, and artist. The workshops owned by the community made furniture, metalware, leatherwork, embroidery, and jewelry. A printshop
produced many signs, books, and the magazines that promoted the sayings of Elbert Hubbard. Furniture by the Roycroft community is listed
in the Furniture category.

Bookends, Copper, Hammered, Brass Wash, Marked, 5 x 2 3/4 In. 200.00
Bookends, Copper, Hammered, Brass Wash, Stylized Flowers, Marked, 4 1/2 x 5 In. 200.00
Bookends, Copper, Hammered, Owl, Original Patina, Cross Mark, 5 x 5 1/2 In. . . .290.00 to 430.00
Bookends, Copper, Hammered, Poppies, Original Medium Patina, 5 1/2 x 5 In. 750.00
Bookends, Copper, Hammered, University Of Illinois Insignia, Impressed Mark, 5 In. . . . 240.00
Bookstand, 11 Copies Of The Philistine, Leather Bound, 19 1/2 x 8 1/2 In. 290.00
Bowl, Copper, Hammered, Original Brass Patina, Impressed Mark, 10 In. 520.00
Box, Copper, Hammered, Gumwood, Handles, Marked, 9 1/4 x 23 x 12 In. 1265.00
Box, Copper, Hammered, Overhanging Lid, Squares, Dard Hunter, 2 1/4 x 6 1/2 In. 16450.00
Candelabrum, 6-Light, Copper, Hammered, Low Line Form, 15 1/2 In. 375.00
Candleholder, Copper, Hammered, Patina, Flowers, Wall Mount, 10 In. 980.00
Candlestick, Copper, Hammered, Brass Wash, Flower Form Base, Cross Mark, 8 In., Pair 500.00
Candlestick, Copper, Hammered, Dark Patina, Flower Form Base, 8 In. 230.00
Candlestick, Copper, Hammered, Impressed Mark, 6 1/2 In., Pair 575.00
Candlestick, Copper, Hammered, Medium Patina, Cross Mark, 8 In. 1380.00
Candlestick, Copper, Hammered, Princess, Wood Grain, 7 3/4 x 3 1/4 In., Pair 690.00
Lamp, Copper, Hammered, Acanthus Leaf, Helmet Shade, Orb & Cross Mark, 15 x 10 In. 3450.00
Letter Holder, Calendar, Copper, Etched Border, Cross Mark, 3 1/2 x 4 3/4 In. 115.00
Letter Holder, Pen Tray, Copper, Patina, Hammered, Marked, 5 In. 240.00
Scone, Brass, Hammered, Glass Candleholder, Stamped, 10 1/4 In. 185.00
Tray, Copper, Hammered, Cleaned Patina, 8 Sides, Handles, Cross Mark, 17 In. 288.00
Tray, Copper, Hammered, Flowers, Dark Patina, Oval, Handles, Cross Mark, 22 In. 430.00
Tray, Copper, Hammered, Orb & Cross Mark In Center, 8 In. 520.00
Tray, Copper, Hammered, Oval, Riveted Handles, Cross Mark, 10 x 20 In. 375.00
Umbrella Stand, Copper Straps, Hammered, William Roth, 1910, 30 x 12 In. 2415.00
Vase, Bronze, Hammered, Spade Shape, Stamped Base, 4 1/2 In. 207.00
Vase, Brown High Glaze, Handles, Impressed Mark, 6 3/4 In. 90.00
Vase, Copper, Hammered, American Beauty, Brass Wash, Orb & Cross, 7 x 3 1/4 In. 1495.00
Vase, Copper, Hammered, American Beauty, Orb & Cross, 18 1/2 x 7 1/2 In. 4315.00
Vase, Copper, Hammered, Brass Patina, Impressed Mark, 4 1/2 In. 138.00
Vase, Copper, Hammered, Flared, Rolled Rim, Bulbous, Original Patina, 15 x 6 3/4 In. . . . 3220.00
Vase, Copper, Hammered, Original Dark Patina, 7 x 3 1/4 In. 1955.00
Vase, Copper, Hammered, Original Dark Patina, Quatrefoils, Cylindrical, 10 x 3 1/4 In. . . 2185.00
Vase, Copper, Hammered, Pinched Edge, Flared Rim, Base, 7 1/2 In. 690.00
Vase, Copper, Hammered, Shouldered Form, Impressed Mark, 5 In. 405.00
Vase, Silver Finish, Acid Etched, Squat Base, Flared, 16 x 9 In. 1095.00

ROZANE, see Roseville category.

ROZENBURG worked at The Hague, Holland, from 1890 to 1914. The
most important pieces were earthenware made in the early twentieth
century with pale-colored Art Nouveau designs.

Bottle, Liqueur, Brown, Boat, Windmill, Farmhouse, 11 x 4 1/2 In. 88.00
Bowl, 3-Leaf Clovers, Blue, Brown, Cobalt Blue, 1904, 4 1/4 x 7 In. 248.00
Bowl, Stars, Green, Purple, Brown, Black, 1900, 3 1/4 x 8 In. 165.00
Clog, Pansy, Leaves, Yellow, Green, Purple, 1900-1904, 4 1/2 In. 140.00
Cup & Saucer, Birds, Poppies, 8 Sides, 1902 . . . . 1909.00
Cup & Saucer, Purple Chrysanthemums, Eggshell, Cylindrical, 1900 . . . . 786.00
Dish, Yellow Iris, Green & Brown Ground, Oval, Rozenburg, 1908, 10 x 4 In. 786.00
Plate, Dutch Royal House, Queen Holds Orb, Palm Frond, 1913, 10 3/4 In. 999.00

Plate, Stylized Poppies & Daisies In Landscape, Stepped Rim, J.C. Heijtze, 1902, 17 In. . 4495.00
Tile, Dutch Woman, Carrying Basket, Painted, Frame, 6 x 6 In. 460.00
Tile, Figure Walking On Snowy Path, Painted, Marked, Frame, 6 x 6 In. 748.00
Tile, Stylized Flowers, Red, Yellow, Green, Underglaze Painted, Frame, 6 In. 115.00
Urn, Cover, Stylized Vines, Green, Blue, Ivory, White Ground, 1902, 20 1/4 x 10 In. 880.00
Vase, Birds On Oak Branches, Eggshell, Baluster Shape, 8 Sides, 1902, 10 1/2 In. 6740.00
Vase, Blossoms, Leaves, Handles, Multicolored, Eggshell, 1907, 8 In., Pair 9775.00
Vase, Butterfly, Insects, Flowers, 1896, 15 3/4 x 7 1/2 In. 660.00
Vase, Daisies, Khaki Green, Bulbous, 1900, 3 3/4 In., Pair 248.00
Vase, Earthenware, Blue, Green, Gold, Flowers, Art Nouveau, c.1916, 15 1/2 In. 2243.00
Vase, Eggshell, Violets, White Ground, Rectangular, Square Rim, 1902, 3 1/2 In. 2470.00
Vase, Flowers, Purple, Violet, White, 1909-1910, 6 3/4 x 3 In. 525.00
Vase, Flowers, Stems, Brown, Yellow, Green, c.1899, 15 1/2 x 6 1/2 In. 440.00
Vase, Flowers, Yellow, Green, Looped Handles, Brown Ground, 1897, 15 x 14 In. 935.00
Vase, Iris, Stylized Leaves, Blue, Brown, White, 8 1/4 x 4 In. 550.00
Vase, Iris, White, Brown, c.1890, 9 1/2 x 3 1/2 In. 140.00
Vase, Lily, Leaves, Purple, Brown, Green, Drip Glaze, Signed, 1895, 15 1/2 x 6 1/2 In. . . . 385.00
Vase, Orchids, Blue, Yellow, Blue Ground, 1894, 8 1/2 x 2 In. 220.00
Vase, Purple, Yellow Violets, Globular, Flattened, Loop Handles, Rozenburg, 1902, 6 In. . . 900.00
Vase, Robin, Branch, Berries, Bulbous, Signed, 1900-1902, 8 3/4 x 4 In. 1210.00
Vase, Stylized Mushrooms, Green, Yellow, Brown, Baluster, 1899, 12 In. 1067.00

RRP, or RRP Roseville, is the mark used by the firm of Robinson-Ransbottom. It is not a mark of the more famous Roseville Pottery. The Ransbottom brothers started a pottery in 1900 in Ironspot, Ohio. In 1920, they merged with the Robinson Clay Product Company of Akron, Ohio, to become Robinson-Ransbottom. The factory is still working.

R. R. P. Co
U.S.A.
Roseville. O.

Bean Pot, Brown Drip Glaze, 2 Handles, 7 1/2 x 8 1/2 In. 15.00
Bean Pot, Brown Rim, Cream Bottom, 6 x 8 In. 12.00
Bowl, Brown, 3 3/4 x 2 1/4 In. 4.00
Bowl, Pasta, Yellow, Blue Sponged Rim, Blue Wheat Sheaves, 11 1/2 x 3 In. 18.00
Bowl, Yellowware, No. 305, 6 1/2 x 10 1/2 In. 225.00
Casserole, Blue, Cream, Lid, 1 1/2 Qt., 4 x 9 3/4 In. 25.00
Cookie Jar, Hey Diddle Diddle, Gold Trim, No. 317, 1940s, 9 3/4 In. . . . . .110.00 to 395.00
Cookie Jar, Peter Peter Pumpkin Eater, No. 1502, 8 3/4 In. 475.00
Cookie Jar, Tiger, Striped Cylinder Jar, Tiger Cubs On Top 150.00
Creamer, Stoneware, Brown Top, Cream Bottom, 4 3/4 x 5 1/4 In. 18.00
Jardiniere, Blended Green Glaze, 6 x 4 3/4 In. 50.00
Jardiniere, White Matte Glaze, c.1970s 46.00
Jardiniere, Yellow, Green Drip Glaze, No. 1420, 7 In. 45.00
Mixing Bowl, Ivory, Black, Yellow Bands, 9 In. 25.00
Pitcher, Brown Top, Cream Colored Bottom, 6 1/2 x 6 In. 25.00
Plant Holder, Burnt Orange, Windowsill, Holds 2 Size Clay Pots, 12 x 4 1/2 In. 42.00
Planter, Baby Shoes, Pink, Button-Up Booties, 1950s, 4 x 4 x 2 3/4 In. 18.00
Planter, Gray, Blue, No. 355, c.1950 . . . . 25.00
Planter, White, 6 x 4 1/4 In. 20.00
Vase, Deer Insert, Aqua Gloss, Dry Bottom Rim, 1940s, 5 1/2 x 7 3/4 In. 48.00

RS GERMANY is part of the wording in marks used by the Tillowitz, Germany, factory of Reinhold Schlegelmilch from 1914 until about 1945. The porcelain was sold decorated and undecorated. The Schlegelmilch families made porcelains marked in many ways. See also ES Germany, RS Poland, RS Prussia, RS Silesia, RS Suhl, and RS Tillowitz.

RS
Germany

Basket, Flower Border, Signed, 1926, 4 1/2 In. 28.00
Bowl, 10 1/8 x 3 1/8 In. 350.00
Bowl, Baroque Style, Flowers, Lavender Ribbon, Open Handle, 11 1/2 In. 600.00
Bowl, Bird, Clouds, Lake Trees, Mark, Prov Saxe, 7 1/2 x 1 1/4 In. 65.00
Bowl, Pink Roses, Stylized Geometric Gilt Border, 3 Handles, Marked, 10 1/2 In. 225.00
Bowl, Satin Finish, Scenic Water Lilies, 10 In. 145.00
Bowl, Trees & Boat, 3 Sections, Handles, Panels, Prov Saxe, 9 1/2 In. 125.00
Cake Plate, Apples, Handles, Signed, 9 3/4 In. 28.00

Cake Plate, Cotton Plant, Light Green, Gold Trim Border, 9 3/4 In. 125.00
Cake Plate, Silver Silhouette, Yellow Border, 2 Handles, 9 3/4 In. 200.00
Candlestick, Gold, Blue, Beading, Mark, Prov Saxe, 3 1/2 x 3 1/4 In., Pair 50.00
Candy Dish, 2 Women & Man With Flowers, Handle, Prov Saxe, 5 1/2 In. 125.00
Chocolate Pot, Yellow Roses 90.00
Cup & Saucer, Stylized Tree, Geometric Planter, Gold, Black, Art Deco 165.00
Pin Dish, Violets, Mark, Reinhold Schlegelmich, c.1910, 5 1/4 In. 35.00
Plate, Parrot, Handles, 1869-1917, Reinhold Schlegelmich, 10 In. 80.00
Tray, Dresser, Lily-Of-The-Valley Border, Multifloral Center, 12 In. 55.00
Tray, Forget-Me-Not, Crescent Moon Shape, Owl Cutout, 9 1/2 In. 175.00
Vase, Victorian Courting, Rose Garland, Red, Green Border, Gold Stencil, 5 In. 175.00

RS POLAND (German) is a mark used by the Reinhold Schlegelmilch
factory at Tillowitz from about 1946 to 1956. After 1956, the factory
made porcelain marked PT Poland. This is one of many of the RS
marks used. See also ES Germany, RS Germany, RS Prussia, RS
Silesia, RS Suhl, and RS Tillowitz.

Bowl, White Rose, Footed, Brown, 7 x 6 In. 175.00
Vase, Chinese Pheasant, Light Green, 2 Handles, 4 In. 275.00
Vase, Tiger Design, White, Gray, Yellow, 2 Handles, 4 In. 750.00

RS PRUSSIA appears in several marks used on porcelain before 1917.
Reinhold Schlegelmilch started his porcelain works in Suhl, Germany,
in 1869. See also ES Germany, RS Germany, RS Poland, RS Silesia,
RS Suhl, and RS Tillowitz.

Berry Set, Magenta Flower Buds, Green Ground, Gold Trim, Reticulated, 4 Piece 200.00
Biscuit Barrel, Cover, French Couple, 2 Handles, 8 1/2 In. 115.00
Bowl, Celadon Green, Flower Sprays, 5 Sections, Intricate Handle, 11 x 10 In. 250.00
Bowl, Centerpiece, Flowers, Green & White Iridescent, Open Handles, 11 1/2 In. 125.00
Bowl, Daffodils, Sky Blue Center, 3 Scalloped Sections, 3 Handles, 9 3/4 In. 175.00
Bowl, Dresden Flowers, Gold Trim & Tracery, Reticulated, 6 1/2 In. 175.00
Bowl, Flowers, Beaded, Scalloped Rim, Wreath Mark, 10 1/4 In. 425.00
Bowl, Flowers, Cream, Dark Aqua Panels, Molded, Shamrocks, Wreath Mark, 3 x 11 In. . 425.00
Bowl, Footed, Woman With Floral Wreath In Hair, Flowers, 11 1/2 x 3 In. 495.00
Bowl, Josephine & Marie Antoinette, Open Handle, Divided, 10 1/2 x 9 In. 500.00
Bowl, Josephine, Scalloped, 12 Circles, Flowers, Gold Frame, 11 In. 275.00
Bowl, Melon Eaters, Magenta Flowers, Gold, Green Ground, 10 1/2 In. 600.00
Bowl, Pink Roses, Gold Leaves, Satin, 11 In. 220.00
Bowl, Pink Roses, Green Leaves, Gilt, Beaded Scallop, Point Rim, Footed, 3 x 5 3/4 In. . . 75.00
Bowl, Roses, Pink, White, Purple Bands, Wreath Mark, 3 x 10 1/2 In. 400.00
Bowl, Snowdrops, Green Ground, 2 Sections, Handles, 10 In. 135.00
Bowl, White Satin, Swans, Red Mark, 11 In. 345.00
Bowl, White, Lavender, Flower Spray, Gold Trim, 10 1/2 In. 300.00
Bowl, Woman With Rose, Scalloped, Iridescent Green Ground, 9 1/4 In. 295.00
Bowl, Woman, Flowers In Hair, Turquoise & Gold Trim, 8 3/4 In. 175.00
Bread Tray, Roses, Flowers, 12 1/2 In. 225.00
Bread Tray, Woman With Flowers, Iridescent, Handles, 14 x 10 In. 300.00
Cake Plate, Flower Center, Blown-Out Floral Mold, Green Border, Gilt, 10 1/4 In. 150.00
Cake Plate, Flowers, 6-Panel Cream Ground, Magenta, Gilt, 10 1/2 In. 275.00
Cake Plate, Pink Lily Center, Mauve Ground, Molded Border, 10 1/4 In. 300.00
Cake Plate, Pink Poppies, Strawberry Mold, Green Border, 11 3/4 In. 175.00
Cake Plate, Rose & Daisy Center, Purple Molded Flower, Beaded Swag, Gilt, 10 1/4 In. . 125.00
Cake Plate, White Lily, Flowers, Fleur-De-Lis Panels, Scalloped Edge, 10 3/4 In. 150.00
Cake Set, Plates, Flowers, Purple, Orange, Yellow, Green, 10 1/4 & 7 In., 7 Piece 225.00
Candlestick, Orchids, Blue Bands, Gold Trim, Handle 125.00
Candy Dish, Dogwood Blossoms, Gold Tracery, Open Handles, 6 1/2 In. 125.00
Celery Dish, Flower Spray, Grapes & Leaves, Etched Gold Trim, 12 x 6 1/2 In. 250.00
Celery Dish, Pink & White Chrysanthemums, Blown-Out Mold, Gold Trim, 12 In. 275.00
Celery Tray, Flowers, Pink, White, Green Leaves, Blue, Cream, Gilt, 6 3/4 x 12 1/2 In. . . . 175.00
Celery Tray, Green Leaves, Berry Clusters, Gilt, Wreath Mark, 2 x 6 1/4 x 12 1/2 In. 75.00
Celery Tray, Medallions, Josephine, Napoleon, Recamier, Maria Louise, 12 In. 325.00
Chamberstick, Gold Flowers, Leaves, Designs, Blue Trim, 6 In. 165.00
Charger, Cartouches, Colonial Lovers, Roses, Gold Tracery Band, Open Handles, 11 In. . . 150.00

Charger, Portrait, Woman With Brown Hair, Signed, Hortense, 11 1/2 In. 275.00
Chocolate Pot, Rose Decoration, Scalloped Footed Base, 10 In. 315.00
Chocolate Set, Flowers, Pearlized Luster, Scalloped Base, 9-In. Pot, 7 Piece 1250.00
Clock, Flowers, White, Mauve, 8 1/2 In. 595.00
Condiment Set, Flowers, Tray, Toothpick Holder, Salt, Pepper, Mustard, 6 Piece 395.00
Condiment Set, Landscape, Mustard, Sat & Pepper, 3 Piece 250.00
Cracker Jar, Ivory Roses, Green, Beige, Gilt, Pedestal, Wreath Mark, 7 x 7 1/2 In. 500.00
Cracker Jar, Pink Roses, Green Leaves, Gilt, Pearl Finish, Footed, 3 x 5 3/4 In. 325.00
Cup & Saucer, 5 Maidens, Gold & Green 200.00
Cup & Saucer, Marie Antoinette & Mme. Recamier, Gold Trim 175.00
Cup & Saucer, Pedestal, Turquoise Beads, Flowers 400.00
Cup & Saucer, Red, Green, Mark, Beehive, 1 1/2 In. 200.00
Cuspidor, Woman's, Flowers, 2 Handles, 7 3/4 x 5 In. 425.00
Ewer, Gold Tracery Vines, Leaves, Flowers, 9 In. 150.00
Frame, Peach Poppies, Gold Trim, 6 3/4 x 9 1/2 In. 145.00
Mug, Mythological Scene, Gold Trim, Beehive Mark, 2 1/2 x 4 In. 125.00
Pin Tray, Blond Woman, Purple Trim, Gold Beads, 7 x 7 In. 325.00
Pitcher, Flowers, Cream, White, Green Ground, 4 1/2 In. 125.00
Pitcher, Milk, Swallow & Plants, Square Spout, 5 1/2 In. 125.00
Pitcher, Roses, White, Yellow, Peach, Gold Trim, 4 In. 75.00
Plate, Cavalier, Ladies, Magenta Band, Gold Tracery, 10 In. 150.00
Plate, Embossed Grapes, Leaves, Gold Trim, 2 Handles, 7 1/4 In.   250.00
Plate, Flower Mold, Decor, Cobalt Blue Open Handle, 1870, 9 1/2 In. 358.00
Plate, King Lear, Scalloped, Turquoise, Gold Beads, Signed, Walter Paget, 9 1/4 In. 350.00
Plate, Leaf Mold, Multicolored, Poppies Center, Open Handles, 10 1/2 In. 105.00
Plate, Portrait, Diana, Cherub, Birds, Garlands Of Roses, Gold Beading, 9 7/8 In. 225.00
Plate, Portrait, Women, Cherub, Flowers, Gold Beading & Trim, 9 In. 225.00
Plate, Roses, Peach Ground, 8 1/2 In. 125.00
Relish, Scalloped, Beaded Rim, Pink, Purple, Gilt, 4 1/4 x 9 1/2 In. 100.00
Sauceboat, Undertray, Pink Roses, Green, Yellow, Gold, Marked, Wreath, 3 x 6 1/2 In. . .   175.00
Sugar, Apple Blossoms, Blue, Gilt, Handles, Stem Base, 5 x 6 In.   200.00
Sugar, Roses, Satin 90.00
Sugar & Creamer, Courting Scene Cartouches, Gold Trim 200.00
Sugar & Creamer, Gold & Blue Raised Dots, Gold Handles & Finial 200.00
Sugar & Creamer, Indian Portraits, Bear, Spotted Horse, Child's 250.00
Sugar & Creamer, Pink, Creamer, Roses, Green, Gilt, Wreath Mark, 4 1/2 To 5 1/4 In. . . .   225.00
Tankard, Hand Painted, 7 1/2 In. 259.00
Tankard, Roses, Gold Tracery, Green, White Ground, 10 1/2 In. 425.00
Tea Set, Tea Pot, Sugar & Creamer, 6 & 5 & 4 3/4 In., 3 Piece 750.00
Tea Set, Tray, Pot, Dish, Cups, Saucers, 7 Piece 150.00
Toothbrush Holder, Forget-Me-Nots, Magenta Roses, Leaves, 5 Bays, 9 1/4 In. 175.00
Toothbrush Holder, Peach Fruit, Flowers, 3 Bays, 4 x 4 In. 125.00
Toothpick, Roses, Cream & Pink, 2 Handles 150.00
Tray, 2 Women & A Man With Flowers, Open Handle, 12 In. 500.00
Tray, Dresser, 3 Graces Dancing, Pink & Maroon Bands, Gold Tracery, 10 1/2 In. 225.00
Tray, Dresser, Basket, Orange, White Roses In Center, Gilt, 7 x 12 In. 125.00
Tray, Dresser, Violets, Celadon Green Twisted Ribbon Trim, 8 x 11 In. 225.00
Tray, Goddess Of The Sea, White, Magenta, Gold Beads, 2 Handles, 10 In. 250.00
Tray, Josephine In Medallion, Flowers, Dotted Geometrics, Oval, 11 x 8 In. 250.00
Tray, Leaf Shape, Landscape, 7 In. 125.00
Tray, Portrait, French Nobleman, Open Handles, 7 In. 155.00
Trinket Box, Cover, Mark, 3 3/4 x 2 In. 28.00
Vase, 5 Women, 2 Handles, Flowers, 7 In. 325.00
Vase, Cartouches, Pink & Purple Flowers, Purple Ribbon, 2 Handles, 6 In. 175.00
Vase, Cupid, 3 Women, Green Iridescent, Gold Beading, 5 In. 275.00
Vase, Portrait, Woman In Green Dress, Opalescent, Turquoise Beads, Gold Trim, 6 In. . . .   275.00
Vase, Portrait, Woman With Clematis In Hair, Gold Beads, Handles, 11 In. 1275.00
Vase, Portrait, Woman, Flowers In Hair, Green Ground, Bulbous, Gold Handles, 5 In. 250.00
Vase, Swallows On Branches, Flowers, 2 Mock Handles, 7 1/4 In. 250.00
Vase, Vase, Woman With Flowers, 2 Handles, Iridescent Green, 13 In. 575.00
Vase, White, Magenta Flowers, Green, 2 Handles, 7 1/4 In. 300.00
Vase, White, Pink Flowers, Green Ground, 7 x 7 In. 300.00
Vase, Woman With Doves, Gold Trim, Gold Dots, 11 In. 375.00

Vase, Woman With Doves, Iridescent, 3 Handles, Mark, ES Clermont, 7 1/2 In. 500.00

RS SILESIA appears on porcelain made at the Reinhold Schlegelmilch factory in Tillowitz, Germany, from the 1920s to the 1940s. The Schlegelmilch families made porcelains marked in many ways. See also ES Germany, RS Germany, RS Poland, RS Prussia, RS Suhl, and RS Tillowitz.

Biscuit Jar, Flowers, Light Blue, Stamped, 7 1/2 x 5 In.	95.00
Bowl, Footed, Willow Tree & Medieval Building, 6 1/4 In.	400.00
Cake Plate, White Wild Roses, Gold Rim, 8 1/2 In.	65.00
Cake Set, Flowers, Cream Ground, Gold Trim, 7 Piece	225.00
Celery Tray, Rose, 15 1/4 x 5 1/4 In.	150.00
Sugar & Creamer, Cover, 2 1/2 x 4 1/2 & 2 3/4 x 5 In.	75.00
Sugar & Creamer, Morning Glories, Blue Mark	25.00
Tea Set, Pedestal, Orange, Beige Flowers, Egg Shape, 3 Piece	375.00
Tray, Old Ivory, Roses, 6 1/4 In.	75.00

RS SUHL is a mark used by the Reinhold Schlegelmilch factory in Suhl, Germany, between 1900 and 1917. The Schlegelmilch families made porcelains in many places. See also ES Germany, RS Germany, RS Poland, RS Prussia, RS Silesia, and RS Tillowitz.

Bowl, Dice Throwers, Green, Mold 181, 10 In.	1000.00
Bowl, Victorian Courting, 3-Footed, Brown, Beehive Mark, 7 1/4 In.	125.00
Box, Lid, Night Watch, Square, Brown, 6 In.	175.00
Clock, Melon Eaters, Green, Red Border, Gold Stencil, 6 1/2 In.	575.00
Cup & Saucer, Hunt Scene, Yellow Border, Fox Hound	110.00
Inkwell, Lid, Tray, Well, Night Watch, Brown, 6 In.	275.00
Pin Dish, Lid, Classical Kauffman, Beehive Mark, 5 In.	225.00
Plate, Peace Bringing Plenty, Cobalt Blue Border, Gold Trim, Beehive Mark, 9 In.	1000.00
Tea Set, Night Watch, Brown, 4 Piece	150.00
Vase, Dice Throwers, Green, Mold No. 2, 7 In.	350.00
Vase, Melon Eaters, Bowling Pin Shape, Red Border, Green Beehive Mark, 9 In.	400.00
Vase, Melon Eaters, Dice Throwers, Bowling Pin Shape, Tiffany, Gold Trim, 9 In., Pair	1300.00
Vase, Melon Eaters, Green, Mold No. 2, 7 In.	375.00
Vase, Night Watch, 2 Handles, Brown, 14 1/2 In.	500.00
Vase, Night Watch, Bowling Pin Shape, Brown, 6 1/4 In., Pair	200.00
Vase, Night Watch, Brown, 5 1/2 In.	100.00
Vase, Night Watch, Brown, 7 In., Pair	275.00
Vase, Peace Bringing Plenty, Green, 6 1/2 In.	700.00
Vase, Renaissance Music, Brown, 12 In.	500.00
Vase, Shepherdess, 2 Handles, Green, Mold No. 3, 9 In.	1400.00

RS TILLOWITZ was marked on porcelain by the Reinhold Schlegelmilch factory at Tillowitz from the 1920s to the 1940s. Table services and ornamental pieces were made. See also ES Germany, RS Germany, RS Poland, RS Prussia, RS Silesia, and RS Suhl.

Cake Plate, White Roses, Gold Rim, Silesia, 8 1/2 In.	65.00
Celery Dish, Fuchsia, Cream & Peach, Beige Ground, 2 Open Handles, 10 1/2 In.	125.00
Cheese Server, Pink Wild Roses, Fire Gold Trim, Signed C. Ostmann	145.00
Chocolate Pot, Apple Blossoms, Gold Trim, 9 3/4 In.	225.00
Jam Jar, Cover, Underplate, Shrimp Roses & Buds, Gold Trim, 4-In. Jar	145.00
Plate, 2 Chinese Pheasants, Wide Gold Band, 8 1/4 In.	400.00
Plate, 2 Parrots, Flowers, Blue Ground, 3 Handles, 7 7/8 In.	185.00
Plate, 2 Parrots, Wide Gold Band, Blue Mark, 8 1/2 In.	350.00
Plate, Bird Of Paradise, 8 Sides, 8 In., 4 Piece	1400.00
Plate, Owl, Gold Trim, 9 1/2 x 5 In.	250.00
Plate, Portrait, Brown-Haired Maiden, Chocolate Ground, Gold Trim, Gold Crown, 8 In.	300.00
Powder Jar, Cover, Melon Eaters, Shadow Flowers, Gold Trim, 4 x 3 In.	350.00
Salt Set, Green & Gold Leaves, Fire Gold Trim, Open Handled Plate, 3 Piece	75.00
Sugar, Cover, Yellow Flowers, Green Leaves, Wide Gold Trim	25.00
Sugar & Creamer, Cover, Morning Glories	25.00
Syrup, Cover, Underplate, Lavender & White Flowers, Gold Trim	125.00
Vase, Chinese Pheasant, Brown, 5 1/4 In.	300.00

RUBINA is a glassware that shades from red to clear. It was first made by George Duncan and Sons of Pittsburgh, Pennsylvania, about 1885. This coloring was used on many types of glassware. The pressed glass patterns of Royal Ivy and Royal Oak are listed under Pressed Glass.

Bowl, Metal Frame, 9 In.	127.00
Creamer, Inverted Thumbprint, Applied Reeded Handle, 5 In.	88.00
Creamer, Inverted Thumbprint, Clear Applied Handle, 4 1/2 In.	80.00
Pitcher, Clear, Melon Ribbed, Shaded Clear To Rose, 8 1/2 In.	58.00
Pitcher, Hobnail, Satin Handle, 8 In.	364.00
Pitcher, Ribbed, Applied Fruit, Squared Handle, 5 1/2 In.	140.00
Rose Bowl, Clear Overshot, Applied Spattered Flowers, Leafy Stem, 3 1/2 In.	160.00
Shade, Ground, Rim, 5 1/2 In.	90.00
Tumbler, Mica Flakes, White Interior, 3 7/8 In.	66.00
Vase, Enameled, Raised Gold Spider Mum, Polished Pontil, 9 3/4 In.	145.00
Vase, Jack-In-The-Pulpit, Clear, Spiral Stem, 13 1/2 In.	150.00
Vase, Trumpet, Enameled Scroll, Flowers	195.00
Water Set, Enameled, Palm Trees, Signed, Moser, 5 Piece	330.00

RUBINA VERDE is a Victorian glassware that was shaded from red to green. It was first made by Hobbs, Brockunier and Company of Wheeling, West Virginia, about 1890.

Basket, Opalescent, Applied Lime Flower Feet, Twisted Thorn Handle, 11 1/4 In.	403.00
Bride's Basket, Vaseline Shaded To Pink, Enameled Flowers, c.1900, 12 1/2 In.	400.00
Finger Bowl, Inverted Thumbprint, 2 1/2 x 4 1/2 In.	80.00
Pitcher, Inverted Thumbprint, Enameled, Flowers, Applied Handle	85.00
Pitcher, Inverted Thumbprint, Polished Pontil, Victorian, 7 In.	345.00
Pitcher, Inverted Thumbprint, Rope Twist Handle, Square Mouth, 7 In.	600.00
Pitcher, Reeded Green Tinted Handle, Polished Pontil, Victorian, 8 3/4 In.	258.00
Salt, Rigaree, Ribbed, Scalloped Rim, Beaded Border, 2 1/2 x 5 In.	85.00
Vase, Flowers, Enameled, Applied Rope, Hobbs, Brockunier & Co., 8 1/4 In.	130.00
Vase, Jack-In-The-Pulpit, Swirl, Applied Feet, 7 1/2 In.	200.00
Vase, Opalescent, Applied Pink Flower, c.1900, 8 1/2 In.	175.00

RUDOLSTADT was a faience factory in the Thuringia region of Germany from 1720 to about 1791. In 1854, Ernst Bohne began working in the area. From about 1887 to 1918, the New York and Rudolstadt Pottery made decorated porcelain marked with the RW and crown familiar to collectors. This porcelain was imported by Lewis Straus and Sons of New York, which later became Nathan Straus and Sons. The word *Royal* was included in their import mark. Collectors often call it *Royal Rudolstadt*. Most pieces found today were made in the late nineteenth or early twentieth century. Additional pieces may be listed in the Kewpie category.

Biscuit Jar, Yellow Roses	39.00
Bowl, Rose, Gold Rim, Roses In Relief, Hand Painted, 9 1/2 x 2 1/4 In.	98.00
Bowl, Serving, White, Green & Gold Border, Schwarzburg, Mark, 1900s, 11 In.	35.00
Charger, Flowers, Open Handles, Gold Accents, 12 In.	310.00
Cookie Jar, Gilt Bow Lid Handle, Swirl Pattern, Flowers, c.1900, 6 3/4 x 5 1/4 In.	395.00
Dish, Shell, Flowers, Hand Painted, 5 1/4 x 5 In.	45.00
Ewer, Flowers, Gold Accents, Scroll Handle, Ruffled Edge Top, 1880s, 10 1/2 In.	220.00
Ewer, Jeweled Handle, Metal Center Band, Cream Ground, Flowers, 1904, 14 In.	175.00
Ewer, Oval, Cream Ground, Flowers, Gold Trim, 10 1/2 In.	195.00
Figurine, Chicken Eggcup, Kammer, Dresden, 2 1/2 In.	20.00
Figurine, Man, Woman, Pastel Colors, c.1900, 15 In., Pair	395.00
Figurine, Victorian Sailor Boy, Rudolf Kammer, Dresden, 3 1/2 In.	15.00
Garniture Set, Urn, Dancing Women, Classical Attire, c.1920, 5 Piece	290.00
Hair Receiver & Powder, Deep Blue, White Cornflower, Lilac Ground, 3 5/8 x 2 In.	200.00
Pitcher, Flow Blue, Gold Trim, Late 1800s, 12 In.	400.00
Plate, 18 Pink Roses, Green Trim, Gold Edge Design, c.1900, 6 1/8 In.	20.00
Plate, Dessert, Roses, Gold Band Design, 6 1/8 In., 4 Piece	80.00
Plate, Green Border, Yellow Roses, Hand Painted, E. Beyer, Early 1900s, 6 1/8 In.	20.00
Plate, Hand Painted, Signed, 10 1/2 In.	50.00

Plate, Peach, Orange Roses, Apples, Gold, Early 1900s, 8 3/8 In.   35.00
Plate, Roses, Gold Trim, 8 1/2 In. 65.00
Plate, Yellow Roses, Hand Painted, E. Beyer, 8 1/2 In. 38.00
Plate, Yellow, White Roses, Hand Painted, 8 5/8 In. 45.00
Relish, Triple Gold Edging, 13 x 5 3/4 In. 40.00
Vase, Arts & Crafts, Peacock Feather Glaze, Purple Body, 3 3/4 In. 120.00
Vase, Flowers, Beige Ground, Gold Handles, Narrow Neck, c.1900, 11 In. 210.00

RUGS have been used in the American home since the seventeenth century. The oriental rug of that time was often used on a table, not on the floor. Rag rugs, hooked rugs, and braided rugs were made by housewives from scraps of material.

Afghan, Flowers, Medallions, Blue, Red Ground, 1950s, 6 Ft. 8 In. x 5 Ft. 2 In. 520.00
Afshar, Diamond Medallions, Flowerhead Groups, Blue Field, 6 Ft. 4 In. x 4 Ft. 6 In. 529.00
Afshar, Flowers, Urn, Medallion, Red Ground, Vine Guard Border, 1950s, 7 x 5 Ft. 1380.00
Afshar Soumak, 5 Hooked Cross Medallions, Red, Blue, Ivory, Olive, 7 Ft. 5 In. x 5 Ft. . . 470.00
Agra, Allover, Herati, Green Field, Palmette & Vine Border, 1880s, 7 Ft. 4 In. x 5 Ft. 418.00
Art Deco, Daisies, Chrysanthemums, Paul Poiret, Wool, c.1930, 8 Ft. 9 In. x 5 Ft. 11 In. . . 5079.00
Arts & Crafts Style, Flowers, Celadon, Sage, Peach, Off-White, 12 Ft. x 8 Ft. 9 In. 880.00
Bagface, Baluchi, Octagonal Medallion, Star-In-Octagon, 2 Ft. 9 In. x 2 Ft. 7 In. 380.00
Bagface, Caucasian, Stylized Flowers, Red, Blue, Brown, Ivory, 20 x 15 In. 290.00
Bagface, Kurd, Midnight Blue Memling Gul, Stripe Border, c.1910, 1 Ft. 5 In. x 1 Ft. 118.00
Bagface, Kurd, Octagonal Memling Gul, Brown Field, Ivory Border, 2 Ft. x 1 Ft. 9 In. . . . 265.00
Bagshaish, Flowers, Animals, Geometric Border, Red, Blue, Rust, Brown, 5 x 6 Ft. 1955.00
Bahktiari, Flowers, Vases, Blue Field, Ivory Border, Early 20th Century, 13 x 6 Ft. 2235.00
Bakhtiari, Flowers In Field, Rosette, Vine Guard Border, 1950s, 11 Ft. 6 In. x 11 Ft. 1955.00
Bakhtiari, Rosette, Trellising Vine Field, Red Ground, Mid 20th Century, 11 x 8 Ft. 920.00
Bakhtiari, Salmon Spandrels, Blue, Orange Rust Ground, Ivory Border, 7 x 10 Ft. 440.00
Bakhtiari, Star Medallion, Vine Field, Flowers, Red Ground, 14 Ft. 9 In. x 10 Ft. 6 In. . . . 1035.00
Baluchi, 6 Serrated Medallions, Midnight Field, Multicolored S Border, 6 Ft. x 3 Ft. 2 In. . . 1175.00
Baluchi, 8 Columns, Meandering Vines, Blue, Red, Brown, Ivory Field, 4 Ft. 4 In. x 3 Ft. . 590.00
Baluchi, Concentric Serrated Diamond Medallion, Blues, Reds, 4 Ft. 2 In. x 3 Ft. 590.00
Baluchi, Octagonal Lattice, Hooked Squares, Curled Leaf Border, 5 Ft. 2 In. x 2 Ft. 10 In. 235.00
Belgian, Geometric, Blank, Red, Gray, Wool, Louis De Poorter, 5 Ft. 8 In. x 7 Ft. 6 In. . . . 470.00
Belouchistan, Blue Ground, Orange, Green Accents, Beige Border, 4 x 6 Ft. 330.00
Beshir, Circular Medallion, Red Star In Octagon Border, 15 Ft. 6 In. x 7 Ft. 9106.00
Bidjar, Allover Herati, Plum, Camel, Blue Field, Red Spandrels, 8 Ft. x 4 Ft. 2 In. 2235.00
Bidjar, Herati Design, Blue Field, Turtle Border, 10 Ft. 6 In. x 7 Ft. 8 In. 1765.00
Bidjar, Medallion Center, Blue Field, 13 Borders, Red, Ivory, Blue, 12 Ft. x 15 Ft. 4 In. . . 865.00
Bidjar, Red, Orange, White, Blue Ground, Early 20th Century, 5 Ft. 2 In. x 9 Ft. 3 In. 1265.00
Bidjar, Terra-Cotta Field, Meandering Vine Borders, Late 1800s, 9 Ft. 6 In. x 4 Ft. 3 In. . . 558.00
Bijar, Black Border, Blue Ground, Runner, 2 Ft. 6 In. x 10 Ft. 2 In. 248.00
Bokhara, Red Ground, White, Tan, Black, Runner, 2 Ft. 8 In. x 11 Ft. 6 In. 275.00
Caucasian, Column Of 9 Serrated Palmettes, Blues, Reds, Browns, 9 Ft. 2 In. x 3 Ft. 1116.00
Caucasian, Geometric Design, Multicolored, Salmon & Green Bands, Mat 750.00
Caucasian, Mat, Geometric Design, Multicolored, 24 x 24 In. 805.00
Caucasian, Medallions, Geometric Field, Red Ground, Rosette, c.1940, 6 Ft. x 4 Ft. 8 In. . 460.00
Caucasian, Prayer, Blue Medallion, Geometric Ivory & Salmon Border, 3 Ft. 9 In. x 5 Ft. . 3740.00
Caucasian, Repeating Diamond, Blue Field, Camel Border, 5 Ft. 10 In. x 3 Ft. 11 In. 518.00
Caucasian, Rosette, Medallions, Red Ground, c.1940, 6 Ft. 9 In. x 3 Ft. 4 In. 863.00
Caucasian, Salmon, Red, Brown & Ivory, Medallion, 4 Ft. x 7 Ft. 5 In. 660.00
Chinese, Blue, Flower, Flowers Border, Red, Blue, Green, Brown, Off-White, 9 x 12 Ft. . . . 1150.00
Chinese, Cobalt Blue, Birds, Flowers, Border, Nichols, c.1925, 11 Ft. 9 In. x 9 Ft. 1058.00
Chinese, Flower, Birds, Blue Field, Red, Ivory, Silk, Late 20th Century, 6 Ft. 1 In. x 9 Ft. . 865.00
Chinese, Flowers, Bamboo Stalks, Vines, Butterfly, Nichols, 13 Ft. 5 In. x 9 Ft. 8 In. 1645.00
Chinese, Flowers, Maroon Field, Red, Blue, Ivory, Gold, Silk, 20th Century, 6 x 9 Ft. 1035.00
Chinese, Ivory Field, Medallion, Indigo Border, Wildlife, Silk, Contemporary, 3 x 2 Ft. . . 896.00
Chinese, Ivory, Blue, Runner, c.1985, 2 Ft. 3 In. x 11 Ft. 8 In. 450.00
Chinese, Serpents, Trees, Birds, Shades Of Blue, Camel Ground, 5 Ft. x 7 Ft. 10 In. 440.00
Chinese, Trees, Vase, Animals, Angels, Maroon Ground, 20th Century, 5 Ft. 1 In. x 8 Ft. . 865.00
Daghestan, Rows Of Flowering Plants, Dark Red Rosette Border, 5 Ft. 2 In. x 3 Ft. 6 In. . 2115.00
Ersari, Blue Guls, Red Field, Early 20th Century, 5 Ft. 10 In. x 3 Ft. 6 In. 355.00
Ersari Torb, Geometric Designs, Red, Ivory, Blue, Multicolored Border, 6 Ft. x 1 Ft. 3 In. 823.00

Fereghan, Allover Flowers, Red, Rose, Blue, Blue Flowerhead Border, 10 Ft. 4 In. x 7 Ft.   14100.00
Fereghan-Sarouk, Oval Medallion, Midnight Blue Palmette Border, 12 Ft. x 8 Ft. 4 In. . . .   7345.00
Fereghan-Sarouk, Prayer Design, Blue Spandrels, Rosette Border 9 Ft. 8 In. x 7 Ft. 5 In. . 12925.00
Ferraghan, Blue Medallion, Ivory Diamond, Salmon Border, Trellis, 6 Ft. 10 In. x 3 Ft. . .   360.00
Grenfell, Dog Sled, Rescue, Brown Border, 38 x 61 1/2 In. 1410.00
Grenfell, Eskimo, Dogs, Houses, Striped Border, 14 x 18 In. 600.00
Grenfell, Gulls In Flight & Floating, Original Label, c.1920, 8 In. 550.00
Grenfell, Labrador Industries, Eskimo, Dog, Moon, Cabin, Burlap, 24 x 37 In. 1645.00
Grenfell, Polar Bear, Seal, On Icebergs, 17 1/2 x 22 1/2 In. 575.00
Grenfell, Puffin, Label, 12 x 9 1/2 In. 1265.00
Hamadan, Animal & Bird Medallions On Red, Blue Border, 4 Ft. x 6 Ft. 10 In. 440.00
Hamadan, Black, Blue, Salmon Medallions, Blue & Gray Border, 4 Ft. 6 In. x 6 Ft. 4 In. .   275.00
Hamadan, Blue Ground, Camel Center, Ivory & Blue Borders, 3 x 15 Ft. 550.00
Hamadan, Blue Medallions, Salmon Border, Runner, 3 Ft. 4 In. x 9 Ft. 7 In. 385.00
Hamadan, Blue Spandrels, Red Ground, Ivory Border, 4 Ft. 2 In. x 6 Ft. 7 In. 468.00
Hamadan, Dark Blue Spandrels, Salmon Ground, Slate Blue Border, 3 Ft. x 6 Ft. 5 In. . . .   220.00
Hamadan, Diamond Medallion, Terra-Cotta Field, Blue Border, 4 Ft. 6 In. x 3 Ft. 4 In. . .   355.00
Hamadan, Flower Field, Beige Ground, Palmette, Vine Guard Border, c.1940, 12 x 9 Ft. .   978.00
Hamadan, Herati, Blues, Camel Rose, Red, Ivory Boteh Border, Runner, 24 x 3 Ft. 2115.00
Hamadan, Ivory Field, Flowers, Runner, c.1950, 2 Ft. 5 In. x 6 Ft. 8 In. 450.00
Hamadan, Medallion, Beige Field, Flowers Border, Runner, 3 Ft. 6 In. x 6 Ft. 11 In. 275.00
Hamadan, Medallion, Geometric, Ivory Field, Flowers, 7 Ft. 10 In. x 16 Ft. 2200.00
Hamadan, Millefleur Field, Blue Ground, Vine Border, c.1950, 5 Ft. x 3 Ft. 6 In. 345.00
Hamadan, Palmettes, Large Leaves, Animals, Red Field, Border, 6 Ft. 2 In. x 3 Ft. 4 In. . .   440.00
Hamadan, Wool, Handmade, Red Field, Blue Diamond Center, c.1930, 3 Ft. 3 In. x 5 Ft. .   420.00
Heriz, Allover Diamonds, Rosettes, Leaves, Blues, Tans, Red, 12 Ft. 8 In. x 9 Ft. 8 In. . . .   3819.00
Heriz, Allover Rosettes, Abrash, Red Rosette Border, 3 Ft. 10 In. x 2 Ft. 8 In. 1410.00
Heriz, Blue, Medallion, Spandrels, Millefleur Field, c.1930, 18 Ft. 2 In. x 12 Ft. 7 In. 2990.00
Heriz, Burgundy Field, Ivory, Blue, Tan, Black, c.1950, 7 Ft. 7 In. x 9 Ft. 9 In. 1680.00
Heriz, Flowerhead Medallion, Palmette, Leaf, Red Field, Turtle Border, 14 Ft. x 9 Ft. 4 In.   5525.00
Heriz, Flowers, Ivory Ground, Red, Blue, Yellow, Early 20th Century, 7 Ft. 4 In. x 10 Ft. .   575.00
Heriz, Gabled Square Medallion, Flowering Vine, Turtle Borders, 12 Ft. x 8 Ft. 2 In. 4115.00
Heriz, Geometric, Red Field, Borders, Red, Blue, Brown, Off-White, 9 x 11 Ft. 690.00
Heriz, Herati Field, Ivory Ground, Medallion, Rosette & Vine Border, 17 Ft. 3 In. x 10 Ft.   750.00
Heriz, Ivory Spandrels, Red Ground, Black Border, 7 Ft. 6 In. x 10 Ft. 6 In. 880.00
Heriz, Ivory Spandrels, Red Ground, Dark Brown Border, 8 Ft. 8 In. x 11 Ft. 4 In. 825.00
Heriz, Lobed Circular Medallion, Red, Rust, Rose, Green, Blue Field, 10 Ft. x 6 Ft. 2 In. .   3410.00
Heriz, Medallion, Red Field, Ivory Spandrels, Turtle Border, 12 Ft. 5 In. x 9 Ft. 5 In. 3055.00
Heriz, Palmettes, Flowers, Leaves, Red, Rose, Gold, Ivory, Blue, 12 Ft. 8 In. x 9 Ft. 8 In. . .   1763.00
Heriz, Persian, Geometric Medallion, Rose Ground, 9 Ft. 2 In. x 12 Ft. 9 In. 1650.00
Heriz, Red Ground, Herati Field, Medallion, Vine Border, c.1960, 12 Ft. 2 In. x 9 Ft. 1 In.   2300.00
Heriz, Red, Green, Cream, Ivory Center Medallion, 9 Ft. 7 In. x 12 Ft. 8 In. 1610.00
Heriz, Red, Navy Blue, Ivory, Light Blue, c.1950, 9 Ft. 6 In. x 13 Ft. 3 In. 2800.00
Heriz, Star Medallions, White, Red, Brown, Persian, 7 Ft. 5 In. x 9 Ft. 10 In. 805.00
Hooked, 2 Deer, Rainbow Border, Dated 1912, Initials, IMS, 44 x 27 In. 340.00
Hooked, 2 Partridges, Landscape, Wool, Cotton, Wooden Frame, 33 1/2 x 46 3/4 In. 825.00
Hooked, 2 Roosters, Peck & Peck, Maude Pall, Cedarburg, Wisc., 1984, 21 x 13 In. 138.00
Hooked, 2-Masted Schooner, Blue, Green Border, 23 x 36 In. 280.00
Hooked, 3 Center Medallions, Stepped Blue & Gray Border, Gray Ground, 30 x 51 In. 550.00
Hooked, 3 Horses, Brown, Tan, Black, Earth Tone Ground, 29 x 40 In. 990.00
Hooked, Abstract Flowers, c.1930, 67 x 30 In. 1700.00
Hooked, Alternating Squares Of Stripes & Schoolhouses, Blue Ground, 30 x 45 In. 770.00
Hooked, Bats, Chinese Symbol, Butterflies, Urns, Flowers, Magenta Ground, 35 x 51 In. .   165.00
Hooked, Bird On Branch, Greek Key Border, 28 x 45 In. 275.00
Hooked, Bird Tree, Flowers, Multicolored, Black Ground, 34 x 48 In. 440.00
Hooked, Birds, Flowers, Figures On Horseback, Claire Murray, 63 x 88 In. 460.00
Hooked, Birds, On Flowerpot, Diamond Border, Wool, Cotton, Frame, 24 x 36 In. 1530.00
Hooked, Black Labradors, Picket Fence, Cloth Mounted, Early 20th Century, 23 x 43 In. . .   690.00
Hooked, Blue Swan, Water, Flower Border, Burlap Back, 38 x 20 1/2 In. 62.00
Hooked, Braided, Welcome, Black Border, Roses, 44 x 32 In. 230.00
Hooked, Broken Line, Brown Field, 55 x 77 In. 230.00
Hooked, Canadian Provincial Flags, Signed, Mrs. Agnes Kedhan, c.1969, Mat 1050.00
Hooked, Cat On Pillow, Brown Ground, Tassels, 26 1/2 x 42 In. 896.00

Hooked, Center Medallion, Flowers, Leaf Border, Mauve Ground, 127 x 92 In. 920.00
Hooked, Center Oval, Lakeside Cottage, Flower Border, c.1930, 28 x 49 In. 207.00
Hooked, Center Wheel, Multicolored Diamonds, 31 1/4 x 51 In. 248.00
Hooked, Central Chicken, Sprigs, Rosettes, Orange, Brown, Tan Ground, 36 x 52 In. 5500.00
Hooked, Clipper Ship, White Sails, Green Sea, Blue Sky, Black Border, 24 x 36 In. 413.00
Hooked, Coastal Landscape, Multicolored, Early 1900s, 31 1/2 x 53 In. 382.00
Hooked, Conestoga Wagon, 4-Horse Team, Landscape Ground, 22 1/2 x 42 In. 357.00
Hooked, Cornucopias, Flowers, Red Scrolls, Tan & Brown Ground, c.1880, 43 x 73 In. . . . 4113.00
Hooked, Cottage, Flower Border, 24 3/4 x 36 In. 55.00
Hooked, Courting Couple, Flower Border, 24 x 37 In. 288.00
Hooked, Dog, Multicolored, Striped, 32 x 40 In. 1100.00
Hooked, Dove, Heart, Wreath, Sunburst, Flowers, Circle Border, Runner, 22 x 68 In. 935.00
Hooked, Flowers & Leaves, Reds, Blues, Greens, Signed Mary, Dated 1874, 41 x 27 In. . . 85.00
Hooked, Flowers, Blossoms, Buds, Ocher Ground, Fan Border, Wool, 28 1/2 x 62 In. 355.00
Hooked, Flowers, Blue Ground, 34 x 62 In. 210.00
Hooked, Flowers, Blue, Pink & Yellow, Tan Ground, Black Border, 28 x 46 In. 138.00
Hooked, Flowers, Flower Blossoms, Border, Wool, 19th Century, 32 x 50 In. 470.00
Hooked, Flowers, Lined Squares, 54 x 71 In. 175.00
Hooked, Flowers, Ribbon Border, 28 x 37 1/2 In. 99.00
Hooked, Flowers, Urn, Black Ground, 29 x 51 In. 276.00
Hooked, Geometric Blocks, Multicolored Rows, Black Outline, 39 x 28 In. 340.00
Hooked, Geometric Medallion, Black, Teal, Red, White, Gray Border, 58 x 34 In. 220.00
Hooked, Geometric Stepped Blocks, Shades Of Red & Green, Brown Ground, 30 x 59 In. 110.00
Hooked, Geometric, Blocks, Multicolored Border, Wool, 67 1/2 x 36 1/2 In. 470.00
Hooked, Geometric, Blue, Black, Orange, Red, Green, 9 x 14 In., Pair 205.00
Hooked, Geometric, Flower Border, Earth Tones, Butterflies, Flowers, 53 x 72 In. 110.00
Hooked, Geometric, Multicolored Squares, Early 20th Century, 36 x 58 In. 70.00
Hooked, Geometric, Multicolored, Rainbow Border, 26 x 39 1/2 In. 140.00
Hooked, Geometric, Rows Of Squares, Triangles, Black Border Ends, 50 x 40 In. 180.00
Hooked, Geometric, Star, Tumbling Block, Wool, Cotton, Wooden Stretcher, 29 x 38 In. . 590.00
Hooked, Gold, Black, Red, Masonic Symbols, Cotton, 34 1/2 x 70 1/4 In. 1076.00
Hooked, Green & Orange Pinwheel, Multicolored Blocks, Blue Border, 42 x 37 In. 220.00
Hooked, Hearth, Red, Mauve Poppies, Green Leaves, Brown, Black Ground, 22 x 37 In. . 138.00
Hooked, Hearts & Stars, Multicolored Striped Field, Cotton Backing, 30 3/4 x 40 In. 2115.00
Hooked, Home Sweet Home, Early 20th Century, 34 x 20 In. 115.00
Hooked, Horses Facing, 2 Stars, Hearts, Multicolored, 1800, 24 x 39 1/2 In. 1075.00
Hooked, House, Covered Bridge, Black Border, Orange House, 45 x 26 In. 115.00
Hooked, House, Red Brick, Blue Door, Green Trees, Black, Burgundy Border, 21 x 33 In. 220.00
Hooked, House, Red, Green, White Ground, Scalloped Borders, 22 x 33 In. 330.00
Hooked, Ivory Border, Red Ground, Flowers, Runner, 42 x 156 In. 195.00
Hooked, Large Smiling Sheep, White & Beige, Black Legs, Green Ground, 30 x 40 In. . . . 1210.00
Hooked, Lion, Palm Tree, Pyramid, Crescent Moon, 33 x 58 In. 575.00
Hooked, Marbelized, Geometric Flowers, Maroon Borders, Runner, 65 x 27 In. 55.00
Hooked, Medallion, 2 Horses, Horseshoe, Black & Olive Field, 30 x 68 In. 275.00
Hooked, Mimosa, Yellow, Black, Blue, Red, Henri Matisse, Designer, 1951, 36 x 58 In. . . 1175.00
Hooked, Monument, Eagle On Top, Flags On Sides, Surrounded By Wreath, 32 x 27 In. . . 495.00
Hooked, Multicolored Lines, 5 Striped Borders, Cloth Binding, Maine, 53 1/2 x 67 In. . . . 220.00
Hooked, Oak Leaves, Scrolled Leaf Border, Gray, Green, Red, Pink, Black, 62 x 62 In. . . . 1175.00
Hooked, Old St. Nick, Holly Border, Early 20th Century, 19 1/2 x 29 1/2 In. 980.00
Hooked, Oval Center, Striped Borders, Crossbands, Multicolored, 27 x 41 In. 330.00
Hooked, Red Barn, House, Picket Fence, Patterned Border, Frame, 30 x 53 In. 353.00
Hooked, Red Horse, Striped Mane, Tail, Medallion, Brown & Gold, 24 1/2 x 41 In. 303.00
Hooked, Red Roses, White Ground, 32 x 45 In. 92.00
Hooked, Retriever Dog, c.1935, 30 x 58 In. 1100.00
Hooked, Robin On Branch, Dog, Scrolled Border, 25 x 38 1/2 In. 1293.00
Hooked, Roses, White Ground, Borders, Initialed, E.H.C., Sheared, 1896, 28 1/4 x 37 In. . 110.00
Hooked, Ship, Sailing High Seas, Blues, Greens, 2 Tone Gold Border, 36 x 38 In. 220.00
Hooked, Square-Rigged Sailing Ship, Gold Sails, Green Ship, High Seas, 36 x 38 In. 220.00
Hooked, USS Monitor, American Flag, Black Border, c.1865, 33 x 56 In. 7768.00
Hooked, Vase, Flowers, Black Ground, Late 19th Century, 43 x 35 In. 140.00
Hooked, Verse, Sailor, Black Border, Initials JEB, c.1946, 34 x 43 In. 4315.00
Hooked, Waldoboro Lion, Reclining, Palm Trees, Flowers, 30 x 62 1/2 In. 900.00
Hooked, Winter Cottages, Horses, Green, Black, Brown, Blue Border, 29 1/2 x 37 In. 448.00

Hooked, Winter Scene, House, Figures, Horse, Ox Cart, Black Border, 30 x 46 In. 295.00
Isfahan, Celadon Field, Indigo Medallion, Leaf Border, 3 Ft. 11 In. x 2 Ft. 3 In. 418.00
Isfahan, Ivory Ground, Palmette, Vine, Medallion, c.1950, 17 Ft. x 11 Ft. 5 In. 7475.00
Karabagh, Camel Spandrels, Blue Ground, Salmon Borders, 3 Ft. x 5 Ft. 8 In. 250.00
Karabagh, Multicolored Medallions, White Border, Blue Ground, 3 Ft. 7 In. x 6 Ft. 5 In. . 1760.00
Karabagh, Octagonal Medallions, Blue, Red, Gold, Green, Ivory Border, 7 Ft. x 4 Ft. 6 In. 1645.00
Karaja, Medallions, Flowers, Blue, Rose, Ivory, Green, Red, 6 Ft. 2 In. x 4 Ft. 8 In. 999.00
Karaja, Red Ground, Dark Brown Border, 3 Ft. 1 In. x 11 Ft. 330.00
Kashan, Blue Border, Blue Diamond Center, Red Ground, 9 Ft. 9 In. x 13 Ft. 7 In. 1955.00
Kashan, Central Flowers, Sprays, Rose Field, Vase Border, 1950s, 6 Ft. 8 In. x 4 Ft. 3 In. .. 6180.00
Kashan, Ivory Spandrels, Blue Border, Burgundy Ground, 9 Ft. 6 In. x 13 Ft. 1210.00
Kashan, Ivory Spandrels, Blue, Burgundy Ground, Multiple Borders, 8 Ft. x 11 Ft. 7 In. ... 770.00
Kashan, Medallion, Red Field, Iran, c.1985, 9 Ft. 8 In. x 12 Ft. 8 In. 1960.00
Kashan, Red, Allover Flowers, Flower Border, 12 x 18 Ft. 4600.00
Kazak, Blue Ground, Camel Border, Red Spandrels, Red Tulips, 5 Ft. 8 In. x 6 Ft. 7 In. .. 385.00
Kazak, Camel & Blue Star Medallions, Dark Blue Border, Runner, 2 Ft. 8 In. x 9 Ft. 7 In. 220.00
Kazak, Diamond Lattice, Hooked Diamonds, Blue, Rose, Green, Ivory, 8 Ft. 4 In. x 4 Ft. . 705.00
Kazak, Medallions, Blue & Green Field, Ivory Flowers, Geometric Borders, 4 x 6 Ft. 2090.00
Kazak, Prayer, Diamond Medallions, Navy Blue, Ivory, Gold, Trefoil Border, 4 x 3 Ft. ... 2940.00
Kazak, Square Medallions, Navy Blue, Ivory, Gold, Ivory Star Border, 6 Ft. 6 In. x 4 Ft. . 1880.00
Kerman, Allover Flowers, Vines, Ivory Field, Vine, Early 1900s, 12 Ft. 2 In. x 8 Ft. 8 In. . 840.00
Kerman, Beige Ground, Millefleur Field, Mid 20th Century, 18 Ft. x 11 Ft. 9 In. 3910.00
Kerman, Blue, Tan, Blue Spandrels, Burgundy Ground, Floral Border, 9 Ft. 6 In. x 13 In. . 1100.00
Kerman, Burgundy Field, Vines, Blue Flower Border, c.1950, 18 Ft. 6 In. x 13 Ft. 6 In. .. 10158.00
Kerman, Dark Blue, Light Blue, Green, Pink Floral, Red Field, 8 Ft. 6 In. x 11 Ft. 5 In. .. 345.00
Kerman, Ivory Field, Floral Sprays, Shades Of Blue, Rose, Green, 12 Ft. 5 In. x 9 Ft. 9 In. 1530.00
Kerman, Ivory Ground, Blue, Gold, Green, Late 20th Century, 6 Ft. 10 In. x 9 Ft. 1 In. ... 430.00
Kerman, Medallion, Ivory Field, Vase Border, Mid 20th Century, 13 Ft. 10 In. x 9 Ft. 8 In. 1795.00
Kerman, Millefleur Field, Flowers, Vine Border, 20th Century, 14 Ft. 10 In. x 8 Ft. 8 In. . 2990.00
Kerman, Oval Medallion, Ivory Ground, c.1950, 24 Ft. 3 In. x 13 Ft. 8 In. 2330.00
Kerman, Red Borderless Ground, Ivory, Wool, Late 20th Century, 8 Ft. 8 In. x 11 Ft. 9 In. 575.00
Khorasan, Spandrels, Wine Red Ground, Dark Blue Border, 9 Ft. 9 In. x 12 Ft. 8 In. 715.00
Kilim, 2 Diamond Medallions, Red, Green, Blue, Mauve, Ivory, 5 Ft. 6 In. x 7 Ft. 11 In. .. 259.00
Kilim, Anatolian, Wide Vertical Stripes, Star-In-Diamond Motifs, 11 Ft. 4 In. x 5 Ft. 7 In. . 470.00
Kilim, Blue, Geometric Field, Rosette Guard Border, Mid 20th Century, 9 Ft. 3 In. x 3 Ft. . 430.00
Kuba, Stepped Diamonds, Boteh In Square, Red, Rose, Ivory, Black, 5 Ft. 4 In. x 3 Ft. ... 765.00
Kurdish, Multicolored Diamonds, Triangles, Tan Ground, Ivory Border, 4 x 6 Ft. 605.00
Kurdish, Staggered Rows Of Boteh, Red Field, Ivory Border, 10 Ft. x 3 Ft. 3 In. 470.00
Ladik, Prayer, Red Ground, Yellow Border, Blue, 3 Ft. 1 In. x 6 Ft. 2 In. 1210.00
Lakai, Panel, 6 Rosette Medallions, Serrated Diamonds, Geometric Border, 2 x 1 Ft. 590.00
Laver Kerman, Birds Of Paradise, Flower Vase, Peacocks, 7 Ft. 1 In. x 4 Ft. 6 In. 5175.00
Laver Kerman, Medallion, Blue Field, Spandrels, Red Ground, c.1920, 7 Ft. x 4 Ft. 5 In. . 575.00
Laver Kerman, Tiger, Peacock, Flowers, Figural Ivory Border, 11 Ft. x 14 Ft. 3 In. 3850.00
Leghi, Stars, Red, Blue, Ivory, Gold, Green, Navy, Ivory Borders, 4 Ft. 10 In. x 3 Ft. 9 In. 1295.00
Lenkoran, Calyx Medallions, Rectangular Medallions, Browns, Ivory, 10 Ft. x 4 Ft. 4 In. . 705.00
Lillahan, Salmon Ground, Dark Blue Border, 4 Ft. 3 In. x 6 Ft. 9 In. 1265.00
Lillihan, Red Ground, Green, Blue, Ebony, Wool, Late 20th Century, 3 Ft. 3 In. x 5 Ft. 375.00
Lillihan, Stylized Flowers, Vines, Blue, Rose, Multiple Border, c.1925, 39 x 69 In. 690.00
Mahal, Dark Blue Field, Salmon, Olive Border, 11 Ft. 7 In. x 17 Ft. x 8 In. 4400.00
Mahal, Indented Diamonds, Snowflakes, Flower Heads, Turtle Border, 12 x 9 Ft. 8225.00
Mahal, Red Ground, Palmette, Trellising Vine Guard Border, c.1940, 13 x 8 Ft. 2530.00
Mahal Sarouk, Flowers, Salmon Ground, Midnight Blue Border, 4 Ft. 3 In. x 6 Ft. 8 In. .. 495.00
Malayer, Blue Field, Flowers, Floral Border, Red, Blues, Greens, 9 x 13 Ft. 1150.00
Malayer, Flower Heads, Vines, Red, Camel, Olive, Blue, Ivory, 4 Ft. 10 In. x 3 Ft. 6 In. .. 999.00
Malayer, Quatrefoil Center, Flowering Plants, Blue Border, 20th Century, 5 x 3 Ft. 440.00
Marasali, Staggered Rows Of Boteh, Blue, Red, Ivory, Tan, Green, Blue, 4 Ft. x 3 Ft. 6 In. 1175.00
Meshed, Beige, Blue Spandrels, Burgundy Ground, Blue Border, 9 x 12 Ft. 220.00
Meshed, Palmettes, Rosettes, Vines, Blues, Red, Brown, Red Field, 16 Ft. 4 In. x 11 Ft. .. 4465.00
Moghan, 4 Columns Of 7 Octagonal Memling Guls, Dragon Tooth Border, 8 x 5 Ft. 3878.00
Musel, Flowers, Pink, Rose, Brown On Blue Ground, 4 Ft. 6 In. x 6 Ft. 10 In. 230.00
Oriental, Tea Washed, Tufted, Poppies, Tan, Salmon, Green, Burgundy Ground, 5 x 8 Ft. . 110.00
Penny, Violet Ground, Red, White Circles, Yellow, Black Bars, Yellow Border, 43 x 33 In. 265.00
Persian, 5 Lobed Medallions, Blue & Red, Camel Field, Runner, 3 Ft. 8 In. x 11 Ft. 4 In. . 405.00

Persian, Archers On Horseback, Deer, Boars, Lions, Red Ground, Blue Border, 4 x 6 Ft. . . 470.00
Persian, Flowering Plant Rows, Red Field, Ivory Meander Border, 5 Ft. 8 In. x 4 Ft. 3 In. 353.00
Persian, Geometric, Red Field, Red, Blue, Green, Off-White, 2 Ft. 5 In. x 9 Ft. 7 In. 288.00
Persian, Herati, Red, Blue, Gold, Ivory, Blue Field, Red Border, Runner, 13 x 3 Ft. 650.00
Persian, Maroon Field, Ivory, Blue, Browns, Green, c.1980, 4 Ft. 11 In. x 8 Ft. 5 In. 896.00
Persian, Navy Blue Field, Urns, Animal Head Border, c.1985, 4 Ft. 9 In. x 7 Ft. 9 In. 1456.00
Persian, Northwest, 6 Bold Crosses, Figures, Red Field, 10 Ft. 4 In. x 3 Ft. 345.00
Persian, Tribal, Red, Ivory Medallions, Black Ground, Blue Border, 5 Ft. x 9 Ft. 11 In. . . 305.00
Pile, Geometric, Rust Spirals, Tan, Gray, 1950s, 13 Ft. 4 In. x 10 Ft. 8 In. 2056.00
Qashgai, Ivory Field, Red, Green, Blue, Wool, Late 20th Century, 8 Ft. x 10 Ft. 10 In. . . . 920.00
Qashqai, 3 Medallion, Red, Black, Ivory, 5 Ft. 10 In. x 9 Ft. 2 In. 670.00
Qashqai, Hooked Diamond Medallion, Overall Herati, Spandrels, 5 Ft. 9 In. x 3 Ft. 6 In. . 500.00
Qum, Birds, Deer, Corner Medallions, Ivory Ground, Blue Border, 5 x 7 Ft. 440.00
Qum, Four Seasons, Silk, 8 x 10 Ft. 1750.00
Rag, 3 Panels, Blue, Brown, Salmon, Yellow, 8 Ft. 6 In. x 11 Ft. 3 In. 195.00
Rag, Blue, Rainbow Stripes, Penna., Runner, 2 Ft. 10 In. x 10 Ft. 9 In. 116.00
Rag, Braided, Shape & Color Of Watermelon, c.1900, 4 Ft. 1 In. x 2 Ft. 1 In. 485.00
Rag, Brown, Tan, Blue, Orange Stripes, Runner, 3 Ft. 1 In. x 12 Ft. 11 In. 85.00
Runner, Arts & Crafts, Brown Velour, Needlework Corners, 4 Ft. 6 In. 230.00
Runner, Black, Brown, Flowers, Floral Border, Red, Brown, Green, Off-White, 3 x 11 Ft. . . 230.00
Rya, Free Form Abstract, Brown, Orange, 11 Ft. 5 In. x 8 Ft. 650.00
Rya, Sunburst Design, Brown, Orange, Yellow, Fringe, 8 Ft. 1 In. x 5 Ft. 7 In. 295.00
Saddlebags, Kurd, Sumak, Lattice, Hooked Diamonds, Blue Border, 3 Ft. 10 In. x 2 Ft. . . 265.00
Salian, Prayer, Diamond Medallion, Navy Blue, Wine Glass Border, 5 Ft. x 3 Ft. 6 In. . . . 1765.00
Samarkand, Rust Field, Gray Medallion, Vase, Vine Border, 9 Ft. 6 In. x 5 Ft. 3 In. 499.00
Saph, Prayer Niches, Vase Border, Silk, China, Contemporary, Runner, 8 Ft. x 2 Ft. 6 In. . 2868.00
Sarab, Red Ground, Blue, Brown, Green, Ivory, 20th Century, 3 Ft. 3 In. x 15 Ft. 6 In. . . . 635.00
Sarouk, Blue, Yellow, Green, Red Field, Mid 20th Century, 10 Ft. 2 In. x 14 Ft. 3 In. 750.00
Sarouk, Center Medallion, Allover Floral Sprays, Red, 11 Ft. 11 In. x 8 Ft. 7 In. 1265.00
Sarouk, Center Medallion, Palmette Border, Madder Field, 18 Ft. 11 In. x 11 Ft. 11 In. . . . 2988.00
Sarouk, Center Medallion, Rust Field, Celadon Spandrels, c.1900, 9 Ft. 9 In. x 8 Ft. 8 In. . 418.00
Sarouk, Central Flowers, Sprays, Crimson Field, Vase Border, c.1925, 11 Ft. 10 In. x 8 Ft. 705.00
Sarouk, Central Leaf Medallion, Sprays, Madder Field, Blue Border, 17 Ft. 7 In. x 12 Ft. . 2938.00
Sarouk, Central Rosette, Flowering Plants, Blue, Dark Red, Vine Border, 4 Ft. 8 In. x 3 Ft. 2470.00
Sarouk, Floral Sprays, Leafy Vines, Red, Blue, Tan, Dark Blue Field, 12 Ft. x 9 Ft. 9 In. . 2175.00
Sarouk, Ivory Palmette, Madder Field, Vine Border, 19 Ft. 4 In. x 9 Ft. 5 In. 1600.00
Sarouk, Overall Floral, Dark Blue, Green, Tan, Burgundy Field, 2 Ft. 2 In. x 4 Ft. 288.00
Sarouk, Persian, Burgundy Field, Allover Trees, Flowers, 6 Ft. 8 In. x 4 Ft. 3 In. 1150.00
Sarouk, Red, Blue, White, 13 Ft. 5 In. x 9 Ft. 10 In. 863.00
Sarouk, Rosette, Sprays, Crimson Field, Palmette, Vine Border, 11 Ft. 6 In. x 8 Ft. 8 In. . . 1554.00
Sarouk, Salmon Spandrels, Midnight Blue Ground, Black Border, 4 Ft. 3 In. x 6 Ft. 9 In. . 1430.00
Sarouk, Stylized Flower Design, Multicolored, 1 Ft. 10 In. x 2 Ft. 3 In. 518.00
Sennah, Red, Allover Geometric, Geometric Border, 4 Ft. 3 In. x 6 Ft. 3 In. 690.00
Seraband, Cartouche Of Vines, Stylized Borders, Red, Brown, 3 Ft. 9 In. x 9 Ft. 9 In. . . . 315.00
Seraband, Rows Of Boteh, Blues, Apricot, Blue Green, Red Field, 12 Ft. x 9 Ft. 4 In. 3175.00
Shiraz, Red Ground, Blue, Orange, Ivory, Late 20th Century, 3 Ft. 11 In. x 6 Ft. 7 In. 316.00
Shirvan, 3 Serrated Hexagonal Medallions, Wine Glass Border, 5 Ft. 4 In. x 3 Ft. 3 In. . . . 295.00
Shirvan, Lesghi Stars, Blue Field, Hexagon Border, Late 1800s, 3 Ft. 5 In. x 2 Ft. 5 In. . . . 645.00
Shirvan Kazak, 3 Medallions, Cream, Brown, c.1985, 8 Ft. 11 In. x 11 Ft. 6 In. 1960.00
Sivas, Rows Of Small Boteh, Burgundy Field, Rosette Border, 5 Ft. 10 In. x 3 Ft. 7 In. . . . 353.00
Soumak, 3 Medallions, Brick Red Field, 6 Ft. 10 In. x 9 Ft. 6 In. 1555.00
Soumak, Animal, Flower Field, Gold Ground, Early 20th Century, 5 Ft. 4 In. x 3 Ft. 6 In. 316.00
Soumak, Diamond Medallions, Blue, Black, Rose, Red, Maroon, Black, 9 Ft. x 8 Ft. 6 In. 2468.00
Sultanabad, Herati, Gray, Blue, Rose, Blue Turtle Border, 17 Ft. 6 In. x 10 Ft. 4 In. 8225.00
Tabriz, Allover Cypress & Willow Trees, Blue Ground, 8 Ft. 7 In. x 11 Ft. 7 In. 546.00
Tabriz, Allover Medallion & Flowers, Red Field, Reds, Blues, Greens, 4 Ft. x 7 Ft. 5 In. . 316.00
Tabriz, Blue, Peach & Blue Spandrels, Red Ground, Multiple Borders, 9 Ft. 6 In. x 12 Ft. 385.00
Tabriz, Central Flower Medallion, Madder Field, Vine Border, 5 Ft. 7 In. x 4 Ft. 3 In. 940.00
Tabriz, Flowers, Medallion, Spandrels, Red Ground, c.1950, 7 Ft. x 4 Ft. 9 In. 635.00
Tabriz, Flowers, Tan, Black, Gray, Iran, c.1985, 8 Ft. 6 In. x 12 Ft. 3640.00
Tabriz, Garden Scene, Silk, 11 Ft. 4 In x 15 Ft. 2300.00
Tabriz, Landscape, Birds, Deer, Beige Ground, c.1950, 10 Ft. 7 In. x 7 Ft. 7 In. 1095.00
Tabriz, Medium Blue Spandrels, Red Border, 8 x 11 Ft. 660.00

Tabriz, Millefleur Field, Stepped Medallion, Blue Ground, c.1950, 13 Ft. x 9 Ft. 10 In. . . .   345.00
Tabriz, Persian, Red Ground, Ivory Border, Flowers, Leaves, 10 Ft. 4 In. x 14 Ft. 8 In. . . .   1725.00
Tabriz, Rust, Blue Spandrels, Red Ground, Blue Border, 9 Ft. x 12 Ft. 6 In. 440.00
Tekke, Columns Of Guls, Blue, Apricot, Green, Rust Field, 5 Ft. 2 In. x 3 Ft. 6 In. 825.00
Tekke, Columns Of Guls, Blue, Ivory, Apricot, Green, Rust Field, 3 Ft. 10 In. x 3 Ft. 2 In.   646.00
Tekke Chuval, Octagonal Turret Guls, Rust Field, Late 19th Century, 4 Ft. x 2 Ft. 6 In. . . .   590.00
Tibetan, Geometric Patterns, Blue, Green, Orange, Off-White, 7 Ft. 10 In. x 10 Ft. 345.00
Turkish, Red Ground, Flowers, Star Medallion, Silk, c.1950, 3 Ft. 1 In. x 2 Ft. 175.00
Turkoman, Rosette Field, Red Ground, Vine Guard Border, c.1950, 9 Ft. 7 In. x 7 Ft. 865.00
Woven, 8 Seated Cats, Star Corners, Wool, 57 1/2 x 26 1/2 In. 2420.00
Woven, Flowers, Yellows, Fringe, Edward Fields, c.1967, 180 x 140 In. 470.00
Woven, Scrolls, Allover, Red, Beige, K.P.C. Debazel, 1912, 288 x 156 In. 5620.00
Woven, Tuschinsky Style, Purple, Blue, Green, Yellow, Black Ground, 1920s, 132 x 96 In.   5390.00
Yastik, Diamond Medallion, Leaves, Blue, Dark Red, Ivory Border, 3 Ft. 2 In. x 2 Ft. 380.00
Yomud, 9 Chuval Guls, Blue, Red, Ivory, Green, Multicolored Border, 4 Ft. x 2 Ft. 6 In. . .   940.00

RUMRILL Pottery was designed by George Rumrill of Little Rock, Arkansas. From 1933 to 1938, it was produced by the Red Wing Pottery of Red Wing, Minnesota. In 1938, production was transferred to the Shawnee Pottery in Zanesville, Ohio. It was moved again in December of 1938 to Florence Pottery Company in Mt. Gilead, Ohio, where Rumrill ware continued to be manufactured until the pottery burned in 1941. It was then produced by Gouda Ceramic Arts in South Zanesville until early 1943.

Figurine, Seal, Bowl On Nose, Glossy Black Glaze, 12 In. 250.00
Jug, Cover, Light Green, 8 In. 125.00
Jug, Lid, Indian, No. 50, Light Green, 8 In. 125.00
Jug, Matte Finish, Blue, Sponge Design, Crackled Ivory Interior, 6 x 7 1/2 In. 399.00
Jug, Tilted, Handle, Cork, Yellow, No. 50, 5 1/2 x 8 1/2 In. 125.00
Planter, Swan, Aqua, Green, 5 1/4 x 5 1/2 In. 40.00
Planter, Wishing Well, Mottled Green, Brown Glaze, 9 3/8 In. 63.00
Vase, Athenia Nudes, 11 1/8 x 6 In. 795.00
Vase, Athenia Nudes, Seafoam Green Outside, White Gloss Inside, 9 1/8 x 6 5/8 In. 695.00
Vase, Dutch Blue, Handles, c.1933, 8 3/4 x 5 In. 125.00
Vase, Grecian, Handles, Blue, Thick Matte Glaze, 9 1/2 In. 85.00
Vase, Grecian, Handles, No. 506, 7 1/4 In. 75.00
Vase, Green, Novelty, 4 1/4 In. 110.00
Vase, Light Blue, Semimatte Glaze, Handles, 6 1/2 In. 75.00
Vase, Opalescent Green, Light Matte, No. 504, 7 1/2 In. 60.00
Vase, Swan, 3 Handles, Green Glaze, 1930s, 7 1/2 x 4 1/2 In. 250.00
Vase, Swan, Creamy White, Lavender Mauve Shading, Crackling, 8 1/8 x 6 3/4 In. 155.00
Vase, Turquoise, Handle, Footed, Semimatte Glaze, White Lining, 7 In. 75.00
Vase, Turquoise, Matte Glaze, White Line, Handle, Footed, 7 In.   80.00
Vase, White, Green, Handles, Wide Flare Top, No. 638, 5 3/8 In.   100.00

RUSKIN is a British art pottery of the twentieth century. The Ruskin Pottery was started by William Howson Taylor, and his name was used as the mark until about 1899. The factory, at West Smethwick, Birmingham, England, stopped making new pieces in 1933 but continued to glaze and sell the remaining wares until 1935. The art pottery is noted for its exceptional glazes.

Vase, Barrel Shape, White, Blue, Rose Mottled Glaze, 5 1/2 x 3 3/4 In. 2350.00
Vase, Tapered, Silver Overlay Poppies, Red, Purple Mottled Ground, 9 1/4 x 3 3/4 In. 2350.00

RUSSEL WRIGHT designed dinnerwares in modern shapes for many companies. Iroquois China Company, Harker China Company, Steubenville Pottery, and Justin Tharaud and Sons made dishes marked *Russel Wright*. The Steubenville wares, first made in 1938, are the most common today. Wright was a designer of domestic and industrial wares, including furniture, aluminum, radios, interiors, and glassware. Dinnerwares and other pieces by Wright are listed here. For more information, see *Kovels' Depression Glass & Dinnerware Price List*.

American Modern, Bowl, Fruit, Lug, Coral, 5 1/2 In. . . . . .15.00 to 18.00

American Modern, Bowl, Vegetable, Coral 20.00
American Modern, Bowl, Vegetable, Divided, Granite Gray 105.00
American Modern, Celery Dish, Coral 23.00
American Modern, Chop Plate, Chartreuse 35.00
American Modern, Cup & Saucer, Coral 9.00
American Modern, Cup & Saucer, Granite Gray 13.00
American Modern, Cup, Cedar Green 10.00
American Modern, Cup, Coral ....7.00 to 8.00
American Modern, Flatware Set, John Hull Cutlery, 1951, 56 Piece 1645.00
American Modern, Flatware, Stainless Steel, 1951, 56 Piece 1645.00
American Modern, Goblet, Water, Smoke, Morgantown, 4 In. 30.00
American Modern, Pitcher, Water, Chartreuse 95.00
American Modern, Pitcher, Water, Granite Gray 95.00
American Modern, Plate, Chartreuse, 6 In. 5.00
American Modern, Plate, Coral, 6 In. ....2.50 to 5.00
American Modern, Plate, Coral, 8 In. 14.00
American Modern, Plate, Coral, 10 In. 12.00
American Modern, Plate, Granite Gray, 6 In. 5.00
American Modern, Plate, Granite Gray, 10 In. 12.00
American Modern, Platter, Coral, 13 x 8 3/4 In. 22.00
American Modern, Saucer, Coral 10.00
American Modern, Saucer, Granite Gray 3.00
American Modern, Soup, Dish, Lug, Coral ....15.00 to 16.00
American Modern, Sugar, Cover, Coral 18.00
Free-Form, Dish, Mottled Beige Exterior, Brown Interior, Bauer, 4 1/4 x 8 In. 294.00
Iroquois, Sugar & Creamer, Stacking, Parsley Green 45.00
Iroquois Casual, Bowl, Cereal, Avocado Yellow, 5 In. 10.00
Iroquois Casual, Bowl, Cereal, Ice Blue, 5 In. 11.00
Iroquois Casual, Bowl, Cereal, Lemon Yellow 11.00
Iroquois Casual, Bowl, Fruit, Avocado Yellow 12.00
Iroquois Casual, Bowl, Fruit, Ice Blue, 5 1/2 In. 11.00
Iroquois Casual, Bowl, Fruit, Lemon Yellow 13.00
Iroquois Casual, Bowl, Fruit, Parsley Green, 5 1/2 In. 12.00
Iroquois Casual, Bowl, Vegetable, Divided, Ice Blue, 10 In. 38.00
Iroquois Casual, Bowl, Vegetable, Round, Parsley Green, 8 In. 55.00
Iroquois Casual, Carafe, Nutmeg Brown 175.00
Iroquois Casual, Casserole, Cover, Divided, Avocado Yellow 50.00
Iroquois Casual, Casserole, Cover, Divided, Sugar White 75.00
Iroquois Casual, Casserole, Ice Blue, 8 In. 25.00
Iroquois Casual, Casserole, Open, Ice Blue, 8 In. 25.00
Iroquois Casual, Coffeepot, Nutmeg Brown 75.00
Iroquois Casual, Creamer, Stacking, Avocado Yellow 15.00
Iroquois Casual, Cup & Saucer, Avocado Yellow 10.00
Iroquois Casual, Cup & Saucer, Ice Blue 8.00
Iroquois Casual, Cup & Saucer, Lemon Yellow 20.00
Iroquois Casual, Cup, Ice Blue 6.00
Iroquois Casual, Plate, Avocado Yellow, 6 In. 5.00
Iroquois Casual, Plate, Avocado Yellow, 7 1/2 In. 8.00
Iroquois Casual, Plate, Avocado Yellow, 10 In. 10.00
Iroquois Casual, Plate, Ice Blue, 6 In. 4.00
Iroquois Casual, Plate, Ice Blue, 9 In. 12.00
Iroquois Casual, Plate, Parsley Green, 6 1/2 In. 6.00
Iroquois Casual, Plate, Parsley Green, 9 1/2 In. 10.00
Iroquois Casual, Platter, Avocado Yellow, 12 3/4 In. 25.00
Iroquois Casual, Platter, Avocado Yellow, 14 1/2 In. 35.00
Iroquois Casual, Platter, Ice Blue, 12 3/4 In. 30.00
Iroquois Casual, Platter, Ice Blue, 14 1/2 In. 30.00
Iroquois Casual, Platter, Pink Sherbet, 14 1/2 In. 38.00
Patio Set, White, Coral Steel, Samsonite, Shwayder Bros., c.1950, 3 Piece 764.00
Pitcher, Devonshire, Art Deco, 6 1/8 x 6 In. 50.00
Relish, Snail Form, Maple, Original Finish, Burned Signature, 11 1/2 In. 2300.00
White Clover, Cup & Saucer, Meadow Green, Harker 15.00
White Clover, Plate, Bread & Butter, Meadow Green, Harker 5.00

White Clover, Plate, Dinner, Meadow Green, Harker 15.00
White Clover, Platter, Barbecue, Coral, Harker, 11 In. 20.00

SABINO glass was made in the 1920s and 1930s in Paris, France. Founded by Marius-Ernest Sabino (1878–1961), the firm was noted for Art Deco lamps, vases, figurines, and animals in clear, colored, and opalescent glass. Production stopped during World War II but resumed in the 1960s with the manufacture of nude figurines and small opalescent glass animals. The new pieces are a slightly different color and can be recognized.

Sabino France

Figurine, 4 Birds On Branch, 1 Bird On Ground, White Opalescent, Signed, 7 1/2 In. 403.00
Vase, Art Deco Design, Satin, 12 In. 265.00

SALOPIAN ware was made by the Caughley factory of England during the eighteenth century. The early pieces were blue and white with some colored decorations. Another ware referred to as *Salopian* is a late nineteenth-century tableware decorated with color transfers.

Salopian

Bowl, Oriental Design, Flower Border, Polychrome Transfer, 7 7/8 In. 294.00
Jug, Milk, Chinese Figural Landscape, Flower Borders, 6 5/8 In. 410.00
Plate, Black Transfer, Deer, Flower Border, Pearlware, Scalloped Rim, 7 1/4 In. 330.00
Saucer, Stag, Blue, Green, Yellow, Orange, Enamel, 5 1/2 In. 250.00

SALT AND PEPPER SHAKERS in matched sets were first used in the nineteenth century. Collectors are primarily interested in figural examples made after World War I. *Huggers* are pairs of shakers that appear to embrace each other. Many salt and pepper shakers are listed in other categories and can be located through the index at the back of this book.

Bear, Hugger, Green, Van Tellingen, Regal China, 3 1/2 In. 14.00
Black Boy & Dog, Hugger 125.00
Black Chef & Mammy, 4 1/2 In. 125.00
Black Chef & Mammy, New Orleans, La., 4 In. 65.00
Bonzo, China, Cork, Japan, c.1930, 3 In. 15.00
Bonzo, Dog, I'm Salt, I'm Pep, Gold Trim, Japan, 3 In. 45.00
Bugs Bunny, Warner Bros., c.1960, 4 1/8 In. 50.00
Bunny, Yellow, Black Tail, Hugger 30.00
Cable Car, San Francisco, 2 x 2 3/4 In. 10.00
Carrot, Souvenir Of Florida's Silver Springs, Japan, 3 x 3/4 In. 10.00
Cat, Black, Polka Dot Tie, Shafford Type, 6 In. 40.00
Cat, Bow, Flowers On Base, Nodder 45.00
Cat, Dark Gray, 9 1/2 x 1 1/2 In. 14.00
Chinese Man, Woman, Playing Mandolin, Reading Book, 3 1/4 In. 14.00
Clown, Ceramic, White, China, c.1920, 2 1/2 In. 35.00
Conoco, Plastic, 2 3/4 In. 44.00
Currier & Ives, Blue, White, Royal China Co. 40.00
Daisy Mae & Dogpatch, U.S.A., Ceramic, c.1970, 3 1/2 In. 20.00
Deer, 8 1/4 In., Pair 14.00
Dog, Cat Up Tree, Japan, F & F, 6 1/4 In. 50.00
Dog & Fire Hydrant, 2 In. 10.00
Dog Playing Violin, Red, Brown Bisque 16.00
Dragon, Green, 3 In., 1 Piece 8.00
Dutch Boy & Girl, Hugger 45.00
Esso, Plastic, 2 3/4 In. 17.00
Fruit Basket, Grapes, F & F, 3 1/2 In. 25.00
Hun, Cluckers, Blue Ridge, 3 1/2 In., 1 Piece 70.00
Imari Fan, Arita, Japan, 2 x 3 1/4 In. 16.00
Kangaroo, F & F 20.00
Lamb, American Bisque, 3 1/4 In. 12.00
Lennie Lennox, Composition, Cork, Painted, c.1950, 4 1/2 In. 125.00
Little Owl, Metal Head Lid, Circular Base, 3 1/4 In. 130.00
Little Red Riding Hood, Hull, 3 1/4 In. 70.00
Mary, Yellow Lamb, Hugger 60.00
Mobil, Gas Pump, Logo, Red & White, 1955, 2 3/4 In. 605.00
Monk, 3 3/4 In. 16.00

To loosen a silver saltshaker lid that is stuck to the glass shaker, immerse the top in white vinegar. Soak overnight.

Salt & Pepper,
Refrigerator, Milk
Glass, G.E., 3 In.

Mrs. Gamp & Sam Weller, c.1930, 3 In.	12.00
Nipper, RCA Dog	25.00
Oriental Man & Woman, Playing Mandolin, Reading Book, 3 1/4 In.	14.00
Owl On Stump, 4 1/4 In.	12.00
Panda, Andy & Miranda, Ceramic, 1958, 3 7/8 In.	100.00
Peek-A-Boo, Red Dots, Regal, 5 1/2 In.	500.00
Pheasant, Rose, Gold, Grindley, 6 In.	20.00
Pink Flamingos, Bisque	20.00
Prayer Lady, Pink	25.00
Rabbit, Hugger, Yellow, Black Tails, Van Tellingen, Regal China	30.00
Refrigerator, Milk Glass, G.E., 3 In. *Illus*	80.00
Rocket & Astronaut, Enesco, Ceramic, 1950, 3 1/2 In.	45.00
Santa, Holding Bell, Candy Cane, 4 3/4 In.	12.00
Santa, Seated, 3 In.	12.00
Santa & Mrs. Claus Waving, 3 3/4 In.	14.00
Shell, Gas Pump, Logo, Yellow & Red, 2 3/4 In.	110.00
Shell, Gasoline, Premium, Plastic, 2 3/4 In.	77.00
Shmoo Couple, Boy, Girl, Glazed Ceramic, 3 1/2 In.	95.00
Shortcake, W.S. George, 3 1/2 In.	20.00
Smokquee, Chef, Black, China, Cork, c.1950, 3 3/4 In.	145.00
Spice Of Life, Milk Glass, Gemco, 3 1/2 In.	6.00
Stein, Metal Lid, Gainsborough Woman's Portrait	16.00
Sunshine, Baker, China, Japan, 2 1/2 In.	24.00
Telephone & Directory, 1 1/2 x 2 x 2 In.	5.00
Texaco, Sky Chief, Fire Chief, Plastic, 2 3/4 In.	17.00
Texaco Gas Pump, Plastic, Box, 1950s	65.00
Tower, Shamrock, Carrigal Pottery, Ireland	18.00
Trout, Souvenir Of Atlantic City, Decal, Japan, 5 In.	20.00
Wheelbarrow, Japan, 2 In.	12.00
Wine Bottle In Raffia, 3 1/2 In.	12.00
Woody Woodpecker, 3 1/4 In.	95.00
Yellow Ball, Mexican Decal, Red Stripe, Zephyr, Cronin	45.00

SALT GLAZE has a grayish white surface with a texture like an orange peel. It is a method of decoration that has been used since the eighteenth century. Salt-glazed pieces are still being made.

Dish, Leaf Shape, Molded, Applied Floret Feet, White, 3 1/2 In., Pair	176.00
Figurine, Foo Dog, White, Brown Slip Eyes & Tongue, 6 1/4 In.	1880.00
Jug, Cream, Ruins In Landscape, White, Polychrome Enamel, 2 7/8 In.	1645.00
Teapot, Oval, Blue Borders, Eagle, Clouds, Scalloped Edge, Hinged Lid, 5 1/2 In.	345.00
Teapot, Twig Finial, Ruins In Landscape, Globular, Crabstock Handle, 4 3/4 In.	1528.00

SAMPLERS were made in America from the early 1700s. The best examples were made from 1790 to 1840. Long, narrow samplers are usually older than square ones. Early samplers just had stitching or alphabets. The later examples had numerals, borders, and pictorial decorations. Those with mottoes are mid-Victorian. A revival of interest in the 1930s produced simpler samplers, usually with mottoes.

ABCDE

2 Boys, Seated, Dog, Elizabeth Kendall, Nov. 6, 1847, Flower Border, Frame, 24 In.	250.00
9 Crosses, Sarah Batchelor, October 14th 1805, Darning, 13 1/4 x 13 1/4 In.	1760.00

Adam & Eve, 10 Commandments, Vine Border, Frame, 19th Century, 24 x 22 In. 980.00
Alphabet, 2 Different Sizes, A. Schermerhorn, 8 Years Old, 1808, 16 1/2 x 11 In. 489.00
Alphabet, Adeline Gillet April 8th 1826, Fair Haven, On Linen, 8 1/2 x 9 In. 495.00
Alphabet, Arabic, Urn, Flowers, Candelabra, Candlesticks, 1864, Frame, 14 3/4 x 14 In. . . 490.00
Alphabet, Arrows, Buildings, Marie Palaquier, 12 3/8 x 15 1/2 In. 550.00
Alphabet, Birds, Flower Baskets, Fruit, Verse, 3/4 Vine Border, 22 x 16 1/2 In. 635.00
Alphabet, Children's Initials, Bible Verse, Adam & Eve, c.1794, 13 3/8 x 13 3/8 In. 646.00
Alphabet, Ephrata, Birds, Flowers, Vine Border, c.1838, 18 1/2 x 18 1/2 In. 770.00
Alphabet, Family Record, Cobb Family, Olive Cobb, Portland, 1809, Frame, 12 x 12 In. . . 835.00
Alphabet, Flower Basket, Verse, Flower Border, Cross-Stitch, 1823, Frame, 18 x 19 In. . . 525.00
Alphabet, Flowers, Mary Jane Hill, Frame, 16 1/2 x 17 1/2 In. 805.00
Alphabet, Flowers, Numbers, Charlotte B., 1837, 17 x 16 In. 145.00
Alphabet, Fruit, Trees, Animals, Marion Brackenridge, Aged 10, 1823, 17 1/2 x 12 In. . . 430.00
Alphabet, House, Birds, Strawberry, Vine, Margaret E. Wilson, Frame, 22 1/2 x 22 In. . . . 2090.00
Alphabet, Jesus Verse, Betsey Sears, Plymouth, Mass., 1829, 17 1/2 x 14 1/2 In. 8400.00
Alphabet, Landscape, Church, Soldier, Animals, c.1826, Frame, 17 1/2 x 20 In. 1100.00
Alphabet, Mary Ann Lightoaps Sampler Worked In Her 14th Year, Frame, 14 x 9 In. 130.00
Alphabet, Numbers, Amelia Grant, 1827, 17 x 9 1/2 In. 288.00
Alphabet, Numbers, Christinah Haner, 1813, Cross-Stitch, Linen, 16 1/2 x 18 1/2 In. . . . 495.00
Alphabet, Numbers, Flower, Rosettes, Mary Megal, 1801, 18 3/8 x 16 1/4 In. 275.00
Alphabet, Numbers, Flowers, Birds, Margaret, 1840, 17 x 7 In. 200.00
Alphabet, Numbers, Flowers, Geometric, Silk, On Linen, c.1746, 10 x 19 In. 10158.00
Alphabet, Numbers, Flowers, Verse, Rosamond Grand Born, 1781, Frame, 15 x 9 1/2 In. . 518.00
Alphabet, Numbers, Flowers, Vines, Margaretta Shrom, Age 8, 1827, 10 1/2 In. 445.00
Alphabet, Numbers, Poetry, Mary Whitton, England, 1741, Linen, 13 3/4 x 8 In. 500.00
Alphabet, Phebe Edwards, Early 19th Century, Frame, 10 1/2 x 12 In. 115.00
Alphabet, Pine Trees, Landscape, Eliza Shipton, 1807, Maple Frame, 21 x 17 In. 1155.00
Alphabet, Plants, Animals, Strawberry Border, Ann Parnell, 1799, Frame, 19 x 15 In. . . . 2475.00
Alphabet, Psalm 134, Multicolored, Susanna Pace, Oct. 14, 1737, 4 x 14 In. 1450.00
Alphabet, Silhouette Of Girl's Head, Mary Alice Su, 17 x 7 In. 230.00
Alphabet, Trees, Fruit, Building, American, 1777, 23 x 12 1/2 In. 1195.00
Alphabet, Verse, Clarissa Mellen, Aged 11 Yrs., 1824, 16 5/8 x 16 3/8 In. 2233.00
Alphabet, Verse, Deer, Cherubs, Flowers, Elizabeth Millard, Aged 12, 1816, 13 x 17 In. . . 990.00
Alphabet, Verse, Flower Basket, Elizabeth Folder, 11 Yrs, 1807, Linen, 20 1/2 x 17 In. . . . 1430.00
Alphabet, Verse, Flowers, Birds, Hannah Greaves, 1789, Silk, Frame, 21 x 16 In. 730.00
Alphabet, Verse, Flowers, Isabella Hill, March 31, 1834, Frame, 17 x 16 1/2 In. 1150.00
Alphabet, Verse, Flowers, Vine, Rebecca H. Bowers, 1824, Silk, Frame, 19 x 19 1/2 In. . . 1870.00
Alphabet, Verse, House, Trees, Sally Hunt, Age 13, 1795, Curly Maple Frame, 15 x 11 In. . 1870.00
Alphabet, Verse, Mahala S. Hamblen, Aged 11 Years, Wareham, c.1836, 21 x 17 5/8 In. . . 8815.00
Alphabet, Verse, Mary P. French, Aged 11, Multicolored, 17 x 16 In. 4600.00
Alphabet, Verse, Numbers, Elizabeth Norris, 1730, Curly Maple Frame, 21 x 14 In. 1760.00
Alphabet, Verse, Vines, Elizabeth M. Mortimer, May 6th 1852, 17 x 17 In. 115.00
Alphabet & Flowers, Dated 1908, Green, Brown, Blue, Linen, 16 1/2 x 10 1/2 In. 575.00
Alphabet & Numbers, Green, Sarah Ann Gresson, On Linen, 8 x 8 In. 115.00
Alphabet & Numbers, Hearts, Stags, Urns, Flowers, BK, 1856, 12 x 10 1/4 In. 360.00
Alphabet & Numbers, Lavender, Blue, Brown, 5 1/2 x 5 In. 360.00
Alphabet & Numbers, Verse, Abigail H. Cheney, Aged 15, June 8, 1830, 13 x 15 In. 315.00
Alphabet & Verse, House, Trees, Flower Border, M.C. Curtz, 1847, 19 1/2 x 16 3/4 In. . . . 3740.00
Alphabet Panels, Geometric Border, Silk, On Linen, c.1830, 8 x 7 In. 295.00
Alphabets, House, Shepherdess, Mary C. Root Royalton, Born 1822, 18 x 20 In. 525.00
Alphabets, Lord's Prayer, Abigail Wilson, 1780, 8 Various Stitches, Frame, 15 x 11 In. . . . 1980.00
Alphabets, Numbers, House, Trees, Flowers, American, Frame, c.1810, 11 x 14 1/2 In. 690.00
Alphabets, Numbers, Verse, Nancy Ann B. Ditto, Strawberry Border, 20 1/2 x 19 1/2 In. . . 495.00
Alphabets, Verse, Made By Rebekah Sage, 10th Year Of Her Life, A.D. 1808, 16 x 14 In. . . 260.00
Alphabets, Verse, Parthenia Browne Davis, Aged 10, Homespun, c.1814, 12 x 16 In. 635.00
Basket, House, Birds, Trees, Insects, Vines, Wrought By Maria Worts, 1838, 18 x 17 In. . . 2595.00
Birds, Butterflies, Windmill, Flower Border, Mary Ann Jones, Linen, 1826, 15 x 18 In. . . 990.00
Birds, Flowers, Initials, E.W., Penn., c.1834, Mennonite, 14 1/4 x 10 1/2 In. 10755.00
Birds, Tulips, Hearts, Crown, Deer, H. H. Chrismanis, 1841, Cross-Stitch, 21 x 20 In. . . . 550.00
Birds On Branch, Deer, Flowers, 16 1/2 x 13 3/4 In. 158.00
Building, Angels, Man, Woman, M. Winterbottom, 1842, Silk, Wool, Linen, 16 x 14 In. . . 2630.00
Buildings, Bird, Flowers, Mary Jane Hendrick, 11 Years, 1835, 20 x 21 In. 2600.00

Crown, Flowers, Birds, Verse, Susan Caroline Seeley, American, 1835, 17 x 17 In. 2070.00
Dogs, Trees, Baskets, Sarah Gove, Lincoln, Mass., August 16, 1741, 14 x 13 In. 980.00
Family Record, Cleaver Family, Flower, House, Grapevine, Willow, 1800s, 16 x 14 In. ... 800.00
Family Register, French Family, 1778 To 1823, P. Payson, 1934, 9 1/2 x 7 1/4 In. 575.00
Flowers, 2 Stars, 8-Point, Signed, Deborah H. Yorgy, Frame, 1851, 18 x 17 In. 154.00
Flowers, Birds, Flower Border, Linen, Martha Wright, 23 x 20 In. 770.00
Flowers, Leaf, Cardinal, Parrot, Butterfly, 1835, Frame, 9 1/4 x 8 3/4 In. 1870.00
Geometric Bands, Trees, Alphabets, C. Quigley, Aged 11, Linen, c.1810, 18 1/4 x 19 In. . . 1240.00
House, Adam & Eve, Birds, Animals, Hannah Hargrove Work Aged 13 1833, 16 x 14 In. . . 5500.00
Manor House, Sheep, Vines, Elizabeth Smith, 1836, Frame, 14 x 13 In. 520.00
Map, United States, State Flowers, Dated 1938, Frame, 25 x 35 In. 430.00
Potted Flowers, Birds, Trees, Caroline Galbreath, c.1835, 17 x 17 In. 1410.00
Prayer, Flower Border, Sarah Pain, 11 Years, March, 1754, 15 1/2 x 11 In. 1320.00
Sarah Batt, Memorial, The Absent Yet Beloved, Linen, 1821, 12 x 12 In. 2310.00
Schoolgirl, Brown, Green, Gold, Red, England, 1847, Linen, 13 1/4 x 7 1/2 In. 170.00
Seek God, Ann Tyers, Aged 11, 1822, Silk, Linen, Frame, 18 x 12 3/4 In. 7200.00
Tell Me Ye Knowing & Discerning Few, Isabella Behham, 1799, Age 9 .... 870.00
Tree Of Life, Funeral Thought, Flowers, Elizabeth Billing Work, c.1808, 18 1/2 x 14 In. ... 1100.00
Verse, Adam & Eve, Apple Tree, Serpent, Mary Chandler, 1809, 12 x 16 1/2 In. 1035.00
Verse, Adam & Eve, Elizabeth Ann Hollow, 1838, 17 5/8 x 13 In. 5280.00
Verse, Adam & Eve, Elizabeth Page, 1804, Cross-Stitch, Frame, 19 x 24 In. 2090.00
Verse, Adam & Eve, Henriette Maria Love, Silk, On Linen, 1792, 16 x 12 In. 765.00
Verse, Alice Drinkwater's Work, 1827, Linen, Wool Petit Point Border, 21 x 20 In. 770.00
Verse, Angels, Shepherd, Shepherdess, Maria H. Rison, Linen, Frame, 23 1/2 x 17 In. ... 440.00
Verse, Bird, Fruit Tree & Basket, Esther Beaulah, Aged 11 Years, 1842, Frame, 26 x 24 In. 990.00
Verse, Building On Hill, Flowers, Birds, Margaret, 1820, 18 x 18 In. 440.00
Verse, Building, Bird, Tree, Abigail Woolman, 18 1/2 x 17 1/4 In. 605.00
Verse, Butterfly, Birds, Flowers, Dog, Mary Jane Hendrick, 9 Years, 14 3/4 x 15 1/4 In. ... 2300.00
Verse, Church, Landscape, Vining Flowers, Mary Ann Oram, Frame, 18 x 20 In. 1045.00
Verse, Corner Flowers, Maidencreek, 1804, Blue, Ivory, Gold Thread, 14 x 13 1/4 In. 2970.00
Verse, Cross, Ann Johnson, 1729, Satin Stitches, Gilt Frame, 23 1/2 x 14 In. 1650.00
Verse, Emblem Of Innocence, Quaker, Homespun Linen, Frame, c.1809, 19 x 23 In. 2310.00
Verse, Figures, Animals, Flowers, Mary Ann Morris, Age 10, 1793, 16 x 10 In. 375.00
Verse, Figures, House, Sarah Taylor, 1802, Silk, On Linen, 24 x 20 In. 16730.00
Verse, Flower Border, Landscape, Emma Bayles, Aged 10 Years, 1833, 27 x 23 In. 3300.00
Verse, Flower, Geometric Borders, Eliz Berg, 1735, 16 1/2 x 10 1/2 In. 1645.00
Verse, Flowers, Geometric Border, Susan Jones, Aged 14 Years, Frame, 17 x 14 In. 315.00
Verse, House, Flower Border, Caroline Burdett, Age 11 Years, 1831, Frame, 18 x 16 In. ... 1950.00
Verse, On Virtue, Brick House, Eliza Henrson, c.1806, Silk, On Linen, 19 1/2 x 15 In. 1045.00
Verse, Shepherd & Shepherdess, Vines, Ship, Trees, Animals, Frame, 16 x 8 In. 2585.00
Verse, Shepherd, Sheep, Dog, Mary Ann Edmonds, Age 8, Frame, 14 1/2 x 12 In. 750.00
Verse, Spies Of Canaan, Strawberry Border, Sary Burditt, 1755, Silk, 21 x 13 In. 1430.00
Verse, Tis To Sovereign Grace I Owe, Born On British Ground, c.1766, 13 x 11 In. 1540.00
Verse, Unusual Lettering, Jane Ogle, Linen, England, Frame, 1700, 21 x 15 In. 1540.00
Verse, Vine Border, House, Elizabeth Eland, Age 12, Silk, On Silk, c.1849, 14 x 13 In. ... 956.00

SAMSON and Company, a French firm specializing in the reproduction
of collectible wares of many countries and periods, was founded in
Paris in the early nineteenth century. Chelsea, Meissen, Famille Verte,
and Chinese Export porcelain are some of the wares that have been
reproduced by the company. The firm uses a variety of marks on the
reproductions. It is still in operation.

Bowl Set, Armorial, Flowers, Coat Of Arms, 7 5/8 In., 3 Piece 66.00
Figurine, Boy Wearing Fig Leaf Hat, 20th Century, 8 1/2 In. 590.00
Figurine, Couple, Drum, Scroll Foot Base, Gold Anchor Mark, c.1890, 9 1/2 In., Pair 550.00
Figurine, Couple, Trellis, Floral Vines, Scroll Foot Base, c.1890, 8 1/2 In., Pair 575.00
Jar, Cover, Gilt Metal Mounted, Famille Verte, 12 In., Pair 3286.00
Plate, Armorial, Blue, Mauve, Gilt, c.1900, 10 In. 115.00
Plate, Heraldic Design, Late 19th Century, 9 1/2 In. 260.00
Plate Set, Reticulated, Center Crest, Flowers, Enameling, 9 1/4 In., 12 Piece 1495.00
Urn, Classical Figures, Rolled Rim, Scroll Handles, Marble Plinth, 25 In., Pair 635.00
Urn, Cover, Armorial, Polychrome, Famille Rose, Late 19th Century, 14 1/4 In., Pair 920.00

SANDWICH GLASS is any of the myriad types of glass made by the Boston and Sandwich Glass Works in Sandwich, Massachusetts, between 1825 and 1888. It is often very difficult to be sure whether a piece was really made at the Sandwich factory because so many types were made there and similar pieces were made at other glass factories. Additional pieces may be listed under Pressed Glass and in related categories.

Basket, Yellow, Tomato Interior, Clear Ruffled Edge, Thorn Handle, Leaf Feet, 10 In. . . .	335.00
Bottle, 24 Ribs, Twisted, Amber, Globular, 1810-1830, 8 In.	1175.00
Bottle, 24 Spiral Ribs, Collared Lip, Globular, c.1830, 9 In.	1175.00
Bottle, Cologne, Horn Of Plenty, 3-Piece Mold, 1849-1862, 10 3/4 In.	170.00
Bowl, Cover, Loop Base, 1830-1840, 11 x 6 1/4 In.	1000.00
Bowl, Diamond Diaper, 3-Piece Mold, 2 x 5 In.	175.00
Bowl, Diamond Diaper, Sunburst In Square, 3-Piece Mold, 1825-1835, 2 x 7 In.	145.00
Bowl, Log Cabin, Stippled Background, Lacy, c.1840, 6 1/4 In. . . . . 165.00 to 205.00
Bowl, Vegetable, Peacock Eye & Strawberry, Lacy, 1835-1850, 10 1/4 x 7 1/2 In.	1115.00
Bowl, Waffle Sunburst, Blue Tint, Folded Rim, 3-Piece Mold, 1825-1835, 3 3/4 x 6 In. . . .	825.00
Candlestick, 6-Sided Socket Loop, 7 In.	90.00
Candlestick, 6-Sided Socket, Amethyst, 9 1/8 In.	410.00
Candlestick, Acanthus Leaf, Blue & White, 6-Sided Base, 1940-1965, 7 1/2 In.	1175.00
Candlestick, Acanthus Leaf, Blue, White, 6-Sided Base, 1840-1865, 9 1/2 In., Pair	1000.00
Candlestick, Acanthus Leaf, Clambroth, Blue, 6-Sided Base, 1840-1865, 11 In., Pair	1530.00
Candlestick, Acanthus Leaf, Translucent Starch Blue, Wafer Construction, 9 1/4 In.	770.00
Candlestick, Amethyst, Petal, 7 1/2 In., Pair	460.00
Candlestick, Canary, Loop Design, Petal Socket, Round Base, 7 In., Pair	385.00
Candlestick, Canary, Paneled Stem, Socket, Round Base, 7 In., Pair	415.00
Candlestick, Clambroth, Loop Pattern, Petal Socket, Circle Base, 7 In., Pair	353.00
Candlestick, Clambroth, Petal Socket, Hexagonal Base, 7 3/8 In., Pair	235.00
Candlestick, Column, Clambroth, Blue 6-Sided Petal Socket, 9 In., Pair	715.00
Candlestick, Column, Petal Socket, Clambroth Top, Translucent Blue Stem, 9 1/4 In.	415.00
Candlestick, Dolphin, Blue & White, 1845-1870, 9 3/4 In.	1530.00
Candlestick, Dolphin, Blue, 1845-1870, 10 1/4 x 3 3/8 In., Pair	10000.00
Candlestick, Dolphin, Dolphin & Shell Socket, Square Stepped Base, 9 1/2 In.	1320.00
Candlestick, Dolphin, Petal Socket, Stepped Base, Blue, 1845-1870, 10 1/4 In.	2940.00
Candlestick, Dolphin, Petal Socket, Stepped Base, Clambroth, 10 1/4 In., Pair	825.00
Candlestick, Free Blown, Knopped Standard, Stepped Base, 1835-45, 10 x 3 In., Pair	645.00
Candlestick, Paneled Stem, Stepped Base, Pewter Socket, 8 3/4 In.	385.00
Candlestick, Petal & Loop, Canary, 7 In., Pair . . . . 350.00 to 415.00
Candlestick, Petal & Loop, Clambroth, 7 In., Pair . . . . 230.00 to 470.00
Candlestick, Petal & Loop, Opaque White, 6 3/4 In. . . . . 150.00 to 209.00
Candlestick, Petal Socket, Blue, White, 1850-1865, 9 In., Pair	1000.00
Candlestick, Petal Socket, Translucent, Pale Green, 1850-1865, 9 1/4 In., Pair	3055.00
Candlestick, Stepped Quatrefoil Base, Lacy, 5 5/8 x 3 1/8 In., Pair	560.00
Candlestick, Vaseline, Petal, 7 1/2 In., Pair	288.00
Celery Vase, Blue-Violet, Paneled Sides, Flaring Rim, 10 In.	1095.00
Celery Vase, Sunburst, Double Ring Bull's-Eye, 3-Piece Mold, 1825-1835, 7 1/8 x 5 In. . .	1175.00
Creamer, Ashburton, Canary, Applied Handle, 5 3/4 In.	7000.00
Creamer, Diamond Diaper, Applied Handle, 3-Piece Mold, 3 x 2 1/8 In.	355.00
Creamer, Overshot, Bulbous, Applied Reeded Handle, 4 7/8 In.	80.00
Creamer, Sunburst In Square, Cobalt Blue, 3-Piece Mold, 3 x 2 1/2 In.	4115.00
Creamer, Sunburst In Square, Cobalt Blue, Folded Rim, Handle, 3-Piece Mold, 4 x 3 In. .	3525.00
Cruet, 20 Ribs, Swirled To Left, Cobalt Blue, Tam-O-Shanter Stopper, 6 1/2 In.	300.00
Cruet, Ribbed, Blue, Tam-O-Shanter Stopper, 3-Piece Mold, Flared Rim, 6 x 2 In. . 300.00 to 410.00
Decanter, Bar, Ashburton, Pewter Stopper, 1940-1960, 11 5/8 In.	1410.00
Decanter, Cobalt Blue, Cased, Stopper, 1850-1880, 11 1/2 In.	205.00
Decanter, Diamond Diaper, 3-Piece Mold, Stopper, 8 1/2 In. , . .	120.00
Decanter, Needle Etched, Fluted Neck, Applied Foot, 11 3/4 In.	530.00
Decanter, Stopper, Overlay Glass, Vintage Grape, 1850-1870, 11 1/2 In.	265.00
Dish, Acanthus Leaf, Scalloped Rim, Lacy, 1845-1860, 4 1/8 In.	205.00
Dish, Amethyst, Open Work, Low Foot, 2 1/2 x 6 In.	1265.00
Dish, Beehive & Thistle, 8 Sides, Lacy, 1835-1850, 9 1/4 In.	105.00
Dish, Beehive, Scalloped, 8 Sides, Lacy, 9 1/4 In.	110.00
Dish, Birds In Urn, Oval, Lacy, 8 x 5 3/4 In.	80.00
Dish, Daisy & Peacock Eye, Cobalt Blue, Lacy, 1830-1845, 6 1/4 In.	355.00

Dish, Diamond & Scroll, Amber, Lacy, Toy, 5/8 x 3 In. 700.00
Dish, Diamond & Scroll, Flowers, Lacy, 1830-1840, 8 1/2 x 11 7/8 In. 1115.00
Dish, Diamond Diaper, 3-Piece Mold, 1 1/2 x 7 1/4 In. 175.00
Dish, Eagle, 13 Stars, Alternating Shield & Nectarine Panels, 8 Sides, Lacy, 11 1/2 In. 360.00
Dish, Gothic Arch, Oval, Lacy, 1835-1845, 4 1/2 x 5 7/8 In. 50.00
Dish, Leaf & Gothic Arch, Lacy, 1835-1845, 8 1/4 x 6 1/4 In. ....120.00 to 150.00
Dish, Loop, c.1860, 10 In. 1320.00
Dish, Nectarine, Lacy, 1835-1845, 7 1/4 x 5 In. 120.00
Dish, Pineapple & Gothic Arch, Lacy, 1830-1845, 9 x 6 1/2 In. 205.00
Dish, Princess Feather & Diamond, Green, Lacy, 1845-1860, 4 3/4 In. 325.00
Dish, Roman Rosette, Opalescent, Lacy, 1838-1850, 5 1/2 In. 80.00
Dish, Roman Rosette, Red, Amber, Lacy, 1835-1850, 5 1/4 In. 380.00
Dish, Shield, Lily, Heart, Scalloped Edge, Lacy, 6 3/4 x 5 1/4 In. 325.00
Dish, Sunburst & Diamond Diaper, 3-Piece Mold, 1825-1830, 1 1/8 x 5 5/8 In. 120.00
Goblet, Lily Of The Valley, Facet Teardrop Stem, 6 5/8 In., Pair 90.00
Jug, Arch & Fern, Gin, 3-Piece Mold, Applied Handle, 1825-1835, 5 7/8 x 4 3/4 In. 2350.00
Jug, Cornucopia, Applied Handle, 1825-1835, 8 x 5 In. 3585.00
Jug, Diamond Diaper, 3-Piece Mold, Applied Handle, 1825-1835, 7 x 4 7/8 In. 1645.00
Jug, Fluted, Hoops, 3-Piece Mold, Handle, Blue, 1825-1835, 4 5/8 x 3 1/4 In. 2585.00
Jug, Sunburst In Square, 3-Piece Mold, Applied Handled, 1825-35, 6 3/4 x 4 1/4 In. 1530.00
Jug, Trefoil, Ribbed, 3-Piece Mold, Handle, Footed, 1825-1835, 5 3/4 x 3 1/2 In. 355.00
Lamp, 3-Layer Cut, Overlay, Brass Stem, Marble Base, 10 3/4 In. 1035.00
Lamp, Blackberry, Translucent Font, Clambroth Base, Stand, 10 x 4 In. 1045.00
Lamp, Fluid, Blown Glass, Star, Quatrefoil, Ovals, White Cut To Clear & Green, 14 In. .. 2750.00
Lamp, Fluid, Octagonal Base, Double Burner, c.1830, 10 1/2 In. 125.00
Lamp, Fluid, Pressed Glass Base, Cut Font, c.1850, 9 In. 100.00
Lamp, Fluid, Pressed Glass, Flute, Cone Shape, 11 In. 880.00
Lamp, Fluid, Pressed Glass, Heart & Star, 1840-1860, 10 x 4 1/3 In. 145.00
Lamp, Kerosene, 3 Dolphins, Floral, 11 3/4 In. 940.00
Lamp, Oil, Moon & Star Font, Milk Glass Base, Brass Collar, 10 1/2 In. 99.00
Lamp, Whale Oil, Green Cut To Clear, Marble Base, Newell Burner, 13 In., Pair 3335.00
Lamp, Whale Oil, Horn Of Plenty, c.1860, 9 1/2 x 5 In. 260.00
Nappy, Crossed Peacock Feather, Rayed Center, Lacy, 1835-1850, 4 x 6 1/2 In. 530.00
Nappy, Crossed Peacock Feather, Rayed Center, Lacy, 1835-1850, 5 x 8 1/2 In. 940.00
Nappy, Heart & Lyre, Stippled Rim, Lacy 1828-1830, 9 In. 325.00
Nappy, Heart, Sheaf, Shield, Lacy 1828-1835, 4 1/4 x 6 1/2 In. 1060.00
Nappy, Horn Of Plenty, 3-Piece Mold, Footed, 8 1/2 x 11 1/4 In. 705.00
Nappy, Peacock Eye, Diamond Point Center, Lacy, 1830-1845, 7 1/2 In. 90.00
Nappy, Peacock Eye, Lacy, 1830-1845, 7 1/4 In. 145.00
Nappy, Ring, 3-Piece Mold, 1825-1835, 1 3/8 x 5 1/2 In. 60.00
Nappy, Thistle & Rose, Lacy, 1835-1850, 8 In. 130.00
Nappy, Tulip & Acanthus Leaf, Cobalt Blue, Lacy, 1830-1845, 5 5/8 In. 235.00
Nappy, Tulip & Acanthus Leaf, Cobalt Blue, Lacy, 1830-1845, 6 1/4 In. 380.00
Nappy, Tulip & Acanthus Leaf, Opalescent, Lacy, 1835-1840, 6 1/4 In. 380.00
Pitcher, Overshot, Bulbous, Reeded Handle, 7 1/2 In. 110.00
Plate, Acanthus Leaf, Border, Amethyst, Lacy, 1830-1836, 5 5/8 In. 145.00
Plate, Diamond Check, Fan Border, Pale Blue Green, Lacy, 1828-1832, 6 In. 1300.00
Plate, Roman Rosette, Amber, Lacy, 1838-1850, 6 In. 705.00
Plate, Thistle & Drape, Green, Lacy, 1835-1850, 7 In. 105.00
Plate, Thistle & Drape, Light Amethyst, Lacy, 7 In. 380.00
Plate, Union Ship Of State, Bull's-Eye Border, 13 Stars, 8 Sides, Lacy, 6 5/8 In. 1410.00
Pomade Jar, Cover, Diamond Point, Opalescent Powder Blue 1760.00
Punch Bowl, Base, Drape, 3-Piece Mold, 16 x 13 1/2 In. 590.00
Punch Bowl, Diamond Diaper, 3-Piece Mold, 1825-1835, 7 1/4 x 8 1/2 In. 5300.00
Salt, 6-Sided Urn, Amethyst, 3 3/4 In. 180.00
Salt, 8-Sided Oblong, Cobalt Blue, Lacy, 1 3/8 x 2 1/8 x 3 In. 55.00
Salt, Basket Of Flowers, Lavender Tint, Lacy, 2 x 1 7/8 x 3 In. 40.00
Salt, Beaded Scroll & Basket, Flowers, Light Emerald Green, Lacy, 1 3/4 x 3 1/4 x 2 In. . 560.00
Salt, Beaded Scroll, Lacy, 1 7/8 x 3 1/8 x 2 In. 205.00
Salt, Beaded Strawberry-Diamond, Opalescent, Lacy, 1 1/2 x 3 1/4 x 2 1/2 In. 350.00
Salt, Beaded Strawberry-Diamond, Opaque Purple Blue, Lacy, 1 5/8 x 3 1/2 x 2 3/8 In. ... 940.00
Salt, Boat, Opalescent Blue, Lacy, 1 1/2 x 3 1/2 x 2 In. 2470.00
Salt, Boat, Starburst Stern, Purple Blue, Opalescent, Lacy, 1 1/2 x 3 7/8 x 2 In. 1000.00
Salt, Cover, Basket Of Flowers, Scroll, Lacy, 3 x 3 1/8 x 2 In. 1760.00

Salt, Diamond Heart, Deep Purple Blue, Lacy, 1 7/8 x 3 x 2 1/8 In. 5000.00
Salt, Diamond Star & Scroll, Light Amethyst, Lacy, 1 1/2 x 3 1/2 x 2 1/2 In. 470.00
Salt, Eagle & Shield, Opalescent, Lacy, 2 x 2 x 3 In. 415.00
Salt, Eagle & Ship, Lacy, 1 3/4 x 2 7/8 In. 440.00
Salt, Eagle Sofa, Lacy, 2 x 2 1/2 x 3 3/4 In. 550.00
Salt, Eagle, Lacy, 1 1/2 x 2 3/4 x 3 3/4 In. 470.00
Salt, Flowers, Silver Blue, Lacy, 2 x 3 1/4 In. 645.00
Salt, Flowers, Silver Opaque Violet Blue, Lacy, 2 x 3 1/4 In. 1115.00
Salt, Hat, Sunburst In Square, Folded Rim, 3-Piece Mold, 1825-1835, 2 5/8 x 2 3/4 In. ... 765.00
Salt, Hat, Swag, Diamond, Rib, 3-Piece Mold, 1825-1835, 2 3/8 In. 205.00
Salt, Leaves, Blossom, Oval, Lacy, 1 1/8 x 4 x 2 5/8 In. 940.00
Salt, Shell & Hairpin, Opalescent, Lacy, 1 1/2 x 3 x 2 In. 410.00
Salt, Shell & Leaves, Amber, Lacy, 1 5/8 x 3 x 2 In. 500.00
Salt, Shell, Cobalt Blue, Lacy, 1 3/4 x 1 7/8 x 3 1/8 In. 220.00
Salt, Shell, Dark Green, Lacy, 1 5/8 x 2 x 3 In. 550.00
Salt, Stag's Horn, Cobalt Blue, Lacy, 1 3/8 x 3 1/8 x 2 In. 350.00
Salt, Stag's Horn, Medium Amber, Lacy, 1 3/4 x 2 x 3 In. 175.00
Salt, Strawberry-Diamond, Cobalt Blue, Lacy, 1 7/8 x 2 1/8 x 2 7/8 In. 145.00
Salt, Strawberry-Diamond, Dark Brown Amber, Lacy, 2 x 2 1/8 x 2 7/8 In. 1045.00
Spooner, Engraved SEH, 1860-1880, 6 1/4 In. 60.00
Spooner, Inverted Diamond & Thumbprint, Amethyst, 1850-1870, 3 1/4 x 4 1/8 In. 1300.00
Spooner, Punty & Ellipse, 1840-1865, 5 1/8 x 3 5/8 In. 1175.00
Sugar, Cover, Acanthus Leaf & Eagle-Headed Shield, Lacy, 6 In. 440.00
Sugar, Cover, Gothic Arch, Sapphire Blue, Footed, 1840-1850, 5 1/2 x 5 In. 1880.00
Tray, Hairpin, Peacock Shape, Closed Handle, Lacy, 8 x 9 1/4 In. 4125.00
Tray, U.S.F. Constitution, Heart, 6-Point Star Border, Lady, c.1840, 5/8 x 7 In. 7345.00
Tumbler, 3 Leaf Bands, Cobalt Blue, Handle, Lacy, 1840-1845, 3 3/8 x 2 5/8 In. 325.00
Tumbler, Barrel, Diamond Diaper, Blue Tint, 3-Piece Mold, 1825-1835, 3 1/4 x 2 1/2 In. . 355.00
Tumbler, Diamond Diaper, 3-Piece Mold, 1825-1835, 5 1/2 x 4 3/8 In ....265.00 to 380.00
Tumbler, Diamond Diaper, 3-Piece Mold, 4 3/4 x 4 3/8 In. 300.00
Tumbler, Diamond Diaper, 3-Piece Mold, 6 1/4 x 4 5/8 In. 355.00
Vase, 4 Printie Block, Canary, 1840-1860, 11 1/4 In. ....300.00 to 575.00
Vase, Arch, Amethyst, Gauffered Rim, 6-Sided Base, 11 3/8 x 4 1/4 In., Pair 3055.00
Vase, Arch, Yellow, Gauffered Rim, 6-Sided Base, 1840-1860, 11 1/4 x 4 1/2 In., Pair ... 1175.00
Vase, Ball & Groove, Amethyst, 1845-1865, 6 x 3 3/4 In. 1880.00
Vase, Ball & Groove, Dark Cobalt Blue, 6-Sided Base, 1845-1865, 5 3/4 x 3 3/4 In. 2940.00
Vase, Cobalt Blue, Gauffered Rim, 8-Sided Double Standard, 1840-1860, 11 x 4 1/2 In. .. 3820.00
Vase, Hobnail With Leaf, Opaque Starch Blue, Gold Bands, Lacy, 11 1/2 In. 330.00
Vase, Hyacinth, Amethyst, Bulbous, Funnel Base, Rolled Inward Rim, 9 1/8 In. 470.00
Vase, Leaf, Canary, 1840-1860, 10 1/2 In. 2820.00
Vase, Loop, Canary, 11 1/2 x 3 1/2 In. 130.00
Vase, Loop, Canary, 6-Sided Stem, Round Base, 10 1/4 In., Pair 825.00
Vase, Loop, Gauffered Rim, Canary, Round Base, 10 1/2 In. 380.00
Vase, Loop, Opalescent, 6-Sided Base, 1840-1850, 3 1/8 x 4 3/4 In. 1765.00
Vase, Loop, Teal Green, Tooled, Fluted Rim, 9 1/4 In. 2800.00
Vase, Loop, Violet Blue, 6-Sided Stem, Square Marble Base, 11 1/2 x 4 1/4 In. 220.00
Vase, Panel, Amethyst, 8-Sided Base, 9 1/2 In. 3100.00
Vase, Pillar, Gauffered Rim, 1850-1880, 16 1/8 x 5 1/2 In. 400.00
Vase, Pink Icicle Rim, 3 Pink Feet, 9 1/2 In. 500.00
Vase, Tulip, Amethyst, 8-Sided Base, 9 1/2 In. 3150.00
Vase, Tulip, Amethyst, Scalloped Rim, 8-Sided Base, 10 In. 2200.00
Vase, Tulip, Teal, 10 7/8 x 5 1/4 In. 10450.00
Vase, Twisted Loop, Amethyst, Fluted Rim, Round Base, 9 3/4 x 4 7/8 In. 2420.00
Window Pane, Diamond Scroll & Fan, Lacy, 1835-1850, 10 x 8 In. 2350.00

SARREGUEMINES is the name of a French town that is used as part of a
china mark. Utzschneider and Company, a porcelain factory, made
ceramics in Sarreguemines, Lorraine, France, from about 1775.
Transfer-printed wares and majolica were made in the nineteenth century. The nineteenth-century pieces, most often found today, usually
have colorful transfer-printed decorations showing peasants in local
costumes.

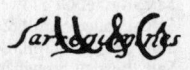

Jardiniere, Majolica, Brown, Green, Cobalt Blue, 3-Footed, c.1880, 12 1/2 In. 315.00

Jug, Face, 18th-Century Gentleman Wearing Wig, Majolica, 1900, 6 1/2 In. 405.00
Plate, G. Washington, 1789-1797, 8 1/2 In. 45.00
Stein, Dachshund, Pewter Lid, Glazed, 1 Liter 480.00
Stein, Fox & Rabbit, Pewter Lid, 1 Liter 320.00
Stein, Munich Child, Pewter Lid, Pewter Strap, 1911, 1 Liter 800.00
Toby Jug, Happy & Sad Face, Verse, Majolica, 8 3/4 In. 50.00

SASCHA BRASTOFF made decorative accessories, ceramics, enamels on
copper, and plastics of his own design. He headed a factory, Sascha
Brastoff of California, Inc., in West Los Angeles, from 1953 until
about 1973. He died in 1993. Pieces signed with the signature *Sascha*
Brastoff were his work and are the most expensive. Other pieces
marked *Sascha B.* or with a stamped mark were made by others in his
company. Pieces made by Matt Adams after he left the factory are
listed here with his name.

Sascha Brastoff

Bank, Piggy, White, Gold, Ceramic, 4 1/2 x 3 3/4 In. 150.00
Bowl, White, Gold Flowers, Silver Leaves, 7 1/4 x 5 1/2 In. 45.00

SATIN GLASS is a late nineteenth-century art glass. It has a dull finish
that is caused by hydrofluoric acid vapor treatment. Satin glass was
made in many colors and sometimes has applied decorations. Satin
glass is also listed by factory name, such as Webb, or in the Mother-of-
Pearl category in this book.

Basket, Pink & White, Vaseline Handle, 7 In. 550.00
Biscuit Jar, Cover, Enameled Scene, Children Playing In Winter, Victorian, 7 In. 205.00
Biscuit Jar, Pink, Diamond-Quilted, Silver Plated Cover & Bail, 8 In. 200.00
Biscuit Jar, Pink, Drape Molded, Enameled, White, Blue Flowers, Amethyst Leaves, 9 In. 480.00
Biscuit Jar, Reverse Swirl, 19th Century, 8 In. 140.00
Biscuit Jar, Shell & Seaweed, Enameled Flowers, Silver Plated Lid & Bail, 8 In. 450.00
Bowl, Cream & Orange Flowers, Green Leaves, Orange Dots, Handkerchief Edge, 3 In. .. 175.00
Bowl, Lime Green, White, Low, Ruffled Edge, 7 In. 30.00
Compote, Blue, Indiana Glass Co., 7 1/2 x 8 1/2 In. 15.00
Ewer, Blue, Cased, Enameled Bird, Coralene Branch, 9 1/2 In. 60.00
Ewer, Blue, Cased, Enameled Flowers, Applied Camphor Handle, 8 In. 35.00
Ewer, Pink, Enameled Flowers, Long Neck, Camphor Handle, 9 1/2 In. 100.00
Ewer, Shaded From White To Pink, Cased, Applied Handle, 9 In. 70.00
Ewer, Shaded Pink, Cased, Enameled Blue Flowers, 12 3/4 In. 100.00
Fairy Lamp, Green & White Swirl, 6 1/2 In. 60.00
Finger Bowl, Blue, Diamond-Quilted, Ruffled Edge, 4 1/2 In. 75.00
Jar, Cover, Pink, Swirl, White Interior, 6 x 4 1/2 In. 115.00
Jar, Pink, Diamond-Quilted, Silver Plated Cover, Beaded Edge, 6 In. 75.00
Lamp, Floral Design, Hanging Miniature Umbrella For Matches, Pink, 20 In. 2300.00
Lamp, Pink, Diamond-Quilted, 10 1/4 In. 230.00
Rose Bowl, Brown, Diamond-Quilted, 2 1/2 In. 60.00
Rose Bowl, Green, Embossed, Flowers, 4 In. 20.00
Sugar, Shaker, Pine Cone Mold, Green, 5 In. 110.00
Tumbler, Pink Over White, 3 1/2 In. 60.00
Tumbler, Rainbow Diamond-Quilted 400.00
Vase, Blue, Enameled Blossoms, 8 In. 60.00
Vase, Blue, Enameled Branch, 4 3/4 In. 30.00
Vase, Blue, Enameled Flowers, 6 In., Pair 80.00
Vase, Light Blue, White Enameled, 2 Cavaliers, 10 In., Pair 175.00
Vase, Peach Shaded To Turquoise, Enameled Cherry Blossoms, Cased, 11 1/4 In. 80.00
Vase, Pink, Enameled Flowers, Butterflies, Handles, 13 In., Pair 600.00
Vase, Pink, Enameled Heart, Vine Collar, Cased, 9 3/4 In. 60.00
Vase, Pink, Enameled Roses, Teardrop Shape, Petal Feet, 9 1/2 In. 50.00
Vase, Pink, Flowers, Birds, Handles, 7 1/2 In., Pair 360.00
Vase, Pink, Ribbed, 6 In. 60.00
Vase, Plum, Enameled Flowers, Cased, Victorian, 13 1/2 In. 60.00
Vase, Raspberry To Pale Pink, White Lining, 5 In. 140.00
Vase, Shaded Yellow, Oval, White Lining, 8 In. 70.00
Vase, Yellow, Enameled, Amethyst & Gold Flowers, Scalloped Rim, 8 1/2 In. 90.00

SATSUMA is a Japanese pottery with a distinctive creamy beige crackled glaze. Most of the pieces were decorated with blue, red, green, orange, or gold. Almost all Satsuma found today was made after 1860. During World War I, Americans could not buy undecorated European porcelains. Women who liked to make hand painted porcelains at home began to decorate plain Satsuma. These pieces are known today as *American Satsuma*.

Bottle, Saki, 2 Samurai Cartouches, 19th Century, 6 In.	115.00
Bowl, Butterflies, Figures, Brocade, 19th Century, 5 In.	470.00
Bowl, Earthenware, Flowering Branches In Interior, 3-Footed, Japan, c.1900, 8 In.	1610.00
Bowl, Earthenware, Scalloped Rim, Brocade Design, Meiji Period, Japan, 5 1/2 In.	750.00
Bowl, Flowers, Lavender, Orange, Yellow Gilt, Kinkozan, 4 1/2 x 9 1/2 In.	4115.00
Bowl, Immortal, Gilt Ground, Brocade Border, Meiji, 5 1/2 In.	235.00
Bowl, Women & Children Viewing Cherry Blossoms, 20th Century, 4 3/4 In.	205.00
Box, Lift-Off Lid, Mule-Colored Flowers, Marked On Base, 1 x 3 1/4 In.	245.00
Cup & Saucer, Detailed Painting, Go Kasen, 19th Century, 5-In. Saucer	550.00
Figurine, Woman On Elephant, Wooden Base, Meiji Period, c.1890, 4 x 4 In.	69.00
Incense Burner, Fan Design In Repeat, Gosu Blue, Oval, 3-Footed, 4 In.	1555.00
Incense Burner, Sparrows, Flowers, Mijo Shrine, Signed, 19th Century, 5 In.	4995.00
Jar, Calligrapher, 8 Musicians, Floral & Lappet, Squat, Ovoid Form, c.1860, 2 In.	400.00
Jar, Cover, 2 Cartouche Panels, Samurai, Birds, Insects, Flowers, 19th Century, 6 x 4 In.	145.00
Jar, Cover, Shouldered Oval, Allover Figures, 18 1/2 In.	2629.00
Koro, Cover, Figural Design, Blue & Gilt Ground, Waisted Form, Box, 5 In.	518.00
Tray, Scrolls, Birds, Flowers, Women, Cobalt Blue Ground, 19th Century, 11 1/2 In.	1528.00
Trinket Box, Butterfly Shape, Tree, Flowers, Birds, 2 1/8 x 4 1/4 x 5 1/4 In.	30.00
Urn, Cover, 2 Foo Dog Handles, Foo Dog Finial, Pedestal Base, 44 In.	1120.00
Vase, 4 Floral Panels, Brocade Ground, Gosu Blue, Globular, 4 1/2 In.	978.00
Vase, Allover Flowers, Urn Shape, Late 19th Century, 9 1/4 In.	140.00
Vase, Birds, Flowers, Branches, Drum Shape, Trumpet Mouth, 19th Century, 18 1/2 In.	825.00
Vase, Eagle, Green & Brown Swirled Ground, Applied Butterflies & Handles, 23 In.	385.00
Vase, Earthenware, Oval, Dragon Chasing Flaming Pearl Of Wisdom, 11 1/2 In.	430.00
Vase, Figural & Flowers, Baluster Shape, Meiji, 20 In.	765.00
Vase, Gamecock, Among Bamboo, c.1930, 9 1/2 In.	160.00
Vase, Iris, White, Leaves, Gold & Mauve, Blue & White Ground, Textured, 20 In.	110.00
Vase, Kishihara, Blue Ground, 3 5/8 In.	20.00
Vase, Oval, Dragon Handles, Figural Decoration, 10 1/2 In., Pair	1195.00
Vase, White Flower Tree, Yellow Ground, 6 1/4 In.	28.00

SATURDAY EVENING GIRLS, see Paul Revere Pottery category.

SCALES have been made to weigh everything from babies to gold. Collectors search for all types. Most popular are small gold dust scales and special grocery scales.

Baby, John Chatillon & Sons, New York, White Wicker Basket, 25 Lb.	58.00
Baby, R.A. Hunter, 25 Lb.	39.00
Balance, Analytical Beam, Becker, Nickeled Fittings, Bowl Pans, Case, London, 14 In.	176.00
Balance, Analytical Beam, Eimer & Amend, Mahogany Case, Weights, New York, 16 In.	150.00
Balance, Analytical Beam, Slate Base, Mahogany Case, England, c.1900, 15 In.	106.00
Balance, Analytical Beam, Thomas, Mahogany Case, Weights, Philadelphia, 16 In.	147.00
Balance, Analytical, Collet A Paris, Longue Suc'r, Marble Base, Case, France, 25 In.	590.00
Balance, Beam, P. Tracento, Plate, Bronze, Iron, Up To 660 Lbs., Italy, 72 In.	775.00
Balance, Brass Shaft, Arms, Copper Pans, Walnut Case, Dovetailed Drawer, 19 In.	125.00
Balance, Candy, Jacobs Bros. Co., N.Y., No. 3, Cast Iron, Countertop	132.00
Balance, Cast Iron, 6 Graduated Weights, 3 3/4 x 12 x 5 In.	70.00
Balance, Cast Iron, Scrolls, Engraved Copper Crossbar & Pans, 58 In.	525.00
Balance, Chemical, Troemner, Cast Iron Base, Philadelphia, c.1900, 10 In.	59.00
Balance, Circular Pans, Lattice Arm, Mahogany Base, England, 2 Lb., 20 In.	148.00
Balance, Fairbanks, Brass Beam, Pan, Cast Iron Turkey Foot Base, 17 In.	68.00
Balance, H. Troemner, Philadelphia, 24 x 24 In.	3520.00
Balance, Portable, Beam, Hernstein, Mahogany Base, New York, 10 1/2 In.	59.00
Balance, Portable, Loetschert, Mahogany Base, 1 Kg, Lacquered Brass, Sweden, 19 In.	88.00
Balance, Salter, Railway Parcel Balance, Iron, Green Paint, 56 Lb., England, 14 In.	80.00
Balance, Sarmiento 3620, Nickel Plated, Marble, Beveled Glass, 2 Pans, 30 In.	525.00

Balance, Torison, New York, Patented Jan. 6-85, 16 x 7 x 9 In. 149.00
Balance, Troemner, Brass, Beveled Glass, Adjustable Feet, Oak Case, 9 x 13 In. 450.00
Balance, Troemner, Brass, Turned Pedestal, Saucer Trays, Signed, 24 x 24 In. 3520.00
Balance, Troemner, No. 4, Iron Base, Brass Pans, 12 1/2 In. 158.00
Balance, Wooden Base, Marble Top, Brass Window & Pans, 21 In. 198.00
Candy, Pelouze, Imperial Computing Confectionery, Tin, Leafy Design, 7 In. 23.00
Computing, Fairbanks, Brass Beam, Brass Bucket, Winchester Bushel On Slide 590.00
Counter, Hunt & Co., Brass Column, Arms & Pan, Cast Iron Base & Crest, 32 1/2 In. ... 169.00
Counter, Marble Top, Ebonized Base, Line Inlay, Marble Pans, 22 3/4 In. 280.00
Diamond, W & T Avery, Steel Beam, Brass Pans, 4 Weights, Fitted Mahogany Case, 5 In. 225.00
Grain, Fairbanks, Patented 1898, 63 In. 500.00
Hanging, Hanson, Texas Cotton, No. 8916, 160 Lbs., 18 In. 23.00
Jockey, Henry Pooley & Son, Rosewood, Blue Seat, England, 36 In. ....*Illus* 3680.00
Jockey, Queen Anne Style, Green Leather, England, 30 In. ....*Illus* 2760.00
Penny, Fortune Telling, Peerless, Floor Model, c.1930s 495.00
Platform, RX Scale Mfg. Co., Art Deco Style, White, Black Pinstripes, 40 In. 290.00
Platform, Salter, Brass Dial, Persian Style, Column Supports, Wheels, 62 In. 259.00
Platform, Toledo, 125 Lb., Cast Iron Pedestal, Wheels, 72 x 41 In. 150.00
Portable, Brass, Iron Balance Arm, Engraved, Weights, Marked, 1776, 1 x 5 x 2 1/2 In. ... 385.00
Postage, Brass, Gesgesch, Late 19th Century, 14 In. 46.00
Postage, Cross Pen Co., Boston, Brass, Iron Base, 19th Century, 7 In. 35.00
Postage, Figural, Kneeling Putto, Bronze, Brass Weight, Oak Base, 5 3/4 In. 175.00
Postage, Mordan & Co., London, Circular Pans, 7 Lb. Capacity, Mahogany Base, 15 In. . 206.00
Postage, Parkins & Gotto, London, 8-Sided Wooden Base, England, 19th Century, 8 In. .. 69.00
Postage, Pelouze Manufacturing Co., Early 20th Century, 6 In. 25.00
Postage, R.W. Winfield, Lighthouse Form, Brass, Birmingham, England, 6 In. 200.00
Produce, Jacobs Bros., Polished Steel, 12 In. 158.00
Seed, Brass, Platform Base, Initialed D.E.L., Early 19th Century, 9 x 16 In. 520.00
Shopkeeper's, No Springs, Honest Weight, Light-Up Milk Glass Top, Toledo 28.00
Sliding, Countertop, Troemner, Weight Bar, Pour Pan, Oak Case, 22 In. 147.00
Sliding, Pelouze, Superb, Candy Computing, Horizontal Beam, 7 In. 65.00
Steel Yard, Fairbanks, Boston, Brass, Copper Pan, Brass Arms, 21 1/2 In. 56.00
Weighing, Bartlett & Son, Bristol, England, Cast Iron, Scrollwork, Painted, 1970, 48 In. .. 920.00
Weighing, Brass, Wood, Leather, Case, 18th Century, 9 x 4 x 1 In. 200.00
Weighing, Chart, Health, Art Deco, Blue & White, Coin-Operated, 53 In. 230.00
Weighing, Chicago Stockyard, Brass, Floor Model, Steer Head Finial, 60 In. 575.00
Weighing, Dr. Fitch's Prescription, Metal Case, Late 19th Century, 3 In. 115.00
Weighing, E. Hoffman's, Pat. Aug. 7, '66, Brown Marble, Brass Pans, 22 In. 298.00
Weighing, E.J. Hoadley, Brass, Iron, Early 20th Century, 6 In. 69.00
Weighing, Health Chart, Blue, White, Art Deco, Coin Operated, 53 In. ....*Illus* 230.00
Weighing, Iron, Porcelain, What You Should Weigh Chart, Penny, 69 x 17 x 30 In. 130.00
Weighing, Mills Novelty Co., 1 Cent, Correct Weight, Blue, White, Red Base, 69 In. *Illus* 978.00
Weighing, Mills, Novelty, Coin-Operated, 1 Cent, Columns, Animal Feet, 69 In. 978.00
Weighing, National Automatic Machine Co., Coin-Operated, Free Slot, Gray Metal, 72 In. 865.00
Weighing, National Automatic Machines, Normandy Chimes, Coin-Operated, 73 In. 2530.00
Weighing, Salter, 50 Family Scale, Cast Iron, 14 Lbs., Silvester's Patent, 10 1/2 In. 80.00
Weighing, Toledo, No Springs, Coin-Operated, Honest Weight, Lollipop Form, 71 In. 1095.00
Weighing, Troemner, Cast Iron, Ball Weights, Brass Pan, Arm, 18 In. 195.00
Weighing, Troemner, Philadelphia, Table Top, Oak, Beveled Glass, 8 1/2 x 13 In. 315.00
Weighing, Watling, Dreams, Quizzes, Fortunes, Coin-Operated, 65 In. 495.00

Scale, Jockey, Queen Anne
Style, Green Leather,
England, 30 In.

Scale, Jockey,
Henry Pooley &
Son, Rosewood,
Blue Seat,
England, 36 In.

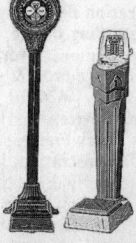

Scale, Weighing,
Health Chart, Blue,
White, Art Deco,
Coin Operated,
53 In.

Scale, Weighing,
Mills Novelty Co.,
1 Cent, Correct
Weight, Blue, White,
Red Base, 69 In.

SCHAFER & VATER, makers of small ceramic items, are best known for their amusing figurals. The factory was located in Volkstedt-Rudolstadt, Germany, from 1890 to 1962. Some pieces are marked with the crown and R mark, but many are unmarked.

Box, Cover, Pink, 3 Sides, 3 1/2 In.	75.00
Figurine, Egyptian Man Playing Horn Next To Obelisk, Pink, 8 In.	150.00
Hair Receiver, Cover, Pink, 3 In.	50.00
Hat Pin Holder, Bronze Color, 5 1/2 In.	150.00
Hat Pin Holder, White, 5 1/2 In.	50.00
Pitcher, Figural Head, Boy, Dimples, Hat & Scarf, Blue & White	150.00
Vase, Bronze Color, Pink, Tubular Shape, 7 In.	70.00

SCHNEIDER Glassworks was founded in 1913 at Epinay-sur-Seine, France, by Charles and Ernest Schneider. Art glass was made between 1913 and 1930. The company still produces clear crystal glass.

Bowl, Emerald Green, Controlled Bubbles, Signed, 2 3/4 x 16 In.	230.00
Bowl, Mottled Yellow, Amber, Brown, Blue, Squat, 5 3/8 x 12 In.	470.00
Bowl, Yellow, Brown Tortoiseshell At Top, Signed, 4 1/2 In.	230.00
Box, Clear Tortoiseshell Cover, Blue, Green, Yellow Tortoiseshell, Clear Handle, 4 In.	240.00
Compote, Mottled Green, Tangerine Base, 3 1/2 x 12 1/4 In.	345.00
Compote, Pulled Cobalt Rim, Yellow, 3 Glass Berries, Iron Vine Base, Signed, 13 In.	460.00
Lamp, Stepped Leaf Base, Domed Shade, Mottled Yellow, Lady By Lake, 14 In.	2470.00
Vase, Applied Carved Grape Clusters, Purple On Orange Mottled Ground, 15 1/2 In.	12075.00
Vase, Curled Stems, Orange, Green, Mottled White Ground, Tapered, Cylinder, 16 In.	3370.00
Vase, Domed Cover, Mottled Blue, Yellow, Signed, 3 3/4 x 6 3/4 In.	325.00
Vase, Intarsia, Grape Clusters, Oval, Signed, 15 In.	8365.00
Vase, Mottled Green Glass, Controlled Bubbles, Dark Green Handles, 5 1/4 In.	200.00 to 240.00
Vase, Mottled Orange, Blue Art Deco Design, Cameo, c.1920, 4 1/2 In.	490.00
Vase, Mottled Orange, Brown Leaves, Signed, 16 x 10 In.	1725.00
Vase, Mottled, Yellow & Orange Flecks, Conical, Signed, 6 1/2 In.	220.00
Vase, Orange, Clear Frosted Glass, Red, White & Blue Latticinio Cane, Cameo, 3 In.	575.00
Vase, Orange, Purple Mottled, Knopped Stem, Footed, 11 In.	470.00

SCIENTIFIC INSTRUMENTS of all kinds are included in this category. Other categories such as Barometer, Binoculars, Dental, Nautical, Medical, and Thermometer may also price scientific apparatus.

Barograph, Friez, Baltimore, Brass Drum, Steel Case, c.1940, 11 In.	235.00
Barometer, G. Muller, Braunschweig, Germany, Brass, 1900, 6 3/4 In.	145.00
Calculator, Keuffel & Esser, Revolving Cylinder, 2 Brass Arms, 1881, 22 In.	690.00
Chronometer, 8 Day, Roman Numerals, Mahogany Case, c.1900, 6 In.	546.00
Chronometer, Hamilton, U.S. Navy, Officer's Clock, Brass Case, 3 In.	520.00
Chronometer, Waltham, Roman Numerals, Mahogany, Brass, Key, c.1910, 5 In.	750.00
Compass, 14K Gold, Aurapole	295.00
Compass, Dry Card, Brass Bowl, Wooden Case, Late 19th Century, 9 In.	206.00
Compass, Surveyor's, E.A. Kutz, New York, Early 19th Century, 14 In.	705.00
Compass, Surveyor's, G. Heisley, Harrisburg, c.1850, 14 In.	2230.00
Compass, Surveyor's, W & Le Gurley, Vernier, Vanes, Levels, Bob, Case, 16 In.	750.00
Composition Of Forces Demonstrator, Max Kohl, Vienna, c.1900, 10 In.	120.00
Cross Head, Surveyor's, Compass, Bate, London, 19th Century, 5 1/2 In.	175.00
Cross Head, Surveyor's, Radiguet, Paris, Silver Nonius Scale, Brass, 1860, 6 1/4 In.	88.00
Demonstration Theodolite, Rabone & Sons, Birmingham, c.1920, 10 In.	90.00
Diamond Cutting Machine, Cast Iron, Brass Fittings, 13 In.	166.00
Electric Demonstration Beam Engine, American, c.1850, 16 In.	2470.00
Electric Power Recording Device, Spring Wound Drum, England, 10 x 15 In.	395.00
Expansion Of Heat Demonstrator, A.L. Robbins, Chicago, c.1900, 15 1/2 In.	90.00
Explorer Transit, Gurley, Frost & Adam's, Boston, 10 1/2 In.	1235.00
Geiger Counter, Philips PW 4010, Manual, Bag	80.00
Geometry Teaching Device, J.L. Hammett & Co., Yellow Box, 17 3/4 In.	210.00
Hourglass, Yellow, Black Frame, c.1800, 7 1/2 In.	1265.00
Hydraulic Press Demonstration, J.M. Wightman, Boston, c.1850, 12 In.	765.00
Kaleidoscope, Brass, Cylindrical Stand, Stepped Base, c.1900, 11 x 7 1/2 In.	1000.00
Kaleidoscope, C.G. Bush & Co., Brass Mounted, Wooden Base, 13 1/2 In.	863.00
Kaleidoscope, England, Brass, c.1890, 6 3/4 In.	350.00

Lamp, Microscope, Bockett, London, 19th Century, 9 In. 355.00
Level, Fr. J. Berg, Stockholm, Sweden, Polished Brass, Case, 1900, 18 1/2 In. 498.00
Level, Transit, B.L. Makepeace, Boston, Loxo No. 3254, Oak Case, 1925, 7 In. 95.00
Logarithm Drum, Albert Nestler, 1935, 24 In. 276.00
Magnifying Glass, Bone Handle, Silvered Metal Mounts, 9 In. 145.00
Micrometer, Lowinson, New York, No. 8072, Thread Counting, 1930s 59.00
Microscope, Arthur Thomas Co., Philadelphia, Brass 288.00
Microscope, Bausch & Lomb Optical Company, Brass, 12 In. 330.00
Microscope, Bausch & Lomb, Enameled Iron, 13 1/2 In 75.00
Microscope, Bausch & Lomb, No. 47240, Mahogany Case, 10 1/4 In 115.00
Microscope, Bausch & Lomb, Nosepiece, Condenser, Accessories, Case, 12 In. 150.00
Microscope, Binocular, Baker, London, Brass, Cased, 18 In. 1840.00
Microscope, Binocular, R. & J. Beck, No. 8683, Mahogany Case, c.1875, 15 In. 1410.00
Microscope, Compound, Mahogany Case, France, Late 19th Century, 4 1/4 In. 90.00
Microscope, Continental Style, L. Schrauer, New York, Late 19th Century, 12 1/2 In. 1175.00
Microscope, Culpepper Pattern, Brass, Mahogany Base, c.1850, 10 1/2 In. 590.00
Microscope, Culpepper, G. Davis, Leeds, England, Brass, c.1840, 10 In. 1060.00
Microscope, Drum, Mahogany Case, France, Late 19th Century, 3 In. 235.00
Microscope, Gilbert & Sons, London, Brass, Fishskin Case, c.1806, 10 1/2 In. 2470.00
Microscope, Gould Pattern, England, Case, c.1825, 9 In. 440.00
Microscope, Gould Pattern, England, Coarse Focusing, Case, 19th Century, 7 3/4 In. 509.00
Microscope, Leitz, No. 2916, Lacquered Brass, Mahogany Case, 1878, 8 1/2 In. 355.00
Microscope, Leitz, No. 53713, Horseshoe Foot, Mahogany Case, 12 In. 150.00
Microscope, Martin Pattern, England, Drum, Walnut Case, c.1850, 9 1/2 In. 500.00
Microscope, Monocular, Pull Tube, Twin Pillars, 19th Century, 9 1/4 In. 235.00
Microscope, Newton, London, Body Tube, Case, c.1875, 13 1/2 In. 176.00
Microscope, R. & J. Beck, London & Philadelphia, Monocular, Brass, 1860, 15 1/2 In. . . . 1090.00
Microscope, Reichert, Vienna, No. 24011, Lacquered Brass, Mahogany Case, 11 In. 265.00
Microscope, Ross, London, No. 230, Lacquered Brass, Late 1840s, 18 In. 2350.00
Microscope, Smith & Beck, Educational, Pull Tube, Fine Focusing, c.1860, 14 In. 235.00
Microscope, Steel Body, Focus Lens, 1937 . . . . 65.00
Microscope, Travel, Monocular, Brass, 1870, 8 3/4 In. 245.00
Microscope, Zeiss, Binocular, Chrome, Eyepiece Mount, Electric Light, 14 In. 235.00
Microscope, Zentmeyer, Dissecting, Rack & Pinion Focusing, 4 1/2 In. 265.00
Observatorium, Dome Shape, Pedestal Base, Derby Spar, 1800s, 4 In. 130.00
Octant, England, Ebony, Ivory Scale, Brass Arm, Oak Case, 13 1/2 In. 590.00
Octant, H.C. Coles, London, Brass, 1850 . . . . 355.00
Octant, Hughes, London, Ebony, Ivory Scale, Brass Arm, Mahogany Case, 8 In. 590.00
Octant, Spencer, Browning & Rust, Ebony, Brass, Green & Black Painted Case 750.00
Periscope, Trench, Micro-Grades, Brass, Nickel, Wooden Handle, Case, c.1920, 20 In. . . . 190.00
Protractor, Cole Course, Marine Compass Co., Massachusetts, 21 In. 90.00
Sextant, Banks, London, Brass, Mahogany Case, c.1810, 5 In. 2700.00
Sextant, Reynolds & Son, Q 749, Brass, Mahogany Case, 9 1/2 x 10 In. 590.00
Sextant, Troughton, London, No. 1259, 2 Frame, Brass, 12 In. 1060.00
Sighting Compass, Stanley, London, Bubble Mechanisms, Brass, 1 1/2 x 3 In. 275.00
Spectroscope, AO Instrument Company, No. 4.680, 1950, 8 3/4 x 16 In. 550.00
Spectroscope, Sighting Tube, Prism Table, Cast Iron Tripod Stand, 9 In. 235.00
Telescope, 3 Draw, Brass, Leather Covered Barrel, 19th Century, 18 In. 150.00
Telescope, 3 Draw, Lacquered Brass Body, Leather Cover, 10 1/2 x 1 3/4 In. 90.00
Telescope, 4 Draw, Brass, Wrapped Fabric Handle, 32 In. 154.00
Telescope, 4 Draw, Dust Slide, Oak, 1887, 10 In. 150.00
Telescope, 5 Draw, Leather, Ray Shade, Dust Slide, 11 1/2 In. 190.00
Telescope, 6 Draw, Cornhill, London, Brass, Blunt, 19th Century, 4 In. 380.00
Telescope, 6 Draw, S & B Solomons, London, Nickel Silver, Baleen, 15 1/2 In. 520.00
Telescope, 7 Draw, Brass, Shagreen, London, 20 In. 920.00
Telescope, 7 Draw, Mother Of Pearl, 2 In. 206.00
Telescope, Brass, Bronze, Aluminum, Oak Tripod Stand, Professional Grade, 84 In. 5085.00
Telescope, Brass, Single Draw, Mahogany, 18th Century, 35 In. 2070.00
Telescope, Cast Iron, Brass Fitting, Tripod Base, 19 3/4 x 11 1/2 In. 275.00
Telescope, G. Bracher, London, Single Draw, Brass, 38 1/2 In. 115.00
Telescope, J.A. O'Donohoe, England, Brass, Engraved, Wooden Tripod 2390.00
Telescope, Marine, Single Draw, Mahogany, England, c.1800, 26 In. 380.00
Telescope, Reflecting, London, Star Finder, 2 Eyepieces, Mirrors, 9 In. 4115.00

Telescope, T. Harris & Sons, London, Mahogany, Brass, Tripod Base, 20 In. 590.00
Telescope, Table, Lacquered Brass Body Tube, Cast Iron Tripod Feet, 40 In. 1880.00
Telescope, Tabletop, S. Johnson, London, Folding, Brass, Late 18th Century, 15 x 22 In. .. 2875.00
Telescope, Thomas L. Ainsley, South Shields, Single Draw, Leather, Brass, 29 In. 60.00
Telescope, Watson & Sons, Brass, Library, Tripod, Pine Case, c.1880, 45 In. 620.00
Theodolite, Morin, Paris, Brass, Telescope, Oak Case & Tripod, c.1890, 8 3/4 In. 295.00
Tool Set, Watchmaker's, Boley, Wooden Case 120.00
Tripod, Instruments De Geodesic, Topographic, Chasselon, Paris, Mahogany, Brass, 57 In. 440.00
Vacuum Pump Demonstration, E.S. Ritchie & Sons, Boston, c.1890, 20 In. 264.00
Weight Set, Laboratory, Graduated, Wood Case, Hinged Lid, c.1900, 2 x 5 In., 10 Piece .. 75.00
Wet Cell, Genet Pattern, Glass Bottle, Ebonite Top, Brass Fittings, 9 In. 235.00
Wye Level, Buff & Buff, No. 15694, Bubble Level, Tripod, Case, 14 In. 150.00
Wye Level, Buff & Burger, Brass, Telescope, Boston, Late 1800s, 17 In. 120.00

SCRIMSHAW is bone or ivory or whale's teeth carved by sailors and others for entertainment during the sailing-ship days. Some scrimshaw was carved as early as 1800. There are modern scrimshanders making pieces today on bone, ivory, or plastic. Other pieces may be found in the Ivory and Nautical categories.

Basket, Panbone, Swing Handles, Silk, Mahogany Bottom, 6 1/2 x 5 1/2 x 8 1/2 In. 5735.00
Birdcage, Whale's Tooth, Panbone, Turned Finials, Feet, Pierced Door, 7 x 6 x 8 In. 4540.00
Block, Double Sheave, Whalebone, Copper Pins, 3 x 2 x 1 1/2 In. 425.00
Bone, Fruitwood, Musicians, Carved, Germany, 19th Century, 8 1/2 In., 4 Piece 1290.00
Box, Baleen, Whalebone, Hardwood, Hinged, Geometric, Stars, 7 1/2 x 9 1/2 x 15 In. 14340.00
Box, Elephant Tusk, 7 1/2 x 4 x 1 1/2 In. 125.00
Busk, Baleen, Heart, Star, Eagle, American Flag, Flowers, 1845, 13 1/2 In. 450.00
Busk, Whalebone, 2 Ships, American Flag, Sailor, Wreath, 19th Century, 12 1/2 In. 4185.00
Busk, Whalebone, Geometric Designs, Flag, Tree Of Life, Flower, Church, 14 In. 960.00
Busk, Whalebone, Pierced Heart, Diamond Design, c.1800, 14 1/8 In. 3080.00
Cane, Bone Shaft, Handle, Ivory, Wood, Spacers, 35 In. 350.00
Cane, Whalebone, Cylindrical Shaft, Turk's Head Handle, 34 1/2 In. 750.00
Cradle, Panbone, Carved, Turned, Scalloped Rails, Stars, Flowers, 3 3/8 In., Pair 1075.00
Cribbage, Caribou Antler, Anchor, Star, Eagle, Hearts, 14 In. 325.00
Cribbage, Walrus Tusk, Board, Carved, Relief, Sea Life, Late 19th Century, 11 In. 350.00
Cribbage, Walrus Tusk, Carved Both Sides, Animals, Fish, Northwest Region, 23 In. 470.00
Cribbage, Walrus Tusk, Goose, Walrus, Reindeer, Newfoundland 1230.00
Crimping Wheel, Fork, Whalebone, Ivory, Half Moon Shape, 3 Baleen Bands, 5 1/2 In. .. 690.00
Ditty Box, Panbone, Engraved, 3-Masted Ship, Flag, Whaling Scene, 3 x 5 In. 3825.00
Dominoes, Whalebone, Ebony 105.00
Door Latch, Whalebone, Nantucket, Mass., 19th Century, 10 3/8 In. 355.00
Fid, Whalebone, 7 3/4 In. 275.00
Flask, Whale's Tooth, Silver, Relief Carved, Only A Toothful, 19th Century, 4 1/2 In. 840.00
Hair Pin, Multifaceted Knob, 2 3/4 In. 50.00
Horn, Covered Goblet, Metal Mounts, Silver-Plated, Lion With Shield Finial, 22 1/2 In. .. 690.00
Hutch, Watch, Mahogany, Ivory, Fireplace Form, Sailor Made, 21 x 13 In. 4025.00
Jackknife, Ivory, Walrus Tusk, Ribbed Handle, Folding, Ivory Blade, American, 5 1/2 In. .. 225.00
Nutcracker, Ivory, Walrus Tusk, Acorn Shape, Threaded Ivory Setscrew, 3 In. 205.00
Pie Crimper, Ivory Whalebone, 4 1/4 In. 1150.00
Pie Crimper, Whale's Tooth, Heart Pierced Handle, Fan Carved Wheel, 7 1/2 In. 960.00
Plaque, A Glorious Victory 1813, Curved, Brass, Wood, 8 In. 325.00
Powder Measure, Bone, Turned, Carved, Drilled Hole, American, 4 In. 735.00
Rolling Pin, Wood, Ivory Handles 750.00
Spool Rack, Whalebone, Ivory, Hardwood, 2 Rotating Tiers, 19th Century, 9 1/4 In. 840.00
Spoon, Whalebone, 3-Masted Ship, Hand-Forged Copper Rivet, Heart-Shaped Head 5500.00
Swift, Whalebone, Baleen Inserts, Carved Center Post, Staves, 18 In. 3200.00
Swift, Whalebone, Carved, Ivory Inlay, Mahogany Pilasters, Turned Knop, 31 x 27 In. ... 4183.00
Swift, Whalebone, Ivory, Copper, 16 In. 880.00
Tooth, Engraved 2-Masted Ship, 4 1/2 In. 115.00
Tusk, Narwhal, 34 In. 4025.00
Walrus Tusk, Whaling Scene, Inscribed, Seeking The Sperm Whale, 19th Century 4540.00
Water Dipper, Coconut, Whale Ivory & Ebony, Curved Handle, 18 In. 1150.00
Whale's Tooth, 3-Masted Ship, American Flag, Woman, c.1800, 8 1/4 In. 13200.00
Whale's Tooth, 3-Masted Ship, Flag, Anchors, Whaling Scene, 4 3/4 In. 935.00

Whale's Tooth, 3-Masted Ship, Flag, Flowers & Leaf, 5 1/2 In.	3575.00
Whale's Tooth, 3-Masted Ship, Rigging, Flag, Woman, 19th Century, 8 In.	7770.00
Whale's Tooth, 3-Masted Ship, Square-Rigged, Flag, BMB 1883, 5 3/4 In.	1045.00
Whale's Tooth, Carved Tiger, Cartouche, Signed, 4 3/4 In.	460.00
Whale's Tooth, Classical Figures, 3-Masted Ships, Choppy Seascape, 6 1/4 In.	990.00
Whale's Tooth, Classical Figures, Kneeling & Standing, 19th Century, 5 1/2 In., Pair	1870.00
Whale's Tooth, Eagle, Clutching Branches, Banner, E Pluribus Unum, Ship, 6 In.	3110.00
Whale's Tooth, Engraved, Color Tinted, Inlaid, Victorian Lady, Fancy Dress, 7 In., Pair . .	15535.00
Whale's Tooth, Engraved, Color Tinted, Man, Woman, 4 1/2 In., Pair	1795.00
Whale's Tooth, Engraved, Color Tinted, Standing Sailor, 19th Century, 6 1/8 In.	3345.00
Whale's Tooth, Engraved, Depicting Ladies Fashionable Dresses, 19th Century, 6 In. . . .	1116.00
Whale's Tooth, Engraved, Figures & Building, 19th Century, 6 1/4 In.	2585.00
Whale's Tooth, Engraved, Goddess Of Liberty, 19th Century, 5 3/4 In.	2585.00
Whale's Tooth, Engraved, Sailor With Saber, 19th Century, 6 7/8 In.	5580.00
Whale's Tooth, Engraved, Ship In Full Sail, British Flag, 19th Century, 5 3/4 In.	1075.00
Whale's Tooth, Engraved, Small, Bearded Man, 19th Century, 4 3/8 In.	765.00
Whale's Tooth, Engraved, Urn, Flowers, 19th Century, 7 1/2 In.	1675.00
Whale's Tooth, Engraved, Woman, Holding Cello, Landscape, 5 1/4 In.	2390.00
Whale's Tooth, Frigate Above 3-Masted Ship, 5 In.	990.00
Whale's Tooth, Ladies In Fancy Dress, Porpoise Shaped Carved Tip, 6 1/4 In.	1675.00
Whale's Tooth, Lady, Fancy Dress, Portrait, George Washington, 19th Century, 7 In.	5380.00
Whale's Tooth, Landscape, Harbor View, New England Screw Co., Providence, 7 1/8 In. . .	7170.00
Whale's Tooth, Liberty, Boy On Reverse, Justice Figure, Commerce Figure, Pair	4315.00
Whale's Tooth, Napoleon On Horse, Neoclassical Structure, Indian, 6 1/2 In.	1760.00
Whale's Tooth, Nude Amorous Couple, 3-Masted Ship, 19th Century, 4 7/8 In.	8605.00
Whale's Tooth, Officer, Mutton Chops, Uniform, Escorting Lady, 6 1/4 In.	990.00
Whale's Tooth, Palm Trees Above 2-Masted Ship, Lighthouse, Weathervane, 5 1/2 In. . . .	1045.00
Whale's Tooth, Port Of Boston, Whaling Scene, Silver Base, 1800s, 4 1/2 In.	1675.00
Whale's Tooth, Portrait, Full-Figured Woman, Nantucket, c.1845	6210.00
Whale's Tooth, Relief Carved, Basket Of Flowers, Leafy Vines, 19th Century, 6 In.	5020.00
Whale's Tooth, Removing Blubber Scene, Ship, American Flag	3910.00
Whale's Tooth, Ship Flying American Flag, 5 1/2 In.	3400.00
Whale's Tooth, Ship, Fox Hound, Full Sail, Harpoon Boats, 19th Century, 7 1/4 In.	15535.00
Whale's Tooth, Ship, Sarah, Banner, 3-Masted Ship, Whale, Anchor, 47 1/4 In.	3346.00
Whale's Tooth, Sleeping Child Inside Shell, Ship, Angel, George Washington, 6 In.	825.00
Whale's Tooth, Whaling Ship, Lighthouse, Marked, Boston, 1842, 5 1/2 In.	530.00
Whale's Tooth, Woman Holding Fan & Letter, 7 3/4 In.	880.00
Whale's Tooth, Woman, 3-Masted Ship, 6 1/2 In.	325.00
Whale's Tooth, Woman, Flowing Dress, Lifeline Chain, Portrait, Engraved, 5 1/2 In.	3825.00
Whale's Tooth, Woman, Victorian Dress, Late 19th Century	1065.00

SEBASTIAN MINIATURES were first made by Prescott W. Baston in 1938 in Marblehead, Massachusetts. More than 400 different designs have been made, and collectors search for the out-of-production models. The mark may say *Copr. P. W. Baston U.S.A.*, or *P. W. Baston, U.S.A.*, or *Prescott W. Baston*. Sometimes a paper label was used.

George & Martha Washington, Standing, Marblehead, 1939, 2 3/4 In., Pair	150.00
Lobsterman, Marblehead, 1947, 2 7/8 In.	60.00
Peter & Annie Stuyvesant, Marblehead, 1940, 2 3/4 & 2 1/2 In., Pair	150.00

SEG, see Paul Revere Pottery category.

SEVRES porcelain has been made in Sevres, France, since 1769. Many copies of the famous ware have been made. The name originally referred to the works of the Royal Porcelain factory. The name now includes any of the wares made in the town of Sevres, France. The entwined lines with a center letter used as the mark is one of the most forged marks in antiques. Be very careful to identify Sevres by quality, not just by mark.

Berry Bowl Set, Server, Flower Border, Gold Rim, Bavaria, 9 & 6 1/2 In., 7 Piece	98.00
Bowl, Centerpiece, Oval, Bronze Dore Handles, Pedestal Base, 1800s, 13 x 24 x 12 In. . . .	4600.00
Box, Blue Opaque, Round, Enameled Butterfly & Floral, Cover, Signed, 3 In.	80.00
Cachepot, Polychrome, Flowers, Cobalt Blue Interlaced L, c.1900, 17 1/2 In.	1380.00

Cake Stand, 2 Tiers, Ormolu Mounts, Gilt Trim, Polychrome Transfer Leaves, 18 3/4 In. . . 1410.00
Clock, Mantel, Louis XVI Style, Gilt Brass, Marble, Roses, Key, c.1885, 38 x 72 In. 345.00
Cooler, Fruit, Cover, Liner, c.1769, 8 3/8 In., Pair 6570.00
Cup, Landscape, Figural Design, Handles, Cover, Undertray, c.1875, 6 1/2 x 5 1/2 In. 138.00
Dresser Box, Bleu De Roi, Hinged Lid, Equestrian Scene, 3 1/4 x 6 x 5 1/4 In. 1325.00
Figurine, Bleu Persian Glaze, Parcel Gilt, Fruit & Brush Vendor, c.1865, 6 In., Pair 748.00
Figurine, Elizabethan Dress, Blue Ground, Gold Accents, Early 19th Century, 8 1/2 In. . . . 635.00
Figurine, L'Amitie Au Coeur, Nymph, Heart, Tree Trunk, Soft Paste, Biscuit, 14 In. 4370.00
Figurine, Marie Antoinette, Sedan Chair, Rococo, 19th Century, 9 1/2 In. 1150.00
Garniture Set, Bleu Celeste, c.1885, 10 1/2 x 8 1/2 In., 3 Piece 1955.00
Garniture Vase, Figures, Landscape, Sevres, 19th Century, 11 1/4 In., Pair 1840.00
Group, L'Amour Nourri Par L'Esperance, Woman Breastfeeding Putti, 9 1/8 In. 3220.00
Lamp, Urn Shape, Gilt Brass Mounts, Lakeside Picnic Scene, c.1880, 38 In. 1019.00
Plate, Boy & Girl Beneath Tree, Mauve, Cobalt Blue Border, Gilt Scrolls, E. Duc, 10 In. . . 45.00
Plate, Cabinet, Chateau Des Rochers, Gilt Scrollwork, c.1900, 9 1/2 In. 218.00
Plate, Portrait, Nicholas Despreaux Boileau, Blue Border, Gilt, 1831, 9 1/4 In. 4830.00
Plate, Portrait, Sebastien Bourdon, Blue Border, Gilt, 1833, 9 1/4 In. 4600.00
Plate, Profile, Man, Mistletoe, White, Green Ground, Gilded, 1911, 8 1/2 In. 2070.00
Plate, Shield, Blue, Multicolored, 10 1/4 In. 250.00
Plate Set, Cabinet, Parcel Gilt, Cobalt Blue Rim, Rural Life Scene, 9 1/2 In., 6 Piece 1500.00
Platter, Oval, Gilt Fleur-De-Lis Rim, c.1880, 15 1/2 In. 400.00
Potpourri, Cobalt, Leaf Cast Lid, Floral Finial, Lion Face Handles, Ormolu, 20 x 13 In. . . 4025.00
Tazza, Napoleon III, Gilt Bronze Mount, Giltwood Stand, Putti, 8 1/2 In. 980.00
Urn, Art Nouveau Woman, Flowers, Bronze Mounts, 25 1/2 In. 2185.00
Urn, Cover, Allegorical Scene, Pink, Blue Ground, 19th Century, 19 In. 1035.00
Urn, Young Lovers Scene, Bronze Mounting, Signed, c.1900, 13 In. 460.00
Vase, Bleu Celeste, 2 Handles, Potpourri, Lamp Mount, France, c.1885, 24 1/2 In., Pair . . 1095.00
Vase, Blue Abstract Peacock Feathers, Mottled Ground, Taxile Doat, 4 1/2 x 1 3/4 In. 560.00
Vase, Campana Form, Restauration Style, Blue Ground, c.1885, 12 1/4 x 9 1/2 In., Pair . . 1725.00
Vase, Cherubs, Flowers, Musical Instruments, White, Ormolu Handles & Base, 13 In. 575.00
Vase, Nort De Pomme, Louis XV Style, Gilt Bronze Mounted, Bottle Form, 12 In., Pair . . 980.00
Vase, Shouldered, Oval, Cobalt Blue, Leaf Gilt Rim, Foot, Mark, c.1901, 13 3/4 In. 470.00
Vase, Silver Mounted, Shouldered Oval, Cobalt Blue, Gold Snowflakes, 19 In., Pair 3585.00

SEWER TILE figures were made by workers at the sewer tile and pipe
factories in the Ohio area during the late nineteenth and early twentieth centuries. Figurines, small vases, and cemetery vases were favored.
Often the finished vase was a piece of the original pipe with added decorations and markings. All types of sewer tile work are now considered
folk art by collectors.

Basin, Rosettes, Applied Ribs, Wide Rim, Center Hole, 3 Loop Handles, 13 3/4 In. 165.00
Doorstop, Eagle, Brown Glaze, Signed, Robert Thompson, 10 In. . . . . *Illus* 175.00
Figurine, Cat, White Clay Eyes, 7 1/2 In. 410.00
Figurine, Dog, Seated, Molded, Hand Tooled, Tan To Brown, Ohio, 11 In. 660.00
Figurine, Dog, Spaniel, Seated, Ohio, 12 In. 550.00
Figurine, Lion, Brown Glaze, Incised Details, Oval Base, Initials, E.J.E., 7 x 13 In. 1210.00
Figurine, Lion, Reclining, Hand Tooled, Molding, Signed, J.C.E., July 28, 1901, 11 x 6 In. 825.00
Figurine, Lion, Reclining, Scalloped Edge Base, Painted Brown, 8 5/8 x 5 1/8 In. 110.00
Figurine, Spaniel, Seated, Incised Face, Wavy Fur, Glazed, 9 3/4 In. 578.00
Figurine, Spaniel, Seated, Manganese Glaze, 11 1/4 In. 395.00
Figurine, Spaniel, Seated, Speckled Glaze, 11 1/2 In. 366.00

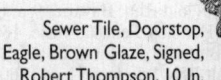

**To remove old gummed labels,
use one of the special solvents
found at artist supply stores.**

Sewer Tile, Doorstop,
Eagle, Brown Glaze, Signed,
Robert Thompson, 10 In.

Planter, Applied Flowers, Shoulder Cutouts, Leaves, Loop Handles, 15 In. 690.00
Planter, Tree Trunk, 5 Open Branches, 21 1/2 In. 600.00
Planter, Tree Trunk, Rough Bark, Applied Snake, 8 1/4 x 6 1/4 In. 55.00
Tile, Signed, Clyde Hochstettler, 1926, 6 x 6 In. 375.00

SEWING equipment of all types is collected, from sewing birds that
held the cloth to tape measures, needle books, and old wooden spools.
Sewing machines are included here. Needlework pictures are listed in
the Picture category.

Bag, Cloth, Striped, 2 1/4 x 7 x 2 In. 120.00
Basket, Woven, Swing Hoop Handle, Turned Bottom, 19th Century, 8 x 8 1/2 In. 956.00
Bird, Brass, Embossed Flowers On Clamp, Pat. 1853, 5 In. 169.00
Bird, Brass, Embossed, Velvet Cushion, Victorian 135.00
Bird, Cast Base, 4 x 2 x 5 In. 355.00
Bird, Iron, Heart Form Thumbscrew, 19th Century, 3 In. 990.00
Bobbin, Lace Tatting, Frame, Bone, Ivory, Brass Wire, Pewter Bands, 22 x 13 In. 385.00
Box, 2 Tiers, Drawer, Pincushion, Victorian, 8 x 7 x 5 In. 56.00
Box, 3 Tiers, Pincushion Top, Spool Holders, Scalloped Sides, 11 In. 155.00
Box, Brass Tack, Hinged Lid, Geometric Applied Carvings, 5 3/4 x 18 3/4 In. 105.00
Box, Burlwood, Brass Bound, Drawers, Compartments, Malachite, Garnets, 11 1/2 In. 1116.00
Box, Hinged Cover, Carved, Cupid, Heart, Flowers, Footed, 8 x 6 1/2 x 13 1/4 In. 600.00
Box, Lacquer, Chinoiserie, Rectangular, c.1890, 5 5/8 x 10 1/4 x 5 3/4 In. 259.00
Box, Lacquer, Scenic Panels, Greek Key Border, Brass Handles, Fitted, 17 1/4 In. 470.00
Box, Lift Top, Wooden, Inlaid, Fitted Interior, 19th Century, 8 x 11 1/2 x 8 In. 290.00
Box, Lozenge Shape, Grain Painted, Flowers, Pinstripe, c.1850, 15 1/2 x 9 1/2 x 6 1/2 In. . . 595.00
Box, Mahogany, Inlaid, Shell Design, Hinged Lid, 19th Century, 5 5/8 x 7 1/4 In. 999.00
Box, Mahogany, Interior Tray, Hinged Top, Inlaid Mother-Of-Pearl, 4 x 10 In. 128.00
Box, Needlework, Petit Point, Seed Pearls, Handles, 17th Century, 10 x 7 x 9 In. 5500.00
Box, Pincushion, Drawer, c.1864 . . . . 265.00
Box, Rosewood, Mother-Of-Pearl, Fitted Interior, Lift-Out Tray, c.1835, 12 x 9 In. 650.00
Box, Spool, Cotton, Oak, Hinged Cover, c.1890, 5 x 3 1/2 In. 28.00
Box, Tortoiseshell, Ivory Pierced Plaques, Sloped Hinged Lid, 8 Sides, 3 1/2 x 6 7/8 In. . . . 410.00
Box, Walnut, Varnish Finish, Compartments, Enfield, Conn., c.1889, 6 1/4 In. 2875.00
Box, Wood, Brass Inlay, Mother-Of-Pearl Accessories, 12 x 9 x 6 1/2 In. 1325.00
Box, Yarn, Silver, Gilt, Repousse Swag & Drape Design, 3 Supports, Victorian, 4 1/2 In. . . 518.00
Button, Luckyday, Men's Sport Shirt, 4 On Card, 3 3/4 In. . . . . *Illus* 8.00
Button, Luckyday, Pearl, Men's, 5 On Card, 3 3/4 In. . . . . *Illus* 12.00
Cabinet, Spool, see also Advertising category under Cabinet, Spool.
Cabinet, 108 Spools, Brainer & Armstrong, c.1890 . . . . 2550.00
Cabinet, Spool, Oak, 2 Drawers, Turned Leg Stand, Embossed Brass Knobs, 23 x 22 In. . . 158.00
Cabinet, Spool, Shaped Gallery, Spool Dowels, 4 Drawers, Pull Rings, 22 1/2 In. 425.00
Cabinet, Victorian, Walnut, Slant Front, 5 Drawers, 13 x 25 x 17 1/2 In. 345.00
Cabinet, Walnut, Ash, 4 Drawers, Spool Caddy On Top, 16 x 10 x 23 In. 990.00
Caddy, Inlaid Wood, Ivory, Cylindrical Base, Inlay, Wafers, Dome, France, 12 In. 110.00

Sewing, Button, Luckyday,
Men's Sport Shirt, 4 On Card,
3 3/4 In.

Sewing, Button, Luckyday,
Pearl, Men's, 5 On Card,
3 3/4 In.

Sewing, Snap, Finery Fasteners,
Woman Dressed As Peacock,
12 On Card, 4 3/4 In.

Caddy, Mahogany, 2 Tiers, Pincushion, Drawer, Thread Holes, Tapered Feet, 6 3/4 In. ... 170.00
Caddy, Wood, Walnut, Red Velvet Pincushion Top, Bowfront Drawer, Ball Feet, 8 In. 110.00
Chest, Micro Mosaic Inlay, Geometric, Ivory, Stone, 19th Century, 5 x 17 x 11 In. 115.00
Chest, Ribbed, Horn, Fitted Compartments, Ivory, 19th Century, 18 x 10 x 8 In. 719.00
Chest, Spool, Cherry, 6 Paneled Drawers, Brass Knobs, 22 x 26 x 19 In. 805.00
Clamp, Ivory, Pair, 3 3/4 In. 428.00
Clamp, Quilting, Thumb Screws, Iron, 4 1/2 In., 4 Piece 35.00
Hoop, Tripod Base, Tilt Adjustment, Mid 19th Century 495.00
Lacemaker's Lamp, Blown Glass, Applied Handle, 10 1/2 In. 1265.00
Lacemaker's Lamp, Bulbous Font, Applied Drip Pan, Handle, Thumb Tab, 9 1/2 In., Pair . 825.00
Lacemaker's Lamp, Free-Blown, Globe Font, Mid Drip Dish, 19th Century, 9 3/8 In. 235.00
Lacemaker's Lamp, Globe Font, Mid Drip Dish, Early 19th Century, 5 1/8 In. 410.00
Loom, Walnut, Tabletop Model, 15 1/2 x 14 3/4 x 12 1/4 In. 85.00
Machine, Baby Lock, Cast Iron, Black Paint, Gilt Flowers, 7 In. 219.00
Machine, Cast Iron, Hand Crank, Gold Stencil, Germany, c.1900, 11 3/4 In. 540.00
Machine, Hurtu, L'Abeille, No. 13, 621, France, c.1875 .... 885.00
Machine, Pocket, Tin Box, Dark Green, Gold Graphics, 8 In. 900.00
Machine, Salter, Ideal, Nickel Stitch Plate, Hand Crank, Cover, 1910 .... 115.00
Machine, Singer, Painted Flowers, Hand Crank, Wooden Base 66.00
Machine, Thabourin, Paris, Cast Iron Cross Arm & Footed Base, c.1880 .... 254.00
Machine, Wanzer, Cast Iron, Black Paint, Gilt Flowers, Marble Base, Brass Label, 10 In. . 230.00
Machine, Wheeler, Wilson, Rosewood Case, Cast Iron Treadle Base, Conn., 36 In. 110.00
Machine, Willcox & Gibbs, Wooden Base, Case, 1871 .... 96.00
Needle Case, Flowers, Avery, 1 3/4 In. 210.00
Needle Case, Ivory, Cylinder, Carved Dragons, Birds, Butterflies, Chinese, c.1880, 6 In. ... 131.00
Needle Case, Silver, Anchor, 3 3/4 In. 428.00
Needle Case, Silver, Flat, Rectangular, Hinged, Arthur J. Stone, 4 1/4 x 3 In. 500.00
Needle Threader, Prudential Has Strength Of Rock Of Gibraltar, Tin 8.00
Needle Threader, Witch, Plastic, Original Box, Germany 20.00
Pincushion, Apple Shape, Velvet, Early 19th Century, 3 1/8 In. 705.00
Pincushion, Apple Shape, Velvet, Satin Ribbon, Velvet Leaf, Early 19th Century, 3 1/2 In. 176.00
Pincushion, Bird, Brass, Molded, Upper & Lower Cushions, Mid 19th Century, 5 In. 200.00
Pincushion, Butterfly, Velvet, Early 19th Century, 5 1/8 x 4 3/8 In. 590.00
Pincushion, Carrot, Velvet, Early 19th Century, 10 In. 880.00
Pincushion, China Doll, Lace Collar & Cushion, Victorian 100.00
Pincushion, Frog, Velvet, Glass Eyes, Painted Details, Early 19th Century, 2 1/2 In. 705.00
Pincushion, Hand Form, Red Heart In Palm, Wooden Spool Base, Machine Stitched 405.00
Pincushion, Peaches, Velvet, Early 19th Century, 2 1/2 In. 355.00
Pincushion, Pear Shape, Velvet, Early 19th Century, 4 1/4 In. 118.00
Pincushion, Pear Shape, Velvet, Early 19th Century, 7 1/8 In. 705.00
Pincushion, Rooster, Make-Do, Wool, Cotton, Wool Yarn, Glass Stand, 14 1/4 In. 440.00
Pincushion, Squash, Velvet, Grosgrain Ribbon, Gourd Stem, Early 1800s, 6 1/4 x 7 In. ... 235.00
Pincushion, Strawberry Form, Cloth, Make-Do, 8 In. 248.00
Pincushion, Strawberry Shape, Red, Cast Iron Base, Urn Shape, 4 x 3 3/4 In. 165.00
Pincushion, Strawberry, 7 Small Around 1 Large Berry, Wool, 8 1/4 In. 440.00
Pincushion, Strawberry, Velvet, Felt Leaves, Glass Pin Seeds, Early 19th Century, 5 In. .. 825.00
Pincushion, Tape Measure, Cloth, Mammy, Red, Dress, Bandanna, Apron, Japan, 5 In. 75.00
Pincushion, Tomato, Velvet, 19th Century, 1 3/4 x 3 5/8 In. 558.00
Pincushion, Wooden Book, Figural Hand Clamp, Victorian, 8 1/2 x 6 x 10 In. 590.00
Pincushion Dolls are listed in their own category.
Pincushion Holder, Poodle, Yellow, Black Accents, 2 1/4 In. 28.00
Pleater, Crown, Counter Model, Cast Iron, Gold & Red Stenciling, Pat. 1880, 9 In. ... 23.00
Snap, Finery Fasteners, Woman Dressed As Peacock, 12 On Card, 4 3/4 In. .... *Illus* 15.00
Spool Caddy, Mahogany, Domed Base, Revolving Tiers, Pegs, Pincushion, 14 1/2 In. ... 105.00
Stool, Lacemaker's, Pine, Birch Stretchers, Bobbins, New Hampshire, c.1850, 31 In. 690.00
Swift, Table, Walnut, Maple, Turned Base, Threaded Oak Screw, 19 1/2 In. 220.00
Swift, Wood, Tabletop, Folding, Pin Cup Finial Top, Thumbscrew Ball, 27 In. 120.00
Tape Measure, 2 Dogs In Basket, Japan, 2 1/4 In. 135.00
Tape Measure, Basket Of Fruit, Celluloid, 1 3/4 In. 95.00
Tape Measure, Basket Of Fruit, Celluloid, 2 In. 130.00
Tape Measure, Basket Of Fruit, Ladybug Handle, Celluloid, Germany, 2 In. 110.00
Tape Measure, Best, 2 1/4 In. 15.00
Tape Measure, Brass, Gristmill, Germany, c.1870, 1 1/2 In. 225.00

Tape Measure, Elephant, Celluloid, Japan, 2 In. 125.00
Tape Measure, Elephant, Cloth, Japan, 3 1/4 In. 35.00
Tape Measure, Flower Basket, Ladybug Handle, Celluloid, Germany, 1 1/2 In. 85.00
Tape Measure, Flower, Celluloid, Germany, 1 3/4 In. 110.00
Tape Measure, Flowerpot, Japan, 2 1/4 In. 85.00
Tape Measure, Indian Head, Cigar, Japan, 1 1/2 In. .... 175.00 to 210.00
Tape Measure, Kingfisher, Sitting On Egg, Celluloid, Ivory, Brown, Germany, 2 1/2 In. .. 138.00
Tape Measure, Lady With Muff, Germany, 2 In. 155.00
Tape Measure, Liberty Bell, Benson's Wild Animal Farm, Celluloid, Germany, 2 In. 110.00
Tape Measure, Lydia Pinkham's, Image Of Lydia, Round, 1 3/4 In. 61.00
Tape Measure, Parrot, On Stand, Butterfly Pull Handle, Bronze, 1 3/4 In. 275.00
Tape Measure, Pig In Boot, Celluloid, Japan, 2 1/4 In. 95.00
Tape Measure, Pig, Celluloid, 2 1/2 In. 40.00
Tape Measure, Snipe, Germany, 2 1/2 In. 280.00
Tape Measure, Terrier & Puppy, Japan, 2 In. 155.00
Thimble, Brass, Elizabethan, Marked, Crotal Bell, England, 1550-1590 .... 185.00
Thimble, Mother-Of-Pearl, Gold Rim, 3/4 In. 525.00
Yarn Winder, Mixed Woods, Cutout Heart, Rose Head Nails, Early 19th Century, 44 In. ... 200.00
Yarn Winder, Panbone, Carved, Turned, Gear Mechanism, Box Base, c.1876, 9 In. 2629.00

SHAKER items are characterized by simplicity, functionalism, and orderliness. There were many Shaker communities in America from the eighteenth century to the present day. The religious order made furniture, small wooden pieces, and packaged medicines, herbs, and jellies to sell to *outsiders*. Other useful objects were made for use by members of the community. Shaker furniture is listed in this book in the Furniture category.

Basket, Gathering, Round, High Sides, Arched Handles, 18 1/4 x 11 1/2 In. 250.00
Basket, Laundry, Woven Splint, 2 Bentwood Handles, Mt. Lebanon, N.Y., 17 1/2 x 14 In. 360.00
Basket, Sewing, Splint, Woven, Round Over Square, Loop Handles, 1 5/8 x 3 1/4 In. 3820.00
Bed, Infirmary, Hickory, Turned Posts, Painted, North Union, Ohio, 81 x 29 x 30 In. 1045.00
Bench, Meeting House, Painted, Lower Shaker Village, Enfield, 96 x 16 x 31 In. 440.00
Bottle Holder, Rectangular Base, Central Post Cutouts, Enfield, N.H., 4 x 15 1/2 x 18 In. 440.00
Box, 2-Finger, Oval, Copper Tacks, 4 x 6 x 2 1/2 In. 580.00
Box, 2-Finger, Oval, Copper Tacks, 6 3/8 x 2 In. 300.00
Box, 2-Finger, Oval, Lid, 2 1/2 x 6 In. 400.00
Box, 3-Finger, Maple & Pine, Copper Tacks, Pencil Inscription, 8 x 5 1/2 In. 340.00
Box, 3-Finger, Oval, Lid, Brown, Copper Tacks, 9 x 6 x 3 1/2 In. 550.00
Box, 3-Finger, Oval, Lid, Pine, Maple, Gray Paint, Mid 19th Century, 4 3/4 x 12 In. 650.00
Box, 3-Finger, Painted Blue, Lid, Oval, Copper Tacks, 11 7/8 x 4 1/4 In. 770.00
Box, 4-Finger, Lid, Painted, Ocher 9075.00
Box, 4-Finger, Maple, Swing Handles, c.1880, 10 In. 1380.00
Box, 4-Finger, Oval, Lapped, Jennet Angus, Watervliet, 1832, 5 x 10 x 7 In. 7050.00
Box, 4-Finger, Pantry, Lid, Painted, Ocher 6875.00
Box, Herb Carrier, Pine, Rectangular, Hoop Handles, Canterbury, N.H., c.1850 .... 1150.00
Box, Maple, Dark Brown Stain, Oval, New Lebanon, N.Y., c.1840, 5 1/2 In. 2070.00
Box, Oval, Ocher Wash, Crazed Varnish, Label, Watervliet 1832, 10 1/2 In. 7050.00
Box, Pine, Maple, Oval, Dark Orange Stain, 4 In. 2185.00
Box, Pine, Maple, Oval, Original Green, 7 3/4 In. 1150.00
Box, Sewing, 3 Tiers, Whalebone Mounts, Walnut Veneers, 8 1/2 x 9 In. 315.00
Box, Sewing, Maple, Pine Lid, Swing Handle, 5 Lapped Fingers, Silk Lined, 11 x 15 In. . 1880.00
Box, Spit, Maple, Pine, 4-Finger, Copper Tacks, New Lebanon, N.Y., c.1850, 11 1/2 In. .. 520.00
Box, Storage, Pine, Original Stain, 4 Compartments, New Lebanon, N.Y., c.1840, 2 1/2 In. 1955.00

Shaker, Brush,
Shoe, Horsehair,
Wooden Handle,
8 1/4 In.

Box Set, Mt. Lebanon, Mid 19th Century, 3 Piece 1325.00
Brush, Shoe, Horsehair, Wooden Handle, 8 1/4 In. .... *Illus* 55.00
Bucket, Painted, Green, Wire Bail, Tongue & Groove Staves, 7 x 10 1/2 In. 499.00
Bucket, Stave Construction, Maple, Painted, Red, Bentwood Handle, 11 1/2 In. 145.00
Bucket, Yellow, Red, Green, Blue, c.1870 .... 650.00
Carrier, 3-Finger, Bentwood, Copper Tacks, Swing Handle, 4 7/8 x 7 x 2 1/2 In. 330.00
Carrier, 3-Finger, Bentwood, Lid, Copper Tacks, Handle, 11 1/4 x 4 1/4 In. 385.00
Medicine Chest, Dovetailed, Green Paint, Brass Hinges, Original Key, c.1800 .... 5995.00
Spinning Wheel, Oak, Maple & Pine, Original Finish, Canterbury, N.H., c.1830, 33 In. .. 690.00
Swift, Yellow Wash, Wood Thread Thumbscrews, 18 1/2 In. 220.00
Tool Chest, 5 Drawers, 6 1/2 x 46 In. 635.00

SHAVING MUGS were popular from 1860 to 1900. Many types were
made, including occupational mugs featuring pictures of men's jobs.
There were scuttle mugs, silver-plated mugs, glass-lined mugs, and
others.

Bicycle, High Wheeled, W.A. Trembly, 3 7/8 In. .... *Illus* 1456.00
Clover, Lucky Horseshoe, Perry Knoblock, Limoges, c.1905, 3 1/2 In. 45.00
Horse, Hand Painted, China, 3 5/8 x 3 5/8 In. 172.00
Hunter, 2 Dogs, Frank Parks, Limoges, c.1905, 3 1/2 In. 235.00
Hunter, Bird In Dog's Mouth, Oar, Rifle, R.F. Addy, c.1905, 4 In. 90.00
Hunter, Bird In Dog's Mouth, W.H. Jaeger, c.1905, 4 In. 170.00
Hunter & Dog, China, 3 5/8 x 3 5/8 In. 221.00
Irish National, Leprechaun Playing Harp, White Insert, Green Ground, 3 1/2 In. 960.00
Man, Photographic, J.E. Neville, 1890-1925, 4 In. 1000.00
Man, Photographic, Wm. K. Jones, Germany, 1890-1925, 4 In. 615.00
Occupational, 2 Plumbers, Working Under Vanity, Dibble, 3 5/8 In. 784.00
Occupational, Barber Tools, E.E. Farrow, c.1905, 4 In. 280.00
Occupational, Brewery Truck, Beer Kegs, Greg Ruppert, 3 3/4 In. .... *Illus* 1792.00
Occupational, Butcher, Cutting Meat, S.H. McKee, c.1905, 3 7/8 In. 1008.00
Occupational, Butcher, Limoges, France, 3 3/4 In. 225.00
Occupational, Butcher, Steer, Tools, China, 3 5/8 x 3 5/8 In. 109.00
Occupational, Dentist, Pulling Tooth, C.F. Becker, 3 5/8 In. 1725.00
Occupational, Dry Cleaning Wagon, Horse Drawn, John Doherty, 3 3/4 In. .... *Illus* 1064.00
Occupational, Fabric Shop, Victorian Woman, Male Clerk, Gilt Lettering 848.00
Occupational, Farmer, Plowing Field, N. Palmer, Hopperstead, c.1905, 4 In. 308.00
Occupational, Farrier Shoeing A Bay, Polychrome, Gilt Letters 735.00
Occupational, Farrier's Shop, Shoeing Horse, Porcelain, J.F. Stewart 734.00
Occupational, Governor, William C. Sproul, P.A., Gilt 700.00
Occupational, Grinding Machine, Hand Painted, Golf Trim, China, 4 x 3 7/8 In. 523.00
Occupational, Hotel Clerk, Interior Of Hotel, Hand Painted, China, 3 7/8 x 3 7/8 In. 715.00
Occupational, Locomotive, Camel Back, G.O. Stone, 1890-1925, 3 7/8 In. 336.00
Occupational, Locomotive, Man In Boxcar, Ice Tongs, Gable, 3 3/4 In. 504.00
Occupational, Man, Driving Cleaning Wagon, J.J. Doherty, 3 3/4 In. 1065.00
Occupational, Man, Driving Horse Drawn Delivery Wagon, c.1910, 3 3/4 In. 728.00
Occupational, Man, Driving Horse Drawn Sulky, J.F. Fullerton, 4 1/8 In. 532.00
Occupational, Man, Driving Horse Drawn Wagon, T.J. Murphy, 1890-1925, 4 In. 308.00

Shaving Mug, Bicycle,
High Wheeled,
W.A. Trembly,
3 7/8 In.

Shaving Mug,
Occupational, Brewery
Truck, Beer Kegs, Greg
Ruppert, 3 3/4 In.

Shaving Mug, Occupational,
Dry Cleaning Wagon,
Horse Drawn, John
Doherty, 3 3/4 In.

Shaving Mug,
Occupational, Sailing
Ship, Stamped,
N. Aeillo, 3 1/2 In.

Occupational, Man, Horse Drawn Delivery Wagon, E.J. Sullivan, c.1905, 3 5/8 In.	280.00
Occupational, Man, On Scaffolding, L.G. Breitenbnch, 1890-1925, 3 5/8 In.	2690.00
Occupational, Man, Photographing Woman, C.J. Peelstrom, 1890-1925, 4 In.	1456.00
Occupational, Man, Plowing Fields, Farm, P.W. Harris, c.1905, 3 5/8 In.	450.00
Occupational, Man, Riding Racing Bicycle, H.K. Shrom, 1890-1925, 3 7/8 In.	1345.00
Occupational, Man, Selling Fabric, Shop, Victorian Woman, W.A. Bowermaster, Vienna	848.00
Occupational, Man, Standing, Inside Railroad Car, R. Gable, 1890-1925, 3 3/4 In.	500.00
Occupational, Metal Lathe, W. Zernick, American, c.1905, 3 1/8 In.	235.00
Occupational, Oyster Shell, N.W. Hoaster, American, c.1905, 3 5/8 In.	840.00
Occupational, Painter, On Scaffold, T & V Limoges, Breitenbunch, 3 5/8 In.	2688.00
Occupational, Railroad Boxcar, P. Gilhards, American, c.1905, 3 3/4 In.	196.00
Occupational, Sailing Ship, Stamped, N. Aeillo, 3 1/2 In. *Illus*	1725.00
Occupational, Sewing Machine, Davis, 1890-1925, 3 3/4 In.	560.00
Occupational, Shoe Store Clerk, G.E. Wersen, Limoges, France, 3 3/4 In.	3920.00
Occupational, Stake Wagon, Hand Painted, China, 3 3/4 x 3 5/8 In.	440.00
Occupational, Steer, Jo Williams, American, c.1900, 3 1/4 In.	179.00
Occupational, Steers Head, W.F. Muller, Kern Barber Supply, c.1905	225.00
Occupational, Touring Car, H. Ratzenberg, 1890-1925, 3 1/2 In.	280.00
Occupational, Truck, Filled With Beer Kegs, G. Ruppert, 1890-1925, 3 3/4 In.	1790.00
Occupational, Woodsmen Of The World, Fraternal, Green Leaf, Gold Trim, 4 x 3 5/8 In.	121.00
Snare Drum, 2 American Flags, A. Suttlerlin, c.1905, 3 5/8 In.	615.00
Stone Obelisk, Eagle, John W. Conroy, c.1905, 3 5/8 In.	56.00
Watermelon, Hand Painted, China, 3 5/8 x 3 1/2 In.	415.00

SHAWNEE POTTERY was started in Zanesville, Ohio, in 1937. The company made vases, novelty ware, flowerpots, planters, lamps, and cookie jars. Three dinnerware lines were made: Corn, Lobster Ware, and Valencia (a solid color line). White Corn pattern utility pieces were made in 1945. Corn King was made from 1946 to 1954; Corn Queen, with darker green leaves and lighter colored corn, from 1954 to 1961. Shawnee produced pottery for George Rumrill during the late 1930s. The company closed in 1961.

Bowl, Console, Cameo, Blond Satin, 15 In.	15.00
Candlestick, Confetti, White On Black, Pair	25.00
Condiment Set, Black, White, Brass Frame, Saucy Susan	125.00
Condiment Set, Saucy Susan, Black & White, Revolving Brass Frame, 9 Piece	125.00
Cookie Jar, Dutch Girl, Tulip	325.00
Cookie Jar, Dutch Girl, Yellow Skirt	110.00
Cookie Jar, Great Northern Girl	350.00
Cookie Jar, Jack & Jill, October 9, 1942, Pair	525.00
Cookie Jar, Muggsy	550.00
Cookie Jar, Smiley Pig, Green Neckerchief & Clover	135.00
Cookie Jar, Winnie & Smiley Pig, Bank	500.00
Creamer, Puss 'n Boots	65.00
Lamp, Harvest Queen, Green, Yellow, 9 1/2 In.	60.00
Pitcher, Bo Peep, Blue Hat, Peach Trim, Marked	95.00
Planter, Ancient Chinese Man, Basket	18.00
Planter, Blue Flower, 8 x 2 1/2 In.	14.00
Planter, Dog, On 3-Button Shoe, Light Blue	25.00
Planter, Planter, Pig, Yellow	16.00
Salt & Pepper, Sailor Boy, Single	14.00
Salt & Pepper, Smiley & Winnie Pig, Clover, 3 1/4 In., Pair	75.00
Salt & Pepper, Smiley & Winnie Pig, Heart, 3 1/4 In., Pair	60.00
Shaker, Puss 'n Boots, Pair	45.00
Teapot, Cover, Red Flower	35.00
Teapot, Pennsylvania Dutch, Lid, Boston Shape, U.S.A. Mark, 32 Oz., 5 In.	150.00
Vase, Bud, Leaf, 7 3/4 In.	18.00

SHEARWATER pottery is a family business started by Mr. and Mrs. G. W. Anderson, Sr., and their three sons. The local Ocean Springs, Mississippi, clays were used to make the wares in the 1930s. The company is still in business.

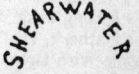

Pitcher, Green, 5 1/4 In.	173.00

SHEET MUSIC from the past centuries is now collected. The favorites are examples with covers featuring artistic or historic pictures. Early sheet music covers were lithographed, but by the 1900s photographic reproductions were used. The early music was larger than more recent sheets, and you must watch out for examples that were trimmed to fit in a twentieth-century piano bench.

'57 Chevrolet, Billie Jo Spears, 1978	4.00
Ac-Cent-Tchu-Ate The Positive, J. Mercer, H. Arlen, E.H. Morris & Co., 1944, 4 Pages	7.00
All My Life, Laughing Irish Eyes, 1936	8.00
Amazon Rag, River Scene, 1904	83.00
Amelia Earhart's Last Flight, Earhart & Airplane, 1939	28.00 to 55.00
American Scene Magazine, Background Theme, Jackie Gleason, 1963	11.00
At Supper Time, Charles Hart, Avery & Hart	82.00
Babe Perfume, Margaux Hemingway Holding Perfume Bottle, 1978	4.00
Ben Casey, Theme, Vince Edwards, 1961	7.00
Billy-Boy The Kidnapped Child, Beekey Music Co., 1909, 11 x 13 1/2 In.	4.00
Black Beauty, Art Cover, c.1910	38.00
Blind Boon's Southern Rag Medley No. 1, Strains From The Alleys, 1908	28.00
Blind Boon's Southern Rag Medley No. 2, Strains From The Flat Branch, 1909	105.00
Bonanza, The Man, Lorne Greene, 1965	9.00
Bonanza Theme, Ben, Hoss, Adam, Little Joe, 1959	9.00
Bowery Buck, Rag Time 2-Step, Tom Turpin	63.00
Brain Storm Rag, Pianist Wailing The Piano, 1907	30.00
Brazil, Josephine Baker	47.00
Brown Skin Who You For, Pretty Woman On Cover, 1915	44.00
Cigar Makers, Local Union No. 431, Label Of Blue	10.00
Cinderella, Vocal Selection, CBS Network Production, Folks In Shoe, 1957	19.00
Cleopha, Scott Joplin, Woman, Flowers On Cover	158.00
College Cuts, Imperial Tobacco Cigarette Co., Cigarette Pack, 1895	56.00
Come Take A Trip In My Automobile, Man Invites Woman For Ride, 1912	66.00
Cow Cow Boogie, Raye, De Paul, Leeds Music, W. Lantz Illustration, 1942, 4 Pages	12.00
Dark Shadows, Quentin's Theme, Black Background, White Text, 1969	9.00
De Glory Road, 15 Page, 1928, 9 x 12 In.	15.00
Do Your Duty Doctor, Irving Berlin, Rag	46.00
Dom Deluise Show, Barrump-Bump, 1968	13.00
Don't Fence Me In, C. Porter, Harms, 1944, 2 Pages	6.00
Dr. Kildare Theme, Chamberlain, 1962	8.00
Dragnet Theme, Jack Webb, 1953	8.00
Euphonic Sounds, S Syncopated Novelty, Scott Joplin	395.00
Father Of The Land We Love, George M. Cohan, 1931	45.00
Felix The Cat, Felix Playing Banjo On Cover	29.00
Free & Easy	161.00
Friend & A Lover, Partridge Family, 1973	8.75
Frisky, Old Man With Dog, 1919	38.00
General Scott's Grand Review March, Stone Lithograph	285.00
God Bless America, Irving Berlin Inc., Published New York, 1939	13.00
Hair, Natoma Productions, Colorful Psychedelic Cover, Copyright 1968, 9 x 12 In.	12.00
Hang On To Me, Lady Be Good, Fred & Adele Astaire On Cover, c.1924	205.00
Hazel, Caricatures Of Shirley Booth & Cast, 1965	20.00
Hee Haw, Folio Of Songs & Photos, Clark & Owens, 1970	10.00
Hilarity Rag, James Scott	130.00
Hot Air Rag, Art Cover, 1900	330.00
Hypnotic Rag, Man, Sparks Fly From Fingertips, 1912	36.00
I Think I Love You, Partridge Family, 1970	6.00
I'll Walk Alone, Dinah Shore Cover, Cahn, Styne, Mayfair Music, 1944, 4 Pages	7.00
I'm In Love With The Gal In The Goldfish Bowl, At Bimbo's 365, Life Magazine	26.00
Idol Of My Heart, My Wife, Uncle Sam Shoes, Latest Shoe Fashion, 1901	46.00
In My Heart, On My Mind, All Day Long, Cupid, Yellow Heard, c.1921	12.00
It's A Long Long Way To Tipperary, Judge, Williams, Chappell & Co., 1912, 4 Pages	9.00
It's Mather's, The Way To My Heart, Mather Store, Atlanta, 1925	38.50
Jeanie With Light Brown Hair, Lithographed, 1854	36.00
Kaufmann's 62nd Anniversary, Bride, Groom, 1933	16.50

Keep Away From The Fellow Who Owns An Automobile, Couple In Auto, 1912 . . . . 3.50
Kerry Mills Medley, Art Cover, 1900 . . . . 110.00
Kismet Rag, Sphinx, Asp, Cleopatra, 1913 . . . . 410.00
Last Night, Michigan Stove Company, Will Bradley Artwork 56.00
Little Nemo, A Fair Tale, Graul Publishing Co., 1906 . . . . 40.00
Love At Home, King Family Show, King Sisters, 1965 . . . . 5.00
Mack's Swell Car Was A Maxwell, Woman, Maxwell Car, 1915 . . . . 18.00
Mah Little Black Angel, F.R. Sweetland 87.00
Mama's Blues, Pretty Woman, Geeky Man, 1917 . . . . 35.00
Mannix, Michael Connors, 1968 . . . . 10.00
Melancholy Serenade, Jackie Gleason, 1953 . . . . 28.00
Miller Beer, Camping Scene, Beer Drinkers, 1970 . . . . 8.00
Mission Impossible Theme, Graves, Landau, Bain, Morris, 1967 . . . . 8.00
Moonlighting, Bruce Willis, Cybill Shepherd, 1985 . . . . 6.00
Mournin' Blues, Original Dixieland Jazz Band, 1918 . . . . 39.00
Moxie, Boy Pointing At You, Boston, 1921 . . . . 33.00
New Sun In The Sky, The Band Wagon, Top Hat On Cover 76.00
Nig-Er, Nig-Er, Never Die 134.00
Nigger War Bride Blues 61.00
Oh Mr. Dream Man, Cy Morgan, Coombs & Bender, 1911 . . . . 150.00
Oh! Lady Be Good, Fred & Adele Astaire On Cover, c.1924 . . . . 285.00
Old Pal Of Mine, Woman By Radio Horn, Music Master, 1925 . . . . 18.00
Onondaga Polka, Head Chief Os-Sa-Hin-Ta, Pipe, Tomahawk, 1852 . . . . 100.00
Pave Your Way Into Tomorrow, Glen Campbell TV Goodtime Hour, 1970 . . . . 6.00
Peter Gunn Theme, Man Show Logo, 1959 . . . . 6.50
Photographic Polka, Walter Dinmore Dedication, 1858 . . . . 300.00
Precious Little Thing Called Love, Gary Cooper, 1928 . . . . 135.00
Quick March, Robert E. Lee, Black, White, 1865 . . . . 325.00
Rag Time Nightmare, Art Cover, 1900 . . . . 155.00
Rag-Knots, Art Cover, 1899 . . . . 39.00
Raggy Rag, Art Cover, 1909 . . . . 105.00
Ragtime Riggles, 1902 . . . . 44.00
Razzle Dazzle, Text Cover, 1905 . . . . 110.00
Red Stockings, Harry & George Wright, 7 Players, 1869 . . . . 2450.00
Refuse All Substitutes, Paul & Marion Stone 35.00
Roaring Twenties, Dorothy Privine, Male Co-Stars, 1960 . . . . 6.00
Shovel Fish, Frog Band Plays For Shovel Fish, 1907 . . . . 55.00
Siberian Dip, Girl Doing Russian Dance, 1911 . . . . 27.00
Sigloo Bigloo, Monitor Stove Co., Eskimo Couple, 1921 . . . . 18.00
Sing Out For Falstaff, Couple At Piano Dream Of Falstaff, 1952 . . . . 13.00
Slam Bank, Art Cover, 1910 . . . . 880.00
Slippery Bill, Trombonist, 1911 . . . . 55.00
Some Enchanted Evening, South Pacific, Rodgers & Hammerstein, 1949 . . . . 11.00
Squirrel Food, Squirrel With Nut, 1916 . . . . 127.00
Star Spangled Banner, Eagle On Banner, F.S. Key, Calumet Music, 1942, 2 Pages 8.00
Sunflower Slow Drag, Sunflower On Cover 141.00
Tarzan's March, Ron Ely, 1966 . . . . 30.00
The Continental, Ginger Rogers, Fred Astaire Dancing On Cover 82.00
They Can't Take That Away From Me, Fred Astaire, Ginger Rogers Smile On Cover 122.00
Till Then, Gershwin & Gershwin, T.B. Harms Co., 1933, 4 Pages 7.00
Tokio, Japanese Geisha, 1912 . . . . 42.00
Treat Me Like A Baby Doll, Trixie McCoy In Blackface, Period Dress, 1914 . . . . 84.00
Uncle Jasper's Jubilee, E.T. Paull, Black Family On Cover 208.00
Washington Evening Star March, Berryman, 1924, 9 x 12 In. 15.00
What Do I Care, Cupid, Arrows, Raymond Klages, Jesse Greer, Harry Carroll, c.1929 . . . 12.00
When Your Hair Has Turned To Silver, Joplin 686.00
With A Little Love, Debbie Reynolds, 1969 . . . . 15.00
With My Head In The Clouds, I Berlin, This Is The Army Inc., 1944 . . . . 6.00
Workers Battle Songs, Internationale, 1934, 9 x 12 In. 215.00
Your Credit Is Good, Henry Messersmith, 1905 . . . . 56.00
Ziegfield Follies Of 1914, The Vampire, 1913 . . . . 44.00

SHEFFIELD items are listed in the Silver Plate and Silver-English categories.

SHELLEY first appeared on English ceramics about 1912. The Foley China Works started in England in 1860. Joseph Ball Shelley joined the company in 1862 and became a partner in 1872. Percy Shelley joined the firm in 1881. The company went through a series of name changes, and in 1910 the then Foley China Company became Shelley China. In 1929 it became Shelley Potteries. The company was acquired in 1966 by Allied English Potteries, then merged with the Doulton group in 1971. The name *Shelley* was put into use again in 1980. A trio is the name for a cup, saucer, and cake plate set.

Ashtray, Lily Of The Valley, Pattern No. 13822, 3 3/4 In.	25.00
Cake Plate, Maytime, Chintz, Center Metal Handle, 8 1/4 In.	155.00
Cake Plate, Maytime, Chintz, Tab Handles, 9 3/4 In.	225.00
Coffeepot, Blue, Dainty, 8 In.	595.00
Cream Soup, Liner, Blue, Dainty	125.00
Creamer, Begonia, Dainty	30.00
Cup, Begonia, Dainty, Demitasse	35.00
Cup, Crestware, Demitasse	12.00
Cup, Queen Anne	20.00
Cup & Saucer, Begonia, Dainty	45.00
Cup & Saucer, Blue Rock	48.00
Cup & Saucer, Blue Rock, Dainty	48.00
Cup & Saucer, Blue Rock, Dainty, Demitasse	75.00
Cup & Saucer, Forget-Me-Not, Rose, Pansy, Dainty	55.00
Cup & Saucer, Melody, Chintz	95.00
Cup & Saucer, Orange, White, Gold Snowflakes	105.00
Cup & Saucer, Stocks, Dainty	48.00
Cup & Saucer, Warwick, Pattern No. 2504	75.00
Eggcup, Bridal Rose, Dainty, 2 1/2 In.	75.00
Plate, Blue Rock, 8 In.	32.00
Plate, Blue, Dainty, 6 In.	450.00
Plate, Fairy Boat, Mabel Lucie Attwell, 7 In.	256.00
Plate, Harebell, No. 13590, 13 In.	175.00
Saucer, Begonia, Dainty	12.00
Saucer, Begonia, No. 134, 5 1/2 In.	23.00
Saucer, Stocks, Dainty	15.00
Saucer, Violets, Dainty	15.00
Sugar, Hulmes Rose, Dainty	45.00
Sugar & Creamer, Serenity	65.00
Trio, Wind Flower, Dainty, 8 In.	125.00
Vase, Melody, Chintz, 7 1/2 In.	275.00

SHIRLEY TEMPLE, the famous movie star, was born in 1928. She made her first movie in 1932. Thousands of items picturing Shirley have been and still are being made. Shirley Temple dolls were first made in 1934 by Ideal Toy Company. Millions of Shirley Temple cobalt blue glass dishes were made by Hazel Atlas Glass Company and U.S. Glass Company from 1934 to 1942. They were given away as premiums for Wheaties and Bisquick. A bowl, mug, and pitcher were made as a breakfast set. Some pieces were decorated with the picture of a very young Shirley, others used a picture of Shirley in her 1936 *Captain January* costume. Although collectors refer to a cobalt creamer, it is actually the 4 1/2-inch-high milk pitcher from the breakfast set. Many of these items are being reproduced today.

Book Set, 5 Books About Me, Box, Akron, Saalfield, 1936	225.00
Doll, Composition, Photo Pin, The World's Darling, 13 In.	688.00
Doll, Ideal, Composition Head & Body, Hazel Sleep Eyes, 6 Teeth, 27 In.	1025.00
Doll, Ideal, Composition, Flirty Eyes, 1930s, 27 In.	1800.00
Doll, Ideal, Composition, Sleep Eyes, Organdy Dress, c.1940, 20 In.	650.00
Doll, Ideal, Hazel Sleep Eyes, Open Mouth, 6 Teeth, Blue Dress, Box, 16 In.	1100.00
Doll, Ideal, Vinyl, Hazel Sleep Eyes, 6 Teeth, Hair, Jointed, 1957, 17 In.	200.00
Doll, Ideal, Vinyl, Hazel Sleep Eyes, 6 Teeth, Hair, Pink Dress, 1957, 15 In.	200.00 to 250.00
Doll, Ideal, Vinyl, Sleep Eyes, Hair, Scottie Dress, 1957, Box, 12 In.	250.00
Dress, Child's, White Linen, Red Collar, Cinderella, Size 8, c.1930, 30 In.	35.00

Sheet Music, Honeymoon, Guy Madison 85.00
Tea Set, Plastic, 6 Piece 90.00

SHRINER, see Fraternal category.

SILVER DEPOSIT glass was first made during the late nineteenth century. Solid sterling silver is applied to the glass by a chemical method so that a cutout design of silver metal appears against a clear or colored glass. It is sometimes called silver overlay.

Bowl, Flower Frog, Green Glass, Flowers & Leaves, 3-Footed, 6 In. 80.00
Bowl, Vaseline Glass, Flowers & Scrolling, 8-Sided Rim, 8 1/4 In. 50.00
Celery Dish, Clear Glass, Flowers & Baskets, Scalloped Rim, 10 1/4 In. 40.00
Decanter, Emerald Green, 9 In. 20.00
Pitcher, Clear Glass, Spring Flowers & Bow, 1950s, 4 1/2 In. 30.00
Vase, Cobalt Blue Glass, Flower & Leaves, Marked, London, 1904, 5 3/4 In. 65.00
Vase, Cobalt Blue Glass, Medallions & Woman Overlay, 10 1/2 In. 190.00
Vase, Etched Green Floral, Swag Overlay At Rim, Oval, 1900s, 9 In. 145.00
Vase, Fan, Black Amethyst Glass, Flowers & Scrolling, Footed, 8 3/4 In. 50.00
Vase, Green Glass, Applied Silver Overlay Style Flowers, 14 In. 3910.00
Vase, Iridescent Amethyst Glass, Scrolled Overlay, 3-Bulb Base, 1900s, 4 In. 500.00

SILVER FLATWARE includes many of the current and out-of-production silver and silver-plated flatware patterns made in the past eighty years. Other silver is listed under Silver-American, Silver-English, etc. Most silver flatware sets that are missing a few pieces can be completed through the help of one of the many silver matching services that advertise in many of the national publications.

SILVER FLATWARE PLATED, Always, Dinner Knife, Oneida, Rogers, 1958 .... 4.00
Always, Soup Spoon, Round, Oneida, Rogers, 1958 .... 4.00
Always, Tablespoon, Oneida, Rogers, 1958 .... 4.00
American Beauty Rose, Dinner Fork, Holmes & Edwards, 1909 .... 7.50
American Beauty Rose, Dinner Knife, Holmes & Edwards, 1909 .... 7.50
Angelica, Dinner Fork, Paragon, 1912 .... 4.00
Anniversary, Dinner Fork, Rogers, 1923 .... 8.00
Arcadian, Dinner Fork, Rogers, 1884 .... 7.50
Ardsley, Dinner Fork, Oneida, 1921 .... 4.50
Ardsley, Teaspoon, Oneida, 1921 .... 2.50
Arlington, Berry Spoon, Rogers, 1938 .... 4.00
Arlington, Cake Server, Rogers, 1938 .... 7.00
Attica, Teaspoon, Rogers, 1892 .... 2.50
Avalon, Bouillon Spoon, Community, 1901 .... 7.50
Ballad Or Country Lane, Teaspoon, Oneida, 1953 ....2.50 to 5.00
Belmont, Dinner Knife, Reed & Barton, 1906 .... 3.75
Berkshire, Gravy Ladle, Rogers, 1897 .... 28.00
Bernice, Sugar Spoon, Oneida, 1900 .... 5.00
Bouquet, Salad Fork, Derby Silver, 1875 .... 10.00
Bridal Wreath, Butter Knife, Oneida, 1915 .... 3.50
Bridal Wreath, Cream Ladle, Oneida, 1915 .... 10.00
Bridal Wreath, Dinner Knife, Oneida, 1915 .... 4.00
Bridal Wreath, Gravy Ladle, Oneida, 1915 .... 10.00
Bridal Wreath, Salad Fork, Oneida, 1915 .... 5.00
Bridal Wreath, Sugar Spoon, Oneida, 1915 .... 3.50
Camelot, Grill Fork, Rogers, 1964 .... 4.00
Camelot, Grill Knife, Rogers, 1964 .... 4.00
Camelot, Iced Tea Spoon, Rogers, 1964 .... 4.00
Camelot, Salad Fork, Rogers, 1964 .... 4.25
Camelot, Tablespoon, Rogers, 1964 .... 4.00
Camelot, Teaspoon, Rogers, 1964 .... 2.50
Caprice, Butter Knife, Master, Oneida, 1937 .... 6.00
Caprice, Cake Server, Oneida, 1937 .... 20.00
Caprice, Coffee Spoon, Oneida, 1937 .... 7.50
Caprice, Dinner Fork, Oneida, 1937 .... 7.50
Caprice, Gravy Ladle, Oneida, 1937 .... 20.00
Caprice, Iced Tea Spoon, Oneida, 1937 .... 7.00
Caprice, Pickle Fork, 3 Tines, Oneida, 1937 .... 9.00

Caprice, Serving Fork, Oneida, 1937	12.00
Caprice, Serving Spoon, Oneida, 1937	8.00
Caprice, Soup Spoon, Oval, Oneida, 1937	7.00
Caprice, Teaspoon, Oneida, 1937	5.00
Cavalcade, Soup Spoon, Round, National, 1946	4.50
Celebrity, Teaspoon, Rogers, 1939	2.50
Centennial, Sugar Spoon, Rogers, 1972	7.50
Century, Teaspoon, Holmes & Edwards, 1923	2.50
Charmion, Dinner Fork, Oneida, 1933	3.75
Chatelaine, Butter Knife, Oneida, 1957	3.75
Chatelaine, Dinner Fork, Oneida, 1957	4.00
Chatelaine, Soup Spoon, Oval, Oneida, 1957	4.00
Chautauqua, Gravy Ladle, Oneida, 1916	10.00
Chautauqua, Salad Fork, Oneida, 1916	4.50
Cheshire, Butter Knife, Rogers, 1925	4.00
Cheshire, Sugar Spoon, Rogers, 1925	4.00
Chester, Teaspoon, Towle, 1888	2.75
Chippendale, Dinner Fork, Rogers, 1919	4.50
Chippendale, Soup Spoon, Oval, Rogers, 1919	4.50
Chippendale, Teaspoon, Rogers, 1919	2.50
Clarion, Gravy Ladle, Oneida, 1931	10.00
Continental, Teaspoon, Rogers, 1914	2.50
Coronet, Teaspoon, Rogers, 1933	2.50
Cotillion, Grill Knife, Rogers, 1937	4.00
Cotillion, Salad Fork, Rogers, 1937	5.00
Cotillion, Tablespoon, Rogers, 1937	4.50
Cuban, Teaspoon, International, 1911	2.50
Danish Queen, Butter Knife, Harmony House, 1944	4.00
Danish Queen, Dinner Fork, Harmony House, 1944	4.00
Danish Queen, Jelly Server, Harmony House, 1944	4.00
Danish Queen, Sugar Spoon, Harmony House, 1944	3.75
Danish Queen, Teaspoon, Harmony House, 1944	2.50
Daybreak, Dinner Fork, Rogers, 1952	4.25
Daybreak, Salad Fork, Rogers, 1952	4.75
Daybreak, Serving Fork, Rogers, 1952	7.50
Daybreak, Soup Spoon, Oval, Rogers, 1952	4.50
Daybreak, Teaspoon, Rogers, 1952	2.50
Devonshire, Butter Knife, Rogers, 1938	4.25
Devonshire, Grill Fork, Rogers, 1938	4.50
Devonshire, Salad Fork, Rogers, 1938	4.50
Devonshire, Soup Spoon, Oval, Rogers, 1938	4.00
Devonshire, Teaspoon, Rogers, 1938	2.50
Dorothy Q, Dinner Fork, Wallace, 1931	3.75
Dorothy Q, Gravy Ladle, Wallace, 1931	10.00
Drexel, Sugar Spoon, Rogers, 1929	5.00
Enchantment, Butter Knife, Rogers, 1952	4.50
Enchantment, Dinner Knife, Rogers, 1952	5.00
Enchantment, Gravy Ladle, Rogers, 1952	7.50
Enchantment, Iced Tea Spoon, Rogers, 1952	4.50
Enchantment, Salad Fork, Rogers, 1952	5.50
Enchantment, Soup Spoon, Oval, Rogers, 1952	5.00
Enchantment, Tablespoon, Rogers, 1952	6.00
Enchantment, Youth Fork, Rogers, 1952	7.50
Enchantment, Youth Spoon, Rogers, 1952	7.50
Encore, Butter Knife, Rogers, 1934	4.00
Encore, Dinner Fork, Rogers, 1934	4.00
Encore, Gravy Ladle, Rogers, 1934	12.50
Encore, Jelly Knife, Rogers, 1934	5.00
Encore, Serving Fork, Rogers, 1934	7.50
Encore, Soup Spoon, Oval, Rogers, 1934	4.50
Encore, Sugar Spoon, Rogers, 1934	4.00
Fair Oak, Sugar Spoon, Rogers, 1913	3.50
First Colony, Cake Server, Pierced, Oneida, 1975	10.00

Flair, Dinner Fork, Rogers, 1956 .... 8.00
Flair, Dinner Knife, Rogers, 1956 .... 8.00
Flair, Pickle Fork, Rogers, 1956 .... 11.00
Flair, Salad Spoon, Rogers, 1956 .... 25.00
Flair, Serving Spoon, Rogers, 1956 .... 13.00
Flair, Soup Spoon, Oval, Rogers, 1956 .... 6.50
Flair, Teaspoon, Rogers, 1956 .... 5.00
Fleur De Luce, Dinner Fork, Community, 1904 .... 7.50
Flirtation, Dinner Fork, Rogers, 1959 .... 4.00
Flirtation, Dinner Knife, Rogers, 1959 .... 4.00
Flirtation, Salad Fork, Rogers, 1959 .... 4.50
Florette, Dinner Knife, Rogers, 1909 .... 6.00
Florette, Teaspoon, Rogers, 1909 .... 2.50
Forever, Butter Knife, Community, 1939 .... 7.00
Forever, Cake Server, Community, 1939 .... 20.00
Forever, Dinner Knife, Community, 1939 .... 7.50
Forever, Salad Fork, Community, 1939 .... 8.00
Forever, Soup Spoon, Oval, Community, 1939 .... 7.00
Forever, Teaspoon, Community, 1939 .... 5.00
Franklin, Sugar Spoon, Oneida, 1901 .... 5.00
Garland, Butter Knife, Rogers, 1937 .... 3.75
Garland, Dinner Fork, Rogers, 1937 .... 4.00
Garland, Gravy Ladle, Rogers, 1914 .... 7.50
Garland, Jelly Server, Rogers, 1914 .... 6.00
Garland, Salad Fork, Rogers, 1937 .... 4.50
Garland, Soup Spoon, Oval, Rogers, 1937 .... 4.00
Garland, Sugar Spoon, Rogers, 1937 .... 3.75
Garland, Teaspoon, Rogers, 1937 .... 2.50
Gay Adventure, Butter Knife, Master, Oneida, 1955 .... 7.50
Gay Adventure, Dinner Fork, Oneida, 1955 .... 8.00
Gay Adventure, Teaspoon, Oneida, 1955 .... 2.50
Grenoble, Dinner Fork, Oneida Prestige, 1938 .... 7.50
Grenoble, Grill Fork, Oneida Prestige, 1938 .... 7.50
Grenoble, Grill Knife, Oneida Prestige, 1938 .... 7.50
Grenoble, Sugar Spoon, Oneida Prestige, 1938 .... 6.00
Grenoble, Teaspoon, Oneida Prestige, 1938 .... 5.00
Jasmine, Serving Spoon, Rogers, 1939 .... 7.50
Jewell, Cream Ladle, International, 1916 .... 10.00
June, Butter Knife, Master, Community, 1932 .... 4.00
June, Dinner Fork, Community, 1932 .... 4.25
June, Dinner Knife, Community, 1932 .... 4.25
June, Salad Fork, Community, 1932 .... 4.75
June, Sugar Spoon, Community, 1932 .... 4.00
June, Teaspoon, Community, 1932 .... 2.50
Justice, Salad Fork, Rogers, 1916 .... 4.50
Kensington, Gravy Ladle, Rogers, 1912 .... 8.00
La Concorde, Tablespoon, Rogers, 1910 .... 8.00
La Concorde, Teaspoon, Rogers, 1910 .... 8.50
La Ronnie, Cocktail Fork, 3 Tine, Oneida, Rogers, 1945 .... 4.50
La Ronnie, Iced Tea Spoon, Oneida, Rogers, 1945 .... 4.50
La Ronnie, Salad Fork, Oneida, Rogers, 1945 .... 4.50
La Ronnie, Soup Spoon, Round, Oneida, Rogers, 1945 .... 4.00
La Ronnie, Teaspoon, Oneida, Rogers, 1945 .... 2.50
Lady Barbara, Gravy Ladle, Rogers, 1959 .... 20.00
Lady Joan, Salad Fork, National, 1931 .... 4.50
Lincoln, Berry Spoon, Rogers, 1917 .... 7.50
Lincoln, Iced Tea Spoon, Rogers, 1917 .... 4.50
Lincoln, Tablespoon, Rogers, 1917 .... 4.75
Linda, Gravy Ladle, Oneida, 1949 .... 10.00
Linda, Sugar Spoon, Pierced, Oneida, 1949 .... 5.00
Longchamps, Butter Knife, Oneida, 1935 .... 4.00
Longchamps, Dinner Fork, Oneida, 1935 .... 4.50
Longchamps, Dinner Knife, Oneida, 1935 .... 4.50

Longchamps, Sugar Spoon, Oneida, 1935 .... 4.00
Louisiane, Grill Knife, Rogers, 1938 .... 4.00
Louisiane, Soup Spoon, Oval, Rogers, 1938 .... 4.00
Louisiane, Tablespoon, Rogers, 1938 .... 4.00
Louisiane, Teaspoon, Rogers, 1938 .... 2.50
Lovely Lady, Dinner Fork, Holmes & Edwards, 1937 .... 8.00
Lovely Lady, Dinner Knife, Holmes & Edwards, 1937 .... 8.00
Lovely Lady, Teaspoon, Holmes & Edwards, 1937 .... 5.00
Lufberry, Butter Knife, Rogers, 1915 .... 3.50
Lufberry, Dinner Fork, Rogers, 1915 .... 3.50
Lufberry, Salad Fork, Rogers, 1915 .... 4.00
Lufberry, Soup Spoon, Oval, Rogers, 1915 .... 3.50
Lufberry, Sugar Spoon, Rogers, 1915 .... 3.50
Marseilles, Meat Fork, Williams Brothers, 1906 .... 5.00
Martinique, Butter Knife, National, 1935 .... 4.00
Martinique, Dinner Fork, National, 1935 .... 4.00
Martinique, Fruit Spoon, National, 1935 .... 7.50
Martinique, Gravy Ladle, National, 1935 .... 12.00
Martinique, Salad Fork, National, 1935 .... 4.50
Martinique, Serving Fork, National, 1935 .... 7.00
Martinique, Sugar Spoon, National, 1935 .... 4.00
Martinique, Teaspoon, National, 1935 .... 2.50
Mary Stuart, Butter Knife, Oneida, 1927 .... 4.00
Mary Stuart, Sugar Spoon, Oneida, 1927 .... 4.00
Mary Stuart, Teaspoon, Oneida, 1927 .... 2.50
Modern Living, Salad Fork, International Supreme, 1956 .... 4.50
Moss Rose, Butter Knife, Master, National, 1949 .... 4.00
Moss Rose, Dinner Knife, National, 1949 .... 4.25
Moss Rose, Salad Fork, National, 1949 .... 4.00
Moss Rose, Sugar Spoon, National, 1949 .... 4.00
Moss Rose, Teaspoon, National, 1949 .... 2.50
Narcissus, Dinner Fork, Oneida, 1908 .... 8.00
Noblesse, Grill Fork, Community, 1930 .... 3.50
Norfolk, Dinner Fork, Rogers, 1905 .... 5.00
Oakland, Dinner Fork, Rogers, 1929 .... 4.00
Oakland, Soup Spoon, Rogers, 1929 .... 4.50
Paris, Iced Tea Spoon, Rogers, 1931 .... 4.00
Persian, Dinner Fork, Rogers, 1871 .... 8.00
Persian, Mustard Spoon, Rogers, 1871 .... 10.00
Portland, Dinner Fork, Rogers, 1891 .... 6.00
Precious, Berry Spoon, Rogers, 1941 .... 8.50
Precious, Cake Server, Rogers, 1941 .... 7.00
Precious, Gravy Ladle, Rogers, 1941 .... 8.00
Precious, Soup Spoon, Round, Rogers, 1941 .... 4.00
Precious, Teaspoon, Rogers, 1941 .... 2.50
Precious Mirror, Dinner Knife, Rogers, 1950 .... 5.00
Queen Bertha, Berry Spoon, Oneida Glastonbury, 1910 .... 7.50
Remembrance, Butter Knife, Master, Rogers, 1948 .... 6.00
Remembrance, Dinner Fork, Rogers, 1948 .... 8.00
Remembrance, Grill Knife, Rogers, 1948 .... 8.00
Remembrance, Salad Fork, Roger, 1948 .... 8.50
Remembrance, Soup Spoon, Oval, Rogers, 1948 .... 7.50
Remembrance, Tablespoon, Rogers, 1948 .... 6.00
Remembrance, Teaspoon, Rogers, 1948 .... 5.00
Rendezvous, Butter Knife, Community, 1938 .... 4.00
Rendezvous, Dinner Fork, Community, 1938 .... 4.50
Rendezvous, Jelly Knife, Community, 1938 .... 6.00
Rendezvous, Soup Spoon, Oval, Community, 1938 .... 4.50
Rendezvous, Sugar Spoon, Community, 1938 .... 4.00
Revelation, Butter Knife, International, 1953 .... 3.75
Revelation, Dinner Fork, International, 1953 .... 4.00
Revelation, Meat Fork, International, 1953 .... 5.00
Revelation, Salad Fork, International, 1953 .... 4.50

Revelation, Soup Spoon, Oval, International, 1953 .... 4.00
Revelation, Teaspoon, International, 1953 .... 2.50
Revere, Sugar Spoon, Rogers, 1905 .... 5.00
Rhinebeck, Dinner Fork, Rogers, 1900 .... 4.00
Rhinebeck, Teaspoon, Rogers, 1900 .... 2.50
Rose & Leaf, Butter Knife, National, 1937 .... 4.00
Rose & Leaf, Cake Server, Pierced, National, 1937 .... 7.50
Rose & Leaf, Dinner Fork, National, 1937 .... 4.00
Rose & Leaf, Dinner Knife, National, 1937 .... 4.00
Rose & Leaf, Soup Spoon, Round, National, 1937 .... 4.50
Roseanne, Dinner Fork, Wallace, 1938 .... 4.00
Roseanne, Soup Spoon, Oval, Wallace, 1938 .... 4.50
Roseanne, Sugar Spoon, Wallace, 1938 .... 3.50
Royal, Punch Ladle, Partially Reeded Bowl, Gorham, 1888, 13 In. 118.00
Royal Rose, Soup Spoon, Oval, Oneida, 1939 .... 7.50
Royal Rose, Tablespoon, Oneida, 1939 .... 8.50
Royal Rose, Teaspoon, Oneida, 1939 .... 5.00
Shakespear, Butter Knife, Stratford, 1924 .... 2.00
Shakespear, Dinner Knife, Stratford, 1924 .... 2.50
Shakespear, Sugar Spoon, Stratford, 1924 .... 2.00
Southern Splendor, Salad Fork, Rogers, 1962 .... 5.00
Southern Splendor, Soup Spoon, Oval, Rogers, 1962 .... 5.00
Southern Splendor, Teaspoon, Rogers, 1962 .... 2.50
Sovereign, Salad Fork, Rogers, 1939 .... 5.00
Starlight, Butter Knife, Rogers, 1950 .... 4.00
Starlight, Dinner Fork, Rogers, 1950 .... 4.50
Starlight, Dinner Knife, Rogers, 1953 .... 4.50
Starlight, Salad Fork, Rogers, 1950 .... 5.00
Starlight, Soup Spoon, Oval, Rogers, 1953 .... 4.50
Starlight, Teaspoon, Rogers, 1950 .... 2.50
Sunburst, Salad Fork, International Supreme, 1938 .... 4.50
Sunkist, Teaspoon, Rogers, 1910 .... 3.00
Sweet Briar, Butter Knife, Oneida, Tudor Plate, 1948 .... 4.50
Sweet Briar, Dinner Fork, Oneida, Tudor Plate, 1948 .... 4.50
Sweet Briar, Dinner Knife, Oneida, Tudor Plate, 1948 .... 4.50
Sweet Briar, Gravy Ladle, Oneida, Tudor Plate, 1948 .... 8.00
Sweet Briar, Iced Tea Spoon, Oneida, Tudor Plate, 1948 .... 5.00
Sweet Briar, Serving Fork, Oneida, Tudor Plate, 1948 .... 8.00
Sweet Briar, Sugar Spoon, Oneida, Tudor Plate, 1948 .... 4.50
Sweet Briar, Teaspoon, Oneida, Tudor Plate, 1948 .... 2.50
Terrace, Dinner Fork, Rogers, 1932 .... 5.00
Terrace, Salad Fork, Rogers, 1932 .... 6.00
Terrace, Tablespoon, Rogers, 1932 .... 4.00
Terrace, Teaspoon, Rogers, 1932 .... 3.00
Triumph, Cake Server, Rogers, 1925 .... 13.00
Tupperware Rose, Dinner Fork, Rogers, 1955 .... 4.00
Tupperware Rose, Dinner Knife, Rogers, 1955 .... 4.00
Tupperware Rose, Iced Tea Spoon, Rogers, 1955 .... 4.25
Tupperware Rose, Salad Fork, Rogers, 1955 .... 4.50
Tupperware Rose, Soup Spoon, Oval, Rogers, 1955 .... 4.00
Tuxedo, Dinner Fork, Rogers, 1890 .... 9.00
Verona, Cocktail Fork, Rogers, 1910 .... 5.00
Verona, Meat Fork, Rogers, 1910 .... 7.50
Viking, Berry Spoon, Oneida, 1931 .... 7.50
Viking, Butter Knife, Master, Oneida, 1931 .... 3.75
Viking, Dinner Fork, Oneida, 1931 .... 4.00
Viking, Salad Fork, Oneida, 1931 .... 4.50
Viking, Sugar Spoon, Oneida, 1931 .... 3.75
Viking, Teaspoon, Oneida, 1931 .... 2.50
Viking, Youth Fork, Oneida, 1931 .... 5.00
Virginia, Butter Knife, Master, Stratford, 1917 .... 5.00
Vista, Gravy Ladle, Rogers, 1940 .... 8.50
Wildwood, Sugar Spoon, Oneida, 1908 .... 6.50

Yale, Soup Spoon, Oval, Rogers, 1894	5.00
Yale, Teaspoon, Rogers, 1894	4.00
SILVER FLATWARE STERLING, Acorn, Serving Set, Georg Jensen, 3 Piece	633.00
Beaded, Marrow Scoop, Georg Jensen	145.00
Beaded, Pie Server, Georg Jensen	175.00
Beaded, Soup Ladle, Georg Jensen	405.00
Buckingham, Salad Servers, Spoon & Fork, Monogram, Gorham, c.1910, 8 1/2 In., Pair . .	230.00
Buttercup, Demitasse Spoon, Opal Stone, Gorham, c.1900, 13 Piece	259.00
Buttercup, Serving Spoon, Tapered Oval Bowl, Gorham, 1899, 10 1/2 In.	88.00
Fiddleback, Pie Server, Spade Form, Beveled, Old Newbury Crafters, 8 3/4 In.	245.00
Florentine, Serving Spoon, Gorham	200.00
Imperial Queen, Ladle, Monogram L, Whiting, c.1893, 10 1/2 In.	316.00
King George, Salad Servers, Pierced, Gorham, 1894, Pair	460.00
King's Pattern Variant, Punch Ladle, Shaped Bowl, Shell Handle, Gorham, 13 In.	605.00
La Parsienne, Ice Cream Slice, Pierced Blade, Reed & Barton, 1902, 12 3/4 In.	560.00
Les Six Fleurs, Serving Spoon, Monogram, Reed & Barton, 1901, 9 3/4 In.	294.00
Lily, Salad Set, Whiting, Gorham, c.1902, 11 3/4 In., 2 Piece	375.00
Lily, Salad Set, Whiting, New York, 11 1/2 x 2 1/4 In.	920.00
Lily, Serving Fork, Whiting, c.1902	155.00
Lotus, Butter Spreader, Porter Blanchard, 5 1/2 In.	45.00
Lotus, Coffee Spoon, George P. Blanchard, 5 1/2 In.	45.00
Lotus, Macaroni Server, Engraved Serrated Blade, Monogram, Gorham, 1865, 10 In.	470.00
Lotus, Serving Spoon, Porter Blanchard, 8 1/2 In.	195.00
Love Disarmed, Fish Set, Reed & Barton, 2 Piece	545.00
Marie Antoinette, Ladle, Gorham, 1890, 10 3/4 In.	200.00
Medallion, Dinner Set, Youth, Oval Leathered Case, Gorham	470.00
Merrimack, Salad Fork & Spoon, Towle Silversmiths, 8 In., Pair	135.00
Narragansett, Coffee Spoon, 2 Fish Handle, Gorham	575.00
Narragansett, Coffee Spoon, Cockleshell Handle, Gorham	575.00
Narragansett, Coffee Spoon, Crab Handle, Gorham	690.00
Narragansett, Coffee Spoon, Fish Handle, Gorham . . . . .460.00 to 635.00
Narragansett, Coffee Spoon, Oyster Handle, Gorham	460.00
Onslow, Bonbon Spoon, Scrolling Handle, Arthur J. Stone, 5 In.	350.00
Onslow, Ladle, Oval Bowl, Slender Handle, Arthur J. Stone, 7 In.	395.00
Persian, Gravy Ladle, Tiffany & Co., 1872, 7 1/8 x 2 In.	460.00
Persian, Serving Fork, Tiffany & Co., 1872, 9 x 1 1/2 In.	489.00
Pomona, Punch Ladle, Towle, 1887	430.00
Prince Albert, Ladle, Shreve Brown & Co., c.1860, 11 In.	260.00
Repousse, Salad Servers, S. Kirk & Son, 1828, 9 1/2 In., Pair	748.00
Repousse, Serving Set, Asparagus Fork, Spoon, Embossed Fruits, Flowers, Kirk & Son . .	323.00
Royal Windsor, Service Set, Mid 20th Century, Towle, 6 Piece	920.00
Sardine Fork, Figural, Stylized Octopus On Tines, Seaweed Handle, Shiebler, 6 1/2 In. . .	1998.00
Trianon, Serving Fork, Pierced, Dominick & Haff	63.00
Violet, Butter Spreader, Wallace, 9 Piece	115.00
XIV Century, Asparagus Server, Broad, Pierced Tines, Hammered, Shreve, 10 1/4 In.	850.00
XIV Century, Berry Spoon, Hammered, Pierced S, Shreve, 10 1/2 In.	675.00
XIV Century, Cake Trowel, Strap Work, Hammered, Engraved, Shreve, 10 1/4 In.	675.00
XIV Century, Serving Spoon, Engraved CF, Shreve & Co., 9 In.	375.00

SILVER PLATE is not solid silver. It is a ware made of a metal, such as nickel or copper, that is covered with a thin coating of silver. The letters *EPNS* are often found on American and English silver-plated wares. Sheffield is a term with two meanings. Sometimes it refers to sterling silver made in the town of Sheffield, England. In this section, Sheffield refers to a type of silver plate, usually English.

Asparagus Server, Dome Top, England, 20th Century, 14 x 9 In.	345.00
Basket, Handles, Leaves, Grape, Scalloped Edges, 19th Century, Sheffield, 12 x 4 In.	115.00
Basket, Holder, Glass, Victorian, c.1880, 14 x 12 In.	460.00
Basket, Lobed, Cast & Chased Leaves On Rim & Handle, Round Base, 3 1/2 x 11 In.	83.00
Basket, Woven Sides, Bottom, Handles, 15 In.	269.00
Beverage Server, Tilting, Simpson, Hall & Co., 17 1/2 In.	288.00
Biscuit Barrel, England	176.00
Biscuit Barrel, Greek Key, Cut, Frosted Glass, Late 19th Century, 6 1/2 In.	173.00

Biscuit Box, Oval, England, First Half 20th Century, 7 3/4 x 8 1/4 In. 315.00
Biscuit Box, Oval, Hinged Lid, Urn Shape Finial, Ball & Claw Feet, 7 3/4 x 8 In. 219.00
Bottle, Fruitwood Base, Gadroon Edge, Sheffield, 19th Century, 2 1/2 x 7 In. 92.00
Bowl, Hammered, Stag Head Handles, Footed, Fan & Diamond Insert, 6 In., Pair 66.00
Bowl, Repousse, Britannia, Teardrop Sides, Flower, Vine Rim, Meriden, 8 1/2 In. 125.00
Bowl, Vegetable, Cover, Engraved, Gadroon Border, Pair 69.00
Box, Sugar, Hermann Suedfeld, Austria, c.1890, 5 1/2 In. 588.00
Butter, Cover, Cow Finial, Meriden 450.00
Candelabrum is listed in its own category.
Candlesticks are listed in their own category.
Carving Set, 2 Forks, 2 Knives, Ivory Handle, c.1870, 8 3/4 x 17 3/4 In. 575.00
Castor, Queen Anne Britannia, Pear Shape, Charles Adams, London, 1707, 7 1/2 In. 2070.00
Cigar Holder, Figural, Carriage, Mother-Of-Pearl Trim, Matchbox Under Seat, 8 1/2 In. . . 338.00
Coffee Urn, Double, Siphon, Vacuum, Inset Burner, Sheffield, 14 1/2 x 11 In. 672.00
Coffee Urn, Engraved Crest & Shield, Adam-Style, Sheffield, 14 1/2 In. 517.00
Coffeepot, Rogers Smith Co., Hartford, 19th Century, 12 1/2 In. 35.00
Cooler, Bottle, Ribbed, Lion Mask Handles, Detachable Sleeve & Collar, 9 1/2 In. 748.00
Cooler, Wine, Neoclassical, Heraldic, Sheffield, 9 1/2 In., Pair 2415.00
Cover, Entree, Oval, Domed, Handles, Walker & Hall, Sheffield, England, 20 x 13 x 16 In.   125.00
Cover, Meat, Fruit Form Final, 19 x 12 In. 400.00
Creamer, Flowers, Feathers, Embossed, Handle, Lid, Pairpoint, 3 In. 20.00
Dish, Breakfast, Domed Top, Swivel Cover, Eagle Crest, England, Footed, 8 x 8 x 12 In.   50.00
Dish, Entree, Domed Cover, Handles, Footed, Heater Base, Sheffield, 9 3/4 x 9 x 14 In. . . 300.00
Dish, Entree, Rounded Rectangle, Sheffield, George IV, c.1830, 7 x 9 In., Pair 575.00
Dish, Round, Revolving Top, Marked, Mappin & Webb, England, c.1900, 8 x 11 In. 345.00
Epergne, 4 Arms, Cut Glass, Footed Base, Scroll, Shell, 15 x 15 1/2 x 11 1/2 In. 1035.00
Epergne, 4 Scroll Arms, Cut Crystal Bowls, Mappin & Webb, c.1900, 15 In. 1840.00
Epergne, 4 Trumpet Shaped Vases, Reticulated & Scalloped Base, 3-Footed, 14 In. 220.00
Epergne, 4 Trumpet, Edwardian, Antique Beaded, c.1900, 10 1/2 In. 175.00
Epergne, Scrolling, Trelliswork, Repousse, Elkington & Co., c.1908, 13 1/4 In. 1095.00
Figurine, Bird, Roadrunner, Jennings Bros., 15 In., Pair 58.00
Figurine, Gamecock, Fighting Pose, Italy, 9 In., Pair 315.00
Fish Serving Set, Ivory, Victorian, Walker & Hall, Sheffield, Case, c.1880, 2 Piece 259.00
Fish Serving Set, Pierced & Engraved Blade, Ivory Handle, Fitted Case, 13 In., 2 Piece . . 176.00
Flask, Engraved, Dry As, Trout Jumping, Cattails 440.00
Flask, Fish In Net, Meriden Silver Plate Co., Quadruple Plate 580.00
Goblet, Sheffield, Pedestal, Beaded, Engraved Coat Of Arms, c.1780, 6 1/4 In., Pair 460.00
Hot Water Urn, England, 19th Century, 21 1/2 In. 765.00
Inkwell, Stand, Satinwood, Inlaid, Ebonized Wood, Sheffield, 3 1/8 x 11 In. 1265.00
Jug, Claret, Bulbous Base, Handle, Grapevines, 11 1/4 x 5 1/4 In. 400.00
Kettle, Hot Water, Bulbous, Handle, Lid, Spout, Burner Stand, Reed & Barton, 13 In. 230.00
Kettle, Hot Water, Dome Lid, Bulbous, Floral Form Handle, England, c.1860, 19 In. 750.00
Kettle, Stand, Flowers, Scroll Work, Fixed Handle, Side Hinged Lid, 14 In. 630.00
Lamp, Hurricane, Sheffield, Matthew Boulton, c.1810, 17 3/4 In. 7500.00
Meat Cover, Grape Cluster Handle, England, Early 20th Century, 10 x 18 x 13 In. 460.00
Mirror, Plateau, Flowers, Vines, Sheffield, c.1820, 33 7/16 In. 2390.00
Napkin Rings are listed in their own category.
Oil Filler, Long Spout, Pump, Manning Bowman & Co., 5 1/2 x 8 1/4 In. 40.00
Pitcher, Cover, Embossed Medallions, Leaf Thumbpiece, Sheffield, 1857, 7 In. 665.00
Pitcher, Water, Gadroon, Art Silver Co., 8 1/2 In. 35.00
Plate, Dinner, Set, Engraved Crown Crest, Gadroon Rim, Sheffield, 9 5/8 In., 12 Piece . . . 1175.00
Platter, Bellflower Swags, Leaves, 3 Pad Feet, c.1925, 11 x 14 In. 104.00
Platter, Warming, Oval, England, Early 20th Century, 3 1/2 x 17 1/2 x 24 In. 575.00
Platter, Well & Tree, Oval, Grapevine Border, England, c.1900, 22 x 15 1/2 In. 104.00
Punch Bowl, Elkington & Co, c.1904, 12 1/2 In. 7050.00
Punch Set, Repousse, Bowl, Ladle, 24 Cups, Mid 20th Century 690.00
Salt, Scroll Cartouches, Lion's Head Corners, Paw Feet, Wood & Hughes, 3 In., Pair 288.00
Salver, Shell & Flower Ring, Piecrust Border, c.1925, 10 In. 115.00
Serving Dish, Dome, Scroll Leaf Handle, Benetfink & Co., c.1900, 11 x 13 x 18 In. 375.00
Serving Dish, Dome, Scroll Leaf Handle, Benetfink & Co., c.1906, 9 x 10 x 14 In. 316.00
Serving Tray, Flowers, Scrolling Feet, Poole, 2 1/4 x 20 1/4 x 30 1/2 In. 345.00
Spoon, Souvenir, see Souvenir category.
Stirrup Cup, Fox Head, England, London Marks, c.1803 . . . . 353.00

Silver Plate, Sugar, Coal Scuttle Shape,
Intaglio Design, E.P. Sheffield 5 x 7 1/2 In.

Silver-American, Creamer,
Coin, Squat Urn Shape,
Gadroon Rim, Scroll
Handle, c.1834, 5 1/2 In.

Sugar, Coal Scuttle Shape, Intaglio Design, E.P. Sheffield 5 x 7 1/2 In. . . . . *Illus*	45.00
Sugar, Lilies, Embossed, Pairpoint	10.00
Tankard, Scroll Thumbpiece, Curved Handle, Heart End, Domed Lid, 8 In.	110.00
Tankard, Tapered, Cylindrical, Dome Cover, Marked, WBB, E.P.N.S., 7 1/4 x 4 7/8 In. . .	50.00
Tankard, Wooden Bottom, Sheffield, Matthew Boulton, c.1790, 8 In.	1950.00
Tantalus, 3 Bottles, Stoppers, 12 In.	359.00
Tea & Coffee Set, Art Deco, Polygon Shape, Rosewood Handles, c.1930, 5 Piece	518.00
Tea & Coffee Set, Gadroon, Domed Lid, Daniel & Arter Globe Works, England, c.1900 . .	230.00
Tea & Coffee Set, Lancaster Rose Pattern, 11 3/4 In., 4 Piece	520.00
Tea & Coffee Set, Monogram, England, 20th Century, 5 Piece	403.00
Tea & Coffee Set, Scrolled, Acanthus Design, DeMontfort Plate, England, 7 Piece	345.00
Tea & Coffee Set, Tray, Poole, 5 Piece	176.00
Tea Set, Art Deco, Mappin & Webb, 5 1/2 In., 3 Piece	106.00
Tea Set, Art Nouveau, Rogers, 4 Piece	308.00
Tea Set, Birmingham Silver Co., Tray 20 x 32 In., 7 Piece	250.00
Tea Set, Chevron Finials, Leather Wrapped Handles, Reed & Barton, 4 Piece	206.00
Tea Set, Floral, Pairpoint, 4 Piece	90.00
Tea Set, Grape, Vine, Flower Finials, Birmingham Silver Co., 7 Piece	523.00
Tea Urn, Engraved, Armorial Crest, Ram's Head, Ring Handles, Sheffield, c.1860, 20 In. .	575.00
Tea Urn, Vase Shape, Swags, Flowers, Reeded Loop Handles, Spout, Bud Finial, Sheffield	3290.00
Teapot, Gadroon Decoration, Beaded Borders, Wood Handle, 19th Century	105.00
Teapot, Sheffield, Bulbous, Hinged, Gadroon, Leaves, M. Boulton, c.1810, 5 3/4 In.	460.00
Teapot, Squat Shape, Flat Top, Scroll Handle, Diamond Decoration, 4 x 11 In.	60.00
Toothpick, Chicken Next To Barrel, 2 1/2 In.	75.00
Toothpick, Cupid Standing Next To Top Hat, M.S.P. Co., 4 In.	230.00
Toothpick, Silver, Flowers, Embossed, Pairpoint, 2 In.	10.00
Tray, Handles, Martin & Half, c.1894, 23 3/4 In.	2820.00
Tray, Rectangular, Handles, Footed, E.P.N.S., W.M.M., 16 1/2 x 28 In.	175.00
Tray, Reticulated Galleried Sides, Cutout Handles, 19th Century, 3 3/4 x 25 x 19 In.	920.00
Tray, Round, Shell & Scroll Border, Acanthus Handles, England, c.1900, 15 1/2 In.	145.00
Tray, Serving, Shell, Grape Vine Border, Footed, Wilcox, 15 1/2 In.	75.00
Trumpet, Presentation, Capt. James L. Mills, Boston Vet Fire Assoc., 1889, 24 In.	2310.00
Tureen, Cover, Gadroon Rim, Scroll & Shell Handle, Paw Feet, Sheffield, 15 In.	1998.00
Tureen, Cover, Sheffield, Matthew Boulton Plate Co., c.1820, 16 7/16 In.	4180.00
Tureen, Gadroon, Leaf Handles, Oval, 12 1/2 x 10 x 8 1/2 In.	805.00
Tureen, Oval, Ram's Head Handles, Engraved, Semper Eadem, 11 x 17 x 9 1/2 In.	180.00
Tureen, Sauce, Matthew Boulton Plate Co., c.1820, 8 7/16 In., 2 Pair	2990.00
Tureen, Soup, Cover, Oval, Artichoke Finial, Reeded Acanthus Handles & Feet, 16 In. . . .	529.00
Urn, Hinged Cover, Handles, Footed, Reed & Barton, Late 19th Century, 14 1/4 In.	175.00
Urn, Ram's Head, Loose Ring Handle, Square Base, Sheffield, 10 1/4 In.	200.00
Vase, Double Trumpet, Stand, Figural, Pup Barking At Large Dog, Reed & Barton, 15 In. .	200.00
Vase, Gino Sabatini, Elliptical Forms, Signed, 1979-1988, 8 x 10 In.	999.00
Vase, Josef Hoffmann, Faceted Body, Foot, Stamped, Wiener Werkstatte, 4 1/2 x 5 In. . . .	3819.00
Vase, Mounted, Oval, Tall Flaring Neck, Swirl Pattern, 21 In., Pair	1175.00
Wall Bracket, Art Deco, Veneer, Ribbed, Flared, Acorn Finial, 17 x 24 x 9 In., Pair	5825.00
Wine Cannon, Scroll Shape Carriage, 7 1/2 x 12 In., Pair	2467.00
Wine Coaster, Applied Exterior Grape & Leaves, England, 6 In., Pair	275.00

Wine Coaster, Armorial Plaque, Embossed Grapevine, Wood Base, 2 x 6 1/2 In., Pair ... 259.00
Wine Coaster, Crest, Gadroon Side, Rim, Wood Base, Sheffield, 2 x 6 7/8 In. 125.00
Wine Coaster, Cylindrical Body, Wood Base, Sheffield, Boulton, c.1825, 2 x 7 In. 690.00
Wine Coaster, Grapevines, Border, Wooden Base, c.1900, 2 1/2 x 5 1/2 In., Pair 144.00
Wine Coaster, Quatrefoil, Flaring Sides, Scroll Borders, 4 x 17 1/4 x 6 3/4 In., Pair 805.00
Wine Coaster, Turned Wood Base, 19th Century, Sheffield, 6 1/2 In. 150.00
Wine Coaster, Vintage Decoration, Turned Wood Base, England, 7 In., Pair 265.00
Wine Cooler, Lion Ring Handles, Wallace, 10 x 8 3/4 In. 69.00
Wine Server, Meriden Co., c.1900 .... 86.00

SILVER, SHEFFIELD, see Silver Plate; Silver-English categories.

SILVER SPRINGS refers to a marbleized pottery that has been made at
Silver Springs, Florida, since 1938. The name is impressed on the bottom of the piece.

Vase, Marbleized Cream, Green, Burgundy, Waisted Neck, Flared, 5 1/2 In. 35.00
Vase, Marbleized Rust, Cream, Urn Shape, Footed, Flared, 3 1/2 In. 25.00

SILVER-AMERICAN. American silver is listed here. Coin and sterling
silver are included. Most of the sterling silver listed in this book is sub-
divided by country. There are also other pieces of silver and silver
plate listed under special categories, such as Candelabrum, Napkin
Ring, Silver Flatware, Silver Plate, Silver-Sterling, and Tiffany Silver.
For information about makers and marks, see *Kovels' American Silver
Marks: 1650 to the Present.*

SILVER-AMERICAN, Baby Fork, Rounded End, 4 Tines, Engraved, Arthur J. Stone, 4 1/8 In. .. 195.00
Baby Spoon, Round End, Pierced & Chased Bunny, Arthur J. Stone, 4 1/4 In. 335.00
Basket, Applied Leaf Design, Handle, Oval, Gorham, c.1872, 11 3/4 In. 545.00
Basket, Beaded Handle, Coin, A. Coles, New York, c.1850, 4 1/2 x 6 1/2 In. 1595.00
Basket, Fenestrated, Chased Design, 3-Footed, W. Dawson, Gorham, 2 1/2 x 7 1/4 In. ... 130.00
Basket, Fenestrated, Footed, Bailey, Banks & Biddle, 9 In. 660.00
Basket, Hammered, Chased Flowers, Pierced Border, Footed, Handles, Gorham 57.00
Basket, Monogram, First Quarter 20th Century, 6 1/4 x 7 1/2 In. 175.00
Basket, Shallow Dish, Articulated Handle, Ring Foot, Gorham, 5 1/2 x 7 In. 335.00
Basket, Sweetmeat, Fluted, Webster Company, c.1920, 6 x 5 1/2 x 4 1/4 In. 175.00
Bonbon Spoon, Pointed End, Chased Design, Arthur J. Stone, 4 1/2 In. 375.00
Bonbon Spoon, Pointed End, Round Bowl, Arthur J. Stone, 4 1/4 In. 195.00
Bonbon Spoon, Pointed, Pierced & Chased Iris, Arthur J. Stone, 4 1/2 In. 375.00
Bonbon Spoon, Round, Pierced Bowl, Molded End, L.S. Wood, 4 1/4 In. 85.00
Bowl, 12 Paneled Sides, Ring Foot, Old Newbury Crafters, 2 1/2 x 8 In. 495.00
Bowl, 12 Paneled Sides, Scalloped Rim, Old Newbury Crafters, 2 1/4 x 6 In. 325.00
Bowl, Applied Border, Hammered, Marked, Shreve, 12 In. 175.00
Bowl, Basket Shape, Apple Blossom, Shreve, Crump & Low Co., 6 x 7 In. 225.00
Bowl, Centerpiece & Mirror Plateau, Kirk & Son, c.1905, 15 In. 9000.00
Bowl, Centerpiece, Flower Shape, William Waldo Dodge, c.1935, 14 In. 2868.00
Bowl, Centerpiece, Oval, Orchids, Iris, Gorham, No. A967M, c.1901, 18 1/4 In. 2160.00
Bowl, Centerpiece, Pierced, Engraved Flowers & Leaves, c.1930, 4 x 16 In. 1150.00
Bowl, Centerpiece, Rose Point, Wallace Silversmiths, 1934, 3 x 12 In. 575.00
Bowl, Centerpiece, Round, 4-Footed, Flowers, Lobed, Gilt, Reed & Barton, 12 In. 600.00
Bowl, Centerpiece, Shell & Scroll Feet, Gorham Mfg. Co., c.1903, 22 In. 4780.00
Bowl, Centerpiece, Shells, Seaweed, 4-Footed, Whiting, c.1885, 13 3/8 In. 8400.00
Bowl, Centerpiece, Shreve & Co., Early 20th Century, 4 x 14 In. 920.00
Bowl, Flared Rim, Floral Reticulated Designs, Gorham, 15 In. 3230.00
Bowl, Flared, Applied Wire Rim, 5 Flutes, Flat Bottom, Kalo, 1 7/8 x 7 1/4 In. 650.00
Bowl, Flared, Ring Foot, Roses, Vines, Leaves, Arthur J. Stone, 4 1/8 x 9 5/8 In. 5200.00
Bowl, Floral Border, Open, Gorham, 10 In. 230.00
Bowl, Fluted, Arts & Crafts Pattern, Marked, Whiting, 1908, 10 1/2 In. 125.00
Bowl, Footed, Applied Tab Handles, Hammered, Marshall Field, 4 x 9 1/2 In. 495.00
Bowl, Francis I, Reed & Barton, 8 In., Pair 500.00
Bowl, Fruit, Allan Adler, 12 In. 575.00
Bowl, Fruit, Grape Leaves, Oval, Shaped Rim, Grapevines, Frank W. Smith, 11 In. 470.00
Bowl, Fruit, Salem Pattern, Reed & Barton 118.00
Bowl, Hammered, Dragonflies, Loop Handles, Footed, Dominick & Haff, 10 In. 3525.00
Bowl, Hand Hammered, Marked Hand Wrought At The Kalo Shop, 2 x 8 1/2 In. 518.00

Bowl, Japanese Style, Mixed Metal, Quatrefoil, Gorham, c.1879, 11 3/4 In. 7200.00
Bowl, Lobed Shape, Floral Border, Shreve, Crump & Low, 9 1/2 In. 705.00
Bowl, Mixed Metal, Grape Leaves, Vine, George W. Shiebler & Co., c.1910, 11 In. 8963.00
Bowl, Mixed Metal, Japanese Style, Copper Cherry Branch, c.1882, 8 3/8 In. 6600.00
Bowl, Mixed Metal, Japanese Style, Maple Leaves, Gorham, c.1879, 11 1/8 In. 6600.00
Bowl, Monogram LDT, Leinonen, 2 x 5 In. 325.00
Bowl, Open, Unger Bros., c.1940, 10 In. 86.00
Bowl, Oval, Repousse, Poppy & Leaves, International, 17 In. 840.00
Bowl, Pedestal Base, Chased Panels, Gyllenberg, 5 1/4 x 11 In. 2900.00
Bowl, Pedestal, Engraved, John & Peter Targee, New York, c.1805, 4 1/2 x 7 In. 5500.00
Bowl, Pierced & Applied Scrolls & Flowers, Oval, Black, Starr & Frost, 15 In. 2115.00
Bowl, Pierced, Scroll Legs, Engraved, Graff, Washbourne & Dunn, 3 3/4 x 15 1/4 In. 1095.00
Bowl, Presentation, Footed, Monogram, Arthur J. Stone, c.1927, 5 3/4 x 8 1/4 In. 1095.00
Bowl, Reticulated Border, Oval, Theodore E. Starr, New York, 10 1/2 In. 250.00
Bowl, Round, Beaded Rim, Joseph Lownes, c.1800, Marked, 6 1/2 In. 4540.00
Bowl, Round, Flat Bottom, Flared, Tapered Sides, Leinonen, 1 5/8 x 3 7/8 In. 225.00
Bowl, Round, Fluted Edge, Monogram, Gorham, 9 1/2 In. 90.00
Bowl, Round, Footed, Ridged Rim, Arthur J. Stone, c.1940, 8 1/8 In. 590.00
Bowl, Scalloped Rim, Stamped, Arthur J. Stone, 1 1/4 x 8 1/2 In. 230.00
Bowl, Scrolling Leaves, Flowers, Swags, Bulbous, Flared Rim, S. Wilmot, 4 x 5 In. 4830.00
Bowl, Shallow Shape, Floral Repousse Decoration, Whiting, 6 In., Pair 235.00
Bowl, Shallow, Swags, Flutes, Ovals, Bellflowers, Gorham, 1927, 15 Oz., 11 In. 184.00
Bowl, Spherical Shape, Applied Shell & Scroll, S. Kirk & Sons, 5 x 10 1/2 In. 1610.00
Bowl, Strawberries, Monogram, Gorham, c.1902, 13 1/2 In. 9000.00
Bowl, Theodore B. Starr, Hammered, Round, Scrolled, c.1916, 7 1/2 In. 325.00
Bowl, Trefoil Shape, Planished, J.O. Randahl, 1 3/4 x 10 In. 575.00
Bowl, Vegetable, Oval, Loop Handles, Hammered, C.H. Didrich, 3 x 16 1/2 In. 2100.00
Bowl, Vegetable, Royal Danish, International Silver Co., 12 In., Pair 345.00
Bowl, Vegetable, Shaped Border, Reed & Barton, 12 1/2 In. 92.00
Bread, Basket, Scenic Repousse, Gorham, 3 x 10 x 8 In. 280.00
Bread Tray, Flowers, Leaves, Monogram, Alvin Corp., c.1910, 1 3/4 x 6 3/4 x 12 1/2 In. . . 460.00
Bread Tray, Francis I, Reed & Barton, 1907, 7 1/2 x 11 1/4 In. 489.00
Bread Tray, Repousse, Chased, Embossed, Scrolled Flowers, Oval, Gorham, 11 In. 295.00
Butter, Round, Banded Rim, Armorial, Pierced Drain Plate, Kirk & Son, 6 1/4 In. 175.00
Butter Knife, MB Style, Engraved, Arthur J. Stone, 6 3/8 In. 85.00
Butter Pick, Celtic Design, Arthur J. Stone, 6 1/8 In. 250.00
Caddy Spoon, Balloon Shape, Concave Handle, James T. Woolley, 4 1/2 x 2 1/4 In. 235.00
Caddy Spoon, Broad Bowl, Pointed Handle, Engraved, Arthur J. Stone, 4 1/2 In. 175.00
Caddy Spoon, Sculpted End, Engraved, Arthur J. Stone, 5 1/8 In. 175.00
Cake Dish, Swing Handles, Gorham, No. 63A 60.00
Cake Plate, Pierced Leaves, Flower Heads, Scroll & Shell Rim, Whiting, 1911, 10 3/8 In. 150.00
Cake Stand, Rolled Rim, Leaf Edge & Foot, Howard & Co., 9 1/2 In. 705.00
Candelabrum is listed in its own category.
Candlesnuffer, Bell, Twisted Wire Handle, Loop End, Julius O. Randahl, 9 In. 95.00
Candlesticks are listed in their own category.
Candy Dish, Rose Point, Glass Liner, Wallace, 7 1/2 In. 58.00
Canister, Flowers, Leaves, Gorham, 19th Century, 3 Oz., 4 In. 140.00
Cann, Cup, Baluster Shape, Capped Scroll Handle, John Brevoort, c.1750, 5 1/4 In. 3585.00
Cann, Cup, Baluster Shape, Scroll Handle, Samuel Tingley, c.1765, 4 1/8 In. 2630.00
Cann, Cup, Baluster, Molded Rim, Double Scroll Handle, B. Burt, c.1780, 5 1/4 In. 3900.00
Cann, Cup, Flared Rim, Mold Foot Rim, A. Bancker, c.1735, 3 7/8 In. 5700.00
Cann, Cup, Keg Form, R. & W. Wilson, c.1825-1846, 3 In. 250.00
Cann, Cup, Wide Baluster Shape, Capped Scroll Handle, Jacob Hurd, c.1750, 5 In. 4780.00
Carafe, Wine, Scroll Handle, Clover Terminations, Gorham, Early 20th Century, 10 1/2 In. 865.00
Charger, Heritage, Monogram, Reed & Barton, 20th Century, 14 In. 575.00
Charger, Rose Point Pattern, Wallace, 13 1/2 In. 210.00
Cheese Scoop, Pointed Handle, U Shape Bowl, Arthur J. Stone, 7 In. 250.00
Child's Set, Little Jack Horner, William Allen Putnam Jr., Whiting, 7 In., 3 Piece 200.00
Chop Serving Set, Round End, Elongated, Old Newbury Crafters, 10 1/4 In., Pair 395.00
Cigarette Case, Monogram, First Half 20th Century, 3 x 5 1/4 In. 90.00
Coaster Set, Glass Base, Silver Rim, Frank M. Whiting Co., 6 Piece 40.00
Cocktail Shaker, Boston Lighthouse, International Silver, c.1928, 14 In. 7768.00
Coffee Set, After Dinner, Footed, Shaped Handles, Black, Starr & Frost, 3 Piece 323.00

Coffee Set, Floral Repousse, S. Kirk & Son, c.1910, 8 In., 3 Piece 999.00
Coffee Set, Gilt Interior, Francis I, Reed & Barton, c.1930, 3 Piece 1955.00
Coffee Set, Gold Wash Interiors, Chased Vine & Flowers, Gorham, c.1890, 3 Piece 980.00
Coffee Set, Incised Floral Garlands, Baluster Shape Pot, Oval Tray, Whiting, 4 Piece 1265.00
Coffee Set, Octagonal Panel Form, Geometric Rim Design, Hallmark, 3 Piece 2500.00
Coffee Spoon, Square, Cut-Corner Ends, Chased Tulip Design, Arthur J. Stone, 5 1/8 In. .. 265.00
Coffeepot, Baluster Shape, Hinged Lid, Gale, Wood & Hughes, c.1844, 13 In. 2150.00
Coffeepot, Demitasse, Ribbed, Wood Handle, Gorham, Marked #2705, 7 1/2 In. 260.00
Coffeepot, Oval Urn, Reeded Borders, J. & P. Targee, c.1800, 12 1/2 In. 3000.00
Coffeepot, Repousse, Baltimore, S. Kirk & Son, Mid 19th Century, 16 1/2 In. 980.00
Compote, Deep Bowl, Pedestal Base, Kirk & Son, 4 3/4 x 10 In. 290.00
Compote, Lady Diana Pattern, Towle, Engraved, Tennis Trophy, 1933 .... 145.00
Compote, Rose Pattern, No. 120B, Footed, Stieff Company, c.1927, 3 1/2 x 7 1/4 In. 230.00
Compote, Sterling, Impressed Underside, Reed & Barton, c.1950, 6 x 8 In., Pair 575.00
Cordial Set, Floral Form Bowl, Monogram, International, 3 1/2 In., 8 Piece 290.00
Cream Jug, Repousse Decoration, Coin, Osmon Reed, c.1835, 6 1/2 In. 295.00
Cream Pot, Pear Form, 3 Trifid Feet, Z. Brigden, c.1760, 4 In. 3300.00
Cream Pot, Pear Form, Waved Rim, 2 Scroll Handle, Z. Brigden, c.1775, 4 5/8 In. 3300.00
Creamer, Coin, Squat Urn Shape, Gadroon Rim, Scroll Handle, c.1834, 5 1/2 In. .... *Illus* 365.00
Creamer, Helmet Form, Husk Swags, Isaac Anthony, c.1790, 6 7/8 In. .... *Illus* 1800.00
Creamer, Pear Form, Beaded Border, A. Carlisle, c.1785, 5 1/4 In. .; 3900.00
Cup, Coin, Pigeon Shoot Award, Engraved, E. Kinsey, c.1836, 9 1/2 In. 4025.00
Cup, Presentation, Etched Stag, Inscription, Gorham, c.1901, 12 3/8 In. 2160.00
Cup, Trophy, Shinnecock Hills Golf Club, 1913, W. Allen Putnam, Tournament, 4 In. 175.00
Cup Set, Tapered, Round Base, Silhouette Mark, Porter Blanchard, c.1950, 12 .... 5378.00
Decanter, Flowers, Leaves, Gilt Handle, Stopper, Gorham, 19th Century, 12 In. 1093.00
Demitasse Set, Gorham, 3 Piece 410.00
Demitasse Set, Hepplewhite Style, Coffeepot, Creamer, Sugar, Gorham 242.00
Demitasse Set, Plymouth, Gorham, 11-In. Pot, 3 Piece 323.00
Desk Set, Art Nouveau, Flowers, Marked, Gorham, 1901-1903, 6 Piece 4780.00
Dessert Set, Gilt Metal, Japanese Style, 12 Forks & Knives, c.1880 .... 4541.00
Dish, Bellflowers, Panels, 2 Handles, Oval, Tiffany & Co., Monogram, c.1907, 9 1/4 In. .. 431.00
Dish, Condiment, Handle Joins 2 Bowls, Mulholland Brothers, 3 1/2 x 9 In. 475.00
Dish, Fruit, Art Nouveau, Monogram, Gorham, Rhode Island, 1903, 20 In. 3286.00
Dish, Leaves, Scroll, Pedestal Foot, Lebkuecher & Co., c.1900, 6 Oz., 8 1/2 In. 288.00
Dish, Oval, Chippendale Style Border, Gorham, 12 In. 104.00
Dish, Oval, Pointed Ends, Ring Foot, Mulholland Brothers, 1 3/8 x 12 1/8 In. 575.00
Dish, Oval, Potato, Dimpled, Leaves, Handle, Gorham, 1886, 6 In. 717.00
Dish, Round, Flowers, Leaves, Berries, M.C. Knight, 1902, 5/8 x 8 In. 1400.00
Dish, Round, Raised Border, Applied Wire Rim, Merrill, 6 In. 125.00
Dish, Scallop Shape, 3-Footed, Hammered, Cellini, 1 1/4 x 8 3/8 In. 375.00
Dresser Set, Art Nouveau, Blackington, Massachusetts, 1905, 11 Piece 502.00
Dresser Set, Sterling Mounted, Marked, c.1900, 8 Piece 400.00
Ewer, Baluster Shape, Repousse, Flowers, Eoff & Shepherd, c.1861, 19 In. 8365.00
Ewer, Baluster, Flowers, Hinged Lid, John Chandler Moore, 1848-1878, 10 In. 1195.00
Ewer, Gilt, Enamel, Jewels, Gorham Mfg., c.1893 .... 32862.50
Ewer, Melon Shaped, Handle, Coin, Jones, Ball & Poor, 9 1/2 x 5 1/2 In. 431.00
Ewer, Tray, Persian Style, Baluster Shape, Repousse Flowers, 11 1/2 In., 8-In. Tray 2070.00
Fish Set, Gilt, Ivory, Scrolled Tendril, Spiral Carved Handles, 13 Piece 2820.00
Fish Set, Ivory Handled, Victorian, Cased, Slice & Fork, Knives, 6 Piece 115.00
Flask, Drinking Cup Top, Wilber F. Parker, 1870, 7 3/8 x 3 In. 920.00
Glass Set, Martini, Hand Hammered, Lebolt & Co., c.1910, 4 1/2 In., 12 Piece 837.00
Goblet, Coin, Beadwork Border, Grape & Vine, Inscribed, c.1856, 5 1/4 In. .... *Illus* 280.00
Goblet, Coin, Flowers, Cartouche, Inscribed, Early 19th Century, 5 1/8 In., Pair .... *Illus* 560.00
Goblet, Coin, Flowers, Cartouche, Inscribed, John Kitts, c.1838, 6 1/4 In. .... *Illus* 532.00
Goblet, Coin, Landscape Decoration, Presentation, Inscribed, 19th Century, 6 1/2 In. 288.00
Goblet, Coin, Wheat Design, Cartouche, Pedestal Base, Inscribed, c.1840, 6 In. ..... *Illus* 280.00
Goblet Set, Stem, S. Kirk & Son, Mid 20th Century, 6 3/4 In., 12 Piece 920.00
Goblet Set, Sterling Stem, Marked, Gorham, 6 1/2 In., 10 Piece 800.00
Goblet Set, Sterling, Impressed Mark, Gorham, c.1960, 6 1/2 In., 11 Piece 920.00
Gravy Boat, Tray, Dublin Pattern, Reed & Barton, 7 1/2 In. 103.00
Gravy Boat, Undertray, Repousse, Engraved Monogram, S. Kirk & Son 920.00
Hot Water Urn, Aesthetic Style, Barbour Silver Co., c.1885, 13 In. 1150.00

Ice Cream Slice, Shaped Blade, Beaded Handle, Horse Head Mark, 11 1/2 In. 120.00
Ice Tongs, Pierced, Chased, Grapevine Design, Arthur J. Stone, 6 5/8 In. 4200.00
Iced Tea Set, Pitcher Spoon, Teaspoons, Engraved Y, Porter Blanchard, 7 Piece 625.00
Iced Tea Spoon, Arched Handle, Pointed End, Engraved, Arthur J. Stone, 8 In., 8 Piece . .   1800.00
Iced Tea Spoon, Teardrop Shape, Thistle Design, Pointed Handle, Arthur J. Stone, 8 In. . .   300.00
Inkstand, Pen Tray, Pierced Gallery, Glass Wells, Gorham Mfg. Co., c.1890, 8 In. 1675.00
Inkstand, Sterling Silver, Crystal Inkpot, Pen, Scroll Border 374.00
Jam Spoon, Straight Handle, Scalloped End, George C. Gebelein, 6 1/2 In. 75.00
Jardiniere, Swan, Removable Grid, Durgin Division, Gorham, c.1900, 13 In. 7800.00
Jelly Knife, Medallion Head Handle, Inscribed 1869, Albert Coles, 7 1/4 In. . . . . *Illus*   250.00
Jelly Spoon, Pierced & Chased Grape Design, Monogram, Arthur J. Stone, 1918, 5 1/8 In.   350.00
Jelly Spoon, Teardrop Bowl, Spade Handle, Grape Cluster, Arthur J. Stone, 7 In. 395.00
Jug, Thermos, Mercury Glass Bottle, Monogram, Stopper, Lebolt, 6 7/8 x 5 In. 1800.00
Julep Cup, Beaker Form, Monogram, Alvin, 3 3/4 In., 12 Piece . . . . .1380.00 to 1495.00
Julep Cup, Shaped, Beaded, 3 3/4 In., 6 Piece 1380.00
Kettle, Hot Water, Bulbous, Handle, Lid, Spout, Stand, Whiting, c.1890 . . . .   690.00
Ladle, Curved Handle, Broad Bowl, Engraved F.H., Lebolt & Co., 5 1/2 In. 125.00
Ladle, Egyptian Style, Woman, Raised Arm, c.1870, 15 In. 2160.00
Ladle, Medallion Tip, Woman, Lobed Bowl, Coin, Hotchkiss & Schreuder, c.1860, 14 In. .   600.00
Ladle, Monogram, J.W. Forbes, c.1830 . . . .   675.00
Ladle, Naturalistic, Twig Stem, Grape Clusters, c.1870, 11 1/2 In. 1560.00
Ladle, Pointed End, Pierced, Chased Frond Design, Arthur J. Stone, 6 In. 425.00
Lemon Fork, 3 Tines, Chased Tulip, Cut Corner Square Handle, Arthur J. Stone, 5 1/2 In.   365.00
Lemon Fork, Slender Handle, Splayed Tines, Hammered, Wallace Silversmiths, 4 3/8 In. .   35.00
Lemon Squeezer, Rounded Triangle, Scroll, Gorham, 1910, 4 3/4 x 2 3/4 In. 630.00
Lemon Squeezer, Triangular, Engraved Scroll, Gorham, 1910, 1/2 x 4 3/4 x 2 3/4 In. 630.00
Letter Knife, Straight Blade, 4 Leaf Clover At End, Leonore Doskow, 7 In. 65.00
Lettuce Server, Hammered, Monogram B, Lebolt & Co., 8 3/4 In., Pair 85.00
Martini Set, Shaker, 6 Goblets, Dragon Relief, 11 In. 1175.00
Meat Fork, 3 Tines, Pointed End, George C. Erickson, 9 1/8 In. 155.00
Meat Fork, 3 Tines, Pointed Handle, Monogram, Hammered, Marcus & Co., 8 In. 85.00
Meat Fork, 3 Tines, Round End, George C. Erickson, 9 1/8 In. 155.00
Meat Fork, Flowers, Hammered, Engraved S, Barbour Silver Co., 8 3/4 In. 175.00
Mirror, Dressing Table, Chased, Embossed, Birds, Insects, Flowers, 15 1/2 x 19 1/2 In. . .   1035.00
Mote Spoon, Pierced Bowl, Cross & Scroll, Monogram, 18th Century 425.00
Mug, Castle, Tapered, Scrolled Handle, Coin, Gale, Wood, & Hughes, 4 1/4 x 4 In. 345.00
Mug, Engine-Turned Design, Cartouche, Scroll Handle, Coin, c.1835, 3 In. . . . . *Illus*   213.00
Mug, Repousse Cottage Scene, Leonard & Wilson, 1850, 3 7/8 In. . . . . *Illus*   250.00
Mustard Pot, Squat, Hammered, Lid, Spoon, Dominick & Haff, 1881, 3 1/2 In. 1315.00
Napkin Rings are listed in their own category.
Nut Dish, Gorham, Oval, 7 x 6 In. 58.00
Nut Dish, Heart Shape, Footed, 1897, Gorham, 1 3/4 x 6 x 6 1/2 In. 125.00
Nut Dish, Round, Low Ring Foot, Tudor Rose, Arthur J. Stone, 3/4 x 3 5/8 In. 50.00
Nut Dish Set, Impressed Mark, Gorham, Dated 1892, 5 1/2 In., 9 Piece 430.00

Left to right:
Silver-American, Goblet, Coin, Flowers, Cartouche,
Inscribed, Early 19th Century, 5 1/8 In., Pair

Silver-American, Goblet, Coin, Wheat Design,
Cartouche, Pedestal Base, Inscribed, c.1840, 6 In.

Silver-American, Mug, Engine-Turned Design,
Cartouche, Scroll Handle, Coin, c.1835, 3 In.

Silver-American, Goblet, Coin, Flowers,
Cartouche, Inscribed, John Kitts, c.1838, 6 1/4 In.

Silver-French, Beaker, Cylinder, Tapered,
Arrowhead Band, Inscribed, c.1850, 2 1/2 In.

Silver-American, Goblet, Coin, Beadwork Border,
Grape & Vine, Inscribed, c.1856, 5 1/4 In.

Olive Spoon, Pierce, Elongated Bowl, Hammered, 6 5/8 In. 60.00
Pickle Fork, Hammered, Pierced Tines, International Silver Co., 5 7/8 In. 60.00
Picture Frame, Rectangular, Lebolt, 6 3/4 x 4 1/8 In. 365.00
Pie Server, Karl F. Leinonen, c.1940, 9 5/8 In. 206.00
Pitcher, Art Nouveau Design, Hammered, Stamped Martele, Gorham, 1906 . . . . 17250.00
Pitcher, Baluster Shape, Chased, Flower Sprays, c.1903, 9 1/2 In. 5378.00
Pitcher, Baluster Shape, Gadroon Foot, William B. Heyer, c.1815, 7 3/8 In. 1912.00
Pitcher, Baluster, Scrolling Handle, International, Mid 20th Century, 9 In. 250.00
Pitcher, Bucket, Swags, Cartouches, International, 9 1/2 x 5 1/4 In. . . . : 546.00
Pitcher, Engraved, Monogram, Randahl Shop, Early 20th Century, 8 7/8 In. 635.00
Pitcher, Flattened Oval, Monogram, Coin, John Lynch, Baltimore, c.1786, 5 In. 2300.00
Pitcher, Flowers, Vines, Repousse, Stippled Ground, Kirk & Son, 1853, 21 Oz., 8 5/8 In. . 1725.00
Pitcher, Repousse, Inverted Pear Shape, Footed, Jenkins & Jenkins, 14 3/4 In. 3038.00
Pitcher, Slender, Hollow Handle, Hammered, Stylized H, Bellis, 11 1/4 In. 3700.00
Pitcher, Water, Baluster Form, No. 250, Gorham, Rhode Island, c.1860, 11 3/4 In. 1675.00
Pitcher, Water, Baluster Shape, Floral, Scroll, Lincoln & Reed, c.1835, 11 In. 1675.00
Pitcher, Water, Baluster Shape, Peter L. Krider, c.1860, Marked, 12 In. 840.00
Pitcher, Water, Baluster Shape, Scroll, Flowers, Gorham, Marked, 1900, 14 In. 2150.00
Pitcher, Water, Bean Pot Shape, Hollow Loop Handle, Kalo, 7 x 8 1/2 In. 2500.00
Pitcher, Water, Bulbous, Ring Foot, Monogram, Arthur J. Stone, 7 3/4 x 9 In. 3500.00
Pitcher, Water, Hand Hammered, Arts & Crafts Design, Kalo Shop, Chicago, N.Y. 1008.00
Pitcher, Water, Inverted Pear Form, Domed Foot, Alvin, c.1920, 11 x 8 1/2 x 6 In. 430.00
Pitcher, Water, Old Newbury Crafters 219.00
Pitcher, Water, Paneled Sides, Monogram, Kalo, 10 In. 2629.00
Pitcher, Water, Revere Style, Engraved, Richard Dimes, 7 x 7 1/2 In. 765.00
Pitcher, Water, Ring Foot, Ebony Handle, Hammered, DeMatteo, 10 x 6 3/4 In. 2300.00
Pitcher, Watson, 8 1/2 In. 259.00
Plate, Bread & Butter, Shell & Scroll Border, Gorham Corp, 1912, 6 1/4 In., 12 Piece . . . 345.00
Plate, Etched Rim, Dominick & Haff, 11 In. 39.00
Plate, Wolcott, Square, Wallace, c.1913, 5 1/2 In., 12 Piece 750.00
Platter, Leaf & Dart, Coin, Newell Harding & Co., 1857, 1 x 13 x 16 In. 1840.00
Platter, Oval, Gorham, 18 In. 175.00
Platter, Rectangular, Flowers, Cast Leaf Border, S. Kirk & Sons, c.1915, 13 1/2 x 9 In. . . 520.00
Porringer, Arthur J. Stone, Pierced Leaf Handle, 1907, 7 In. 1295.00
Porringer, Engraved MSCGH, IC On Handle, John Edwards, Boston, c.1746 . . . . 1570.00
Porringer, Keyhole Handle, J. Hancock, c.1765, 5 1/4 In. 4440.00
Porringer, Keyhole, John Edwards, Boston, c.1725, 7 3/4 In. 7500.00
Porringer, Pierced Handle, Mark, Simpkins, Engraved Initials, 5 1/4 x 2 1/2 In. 2875.00
Porringer, Wide Body, Pierced Handle, G. Hanners Sr., c.1720, 5 3/8 In. 5700.00
Porringer & Spoon, Wheat Ears, Flower, Scroll Spoon, Gorham, c.1898, 5 In. 6600.00
Punch Bowl, Domed Round Foot, Leaf Border, Hyde & Goodrich, c.1850, 9 In. 3825.00
Punch Bowl, Incised Molding, Engraved, John Moulinar, c.1750, 8 3/4 In. 4780.00
Punch Bowl, Monteith Form, Women On Swags, Kirk & Son, c.1890, 10 3/8 In. 8400.00
Punch Bowl, Thistle Form, Gadroon Rim, Marcus & Co., 6 1/4 x 12 x 14 1/4 In. 3680.00
Punch Ladle, Birds, Flowering Trees, Hale, Houston & Brower, Albany 255.00
Punch Ladle, Gold-Washed Bowl, Grapevine Handle, Frank W. Smith, 13 1/2 In. 380.00
Punch Ladle, Marked SW, Boston, 1780 . . . . 500.00
Salad Servers, Acanthus Style Handle, J.O. Randahl, 9 1/2 In., Pair 495.00
Salad Servers, Arts & Crafts Style, Fessenden & Co., 7 1/2 In., Pair 350.00
Salad Servers, Scrolled Handle, Karl F. Leinonen, 9 In., Pair 450.00
Salad Servers, Spade Bowls, Pierced Tines, Kalo, 9 3/4 In., Pair 535.00
Salad Set, Handwrought, Shreve, Crump & Low, California, 2 Piece 150.00
Salt, Open, Repousse, Black, Starr & Frost, N.Y., c.1908, 1 1/2 x 2 1/2 In., Pair 259.00
Salt, Oval, Pierced Balusters, Rosettes, John Burger, c.1790, 3 1/4 In., Pair 4500.00
Salt & Pepper, Cylindrical, Plugs, Allan Adler, 1 1/4 x 1 1/8, Pair 125.00
Salt & Pepper, Steeple Shape, Gorham, 4 Piece 200.00
Saltshaker, Rose Pattern, Bulbous Shape, 3-Footed, Stieff Company, c.1927, 4 1/2 In. . . . 200.00
Salver, Charters, Cann & Dunn, New York, 8 In. 3250.00
Salver, Circular, Shell & Flower Borders, Harvey Lewis, c.1825, 14 In. 3000.00
Salver, Flowers, Ball & Claw Feet, Cast Leaf Rim, S. Kirk & Sons, c.1925, 7/8 x 7 In. . . . 196.00
Salver, Flowers, Scrolls Repousse, Ball & Claw Feet, Howard & Co., 19th Century, 10 In. 1150.00
Salver, Leaf Rim, Grapevine, Tripod Ball & Claw Feet, S. Kirk & Son, 8 In. 505.00
Salver, Pierced Rim, Single Stylized Fleur-De-Lis, Arthur J. Stone, 10 3/8 In. 590.00

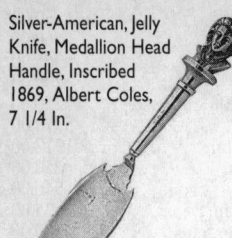

Silver-American, Jelly
Knife, Medallion Head
Handle, Inscribed
1869, Albert Coles,
7 1/4 In.

Silver-American, Mug, Repousse
Cottage Scene, Leonard & Wilson,
1850, 3 7/8 In.

Silver-American, Tureen,
Neoclassical, Oval, Revolving Cover,
Early 20th Century, 9 In.

Salver, Rectangular, Gadroon Rims, Hugh Wishart, c.1805, 10 3/4 In.	6600.00
Salver, Round, Floral Border, Diaperwork, Kirk & Son, 1903-1924, 11 1/4 In.	1195.00
Salver, Salem, Dominick & Haff, 13 1/2 In.	145.00
Sandwich Server, Scissor Form, Hinged Halves, c.1890, 7 3/4 x 2 3/4 In.	115.00
Sandwich Tray, Circular, Blossoms, Monogram, Gorham, c.1925, 12 3/8 In.	5400.00
Sauce Bowl, Underplate, Stylized Flower Form, Hammered, Rolled Rim, Kalo, 4 In.	764.00
Sauceboat, Coin, Alexander Gordon, New York City, c.1798	2500.00
Server, Vegetable, Hammered, Bowls, Tray, Cellini, 10 1/2 x 7 1/8 In., 3 Piece	1200.00
Serving Spoon, Long Handle, Arthur J. Stone, 12 In.	242.00
Serving Spoon, Pear Shape, Hammered, Engraved L, Lebolt & Co., 9 1/8 In.	180.00
Shears, W. Meyers, N.J., Early 20th Century, 7 In.	235.00
Soup Ladle, Fiddle Handle, Monogram, Ebenezer Whitney, N.Y., c.1830	375.00
Spoon, Shell Form Bowl, Coin, Bailey & Co., c.1849, 11 In.	145.00
Spoon, Shell Form Bowl, Coin, c.1849, 11 In.	144.00
Stuffing Spoon, Coin, G In Circle, IF In Oval, 12 1/4 In.	115.00
Sugar, Coin, Repousse, Cover, Fruit Finial, R&W Wilson, c.1835, 8 In.	750.00
Sugar & Creamer, Allan Adler, Signed, 2 1/5 & 3 1/2 In.	1200.00
Sugar & Creamer, Baluster Shape, Cover, Reeded Pedestal, Ensko, 4 In.	460.00
Sugar & Creamer, Bean Pot Shape, Engraved, Gorham, 2 1/2 x 5 In.	295.00
Sugar & Creamer, Leaves, Flowers, C-Scrolls, T.B. Starr, 19th Century, 9 Oz., 6 1/2 In.	431.00
Sugar & Creamer, Rose, Stieff, No. 26	506.00
Sugar & Creamer, Round, Flat Top Strap Handles, Marshall Field, 2 1/2 In.	350.00
Sugar & Creamer, Tapered Body, Flowering Vines, Scrolls, Starr & Marcus, 3 1/2 In.	150.00
Sugar Basket, Creamer, Flowers, Paw Supports, Monogram, Ball, Tompkins & Black	805.00
Sugar Scoop, 10 Sides, Ebony Handle, Arthur J. Stone, 4 1/8 In.	495.00
Sugar Shovel, Square Bowl, Enameled, Hammered, Marcus & Co., 5 In.	145.00
Sugar Spoon, Pierced & Chased Celtic Design, Pierced Bowl, Arthur J. Stone, 6 In.	375.00
Sugar Spoon, Pierced & Chased Rose Design, Arthur J. Stone, 6 In.	375.00
Sugar Spoon, Pointed Handle, Hammered, Engraved, Marshall Field, 6 1/4 In.	69.00
Sugar Tongs, Chased Twig Edge, Hammered, Marshall Field Craft Shop, 4 In.	125.00
Sugar Tongs, Claw Form, Hammered, Engraved A, Lebolt & Co., 4 In.	85.00
Sugar Tongs, Lewis & Smith, Philadelphia, c.1895	35.00
Sugar Tongs, Nips, Shell Form, Initials RET, Daniel Dupuy, Philadelphia	1238.00
Sugar Tongs, Spoon Shaped Graspers, Old Newbury Crafters, 3 In.	75.00
Sugar Urn, Beaded Borders, Arched Gallery, J. Richardson Jr., c.1790, 10 In.	2400.00
Syrup Jug, Hinged Lid, Impressed Hearts, Shaw, 1900s	1295.00
Tablespoon, Coin James Munroe, Barnstable, Mass., Pair	201.00
Tablespoon, Monogram, Coin, A. Johnston, c.1835, 9 1/4 In., 6 Piece	144.00
Tazza, Pierced, Monogram, 1907-1938, Tiffany, 3 1/4 In.	400.00
Tazza, Pierced, Oval, Marked, 20th Century, 3 1/4 x 11 3/8 In.	345.00
Tazza, Repousse, Pedestal, Round Base, Black Starr & Frost, 8 x 3 In., Pair	785.00
Tazza, Simple Foot, Concave Top, Scalloped, International No. 730, 4 x 10 In.	170.00
Tea & Coffee Set, Berry & Co., Meriden, Ct., 5 Piece	1495.00
Tea & Coffee Set, Cartouches, Forbes For Ball, Tomkins & Black, c.1845, 5 Piece	3000.00
Tea & Coffee Set, Chased Flowers, No. A2341, Gorham, 5 Piece	865.00
Tea & Coffee Set, Engraved Flowers, Monogram, Gorham, 5 Piece	690.00
Tea & Coffee Set, Engraved, Monogram, S. Kirk & Son Co., Early 1900s, 5 Piece	1380.00

Tea & Coffee Set, Floral Band, Joseph Shoemaker, c.1825, 5 Piece 7770.00
Tea & Coffee Set, Flowers, Matte Ground, S. Kirk & Son, c.1885, 5 Piece 7200.00
Tea & Coffee Set, Hampton Court Pattern, Reed & Barton, 6 Piece 4250.00
Tea & Coffee Set, Heavily Carved, Gorham, 6 Piece 1380.00
Tea & Coffee Set, La Paglia, Beaded, Wood Trim, 4 Piece 2015.00
Tea & Coffee Set, Lobed Sides, Scrolling Feet, 5 Piece 837.00
Tea & Coffee Set, No. 2300, Wallace, 7 Piece 1725.00
Tea & Coffee Set, Octagonal Vase Form, c.1900, 11 In., 5 Piece 1675.00
Tea & Coffee Set, Plymouth, Classical Revival, Oval, Paneled, Gorham, 1909, 4 Piece ... 590.00
Tea & Coffee Set, Plymouth, Gorham, Hallmark 1909, 5 Piece 2150.00
Tea & Coffee Set, Prelude Pattern, International, 6 Piece 980.00
Tea & Coffee Set, Rectangular, Round Corner, Mulholland Brothers, 6 Piece 19500.00
Tea & Coffee Set, Rose Pattern, No. 800, Stieff Co., c.1925, 5 Piece 8400.00
Tea & Coffee Set, Rose Point, Wallace, 5 Piece 2070.00
Tea & Coffee Set, Royal Danish Pattern, International, 9 In., 5 Piece 1035.00
Tea & Coffee Set, Scrolling Leaves, Watson Company, 8 Piece 4540.00
Tea & Coffee Set, Tray, 10 1/4 & 24 In., 5 Piece 1495.00
Tea & Coffee Set, Viking, Reed & Barton, Marked, c.1873, 5 Piece 720.00
Tea Set, Baluster Shape, Paneled, Anthemion Band, Hall, Hewson & Co., 3 Piece 1528.00
Tea Set, Champlain, Early 20th Century, 5 Piece 1680.00
Tea Set, Embossed, Flowers, Leaves, Swing Handles, Oval, Squat, Whiting, 3 Piece 880.00
Tea Set, Federal Style, Bailey, Banks & Biddle, 4 Piece 506.00
Tea Set, Floral Repousse, Pedestal Base, R. Gardiner, New York, 3 Piece 3900.00
Tea Set, Grape & Vine, Jones, Shreve & Ball Co., Boston, 1800s, 5 Piece 2910.00
Tea Set, Hampton Court Design, Reed & Barton, 6 Piece 4950.00
Tea Set, Ivory Trim, Jarvie, 4 Piece 6900.00
Tea Set, Repousse, Scroll Handles, Flowers, Kirk, 6 Piece 7475.00
Tea Set, Repousse, Trumpet Urns, Gorham, c.1905, 6 Piece 4675.00
Tea Set, Urn Form, Bud Finials, Thomas Fletcher, c.1820, 9 1/4 In., 3 Piece 3900.00
Tea Set, Wood Handle, John Vernon, N.Y., Marked, c.1792, 3 Piece 8365.00
Tea Strainer, Chased Twig & Vine, Hammered, Marshall Field, 1919, 5 1/2 In. 285.00
Tea Strainer, Flared Edge, Pierced Handle, Enameled Iris, Mary Winlock, 1901, 5 1/2 In. 1410.00
Tea Tray, 2 Handles, Gadroon Border, William B. Heyer, c.1815, 25 In. 5380.00
Tea Tray, 2 Handles, Rectangular, Gadroon Edge, 26 In. 1555.00
Tea Tray, Oval, Stylized Trefoil Border, Islamic Style, Gorham Mfg. Co., 24 In. 4185.00
Teapot, Acanthus, Woman Finial, Coin, W.G., Jones, Ball, Poor, Boston, 19th Century ... 863.00
Teapot, Basketry Bands, Eagle Head Spout, Serpent Handle, Rose Finial, Pedestal, 11 In. . 1035.00
Teapot, Oval Body, Strawberries, Cartouches, Jabez Halsey, c.1790, 6 1/2 In. 4800.00
Teapot, Scrolling Strapwork, Domed Lid, Ear Handle, Leaf Tip, Oval, Gorham, 6 In. 325.00
Teapot, Side Handle, Elgin Silversmith Co., Inc., New York, N.Y., 5 1/2 In. 90.00
Teaspoon, 5 O'Clock, Pointed End, Arthur J. Stone, 4 3/4 In. 75.00
Teaspoon, Chased Double Line Handle, Engraved, Arthur J. Stone, 6 In., 6 Piece 480.00
Teaspoon, Coin, Down Turned Ends, Baltimore, Aiken, 6 Piece 281.00
Teaspoon, Coin, Farrington & Hunnewell, Boston, Early 19th Century, 6 Piece 58.00
Teaspoon, Coin, Fitted Case, Downward Ends, Baltimore, A.E. Warner, 6 Piece 158.00
Teaspoon, Fiddle, Coin, R & W Wilson, c.1840, 5 1/2 In. 259.00
Teaspoon, Stylized Palmette & Leaves, F.W. Cooper, Monogram, c.1865, 8 Oz., 12 Piece . 115.00
Tongs, Shell Design, Marked, Motts 225.00
Tongs, Shell Ends, Embossed, Baskets Of Flowers, A. Mathey, c.1824-1835, 6 1/2 In. 165.00
Toothpick Holder, Quatrefoil, 2 Griffins, Ball, Black & Co., c.1875, 1 1/2 x 2 3/4 In. 230.00
Tray, Fenestrated, Chased Decoration, Gorham, 11 In. 145.00
Tray, Flowers, Leaves, Fruit & Leaf Rim, F.M. Whiting, c.1896, 19 Oz., 12 1/4 In. 140.00
Tray, Handles, Engraved, Monogram, Cowell & Hubbard, Dominick & Haff, 28 1/2 In. .. 3220.00
Tray, Italian Renaissance, Eleder-Hickok, c.1925, 13 1/2 In., Pair 8050.00
Tray, Lobed, Shallow, Ridged Rim, Arthur J. Stone, c.1924, 13 In. 1645.00
Tray, Octagonal, Greek Key Border, Medallions, Urns, Gorham, 20 In. 1315.00
Tray, Oval, Flared Border, Pierced Handles, Clemens Friedell, 19 1/4 x 12 In. 2900.00
Tray, Oval, Gadroon Border, No. 1050, Dominic & Haff, 20th Century, 16 In. 575.00
Tray, Oval, Leaf Tip Border, Engraved, Coin, N. Harding & Co., 16 1/4 In. 1015.00
Tray, Oval, Pierced Handles, Arthur J. Stone, c.1924, 11 3/4 In. 1295.00
Tray, Oval, Raised Border, Applied Rim Wire, G.C. Gebelein, 19 x 13 In. 1350.00
Tray, Rectangular, 4-Footed, Harbor Scene, Japanese, Gorham, 1881, 27 In. 21500.00
Tray, Rectangular, Oval Handles, Black, Starr & Frost, New York, 1910, 26 In. 3345.00

Tray, Repousse, Flower Border, 3 Claw Feet, Round, S. Kirk & Son Co., 11 In. 575.00
Tray, Roll, Leaf Scroll Design, William B. Durgin Co., H.H., 12 3/4 In. 201.00
Tray, Sandwich, Keyhole Pierced Handles, Gyllenberg, 1 1/4 x 12 1/2 In. 625.00
Tray, Serving, Circular, Flowers, Handles, J.E. Caldwell, 12 1/2 In. 633.00
Tureen, Neoclassical, Oval, Revolving Cover, Early 20th Century, 9 In. . . . . *Illus* 616.00
Tureen, Oval, Ram Head Handles, Repousse Flowers, Ring Cover Handle, 11 x 15 x 9 In. 1670.00
Urn, Cover, Reticulated, Repousse, Cobalt Glass Liner, Howard & Co., 16 In., Pair 3640.00
Vase, 3 Stag Horn Handles, Gorham, 5 3/4 In. 598.00
Vase, 8 Sides, Etched Leaf, No. 503, Reed & Barton, Taunton, c.1930, 24 1/2 In. 6000.00
Vase, Baluster Form, Poppy Plants, Flared Rim, Squared Base, Gorham, c.1903 . . . . 11400.00
Vase, Engraved, Square Tapered Shape, Square Foot, Towle, 12 1/2 In. 290.00
Vase, Etched Octagonal Shaft, Flowers, Flared Rim, Watson, 18 In. 759.00
Vase, Glass, Trumpet, Geometric, Flowers On Rim, 14 3/4 In. 940.00
Vase, Trumpet, Flower Repousse, Gorham, 10 1/2 In. 2868.00
Vase, Vines, Leaves, Engraved, Handles, Marked, Dominick & Haff, 1879, 4 In. 600.00
Waste Bowl, Coin, Repousse, Monogram, R&W Wilson, c.1835, 4 3/4 In. 500.00
Wine Coaster, Birds On Branches, Engraved, George Shreve, c.1890, 5 x 3 In. 1295.00
Wine Coaster, Gorham, c.1900, 6 In. 86.00
Youth Fork, Blunt Tines, Chased & Pierced Terrier Design, Arthur J. Stone, 4 1/4 In. 335.00
Youth Fork, Concave Handle, Round End, Hammered, Lebolt & Co., 4 1/2 In. 75.00
Youth Set, Cut Corner Handles, Hammered, Engraved, Frank Smith, 3 3/4 In., 3 Piece . . . 225.00
Youth Spoon & Knife, Hammered, Pointed Handle, Karl F. Leinonen, Pair 250.00
SILVER-AUSTRIAN, Tureen, Oval, Stepped Sides, Dome Cover, Hoffman, c.1910, 12 In. 2510.00
Vase, Lotus Shape, Flared Foot, Hammered, Hoffman, c.1920, 4 1/2 In. 4180.00
SILVER-CHINESE, Card Case, Hinged, Cartouche, Engraved Initials, Box, 3 1/2 x 2 1/2 In. . . 235.00
Cigarette Case, Dragon, 3 x 3 In. 175.00
Compote, Chased & Embossed Cartouches, Dragons, Leaves, Domed Foot, 6 1/2 In. 590.00
Fingernail Extension, Floral Scrollwork, 2 1/2 In. 195.00
Incense Burner, Cover, Chalice, Claw Feet, Engraved Flowers, China, 1800s, 6 In. 470.00
Tea & Coffee Set, Impressed Old Friend, c.1950, 5 Piece 1092.00
Tea Set, Chrysanthemum Blossoms, Faux Bamboo Handles, Oval, 6-In., Pot, 3 Piece 588.00
Tea Set, Embossed Bamboo, Square Shape, Bamboo Handles, 5 1/2-In. Pot, 5 Piece 3585.00
SILVER-CONTINENTAL, Basket, Cupids, Glass Liner, 19 In. 1116.00
Basket, Oval, Ribbon, Flowers, 19th Century, 2 1/2 x 5 1/2 x 3 3/4 In. 230.00
Basket, Pierced, 800, 18 x 11 In. 1035.00
Bowl, Mounted, Cut Glass, Dolphin Shape Base, 6 In., Pair 359.00
Bowl, Mounted, Cut Glass, Rose, Winged Dragon Handle, 10 In. 720.00
Coffeepot, Bulbous, Wood Handle, 3 Cabriole Legs, 18th Century, 11 In. 1380.00
Compote, Chased, Embossed, Fruits, Leaves, Fluted Trumpet Foot, 5 x 8 1/2 In. 325.00
Ewer, Mounted Glass, Scrolling, Leaves, Swirl Pattern, 12 3/4 In. 1175.00
Jewelry Box, Rococo Style, Engraved, Scrolling Leaves, Late 19th Century, 7 3/4 In. 635.00
Pomander, Urn Shape, c.1750, 2 In., 3 Piece 230.00
Tray, Oval, Leafy Panel Edge, 23 1/2 In. 720.00
Tray, Ribbed Border, Chased Decoration, Monogram, 12 In. 259.00
Wine Coaster, Dionysian Cherubs, Lions, Grapevines, Pierced, Reeded Rim, 5 In., Pair . . 999.00
SILVER-DANISH, Bowl, 2 Scrolled Handled, Flared Shape, Georg Jensen, 10 In. 4480.00
Bowl, Centerpiece, Leaf, Berry Stem, No. 160, G. Jensen, J. Rohde, c.1928, 11 1/8 In. . . . 5019.00
Bowl, Centerpiece, Openwork Leaf & Berry Stem, Georg Jensen, c.1920, 8 In. 3585.00
Bowl, Centerpiece, Shallow, Openwork Leaf, Tendril Handles, c.1950, 13 In. 8365.00
Bowl, Flaring Shape, Pierced Leaf Standard, Oval Base, Georg Jensen, 6 1/2 In. 1645.00
Bowl, Hammered, Oval, Tapered, Openwork Leaf Stem, Georg Jensen, 7 5/8 In. 2820.00
Bowl, Oval, Irregular Wavy Rim, Low Foot, E. Dragsted, 10 1/8 In. 353.00
Bowl, Round, Beaded Border, Georg Jensen, 9 In. 764.00
Cigarette Case, Men, Women, Sitting Around Barrel, Denmark, 3 1/2 x 2 1/4 In. 460.00
Coffee Set, Hammered, Ivory Handles, Georg Jensen, 1900, 3 Piece 2750.00
Fish Server Set, Twisted Fish Handle, Shell, Pierced, Georg Jensen, 1945, Pair 2390.00
Jelly Server, Curled Beaded Stem, Georg Jensen, 4 In. 90.00
Pitcher, Baluster, Lightly Hammered, Johan Rohde, c.1950, 11 3/8 In. 7768.00
Pitcher, Lobed, Flower Motif, Carved Wood Handle, Georg Jensen, 10 In. 4406.00
Pitcher, Shouldered, Oval Shape, Base, Wood Handle, Johan Thode, Georg Jensen, 9 In. . . 2938.00
Platter, Fruit, Georg Jensen, 14 3/8 In. 6050.00
Salad Servers, Plastic, Accents, Georg Jensen, c.1957 . . . . 1265.00
Salad Set, Weighted Handles, Georg Jensen, Marked 54, 8 1/2 In. 546.00

Sauceboat, Leaf Band, Ladle, Blossom Pattern, Georg Jensen, 8 In. 2629.00
Serving Spoon, Stylized Leaf & Berry Handle, No. 141, Georg Jensen, 1936, 10 In. 529.00
Spoon, Demitasse, Blossom, Georg Jensen, 3 1/2 In., 7 Piece 558.00
Spoon, Demitasse, Georg Jensen, 6 Piece 150.00
Sugar Castor, Spherical, Georg Jensen, 5 In. 1795.00
Tazza, Grapevine Pattern, Georg Jensen, Copenhagen, c.1950, 7 1/2 In. 8962.00
Tray, Oval, Fluted Rim, Georg Jensen, c.1950, 22 7/8 In. 4780.00
SILVER-DUTCH, Biscuit Box, Cover, Round, Ebony Finial, C. Ehrlich, 1928, 5 In. 3145.00
Charger, Openwork Squares, Circular, Loop Handle, 4 Ball Feet, Glass Liners, 11 x 7 In. . 1909.00
Pitcher, Dutch Village, Bagpipe Player, Branch Form Handle, 19th Century, 7 In. 1035.00
Salver, Openwork Waves & Circles, Rounded 3 Sides, 3 Open Feet, 3 x 6 In. 1011.00

SILVER-ENGLISH. English sterling silver is marked with a series of four
or five small hallmarks. The standing lion mark is the most commonly
seen sterling quality mark. The other marks indicate the city of origin,
the maker, and the year of manufacture. These dates can be verified in
many good books on silver.
SILVER-ENGLISH, Basket, Fruit Branches, Gilt Liner, Marked, William Pitts, 1801, 7 1/2 In. . 5079.00
Basket, Handles, Fruit, Leaves, Oval, James Dixon, Sheffield, 11 1/2 x 8 3/4 x 3 In. 230.00
Basket, Leaves, Swags, Maple & Co., George V, 1911, 9 1/4 In. 460.00
Basket, Oval, Scroll, Diaper, Shell Rim, Marked, Edward Aldridge, 1761, 13 1/2 In. 2390.00
Beaker, Flared, Fruit, Leaves, Marked, London, 1597, 6 1/2 In. 16730.00
Bottle Coaster, Georgian Style, Reticulated, E. & Co., Birmingham, 2 x 5 In., Pair 288.00
Bowl, Band Of Peaked Reeding, Domed Reeded Foot, George IV, 1820, 9 In. 705.00
Bowl, Boat Shape, Foliate Swag Motif, 6 In., Pair 359.00
Bowl, Boat Shape, Reticulated Sides, Leaf Relief, Mappin & Webb, c.1905, 10 In. 1673.00
Bowl, Centerpiece, Flowers, Scrolls, Handles With Cherubs, Gilt Interior, 19 x 11 In. 2588.00
Bowl, Centerpiece, Oval, Fluted, Pierced Balustrade, Roses, c.1931, 21 1/4 In. 2988.00
Bowl, Round Pedestal, Birmingham, c.1919-1920, 10 In. 115.00
Box, Counter, Tubular Form, Crest Of Balfour Of Dunbog, 1780, 3 In. 126.00
Box, Hedgehog, Semper Paratus Motto, George V, c.1913, 2 1/4 x 7 1/4 x 5 In. 115.00
Box, Lid, Cartouche Shape, Engraved, Henry Greenway, 1778, 1 In. 161.00
Box, Toilet, Arms Of Edmund Rolfe, Norfolk, R.B., 1806, 1 3/4 In. 170.00
Caddy Spoon, Daisy-Form, Gilt Leaf Handle, Birmingham, 1852, 3 1/2 In. 460.00
Caddy Spoon, Floral Chased Handle, J. Willmore, Birmingham, 1810, 2 1/2 In. 259.00
Caddy Spoon, Scoop Handle, Birmingham, Thomas Willmore, 1800, 3 1/2 In. 288.00
Caddy Spoon, Shell Form, Bright Cut Handle, Hester Bateman, 1783-1784 . . . . 630.00
Caddy Spoon, Shovel, Chased Loop, Birmingham, J. Taylor, 1818, 2 3/4 In. 160.00
Cake Basket, Embossed Floral & Fruit, Swing Handle, William IV, 1835, 12 In. 690.00
Cake Basket, Wheat & Floral Branch Handle, Engraved, 1846, 14 In. 1840.00
Candelabrum is listed in its own category.
Candlesticks are listed in their own category.
Candy Dish, Reticulated, Scrolls, Floral Rims & Feet, W. Comyns, 1890, 6 In., Pair 415.00
Card Tray, Shell & Scroll Borders, 3-Footed, George III, 1763, 1 1/4 x 7 1/2 In. 715.00
Card Tray, Victorian, Flowers, Figural, Scroll, 1885, 17 In. 460.00
Carving Set, Ivory Handle, Sheffield, Oak Case, Edwardian, c.1910, 14 In. 259.00
Carving Set, Stag Antler Handles, 4 Piece 115.00
Cheese Dome, Fluted, Wood Mushroom Finial, C.S. Harris & Son, 1905, 5 x 5 3/4 In. 169.00
Claret Jug, Waved, Scalloped Rim, Border, Strapwork, Hunt & Roskell, c.1848, 15 3/4 In. 7770.00
Coaster, Pierced Grapevine, Marked, 20th Century, 7 Piece 405.00
Coffee Set, C.S. & F.S., 1911, Miniature, 5-In. Tray, 9 Piece 520.00
Coffeepot, Cylindrical, Swan Spout, Marked, John Penfold, 1725, 10 3/8 In. 4180.00
Coffeepot, Engraved, Bell Finial, John Swift, George II, c.1738, 8 1/4 In. 2689.00
Coffeepot, Flowers & Leaves, Coat Of Arms, W. Kidney, 1798, 9 1/2 In. 1495.00
Coffeepot, Lighthouse Form, Domed Lid, Ribbed Ball Finial, Charles Wright, 8 In. 1175.00
Coffeepot, Oval, Footed, Lobed, Wooden Handle, Late 18th Century, 9 1/2 In. 250.00
Compote, Reticulated Edge, Engraved Flowers, Scroll, Footed, 4 x 9 In., Pair 220.00
Cream Jug, Hester Bateman, London, George III, 1782 . . . . 2500.00
Creamer, Baluster Form, Pedestal Base, Drapery, Vacant Cartouche, 1777, 4 In. 520.00
Creamer, Chased Swags, Leaf Tips, Inverted Pear Shape, Beaded, George III, 5 In. 205.00
Creamer, Leaf Design, Pedestal Base, Beaded Rim, C.H., 1778, 4 1/4 In. 375.00
Creamer, Leaves, Baluster, Serpentine Lines, London, George III, 1799, 4 1/8 In. 375.00
Creamer, Sterling, Squat, Gadroon Border, Ball Feet, London, 1821, 3 1/2 x 5 In. 110.00

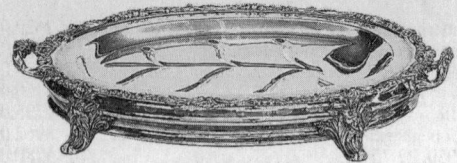

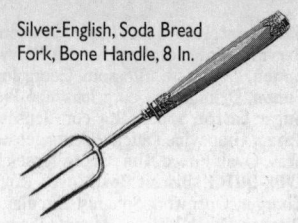

Silver-English, Soda Bread
Fork, Bone Handle, 8 In.

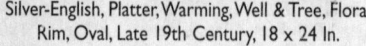

Silver-English, Platter, Warming, Well & Tree, Floral
Rim, Oval, Late 19th Century, 18 x 24 In.

Cruet, Crystal, Hamilton & Inches, Victorian, 1880-1881, 7 1/2 In., Pair 345.00
Cruet Set, Oval Stand, Pierced, 8 Bottles, Thomas Jackson, London, 1777, 7 1/2 In. 1265.00
Cup, Cover, Handles, David Willaume, Queen Anne, London, 1713 .... 10755.00
Cup, Georgian Style, 2 Handles, Harp Shape, London, c.1938, 11 1/2 In. 1315.00
Cup, Wine, Egg Shape, London, George III, c.1767, 5 x 3 1/2 In., Pair 1610.00
Dessert Spoon, Berry Design On Chased Bowl, Acanthus Carved Handle, 1763 .... 105.00
Dish, Cover, Reeded Base & Rim, Domed Lid, Ball Finial, E. Coker, 6 1/2 In., Pair 2350.00
Dish, Entree, Cover, Cushion Shape, Incurved Angles, George IV, c.1823, 11 3/4 In., Pair . 5375.00
Dish, Entree, Cushion Shape, Engraved, George IV, c.1823, 11 In. 13145.00
Dish, Strawberry, Fluted, Scalloped Rim, Marked, John Edwards II, 1738, 9 In. 2390.00
Dish Cross, Pear Shape Lamp, Beaded Borders, George III, c.1782, 12 1/2 In. 2990.00
Egg Spoon, Teardrop Shape, Enamel Highlights, Liberty & Co., 5 In. 225.00
Epergne, 5 Baskets, Flowers, Scroll Arms, Emick Romer, 1771, 14 x 27 x 25 In. 11950.00
Epergne, Chevron Support, Mask, Matthew Boulton, George III, c.1807, 14 In. 5080.00
Epergne, Sterling, Scrolling Standard, Lobed Base, c.1906, 16 1/2 In. 4185.00
Epergne, Walker & Hall, Sheffield, Edward VII, 1909, 100 Troy Oz., 20 In. 6050.00
Ewer, Fluted Neck, Sterling, A. Fogelberg, George III, 12 1/2 x 7 1/2 In. 1610.00
Fish Server, Flowers, Leaves, W.G.S. & Co., Monogram 290.00
Fish Server, Pierced, W. Eley, W. Fearn, W. Chawner, 1811 .... 175.00
Fish Set, Rococo Style, Knife, 5 Tine Fork, Leaf Engraved, Marked, 1869, 2 Piece 345.00
Fish Slice, Fiddle End, Relief Shell, Pierced, W. Chawner, c.1815, 12 In. 180.00
Flask, Double, Suede Case, Abercrombie & Fitch, 1985, 7 1/2 x 10 x 1 1/4 In. 190.00
Frame, Picture, Rectangular, Art Nouveau Style, Repousse Flower, Woman, 6 x 8 In. 80.00
Fruit Set, Shears, Spoons, Acanthus Scroll, 3 Piece, Sheffield, 1898, 7 1/2 x 12 1/2 In. ... 980.00
Funnel, Wine, George Smith, Thomas Hayter, 5 3/4 In. 260.00
Gravy Boat, Trefoil, Pad Feet, Scalloped Rim, Spout, George II, 1747-1748 .... 660.00
Inkstand, Inkpot, Sander, Candleholder, Snuffer, Tray, Barnard, William IV, 1836 ...... 1610.00
Inkstand, Navette Shape, Scrolled Rim, Pierced Border, H. Wilkinson & Co., 9 5/8 In. 764.00
Jug, Scroll Handle, Bud Finial, Paul Storr, 1812, 10 In. 5975.00
Kettle, Lampstand, Pear Shape, Rococo, E & J Barnard, 1853, 17 1/2 In. 2030.00
Kettle, Lampstand, Shells, Husks, Gabriel Sleath, c.1730, 14 1/2 In. 8605.00
Kettle, On Stand, Floral & Scroll Chasing, Carrington, London, 1910 ....1725.00 to 2900.00
Label, Decanter, Embossed, Engraved, George IV, 1 1/2 x 2 1/4 In. 315.00
Ladle, Fiddle Pattern, T. Wallis & J. Hayne, London, George III, 1817, 13 In. 265.00
Ladle, Oval Stylized Shell Shaped Bowl, R. Cruickshank, George III, 1787, 14 In. 350.00
Memo Pad, Telegram, Sterling, Goldsmiths & Silversmiths Co., London, 1905 .... 1500.00
Mug, Baluster Form, Leaf-Capped Double-Scroll Handle, Thomas Evans, 1775, 4 In. 675.00
Mustard Pot, Owl, Hinged Head, Chased & Engraved Feathers, Glass Eyes, 3 3/8 In. 1880.00
Mustard Pot, Triangular, Cobalt Blue Liner, Hinged Lid, Asprey, London 135.00
Napkin Rings are listed in their own category.
Page Turner, Simulated Tortoise Blade, Hallmarks, 1902, 17 3/4 In. 259.00
Pill Box, Bright-Cut Top, Samuel Pemberton, Birmingham, 1789, 1 In. 138.00
Pill Box, Cover, Applied Lion, 17th Century 550.00
Pill Box, Hatchwork Top, Joseph Taylor, Birmingham, 1804, 1 In. 115.00
Pill Box, Oval Shell Form, T.W., c.1810, 1 In. 105.00
Plate Set, J. Young, O. Jackson, London, George III, 1774, 9 1/4 In., 12 Piece 7768.00
Plate Set, Pierced, Scrolling Leaves, 4 Seasons Masks, c.1931, 18 Piece 5980.00
Platter, Meat, Oval, Coat Of Arms, Marked, Charles Kandler, 1769, 20 1/4 In. 3585.00
Platter, Meat, Oval, Gadroon Rims, Fox Crest, George III, c.1805, 13 1/4 In., Pair 2630.00
Platter, Meat, Oval, Molded Rim, Marked, William Pitts, 1787, 23 In. 4480.00
Platter, Warming, Well & Tree, Floral Rim, Oval, Late 19th Century, 18 x 24 In. ... *Illus* 560.00
Porringer, Cover, Chased, Embossed, Reeded & Fluted Band, Oval, Crump, 1767, 5 In. .. 1880.00
Punch Bowl, Art Nouveau, Stylized Fans & Iris, Shaped Rim, Lee & Wigfull, 7 In. 1058.00

Punch Bowl, Sterling, Footed, Impressed, Goodnow & Jenks, c.1900, 8 x 12 In. 633.00
Punch Ladle, Leaf & Shell Terminal, Lewis Samuel, William IV, 1835, 14 In. 375.00
Rattle, Child's, Whistle, Coral End, Balls, Scrollwork, G & N, Birmingham, 1861, 4 In. . . . 790.00
Rattle, Whistle, 6 Bells, Ivory Ring, 5 In. 520.00
Saltcellar Set, 10 Spoons, Gilt Washed Interior, Rope Handles, c.1864, 3 In., 6 Piece 1955.00
Saltcellar Set, Thomas Robbins, Rectangular, Pedestal, c.1807, 5 1/8 In., 4 Piece 1315.00
Salver, Border, Francis Pages, London, 1731, 8 In. 4800.00
Salver, Gadroon Rim, Richard Rugg, London, George III, 1771, 18 3/8 In. 4180.00
Salver, George II Style, Lapped-On Border, Masks, Shell Feet, c.1928, 22 In. 6275.00
Salver, Heraldic Crest, Molded Rim, Trumpet Foot, T. Mason, 1718, 3 1/4 x 8 1/2 In. 3410.00
Salver, Lions, Boars, Rams, Barnard Brothers, London, Victorian, 1898, 23 In. 3585.00
Salver, Molded & Gadroon Rim, Engraved Lion Crest, John Carter, 1774, 10 In. 705.00
Salver, Peter, Ann & William Bateman, London, George III, c.1803, 16 In. 5380.00
Salver, Robert Abercrombie, London, 1741, 6 1/2 In. 3500.00
Salver, Scroll Feet, William Peaston, London, George II, c.1754, 11 1/2 In. 1435.00
Salver, Shell, Scroll, Rim, 3-Footed, Rococo, Richard Rugg, 1764, 12 7/8 In. 3585.00
Salver, Thomas Hannam & John Crouch, George III, c.1800, Reeded Rim, 9 3/4 In., Pair . 2070.00
Sauce Ladle, Fiddle, Monogram, William Eaton, London Hallmarks, 1842 . . . . 69.00
Sauce Pan, Baluster Shape, Wood Handle, George II, c.1738, 13 In. 5080.00
Sauceboat, Bombe Oval Shape, Engraved, Scroll Handle, George II, c.1742, 7 In., Pair . . 2760.00
Sauceboat, Chased Gadroon Rims, Shell & Hoof Feet, c.1788, 6 3/4 In., Pair 4180.00
Sauceboat, Engraved, Contemporary Arms, Shell & Hoof Feet, 7 1/2 In., Pair 3285.00
Sauceboat, Engraved, Marked, George III, 1764, 7 1/4 In. 635.00
Soda Bread Fork, Bone Handle, 8 In. . . . . *Illus* 75.00
Soup Ladle, Shell Shape Handle, Engraved Bird, William Eley, William Fearn, c.1797 . . . 380.00
Spoon, Medicine, Tooled Cylindrical Handle, Tip Unscrews, George Adams 335.00
Spoon, Silver, Enamel, Celtic Style, No. 355, Liberty & Co., 7 3/4 In. 2070.00
Stuffing Spoon, Fiddle Handle, Monogram, W. Bateman, 1869 . . . . 175.00
Stuffing Spoon, Fiddle, James Beebe, George IV, 1822, 11 3/4 In. 175.00
Stuffing Spoon, Fiddleback, Lion Crest, Fennell, London, 1820, 12 1/4 x 2 1/8 In. 195.00
Stuffing Spoon, Monogram H, Dated 1806, London, 12 In. 230.00
Stuffing Spoon, Peter, Anne & William Bateman, George III, 1800 . . . . 160.00
Sugar Basin, Nautilus Shell, Hutton, London, Edwardian, c.1904, 5 x 3 1/2 In. 2300.00
Sugar Castor, Globe Form, Sterling, W. Peaston, London, 1804 . . . . 1200.00
Sugar Sifter, Fiddle, Thread, Shell, Boyton, London, c.1860, 6 x 2 1/4 In. 69.00
Sugar Tongs, Fluted Decoration, Late 18th Century, 5 1/2 In. 75.00
Sugar Tongs, Sterling, Thomas Law, Sheffield, c.1793, 5 1/2 In. 115.00
Sugar Tongs, Threaded Pattern, Stephen Adams Mark, George III, 5 3/8 In. 80.00
Tablespoon, King's Shell, George Angell, London, 9 In., Pair 175.00
Tankard, Baluster Shape, John Langlands, Newcastle, George III, c.1769, 7 1/2 In. 2390.00
Tankard, Baluster, Inscribed, Gurney, Cook, London, George II, 1749, 7 3/4 In. 3346.00
Tankard, Cover, Molded Borders, Arms Between Palms, London, 1674, 5 7/8 In. 3884.00
Tankard, Cylinder Form, W. & J. Priest, London, George III, 1766, 7 1/2 In. 1725.00
Tankard, Peg, Tapered Cylinder, PR Coronet, London, Charles II, 1683, 6 1/2 In. 5019.00
Tankard, Slight Baluster Form, R. Bayley, London, George II, 1734, 7 1/2 In. 3884.00
Tankard, Tapered Cylinder, Inscribed, Darker, London, George II, 1731, 6 3/4 In. 2270.00
Tea & Coffee Set, Elizabeth II Pattern, Pyriform, Gadroon Trim, 5 Piece 1528.00
Tea & Coffee Set, Oval, Paneled, Angular Handles, Ball Feet, Sheffield, 1926, 5 Piece . . . 588.00
Tea Set, Chased, Embossed, Squat Oval Shape, Barnard, William IV, 1833, 3 Piece 470.00
Tea Set, Indian Design, London Hallmarks, 19th Century, 3 Piece 345.00
Tea Set, Oval, Tapered, Ivory Handle & Finial, J. Schofield, George III, 6-In. Pot, 3 Piece 2585.00
Tea Urn, Reeded Supports, Paw Feet, Mask & Ring Handles, c.1797, 18 1/4 In. 3885.00
Tea Urn, Vase Shape, Lion's Head Ring Handles, George III, c.1802, 18 In. 6900.00
Teapot, Engraved, Lion Crest, Ebony Finial, G. Smith, T. Haytor, George III, 10 In. 850.00
Teapot, Inverted Pear, Spiral Gadroon, William Grundy, George II, c.1758, 6 1/2 In. 1910.00
Teapot, Monogram, Wreath, Finial, Wood Handle, George III, 6 1/2 In. 748.00
Teapot, Oval, Straight Sides, Hester Bateman, London, George III, 1789, 6 In. 2091.00
Teapot, Repousse Garlands, Hand Holding Shell Spout & Handle, G & M . . . . *Illus* 850.00
Teapot, Treen Handle, Maker's Mark, George II, 6 In. 1495.00
Teapot, Wooden Handle, Ribbed & Plain Panels, Octagonal, 6 In. 431.00
Toddy Ladle, Coin Inlay, Twisted Horn Handle, George III, 1787 . . . . 113.00
Tongs, Kings Honeysuckle, Shell Heel, W. Theobalds, London, 1828, 6 In., Pair 196.00
Tray, Octagonal, Swags, Flowers, Handles, Marked, Job Frank Hall, 1894, 26 In. 8365.00

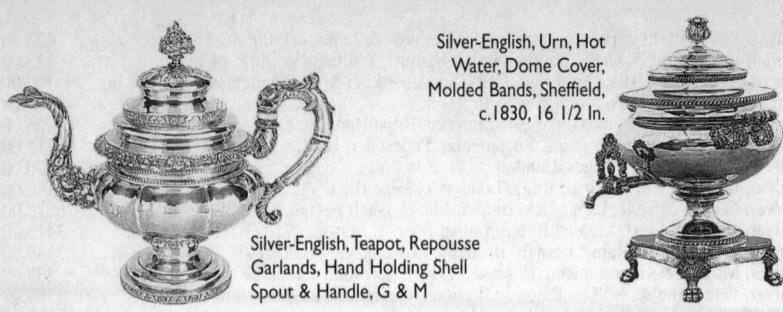

Silver-English, Urn, Hot
Water, Dome Cover,
Molded Bands, Sheffield,
c.1830, 16 1/2 In.

Silver-English, Teapot, Repousse
Garlands, Hand Holding Shell
Spout & Handle, G & M

Tray, Oval, Grapevine Rim, Handles, Benjamin Smith III, 1847, 27 3/4 In. 11352.00
Tray, Round, c.1900, 19 1/2 In. 1725.00
Tray, Scrolls, Flowers, Leaves, Circular, Mappin & Webb, George V, 1913, 14 In. 633.00
Tray, Waved, Raised Border, Shell, Scroll Rim, 2 Handles, Edward VII, c.1903, 30 3/4 In. 3885.00
Trophy, Rowing, R. Emes & E. Barnard, London, William IV, 1831, 8 In. 1195.00
Tureen, Cover, Regency, Oval, Gadroon Border, Lion Mask Handles, 8 1/4 In., Pair 4780.00
Tureen, Soup, Cover, Oval, Leaves, Flower Finial, Marked, Halford, 1808, 17 3/4 In. 9560.00
Urn, Cover, Gilt, Amphora Form, Handles, Wood Base, D & J Welby, 1911, 22 In. 4180.00
Urn, Hot Water, Dome Cover, Molded Bands, Sheffield, c.1830, 16 1/2 In. . . . . *Illus* 840.00
Urn, Regency, Fluted Supports, Acanthus Headers, John Edwards, c.1810, 16 1/2 In. 7470.00
Vase, Hammered, Stylized Buds In Relief, Cylindrical, 4 Applied Feet, W. Comyns, 10 In. 3930.00
Vinaigrette, Gold Wash Interior, Birmingham, T.F., 1826, 1 In. 170.00
Vinaigrette, Gold Wash Interior, Feathered Grill, Inscribed, J. Willmore, 1819 . . . . 230.00
Vinaigrette, Gold Wash Interior, Flowers & Ribbed, Birmingham, 1838, 2 In. 230.00
Waste Bowl, Ribbed Scroll Repousse, Mappin & Webb, London, 1891, 3 x 3 3/4 In. 118.00
Wine Coaster, Cymric, Round, 3 Ear Handles, Openwork Sides, Liberty & Co., 5 In. 380.00
Wine Coaster, Gothic Openwork, Turned Wood Base, 7 In., Pair 320.00
Wine Coaster, Leaf Scroll Rim, George III, c.1797, 6 1/2 In., Pair 1265.00
Wine Cooler, Campana, Vine Border, Marked, Emes & Barnard, 1826, 10 1/2 In. 9560.00
Wine Cooler, Urn Shape, 2 Ring Handles, Gadroon Edge, Footed, 11 3/4 In., Pair 806.00
Wine Cooler, William IV, Sterling, Barnard, London, c.1830, 11 1/2 x 9 3/4 In. 10060.00
Wine Funnel, Beaded Border, Detachable Bowl, George III, 1790 . . . . 1673.00
SILVER-FRENCH, Aspic Set, E. Puiforcat, Case, c.1885, 14 Piece 3200.00
Beaker, Cylinder, Tapered, Arrowhead Band, Inscribed, c.1850, 2 1/2 In. . . . . *Illus* 90.00
Bonbon Set, Fitted Case, Fanniere Freres, 4 Piece 2160.00
Bowl, Cover, Flowers, Leaves, Ivory Finial, Cardeilhac, 5 1/8 x 7 In. 5400.00
Bowl, Cover, Round Ivory Handle, Jean Puiforcat, 8 In. 10158.00
Bowl, Lily Leaf, Christofle, 4 1/2 x 12 5/8 In. 3000.00
Bowl, Vegetable, Gustav Odiot, 3rd Republic, Cover, c.1880, 6 1/2 x 12 In. 1380.00
Box, Card, Floral Chased Top, Ribbed Sides, Gold Wash Interior, 3 In. 115.00
Chalice, Gilt, Ivory Stem, 4 Fish On Stem, Bowl Foot, Puiforcat, c.1937, 6 In. 5975.00
Chalice, Trefoil Foot, Leaves, Branches On Stem, Gilt Interior, Husson, 5 1/2 In. 6000.00
Chalice & Paten, Gilt, Engraved, 19th Century, 7 1/2 In. 1035.00
Chalice & Paten, Pierced Flower Basket Shape, 19th Century, 8 1/4 In. 1150.00
Chalice & Paten, Repousse, Engraved, Maker Marks, 19th Century, 9 In. 1035.00
Chalice & Paten, Shamrock Sculpted Base, Medallions, 19th Century, 8 1/2 In. 1265.00
Chalice & Paten, Wheat Motif, Hallmarked, 19th Century, 9 In. 805.00
Cigarette Case, Art Deco, Enamel, Black, 3 In. 705.00
Coffee Set, Moka, Japonism Design, Hammered Surface, Lagarde & Fortin, 3 Piece 1080.00
Coffeepot, Demitasse, Acanthus Design Cover, Corn-Husk Finial, Handles, Monogram . . 460.00
Coffeepot, Pear Shape, 4 Serpentine Feet, .950, Ivory Handle, c.1885, 9 In. 920.00
Communion Set, Gilded, Bishops, Chased Base, Wheat, Grapes, c.1890, 5 Piece 9200.00
Crumb Scoop & Brush, Leaf Form, Christofle 1560.00
Crumb Scoop & Tray, Ivory Handle, Bonvallet Design, Cardeilhac, 7 7/8 In. 1680.00
Cup, Cover, Coconut, Silver Mount, L.R. Ruchmann, c.1825, 8 1/2 In. 540.00
Cup, Dragonfly, Pansies, 4 1/3 In. 240.00
Cup, Wine Tasting, Inset Coin, Mark, c.1880, 4 1/4 In. 290.00
Cup & Saucer, Silver Gilt Interior, Applied Hawthorn Branch, Debain 720.00
Decanter, Flat Pear, Bust, .950, First Standard, E. Puiforcat, c.1900, 7 1/2 In. 1035.00

Dish, Cover, Gold Details, Bonvallet Design, Cardeilhac, 1 1/5 x 7 3/4 In. 1200.00
Dish, Mother Of Pearl, Bonvallet Design, Cardeilhac, 1 1/5 x 8 5/8 In. 7800.00
Dish, Shell Form, First Standard, c.1910, 6 1/4 x 6 x 1 In. 115.00
Egg Coddler & Spoon, Silver Gilt Bowl, 3 In. 336.00
Epergne, Neoclassical Style, Round, Reeded Frame, Swags, c.1900, 13 1/4 In. 635.00
Ewer, Basin, Baluster, Scrolling Foliage, Nymph Handle, Paris, c.1865, 12 5/8 In. 5975.00
Figurine, Porcupine, Reticulated,.950, Collier, c.1828, 4 1/4 In. 375.00
Figurine, Saint George, Dragon, Hallmark, 20th Century, 11 x 8 1/2 In. 520.00
Ice Cream Spoon Set, Japonism, Silver Gilt, Fitted Case, Merite, 13 Piece 600.00
Inkstand, Sterling, Enamel, Yellow, Engine Turned, 7 In. 3585.00
Jar, Cover, Geranium, Bonvallet Design, Cardeilhac, c.1898, 7 1/4 In. 4800.00
Medal, Doll On Hill, Exposition De La Poupee, Lyon 1933, 3 In. 200.00
Mirror Plateau, 2 Matching Round, Wood Base, c.1900, 35 x 22 1/2 In. 6570.00
Opium Lamp, c.1900, 7 7/8 In. 840.00
Pill Box, Cover, Green Enamel, Silver Stars, 20th Century, 1 Oz., 2 3/8 In. 195.00
Pill Box, Perforated Figures, Panels, c.1900, 1 1/4 In. 35.00
Porringer, Cover, Flower, Ivory Handle, Bonvallet, Cardeilhac, 6 x 12 1/2 In. 6600.00
Reliquary, Cased, St. Vincent De Paul Relic, Hinged, Velvet, 19th Century, 3 x 3 In. 520.00
Salad Servers, Clover Decorations, Maillard, 10 1/4 In. 300.00
Salt Set, Shell Shape, Ring Handles, Charles-Antoine-Amand Lenglet, 7 7/16 In., 6 Piece 5079.00
Spoon, Poppy Form Bowl, Gauthier, 9 1/4 In. 840.00
Spoon, Strawberry Form Bowl, Leaves Handle, L'Hericart De Thoury, 6 1/2 In. 480.00
Sugar Bowl & Sifter, Gilt Interior, Fitted Case, Monogram, Henin, 6 x 6 1/4 In. 1200.00
Sugar Sifter, Paris, c.1775 . . . . 1850.00
Tazza, Open Flower Shape, Partially Gilt, G. Gueyton, 3 1/2 In. 240.00
Tea & Coffee Set, Octagonal, Angular Handles, Fountain Finials, Puiforcat, 6 Piece 15535.00
Tray, Circular, Molded Rim, Cartier, 20th Century, 44 Oz., 15 In. 865.00
Tray, Hammered, Iris Handles, Jean Puiforcat, 1 1/2 x 16 1/8 In. 2160.00
Tray, Visiting Card, Orchid Flower On Grip, Kidney Bean Shape, C. Forgelot, 6 In. 480.00
Tureen, Soup, Cover, Hexagonal Shape, Hammered, Lefebvre, 8 1/4 x 16 1/8 In. 2160.00
Tureen, Soup, Oval, Reeded Borders, Handles, Bud Finial, Cheret, 1785, 18 In. 4780.00
Vide Poche, Change Receiver, Leaf Form, 4 1/3 In. 460.00
SILVER-GERMAN, Beaker, Maker's Mark, Augsburg, 18th Century, 3 1/2 In., Pair 575.00
Bell, Table, Girl, Muti-Hooped Skirt, Feather Hat, Early 20th Century, 5 3/4 In. 780.00
Bowl, Handle, Art Nouveau Style, Silver Insert, Rosenau, Oval, 12 In. 300.00
Bowl, Rococo Style, Putti, Openwork, Pedestal Base, c.1900, 6 1/4 x 9 In., Pair 1265.00
Bowl, Sauce, Rococo Style, Circular Footed, Shaped Sides & Lip, c.1900, 7 1/2 In. 259.00
Bread Tray, Repousse, Courtship Scene, c.1920, 15 x 10 1/2 In. 920.00
Chalice, Cover, Gilt, Dated 1885, 13 In. 170.00
Claret Jug, .800 Silver Mounted, Glass Body, Egg Shape, 1800s, 11 In. 1610.00
Claret Jug, Lid, Monogram, Stylized Leaf, Handle, Stamped, c.1900, 10 1/4 In. 315.00
Coffee & Tea Set, Hammered, Globular, Loop Handles, Ball Finial, 1920s, 5 Piece 2250.00
Cup, Cover, Nautilus Shell, Marked, 19th Century, 15 In. 3910.00
Dish, Fruit, Gilt Interior, Pail Form, C.G. Schrodel, 18th Century, 11 In. 4180.00
Dish, Upright Shell Form, Wollenweber, 11 3/4 x 13 3/4 In. 960.00
Figure, Pheasant, Cock & Hen, Hinged Wings, 21 In., Pair 5380.00
Lobster Pick Set, Spatulate Handle, Threaded Leaf, Gilt, c.1920, 8 In., 12 Piece 980.00
Pitcher, Strap Handle & Lip, Oval, 18th Century, 6 In. 127.00
Salt & Pepper, Dutch Girl, Boy, Hinged Hats, Wooden Shoes, 5 In. 345.00
Stein, 21 Coins, Silver, Dresden H. Mau, 1907, 8 1/2 In., Liter 4945.00
Tankard, Baroque, Embossed, Marriage Scene, Gilded Interior, Hamburg, 1711, 7 3/4 In. . . 1610.00
Tankard, Parcel Gilt Silver, Fleur-De-Lis, Scroll Thumb Plate, c.1675, 8 3/4 In. 8365.00
Tankard, Parcel Gilt Silver, Squat, Cylindrical Shape, 3 3/4 In. 5080.00
Tea & Coffee Set, Iris & Scroll, Openwork Border Tray, 4 Piece 7170.00
Tea & Coffee Set, Pear Shape, Scroll Neck, Handle & Foot, Rosebud Finial, 4 Piece 825.00
Tea Set, Tray, Rococo Style, 20th Century, 3 Piece 290.00
Tray, Round, Hand Hammered Border Panels, H. Schaper, Berlin, 10 1/2 In. 175.00
Vase, 2 Lion Masks, Ring Handles, Leaf Tip Borders, 19th Century, 21 Oz., 7 In. 430.00
Wine Cooler, Urn Shape, Quarter Lobed, Ringed Lion's Head Handles, 7 1/4 In. 805.00
SILVER-IRAQI, Cigarette Case, Cityscape, Inscribed Florence Taylor, c.1910, 3 x 2 In. 200.00
Cigarette Case, Shatt Al Arab River & Camel Designs, c.1910, 2 1/4 x 3 In. 230.00
Cigarette Case, Shatt Al Arab River Decoration, Signed, c.1910, 3 1/4 x 3 3/4 In. 175.00
SILVER-IRISH, Bowl, Footed, Ribbed, Scalloped Edge, Dublin, No. 453, 5 x 11 In. 448.00

Bowl, Pierced, Rococo Style, Embossed, West & Son, Dublin, c.1899, 10 1/2 In. 1790.00
Cream Jug, Chased, Embossed Birds, Snake, Hound, Oval, J. Scott, Dublin, 6 1/2 In. 295.00
Marrow Scoop, George III Style, Double End, William War, Dublin, 1901, 9 7/8 In. 325.00
Tray, Oval, Gadroon Edge, Engraved, Motto, George III, c.1760, 24 In. 5175.00
Trophy, Stippled Stars, Flowers, Shield On Bowl, Handle, 1813, Dublin, 9 3/4 In. 635.00
Tureen, Cover, Boat Shape, Reeded Handles, Leaves, Gadroon Rim, c.1802, 19 3/4 In. . . . 3885.00
Wine Cooler, Campana Shape, Egg & Dart Borders, Double Scroll Handles, 10 1/4 In. . . . 4180.00
SILVER-ITALIAN, Centerpiece, Oval, Fish, Crabs, Mussels, Fishnet, Buccellati, 1900s, 32 In. 14340.00
Dish, 3 Grape Leaves, Mario Buccellati, Rome, 1900s, 17 In. 5380.00
Ewer, Urn Form, Carved Rosewood Handle, Figural Female Head, c.1945, 16 In. 2250.00
Figure, Fox, Full Tail, Pricked Ears, Signed M. Buccellati, 1900s, 13 In. 4480.00
Figure, Pheasant, Cock & Hen, 20th Century, 10 7/8 In., 2 Pair 8365.00
Goblet Set, Grapevine Stem, Satyrs, Rococo Base, 4 7/8 In., 12 Piece 2689.00
Inkstand, Gilt, 4 Piece, Wreath Finials, Paw Feet, Franceshini, c.1840, 9 1/2 In. 3585.00
Tea & Coffee Set, Art Deco, Hammered, Knob Finials, Lacquered Tray, Ronchi, 5 Piece . 470.00
Vase, Baluster, Satyr Masks, Scroll Handles, Corbella, c.1830, 19 In. 3585.00
Wine Cooler, Partly Fluted, Campana Shape, Fixed Collars, 20th Century, 9 9/16 In., Pair 4180.00
Wine Pail, Double, Flared Oval, Applied Pierced Handles, Brandi Marte, 13 In. 3885.00
SILVER-JAPANESE, Bowl, Embossed, Chrysanthemum, 4 1/2 x 7 1/4 In. 920.00
Bowl, Scalloped Rim, Reeded Round Body, c.1900, 3 x 7 In. 345.00
Bowl, Sterling, Chrysanthemum, Footed, Impressed Base, 4 1/2 x 7 1/4 In. 575.00
Box, Spiral Design, Signed, Koeki, 20th Century, 6 3/4 In. 160.00
Cocktail Set, Applied Dragons, Ice Bucket, Faux Bamboo Swing Handle, 14 Piece 999.00
Pitcher, Bamboo Form, Wisteria Design, Enamel, Signed, 6 In. 660.00
Sword Guard, Openwork, Dragon Design, Meiji Period, Signed 1035.00
Tazza, Circular, Center Paulownia Crest Mark, 20th Century, 2 x 6 In., Pair 690.00
Tea Set, Coffeepot, Teapot, Creamer, Sugar, Sterling, Impressed Mark, Maita 1495.00
Tea Set, Naturalistic, Tree Trunk Form, Twig Handles, c.1885, 5 Piece 8400.00
Tray, Ivory Center, Tortoise Shell Inlay, 4 Figures Under Tree, Shibayama Style, 9 1/2 In. . 1495.00
Tray, Sterling, 2 Handles, Impressed Kuyeda, Imperial Hotel, c.1950, 25 In. 805.00
Urn, Filigree, Enamel, Lacquer, Mother-Of-Pearl Birds, Cover, c.1885, 11 3/4 In. 19200.00
Vase, Inverted Pear Shape, 2 Men, Landscape, Carved, Gilt, Signed, 8 1/2 In. 3680.00
SILVER-MEXICAN, Belt Buckle, Square, Crescent Links, Circles, Hector Aguilar 529.00
Coffee & Tea Set, Tray, Mid 20th Century, 4 Piece 748.00
Dish, Cover, Oval, Gadroon Border, Removable Interior, 2 Handles, c.1950, 15 In. 345.00
Goblet, Sterling, Stem, Marked, 6 3/4 In, 8 Piece 520.00
Sauceboat, Undertray, Applied Scroll Molding, Mid 20th Century, 7 In. & 13 3/4 In. 405.00
Tea & Coffee Set, Scroll Handles, Ball Finial, Tray, 2 Handles, Spratling, 4 Piece 11950.00
Tea & Coffee Set, Shaped Body, Scalloped Rim, Scroll Feet, 5 Piece 805.00
Tray, Oval, Broad Rim, Monogram, 2 Handles, Mid 20th Century, 26 1/4 In. 430.00
Tray, Scalloped Flowers, Leaf Cluster Borders, Maciel No. 844/8, 17 In. 165.00
SILVER-PERUVIAN, Tea Set, Swirled Ribs, Roses, 7 Piece 2200.00
SILVER-PORTUGUESE, Nef, Sails Set With Enamel Crosses, Filigree Wire, 17 In. 1763.00

SILVER-RUSSIAN. Russian silver is marked with the Cyrillic, or
Russian, alphabet. The numbers 84, 88, or 91 indicate the silver con-
tent. Russian silver may be higher or lower than sterling standard.
Other marks indicate maker, assayer, or city of manufacture. Many
pieces of silver made in Russia are decorated with enamel. Faberge
pieces are listed in their own category.

SILVER-RUSSIAN, Altar Gospel, Repousse, Velvet, Cloisonne Enamel Medallions, 17 x 12 In. 4600.00
Bowl, Fruit, Shell Form, Eagle, Grip, Grachev, St. Petersburg, c.1900, 12 1/2 In. 2270.00
Box, Dragons, Flowers, City, Enamel, Khlebnikov, Moscow, c.1910, 10 In. 15535.00
Box, Reclining Dog, Red Glass Eyes, Collar, 3 3/8 In. 978.00
Box, Sewing, Fringed Sides, Gilded, Trompe L'Oeil, Moscow, 1885, 5 3/4 In. 3885.00
Chalice, Engraved, Evangelists, Deisis, 19th Century, 12 3/4 In. 1035.00
Cheroot, Case, Tsarist, Napoleon Bonaparte On Horseback, 5 x 3 5/8 In. 1095.00
Cigar Case, Man On Horse, Landscape, Enamel, Feodor Ruckert, c.1910, 6 In. 23900.00
Cigarette Case, Art Nouveau Ribbon Design, c.1890, 3 x 2 1/4 In. 259.00
Cup Set, Gilt, Cloisonne Enamel, For Tiffany & Co., c.1895, 2 1/4 In., 4 Piece 4025.00
Dagger, Kinjal, Leather Sheath, Silver, Niello Mount, Ivory Handle, 20th Century, 21 In. . 750.00
Drink Set, Etched Architectural Scenes, Cut Work On Tray, St. Petersburg, 1882, 8 Piece . 550.00
Group, Mounted Officer, Tsar Nicholas II Cipher, c.1908, 9 x 8 In. 4600.00

Knife Rest, Shield & Garland Design, Twist Support, Faberge, 2 7/8 In., 6 Piece 2185.00
Kovsh, Geometric Border, Grachev, St. Petersburg, c.1890, 11 3/8 In. 2990.00
Kovsh, Peacock, Enamel, Gilded, Ovchinnikov, Moscow, c.1910, 9 1/2 In. 20315.00
Kovsh, Shaded Enamel, Moscow, c.1896, 4 In. 865.00
Liquor Set, Flowers, Enamel, Gilded, Blue Beads, Moscow, 1892, 7 Piece 7170.00
Punch Bowl, Scrolling Foliage, Stand, Ovchinnikov, Moscow, c.1900, 11 In. 11950.00
Punch Ladle, Shaded Enamel, Scrolling Foliage, Red Cabochon, c.1899, 10 In. 2530.00
Punch Set, Flowers, Enamel, Gilded, Ovchinnikov, Moscow, c.1900, 11 Piece 71700.00
Salver, Cloisonne, Stylized Floral & Geometric Designs, Enameled, 6 1/2 In. 940.00
Samovar, Award Stampings, Imperial, Ivana Kaprzina, c.1905, 22 In. 575.00
Samovar, Under Tray, Bowl, 19th Century, 14 In. 405.00
Serving Spoon, Gilt, Shaded Enamel, Beaded Border, c.1900, 7 1/4 In. 865.00
Serving Spoon, Niello, Scrolls, Greek Key, Initials, 6 7/8 In. 58.00
Spoon, Enamel, Gilded, Oak Case, Moscow, c.1900, 13 Piece 2150.00
Tea & Coffee Set, Lobed Border, St. Petersburg, c.1825, 7 Piece 7768.00
Tongs, 2 Headed Eagle, Fiddle Handle, Pierced Ends, Coat Of Arms, 11 In. 280.00
Vase, Champleve Enamel, Cartouche, 2 Headed Eagle, c.1874, 11 1/2 In. 5720.00
Vodka, Caviar Set, Oval Tray, Gilded, Semyonov, Moscow, c.1860, 11 Piece 11352.00
Wine, Enamel Nephrite, Impressed Bowl, c.1892, 4 3/4 In. 1265.00
Writing Set, Cased, Letter Opener, Pencil, Pen, Marked 84 . . . . 290.00
SILVER-SCANDINAVIAN, Coffeepot, Ivory Heat Stops, Marked Jor, Sterling 925, 8 In. . . 260.00
   Stein, Repousse Leaf, Berry, 3 Ball Feet, Coin In Lid, 3 1/2 In. 575.00
SILVER-SCOTTISH, Cream Jug, Edinburgh, 1881 . . . . 800.00
   Letter Opener, Edinburgh, 1893 . . . . 1500.00
   Marrow Scoop, Armorial Hearth Engraving, H.C. & Co., Scotland, 8 In. 316.00
   Sauce Ladle, Fiddle & Shell Pattern, John McDonald, George III, c.1817, 5 1/2 In., Pair . . 547.00
   Spoon, Condiment, Pear-Shaped Bowl, Fiddle Handle, F & S, 1826, 4 1/2 In. 58.00
   Sugar Tongs, Sterling, Monogram, Glasgow, c.1859, 6 1/4 In. 69.00
   Sugar Tongs, Sterling, Victorian, Marshall & Son, Edinburgh, c.1848, 6 1/2 In. 104.00
SILVER-SOUTH AMERICAN, 2 Mugs, Brazier, Cartouche Traces, Early 20th Century, 4 1/4 In. 538.00

SILVER-STERLING. Sterling silver is made with 925 parts silver out of
1,000 parts of metal. The word *sterling* is a quality guarantee used in
the United States after about 1860. The word was used much earlier in
England and Ireland. Pieces listed here are not identified by country.
Other pieces of sterling quality silver are listed under Silver-American,
Silver-English, etc.

SILVER-STERLING, Bottle, Figural, Peacock, Hallmarks, Late 20th Century, 15 1/2 In. 690.00
   Bowl, Arts & Crafts, Hammered, Lobed, Footed, Rolled Rim, c.1927, 2 1/4 In. 295.00
   Bowl, Flared, Lobed Shape, Reticulated Border, Leaf Motifs, 13 1/2 In. 480.00
   Bowl, Oval Body, Grape Cluster Handles, 20th Century, 4 1/2 x 11 x 7 3/4 In. 430.00
   Bowl, Round, 3 Sections, 15 In. 230.00
   Bowl, Round, Open, S. Marsh & Sons, c.1940, 10 In. 115.00
   Bowl, Vegetable, Cover, Engraved, Monogram, Early 20th Century, 6 x 12 1/2 In., Pair . . . 1035.00
   Box, Tobacco, Leaf Collar, Cover, Hinged, Urn Finial, Marked, c.1800, 6 In. 1673.00
   Box, Tortoise Cover, Openwork Border, 1 1/2 x 5 1/2 x 3 1/2 In. 375.00
   Bread Tray, Oval, 6 1/2 x 11 In. 115.00
   Candelabrum is listed in its own category.
   Candlesticks are listed in their own category.
   Candy Dish, Square, Scalloped Rim, Center Handle, Bakelite Finial, c.1940, 7 In. 90.00
   Centerpiece, Hepplewhite, Swags, Cartouches, 6 x 14 In. 431.00
   Chalice, Cover, Diamonds, Sapphires, Opals, E.B. McGlynn, No. 7215, 8 1/2 In. 2300.00
   Charger, Circular, D'Orleans, Monogram, 13 1/4 In. 460.00
   Cigarette Box, Cover, Cabochon, Copper Base, c.1910, 3 1/4 x 3 1/8 x 4 3/4 In. 46.00
   Cigarette Case, Enameled, Deco, Daimler Race Car, Black Ground, 4 1/4 x 3 In. 2365.00
   Coaster Set, Glass, Openwork Overlay, Daffodils, Leaves, 3 In., 6 Piece 138.00
   Cordial Set, Floral Form Bowl, Simple Stem, 3 In., 24 Piece 400.00
   Cover, Meat, Detachable Handle, Crest On Griffin Holding Sword, 1820, 14 x 11 x 9 In. . 600.00
   Creamer, Flatted Oval, Gadroon Sides, Charles A. Burnett, c.1793, 6 1/2 In. 805.00
   Decanter, Overlay, Stopper, Scroll Design, Shaped Bottle, 12 In. 1150.00
   Demitasse Pot, Rococo-Style, Repousse 150.00
   Dresser Set, Brushes, Comb, Mirror, Case, Art Deco, c.1930, 6 x 10 In., 13 Piece 978.00
   Ewer, Wine, Dragon & Leaves, 8 1/2 In. 748.00

Figure, Pheasant, Standing, Intricate, Feather Design, 7 1/4 x 18 x 16 In., Pair 978.00
Flask, Hip, Leather, Covered, Engraved, William Allen Putnam Jr., 5 1/2 In. 105.00
Flask, Randahl, Hammered, Flattened, Curved, c.1920, 5 7/8 In. 355.00
Flask, Scrolling Leaves Design, 7 1/2 In. 480.00
Frame, On Wood, Arts & Crafts, 9 1/2 x 12 1/4 In. 175.00
Glass Holder Set, 3 1/2 In., 6 Piece 90.00
Glass Set, Iced Tea, Engraved As Tennis Trophies, 9 Piece 290.00
Goblet Set, Stem, Cased, Marked, Mid 20th Century, 6 5/8 In., 12 Piece 690.00
Ladle, Repousse Pattern, Engraved Bowl 175.00
Mirror, Dressing, Rococo Style, Heart Shape, Putti, Flowers, 17 In. 805.00
Mirror, Rococo Style, Sterling Mount, Blue Velvet, Impressed, 13 In., Pair 489.00
Mirror, Table, Repousse, Allover Chased, Embossed, Twig Border, 19 1/2 In. 690.00
Napkin Rings are listed in their own category.
Page Turner, Shell Blade, Silver Handle, Repousse, W. Comyns, Victorian, 16 In. 675.00
Pill Box, Floral Repousse, c.1905, 1 3/4 In. 80.00
Pin Tray, Guilloche, Enamel, Oblong, Footed, Machine Tooling, 2 x 4 5/8 In., Pair 110.00
Pitcher, Rope Borders, Scrolled Handle, Engraved Crest, Marked, 10 1/2 x 7 x 5 1/2 In. .. 770.00
Pitcher, Scrolled Handle, Incised Pin Stripes On Shoulder, 8 In. 295.00
Plate Set, Bread & Butter, Leaf Border, 6 1/4 In., 8 Piece 896.00
Punch Bowl, Floral Repousse, Crest, Banner, Deus Amici Et Nos, 8 x 13 In. 2250.00
Salver, Circular, Serpentine Shape, Shell & Leaf Moldings, 4 Claw & Ball Feet, 17 In. 1150.00
Serving Dish, Cover, Plain Design, Emma Haig, Miniature, 1 1/4 In., Pair 175.00
Spoon, Souvenir, see Souvenir category.
Stuffing Spoon, Flowers, Late 19th Century, 13 3/4 In. 100.00
Sugar & Creamer, Colonial Style, Monogram 58.00
Table Knife Set, Beaded Handles, Shell Ends, Late 18th Century, 14 Piece 250.00
Tea & Coffee Set, Miyata, Black Plastic Finials, Mid 20th Century, 4 Piece 690.00
Tea Set, Chased Floral Design, Coffeepot, Teapot, Sugar, Creamer, W.H., 1826 .... 1840.00
Tray, Repousse, Ball & Claw Feet, Engraved Monogram, Early 20th Century, 8 In., Pair .. 632.00
Vinaigrette, Art Nouveau, Sea Monster, Vermeil, Chain, c.1890, 3 In. 785.00
SILVER-SWEDISH, Toddy Ladle, Turned Wood Handle, .830 Silver 88.00
SILVER-THAI, Smoking Stand, Tiger Head Mount, Figural Panels, 12 In. 1915.00
SILVER-TURKISH, Tablespoon, Monogram, Marked, c.1890, 7 Piece 290.00

SINCLAIRE cut glass was made by H.P. Sinclaire and Company of
Corning, New York, between 1905 and 1929. He cut glass made at
other factories until 1920. Pieces were made of crystal as well as
amber, blue, green, or ruby glass. Only a small percentage of Sinclaire
glass is marked with the S in a wreath.

Bowl, Bristol Yellow, Engraved Flower Band, Signed, 13 x 3 In. 460.00
Bowl, Crosscut Diamonds, Medallions, Grapes & Floral, Fluted, c.1920, 9 In. 350.00
Cake Plate, Cut Hobstars, Engraved Floral & Leaf Border, 10 In. 280.00
Vase, Amber, Engraved Poppies & Butterflies, 8 1/4 In. 225.00
Vase, Yellow Green, Gallery Rim, Footed, 6 3/4 In. 195.00

SKIING, see Sports category.

SLAG GLASS resembles a marble cake. It can be streaked with different
colors. There were many types made from about 1880. Caramel slag is
the incorrect name for Chocolate glass. Pink slag was an American
Victorian product made by Harry Barstow and Thomas E.A. Dugan at
Indiana, Pennsylvania. Purple and blue slag were made in American
and English factories. Red slag is a very late Victorian and twentieth-
century glass. Other colors are known but are of less importance to the
collector. New versions of chocolate glass and colored slag glass are
being made.

Pink, Punch Bowl, Cups, Inverted Fan & Feather, Satin, 13 1/2 In., 13 Piece 5865.00
Pink, Tumbler, Inverted Fan & Feather 80.00
Purple, Bowl, Basket Weave, Open Edge, Sowerby, Marked, 10 In. 125.00
Vase, Red, Urn Shaped, Ruffled Edge, Footed, 9 1/2 In. 125.00

SLEEPY EYE collectors look for anything bearing the image of the nineteenth-century Indian chief with the drooping eyelid. The Sleepy Eye
Milling Co., Sleepy Eye, Minnesota, used his portrait in advertising

from 1883 to 1921. It offered many premiums, including stoneware and pottery steins, crocks, bowls, mugs, and pitchers, all decorated with the famous profile of the Indian. The popular pottery was made by Western Stoneware, Weir Pottery Company, and other companies long after the flour mill went out of business in 1921. Reproductions of the pitchers are being made today. The original pitchers came in only five sizes: 4 inches, 5 1/4 inches, 6 1/2 inches, 8 inches, and 9 inches. The Sleepy Eye image was also used by companies unrelated to the flour mill.

Apron, Clothespin	400.00
Bowl, Fleur-De-Lis, Scrolls, Blue & White, 6 3/8 In.	450.00
Cookbook, Indian Chief, Loaf Of Bread Shape	99.00
Cookbook, Loaf	60.00 to 85.00
Label, Barrel	60.00 to 90.00
Mug, Blue & White, 4 In.	88.00
Mug, Blue & White, Blue Rings, 4 In.	220.00
Mug, Chestnut Brown, Teepees, Embossed Maple Leaf, Mark, Monmouth, 1952	45.00
Mug, Solid Blue, 4 In.	600.00
Pitcher, Blue & Gray, No. 3	380.00
Pitcher, Blue & Gray, No. 5	550.00
Pitcher, Blue & White, Blue Rim, No. 1, 4 In.	500.00
Pitcher, Blue & White, Blue Rim, No. 2	320.00
Pitcher, Blue & White, No. 3, 6 1/2 In.	200.00 to 210.00
Pitcher, Blue & White, No. 4, 8 In.	250.00 to 325.00
Pitcher, Blue & White, No. 5, 9 In.	410.00
Pitcher, Blue & White, Shaped Handle, No. 5, 9 In.	150.00 to 165.00
Pitcher, Brown & White, No. 4	400.00
Pitcher, Creamer, Blue & Gray, No. 1, 4 In.	160.00 to 225.00
Pitcher, Creamer, Blue & White, No. 1, 4 In.	150.00 to 160.00
Pitcher, Green, No. 4	425.00
Pitcher, Standing Indian, Qt.	1200.00
Pitcher, Teepees, Shaped Handle, Blue & White, No. 2, 5 In.	150.00 to 160.00
Salt Crock	250.00 to 450.00
Sign, Sleepy Eye Milling Co., Indian Chief, Lithograph, Round, c.1900, 16 In.	468.00
Stein, Flemish, Blue & White, 7 3/4 In.	635.00
Sugar, Blue & White, Teepees, Flared Top, Marked, Monmoth, 3 1/4 In.	325.00
Vase, Blue, Gray, Indian, Cylinder Shape, 8 1/2 In.	200.00
Vase, Cat-O'-Nine Tails, Indian Head, Blue, White, Cylindrical, 8 In.	405.00
Vase, Cattail, Flemish, 9 In.	230.00 to 525.00
Vase, Cattail, Green	425.00 to 475.00

SLOT MACHINES are included in the Coin-Operated Machine category.

SMITH BROTHERS glass was made after 1878. Alfred and Harry Smith had worked for the Mt. Washington Glass Company in New Bedford, Massachusetts, for seven years before going into their own shop. They made many pieces with enamel decoration.

Smith Bros. Co.

Biscuit Jar, Blue Flowers, Yellow Leaves, Square, Silver Plated Cover & Bail, 7 1/2 In.	550.00
Biscuit Jar, Cover, Melon Ribbed, Flowers, Cream Ground, 7 1/2 In.	50.00
Biscuit Jar, Cream, Pansies, Silver Plated Cover, Signed, 7 In.	100.00
Biscuit Jar, Diagonal Swirl, Enameled, Flowers, 7 In.	288.00
Biscuit Jar, Gold Flowers, Leaves, Branches, Butterfly, 9 1/4 In.	400.00
Biscuit Jar, Melon Ribbed, Cream Body, Oak Leaves, Acorns, 7 In.	400.00
Biscuit Jar, Melon Ribbed, White To Blue, Enameled Flowers, Victorian, 6 In.	144.00
Biscuit Jar, White & Gold Flowers, Blue Ground, Original Hardware, 10 1/2 In.	575.00
Jar, Cover, Melon Ribbed, Amber Roses, Lion Trademark, 5 In.	150.00
Jar, Cover, Melon Ribbed, Blue & Pink Chrysanthemums, Gold Outline, 3 In.	390.00
Jar, Cover, Melon Ribbed, Cream Body, White Daisies, 4 In.	144.00
Jar, Dresser, Melon Ribbed, Yellow Daisies, Green Leafy Stems, 3 1/4 x 4 In.	308.00
Jar, Sweetmeat, Melon Ribbed, Daisies, Lion Trademark, 5 In.	210.00
Jar, Temple, Melon Ribbed, Chrysanthemum, Pastel Green Ground, Gold Beads, 8 1/2 In.	98.00
Sugar, Cover, Melon Ribbed, Enameled, Gold Flowers, Metal Hardware, 4 1/4 In.	230.00
Sugar Shaker, Cream, Pansies, Silver Plated Top, 5 In.	275.00
Vase, Daisies, Leaves, Vines, Beige Ground, Pinched, Beaded Top, Signed, 4 3/4 In.	175.00

SNUFF BOTTLES are listed in the Bottle category.

SNUFFBOXES held snuff. Taking snuff was popular long before cigarettes became available. The gentleman or lady would take a small pinch of the ground tobacco or snuff in the fingers, then sniff it and sneeze. Snuffboxes were made of many materials, including gold, silver, enameled metal, and wood. Most snuffboxes date from the late eighteenth or early nineteenth centuries.

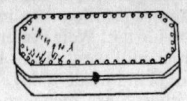

America Forever, Black, Gilt Anchor, c.1790-1820, 3 1/2 In.	450.00
Brass, Leaf Engraved Lid, England, 17th Century	495.00
Burlwood, 8-Sided, Hinged Lid, 4 In.	138.00
Carved Horn, Boot Shape, Hinged Lid, 1800s, 3 In.	235.00
Cherry Amber, Carved, Ducks, Lotus, Bird, Relief Foo Dogs, 2 3/4 In.	260.00
Coin Silver, Central Lion Crest, Oval, Hinged Cover, Marked PS, 1/2 x 2 x 3 1/8 In.	400.00
Copper, Gilt, Rectangle, Engraved, Flowers, Hunt Scene, England, c.1825, 2 1/2 In.	400.00
Copper, Hinged Lid, Oval, Engraved AH 1793	395.00
Enamel, Flowers Inside & Out, 2 Lids, 3 3/8 x 2 x 1 5/8 In.	2415.00
Enamel, Flowers, White Base, Raised Lid, 3 1/8 In.	185.00
George III, Varicolored, A.J. Starachan, Red Gold, Oak Leaves, Acorns, 2 7/8 In.	3585.00
Gold, Enamel, Amber, White, Switzerland, 19th Century, 3 1/4 In.	6570.00
Gold, Enamel, Blue, Gilded, Stars, Lozenges, Switzerland, Late 18th Century, 3 1/4 In.	6570.00
Gold, Enamel, Varicolored, Alpine Scene, Leaves, Switzerland, c.1820, 3 7/16 In.	5380.00
Ivory, Painting Of Hercules & Omphale, Tortoiseshell Lining, Oval, Case, 3 1/2 In.	1115.00
Papier-Mache, Isaac Chauncy Of The U.S. Navy, 3 1/2 In.	300.00
Papier-Mache, Victory Over The Lake Champlain, Naval Battle, 3 1/2 In.	1000.00
Pottery, Raised Flowers, Women Using Snuff, Pewter Neckband, Screw Lid, 6 3/4 In.	179.00
Silver, Fish Shape, Articulated Body, Head Forms Lid, Red Cabochon Eyes, 3 3/4 In.	295.00
Silver, Rectangular, Canted Corners, Hallmarked, Engraved, Kalmar Anno 1802, 3 x 1 In.	69.00
Tin, Victoria & Albert	100.00
Tortoiseshell, Oval, Cupid Engraved Lid, Silver Mount, France, c.1800, 2 3/4 In.	260.00
Wood, Lacquered, Hand Painted, Man With Baby In Cradle, 1 1/4 x 1 7/8 x 4 1/2 In.	2235.00
Wood & Horn, Carved, Woman's Shoe, Cover, Mid 19th Century, 3 3/4 In.	147.00

SOAPSTONE is a mineral that was used for foot warmers or griddles because of its heat-retaining properties. Soapstone was carved into figurines and bowls in many countries in the nineteenth and twentieth centuries. Most of the soapstone seen today is from China or Japan. It is still being carved in the old styles.

Carving, 3 Dragons, Beige, Ocher, Russet, Chinese, Qing Dynasty, 3 3/4 In.	175.00
Seal, Carved, Chinese, 11 In.	1792.00
Seal, Scholars & Animals Under Pine Trees, Chinese, 11 In., Pair	880.00
Vase, Tiger, Monkeys, Birds Around 2 Urns, 19th Century, 6 1/3 x 11 In.	58.00

SOFT PASTE is a name for a type of pottery. Although it looks very much like porcelain, it is a chemically different material. Most of the soft-paste wares were made in the early nineteenth century. Other pieces may be listed under Gaudy Dutch or Leeds.

Cup & Saucer, Strawberry Pattern, Handleless	50.00
Plate, King's Rose, England, 10 In.	299.00
Plate, Yellow Strawberry, Scalloped, Blue Feather Edge, 9 1/2 In.	330.00
Platter, Flowers On Border, Cobalt Blue Scalloped Feather Edge, 15 x 19 In.	440.00
Tankard, Vincennes, Bleu Celeste, Blue Enamel, Framed Flowers, 4 1/2 In.	7820.00
Tea Caddy, King's Rose, Red, Green Pink, 5 1/8 In.	605.00

SOUVENIRS of a trip—what could be more fun? Our ancestors enjoyed the same thing and souvenirs were made for almost every location. Most of the souvenir pottery and porcelain pieces of the nineteenth century were made in England or Germany, even if the picture showed a North American scene. In the twentieth century, the souvenir china business seems to have gone to the manufacturers in Japan, Taiwan, Hong Kong, England, and America. Another popular souvenir item is the souvenir spoon, made of sterling or silver plate. These are usually made in the country pictured on the spoon. Related pieces may be found in the Coronation and World's Fair categories.

Ashtray, Hotel Reina Cristinas, Algeciras, No Perder Ganancia Es, Stoneware, 5 In. . *Illus* 6.00
Ashtray, Hotel Ritz, Guatemala, Clay, Hand Painted, 4 1/2 In. . . . . *Illus* 10.00
Ashtray, Restaurante Castillo De La Albaida, Cordoba, Majolica, Spain, 4 In. . . . . . . *Illus* 10.00
Auto Grill Plaque, Olympic, 1936, Berlin, Brandenburg Gate, 3 x 2 3/4 In. 200.00
Badge, Olympic, 1936 Winter Games, Garmisch Partenkirchen, 1 3/8 In. 185.00
Bandanna, Queen Victoria, Memorial, Black, White, 1901, 19 In. 175.00
Bracelet, Olympic, 1976, Innsbruck, Silver Snowflake Logo 95.00
Desk Set, Gettysburg, Iron Ball Engraved Gettysburg 1863, Cemetery Ridge, 3 Piece 590.00
Dish, Union Station, Portland Me., Leaf, Gold, Germany, 4 In. 45.00
Insignia, Blazer, Olympic, 1936, Berlin, Eagle, Swastika, Wool, 3 1/8 x 2 7/8 In. 114.00
Jug, Cylinder, Hand Painted, Looking Down Sawkill, Milford, Pa., Germany, 4 1/2 In. . . . 60.00
Medal, Olympic, 1908, London, Participants, Pewter, Hinged Case, 2 In. 375.00
Mirror, Jerusalem, Damascus, Pyramids, Rochester, Falls, Celluloid, 1911, 2 x 3 In. 125.00
Mirror, North Dakota, Celluloid, 1 3/4 x 2 7/8 In. 300.00
Mirror, Olympic, 1980, Lake Placid, XIII Winter Games, 3 In. 7.00
Mug, Clock Design, Ladies Beefstock Social, February 5th, 1914 . . . . 55.00
Nut, Carved, Panama Canal, Commenced 1904-Completed 1915 . . . . 35.00
Pen, Float About, Olympic, 1996, Atlanta, Basketball, No. 17 Jumps To Hoop 2.75
Pennant, Chattanooga, Tenn., Incline Railway, Blue Flannel, 26 In. . . . . *Illus* 10.00
Pennant, Fontana Dam, Dark Green, White Border, North Carolina, 1950s, 26 In. 10.00
Pennant, Golden Gate Bridge, Centennial, Submarine Passing Under, 1945, 26 In. 45.00
Pennant, Harper's Ferry, W. Va., Blue Felt, 11 1/2 In. . . . . *Illus* 10.00
Pennant, New Mexico, Blue, White Lettering, Indian Chief, 1940s, 1952, 25 In. 15.00
Pennant, Pennsylvania Turnpike, Purple, White Lettering, Kittatinny Tunnel, 1952, 27 In. 13.00
Pennant, Snowquaimie Falls, Washington, Brown, Multicolored Graphics, 1940, 26 In. . . 12.00
Pennant, St. Andrews By The Sea, N.B., Canada, Maple Leaf, Red Felt, 17 In. . . . . . *Illus* 15.00
Pennant, Statue Of Liberty, Centennial, Black, Clouds, 1930s, 29 1/2 In. 22.00
Photograph, Niagara Falls, Mother-Of-Pearl, Aluminum Frame, 6 x 11 In. . . . . *Illus* 40.00
Pin, Blossom Festival, Wenatchee, Multicolor, Celluloid, 1924, 1 3/4 In. 30.00
Pin, Cuyahoga County, Cleveland, 1910 Centennial, Celluloid, 1 1/4 In. 110.00
Pin, Fiesta De La Flores, Multicolor Celluloid, Los Angeles, 1907, 1 1/4 In. 40.00
Pin, Fort Worth, Exposition, Red, White, Blue, Celluloid, 1919, 1 1/4 In. 45.00
Pin, Indian Show, Horton, Kansas, Multicolor, Celluloid, 1 1/4 In. 45.00
Pin, Mena, Ark., Street Fair, Multicolor, Celluloid, 1 1/4 In. 55.00
Plaque, Maine, Natures Own Wonderland, Fish, Anglers, Scenes, 8 x 15 In. 105.00
Plate, Blue Hole Trout Hatchery, Castalia, Ohio, 7 In. 39.00
Plate, French Lick Springs Hotel, French Lick, Ind., 8 In. 80.00
Plate, Fry's Hotel, Colfax, Iowa, Wheelock, Austria, 6 In. 55.00
Plate, Niagara Falls, Maid Of The Mist, Green, Cream Ground, England, 11 In. 44.00
Plate, Olympic, 1936, Berlin, Glass, Smoke Color, Olympic Rings, Oak Leaf, 7 1/2 In. . . . 109.00
Scarf, Silk, Flying, Embroidered Dragon, Theatre Made, US Army AAF CBI 29.00
Sign, Howey, Florida, Black Bird, Celluloid, Over Tin, Over Cardboard, 10 x 10 In. 120.00
Spoon, Silver Plate, Point Wilson Light, Ft. Townsend, Scene & Fish Handle 105.00
Spoon, Sterling Silver, Admiral Dewey, 4 Enamel Colors, 5 1/2 In. 110.00
Spoon, Sterling Silver, Alamo, 5-Point Star, Longhorn, Cowboy, Roping Steer, 5 3/4 In. . . 70.00

Souvenir, Ashtray, Hotel Reina Cristinas, Algeciras, No Perder Ganancia Es, Stoneware, 5 In.

Souvenir, Ashtray, Hotel Ritz, Guatemala, Clay, Hand Painted, 4 1/2 In.

Souvenir, Ashtray, Restaurante Castillo De La Albaida, Cordoba, Majolica, Spain, 4 In.

Souvenir, Pennant, Chattanooga, Tenn., Incline
Railway, Blue Flannel, 26 In.

Souvenir, Pennant, Harper's Ferry,
W.Va., Blue Felt, 11 1/2 In.

Souvenir, Pennant, St. Andrews
By The Sea, N.B., Canada, Maple
Leaf, Red Felt, 17 In.

Souvenir, Photograph,
Niagara Falls,
Mother-Of-Pearl,
Aluminum Frame,
6 x 11 In.

Spoon, Sterling Silver, Bear, Elk, Bison, Cowboy, Roping Steer, Wyoming, 5 7/8 In.	80.00
Spoon, Sterling Silver, Cowboy On Horse, Revolver, Spur, Tijuana, Mexico, 5 1/4 In.	70.00
Spoon, Sterling Silver, Cowboy, State Seal, Miner, Pears, Indian Symbols, Montana	60.00
Spoon, Sterling Silver, Cowboy, Texas Star, Wreath, Steer, Bale Of Cotton, 5 1/2 In.	90.00
Spoon, Sterling Silver, Indian Wearing Chief's War Bonnet, Indian On Horseback, 6 In. . .	90.00
Spoon, Sterling Silver, Lincoln, Flags, Map, Eagle, Cannon, International, 5 7/8 In.	35.00
Spoon, Sterling Silver, Luverne, Minnesota, Indian On Globe Handle	33.00
Spoon, Sterling Silver, Mining, Standing Miner, Pan Of Gold, Skagway, Alaska, 5 3/4 In. .	120.00
Spoon, Sterling Silver, Spirit Lake, Iowa, Indian Handle	50.00
Spoon, Sterling Silver, State Seal, Miner With Pick, Sioux Falls, South Dakota, 5 3/8 In. .	110.00
Spoon, Sterling Silver, Stonewall Jackson Beard & 3 Stars, 1891, 5 3/4 In.	125.00
Sprinkler Bottle, Lake George, New York, Ceramic, 2 2/3 x 2 2/3 x 8 1/4 In.	295.00
Stein, Miniature, Shakespeare's House, c.1897, 1 1/4 In.	20.00
Tumbler, Carlsbad Caverns, N.M., Frosted, Brown Images, Tapered, 3 3/4 In.	7.00
Tumbler, Chinatown, New York, Dragon, Frosted, 4 3/4 In.	6.00
Tumbler, Kentucky The Blue Grass State, Scenes, Frosted, 5 In.	6.00
Tumbler, Olympic, 1936, Munich, Amber, Etched Munich Cathedral, 5 1/2 In.	460.00
Virginia, Red, White Letters, Scenic, White Streamers, 1940s, 25 In.	15.00

SPANGLE GLASS is multicolored glass made from odds and ends of colored glass rods. It includes metallic flakes of mica covered with gold, silver, nickel, or copper. Spangle glass is usually cased with a thin layer of clear glass over the multicolored layer. Similar glass is listed in the Vasa Murrhina category.

Creamer, Cased Pink, Mica Flakes, Swirled Rib Body, 4 1/2 In.	100.00
Ewer, Clear Over White, Applied Clear Handle, Victorian, 9 1/2 In.	540.00
Pitcher, Tumbler, Ruby, White, Mica Flakes, Ribs, Ruffles, 8 3/4 x 7 1/2 In.	395.00
Vase, Blue Over Clear, Mica Flakes, 7 3/4 x 5 1/4 In.	245.00

SPATTER GLASS is a multicolored glass made from many small pieces of different colored glass. It is sometimes called *End-of-Day* glass. It is still being made.

Cruet, Deep Ruby & White On Clear, Cut Stopper, Applied Handle, 6 In. . . . . *Illus*	175.00
Pitcher, Amber Over Cranberry, Red, Opal, Mica Flakes, Tricornered Rim, 8 1/2 In.	250.00
Pitcher, Blood Red & Opal, Tricornered Rim, Clear Reeded Handle, 7 3/4 In.	130.00
Pitcher, Blue & White, Applied Clear Handle, 7 3/4 In.	160.00
Pitcher, End Of Day, White Interior, Applied Clear Reeded Handle, 8 1/2 In.	200.00
Pitcher, Flared, Applied Clear Handle, Tricorner Spout, 8 3/4 In.	75.00
Pitcher, Ribbed Swirl, Multicolored, Bulbous, Clear Reeded Handle, 7 1/2 In.	150.00
Pitcher, Sapphire Blue & White, Octagonal Shape, Clear Handle, 8 1/4 x 5 In.	165.00
Tumbler, Multicolored, Mica Flakes, White Interior, 3 3/4 In.	55.00
Vase, Blue & White Over Clear, 9 3/4 In.	15.00

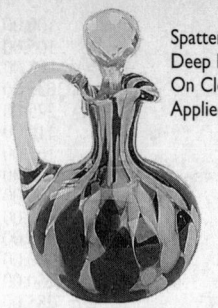

Spatter Glass, Cruet,
Deep Ruby & White
On Clear, Cut Stopper,
Applied Handle, 6 In.

Don't ask for a personalized autograph if you plan to sell. Buyers prefer a plain signature over "Best Wishes to Mike." Some sports figures, however, always personalize their autographs.

Vase, Pink, Yellow Spatter, Tricornered, 8 In.	28.00
Vase, Trumpet, Orange & White, Triple Cased, Black Rim, Czechoslavakia, 7 In.	95.00
Water Set, Cranberry & Opal, Ruffled Edge, Clear Handle, 7 Piece	350.00

SPATTERWARE is the creamware or soft paste dinnerware decorated with colored spatter designs. The earliest pieces were made in the late eighteenth century, but most of the spatterware found today was made from about 1800 to 1850, or it is a form of kitchen crockery with added spatter designs, made in the late nineteenth and twentieth centuries. The early spatterware was made in the Staffordshire district of England for sale in America. The later kitchen type is an American product.

Bowl, Holly Berry, Blue Sunburst, Paneled, 5 In.	275.00
Bowl, Holly Berry, Blue, Green, Red Border, 9 1/2 In.	330.00
Bowl, Pansy, Blue Bow Border, Red Stripes, 6 1/2 In.	495.00
Bowl, Pansy, Brown, Yellow, Green Leaves, Brown Border, 2 1/4 x 7 In.	220.00
Bowl, Rose, Red, Blue Leaf, Green Leaves, Purple Border, Fluted, 2 x 10 In.	300.00
Bowl, Rose, Red, Green Leaves, Brown Body, 3 x 5 1/2 In.	110.00
Bowl, Vegetable, Adam's Rose, Oval, 9 3/4 In.	80.00
Bowl, Zigzag, Brown, Blue, Brown Band, 3 x 6 In.	2100.00
Coffeepot, Thistle, Red Flower, Green Leaves, Purple, Both Sides, 9 1/2 In.	770.00
Creamer, Blue On White, 5 1/4 x 5 1/2 In.	190.00
Creamer, Buds, Red, Bulbous, 3 1/2 In.	330.00
Creamer, Fort, Green Trees, Yellow, Red, Black, Blue, 4 In.	250.00
Creamer, Peafowl, Blue, Red, Green, Both Sides, 4 1/4 In.	715.00
Creamer, Peafowl, Blue, Red, Yellow, Green, 3 1/2 In.	130.00
Creamer, Peafowl, Green, 3 3/4 In.	3740.00
Creamer, Rainbow, Red, Blue, Bulbous, Loop Handle, 3 1/2 In.	165.00
Creamer, Rose, Red, Green Leaves, Blue Body, 3 1/4 In.	330.00
Creamer, Rose, Red, Green Leaves, Bulbous, Red Body, 3 1/2 In.	190.00
Cup, Chocolate, Blue Border, Paneled, Shaped Handle, 3 In.	50.00
Cup, Festoons, 4 Colors, Child's, 1 1/2 x 2 In.	745.00
Cup, Peafowl, Blue, Yellow, Red, Green, Handleless, 2 1/3 In.	275.00
Cup, Peafowl, Red, 2 1/4 x 3 7/8 In.	65.00
Cup, Rainbow, Blue & Yellow Stripes, Handleless	275.00
Cup, Rose, Red, Green Leaves, Green & Blue Body, 3 In.	220.00
Cup, Tree, Black, Green Leaves, Purple, Handleless	300.00
Cup & Saucer, 4-Petal Flower, Blue, Red Border, Handleless	85.00
Cup & Saucer, 6-Point Star, Red, Blue, Green, Sunburst, Handleless	800.00
Cup & Saucer, Acorn, Purple, Flared Rim, Handleless	2025.00
Cup & Saucer, Adam's Rose, Handleless, 6 Sets	220.00
Cup & Saucer, Adam's Rose, Purple Flowers, Red, Blue Buds, Leaves, Handleless	85.00
Cup & Saucer, Adam's Rose, Red, Handleless	85.00
Cup & Saucer, Basket Of Flowers, Brown, Red, Gray, Blue Ribbon, Handleless	165.00
Cup & Saucer, Blue & Green, Cluster Of Buds, Handleless	275.00
Cup & Saucer, Blue, Handleless	55.00
Cup & Saucer, Blue, Straight-Sided, 3 1/8 x 4 3/4 In.	250.00
Cup & Saucer, Blue, Tan	300.00
Cup & Saucer, Bud, Green, Handleless	190.00

Cup & Saucer, Christmas Balls, Green Star, Handleless 3100.00
Cup & Saucer, Drape & Rosette, Red, Handleless, Child's 105.00
Cup & Saucer, Floral, Red, Handleless 85.00
Cup & Saucer, Forget-Me-Not, Blue, Handleless 3630.00
Cup & Saucer, Grapes, Red, Green Leaves, Handleless 275.00
Cup & Saucer, Green Border, Bull's-Eye Center, Handleless 110.00
Cup & Saucer, Hex Sign, Red Border, Handleless 165.00
Cup & Saucer, Holly Berry, Blue, Handleless 250.00
Cup & Saucer, Holly Berry, Purple Border, Handleless ....200.00 to 300.00
Cup & Saucer, Mush, Blue Sponge 105.00
Cup & Saucer, Parrot, Perched On Branch, Red 745.00
Cup & Saucer, Peafowl, Blue, Yellow, Red, Green Border, Child's Size 360.00
Cup & Saucer, Peafowl, Blue, Yellow, Red, Handleless 250.00
Cup & Saucer, Peafowl, Green, Blue, Yellow, Red, Handleless 285.00
Cup & Saucer, Peafowl, Green, Handleless 415.00
Cup & Saucer, Peafowl, Red, Blue, Yellow, Green Border, Handleless 250.00
Cup & Saucer, Peafowl, Red, Green, Blue, Green Ground, Handleless 275.00
Cup & Saucer, Peafowl, Red, Handleless 165.00
Cup & Saucer, Pinwheel, Black, Green, Red, Yellow, Alternating, Handleless 14300.00
Cup & Saucer, Rainbow, Red & Blue, Handleless 6325.00
Cup & Saucer, Rainbow, Red, Blue, Green, Handleless 275.00
Cup & Saucer, Rainbow, Red, Green, Handleless 770.00
Cup & Saucer, Rainbow, Red, Green, Handleless, Adams 210.00
Cup & Saucer, Red Border, Pinched Waist, Handleless 140.00
Cup & Saucer, Rooster, Blue, Yellow, Red, Purple Rim, Handleless 935.00
Cup & Saucer, Rose, Blue, Handleless ....190.00 to 220.00
Cup & Saucer, Rose, Purple, Blue, Rainbow, Handleless 800.00
Cup & Saucer, Rose, Rainbow, Red, Green, Handleless, W. Adams & Sons 250.00
Cup & Saucer, Rose, Red Flower, Green Leaves, Blue, Handleless 130.00
Cup & Saucer, Rose, Red Flowers, Green Leaves, Handleless 460.00
Cup & Saucer, Rose, Red, Green Leaves, Black, Brown Border 130.00
Cup & Saucer, Rose, Red, Green Leaves, Red, Blue, Rainbow 495.00
Cup & Saucer, Star, Red & Green, Handleless 440.00
Cup & Saucer, Tulip, Blue, Red, Green Leaves, Black Stem, Blue Border 140.00
Cup & Saucer, Tulip, Blue, Yellow Highlights, Leaves, Handless 50.00
Cup & Saucer, Tulip, Blue, Yellow, Green, Red Leaves, Black Stem, Handleless 275.00
Cup & Saucer, Tulip, Red Flower, Green Leaves, Handleless 385.00
Mug, Crisscross Strawberry Thumb Print, Blue, Straight Sides, 1 7/8 In. 2475.00
Mug, Peafowl, Blue, Straight Sides, Loop Handle, Child's, 2 1/2 In. 715.00
Pitcher, Acorn, Red, Brown Acorns, Teal Caps, Bulbous, 4 1/4 In. 880.00
Pitcher, Adam's Rose, Flowers, Springs, Leaves, Read, Blue, Green, Embossed, 8 In. 305.00
Pitcher, Black, Blue, Red, Green, Yellow Bands, Double C-Scroll Handle, 11 In. 2090.00
Pitcher, Bull's-Eye, Red, Blue, 2 Bands, 9 1/4 In. 300.00
Pitcher, Crisscross Strawberry Thumbprint, Blue 330.00
Pitcher, Daisy, Red, Red & Blue, Vertical Bands, Helmet Shape, 4 1/4 In. 330.00
Pitcher, Fort, Blue, Both Sides, 11 3/4 In. 2090.00
Pitcher, Milk, Rosette, Red, Black, Yellow Flowers, Purple Body, 5 1/4 In. 715.00
Pitcher, Peafowl, Blue, Green, Red, Blue Mouth & Base, 6 Sides, Bulbous, 7 x 8 In. 880.00
Pitcher, Peafowl, Blue, Red, Paneled, Red, Green, 7 7/8 In. 880.00
Pitcher, Peafowl, On Branch, Blue, Brown, Yellow, Green, Green Body, 4 1/2 x 5 In. 880.00
Pitcher, Pineapple, Pink, Black, Green Border, 3 1/2 In. 3850.00
Pitcher, Primrose, Blue, Red Flower, Bud, Leaves, Bulbous, 4 1/4 In. 965.00
Pitcher, Rainbow, 5 Colors, 7 1/2 In. 6050.00
Pitcher, Rainbow, Red, Blue, Green, Bulbous, 4 1/2 In. 2860.00
Pitcher, Red, Blue, Green, Helmet Shape, 4 3/4 In. 275.00
Pitcher, School House, Red, Yellow Roof, Green Tree, Blue, 10 1/4 In. 5390.00
Pitcher, Wash, Blue, Shaped Handle, 12 In. 145.00
Plate, Acorn, Green Leaves, Blue Border, Paneled, 9 1/4 In. 1265.00
Plate, Acorn, Purple, Leaves, Vines On Center, Flared Rim, 8 1/4 In. 1180.00
Plate, Acorns, Yellow, Teal Caps, Purple, Paneled, 9 1/4 In. 5500.00
Plate, Adam's Rose, 8 1/4 In., Pair 39.00
Plate, Adam's Rose, 8 3/4 In., 3 Piece 72.00
Plate, Adam's Rose, 9 1/4 In., Pair 60.00

Plate, Adam's Rose, Purple Flowers, 9 In. 39.00
Plate, Adam's Rose, Red & Green, Scalloped Edge, Impressed, 9 1/2 In. 165.00
Plate, Adam's Rose, Red, Blue, Green Rainbow Pattern, Scalloped Edge, 8 In. 1540.00
Plate, Adam's Rose, Scalloped Edge, 9 3/8 In. 165.00
Plate, American Eagle, Shield, Blue Transfer, Blue Border, Paneled, 7 In. 415.00
Plate, Blue, Leaf Border, Scalloped Edge, 9 1/2 In. 415.00
Plate, Bull's-Eye, Blue, 8 1/2 In. 110.00
Plate, Bull's-Eye, Overlapping Red & Blue, 8 5/8 In. 220.00
Plate, Bull's-Eye, Rainbow, Green, Blue, 9 1/4 In. 880.00
Plate, Bull's-Eye, Rainbow, Red, Green, 9 1/2 In. 385.00
Plate, Cockscomb, Blue Flower, Green Leaves, Red Border, 9 1/2 In. 385.00
Plate, Crisscross, Red & Blue Rainbow, Paneled, 8 1/2 In. . . . . .660.00 to 1100.00
Plate, Dahlia, Red, Blue Flower, Sprigs, Blue, Paneled, 8 1/4 In.   2200.00
Plate, Dahlia, Red, Blue, Green Sprigs, Blue Border, 8 1/4 In. 745.00
Plate, Flower, Red, Blue Bud, Green Leaves, Red Border, 8 1/4 In. 360.00
Plate, Fort, Blue, Paneled, 8 3/8 In. 360.00
Plate, Holly Berry, Green Leaves, Purple Border, 9 1/2 In. 220.00
Plate, Kids Fishing, First Nibble, Red, Blue Border, Blue Transfer, 8 In. 360.00
Plate, Peafowl, Blue, Black, Green, Red Border, Paneled, 8 3/4 In. 300.00
Plate, Peafowl, Blue, Green Red, 9 In. 275.00
Plate, Peafowl, Blue, Green, Red, Brown Branch, Adams, 6 1/4 In. 195.00
Plate, Peafowl, Blue, Yellow, Red, Green Body, 7 In. 495.00
Plate, Peafowl, Blue, Yellow, Red, Green, Paneled, 8 1/2 In. 415.00
Plate, Peafowl, Green, Yellow, Blue, Red Body, Border, 7 1/4 In.   360.00
Plate, Peafowl, Green, Yellow, Red, Black, Blue Border, 10 1/2 In. 880.00
Plate, Peafowl, Red, 8 3/4 In. 225.00
Plate, Peafowl, Red, Blue & Green, Red Body, 9 1/2 In. 415.00
Plate, Peafowl, Red, Yellow & Green, Blue Body, Blue Border, 10 3/4 In. 220.00
Plate, Peafowl, Red, Yellow, Blue, Blue Body, 8 In. 470.00
Plate, Peafowl, Red, Yellow, Blue, Blue Body, Venable Royal Patent, 8 In. 385.00
Plate, Peafowl, Yellow, Green, Red, Blue Body, Blue Border, 6 1/4 In. 620.00
Plate, Pinwheel, Rainbow, Feather Molded Edge, 8 1/4 In. 9900.00
Plate, Primrose, Red, Green, Blue Border, 8 5/8 In. 250.00
Plate, Red, Blue, Green, Scalloped Edge, Impressed Adams, 8 In. 285.00
Plate, Red, Blue, Green, Scalloped Edge, Impressed Adams, 10 1/2 In. 200.00
Plate, Red, Peafowl Pattern, Yellow, Green, 8 1/4 In. 415.00
Plate, Rooster, Red & Blue, Green Grass, Red Border, 8 1/2 In. 715.00
Plate, Rose Bud, Red Bud, Cobalt Blue Foliage, Leaves, Blue, Paneled, 9 1/2 In. 660.00
Plate, Rose, Blue, Red Rose, Green Leaves, Paneled, 6 1/4 In. 220.00
Plate, Rose, Buds, Red, Green, Black Leaves, Red Border, Green Body, 9 In. 2860.00
Plate, Rose, Flowers, Leaves, Red, Green, 8 1/2 In. 220.00
Plate, Rose, Red Flower, Green Leaves, Blue, 4 1/4 In. 220.00
Plate, Rose, Red, Green Leaves, Blue Border, 9 1/4 In. 190.00
Plate, Rose, Red, Green Leaves, Green, Blue Border, 8 3/4 In. 175.00
Plate, Rosebud, Red, Green Leaves, Blue Border, 7 In. 165.00
Plate, School House, Blue, 8 3/8 In. 965.00
Plate, Toddy, Peafowl, Blue, Green, Red Border, Impressed Adams, 6 1/4 In. 230.00
Plate, Toddy, Tulip, Blue, Green, 6 1/2 In. 200.00
Plate, Tulip, Orange, Brown Flower, Green Leaves, Blue Border, 8 1/4 In. 110.00
Plate, Tulip, Red, Green Leaves, Blue Border, 8 3/4 In. . . . . .220.00 to 250.00
Plate, Tulip, Red, Yellow, Green Leaves, Blue Border, Cotton & Barlow, 8 3/4 In. 175.00
Plate, Tulip, Yellow, Green Leaves, Blue Border, Cotton & Barlow, 8 3/4 In. 330.00
Plate, Yellow Tulip, Red Buds, Green Leaves, Blue Border, 7 1/4 In. 770.00
Plate, Zigzag, Red, 8 3/8 In. 250.00
Plate Set, Adam's Rose, 7 In., 6 Piece 165.00
Platter, Adam's Rose, Oval, 10 3/4 In. 85.00
Platter, Bull's-Eye, Rainbow, Purple, Blue, 8 1/4 x 11 In. 2200.00
Platter, Bull's-Eye, Rainbow, Purple, Blue, 10 1/4 x 13 1/2 In. 3080.00
Platter, Dragoon Guards, Rifle Band, Red Border, Oval, 9 x 12 1/2 In. 580.00
Saucer, Blue, 6-Petal Flower, Red, Green, Blue 120.00
Saucer, Rainbow, Red, Blue, Child's, 4 1/4 In. 55.00
Saucer, Red, Green Spatter 220.00
Saucer, Rose, Red & Green Rims, Red Rose, Green Leaves, 5 5/8 In. 55.00

Saucer, Thistle, Red Flower, Green Leaves, Purple Border	190.00
Soup, Dish, Tulip, Blue, Red, Black Stem, Green Leaves, Blue Border, 10 1/2 In.	165.00
Sugar, Bud, Red, Blue, Shell Handles, 8 In.	300.00
Sugar, Cover, Adam's Rose, 4 3/4 In.	176.00
Sugar, Cover, Rainbow, Red, Blue, 4 In.	80.00
Sugar, Cover, Rainbow, Red, Green, 4 1/2 In.	165.00
Sugar, Cover, Rose, Green, Rainbow, Leaf End Handles, 4 1/4 In.	470.00
Sugar, Cover, Rose, Red, Green & Blue Leaves, Red Striped Finial, 4 x 4 1/2 In.	190.00
Sugar, Cover, Rose, Red, Green Leaves, Blue Body, 8 Sides, Shaped Rim	550.00
Sugar, Cover, Rose, Red, Green Leaves, Both Sides, 5 In.	85.00
Sugar, Cover, Thistle, Red Flower, Green Leaves, Blue, Both Sides, 7 In.	360.00
Sugar, Cover, Tulip, Blue Border, Cover, Red, Yellow, Green, 4 1/2 In.	190.00
Sugar, Cover, Tulip, Blue, Paneled, Handles, 6 In.	80.00
Sugar, Cover, Tulip, Yellow Flower, Green Leaves, Red, Purple, 3 1/2 In.	165.00
Sugar, Rainbow, Blue & Green Stripes, 4 1/2 In.	330.00
Sugar, Rainbow, Red, Blue, Green Bands, Cover, 4 1/4 In.	220.00
Sugar, Red, Blue, 8 Sides, Paneled, 5 1/4 x 6 In.	300.00
Sugar, Rose, Red, Green Leaves, Blue, 2 3/4 In.	50.00
Sugar, Tulip, Red, Paneled, Scrolled Handles, 7 1/2 In.	360.00
Sugar & Creamer, Blue, Cover, 5 In.	70.00
Tea Set, Peafowl, Green, Teapot, Child's, 3 Piece	550.00
Teapot, Peafowl, Blue, Green, Red	1540.00
Teapot, Peafowl, Blue, Leaf & Twig, Green & Black, 4 1/2 In.	900.00
Teapot, Rose, Red, Green Leaves, Blue Body, 4 1/2 x 6 1/2 In.	660.00
Tureen, Cover, Blue, 8 Sides, 6 1/4 x 7 In.	440.00
Tureen, Cover, Rainbow, Footed, Paneled Body, 5 3/4 x 6 1/2 In.	1100.00
Wash Set, Bowl, Pitcher, Blue, Paneled, 10 1/4 In., 4 x 12 In.	660.00
Waste Bowl, Adam's Rose, 3 x 6 1/4 In.	85.00
Waste Bowl, Adam's Rose, Red & Green, Impressed 6, 3 1/4 x 6 1/2 In.	44.00
Waste Bowl, Holly Berry, Purple, Paneled, 4 In.	275.00
Waste Bowl, Peafowl, Yellow, Blue, Green Leaves, Red, 4 1/2 x 2 1/2 In.	770.00
Waste Bowl, Rainbow, 5 Colors, Wood, 5 1/2 x 3 In.	3900.00

SPELTER is a synonym for a zinc alloy. Figurines, candlesticks, and other pieces were made of spelter and given a bronze or painted finish. The metal has been used since about the 1860s to make statues, tablewares, and lamps that resemble bronze. Spelter is soft and breaks easily. To test for spelter, scratch the base of the piece. Bronze is solid; spelter will show a silvery scratch.

Clock, Figural Horse Standing, Copper Patina, Horseshoe Frame, Wooden Base	35.00
Lamp, Reclining Woman With Globe, Art Deco, c.1920	86.00

SPINNING WHEELS in the corner have been symbols of earlier times for the past 100 years. Although spinning wheels date back to medieval days, the ones found today are rarely more than 200 years old. Because the style of the spinning wheel changed very little, it is often impossible to place an exact date on a wheel.

Flax, Mixed Woods, Bold Turnings, Mid 19th Century, 46 x 20 1/2 In.	200.00
Flax, Turned Legs & Spokes, Marked I Leicht 1817, N.C., 34 1/4 x 32 x 20 In.	605.00
Fruitwood, Turned, Ivory Mounts, 1700s, 36 In.	235.00
Maple, Oak, Flax Wheel, 50 In.	1150.00
Maple, Oak, Natural Finish, Adjustable Arm, Bone Collar At Neck Of Flyer	230.00
Oak, All Attachments, 37 In.	165.00
Oak, Walking Wool Wheel	690.00
Treadle Model, Black Paint, Iron Hardware, AM Stamp, Child's, 24 x 23 In.	330.00
Upright, Cherry, Ivory Buttons, Turned Legs, Tripod Base, 9 1/2-In. Wheel, 38 In.	305.00
Upright, Hardwood, Tuned Posts, Ivory Pegs, Black Paint, 35 In.	275.00
Upright, Hardwood, Turned Posts, Ivory, Ebonized Wood Details, 34 1/2 In.	415.00
Wool Wheel, Mixed Woods, Mid 19th Century, 57 1/2 x 44 In.	225.00
Yarn Winder, Turned Feet, Mahogany Platform, Goodbrand & Co., 28 x 16 x 29 1/2 In.	550.00

SPODE pottery, porcelain, and bone china were made by the Stoke-on-Trent factory of England founded by Josiah Spode about 1770. The firm became Copeland and Garrett from 1833 to 1847, then W.T.

Copeland or W.T. Copeland and Sons until 1976. It then became Royal
Worcester Spode Ltd. The word *Spode* appears on many pieces made
by the factories. Most collectors include all the wares under the more
familiar name of Spode. Porcelains may be listed in this book by the
name that appears on the piece. Related pieces may be listed under
Copeland, Copeland Spode, and Royal Worcester.

Stone-China

Bowl, En Griselle, Transfer Design, Italian Landscape, Gilt Rim, c.1900, 9 1/2 In.	175.00
Butter Chip, Cowslip	35.00
Butter Chip, Gainsborough	30.00
Butter Chip, Reynolds	20.00
Creamer, Gaudy Design, Gilt & Polychrome Flowers, c.1810, 5 1/2 x 4 In.	135.00
Dessert Service, 967 Pattern, Flowering Peony, Bamboo, c.1815, 13 Piece	2510.00
Dessert Service, 2472 Pattern, Dragon & Phoenix, Flaming Pearl, c.1820, 26 Piece	4180.00
Dessert Service, Blue, Pink Peonies, Green Leaves, c.1820, 12 1/2 In., 14 Piece	7770.00
Dessert Set, Imari Pattern, Gilt Edge Panels, c.1815, 11 1/8 In., 4 Piece	2035.00
Plate, Dinner, Chinese Export Style, Prunus & Peony, c.1820, 9 5/8 In., 12 Piece	1675.00
Plate, Dinner, Feldspar, Armorial, Motto, Green Border, 1825, 10 In., 12 Piece	2748.00
Plate, Gold Classical Design, Cobalt Blue Rim, White Center, 9 In., 11 Piece	405.00
Plate, Soup, Chinese Export Style, Prunus & Peony, c.1820, 8 1/4 In., 12 Piece	1435.00
Plate, Soup, Imari Pattern, Cobalt Blue, Red, Gold Rim, 9 7/8 In., Pair	345.00
Punch Bowl, Stone, Factory Mark, 20th Century, 14 3/4 In.	316.00
Sugar, Newton Pattern, Open, Blue, Rust, Green, c.1850, 2 1/2 x 3 3/4 x 7 1/2 In.	90.00
Tea Service, Imari Pattern, Flower, Rockwork Panels, c.1820, 13 Piece	1315.00
Tureen, Stand, Imari Style, Oval, 2 Grotesque Handles, Artichoke Finial, Ironstone, 15 In.	410.00

SPONGEWARE is very similar to spatterware in appearance. The
designs were applied to the ceramics by daubing the color on with a
sponge or cloth. Many collectors do not differentiate between spongeware and spatterware and use the names interchangeably. Modern pottery is being made to resemble the old spongeware, but careful
examination will show it is new.

Baking Dish, Blue, 9 In.	70.00
Bowl, 2 Blue Bands, 5 1/4 x 11 In.	175.00
Bowl, Allover Cobalt Blue, Green, Brown, Cream Ground, 2 3/4 x 10 In.	115.00
Bowl, Blue, Cover, 2 x 3 1/4 In.	250.00
Bowl, Blue, Red, Blue Band, 4 x 9 In.	105.00
Bowl, Blue, White, Molded, 2 1/2 x 4 1/4 In.	70.00
Chamber Pot, Blue Center Band, Pin Stripes, Blue Edge, 9 1/4 In. Diam.	90.00
Chamber Pot, Blue, Cover, Blue Band, 7 1/2 In. Diam.	145.00
Coffeepot, Pansy, Bulbous, Blue 8-Point Star Border, Ironstone, 8 3/4 In.	95.00
Creamer, Blue, Paneled, Shaped Handle, 5 3/4 In.	120.00
Crock, Butter, Cover, Blue, 4 3/8 x 6 3/8 In.	470.00
Crock, Butter, Cover, Blue, Wire Bail Handle, 4 x 5 5/8 In.	40.00
Crock, Butter, Stenciled, Blue, White, 4 1/4 x 6 1/2 In.	110.00
Cup & Saucer, Black & Red, Handleless	300.00
Cup & Saucer, Blue & Green, Handleless	120.00
Cup & Saucer, Blue, Flared Rim, Handleless	40.00
Cup & Saucer, Blue, Red, Handleless, Child's	165.00
Cup & Saucer, Brown, Purple Flowers, Leaves, Handleless, Child's	165.00
Cup & Saucer, Crisscross, Handleless, Purple Daisy, Brown	300.00
Cup & Saucer, Red & Blue, Handleless, Bulbous	130.00
Cup & Saucer, Red, Green	60.00
Cup & Saucer, Red, Handleless	165.00
Cup & Saucer, Rosette, Blue Center, Green Rays, Handleless	140.00
Cuspidor, Blue, 7 1/4 In.	60.00
Jar, Cover, Blue, Flat, Handles	140.00
Jar, Vanity, Cover, 3 Blue Bands, 3 1/4 x 6 1/2 In.	470.00
Jug, Blue, White, Handle, Freehand Script Initials J.E.W., 11 1/2 In., 2 Gal.	1815.00
Jug, Stepped Shoulder, Straight Sides, Blue, 8 3/4 In.	550.00
Mixing Bowl, 2 Blue Bands, Flared, 3 3/4 x 8 In.	220.00
Mixing Bowl, Blue, 10 1/4 In.	70.00 to 105.00
Mixing Bowl, Blue, 12 1/4 In.	80.00 to 105.00
Mixing Bowl, Blue, Banded, 9 In.	175.00

Mixing Bowl, Blue, Banded, Molded Flare Top, 6 1/4 x 14 In. 250.00
Mixing Bowl, Blue, Heart Shaped Panels, 3 3/4 x 8 In. 165.00
Mug, Blue, Straight Sides, Applied Loop Handle, 3 In. 70.00
Mug, Blue, White, 3 Blue Bands, Handle, 3 1/2 In. 300.00
Pepper Pot, Tin Cover, Blue, Bulbous, 4 1/4 In. 440.00
Pitcher, Blue Bands, Cylindrical 165.00
Pitcher, Blue, 8 3/4 In. 105.00
Pitcher, Blue, 9 1/4 In. 55.00
Pitcher, Blue, Bulbous, 8 1/2 In. 250.00
Pitcher, Blue, Bulbous, 9 x 7 3/4 In. 495.00
Pitcher, Blue, Tapered Base, 8 3/4 x 7 In. 330.00
Pitcher, Blue, White, 9 In. 130.00
Pitcher, Blue, White, Blue Rose, 9 In. 275.00
Pitcher, Blue, White, Cobalt Blue, 9 In. 300.00
Pitcher, Bowl, Blue, Banded, 11 3/4 & 14 In. 165.00
Pitcher, Cream, Lily Of The Valley, Green Daisy, Red, Paneled, 5 1/2 In. 690.00
Pitcher, Cream, Purple, Green Vines, Bulbous, 4 In. 110.00
Pitcher, Hot Water, Blue, Banded, Handle, 7 1/4 In. 210.00
Pitcher, Water, Blue, Banded, 11 In. 110.00
Plate, 5-Petal Flower, Red, Green Leaves, Butterfly Border, 8 1/2 In. 275.00
Plate, Adam's Rose, Green Bow Border, Blue Stripes, 8 1/2 In. 60.00
Plate, Adam's Rose, Red Rose, Blue Bud, Green Leaves, Green Bow Border, 10 In. 385.00
Plate, Adam's Rose, Red Rose, Blue Bud, Green Leaves, Red Bow, Blue Stripes, 8 3/4 In. 440.00
Plate, Adam's Rose, Red, Blue, Green, Flower, Leaves, Red Bow, Blue Stripes, 10 In. 415.00
Plate, Adam's Rose, Running Rabbit Border, 9 1/4 In. 280.00
Plate, Blue Spring, Red & Green Vine, Teal Striped Border, 8 7/8 In. 248.00
Plate, Blue, 9 1/4 In. 80.00
Plate, Columbine, Rose & Thistle, Purple Daisy Border, Red Stripes, 8 3/4 In. 413.00
Plate, Daisy, Roses, Blue, Green, Red Striped Border, 10 1/2 In. 138.00
Plate, Dogwood, Maroon Flower, Green Leaves, Blue Rosette Border, Stripes, 9 3/4 In. .. 358.00
Plate, Dogwood, Maroon Flower, Leaves, Purple Bow Border, Blue Stripes, 8 5/8 In. 413.00
Plate, Dogwood, Maroon Flower, Leaves, Purple Bow Border, Red Stripes, 8 5/8 In. 413.00
Plate, Dogwood, Purple Bow Border, Blue Stripes, 10 3/8 In. 440.00
Plate, Flowers, Red, Blue, Green Leaves, Blue Butterfly Border, 9 3/4 In. 330.00
Plate, Green, Blue Vine Band, Red Stripe Border, 8 1/2 In. 50.00
Plate, Orphan Child, Transfer, Red, Blue Border, Scalloped Edge, 8 1/4 In. 165.00
Plate, Pansy, Purple, Yellow, Flowers, Leaves, 8-Point Star Border, 8 3/4 In. 330.00
Plate, Pansy, Purple, Yellow, Leaves, Red 8-Point Star Border, Stripes, 8 1/2 In. ....275.00 to 385.00
Plate, Polychrome Flowers, Leaves, Purple Rosette, 10 1/2 In. 132.00
Plate, Purple, Green Vine Border, Blue Stripes, 9 1/2 In. 60.00
Plate, Red, Blue, Paneled, 8 1/4 In. 40.00
Plate, Rose, Bud, Leaves, Red Bow Border, Blue Stripes, 8 3/4 In. 220.00
Plate, Soup, Blue Stripes, Green, Purple Vine Border, 10 3/4 In. 28.00
Plate, Soup, Dogwood, Maroon Flower, Green Leaves, Blue Rosette, Red Stripes 385.00
Plate, Soup, Fruit, Blue Daisies, Green Leaves, Basket Weave Border, 10 1/4 In. 55.00
Plate, Soup, Red Roses, Blue Sprigs, Leaves, Blue Ring Border, Red Stripes, 9 In. 85.00
Plate, Soup, Roseate, Blue Center, Purple Ray, 9 1/4 In. 248.00
Plate, Soup, Tulip, Purple, Flowers, Leaves, Red Bow, Blue Stripes, 10 3/8 In. 220.00
Plate, Starflower, Chrysanthemum Wreath, Rabbit & Frog Border, 9 1/4 In. 340.00
Plate, Thistle & Lily Of The Valley, Paneled, Red Smoke Rings Border, 8 1/2 In. 495.00
Plate, Toddy, Dogwood, Maroon Flower, Leaves, Rosette Border, Blue Stripes, 6 1/2 In. . 275.00
Plate, Toddy, Pansy, Purple, Yellow, Leaves, Green 8-Point Star Border, 6 5/8 In. 330.00
Platter, Dark Blue, Oval, 8 1/2 x 12 3/4 In. 50.00
Salt Jar, Cover, Blue, 5 3/4 x 6 In. 550.00
Saucer, Blue & White, 8 1/4 In. 85.00
Shaving, Mug, Blue, Banded, Handle, 3 3/4 In. 250.00
Soup, Dish, Oval Platter, Blue, Shaped, Molded Rim, 9 1/4 x 13 1/4 x 8 In. 100.00
Soup, Dish, Underplate, Dark Blue, 9 1/2 x 9 In. 50.00
Sugar, Cover, Pansy, Bulbous, Blue 8-Point Star Border, 7 1/4 In. 990.00
Teapot, Blue, Bulbous, 5 3/4 x 8 In. 275.00
Teapot, Pansy, Bulbous, Blue 8-Point Star Border, 8 In. 1210.00
Toothbrush Holder, Blue, Banded, 5 In. 110.00
Vase, Blue, White, 3 Blue Accent Lines, 5 In. 360.00

Wash Set, Blue Band, Pitcher, Bowl, Mug, Soap Dish, 7 Piece 1540.00
Water, Cooler, Blue, White, 20 In., 2 Gal., 3 Piece 470.00

SPORTS equipment, sporting goods, brochures, and related items are
listed here. Items are listed by sport. Other categories of interest are
Bicycle, Card, Fishing, Sword, Toy, and Trap. Kentucky Derby glasses
are listed in the Decorated Tumblers category.

Baseball, Ball, 1933 World Series, Pair 1495.00
Baseball, Ball, Autographed, Babe Ruth 6900.00
Baseball, Ball, Autographed, Babe Ruth, 1920 .... 1755.00
Baseball, Ball, Autographed, Babe Ruth, 1934 .... 4715.00
Baseball, Ball, Autographed, Babe Ruth, Letter, Presented To Umpire J. Quinn 4675.00
Baseball, Ball, Autographed, Babe Ruth, New Orleans, 1923 .... 2990.00
Baseball, Ball, Autographed, Billy Sunday 5750.00
Baseball, Ball, Autographed, Buck Harris 1150.00
Baseball, Ball, Autographed, Charles Comiskey 6325.00
Baseball, Ball, Autographed, Detroit & Pittsburgh, 1909 World Series 1495.00
Baseball, Ball, Autographed, Detroit Tigers, 1968 .... 375.00
Baseball, Ball, Autographed, Gehringer, Row, Newhouser, Detroit Tigers, c.1930 .... 1150.00
Baseball, Ball, Autographed, George Moriarity, Chicago White Sox, 1916 .... 1840.00
Baseball, Ball, Autographed, Hank Aaron, 660th Home Run, August 6, 1972 .... 2396.00
Baseball, Ball, Autographed, Hank Aaron, 719th Home Run, 15th Grand Slam 4285.00
Baseball, Ball, Autographed, Hank Greenberg .... Illus 3045.00
Baseball, Ball, Autographed, Harry Heileman, April 17, 1927, Triple Play 1725.00
Baseball, Ball, Autographed, Herbert Hoover, U.S. President 2070.00
Baseball, Ball, Autographed, Jackie Robinson & 4 Players, Brooklyn Dodgers, c.1950 ... 765.00
Baseball, Ball, Autographed, Jim Thorpe 1045.00
Baseball, Ball, Autographed, John J. Pershing, U.S. General, April 13, 1921 .... 1150.00
Baseball, Ball, Autographed, Larry Lajoie, 1934 .... 2185.00
Baseball, Ball, Autographed, Mickey Cochrane, 1935 World Series 3220.00
Baseball, Ball, Autographed, Ray Schalk, c.1920 .... 1725.00
Baseball, Ball, Autographed, Red Grange 295.00
Baseball, Ball, Autographed, Stan Musial 75.00
Baseball, Ball, Autographed, Stan Musial, 1982 .... 28.00
Baseball, Ball, Autographed, Ted Williams & 5 Players, Boston Red Sox, c.1950 .... 380.00
Baseball, Ball, Autographed, Ted Williams & 6 Players, Boston Red Sox, c.1960 .... 440.00
Baseball, Ball, Autographed, Walter Johnson 1150.00
Baseball, Ball, Autographed, Walter Johnson, 1937 .... 2530.00
Baseball, Ball, Autographed, Walter Johnson, Opening Day, 1919 .... 3146.00
Baseball, Ball, Thrown By President Coolidge, World Series, 1920s 3335.00
Baseball, Base, 1996 World Series 980.00
Baseball, Bat, 1945 World Series, Black, Chicago Cubs 950.00
Baseball, Bat, Autographed, New York Yankees, 1968 .... 930.00
Baseball, Bat, Autographed, Willie Mays, 1965-1968, 34 Oz., 35 In. 5704.00
Baseball, Bat, Billy Williams, 1969-1972, 32 Oz., 34 1/2 In. 645.00
Baseball, Bat, Chicago Cubs, Hillerich & Bradsby, 1935 .... 2830.00
Baseball, Bat, Giveaway, Louisville Slugger, Schoolboy Rowe Model, 22 In. 80.00
Baseball, Batting Helmet, Cal Ripken Jr., 1980s 2572.00
Baseball, Booklet, 1924 World Series, Washington Baseball Club 28.00

A baseball signed on the sweet spot sells for
twice as much as one that's not. And single-
signed balls can go for three times as much
as baseballs signed by two players—
even if both are Hall of Famers.

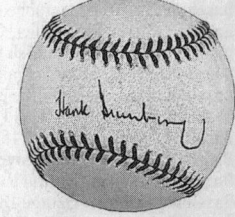

Sports, Baseball, Ball,
Autographed, Hank Greenberg

Baseball, Booklet, How To Play Outfield, Babe Ruth, Quaker Cereal, 3 1/4 x 4 1/2 In. ...   48.00
Baseball, Button, Babe Ruth Club, Black, White, Celluloid, 7/8 In. 28.00
Baseball, Button, Babe Ruth Club, Black, White, Jordan Marsh, 7/8 In. 99.00
Baseball, Button, Harry Hooper, Boston Red Sox, Celluloid, Sweet Caporal 18.00
Baseball, Button, N.Y. Giants, N.L. Champions, Plastic Ball, Purple Ribbon, Celluloid ...   30.00
Baseball, Button, Nap Rucker, Brooklyn Superbas, Celluloid, Sweet Caporal 16.00
Baseball, Button, New York Yankees, American League Champions, Ball, Bat, Ribbon ...   60.00
Baseball, Cane, Nickel Plated, Hollow, Pennant Inside, American League Champs, 1934 .   1250.00
Baseball, Cap, Chicago Cubs, Wishbone C, 1957 ....   710.00
Baseball, Cap, Dodger's, Blue, Red & White Stripe, c.1940 ....   125.00
Baseball, Cap, New York Yankees, 1932 ....   1735.00
Baseball, Card Vending Machine, 2 Tiers, 1962 ....   1300.00
Baseball, Collier's Book Of Baseball, W. Patten & J. Walker Mcspadden, N.Y., 1911 ....   382.00
Baseball, Coloring Book, Hank Aaron 15.00
Baseball, Figure, 2 Angry Players, Indignant Umpire, 1940s, 3 Piece 843.00
Baseball, Figure, Babe Ruth, Hartland Plastics, Original Box & Tag 790.00
Baseball, Glove, Autographed, Barry Bonds 2338.00
Baseball, Glove, Autographed, Cal Ripken Jr. 1198.00
Baseball, Glove, Autographed, Randy Johnson 7345.00
Baseball, Glove, Batting, Ken Griffey Jr. Model, 2 Pairs 165.00
Baseball, Glove, Catcher's, Pat Collins, New York Yankees, 1926-1927 ....   3808.00
Baseball, Glove, Ferguson Jenkins, Game Used, Cy Young Model, 1971 ....   1735.00
Baseball, Glove, Pedro Martinez, Game Used 1089.00
Baseball, Glove, Ted Williams Model, Sears, Japan 60.00
Baseball, Invitation, Boston Red Sox, Opening Game, 1906, 10 x 8 In. 159.00
Baseball, Jersey, Billy Williams, Chicago Cubs, Game Worn, 1974 ....   4608.00
Baseball, Jersey, Don Kessinger, Chicago Cubs, Game Worn, 1970 ....   6127.00
Baseball, Jersey, Glenn Becker, Chicago Cubs, Game Worn, 1966 ....   4185.00
Baseball, Jersey, Joe Pepitone, Chicago Cubs, Game Worn, 1973 ....   977.00
Baseball, Jersey, Leo Durocher, Chicago Cubs, Game Worn, 1968 ....   3460.00
Baseball, Jersey, Ron Santo, Rookie, Chicago Cubs, Game Worn, 1960 ....   8365.00
Baseball, Magazine, Play Ball, Connie Mack, Liquor Injures, 16 x 22 In. 225.00
Baseball, Pants, Moe Berg, Game Worn, 1930s 3425.00
Baseball, Payroll Check Collection, Chicago Cubs, 14 Piece 1044.00
Baseball, Pennant, Jackie Robinson, Brooklyn Dodgers, Green Ground, 1947, 17 In. 500.00
Baseball, Pennant, Negro League, Team Names, Catcher, Batter, 1930s, 26 In. 235.00
Baseball, Photograph, Boston Red Sox, Stuffy McGinnis Insert, 1921, 6 x 8 In. 264.00
Baseball, Plaque, Batter, Cracking Bat Over Head Of Another, Umpire, 1947, 12 x 9 In. ...   1420.00
Baseball, Postcard, Mickey Mantle, Holiday Inn, 1960s 25.00
Baseball, Ring, Andy Pafko, Muffets Cereal Premium 395.00
Baseball, Ring, Championship, L.A. Dodgers, 1963 ....   5705.00
Baseball, Ring, Gil Hodges, N.Y. Mets, 1969 World Series 1735.00
Baseball, Seat, Comiskey Park, Chicago, 1 Row, 5 Connected Seats 1500.00
Baseball, Seat, Griffith Stadium Trio, Washington, D.C. 1410.00
Baseball, Seat, Shibe Park Quadruple, Philadelphia 949.00
Baseball, Seat, Single, Yankee Stadium Single, New York 3384.00
Baseball, Seat, Yankee Stadium Triple, New York 4900.00
Baseball, Sheet Music, Root Root Root For The Reds, Cincinnati Reds Photo On Cover ..   255.00
Baseball, Shirt, Usher, Yankee Stadium, 1960 ....   240.00
Baseball, Shoes, Autographed, Randy Johnson, Game Worn 1242.00
Baseball, Shoes, Autographed, Tony Kubek, Game Worn, 1960s 1367.00
Baseball, Shoes, Bob Feller, Game Worn, 1955 ....   2310.00
Baseball, Shoes, Jim Catfish Hunter, Game Worn 847.00
Baseball, Shoes, Mike Schmidt, Game Worn, Rookie Era 1265.00
Baseball, Sunglasses, Willie Mays, Game Worn 6599.00
Baseball, Ticket, 1955 World Series, Game 5, Brooklyn, Unused 795.00
Baseball, Ticket, Aaron's 715th Home Run, 4/8/74, Fulton Co. Stadium, Atlanta, Full 1129.00
Baseball, Trophy, Gold Glove Award, Joe Pepitone, 1969 ....   4608.00
Baseball, Tumbler, Boston Red Sox, Carl Yastrzemski, Papa Gino's Pizza 18.00
Baseball, Tumbler, George Brett, Super Action Baseball, Pepsi-Cola, 1981 ....   5.00
Baseball, Uniform, Barry Bonds, Throwback, San Francisco Seals, Game Worn, 1994 ...   2310.00
Baseball, Uniform, Bob Rush, Chicago Cubs, Game Worn, 1954 ....   3425.00
Baseball, Uniform, Charlie Grimm, Chicago Cubs, Game Worn, 1948 ....   6748.00

Baseball, Uniform, San Francisco Giants, 1959 .... 636.00
Baseball, Yearbook Collection, Chicago Cubs, 18 Piece 860.00
Basketball, Ball, Autographed, Michael Jordan, Wizards, Hawks, Nov. 1, 2001 .... 1089.00
Basketball, Button Collection, Michael Jordan, 1980s, 1990s, 445 Piece 710.00
Basketball, Figure Set, Player Rebounding, Headless Opponent, Basket, 1949, 3 Piece 4830.00
Basketball, Photograph, Autographed, Michael Jordan, 1982 .... 324.00
Basketball, Print, Michael Jordan, Silk Screened, 1959, 3 Piece 1774.00
Basketball, Trophy, Field Goal, Artis Gilmore, 1982-1983 .... 780.00
Basketball, Uniform, Artis Gilmore, NBA All Star Game, Game Worn, 1970 .... 1264.00
Billiards, Ball Holder, Edwardian, Oblong, Scroll Handle Ends, 18 Ball Indents, 6 x 40 In. 520.00
Billiards, Cue Stick Rack, Wood, Marked Brunswick Balke-Collender, 56 In. 358.00
Billiards, Table, Burl Veneer, J.M. Brunswick & Balke, 19th Century, 50 x 96 In. 5000.00
Bowling, Ball, Ronald McDonald, Red, Ebonite, c.1970, 9 Lb., 9 In. 40.00
Boxing, Button, Joe Louis, Photo, Black, White, Celluloid, 1 3/4 In. 65.00
Boxing, Envelope, Jack Sharkey, Mickey Walker, Red, White, Blue, 1931 .... 135.00
Boxing, Figure Set, Boxer, Opponent Ducking, Black-Eyed Referee, 1942, 3 Piece 518.00
Boxing, Gloves, Autographed, Cassius Clay, Signed, 1964 .... 6275.00
Boxing, Gloves, Joe Louis Distilling Co., Miniature 110.00
Boxing, Gloves, Reach, 1930s 150.00
Boxing, Program Collection, Muhammad Ali, 1965-1978 .... 1240.00
Boxing, Protective Cup, Autographed, Muhammad Ali, 1970s 590.00
Boxing, Robe & Glove, Autographed, Muhammad Ali 1530.00
Boxing, Shoes, Training, Muhammad Ali, Pair 4715.00
Boxing, Sweater, Entourage, Muhammad Ali 2600.00
Football, Ball, Autographed, Chicago Bears, Western Conference Champions, 1956 ..... 1655.00
Football, Ball, Autographed, Kansas City Chiefs, Super Bowl Champions, 1969 .... 578.00
Football, Ball, Autographed, Notre Dame, Includes Rockne, 1929 .... 485.00
Football, Figure, Tackler, Pulling Pants Of Ball Carrier, 1941, 2 Piece 275.00
Football, Helmet, Jim Thorpe, Game Worn 2750.00
Football, Helmet, Leather, Dog Ear, Horace Partridge 270.00
Football, Helmet, Leather, Pro Model, Wing Front, Goldsmith, 1930s 325.00
Football, Jacket, Warm-Up, Buffalo Bills, 1970s 180.00
Football, Jacket, Warm-Up, Cleveland Browns, 1960s 325.00
Football, Jersey, Dallas Cowboys, Game Worn, 1960s 785.00
Football, Jersey, Gale Sayers, Chicago Bears, Game Worn, 1971 .... 2830.00
Football, Pennant, New York Giants, Dark Blue, Football Player, Ball, 1950s, 12 x 29 In. . 60.00
Football, Pennant, Rose Bowl, Michigan State, Green, White, 29 In. 75.00
Football, Pennant, Saskatchewan Rough Riders, Grey Cup Champs, 1989, 26 In. 15.00
Football, Pillow, U. Of Chicago, Burgundy, Player Running With Ball, 1910, 21 x 21 In. . 355.00
Football, Program, Tournament Of Roses, Pasadena Star, 1910 .... 60.00
Football, Program, Tournament Of Roses, Pasadena Star, Woman, American Flag, 1936 .. 40.00
Football, Ring, Dante Lavelli, Hall Of Fame, 1975 .... 2659.00
Football, Sweater, Tommy McDonald, Philadelphia Eagles, 1961-1964 .... 1735.00
Football, Ticket, Super Bowl I, January 15, 1967, Los Angeles Memorial Coliseum 1735.00
Football, Tumbler, Dallas Cowboys, Mobil, Single Line, Tall 4.00
Golf, Ball, Autographed, Babe Ruth 733.00
Golf, Figure, Frustrated Golfer, Black Caddie, 1948, 2 Piece 1087.00
Hockey, Goalie Pads, Gerry Cheevers, Game Used, 1960 .... 711.00
Hockey, Mug, Bobby Smith, Les Canadiens Une Tradition, Nescafe 4.00
Hockey, Pennant, Soviet All Stars, Red, White, Crossed Sticks, C.C.C.P., 1950s, 29 In. ... 250.00
Hockey, Stick, Autographed, Bobby Orr, Northland, Game Used, Nov. 13, 1966 .... 6409.00
Hockey, Stick, Autographed, Harry Howell, New York Rangers, 1953-1954 .... 540.00
Hockey, Stick, Wayne Gretzky, Titan 1149.00
Horse Racing, Tumbler, Indiana Derby, 1995 .... 3.00
Horse Racing, Tumbler, Jim Beam Stakes, 1983 .... 10.00
Horse Racing, Tumbler, Jim Beam Stakes, 1989 .... 3.00
Horse Racing, Tumbler, Kentucky Derby, 1951 .... 550.00
Horse Racing, Tumbler, Kentucky Derby, 1952 ....100.00 to 190.00
Horse Racing, Tumbler, Kentucky Derby, 1964 .... 26.00
Horse Racing, Tumbler, Kentucky Derby, 1978 .... 4.00
Horse Racing, Tumbler, Kentucky Derby, 1983 .... 10.00
Horse Racing, Tumbler, Kentucky Derby, 1986 .... 10.00
Horse Racing, Tumbler, Kentucky Derby, 1987 .... 10.00

Horse Racing, Tumbler, Kentucky Derby, 1988 .... 10.00
Horse Racing, Tumbler, Preakness, 1983 .... 21.00
Hunting, Box, Red Head Shot Shells, Montgomery Ward Co., 4 x 4 x 2 1/2 In., 2 Piece .. 290.00
Hunting, Box, Remington UMC, Nitro Club, Cartridge, 1912, 4 x 4 x 2 1/2 In., 2 Piece .. 230.00
Hunting, Box, Western Shotgun Shells, Xpert, 4 x 4 x 2 3/4 In., 2 Piece 305.00
Hunting, Box, Winchester, Repeater, Paper Shot Shells, 1903, 4 x 4 x 2 1/2 In., 2 Piece .. 230.00
Hunting, Box, Winchester, Repeater, Speed Loads, Smokeless, 12 Gauge, 4 x 4 x 2 1/2 In. 165.00
Hunting, Button, Peters Cartridges, Experts Use, Celluloid, 7/8 In: 66.00
Hunting, Button, Winchester Rifle, Jr. Rifle Corps, Red, White, Blue, Celluloid, 1 In. 25.00
Hunting, Display, Gee, I Wish I Had Dad's Winchester, Boy, Dog, 31 x 42 In. 495.00
Hunting, Display, Peters Rustless Metallic Ammunition, Die Cut, Easel Back, 13 x 9 In. . 275.00
Hunting, Display, Remington, Sporting Rifles, Buck, Cardboard, Die Cut, 13 x 31 In. 210.00
Hunting, Display, Savage, Stevens & Fox Firearms, Squirrel, Cardboard, 18 x 13 1/2 In. . 60.00
Hunting, Display, Savage, Stevens & Fox, Firearms, Men Duck-Hunting, 20 x 22 In. 65.00
Hunting, Display, Western Cartridge Co., Man, Boy, Dogs, 5 Piece, Box, 1929 .... 2255.00
Hunting, Display, Winchester, Illustrated By Frank Stick, 1926, 54 1/2 x 31 In. 4070.00
Hunting, License, Button, N.C. County Resident, Orange Ground, 1927, 2 In. 165.00
Hunting, License, California, Expires June 30, 1925, 4 1/2 x 2 1/2 In. 80.00
Hunting, License, California, Pheasants, Expires June 30, 1913, 2 1/2 x 4 1/4 In. 259.00
Hunting, License, State Of California, $1.00, Expires June 30, 1915, 4 1/4 x 2 3/4 In. 170.00
Hunting, Poster, Marlin Rifles, Shotguns, Gun For Man Who Knows, 1908, 15 x 24 In. .. 1430.00
Hunting, Poster, Peters Big Game Ammunition, Elk, 20 x 30 In. 3630.00
Hunting, Poster, Remington UMC, 2 Men, Dog, Log Cabin, 18 x 26 1/2 In. 726.00
Hunting, Poster, Transaerienne, Paris, Dirigible Over Paris, Lithograph, 1915, 31 x 46 In. 1658.00
Hunting, Poster, Winchester, 4 Deer Going Up Snowy Mountain, 1912, 16 1/2 x 30 In. .. 2365.00
Hunting, Poster, Winchester, World Standard Shot Shells, 1937, 13 x 21 1/2 In. 204.00
Hunting, Poster, Winter Sports In France, Skiers, Birdhouse, c.1930, 39 x 25 In. 206.00
Hunting, Sign, American Powder Mills, Dead Shot, Duck Falling, Frame, 24 x 30 In. 3740.00
Hunting, Sign, Austin Powder Co., 2 Hunting Dogs, Paper, 23 x 19 In. 468.00
Hunting, Sign, Federal Ammunition, North American Ducks, Box, c.1950, 23 x 16 In. ... 110.00
Hunting, Sign, Marlin Rifles & Shotguns, G. Muss-Arnolt, 24 1/2 x 15 In. 3135.00
Hunting, Sign, Remington Guns, Duck, Shotguns, Paper, Roll-Up, 25 x 21 In. 578.00
Hunting, Sign, Remington, Solves Northwest Hunger, Oilcloth, 1909, 29 x 19 In. 3220.00
Hunting, Sign, Shoot Western World's Champion Ammunition, Matted, Frame, 1935 .... 230.00
Hunting, Sign, U.S. Ammunition, Soldiers, Salesman, Tin, Frame, 28 1/4 x 22 1/4 In. 1980.00
Hunting, Sign, Union Metallic Cartridge Co., Dock Workers, 29 x 17 In. 2360.00
Hunting, Sign, Union Metallic Cartridges, Paper, c.1870, 11 x 15 In. 240.00
Hunting, Sign, Winchester Junior Rifle Corp., Join The W.J.R.C., 2 Sides, 5 1/2 x 7 In. .. 2035.00
Hunting, Stickpin, DuPont Powders, Bird, On Tree Branch, Gold Wash, 5/8 x 2 1/4 In. 495.00
Hunting, Stickpin, DuPont Powders, Dog, Gold Plated, 3/4 x 5/16 x 2 In. 523.00
Hunting, Tin, Golden Pheasant Gun Powder, 2 Birds, A.F. & Co., c.1880, 4 x 6 x 1 1/2 In. 1540.00
Hunting, Tin, Hazard Powder Company, Red Paint, Labels, 19th Century, 7 1/2 In. 46.00
Hunting, Tin, Lalflin & Rand Gunpowder Orange, Hercules Powder Co., 4 x 6 x 1 1/2 In. 100.00
Hunting, Tin, Winchester No. 9114, Split BB Shot, Metal, Celluloid, 1 1/2 x 1/4 In. 132.00
Pennant, Auto Racing, Indianapolis 500, Green, Car, Red Border, Driver, 1914 .... 250.00
Pool, Table, Mahogany, Inlaid, Reverse Tapered Legs, Arts & Crafts, 32 x 111 x 60 In. ... 952.00
Rugby, Ball, Winchester American, No. 912 .... 4305.00
Snowshoes, Bear Paw, Leather Bindings, 13 x 28 In. 110.00
Snowshoes, Kidney Shape, Rope, Canvas Webbing, 18 In. 51.00
Snowshoes, Wood, Cloth, Hide, Fiber Netting, Wool Tufts, c.1900, 18 1/2 In. 235.00
Table Tennis, Paddles, Balls, Net, McLoughlin Bros., Box, 6 1/2 x 19 In. 165.00
Wrestling, Figure, Gorgeous George, Frightened Trainer, Big Wrestler, 1952, 3 Piece 1490.00
Wrestling, Figure, Wrestler, Twisted Opponent, Referee, Ring, 1941, 4 Piece 1670.00

STAFFORDSHIRE, England, has been a district making pottery and porcelain since the 1700s. Hundreds of kilns are still working in the area.
Thousands of types of pottery and porcelain have been made in the
many factories that worked and still work in the area. Some of the most
famous factories have been listed separately, such as Adams, Davenport, Ridgway, Rowland & Marsellus, Royal Doulton, Royal Worcester,
Spode, Wedgwood, and others. Some Staffordshire pieces are listed
under categories like Fairing, Flow Blue, Mulberry, Shaving Mug, etc.

Basin, Ship Of The Line In The Downs, Blue & White Transfer, 3 x 12 5/8 In. 2585.00

Basket, Stand, Landscape, Blue Transfer, Pierced Border, Leaf Handle, 11 In., Pair 880.00
Bird Whistle, Bird Perched On Tree Trunk, Applied Flowers, c.1820, 3 1/2 In. 410.00
Bowl, Oriental Pine Tree, Paper Lanterns, Wilkinson Ltd., 9 1/2 In. 45.00
Bowl, Underplate, Figures, Cows, Rural Landscape, Flower Border, Oval, 10 1/2 In. 764.00
Bowl, Vegetable, Cover, Canova, Handles, 12 1/2 In. 320.00
Bowl, Vegetable, Cover, Parisian Chateau Pattern, Black & White, 12 1/2 In. 275.00
Bowl, Vegetable, Cover, Parisian Chateau, 12 1/2 In. 275.00
Bowl, Vegetable, Cover, Undertray, Patriot's Departure, Maroon, Phillips, 15 1/2 In. 290.00
Bowl, Vegetable, Oxfordshire, Whitney Semi China, Dark Blue Transfer, 11 1/2 In. 135.00
Bust, John Wesley, Waisted Round Socle, Table Base, c.1830, 11 1/4 In. 1195.00
Bust, Shakespeare, Polychrome Enamel, Marble Waisted Base, 8 1/2 In. 305.00
Charger, Baltimore & Ohio, 7 Locomotives, Facts On Back, 10 1/2 In. 75.00
Charger, Baltimore & Ohio, 8 Locomotives, Harper's Ferry, 10 1/2 In. 150.00
Coffeepot, Lafayette At Franklin's Tomb, Blue & White Transfer, 11 1/8 In. 1060.00
Coffeepot, Pilgrim, Floral, Flow Blue, 11 In. 600.00
Creamer, Locomotive Pulling Carriage, Blue & White Transfer, 4 3/4 In. 380.00
Cup, Billy Button, Man Riding Backwards On Horse, Polychrome, Child's, 2 5/8 In. 115.00
Cup, Llama, Floral Border, Scalloped Rim, Handleless 99.00
Cup & Saucer, American Eagle On Urn, Dark Blue, 5 3/4 In. 195.00
Cup & Saucer, Baltimore & Ohio, 3 Locomotives, Handleless 40.00
Cup & Saucer, Blue Flowers, Red, Green Leaves, Blue Buds, Handleless ....39.00 to 50.00
Cup & Saucer, Blue Flowers, Red, Green, Blue Leaves, Handleless, 6 Sets 195.00
Cup & Saucer, Lafayette At Franklin's Tomb, Blue & White Transfer, 2 3/4 In. 176.00
Cup & Saucer, Napoleon, Driving Russian Sled, Blue & White Transfer, 2 3/4 In. 118.00
Cup & Saucer, Red & Green Flowers, Scroll Handle 22.00
Cup & Saucer, Spread Wing Eagle & 13 Stars, Red Transfer, 16 In. 330.00
Cup & Saucer, Washington, Standing, Scroll, Blue & White Transfer, 2 3/4 In. 382.00
Cup Plate, Cows In Stream, Bridge, Castle Ruins, Blue Transfer, Scalloped Rim, 3 1/2 In. 50.00
Cup Plate, Creature, Blue & White Transfer, Urn Border, 4 1/4 In., 6 Piece 499.00
Cup Plate, Eagle & Shield, Blue Transfer & Border 90.00
Cup Plate, Experience Keeps A Dear School, Gray, Green Transfer, 4 1/2 In. 68.00
Cup Plate, For Age & Want Save While You May, Black Transfer, 3 1/2 In. ....73.00 to 79.00
Dish, Hen On Nest Cover, Basket, Mustard Glaze, 8 1/2 x 7 1/2 x 10 In. 700.00
Dish, Hen On Nest Cover, White, Enamel Design, S & S, 6 In. 28.00
Dish, Hen On Nest Cover, White, Yellow Basket, 6 1/4 In. 90.00
Figurine, Baden Powell On Horse, 11 1/2 In. 500.00
Figurine, Bagpiper & Lady Above Clock Face, c.1850, 14 In. 800.00
Figurine, Bird, Raised Wing, Perched Above Nest, 3 Eggs, Applied Grass, 6 1/2 In. 220.00
Figurine, Boy, Riding Elephant, White, Gilt, 7 1/2 In. 489.00
Figurine, Camel, Recumbent, Light Olive Body, Oval Lined Base, 3 In. 385.00
Figurine, Camel, Recumbent, Oval Mound Base, c.1850, 3 1/2 In., Pair 1195.00
Figurine, Cat, Brown, Gray, White, Eyes, Green, 9 In., Pair .... *Illus* 206.00
Figurine, Cat, Seated, Black & Brown Sponged Enamel, 3 3/4 In. 165.00
Figurine, Cherub, Seated On Drum, Holding Dove, 19th Century, 7 In. 145.00
Figurine, Classical Woman, Floral Robe, Comedy Mask, Early 1800s, 6 1/4 In. 305.00
Figurine, Cobbler, Seated On Stool, With Dog, Square Gilt Lined Base, 12 3/4 In. .:.... 120.00
Figurine, Cottage, Stanfield Hall, 6 In. 69.00
Figurine, Couple, Courting, 19th Century, 11 1/2 In. 196.00
Figurine, Cradle, Yellow, Basket Weave, 2 3/4 x 4 3/4 In. 175.00

Staffordshire, Figurine,
Cat, Brown, Gray, White,
Eyes, Green, 9 In., Pair

Think about the problems of
owning a cat and a large
collection of ceramics.

Figurine, Cribb & Milineux, Fists Raised, Oval Base, c.1815, 8 1/4 & 8 1/2 In., Pair 7770.00
Figurine, Deer, Black & White Spotted, Oval Flower Base, 1800s, 3 3/4 x 6 In. 978.00
Figurine, Dog, Copper, Green & Pink Yellow Eyes, 12 In., Pair 440.00
Figurine, Dog, Gold Ears, Tail, Spots, Pair 450.00
Figurine, Dog, Greyhound, Standing, Black, M. Grath, 9 3/4 In. 575.00
Figurine, Dog, Greyhounds, Rabbits In Mouth, Cobalt Blue Base, 1800s, 5 3/4 In. 750.00
Figurine, Dog, King Charles Spaniel, On Cushion, 19th Century, 12 1/2 x 8 1/2 In. 865.00
Figurine, Dog, Luster Collar, Brown Markings, Muzzle, Pair 500.00
Figurine, Dog, Pekinese, Standing, Tan & White, Rhomboid Base, 8 1/2 In., Pair 110.00
Figurine, Dog, Pekingese, Ribbons, Russet, Ivory, c.1900, 7 1/2 x 8 In. 50.00
Figurine, Dog, Poodle, Mother & Puppy, Cobalt Blue Base, 7 In. 180.00
Figurine, Dog, Spaniel, Holding Yellow Flower Basket, 8 In., Pair 880.00
Figurine, Dog, Spaniel, Painted Face, Gilt Trim, 19th Century, 14 3/8 x 15 In., Pair 410.00
Figurine, Dog, Spaniel, Seated, Chain & Lock, White, Gilt, 15 In. 400.00
Figurine, Dog, Spaniel, Seated, Copper, Yellow Eyes, 9 1/2 In., Pair 440.00
Figurine, Dog, Spaniel, Seated, Pink & Copper Luster, Amber Glass Eyes, 13 In., Pair ... 138.00
Figurine, Dog, Spaniel, Seated, Russet, Glass Eyes, Edwardian, c.1900, 13 1/2 In., Pair .. 345.00
Figurine, Dog, Spaniel, White, Black Nose, Gilt Trim, 10 In., Pair 300.00
Figurine, Dog, Whippet, 19th Century, 8 In. 58.00
Figurine, Dog, Whippet, Recumbent, Shaped Scroll Base, 3 In. 220.00
Figurine, Dog, White, Black Nose, Gilt Accented Fur, 15 In., Pair 470.00
Figurine, Dog, White, Copper Luster Spots, Collars & Chains, 8 1/2 In., Pair ... 275.00
Figurine, Donkey, Beesums, Sand, c.1845, 10 In., Pair 1495.00
Figurine, Donkey, Fruit Baskets On Back, Cole Slaw Edge, 9 In., Pair 489.00
Figurine, Elephant Of Siam, Rose Colored Castle, c.1840 .... 1495.00
Figurine, Equestrian, Duke & Duchess Of Cambridge, On Horseback, 14 In., Pair 480.00
Figurine, Fisherman & Wife, 8 In. 170.00
Figurine, Gentleman Wearing Green Coat, 13 In. 40.00
Figurine, Gypsy, Polychrome Design, Pair 470.00
Figurine, King Edward VII, 12 1/2 In. 135.00
Figurine, Lamb, Recumbent, White, Applied Fur, Scrolled Base, 2 1/2 In., Pair 120.00
Figurine, Lion, Forepaw Resting On Globe, c.1820, 11 1/2 & 11 3/4 In., Pair 11350.00
Figurine, Lion, Forepaw Resting On Yellow Ball, Grinning, c.1815, 5 1/4 In. 1435.00
Figurine, Lion, Left Forepaw On Ball, 19th Century, 10 x 12 3/4 In. 546.00
Figurine, Lioness, Head Tuned Over Shoulder, c.1815, 5 1/2 In. 1434.00
Figurine, Man & Woman, Red Hair, 18th Century Costume, 9 In., Pair 150.00
Figurine, Man Leaning On Anchor, Woman, Green Coats, Birds, 7 3/8 & 8 1/4 In., Pair .. 385.00
Figurine, Moody & Sankey, 19th Century Ministers, 12 In., Pair 450.00
Figurine, Neptune, Venus, Standing Before Dolphins, c.1830, 10 In., Pair 1790.00
Figurine, Parrot, Tree Stump, c.1890, 12 3/4 In., Pair 1495.00
Figurine, Pigeons Perched On Branch, 3 Eggs, 19th Century, 8 1/2 In., Pair 1955.00
Figurine, Prepare To Meet Thy God, Masonic, Clock Face, c.1830, 10 3/4 In. 2150.00
Figurine, Queen Victoria, Prince Albert, 6 In., Pair 460.00
Figurine, Scotsman, Leaning On Rocky Crag, 12 In. 345.00
Figurine, Scotsman, With Dog, Rifle, Horn, Deer At Feet, 13 1/4 In. 460.00
Figurine, Sir Wm. Gordon-Cumming, Rifle & Dog, Early 19th Century 115.00
Figurine, Venus & Neptune, Dolphin At Base, c.1770, 9 In., Pair 678.00
Figurine, Village Maid, Seating On Tree Stump, Reading Book, c.1830, 11 1/2 In. 956.00
Figurine, Zebra, Standing, Applied Grass, Ground-Like Base, 4 3/4 In. 110.00
Gravy Boat, Baltimore & Ohio, 7 In. 170.00
Group, Abra Stop, Sacrifice Of Isaac, c.1830, 11 1/8 In. 2390.00
Group, Bull Baiting, Bull Terrier, Mound Base, c.1815, 5 In. 1195.00
Group, Bull Baiting, Reddish Brown Bull, Dog, Trainer, c.1830, 12 1/2 In. 9560.00
Group, Couple Seated On Garden Bench, 2 Children, 7 1/2 In. 2990.00
Group, Cross Legged Man, Woman With Sticks, White, 12 1/2 In. 100.00
Group, Death Of Munrow, Yellow & Black Tiger, Man In Mouth, 14 In. 25095.00
Group, Gretna Green Marriage, Blacksmith, c.1825, 7 3/4 In. 2390.00
Group, Jolly Traveler, 6 1/4 In. 440.00
Group, Man & Woman, In Highland Dress, 19th Century, 14 In. 230.00
Group, Pastoral, Couple Under Flowering Tree, c.1830, 11 1/2 In. 6570.00
Group, Polito's Menagerie, Fairground Booth, c.1835, 12 3/4 In. 14340.00
Group, Romulus & Remus, c.1830, 5 5/8 In. 956.00
Group, Scolding Wife, Fallen Husband, Ale Bench, c.1835, 7 1/2 In. 5675.00

Group, Sheep, Lamb, Green Washed Base, c.1810, 4 1/8 In. 1195.00
Group, St. Peter & The Lame Man, c.1830, 10 3/4 In. 2390.00
Group, Tam O'Shanter & Souter Johnny, c.1830, 8 1/4 In. 2990.00
Group, Tee Total, Woman Holding Baby, Man At Table, c.1835, 8 1/4 In. 7770.00
Group, Virgin Mary, Seated On Tree Stump, c.1830, 12 In. 1675.00
Group, Vivandiere, Mounted Soldier, Lass, 19th Century, 13 1/4 In. 375.00
Group, Who Shall Ware The Breeches, c.1830, 8 1/4 In. 6570.00
Incense Burner, Cottage Shape, Blue Thatched Roof, 6 x 5 1/2 In. 110.00
Jar, Condiment, Glass Spoon, Transfer Ware Flowers, Thorley 35.00
Jardiniere, Pedestal, Relief Flowers, Yellow Glaze, G. Jones, Melrose Ware, 22 In. 105.00
Jug, Cow, Jackfield Type, Black Underglaze, Gilt Trim, Oval Base, 5 In. 39.00
Jug, Cream, Hound & Game Scenes, Green Bands, Scallops, Hound Handle, 4 1/2 In. 65.00
Jug, Embossed Rows Of Pink & Green Daisies, Bulbous, Scroll Handle, 6 1/2 In. 55.00
Jug, Hunt Scenes, River Landscape, Black Transfer, Shaped Handle, 5 1/2 In. 440.00
Jug, Tropical Birds, Farm Birds, River Landscape, Black Transfer, 4 1/4 In. 380.00
Matchbox, Boy, Holding Yarn At Spinning Wheel, Gilt Trim, 4 1/2 In. 55.00
Mug, Franklin's Maxims, Industry Needs Not, Blue Transfer, 2 1/4 In. 90.00
Mug, Franklin-Type Maxim, Diligence Is The Mother, Green Transfer, 2 3/4 In. 56.00
Mug, Man With Mustache, Beard, Turban, 4 3/4 In. 130.00
Mug, Mule Dancing To Flute Player, Spilling Contents, 2 1/2 In. 158.00
Mug, Temperance Design, Early 1800s, 2 3/4 In. 85.00
Mug, To Washington The Patriot Of American, Black Transfer, 2 1/2 In. 480.00
Pitcher, Blue & White, Floral, American Eagle Mark, 19th Century, 10 3/4 In. 575.00
Pitcher, Commemorative, Nelson & Berry, c.1805, 5 In. 395.00
Pitcher, Cow, Landscape, Blue, White, 7 x 5 In. 520.00
Pitcher, Dog & Stag Scene, Embossed, Blue & White, Twig Handle, 7 In. 70.00
Pitcher, Flowers, Pink, Green Flowers, Leaves, Blue Highlights, 5 In. 85.00
Pitcher, Fruit & Birds Panel, Dark Blue Ground, Bulbous, Handle, 6 1/2 In. 475.00
Pitcher, John Wesley, Figure, Royal Blue, Polychrome, 9 x 7 1/4 x 5 1/2 In. 115.00
Pitcher, Lafayette At Franklin's Tomb, Blue & White Transfer, c.1846, 5 7/8 In. 590.00
Pitcher, Milk, Urn Form, Eagle, Shield, 14 Stars, Blue & White, 6 1/4 In. 2300.00
Pitcher, Quilted, Brown Flowers, Leaves, Canary Yellow, 4 In. 165.00
Pitcher, Spaniel Shape, 19th Century, 8 In. 230.00
Pitcher, View Of Erie Canal, Blue & White Transfer, Scrolled Terminals, 5 7/8 In. 825.00
Pitcher, Water Girl, Floral Ground, Deep Blue Transfer, 7 1/4 In. 580.00
Pitcher & Bowl, Baltimore & Ohio, 7 Locomotives, Thomas Viaduct, 1835 .... 250.00
Pitcher & Bowl, Embossed, Polychrome Flowers, Flared, Footed, 9 1/2 x 13 In. 155.00
Plaque, Prepare To Meet Thy God, Angel With Wings, 7 In. 489.00
Plate, America & Independence, Fisherman, Blue, 10 1/2 In. 358.00
Plate, Baltimore & Ohio, 7 Locomotives, Thomas Viaduct, 1835, 6 3/4 In. 60.00
Plate, Cabbage Rose, 7 In. 39.00
Plate, Canovian, Purple, Scalloped Edge, 9 1/4 In., Pair 110.00
Plate, Chief Justice Marshall, Shell Border, Enoch Wood & Sons, 10 1/8 In. 700.00
Plate, City Hall, New York, Blue, 10 In. 305.00
Plate, Commodore MacDonnough's Victory, Blue & White Transfer, 10 1/8 In. 470.00
Plate, Dam & Waterworks, Philadelphia, Fruit & Flower Border, 1800s, 9 7/8 In. 645.00
Plate, Don Quixote & The Shepherdess, Blue, 10 In. 275.00
Plate, Dr. Syntax Disputing Bill With Landlady, 1818-1834, 10 1/4 In. 175.00
Plate, Entrance Of Erie Canal, Locks In Border, Medium Blue Transfer, 10 In. 220.00
Plate, Erstes Theater, Hamburg, Blue Transfer, Floral Border, 7 In. 125.00
Plate, Exchange, Baltimore, Fruit & Flower Border, 10 In. 385.00
Plate, Figure, Verses, Molded Leaf Border, Polychrome Transfer, Meakin, 6 1/4 In. 100.00
Plate, Fisherman Pattern, Scalloped, Blue Border, Enoch Wood & Sons, 10 3/8 In. 248.00
Plate, Flowers, Red, Sprigs, Blue Buds, Green Leaves, 10 1/2 In. 85.00
Plate, Historical, Valkyries, Burslem, Blue, Enoch Wood & Sons, 9 1/4 In. 275.00
Plate, Landing Of General Lafayette, Blue, 10 In. 525.00
Plate, Landing Of The Fathers At Plymouth, Blue, Enoch Wood, 10 In. 185.00
Plate, Masonic Emblems, Blue Transferware, Swag Borders, 10 5/8 In. 550.00
Plate, Municipality No. 1, Jackson Square, New Orleans, 9 In. 1700.00
Plate, Pastoral Scene, Cattle In Field, Blue, 10 1/4 In. 275.00
Plate, Polychrome, Flowers, Leaves, 10 1/4 In. 28.00
Plate, Rainesvilles Gardens, Hamburg, Green Transfer, Floral Border, 7 In. 125.00
Plate, River Scene, Blue, 10 In., Pair 230.00

Plate, Rose & Blue Flowers, Yellow Centers, Green & Black Leaves, 10 1/4 In.	55.00
Plate, Rural Landscape, Bridge, People, House, Church, Blue Transfer, 8 1/2 In.	146.00
Plate, Scene Of Travelers, Classical Buildings, Blue, 10 1/4 In.	140.00
Plate, States, Observatory, Blue Transfer, Scalloped Edge, 10 3/4 In.	385.00
Plate, Strawberry, Purple Sprigs, Green Leaves, Scalloped Edge, 8 3/4 In.	132.00
Plate, Union Line, Blue & White Transfer, Shell Border, c.1846, 10 1/4 In.	558.00
Plate, Verse, Employ Time Well, Molded Leaves, Blue Transfer, Pink Border, 7 1/8 In. . .	75.00
Plate, View Of Trenton Falls, Blue Transfer, Impressed E. Wood & Sons, 7 1/2 In.	282.00
Plate, Vue D'Une Ancienne Abraye, Dark Blue Transfer, E. Wood & Sons, 9 In.	226.00
Plate, W. Penn's Treaty, Geometric Patterns, Brown Transfer, 10 5/8 In.	275.00
Plate, Water Works, Philadelphia, Floral Border, Green, Scalloped, 9 In.	405.00
Plate, Wells Cathedral, 10 In.	160.00
Plate, White Boy Gives Money To Shoeless Black Beggar, Poem, c.1855, 8 In.	375.00
Plate, Winter View Of Pittsfield, Mass., Blue & White Transfer, c.1836, 8 1/2 In.	175.00
Plate, Winter View Of Pittsfield, Mass., Dark Blue Transfer, 8 1/2 In.	395.00
Plate Set, Buildings, Ships, Blue & White, Transfer, Early 1800s, 5 In., 5 Piece	1175.00
Platter, 3-Story Building, Blue & White Transfer, 2 Wings, 16 1/2 In.	2585.00
Platter, Antiquarian, Pale Blue, Scalloped Rim, 17 1/2 In.	338.00
Platter, Baltimore & Ohio, Locomotives, Indian Creek, Oval, 14 x 10 In.	275.00
Platter, Bywell Castle, Northumberland, Blue Transfer, 10 x 13 In.	385.00
Platter, Cape Coast Castle On Gold Coast Africa, Blue & White Transfer, 16 5/8 In.	2820.00
Platter, Chinese, Blue Transfer, 15 x 18 1/2 In.	75.00
Platter, Commerce-Free Trace Pattern, Black Transfer, Scalloped, 17 x 19 1/4 In.	550.00
Platter, East Cowes, Isle Of Wight, Shell Border, Enoch Wood & Sons, 10 1/2 In.	764.00
Platter, Foley, Brown Transfer, 14 1/2 In.	28.00
Platter, Fruit, Flower, Acanthus Leaf Border, Blue Transfer, 13 x 16 1/2 In.	990.00
Platter, Gryn Castle, Flintshire, Wales, Blue & White Transfer, 1822-1836, 17 In.	940.00
Platter, Junction Of Sacandaga & Hudson Rivers, Blue & White Transfer, 14 In.	3055.00
Platter, Lake George, State Of New York, Enoch Wood & Sons, 16 1/2 In.	2585.00
Platter, Landing Of General Lafayette At Castle Garden, 14 1/2 In.	1800.00
Platter, New York, Brown, Thomas Dimmock, c.1840, 19 In.	850.00
Platter, Niagara Falls From American Side, Blue & White Transfer, 14 3/4 In.	2820.00
Platter, Rome, St. Peter's, Castel Sant Angelo, Bridge, Tiber River, 1820, 19 x 14 In.	650.00
Platter, Royal Exchange London, Dark Blue Transfer, 16 x 12 3/4 In.	295.00
Platter, Shell Pattern, Flowers, Fruit, Urn, Blue & White Transfer, 20 1/2 In.	2115.00
Platter, Tiger Hunting Scene, Hunters On Elephants, Blue & White, 20 x 16 In.	805.00
Platter, View Of Dublin, Shell Border, Blue & White Transfer, 14 3/4 In.	1765.00
Platter, Washington, Capitol, Blue, Well & Tree 20 1/2 x 15 1/2 In.	1315.00
Platter, White House Washington, Blue & White Transfer, 14 3/4 In.	1880.00
Saucer, English Scenery, Blue, White, Enoch Wood, 5 3/4 In.	19.00
Soup, Dish, Blue Transferware, Ralph Stevenson, 7 In.	525.00
Soup, Dish, Cuba, Spanish Verse, Classical Columns, Blue Transfer, 8 3/4 In.	605.00
Soup, Dish, Don Quixote, Meeting Of Sancho & Dapple, Blue Transfer, 7 5/8 In.	195.00
Soup, Dish, Mitchell & Freeman, Blue & White Transfer, c.1834, 10 1/4 In.	705.00
Spill Holder, Castle, 5 1/2 In.	115.00
Spill Holder, Castle, Peach, 3 Turrets, Cole Slaw Trim, 7 In.	230.00
Spill Holder, Cat, Puss In Boots, Black Boot Spill, c.1860, 4 3/4 In.	375.00
Spill Holder, Clock Face, Garter Flanked By Royal Supporters, c.1835, 10 1/8 In.	2990.00
Spill Holder, Dog, Spaniel, 14 In.	375.00
Spill Holder, Lion, Standing, Applied Leaves, Shaped Gilt Lined Base, 5 1/2 In.	385.00
Sugar, Cover, 2 Boats On River, Town, Blue Transfer, Impressed, 4 1/2 x 6 1/4 In.	75.00
Sugar, Cover, Green Band, Red Flowers, Blue Drape, Black, Bulbous, 5 1/4 In.	138.00
Sugar, Cover, Wadsworth Tower, Scalloped Handles, Enoch Wood & Sons, 6 In.	264.00
Sugar, Lafayette At Franklin's Tomb, Olive Green, Blue Rim, 6 3/4 In.	495.00
Sugar, Man In Low Sled Pulled By Horses, Dark Blue, 6 1/2 In.	770.00
Sugar, Thistle Cover, Man On Horse Drawn Sled, Deer, Woods, Blue Transfer, 6 1/2 In. . .	770.00
Sugar & Creamer, 2 Women With Parasols, Lake, Oriental Tents, Dark Blue Transfer	330.00
Sugar & Creamer, Blue & White Flowers, Stippled Blue Ground, Scalloped Rims	305.00
Tea Set, Agrarian Scenes, Black, White Transfer, 16 Piece	489.00
Tea Set, May Pattern, Brown Transfer, Girl With Roses, Cottage, Child's, 11 Piece	395.00
Tea Set, Pointer & Quill Pattern, Teapot, Sugar, Milk Jug, Waste Bowl, 1825, 12 Piece . . .	1700.00
Teapot, Button Finial, Floral, Bulbous, Footed, Flared Rim, Inset Lid, 5 1/2 In.	145.00

Teapot, Courtyard & Floral, Blue, 7 In. 200.00
Teapot, Napoleon, Driving Russian Sled, Blue & White Transfer, c.1846, 7 3/4 In. 825.00
Teapot, Oriental Flower Garden, Green Base, Ball Shape, Square C Handle, 5 In. 635.00
Teapot, Romantic View, Red Transfer, T. Mayer, 6 1/4 In. 50.00
Teapot, Scenic, Marked Stone China, Rose Border, Blue & White, 6 1/2 x 10 In. 920.00
Toby Jugs are listed in their own category.
Toddy Plate, Winter View Of Pittsfield, Mass., Blue, Scalloped Edge, 5 3/4 In. 385.00
Toothbrush Holder, Daisy Bell, 2 Holes, Incised, England, 5 3/4 x 5 1/2 In. 55.00
Tray, Baltimore & Ohio, 5 Locomotives, Viaduct, Oval, c.1835, 8 x 5 In. 100.00
Tureen, Cover, Flowers, Gondolas, Blue, 2 Handles, Pedestal Base, Flower Finial 660.00
Tureen, Soup, Romantic Scene, Shepherd, Woman, Black Transfer, 7 x 5 1/2 In. 385.00
Tureen, Underplate, Ladle, Hudson River View, Light Blue Transfer, Beaded, 6 x 8 In. ... 578.00
Vase, Boy, Feeding Swan, Pink, Orange & Yellow Coleslaw, 5 In. 495.00
Vase, Cow & Calf, Rust & White, Black & Gold Trim, 11 In., Pair 635.00
Vase, Cow, Over Thistle Sprig, Embossed Base, Milk Sold Here, 14 In. 2035.00
Vase, Dog, Mastiff, Black Muzzle, Tree, 6 In., Pair 1650.00
Vase, Dog, Spaniel, Seated, Gilt Spots & Collar, Tree, 13 In., Pair 690.00
Vase, Elephant, Tree, 19th Century, 6 In. 115.00
Vase, Family Of 3 White Swans, Gilt Highlights, Orange Tree, 5 In. 275.00
Vase, Man Holding Bow, Stag At Side, 19th Century, 17 1/4 In. 1410.00
Vase, Swans, White, Orange, Light Blue, Gold Highlights, 5 In. 275.00
Waste Bowl, Floral Vines, Red Band & Rim, Round, Flared Foot, 3 x 6 1/2 In. 22.00
Waste Bowl, Homestead Scene, Blue Transfer, Flared Edge, 2 3/4 x 5 5/8 In. 165.00

STANGL Pottery traces its history back to the Fulper Pottery of New
Jersey. In 1910, Johann Martin Stangl started working at Fulper. He
left to work at Haeger Pottery from 1915 to 1920. Stangl returned to
Fulper Pottery in 1920, became president in 1926, and changed the
company name to Stangl Pottery in 1929. Stangl acquired the firm in
1930. The pottery is known for dinnerware and a line of bird figurines.
Martin Stangl died in 1972, and the pottery was sold to Frank
Wheaton, Jr., of Wheaton Industries. Production continued until 1978,
when Pfaltzgraff Pottery purchased the right to the Stangl trademark,
and the remaining inventory was liquidated. A single bird figurine is
identified by a number. Figurines made up of two birds are identified
by a number followed by the letter "D" indicating "Double."

ABC, Dish, 3 Sections 75.00
Amber-Glo, Bowl, 8 In. 22.00
Amber-Glo, Gravy Boat ....18.00 to 19.00
Apple Delight, Pitcher, 1 1/2 Pint, 5 In. 30.00
Basket, Blue, 7 In. 50.00
Bird, Allen Hummingbird, No. 3634, 3 1/2 In. 120.00
Bird, Bird Of Paradise, No. 3625, 13 3/4 In. 3220.00
Bird, Bluebird, No. 3276, 5 In. 110.00
Bird, Bluejay, No. 3715, With Peanut, 9 3/4 In. 920.00
Bird, Bluejay, No. 3716, With Leaf, 10 1/2 In. ....460.00 to 489.00
Bird, Cerulean Warbler, No. 3456, 4 1/4 In. 90.00
Bird, Cockatoo, No. 3580, Medium, 8 3/4 In. ....148.00 to 190.00
Bird, Cockatoo, No. 3584, Large 259.00
Bird, Drinking Duck, No. 3250E, Granada Gold, 2 In. 45.00
Bird, European Finch, No. 3922, 4 3/4 In. 2530.00
Bird, Flying Duck, No. 3443, Blue & Gray, 9 In. 173.00
Bird, Hummingbird, Double, No. 3599D, 8 3/4 In. 230.00
Bird, Key West Quail Dove, No. 3454, Wings Spread 748.00
Bird, Magpie Jay, No. 3758, 10 3/8 In. 1725.00
Bird, Oriole, Double, No. 3402D, 5 1/2 In. 125.00
Bird, Penguin, No. 3274, 5 1/2 In. 748.00
Bird, Scarlet Tanager, Double, No. 3750D, Apple Blossoms, 7 1/2 In. 4406.00
Bird, Shoveler Duck, No. 3455, 12 5/8 In. 1150.00
Bird, Western Tanager, Double, No. 3750D, 8 In. ....*Illus* 489.00
Bird, Western Tanager, No. 3749, 5 In. 2530.00
Bird, White Wing Crossbill, No. 3754, 8 In. 4600.00

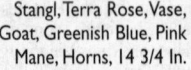

Stangl, Bird, Western
Tanager, Double,
No. 3750D, 8 In.

Stangl, Terra Rose, Vase,
Goat, Greenish Blue, Pink
Mane, Horns, 14 3/4 In.

Bird, Wren, Double, No. 3401D	1035.00
Bird, Wren, No. 3401, Granada Gold, Original Shape, 3 1/2 In.	50.00
Blueberry, Casserole, 8 In.	35.00
Blueberry, Cup	10.00
Candleholder, Green, No. 2049	20.00
Chicory, Cake Plate, Metal Base, 10 In.	20.00
Chicory, Plate, 10 In.	30.00
Christmas Tree, Tidbit, Metal Handle, 10 In.	35.00
Circus Clown, Plate, 8 1/4 In.	180.00
Colonial, Plate, Dinner, Blue	10.00
Colonial, Plate, Silver Green, 8 In.	15.00
Colonial, Saucer, Tangerine	5.00
Colonial, Sugar, Cover, Blue	10.00
Country Garden, Bread Tray	40.00
Country Garden, Plate, Dinner, 10 In.	25.00
Country Garden, Platter, 14 In.	80.00
Festival, Chop Plate, 14 1/2 In.	90.00
Fruit, Bowl, Vegetable, Oval, Divided, 10 In.	45.00
Fruit & Flowers, Bowl, Vegetable, Divided, 10 1/2 In.	50.00
Fruit & Flowers, Cup & Saucer	18.00
Fruit & Flowers, Gravy Boat	25.00
Fruit & Flowers, Tidbit, 10 In.	15.00
Jug, Miniature, Peach, 1 3/4 In.	20.00
Jug, Miniature, White, Blue Flower, 1 3/4 In.	24.00
Jug, Miniature, White, Red Flower, 1 3/4 In.	24.00
Kiddieware, Circus Clown, Plate, 8 1/4 In.	180.00
Kiddieware, Indian Campfire, Plate, 9 In.	200.00
Kiddieware, Little Quackers, Plate, 9 In.	350.00
Kiddieware, Mother Hubbard, Plate, 9 In.	200.00
Kiddieware, Musical, Toy Soldiers, Mug	250.00
Kiddieware, Playful Pups, Cup	55.00
Lamp, Apple Green, Scroll Handles, c.1933	150.00
Oyster Plate Set, 9 In.	2070.00
Pansy, Ashtray, Yellow, Brown Edge, 4 In.	14.00
Pansy, Ashtray, Yellow, Gold, 4 In.	20.00
Poppy, Ashtray, 4 In.	35.00
Poppy, Ashtray, Flower, 4 In.	35.00
Provincial, Bowl, 5 1/2 In.	10.00
Provincial, Plate, 6 In.	5.00
Provincial, Plate, 8 In.	10.00
Provincial, Plate, 10 In.	15.00
Rhythmic, Wall Pocket, Satin White, 6 x 9 In.	120.00
Sportsmen's Giftware, Pheasant, Ashtray, Oval, 10 5/8 In.	35.00
Terra Rose, Candle Warmer, Blue	12.00
Terra Rose, Vase, Goat, Greenish Blue, Pink Mane, Horns, 14 3/4 In. . . . . *Illus*	450.00
Thistle, Bowl, Vegetable, 8 In.	45.00
Thistle, Plate, 8 In.	12.00
Thistle, Plate, 10 In.	22.00
Toastmaster, Tray, Persian Yellow, Square, Divided, 8 In.	12.00

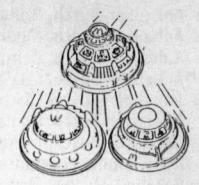

STAR TREK AND STAR WARS collectibles are included here. The television series *Star Trek* ran from 1966 through 1969. The TV show *Next Generation,* a sequel, ran from 1987 to 1994. The first Star Trek movie was released in 1979 and 8 others followed, the most recent in 1999. The movie *Star Wars* opened in 1977 and sequels and prequels were released in 1980, 1983, and 1999, and 2002. Other science fiction and fantasy collectibles can be found under Batman, Buck Rogers, Captain Marvel, Flash Gordon, Superman, Movie, and Toy.

STAR WARS, Bracelet, Navigation, McDonald's, Blue, Plastic, Sticker, Bag, 1979, 3 x 11 In.	15.00
Card, Greeting, Birthday, Captain Kirk, Punch-Out Figure, Color, Photo, 1976	8.00
Coloring Book, Rescue At Raylo, 1978	5.00
Costume, Captain Kirk, Wrath Of Khan, Collegeville, Box, 1982	15.00
Figure, Captain Jean-Luc Picard, First Contact, On Card	8.00
Figure, Q, The Next Generation, On Card	8.00
Figure, Quark, Deep Space Nine, On Card	8.00
Game, Board, Ideal, 1967, 19 In.	70.00
Game, Board, Star Fleet, McDonald's, 1979, 5 x 10 In.	15.00 to 20.00
Ring, McDonald's, Blue, Plastic, Compartment, 1979, 1 1/4 In.	20.00
Toy, Communicators, Blue, Plastic, Battery Operated, 1974, 2 1/2 x 7 In.	15.00
Tumbler, Dr Pepper, Mr. Spock, 1976	30.00
TV Guide, Cast Of Star Trek, March 1967	65.00
STAR WARS, Bank, Darth Vader, Figural, Vinyl, 1983, 9 1/2 In.	20.00
Cookie Jar, Darth Vader, C-3PO, R2-D2, Hexagonal, Ceramic, c.1980, 5 x 9 x 11 In.	75.00
Display, Jar Jar Binks, 84 In.	550.00
Figure, 4-LOM, Admiral Ackbar, Blister Card, 1982, 3 1/4 In.	85.00
Figure, C-3PO, Blister Card, Kenner, 1977, 3 3/4 In.	190.00
Figure, Han Solo, Blister Card, Kenner, 1977, 3 3/4 In.	295.00
Figure, Luke Skywalker, Stormtrooper Disguise, Green, No. 1, On Card	10.00
Figure, Max Rebo, Pewter, Rawcliffe	25.00
Figure, Obi-Wan Kenobi, Green, No. 1, Pack No. 521791.02, On Card	10.00
Figure, Princess Leia, Pewter, Rawcliffe	15.00
Figure, Princess Leia, Prisoner, Green Card, No. 1, On Card	10.00
Figure, Yoda, Prepares To Attack Count Dooku, Attack Of Clones, Life Size	595.00
Figure, Yoda, Red, No. 2, Pack No. 527603.01, On Card	10.00
Helmet, Clone Trooper	60.00
Lightsaber, Count Dooku, Christopher Lee Autograph, Display Case	395.00
Lightsaber, Darth Vader, James Earl Jones, David Prowse Autograph, Case	495.00
Lightsaber, Obi Wan Kenobi, Collector's Edition, Master Replicas LLC	295.00
Lunch Box, Return Of The Jedi, Thermos Co., c.1983	40.00
Model Kit, AT-AT, Jedi, Photo, Box, 1983, 8 In.	12.00
Model Kit, R2-D2, PMC Plastic Scale Model, Unassembled, Box, 1977, 6 In.	95.00
Model Kit, Speeder Bike Vehicle, Return Of Jedi, Box, 1983	47.00
Toothbrush, Battery Powered, Plastic, Kenner, 1977, 7 1/2 In.	20.00
Toy, Fighter Vehicle, B-Wing, Laser Sounds, Box, 1984, 12 x 23 x 5 In.	75.00

STEINS have been used by beer and ale drinkers for over 500 years. They have been made of ivory, porcelain, stoneware, faience, silver, pewter, wood, or glass in sizes up to nine gallons. Although some were made by Mettlach, Meissen, Capo-di-Monte, and other famous factories, most were made by less important German potteries. The words *Geschutz* or *Musterschutz* on a stein are the German words for *patented* or *registered design,* not company names. Steins are still being made in the old styles. Lithophane steins may be found in the Lithophane category.

3 Jockeys On Horseback, Crest With Student Society Sword, Relief, 1/2 Liter	240.00
3 Military Scenes, W. I Deutscher Kaiser, Relief, Pottery, Bavaria Inlaid Lid, 1/2 Liter	310.00
3 Scenes, People, No. 234, Pewter Lid, Pottery, 1/2 Liter	109.00
Amber, Glass, Inlaid Lid, Dwarf Thumblift, c.1860, 1/2 Liter	300.00
Anheuser-Busch, Adolphus Busch, 1/2 Liter	100.00
Anheuser-Busch, Americano, Ceramarte, 1/2 Liter	320.00
Anheuser-Busch, August A. Busch, Jr., 1/2 Liter	130.00
Anheuser-Busch, Bud Frog, 1/2 Liter	110.00
Anheuser-Busch, Bud Man 30th Anniversary, Ceramarte, 5 Liter	100.00

Anheuser-Busch, Budweiser 100 Years, Ceramarte, 1/2 Liter 215.00
Anheuser-Busch, Ceramic, 25 Years Of Safe Service, St. Louis, 1978, 12 1/2 In. 235.00
Anheuser-Busch, Ceramic, 35 Years Of Service, St. Louis, 14 1/2 In. 360.00
Anheuser-Busch, City Series, Frankfurt, Ceramarte, 1/2 Liter 230.00
Anheuser-Busch, Clydesdales, Ceramarte, 1/2 Liter 175.00
Anheuser-Busch, Louie The Lizard, Ceramarte, 1/2 Liter 80.00
Anheuser-Busch, United States Of America 200 Years, 1776-1976, Ceramarte, 1/2 Liter .. 215.00
Automobile, German Automobile Club, Pressed Glass, Pewter Lid, 1/2 Liter 518.00
Baseball, Pitcher, Batter, Catcher, Hand Painted, Porcelain, Inlaid Lid, 1/2 Liter 2185.00
Bearded Man, Large Face, Stoneware, 6 1/2 In. 300.00
Bird, Holding Sausage, Perched On Beer Stein, Engraved, F. Ringer, 1/2 Liter 360.00
Blue Flowers, Birds, Hand Painted, Faust, Transfer, Porcelain, Inlaid Lid, 1/2 Liter 400.00
Brewery, St. Georgenbrau Buttenheim, Stoneware, 1/2 Liter 111.00
Brewery, Tigerbrau, Pottery, Relief Pewter Lid, 1/3 Liter 230.00
Bunzlau, Brown Glaze, Stoneware, Pewter Ring, Lid, Strap, c.1820, 1/4 Liter 775.00
Castle Scene, Faience, Pewter Lid, 10 1/2 In. 345.00
Cats, Relief, Bear Handle, Inlaid Monkey & Boot Lid, Relief, Stoneware, 1/2 Liter 300.00
Cats, White, Wearing Hats, Pottery, Transfer, Enameled, Pewter Lid, 1/2 Liter 115.00
Character, Alligator, Porcelain, Inlaid Lid, E. Bohne & Sohne, 1/2 Liter 575.00
Character, Artillery Shell, Eagle, Flags, Stoneware, Pewter Lid, M.P. Munchen, 1 Liter .. 690.00
Character, Artillery Shell, Stoneware, Inlaid Lid, Wilhelm Conze, 1906, 1/2 Liter 660.00
Character, Bear, Pottery, Inscribed Berlin 1890, Marked RM, No. 731, 1/2 Liter 720.00
Character, Bismarck, Porcelain, Porcelain Lid, 1/2 Liter 130.00
Character, Black Boy, Pottery, Inlaid Lid, 1/2 Liter 335.00
Character, Bustle Lady, Stoneware, Pewter Lid, Hauber & Reuther, 1/2 Liter 805.00
Character, Cat, With Bottle, Pottery, Music Box Base, Inlaid Lid, 1/2 Liter 725.00
Character, Clown, Pottery, Inlaid Lid, 1/2 Liter 360.00
Character, Fox, Wearing Lounging Wear, No. 8672, 7 1/4 In. 198.00
Character, Graf Zeppelin, Porcelain, Porcelain Lid, 1/2 Liter 2530.00
Character, Kathreiner's Kneipp Malz Kaffee, Coffee Bag, Porcelain, 1/2 Liter 6325.00
Character, Monk, Pewter, Pewter Lid, 1 Liter 185.00
Character, Monk, Pottery, Marked Made In Munchen, 1/2 Liter 230.00
Character, Monk, Red Robe, Lithophane, Porcelain, 1/2 Liter 220.00
Character, Monkey, Black Hat, Germany, No. 1261, 1/2 Liter 230.00
Character, Munich Child, Porcelain, 1/4 Liter 200.00
Character, Munich Child, Pottery, 1/8 Liter 290.00
Character, Nurnberg Tower, Stoneware, Blue Salt Glaze, Pewter Lid, 1/2 Liter 299.00
Character, Owl, Marked Germany No. 740, 8 In. 100.00
Character, Skull On Book, Inlaid Lid, Pottery, 1/2 Liter 220.00
Character, Skull, Porcelain, Inlaid Lid, E. Bohne Sohne, 1/2 Liter 360.00
Character, Smoking Pig, Porcelain, Inlaid Lid, Schierhold, 1/2 Liter 299.00
Character, Soldier, Stoneware, Inlaid Lid, Marked LB & C, 1/2 Liter .... .920.00 to 1725.00
Character, Student Frog, Porcelain, 1/2 Liter 665.00
Cherub & Woman, Pewter Lid, Martin Pauson, 1 Liter 145.00
Chicken, Inlaid Bird Lid, Pottery, Relief, Dumler & Breiden, 1/2 Liter 375.00
Choir, Pottery, V Deutsche Sangerfest I. Stuttgart, 1/2 Liter 210.00
Christopher Columbus, Relief, Pottery, Inlaid Lid, Reinhold Hanke, 1/2 Liter 345.00
Copper, Classical Figure, Embossed, Early 20th Century, 10 1/2 In., Pair 210.00
Deer, Magdeburg, S. German, Creamware, c.1900, 1 Liter 410.00
Delft Blue, Purple, Pewter Mounted, Armorial Crown, Angels, Initials, c.1730, 9 In. 520.00
Diamond Pattern, Westerwald, Pewter Lid, Stoneware, 1/4 Liter 240.00
Evolution, Monkeys Read Books, Skull, Relief, No. 1257, Pottery, 1/2 Liter 460.00
Festive Scene, Pewter Lid, Pottery, Dumler & Breiden, 1 Liter 259.00
Flower, Leaf, Gray Crockery, Pewter Lid, Indian Maid Thumblift, 1/2 Liter 98.00
Flowers, Art Nouveau, Hand Painted, Pottery, Relief Silver Plated Lid, 1/2 Liter 405.00
Fox, Grape Vines, Transfer, Enameled, Stoneware, Pewter Lid, 1/2 Liter 185.00
Germans Meet Romans, Relief, No. 378, Pottery, Pewter Lid, 1/2 Liter 375.00
Glass, Amber, Enameled, Child, Holding Book, Pewter Lid, 1/4 Liter 160.00
Glass, Amber, Enameled, Deer At River, Pewter Base Ring & Lid, 1/2 Liter 360.00
Glass, Amber, Enameled, Woman, Glass Prunts, Pewter Lid, 1/2 Liter 230.00
Glass, Amber, Munich Child, Enameled, Pewter Lid, 2 Liter 460.00
Glass, Amber, Pewter Overlay, Inlaid Lid, Serpent Finial, 1 Liter, 9 1/2 In. 750.00
Glass, Amber, Ribbed, Enameled, Munich Child, Pewter Base Ring & Lid, 1/2 Liter 365.00

Glass, Blue To Clear, Threaded, Pewter Top, Foot, Clear Applied Handle, 14 1/2 x 5 In. ... 375.00
Glass, Clear To Vaseline, Ribbed, Pewter Overlay, Cherub, Pewter Lid, 1/2 Liter 349.00
Glass, Clear, Enameled Flowers, Pewter Base Ring & Lid, 1839, 9 1/2 In. 845.00
Glass, Clear, Enameled Flowers, Pewter Base Ring & Lid, 1854, 9 1/2 In. 835.00
Glass, Clear, Enameled Flowers, Pewter Base Ring & Lid, 1864, 9 In. 345.00
Glass, Clear, Fluted, Pewter Lid, Carved Horn, Fox, Stump, 10 1/2 In., 1 Liter 575.00
Glass, Clear, Red Overlay, Cut Circles, Striped Handle, Matching Inlaid Lid, 1/2 Liter ... 725.00
Glass, Cobalt Blue, Blown, Pewter Lid, Closed Hinge, c.1840, 1/2 Liter, 4 3/4 In. 375.00
Glass, Cut Panels, Blown, Clear, Blue Glass Overlay, Glass Lid, c.1840, 1/2 Liter 660.00
Glass, Deer Decoration, Amber, Silver Band, Lid, c.1850, 12 In., 1 Liter 3450.00
Glass, Enameled Crest, Anno 1667, Amber, Inlaid Lid, c.1890, 1/2 Liter 260.00
Glass, Gold Iridescent, Pewter Lid, Rigaree Around Bottom, 1/2 Liter, 6 In. 145.00
Glass, Man Taking Off Shoes & Lady Peeking In Door, Ceramic Lid, 5 In. 45.00
Glass, Military Scene, Blown, Pewter Lid, F. Ringer, 1/2 Liter 605.00
Glass, Military, Lions On Crest, Green Wreaths, Munchen, Beaded Pewter Lid, 1918 .... 140.00
Glass, Munich Child, Beer Stein, Amber, Pewter Lid, L. Hohlwein, 1/2 Liter 405.00
Glass, Skull & Crossbones, Gray Metal Lid, Porcelain Bier Ist Gift, 1/2 Liter 405.00
Glass, Waterfall, Inlaid Lid, 1/2 Liter 115.00
Glass, Woman & Cupid, Polychrome, Pewter & Glass Lid, Germany, 6 In. 170.00
Golf, Clubhouse In Distance, Pottery, 1/2 Liter 300.00
Hannoverisch Munden, Hand Painted, Faience, Pewter Lid, c.1847, 1 Liter, 8 1/4 In. 375.00
Hermann's Departure, No. 93, Pewter Lid, Pottery, 1/2 Liter 97.00
Horse, Flowers, Hand Painted, Faience, Pewter, c.1811, 1 Liter, 10 1/4 In. 2415.00
Hunter, Wife, Dog, Enameled, Lithophane, 1/2 Liter 140.00
Hunter Departing, No. 36, Pewter Lid, Stoneware, 1/2 Liter 100.00
Hunters Cleaning Deer, Pewter Lid, Pottery, 3 1/2 Liter 305.00
Innkeeper, Porcelain, Pewter Lid, 1/2 Liter ....'............. 80.00
Karl Melham, Art Nouveau, No. 3855, Stoneware, Pewter Lid, Merkelbach, 1/2 Liter 300.00
Koln Cathedral, Regensburg, Stoneware, Pewter Lid, 1/2 Liter 130.00
Lohengrin Opera Scene, Relief, No. 390, Pottery, Pewter Lid, 1/2 Liter 400.00
Man, Wearing Large Yellow Pants, Stoneware, Pewter Lid, F. Ringer, 1/2 Liter 330.00
Man, Woman, Flower Urns, Faience, Pewter Lid, Inset Coin, 10 In. 525.00
Man Dancing, No. 442, Pottery, Pewter Lid, 3 Liter 120.00
Man In Green Jacket, Stoneware, Pewter Lid, F. Ringer, 1/2 Liter 460.00
Man In Red Jacket, Enameled, Stoneware, Pewter Lid, Riemerschmid, Ringer, 1 Liter ... 490.00
Man Sitting At Table, Barmaid, Transfer, Enameled, Stoneware, 1/2 Liter 115.00
Marzi & Remy, No. 881, Pewter Lid, Stoneware, 1 Liter 215.00
Men Drinking, JWR, Pottery, 1/4 Liter 120.00
Mettlach steins are listed in the Mettlach category.
Military, Erholungs Park Fur, 3 Soldier Scenes, Stoneware, 1/2 Liter 605.00
Military, Unteroffz-Korps Reiter Rgt. 14 Standort Ludwigslust, Pottery, 1/2 Liter 216.00
Mountains, Faces, Turtlenecks, Hikers, Relief, No. 1264, Pottery, Pewter Lid, 1/2 Liter .. 375.00
Munich Child, Pottery, Inlaid Lid, 3 Liter 2530.00
Munich Child, Pottery, J. Reinemann Munchen, 1 Liter 240.00
Munich Child, Pottery, Lion Thumblift, Relief Pewter Lid, 1/2 Liter 460.00
Munich Child, Stoneware, Pewter Lid, Transfer, Enameled, F. Ringer, 1/8 Liter, 4 1/2 In. . 275.00
Munich Child, Transfer, Enameled, Pottery, Pewter Lid, 1/2 Liter 95.00
Musical Band, Pottery, Pewter Lid, Stamped HR457, Germany, 11 In. 138.00
Musical Instruments, Blown, Clear, Glass, Pewter Lid, c.1800, 1 Liter, 7 3/4 In. 1325.00
Nordic King, Seated, Beer Barrel, Scene On Porcelain Cover, Salt Glaze, 1800s, 8 1/2 In.. 80.00
Nurnberg, Albrecht Durer, Pewter Lid, Pewter, 1 Liter 440.00
Nurnberg, Etched, Relief, No. 531, Pottery, Pewter Lid, Hauber & Reuther, 1/2 Liter 310.00
Occupational, Baker, People, Porcelain, Pewter Lid, 1/2 Liter 195.00
Occupational, Blacksmith, Porcelain, Pewter Lid, Horse Finial, 1914, 1/2 Liter 400.00
Occupational, Coal Shoveler, Large Scene, Porcelain, Pewter Lid, 1/2 Liter 660.00
Occupational, Fireman, Stoneware, Inlaid Lid, 1/2 Liter 635.00
Occupational, Jockey, Man & Woman, Stoneware, Pewter Lid, 1 Liter 345.00
Occupational, Mason, Stoneware, Pewter Lid, 1/2 Liter....................... 285.00
Occupational, Miner, Lion & Shield, Pottery, Pewter Lid, 1/2 Liter 290.00
Occupational, Ornamental Plasterer, Porcelain, Pewter Lid, Lion Finial, 1/2 Liter 485.00
Occupational, Wagon Wheel Builder, Scene, Porcelain, Pewter Lid, 1/2 Liter 575.00
People Playing Cards, Pottery, Inlaid Lid, 1 1/2 Liter 230.00
Pewter, Beveled Glass, Domed Lid, Painted King, Germany, Late 19th Century, 12 In. 105.00

Pewter, Prussian Eagle, State Crests, Wilhelm II Lid, Kayserzinn No. 4095, 3 Liter 490.00
Post Telegraph, Post Horn Handle, Eagle Thumblift, Pottery, Pewter Lid, 1/2 Liter 375.00
Pottery, Dancing Scene, Relief, Pewter Lid, Hauber & Reuther, 1/2 Liter 150.00
Pottery, Landscape Background, Pewter Top, Ball Thumb Rest, Inscribed, c.1735, 10 In. . 690.00
Pottery, Marching Band, Relief, Pewter Lid, Hauber & Reuther, 1/2 Liter 180.00
Proud Rider, Der Stolze Reiter, Boy On Toy Horse, Stoneware Pewter Lid, 1/8 Liter 185.00
Regimental, 2 Comp. Infantry Rgt. N. 67 Metz 1899, Porcelain, 1/2 Liter, 9 3/4 In. 345.00
Regimental, 2-Sided, Eagle Thumblift, Helmet Finial, Pottery, 1/2 Liter 2029.00
Regimental, 2-Sided, Eagle Thumblift, Porcelain, c.1905, 1/2 Liter 515.00
Regimental, 2-Sided, Infantry No. 32, Eagle Thumblift, Porcelain, c.1900, 1/2 Liter 380.00
Regimental, 2-Sided, Roster, Esk. Husar Regt. Don Zieten, Pottery, 1/2 Liter, 15 In. 1725.00
Regimental, 2-Sided, Roster, Esk. Husar Rgt. Landgr., Pottery, 1/2 Liter, 14 1/2 In. 720.00
Regimental, 2-Sided, Roster, Garde Jager Battalion, Porcelain, 1/2 Liter, 11 1/2 In....... 2760.00
Regimental, 2-Sided, Roster, Garde Schutzen, Stoneware, 1907-1909, 1/2 Liter, 6 1/2 In. . 520.00
Regimental, 2-Sided, Sachsen Thumblift, Porcelain, 1/2 Liter 485.00
Regimental, 2-Sided, Schaffenburg, Porcelain, 1902-1904, 1/2 Liter 460.00
Regimental, 2-Sided, Soldier Meeting Guard, Walking With Girl, 11 1/2 x 5 1/2 In. 715.00
Regimental, 2-Sided, Soldiers Loading Canon, Germany, 1934, 6 x 5 1/2 In............ 550.00
Regimental, 4-Sided, Maschinengewehr, Porcelain, 1/2 Liter, 11 1/4 In. 3105.00
Regimental, 4-Sided, Roster, 10 Feld. Artillerie Regt., Porcelain, 1/2 Liter, 10 In. 800.00
Regimental, 4-Sided, Roster, 4 Battr. Fuss Artillerie, 1908-1910, 1/2 Liter, 11 1/2 In. ... 575.00
Regimental, 4-Sided, Roster, 4 Comp. 2 Kgl. Sachs. Pionier, 1/2 Liter, 11 1/2 In. 1035.00
Regimental, 4-Sided, Roster, Artillerie Regt. 1912-1914, Porcelain, 1/2 Liter, 12 1/2 In. .. 605.00
Regimental, 4-Sided, Roster, Infantry Rgt., Metz 1909-1911, Porcelain, 1/2 Liter, 12 In. .. 605.00
Regimental, 4-Sided, Roster, Wurtt Grenadier Rgt. Nr. 119, Porcelain, 1/2 Liter, 12 In. ... 775.00
Regimental, Baden 6th Comp. Inf., Kasier Friedr. III, Griffin Thumblift, 11 1/2 In. 445.00
Regimental, Hessian, Offenback 168th Infantry, Hessian Lion Thumblift, 1912, 11 1/2 In. 400.00
Regimental, Roster, S.M. Reserve Kaiser Friedrich III, Pottery, 1/2 Liter, 10 In. 660.00
Regimental, Roster, S.M.S. Kurfurst Friedrich Wilhelm, Porcelain, 1/2 Liter, 11 In. 1495.00
Regimental, Roster, Telegrathen Bataillon, 1907-1909, Stoneware, 1/2 Liter, 6 1/2 In. 518.00
Regimental, Schneider, Cavalry, Riding Into Town, Pewter Lid 440.00
Repeating Design, Relief, Stoneware, Pewter Lid, Merkelbach, 1 Liter 160.00
Sailboat, Rowing, Oarsmen, Inlaid Buoy Lid, Relief, No. 984, Pottery, 1/2 Liter 460.00
Schutzenliesl, Transfer, Enameled, Porcelain, Pewter Lid, 1/2 Liter 345.00
Ship, Relief, Transfer, Enameled, Pottery, Pewter Lid, No. 1411, 1/2 Liter 345.00
Shooting Festival, People & Rifles, Pewter Lid, Pottery, 1/2 Liter 335.00
Silver Plate, Outdoor Scene, Denmark, 5 1/2 In. 65.00
Smoking Club, Transfer, Enameled, Porcelain, Pewter Lid, Biebrich, 1903, 1/2 Liter 375.00
Soldiers, Regensburg, Westerwald, Porcelain Inlaid Lid, Stoneware, 1/2 Liter 146.00
Stoneware, Blue & Purple Salt Glaze, Pewter Lid, 1 1/2 Liter 110.00
Stoneware, Pewter Mounted, Cobalt Blue Boar, Geometric, 8 1/2 In. 360.00
Student Society, Silesia Und Thuringia, Pressed, Glass, 1/4 Liter 630.00
Tankard, Monk Drinking Beer, Animal Head Handle, 11 1/2 In. 225.00
Tankard, Pewter, Goat's Head, Flowers, Scroll Work, 13 1/2 In. 190.00
Third Reich, Landes Polizei Ausburg, Pottery, Pewter Helmet Lid, 1935, 1/2 Liter 545.00
Third Reich, Soldier On Motorcycle, Stoneware, Pewter Lid, 1940, 1/2 Liter 460.00
Third Reich, Stoneware, Transfer, Soldier Carrying Machine Gun, 1935, 1/2 Liter 360.00
Trains, Railway Bridge, Pottery, Pewter Lid, Crown Finial, Eisenbahn, 1/2 Liter 575.00
Trumpeter Of Sackingen, No. 18, Pewter Lid, Pottery, 1/2 Liter 150.00
Turner, Stoneware, Transfer, Enameled, Pewter Lid, 1/2 Liter 255.00
University, Remembering My University, Konigsbergnm, Porcelain, 1898-1901, 1 Liter .. 375.00
US 11th ACR, McPheeters Barracks, Silver Plated Metal Lid, Germany, 1/2 Liter, 6 1/2 In. 45.00
US Third AF, F-111, Lakenheath, Right People, Germany, 1/2 Liter, 5 1/2 In. 178.00
Warrior Scene, Relief, No. 555, Pottery, Pewter Lid, Dumler & Breiden, 1 Liter 345.00
Westerwald, Dragonfly, Circle, Wild Boar, Flowers, Stoneware, c.1800, 1 Liter 845.00
Westerwald, Knibis Design, Stoneware, Pewter Lid, c.1700, 1/2 Liter, 7 3/4 In. 834.00
Westerwald, Line Design, Stoneware, Pewter Lid, c.1800, 1/2 Liter, 7 1/2 In. 405.00
Westerwald, Village Relief, Fairies, Stoneware, Pewter Lid, c.1840, 1 Liter, 9 In. 835.00
Woman Serves Dinner, Transfer, Enameled, Stoneware, Pewter Lid, F. Ringer, 1 Liter ... 489.00
Woman Serving Beer & Chicken, Transfer, Enameled, Pewter Lid, F. Ringer, 1 Liter 455.00
Woman With Machine, St. Louis, Pewter Lid, Pottery, c.1904, 1 Liter 240.00
XV Deutsches Bundesschiessen Hamburg, Stoneware, Pewter Lid, 1909, 1/2 Liter 660.00
XVI Deutsches Bundesschiessen Munchen, Stoneware, Pewter Lid, 1906, 1/2 Liter 575.00

STEREO CARDS that were made for stereoscope viewers became popular after 1840. Two almost identical pictures were mounted on a stiff cardboard backing so that, when viewed through a stereoscope, a three-dimensional picture could be seen. Value is determined by maker and by subject. These cards were made in quantity through the 1930s.

2 Prospectors In Mountains, Lighting Pipe, No. 114, Thurlow	125.00
5th Penn Cavalry, October 29, 1864	250.00
Admiral Sampson's Fleet At The Blockade, Havana, Davis, Kilburn, c.1898	12.00
American Indian Chiefs, S.J. Morrow	500.00
American Indian Woman & Child, C.B. Brubaker, Marquette, Michigan	50.00
American Indian Women Guard Corn From Birds, Whitney's Gallery, 1862	100.00
Army On Hill, Alex Gardner, c.1863	275.00
Artists At Work, Prospect Park	65.00
Bandits At Dinner, Mammoth Cave, Waldack, Cincinnati	60.00
Battleship Missouri, Polychrome, c.1907	8.00
Black Woman Servant	125.00
Camouflaged Artillery Before Jablonka, Germany, c.1940	6.00
Cathedral Interior, Crystal Palace	350.00
Chinese Government Official, 2 Students, Palmquist, 3 Piece	150.00
Civil War Steamboat, Alex Gardner, c.1863	300.00
Connecticut St., S. Norwalk	45.00
Covered Wagons, Crook City, S.D., F. Jay Haynes	150.00
Danville Iron Works, Pennsylvania	90.00
Dead Soldier, Petersburgh, Virginia, April 3, 1865	100.00
Dedication Of Grant's Tomb, USS Maine, Griffith & Griffith	14.00
Family In Front Of Gingerbread House, Long Branch, N.J., G.W. Pach	45.00
Family Posing On Veranda, Sea Cliff, Long Island, Rutherford	45.00
Georgetown Village, Rocky Mountain	90.00
Girls & Women Teachers In Shaker School, Julius Hall, Great Barrington, Mass.	350.00
Greek Statues, Crystal Palace, Negretti & Zambra	400.00
Gun Ship, New Orleans, Hart, Watertown, N.Y.	90.00
Hampton, Steamer, Upton	75.00
Hot Springs, S.D., W.R. Cross	50.00
Indian Camp, Montana	275.00
Japanese Soldier On His Way For Water, Polychrome, T.W. Ingersoll, 1905	7.00
London Bridge, London, England, Underwood, 1901	12.00
Man & Decoy Sheep, Houseworth	40.00
Marching German Troops Cross Border, Germany, c.1940	6.00
Merry Bootblacks, Inauguration, Washington, D.C., 1889	59.00
Military Prison, Fort Lafayette, New York Bay, D. Barnum	45.00
Mountain Top View, Gurnsey	60.00
Mountain Top View, James Peak Trail, F. Collier, Denver	60.00
Nude Woman Leaning On Blue Cushion, c.1850	7500.00
NYC Military Parade, Chambers St., July 4, 1860	125.00
People Pose In Front Of Tent, Upton	90.00
Pirates Fight Sailors On Ship	65.00
Rebel Prisoners, Gen. Sheridan At 5 Forks, April 2, 1865	585.00
Royal Guards, Entrance To Windsor Palace, Windsor, England, Travel Co., 1908	12.00
Savannah, Georgia	50.00
Sculpture Display, Mechanics Institute Fair, 3 3/8 In x 3 3/4 In.	50.00
Shaft Of Mines, Men Working, Little Pittsburgh, Thurlow	95.00
Sheep Ranch, Templetons Gap, Gurnsey	50.00
Sioux Chief With Wife, Dakota Territory, S.J. Morrow, c.1880	375.00
Sioux Graves, Ceremonial Burial, S.J. Morrow	300.00
Sitting Bull, S.J. Morrow	300.00
Statue Of Selenus, Crystal Palace, Negretti & Zambra	350.00
Teddy Roosevelt, Sitting At Desk, White House	28.00
Uncle Sam Remembers Dewey Day, Griffith & Griffith, 1898	14.00
United States Military Railroad, City Point, Virginia	100.00
Urns & Nymphs, Crystal Palace, Negretti & Zambra	350.00
Venison Island, Harbor & Boats, H.N. Robinson, Reading, Mass.	50.00
Views Of Early Russia, Calotype, Mounted, Zuccamaglio, Moscow, 9 Piece	1030.00
Volcanic Explosion, Mount Pelee, Underwood, June 5, 1902	10.00

Washoe Indian Children, Lake Tahoe, Palmquist, 3 Piece 235.00

STEREOSCOPES were used for viewing stereo cards. The hand viewer was invented by Oliver Wendell Holmes, although more complicated table models were used before his was produced in 1859. Do not confuse the stereoscope with the stereopticon, a magic lantern that used glass slides.

    Mahogany, Stereopticon, Victorian, Carved Wave, Cards, c.1880, 18 x 7 x 11 In. 259.00
    Rosewood, Hinged Door, Late 19th Century, 6 1/2 x 7 1/2 In. 15.00
    Sculptoscope, Lithographed Stereo Cards, Coin-Oeprated, Metal, Glass, 14 1/4 In. 330.00
    Stereo-Graphoscope, Wooden Viewer, Brass Eye Openings, 1896 .... 60.00
    Underwood & Underwood, 30 View Cards 143.00
    Wood, 10 Images, Patent 1898 .... 125.00
    Wood, Unis France, Standard, Stereoscopes Mattey, Paris, 3 3/4 x 5 1/2 In. 80.00

STERLING SILVER, see Silver-Sterling category.

STEUBEN glass was made at the Steuben Glass Works of Corning, New York. The factory, founded by Frederick Carder and T.G. Hawkes, Sr., was purchased by the Corning Glass Company. They continued to make glass called *Steuben*. Many types of art glass were made at Steuben. The firm is still making exceptional quality glass but it is clear, modern-style glass. Additional pieces may be found in the Aurene, Cluthra, and perfume bottle categories.

    Ashtray, Clear, Applied Rests, Marked, 8 3/4 In. 90.00
    Bowl, Amber, Celeste Blue, Lattice, 3 1/2 x 8 1/4 In. 748.00
    Bowl, Bristol Yellow, Swirl Pattern, 11 1/4 In. 115.00
    Bowl, Bristol Yellow, Wide Rim, 2 x 13 1/2 In. 170.00
    Bowl, Calcite, Gold Aurene Interior, 5 3/4 In. 145.00
    Bowl, Calcite, Gold Aurene Interior, 8 In. 200.00
    Bowl, Calcite, Gold Aurene Interior, Flared Rim, Round Foot, 2 1/2 x 10 In. 265.00
    Bowl, Calcite, Gold Aurene Interior, Footed, 3 1/2 x 10 In. 345.00
    Bowl, Calcite, Gold Aurene Interior, Footed, c.1915, 8 In. 230.00
    Bowl, Centerpiece, Clear, Garland Design, Signed, 12 In. 40.00
    Bowl, Centerpiece, Clear, Scroll Handles, George Thompson, 1937, 10 In. 288.00
    Bowl, Grotesque, Green Edge, Clear, c.1933, 6 5/8 x 12 3/4 In. 200.00
    Bowl, Lily Pad, Ivrene, Interior Rainbow, Ribbed, Footed, Marked, 6 x 14 In. 374.00
    Bowl, Plum Jade, Acid-Cut Flowers, Scrolls, Ground Pontil, 8 x 4 In. 5175.00
    Bowl, Plum Jade, Acid-Cut Murillo Design, 6 1/4 In. 2590.00
    Bowl, Rosaline Over Alabaster, Acid-Cut Murillo Design, 5 3/4 x 3 In. 1725.00
    Bowl, Rosaline, Shaded To Opal Foot, 9 3/4 In. 196.00
    Bowl, Rose, Controlled Bubbles, Applied Threading, Wide Rim, 14 1/4 x 2 1/8 In. 220.00
    Bowl, Ruby, Footed, 13 In. 316.00
    Bowl, Ruby, Tricornered, 9 In. 260.00
    Bowl, Topaz, Celeste Blue Rim, 8 Swirled Cabochons, Footed, 8 x 14 In. 374.00
    Candelabrum, 2-Light, Disc Base, Scroll Supports, Orb Finial, Engraved, 6 x 8 In. 890.00
    Candlestick, Amber, Celeste Blue Rims On Foot & Cup, 10 In., Pair 860.00
    Candlestick, Baluster, Clear, No. 7746, c.1934, 10 1/2 In., Pair 690.00
    Candlestick, Celeste Blue, Tulip Cup, Lily Pad Foot, Amber Stem, 12 In. 1495.00
    Candlestick, Cranberry Swirl, Clear Twist Stems & Foot, Flat Cup Rim, 6 In., Pair 728.00
    Candlestick, Ruby, 12 In., Pair 1090.00
    Candlestick, Selenium Red, Marked, 2 1/4 In., Pair 210.00
    Champagne, Amber, Marked, 4 In., 8 Piece 315.00
    Chandelier, 4-Light, Brass, Iridescent Gold Shades, Tassels, 15 x 36 In. 863.00
    Cocktail, Conical Cup, Tear Drop Base, 4 In., 6 Piece 530.00
    Compote, Amber Bowl, Celeste Blue Stem, 7 In. 195.00
    Compote, Bristol Yellow, Ribbed, Pedestal Base, Reeding, Carder, 1900s, 6 7/8 In. 295.00
    Compote, Calcite, Amber, Red, Gold Iridescent, Rope Twist Stem, 8 In. 1840.00
    Compote, Clear, Applied Green Threading, Controlled Bubbles, 7 In. 173.00
    Compote, Clear, Broad, Flaring Rim, 4-Lobed Base, 7 In. 558.00
    Compote, Clear, Shallow, 4 Open Scroll Supports, Round Base, 10 In. 169.00
    Compote, Cobalt Blue, 8 1/4 In. 201.00
    Console, Amethyst, Matching Flower Frog, 2 x 12 In. 403.00
    Console, Clear, Looped Base, 3 1/2 x 13 In. 220.00

Cruet, Rosaline, Stopper, Alabaster Handle, 6 In. 230.00
Decanter, Ship's, Clear, 4-Ring Neck, Stopper, Engraved Signature, 9 1/2 In., Pair 805.00
Dish, Molded, Clear, Circular, Inscribed, c.1925, 12 In. 705.00
Ewer, Clear, Petal-Like Top, Bulbous Base, 10 1/2 In. 140.00
Figurine, Apple, Signed, Angus McDougal, 1940, 4 In. 295.00
Figurine, Disk, Carved Ram, Stars, Aluminum Display Stand, Box, 9 3/4 In. 360.00
Figurine, Elephant, Trumpeting, Signed, 5 1/2 x 4 1/2 x 6 1/2 In. 695.00
Figurine, Fox, Marked, 6 1/4 In. 805.00
Figurine, Gazelle, Leaping, Marked, 6 1/2 In. 130.00
Figurine, Horse Head, Marked, 4 In. 185.00
Figurine, Mouse, Marked, Box, 2 1/2 In. 130.00
Figurine, Phoenix, Lloyd Atkins, 1965, 13 In. 805.00
Figurine, Porpoise, Lloyd Atkins, 1964, 9 1/4 In., 2 Piece 375.00
Figurine, Rabbit, Marked, 1942, 3 In. 70.00
Finger Bowl, Flared, 4 1/2 In., 6 Piece 85.00
Flower Frog, Green Jade, 2 Tiers, 2 1/4 x 4 In. 60.00
Goblet, Celeste Blue Cut To Amber, Clear Stem, Footed, Marked, 5 3/4 In. 865.00
Goblet, Cranberry Swirl, Clear Stem, 8 In., 12 Piece 675.00
Goblet, Eagle Cutting, Wreath, Pointed Rosette, Clear, Flared, Square Foot, 6 1/4 In. 190.00
Goblet, Green Jade, York Etching Trumpet Bowl, 1903-1932, 6 In. 180.00
Goblet, Oriental Poppy, Rosaline, Bell Shape, Green Stem 2465.00
Lamp, Cintra, Opal Wheat Stalks, Green Ground, Silvered Base, 32 In. 1725.00
Lamp, Figural Quan Yen, Wisteria, Orange Base, 7 In. 615.00
Plate, Jade Green, 8 1/2 In., 6 Piece 300.00
Platter, Rosaline, Cut To Alabaster, Flowers, Ladder Design, Marked, 14 In. 1035.00
Sculpture, Counterpoise, Donald Pollard, Fitted Case, 21 1/4 In. 2390.00
Shade, Calcite Quilted, Acorn Shape, 4 1/2 In. 25.00
Shade, Calcite, Blue Pulled Feathers, Gold Aurene Tipped, 5 In., Pair 605.00
Shade, Calcite, Gold Aurene Hooked Border, Fleur-De-Lis Mark, 5 1/4 In. 145.00
Shade, Calcite, Gold Aurene Paneled Fishnet, 4 1/4 In. 230.00
Shade, Calcite, Gold Aurene Pulled Feathers, Fleur-De-Lis Mark, 4 1/2 x 4 3/4 In. 588.00
Shade, Calcite, Gold Aurene Pulled Loops, Fleur-De-Lis Mark, 4 x 5 3/4 In., Pair 400.00
Shade, Calcite, Green Pulled Decoration, Gold Aurene Florets, 4 1/2 In. 260.00
Shade, Calcite, Green Pulled Drape, Gold Aurene Tipped, 4 1/4 In. 145.00
Shade, Calcite, Green Pulled Feather, Gold Interior, Fleur-De-Lis, 4 1/2 x 5 In. 200.00
Shade, Calcite, Green Pulled Feathers, Gold Aurene Tipped, Silver Fleur-De-Lis, 4 3/4 In. 170.00
Shade, Calcite, Platinum, Gold Fishnet, Fleur-De-Lis Mark, 6 In. 260.00
Shade, Domed, Calcite, Scrolling Ivy & Acanthus, Leaves, Etched, c.1915, 12 In. 230.00
Shade, Egg Shape, Calcite, Gold, Pulled Hearts & Vines, 6 1/2 In. 92.00
Shade, Morning Glory, Iridescent Blue Gold, Ribbed, Gas, 4 7/8 In., Pair 260.00
Shade, Patterned Green Aurene, Calcite, Fleur-De-Lis Mark, 4 3/4 In. 920.00
Sherbet, Rosaline, Alabaster Foot, 5 In., 12 Piece 1400.00
Sherbet, Underplate, Calcite, Gold Aurene Interior, c.1920, 4 x 6 In., 4 Sets 575.00
Toothpick Holder, Clear, Urn, Pedestal Base, 3 3/8 x 2 3/4 In., Pair 200.00
Torchere, Wrought Iron, Figural Glass Insert, Signed, Frederick Carder, 70 In. 3360.00
Tray, Amber, Celeste Blue Rim, 16 In. 219.00
Tray, Topaz, Applied Pomona Green Leaves, Honeycomb Pattern, 6 In. 115.00
Vase, 3 Prong, Optic Ribbed, Green Jade, Alabaster Foot, 10 1/2 In. 1840.00
Vase, Amethyst To Clear, Clear Foot, Marked, 11 1/4 In. 520.00
Vase, Black, On Deep Green, Indian Design, Shouldered, Cameo, 10 In. 5935.00
Vase, Blue Jade, Ribbed, Fluted Top, 5 1/2 In. 4025.00
Vase, Clear, Controlled Bubbles, Applied Pink Threading, 8 In. 290.00
Vase, Clear, Flared Sides, Applied Pillars At Base, 10 In. 275.00
Vase, Clear, Horizontal Etched Design, Walter Dorwin Teague, 6 In. 489.00
Vase, Clear, Layered Side Ornaments, c.1940, 5 1/2 x 14 In. 490.00
Vase, Clear, Scrolled Stem, Bell Shaped, Footed, Marked, 8 3/8 In. 200.00
Vase, Cobalt Blue Cut To Clear, Flared, Marked, 8 In. 1020.00
Vase, Cornucopia, Pomona Green, Applied Amber Foot, Ruffled Edge, 8 1/4 In. 260.00
Vase, Cyprian, Aquamarine, Celeste Blue Rim, Urn, Footed, 10 3/4 In. 110.00
Vase, Fan, Pomona, Green, Engraved Ship, Marked, 8 1/2 In. 201.00
Vase, Fan, Ruby To Clear, Applied Clear Foot, 11 1/4 In. 518.00
Vase, Fan, Topaz, Pomona Green Base, Ribbed, Marked, 8 5/8 In. 173.00
Vase, Frosted Flowers, Swirls, Ovals, Footed, G. Thompson, No. 7913, 8 1/2 In. 230.00

Vase, Green Iridescent, Gold Hooked Feathers, Fishnet Rim, 11 In. 5750.00
Vase, Green Jade On Alabaster, Dragons, Stalactite Rim, Foot, Shouldered, 9 1/2 In. 3080.00
Vase, Green Jade On Alabaster, Japanese, Flowering Trees, Clouds, 7 In. 1300.00
Vase, Green Jade, Fan, Ribbed, Applied Alabaster Foot, 11 1/4 In. 300.00
Vase, Green Jade, Matsu Design, Oval, 8 x 8 In. 1345.00
Vase, Green Jade, Morning Glory, Pillared, Fleur-De-Lis Mark, 9 In. 400.00
Vase, Green, Gold Iridescent, Silver Pulled Heart & Vines, Marked, 10 In. 4025.00
Vase, Grotesque, Ivrene, 7 x 12 In. 450.00
Vase, Grotesque, Ivrene, Black, Applied Black Foot, 6 1/4 In. 460.00
Vase, Ice Bucket Shape, 3 Bands Of Alabaster Threading, Marked, 6 1/4 In. 365.00
Vase, Ivory, Ribbed, Black Foot, 9 1/4 In. 575.00
Vase, Ivory, Ribbed, Flared, 5 1/4 In. 540.00
Vase, Ivrene, Ribbed, 3 Applied Handles, 11 1/2 In. 175.00
Vase, Ivrene, Ribbed, Marked, 5 1/4 In. 345.00
Vase, Jack-In-The-Pulpit, 3 Prongs, Ivrene, Marked, 12 In. 1265.00
Vase, Lotus, Clear, George Thompson, 1940, 14 In. 460.00
Vase, Rope Twist, No. 7858, George Thompson, Marked, 1939, 10 1/2 In. 170.00
Vase, Rosaline, On Alabaster, Chinese Design, Shouldered, 10 In. 5600.00
Vase, Rosaline, Urn, Alabaster Disk Foot, 9 In. 675.00
Vase, Rose Quartz, Alabaster Handles, c.1927, 11 1/8 In. 1555.00
Vase, Ruby, Sculptured Swirl Pattern, Marked, 9 3/4 In. 430.00
Vase, Selenium, Red, Flowers, Leaves, Heaton Design, 12 In. 4025.00
Vase, Selenium, Red, Spiral Ribbing, Oval Footed, Fleur-De-Lis Mark, 6 1/2 In. 235.00
Vase, Silverina, Blue, Mica Flecks, Flared Rim, Fleur-De-Lis Mark, 7 5/8 In. 825.00
Vase, Stick, Green Jade, Applied Alabaster Foot, 10 In. 300.00
Vase, Stick, Rosaline, Alabaster Base, Marked, 8 In. 200.00
Vase, Tree Trunk, Clear, 3 Prongs, 8 In. 290.00
Vase, Tree Trunk, Plum Jade, 3 Prongs, 8 1/2 In. 575.00
Vase, Tree Trunk, Topaz, 3 Prongs, 6 In. 219.00
Vase, Tree Trunk, Topaz, 3 Prongs, Marked, 7 In. 470.00
Vase, Trumpet, Calcite Exterior, Gold Aurene Interior, 6 In. 400.00
Vase, Tyrian, Turquoise Body, Gold Aurene Bands, Shouldered, Marked, 8 1/2 In. 14000.00

STEVENGRAPHS are woven pictures made like fancy ribbons. They were manufactured by Thomas Stevens of Coventry, England, and became popular in 1862. Most are marked *Woven in silk by Thomas Stevens* or were mounted on a cardboard that tells the story of the Stevengraph. Other similar ribbon pictures have been made in England and Germany.

Picture, Children Cross River, Hold Hands, P. Tarrant, 12 1/4 x 10 In. 675.00
Picture, Crystal Palace, Gold Frame, 1880s, 2 1/2 x 5 1/4 In. 300.00
Picture, Family Plays Tug Of War, Fred Morgan, 17 x 12 1/2 In. 675.00
Picture, Tea Party, Children, Near Dock, Neyret Fre'res, F. Morgan, 17 x 12 1/2 In. 675.00
The Old Oak Bucket, T. Stevens, 11 x 2 1/2 In., 18 x 10-In. Frame 165.00

STEVENS & WILLIAMS of Stourbridge, England, made many types of glass, including layered, etched, cameo, and art glass, between the 1830s and 1930s. Some pieces are signed *S & W.* Many pieces are decorated with flowers, leaves, and other designs based on nature.

Basket, Amber, Applied Strawberries, Feet, Handle, 5 x 5 1/2 In. 403.00
Basket, Blue, Applied Red & White Flower, Clear Rigaree, Thorn Handles, 6 x 11 In. ... 532.00
Basket, Double Cornucopia, Pink, Clear Rigaree Petals, Rope Twist Handle, 12 In. 1456.00
Basket, Mother-Of-Pearl, Herringbone, Translucent Aqua, Over Crimson, 2 1/2 x 4 1/2 In. 504.00
Bowl, Mother-Of-Pearl, Turquoise, Zipper, 19th Century, 3 1/2 x 4 1/2 In. 690.00
Bowl, Rose Over Cream, Over Rose, Applied Fern Leaves, Footed, 3 x 5 1/2 In. 144.00
Creamer, Underplate, Rosaline, 2 3/4 x 4 In. 104.00
Ewer, Opalescent, Green Handle, Applied Pink Flower, 8 3/4 In. 127.00
Parfait, Green Jade, Alabaster Foot, Waffer Connector, 6 In. 58.00
Rose Bowl, Apricot Over Blue, Mother-Of-Pearl, Swirl Satin, Ruffled Edge, 4 3/4 In. 1680.00
Rose Bowl, Pink, Cased Swirl, Clear Applied Feet, Ruffled, 4 1/2 In. 210.00
Vase, Amberina, Swirled Cone, Applied Coiled Snakes, c.1890, 14 3/4 In., Pair 575.00
Vase, Blue Plums, Pink Leaves On Applied Amber Handle, Oval, Ruffled Edge, 5 In. 123.00
Vase, Cylinder, Shore Birds & Geometric Cutting, Signed, 12 In. 980.00

Vase, Green Mother-Of-Pearl, Diagonal Swirl, 19th Century, 8 In. 2530.00
Vase, Light Green & Pink Swirled Stripes, Clear Base, 8 In. 200.00
Vase, Mother-Of-Pearl, Pink & Green, Diagonal Swirl, Pink Interior, Shouldered, 7 In. . . . 1790.00
Vase, Mother-Of-Pearl, Rose To Yellow, Diagonal Swirl, 1800s, 7 In. 1150.00
Vase, Pink Over Opal, Applied Clear Leaf, 5 In. 60.00
Vase, Tree Trunk, Opalescent Chartreuse, Applied Roots At Base, 4 In., Pair 90.00
Vase, White Over Pink, Applied Amber Rigaree, 6 1/2 In., Pair 120.00

STIEGEL TYPE glass is listed here. It is almost impossible to be sure a
piece was actually made by Stiegel, so the knowing collector refers to
this glass as *Stiegel type*. Henry William Stiegel, a colorful immigrant
to the colonies, started his first factory in Pennsylvania in 1763. He
remained in business until 1774. Glassware was made in a style popular in Europe at that time and was similar to the glass of many other
makers. It was made of clear or colored glass and was decorated with
enamel colors, mold blown designs, or etching.

Bottle, Multicolored, Bird With Blue Wings, Pewter Collar, Pontil, 6 In. 300.00
Bottle, Multicolored, Building, Bird, Flag, Sheared Mouth, Pewter Collar, Pontil, 7 In. 240.00
Bottle, Multicolored, Man In Coat, Pewter Collar, Pontil, 7 In. 190.00
Bottle, Multicolored, Man With Glass, Sheared Mouth, Pewter Collar, 6 3/4 In. 1400.00
Bottle, Multicolored, Man With Glass, Sheared Mouth, Pontil, 5 In. 160.00
Cologne, Multicolored Enamel, Birds On Heart, Flowers, 4 1/2 In. 165.00
Flask, Deep Amethyst, Pattern-Molded, Diamond & Daisy, 5 1/4 In. 4510.00
Tankard, Engraved Sunflowers, Applied Handle, Flared Foot, 6 1/2 In. 600.00
Tankard, White Opalescent, Enameled Man Holding Cane & Flowers, 6 1/2 In. 675.00
Tumbler, Engraved Band Of Flowers, Sheared Rim, Pontil, 18th Century, 5 3/4 In. 240.00
Tumbler, Engraved Basket & Flowers, Sheared Rim, Pontil, 18th Century, 6 1/8 In. 275.00
Tumbler, Engraved Bird With Sunburst, Sheared Rim, Pontil, 18th Century, 5 1/2 In. 500.00

STONE includes those articles made of stones not listed elsewhere in
this book. Micro mosaics (small decorative design, made by setting
pieces of stone into a pattern), urns, vases, and other pieces made of
natural stones are listed here. Alabaster, Jade, Malachite, Marble, and
Soapstone are in their own categories. Stoneware is pottery and is
listed in the Stoneware category.

Bust, Woman, Flowing Hair, Signed, Lembke, c.1935, 15 x 10 x 8 In. 3825.00
Figure, Krishna, Playing Flute, India, c.1900, 20 In. 290.00
Figure, Lion, Seated, Holding Shield, Hand Carved, c.1890, 42 In., Pair 6720.00
Figure, Squirrel, c.1900, 22 In., Pair 546.00
Frame, Carved, Border, Pierced Designs, Birds, Flowers, Chinese, 12 x 9 In. 325.00
Head, Bodhisattva, Limestone, Ebonized Wood Plinth, Chinese, c.1900, 12 1/2 In. 1610.00
Head, Buddha, Sandstone, Ayuthia Style, 20th Century, 15 In. 3884.00
Head, Guanyin, Gray, Chinese, c.1900, 11 1/2 In. 633.00
Mosaic, Venice Canal Scene, Glass, Carved Frame, Gilt, 19th Century, 4 x 7 In. 920.00
Owl, Limestone, Carved, Square Crossed-Out Eyes, Signed E. Reed, 5 3/8 In. 250.00
Panel, Round, Flowers, Pietra Dura, 38 In. 4183.00
Plaque, Bird On Fruited Branch, Pietra Dura, Gilt Wood Frame, 16 x 12 In., Pair 4481.00
Plaque, Urn Of Tulips, Painted, 9 1/2 x 11 3/4 In. 8800.00

STONEWARE is a coarse, glazed, and fired potter's ceramic that is used
to make crocks, jugs, bowls, etc. It is often decorated with cobalt blue
decorations. In the nineteenth and early twentieth centuries, potters
often decorated crocks with blue numbers indicating the size of the
container. A "2" meant 2 gallons. Stoneware is still being made.

Amphora, Celadon Glazed, Dragon Head Handles, Chinese, Tang Dynasty, 16 In. 1840.00
Basket, Lead Glaze, Earthenware, Blue, Green, Signed, Teague's Pottery, c.1915, 7 In. 415.00
Batter Jar, Sponge, Lid, 2 Qt. 450.00
Batter Jug, Cobalt Blue Flowers, Signed, Evan R. Jones, Pittston, Pa., 6 Qt. 550.00
Batter Jug, Cobalt Blue Tulip, Salt Glaze, Wire Bail Handle, 8 1/2 In. 440.00
Batter Jug, Cover, Cobalt Blue Wreath, Leaf Slip, Gal. 825.00
Bean Pot, Lid, Embossed Boston Baked Beans, Blue, White Salt Glaze, 7 1/2 In. 305.00
Bean Pot, Relief, Boston Baked Beans, Children Eating Beans, Handle, 10 In. 110.00
Bottle, Alkaline Glaze, Cone Shape, 8 In. 66.00

Bottle, Alkaline Glaze, Impressed Newton & Co., California Beer, 10 In. 44.00
Bottle, Blue Accent, Impressed, George Stang, Ribbed, 10 1/2 In.   44.00
Bottle, Blue Accents, Jones & Co., Impressed, 11 1/2 In. 33.00
Bottle, Bristol Glaze, Impressed, Blue Accent, G.A. Potter, 9 1/2 In. 55.00
Bottle, Bristol Glaze, Red Sponge, Impressed Mohawk, Handle, 9 In. 66.00
Bottle, Brushed Blue Accents, 10 In. 55.00
Bottle, Cobalt Blue, Stoneware, Qt. 72.00
Bottle, Impressed, Blue Accents, John Fields 77.00
Bottle, Impressed, Blue Accents, McHeald, 9 1/2 In. 33.00
Bottle, Impressed, Gardner, Brown Alkaline Glaze, 6 1/2 In. 44.00
Bottle, Ocher Accents, 10 1/2 In. 77.00
Bowl, Basket Weave & Flower, Blue & White 88.00
Bowl, Blue & White Sponge, 9 In. 155.00
Bowl, Celadon, Leaves, 4 Flying Cranes, Medallion, Chrysanthemum, Korea, 7 1/2 In. . . .   2645.00
Bowl, Chinese Blue Glaze, Signed, Ben Owen, 1940, 3 x 9 1/4 In. 440.00
Bowl, Cream, Cobalt Blue Edge, Crush Glass, E. A. Hilton Shop, 1920s, 1 3/8 x 5 1/2 In. .   145.00
Bowl, Fruit, Glazed & Sponged, Cream, Green & Brown, 12 1/2 x 3 1/2 In. 120.00
Bowl, Leaf, Flower Band, Brown, Green, Black, Ivory, Charles M. Hauder, 3 x 6 In. 560.00
Bowl, Milk, Flowers, Solomon Bell, 2 Qt. 1155.00
Bowl, Salt Glaze, Blue & White, Apricot, 3 3/4 x 9 1/4 In. 99.00
Bowl, Wheel Thrown, Umber Underglaze, Sponged Spiral, John Foster, 4 x 10 1/2 In. . . .   410.00
Canister, Sugar, Wildflowers, Blue, White Salt Glaze, 5 3/4 In.   110.00
Chamber Pot, Coiled Snake, Fangs, Brown Glaze, Albert Hodge, N.C., 4 x 12 In. 275.00
Churn, Blue Flower, Blue Swags, Wooden Dasher, Cylinder, c.1850, 2 Gal., 15 1/2 In. . . .   440.00
Churn, Cobalt Blue Bird, Stylized Flower Banner, Boston, Mass., 3 Gal. 1060.00
Churn, Cover, Cobalt Blue Squiggled Line, 5 Gal. 305.00
Churn, Cylinder, Fern, Wooden Dasher, Burger & Co., Rochester, c.1877, 4 Gal., 16 In. . . .   580.00
Churn, Dotted Goose Sitting On Flower, Ithaca, c.1880, 5 Gal., 18 1/2 In. 1870.00
Churn, Double Flower, Navy Blue, John Burger, Rochester, c.1865, 3 Gal., 16 In. 3410.00
Churn, Olive, Alkaline Glaze, 3 Handles, Early 20th Century, 19 In. 99.00
Churn, Orchid, White's, Utica, c.1865, 3 Gal., 15 In. 990.00
Churn, Ribbed Flower, Blue, J. Burger, Rochester, c.1880, 6 Gal., 21 In. 963.00
Churn, Stylized Dotted Flowers, White's, Utica, c.1865, 5 Gal., 17 1/2 In. 530.00
Cookie Jar, Lid, Bristol Glaze, Blue Accent Bands, 8 In. 55.00
Cookie Jar, Red, White Flowers, Blue, Handles 68.00
Cream Riser, Masonic Emblem, Salt Glaze, J.F. Brower, 19th Century, 9 1/8 x 11 1/2 In. .   305.00
Cream Riser, Salt Glaze, White Gray, Early 20th Century, 7 x 9 1/2 In. 22.00
Crock, 2 Bands, Brown Spatter, Streaked, Lug Handles, 19 1/2 In. 470.00
Crock, Ayers Bros., Jobbers Crockery & Glass, Stamford, Conn., c.1870, 2 Gal., 9 In. 175.00
Crock, Bird On Branch, Cobalt Blue, New York Pottery, 2 Gal.   195.00
Crock, Bird On Branch, New York Stoneware, 3 Gal. 330.00
Crock, Bird On Branch, Stamped, New York Stoneware Co., c.1880, 5 Gal., 12 In. 525.00
Crock, Bird On Plume, Tail, Dots, Adam Claire, Poughkeepsie, c.1880, 3 Gal., 10 In. 305.00
Crock, Bird On Stump, Riedinger & Caire, Poughkeepsie, c.1870, 2 Gal., 11 1/2 In. 1020.00
Crock, Bird On Twig, Blue, Haxstun, Ottman & Co., Ft. Edward, c.1870, 3 Gal., 10 In. . . .   220.00
Crock, Bird On Twig, Haxstun, Ottman & Co., Ft. Edward, N.Y., c.1880, 4 Gal., 11 1/2 In.   495.00
Crock, Bird, J. Fisher & Co., Lyons, c.1880, 2 Gal., 9 In. 715.00
Crock, Bird, Taunton, Mass., 19th Century, 1 1/2 Gal. 1210.00
Crock, Bird, White's, Utica, N.Y., 5 Gal. 440.00
Crock, Blue Bands, Salt Glaze, Qt. 50.00
Crock, Blue Crowing Rooster, Cinnamon, c.1865, 4 Gal., 11 In.   688.00
Crock, Blue Dandelion, A.K. Ballard, Burlington, Vt., 2 Ear Handles, 2 Gal. 185.00
Crock, Blue Dotted Flowers, S. Hart & Son, Fulton, c.1877, 2 Gal., 9 1/2 In. 150.00
Crock, Blue Flower, Semi-Oval Shape, Newport, 1 1/2 Gal. 605.00
Crock, Blue Flowers, John Burger, Rochester, N.Y., 3 Gal. 4125.00
Crock, Blue Orchids, Leaf, N.A. White & Son, Utica, c.1870, 2 Gal., 8 1/2 In. 210.00
Crock, Blue Rose Petal, c.1880, 5 Gal., 12 1/2 In. 305.00
Crock, Blue Wreath, Marked S & M, c.1870, 2 Gal., 9 1/2 In. 305.00
Crock, Blue, 5-Leaf Fern, J. Burger, Jr., Rochester, c.1885, 4 Gal., 11 In. 275.00
Crock, Blue, Crushed Vine Flowers, N. Clark Jr., Athens, c.1850, 3 Gal., 10 In. 305.00
Crock, Blue, Dotted Bird, J. Burger, Jr., Rochester, c.1885, 3 Gal., 10 1/2 In. 7425.00
Crock, Blue, Dotted Leaf, Bullard & Scott, Cambridge, Mass., c.1870, Gal., 7 1/2 In. 360.00
Crock, Blue, Flowers, N. Clark Jr., Athens, c.1850, Gal., 7 In. 580.00

Crock, Bull's-Eye, Blue Slip, Lamson & Swasey, Portland, Me., c.1881, 6 Gal., 13 1/2 In.   220.00
Crock, Butter, Flowers, Blue, Gal. 495.00
Crock, Butter, Lid, White Bristol Glaze, Blue Accent, Stenciled Butter, 9 1/2 x 4 In. 120.00
Crock, Butterfly, Salt Glaze, Blue & White 99.00
Crock, Cabbage Flower, Pail Shape, John Burger, Rochester, c.1865, 4 Gal., 12 1/2 In. ... 1760.00
Crock, Cake, Cobalt Blue Flowers, Leaf, 2 Handles, Signed, John Bell, 4 1/4 x 7 In. 1595.00
Crock, Cake, Flowers, Leaf Border, Cobalt, Salt Glaze, Lug Handles, 5 1/4 In. 440.00
Crock, Cake, Lid, Flowers, Blue 415.00
Crock, Cherry & Leaves, Ear Handles, Pottery Works, N.Y., 11 In. 690.00
Crock, Chicken Pecking Corn, 3 Gal. ....470.00 to 495.00
Crock, Chicken Pecking Corn, 4 Gal. 1045.00
Crock, Chicken Pecking Corn, Riedinger & Caire, Poughkeepsie, c.1870, 3 Gal., 9 1/2 In.   605.00
Crock, Cobalt Blue Bird On Branch, Salt Glaze, Lug Handles, N.Y., c.1870, 3 Gal., 9 In. . 765.00
Crock, Cobalt Blue Bird On Stump, Riedinger & Caire, N.Y., 2 Gal. 1100.00
Crock, Cobalt Blue Bird, F.T. Wright, Taunton, Mass., 19th Century, 6 Gal. 920.00
Crock, Cobalt Blue Bird, Flowering Branch, Late 19th Century, 5 Gal. 560.00
Crock, Cobalt Blue Bird, West Troy Pottery, 3 Gal., 10 1/2 In. 370.00
Crock, Cobalt Blue Butterfly, Salt Glaze, Lug Handles, New York City, c.1873, 8 In. 1060.00
Crock, Cobalt Blue Double Flower, N. Clark, Jr., Athens, c.1850, 3 Gal., 10 In. 175.00
Crock, Cobalt Blue Fern, Fuchsia Slip, Oval, Ear Handles, Remmy, Philad., 3 Gal. 440.00
Crock, Cobalt Blue Floral Sprig, Salt Glaze, Lug Handles, c.1870, 7 5/8 In. 325.00
Crock, Cobalt Blue Flower, Gray, c.1870, Gal., 9 In. 200.00
Crock, Cobalt Blue Flower, Tan, Free-Form, Incised Lines, Impressed 2, 8 x 11 1/2 In. ... 220.00
Crock, Cobalt Blue Flowers, Applied Handles, Salt Glaze, 19th Century, 12 In. 480.00
Crock, Cobalt Blue Flowers, Buds, Leaves, Bulbous, Ear Handle, Utica, N.Y., 9 1/4 In. ... 385.00
Crock, Cobalt Blue Flowers, Bulbous, Ear Handles, 2 Gal., 9 3/4 In. 715.00
Crock, Cobalt Blue Flowers, Leaves, Ear Handles, Signed, Cowden & Wilcox, Gal. 470.00
Crock, Cobalt Blue Flowers, Leaves, Ear Handles, Rochester, N.Y., 2 Gal., 11 In. 1320.00
Crock, Cobalt Blue Flowers, Plumes, Handles, H.C. Smith, Gal., 7 3/8 x 7 In. 2100.00
Crock, Cobalt Blue Flowers, Splayed Edge, Ear Handles, 5 3/4 x 9 1/4 In. 660.00
Crock, Cobalt Blue Leaf Slip, Ear Handles, Remmy, Philad., 3 Gal. 220.00
Crock, Cobalt Blue Leaf Stencil, James Hamilton & Co., Greensboro, Pa., 6 x 9 1/2 In. .. 195.00
Crock, Cobalt Blue Lovebirds, S. Hart, Fulton, New York, 3 Gal. 825.00
Crock, Cobalt Blue Oval, W. Roberts, 2 Gal. 660.00
Crock, Cobalt Blue Palm Tree, 3 Gal. 760.00
Crock, Cobalt Blue Slip Bird On Branch, Salt Glaze, 2 Closed Handles, 3 Gal., 10 1/4 In. . 475.00
Crock, Cobalt Blue Slip House, 2 Closed Handles, A.O. Whittemore, Havana, N.Y., 2 Gal. 1680.00
Crock, Cobalt Blue Slip, Quilled, Wilcox & Cowden Harrisburg, Pa., 20 In. 575.00
Crock, Cobalt Blue Stencil, Salt Glaze, Qt. 500.00
Crock, Cobalt Blue Stylized Feather, Bullard & Scott, Cambridgeport, Ma., 2 Gal. 160.00
Crock, Cobalt Blue Stylized Flowers, 2 Ear Handles, Albany, N.Y., 13 x 13 In. 250.00
Crock, Cobalt Blue Stylized Flowers, Salt Glaze, Lug Handles, 3 Gal. 440.00
Crock, Cobalt Blue Triple Orchid, N.A. White & Son, Utica, c.1870, 5 Gal., 12 1/2 In. ... 745.00
Crock, Cobalt Blue Tulip, Freehand, 2 Handles, Inscribed, Damson, 5 3/4 In. 5060.00
Crock, Cobalt Blue Tulips, Swags, 2 Ear Handles, R.C.R., Philadelphia, 1859-1900, 16 In. 1100.00
Crock, Cobalt Blue, Gray Tan, Open Handles, Germany, c.1890, 10 In. 180.00
Crock, Cobalt Blue, Handles, OL & AK Ballard, Burlington, VT., 1800s, 3 Gal. 230.00
Crock, Dotted Long Fish, W. Hart Odgensburg, c.1860, 5 Gal., 12 1/2 In. 3740.00
Crock, Fern, Fuchsia, Cobalt Blue Slip, Signed, D.P. Shenfelder, Reading, Pa., 3 Gal. 250.00
Crock, Fish Incised, New York, c.1830, 2 Gal., 11 1/2 In. 1320.00
Crock, Flower & Fern Leaf, Sugar Valley, Pa., 1 1/2 Gal. 330.00
Crock, Flowers, Blue, Brushed Plumes, Ingell Pottery, Taunton, c.1850, Gal., 7 1/2 In. ... 165.00
Crock, Flowers, E.W. Farrington & Co., Elmira, c.1880, 2 Gal., 9 In. 210.00
Crock, Flowers, Lug Handles, J.H. Dipple, 5 Gal. 550.00
Crock, Flowers, Semi-Oval, Manson & Russel, Gal. 495.00
Crock, Flowers, Semi-Oval, Stamped R.C.R., Phila., 4 Gal. 330.00
Crock, Flowers, Slip Blue Face, Albany, c.1860, 2 Gal., 9 1/2 In. 910.00
Crock, Flowers, Vine Design, Prudent & Olcott, N.Y., c.1870, 4 Gal., 10 1/2 In. 200.00
Crock, Grape, Cowden & Wilcox, 2 Gal. 495.00
Crock, Paddletail Bird, N. A. White & Son, 2 Gal. 715.00
Crock, Patriotic, The Union Forever, 3 Gal. 825.00
Crock, Ribbed Flower, Arrows, c.1860, 5 Gal., 12 1/2 In. 120.00
Crock, Roadrunner Bird On Branch, Number 4 In Wreath, 4 Gal. 1045.00

Crock, Slip Blue Thistle Flower, Blue, C.W. Braun, Buffalo, c.1870, 4 Gal., 11 In. 275.00
Crock, Slip, Fruit, Arrows, A.O. Whittemore, Havana, c.1870, 5 Gal., 11 1/2 In. 635.00
Crock, Stemmed Thistle, White's, Utica, c.1865, Gal., 7 1/2 In. 165.00
Crock, Storage, Cobalt Blue Flowers, Leaves, 10 1/4 In. 220.00
Crock, Storage, Cobalt Blue Leaves, Flowers, Bulbous, Ear Handles, Gal., 9 In. 605.00
Crock, Storage, Stenciled, Hasslebeck, Cheese Co., Buffalo, N.Y., c.1900, 6 In. 11.00
Crock, Triple Flowers, 1 1/2 Gal. 1320.00
Crock, Trotting Horse, N.Y., 2 Gal. 2530.00
Crock, Tulip, Burger & Co., Rochester, c.1877, 4 Gal., 11 1/2 In. 415.00
Crock, Tulips, 3, Incised Lines, Ear Handles, 10 1/2 In. 330.00
Crock, Wreath, Pail Shape, John Burger, Rochester, c.1865, 2 Gal., 8 1/2 In. 220.00
Cuspidor, Blue, White, Rose Panels 83.00
Cuspidor, Cobalt Blue Leaves, Signed, Cowden & Wilcox, Pa., 3 1/2 x 6 3/4 In. 470.00
Figurine, Dog, Spaniel, Sitting, Albany Slip Glaze, Peoria Pottery, 7 In. 88.00
Figurine, Lion, Reclining, Brown Alkaline Glaze, c.1870, 5 In. 145.00
Figurine, Pig, Olive Glaze, Marked, Graduation Pig, Clete Meaders, 8 1/4 x 9 1/4 In. 360.00
Figurine, Rooster, Cobalt Glaze, Speckled Green, Edwin Meaders, 15 1/2 In. 1210.00
Figurine, Rooster, Pedestal, Feldspathic Glaze, Clay Eyes, 1900s, 12 5/8 x 11 In. 360.00
Figurine, Rooster, Red, White, Green, Brown Glaze, R. Meaders, 8 3/4 x 14 1/2 In. 470.00
Flowerpot, Underplate, Blue Band, Cowden & Co., 2 Gal. 275.00
Glass, Pilsner, Blue Accent Bands, Salt Glaze, Impressed Crystal Spring Lager, 5 3/4 In. ... 155.00
Humidor, Lid, Relief Hunting Dog, Blue Accent, Bristol Glaze, 6 1/2 In. 250.00
Inkwell, Desk Top, 3 Hole, Cobalt Blue, c.1839, 1 1/2 x 3 In. 440.00
Jar, 2 Swirled Bands, Oval, Flared Rim, Lug Handles, c.1850, 16 In. 690.00
Jar, Alkaline Glaze, Applied Lug Handles, Stamped DS, Mid 1800s, 14 1/4 In. 2970.00
Jar, Alkaline Glaze, Egg Shape, Dragon Design, Chinese, c.1860, 27 x 24 In. 635.00
Jar, Blue Floral, Oval, Lug Handles, 2 Gal. 495.00
Jar, Blue Flower, Oval, P. Mugler & Co., Buffalo, c.1870, 2 Gal., 14 In. 825.00
Jar, Blue Highlights, Bulbous Shape, Ear Handle, 8 1/4 In. 305.00
Jar, Blue Impressed Name, Swan & States, Stonington, c.1830, Gal., 9 In. 190.00
Jar, Blue Leaf Design, Cylinder Shape, Mottled Clay, c.1830, 2 Gal., 13 In. 33.00
Jar, Blue Leaf, Blue, c.1850, 1/2 Gal., 11 1/2 In. 210.00
Jar, Blue Script, Lyons Oval, 2 Gal. 200.00
Jar, Blue Swags, c.1850, 2 Gal., 13 In. 77.00
Jar, Blue, Bowers Three Thistles Snuff, c.1880, 3 Gal., 14 In. 470.00
Jar, Bulbous, Vine, Lug Handles, Gal. 470.00
Jar, Cactus, Gal., 11 In. 88.00
Jar, Canning, Bird Amidst Sweeping Branches, Blue, Charlestown, c.1850, 3 Gal., 13 In. .. 825.00
Jar, Canning, Blue Flower, Blue Accents, Lyons, c.1860, Gal., 10 In. 145.00
Jar, Canning, Blue Lines, 2 Qt., 8 1/2 In. 365.00
Jar, Canning, Blue Swag, Flowers, c.1840, Qt., 7 In. 360.00
Jar, Canning, Chocolate Brown Glaze, c.1850, 1/2 Gal., 7 In. 175.00
Jar, Canning, Cobalt Blue, Lattice, Dots, Hannah Machet, 1811, 3 3/4 In. 3575.00
Jar, Canning, Cobalt, Salt Glaze, Commeraws Stoneware, N.Y.C., c.1790, 9 5/8 In. 2230.00
Jar, Canning, Comb, Elephant Head, Blue, Cortland, c.1860, 2 Gal., 11 In 440.00
Jar, Canning, Cover, Lion Face, W.A. MacQuoid & Co., N.Y., c.1850, 1 1/2 Gal., 11 In. .. 2420.00
Jar, Canning, Dancing Flowers, John Burger, Rochester, c.1865, 2 Gal., 11 1/2 In. 385.00
Jar, Canning, Fat Bird On Twig, Stamp, E.W. Hall, Boston, c.1870, 4 Gal., 16 In. 415.00
Jar, Canning, Flower, Cobalt Blue Accent, Bristol Glaze, c.1870, Gal., 10 In. 99.00
Jar, Canning, Flower, Ribbed, Blue, F. Stetzenmeyer & Co., Rochester, 2 Gal., 12 In. 4070.00
Jar, Canning, Flying Eagle, Blue, c.1850, 11 In. 1485.00
Jar, Canning, Oval, 4 Cobalt Blue Lines, 7 7/8 In. 220.00
Jar, Canning, Salt Glaze, Aqua Kiln Arch Drips, Late 19th Century, 10 7/8 In. 195.00
Jar, Canning, Stenciled, Bell Shape, Conrad & Co., Gal. 250.00
Jar, Canning, Stenciled, Hamilton & Co., Gal. 145.00
Jar, Canning, Stenciled, Western Pa., Wax Seal, Qt. 630.00
Jar, Canning, Swag, c.1850, 1/2 Gal., 8 1/2 In. 110.00
Jar, Canning, Tulip, Blue, J. Mantel, Penn Yan, c.1860, 2 Gal., 11 In. 165.00
Jar, Cobalt Blue Leaves, Qt., 7 1/4 In. 255.00
Jar, Cobalt Blue, Cover, Applied Handles, Cowden & Wilcox, 3 Gal. 13860.00
Jar, Cobalt Blue, Salt Glaze, 2 Groove Top Lug Handles, 11 1/2 In. 165.00
Jar, Cobalt Blue, Salt Glaze, 3 Rows Loops, Cortland Factory, c.1870, 7 3/8 In. 440.00
Jar, Cobalt Blue, Salt Glaze, Bird On Branch, Wide Mouth, Lug Handles, 2 Gal., 9 In. 590.00

Jar, Cobalt Blue, Salt Glaze, Bird On Branch, William Roberts Pottery, c.1882, 7 In. 2000.00
Jar, Cobalt Blue, Salt Glaze, N. Loundes Manufactor Petersburg Va., c.1840, 17 In. 7050.00
Jar, Cobalt Blue, Salt Glaze, Ottoman Bros. & Co., Fort Edward, N.Y., c.1860, 11 3/8 In. . . 295.00
Jar, Cobalt Blue, Salt Glaze, Triple Circle, Leaves, Open Loop Handle, 11 3/8 In. 2230.00
Jar, Cover, Pig Figure, Eating From Trough, Germany, 6 1/2 x 6 In. 115.00
Jar, Double Groove Pattern, Cylindrical, Flared Rim, Sloping Shoulder, 9 1/2 In. 160.00
Jar, Floral Star, Fenton & Hancock, Vermont, 3 Gal. 5500.00
Jar, Flowers, Bulbous, Wm. Moyer, Harrisburg, 2 Gal. 3300.00
Jar, Flowers, Cowden & Wilcox, Gal. 745.00
Jar, Freehand Decoration, Soldier Holding Rifle, 5 Gal., 15 3/4 In. 15400.00
Jar, Freehand Decoration, Woman Holding Garment, Peacock, 5 Gal., 15 3/4 In. 20900.00
Jar, Hamilton & Jones Star Pottery, Greensboro, Pa., 20 Gal. 9350.00
Jar, Lid, Brown Mottled Glaze, c.1870, Qt., 7 In. 44.00
Jar, Lid, Salt Glaze, 19th Century, 11 1/2 In. 880.00
Jar, Lid, Salt Glaze, Lug Handles, Incised Rings, Arched Rim Top, 20th Century, 6 1/2 In. 110.00
Jar, Olive, Alkaline Glaze, 2 Handles, James Franklin Seagle, c.1880, 13 1/4 In. 1760.00
Jar, Pot Of Flowers, Barrel Shape, Gal. 385.00
Jar, Ribbed, Drooping Orchid, White's Utica, c.1865, 3 In. 525.00
Jar, Rolled Rim, Lug Handles, Stamped, 4 Gal., 14 1/4 In. 2970.00
Jar, Salt Glaze, 2 Handles, Signed, N. Fox, Mid 19th Century, 14 1/2 In. 1045.00
Jar, Salt Glaze, Lug Handles, E.S. Craven, 19th Century, 16 3/4 x 39 In. 825.00
Jar, Slip Blue Daisy, C.W. Braun, Buffalo, c.1870, 2 Gal., 11 In. 110.00
Jar, Slip Flowers, John Burger, Rochester, 2 Gal. 605.00
Jar, Soda, Brownish Olive, Alkaline Glaze, Joseph D. Johnson, 1870s, 11 In. 825.00
Jar, Stamped, Oval, Humiston & Cummings, Gal. 440.00
Jar, Tulip, Oval, c.1850, 1/2 Gal., 6 1/4 In. 800.00
Jug, 3 Incised Hearts, Egg Shape, Marked, Charlestown, 15 1/2 In. 660.00
Jug, A.B. Wheeler & Co., 69 Broad St., Boston, Mass., c.1870, Gal., 11 In. 470.00
Jug, Abstract Finger Leaf, Brown, 5 Gal. 495.00
Jug, Albany Glaze, Little Brown Jug, Handle, 1876, 3 In. 165.00
Jug, Bird In Rain, 2 Gal. 330.00
Jug, Bird On Branch, Cherries, c.1880, 4 Gal., 18 In. 330.00
Jug, Bird On Branch, White Bristol Glaze, c.1880, 2 Gal., 14 In. 275.00
Jug, Bird On Dotted Plume, Blue, New York Stoneware Co., c.1880, 4 Gal., 17 In. 1155.00
Jug, Bird On Scrolled Branch, Cobalt Blue, Fort Edwards, New York, Gal., 12 In. 440.00
Jug, Bird On Twig, J.A. & C.W. Underwood, Ft. Edward, c.1870, Gal., 12 In. 360.00
Jug, Bird, Dean Foster & Co., 2 Gal. 580.00
Jug, Bird, Paddle-Tail, Handle, N.A. White, Utica, N.Y., 4 Gal. 1265.00
Jug, Blue & Slip Plume, Blue Accents, F. Norton, Worcester, Ma., c.1870, 2 Gal., 15 In. . . 165.00
Jug, Blue Slip, Marked 1867, Gal., 11 1/2 In. 415.00
Jug, Blue Slip, Wreath, Marked 1866, C. Hart & Son, Sheburne, c.1866, 2 Gal., 13 In. . . . 855.00
Jug, Blue Wash, Stamped, Oval, Dickinson & Bigelow, Gal. 120.00
Jug, Brown & White Glaze, Blue Letters, Edwin T. Moul, York, Pa., 3 In. 440.00
Jug, Brown & White Glaze, W. Foust Distiller, Glen Rock, Pa., 4 1/4 In. 190.00
Jug, Brown & White, Patented Closure Top, Gal. 33.00
Jug, Brown, Speckled, Country House, Vermont Onion River 9.00
Jug, Cabbage Flower, Blue, N. Clark & Co., Rochester, c.1850, 3 Gal., 17 In. 580.00
Jug, Caramel, Straw, Feldspathic Glaze, Edith Harwell, c.1936, 3 3/4 In. 220.00
Jug, Cobalt 3, Wreath, Handle, Harrington & Berger, Rochester, 19th Century, 3 Gal. 490.00
Jug, Cobalt Blue Bird, Full-Bodied, Leaf, Cowden & Wilcox, Harrisburg, Penna., 2 Gal. . . 4400.00
Jug, Cobalt Blue Bird, Long Tail, Perched On Tree Stump, White's, Utica, 10 3/4 In. 935.00
Jug, Cobalt Blue Bird, New York Pottery, 2 Gal. . . . . 195.00 to 385.00
Jug, Cobalt Blue Bird, On Tree, Cowden & Wilcox, Harrisburg, Penna., 3 Gal. 3575.00
Jug, Cobalt Blue Blooming Flower, T. Harrington, c.1860, 3 Gal., 16 In. 440.00
Jug, Cobalt Blue Feather Wreath, Salt Glaze, Impressed 6l, 6 Liters, 15 In. 340.00
Jug, Cobalt Blue Floral, Salt Glaze, Oval, Impressed 6, 15 In. 225.00
Jug, Cobalt Blue Flower, B. Lent Caldwell, c.1825, 2 Gal., 14 In. 2640.00
Jug, Cobalt Blue Flower, Feathery Leaves, Strap Handle, Egg Shape, 11 In. 275.00
Jug, Cobalt Blue Flowers & 8, Oval, Signed, Wm. Moyer, Harrisburg, 3 Gal. 4290.00
Jug, Cobalt Blue Flowers, Burger Bro's. & Co., Rochester, N.Y., 2 Gal., 14 1/4 In. 550.00
Jug, Cobalt Blue Flowers, Egg Shape, Signed, Moyer, Harrisburg, Pa., Gal. 1045.00
Jug, Cobalt Blue Flowers, J. Burger, Rochester, N.Y., 3 Gal., 15 1/2 In. 715.00
Jug, Cobalt Blue Flowers, J.B. Magee, Ithaca, N.Y., Gal., 10 1/4 In. 525.00

Jug, Cobalt Blue Flowers, JH, Ottman Bros. & Co., Fort Edward, N.Y., 2 Gal. 260.00
Jug, Cobalt Blue Flowers, Leaves, E.W. Farrington & Co., Elmira, N.Y., 2 Gal., 13 In. ... 495.00
Jug, Cobalt Blue Flowers, Leaves, S.T. Brewer, Havana, N.Y., Gal., 10 3/4 In. 305.00
Jug, Cobalt Blue Flowers, Marked Frank B. Norton, Worcester, Mass., 2 Gal. 315.00
Jug, Cobalt Blue Highlights, Bulbous, Gibson & Co., Reading, Penna., 2 Gal., 13 In. 770.00
Jug, Cobalt Blue Leaf, Egg Shape, T. Harrington, Lyons, 18 1/2 In. 220.00
Jug, Cobalt Blue Leaves, Beescape, Stamped F.B. Norton & Co., Worcester, Mass., 4 Gal. 450.00
Jug, Cobalt Blue Leaves, Signed, Cowden & Wilcox, Harrisburg, Pa., Gal. 440.00
Jug, Cobalt Blue Plume, F. Norton, Worcester, Ma., c.1870, Gal., 11 In. 220.00
Jug, Cobalt Blue Running Bird, Fan Tail, Impressed, White's, Utica, 2, 14 1/2 In. 550.00
Jug, Cobalt Blue Script, J.D. Clasky, 98 Fulton St., Brooklyn, N.Y., c.1870, 3 Gal., 16 In. . 165.00
Jug, Cobalt Blue Slip Bird, Flower, Handle, Impressed, 4 Gal., 17 3/8 In. 895.00
Jug, Cobalt Blue Slip Flower, Dark Gray, Stamped, Oval, 1842, 3 Gal., 14 In. 505.00
Jug, Cobalt Blue Slip Letters, Salt Glaze, C. Person's Sons, Buffalo, N.Y., 10 1/2 In. 235.00
Jug, Cobalt Blue Stencil, John Lyons, Corner Beach & South Streets, c.1870, 2 Qt., 9 In. . 210.00
Jug, Cobalt Blue Sunflower Slip, Signed J.H., Easton Pa., 2 Gal. 220.00
Jug, Cobalt Blue Swag, Blue Accent, Oval, G. Heiser, Buffalo, c.1838, 4 Gal., 16 In. 190.00
Jug, Cobalt Blue Swirled Beescape & 4, Salt Glaze, Handle, 4 Gal. 57.00
Jug, Cobalt Blue, Flowers In Urn, Salt Glaze, Lug Handles, c.1829, 11 1/2 In. 1470.00
Jug, Cobalt Blue, Grape Bunch, Applied Strap Handle, 10 1/2 In. 88.00
Jug, Cobalt Blue, Hartford, Conn., 19th Century, 5 Gal. 230.00
Jug, Cobalt Blue, I. Seymour & Co., Troy, c.1825, Gal., 13 1/2 In. 200.00
Jug, Cobalt Blue, Incised Cherry Cluster, Salt Glaze, Strap Handle, c.1820, 13 1/2 In. 825.00
Jug, Cobalt Blue, Incised Male Profile, Salt Glaze, Strap Handle, 1800s, 15 5/8 In. 6463.00
Jug, Cobalt Blue, Incised Tulip, Salt Glaze, Strap Handle, Early 19th Century, 11 1/4 In. ... 1410.00
Jug, Cobalt Blue, Jacob Bennett 122 3rd Ave. Brooklyn, 2 Gal., 14 1/2 In. 175.00
Jug, Cobalt Blue, Leaves, Salt Glaze, F.H. Cowden, 15 In. 235.00
Jug, Cobalt Blue, Salt Glaze, Strap Handle, Ballard & Brothers, c.1872, 11 1/2 In. 480.00
Jug, Devil, Horns, Black Painted Eyebrows, Mustache, Beard, N.C., 16 In. 495.00
Jug, Dotted Bird On Branch, Roberts, Binghamton, N.Y., c.1860, Gal., 11 In. 470.00
Jug, Dotted Leaf, Blue, New York Stoneware Co., c.1880, 2 Gal., 14 In. 210.00
Jug, Dotted Leaf, Blue, New York Stoneware Co., Ft. Edward, c.1880, 3 Gal., 16 In. 525.00
Jug, Dotted Plume, Blue, Ft. Edward Pottery, c.1860, Gal., 11 1/2 In. 220.00
Jug, Double Face, Applied Eyes & Ears, Teeth, 16 In. 1180.00
Jug, Double Flower, Nicholas & Co., 2 Gal. 1100.00
Jug, Double Flowers, Beehive Shape, A. Whittemore, Havana, c.1870, 3 Gal., 14 In. 525.00
Jug, Double Flowers, Blue, Handle, N. Clark Jr., Athens, c.1843, 2 Gal., 13 In. 415.00
Jug, Face, Applied Handles, Teeth, Stamped, 12 1/4 In. 935.00
Jug, Face, Bulging Eyes, Ceramic Teeth, Brown Glaze, Flossie Meaders, 9 1/4 In. ... *Illus* 358.00
Jug, Face, China Teeth, Matte Brown Glaze, A. Teague, Seagrove, N.C., 8 1/4 In. 415.00
Jug, Face, Crushed Glass Glaze, 2 Sides, 2 Handles, Craig, 11 1/2 In. 3700.00
Jug, Face, Crying Eyes, Teeth, Applied Ears, Alkaline-Glaze, Impressed, 10 In. 2200.00
Jug, Face, Ears, Holes, Pursed Lips, Mottled Olive Glaze, Anita Meaders, 10 1/2 In. 200.00
Jug, Face, Eyebrows, Pinched Nose, 5 Teeth, Beard, Mustache, Cole Pottery, 10 1/4 In. .. 660.00
Jug, Face, Pointed Ears, Red Horns & Eyes, Teeth, Brown Glaze, R. Meaders, 9 1/2 In. .. 165.00
Jug, Face, Red Devil, Black Bear, Mustache, 16 In. .... *Illus* 495.00
Jug, Face, Snake, Ceramic Teeth, Bulging Eyes, Man Hanging, Inscribed, 20 In. 605.00
Jug, Face, Wrinkled Loop Ears, Exaggerated Eyebrows, Brown Glaze, N.C., 8 3/4 In. 220.00
Jug, Fat Bird On Twig, Blue, Ottman Bros., Ft. Edward, c.1870, 2 Gal., 14 1/2 In. 745.00
Jug, Fat Bird On Twig, West Troy, c.1880, 2 Gal., 13 In. 155.00
Jug, Flared Mouth, Sloping Shoulder, Handle, c.1860, 7 In. 635.00
Jug, Flower Basket, Cobalt Blue, A.O. Whittemore, Havana, N.Y., 2 Gal. 910.00
Jug, Flower, Blue, White's, Utica, c.1865, Gal., 11 1/2 In. 145.00
Jug, Flower, Havana, N.Y., c.1870, Gal., 12 1/2 In. 99.00
Jug, Flower, J. Fisher & Co., Lyons, c.1880, 2 Gal., 13 In. 165.00
Jug, Flowers, Blue, J. Clark & Co., Troy, c.1824, Gal., 11 1/2 In. 470.00
Jug, Flowers, Blue, Pink, E.W. Farrington & Co., Elmira, c.1890, 2 Gal., 14 In. 495.00
Jug, Flowers, Cowden & Wilcox, 2 Gal. 2200.00
Jug, Flowers, Crow's Foot Spider, Slip, G.O. Delorme, Toronto, c.1870, Gal., 11 In. 415.00
Jug, Flowers, H. Weston, 2 Gal. 745.00
Jug, Flowers, Nichols & Co., 2 Qt. 305.00
Jug, Flying Song Bird, Egg Shape, Hayes & Co., Manchester, N.H., 14 1/2 In. 935.00
Jug, Fruit, Beehive Shape, A.O. Whittemore, Havana, c.1870, 3 Gal., 14 In. 580.00

Jug, Gray, Brown, Salt

Stoneware, Jug, Face,
Red Devil, Black Bear,
Moustache, 16 In.

Stoneware, Jug, Face, Bulging
Eyes, Ceramic Teeth, Brown
Glaze, Flossie Meaders, 9 1/4 In.

Glaze, N.C., 11 1/2 In.	250.00
Jug, Gray, Stamped, Lewistown Pottery, 2 Gal.	130.00
Jug, Handle, Salt Glaze, Wide Bottom, 20th Century, 10 In.	130.00
Jug, Hearts & Flower, Nichols & Co., 2 Gal.	1075.00
Jug, Horse Hitched To Tree, Stencil, J.S. Waelde, North Bay, c.1855, 2 Gal., 13 1/2 In.	8525.00
Jug, Horse, Rabbit, Deer, Vines, Leaves, Wide Incised Band, Oval, Westerwald, 15 1/2 In.	395.00
Jug, Impressed Head, Salt Glaze, Bellarmine, Continental, 18th Century, 16 1/2 In.	1045.00
Jug, Incised Bird, Blue, Handle, I. Seymour & Co., Troy, 1830, Gal., 11 In.	1595.00
Jug, Incised Bird, Oval, Troy, Gal.	2420.00
Jug, Leaf, Lyons, c.1870, 2 Gal., 14 1/2 In.	155.00
Jug, Maroon, Brown, Albany Slip Glaze, Signed, Jos. L. Friedmann, 19th Century, 3 In.	110.00
Jug, Olive, Black, Blue Rutile, Alkaline Glaze, Early 20th Century, 16 3/4 In.	145.00
Jug, Olive, Streaked Alkaline Glaze, Handle, Early 20th Century, 13 1/2 In.	415.00
Jug, Oval, Handle, Incised Neck Lines, Brown Glaze, Early 19th Century, 10 In.	380.00
Jug, Oval, Handles, 2-Tone Brown Glaze, Marked Charleston, 19th Century, 2 Gal.	340.00
Jug, Paddeltail Bird, N.A. White & Son, 2 Gal.	1430.00
Jug, Parrot, O.L. & A.K. Ballard, Burlington, Vt., c.1870, 2 Gal., 14 In.	470.00
Jug, Perky Little Bird, West Troy Pottery, Gal.	495.00
Jug, Pinwheel Flower, Blue Handle, Cowden & Wilcox, 3 Gal.	605.00
Jug, Plume, Blue, New York Stoneware, Ft. Edward, c.1880, Gal., 11 In.	130.00
Jug, Plume, West Troy, c.1880, 2 Gal., 14 In.	110.00
Jug, Poppy Flower, Blue Accents, Oval, c.1850, 3 Gal., 15 In.	220.00
Jug, Ring, Salt Glaze, 19th Century, 9 In.	220.00
Jug, Rooster, Flowers, W.H. Farrar & Co., Geddes, N.Y., 4 Gal.	12925.00
Jug, Running Bird, Navy Blue, White's, Utica, c.1865, 2 Gal., 13 In.	580.00
Jug, Rust Brown, Alkaline Glaze, Handles, Tapered Ends, Mid 19th Century, 15 In.	275.00
Jug, Salt Glaze, Applied Handle, Rolled Rim, 20th Century, 10 3/4 In.	145.00
Jug, Salt Glaze, Enhanced Rim, Handle, Signed, A. Teague, 19th Century, 14 3/4 In.	770.00
Jug, Salt Glaze, Handle, Nicholas Fox, Late 19th Century, 12 1/4 In.	415.00
Jug, Salt Glaze, Handles, Signed, W.T. Macon, 19th Century, 19 1/4 In.	1870.00
Jug, Salt Glaze, Oval, Incised Lines, C. Corlius, New York, c.1840s, 14 3/4 In.	1410.00
Jug, Script, Gray, James Ryan, Gal.	195.00
Jug, Script, H. Kelley & Co., Gal.	245.00
Jug, Slip Blue Bird, Navy Blue, Haxstun & Co., Ft. Edward, c.1870, 2 Gal., 14 In.	635.00
Jug, Slip Blue Flower, Oval, J. Heiser, Buffalo, c.1852, Gal., 11 1/2 In.	110.00
Jug, Slip Blue Flowers, John Burger, Rochester, c.1865, 2 Gal., 14 In.	275.00
Jug, Smith & Brown, 40 Charlotte St., Utica, N.Y., c.1870, 2 Gal., 13 1/2 In.	360.00
Jug, Stamped, Fenderson & Rudd, 2 Gal.	210.00
Jug, Stylized Bird, Beehive Shape, S. Hart Fulton, c.1875, 2 Gal., 12 In.	580.00
Jug, Tan, Brown, Matawan's Old Time Maple Syrup, Blue Stencil, Oval, Handle, 6 1/2 In.	140.00
Jug, Tobacco Leaf, Sipe Nichols & Co., 2 Gal.	990.00
Jug, Tornado, Blue, D.W. Graves, Westmoreland, c.1860, 2 Gal., 12 In.	155.00
Jug, Triple Floral, Cowden & Wilcox, Harrisburg Pa., 3 Gal.	880.00
Jug, Tulip, Lyons, c.1870, 2 Gal., 13 1/2 In.	130.00
Jug, White, Salt Glaze, Polychrome, Strap Handle, England, c.1760, 10 1/4 In.	5080.00
Jug, Wreath, Incised & Blue, 11 1/2 In.	715.00
Jug, Wreath, T.G. Daub, Easton, Pa., Gal.	120.00
Mixing Bowl, Blue Sponge, 6 x 12 In.	275.00

Mixing Bowl, Salt Glaze, Blue Band, 2 1/4 x 4 1/4 In. 105.00
Mug, Impressed, Blue Accent Greek Key, Impressed Gesundheit, Handle, 6 1/2 In. 120.00
Mug, Impressed, Blue Accent, Souvenir Endicott Hotel, Bristol Glaze, 2 1/2 In 55.00
Mug, Relief, Blue Accented Monk Drinking, Bristol Glaze, Handle, 4 1/2 In. 22.00
Mug, Shaving, Slipware, Brown Glaze, 1805-1825 .... 3630.00
Mug, St. Louis Souvenir, Impressed, Blue Accented, Bristol Glaze, Handle, 3 In. 175.00
Pail, Batter, Blue Slip, Ribbed Orchid, Bail Handle, c.1865, Gal., 9 1/2 In. 1155.00
Pail, Milk, 5 Sprays Cobalt Blue Flowers, 4 1/2 x 11 In. 440.00
Pail, Milk, Cobalt Blue Leaves, Spout, 4 1/4 x 11 In. 330.00
Pitcher, 3 Cherries On Branch, Gal., 10 1/4 In. 605.00
Pitcher, 3 Rose Blossoms, Blue Neck Band, Cobalt Blue, Salt Glaze, c.1870, 10 3/4 In. .. 940.00
Pitcher, Alkaline Glaze, Dark Olive, 19th Century, 10 In. 195.00
Pitcher, Alkaline Glaze, Medium Olive, Handle, 19th Century, 11 1/4 In. 165.00
Pitcher, Blue & Gray, Leaf Mold, 8 1/2 In. 130.00
Pitcher, Blue, Green, Sponge, Blue Trim, 19th Century, 6 3/4 In. 295.00
Pitcher, Brown, Stamped Vinegar, 2 Qt. 99.00
Pitcher, Brown, Star On Bottom, 2 Qt. 55.00
Pitcher, Buttermilk, Dogwood Blossoms, Brown Field, Marked, 20th Century, 7 In. 825.00
Pitcher, Buttermilk, Salt Glaze, Handle, Signed, Ben Owen, 1920s, 8 1/4 In. 130.00
Pitcher, Cobalt Blue, Richard C. Remmey, 3 Gal. 4400.00
Pitcher, Cobalt Blue, Salt Glaze, Flared Rim & Spout, Applied Handle, 12 1/2 In. 220.00
Pitcher, Cobalt Blue, Salt Glaze, Strap Handle, Clara Hindman 1877, 3 1/8 In. 825.00
Pitcher, Colonial Log Cabin, Molded, Qt., 7 In. 99.00
Pitcher, Cow Design, Blue & White, Salt Glaze, 8 In. 120.00
Pitcher, Cream, Blue Flowers, Slip, Blue Accents, Qt., c.1860, 7 In. 495.00
Pitcher, Dogwood Blossom, Auburn Feldspathic Glaze, 1950s, 3 1/4 In. 120.00
Pitcher, Dotted Flowers, c.1870, 2 Gal., 12 In. 185.00
Pitcher, Draped, Tall Neck, c.1850, Gal., 11 In. 855.00
Pitcher, Floral & Leaf, Cobalt Blue, Bulbous, 1 1/2 Gal., 12 In. 495.00
Pitcher, Flowers, Leaves, Cobalt Blue, Bulbous, Richard C. Remmey, Phila., 3 Gal. 3575.00
Pitcher, Flowers, Leaves, Cobalt Blue, Bulbous, Signed, R.C.R., Phila., 2 Gal. 2090.00
Pitcher, Frogskin, Albany Slip, Signed, Mcg. Bishop Ronda, N.C., c.1930, 9 3/4 In. 440.00
Pitcher, Girl & Dog, Allover Blue Sponge, Relief Molded Oval Panels, 9 In. 180.00
Pitcher, Grape, Brown, Gal., 7 In. 55.00
Pitcher, Incised Blue Flowers, Alkaline Glaze, David Meaders, 10 In. 165.00
Pitcher, Men, Bulldogs & Word Prosit, Bulbous, No. 3 On Bottom, Gal. 440.00
Pitcher, Molded Figure, Brown, C. Hart, Sherburne, 2 Qt. 66.00
Pitcher, Multicolored Sponge, Barrel Shape, 2 Qt. 155.00
Pitcher, Paul Revere, White's, Utica, Qt. 220.00
Pitcher, Relief Country Scenes, Bristol Glaze, 6 1/2 In. 66.00
Pitcher, Salt Glaze, Green, Groove Top, Flat Handle, Signed, 1920, 8 In. 195.00
Pitcher, Shaped Spout, Bulbous, Loop Handle, Gal. 440.00
Pitcher, Singing Bird, Cobalt Blue, Salt Glaze, Applied Handle, c.1880, 1 1/2 Gal. 880.00
Pitcher, Spoutless Face, Teeth & Eyes, Eyebrows, Alkaline Glaze, Marked, 9 3/4 In. 275.00
Pitcher, Tulips, Blue Accent Leaves, Cylinder, Handle, c.1850, 2 Gal., 13 1/2 In. 2200.00
Pitcher, Vine, Flowers, Cobalt Blue, Blue Accents, c.1850, Gal., 10 In. 1320.00
Planter, Cobalt Blue Slip, Flared Top, Saucer Base, 9 1/4 x 10 In. 415.00
Plaque, Daniel & Lion, Embossed, 5 x 6 In. 1980.00
Plate, Black Bears & Shield, Incised, Redware, Dated 1905, 10 1/4 In. 88.00
Plate, Green Glaze, Black Design, Redware, 10 1/4 In. 61.00
Pot, Cover, Embossed, Boston Baked Beans In Blue Glaze, 8 x 8 In. 135.00
Pot, Cream, Blue, Henry & Van Allen, Albany, c.1845, 2 Gal., 8 1/2 In. 385.00
Pot, Cream, Dotted Pinwheel, c.1860, 2 Gal., 11 In. 305.00
Pot, Cream, Double Grape, Blue, Geddes, c.1870, 4 Gal., 11 1/2 In. 385.00
Pot, Cream, Flowers, Blue, White's, Utica, c.1865, Gal., 8 In. 120.00
Pot, Cream, Flowers, Cowden & Wilcox, Harrisburg, Pa., 4 Gal. 690.00
Pot, Cream, Footed, Brown Albany Glaze, Inscribed J.M. Loomis, c.1840, 2 Gal., 9 In. .. 66.00
Pot, Cream, Slip, Blue Flowers, Ithaca, N.Y., c.1880, 3 Gal., 11 In. 250.00
Pot, Cream, Slip, Blue Plume, Jordan, c.1850, Gal., 8 1/2 In. 360.00
Pot, Flower, Incised, Brown Ocher Accent, c.1860, 1/2 Gal., 6 In. 220.00
Pot, Flower, Wreath, West Troy, c.1880, 4 Gal., 11 1/2 In. 385.00
Pot, Lid, Alkaline Glaze, Dark Olive, 1960s, 2 3/4 In. 99.00
Pot, Lid, Aqua, Feldspathic Glaze, Slope Handle, Early 1960s, 3 1/2 In. 470.00

Pot, Squat, Cover, Handles, Blue Leaves, Andrew Coffman, 6 3/4 x 4 1/2 In. 3500.00
Salt, Lid, Hanging, Stenciled Flower, Blue, White Salt Glaze, 6 In. 99.00
Soap Dish, Relief Indian Head, Blue, White, 4 3/8 In. 415.00
Sugar & Creamer, Cobalt Blue, Salt Glaze, Ben Owen, c.1960, 3 1/2 In. 99.00
Tankard, Gray, Blue GR & Incised Scroll, Turned Bands, Westerwald, 5 7/8 In. 325.00
Teapot, Figural, Peafowl, Tail Handle, Spout Neck, Red, J.F. Bottger, c.1720, 6 In. 565.00
Tobacco Jar, Applied Egyptian Motif, Brown Ground, c.1890, 6 x 5 In. 125.00
Urn, Vine & Bird, Gray, Brown Glazing, Impressed, c.1885, 7 5/8 In. 170.00
Vase, 3 Handles, Bulbous, Flat Rim, Salt Glaze, Cobalt Blue, C.R. Auman, 5 x 8 In. 360.00
Vase, Bottle, Crane, Cloud, Bamboo, Blue & White, Pear Shape, Korea, 8 1/2 In. 2300.00
Vase, Chinese White Over Frogskin, 1930s-1940s, 4 In. 220.00
Vase, Cobalt, Salt Glaze, Branches, Jonathan Fenton, Boston, c.1796, 6 3/8 In. 2230.00
Vase, Double Grape Cluster, Stems, Leaves, Alkaline Glaze, Oval, 1960s, 5 1/2 In. 2090.00
Vase, Dragon Head, Chinese White, Ben Owen, Late 1930s, 15 In. 1870.00
Vase, Egg, Chinese White Glaze, Ben Owen, c.1960, 4 5/8 In. 77.00
Vase, Egg, Chinese White, Signed, Ben Owen, 1930s, 3 1/2 In. 120.00
Vase, Egg, Low Gloss Chinese Blue Glaze, Signed, Ben Owen, 4 In. 275.00
Vase, Green, Impressed Monogram, Emile Lenoble, c.1900, 8 3/4 In. 4780.00
Vase, Matte Blue, Brown, Green Glaze, Zanesville Pottery, 4 3/4 In. 195.00
Vase, Toothed Rim, Green, Blue Glazes, Carl Harry Stalhane, Rorstrand, 6 x 4 In. 145.00
Water Cooler, Floral, Cowden & Wilcox, 3 Gal. 5170.00
Water Cooler, Flowers, Blue Bands, 3 Gal. 130.00
Water Cooler, Lid, Wreath, Blue Slip, New York Stoneware Co., c.1868, 4 Gal., 16 In. .. 578.00
Water Cooler, Swan, Blue, 6 Gal. 440.00
Watermelon Slice, Painted, c.1900, 7 In. 6050.00
Window Stop, Man, Long Sideburns, 19th Century, 3 3/4 x 2 1/2 x 4 In., Pair 1380.00

STORE fixtures, cases, cutters, and other items that have no advertising
as part of the decoration are listed here. Most items found in an old
store are listed in the Advertising category in this book.

Backbar, Tavern, Mahogany, 16 Ft. 2500.00
Bag Holder, Metal & Wire, Painted, 29 In. 285.00
Bin, Spice, Roll Top, Scrolling Spice Names, Battleship, 12 1/4 x 9 3/8 x 9 In. 165.00
Cabinet, Display, Tobacco, 9 Beveled Glass Doors, 96 x 72 In. 3400.00
Cabinet, Hardware, Oak, 40 Drawers, A.R. Brown, Erwin, Tenn., 36 x 23 In. 400.00
Cabinet, Oak, Glass Door, Cubbyhole Interior, Scalloped Skirt, Countertop, 22 x 15 In. .. 330.00
Case, Display, Curved Glass, Front, Wood Frame, Hinged Mirror Back, 9 3/4 x 18 1/2 In. . 660.00
Case, Display, Glass, Silver, Mirrored Door, Slant Front, Countertop, 18 x 12 x 9 1/2 In. .. 345.00
Case, Display, Mahogany, 12 1/2 x 10 x 18 1/2 In. 115.00
Case, Display, Nickel Frame, 2 Doors, Mirrors, Countertop, 13 x 35 1/2 x 27 In. 190.00
Case, Display, Nickel Frame, Slant Front, Fold-Down Door, 12 1/2 x 24 x 19 1/2 In. 240.00
Case, Display, Oak, 2 Sliding Doors, Mirrors, Countertop, 17 x 32 x 26 1/2 In. 130.00
Case, Display, Oak, 4 Fold-Down Glass Doors, Ribbon Rack, Late 1800s, 26 x 14 x 28 In. . 800.00
Case, Display, Oak, 4 Shelves, Hinged Door, Countertop, 30 x 28 x 16 1/2 In. 300.00
Case, Display, Oak, Inset Beveled Glass Top, 2 Sliding Doors, Mirrors, 40 x 60 In. 220.00
Case, Display, Oak, Slant Front, 2 Doors, Glass, Shelf, 23 x 13 x 24 1/2 In. 250.00
Case, Display, Oak, Slant Front, Adjustable Shelf, 3 Sliding Glass Doors, 23 x 72 In. 385.00
Case, Display, Oak, Wall, Cornice, Glass Door, 34 x 28 x 16 In. 150.00
Case, Wood Frame, 4 Glass Shelves, Waddel, Greenfield, Ohio, 21 1/4 x 39 In. 200.00
Cash Drawer, Wooden, Divided Interior, Alarm Till, Tucker & Dorsey, 5 x 16 x 18 In. ... 40.00
Chest, Seed, Softwood, 20 Drawers, Cutout Cornice, Porcelain Pulls, Gilt, 16 x 17 x 5 In. 880.00
Coffee Grinders are listed in their own category.
Coin Till, Shopkeeper's, Pine, 6 Wells, Red Paint, 19th Century 185.00
Counter, Oak, Recessed Panel Front & Ends, 31 x 61 In. 1045.00
Counter, Pine, Recessed Panel Ends, 32 x 79 In. 525.00
Counter, Wooden, Panel Front, 16 Ft. 2420.00
Cupboard, Double 6 Glass Pane Doors, 2 Sections 930.00
Display, Advertising, Globe, Apothecary, Deco, Stopper, Colored Water, Hanging, 18 In. . 360.00
Display, Cowboy, Plastic, Removable, 15 1/2 In. 115.00
Display, Shoe Stretcher, c.1897, 19 3/4 x 22 In. 29.00
Light, Exit Light Globe, Red Glass, 6 In. 175.00
Mannequin, Boy, Composition, Painted, Late 19th Century, 42 1/2 In. 2938.00
Mannequin, Dress Form, Wood Tripod Base, E. Girard, Marked, 69 In. 60.00

Money Box, Wood, Paper Money Slot, Semicircular Coin Cutouts 89.00
Paper Cutter, Metal, Vertical, 24 1/2 In. 110.00
Post Office, 75 Cubby Holes, 2 Lower Drawers, Refinished, 51 x 60 In. 715.00
Rack, Display, Hat, Wood, Wire, 19th Century, 35 x 40 1/2 In. 90.00
Safe, Black, Gold Highlights, Drawer, Baum, Cincinnati, Victorian, 28 x 18 In. 168.00
Safe, York Safe & Lock Company, Painted Door, Fitted Interior, Carpet Lining, 27 In. . . . 660.00
Shelf, Country Store, Folding, Oak, 5 Shelves, Folds Into Table, 36 x 54 x 12 In. 440.00
Shelf, Display, Softwood, Scallop Cutouts, Shelves, York County, Penn., 59 x 57 x 16 In. . 2200.00
Shelving, Oak, Metal Frame, Converts To Table, 57 In. 495.00
Showcase, Slant Front, Wood Trim, Glass Divided Interior, Countertop, 11 x 47 In. 248.00
Sign, Black Woman Holds High-Top Shoe, Pine, Carved, 1900s, 60 1/2 In. 5463.00
Sign, Frog, Frog Legs In Red Letters, Wooden Body, Tin Arms, Feet, 41 x 27 In. 1210.00
Soda Fountain, 2 Spigots, Leaded Glass Shade, Footed Marble Base, Bishop, c.1900 . . . . 2750.00
Soda Fountain, Root Beer, Amber Glass, Cover, Spigot, Nickel Plated, 12 In. 300.00
Strawholder, Soda Fountain, Glass, Metal Lifter Lid, Flared Bottom, 11 3/4 In. 396.00
Strawholder, Soda Fountain, Pressed Glass, Green, Metal Lifter Lid, 13 1/2 In. 195.00
Strawholder, Soda Fountain, Pressed Glass, Metal Lifter Lid, 11 In. 155.00
Strawholder, Soda Fountain, Square, Pressed Glass, Geometric Fan & Panel, 12 1/4 In. . . 175.00
Strong Box, Vandeman, Steel, Oak Bound, Steel Handles, c.1900, 20 x 20 x 38 In. 575.00
Tobacco Caddy, Walnut, 6 Drawers, 1906 . . . . 300.00
Tobacco Cutter, Cast, Brighton, Molded Handle, Boy Thumbing Nose, Iron, 10 In. 81.00

STOVES have been used in America for heating since the eighteenth
century and for cooking since the nineteenth century. Most types of
wood, coal, gas, kerosene, and even some electric stoves are collected.

Camp, Kerosene, Taylor & Bogg Foundry Company, Cleveland, 1 Burner 110.00
Cook, Jewel Range Jr., Detroit Stove Works, Salesman's Sample, 15 x 19 x 9 In. 3950.00
Cook, Kalamazoo, Regal, Oak Wood, Coal, 1890s 350.00
Cook, Range, Gas, Wood, Coal, Manifest No. 182, Enamel, Wehrle, c.1925, 33 x 66 In. . . 3000.00
Cook, Royal Princess, No. 29, Ceramic, Brown & Cream Heads, Water Urn On Top 1000.00
Cook, Superior, Light Blue, Beige, Grape Pattern On Reservoir 800.00
Cook, Thomas White, Royal Princess No. 30 . . . . 1600.00
Cook, Wood & Coal, Porcelain On Steel, Salesman's Sample, c.1910, 4 Piece 20000.00
Heating, Frostproof, Dance Hall, Cast Iron, 1875 . . . . 800.00
Heating, Treadwell & Perry, No. 2, Cast Iron, 30 x 21 x 45 In. 805.00
Heating, Zoar Furnace, Cast Iron, Wood Burning, Removable Paw Feet, 31 x 19 x 25 In. . 3190.00
Laundry, Cast Iron, Fits 5 Irons, Lamans, No. 6, 20 In. 192.00
Parlor, Cylindrical, Art Nouveau Design, 3-Footed, Cast Iron, Germany, 33 1/2 In. 243.00
Potbelly, Cast Iron, Nickel, F & L Kahn & Bros., Hamilton, Ohio, 61 x 24 In. 50.00
Potbelly, Cast Iron, Nickel, Great Western, Late 19th Century, 64 x 24 In. 60.00

STRETCH GLASS is named for the strange stretch marks in the glass. It
was made by many glass companies in the United States from about
1900 to the 1920s. It is iridescent. Most American stretch glass is
molded; most European pieces are blown and may have a pontil mark.

Bowl, Blue, Cupped Rim, Flared Foot, Cupped, Diamond Glass Co., 1920s, 6 1/2 x 3 In. . 50.00
Bowl, Blue, Cupped, Diamond Glass Co., 8 x 3 3/4 In. . . . . .40.00 to 50.00
Bowl, Blue, Flared Rim, Footed, 4 1/4 x 7 1/4 In. 40.00
Bowl, Blue, Wide Flare, Diamond Glass Co., 1920s, 9 1/4 x 1 3/4 In. 50.00
Bowl, Gold Iridescent, Round, Waffle Pontil, c.1910, 12 1/4 In. 300.00
Bowl, Iridescent, Vaseline, 9 1/2 x 3 1/4 In. 75.00
Bowl, Iris Ice, 10 1/2 In. 55.00
Bowl, Lancaster Lily, Green, 5 x 2 1/2 In. 20.00
Bowl, Marigold, 3-Footed, Flared, Jeannette Glass Co., 10 x 3 3/4 In. . . . . .45.00 to 50.00
Bowl, Mayonnaise, Green, 6 1/4 x 3 1/4 In. 40.00
Bowl, Pearl Ruby, 9 3/4 x 3 1/2 In. 90.00
Bowl, Pearl, Diamond Glass Co., 1920s, 3 x 9 3/4 In. 50.00
Compote, Iridescent, U.S. Glass Co., 7 x 6 1/2 In. 60.00
Compote, White, 12-Panel Interior, 4 x 6 1/2 In. 45.00
Compote, White, Iridescent, Enameled, Blue Floral Rim, Lancaster, 1920s, 9 x 4 In. 65.00
Compote, Yellow, 3 7/8 x 7 1/4 In. 80.00
Plate, Amberina, 6 1/4 In. 18.00
Sherbet, Underplate, Green, Diamond Glass Co. 35.00

Sugar, Green, Trophy Shape, Handles, Swirled Foot, 4 1/8 x 5 1/4 In. 40.00
Tidbit, Yellow, Cupped Rim, 3 1/2 x 9 1/2 In. 70.00
Vase, Amber, Light Iridescence, 5 In. 140.00
Vase, Fan, Green, 5 1/4 x 6 In. 40.00
Vase, Iridescent Red, Yellow, Blue, Green Highlights, Vaseline, 10 1/2 x 3 3/4 In. 230.00

SUMIDA is a Japanese pottery that was made from about 1870 to 1941. Pieces are usually everyday objects—vases, jardinieres, bowls, teapots, and decorative tiles. Most pieces have a very heavy orange-red, blue, brown, black, green, purple, or off-white glaze, with raised three-dimensional figures as decorations. The unglazed part is painted red, green, black, or orange. Sumida was sometimes called *Poo Ware* in the past.

Bowl, Fishing Hut, Men On Rim Peering In, Unglazed Red Ground, 1920s, 7 1/2 In. 125.00
Chocolate Pot, Cover, Figural Monk, Red & Blue Robe, Inoue Ryosai, 8 3/4 In. 300.00
Loving Cup, Man Sitting On Handle, Dog Below, Red Unglazed Ground, 5 3/4 In. 1095.00
Pitcher, Man, Koi, Green Mottled Ground, 11 In. 850.00
Vase, 2 Men, Unglazed Shield Shape Base, Drip-Glazed Neck, Handles, Ryosai, 9 3/4 In. . .   350.00
Vase, Cover, Drip-Glazed Foo Dog Finial, Men On Handles, Unglazed Base, 6 In. 450.00
Vase, Dragon, Embossed Waves, Red Ground, Blue Drip-Glazed 4-Sided Neck, 8 1/2 In. . .   550.00
Vase, Dragon, Red Ground, Applied White Glaze Seal, c.1926, 18 In. 978.00
Vase, Man, Children, Horizontal Ribs, Dark Red Ground, Drip Glazed, Flared, 12 In. 1100.00
Vase, Plum Tree Branch, Glazed Dark Red Ground, 1920s, 6 In.   375.00
Vase, Sage Taking Tea, Glazed Red Ground, Signed, 2 1/2 In. 220.00

SUNBONNET BABIES were first introduced in 1900 in the book *The Sunbonnet Babies*. The stories were by Eulalie Osgood Grover, illustrated by Bertha Corbett. The children's faces were completely hidden by the sunbonnets. The children had been pictured in black and white before this time, but the color pictures in the book were immediately successful. The Royal Bayreuth China Company made a full line of children's dishes decorated with the Sunbonnet Babies. Some Sunbonnet Babies plates have been reproduced, but are clearly marked.

Book, A-B-C Book, Rand McNally, 1929 . . . .   400.00
Creamer, Friday, Sweeping, Royal Bayreuth, 3 1/2 In. . . . . .225.00 to 365.00
Nappy, Wash Day, Handles, 6 In. 230.00
Plate, Sunday, Fishing, Royal Bayreuth, 1974, 7 1/4 In. 200.00
Postcard, Wednesday, Mending, Ullman, c.1905 . . . .   15.00
Rug, Hooked, Sweeping Leaves With Broom, Brown Border, Early 20th Century 115.00

SUNDERLAND luster is a name given to a special type of pink luster made by Leeds, Newcastle, and other English firms during the nineteenth century. The luster glaze is metallic and glossy and appears to have bubbles in it. Other pieces of luster are listed in the Luster category.

Jug, Pink Luster, Ship, View Of Cast Iron Bridge, Moore & Co., Southwick, 9 1/2 In. 1765.00
Jug, Pink Luster, South East View Of Iron Bridge, Verse In Floral Frame, 9 1/4 In. 940.00
Pitcher, Luster, Enameled Gray Transfer, 2 Verses, Floral Wreaths, c.1820, 8 1/2 In. 546.00
Pitcher, Pink Luster, Black Transfer, Enameled, Ship, Peace & Plenty Verse, 9 3/8 In. . . .   646.00
Pitcher, Pink Luster, Black Transfer, Sailor's Farewell, Puzzle Verse, 9 3/8 In. 3290.00
Pitcher, Pink Luster, Verse In Wreath, Inscribed Auther Rutter 1840, 10 1/8 In. 1645.00
Plaque, Pink Luster, Copper Border, Motto, Wreath Of Flowers, 8 x 9 In. 720.00
Plaque, Pink Luster, Northumberland 74, Sailing Ship, Rectangular, Self-Framed, 8 x 9 In.   355.00
Wall Plaque, Pink Luster, Prepare To Meet Thy God, Mid 19th Century, 8 1/4 x 9 1/2 In. . .   1725.00

SUPERMAN was created by two seventeen-year-olds in 1938. The first issue of *Action* comics had the strip. Superman remains popular and became the hero of a radio show in 1940, cartoons in the 1940s, a television series, and several major movies.

Mold, For Bubble Bath Bottle, Bronze, Avon, 1970, 4 1/2 In. 345.00
Movie Viewer, Chemtoy, Card, 1965, 5 x 7 In. 70.00
Playsuit, 3-Piece Cotton, Red & Blue Silk Shirt, Emblem, Funtime Inc., 1950 . . . .   165.00
Toy, Tank, Rollover, Superman Lifts Tank, Tin, Linemar, Japan, 4 In. 300.00

SUSIE COOPER began as a designer in 1925 working for the English firm A.E. Gray & Company. In 1932 she formed Susie Cooper Pottery, Ltd. In 1950 it became Susie Cooper China, Ltd., and the company made china and earthenware. In 1966 it was acquired by Josiah Wedgwood & Sons, Ltd. The name Susie Cooper appears with the company names on many pieces of ceramics.

Coffee Set, Kestral, Green, Tan, 7 3/4 & 2 1/2 & 4 3/4 In., 13 Piece	300.00
Jam Jar, Leaves, Lavender, Peach, Green, 2 1/2 In.	66.00
Pitcher, Incised Stag, Abstract Design, Charging Ram, Green Glaze, Marked, 21 In.	420.00
Pitcher, Stag, Charging Ram, Abstracts, Green Glaze, 8 1/2 x 7 In.	300.00
Vase, Fox, Abstracts, Blue Glaze, 1930, 6 1/4 x 5 In.	300.00

SWANKYSWIGS are small drinking glasses. In 1933, the Kraft Food Company began to market cheese spreads in these decorated, reusable glass tumblers. They were discontinued from 1941 to 1946, then made again from 1947 to 1958. Then plain glasses were used for most of the cheese, although a few special decorated Swankyswigs have been made since that time. A complete list of prices can be found in *Kovels' Depression Glass & Dinnerware Price List*.

Antique No. I, Brown, 3 1/2 In.	6.00
Bustlin' Betsy, Red, 3 3/4 In.	8.00
Checkerboard, Green & White, 3 1/2 In.	10.50
Galleon, Red, 3 1/8 In.	10.50
Posy Tulip No. 3, Red, 4 1/2 In.	10.00
Posy Violet, 3 1/2 In.	9.00
Stars, Blue, 4 3/4 In.	15.00

SWASTIKA KERAMOS is a line of art pottery made from 1906 to 1908 by the Owen China Company of Minerva, Ohio. Many pieces were made with an iridescent glaze.

Vase, Bulbous, Gold Swastika Bands, Gray Panels, 7 x 5 In.	353.00
Vase, Flowers, Gilt Ground, Own China Co., c.1900, 8 In.	86.00
Vase, Gold Trees, Gold, Red Ground, 11 3/4 x 4 1/2 In.	235.00

SWORDS of all types that are of interest to collectors are listed here. The military dress sword with elaborate handle is probably the most wanted. Be sure to display swords in a safe way, out of reach of children.

Artillery, Infantry, American Eagle Head, Metal Scabbard, 36 In.	1410.00
Artillery, Roman Pattern, Feathered Grip, Straight, Rectangular Guard, 31 In.	175.00
Artillery Saber, Scroll Engraved, Gilt Finish, Steel Scabbard, 30 1/2-In. Blade	275.00
Backsword, Basket Hilt, Leather Grip, England, c.1645, 32 1/4-In. Blade	3850.00
Backsword, Double Back Fullers, Scalloped, Chinese, c.1850, 21 3/4-In. Blade	575.00
Bayonet, Army, For JD Greene Breech Loading Rifle, American, c.1855, 21 In.	112.00
Bayonet, Scabbard, Blue Webbing, Leather Straps, Rubber, M1968 SVD, Soviet Union	40.00
Bayonet, Scabbard, Germany, 1898, 20 In.	92.00
Bayonet, Type 30, Wood Grip, Steel Scabbard, Leather Frog, 15-3/4 In. Blade	195.00
Bayonet, U.S. Navy, Dahlgren, Original Scabbard	2500.00
Bayonet, U.S., Scabbard, Frog, Krag, 1892	127.00
Bayonet, Wehrmacht, NCO Dress, Black Scabbard, Eickhorn, 7 3/4-In. Blade	520.00
British Officer's, 2nd Volunteer Battery, East Kent Regiment, Metal Scabbard, 39 In.	470.00
British Officer's, Victoria Rifles, Metal Scabbard, Busain & Co., London, 38 In.	470.00
Bullfighter's, Straight, Diamond Section Blade, Cloth Wrap, Spain, c.1885, 33 1/4 In.	245.00
Capt. Samuel Storer, Ivory Grip, Silver Hilt, S. Drowne, New Hampshire, c.1780	9200.00
Cross & Crown Device, Gilt Guard, Helmet Device Pommel, Black Grip Scabbard, 32 In.	210.00
Cross & Crown Device, Gilt Guard, Helmet Device Pommel, Black Grip, Scabbard, 28 In.	260.00
Cutlass, Navy, Iron Guard, Scabbard, Reeves & Co., England, c.1855, 28 1/4-In. Blade	735.00
Dagger, Barbary Coast Pirate, Curved Blade, Horn Grip, 14 1/2 In.	325.00
Dagger, Brass Handle, Mideast, 8 1/2 In.	60.00
Dagger, Brass Hilt, Sun God, Surya, Tigers & Prey, India, 15 In.	411.00
Dagger, Cossack Kindjahl, Nickel Plate, Wood Scabbard, Sterling Grip Cover, 13 1/2 In.	140.00
Dagger, Fascist, Aluminum Handle, Steel Scabbard, Gold Brocade Strap, Italy, 12 In.	980.00
Dagger, Iron Pommel, Leather-Covered Hilt, Leather Scabbard, Sahara, c.1870, 7 1/2 In.	80.00

Dagger, Judi Tranchang, Wood Scabbard, Iron Hilt, Indonesia, 18th Century 175.00
Dagger, Luftwaffe, Wire-Wrapped Handle, Leather-Covered Scabbard, 12 1/4-In. Blade . . 600.00
Dagger, Pesh Kabz, Steel Blade, Ivory Hilt, Wood, Indo-Persia, 19th Century, 17 In. 500.00
Dagger, Teno EM Hewer, Nazi Eagle, Celluloid Grip, Scabbard, Gesch & Eickhorn 1360.00
Dirk, Wavy Blade, Naval, Ebony Handle, Leather Scabbard, 11 In. 235.00
Eagle Hilt, Bone Handle, American, c.1810, 31 In. 230.00
Ecle De Mars Style, Theatrical, Scabbard, Cast Brass Grip, 24 3/4 In. 90.00
Folk Art, Swordfish Bill, Carved Wood Handle, Painted Swordfish, 39 1/2 In. 165.00
German, Junior Officer, Scabbard, World War I, 28 In. 80.00
Horseman's, Iron Hilt, Broad, Flat Pommel, India, 18th Century, 30 1/2 In. 525.00
Imperial, German Officer's, Curved, Brass Hilt, P Form Guard, Leather Grip, 33 In. 345.00
Infantry Officer's, Scabbard, Prussia, 32 In. 138.00
Katana, Japan, Blade, Grooved, Partial Mounts, 19th Century, 21 In. 206.00
Kris, 11-Wave Blade, Damascus Steel, Silver Ferrule, Cord-Wrapped Grip, Moro, 20 In. . . 395.00
Kris, Iron, Wood Grip, Scabbard, Gilt Mendak, Plain Brass, Java, 13-In. Blade 425.00
Military, Bronze Hilt, Flattened Diamond Section Blade, Germany, c.1760, 31 1/2 In. 1125.00
Military, Sharkskin Grip, Firmin & Sons, England, c.1855, 20 1/2 In. 325.00
Naval, Ceremonial, Leather Case, Portapee, Hilborn & Hamburger, American, 29-In. Blade 430.00
Naval, Lion Head Pommel, Brass Mounted, Leather Scabbard, Germany, 35 In. 235.00
Naval, Officer's, Leather Scabbard, W.H. Horstmann & Sons, Philadelphia, 36 In. 1410.00
Naval, U.S. Officer's, Model 1852, Dolphin Mount, Leather Scabbard, 37 In. 1528.00
Rapier, Flattened Diamond-Sectioned Blade, Inscription, Italy, c.1600, 44 3/4 In. 1650.00
Saber, Artillery, Infantry, American Eagle Head, Leather Scabbard, c.1820, 33 In. 765.00
Saber, Cavalry Officer's, Metal Scabbard, Alex. Coopel, Solingen, 35 In. 295.00
Saber, Cavalry Officer's, Steel Scabbard, Collins & Co., 1862, 40 1/2 In. 2115.00
Saber, Cavalry, Brass Guard, Steel Scabbard, M1860, C. Roby & Co., 1865, 41 In. 558.00
Saber, Cavalry, Nickeled Guard & Scabbard, Blued, Etched Blade, Continental, 40 In. . . . 558.00
Saber, Cavalry, U.S., Brass Guard, Etched Blade, Metal Scabbard, 37 1/2 In. 235.00
Saber, Eagle Hilt, Brass Scabbard, Bone Grip, Flowers, Berger, Germany, 36 In. 6325.00
Saber, Georgian, Lion Head Pommel, Pierced Hilt, Metal Scabbard, 37 In. 588.00
Saber, Horseman's, Triple Fuller, Wire & Leather Wrap, Revolutionary War 2200.00
Saber, Imperial Russian Cavalry, Nicholas II Crest, Leather Scabbard, c.1900, 37 In. 410.00
Saber, Infantry Officer's, Curved, Bern Canton, Switzerland, 1750, 28 1/4-In. Blade 1550.00
Saber, Light Artillery Officer, Engraved, Leather Scabbard, Hortsmann Bros., 35 1/2 In. . . . 6460.00
Saber, Simple, Cast Brass Handle, Stamped 745, Leather Scabbard, 33 In. 147.00
Scabbard, Bone Handle, American, c.1810, 31 In. . : 345.00
Shashka, Silver Gilt, Niello, Russia, Georgian, 20th Century, 21 In. 690.00
Staff & Field, Officer's, Presentation, Brass Scabbard, Ames Model 1860, 37 1/2 In. 2470.00
Talwar, India, Dished Pommels, Iron Grip, Leather Scabbard, 19th Century, 36 In., Pair . . 380.00
Tsuba, Iron, Inlaid, Carved, Chased, Signed, c.1868, 3 1/2 In., 9 Piece 1725.00
Yataghan, Turkey, Silver Hilt, Coral, Niello Plaques, Silver Mount, 19th Century, 28 In. . . 529.00
Yataghan, Turkey, Walrus Ivory Grips, Gilt Copper Mounts, 19th Century, 32 In. 499.00

SYRACUSE is a trademark used by the Onondaga Pottery of Syracuse, New York. The company was established in 1871. It is still working. The name became the Syracuse China Company in 1966. It is known for fine dinnerware and restaurant china.

SYRACUSE
ⅲⅲ China

Appleton, Plate, Federal Shape, Blue, Yellow Flowers, Metallic Gold Trim, 6 1/2 In. 8.00
Appleton, Sugar & Creamer, Federal Shape, Blue, Yellow Flowers, Gold Trim, Cover . . . 45.00
Arcadia, Plate, Winchester Shape, Blue, Red Garlands, Gold Trim, 9 3/4 In. 13.00
Arcadia, Soup, Dish, Winchester Shape, Swags, Pink Flowers, Gold Trim 8.00
Bracelet, Saucer, Virginia Shape, Embossed Gold Band 6.00
Bracelet, Saucer, Virginia Shape, Embossed Gold Band, Demitasse 8.00
Briarcliff, Cup & Saucer, Federal Shape, Pastel Flowers, Gold Trim 18.00
Briarcliff, Sugar, Cover, Federal Shape, Pastel Flowers, Metallic Gold Trim 7.00
Coralbel, Bowl, Fruit, Pink, Green Flowers, Platinum Trim, 5 1/8 In. 10.00
Coralbel, Cup & Saucer, Virginia Shape, Pink, Green Floral, Platinum Trim 18.00
Coralbel, Plate, Virginia Shape, Pink, Green Flowers, Platinum Trim, 6 1/4 In. 8.00
Coralbel, Plate, Virginia Shape, Pink, Green Flowers, Platinum Trim, 8 In. 18.00
Coralbel, Soup, Dish, Virginia Shape, Pink & Green Flowers, Platinum Trim 20.00
Diane, Cup & Saucer, Virginia Shape, Embossed Gold Band 18.00
Diane, Plate, Virginia Shape, Embossed Gold Band, 6 1/4 In. 8.00
Diane, Plate, Virginia Shape, Embossed Gold Band, 8 In. 18.00

Diane, Plate, Virginia Shape, Embossed Gold Band, 9 In. 25.00
Monticello, Cup & Saucer, Winchester Shape, Metallic Gold Bands 18.00
Monticello, Plate, Winchester Shape, Metallic Gold Bands, 6 1/4 In. 8.00
Monticello, Plate, Winchester Shape, Metallic Gold Bands, 8 In. 15.00
Orchard, Plate, Federal Shape, Apple Blossom Wreath, Gold Trim, 6 1/2 In. 8.00
Orchard, Plate, Federal Shape, Apple Blossom Wreath, Gold Trim, 8 In. 18.00
Orchard, Plate, Federal Shape, Apple Blossom Wreath, Gold Trim, 10 1/2 In. 30.00
Portland, Sauceboat, Federal Shape, Attached Stand, Pink Roses, Flowers, Gold Trim ... 35.00
Sherwood, Cup & Saucer, Virginia Shape, Blue Laurel Wreath Border, Gold Trim 18.00
Sherwood, Plate, Virginia Shape, Blue Laurel Wreath Border, Gold Trim, 8 In. 18.00
Sherwood, Plate, Virginia Shape, Blue Laurel Wreath Border, Gold Trim, 10 1/4 In. 30.00
Sherwood, Sugar & Creamer, Virginia Shape, Blue Laurel Wreath, Gold Trim, Cover 45.00
Suzanne, Plate, Federal Shape, Yellow, Blue, Pink Flowers, Gold Trim, 6 3/8 In. 13.00
Webster, Plate, Virginia Shape, Tan, Black Border, Gold Trim, 9 In. 13.00
Windsor, Cup & Saucer, Winchester Shape, Flowers, Aqua Band, Gold Trim 18.00
Windsor, Plate, Winchester Shape, Flowers, Aqua Band, Gold Trim, 6 1/2 In. ....8.00 to 13.00
Windsor, Plate, Winchester Shape, Flowers, Aqua Band, Gold Trim, 9 In. 23.00
Windsor, Platter, Winchester Shape, Flowers, Blue Band, Gold Trim, 12 In. 23.00

TAPESTRY, PORCELAIN, see Rose Tapestry category.

TEA CADDY is the name for a small box made to hold tea leaves. In the
eighteenth century, tea was very expensive and it was stored under
lock and key. The first tea caddies were made with locks. By the nineteenth century, tea was more plentiful and the tea caddy was larger.
Often there were two sections, one for green tea, one for black tea.

Applewood, Apple Shape, Wood Stem, Oval Escutcheon, 4 1/8 In. 1870.00
Banded Burlwood, 8 Sides, Ivory Escutcheon, Georgian, 5 x 5 1/2 In. 460.00
Black Lacquer, Abalone & Mother-Of-Pearl Inlay, 2 Sections, 8 x 5 1/2 In. 489.00
Blond Tortoiseshell, 2 Compartments, William IV, c.1835, 5 1/4 x 7 3/4 In. 2760.00
Blond Tortoiseshell, Brass Mounted, 2 Sections, Georgian, 5 1/2 x 4 3/4 x 3 1/4 In. 2300.00
Brass Inlay, Hinged Lid, Handle, Spoon Keeper, Regency, c.1820, 6 x 10 x 6 1/2 In. 1495.00
Burlwood, Banded, 2 Compartments, Georgian, Oblong, c.1815, 5 x 7 1/2 In. 460.00
Burlwood Veneer, Domed Lid, Flared Sides, Inlaid Bird, Bun Feet, 13 x 8 1/2 In. 529.00
Chinoiserie, Coffin Shape, Hinged Lid, Landscapes, Gilt, Paw Feet, 19th Century 1035.00
Double, Walnut, Silver Handle, Domed Lid, 2 Glass Caddies, Georgian, c.1820 .... 805.00
Fruitwood, Apple Shape, George III, Early 19th Century, 4 1/4 In. 2990.00
Fruitwood, Apple Shape, George III, Early 19th Century, 4 7/16 In. 6570.00
Fruitwood, Apple Shape, George III, Early 19th Century, 4 9/16 In. 3585.00
Fruitwood, Apple Shape, George III, Early 19th Century, 5 In. 5970.00
Fruitwood, Melon Shape, George III, Early 19th Century, 5 1/4 In. 7768.00
Fruitwood, Pear Shape, George III, 19th Century, 7 In. 5676.00
Fruitwood, Pear Shape, George III, Early 19th Century, 5 7/16 In. ....3585.00 to 5079.00
Fruitwood, Pear Shape, George III, Early 19th Century, 6 7/16 In. 3585.00
Fruitwood, Pear Shape, George III, Early 19th Century, 7 7/16 In. 6570.00
Fruitwood, Treen, Late 18th Century, 5 In. 1540.00
Fruitwood Veneers, 19th Century, 4 1/2 x 4 1/2 x 4 1/2 In. 127.00
Lacquer, Pewter, Oriental, Lift Lid, 2 Interior Containers, 8 Sides, 5 1/2 x 9 x 6 In. 145.00
Lacquer, Troika, 3 Horses, Man, Maids, Russia, 19th Century, 10 x 5 1/2 x 5 1/2 In. 1323.00
Mahogany, 2 Compartments, Bone Escutcheon, George IV, c.1835, 7 3/4 x 14 In. 405.00
Mahogany, 3 Lidded Tin Containers, George III, c.1800, 5 1/2 x 9 1/2 x 5 In. 460.00
Mahogany, Brass Bands, Corners & Quatrefoil Inlay, 4 x 7 x 5 In. 330.00
Mahogany, Brass Inlay, Chamfer Corners, Ogee Body, George III, c.1810 .... 2415.00
Mahogany, Brass, Hinged Lid, Greek Key, Floral, Regency, c.1815, 7 x 13 x 6 In. 1035.00
Mahogany, Coffin Shape, 8 Sides, 2 Compartments, Divided Well, 5 x 10 1/2 In. 185.00
Mahogany, Domed Lid, Fluted Tapered Pedestal, Triangular Base, 30 In. 688.00
Mahogany, Hinged Lid, 2 Compartments, England, c.1800, 12 In. 277.00
Mahogany, Hinged Lid, Chamfered Corners, William IV, c.1830, 6 x 12 x 6 In. 430.00
Mahogany, Inlaid Bat's-Wing Roundel, Checker-Band Edge, Georgian, 5 x 5 In. 325.00
Mahogany, Inlaid, Coffin Shape, Hinged Lid, Georgian, c.1830, 6 1/2 x 12 x 6 In. 345.00
Mahogany, Inlaid, Hinged Lid, Conforming Body, Georgian, 30 x 36 x 18 1/2 In. 345.00
Mahogany, Inlaid, Interior Sections, Lids, George IV, c.1825, 5 x 8 1/2 x 5 1/2 In. 259.00
Mahogany, Inlaid, Veneer, Domed Lid, 19th Century, 5 x 7 1/4 x 4 1/4 In. 1410.00
Mahogany, Inlay, Sarcophagus Style, Brass Ball Feet, Regency, c.1810, 11 1/2 In. 1450.00

Mahogany, Marquetry, 3 Compartments, Georgian, c.1785, 6 3/4 x 12 In. 1035.00
Mahogany, Marquetry, 3 Compartments, Seashells, Georgian, c.1785, 6 x 12 In. 690.00
Mahogany, Mounded Coffin Shape, Hinged Lid, Georgian, c.1770, 5 x 9 In. 210.00
Mahogany, Rectangular, Chamfered Corners, William IV, c.1830, 6 x 12 x 6 In. 316.00
Mahogany, Regency, 2 Sections, 1800s, 6 1/4 x 7 3/4 x 4 1/2 In. 290.00
Mahogany, Satinwood Inlay, Rectangular, Fitted Interior, England, c.1800, 12 In. 260.00
Mahogany, Silver Handle, 4 Compartments, Georgian, c.1830, 6 1/4 x 11 x 9 In. 1265.00
Mahogany, Silver Mounted, 2 Sections, 19th Century, 5 3/4 x 8 x 5 1/2 In. 920.00
Mahogany Veneer, Brass Bail Handle, Keyhole Escutcheon, 9 1/2 x 5 1/2 x 6 In. 248.00
Mahogany Veneer, Ivory Keyhole Escutcheon, Mixing Bowl Opening, 12 x 6 In. 165.00
Mother-Of-Pearl, Bowfront, Inlaid, 2 Lids, Anglo-Dutch, 19th Century, 4 x 7 x 4 1/2 In. . . . 1495.00
Mother-Of-Pearl, Ivory Bun Feet, 2 Lids, Anglo-Dutch, 19th Century, 5 x 8 x 4 1/2 In. 1495.00
Mother-Of-Pearl Inlay, Tortoiseshell, George IV, Mid 19th Century, 6 x 8 x 5 In. 3286.00
Nickel, Brass Mounted, Tigerskin Tortoiseshell, Bone Grips, Regency, 5 x 7 x 4 In. 3450.00
Painted, Cameo Mount, Henry Clay, George III, c.1775, 4 1/2 x 4 3/4 x 3 1/2 In. 4180.00
Painted, Faceted Outline, Lidded Compartment, George III, c.1790, 7 In. 1435.00
Papier-Mache, Mother-Of-Pearl Inlay, Bun Feet, c.1890, 5 x 7 3/4 x 5 1/2 In. 1095.00
Porcelain, Japanese Hosan Style, Red, Turquoise, Yellow, Chrysanthemum Lid, 7 In. 1575.00
Porcelain, Maritime Decoration, Naval Coat Of Arms, Inscribed Nelson, 4 1/8 In. 920.00
Regency, Hollywood Banded, Mahogany, Double Compartment, 7 1/2 x 12 1/2 x 6 In. . . . 690.00
Rosewood, 2 Sections, Mother-Of-Pearl Inlay, 19th Century, 5 x 8 x 5 In. 200.00
Rosewood, Bird's-Eye Maple, Sarcophagus, Ebony Stringing, Bun Feet, c.1810, 25 In. . . . 475.00
Rosewood, Brass & Mother-Of-Pearl Inlay, Coffin Shape, 7 x 9 x 6 In. 173.00
Rosewood, Brass Inlay, Hinged Top, Glass Bowl, Regency, c.1815, 8 x 15 x 7 In. 2390.00
Rosewood, Coffin Shape, 2 Compartments, Bowl, Bun Feet, Regency, 7 1/2 x 12 In. 345.00
Rosewood, Coffin Shape, 2 Compartments, Bowl, c.1820, 7 1/2 x 12 x 6 In. 290.00
Rosewood, Coffin Shape, 2 Compartments, Glass Insert, Regency, 8 x 12 x 7 In. 1150.00
Rosewood, Coffin Shape, Brass Ball Feet, Regency, c.1815, 6 x 8 x 4 In. 375.00
Rosewood, Coffin Shape, Hinged Lid, 2 Compartments, Ring Handle, Regency, 8 In. 690.00
Rosewood, Coffin Shape, Inlaid, Mother-Of-Pearl, Bun Feet, Regency, 6 x 8 x 5 In. 635.00
Rosewood, Coffin Shape, Lid, Inlay, Brass Feet, Regency, c.1815, 5 x 8 x 4 1/2 In. 460.00
Rosewood, Sarcophagus, Satinwood Inlay, Gilt Brass, Ring Handles, c.1810, 8 1/2 In. . . . 365.00
Rosewood, Tapering Sides, Hinged Lid, 2 Compartments, Bun Feet, 1820, 9 x 6 x 5 In. . . 400.00
Satinwood, 3 Compartments, Pinwheels, Georgian, c.1785, 6 3/4 x 12 In. 1380.00
Satinwood, Burl Walnut Inlay, Hinged Lid, c.1790, 5 1/4 x 7 3/4 x 4 3/8 In. 690.00
Satinwood, Burl Walnut Inlay, Hinged Lid, c.1800, 5 1/8 x 8 1/8 x 4 5/8 In. 805.00
Satinwood, Chamfered Corner, Hinged Lid, George III, c.1810 . . . . 980.00
Satinwood, Inlay, Coffin Shape, Hinged Lid, c.1840, 5 x 7 3/4 x 4 3/8 In. 518.00
Satinwood, Marquetry, 2 Compartments, Georgian, Early 1800s, 6 x 8 x 4 1/2 In. 1150.00
Satinwood, Rectangular, Burl Walnut Inlay, George III, c.1810, 5 x 9 x 5 In. 1150.00
Satinwood, Shell Inlay, Harewood Ground, Domed Top, Foil-Lined Interior, 7 x 5 In. 355.00
Silver, Armorial Engraving, George II, c.1734, 4 1/8 In. 3525.00
Silver, Copper, Fish, Seaweed, Crab, Dome Cover, Gorham Mfg. Co., c.1882, 4 1/2 In. . . . 5378.00
Silver, Flat Lid, Pineapple Finial, Engraved Coat Of Arms, George III, 4 In., Pair 1175.00
Silver, Mixed Metal, Woven Basket Shape, Whiting Mfg. Co., c.1880, 3 1/4 In. 5378.00
Silver, Rectangular, Canted Corners, Domed Cylindrical Cap, George I, 4 3/4 In. 1880.00
Silver Plate, 2 High Relief Panels, Horses & Hunters, Divided Compartment, 5 In. 635.00
Silver Plate Over Copper, Basket Shape, 2 Lift Lids, Ribbed Swing Handle, 3 x 6 In. . . . 110.00
Tin, Black Enamel, Gilt Bands, Rectangular Lid, c.1845, 5 3/4 x 5 1/2 x 3 3/4 In. 90.00
Tole, Flowers, Scrolls, Gilt Accents, Black Ground, Rectangular, Ball Feet, 7 3/4 In. 825.00
Tortoiseshell, Ivory, Satinwood Bun Feet, Quadrupled Hopes, Early 1800s 2600.00
Tortoiseshell, Mahogany, 3 Compartments, William IV, c.1835, 6 x 12 1/4 In. 2760.00
Tortoiseshell, Mother-Of-Pearl Bands, Cover, Bone Grip, William IV, 6 x 7 In. 1095.00
Tortoiseshell, Rectangular, Domed Lid, Sunburst Reed Carving, Ball Feet & Finial, 7 In. . . 3819.00
Tortoiseshell, Sarcophagus Lid, Silver Inlay, 2 Sections, Brass Ball Feet, 6 x 7 1/2 x 4 In. 1045.00
Tortoiseshell, Silver Escutcheon, Silver Plated Lid, Domed 460.00
Tortoiseshell, Silver Mounted, Bone, 2 Sections, 19th Century, 6 x 7 x 4 1/2 In. 3680.00
Tortoiseshell, Veneered, Hinged Lid, Brass Plate, England, 19th Century, 4 3/4 In. 880.00
Tortoiseshell, Walnut, Silver, Ivory, Feather Band, George III, c.1760, 6 x 11 x 7 In. 3885.00
Tulipwood, Ivory, Brass, Mother-Of-Pearl Inlay, 2 Compartments, Hinged, 9 In. 420.00
Walnut, Bird's-Eye Maple Flowers, c.1830, 5 1/2 x 9 x 5 In. 460.00
Walnut, Coffin Shape, Hinged Lid, Brass Handles, Regency, c.1815, 7 x 12 x 6 In. 750.00
Wood, Crossbanded Inlay, Starfish-Like Shells In Ovals, 8 Sides, 5 x 5 x 8 In. 770.00

Wood, Slant Front, Children, Stream, Polychrome, Porcelain Knob, Edwardian, 19 In. ...   90.00
Yew, Turned, Apple Form, Georgian Style, Bone Escutcheon, England, 6 1/2 In. 460.00

TEA LEAF IRONSTONE dishes are named for their decorations. There was a superstition that it was lucky if a whole tea leaf unfolded at the bottom of your cup. This idea was translated into the pattern of dishes known as *tea leaf*. By 1850, at least twelve English factories were making this pattern, and by the 1870s, it was a popular pattern in many countries. The tea leaf was always a luster glaze on early wares, although now some pieces are made with a brown tea leaf.

Baker, Grape Octagon, Walley	70.00
Basin, Meakin, 2 Piece	150.00
Bowl, Vegetable, Cover, Cable, Shaw	60.00
Bowl, Vegetable, Cover, Chelsea, Meakin	40.00
Bowl, Vegetable, Cover, Dignity, Hughes	135.00
Bowl, Vegetable, Cover, Gentle Square, Furnival	60.00
Bowl, Vegetable, Cover, Sunburst, Wilkinson ....60.00 to	70.00
Bowl, Vegetable, Open, Dignity, Hughes	30.00
Brush Vase, Cylindrical, Scalloped, Meakin	205.00
Butter, Fishhook, Meakin, 3 Piece	85.00
Butter, Gothic, Livesley & Powell, 3 Piece	150.00
Butter, Iona, Bishop & Stonier, 3 Piece	70.00
Cake Plate, Basketweave, Shaw	500.00
Cake Plate, Chelsea, Meakin	190.00
Cake Plate, Daisy, Shaw	50.00
Cake Plate, Hexagon, Shaw	60.00
Chamber Pot, Cover, Cable, Shaw	170.00
Coffee Set, Morning Glory, Mid 19th Century, 4 1/4 To 11 1/4 In., 5 Piece	1200.00
Coffeepot, Bamboo, Meakin	50.00
Compote, Hexagon, Shaw	375.00
Compote, Pedestal, Wilkinson	325.00
Creamer, Ceres, Elsmore & Forster	210.00
Creamer, Chelsea, Meakin	290.00
Creamer, Elegance, Clementson Bros.	600.00
Creamer, Gothic, Livesley & Powell, 5 In.	110.00
Creamer, Laurel Wreath, Copper Luster Trim, Elsmore & Forster	625.00
Creamer, Lenoir, Laughlin	130.00
Creamer, Portland, Elsmore & Forster	190.00
Cup, Clementson	25.00
Cup & Saucer, Balanced Vine, Clementson Bros.	30.00
Cup & Saucer, Ceres, Elsmore & Forster	30.00
Cup & Saucer, Clementson, Child's	350.00
Cup & Saucer, Cone, Meakin	25.00
Cup & Saucer, Fanfare, Elsmore & Forster	95.00
Cup & Saucer, Fanfare, Tobaco Leaf, Handleless, Elsmore & Forster	95.00
Cup & Saucer, Niagara, Walley	55.00
Eggcup, Boston, Meakin	250.00
Ewer & Basin, Beaded Band, Teaberry, Clementson Bros., 2 Piece	475.00
Ewer & Basin, Cable, 2 Piece	325.00
Ewer & Basin, Cable, Shaw, 2 Piece	325.00
Ewer & Basin, Lion's Head, Mellor Taylor, 2 Piece	225.00
Ewer & Basin, Maidenhair Fern, Wilkinson, 2 Piece	250.00
Gravy Boat, Bamboo, Grindley	20.00
Gravy Boat, Bathtub, Mayer	70.00
Gravy Boat, Daisy & Chain, Wilkinson	70.00
Gravy Boat, Gothic, Livesley & Powell	70.00
Gravy Boat, Grand Loop, Furnival	350.00
Jug, Burgess, 6 5/8 In.	170.00
Ladle, Sauce, Shaw	250.00
Pitcher, Bamboo, Meakin, 7 3/4 In.	110.00
Pitcher, Daisy, Shaw, 5 1/2 In.	90.00
Pitcher, Grape Octagon, Livesley & Powell, 11 In. ....85.00 to	250.00
Pitcher, Maidenhair Fern, Wilkinson, 6 In.	225.00

Pitcher, Maidenhair Fern, Wilkinson, 8 1/2 In. 425.00
Pitcher, Oval, Cartwright, 6 3/4 In. 55.00
Pitcher, Peerless, Edwards, 8 In. 400.00
Platter, Brocade, Meakin, 12 x 17 In. 70.00
Platter, Ceres, Elsmore & Forster, 16 In. 90.00
Potty, Cover, Grape Octagon, Livesley & Powell 160.00
Potty, Maidenhair Fern, Wilkinson 450.00
Relish, Cable, Furnival 90.00
Relish, Chinese, Shaw 220.00
Relish, Daisy & Chain, Wilkinson 30.00
Relish, Elegance, Mitten Shape, Teaberry, Clementson 625.00
Relish, Gentle Square, Furnival 220.00
Relish, Lily Of The Valley, Mitten Shape, Shaw 250.00
Relish, Oval, Burgess 45.00
Sauce, Bamboo, Meakin, 3 Piece 60.00
Shaving Mug, Chinese, Shaw 120.00
Shaving Mug, Niagara, Shaw 750.00
Shaving Mug, Portland, Elsmore & Forster 1250.00
Shaving Mug, Square Ridge, Mellor Taylor 600.00
Soap Dish, Cable, Shaw 325.00
Soap Dish, Fishhook, Meakin, 3 Piece 105.00
Soup, Cream, Undertray, Sayres 80.00
Sugar, Cover, Ceres, Copper Luster Wheat Band, Elsmore & Forster 250.00
Sugar, Elsmore & Forster 55.00
Sugar & Creamer, Fishhook, Meakin 70.00
Teapot, Grape Octagon, Walley 100.00
Teapot, Niagara, Walley 140.00
Teapot, Ring Of Hearts, Livesley & Powell 150.00
Teapot, Tulip, Elsmore & Forster 200.00
Tureen, Soup, Cover, Wedgwood, 3 Piece 200.00
Tureen, Soup, Red Cliff, 4 Piece 175.00
Undertray, Hexagon, Shaw 50.00
Vase, Toothbrush, Footed, Shaw 425.00
Vase, Toothbrush, Scalloped, Meakin ....150.00 to 205.00
Waste Bowl, Portland, Morning Glory, Elsmore & Forster 260.00

TECO is the mark used on the art pottery line made by the American
Terra Cotta and Ceramic Company of Terra Cotta and Chicago,
Illinois. The company was an offshoot of the firm founded by William
D. Gates in 1881. The Teco line was first made in 1885 but was not
sold commercially until 1902. It continued in production until 1922.
Over 500 designs were made in a variety of colors, shapes, and glazes.
The company closed in 1930.

T€co

Bowl, Holly, Round, Low, Green Matte Glaze, Marked, 9 In. 173.00
Bowl, Low Shape, Green Matte Glaze, Impressed Marks, 7 In. 345.00
Chamberstick, Green Matte Glaze, Marked, 5 In. 240.00
Vase, 2 Handles, Green Matte Glaze, 5 1/2 x 8 1/2 In. 1998.00
Vase, 2 Handles, Green Matte Glaze, Impressed Marks, 5 1/2 In. 316.00
Vase, 4 Buttress Form, Organic Design, Green Matte Glaze, Moreau, Marked, 14 1/2 In. . 4025.00
Vase, 4 Buttresses, Green Matte Glaze, Ivory Interior, Holmes Smith, 12 x 6 In. . 5465.00
Vase, 4 Cutout Buttresses, Green Matte Glaze, W.D. Gates, Impressed Mark, 7 In. 2875.00
Vase, 4 Whiplash Handles, Green Matte Glaze, Charcoal, Stamped, 12 x 4 3/4 In. 2760.00
Vase, Bud, Raised Rim, 4 Dimples, Impressed, c.1910, 2 3/4 In. 410.00
Vase, Bulbous, 3-Sided Rim, Buff Matte Glaze, Stamped, 4 1/2 x 4 In. 460.00
Vase, Bulbous, Buttressed Handles, Mottled Green, Charcoal Matte Glaze, 7 x 4 In. 2415.00
Vase, Bulbous, Green, Brown Matte Glaze, Handles, Stamped, 4 x 4 In. 920.00
Vase, Bulbous, Green, Brown Speckled Matte Glaze, Stamped, 5 1/2 x 5 1/4 In. 1495.00
Vase, Buttressed Rim, Charcoal Matte Green Glaze, 4 Sides, Stamped, 9 1/4 x 4 1/4 In. . 2990.00
Vase, Buttresses, Bulbous, Flared Rim, Green Matte Glaze, Charcoaling, 6 3/4 x 3 1/4 In.. 1955.00
Vase, Cylindrical, Molded Lily Shape, Green Matte Glaze, Fritz Albert, 13 In. 1095.00
Vase, Double Gourd, Handles, Green Matte Glaze, Charcoaling, Stamped, 6 3/4 x 6 In. .. 3335.00
Vase, Egg Shape, 2 Buttressed Handles, Green Matte Glaze, 5 1/4 x 3 In. 1410.00
Vase, Flared Rim, 12 Applied Leaves, Green Matte Glaze, Charcoaling, Stamped, 12 In. .. 10350.00

Vase, Flared, Green Matte Glaze, Charcoaling, Oval, Mark, 11 1/2 x 4 3/4 In. 1210.00
Vase, Flaring Organic Shape, Leaves, Green Matte Glaze, William Dodd, 12 In. 8625.00
Vase, Gourd, Handles, Green Matte Glaze, Stamped, 6 3/4 x 5 1/2 In. 2760.00
Vase, Green Matte Glaze, Ivory Interior, Holmes, Smith, 12 x 6 In. 5465.00
Vase, Handles, Footed, Green Matte Glaze, Stamped, 3 1/4 x 4 3/4 In. 489.00
Vase, Handles, Green Matte Glaze, 3 3/4 In. 546.00
Vase, Handles, Green Matte Glaze, Impressed Mark, 4 In. 635.00
Vase, Lobed, Ivory Matte Glaze, Leathery, Stamped, 13 x 6 In. 4025.00
Vase, Pinched Waist, Green Matte Glaze, Charcoaling, 7 In. 978.00
Vase, Shouldered Shape, Green Matte Glaze, 4 1/2 In. 374.00
Vase, Shouldered Shape, Green Matte Glaze, Marked, 4 In. 374.00
Vase, Tapered, 2 Open Buttresses, Green Matte Glaze, W.B. Mundie, 11 In. 1495.00
Vase, Tapered, 4 Triangular Buttresses, Green Matte Glaze, Fernand Moreau, 9 In. 2415.00
Vase, Tulip Shape, 4 Buttresses, Blue Matte Glaze, Fernand Moreau, 12 In. 1955.00
Vase, Tulips, Green Matte Glaze, Charcoaling, Stamped, 11 3/4 x 4 3/4 In. 3450.00

TEDDY BEARS were named for a president of the United States. The
first teddy bear was a cuddly toy said to be inspired by a hunting trip
made by Teddy Roosevelt in 1902. Morris and Rose Michtom started
selling their stuffed bears as *teddy bears* and the name stayed. The
Michtoms founded the Ideal Novelty and Toy Company. The German
version of the teddy bear was made about the same time by the Steiff
Company. There are many types of teddy bears and all are collected.
The old ones are being reproduced. Other bears are listed in the Toy
section.

Mohair, Brown, Swivel Head, Humpback, Brown Glass Eyes, Blue Bow, 30 In. 600.00
Mohair, Elongated Limbs, Felt Pads, Shoebutton Eyes, Stuffed, Straw, 14 1/2 In. 1295.00
Mohair, Gold, Jointed, Early 20th Century, 17 In. 290.00
Mohair, Jointed, Humpback, Early 20th Century, 21 In. 120.00
Mohair, Long Fur, White, Woven Nose, Stitched Mouth, Glass Eyes, 1920s, 23 In. 265.00
Plush, Ocher, Jointed, Glass Eyes, Early 20th Century, 11 In. 50.00
Schuco, Mohair, Yes-No, Music Box, Molded Nose, Glass Eyes, 1940s, 16 In. 999.00
Steiff, Dicky, Mohair, Golden, Fully Jointed, Box, 12 In. 400.00
Steiff, Mohair, Blond, Brown, Peach Felt Mouth, Sleeping, Brown Eye, 7 1/4 In. 30.00
Steiff, Mohair, Blond, Jointed, Steel Eyes, Felt Pads, Stitched Face, c.1910, 10 In. 1528.00
Steiff, Mohair, Blond, Rod Joints, Felt Paws, 5 Claws, Button Eyes, 1905, 20 In. 4700.00
Steiff, Mohair, Dark Brown, Jointed, Humpback, 5 In. 800.00
Steiff, Mohair, Gold, Fully Jointed, Ear Button, 12 1/2 In. 920.00
Steiff, Mohair, Gold, Humpback, Brown Glass Eyes, 14 In. 375.00
Steiff, Mohair, Light Brown, Padded Paws, Brown Glass Eyes, 8 1/2 In. 33.00
Steiff, Mohair, White, Fully Jointed, Button In Left Ear, 17 In. 8200.00
Steiff, Mohair, White, Humpback, Black Button Eyes, Leather Collar, Chain, 16 In. 2600.00
Steiff, Zotty, Curly Mohair, Open Mouth, Glass Eyes, Ear Button & Tag, 1950, 22 In. 270.00

TELEPHONES are wanted by collectors if the phones are old enough or
unusual enough. The first telephone may have been made in Havana,
Cuba, in 1849, but it was not patented. The first publicly demonstrated
phone was used in Frankfurt, Germany, in 1860. The phone made by
Alexander Graham Bell was shown at the Centennial Exhibition in
Philadelphia in 1876, but it was not until 1877 that the first private
phones were installed. Collectors today want all types of old phones,
phone parts, and advertising. Even recent figural phones are popular.

Bauhaus, Metal & Bakelite, c.1929 . . . . 14950.00
Booth, Wood, Pressed Tin Interior, Porcelain Bell Telephone Sign, Original Pay Phone . . . 2750.00
G. Hasler, Wall, Fixed Microphone, Side Crank, Bern, Switzerland, 1925 . . . . 409.00
Garfield, Figural, Tyco, 1988, 5 x 9 3/4 x 5 In. 25.00
Grammont, Wooden Case On Marble Socket, Paris, France, 1917 . . . . 995.00
Kellogg, Candlestick, S. & S. Co., 1908 . . . . 175.00
L.M. Ericsson, Wall, Turntable Microphone, Sweden, 1900 . . . . 2300.00
L.M. Ericsson, Wood, Brass Autodial, Clockwork Mechanism, Stockholm, Sweden 420.00
Sign, Bell System Underground Telephone Cable Plaque, Porcelain, 7 x 3 1/2 In. 11.00
Sign, Bell System, Public Telephone, Porcelain, 2 Sides, 11 x 11 In. . . . . .95.00 to 120.00
Sign, Independent Telephone Pay Station, Porcelain, Flange, 18 x 8 In. 215.00

Table, Ader, Wooden Case, Marble Socket, Bullring Receivers, France, 1880 . . . . 5638.00
Toy, Truck, Bell, 5 1/4 In. 200.00
Toy, Truck, Bell, Olive Green, Hubley, Box, 1950s, 8 In. 250.00
Western Electric Wall, Oak Case, 24 In. 242.00

TELEVISION sets are twentieth-century collectibles. Although the first
television transmission took place in England in 1925, collectors find
few sets which pre-date 1946. The first sets had only five channels, but
by 1949 the additional UHF channels were included. The first color
television set became available in 1951.

    JVC, Model 3240, Table, Red, Orange, Circular, Plastic Case, Carton 176.00

TEPLITZ refers to art pottery manufactured by a number of companies
in the Teplitz-Turn area of Bohemia during the late nineteenth and
early twentieth centuries. Two of these companies were the Alexandra
Works and The Amphora Porcelain Works, run by Reissner,
Stellmacher, and Kessel, Ernst Wahliss, connected with the RS & K
wares, started his own factory after 1900.

Basket, Grapes, Leaves, Cross-Type Handle, Gold, Blue Beads, Amphora, 7 In. 834.00
Bowl, Mottled Blue, Green Ground, Gold Trim, Butterfly Wing Supports, Amphora, 7 In. . . 405.00
Bowl, Multicolored Birds, Footed, 5 x 8 In. 35.00
Bust, Elegantly Dressed Woman, Printed Marks, 20 In. 2270.00
Bust, Young Girl, Gold & Metallic Iridescent, Amphora, 16 In. 1230.00
Candlestick, Open Flower, Supported By Fairy, Gold Matte Glaze, Ernst Wahliss, 5 In. . . 805.00
Candlestick, Organic Form, Shaped Handle, Green, Blue, Amphora, 11 In. 1150.00
Compote, Jeweled, Carved, Mottled Green, Rose, Pedestal, 4 Legs, Amphora, 7 In. 1320.00
Ewer, Globular, Flower Decoration, Gilt Details, Marked, 8 1/2 In. 896.00
Ewer, Polychrome & Gilt, Floral & Mask, Leaf Handle, Stellmacher, 18 In. 288.00
Figurine, Bust Of Lady, Signed E. Stelmacher, 22 In. 575.00
Figurine, Maiden, Extended Arms On Leaves, Amphora, Signed Stellmucher, 19 1/2 In. . . 9315.00
Pitcher, Boy, Straw Hat, Green Matte Glaze, Impressed 2116, 5 3/4 In. 80.00
Pitcher, Red Flower Sprigs, Dragon Handle, Fish Spout, Stamp, 12 In. 345.00
Vase, 2 Girls, Bathtime, Green Matte Glaze, 2 Handles, Amphora, 7 3/8 In. 105.00
Vase, Applied Grapes, Vines, Amphora, Amphora, Marked Edda, 9 1/2 In. 405.00
Vase, Art Nouveau, Portrait, Floral, Amphora, 14 1/2 In. 2800.00
Vase, Blown-Out Trees, Pinecones, Amphora, 9 In. 978.00
Vase, Bottle Shape, High Relief Dragon, Marked, 20 In. 15535.00
Vase, Cover, Egyptian, Winged Heads, Jeweled, Blue, Brown, Amphora, 12 In. . . . . . *Illus* 1225.00
Vase, Female, Dress Wrapped Around Bottom, Art Nouveau, Lavender, Beige, 9 1/8 In. . . 290.00
Vase, Flattened Square Form, Bust Of Woman, Gilt Details, Mark, 6 In. 5875.00
Vase, Insect, Blue, Black, Green, Ivory, Gold Trim, Amphora, 8 1/2 In. 690.00
Vase, Leaves, Acorns, Purple, Gilded, Gourd, Handles, Amphora, 7 1/4 x 6 In. 300.00
Vase, Luster Crystalline Bronze Glaze, Stamped Austria, 8 In. 400.00
Vase, Multicolored Flowers, Amphora, 17 1/2 In. 322.00
Vase, Oval, Enamel, Stylized Flower Bands, Green Ground, Amphora, 18 x 10 In. 325.00
Vase, Owl, Flowers, Brown Ground, High Glaze, Amphora, 8 1/2 In. 290.00
Vase, Pearlescent Berries, Reticulated Rim, Impressed Dachsel, Austria, 6 In. 2875.00
Vase, Poppies Against Shaded Blue Ground, Gilt, Egg Shape, 7 In. 529.00

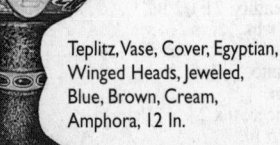

Teplitz, Vase, Cover, Egyptian,
Winged Heads, Jeweled,
Blue, Brown, Cream,
Amphora, 12 In.

**It is said creativity comes from a
messy, cluttered environment. It
inspires ideas. Remember that
the next time you rearrange
your collectibles.**

Vase, Pottery, Swollen Cylindrical, Landscape, Deer, Flowers, Iridescent Red, 17 3/4 In. . . . 764.00
Vase, Raised Jewel, Gilt Details, Egg Shape, Amphora, Mark, 6 In. 2938.00
Vase, Raspberry Clusters Hanging From Green Stalks, Marked, Paul Dachsel, 16 In. 2530.00
Vase, Red, Green & Ivory Design, Gold Highlights, Pedestal Base, Amphora, 6 In. 35.00
Vase, Roses, Yellow, Mottled Blue, Cream, Gold Ground, Handles, Amphora, 13 1/2 In. . . . 860.00
Vase, Sea Serpent, Water Lily, Maiden Emerges From Top, Amphora, 16 1/2 In. 1090.00
Vase, Shouldered, Oval Shape, Continuous River Landscape, Gilt Details, Mark, 4 1/2 In. . . 558.00
Vase, Trees, Painted, Applied Flowers & Leaves, Amphora, 12 In. 489.00
Vase, Urn Form, 2 Handles, Stylized Flowers, Amphora, 1900s, 10 5/8 In. 350.00
Vase, Woman, Child, Spring Clothes, Baskets, Square, Green, Pink Drapery, 6 In. 115.00
Vase, Woman, Flowing Hair, Grapes, Vine, Trees, Art Nouveau, Amphora, 16 In. 1295.00

TERRA-COTTA is a special type of pottery. It ranges from pale orange to
dark reddish-brown in color. The color comes from the clay, which is
fired but not always glazed in the finished piece.

Bowl, Dinner Set, Traditional Style, Pie Crust Crimp Edge, France, 11 1/2 In., 10 Piece . . 230.00
Bowl, Salad, Yellow Gloss Glaze, France, 12 In., 8 Piece 145.00
Bust, Baby, Onyx Base, 9 3/4 In. 430.00
Bust, George Washington, After Houdon, 23 x 11 x 12 In. 5019.00
Bust, Indian, Hollow, Red Patina, 10 x 10 1/2 In. 110.00
Bust, Lady, Marble Base, 19th Century, 28 1/2 In. 1265.00
Bust, Venus, Weathered, Louis XVI, 27 In. 978.00
Bust, Woman Amid Bulrush Reeds, Taupe, Self Socle, Art Nouveau, 1900, 25 In. 880.00
Figurine, Cat, Painted, Wood Base, c.1900, 5 1/4 x 5 1/4 In. 290.00
Figurine, Dog, Pug, Painted, Austria, 16 1/2 In. 1555.00
Figurine, Dwarf Holding Apron, Radish, No. 1713, 17 In. 920.00
Figurine, Eagles Perched, Open Wings, French Glazed, 28 1/2 x 22 1/2 In., Pair 1840.00
Figurine, Jester, Man, Woman, Polychrome Glazes, Italy, 56 1/2 In., Pair 2875.00
Figurine, Lion, Hand Tooling, Pink Gray, Black, White, 4 1/2 x 10 1/4 x 5 1/4 In. 90.00
Figurine, Munich Child Sitting On Barrel, 10 In. 949.00
Figurine, Reclining Nude, Etienne Leroux, Impressed, 1867, 31 x 20 x 9 1/2 In. 2990.00
Figurine, Sheep, White, Glass Eyes, 13 x 20 In. 805.00
Hair Grower, Smiling Man's Head, Germany 45.00
Humidor, Terrier, Smoking Pipe, Red Hat, Late 19th Century, 6 In. 210.00
Jar, Confit, Demi Citron Glaze, 2 Handles, France, 12 1/2 x 8 1/2 In. 175.00
Jar, Confit, Demi Ocher Glaze, 2 Handles, 14 In. 316.00
Jar, Confit, Demi Ocher Glaze, Buff, 2 Handles, France, 13 3/4 x 8 1/4 In. 175.00
Jar, Oil, Ming Dynasty Style, Pyriform, Green, 3 Frogs, Chinese, 37 1/4 x 29 1/2 In. 460.00
Jar, Oil, Storage, Green Glaze, Pyriform, France, 18 1/2 In., Pair 144.00
Mixing Bowl, Cobalt Blue Glaze, France, 15 In., Pair 145.00
Mixing Bowl, Green Glaze, France, c.1900, 15 In., Pair 144.00
Planter, Figural, Donkey, 25 1/2 x 31 In. 104.00
Planter, Wall, Ancient Greek Man's Head, England, 8 1/2 In. 35.00
Planter, Wall, Art Nouveau Head, Continental, 13 1/2 In. 35.00
Plaque, B. Franklin American, Nini, 1777, 4 1/2 In. 1375.00
Plaque, Continental, 2 Putto Heads, Continental, 10 1/2 In. 69.00
Plaque, Flora, Classical Dress, Bearing Traditional Attributes, Oval, 20 1/2 x 15 In. 69.00
Plaque, Head Of Triton, Seashells, Kelp, Crab Crawling, France, 23 1/2 In. 259.00
Plaque, Louis XVI Style, Haut Relief, Putto, Oval, France, 9 1/2 In. 29.00
Plaque, Napoleon III Style, Woodland Sprite, Child Satyr, Circular, 20 1/4 In. 90.00
Plaque, Relief, Round, Depicting Venus & Cupids, Leaf Border, 25 In. 529.00
Pot, Strawberry, 3 Handles, Pyriform, c.1900, 25 1/2 x 24 1/2 In. 145.00
Reliquary, Figural, Bishop, Chest Area Window, Italy, 18th Century, 22 In. 748.00
Sculpture, Figurine, 3 Cherubs, Painted, France, 18th Century, 10 1/2 In. 855.00
Sculpture, Jancerrs, Moses, After Michelangelo, 19th Century, 21 1/2 In. 855.00
Tobacco Jar, Dwarf Standing With Champagne Bottle, 11 In. 604.00
Tobacco Jar, Turkey, 9 1/2 In. 754.00
Tondo, Nymph Playing Pipes, Dancing Satyr, Winged Putto, France, 20 In. 115.00
Vase, Dragon Encircling, Incised, J.M., Austria, 16 3/4 In. 316.00
Vase, Louis XVI Style, Monumental, Ram Masque, France, 90 x 24 In., Pair 2990.00
Vase, Square Pedestals, Ribbon Wreaths, 21 x 14 1/2 x 15 In. 865.00
Wall Bracket, Female Heads, Scroll, Palmate, Concrete Interior, 11 x 8 x 8 In., Pair 201.00
Wall Pocket, Cherub, Reeded, France, 10 1/4 x 16 In., Pair 144.00

TEXTILES listed here include many types of printed fabrics and table and household linens. Some other textiles will be found under Clothing, Coverlet, Quilt, Rug, etc.

Altar Cloth, Gold Brocade, Rose Pattern, 54 x 25 In.	60.00
Altar Cloth, Velvet, Embroidered Crucifix, Wreaths, Scalloped Edge, Silver Fringe, 1900 .	405.00
Bag, Eagle, 26 Stars In Sky, Floral, Silk Lining, Anna Whitemore, Gold Beads, 1837	1350.00
Bagface, Sumak, Medallions, Red Field, 38 x 18 In.	118.00
Banner, Sacred Heart, Burgundy Velvet, Silver Embroidery, Heart, Scrolls	920.00
Bell Pull, Needlepoint, Ship, Beads, Inset Mirrors, Elliptical, Tapered, Frame, 18 x 6 In.	265.00
Bell Pull, Needlepoint, White, Yellow Lilies, Brown Ground, Brass, 5 1/2 x 70 In.	120.00
Blanket, Saddle, 1920s, 29 1/2 x 58 In.	825.00
Blanket, Wool, White, Pine Tree Border, 2 Panel, 70 x 42 In.	205.00
Curtains, Linen, Eclipse Pattern, Warren Platner, Jack Lenor Larsen, Mid 1960s, 2 Pair	235.00
Doily, Crocheted, Starburst, Cotton, 10 In. . . . . *Illus*	25.00
Fabric, Mexicotton Stripe, Alexander Girard, Herman Miller, Gold, Ocher, 15 Yds.	4312.00
Flag, American, 13 Stars, 10 Stars In Circle, 3 Stars Triangle, c.1876, 57 x 92 In.	4780.00
Flag, American, 13 Stars, 12 Stars Circle 1 Star, Mid 19th Century, 45 x 60 1/2 In.	7770.00
Flag, American, 13 Stars, 1876 Centennial, 33 x 72 In.	176.00
Flag, American, 13 Stars, 1876, 49 x 101 In.	2689.00
Flag, American, 13 Stars, Centennial 1876, 52 x 75 In.	3885.00
Flag, American, 13 Stars, Diamond Configuration, c.1876, 49 x 116 In.	5975.00
Flag, American, 13 Stars, Silk, Rachel Albright, Ross' Granddaughter, 1908, 7 x 10 3/4 In.	4888.00
Flag, American, 13 Stars, Stars In 3 Rows, 5, 4, 4, c.1840, 35 x 58 3/4 In.	5079.00
Flag, American, 17 Stars, Commemorates Ohio Statehood, 1860-1890, 118 x 228 In.	8960.00
Flag, American, 19 Stars, 11 Stripes, For Indiana Statehood, 1861-1865, 48 x 91 In.	7170.00
Flag, American, 30 Stars, Commemorates Wisconsin Statehood, 1848, 59 x 65 1/2 In.	5975.00
Flag, American, 31 Stars, Commemorates California Statehood, 1850, 36 x 22 In.	5079.00
Flag, American, 32 Stars, Commemorates Minnesota Statehood, May 11, 1858, 5 x 7 In.	4180.00
Flag, American, 34 Stars, Civil War	8500.00
Flag, American, 34 Stars, Concentric Circle Stars, Bunting, c.1861, 53 x 65 In.	2300.00
Flag, American, 34 Stars, Double Medallions, Grant's Campaign, 1868, 22 x 33 In.	9560.00
Flag, American, 34 Stars, Handmade, Canton Sits On Red, 33 x 41 1/2 In.	3190.00
Flag, American, 35 Appliqued White Cotton Stars, Twill Hoist, c.1863, 70 x 100 In.	588.00
Flag, American, 35 Stars, Commemorates West Virginia Statehood, 1863, 61 x 73 In.	3585.00
Flag, American, 36 Stars, 1864-1867, 48 x 70 In.	2090.00
Flag, American, 37 Stars, Equal Taxation, 1868, 134 x 131 In.	4180.00
Flag, American, 38 Stars, c.1860, 54 x 78 In.	5975.00
Flag, American, 38 Stars, Rope Grommets, 1877-1890, 70 x 100 In.	118.00
Flag, American, 38 Stars, Wool Bunting, 12 x 6 1/2 In.	3737.00
Flag, American, 42 Stars, Walnut Frame, Under Glass, 12 x 17 In.	195.00
Flag, American, 44 Stars, Commemorates Wyoming Statehood, c.1890, 66 x 99 In.	3585.00
Flag, American, 47 Stars, Commemorates New Mexico Statehood, 66 x 105 In.	5975.00
Flag, American, 48 Stars, Marked Betsy Ross Bunting, 24 x 36 In.	45.00
Flag, American, 48 Stars, Silk, Frame	325.00
Flag, American, Centennial, 36 Stars, Blue Eagle, 1876, 42 1/2 x 28 In.	1434.00
Flag, American, Sitting Bull, Osceola, Black Hawk, Embroidered Borders, 22 In.	375.00
Flag, East Germany, 2 Sides, Printed, 28 x 15 In.	28.00
Flag, Old Glory Free Cuba, Sampson, Lee, Hobson, Red, White, Blue, 19 x 23 In.	1200.00

Textile, Doily, Crocheted, Starburst, Cotton, 10 In.

Textile, Mandarin Square, Panther, Buddhist Symbols, Male, Military, Late 1800s, Pair

Flag, Parade, 36 Stars, Cotton, Flag Staff, Holder, Mounted, Frame, 14 1/4 x 16 1/4 In. . . . 235.00
Flag, Uncle Sam Spanks Spaniard, Equity To All Nations, 2 1/2 In. 150.00
Handkerchief, Ol' King Cole Nursery Rhyme, Verse, Early 20th Century 24.00
Handkerchief Set, Flowers, Blue, Red, White Ground, Sears Roebuck, Original Box 12.00
Hot Pad, Patchwork, Basket Pattern, 6 x 6 In., 2 Piece 220.00
Hot Pad, Patchwork, Block Pattern, Round, 5 1/2 To 6 In., 3 Piece 175.00
Hot Pad, Patchwork, Block Pattern, Square, 5 x 5 In., 3 Piece 110.00
Lap Throw, Fur, Gray Wool Backing, Hermes, 64 1/4 x 76 In. 1645.00
Mandarin Square, Crane, Buddhist Symbols, Male, Civil 1st Rank, c.1800, Pair 2645.00
Mandarin Square, Embroidered, Tiger, Flowers, Bats, Female, Military 4th Rank, Pair . . . 805.00
Mandarin Square, Golden Pheasant, Bats, Clouds, Male, Civil 2nd Rank, c.1800, Pair . . . 1150.00
Mandarin Square, Panther, Buddhist Symbols, Male, Military, Late 1800s, Pair . . . . *Illus* 1323.00
Mandarin Square, Phoenix, Serrated Tail, Male, Civil Imperial Rank, Pair 489.00
Mandarin Square, Quail, Buddhist Symbols, Female, Civil 8th Rank, Pair 605.00
Mandarin Square, Tiger, Black Cloud-Filled Ground, Female, Military, Pair 375.00
Mattress Cover, Blue On White Stripe, 60 x 86 In. 28.00
Mattress Cover, Homespun, Blue Check 120.00
Napkin, Cotton, Daffodils & Daisies, Printed Signature Vera, Ladybug, 15 1/2 In. . . . *Illus* 20.00
Needlework, Tapestry, Seat Cover, Animals, Flowers, Birds, 19 x 23 In. 29.00
Needlework, Woman Plays Mandolin, Man Dances, M.A. Palmer, 1779, 9 x 11 1/2 In. . . . 2800.00
Panel, Alexander Girard, Environmental Enrichment, H. Miller, c.1971, 46 1/2 x 58 In. . . 805.00
Panel, Altar, Embroidered, Dragons, Butterflies, Gold, Chinese, 19th Century, 48 x 32 In. 355.00
Panel, Embroidered, Gold, Mica Inlay, Indonesia, 19th Century, 47 1/2 In. 588.00
Panel, Embroidered, Immortals, Deities, Chinese, 19th Century, 116 x 52 In. 2115.00
Panel, Embroidered, Peacock & Flowers, Yellow, Gold Thread Work, Chinese, 25 x 20 In. 115.00
Panel, Embroidered, Peacocks, Peonies, Gold Ground, Chinese, 32 x 35 In. 489.00
Panel, Embroidered, Roses, Wild Flowers, Oval, India, Mid 19th Century, 14 x 28 In. . . . 175.00
Panel, Flowers, Brocade Ground, Embroidered Panels, Sleeve Borders, c.1900, 56 x 88 In. 375.00
Panel, Foo Dogs, Mirror Pieces, Blue Ground, Gold Thread Work, Chinese, 36 x 36 In. . . 920.00
Panel, Old Sun Environmental Enrichment, Alexander Girard, c.1972, 47 x 47 In. 460.00
Panel, Silk, Embroidered, Elephant Carrying Vase, Chinese, 19th Century, 19 x 18 In. . . . 176.00
Panel, Silk, Embroidered, Gold Bullion Thread Cross, Flowers, Leaves, 24 x 34 In. 175.00
Pillow, Dog, Lying Down, Tufted Wool Needlework, Floral Jacquard, Braid Trim, 21 In. . . 176.00
Pillow, Tapestry, Camel, Pink, Flowers, Fringe, 18 x 18 In., Pair 546.00
Pillow, Tapestry, Cherubs, Flower Vase, Red Back, Flemish, 22 x 14 In. 575.00
Pillow, Tapestry, Taupe, Flowers, Linen Backing, Green, 17 x 15 In., Pair 375.00
Pillow, Velvet, Painted Silk, Embroidered, Terra-Cotta Brocade, Foo Dog, 21 x 25 In. . . . 1150.00
Pillow Case, Linen, Pink Poppies, Arts & Crafts, 24 x 16 1/2 In. 29.00
Playboy Bunny Outfit, Multicolored, Ears, Tail, Bowtie, Neck Collar, Wrist Cuffs, 1960s . 1235.00
Ribbon, Embroidered, Peacocks, Frame, India, c.1900, 40 x 27 In. 69.00
Sham, Bolster, Homespun, Blue Check, 21 x 62 In. 175.00
Sheet, Top, Embroidered, Buon Ripuso, Victorian, 108 x 120 In. 215.00
Show Towel, Birds, Flowers, Elizabeth Buchwalter, 1846, 57 x 17 In. 2310.00
Show Towel, Cross-Stitch, Birds, Flowers, Susana Brubacker, 1844, 65 x 17 1/2 In. 2860.00

Textile, Napkin, Cotton,
Daffodils & Daisies, Printed Signature
Vera, Ladybug, 15 1/2 In.

Textile, Towel, Linen, Appliqued
Oak Leaves, Acorns, Hand
Rolled, Marghab, 20 In.

Textile, Towel, Linen, Blue
Printed Poodle, Crewel Work
Puffs, Faux Pearl Eye, 19 1/2 In.

Show Towel, Heart, Star, Geometric, Flowers, Magaretha Arnold, c.1855, 61 x 15 1/2 In. . . 2090.00
Table Pad, Hooked, Blocks, Multicolored, 10 1/2 x 10 1/2 In. 165.00
Table Rug, With Scalloped Skirt, Flowers, 18th Century, 18 In. 495.00
Table Topper, Linen, Embroidered, Dragonfly Corners, Square, Victorian, 34 In. 75.00
Tablecloth, Penny, Wool, Blocks, Black, Green, Flowers, 40 x 71 In. 605.00
Tablecloth, Silk, Needlework, Star & Peacock, Purple, Red Saffron, Chinese, 66 x 88 In. . . 145.00
Tablecloth, White Damask, Yellow, Geometric, 1902, 53 x 70 In. 280.00
Tablecloth, Woven, Owens Corning Fiberglass, Numbered 94/500, Cased, 1940s 40.00
Tapestry, Aubusson, King, Queen On Throne, Servants, Followers, 112 x 116 In. 1434.00
Tapestry, Dancing Couples In Courtyard, 19th Century, 52 x 67 In. 920.00
Tapestry, Distant Castle In Woodland Scene, Fruit & Flowers, Wool, France, 134 x 93 In. 3290.00
Tapestry, Garden, 2 Cranes By Pond, Flower Border, 105 x 111 1/2 In. 4180.00
Tapestry, Hooked, Hemisphere, Evelyn Ackerman, c.1970, 50 x 27 In. 705.00
Tapestry, Hundred Children, Frame, Chinese, 19th Century, 80 x 55 In. 3055.00
Tapestry, Hunting Dogs Chasing Boar, Trees, Fringe, Arts & Crafts, 62 x 81 In. 1410.00
Tapestry, Pastoral, Shepherd & Shepherdess, Belgium, Late 17th Century, 118 x 123 In. . 5975.00
Tapestry, Screen, Velvet, Brocade, 3 Panel, Late 17 Century, 71 x 24 1/2 In. 4180.00
Tapestry, Warriors In Combat, Chinese, 19th Century, 53 x 13 In. 705.00
Tapestry, Wooded Landscape, Church, Flowers, Belgium, 17th Century, 104 x 88 In. 6570.00
Tapestry, Wool, Castle In Woodland Scene, Fringe, France, 134 x 93 In. 3290.00
Tapestry, Wool, Geometric, Red, Blue, Black, Green, Cream, Sonia Delaunay, 81 x 56 In. 2350.00
Tapestry Set, Aubusson, Birds & Pheasants, Landscape, 1800s, 20 x 15 In., 7 Piece 3236.00
Towel, Hand, Linen, Cotton, Verse, Birds, Flowers, Catherine Derr, c.1866, 54 x 18 In. . . . 2868.00
Towel, Homespun, Needlework, Peacock, Geometric, Rebeca Hishin, 1828, 16 x 52 In. . . . 660.00
Towel, Linen, Appliqued Oak Leaves, Acorns, Hand Rolled, Marghab, 20 In. . . . . . . *Illus* 20.00
Towel, Linen, Blue Printed Poodle, Crewel Work Puffs, Faux Pearl Eye, 19 1/2 In. . . *Illus* 18.00
Towel, Linen, Blue, Red Vine Border, Signed, Christian Bomberger, 1839, 16 1/2 x 52 In. 165.00
Waistpocket, Cotton, Patchwork, Flying Geese Variation, Centennial, 12 x 12 In. 499.00
Wall Hanging, 3 Figures, 2 Horses, Yellow, Orange, Brown, Rya, c.1950, 26 x 69 In. 206.00
Wall Hanging, Clipped Wool, Beadwork, Parrot, Flowers, Ebonized Frame, 18 x 18 In. . . . 764.00
Wall Hanging, Crocheted, Flowers, Red, Rose, Blue, Green, Bokaran Susani, 103 x 86 In. . 805.00
Wall Hanging, Jute, Turquoise, Signed, A. Calder, c.1975, 78 x 56 In. 3819.00
Wall Hanging, Linen, Turtle, Crab, Fish, Wood Fasteners, Ross Littell, c.1960, 12 x 36 In. 46.00
Wall Hanging, Needlepoint, Garden, Evelyn Ackerman, c.1963, 24 x 36 In. 823.00
Wall Hanging, Wool, Cotton, Goblins, Ada Kierzkowska, 1964, 86 1/2 x 69 In. 558.00
Weaving, Coptic Style, Animals, Wooded Landscapes, Fringe, 20th Century, 41 x 57 In. . . 374.00
Window Shade, Venini, Fixture With Ceiling Cap, Label, 19 1/2 In. 1725.00

THERMOMETER is a name that comes from the Greek word for heat.
The thermometer was invented in 1731 to measure the temperature of
either water or air. All kinds of thermometers are collected, but those
with advertising messages are the most popular.

Abbotts Bitters, San Francisco, Ca., Round, 1899, 9 In. 190.00
Camel Cigarettes, Camels, Have A Real Cigarette, Sold Here, 13 1/2 x 5 3/4 In. 70.00
Casite, Better & Smoother Performance, Tin, 10 x 26 In. 200.00
Chesterfield Cigarettes, They Satisfy, Tin, Embossed,, 6 x 13 In. 120.00
Chesterfield Cigarettes, Tin Lithograph, Embossed Pack, 13 x 6 In. 88.00
Chocolait Royale, Its Refreshing, Hot Or Cold, Tin Lithograph, 5 1/2 x 13 In. 90.00
Double Cola, You'll Like It Better, Blue Ground, Tin, 8 x 26 In. 165.00
Dr Pepper, Hot Or Cold, Plastic Face, Dial, 1950-1960, 12 In. 140.00
Ex-Lax, Chocolate Laxative, Keep Regular, Porcelain, 36 x 8 1/4 x 1 3/8 In. 145.00
Farnham, Horse Care Products, Horses, Pam Clock, Square, 12 In. 110.00
Gaerdner & Co. Morticians, Hearse, 9 1/4 In. 80.00
Geffinger Scientific Optician, Eyes Examined Free, Wooden, 12 x 3 1/8 In. 135.00
Hires Root Beer, Figural, Embossed, Die Cut, Metal, 8 x 28 1/2 In. 80.00
Hires Root Beer, Tin Ad Face, Aluminum Case, 12 In. 90.00
Hobo, Mounted On Base, 5 3/4 x 4 1/2 In. 16.00
M.J. O'Hara & Sons Sales, Amoco, White Ground, 24 x 8 In. 138.00
Mail Pouch Tobacco, Treat Yourself To The Best, 39 x 8 In. 80.00
Mason's Root Beer, Tin Ad Face, Aluminum Case, Dial, 12 In. 130.00
Mo-Ko, Wooden, John F. Bauer Co., Elmira, N.Y., Box, 3 x 12 In. 45.00
Mobil, Sanilac Cattle Spray, Field With Cows, Riber, 18 x 8 In. 410.00
Neuhuser Hatcheries, Hy-Line Chicks, Metal, Glass, Round, 12 In. 110.00

Obelisk, Pietra Dura, Inset In Base, 33 In.	1645.00
Orange Crush, Metal, 16 x 5 3/4 In.	90.00
Pink Rose, Lucite, 2 1/8 x 1 x 2 5/16 In.	12.00
Prestone Anti-Freeze, Porcelain, Gray, Blue, Red, 36 x 8 In.	100.00
Red Crown Gasoline, Porcelain, 20 x 73 In.	1140.00
Red Goose Shoes, Porcelain, 27 In.	468.00
Red Rock Cola, Soda Bottle, Metal, 27 x 7 In.	330.00
Reynolds Coal, Wood, Painted, Glass, 21 In.	55.00
Royal Crown Cola, Red Ground, Tin, 10 x 25 In.	195.00
Shur-On Eyeglasses, Wood, Painted, 24 In.	230.00
Sparkling Champale, Tin Lithograph, Permanent Sign & Display Co., c.1950, 8 x 8 In.	20.00
Sun Drop Cola, 24 In.	149.00
USS American Fence & Posts, Buy The Fence, Porcelain, 19 x 6 1/2 In.	220.00
White Metal, Marble Base, Brass Plate, Late 19th Century, 8 In.	150.00

TIFFANY is a name that appears on items made by Louis Comfort Tiffany, the American glass designer who worked from about 1879 to 1933. His work included iridescent glass, Art Nouveau styles of design, and original contemporary styles. He was also noted for stained glass windows, unusual lamps, bronze work, pottery, and silver. Other types of Tiffany are listed under Tiffany Glass, Tiffany Gold, Tiffany Pottery, or Tiffany Silver. The famous Tiffany lamps are listed in this section. Tiffany jewelry is listed in the jewelry and wristwatch categories. Some Tiffany Studio desk sets have matching clocks. They are listed here. Clocks made by Tiffany & Co. are listed in the Clock category. Reproductions of some types of Tiffany are being made.

Louis C. Tiffany

Ash Stand, Bronze, Copper Insert, Swirled Base, 26 In.	980.00
Ash Stand, Bronze, Gold Dore, Removable Tray, 28 x 8 1/2 In.	1150.00
Ashtray, Bronze, Footed, Gold Dore, Pedestal Base, 3 1/4 In.	400.00
Ashtray, Match Safe, Bronze, Gold Dore, Round, Footed, Signed, 4 In.	560.00
Ashtray, Match Safe, Venetian, Sculptured Minks, Bronze, Gold Dore, 5 x 3 1/2 x 3 In.	450.00
Ashtray, Spanish, Bronze, Gold Dore, 8 Sides, Signed, 4 1/2 In.	750.00
Ashtray Set, Bronze, Gold Dore, Nested, Round, 4 1/2, 3 3/4 & 3 In., 3 Piece	225.00
Bill File, Bookmark, Bronze, Gold Dore, 8 Sides, 3 3/4 x 6 1/2 In.	650.00
Bill File, Byzantine, Bronze, Gold Dore, Turquoise Stones, Mother-Of-Pearl Beads, 8 In.	1500.00
Bill File, Zodiac, Bronze, Curved Spindle, Signed, 7 3/4 In.	750.00
Blotter, Graduate, Bronze, Gold Dore, Knob Handle, Signed, 2 3/4 x 5 1/2 In.	250.00
Blotter, Louis XVI, Wreath, Ribbon, Bronze, Knob Handle, Signed, 5 1/4 x 2 3/4 In.	450.00
Blotter, Pine Needle, Slag Glass, Bronze, Gold Dore, Knob Handle, 6 x 3 x 2 In.	400.00
Blotter, Venetian, Bronze, Knob Handle, Signed, 5 1/4 x 2 3/4 In.	350.00
Blotter, Zodiac, Bronze, Gold Dore, Knob Handle, 5 1/2 x 2 3/4 x 2 In.	400.00
Blotter, Zodiac, Bronze, Knob Handle, Signed, 5 1/4 In.	350.00
Blotter Ends, American Indian, Bronze, Gold Dore, Signed, 12 x 2 In., Pair	300.00
Blotter Ends, Chinese, Bronze, Dark Patina, Signed, 19 x 2 In., Pair	250.00
Blotter Ends, Graduate, Bronze, Gold Dore, Signed, 19 x 2 1/4 In., Pair	250.00
Blotter Ends, Grapevine, Corner, Bronze, Signed, 5 3/4 x 5 3/4 x 8 In., 4 Piece	500.00
Blotter Ends, Louis XVI, Wreath, Bronze, Signed, 12 1/4 x 1 1/4 In., Pair	350.00
Blotter Ends, Pine Needle, Bronze, Dark Patina, Signed, 12 x 2 In., Pair	450.00
Blotter Ends, Pine Needle, Bronze, Green Patina, Corner, 5 3/4 In., 4 Piece	390.00
Blotter Ends, Pine Needle, Dark Patina, Signed, 19 x 2 In., Pair	450.00
Blotter Ends, Venetian, Raised Minks, Bronze, Gold Dore, 19 1/4 x 2 1/2 In., Pair	400.00
Blotter Ends, Zodiac, Bronze, Gold Dore, Signed, 12 1/4 In., Pair	175.00
Blotter Ends, Zodiac, Bronze, Gold Dore, Signed, 19 x 2 In., Pair	250.00
Bonbon, Bronze, Gold Dore, Scalloped, Pedestal, 1 1/2 x 3 3/4 In.	150.00
Bookends, Bronze, Zodiac, Stamped, 5 3/4 x 4 3/4 In.	460.00
Bookends, Buddha, Raised Platform, Bronze, Gold Dore, 6 x 3 In., Pair	750.00
Bookends, Engraved Art Nouveau Design, Bronze, No. 1765, Pair	520.00
Bookends, Graduate, Bronze, Gold Dore, Signed, 5 x 5 3/4 In., Pair	750.00
Bookends, Grapevine, Amber Slag Glass, Bronze, Gold Dore, 5 1/2 In., Pair	1500.00
Bookends, Hieroglyphic Symbols, Birds, Trees, Rectangular, Bronze, 5 3/4 In., Pair	2500.00
Bookends, Jewels, Enamel, Bronze, Gold Dore, Signed, 5 In., Pair	1500.00
Bookends, Peacock Portal, Bronze, Gold Dore, Signed, 4 1/2 In., Pair	1200.00
Bookends, Venetian, Bronze, Gold Dore, Signed, 5 x 6 In., Pair	1500.00

Bookends, Zodiac, Gold Dore, Signed, 5 x 6 In., Pair . . . . .575.00 to 800.00
Bookrack, Grapevine, Green Slag Glass, Bronze, 14 In. Extends To 23 In. 2500.00
Bowl, Abalone Insets, Flowered Rim, Bronze, Gold Dore, Signed, 8 3/4 In. 316.00
Bowl, Carved Wood, Glass, Favrile, c.1908, 3 1/8 In. 7768.00
Bowl, Gilt Brass, Mottled Texture, Tallship Medallion, No. 406, Signed, Favrile, 8 In. 190.00
Box, Card, Hinged Cover, Pine Needle, Green Slag Glass, 2 Sections, Bronze, 3 x 4 In. . . 1500.00
Box, Enameled Design, 4 Ball Feet, Bronze, Gold Dore, 4 x 6 1/2 In. 730.00
Box, Geometric Design, Bronze, Patina, Signed, 5 In. 370.00
Box, Grapevine, Amber Slag Glass, Bronze, Gold Dore, Signed, 4 1/4 x 3 x 1 3/4 In. 450.00
Box, Hinged Cover, Adam, Bronze, Gold Dore, Oval, 4 x 3 x 1 1/2 In. 500.00
Box, Hinged Cover, Adam, Wreath, Ribbon, Urn, Bronze, Gold Dore, 5 x 3 3/4 x 1 3/4 In. 750.00
Box, Hinged Cover, Beaded, Star, Enameled, Bronze, Gold Dore, 6 1/4 x 4 In. 900.00
Box, Hinged Cover, Bookmark, Bronze, Gold Dore, 5 x 3 In. 800.00
Box, Hinged Cover, Bookmark, Gold Dore, Cedar Liner, Signed, 6 1/4 x 5 3/4 x 2 1/2 In. . 1200.00
Box, Hinged Cover, Fleur-De-Lis, Enamel, Bronze, Ball Feet, Signed, 6 x 5 x 2 3/4 In. . . . 1200.00
Box, Hinged Cover, Graduate, Bronze, Gold Dore, 5 1/2 x 3 1/2 x 1 In. 450.00
Box, Hinged Cover, Pine Needle, Green Slag Glass, Bronze, 9 1/2 x 6 3/4 In. . . .1600.00 to 1955.00
Box, Hinged Cover, Zodiac, Bronze, Dark Patina, Signed, 4 1/4 x 3 1/2 x 2 In. 650.00
Box, Hinged Cover, Zodiac, Bronze, Gold Dore, 5 1/4 x 3 1/2 x 1 In. 450.00
Box, Jewel, Enameled Floral Relief, Bronze, Gold Dove, Signed, c.1900, 4 x 6 1/4 x 2 In. 635.00
Box, Jewel, Hinged Cover, Grapevine, Amber Slag Glass, Bronze, Signed, 6 x 4 x 3 In. . . 1500.00
Box, Jewel, Hinged Cover, Venetian, Bronze, Gold Dore, 6 1/4 x 3 3/4 x 3 In. 1800.00
Box, Letter, Chinese, Bronze, Gold Dore, No. 1774, 10 In. 1495.00
Box, Pine Needle, Amber Slag Glass, Bronze, Gold Dore, 6 1/2 x 4 x 2 1/4 In. 800.00
Box, Pine Needle, Amber Slag Glass, Bronze, Gold Dore, Signed, 4 1/4 x 3 x 1 3/4 In. . . . 450.00
Box, Stamp, Bookmark, Bronze, Gold Dore, Hinged Cover, 1 1/4 x 2 x 2 1/4 In. 550.00
Box, Stamp, Grapevine, Amber Slag Glass, Bronze, Ball Feet, 4 x 2 x 1 1/2 In. 550.00
Box, Stamp, Hinged Cover, Graduate, Bronze, Gold Dore, 3 Sections, 4 x 2 x 1 1/4 In. . . . 400.00
Box, Stamp, Hinged Cover, Venetian, Sculptured Minks, Bronze, Gold Dore, 4 x 2 x 2 In. 650.00
Box, Stamp, Hinged Cover, Zodiac, Bronze, Gold Dore, 3 Sections, 3 3/4 x 2 1/4 In. 550.00
Box, Stamp, Venetian, Bronze, Gold Dore, Chain Links, Chest Shape, 2 x 4 In. 650.00
Box, Twine, Bookmark, Bronze, Gold Dore, 5 Sides, 3 x 4 In. 1500.00
Box, Twine, Hinged Cover, Grapevine, Amber Slag Glass, Bronze, 6 Sides, 3 1/4 x 4 In. . . 1500.00
Calendar, Adam, Bronze, Gold Dore, Easel, Signed, 6 1/2 x 6 In. 850.00
Calendar, Paperweight, Abalone, Bronze, Gold Dore, Signed, 4 1/2 x 3 1/2 In. 650.00
Calendar, Pine Needle, Amber Slag Glass, Bronze, Gold Dore, 3 3/4 x 4 1/4 In. 600.00
Calendar, Venetian, Raised Minks, Bronze, Gold Dore, Easel, Signed, 6 1/2 x 6 In. 900.00
Candelabrum, 2-Light, Bronze, Green Glass, c.1910, 4 In. 3110.00
Candelabrum, 4-Light, Removable Bobeches, Curved Arms, Gems, Bronze, c.1910, 11 In. 2940.00
Candelabrum, 7-Light, Reticulated Glass, Bronze, Green Patina, c.1915, 13 1/4 In. 4185.00
Candelabrum, 8-Light, Bronze, Snuffer, No. 9964, c.1910, 15 1/2 In. 9560.00
Candle Lamp, Blue Iridescent Swirl, Signed, Favrile, 5 1/2 In. 450.00
Candle Lamp, Gold Iridescent, Purple, Ruffled Turtleback Shade, Swirled Base, 15 In. . . . 1840.00
Candle Lamp, Gold Iridescent, Twisted Rib, Shade, Favrile, Signed, 12 1/2 In. 2400.00
Candle Lamp, Peacock Blue, Iridescent Base, Quilted Shade, Signed, Favrile, 14 In. 6000.00
Candle Lamp, Twisted, Bronze, Blue Iridescent Glass, Favrile, 14 In. 6000.00
Candlestick, 2-Light, Green Glass Blown Into Bronze Frame, Handle, Signed 3360.00
Candlestick, 3-Light, Bronze, Apple Green Glass, Snuffer, 9 In., Pair 2000.00
Candlestick, Bronze Root, Base Signed, 13 In. 1910.00
Candlestick, Bronze, 3 Curved Feet, Blown Glass Cup, Bronze, Dark Patina, Signed, 8 In. 2000.00
Candlestick, Bronze, Bobeche, 3 Curved Legs, Sphere Feet, 6 In. 940.00
Candlestick, Bronze, Commemorative, Tripod, Triangular Base, Signed, 8 In. 750.00
Candlestick, Bronze, Favrile Glass, Bobeches, Tripod Base, Signed, 8 1/2 In., Pair 4405.00
Candlestick, Bronze, Gold Dore, Enameled, Iridescent Circular Foot, c.1910, 10 In., Pair . 2870.00
Candlestick, Bronze, Green Glass Insert, 3 Legs, Favrile, c.1910, 10 1/4 In. 2870.00
Candlestick, Bronze, Green Glass Insert, No. 11477, Favrile, c.1910, 7 7/8 In. 3345.00
Candlestick, Bronze, Green Glass Insert, No. 21100, Favrile, c.1910, 17 1/2 In., Pair 5975.00
Candlestick, Bronze, Green Glass Insert, Snuffer, No. 8606, Favrile, c.1910, 10 1/4 In. 3346.00
Candlestick, Bronze, Stick Body, Green Glass Insert, 17 3/4 In., Pair 4145.00
Candlestick, Glass Cabochon, Bronze, Green & Brown Patina, 13 In. 1645.00
Canister, Geometric, Enameled, Bronze, Gold Dore, Signed, 4 1/4 x 3 1/4 In. 550.00
Chamberstick, Bronze, Dark Patina, Glass Insert, Handles, 6 1/4 x 7 In. 4000.00
Charger, Bronze, Dore, Geometric Rim Design, 12 In. 330.00

Charger, Linear Floral, Low Relief, Raised Rim, Bronze, Gold Dore, 14 In. 220.00
Clock, Carriage, Grape Vine, Green Slag Glass, Bronze, Patina, 7 1/2 In. 2115.00
Clock, Carriage, Pine Cone, Bronze, Green Slag Glass, Beaded, Twisted Handle, 5 In. . . . 1645.00
Clock, Desk, Adam, Bronze, Gold Dore, 8 Sides, Signed, 4 x 4 1/4 x 2 In. 1800.00
Compote, Bronze, Jewels, Footed, Gold Dore, Flowers, Signed, 10 In. 1200.00
Compote, Peacock Eye & Trailing Border, Bronze, Gold Dore, Signed, 8 x 4 In. 550.00
Compote, Raised Floret Border, Red Jewels, Bronze, Gold Dore, Signed, 10 x 2 1/2 In. . . 1200.00
Desk Set, Bookmark, Bronze, Gold Dore, Signed, 7 Piece 1880.00
Desk Set, Bronze, Abalone Inserts, 5 Piece 2640.00
Desk Set, Grapevine, Etched, Brass, Abalone Inlay, 8 3/4 In., 4 Piece 1380.00
Desk Set, Pine Needle, Etched Metal, Green Slag Glass, c.1910, 10 Piece 2585.00
Desk Set, Pine Needle, Green Opalescent, Bronze, 4 Piece 2760.00
Desk Set, Zodiac, Bronze, Brown & Green Patina, c.1910, 7 Piece 1410.00
Desk Set, Zodiac, Bronze, Signed, 10 In., 4 Piece 345.00
Desk Set, Zodiac, Bronze, Signed, c.1900, 9 Piece 5975.00
Dish, Flower Border & Center, Enameled, Bronze, Gold Dore, Signed, 8 1/4 In. 550.00
Easel, Heraldic, Bronze, Gold Dove, Signed, 10 x 12 In. 1500.00
Frame, Abalone, Bronze, Gold Dore, Leaf, Flowers, Easel, Signed, 7 1/2 x 10 1/4 In. 3000.00
Frame, Adam, Bronze, Gold Dore, Easel, Signed, 9 1/2 x 6 1/4 In. 1200.00
Frame, Bronze, Blue, c.1910, 8 5/8 x 7 1/8 In. 4780.00
Frame, Chinese, Bronze, Dark Patina, Easel, Signed, 8 3/4 x 7 1/4 In. 950.00
Frame, Grapevine, Amber Slag Glass, Bronze, Gold Dore, Signed, 12 x 14 In. 3500.00
Frame, Grapevine, Etched Metal, Slag Glass, Favrile, 1902-1918, 7 3/4 x 6 1/2 In. 880.00
Frame, Grapevine, Green Slag Glass, Bronze, 12 x 14 In. 3500.00
Frame, Grapevine, Green Slag Glass, Bronze, Gold Dore, Easel, 7 1/2 x 9 1/2 In. 1735.00
Frame, Ninth Century, Bronze, Gold Dore, Jewels, Easel, 7 x 8 In. 1800.00
Frame, Pine Needle, Amber Slag Glass, Bronze, Gold Dore, 9 1/2 x 7 1/2 In. . . .2000.00 to 2520.00
Frame, Pine Needle, Bronze, Green Slag Glass, Signed, 8 1/4 x 7 In. 1800.00
Frame, Pine Needle, Green Slag Glass, Bronze, 2 Oval Openings, c.1915, 10 x 16 In. 7170.00
Frame, Pine Needle, Green Slag Glass, Bronze, Signed, 8 x 10 In. 1840.00
Frame, Zodiac, Bronze, Brown Patina, Signed, 7 x 8 In. 1200.00
Humidor, Grapevine, Amber Slag Glass, Bronze, Gold Dore, Signed, 6 1/2 In. 3000.00
Humidor, Leaf & Vine, Gold Iridescent, Bronze, Cylindrical, Signed, 9 1/2 In. 2500.00
Humidor, Pine Needle, Bronze, Dark Patina, Signed, 6 1/2 x 5 In. 2500.00
Inkstand, Hinged Cover, Zodiac, Glass Insert, Signed, 3 1/2 In. 375.00
Inkwell, American Indian, Bronze, Gold Dore, Alligator Etching, Signed 750.00
Inkwell, Bronze, Gold Dore, Glass Insert, Square, Signed, 3 x 2 1/2 In. 550.00
Inkwell, Byzantine, Bronze, Gold Dore, Jeweled, Mother-Of-Pearl, 4 1/2 x 2 1/2 In. 2000.00
Inkwell, Cover, Zodiac, Crab, Bronze, Stylized Chain, Square, Insert, 4 1/4 In. 480.00
Inkwell, Double, Venetian, Sculptured Minks, Bronze, Gold Dore, 5 x 3 x 2 In. 1500.00
Inkwell, Glass Insert, Bronze, Blue, Amber Swirls, Square, Favrile, 3 1/2 In. 4406.00
Inkwell, Grapevine, Bronze, Green Slag Glass, Square, Signed, 4 x 3 In. 800.00
Inkwell, Grapevine, Green Slag Glass, Bronze, Beaded, Leaf, 3 1/2 x 4 In. 690.00
Inkwell, Hinged Cover, Abalone, Bronze, Gold Dore, Insert, Signed, 3 1/2 x 3 1/2 In. 750.00
Inkwell, Hinged Cover, Adam, Bronze, Gold Dore, Oval, Signed, 4 x 3 x 2 1/2 In. 550.00
Inkwell, Hinged Cover, American Indian, Bronze, Gold Dore, Glass Insert, 5 1/2 In. 750.00
Inkwell, Hinged Cover, Bookmark, Bronze, Gold Dore, 8 Sides, 4 1/2 x 2 1/2 In. 750.00
Inkwell, Hinged Cover, Bronze, Salmon Enameled Leaves, Signed, 7 x 4 In. 1200.00
Inkwell, Hinged Cover, Graduate, Bronze, Gold Dore, Glass Insert, 4 x 2 In. 450.00
Inkwell, Hinged Cover, Grapevine, Bronze, Green Slag Glass, Glass Insert, 7 In. 1800.00
Inkwell, Hinged Cover, Grapevine, Green Slag Glass, Bronze, 7 In. 1800.00
Inkwell, Hinged Cover, Heraldic, Bronze, Green Enameled, Signed, 3 1/2 x 3 In. 950.00
Inkwell, Hinged Cover, Louis XVI, Bronze, Gold Dore, Glass Insert, Signed, 3 x 4 x 3 In. 1200.00
Inkwell, Hinged Cover, Pine Needle, Amber Slag Glass, Bronze, Gold Dore, 3 In. 1800.00
Inkwell, Hinged Cover, Pine Needle, Green Slag Glass, Bronze, Signed, 7 In. 1800.00
Inkwell, Hinged Cover, Spanish, Handle, Gold Dore, Signed, 4 1/2 x 6 In. 2200.00
Inkwell, Hinged Cover, Zodiac, Bronze, Gold Dore, 5 Sides, 6 1/2 x 4 In. 750.00
Inkwell, Hinged Cover, Zodiac, Bronze, Gold Dore, 8 Sides, Glass Insert, 2 x 4 In. 550.00
Inkwell, Pine Needle, Green Slag Glass, Bronze, Dark Patina, 3 3/4 x 4 In. . . . . . . .633.00 to 750.00
Lamp, 3-Light, Gold Iridescent Shades, Twisted Standard, Bronze, Favrile, 17 In. 8365.00
Lamp, 3-Light, Lily, Amber Violet Quezal Shades, Bronze Base, 8 1/2 x 5 1/2 In. 1840.00
Lamp, 3-Light, Lily, Fluted Iridescent Shades, Bronze, Signed, 13 In. 3080.00
Lamp, 3-Light, Lily, Gold Iridescent With Silver, Blue & Red Highlights, Bronze, 13 In. . 5500.00

Lamp, 3-Light, Lily, Iridescent, Bronze, Favrile, c.1910, 8 3/4 In. 5736.00
Lamp, 3-Light, Lily, Lobed Base, Bronze, Favrile, c.1910, 23 In. 5875.00
Lamp, 3-Light, Lily, Trumpet Shades, Favrile, 12 1/2 x 10 In. 2070.00
Lamp, 7-Light, Lily, Bronze, Gold Dore, Favrile, c.1910, 21 In. 8963.00
Lamp, 10-Light, Lily, 21 In. 45920.00
Lamp, 12-Light, Lily, Bronze, Gold Dore, Iridescent, Favrile, c.1910, 21 In. 8365.00
Lamp, Acid-Etched Gold Tone, Swivels, Harp Arm, Quezal Shade, 16 1/2 x 9 1/2 In. 1610.00
Lamp, Acorn, 5-Footed Bronze Base, Signed, 57 In. 16240.00
Lamp, Acorn, Caramel, Amber, Bronze Base, Removable Font, 21 x 15 In. 9775.00
Lamp, Acorn, Green Striated Glass, Urn Base, 3 Curved Arms, 4 Legs, Round Foot, 17 In. 8120.00
Lamp, Acorn, Mottled Orange, Green Slag Acorns, Bronze Base, Signed, 17 In. 3165.00
Lamp, Aladdin's Lamp Shape, Gold Iridescent, Signed, 54 In. 6720.00
Lamp, Amber Glass, Raised Leaf Edge On Base, Pierced Shade, Bronze, Harp Arm, 15 In. 6000.00
Lamp, Arabian, Brown, Iridescent Silver Dots, Applied, Buttons, Bronze Base, 16 In. 2415.00
Lamp, Arabian, Conical Shade, Carmel, Gold Iridescent Pulled Zipper, Favrile, 15 In. . . . 5000.00
Lamp, Arabian, Conical Shade, Orange & Yellow Iridescent, Dots, Favrile, 15 In. 4480.00
Lamp, Arabian, Conical, Shade, Gold Iridescent Pulled Zipper, Favrile, 15 In. 5000.00
Lamp, Base, Favrile, Shaped Like Candle Lamp, Swirled Ribs, 7 1/4 In. 468.00
Lamp, Brass, Reeded Columns, Quatrefoil Base, Rosettes, 56 1/4 In., Pair 715.00
Lamp, Bronze, Gold Dore, Gold Shade, Favrile, c.1910, 17 In. 8965.00
Lamp, Butterflies, Blue Iridescent, Ribbed Shade, Round Foot, Favrile, Signed, 15 In. . . . 13440.00
Lamp, Colonial, Golden Green Shade, Bronze Reeded Stem, Signed, 1901, 23 In. 9200.00
Lamp, Daffodil, Bronze, Favrile, Signed, 21 x 16 In. 34655.00
Lamp, Damascene, Bridge, Gold & Pink, Bronze, Gold Dore, Signed, 56 In. 9632.00
Lamp, Damascene, Green & Gold, Curved Stem, Bronze Base, 7 In. 5320.00
Lamp, Damascene, Green, Murano Design, Bronze, Favrile, c.1910, 19 x 12 In. 11950.00
Lamp, Damascene, Opal Ground, Gold Iridescent Swirl, Bronze Base, 15 In. 7500.00
Lamp, Fabrique Glass, Green, Bronze, Harp, Signed, Favrile, 19 1/2 In. 6500.00
Lamp, Fabrique Glass, Green, Harp Arm, Bronze, 7 1/2 In. 6500.00
Lamp, Flower-Form Shade, Acid-Etched Base, Swivels, Favrile, 14 x 10 In. 2530.00
Lamp, Geometric, Leaded, Domed Shade, Green, Bronze, c.1910, 24 1/2 In. 9560.00
Lamp, Glass, Pulled Feather Shade, Bronze, Favrile, c.1910, 56 x 10 In. 7170.00
Lamp, Gold Diagonal Ribs, White Cased, Bronze, Patina, 3 Arms, 15 In. 7600.00
Lamp, Gold Iridescent, Adjustable, Harp Arm, Bronze, Stick Body, 19 In. 4000.00
Lamp, Gold To Amber Wave, Bronze, 5-Footed Base, Signed, Favrile, 53 In. 8050.00
Lamp, Grapevine, Bell Shape, Bronze, Harp Arm, c.1910, 8 3/4 x 3 In. 3824.00
Lamp, Grapevine, Bell Shape, Slag Glass, Bronze, Harp Arm, Stick Body, 18 In. 4500.00
Lamp, Greek Key, Leaded, Bronze, Favrile, c.1899-1928, 20 3/4 x 16 In. 21150.00
Lamp, Green & White, Domed Shade, Bronze, Gold Dore, Favrile, c.1910, 15 1/2 x 7 In. . 8365.00
Lamp, Green & Yellow Iridescent, Domed Shade, Bronze, Favrile, 56 x 12 In. 6575.00
Lamp, Green Glass Base, Shade, Gold Iridescent Loop, 3 Amber Punts, Favrile, 15 In. . . . 4000.00
Lamp, Green Shade, Iridescent Blue Waves, Bronze, Harp Arm, 13 1/2 In. 4715.00
Lamp, Hanging, Acorn, Green, Leaded, 3 Hooks, 26 In. 10640.00
Lamp, Iridescent, Dome Shade, Bifurcated Stem, Bronze, Favrile, c.1910, 13 3/4 In. 2910.00
Lamp, Leaded Shade, Green Opalescent Glass, Bronze, Bell Shape Harp, Signed, 55 In. . . 3450.00
Lamp, Lime Green Pulled Feathers, Iridescent Gold, Harp Arm, Bronze, Gold Dore, 7 In. . 4760.00
Lamp, Linenfold, Green Panels, Peach Borders, Bronze Base, Signed, 24 1/2 In. 7475.00
Lamp, Mosque, Pulled Feathers, Wood Base, Bronze, Gold Dore Finial, Signed, 8 1/2 In. . 5040.00
Lamp, Neoclassical, Bronze, Favrile Glass, Signed, 30 1/2 In. 8000.00
Lamp, Oil, Pulled Green Feather Design, Shade, Favrile, 6 x 14 In. 2070.00
Lamp, Pulled Green Feather, Gold Trim, Bronze Base, Harp Arm, Signed Favrile, 7 In. . . 3920.00
Lamp, Tripod Shape, Adjustable Standard, Bronze Base, Tiffany Studios, 14 In. 3525.00
Lamp, Turtleback, Bronze, Tile, Favrile, Signed, c.1905, 14 In. 8365.00
Lamp, Turtleback, Swivel, Hobnail & Favrile Shade, Bronze Base, Harp Arm, 14 x 6 In. . 5750.00
Lamp, Vine Border, Leaded, Bronze, No. 1435, c.1910, 21 1/4 x 15 3/4 In. 14340.00
Lamp, Weight-Balance, Bulbous Stylized Leaves, Circular Ruffled Foot, 55 In. 3080.00
Lamp, Weight-Balance, Green Shade, Leaf Pattern, c.1910, 16 1/4 x 8 In. 10755.00
Lamp, Weight-Balance, Leaf, Mustard, Bronze, Favrile, c.1910, 15 1/2 x 7 1/4 In. 7768.00
Lamp, Zodiac, 6-Sided Bronze Base, Gold Dore, Adjustable, 13 1/2 In. 5500.00
Lamp, Zodiac, Gold Iridescent, Bell Shade, Bronze Base, 2 Curved Arms, Favrile, 18 In. . 4500.00
Lamp Base, Arabian, Brown Iridescent, Silver Dots, Glass Buttons, Favrile, 9 1/4 In. 460.00
Lamp Base, Gold Iridescent, Twisted Ribs, Favrile, Signed, 5 1/2 In. 480.00
Letter Holder, American Indian, Bronze, Gold Dore, 2 Sections, 6 x 4 1/2 x 2 3/4 In. 750.00

Letter Holder, Blue Enamel, Bronze, Gold Dore, 2 Sections, 6 1/2 x 3 x 3 1/2 In. 900.00
Letter Holder, Grapevine, Green Slag Glass, Bronze, 2 Sections, 4 1/2 x 6 1/4 In. 1200.00
Letter Holder, Ninth Century, Jeweled, 2 Sections, 4 1/2 x 6 x 2 1/2 In. 1200.00
Letter Holder, Pinecone, Green Slag Glass, Bronze, No. 1008, Signed, 10 x 6 1/2 In. 750.00
Letter Opener, Abalone, Bronze, Gold Dore, Signed, 10 In. ....350.00 to 450.00
Letter Opener, Abalone, Iridescent Discs, Bronze, Gold Dore, Signed, 10 In. 350.00
Letter Opener, Adam, Bronze, Gold Dore, Curved Handle, Signed, 10 In. 350.00
Letter Opener, Chinese, Bronze, Gold Dore, Signed, 11 In. ....250.00 to 350.00
Letter Opener, Grapevine, Amber Slag Glass, Bronze, Gold Dore, Signed, 9 1/4 In. 550.00
Letter Opener, Louis XVI, Berry, Leaf, Fan, Bronze, Gold Dore, Signed, 10 In. 500.00
Letter Opener, Nautical, Fish & Rope, Bronze, Dark Patina, Signed, 10 In. 650.00
Letter Opener, Pine Needle, Bronze, Gold Dore, Signed, 7 In. 550.00
Letter Opener, Zodiac, Bronze, Gold Dore, Signed, 10 1/2 In. 250.00
Letter Rack, Abalone, Leaf & Line, Bronze, Gold Dore, 2 Sections, Signed, 9 1/4 In. 1200.00
Letter Rack, Adam, Bronze, Gold Dore, 2 Sections, 9 1/4 x 2 1/4 x 6 In. 700.00
Letter Rack, American Indian, Bronze, Gold Dore, 2 Sections, 11 x 5 3/4 x 2 3/4 In. 950.00
Letter Rack, Bookmark, Bronze, Gold Dore, 2 Sections, Signed, 9 1/4 x 2 1/4 x 5 1/2 In..   950.00
Letter Rack, Chinese, Bronze, Dark Patina, 3 Sections, Signed, 8 x 12 x 3 1/2 In. 1500.00
Letter Rack, Graduate, Bronze, Gold Dore, 2 Sections, Signed, 9 1/2 x 2 3/4 x 5 1/4 In. ..   750.00
Letter Rack, Grapevine, Green Slag Glass, Bronze, 3 Sections, 12 1/2 x 8 1/2 x 3 1/2 In. .   1800.00
Letter Rack, Pine Needle, Bronze, 2 Sections, 6 1/8 x 10 x 2 1/4 In. 450.00
Letter Rack, Pine Needle, Green Slag Glass, Bronze, 3 Sections, 10 x 6 x 2 1/4 In. 1500.00
Letter Rack, Spanish, Bronze, Gold Dore, 2 Sections, Signed, 10 x 8 x 3 1/3 In. 1500.00
Letter Rack, Zodiac, Bronze, 2 Sections, Signed, 9 1/2 x 6 1/4 In. 863.00
Letter Rack, Zodiac, Bronze, Gold Dore, 3 Sections, 12 x 3 x 3 1/2 In. 1500.00
Magnifying Glass, Abalone, Bronze, Gold Dore, Signed, 4 x 8 3/4 In. 1500.00
Magnifying Glass, Adam, Bronze, Dark Patina, Beaded Edge, 8 1/4 In. 1500.00
Magnifying Glass, Adam, Bronze, Gold Dore, Beaded Edge, 8 1/4 In. 1500.00
Magnifying Glass, Bookmark, Bronze, Gold Dore, Signed, 4 x 8 3/4 In. 1500.00
Magnifying Glass, Venetian, Bronze, Gold Dore, Signed, 9 In. 1500.00
Magnifying Glass, Zodiac, Bronze, Gold Dore, Signed, 8 3/4 In. 1500.00
Match Safe, Bookmark, Bronze, Gold Dore, Emblem, Signed, 2 1/2 x 1 1/2 In. 550.00
Matchbox Holder, Grapevine, Green Slag Glass, Bronze, Signed, 2 3/4 x 1 3/4 In. 520.00
Mirror, Grapevine, Amber Slag Glass, Bronze, 7 1/2 x 1 3/4 In. 1800.00
Nested Ashtray, Bronze, Gold Dore, Raised Ruffled Rim, 4 Piece 350.00
Notepad Holder, Bookmark, Bronze, Wood Back, Signed, 4 1/4 x 8 1/2 In. 550.00
Notepad Holder, Cover, Zodiac, Bronze, Dark Patina, Signed, 6 x 4 In. 850.00
Notepad Holder, Hinged Cover, Graduate, Bronze, Gold Dore, 7 1/2 x 4 3/4 In. ...300.00 to 325.00
Notepad Holder, Zodiac, Bronze, Gold Dore, 7 1/2 x 4 1/2 In. 550.00
Paper Clip, Bookmark, Bronze, Gold Dore, 2 1/4 x 3 1/4 In. 450.00
Paper Clip, Grapevine, Amber Slag Glass, Bronze, Beaded, Signed, 2 x 3 3/4 In. 450.00
Paper Clip, Iridescent Abalone Discs Leaf & Flowers, Bronze, Gold Dore, 2 x 2 In. 550.00
Paper Clip, Zodiac, Bronze, Gold Dore, Signed, 2 1/2 x 3 3/4 In. 450.00
Paperweight, Beetle, Bronze, Gold Dore, 2 x 4 1/2 In. 1430.00
Paperweight, Glass, Bronze, Dark Patina, Favrile, 2 3/4 x 1/2 In. 3500.00
Paperweight, Gold, Iridescent, Millefiori, Squat Form, c.1915, 6 1/2 In. 690.00
Paperweight, Grapevine, Amber Slag Glass, Bronze Knob Handle, 3 1/2 In. 450.00
Paperweight, Lion, Bronze, Signed, 5 In. 575.00
Paperweight, Turtleback Tile, Bronze, Favrile, c.1910, 6 x 4 3/4 In. 2629.00
Paperweight, Turtleback, Bronze, Dark Patina, Squat Feet, 6 x 4 3/4 x 1 1/2 In. 1500.00
Pen Brush, Abalone, Bronze, Gold Dore, Iridescent Discs, Signed, 2 1/4 x 2 In. 650.00
Pen Brush, Abalone, Bronze, Gold Dore, Pattern Border, Signed, 2 1/4 x 2 In. 650.00
Pen Brush, Bookmark, Bronze, Gold Dore, Signed, 2 1/4 x 2 In. 450.00
Pen Brush, Pine Needle, Bronze, Urn Shape, 2 1/4 x 2 1/4 In. 450.00
Pen Brush, Venetian, Sculptured Minks, Bronze, Gold Dore, 8 Sides, 3 x 2 1/4 In. 450.00
Pen Holder, Geometric Pattern, Red & Black Enamel, Bronze, Gold Dore, 3 x 4 In. 550.00
Pen Holder, Grape & Leaf, Green Slag Glass, Bronze, Signed, 9 1/2 x 2 3/4 In. 316.00
Pen Tray, Adam, Bronze, 3 Sections, Signed, 9 1/4 x 2 3/4 In. 250.00
Pen Tray, Chinese, Raised Center, Border, Bronze, Signed, 9 1/4 x 3 In. 250.00
Pen Tray, Graduate, Bronze, Gold Dore, 3 Sections, Ball Feet, Signed, 8 1/2 x 2 1/2 In. ..   225.00
Pen Tray, Grapevine, Green Slag Glass, Bronze, Ball Feet, Signed, 9 1/2 x 2 3/4 In. 550.00
Pen Tray, Louis XVI, Oval, Ribbed, Bronze, Signed, 8 1/4 x 3 1/2 In. 450.00
Pen Tray, Pine Needle, Bronze, Gold Dore, 3 Sections, Ball Feet, 9 3/4 x 2 1/4 In. .550.00 to 650.00

Pen Tray, Spanish, Bronze, Gold Dore, Signed, 9 3/4 x 3 3/4 In. 850.00
Pen Tray, Zodiac, Bronze, Gold Dore, Signed, 3 x 9 3/4 In. 300.00
Planter, Grapevine, Amber Slag Glass, Bronze, Gold Dore, Signed, 10 1/2 In. 2500.00
Plate, Classical Relief, Green Enamel, Bronze Gold Dore, Footed, Signed, c.1910, 8 In. . . . 440.00
Plate, Embossed Block Design, Bronze, Gold Dore, Footed, 9 3/4 x 1 In. 468.00
Plate, Gold Flower, Favrile, Signed, 8 1/2 In. 705.00
Plate, Linear Scrolled Design, Raised Rim, Bronze, Gold Dore, 12 In. 110.00
Plate, Shallow, Raised Floral & Leaf Design, Bronze, Gold Dore, c.1910, 10 1/8 In. 106.00
Plate, Spun Bronze, Etched Border, Signed, 7 3/4 In. 403.00
Platter, Raised Flowers, Red Enamel Centers, Bronze, Gold Dore, 11 In. 550.00
Platter, Raised Geometric Border, Iridescent Abalone Discs, Bronze, Gold Dore, 9 In. . . . 550.00
Scale, Postage, Grapevine, Green Slag Glass, Bronze, 3 x 3 In. 1500.00
Scale, Postage, Pine Needle, Green Slag Glass, Bronze, 6 1/2 In. 3500.00
Scale, Postage, Pine Needle, Green Slag Glass, Bronze, Signed, 1 1/2 x 3 x 3 In. 1500.00
Scale, Postage, Zodiac, Bronze, 3 1/4 In. 1500.00
Sconce, Tulip Shape, Pulled Feather, Curved Arms, Signed, 12 In., Pair 7000.00
Screen, Tea, 3-Panel, Green Slag Glass, Bronze, Ball Feet, Signed, 4 1/2 x 7 1/2 In. 3500.00
Smoking Stand, Bronze, Gold Dore, Green Enameled, Stick Body, Signed, 25 In. 1800.00
Thermometer, Byzantine, Bronze, Gold Dore, Turquoise Stones, 8 1/4 In. 2000.00
Thermometer, Grapevine, Green Slag Glass, Bronze, Easel, 8 1/4 x 3 3/4 In. 1800.00
Thermometer, Pine Needle, Green Slag Glass, Bronze, Signed, 8 1/4 x 3 3/4 In. 1800.00
Thermometer, Zodiac, Easel, Signed, 8 x 4 In. 1200.00
Tray, Bookmark, Bronze, Gold Dore, Signed, 13 3/4 x 8 In. 1200.00
Tray, Bronze, Abalone Disc, Round, 12 In. 335.00
Tray, Card, Bronze, Figural Reclining Woman Reclining With Waves, 5 3/4 x 4 In. 950.00
Tray, Enameled, Bronze, Gold Dore, Flowers, Leaf, Handle, 8 1/4 In. 550.00
Tray, Geometric, Bronze, Gold Dore, Signed, 12 In. 300.00
Tray, Glass Scarabs, Bronze, Patina, Footed, Favrile, Signed, 14 In. 1400.00
Tray, Venetian, Sculptured Minks, 2 Sections, Signed, 10 x 3 3/4 In. 350.00
Vase, Amber Iridescent, 2 Handles, No. 2089, Paper Label, c.1900, 3 1/4 In. 545.00
Vase, Bud, Green Stem, Glass, Bronze, Gold Dore, Favrile, 1900-1902, 11 1/4 In. 2115.00
Vase, Bud, Pointed Rim, Iridescent Glass Insert, Bulbous Base, Footed 15 In., Pair 1400.00
Vase, Glass Insets, Raised Leaves, Handle, Bronze, Gold Dore, Signed, 8 1/2 In. 2500.00
Vase, Orchid Holder, Bronze, Gold Dore, 6 Flower-Form Cups, Signed, 22 In. 3500.00
Vase, Raised Linear Pattern, Bulbous, Bronze, Gold Dore, Signed, 6 1/2 In. 450.00
Vase, Trumpet, Enameled, Blue, Gold Foot, Bronze, Signed, 13 1/2 In. 1150.00
Wine Coaster, Bronze, Japonesque, Basketweave, No. 0534M70, Signed 411.00
TIFFANY GLASS, Bowl, Amber Iridescent, Flared, Ivy Leaf Cutting, Favrile, 10 In. 655.00
Bowl, Amber, Gold Iridized Finish, Signed, Favrile, c.1892, 5 In. 1095.00
Bowl, Amber, Pulled Swirls, Flared Rim, Signed, Favrile, 4 1/2 In. 529.00
Bowl, Blue Iridescent, Purple Highlights, Ribbed, Scalloped Rim, Signed, 1 1/8 In. 546.00
Bowl, Blue Iridescent, Etched, Flowers, Footed, Signed, Favrile, 4 x 11 In. 4100.00
Bowl, Blue Iridescent, Footed, Flared, Favrile, c.1910, 2 x 7 1/2 In. 2870.00
Bowl, Blue Iridescent, Scalloped Rim, Signed, Favrile, 3 1/2 x 6 In. 805.00
Bowl, Blue Iridescent, Shallow, Signed, c.1910, 11 3/4 In. 470.00
Bowl, Blue, Etched Vines & Floral, Pedestal Base, Signed, Favrile, 5 3/4 In. 5600.00
Bowl, Blue, Purple Iridescent, Scalloped Rim, c.1910, 4 3/8 x 9 3/4 In. 1020.00
Bowl, Butterscotch, Scalloped Rim, Signed, Favrile, 1 1/2 x 5 5/8 In. 375.00
Bowl, Clear Opalescent, Yellow Rolled Rim, Cupped Foot, Signed, 10 In. 2820.00
Bowl, Flower, Gold, Favrile, c.1917, 11 x 11 1/4 In. 2390.00
Bowl, Gold Iridescent, Blue Highlights, Applied Foot, Signed, 6 In. 200.00
Bowl, Gold Iridescent, Blue Highlights, Ruffled Edge, Signed, 4 3/4 In. 360.00
Bowl, Gold Iridescent, Broad, Ribbed, Favrile, 7 In. 520.00
Bowl, Gold Iridescent, Flared, Ribbed, Applied Rim, Favrile, 3 1/4 x 4 1/2 In. 950.00
Bowl, Gold Iridescent, Lily Pad, Flower Frog Insert, Signed, 10 In. 2015.00
Bowl, Gold Iridescent, Ribbed, Pinched Ruffled Rim, 3 1/2 x 7 In. 1010.00
Bowl, Gold Iridescent, Ruffled Edge, Applied Foot, Signed, 6 In. 750.00
Bowl, Gold Iridescent, Ruffled Steel Blue Edge, Favrile, 4 x 2 In. 325.00
Bowl, Gold Iridescent, Ruffled, Fluted Edge, Ribbed, 7 In. 520.00
Bowl, Gold Iridescent, Scalloped Edge, Favrile, 8 In. 440.00
Bowl, Gold Iridescent, Scalloped Edge, Signed, Favrile, 4 In. 290.00
Bowl, Green, Diamond Optic, Stretch Rim, Signed, Favrile, 10 1/4 In. 840.00
Bowl, Opalescent Light Blue Optic Pattern, Leaves, Electric Blue Rim, 6 1/4 In. 950.00

Candlestick, Citron Yellow, Vertical Ribbing, Hollow Ball Stem, 12 In. 1325.00
Candlestick, Gold Iridescent, Diagonal Twisted Stem, 7 In. 870.00
Candlestick, Gold Iridescent, Raised Ribbed Base, Signed, Favrile, 7 In., Pair 1000.00
Candlestick, Gold Iridescent, Ribbed & Twisted Stem, Signed, 7 In. 460.00
Candlestick, Gold Iridescent, Twisted Ribs, Stand-Up Flanged Cup, 5 In., Pair 1200.00
Candlestick, Pastel Blue, Stretched, Applied Clear Foot, Signed, 4 In., Pair 978.00
Candlestick, Pink Candle Cup, White Ribbed Stem, Satin Foot, Signed, 12 In., Pair 4313.00
Candlestick, Yellow, White Opalescent, Twisted Stem, 12 In., Pair 2520.00
Claret Jug, Cut, Sloping Flutes, Roundels, Silver Cover, c.1895, 8 3/4 In. 2280.00
Claret Jug, Cut, Swirled Flowers, Leaves, Silver Mounted, c.1895, 10 3/4 In. 3000.00
Compote, Blue Iridescent, Ruffled Edge, Signed, Favrile, 5 3/4 In. 2390.00
Compote, Blue, Gold, Ribbed, Signed, Favrile, 3 1/4 x 5 In. 635.00
Compote, Chinese Gold, Rolled Ruffled Edge, Pedestal, Favrile, 6 In. 900.00
Compote, Cover, Blue Iridescent, Purple Highlights, Signed 9 1/2 In. 2400.00
Compote, Diamond Optic Center, Pink Iridescent, Bright Pink Foot, 8 x 2 1/2 In. 1500.00
Compote, Diamond Optic, Gold Iridescent, Favrile, 8 In. 1500.00
Compote, Double Ribbed Body, Scalloped, Short Pedestal, Signed, 3 3/4 In. 750.00
Compote, Gold Iridescent, Intaglio Grape Leaves, Green Border, 2 x 8 In. 3808.00
Compote, Gold Iridescent, Magenta, Blue, Ribbed, Signed, Favrile, 3 1/2 x 4 In. 405.00
Compote, Gold Iridescent, Ruffled Edge, Green Pulled Feathers, Favrile, 7 In. 2235.00
Compote, Gold Iridescent, Scalloped Rim, Pedestal Base, Signed, Favrile, 7 1/2 In. 900.00
Compote, Gold Iridescent, Stretched, Applied Pedestal & Foot, Signed, 8 In. 920.00
Compote, Gold Iridescent, Waisted Stem, Ruffled Edge, Ribbed Foot, Favrile, 4 In. 560.00
Compote, Green, Reactive Iridescent, Favrile, Signed, 2 1/4 x 5 In. 480.00
Compote, Iridescent Blue To Purple, Signed, Favrile, 4 x 6 In. 865.00
Compote, Pastel Gold Iridescent, Oyster White Exterior, Signed, 8 1/4 In. 805.00
Compote, Pastel Green, Ruffled Edge, Signed, 8 1/2 In. 980.00
Compote, Pink, Satin Bowl, Stretched Rim, Signed, Favrile, 7 In. 1200.00
Compote, Pink, White Opalescent, Applied Foot, Signed, 7 3/4 In. 1020.00
Compote, Stars, Opal Iridescent, Turquoise Stretched Edge, Favrile, 4 In. 1800.00
Cordial, Amber Iridescent, Dimpled Sides, Signed, Favrile, 1 3/4 In., 10 Piece 825.00
Cordial, Blue Gold Iridescent, Dimpled, Signed, 1 7/8 In. 185.00
Decanter, Gold Iridescent, Bulbous Body, Stopper, Finial, Favrile, 10 In. 1495.00
Decanter, Gold Iridescent, Squat, Elongated Neck, Balled Finial Stopper 1510.00
Decanter, Pinched Knop Stem, Opalescent, Favrile, 10 In. 2000.00
Decanter Set, Gold Iridescent, Rose Highlights, Favrile, 10 In., 11 Piece 4315.00
Dish, Gold Iridescent, Ruffled Edge, Footed, 2 1/4 In. 800.00
Dish, Gold Iridescent, Ruffled Edge, Pedestal, Favrile, 4 x 2 1/2 In. 400.00
Finger Bowl, Underplate, Gold Iridescent, Ruffled Edge, Signed, 6 1/2 In. 900.00
Finger Bowl, Yellow, White, Opalescent, Flared, Signed, Favrile, 5 In. 460.00
Fruit Bowl, Etched, Grapevine, Lobed Body, Monogram, Silver Rim, c.1915, 9 5/8 In. 2160.00
Goblet, Etched Leaves, Green Tint, Favrile, 8 In., 4 Piece 1960.00
Goblet, Favrile, Opalescent Pink, Gold Iridescent, Disk Foot, c.1896, 7 1/2 In. 1380.00
Goblet, Gold Favrile, Blue, Green Highlights, Etched Grapes Rim, 7 In., 6 Piece 3335.00
Goblet, Gold Iridescent, Signed, Favrile, 7 In. 865.00
Loving Cup, 3 Applied Handles, No. 2684, Favrile, 7 1/4 In. 1765.00
Nightlight, Green Pulled Feathers, Cover, Finial, Signed, Favrile, 17 1/2 In. 4200.00
Ornament, Dragonfly, Bronze, Favrile, Signed, c.1910, 6 5/8 x 10 1/8 In. 5975.00
Ornament, Scarab, Red Iridescent, Favrile, 3/4 In. 150.00
Parfait, Aqua-Turquoise, Heat Reactive Striping, Signed, Favrile, 6 1/4 In. 1150.00
Parfait, Lavender, White Heat Reactive Feathering, Signed, Favrile, 5 1/2 In. 840.00
Punch Bowl, Gold, Favrile, Scalloped Sides, Pedestal Base, 11 1/4 In. 2800.00
Punch Cup, Gold Iridescent, Applied Pods & Vines, Handle, Favrile, 2 1/2 In. 750.00
Salt, Blue Gold, Iridescent, Ribbed, Scalloped Rim, Signed, 7/8 x 2 1/2 In. 175.00
Salt, Blue Iridescent, Oval, Footed, Favrile, 2 In. 450.00
Salt, Gold Iridescent, Applied Pods & Vines, Signed, Favrile, 1 1/4 x 2 1/4 In. 660.00
Salt, Gold Iridescent, Blue & Silver Tones, Ribbed, Pedestal, Favrile, 1 1/2 x 2 1/4 In. . . . 350.00
Salt, Gold Iridescent, Blue Iridescent Interior, Favrile, 1 3/4 In. 300.00
Salt, Gold Iridescent, Blue, Green & Violet, Twisted Prunts, Favrile, 1 1/4 x 2 In. 350.00
Salt, Gold Iridescent, Flared Lip, Footed, Signed, 2 1/4 In. 259.00
Salt, Gold Iridescent, Flat Bottom, Ruffled Edge, Signed, Favrile, 2 1/2 In., Pair 200.00
Salt, Gold Iridescent, Green & Violet, Round, Stand-Out Twists, Favrile, 1 1/2 In. 350.00
Salt, Gold Iridescent, Oval, 8 Pigtail Prunts, Signed, 2 1/2 In. 200.00

Salt, Gold Iridescent, Pods & Trailing Vines, Signed, Favrile, 1 1/4 x 2 1/4 In.	550.00
Salt, Gold Iridescent, Purple Highlights, Ribbed, Signed, 2 1/2 In.	420.00
Salt, Gold Iridescent, Ribbed, Stand-Up Collar, Signed, Favrile, 1 1/2 x 2 1/4 In.	350.00
Salt, Gold Iridescent, Ruffled Edge, Signed, Favrile, c.1910, 2 1/2 In.	405.00
Salt, Gold Iridescent, Twisted Prunts, Signed, Favrile, 1 1/4 x 2 In.	350.00
Sconce, Turtleback, Green Iridescent, Amber Ground, 6 1/4 x 7 1/4 In.	2875.00
Shade, Gold Feathers, Closed Bottom, Upside Down Pear Shape, Favrile, 12 In.	4760.00
Shade, Gold Iridescent, Ruffled Edge, Onion Skin Rim, Signed, c.1910, 7 1/4 In.	880.00
Shade, Opal, Gold Pulled Feathers, Iridescent, Favrile, 3 In.	230.00
Shade, Pine Needle, Domed, Bronze, Gold Dore, Yellow Ground, Favrile, c.1910, 14 In. . .	6575.00
Toothpick, Amber Iridescent, Stem Pods, Signed	315.00
Tumbler, Blue Gold Iridescent, Lily Pad Trailings, Handles, Favrile, c.1903, 2 1/4 In.	865.00
Tumbler, Gold Iridescent, Applied Lily Pad Trailings, Favrile, c.1904, 3 1/4 In.	1265.00
Tumbler, Gold Iridescent, Grapes & Leaves, Intaglio, Pinched, 4 In.	785.00
Tumbler, Whiskey, Gold Iridescent, Blue Highlights, Signed, 3 In.	460.00
Tumbler, Whiskey, Gold Iridescent, Twisted Prunts, Signed, Favrile, 1 3/4 In.	300.00
Urn, Blue, Shell Handles, Pedestal Base, Favrile, 6 1/2 In.	2500.00
Urn, Gold Iridescent, Handles, Signed, Favrile, c.1918, 2 3/4 In.	1035.00
Vase, Amber Iridescent, Cylindrical, Bronze, Gold Dore, Favrile, 13 In.	1675.00
Vase, Amber Iridescent, Leaf Cutting, Baluster Shape, 18 In.	4185.00
Vase, Amber, Applied Lily Pads, Favrile, c.1910, 2 1/2 In.	2070.00
Vase, Amber, Gold Iridescent, Footed, Sculptured, Favrile, c.1910, 8 1/4 In.	1725.00
Vase, Amber, Gold Iridescent, Pinched Prunts, Signed, Favrile, c.1905, 9 1/4 In.	2415.00
Vase, Amber, Gold Iridescent, Signed, Favrile, c.1895, 2 3/4 In.	1380.00
Vase, Blue Gray, Silvery Pulled Leaves & Vines, Signed, 21 In.	9775.00
Vase, Blue Iridescent, Favrile, 10 1/2 In.	4025.00
Vase, Blue Iridescent, Globular Base, Cylindrical Neck, Favrile, c.1916, 6 In.	5020.00
Vase, Blue Iridescent, Gold Leaves, Globular, Favrile, c.1910.	2868.00
Vase, Blue Iridescent, Impressed Leaves, Cylindrical, Footed, Favrile, 8 3/4 In.	2465.00
Vase, Blue Iridescent, Ribbed Shape, No. 4311L, Signed, Favrile, 2 In.	805.00
Vase, Blue Iridescent, Ribbed, Elongated Cylindrical, Favrile, c.1910, 12 In.	2390.00
Vase, Blue Iridescent, Ribbed, Globular, Favrile, 3 3/4 In.	673.00
Vase, Blue Iridescent, Ribbed, Prunts, Favrile, 3 1/2 In.	920.00
Vase, Blue Iridescent, Scalloped Rim, Applied Button, Signed, 5 1/2 In.	1668.00
Vase, Blue Iridescent, Shouldered, Ribbed Shape, No. 4484N, Favrile, 3 In.	980.00
Vase, Blue Iridescent, Shouldered, Ribbed Shape, No. Y4050, Favrile, 3 3/4 In.	1150.00
Vase, Blue Iridescent, Urn Shape, Applied Button Pontil, Signed, Favrile, 7 1/4 In.	1955.00
Vase, Blue, Pulled Feather, Flares To Base, Signed, Favrile, c.1902, 10 1/8 In.	1530.00
Vase, Bud, Blue & Purple Iridescent, Green Pulled Leaves, Bulbous Top, 8 1/2 In.	2745.00
Vase, Bud, Blue Iridescent, Trumpet, Narrow Flared Neck, Disc Foot, 6 In.	1000.00
Vase, Bud, Gold Iridescent, Vertical Ribbing, Signed, Favrile, 8 1/2 In.	1095.00
Vase, Cypriote, Gold Iridescent, Signed, Favrile, 3 In.	1790.00
Vase, Cypriote, Iridescent Pink, Yellow, No. H1808, c.1897, 7 1/2 In.	9560.00
Vase, Double Gourd, Gold Iridescent, Rainbow, No. N1573, Signed, 7 3/4 In.	575.00
Vase, Double Gourd, Peacock Blue, Bulbous, Favrile, 1 3/4 In.	1200.00
Vase, Flower Form, Amber, Iridescent Gold, Flared Rim, Favrilec.1905, 2 1/2 In.	865.00
Vase, Flower Form, Aqua Pastel, Scalloped Rim, Signed, Favrile, 6 In.	1095.00
Vase, Flower Form, Blue Opalescent, Bronze Base, Slim Stem, Signed, 17 1/2 In.	2520.00
Vase, Flower Form, Gold Iridescent, Circular Foot, Favrile, c.1905, 10 3/4 In.	1795.00
Vase, Flower Form, Gold Iridescent, Green Highlights, Ribbed, Favrile, 9 In.	1438.00
Vase, Flower Form, Gold Iridescent, Green Pulled Feather, Signed, 17 In.	8050.00
Vase, Flower Form, Gold Iridescent, Pulled Leaves, Footed, Favrile, c.1905, 15 In.	5750.00
Vase, Flower Form, Gold Iridescent, Ribbed, Knopped Stem, Signed, 18 In.	1840.00
Vase, Flower Form, Gold Iridescent, Scalloped Rim, Footed, Signed, Favrile, 12 In.	1725.00
Vase, Flower Form, Gold Iridescent, Short Stem, Pedestal Base, Favrile, 4 In.	1800.00
Vase, Flower Form, Green Leaf, Fluted, Gold Iridescent Interior, Favrile, 4 1/2 In.	1800.00
Vase, Flower Form, Green Pulled Feathers, Signed, Favrile, 11 In.	7170.00
Vase, Flower Form, Olive Green, Gold Iridescent, Favrile, c.1906, 15 1/4 In.	7768.00
Vase, Flower Form, Peacock Blue, Iridescent, Red, Purple Interior, 4 3/4 In.	2500.00
Vase, Flower Form, Peacock Blue, Pedestal, Favrile, 5 1/2 x 4 3/4 In.	2500.00
Vase, Flower Form, Pulled Green & Amber Leaves, Bronze Base, Favrile, 12 x 5 In.	1668.00
Vase, Flower Form, Pulled Green Feather, White Ribbed Foot, 12 In.	7480.00
Vase, Flower Form, Red, Gold, Signed, Favrile, 15 In.	1495.00

Vase, Gold Iridescent & Prunts, Signed, Favrile, 1 1/4 In. 375.00
Vase, Gold Iridescent, 3-Part Body, Prunts, Signed, 7 x 3 1/2 In. 1500.00
Vase, Gold Iridescent, 6 Sides, Ribs, Purple, Blue Rim, Favrile, 6 3/4 In. 800.00
Vase, Gold Iridescent, 6 Sides, Signed, Favrile, 6 3/4 In. 800.00
Vase, Gold Iridescent, Baluster Shape, Flared Curved Top, Handles, Favrile, 5 In. 790.00
Vase, Gold Iridescent, Blue, Red Highlights, Flared, Ruffled Edge, Ribs, Favrile, 18 In. . . . 2500.00
Vase, Gold Iridescent, Bottle Shape, Favrile, c.1897, 4 1/2 In. 1840.00
Vase, Gold Iridescent, Bulbous Bottom, Curved, Flared, Raised Prunts, 7 In. 1500.00
Vase, Gold Iridescent, Chain Pattern, Raised Punts, Signed, Favrile, 7 In. 1500.00
Vase, Gold Iridescent, Globular, Ribbed, Flared Cylindrical Neck, Favrile, 8 1/2 In. 825.00
Vase, Gold Iridescent, Green Heart & Vine, Signed, Favrile, 2 1/2 x 3 1/2 In. 1985.00
Vase, Gold Iridescent, Handles, No. 4944K, Signed, Favrile, 2 In. 460.00
Vase, Gold Iridescent, Lily Pads, Signed, Favrile, c.1913, 10 1/2 In. 3525.00
Vase, Gold Iridescent, Pinched Body, Triangular, Favrile, 1 1/2 In. 650.00
Vase, Gold Iridescent, Pulled Tendrils, Favrile, 3 1/4 In. 920.00
Vase, Gold Iridescent, Pulled, Hooked Ribs, Favrile, 2 In. 276.00
Vase, Gold Iridescent, Ribbed, Dimpled, Flared Rim, Favrile, 4 In. 750.00
Vase, Gold Iridescent, Scalloped, Paneled, Signed, Favrile, 8 1/2 In. 1150.00
Vase, Gold Iridescent, Stretched Ruffled Edge, Applied Gold Foot, Signed, 11 In. 3105.00
Vase, Gold Iridescent, Twisted Pigtail Prunts, Favrile, 2 In. 1000.00
Vase, Gold Iridescent, Urn Shape, Bulb Rim, Dome Base, c.1910, 15 1/4 In. 2585.00
Vase, Gold, Blue, Pink, Iridescent Neck, Bulbous, Favrile, c.1916, 11 1/2 In. 1150.00
Vase, Gold, Blue, Pink, Iridescent, Signed, Favrile, c.1904, 6 3/4 In. 999.00
Vase, Gold, Melon Ribbed, Looped Swags, Squat, Footed, 4 1/2 x 6 1/2 In. 1960.00
Vase, Gold, Millefiori, Wide Rim, Bulb Base, Leaves, Vines, Signed, Favrile, 1902, 4 In. . . 940.00
Vase, Gold, Pink, Green, Blue, Pulled Drape, Ribbed, Favrile, 4 x 5 1/2 In. 1725.00
Vase, Gold, Pulled Leaves, Vines, White, Red Millefiori, Baluster Shape, Favrile, 7 1/2 In. . 5040.00
Vase, Gold, Trumpet, Gold, Disk Base, Signed, Favrile, 1900s, 6 In. 560.00
Vase, Green Heart & Vine, Gold Iridescent Ground, Signed, Favrile, 18 1/4 In. 6325.00
Vase, Green, White, Cameo, Wheel Carved, Favrile, Metal Collar, 11 3/4 In. 2868.00
Vase, Iridescent, Brown, Gold, Allover Striped Decoration, Signed, 11 1/4 In. 4315.00
Vase, Iridescent, Pinched Bulbous Body, Short Flared Rim, No. 6017, 1 7/8 In. 295.00
Vase, Jack-In-The-Pulpit, Gold Iridescent, Twisted Stem, Favrile, 14 In. 6720.00
Vase, Lava, Gold Iridescent, Cylindrical, Favrile, 9 1/2 In. 1150.00
Vase, Lava, Yellow, Pink Tones, Favrile, c.1906, 5 3/4 In. 7170.00
Vase, Leaf, Green, White, Ruffled Edge, Signed, Favrile, 5 1/2 x 4 1/2 In. 1800.00
Vase, Lily, Gold Over Opal, Green Pulled Leaves, Signed, Favrile, 7 In. 748.00
Vase, Paperweight, Blue Flowers, Leaves, Egg Shape, Signed, Favrile, 7 3/4 In. 29375.00
Vase, Paperweight, Green Iridescent, Globular, Flared Rim, Favrile, c.1910, 6 In. 8365.00
Vase, Paperweight, Orange Flowers, Green, Yellow, Signed, Favrile, 6 In. 940.00
Vase, Paperweight, Violets, Green Leaves, Favrile, Inscribed, c.1904, 4 1/4 x 6 In. 9560.00
Vase, Paperweight, White Millefiori, Gold Iridescent, Green Leaves, Favrile, 7 In. 4030.00
Vase, Peacock Blue, Favrile, Green Leaves & Vines, Signed, 4 x 6 In. 2500.00
Vase, Peacock Blue, Green Pulled Leaves & Vines, Bronze Mount, 4 x 6 In. 2500.00
Vase, Peacock Feather, Oval, Ribs, Blue, Favrile, 4 In. 2800.00
Vase, Pulled Heart, Lustered Gold, Purple, Green Ground, Favrile, 7 1/2 In. 3220.00
Vase, Red Iridescent, Oval, Shouldered, Cylindrical Neck, Favrile, 6 In. 4145.00
Vase, Red, Black Rim, Favrile, c.1917, 9 1/2 In. 8965.00
Vase, Red, Favrile, 1910, 6 1/2 In. 8965.00
Vase, Tel-El-Amarna, Blue, No. 7237, Favrile, c.1910, 5 3/4 In. 7170.00
Vase, Tel-El-Amarna, Favrile, c.1910, 8 3/4 In. 6575.00
Vase, Tel-El-Amarna, Green Iridescent, Gold Bulbous Neck, Egyptian Trailings, 7 In. 6830.00
Vase, Trumpet, Blue Iridescent, Butterfly, Rolled-On Collar, Favrile, 15 In. 3585.00
Vase, Trumpet, Blue, Signed, Favrile, 13 1/2 In. 3080.00
Vase, Trumpet, Gold Iridescent, Pulled Green Feather, Bronze Holder, Signed, 14 1/2 In. . 1840.00
Vase, Trumpet, Lavender, c.1910, 7 1/4 In. 1610.00
Vase, Turquoise, Green, Striped, Fluted, Favrile, Signed, 7 1/2 In. 1265.00
Vase, Turquoise, Iridescent Dark Blue Bands, Signed, 7 1/4 In. 4025.00
Vase, White Pulled Leaves, Gray Blue Iridescent, Bulbous, Flared, Favrile, 3 In. 2128.00
Vase, White To Gold Opalescent, Calyx Shape, Green To Blue Pulled Leaves, 7 In. 2140.00
Vase, Yellow, Gold Iridescent, Pulled, Hooked Feather, Bulbous, Signed, Favrile, 4 In. . . . 1725.00
Window, Leaded, Stained Glass, Tulips, Magnolias, 50 x 27 In. 12880.00
Wine, Gold Favrile, Green, Purple Highlights, Signed, 4 In., 4 Piece 1725.00

Wine, Gold Iridescent, Applied Pods & Vines, Signed, Favrile, 3 1/2 In. 750.00
Wine, Gold, Opalescent Cup, Iridescent Stem & Base, Signed, Favrile 7 1/2 In., Pair 1500.00
Wine, Lavender, Opalescent Reactive, Stretched, Signed, Favrile, 7 3/4 In. 1380.00
TIFFANY GOLD, Dressing Table Set, Gold, Reeded Borders, Engraved, 18K, c.1930, 6 Piece 3585.00
TIFFANY POTTERY, Bowl, Fish & Shell, Black, Green, Brown Glaze, Green Interior, 8 x 3 In. 2000.00
Ginger Jar, Cover, Leaves & Vines, Berries, Allover Glaze, Signed, 9 x 5 In. 3500.00
Pitcher, Olive Green Glaze Interior, c.1905, 10 1/4 In. 5019.00
Vase, Agate, Green, Brown, Beige, Faceted, Exhibition Piece, 4 1/2 In. 11730.00
Vase, Blossoms & Vines, Raised, Green Glaze Interior, Signed, 13 1/4 In. 2000.00
Vase, Caramel, Beige, Flambe Glaze, Bulbous, Porcelain, 6 x 4 In. 920.00
Vase, Carved Leaves, Bulbous, Green Glaze, Signed, 4 1/2 In. 950.00
Vase, Chartreuse, Yellow Glaze, Raised Bands, Signed, 20 1/2 x 10 In. 2420.00
Vase, Cobalt, Turquoise Glaze, Short Rim, Flared Base, c.1910, 17 In. 2350.00
Vase, Fern Tendrils, Green Crackle Glaze, Green To Yellow Interior, 10 In. 3500.00
Vase, Green Leaf, Mottled Yellow & Brown Ground, Signed, 3 1/4 x 4 1/4 In. 3600.00
Vase, Green Raised Leaf, Molted Yellow & Brown Ground, 3 1/4 In. 3600.00
Vase, Hanging Pods Center, Leaves Top, Blue, Green Glaze, 6 1/2 x 4 In. 2000.00
Vase, Leaves & Vines, Green Glazed Interior, Signed, 5 1/2 x 9 1/2 In. 2500.00
Vase, Raised Carved Leaves, Pale Green, Signed, 4 1/2 In. 2000.00
Vase, Tel-El-Amarna, Cobalt Blue, Iridescent Collar, Footed, Bulbous 12320.00
TIFFANY SILVER, Asparagus Server, Pierced Lift-Out Tray, Handles, 13 x 10 1/2 In. 1440.00
Basket, Mint, Geometric Piercings, Hinged Handle, 3 1/2 In. 125.00
Berry Bowl, Pierced, Chased, Blackberries, Leaves, Monogram, c.1905, 11 1/4 In. 3900.00
Berry Spoon, Saratoga, Pair 575.00
Bowl, 6 Serpentine Shaped Panels, 6 Flutes, 3 1/2 x 9 1/4 In. 1035.00
Bowl, Centerpiece, Oval, Lobed Rim, Applied C-Scroll & Leaf, Footed, 13 5/8 In. 2000.00
Bowl, Centerpiece, Stepped Round Foot, Pierced Leaf Band, c.1947, 16 In. 7170.00
Bowl, Chased Leaf Rim, 8 1/2 In. 345.00
Bowl, Chrysanthemum, 4-Leaf Clover, Monogrammed, c.1900, 9 x 2 1/2 In. 690.00
Bowl, Clover, Engraved, Conjoined Script Monogram, c.1938, 2 3/4 x 10 In. 635.00
Bowl, Clover, Oval, 10 1/4 In. 700.00
Bowl, Flared, Oval, 12 1/4 In. 660.00
Bowl, Footed, Flower Band, 10 3/4 In. 2270.00
Bowl, Gadrooned Sides, Floral Border, 8 1/4 In. 590.00
Bowl, Revere, c.1955, 4 x 7 1/2 In. 345.00
Bowl, Revere, Everted Rim, Low Spreading Foot, Monogram, 7 3/4 In. 325.00
Bowl, Short, Squatty, Bulbous Body, Flared Rim, 3 1/2 In. 169.00
Bowl, Trefoil Pierced Rim, Shallow, Oval, 9 In. 150.00
Box, Cover, Apple Shape, Monogram M.H., 4 In. 120.00
Box, Spool, Repousse Design, Inscribed A.E.K., 1 3/4 In. 105.00
Bread Tray, Fenestrated, Engraved, Monogram, 11 1/4 In. 200.00
Bread Tray, Oval, 10 1/2 In. 140.00
Bread Tray, Stylized Shell Design, Oval, Squared Ends, 5 1/2 x 12 In. 290.00
Butter, Domed Cover, Button Finial, Floral Rim, Marked, 1875-1891, 6 In. 1554.00
Calendar, Heraldic, Hobnail Around Edges, Easel, 6 x 5 3/4 In. 750.00
Candelabrum, 3-Light, Georgian, Baluster Stems, Shaped Base, 14 3/4 In., Pair 4480.00
Candlestick, Column Stem, Rib At Drip Pan, Trumpet Foot, 6 In., 1908-1938, 4 Piece ... 380.00
Candlestick, Panels Of Chased & Pierced Flower Sprays, Art Deco, 9 In., Pair 5975.00
Candlestick, Trumpet, 8 Sides, Chased Leaves, Buds, 9 1/2 In., Pair 1790.00
Candy Dish, Elliptical, Shallow, Center Monogram, 4 Ball Feet, 10 In. 175.00
Chafing Dish, Feathered, Scalloped Edge, Ivory Handles, 3 Cabriole Legs, Plated, 10 In. . 220.00
Coffee Set, Barrel Shape, Inverted Acorn Finial, Fruitwood Handle, 9-In. Pot, 3 Piece ... 2350.00
Coffee Set, Demitasse, Stylized Leaf Knop & Handle, 3 Piece 1075.00
Coffee Set, Demitasse, Tray, Rectangular, Marked, 1935-1938, 4 Piece 33460.00
Coffee Set, Tray, Angular Wood Handle, Floral Scroll, c.1956, 12 1/4 In. 7770.00
Coffeepot, Flattened Sphere Shape, 8 1/2 In. 645.00
Coffeepot, Hammered, Applied Dandelion, Curved Handles, c.1891, 7 1/4 In. 19120.00
Cold Meat Fork, San Lorenzo, Sterling 175.00
Compote, Danish Design, 3 x 5 1/2 In. 140.00
Compote, Scroll & Fan Shape, 5 In. 575.00
Creamer, Marsh Scene, Copper, Hammered, Marked, c.1880, 5 1/2 In. 33460.00
Creamer, Scalloped Rim, Scrolled Handle & Feet, Monogram, 4 In. 55.00
Dish, Entree, Cover, Ferns, Flowers, Monogram, Rectangular, c.1885, 8 5/8 In., Pair 3000.00

Dish, Jam, Sterling Silver, 4 In. 805.00
Dish, Leaf, Pierced Scroll & Bead Handle, Art Deco, 10 1/2 In. 310.00
Dish, Leaves, Flowers, c.1902, 12 Oz., 11 In. 431.00
Dish, Lobed Sides, Scalloped Rim, Monogram, 18 Oz., 11 In. 403.00
Dish, Molded Edge, Monogram, c.1907, 13 Oz., 10 1/2 In. 403.00
Dish, Navette Form, Handles, Conical Foot, 8 x 16 1/2 x 8 In. 920.00
Dish, Shell, No. 22478, 5 1/4 In. 110.00
Dresser Set, Chrysanthemum, Gilt, Box, 5 Piece 2300.00
Flatware Set, Audubon, Sterling, Gilt, Mahogany Box, 81 Piece 11500.00
Flatware Set, Olympian Pattern, 47 Piece 4113.00
Frame, Stamped Geometric Bands, Monogram, Mahogany Back, 14 x 11 In. 2350.00
Goblet, Engraved Gothic Interlace, Matte, Rolled Band, Gilt Interior, 7 In., Pair 2988.00
Goblet, Engraved, Chased Flowers, Monogram, Sterling, c.1865, 6 3/4 In. 415.00
Gravy Boat, Oval, Molded Beaded Rim, 3 Paw Feet, Shells, Monogram, 7 1/8 In. 176.00
Gravy Boat, Ram's Head Handle, Flowers, Leaves, 7 1/2 In. 880.00
Gravy Ladle, San Lorenzo, Sterling 201.00
Inkwell, Traveling, Screw-Lock Cap, Glass Insert, 2 5/8 In. 385.00
Jardiniere, Flowers, Scroll, Rim, Oval, 4-Footed, 1875-1891, 10 3/4 In. 3346.00
Jug, Baluster, Hammered, Bamboo, Butterfly, Mixed Metal, c.1880, 7 In. 5378.00
Knife, Carving, Chrysanthemum, Monogram, 11 In. 206.00
Knife, Child's, Little Red Riding Hood, Monogram, 7 1/2 In. 235.00
Ladle, Chrysanthemum, Diagonally Fluted Bowl, Monogram, 12 1/2 In. 1645.00
Ladle, Embossed Tomato Vines, 15 In. 700.00
Loving Cup, Copper, Urn Shape, Molded Foot, Angular Handles, c.1947, 7 In. 2270.00
Mirror, Japanese Style, Oval, Spot Hammered, Monogram, Easel, c.1881, 8 1/2 In. 2700.00
Mug, Paris Exposition, Old Testament Scene, c.1900, 3 3/4 In. 3300.00
Nut Dish, Sterling, Ball Feet, Pierced Sides, 4 In., Pair 104.00
Nutcracker, Wave Edge Handles 489.00
Pitcher, Boar Hunt, Repousse, 8 1/4 In. 3770.00
Pitcher, Colonial Revival, Oval, Squat, Square Handle, Monogram, 6 1/4 In. 880.00
Pitcher, Floral, Geometric, Bands, 1873-1891, 7 3/4 In. 1912.00
Pitcher, Japanese Style, Baluster Form, c.1880, 8 1/2 In. 13145.00
Pitcher, Raised Figural Band, No. 4706 7134, c.1885 . . . . 1495.00
Pitcher, Rolled Bands Of Scrolls & Leaves, Monogram, 7 1/2 In. 4480.00
Pitcher, Spiraled Flutes, Grape Clusters, Monogram, c.1898, 10 7/8 In. 6000.00
Platter, Meat, Chippendale Style Border, 16 In. 430.00
Porringer, Handles, Monogram, 6 In. 240.00
Punch Bowl, Wedding, Scroll & Keys, Society Names, 1938, 6 x 10 In. 1380.00
Salad Set, Pomegranates, Leaves, Art Deco, c.1944, 9 1/4 In., 3 Piece 2400.00
Salt & Pepper, Dunsten, Vase Shape, Domed Lid, Trefoils, Stepped Foot, 2 1/2 In. 470.00
Salver, Engraved Cornucopia, Shells, Flowers, Scroll Edge, 12 x 12 In. 2115.00
Salver, Round, 3-Footed, Hammered, 1879-1891, 8 In. 5975.00
Sandwich Server, Chippendale Style, Monogrammed SW, 4 Scrolled Feet, 12 In. 835.00
Sauceboat, Monogram, E.C. Moore, French Import Mark, c.1865, 9 1/4 In., Pair 2400.00
Scoop, Bonbon, Pierced Bowl, Holly Handle, Columbian Exposition, 1893, 3 3/4 In. 560.00
Serving Spoon, Medallion End, Monogram D.C., 1905, 8 In., Pair 150.00
Serving Spoon, Molded Edge Handles, Leaf, Monogram, 6 Oz., Pair 115.00
Serving Spoon, Royal Crown Design Handles, Gilt, Case, 12 1/4 In., Pair 2400.00
Serving Spoon, San Lorenzo, Sterling 175.00
Serving Spoon, Strawberry, 9 1/2 In. 288.00
Spoon, Strawberry, 9 1/2 In. 400.00
Spoon, Sugar Sifter, Chrysanthemum, 6 In. 635.00
Spoon Set, Grapefruit, Chrysanthemum, Gold Washed Bowls, 5 7/8 In., 6 Piece 646.00
Spoon Set, Ice Tea, Bamboo, Blue Cloth Bag, Mid 20th Century, 8 In., 4 Piece. 175.00
Sugar & Creamer, Cover, Gourd, Peonies, Twig Handles, Gilt, c.1885, 3 1/4 In. 2400.00
Sugar & Creamer, Engraved Initial, New York, c.1938, 5 In. 345.00
Tazza, Scrolls, Rose Sprigs, Shaped Rim, Ribbed Knop, Trumpet Foot, 4 5/8 In. 880.00
Tazza, Stylized Heart-Shape Piercing, Molded Shell Rim, Trumpet Foot, 9 In. 880.00
Tea & Coffee Set, Cartouches, Flower Sprays, Stag Finials, Straight, 7 Piece 8960.00
Tea & Coffee Set, Coffeepot, Stand, Teapot, Creamer, Waste Bowl, c.1915, 5 Piece 2760.00
Tea Set, Bulbous Bodies, Flowers, Vermicelli Borders, c.1895, 3 Piece 2390.00
Tea Set, Classical Revival, Partially Reeded, Lion's Head Pendant Handles, 5 Piece 2705.00
Tea Set, Coffee Set, Geometric Band, Bud Finial, Marked, 1873-1891, 5 Piece 7170.00

Tea Set, Reeded Body, Floral Rim Bands, Angular Leaf Handles, 1880-1891, 3 Piece 2820.00
Tea Set, Shield Shape Body, Spreading Oval Foot, 5 Piece 1675.00
Tea Strainer, Sterling Bead & Scroll Design Rim, Ivory Handle, c.1880, 6 1/2 x 3 In. 350.00
Tea Tray, Marquise Pattern, Oval, Handles, c.1895, 30 1/2 In. 4780.00
Teapot, Paneled Sides, 7 In. 717.00
Toast Rack, Wire Frame, 4 Stylized Acanthus & Paw Feet, Center Handle, 6 1/4 In. 558.00
Tongs, Ice & Sandwich, Kings Pattern, Sterling 2868.00
Tray, Flower Basket Cartouches, Diapering, Reeded Rim, Round, 12 In. 325.00
Tray, Oval, Reeded Border, 20 In. 2235.00
Vase, 3 Pierced Scroll & Flower Panels, Everted Rim, c.1956, 11 In. 2150.00
Vase, Japanese Style, 5 Silver, Copper Butterflies, Mixed Metal, c.1878, 8 1/2 In. 8400.00
Vase, Laurel Band At Top, Monogram, Art Deco, 1930-1950, 14 In. 1985.00
Vase, Pine Boughs, Arts & Crafts, Hammered, Cylindrical, Rim & Foot, 9 1/4 In. 3525.00
Vase, Pomegranate, Hand Hammered, 3 1/2 x 4 In. 288.00
Vase, Scrolling Leaf Strapwork, Tendril Handles, Flared, c.1896, 14 3/4 In. 6600.00
Vase, Stepped, Round, Flared Rim, Teardrop Finial, 16 3/4 In., Pair 2530.00
Vase, Trumpet, Greek Key Band, Husk Swags, Scalloped Rim, Spreading Foot, 18 In. 1058.00
Vase, Trumpet, Round Foot, Floral Scrolls, Frank W. Smith, 21 In. 3107.00
Vase, Trumpet, Spreading Round Foot, 10 In. 590.00
Waffle Server, St. Dustan, 2 3/4 In. 180.00

TIFFIN Glass Company of Tiffin, Ohio, was a subsidiary of the United
States Glass Co. of Pittsburgh, Pennsylvania, in 1892. The U.S. Glass
Co. went bankrupt in 1963, and the Tiffin plant employees purchased
the building and the inventory. They continued running it from 1963 to
1966, when it was sold to Continental Can Company. In 1969, it was
sold to Interpace, and in 1980, it was closed. The black satin glass,
made from 1923 to 1926, and the stemware of the last twenty years are
the best-known products.

Alexandrite, Parfait Set, 8 Piece 400.00
Amberina, Candlestick, Twisted Stem, No. 315, Pair 45.00
Amberina, Sugar & Creamer 75.00
Canterbury, Goblet, Amber, 10 Oz., 7 In. 10.00
Canterbury, Sherbet, Amber 7.50
Cherokee Rose, Tumbler, Footed, 8 Oz. 25.00
Crystal Nudes, Candy Dish, Black & Clear, 8 7/8 x 3 1/2 In. 190.00
Dahlia, Vase, Black Satin, Iris Design Silver Overlay, Cupped, 1920s, 10 1/2 In. 395.00
Dahlia, Vase, Sky Blue, Satin, Flowers Silver Overlay, Flared, 1920s, 6 In. 185.00
Dolores, Compote, Graduated Bead Stem, 6 1/2 In. 49.00
Dolores, Console, Beaded & Scalloped Edge, 13 x 3 In. 85.00
Dolores, Pitcher, Water 250.00
Dolores, Relish, 3 Sections, Beaded & Scalloped Edge, 12 1/2 x 10 1/2 In. 65.00
Dolores, Sugar & Creamer 49.00
Draped Nude, Wine, Green, 7 1/4 In. 245.00
Draper Nude, Cordial, Frosted Stem 180.00
Flanders, Goblet, Water, 4 3/4 In. 40.00
Forever Yours, Goblet, Water 20.00
Forever Yours, Sherbet 18.00
Franciscan Ondine, Goblet, Water 100.00
Franciscan Ondine, Tumbler, Iced Tea 100.00
Franciscan Ondine, Wine 100.00
Frog, Candy Dish, Cover, Ice Green 625.00
Fuchsia, Candlestick, 2-Light 70.00
Fuchsia, Relish, 3 Sections, 9 1/4 x 9 In. 25.00
King's Crown, Ashtray, Square, 5 1/2 In. 45.00
King's Crown, Bowl, Cobalt Blue, 4 1/4 In. 23.00
King's Crown, Bowl, Scalloped Rim, Engraved Leaf, Berry, Ruby Stain, 3 1/4 x 8 3/4 In. .. 120.00
King's Crown, Claret, Cranberry Stain, 4 Oz. 12.00
King's Crown, Compote, Platinum, 7 In. 40.00
King's Crown, Cup & Saucer, Ruby Stain, 2 1/2 x 5 In. 25.00
King's Crown, Goblet, Water, Ruby Stain, 9 Oz. ....8.00 to 13.00
King's Crown, Pitcher, Milk, Ruby Stain, 8 3/8 In. 110.00
King's Crown, Pitcher, Water, Bulbous, Ruby Stain, 8 1/4 x 6 3/4 In. 200.00

King's Crown, Pitcher, Water, Engraved Leaf, Berry, Ruby Stain, 11 3/4 In.	240.00
King's Crown, Water Set, Ruby Stain, 8-In. Pitcher, 3 3/4-In. Tumblers, 4 Piece	275.00
Lamp, Owl, 8 1/2 x 5 In.	496.00
Lamp, Santa Claus, Coming Out Of Chimney, 1920s, 10 In.	1845.00
Melrose, Cordial, Etched Bowl, Platinum Band	65.00
Melrose, Goblet, Water, Platinum Band	50.00
Modern, Basket, Flower, Blue Base, Crystal Flared Top, 13 In.	125.00
Modern, Basket, Flower, Blue Flared Top, 17 In.	150.00
Modern, Bowl, Handles, 4 x 11 1/2 In.	135.00
Modern, Vase, Copen Blue, Cylindrical, 12 x 4 In.	140.00
Opaque Coral, Vase, Flared, 11 1/2 In.	119.00
Palais Versailles, Champagne	95.00
Palais Versailles, Goblet, Water	95.00
Palais Versailles, Wine	95.00
Persian Pheasant, Goblet, Wide Optic Blank, 8 5/8 In.	48.00
Rotterdam, Champagne, 6 In.	85.00
Swedish Optic, Rose Bowl, Citron Green, 5 1/2 x 5 In.	145.00
Swedish Optic, Vase, Copen Blue, Clear Stem, 7 x 5 In.	60.00
Thistle, Sherbet, 4 5/8 In.	30.00
Twilight, Basket, 3 x 5 In.	140.00
Twilight, Bowl, Crimped, 4 1/4 x 9 1/2 In.	90.00
Twilight, Bowl, Square, 4 Scroll Feet, 4 x 10 In.	290.00
Twilight, Vase, 4 3/4 x 5 3/4 In.	70.00
Twilight, Vase, 7 x 5 1/2 In.	240.00
Twilight, Vase, Orchid Pink Stain, Manzoni Style Curved Feet, 9 In.	695.00
Velva, Bowl, Blue & Clear, 2 1/4 x 8 1/2 In.	50.00
Wisteria, Compote, Cover, Cellini Foot	395.00
Wisteria, Vase, 4-Footed, 7 5/8 x 4 1/4 In.	145.00

TILES have been used in most countries of the world as a sturdy building material for floors, roofs, fireplace surrounds, and surface toppings. Many of the American tiles are listed in this book under the factory name.

Alpine Village, Matte Glaze, Tudor, Arts & Crafts Frame, 7 1/2 x 3 3/4 In.	375.00
Angel Fish, Blue, Pink Ground, Franklin, Frame, 4 In.	45.00
Architecture, Music, Painting, Ivory & Blue Glaze, Moravian, Frame, 3 3/4 In., 3 Piece . .	2070.00
Bird, Embossed, Maroon Metallic Glaze, 11 1/2 x 19 1/8 In.	375.00
Bookends, 2 Women, Holding Pots, Unglazed Outline, Turquoise, San Jose, 7 x 6 x 3 In. .	750.00
Bridge, Covered, Pond, Trees, Raised Mark, Wheeling, 6 In.	77.00
Brown Berries On Blue, Solid Ivory, Gilliot & Cie, 6 In., 5 Piece	175.00
Cabin, Indian, Man, Woman, Landscape, Marked, Lucille Schoenfeld, Frame, 1926, 6 In. .	220.00
Calendar, Boston Custom House, 1915, 4 1/2 x 3 1/8 In.	55.00
Calendar, Cunard Line Dock Boston, 1912, 4 3/4 x 3 1/4 In.	55.00
California Mission Scene, Earth Tone Matte Glazes, Claycraft, Frame, 8 x 4 In.	635.00
Calla Lily, Blue Heart, Green, Raised Outline, Boizenburg, Germany, 6 In., 4 Piece	375.00
Calla Lily, Brown & Green Ground, Unglazed Outline, San Jose, Frame, 6 In., 3 Piece . . .	175.00
Cherub's Head, Ceramic, Blue Glaze, 14 In. . . . . *Illus*	800.00
Clock Tower Rising Through Trees, California Faience, 5 3/8 In.	460.00
Cottage, Lush Garden, Painted, Polychrome Glaze, Faience, Byrdcliffe, 5 1/2 x 5 1/2 In. .	1095.00
Cottage, Thatched Roof, Bridge, Stamped, Claycraft, Frame, 4 x 4 In.	460.00
Covered Wagon, Mountainside, Multicolored, Frame, Dec Art, 6 In.	138.00
Doctor, From Canterbury Tales, Ivory & Green Semimatte Glaze, Moravian, 4 In.	230.00
Dogwood Blossom, On Oval Cushion, Glossy Pink Glaze, Old Bridge, 3 x 6 In., 4 Piece . .	60.00
Dutch Cook, Geese, Polychrome Matte & Semimatte, Empire, 6 x 6 In.	290.00
Fish, Framed, Recessed Eye, Tooled Fins, Green Ground, Arts & Crafts, 7 1/4 x 7 1/4 In. .	248.00
Fish, Whimsical, Blue Ground, Matte Glaze, Red Clay, Incised, Mueller, Frame, 6 In.	345.00
Fleur-De-Lis, Gold, Cobalt, Coat-Of-Arms Shape, Franklin Pottery Faience, 9 x 7 In. . . .	90.00
Flower, Red, Stylized, Geometric Indigo & Blue Ground, Raised Outline, Grohn, 6 In., Pair	316.00
Flowers, Stylized, Blue & Ivory, Arts & Crafts Oak Frame, 3 x 11 In., Pair	520.00
Forest, Castle, Winding Road, Sandy Textured Glaze, California Art Tile, Frame, 5 1/2 In.	140.00
Frieze, Stylized Flower, Embossed, White, Clear Glaze, Belgium, 6 In., 6 Piece	175.00
Frieze, Stylized Woman's Head, Poppies, Green Ground, E. Teichert, 6 In., 3 Piece	460.00
George Washington, Profile, Clear Burgundy Glaze, I. Broome, Beaver Falls, 11 x 11 In. .	259.00

Some types of stone and metal garden urns and statues remain free of organic stains if they're left in partial sunlight and heat, but not if in deep shade.

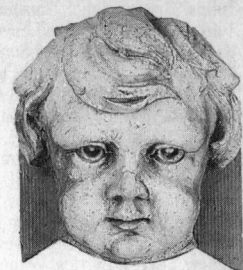

Tile, Cherub's
Head, Ceramic,
Blue Glaze, 14 In.

Gibbon Faces, Embossed, Green Glaze, Ernst Teichert, 6 In., 4 Piece 489.00
Hibiscus Blossoms, White, Gray, Turquoise Ground, Gilliot & Cie, 6 x 6 In., 3 Piece 290.00
Horse Racing, Riders, Multicolored, Frame, Wheeling, 6 In., 3 Piece 415.00
Jester, Brocade, Mounted On Walnut Board, Harris Strong, 41 x 9 1/2 In. 200.00
Joker Face, Gray Glaze, Flint, Frame, 4 In. 66.00
Knight On Horseback, Dead-Matte Polychrome Glaze, Framed, Claycraft, 3 3/4 In. 230.00
Knight On Horseback, Fortress, Blue, Brown, Black, California Art Tile, 5 1/2 x 5 1/2 In. 200.00
Lady, Pink, Green Dress, Flower, Raised Outline, Art Nouveau, 14 1/2 x 4 1/2 In. 518.00
Landscape, Trees, River, Barbotine Painted, Chas. Volkmar, Frame, c.1880, 9 1/4 x 16 In. 8625.00
Lily, Spotted, Pink, Green, Blue Ground, Raised, Franklin, Frame, 4 In. 35.00
Log Cabin, Landscape, Pilgrims, Signed, Prins, Wheeling, 6 In. 77.00
Magnolia, White & Yellow, Green Leaves, Unglazed Outline, San Jose, Frame, 6 In. 200.00
Man In Bowtie, Long Jacket, White, Blue & Black Glaze, Unitile, Frame, 8 1/2 x 6 In. .. 460.00
Musician, Girl Next To Bubbling Fountain, Impressed, California Art Tile, 8 x 12 In. 700.00
Ohio Brick, Lion Head, High Relief, Fleur-De-Lis Corners, Tuscarawas County, 5 x 5 In. . 116.00
Panel, Bright Flowers In Pitcher, Squeezebag, Harris Strong, Frame, 6 In., 4 Piece 200.00
Panel, Colonial Landscape, Framed, Harris Strong, 6 In., 5 Piece 58.00
Panel, Houses, Orange, Yellow, Black Tree, Harris Strong, 6 In., 2 Piece 145.00
Panel, Yellow Water Lilies, Lily Pads, Blue Sky, Saint-Amand, France, 6 In., 9 Piece 200.00
Papyrus Plant, Amber & Gray Raised Outline, White Ground, Raised T.A.W., 6 In., Pair . 115.00
Parrot, Leaves, Flowers, Multicolored, Black Ground, Catalina, Frame, 6 In. 275.00
Parrots, On Branch, Multicolored, Pale Blue Ground, Incised, Smith & Johnson, 5 1/2 In. 165.00
Peacock Feather, Blue, Green, Amber, White Raised Outline, Germany, 6 x 6 In., 2 Piece 635.00
Peacock Feathers In Chain, Turquoise, Amber, Outline, Art Nouveau, 6 In., 2 Piece 115.00
Pine Tree, Oak Tree, Claycraft, Frame, 16 x 4 In., Pair 2070.00
Pine Trees, Mountain Peak, Light Green Ground, Handcraft, 7 1/2 x 8 In. 220.00
Pink Fruit, Green Leaves, White Ground, Trail-Slip Decorated, Gilliot & Cie, 6 In. 115.00
Purple Wisteria, Green Leaves, White Ground, Gilliot & Cie, 6 x 6 In., 8 Piece 290.00
Queen, Brocade, Mounted On Walnut Board, Harris Strong, 41 x 9 1/2 In. 200.00
Red Thistles, Green Leaves, Ivory & Brown, Raised Outline, Stamped FP, 6 In., 4 Piece .. 200.00
Road, Through Mountains, Brown Matte Glaze, California Art Tile, Frame, 6 In. 259.00
Roof, Relief Molded Dragon, Glazed, Chinese Ming Dynasty, 40 1/2 In., Pair 7000.00
Roses On Medallion, Brown & Ivory, Brown Leafy Ground, BFK, Belgium, 6 In., 9 Piece 230.00
Scene, Raised & Painted, Mission, Claycraft, Arts & Crafts Frame, 4 x 12 In. 1150.00
Seahorse, Black, Pink, Orange, Green, Art Deco, Mark, Wheeling, Frame, 5 3/4 In. 110.00
Shepherd Boy, Lamb, Trent Tile Co., Frame, 18 x 6 In., 3 Piece 1610.00
Shepherd Boy, Playing Flute, Sheep, Green, Brown, Trent Tile, Frame, 18 x 6 In., 3 Piece 2015.00
Shepherdess, Sheep, Staff, Green To Mottled Brown, Trent, Frame, 18 x 6 In., 3 Piece ... 1035.00
Ship, 2-Masted, Green Waves, Pink Clouds, Arts & Crafts Frame, 1930s, 6 x 6 In. 575.00
Ship, Brown Glaze, Blue Waves, Moravian, Frame, 4 In. 99.00
Ship, Flying Dutchman, Brown Glaze, Moravian, Frame, 4 In. 110.00
Ship, Sky, Brown, Blue, White, Outline, Gladding & McBean, Frame, 6 In., 4 Piece 1495.00
Smoker, Tired, Gio Ponti, Polychrome, Ivory Ground, Richard Ginori, Frame, 6 x 6 In. .. 550.00
Stag, Glossy Pink Glaze, Framed, Hamilton, 1880s, 6 x 6 In. 290.00
Swan Scene, Water Lilies, Cattails, Dragonfly, Polychrome, Germany, 6 x 6 In., 4 Piece .. 405.00
Taupe Iris, Trefoils, Blue Ground, Raised Outline, Gilliot & Cie, Belgium, 6 In., 8 Piece . 230.00
Tree, Blue, Yellow Ground, Impressed, Walrich, Frame, 5 1/3 In. 660.00
Triple Blossoms, Stylized, Red & Amber, Celadon Stems, Blue Ground, 6 In., 6 Piece ... 259.00
Trivet, 3-Masted Tall Ship, Cobalt Blue Glossy Glaze, Paul Bogatay, 6 In. 175.00

Tulips, Green, White, Transfer Decorated, Belgium, 3 x 6 In., 8 Piece 115.00
Tulips, Lavender, Green Leaves, Ivory Ground, Marked, Wheeling, Frame, 4 In. 138.00
Urn, Scrolling Vines, Sea Serpent, Pink, Green, Gray, Blue, 18 x 9 In. 58.00
Venus & Cupid, Over Coal Fire, Clear Burgundy Glaze, Gilded Frame, 6 In., 6 Piece 690.00
Viking Ship On Stormy Sea, Crystalline Polychrome Glaze, De Porceleyne Fles, 8 x 8 In. 345.00
Water Lily, White, Yellow, Green Leaves, Blue, Impressed, Claycraft, Frame, 1 3/4 In. . . . 195.00
Windmill, Farm House, Blue, White, Marked, Gladding & McBean, Frame, 6 In. 80.00
Woman, Red Hair, Green Dress, Raised Outline, Arm Up, J. Von Schwarz, 14 x 5 In. . . . 1380.00
Woman In Garden, Daffodil, Landscape, Raised Outline, J. Von Schwarz, 6 1/2 x 11 In. . 1610.00
Woman's Head, Water Lilies, Green Glaze, Ernst Teichert, 6 x 6 In., 3 Piece 690.00
Women, Picking & Watering Flowers, Johann Von Schwarz, 11 x 6 1/2 In., 4 Piece 5290.00
Yellow Flowers, Green Leaves, Green Ground, Raised FP, Germany, 3 x 6 In., 7 Piece . . . 200.00
Yellow Leaves, Berries, Within Brown Medallion, Trail-Slip, Gilliot & Cie, 6 In. 175.00
Zebra Finch & Thistle, Yellow, Pink, Blue Ground, Franklin, 4 In. 110.00

TINWARE containers for household use have been made in America
since the seventeenth century. The first tin utensils were brought from
Europe, but by 1798, tin plate was imported and local tinsmiths made
the wares. Painted tin is called tole and is listed separately. Some tin
kitchen items may be found listed under Kitchen. The lithographed tin
containers used to hold food and tobacco are listed in the Advertising
category under Tin.

Birdhouse, Cupola, Horse Shape Weather Vane, Green Paint, 19th Century, 24 In. 490.00
Box, Storage, Grain Painted, 19th Century, 13 1/2 x 18 x 12 1/2 In. 175.00
Bull's Head, Hanging, Gilt, 12 x 14 In. 1035.00
Canister, Green Ground, Smoke Decoration, 23 x 18 1/2 In. 39.00
Canister, Storage, Smoke Decorated, 16 x 12 In. 715.00
Canister, Storage, Smoke Decorated, Applied Loop Handles, 9 x 6 1/4 In. 440.00
Chandelier, 4-Light, Strap Arms, Round Drip Pans, Stamped C. Wilson, 19 1/2 In. 550.00
Coach Horn, 5 Tube, Tapered, Funnel-Like Mouthpiece, 19th Century, 16 In. 880.00
Coffeepot, Gooseneck, Punched Tulip, C-Scroll Handle, 20th Century, 11 1/4 In. 360.00
Coffeepot, Painted Flowers & Leaves, Yellow, Green, Red, Black Ground, 10 5/8 In. 765.00
Coffeepot, Punched Tulip, Raised Lines, Beaded, Domed Lid, Brass Finial, 11 1/2 In. . . . 770.00
Coffeepot, Punched, Tulips, Flowerpot, Wavy Bands, Heart, 10 3/4 In. 4125.00
Coffeepot, Wrigglework, Sheet Metal, Baluster Shape, Cone Shape Cover, 14 In. 2870.00
Coffeepot, Wrigglework, Sheet Metal, Baluster Shape, Domed Cover, 11 1/2 In. 3585.00
Figure, Silhouette, Man, Articulated Limbs, Black Hair, Blue Arms, Legs, 10 1/2 In. 195.00
Foot Warmer, Punched Circles, Wood Frame, Turned Posts, Bail Handle, 9 x 8 x 6 In. . . . 305.00
Foot Warmer, Punched, Circle Design, Wood Frame, Wire Bail Handle, 9 x 7 1/2 x 6 In. . 180.00
Foot Warmer, Punched, Diamond Design, Mortise Frame, Bail Handle, 7 3/4 x 9 x 6 In. . 110.00
Infant Feeder, Conical, Hinged Lid, Loop Handle, Tapered Spout, 19th Century, 3 3/4 In. 365.00
Lamp Fillers, Conical Shaped, Angled Spouts, 8 In. 230.00
Lantern, Candle Socket, Cutouts, Stars, Onion Globe, Rim Handle, 8 1/4 In. 580.00
Lantern, Paul Revere, Black Paint, Punched Circular Designs, Ring Handle, 17 In. 165.00
Lard Container, Smoke Decorated, Applied Handles, 9 In. 195.00
Mold, Candle, 6 Tube, Folded Rim Handle, 6 x 5 In. 770.00
Mold, Candle, 12 Tube, 11 1/2 In. 58.00
Mold, Candle, 12 Tube, Arched Foot, Side Handle, Mid 19th Century, 9 1/4 In. 100.00
Mold, Candle, 13 Tube, Round 495.00
Mold, Candle, 24 Tube, 2 Handles, Late 19th Century, 11 3/4 x 5 x 13 In. 70.00
Mold, Candle, 50 Tube, Tapered Sides, Tab Handles, 15 x 7 x 11 In. 220.00
Mold, Candle, Side Handle, Late 19th Century, 10 In. 60.00
Ornament, Eagle, Holding Arrow, Flag, Painted, Red, White, Blue, 24 x 19 In. 275.00
Ornament, Eagle, Punched, Raised Wings, Pine Cutting Board Mount, 25 x 19 In. 195.00
Panel, Applied Decoration, Painted, White, Early 20th Century, 12 In. 80.00
Sconce, Candle, Air, Rounded Base, Scalloped Crests, Marietta, Penn., 14 In., Pair 220.00
Sconce, Candle, Crimped Crest, Socket Base, 3 1/2 x 11 In. 255.00
Sconce, Candle, Radiating Crimped Round Reflector, Early 19th Century, 14 1/2 In. 500.00
Sconce, Candle, Rounded Base, Ribbed Back, Crimped Crest, 14 In., Pair 525.00
Sconce, Single Socket, Mirrored, Round Reflector, Crimped Drip Pan, 9 1/2 In., Pair 1116.00
Sconce, Stamped Rosettes & Border, Double Arched Back Reflector, Shelf, 9 3/4 In. 205.00
Sprinkler, Lithograph, Black Boys 150.00
Tray, Indian With 3 Horses, Oval, 17 In. 210.00

TOBACCO CUTTERS may be listed in either the Advertising or Store categories.

TOBACCO JAR collectors search for those made in odd shapes and colors. Because tobacco needs special conditions of humidity and air, it has been stored in special containers since the eighteenth century.

Boy, Crawling Out Of Doghouse, Terra-Cotta, 6 1/2 In.	127.00
Cowboy On Box, Terra-Cotta, 8 x 6 In.	865.00
Dog, Ceramic, Fidele, 5 In.	115.00
Dwarf, In Bag, Terra-Cotta, Set On Lid, 8 In.	345.00
Lumberjack, Seated On Stump, Terra-Cotta, 9 3/4 In.	785.00
Man Playing Guitar On Crate, Terra-Cotta, 10 In.	949.00
Mother & Daughter, Terra-Cotta, 9 In.	835.00
Munich Child Leaning On Barrel, Terra-Cotta, 10 1/2 In.	1065.00
Pig, Seated, Terra-Cotta, J. Marasch, Austria, c.1890, 6 1/4 In.	550.00
Pig Fraternity Student, Terra-Cotta, 8 1/2 In.	725.00
Stag Horn & Boar's Head Design, Cheroot, c.1890, 10 In.	431.00
Uncle Sam, Terra-Cotta, Austria, c.1900, 4 1/3 x 7 1/2 In.	350.00
Woman, Dancing, Porcelain, Conta & Bohme, 7 1/2 In.	535.00
Woman, Yelling, I Say Down With The Trousers, Hat, Sash, Porcelain, 4 3/4 In.	1350.00

TOBY JUG is the name of a very special form of pitcher. It is shaped like the full figure of a man or woman. A pitcher that shows just the top half of a person is not correctly called a toby. More examples of toby jugs can be found under Royal Doulton and other factory names.

Black Woman, Kneeling In Prayer, c.1850 .... *Illus*	850.00
Chef, Black, Borough Of Gosport, England, 2 1/2 x 1 1/2 In.	50.00
Hearty Good Fellow, Pearlware Body, 11 1/2 In.	411.00
Man, Seated, Rust, Yellow, Gray, Blue, Blue Willow Transfer On Back, 5 1/2 In.	275.00
Man, Seated, Tricorner Hat, Pitcher Of Ale, Lid, Staffordshire, 1800s, 10 1/2 In.	735.00
Man, Standing, Cobalt Blue Coat, Red Pants, Sponged Green Base, 9 7/8 In.	385.00
Martha Gunn, Woman, Seated, Holding Bottle, Cup, Prattware Style, c.1800, 8 3/4 In.	1058.00
Pitcher, Seated, Stoneware, Blue, Green, Yellow, 6 1/2 In.	69.00
Seated Woman Holding Bottle, Prattware Style, c.1800, 9 5/8 In.	999.00
Woodrow Wilson, Sitting With Biplane, China, Carruthers Gould, 12 In.	1375.00
Zeus, Polychrome Enamel, Staffordshire, 7 1/2 In.	121.00

TOLE is painted tin. It is sometimes called *japanned ware*, *pontypool*, or *toleware*. Most nineteenth-century tole is painted with an orange-red or black background and multicolored decorations. Many recent versions of toleware are made and sold. Related items may be listed in the Tinware category.

Bowl, Classical Figures, Steel, Scalloped Edge, Bail Handles, Late 1700s, 11 x 7 In.	735.00
Bowl, Monteith Regency, Painted, Early 19th Century, 4 7/16 x 13 x 8 7/16 In., Pair	2988.00
Box, Black, Colorful Front Panel, Fruit, Flowers, Vine Border, 5 1/2 x 8 3/4 x 4 3/4 In.	1438.00
Box, Black, Swags & Drapes, 10 x 4 1/2 x 7 In.	375.00
Box, Document, Dome Top, Flower, Fruit Designs, Wire Bail Handle, 9 1/4 x 5 x 6 3/8 In.	1705.00
Box, Document, Dome Top, Japanning, Fruit Decoration, Red, Yellow, 4 x 2 3/4 x 3 In.	533.00
Box, Document, Dome Top, Leaves, Ring Handle, Pa., 1800s, 6 3/8 x 9 1/2 x 6 In.	1650.00
Box, Document, Dome Top, Scroll Hasp, Fruit, Pa., 1800s, 6 3/4 x 9 1/2 x 6 In.	880.00
Box, Document, Flowers, Swags, Polychrome, Early 1800s, 4 3/4 x 3 3/4 x 8 In.	70.00
Box, Document, Salmon Ground, Stenciled Silver Leaves, Gold Trim, 7 x 4 1/4 x 3 3/4 In.	140.00
Box, Document, Salmon, Red, Yellow Draped Leaves, 19th Century, 4 1/4 x 8 x 4 In.	330.00
Box, Document, Tin, Dome Top, Flowers, Leaves, Sprigs, 19th Century, 9 x 5 x 4 In.	405.00
Box, Dome Top, Multicolored Flowers, Crosshatching, Pinwheels, 4 x 3 x 8 In.	1430.00
Box, Dome Top, White Band, Red Flowers, Green Leaves, 6 1/2 In.	125.00
Box, Dome Top, Yellow Vine, Red & Black Flowers, Bail Handle, 8 3/4 x 4 3/4 x 5 1/2 In.	1430.00
Box, Swags, Stripes, Wavy Lines, Red Band, Brass Bail Handle, 4 x 4 x 8 In.	990.00
Box, Tulips, Leaves, Buds, Black, Yellow Interior, Oval, Wire Bail Handle, 4 x 7 x 5 In.	110.00
Cachepot, Gilt, Brass Mounted, Paisley Blooms, France, 11 1/2 x 11 1/4 In., Pair	863.00
Canister, Storage, Slant Front, Chinoiserie, Maker Stencil, Troemner, 22 x 19 In.	450.00
Canister, Tea, 8 Sides, Chinoiserie Decoration, England, c.1850, Pair	7500.00
Canister, Tea, Painted, Oval, Black Ground, Red Stylized Flower, 19th Century, 5 In.	239.00
Chandelier, 4-Light, Shades, Painted, U-Shaped Center, Late 18th Century	3248.00

Coal Scuttle, Flower Sprays, Gold Edging, Sloped Hinged Lid, Top Handle, 15 x 12 In. . .   235.00
Coal Scuttle, Gilt, Floral Painted, Lion Ring Handles, Cast Paw Feet, 15 x 13 x 17 In. 875.00
Coffeepot, Dome Top, Gooseneck, Apple, Bud, Yellow Leaf, Pa., 1800s, 10 1/4 In. 495.00
Coffeepot, Dome Top, Gooseneck, Finial, Polychrome Flowers, Pa., 1800s, 11 In. 605.00
Coffeepot, Dome Top, Gooseneck, Pomegranate, Fruit Design, 19th Century, 10 1/2 In. . . .   770.00
Coffeepot, Dome Top, Strap Handle, Curved Spout, 10 1/2 In. 2270.00
Coffeepot, Dome Top, Tapered Cylindrical Body, 11 In. 2270.00
Coffeepot, Fruit, Flowers, Blue, Red, Yellow, Tan, Olive Green, Brass Finial, 10 3/4 In. . . .   1100.00
Coffeepot, Yellow & Gold Fruit & Leaves, White Wavy Lines, Red Band, 10 1/2 In. 275.00
Cup, Red, Gold Lettering, Child's, My Girl, 2 In. 45.00
Flower Stand, Painted, Plaited, Wire, Flower Shape, Louis Philippe Style, 6 x 16 1/4 In. .   145.00
Jardiniere, Giltwood, Carved, Eagle Uprights, Pair, 23 x 16 In. 620.00
Lamp, Desk, Painted Shade, Paw Feet, 13 In. 748.00
Lantern, Wall, Green, Flowers, 3 Glass Sides, France, 1890, 19 In. 1675.00
Pot, Dome Top, Red Flowers, Fruit, Yellow, Green, Brass Final, 10 1/4 In. 3135.00
Sconce, Painted Red, Crimped Top, 7 x 2 In., Pair 1380.00
Sugar, 4-Petal Flowers, Leaves, Sunburst On Lid, Scrolled Handle, 3 3/8 In. 110.00
Tea Caddy, Curved Sides, Undulating Lid, Paw Feet, Yellow & White, Heart, 3 x 4 3/8 In.   1100.00
Tea Caddy, Red Flower, Green Leaves, Yellow Trim, 6 1/2 In. 55.00
Tray, 2 Women & Child In Garden, 23 In. 290.00
Tray, Apple, Amber Crystallized Center, Flower Border, Canted Sides, 1860, 8 x 12 In. . . .   660.00
Tray, Apple, Japanning, Gold, Red Stenciled Flower Baskets, 10 3/4 x 10 1/2 x 2 1/4 In. . . .   110.00
Tray, Apple, White Bands, Feathered Tulips & Leaves, Red, Yellow, Green, 12 x 7 In. . . .   660.00
Tray, Battle Scene, Constitution, Guerriere, Angel With Trumpet, c.1812, 26 x 19 1/4 In. .   1680.00
Tray, Battle Scenes, Vines, Red Ground, Gallery, Cutout Handles, Scalloped Rim, 19 In. . .   380.00
Tray, Black, Center Bouquet, Parcel Gilt Border, 25 x 20 In. 40.00
Tray, Busy Harbor Scene, Yellow, Pierced Gallery, Rectangular, 24 In. 355.00
Tray, Canted Corner, Rectangular, Berries, Yellow Drape Border, 6 x 8 3/4 In. 385.00
Tray, Courting Couples, Black, Pierced Gallery, Gilt Scroll Border, Oval, 21 In., Pair 1116.00
Tray, Crags Beside Village, Farmer, Livestock, Oval, 2 Cutout Handles, 28 In. 499.00
Tray, Elongated Tulips, Leaves, Black, Mustard, Octagonal, Gallery Rim, 12 x 9 In. 110.00
Tray, Feathered Tulips & Leaves, Red, Yellow, Green, 12 5/8 x 7 3/4 In. 660.00
Tray, Flowers, Black Ground, Pierced Gallery, Cutout Handles, Oval, 25 In. 150.00
Tray, Flowers, Gilt, Red Wreath Border, Round, France, 19th Century, 15 1/2 In. 345.00
Tray, Flowers, Orange, Tan, Green, Black & Gold, Scalloped Edges, 18 3/4 x 24 In. 99.00
Tray, Fruit Bowl On Table, Leaves & Berries On Rim, Black Ground, Oval, 24 In. 495.00
Tray, Gold, Birds, Trees, Figures, Folding Metal Base, 46 x 22 In. 690.00
Tray, Hot Air Balloon Center, House Border, Green Ground, Early 1800s, 33 1/2 In. 7050.00
Tray, Oval, Floral & Leaf, Gilt Fruit, Vine Border, France, c.1900, 12 In. 190.00
Tray, Oval, Military Portraits, Leaf Border, France, 1800s, 24 1/2 In. 235.00
Tray, Red, Ground, Canted Corners, Fruit, Flowers, Pa., 19th Century, 6 x 8 3/4 In. 415.00
Tray, Serpentine Shape, Black, Gold Fruit & Flowers, Leaf Border, 31 1/2 In. 1035.00
Tray, Soldier Scene, Fighting, Horses, Carriage, 21 x 26 In. 690.00
Tray, Yellow Swags, Flower In Red, Orange, Green, Black Ground, Octagonal, 8 x 12 In. .   220.00
Tray, Yellow Swags, Flower, Red, Orange, Green, Octagonal, 8 3/4 x 12 1/2 In. 220.00
Umbrella Stand, Dummy Board, Dog, Late 19th Century, 25 In. 1315.00
Washstand, Flowers, Gold Borders, Hinged Top, England, Mid 1800s, 36 x 17 x 16 In. . .   2495.00
Wastebasket, Courting Couple, Ball Feet, Square Base, Flared Rim, 12 1/2 In. 235.00

Toby Jug, Black Woman,
Kneeling In Prayer, c.1850

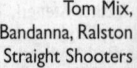

Tom Mix,
Bandanna, Ralston
Straight Shooters

TOM MIX was born in 1880 and died in 1940. He was the hero of over 100 silent movies from 1910 to 1929, and 25 sound films from 1929 to 1935. There was a Ralston Tom Mix radio show from 1933 to 1950, but the original Tom Mix was not in the show. Tom Mix comics were published from 1942 to 1953.

Bandanna, Ralston Straight Shooters . . . . *Illus*	175.00
Cap Gun, White Grip, Branded Signature, 9 In.	130.00
Ring, Whistle, Premium, Gold Metal, Aluminum	45.00
Ring, Whistle, Premium, Gold Metal, Aluminum, Box	80.00
Rocking Horse, Tony The Pony, Pictures Tom Mix, Painted Wood, 40 In.	145.00
Spurs, Glow-In-The-Dark, Plastic, Aluminum, 1940s	40.00
Viewer, RCA Television Shape, 9 Picture Wheels, Brown Plastic, 1 1/4 In.	35.00
Watch Fob, Gold Ore, Plastic, Ralston Straight Shooters, c.1940	20.00

TOOLS of all sorts are listed here, but most are related to industry. Other tools may be found listed under Iron, Kitchen, Tinware, and Wooden.

Adze, Hand, Stirrup	80.00
Ax, Fanning Blade, Hand Forged, Late 18th Century, 28 1/2 x 4 1/2 In.	110.00
Ax, Iron, c.1720, 7 In.	165.00
Ax, Naval, Boarding, Wooden Handle, Belt Hook, 18th Century, 23 3/4 In.	750.00
Ax, Throwing, Double Blade, Hand Forged, Revolutionary War, 3 1/2 x 1 3/4-In. Blade . .	850.00
Ax, Trade, Hand Forged, Stamped, Dug At Lake George, Late 18th Century, 19 x 3 In. . .	140.00
Bank Vault Timer, Alarm, Microphone System, Duplex Electric Co., c.1928, 24 In.	696.00
Bootjack, Walnut, Lip-Molded Edge, 14 1/2 x 6 In.	11.00
Box, Conestoga Wagon, Iron Mounted, Tacked & Pegged, 35 x 42 In.	4675.00
Box, Conestoga Wagon, Wrought Iron, Ram's-Horn Keeper, 18 x 22 x 7 In.	2420.00
Box, Lift Top, Pine, Blue, American, 19th Century, 14 x 25 x 15 In.	150.00
Box, Walnut, Dovetail, Cutout Handle, Highland County, Virginia, 8 1/2 x 10 1/2 x 14 In. .	250.00
Branding Iron, Whale, Stamped, STMR, Wanderer, 19th Century, 30 In.	1195.00
Brush, Clothes, Strapwork, Oval, England, 1760	550.00
Bucket Yoke, Carved, Primitive, Child's	35.00
Caddy, Farriers, Softwood, Turned Handle, Interior Tray, Tar Bucket, Faring Tools	124.00
Cage, Poultry, Iron Mounted, Oak, Elm, England, 1800s, 24 1/2 x 39 1/2 x 30 In.	1150.00
Caliper, Double Lady, Red Japanning, 15 1/2 In.	155.00
Chest, Nuts & Bolts, 8 Sides, Revolving, 72 Drawers, Stenciled	3850.00
Chest, Poplar, Birch, Ash, Red Paint, Raised Panel, Steel Handles, Hasp, 36 x 17 x 14 In. . .	220.00
Cobbler's Bench, Leather Padded Back, c.1840, 42 x 20 In.	1395.00
Coin Changer, Kwik-Koin, Cast Metal, 19 1/4 In.	22.00
Combination, Level, Rule, Square, Brass, Plumb Bob Window, Hinged, 7 1/2 x 7/8 In.	265.00
Combination, Saw, Rule, Level, Scribe, Henry Disston, No. 43	1815.00
Cork Press, Cast Iron, 10 In.	50.00
Cranberry Scoop, Branded Hatch Sides	230.00
Cranberry Scoop, Cape Cod, G.S. Sampson, Plymouth	345.00
Cranberry Scoop, Steel Tines, Wood Body, 18 x 19 In.	250.00
Cranberry Scoop, Wood Tines, Original Label Remains, 22 In.	315.00
Cranberry Scoop, Wood, 15 In.	105.00
Damp Detector, Circular Case, Enamel Dial, Leather Case, England, 1920s, 1 1/2 In. . . .	60.00
Drill, Hand, Whitney's, No. 10, 15 Drill Points, Wrench, Wood Box, Patent May 4, 1876 .	1650.00
Flax Break, Ceremonial, Wedding, Green, Pink Tulips, Roses, Leaves, Scandinavia, 24 In. .	85.00
Flax Break, Wood Panel, Handle, Tulips, Orange, Salmon, White, Red, 1888, 23 In.	85.00
Froe, Shingle, Forged	35.00
Gauge, Marking, George Kenny, New Hampshire, Patent Jan. 4, 1870	475.00
Gimlet, Ivory Handles, c.1861	60.00
Hackle, Pine, Dovetailed Cover, Molded Base, Shaker, New Lebanon, c.1830, 6 In.	520.00
Hackle, Wooden, Iron Spike, Incised Leaf Carving, Signed I.M., 5 x 34 1/2 x 7 1/2 In. . . .	275.00
Hackle, Wooden, Iron Spike, Signed, T. Gowell, 1776, 6 1/2 x 23 x 6 In.	275.00
Hacksaw, Pattern, Lancashire	30.00
Handsaw, Winchester, Old Trusty	1575.00
Hatchet, Winchester, Broad Pattern, No. F5343C, 5 1/2 x 16 In.	155.00
Hay Fork, Wooden, 3 Tines, White Paint, 58 In.	96.00
Hay Fork, Wooden, 4 Tines	56.00
Hay Fork, Wooden, 7 Tines	68.00
Hay Fork, Wooden, Signed, M. B. Young, 67 1/2 In.	195.00

Brush fur in the direction it grows. If brushed the other way, the hairs will break off. Furs should never be stored in sealed plastic bags. They need to breathe.

Tool, Mold, Shank Button,
Iron, 2 1/2 In.

Jack, Conestoga Wagon, Punched Dot, Crossed Line, Red Paint Remnants, c.1855, 18 In. .	300.00
Key, Winchester, Padlock	70.00
Ladder, English Pine, Mahogany, Folding Hinge, 6 Tapered Rungs, 19th Century, 45 In. . .	405.00
Leather Slitter, C.P. Bursch, Marked, N.J., c.1837	110.00
Leather Slitter, Nichols Patented	65.00
Level, Gravity, T.F. Deck, Patent February 4, 1905	2200.00
Level, Inclinometer, Pendulum, T. Deck, No. 5, Toledo Gravity Level, Type 1, c.1895	2970.00
Linen Smoother, Maple, 27 In.	125.00
Measure, Bentwood, Green, Chamfered Edge, Iron Nails, EB, Rye, Wilton, N.H., 9 x 5 In.	195.00
Measurer, Rope, Columbian Pure Manila Rope, Tin, 16 In.	275.00
Mold, Shank Button, Iron, 2 1/2 In. . . . . *Illus*	95.00
Padlock, Best Logo, LA Coliseum, Brass Body, Steel Shackle, 2 3/4 In.	40.00
Padlock, Brass, Attached To Hindu Ganesha Figure, 4 1/2 In.	25.00
Padlock, Bull & Dog, Brass, Original, Key, 2 1/2 In.	170.00
Padlock, Combination, American Keyless Lock Co., Chicago, Box, Instructions, 2 3/4 In.	200.00
Padlock, Corbin USA, Brass, 6 Lever, Push Key, Round, 2 3/4 In.	325.00
Padlock, Corbin, Cut Away, Rim Lock, Brass, 3 Keys, 1 5/8 In.	100.00
Padlock, Eagle On Both Sides, Brass, Pin Tumbler Push Key, 2 Original Keys, 2 1/4 In. . .	50.00
Padlock, Eagle, Brass, Steel Chain, Original Key, 1 1/8 In.	25.00
Padlock, Eagle, Die-Cast Body, Steel Shackle, 2 Original Keys, Original Box, 2 1/2 In. . .	48.00
Padlock, Eagle, Eagle Lock Co., Terryville, U.S.A., Brass, Lever, Key, 3 In.	40.00
Padlock, Figural, Anti-Chinese Design, Iron, 1872 Patent	1725.00
Padlock, Fraim, Smokehouse, Steel Body, Brass Trim, F Logo, Original Key, 3 1/4 In. . . .	15.00
Padlock, Gamma, Tin, Steel, Lever, Key, 3 In.	26.00
Padlock, Hawkeye Six Lever, Steel, Warded, 3 1/8 In.	39.00
Padlock, Ideal 6 Lever, Steel, Round, Key, 2 1/2 In.	800.00
Padlock, Keen Kutter On Both Sides, Red Paint, Brass, Key, 4 In.	155.00
Padlock, Lock O' Fortune, Brass Body, Steel Shackle, Warded, 2 3/4 In.	20.00
Padlock, Mystery Lock, Brass Body, Steel Shackle, Warded, 2 3/4 In.	35.00
Padlock, Sargent, Oliver, Steel Body, Brass Shackle, Pin Tumbler, Push Key, 2 3/4 In. . . .	325.00
Padlock, Steel, Laminated Construction, Squire Defiant, 3 Original Keys, 4 In.	28.00
Padlock, Werewolf, Steel, Key, 4 1/2 In.	805.00
Padlock, Wheel, Nickel Plated, Brass, Chain, 1 3/4 In.	45.00
Padlock, Winchester, Cast Brass, No. W33, 2 x 2 1/2 x 3/4 In.	99.00
Padlock, Winchester, Tin, Key, 2 3/4 In.	210.00
Padlock, Yale, University Of Colorado, Brass Body, Steel Shackle, 2 3/4 In.	200.00
Pile Driver, Horse Drawn, Red Paint, T.W. Loveless, Patent Model, 1858, 25 1/2 In.	3450.00
Plane, Bed Rock Smooth, Stanley, No. 603, Red Label, Box	935.00
Plane, Birmingham Plane Manufacturing Co., Conn., 1880s, 7 5/16 x 1 1/2 In.	2600.00
Plane, Block, Bailey, Woods & Co., No. 3, Vertical Post Adjuster, Stamped	5500.00
Plane, Block, Leonard Bailey, Victor No. 51, Patent, Oct. 16, 1877, 3 3/16 x 1 1/4 In.	950.00
Plane, Butcher Block, Stanley, No. 64, Type II Trademark, c.1915	1870.00
Plane, Dovetail, Stanley, No. 444, Nickel Plated, Instructions, Cardboard Box	1760.00
Plane, Jack, Ohio Tool, No. 05	60.00
Plane, Jack, Stanley, No. 62, Low Angle, Box	1070.00
Plane, Plow, Coach Maker's, France	350.00
Plane, Plow, Ohio Tool Co., Boxwood Center Wheel, Columbus	60.00
Plane, Plow, Sandusky Tool Co., No. 141, Center Wheel, Self-Regulating, 6 Ivory Tips . .	9350.00
Plane, Plow, Stanley Rule & Level Co., No. 44, Miller's Patent, No. 44, c.1870	3520.00

Plane, Plow, Stanley, No. 42, Gunmetal, Rosewood Handle, Miller's Patent, c.1880	765.00
Plane, Smooth, Stanley, No. 1, Japanned, Tapered Box, 5 15/16 In.	1870.00
Plane, Tongue & Groove, Stanley, No. 48	45.00
Press, Cast Iron, Dolphin Supports, Screw Mechanism, 12 x 21 In.	310.00
Press, Cast Iron, Green Paint, Gage, Warner & Whitney, 18 x 16 In.	70.00
Press, Cast Iron, Pridmore Automatic Screw Press, Chicago, Work Slide, Drawer, 41 In. . .	56.00
Rack, Drying, Pine, 3 Slats, Feet, Late 19th Century, 35 1/2 x 22 1/2 In.	100.00
Rack, Drying, Shaker, Cherry, Tapered Sides, Enfield, Ct., c.1860, 32 1/2 In.	3910.00
Reamer, Forged	15.00
Rope Bed Tightener, Man Standing Form, Extended Arms, 13 In.	3025.00
Rule, Sector, Bleuler, Ivory & Brass, London, 6 x 1 1/2 In.	220.00
Shave, Stair Rail, 2-Way	50.00
Shears, Forged Iron, Spring, Blades Stamped, Late 18th Century, 4 5/8 In.	60.00
Shears, Forged Steel, Ornamental Brass Turnings, c.1887	150.00
Shoe Stretcher, Turn Screw, Mortised, Pegged, 12 1/2 In.	130.00
Shoemaker's Last, Cast Iron, Wood Base, 19th Century	45.00
Shovel, Grain, Hand Turned, Wood, Natural Finish, 1700s, 36 1/2 x 11 1/2 In.	250.00
Shovel, Snow, Phillip's No. 22, Wooden	65.00
Shovel, Wooden, 1 Piece, D-Handle, American, 12-In. Wide Blade, 36 In.	200.00
Tar Bucket, Wooden, Conestoga Wagon, Applicator, Leather Strap Handle, 9 In. . .110.00 to 220.00
Tin Shears, Forged	50.00
Trencher, Pine, Rectangular, Canted Sides, 10 3/4 x 23 x 3 1/4 In.	55.00
Wagon Jack, Conestoga, Red Wash, Initialed FN, 1810	215.00
Wheel Barrow, Wooden, Chamfered Slats, Chip-Carved Ends, Green Paint	112.00
Wood Thread Cutter, Forged	10.00
Workbench, Cabinetmaker's, 2 Vises, Mortised Openings, 1840s, 7 Ft.	1395.00
Yoke, Ox, Iron Strap, 1800s, 24 In.	85.00

TOOTHBRUSH HOLDERS were part of every bowl and pitcher set in the late nineteenth century. Most were oblong covered dishes. About 1920, manufacturers started to make children's toothbrush holders shaped like animals or cartoon characters. A few modern toothbrush holders are still being made.

3 Little Pigs, 3 Holes, Paste Holder, Goldcastle, Japan, 1930s, 4 In.	121.00
Begging Dog, Brush Held In Mouth, Countertop, Japan, 5 1/8 In.	175.00
Boy By Postbox, Large Slot, Countertop, Japan, 4 1/4 In.	65.00
Boy In Knickers, Red & Green Outfit, Japan, 4 1/4 In.	65.00
Boy Playing Flute, Japan, 2 1/2 x 4 1/4 In.	75.00
Bulldog, Large Hole, Countertop, Japan, 3 1/2 In.	135.00
Candlestick Maker, Pottery, Goldcastle, Japan, 5 1/4 In.	90.00
Cat, 2 To 3 Brushes, Hanging, Incised, Norwood, Ohio, Germany, 5 3/4 In.	200.00
Chef, Big Feet, Feet Hold Toothpaste Tube, Japan, 5 1/8 In.	130.00
Clown, 1 Hand Holds Brush, 1 Hand Holds Tube, Countertop, 5 In. . . . . .65.00 to 95.00
Duck, 1 Hole, Countertop, Hand Painted, Japan, 4 1/2 In.	125.00
Duck, Large Bill, Holds 4 Brushes, Countertop, Japan, 4 1/4 In.	100.00
Dutch Boy & Girl Kissing, 3 Holes, Paste Holder, Japan, 5 1/2 In.	85.00
Dutch Girl, Big Feet, Feet Hold Toothpaste Tube, Japan, 5 1/2 In.	125.00
Dutch Girl With Water Jug, 2 Holes, Paste Holder, Japan, 3 3/8 In.	95.00
Genie, 2 Holes, Base Holds Paste, Hand Painted, Japan, 5 3/4 In.	130.00
Girl & Doll, 1 Hole, Base Holds Paste, Japan, 5 5/8 In.	95.00
Moon Mullins With Feet, 2 Holes, Feet Hold Paste, 5 1/8 In.	151.00
Old Woman In Shoe, 3 Brushes, Paste Holder, Japan, 4 7/8 In.	90.00
Peter Rabbit, Base Holds Toothpaste Tube, Incised, Japan, 5 In.	200.00
Soldier, 1 Hole, Paste Holder, Japan, 6 3/4 In.	110.00
Swami, No. 2991, 2 Holes, Countertop, Germany, 3 7/8 In.	150.00
Turtle Wearing Hat, 4 Holes, Countertop, 5 1/2 x 2 1/2 In.	65.00

TOOTHPICK HOLDERS are sometimes called *toothpicks* by collectors. The variously shaped containers used to hold small wooden toothpicks are made of glass, china, or metal. Most of the toothpick holders are Victorian. Additional items may be found in other categories, such as Bisque, Silver Plate, Slag Glass, etc.

Beaded Grape, Green . . . . .35.00 to 55.00

Buckingham	45.00
Button & Bulge, Enameled, Pansy, Green Ground	150.00
Corona, Ruby Stain, Engraved, 2 1/4 x 2 In.	20.00
Delaware, Emerald Green, Gold Trim	45.00
Diamond Panels, Green	22.00
Esther, Green, Gold Trim	85.00
Eureka, Ruby Stain, 2 1/2 x 2 1/4 In.	70.00
Frisco, Milk Glass	12.00
Guttate, Green	135.00
Hanging Flowers, Enameled, Yellow, Green, Milk Glass, Germany, 2 1/4 In.	250.00
Inverted Thumbprint, Cranberry	70.00
Iowa, Clear	30.00
Iris With Meander, Electric Blue	50.00
Kentucky, Green, Gold Trim	90.00
Klondike, Frosted, Stained, 2 3/8 x 1 3/4 In.	350.00
Ladder With Diamond	40.00
Lattice Leaf, Gold Trim	75.00
Monkey, Glass, Basket Pattern Cup On Back, Frosted, Brass Frame, 4 x 3 In.	900.00
Naomi, Ruby Stain, 2 1/2 x 1 7/8 x 2 1/4 In.	25.00
Opaline, Pink	25.00
Palm Leaf, Opal, Footed	30.00
Paneled 44, Gold Flash, U.S. Glass	50.00
Peek-A-Boo, Gold Trim	50.00
Porcelain, Flowers, Art Deco, Germany	30.00
Porcelain, Flowers, Cobalt Trim, Germany, 2 3/8 In.	65.00
Porcelain, Flowers, Purple, Germany	30.00
Porcelain, Roses, Germany	30.00
Portland, Maiden's Blush	45.00
Pretty Maid, Figural, Woman Beside Basket, Square Base, 5 1/4 x 3 1/8 In.	60.00
Ramona	45.00
Rising Sun, Gold Trim	28.00
Scalloped Panel, Green	35.00
Shell & Seaweed, Opal	65.00
Shoshone	30.00
Stippled Fans	30.00
Swirl, Amber	60.00
The States, Gold	38.00
Vermont, Green, Gold Trim	55.00
Windermere's Fan, Blue Iridescent	30.00
X-Bull's-Eye	50.00

TORQUAY is the name given to ceramics by several potteries working near Torquay, England, from 1870 until 1962. Until about 1900, the potteries used local red clay to make classical-style art pottery vases and figurines. Then they turned to making souvenir wares. Items were dipped in colored slip and decorated with painted slip and sgraffito designs. They often had mottoes or proverbs, and scenes of cottages, ships, birds, or flowers. The *Scandy* design was a symmetrical arrangement of brushstrokes and spots done in colored slips. Potteries included Watcombe Pottery (1870–1962); Torquay Terra-Cotta Company (1875–1905); Aller Vale (1881–1924); Torquay Pottery (1908–1940); and Longpark (1883–1957).

TORQUAY

Bowl, Blue Flowers, Mottled Black, Brown Exterior, Rusty Brown Interior, 6 1/2 x 3 In. ...	79.00
Bowl, Motto Ware, Early Sow Early Mow, 4 1/2 x 1 1/2 In.	70.00
Bowl, Motto Ware, Good Courage Breaks Ill Luck, 4 1/2 x 1 1/2 In.	70.00
Bowl, Motto Ware, Time Ripens All Things, 4 1/2 x 1 1/2 In.	70.00
Cheese Dish, Motto Ware, Comfort Is Better Than Pride, 6 1/2 x 5 1/4 In.	175.00
Cup, Demitasse, Clover	35.00
Cup, Motto Ware, Speak Little Speak Well, Child's, 3 1/2 x 2 3/4 In.	85.00
Eggcup, Motto Ware, Fresh To Day, 2 x 2 3/4 In.	65.00
Eggcup, Motto Ware, Waste Not Want Not, 2 x 2 3/4 In.	65.00
Inkwell, Motto Ware, Redware, Us Be Always Glad Tu Wer Frumee, Rooster	100.00
Jug, Motto Ware, Kind Words Are The Music Of The World, Cover, 5 3/4 x 4 1/2 In.	180.00

Pitcher, Motto Ware, Say Well Is Good Do Well Is Better, 4 x 4 In. 125.00
Plate, Motto Ware, Action Speaks Louder Than Words, 7 1/4 In. 79.00
Plate, Motto Ware, May The Hinges Of Friendship Never Go Rusty, 7 1/4 In. 79.00
Teapot, Motto Ware, Don't Worry It May Never Happen, 7 x 4 1/2 In. 250.00
Teapot, Motto Ware, Weel Take A Cup O Kindness For Auld Lang Syne, 6 1/4 x 3 1/4 In. 195.00
Vase, Peacock, 3 Handles, 9 1/2 In. 125.00

TORTOISESHELL is the shell of the tortoise. It has been used as inlay
and to make small decorative objects since the seventeenth century.
Some species of tortoise are now on the endangered species list, and
old and new objects made from these shells cannot be sold legally.

Bottle, 4 Sides, Mushroom-Shaped Threaded Lid, Nickel & Cork Stopper, 5 In. 170.00
Box, Arched & Hinged Lid, Leaf-Shape Brass Mounts, 4 x 6 3/4 x 2 7/8 In. 460.00
Box, Engraved Oval Silver Crest, 5 1/2 x 2 3/4 In. 315.00
Box, Intricate Figural Carving, Round, c.1800, 4 1/2 In. Diam. 430.00
Box, Writing, Hinged Dome Top, Mirror, Interior Compartments, 2 3/4 x 1 3/4 In. 825.00
Cabinet, Jewelry, Bombe Form, Handles, Brass Feet, 18 x 13 x 14 In. 8225.00
Card Case, Bone Banded, England, Mid 19th Century, 3 1/2 x 2 x 1/2 In. 259.00
Page Turner, Sterling Handle, Engraved Viking Ship Chester Mark, 14 In. 260.00
Tea Caddy, 2 Compartments, Ivory Surround, Bun Feet, c.1820, 4 x 6 x 4 In. 2600.00
Watchcase, Gold & Silver Pique Inlaid Top, Key Wound Watch, 4 x 2 In. 240.00

TOY collectors have special clubs, magazines, and shows. Toys are
designed to entice children, and today they have attracted new interest
among adults who are still children at heart. All types of toys are collected. Tin toys, iron toys, battery operated toys, and many others are
collected by specialists. Dolls, Games, Teddy Bears, and Bicycles are
listed in their own categories. Other toys may be found under company
or celebrity names.

Accordion, Germany, 5 In. 44.00
Acrobat, Celluloid Figure, Steel Frame, Spring Motor, Instructions, Branko, Box 118.00
Acrobat, Tik-Tak, Boy On Trapeze, Windup, Tin, Japan, 11 In. 44.00
Air Control Tower, Helicopter, Airplane, Tin, Cragstan By Bandai, 1960s, 11 x 37 In. 650.00
Aircraft Carrier, Moves As Helicopter Blade Spins, Tin, Friction, Bandai, Box, 7 In. 310.00
Aircraft Carrier, Planes, Tin, Plastic, Wolverine, Box, 18 In. 250.00
Aircraft Carrier, Ventura, Plastic, Battery Operated, Italy, 1950s, 33 In. 121.00
Airplane, Air Force Jet, Tin Lithograph, Friction, Star Fire, Japan, 18-In. Wingspan 220.00
Airplane, Air Mail, Pressed Steel, Keystone, 1920s, 32 In. 495.00
Airplane, American Airlines, Electra, 4 Propellers, Wing Lights, Linemar, 18 In. 90.00
Airplane, American Flyer, Green, Yellow, Steel, Motor, c.1920, 23 1/2-In. Wingspan 635.00
Airplane, Army Scout, Tri-Motor, Pressed Steel, Steelcraft, 1920, 22 1/2-In. Wingspan . . . 690.00
Airplane, Biplane German Fighter, Tippco, 1938, 11 In. 2650.00
Airplane, Biplane, Pilot, White, Tin, Penny Toy, 3 In. 1155.00
Airplane, Biplane, Sea, 1723, Red, Yellow, Clockwork, 21-In. Wingspan 1760.00
Airplane, Biplane, Steel, Cor-Cor, c.1920, 17-In. Wingspan 255.00
Airplane, Biplane, Windup, Yellow, Tin Lithograph, Distler, Germany, 20-In. Wingspan . . 2420.00
Airplane, Boeing 747, Thai Airlines, Composition, Wire Stand, 24-In. Wingspan 99.00
Airplane, Boeing B-50, Props Spin, Tin, Friction, Yonezawa, Box, 19-In. Wingspan 1485.00
Airplane, Bomber, Camouflage, Guns On Wing, Marx, 19 In. 550.00
Airplane, Bomber, Green, Tin Lithograph, 18 1/2-In. Wingspan 375.00
Airplane, Cargo, Air Force, Tin Lithograph, Modern Toys, Japan, 22 1/2-In. Wingspan . . . 525.00
Airplane, Cargo, Metal, Red & Green, Wyandotte, 1930s, 10 In., 13-In. Wingspan 235.00
Airplane, Catapult, Hangar, Lever, Steel, Buddy L, c.1920, 8 x 12 In. 3080.00
Airplane, Circles Tower, Germany, Box, 12 In. 403.00
Airplane, Commercial, 2 Propellers, Huki, Germany, 6 3/4-In. Wingspan 175.00
Airplane, Commercial, 4 Propellers, Friction, Silver, Black, 10-In. Wingspan 165.00
Airplane, Condor, Circles, Lights Flash, Tin, Japan, Battery Operated, Box, 9 In. 195.00
Airplane, Conveyor, B36, U.S. Air Force, Tin, Friction, Japan, 26-In. Wingspan 230.00
Airplane, DC-3, Douglas Die Cast, Propeller, Landing Gear, Ertl, Box, 15 1/2 In. 65.00
Airplane, DC-6, Pan Am Marx, 1950, 25-In. Wingspan 209.00
Airplane, DC-7, TWA, Stairs, Tin Lithograph, Battery Operated, Cragstan, Box, 24 In. . . . 660.00
Airplane, DC-10, Passenger, UTA, France, 1960, 20-In. Wingspan 35.00
Airplane, Douglas Sky Rocket, Cockpit Opens, Pilot Ejects, Tin, Friction, Bandai, 11 In. . 195.00

Airplane, F-611 Jet, Black & Yellow, U.S. Air Force, Y, 1960s, 14 1/2 In. 225.00
Airplane, F100 Super Sabre, Sparks, Tin, Friction, Yonezawa, Box, 7 In. 195.00
Airplane, Float, Pilot, Beige, Tin Lithograph, Windup, Paya, 12-In. Wingspan 145.00
Airplane, Ford, Tri-Motor, Steel, U.S. Mail, Steelcraft, c.1920, 22-1/2 In. Wingspan 2200.00
Airplane, German Monoplane, Windup, Fold Back Wings, Tin, Tippco, 16 In. 3740.00
Airplane, Heddon, Curtis Jenny, Fish On Sides, Aviator, Propeller, Motor, 1918, 11 In. . . .   740.00
Airplane, Heinkel, He111, Swastika On Tail, Tin Lithograph, Lehmann, Box, 7 1/4 In. . . .   230.00
Airplane, Helicopter, Army, Tin, Linemar, 1950, 10-In. Wingspan 385.00
Airplane, Japan International Airlines, Tin, Friction, 14 In. 150.00
Airplane, Jet, Supersonic, Stairs, Tin Lithograph, Battery, Sears, Box, 19-In. Wingspan . . .   248.00
Airplane, LM-59, Tin, Friction, Linemar, Box, 6 1/2 In. 120.00
Airplane, Lufthansa, Propeller, Tin, Friction, Tippco, West Germany, 12 In. 195.00
Airplane, ME 109, Windup, Tin, Tippco Germany, 14 In. 1375.00
Airplane, Military Transport, Wyandotte, Box, 1940s, 13 In. 385.00
Airplane, Military, Transport, 4 Propellers, Wyandotte, 1950s, 10 In., 13-In. Wingspan . . .   295.00
Airplane, Monoplane, Cast Iron, C.A. Wood, 1930s, 3 1/2 In. 75.00
Airplane, Monoplane, CR-505, Windup, Tin, Rossignol, France, c.1928, 15 In. 2200.00
Airplane, Mystoplane, Remote Control, Box, 6 x 21 In. 66.00
Airplane, Pan Am, Air France, Lights, Windup, Tin, Battery Operated, 25-In. Wingspan . .   690.00
Airplane, Pan Am, Tin Lithograph, 4 Propeller Engines, Light, Electric, Gama, 15 In. 220.00
Airplane, Pan American Sky Chief, Props Spin, Tin, Friction, Hadson, 14 1/2 In. 275.00
Airplane, Pioneer Air Express, Tin, Indian On End, Marx, 1920s, 25 In. 395.00
Airplane, Piper, Sport Plane, Red, Tin, Friction, Cragstan, Japan, 20-In. Wingspan 190.00
Airplane, Pressed Steel, Ford Tri-Motor, Kingsbury, 1920s, 14 1/2 In. 330.00
Airplane, Propeller Spins When String Is Pulled, Tin, Chein Nifty Logo, 7 In. 275.00
Airplane, Red Cross, 2 Propellers, Tekno, Denmark, 5 In., 8-In. Wingspan 225.00
Airplane, Ride 'Em, Red Wings, Keystone, 1941, 36-In. Wingspan 1540.00
Airplane, Seaplane, Prop Spins, Tin, Chein, c.1938, 9 In. 248.00
Airplane, Shooting Rocket, Remote, Automatic, Japan, 13 In. 395.00
Airplane, Spirit Of St. Louis, Rubberized Wheels, Steelcraft, 1930s, 24 x 24 In. 225.00
Airplane, Spirit Of St. Louis, Windup, Tin, Strauss, 7-In. Wingspan 330.00
Airplane, Swissair, Aluminum, On Stand, Coronado HB-ICA, 34 In. 635.00
Airplane, Tiger X-15, Props Spin, Tin, Friction, Usagiya, Box, 8-In. Wingspan 198.00
Airplane, Tin, Battery Operated, Remote Control, Linemar, Japan, 1950s, 14 In. 110.00
Airplane, Tin, Plastic, Battery Operated, Remote Control, Schuco, Box, 19 In. 205.00
Airplane, Tootsietoy, Box, 12 x 13 In., 12 Piece 415.00
Airplane, Tower Aeroplane, Windup, Spins, Tin, Marx, Box, c.1930, 9 In. 275.00
Airplane, Trans Canada, Cast Aluminum, 1950s, 24-In. Wingspan 2090.00
Airplane, Trans World Flyer, Circles Globe, Windup, Tower, Biller, W. Germany, 12 In. . . .   240.00
Airplane, Tri-Motor, Army Scout, Steel, Steelcraft, c.1920, 22 1/2-In. Wingspan 690.00
Airplane, Tri-Motor, Ford, Nickel Plated Props & Motor, Cast Iron, Kilgore, 13 1/2 In. . . .   2070.00
Airplane, U.S. Mail, Windup, Tin, Marx, Box, c.1930, 18-In. Wingspan 900.00
Airplane, USAF F104, Tin, Friction, Japan, 14-In. Wingspan 95.00
Airplane, Whirligig, Wood, Steel, Blue, Silver, Red, Wood Base, 18 1/2 x 9 3/4 In. 120.00
Airplane, Windup, Tin, Yellow, Blue, Red, Cast Metal Pilot, 16 1/4 x 12 In. 470.00
Airplane, Yellow, Blue, Cast Iron, Arcade, 6 1/2 In., 10 1/2-In. Wingspan 375.00
Airplane, Zero Fighter, Green, Tin, Plastic, 16 In. 90.00
Airplane Set, 3 Super Jets, No. 415, Fisher-Price, Box, c.1950 . . . .   950.00
Airplane Set, Biplane, Pilot, Hanger, Aircraft Series, Box, Britains 1525, c.1938 . . . .   3300.00
Airport, American Airlines, Airplane, Tin, Battery Operated, Wyandotte, 12 x 16 In. 300.00
Airport, Hanger, Wood, 2 Cast Iron Planes, Arcade, 12 In. 962.00
Airship, Windup, Aluminum, Schylling, 10 In. 75.00
Alligator, Wally Gator, Stuffed, Cloth, c.1970, 7 1/2 In. 40.00
Alpine Boy, Beer Mug, Tan Shorts, Green Hat, Schuco, 5 In. 150.00
Alpine Boy, Dancing With Girl, Schuco, 5 In. 155.00
Ambulance, Buick, Friction, Japan, 15 In. 325.00
Ambulance, Open Rear Door, White, Steel, Wyandotte, c.1940, 11 1/2 In. 120.00
Ambulance, Plymouth, White, Ichiko, 1961, 12 In. 395.00
Ambulance, Steel, Rubber, Sturdi-Toy, c.1920, 26 In. 6600.00
Ambulance, Superior, Tin, Battery Operated, Box, 11 In. 110.00
Ambulance, Tin, Friction, Cragstan, Box, 8 1/2 In. 88.00
American Cuzner Trotter, Tan Horse, Tin, Red Wagon, Clockwork, 1872, 10 In. 6600.00
Amusement Park, Sportsland, Windup, Tin, Japan, 6 x 6 In. 635.00

Amusement Park, Whip, Tin, Germany, Box, 9 In. 1595.00
Arcade, Shooting Gallery, Gun, Tin Lithograph, Revolving Ducks, 20 In. 65.00
Army Set, Paint Your Own, 3 Vials Of Paint, Dried Up, Barclay 365.00
Arnold Monkey On Tricycle, Tin Lithograph, 3 3/4 In. 99.00
Astronaut, Astro Scout, Walks, Chest Meter Moves, Tin, Crank, Yonezawa, 10 In. 2200.00
Astronaut, Cragstan, Walks, Tin, Crank, Yonezawa, 10 In. 550.00
Astronaut, Doll, 8 Accessories, Hong Kong, Box, 8 1/2 In. 85.00
Astronaut, Kamen Flyer, Moves On Chest, Windup, Vinyl, Yonezawa, Box, 9 1/2 In. 330.00
Astronaut, Moonlight, Walks, Tin, Vinyl, Battery Operated, Bullmark, 12 1/2 In. 690.00
Astronaut, NASA, Walks, Light, Plastic, Tin, Battery Operated, Marx, 12 In. 385.00
Astronaut, Rotate-O-Matic, Walks, Lights, Tin, Battery Operated, Japan, Box, 12 In. 99.00
Astronaut, Ultraman, Walks, Arms Move, Windup, Tin, Vinyl, Bullmark, Box, 9 1/2 In. .. 605.00
Astronaut, Video, Tin Body, Plastic Limbs, S.H. Japan, 11 In. 60.00
Astronaut, Walks, Lights, Sound, Tin, Battery Operated, Nomura, Japan, 13 1/2 In. 880.00
Astronaut, Walks, Lights, Tin, Battery Operated, Remote, Linemar, 8 In. 1210.00
Astronaut, Walks, Moves Arms, Battery Operated, Tin, Plastic Arms, Marx, 12 In. 210.00
Atom Rocket, Space Vehicle, Battery Operated, Lights, Modern Toys, Japan, 9 1/2 In. ... 90.00
Auto Runabout, Red Devil Tiller, Jones & Bixler, 1912, 5 In. 350.00
Baby, Pip-Squeak, Papier-Mache Doll, Wood Cradle, Rocking, c.1870, 2 x 2 3/4 In. 235.00
Baby, Pip-Squeak, Swaddled, In Cradle, Leatherized Paper Bellows, 4 1/2 In. 495.00
Baby Haymaker Set, Tin Tractor, Mowing Machine, Rake, Wagon, 9 x 9 In. 285.00
Baggage Man, Windup, Distler, Germany, 1920s, 4 In. 675.00
Balloon, Jack Skellington, Nightmare Before Christmas, Bionic Air Walker, 7 Ft. 85.00
Balloon Blower, Gino Neapolitan, Tomiyama, Japan, Box 295.00
Balloon Seller, Monkeys Under Hurdy-Gurdy, Mechanical, 6 In. 240.00
Barn, Stock, Removable Roof, Doors Slide, Wood, Paper, Roosevelt, 20 In. 145.00
Barnacle Bill, Windup, Tin, Chein, 6 In. ....145.00 to 305.00
Barney Google, On 4-Wheeled Platform, Tin, Pull Toy, 1920s .... 950.00 to 1150.00
Barrel, Hires Root Beer Soda Fountain, Box, 7 In. 28.00
Barrel Dray, 2 Horses, Driver, Steel, Cast Iron, Stenciled, Wilkins, Kingsbury, 22 1/2 In. . 748.00
Baseball Bat, Flintstones, Vinyl, c.1960, 25 In. 12.00
Baseball Bat, Peter's Weatherbird Shoes, Diamond Brand, 33 In. 144.00
Bears are also listed in the Teddy Bears category.
Bear, Bar B Q, Windup, Tin, Plush, Composition, Alps Of Japan, 1950s 125.00
Bear, Busy Housekeeper, Pushes Vacuum, Plush, Plaid Skirt, Alps, Box, 1958, 8 In. 275.00
Bear, Fishing, 2 Fish, Battery Operated 175.00
Bear, Head Turns, Mouth Opens & Closes, Clockwork, Ives, 8 In. 200.00
Bear, Musical Marching, Blows Horn & Bangs On Drum, Alps Toys, 1950s 950.00
Bear, Papa Smoking, Battery Operated, Felt, Tin, San In Circle Mark, Japan, 8 1/4 In. *Illus* 72.00
Bear, Popcorn Vendor, Pushes Cart, Battery Operated, Japan, Box, 8 In. 226.00
Bear, Tippy Joe, Metal, Windup, U.S. Zone Germany, 15 In. 295.00
Bear, VIP The Busy Boss, Telephone Remote, Battery Operated, Box, 7 In. .... *Illus* 150.00
Bear, Washing, Bubbles, Washes Clothes, Battery Operated, Instructions, Box 475.00
Bed, Doll's, Brass, Wooden Rails, Springs, Early 20th Century, 16 1/2 x 14 x 26 In. 130.00
Bed, Doll's, Renaissance Revival, Woman's Head On Headboard, 27 x 30 x 17 In. 275.00
Bed, Doll's, Walnut, Turned Posts, Cutout Headboard 365.00
Bed, Doll's, Wood, Painted, Blue, Pierced Heart, Mattress, Quilt, c.1845, 8 x 10 x 14 In. . 239.00
Beetle, Crawling, Lehmann, c.1900, 4 1/2 In. 325.00
Bell Ringer, Bear Riding Tricycle, Iron, 4 In. 145.00
Bell Ringer, Horse Drawn, Cast Iron, Pressed Steel, Nickel Plated, 16 In. 90.00

Toy, Bear, Papa Smoking, Battery
Operated, Felt, Tin, San In
Circle Mark, Japan, 8 1/4 In.

Toy, Bear, VIP The
Busy Boss, Telephone
Remote, Battery
Operated, Box, 7 In.

Bell Ringer, Horse Race, 2 Horses, Riders, 4 Bells, Wheels, Iron, 11 In. 205.00
Bell Ringer, Horse, Derby, Wheels, Iron, 7 In. 130.00
Bell Ringer, Pony On Wagon, Iron, No. 39, 8 In. 715.00
Bell Ringer, Trick Elephant, Cast Iron, Gong 605.00
Bicycle, Bell, Rabbit Holding Balloon, Celluloid, Japan 100.00
Bicycle, E.T. & Elliot, Plastic, Pull & Go, 1982, 3 1/2 In. 15.00
Bicycle, Wagon, Humphrey Mobile, Windup, Tin, Wyandotte, 8 In. 265.00
Bicycles that are large enough to ride are listed in their own category.
Big Joe Chef, Windup, Tin Lithograph, Yone, Japan, Box, 6 1/2 In. 95.00
Big Parade, Windup, Tin, Marx, 24 In. 520.00
Billiard Player, Hits Ball In Hole, Windup, Tin, Kico Germany, 6 In. . . . . .250.00 to 350.00
Billiard Table, Mechanical, 2 Players, Windup, 14 In. 250.00
Billy The Cowboy, Tin, Plastic, Windup, Japan, 4 1/2 In. 35.00
Bird, Hekyl & Jekyl, Hops, Windup, Tin, Linemar & Marx, 4 1/2 In. 275.00
Black Boy Pete, Shaking Dog, Celluloid, Windup, Japan, 6 In. 460.00
Black Oscar The Porter, Peddles 3-Wheel Baggage Cart, Head Goes Up, Down, France . .   550.00
Black Porter, Pushes Trunk, Dog Lurches Out Of Trunk, Strauss, 6 In. 600.00
Blocks, Alphabet, Safety, Wood, Box, 5 1/2 x 5 1/2 In. 80.00
Blocks, At The Circus, Animals, Figures, Children, Lithograph, 9 1/2 x 4 1/2 x 6 In. 345.00
Blocks, Building, Gilbert, Box, 10 x 18 In. 40.00
Blocks, Building, Wood, Instructions, Crandall's, Box, c.1880 . . . .   65.00
Blocks, Ole Million Faces, Changeable, Face Corp., Philadelphia, 1920s, 11 Piece 59.00
Blocks, Picture, Lithograph, 6 Animals, Box, 2 1/2 x 8 x 6 3/4 In. 40.00
Boat, Amphibian, Tin, Friction, Japan, 10 In. 395.00
Boat, Battleship, 6 Gun Turrets, 2 Masts, 2 Lifeboats, Germany, 14 In. 1495.00
Boat, Battleship, Green, Tin, Clockwork, Carrete, 14 In. 360.00
Boat, Battleship, Lifeboats, Tin, Clockwork, Ives, 14 In. 745.00
Boat, Battleship, New York, Black, Steel, Clockwork, Orkin, c.1920, 25 In. 990.00
Boat, Battleship, Red, White, Tin, Clockwork, 10 In. 99.00
Boat, Battleship, Tin Lithograph, Penny, Germany, c.1810, 4 x 2 In. 110.00
Boat, Battleship, Tin, Arnold Sparking, U.S. Zone Germany 800.00
Boat, Blue Bird, Prop Spins, Engine Noise, Tin, Crank, Japan, Box, 6 In. 165.00
Boat, Cabin Cruiser, Commodore Clockwork, Tin, Sutcliffe, England, Box, 13 In. 80.00
Boat, Cabin Cruiser, Radio-Controlled, Handmade, Wood, 2 Electric Motors, 42 x 17 In. . .   1650.00
Boat, Captain, Speedboat, Friction, Tin, Mitsuhashi, Box, 1960s, 10 1/2 In. 195.00
Boat, Carrier, Aircraft, 2 Planes, Guns, Wooden, Spring-Loaded, Keystone, Box, 16 In. . .   360.00
Boat, Carrier, Aircraft, Wood, Battery Operated, Japan, c.1950, 13 In. 130.00
Boat, Dayton, Lifeboats, Yellow, Tin, Friction, 12 1/2 In. 255.00
Boat, Diamond, Battery Operated, Tin, Japan, 8 In. 325.00
Boat, Electric, Lang Craft, L-912, Box, 15 In. 225.00
Boat, Flywheel Drive, Germany, c.1912, 7 In. 265.00
Boat, Green, Steel, Electric, Lepage Outboard Motor, 1920, 23 In. 77.00
Boat, Greist, Wood, Battery Powered Motor, 22 1/2 In. 110.00
Boat, Gun, Brown, Black, Tin, Clockwork, Marklin, Germany, 11 1/2 In. 495.00
Boat, Gun, White, Red, Tin, Clockwork, Carette, 11 In. 358.00
Boat, KronPrinz, Paddlewheel, Painted, Germany, 17 In. 3160.00
Boat, Launch, Cream, Green, Red, Lithograph Skipper, Windup, Germany, 7 In. 750.00
Boat, Live Steam Launch, Schonner, 12 1/2 In. 825.00
Boat, Luxury Liner, Sparks, Tin, Friction, Marx, Box, 14 1/2 In.   350.00
Boat, Metal, Windup, Wolverine, American, 1950s, 13 In. 135.00
Boat, Model, Commodore Cruiser, Clockwork, Box 120.00
Boat, Model, Hawk, Clockwork, Box 105.00
Boat, Model, Valiant, Clockwork, Metal, Box 365.00
Boat, Model, Victor, Motor Torpedo Boat, Clockwork, Box 139.00
Boat, Mouse Driver, Tin, Vinyl, Crank, Tada, Box, 9 1/2 In. 330.00
Boat, Ocean Liner, 2 Masts, 2 Funnels, 8 Lifeboats, Marklin, Germany, 24 In. 1670.00
Boat, Ocean Liner, 3 Stacks, Lifeboats, White, Black, Red, Bing, 40 In. 3080.00
Boat, Ocean Liner, 4 Stacks, Lifeboats, Masts, 2 Smokestacks, Clockwork, Bing, 21 In. . .   3740.00
Boat, Ocean Liner, Battery Operated, Modern Toys, Japan, 22 In.   65.00
Boat, Ocean Liner, Friction, Red, White, Pressed Steel, Hillclimber, 1920s 250.00
Boat, Ocean Liner, Lifeboats, White, Red, Tin, Clockwork, Carette, Germany, 12 1/2 In. . .   360.00
Boat, Ocean Liner, White, Red, Tin, Clockwork, Ives, Germany, 13 1/2 In. 415.00
Boat, Ocean Liner, Windup, Tin, Bing, Germany, 20 In. 1760.00

Boat, Paddlewheel Lake, 3 Smokestacks, 4 Funnels, Bull Nose Bow, Germany, 17 In. ... 3165.00
Boat, Patrol, Crank, Tin, Japan, 10 In. 145.00
Boat, Pond, 2-Masted, 4 Sails, Rudder, Wood, Cloth, 27 1/2 In. 150.00
Boat, Pond, Black, Red Painted Hull, Early 20th Century, 18 In. 219.00
Boat, Pond, Wooden Hull, Metal Fittings, Clockwork, 21 In. 865.00
Boat, Racing Scull, Coxswain, Rowers, Oars, Issmayer, 20 1/2 In. 4400.00
Boat, Racing, Painted, Tin, Sutcliffe, England, 10 In. 44.00
Boat, Racing, Red, Windup, Tin, Lindstrom, 14 1/2 In. 22.00
Boat, Rowboat, Wood, Clockwork Outboard Motor, 11 In. 77.00
Boat, Sail, Wood, 2 Masts, Full Spinnaker, Rigging, Tiller, 1940s, 72 x 65 x 11 In. 920.00
Boat, Sailing, Galleon Espanol, 3-Masted, Wood, c.1940, 23 x 23 In. 15.00
Boat, Sea Elizabeth, Tin, Friction, Japan, c.1950, 8 1/2 In. 33.00
Boat, Ship, Cargo, 2 Masts, Smokestack, 2 Lifeboats, Fleischmann, c.1930, 20 In. 635.00
Boat, Slo Moshin, Plastic, Crank Action, Ideal, Box, c.1950, 13 In. 220.00
Boat, Speedboat, Ideal, Plastic, Crank Operated, 13 In. 95.00
Boat, Speedboat, Japanese Riverstreak, Friction, 5 In. 275.00
Boat, Speedboat, Lionel, Tin, Clockwork Motor, Stand, 18 In. 330.00
Boat, Speedboat, Mercury, Prop Spins, Tin, Lever, Marusan, Box, 6 In. 165.00
Boat, Speedboat, Outboard Motor, Red, Yellow, Windup, Tin, 20 In. 144.00
Boat, Speedboat, Penn Yan, 3 Cast Iron Figures, Johnson Outboard Motor, Hubley, 1929 . 2875.00
Boat, Speedboat, Robot, Tin, Friction, Japan, 13 In. 495.00
Boat, Speedboat, Sea Queen, Crank Action, Japan, 9 1/2 In. 75.00
Boat, Speedboat, Wood, Brass Boiler, 1918, 30 In. 375.00
Boat, Speedboat, Wood, Display Model, Box, 24 In. 90.00
Boat, Steam Powered, Wood Top, Yellow Body, Black Bottom, Box, 38 In. 1430.00
Boat, Steam, Launch, Painted, Tin, Brass, Schoenner, 12 1/2 In. 825.00
Boat, Steamship, Passenger, Revolving Planes, Windup, Japan, 9 In. 300.00
Boat, Steamship, Tin Lithograph, Germany, 7 In. 198.00
Boat, Torpedo, 4 Guns, 3 Masts, 3 Lifeboats, Clockwork, Bing, c.1910, 21 In. 1380.00
Boat, Torpedo, Blue, Wood, Battery Operated, Japan, c.1950, 17 In. 145.00
Boat, Torpedo, Blue, Wood, Battery Operated, Japan, c.1950, 32 In. 305.00
Boat, Torpedo, Tin, Battery Operated, Linemar, Japan, Box, c.1950, 11 In. 200.00
Boat, USA Coast Guard, Metal, Friction, Japan, 1950s, 7 1/2 In. 145.00
Boat, Voyager, Red, Plastic, Hess, Box, c.1960, 18 In. 250.00
Boat, Whaling, Radar Dish, Lifeboats, Harpoon, Windup, Japan, Box, 13 In. 240.00
Boat, Zoom Boat, Tin, Forward & Reverse, Pistons Move, Box, 1950s, 12 In. 365.00
Bottle, Baby Set, Bottle, Glass, Embossed, C.B., Teething Ring, Rattle, Box, c.1910, 3 In. 425.00
Box, Cardboard, Limping Lizzie, Marx, c.1930, 7 In. 200.00
Box, Pencil, Felix The Cat, 1950s 25.00
Boxers, Moves Back & Forth, Windup, Celluloid & Tin, Japan, Box, 6 1/2 In. 275.00
Boy, Crying, Windup, Tin, c.1920-1930s, 4 1/2 In. 145.00
Boy, Eating Watermelon, Celluloid, Tin, Windup, Japan, 6 In. 143.00
Boy, Naughty, Father Drives Car, Boy Grabs Tiller, Windup, Lehmann, 5 In. 1000.00
Boy, On Horse, Wooden, Paper, Tin, Pull Toy, 8 In. 205.00
Boy, On Scooter, Kid Flyer, Tin Lithograph, Marked, B & R, 8 1/2 In. 220.00
Boy, On Tricycle, Cloth, Metal, Pull Toy, Steiff, c.1918, 8 In. 5600.00
Boy, On Velocipede, Spring Motor, Steering Rod, Stevens & Brown, 11 In. 2350.00
Boy, Wood, Moving Head, Arms, Kobe, Japan, c.1890, 5 In. 575.00
Bridge, 6 Cars Crossing Bridge, Lithograph, Windup, Marx, 24 In. 300.00
Bubble Gum Machine, Plastic, 1 Cent, Jaw Teasers, 12 In. 145.00
Bucking Bronco, White, Rider, Lehmann, 6 In. 480.00
Building Set, Anchor Blocks, No. 3, Richter, Box, 6 1/2 x 10 In. 55.00
Building Set, Anchor Blocks, No. 3A, Richter, Box, 7 1/2 x 11 1/2 In. 55.00
Building Set, Boy Toymaker, Wood Novelties, Material, Tools, M. Carlton Dank, Box ... 165.00
Building Set, Brick, Mortar, Masonry Tools, Instructions, Box, 8 x 12 In. 66.00
Building Set, Lumber, Roofs, Doors, Windows, Wood, Falcon, Box, 11 1/2 x 16 In. 40.00
Bulldog, Papier-Mache, Glass Eyes, Head Nods, Mouth Opens, Pull Chain, c.1890, 18 In. 2500.00
Bulldozer, Cast Aluminum, Caterpillar, 24 In. 1980.00
Bulldozer, Driver, Blue, Tin, Battery Operated, Japan, Box, 10 In. 110.00
Bulldozer, Driver, International Diesel, Arcade, 7 1/2 In. 950.00
Bulldozer, Driver, Piston, Tin Lithograph, Battery Operated, Linemar, Box, c.1959, 7 In. . 450.00
Bulldozer, John Deere, Model 554, Box, c.1967 ....300.00 to 350.00
Bulldozer, Yellow, Black, Tonka, 1963, 12 In. 65.00

Bus, Autobus, Windup, Tin, Lehmann, Germany, Box, 1907, 8 In. 3080.00
Bus, Battery Operated, Radio Control, Silver, Tin, Radicon, Japan, Box, 14 In. 250.00
Bus, Buddy L, Pressed Steel, 28 1/4 In. 4180.00
Bus, Continental Trailways, Tin, Friction, Japan, 11 In. 110.00
Bus, Dinky Continental, Tour, Green, Die Cast, England, 8 1/2 In. 110.00
Bus, Double-Decker, Red, Tin Lithograph, Friction, Japan, 7 1/2 In. 20.00
Bus, Double-Decker, Tin Lithograph, Windup, Wells, England, 7 In. 190.00
Bus, Double-Decker, Utilice Este Omnibus Para Teatro, Windup, Tin, 3 3/4 x 9 In. 770.00
Bus, Double-Decker, Yellow, Iron, Rubber Driver, Tin Seats, Arcade, 13 1/2 In. 1265.00
Bus, Greenline, Tin Lithograph, Windup, London, England, 7 1/2 In. 99.00
Bus, Greyhound Lines, Century Of Progress, Arcade, Box, 1933, 8 In. . . . . .185.00 to 220.00
Bus, Greyhound, Cast Iron, Blue Cab, White Trailer, Logo, Arcade, No. 3220, 10 1/4 In. . 140.00
Bus, Greyhound, Cast Iron, Nickel, Arcade, 9 In. 350.00
Bus, Greyhound, Clockwork Motor, Buddy L, 1930s, 16 1/2 In. 385.00
Bus, Greyhound, People Move, Tin, Friction, Miyamae, 11 1/2 In. 180.00
Bus, Greyhound, Pop-Up Passengers & Driver, France, 5 In. 175.00
Bus, Greyhound, Tin, Friction, Daiya, Box, 8 1/2 In. 140.00
Bus, Inter-State, Windup, Green, Yellow, Tin Lithograph, Strauss, c.1920, 11 In. 580.00
Bus, Jack Rabbit, Holgate, 12 In. 145.00
Bus, Metal, Friction, Arnold, Germany, 1950s, 8 1/2 In. 195.00
Bus, Motor Coach, Driver, Windup, Lehmann 425.00
Bus, O-Gan-Bat, Tin, Friction, Japan, Box, 8 In. 470.00
Bus, Panoramic Overland, Tin, Friction, Marusan, Box, 12 1/2 In. 1100.00
Bus, Pressed Steel, Windup, Door Opens, Buddy L, American, 16 1/2 In. 275.00
Bus, Red & White, Bandai, 1960, 14 In. 285.00
Bus, Robot, Tin Lithograph, Clockwork Motor, Woodhaven, 14 In. 90.00
Bus, Safety, Cast Iron, Painted Green, Kilgore, 8 In. 440.00
Bus, School, Tin, Friction, Daiya, Box, 13 In. 185.00
Bus, Sonicon, Whistle, Antenna Spins, Tin, Battery Operated, Remote, Japan, Box, 14 In. . 330.00
Bus, Tin, Sliding Roof, Tipp, Germany, 8 In. 150.00
Bus, Tootsietoy, Greyhound, Scenic Cruiser, Box, 1940s, 7 In. 99.00
Bus, Travels Road, Plastic, Windup, Technofix, West Germany, Box, 33 In. 149.00
Bus, Trolley, Buy British, Tin Lithograph, Windup, England, 7 In. 110.00
Bus, Trolley, Set, Accessories, Plastic, West Germany, Box, 7 1/2 x 16 In. 55.00
Bus, Volkswagen, TV, Tin, Remote Control, Box, 7 1/2 In. 176.00
Busy Lizzie Sweeps Floor, Windup, Germany, 1920s 575.00
Buttercup & Spareribs, Pull Toy, Nifty, 1920s 590.00
Butterfly, Flaps Wings, Tin, Friction, Alps, Box, 5 In. 120.00
Cabinet, Kitchen, 2 Doors, 2 Drawers, Breadboard, Cast Iron, Early 1900s, 8 x 5 1/2 In. . 40.00
Caisson, Horse, Soldiers, Drop-Down Door, Germany, c.1930, 15 In. 265.00
Calypso Joe The Drummer, Battery Operated, Linemar, Box, 1950s, 11 In. . . . . .545.00 to 770.00
Camel, Brown, Stuffed, Steiff, 10 1/2 In. 248.00
Canary, Pip-Squeak, Tree, Vines, Embossed Cloth Leaves, Leather Bellows, 5 1/2 In. 440.00
Cane, Bat Masterson, Black With Silver Engraved Top, Carrnell, 1958, 30 In. 45.00
Cannon, 25 Pounder Howitzer Military, Metal, Rubber Tires, Box, 1950s 125.00
Cannon, Big Bang, Tin, Premier Toy Co., 24 1/2 In. 35.00
Cannon, Cast Iron, Big Bang, 9 In. 77.00
Cannon, Metal, Shooting Device, Rolling Wheels, 3 x 6 In. 28.00
Cannon Truck, Electronic, Olive Green, Steel, Yellow Decals, Battery, Ny-Lint, 23 In. . . . 125.00
Cap Firing Bomb, Wood, Red, Metal Firing Nose, Paper Fins, Fliegerbom, 4 1/2 In. 40.00
Cap Gun Play Set, Al Capone, Die Cast Metal, FBI Badge, Spain, 1950s 175.00
Car, 3 Wheels, Man Driver, Windup, Germany, c.1920, 5 1/2 In. 460.00
Car, Adenauer's, Metal, Windup, Germany, 9 1/2 In. 395.00
Car, Andy Gump, Driver, Iron, Arcade, 7 In. . . . . .605.00 to 950.00
Car, Army Staff, Siren, Tin Lithograph, Mechanical, Marx, Box, c.1947, 11 In. 695.00
Car, Bayby Sport, Windup, Tin, Prewar, Japan, Box, 4 1/4 In. 220.00
Car, Benz, Go Stop, Lights Flash, Tin, Battery Operated, Marusan, Box, 10 In. 385.00
Car, Big Friction, Japan, 1950s, 13 In. 275.00
Car, BMW, 200CS, Tin, Battery Operated, Remote, Yonezawa, Box, 11 In. 385.00
Car, BMW, Convertible, Transmission, Gold, Windup, Tin, Distler, Box, 10 In. 165.00
Car, BMW, Red, Yellow, Windup, Tin, Multiple Speed, Distler, Box, 10 In. 275.00
Car, Borgward-Cabrio, Convertible, Tin Lithograph, Friction, Germany, 11 In. 145.00
Car, Bugatti, Type 35, 1924, Tin, Working Brake, Blue, P. Fontanelle, 19 In. 4645.00

Car, Buick, 1927, Coupe, Blue, Black, Tootsietoy 65.00
Car, Buick, Blue, Tin, Friction, Asahi, Japan, Box, c.1950, 8 1/2 In. 120.00
Car, Buick, Blue, Tin, Friction, TN, Japan, 1962, 12 In. 120.00
Car, Buick, Fire Dept. Chief, Plastic & Metal, Battery Siren & Light, 12 In. 95.00
Car, Buick, Future, Friction, Japan, 1950s, 14 In. 375.00
Car, Buick, Next Year's Model, Alps, Japan, Box, 1954, 9 1/4 In. 350.00
Car, Buick, Red, Tin, Friction, Japan, Box, 10 1/4 In. 990.00
Car, Buick, Riviera, Doors Open, Roof Removable, Tin, Friction, Haji, Box, 11 1/4 In. 465.00
Car, Buick, Tin, Battery Operated, Japan, Box, 1954, 7 1/2 In. 275.00
Car, Buick, Tin, Friction, Ichiko, 1960, 17 1/2 In. 116.00
Car, Buick, Touring, Driver, Red, Black, Iron, Lewis, 8 In. 305.00
Car, Cadillac Eldorado Brougham, 1957, 15 In. 280.00
Car, Cadillac, 1950s Model, Black, Box, Marusan, 12 In. 200.00
Car, Cadillac, 1957 Model, Marusan, 13 In. 280.00
Car, Cadillac, 2 Door, Hard Top, Tin, Friction, Marusan, Japan, 1960, 12 In. 300.00
Car, Cadillac, Blue, Tin, Battery Operated, Gama, West Germany, 1952, 12 In. 240.00
Car, Cadillac, Blue, Tin, Friction, ATC, Japan, 1965, 17 In. 385.00
Car, Cadillac, Boat, Trailer, Tin, Friction, Battery Operated, Japan, Box, 10 In. 500.00
Car, Cadillac, Convertible, Gold, Battery, Japan, 17 In. 375.00
Car, Cadillac, Convertible, Purple, Tin, Friction, Bandai, 1959, 11 1/4 In. 165.00
Car, Cadillac, Convertible, Red, Alps, Box, 11 1/2 In. 1155.00
Car, Cadillac, Convertible, White, Tin, Friction, Bandai, Box, 17 In. 1070.00
Car, Cadillac, Coupe, Blue, Yellow, Tin Lithograph, Windup, Marx, 11 1/2 In. 275.00
Car, Cadillac, Red, Convertible, Tin, Friction, Bandai, 1960, 17 In. 496.00
Car, Cadillac, Tin, Black, Remote Control, Marusan, Japan, 1954, 13 In. 550.00
Car, Cadillac, Tin, Plastic, Lithograph, Blue, Friction, Japan, 1953, 3 x 4 x 11 In. 160.00
Car, Carette Touring, Early 20th Century, 12 In. 2015.00
Car, Champion, Driver, Red, Tin, Battery Operated, Japan, Box, 5 3/4 In. 270.00
Car, Chevrolet, 1954 Model, Red, Yellow, Tin Friction, Japan, 11 1/2 In. 440.00
Car, Chevrolet, 1955 Model, Convertible, Tin, Bandai, Japanese, 10 In. 550.00
Car, Chevrolet, Camaro, Blue, Rubber Bumper, ATC, 9 1/2 In. 235.00
Car, Chevrolet, Convertible, Tin, Friction, Bandai, Box, 10 In. 420.00
Car, Chevrolet, Impala, Convertible, Tin, Friction, Bandai, 1962, 11 In. 315.00
Car, Chevrolet, Police, Battery Operated, 1962, 14 In. 245.00
Car, Chevrolet, Police, Battery Operated, Tin Lithograph, Marusan, Japan, 1954, 10 In. .. 550.00
Car, Chevrolet, Police, Tin, Friction, Siren, Japan, 1964, 17 1/4 In. 295.00
Car, Chevrolet, Sedan, Tin, Friction, Bandai, Box, 1958, 6 1/4 In. 220.00
Car, Chrysler Airflow Sedan, Pressed Steel, Electric Lights, Cor-Cor, 16 1/2 In. 2860.00
Car, Chrysler, Air Flow, Pressed Steel, Windup, Kingsbury, 13 1/2 In. 250.00
Car, Citroen, 2CV, Clicking Noise, Tin, Friction, Daiya, 8 1/2 In. 165.00
Car, Citroen, DS19, Green, Cream, 1960s, 8 In. 185.00
Car, Citroen, DS19, Tin, Friction, Bandai, Box, 8 In. 255.00
Car, Clockwork, Tiller Steering, Driver, Cast Iron, Ives, 6 3/4 In. 715.00
Car, Convertible, Blue, Tin, Red Seats, Lithograph, Friction, Marx, 11 In. 55.00
Car, Convertible, No. 65, Tin Lithograph, Lupor 195.00
Car, Coo Coo, Driver, Windup, Tin, Marx, 1931, 9 In. ....145.00 to 175.00
Car, Corvette Stingray, Lights, Horn, Tin, Battery Operated, Ichida, Box, 12 In. 305.00
Car, Corvette Stingray, White, Tin, Battery Operated, Japan, Box, 12 In. 145.00
Car, Corvette, 1958, White, Convertible, Tin, Friction, Yonezawa, 8 In. 250.00
Car, Corvette, Fire Dept., Chief, Tin, Friction, Japan, 10 In. 145.00
Car, Corvette, Silver, Friction, Bandai, 1962, 8 In. 120.00
Car, Coupe, Metal, Windup, Box, 1947, 9 1/2 In. 595.00
Car, Coupe, Pressed Steel, Spoke Wheels, Buddy L, 10 1/2 In. 880.00
Car, Coupe, Take Apart, Cast Iron, A.C. Williams, 6 1/2 In. 3430.00
Car, Cragstan, Airport Fuel, Lights, Meter, Tin, Battery Operated, Japan, c.1950, 11 In. ... 1265.00
Car, Datsun, 240Z, Tin, Friction, Ichiko, Box, 17 In. 140.00
Car, Dodge, Dart, Forward & Reverse Sidelights, 12 In. 285.00
Car, Door Opens, Men Come Out, Windup, Germany, 1950, 6 In. 195.00
Car, Dragster, Front Motor, Japan, 1950s, 9 1/2 In. 295.00
Car, Dragster, Tin, Battery Operated, Plastic, Japan, Box, 13 In. 300.00
Car, Electromobile, Green, Tin, Battery Operated, Japan, Box, 8 1/2 In. 275.00
Car, F.B.I, Godfather, Roof Light, Tin, Plastic, Battery Operated, Taiyo, Box, 10 In. 110.00
Car, Fairlady Z, Tin, Friction, Ichiko, Box, 11 1/2 In. 70.00

Car, Ferrari, Berlinetta 250, Red, Tin, Battery Operated, Box, 11 1/2 In. 110.00
Car, Ferrari, British Flag On Hood, Tin, Friction, Vinyl, Windup, Bandai, 8 In. 175.00
Car, Ferrari, Red, FCS, Italy, 1960s, 11 In. 385.00
Car, Fiat, 600, Rollback Roof, Tin, Friction, Bandai, 7 In. 95.00
Car, Field, Trailer, Soldiers, Windup, Tin, Tipp, Germany, 11 In. 360.00
Car, Fire Chief, Lights, Tin, Battery Operated, Remote, Yonezawa, Box, 11 In. 275.00
Car, Fire Chief, Pressed Steel, Clockwork Motor, Wyandotte Cord, 1940s, 13 1/2 In. 385.00
Car, Fire Chief, Siren, Pressed Steel, Windup, 1930, 14 1/2 In. 145.00
Car, Fire Chief, Siren, Steel, Mechanical, Coupe, Girard, Box, 1933, 14 1/2 In. 1495.00
Car, Flintmobile, Fred Flintstone, Vitamin Premium, Brown, Plastic, Snap, c.1972 . . . . . . 18.00
Car, Flivver, Contractor's Dump, Aluminum Spoke Wheels, Buddy L, 1920s, 12 1/2 In. . . 1760.00
Car, Flivver, Funny, Windup, Louis Marx & Co., c.1925, 3 1/2 x 6 x 7 1/2 In. 405.00
Car, Ford Ranch, Wagon, Red, Tin, Friction, Bandai, Box, c.1950, 12 In. 385.00
Car, Ford, 1930 Model, Red, Black, Bandai, 7 In. 95.00
Car, Ford, 1956 Model, Red & White, Marusan, Japan, 13 In. 1320.00
Car, Ford, 1958 Model, Battery Operated, 9 1/2 In. 295.00
Car, Ford, 1959 Model, Battery Operated, Japan, 11 In. 375.00
Car, Ford, Capri Rally, Blue, Yone, 1960s, 8 1/2 In. 185.00
Car, Ford, Country Wagon, Tin, Friction, Bandai, 1960, 10 1/2 In. 110.00
Car, Ford, Falcon Country Squire, Cream & Orange, Alps, 1960s, 9 In. 185.00
Car, Ford, G.T. 40, Spin Out Action, Lights, Tin, Battery Operated, Alps, Box, 10 In. 145.00
Car, Ford, Gyron, Roof Opens, Tin, Friction, Japan, 9 1/2 In. 220.00
Car, Ford, Ice Cream, Door Opens, Bell Rings, Tin, Friction, Bandai, Box, 7 1/2 In. 440.00
Car, Ford, Irwin, Convertible, Wipers, Engine Noise, Plastic, Friction, Irwin, Box, 9 In. . . 485.00
Car, Ford, Matra, Formula 1, Blue, Tin, Plastic, Windup, Schuco, Box, 9 1/2 In. 60.00
Car, Ford, Model T, Sedan, Driver, Woman, Black, Clockwork, Bing, c.1924, 6 1/4 In. . . . 800.00
Car, Ford, Model T, Sedan, Nickel Driver, Cast Iron, Arcade 360.00
Car, Ford, Model T, Sedan, Nickel Wheels, Driver, Cast Iron, Arcade 800.00
Car, Ford, Model T, Tin Lizzy, Gas Powered, Red, Briggs & Stratton Engine, 52 x 37 In. . 2765.00
Car, Ford, Model T, Touring, Rubber Tires, Nickel-Plated Driver, Arcade, 6 In. 250.00
Car, Ford, Monkeys, Singing Group, Tin, Battery Operated, Rico, Spain, 1960, 19 In. 460.00
Car, Ford, Mustang, 1966 Model, Plastic, Battery Operated, WPN Mac, 16 In. 135.00
Car, Ford, Police, Driver, Passenger, Battery Operated, Tin, Marusan, Japan, 1954, 10 In. . 385.00
Car, Ford, Station Wagon, 1959, Red & Cream, 11 In. 285.00
Car, Ford, Station Wagon, Friction, SAN, Japan, Box, 12 1/2 In. 575.00
Car, Ford, Thunderbird, 1960s Model, Blue & White, Bandai, 8 In. 90.00
Car, Ford, Thunderbird, 1964 Model, Tin, Friction, ATC, Box, 13 1/4 In. 660.00
Car, Ford, Thunderbird, Convertible Roof, Tin, Friction, Japan, 1964, 15 In. 305.00
Car, Ford, Thunderbird, GT, Tin, Battery Operated, Bandai, Box, 11 In. 110.00
Car, Ford, Thunderbird, Hood Opens, Battery Operated, Remote, Yonezawa, 1963, 11 In. . 220.00
Car, Ford, Thunderbird, Man, Wipers Move, Tin, Friction, West Germany, Box, 13 In. . . . 220.00
Car, Ford, Thunderbird, Red, Convertible, Tin, Friction, Haji, Japan, 8 In. 50.00
Car, Ford, Tin, Friction, 7-Up, Japan, 1962, 10 1/2 In. 395.00
Car, Ford, Tin, Friction, Ichiko, Japan, 9 1/2 In. 295.00
Car, French Floride, Friction, Ichiko, Japan, 1950s, 7 1/2 In. 175.00
Car, Funny Flivver, Tin Lithograph, Windup, 1926, 7 In. . . . . *Illus* 303.00
Car, Futuristic Roadster, Bubble Top, Friction, Sparks, Motor Sound, Box, 1956 . . . . 2000.00
Car, GAMA, Metal, Windup, Germany, 1950s, 6 1/2 In. 145.00
Car, Gang Busters, Tin Lithograph, Windup, Marx, 15 In. 687.00
Car, Go-Cart, Driver, Engine Noise, Friction, Tin, Japan, Box, 5 In. 145.00
Car, Go-Cart, Modern Toys, Japan, 6 In. 75.00

Toy, Car, Funny
Flivver, Tin Lithograph,
Windup, 1926, 7 In.

Toy, Car, Jalopy,
4 People, Tin
Lithograph, Windup,
Marx, 1950, 6 In.

Car, Go-Cart, Tin, Windup, Rubber Head, Japan, 5 In. 27.00
Car, Graham, Pressed Steel, Dealer Model, 1930s, 21 In. 1320.00
Car, Green Hornet Black Beauty, 3 Missiles, 4 Radar Scanners, Corgi, No. 268, Box 425.00
Car, Hagi Ford, Tin, Friction Powered, Japan, 1950s, 12 In. 1650.00
Car, Happy Chick, Tin, Friction, Japan, 5 1/2 In. 110.00
Car, Happy Pup, Dog Drives Car, All Metal Friction, Alps, Japan, 8 In. 295.00
Car, Hi-Way Henry, Mechanical, Geo. Borgfeldt & Co., Box, 6 x 9 In. 175.00
Car, Hot Rod, Propeller Spins, Pistons Move, Tin, Friction, Japan, 9 In. 443.00
Car, Humphrey Mobile, Windup, Tin, Wyandotte, 7 1/2 In. 259.00
Car, Humphrey, Man Peddles, Waves, Windup, Tin, Wyandotte, Box, 10 1/2 In. 798.00
Car, Ito, No. 679, Driver, Windup, Lehmann, 1914 . . . . 485.00
Car, Jaguar XK 120, Gold, Key In Shape Of Driver, Windup, Germany, 6 In. 210.00
Car, Jaguar XK-E, Metal, Battery Operated, Japan, 10 1/2 In. 295.00
Car, Jaguar, 2 Speed, Friction, Alps, Japan, 8 1/2 In. 195.00
Car, Jaguar, Convertible, Red, Tin, Bandai, Japan, 9 1/2 In. 99.00
Car, Jaguar, Convertible, Transmission, Yellow, Windup, Tin, Distler, Box, 10 In. 230.00
Car, Jaguar, Gas Station, Tin Lithograph, Battery Operated, Distler, 1958 . . . . 310.00
Car, Jaguar, Hippy Flower, Tin, Friction, Japan, 1950s, 11 In. 375.00
Car, Jaguar, Red, No. 2018, Doepke, 1955, 17 1/2 In. 525.00
Car, Jaguar, Yellow, Tin, Battery Operated, Remote Control, Japan, Box, 11 In. 195.00
Car, Jalopy, 4 People, Tin Lithograph, Windup, Marx, 1950, 6 In. . . . . *Illus* 255.00
Car, Jalopy, Hop Inn, 100 Miles To A Gal., Windup, Tin, Marx, American, 1930s, 7 In. . . . 225.00
Car, Jalopy, Tin, Windup, Louis Marx & Co., 1930-1940, 4 x 4 x 7 In. 460.00
Car, Jet Race Y-55, Tin, Friction, Yonezawa, Box, 12 In. 660.00
Car, Joy Rider, Tin Lithograph, Windup, Marx, 7 In. 265.00
Car, Kojak, Buick With Figure, Die Cast, Corgi, 1975, 6 In. 110.00
Car, Leaping Lena, Driver, Black, Windup, Tin, Strauss, 1920, 8 In. . . . . .55.00 to 115.00
Car, Limousine, Cast Iron, Chauffer, Lady, Kenton, 8 In. 660.00
Car, Limousine, Driver, Brown, Green, Windup, Tin, Japan, 7 In. 495.00
Car, Limousine, Driver, Cast Iron, Pressed Steel, Spoke Wheels, Hill Climber, 12 In. 294.00
Car, Limousine, Driver, White, Windup, Tin, Carette, Germany, 9 In. 715.00
Car, Limousine, Driver, Windup, Carette, Germany, 14 In. 1800.00
Car, Limousine, Top Rack, Driver, Clockwork, Tin Lithograph, Richter & Co, 6 In. 863.00
Car, Lincoln & House Trailer, Furniture, Smith-Miller, 1950s, 38 In. 1155.00
Car, Lincoln, 1960 Model, Convertible, Tin, Driver, Bandai, Japanese, 12 In. 475.00
Car, Lincoln, Honk-A-Long, Tin, Friction, Ichiko, Box, 7 1/2 In. 138.00
Car, Lincoln, Lite-O-Wheel, Bump & Go, Tin, Battery Operated, Japan, Box, 10 1/2 In. . . 550.00
Car, Lincoln, Red, Plastic, Ichiko, 1956, 17 In. 605.00
Car, Lincoln, XL500, Tin, Friction, Yonezawa, 7 1/2 In. 495.00
Car, Lucky Racer, Driver, Tin, Friction, Japan, Box, 5 1/2 In. 303.00
Car, Mazda, Coupe, R360, Tin, Friction, Bandai, 7 In. 528.00
Car, Mazda, Familia, Red, Mirrors, Tin, Friction, Bandai, 9 In. 293.00
Car, Mazinga, Crank Siren, Tin, Japan, Box, 11 In. 303.00
Car, Mercedes 220S, Trunk Opens, Change Tire, Tin, Friction, Japan, Box, 12 In. 193.00
Car, Mercedes 230SL, Shift Lever, Driver, Tin, Battery Operated, Alps, Box, 10 1/4 In. . . . 396.00
Car, Mercedes 250SL, Red, Tin, Battery Operated, Bandai, Box, 10 In. 66.00
Car, Mercedes Benz, Different Speeds, Chrome, Windup, Prameta, Germany, 5 1/2 In. 110.00
Car, Mercedes, Orange, Plastic, Battery Operated, Schuco, Box, 10 1/2 In. 39.00
Car, Mercedes, Red, Ichiko, Box, 24 In. 220.00
Car, Messerschmitt, Tin, Friction, Japan, 8 1/2 In. 523.00
Car, MG, Sports, Blue, Tin, Friction, Japan, 6 1/2 In. 44.00
Car, MGA 1600, Forward & Reverse Headlights, 8 In. 375.00
Car, MGA, Mark II, Red, Tin, Friction, Bandai, 8 In. 66.00
Car, Military Police, Machine Gun, Japan, Box, 1950s, 5 1/2 In. 110.00
Car, Monorail, Electric, Red & White, Motor Above, Leland-Detroit 176.00
Car, Nash, Station Wagon, Door Opens, Tin, Friction, Marusan, Box, c.1950, 10 In. 400.00
Car, NBC TV, Camera & Man Move, Tin, Friction, Japan, 8 In. 1100.00
Car, O-Gan Driver, Tin, Vinyl, Friction, Yonezawa, 15 1/2 In. 910.00
Car, Old Timers, No. 1, TM, Tin Lever Action, Japan, 5 1/2 In. 48.00
Car, Oldsmobile, Convertible, Tin, Friction, Metal, Red, 1958, 7 In. 75.00
Car, Oldsmobile, Gold, Tin, Friction, Japan, 1958, 12 In. 520.00
Car, Oldsmobile, Radicon, Tin, Battery Operated, Remote, Japan, Box, 14 In. 1100.00
Car, Oldsmobile, Toronado, Red, Tin, Friction, Japan, Box, 15 1/2 In. 305.00

Car, Open, Gentleman Driver, Windup, Tin, Germany, 1903, 6 1/2 In. 975.00
Car, Packard, Black, Tin, Alps, 1953, 16 1/4 In. 4400.00
Car, Packard, Convertible, Tin, West Germany, Schuco 5700 Electro Synchromatic, 11 In. 528.00
Car, Phaeton, Canopy, Chauffeur, Passenger, Cast Iron, Dent, 9 In. 950.00
Car, Phantom, Blue, Whitewall Tire, Tin, Tippco Germany, 14 In. 1210.00
Car, Pinkee The Farmer, Driver, Tin Lithograph, Japan, Box, 9 1/2 In. 39.00
Car, Plymouth, 4 Door, Tin, Japan, 1959, 11 In. 577.00
Car, Plymouth, Sedan, Windler Motor Sales, Cast Iron, Arcade, 4 1/2 In. 3080.00
Car, Plymouth, Station Wagon, Woody, Tin, Friction, Japan, 9 1/2 In. 275.00
Car, Police Patrol, Buick, Friction, Japan, 1961, 16 In. 375.00
Car, Police, Chevy, Black & White, Bandai, 1958, 8 In. 360.00
Car, Police, Highway Patrol, Tin, Friction, Japan, Box, 9 In. 45.00
Car, Police, Plymouth, Roof Light, Siren, Tin, Battery Operated, Alps, Box, 1959, 11 In. . 290.00
Car, Police, Siren, Lights, Plastic, Battery Operated, Alps, Box, 13 In. 28.00
Car, Pontiac Roadster, Cast Iron, Nickel Plated Iron Trim, Kilgore, 10 1/2 In. 935.00
Car, Pontiac, Black, Windup, Tin, Kosuge, Japan, 1926, 11 1/2 In. 2805.00
Car, Pontiac, Driver, Tin, Friction, Japan, 1954, 15 In. 305.00
Car, Pontiac, Fat, Tin, Friction, Japan, 1954, 9 In. 248.00
Car, Pontiac, Green, Tin, Friction, Japan, 1958, 8 1/4 In. 160.00
Car, Porsche 911, Red, Tin, Battery Operated, Bandai, Box, 10 In. 105.00
Car, Porsche 911, Tin, Remote Control, Bandai, Box, 10 In. 110.00
Car, Porsche 914, Kamen Rider, Tin, Friction, Japan, Box, 11 In. 635.00
Car, Porsche 914, Tin, Battery Operated, Daiya, Box, 9 1/2 In. 130.00
Car, Porsche Carrera, Lights, Tin Friction, Battery Operated, Japan, Box, 9 In. 190.00
Car, Porsche Carrera, Plastic, Windup, Schuco, Box, 11 1/2 In. 45.00
Car, Porsche, Police, Tin, Battery Operated, Aoshin, Box, 11 In. 85.00
Car, Porsche, Red, Tin, Battery Operated, Remote, Distler, Box, 10 In. 275.00
Car, Porsche, Red, Tin, Friction, Joustra, Box, 8 1/2 In. 155.00
Car, Press & Go, Mystery, Steel, Yellow, 10 In. 300.00
Car, Pressed Steel, Scarab Windup, Key, Buddy L, 1930s, 3 1/2 x 9 1/2 In. 450.00
Car, Prince Skyline Sport, White, 1960s, 10 In. 950.00
Car, Racing, Bluebird, Land Speed, Steel, Windup, Kingsbury, c.1920, 18 In. 1375.00
Car, Racing, BMW, Formel 2, Tin, Plastic, Windup, Schuco, Box, 10 In. 55.00
Car, Racing, Boattail, Spoke Wheels, Cast Iron, Driver, 6 In. 380.00
Car, Racing, Boattail, Tin Lithograph, Windup, England, 12 In. 330.00
Car, Racing, Cast Iron, White Rubber Tires, Driver, Champion, 9 In. 190.00
Car, Racing, Driver, Helmet, Goggles, Nickel-Plated Wheels, Cast Iron, Hubley, 10 1/4 In. 600.00
Car, Racing, Driver, Painted Tin, No. 98, Friction, Champions Racer Logo, Japan, 1950s . 1600.00
Car, Racing, Driver, Rubber Tire, Cast Iron S, Hubley, 6 In. 1375.00
Car, Racing, Flame Exhaust, Green, Cast Iron, Hubley, 9 In. 935.00
Car, Racing, Gilbert, Tin Lithograph, Crank Windup, 10 In. 540.00
Car, Racing, Golden Jet Racer, Tin, Friction, Japan, Box, 1950, 12 In. 295.00
Car, Racing, Hess Mobile, Tin, Flywheel Power, Germany, 9 In. 550.00
Car, Racing, Hood Opens, Cast Iron, Hubley, 9 1/2 In. 580.00
Car, Racing, Indianapolis 500, Tin Lithograph, Battery Operated, Sears, Box, 15 In. 440.00
Car, Racing, King Racer, Tin, Friction, Alps, Box, 5 1/2 In. 105.00
Car, Racing, La Piloto, Red, Tin, Composition Driver, Remote Control, Box, 10 1/2 In. . . . 715.00
Car, Racing, Lotus, Green, Tin, Plastic, Battery Operated, Bandai, Box, 9 1/2 In. 90.00
Car, Racing, Midget, No. 63, Tin, Friction, Yonezawa, Japan, 1950s, 7 In. 1045.00
Car, Racing, No. 3, Cast Iron, Hubley, 7 1/4 In. 195.00
Car, Racing, No. 4, Windup, Tin, U.S. Zone Germany, 6 1/2 In. 155.00
Car, Racing, No. 8, Tin, Orange, Black, Rubber Tires, 1930s, 11 1/2 In. 125.00
Car, Racing, No. 19, Blue, Driver, Tin, Friction, Tippco West Germany, Box, 11 1/2 In. . . 250.00
Car, Racing, No. 21, Tin, Friction, Japan, 1950s, 9 1/2 In. 95.00
Car, Racing, No. 24, Moving Tin Fan & Piston, TN, Japan, 1950s, 8 In. 245.00
Car, Racing, No. 31, Metal, Germany, Prewar 195.00
Car, Racing, No. 158, Battery Operated, TN, Japan, 1950s, 10 In. 375.00
Car, Racing, No. 1790, Cast Iron, Hubley, 5 In. 245.00
Car, Racing, Red Streak, Mechanical, Tin Lithograph, 22 1/2 In. 450.00
Car, Racing, Rocket, Driver, Windup, Tin Lithograph, Marx 475.00
Car, Racing, Special 6, Mobile Pegasus Advertising, Tin, Japan, 7 In. 825.00
Car, Racing, Speed Control, Travels In 4 Gears, Tin, Battery Operated, Box, 12 In. 670.00
Car, Racing, Steel, Enamel, Red, Rubber Wheels, Electric Lights, Wyandotte, 1934 . . . . . 400.00

Car, Racing, Strato, No. 18, Moving Spoiler, Friction, Japan, 1950s, 11 In. 395.00
Car, Racing, Stutz, Cast Iron, 8 In. 230.00
Car, Racing, Ventura Freccia, No. 7, Aluminum & Wood, 18 1/2 In. 880.00
Car, Racing, White, Gear Shift, Tin, Friction, Japan, Box, 6 1/2 In. 385.00
Car, Racing, X-3 Race, Driver, Tin, Friction, Bandai, Box, 7 1/2 In. 130.00
Car, Radio, Open Top, Music, Schuco 4012 .... 210.00
Car, Renault, Floride, Removable Roof, Tin, Friction, Japan, Box, 9 1/2 In. 400.00
Car, Renault, Viva Sport Decal, Blue, Mechanical, Steel, France, c.1935 .... 1300.00
Car, REO Coupe, Green, Cast Iron, Rubber Tires, Rumble Seat, Arcade, 7 1/2 In. 950.00
Car, Roadster, Cast Iron, Iron Spoke Wheels, Hubley, 7 1/4 In. 65.00
Car, Roadster, Driver, Chein, 8 1/2 In. 460.00
Car, Roadster, Driver, Orange, Cast Iron, Kilgore, 7 1/2 In. 550.00
Car, Roadster, Metal, Windup, Kingsbury, 11 In. 250.00
Car, Roadster, Motor, Steering, Doors Open, Blue, Steel, C.I.J., France, c.1930, 12 1/2 In. 690.00
Car, Roadster, Pressed Steel, Friction, Schieble, 17 1/2 In. 235.00
Car, Roadster, Yellow, Black, Ny-Lint, 1968, 10 In. 45.00
Car, Rocket Racer, Metal, Windup, Marx, 1930s, 16 1/2 In. 375.00
Car, Rolls-Royce, Silver Cloud, Tin, Friction, Bandai, Box, 11 1/2 In. 300.00
Car, Rubble's Wreck, Flintstones, Barney, Tin, Friction, Hanna-Barbera, Marx, 1962 ..... 450.00
Car, Sedan, 2 Doors Open, Windup, Tin, Orobr, 6 In. 230.00
Car, Sedan, Cast Iron, Skoglund & Olson, 7 1/2 In. 825.00
Car, Sedan, Driver, Cable, Plunger, Windup, Gunthermann, 1930s, 9 1/2 In. 650.00
Car, Sedan, Driver, Doors Open, Lights, Motor, Black, Tin, Distler, Germany, 14 1/2 In. .. 1620.00
Car, Sedan, Driver, License Plate, Windup, Tin, Bing, 6 1/2 In. 345.00
Car, Sedan, Metal, Painted, Patented, c.1907, 12 In. 200.00
Car, Sedan, Remote Steering, Windup, Tin, Gunthermann, 9 1/2 In. 149.00
Car, Sedan, Silver Arrow, Nickel Grille, Rubber Tires, Arcade, 7 In. 440.00
Car, Sedan, Touring, Tin, Push, c.1950, 10 In. 80.00
Car, Service, 3 Wheel, Plastic Tires, Handlebar Steering, Pressed Steel, Tonka, 9 In. ... 65.00
Car, Space Patrol, Astronauts, Silver, Tin, Plastic, Battery Operated, Bandai, Box, 13 In. ... 330.00
Car, Space Patrol, Robot, Silver, Red, Tin, Friction, ATC, Japan, 8 In. 300.00
Car, Space, Planeteer, Plastic, Battery Operated, Remote, Mormac Toys USA, 9 In. 99.00
Car, Space, Satellite, Tin, Battery Operated, Japan, Box, 9 In. 360.00
Car, Speedster, Converse, Clockwork Motor, Green, Red, Tin, 15 In. 1075.00
Car, Sports, Open, Cream, Man In Sweater, Plastic Cap, Schuco Texi 5735, 9 3/4 In. 420.00
Car, Sports, Open, Red, Woman In Sweater, Schuco Texi 5745, Germany, 9 3/4 In. 375.00
Car, Sports, Removable Hard Plastic Top, Friction, Japan, Box, 8 In. 495.00
Car, Sports, Tin, Friction, Green, Japan, Box, 7 1/2 In. 305.00
Car, Staff, Tin, Compression Soldiers, Windup, Tipp, 6 1/2 In. 330.00
Car, Super Racer, Driver, No. 42, Tin, Plastic, Friction, Japan, 19 In. 1925.00
Car, Take-A-Part Coupe, Cast Iron, Rubber Tires, Hubley, 6 1/2 In. 220.00
Car, Tammy's, Aqua Convertible, Orange Interior, Tammy Flag, Ideal, Box, c.1963 ..... 140.00
Car, Tin Lizzie, 4 Composition Figures, Remote Control, Arnold, Germany, 10 In. 190.00
Car, Tin Lizzie, Flip Down Shield, Tin, Remote Control, Arnold, West Germany, 9 1/2 In. 580.00
Car, Tom & Jerry, Bell, Noise, Tin, Battery Operated, MGM, Box, 8 In. 149.00
Car, Tom & Jerry, Bump & Go, Tin, Battery Operated, Rico Hanna-Barbera, 13 In. 655.00
Car, Touring, 2 Cast Iron Passengers, Clark Co., 1909, 13 In. 350.00
Car, Touring, 2 Side Lamps, Clockwork, Gray, Carrette, 12 In. 2015.00
Car, Touring, Antique Deluxe, Friction, Cragstan, Box, 9 1/4 In. 39.00
Car, Touring, Cast Iron, A.C. Williams, 7 In. 1430.00
Car, Touring, Cast Iron, Jones & Bixler, 9 1/4 In. 1045.00
Car, Touring, Chauffer, Female Passenger, Arms Move, Cast Iron, Kenton, 9 In. 850.00
Car, Touring, Driver, Adolf Schumann, c.1915 .... 750.00
Car, Touring, Driver, Black, Windup, Tin, Germany, 11 In. 550.00
Car, Touring, Figures, Cast Iron, Dent, 9 1/2 In. 825.00
Car, Touring, Friction, Orange, Steel, Dayton, c.1920, 13 1/2 In. 550.00
Car, Touring, Model T, Nickel Driver, Cast Iron, Arcade 385.00
Car, Touring, Open, 2 Cowl Lamps, Chauffeur, Doors Open, 11 In. 840.00
Car, Touring, Ragtop, Tin, Man Driver, License Plate, Windup, Bing, 6 1/2 In. 400.00
Car, Touring, Red, Windup, Tin, Germany, 6 In. 145.00
Car, Toyota, Crown Deluxe Police, 1960s, 11 In. 365.00
Car, Toyota, Tin, Friction, ATC, Box, 1962, 10 In. 440.00
Car, Traffic, Red, Windup, Tin, England, Box, 6 1/4 In. 55.00

Car, Tut-Tut, Man In Car, Windup, Tin, Lehmann, c.1910, 4 x 7 x 6 3/4 In. . . . . . . .575.00 to 975.00
Car, U Control No. 4 Racer, Tomiyama Cragstan, Bronze, 1960s, 15 In. 865.00
Car, Versailles, Lights, Key, Plastic, Windup, Gege, Plastic Showcase Box, 9 3/4 In. 165.00
Car, Volkswagen 1500, Tin, Windup, Ichiko, Box, 7 1/2 In. . . . . .275.00 to 285.00
Car, Volkswagen, 1960s Model, Sunroof, Maroon, Bandai, 14 In. 185.00
Car, Volkswagen, Beetle, Red, Steel, Plastic, Friction, Box, 8 1/2 In. 55.00
Car, Volkswagen, Doors Open, Engine Cover, Storage, Steerable Wheels, Germany 50.00
Car, Volkswagen, Driver, Tin, Battery Operated, Bandai, Box, 10 1/2 In. 65.00
Car, Volkswagen, Herbie The Love Bug, Tin, Battery Operated, Box, 9 1/2 In. 220.00
Car, Volkswagen, Karmann Ghia, Tin, Friction, Alps, Box, 6 In. 250.00
Car, Volkswagen, Revolving Light, Tin, Remote Control, Ko, Box, 6 1/2 In. 55.00
Car, Volkswagen, Tin, Friction, Cragstan, Japan, 8 In. 55.00
Car, Volkswagen, Tin, Friction, Japan, Box, c.1950, 7 3/4 In. 195.00
Car, Volkswagen, Tin, Remote Control, Bandai, Box, 7 1/2 In. . . . . ˋ   80.00
Car, Volvo, P-1800, Red, SSS, 1960s, 11 In. 1275.00
Car, Whoopee, Uncle Wiggily, Windup, Tin, Marx, 7 1/2 In. 1020.00
Car, Windup, Tin Lithograph, G & K, 7 In. 880.00
Car, With Trailer, Tin, Friction, Japan, 1950s, 8 In. 75.00
Car, X-Car, Lady Driver, Windup, Tin, Occupied Japan, Box, 5 In. 170.00
Car, Yell-O-Taxi, With Driver, Windup, Strauss, 8 In. 650.00
Car, Zone, Windup, Metal, Germany, 5 1/2 In. 95.00
Car & Trailer, Tin Friction, Blue, Red, Japan, 1950s, 16 In. 175.00
Car & Trailer, Tin Friction, Japan, 1950s, 11 1/2 In. 175.00
Carnival Round-A-Bout, Passengers, Suspended By Wires, Windup, Germany, 1900 . . . . .   850.00
Carousel, 3 Zeppelins, French Flag On Top, Tin Lithograph, Windup, 1910, 16 In. 1150.00
Carousel, Airplanes, Children On Horses, Windup, Wolverine, 1940s 350.00
Carousel, Bluebird, 3 Birds Revolve Around Tower, Lever Action, Reeves, 10 In. 175.00
Carousel, Rockets, Flying, Props Spin, Tin, Lever Action, Japan, 7 In. 210.00
Carousel, Swans, Airplanes, Windup, Wyandotte, 6 In. 375.00
Carriage, 2 Horses, Red Driver, Yellow Passenger, Cloth Canopy, 1920s, 12 1/2 x 6 In. . .   225.00
Carriage, 3 Wheels, Wood, Red Velvet, Gilt, France, c.1865, 14 In. 1500.00
Carriage, Baby, Mother Walks, Windup, Tin, Haji, Box, 6 In. 280.00
Carriage, Doll's, Fringe Top, Leather Seat, Wood Wheels, Stenciled, c.1870, 38 x 28 In. . . .   500.00
Carriage, Doll's, Push, 3 Wheels, Wood, 12 In. 190.00
Carriage, Doll's, Red Paint, Wood Frame, Spokes, Yellow, White Stenciling, Lace Fringe .   85.00
Carriage, Doll's, Red, Painted Wheels, Fringe, White & Yellow Designs, Vermont, c.1870   390.00
Carriage, Doll's, Stick & Ball, Fabric, Wood Wheels, Parasol, Late 1800s, 24 x 32 In. 160.00
Carriage, Doll's, Victorian, Natural, Wicker, Upholstered, 39 In.   230.00
Carriage, Doll's, Wicker, Corduroy Interior, 36 In. 120.00
Carriage, Doll's, Wicker, Upholstered, Parasol, Rubber Wheels, Victorian, 49 In. 316.00
Carriage, Doll's, Wicker, Upholstered, Wood Wheels, Curve Handle, c.1910, 32 In. 176.00
Carriage, Horse Drawn, Driver, Rider, Cast Iron, 20th Century, 16 In. 290.00
Carriage, Landau, Horses, Driver, Cast Iron, Wilkins 3960.00
Carriage, Wicker, Fabric Interior, Gray Paint, Traveler, Wire Spoke Wheels, 27 x 28 In. . . .   170.00
Cart, Black Boy Riding, Oranges, Windup, Martin, France, 1910 . . . . ˙ . .   950.00
Cart, Coal, Mule, Driver, Early 1900s, 13 1/2 In. 995.00
Cart, Donkey & Clown, Tin Lithograph, Lever, Gama, 8 In. 130.00
Cart, Hood's Milk, Wooden, Articulated Horse, Sign On Top, Cow Logo, 21 In. 470.00
Cart, Horse Drawn, 4 Horses, Delivery Cart, Driver, Barrels, Leather Harness, 39 In. 1000.00
Cart, Horse Drawn, Black, Brown, Tin, 10 In. 65.00
Cart, Horse Drawn, Woman Driver, Shimer, 1890s, 10 1/4 In. 1195.00
Cart, Ice Cream, Tin, Spain, 1926, 4 1/2 In. 995.00
Cart, Plantation, Donkey, Cast Iron, 10 In. 150.00
Cart, Sam The City Gardener, Tools, Windup, Marx, Box 350.00
Case, Barbie, Vinyl, Graphics, Handle, Snap Closure, Plastic Hangers, 1963 . . . .   95.00
Case, Major Matt Mason, Vinyl, Figure Storage, 1967, 3 x 12 x 8 In. 35.00
Casey The Cop, Walks, Windup, Unique Art, 1930s, 9 In. 575.00
Casper, Toots, Baby Buttercup, Dog, Rattles, Rolls, Wood, Pull Toy, c.1930, 15 x 8 In. . . .   195.00
Cat, 3 Musical, Instruments, Tin, Windup, Germany, 9 In. 2640.00
Cat, Felix, Bounces, Tin, Cloth, Windup, Pat Sullivan, Box, 1922, 12 In. 715.00
Cat, Felix, On Scooter, Tin, Mechanical, Nifty, c.1925, 8 In. 3800.00
Cat, Pip-Squeak, White & Gray Tabby, Felt, Brass Bell, Button Eyes, 5 7/8 In. 110.00
Cat, Playing With Ball, Tin Lithograph, Windup, Marx, 5 In. 39.00

Cat, Push Toy, Wood Handle, Iron Wheels 700.00
Cat, Pushing Cage With Mice, Mice Jumps, Windup, 8 In. 1095.00
Cat, Rollover, Tail Moves, Windup, Tin, Marx, Box, 5 1/2 In. 99.00
Cat, Tiger Striped, Push, Wood, Tin, 27 In. 255.00
Cathedral, Musical, Tin, Twin Towers, Crank Action, Germany, Box, 7 1/2 In. 240.00
Cement Mixer, Cast Iron, Aluminum Mixer & Scoop, Kenton, 8 In. 380.00
Cement Mixer, Mechanical, Orange, Green, Jaeger, 9 3/4 In. 700.00
Cement Mixer, Red, White, Tonka, 1969, 14 In. 60.00
Chair, Rocking, Doll's, Carved Wood, Spindle Back, Lithographed Seat, Back, 12 In. 300.00
Charleston Trio, 2 Men, Dog, Tin, Windup, Marx, 8 In. 385.00
Charlie McCarthy, Tractor, Windup, Tin, Louis Marx & Co., c.1940, 3 x 6 1/2 x 7 In. 750.00
Charlie Weaver Bartender, Battery Operated, Smokes, Resko, 1960 .... 350.00
Chest, Walnut, Molded Top Edge, Iron Handles, 19th Century, 8 x 20 1/2 x 10 In. 115.00
Chicken Pulling Cart, Windup, Tin, Germany, 10 In. 175.00
Chicken Snatcher, Black Man Waddles, Swinging Arms, Swaying Head, 8 1/2 In. 400.00
Child, Crawling, Articulated Arms, Iron, 5 In. 360.00
Chinese Man, Nu-Nu, Pulls Tea Cart, Lehmann, 1924 .... 750.00
Chinese Men, Carrying Tea Chest, Kadi, Windup, Lehmann, 1917 .... 1100.00
Church Organ, Tin Lithograph, Hand Crank, Chein, 9 In. 75.00
Circus, Ring-A-Ling, Ringmaster Center, 4 Animals, Marx, Box, 8 In. .... *Illus*   935.00
Circus Monkey, Acrobat On Chairs, Windup, Metal, Felt, Japan 175.00
Circus Set, Big Top, Lithograph, Woodette, Contents, 1940s 75.00
Circus Set, Ringling Circus, Tin, Windup, Ringmaster, Animals, Marx, 8 In. 935.00
Circus Wagon, Band, 9 Figures, Chain Reins, Cast Iron, Kenton, 15 1/2 In. 575.00
Circus Wagon, Band, Horses, Band Members, Overland Circus, Cast Iron, Kenton, 16 In. .. 605.00
Circus Wagon, Bear, Kenton, 14 1/2 In. 675.00
Circus Wagon, Black Bear, 2 Horses, Men, Overland Circus, Cast Iron, Kenton, 14 In. 415.00
Circus Wagon, Cage, Push Cart, Metal Bars, Spoke Wheels, 56 In. 305.00
Circus Wagon, Cast Iron, Monkey On Trapeze, 12 In. 2420.00
Circus Wagon, Horses, Band, Cast Iron, Overland, c.1930, 16 In. 172.00
Circus Wagon, Polar Bear, 2 Horses, Men, Overland Circus, Cast Iron, Kenton, 14 In. 330.00
Clock, Cuckoo, Girl Swing, Windup, Tin, Bandai, Box, 12 In. 418.00
Clown, Artie, Tractor, Windup, Tin, Unique Art, 8 In. 255.00
Clown, Artist, Draws Picture On Paper, Discs, Windup, Germany, 5 x 5 x 5 In. 2015.00
Clown, Balancing Whirligig On Nose, Windup, Gely, Germany, 1920s, 10 In. 350.00
Clown, Balancing, Waddles, Windup, Tin, Issmayer, Germany, 7 In. 460.00
Clown, Bimbo, Drumming, Battery Operated, Alps, Rock Valley, Japan, Box, 12 In. 485.00
Clown, Blinky, Tin, Cloth, Battery Operated, Japan, Box, 12 In. 340.00
Clown, Bozo, Dancing, Mechanical, Vinyl, Lakeside Toys, No. 8612, c.1970, 2 x 3 x 5 In. 40.00
Clown, Bozo, Sways, Plays Drum, Windup, Tin, Alps, Box, 8 1/2 In. 690.00
Clown, Dancing, Mechanical, T.P.S., Japan, Box, 7 1/2 In. 75.00
Clown, Dozo, Sweeps, Smokes, Rolls Eyes, Battery Operated, Japan, Box, 13 1/2 In. 275.00
Clown, Hits Golliwog With Mallet, Tin, 9 In. 195.00
Clown, In Sulkie, Pulled By Mule, Windup, Tin, Lehmann, Germany, 7 1/2 In. 255.00
Clown, Juggler, Red Coat, Plaid Pants, Plastic Top Hat, Germany, 4 3/4 In. 145.00
Clown, Lester The Mechanical Jester, Box, 1959, 10 In. 375.00
Clown, Magic Man, Battery Operated, Marusan, Insert, Box, 12 In. 365.00
Clown, Moves Hand Over Rope, Pipe Smokes, Tin, Celluloid, Windup, Japan, Box, 9 In. . 250.00
Clown, Musical Clown, Windup, Nomura, Box, 7 In. 95.00
Clown, Nods Head & Beats Drum, Cone Hat, Japan, Box, 12 1/2 In. 430.00
Clown, On Donkey, Moves Back & Forth, Windup, Gama, Germany, 1930s 450.00
Clown, On Pig, Windup, Tin, 5 In. 187.00
Clown, Pinky, Juggling Clown, Inserts, Alps, Japan, Box, 1960s, 19 In. .... 206.00 to 450.00
Clown, Plays Saxophone, Music Box In Base, Distler, Germany, 1950, 8 1/2 In. 510.00
Clown, Plays Xylophone, Zilotone, Wolverine, Windup, 1930s 450.00
Clown, Roller Skating, Japan, Box, 5 1/2 In. 180.00
Clown, Roly Poly, Papier-Mache, Polychrome Decorated, Early 20th Century, 8 1/2 In. 90.00
Clown, Silly Clown, Celluloid, Alps, Japan, Box, c.1950, 6 1/2 In. 850.00
Clown, Skipping Rope, Ceramic, Cloth, 16 In. 66.00
Clown, Smiling Sam, Windup, Up & Down Action, Torn Box, 10 In. 200.00
Clown, Squeeze, Plaster Head, Wood Body, Felt Clothes, Tambourine, Germany, 10 In. 90.00
Clown, Toe Joe, Tin Lithograph, Acrobatic Clown, Ohio Art, 14 In. 22.00
Clown, Tumbling, Bisque, Chair, Wood, Bellows, Base, Acrobatic, France, c.1890, 16 In. . 2200.00

Clown, Violinist, Gray Coat, Yellow Pants, Schuco, 4 1/4 In. 60.00
Clown, Violinist, Red Coat, Plaid Pants, White Face, Tin, Schuco, 4 1/2 In. 150.00
Clown, Waddles, Windup, Tin, Distler, Germany, 7 In. 195.00
Clown, Weight Lifter, Picks Up Weight With Teeth, Windup, 1920s 1250.00
Clown, White Face, Bends To Skate, Windup, Tin, Japan, 6 1/2 In. 385.00
Coach, Processional, Cast Iron, King, Queen, 8 Horses, 4 Drivers, Britains, 20 In. 130.00
Cocks, Pip-Squeak, 2 Fighting, Papier-Mache, Feather Tails, Spring Legs, Painted, 6 In. ... 110.00
Colorforms, E.T., Dress Up, 1982, 10 x 16 In. 15.00
Colorforms, Rocky & His Friends, No. 146, Box, 1961, 8 1/4 x 13 In. 60.00
Communication Set, Elex, Marklin, Box, 9 1/2 x 14 In. 35.00
Construction Set, Anker, No. 10, Wooden Blocks, Germany, Box, 1900, 400 Piece 120.00
Construction Set, Hi-Lift, Die Cast & Steel, Reuhl, 34 In. 850.00
Construction Set, Instruction Booklet, Meccano, Box 226.00
Construction Set, War Tank, U.S. Alligator, Wooden, Box, 1950s, 8 In. 45.00
Contractor Set, Tootsietoy, Mack Truck, 3 Construction Trailers, Box, 12 In. 605.00
Country Station, Painted, Side Ramps, Candles, Marklin, England 6600.00
Cow, Composition, Leatherette Collar, Green Wood Base, Wheels, Germany, 5 In. 28.00
Cow, On Wheels, Brown, White, Growler, Bell, Straw Filled, Steiff, 12 In. 605.00
Cow, Wood Platform, Steel Wheels, Felt, 8 In. 145.00
Cowboy, Bounces, Click Noise, No. 430, Fisher-Price, c.1938 .... 715.00
Cowboy, Juggler, Windup, Schuco, Box, 4 3/4 In. 1350.00
Cradle, Doll's, Pine, Painted, Green, Flowers, 19th Century, 3 1/4 x 11 x 23 In. 147.00
Cradle, Doll's, Softwood, Red Graining, Scrolled Ears, Scalloped Head, Footboard 45.00
Crane, Mechanical, Battery Operated, Sound, Lumber, Buddy L, Box, 1950, 27 In. 565.00
Crane, Railroad, Flatbed, Crank Lift, Cast Iron, 8 In. 420.00
Cycle, Halloh, Black Coat, White Pants, Windup, Lehmann, 6 3/4 x 9 x 1 3/4 In. 935.00
Cyclist, Bear, Peddles, Tin, Lever, Marx, Box, c.1920, 6 In. 390.00
Cyclist, Boy, Peddles Figure 8, Windup, Tin, Unique Art, 9 In. 205.00
Cyclist, Rides Around Base, Windup, Tin, 4 In. 740.00
Dancing Couple, Wood, Carved, Brass Floor, Arkansas Trav & Eliza Jane, 21 In. 2300.00
Dancing Dude, Music Box, Cardboard Base, Crank, Mattel, 9 3/4 x 8 1/4 x 5 1/2 In. 140.00
Dancing Hawaiian, Windup, Celluloid, Tin, Occupied Japan, Box, 6 1/2 In. 110.00
Delivery Truck, Finnegan, Bump & Go, Windup, Tin, Unique Art, 13 1/2 In. 259.00
Detector, Ore, Sergeant Preston, Compass, Needle Jumps, Quaker, 1952, 4 1/2 x 2 In. ... 95.00
Dinosaur, Juras, Walks, Growls, Smoke, Tin, Battery Operated, Bullmark, Box, 11 In. ... 1210.00
Dinosaur, Tysus, Steiff, 15 1/2 In. 1300.00
Disc Barrow, Metal, John Deere, Box, 8 In. 175.00
Diver, Tin, Green, Blue, Electric Lantern, Pickaxe, Germany, 20th Century, 7 1/4 In. 1175.00
Diver, Windup, Tin, Red Flippers, Chein, 12 In. 295.00
Dog, Bazi, Plush, Steiff, 10 In. 65.00
Dog, Bulldog, Beige Velvet, Black Eye Patch & Spots, Button Ear, Steiff, 1905, 4 x 3 In. .. 650.00
Dog, Bulldog, Cast Iron, Hubley, 9 x 10 In. 199.00
Dog, Bulldog, Pull Toy, Papier-Mache, Hinged Mouth, Growls, France, c.1900, 18 In. ... 1400.00
Dog, Flipo The Jumping Dog, Windup, Tin, Marx, Box, 4 In. 77.00
Dog, In Basket, Windup, Dog Rises & Barks, Alps, 1958, 10 In. 85.00
Dog, Lady Pup Gardener, Bends, Tulips Light, Battery Operated, Japan, Box, 8 In. 195.00
Dog, Robot, Ears Flap, Eyes Roll, Tin, Friction, Japan, 7 In. 195.00
Dog, Sandy, Windup, Tin, Marx, 5 In. 86.00

Toy, Circus, Ring-A-Ling,
Ringmaster Center,
4 Animals, Marx,
Box, 8 In.

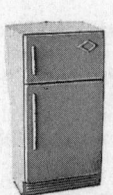

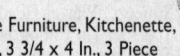

Toy, Dollhouse Furniture, Kitchenette,
Pink, Plastic, 3 3/4 x 4 In., 3 Piece

Dog, Space, Windup, Tin, Japan, Box, 7 1/2 In. 650.00
Dogpatch Band, Tin Lithograph, Windup, Figures Playing & Dancing, 10 In. 330.00
Dolls are listed in their own category.
Dollhouse, 2 Porches, Lithograph, Early 20th Century, 16 x 10 x 7 1/2 In. 90.00
Dollhouse, 2 Story, Dormer, 2 Rooms, Door, Lithograph, Bliss, 10 1/2 x 7 1/2 x 4 In. 280.00
Dollhouse, 2 Story, Dormers, Porch, Balcony, 4 Rooms, Gottschalk, 29 x 22 x 15 In. 1560.00
Dollhouse, 2 Story, Dutch Colonial, Wood, Wallpaper, Gottschalk, c.1925, 20 x 17 In. . . 900.00
Dollhouse, 2 Story, Elevator, Paper Lithograph, Porch, Gottschalk, c.1900, 11 x 19 x 8 In. 7000.00
Dollhouse, 2 Story, English Tudor, Porch, 2 Rooms, Lithograph, Bliss, 13 x 6 x 9 1/2 In. . 550.00
Dollhouse, 2 Story, Porch, Door Knocker, Paper Brick, 4 Rooms, 23 x 19 x 11 In. 575.00
Dollhouse, 2 Story, Porch, Filigree, Paper Lithograph Brick, Gottschalk, 26 x 15 x 13 In. . 345.00
Dollhouse, 2 Story, Stone, Brick, Clapboard, Windows, Paper Lithograph, Bliss, 13 In. 600.00
Dollhouse, 2 Story, Wood, Blue Roof, Elevator, Porch, Gottschalk, c.1910, 27 x 17 In. ... 950.00
Dollhouse, 2 Story, Wood, Gable Attic, Porches, Glass Windows, Gottschalk, 1902 ...... 2500.00
Dollhouse, 2 Story, Wood, Lithograph, Furnishings, Gottschalk, c.1910, 23 x 20 In. 5000.00
Dollhouse, 3 Porches, Balcony, 2 Chimneys, Victorian, Paper, Bliss, 19 x 12 x 23 In. 1115.00
Dollhouse, 3 Story, 2 Porches, 2 Rooms, Paper Lithograph, Gottschalk, 25 x 18 x 11 In. ... 1035.00
Dollhouse, 3 Story, Colonial Style, Furniture, Accessories, Figures, 32 x 19 x 29 In. 230.00
Dollhouse, 4 Rooms, Hinged Doors, Wallpaper, 2 Chimneys, 34 1/2 x 18 x 13 1/2 In. 600.00
Dollhouse, Clapboard, Shingled Roof, 2 Porches, Dormer, Cupola, 25 x 24 x 17 In. 635.00
Dollhouse, Clapboard, Simulated Brick Base, Latticework, Porches, c.1910, 24 x 48 In. ... 1200.00
Dollhouse, Hinged Door, Lithograph, 20th Century, 10 x 7 3/4 x 4 In. 80.00
Dollhouse, Kitchen, Tin, Canister Set, 6 Containers, Lids, 1895 .... 355.00
Dollhouse, Lithograph Wood, Front Opens, 1 Room, Red Tile Roof, 12 x 12 x 12 In. 345.00
Dollhouse, Porch, Balcony, Chimney, Victorian, Paper, Accessories, 18 x 10 x 24 In. 2115.00
Dollhouse Furniture, Bed, Canopy, Sheraton Style, Maple, 1828, 18 x 15 x 11 In. 460.00
Dollhouse Furniture, Bed, Four-Poster, Barbie, Susy Goose, Original Sealed Box, 1962 .. 120.00
Dollhouse Furniture, Canopy Bed, Table, Piano, Settee, Chairs, Gottschalk, c.1885 ..... 550.00
Dollhouse Furniture, Chairs, Cabinet Table, Settee, Fireplace Screen, Magenta, c.1890 .. 2000.00
Dollhouse Furniture, Kitchenette, Pink, Plastic, 3 3/4 x 4 In., 3 Piece .... *Illus* 9.00
Dollhouse Furniture, Salon Set, Ebony Painted, Upholstered, France, c.1870, 6 Piece 900.00
Dollhouse Furniture, Toilet Set, Tub, Pedestal Sink, Stool, Toilet, Green, 1930s, 3 In. ... 320.00
Dollhouse Furniture, Toilette, Mirror, Shelf, Lace Trimmed, France, c.1895, 16 In. 650.00
Dollhouse Furniture, Toilette, Wood, Marble, Drawer, Shelves, Mirror, c.1875, 15 In. 1050.00
Dolphin, Windup, Floats, Tail Moves, France, 1890s, 15 In. 650.00
Donkey, Stubborn, Driver, Lehmann, Box, 7 In. 520.00
Donkey, Wood, Carved, Painted Features, Jointed Body, Seated, Grodner Tal, c.1840, 2 In. 500.00
Drum, Wood, American Flag, Cannon, 12 In. 475.00
Drummer, Black Beret, Red, Brown Hair, Schuco, 4 1/4 In. 90.00
Duck, Pulling 3 Ducklings In Basket, Windup, Lehmann, 7 In. 360.00
Duck, Steel, Friction, Dayton, 9 In. 176.00
Duck, Waddles, Opens Mouth, Celluloid, Windup, Japan, Box, 4 In. 95.00
Duck, Windup, Tin, Key, Japan, 4 In. 65.00
Dune Buggy, Battery Operated, Tin, Japan, 9 1/2 In. 50.00
Dutch Girl, Holding Baby, Windup, Schuco, 5 1/2 In. 315.00
Dutch Girl, Vinyl, Plastic, Windup, Japan, Box, 4 In. 90.00
Elephant, Circus, Pushes Ball, Umbrella Spins, Windup, Tin, Japan, Box, 7 In. 85.00
Elephant, Felt, Glass Eyes, White Tusks, Embroidered, Early 20th Century, 24 In. 175.00
Elephant, Mohair, Steel Eyes, Excelsior Stuffed, Wheels, Steiff, 1930, 17 x 13 In. 380.00
Elephant, Polychrome, Indian Style, Zanzibar, Pull Toy, 11 1/2 In. 750.00
Elephant, Red Felt, Bells On Back, Button In Ear, Chest Tag, Steiff, 8 1/2 In. 190.00
Elephant, Riding, Felt Blanket, Button Eyes, Cast Iron Wheels, Signed, Steiff, 31 x 32 In. 895.00
Elephant, Wooden Platform, Wheels, Tin, 10 In. 45.00
Elephant, Wool Felt, Button Eyes, Excelsior Stuffed, Red Blanket, Steiff, c.1890, 4 In. ... 175.00
Elf, Windup, Schuco, 5 1/2 In. 430.00
Engine, Gas, Clockwork, Painted, 6 1/2 x 9 In. 575.00
Engine, Horizontal, Electric, No. 44, Wooden Base, Weeden, 9 x 10 In. 72.00
Engine, Hot Air, Black, Brown, Vertical, Wooden Base, Ernst Plank, 21 In. 4620.00
Engine, Hot Air, Cast Iron Base, Black, Carette, 12 In. 470.00
Engine, Overtype, Black, Double Flywheel, Cup, Funnel, Burner, Doll, 8 1/2 In. 145.00
Engine, Vertical, No. 4112/12, Cans, Funnels, Cups, Marklin, Wooden Box, 21 1/2 In. ... 4400.00
Erector Set, Electric Motor, Power Plant Tower, Screws, Bolts, Gears, Box, 1938 .... 120.00
Farm Set, Barn, Out Buildings, Wood Farm Animals, Hay Wagons, 16 In. 29.00

Farm Set, Cutouts, Wood, Japan, Box, 9 x 12 In. 55.00
Ferdinand The Bull, Bullfighter, Windup, Tin, Marx, 7 In. 240.00
Ferdinand The Bull, Vibrates, Tail Spins, Windup, Tin, Marx, Box, 1938, 6 In. 990.00
Ferris Wheel, 6 Gondolas, Lithographed Figures, Painted, Germany, 11 In. 375.00
Ferris Wheel, Hercules, Carnival Scenes, Bell, Gondolas, Children, Chein, Windup, 17 In. 345.00
Ferris Wheel, Tin, Plastic Seats, Windup, Ohio Art, 1950s, 15 1/4 In. 75.00
Fire Patrol, Phoenix, 2 Articulating Horses, Ives, 1893, 20 1/2 In. 2195.00
Fire Pumper, 2 Horses, Cast Iron, 16 1/2 In. 295.00
Fire Pumper, 3 Horses, 2 Firemen, Gong Bell, Hubley, 1915, 18 1/2 In. 850.00
Fire Pumper, 3 Horses, Bell, Cloth Hose, Boiler, Cast Iron, Kenton, 1929, 19 x 7 3/4 In. . 1650.00
Fire Pumper, 3 Horses, Bell, Rubber Hoses, Boiler, Hubley, 1906, 21 1/2 x 8 3/4 In. 3600.00
Fire Pumper, 3 Horses, Driver, Boiler, Dent, 21 In. 355.00
Fire Pumper, 3 Horses, Driver, Cast Iron, Hubley, 21 1/2 In. 495.00
Fire Pumper, 3 Horses, Driver, Cast Iron, Wilkins, 12 1/2 In. 375.00
Fire Pumper, Cast Iron, 2 Hoses, Wooden Plugs, Rubber Tires, Wilkins, 20 In. 155.00
Fire Pumper, Cast Iron, A.C. Williams, 6 1/2 In. 135.00
Fire Pumper, Driver, Cast Iron, Hubley, 13 1/2 In. 775.00
Fire Pumper, Driver, Cast Iron, Kenton, 10 1/2 In. 275.00
Fire Pumper, Packard, Turner, 36 In. 1900.00
Fire Pumper, Red, Iron, Nickel Plated, 6 In. 44.00
Fire Pumper, Roof Light, Hoses, Decals, Structo, 24 In. 145.00
Fire Pumper, Water Pump, Single Pump, Engine, Buckman, c.1890 . . . . 3190.00
Fire Truck, 2 Ladders, Pressed Steel, Gerard, 1920s, 11 1/2 In. 195.00
Fire Truck, 2 Riders, Cast Iron, Windup, Tin, 11 1/2 In. 420.00
Fire Truck, Bear, Battery, Tin, Japan, 1950s, 16 In. 195.00
Fire Truck, Chemical, Smokes, Tin, Battery Operated, Japan, Box, 10 1/2 In. 120.00
Fire Truck, Driver, Ladders, Bell Ringer, Hubley, 14 In. 600.00
Fire Truck, Driver, Ladders, Hose, Bell Ringer, Motorized, Cast Iron, 21 In. 1500.00
Fire Truck, Electric Headlights, Buddy L, 1930s, 20 In. 155.00
Fire Truck, Engine Pumper, 3 Horses, 2 Men, Gong Bell, Hubley, 1915, 18 1/2 In. 925.00
Fire Truck, Fireman, Friction, Japan, 1950s, 9 In. 110.00
Fire Truck, Hook & Ladder, Doepke America La France, Label, 33 In. 259.00
Fire Truck, Hook & Ladder, Hose, Rope, Hook, Decals, Buddy L, No. 205, 1923, 26 In. . . 2950.00
Fire Truck, Hook & Ladder, Transitional Windup, Wilkins, 1905, 13 In. 1295.00
Fire Truck, Hose Reel, Horse Drawn, Cast Iron, Pratt & Letchworth, 15 1/2 In. 805.00
Fire Truck, Ladder, Aerial, Driver, Automatic Ladder Mechanism, Kingsbury, 18 In. 325.00
Fire Truck, Ladder, Aerial, Pressed Steel, Buddy L, 29 In. 825.00
Fire Truck, Ladder, Cast Iron, 2 Horses, Firemen, Bell, Wooden Ladders, 20 In. 206.00
Fire Truck, Ladder, Friction, 13 1/2 In. 395.00
Fire Truck, Ladder, Hose Reel, Marx, 1930s, 14 1/2 In. 1020.00
Fire Truck, Ladder, Tippco, Germany, 13 In. 595.00
Fire Truck, Lights, Bell, Ladder Extends, Tin, Battery Operated, Yonezawa, Box, 12 In. . . 165.00
Fire Truck, Metal, Rubber Tires, Red, Silver, Manoil, 4 1/2 In. 44.00
Fire Truck, P.S. Hose & Ladder, Marked, Rossmoyne, Doepke, 1950s, 19 In. 300.00
Fire Truck, Packard, Red, Accessories, Balloon Tires, Bell, Steel, Keystone, c.1920, 29 In. 4400.00
Fire Truck, Pressed Steel, Boiler, Hose Reel, Friction, Clark, 14 1/2 In. 118.00
Fire Truck, Pressed Steel, Reel, Boiler, Friction, 2 Firemen, Hill Climber, 14 In. 295.00
Fire Truck, Steam Boiler, Cast Iron, 8 1/2 In. 115.00
Fire Truck, Texaco, Pressed Steel, Plastic, Buddy L, 25 In. 65.00
Fire Truck, Windup, Penny Toy, 4 In. 200.00
Fire Truck, Windup, Tin, 4 Firemen, England, 1950s, 15 In. 395.00
Fire Truck, Wooden Ladders, Kelmet White, 6 1/2 In. 1200.00
Fire Wagon, 2 Horses, Driver, 3 Firemen, Bell Ringer, 18 1/2 In. 1250.00
Fire Wagon, Fire Hose Reel, Horse, Driver, Painted, Cast Iron, Carpenter Toys, c.1883 . . . 3800.00
Fire Wagon, Hook & Ladder, 2 Drivers, Bell Ringer, Cast Iron, 23 1/2 In. 1600.00
Fire Wagon, Hose Reel, Horse, Driver, Brass Nozzle, Shimer, 1890s, 10 In. 1150.00
Fire Wagon, Ladders, 3 Horses, Drivers, Bell Ringer, Cast Iron, 28 In. 1200.00
Fire Wagon, Patrol, 2 Horse Team, Figures, Cast Iron, 17 In. 825.00
Fire Wagon, Patrol, 2 Moving Horses, 7 Firemen, Driver, 1893, 20 1/2 In. 2195.00
Fire Wagon, Patrol, 3 Horse Team, Figures, Cast Iron, Ives, 22 In. 1210.00
Fire Wagon, Patrol, 3 Horses, Firemen, Dent, 1905, 21 In. 1295.00
Fire Wagon, Patrol, Horses, Gong Bell, Firemen, Driver, Kenton, 1910, 16 3/4 In. 1495.00
Fireman, On Ladder, Hook & Wagon, Tin Lithograph, Windup, Marx, 9 In. . . . . *Illus* 1870.00

Toy, Fireman,
On Ladder,
Hook & Wagon,
Tin Lithograph,
Windup, Marx, 9 In.

Toy, Grasshopper, Bride &
Groom, Felt, Floss Covered
Arms & Legs, 1930s, 15 In., Pair

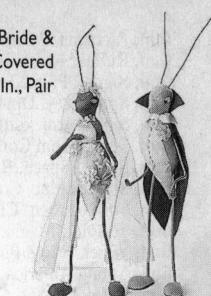

**Rusted toys have very
low value.
Remove the batteries
from a stored toy.**

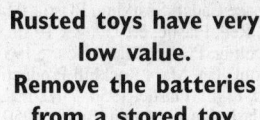

Fireman, On Yellow Ladder, Red Jacket, Tin, Plastic, Marx, Box, 22 In.	135.00
Flashlight, Porky Pig, Figural, Warner Bros., c.1950, 2 1/2 x 4 7/8 In.	35.00
Flashlight, Ringling Bros & Barnum & Bailey, Tiger Head, 9 1/2 In.	5.00
Flying Circus, Elephant Balancing Plane, Clown, Tin, 12 x 30 In.	480.00
Football, Bladder, Blow Up, Peppy, Yellow, Brown, Rubber, Occupied Japan, 6 In.	85.00
Football, Touchdown Pete, Windup, Bends Over, Tin, Linemar, 6 In.	245.00
Frankenstein, Monster, Arms Wave, Hands Light Up, Vinyl, Cloth, Japan, Box, 7 1/2 In.	140.00
Fred Astaire, Dances Under Hollywood & Vine, Celluloid, Windup, Japan, 8 In.	170.00 to 275.00
Frog, Dakin Dream Pets, Cloth, Felt, Stuffed, c.1960, 8 In.	10.00
Frog, Pepper, Smiling, Squeeze, Rempel, Box, c.1940, 6 In.	45.00
Fruit Vendor, Spring Motor, Red, White Striped Trousers, Cart, 7 In.	325.00
G.I. Joe, Carries Cages With K-9 Pups, Mechanical, Unique Art, Box, 1941	500.00
G.I. Joe, Jeep, Bounces, Red, Windup, Tin, Unique Art, Box, 7 In.	165.00 to 385.00
Games are listed in their own category.	
Garage, Magic, Car, Windup, Tin, Box, 5 In.	80.00
Garage, Single Car, Tin Lithograph, Green Sedan, Lehmann, 6 In.	300.00
Garage & Car, Tin Lithograph, Windup, Woody Sedan, 10 1/2 In.	275.00
Garden Set, Floral Miniature, Painted, No. 7530, Britains Ltd., England	260.00
Gas Pump, Gulf, Plastic, Box, 18 In.	225.00
Gas Pump, Tin, Hullco Toys, 7 1/2 In.	110.00
Gas Pump, Tin, Marked DRGM, Germany, 8 1/2 In.	210.00
Gas Station, Car, Hose & Pump, Tin, Battery Operated, West Germany, Box, 6 In.	140.00
Geccha Man, Walks, Arms Move, Tin, Vinyl, Ansonii, Box, 9 1/2 In.	330.00
Geese, Feeding, Heads Stick Out Coop, Peck Feed Basket, Windup, Penny Toy, 2 In.	115.00
General Alarm Fire House, Base, Headquarters, 2 Cars, Winder, Box, 1930s	1650.00
George Washington, Rides Galloping Horse, Windup, Tin, 1920s, 6 1/2 In.	325.00
George Washington, Riding Horse, Bisque Head, Windup, Decamp, 8 x 8 1/2 In.	1380.00
Gilbert Lab Set For Girls, No. 13120, Complete With Booklet, c.1950	115.00
Ginny's Pup, Terrier, Mohair, Glass Eyes, Felt Ears, Bell, Steiff, 1954, 3 1/2 In.	110.00
Giraffe, Ear Button, Steiff, 1950s, 25 1/2 In.	350.00
Girl, Rocking At Beachside, Umbrella Spins, Tin, Celluloid, Windup, Japan, c.1940, 9 In.	345.00
Girl, Staff & Flowers, Green Velvet Dress & Apron, Schuco, Germany, 5 In.	480.00
Girl, Waltzing, Celluloid Head, Tin, 9 In.	520.00
Globe, Earth Spins, Ball Floats, Tin, Battery Operated, Japan, Box, 10 In.	635.00
Goat, Bow With Bell, Button In Ear, Steiff, 4 In.	120.00
Godzilla, Walks, Growls, Smoke, Lights, Tin, Battery Operated, Bullmark, Box, 10 In.	1045.00
Golfer, Hits Ball, Windup, Tin, Strauss, Box, c.1920, 12 In.	330.00
Gorilla, King Kong, Opens Mouth, Thumps Chest, Windup, Tin, 7 1/2 In.	240.00
Gorilla, Magilla, Stuffed, Vinyl, Cloth, Ideal, c.1960, 7 1/2 In.	40.00
Gorilla, Walks, Beats Chest, Windup, Growls, Plush Over Tin, Marx, Box, 8 In.	255.00
Grasshopper, Bride & Groom, Felt, Floss Covered Arms, Legs, 1930s, 15 In., Pair . . *Illus*	200.00
Grasshopper, Hubley, 11 In.	875.00
Grasshopper, Windup, Marusan, Japan, Box, 9 In.	540.00
Gun, Air Rifle, BB, Daisy Double Barrel, Plastic Grip & Stock, 37 In.	495.00
Gun, American Bull Dog, Nickel Plated, c.1900, 8 1/2 In.	85.00
Gun, Anti-Aircraft, Astra, Aluminum, Steel, England, 10 In.	120.00
Gun, Astro Ray Flashlight Target, Dart Shooting, Tin Target Board, 13 x 13 In.	110.00
Gun, Bubble, Jetsons, Plastic, Card, Imperial Toy Co., 1976, 6 1/2 x 12 In.	50.00
Gun, Popgun, 2 Barrel, Box, 21 In.	165.00

Gun, Ricochet Carbine, Marx, Box, c.1955, 34 In. 485.00
Gun, Rubber Band, Targets, Bull's Eye Pistol Mfg., Rawlins, Wyoming, Box, 9 In. 345.00
Gun, Signal, Painted, Marx, c.1935, 7 In. 489.00
Gun, Space Ray, Double Barrel, Sparking, Tin, Plastic, Japan, Box, 15 In. 305.00
Gun, Space, Knickerbocker, Dart, Belt, Plastic, Vinyl, c.1950, 5 x 11 x 3 In. 60.00
Gun, Space, Tom Corbett Space Cadet, Sparking, Plastic, Marx, 1952, 21 In. 500.00
Gun, Squirt, Space, Bicycle, Red, Plastic, c.1950, 4 x 10 In. 20.00
Gun, Submachine, Cork Shooting, Plastic, Marx, Box, c.1951, 19 1/2 In. 270.00
Gun, Tom Corbett, Click Pistol, Tin, Marx Rockhill Production, 10 In. 525.00
Gun, Tricolor, Magic, Sound, Light, Plastic, 1950, 7 1/2 In. 25.00
Gun, Water, Rapid Firing, Blask, Plastic, Arpin, Box, c.1950, 7 In. 75.00
Gun, Young America Rapid Fire, Cast Iron, Painted, Mechanical, 15 In. 130.00
Gun & Holster Set, Cap Gun, Deputy Dog, Leather, Brown, c.1960, 2 1/2 x 5 1/2 x 24 In.   60.00
Gun & Holster Set, Wyatt Earp, Guns, Bullets, Esquire 685.00
Gun Boat, Windup, Tin, Japan, 13 In. 130.00
Ham & Sam, Entertainers, Dance, Play Piano, Windup, Linemar, 1921, 7 1/2 In. 360.00
Hansom Cab, Driver, Pratt & Letchworth, 1888, 13 In. 1725.00
Hansom Cab, Lavender Horse Blanket, Driver, Pratt & Letchworth, c.1885, 12 x 7 1/2 In.   2350.00
Hansom Cab, Wood, Pressed Steel, Cast Iron, Friction, Dayton Hill Climber, 11 In. 325.00
Happy Hooligan, Police Patrol, 2 Horse Team, Accessory Figures, Kenton, 18 In. 2200.00
Helicopter, Air Force, Tin, Friction, TN, Japan, 10 1/2-In. Wingspan 35.00
Helicopter, Army, Tin, Friction, Haji, 16 In. 55.00
Helicopter, G-AMHK, Green, Tin, Battery Operated, Alps, Box, 13 In. 205.00
Helicopter, Hughes 500, Blue, Tin, Plastic, Battery Operated, Box, 16 In. 110.00
Helicopter, Marine, Tin, Battery Operated, Marx, Japan, 17 In. 45.00
Helicopter, Moon Scout, Battery Operated, Tin, Plastic, Japan, Box, 16 In. 95.00
Helicopter, Moves As Propeller Spins, Windup, Tin, Japan, 10 In.   95.00
Helicopter, Pioneer Airways, Red, Tin Lithograph, Friction, Windup, 11 In. 65.00
Helicopter, Rettungsdienst, Yellow, Tin, Plastic, Battery Operated, Japan, Box, 14 In. 85.00
Helicopter, Sky Patrol, Tin Lithograph, Battery Operated, Japan, Box, 10 1/2 In. 65.00
Helicopter, Streamlined, Steel, Pull Toy, Wyandotte, Box, c.1940, 8 In. 320.00
Helicopter, Super Copter, Blue, Plastic, Battery Operated, Japan, Box, 15 In. 55.00
Helicopter, U.S. Air Force, Friction, Japan, 1950s, 8 In. 295.00
Helicopter, U.S. Army Air Rescue, Windup, Tin, Marx, Box, 10 In.   145.00
Helicopter, U.S. Army, Tin, Friction, Linemar, Japan, 1950s, 10 In.   130.00
Helicopter, Vertol 107, New York Air, Tin, Battery Operated, Japan, Box, 13 1/2 In. 85.00
Hen, Mechanical, Egg Laying, Clucking, Tin, 5 1/2 In. 98.00
Hen, On Large Egg, Multicolored, Tin Lithograph, Chein, 4 3/4 In. 45.00
Henry, Brother, Prewar Japan, 7 In., 4 1/2 In. 1095.00
Henry, On Pink Elephant, Celluloid, Windup, Borgfeldt, Box, 8 In. 1250.00
Henry, Riding Elephant, Head Sways Side To Side, Celluloid, Windup, 3 1/2 In. 520.00
Highchair, Doll's, Maple, Spindle Back, Cane Seat, Bamboo Shape, France, c.1890, 17 In.   450.00
Highchair, Doll's, Maple, Spindle Back, Cane Seat, Bamboo Shape, France, c.1900, 24 In.   300.00
Hippo, Man On Back, Windup, Moves While Opening Mouth, Tin, Japan, Box, 6 In. 800.00
Hippo, Missing Button, Steiff, 3 In. 80.00
Hobbyhorse, Stick, Carved, Horse Head Mounted, Cast Iron Wheels, 38 1/2 In. 145.00
Horse, Black, Red Saddle, Green Base, Wheels, Tin, Pull Toy, Late 19th Century, 8 x 9 In.   110.00
Horse, Felt, On Wheels, Steiff, 15 In. 695.00
Horse, Glider, Dapple Painted, Red Stand, 36 In. 325.00
Horse, Glider, Hide Covered, Turned Columns, Painted Stand, F.A.O. Schwarz, 45 In. . . .   825.00
Horse, Glider, Leather Covered, 19th Century, 28 1/2 x 38 In. 260.00
Horse, Moving Woman Rider, Cast Iron, Push Or Pull, 1950s, 6 3/4 In. 245.00
Horse, Platform, Dapple Gray, Galloping, Saddle, Stirrups, Iron Wheels, 16 In. 2145.00
Horse, Platform, Wheels, Wagon, Hide Covered, Pull Toy, Horse, 5 x 27-In. Wagon 240.00
Horse, Platform, Wheels, Wood, Pull Toy, 11 1/2 In. 275.00
Horse, Platform, White, Wheels, Tin, Pull Toy, 9 1/2 In. 250.00
Horse, Platform, Wood, Felt, Metal Wheels, Pull Toy, 15 In. 155.00
Horse, Platform, Wooden, Horsehide Cover, 4 Wheels, 14 x 21 In.   550.00
Horse, Push, Cast Iron Jockey, 33 In. 745.00
Horse, Rocking, Canvas Covered, Glass Eyes, Leatherette Harness, 34 In. 355.00
Horse, Rocking, Carved Wood, Painted, Gray, Swing Base, Leather Saddle, 36 x 39 In. . .   870.00
Horse, Rocking, Hide Covered, Red Painted Platform, Heel, 28 x 27 x 49 In. 480.00
Horse, Rocking, Hide Covered, Trestle Base, Leather Mounts, 34 x 37 In. 520.00

Horse, Rocking, Hide Covered, White, Leather Saddle, Late 19th Century, 30 x 63 In. ...   350.00
Horse, Rocking, Platform Base, Wood, Painted, 10th Century, 29 x 31 1/2 x 14 In. 415.00
Horse, Rocking, Wood, Black Ground, Polychrome, 28 1/2 x 50 1/2 In. 1375.00
Horse, Spark Plug, Pull Toy, Wooden, Painted, Articulated Body, 10 In.   355.00
Horse, Trotter, Red Wagon, Rider, Tin, Clockwork, Cuzner, American, 1871, 10 In. 6600.00
Horse, Wood, Cloth, Wooden Base, Painted Red, 4 Iron Wheels, 27 x 29 In. 345.00
Horse, Wood, Painted, Leather Harness, Wheels, Push, 20th Century, 19 x 20 In. 431.00
Horse & Cart, Hide Covered, China Head Doll, Painted, Pull Toy, 19th Century, 20 In. ..   715.00
Horse & Wagon, 2 Horses, Bell, No. 171, Fisher-Price, 1942, 19 In. 69.00
Horse & Wagon, Ambulance, 2 Horses, Metal, Tin, Lineol, 9 1/2 In. 175.00
Horse & Wagon, Buckboard, Pressed Metal, Cast Iron Legs, 30 In. 646.00
Horse & Wagon, Cast Iron, Stanley, 20th Century, 11 1/2 In. 69.00
Horse & Wagon, Covered Wagon, Tin, Composition Men, Horses, Germany, 9 1/2 In. ...   275.00
Horse & Wagon, Covered, 2 Horse Team, Canvas, Cast Iron, Kenton, 15 In. 470.00
Horse & Wagon, German Soldier, Spiked Helmet, Medical, 2 Horses, Tin, 4 1/2 In. 250.00
Horse & Wagon, Milk, Cast Iron, Painted, 11 In. 315.00
Horse & Wagon, Milk, Driver, Spoke Wheels, Cast Iron, Kenton, 19 In. 430.00
Horse & Wagon, Police Patrol, Cast Iron, 3 Horses, Figures, Dent, 17 1/2 In. 935.00
Horse & Wagon, Police, 2 Horses, Driver, Cast Iron, 14 In. 90.00
Horse & Wagon, Pull Toy, Cloth Body, Wheeled Platform, c.1885, 29 x 10 In., 2 Piece ...   785.00
Horse & Wagon, RR Transfer, 2 Brown Horses, Covered Bed, Tin, Iron, 21 In. 910.00
Housekeeper, Black, Broom, Sweeps, Windup, Lindstrom, 1930s 275.00
Hum-A-Zoo, Plastic, Round, Box, 3 Dozen, 2 In. .... *Illus*   25.00
Ice Cream Parlor Set, Wire, Wooden Table, Chairs, Child's, 18 x 18 In., 3 Piece 115.00
Iceman, Waddles, Swings Ice, Windup, Tin, Marx, Box, c.1930, 8 1/2 In. 3960.00
Indian, Horse, Hops, Windup, Tin, Japan, Box, 5 In. 155.00
Indian, Plays Drum, Nutty Mad, Battery Operated, Marx, Japan, Box, 14 In. 80.00
Jack-In-The-Box, Papier-Mache, Wood, Lithograph, Blue Beard, France, c.1885, 5 In. 300.00
Jack-In-The-Box, Striped Cloth Body, Peaked Cap, Leather Trim, Wooden Box, 7 In. 330.00
Jeep, Army, Two Soldiers, Tin, Friction, Japan, Box, 8 1/2 In. 210.00
Jeep, Beetle Bailey, Bounces, Windup, Tin, Plastic Figure, Brazil, Box, c.1950, 7 In. 165.00
Jeep, Bump & Go, Tin, Battery Operated, Japan, Box, 10 In. 110.00
Jeep, Magnetic Crane, Tin, Friction, Bandai, 9 1/2 In. 290.00
Jeep, Patrol, Seat Flips, Tin, Friction, Japan, Box, 8 In. 110.00
Jeep, Willys, Movable Windshield, Pressed Tin, Marx, 11 In. 200.00
Jeep, Willys, Silver Gray, Japan, 1960s, 8 In. 90.00
Joe Penner, Cigar Smoking, Bowler Hat, Check Jacket, Tin Lithograph, Windup, 8 In. ...   460.00
Joe Penner, Holding Duck & Cage, Tipping Hat, Moving Cigar, Windup, 8 1/4 In. 460.00
Kaleidoscope, Table, G.C. Bush & Co., Providence, Late 19th Century, 8 1/2 In. 1293.00
Kazoo, Woody Woodpecker, Plastic, Kellogg Cereal, c.1960, 6 1/2 In. 20.00
King Kong, Battery Operated, 12 In. 325.00
Knife Sharpener, Sparks, Windup, Tin, Girard, c.1930, 4 1/2 In. 99.00
Knight, On Horse, Turns, Windup, Tin, Haji, Box, 4 1/2 In. 331.00
Ladybug, Windup, Tin, Nurnberg, Bavaria, 7 1/2 In. 165.00
Lamb, Papier-Mache, Painted Face, Mohair, Wood Base, Squeeze Toy, c.1890, 6 In. 550.00
Li'l Abner Dogpatch Band, Tin, F.S. Mfg, By Unique Art, 1945, 9 In. ....400.00 to 600.00
Li'l Abner Dogpatch Band, Tin, F.S. Mfg, By Unique Art, Box, 1945, 9 In. 750.00
Light, Finger, E.T., Vinyl, Battery Operated, 1982, 5 In. 20.00

Toy, Hum-A-Zoo,
Plastic, Round, Box,
3 Dozen, 2 In.

Toy, Merrymakers Band, Mice Play Instruments,
Windup, Tin, Marx, Box, c.1931, 9 1/2 In.

Lion, Circus, Mat, Whip, Battery Operated, Inserts, Box, 1960s, 10 In. 575.00
Lunar Expedition, Tank, Plastic, Windup, Tin, Technofix, 11 x 16 In. 80.00
Magic Slate, Deputy Dawg, Terrytoons, 1977, 9 x 13 In. 18.00
Magic Slate, Skyhawk, Ken Snyder Enterprises, 1969, 8 x 14 In. 8.00
Maid, Chasing Mouse With Broom, Clockwork, Martin, 8 In. 1140.00
Man, Black, Driver, Horse, Wagon, Cast Iron, 20th Century, 15 1/2 In. 1000.00
Man, Black, Driver, Wagon, 2 Horses, Red, Yellow, Cast Iron, 15 In................ 950.00
Man, Luggage Cart, Suitcases, Girard, Woods, 6 In. 420.00
Man, Sailor, Pretends To Pull On Stick, Irish Male, Penny Toy, Germany, 3 In. 518.00
Man, Sawing Log, Windup, 7 1/2 In. 350.00
Man, Sharpening Scissors, Windup, Tin, 5 1/2 In. 145.00
Man, Traveler, Walks, 2 Suitcases, Windup, Distler, Germany, 1920s, 7 1/2 In. 675.00
Man, Violinist, Stands On Corner Playing Violin, 8 In............................ 480.00
Man, Zebra, Lehman Daredevil, Windup, 5 1/2 x 7 x 3 1/2 In...................... 660.00
Mandarin, Umbrella Spins When Rolled, Penny Toy, Germany, 2 1/2 In. 415.00
Marionette Theater, Windup, Celluloid, Japan, Box, 5 1/2 x 14 In. 440.00
Mary & Little Lamb, Celluloid, Windup, Tin, C.K., Japan, 6 1/2 In. .... .175.00 to 540.00
Merry-Go-Round, Horses, Children, Lever Operated, Wolverine, 12 x 11 In. 230.00
Merrymakers Band, Mice Play Instruments, Windup, Tin, Marx, Box, c.1931, 9 1/2 In. *Illus* 2530.00
Microscope, Set, Reg'lar Fellers, L.H. & H., New York City, Japan, Box, c.1930 .... 25.00
Microscope, Space Patrol, J.V.Z. Co., c.1950, 3 1/2 In............................ 55.00
Minstrel, Plays Sax, Bangs Drum, Hits Cymbal, Tin, Pull String, Germany, 1900s, 5 In. ... 333.00
Missile Launcher, 3 Missiles, 1950s, 21 In. 255.00
Missile Launcher, Naval Defense Coastal Unit, Blue, Ny-Lint, 1950s, 21 In. 105.00
Mister Machine, Ideal, 1960 .... 500.00
Model, Grumman Type X-29A, White Body, Stand, Grumman, USAF, NASA, 7 In. 175.00
Model, Jet, Fighter, U.S. Air Force F-15, Upright, Plastic, Missiles, Wooden Base, Box ... 37.00
Model, Jet, Fighter, U.S. Navy, Silver Plastic, Decals, Wooden Base, 1970s, 10 x 10 In. .. 200.00
Model, Ship, Pilot Cutter, Glass Case, Hitchcox, France, 32 In. 3000.00
Monkey, Baseball, Raises Hat, Tail Spins, Windup, Tin, Japan, 7 1/2 In. 305.00
Monkey, Batter, Windup, Tin, Painted, Cragstan, Box, 7 1/2 In. 745.00
Monkey, Bellhop, Yes-No Action, Schuco, 12 In. 415.00
Monkey, Climbing, Tin Lithograph, Lehmann, 8 In. 35.00
Monkey, Drummer, Red Beret, Coat, Yellow Pants, Schuco, 4 1/2 In. 150.00
Monkey, Elephant, Jungle Trio, Tin, Battery Operated, Linemar, Box, 7 In. 204.00
Monkey, Jointed, Stuffed, Chest Tag, Clemens, West Germany, 8 1/2 In. 45.00
Monkey, Mungo, Chest Tag, Steiff, 8 In. 175.00
Monkey, Playing Banjo, Red Pants, Green Shirt, Tin Lithograph, Schuco, 6 In. 290.00
Monkey, Playing Banjo, Sitting, Musical, Celluloid, Tin, 8 In. 99.00
Monkey, Rock & Roll, Plays Guitar, Battery Operated, Alps, Box, 12 In. 145.00
Monkey, Stuffed, Celluloid, 1940s, 12 In...................................... 225.00
Monkey, Violinist, Green Coat, Yellow Pants, Red Beret, Schuco, 4 1/4 In. 115.00
Monkey, Yes-No Tricky Monkey, Tag, Ribbon, Schuco, 14 In....................... 180.00
Monkey, Yes-No, Blue Short Jacket, Schuco, 15 In. 518.00
Monkey & Ballerina, Red, Yellow Pants, Dance, Schuco, 4 1/2 In. 210.00
Monkey Swing, Tin, Wood, Japan, 1950s, 6 1/2 In. 175.00
Monkeys, Teeter-Totter, Flag, Windup, Tin, Germany, 10 1/2 In. 330.00
Mother Goose, Cat Rides Hopping Goose, Windup, 9 /2 In. 375.00
Mother Goose, Windup, Tin, Nursery Rhyme Character & Cat Ride Aboard, 9 In. 540.00
Motor, Atom, Power Accessories, Wilson, Cleveland, Box, 7 x 9 In. 22.00
Motor, Outboard, Electric Starting, Evinrude, 5 1/2 In. 230.00
Motorcycle, Curvo 1000, Tin Lithograph, Windup, Schuco, Box, 5 In................. 360.00
Motorcycle, Delivery, Speed Boy, Windup, Electric Lights, Tin, c.1932, 10 In. ..... *Illus* 550.00
Motorcycle, Deliveryman, Bump & Go, Tin, Crank, Japan, 6 1/2 In. 220.00
Motorcycle, Driver, Sidecar, Cast Iron, Iron Spoke Wheels, 4 In..................... 145.00
Motorcycle, Driver, Sidecar, Cast Iron, Rubber Tires, 4 In. 145.00
Motorcycle, Echo, Tin Lithograph, Blue Frame, Uniformed Rider, Lehmann, 9 In. 1610.00
Motorcycle, Harley-Davidson, Friction, Japan, 1950s, 9 In......................... 295.00
Motorcycle, Harley-Davidson, Parcel Post, Rider, Cast Iron, Hubley, 9 In. 1700.00
Motorcycle, Harley-Davidson, Policeman, Movable Head, Tires, Headlights, Hubley, 7 In. 145.00
Motorcycle, Harley-Davidson, Tin, Friction, Japan, 9 In. 385.00
Motorcycle, Indian, Friction, Japan, 8 In. 450.00
Motorcycle, Mac 700, Windup, Tin Lithograph, West Germany, 5 x 7 1/2 In. .... .575.00 to 910.00

Toy, Motorcycle, Delivery,
Speed Boy, Windup,
Electric Lights, Tin,
c.1932, 10 In.

Toy, Motorcycle, Police,
Sidecar, Siren, Tin Lithograph,
Windup, Late
1930s, 8 1/2 In.

Motorcycle, Military, Camouflaged, Headlight, Tin, Embossed, Germany, KAO, 7 1/2 In. . . 480.00
Motorcycle, Mystic, Advances As He Rocks Back & Forth, Marx, Box, 1930s, 4 1/2 In. . . . 295.00
Motorcycle, Mystic, Marx, 1930s, 4 1/2 In. 250.00
Motorcycle, No. 2, Rider, Windup, Tin, Technofix, US Zone Germany, 7 In. 450.00
Motorcycle, No. 4, Windup, Tin, Technofix, US Zone Germany, 7 In. 175.00
Motorcycle, No. 15, Windup, Tin, Technofix, US Zone Germany, 7 In. 226.00
Motorcycle, Police, Blue, White Rubber Tires, Hubley, 1920s, 4 In. 250.00
Motorcycle, Police, Metal, Siren, Friction, Japan, 1960, 10 In. 295.00
Motorcycle, Police, Painted, Whitewall Ties, Cast Iron, Champion, 1930s, 7 In. 695.00
Motorcycle, Police, Patrol, Sparks, Tin, Friction, Japan, Box, 8 In. 160.00
Motorcycle, Police, Rider, Plastic, Battery Operated, Bandai, Box, 11 In. 45.00
Motorcycle, Police, Rubber Tires, Tin, Friction, Usagiya, Box, c.1950, 8 In. 495.00
Motorcycle, Police, Sidecar, 2 Policemen, Hubley, 8 1/2 In. 975.00
Motorcycle, Police, Sidecar, Harley-Davidson, Cast Iron, Hubley, 5 In. 450.00
Motorcycle, Police, Sidecar, Siren, Tin Lithograph, Windup, Late 1930s, 8 1/2 In. . . . . *Illus* 330.00
Motorcycle, Police, Tin Lithograph, Windup, Sidecar, Siren, Marx, 8 1/2 In. 330.00
Motorcycle, Police, Tin, Battery Operated, Box, 1930s, 12 In. 1250.00
Motorcycle, Police, Windup, Marx Tin, Working Siren, 1940, 8 1/2 In. 170.00
Motorcycle, Police, Windup, Tin, Unique Art, 8 1/2 In. 275.00
Motorcycle, Rider In Orange Jacket & Cap, Ivory Pants, Clockwork, KiCo, 8 In. 2360.00
Motorcycle, Rider, Arnold, U.S. Zone Germany, 8 1/4 In. 675.00
Motorcycle, Rider, Headlamp, Luggage Rack, Embossed, Windup, Tin, Germany, 7 1/2 In. 480.00
Motorcycle, Sidecar, 2 Passengers, Battery Operated, Cast Iron, Hubley, 9 In. 1100.00
Motorcycle, Sidecar, Balloon Tires, Tin, Original Key, Russia, 8 3/4 In. 225.00
Motorcycle, Sidecar, Cop Logo, Yellow, Cast Iron, 4 In. 85.00
Motorcycle, Sidecar, Driver In Orange Suit, Yellow Belt, Leggings, Box, G & K, 7 In. . . . 1320.00
Motorcycle, Sidecar, Sparks, Siren Noise, Windup, Tin, Marx, 8 1/2 In. . . . . .395.00 to 440.00
Motorcycle, Siren, Police Officer, Marx, 8 1/2 In. 180.00
Motorcycle, Soldier, Sparks, Windup, Tin, Marx, Box, 8 1/4 In. 580.00
Motorcycle, Speedy Gonzalez, Stuffed, Mighty Star, 1971, 14 In. 15.00
Motorcycle, Travels On Spring Cable, Windup, Tin, Box, 5 In. 155.00
Motorcycle, Windup, Tin Lithograph Man On Racing Cycle, 1940s, 7 In. 315.00
Motorcycle, Windup, Tin, c.1920, 7 1/2 In. 520.00
Motorcycle, Zabitan, Rider, Tin, Vinyl, Bullmark, Japan, Box, 9 1/2 In. 250.00
Mouse, Drinking Beer, Red Britches, Gray Felt Top, Schuco, 4 1/4 In. 145.00
Mule & Wagon, Medical, World War I, Elastolin, Germany, 1920s, 15 In. 295.00
Mule & Wagon, Milk, Hee Haw, Driver, Milk Cans, Tin Lithograph, 10 3/4 In. 300.00
Musicians, Hott & Tott, Black, Piano & Banjo, Unique Art Co., Windup, 1921 . . . . 965.00
Naughty Boy, Father Drives Car, Boy Grabs Tiller, Windup, Lehmann, 5 In. 690.00
Noah's Ark, Carved, Wood, 116 Figures, Germany, c.1870, 17 In. 4000.00
Noah's Ark, Figures, Animals, Wood, Carved, 96 Figures, Germany, 21-In. Ark 2100.00
Noah's Ark, Pine, Salmon Paint, Stenciled Details, 13 x 5 1/2 In. 360.00
Nodder, Andy Gump, Bisque, Germany, 1920s 125.00
Nodder, Buttercup, Bisque, 1920s 185.00
Nodder, Pat Finnegan, Bisque, 1920s 185.00
Nodder, Uncle Walt, Boardinghouse Gang, Bisque, Germany 100.00
Noisemaker, Mardi Gras, 5 Figures, Dancing, Wood, Fabric, Composition, 24 In. 195.00
Organ Grinder, Dancing Dogs, Mechanical, Musical, France, c.1865, 12 In. 3100.00
Paddy & Pig, Animated, Ears Flop, Paddy Sways, Lehmann, 1903, 6 In. . . . . . . .540.00 to 970.00
Pail, 3 Little Pigs, Mayfair Candies, Chein, 3 1/2 In. 275.00

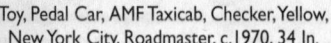

Toy, Pedal Car, AMF Taxicab, Checker, Yellow,
New York City, Roadmaster, c.1970, 34 In.

Toy, Pedal Car, Fire Truck, Pontiac, Red,
Wooden Ladder, Padded Seat, 1949, 45 In.

Pail, Felix The Cat, Tin, 6 x 7 In. 165.00
Pail, Patriotic Images, Lid, Tin Lithograph, Lovell & Covel, 3 x 2 7/8 In. 450.00
Pail, Queen Of Hearts, Nursery Rhyme Images, Tin Lithograph, 3 x 2 7/8 In. 196.00
Pail, Seaside, Eagle, Airplane, Drum Soldier, Handle, Tin Lithograph, 5 1/4 x 5 3/8 In. 297.00
Pail, Teddy Roosevelt On Bear, Bears Drumming, Playing Trumpet, Flag, Tin, 4 x 3 In. . . 1210.00
Pail, Uncle Wiggily, Cartoon Characters, Tin Lithograph, 1920s, 3 x 3 3/4 In. 385.00
Pail & Shovel, Atlantic City, Children Playing, Beach Scenes, Germany, c.1920, 6 In. 375.00
Panda, Grandpa, Moves Arms, Chews, Plush, Tin, Battery Operated, Japan, Box, 10 In. . . 195.00
Parade, Bandsman, Soldier, Cannon, Plane Circles, Windup, Tin, Marx, Box, 24 In. 715.00
Parade, Circus, Elephant Pulls Clown, Spin, Windup, Tin, Japan, Box, 12 In. 305.00
Parade, Circus, Elephant Pulls Wagon, Tin, Courtland, 12 In. 110.00
Parade, Military, Circling Plane, Windup, Tin, Marx, Box, 24 In. 120.00
Parrot, In Carrying Case, Metal Lithograph, Battery Operated, 19 In. 175.00
Parrot, Pip-Squeak, On Stump, Yellow Tail Coat, Black Top Hat, 5 3/4 In. 110.00
Parrot, Talking, Lighted Eyes, Flapping Wings, Tin Lithograph, Marx, 19 In. 175.00
Peacock, Windup, Tin, 8 In. 55.00
Pedal Car, Airplane, U.S. Army Pursuit, Pressed Steel, Silver, Red, Blue, 46 In. 880.00
Pedal Car, AMF Taxi, Checker, Yellow, New York City, Roadmaster, c.1970, 34 In. . *Illus* 305.00
Pedal Car, Boat, Murray Jolly Roger, Plastic Flag & Light, Seat Pad, 38 In. 770.00
Pedal Car, Buick Skylark, Garton Toy Co., 33 In. 470.00
Pedal Car, Bulldozer, Pressed Steel, Working Blade, Caterpillar D6, 1950s, 41 In. 1430.00
Pedal Car, Bus, Coast To Coast, Pressed Steel, Rubber Tires, Keystone, c.1920, 32 In. . . . 4620.00
Pedal Car, Bus, Packard, Pressed Steel, Greyhound, Keystone, 1920s, 32 In. 5720.00
Pedal Car, Chief City Fire Department, Red Paint, Stripes, 35 In. 115.00
Pedal Car, Chrysler, Airplane Hood Ornament, Chrome Hubs, Bumpers, 1941, 39 In. 1650.00
Pedal Car, Dump Truck, Mack, Steelcraft, 46 In. 1560.00
Pedal Car, Dump Truck, Pressed Steel, Lever Operated Bed, Tailgate, Steelcraft, 64 In. . . . 1880.00
Pedal Car, Fire Truck, Pontiac, Red, Wooden Ladder, Padded Seat, 1949, 45 In. . . . . *Illus* 415.00
Pedal Car, Fire Truck, Water Tower, Pump, Ladders, Keystone, 1930, 24 In. 840.00
Pedal Car, Fire Truck, Wooden Ladders, Chrome Hubs & Bell, 42 In. 470.00
Pedal Car, Good Humor Ice Cream Truck, White, Blue, Red, Murray, 1955, 36 In. . . *Illus* 880.00
Pedal Car, Jeep, Pressed Steel, Windshield, Lights, Grille, Mercury Industrial, 40 In. 205.00
Pedal Car, Locomotive, Pressed Steel, Bell, Whistle, Keystone, 1920s, 27 In. 880.00
Pedal Car, Missle, Chain Drive, Green, Red, White, Murray Atomic, c.1950, 40 In. . *Illus* 1650.00

Toy, Pedal Car, Good Humor Ice Cream Truck,
White, Blue, Red, Murray, 1955, 36 In.

Toy, Pedal Car, Missle, Chain Drive, Green, Red,
White, Murray Atomic, c.1950, 40 In.

Pedal Car, Murray Comet Super Sport, Headlights, Bumpers, Chrome Hubs, 38 In. 715.00
Pedal Car, Murray Dip Side, Red, Marked Coca-Cola Catch The Wave, 37 In. 300.00
Pedal Car, Murray Tee Bird, Blue, Steering Wheel & Hubcaps, 1961, 33 In. 200.00
Pedal Car, Murray Torpedo, Burgundy, 40 In. 475.00
Pedal Car, Murray, Comet, Hood Ornament, Chrome Hubs, Padded Seat, 37 In. 660.00
Pedal Car, Mustang, 1965 Model, Red, Junior Toy Division, AMF, 40 In. 400.00
Pedal Car, New York City Checker Cab, Pressed Steel, Studebaker, 35 In. 575.00
Pedal Car, Stamped S.A. Smith Mfg. Co., Brattleboro, Vt., 1910 .... 3500.00
Pedal Car, Steam Shovel, Pressed Steel, Wooden Handles, 14 In. 315.00
Pedal Car, Steamroller, Decals, Bell, Steerable, Pressed Steel, Keystone, 20 In. 240.00
Pedal Car, Steelcraft, Chrysler, Green, Ivory, Pleated, Rolled, Vinyl Seat, 1941, 40 In. ... 1725.00
Pedal Car, Train Engine, Pioneer Express, 28 In. 165.00
Pedal Car, Train, Engine, Metal, Keystone, c.1930, 8 x 26 x 13 In. 475.00
Pencil Box, Felix The Cat, Red, 5 1/2 x 8 1/2 In. 50.00
Piano, 7 Keys, Schoenhut, Early 20th Century, 7 x 8 1/4 In. 45.00
Piano, Upright, Natural Finish, Schoenhut, 20 In. 60.00
Piano, Upright, Yellow, Stenciled Scene Over Keyboard, Schoenhut, 10 x 15 In. 225.00
Pig, Mohair, Excelsior, Bead Eyes, Embroidered Mouth, Ear Button, Steiff, 1920, 9 In. 650.00
Pig, Pulling Man On Cart, Windup, Tin, Lehmann, Germany, 8 In. 305.00
Pig, Walker, Tin Lithograph, Windup, Chein, 4 1/2 In. 55.00
Pigeon, Pip-Squeak, Blue Wings, Sitting On Bellows, 3 1/4 In. 430.00
Pile Driver, Buddy L, Corrugated Roof, Fire Box, Buddy L, 22 1/2 In. 4700.00
Pinocchio, Plays London Bridge, Battery Operated, Rosco, TN, Japan, Box, 1962, 10 In. . 375.00
Pirate, Raises Pistol, Shoots, Vinyl Head, Battery Operated, Marusan, 8 In. 570.00
Plane, Zeppelin, Fly Around Tower, Sky Rangers, Windup, Unique Art 375.00
Planetarium, Junior, Spitz, Box, 1950, 15 In. 45.00
Play Set, Barney Google & Spark Plug, 1920s, 7-In. Barney, 8-In. Spark Plug 1500.00
Plow, Metal, Rubber Wheels, John Deere, Box, 6 3/4 In. 300.00
Police Officer, Stop & Go Street Sign, Tin Lithograph, 5 1/2 In. 120.00
Policeman, Raises Arm, Tin, Lever, Prewar Germany, 5 1/2 In. 176.00
Pool Player, Windup, Tin, Clock Work, Germany, 6 In. 480.00
Porch Set, Sofa, 2 Chairs, Wicker, Fabric Seats, 19 x 13 1/2 In. 115.00
Porky Pig, Spins Umbrella, Tin, Marx, 8 In. ....120.00 to 375.00
Porter, Black, Wagon, Red Cap, Windup, Pressed Steel, 6 1/2 In. 375.00
Porter, Pushing Wheelbarrow, 2 Ducks, Windup, G & K, 7 In. 480.00
Powerful Katrinka, Jimmy In Wheelbarrow, Windup, Tin, Fontaine Fox, 5 In. ...800.00 to 1045.00
Precursor Tank Engine, 4-4-0, Midland Red, Clockwork, Bing, Basset Lowke, 1920s 870.00
Printing Set, Daisy, Instructions, Box, 5 x 10 In. 145.00
Prize Fighters, Knock-Out, Red Mike Fights Battling Jim, Windup, Strauss, 1920s 475.00
Purse, Change, Blondie, Cookie, Red, Vinyl, Brass, c.1950, 2 3/4 x 3 3/8 In. 25.00
Puss In Boots, White, Wool, Standing, Green Glass Eyes, Black Boots, c.1915, 9 In. 325.00
Rabbit, Bounces, Ears Flop, Decamp, Windup, 11 In. 145.00
Rabbit, Pip-Squeak, White Chest, Red Eyes, Movable Ears, Leather Bellows, 4 5/8 In. ... 550.00
Rabbit, Pulling Wagon, Tin, Courtland, 12 In. 110.00
Rabbit, Sitting Playing Banjo, Windup, Musical, Celluloid, Tin, 8 In. 120.00
Rabbit, Tin Lithograph, Grey, Pink Rabbit On Back, Windup, 5 In. 45.00
Radio, Cavalcade, Bakelite Case, 8 In. 120.00
Railcar, Streamline Railway, No. 129, Tin Lithograph, Wolverine, Box, 1933 .... 495.00
Railcar, Zephyr, No. 0117, Blue, Tootsietoy, 1935, 2 1/4 In. 35.00
Record Player, Baby Cabinet, Hand Crank, Wood, Tin, 8 Records, Hegarford Mfg., 18 In. 340.00
Reindeer, Renny, Glass Eyes, Steiff, 10 In. 285.00
Reindeer, Renny, Glass Eyes, Steiff, Paper Label, 6 In. 165.00
Rifle, Land Of The Giants, Shoot'n Stick, Remco, 1969 .... 410.00
Ring, Flicker, Cowboy Shooting, Silver Plastic ....*Illus* 7.00
Road Grader, Cast Iron, Kenton, 7 3/4 In. 250.00
Road Grader, Orange, Adam's, 28 x 8 In. 110.00
Road Race, Mini-Sport, 2 Cars, Track, 2 Mechanical Hand Controls, Biller, Box, 1960 ... 85.00
Road Scraper, Highway, Tonka, 17 In. 55.00
Robot, Astronaut Rolls Forward, Windup, Tin, Japan, 7 In. 290.00
Robot, Astronaut, Tin, Walks Forward, Fires Gun, Plastic, S.H., Japan, 11 In. 60.00
Robot, Astronaut, Walks, Arms Swing, Light, Battery Operated, Japan, 8 In. 1540.00
Robot, Atom, Bump & Go, Arms Swing, Tin, Crank, Japan, 6 1/2 In. 200.00
Robot, Atomic, Windup, Walks, Swivels, Tin, Japan, 6 1/2 In. 440.00

Toy, Ring, Flicker, Cowboy
Shooting, Silver Plastic

**Don't let plastic toys or dishes touch
each other. Different types of plastic may
react to each other and be damaged.**

Robot, Aztecaser, Walks, Arms Move, Tin, Vinyl, Windup, Yonezawa, Box, 9 1/2 In.	220.00
Robot, Baby, Swinging, Windup, Tin, Japan, Box, 12 In.	440.00
Robot, Bump & Go, Arms Swing, Lights, Battery Operated, Remote, Japan, 11 In.	440.00
Robot, Bump & Go, Head Spin, Light, Tin, Battery Operated, Yonezawa, 11 In.	425.00
Robot, Bump & Go, Head Turns, Light, Noise, Tin, Battery Operated, Japan, 12 In.	440.00
Robot, Change Man, Walks, Head Splits, Tin, Battery Operated, Remote, Japan, 14 In. . . .	5940.00
Robot, Chief Robot Man, Battery Operated, Silver, K.O., Japan, 11 3/4 In.	170.00
Robot, Chief Smoky, Bump & Go, Smokes, Tin, Battery Operated, Japan, Box, 12 In. . . .	1458.00
Robot, Daipalon, Transforms, Tin, Vinyl, Windup, Bullmark, Box, 8 1/2 In.	248.00
Robot, Daitersujin, Walks, Arms Move, Tin, Vinyl, Popy, Japan, Box, 9 1/2 In.	275.00
Robot, Drummer, Remote Control, Tin, Japan, Box, c.1950, 8 1/2 In.	2750.00
Robot, Dux Astroman, Plastic, Battery Operated, Germany, Box, 11 1/2 In.	880.00
Robot, Fights On Platform, Vinyl, Windup, Japan, Box, 7 In.	138.00
Robot, Flashy Jim, Walks, Arms Move, Sparks, Windup, Tin, Japan, 8 In.	650.00
Robot, Gaikingu, Walks, Tin, Vinyl, Windup, Popy, Box, 9 In.	240.00
Robot, Getta 1, Walks, Arms Move, Tin, Vinyl, Windup, Popy, Box, 9 1/2 In.	220.00
Robot, Great Mazinga, Walks, Arms Move, Tin, Vinyl, Windup, Japan, Box, 9 1/2 In. . . .	225.00
Robot, Gurendaiza, Walks, Tin, Vinyl, Popy, Box, 9 In.	220.00
Robot, High Wheel, Box, Japan, 10 In.	550.00
Robot, High Wheel, Walks, Light, Tin, Battery Operated, Remote, Japan, Box, 9 In.	880.00
Robot, Jetmouse, Walks, Tin, Vinyl, Windup, Japan, Box, 9 1/2 In.	330.00
Robot, Jupiter, Plastic, Windup, Japan, Box, 7 1/2 In.	110.00
Robot, Lilliput, Walks, Claw Spring Hands, Windup, Tin, Japan, 6 In.	3960.00
Robot, Lost In Space, Plastic, Light In Chest, Clear Dome, Battery, Remco, 1966, 13 In. .	630.00
Robot, Mach Baron, Walks, Tin, Vinyl, Windup, Popy, Box, 9 1/2 In.	280.00
Robot, Magician, Cars, Motor Turns, Lifts Cars, Electric, Meccano, 19 x 14 x 19 In.	3960.00
Robot, Martian, Walks, Guns, Lights, Tin, Plastic, Battery Operated, Japan, Box, 9 1/2 In.	195.00
Robot, Mazinga Z, Tin, Arms Move, Vinyl, Windup, Japan, Box, 11 1/2 In.	495.00
Robot, Mighty, Walks, Flexes, Tin, Plastic, Windup, Yonezawa, Box, 19 1/2 In.	2560.00
Robot, Mighty, Windup, Tin, Japan, Box, 5 1/2 In.	90.00
Robot, Moon, Spring Motor, Robby-Style, Gray, Yonezawa, Box, 10 In.	2585.00
Robot, Moon, Walks, Sparks, Face Shield Moves, Windup, Tin, Yonezawa, Box, 11 In. . .	2530.00
Robot, Radar, Walks, Lights, Tin, Battery Operated, Remote, Japan, Box, 9 In.	1595.00
Robot, Ratchet, Walks, Sparks, Windup, Tin, Japan, 8 In.	479.00
Robot, Robby, Black, Bubble Dome, Battery Operated, TN, Japan, 13 In.	460.00
Robot, Robby, Walks, Mechanical, Tin, Yonezawa, Box, 8 1/4 In.	2420.00
Robot, Robokon, Walks, Propeller Spins, Plastic, Windup, Japan, 8 In.	120.00
Robot, Rusher, Walks, Moves On Chest, Tin, Plastic, Friction, Japan, Box, 6 In.	250.00
Robot, Secret Weapon Space Scout, Face, 6 Actions, Black, Red, Horikawa, 8 In.	805.00
Robot, Spaceman, Smoke, Walks, Light, Tin, Battery Operated, Linemar, Box, 12 In.	2035.00
Robot, Sparking, Walks, Windup, Lithograph, Japan, 7 1/2 In.	805.00
Robot, Sparky, Walks, Sparks, Tin, Friction, Yonezawa, Box, 8 In.	495.00
Robot, Super Space Giant, Tin, Plastic, Battery Operated, Box, 18 In.	385.00
Robot, Talking, 4 Sentences, Tin, Friction, Yonezawa, Box, 9 1/2 In.	1760.00
Robot, Ultraman, Arms Move, Tin, Vinyl, Windup, Japan, Box, 9 1/2 In.	550.00
Robot, Video, Walks, TV Screen, Tin, Plastic, Battery Operated, Japan, Box, 9 1/2 In. . . .	255.00
Robot, Walks, Gears Spin, Chest Spark, Plastic, Windup, Japan, 8 1/2 In.	85.00
Robot, Walks, Lights, Spins, Tin, Mechanized, Battery Operated, Japan, Box, 13 In.	990.00
Robot, Walks, Sparks, Needle Moves, Windup, Tin, Yonezawa, 10 In.	1130.00
Robot, Walks, Tin, Vinyl, Bullmark, Box, 8 1/2 In.	440.00
Robot, Windup, Tin, Walks, Antenna, S.Y., Japan, 8 1/2 In.	420.00

Robot, X-27 Explorer, Friction, Crank, Tin, Yonezawa, Box, 9 In. 7700.00
Robot, Zoomer, Blue, Silver, Walks, Eyes Light, Tin, Battery Operated, Japan, 8 In. 550.00
Robot, Zoomer, Purple, Black, Walk, Light, Tin Battery Operated, Japan, Box, 8 In. 965.00
Rocket, 3 Stage, U.S. Air Force, Tin, Plastic, Battery Operated, Japan, Box, 21 In. 495.00
Rocket, Apollo Lunar Module, Battery Operated, Tin, Plastic, Japan, Box, 6 In. 230.00
Rocket, Booster, Lights, Plastic, Friction, Battery Operated, Hong Kong, Box, 18 In. 140.00
Rocket, Bus, Tin, Friction, Japan, 13 In. 195.00
Rocket, GE-268, Sparks, Tin, Friction, U.S. Zone Germany, 9 1/2 In. 159.00
Rocket, Moon, Rises, Ladder Flips, Tin, Friction, Masuya, 16 In. 112.00
Rocket, NASA Gemini, Lights, Noise, Spins, Tin, Battery Operated, Japan, Box, 9 In. ... 330.00
Rocket, Pilot, Click Noise, Tin, Friction, Vinyl, Japan, 7 In. 99.00
Rocket, Planet Explorer, Battery Operated, Tin, Plastic, Japan, Box, 9 1/2 In. 195.00
Rocket, Robot, Jumps, Windup, Tin, Japan, 6 In. 235.00
Rocket, Solar-X, Battery Operated, Tin, Plastic, Japan, Box, 15 In. 155.00
Rocket, Space Frontier, Apollo 12, Tin, Plastic, Battery Operated, Japan, Box, 18 In. ... 145.00
Rocket, Twirls, Trains Circles Base, Windup, Tin, Bullmark, Box, 6 In. 385.00
Rocket, Twirly Whirly, Spin & Rise, Tin, Battery Operated, Alps, Box, 12 In. 798.00
Rocket, USAF Gemini X-5, Astronaut, Tin, Battery Operated, Japan, Box, 9 1/2 In. 165.00
Rocket, X-6, Moves, Tin, Friction, Japan, 4 In. 110.00
Rocket, XB115, Tin, Plastic, Friction, Harikawa, Japan, Box, 11 1/2 In. 145.00
Rocket, XY Moon Express, Tin, Friction, Japan, Box, 5 1/2 In. 730.00
Roller Coaster, Circus, Carousels, Animals, Sideshows, Tin, Mechanical, Germany, 15 In. 180.00
Roller Coaster, Coney Island, Windup, Towers, Tin Lithograph, 16 In. 240.00
Roller Skates, Buck Rogers, Pressed Steel, Streamlined Style, Marx, 10 1/2 In. 2860.00
Roller Skates, Winchester, No. 50, Double Ball Bearing, Box, 11 x 5 x 4 In. 300.00
Room Setting, French Pictures, Mirror, Clock, Fireplace, Folds, 13 x 10 x 9 In. 460.00
Room Setting, Germany, Wallpaper, Flooring, Curtains, 26 x 18 x 15 In. 920.00
Room Setting, Paintings, Clock, Fireplace, McLaughlin Bros., 12 x 17 x 10 In. 201.00
Rooster, Pip-Squeak, Papier-Mache, Painted, Gray, Orange, Red, Black, Green Base, 7 In. 130.00
Rooster, Pip-Squeak, Spring Legs, Polychromatic, 7 In. 405.00
Rooster, Pip-Squeak, White, Yellow, Orange Comb, Feathers, Cloth Bellows, 5 3/4 In. ... 275.00
Sailor, Walks, Hat Band Marked Columbia, Lehmann, 7 1/2 In. 460.00
Sailor Boy & Girl, Dancers, Blue & White Uniform, Schuco, 5 1/2 In. 315.00
Sand, Dandy Sandy Andy, Tin, Wolverine Supply, 11 In. 75.00
Sand, Teeter-Totter, Tin, 10 1/2 In. 55.00
Sand, Windmill, Tin Lithograph, Poured Sand Activates Blade, 12 In. 88.00
Sand Crane, Automatic, Tin, Wolverine, Box, 13 1/2 In. 55.00
Sand Loader, Red, Tin, Battery Operated, Electrotoy, Japan, Box, 11 In. 145.00
Sand Loader, Swings, Tin, Wolverine, Box, 11 In. 145.00
Sand Screener, Pressed Steel, Construction, Buddy L, 1920s, 22 In. 1100.00
Sandy & Yankee Tank, Metal, Wyandotte, 1930s, 14 1/2 In. 175.00
Satellite, Zooming, Windup, Tin, Gama, West Germany, Box, 12 In. 99.00
School Set, Wooden Figures, Crandall, Box, 1876, 6 x 10 In. 525.00
Science Kit, Electric, Old Stone Stock, Remco, 1950s 195.00
Scoop-N-Load, Conveyor Belt Action, Pressed Steel, Rubber Tires, Buddy L, 8 In. 160.00
Scooter, Chief Scooting Star, Pressed Steel, Labels, 1930s 325.00
Scooter, Driver, Rubber Tires, Tin, Friction, Japan, 7 1/2 In. 330.00
Scooter, Silver Pigeon, Friction, Tin, Bandai, Box, 9 In. 880.00
Scooter, Space, Astronaut, Engine, Light, Tin, Plastic, Battery Operated, Japan, Box, 9 In. 105.00
Scooter, Vespa, Blue, Tin, Friction, Bandai, 8 1/2 In. 165.00
Scuba Diver, Navy, Moves Flippers, Windup, Tin, Display Card, Chein, 12 In. 165.00
Seal, Rolls On Floor, Front Flippers, Tail Move, 7 1/2 In. 180.00
Service Station, Jaguar, Tin, Distler Of West Germany, Marx, Box, 8 1/2 In. 305.00
Service Station, Model, Wood, Esso Sign, Tin Roof, 30 x 14 In. 468.00
Service Station Set, Windup, Tin, Auto & Traffic Light, Marx, 1920s, 9 x 12 In. 2310.00
Sewing Basket, Felt, Flowers, Wood Frame, Folds, Lenci, c.1935, 10 In. 800.00
Sewing Machine, American Girl 150.00
Sewing Machine, Casige 175.00
Sewing Machine, Hand, Metal, Little Comfort, c.1920, 7 In. 170.00
Sewing Machine, Lindstrom Little Miss, Black Steel, Iron Wheel, Wooden Knob 65.00
Sewing Machine, Lindstrom, Steel, Electric, Retrofit Motor, 8 In. 22.00
Sewing Machine, Singer, Cast Iron, Electric Motor, 7 In. 66.00
Sewing Machine, Straco Electra-Matic 175.00

Sewing Machine, Wamzer, Black Paint Floral Gilt Design, Brass Label, 10 In. 230.00
Shed On Tricycle, Humphrey, Metal, Windup, Metal, Wyandotte, American, 1950s, 10 In. 495.00
Sheriff, Draws Gun & Flips Hat, Tin, Japan, Box, 8 1/2 In. 210.00
Shield, Pinback, G-Man, Celluloid, Premium Of Pep Comics, 1944 . . . . 145.00
Skillet, Cast Iron, Griswold, No. 411 . . . . 4600.00
Skip Rope, Animals, Twirl, Jump, Windup, Tin, Japan, Box, 8 In. 205.00
Sled, Bent Oak, Iron Runner, Red Paint, Victorian, 45 In. 145.00
Sled, Black & Red Paint, Gold Horseshoe, Bentwood, Iron Bracing & Trim, 56 In. 440.00
Sled, Blue Paint, Iron Runners, 19th Century, 39 x 15 In. 200.00
Sled, Boy Riding, Spins Out, Celluloid, Windup, Occupied Japan, Box, 4 In. 149.00
Sled, Child, Wood, Metal, Maroon, 33 x 12 1/2 In. 85.00
Sled, Eagle, Stars, Stripes, Red, White, Blue, 45 1/2 In. 2310.00
Sled, Iron Runners, Red Paint, England, 48 In. 495.00
Sled, Polychrome, Iron Bound Runners, Germany, 41 x 11 In. 895.00
Sled, Red Paint, Stenciled, Bird On Branch, Bentwood Hickory Runners, 34 In. 415.00
Sled, Red, Black & Gold Scrolls, Wood Sides, Iron Runners & Handrail, 49 3/4 In. 385.00
Sled, Red, Blue, Green Daisies, Wood, Iron, Oak Runners, 12 x 9 7/8 x 29 3/8 In. 470.00
Sled, Turned Rails On Side, American, 19th Century, 72 x 14 In. 115.00
Sled, Wood, Painted, Re-Enforced Scrolled Iron Runners, 33 1/2 In. 440.00
Slugger Champions, Based On Louis Schmelling Fight, Metal, Windup, 1950s 450.00
Soldier, Imperial Machine Gunner, Composition, Blue Tone, Elastolin, Germany, 5 In. . . . 69.00
Soldier, On Horses, Wooden Crank, Polychrome, 19th Century, 8 1/2 In. 4070.00
Soldier, SA Standard Bearer, Composition, Painted, Swastika Flag, Elastolin, 7 1/2 In. . . . 180.00
Soldier, Take Apart, Doepke, Wood, 1956, 9 In. 175.00
Soldier, Tin, Celluloid Head, Windup, Japan, 6 In. 50.00
Soldier, With Drum, Germany, Schuco, Windup, 5 1/2 In. . . . . .240.00 to 300.00
Soldier Of Fortune, Tin Lithograph, Marx, Box, 1930s 680.00
Soldier Set, 25 On Parade, No. 3, McLoughlin, Box 250.00
Soldier Set, Band Of Life Guards, Blue Version, Britains, c.1905, 12 Piece 3575.00
Soldier Set, Civilians, Men & Women, No. 168, Britains, Box, 8 Piece 3025.00
Soldier Set, Confederate Infantry, No. 2060, Britains, 8 Piece 29.00
Soldier Set, French Infantry, No. 215, Britains, 14 Piece 175.00
Soldier Set, German Infantry, No. 432, Britains, 8 Piece 46.00
Soldier Set, Irish Infantry, No. 1603, Britains, 7 Piece 29.00
Soldier Set, King's Royal Rifle Corps, Britains, 1953, 8 Piece 485.00
Soldier Set, Naval Landing Party, Britains, 1950s, 11 Piece 475.00
Soldier Set, Salvation Army Musicians, Red Jackets, Britains No. 1317, c.1934, 24 In. 6050.00
Soldier Set, Soldier Of Fortune Set, Tin Lithograph, Box, Marx, 1930s 675.00
Soldier Set, Soldier Of Fortune, Contents, Marx, 1940s, 8 Piece 165.00
Sonny Parcel Post, Pressed Steel, Daytona Toy & Specialty, Co., 1920, 26 In. 1760.00
Space, Whale, Black, Red, Windup, Tin, Pioneer, 9 1/2 In. 248.00
Space Capsule, Astronaut, Friendship 7, Sparks, Tin, Friction, Japan, Box, 6 1/2 In. 155.00
Space Car, Gravity, Tin, Plastic, Battery Operated, Box, 13 In. 105.00
Space Station, Planet Y, Battery Operated, Tin, Japan, Box, 9 In. 250.00
Space Station, Refuel, Tin, Rocket, Satellite, Battery Operated, Tin, Japan, Box, 14 In. . . 1870.00
Space Trooper, Battery Operated, 7 In. 750.00
Spaceman, Walks, Tin & Plastic, Battery Operated, Bandai, Box, 5 In. 85.00
Spaceship, 3 Spin Around Globe, Tin, Plastic, Lever, West Germany, 10 In. 95.00
Spaceship, Astronaut Moves, Plastic, Friction, Hong Kong, Box, c.1960, 5 In. 110.00
Spaceship, Bump & Go, Lights, Noise, Plastic, Tin, Battery Operated, Japan, Box, 8 In. . . 110.00
Spaceship, Explorer, Battery Operated, Japan, 8 In. 275.00
Spaceship, Frog, Engine Noise, Tin, Friction, Japan, Box, 7 In. 330.00
Spaceship, Mercury, Plastic, Battery Operated, Mego, Hong Kong, Box, c.1959, 8 In. 248.00
Spaceship, Sky Patrol, Tin, Plastic, Battery Operated, Japan, Box, 13 In. 275.00
Spaceship, Skyro-Plane, Kite, Plastic, Box, c.1950, 9 x 18 x 2 In. 5.00
Spaceship, UFO-X2, Tin, Plastic, Battery Operated, Japan, Box, 5 1/2 In. 85.00
Spaceship, X-15, Sparks, Tin, Crank, Japan, 6 In. 110.00
Spaceship, Z-26, Astronaut, Tin, Friction, Japan, 6 In. 165.00
Sparkler, Felix The Cat, Tin, Push Handle, Pat Sullivan, c.1920, 5 In. 222.00
Sparkler, Fireman, Sparks, Tin, Japan, Bag, 5 1/2 In. 145.00
Sparkler, Old Witch, Tin, Range Steel Products, New York, Box, 6 In. 215.00
Speedway, Cars, Windup, Tin, McDowell, Box, 14 In. 415.00
Speedy Boy Delivery, Windup, Tin, Electric Headlight & Taillight, Marx, 10 In. 550.00

Spreader, Metal, Rubber Wheels, John Deere, Box, 10 1/4 In. 176.00
Squirrel, Black Glass Eyes, Long Bushy Tail, Steiff, 6 3/4 In. 36.00
Squirrel, Runs In Cage, Le Petit Ecureuil Vivan, Windup, Martin, France, Box, 1908 . . . . 1450.00
Stagecoach, Cowboys, Indians, Brakes, Brake Handle, Tin Lithograph, 12 In. 195.00
Stagecoach, Pull Toy, Paper Lithograph, Wooden, Fisher-Price, 15 x 8 3/4 In. 690.00
Stagecoach, Women, Dog Move, Windup, Tin, Germany, 1907, 6 In. 1540.00
Steam Accessory, Bandsaw, Black, Gold, Cast Iron, Blade, 6 3/4 In. 470.00
Steam Accessory, Drill Press, Black, Gold, Bing, 9 In. 495.00
Steam Accessory, Grindstone, Cast Iron, 6 In. 330.00
Steam Accessory, Lathe, Black, Cast Iron, 8 In. 470.00
Steam Accessory, Lathe, Black, Gold, Marklin, 4 1/2 In. 155.00
Steam Engine, Accessories, Instructions, Weeden, No. 500, 11 In. . . . . .350.00 to 425.00
Steam Engine, Bing, Tin, Enameling, Brass Boiler, Bavaria, 9 x 9 1/2 x 14 1/2 In. 110.00
Steam Engine, Cast Iron Base, Vertical, No. 57, Weeden, 12 In. 550.00
Steam Engine, Holly, Buckman, c.1886, 10 In. 415.00
Steam Engine, Marklin, Germany, 21 1/2 In. 4400.00
Steam Engine, Uranus, No. 13264, Bing, c.1902, 11 In. 2090.00
Steam Engine, Vertical, Bing, 14 1/2 In. 305.00
Steam Engine, Vertical, Marklin, Model 4112/14, 21 1/2 In. 4400.00
Steam Engine, Vertical, No. 354, Cast Iron Base, Doll, 13 1/4 In. 275.00
Steam Shovel, On Tracks, Buddy L, 24 In. 630.00
Steam Shovel, Pressed Steel, Loading Ramp, Steam Shovel, 1940s, 18 In. 180.00
Steam Shovel, Pressed Steel, Steelcraft, 25 In. 58.00
Steam Shovel, Red, Wood, Handmade, 23 In. 28.00
Steamroller, Driver, Cast Iron, Huber, Hubley, 8 In. 295.00
Steamroller, No. 644, Weeden, 10 1/2 In. 440.00
Steamroller, Pressed Steel, Keystone, 1920s, 20 In. 180.00
Steamroller, Red, Clockwork, Tin Lithograph, Germany, 13 In. 120.00
Steamroller, S.R. 1, Mamod, Box, 10 In. 120.00
Stencil Set, Felix The Cat, Smoking Pipe, Box, c.1920, 5 1/2 x 7 x 3/4 In. 80.00
Stove, Arcade, Burners, Grates, Cast Iron, Decal, 6 In. 465.00
Stove, Baby Hazel, Cast Iron, Nickel, Rome Stove & Range Co., c.1910, 15 x 17 In. 7480.00
Stove, Baby, Embossed Leaves, Cast Iron, 6 Burners, Ives Toy Co., 9 x 15 x 7 In. 690.00
Stove, Cast Iron, Flattop, Charter Oak, No. 503, 1885, 25 x 12 x 14 In. 460.00
Stove, Cast Iron, Nickel Plated, Ornately Decorated, 4 Pots, Acme, 11 1/4 In. 110.00
Stove, Charter Oak, Cast Iron, Removable Hearth Plate, G.F. Filley, c.1885, 14 x 12 In. . . 578.00
Stove, Cotton Plant, Cast Iron, Paneled Burners, Abendroth Brothers, c.1880, 9 x 12 In. . . 2200.00
Stove, Crescent, Embossed Moon & Star, Cast Nickel, c.1900, 12 x 13 x 6 In. 2090.00
Stove, Eagle, Cast Iron, 11 In. 61.00
Stove, Eagle, Cast Iron, Pan, Pot, Coal Bucket, Lid Handle, 10 1/2 x 11 1/2 x 5 1/4 In. . . . 275.00
Stove, Eagle, Nickel Plated, Fretwork, Lancaster Brand, c.1890, 22 x 23 In. 1320.00
Stove, Eclipse, Gas Range, Black Steel, Porcelain, Tappan Stove Co., c.1935, 17 x 16 In. . . 1650.00
Stove, Globe, Cast Nickel Plated, Elaborately Embossed, Kenton, c.1900, 18 x 23 x 9 In. . . 1980.00
Stove, Ideal No. 5, Cast Iron, 6 Burners, Embossed Scrolls, c.1895, 16 x 10 In. 1650.00
Stove, Lionel, Chrome, Baked Enamel, Cream, Green & Black, Winking Chef, 33 x 26 In. . 2750.00
Stove, Little Chef, Electric, Yellow, Aluminum, Decal, American c.1950, 11 In. . . . . . . *Illus* 99.00
Stove, Little Willie, Cast Iron, 4 Burners, Abbott & Noble, c.1885, 8 x 9 In. 935.00

Toy, Stove, Little Chef, Electric, Yellow,
Aluminum, Decal, American c.1950, 11 In.

Toy, Stove, Rival, Nickel-Plated Cast Iron,
J. & E. Stevens, American, 1895, 13 In.

Toy, Stove, Tin, Embossed,
Copper Utensils, Claw Feet,
Germany, c.1890, 16 In.

Toy, Stove, Tin,
Cookware, Embossed,
Red & Blue Paint, Bowls,
Germany, c.1910, 11 In.

Stove, Mechanic, Cast Iron, 3-Step Style, Embossed, P & G Brecher, 1860, 6 x 8 x 12 In. .	660.00
Stove, Midget, Cast Iron, Sheet Metal, Art Nouveau, Belleville Stove Works, 12 In.	9900.00
Stove, Nickel Plated, Enamel Door Ovens, Porcelain Knobs, Electric, c.1925, 15 x 19 In. .	55.00
Stove, Nickel Plated, Victorian, Embossed, 25 x 20 x 9 In.	575.00
Stove, Potbelly, Cast Iron, 13 1/2 In.	138.00
Stove, Qualified Range, Blue Enamel, Nickel Plated, 21 x 12 x 8 In.	4840.00
Stove, Rival, Nickel-Plated Cast Iron, J. & E. Stevens, American, 1895, 13 In. ...... *Illus*	3080.00
Stove, Ruby, Embossed Wildflowers, Beaded Edges, J. & E. Stevens, c.1890, 4 1/2 x 7 In.	358.00
Stove, Tin, Cookware, Embossed, Red, Blue Paint, Bowls, Germany, c.1910, 11 In. . *Illus*	248.00
Stove, Tin, Embossed, Copper Utensils, Claw Feet, Germany, c.1890, 16 In. .... *Illus*	2420.00
Stove, Tin, Turquoise, Embossed Bricks, Nickel-Plated Cookware, JEP, France, 10 In. ...	1045.00
Stove, Tiny Tot, Cast Iron, Embossed Girl, Cylindrical, Fatsco, c.1890, 12 In.	635.00
Stove, Triumph Range, Cast Iron, Nickel Plated, 3 Pots, Gallery, Pipe, 16 In.	605.00
Stratowagon, Rocket Ship Design, Tin, Wyandotte, Box, 6 In.	265.00
Streetcar, Dayton, 15 In.	350.00
Streetcar, Push, Penny Toy, 3 In.	30.00
Stroller, Baby, Plastic, Box, 3 1/2 In.	60.00
Stroller, Doll's, Victorian, Wicker, Natural, Metal Wheels, 36 In.	259.00
Stroller, Doll's, Wicker, Curved Sides, 4 Wheels, Spokes, Metal, American, c.1890, 33 In.	525.00
Stroller, Doll's, Wicker, Rubber Wheels, Gray, 28 In.	98.00
Submarine, Diving, Windup, Tin, Wolverine, Box, 13 In.	140.00
Submarine, Diving, Wyandotte, 15 In.	295.00
Submarine, Tin Lithograph, Windup, Wolverine, Box, 1950s, 13 1/2 In. ....130.00 to	145.00
Submarine, Tin, Marklin, 16 In.	990.00
Supermarket, Shelves Fold Out, Accessories, Tin, Wolverine, c.1930, 12 x 30 In.	730.00
Surrey, Driver, Woman Passenger, Cast Iron, Kenton, 12 1/2 In.	550.00
Surrey, Horse Drawn, Passenger, Red Wheels, Cast Iron, Nickel Plated, 13 1/2 x 5 1/2 In.	750.00
Suspenders, Captain Marvel, Mint On Card	550.00
Susy Bouncing Ball, Windup, Tin Lithograph, Japan, Box	395.00
Swing, Doll's, Suspended Rocking Chair, Swing Frame, Wood, 29 In.	316.00
Swing, Wicker Wrapped, 24 In.	85.00
Tank, 964, Tin Lithograph, Windup, Gama, Box, 4 3/4 x 2 3/4 x 2 1/2 In.	80.00
Tank, Army, Windup, Tin, 8 In.	259.00
Tank, Camouflage, Electric, Tin, Rubber, France, 17 1/2 In.	230.00
Tank, Camouflaged, Sparks, Windup, Tin, Yonezawa, Occupied Japan, Box, 5 In.	330.00
Tank, Crusader, Tin Lithograph, Battery Operated, Great Britain, Box, 8 1/2 In.	35.00
Tank, Die Cast, Turning Turret, Dinky Toys, 3 1/2 In.	35.00
Tank, Dual Control, Arnold, Germany, 1950s, 7 In.	240.00
Tank, Flintstone Turnover, Windup, Tin, Linemar, 1950s, 4 In.	550.00
Tank, Flips, Windup, Tin, Marx, Box, 4 In.	100.00
Tank, Gama, Tin, Rubber, Windup, Germany, Box, 5 1/2 In.	99.00
Tank, Gama, Tin, Rubber, Windup, Germany, Box, 8 In.	190.00
Tank, Gun Sparks, Soldier Moves, Windup, Tin, Marx, Box, 10 In.	495.00
Tank, Gun Turrets, Friction Wood Wheels, Tin Lithograph, Japan, 6 1/4 In.	50.00
Tank, M-35, Soldier, Tin, Battery Operated, Linemar, 9 In.	65.00
Tank, MF-721, Tin, Friction, 6 In.	10.00
Tank, Military, Tin, Rubber, Windup, Gama, 8 In.	39.00
Tank, Missile, Green, Tin, Plastic, Battery Operated, Japan, Box, 9 In.	66.00
Tank, Panther, Windup, Key, Germany, 7 In.	295.00

Tank, Planet Patrol, Blue, Windup, Tin, Marx, Box, 10 In. 440.00
Tank, Rollover, Windup, Tin, Marx, 4 In. 45.00
Tank, Sandy & Yankee, Heavy Metal Gauge, Wyandotte, 1930s, 14 1/2 In. 175.00
Tank, Space, Advances, Guns Fire, Robot Driver, Tin, Friction, Japan, Box, 9 In. 690.00
Tank, Tin, Germany, Box, 5 1/2 In. 160.00
Tank, Tin, Rubber, Windup, Gama, Box, 5 1/2 In. 75.00
Tank, U.S. Tank Division, Gun Firing, Tin, Rubber, Windup, Marx, 11 In. 110.00
Tank, U.S. Tank Division, Gun Noise, Sparks, Tin, Plastic, Marx, Box, 7 1/2 In. 116.00
Tank, Wonder Sparking Tank, Windup, Japan, Box, 1930s, 3 In. 125.00
Tank Car, Railroad, Pressed Steel Outdoor, Buddy L, 18 In. 385.00
Tanker, Pressed Steel, Tractor, Plastic Trailer Tanker, Tonka, 1960s, 28 In. 300.00
Tap Dancer, Black Man, Street Sign, Windup, Tin, Box, Alps, Occupied Japan, 9 In. 336.00
Tarzan, King Of Jungle, Battery Operated, Remote Control, Marusan, Box, 13 1/2 In. 1495.00
Taxi, Amos 'n' Andy, Windup, Tin Lithograph, 1932, 8 1/2 In. . . . . *Illus* 660.00
Taxi, Amos 'n' Andy, Windup, Tin, Eccentric Shaking & Rolling, Correll & Gosden, 8 In. 200.00
Taxi, Amos 'n' Andy, Windup, Tin, Marx, Box, 1930, 11 In. 3355.00
Taxi, Clockwork Yell-O, No. 59, Driver, Tin Lithograph, c.1919, 8 1/2 In. 1050.00
Taxi, Coin, Red, Tin, Plastic, Battery Operated, Japan, 7 In. 35.00
Taxi, Girl Shifts Gear, Tin, Vinyl, Windup, Remote, Schuco, West Germany, Box, 9 1/2 In. 585.00
Taxi, Red Top Cab, Cast Iron, Arcade, 8 In. 495.00
Taxi, Tin Lithograph, Windup, Chein, 6 In. 45.00
Taxi, Yellow Cab, Cast Iron, Driver, Dent, 8 1/4 In. 385.00
Taxi, Yellow Cab, Cast Iron, License Plate 330, Arcade, 8 1/4 In. . . . . .1045.00 to 2530.00
Taxi, Yellow Cab, Cast Iron, Rubber Tires, Spare, Arcade, 5 1/4 In. 590.00
Taxi, Yellow Cab, Thompson Transportation On Door, Arcade, 7 1/4 x 4 1/2 In. 2655.00
Taxi, Yellow Cab, With Driver, Arcade, 9 In. 750.00
Taxi, Yellow, Tin, Friction, Japan, Box, 7 1/2 In. 135.00
Taxi, Yellow, Tin, Friction, Marusan, Japan, 1954, 10 In. 630.00
Tea Set, Barbie, Plastic Plates, Teacups, Sugar & Creamer, Spoons, Forks, Knives, 1961 . 55.00
Tea Set, Little Hostess, China, Made In Japan, Box, 9 x 12 In. 165.00
Tea Set, Molded Googly Face Cups, Green Saucers, No. 113/45, Japan, 1930s 380.00
Tea Set, Smurf, Plastic, Worcester Toy Corp., Box, 1981 . . . . 30.00
Tea Set, Soft Paste, Blue Feather, 4 1/2-In. Teapot, 7 Piece 635.00
Teddy Bears are listed in the Teddy Bear category.
Theater, Comic, Tin, Revolving Paper Roll, Box, 11 In. 310.00
Theater, Fairy Tales, Les Contes Des Fees, Chez Pintard, c.1820, 7 1/8 x 5 In., 30 Pieces . 4500.00
Tool Set, Boy's Union Tool Chest, Wood, Box, Bliss 7 1/2 x 20 In. 265.00
Toonerville Trolley, Erratic Motion, Maker's Box, Nifty 1175.00
Toonerville Trolley, No. 280098, Windup, Tin, Fontaine Fox, c.1922, 6 5/8 x 5 In. .688.00 to 695.00
Tootsietoy Set, Autos, Trucks, Airplane, Box, 8 x 12 In. 165.00
Top, Choral, Animal Orchestra Lithograph, Chords Play When Spinning, Box, 1950s, 9 In. 85.00
Top, Dancing Ballerina, Tin Lithograph, 5 1/2 In. 65.00
Top, Tin Lithograph, Maerklin, Germany, Box, c.1900, 7 x 3 In., 4 Piece 50.00
Tractor, Arcade No. 274 Fordson, Green & Red Paint, 1928, 4 3/4 In. 210.00
Tractor, Climbing, Driver, Red, Yellow, Tin Lithograph, Mechanical, Marx, Box, c.1948 . 495.00
Tractor, Farmer Driver, Windup, Tin, Courtland Toy, Box, 6 In. 176.00
Tractor, Fordson No. 273, Driver, Gray, Red Lug Wheels, Cast Iron, Arcade, 1923, 4 In. . 175.00
Tractor, Fordson, Driver, Iron, Nickel Plated, Arcade, 5 1/2 In. 105.00
Tractor, Hessmobil, Tin, Crank, Sanko, Japan, Box, 1930s, 11 In. 300.00

Toy, Taxi, Amos 'n' Andy,
Windup, Tin Lithograph,
1932, 8 1/2 In.

**If the batteries in a battery toy
have corroded, remove them and
rub an emery board or 0000
steel wool on the contact points.
Then put new batteries in the
toy and it should work.**

Tractor, John Deere, Metal, Rubber Wheels, Box, 8 In. 415.00
Tractor, Yellow, Accessories, Tin, Friction, Marusan, Box, 6 In. 95.00
Trailer, Vacationers No. 3, Car, Tin, Friction, Japan, Box, 9 3/4 In. 220.00
Train, Billy Loco, Blue, Red, Plastic, Battery Operated, Japan, Box, 7 In. 6.00
Train, Bing, 2B Clockwork Locomotive 800.00
Train, Buddy L, Engine & Tender, Outdoor Railway Train, On Track Section, 1927 ..... 1100.00
Train, Buddy L, Industrial, Locomotive, Coal Rack, Stake, Rocker Dump, Tracks, 50 In. . 825.00
Train, Buddy L, Roundhouse, 3 Sections, Switches, Tracks, Rocker Dump, 33 In. 2820.00
Train, Bullet Nose, Tin, Friction, Ichiko, Box, 19 In. 149.00
Train, Car Hopper, Buddy L Outdoor, 22 In. 220.00
Train, Engine, 2 Tenders, Passenger Cars, Caboose, Wood, Tin, Found Objects, 12 x 41 In. 330.00
Train, Floor, Locomotive, Passenger, Observation, Cast Iron, 36 In. 190.00
Train, Hobo, Dog Bites Seat Of Hobo, Train Moves, Windup, Unique Art, 1930s . .425.00 to 550.00
Train, Hornby, No. 501, Windup, Tin, Key, Box, 1930s 1200.00
Train, Ives & Blaklee, Locomotive, 287 Tender, CPRR Freight, Cast Iron, Windup, 18 In. 3500.00
Train, Jetsons, Linemar, 12 In. 475.00
Train, Kemtron, Locomotive, Tender, Brass, Track, 15 In. 410.00
Train, Lionel, Freight, Lumber, Baby Ruth, Crane, 2 Tanks, Caboose, Hopper 235.00
Train, Lionel, Locomotive, No. 390E, Coal Car, Caboose, 13 In. 490.00
Train, Lionel, Locomotive, No. 2026, Tender, 3 Plastic Cars, 9 In. 145.00
Train, Lionel, Locomotive, No. 2333-20, Santa Fe, Silver, Red, O Gauge, Box, 3 x 13 In. . 545.00
Train, Lionel, New York Central Lines, 150, O Gauge, Track, Electric, 6 In. 165.00
Train, Lionel, Pullman Car, Manhattan, No. 2628, O Gauge, Box, 1948, 3 1/4 x 14 1/2 In. 460.00
Train, Locomotive & Coach, Lithograph, 4 Wheels, Passenger, Penny Toy, Germany 145.00
Train, Locomotive & Tender, Red, Black, Lithograph, Lead Wheels, Germany 149.00
Train, Locomotive, Ernst Plank, Steam, Cab, Tender, Coach 1020.00
Train, Locomotive, Red, Green, Cowcatcher, Clockwork, Lithograph, Germany 385.00
Train, Locomotive, Steam, The Victor, Maroon Livery, Large Gauge 1650.00
Train, Locomotive, Tender, Wood, Green, Black, Red Trim, Cast Iron Wheels, 31 x 11 In. 525.00
Train, Marklin, Coupe Vent Clockwork, Tender, Painted 11220.00
Train, Marklin, Locomotive & Tender, Clockwork, 4 Wheels, No. 1 Gauge 770.00
Train, Marklin, Windup, 5 Cars, Gebrauchs Muster, Germany, 8-In. Engine 4400.00
Train, Marklin, Zeppelin, Electric Rail, O Gauge, Red Prop, No. SZ1297 .... 798.00
Train, Military, Push Toy, Japan, 1933, 13 In. 250.00
Train, Pennsylvania, Tin, Friction, Japan, Box, 10 1/2 In. 88.00
Train, Rail Car, Penny Toy, 1 In. 65.00
Train, Ranger, Locomotive, O Gauge, Sweden, Box, 8 1/2 In. 411.00
Train, Swiss Railways, Passenger, Green, Silver, Tracks, Signed, 38 In. 294.00
Train, Tasty Food, Locomotive, Tin, 3 Cars, Limited Brand Coffee, 50 In. 467.00
Train, Tin, Red, Black, Lithograph, Removable Roof On Baggage, Pullman Car, 15 1/2 In. 468.00
Train Accessory, American Flyer, Crossing Signals, Signal Tower, 5 Piece 70.00
Train Accessory, Bassett-Lowke, Depot, World War II Goods, Wood, Tin Signs, 13 In. 105.00
Train Accessory, Bing, Kiosk, Newspaper, Zeitungen, No. 1 Gauge, White, Red 165.00
Train Accessory, Bing, Semaphore, Red, White, Dual, No. 1 Gauge 99.00
Train Accessory, Bing, Signal Tower, Twin, Painted, Oil Pots, 16 In. 248.00
Train Accessory, Destination Board, Yellow, Brown, City Signs, Germany 190.00
Train Accessory, Hornby Series, Station, No. 2, Red, Blue, White Fence, Wooden Box ... 305.00
Train Accessory, Ives, Station, Union, Wood Poles, Glass Dome Canopy 1430.00
Train Accessory, Lighthouse Shines, Tin, Battery Operated, Japan, Box, 7 1/2 In. 415.00
Train Accessory, Lionel, Passenger Station, No. 115, Box 506.00
Train Accessory, Marklin, Railway Crossing, No. 2192 .... 400.00
Train Accessory, Marklin, Station, English Country, Side Ramps, 2 Signs, No. 2846 ..... 6600.00
Train Accessory, Marklin, Station, Painted, Candlelit, Side Ramps, 2 Signs, England 6600.00
Train Accessory, Marklin, Ticket Dispenser, White, 8 In. 88.00
Train Accessory, Marx, Station, Universal Freight, Crossing Gate, Tin, Box, 12 In. 175.00
Train Accessory, Shed, Steam Engine, Tin Lithograph, Friction, D.R. Patent, 5 3/4 In. 330.00
Train Accessory, Station, Tin Lithograph, 10 3/4 x 9 In. 300.00
Train Accessory, Station, Tin, Painted, Electric Lights, 9 x 4 In. 410.00
Train Accessory, Tunnels, Buildings, Windup, Tin, Germany, 10 1/2 In. 300.00
Train Car, Barrel, Flat Car, Gargoyle, BP, BMX, Barrels, O Gauge 330.00
Train Car, Bing, Baggage, 8 Wheels, Hinged Roof, Lithograph, O Gauge 70.00
Train Car, Bing, Boxcar, Green, Open Door, No. 2 Gauge 145.00
Train Car, Bing, Freight, Yellow, Jamaica Banana, Guardhouse, No. 1992 .... 330.00

Train Car, Bing, Stock, Cattle, Brown, No. 2 Gauge 80.00
Train Car, Bowman, Coach, No. 550, Brown, White, 12 Doors, Wooden Box, 16 In. 230.00
Train Car, Buddy L, Side Dump Ballast, No. 70836, Twin Compartments, 10 In. 2700.00
Train Car, Buddy L, Steam Shovel, No. 1023, Hand Operated Windlass, Shovel, 22 1/2 In. 530.00
Train Car, Buddy L, Wrecking Crane, No. 1020, Corrugated Roof, Firebox, 22 1/2 In. ... 2235.00
Train Car, Engine, L.M.S.R. Royal Scot, Tin Lithograph Cutout, 1928, 4 1/2 In. .... *Illus* 25.00
Train Car, Engine, L.N.E.R. Flying Scotsman, Tin Lithograph Cutout, 1927, 4 1/2 In. *Illus* 25.00
Train Car, Ernst Plank, Engine, Vertical Hot Air, 21 In. 4620.00
Train Car, Fandor, Illinois Central, 4 Wheels, Box 99.00
Train Car, KBN, Bayr Bier Transport AG, Munchen, Kulmbach, Nuremberg 200.00
Train Car, Lionel, Dining Car, Hinged Roof, No. 431, Standard Gauge 2530.00
Train Car, Lionel, Metropolitan Express Boxcar, Barred Windows, No. 800, 1904-1905 .. 7150.00
Train Car, Locomotive, Ives, No. 3241, 1925 .... 4290.00
Train Car, Locomotive, Steam, Penny Toy, 3 In. 185.00
Train Car, Marklin, Baggage, Blue, Gold, No. 1 Gauge, Coluzzi, Fulgurex 300.00
Train Car, Marklin, Carrier, Log, Gray, Black, No. 1 Gauge 145.00
Train Car, Marklin, Combination, No. 1895, Postal, Passenger, 3 Figures, No. 1 Gauge ... 220.00
Train Car, Marklin, Freight, Stake, Red, Black, No. 1772 .... 35.00
Train Car, Marklin, Open Passenger Car, Painted, Yellow, Blue Curtains, Black Roof, 5 In. 1540.00
Train Car, Marklin, Passenger, Green, Red, No. 1888, Hinged Roof 275.00
Train Car, Marklin, Tip, Brown, Orange, No. 1 Gauge 120.00
Train Car, Stock Car, Pressed Steel, Buddy L Outdoor, 1920s, 21 In. 605.00
Train Car, Tank Car, Buddy L Outdoor, 20 In. 385.00
Train Set, American Flyer, Clockwork Powered, Box, c.1923 .... 415.00
Train Set, American Flyer, No. 20610, The Dispatcher, S-Gauge, Box, 5 Piece 285.00
Train Set, American Flyer, President's Special, 5 Piece 10350.00
Train Set, Buddy L, Industrial, 6 Cars, Cast Iron Wheels, 45 In. 480.00
Train Set, Buddy L, Industrial, Pressed Steel, Locomotive, 5 Cars, Track, 1920s 2090.00
Train Set, Ives, Parlor, Chair, Baggage, Stake Bed Cars, Tracks, Box 520.00
Train Set, KTM, Locomotive, Tender, Brass, Track, Japan, 12 1/2 In. 410.00
Train Set, KTM, Santa Fe Northern, Locomotive, Tender, O Gauge, Japan, Box, 28 In. 940.00
Train Set, Lionel, Electric, Union Pacific, 39 In., 4 Piece 1045.00
Train Set, Lionel, Locomotive, Tender, No. 249E, Tank, Coal, Lumber Cars, Box 990.00
Train Set, Lionel, Locomotive, Tender, Passenger, Parlor, Observation Cars 1650.00
Train Set, Lionel, No. 11600,027 Steam Freight, 7 Cars, Box, 1968 .... 3410.00
Train Set, Lionel, State Set, Standard Gauge, Brown, 1932 ....11000.00
Train Set, Marx, Sears, Allstate Electric, Box, 1950s 150.00
Tricycle, Boy, Bell Noise, Tin, Vinyl, Plastic, Windup, Japan, Box, 5 In. 110.00
Tricycle, Flintstones, Barney Rides Tricycle, Windup, Box 495.00
Tricycle, Flintstones, Wilma Peddles, Tin, Celluloid, Marx, Hanna-Barbera, Box, 4 1/2 In. 550.00
Tricycle, Patrol, Police, Driver, Tin Lithograph, Battery Operated, Nomura, Box, c.1950 .. 795.00
Tricycle, Police, Bump & Go, Lights, Noise, Tin, Battery Operated, Japan, Box, 9 In. 441.00
Tricycle, Robbie, Tin, Vinyl Robot, Japan, 4 1/2 In. 303.00
Tricycle, Superhero, Tin, Vinyl, Windup, Japan, Box, 4 1/2 In. 468.00
Trolley, Kingsbury, 14 In. 395.00
Trolley, Metal, Germany, c.1900, 10 In. 495.00
Trolley, No. 45 Streetcar, Bell Ringer, Friction, Tin 400.00
Trolley, Open, Tin, Alps, Japan, 10 In. 195.00
Trolley, Pressed Steel, Friction, Dayton, 1930s, 16 In. 140.00
Trolley, Tin Lithograph, Clockwork Motor, Doors Open, Operator, Germany, 13 In. 1100.00
Trolley, Tin, Embossed, Side Doors, Bell Rings, Trolley Reverses, Germany, 9 In. 144.00

Toy, Train Car, Engine, L.M.S.R. Royal Scot,
Tin Lithograph Cutout, 1928, 4 1/2 In.

Toy, Train Car, Engine, L.N.E.R. Flying Scotsman,
Tin Lithograph Cutout, 1927, 4 1/2 In.

Trolley, Windows Open, Penny Toy, 4 In. 55.00
Truck, 3 Wheels, Yellow, Tin, Friction, Marusan, 6 In. 550.00
Truck, A.C.E., Doors Open, Tin, Momentum, Marx, c.1950, 22 In. 255.00
Truck, Aerial Ladder, Mack, Red, Smith-Miller, 1953, 35 In. 675.00
Truck, Aerial Ladder, Pressed Steel, Buddy L, 39 In. 765.00
Truck, Airport Lift, Metal, Friction, Japan, 1950s, 14 In. 295.00
Truck, Airport Mail, Tractor, Trailer, Airplane Decals, Structo, 1920s, 23 In. 770.00
Truck, Allied Van Lines, Little Beaver, Canada, 1950s 595.00
Truck, Allied Van Lines, Steel Trailer, Die Cast, B Model, Smith-Miller, 38 In. 1155.00
Truck, Allied Van, Pressed Steel, Tonka, 1960s, 24 In. 220.00
Truck, American Railway Express, Pressed Steel, Keystone, 26 In. 745.00
Truck, Anti-Aircraft, Plane Overhead, Windup, Tin, Alps, Box, 5 1/2 In. 2450.00
Truck, Army, Covered, Tin, Canvas, Friction, Marx, 5 1/2 In. 220.00
Truck, Army, Mack, Steerable, Decals, Steelcraft, 1927, 24 In. 2000.00
Truck, Army, Packard, Steel, Canvas, Keystone, c.1920, 27 In. 1210.00
Truck, Army, Personnel Carrier, Removable Roof, Metal, Rubber, Britains, 5 In. 90.00
Truck, Army, Pressed Steel, Army Bulldog, Steelcraft, 1930s, 23 In. 330.00
Truck, Army, Pressed Steel, Disk Wheels, Sonny, 1920s, 24 In. 275.00
Truck, Army, Pressed Steel, Marx, 10 In. 250.00
Truck, Army, Pressed Steel, Searchlight Trailer, Marx, 1950s, 32 In. 130.00
Truck, Army, Search Light, 3 Soldiers, Windup, Box, Wells Of London, 1940s, 9 In. 485.00
Truck, Army, Tin, Bulldog Mack, Chein, 1920s, 20 In. 330.00
Truck, Army, Truck & Trailer, Canvas Covered, Buddy L, 1930s, 32 In. 198.00
Truck, B Model, Cleveland Wrecking, Wood & Aluminum Trailer, Smith-Miller, 36 In. . . 1430.00
Truck, Baggage, Buddy L, 26 1/2 In. 880.00
Truck, Bank Of America, Cab Over, Die Cast, Smith-Miller, 1940s, 14 In. 300.00
Truck, Bedford Fire, Red, 1960s, 8 1/2 In. 125.00
Truck, Big Metal, Marx, 1950s, 20 In. 120.00
Truck, Blue Diamond Cement Mixer, Pressed Steel, Model D, Smith-Miller 3960.00
Truck, Bonner Ice Cream, 9 In. 75.00
Truck, Borden's Ice Cream, Japan, 1955, 6 In. 375.00
Truck, Bus, Green, Steel, Aluminum, Buddy L, c.1920, 29 In. 3850.00
Truck, Camtoy Lorrie, Windup, Tin, England, 1950s, 6 1/2 In. 175.00
Truck, Cannon, No. 2400, Green Yellow Decals, Battery, Radar, Ny-Lint, 23 In. 125.00
Truck, Cannon, Steel, Clockwork Motor, Missiles, Kingsbury, c.1940, 15 1/2 In. 145.00
Truck, Cannon, Tin, Composition Soldiers, Tipp, Germany, 11 In. 415.00
Truck, Car Carrier, 2 Plastic Cars, Box, SSS, Japan, 1950s, 7 In. 125.00
Truck, Car Carrier, 3 Cars, 4 Piece, USA Structo, 1950s 195.00
Truck, Car Carrier, 9 Cars, Metal, Friction, Japan, 1950s, 24 In. 345.00
Truck, Car Carrier, 12 Cars, Plastic, Metal, Japan, Box, 1960s, 19 In. 295.00
Truck, Car Carrier, 3 Austin Coupes, Cast Iron, A.C. Williams, 12 1/2 In. 410.00
Truck, Car Carrier, 3 Cars, Cast Iron, Hubley, 15 1/2 In. 770.00
Truck, Car Carrier, Cars, Tin, Wyandotte, 8 1/2 In. 95.00
Truck, Car Carrier, Trailer, 2 Sedans, 1 Coupe, Cast Iron, Arcade, 19 In. 1155.00
Truck, Car Carrier, White Rubber Tires, 2 Cars, Cast Iron, Hubley, 10 In. 385.00
Truck, Cargo Liner, All-American Toy Co., 38 In. 2200.00
Truck, Carnival Ride, Kids Spin, Tin, Friction, Japan, 7 In. 95.00
Truck, Cattle, Metal, Marx, 14 In. 75.00
Truck, Cattle, Trailer, Wyandotte, 1950s, 22 1/2 In. 65.00
Truck, Cement Mixer, Buddy L, 16 In. 1320.00
Truck, Cement Mixer, Buddy L, 1920s, 18 In. 275.00
Truck, Cement Mixer, Buddy L, 24 In. 750.00
Truck, Cement Mixer, D Model, Blue Diamond, Die Cast, Steel, Smith-Miller, 21 In. 3960.00
Truck, Cement Mixer, Pressed Steel, Hood Opens, Structo, 23 In. 70.00
Truck, Cement Mixer, Tin, Painted, Girard, 8 In. 190.00
Truck, Circus Bandwagon, Drum Player, Tin, Friction, Japan, 8 In. 110.00
Truck, Circus, Lion In Cage Moves, Tin, Friction, Linemar, 5 1/2 In. 99.00
Truck, Circus, Managerie, Lions Seesaw, Tin, Friction, Japan, 10 In. 250.00
Truck, Circus, Menagerie, Friction, Box, 9 1/2 In. 415.00
Truck, Circus, Trailer, Steel, Wyandotte, c.1940, 20 In. 525.00
Truck, Cities Service, Litchfield Oil Co., Cast Metal, Green Paint, Decals, 4 1/2 In. 176.00
Truck, City Sanitation Dept., Marx, 13 In. 110.00
Truck, Civilian Defense, Cannon, Tin Lithograph, Mechanical, Marx, Box, c.1952, 13 In. . 400.00

Truck, Coal, Driver Iron Spoke Wheels, Lever Activated, Kenton, 8 1/2 In. 690.00
Truck, Coal, Pressed Steel, Front Crank Noisemaker, American National, 1920s, 27 In. . . .   9020.00
Truck, Continental Express, Fast Freight, Yellow, Blue, Tin, Friction, Japan, 14 In. 70.00
Truck, Corvair, Bakery, 9 In. 225.00
Truck, Courtland Fire, Red, Windup, 1960s, 9 In. 40.00
Truck, Crane, Red & Yellow Paint, Sturdi-Bilt, 1950s, 23 In. 5170.00
Truck, Delivery, 2 Horses, Tin Lithograph, Converse, 18 In. 235.00
Truck, Delivery, Cast Iron, J.L. Hudson, c.1960, 8 In. 290.00
Truck, Delivery, Hillclimber, Green, Friction, 12 In. 265.00
Truck, Delivery, Motor, Lights, Steel, Antar, France, 13 1/2 In. 635.00
Truck, Delivery, Nickel Grill, Bumper, Arcade International, 9 1/4 x 3 1/4 In. 2012.00
Truck, Delivery, Pressed Steel, Driver, Friction, Clark, 10 3/4 In. 325.00
Truck, Delivery, Sit & Ride, Red, Green, Steel, Marx, c.1940, 26 In. 605.00
Truck, Delivery, Steel, Friction Motor, Clark, 10 1/2 In. 206.00
Truck, Delivery, Sun Bread, Orange, Yellow, 1960s, 6 In. 115.00
Truck, Delivery, Sunshine Produce Fruit Grower, Plastic, Metal, Marx, 14 In. 80.00
Truck, Delivery, Tin, Old Timer, Japan, 6 1/2 In. 30.00
Truck, Dodge, Dumping Action, Tin, Marx, Box, 10 In. 350.00
Truck, Dump, Aluminum Cab, Steel Hydraulic Body, All-American Toys, 1950s, 20 In. . .   385.00
Truck, Dump, Cast Iron, Anthony, 1927, 8 1/4 In. 1070.00
Truck, Dump, Cast Iron, Kenton, 9 In. 715.00
Truck, Dump, Dan Dee, Lever Action, Windup, Chein, Box, 1920s-1930s, 8 1/2 In. 480.00
Truck, Dump, Dept. Of Street Cleaning, Steel, Marx, c.1930, 11 In. 110.00
Truck, Dump, Flivver, Pressed Steel, Buddy L, 1920s, 11 In. 880.00
Truck, Dump, Friction, Japan, 1950s, 18 In. 245.00
Truck, Dump, Front Loader, Wyandotte, Box, 12 In. 495.00
Truck, Dump, Green Body, Cast Iron, Nickel Plated, White, Rubber Wheels, Hubley 100.00
Truck, Dump, Hubley, 1930s, 7 1/2 In. 1150.00
Truck, Dump, Hydraulic Body, International Harvester, Steel, c.1960, 15 In. 220.00
Truck, Dump, Lincoln, Pressed Steel, Canada, 1950s, 16 In. 295.00
Truck, Dump, Little Jim, Pressed Steel, Steelcraft, 1930s, 23 In. 440.00
Truck, Dump, Mandy's Trucking, Tin, Friction, Yonezawa, 6 In. 220.00
Truck, Dump, Marx, 1950s, 11 In. 75.00
Truck, Dump, Pressed Steel, Buddy L, 24 In. 1045.00
Truck, Dump, Pressed Steel, Buddy L, c.1920, 24 In. 605.00
Truck, Dump, Pressed Steel, Electric Headlights, Structo, 1920s, 17 In. 275.00
Truck, Dump, Pressed Steel, Hydraulic Dump Body, Big Mike, Tonka, 1950s, 15 In. 660.00
Truck, Dump, Pressed Steel, Marx, 18 1/2 In. 275.00
Truck, Dump, Pressed Steel, Ratchet Dump, Sturditoy, 1920s, 27 In. 275.00
Truck, Dump, Pressed Steel, Steelcraft, 1930s, 23 In. 385.00
Truck, Dump, Pressed Steel, Sturditoy, American, 1928 . . . .   3630.00
Truck, Dump, Pressed Steel, Tailgate Opens, Keystone, 27 In. 240.00
Truck, Dump, Pressed Steel, V Snow Plow, Tonka, 1960s, 17 1/2 In. 176.00
Truck, Dump, Red, Orange, Steel, Wood Wheels, Wyandotte, c.1930, 10 In. 60.00
Truck, Dump, Steel, Wyandotte, Box 425.00
Truck, Dump, Tan, Red, Steel, Wyandotte, Box, c.1940, 21 In. 770.00
Truck, Dump, Tin, Friction, Japan, 8 In. 20.00
Truck, Dump, Tin, Japan, 11 In. 65.00
Truck, Dump, Tin, Paya, Spain, 10 In. 110.00
Truck, Dump, Turner, Pressed Steel, Rubber Wheels, 27 In. 880.00
Truck, Dump, Turner, U.S.A, 1930s, 27 In. 195.00
Truck, Dump, Windup, Crane, Scoop, Tin, 12 In. 50.00
Truck, Express, Open Cab, Spoke Wheels, Buddy L 295.00
Truck, Fanny Farmer, Rear Door Opens, Tin, Friction, Tada Tokyo, Box, 8 In. 220.00
Truck, Farm, Cottonwood International, Cast Aluminum, 15 In. 330.00
Truck, Farm, Cow Head Pops Up From Top Of Van, Tin, Alps, Japan, 1960s, 11 In. 195.00
Truck, Fast Freight, Japan, Friction, Ford, 10 In. 140.00
Truck, Fire Pumper, Driver, Ladder, Mohawk, 10 In. 295.00
Truck, Ford, 1960 Model, Doors Open, Tin, Friction, Japan, 19 In.   699.00
Truck, Ford, Brown, Tonka, 1960, 12 In. 165.00
Truck, Ford, Cast Metal, Smith & Wesson, 1951, 8 1/4 x 3 x 3 3/4 In. 30.00
Truck, Ford, Ice Cream, Bandai, 1930s, 6 In. 145.00
Truck, Fruehauf, Tractor, Trailer, Cab Over, Smith-Miller, 1940s, 26 In. 330.00

Truck, G.M., Experimental, Door Opens, Tin, Friction, Linemar, 8 In. 110.00
Truck, Gas, Mobile, Red, Toymaster, 1960s, 8 1/4 In. 185.00
Truck, Good Humor, Tin, Friction, Linemar, 4 1/4 In. 415.00
Truck, Gravel, Lumar, Tin Lithograph, Marx, 15 1/2 In. 150.00
Truck, Gravel, Red, Rubber Wheels, Cast Iron, Champion, 8 In. 250.00
Truck, Green Giant, 2 Piece, Tonka, 1950s, 23 In. 245.00
Truck, Gun, Adjustable Guns, Tin, Friction, Japan, Box, 7 In. 70.00
Truck, Heavy Machinery, Buddy L, 1950s, 23 In. 1045.00
Truck, Heinz 57, Decals, Battery Operated Headlights, Pressed Steel, Metalcraft, 12 In. . . 120.00
Truck, Heinz, Lights, Rubber Tires, Metalcraft, 1930s, 12 In. 495.00
Truck, Hillclimber, Green, Gold, Pressed Steel, 1920s 250.00
Truck, Hollywood Searchlight, Die Cast, Battery, Cab Over, Smith-Miller, 1940s, 25 In. . . . 1100.00
Truck, Horse, 2 Movable Horses, Japan, 8 In. 75.00
Truck, Hospital, Hausser, 11 In. 2800.00
Truck, Hydraulic Dump, Blue & White, Buddy L, No. 3859, 1953, 20 In. 195.00
Truck, Ice Cream, Cream & White, 1929 Model, SSS, Box, 1960s, 8 In. 195.00
Truck, Ice Cream, Friction, Japan, 6 1/2 In. 125.00
Truck, Ice Cream, International, Buddy L, 1950s, 23 In. 165.00
Truck, Ice Cream, Tin, Bandai, 7 In. 150.00
Truck, Ice Cream, Tin, Bell On Hood, Japan, 7 In. 100.00
Truck, Ice, Rubber Wheels, Cast Iron, Arcade, 7 In. 225.00
Truck, Ice, Wooden, World War II, Decal, Marked, Buddy L, 16 In. 29.00
Truck, Insurance Patrol, Aluminum Wheels, Buddy L, 1920s, 26 In. 6050.00
Truck, Junior Dray, Milk Cans, Buddy L, 1920s 11550.00
Truck, Ladder, Aerial, Hydraulic, Red, Buddy L, 1926, 39 In. 1250.00
Truck, Ladder, Aerial, Yellow, Steel, Doepke, c.1940, 33 In. 165.00
Truck, Ladder, Cast Iron, Bulldog Mack, Nickel Plated Wheels, Arcade, 19 In. 580.00
Truck, Ladder, Pressed Steel, Steel Wheels, 36 In. 385.00
Truck, Livestock Carrier, Cragstan, Tin, Box, 12 In. 150.00
Truck, Loader & Dump, Red, Black, Steel, Tonka, c.1950, 25 In. 305.00
Truck, Loader, Orange, Adam's Travel, 30 x 11 In. 85.00
Truck, Lumber Carrier, USA, Cast, 1930s, 10 In. 395.00
Truck, Lumber, Timber Toter, All-American Toy Co. 1980.00
Truck, Lumber, Trailer, Aluminum, Allen Toy Co., 36 In. 550.00
Truck, Lumber, Trailer, Die Cast, Sturdi-Bilt, 1950s, 43 In. 1980.00
Truck, Mail, Royal, Wood, Pressed Steel, Triang, 1930s, 20 In. 1430.00
Truck, Mail, Tractor Trailer, Pressed Steel, Marx, 1950s, 25 In. 70.00
Truck, Military, Camouflage, Windup, Searchlight, Tin, England, 9 1/2 In. 150.00
Truck, Milk & Cream, Orange, Paper Sticker, Hubley, 1928, 3 3/4 In. 550.00
Truck, Milk, 2 Tin Milk Cans, Pressed Steel, England, 1950s, 16 In. 275.00
Truck, Mobile Communications, Pressed Steel, Structo, 1950s, 20 In. 165.00
Truck, Motor Express, Door Slide, Cab Lifts, Die Cast, Hubley, Box, 19 In. 440.00
Truck, Moving Van, Sonny, Pressed Steel, Disk Wheels, Rear Gate, 1920s, 26 In. 1045.00
Truck, Moving Van, World Van Lines, 12, Tin, Plastic, Japan, 4 In. 315.00
Truck, Overland Transport Express, Battery, Light, Horn, Japan, Box, 1950, 18 In. 375.00
Truck, Panel, Citroen, Pressed Steel, Electric Headlights, Motor, 1920s, 22 In. 660.00
Truck, Pickup, Enamel, Red, Yellow, Structo, Box, 1948 . . . . 1100.00
Truck, Plumbers, Revell, Box 275.00
Truck, Polar Ice Company, Tin, Plastic, Marx, 14 1/2 In. 195.00
Truck, Pontiac, Pickup, Blue, Tin, Friction, Bandai, Box, c.1950, 6 1/4 In. 250.00
Truck, Power Shovel, Green, Yellow, Tin Lithograph, Friction, Linemar, Box, 11 In. 155.00
Truck, Power Shovel, Yellow & Black, Daiya No. 25, 1960s, 9 In. 185.00
Truck, Power Shovel, Yellow & Black, Friction, Diaya No. 257, Box, 1960s, 13 In. 285.00
Truck, Railway Express, Buddy L, 24 In. 880.00
Truck, Ranger, Windup, Tin, 1950s, 7 In. 55.00
Truck, RCA Service Company, Marx, 1950s 150.00
Truck, Refreshment, Windup, Mettoy, England, 1950s, 9 1/2 In. 395.00
Truck, Robot, Lights, Guns Move, Tin, Battery Operated, Yonezawa, 9 1/2 In. 1980.00
Truck, Roller, Dump Trailer, Driver, Iron, Arcade, 11 In. 165.00
Truck, Sand & Gravel, Buddy L, 26 1/2 In. 880.00
Truck, Sand Loader & Dump, Tonka, 1940s, 26 In. 240.00
Truck, Satellite Launching, Blue, Tin Lithograph, Friction, Windup, Japan, 12 In. 220.00

Truck, Searchlight, B-Model, Battery Operated, Smith-Miller, c.1950, 14 In. 800.00
Truck, Searchlight, Clockwork, Battery, Soldiers, Lineol, Germany 3000.00
Truck, Searchlight, Lithograph, Battery, Friction, Marx, Box, 1957, 17 In. 895.00
Truck, Searchlight, P.S. American LaFrance, Doepke, 1950s, 19 In. 910.00
Truck, Semi-Trailer, Continental Express, Fast Freight, Tin, Friction, 15 1/2 In. 85.00
Truck, Semi-Trailer, Sears, 22 x 8 In. 30.00
Truck, Semi-Trailer, Valley Farms, Tin, Wyandotte, Box, 8 1/2 In. 300.00
Truck, Sprinkler, Street, Tin, Friction, Box, 9 1/2 In. 105.00
Truck, Stake, Iron, Red, Yellow Wheels, 5 1/2 In. 110.00
Truck, Structo Ready Mix, Blue & White, 1960, 17 In. 95.00
Truck, Structo Refrigerated Express, Blue, Yellow, Steel, Box, 1957, 21 In. 795.00
Truck, Take-Apart Stakes, Black & Blue, Rubber Tires, A.C. Williams, 1932, 7 In. 350.00
Truck, Tanker, Campsa, Red, Yellow, Windup, Tin, 7 In. 120.00
Truck, Tanker, Coreco Pennsylect, Pressed Steel, Rubber Wheels, 26 In. 360.00
Truck, Tanker, Gasoline, Mack, Hose & Driver, Cast Iron, Arcade, 1929, 12 1/2 In. 1750.00
Truck, Tanker, Mobilgas, Metal, Smith-Miller, 23 In. 470.00
Truck, Tanker, Shell, 8 Oil Barrels, Metalcraft, 1930s 1595.00
Truck, Tanker, Shell, England, 1950s, 17 In. 895.00
Truck, Tanker, Sinclair, Metal, 17 1/2 In. 145.00
Truck, Tanker, Sunoco Oil, Buddy L, 1930s, 13 In. 660.00
Truck, Tanker, Terrible Herbst, Trailer, Pressed Steel, Smith-Miller 2310.00
Truck, Tanker, Texaco, Metal, Buddy L, 24 In. 95.00
Truck, Tanker, Texaco, Trailer, Plastic, Metal, 23 In. 28.00
Truck, Telephone Maintenance, Accessory Trailer, Poles, Ladder, Box, Buddy L, 17 In. . . 660.00
Truck, Television, NBC, Camera, Tin Lithograph, Battery Operated, Cragstan, Box, 9 In. . 605.00
Truck, Texaco, Cast Iron, Allen's Toy Company, 18 In. 220.00
Truck, Texaco, Logo On Tank, Tin, Friction, Japan, 9 In. 85.00
Truck, Tool, Blue, Yellow, Irco, 1960s, 7 1/2 In. 175.00
Truck, Tow, Aluminum, All-American Toy Co., 1950s, 24 In. 1760.00
Truck, Tow, Japan SSS, 1950s, 10 1/2 In. 195.00
Truck, Tow, Packard Wrecker, Pressed Steel, Keystone, 1920s, 27 In. 330.00
Truck, Tow, Plastic, Rubber Tires & Tow Hook, Hubley, 1950s, 6 3/4 In. 15.00
Truck, Tow, Pressed Steel, Marx, 10 In. 275.00
Truck, Tow, Pressed Steel, Painted, Red & Black, Buddy L, 28 In. 2240.00
Truck, Tow, Pressed Steel, Rubber Wheels, Keystone Packard, 27 In. . . . . .825.00 to 990.00
Truck, Tow, Rear Crank, Battery Operated Lights, Buddy L, 20 In. 120.00
Truck, Tow, Weaver Boom, Iron, Nickel Plated, Arcade, 11 In. 470.00
Truck, Tow, Wooden Wheels, Crank Handle Boom, Pressed Steel, Wyandotte, 20 In. 230.00
Truck, Trailer, Bekins Van Lines, White, Steel, Smith-Miller, c.1940, 27 In. 690.00
Truck, Trailer, Continental Express, Tin, Friction, Utaka, Box, 12 In. 165.00
Truck, Trailer, Grey Van Lines, Aluminum, Wyandotte, c.1940, 24 In. 145.00
Truck, Trailer, L Mack, Hostess Advertising, Smith-Miller, 40 In. 990.00
Truck, Trailer, Marshall Field's & Co., Tonka, 1940s, 22 In. 1485.00
Truck, Trailer, Orange Mack Cab, A & P Trailers, Tootsietoy 440.00
Truck, Trailer, Plastic, Rubber Tires, Marx, Box, 9 1/2 In. 115.00
Truck, Trailer, Wood, Red, Green, Grand Dad's Toy Shop, No. Thetford, Vt., 1953, 32 In. . 65.00
Truck, Trailer, Wrigley's Chewing Gum, Green, Steel, Buddy L, c.1930, 23 In. 495.00
Truck, Transport, 6 Cars, Tin, Friction, Sanyo, Box, 13 In. 175.00
Truck, Trash, Pressed Steel, Hydraulic Front Scoop, Tonka, 1950s, 17 In. 360.00
Truck, U.S. Army, Cast Metal, Green Paint, Canvas Canopy, Keystone Packard, 26 1/2 In. 690.00
Truck, U.S. Mail, Olive Green, Decals, Buddy L, 1940, 21 In. 950.00
Truck, Volkswagen, Doors Open, Sliding Roof, Tin, Friction, Mexico, 9 1/2 In. 220.00
Truck, Volkswagen, Doors Open, Sliding Roof, Tin, Friction, Tippco, West Germany, 9 In. 305.00
Truck, Volkswagen, Driver, Blinkers Light, Tin, Battery Operated, Bandai, 10 In. 330.00
Truck, Walgreen's Ice Cream, Marx, 1960s, 20 In. 395.00
Truck, Washington Daily News Wagon, Oak, Stenciled Letters, Spoke Wheels, 42 In. 1045.00
Truck, Water Sprayer, New York, Tin Lithograph, Friction, Japan, Box, 6 1/2 In. 130.00
Truck, Water Tower, Pressed Steel, Pump, Seat, Keystone, 30 In. 1060.00
Truck, Water Tower, Pump, Keystone, 1920s, 32 In. 820.00
Truck, Water, Tower, Dayton, Flywheel, Motor, Yellow, Steel, c.1920, 20 In. 360.00
Truck, White Panel, Nickel Plated Wheels, Arcade, 8 1/2 In. 3630.00
Truck, Wrecker, Cab Over, Smith-Miller, 1940s, 15 In. 175.00

Truck & Trailer, Cars, Die Cast, 1950s, 21 In. 225.00
Truck & Trailer, Rubber Tire, Plastic, Marx, 9 1/2 In. 115.00
Trumpet Player, Louis Armstrong, TN, Japan, 10 1/2 In. 260.00
Typewriter, Buddy L, No. 200, Blue, Box, 1976 .... 45.00
Typewriter, Dial, Steel, Black Enamel, Red & Gold Applied Decoration 85.00
Van, Maple Leaf, Value, Pressed Steel, Minnitoy, 1950s, 30 In. 395.00
Vehicle, Circus Set, Corgi, 1960s 275.00
Vending Machine, Candy, Clown, Tin, Battery Operated, Wakasuto, Box, 10 In. 1570.00
Vendor, Cart, Friction Motor, Woman, Rossingnal, France, c.1900, 5 In. 205.00
Vendor, Ice Cream, Drives Cart, Windup, Tin, Frankonia, Box, 4 1/2 In. 140.00
View-Master, Casper The Friendly Ghost, 3 Reels, 1961 .... 15.00
View-Master, Charlotte's Web, 3 Reels, Hanna-Barbera, 1973 .... 5.00
View-Master, Queen Elizabeth II Coronation, 3 Reels, June 2, 1953 .... 20.00
View-Master, Secret Squirrel, Atom Ant, 3 Reels, Story Booklet, 1966 .... 14.00
Village, New Pretty Village, Cardboard Buildings, McLoughlin Bros., Box, 1897 .... 265.00
Wagon, Ambulance, Green, Tin, Composition Soldiers, Lineol, 9 In. 220.00
Wagon, Beer, American Cast Iron, 19th Century, 14 1/2 In. 200.00
Wagon, Dray, Black Driver, Lumber, Cast Iron, 23 In. 1300.00
Wagon, Express, Red, Wood, 14 In. 145.00
Wagon, Farm, Metal, Rubber Wheels, John Deere, Box, 8 In. 165.00
Wagon, Ice, Cast Iron, 11 1/2 In. 300.00
Wagon, Ice, Horse Drawn, Orange, Red, 9 3/4 x 4 1/2 In. 375.00
Wagon, Jetflyer, Steel, Rubber, Tires, c.1950, 16 In. 275.00
Wagon, Military, Horse Drawn, Covered, Driver & Outrider, Elastolin, 1920s, 14 1/2 In. . 220.00
Wagon, Milk, Horse Drawn, Animated Legs, Sheffield Farms, 21 In. 748.00
Wagon, Patrol, Pressed Steel, Friction, Clark, 14 1/2 In. 235.00
Wagon, Sand & Gravel, 2 Horses, Driver, Kenton, 14 In. 350.00
Wagon, Sand & Gravel, Dump Lever, Horse Drawn, Kenton, 10 1/2 In. 147.00
Wagon, Wooden, Buckboard, Green, Yellow, Landscape Panels, 21 x 17 1/2 x 40 In. 1700.00
Wagon, Wooden, Yellow, Red, Iron Banded Wheels, Early 20th Century, 44 In. 290.00
Wagon, Wyandotte, Red, Steel, Art Deco, c.1940, 11 1/2 In. 120.00
Wagon, Yellow Kid, Tin Cart, Cast Iron Goat, 7 1/2 In. 195.00
Walkie-Talkie, Plastic, Magnetic Power, Remco, Box 50.00
Wallet, Barbie, Vinyl, Figures, Zipper, Coin Section, Photo Holders, Mirror, 1962 ...... 120.00
Washing Machine, Blue Delft Scene, Tin Lithograph 55.00
Washing Machine, Laundry Queen Ringer, Metal, Turner Toy, U.S.A., 12 1/2 In. 140.00
Washstand, Wooden, Mirror, Washbowl, Pitcher, Early 20th Century, 15 1/2 In. 60.00
Watch, Bozo, Paper, Cloth, Plastic, Toy, c.1970, 3-In. Diam. 10.00
Water Pistol, Metal, 1917, 5 1/2 In. 45.00
Wheelbarrow, Katrinka Lifts Jimmy, Windup, Nifty, 1920s 1250.00
Wheelbarrow, Maple & Oak, Spoke Wheel, Turned Axle, Child's, 43 In. 75.00
Whirligig, Blue, Orange, Yellow, Tin, Penny Toy, Germany, 4 In. 99.00
Whirligig, Zouave, Pine, Carved, Turned Wood Base, American, c.1885, 11 In. 4500.00
Windmill, 4 Blades, Blue Base, Tin Lithograph, Penny, Germany, 4 1/2 x 2 1/4 In. 56.00
Windmill, Steam Powered, Tin Lithograph, c.1900, 4 5/8 x 8 1/2 x 4 5/8 In. 250.00
Windmill, Steam Water Pump, Ladder, Pressed Steel, 21 In. 175.00
Woman, With Parasol, Windup, France, 6 In. 520.00
Wrestler, Sumo, Celluloid, Air Bulb Movement, Japan, Box, 5 In. 95.00
Xylophone, Animated Clown, Song Disc, Yankee Doodle, Wolverine, 7 1/2 In. 290.00
Xylophone, Pinky Lee, Emenee, 1950s, 14 In. 45.00
Xylophone, Schoenhut, 22 Keys 140.00
Zebu, Schoenhut, Wood, 8 In. 1950.00
Zeppelin, Gondola, 5 Engines, 27 In. 205.00
Zeppelin, Graf, Wheels, Steel, Steelcraft, c.1930, 25 In. 155.00
Zeppelin, Hindenburg, Windup, Tin, Germany, 11 1/2 In. 1400.00
Zeppelin, Mechanical, Windup, Pressed Steel, Germany, 1930s, 17 1/2 In. 1600.00
Zeppelin, Pony Blimp, 6 In. 400.00
Zeppelin, Pressed Steel, Marx, 1930s, 25 In. 295.00
Zeppelin, Tin Lithograph, Pressed Steel, Click Mechanism, Marx Mammoth, 27 In. 505.00
Zeppelin, Tootsietoy 150.00
Zeppelin, Windup, Lehmann 475.00
Zilotone, 1 Cam Disc, Unique Art 325.00
Zylo-P-Ano, Song Sheet, Wood Hammer, Courtland, Box, 14 In. 11.00

TRAMP ART is a form of folk art made since the Civil War. It is usually made from chip-carved cigar boxes. Examples range from small boxes and picture frames to full-sized pieces of furniture.

Altar, Arched Crest, Drawer, Mirrors, Velvet, Lithograph Saint Cards, 19 x 14 x 7 In.	1528.00
Ballot Box, Fraternal Symbols, 3-Link Chain, Crescent Moon, Marbles, 7 x 15 In.	1410.00
Bank, Cathedral, Notch Carved, 3 Slotted Peaks, 6 Drawers, 26 x 14 x 8 1/2 In.	1410.00
Bank, Chip Carved, Pull-Out Slot, Mirrors, Scroll, Geometrics, Inscribed, 11 x 8 In.	1998.00
Birdcage, Chip Carved, Peaked Roof, Metal Feed Openings, 18 1/2 x 13 x 15 3/8 In.	235.00
Birdcage, Peaked Roof, Dormer, Bird Finials, 1900s, 18 3/4 x 15 x 14 3/4 In.	3173.00
Box, 2-Tier Pyramid, Drawer In Each Pyramid, 11 In.	84.00
Box, 5 Drawers, Chip Carved Molding, Geometrics, 14 3/4 x 15 5/8 x 10 3/4 In.	295.00
Box, Applied Brass Stars, Nickel Plate Dolphin Handle, Initials, 8 x 6 x 5 In.	55.00
Box, Comb, Pine, Crossed Leaf Designs, Painted, Hanging, Applied Molding, 13 x 9 In.	220.00
Box, Diamond Shape, Hinged Lid, Applied Stepped Diamonds, 5 x 11 x 6 In.	590.00
Box, Double Pyramid Form On Top & Sides, Hinged Lid, 10 In.	145.00
Box, Jewelry, Chip Carved, Mahogany, Heart Shape, 1800s, 6 1/8 x 9 1/4 x 10 3/8 In.	2585.00
Box, Jewelry, Chip Carved, Mahogany, Heart Shape, 1800s, 6 x 9 1/4 x 10 3/8 In.	2585.00
Box, Keepsake, 4 Drawers, J.A. Williams, 1884	1200.00
Box, Pedestal, Notch Carved, 3 Tiers, Stepped Diamond, Hearts, 14 x 11 x 8 In.	264.00
Box, Pedestal, Pyramidal, Cubed Shape, Stacked Square Segments, Cover, 10 1/2 In.	190.00
Box, Pine, Chip Caved Panels Stacked In Layers, Geometric Design, 7 x 11 x 8 In.	305.00
Box, Stacked, Chipped Carved Moldings, Painted, Brass Pull, 16 x 11 x 9 1/4 In.	330.00
Box, Wall, Masonic Symbols, 10 7/8 x 4 x 16 In.	600.00
Box On Box, 5 Drawers, 11 x 14 x 6 In.	975.00
Bureau, Mirror, Carved Arched Crest, Applied Design, 38 x 23 1/2 x 15 In.	470.00
Bureau, Shaped Crest, Swivel Mirror, 2 Drawers, Compartment, 33 x 14 x 11 In.	380.00
Cabinet, Postcard Display, 2-Part Hinged Doors, Stepped Apertures, 25 5/8 x 12 In.	3175.00
Candlestick, Carved Stars, 8 1/2 In.	350.00
Chair, Doll's, Fruit Box Wood, Dark Blue-Black Stain, Concealed Rattle In Seat, 12 In.	335.00
Chest, Doll's, Mirrored, Arched, 1/2 Round Shelves, 17 3/8 x 9 1/2 x 5 1/2 In.	118.00
Clock, Cathedral, Fretwork, 5 Spires, Gilded Acorn Finials, 40 x 19 x 10 In.	355.00
Cupboard, Carved Pyramid Peaks, Canadian Crate Boards Back, 52 In.	4400.00
Frame, Carved Cruciforms, Nicholas & Alexandra, Early 1900s, 21 3/4 x 13 In.	118.00
Frame, Carved, Fretwork, Star Shaped, 6-Point, 20th Century, 21 3/8 x 21 In.	560.00
Frame, Crown-Of-Thorns, 4 Apertures, High Relief, 20th Century, 27 1/2 x 23 1/2 In.	90.00
Frame, Crown-Of-Thorns, 4 Apertures, Intersecting Notch Carving, 20 x 18 3/4 In.	59.00
Frame, Crown-Of-Thorns, Oval, Painted, Oval Aperture, Girl Portrait, 14 3/4 In.	235.00
Frame, Crown-Of-Thorns, Peaked Crest & Aperture, 20th Century, 30 1/2 x 21 3/8 In.	200.00
Frame, Crown-Of-Thorns, Triple, Chip Carved, Molded, 20th Century, 33 x 39 In.	235.00
Frame, Double Mirrored, Chip Carved, Stacked Geometric Segments, 21 x 30 1/2 In.	141.00
Frame, Double, Tiered Chip Carved Molding, Diamond Blocks, 8 1/4 x 12 3/4 In.	99.00
Frame, Gilt Carved, Pyramidal Geometric Ornamentation, 1800s, 70 x 70 In.	5405.00
Frame, High Relief Carved Spool, Scroll, Geometric, 1800s, 38 1/2 x 35 x 5 In.	5405.00
Frame, Mirrored, 9 Apertures Surrounding Photos, Carved, 33 x 34 1/4 In.	2233.00
Frame, Notch Carved, Mirrored, Stacked Geometric, 20th Century, 22 x 16 1/2 In.	118.00
Frame, Oak Leaves, Acorns, Notch Carved, Applied Flowers, 19th Century, 30 x 26 In.	500.00
Frame, Pierced Hearts, Scallops, Chromolithograph Of Saint, 1896, 32 x 21 In.	410.00
Frame Tower, Crown-Of-Thorns, Puzzle-Like Segments, 1800s, 40 x 23 x 23 In.	825.00
Lamp, Chip Carved, Geometric Segment Shaft, Paper Shade, Early 1900s, 59 In.	1765.00
Lamp, Foliate Cutouts, Fretwork Shade, Figural Brackets, Baluster Base, 20 x 13 In.	29.00
Lamp Base, Calendar, Geometric Inlay, Cigarette Dispenser, 13 x 12 x 11 In.	59.00
Match Safe, Wall Mounted, Civil War Soldier, Lamp, 19h Century, 13 3/4 x 7 In.	1870.00
Mirror, Anchor, Chip Carved, Oval Aperture, Cross, Heart, Gilt Highlights, 15 x 12 In.	2820.00
Mirror, Shaving, Drawer, Late 19th Century, 17 x 7 x 21 In.	175.00
Mirror Frame, Notch Carved, Stacked Geometric, Heart Shapes, 26 x 22 In., Pair	118.00
Model, Church, Notched, Gothic Arch, Painted, Early 20th Century, 14 x 10 x 8 In.	176.00
Piano Bench, Notch Carved, Stepped Designs, Hinged Lid, 8 x 11 x 5 1/2 In.	499.00
Planter, Stand, Chip Carved, Elongated, Galvanized Steel Liner, 31 1/2 x 50 x 11 In.	2235.00
Purse, Notch Carved, Oval, Upright Handle, Heart, Geometric, 11 x 7 x 10 1/2 In.	1645.00
Radio, Case, Faux Organ Pipes, Eagle Finial, 1930s, 52 1/2 In.	12500.00
Sewing Box, 2 Tiers, 9 3/4 In.	395.00
Sideboard, Mirrored, Oval, Shelf, 1 Long Over 3 Short Drawers, 67 x 42 x 23 In.	3055.00
Stand, Dressing, Notch Carved, Mirrored Cube, Deep Drawer, 1 7/8 x 14 x 8 In.	176.00

Stand, Mirrored, 2 Side Stands, Medial Shelves, 19th Century, 47 x 38 x 12 5/8 In. 590.00
Stand, Plant, Openwork, Carved, Stacked, Painted, Splayed Legs, 34 x 15 x 15 In. 265.00
Table, Sewing, Notch Carved, Lift Top, Hinged Top, Carved Mother, 31 x 33 x 17 In. 2350.00
Wall Pocket, 3 Tiers, Wheel-Like Drives, Pierced, X-Motifs, 1800s, 21 x 17 x 7 In. 105.00
Wall Pocket, Diamond & Circles, Heart Crest, Blue, Yellow, 8 x 3 1/2 x 14 In. 275.00
Wall Pocket, Stepped Latticework Back, Rosettes, Pocket Sides, Mirrored, 17 x 38 In. . . . 440.00
Wall Rack, Notched, Painted, Chip Carved, Mother-Of-Pearl Buttons, 11 x 14 x 4 In. 470.00

TRAPS for animals may be handmade. One of the most unusual is the
mousetrap made so that when the mouse entered the trap, it was hit on
the head with a mallet. Other traps were commercially manufactured
and often are marked with the name of the manufacturer. Many traps
were designed to be as humane as possible, and they would trap the
live animal so it could be released in the woods.

Fly, Aqua Glass, Bulbous Base, Cork Stopper, Wire Bail Handle, 5 In. 45.00
Mole, 8 Prongs, Spring Loaded, 7 1/4 In. 20.00
Rabbit, Leghold, Ground Stake & Chain, No. 10, Victor, Australia, 10 1/2 In. 17.00
Rodent, Wire, 15 In. 25.00
Weasel, Printed Wood Base, Spring Loaded, Animal Trap Company, 7 In. 30.00
Wolf, Leghold, No. 114, Newhouse, 22 In. 200.00

TREEN, see Wooden category.

TRENCH ART is a form of folk art made by soldiers. Metal casings from
bullets and mortar shells were cut and decorated to form useful objects,
such as vases.

Ashtray, Brass, Letters, Flowers, 3 x.30 Caliber Bullet Legs, World War I, 2 1/2 In. 35.00
Ashtray, Brass, Russian Artillery Shell, Luga, Petersburg, 5 1/8 In. 87.00
Ashtray, Hammered Copper, On 4 U.S. Rifle Cartridges, Chinese Coin Trim 63.00
Ashtray, P-38, 90 mm M-19 Shell Base, 1943, 7 1/2 In. 70.00
Ashtray, Shell, British Penny Cigarette Holders, Canada, World War II 70.00
Candleholder, Brass Ammo Shell, Square Copper Base, Engraved, 1940s, 3 x 5 In., Pair . 75.00
Cigar Trimmer, 37mm Cannon Projectile, Copper Bands, Eagle Top 81.00
Cigarette Case, Engraved Flags, Planes, P.O.W. Made, 1945, 4 x 3 In. 29.00
Cigarette Lighter, Figural, Gun, 2 3/8 x 4 1/16 In. 200.00
Hate Belt, Leather, Various Armys' Buttons, Brass Buckle, World War I, 1918 . . . . 225.00
Lamp, Military Shell, 14 In. 39.00
Letter Opener, 303 Bullet Handle, Brass Shell Cut For Blade, World War II, 6 In. 70.00
Letter Opener, Shrapnel Handle, 6 1/2 In. 45.00
Lighter, Floral Band, Silver Band, World War I, 3 In. 50.00
Pencil Holder, Shells, World War I, 4 3/8 x 3 1/2 In. 95.00
Ring, Etched, 6-Point Star, Sun Peeking Through Clouds, Korea, 1947, 3/4 x 5/8 In. 25.00
Sailing Ship, Hand Hammered, Butterflies, Scalloped, 27 x 3 In. 85.00
Shell Casing, Etched Ship, German Style Flag, 1943, 11 1/2 x 4 1/8 In. 50.00
Shell Casing, Flowers, Brass Body, Hammered, 1917, 9 x 1 3/4 In. 46.00
Tobacco Lighter, Copper Band, World War I, 3 1/4 In. 50.00
Vase, Brass Shell, Flowers, Pinpoint Hammered Background, World War II, 13 3/4 In. 80.00
Vase, Brass Shell, Scalloped Top, Hammered Flowers, World War I, 11 1/4 In. 100.00
Vase, Brass Shell, Scalloped Top, Hammered, Flowers, Metz 1918, World War I, 9 In. . . . 100.00
Vase, Brass Shell, Scalloped, Fluted Top, 7 x 1 x 2 1/4 In. 75.00
Vase, Brass Shell, Sculptured Hammered Scene, Horse Head, Flowers, World War I, 23 In. 220.00
Vase, Flowers, Intertwined Vine, Hammered, Verdun, World War I, 1918, 11 1/4 In. 145.00
Vase, Hammered, Flowers, Brass, Canada, World War I, 12 x 3 1/2 In. 90.00
Vase, Shell Casting, Ivy Leaf Design, Hammered, France, World War I, 14 In., Pair 180.00

TRIVETS are now used to hold hot dishes. Most trivets of the late nineteenth and early twentieth centuries were made to hold hot irons. Iron
or brass reproductions are being made of many of the old styles.

Aluminum, Tree Of Life, Chrome Frame, Farberware, 7 1/4 In. 25.00
Brass, Bedside, Iron Frame, Celtic Cross Design, 1800s, 4 1/2 x 16 1/2 In. 56.00
Brass, Lion, Ball & Claw Feet, 4 x 10 x 6 In. 150.00
Brass, Pierced, Victorian, 19th Century, 14 x 14 x 12 In. 358.00
Brass, Wrought Iron, Openwork Design, Sliding Shelf, Hanging, Shelf Rods, 16 x 8 In. . . 55.00
Cast Iron, Griswold, No. 5, Oval Roaster 85.00

Cast Iron, Griswold, No. 7 .... 45.00
Cast Iron, Oval Roaster, Griswold, No. 3 .... 295.00
Iron, Cabriole Legs, Arrow Feet, 2 Shelves, Black Paint, England, 1800s, 13 x 15 In. 125.00
Iron, Duck, Figural, Painted, 4 1/2 In. 165.00
Iron, Heart Shape, Handle, 12 1/2 In. 110.00
Iron, Holder, Embossed, Thurston-London, 9 In. 110.00
Iron, Reticulated Sheet Metal, Hand Forged Legs, 1800s, 11 1/2 x 12 In. 56.00
Iron, Sadiron, Griswold, Classic 55.00
Pottery, Flow Blue, Flowers, Leaves, Wooden Frame, Germany 28.00
Pottery, Magenta Shading, White, Sculpted, Square, 6 1/2 In. 50.00
Pottery, Maroon, Round, Hall, 6 In. 25.00
Pottery, Niagara Falls, American Falls From Goat Island, Molded Rim, Round, 6 1/2 In. . 50.00
Pottery, Pink Cabbage Rose & Green Leaf Border, Cobalt, Lace Swags, Round, 6 1/2 In. . 45.00
Pottery, White, Art Glaze Red Edge, 8 Sides, Hall, No. DEC T 143, 6 In. 35.00
Pottery, Woman, Flowers, No. 615, Blue, Tan, Sponge, Square, Pfaltzgraff, 7 3/4 In. 30.00
Pottery, Yellow Flowers, Brown Leaves, Hand Painted, Round, 6 1/2 In. 25.00
Tile, 8-Point Star, Pink, Burgundy, Gray, Metal Band, Round, No. 4951M, 6 3/4 In. 45.00
Tile, Blue, White, Dresden, Villeroy & Boch 50.00
Wrought Iron, Fireplace, Diamond-Shaped Rods, Petal Ends, 2 3/4 x 23 x 9 In. 60.00
Wrought Iron, Folding, Platform Top, Tripod Base, Rod, Catch, 1900s, 20 x 14 x 13 In. . 440.00
Wrought Iron, Handle, 19th Century, 26 In. 160.00
Wrought Iron, Heart Shape, 2 Splayed Legs, Turned Up Feet, 6 1/4 x 4 3/4 x 1 1/2 In. 325.00
Wrought Iron, Hearth, Revolving Round Grill, Heart Shape, 5 1/2 x 33 1/2 x 17 In. 275.00
Wrought Iron, Square Grilling Surface, Penny End, 5 1/4 x 28 1/4 x 14 In. 95.00

TRUNKS of many types were made. The nineteenth-century sea chest
was often handmade of unpainted wood. Brass-fitted camphorwood
chests were brought back from the Orient. Leather-covered trunks
were popular from the late eighteenth to mid-nineteenth centuries. By
1895, trunks were covered with canvas or decorated sheet metal.
Embossed metal coverings were used from 1870 to 1910. By 1925,
trunks were covered with vulcanized fiber or undecorated metal.
Suitcases are listed here.

Camphorwood, Black Leather Covering, Painted Flowers, Brass Tacks, 10 x 12 x 25 In. . 550.00
Camphorwood, Black Leather, Brass Binding & Tacks, 2 Bail Handles, 10 x 25 In. 360.00
Dome Top, Iron Straps, Original Paint, Hand Cut Nails, 20 x 14 1/2 x 12 In. 650.00
Dome Top, Pine, Painted, Plank Sides, Bracket Feet, Till Inside, 34 x 51 In. 805.00
Dome Top, Pine, Wrought Iron Bindings, Handle, Painted, 45 x 20 1/2 x 21 1/2 In. 305.00
Dome Top, Poplar, Sponge Flowers, 1870s Newspaper Lining, 24 x 12 x 10 1/2 In. 110.00
Dome Top, Portmanteau, Wood, Black, Brass Tacking, 19th Century, 10 x 23 In. 184.00
Dome Top, Softwood, Grain Painted, Banded Highlights, 12 1/2 x 28 1/2 x 14 In. 190.00
Hide Covered, Wood, Brass Tacks, Center Brass Bale Handle, Label, c.1825, 15 x 8 In. .. 90.00
Immigrant's, Paneled, Painted, Flowers, Dovetailed, Iron Hinges, 1840, 21 x 54 In. 280.00
Leather Bound, Brass Studded, Inscribed Francis W. Upham, 19th Century, 7 x 16 In. 255.00
Leather Bound, Brass Tack Decoration, Peafowl, 19th Century, 16 x 38 x 16 In. 115.00
Leather Covered, Paper Interior, Early 19th Century, 19 x 14 1/2 x 28 In. 50.00
Leather Covered, Studwork Cartouches & Edges, Brass Handles, Ball Feet, 24 x 14 In. .. 295.00
Leather Covered, Tooled, Iron Mounted, Baroque, Spain, 18th Century, 13 x 34 In. 635.00
Louis Vuitton, Steamer, Drawers, Hangers, 16 x 44 x 15 1/2 In. 2990.00
Louis Vuitton, Steamer, Fitted, Leather, Early 20th Century 4500.00
Louis Vuitton, Vanity Case, Blue Leather, Fall Front, Accessories, 1925, 28 x 11 In. 4115.00
Mahogany, Painted, Demilune Top, Hinged, 19th Century 7170.00
Pine, Red Over Mustard Vinegar, Fan Sponging, P.M.S. 1862, 21 x 48 In. 605.00
Rawhide, Civil War, Robert Burr, Saddle & Trunk Makers, 13 7/8 x 8 3/4 x 6 1/2 In. 94.00
Wood, Carved, 2 Armorials On Top & Front, Painted Leaves On Sides, 15 x 24 x 16 In. .. 765.00
Wood, Painted, Lift Top, Printed Shawls, Canvas Top, 18 x 37 x 22 In. 1265.00

TYPEWRITER collectors divide typewriters into two main classifica-
tions: the index machine, which has a pointer and a dial for letter selec-
tion, and the keyboard machine, most commonly seen today. The first
successful typewriter was made by Sholes and Glidden in 1874.

Braille, Frank H. Hall, Coopering & Mfg. Co., Chicago, 1892 .... 387.00
Crown, Straight Index, Type Wheel, Ink Roller, Wooden Base, 1890s, 11 1/2 In. 6465.00

E. Sottsass Jr, P. King, Valentine, Red, Case, Olivetti, c.1969, 4 x 13 x 13 In. . . . . .118.00 to 176.00
Hammond, Multiplex, Wooden Case, 14 In. 255.00
Hammond, No. 12, 3 Type Sleeves, Wooden Case, 1893 . . . . 365.00
Imperial Portable, Model D, Green, England, 1919 . . . . 245.00
Kanzler, Model 1 B, Serial No. 1.184, Germany, 1903 . . . . 2210.00
Lambert, No. 3.543, 1896 . . . . 940.00
Moya Visible No. 2, 1905 . . . . 3680.00
Odell's Typewriter, Chicago, 1890 . . . . 970.00
Pittsburgh Visible No. 10, 1902 . . . . 440.00
Royal Bar-Lock, Wooden Hood, 1902 . . . . 310.00
Smith Premier No. I, 1889 . . . . 330.00
Underwood, Elliott Fisher, Bookkeeping, Electric, 1903 . . . . 390.00
World Typewriter Model 2, 1886 . . . . 610.00

TYPEWRITER RIBBON TINS are now being collected. The lithographed
tin containers have been used since the 1870s. Most popular with collectors are tins with pictorial graphics.

Addressograph, J.S. Duncan, Rounded Square 75.00
Bay State Brand, Non-Filling, Rounded Square 50.00
Bradford's Best, Barnsdall Printing Co., Bradford, Pa., Art Deco Design, Round 16.00
Cello-Seal, Shrec-Rich, Weyers Cave, Virginia, Rounded Square 160.00
Daisy Brand, Rounded Square 80.00
Durite, Excels, Secretary Typing, 2 1/2 x 2 1/2 x 7/8 In. 70.00
Ebony, Image Of Black Man, Green, White, Black, Rounded Square 210.00
H.M. Stroms, American Brand, Indian, 2 5/8 x 2 5/8 In. 165.00
Just Rite, Ryan & Williams, Buffalo, N.Y., Art Deco Design, Round 51.00
Kangaroo, White Kangaroo, Black Ground, Cardboard, Round 269.00
Kopy-Rite, Carbon & Ribbon Co., Dark & Light Green, Round 227.00
Marvel Brand, Carbon Paper & Ribbon Co., Pittsburgh, Buffalo, Boston, Square 69.00
Niagara, Metal, 2 1/4 x 2 1/4 x 3/4 In. 55.00
Penguin, Image Of Penguin, Green, Yellow, Embossed, Round 56.00
Queen Of Hearts, Black, Green & Red, Queen On Cover 455.00
Silhouette, Blue Box, Silhouette Of Woman, Turquoise, White, Black, Round 70.00

UHL pottery was made in Evansville, Indiana, in 1854. The pottery
moved to Huntingburg, Indiana, in 1908. Stoneware and glazed pottery
were made until the mid-1940s.

Canteen, Advertising, Colonial Mineral Springs, Martinsville, Indiana, Blue 150.00
Crock, Advertising, Riverside Ice & Oyster Co., Evansville, 3 Gal. 490.00
Jug, Christmas, 1939 . . . . 175.00
Jug, Evansville, 3 Gal. 155.00
Jug, Evansville, 5 Gal. 225.00
Jug, Shoulder, Acorn, 3 Gal. 95.00
Mug, Home Sweet Home, Blue & White 300.00
Mug, Honey Brown, Blue Stamp, 1940s, 4 1/2 In. 45.00
Pitcher, Christmas, 1943, Paper Label, Miniature 1250.00
Pitcher, Home Sweet Home, Blue & White 800.00
Pitcher, Iced Tea, Maroon, 7 1/2 In. 50.00
Vase, Flower, Terra-Cotta, Greek Key Design, 15 In. 240.00
Vase, Milk White, Tapered Neck, Flared Top, Blue Mark, 7 x 5 In. 45.00

UMBRELLA collectors like rain or shine. The first known umbrella was
owned by King Louis XIII of France in 1637. The earliest umbrellas
were sunshades, not designed to be used in the rain. The umbrella was
embellished and redesigned many times. In 1852, the fluted steel rib
style was developed, and it has remained the most useful style.

Silk, Red, White & Blue, 1890s 275.00

UNION PORCELAIN WORKS was established at Greenpoint, New York,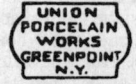
in 1848 by Charles Cartlidge. The company went through a series of
ownership changes and finally closed in the early 1900s. The company
made a fine quality white porcelain that was often decorated in clear,
bright colors.

Cup & Saucer, White, Relief Of Justice, Hermes, Liberty Figure Handle, c.1880 . . . . 705.00

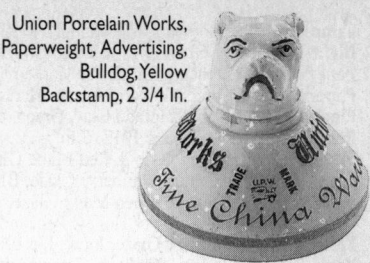

Union Porcelain Works,
Paperweight, Advertising,
Bulldog, Yellow
Backstamp, 2 3/4 In.

Paperweight, Advertising, Bulldog, Yellow Backstamp, 2 3/4 In. . . . . *Illus*	765.00
Paperweight, Eagle, Tapered Rectangular Base, White Glaze, 2 3/4 In.	235.00
Pitcher, Figural Bear Handle, Walrus Spout, Card Scene, Marked, 10 In.	700.00
Vase, Figural, Tortoise Grasping Pitcher Plant, White, 8 1/2 In.	825.00

UNIVERSITY CITY POTTERY, of University, Missouri, worked from 1909 to 1915. Well-known artists, including Taxile Doat, Adelaide Alsop Robineau, and Frederick Hurten Rhead, worked there.

Dish, Fish, Embossed Shell, 3-Footed, Taxile Doat, 1914, 2 3/4 x 5 1/4 In.	940.00

UNIVERSITY OF NORTH DAKOTA, see North Dakota School of Mines category.

VAL ST. LAMBERT Cristalleries of Belgium was founded by Messieurs Kemlin and Lelievre in 1825. The company is still in operation. All types of table glassware and decorative glassware have been made. Pieces are often decorated with cut designs.

Val St Lambert

Bowl, Cobalt Blue Cut To Clear, Gold Enameled, c.1900, 9 3/4 x 12 1/2 In.	635.00
Candlestick, Cut, Cobalt Blue Cup, Gold Enameled, c.1900, 12 3/4 In., Pair	635.00
Decanter, Cut, Cobalt Blue Top, Square, Gold Enameled, c.1900, 10 In.	374.00
Vase, Cobalt Blue, Copper Overlay, Gilt Bronze Base, Rosettes, c.1910, 11 In.	575.00
Vase, Cranberry Cut To Clear, Columbine Blossoms, Signed, 7 In.	520.00
Vase, Green, Chrysanthemums, Enamel Cameo, c.1900, 14 In.	460.00

VALLERYSTHAL Glassworks was founded in 1836 in Lorraine, France. In 1854, the firm became Klenglin et Cie. It made table and decorative glass, opaline, cameo, and art glass. A line of covered, pressed glass animal dishes was made in the nineteenth century. The firm is still working.

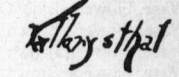

Vase, Grapevine, Berries, Insects, Gold Highlights, Cylindrical, Flared Foot, Rim, 14 In. .	3136.00
Vase, Pink Thistles, Leaves, Gold Highlights, Cameo, Signed, 8 In.	1035.00

VAN BRIGGLE pottery was made by Artus Van Briggle in Colorado Springs, Colorado, after 1901. Van Briggle had been a decorator at Rookwood Pottery of Cincinnati, Ohio. He died in 1904. His wares usually had modeled relief decorations and a soft, dull glaze. The pottery is still working and still making some of the original designs.

Bookends, Elephant, Purple Glaze, Burgundy, 4 1/4 x 7 1/4 In.	220.00
Bookends, Owl, Persian Rose Matte Glaze, 5 In.	206.00
Bookends, Rams, Maroon & Blue Matte Glaze, Incised Marks, c.1922, 4 1/2 In.	115.00
Bookends, Ship, Embossed, Persian Rose Glaze, 3 1/2 In.	115.00
Bowl, Arrowroot, Green Matte Glaze, c.1920, 6 1/2 In.	259.00
Bowl, Flower Frog, Lady Of The Lake, Blue & Green Matte Glaze, 14 x 10 In.	290.00
Bowl, Flower Frog, Siren Of The Sea, Seashell, Mermaid, Relief Fish, 1904, 8 In. .470.00 to	920.00
Bowl, Flowers, Leaves, Aqua, Marked, 2 1/4 x 5 1/2 In.	90.00
Bowl, Leaves, Maroon & Blue Matte Glaze, c.1915, 10 1/2 In.	460.00
Bowl, Mermaid On Side, Red & Blue Matte Glaze, 14 In.	255.00
Bowl, Rolled Rim, Maroon Glaze, Blue Overspray, c.1916, 7 In.	145.00
Creamer, Heart, Ming Turquoise	35.00
Dish, Spider, Dark Green Matte Glaze, Round, Marked, 1906, 5 1/2 In.	920.00
Figurine, Indian Maiden Grinding Corn, Ming Turquoise Glaze, 5 3/4 In.	149.00
Jug, Fire Water, Spider, Purple, Teal Matte Glaze, c.1900, 6 1/2 x 5 1/4 In.	1495.00
Lamp, Bird Perched On Tree Trunk, White Matte Glaze, Impressed, 10 1/2 In.	120.00

Lamp, Embossed Flowers, Maroon Glaze, Blue Overspray, c.1920, 9 In. 115.00
Night-Light, Owl, Glass Eyes, Blue & Green Matte Glaze, 7 1/4 In. 316.00
Paperweight, Elephant, Turquoise, Marked, 3 In. 35.00
Paperweight, Rabbit, Mulberry Glaze, Marked, 2 1/2 In. .115.00 to 138.00
Plaque, Advertising, Colorado Clay, Green, c.1930, 5 3/4 x 11 1/2 In. 2300.00
Plate, Blue Matte Glaze, c.1912, 6 In. 276.00
Plate, Leaves, Grapes, Blue & Red Matte Glaze, 1907-1912, 9 1/2 In. 805.00
Sugar & Creamer, Plum, Mulberry Glaze, Blue Overspray 193.00
Tray, Shell Girl, Blue & Green Matte Glaze, 8 1/2 In. 175.00
Vase, 2 Bears, Climbing For Honey, Persian Rose Matte Glaze, c.1920, 15 In. 2185.00
Vase, 2 Bears, Mulberry Glaze, Incised, c.1926, 15 1/2 In. 1840.00
Vase, 3-Headed Indian, Brown & Green Matte Glaze, 11 In. 430.00
Vase, 3-Headed Indian, Maroon & Blue Matte Glaze, c.1930, 12 In. 518.00
Vase, 3-Headed Indian, Mulberry Glaze, Marked, 11 1/8 In. 150.00
Vase, Berries & Leaves, Caramel & Indigo Matte Glaze, Bulbous, 8 1/2 In. 6900.00
Vase, Black, Green Leathery Matte Glaze, Oval, Marked, 1903, 8 x 23 1/2 In. 1610.00
Vase, Blue & Purple Matte Glaze, Incised Marks, 1915-1918, 6 3/4 In. 400.00
Vase, Brown Clay Body, Green Matte Glaze, c.1906, 4 1/2 In. 750.00
Vase, Bud, Flower Buds, Green Frothy Matte Glaze, 1907-1911, 8 x 2 1/2 In. 1093.00
Vase, Bud, Mulberry Glaze, Cylindrical, Tapered, Incised Marks, 1915, 7 1/2 In. 230.00
Vase, Buds, Ribs, Persian Rose Glaze, Handles, Bulbous, Marked, c.1930, 6 1/2 In. 230.00
Vase, Clovers, Blue & Maroon Matte Glaze, Marked, c.1920, 4 In. 115.00
Vase, Clovers, Mountain Craig Brown Glaze, Marked, 6 1/4 In. 175.00
Vase, Cornflowers, Persian Rose Glaze, 1930, 11 1/2 In. 546.00
Vase, Crocus, Green, Gray Matte Glaze, Squat, 1904, 3 1/2 x 4 In. 1150.00
Vase, Crocus, Multitone Blue Matte Glaze, c.1903, 3 1/2 In. 660.00
Vase, Daffodils, Blue & Green Matte Glaze, 10 1/2 In. 175.00
Vase, Daffodils, Multitone Blue Matte Glaze, c.1916, 9 In. 978.00
Vase, Despondency, Blue & Green Matte Glaze, c.1930, 13 1/2 In. 635.00
Vase, Dos Cabezas, 2 Art Nouveau Maidens, Mustard Matte Glaze, 7 1/2 x 5 In. 6900.00
Vase, Dragonfly, Brown & Green Matte Glaze, Incised Mark, 1920-1930, 7 1/4 In. 405.00
Vase, Flowers, Blue & Green Matte Glaze, Broad Form, c.1920, 7 In. 175.00
Vase, Flowers, Blue Gray Glaze, Turquoise Overspray, c.1920, 6 In. 375.00
Vase, Flowers, Blue Matte Glaze, Maroon Highlights, c.1916, 7 In. 690.00
Vase, Flowers, Blue Matte Glaze, Tapered, Incised Mark, c.1920, 8 1/2 In. 290.00
Vase, Flowers, Blue, Oatmeal Glaze, 1903, 9 3/8 In. 1610.00
Vase, Flowers, Brown & Green Matte Glaze, Incised Mark, 1920-1930, 7 1/2 In. 345.00
Vase, Flowers, Brown Glaze, Green Overspray, c.1920, 5 1/2 In. 230.00
Vase, Flowers, Brown Matte Glaze, 2 1/2 x 3 1/4 In. 110.00
Vase, Flowers, Buds, Blue, Green Crystalline Matte Glaze, Cylindrical, 10 In. 1725.00
Vase, Flowers, Curved Panels, Dark Teal Matte Glaze, 1904, 4 1/4 x 2 1/2 In. 1610.00
Vase, Flowers, Deep Purple Glaze, Maroon Ground, 1921, 2 3/4 x 2 3/4 In. 165.00
Vase, Flowers, Frothy Blue & Green Matte Glaze, Bell Shape, 1903, 6 1/2 In. 2185.00
Vase, Flowers, Gray & White Matte Glaze, Shouldered, c.1906, 4 1/2 In. 290.00
Vase, Flowers, Gray Matte Glaze, Incised, 1900s, 10 3/4 In. 1295.00
Vase, Flowers, Green & Yellow Matte Glaze, c.1905, 7 In. 2185.00
Vase, Flowers, Leaves, Mulberry Glaze, Incised AA, 5 3/4 In. 375.00
Vase, Flowers, Leaves, Purple, Blue, Green Matte Glaze, Tapered, 1907-1911, 10 In. 3738.00
Vase, Flowers, Leaves, Purple, Green, Blue Matte Glaze Ground, Bulbous, 1905, 5 1/4 In. 2760.00
Vase, Flowers, Leaves, Turquoise Matte Glaze, Gourd, Marked, 4 5/8 In. 90.00
Vase, Flowers, Maroon Glaze, Blue Overspray, c.1920, 4 In. 115.00
Vase, Flowers, Matte Mustard Glaze, Bulbous, Marked, 6 x 3 1/2 In. 2415.00
Vase, Flowers, Ming Turquoise, 5 In. 55.00
Vase, Flowers, Multitone Blue Matte Glaze, Marked, c.1918, 2 1/2 In. 375.00
Vase, Flowers, Persian Rose, Marked, 3 3/8 In. 115.00
Vase, Half Moons, Cerulean Blue, Mottled, 7 1/2 x 6 1/2 In. 385.00
Vase, Iris, Ming Turquoise, 6 In. 115.00
Vase, Iris, Persian Rose Glaze, Bulbous, Marked, c.1920, 13 1/4 In. 546.00
Vase, Iris, Purple, Green, 1906, 13 1/2 x 5 1/2 In. 3220.00
Vase, Iris, Turquoise Matte Glaze, Marked, 14 In. 465.00
Vase, Lady Of The Lily, Maroon & Blue Matte Glaze, 11 1/2 In. 345.00
Vase, Leaves & Stems, Blue & Green Matte Glaze, Marked, 1930s, 13 In. 230.00
Vase, Leaves Around Base, Purple & Green Matte Glaze, Handles, 1903, 9 1/2 In. 3738.00

Vase, Leaves, Blue & Green Matte Glaze, 2 Handles, c.1922, 9 In. 175.00
Vase, Leaves, Blue & Green Mottled Matte Glaze, 1907-1912, 7 In. 690.00
Vase, Leaves, Blue Green Matte Glaze, Marked, 1907-1912, 3 In. 375.00
Vase, Leaves, Blue, Green Matte Glaze, Squat, Ribbed, 1915, 5 x 9 1/2 In. 1035.00
Vase, Leaves, Brown & Green Matte Glaze, 2 Handles, 8 1/2 In. 200.00
Vase, Leaves, Brown & Green Matte Glaze, Low Form, Incised, c.1925, 7 In. 185.00
Vase, Leaves, Frothy Green Matte Glaze, Squat, 1904, 3 x 5 In. 1495.00
Vase, Leaves, Gray Green Matte Glaze, 1907-1912, 5 In. 748.00
Vase, Leaves, Green Matte Glaze, Low, Marked, 6 1/2 In. 489.00
Vase, Leaves, Leathery Raspberry Matte Glaze, Gourd Shape, 1903, 10 1/4 x 5 In. 2300.00
Vase, Leaves, Leathery Turquoise, Plum Matte Glaze, Bulbous, 1905, 9 3/4 x 5 In. 1840.00
Vase, Leaves, Lime Green & Purple Matte Glaze, Low, 1908-1912, 5 1/2 In. 430.00
Vase, Leaves, Maroon & Blue Matte Glaze, Cylindrical, Marked, c.1925, 8 In. 160.00
Vase, Leaves, Maroon & Blue Matte, Gourd Shape, Incised Marks, c.1925, 13 In. 345.00
Vase, Leaves, Mottled Purple Over Green Matte Glaze, Bulbous, 1907-1911, 8 In. 1095.00
Vase, Leaves, Mulberry Glaze, Dark Blue Overspray, Incised, 6 3/4 In. 140.00
Vase, Leaves, Multitone Blue Matte Glaze, Incised Mark, c.1918, 8 In. 460.00
Vase, Leaves, Panels, Leathery Yellow, Green Matte Glaze, Oval, 1908-1911, 5 In. 920.00
Vase, Leaves, Persian Rose Glaze, Squat, 1920, 4 1/2 In. 200.00
Vase, Leaves, Persian Rose Glaze, Squat, 1940, 4 3/4 x 7 1/2 In. 290.00
Vase, Leaves, Turquoise Blue, Marked, 4 3/4 x 7 3/4 In. 175.00
Vase, Lorelei, Blue, Turquoise Glaze, 1901, 10 In. 325.00
Vase, Maroon Matte Glaze, Crystalline Black Highlights, 1916, 5 7/8 In. 430.00
Vase, Maroon Matte Glaze, Low, c.1920, 4 In. 230.00
Vase, Mistletoe, Frothy Sky Blue Glaze, 1907-1911, 2 1/2 In. 518.00
Vase, Mottled Green Matte Glaze, 2 Handles, Incised Mark, 1907-1912, 5 1/2 In. 460.00
Vase, Mountain Craig Brown, 7 3/8 In. 195.00
Vase, Mulberry Glaze, Blue Overspray, 6 1/2 In. 140.00
Vase, Pinecones, Needles, Matte Glaze, c.1913, 10 In. 978.00
Vase, Pink & Blue Matte Glaze, 1907-1912, 2 1/2 In. 345.00
Vase, Poppies, Blue & Green Matte Glaze, Incised Mark, 8 1/4 In. 138.00
Vase, Poppies, Whiplash Stems, Green, Brown, Tobacco Matte Glaze, c.1918, 8 In. 546.00
Vase, Poppy Pods, Blue, Green Leathery Matte Glaze, Bulbous, 1903, 9 x 6 In. 4888.00
Vase, Poppy Pods, Leaves, Lime Green Matte Glaze, 10 1/4 x 4 1/2 In. 4715.00
Vase, Red & Blue Matte Glaze, Incised Marks, 1908-1912, 2 1/2 In. 430.00
Vase, Red, Green Matte Glaze, Handles, Oval, 1903, 8 x 3 1/2 In. 1095.00
Vase, Spider, Matte Apple Green, 1902, 5 In. 2185.00
Vase, Stylized Flowers, Maroon Glaze, Blue, c.1921, 4 In. ....•.... 200.00
Vase, Sunflowers, Blue & Green Matte Glaze, Marked, 9 1/2 In. 175.00
Vase, Swirling Leaves, Cerulean Blue, Aqua Matte, 7 1/4 x 3 In. 360.00
Vase, Tobacco Leaves, Yellow, Brown Matte Glaze, Tapered, 1915, 10 x 4 1/4 In. 1380.00
Vase, Trefoil, Blue, Purple Glaze, 1907-1911, 3 x 3 In. 316.00
Vase, Trefoil, Green Glaze, Bulbous, 1907-1911, 5 x 3 1/4 In. 980.00
Vase, Trefoil, Yellow, Green Matte Glaze, Cylindrical, 1905, 7 3/4 x 3 3/4 In. 460.00
Vase, Tulips, Brown Glaze, Green Overspray, 4 1/2 In. 195.00
Vase, Tulips, Deep Blue To Pale Blue Glaze, Oval, 2 3/4 x 2 1/2 In. 195.00
Vase, Tulips, Ming Turquoise, 3 1/2 In. 72.00
Vase, Tulips, Plum, Mulberry Glaze, Blue Overspray, 4 1/2 In. 110.00
Vase, Tulips, Yellow Matte Glaze, Closed Rim, 1904, 8 x 3 In. 2300.00
Vase, Turquoise Blue Glaze, Handles, Marked, 8 In. 316.00
Vase, Yellow Matte Glaze, Incised Mark, 1920-1930, 6 In. 260.00
Vase, Yucca Leaves, Dusty Rose Glaze, Marked, c.1920, 4 1/2 In. 400.00

VASA MURRHINA is the name of a glassware made by the Vasa
Murrhina Art Glass Company of Sandwich, Massachusetts, about
1884. The glassware was transparent and was embedded with small
pieces of colored glass and metallic flakes. The mica flakes were
coated with silver, gold, copper, or nickel. Some of the pieces were
cased. The same type of glass was made in England. Collectors often
confuse Vasa Murrhina glass with aventurine, spatter, or spangle glass.
There is uncertainty about what actually was made by the Vasa
Murrhina factory. Related pieces may be listed under Spangle Glass.

Basket, Silver Mica Flakes, Blue Overlay, Ruffled Edge, Clear Handle, 9 In. 125.00

Jar, Sweet Meat, Pink, Silver Mica Flecks, Silver Plated Lid, Twist Handle, 7 In. 700.00
Vase, Jack-In-The-Pulpit, Blue, Multicolored, 8 1/2 In. 168.00

VASELINE GLASS is a greenish-yellow glassware resembling petroleum jelly. Some vaseline glass is still being made in old and new styles. Pressed glass of the 1870s was often made of vaseline-colored glass. Additional pieces of vaseline glass may also be listed under Pressed Glass in this book.

Basket, Yellow, 9 3/4 In. 60.00
Bowl, Centerpiece, Gilt Brass, Frame, Oval, Scroll Handles, France, c.1880, 19 In. 620.00
Candlestick, 6-Sided Base, c.1870, 7 1/2 In. 345.00
Candlestick, Dolphin, Petal Socket, 2 Step Square Base, 9 3/4 In., Pair 825.00
Candlestick, Paneled & Fluted, Scalloped Domed Base, Flint, 10 In., Pair 270.00
Celery Dish, Daisy & Button, Canoe Shape, 8 In. 25.00
Compote, Alternating Quilted & Clear Panes, 8 x 8 In. 45.00
Epergne, 3 Lilies, Opalescent, Brass Base, 17 In. 375.00
Pitcher, Water, Sunflower Base, Skirted Base, 8 In. 150.00
Tea Caddy, Paneled, Diamond, Cork Stopper, Brass Cap, 5 1/4 In. 660.00
Tray, Ice Cream, English Hobnail Type, Serpentine, 10 x 16 1/2 In. 160.00
Tumbler, Opalescent, Ribbed Spiral, 3 3/4 In. 75.00
Water Set, Everglades, Opalescent, 7 Piece 575.00

VENETIAN GLASS, see Glass-Venetian category.

VERLYS glass was made in France after 1931. It was made in the United States from 1935 to 1951. The glass is either blown or molded. The American glass is signed with a diamond-point-scratched name, but the French pieces are marked with a molded signature. The designs resemble those used by Lalique.

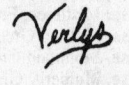

Vase, Blue Ground, Flowers, 10 In. 690.00
Vase, Chinoiserie, Figure, Trees, Molded, Frosted, Cylinder, Inscribed, c.1935, 9 1/4 In. ... 430.00

VERNON KILNS was the name used by Vernon Potteries, Ltd. The company, which started in 1931 in Vernon, California, made dinnerware and figurines until it went out of business in 1958. The molds were bought by Metlox and they continued to make some patterns. Collectors search for the brightly colored dinnerware and the pieces designed by Rockwell Kent, Walt Disney, and Don Blanding. For more information, see *Kovels' Depression Glass & Dinnerware Price List.*

Bits Of Old New England, Chop Plate, Tapping For Sugar, 12 In. 55.00
Casual California, Butter, Dawn Pink 30.00
Coronado, Soup, Dish, Turquoise, 7 1/2 In. 20.00
Early California, Eggcup, Turquoise 20.00
Early California, Plate, Blue, 6 In. 3.50
Early California, Saucer, Blue 3.00
Fantasia, Figurine, Elephant, Dancing 245.00
Gingham, Pitcher, Streamline, 11 In. 65.00
Gingham, Plate, 7 1/2 In. 6.00
Hawaiian Flower, Chop Plate, Blue, 12 In. 180.00
Homespun, Bowl, 8 1/2 In. 24.00
Homespun, Bowl, Vegetable, Divided, 10 In. 25.00
Homespun, Butter Chip, 2 1/2 In. 36.00
Homespun, Creamer 12.00
Homespun, Cup & Saucer 12.00
Homespun, Jug, Bulb Bottom, Pt. 35.00
Homespun, Plate, 6 1/2 In. 3.00
Homespun, Plate, 7 1/2 In. 7.00
Homespun, Plate, 9 1/2 In. 9.00
Homespun, Platter, 12 In. 19.00
Homespun, Saucer, 6 In. 3.00
Homespun, Soup, 8 1/2 In. 24.00
Modern California, Creamer 15.00
Monterey, Cup & Saucer 30.00
Native California, Chop Plate, Yellow, 12 In. 20.00

Native California, Plate, Dinner, Aqua, 10 1/2 In. 16.00
Native California, Plate, Dinner, Blue, 10 1/2 In. 16.00
Native California, Plate, Dinner, Pink, 10 1/2 In. 16.00
Native California, Plate, Salad, Aqua, 7 1/2 In. 8.00
Native California, Relish, 4 Sections, Leaf Shape, 14 In. 60.00
Native California, Saucer, Aqua 5.00
Organdie, Bowl, Round, 8 1/2 In. 17.50
Organdie, Casserole, Round, 2 Handles 40.00
Organdie, Chop Plate, 12 In. 24.00
Organdie, Creamer, Round 12.00
Organdie, Cup 10.00
Organdie, Cup & Saucer 7.00
Organdie, Cup & Saucer, After Dinner 25.00
Organdie, Mug, Straight Sides, 3 1/2 In. 26.00
Organdie, Plate, 7 1/2 In. 5.00
Organdie, Plate, 9 1/2 In. 7.00
Organdie, Plate, Dinner, 10 1/2 In. 5.00
Organdie, Salt & Pepper 18.00
Our America, Ashtray, Maine, Round, Maroon 15.00
Our America, Plate, Arkansas, Maroon, 10 1/2 In. 15.00
Santa Anita, Casserole, Cover, 9 1/2 In. 75.00
Souvenir, Plate, Arkansas, Maroon, Picture, 10 1/2 In. 15.00
Souvenir, Plate, California, Brown, Picture, 10 1/2 In. 15.00
Souvenir, Plate, Excelsior Springs Missouri, Maroon, 10 1/2 In. 25.00
Souvenir, Plate, Historic Places, Massachusetts, Brown, Picture, 10 1/2 In. 30.00
Souvenir, Plate, Maine, Maroon, Map, 10 1/2 In. 15.00
Souvenir, Plate, North Carolina, Multicolored, Picture, 10 1/2 In. 25.00
Souvenir, Plate, Oregon, Multicolored, Picture, 10 1/2 In. 25.00
Souvenir, Plate, Pennsylvania, Multicolored, 10 1/2 In. 25.00
Tam O'Shanter, Chop Plate, 12 In. 35.00
Tam O'Shanter, Jug, Pt. 15.00
Tam O'Shanter, Pepper Shaker 8.00
Tam O'Shanter, Plate, 7 1/2 In. 7.00
Tam O'Shanter, Sugar, Cover 15.00
Tickled Pink, Pepper Shaker 10.00
Ultra California, Coffeepot ....100.00 to 110.00

VERRE DE SOIE glass was first made by Frederick Carder at the
Steuben Glass Works from about 1905 to 1930. It is an iridescent glass
of soft white or very, very pale green. The name means *glass of silk*,
and it does resemble silk. Other factories have made verre de soie, and
some of the English examples were made of different colors. Verre de
soie is an art glass and is not related to the iridescent, pressed, white
carnival glass mistakenly called by its name. Related pieces may be
found in the Steuben category.

Bowl, Underplate, Steuben 6 In. 90.00
Compote, Blue Threading, Steuben, 1 3/8 x 3 1/8 In. 316.00
Compote, Cover, Lime, Early 20th Century, 6 3/4 In. 80.00
Compote, Steuben, 6 1/4 x 4 1/4 In. 290.00
Console, Flared Rim, Stretched Edge, Steuben, 12 x 4 1/2 In. 230.00
Jar, Cover, Underplate, Lime, Leafy Pear Finial, Steuben, 4 1/2 In. 70.00
Marmalade, Disc Cover, Pear Finial, Underplate, Steuben, 4 1/2 In. 185.00
Shade, Horizontal Etched Flowers, Blue Threading, 4 In., Pair 315.00
Sherbet, Underplate, Iridescent, S Monogram, 3 Sets 240.00
Tumbler, Love Knots, Swags, Wreath, Flared Rim, Hawkes, 4 3/4 In. 121.00
Vase, Lily, Steuben, 6 In. 259.00
Vase, Lime, Footed, Steuben, 6 3/4 In. 173.00
Vase, Neoblue, Orange Anthuriums, Blue Feathered Leaves, Signed, Lotton, 1994, 6 In. . 403.00
Vase, Neoblue, Pulled Leaves, Cascading From Vines, Signed, Lotton, 1986, 10 In. 545.00
Vase, Stick, Spiraling Flower Vine, Steuben, 8 In. 185.00
Water Set, Celeste Blue, Applied Prunts, Opaque, Steuben, 10 1/2 In., 5 Piece 1150.00

VIENNA, see Beehive category.

VIENNA ART plates are round metal serving trays produced at the turn of the century. The designs, copied from Royal Vienna porcelain plates, usually featured a portrait of a woman encircled by a wide, ornate border. Many were used as advertising or promotional items and were produced in Coshocton, Ohio, by J.F. Meeks Tuscarora Advertising Co. and H.D. Beach's Standard Advertising Co.

Plate, Girl, Cobalt Blue Border, Tin, 1905, 10 In.	80.00
Plate, Queen Louisa, Fruit Border, Tin, 1905, 10 In.	60.00

VILLEROY & BOCH Pottery of Mettlach was founded in 1836. The firm made many types of wares, including the famous Mettlach steins. Collectors can be confused because although Villeroy & Boch made most of its pieces in the city of Mettlach, Germany, they also had factories in other locations. The dating code impressed on the bottom of most pieces makes it possible to determine the age of the piece. Additional items, including steins and earthenware pieces marked with the famous castle mark or the word *Mettlach,* may be found in the Mettlach category.

Ashtray, Frog Bandleader, Dresden, 8 In.	485.00
Ashtray, Monkey Holding Bowl, Glazed Relief, 5 x 7 1/2 In.	360.00
Figurine, Pigeon, Sheer Pink Semimatte Glaze, 8 In., Pair	45.00
Mug, Eagle, American Flag, E Pluribus Unum Banner, Marked, 5 In.	105.00
Plate, 4 Designs, White Ground, Wladimir Njemuchin, c.1921, 12 In., 4 Piece	1116.00
Plate, Rheinstein, Lauffenburg, Delft Style, Hand Painted, c.1890, 20 In., Pair	1595.00
Terrine, Lid, Vegetables, Luxembourg No. 5, 8 x 5 1/2 In.	95.00
Tile, Carp Swimming, Water Lilies, Green Ground, 6 x 6 In., 4 Piece	545.00
Tile, Daisies, White & Yellow, Green Leaves, Blue Sky, 6 x 6 In., 5 Piece	520.00
Tray, Flowers, Green Ground, Art Deco Handles, Oval, 12 3/8 In.	235.00
Tray, Flowers, White, Green, Dark Green Ground, Handles, 12 In.	235.00
Tray, Flowers, White, Green, Oval, Raised Rim, Handles, c.1940, 13 In.	235.00
Tray, Oval, Flowers, White, Dark Green, Green Ground, Silver Sides, 12 In.	325.00
Vase, Cameo Landscape, Purple Over Frost, Signed, E. Rigot, 3 1/4 In.	230.00
Vase, Landscape, Olive Green On Pumpkin Ground, Signed, E. Rigot, 3 1/2 In.	207.00

VOLKMAR pottery was made by Charles Volkmar of New York from 1879 to about 1911. He was associated with several firms, including the Volkmar Ceramic Company, Volkmar and Cory, and Charles Volkmar and Son. Volkmar had been a painter, and his designs often look like oil paintings drawn on pottery.

VOLKMAR
Corona N.Y

Vase, Gourd Shape, Mottled Olive Green Glaze, 5 In.	230.00
Vase, Spherical, Frothy Sky Blue Glaze, 5 1/2 In.	316.00

VOLKSTEDT was a soft-paste porcelain factory started in 1760 by Georg Heinrich Macheleid at Volkstedt, Thuringia. Volkstedt-Rudolstadt was a porcelain factory started at Volkstedt-Rudolstadt by Beyer and Bock in 1890. Most pieces seen in shops today are from the later factory.

Figurine, Marchand De Chansons, Peddler Family, Musicians, c.1940, 10 x 10 In.	460.00
Figurine, Visit To Grandmother, Women, Men, Children, c.1900, 15 1/4 x 21 1/2 In.	1840.00

WADE pottery is made by the Wade Group of Potteries started in 1810 near Burslem, England. Several potteries merged to become George Wade & Son, Ltd. early in the twentieth century, and other potteries have been added through the years. The best-known Wade pieces are the small figurines given away with Red Rose Tea and other promotional items. The Disney figures are listed in this book in the Disneyana category.

c. 1936 +

Bottle, Chivas Royal Salute, Blue, Gold Labels, Velvet Bag, 750 Ml	40.00
Bottle Pourer, Burroughs, Figural, Smiling Elizabethan Head, Collar & Hat, 1 3/4 In.	28.00
Creamer, Luster, Blue Flowers, White Ground, Copper Luster Trim, 3 In.	37.00
Dish, Bramble Ware, 1950, 7 In.	25.00
Dish, Child's, Quack Quacks Ware, 1930, 7 In.	85.00
Figurine, Alsatian Puppy, 1973, 1 1/4 In.	8.50

Figurine, Bear Cub, 1972, 1 1/4 In.	7.50
Figurine, Beaver, 1972, 1 1/4 In.	7.50
Figurine, Bluebird, 1979, 1 1/4 In.	13.00
Figurine, Boy Blue, Box, 1974, 2 7/8 In.	52.00
Figurine, Butterfly, 1975, 1 3/4 In.	8.00
Figurine, Cat, Lying Down, Gray, 1996, 1 3/4 In.	13.00
Figurine, Circus Clown, Water Bucket, 1996, 1 1/2 In.	7.50
Figurine, Circus Pony, 1978, 1 3/4 In.	7.50
Figurine, Circus Set, Ringmaster, Human Cannonball, Clowns, Animals, 1996, 15 Piece	50.00
Figurine, Cock-A-Teel, 1990, 1 1/2 In.	13.00
Figurine, Dog, Irish Setter, Standing, 1984, 2 1/4 In.	28.00
Figurine, Duck, 1972, 1 1/4 In.	13.00
Figurine, Human Cannonball, 1993, 1 1/4 In.	7.50
Figurine, Humpty Dumpty, 1971, 1 1/2 In.	13.00
Figurine, Jack, Box, 1971, 2 7/8 In.	50.00
Figurine, Jill, Box, 1971, 2 7/8 In.	40.00
Figurine, Kathleen, 1986, 3 1/2 In.	35.00
Figurine, King Cole, Box, 1971, 2 1/2 In.	50.00
Figurine, Leopard, 1996, 1 7/8 In.	3.00
Figurine, Mary Mary, Box, 1973, 2 7/8 In.	56.00
Figurine, Orangutan, 1994, 1 1/4 In.	5.00
Figurine, Otter, 1972, 1 1/4 In.	7.50
Figurine, Papa Tortoise, Removable Shell Lid, 1958, 4 In.	15.00
Figurine, Pied Piper, 1971-1979, 2 In.	13.00
Figurine, Polly, Kettle, Box, 1973, 2 7/8 In.	48.00
Figurine, Sea Lion, 1973, 1 1/2 In.	7.50
Figurine, Soldier, Nursery Rhyme, 1958, 3 In.	200.00
Figurine, Squirrel, Blue, 1985, 1 1/2 In.	12.00
Figurine, Tiger, 1985, 1 7/16 In.	3.00
Figurine, Tom Piper, Box, 1972, 2 3/4 In.	52.00
Figurine, Tom, 1997, 3 5/8 In.	75.00
Figurine, Tommy Tucker, Box, 1972, 3 In.	42.00
Figurine, Willie Winkie, Box, 1972, 2 7/8 In.	25.00
Mug, Family Riding In 2-Wheeled Horse-Drawn Cart, Ireland, 3 In.	15.00
Mug, Shamrocks, Ireland, 4 1/4 In.	22.00
Table Set, Salt & Pepper, Toothpick, Shamrock, Ireland, 2 1/2 In., 4 Piece	60.00
Tankard, Barrel, Metallic Accents, Pt.	40.00
Tankard, Rhinoceros, Figural, 9 1/2 In.	235.00
Teapot, Shamrocks, Ireland, 6 x 9 1/2 In.	295.00

WAHPETON POTTERY, see Rosemeade category.

WALL POCKETS were popular in the 1930s. They were made by many
American and European factories. Glass, pottery, porcelain, majolica,
chalkware, and metal wall pockets can be found in many fanciful
shapes.

Apple, Red, Treasure Craft	25.00
Apple, Yellow, Treasure Craft	25.00
Bird, Aqua, 3-D, Green, 5 x 3 3/4 In.	45.00
Bird, Aqua, Green Planter, 5 x 3 3/4 In.	45.00
Bird, Birdhouse, Czechoslovakia, 5 In.	35.00
Bird Of Paradise, Flowers, Bullet Shape, 6 In.	25.00
Chocolate Albany Slip Glaze, Pottery, c.1920, 10 3/4 In.	55.00
Deer, In Pink Slipper, 3-D Bells, Holly, Arnart Creation, No. 7705, Japan, 7 1/4 In.	40.00
Emerald, Rust, Albany Slip Glaze, Bird, Signed Owens, Late 1970s, 7 In.	99.00
Faience, Polychrome, Bellows Shape, 4 1/2 In.	30.00
Hanging, Pine, Chipped, Line Carving, Stippling, 11 x 3 1/2 x 16 In.	166.00
Maple Leaf, Yellow, 6 x 6 In.	30.00
Molded Grapes, Green Matte Glaze, Shawsheen, Pottery, 13 In.	518.00
Parrot, White, Multicolored Feathers, Morton	30.00
Peacock, Green, West Coast Pottery, No. 411	50.00
Pitcher, 3-D Fruit, Green, White, 5 1/4 In.	25.00
Pitcher, Fruit, Green, White, 5 1/4 In.	25.00

Pumpkin, Lead Glaze, Earthenware, 1920s, 6 1/2 In. 88.00
Red Apple, Pottery, Treasure Craft 25.00
Southern Pine, Multicolored Flowers, Folk Art, Ohio, 1937, 15 x 5 x 9 In. 110.00
Walnut, Painted, Pierced Heart, Geometric, c.1820, 14 1/2 x 10 1/2 In. 1435.00
Yellow Apple, Pottery, Treasure Craft 25.00

WALLACE NUTTING photographs are listed under Print, Nutting. His reproduction furniture is listed under Furniture.

WALRATH was a potter who worked in New York City; Rochester, New York; and at the Newcomb Pottery in New Orleans, Louisiana. Frederick Walrath died in 1920. Pieces listed here are from his Rochester period.

Walrath
Pottery

Bowl, Flower, Kneeling Nude, Mottled Green Glaze, 6 1/4 x 7 1/4 In. 825.00
Bowl, Flower, Seated Nude Figure, Mottled Green, Terra-Cotta Glaze, 8 1/2 x 6 1/2 In. 1058.00
Paperweight, Frog, Green, Marked, 2 3/8 x 3 5/8 In. 430.00
Vase, Orange Blossoms, Speckled Green Matte Glaze, Bulbous, 6 x 3 3/4 In. 4406.00
Vase, Painted Design, Green & Brown Matte Glaze, Shouldered, 7 1/2 In. 4315.00

WALT DISNEY, see Disneyana category.

WALTER, see A. Walter category.

WARWICK china was made in Wheeling, West Virginia, in a pottery working from 1887 to 1951. Many pieces were made with hand painted or decal decorations. The most familiar Warwick has a shaded brown background. The name *Warwick* is part of the mark and sometimes the mysterious word *IOGA* is also included.

Bowl, Painted Flowers, Pink, Violet, Blue, Gold Branches, Swirled Edge, 8 In. 35.00
Bowl, Vegetable, 9 In. 13.00
Casserole, Cover, Flowers 57.00
Cup, Flowers 9.00
Gravy Boat, Faststand, Flowers 29.00
Mustard, Virginia, Black Transfer 9.00
Pitcher, Embossed, Brown To Orange, Flowers & Leaves, IOGA, 9 1/2 In. 50.00
Plate, Flowers, 8 In. 10.00
Plate, Flowers, 10 In. 14.00
Plate, GH Monogram, Green Trim, Restaurant Ware, 9 3/4 In. 10.00
Plate, Palm Trees, Red Band Border, 7 1/4 In. 24.00
Plate, Shaded Brown To Tan, Monk Portrait, IOGA, 10 In. 30.00
Soup, Dish, Flowers, 8 In. 14.00
Tankard, Shaded Brown To Tan, Monk Portrait, IOGA, 5 1/8 In. 30.00
Teapot, Lid, Pink Rose 75.00
Tray, Dresser, Flowers, Gold Trim, c.1900, 11 1/4 x 7 1/2 In. 50.00
Vase, Shaded Brown, Portrait Of Young Woman, Squat, IOGA, 4 x 6 1/2 In. 130.00

WATCH pockets held the pocket watch that was important in Victorian times because it was not until World War I that the wristwatch was used. All types of watches are collected: silver, gold, or plated. Watches are arranged by company name or by style. Wristwatches are a separate category.

A. Favre Brandt, Hunting Case, Flowers, Geometric, Gold, No. 4012, Switzerland, Pocket   135.00
Auguste Saltzman, Hunting Case, Chouise De Fonds, 18K Gold, c.1860, 14-In. Chain ...   315.00
B. Vaayu, Hunting Case, 14K Yellow Gold, Russia, 19th Century, Pocket 405.00
Ball Watch Co., Railroad, Official Standard, Open Face, No. B551535, Pocket 270.00
Beefield, Open Face, Enamel Face, Arabic Numerals, Silver Nested Case, England 825.00
Breguet, Open Face, Mother & Child In Garden, Enamel Face, Arabic Numerals, Paris ..   660.00
Breitling, Chronomat, Aviator, 3 Dials, Stopwatch 950.00
Bucherer, Hunting Case, Self Winding, 18K White Gold, Ultra Thin 430.00
Chas E. Jacots, Hunting Case, 18K Gold, Key Wind, Shield, Star Motif, c.1865 ....   230.00
Chase, Lapel, 10K Rolled Gold Plate, Gold-Toned Ribbon, 5 In. 38.00
Chatelaine, Ivory Enamel Dial, Arabic Numerals, Swiss, Art Nouveau, 14K Gold 646.00
Chatelaine, White Enamel Dial, Roman Numerals, Victorian, 14K Gold 210.00
Dennison Howard & Davis, Hunting Case, Eagle Stamped, Roman Numeral Dial 1700.00
Elgin, 17 Jewel, Enamel Dial, Arabic Numerals, Second Hand, 14K Gold, c.1900 ....   175.00

Elgin, Gold Filled, Open Face, White Enamel Dial, B.W. Raymond, No. 2837324, Pocket .	84.00
Elgin, Hunting Case, Engraved, Flowers, No. 21547389, Pocket	11.00
Elgin, Hunting Case, Sterling, Gold Birds, Flowers, No. 11519039, Pocket	95.00
Elgin, Open Face, Octagonal, Engraved Leaves, Bows, Arabic Numerals, Sundial	55.00
Elgin, Presentation B.W. Raymond, 19 Jewel, Up-Down Indicator Dial	650.00
Girard-Perregaux, Shell Oil, Skeleton, Base Metal, A.Schild Movement, 1940	250.00
Gregson, Open Face, Silver, Enamel Face, Lady By River, Roman Numerals, Paris	990.00
Gruen, White Dial, 17 Jewel, 14K Gold, Smith, Patterson Co., 10K Gold Chain, 1 1/2 In. .	127.00
Half Hunting Case, 18K Yellow Gold, London, c.1870	345.00
Hampden Watch Co., Dueber Coin Silver Case, Baseball Player, Bat, c.1880	1200.00
Hebomas, Open Face, Inner Dial, Open Escapement	160.00
Hunting Case, Engraved Eagle, Enamel Face, Roman Numerals, Fleur-De-Lis Hands	385.00
Hunting Case, Woman's, White Enamel Dial, Arabic Numerals, Pocket, 14K Gold .176.00 to	294.00
Illinois, Hunting Case, Engraved, White Enamel Dial, 14K Gold, No. 1064327	250.00
J. Charlson, Enamel Dial, Roman Numerals, Brass Plique Border, Tortoiseshell Case	1058.00
James Williams Movement, No. 7219, Open Face, Silver, England	115.00
Key Wind, Brass, Swing-Out Pair Case, Thomas Harrison, Silversmith, Chain	1870.00
Lapel, Enamel, Rose Cut Diamonds, 18K Gold, c.1895	1955.00
Lapel, White Porcelain Dial, Roman Numerals, Edwardian, 18K Gold	705.00
Longines, Pendant, Ivory Guilloche, Arabic Numerals, Flowers, Edwardian, 18K Gold . . .	1175.00
M.J. Tobias, Yellow Gold, Key Wind, Open Face, Chain, Gold Coin Fob, 1911, Pocket . . .	430.00
Meister, Pendant, Black, Gold Enamel, Silver, Gold-Filled Chain, c.1920	230.00
Molton, Open Face, 18K Yellow Gold, Mid To Late 19th Century	200.00
Movado, Open Face, Gold, Ivory Dial, Arabic Numerals, Art Deco, 18K Gold, Signed . . .	764.00
Omega, Inset Second Face, Top Winding Mechanism, Swiss	259.00
Open Face, 18K Gold, Multicolored, England	765.00
Open Face, Erotic Scene, Silver, Roman Numerals, Swing-Out Movement, Silver Case . .	1265.00
Open Face, Lever Movement, Gold Tone Dial, 14K Gold, Swiss, Pocket	50.00
Open Face, Moon Phase, White Enamel, Gun Metal Case, Swiss, Pocket	169.00
Patek Philippe, Woman's, Open Face, 18K Gold, Enamel, Fleur-De-Lis, c.1868	1115.00
Rockford Watch Co., Hunting Case, 14K Yellow Gold, Engine Turned, Illinois, c.1888 . .	345.00
Samuel Curtis, Roxbury, No. 418, Original No. 101 Case, Anchor & Eagle Hallmark . . .	6100.00
Schaffhausen, Turler, Open Face, 14K Gold, Self-Winding, 10K White Gold Chain, 1948 .	320.00
Stephen & Maurice Hart, Chain, Fob, Key, 18K Yellow Gold, England, 1794, Pocket . . .	865.00
Swiss Coach, Travel, Pin Set, Day, Month, Moonphase, Nickel Case, c.1890, 4 3/4 In. . . .	1265.00
T.B. Starr, Art Deco, Silvertone, Platinum, Diamond, 17 Jewel, Size 10	765.00
T.J. Tobias, Hunting Case, Key Wind, Vest Chain, 14K Yellow Gold, 1800, Pocket	720.00
Tiffany, Hunting Case, 18K Gold, White Enamel Dial, Arabic, Jewel Movement, 14 In. . . .	1410.00
Tiffany, Woman's, Open Face, 18K Gold, No. 71063, c.1892	355.00
Waltham, Hunting Case, Engraved Flowers, No. 9493990 Movement, 10K Gold, Pocket . .	169.00
Waltham, Hunting Case, White Enamel Dial, No. 4472163, 14K Gold, Size 14, Pocket . .	160.00
Waltham, Open Face, Enamel Dial, Arabic, 17 Jewel, Ribbed Edge, 14K Gold, 1903	265.00
Waltham, Woman's, Hunting Case, Enamel Dial, Roman, Leaves, Flowers, 14K Gold . . .	265.00
Westclox, Combination Pocket Watch & Pistol, Nickel Finished Case, 1890, 3 x 2 In. . . .	4100.00
Woman's, Silver, Enamel, Relief Case, Lady's Head In Flower, Art Nouveau, Swiss	203.00
Zenith, No. 1696300, 14K Gold, Open Face, White Enamel Dial, Swiss, Pocket	100.00

WATCH FOBS were worn on watch chains. They were popular during
Victorian times and after. Many styles, especially advertising designs,
are still made today.

Bradstreet & Clemens, Nebraska Horse Auction, Horseshoe Shape, 2 Horses, 1912	70.00
Bryan, Sepia Celluloid	40.00
Cowboy, On Bronco, Gilt, Strap, Los Angeles, 1915	160.00
Dempsey-Gibbons, Championship Fight, 2 Boxers In Ring, Bronze, Gilt, 1 1/4 In.	150.00
Echo Springs Rye Whiskey, Silver Plated, Scalloped Edges, Louisville, Kentucky	75.00
Family Crest, Sardonyx Intaglio, Vest Chain, 14K Yellow Gold	1095.00
Filigree, Gold Filled, Clasp, Chain, 3 Scrolls	125.00
Keystone Lumber Co., Running Elephant, Carrying 2 x 4 Board	75.00
Musical, Shell & Bellflower Design, 18K Gold	1540.00
Nabisco Co., Enameled Sterling Silver, Uneeda Biscuit Box	170.00
Pine Tree Manufacturing Co., Swan Swimming In River, Trees, White Metal, Oval	75.00
Red Diamond Overalls, Man With Oil Can, Red, White, Blue Celluloid	85.00
Standard Horseshoe Co., Horse Head In Horseshoe, Round, Silver Plated	89.00

Taft, Brass, White House Lock, 1908 .... 25.00
U.S. Tires, Be One Of The Satisfied Family, Race Driver, Celluloid, 2 In. 500.00
Whitewater Falls Stock Farm, Standing Percheron Horse, Shield Shape 65.00

WATERFORD type glass resembles the famous glass made from 1783 to 1851 in the Waterford Glass Works in Ireland. It is a clear glass that was often decorated by cutting. Modern glass is being made again in Waterford, Ireland, and is marketed under the name *Waterford*.

Basket, Diamond Cutting, 13 x 14 In. 750.00
Bowl, Salad, Diamond & Arched Fan Rim, Oval, 11 x 7 1/2 x 3 1/2 In. 260.00
Candlestick, Baluster Stem, 8 In., Pair 185.00
Ice Bucket, Diamond & Leaf, 6 1/2 In. 230.00
Ice Pail, Tapered Body, 2 Fitted Scrolling Handles, 7 x 8 1/2 In. 290.00
Parfait, Kylemore, 6 1/2 In., 8 Piece 250.00
Tumbler, Water, Kylemore, 6 3/4 In., 8 Piece 250.00
Vase, Diamond Cutting, 10 In. 175.00
Vase, Scroll & Checker Bands, Urn Shape, 9 In. 230.00
Wine, Kylemore, 6 In., 8 Piece 250.00

WATT family members bought the Globe pottery of Crooksville, Ohio, in 1922. They made pottery mixing bowls and tableware of the type made by Globe. In 1935 they changed the production and made the pieces with the freehand decorations that are popular with collectors today. Apple, Starflower, Rooster, Tulip, and Autumn Foliage are the best-known patterns. Pansy, also called Rio Rose, was the earliest pattern. Apple, the most popular pattern, can be dated from the leaves. Originally, the apples had three leaves; after 1958 two leaves were used. The plant closed in 1965. For more information, see *Kovels' Depression Glass & Dinnerware Price List.*

American Red Bud, Baker, Square, No. 84 .... 800.00
American Red Bud, Salt & Pepper, Barrel 300.00
Apple, Bowl, 3-Leaf, Advertising, W.O. Kienas Markesan, 5 x 9 In. 125.00
Apple, Bowl, 4 x 6 1/2 In. 100.00
Apple, Bowl, 5 x 9 In. 175.00
Apple, Bowl, Cereal, 5 1/2 In. 40.00
Apple, Bowl, Ribbed, 3 1/4 x 6 1/4 In. ....90.00 to 95.00
Apple, Bowl, Spaghetti, No. 39 .... 150.00
Apple, Casserole, Cover, No. 110 .... 300.00
Apple, Casserole, Cover Only 90.00
Apple, Mixing Bowl, Ribbed, 3 3/4 x 7 3/4 In. 110.00
Apple, Nappy, 3-Leaf, No. 05 .... 70.00
Apple, Pitcher, 3-Leaf, No. 16 .... 120.00
Apple, Pitcher, 5 1/4 In. 100.00
Apple, Pitcher, No. 15, Beemer Lumber Co., Beemer, Neb. 95.00
Autumn Foliage, Bowl, 4 x 6 1/4 In. 50.00
Autumn Foliage, Bowl, 9 1/4 In. 115.00
Autumn Foliage, Nappy, No. 05 .... 57.00
Autumn Foliage, Pitcher, 5 1/4 In. 107.00
Bands, Bowl, Blue, White, Impressed Oven Ware U.S.A., 12, 6 x 12 In. 20.00
Basket Weave, Bowl, 5 x 9 In. 50.00
Bleeding Heart, Bean Pot, Cover, 6 1/2 In. 140.00
Bleeding Heart, Bowl, No. 75, 2 1/2 In. 30.00
Blue & White Banded, Bowl, Yellow, 9 In. 45.00
Brown, Bean Pot, Cover, 10 In. 20.00
Brown, Bowl, Cinnamon Drip, 3 1/2 x 9 1/4 In. 30.00
Brown, Dog Dish, 7 3/4 In. 65.00
Butterscotch, Casserole, Cover, 6 x 8 1/2 In. 39.00
Dutch Tulip, Saltshaker, 4 In. 450.00
Eagle, Canister, 7 1/4 In. 465.00
Kitch-N-Queen, Mixing Bowl, Ribbed, No. 8 .... 36.00
Kla-Hammered, Pitcher, Cover, 4 7/8 x 3 1/2 In. 23.00
Pansy, Bowl, Spaghetti, Cut-Leaf, No. 39, 13 x 3 In. 80.00
Pansy, Platter, Cut-Leaf, 15 In. 105.00

Rio Rose, Bowl, 13 In.	110.00
Rio Rose, Bowl, Spaghetti, Lipped	90.00
Rio Rose, Pie Plate, 9 In.	85.00
Starflower, Bowl, 3 5/8 x 7 3/4 In.	40.00
Starflower, Bowl, 12 In.	100.00
Starflower, Bowl, No. 06, 3 1/2 In.	55.00
Starflower, Bowl, Salad, 5-Petal, 11 3/4 x 4 1/4 In.	75.00
Starflower, Casserole, Cover, 6 x 8 1/2 In.	245.00
Starflower, Cookie Jar, 5-Petal	225.00
Starflower, Ice Bucket, Cover, 5-Petal	185.00
Starflower, Pitcher, 8 In.	110.00
Starflower, Platter, 5-Petal, Chartreuse, Brown Ground	125.00
Tear Drop, Bowl, No. 74	45.00
Tulip, Bowl, 5 3/4 x 8 1/2 In.	190.00
Tulip, Bowl, 5 x 7 1/2 In.	175.00

WAVE CREST glass is an opaque white glassware manufactured by the Pairpoint Manufacturing Company of New Bedford, Massachusetts, and some French factories. It was decorated by the C.F. Monroe Company of Meriden, Connecticut. The glass was painted in pastel colors and decorated with flowers. The name *Wave Crest* was used after 1898.

WAVE CREST WARE

Biscuit Jar, Crescent Moon, Cream Top, Blue Base, Silver Plated Cover & Bail, 8 In.	400.00
Biscuit Jar, Enameled Flowers, White, Green, Silver Plated Cover & Bail, 6 In.	175.00
Biscuit Jar, Fern Bows, Forget-Me-Nots, Hinged Cover, 7 1/2 In.	460.00
Biscuit Jar, Ferns, Yellow, Silver Plated Cover & Bail, 8 In.	225.00
Biscuit Jar, Helmschmied Swirl, Pink Flowers, Metal Hardware, Label, 10 In.	345.00
Biscuit Jar, Helmschmied Swirl, White, Tan, Red Enamel, 6 1/2 In.	460.00
Biscuit Jar, Irises, Gold, Purple, 7 1/2 In.	345.00
Biscuit Jar, Opaque White, Blue Sculptured Panels, Mums, Collar, 7 1/2 In.	175.00
Biscuit Jar, Robin On Branch, Orange Ground, Silver Plated Cover & Bail, 8 In.	125.00
Biscuit Jar, Roses, Pink, Cream Ground, Square, 6 In.	260.00
Biscuit Jar, Scroll, Yellow, Flowers, Silver Plated Cover & Bail, 8 1/2 In.	325.00
Biscuit Jar, White, Yellow, Pink & Blue Flowers, Ruffled, Brass Cover, 7 1/2 In.	175.00
Box, Cigar, Blown-Out Pink Flowers, Royal Blue Ground, Script Word Cigars, 6 In.	2300.00
Box, Cigarette, White, Green, Gold Enameled Trim, 6 In.	325.00
Box, Collars & Cuffs, Pink Poppies, Hinged Cover, Egg Crate Shape, 7 In.	1200.00
Box, Glove, Rococo, Enameled Daisies, Cover	1175.00
Card Holder, Pink Flowers, Blue Ground, 2 3/4 x 4 In.	300.00
Creamer, Pink Blown-Out Flowers, Square	335.00
Dresser Box, Baroque Shell, Blue & White Flowers, Pink Ground, 4 In.	345.00
Dresser Box, Baroque Shell, Flowers, Blue, Maroon, Red Mark, 4 In.	145.00
Dresser Box, Baroque Shell, Flowers, Yellow, Brown, Cover, Stamped, 4 1/4 In.	175.00
Dresser Box, Baroque Shell, Lavender, Field Of Daisies, 7 In.	670.00
Dresser Box, Baroque Shell, Pink, Beaded Design, 7 In.	520.00
Dresser Box, Baroque Shell, Red Flowers, Scrolling, 7 In.	805.00
Dresser Box, Blown-Out Flowers, Border, Hinged Cover, Oval, 3 1/2 x 8 In.	2000.00
Dresser Box, Blown-Out Flowers, Border, Hinged Cover, Oval, 4 1/2 x 8 In.	2300.00
Dresser Box, Blown-Out Flowers, Green & Blue, Enameled Mill Scene, 4 In.	260.00
Dresser Box, Blown-Out Robins & Branches, Hinged Cover, Square, 6 1/2 x 7 In.	4400.00
Dresser Box, Blue & Pink Flowers, Hinged Clock Cover, 5 In.	2000.00
Dresser Box, Blue Flowers, White Ground, Hinged Cover, Casket Shape, 3 1/2 In.	700.00
Dresser Box, Enameled Puffy Daisies, Cream Ground, Hinged Cover, 7 In.	300.00
Dresser Box, Enameled, Pink Flowers, Hinged Clock Cover, 5 In.	1782.00
Dresser Box, Flowers, Egg Crate Shape, 3 1/4 In.	165.00
Dresser Box, Flowers, Turquoise, Opal Panels, Egg Crate Shape, Footed, 5 1/2 In.	1265.00
Dresser Box, Helmschmied Swirl, Blue To White Opaque, 6 3/4 In.	489.00
Dresser Box, Mums, Brown, Tan, Mums, Egg Crate Shape, Ormolu Stand, 6 3/4 In.	3800.00
Dresser Box, Pastel Pansies, Banner, Shield, Hinged Cover, Oval, Marked, 3 x 5 In.	260.00
Dresser Box, Pink, Gold Enameled, Flowers, Scrolls, Portrait, Hinged Cover, 7 In.	776.00
Dresser Box, Pink, Starburst Beading, Cover, 5 1/2 In.	650.00
Dresser Box, Ships, Waves, Shore, Cut Stars Around Base, Cameo, 3 3/4 In.	1550.00
Dresser Box, Swirl, Cream, Blue Flowers, Jeweled, Hinged Cover, Square, 3 1/4 In.	175.00

Dresser Box, White & Yellow, Pink Flowers, Hinged Cover, Label, 5 In. 350.00
Ewer, Blue, Pink Flowers, Serpentine Metal Handles, Spout & Base, 16 In., Pair 500.00
Fernery, Enameled, Flower, Lion-Footed, Liner, Egg Crate Shape, 6 3/4 In. 520.00
Fernery, Hobstar, Prism & Fan, Silver Rim, 8 Sides, 10 In. 350.00
Fernery, Landscape Scene, Yellow, Blue, 8 Sides, 8 In. 850.00
Humidor, Bulldog Scene, Old Sport, Browns, Metal Cover, 7 In. 950.00
Humidor, Fisherman With Pipe, Brown, Yellow, Metal Cover, Embossed Poppy, 6 In. 175.00
Humidor, Golfer Scene, Rust Ground, Metal Cover, 6 In. 225.00
Humidor, Monk Scene, Brown & Yellow, Metal Cover, 7 In. 175.00
Humidor, Tavern Scene, Brown, Tavern Scene, Metal Cover, 7 In. 300.00
Jewelry Box, Blown-Out Dahlia, Hinged Cover, 4 In. 800.00
Jewelry Box, Helmschmied Swirl, Daisies, White, Hinged Cover, Round, 4 In. 180.00
Jewelry Box, Helmschmied Swirl, Pink, Blue Flowers, Square Cover, 3 In. 120.00
Jewelry Tray, Flower Mold, Green, Pink Flowers, Mirror, Marked, 7 x 5 In. 350.00
Lamp, Flowers, Pink, 17 In. 350.00
Lamp, Kerosene, School In Wintertime, Leaf & Berry, Blue, 16 1/2 In. 500.00
Letter Holder, Cream, Orange Flowers, 5 x 6 1/2 In. 275.00
Letter Holder, Light Green, Pink Flowers, Scroll Shape, Brass Rim, 4 x 6 In. 375.00
Letter Holder, White, Pink Flowers, Egg Crate Shape, 4 x 6 In. 175.00
Memo File, Blue Flowers, Pink & Yellow, Spindle, 3 x 7 In. 350.00
Paperweight, Cupid Playing Cymbals, Yellow & Blue Flowers, 4 In. 800.00
Photo Receiver, Cream, Blue Flowers, Brass Rim, Puffy, 4 1/4 x 5 1/2 In. 275.00
Photo Receiver, Lavender Flowers, Cream, White, Egg Crate Shape, 4 x 6 In. 400.00
Photo Receiver, Scroll, Enameled Daisies, Yellow, Blue, 4 x 6 In. 375.00
Pin Tray, Blue Flowers, Pink & White, Ormolu Top, 3 1/2 In. 75.00
Pin Tray, White, Fields Of Flowers, Scroll Shape, Gilt Feet, 6 1/2 In. 375.00
Plaque, Girl Calling, Green Border, Gold Highlights, Metal Frame, Round, 9 1/2 In. 6000.00
Plaque, Woman Among Flowers, Green Border, Gold, Frame, 11 1/2 x 8 1/2 In. 5800.00
Powder Jar, Helmschmied, Yellow Flowers, White & Blue, Silver Plated Cover, 3 In. 100.00
Salt & Pepper, Birds & Flowers, White, Brown, Tulip Shape, 2 3/4 In. 100.00
Salt & Pepper, Blossoms & Branches, Ribbed, White, 4 In. 175.00
Saltshaker, Erie Swirl, White & Peach, Blue Floral 30.00
Smoking Set, Delft Pattern, Bird's-Eye Maple Base, 4 x 12 In. 250.00
Sugar & Creamer, Helmschmied Swirl, Yellow, Pink Flowers, Silver Plated Covers 275.00
Sugar Shaker, Helmschmied Swirl, White, Brown, Pink Flowers, Silver Cover, 3 In. 250.00
Syrup, Pink Roses, Cream Ground, Swirl, Silver Plated Spout & Handle, 3 1/2 In. 275.00
Toothpick, Pink Flowers, Light Green, Footed, 2 1/4 In. 150.00
Tumbler, Yellow, Pink & Lavender Flowers, 3 7/8 In. 170.00
Vase, Blown-Out Wildflowers, Blue Ground, Ormolu Foot & Collar, 8 In. 335.00
Vase, Blue Flowers, Pink & White, Ormolu Base & Rim, 7 1/2 In. 400.00
Vase, Blue, Pink Flowers, Squat, Handles, Marked, 3 In. 200.00
Vase, Bud, Pink, Blue Flowers, Brass Rim, 3 In. 150.00
Vase, Daisies, Light Aqua, Ormolu Base, 10 1/2 In. 450.00
Vase, Green, Blown-Out Pink Flowers, Silver Plated Handles, Dolphin Feet, 17 In. 2100.00
Vase, Pink Daisies, Shaded Pink To Yellow, Metal Rim, Marked, 8 In. 150.00
Vase, Pink Mums, Enameled, Rococo Cartouches, Beaded Rim, 9 1/2 In. 115.00
Vase, Pink, Blue Flowers, Brass Handles & Base, Footed, 5 In. 125.00
Vase, White Flowers, Red To Rust & Green, Gold Ormolu Handles & Feet, 12 In. 3250.00
Whiskbroom Holder, Light Blue, Pink Flowers, Brass Rim & Holder, 10 x 6 In. 550.00

WEAPONS listed here include instruments of combat other than guns,
knives, rifles, or swords. Firearms are not listed in this book. Knives
and Swords are listed in their own categories.

Arrow, Armor Piercing, Leaf-Shape Head, Cane Shaft, Japan, c.1750, 36 1/2 In. 255.00
Ax, Steel Wedge Blade, Animals, Wood Shaft, Indo-Persia, 19th Century, 26 In. 294.00
Ax, Wedge Blade, Silver Inlay, Steel Spike, Wood Shaft, Indo-Persia, 1800s, 29 In. 35.00
Billy Club, British Bobby's, Polychrome, Gold Crown, Wooden, G III R, 16 1/2 In. 195.00
Blow Pipe, Hardwood Core, Flared Mouthpiece, British Guiana, 71 In. 545.00
Blunderbuss, Turkish Market, Inlaid Silver & Gold, France, 19th Century, 20 In. 1880.00
Boomerang, White, Dark Wood, Aboriginal, Australia, c.1935, 25 1/2 In. 275.00
Cannon, Deck, Bronze, Heraldic Relief, Oak Frame, Brass, Wheels, Bronze, 1671, 41 In. . 775.00
Club, Gunstock, Curved Bi-Partite Head, Striations, Wooden, Fiji, 41 In. 411.00
Club, Knobkerry, Elongated Spherical Head, Tapered Haft, Zulu, 1870s, 3 x 30 1/2 In. ... 325.00

Club, Lanceolate Blade Shape, Wooden, Geometric Carving, Samoa, 47 In. 2233.00
Club, Pole, Wood, Fine Heavy Grain, Red Brown, Fiji, 48 1/2 In. 275.00
Club, Throwing, Wood, Carved, Curved, Faceted Head, Pointed Dome, Fiji, 1800s, 14 In. . 1295.00
Golok, Broad Wedge Blade, Wood Grip, Scabbard, Malay, 18-In. Blade 145.00
Jambiya, Silver Mounted, Wood Grip, Morocco, 8 3/4-In. Blade 385.00
Shield, Figures In Garden Scenes, Koranic Cartouches, Indo-Persia, 1800s, 18 In. 325.00
Spear, Masai, Leaf-Shape Head, Cylindrical Bolster, Wood Shaft, Hide Sheath, 77 In. . . . 265.00

WEATHER VANES were used in seventeenth-century Boston. The direction of the wind was an indication of coming weather, important to the
seafaring and farming communities. By the mid-nineteenth century,
commercial weather vanes were made of metal. Today's collectors
often consider weather vanes to be examples of folk art, even though
they may not have been handmade.

Angel, With Trumpet, Zinc, American, 19th Century, 30 3/4 In. 3820.00
Arrow, Cast Iron, 32 In. 58.00
Arrow, Copper, Belted Ball Finial, Verdigris, 19th Century, 29 x 60 In. 940.00
Arrow, Copper, Gilded Surface, Ball Finial, 19th Century, 17 x 31 In. 560.00
Arrow, Iron, Copper Spire & Ball Finial, 17 x 25 In. 560.00
Arrow, Iron, Copper Strips, Ball, Geometric Designs, 115 In. 330.00
B-50 Bomber, U.S. Air Force, Copper, Virginia, c.1950 . . . . 6800.00
Banner, Oval Cutouts, Ball Finial, Black Paint, Iron, 37 x 15 3/4 In. 1645.00
Banner, Pierced, Scrolled, Gilt Traces, Sheet Copper, Mid 1800s, 71 1/2 In. 2700.00
Battleship Maine, Painted, Sheet Metal, 27 x 24 In. 1725.00
Blacksmith, Rooster, Crescent Moon, Painted, Iron, American, 1800s, 19 In. 8400.00
Cow, Full-Bodied, Molded, Copper, New England, Late 1800s, 23 x 38 In. 11950.00
Cow, Green Patina, Gilt Detail, Copper, Bullet Holes, 19th Century, 16 x 25 In. 1495.00
Cow, Molded, Copper, Wrought Iron Horns, 25 x 25 1/2 In. 10755.00
Cow, Standing, Arrow, Gilt Metal, 15 In. Cow, 28 1/2 In. 460.00
Dog, Walking, Pointing Tail, Copper, American, 20th Century, 16 x 35 In. 6573.00
Dolphin, Leaping, Scrolled Wire Directionals, Copper, 22 1/2 x 34 1/2 In. 440.00
Duck, Flying, Arrow, Directionals, Sheet Copper, 21 3/4 In. 85.00
Eagle, Full-Bodied, Arrow, Copper, Cast Zinc Feet, 21 x 18 1/2 In. 330.00
Eagle, Perched, Ball, Arrow, Directionals, Copper, Stand, 20 x 25 5/8 In. 440.00
Eagle, Spread Wings, Gilt Copper, Brass, Late 1800s, 36 1/2 x 15 x 21 1/2 In. 700.00
Eagle, Spread Wings, Perched, Arrow, Directionals, Copper, Verdigris, 15 1/2 In. 1058.00
Fire Wagon, Horse Drawn, Copper, Brushed Verdigris, 20th Century, 42 1/2 In. 770.00
Firemen, On Horse-Drawn Wagon, Iron, 30 In. 6000.00
Fish, Iron, Copper, 25 x 42 In. 165.00
Fisherman, In Rowboat, Copper, H.J. White, 20th Century, 18 x 28 1/2 In. 325.00
Fox, Leaping, Extended Tail, Molded Copper, Early 1900s, 26 1/2 x 14 1/2 In. 14340.00
Fox, Running, Copper, Zinc, American, 19th Century, 15 1/8 x 29 1/4 In. 4700.00
Fox, Running, Painted, Wood, 49 x 11 In. 430.00
Gamecock, Embossed, Gilt Surface, Copper, Sheet, 19th Century, 18 x 17 In. 4995.00
Hand, Pointing, Sunburst, Iron, 2 Wooden Finials, 35 1/4 x 23 In. 2235.00
Horse, Blackhawk, Copper, American, 19th Century, 24 7/8 x 34 1/4 In. 3820.00
Horse, Copper, Wooden Base, 1860-1880, 33 In. 2800.00
Horse, Copper, Zinc Torso, J. Howard & Co., 18 1/2 x 24 In. 7640.00
Horse, Jockey, Molded, Copper, Iron, Zinc, Verdigris, 19th Century, 19 x 34 In. 8813.00
Horse, Jockey, Yellow Glazed Surface, Copper, Late 19th Century, 23 x 31 In. 9400.00
Horse, Molded, Painted, Gilt, Copper, Verdigris, 19th Century, 24 x 26 3/4 In. 2585.00
Horse, Painted, Copper, A.J. Harris & Co., 18 1/2 x 32 1/2 In. 2350.00
Horse, Painted, Wooden Arm, Propeller, Sheet Iron, Tin Flag, 20 1/2 x 25 1/2 In. 305.00
Horse, Prancing, Weathered Gilt Surface, Copper, 25 1/2 x 34 In. 4115.00
Horse, Rider, Hollow, Mustard Paint, Sheet Iron, 28 3/4 x 36 In. 6465.00
Horse, Running, 2 Scrolled Directionals, Zinc, Mounted On Rod, 26 1/2 x 41 In. 7770.00
Horse, Running, Ball Finial, Directionals, Copper, Bullet Holes, 25 In. 575.00
Horse, Running, Cast Iron Head, Traces Of Gilt, Copper, 20 x 38 In. 7770.00
Horse, Running, Copper, Zinc, A.L. Jewell & Co., c.1850s, 14 x 29 In. 4700.00
Horse, Running, Double-Ball Rod, Directionals, Molded Copper, American, 65 In. 9600.00
Horse, Running, Full-Bodied, Ball, Directionals, Copper, Zinc, 67 x 43 5/8 In. 2350.00
Horse, Running, Full-Bodied, Copper, Molded, Early 20th Century, 28 x 44 In. 10755.00
Horse, Running, Molded, Copper, Verdigris, Zinc, 19th Century, 19 x 32 In. 2235.00

Horse, Running, Molded, Gold Leaf, Sheet Metal, Verdigris, 23 In. 920.00
Horse, Running, Painted, Copper, 19th Century, 18 x 32 In. 1410.00
Horse, Running, Painted, Copper, 25 In. 1035.00
Horse, Running, Zinc, 36 1/2 x 19 In. 115.00
Horse, Running, Zinc, Lead, Tripod, 91 In. 1530.00
Horse, Sheet Metal, Cast Iron Arrow, Wooden Base, 14 x 20 In. 340.00
Horse, Standing, Sheet Metal, Pennsylvania, 1913, 17 1/4 x 20 In. 1665.00
Horse, Zinc Head, Copper Body, J. Howard & Co., 19 x 25 In. 12925.00
Horse & Sulky, Copper, American, 19th Century, 18 1/2 x 34 In. 4405.00
Indian, Pontiac Dealership, Die Cut, c.1950, 52 x 37 In. 865.00
Indian, Salmon Paint Trace, Tin, Iron, 64 3/4 In. 2090.00
Locomotive, Polychrome, Sheet Metal, Early 20th Century 9350.00
Pen, Quill, Iron, Spire, Ball Finial, Copper, L.W. Cushing & Sons, 23 x 36 In. 2470.00
Plow, Iron, Bronze, 19th Century, 13 1/2 x 38 1/4 In. 3410.00
Rooster, Ball Finial, Directionals, Copper, Verdigris, 18 1/2 x 49 1/2 In. 468.00
Rooster, Copper, Tin, 13 In. 1760.00
Rooster, Copper, Verdigris, 27 In. 5980.00
Rooster, Full-Bodied, Flattened, Painted, Zinc, Copper, Verdigris, 30 1/4 In. 16450.00
Rooster, Full-Bodied, Gilded, Sheet Copper, 19th Century, 31 x 34 In. 1580.00
Rooster, Gilt Traces, Sheet Copper, Verdigris, 26 1/2 x 42 In. 5580.00
Rooster, Painted, White, Red, Sheet Metal, 18 x 18 In. 460.00
Rooster, Polychrome, Pine Stand, Late 19th Century, 26 1/2 In. 2115.00
Schooner, Painted, Red, Black, Off-White, Wood, Wire Rigging, 23 x 39 In. 265.00
Sea Serpent, Painted, White, Sheet Iron, 19th Century, 15 1/2 In. 345.00
Ship, 2 Masted, Painted Hull, Wood, Metal Sail, 31 x 38 In. 1668.00
Ship, 3 Masted, Painted, Wood, Early 20th Century, 18 x 23 In. 1095.00
Ship, Copper, Carved Pine, American, c.1885, 17 In. 9600.00
Sloop, Gaff-Rigged, Copper, Verdigris, 20th Century, 20 3/4 x 20 5/8 In. 4406.00
Soldier, Civil War, Blowing Trumpet, Holding Flag, Sheet Iron, Painted, 47 In. 15535.00
Stag, Full-Bodied, Tucked Front Legs, Molded Copper, 1800s, 24 x 29 In. 14340.00
Stag, Leaping, Copper, Regilded Surface, Wooden Stand, 18 x 21 1/2 In. 5290.00
Steer, Zinc Head, Painted, Gilt Traces, Copper Body, 20 x 29 1/2 In. 6463.00
Sword, Spire Finial, Copper, American, 19th Century, 10 1/4 x 22 7/8 In. 2470.00
Whale, Copper, Early 20th Century, 33 x 8 In. 1150.00

WEBB glass is made by Thomas Webb & Sons of Ambelcot, England.
Many types of art and cameo glass were made by them during the
Victorian era. Production ceased by 1991, and the factory was demol-
ished in 1995. Webb Burmese and Webb Peachblow are special colored glasswares of the Victorian era. They are listed at the end of this
section. Glassware that is not Burmese or Peachblow is included here.

Webb

Bowl, Clover Shape, Brown, White Interior, Enameled, 9 1/2 In. 75.00
Dish, Gold Prunus Blossoms, Gold Butterfly, White Interior, 3 In. 225.00
Epergne, Tear-Drop Horn, Flowers, Grass, Silver Plated Lion Holder, 8 1/2 In. 2860.00
Ewer, Orange Shaded To Lavender, Flowers, Gold Highlights, Thorny Handle, 7 1/2 In. . . 560.00
Finger Bowl, Pastel Blue, Turquoise, Pink, Amber, Pinched, Fluted, c.1880, 3 In., 6 Piece . 2025.00
Jar, Cover, Yellow Satin, Gold Enameled Ginkgo, Butterfly, Cased, Ground Pontil, 5 In. . . 100.00
Lamp, Rose Over White Sprig, Flowers, Camphor Feet, Cameo, 19th Century, 4 3/4 In. . . 1265.00
Perfume Bottle, Cameo, Lay Down, White Over Yellow Swan's Head, 5 3/4 In. 9184.00
Perfume Bottle, Pink Mums, Vines, Butterfly, Yellow Satin, Cased, Screw Lid, 4 1/2 In. . . 500.00
Perfume Bottle, Swan's Head Form, White Cameo Over Yellow, Silver Cap, c.1888, 6 In. . 9185.00
Rose Bowl, Butterfly, Gold Enameled Cascades, Ruffled Edge, 3 In. 225.00
Vase, Bird, Butterfly, Flowers, Branch, White Over Yellow, Cameo, 11 x 7 In. 1060.00
Vase, Blossom & Butterfly, Pink, White Enamel, 7 In. 200.00
Vase, Blue Satin, Gold Flower Branches & Insects, 6 In. 350.00
Vase, Blue Tulips, Overall Crystal Stippling Effect, Cameo, 19th Century, 9 In. 660.00
Vase, Carved Birds, Almond, Branches, Flowers, Green Over Yellow, Cameo, 4 In. 5175.00
Vase, Cockleshells, Ginkgo Leaves, White Over Red, Double Stalactite Rim, 10 1/2 In. . . 9200.00
Vase, Flowers, Bird, Blue, White, Spatter, Handles, Gold, 10 1/2 In. 110.00
Vase, Ivory, Applied Raspberries, Gold Flowers, Spider Web Mark, 7 1/2 In. 165.00
Vase, Jonquil Flowers, Lime Green Over Clear, Signed, 6 1/2 x 8 1/2 In. 150.00
Vase, Lemon Yellow Satin, Enameled Gold, Cased, 6 1/2 In. 90.00
Vase, Mother-Of-Pearl, Purple Over Black, Melon Ribbed, Applied Handles, 7 In. 2680.00

Vase, Pink Fishscale, Gold Rim, Underwater Scene, Cameo, 19th Century, 4 x 7 In. 865.00
Vase, Red Grapes, Green Leafy Vines, Crimped 5-Point Star Rim, Pedestal, 4 3/4 In. 560.00
Vase, Rose Over Citron, Flower Branch, Cameo, England, 19th Century, 4 1/4 In. 1265.00
Vase, Shaded Yellow To Caramel, Satin, Morning Glories, 19th Century, 8 3/4 In. 145.00
Vase, Shells, Stalactite Feathers, White Over Citron, Bulbous, Round Flared Neck, 14 In. . . 6720.00
Vase, Stick, Citron, Horizontal Scrolls, Flowers, Stalactite Feathers, Bulbous, 4 1/4 In. . . . 1960.00
Vase, Stick, Flowers, Buds, Grasses, Butterfly, Red Ground, Bulbous, Footed, 10 In. 3025.00
Vase, Stick, Flowers, Leaves, Butterfly, White Over Red, Yellow Ground, Bulbous, 6 In. . 2630.00
Vase, Yellow Over Red & White, Flowers, Cameo, Spherical, 3 1/2 In. 1900.00

WEBB BURMESE is a colored Victorian glass made by Thomas Webb
& Sons of Stourbridge, England, from 1886.

Rose Bowl, Amethyst Flower, 3 1/4 In. 260.00
Rose Bowl, Amethyst Flowers, Buds, Green Leaves, Globular, 6-Sided Rim, 2 In. 335.00
Rose Bowl, Brown Pinecones, Green Needles, 6-Sided Rim, 3 x 4 In. 500.00
Rose Bowl, Pinecones, 3 x 3 3/4 In. 200.00
Toothpick, Red Berries, Green Leafy Stems, 5-Point Star Crimped Rim, 3 In. 785.00
Vase, Red Berry, Green Leaves, Trumpet, 5-Point Star Crimped Rim, Footed, 4 In. 335.00
Vase, Vines, Raspberry Prunts, 4-Fold Rim, Oval, Shouldered, 3-Footed, 7 In. 1450.00

WEBB PEACHBLOW is a colored Victorian glass made by Thomas
Webb & Sons of Stourbridge, England, from 1885.

Basket, Rose To Pink, Amber Stem, Leaves, Cased, Applied Feet, 10 1/2 In. 145.00
Bowl, Rose To Pink, Applied Amber Stem, White Flowers, Cased, Footed, 6 In. 200.00
Rose Bowl, Gold Overlay, Flower & Leaves, 10 1/2 In. 470.00
Vase, Applied Clear Raspberries, Cased, 12 In. 195.00
Vase, Applied White Flowers, Amber Stems, Enameling, 5 1/2 In. 69.00
Vase, Birds On Branches, 9 1/2 In., Pair 475.00
Vase, Classical Shape, Satin Handles, 7 1/2 In. 200.00
Vase, Enameled Gold Leafy Vines, Cased, 5 In. 70.00
Vase, Flowers, Amber Feet, Flat Sides, 19th Century, 8 1/2 In.   690.00
Vase, Gold Cascading Branch, Cased, 19th Century, 10 In. 1265.00
Vase, Gold Enameled Flowers, 5 In., Pair 210.00
Vase, Gold Floral, Candlestick Top, Gold Loop Handles, Footed, 13 In. 335.00
Vase, Gold Scrolls Top & Base, Gold Handles, Bulbous, Long Neck, 11 In. 392.00
Vase, Gold, Gray Cascading Vine, Insect, Cased, 10 1/2 In. 175.00
Vase, Satin, Enameled Branches, Butterfly, Cased, 9 In. 125.00
Vase, Stick, Pink & White Flower, Amber Branch Handle, Bulbous, 9 In. 280.00

WEDGWOOD, one of the world's most successful potteries, was
founded by Josiah Wedgwood, who was considered a cripple by his
brother and was forbidden to work at the family business. The pottery
was established in England in 1759. A large variety of wares has been
made, including the well-known jasperware, basalt, creamware, and   WEDGWOOD
even a limited amount of porcelain. There are two kinds of jasperware.
One is made from two colors of clay, the other is made from one color
of clay with a color dip to create the contrast in design. The firm is still
in business. Other Wedgwood pieces may be listed under Flow Blue,
Majolica, Tea Leaf Ironstone or in other porcelain categories.

Basket, Cream, Green Bands, Polychrome Flowers, Oval, Impressed 3UL, 4 x 6 In. 55.00
Biscuit Jar, Cover, Jasper Dip, Black Relief Muses, Lion Masks, Yellow Ground, 6 In. . . .   765.00
Biscuit Jar, Cover, Jasper Dip, Blue Ground, Classical Figures, Silver Plated Rim, 6 In. . .   645.00
Biscuit Jar, Cover, Jasper Dip, Light Blue, White Relief Muses, Stand, 6 3/8 In. 410.00
Biscuit Jar, Cover, Jasper Dip, White Classical Relief, Green, Lilac Border, 5 In. 645.00
Biscuit Jar, Cover, Majolica, Elephants, Plated Rim, Bail Handle 1115.00
Bottle, Scent, Jasper, Blue, Woman, Green Oval, White Flowers, Case, 3 1/4 In. 1035.00
Bowl, Butterfly Luster, Mother-Of-Pearl, Mottled Orange Interior, 8 Sides, 4 In. 560.00
Bowl, Butterfly Luster, Mottled Orange & Green, 8 5/8 In. 1645.00
Bowl, Cover, Black & White, Basket Weave, Leaf & Flower Border, 5 1/4 In. 3970.00
Bowl, Cover, Carved, Black, White, Basket Weave, Marked, 5 1/4 In. 3970.00
Bowl, Cover, Raised Chain & Flowers, Scalloped, Footed, Leaf Handle, 11 x 9 In. 690.00
Bowl, Drab Ware, Molded Arabesque Relief Flowers, Orange Peel Ground, 7 5/8 In. 940.00
Bowl, Dragon Luster, Mottled Blue, Mother-Of-Pearl Interior, 8 Sides, 7 3/8 In. 880.00

Bowl, Egyptian, Rosso Antico, Black Basalt Meander Band, 7 7/8 In. 1295.00
Bowl, Fairyland Luster, Blue Glaze, Man In Waves, 10 3/4 x 6 In. 4890.00
Bowl, Fairyland Luster, Castle On Road, 8 Sides, c.1930, 9 In. 4180.00
Bowl, Fairyland Luster, Imperial, Trees, Woodland Elves, Bridge, c.1925, 11 In. 6570.00
Bowl, Fairyland Luster, Jumping Faun, Leaf Medallion, Fish, Paisley, 1920s, 8 In. 5975.00
Bowl, Fairyland Luster, Moorish, Smoke Ribbons, 8 Sides, 1920s, 8 1/8 In. 5380.00
Bowl, Fairyland Luster, Woodland Elves, Ship, Mermaid, 8 Sides, 1920s, 8 In. 5380.00
Bowl, Hummingbird Luster, Mottled Blue, Orange Interior, 8 Sides, 8 1/8 In. 1295.00
Bowl, Jasperware, Blue & White, Dancing Classical Women, 10 1/8 In. 265.00
Bowl, Luster, Border, Mottled Blue & Green Ground, Fish, c.1929, 8 1/2 In. 2270.00
Bowl, Oriental, Mottled Orange, Mottled Purple Interior, Phoenix, 4 In. 500.00
Bowl, Queen's Ware, Molded Crab Shell, 3 Shell Feet, 2 Shell-Handle Servers, 9 In. 825.00
Bowl, Vegetable, Cover, Molded, Flowers, Gold, 12 1/4 In. 105.00
Bowl Set, Majolica, Tan Mottled Glaze, Shell Shape, 10 1/2 To 12 1/2 In., 5 Piece 480.00
Box, Cover, Queen's Ware, Leaves, Green Transfer, Gilt, Cylindrical, Flat, 3 3/4 In. 500.00
Bust, Byron, Carrara, Waisted Circular Socle, 15 In. 1295.00
Bust, Minerva, 19 In. 2310.00
Bust, Robert Stephenson, Carrara, Waisted Circular Socle, 1858, 14 3/4 In. 1295.00
Bust, Scott, Carrara, Waisted Circular Socle, 15 In. 1115.00
Cabaret Set, Creamware, Red Transfer, c.1872, 5 Piece 1350.00
Candlestick, Black Basalt, Triton, Bearded Male, 19th Century, 11 In., Pair 2510.00
Candlestick, Jasperware, Blue, White Relief Figures, Ormolu, Pair 245.00
Candlestick, Jasperware, Green, Grapevines, 1 1/2 In., Pair 125.00
Casserole, Cover, Grapevine Border, Cabbage Finial, Brown Clay, 7 x 10 In. 110.00
Cheese Dish, Cover, Jasperware, Blue, White, England, 19th Century, 8 In. 350.00
Cigarette Lighter, Jasperware, Churchill Bust, Blue, White 60.00
Coffee Set, Black Basalt, Wide Fluted Band, Footed Sugar Bowl, 3 Piece 1175.00
Compote, Majolica, Shell Shape, Raised On 3 Dolphins, 7 In., Pair 1135.00
Compote, Shepherdess, Gold Trim, Low Pedestal, 8 3/4 In. 150.00
Compote, Woman Seated On Rock, Gold Trim, Low Pedestal, 8 3/4 In. 125.00
Compote Set, Majolica, Shell Shape Bowl, Raised On 3 Dolphins, 9 1/2 In., 4 Piece 1135.00
Cracker Jar, Cover, Allegorical Figures, Blue Ground, Silver Plated Bail, 4 3/4 In. 150.00
Cup, Cover, Creamware, Red Trim, c.1820, 2 1/2 In. .... *Illus* 20.00
Dinner Service, Ivory, Lavender Transfers, Sailboats, Flowers, 79 Piece 330.00
Dish, Game, Cover, Terra-Cotta, Molded Game, Rabbit On Cover, 14 In. 600.00
Dish, Majolica, Green Ground, Fern, 1868, 11 In. 230.00
Figurine, Greek Woman, Jasperware, Gilt Bronze, 1800s, 23 x 12 1/2 In., Pair 1095.00
Inkstand, Black Basalt, Molded Leaves, Oil Lamp Shape, Attached Tray, 7 In. 355.00
Jardiniere, Jasper Dip, Dark Blue, White Relief Muses, Lion Heads, 8 x 9 In. 415.00
Jug, Caneware, Rabbit Hunt In Relief, Applied Blue Grapevine Border, 7 1/2 In. 645.00
Jug, Cream, Jasperware, White, Blue Classical Figures, Baluster Shape, 4 1/2 In. 39.00
Jug, Jasper Dip, Etruscan, Crimson, Applied White Classical Relief, 4 1/2 In. 1000.00
Jug, Jasperware, White, 2-Tone Green Classical Relief, Rope Handle, 5 1/4 In. 28.00
Jug, Longfellow's Poem Keramos, Potter Scene, 6 1/2 In. 175.00
Jug, Majolica, Applied Relief Grapevine Band, 8 3/4 In., Pair 1295.00
Jug, Queen's Ware, Roger Williams, Black Transfer, Flower Band Border, 7 3/4 In. 120.00
Kettle, Rum, Black Basalt, Bacchanalian Boys In Relief, Bail Handle, 5 3/4 In. 590.00
Lamp, Oil, Cover, Jasper Dip, Dark Blue, White Classical Relief Figures, Leaves, 5 In. .. 1000.00
Mold, Queen's Ware, Fruit & Flowers In Ribbed Pot, Oval, Scalloped Rim, 11 In. 1295.00
Mustard Pot, Cover, Monochromatic, Black, White Ground, Exotic Birds, 3 1/2 In. 75.00

Wedgwood, Cup, Cover,
Creamware, Red Trim,
c.1820, 2 1/2 In.

Never use commercial window cleaner on a stained glass window. It could remove the color or damage the lead.

Pie Dish, Cover, Caneware, Dead Game, Fruiting Festoons, Hare Finial, Oval, 11 In. 380.00
Pie Dish, Cover, Caneware, Dead Game, Grapevine Festoons, Oval, 9 1/2 In. 325.00
Pie Dish, Cover, Caneware, Fruiting Grapevine, Cauliflower Finial, Oval, 9 In. 295.00
Pitcher, Helmet, Etruria, England 325.00
Pitcher, Leaf & Berry, Embossed, Green, Yellow, Branch Handle, Blue Glaze, 8 In. 305.00
Pitcher, Sailboats At Port, Flow Blue, 5 1/2 In. 90.00
Pitcher, Sunflower & Lily, Impressed, 6 Sides, 8 1/4 In. 4475.00
Plaque, Jasper Dip, Blue, White Classical Figure, Laurel Frame, Oval, 6 3/4 In. 1115.00
Plaque, Jasperware, Blue & White, Mahogany Frame, 6 1/2 x 11 1/2 In. 81.00
Plaque, Jasperware, Blue, Neoclassical, Giltwood Frame, Moire Mat, 14 x 17 1/2 In. 175.00
Plate, Abraham Lincoln Memorial, Flow Blue, 10 In., Pair 90.00
Plate, Captain George Vancouver, Etruria, 10 In. 60.00
Plate, Clytie, Flow Blue, 10 1/4 In. 100.00
Plate, Dessert, Majolica, Birds, Fans, Pale Blue Ground, 1879, 9 In. 200.00
Plate, Ferrara, Flow Blue, 10 In. 110.00
Plate, Peter Rabbit, 7 In. ....12.00 to 30.00
Plate, Shepherdess, Gold Trim, 8 3/4 In. 99.00
Plate, Trophy, Jasper Dip, Green, White Classical Figures, Vines, Festoons, 8 3/4 In. 940.00
Plate, Woman Holding Hat, Spring, Gold Trim, 8 3/4 In. 99.00
Plate Set, Wellesley, Center Flower Spray, Butterfly, Ivory Ground, 11 In., 12 Piece 230.00
Platter, Brown, Blue, Green Mottled, Oval, 12 x 9 1/4 In. 175.00
Platter, Chapoo, Flow Blue, 13 1/2 x 10 In. 225.00
Platter, Majolica, Coral, Shells, Blue & Yellow Border, Molded Edge, 19 x 8 3/4 In. 780.00
Punch Bowl, Luster, Mottled Blue, Mother-Of-Pearl Interior, Footed, 11 In. 2235.00
Punch Set, Harvard Tercentenary, Red Transfers, 25 Piece 200.00
Sugar, Jasperware, Grecian Scene, Crimson Ground, Handles, 3 1/2 In. 1095.00
Tankard, Black Basalt, Classical Figures, Cylindrical, 4 1/4 In. 355.00
Tea Set, Jasperware, Terra-Cotta, White Classical Relief, 3 Piece 355.00
Teapot, Cover, Black Basalt, Enameled Flowers, Red Trim, 6 3/4 In. 1495.00
Teapot, Cover, Rosso Antico, Black Basalt Relief Hieroglyphs, 8 Sides, 3 In. 380.00
Tile, Blue, White, Red Riding Hood, Wolf, c.1890, 6 x 6 In. 295.00
Tureen, Cover, Blue, White, Raised Flowers, Handles, 11 1/2 x 9 In. 805.00
Urn, Fairyland Luster, Marked, Mounted As Lamp, c.1925, 10 In. 3450.00
Vase, Cover, Agate, White Festoons, Handles, Wedgwood & Bentley, 11 1/2 In. 1060.00
Vase, Cover, Jasper Dip, Dark Blue, White Classical Relief, Loop Handles, 13 In., Pair ... 1115.00
Vase, Cover, Jasperware, Pink, Green, White Relief, c.1900, 14 In. 1530.00
Vase, Dragon Luster, Dragons, Mottled Blue, c.1920, 7 1/2 In. 500.00
Vase, Fairyland Luster, Flame, Imps On Bridge, Flaming Wheel Border, 1925, 9 In. 6570.00
Vase, Hummingbird Luster, Polychrome Birds, Blue Ground, Orange Interior, 8 In. 880.00
Vase, Hummingbird Luster, Polychrome Enameled Birds, Mottled Blue, 5 In., Pair 705.00
Vase, Jasper Dip, Classical Maidens, Royal Blue, Long Neck, 6 1/2 In. 200.00
Vase, Jasper Dip, Crimson, White Classical Relief, Grapevine Borders, 5 7/8 In. 1000.00
Vase, Jasper Dip, Portland, Dark Blue, Applied White Relief Figures, 6 3/4 In. 440.00
Vase, Jasper Dip, Portland, Royal Blue, 6 In. 575.00
Vase, Jasper Dip, White & Olive Green, 2 Handles, Greek Cup Form, 5 1/2 x 7 In. 345.00
Vase, Jasperware, 3 Ladies, Soldier, Angel, White Decoration, England, 5 x 3 In., Pair 165.00
Vase, Jasperware, Pastel Blue, Classical Vignettes, 5 In. 24.00
Vase, Luster, Mother-Of-Pearl, Butterflies, c.1920, 7 1/2 In. 645.00
Vase, Powder Blue Luster, Gilt Dragon, Greek Key Border, Trumpet Shape, 9 5/8 In. 470.00
Vase, Rosso Antico, Black Basalt Relief Leaves & Medallions, Tripod, 6 1/2 In., Pair 1175.00
Vase, Spill, Jasperware, Blue & White, 6 In. 52.00
Vase, Victoria Ware, Blue, Gilt Flowers, Grapevine Bands & Festoons, 5 3/8 In. 1115.00

WELLER pottery was first made in 1872 in Fultonham, Ohio. The firm
moved to Zanesville, Ohio, in 1882. Artwares were introduced in
1893. Hundreds of lines of pottery were produced, including
Louwelsa, Eocean, Dickens Ware, and Sicardo, before the pottery
closed in 1948.

LOUWELSA
WELLER

Ardsley, Umbrella Stand, Cattails, Water Lilies On Base, 19 1/2 In. 315.00
Ardsley, Vase, Cattails, Double, 10 In. 200.00
Ardsley, Vase, Figural Water Lily, Leaves, 7 In. 430.00
Ardsley, Vase, Flower Frog, Iris, Long Leaves, 9 1/2 In. 430.00
Art Nouveau, Vase, Molded Pansies, Pink, Green, 11 1/2 In. 920.00

Atlas, Bowl, Yellow, Squat, 4 x 6 In. 175.00
Aurelian, Ewer, Orange Roses, Stamped, 11 1/2 In. 545.00
Aurelian, Jardiniere, Fruit, Leaves On Branch, Brown Glaze, 18 x 16 In. 1265.00
Aurelian, Oil Lamp, Clematis, Signed, 12 3/8 In. 2645.00
Aurelian, Oil Lamp, Heart-Shape Panels, Flowers, 10 1/8 In. 865.00
Aurelian, Oil Lamp, Iris, William Hall, Marked, 6 3/4 x 13 In. 920.00
Aurelian, Vase, Blackberries, 3 Sides, Frank Ferrell, 11 5/8 In. 575.00
Aurelian, Vase, Blackberries, 8 5/8 In. 490.00
Aurelian, Vase, Leaves, 3 Handles, 7 In. 115.00
Aurelian, Vase, Roses, Orange, Lillie Mitchell, 24 5/8 In. 2530.00
Auroro, Vase, Brown Blossom, Light Blue, White, Egg Shape, 6 1/2 In. 765.00
Baldin, Vase, Apples, Stems, Leaves, Blue Ground, 2 Handles, 10 1/2 In. 290.00
Barcelona, Vase, Stylized Flower, Hand Painted, Yellow Slip, Handles, 9 1/4 In. 205.00
Blue Drapery, Vase, Dark Red, 6 1/2 In. 150.00
Blue Ware, Jardiniere, 2 Classical Figures, Blue Matte Ground, Footed, 9 1/2 In. 260.00
Blue Ware, Vase, Grecian Women, Lyre, Grapes, 11 In. 220.00
Bonito, Vase, Pink, Amber Columbine, Egg Shape, 2 Handles, 11 x 5 1/2 In. 235.00
Brighton, Figurine, Bluebird, Double-Stump Base, High Gloss, 1915, 6 In. 295.00
Brighton, Figurine, Woodpecker, Blue, White, Rust, Base, 6 In. 230.00
Brighton, Flower Frog, Kingfisher, Blue, Rust, Green, 8 5/8 In. 405.00
Brighton, Wall Pocket, Double Bud, Kingfisher Perched On Tree, Gray, Green, 12 In. . . . 805.00
Burntwood, Vase, Mice, 2 In. 10.00
Burntwood, Vase, Peacocks In Forest, Cream, Brown, 11 5/8 In. 220.00
Burntwood, Vase, Stylized Flowers, 3 1/4 In. 25.00
Cactus, Figurine, Duck, Ocher To Brown, 4 1/2 In. 225.00
Camelot, Vase, Matte, Glossy Glazes, Bottle Shape, Marked, 10 In. 920.00
Chase, Vase, White Molded Rider On Horseback, Dark Blue Ground, 6 5/8 In. 315.00
Chelsea, Pitcher, Ivory Matte, 5 1/4 In. 70.00
Cloudburst, Vase, Bud, Lavender, Pink Luster, 6 1/4 In. 105.00
Cloudburst, Vase, Lavender, White Luster Glaze, 4 3/4 In. 90.00
Coppertone, Bowl, Flower Frog, Lily-Pad Handles, 15 1/2 In. 460.00
Coppertone, Figurine, Frog, 2 In. 165.00
Coppertone, Figurine, Frog, Orange Ground, 4 x 5 In. 325.00
Coppertone, Figurine, Turtle, Brown, 6 1/2 In. 460.00
Coppertone, Lawn Sprinkler, 2 Ducks, Yellow, Green Grass, 14 1/2 In. 1495.00
Coppertone, Lawn Sprinkler, Frog, 8 1/4 x 10 In. 2750.00
Coppertone, Paperweight, Frog, Green, Yellow, Brown, 3 3/4 In. 315.00
Coppertone, Paperweight, Turtle, Green, 1 3/4 x 5 1/2 In. 415.00
Coppertone, Paperweight, Turtle, Green, Rust, 1 7/8 x 5 1/8 In. 230.00
Coppertone, Pitcher, Mottled Green, Fish Handle, 8 In. 2415.00
Coppertone, Vase, 2 Handles, Floor, 18 In. 1380.00
Coppertone, Vase, Molded Leaves, Frogs, 2 Frog Handles, 8 In. 1380.00
Coppertone, Vase, Mottled Texture, Green, Copper, Flared, 8 1/2 x 6 In. 325.00
Dickens Ware, Jardiniere, Yellow Roses, Stamped Mark, 10 1/2 x 11 1/2 In. 190.00
Dickens Ware, Lamp Base, Shoreline, Ships, Brown Glaze, Impressed, 27 In. 2300.00
Dickens Ware, Vase, 2 Men Playing Checkers, Green Ground, 2 Angular Handles, 5 In. . . . 175.00
Dickens Ware, Vase, 2 Women, Landscape, Incised, Cylindrical, 17 1/2 In. 1610.00
Dickens Ware, Vase, Cover, Figural, Oriental Man's Head, 6 In. 2875.00
Dickens Ware, Vase, Dragonfly, Green, Brown & Tan Matte, 9 In. 290.00
Dickens Ware, Vase, Ducks, Water, Incised, Brown, Blue, Ivory, Flattened, 5 In. . . 230.00 to 430.00
Dickens Ware, Vase, Flying Duck, Fish, Blue, Yellow, Footed, 9 3/4 In. 2310.00
Dickens Ware, Vase, Matte Blue, Green Glaze, 3 Handles, Fish Form, No. 354, 6 1/4 In. . . 545.00
Dickens Ware, Vase, Monk Drinking Ale, 9 x 4 1/4 In. 405.00
Dickens Ware, Vase, Monk, Painted & Incised, 3 Sides, 6 3/4 In. 115.00
Dickens Ware, Vase, Shepherd, Sheep, Incised, Tapered, Impressed Mark, 11 In. 230.00
Dickens Ware II, Vase, Dutch Girl, Vines On Sides, 10 5/8 In. 230.00
Dickens Ware II, Vase, Golfer, 8 1/8 In. 1495.00
Dickens Ware II, Vase, Nudes, Children Dancing In Woods, 9 3/8 In. 520.00
Dresden, Vase, Windmills, Sailboats, 4 1/2 In. 260.00
Drunken Ducks, Lawn Sprinkler, 15 In. 5635.00
Duck, Flower Frog, Brown Matte Glaze, Impressed Mark, 11 1/2 In. 690.00
Dupont, Planter, Round, 6 1/2 In. 45.00
Eocean, Flask, Pilgrim, Gray, Pink, Red Mushrooms, 7 1/2 x 6 In. 590.00

Eocean, Mug, Handles, 4 In. 115.00
Eocean, Mug, Mushrooms, 5 1/4 In. 90.00
Eocean, Pitcher, 2 Cranes, Lavender, Charles Chilcote, 6 1/4 In. 1265.00
Eocean, Vase, Lilac, Floral Decoration, 7 In. 70.00
Eocean, Vase, Nasturtiums, Wine, Green Ground, 3 1/8 x 5 3/4 In. 185.00
Eocean, Vase, Painted Flowers, Blue Ground, Cinch Waist, 8 1/2 In. 315.00
Eocean, Vase, Pansies, 7 5/8 In. 750.00
Eocean, Vase, Trillium, White, Green Ground, 11 7/8 In. 690.00
Etched Matte, Vase, Woman's Profile, Green Ground, Impressed Mark, 10 1/4 In. 633.00
Etna, Mug, Grapes, Embossed, Purple, 5 5/8 In. 60.00
Etna, Vase, Buckeyes, Embossed, Yellow, Marked, 8 3/8 In. 315.00
Etna, Vase, Flowers, Underglaze, Slip, c.1915, 8 1/2 In. 260.00
Etna, Vase, Morning Glory, Aubergine Slip Fading To Green, 5 In. 140.00
Etna, Vase, Pink Roses, Gray Ground, Slip, 10 1/4 x 4 In. 440.00
Etna, Vase, Pink Roses, Shaded Gray Ground, 14 In. 575.00
Etna, Vase, Raised Chrysanthemums, Gray Ground, Impressed Mark, 15 1/2 In. 490.00
Etna, Vase, Red Poppies Around Rim, Impressed Mark, 6 In. 200.00
Etna, Vase, Yellow Flower, Gray Ground, Cinch Waist, Handles, 4 1/4 In. 90.00
Fairfield, Wall Pocket, Cherubs, Green, Brown, Ribbed, 10 In. 185.00
Flemish, Jardiniere, Pedestal, Parrots, Flowers, 31 7/8 In. 3220.00
Flemish, Jardiniere, Trees, Birds, Path, Incised, Green, Pink, c.1915, 8 1/4 In. 205.00
Floretta, Tankard, Apples, Leaves, Scalloped Rim, Handle, 13 1/8 In. 460.00
Floretta, Vase, Pink Poppies, Green Ground, Bulbous, 11 1/2 x 5 1/2 In. 295.00
Forest, Jardiniere, Footed, 5 3/8 In. 175.00
Forest, Vase, Flared, Footed, 10 3/8 In. 316.00
Forest, Vase, Oval, 8 In. 195.00
Fru Russet, Vase, Brown Scarabs, Red Acanthus Leaves, Blue, Green, 5 x 4 3/4 In. 2940.00
Fru Russet, Vase, Green Leaves, Blue, Rose, Curdled, Gourd Shape, 2 Handles, 6 x 6 In. . 1410.00
Fru Russet, Vase, Salamander, Vein, Raspberry Matte Glaze, 4 3/4 x 3 In. 1530.00
Fruitone, Jardiniere, Stippled Matte Green, Red Glaze, Squat, 5 1/2 x 9 In. 260.00
Garden Ornament, Scottie, Rose Cast, Magenta Patches, 11 In. 27600.00
Glendale, Vase, Bird & Nest, Cylindrical, Stamped Mark, 8 In. 575.00
Glendale, Vase, Bird, Sitting Next To Nest, 9 3/4 In. ....460.00 to 750.00
Greora, Jar, Incised, Cover, Red, Green, 6 1/4 x 5 In. 530.00
Greora, Vase, Green, Brown, Bulbous, 5 x 4 In. 145.00
Greora, Vase, Orange, Green, Flared, Footed, 5 In. 105.00
Greora, Vase, Rust, Green, Twisted, 4 3/4 In. 105.00
Hobart, Flower Frog, Female Nude Reclining On Rock, Ivory Glaze, 5 3/4 In. 90.00
Hudson, Basket, Flowers, White, Pink, Brown & Green Ground, 14 x 8 1/4 In. 470.00
Hudson, Pitcher, Leaves & Berries, White, Blue, 9 3/4 In. 375.00
Hudson, Tile, Cornstalks, Pumpkins, Pink Sky, Timberlake, 5 7/8 In. 4140.00
Hudson, Tile, Elephant, Standing In Water, Palm Tree, Mae Timberlake, 8 1/2 In., 4 Piece 6325.00
Hudson, Urn, White, Pink, Blue Poppies, Spherical, Mae Timberlake, 9 1/2 x 9 1/2 In. ... 1880.00
Hudson, Vase, Azure, Teal, Blue, Mauve Flowers, Green Leaves, 7 1/4 x 3 1/2 In. 650.00
Hudson, Vase, Banded Flowers, 7 7/8 In. 490.00
Hudson, Vase, Blue & Decorated, Berries, Leaves, Pastel, Bullet Shape, 9 x 4 1/4 In. 440.00
Hudson, Vase, Blue, Painted Flowers, 8 In. 230.00
Hudson, Vase, Blue, Yellow Flowers, Blue, Green Ground, Dorothy England, 8 x 4 In. ... 1100.00
Hudson, Vase, Bud, Flowers, Blue, 10 1/2 In. 230.00
Hudson, Vase, Clover Blossoms, 6 3/4 x 3 1/4 In. 405.00
Hudson, Vase, Daffodils, White, Magenta, 9 1/4 In. 290.00
Hudson, Vase, Daisies, Incised, Impressed Mark, 7 1/4 In. 690.00
Hudson, Vase, Dogwood Blossoms, 9 In. 805.00
Hudson, Vase, Dogwood Blossoms, Yellow, Pale Blue, Flared, 6 Sides, 11 5/8 In. 230.00
Hudson, Vase, Flowers, White, Pink, Purple, Green, Blue Ground, 10 In. 70.00
Hudson, Vase, Forget-Me-Nots, Blue, Green Leaves, Flared, Timberlake, 9 x 5 In. 935.00
Hudson, Vase, Irises, Blue, Pink & Blue Ground, Mae Timberlake, 9 1/4 In. 690.00
Hudson, Vase, Irises, Blue, White, Blue Ground, McLaughlin, 15 x 7 In. 2585.00
Hudson, Vase, Irises, Lavender, Pink, Yellow Ground, Cone Shape, 11 3/8 In. 315.00
Hudson, Vase, Irises, McLaughlin, 15 In. 1150.00
Hudson, Vase, Irises, Pink & Blue, Mae Timberlake, 9 1/4 In. 1610.00
Hudson, Vase, Ivory Water Lilies, Cream & Tan Ground, 9 1/2 In. 145.00
Hudson, Vase, Lilies Of The Valley, White, Blue Ground, 8 3/4 In. 865.00

Hudson, Vase, Lilies Of The Valley, White, Green To Yellow Ground, D. England, 9 In. . . . 315.00
Hudson, Vase, Milkweed Pods & Seedlings, 7 1/8 In. 980.00
Hudson, Vase, Nasturtium, Pink, Green, Blue Ground, Handles, McLaughlin, 9 1/2 In. . . . 920.00
Hudson, Vase, Pink & White Forget-Me-Nots, 5 3/4 In. 130.00
Hudson, Vase, Poppies, Pastel, Stamped Mark, 22 1/2 x 9 In. 3525.00
Hudson, Vase, Poppies, Pink, White, Black Outline, Mae Timberlake, Handles, 9 3/8 In. . . 2760.00
Hudson, Vase, Poppies, Red, White, 13 1/2 In. 2990.00
Hudson, Vase, Rose Hips, Gray To Pink Ground, Hester Pillsbury, 7 1/4 In. 520.00
Hudson, Vase, Rose, White Nasturtium Vine, 9 1/2 In. 860.00
Hudson, Vase, Ship At Full Sail, 3 Boats, Green Slip Ground, 8 3/4 In. 5750.00
Hudson, Vase, Stylized Hanging Flowers, Green To Pink Ground, Sarah Timberlake, 7 In. 750.00
Hudson, Vase, Thistles, Mauve, White, Pale Blue, Yellow Ground, 13 1/2 In. 290.00
Hudson, Vase, Water Lily, Cream & Green Ground, 2 Handles, 8 In. 520.00
Hudson, Vase, Water Lily, White, Buds, Blue To Tan Ground, Mae Timberlake, 7 3/4 In. . 1035.00
Hudson, Vase, White, Pink Nasturtiums, Celadon Ground, McLaughlin, 9 1/2 x 5 1/4 In. . 530.00
Hudson, Vase, Wild Roses, Edith Hood, 8 7/8 In. 920.00
Hudson, Vase, Wild Roses, Mae Timberlake, 6 In. 230.00
Hudson, Vase, Wisteria, White, Pink, Pale Blue, Yellow Ground, 6 Sides, 11 1/2 In. 260.00
Hudson Perfecto, Vase, Apple Blossoms, White, Blue Ground, Bulbous, Pillsbury, 6 In. . . 410.00
Hudson Perfecto, Vase, Roses, Ivory Ground, 5 1/4 x 5 In. 380.00
Ivory, Jardiniere, Lion, Flowers, Fence, Ivory, Taupe, Bisque, 9 1/4 x 10 1/2 In. 110.00
Jap Birdimal, Vase, Trees, Teal Ground, Sqeezebag, 3 Handles, 8 1/4 x 5 1/2 In. 2115.00
Jewel, Vase, Embossed Man, Woman, Impressed, 10 3/4 x 5 1/2 In. 2350.00
Kingfisher, Flower Frog, Blue, Pink, 3 1/2 In. 175.00
Knifewood, Jar, Hunting Dog Scene, 5 1/2 In. 140.00
Knifewood, Vase, Daises, Butterflies, 4 1/2 In. 145.00
Lamar, Vase, Black Trees, Red Ground, Tapered, 11 1/2 In. 260.00
Lamar, Vase, Palm Trees, Red, Pink Ground, 13 1/8 In. 150.00
Lamar, Vase, Pansies, Tapered, 4 In. 70.00
LaSa, Vase, Lake, Tall Trees, Hills, Brown, Gold, 4 7/8 In. 405.00
LaSa, Vase, Landscape, Painted & Etched, Iridescent Glaze, 7 In. 3565.00
LaSa, Vase, Pine Trees, Hillside, Clouds, Red, Gold, Polychrome, 9 3/4 x 4 1/2 In. 385.00
Louwelsa, Charger, Nasturtium, Gold, Rust, Minnie Mitchell, 10 3/4 In. 175.00
Louwelsa, Clock, Mantel, Brown, Flowers, 10 x 11 In. 675.00
Louwelsa, Ewer, Pansies, Red, Yellow, William Hall, 9 1/4 In. 175.00
Louwelsa, Ewer, Rose, Squat, Impressed Mark, 4 1/4 x 5 1/2 In. 205.00
Louwelsa, Ewer, Wild Rose, Short Neck, 3 1/4 x 5 3/4 In. 80.00
Louwelsa, Ewer, Yellow Rose, Teardrop Handle, 7 1/8 In. 140.00
Louwelsa, Jardiniere, Pedestal, Flowers, Red, Yellow, Marked, 25 3/4 In. 460.00
Louwelsa, Jug, Oak Branches, Leaves, 3 1/4 x 5 3/4 In. 205.00
Louwelsa, Mug, Blackberries, Marked, 5 3/4 In. 60.00
Louwelsa, Mug, Cherry, Red, Split Handle, Helen Windle, 5 1/4 In. 375.00
Louwelsa, Pitcher, Cherry, 5 3/4 In. 260.00
Louwelsa, Vase, Autumn Leaf Branches, Buckeyes, Signed, 18 1/4 In. 1955.00
Louwelsa, Vase, Berries, 4 1/2 x 6 1/2 In. 230.00
Louwelsa, Vase, Blue, Rose Branch, Egg Shape, 11 x 4 In. 1175.00
Louwelsa, Vase, Bud, Iris, Marked, 4 3/4 In. 160.00
Louwelsa, Vase, Carnations, Ivory, Rust, 3 Sides, Marked, 11 3/8 In. 290.00
Louwelsa, Vase, Clovers, Red, Charles Dibowski, Marked, 4 3/4 In. 105.00
Louwelsa, Vase, Flowers, Brown Glaze, Squat, 4 In. 70.00
Louwelsa, Vase, Full Moon, Rising Over Lake, Blue, White, Claude Leffler, 1898, 10 In. . 1610.00
Louwelsa, Vase, Leaves & Berries, Blue, 9 In. 805.00
Louwelsa, Vase, Lily, Blue, White, 11 3/4 In. 1725.00
Louwelsa, Vase, Pansies, Gold, Rust, Slim Neck, Josephine Imlay, Marked, 11 3/4 In. 315.00
Louwelsa, Vase, Poppy, Yellow, Brown To Green Ground, 19 1/2 x 6 In. 1100.00
Louwelsa, Vase, Portrait, Oval, Man, Marked, 17 1/2 In. 1195.00
Louwelsa, Vase, Roses, Brown Glaze, Cylindrical, 14 In. 200.00
Louwelsa, Vase, Roses, Madge Hurst, 4 1/4 x 6 3/4 In. 265.00
Louwelsa, Vase, Stick, Blackberries, Heavy Slip, Elizabeth Ayers, Marked, 10 1/8 In. 160.00
Louwelsa, Vase, Wild Clover, Red, Bell Shape, 4 1/2 In. 115.00
Louwelsa, Vase, Wild Rose, Pillow, 4 x 5 1/4 In. 175.00
Louwelsa, Vase, Wild Rose, Red, Marked, 4 1/8 In. 70.00

Louwelsa, Vase, Yellow Daffodils, Teardrop, 2 Handles, M. Mitchell, 10 In. 265.00
Mammy, Tea Set, Marked Weller Pottery Since 1872, 8-In. Teapot, 3 Piece 1380.00
Manhattan, Vase, Stylized Leaves, Mottled Blue Matte Glaze, 8 1/2 In. 230.00
Marbleized, Bowl, Pink, Black, Tan, Bulbous, 4 1/4 In. 60.00
Marbleized, Vase, Gourd Shape, 7 In. 70.00
Marengo, Vase, Tree, Mountains, Blue, Luster Glaze, 8 In. 160.00
Marengo, Wall Pocket, Stylized Tree, Brown, Orange Ground, 8 3/4 In. 375.00
Marvo, Jardiniere & Pedestal, Brown, Ink Mark, 22 1/4 x 10 1/2 In. 705.00
Marvo, Umbrella Stand, Green, Orange Leaves, Branches, 20 In. 290.00
Minerva, Vase, Amber Trees, Brown Ground, 13 1/2 In. 2070.00
Muskota, Figurine, Bird, Brown, Blue, Black High Glaze, 6 In. 225.00
Muskota, Figurine, Fisherman, 7 In. 115.00
Muskota, Figurine, Woman Kneeling, 8 In. 230.00
Muskota, Fishbowl Holder & Bud Vase, Playful Cat, 11 x 11 1/4 In. 1880.00
Muskota, Flower Frog, Frog Inside Lotus Blossom, 4 1/2 In. . . . . .115.00 to 160.00
Muskota, Flower Frog, Lobster, 1 1/2 x 5 3/4 In. 115.00
Muskota, Flower Frog, Starfish, 5 In. 150.00
Muskota, Lamp Base, Fisherman, 11 1/4 In. 920.00
Orris, Vase, Daffodils, Green, Rust, 10 1/8 In. 260.00
Pelican, Garden Figure, Weller Ink Stamp, 19 1/8 In. 16415.00
Perfecto, Vase, Flowers, Lavender Ground, Leffler, 5 1/2 In. 290.00
Rhead Faience, Vase, Geisha, Instrument, Under Trees, 8 1/8 In. 1725.00
Rochelle, Vase, Daisies, Ivory, Squat, 3 1/2 x 4 In. 150.00
Roma, Umbrella Stand, Flowers, Ivory, 22 In. 105.00
Rosemont, Vase, Birds, Flowers, Incised, Painted, Black High Glaze, 7 In. 115.00
Sabrinian, Vase, Shell Design, 2 Seahorse Handles, 7 In. . . . . .230.00 to 460.00
Sicardo, Jardiniere, 10 1/2 x 11 1/2 In. 1955.00
Sicardo, Jardiniere, Tulips, Art Nouveau, 10 3/4 x 11 3/4 In. 690.00
Sicardo, Vase, Butterflies, Stars, Iridescent, Multicolored, c.1901-1907, 7 3/8 In. 145.00
Sicardo, Vase, Flower Sprays, Tapered, Unmarked, 7 3/4 In. 345.00
Sicardo, Vase, Flowers, Purple, Green & Blue Iridescent, Twisted, 5 In. 575.00
Sicardo, Vase, Pillow, Chrysanthemums, Cockscomb, 10 1/2 x 5 1/2 In. 1840.00
Sicardo, Vase, Spider Mums, Vines, Stylized, 4 Sides, Signed, 10 1/2 In. 865.00
Silvertone, Vase, Bearded Iris, Yellow, Purple, Green Leaves, 5 3/4 In. 230.00
Silvertone, Vase, Blackberry, 7 1/8 In. 690.00
Silvertone, Vase, Daisies, 2 Handles, 6 1/2 In. 260.00
Silvertone, Vase, Flowers, Pink, White, Handles, Hester Pillsbury, 9 3/4 In. 460.00
Silvertone, Vase, Hawthorne, 2 Handles, 7 5/8 In. 345.00
Silvertone, Vase, Lily, 11 5/8 In. 635.00
Silvertone, Vase, Magnolia, 2 Twig Handles, 8 1/8 In. 375.00
Silvertone, Vase, Magnolias, Yellow, Lavender Ground, Tree-Branch Handles, 11 1/2 In. . . 460.00
Silvertone, Vase, Narcissus, 7 7/8 In. 345.00
Silvertone, Vase, Tulips, 2 Handles, 8 In. 250.00
Souevo, Vase, American Indian Design, Flared Rim, 6 3/4 In. 130.00
Souevo, Vase, American Indian Design, Lightning Bolts, 3 5/8 In. 70.00
Stellar, Vase, Stars, White, Blue Ground, 5 5/8 In. 160.00
Turada, Bowl, Latticework Cover, Blue Flowers, Ivory Vines, Impressed Mark, 6 In. 200.00
Turada, Jardiniere, Orange & Ivory Squeezebag Bands, Olive Green Ground, 17 x 18 In. . . 920.00
Warwick, Vase, Branch Handles, Ink Stamp, 10 6 1/2 In. 235.00
Warwick, Wall Pocket, 12 In. 230.00
Wild Rose, Vase, Cornucopia, Salmon, Aqua Wash, 6 In., Pair 55.00
Woodcraft, Bowl, Oak Leaves, Perched Squirrel On Rim, 8 In. 315.00
Woodcraft, Bowl, Squirrels, Forest, 7 In. 235.00
Woodcraft, Jardiniere, Apple Tree Branches, Applied Figural Bird, 8 In. 546.00
Woodcraft, Jardiniere, Hollowed Tree Trunk, Relief Owl, 16 1/2 In. 1725.00
Woodcraft, Vase, Embossed Wild Roses, 10 1/8 In. 290.00
Woodcraft, Vase, Owl, Peeking Out Of Knothole, 13 1/2 In. 516.00
Woodcraft, Wall Pocket, Applied Figural Squirrel, Impressed Mark, 9 In. 345.00
Woodcraft, Wall Pocket, Owl, Brown, 11 In. 375.00
Woodrose, Wall Pocket, 2 Roses, Burnt Orange, Green, Brown, 10 1/4 In. 140.00
Xenia, Vase, Green Leaves & Berries, Blue Ground, Handles, 10 In. 1150.00
Zona, Vase, Carved Birds, Wolves, Grapevines, 10 In. 1035.00

WESTMORELAND GLASS was made by the Westmoreland Glass Company of Grapeville, Pennsylvania, from 1890 to 1984. They made clear and colored glass of many varieties, such as milk glass, pressed glass, and slag glass.

Argonaut Shell, Candy Dish, Cover, Golden Sunset	75.00
Beaded Edge, Bowl, Enameled Blackberries, Oval, Crimped, Milk Glass, 6 In.	20.00
Beaded Edge, Cup, Enameled Cherry, Milk Glass	13.00
Beaded Edge, Plate, Enameled Peach, Milk Glass, 7 In.	15.00
Cavalier, Mug, Milk Glass	10.00
Della Robbia, Bowl, Salad, Flat, Flared, 12 In.	110.00
Della Robbia, Cake Salver, 14 In.	150.00
Della Robbia, Plate, Luncheon, 9 In.	25.00 to 30.00
Della Robbia, Torte Plate, 14 In.	90.00
Doric, Bowl, Footed, Milk Glass, 12 In.	35.00
English Hobnail, Basket, Ruby Stain	165.00
English Hobnail, Bowl, Ivy, No. 106	25.00
English Hobnail, Bowl, Oval, Crimped, Milk Glass, 10 In.	20.00
English Hobnail, Cordial	17.00
Figurine, Bulldog, Crystal, Satin	35.00
Lotus, Bowl, Footed, Milk Glass, 11 In.	30.00
Lotus, Bowl, Oval, Crimped, Bermuda Blue, 1967, 10 x 12 In.	20.00
Lotus, Plate, Flared, Green, 13 In.	45.00
Old Quilt, Bowl, Iridescent Blue	185.00
Old Quilt, Cake Plate, Footed, Milk Glass, 12 1/2 In.	40.00
Old Quilt, Celery Vase, Milk Glass	20.00
Old Quilt, Pitcher, Milk Glass, 8 1/2 In.	40.00
Old Quilt, Sugar & Creamer, Milk Glass, 4 In.	55.00
Old Quilt, Vase, Fan, 8-Sided Foot, Milk Glass, 9 In.	25.00
Paneled Grape, Basket, Split Handle, Milk Glass, 6 1/2 In.	30.00
Paneled Grape, Bowl, Lipped, Skirted Foot, Milk Glass, 9 In.	65.00
Paneled Grape, Candlestick, Milk Glass, 4 In., Pair	25.00
Paneled Grape, Cup & Saucer, Milk Glass	23.00
Paneled Grape, Dish, Mayonnaise, Milk Glass	30.00
Paneled Grape, Dish, Sleigh, Milk Glass, 9 In.	55.00
Paneled Grape, Goblet, Milk Glass, 8 Oz.	20.00
Paneled Grape, Jardiniere, Milk Glass, 4 In.	30.00
Paneled Grape, Jardiniere, Milk Glass, 5 In.	40.00
Paneled Grape, Jardiniere, Milk Glass, 6 1/2 In.	45.00
Paneled Grape, Nut Dish, Oval, Footed, Milk Glass, 6 1/2 In.	30.00
Paneled Grape, Pitcher, Footed, Milk Glass, Qt.	40.00
Paneled Grape, Planter, Milk Glass, 5 x 9 In.	35.00
Paneled Grape, Plate, Salad, Milk Glass, 8 1/2 In.	25.00
Paneled Grape, Vase, Ivy Ball, Footed, Milk Glass	50.00
Paneled Grape, Vase, Milk Glass, 9 1/2 In.	40.00
Princess Feather, Champagne	9.00
Princess Feather, Sherbet	5.00
Ring & Petal, Candlestick, Milk Glass, Pair	20.00
Santa On Sleigh, Dish, Cover, Milk Glass, 5 1/2 In.	100.00
Sitting Bull, Vase, Opal Glass, 1910, 7 1/4 In.	10.00
Toothpick, Owl, Spread Wings, Milk Glass, 3 In.	20.00

WHEATLEY Pottery was established in 1880. Thomas J. Wheatley had worked in Cincinnati, Ohio, with the founders of the art pottery movement, including M. Louise McLaughlin of the Rookwood Pottery. Wheatley Pottery was purchased by the Cambridge Tile Manufacturing Company in 1927.

Humidor, Green Matte Glaze, Flared Lip, Cylindrical Base, 7 1/2 x 5 In.	470.00
Pitcher, Landscape, c.1880, 6 1/4 x 5 1/2 In.	495.00
Pitcher, Warlord, Panels, Raised Dots, Green, Marked, 1882, 7 1/2 x 6 In.	165.00
Tile, Ship, 4 Masts, Multicolored, Marked Cambridge, 8 x 12 1/2 In., 6 Piece	1100.00
Vase, Applied Leaves, Flowers, Green Matte Glaze, Tapered, 12 1/2 In.	1150.00
Vase, Bud, Oatmeal Matte Glaze, Leaves, Tooled, 11 1/2 x 8 1/2 In.	1980.00
Vase, Curdled Green Glaze, 4 Flaring Buttresses, 8 1/4 x 9 In.	1840.00

WHEELING Pottery Company of Wheeling, West Virginia, worked from 1879 to about 1923. The firm went through a number of mergers and name changes during that time. Pottery, semiporcelain, artware, and sanitary wares were made.

Pitcher, LaBelle, Flow Blue, Blue Flowers, Gold Trim, 7 In.	395.00
Plate, Dessert, Floral Transfer, Pink, Yellow, Gold Trim, Adamantine China, 7 In.	7.50
Sugar & Creamer, LaBelle	595.00
Tile, Tulips, Lavender, Green, Ivory Ground, Mark, 4 In.	220.00
Tile, Viking Ship, Yellow, Lavender Mast, Blue Sky, Green Waves, Frame, Mark, 6 In.	140.00

WHIELDON was an English potter who worked alone and with Josiah Wedgwood in eighteenth-century England. Whieldon made many pieces in natural shapes, like cauliflowers or cabbages.

Plate, Feather Medallion, Diamond Grid, Mottled, Brown, Green, Scalloped, 9 1/4 In.	523.00
Plate, Multicolored, Embossed, Ruffled, 9 1/2 In.	115.00
Plate, Rope Border, Mottled Brown, Octagonal, 8 3/4 In.	138.00
Teapot, Cover, Agateware, Globular Body, Crabstock Handle, c.1760, 5 3/4 In.	4180.00

WILLETS Manufacturing Company of Trenton, New Jersey, began work in 1879. The company made Belleek in the late 1880s and 1890s in shapes similar to those used by the Irish Belleek factory. They stopped working about 1912. A variety of marks were used, all including the name Willets.

Basket, Woven, Applied Flowers, 2 Branch Handles, 3 1/2 x 9 In.	2070.00
Basket, Woven, Applied Leaves, Berries, Belleek Mark, 2 1/4 x 8 1/2 In.	1495.00
Basket, Woven, Cream, Applied Flowers, Stamped, 3 1/2 x 9 In. .... *Illus*	2070.00
Tankard, Daisies, Dragon Handle, Gilt, Belleek, 10 In.	896.00
Tankard, Monks, Red Ground, Gilt, Ornate Handle, Belleek, 14 1/2 In.	1120.00
Tea Set, Burgundy, Sterling Silver Leaf Overlay, Bamboo Handles, Belleek Mark, 3 Piece	978.00
Tea Set, Thistle, Bone Ground, Gilt Trim, Figural Dragon Handles, 8-In. Teapot, 3 Piece	1035.00
Urn, Roses, Pink, Yellow, Gilt, G.G. Houghton, Belleek Mark, 1903, 17 1/2 x 9 In. ... *Illus*	1840.00
Vase, Butterfly, Wheat, Gilt Trim, Cobalt Blue Ground, Oval, 15 1/2 In.	518.00
Vase, Flowers, Mottled Blue, Green Ground, Gilt Rim, Belleek Mark, 1904, 20 3/4 In.	2689.00
Vase, Pink Glaze, Gilt, Ivory Ground, Coral Handle, Shell Shape, Belleek Mark, 8 In.	1955.00
Vase, Rose, Hand Painted, Snake Mark, 12 1/2 In.	115.00
Vase, Wild Roses, Gold Dragon Handles, Belleek Mark, c.1880, 9 x 4 In. .... *Illus*	300.00

WILLOW pattern has been made in England since 1780. The pattern has been copied by factories in many countries, including Germany, Japan, and the United States. It is still being made. Willow was named for a pattern that pictures a bridge, birds, willow trees, and a Chinese landscape. Most pieces are blue and white.

Bowl, 12 x 2 1/2 In.	20.00
Bowl, Cereal, Japan, 6 1/4 In.	11.00
Bowl, Cereal, Royal Cavalier, D. Schreckengost, 6 1/2 In.	6.00
Bowl, Gold Trim, Willow Duchess Bone China, 9 x 2 1/2 In.	50.00
Bowl, Marked Societe Creme Que Maestright, Holland, 5 1/4 In.	25.00

Willets, Basket, Woven, Cream, Applied Flowers, Stamped, 3 1/2 x 9 In.

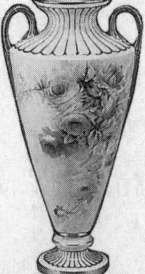

Willets, Urn, Roses, Pink, Yellow, Gilt, G.G. Houghton, Belleek Mark, 1903, 17 1/2 x 9

Willets, Vase, Wild Roses, Gold Dragon Handles, Belleek Mark, c.1880, 9 x 4 In.

Bowl, Midwinter, 10 x 8 1/4 In.	47.00
Bowl, Norcrest, 4 1/2 In.	15.00
Bowl, Oval, Homer Laughlin	50.00
Bowl, Salad, 9 1/2 In.	60.00
Bowl, Vegetable, Cover, 1891-1900	195.00
Bowl, Vegetable, Grimwades, England, 9 x 6 3/4 In.	25.00
Bowl, Vegetable, Oval, 8 3/4 In.	40.00
Bowl, Wash, Ironstone, 16 x 4 1/4 In.	395.00
Bowl, Ye Old Willow, Myott Son & Co., 1936, 5 1/2 x 3 1/2 In.	40.00
Bread Plate, William Adams & Sons, 1893-1917, 6 In.	18.00
Butter, Dark Blue, Japan, 1930, 6 1/8 In.	14.00
Butter, Dark Blue, William Adams & Son, 1893-1917, 6 In.	14.00
Butter, Green, Royal Grafton Bone China, England, 6 1/4 In.	22.00
Butter, Myott Sons & Co., 1910, 6 In.	10.00
Butter Chip, Allerton, c.1903	25.00
Butter Chip, Allerton, England, c.1907	25.00
Cake Plate, Blue & Pink, 9 1/2 x 4 1/2 In.	20.00
Cake Plate, England, Box	40.00
Cake Plate, Multicolored, Silver Plate Stand, Newport Pottery Co., 1920	299.00
Canister, Cover, Set Of 4	480.00
Casserole, Child's, 5 x 3 In.	50.00
Casserole, Cover, Gold Trim, 6 1/8 x 10 3/8 In.	249.00
Chop Plate, Royal Cavalier, 11 1/2 In.	18.00
Creamer, 2 In.	35.00
Creamer, Cross-Shaped Cover, 4 1/2 x 3 x 2 1/2 In.	40.00
Creamer, Individual, Handle, Restaurant, Shenango	35.00
Creamer, Japan, Child's	20.00
Creamer, Multicolored, 4 In.	25.00
Crumb Tray, 6 x 5 1/2 In.	10.00
Cup, 8 3/4 x 5 In.	75.00
Cup, Custard, Red, Restaurant, Sterling China	10.00
Cup, Tea, Black, Germany, 3 x 1 1/2 In.	35.00
Cup & Saucer, Box & Display Stand, Child's	20.00
Cup & Saucer, Child's, 2 1/4 x 3 1/2 In.	33.00
Cup & Saucer, Child's, 2 1/4 x 3 1/4 In.	25.00
Cup & Saucer, Impressed U.S.A, 3 In.	20.00
Cup & Saucer, Japan	6.00
Cup & Saucer, Light Blue, Child's, 2 1/4 x 1 1/4 In.	25.00
Cup & Saucer, Multicolored, 2 3/4 x 5 1/2 In.	25.00
Cup & Saucer, Royal Cavalier, D. Schreckengost	7.00
Cup & Saucer, Swinnertons Old Willow, 2 1/2 x 3 1/2 In.	50.00
Gravy Boat, Child's, 3 x 1/2 In.	25.00
Mug, U.S.A.	25.00
Pitcher, Milk, 5 1/2 x 3 7/8 In.	28.00
Pitcher, Milk, 6 1/2 In.	35.00
Pitcher, Newport Pottery Co., 6 In.	98.00
Pitcher, Pink, Regal Of England, 7 x 3 1/2 In.	77.00
Plate, England, 10 In.	20.00
Plate, Flow Blue, Allerton, England, 6 In.	16.00
Plate, Gold Trim, Shetlonian Bone China, 3 In.	15.00
Plate, Green, Jackson Vitrifield, 1950-1960, 10 In.	30.00
Plate, Japan, 6 In.	6.00
Plate, Japan, 7 In.	7.00
Plate, Japan, 7 1/2 In.	7.00
Plate, Japan, 7 3/8 In.	7.00
Plate, Japan, 9 In.	10.00
Plate, Japan, Child's, 3 3/4 In.	20.00
Plate, Multicolored, 6 In.	16.00
Plate, Oriental Canton Design, Ashworth Hanley, 1900-1920, 10 1/2 In.	60.00
Plate, Pink, Japan, 6 1/2 In.	22.00
Plate, Royal Cavalier, 6 1/2 In.	4.00
Plate, Royal Cavalier, 10 In.	10.00
Plate, Royal China, 10 In.	40.00

Plate, Salad, Royal Grafton Bone China, 7 In. 25.00
Platter, Brown Transfer, Octagonal, J & G Meakins, 15 3/4 x 12 1/2 In. 110.00
Platter, England, 12 1/2 x 15 1/2 In. 55.00
Platter, Handles, Child's, 5 1/4 In. 30.00
Platter, Handles, Royal Sebring, 11 1/2 In. 50.00
Platter, Ironstone, Barker & Son Stoneware, 10 x 12 1/2 In. 110.00
Platter, Mahogany Stand, Mid 19th Century, 19 x 21 x 15 3/4 In. 635.00
Platter, Oval, 13 1/2 x 18 1/2 In. 60.00
Platter, Pink, Oval, 18 1/2 In. 46.00
Platter, Royal Sebring, 12 1/4 In. 25.00
Platter, Staffordshire, 19th Century, 18 In. 115.00
Ramekin, 2 x 3 3/4 In. 16.00
Salt & Pepper, 3 In. 32.00
Salt & Pepper, Blue & Pink, 3 In. 11.00
Sauce, Red, Jackson, Restaurant Ware, 4 In. 6.00
Saucer, Allerton, England 5.00
Saucer, Brown, Japan 3.00
Saucer, Gold Trim, Royal Grafton Bone China, 5 1/2 In. 20.00
Saucer, Japan, Child's, 3 1/2 In. 20.00
Saucer, Red 3.00
Shaving Mug, Victoria Ironstone, 3 3/4 x 7 In. 35.00
Sherbet Set, Homer Laughlin, 5 Piece 70.00
Skillet, Porcelain On Steel, 11 1/2 In. 50.00
Soup, Dish, Baker, England, 7 3/4 In. 20.00
Soup, Dish, Dudson Wilcox & Till Ltd., 1902-1926, 8 In. 14.00
Soup, Dish, Japan, 7 1/2 In. 30.00
Sugar, 2 3/4 In. 35.00
Sugar, Cover, Japan, 4 1/2 In. 15.00
Sugar, Japan, Child's 20.00
Sugar, Multicolored, 2 1/4 x 5 In. 25.00
Tea Set, Child's, 25 Piece 75.00
Teapot, Christopher Johnson, 7 x 4 1/2 x 3 1/2 In. 69.00
Teapot, Gold Design, Gold Rim, Gold Ring-Shaped Finial, 4 3/4 x 6 1/2 In. 58.00
Teapot, Pink, 5 3/4 x 9 In. 17.00

WINDOW glass that was stained and beveled was popular for houses during the late nineteenth and early twentieth centuries. The old windows became popular with collectors in the 1970s; today, old and new examples are seen.

Leaded, Cockatoo, Red, Yellow, Black, Rectangular, Dutch, 1920s, 36 x 22 In. 505.00
Leaded, Green Slag Glass, Painted Girl & Dog, Jewels, Signed CM 95, 24 x 28 In. 3910.00
Leaded, Green, Caramel Swirl, Pink, Amber, Geometric & Floral, 32 x 34 In. 300.00
Leaded, Jeweled, Lavender Braided Border, Round, Frame, 43 x 39 In. 2185.00
Leaded, Mission Style, Caramel, Green, Purple, 43 x 19 In. 250.00
Leaded, Nude Woman, Shawl, Green, Brown Slag Glass, 19 1/2 x 46 In. 3450.00
Leaded, Prairie School, 3 Stylized Flowers, Green, 18 x 38 In., Pair 750.00
Leaded, Prairie School, Geometric, Amber Glass Field, 16 x 30 In., Pair 520.00
Leaded, Stained Glass, 2 Fish, Circular, Favrile Balls On Perimeter, 17 In. 450.00
Leaded, Stained Glass, Art Nouveau, Flowers & Leaves, Arched, c.1915, 48 x 36 In. ... 670.00
Leaded, Stained Glass, Billiards, Purple Flowers, 40 x 28 In. 550.00
Leaded, Stained Glass, Bull's-Eye Border, Intertwined Ovals, 20 x 34 1/2 In. 835.00
Leaded, Stained Glass, Butterfly, Frosted, Rippled, Vine, Flowers, 21 x 32 1/2 In., Pair .. 230.00
Leaded, Stained Glass, Etched, Calla Lilly, Green Borders, 53 1/2 x 31 In., Pair 575.00
Leaded, Stained Glass, Flower, Leaves, Jewels, 51 In. 2875.00
Leaded, Stained Glass, Flowers, Ribbons, Jewels, Fleur De Lis, 3 Panels, 32 x 47 1/2 In. . 1725.00
Leaded, Stained Glass, Hunter, Trees, Birds, Snow, Jewels, 27 1/2 x 34 In. 1150.00
Leaded, Stained Glass, Irises, Rolling Hills, 28 x 24 In. 2010.00
Leaded, Stained Glass, Mosaic, Flowers, c.1890, 43 x 46 In. 4760.00
Leaded, Stained Glass, Peacock, Watson, 35 x 25 In. 4310.00
Leaded, Stained Glass, Putti, Faceted Jewels On Sides, 16 x 107 In., 3 Piece 3920.00
Leaded, Stained Glass, Tulips, Arts & Crafts, Demilune, c.1888, 33 1/2 x 44 1/2 In. 920.00
Leaded, Stained Glass, Woman Dancing, Tambourine, Ewels, Frame, 37 1/2 x 68 In. 6900.00
Leaded, Urn With Flowers, Blue Sky Ground, Gothic Arch, 23 1/2 x 41 1/4 In. 1725.00

Stained Glass, Art Deco, Engraved, Cameo, Flamingos, 50 x 56 x 1/2 In. 950.00
Stained Glass, Dove, Crosses As Feet, Frame, Pre 1900, 57 x 53 In. 2850.00
Stained Glass, Our Lady Of Perpetual Help, 19th Century, 12 3/4 x 9 In. 85.00
Stained Glass, Scrolled, Beveled Panels, Amber Ground, Lavender Border, 44 x 29 In. 1265.00
Stained Glass, Seashells, Cabochon Jewels, Amber Geometric Border, 28 x 32 In. 1035.00
Stained Glass, Urns, Swags, Walnut Edges, c.1890, 41 x 73 In. 1100.00
Stained Glass, Yellow Stippled, Painted Cherub & Grapes, Jewels, 16 x 35 In. 575.00

WOOD CARVINGS and wooden pieces are listed separately in this book.
Many of the wood carvings are figurines or statues. There are also
wooden pieces found in other categories, such as Kitchen.

2 Deer, Locked In Battle, Switzerland, c.1890, 13 In. 690.00
Acrobat, Jointed Arms & Legs, Smiling Face, North Carolina, c.1909, 18 In. 187.00
African Man, Seated With Spear, Hagenauer, 10 3/4 In. 230.00
African Man's Head, Hagenauer, 4 1/4 In. 345.00
Altar, Christ, Virgin, Apostle John, God The Father, Polychrome, 1700s, 16 In. 2875.00
Amazon, Greco-Roman Dress, Carnival, 1880-1900, 96 In. 8625.00
American Indian's Head, Hagenauer, 5 3/4 In. 920.00
Angel, Polychrome, Gilt, Gold Leaf, Italy, 18th Century, 41 In. 2990.00
Angel, Praying, Polychrome, Gold Leaf, 19th Century, 27 x 20 1/2 In. 1900.00
Barn Owl, Painted, Glass Eyes, Mounted On Stand, 20th Century, 15 1/2 In. 2938.00
Bear, Glass Eyes, Holding Large Basket, Switzerland, c.1890, 16 1/2 In. 3680.00
Bear, Glass Eyes, Switzerland, c.1930, 10 x 16 1/2 In. 1330.00
Bear, Seated, Glass Eyes, Holding Glass Bowl, Switzerland, c.1890, 14 In. 2300.00
Beaver, Inlaid Abalone Eyes, c.1950, 4 x 9 1/2 In. 259.00
Bird, Painted, Black, Red, White Eyes, Green Grass, Aaron Mountz Style, 5 3/4 In. 375.00
Bird, Pine, Green Paint, Glass Eyes, Rocking Legs, W. Parks, Pa., c.1935, 5 In. 1800.00
Bird Tree, Painted, 6 Polychrome Birds, Wire Legs, 1800s, 10 1/2 x 19 In. 2390.00
Black Man's Head, Painted, 19th Century, 19 1/4 In. 3175.00
Blackamoor, Carved, Painted, Standing, Costumed, Holding Urn, Italy, 72 In. 1410.00
Blackamoor, Crouching, Arm Above Head, Scroll-Carved Sarong, 38 In., Pair 764.00
Blackamoor, Holding Bowl, Mother Of Pearl, Carved Bone, c.1900, 64 In. 5060.00
Blackamoor, Italian Gilt, Painted, Holding Torch, 81 In. 16730.00
Bottle Stopper, Couple Dance, Stamped Depose, 6 1/4 In. . . . . *Illus* 40.00
Bracket, Pine, Console, Louis XVI Style, 19th Century, 27 1/2 x 9 1/2 In., Pair 405.00
Buddha, Gilt, Standing On Lotus Throne, Japan, 19th Century, 33 In. 3450.00
Buddha, Lacquer, Seated On Lotus Throne, Chinese, 18th Century, 13 In. 380.00
Buddha, Seated On Lotus Throne, 8 1/2 In. 430.00
Bull, Mahogany, Removable Tail & Horns, Dennis Smith, 14 1/2 x 26 In. 415.00
Caged Ball, Green, Brown Paint, 16 In. 60.00
Cat, Pine, Painted, Relaxed Crouch, Weathered, 10 3/8 x 31 5/8 In. 10575.00
Cat, Resting, 16 In. 370.00
Chinese Man, Giltwood, Rouge Lacquer, Stand, Chinese, c.1800, 12 1/2 In. 230.00
Christ, Going To Calvary, Iron Crown Of Thorns, 19th Century, 27 1/2 In. 690.00
Christ, Sacred Heart, Germany, 19th Century, 67 In. 690.00
Christ, Standing, Red & Blue Robes, Painted, Gesso, 21 In. 355.00
Cobra, Coiled, Rosewood, Opalescent White Glass Eyes, 11 1/2 In. 575.00
Corpus, Mounted On Polished Cross, Southern Germany, 35 x 15 In. 290.00
Corpus, Polychrome, Carved In Round, 19th Century, 20 x 13 In. 690.00
Corpus, Polychrome, Continental, 19th Century, 28 x 17 1/2 In. 460.00
Crest, Painted, Saint John Woodcarver, Lion, Unicorn, 16 x 53 In. 2300.00
Crucifix, Burnt Wood, Inscription, Provincial, France, c.1941, 24 In. 115.00
Crucifix, Corpus, Polychrome, Colonial, Spain, c.1850, 28 x 16 3/4 In. 288.00
Crucifix, Corpus, Polychrome, South Germany, 19th Century, 39 x 19 In. 345.00
Crucifix, Polychrome, Spanish Colonial, 19th Century, 17 In. 200.00
Curtain Tieback, Caricature, Comic, Walnut, 19th Century, 7 In., Pair 175.00
Dance-Hall Woman, No Arms, Pine, American, c.1890, 33 In. 9600.00
Demon, Chinese, 19th Century, 20 In. 410.00
Diorama, Ship, 3-Masted, Paddle Wheel, 2 Smokestacks, 25 1/2 x 7 x 11 In. 825.00
Dog, Articulated Face, Ears, Tail, Aaron Mountz, Pa., c.1900, 6 3/4 In. 359.00
Dog, Articulated Face, Ears, Tail, Holding Basket, Aaron Mountz, 4 3/4 In. 2629.00
Dog, Crosshatched Upper Body, Polychrome, Square Base, 4 In. 340.00
Dog, Reclining, Head On Paws, Shaggy, Walnut, 11 In. 1840.00

Dog, Spaniel, Reclining, Brown, Painted, 12 x 24 In. 635.00
Dwarf, Feeding Squirrel, Engraved, Schran Fec, c.1910, 7 1/2 In. 290.00
Eagle, Bellamy Style, California Sugar Pine, Janet Weaver, 1956, 29 In. 690.00
Eagle, Flying, Gray Paint Over Gilt, 13 In. 2875.00
Eagle, Giltwood, Perched On Rockery, Pilot House, c.1875, 25 x 31 x 26 In. 2470.00
Eagle, Giltwood, Pilot House, Early 20th Century, 15 3/4 x 21 In. 1725.00
Eagle, On Post, Painted, Weathered, 19th Century, 45 1/2 In. 2115.00
Eagle, Painted, White, Black Spots, Wilhelm Schimmel, 1800s, 6 3/8 In. 4780.00
Eagle, Painted, Wilhelm Schimmel Style, Early 1900s, 8 1/2 x 20 In. 580.00
Eagle, Pine, Painted, Standing, Outstretched Wings, Early 1900s, 24 x 23 In. 1410.00
Eagle, Spread Wing, Polychrome, Schimmel Style, Signed, Pa, 11 x 23 In. 580.00
Eagle, Spread Wings, Glass Eyes, Gilded, c.1860, 35 1/2-In. Wingspan 9900.00
Eagle, Spread Wings, Head Facing Left, Shield, Arrows, 42 1/2 x 14 1/2 In. 1725.00
Eagle, Spread Wings, Louis Gansell, Montour, Pa., Mid 1900s, 9 x 36 In. 440.00
Eagle, Spread Wings, Pine, Gilded, U.S. Shield, 19th Century, 4 x 20 In. 10158.00
Eagle, Spread Wings, Walnut, Cherry Base, Brass Plate, June 1782, 31 x 15 In. 550.00
Eagle, Spread Wings, West Virginia, 60 In. 475.00
Eagle, White, Red, Blue Shield, 25 In. 150.00
Eagles, Relief Detail, Shield, 19 Stars, Paint Traces, 18 1/2 x 29 1/2 In. 275.00
Elephants Working, Polychrome, India, 20th Century, 63 x 32 x 3 1/2 In. 980.00
Elf, Pulling Up Boots, Applied Goat Horns, Hat Rack, Wall Mounted, 16 In. 980.00
Female Nude, Full Round, American, c.1931, 18 1/2 In. 1725.00
Finial, Newel, Swirling Flame, 19th Century, 14 In. 315.00
Fish, Pine, Brass Tack Eyes, Red Painted Base, 35 1/4 x 22 1/4 In. 715.00
Foo Dog, Red, Gold Lacquer, Chinese, 19th Century, 10 1/2 x 11 In. 530.00
Goddess, Meditative Stance, Rosewood, Japan, 14 In. 175.00
Goddess, Watermoon Viewing Kuan Yin, Lacquer, Vietnam, 1800s, 14 1/2 In. 500.00
Gondola, Dragon Shape, 8 Oriental Passengers, 1900s, 8 1/2 x 32 In. 85.00
Guanyin, Parcel Rouge, Painted Blue, Gesso, Chinese, 24 In. 1725.00
Guinea Fowl, W, & J, Sloane, 20th Century, 20 3/4 In. 265.00
Human Skull, Pine, Silver Plated Lower Mandible, 17th Lancers 175.00
Humidor, Bear, Walnut, Black Forest, Glass Eyes, Hinged Cover, 13 In. 3165.00
Humidor, Presentation, Walnut, Knotty Tree Trunk, c.1871, 6 1/2 x 7 In. 316.00
Indian Maiden, Comic, Hands On Hips, Multi-Products, c.1954, 6 1/2 In. 27.00
Jockey, Racehorse, Painted, Horsehair Tail, Stand, Scroll Feet, 17 In. 1645.00
Kwan Ti, Seated On Dragon Throne, Foo Lions, 19th Century, 16 1/2 In. 520.00
Lion, Glass Eyes, Pointed Teeth, Japan, 14 1/2 In. 1440.00
Lion, Schimmel Style, Painted, Yellow, Black Highlights, 1900s, 6 x 4 1/2 In. 58.00
Madonna & Child, Gilt, Painted, Italy, c.1800, 33 In. 1610.00
Madonna & Child, Polychrome, Continental, 18th Century, 19 1/4 In. 1495.00
Madonna & Child, Standing On Dragon, c.1900, 39 In. 805.00
Man, Cloth Coat, Handlebar Mustache, Carved, Jointed, Glass Eyes, 29 In. 1125.00
Man Reading Book, Polychrome, Korea, 14 1/2 In. 4680.00
Mannequin, Painted, Articulated, Back Brace, Platform, 51 In. 1200.00
Mask, African Warrior, Painted, Braided Grass Hair, 14 In. 690.00
Mask, Daruma, Polychrome, Damban Style, Japan, 20th Century, 23 In. 35.00
Mask, Helmet, Serpent-Form Nose, Headdress, Africa, Early 1900s, 28 In. 259.00
Mask, Round Eyes, Square Mouth, White Paint, Raffia Beard, Africa, 18 1/2 In. 85.00
Monk, Holding Bust Of Woman, Black Forest, 22 1/2 In. 1150.00
Monk, Lacquered, 20th Century, 10 3/4 In., Pair 956.00
Monkey, Root, Upstretched Arm, Leg, 34 In. 345.00
Monkey, Seated, Applied Glass Eyes & Nose, 6 1/2 In. 165.00
Nativity Scene, Wise Men's Heads Over Mary & Joseph, Star, Pine, 51 In. 55.00
Neptune, Standing, Holding Triton, Sea Monster, Painted, 46 In. 4700.00
Ornament, Happy Hog Face, Gold Paint, Green Scalloped Leaves, 16 x 25 In. 330.00
Our Lady Of Mt. Carmel, Polychrome, Gesso, Spain, Colonial, 15 1/4 In. 1035.00
Owl, Perched, Reading Book, c.1890, 17 In. 670.00
Oxen, Painted, Brown, White Spots, New England, c.1930, 8 1/4 In., Pair 1555.00
Panel, Deity, 4 Hands Holding Attributes, 21 x 12 In. 170.00
Panel, Oak, Queen Elizabeth, Ruffled Collar, Notched Frame, 26 x 23 1/2 In. 540.00
Panel, Peacocks, On Tree, Rosewood, Chinese, 20th Century, 23 x 16 In. 104.00
Panel, Peonies & Shishi, Cloth Eyes, Japan, 19th Century, 5 1/2 x 23 In. 400.00
Panel, Phoenix In Flight, Above Flowers & Grasses, Japan, 30 x 63 In. 1150.00

Panel, Woman Holding Child, Angels, Crown, Polychrome, 51 1/2 x 24 In. 920.00
Parrot, Green & Red Decoration, On Stand, 12 In. 315.00
Parrot, Painted, Twisted Copper Wire Legs, On Stand, 19th Century, 16 1/2 In. 500.00
Parrot, Polychrome Painted, Wire Hoop, Perched On Bar, 15 1/2 In. 1870.00
Parrot, Schimmel Style, Painted, Red, Green, Black, Yellow, On Green Base, 8 In. 230.00
Pieta, Painted, Lithuania, 19th Century, 3 Piece 690.00
Pieta, Polychrome, 19th Century, 15 In. 345.00
Plaque, Eagle, Holding Banner, Live & Let Live, Painted, Gilt, 15 x 36 In. 345.00
Plaque, Eagle, Spread Wings, Holding Shield, Arrows In Talons, Giltwood, 42 In. 3525.00
Plaque, Eve Reaching For Apple, c.1935, 58 x 11 1/2 In. 6325.00
Plaque, Girl Picking Fruit, Oak, 17 1/2 x 9 5/8 In. 385.00
Plaque, Man, Woman, Walnut, Arts & Crafts, Goldberg, Phila., c.1936, 10 In., Pair 470.00
Plaque, Vase Of Tulips, 9 1/2 x 11 3/4 In. 8800.00
Plate, Birthday, 1972, Boy, Playing Cello, Bird, Cat, Fish, Schmidt, Box 75.00
Putto, Draped, Glass Eyes, Weathered Gray, Spanish Colonial, 30 In. 490.00
Putto, Painted Wood, Parcel Gilt, Continental, 1900s, 29 1/2 In., Pair 1035.00
Quail, Painted, Next To Rocks, Tree, Wood Base, 11 x 9 In. 260.00
Resurrected Christ, Foot On Skull, Serpent, 19th Century, 27 1/2 In. 1150.00
Resurrected Christ, Painted White, Germany, 19th Century, 60 In. 1035.00
Romulus & Remus, Suckled By She Wolves, Continental, 22 In. 1765.00
Santos, Apostle, 19th Century, 32 1/2 In. 2705.00
Santos, Franciscan Monk, Portugal, 18th Century, 13 In. 430.00
Snake, Open Mouth, 10 Joined Body Sections, Polychrome Paint, 17 In. 80.00
Sperm Whale, Painted Eyes, Teeth, 23 In. 468.00
Sphinx, Full-Bodied, Initialed, 20th Century, 16 x 10 In. 798.00
Spoon, Wedding, Carved Hex Signs, Potted Flower, Bird, 20 1/4 In. 25.00
Squirrel, Seated On Stump, Holding Nut, 11 3/4 In. 1870.00
St. Elizabeth Of Hungary, Oak, Signed E. Sund, c.1900, 18 In. 865.00
St. George, Slaying Dragon, 19th Century, 22 x 19 In. 1955.00
Standing Guanyin, Yuan Ming, Polychrome, Chinese, 37 1/2 In. 3285.00
Swallowtail, Pine, Black, Rocking Spring Legs, W. Parks, Pa., c.1935, 7 1/4 In. 1080.00
Toad, Silver, Red Pigment, Southeast Asia, 19th Century, 13 3/4 In. 480.00
Tree, 24 Fanciful Birds & Squirrel On Trunk, Painted, 54 In. 2750.00
Uncle Sam, Double-Sided, Painted, Early 20th Century, 76 1/2 In. 380.00
Veronica's Veil, Germany, 19th Century, 20 x 12 1/2 In. 1035.00
Virgin, Miraculous Medal Depiction, 19th Century, 19 1/2 In. 575.00
Virgin, Polychrome, Flowing Hair, Germany, 19th Century, 24 1/2 In. 1150.00
Virgin & Child, French Gothic Style, 19th Century, 27 In. 1093.00
Virgin & Child, Germany, 18th Century, 23 1/2 In. 690.00
Whistler, Accordion Player, Guitarist, Germany, c.1960, 13 1/2 In. 1375.00
Whistler, Accordion Player, Key Wind, Clockwork, Germany, c.1935, 13 1/4 In. 1210.00
Whistler, Dark Man, Top Hat, Umbrella, Key Wind, Germany, c.1910, 13 1/2 In. 1595.00
Whistler, Old Friends, 2 Tunes, Karl Griesbaum, Germany, c.1910, 13 3/4 In. 1375.00
Woman, Driving Surrey, William Dupre, Mass., 11 x 16 1/2 In. 260.00
Woman, Green Dress, Magenta Sash, Shoes, 20 3/4 In. 305.00
Woman, Wearing Beadwork Jewelry, Ibeji, 11 1/2 In. 80.00
Woman, Wearing Dress, Full-Bodied, Feather Quill Holder, 1800s, 6 1/2 In. 440.00
Woman's Head, Carved Face, Ears, Hair, Stepped Base, Dentil, Stamped, 8 In. 645.00

WOODEN wares were used in all parts of the home. Wood was used for
many containers and tools. Small wooden pieces are called *treenware*
in England, but the term woodenware is more common in the United
States. Additional pieces may be found in the Advertising, Kitchen,
and Tool categories.

Altar, Tabletop, Cross, Spanish Colonial, 28 In. 700.00
Altar, Tabletop, Flowers, Portugal, 38 1/2 In. 1528.00
Backstaff, Davis Style, Mahogany, Holly, Ivory Plaque, Diamonds, 20 1/4 In. 1840.00
Barrel, Oak, Green Paint, Stave Construction, 29 1/4 In. 965.00
Barrel, Rum, Oak, Metal Banding, c.1900, 20 In. 104.00
Basket, Bombe, Square, Handle, Provincial, c.1900, 8 3/4 x 13 x 13 In. 60.00
Basket, Flared, Square, Arched Handle, Provincial, c.1900, 11 1/4 x 15 1/4 x 15 1/2 In. ... 60.00
Basket, Smoked Split Bamboo, Gnarled Branch Handle, Ikebana, Japan, 12 1/2 In. 230.00
Birdhouse, 2 Drawers In Base, Peaked Roof, Wire, Zoar, Ohio, 36 x 17 x 20 3/4 In. 440.00

Wooden,
Figurine, Russian
Dancers, Native
Dress, 5 3/4 In.

Wood Carving,
Bottle Stopper,
Couple Dance,
Stamped Depose,
6 1/4 In.

**Don't store wooden
bowls and other pieces
on their sides. This can
cause them to warp.**

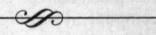

Birdhouse, 8 Sides, 4 Gables, Michigan, 20th Century, 25 x 23 x 23 In.	1540.00
Book Cover, Sandalwood, 5 Heads, 4-Armed Deity, Mysore, 19th Century, 15 In.	230.00
Bowl, Amber, Brown, Initials, Hawaii, 6 3/4 x 12 In.	5500.00
Bowl, Burl, 5 1/2 x 14 In.	805.00
Bowl, Burl, Ash, Dark Patina, 4 x 11 In.	990.00
Bowl, Burl, Ash, Incised Decoration, 6 1/2 x 18 1/2 In.	3080.00
Bowl, Burl, Ash, Straight Sloping Sides, 3 3/8 In.	495.00
Bowl, Burl, Carved Handle, Oblong, Hanging Hole, 11 1/2 x 4 3/4 x 15 In.	935.00
Bowl, Burl, Deep, Molded Flattened Base & Rim, 4 x 8 1/4 In.	340.00
Bowl, Burl, Indian Head, Mohawk Handle, Oblong, 11 1/2 In.	1870.00
Bowl, Burl, Oval, 4 1/2 x 15 x 12 In.	990.00
Bowl, Burl, Oval, 10 x 7 1/2 x 3 1/2 In.	460.00
Bowl, Burl, Splayed Edge, 3 1/4 x 8 3/4 In.	145.00
Bowl, Burl, Thin Tapering Sides, Rim Handles, 5 x 12 In.	1815.00
Bowl, Butter, Incised Lip, Butter Paddle, Hook Handle, 6 x 18 In.	165.00
Bowl, Butter, Lip Edge, Blue Paint, 7 x 24 In.	440.00
Bowl, Butter, Oblong, 1-Piece Scoop, 4 1/2 x 23 x 13 In.	190.00
Bowl, Chopping, Oval, Notch-Cut Handles, 19th Century, 21 x 11 x 4 In.	70.00
Bowl, Chopping, Trencher, Softwood, Lip Stamped L. Goodard, 20 1/2 x 12 x 5 In.	226.00
Bowl, Deep, James Prestini, 10 In.	2350.00
Bowl, Dough, Oval, Carved Handles, 19th Century, 3 1/2 x 11 1/4 x 21 1/2 In.	170.00
Bowl, Finn Juhl, Denmark, 14 In.	2645.00
Bowl, Hardwood Trough, Pedestal, Cook Islands, 19th Century, 17 1/2 In.	590.00
Bowl, Painted, Red, Scrubbed, 1-Board, Rectangular, 22 1/2 x 6 3/4 x 2 1/2 In.	110.00
Bowl, Painted, Salmon, 19th Century, 4 1/2 x 15 5/8 In.	1530.00
Bowl, Pine, Yellow Painted, 19th Century, 1 3/4 x 5 7/8 In.	499.00
Bowl, Red Paint, Thick, 18 1/2 x 6 In.	525.00
Bowl, Red, Molded Lip, 8 1/2 x 24 In.	1375.00
Bowl, Round, 2 Handles, Applied With Pegs, Early 19th Century, 7 x 21 In.	646.00
Bowl, Salad, 16 In.	80.00
Bowl, Salad, Oval, 23 x 13 In.	80.00
Bowl, Spice, Cover, Pennsylvania, 19th Century	350.00
Bowl, Walnut, Grape & Grapevine, 1930, 3 3/4 x 9 1/2 In.	770.00
Brushpot, Bamboo, Carved Calligraphy & Flowers, Cylindrical, Chinese, 4 3/4 In.	175.00
Brushpot, Bamboo, Carved Goddess, 19th Century, 4 3/8 In.	175.00
Brushpot, Burl, Tree Stump Form, 7 In.	150.00
Brushpot, Tree Stump Shape, Phoenix, Peonies & Butterflies, Chinese, c.1800, 7 In.	550.00
Bucket, 2 Wooden Bands, Mid 19th Century, 4 1/2 x 10 1/2 In.	190.00
Bucket, Kerosene, Iron Banding, Painted, 19th Century, 10 In.	200.00
Bucket, Kerosene, Red Paint, Black Iron Handle, 13 1/2 In.	145.00
Bucket, Mahogany, Laminated, Round Base, Brass Bail Handle, 13 x 12 In.	440.00
Bucket, Oak, Brass Bound, Tapered, Copper Lining, Handle, c.1850, 10 1/2 x 12 In.	460.00
Bucket, Sugar, Lid, Red Wash, Iron Tacks, Bentwood Handle, 17 In.	385.00
Bucket, Sugar, Lid, Stave Construction, Bentwood, Swing Handle, 11 1/2 x 11 3/4 In.	360.00
Canteen, 2 Iron Bands, 2 Spouts, 10 x 5 3/4 In.	175.00
Canteen, Arrow Mark, England, 1854, 7 1/4 In.	295.00
Canteen, Bentwood, Stave Construction, Interlocking Bands, 9 1/2 x 7 In.	120.00
Canteen, Blue Gray Paint, Initialed I.F.W., Early 19th Century, 7 x 3 In.	440.00

Canteen, Inscribed E.L.H. & G.L.H., 5 In. 323.00
Canteen, Painted, Blue, Metal Straps, Cork, Round, Initialed W.D., 1856, 7 1/4 In. 405.00
Canteen, Pine, 4 Split-Ash Bands, 18th Century, 8 1/4 x 7 1/2 In. 460.00
Card Case, Sandalwood, Chinese Export, c.1830 .... 80.00
Carrier, Stave Construction, Bentwood Bands, Swing Handle, Lid, 12 1/2 x 6 1/2 In. 220.00
Carrier, Utensil, Bottle, Softwood, Hand-Hold Cutouts, Painted, 7 x 17 1/2 x 11 1/2 In. .. 410.00
Chalice, Carved, Gilded, 18th Century, 11 In. 520.00
Comb, Sycamore, Hatchwork Initials, Date, New England, 18th Century 295.00
Compote, Black Forest, Carved Birds, Leaves, Vines, c.1885, 8 1/2 x 15 x 10 In. 728.00
Compote, Painted Decoration, Initials M.H.D.H., 6 In. 1650.00
Compote, Rosewood, 18th Century, 10 x 6 1/4 In. 595.00
Container, Cover, Oval, Relief Faces, Serpents, Polynesian, Maori, 19th Century, 9 In. ... 2350.00
Cup, Painted, Flowers, Initials, Lehnware, Pennsylvania, c.1878, 3 1/4 In. 598.00
Cup, Rhyton, Bamboo, Carved Relief, Pine Tree, Wood Stand, Chinese, 1700s, 3 3/4 In. ... 3565.00
Dish, Laminated Birch, Tapio Wirkkala, 1954, 11 x 8 1/2 In. 4025.00
Feed Bin, Softwood, Yellow, Brown, Graining, Dovetailed, Turned Feet, 36 1/2 In. 845.00
Figurine, Russian Dancers, Native Dress, 5 3/4 In. .... *Illus* 6.00
Firkin, 4 Bands, Red Paint, Forged Iron Bail Handle, Stopper, 7 x 9 In. 265.00
Firkin, Bail Handle, 6 3/4 In. 115.00
Firkin, Gray Green, Wire Bail Handle, Late 19th Century, 7 1/2 x 8 In. 440.00
Firkin, Gray Paint, Round, Copper Tacks, Arched Bentwood Handle, 16 1/2 In. 715.00
Firkin, Painted, Green, Finger Joint Construction, Bail Handle, 7 3/4 In. 215.00
Firkin, Painted, Swing Handle, Lapped Finger & Stave, 19th Century, 4 In. 940.00
Firkin, Pine, Bent Ash Swing Handle, Buttermilk Blue Paint, 14 x 15 In. 175.00
Firkin, Pine, Green Paint, C. Milder & Son, Hingham, Mass. 90.00
Firkin, Salmon Paint, Wire Bail Handle, Late 19th Century, 6 3/4 In. 440.00
Firkin, Stave Construction, Bentwood, Buckwheat, Bail Handle, 7 x 6 1/2 In. 385.00
Firkin, Stave Construction, Bentwood, Swing Handle, 10 x 9 1/2 In. 145.00
Firkin, Stave Construction, Red, Green Bands, Swing Handle, 12 1/2 x 12 In. 529.00
Humidor, Bear, Glass Eyes, Hinged Lid At Neck, c.1890, 11 1/2 In. 1840.00
Humidor, Deer, Standing At Stump, Hinged Lid On Stump, Switzerland, 1890, 10 1/2 In. .. 290.00
Humidor, Mahogany, Brass Plaque, Zinc Lined, Late 19th Century, 4 3/4 x 8 x 11 In. 70.00
Humidor, Pine, Painted, Blue, Gilt, Landscape Design, Hinged Lid, c.1910, 3 x 9 x 6 In. . 294.00
Indian Club, Turned Maple, 14 & 16 In., 3 Piece 125.00
Jar, Cover, Maple, Lathe Turned, 3 1/2 In. 280.00
Keg, Powder, Open Top, Steel Bands, Painted Slats, 24 x 10 1/2 x 8 1/2 In. 230.00
Knife Tray, Walnut, Dovetailed, Pegged Construction, 1800s, 3 3/4 x 14 1/2 x 8 1/4 In. ... 106.00
Ladder, Blue Green Paint, Folds Flat, Serpentine Sides, 3 Steps, 43 In. 275.00
Mirror Case, Polychrome, Inlay, Hinged Scenic Doors, India, 19th Century, 19 In. 259.00
Pail, Food, Lacquered, Stackable Compartments, Bamboo Handle, Brass, 15 x 17 In. 104.00
Pail, Lid, Wilder P. Clark, 10 In. 80.00
Pail, Tin Lid, Old Salmon Paint, Wire Bail Handle, 12 x 13 1/2 In. 70.00
Panel, Prim Girl Seated In Chair, Pyrograph, Painted, c.1910, 10 3/4 x 19 1/2 In. 431.00
Plate, Treen, James Prestini, 10 1/2 In. 1645.00
Platter, Laminated Birch, Leaf Shape, Veined, Tapio Wirkkala, Finland, 1951, 17 x 10 In. 8625.00
Platter, Leaf, Laminated, Tapio Wirkkala, Soinne Et Kni, c.1954, 17 7/8 x 9 1/2 In. 6670.00
Rice Measure, Brass Binding, Chinese, 19th Century, 6 1/2 x 21 In. 115.00
Salt, Master, Painted, Salmon Ground, Tulip, Pedestal, Footed, 3 In. 3850.00
Salt Dip, Salmon Ground, Strawberries & Leaves, 1 1/4 x 3 In. 440.00
Sieve, Hinged Frame, Movable Slats, A.S. Clough, Meredith, N.H., 18 x 18 In. 165.00
Spoon, Wedding, Carved, Geometric, Cross, Hearts, Will Reese, 1845, 8 3/4 x 2 3/4 In. .. 220.00
Tray, Carrying, Walnut, Hand-Hold Cutouts, 19th Century, 4 1/4 x 30 x 18 In. 165.00
Tray, Glass Top, Flower Still Life, Gold Painted Frame, 33 In. 50.00
Tray, Hand Painted, Farmyard Scene, 18 x 24 In. 345.00
Tray, Mahogany, Marquetry, Kidney Shape, Serpentine Gallery, Brass Handles, 24 In. 175.00
Tub, 3 Tiers, Bentwood, Green, 9 x 8 In. 105.00
Utensil Carrier, Mahogany, Carved, Splayed Edge, 4 1/4 x 14 1/2 x 8 1/2 In. 85.00
Vase, Olive Wood, Flared, 8-Petaled Flowerhead, Domed Foot, Italy, 19 x 11 1/2 In. 1380.00
Vase, Root, Hollow Gnarled Branch, Chinese, 15 1/2 In. 175.00
Wagon Seat, Split, Double Ladder Back, Turned Arms, Box Stretcher, 28 x 12 In. 200.00
Wash Tub, Shaker Style, Red Finish, 20 x 26 1/2 In. 460.00
Watch Holder, Softwood, Orange Paint, Pin Locking Hinged Door, 8 x 4 x 2 1/2 In. 4510.00

WORCESTER porcelains were made in Worcester, England, from 1751. The firm went through many name changes and eventually, in 1862, became The Royal Worcester Porcelain Company Ltd. Collectors often refer to *Dr. Wall*, Barr, *Flight*, and other names that indicate time periods or artists at the factory. It became part of Royal Worcester Spode Ltd. in 1976. Related pieces may be found in the Royal Worcester category.

Basket, Pinecone, Blue & White, Reticulated, 1 Round, Other Oval, c.1780, 2 Piece	1610.00
Basket, Pinecone, Oval, Pierced, Blue, White, 8 1/2 In.	345.00
Beaker, Flowers, 18th Century, 4 In.	230.00
Beaker, Sepia, Figures, Buildings, Salmon Ground, Flight & Barr, c.1804, 4 In., Pair	2270.00
Butter, Cover, Stand, Imari Pattern, Barr, Flight & Barr, c.1813, 8 1/4 In.	4480.00
Can, Cylindrical, Dr. Wall, 4 1/2 In.	400.00
Dish, Dessert Set, Botanical, Shell Shape, Chamberlain, 1815-1830, 10 In., 3 Piece	2990.00
Dish, Dessert, Armorial, Shell Shape, Flight & Barr, c.1804, 7 7/8 In., Pair	1555.00
Dish, Dessert, Crest, Square, Poppy Border, Barr, Flight & Barr, c.1810, 8 1/2 In., Pair	5079.00
Dish, Dollar Pattern, c.1825, 6 1/4 In.	175.00
Dish, Sweetmeat, Flowers, Green Border, Shell Shape, 1800s, 8 x 10 In., 4 Piece	290.00
Dish, Thumb & Finger, c.1807, 8 1/2 In.	460.00
Eggcup Stand, 6 Eggcups, Imari Pattern, Flight, Barr & Barr, c.1813, 8 1/2 In.	2510.00
Figurine, Man In Top Hat, 1875, 6 1/4 In.	106.00
Jar, Cover, Kakiemon Style, c.1770, 6 1/2 In.	1000.00
Pitcher, Flowers, Matte Glaze, 7 1/2 In.	90.00
Plate, Brocade Pattern, Scalloped, Dragon Border, c.1775, 8 5/8 In.	1790.00
Plate, Dessert, Dollar Pattern, Blue & Red Leaves, Gold Rim, 8 5/8 In., Pair	230.00
Plate, Dessert, King Pattern, Red, Gold & Blue Scrolls, Plants, 8 7/8 In.	175.00
Plate, Dessert, Polychrome, Gilt Leaf Border, Continental, c.1900, 9 1/2 In., 12 Piece	920.00
Plate, Dragon In Compartments, A. Chamberlain, c.1797	375.00
Plate, Overall Blue Flowers, Off-White Ground, Dr. Wall, 9 3/4 In.	85.00
Plate Set, Commemorative, Chamberlain, c.1820, 9 3/8 In., 3 Piece	1910.00
Platter, Armorial, Stowe, Bellflower, Palmette Edge, Flight, Barr & Barr, 1813, 14 In.	9560.00
Platter, Crest, Motto, Green Border, Gilt Edge, Flight, Barr & Barr, c.1825, 19 In.	956.00
Platter, Oval, 2 Birds In Flight, Peony, Flight, Barr & Barr, c.1820, 18 In.	956.00
Platter, Oval, Oriental Flowers, Flight, Barr & Barr, c.1820, 22 1/4 In.	1434.00
Sugar, Open, Flowers, Gilt, c.1825, 3 x 4 x 6 In.	230.00
Teabowl, Saucer, Brocade Pattern, Gilt Edge, Fluted, Flight Barr, c.1795, 2 In.	1315.00
Teapot Stand, Puce Camieu, 2 Oriental Figures, Landscape, c.1760, 5 1/2 In.	2150.00
Tureen, Soup, Cover, Stand, Commemorative, Chamberlain, c.1820, 15 1/4 In.	7170.00
Vase, Imari Pattern, Jabberwocky & Phoenix, c.1770, 5 1/2 In.	1910.00

WORLD WAR I and World War II souvenirs are collected today. Be careful not to store anything that includes live ammunition. Your local police will tell you how to dispose of the explosives. See also Sword and Trench Art.

WORLD WAR I, Badge, U-Boat, Die Struck, Hallmarked Walter Schot, 2 In.	430.00
Badge, War Service, Ship Building, Bronze, Die Struck, 2 1/4 x 1 5/8 In.	40.00
Banner, Son-In-Service, 2 Stars, Red & White Satin, 58 x 36 In.	3286.00
Belt, Sentry, U.S. Army, 2 Pockets, Tan, Dot Type Snaps	95.00
Binoculars, Field, Gray, Carl Zeiss Jena, Dienstaglas 08, Germany	112.00
Binoculars, Field, Leitz Fernglas 08, Leather Case, Germany, 1916	230.00
Binoculars, Navy, 6 x 30 Marine-Trieder, Leather Case, C.P. Goerz, Germany	258.00
Boots, Riding, U.S. Officer, Leather Cap Toed, Lace Up, Speed Hooks, Size 5, 14 In.	115.00
Button, Army Combat Uniform, Raised Rim, Blackened Brass, 3/5 In.	2.00
Button, General Black Jack Pershing, Celluloid, 1 1/4 In.	66.00
Canteen, Aluminum, U.S. Army	12.00
Canteen, Cup, Field, U.S. Marine Corps, Emblem, Canvas Carrier, Snaps	310.00
Canteen, Cup, Khaki Cover, U.S. Army	24.00
Epaulettes, U.S. Navy, Cream, Brass Anchor, 4 Bars, Metal Case, Patent 1915	230.00
Funeral Card, Bernhard Bushner, Soldat, Photograph, Germany, 1917, 5 3/8 x 4 In.	16.00
Helmet, Camouflage Paint, Germany	130.00
Helmet, Spike, Prussian Enlisted, Eagle Crest, Black Leather Body, Chinstrap, Size 56	997.00
ID Papers, Luftschiff Btn No. 3, Crewman Militarpass, Zeppelin Crewman	110.00

Iron Cross, 1st Class, Struck Silver Frame, Painted Center, Pin Back, Germany, 1914 ....   105.00
Plaque, Lion's Head, Honor Fortitudo Fiedes, Cast Brass, 1916, 11 x 7 1/2 In. 60.00
Plate, Commemorative, Pro Patria, Soldier's Grave, Kjobenhavn, c.1915, 8 In. 58.00
Poster, Avec Toutes Vos Resources, Linen Back, B. Chavannaz, 46 x 32 In. 195.50
Poster, Beat Back The Hun, Strothman, 28 x 20 In. 35.00
Poster, Debout Dans La Tranchee, Linen Back, Jean Droit, 31 x 44 In. 172.00
Poster, Emprunt De La Defense Nationale, Linen Back, 31 1/2 x 45 In. 35.00
Poster, Emprunt De La Liberation, Lonoy, Linen Back, 47 x 30 In. 316.00
Poster, Follow The Boys In Blue For Home & Country, G. Wright, 20 1/2 x 29 In. 150.00
Poster, Hatons Leur Retour, France, 24 x 36 1/2 In. 85.00
Poster, Have You A Red Cross Service Flag, Jessie Wilcox Smith, 1918, 21 x 28 In. 200.00
Poster, Help, Nurse On Battlefield, Injured Soldier, 28 x 22 In. 85.00
Poster, It Is Here, Hoover, Squirrels With Spiked Helmets, 13 x 28 In. 275.00
Poster, Keep Him Smiling, United War-Work Campaign, 11 x 21 In. 57.50
Poster, Lend Him A Hand, Buy Liberty Bonds, 21 x 13 In. 92.00
Poster, Liberty Bonds, Immigrants At Ellis Island, 1917, 22 1/2 x 33 In. 175.00
Poster, Make This The Glorious 4th, Buy Your Bonds Here, 27 x 40 In. 135.00
Poster, Our Flags, Adolph Treidler, 21 1/2 x 14 In. 40.00
Poster, Pour La France Versez Votre, Combat Pour La Victoire, 45 x 31 In. 57.00
Poster, Remember Your First Thrill Of American Liberty, 30 x 20 In. 51.00
Poster, U.S. Navy, Here He Is, Sir, Uncle Sam, Recruiting, 28 x 41 In. 400.00
Poster, USA Bonds, 3rd Liberty Loan Campaign, J. Leyendecker, 30 x 20 In. 325.00
Poster, Where Columbia Sets Her Name, J. Blushfield, 1918, 28 x 19 In. 200.00
Poster, Y.W.C.A., For Every Fighter A Woman Worker, Linen, Baker, N.Y., 27 x 41 In. ..   275.00
Pouch, Equipment, U.S. Army, Tan, 3 Snap Closure Flap, 1918, 8 x 12 In. 50.00
Sheet Music, After The War Is Over Will There Be Home Sweet Home?, 1917 ....   7.00
Sheet Music, Au Revoir, But Not Goodbye, Brown, Von Tilzer, Broadway Music, 1917 ..   7.00
Sheet Music, Billy Boy, Col. William Hayward Of The 15th N.Y. Infantry, 1917 ....   40.00
Sheet Music, Break The News To Mother, C.K. Harris, 1917, 2 Pages 6.00
Sheet Music, Everything Is Peaches Down In Georgia, War Ed., Clark, Ager, 1918 ......   7.00
Sheet Music, First To Berlin, Doughboy With Rifle, 1918 ....   28.00
Sheet Music, Hero Of The European War, Woodrow Wilson, 1916 ....   48.00
Sheet Music, Hoe Your Little Bit In Your Own Back Yard, Cahill, 10 1/2 x 13 1/2 In. .,..   22.00
Sheet Music, I Want To Be Loved By A Soldier, Fink, Silver, Joe Morris Music, 1918 ...   8.00
Sheet Music, K-K-K-Katy, War Edition, G. O'Hara, Feist, 1918, 2 Pages, 7 x 10 1/2 In. ...   6.00
Sheet Music, Sammy Rag, Frolicking Doughboys, 1918 ....   38.00
Sheet Music, Song Of Separation, Ralph Chapin, 1920, 10 1/4 x 13 1/4 In. 120.00
Shovel, U.S. Army, Large Spade Shape, Wooden T-Handle, Marked US 69.00
Sidecap, Machine Gun Officer, U.S. Army, Piped Blue & Red, Coffin Lid Lt. Bar 106.00
Stereo Card, Father At Son's Grave, France, Troutman, New York 8.00
Stereo Card, German Submarines, U139, U159, Cherbourg Harbour, Troutman 11.00
Stereo Card, Victory Day Celebration, Arch Of Triumph, July 14, 1919, Keystone 8.00
Telephone, Prussian Official, Crank Handle, Eagle Decals, 12 x 8 x 5 In. 880.00
Uniform, Artillery, British Army, No. 1 Dress Tunic, Red Stripes, Size 30-32 ....   200.00
WORLD WAR II, Armband, Belgian Forced Labor, Dornier Werke Factory, 5 x 17 In. ..   58.00
Armband, Deutsche Wehrmacht, Screened, Black On Yellow, Germany 30.00
Armband, SS, Red Cotton, White Center, 2 Piece Swastika, RZM Paper Tag 86.00
Artillery Barrel Cover, Wehrmacht, Leather, Khaki, Canvas Straps 127.00
Artillery Inclinometer, Wehrmacht, Metal Hinged Box, W.M., 35 In. 98.00
Badge, Deutsche Jagerschaft, Deer Antlers, Swastika, Germany, 2 x 2 In. 285.00
Badge, Expert Bayonet, USMC, Wreathed Target, EG&A, Ex-Bayonet Bar 60.00
Badge, Hitler Youth, Gausieger, Made By Brehmer, 1938, 1 7/8 In. 403.00
Badge, Imperial Austria Sea Battle, Copper Bird, Gilt Anchor, Crown, 1 3/4 x 1 In. 253.00
Badge, Red Cross, German Nurse, Nickeled Silver, Swastika Border, Enamel, 1 1/2 In. ..   98.00
Bag, Drawstring, Olive Drab, Marked Shirts, U.S. Army 7.00
Bayonet, Tapered, No. 4, MK 2, Spike, Scabbard, Great Britain 15.00
Beaker, Third Reich, Troops Marching, Reichsparteitag, Pottery, 4 1/2 In. 374.00
Belt, Wehrmacht Enlisted, Combat, Black Rough Leather, White Stitching, 1938, 45 In. ..   78.00
Belt & Buckle, Kriegsmarine Officer, Parade, Silver Brocade, Wool, 34 1/2 In. 185.00
Belt & Buckle, Lut Und Ehre Motto, Leather Belt, Steel Buckle, HJ, 1939, Size 85 ......   80.00
Belt & Buckle, Wehrmacht Enlisted, Sword Hanger, Leather, Steel, Size 100, 2 x 3 In. ...   81.00
Belt Buckle, Luftwaffe Enlisted, Aluminum, Pebbled Silver Finish, Wreath, Eagle 56.00

Belt Buckle, Niedersachsen Forestry Officer, Brass, Horse Over Swastika, 1 7/8 In.	127.00
Belt Buckle, SS Enlisted, Eagle, Swastika, RZM 155/43, Silver Finish, 2 x 2 1/2 In.	242.00
Belt Buckle, SS Officer, Die-Struck Aluminum, RZM Mark, 2 In.	380.00
Binoculars, Military, Barr & Stroud 7X, British Arrows, Leather Case, England	230.00
Boots, Cavalry Officer, U.S. Army, Brown Leather, Lace Bottom, Size 10	180.00
Boots, Knee Wader, U.S. Army, Canvas Uppers, Black Rubber Soles, 1945, Size 10	40.00
Boots, Luftwaffe Officer's, Brown Leather, Hobnails, Toe & Heel Plates, 16 In.	230.00
Boots, Luftwaffe, Fighter Pilots, Black Leather, Suede Uppers, Wilo, 16 1/2 In.	575.00
Boots, Riding, Officer's, U.S. Army, Red Brown, Leather Soles, Heel, Size 9 1/2 In.	65.00
Boots, Wehrmacht Officer's, Black, Leather, No. 12508 6 10, Nailed Soles, Size 6	98.00
Boots, Winter, Brown Leather Lower, Felt Uppers, Rubber Sole, 1942, Size 30	60.00
Bowl, Vegetable, Luftwaffe, Swastika, Porcelain, Finland, 1943, 10 In.	175.00
Bracelet, Home Front, Enamel, Dagger Through Hitler & Tojo Heads, Stamped	290.00
Breeches, Khaki Twill, Plastic Buttons, U.S. Army, 29 x 24 In.	22.00
Buckle, Wehrmacht Enlisted Army, Eagle, Assmann A&S, Leather Tongue, SRM 37	95.00
Button, Let's Pull Together, Uncle Sam, Anti Hitler, Mechanical	70.00
Button, Mussolini The Ill Duce, Red, White, Blue, Lithograph	37.00
Button, Navy Service Cap, Gilt, Eagle Facing Left, 3/5 In.	2.00
Canteen, Aluminum, U.S. Army	8.00
Cap, Field, Wehrmacht, M-43, 2 Buttons, RBNR Mark, Size 57	181.00
Cap, Flying, USAAF, Summer, Type B-1, 2 Panel Style, False Ear Flaps, Size 7	115.00
Cap, Hitler Youth, Wool, Gray, Diamond Emblem, Size 55	378.00
Cap, Mechanic's, USAAF, Type A-3, 6 Panel Style, Blue Stamp Logo, Size 7 1/2	259.00
Cap, Red Cross Worker, Female, Cotton, Embroidered Patch, 1 3/4-In. White Base	45.00
Cap, Red Cross, Overseas, Wool, Blue, German Red Cross Patch, 6 3/4 In.	155.00
Cap, Visor, Navy Officer, Blue Top, Blue Body, Gold Chinstrap, Navy Eagle	100.00
Cap, Wehrmacht Transportation, Wool, Aluminum Eagle Bullion Wreath, Size 55	485.00
Chronometer, U-Boat, Kriegsmarine, Roman Numerals, Wooden Case, 3 x 3 In.	1390.00
Coaster, Keep 'Em Flying, 3 Planes, Red, White, Blue, 5 In.	20.00
Coaster, Let's Go USA, Keep 'Em Flying, Esslinger's, Philadelphia	17.00
Coat, Jeep, Mackinaw, U.S. Army, Cotton, Plastic Buttons, Wool Liner, Medium	138.00
Coat, Wool, Officer's, Dark Olive Drab, U.S. Army, Size 32S	45.00
Compass, Kriegsmarine, Aluminum Housing, Brass Ball Mount, 1943, 4 1/8 In.	146.00
Compass, Luftwaffe Air Crew, Black Bakelite Case, Oil Fill, Leather Wrist Strap	175.00
Compass, Luftwaffe Pilot's, Bakelite, Liquid Fill, Black Leather Wrist Strap, 1939	108.00
Compass, Luftwaffe, Metal Rim, FL 23825, Dennert & Pape, 1940, 5 7/8 In.	105.00
Compass, Wrist, Brown Leather, Helsinka Marker, Alum, Celluloid, Finland, 1 3/4 In. ...	48.00
Coveralls, Field, Cotton Shell, Wool Lining, U.S. Army, Medium	60.00
Coveralls, Pilot's, AAF, Summer Weight, Wool, Zipper Front, Size M42	55.00
Coveralls, U.S. Army, Star Metal Buttons, Olive Drab, Cotton, Size 36R	29.00
Dog Coat, Wool, U.S. 8th Air Force Insignia, Sergeant Rank Patch	175.00
Duffle Bag, U.S. Navy Nurse's Corps	45.00
First Aid Packet, Olive Drab, Carlisle Model, U.S. Army	8.00
Fishing Kit, Survival, Canvas, 12 Pockets, Contents, American	80.00
Flag, Japanese National, White Cotton, Stitched Red Dot, 28 x 31 In.	85.00
Flag, Kriegsmarine, Red Ground, Iron Cross, Swastika, Germany, 51 x 93 In.	690.00
Flak Spotting Scope, Steel Tube, Rubber Eyepiece, Hensoldt Wetzlar, 5 1/4 In.	64.00
Flare Gun, U.S. Navy, Chrome, Marked Intl. Flare Signal Div.	70.00
Flashlight, Wehrmacht, Soldiers, Gray, Color Filters, Box, Daimon, Czechoslovakia	86.00
Fuel Can, SS Runes, Pressed Steel, Square, 20 Liter, 18 1/2 In.	80.00
Funeral Card, Anton Frankl, Gefreiter, Photograph, Germany, 1941, 4 x 2 1/2 In.	14.00
Gas Mask, Luftschutz, Treated Fabric Facemask, Fluted Container, Marked	65.00
Gas Mask, Luftwaffe, Rubber Back, Gray Canvas, Leather Trim, FE 41 Filter, Carrier ...	139.00
Gas Mask, Rubber, Filter, Tin Box, Germany, 1940	90.00
Gloves, Flying, Luftwaffe, Brown Leather Shell, Suede Lining, 1941, Size 8	230.00
Gloves, Flying, U.S. Navy, Brown Leather, Marked USN, Size 9	118.00
Goggles, Pilot, Luftwaffe, Hinged, Plastic Frames, Tinted, Strap, Booklet, Box, 1938	460.00
Handkerchief, Fort McDowell, Angel Island, California, Great Seal, Flesh Satin	16.00
Handkerchief, USAA, 8th AF, Embroidered, Purple, White Trim, 1944, 8 x 11 In.	40.00
Hat, Cossack, Wehrmacht, Pill Box, Black Fleece, Red Wool Top, Silver Eagle	175.00
Hat, SS Police, Overseas, Blue Gray, White On Black Eagle, Inverted V, Size 58	253.00
Hat, Visor, U.S. Navy Officer's, Great Cover, Sterling Cap Device, Commodore	120.00

Head Scarf, Pendleton Field, Oregon, U.S. Army Air Forces, Purple Fringe, Flocked 20.00
Helmet, Combat, Luftwaffe M 40, Blue, Gray Liner, Size 68 .... 369.00
Helmet, Deep Sea Diving, U.S. Navy, Brass, Bubble, Mark V, Morse Diving Co. 2655.00
Helmet, Flight, Brown Leather, Fleece Lining, Label, Japan 325.00
Helmet, Flight, Luftwaffe, Leather, Chinstrap, Bakelite Throat Microphones, Label 210.00
Helmet, Flight, Navy, Leather, Chamois Lining, Type NAF-1092, American, Size 7 ..... 75.00
Helmet, Kreigsmarine, M-35, Gold Eagle Decal, Colors, Liner, Chinstrap, Size 59 ..... 2875.00
Helmet, Leather Liner, Green Chinstrap, Italy 86.00
Helmet, Luftwaffe, M-35, Steel, Eagle, Double Decal, Leather Liner, Size 59 .... 1015.00
Helmet, Luftwaffe, Parade Dress, M-35, Aluminum, Double Decal, Liner, Size 57 ...... 2070.00
Helmet, Luftwaffe, Paratrooper, Camouflage, Eagle Decal, Chinstrap, Size 56 .... 2530.00
Helmet, Steel Shell, Canvas Chinstrap, Camouflage Net Cover, 1943 .... 60.00
ID Disk, Criminal Police, Brass, Oval, No. 10666, Original Chain, 1 1/2 x 2 In. 1095.00
Instrument Panel, Cockpit, From Spitfire Combat Aircraft, 6 Dials, 1942 .... 640.00
Jacket, 7th Army, Wool, Patches, Ribbon Group, American, 1944, Size 36S 50.00
Jacket, 9th Air Force Glider Pilot, Gabardine, Patch, Sterling Wings, 1942 .... 420.00
Jacket, Flight, U.S. Air Force, A-2, Brown Leather, Sleeve Decal, Size 38 .... 978.00
Jacket, Flight, U.S. Navy, Goatskin, Brown, Fur Collar, Size 38 .... 144.00
Jacket, Ike, Glider Assault, U.S. Army, Corporal Stripes, 17th Airborne, 1944 .... 190.00
Jacket, Tanker, Flight Crew, U.S. 8th Air Force, 381st Bomb Group, Cotton Twill 1149.00
Jacket, Uniform, U.S. Army, Brass Buttons, Partial Cotton Lining, 1942, Size 40L 32.00
Jacket, USMC, Vandergriff, Green Wool, Cotton Lining, Sgt. Chevrons, Size 38 .... 58.00
Jumper, USN, Amphibious Unit, Blue Wool, CPO 1st, Water Tender Rate, 1945, Small .. 65.00
Lamp, Candlelight, Nazi Swastika, Red Globe, 8 1/4 In. 86.00
Lantern, Blackout, Metal, Battery Powered, Frosted Glass Lens, Extra Bulb 40.00
Mailer, Liquidate Rats, Put 10% In War Bonds, Hitler, Mussolini, Tojo Rats, 3 x 5 In. 25.00
Mailer, Stamp 'Em Out, Buy More Savings Bonds, Foot Stomps Snakes, 3 x 5 In. 20.00
Manual, Soldier's First Aid, U.S. Army, Government Printing, 1943, 119 Pages 6.00
Map Case, Army Officer, Brown Leather, D-Ring, Roller Style Buckle, Japan, 11 x 8 In. . 48.00
Mess Tray, Bakelite, 6 Sections, American, 1945, 15 x 12 In. 30.00
Meter, Oxygen Flow Check, AAF, Original Carton, Never Opened, 12 x 5 1/2 In. 30.00
Model, Fighter Plane, Brass, 5 x 6 In. 165.00
Model, Plane, German 109, 56 x 62 In. 450.00
Motor, Starter, From German Turbo Jet, 1944 .... 720.00
Musette Bag, U.S. Army, Tan Canvas, Marked Langdon Tent & Awning, 1942 .... 85.00
Overcoat, Officer's, Wehrmacht, Green Wool, Braided Cord, Labels 320.00
Pamphlet, Going Back To Civilian Life, American, 1944, 58 Pages 6.00
Pamphlet, WAC, Recruitment, Facts You Want To Know About The War, 32 Pages 30.00
Pants, Deck, USN, Twill Wool Lined, Talon Zipper, Size Medium 40.00
Pants, HBT, Army, 13-Star Metal Buttons, Cargo Pockets, Flaps, 34 x 31 In. 65.00
Patch, 7 CAV, Yellow, Blue, Red 106.00
Patch, Navy, Third Class Corpsman, Fully Embroidered, Eagle, Red Cross, Tan Twill 29.00
Patch, U.S. Army, 306th Armored, Tan Twill, Cut Edge, Embroidered, Multicolored 37.00
Patch, U.S. Army, 351st RCT Unit, Red, White, Blue, Fully Embroidered 100.00
Patch, U.S. Army, Europe, Bullion, Gold, Silver, Blue Felt, Flaming Sword 30.00
Pennant, North, South Carolina Army Maneuvers, Felt, Great Seal, 1941, 28 x 10 In. 16.00
Pennant, Target For 1943, U.S., Aussie Soldiers, Kangaroo, 25 In. 200.00
Phonograph Record, Patriotic Songs, Columbia Label, Japan 40.00
Photograph, Raising The Flag On Iwo Jima, Joe Rosenthal, Signed, 11 x 14 In. 1998.00
Pillowcase, Camp Blanding, U.S. Army, Mother Poem, Soldiers, Satin 18.00
Plaque, Adolf Hitler Profile, Black Iron, Fischer Bulle Hemelinger, 11 x 8 In. 138.00
Plaque, Adolf Hitler Profile, Quote, Sheet Metal On Wood, 9 1/4 x 6 In. 120.00
Plate, Luftwaffe, Christmas, Fliegerhorst Bologna, 2 Towers, Italy, 1943, 9 1/2 In. 185.00
Postcard, I'm Bringing Home The Bacon, WAC Leads Leashed Hitler 9.00
Postcard, Victory, Let's Go Forward Together, 3 Vs, Soldier, Sailor, Worker, 1941 ...... 9.00
Poster, Committee For American War Work, J. Pages, 31 x 25 In. 69.00
Poster, Fire Away, Buy Extra Bonds, George Schreiber, 27 x 20 In. 125.00
Poster, French Workers Warn, Defeat Means Slavery, Ben Shahn, 28 x 40 In. 300.00
Poster, Gerade Du, Uniformed HJ Boy, SS Flag, Anton, Berlin, 16 1/2 x 23 In. 520.00
Poster, Let 'Em Have It, Buy Extra Bonds, 1943, 10 1/4 x 14 1/4 In. 51.00
Poster, Occupied Belgium, Denounce Belgian Terrorists, Reward, 37 x 26 In. 165.00
Poster, Recruiting, Panzer Grenadier Division, 2 Men, Tank, 16 1/2 x 11 1/2 In. 645.00
Poster, Share The Meat, Americans, 21 x 28 In. 25.00

Poster, Soldiers Beware Of Spies!, Black Print, Germany, 20 x 28 In. 56.00
Poster, U.S. Army Enlistment, Uncle Sam Pointing, J.M. Flagg, 1941, 38 x 25 In. 488.00
Poster, We Caught Hell, Someone Must Have Talked, 40 x 28 In. 92.00
Poster, You Buy 'Em We Fly 'Em, Norman Wilkinson, 31 x 20 In. 145.00
Poster, You Can Lick Runaway Prices, James Montgomery Flagg, 20 x 28 In. 46.00
Pouch, Dispatch, Leather, 2 Pockets, Strap, Buckles, Japan, 10 x 8 1/2 x 1 1/2 In. 46.00
Pouch, Field Medic's Assistant, Wehrmacht, Leather, Partial Contents, 1942 .... 89.00
Radio, Marine, Philips, 78, 11 Valves 4200.00
Radio Set, Telefunken, Koln, E 52a-1, Used For French Troop Care, 1940 .... 2760.00
Ration Tin, Emergency, Pressed Steel, Embossed, England, 3 x 4 1/4 x 1 In. 30.00
Ration Tin, Tea, Tea, Sugar, Milk Powder, Full, England, 1943, 14 1/2 Oz., 5 x 3 In. 130.00
Record Player, Field, Portable, Carry Handle, Japan, 15 x 9 x 13 In. 235.00
Ring, Hitler Youth Leader, Nickel, Stylized Eagle & Swastika, Slanted Ends 219.00
Ring, SS, Rune On Front, SS Motto Along Band, Marked DRGM, Size 9 1/4 .... 160.00
Ring, Swastika, 800 Silver, 3/4 In. 98.00
Saddle Bag, Wehrmacht, Brown Leather, Pouch, Front Flap, Steel Slot, 15 x 8 In. 115.00
Sextant, Luftwaffe, Blue Gray Wooden Case, FL 23750, 12 x 9 x 5 In. 259.00
Sheet Music, Anchors Aweigh, Zimmerman, Robbins Music Corp, 1942, 2 Pages 7.00
Sheet Music, Hot Time In Town Of Berlin, Sinatra Cover, Bushkin, De Vries, 1943 ..... 8.00
Shirt, Brown, Swastika Arm Band, Black Collar Tabs, NSDAP, Medium 345.00
Shirt, Flannel, Coat Style, Olive Drab, U.S. Army, 14 x 32 1/2 In. 18.00
Shirt, U.S. Army, HBT, 13 Star Metal Button Fasteners, Size 34R 37.00
Siren, Air Raid, Brass Bell Mouth Horn, Crank, Bakelite Handle, Japan, 5 In. 175.00
Siren, Air Raid, German, Aluminum, Crank Operated, Steel Tripod, 32 In. 390.00
Sleeping Bag, Wool, Olive Drab, Case, U.S. Army 45.00
Statue, Wehrmacht Service, Eagle, Nazi Soldier, Marble Base, UFFZ Korps, 6 x 9 In. ... 290.00
Stick Pin, SS, Bronze Disk, SS Rungs In Wreath Over Swastika, 1 In. 110.00
Sticker, Window, Keep U.S. Out Of War, Be Neutral, Red, White, Blue, Times Union 12.00
Stopwatch, White Face, Wehrmacht Eagle, Second Hand, Junghans, 2 In. 1381.00
Sunglasses, Aviator's, USAAF, B-2 Style, Green, Gilt Plate Frame, Nose Pads, Case 83.00
Sweater, V Neck, 5 Buttons, Olive Drab, U.S. Army, Size 38 .... 28.00
Sword, Police, Scabbard, Japan, 27 In. 80.00
Table Mat, Great Seal, Rose Satin, Flocked, Gold, Rose, Gold Fringe, 9 x 6 In. 8.00
Tin, Chocolate, High Energy, White, Red Lithograph, Germany, 1941, 3 1/4 In. 85.00
Tool Kit Bag, Flame Thrower, U.S. Army, Canvas, Stenciling 38.00
Trousers, Flight, U.S. Navy, Brown Leather, Fleece Lining, M-446-A, Size 40M 36.00
Trousers, U.S. Army, Wool, Button Fly, Large Size, 42 x 33 In. 55.00
Tunic, Camouflage Gray, U.S. Navy, Black, Plastic Buttons, Aviator Wings 125.00
Tunic, SS Signal Untersturmfuhrer Officer, Gray Wool, Eagle Patch, 6 Buttons 196.00
Tunic, Summer, Navy Line Lieutenant, White, Ribbon Bar, Size 38 .... 190.00
Underpants, Silk, Before You Ask, Answer Is No, V For Victory, 8 x 5 In. 40.00
Undershirt, Sleeveless, U.S. Army 29.00
Uniform, General's, Wehrmacht, Tunic & Trousers, Wool Twill, Stripes, Braids 4140.00
Uniform, INF Officers, Lt., Wool, 4 Pocket, US & INF Insignia, 1944, Size 38R 46.00
Uniform, U.S. Navy, Petty Officer 3rd Class, Rank Insignia, Seebee Patch, Wool 58.00
Uniform, Wehrmacht General Tunic, Ribbon Bar, Green Wool, Small 2870.00

WORLD'S FAIR souvenirs from all of the fairs are collected. The first fair was the Great Exhibition of 1851 in London. Some other important exhibitions and fairs include Philadelphia, 1876 (Centennial); Chicago, 1893 (World's Columbian); Buffalo, 1901 (Pan-American); St. Louis, 1904 (Louisiana Purchase); San Francisco, 1915 (Panama-Pacific); Philadelphia, 1926 (Sesquicentennial); Chicago, 1933 (Century of Progress); Cleveland, 1936 (Great Lakes); San Francisco, 1939 (Golden Gate International); New York, 1939 (World of Tomorrow); Seattle, 1962 (Century 21); New York, 1964; Montreal, 1967; New Orleans, 1984; Tsukuba, Japan, 1985; Vancouver, B.C., 1986; Brisbane, Australia, 1988; Seville, Spain, 1992; and Genoa, Italy, 1992; Seoul, Korea, 1993; and Lisbon, Portugal, 1998. Memorabilia of fairs include directories, pictures, fabrics, ceramics, etc. Memorabilia from other similar celebrations may be listed in the Souvenir category.

Bank, 1893, Chicago, Mechanical, Columbus & Indian, Cast Iron, J. & E. Stevens, 1893 . 2900.00
Bell, 1893, Chicago, Glass, Swirled Handle, Etched, 4 1/4 x 3 In. 60.00

Book, 1893, Chicago, Columbia's Courtship, Prang, Cloth, c.1893 .... 600.00
Booklet, 1939, San Francisco, Magic In The Night, 18 Pages 20.00
Button, 1904, St. Louis, Red, White, Blue, Celluloid, 1 1/4 In. 40.00
Card, Mechanical, 1901, Buffalo, Man Shaving, Williams Soap 100.00
Cigarette Case, 1939, New York, Manhattan Map, Sterling Silver 250.00
Darner, 1893, Chicago, Peachblow, Etched, New England 196.00
Flag, 1904, St. Louis, St. Louis Car Co., American Street Railroad Assn., 12 x 8 In. . 600.00
Guide, 1964, New York, Illustrated, Soft Bound, Time Inc., 280 Pages 12.00
Handkerchief, 1893, Chicago, Silk, 11 x 11 In. 45.00
Jug, 1893, Chicago, Stoneware, Cobalt Blue, 2 1/2 In. 175.00
Paperweight, 1901, Buffalo, Nile Green, 3 In. 800.00
Paperweight, 1904, St. Louis, Gold Brick, 2 1/2 x 1 In. 75.00
Paperweight, 1904, St. Louis, Iron, Painted Gold, Brick Shape, 2 x 1 In. 75.00
Paperweight, 1933, Chicago, Dog, Holding Pencil, Cast Iron, Pair 127.00
Paperweight, 1939, New York, Trylon & Perisphere, Syroco Wood, Label, N.Y 40.00
Pennant, 1876, Philadelphia Centennial Exhibition, Linen, Eagle, Flag 225.00
Plate, 1939, New York, Potter At His Wheel, Ivory, Fiesta, 8 In. 80.00
Plate, 1939, New York, Potter At His Wheel, Turquoise, 8 In. 35.00
Plate, 1969, New York, Shell, Fire-King, Gold 45.00
Postcard, 1904, St. Louis, Palace Of Agriculture, Hold-To-Light 12.50
Purse, 1893, Chicago, Agriculture Bldg, Mother-Of-Pearl, 2 1/2 In. 85.00
Salt & Pepper, 1939, New York, Chrome, Miniature Coffeepot, Tray 60.00
Scarf, 1876, Philadelphia, Fairmount Park, Sepia Tones, 24 x 26 In. 169.00
Sheet Music, 1904, St. Louis, Cascades, Cascading Fountains 33.00
Sheet Music, 1904, St. Louis, St. Louis Tickle, Smiling Black Kids 41.00
Spoon, 1939, New York, Silver Plate, William Rogers, Box, 9 Piece 29.00
Spoon Set, 1893, Chicago, World's Columbian, Silver Plate, 12 Piece 75.00
Tag, 1939, San Francisco, License Plate, Tin, Die Cut, Pegasus, Embossed, 6 x 5 In. ... 154.00
Tip Tray, 1901, Buffalo, Kings, Maid, Holding Tray, Tin Lithograph, 4 1/4 x 6 In. 55.00
Tip Tray, 1901, Buffalo, Roltairs, House Of Up Side Down, Pan-Am Expo, 7 x 5 In. 220.00
Tip Tray, 1915 Pan-Pacific, Buffalo Brewing, San Francisco, Sacramento, 1915, 4 1/4 In. . 490.00
Tip Tray, 1915 Pan-Pacific, California Invites The World, Ruhstaller 175.00
Toy, 1933, Chicago, Bus, Cast Iron, Arcade, 10 1/2 In. 350.00
Toy, 1933, Chicago, Cab, Trailer, Cast Iron, 10 1/4 In. 295.00
Toy, 1933, Chicago, Wagon, Radio Flyer, Metal, 2 1/2 x 4 3/4 x 2 1/8 In. 85.00
Toy, 1939, New York, Trolley, Arcade 295.00
Toy, 1958, Brussels, Helicopter, Flies Around Satellite On Base, Windup, Germany 95.00
Tumbler, 1962, Seattle, Pepsi-Cola, 20th Anniversary, Herfy's 12.00
Tumbler, 1964, New York Central Railroad System, Black, Gold, 4 1/2 In. 8.00
Tumbler, 1984, New Orleans, Pelican Mascot Playing Instruments, 6 1/4 In. 4.00
Tumbler Set, 1892, Chicago, Arched Logo, Buildings & Titles, 3 1/2 In., 13 Piece 209.00

WPA is the abbreviation for Works Progress Administration, a program
created by executive order in 1935 to provide jobs for millions of
unemployed Americans. Artists were hired to create murals, paintings,
drawings, and sculptures for public buildings. Pieces are marked WPA
and may have the artist's name on them.

Diorama, Indian In Canoe, 8 x 12 In. 670.00
Figure, Outhouse, Skeleton, The Lost WPA Worker, Wood, Kansas City, 4 1/2 In. 100.00
Painting, Oil On Canvas, Mother & Child With Sunflowers, Topeka, c.1935, 27 x 17 In. . 3220.00
Textile, Little Black Sambo, Tiger, Milwaukee State Teachers College, 32 1/2 x 42 In. 1320.00

WRISTWATCHES came into use during World War I. Wristwatches are
listed here by manufacturer or as advertising or character watches.
Pocket watches are listed in the Watch category.

Advertising, Charlie The Tuna, 25 Anniversary, Certificate, Carton, 1 1/4 In. 35.00
Advertising, Charlie The Tuna, Pink Plastic Box, 1971 .... 25.00
Advertising, Hawaiian Punch, Punchy, White Face, Red Strap, 1971 .... 19.00
Advertising, Peter Pan Peanut Butter, Child's, 1980s 22.00
Advertising, Reddy Kilowatt, Leather, Metal, Case, c.1970, 3/4 x 2 x 9 1/2 In. 75.00
Advertising, Ritz Cracker, 1976 .... 86.00
Advertising, Ronald McDonald, Leather Strap, Case, Chinese, c.1980, 1 1/4 In. Diam. ... 40.00

Babe Ruth, Exacta, Original Baseball Box, 1948 . . . . 325.00
Baume & Mercier, Woman's, Diamond Bezel, 14K Gold, 6 1/4 In. 590.00
Boucheron, Woman's, Gold Dial, 18K Gold, Brown Leather Cartier Strap, 8 In. 265.00
Bulgari, 18K Gold, Flexible Band, Watch Face Terminal 8225.00
Bulgari, Silvertone Dial, Arabic & Abstract Indicators, Signed, c.1998, 9 1/2 In. 940.00
Bulova, Brushed Stainless Case, Scroll Borders, Black Cord Band, 1 x 5/8 In. 75.00
Bulova, Woman's, Gold Face, 24 Diamonds, 14K Yellow Gold Bar, Bracelet, 7 1/4 In. . . . 75.00
Cartier, Lapel, Woman's, 18K Yellow Gold 470.00
Cartier, Square Ivory Dial, Roman Numerals, Quartz Movement, Sapphire Crown 2350.00
Cartier, Woman's, 18K White Gold, Diamond, c.1950, 6 1/2 In. 2820.00
Cartier, Woman's, Diamond, 14K White Gold 1035.00
Character, Andy Panda, Chrome 75.00
Character, Bugs Bunny, Warner Bros., Box, Lafayette Watch Co., c.1974, 1 1/8 In. 50.00
Character, Cool Cat, Gold, Case, Leather, Sheraton, c.1970, 1 1/4 In. 95.00
Character, Curious George, Silvertone 27.00
Character, E.T., Digital, Blue, Vinyl, Case, 1982 . . . . 25.00
Character, Humpty Dumpty, Time Distributors, 1967 . . . . 60.00
Character, Lil Abner, Saluting American Flag, New Haven, Box, 1947 . . . . 1238.00
Character, Mighty Mouse, Articulated Arms, Bradley, Box 150.00
Character, Peace Mouse, Stars, c.1968 . . . . 60.00
Character, Simpsons, Butterfinger, 1980s 11.00
Character, Smokey The Bear, Only You Can Stop Forest Fires, Case, c.1970, 1 1/4 In. 50.00
Concord, Impresario, Stainless Steel, Roman, Quartz Movement, Box 470.00
Concord Watch Co., Ayre & Taylor Co., Bangle, 14K Gold, c.1950 . . . . 320.00
Croton Watch Co., Self-Winding, Platinum & Diamonds, c.1920 . . . . 1380.00
Emewo, Self-Winding, Platinum & Diamonds, Swiss, c.1957 . . . . 2185.00
Girard-Perregaux, Woman's, 20 Diamonds, 14K White Gold, c.1940, 5 3/4 In. 200.00
Grogan, Woman's, Art Deco, Diamond, Silvertone Dial, Meylan Movement, Box 1058.00
Gruen, Woman's, Diamonds, Rectangular Dial, Platinum, Mesh Strap 4113.00
Gubelin, Woman's, 18K Yellow Gold, Self-Winding, c.1950, 7 In. 259.00
Gucci, Woman's, Lucite, Round Dial, Bezel, Bangle, 17 Jewel Swiss Movement 441.00
Hamilton, Woman's, Diamond, Graduating, Arabic, Diamond Band, 6 1/2 In. 1998.00
Hamilton, Woman's, Platinum, Diamond, 17 Jewel, 7 In. 353.00
Hamilton, Woman's, White Gold, 40 Diamonds, Self-Winding, 14K Gold, 1950 . . . . 546.00
Helbros Watch Co., Platinum, Diamond, Sapphire, 17 Jewel, Art Deco 990.00
Hermes, Woman's, Rectangular, Tan Leather Strap, Box, 9 In. 1116.00
Longines, 14K Gold, Square, Seconds Dial, Mesh Band, Box, 1962 . . . . 823.00
Longines, Gold Filled, Self-Winding, 14K Yellow Gold Band, c.1930 . . . . 1265.00
Lucien Piccard, Woman's, 14K White Gold, Pearl, Gold Bars, Pearl Clasp, 8 In. 764.00
Movado, 14K & 18K Yellow Gold, Self-Winding, c.1950 . . . . 431.00
Movado, 14K Yellow Gold, Self-Winding, Swiss, c.1940 . . . . 748.00
Omega, Seamaster, Goldtone Dial, Abstract Indicators, Brown Leather Band, 9 In. 470.00
Omega, Seamaster, Self-Winding, 18K Yellow Gold 575.00
Patek Philippe, 18K Gold, Large Format, Second Hand, Leather Band, Box 4700.00
Patek Philippe, Silvertone Dial, 18 Jewel, 18K Gold, 1940, 8 In. 6110.00
Patek Philippe, Woman's, Platinum, Diamonds, Enamel Face, Art Deco, 1925 . . . . 1430.00
Pathe Swiss, 14K Gold, Diamond, Sapphires, Bow Topped Oval Bezel, Link Bracelet . . . 338.00
Pery, Woman's, Diamond, Square Dial, 70 Baguettes, Platinum Mount, 6 In. 881.00
Pilot's, Vietnam, Type DTU-2A/P, Nickel Case, Black Dial Face, 1964 . . . . 175.00
Rolex, 14K Yellow Gold, Chronometer, No. E34994, Alligator Band 1200.00
Rolex, Oyster Perpetual, Explorer, Stainless 1400.00
Rolex, Presidential, Oyster, 18K Gold, Box, c.1970 . . . . 7190.00
Rolex, Presidential, Oyster, Perpetual Datejust 4315.00
Rolex, Woman's, 14K Yellow Gold, Self-Winding, c.1960, 6 1/4 In. 1100.00
Rolex, Woman's, Bracelet, Yellow Gold, Diamonds, Silver Matte Dial, 18K Gold 2990.00
Rolex, Woman's, Oyster Perpetual Datejust, Polished Steel, Flex Band, Swiss 299.00
Tiffany, Woman's, Trapezoid, Emerald, Diamond, 14K Gold, 6 1/4 In. 1880.00
Ultime, Woman's, 14K Yellow Gold, Quartz, c.1980 . . . . 290.00
Vacheron & Constantin, 18K Gold, 14K Band, Self-Winding, c.1950, 7 1/2 In. 1840.00
Vacheron & Constantin, Platinum, Sapphires, 18 Jewel, Arabic Numerals, c.1920 . . . . . . 1265.00
Whiteside & Blank, Woman's, Art Deco, Platinum, Diamond, 18 Jewel Movement 880.00
Wittnauer, Aviator, Stainless Steel, Arabic, Curved Lugs, Bakelite Box 2703.00

YELLOWWARE is a heavy earthenware made of a yellowish clay. It varies in color from light yellow to orange-yellow. Many nineteenth- and twentieth-century kitchen bowls and jugs were made of yellowware. It was made in England and in the United States. Another form of pottery that is sometimes classed as yellowware is listed in this book in the Mocha category.

Bowl, 3 Blue Accent Bands, 2 1/2 x 6 In.	45.00
Bowl, Applied Brown Sponge Design, 11 x 5 1/2 In.	110.00
Bowl, Blue, White Accent Bands, 5 x 9 1/2 In.	75.00
Bowl, Brown Band, 15 1/2 In.	475.00
Bowl, Brown, White Accent Band, 4 1/2 x 10 In.	75.00
Bowl, Brown, White Slip Accent Bands, 5 x 10 1/2 In.	35.00
Bowl, Girl With Watering Can By Window, Impressed 166 U.S.A, 5 1/4 x 10 In.	88.00
Bowl, Rockingham Glaze, 7 1/2 x 3 1/4 In.	44.00
Bowl, Tea, 3 White Accent Bands, Footed, 3 1/2 x 6 3/4 In.	77.00
Canister, Cover, Brown, White Banded, 8 1/2 x 8 1/2 In.	1073.00
Chamber Pot, 3-Line Annular Design, Applied Handle	80.00
Chamber Pot, Wheel Thrown, Annular Design, Applied Handle, Ohio, 7 1/2 In.	100.00
Cigar Stand, Match Holder & Striker, Figural, Bunny, 4 1/4 In.	355.00
Colander, Pierced Star, 4 3/4 x 9 3/4 In.	523.00
Creamer, Cow, Figural, Rockingham Glaze, 10 x 5 1/2 In.	80.00
Crock, Butter, White Slip Accent Bands, 4 x 6 In.	175.00
Figurine, Lion, Recumbent, Cobalt Highlights, 8 In.	2000.00
Flask, Eagle Perched On Flags, Flower, Rockingham Glaze, c.1850, 7 In.	440.00
Jar, Canning, 6 1/2 In.	99.00
Lamp Base, Brown, Yellow Green Ring, 8 1/2 In.	110.00
Milk Pan, 19th Century, 3 x 10 1/2 In.	80.00
Mixing Bowl, 2-Color Sponge, Ribbed, Impressed 10, 10 3/4 x 5 In.	120.00
Mixing Bowl, 3 White Bands, 8 1/2 In.	95.00
Mixing Bowl, Annular Band, White & Red Border, Ohio, Mid 1800s, 16 3/4 In.	260.00
Mixing Bowl, Brown & White Banded, 12 3/4 In.	165.00
Mixing Bowl, Brown Banding, 9 1/2 x 10 1/2 In., 2 Piece	98.00
Mixing Bowl, Embossed, Scrollwork, Mid 1800s, 13 1/2 In.	190.00
Mixing Bowl, Graduated, Blue Banding, 19th Century, 6 To 8 1/2 In.	140.00
Mixing Bowl, White & Brown Band, 9 1/4 In.	165.00
Mixing Bowl, White Band, 9 1/4 In.	95.00
Mold, Fish, Mottled Green, Brown, Tan Glaze Interior, 13 In.	165.00
Mold, Lion, Holland, 9 1/2 x 3 1/2 In.	300.00
Mug, Brown Alkaline Glaze, Handles, Morton Pottery, 4 3/4 In., 4 Piece	55.00
Mug, Slip Cast, 4 Blue Line Annular Design, Late 1800s, 5 x 3 1/4 In.	100.00
Nappy, Rockingham Glaze, 7 x 2 In.	55.00
Pitcher, 4 Apple Green Accent, Impressed 133/5, 4 1/2 In.	55.00
Pitcher, Bristol Glaze, Brown, Blue Sponge Accent Design, 8 1/2 In.	165.00
Pitcher, Bulbous, Blue & Brown Band, 7 3/4 In.	745.00
Pitcher, Milk, Applied Grapes & Leaves, Brown Glazed Rim, 5 1/2 In.	248.00
Pitcher, Paneled, Rockingham Type Glaze, Floral Scrollwork, William Bromley, 9 In.	1580.00
Pitcher, Rockingham Glaze, Eagle In Flight, Olive Branch, W. Bromley, 8 In.	1920.00
Pitcher, Rockingham Glaze, Flowers, Woman With Harp, Bromley & Co., 9 1/2 In.	1580.00
Pitcher, Rockingham Glaze, Impressed 345, 5 1/2 In.	66.00
Pitcher, White, Brown Bands, Dendritic Decoration, White Field, 8 1/8 In.	440.00
Tumbler, Rockingham Glaze, c.1900, 4 1/2 In., 5 Piece	410.00
Vase, Advertising, Stenciled Meyers' Dairy Grade A Milk, Pierz, Minn., 4 1/2 In.	90.00

ZANE Pottery was founded in 1921 by Adam Reed and Harry McClelland in South Zanesville, Ohio, at the old Peters and Reed Building. Zane pottery is very similar to Peters and Reed pottery, but it is usually marked. The factory was sold in 1941 to Lawton Gonder.

Vase, Ivory Glaze, 8 In.	65.00
Vase, Leaf & Berry Design, Carved, Blue Matte Glaze, 7 1/2 In.	115.00
Vase, Shadow Ware, Blue, Olive, Cream, 8 5/8 In.	150.00
Vase, Shadow Ware, Brown, Tan, Blue, Marked, 8 3/4 In.	150.00
Vase, Shadow Ware, Green, Black, Mirror Finish, 6 7/8 In.	127.00

ZANESVILLE Art Pottery was founded in 1900 by David Schmidt in Zanesville, Ohio. The firm made faience umbrella stands, jardinieres, and pedestals. The company closed in 1962. Many pieces are marked with just the words *La Moro*.

LA MORO

Bowl, Green Matte, 6 3/4 x 3 1/2 In.	145.00
Figurine, Elephant, Green Drip Iridescent Glaze, 1917, 6 x 9 In.	550.00
Jardiniere, Aqua, 8 1/4 x 7 In.	95.00
Jardiniere, Aqua, Footed, c.1951, 6 1/2 x 6 3/4 In.	95.00
Jardiniere, Leaves & Berries, 8 x 8 1/2 In.	45.00
Vase, Pansy, Impressed La Moro, Artist Signed, 7 5/8 In.	140.00

ZSOLNAY pottery was made in Hungary after 1862 and was characterized by Persian, Art Nouveau, or Hungarian motifs. A series of new Zsolnay figurines with green-gold luster finish is available in many shops today. Early Zsolnay was not marked, but by 1878 the tower trademark was used.

Ashtray, Lobster Shape, Blue, Gold Iridescent Glaze, Mark, 7 In.	325.00
Figurine, 2 Bears Playing, c.1950, 11 1/4 x 7 In.	110.00
Figurine, Buffalo, c.1950, 4 1/2 x 8 In.	55.00
Figurine, Dog, Hound, Seated, c.1950, 10 1/4 x 8 3/4 In.	110.00
Figurine, Lady Dancer, Gold & Luster Glaze, 1873 Sydney International Expo, 27 In. ...	3410.00
Pitcher, Pottery, Flattened Oval Shape, Nude Handle, Blue Iridescent Glaze, 8 In.	645.00
Sculpture, Figure, Girl Standing, Holding Jug, Blue Iridescent Glaze, Mark, 12 3/4 In.	645.00
Vase, Baluster Form, Iridescent Glaze, 10 1/2 In.	345.00
Vase, Bird, Foliage, Double Gourd Shape, 7 1/2 In.	405.00
Vase, Carp Leaping From Water, Flowers, Opaque Rosin Glaze, Marked, 14 3/4 In.	4600.00
Vase, Cream, Cobalt Swirls, Flowers, Reticulated, 9 3/4 In.	275.00
Vase, Iridescent Blue, Purple, Gold Glaze, Inverted Paneled Body, Waisted, 6 1/2 In.	413.00
Vase, Nacreous Chartreuse Glaze, Stylized Suns & Flowers, Flared Rim, 11 x 5 In.	489.00
Vase, Shouldered, Oval Shape, Tall Neck, Reclining Woman, 9 1/4 In.	355.00

INDEX

This index is computer-generated, making it as complete as possible. References in uppercase type are category listings. Those in lowercase letters refer to additional pages where pieces can be found. There is also an internal cross-referencing system used in the main part of the book, so if you look for a Kewpie doll in the Doll category, you will be told it is in its own category. There is additional information at the end of many paragraphs about where to find prices of pieces similar to yours.

KOVELS' DEPRESSION GLASS & DINNERWARE

PRICE LIST · 7TH EDITION

LEARN FROM AMERICA'S ANTIQUES EXPERTS!

- *More than 8,000 actual appraiser-approved prices*

- *More than 200 Depression glass patterns,*
  with photos and line drawings

- *Ceramic dinnerware patterns from the 1920s to the 1980s—*
  the patterns seen most often at shops and flea markets

- *Prices and histories of collectible plastic dinnerware—*
  included here for the first time

- *Special sixteen-page full-color report*

- *Factory histories, makers, dates, and marks*

256 PAGES, PAPERBACK, $16.00 · ISBN: 0-609-80640-8